W9-CEQ-366

# Shakespeare Lexicon
# and Quotation Dictionary

---

## A COMPLETE DICTIONARY
### OF ALL THE ENGLISH WORDS, PHRASES AND CONSTRUCTIONS
## IN THE WORKS OF THE POET
BY
## ALEXANDER SCHMIDT

THIRD EDITION
REVISED AND ENLARGED
BY
**GREGOR SARRAZIN**

IN TWO VOLUMES
## VOLUME II
## N–Z

DOVER PUBLICATIONS, INC.
NEW YORK

# Abbreviations.

| | | | | |
|---|---|---|---|---|
| Ado | Much Ado about Nothing. | | Lr. | King Lear. |
| All's or Alls | All's well that ends well. | | Lucr. | the Rape of Lucrece. |
| Ant. | Antony and Cleopatra. | | Mcb. | Macbeth. |
| Arg. | Argument. | | Meas. | Measure for Measure. |
| As | As you like it. | | M. Edd. | Modern Editors. |
| Caes. | Julius Caesar. | | Merch. | the Merchant of Venice. |
| Chor. | Chorus. | | Mids. | a Midsummer-night's Dream. |
| Compl. | A Lover's Complaint. | | O. Edd. | Old Editions (i. e. the Folios as well as the Quartos; or the Folios or Quartos alone, if there are no other old editions extant). |
| Cor. | Coriolanus. | | | |
| Cymb. | Cymbeline. | | | |
| Ded. | Dedication. | | | |
| Epil. | Epilogue. | | Oth. | Othello. |
| Err. | Comedy of Errors. | | Per. | Pericles. |
| F1 | the Folio Edition of 1623. | | Phoen. | the Phoenix and the Turtle. |
| F2 | the Folio Edition of 1632. | | Pilgr. | the Passionate Pilgrim. |
| F3 | the Folio Edition of 1663. | | Prol. | Prologue. |
| F4 | the Folio Edition of 1685. | | Qq | the old Quarto Editions, as differing from the Folios. |
| Ff | all the four Folios, as differing from the existing Quarto Editions. | | | |
| | | | R2 | Richard II. |
| Gent. | the two Gentlemen of Verona. | | R3 | Richard III. |
| H4A | First Part of Henry IV. | | Rom. | Romeo und Juliet. |
| H4B | Second Part of Henry IV. | | Shr. | the Taming of the Shrew. |
| H5 | Henry V. | | Sonn. | Sonnets. |
| H6A | First Part of Henry VI. | | Tim. | Timon of Athens. |
| H6B | Second Part of Henry VI. | | Tit. | Titus Andronicus. |
| H6C | Third Part of Henry VI. | | Tp. | Tempest. |
| H8 | Henry VIII. | | Troil. | Troilus and Cressida. |
| Hml. | Hamlet. | | Tw. | Twelfth Night. |
| Ind. | Induction. | | Ven. | Venus and Adonis. |
| John | King John. | | Wint. | the Winter's Tale. |
| LLL | Love's Labour's Lost. | | Wiv. | the Merry Wives of Windsor |

The different Quarto editions are designated in the same manner as in the great Cambridge edition of Messrs. Clark and Wright.

By the initials the unchanged forms and words are meant, as they stand in the respective headings; inflected forms are denoted by their terminations preceded by a dash; f. i. under the article Grow g. means grow, —s grows, —ing growing, etc.

The quotations are from the Globe edition.

**Asterisks inserted behind some articles or quotations refer to the Supplement.**
Names of Authors quoted in the Supplement indicate, as a rule, editions of Shakespeare's Plays and Poems, or other well-known books connected with Shakespeare, f. i. Wyndham = Shakespeare's Poems by George Wyndham; D. H. Madden = The Diary of Master William Silence by D. H. Madden; S. Lee = A Life of Shakespeare by Sidney Lee.

---

This Dover edition, first published in 1971, is an unabridged republication of the third revised and enlarged edition as published by Georg Reimer in Berlin in 1902 under the former title *Shakespeare-Lexicon*.

*International Standard Book Number: 0-486-22727-8*
*Library of Congress Catalog Card Number: 70-150407*

Manufactured in the United States of America
Dover Publications, Inc.
180 Varick Street
New York, N. Y. 10014

# N.

**Nabuchadnezzar** (M. Edd. *Nebuchadnezzar*) the famous Babylonian king: All's IV, 5, 21 (cf. Daniel IV, 33).

**Nag,** a worthless horse: *the forced gait of a shuffling n.* H4A III, 1, 135. Term of contempt for a loose woman: *know we not Galloway —s?* H4B II, 4, 205. *you ribaudred n. of Egypt,* Ant. III, 10, 10.

**Naiad,** a water nymph: Tp. IV, 128.

**Nail,** subst. 1) a pointed piece of metal by which things are fastened together: Tp. III, 2, 69. Gent. II, 4, 193. All's II, 2, 26. Cor. IV, 7, 54. Lr. II, 3, 16. Proverbial phrase: *is the old king dead? as n. in door,* H4B V, 3, 126 (cf. *Door-nail*).

2) the horny substance covering the ends of the fingers and toes: Lucr. 739. 1472. 1564. Tp. II, 2, 172. Err. IV, 4, 107. Mids. III, 2, 298. IV, 2, 41. All's V, 2, 31. Tw. IV, 2, 140. Wint. II, 3, 103. R2 V, 5, 19. H5 IV, 4, 76. H6A I, 4, 45. H6B I, 3, 144. R3 I, 2, 126. IV, 4, 231. Troil. II, 1, 115. Lr. I, 4, 329. Ant. IV, 12, 39. V, 2, 223. *the parings of one's n.* (a trifle) Err. IV, 3, 72. *the very parings of our —s shall pitch a field when we are dead,* H6A III, 1, 102. *to blow one's n.* (in order to warm one's hands) LLL V, 2, 923. = to take patience: *their love is not so great, but we may blow our —s together and fast it fairly out,* Shr. I, 1, 109. cf. H6C II, 5, 3.

3) a measure of about two inches: *thou yard, three-quarters, half-yard, quarter, n.* Shr. IV, 3, 109.

**Nail,** vb. to fasten with spikes of iron: *—ed on the bitter cross,* H4A I, 1, 26.

**Naked,** 1) not covered with clothes: Pilgr. 80. Compl. 317. Wint. III, 2, 212. R2 I, 3, 298. III, 2, 46. H4B III, 2, 333. H5 III, 3, 38. V, 2, 321. 324. 325. H6B III, 2, 336. R3 II, 1, 117. Cor. II, 2, 141. Mcb. I, 7, 21. II, 3, 132. Lr. III, 4, 28. IV, 1, 42. 46. Oth. IV, 1, 3. IV, 2, 143. Ant. V, 2, 59. *who sees his true love in her n. bed,* Ven. 397 ("a person undressed and in bed was formerly said to be in naked bed. It may be observed that, down to a certain period, those who were in bed were literally naked, no night linen being worn." Nares). *he doth despise his n. armour of still slaughtered lust,* Lucr. 188 (a play upon the word).

2) not sheathed, drawn: *with n. swords,* Err. IV, 4, 148. Tw. III, 4, 275. H4B II, 4, 222. H5 IV, 2, 21. Rom. I, 1, 39.

3) unarmed: *he but n., though locked up in steel,* H6B III, 2, 234. *n. as I am, I will assault thee,* Oth. V, 2, 258. H6C V, 4, 42. R3 I, 2, 178. Cor. I, 10, 20. Cymb. V, 5, 4.

4) unprovided, unfurnished, destitute: *some good conceit of thine in thy soul's thought, all n., will bestow it* (my duty) Sonn. 26, 8. Meas. III, 1, 73. LLL V, 2, 805. John II, 387. R2 I, 2, 31. H4A IV, 3, 77. H4B I, 3, 61. H5 V, 2, 34. H8 III, 2, 458. Tim. II, 1, 31. IV, 3, 228. Caes. IV, 3, 101. Hml. IV, 7, 44.

5) open, plain, undisguised: *the n. truth,* LLL V, 2, 716. H6A II, 4, 20. *I clothe my n. villany with old odd ends,* R3 I, 3, 336. *let it go n., men may see't the better,* Tim. V, 1, 70.

6) mere, bare, simple: *the very n. name of love,* Gent. II, 4, 142.

**Nakedness,** 1) want of clothing: Lr. II, 3, 11.

2) state of being unfurnished with what is wanted: *in his n. he appears but a man,* H5 IV, 1, 109. *nothing I'll bear from thee but n.* Tim. IV, 1, 33.

3) plainness, openness to view: *to cover with excuse that which appears in proper n.* Ado IV, 1, 177.

**Name,** subst. 1) individual appellation: *naming thy n. blesses an ill report,* Sonn. 95, 8. *what is your n.?* Tp. III, 1, 36; Meas. II, 1, 45; Ado IV, 2, 11; Tw. I, 2, 26; III, 1, 106 etc. *repeat their —s,* Gent. I, 2, 7. *his n.* 16. 111. 120. *what do you call your knight's n.?* Wiv. III, 2, 21; Err. III, 1, 53; V, 286; Shr. IV, 5, 55; H5 IV, 7, 13. *could not be distinguished but by —s,* Err. I, 1, 53. *call us by our —s,* II, 2, 168; IV, 3, 3; Cor. V, 1, 9; Tim. I, 1, 187. *give a name* (like a godfather) *to every fixed star,* LLL I, 1, 89; 93; R2 IV, 256. *friend Simple by your n.* Wiv. III, 1, 3. *which Lion hight by n.* Mids. V, 140. *one Snout by n.* 157; H5 II, 1, 81. *a very valiant rebel of the n.* H4A V, 4, 62 etc. etc. With *of: the n. of Prosper,* Tp. III, 3, 99. Wiv. II, 1, 72. As III, 2, 381. John V, 2, 19. R3 I, 1, 58 etc. *Of* omitted: *thy stolen n.* Coriolanus, Cor. V, 6, 89.

2) common or generic appellation: *thou dost usurp the n.* (of king) Tp. I, 2, 454. *he couples it to his com-*

*plaining —s,* Gent. I, 2, 127. *had I more n. for badness* (than villain) Meas. V, 59. *a noble duke, in nature as in n.* Tw. I, 2, 25. *I have no n., no title,* R2 IV, 255. *know not what n. to call myself,* 259. *had his great n.* (of king) *profaned with their scorns,* H4A III, 2, 64. *gave his countenance, against his n., to laugh at gibing boys,* 65. *called me all these bitter —s,* R3 I, 3, 236. *a traitor to the n. of God,* I, 4, 210. *let life bear his n.* Tit. III, 1, 249. *be thy thoughts imperious, like thy n.* (of emperor) IV, 4, 81 etc. etc. With *of: our dear love lose n. of single one,* Sonn. 39, 6. *the n. of king,* Tp. I, 1, 18. *no n. of magistrate,* II, 1, 149. Gent. II, 4, 142. Wiv. V, 5, 239. Meas. III, 1, 39. Err. II, 2, 137. Ado I, 1, 302. John V, 2, 67. Mcb. III, 1, 58. Lr. IV, 3, 27 etc.

*By the n. of* = in the quality of, as being; *I have wooed Margaret by the n. of Hero,* Ado III, 3, 155. *I arrest thee by the n. of Richard Earl of Cambridge,* H5 II, 2, 145. 147. 149. *and by that n.* (of traitor) *must die,* H8 II, 1, 59. *this diamond he greets your wife withal by the n. of most kind hostess,* Mcb. II, 1, 16. *In the n. of* or *in n. of* = under the title, as: *to carry me in the n. of foul clothes to Datchet-lane,* Wiv. III, 5, 101. *I'll to him again in n. of Brook,* IV, 4, 76. *thus answer I in n. of Benedick,* Ado II, 1, 179. *now take upon me, in the n. of Time, to use my wings,* Wint. IV, 1, 3. *which comes to me in n. of fault,* III, 2, 61. *received eight thousand nobles in n. of lendings,* R2 I, 1, 89. = by virtue of, by means of: *and in the lawful n. of marrying, to give our hearts united ceremony,* Wiv. IV, 6, 50. cf. *wretched shall France be only in my n.* H6A I, 4, 97. *Under n.* = under pretence: *he does it under n. of perfect love,* Shr. IV, 3, 12.

3) reputation, character: *my good n.* Lucr. 820. *no man that hath a n., by falsehood and corruption doth it shame,* Err. II, 1, 112. *he hath an excellent good n.* Ado III, 1, 98. III, 3, 14. H4A I, 2, 94. *I am in good n. and fame,* H4B II, 4, 81. *you are in an ill n.* 98. *let our nation lose the n. of hardiness and policy,* H5 I, 2, 220. *expected to prove so worthy as since he hath been allowed the n. of,* Cymb. I, 4, 3 etc.

4) renown, honour, eminence: *and for a n., now puts the drowsy and neglected act freshly on me, 'tis surely for a n.* Meas. I, 2, 173. 175. *none of n.* Ado I, 1, 7. R2 II, 3, 56. H5 IV, 8, 110. R3 IV, 5, 8. V, 5, 12. *great n. in arms,* H4A III, 2, 108. V, 1, 98. *that, Talbot dead, great York might bear the n.* H6A IV, 4, 9 (= have all the glory of the war). *he gives my son the whole n. of the war,* Cor. II, 1, 149 etc. Abstr. pro concr.: *our battle is more full of —s than yours,* H4B IV, 1, 154. *Tullus Aufidius, the second n. of men,* Cor. IV, 6, 125.

5) descent, ancestry: *I am from humble, he from honoured n.* All's I, 3, 162. *good alone is good without a n.* II, 3, 136. *thou dislikest of virtue for the n.* 131. *the honour of a maid is her n.* III, 5, 13.

6) authority, behalf, part: *I did in your n. receive it,* Gent. I, 2, 40. *charge you in the duke's n. to obey me,* Err. IV, 1, 70. *I have wooed in thy n.* Ado II, 1, 310. III, 3, 177. IV, 2, 40. Shr. V, 1, 92. Wint. III, 2, 119. John III, 1, 140. H6A II, 1, 26 etc. Common phrases of exhortation or obsecration: *a God's n.* H6A I, 2, 102. *i' God's n.* Ado I, 1, 144. V, 1, 319. Shr. I, 2, 195. IV, 5, 1. H4B IV, 1, 227. R3 V, 2, 14 etc. *in the —s of all the Gods at once,* Caes. I, 2, 148.

*i' devil's n.* Shr. IV, 3, 92. *i' the n. of Beelzebub,* Mcb. II, 3, 4. *i' the n. of something holy,* Tp. III, 3, 94. *close, in the n. of jesting,* Tw. II, 5, 23. *in the n. of sanctity,* III, 4, 93. *i' the n. of truth,* Mcb. I, 3, 52. *i' the n. of me,* Wint. IV, 3, 54 (the clown's speech. Anon. *me-,* as abbreviated from *mercy*). *n. of mercy, when was this?* III, 3, 105. *what an unweighed behaviour hath this Flemish drunkard picked — with the devil's n. — out of my conversation?* Wiv. II, 1, 24.

**Name,** vb. 1) to call: *teach me how to n. the bigger light,* Tp. I, 2, 335. *do not n. Silvia thine,* Gent. V, 4, 128. *which we may n. tough,* LLL I, 2, 18. *fairer than tongue can n. thee,* R3 I, 2, 81. *a servant —d Lucilius,* Tim. I, 1, 111.

2) to give a name or appellation to: *my father —d me Autolycus,* Wint. IV, 3, 24. *we will not n. desert before his birth,* Troil. III, 2, 101. *he whom my father —d? your Edgar?* Lr. II, 1, 94. = to give a title to: *nobly —d so,* Cor. II, 3, 251. *henceforth be earls, the first that ever Scotland in such an honour —d,* Mcb. V, 8, 64.

3) to mention by name, to specify: *when thou didst n. the boar, I feared thy fortune,* Ven. 641. *—ing thy name blesses an ill report,* Sonn. 95, 8. *I guess the sequel; and yet I will not n. it,* Gent. II, 1, 123. *never n. her, if she be a whore,* Wiv. IV, 1, 65. Meas. III, 1, 102. Ado III, 1, 18. LLL I, 2, 71. III, 167. Mids. I, 2, 20. 41. III, 1, 37. Merch. I, 2, 40. As V, 4, 96. Tw. I, 2, 28. III, 4, 414. Wint. I, 2, 386. IV, 1, 23. IV, 2, 24. H4A IV, 3, 48. H4B II, 2, 120. H8 I, 2, 60. Mcb. II, 3, 70. Lr. I, 1, 73 etc.

4) to appoint, to designate, to nominate: *n. the day of marriage,* Ado II, 1, 311. *you may n. the time,* R3 III, 4, 19. *the event is yet to n. the winner,* Cymb. III, 5, 15. *Marcius, whom late you have —d for consul,* Cor. III, 1, 196. *and n. thee in election for the empire,* Tit. I, 183. *he is already —d,* Mcb. II, 4, 31.

**Nameless,** 1) having no name: *thy issue blurred with n. bastardy,* Lucr. 522. *the secret n. friend of yours,* Gent. II, 1, 111.

2) inexpressible: *she hath many n. virtues,* Gent. III, 1, 319. *what I cannot name; 'tis n. woe, I wot,* R2 II, 2, 40.

**Namely,** to mention by name; that is to say: *n., no time to recover hair lost by nature,* Err. II, 2, 103. *except it be the last, n. some love,* V, 56. *to him that owes it, n. this young prince,* John II, 248. *as well appeareth by the cause you come, n. to appeal each other,* R2 I, 1, 27. *the borrowed glories ... n. the crown,* H5 II, 4, 81. *to many simple gulls, n. to Hastings, Derby, Buckingham,* R3 I, 3, 329.

**Nan,** diminutive of Anne: Gent. II, 3, 23. Wiv. I, 4, 160. III, 4, 2. 98. 104. IV, 4, 47. 71. 74. 85. IV, 6, 20. V, 3, 12.

**Nap,** the woolly substance on the surface of cloth: *Jack Cade the clothier means to dress the commonwealth, and turn it, and set a new n. upon it,* H6B IV, 2, 7.

**Nap,** a short slumber: Shr. Ind. 2, 83. *take a n.* Tw. V, 52. R3 V, 3, 104.

**Nape,** the joint of the neck behind: *turn your eyes toward the —s of your necks,* Cor. II, 1, 43.

**Napkin,** handkerchief: *oft did she heave her n. to her eyne,* Compl. 15. *and to that youth he sends this bloody n.* As IV, 3, 94. 139. 155. *an onion ... in a n.* close conveyed, Shr. Ind. 1, 127. Wiv. III, 5, 92. H4A IV, 2, 47. H6C I, 4, 79. 159. II, 1, 62. Tit. III, 1,

140. 146. Caes. III, 2, 138. Mcb. II, 3, 6. Hml. V, 2, 299. Oth. III, 3, 287. 290. 321.

**Naples,** 1) kingdom in the south of Italy: Tp. I, 2, 112. 121. 235. 431. 448. II, 1, 112. 245. 247. 256. 259. 262. 292. II, 2, 72. III, 3, 27. V, 149. 206. Epil. 5. H6A V, 3, 52. 94. V, 4, 78. V, 5, 40. H6B I, 1, 48. V, 1, 118. H6C I, 4, 121. II, 2, 139. Oth. III, 1, 4 (the venereal disease appeared first in Naples). 2) king of Naples: *myself am N.* Tp. I, 2, 434.

**Napless,** threadbare: *the n. vesture of humility,* Cor. II, 1, 250.

**Napping;** *to take n.* = to take or surprise in the very act, in committing an offence: *I should blush to be o'erheard and taken n. so,* LLL IV, 3, 130. *I have ta'en you n.* Shr. IV, 2, 46.

**Naps,** name: *John N. of Greece,* Shr. Ind. 2, 95.

**Narbon,** French name: All's I, 1, 31. 43. II, 1, 104.

**Narcissus,** a fabulous youth, who fell in love with his own shadow in a brook: Ven. 161. Lucr. 265. Ant. II, 5, 96.

**Narrow,** 1) not broad, having but a small distance from side to side: Err. IV, 2, 38. Merch. II, 8, 28. III, 1, 4.\* All's IV, 5, 53. R2 V, 3, 8. H4A II, 2, 63. H5 Prol. 22. I, 2, 201. H6C I, 1, 239. IV, 8, 3. Troil. III, 3, 154. Rom. II, 4, 88 *(from an inch n. to an ell broad).* Caes. I, 2, 135. II, 4, 33. Cymb. V, 3, 52. 2) not wide, very limited: *'tis too n. for your mind,* Hml. II, 2, 259; cf. Caes. I, 2, 135. *most n. measure lent me,* Ant. III, 4, 8.

**Narrowly,** closely, with minute scrutiny: *if my cousin do not look exceeding n. to thee,* Ado V, 4, 118. *doth watch Bianca's steps so n.* Shr. III, 2, 141. *search the market n.* Per. IV, 2, 3.

**Narrow-mouthed,** having a small opening: *a n. bottle,* As III, 2, 211.

**Narrow-prying,** watching closely: Shr. III, 2, 148.

**Naso,** family name of the poet Ovid: LLL IV, 2, 127.

**Nasty,** dirty, filthy, nauseous: H5 II, 1, 53. Hml. III, 4, 94.

**Nathaniel,** name of 1) the curate in LLL IV, 2, 11. 50. 140. 156. 2) a servant in Shr. IV, 1, 91. 125. 135.

**Nation,** a people: Err. IV, 4, 158. Merch. I, 3, 49. III, 1, 59. 89. III, 3, 31. As I, 1, 49. All's IV, 3, 363. IV, 5, 4. John V, 2, 33. 144. R2 II, 1, 22. H4B I, 2, 241. V, 2, 137. H5 I, 2, 219. II, 4, 80. III, 2, 131. H6A III, 3, 23. 62. IV, 1, 138. IV, 2, 16. V, 4, 99. H8 V, 5, 53. Troil. II, 2, 180. 185. Cor. III, 3, 132. IV, 5, 186. Tit. I, 30. Tim. IV, 3, 43. Mcb. IV, 3, 103. Hml. I, 4, 18. II, 2, 370. IV, 7, 95. 101. Lr. I, 2, 4. Oth. I, 2, 68. Per. I, 4, 65. IV, 2, 123.

**Native,** 1) produced by nature, natural, genuine: *her cheeks possess the same which n. she doth owe,* LLL I, 2, 111. *n. blood is counted painting now,* IV, 3, 263. *chase the n. beauty from his cheek,* John III, 4, 83. *in his true, n. and most proper shape,* H4B IV, 1, 37. *titles miscreate, whose right suits not in n. colours with the truth,* H5 I, 2, 17. *no pulse shall keep his n. progress,* Rom. IV, 1, 97. *if thou path, thy n. semblance on,* Caes. II, 1, 83. *the n. hue of resolution,* Hml. III, 1, 84. *the n. act and figure of my heart,* Oth. I, 1, 62. *base men being in love have then a nobility in their natures more than is n. to them,* II, 1, 218. 2) resulting from birth, hereditary, legitimate: *ere her n. king shall falter under foul rebellion's arms,*

R2 III, 2, 25. *your crown and kingdom, indirectly held from him the n. and true challenger,* H5 II, 4, 95. *let us fear the n. mightiness and fate of him,* 64 (innate in his race). *did I put Henry from his n. right,* H6C III, 3, 190. *the senator shall bear contempt hereditary, the beggar n. honour,* Tim. IV, 3, 11. 3) pertaining to home, or to the place of birth: *thy n. home,* Err. I, 1, 30. *her n. bay,* Merch. II, 6, 15. *in their assigned and n. dwelling-place,* As II, 1, 63. *bring this instrument of honour again into his n. quarter,* All's III, 6, 70. *at their n. homes,* John II, 69. *shall leave his n. channel,* 337. *my n. English now I must forego,* R2 I, 3, 160. *breathing n. breath,* 173. *chasing the royal blood from his n. residence* (i. e. the cheeks) II, 1, 119. *to fright our n. peace with self-borne arms,* II, 3, 80 (= domestic). *bear our civil swords and n. fire as far as France,* H4B V, 5, 112. *if these men have defeated the law and outrun n. punishment,* H5 IV, 1, 176 (i. e. inflicted at home). *a many of our bodies shall find n. graves,* IV, 3, 96 (i. e. at home). *he could not speak English in the n. garb,* V, 1, 80 (like a born Englishman). *my n. clime,* H6B III, 2, 84. *your n. coast,* IV, 8, 52. *in our n. place,* Troil. II, 2, 96. *your n. town,* Cor. V, 6, 50. *back to your n. spring,* Rom. III, 2, 102. 4) born in a place, being at home: *being n. burghers of this desert city,* As II, 1, 23. *their n. lords,* H5 III, 5, 26. *I am n. here,* Hml. I, 4, 14. *like a creature n. and indued unto that element,* IV, 7, 180. With *of:* *are you n. of this place?* As III, 2, 356. 5) cognate, congenial, kindred: *adoption strives with nature, and choice breeds a n. slip to us from foreign seeds,* All's I, 3, 152. *to join like likes and kiss like n. things,* I, 1, 238. *the head is not more n. to the heart,* Hml. I, 2, 47.\*

**Native,** subst. natural origin, source: *the accusation which they have often made against the senate, all cause unborn, could never be the n. of our so frank donation,* Cor. III, 1, 129 (some M. Edd. *motive*).

**Nativity,** birth: *I have served him from the hour of my n. to this instant,* Err. IV, 4, 31. *you the calendars of their n.* V, 404. *after so long grief such n.* 406 (some M. Edd. *festivity*). *be out of love with your n.* As IV, 1, 36. *cursed be the time of thy n.* H6A V, 4, 27. Especially = birth or coming into life under particular circumstances bearing on the destiny of the person born: *marks descried in men's nativity are nature's faults, not their own infamy,* Lucr. 538. *n., once in the main of light, crawls to maturity,* Sonn. 60, 5. *there is divinity in odd numbers, either in n., chance, or death,* Wiv. V, 1, 4. *vows so born, in their n. all truth appears,* Mids. III, 2, 125. *mark prodigious, such as are despised in n.* V, 420. *at my n. the front of heaven was full of fiery shapes,* H4A III, 1, 13. cf. 26. *to whom the heavens in thy n. adjudged an olive branch,* H6C IV, 6, 33. *thou that wast sealed in thy n. the slave of nature,* R3 I, 3, 229. *my n. was under Ursa major,* Lr. I, 2, 140. *thou hast as chiding a n. as fire, air, water, earth and heaven can make,* Per. III, 1, 32.

**Natural,** adj 1) pertaining to nature, being an effect or forming part of nature: *nothing n. I ever saw so noble,* Tp. I, 2, 418. *a n. perspective,* Tw. V, 224. *children of divers kind we sucking on her* (earth's) *n. bosom find,* Rom. II, 3, 12. *the n. gates and alleys of the body,* Hml. I, 5, 67. *thy n. magic and dire property,*

III, 2, 270. *some n. notes about her body*, Cymb. II, 2, 28. *she held the very garment of Posthumus in more respect than my noble and n. person*, III, 5, 140.

2) bestowed by nature, not acquired: *our n. wits*, As I, 2, 55. *our n. goodness*, Wint. II, 1, 164. *her n. posture*, V, 3, 23. *n. graces*, H6A V, 3, 192. *n. gifts*, Hml. I, 5, 51. *a n. and prompt alacrity*, Oth. I, 3, 233. *Caesar's n. vice*, Ant. I, 4, 2. *n. luck*, II, 4, 26. *the n. bravery of your isle*, Cymb. III, 1, 18. *that n. stamp*, V, 5, 366.

3) subject to, or caused by, the laws of nature: *blunt his n. edge*, Meas. I, 4, 60. *a n. guiltiness such as is his*, II, 2, 139. *to make it n. rebellion*, All's V, 3, 6 (= rebellion of nature). *dearer than the n. bond of sisters*, As I, 2, 288. *the thousand n. shocks that flesh is heir to*, Hml. III, 1, 62.

4) consonant to nature and its general or individual laws: *come to my n. taste*, Mids. IV, 1, 179. *his n. scope*, H4A III, 1, 171. *a fair and n. light*, V, 1, 18. *congreeing in a full and n. clause*, H5 I, 2, 182. *as two yoke-devils sworn to either's purpose, working so grossly in a n. cause*, II, 2, 107. *never to lie and take his n. rest*, H6C IV, 3, 5. *none of you may live your n. age*, R3 I, 3, 213. *that n. competency whereby they live*, Cor. I, 1, 143. *the n. ruby of your cheeks*, Mcb. III, 4, 115. *he wants the n. touch*, IV, 2, 9.

5) prompted or governed by nature, not by art or study: *such a one is a n. philosopher*, As III, 2, 33. *the painting is almost the n. man*, Tim.·I, 1, 157. *I am even the n. fool of fortune*, Lr. IV, 6, 195 ("born to be the sport of fortune." Walker).

6) genuine, not artificial or affected: *a n. coward, without instinct*, H4A II, 4, 542. *their n. tears*, H5 IV, 2, 13. *thou art even n. in thine art*, Tim. V, 1, 88. *n. roses*, Per. V Prol. 7.

Adverbially: *I do it more n.* Tw. II, 3, 89 (Sir Andrew's speech).

7) according to the ordinary course of things, not supernatural: *their words are n. breath*, Tp. V, 157. *these are not n. events*, 227. *which is the n. man, and which the spirit*, Err. V, 333 (perhaps to be registered under def. 1). *no n. exhalation*, John III, 4, 153. *his n. cause*, 156. *they are n.* Caes. I, 3, 30. *there is something in this more than n.* Hml. II, 2, 385.

8) native, given by birth, not adopted: *a contriver against me his n. brother*, As I, 1, 151. *whom should he follow but his n. king?* H6C I, 1, 82. *dear divorce 'twixt n. son and sire*, Tim. IV, 3, 383. *myself they take for n. father*, Cymb. III, 3, 107 (Germ. *leiblich*).

9) obedient to the impulse of nature, kind, tender: *in his love toward her ever most kind and n.* Meas. III, 1, 229. *were all thy children kind and n.* H5 II Chor. 19. *loyal and n. boy*, Lr. II, 1, 86.

10) foolish, idiotic: *hath all the good gifts of nature. He hath indeed, almost n.* Tw. I, 3, 30 (some M. Edd. *all most n.*).

**Natural,** subst. an idiot: *that a monster should be such a n.* Tp. III, 2, 37. *when Fortune makes Nature's n. the cutter-off of Nature's wit*, As I, 2, 52. *sent this n. for our whetstone*, 57. *a great n. that runs lolling up and down*, Rom. II, 4, 96.

**Naturalize,** to initiate, to familiarize: *I will return perfect courtier, in the which my instruction shall serve to n. thee*, All's I, 1, 223.

**Naturally,** 1) by nature: *I am not n. honest*, Wint IV 4, 732. *a woman, n. born to fears*, John III,

1, 15. *the cold blood he did n. inherit of his father*, H4B IV, 3, 128.

2) to the life, with just representation: *that part was aptly fitted and n. performed*, Shr. Ind. 1, 87.

**Nature** (usually fem., sometimes neuter, as in Wint. I, 2, 151 and Oth. III, 3, 227) 1) the world around us as created and creating by fixed and eternal laws: *n. that made thee*, Ven. 11. 291. *the curious workmanship of n.* 734. *swear —'s death for framing thee so fair*, 744. *those whom n. hath not made for store*, Sonn. 11, 9. 20, 10. 67, 9. 126, 5. Tp. II, 1, 159. 162. Meas. I, 1, 37. Ado III, 1, 49. 63. IV, 1, 130. LLL II, 10. Mids. II, 2, 104. V, 296. Merch. I, 1, 51. III, 2, 90. As II, 4, 56. III, 2, 149. All's I, 1, 138. 148. 153. V, 3, 103. Tw. I, 2, 48. Wint. II, 3, 104. IV, 4, 89. 489. V, 2, 108. R2 II, 1, 43. H4B I, 1, 153. R3 IV, 3, 18. Rom. II, 3, 9. Caes. V, 5, 74. Per. III, 2, 38 etc. etc. *wisdom of n.* Lr. I, 2, 113 (= natural philosophy).

Denoting spontaneous growth and formation: *a woman's face with —'s own hand painted*, Sonn. 20, 1; cf. Tw. I, 5, 258. *the blots of —'s hand*, Mids. V, 416; cf. Hml. I, 4, 24. *the something that n. gave me*, As I, 1, 18. *n. hath given us wit*, I, 2, 47. *adoption strives with n.* All's I, 3, 151. *in these to n. she's immediate heir*, II, 3, 139. *the affection of nobleness which n. shows above her breeding*, Wint. V, 2, 40. *this fortress built by n.* R2 II, 1, 43 etc. etc. *diminutives of n.* Troil. V, 1, 39 (cf. v. 5; i. e. diminutives from your birth and destined to be so for ever). *the slave of n.* R3 I, 3, 230. *we fools of n.* Hml. I, 4, 54 (cf. *Fool*). *this carl, a very drudge of —'s*, Cymb. V, 2, 5. *by n.:* Lucr. 697. Sonn. 122, 6. Err. II, 2, 74. 104. Ado III, 3, 16. Tw. I, 3, 105. H6A III, 1, 18. H6B III, 1, 258. Opposed to *art:* Ven. 291. Lucr. 1374. Meas. II, 2, 184. Mids. II, 2, 104. As III, 2, 31. All's II, 1, 121. Wint. IV, 4, 91. Rom. II, 4, 95. Caes. IV, 3, 195. Lr. IV, 6, 86. Opposed to *fortune:* Wiv. III, 3, 70. Ado III, 3, 16. As I, 2, 43. 45. All's I, 1, 237. John III, 1, 52. Hml. I, 4, 32. Opposed to the agency of supernatural powers: *there is in this business more than nature was ever conduct of*, Tp. V, 243. Opposed to human institutions or tendencies: *by law of n. thou art bound to breed*, Ven. 171. *by law of n. and of nations*, H5 II, 4, 80. Troil. II, 2, 176. *if we are —'s, these are ours*, All's I, 3, 135. *the show and seal of —'s truth*, 138. *n. craves all dues be rendered to their owners*, Troil. II, 2, 173. *one touch of n. makes the whole world kin*, III, 3, 175. *a fault to n., to reason most absurd*, Hml. I, 2, 102. *o'erstep not the modesty of n.* III, 2, 22. *where n. doth with merit challenge*, Lr. I, 1, 54. *the offices of n.* II, 4, 181. *thou, n., art my goddess*, I, 2, 1. *in the lusty stealth of n.* 11 etc. etc. Implying the idea of necessity: *he's walked the way of n.* H4B V, 2, 4. *when n. brought him to the door of death*, H6C III, 3, 105.

2) native sensation, innate and involuntary affection of the heart and mind: *n. hath charged me that I hoard them not*, Compl. 220. *expelled remorse and n.* Tp. V, 76. *n. dispenses with the deed so far that it becomes a virtue*, Meas. III, 1, 135. *my end was wrought by n., not by vile offence*, Err. I, 1, 35. *n., stronger than his just occasion*, As IV, 3, 130. *the mightiest space in fortune n. brings to join like likes*, All's I, 1, 237. *n. to her bias drew in that*, Tw. V, 267. *how sometimes n. will betray its folly*, Wint. I, 2, 151. *tears which n., love and filial tenderness shall pay thee*, H4B IV, 5,

39. *how quickly n. falls into revolt when gold becomes her object*, 66. *n. makes me relent*, H6A III, 3, 59. *with whom an upright zeal to right prevails more than the n. of a brother's love*, H6C V, 1, 79. *fond n. bids us all lament*, Rom. IV, 5, 82. *n. can bear great fortune, but by contempt of n.* Tim. IV, 3, 8. *my n. could not bear it so*, Caes. IV, 3, 195. *compunctious visitings of n.* Mcb. I, 5, 46. *so far hath discretion fought with n.* Hml. I, 2, 5. *if thou hast n. in thee, bear it not*, I, 5, 81. *O heart, lose not thy n.* III, 2, 411. *n. makes them partial*, III, 3, 32. *I am satisfied in n., but in my terms of honour I stand aloof*, V, 2, 255. *wrenched my frame of n.* Lr. I, 4, 290. *n. erring from itself*, Oth. III, 3, 227. *n. would not invest herself in such shadowy passion*, IV, 1, 40 etc.

3) the physical and moral constitution of man: *our —s do pursue a thirsty evil*, Meas. I, 2, 132. *the weariest life that age ... can lay on n.* III, 1, 131. *so is all n. in love mortal in folly*, As II, 4, 56. *labouring art can never ransom n. from her inaidible estate*, All's II, 1, 121. *all the miseries which n. owes*, III, 2, 122. *so long as n. will bear up with this exercise*, Wint. III, 2, 241. *n. does require her times of preservation*, H8 III, 2, 146. *to repair our n. with comforting repose*, V, 1, 3. *in our own —s frail*, V, 3, 11. *n. to whom all sores lay siege*, Tim. IV, 3, 6. *that n. ... should yet be hungry*, 176. *whose naked —s live in all the spite of wreakful heaven*, 228. *the multiplying villanies of n. do swarm upon him*, Mcb. I, 2, 11. *their drenched —s lie as in a death*, I, 7, 68. *the season of all —s, sleep*, III, 4, 141. *a violet in the youth of primy n.* Hml. I, 3, 7. *to hold the mirror up to n.* III, 2, 25. *n. is fine in love*, IV, 5, 161. *n. finds itself scourged by the sequent effects*, Lr. I, 2, 114. *oppressed n. sleeps*, III, 6, 104. *thou hast one daughter who redeems n. from the general curse*, IV, 6, 210. *the sides of n. will not sustain it*, Ant. I, 3, 16 etc.

4) individual constitution, personal character: *though in my n. reigned all frailties*, Sonn. 109, 9. *my n. is subdued to what it works in*, 111, 6. *in my false brother awaked an evil n.* Tp. I, 2, 93. *that which good —s could not abide to be with*, 359. *my father's of a better n.* 496. *on whose n. nurture can never stick*, IV, 188. *the n. of our people*, Meas. I, 1, 10. *and yet my n. never in the fight to do it slander*, I, 3, 42. *to practise his judgment with the disposition of —s*, III, 1, 165. *music doth change his n.* Merch. V, 82. *I have kept of them tame and know their —s*, All's II, 5, 50. *the younger of our n.* III, 1, 17. *my son corrupts a well-derived n. with his inducement*, III, 2, 90. *there's something in't that stings his n.* IV, 3, 4. *the tenderness of her n. became as a prey to her grief*, 61. *whose n. sickens but to speak a truth*, V, 3, 207. *a noble duke, in n. as in name*, Tw. I, 2, 25. *nor can there be that deity in my n.* V, 234. *not noted but of the finer —s*, Wint. I, 2, 226. *my lord of York, out of his noble n.* H8 III, 1, 62. *I know his noble n.* III, 2, 419. *affairs that walk at midnight have in them a wilder n.* V, 1, 15. *thou hast a cruel n.* V, 3, 129. *all our abilities, gifts, —s, shapes*, Troil. I, 3, 179. *what he cannot help in his n.* Cor. I, 1, 42. *such a n., tickled with good success*, 263. *his gracious n.* II, 3, 195. *his surly n.* 203. *his n. is too noble for the world*, III, 1, 255. *wilt thou draw near the n. of the gods?* Tit. I, 117. *ranked with all deserts, all kind of natures*, Tim. I, 1, 65. *this is in thee a n. but infected*, IV, 3, 202. *I will make thee*

*do thy right n.* 44. *the worm that's fled hath n. that in time will venom breed*, Mcb. III, 4, 30. *when the baser n. comes between mighty opposites*, Hml. V, 2, 60. *a tardiness in n.* Lr. I, 1, 238. *—s of such deep trust*, II, 1, 117. *is this the n. whom passion could not shake?* Oth. IV, 1, 276 etc.

5) quality, sort, kind: *sonnets that did amplify each stone's dear n., worth and quality*, Compl. 210. *love you 'gainst the n. of love*, Gent. V, 4, 58. *a power I have, but of what strength and n. I am not yet instructed*, Meas. I, 1, 80. *the n. of their crimes*, II, 3, 7. *but in what n.?* III, 1, 70. *your capacity is of that n.* LLL V, 2, 377. *distinct offices and of opposed —s*, Merch. II, 9, 62. *of a strange n. is the suit you follow*, IV, 1, 177. *let my officers of such a n. make an extent upon his house*, As III, 1, 16. *the n. of our quarrel yet never brooked parle*, Shr. I, 1, 116. *I con him no thanks for't, in the n. he delivers it*, All's IV, 3, 175. *the n. of his great offence is dead*, V, 3, 23 (almost = cause). *the offence is not of such a bloody n.* Tw. III, 3, 30. *those pearls which heaven shall take in n. of a fee*, John II, 170. *all of one n., of one substance bred*, H4A I, 1, 11. *to know the n. of your griefs*, IV, 3, 42. *this man's brow foretells the n. of a tragic volume*, H4B I, 1, 61. *figuring the n. of the times deceased*, III, 1, 81. *a peace is of the n. of a conquest*, IV, 2, 89. *our vineyards, fallows, meads and hedges, defective in their —s, grow to wildness*, H5 V, 2, 55. *all* (articles) *according to their firm proposed —s*, 362. *the n. of it* (an exaction) H8 I, 2, 53. *thus we debase the n. of our seats*, Cor. III, 1, 136. *all these things change their —s*, Caes. I, 3, 67. *the state of man suffers the n. of an insurrection*, II, 1, 69. *the n. of bad news infects the teller*, Ant. I, 2, 99. *upon importance of so slight and trivial a n.* Cymb. I, 4, 45 etc.

6) human life, vitality: *hath from n. stolen a man already made*, Meas. II, 4, 43. *would have made n. immortal*, All's I, 1, 22. *n. and sickness debate it at their leisure*, I, 2, 74. *I would repent out the remainder of n.* IV, 3, 272. *in me, O n., cesse*, V, 3, 72. *gentle sleep, —'s soft nurse*, H4B III, 1, 6. *wait on —'s mischief*, Mcb. I, 5, 51 (on the destruction of life). *death and n. do contend about them whether they live or die*, II, 2, 7. *in them —'s copy 's not eterne*, III, 2, 38. *the least* (gash) *a death to n.* III, 4, 28. *passing through n. to eternity*, Hml. I, 2, 73. *n. cannot choose his origin*, I, 4, 26. *the foul crimes done in my days of n.* I, 5, 12. *n. in you stands on the very verge of her confine*, Lr. II, 4, 149. *my snuff and loathed part of n. should burn itself out*, IV, 6, 39. *if thou and n. can so gently part*, Ant. V, 2, 297. *n. doth abhor to make his bed with the defunct*, Cymb. IV, 2, 357. *n. awakes*, Per. III, 2, 93.

**Naught** or **Nought** (rhyming to *thought* in R3 III, 6, 13 and Mcb. IV, 1, 70; to *oft* in Pilgr. 340) 1) nothing (usual orthogr. *nought*): Ven. 631 (cf. Gent. III, 1, 83). 911. Lucr. 1092. 1095. Sonn. 15, 3. 44, 13. 57, 11. Tp. I, 2, 18. III, 2, 74. Gent. III, 1, 83 (cf. Ven. 631). V, 4, 64. Err. IV, 1, 91. LLL I, 1, 92. Mids. III, 2, 462. Merch. V, 81. 197. Shr. I, 1, 166. All's III, 7, 21. Tw. I, 1, 11. Wint. II, 1, 177. John III, 4, 111. V, 7, 117. R2 I, 1, 53. II, 1, 83. II, 2, 23. H4B V, 5, 40. H5 I, 2, 251. H6A I, 2, 135. I, 3, 70. H6B III, 1, 216. III, 2, 366. V, 1, 7. R3 I, 1, 97. H8 I, 1, 43. II, 4, 135. Troil. I, 2, 314. I, 3, 19. 249. Cor. V, 3, 93. Tit. I, 146. IV 4, 7. V, 1, 85. Rom.

Prol. 11. II, 3, 17. Tim. III, 6, 121. IV, 3, 376. Mcb. III, 2, 4. IV, 1, 70. Lr. II, 2, 86. Oth. I, 1, 48. 163. IV, 2, 187. V, 2, 295. Ant. III, 5, 23. Cymb. III, 6, 49. V, 5, 9. Per. I, 4, 43. *to set at n.* = to slight, to despise: Gent. I, 1, 68. H4B V, 2, 85. Cor. III, 1, 270. *all to n.* (when all is staked to nothing) Ant. II, 3, 37. *a woman's nay doth stand for n.* Pilgr. 340 (is not meant in earnest). *it was not she that called him all to n.* Ven. 993 (= good for nothing, naughty).

2) naughty, worthless, wicked (usually spelt *naught*): *if I do not carve most curiously, say my knife's n.* Ado V, 1, 157. *the mustard was n.* As I, 2, 68. 69. *in respect that it is a shepherd's life it is n.* III, 2, 15. *his title was corrupt and n.* H5 I, 2, 73. *he that doth n. with her,* R3 I, 1, 99. (the play) *is n.* H8 Epil. 5. *all forsworn, all n., all dissemblers,* Rom. III, 2, 87. *n. that I am,* Mcb. IV, 3, 225. *you are n.* Hml. III, 2, 157. *thy sister's n.* Lr. II, 4, 136. *all's but n.* Ant. IV, 15, 78. *she was n.* Cymb. V, 5, 271. Substantively: *a paramour is, God bless us, a thing of n.* Mids. IV, 2, 14 (a naughty, wicked thing. Flute's speech).

3) lost, ruined: *thy fortune might happily have proved far worse than his. What, worse than n.?* H6B III, 1, 307. *away! all will be n. else,* Cor. III, 1, 231. *n., n., all n.* Ant. III, 10, 1. *be n. awhile* = the devil take you! As I, 1, 39. Substantively, = ruin, perdition: *all will come to n.* R3 III, 6, 13. *this great world shall so wear out to n.* Lr. IV, 6, 138.

**Naughtily,** wickedly, lasciviously: *come again into my chamber: you smile and mock at me, as if I meant n.* Troil. IV, 2, 38 (cf. *naughty* in Meas. II, 1, 77).

**Naughty,** bad, wicked, good for nothing: *a n. house,* Meas. II, 1, 77. *thou n. varlet,* Ado IV, 2, 74. *this n. man,* V, 1, 306. *these n. times,* Merch. III, 2, 18. *thou n. gaoler,* III, 3, 9. *so shines a good deed in a n. world,* V, 91. *a good drum, but a n. orator,* All's V, 3, 254. *thou n. varlet,* H4A II, 4, 474. *a sort of n. persons,* H6B II, 1, 167. *whiles he lived upon this n. earth,* H8 V, 1, 139. *you n. mocking uncle,* Troil. IV, 2, 26. *a n. man,* 34. *thou n. knave,* Caes. I, 1, 16. *'tis a n. night to swim in,* Lr. III, 4, 116. *n. lady,* III, 7, 37.

**Navarre,** a kingdom between France and Spain: LLL I, 1, 12. 222. II, 90. = king of N.: II, 7. 22. 81. 89. 227. 230.

**Nave,** 1) navel: *he unseamed him from the n. to the chaps,* Mcb. I, 2, 22.

2) the middle part of a wheel, in which the spokes are inserted: Hml. II, 2, 518. Quibbling with *knave: would not this n. of a wheel have his ears cut off?* H4B II, 4, 278 (with allusion to Falstaff's roundness).

**Navel,** the centre: *when the n. of the state was touched,* Cor. III, 1, 123.

**Navigation,** voyages by sea: *though the yesty waves confound and swallow n. up,* Mcb. IV, 1, 54.

**Navy,** a fleet: H4B IV, 4, 5. H5 III Chor. 18. R3 IV, 4, 434. 523. H8 III, 2, 383. Ant. II, 6, 20. III, 5, 20. III, 13, 12. 170. IV, 3, 10.

**Nay,** no: *there a n. is placed without remove,* Pilgr. 256. *say thee n.* 318. *a woman's n.* 340. *I say n. to that,* Err. V, 371. *by yea and n.* LLL I, 1, 54. *dares not answer n.* Mids. III, 1, 136. *past all saying n.* Merch. III, 2, 232. *said him n.* John I, 275. *you'll say a beggar n.* R3 III, 1, 119. III, 7, 51. 53. Rom. II, 2, 96.

Used, not simply to deny or refuse, but to reprove, to correct, or to amplify that which has been said before: *n., good, be patient,* Tp. I, 1, 16. *n., good my lord, be not angry,* II, 1, 186. *n., give me not the boots,* Gent. I, 1, 27. *n., now you are too flat,* I, 2, 93. *n., would I were so angered with the same,* 104. *n. then, no matter,* III, 1, 58. *n., hear me,* Meas. III, 1, 148. *n., if there be no remedy ....,* III, 2, 1 etc. *n., that I can deny,* Gent. I, 1, 84. *n., in that you are astray,* 109. 111. 135. *without you? n., that's certain,* II, 1, 37. *n., take them,* 130. *what are you reasoning? N., I was rhyming,* 149. *the tide is now: n., not thy tide of tears,* II, 2, 14. *n., I'll show you the manner of it,* II, 3, 15. *n., that cannot be so,* 18. II, 4, 92. II, 7, 63. *n., but I know 'tis so,* Meas. I, 2, 67. *n., but I bar to-night,* Merch. II, 2, 208. *n., n., Octavia, not only that,* Ant. III, 4, 1 etc. *than you shall find many, n. almost any,* Tp. III, 3, 34. *we are betrothed, n. more,* Gent. II, 4, 179. Err. I, 1, 16. *a wolf, n. worse, a fellow all in buff,* IV, 2, 36. *n., he's a thief too,* 59. *a critic, n. a night-watch constable,* LLL III, 178. *to strike me, spurn me, n. to kill me too,* Mids. III, 2, 313. R3 III, 5, 85. Merch. III, 5, 33 etc. etc.

**Nayward;** *to the n.* = towards nay, towards a negative: *you would believe my saying, howe'er you lean to the n.* Wint. II, 1, 64 (i. e. however you are a lover of contradiction).

**Nayword,** a watch-word: *in any case have a n.* Wiv. II, 2, 131. V, 2, 5. In Tw. II, 3, 146 O. Edd. *an ayword,* most M. Edd. *a n.*\*

**Nazarite,** a native of Nazareth: *your prophet the N.* Merch. I, 3, 35 (Shylock's speech).

**Ne,** nor: *my maiden's name seared otherwise, ne worse of worst extended, with vilest torture let my life be ended,* All's II, 1, 176 (differently and very unhappily corrected by M. Edd. cf. *Extend*). *all perishen of man, of pelf, ne aught escapen but himself,* Per. II Prol. 36.

**Neaf** or **Neif,** fist: *give me your n.* Mids. IV, 1, 20 (Bottom's speech). *I kiss thy n.* H4B II, 4, 200 (Pistol's speech).

**Neapolitan,** native of Naples; subst.: Tp. I, 2, 161. II, 2, 117. Merch. I, 2, 63. Shr. I, 1, 210. H6B V, 1, 117. Adj.: Merch. I, 2, 43. In Troil. II, 3, 20 Ff *the bone-ache,* Qq *the N. bone-ache.*

**Near,** adj. and adv. 1) nigh, not far, at a short distance; of place: *come a little —er,* Wiv. II, 2, 47. *how n. is he?* IV, 2, 39. *a' must shoot —er,* LLL IV, 1, 136. *approach not n.* Mids. II, 2, 22. *a neighbour and n. bred,* Merch. II, 1, 3. *every country far and n.* H6A V, 4, 3. *a —er way* (= a shorter way) R3 IV, 4, 462. *to catch the —est way,* Mcb. I, 5, 19 etc. etc. With *to: to this troop come thou not n.* Phoen. 8. *draw n. to me,* Err. V, 12. *n. to her bower,* Mids. III, 2, 7. *n. to the walls,* H6A II, 1, 3. *n. to the town of Leicester,* R3 V, 2, 12. *your ladyship is —er to heaven than when I saw you last,* Hml. II, 2, 445 (Ff *—er heaven*). *I am n. to the place,* Cymb. IV, 1, 1. *on the mountains n. to Milford,* V, 5, 281 etc. With a noun without *to: do so n. the bottom run,* Tp. II, 1, 227. *we now are n. his cell,* IV, 195. *come not n. her,* Err. IV, 3, 58. IV, 4, 109. Mids. II, 2, 12. 136. V, 170. Merch. III, 4, 80. IV, 1, 233. 254 (—est). As I, 3, 46. III, 5, 32. All's I, 3, 110. H6B I, 3, 144 etc. etc.

Peculiar use: *come n. the house, I pray you,* = enter the house, come in: Wiv. I, 4, 140. *let not that doctor e'er come n. my house,* Merch. V, 223. *pray you,*

N 761

come n. (= come in, go in) Wiv. III, 3, 159. *please you, draw n.* (enter the cell) Tp. V, 318. *will you draw n.?* All's III, 2, 101. *pray, draw n.* Tim. II, 2, 46. *pray you, walk n.; I'll speak with you anon,* 132 (cf. *Approach*).

Used of time: *dreading the winter's n.* Sonn. 97, 14. *when their deaths be n.* 140, 7. *and very n. upon the duke is entering,* Meas. IV, 6, 14 (cf. *Upon*). *that ever may be n.* As III, 5, 28 etc. With *to: I cannot give guess how n. to day,* Caes. II, 1, 3. Without *to: is't n. dinner-time?* Gent. I, 2, 67. *she is very n. her hour,* Meas. II, 2, 16. IV, 2, 97. *thy conceit is —er death than thy powers,* As II, 6, 8. *it is not yet n. day,* R3 V, 3, 220 etc.

2) approaching to, up to, not very short of the thing in question: *how n. the god drew to the complexion of a goose,* Wiv. V, 5, 8. *it draws something n. to the speech we had to such a purpose,* Meas. I, 2, 79. *this comes too n. the praising of myself,* Merch. III, 4, 22. *by the n. guess of my memory,* I, 3, 55. *your coming before me is —er to his* (our father's) *reverence,* As I, 1, 54. *as n. as I could sift him on that argument,* R2 I, 1, 12. *tell me their words as n. as thou canst guess them,* H6C IV, 1, 90. *I aimed so n.* Rom. I, 1, 211. *what things in the world canst thou —est compare to thy flatterers?* Tim. IV, 3, 319. 320. Hence = resembling, like: *he so n. to Hermione hath done Hermione,* Wint. V, 2, 109. *comes it not something n.?* V, 3, 23. And = nearly, almost, within a little: *since I am n. slain, kill me outright with looks and rid my pain,* Sonn. 139, 13. *whose contents shall witness to him I am n. at home,* Meas. IV, 3, 99. *n. twenty years ago,* Shr. IV, 4, 4. *to go n.* = to be like, or to have like: *it will go n. to remove his fit,* Tp. II, 2, 78. *it will go n. to be thought so shortly,* Ado IV, 2, 24. *the death of a dear friend would go n. to make a man look sad,* Mids. V, 294. *there be some women . . . would have gone n. to fall in love with him,* As III, 5, 125. *you shall go n. to call them both a pair of crafty knaves,* H6B I, 2, 102.

3) attached by the ties of blood, or of affection and confidence: *for thee watch I whilst thou dost wake elsewhere, from me far off, with others all too n.* Sonn. 61, 14. *n. allied unto the duke,* Gent. IV, 1, 49. *done my adieu with his* (the duke's) *—est,* All's IV, 3, 101. *my —est of kin,* Wint. III, 2, 54. *my —est and dearest enemy,* H4A III, 2, 123. *n. kinsman unto Charles,* H6A V, 5, 45. *—er in bloody thoughts, but not in blood,* R3 II, 1, 92. *emulation now, who shall be —est,* II, 3, 25. *you and he are n. in love,* III, 4, 14. *I will have none so n. else,* H8 II, 2, 135. *sons, kinsmen, thanes, and you whose places are the —est,* Mcb. I, 4, 36. *who, being born your vassal, am something —er,* Cymb. V, 5, 114. With *to: I love the king and what is —est to him,* Wint. IV, 4, 533. *the lady Blanche is n. to England,* John II, 424 (M. Edd. *niece*). *n. to the king in blood and n. in love,* R2 III, 1, 17. *you twain are n. to Warwick by blood and by alliance,* H6C IV, 1, 136. *I have often wished myself poorer, that I might come —er to you,* Tim. I, 2, 105. *murder's as n. to lust as flame to smoke,* Per. I, 1, 138. With an accus. without *to: a scandalous breath to fall on him so n. us,* Meas. V, 123. *you are very n. my brother in his love,* Ado II, 1, 169. *the son of the king —est his father,* H4B II, 2, 130. *this Percy was the man — est my soul,* III, 1, 61. *I would humour his men with the imputation of*

being n. their master, V, 1, 81. *he is n. you in descent,* H6B III, 1, 21. *a man of his place, and so n. our favour,* H8 V, 2, 30.

4) touching, interesting one's intellect or feelings, coming home to one: *some affairs that touch me n.* Gent. III, 1, 60. *I have heard herself come thus n.* Tw. II, 5, 29. *when his holy state is touched so n.* H6A III, 1, 58. *will touch us all too n.* R3 II, 3, 26. *to touch his growth —er than he touched mine,* II, 4, 25. *Ely with Richmond troubles me more n.* IV, 3, 49. *what —er debt in all humanity than wife is to the husband?* Troil. II, 2, 175. *it does concern you n.* Tim. I, 2, 183. *which many my n. occasions did urge me to put off,* III, 6, 11. *every minute of his being thrusts against my —est of life,* Mcb. III, 1, 118. *touch me not so n.* Oth. II, 3, 220. With *to: whose love of either to myself was —er?* Lucr. 1165. *the —est things to my heart,* Wint. I, 2, 236. With an accus.: *no grief did ever come so n. thy heart,* Gent. IV, 3, 19. *if you do love Rosalind so n. the heart,* As V, 2, 68. *our nearness to the king in love is n. the hate of those love not the king,* R2 II, 2, 128. *do you come n. me now?* Tw. III, 4, 71. *you come n. me now,* H4A I, 2, 14. *so n. mine honour,* H8 III, 1, 71. *am I come n. ye now?* Rom. I, 5, 22. *if it touch not you, it comes n. nobody,* Oth. IV, 1, 210. *they are not n. my conscience,* Hml. V, 2, 58.

5) near, the form of the positive, by contraction for *nearer: nor n. nor farther off,* R2 III, 2, 64 (here the suffix *er* may be considered as belonging to both adverbs). *better far off than n., being ne'er the n.* V, 1, 88 (i. e. being not nearer for being at a small distance). *the n. in blood, the —er bloody,* Mcb. II, 3, 146 (perhaps positive).

**Near-legged,** knock-kneed: Shr. III, 2, 57 (O. Edd. *neere leg'd.* Some M. Edd. *ne'er-legged before,* i. e. foundered in his forefeet, having, as the jockeys term it, never a fore leg to stand on).

**Nearly,** 1) at or to a small distance: *I doubt some danger does approach you n.* Mcb. IV, 2, 67.

2) in a manner approaching to, not falling short of, what is proposed: *as n. as I may, I'll play the penitent to you,* Ant. II, 2, 91 (i. e. as much like a real penitent as it is consistent with my dignity).

3) intimately, pressingly: *a loss in love that touches me more n.* Sonn. 42, 4. *some confidence that decerns you n.* Ado III, 5, 4. *something n. that concerns yourselves,* Mids. I, 1, 126. *what most n. appertains to us both,* Lr. I, 1, 287.

**Nearness,** close alliance by blood or affection: *such neighbour n. to our sacred blood should nothing privilege him,* R2 I, 1, 119. *our n. to the king in love is near the hate of those love not the king,* II, 2, 127.

**Neat,** subst. horned cattle: *the steer, the heifer and the calf are all called n.* Wint. I, 2, 125. *a lion in a herd of n.* H6C II, 1, 14. *what say you to a —'s foot?* Shr. IV, 3, 17. *you dried —'s tongue,* H4A II, 4, 271. Merch. I, 1, 112. *—'s leather,* Tp. II, 2, 73. Caes. I, 1, 29.*

**Neat,** adj. 1) nice, delicate, pretty: *a knight well-spoken, n. and fine,* Gent. I, 2, 10. *is all ready, and all things n.?* Shr. IV, 1, 117. *we must be n.; not n., but cleanly,* Wint. I, 2, 123. *wherein n. and cleanly,* H4A II, 4, 502. *sluttery to such n. excellence opposed,* Cymb. I, 6, 44. *his n. cookery,* IV, 2, 49.

2) spruce, finical, foppish: *a certain lord, n. and*

*trimly dressed,* H4A I, 3, 33. *you n. slave, strike,* Lr. II, 2, 45.

**Neat-herd,** a cow-keeper: Wint. IV, 4, 332. Cymb. I, 1, 149.

**Neatly,** nicely, sprucely: *wearing his apparel n.* All's IV, 3, 168.

**Neb,** the bill of a bird: *how she holds up the n., the bill to him,* Wint. I, 2, 183.

**Nebour,** the usual pronunciation of *neighbour,* blamed by Holofernes: LLL V, 1, 25.

**Nebuchadnezzar,** writing of M. Edd. for *Nabuchadnezzar,* q. v.

**Necessaries,** things indispensable, whether to a certain purpose: *we have culled such n. as are behoveful for our state to-morrow,* Rom. IV, 3, 7. or in daily use: *linens, stuffs and n.* Tp. I, 2, 164. *to safeguard n.* H5 I, 2, 176 (= provisions). = luggage: Gent. II, 4, 188. Hml. I, 3, 1. Oth. II, 1, 292.

**Necessarily,** by unavoidable consequence: Ado II, 3, 201.

**Necessary,** 1) indispensably requisite, needful: *dispossessing all my other parts of n. fitness,* Meas. II, 4, 23. *a harmless, n. cat,* Merch. IV, 1, 55. *a nimble hand is n. for a cutpurse,* Wint. IV, 4, 686. 804. H4A I, 2, 215. H8 I, 2, 77. Troil. III, 3, 230. Cor. II, 1, 91. Caes. II, 1, 178. Hml. III, 2, 47. Lr. IV, 3, 7. Ant. V, 2, 50. Followed by a subjunctive: *it is n. that he keep his vow,* H5 IV, 7, 146. *it were but n. you were waked,* H6B III, 2, 261. By *should:* *'tis n. he should die,* Tim. III, 5, 2.

2) unavoidable: *nor gives to n. wrinkles place,* Sonn. 108, 11. *as horns are odious, they are n.* As III, 3, 52. *by the n. form of this King Richard might create a perfect guess that great Northumberland.... would grow to a greater falsehood,* H4B III, 1, 87. *death, a n. end,* Caes. II, 2, 36. *most n. 'tis that we forget to pay ourselves what to ourselves is debt,* Hml. III, 2, 202.

**Necessitied,** with *to,* = driven by want to, wanting: *I bade her, if her fortunes ever stood n. to help, that by this token I would relieve her,* All's V, 3, 85.

**Necessity,** 1) that which must be, unavoidableness: *to make a virtue of n.* Gent. IV, 1, 62. *she must lie here on mere n.* LLL I, 1, 149. 150. 155. *there is no virtue like n.* R2 I, 3, 278. *one of these two must be —es,* Wint. IV, 4, 38. *thou must think there's a n. in it,* 649. *are these things then —es? then let us meet them like —es,* H4B III, 1, 92. 93. *n. commands me name myself,* Cor. IV, 5, 62. *as if we were villains by n.* Lr. I, 2, 132 (Ff on n.). *such a n. in his death,* Oth. IV, 2, 247. *you could not lack ... very n. of this thought,* Ant. II, 2, 58. *the time, which drives o'er your content these strong —es,* III, 6, 83. *of n.* = necessarily: *he that so generally is at all times good must of n. hold his virtue to you,* All's I, 1, 9.

2) indispensableness, cogency, imperative exigency: *it shall bite upon my n.* Wiv. II, 1, 136. *hiding mine honour in my n.* II, 2, 25. *the fairest grant is the n.* Ado I, 1, 319. *this imposition, the which my love and some n. now lays upon you,* Merch. III, 4, 34. *were there n. in your request,* Wint. I, 2, 22. *yet that is but a crushed n.* H5 I, 2, 175. *his legs are legs for n.* Troil. II, 3, 114. *urged extremely for it and showed what n. belonged to it,* Tim. III, 2, 14. *nature must obey n.* Caes. IV, 3, 227. *n., of matter beggared, will nothing stick our person to arraign,* Hml. IV, 5, 92. *that then*

*n. will call discreet proceeding,* Lr. I, 4, 232. *for n. of present life I must show out a flag and sign of love,* Oth. I, 1, 156. *the strong n. of time commands our services awhile,* Ant. I, 3, 42. With *of:* *there's no further n. of qualities can make her be refused,* Per. IV, 2, 53. Plur. *—es* = absolute wants, imperative demands: *I'll do the service of a younger man in all your business and —es,* As II, 3, 55. *their more mature dignities and royal —es made separation of their society,* Wint. I, 1, 28. *construe the times to their —es,* H4B IV, 1, 104. H8 V, 1, 2. Cor. III, 1, 147. Tim. IV, 3, 377. Caes. IV, 3, 165.

3) extreme indigence, distress, want of what is needed (personified as masc. in R2 V, 1, 21): *I'll rather dwell in my n.* Merch. I, 3, 156. *nor shalt not (eat) till n. be served,* As II, 7, 89. *my n. makes me to ask you for my purse,* Tw. III, 4, 368. *leaving his friend here in n.* 422. *teach thy n. to reason thus,* R2 I, 3, 277. *I am sworn brother to grim n.* V, 1, 21. *n. so bowed the state,* H4B III, 1, 73. *God comfort him in this n.* H6A IV, 3, 15. *deceit bred by n.* H6C III, 3, 68. *urge the n. and state of times,* R3 IV, 4, 416. *some good n. touches his friend,* Tim. II, 2, 236. *had his n. made use of me,* III, 2, 89. *—'s sharp pinch,* Lr. II, 4, 214. *the art of our —es is strange, that can make vile things precious,* III, 2, 70. *till he hath passed n.* Per. II Prol. 6. *in like n.... may defend thee,* II, 1, 134.

**Neck,** the part of the body which connects the head and the trunk: Ven. 99. 539. 592. 627. Tp. I, 2, 461. Meas. III, 2, 42. Err. III, 2, 148. V, 10. 258. Ado II, 1, 196. LLL IV, 1, 114. Mids. III, 1, 38. As I, 2, 131. III, 2, 192. III, 5, 5. Shr. IV, 1, 16. Tw. I, 5, 267. Wint. V, 2, 37. R2 II, 2, 74. V, 2, 19. H5 III, 4, 35. IV, 1, 120. H6A II, 5, 37. H6B III, 2, 106. Troil. III, 3, 223. Cor. II, 1, 43. 167. 225. Tit. IV, 4, 49. Rom. I, 1, 5. I, 4, 82. Caes. V, 1, 44. Mcb. IV, 3, 153. Hml. III, 4, 185. Lr. II, 4, 8. Ant. III, 13, 130. 161. IV, 8, 14. IV, 14, 74. Cymb. V, 4, 173. V, 5, 364. *to break a person's n.,* in a literal sense, or generally = to destroy: LLL IV, 1, 59. As I, 1, 153. R2 V, 5, 88. H6A IV, 4, 91. Troil. III, 3, 259. IV, 2, 79. V, 4, 34 (*a plague break thy n.*). Cor. III, 3, 30. IV, 7, 25. V, 4, 37. Tit. V, 1, 132. Hml. III, 4, 196. Lr II, 4, 74. *to hang about a person's n.:* Merch. II, 2, 14. Shr. II, 310. Wint. I, 2, 308. V, 3, 112. H5 V, 2, 190. H8 II, 2, 33. *to hang on one's n.:* H4B II, 3, 44. *he took the bride about the n.* Shr. III, 2, 179. *she falls me thus about my n.* Oth. IV, 1, 140. *he fastened on my n.* Lr. V, 3, 212. *hang him with his pen and ink-horn about his n.* H6B IV, 2, 117. *be hanged with your pardons about your —s,* IV, 8, 23. *with halters on their —s,* IV, 9, 11. *over Suffolk's n. he threw his wounded arm,* H5 IV, 6, 24. *I'll give thee this n.* = I'll be hanged: H4A II, 1, 68. *let his n. answer for it,* H5 IV, 8, 45. *on the n. of* or *in the n. of* = immediately after: *a thousand groans, one on another's n.* Sonn. 131, 11. *and in the n. of that, tasked the whole state,* H4A IV, 3, 92. *on the n. of* = by the ruin of: *many so arrive at second masters upon their first lord's n.* Tim. IV, 3, 513; cf. *now Margaret's curse falls heavy on my n.* R3 V, 1, 25 (Qq *is fallen upon my head*). *to lay on the n. of* = to lay to the charge of: *men must lay their murders on your n.* Oth. V, 2, 170. Used to express submission by receiving a yoke or any token of servility: Ado I, 1, 203. Tw. II, 5, 205. R2 III, 1, 19.

H6A II, 3, 64. H6B I, 2, 65. H6C III, 3, 16. R3 IV, 4, 111. Cor. I, 3, 50. Cymb. III, 3, 92.

**Necklace**, a string of beads worn on the neck: Wint. IV, 4, 224.

**Nectar**, the drink of the gods; any pleasant liquor: Ven. 572. Gent. II, 4, 171. Troil. III, 2, 23.

**Ned**, diminutive of Edward: H4A I, 2, 123. II, 2, 63. 78. 115. II, 4, 1 etc. H4B II, 2, 150. 173. 196. H6C V, 4, 19. V, 5, 51. V, 7, 16. R3 IV, 4, 146.

**Nedar**, name in Mids. I, 1, 107. IV, 1, 135.

**Need**, subst. 1) occasion for something, want, exigency: *'tis more than n.* LLL IV, 3, 289 and John I, 179 (= there is the most urgent occasion for it; it is absolutely necessary). *the very stream of his life must upon a warranted n. give him a better proclamation*, Meas. III, 2, 152 (on need of a warrant; when a warrant is needed). *what apology you think may make it probable n.* All's II, 4, 52. *my appointments have in them a n. greater than shows itself*, II, 5, 72. *most opportune to our n. I have a vessel*, Wint. IV, 4, 511. *I would your spirit were ... stronger for your n.* 517. *the Lady Constance speaks not from her faith, but from her n.* John III, 1, 211. *whom he hath used rather for sport than n.* V, 2, 175. *never so few, and never yet more n.* H4B I, 1, 215. *if n. were*, R3 III, 7, 166. *what's the n.?* H8 II, 4, 2. *there is no n.* Rom. III, 1, 10. *this same thought did but forerun my n.* V, 1, 53. *immediate are my —s*, Tim. II, 1, 25. *the present n. speaks to atone you*, Ant. II, 2, 101. *O reason not the n.* Lr. II, 4, 267. *Almost* = business: *effected many nicer —s*, All's IV, 3, 105. *for a n.* = in case of necessity: *with five hundred, for a n.* H6C I, 2, 67. *nay, for a n., thus far come near my person*, R3 III, 5, 85. *you could, for a n., study a speech*, Hml. II, 2, 566 (Qq *for n.*). *to have n.:* Shr. I, 1, 215. All's II, 7, 169. H6A I, 1, 157. H6B IV, 2, 8. Tit. IV, 2, 15. Rom. IV, 3, 13. *to have n. of* a person or a thing: Gent. IV, 4, 69. Wiv. III, 3, 193. Ado III, 3, 121. Wint. IV, 2, 13. IV, 3, 57. H4A III, 2, 3. R3 I, 3, 76. 77. Troil. IV, 4, 23. Rom. IV, 3, 3. Tim. I, 2, 100. Mcb. II, 2, 32. Ant. III, 11, 10. *n. of any engine*, Tp. II, 1, 161. *our great n. of him*, Caes. I, 3, 161. *there is no n. of:* Ado III, 3, 22. H4B IV, 1, 97. R3 III, 7, 165. *of posting is no n.* Sonn. 51, 4. *what I stand in n. of*, Gent. II, 7, 84. *God send me no n. of thee*, Rom. III, 1, 8. Followed by an inf. with *to: I have no n. to beg*, R2 IV, 309. *there was no n. to trouble himself with such thoughts*, H5 II, 3, 22. H6B IV, 2, 3. R3 II, 1, 36. Rom. I, 3, 33. Hml. II, 2, 3. Lr. I, 2, 34. I, 4, 211. Cymb. II, 3, 67. Without *to: thou hadst n. send for more money*, Tw. II. 3, 199 (= thou wouldst do well, thou hadst better). *captains had n. look to't*, H4B II, 4, 163. *we had n. pray, and heartily, for our deliverance*, H8 II, 2, 45. *he had n. mean better than his outward show can speak in his commend*, Per. II, 2, 48. cf. *so had you n.* As II, 7, 169 (= you do well). H6A I, 1, 157. H6B IV, 2, 8.

2) indigence, distress, extremity: *he will help thee in thy n.* Pilgr. 424. *your n. to sustain*, Tw. IV, 2, 135. *forced by n. and accident*, Wint. V, 1, 92. *tread down my n.* John III, 1, 215. *we did it for pure n.* H6B II, 1, 157. *in thy n. such comfort come to thee*, H6C I, 4, 165. *lest in our n. he might infect another*, V, 4, 46. *which in his greatest n. will shrink from him*, R3 V, 2, 21. *n. and oppression starveth in thine eyes*, Rom. V, 1, 70. Hml. I, 5, 180. Lr. II, 4, 273. Cymb. III, 6, 13. V, 3, 45.

**Need**, vb. (3 d. pers. pres. *needs; need* only in Gent. II, 1, 158. III, 1, 311. 314. Err. III, 2, 15. Ado I, 1, 318. H4A III, 3, 17. H4B I, 3, 78. IV, 1, 114. H6B IV, 2, 64; never when governing an accusative. In Lr. II, 4, 266 Ff. *n.*, Qq —*s*. —*eth* in Lucr. 31. Impf. —*ed:* Shr. IV, 3, 8. Lr. I, 2, 32. Partic. —*ed:* Mcb. V, 3, 33. Partic. and gerund —*ing:* Sonn. 118, 8. Pilgr. 268). 1) to want, to lack, to require; absol.: *it flows over on all that n.* Ant. V, 2, 25. With an accus.: *truth —s no colour*, Sonn. 101, 6. *that you did painting n.* 83, 1. *nor n. I tallies*, 122, 10. —*s no defence*, Pilgr. 110. *if you should n. a pin*, Meas. II, 2, 45. LLL II, 14. IV, 3, 239. 269. V, 2, 21. Mids. V, 363. Merch. I, 3, 115. As Epil. 4. Shr. V, 1, 4. 25. Wint. II, 1, 155. 189. John IV, 2, 179. R2 III, 2, 176. V, 6, 38. H4A I, 3, 20. II, 2, 74. III, 1, 88. V, 3, 35. V, 4, 10. H4B I, 2, 87. II, 2, 112. H6A V, 1, 191. H6B I, 2, 100. I, 3, 153. H6C V, 4, 49. R3 I, 4, 224. III, 2, 115. H8 V, 4, 45. Troil. I, 2, 93. Cor. II, 3, 209. IV, 5, 248. V, 1, 34. Tit. I, 299. Rom. III, 5, 176. IV, 3, 6. V, 1, 50. Tim. I, 1, 101. I, 2, 70. Caes. II, 1, 123. 136. III, 2, 51. Mcb. III, 3, 2 (*he —s not our mistrust* = we n. not mistrust him). V, 1, 82. V, 3, 33. Hml. III, 2, 217. IV, 2, 21. Lr. II, 1, 117. II, 4, 264. 269. IV, 1, 81. Oth. III, 1, 51. Ant. III, 13, 49. 50. Cymb. II, 4, 66. Per. III, 3, 23. V, 1, 259.

Followed by an inf. with or without *to: I was as virtuously given as a gentleman n. to be*, H4A III, 3, 17. *what thing, in honour, had my father lost, that n. to be revived and breathed in me?* H4B IV, 1, 114. *you n. but plead your honourable privilege*, All's IV, 5, 95. *thou —est but keep that countenance*, Cymb. III, 4, 14. Everywhere else negatively; with *to:* then *n. I not to fear the worst*, Sonn. 92, 5. Wiv. II, 2, 132. Meas. II, 1, 247. Mids. V, 364. Shr. I, 1, 61. All's III, 5, 27. 31. IV, 3, 309. V, 2, 11. Tw. I, 5, 6. Wint. IV, 4, 426. R2 III, 4, 17. H4B III, 2, 125. Rom. III, 5, 16. Per. I, 3, 11. *what n. I my body to anatomize?* H4B Ind. 20. *what —s your grace to be protector?* H6B I, 3, 121. *what shall I n. to draw my sword?* H4A I, 3, 34. Without *to: you n. not fear*, Ven. 1083. *I n. not fear to die*, Lucr. 1052. Tp. III, 3, 43. Gent. I, 3, 17. II, 4, 85. III, 1, 314. Meas. I, 1, 64. I, 2, 111. Err. III, 2, 187. LLL IV, 3, 201. Merch. I, 2, 109. III, 5, 33. All's II, 3, 225. Wint. II, 2, 58. R2 II, 3, 81. H4A IV, 4, 21. H4B I, 3, 78. H5 IV, 7, 118. H6A V, 2, 17. V, 3, 105. H6B IV, 2, 64. H6C V, 4, 70. R3 III, 1, 148. Cor. I, 1, 45. III, 3, 76. IV, 6, 1. Tim. III, 4, 39. III, 6, 83. Hml. III, 1, 187. *what —est thou wound with cunning?* Sonn. 139, 7. *what n. a man care for a stock?* Gent. III, 1, 311. Wiv. V, 5, 202. Err. III, 2, 15. Wint. II, 1, 161. John IV, 1, 76. H4A V, 1, 129. H8 II, 4, 127. Troil. III, 2, 42. Tim. I, 2, 99. Mcb. IV, 1, 82. V, 1, 42. Per. I, 4, 77. II Prol. 16. An inf. understood, not expressed: *what n. she?* (viz write) Gent. II, 1, 158. *she —s not*, V, 2, 21. Wiv. I, 4, 91. John III, 1, 320. H5 III, 7, 118. H6C I, 2, 65. Caes. II, 1, 279.

Followed by a clause: *who never —ed that I should entreat*, Shr. IV, 3, 8.

By *of: we n. no more of your advice*, Wint. II, 1, 168. *what should you n. of more?* Lr. II, 4, 241.

2) to want, not to have, to be without: *their gross painting might be better used where cheeks n. blood*, Sonn. 82, 14. *and much I n. to help you, if need were,*

R3 III, 7, 166. —*ing* = wanting: *heart is bleeding, all help* —*ing*, Pilgr. 268.

3) to be wanted, to be requisite, to be necessary: *to be diseased ere that there was true* —*ing*, Sonn. 118, 8. *so much as it* —*s*, Mcb. V, 2, 29. Negatively: *it shall not n.* Err. V, 390. *to prove that true* —*s no more but one tongue*, H4A I, 3, 96. *it* —*s not*, H6C I, 4, 125. *there* —*s no such apology*, R3 III, 7, 104. *there* — *s none*, Tim. I, 2, 18. *there* —*s no ghost*, Hml. I, 5, 125. *what* —*s a second striking?* Ven. 250. *what — eth then apologies be made?* Lucr. 31. *what* —*s your mum?* Wiv. V, 2, 9. *what* —*s all that?* Err. III, 1, 60. *what n. the bridge much broader than the flood?* Ado I, 1, 318. *what* —*s these hands?* Wint. II, 3, 127. *what n. these tricks?* Troil. V, 1, 14. *what n. these feasts?* Tim. I, 2, 248. *what* —*ed then that terrible dispatch*, Lr. I, 2, 32. *what n. one?* II, 4, 266 (Qq —*s*). *what* —*s this iteration?* Oth. V, 2, 150. *what* —*s more words?* Ant. II, 7, 132.

**Needer**, one who wants a thing: Cor. IV, 1, 44.

**Needful**, 1) requisite, indispensable, necessary: Meas. I, 3, 20. II, 1, 296. II, 2, 24. II, 3, 9. Ado I, 3, 26. LLL II, 25. All's IV, 3, 93. IV, 4, 3. Wint. I, 2, 23. II, 3, 40. John V, 7, 110. H4A IV, 4, 34. H4B IV, 4, 70. H6A IV, 3, 18. H6C IV, 1, 129. IV, 6, 53. H8 II, 4, 231. Tit. V, 1, 39. Rom. IV, 2, 34. Mcb. V, 8, 71. Hml. I, 1, 173. IV, 7, 79. Lr. II, 1, 129. II, 4, 209. Oth. I, 3, 287. Cymb. IV, 3, 8. Per. V, 3, 68.

2) being in want of something, requiring: *with aid of soldiers to this n. war*, H6C II, 1, 147.

3) urgent, important: *leaves unquestioned matters of n. value*, Meas. I, 1, 56 (wanting to be discussed). *give him from me this most n. scroll*, R3 V, 3, 41 (wanting to be delivered). *to our own selves bend we our n. talk*, Troil. IV, 4, 141.

**Needle**, a small instrument of steel used in sewing and embroidery: Lucr. 317. 319. Mids. III, 2, 204. Shr. II, 25. IV, 3, 121. John V, 2, 157. R2 V, 5, 17. H5 II, 1, 37. Troil. II, 1, 87. Oth. IV, 1, 199. Cymb. I, 3, 19. Per. IV Prol. 23. cf. *Neeld*.

**Needless**, 1) not requisite, unnecessary, superfluous: Meas. V, 92. LLL II, 117. John V, 5, 5. Troil. I, 3, 71. Cor. II, 3, 124. Tim. I, 2, 100.

2) without cogency, without sufficient cause, groundless: *sigh at each his n. heavings*, Wint. II, 3, 35. *pray God I prove a n. coward*, R3 III, 2, 90. *n. diffidences*, Lr. I, 2, 161. *n. jealousy*, Cymb. V, 4, 66.

3) not wanting, having enough: *weeping into the n. stream*, As II, 1, 46.

**Needlework**, embroidery: Shr. II, 356.

**Needly**, needs, absolutely: *if sour woe delights in fellowship and n. will be ranked with other griefs*, Rom. III, 2, 117.

**Needs**, indispensably, absolutely; used only with the verbs *must* and *will*; with *must:* Ven. 759. Sonn. 35, 13. 120, 3. Pilgr. 104. Tp. II, 1, 41. II, 2, 4. III, 3, 4. Gent. II, 4, 188. II, 6, 20. II, 7, 53. Wiv. III, 4, 96. Meas. II, 2, 48. II, 4, 30. V, 123. LLL V, 2, 552. Mids. I, 2, 90. III, 2, 119. Merch. II, 4, 30. III, 4, 14. 18. IV, 1, 205. Shr. V, 2, 88. Wint. IV, 4, 498. H6B IV, 2, 58. H6C II, 3, 5. IV, 3, 42. 58. Ant. III, 7, 11 etc. With *will:* Ven. 673. Compl. 167. Tp. I, 2, 108. Meas. III, 2, 2. Ado I, 1, 202. All's I, 3, 22. H4B I, 2, 242. IV, 5, 96. H6B IV, 8, 22. R3 III, 1, 141. Hml. III, 1, 143. IV, 5, 3. Oth. I, 3, 359. With *would:* Sonn. 153, 10. Wiv. III, 3, 94. H8 II, 2, 133.

**Needy**, 1) very poor, indigent: Sonn. 66, 3. Err. V, 240. H6B III, 1, 116. Rom. V, 1, 42. 54. *joy comes well in such a n. time*, Rom. III, 5, 106 (= void of joys).

2) needful, requisite: *stored with corn to make your n. bread*, Per. I, 4, 95 (or = the bread of your need, the bread relieving your distress?).

**Neeld**, a needle; substituted, for the sake of the metre, by some M. Edd. for *needle* of O. Edd. in Lucr. 319. Mids. III, 2, 204. John V, 2, 157. Per. IV Prol. 23. In Per. V Prol. 5 Ff *needle*, Qq *neele*.

**Ne'er**, see *Never*.

**Ne'er-changing**, immutable: *n. night*, R3 II, 2, 46 (Qq *perpetual rest*).

**Ne'er-cloying**, never causing satiety: *your n. sweetness*, Sonn. 118, 5.

**Ne'er-legged**, see *Near-legged*.

**Ne'er-lust-wearied** (O. Edd. *ne'er lust-wearied*), never surfeited with lust: Ant. II, 1, 38.

**Ne'ertheless**, not the less for it, notwithstanding, all the same: Shr. I, 1, 77. Troil. II, 2, 189.

**Ne'er-touched**, inviolate, chaste: *the n. vestal*, Ant. III, 12, 31.

**Ne'er-yet-beaten**, as yet unconquered: Ant. III, 1, 33.

**Neeze**, to sneeze: Mids. II, 1, 56.

**Negation**, declaration that something is not; denial: Troil. V, 2, 127.

**Negative**, subst. a word that denies: *if your four* —*s make your two affirmatives*, Tw. V, 24.

**Negative**, adj. denying: *or else be impudently n.* Wint. I, 2, 274.

**Neglect**, subst. 1) want of care shown by not doing what ought to be done: *which, out of my n., was never done*, Gent. V, 4, 90. *we may (escape), if not through your n.* H6B V, 2, 80. *fines for your n.* H8 V, 4, 84. Per. III, 3, 20 (Qq *neglection*).

2) omission of attention, disregard: *how with my n. I do dispense*, Sonn. 112, 12. *thrown into n. the pompous court*, As V, 4, 188. *nor construe any further my n.* Caes. I, 2, 45. *from their coldest n.* Lr. I, 1, 257. *I have perceived a most faint n.* I, 4, 73. With *of:* thy *n. of truth*, Sonn. 101, 2. *my n. of his dreadful might*, LLL III, 204.

**Neglect**, vb. 1) to pay no attention to, to leave undone or unnoticed: *her* —*ed child holds her in chase*, Sonn. 143, 5. —*ing worldly ends*, Tp. I, 2, 89. *if thou* —*st what I command*, 368. *n. my studies*, Gent. I, 1, 67. *she did n. her looking-glass*, IV, 4, 157. *the drowsy and* —*ed act*, Meas. I, 2, 174. *for your fair sakes have we* —*ed time*, LLL V, 2, 765. *lose and n. the creeping hours of time*, As II, 7, 112. *a beard* —*ed*, III, 2, 395. —*ed my sworn duty*, R2 I, 1, 134. *the means that heaven yields must be embraced, and not* —*ed*, III, 2, 30. *we must n. our holy purpose*, H4A I, 1, 101. *if once it (the opportunity) be* —*ed*, H6A V, 4, 157. *I hope, my absence doth n. no great designs*, R3 III, 4, 25. *n. the visitation of my friends*, III, 7, 107 (Ff deferred). *the* —*ing it may do some danger*, Rom. V, 2, 19. *our* —*ed tribute*, Hml. III, 1, 178. *and both n.* III, 3, 43. *infirmity doth still n. all office*, Lr. II, 4, 107. —*ing an attempt of ease and gain*, Oth. I, 3, 29. —*ed rather*, Ant. II, 2, 89. *jewels lose their glory if* —*ed*, Per. II, 2, 12.

2) to disregard, not to treat with due honour, to set at nought, to slight: *his honour, his affairs, his*

*friends, his state, —ed all*, Lucr. 46. *we do n. the thing we have*, 152. *I conjure thee that thou n. me not*, Meas. V, 50. *n. me, lose me*, Mids. II, 1, 206. *wherefore do you n. them?* Wint. IV, 4, 86. *he loves thee, and thou doest n. him*, H4B IV, 4, 21. *the fatal and —ed English*, H5 II, 4, 13. *what infinite heart's ease must kings n.* IV, 1, 254. *strangely —ed* (peers) H8 III, 2, 11. *n. him not*, 421. *the specialty of rule hath been —ed*, Troil. I, 3, 78. *—ed love*, Hml. III, 1, 186. *that so —ed you*, Oth. V, 1, 95.

**Neglectingly**, slightingly: *answered n. I know not what*, H4A I, 3, 52.

**Neglection**, want of care, disregard: *sleeping n. doth betray to loss the conquest of our scarce cold conqueror*, H6A IV, 3, 49. *if n. should therein make me vile*, Per. III, 3, 20 (Ff *neglect*). With *of: this n. of degree*, Troil. I, 3, 127.

**Negligence**, 1) want of care and attention: Lucr. 1278. Compl. 35. Mids. III, 2, 345. Tw. I, 4, 5. III, 4, 280. Wint. I, 2, 252. 257. H8 III, 2, 213. Troil. V, 6, 17. Lr. I, 3, 12. III, 1, 32. Oth. I, 1, 76.. III, 3, 311. Cymb. I, 1, 66.

2) disregard, slight, contempt: *both the worlds I give to n., let come what comes; only I'll be revenged*, Hml. IV, 5, 134.

**Negligent**, wanting care and attention: LLL III, 36. Wint. I, 2, 247. 250. 255. H6A IV, 2, 44. Troil. III, 3, 41. Ant. III, 7, 26. *till we perceived, both how you were wrong led, and we in n. danger*, III, 6, 81 (= a danger of negligence, i. e. a danger arising from our continued negligence).

**Negotiate**, to hold intercourse by way of transacting business: *let every eye n. for itself and trust no agent*, Ado II, 1, 185. *have you any commission from your lord to n. with my face?* Tw. I, 5, 250.

**Negotiation**, treaty of business: Troil. III, 3, 24.

**Negro**, a female blackamoor: *the getting up of the —'s belly*, Merch. III, 5, 42.

**Neif**, see *Neaf*.

**Neigh**, subst. the cry of a horse: H5 III, 7, 29. IV Chor. 10. Ant. III, 6, 45.

**Neigh**, vb. to utter the voice of a horse: Ven. 262. 265. Sonn. 51, 11. Mids. II, 1, 46. III, 1, 113. Merch. V, 73. Shr. I, 2, 207. H4B IV, 1, 119. Caes. II, 2, 23. Oth. III, 3, 351. Ant. I, 5, 49. Cymb. IV, 4, 17. With *to:* Ven. 307. Oth. I, 1, 112. With *for:* our steeds for present service n.* H5 IV, 2, 8 (express their desire for combat by neighing).

**Neighbour**, subst. 1) one who lives near another: Ado V, 2, 79. LLL V, 1, 25. V, 2, 586. Mids. V, 209. Shr. II, 336. All's III, 5, 15. Wint. I, 2, 195. 196. IV, 2, 45. H4B II, 4, 80. Cymb. I, 4, 134. With *to: the sun, to whom I am a n.* Merch. II, 1, 3.

2) one who lives in an adjacent country: *what think you of the Scottish lord, his n.?* Merch. I, 2, 84. *though France himself and such another n. stand in our way*, H5 III, 6, 166. *our —s, the upper Germany*, H8 V, 3, 29. *a giddy n. to us*, H5 I, 2, 145.

3) one who is standing or sitting near another: *his nose being shadowed by his —'s ear*, Lucr. 1416. *and this my n. too?* Wint. IV, 4, 381. *our bad n. makes us early stirrers*, H5 IV, 1, 6 (i. e. the enemy). *can any of your —s tell?* V, 2, 208. *cheer your —s*, H8 I, 4, 41.

4) one who lives in familiarity with another: *all my —s shall cry aim*, Wiv. III, 2, 45. *the more the pity*

*that some honest —s will not make them friends*, Mids. III, 1, 149. *made her —s believe she wept for the death of a third husband*, Merch. III, 1, 10. *will on the vigil feast his —s*, H5 IV, 3, 45. *sing the merry songs of peace to all his —s*, H8 V, 5, 36. With *to:* *Buckingham no more shall be the n. to my counsel*, R3 IV, 2, 43. Used as a term of familiar address: Ado III, 3, 7. 13. 93. 97. III, 5, 2. 19. 20. 39. 45. V, 1, 336. Shr. II, 39. 40. 76. 401. III, 2, 248. H4A II, 1, 49. II, 2, 82. H4B II, 4, 94. H6B II, 3, 59. 63. 65. R3 II, 3, 1. 6. Cor. I, 1, 63. IV, 6, 20. 24. Caes. I, 2, 231. Per. III, 2, 107.

5) a countryman: *civil wounds ploughed up with —s' sword*, R2 I, 3, 128. *we will home to Rome and die among our —s*, Cor. V, 3, 173.

6) a fellow-creature: *when such a one as she such is her n.* As II, 7, 78. *your wife's wit going to your —'s bed*, IV, 1, 170. *lie with his —'s wife*, R3 I, 4, 141.

**Neighbour**, adj. being in the vicinity: *the n. caves*, Ven. 830. *a n. thicket*, LLL V, 2, 94. *bottom*, As IV, 3, 79. *such n. nearness to our blood*, R2 I, 1, 119. *confines*, H4B IV, 5, 124. *air*, Rom. II, 6, 27. *states*, Tim. IV, 3, 94. *room*, Hml. III, 4, 212. *shepherd*, Cymb. I, 1, 150.

**Neighbour**, vb. 1) intr. to be near, to be in the vicinity: *a copse that —s by*, Ven. 259. Partic. *—ing* adjectively: *all —ing languages* All's IV, 1, 18. *tenants, friends and —ing gentlemen*, H4A III, 1, 90. *—ing ponds*, Cymb. I, 4, 97. *our —ing shore*, Per. I, 4, 60. *some —ing nation*, 65.

2) trans. to be near, to adjoin, to be at the side of: *thy places shall still n. mine*, Wint. I, 2, 449. *wholesome berries ripen best —ed by fruit of baser quality*, H5 I, 1, 62.

**Neighboured**, adj. near intimate, familiar: *so n. to his youth and haviour*, Hml. II, 2, 12. *shall to my bosom be as well n., pitied and relieved*, Lr. I, 1, 121.

**Neighbourhood**, 1) an adjacent country with its inhabitants: *trembled at the ill n.* H5 I, 2, 154.

2) friendly terms, amicableness: *plant n. and Christian-like accord in their sweet bosoms*, H5 V, 2, 381. *domestic awe, night-rest and n.* Tim. IV, 1, 17.

**Neighbouring**, see *Neighbour*, vb.

**Neighbourly**, becoming a neighbour, friendly, kind: *a n. charity*, Merch. I, 2, 85. *is not that n.?* As III, 5, 90.

**Neighbour-stained**, stained by the blood of countrymen: *this n. steel*, Rom. I, 1, 89.

**Neither**, 1) not either, none of two: *n. may possess the claim they lay*, Lucr. 1794. *where n. party is nor true nor kind*, Compl. 186. *excellent in n.* Pilgr. 102. *good night, good rest. Ah, n. be my share*, 181. *to themselves yet either n.* Phoen. 43. Wiv. IV, 6, 15. Err. III, 1, 67. LLL V, 2, 459 (*n. of either*). 822. Merch. V, 103. As I, 2, 283. All's III, 2, 52. John V, 2, 163. R2 III, 4, 12. H5 II, 2, 136. H6C II, 5, 12. R3 I, 1, 113. Lr. I, 1, 6. Ant. III, 2, 50 etc. etc. The verb sometimes following in the plural: *say that he or we, as n. have, received that sum*, LLL II, 133. *Thersites' body is as good as Ajax', when n. are alive*, Cymb. IV, 2, 253. cf. also Pilgr. 181.

Correlative to *nor* (in this case sometimes monosyllable: Merch. I, 1, 178. H6A V, 1, 59. H6C I, 1, 199): *n. eyes nor ears*, Ven. 437. *n. red nor pale,*

Lucr. 1510. Sonn. 16, 11. 86, 7. Pilgr. 86. Tp. II, 2, 18. Gent. III, 1, 70. Meas. II, 2, 50. Err. II, 1, 1. II, 2, 49. III, 1, 66. V, 215. Ado I, 1, 232. LLL I, 2, 119. Merch. I, 1, 178. H6C I, 1, 45. 199 etc. *that's n. here nor there*, Wiv. I, 4, 112 (cf. *Here*). More than two things thus joined: *n. sad, nor sick, nor merry, nor well*, Ado II, 1, 303. *I should n. sell, nor give, nor lose it*, Merch. IV, 1, 443. *I have n. wit nor words nor worth, action, nor utterance, nor the power of speech*, Caes. III, 2, 225 etc. Usually *nor* placed only before the last: *n. sting, knot, nor confine*, Compl. 265. *n. bended knees, pure hands held up, sad sighs, deep groans, nor silver-shedding tears*, Gent. III, 1, 229. *thou hast n. heat, affection, limb, nor beauty*, Meas. III, 1, 37. *n. my coat, integrity, nor persuasion*, IV, 2, 204. *n. maid, widow, nor wife*, V, 177. *n. savouring of poetry, wit, nor invention*, LLL IV, 2, 165. *he hath n. Latin, French, nor Italian*, Merch. I, 2, 74. *n. call the giddiness of it in question, the poverty of her, the small acquaintance, my sudden wooing, nor her sudden consenting*, As V, 2, 6. *has n. leg, hands, lip, nor cap*, All's II, 2, 11. *n. in estate, years, nor wit*, Tw. I, 3, 116. *n. pity, love, nor fear*, H6C V, 6, 68. *n. mother, wife, nor England's queen*, R3 I, 3, 209. *you know n. me, yourselves, nor any thing*, Cor. II, 1, 75 etc. *Neither* omitted: *he, nor that affable familiar ghost*, Sonn. 86, 9. *but my five wits nor my five senses can dissuade one foolish heart from serving thee*, 141, 9. *then, nor now*, Meas. III, 2, 86 (look for more instances sub *Nor*). *Nor* omitted: *n. press, coffer, chest, trunk, well, vault, but he hath an abstract*, Wiv. IV, 2, 62. Or for *nor*: *n. in time, matter, or other circumstance*, Meas. IV, 2, 108. *n. in birth or for authority, the bishop will be overborne by thee*, H6A V, 1, 59. *Coriolanus n. to care whether they love or hate him*, Cor. II, 2, 13. Lr. III, 3, 6 (Qq *nor*).

2) as little, likewise not: *shall she marry him? No. How then? shall he marry her? No, n.* Gent. II, 5, 18. *Valentine? No. Who then? his spirit? N.* III, 1, 196. *which of you saw Sir Eglamour of late? Not I. Nor I. Saw you my daughter? N.* V, 2, 33. *a widow, then. N.* Meas. V, 176. *good people, enter and lay hold on him. No, not a creature enters in my house. Then let your servants bring my husband forth.* N. Err. V, 94. *you know me well. I never saw you in my life. Dost thou not know my voice? N.* 301. *not sad, my lord. How then, sick? N., my lord*, Ado II, 1, 302. *wouldst thou have thy head broken? No. Then be still. N.* H4A III, 1, 245 etc. Double negative: *we'll not run. Nor go n.* Tp. III, 2, 22. *that cannot be so n.* Gent. II, 3, 18. *I care not for that n.* III, 1, 345. *my brows become nothing else, nor that well n.* Wiv. III, 3, 64. Ado II, 1, 323. II, 3, 98. LLL I, 1, 294. IV, 3, 191. V, 1, 158. Merch. I, 1, 47. I, 3, 167. As I, 2, 30. All's II, 1, 94. Tw. II, 5, 203. Caes. I, 2, 238. Oth. V, 2, 243. Ant. V, 2, 51 etc.

Hence = nor: *n. do I labour for a greater esteem*, As V, 2, 61. *n. allied to eminent assistants*, H8 I, 1, 61. *many dream not to find, n. deserve, and yet are steeped in favours*, Cymb. V, 4, 130.

3) Following a negative by way of enforcing it (almost = nevertheless, for all that): *you'll lie like dogs and yet say nothing n.* Tp. III, 2, 23. *and I paid nothing for it n.* Wiv. IV, 5, 63. *I will physic your rankness, and yet give no thousand crowns n.* As I, 1, 93. *let it live. It shall not n.* Wint. II, 3, 158. Simi-

larly after *but*: *the body of your discourse is sometime guarded with fragments, and the guards are but slightly basted on n.* Ado I, 1, 290. *and that is but a kind of bastard hope n.* Merch. III, 5, 9. *it must be an answer of most monstrous size that must fit all demands. But a trifle n.* All's II, 2, 36. *Not so n.* = by no means: *but art not thou thyself giddy with the fashion too, that thou hast shifted out of thy tale into telling me of the fashion? Not so n.* Ado III, 3, 153 *thou art as wise as thou art beautiful. Not so n.* Mids. III, 1, 152 (or = the one as little as the other?). Cor. IV, 5, 175.

**Nell,** diminutive of Eleanor and of Helen: Err. III, 2, 111. H4B II, 2, 140. H5 II, 1, 20. 33. V, 1, 86 (O. Edd. *Doll*). H6B I, 2, 17. 59. II, 4, 10. 26. 58. 67. 74. III, 2, 26 (M. Edd. *Meg*). Troil. III, 1, 56. 150. Rom. I, 5, 11.

**Nemean,** native of Nemea in Argolis: *the N. lion*, LLL IV, 1, 90. Hml. I, 4, 83.

**Nemesis,** the goddess of retributing justice: H6A IV, 7, 78.

**Neoptolemus,** the son of Achilles; somewhat confusedly mentioned in Troil. IV, 5, 142.*

**Nephew,** 1) the son of a brother or sister: Gent. I, 3, 3. Ado V, 1, 297. Merch. I, 2, 91. Tw. V, 66. John I, 15. H4A I, 3, 138. V, 1, 85. V, 2, 1. 16. 47. H5 IV, 8, 81. H6A II, 5, 17. 33. 36. 55. H6B I, 1, 104. I, 2, 20. H6C V, 7, 27. R3 V, 3, 154. H8 II, 2, 26. IV, 2, 110. Tit. I, 172. 356. 376. 480. III, 1, 173. V, 2, 122. Rom. I, 1, 112. Hml. I, 2, 30. II, 2, 62. III, 2, 254. IV, 4, 14.

2) Used with some latitude; = cousin: *Henry the Fourth deposed his n. Richard*, H6A II, 5, 64. Troil. I, 2, 13 (cf. IV, 5, 120). = grandchild: *you'll have your —s neigh to you*, Oth. I, 1, 112.

**Neptune,** the god of the ocean and the seas: Wint. IV, 4, 28. Troil. V, 2, 174. Cor. III, 1, 256. Mcb. II, 2, 60. Hml. I, 1, 119. Ant. II, 7, 139. Cymb. III, 1, 19. Per. V Prol. 17. V, 1, 17. = the sea: *the fire and cracks of sulphurous roaring the most mighty N. seem to besiege*, Tp. I, 2, 204. *chase the ebbing N.* V, 35. *sat with me on —'s yellow sands*, Mids. II, 1, 126. III, 2, 392. Wint. V, 1, 154. John V, 2, 34. R2 II, 1, 63. H4B III, 1, 51. Troil. I, 3, 45. Tim. V, 4, 78. Hml. III, 2, 166. Ant. IV, 14, 58. Per. III Prol. 45. III, 3, 36.

**Nereides** (quadrisyll.) sea-nymphs: Ant. II, 2, 211.

**Nerissa,** female name in Merch. I, 2, 1 etc.

**Nero,** the notorious Roman emperor who set Rome on fire and killed his own mother: John V, 2, 152. H6A I, 4, 95. H6C III, 1, 40. Hml. III, 2, 412. Lr. III, 6, 7.

**Nerve,** that in which the strength of a body lies, rather = sinew, tendon, than an organ of sensation and motion: *needs must I under my transgression bow, unless my —s were brass*, Sonn. 120, 4. *thy —s are in their infancy again and have no vigour in them*, Tp. I, 2, 484. *the strongest —s and small inferior veins from me receive that natural competency*, Cor. I, 1, 142. *my firm —s shall never tremble*, Mcb. III, 4, 102. *makes each petty artery in this body as hardy as the Nemean lion's n.* Hml. I, 4, 83. *a brain that nourishes our —s, and can get goal for goal of youth*, Ant. IV, 8, 21. *strains his young —s and puts himself in posture*, Cymb. III, 3, 94. Metaphorically: *those that know the very —s of state*, Meas. I, 4, 53. *thou great commander, n. and bone of Greece*, Troil. I, 3, 55.

**Nervii**, a people of ancient Gaul: Caes. III, 2, 177.

**Nervy**, sinewy, vigorous: *death in his n. arm doth lie*, Cor. II, 1, 177.

**Nessus**, name of the Centaur who attempted to ravish Deianira and then persuaded her to dye the garment of Hercules with his blood: All's IV, 3, 281. Ant. IV, 12, 43.

**Nest**, 1) the bed formed by a bird for incubation and feeding its young: Ven. 532. Lucr. 849. 1611. Phoen. 56. Tp. II, 2, 173. Err. IV, 2, 27. Ado II, 1, 230. 238. As IV, 1, 208 (allusion to the proverb: *it is a foul bird that defiles her own nest*) All's IV, 3, 319. John V, 2, 150. H4A V, 1, 61. H5 I, 2, 170. H6C II, 2, 31. R3 I, 3, 270. IV, 4, 424. Tit. II, 3, 154. Rom. II, 5, 76. Mcb. IV, 2, 11. Ant. IV, 12, 4. Cymb. III, 3, 28. III, 4, 142.

2) the place where some insects breed: *a wasps' n.* Wint. IV, 4, 814. *a scorpion's n.* H6B III, 2, 86.

3) any place of abode: *see here the tainture of thy n.* H6B II, 1, 188. Used of a grave: *to inter his noble nephew here in virtue's n.* Tit. I, 376. *come from that n. of death*, Rom. V, 3, 151.

4) a pack, a faction: *a n. of traitors*, Wint. II, 3, 81. *France hath in thee found out a n. of hollow bosoms*, H5 II Chor. 21.

**Nestor**, 1) the oldest and wisest hero before Troy: Lucr. 1401. 1420. LLL IV, 3, 169. Merch. I, 1, 56. H6C III, 2, 188. Troil. I, 3, 32 etc. 2) Name of·an attendant of Pericles: Per. III, 1, 66.

**Nestor-like**, like Nestor: H6A II, 5, 6.

**Net**, a texture used to catch fish, birds, and other animals: Ven. 67. Ado II, 3, 221 (*spread*). H6C I, 4, 62. H8 I, 1, 203. Tit. IV, 3, 7. Rom. I, 2, 42. Mcb. IV, 2, 34. Oth. II, 3, 367. Per. I, 1, 40. II, 1, 13. 98. 123. Peculiar use: *and rather choose to hide them in a n. than amply to imbar their crooked titles*, H5 I, 2, 93 (= intricacy).

**Nether**, lower, opposed to upper: *I'll sew n. stocks*, H4A II, 4, 130 (i. e. stockings, Fr. bas-de-chausses). Lr. II, 4, 11. *thy n. lip*, H4A II, 4, 447. Oth. IV, 3, 40. V, 2, 43. *our n. crimes*, Lr. IV, 2, 79 (committed on earth).

**Netherlands**, the Low - Countries: Err. III, 2, 142.

**Nether-stocks**, see *Nether*.

**Nettle**, subst. the plant Urtica urens: Wint. I, 2, 329. R2 III, 2, 18. H4A II, 3, 10. H5 I, 1, 60. Troil. I, 2,191. Cor. II, 1,207. Tit. II, 3, 272. Hml. IV, 7, 170. Lr. IV, 4, 4. Oth. I, 3,325. In Tw. II, 5, 17 the later Ff n., F1 *mettle*, i. e. metal, q. v.

**Nettled**, stung as with nettles, fretted, irritated: H4A I, 3, 240. H6C III, 3, 169.

**Nettle-seed**, seed of the nettle: Tp. II, 1, 144.

**Neuter**, taking no part in a contest: *I do remain as n.* R2 II, 3, 159.

**Neutral**, the same: *loyal and n. in a moment*, Mcb. II, 3, 115. *which came from one that's of a n. heart*, Lr. III, 7, 48. Substantively: *like a n. to his will and matter*, Hml. II, 2, 503.

**Never**, 1) not ever, at no time: Ven. 17. 48. 81. 91. 126. 376. 377. 408. 420. 480. 489. 506. 548. 617. 708. 846. 1042. 1098. 1119 etc. etc. *n. is my day*, Troil. IV, 5, 52 (cf. the Germ. *Nimmertag*). *n. more* = no more in future, never again: *mine appetite I n. more will grind on newer proof*, Sonn, 110, 10. *and*

*n. more abase our sight so low*, H6B I, 2, 15. *but n. more be officer of mine*, Oth. II, 3, 249. Contracted to *ne'er*: Ven. 99. 974. 1107. 1139. Sonn. 17, 8. Pilgr. 238. Tp. II, 1, 111. III, 3, 26. IV, 76. Gent. IV, 4, 65. Wiv. I, 1, 186. Meas. III, 1, 143. V, 184. Err. III, 1, 45. III, 2, 182. V, 48. 210 etc. (As for the use of the indef. article, see *A*).

Compounds (not hyphened in most O. Edd.): *n. conquered*, Lucr. 482. *n. daunted*, H4B I, 1, 110. *n. dying*, H4A III, 2,106. *n. ending*, Lucr. 935. *n. heard of*, Tit. II, 3, 285. *n. quenching*, R2 V, 5, 109. *n. resting*, Sonn. 5, 5. *n. surfeited*, Tp. III, 3, 55. *n. withering*, Cymb. V, 4, 98.

*Never so* or *ne'er so* = more than ever, in the highest degree: *n. so weary, n. so in woe, I can no further crawl, no further go*, Mids. III, 2, 442. (cf. *this so never needed help*, Cor. V, 1, 34). Especially in conditional and concessive sentences; a) *never so: who would give a bird the lie, though he cry cuckoo n. so?* Mids. III, 1, 139. *if thou dost intend n. so little show of love to her, thou shalt aby it*, III, 2, 334. *be his cause n. so spotless*, H5 IV, 1, 167. *new customs, though they be n. so ridiculous, are followed*, H8 I, 3, 3. b) *ne'er so: though n. so black, say they have angels' faces*, Gent. III, 1, 103. *if it be n. so false, a true gentleman may swear it*, Wint. V, 2, 175. *creep time n. so slow, yet it shall come*, John III, 3, 31. *wilt know again, being n. so little urged, another way to pluck him from the usurped throne*, R2 V, 1, 64. *who, n. so tame, will have a wild trick*, H4A V, 2, 10. *be he n. so vile*, H5 IV, 3, 62. *your grudge will out, though n. so cunningly you smother it*, H6A IV, 1, 110. *it shall be so, disdain they n. so much*, V, 3, 98. *I must ever doubt, though n. so sure*, Tim. IV, 3, 514 (cf. *where it draws blood no cataplasm so rare can save the thing from death*, Hml. IV, 7, 144).

2) = not, emphatically; a) *never: forced to content, but n. to obey*, Ven. 61. *n. say that I was false of heart*, Sonn. 109, 1. *then n. dream on infamy, but go*, Gent. II, 7, 64. *where your good word cannot advantage him, your slander n. can endamage him*, III, 2, 43. *n. a woman in Windsor knows more of Anne's mind*, Wiv. I, 4, 135. *n. stand 'you had rather'*, III, 3, 133. *he would n. else cross me thus*, V, 5, 40. *I can n. cut off a woman's head*, Meas. IV, 2, 5. *n. crave him*, V, 432. *let us dine and n. fret*, Err. II, 1, 6. *n. lay thy hand upon thy sword*, Ado V, 1, 54. *n. fleer and jest at me*, 58. *n. paint me now*, LLL IV, 1, 16. *I n. may believe these antique fables*, Mids. V, 2. *n. excuse*, 363. *and n. stays to greet him*, As II, 1, 54. *n. talk to me*, III, 4, 1. *n. make denial*, Shr. II, 281. *his father n. was so true begot*, John II, 130. *I'll be damned for n. a king's son in Christendom*, H4A I, 2, 109. *hast thou n. an eye in thy head?* II, 1, 31. *n. fear me*, IV, 2, 64. H4B I, 1, 54. II, 2, 62. H6B II, 3, 78. III, 2, 215. R3 III, 4, 53. H8 Prol. 22. Troil. IV, 5, 199. V, 10, 2. Tim. V, 1, 96 etc. b) *ne'er: n. repent it, if it were done so*, Gent. IV, 1, 30. *I'll n. put my finger in the fire*, Wiv. I, 4, 90. *hath your grace n. a brother like you?* Ado II, 1, 336. *swear me to this, and I will n. say no*, LLL I, 1, 69. *I have n. a tongue in my head*, Merch. II, 2, 166. *with many vows of faith, and n. a true one*, V, 20. *n. a fantastical knave of them all shalt flout me out of my calling*, As III, 3, 107. *n. a whit*, Shr. I, 1, 240. *with n. a tooth in her head*, I, 2, 80. H4A II, 1, 19. H6A I, 2, 120. H6B II, 4, 72. Troil.

I, 2, 264. Mcb. IV, 3, 208. Hml. I, 5, 123. Ant. I, 4, 43 etc.

Followed by a comparative: *I like it never the better for that*, Wiv. II, 1, 186. *I will love thee ne'er the less*, Shr. I, 1, 77 (cf. *Ne'ertheless*). *better far off than near be ne'er the near*, R2 V, 1, 88 (= not the nearer for being near). *when our throats are cut, he may be ransomed, and we ne'er the wiser*, H5 IV, 1, 206.

**Nevil**, family name of the Earls of Salisbury and Warwick: H4B III, 1, 66. H6B I, 1, 240. I, 3, 76. II, 2, 8. 80. III, 2, 215. IV, 1, 91. V, 1, 202.

**New**, adj. 1) lately made or come into being, recent in origin, novel, fresh: *of the —est Poor-John*, Tp. II, 2, 28. *a n. jerkin*, Wiv. I, 3, 18. *a n. doublet*, III, 3, 35. *fresh and n.* IV, 5, 9. *a n. doublet*, Ado II, 3, 19. *coat*, III, 2, 7. *tire*, III, 4, 13. *nuts*, Mids. IV, 1, 40. *ribbons*, IV, 2, 37. *liveries*, Merch. II, 2, 117. *fustian*, Shr. IV, 1, 49. *map*, Tw. III, 2, 85. *a fine n. prince*, Wint. II, 1, 17. *chimney*, H4A II, 1, 3. *fresh and n.* III, 2, 55. *silk*, H4B I, 2, 222. *petticoat*, II, 2, 89. *link*, V, 1, 23. *snow*, Rom. III, 2, 19. *honours*, Mcb. I, 3, 144. *—est gloss*, I, 7, 34. *n. robes*, II, 4, 38. *this fresh n. sea-farer*, Per. III, 1, 41 etc. etc.

2) lately introduced to our knowledge, unknown before, recently discovered: *what's n. to speak, what n. to register*, Sonn. 108, 3. *thy pyramids built up with —er might*, 123, 2. *O brave n. world*, Tp. V, 183. *'tis n. to thee*, 184. *the remembrance of my former love is by a —er object quite forgotten*, Gent. II, 4, 195. *n. fashion*, LLL I, 1, 165. *all but n. things disdain*, All's I, 2, 61. *what old or —er torture*, Wint. III, 2, 178. *of the —est and finest wear*, IV, 4, 327. *how n. is husband in my mouth*, John III, 1, 305. *so it* (a vanity) *be n.* R2 II, 1, 25. *commit the oldest sins the —est kind of ways*, H4B IV, 5, 127. *n. customs*, H8 I, 3, 2. *opinions*, V, 3, 17. *sect*, 81. *make n. nations*, V, 5, 53. *a n. Gorgon*, Mcb. II, 3, 77 etc.

3) renovated, repaired, additional, repeated: *I will furnish it anon with n. contents*, Tp. II, 2, 146. *a fortnight hold we this solemnity in nightly revels and n. jollity*, Mids. V, 377. *the next n. moon*, I, 1, 83. *there begins n. matter*, As IV, 1, 81. *n. flight*, John V, 4, 60. *with a n. wound in your thigh*, H4A V, 4, 131. *history his loss to n. remembrance*, H4B IV, 1, 204. *n. courage*, H6A III, 3, 87. *to my determined time thou gavest n. date*, IV, 6, 9. *made n. head*, Cor. III, 1, 1. *infuse n. life in me*, Tit. I, 461. *break to n. mutiny*, Rom. Prol. 3. *n. supplies of men*, Mcb. I, 2, 32. *each n. morn*, IV, 3, 4. *n. wars*, Ant. III, 4, 4 etc.

3) recently produced by change, other than before: *to mourn some —er way*, Lucr. 1365. *mine appetite I'll never more will grind on —er proof*, Sonn. 110, 11. *n. faith torn in vowing n. hate after n. love bearing*, 152, 3. 4. *Caliban has a n. master: get a n. man*, Tp. II, 2, 189. *plead a n. state in thy unrivalled merit*, Gent. V, 4, 144. *he hath every month a n. sworn brother*, Ado I, 1, 73. *to seek n. friends*, Mids. I, 1, 219. *try n. master*, Merch. II, 3, 6. II, 4, 18. *seek no n.* (fortune) III, 2, 135. *my n. mistress*, As III, 2, 92. All's II, 3, 258. *a hazard of n. fortunes*, John II, 71. *n. exactions*, R2 II, 1, 249. *as I intend to thrive in this n. world*, IV, 78 (changed by the events lately happened). *n. care won*, 197. *win a n. world's crown*, V, 1, 24. *in this n. spring of time*, V, 2, 50. *God make thee n.* V, 3, 146. *n. broils*, H4A I, 1, 3. *by n. act of parliament*, H6C II, 2, 91. *they have all n. legs*,

*and lame ones*, H8 I, 3, 11. *a n. father*, Mcb. IV, 2, 63. *n. widows*, IV, 3, 5. *a —er friend*, Oth. III, 4, 181.

4) received or instated since a short time: *once more, n. servant, welcome*, Gent. II, 4, 118. *the n. governor*, Meas. I, 2, 161. 169. *the n. gloss of your marriage*, Ado III, 2, 6. *my n. interest here*, Merch. III, 2, 224. *the n. duke*, As I, 1, 105. *my n. mistress*, Shr. IV, 1, 26. *his n. bride*, H6B I, 1, 252. *am become as n. into the world*, Troil. III, 3, 12. *he can report of the revolt the —est state*, Mcb. I, 2, 3. *what's the —est grief*, IV, 3, 174. *here comes —er comfort*, V, 8, 53 etc.

**New**, adv. 1) since a very short time, freshly: *proofs n. bleeding*, Compl. 153. *so they were bleeding n., there's no meat like 'em*, Tim. I, 2, 80. *out of a n. sad soul*, LLL V, 2, 741.

2) so as to restore to a primitive state: *my shame so dead, mine honour is n. born*, Lucr. 1190. *my old age n. born*, 1759. *this were to be n. made when thou art old*, Sonn. 2, 13. *as he takes from you, I engraft you n.* 15, 14. *on Helen's cheek all art of beauty set, and you in Grecian tires are painted n.* 53, 8. *robbing no old to dress his beauty n.* 68, 12. *love's brand n. fired*, 153, 9. *n. dyed*, Tp. II, 1, 63. *mercy then will breathe within your lips, like man n. made*, Meas. II, 2, 79 (i. e. redeemed and regenerated by divine grace. cf. *renewed*, in Sonn. 111, 8). *are you a god? would you create me n.?* Err. III, 2, 39. *a silver bow n. bent in heaven*, Mids. I, 1, 10 (O. Edd. *now bent*). *beauty doth varnish age, as if n. born*, LLL IV, 3, 244. *how much honour picked from the chaff and ruin of the times to be n. varnished*, Merch. II, 9, 49. *furbish n. the name of John of Gaunt*, R2 I, 3, 76. *to line and n. repair our towns of war*, H5 II, 4, 7. *to n. store France with bastard warriors*, III, 5, 31. *a vessel that is n. trimmed*, H8 I, 2, 80. *I feel my heart n. opened*, III, 2, 366. *her ashes n. create another heir*, V, 5, 42. *with a heart n. fired*, Caes. II, 1, 332. *n. added*, IV, 3, 209. *n. built*, Cymb. I, 5, 59. *and shall make your lord, that which he is, n. o'er*, I, 6, 165.

3) in a manner not known before: *to n. found methods and to compounds strange*, Sonn. 76, 4. *all my best is dressing old words n.* 11. *n. fangled ill*, 91, 3. *full of n. found oaths*, Gent. IV, 4, 134. *old Adam n. apparelled*, Err. IV, 3, 14. *in May's n. fangled mirth*, LLL I, 1, 106. *more n. fangled than an ape*, As IV, 1, 152. *so n. a fashioned robe*, John IV, 2, 27. *with n. tuned oaths*, H5 III, 6, 80. *is it his use? or did the letters work upon his blood and n. create this fault?* Oth. IV, 1, 287.

4) in another manner than before: *so love's face may still seem love to me, though altered n.* Sonn. 93, 3. *n. created the creatures that were mine*, Tp. I, 2, 81. *n. formed them*, 83. *you shall be n. christened in the Tower*, R3 I, 1, 50. *I'll be n. baptized*, Rom. II, 2, 50.

5) anew, afresh, again: *his n. appearing sight*, Sonn. 7, 3. *and with old woes n. wail my dear time's waste*, 30, 4. *which I n. pay as if not paid before*, 12. *by n. unfolding his imprisoned pride*, 52, 12. *she was n. lodged*, Compl. 84. *would again betray the forebetrayed, and n. pervert a reconciled maid*, 329. *go back again, and be n. beaten home*, Err. II, 1, 76. *now thou and I are n. in amity*, Mids. IV, 1, 92. *I'll n. woo my queen*, Wint. III, 2, 157. *an ancient tale n. told*, John IV, 2, 18. *before you were n. crowned*, 35. *n. lamenting ancient oversights*, H4B II, 3, 47. *I*

*Richard's body have interred* n. H5 IV, 1, 312. *who set this ancient quarrel* n. *abroach?* Rom. I, 1, 111. *aroused vengeance sets him* n. *at work,* Hml. II, 2, 510.

6) lately, recently, freshly: *n. fallen snow,* Ven. 354. *the* n. *sprung flower,* 1171. *a* n. *killed bird,* Lucr. 457. *lips* n. *waxen pale,* 1663. *where two contracted* n. *come daily to the banks,* Sonn. 56, 10. *till* n. *born chins be rough,* Tp. II, 1, 249. *evils by remissness* n. *conceived,* Meas. II, 2, 96. *this* n. *married man,* V, 405. *my* n. *trothed lord,* Ado III, 1, 38. *a* n. *devised courtesy,* LLL I, 2, 66. *a* n. *crowned monarch,* Merch. III, 2, 50. *a messenger* n. *come from Padua,* IV, 1, 109. *to seal love's bonds* n. *made,* II, 6, 6. *this* n. *fallen dignity,* As V, 4, 182. *as one* n. *risen from a dream,* Shr. IV, 1, 189. *her* n. *built virtue and obedience,* V, 2, 118. *I met with things* n. *born,* Wint. III, 3, 117. *n. made honour doth forget men's names,* John I, 187. *one* n. *burned,* III, 1, 278. *a* n. *untrimmed bride,* 209. *even before this truce, but* n. *before,* 233. *as red as* n. *enkindled fire,* IV, 2, 163. *I am a prophet* n. *inspired,* R2 II, 1, 31. *a gasping* n. *delivered mother,* II, 2, 65. *the* n. *made king,* V, 2, 45. *the* n. *come spring,* 47. *n. lighted from his horse,* H4A I, 1, 63. *his chin* n. *reaped,* I, 3, 34. *your* n. *fallen right,* V, 1, 44. *n. healed wound,* H4B I, 2, 166. *n. dated letters,* IV, 1, 8. *a* n. *married wife,* H5 V, 2, 190. *your honours* n. *begot,* H6A I, 1, 79. *a holy prophetess* n. *risen up,* I, 4, 102. *his* n. *come champion,* II, 2, 20. *a man* n. *haled from the rack,* II, 5, 3. *the* n. *made duke,* H6B I, 1, 109. I, 2, 95. *his* n. *made bride,* H6C III, 3, 207. *n. committed to the bishop of York,* IV, 4, 11. *whiles thy head is warm and* n. *cut off,* V, 1, 55. *the* n. *delivered Hastings,* R3 I, 1, 121. *the* n. *healed wound,* II, 2, 125. *my unblown flowers,* n. *appearing sweets,* IV, 4, 10. *a* n. *ta'en sparrow,* Troil. III, 2, 36. *n. born gawds,* III, 3, 176. *this* n. *made empress,* Tit. II, 1, 20. *n. married ladies,* II, 2, 15. *thy* n. *transformed limbs,* II, 3, 64. *n. shed blood,* 200. *but* n. *struck nine,* Rom. I, 1, 167. *her* n. *beloved,* II Prol. 12 (or adj.?). *a* n. *made grave,* IV, 1, 84. *warm and* n. *killed,* V, 3, 197. *the* n. *made bridegroom,* 235. *n. planted orchards,* Caes. III, 2, 253. *a* n. *born babe,* Mcb. I, 7, 21. *n. hatched,* II, 3, 64. *each* n. *hatched comrade,* Hml. I, 3, 65 (Ff *unhatched*). *n. born babe,* III, 3, 71. *n. lighted,* III, 4, 59. *n. adopted to our hate,* Lr. I, 1, 206. *their precious stones* n. *lost,* V, 3, 190.

Most of the compounds registered below are not hyphened in O. Edd.

**New-added:** Caes. IV, 3, 209.
**New-adopted:** Lr. I, 1, 206.
**New-apparelled:** Err. IV, 3, 14.
**New-appearing:** Sonn. 7, 3. R3 IV, 4, 10.
**New-baptized:** Rom. II, 2, 50.
**New-beaten:** Err. II, 1, 76.
**New-before:** John III, 1, 233.
**New-begot:** H6A I, 1, 79.
**New-beloved:** Rom. II Prol. 12.
**New-bent:** Mids. I, 1, 10 (O. Edd. *now bent*).
**New-bleeding:** Compl. 153.
**New-born:** Lucr. 1190. 1759. Tp. II, 1, 249. LLL IV, 3, 244. Wint. III, 3, 117. Troil. III, 3, 176. Mcb. I, 7, 21. Hml. III, 3, 71.
**New-built:** Shr. V, 2, 118. Cymb. I, 5, 59.
**New-burned:** John III, 1, 278.
**New-christened:** R3 I, 1, 50.

**New-come:** Merch. IV, 1, 109. R2 V, 2, 47. H6A II, 2, 20.
**New-committed:** H6C IV, 4, 11.
**New-conceived:** Meas. II, 2, 96.
**New-create:** Tp. I, 2, 81. H8 V, 5, 42. Oth. IV, 1, 287.
**New-crowned:** Merch. III, 2, 50. John IV, 2, 35.
**New-cut-off:** H6C V, 1, 55.
**New-dated,** of a new date, recently written: *n. letters,* H4B IV, 1, 8.
**New-delivered:** R2 II, 2, 65. R3 I, 1, 121.
**New-devised:** LLL I, 2, 66.
**New-dyed:** Tp. II, 1, 63.
**New-enkindled:** John IV, 2, 163.
**New-fallen:** Ven. 354. As V, 4, 182. H4A V, 1, 44.
**New-fangled,** given to foppish love of fashionable finery: Sonn. 91, 3. LLL I, 1, 106. As IV, 1, 152.
**New-fired:** Sonn. 153, 9. Caes. II, 1, 332.
**New-form:** Tp. I, 2, 83.
**New-found:** Gent. IV, 4, 134. Sonn. 76, 4.
**Newgate,** name of a prison in London: *two and two, N. fashion,* H4A III, 3, 104 (prisoners being fastened two and two together).
**New-haled:** H6A II, 5, 3.
**New-hatched:** Mcb. II, 3, 64. Hml. I, 3, 65 (Ff *unhatched*).
**New-healed:** H4B I, 2, 166. R3 II, 2, 125.
**New-inspired:** R2 II, 1, 31.
**New-killed:** Lucr. 457. Rom. V, 3, 197.
**New-lamenting:** H4B II, 3, 47.
**New-lighted:** H4A I, 1, 63. Hml. III, 4, 59.
**New-lodged:** Compl. 84.
**New-lost:** Lr. V, 3, 190.
**Newly,** 1) in a new manner different from the former: *by deed-achieving honour* n. *named,* Cor. II, 1, 190. *which would be planted* n. *with the time,* Mcb. V, 8, 65.

2) anew, afresh, as in the beginning: *as reproof and reason beat it* (my will) *dead, by thy bright beauty was it* n. *bred,* Lucr. 490. *she was new lodged and* n. *deified,* Compl. 84. *he hath ta'en you* n. *into his grace,* Ado I, 3, 23. *I will have that subject* n. *writ o'er,* LLL I, 2, 120. *the organs ... break up their drowsy grave and* n. *move,* H5 IV, 1, 22.

3) since a very short time, very lately, just now: *as Falstaff, she and I, are* n. *met,* Wiv. IV, 4, 52. *n. in the seat,* Meas. I, 2, 165. *none of Pygmalion's images,* n. *made woman,* III, 2, 48. *friends but* n. *found,* LLL V, 2, 761. *morning roses* n. *washed with dew,* Shr. II, 174. *you are but* n. *come,* IV, 2, 86. *what hath* n. *passed between this youth and me,* Tw. V, 158. *a piece many years in doing and now* n. *performed,* Wint. V, 2, 105. *the statue is but* n. *fixed,* V, 3, 47. *this royal hand and mine are* n. *knit,* John III, 1, 226. *so* n. *joined in love,* 240. *the days but* n. *gone,* H4B IV, 1, 80. *their stings and teeth* n. *ta'en out,* IV, 5, 206. *the Duke of York is* n. *come from Ireland,* H6B IV, 9, 24. *n. preferred from the king's secretary,* H8 IV, 1, 102. *but* n. *planted in your throne,* Tit. I, 444. *who had but* n. *entertained revenge,* Rom. III, 1, 176. *bleeding, warm and* n. *dead,* V, 3, 175. *n. alighted,* Tim. I, 2, 181. *when sects and factions were* n. *born,* III, 5, 30. *here is* n. *come to court Laertes,* Hml. V, 2, 110. *whose breath these hands have* n. *stopped,* Oth. V, 2,

202. *the hated, grown to strength, are n. grown to love,* Ant. I, 3, 49. *three kings I had n. feasted*, II, 2, 76.

**New-made:** Sonn. 2, 13. Meas. II, 2, 79 (see *New*, adv. 2). Merch. II, 6, 6. John I, 187. R2 V, 2, 45. H6B I, 1, 109. I, 2, 95. H6C III, 3, 207. Tit. II, 1, 20. Rom. IV, 1, 84. V, 3, 235.

**New-married:** Meas. V, 405. H5 V, 2, 190. Tit. II, 2, 15.

**Newness,** 1) novelty: *whether it be the fault and glimpse of n.* Meas. I, 2, 162.

2) recentness: *n. of Cloten's death,* Cymb. IV, 4, 9.

3) state differing from the former, change: *new flight, and happy n., that intends old right,* John V, 4, 61.

**New-opened:** H8 III, 2, 366.

**New-pay:** Sonn. 30, 12.

**New-pervert:** Compl. 329.

**New-planted:** Caes. III, 2, 253.

**New-reaped:** H4A I, 3, 34.*

**New-repair:** H5 II, 4, 7.

**New-risen:** Shr. IV, 1, 189. H6A I, 4, 102.

**News** (dissyll. and spelt *newes* in R3 IV, 4, 536; Qq *tidings*), fresh information, tidings: Ven. 658. Lucr. 255. Sonn. 140, 8. Gent. I, 3, 55. III, 1, 205. 284. Meas. III, 2, 86. 90. Ado I, 2, 4. V, 1, 111. LLL II, 255. V, 2, 81. Merch. I, 3, 39. III, 1, 1. III, 2, 241. As I, 1, 102 *(what's the new n.?).* I, 2, 104. Wint. V, 2, 23. H6B I, 1, 237. III, 1, 86. H6C II, 1, 4. Cymb. III, 4, 12 etc. etc. Used as a singular: Tp. V, 221. Gent. I, 1, 58 *(what n. else betideth here).* I, 3, 56. II, 4, 52. Wiv. II, 2, 140. Meas. III, 2, 243. Ado V, 2, 103. LLL V, 2, 726. John III, 1, 164. V, 3, 12. V, 6, 21. R2 III, 1, 74. 82. H4A I, 1, 58. H4B I, 1, 59. IV, 2, 70. IV, 4, 109. H6A V, 3, 167. H6B II, 1, 180. H6C III, 1, 31. Cor. I, 4, 1. Ant. III, 7, 55 etc. As a plural: Gent. III, 1, 289. Ado II, 1, 180. John V, 7, 65. R2 III, 4, 100 (Qq *these n.*, Ff *this n.*). H4A III, 2, 121. H4B I, 1, 137 (Qq *these n.*, Ff *this n.*). IV, 4, 102. H6A I, 1, 67. V, 2, 1. H6B I, 4, 78. III, 2, 380. R3 IV, 4, 536 (Qq *tidings*). H8 II, 2, 39. Oth. II, 2, 7 etc. *what is the n.?* or *what n.?* = what is the matter: Tp. V, 220. Merch. I, 2, 134. Oth. I, 2, 36. *hate me! wherefore? O me! what n., my love?* Mids. III, 2, 272. *what is the n. with you?* or *what n. with you?* = what is the matter with you? what would you have with me? Gent. III, 1, 279. Wiv. III, 3, 23. Meas. I, 2, 86. IV, 3, 44. Mids. I, 1, 21. Merch. II, 4, 9. Shr. IV, 3, 62. John IV, 2, 68. H6B V, 1, 125. R3 IV, 2, 45. IV, 4, 457. Troil. IV, 2, 48. Tit. IV, 4, 61. Hml. I, 2, 42 etc.

**New-sad:** LLL V, 2, 741.

**News-crammed,** stuffed with news to satiety: As I, 2, 101.

**New-shed:** Tit. II, 3, 200.

**News-monger,** talebearer: *by smiling pick-thanks and base —s,* H4A III, 2, 25.

**New-sprung:** Ven. 1171.

**New-store:** H5 III, 5, 31.

**New-struck:** Rom. I, 1, 167.

**Newt,** small lizard: Mids. II, 2, 11. Tim. IV, 3, 182. Mcb. IV, 1, 14. *the wall-n. and the water,* Lr. III, 4, 135.

**New-ta'en:** Troil. II, 2, 36.

**New-told:** John IV, 2, 18.

**New-transformed:** Tit. II, 3, 64.

**New-trimmed:** H8 I, 2, 80.

**New-trothed:** Ado III, 1, 38.

**New-tuned:** H5 III, 6, 80.

**New-unfolding:** Sonn. 52, 12.

**New-untrimmed:** John III, 1, 209 (see Untrimmed).

**New-varnished:** Merch. II, 9, 49.

**New-waxen:** Lucr. 1663.

**New-woo:** Wint. III, 2, 157.

**New-year,** the first day of the year: *a —'s gift,* Wiv. III, 5, 8.

**Next,** adj. 1) nearest, being at the least distance, to be arrived at in the shortest time: *the n. tree,* Tp. III, 2, 40. Mcb. V, 5, 39. *the vicar of the n. village,* As III, 3, 44. *his n. neighbour,* Wint. I, 2, 195. *in the n. room,* R3 I, 4, 161. *in the n. chamber,* H8 I, 4, 102 (= adjoining). *home, home, the n. way,* Wint. III, 3, 129. 131. *'tis the n. way to turn tailor,* H4A III, 1, 264. *I speak the truth the n. way,* All's I, 3, 63 (in a straight-forward way, frankly, openly).

2) immediately following, having no other object of the kind intervening: *the n. advantage will we take throughly,* Tp. III, 3, 13. *the best news is …; the n., our ship is tight and yare,* V, 222. *the n. word that thou speakest,* Gent. III, 1, 237. *what's n.?* 372. *the n. time we have confidence,* Wiv. I, 4, 172. *sleep the sounder all the n. day,* Meas. IV, 3, 50. *the n. morn,* V, 101. *it* (the fashion of his hat) *ever changes with the n. block,* Ado I, 1, 77. *at the n. turning,* II, 1, 160. *n. morning,* III, 3, 171. *upon the n. occasion,* LLL V, 2, 143. *by the n. new moon,* Mids. I, 1, 83. *the n. live creature that it sees,* II, 1, 172. *the n. thing he espies,* 262. *who is n.?* V, 127. *at the n. turning,* Merch. II, 2, 43. *till the n. night,* V, 302. *ere the n. Ascension-day,* John IV, 2, 151. *to-morrow n. we will for Ireland,* R2 II, 1, 217. *on Wednesday n.* IV, 319. *that one day bloomed and fruitful were the n.* H6A I, 6, 7. *in the n. parliament,* II, 4, 117. *n. time,* H6B I, 2, 53. *the n. month,* I, 3, 224. II, 4, 71 etc. etc. With the indef. article: *give me but this* (wife) *I have, and sear up my embracements from a n. with bonds of death,* Cymb. I, 1, 116. *n. day* = the day after to-morrow: *to visit him to-morrow or n. day,* R3 III, 7, 60. *good morrow. Ay, and good n. day too,* Troil. III, 3, 69.

= immediately preceding: *each following day became the n. day's master, till the last made former wonders its,* H8 I, 1, 17.

Substantively: *my n. is 'Most fair Pyramus',* Mids. IV, 1, 206. *hail, noble prince of France! the n. is …,* John V, 2, 69 (cf. Lucr. 1305). *for Humphrey being dead, as he shall be, and Henry put apart, the n. for me,* H6B III, 1, 383 (= what follows, the rest). *bury him, and bury me the n.* Tit. I, 386.

3) nearest in degree or relation: *thou art the n. of blood,* Ven. 1184. H4A I, 3, 146. H6B I, 1, 151. I, 2, 63. *me from myself thy cruel eye hath taken, and my n. self thou harder hast engrossed,* Sonn. 133, 6. *who's the n. heir of Naples?* Tp. II, 1, 245. *I was the n. by birth and parentage,* H6A II, 5, 73.

**Next,** adv. 1) so as to approach nearest in degree: *stood it n. to death,* Gent. V, 4, 41. *before you, and n. unto high heaven, I love your son,* All's I, 3, 199. *n. to thyself and my young rover, he's apparent to my heart,* Wint. I, 2, 176. *n. to whom was John of Gaunt,* H6B II, 2, 13. *which buys a place n. to the king,* H8 I, 1, 66.

2) immediately after, without any other object of the kind intervening: *what impossible matter will he make easy n.?* Tp. II, 1, 89. *the n. ensuing hour,* Gent. II, 2, 11. *what it was that n. came in her eye,* Mids.

Ill, 2, 2. *idly bent on him that enters n.* R2 V, 2, 25. *the thirtieth of May n. ensuing,* H6B I, 1, 49. In enumerations, = secondly: *health to thy person! n. vouchsafe...,* Lucr. 1305. Ant. III, 12, 16. *first ... n.* Meas. V, 108. H6A III, 4, 12. H6B I, 3, 170. *first ... n. ... and last,* Wiv. II, 2, 263. *first ... n. ... and then,* III, 5, 112. *first ... n. ... lastly,* Merch. II, 9, 11.

3) the next time, on the first occasion offering: *I'll make you amends n.* Err. II, 2, 54. *when they n. wake, all this derision shall seem a dream,* Mids. III, 2, 370. *who therewith angry, when it n. came there, took it in snuff,* H4A I, 3, 40. *where is best place to make our battery n.* H6A I, 4, 65. *and so farewell until I meet thee n.* II, 4, 113. *when I did meet thee n.* IV, 1, 14. *come when you are n. prepared for,* Oth. IV, 1, 167.

**Next,** prepos. 1) nearest, close to: *and that a' wears n. his heart,* LLL V, 2, 721. *I have kept you n. my heart,* H8 III, 2, 157.

2) most with the only exception of, second only to, under: *he whom n. thyself of all the world I loved,* Tp. I, 2, 68. *loved him n. heaven,* H8 III, 1, 130. *n. the king he was successive heir,* H6B III, 1, 49.

**Nibble,** to eat in small bits: *—ing sheep,* Tp. IV, 1, 62. *as pigeons bill, so wedlock would be —ing,* As III, 3, 83.

**Nibbler,** one that bites by little, instead of taking a mouthful: *the tender n. would not touch the bait,* Pilgr. 53.

**Nicander,** name in Per. III, 1, 67.

**Nicanor,** name in Cor. IV, 3, 6. 31.

**Nice,** 1) fine, elegant: *despite his n. fence,* Ado V, 1, 75.

2) tender, delicate, dainty: *hence, thou n. crutch,* H4B I, 1, 145.*when mine hours were n. and lucky,* Ant. III, 13, 180.

3) precise, accurate: *the painter was so n.* Lucr. 1412. *to hold your honour more precise and n.* H4B II, 3, 40. *to prenominate in n. conjecture where thou wilt hit me,* Troil. IV, 5, 250. *O relation too n., and yet too true,* Mcb. IV, 3, 174. Hence = precarious: *to set so rich a main on the n. hazard of one doubtful hour,* H4B IV, 1, 48.

4) scrupulous, punctilious, critical: *n. affections wavering stood in doubt if best were as it was, or best without,* Compl. 97. *I am not solely led by n. direction of a maiden's eyes,* Merch. II, 1, 14. *to make n. of* = to be scrupulous about: *he that stands upon a slippery place makes n. of no vile hold to stay him up,* John III, 4, 138.

5) subtile, sophistical: *if you grow so n., metheglin, wort and malmsey,* LLL V, 2, 232. *these n. sharp quillets of the law,* H6A II, 4, 17. *wherefore stand you on n. points?* H6C IV, 7, 58.

6) coy, prudish, delicate to a fault: *she is n. and coy,* Gent. III, 1, 82. *these betray n. wenches, that would be betrayed without these,* LLL III, 24. *we'll not be n.: take hands!* V, 2, 219. *this is the ape of form, monsieur the n.* 325. *sharp occasions, which lay n. manners by,* All's V, 1, 15. *n. customs curtsy to great kings,* H5 V, 2, 293. *upholding the n. fashion of your country in denying me a kiss,* 299.

7) squeamish, not contented with any thing, capricious: *the lady's* (melancholy) *which is n.* As IV, 1, 14. *I am not so n., to change true rules for old inventions,* Shr. III, 1, 80. *n. longing, slanders, mutability,* Cymb. II, 5, 26 (hyphened in O. Edd.).

8) petty, insignificant, trifling: *and between these*

*main parcels of dispatch effected many —r needs,* All's IV, 3, 105. *every idle, n. and wanton reason,* H4B IV, 1, 191. *the respects thereof are n. and trivial,* R3 III, 7, 175. *bethink how n. the quarrel was,* Rom. III, 1, 159. *the letter was not n. but full of charge,* V, 2, 18. *that every n. offence should bear his comment,* Caes. IV, 3, 8. *feed upon such n. and waterish diet,* Oth. III, 3, 15.

**Nice-longing** (not hyphened by M. Edd.), see Nice 7.

**Nicely,** 1) finely, elegantly: *two Cupids ... n. depending on their brands,* Cymb. II, 4, 90.

2) scrupulously, punctiliously: *stretch their duties n.* Lr. II, 2, 110. *what safe and n. I might well delay by rule of knighthood,* V, 3, 144. *let not conscience ... inflame too n.* Per. IV, 1, 6.

3) sophistically, subtilely: *they that dally n. with words may quickly make them wanton,* Tw. III, 1, 17. *can sick men play so n. with their names?* R2 II, 1, 84. *or n. charge your understanding soul with opening titles miscreate,* H5 I, 2, 15. *when articles too n. urged be stood on,* V, 2, 94.

**Nicely-gawded** (not hyphened in O. Edd.), probably = scrupulously treated as a precious thing, carefully guarded and preserved: *our veiled dames commit the war of white and damask in their n. cheeks to the wanton spoil of Phoebus' burning kisses,* Cor. II, 1, 233.

**Niceness,** coyness: *fear and n., the handmaids of all women, or, more truly, woman its pretty self,* Cymb. III, 4, 158.

**Nice-preserved,** coyly guarded: *that n. honesty of yours,* Tit. II, 3, 135.

**Nicety,** coyness: *lay by all n. and prolixious blushes,* Meas. II, 4, 162.

**Nicholas,** name; 1) Saint N., the patron of scholars: *try me in thy paper. There; and Saint N. be thy speed,* Gent. III, 1, 300. *Saint —' clerks* = highwaymen: H4A II, 1, 68. 71. 2) Sir N. Gawsey: H4A V, 4, 45. 58. 3) N. Hopkins: H8 I, 1, 221 (O. Edd. *Michael*). I, 2, 147. 4) Sir N. Vaux: H8 II, 1, 96. 100. 5) a servant in Shr. IV, 1, 92.

**Nick,** diminutive of Nicholas: *N. Bottom,* Mids. I, 2, 18.

**Nick,** subst. *in the n.* = at the right moment: *Iago in the n. came in and satisfied him,* Oth. V, 2, 317 (Ff *interim*). *out of all n.* = excessively: *he loved her out of all n.* Gent. IV, 2, 76.

**Nick,** vb. to cut in notches, to clip, to curtail: *his man with scissors —s him like a fool,* Err. V, 175. *the itch of his affection should not then have —ed his captainship,* Ant. III, 13, 8.

**Nickname,** subst. a name given in derision: Rom. II, 1, 12.

**Nickname,** vb. to name perversely: *you n. virtue; vice you should have spoke,* LLL V, 2, 349. *you lisp, and n. God's creatures,* Hml. III, 1, 151.

**Niece,** the daughter of a brother or sister: Ado I, 1, 34. 46. 61. I, 2, 12. II, 1, 19. II, 3, 93. V, 4, 22 etc. As I, 2, 290. I, 3, 89. V, 4, 153. Tw. I, 3, 1. II, 3, 174 etc. John II, 64. 469. 521. H6C III, 3, 188. Troil. I, 2, 99. 194 etc. Tit. II, 4, 11. 16. III, 1, 138 etc. Rom. I, 2, 70. 72. Oth. V, 2, 201. Per. III, 4, 15. = grand-daughter (cf. *Nephew*): R3 IV, 1, 1.

**Niggard,** subst. a miser: Sonn. 4, 5. H8 I, 1, 70. With *of: why is Time such a n. of hair,* Err. II, 2, 78. *be not a n. of your speech,* Mcb. IV, 3, 180.

**Niggard**, adj. miserly: Lucr. 79. Sonn. 72, 8. Tim. V, 4, 77. With *of*: *n. of question*, Hml. III, 1, 13.

**Niggard**, vb. 1) intr. to be miserly: *makest waste in —ing*, Sonn. I, 12.

2) tr. to supply sparingly: *nature must obey necessity; which we will n. with a little rest*, Caes. IV, 3, 228.

**Niggardly**, adj. miserly: Err. III, 1, 27. Tw. II, 5, 6. H5 II, 4, 46.

**Niggardly**, adv. in the manner of a miser, very sparingly: *every slight occasion that could but n. give me sight of her*, Wiv. II, 2, 205.

**Nigh**, adv. 1) near: *grazed his cattle n.* Compl. 57. *never harm ... come our lovely lady n.* Mids. II, 2, 18. *grapple with him ere he comes so n.* John V, 1, 61. *draw n.* Tit. V, 3, 24. *so n. at least*, Cymb. III, 4, 151. *to be n.*: Ven. 341. 1055. Err. II, 1, 43. Mids. II, 2, 155. Wint. V, 1, 180. H4A IV, 1, 118. H6C II, 2, 56. V, 1, 8. V, 2, 5. Oth. II, 1, 153.

Used as a prepos.: *was not this n. shore?* Tp. I, 2, 216. *which is too n. your person*, Mcb. IV, 2, 72.

2) in a manner touching near, coming home to the heart: *that dost not bite so n. as benefits forgot*, As II, 7, 185.

3) nearly, almost: *n. wrecked upon the sea*, H6B III, 2, 82. *well n. worn to pieces with age*, Wiv. II, 1, 21. *well n. dead for me*, Ado V, 4, 81.

**Night**, the time of darkness between sunset and sunrise: Ven. 122. 154. 531. 583. 717. 727. 841. 847. Lucr. 15. 123. 356 etc. etc. *the n.* = the night-time: *there sleeps Titania some time of the n.* Mids. II, 1, 253. *I have watched the n.* H6B III, 1, 110. *forbear to sleep the n.* R3 IV, 4, 118 (Q1.2. —s). *to walk the n.* Hml. I, 5, 10. See *in the n.* below. *In deep of n.* Wiv. IV, 4, 40. *the dead of n.* Lucr. 162. Tw. I, 5, 290. H4B I, 1, 72. *how goes the n.?* Mcb. II, 1, 1 (= how late is it in the night?). *what is the n.?* in the same sense, Mcb. III, 4, 126. *three —s ago*, John V, 3, 11. *in less than two —s*, Tim. III, 1, 58. *three —s after this*, H8 IV, 2, 25. *day and n.* Ven. 1186. All's V, 1, 1. H4A I, 3, 184. V, 1, 35. H4B V, 5, 21. *by day and n.!* (an oath) H8 I, 2, 213. *O day and n.!* Hml. I, 5, 164. *both day and n.* Tw. V, 99. *days and —s*, Mcb. IV, 1, 7. *day or n.* H6A II, 2, 31. *day nor n.* H6B II, 1, 85. *n. and day*, Troil. III, 2, 122. *nor n. nor day no rest*, Wint. II, 3, 1. *neither n. nor day*, Mcb. I, 3, 19 (rhyming). *n. by n.* H6B III, 1, 111. Rom. I, 4, 70. *good n.!* Ven. 534. 535. 537. Pilgr. 181. Meas. IV, 4, 22. Ado III, 3, 157. Mids. II, 2, 19. Tw. II, 3, 193. H8 V, 1, 54 etc. etc. *many good —s*, H8 V, 1, 55. *good hour of n.* H8 V, 1, 5. *the goodness of the n. upon you*, Oth. I, 2, 35; cf. Meas. IV, 2, 76 and R3 V, 3, 80. *good n.* = farewell for ever, lost for ever: *good n. your vow*, Tp. IV, 54. *good n. to your redress*, Meas. V, 301. *good n. our part*, Shr. II, 303. *and so good n.* Wint. I, 2, 411. *if he fall in, good n.* H4A I, 3, 194. *hath bid the world good n.* R3 IV, 3, 39. *why, then, good n. indeed*, Ant. III, 10, 30. *all n.* (= the whole night) Meas. IV, 3, 47. 49. LLL I, 1, 44. Merch. V, 262. All's IV, 3, 117 etc. *all the n.* Rom. III, 3, 159. *the other n.* (= lately at n.) H4A III, 3, 112. *last n.* Gent. II, 1, 93. Ado IV, 1, 91. 149. All's V, 1, 23. V, 2, 57. Tw. II, 3, 23. II, 4, 3 etc. *this n.* Gent. II, 6, 33. III, 1, 11. III, 2, 89. Ado I, 1, 2. I, 2, 14. Mids. IV, 1, 105. Merch. IV, 1, 403 etc. *at n.* Tp. III, 1, 34. Wiv. II, 2, 277. Mids. I, 2, 7. Merch. III, 2, 279. Mcb. III, 1, 36 etc. *till seven at n.* Mcb. III, 1, 42. *come Lam-*

*mas-eve at n.* Rom. I, 3, 17. *soon at n.* Wiv. I, 4, 9. II, 2, 296. 299. Meas. I, 4, 88. H4B V, 5, 96. Rom. II, 5, 78. Oth. III, 4, 198 (cf. *Soon*). *by n.*: Ven. 492. 732. 755. Sonn. 27, 13. 86, 7. Gent. III, 2, 83. III, 1, 110. Wiv. II, 1, 126. Mids. II, 1, 124. III, 2, 283. V, 141. Wint. III, 2, 22. H4A III, 1, 142. H6B I, 1, 26. *by day and n.* Tp. I, 2, 336. Lr. I, 3, 3. *by day or n.* Wiv. II, 1, 16. *by night and day* (in rhyming): Err. IV, 2, 60. John I, 165. *in n.* Ven. 720. Rom. II, 2, 140 (Q1 *being n.*). Oth. II, 3, 216. *in the n.* Ven. 816. Gent. III, 1, 178. Ado III, 3, 69. 80. V, 1, 241. LLL I, 1, 42. Mids. II, 1, 222. V, 21. All's V, 2, 61. Rom. I, 4, 89 etc. *on n.*: ne'er may I look on day, nor sleep on n.* Err. V, 210. *fighting on days and foining on —s*, H4B II, 4, 252 (Q *a nights*). *o'er n.*: (good rest) as wretches have o'er n. that wait for execution in the morn*, Gent. IV, 2, 133. *what he saw o'er n.* Ado III, 3, 174. *since n.*, see *Since*. *a —s* = at night: Tw. I, 3, 5. H4B II, 4, 252 (Ff *on —s*). Tim. IV, 3, 292. Caes. I, 2, 193. II, 2, 116. *o' —s*, H4B II, 1, 83. *a n.* As II, 4, 48.

*Dian, the goddess of the moon, called* queen of night: Gent. IV, 2, 100. Ado V, 3, 12. As III, 2, 2. Night herself represented as a goddess, drawn by a team of dragons: Mids. III, 2, 379. H6B IV, 1, 4. Troil. V, 8, 17. Cymb. II, 2, 48. *N. a dreary and hateful time*: *ugly n.* Ven. 1041. Lucr. 925. Troil. V, 8, 6. *the merciless and pitchy n.* Ven. 821. *sable n., mother of dread and fear*, Lucr. 117. *comfort-killing n., image of hell*, 764. *hateful, vaporous and foggy n.* 771. *uncheerful n.* 1024. *solemn n. descended to ugly hell*, 1081. *hideous n.* Sonn. 12, 2. *ghastly n.* 27, 11. *dark dismal-dreaming n.* Pilgr. 200. *as sad as n.* John IV, 1, 15. *the tragic melancholy n.* H6B IV, 1, 4. *through the foul womb of n.* H5 IV Chor. 4. *never sees horrid n., the child of hell*, IV, 1, 288. Represented as the nurse of crime: *this blackfaced n., desire's foul nurse*, Ven. 773. *he is but —'s child*, Lucr. 785. *the motions of his spirit are dull as n.* Merch. V, 86. *acts of black n.* Tit. V, 1, 64. *—'s black agents*, Mcb. III, 2, 53. *actions blacker than the n.* Per. I, 1, 135. Image of ugliness: *to change your day of youth to sullied n.* Sonn. 15, 12. *as good to wink as look on n.* Err. III, 2, 58. Of age: *my n. of life*, Err. V, 314. *hath dimmed your infant morn to aged n.* R3 IV, 4, 16. Of distress and sorrow: *the n. of sorrow now is turned to day*, Ven. 481. *our n. of woe*, Sonn. 120, 9. *as thy eye-beams, when their fresh rays have smote the n. of dew that on my cheeks down flows*, LLL IV, 3, 29. *from Richard's n. to Bolingbroke's fair day*, R2 III, 2, 218. *black n. o'ershade thy day*, R3 I, 2, 131. Of death: R3 I, 4, 47. V, 3, 62 etc.

**Night-bird**, a bird singing in the night: *she sung and made the n. mute*, Per. IV Prol. 26 (the nightingale).

**Night-brawler**, one who raises brawls at night: Oth. II, 3, 196.

**Night-cap**, a cap worn in bed or in undress: Caes. I, 2, 247. Oth. II, 1, 316.

**Night-crow**, according to some an owl, to others a night-heron (Ardea nycticorax): *the n. cried, aboding luckless time*, H6C V, 6, 45.

**Night-dog**, a dog hunting by night: *when —s run, all sorts of deer are chased*, Wiv. V, 5, 252.

**Nighted**, dark: *cast thy n. colour off*, Hml. I, 2, 68 (Ff *nightly*). *to dispatch his n. life*, Lr. IV, 5, 13.

**Night-fly**, an insect that flies in the night: *hushed with buzzing —es to thy slumber*, H4B III, 1, 11.

**Night-foe**, an enemy profiting by the night to make an attack: *to defend his person from —s*, H6C IV, 3, 22.

**Night-gown**, a loose gown used for undress: Ado III, 4, 18. Mcb. II, 2, 70. V, 1, 5. 69. Oth. IV, 3, 34.

**Nightingale**, the bird Sylvia luscinia: Pilgr. 380. Gent. III, 1, 179. V, 4, 5. Mids. I, 2, 86. Merch. V, 104. Shr. Ind. 2, 38. II, 172. Tw. III, 4, 38. Rom. III, 5, 2. 7. Lr. III, 6, 32. Ant. IV, 8, 18.

**Nightly**, adj. happening, or acting, or used in the night: *n. linen*, Lucr. 680. *her n. sorrow*, 1080. *n. tears*, Gent. II, 4, 132. *n. revels*, Mids. V, 377. *to give thee n. visitation*, Troil. IV, 4, 75. *the n. owl*, Tit. II, 3, 97. *give me my n. wearing*, Oth. IV, 3, 16. In Hml. I, 2, 68 Ff *n. colour*, Qq *nighted colour*.

**Nightly**, adv. 1) by night: *which n. gulls him with intelligence*, Sonn. 86, 10. *I n. lodge her in an upper tower*, Gent. III, 1, 35. *my thoughts do harbour with my Silvia n.* 140. *and n. look you sing*, Wiv. V, 5, 69. *then n. sings the staring owl*, LLL V, 2, 927. 936. *the owl that n. hoots*, Mids. II, 2, 6. *shut me n. in a charnel-house*, Rom. IV, 1, 81.

2) every night: *day doth daily draw my sorrows longer, and night doth n. make grief's strength seem stronger*, Sonn. 28, 14. *he's drunk n. in your company*, Tw. I, 3, 39. *I have n. since dreamt of encounters*, Cor. IV, 5, 128. *n. she sings on yon tree*, Rom. III, 5, 4. *which with sweet water n. I will dew*, V, 3, 14. *these terrible dreams that shake us n.* Mcb. III, 2, 19. *while this strict watch so n. toils the subject*, Hml. I, 1, 72. *there's millions that n. lie in those unproper beds*, Oth. IV, 1, 69.

**Nightmare**, incubus: *the n. and her nine-fold*, Lr. III, 4, 126.

**Night-oblation**, offering or sacrifice brought in the night: Per. V, 3, 70.

**Night-owl**, an owl screeching and hunting by night: Lucr. 360. Tw. II, 3, 60. R2 III, 3, 183. H6C II, 1, 130.

**Night-raven**, probably the same as *night-crow*, q. v.: *I had as lief have heard the n., come what plague could have come after it*, Ado II, 3, 84.

**Night-rest**, nocturnal quiet and repose: *domestic awe, n. and neighbourhood*, Tim. IV, 1, 17.

**Night-rule**, order of the night, nightly diversion: *what n. now about this haunted grove?* Mids. III, 2, 5.

**Night-shriek**, a scream of anguish heard in the night: *to hear a n.* Mcb. V, 5, 11.

**Night-taper**, a candle used in the night: Mids. III, 1, 172.

**Night-tripping**, tripping about in the night: *n. fairy*, H4A I, 1, 87.

**Night-waking**, being awake in the night: *n. cat*, Lucr. 554.

**Night-walking**, doing one's work by night: *n. heralds*, R3 I, 1, 72.

**Night-wanderer**, one travelling on foot in the night: *stonished as —s often are, their light blown out in some mistrustful wood*, Ven. 825. *mislead —s*, Mids. II, 1, 39.

**Night-wandering**, roving by night: *n. weasels*, Lucr. 307.

**Night-watch**, a guard on duty in the night: *a critic, nay, a n. constable*, LLL III, 178.

**Night-work**, name in H4B III, 2, 211. 222.

**Nile**, the river of Egypt (with one exception, al-ways without the article): Ant. I, 5, 25. II, 5, 78. II, 7, 20. III, 13, 166. V, 2, 356. Cymb. III, 4, 37.

**Nill**, will not: *in scorn or friendship*, n. *I construe whether*, Pilgr. 188. *and, will you, n. you, I will marry you*, Shr. II, 273. *it is, will he, n. he, he goes*, Hml. V, 1, 19. *I n. relate*, Per. III Prol. 55.

**Nilus**, the river of Egypt (used without the article): Tit. III, 1, 71. Ant. I, 2, 49. I, 3, 69. II, 7, 23. V, 2, 58. 243.

**Nimble**, light, quick and lively in motion: *relish your n. notes to pleasing ears*, Lucr. 1126. *n. thought can jump both sea and land*, Sonn. 44, 7. *youth is n., age is lame*, Pilgr. 162. *of such sensible and n. lungs that they always use to laugh at nothing*, Tp. II, 1, 174. *my spirits are n.* 202. *to snare the n. marmoset*, II, 2, 174. *n. jugglers that deceive the eye*, Err. I, 2, 98. *universal plodding poisons up the n. spirits in the arteries*, LLL IV, 3, 306. *of such a merry, n., stirring spirit*, V, 2, 16. *the pert and n. spirit of mirth*, Mids. I, 1, 13. *you have a n. wit*, As III, 2, 293. *with her head n. in threats*, IV, 3, 110. *a n. hand*, Wint. IV, 4, 685. *his n. haste*, John IV, 2, 197. *n. mischance, that art so light of foot*, R2 III, 4, 92. *with n. wing*, H4A V, 1, 64. *full of n. fiery and delectable shapes*, H4B IV, 3, 108. *a n. galliard*, H5 I, 2, 252. *the n. gunner*, III Chor. 32. *dancing shoes with n. soles*, Rom. I, 4, 15. *your n. lightnings*, Lr. II, 4, 167. IV, 7, 34. Per. III, 1, 6. *to make your vessel n.* Cymb. II, 4, 29. *horses have been —r*, III, 2, 74. In LLL V, 2, 747 most M. Edd. *a n. tongue;* O. Edd. *an humble tongue.*

Adverbially: *those jacks that n. leap*, Sonn. 128, 5.

**Nimble-footed**, light of foot: Gent. V, 3, 7. H4A IV, 1, 95.

**Nimbleness**, agility: *full of rest, defence and n.* Caes. IV, 3, 202.

**Nimble-pinioned**, swift-winged: Rom. II, 5, 7.

**Nimbly**, with light and easy motion: Ven. 38. R2 IV, 318. H4A II, 4, 285. R3 I, 1, 12. *the air n. and sweetly recommends itself unto our gentle senses*, Mcb. I, 6, 2 (in a manner enlivening the spirits).

**Nine**, one more than eight: Sonn. 38, 10. Wiv. III, 5, 47. 54. 55. Meas. II, 1, 34. 212. 213. IV, 2, 135. Ado III, 2, 74. LLL V, 2, 488. 492. 496. Merch. II, 2, 171. II, 6, 63. As II, 7, 24. All's I, 3, 81. Wint. I, 2, 1. II, 1, 145. III, 2, 183. H4A II, 4, 236. III, 1, 156. H6B IV, 9, 4. H6C I, 1, 112. III, 1, 76. R3 II, 3, 17. V, 3, 48. Troil. Prol. 5. Cor. II, 1, 168. Rom. I, 1, 167. II, 2, 169. II, 5, 1. 10. Tim. II, 1, 2. III, 4, 8. Hml. V, 1, 183. 184. V, 2, 175. Lr. I, 1, 33. Oth. I, 2, 4. I, 3, 84. 280. IV, 1, 188. Per. III, 2, 85. *the n. men's morris*, Mids. II, 1, 98 (see *Morris*). *the n. Worthies*, LLL V, 1, 124. H4B IV, 4, 238. *the n. sibyls of old Rome*, H6A I, 2, 56. *I was seven of the n. days out of the wonder*, As III, 2, 184 (alluding to the proverb: *a wonder lasts but nine days*; cf. H6C III, 2, 113). Thought to be the usual number of the young of some animals: Troil. II, 1, 77. Mcb. IV, 1, 65 (in Tw. III, 2, 71 M. Edd. *the youngest wren of n.;* O. Edd. *of mine*). A number of magical power: Mcb. I, 3, 22. 36. A cat has nine lives: Rom. III, 1, 81.

**Nine-fold**, nine foals (Tyrwhitt) or nine familiars (Malone): *he met the nightmare and her n.* Lr. III, 4, 126. (*nine-foaled*, sc. *mare*?).

**Ninescore**, nine times twenty: *n. and seventeen pounds*, Meas. IV, 3, 6. *n. and odd posts*, H4B IV, 3, 39.

**Nineteen,** one less than twenty: Meas. I, 2, 172. Wint. III, 3, 65. Ant. III, 7, 59.

**Ninny,** a fool: *what a pied n.'s this!* Tp. III, 2, 71.

Corruption of *Ninus:* Mids. III, 1, 99. V, 204. 268.

**Ninth,** the ordinal of nine: LLL V, 2, 581. H4A II, 3, 29. III, 1, 140. Troil. II, 1, 78. Caes. II, 4, 23. Ant. II, 5, 21. Cymb. IV, 2, 30.

**Ninus,** ancient king of Assyria: Mids. III, 1, 100. V, 139. cf. *Ninny.*

**Niobe,** the wife of Amphion, whom the gods transformed into a stone, after her seven sons and daughters had been killed by Apollo and Dian: Troil. V, 10, 19. Hml. I, 2, 149.

**Nip,** to pinch, to bite, to blast: *whose settled visage and deliberate word —s youth i' the head,* Meas. III, 1, 91. *if frosts and fasts n. not the gaudy blossoms of your love,* LLL V, 2, 812. *when blood is —ed and ways be foul,* 926. *winter with his —ing cold,* H6B II, 4, 3. *a frost —s his root,* H8 III, 2, 357. *these tidings n. me, and I hang the head as flowers with frost,* Tit. IV, 4, 70. *a —ing and an eager air,* Hml. I, 4, 2. Dubious passage: *most heavenly music! it —s me unto listening, and thick slumber hangs upon mine eyes,* Per. V, 1, 235 (Collier *raps*).

**Nip,** subst. cut: *here's snip and n. and cut and slish and slash,* Shr. IV, 3, 90.

**Nipple,** the pap of a woman: Rom. I, 3, 30. Mcb. I, 7, 57.

**Nit,** any thing very diminutive: *it is a most pathetical n.* LLL IV, 1, 150. *thou flea, thou n., thou winter-cricket thou,* Shr. IV, 3, 110.

**No,** pron., not any: Ven. 138. 148. 214. 215. 240. 341. 390. 426. 428. 433. 526. 612. 647. 676. 715. 867. 883 etc. etc. *this no slaughterhouse no tool imparteth,* Lucr. 1039 (this house, which is no slaughterhouse). *no believing you,* Gent. II, 1, 162. *'tis no trusting to yond foolish lout,* IV, 4, 71. *no one,* Lucr. 792. R3 II, 1, 84 etc. *no one,* adjectively, = no single, not even one: *the owner of no one good quality,* All's III, 6, 12. *he is poor in no one fault,* Cor. II, 1, 20. No, ironically, = much: *here's no knavery!* Shr. I, 2, 138. *here's no vanity!* H4A V, 3, 33. *here's no sound jest!* Tit. IV, 2, 26.

Used for *not,* before comparatives: *no better,* Tp. II, 1, 281. Meas. II, 4, 77. Merch. II, 9, 60. H5 III, 6, 156. H6A II, 1, 62. Cor. II, 1, 255. *no bigger,* H4A IV, 2, 23. Lr. IV, 6, 16. *no costlier,* Cymb. III, 2, 78. *no dearer,* Lr. I, 1, 20. *no elder,* Cymb. III, 6, 45. *no farther,* H4A III, 3, 110. *no further,* Ven. 905. Tp. III, 3, 1. Meas. V, 486. Cor. II, 3, 181. III, 3, 87. *no finer,* Tw. I, 3, 10. *no greater,* Tp. I, 2, 21. *no harder,* Lucr. 593. *no higher,* Wiv. V, 5, 109. *no honester,* Ado III, 5, 16. *no less,* Meas. I, 4, 17. Err. IV, 4, 49. Cymb. IV, 2, 375. *no longer,* Ven. 579. Tp. II, 2, 37. III, 3, 8. Meas. V, 371. Err. II, 2, 205. *no mightier,* Caes. I, 3, 76. *no more,* Ven. 185. 504. 563. 577. 819. 899. Tp. I, 2, 14. 246. 478. II, 1, 170. 205. II, 2, 44. 167. 184. III, 1, 61. III, 2, 59. III, 3, 17. IV, 142. V, 162. Gent. I, 2, 47. I, 3, 75. II, 3, 11. II, 4, 47. III, 1, 237. 275. Wiv. IV, 4, 10. Meas. I, 1, 7. 51. II, 1, 221. III, 2, 179. 218. V, 316. Err. I, 1, 95. LLL I, 1, 90. 105. IV, 2, 40. Merch. III, 2, 300. IV, 1, 428. H6B III, 1, 304. Rom. I, 3, 98. *no richer,* LLL V, 2, 159. Wint. III, 2, 171. *no sooner,* Meas. III, 1, 32 (cf. *Soon*). *no straiter,* H6B III, 2, 20. *no stronger,* Sonn. 65, 4. Tp. I, 1, 50. Meas. II, 4, 132. As III, 4, 34. *no wiser,* H6A II, 4, 18. *no worse,* Tp. I, 2, 59. II, 1, 261. Gent. II, 1, 169. *no worthier,* Caes. III, 1, 116 etc. etc. Peculiar use and position of the ind. article: *no better a musician,* Merch. V, 106. *no worse a name,* As I, 3, 126. *with no greater a run,* Shr. IV, 1, 17. *upon no better a ground,* Cor. II, 2, 12. *no worse a place,* Oth. I, 1, 11. *no worse a husband,* Ant. II, 2, 131.

Similarly before *other: it is no other,* Meas. IV, 3, 122 (= exactly so); cf. Mcb. III, 4, 97; Hml. I, 1, 108; Oth. IV, 2, 168. *if she be mad, — as I believe no other,* Meas. V, 60. *being no other but as she is, I do not like her,* Ado I, 1, 177. *can't no other but, I your daughter, he must be my brother?* All's I, 3, 171. *he shall suppose no other,* III, 6, 27. *the duke knows him for no other but a poor officer of mine,* IV, 3, 225. *we hope no other from your majesty,* H4B V, 2, 62. *we do no otherwise than we are willed,* H6A I, 3, 10. *he hopes it is no other but for your health and your digestion sake, an after-dinner's breath,* Troil. II, 3, 119. *we learn no other but ...* Mcb. V, 4, 8 (cf. *Other*).

**No,** the word of denial and refusal, opposed to *Yes:* Ven. 587. 785. 852. 937. 997. Tp. I, 2, 30. 251. 371. 395. III, 2, 143. IV, 48. Gent. I, 1, 56. I, 2, 55. II, 5, 16. 37. Wiv. IV, 2, 16. Meas. I, 3, 1. As III, 3, 57. Wint. IV, 4, 46. R3 IV, 1, 66 etc. etc. Substantively: *love's eye is not so true as all men's no,* Sonn. 148, 8. *by yea and no, I do,* Wiv. I, 1, 88. IV, 2, 202. *the very yea and the no is,* I, 4, 99. *reason dares her no,* Meas. IV, 4, 28. *in russet yeas and honest kersey noes,* LLL V, 2, 413.

Equivalent to *not,* when opposed to affirmations: *if you be maid or no,* Tp. I, 2, 427. Meas. III, 2, 180. *whether you will or no,* Tp. III, 1, 86. V, 111. Wiv. IV, 5, 34. Mids. III, 1, 156. III, 2, 81. Merch. II, 2, 49. III, 1, 45. As III, 2, 130. H6A IV, 7, 25. H6B III, 2, 265. R3 III, 1, 23. III, 7, 214. *had he such a chain or no?* Err. V, 256. *is she wedded or no?* LLL II, 211. *will you or no,* Tw. I, 5, 163 etc.

In other cases: *beg thou or borrow, to make up the sum, and live; if no, then thou art doomed to die,* Err. I, 1, 155. *I had a mighty cause to wish him dead, but thou hadst none to kill him. No had, my lord? why, did you not provoke me?* John IV, 2, 207 (Arrowsmith cites the following parallel passages: *the whole world yields not a workman that can frame the like. No does?* Dekker. *In all my life I knew not this before. No did?* John Bon and Master Parson; etc.).

**No,** one of several inarticulate words imitative of the sound of the wind: *suum, mun, ha, no, nonny,* Lr. III, 4, 103.

**Noah,** the patriarch saved in the great flood: Err. III, 2, 108. Tw. III, 2, 18.

**Nob** (O. Edd. *Nobbe*), diminutive of Robert: *I would not be Sir N. in any case,* John I, 147.

**Nob:** *hob, nob, is his word,* Tw. III, 4, 263 (see *Hob*).

**Nobility,** 1) dignity of mind, greatness: John V, 2, 42. Cor. I, 1, 234. Tit. I, 15. 93. 119. 271. Hml. I, 2, 110 (cf. *nobly* in Cor. IV, 5, 117). Oth. II, 1, 218. Ant. II, 5, 82.

2) high descent (elevated sentiments supposed inherent in it): H4A I, 3, 172. H6B II, 1, 196. III, 1, 50. IV, 1, 129. H8 II, 4, 142.

3) high rank: All's IV, 3, 29. John IV, 3, 86. H4A I, 3, 45. R3 I, 3, 257. H8 III, 2, 281.

4) the persons of high rank collectively, the peerage: All's IV, 5, 52. H4A II, 1, 84. II, 4, 429. V, 4, 13. H5 I, 2, 110. H6A I, 1, 78. IV, 1, 146. 188. V, 3, 96. H6B IV, 2, 13. IV, 8, 29. R3 I, 3, 79. H8 III, 2, 291. Cor. I, 1, 201. III, 1, 39. IV, 2, 2. IV, 7, 29.

**Noble,** adj. 1) magnanimous, elevated, dignified, generous: Compl. 108. Sonn. 151, 6. Tp. I, 2, 7. 161. 299. 419. II, 1, 215. III, 1, 33. 45. III, 2, 43. V, 26. 120. Gent. III, 1, 38. Meas. I, 1, 50. II, 1, 7. III, 1, 13. 88. V, 224. Mids. I, 1,. 24. V, 91. As IV, 3, 129. Tw. II, 4, 84. H8 II, 1, 119. II, 2, 92. Troil. IV, 1, 33. Tit. I, 25. Ant. III, 13, 78. IV, 15, 55. 59 etc. etc. With *to: that I should not be n. to myself*, Ant. V, 2, 192. Used with irony: *here come two n. beasts in*, Mids. V, 220. *O n. fool*, As II, 7, 33. *breaks his staff like a n. goose*, As II, 4, 48. *here comes my n. gull-catcher*, Tw. II, 5, 204 *(notable?).*

2) magnificent, stately, splendid: *you will my n. grapes, an if my royal fox could reach them*, All's II, 1, 74 (perhaps used for the sake of the quibble with *royal*). *the most n. bottom of our fleet*, Tw. V, 60; cf. Oth. II, 1, 22. *a n. plot*, H4A I, 3, 279. *n. horsemanship*, IV, 1, 110. *a n. feast*, Tim. III, 6, 68. *some —r token I have kept apart for Livia*, Ant. V, 2, 168.

3) of an ancient and illustrious family: Compl. 234. Ado II, 3, 35. All's I, 3, 163. II, 3, 68. V, 3, 95. Tw. I, 5, 277. V, 271. Wint. I, 2, 393. R2 II, 1, 240. II, 3, 56. H5 II, 2, 129. H6A V, 4, 22. Cymb. III, 4, 135 etc. etc. *believe not the word of the n.* H4B IV, 3, 59. *the n. and the common*, Cor. III, 1, 29.

= becoming persons of quality: *to be abridged from such a n. rate*, Merch. I, 1, 127. *they do prank them in authority, against all n. sufferance*, Cor. III, 1, 24.

The different significations confounded: Tw. I, 2, 25. R2 IV, 117. H5 III, 1, 17 etc.

Used adverbially: *she is n. born*, H8 II, 4, 141. *you do the —r*, Cor. III, 2, 6. *'tis n. spoken*, Ant. II, 2, 98 (the later Ff *nobly*).

**Noble,** subst. 1) a nobleman: *a beggar's book outworths a —'s blood*, H8 I, 1, 123. *will deserve a right good husband, let him be a n.* IV, 2, 146. Often in the plural: John IV, 2, 243. V, 1, 33. V, 2, 62. R2 II, 1, 247. II, 2, 88. H4B II, 3, 51. V, 2, 17. H5 IV, 7, 77. IV, 8, 96. H6A I, 3, 90. III, 2, 129. V, 4, 172. Troil. II, 2, 209. Cor. II, 1, 255. III, 2, 65. IV, 3, 22. IV, 4, 9. IV, 6, 122. Tim. I, 2, 180. Mcb. IV, 3, 79 etc.

2) a gold coin (worth 6 s. 8 d.): R2 I, 1, 88. H4B II, 1, 167. H5 II, 1, 112. 119. H6A V, 4, 23. R3 I, 3, 82. Quibbling with *royal*: H4A II, 4, 317. 321; and perhaps All's II, 1, 74. With *angel*: Ado II, 3, 35.

**Noble-ending,** making a noble end: *a testament of n. love*, H5 IV, 6, 27.

**Nobleman,** a man of an illustrious family, a peer: Meas. V, 159. All's V, 2, 18. Wint. III, 3, 99. John IV, 3, 87. H4A II, 4, 317. V, 3, 42. V, 4, 169. H4B I, 2, 62. H6B III, 2, 24. H6C IV, 3, 9. H8 III, 2, 308. Rom. II, 4, 213. Per. IV, 6, 147. Plur. *noblemen*: Lucr. Arg. 4. Gent. I, 3, 31. H6B III, 2, 186.

**Noble-minded,** generous: H6A IV, 4, 37. Tit. I, 209.

**Nobleness,** 1) magnanimity, generosity, elevated sentiments: Wint. II, 3, 12. 165. V, 2, 40. R2 IV, 119 (Q1 *nobless*). Cor. V, 3, 72. Tim. V, 1, 66. Ant. IV, 14, 99. V, 2, 45. Cymb. V, 3, 33. *n. of mind*, R3 III, 7, 14. *the n. of life is to do thus*, Ant. I, 1, 36.

2) illustrious descent, or distinguished rank: *regard the stamp of n.* H8 III, 2, 12. *signs of n. shall shine on all deservers*, Mcb. I, 4, 41. *flatterers, foes to n.* Cor. III, 1, 45. *thy gait did prophesy a royal n.* Lr. V, 3, 176. *virtue and cunning were endowments greater than n. and riches*, Per. III, 2, 28. With *of: n. of birth*, Gent. I, 3, 33.

**Nobless,** nobleness; reading of Q1 in R2 IV, 119; the other O. Edd. *nobleness.*

**Noblest-minded,** most generous: Caes. I, 3, 122.

**Noblish,** reading of F1 in H5 III, 1, 17; the later Ff *noblest.*

**Nobly,** 1) magnanimously, generously, with greatness of mind: Tp. III, 1, 3. All's IV, 5, 105. Tw. V, 123. Wint. IV, 4, 528. H4A V, 4, 160. H4B IV, 2, 90. H6B V, 2, 16. H8 III, 2, 199. Troil. II, 3, 201. Cor. I, 3, 27. I, 9, 66. II, 2, 72. II, 3, 94. 139. IV, 5, 117 (cf. Hml. I, 2, 110). Tim. V, 4, 63. Caes. II, 1, 137. Mcb. III, 6, 14. Lr. V, 1, 28. Ant. II, 2, 98 (F1 *noble*). III, 13, 170. IV, 14, 43. Cymb. IV, 2, 51. V, 5, 405. 420.

2) honourably: *to think but n. of my grand-mother*, Tp. I, 2, 119. *hears most n. of him*, All's III, 5, 53. *pestiferous reports of men very n. held*, IV, 3, 341. *I think n. of the soul*, Tw. IV, 2, 59. *receive 'em n.* H8 I, 4, 58. *n. named so*, Cor. II, 3, 251. *will use you n.* Tit. I, 260. *will n. him remunerate*, 398. *speaks n. of her*, Per. V, 1, 189.

3) in a high place, as being of high rank: *thou n. base, they basely dignified*, Lucr. 660. *more n. born*, H6B II, 3, 9. *all such emblems laid n. on her*, H8 IV, 1, 90. *n. trained*, Rom. III, 5, 182.

**Nobody** or **Nobody,** (mostly in two words, sometimes hyphened in O. Edd.) no person, no one: Wiv. I, 4, 14. II, 2, 51. IV, 2, 19. Ado I, 1, 118. III, 4, 34. V, 1, 165. Merch. V, 23. Wint. IV, 4, 645. John IV, 1, 13. H4A V, 4, 129. H4B II, 4, 73. III, 2, 246. H6B IV, 4, 58. H6C II, 5, 55. Troil. II, 3, 75. III, 3, 269. Oth. IV, 1, 210. IV, 3, 52. V, 2, 124. Cymb. II, 1, 24. Per. II, 1, 59. *played by the picture of N.* Tp. III, 2, 136 (allusion to a print prefixed to the comedy of *No-body and Some-body*, or to an engraving on the old ballad of *The Well-spoken Nobody*).

**Nod,** subst. an inclination of the head: *n., ay, why, that's noddy*, Gent. I, 1, 119. *makes fearful action, with wrinkled brows, with —s, with rolling eyes*, John IV, 2, 192. *her winks and —s and gestures*, Hml. IV, 5, 11. Made in drunken drowsiness: *like a drunken sailor on a mast, ready, with every n., to tumble down*, R3 III, 4, 102. By way of a slight obeisance: *duck with French —s*, R3 I, 3, 49. *most rich in Timon's n.* Tim. I, 1, 62. *with certain half-caps and cold-moving —s*, II, 2, 221. *the insinuating n.* Cor. II, 3, 107. *will he give you the n.? You shall see. If he do, the rich shall have more*, Troil. I, 2, 212 (i. e. it will not make you rich. Singer: *"to give the nod* was a term in the game at cards called Noddy. The word also signifies a silly fellow. Cressid means to call Pandarus a noddy, and says he shall by more nods be made more significantly a fool.").

**Nod,** vb. 1) intr. to incline the head: *she did n.* Gent. I, 1, 120. 121. *where oxlips and the —ing violet grows*, Mids. II, 1, 250. *with —ing of their plumes*, Cor. III, 3, 126. *nor wink, nor n., nor kneel*, Tit. III, 2, 43. *if thou canst n., speak too*, Mcb. III, 4, 70. *trees that n. unto the world*, Ant. IV, 14, 6. An effect of drowsiness: *you n.* Shr. I, 1, 254. IV, 1, 209. Caes. IV, 3, 271. Done by way of making a slight salutation: *so he — ed,* Ant. I, 5, 47. With *at: courteous feathers which bow the head and n. at every man,* All's IV, 5, 112. *he —s at us, as who should say, I'll be even with you,* H6B IV, 7, 99. *you shall see him n. at me,* Troil. I, 2, 211. With *on: if Caesar carelessly but n. on him,* Caes. I, 2, 118. With *to: n. to him, elves,* Mids. III, 1, 177. *as if Olympus to a molehill should in supplication n.* Cor. V, 3, 31.

2) trans. a) to bend, to incline: *and n. their heads,* H6B II, 4, 22.

b) with an accus. denoting the result, = to beckon: *Cleopatra hath —ed him to her,* Ant. III, 6, 66.

**Noddle,** the head, in contempt: *to comb your n. with a three-legged stool,* Shr. I, 1, 64. Evans says: *I will smite his —s,* Wiv. III, 1, 128.

**Noddy,** a simpleton: *but what said she? I. Nod-I, why that's n. You mistook, sir; I say, she did nod: and you ask me if she did nod; and I say I. And that set together is n. Now you have taken the pains to set it together, take it for your pains,* Gent. I, 1, 119. 131.

**'Noint,** to anoint: *I have — ed an Athenian's eyes,* Mids. III, 2, 351. *flayed alive; then — ed over with honey,* Wint. IV, 4, 813.

**Noise,** subst. 1) any sound (particularly of voices) attracting attention or causing disturbance, whether it be loud or low: Ven. 919. Lucr. 165. Tp. II, 1, 320. IV, 216. V, 232. Wiv. V, 5, 34. Meas. IV, 2, 72. 91. Mids. III, 1, 93. All's II, 3, 314. Wint. II, 3, 39. John V, 4, 45. R2 III, 3, 51. H4B IV, 5, 7. 15. H6A I, 3, 15. I, 4, 99. II, 1, 2. H6B II, 1, 59. III, 2, 236. IV, 8, 3. H6C III, 1, 6. R3 I, 4, 22. 60. II, 2, 33. H8 Prol. 15. IV, 1, 71. V, 4, 1. Troil. II, 2, 97. Cor. I, 4, 22. II, 1, 175. II, 3, 60. V, 5, 4. V, 6, 52. Tit. I, 155. II, 2, 6. II, 3, 20. V, 1, 25. Rom. I, 1, 82. II, 2, 136. IV, 5, 17. V, 3, 151. 169. 262. Caes. I, 2, 14. 224. II, 2, 22. II, 4, 16. Mcb. II, 2, 15. 58. V, 7, 14. Hml. III, 2, 14. IV, 2, 3. IV, 5, 96. 153. Lr. II, 1, 57. Oth. II, 1, 52. II, 3, 149. V, 2, 86. 93. Ant. V, 2, 233. Cymb. IV, 4, 1. *what is that n.? =* what noise is that? what does that noise mean? Mcb. V, 5, 6. Ant. IV, 14, 104. *darest wag thy tongue in n. so rude against me,* Hml. III, 4, 40. *whose n. is this that cries on murder?* Oth. V, 1, 47. *that keeps all this n.* Err. III, 1, 61 (causes it mischievously). *to make n.:* Lucr. 1329. Meas. IV, 3, 27. Ado III, 3, 36. Mids. III, 2, 116. Merch. IV, 1, 76. V, 3. As IV, 2, 10. H4B IV, 5, 1. Cor. I, 5, 10. Lr. III, 6, 89. Oth. III, 1, 13. Cymb. III, 5, 44. In R3 V, 3, 104 Ff *n.,* Qq. *thoughts.*

2) report, rumour: *the n. goes,* Troil. I, 2, 12. *mark the high —s,* Lr. III, 6, 118. *Cleopatra, catching but the least n. of this, dies instantly,* Ant. I, 2, 145.

3) music: *the isle is full of —s, sounds and sweet airs,* Tp. III, 2, 144. *being but the horn and n. of the monster's,* Cor. III, 1, 95. *what n. is this?* Mcb. IV, 1, 106. *what warlike n. is this?* Hml. V, 2, 360. *peace! what n.?* Ant. IV, 3, 12.

Hence = a company of musicians: *find out Sneak's n.* H4B II, 4, 13.

**Noise,** vb. 1) with *it,* to cause a tumult and disturbance: *gives his potent regiment to a trull, that —s it against us,* Ant. III, 6, 96.

2) to spread by rumour: *all-telling fame doth n. abroad, Navarre hath made a vow,* LLL II, 22. *to n. abroad that Harry Monmouth fell,* H4B Ind. 29. *let it be —d that ...* H8 I, 2, 105. *it is — d he hath a mass of treasure,* Tim. IV, 3, 404.

**Noiseless,** still, silent: All's V, 3, 41. Lr. IV, 2, 56.

**Noisemaker,** one who makes a clamour: Tp. I, 1, 47.

**Noisome,** noxious, offensive, disgusting: Ado V, 2, 53. R2 III, 4, 38. H6A I, 5, 23. Cor. V, 1, 26. Cymb. I, 5, 26.

**Nole** or **Nowl,** noddle, head: *an ass's n. I fixed on his head,* Mids. III, 2, 17.

**Nominate,** 1) to name: *thy young days, which we may n. tender,* LLL I, 2, 16 (Armado's speech). *who is intituled, —d, or called, Don Adriano,* V, 1, 8 (Sir Nathaniel's speech). *can you n. in order now the degrees of the lie?* As V, 4, 92. *sight may distinguish of colours but suddenly to n. them all, it is impossible,* H6B II, 1, 130.

2) to appoint: *let the forfeit be — d for an equal pound of your fair flesh,* Merch. I, 3, 150. *is it so —d in the bond?* IV, 1, 259.

**Nomination,** 1) the act of mentioning by name: *the n. of the party writing,* LLL IV, 2, 138 (Holofernes' speech). *what imports the n. of this gentleman?* Hml. V, 2, 133 (with purposed affectation).

2) the act of appointing: (the day of the coronation) *wants but n.* R3 III, 4, 5.

**Non,** part of the burden of a song: *hey non nonny,* Hml. IV, 5, 165.

**Nonage,** minority: R3 II, 3, 13.

**Nonce,** in the phrase *for the n. =* pat to the purpose, just as occasion requires: *I have cases of buckram for the n.* H4A I, 2, 201. *this is a riddling merchant for the n.* H6A II, 3, 57. *I'll have prepared him a chalice for the n.* Hml. IV, 7, 161.

**Noncome,** abbreviation of the juridical term *non compos mentis,* used nonsensically by Dogberry: Ado III, 5, 67.

**None,** 1) no one, nobody: *thou single wilt prove n.* Sonn. 8, 14. *you like n., n. you, for constant heart,* 53, 14. *who his spoil of beauty can forbid?* O, n. 65, 13. *n. that I more love than myself,* Tp. I, 1, 22. *without you were so simple, n. else would,* Gent. II, 1, 38. *n. better knows than you,* Meas. I, 3, 7. *let n. enter,* Err. II, 2, 220. *else n. at all in aught proves excellent,* LLL IV, 3, 354. *n. so poor to do him reverence,* Caes. III, 2, 125 etc. As a plural: *that n. but fools would keep,* Meas. III, 1, 8. *there's n. but asses will,* Err. II, 1, 14. *there's n. but witches do inhabit here,* III, 2, 161. *it should n. spare that come within his power,* LLL II, 51. *n. offend where all alike do dote,* IV, 3, 126. *n. but minstrels like of sonneting,* 158. *n. are so surely caught as wit turned fool,* V, 2, 69. *n. can cure their harms by wailing them,* R3 II, 2, 103.

2) not one, not any; used to supply a noun: *desire hath n.* (bounds) Ven. 389. *n.* (sorrow) *is best,* 971. *be nurse to n.* (babe) Lucr. 1162. *love hath reason, reason n.* (reason) Phoen. 47. *no marrying? n.* Tp. II, 1, 166. *n. of us,* II, 2, 51. *she gave me n.* (earnest) Gent. II, 1, 164. *that's far worse than n.* (faith) V, 4, 51. *n.* (people) *but mine own people,* Wiv. IV, 2, 14. *and n. of them been worn,* Meas. I, 2, 173. *he did me n.* (right) Err. IV, 2, 8. *he with n.* (ducats) *returned,* V, 232. *he wore n.* (linen) *but a dishclout,* LLL V, 2, 720. *what news with you? n. good, my lord, to please you with the hearing, nor n. so bad ....* R3 IV, 4, 458 (Qq

*none good my lord;* Ff *none, good my lord*) etc. Following the noun emphatically: *two distincts, division* n. Phoen. 27. *riches, poverty, and use of service,* n. Tp. II, 1, 151. *and subjects n. abroad,* V, 167. *other means was* n. Err. I, 1, 76. *satisfaction can be* n. *but by pangs of death,* Tw. III, 4, 262. *he is true-hearted, and a soul* n. *better in my kingdom,* H8 V, 1, 156. Followed by *of* (and then almost = not): *we are their offspring, and they* n. *of ours,* Lucr. 1757. *to force that on you which you knew* n. *of yours,* Tw. III, 1, 128. *she's a changeling and* n. *of your flesh and blood,* Wint. IV, 4, 705. *he must know 'tis* n. *of your daughter nor my sister,* 850. *that fault is* n. *of yours,* R3 I, 1, 47. *our thoughts are ours, their ends* n. *of our own,* Hml. III, 2, 223.

Peculiar use: *he shall be* n.; *we'll keep him here,* R2 V, 2, 99 (= he shall not make one, not be one of the party).

Passages leading over to the following signification: *keep thy Hermia, I will* n. Mids. III, 2, 169 (I will not have her). *I'll* n. *now,* Ant. II, 5, 9 (I will not now play at billiards). *take it, God, for it is* n. *but thine,* H5 IV, 8, 117. *lest it* (her love) *should ravel and be good to* n. Gent. III, 2, 52 (to no suitor; or to nothing?). *means to live; of that there's* n. *or little,* Tp. II, 1, 51 (no means? or nothing?). *poor trespasses...whereof I reckon the casting forth to crows thy baby daughter to be or* n. *or little,* Wint. III, 2, 193. *if you can penetrate her with your fingering, so; we'll try with tongue too: if* n. *will do, let her remain,* Cymb. II, 3, 17.

3) nothing: *forbear, and eat no more. Why, I have eat* n. *yet,* As II, 7, 88. Usually followed by *of*: *away with the rest. I will have* n. *on't,* Tp. IV, 248. *you writ them; but I will* n. *of them,* Gent. II, 1, 133. *eat* n. *of it,* Err. II, 2, 61. *we'll* n. *of that,* Mids. V, 46. *I'll* n. *of it,* Shr. IV, 3, 100. Tw. I, 5, 321. II, 2, 13. H4A II, 1, 69. V, 1, 142. Mcb. V, 3, 47. *I will* n. *of thee,* Merch. III, 2, 102. All's V, 3, 149. Tw. I, 3, 113. II, 2, 9. Wint. II, 1, 3. H4B III, 2, 271. Troil. II, 3, 143. III, 1, 110. *that is the dowry of his wife; 'tis* n. *of his own getting,* As III, 3, 56. *you can eat* n. *of this homely diet,* All's II, 2, 48. *you can say* n. *of this,* Tw. V, 342. *privy to* n. *of this,* Wint. II, 1, 96. *fear* n. *of this,* IV, 4, 601. n. *of this could restrain the action,* H4B I, 1, 175.

4) = no, before a noun: n. *so small advantage shall step forth,* John III, 4, 151. *the late marriage made of* n. *effect,* H8 IV, 1, 33. *your Italy contains* n. *so accomplished a courtier,* Cymb. I, 4, 103 (none that is so accomplished a courtier); cf. n. *our parts so poor, but was a race of heaven,* Ant. I, 3, 36. n. *a stranger there so merry and so gamesome,* Cymb. I, 6, 59.

**None-sparing,** sparing nobody: *the* n. *war,* All's III, 2, 108.

**Nonino,** part of an exclamation expressing joy: *with a hey, and a ho, and a hey* n. As V, 3, 18. 24. 28. 32.

**Nonny,** the same: *converting all your sounds of woe into Hey* n. n. Ado II, 3, 71. *hey non* n., n., *hey* n. Hml. IV, 5, 165 (used preposterously by Ophelia in her madness). *the cold wind says suum, mun, ha, no,* n. Lr. III, 4, 103.

**Nonpareil,** one who has no equal, a paragon: *he himself calls her a* n. Tp. III, 2, 108. *though you were crowned the* n. *of beauty,* Tw. I, 5, 273. *if thou didst it, thou art the* n. Mcb. III, 4, 19. *spake you of Caesar? how, the* n.*!* Ant. III, 2, 11. *my mother seemed the Dian of that time: so doth my wife the* n. *of this,* Cymb. II, 5, 8.

**Non-payment,** neglect of payment: *say, for* n. *that the debt should double,* Ven. 521 ("the poet was thinking of a conditional bond's becoming forfeited for non-payment; in which case the entire penalty — usually the double of the principal sum lent by the obligee — was formerly recoverable at law." Malone).

**Non-performance,** omission: Wint. I, 2, 261.

**Non-regardance,** want of due regard, disregard, contempt: *since you to* n. *cast my faith,* Tw. V, 124.

**Non-suit,** vb. to disappoint in a suit, not to comply with: *and in conclusion —s my mediators,* Oth. I, 1, 16.

**Nook,** a corner, inlet, creek: *in the deep* n. *where once thou calledst me up,* Tp. I, 2, 227. *ly many winding —s he strays,* Gent. II, 7, 31. *to forswear the full stream of the world and to live in a* n. *merely monastic,* As III, 2, 441.

**Nook-shotten,** shooting out into capes and necks of land, abounding in bays: *in that* n. *isle of Albion,* H5 III, 5, 14.

**Noon,** midday: *out-going in thy* n. Sonn. 7, 13. *'fore* n. Meas. II, 2, 160. *love's night is* n. Tw. III, 1, 160. Wint. I, 2, 290. H4A I, 2, 4. Rom. II, 4, 119. Mcb. III, 5, 22. Lr. II, 2, 141. Oth. III, 3, 61 (Qq *morn*). *at* n.: Lucr. 784. John IV, 2, 151. V, 1, 26. Cor. I, 1, 265. Lr. III, 6, 92. Ant. I, 4, 20. Cymb. I, 3, 31.

**Noon-day,** midday: *at* n. Caes. I, 3, 27.

**Noon-tide,** midday: *displease her brother's* n. Mids. III, 2, 55. *makes the* n. *night,* R3 I, 4, 77. Adjectively: *his weary* n. *prick,* Lucr. 781. *the* n. *sun,* Tp. V, 42. *at the* n. *prick,* H6C I, 4, 34.

**Nor,** a particle rendering negative a subsequent part of a proposition: *I could not see,* n. *hear,* n. *touch,* Ven. 440. *knows not parching heat* n. *freezing cold,* Lucr. 1145. Tp. I, 2, 19. 141. II, 1, 202. II, 2, 54. V, 164. Gent. III, 1, 266. Err. III, 2, 68 etc. etc. Double negative: *be not proud,* n. *brag not of thy might,* Ven. 113. *never can blab,* n. *know not what we mean,* 126. *I know not love,* n. *will not know it,* 409. n. *feared no hooks,* Lucr. 103. n. *I to none alive,* Sonn. 112, 7. n. *no man ever,* 116, 14. n. *never woo,* Compl. 182. n. *none falser,* Pilgr. 90. *there is no woe to his correction,* n. *to his service no such joy on earth,* Gent. II, 4, 139. *that I cannot choose one* n. *refuse none,* Merch. I, 2, 28. Sonn. 5, 12. 134, 5. Tp. I, 2, 406. Gent. II, 4, 139. Wiv. IV, 2, 166. Meas. V, 64. 431. Err. III, 2, 68. 43. IV, 2, 17. Ado II, 3, 242. III, 1, 55. V, 1, 6. 310. LLL IV, 3, 135. V, 2, 401. Mids. II, 1, 201. III, 2, 135. V, 2, 227. Merch. III, 1, 98. III, 4, 11. IV, 1, 59. V, 84. As I, 2, 19. II, 3, 50. Shr. I, 1, 31. Wint. I, 2, 360. II, 3, 1. III, 2, 204. R2 V, 5, 39. H5 II, 4, 17. III, 6, 174. H6A I, 3, 21. IV, 5, 40. H6B II, 4, 57. R3 III, 1, 147. Mcb. II, 3, 69 etc. Triple negative: n. *understood none neither,* LLL V, 1, 158. n. *no further in sport neither,* As I, 2, 29. n. *never none shall mistress be of it,* Tw. III, 1, 171.

Used to connect two sentences grammatically independent from each other: *spirits are not finely touched but to fine issues,* n. *nature never lends the smallest scruple of her excellence,* Meas. I, 1, 37. *your honour cannot come to that yet. No, sir,* n. *I mean not,* II, 1, 124. *the law will not allow it,* n. *it shall not be allowed in Vienna,* 241. *and since I have not much importuned you;* n. *now I had not, but that I am bound to Persia,* Err. IV, 1, 3. *he is not* (returned); n. *we have not heard from him*, Merch. V, 35. *these boys know little they are sons to the king; n. Cymbeline dreams that they are alive*, Cymb. III, 3, 81. With inversion of the subject: *n. dare I chide the world-without-end hour*, Sonn. 57, 5. *n. are mine eyes with thy tongue's tune delighted*, 141, 5. *no woman's face remember.... n. have I seen more that I may call men*, Tp. III, 1, 50. *n. needest thou much importune me*, Gent. I, 3, 17. *n. do I think the man of safe discretion*, Meas. I, 1, 72. *n. doth she tempt*, II, 2, 165 etc.

Correlative to *neither*: Ven. 437. Tp. II, 2, 18 etc. etc. (see *Neither*). *Neither* omitted: *but king n. peer (espoused) to such a peerless dame*, Lucr. 21. *since brass, n. stone, n. earth, n. boundless sea, but sad mortality o'ersways their power*, Sonn. 65, 1. *he n. that affable familiar ghost*, 86, 9. *my five wits n. my five senses can dissuade one foolish heart*, 141, 9. *vow, bond, nor space*, Compl. 264. *then, Pompey, n. now*, Meas. III, 2, 86. *more n. less to others paying*, 279. *worm n. snail, do no offence*, Mids. II, 2, 23. *know that I, one Snug the joiner, am a lion fell, n. else no lion's dam*, V, 227. *by taking n. by giving of excess*, Merch. I, 3, 63. *contempt n. bitterness were in his pride or sharpness*, All's I, 2, 36. *if word n. oath prevail not*, Wint. III, 2, 204. *though war n. no known quarrel were in question*, H5 II, 4, 17. *that thou n. none of thine shall be let in*, H6A I, 3, 21. *tongue n. heart cannot conceive n. name thee*, Mcb. II, 3, 69. *the fitchew, n. the soiled horse, goes to't with a more riotous appetite*, Lr. IV, 6, 124. *the shot of accident, n. dart of chance*, Oth. IV, 1, 278. *the queen of audience n. desire shall fail*, Ant. III, 12, 21. *the miserable change now lament n. sorrow at*, IV, 15, 52. *pitied n. hated, to the face of peril myself I'll dedicate*, Cymb. V, 1, 28.

*Nor ... nor* for *neither ... nor: n. sun n. wind will ever strive to kiss you*, Ven. 1082. *n. children's tears n. mother's groans respecting*, Lucr. 431. *grief n. law n. limit knows*, 1120. *n. it n. no remembrance what it was*, Sonn. 5, 12. *n. Mars his sword n. war's quick fire*, 55, 7. 98, 5. 99, 10. 124, 12. Compl. 186. Gent. V, 4, 80. Meas. III, 1, 32. IV, 3, 128. LLL V, 2, 346. Merch. II, 7, 21. Tw. III, 1, 164. Wint. I, 2, 275. 360. II, 3, 1. R2 II, 3, 170. III, 2, 64. V, 5, 39. H6A I, 2, 17. I, 3, 60. H6B V, 2, 74. H6C II, 6, 63. Cor. I, 1, 173. Caes. II, 2, 1. Mcb. I, 7, 51. V, 5, 48. Hml. II, 2, 6. Lr. I, 1, 95. More than two parts of a proposition thus joined: *it is n. hand, n. foot, n. arm, n. face, n. any other part*, Rom. II, 2, 40. *n. my service past, n. present sorrows, n. purposed merit*, Oth. III, 4, 116 (Q *neither my service*). *N.* omitted before the middle parts: *n. tackle, sail, n. mast*, Tp. I, 2, 147. *they'll n. pinch, fright me with urchin shows, pitch me i'the mire, n. lead me out of my way*, II, 2, 4. *n. mother, wife, n. England's counted queen*, R3 IV, 1, 47. cf. *neither sting, knot, n. confine*, Compl. 265. *you know neither me, yourselves, n. any thing*, Cor. II, 1, 75. Hml. III, 2, 34. *I never spake with her, saw her, n. heard from her*, Meas. V, 223. *have you no wit, manners, n. honesty*, Tw. II, 3, 94. *is there no respect of place, persons, n. time in you*, 99. *mine eyes were not in fault, for she was beautiful; mine ears, that heard her flattery, n. my heart, that thought her like her seeming*, Cymb. V, 5, 64. *Nor* omitted before all the subsequent parts: *n. rain, wind, thunder, fire, are my daughters*, Lr. III, 2, 15. cf. *neither press, coffer, chest, trunk, well, vault*, Wiv. IV, 2, 62.

**Norbery**, name in R2 II, 1, 284.

**Norfolk**, 1) English county: H6C I, 1, 156. 208. IV, 8, 12. 2) *Thomas Mowbray Duke of N.*: R2 I, 1, 6 etc. H4B III, 2, 29. IV, 1, 111. *John Duke of N.:* H6C I, 1, 31. I, 2, 38. II, 1, 138 etc. R3 II, 1, 101. IV, 4, 440. V, 3, 4. 296. 304 etc. *Duke of N.*: H8 III, 2, 289. IV, 1, 18. 42. *Duchess of N.* 52. V, 3, 169.

**Norman**, a native of Normandy: H5 III, 5, 10. H6B IV, 1, 87. Hml. IV, 7, 91. 92. In Hml. III, 2, 36 Ff *pagan or N.*, Qq and M. Edd. *pagan nor man.*

**Normandy**, French province: LLL II, 43. H6B I, 1, 87. 114. 215. IV, 7, 30. 70. Hml. IV, 7, 83.

**North**, 1) septentrion: *the sharp wind of the n.* Tp. I, 2, 254. *I from the n.* John II, 411. *from n. to south*, 413. *from the n. to south*, H4A I, 3, 196. *higher toward the n.* Caes. II, 1, 109. *you are now sailed into the n. of my lady's opinion*, Tw. III, 2, 28. *n. from =* to the north of: H4A III, 1, 96. *by east, west, n. and south*, LLL V, 2, 566. *from east, west, n. and south*, Wint. I, 2, 203. *they take their courses east, west, n., south*, H4B IV, 2, 104. Cor. II, 3, 24. Adjectively: *the n. gate*, Gent. III, 1, 258. 382. H6A I, 4, 66. *the n. star*, Ado II, 1, 258. *the n. pole*, LLL V, 2, 699. *on this n. side*, H4A III, 1, 113. Tit. II, 3, 255.

2) the country lying opposite to the south: *the Hotspur of the n.* H4A II, 4, 115. 369. *the Percies of the n.* H6A II, 5, 67. *the lordly monarch of the n.* V, 3, 6 (i. e. Lucifer; cf. Isaiah XIV, 13). *the horsemen of the n.* H6C I, 1, 2. *the frozen bosom of the n.* Rom. I, 4, 101. *I toward the n.* R2 V, 1, 76. R3 III, 2, 17. *news came from the n.* H4A I, 1, 51. H4B II, 4, 386. *at Berwick in the n.* H6B II, 1, 83. R3 IV, 4, 484. 485. H8 II, 2, 4. *nor entreat the n. to make his bleak winds kiss my parched lips*, John V, 7, 39. *the grisly n. disgorges such a tempest forth*, Per. III Prol. 47.

3) the Aquilon: *I will speak as liberal as the n.* Oth. V, 2, 220 (Q *air*). *the tyrannous breathing of the n.* Cymb. I, 3, 36. *the wind was n.* Per. IV, 1, 52.

**Northampton**, English town and county: H6C IV, 8, 15. R3 II, 4, 1. H8 I, 1, 200.

**Northamptonshire**, English county: John I, 51.

**North-east**, coming from between the north and east: *the n. wind*, R2 I, 4, 6.

**Northerly**, coming from the north: *the wind is n.* Hml. V, 2, 99.

**Northern**, 1) coming from the north: *the n. blast*, Lucr. 1335. Wint. IV, 4, 376. *the n. wind*, Tit. IV, 1, 104.

2) lying in the north: *our n. shore*, R2 II, 1, 288. *your n. castles*, III, 2, 201. *the n. star*, Caes. III, 1, 60.

3) living in the north: *I will not fight with a pole like a n. man*, LLL V, 2, 701 (Costard's speech. According to commentators, = a clown; cf. *Sir John of the north country*, in the ballad of the Child of Elle). *this n. youth*, H4A III, 2, 145. *proud n. lord*, H6B V, 2, 6. *the n. lords*, H6C I, 1, 251. I, 2, 49.

**North-gate**, see *North*.

**North-north-east**, between the north and the east, but more towards the former: LLL I, 1, 248.

**North-north-west**, between the north and west, but more towards the former: *I am but mad n.* Hml. II, 2, 396.

**Northumberland**, English county: H4B 1, 2, 230. H5 II Chor. 25. II, 2, 68. 150. H6C I, 1, 4. 54. = the Earl of N.: R2 II, 1, 274. II, 2, 53 etc. H4A I, 1, 79. I, 3, 122. II, 4, 376 etc. H4B Ind. 36. I, 1,

152 etc. H6C I, 4, 27. II, 1, 169 etc. R3 I, 3, 187. V, 3, 68. 271. H8 IV, 2, 12. Mcb. III, 6, 31.

**Northward,** in or to the north: *the fairest creature n. born,* Merch. II, 1, 4. *the remnant n.* H4A III, 1, 79. Adjectively: *threw many a n. look,* H4B II, 3, 13.

**Norway,** the country north-west of Sweden: *Sweno, the —s king,* Mcb. I, 2, 59 *(Norway's* or *Norways'?* O. Edd. *Norwayes). those of N.* I, 3, 112. Hml. I, 1, 82. 97. II, 2, 40. IV, 4, 10.
= king of N.: Mcb. I, 2, 50. Hml. I, 1, 61. I, 2, 28. 35. II, 2, 59. 69. 72. IV, 4, 14. 21.

**Norweyan,** pertaining to Norway: Mcb. I, 2, 31. 49. I, 3, 95.

**Nose,** subst. the organ of smell: Ven. 475. Lucr. 1416. Tp. IV, 177. 200. Gent. II, 1, 142. Err. III, 2, 137. 141. Ado V, 1, 115. LLL V, 2, 934. Mids. V, 338. As II, 1, 39. II, 7, 159. Shr. V, 1, 134. All's II, 3, 267. V, 2, 11. Tw. II, 3, 28. 58. 177. IV, 1, 8. Wint. I, 2, 121. II, 1, 14. 152. II, 3, 99. IV, 4, 223. 686. 757. H4A I, 3, 39. II, 3, 96. II, 4, 340. III, 3, 29. 90. H4B II, 4, 357. H5 II, 3, 17. 43. III, 6, 109. 111. H6B III, 2, 34. H6C IV, 7, 25. H8 I, 3, 9. III, 2, 55. V, 4, 44. 47. Troil. I, 2, 115. III, 1, 139. Cor. I, 9, 48. Rom. I, 4, 58. 77. 80. Tim. IV, 3, 157. Mcb. IV, 1, 29. Lr. I, 5, 19. 23. II, 4, 70, 71. IV, 6, 70. Oth. IV, 1, 42. 146. IV, 2, 77. Ant. I, 2, 63. III, 13, 39. Cymb. III, 1, 14. 37. *your nose says no, you are not* (Alexander), *for it stands too right,* LLL V, 2, 568 (according to ancient writers, the head of Alexander was obliquely placed on his shoulders). *it was not for nothing that my n. fell a bleeding,* Merch. II, 5, 24 (bleeding at the nose being thought ominous). *sing a note, sometime through the n.* LLL III, 16. *when the bagpipe sings i'the n.* Merch. IV, 1, 49. *they speak i'the n.* Oth. III, 1, 4. *liberty plucks justice by the n.* Meas. I, 3, 29. *bite the law by the n.* III, 1, 109 (mock it). *did not I pluck thee by the n. for thy speeches?* V, 343. *tweaks me by the n.* Hml. II, 2, 601. *though authority be a stubborn bear, yet he is oft led by the n. with gold,* Wint. IV, 4, 832. *will as tenderly be led by the n. as asses are,* Oth. I, 3, 407. *to see your wives dishonoured to your —s,* Cor. IV, 6, 83 (= to your faces). *borne her cleanly by the keeper's n.* Tit. II, 1, 94.

**Nose,** vb. to smell: *to leave unburnt and still to n. the offence,* Cor. V, 1, 28. *you shall n. him as you go up the stairs,* Hml. IV, 3, 38.

**Nosegay,** a bunch of flowers: Mids. I, 1, 34. Wint. IV, 3, 44.

**Nose-herb,** herb fit for a nosegay, flower: *they are not herbs, you knave; they are —s,* All's IV, 5, 20.

**Noseless,** having one's nose cut off: Troil. V, 5, 34.

**Nose-painting,** making the nose red: Mcb. II, 3, 31.

**Nostril,** the cavity in the nose: Ven. 273. 296. Tp. II, 2, 65. Wiv. III, 5, 94. Wint. I, 2, 421. H5 III, 1, 15. H6B III, 2, 171. Cymb. V, 5, 477. Per. III, 2, 62.

**Not,** the particle by which a word or sentence is negatived: *I'll smother thee with kisses, and yet not cloy thy lips,* Ven. 19. *governed him in strength, though not in lust,* 42. *be not proud,* 113. 116. 120. 124 etc. etc. No such difference made as in modern English with respect to the periphrasis of the verb by *to do* (see *Do*): *know not,* Ven. 126. 304. 409. 615. 904. Tp. I, 2, 124. *seek not to know me,* Ven. 525. *come*

*not within his danger,* 639. *my heart longs not to groan,* 785. *I hate not love,* 789. *call it not love,* 793. *love surfeits not,* 803. *nature cares not for thy vigour,* 953. *the grass stoops not,* 1028. *thou attendest not,* Tp. I, 2, 87. *whose influence if now I court not,* 183. *my charms crack not,* V, 2. *I find not myself disposed,* II, 2, 201. *hurt not,* III, 2, 145. *I feel not this deity,* II, 1, 277. *that you remember not,* V, 255 etc. etc. *didst thou not mark my face? sawest thou not signs of fear lurk in mine eye? grew I not faint? and fell I not downright?* Ven. 643—645. *knowest thou not his looks are my soul's food?* Gent. II, 7, 15. *went'st not thou to her for a purse of ducats?* Err. IV, 4, 90. *why speak not you?* Ado IV, 1, 64. *standest not thou attainted?* H6A II, 4, 92 etc.

Sometimes placed before the verb: *I not doubt he came alive to land,* Tp. II, 1, 121. *whereof the ewe not bites,* V, 38. *I not know,* 113. *I not doubt,* 303. *I not deny,* Meas. II, 1, 18. *she not denies it,* Ado IV, 1, 175. *which they themselves not feel,* V, 1, 22. *I not acquaint my father of this business,* Wint. IV, 4, 423. *I not purpose it,* 483. *it not belongs to you,* H4B IV, 1, 98. *it not appears to me,* 107. *whose all not equals Edward's moiety,* R3 I, 2, 250. *what not stirs,* Troil. III, 3, 184 (Q *stirs not). and that you not delay the present,* Cor. I, 6, 60. *and not impute this yielding to light love,* Rom. II, 2, 105. *I not desire to know,* Tim. IV, 3, 58. *I marvel our mild husband not met us,* Lr. IV, 2, 2. *that which not enriches him,* Oth. III, 3, 160. *what they do delay, they not deny,* Ant. II, 1, 3. *it not concerned me,* II, 2, 35. *many years not wore him from my remembrance,* Cymb. IV, 4, 23. Lr. II, 1, 77.

The same liberty in placing it, in interrogative, imperative, and conditional sentences: *didst not thou share? hadst thou not fifteen pence?* Wiv. II, 2, 14. *did not I tell thee yea? hadst thou not order?* Meas. II, 2, 8. *would they not wish?* Ven. 447. *are they not quickly told?* 520. 643. 644. 645. Tp. II, 1, 201. 210. 312. III, 2, 82. Gent. II, 7, 15. Err. V, 337. Ado IV, 1, 133. V, 4, 1. LLL V, 1, 86 etc. etc. *is not this true?* Tp. I, 2, 267. *is not this Stephano?* V, 277. *wherefore do not you a mightier way make war?* Sonn. 16, 1. *did not you say,* Meas. V, 261. Err. IV, 4, 90. Ado II, 1, 167. LLL II, 114. V, 2, 433 (Q1 *not you,* Q2 Ff *you not).* 474 (Q2 *you not,* Q1 Ff *not you).* Mids. II, 1, 34 (Q1 *not you,* Q2 Ff *you not).* 42. 63. III, 2, 273. 348. IV, 1, 140. 199. As III, 5, 90. H6A II, 4, 92. III, 1, 129. Troil. III, 1, 1 (Q *you not,* Ff *not you)* etc. etc. *let me not dwell in this island,* Tp. Epil. 5. *give me not the boots,* Gent. I, 1, 27. *let not me play a woman,* Mids. I, 2, 49. *fear you not my part of the dialogue,* Ado III, 1, 31 (cf. *Fear). were I not immortal,* Ven. 197. *had not you come,* R3 III, 4, 27 (Ff *had you not).* Placed before the subject, when there is stress laid on the latter: *and have not they suffered?* Wiv. IV, 5, 113. *and are not you my husband?* Err. V, 370. *why speak not you?* Ado IV, 1, 64. *love you my son? Do not you love him?* All's I, 3, 193. *am I not protector, saucy priest? And am not I a prelate of the church?* H6A III, 1, 46. *tell not me,* Tp. III, 2, 1. Merch. I, 1, 39. III, 3, 1. *were never four such lamps together mixed, had not his clouded,* Ven. 490. cf. *that cannot I help,* Gent. III, 1, 359. *now will not I deliver this letter,* Tw. III, 4, 202. *yet had not we determined he should die,* R3 III, 5, 52 (Ff *we not).*

Followed by *but,* sometimes = not only: *it is not*

*my consent, but my entreaty too,* Meas. IV, 1, 67. *you may salve so not what is dangerous present, but the loss of what is past,* Cor. III, 2, 71. *and that not in the presence of dreaded justice, but on the ministers that do distribute it,* III, 3, 97. *and not your knowledge, your personal pain, but even your purse, still open, hath built Lord Cerimon such strong renown,* Per. III, 2, 46.

Substantively: *to make the not eternal,* All's III, 2, 24.

**Notable,** excellent, remarkable, egregious (oftener in a bad than in a good sense): *my master is become a n. lover,* Gent. II, 5, 44. *a n. lubber,* 47. *we shall find this friar a n. fellow,* Meas. V, 268. *thou wilt prove a n. argument,* Ado I, 1, 258. *he's a most n. coward,* All's III, 6, 10. *on that vice in him will my revenge find n. cause to work,* Tw. II, 3, 166. *come by some n. shame,* II, 5, 6. *turn him into a n. contempt,* 223. *set upon Aguecheek a n. report of valour,* III, 4, 210. *n. pirate,* V, 72. *a n. passion of wonder appeared in them,* Wint. V, 2, 17. *you depend upon a n. gentleman,* Troil. III, 1, 6 (Ff and M. Edd. *noble*): *the fleers, the gibes, and n. scorns,* Oth. IV, 1, 83. *O n. strumpet,* V, 1, 78.

**Notably,** excellently: *it would have been a fine tragedy: and so it is, truly, and very n. discharged,* Mids. V, 368.

**Not-answering,** (O. Edd. in one word, M. Edd. in two), making no answer: *he professes n.* Troil. III, 3, 270.

**Not-appearance,** non-appearance in court: H8 IV, 1, 30.

**Notary,** one authorized to attest contracts or writings of any kind: *dim register and n. of shame,* Lucr. 765. Merch. I, 3, 145. 173.

**Notch,** to cut in small hollows: *he scotched him and —ed him like a carbonado,* Cor. IV, 5, 199.

**Note,** subst. 1) a mark, a sign by which something may be perceived or known: *the greatest n. of it* (his being in love) *is his melancholy,* Ado III, 2, 54. *nine changes of the watery star hath been the shepherd's n.* Wint. I, 2, 2 (by which he measured time). *a n. infallible of breaking honesty,* 287. *the changes I perceived in the king and Camillo were very —s of admiration,* V, 2, 12. *upon his royal face there is no n. how dread an army hath enrounded him,* H5 IV Chor. 35. *lest they should spy my windpipe's dangerous —s,* Tim. I, 2, 52 (where best to cut it). *some natural —s about her body,* Cymb. II, 2, 28. *averring —s of chamber-hanging, pictures,* V, 5, 203.

2) a musical character marking a sound: *one clef, two —s have I,* Shr. III, 1, 77. *would sound me from my lowest n. to the top of my compass,* Hml. III, 2, 383. Hence = tune, melody: *she begins a wailing n.* Ven. 835. *relish your nimble —s to pleasing ears,* Lucr. 1126. *who ... one pleasing n. do sing,* Sonn. 8, 12. *give me a n.: your ladyship can set,* Gent. I, 2, 81. *the nightingale's complaining —s,* V, 4, 5. *that is the very n. of it,* Wiv. I, 1, 172. Err. III, 2, 45. Ado II, 3, 56. 57. 59. LLL III, 14. V, 2, 929. 938. Mids. III, 1, 130. 135. 141. V, 405. As II, 5, 3. 48. V, 3, 36. Shr. V, 2, 1. H5 IV, 2, 35. H6B III, 2, 40. H6C IV, 6, 14. H8 IV, 2, 78. Troil. IV, 5, 3. V, 3, 14. V, 10, 45. Tit. III, 1, 86. Rom. III, 5, 21. Cymb. IV, 2, 237. 241.

3) any paper or writing from which something may be gathered: *I come by n., to give and to receive,* Merch. III, 2, 141 (according to the direction of the scroll). *here is the n. of the fashion to testify,* Shr. IV, 3, 130. 133. *perusing o'er these —s,* John V, 2, 5. *this n. doth tell me of ten thousand French,* H5 IV, 8, 85. *I have a n. from the Volscian state, to find you out there,* Cor. IV, 3, 11. *what doth her beauty serve but as a n. where I may read who passed that passing fair?* Rom. I, 1, 241. *take thou this n.* Lr. V, 3, 27. *left these —s of what commands I should be subject to,* Cymb. I, 1, 171. = letter, billet: Meas. IV, 2, 106. Merch. III, 4, 51. R3 V, 3, 41 (Qq *scroll*). Hml. II, 1, 1. = reckoning, bill: *here's the n. how much your chain weighs,* Err. IV, 1, 27. *the smith's n. for shoeing,* H4B V, 1, 19. *here is a n. of certain dues,* Tim. II, 2, 16. = list, catalogue: *he hath an abstract for the remembrance of such places, and goes to them by his n.* Wiv. IV, 2, 64. *I have perused the n.* Shr. I, 2, 145. *answer to what I shall ask you out of a n.* All's IV, 3, 146. *that's out of my n.* Wint. IV, 3, 49. *the rest that are within the n. of expectation already are in the court,* Mcb. III, 3, 10 (= in the list of expected guests). *who has the n. of them?* Cymb. I, 5, 2. = prescription, receipt: *—s whose faculties ...,* All's I, 3, 232.

4) stigma, brand, reproach: *my posterity, shamed with the n.* Lucr. 208. *would from my forehead wipe a perjured n.* LLL IV, 3, 125 (= a n. of perjury). *folly in fools bears not so strong a n. as foolery in the wise,* V, 2, 75. *the more to aggravate the n., with a foul traitor's name stuff I thy throat,* R2 I, 1, 43.

5) any distinction or eminence: *you must not foil the precious n. of it* (the crown) *with a base slave,* Cymb. II, 3, 127. *of n.* = distinguished, eminent: *make them men of n.* LLL III, 25. *offence of mighty n.* All's V, 3, 14. *some sir of n.* Tw. III, 4, 82. *a daughter of most rare n.* Wint. IV, 2, 48. *creatures of n. for mercy-lacking uses,* John IV, 1, 121. *one of greatest n.* Mcb. V, 7, 21. *a youth that means to be of n.* Ant. IV, 4, 27. *he is of n.* V, 9, 32. *my report was once first with the best of n.* Cymb. III, 3, 58. *he brags as if he were of n.* V, 3, 94. With an adjective denoting the particular kind of distinction: *a nun, or sister sanctified, of holiest n.* Compl. 233. *I did some service, of such n. indeed, that it would scarce be answered,* Tw. III, 3, 27. *there shall be done a deed of dreadful n.* Mcb. III, 2, 44. *he is one of the noblest n.* Cymb. I, 6, 22. *he was then of a crescent n.* I, 4, 2.

6) remark: *a good n.; that keeps you from the blow of the law,* Tw. III, 4, 168.

7) any thing by which something is kept in mind; record: *no n. upon my parents, his all noble,* All's I, 3, 163. *to take n.* (German *sich merken*) = a) to mind, to remember: *take n. of it,* Meas. V, 80. *for which the heavens, taking angry n., have left me issueless,* Wint. V, 1, 173 (remembering, recording it in anger). *take this n.* Lr. IV, 5, 29. *take n., take n., O world, to be direct and honest is not safe,* Oth. III, 3, 377. b) to imprint in the mind: *to take a n. of what I stand in need of,* Gent. II, 7, 84. *I have ta'en a due and wary n. upon't,* Meas. IV, 1, 38. *as I took n. of the place, it cannot be far,* Tim. V, 1, 1.

8) attention, observation: *some precepts worthy the n.* All's III, 5, 104. *O give us n.* H8 I, 1, 63 (M. Edd. *he gives us n.*). *which, without n., here's many else have done,* Cor. I, 9, 49 (without notice taken). *what hath proceeded worthy n.* Caes. I, 2, 181. *give him heedful n.* Hml. III, 2, 89. *three in Egypt cannot make better n.* Ant. III, 3, 26 (be better observers).

*that they will waste their time upon our n.* Cymb. IV, 4, 20 (to mind, to take notice of us). *to take n.* = a) to pay regard, to respect: *my love hath in't a bond whereof the world takes n.* All's I, 3, 195. *high n. is taken of your many virtues,* H8 II, 3, 59. b) to observe: *take good n. what Caesar doth,* Caes. II, 4, 14. *I have taken a n. of it,* Hml. V, 1, 151. *take but good n.* Ant. I, 1, 11. c) to take notice, to care for, to heed: *now 'tis awake, takes n. of what is done,* Meas. II, 2, 94. *take no n. of him,* Ado III, 3, 29. *that they take no n. at all of our being absent,* Merch. V, 120. *to take n. how many pair of silk stockings thou hast,* H4B IV, 2, 17. *take no n. of him,* Rom. I, 5, 73. *where never Roman shall take n. of him,* Caes. V, 3, 50. d) to perceive, to become aware: *taking n. of thy abhorred aspect,* John IV, 2, 224. *they have ta'en n. of us,* Cor. IV, 2, 10. *let the world take n., you are the most immediate to our throne,* Hml. I, 2, 108.

9) intelligence, information, knowledge: *she that from Naples can have no n.* Tp. II, 1, 248. *—s whose faculties inclusive were more than they were in n.* All's I, 3, 233 (= known). *my niece shall take n. of it,* Tw. III, 2, 38 (= be informed of it). *it shall come to n.* IV, 3, 29 (become known). *a gentleman of the greatest promise that ever came into my n.* Wint. I, 1, 40. *the king hath n. of all,* H5 II, 2, 6. *give dreadful n. of preparation,* IV Chor. 14. *whereof my sovereign would have n.* H8 I, 2, 48. *in self-assumption greater than in the n. of judgment,* Troil. II, 3, 134 (than true judges know him to be). *give him n. of our approach,* IV, 1, 43. *the king shall have n. of this,* Tit. II, 3, 85 (O. Edd. *notice*). *such ambiguous giving out to n. that you know aught of me,* Hml. I, 5, 179 (Qq *out, to n.*). *I do know you, and dare upon the warrant of my n. commend a dear thing to you,* Lr. III, 1, 18 (Qq *art*). *his picture I will send far and near, that all the kingdom may have due n. of him,* II, 1, 85. *these present wars shall find I love my country, even to the n. o' the king,* Cymb. IV, 3, 44 (so that the king shall hear of it).

**Note,** vb. 1) to set a mark on; in an ill sense, = to dishonour, to stigmatize: *you have condemned and —d Lucius Pella,* Caes. IV, 3, 2 (the Latin *notare*).

2) to mark with musical characters: *an you re us and fa us, you n. us,* Rom. IV, 5, 122. *any man may sing her, if he can take her cliff; she's —d,* Troil. V, 2, 11 (quibbling in both passages).

3) to set down, to commit to memory in any manner, to keep in remembrance: *I'll n. you in my book of memory,* H6A II, 4, 101. *but my design, to note the chamber; I will write all down,* Cymb. II, 2, 24. *the gravity and stillness of your youth the world hath —d,* Oth. II, 3, 192.

4) to attend to, to observe; a) to do observance, to respect: *whose worth and honesty is richly —d,* Wint. V, 3, 145. *I desire to find him so* (honourable), *that I may worthily n. him,* Per. IV, 6, 56. b) to pay attention, to heed, to take notice of, to listen to, to mark: *what could he see but mightily he —d? what did he n. but strongly he desired?* Lucr. 414. 415. *yet n., their manners are more gentle-kind,* Tp. III, 3, 31. *I —d her not, but I looked on her,* Ado I, 1, 165. *n. this before my notes,* II, 3, 56. *worth the —ing,* 57. *do you n., men?* LLL III, 25 (most M. Edd. *n. me*). *but n. me, signior,* Merch. I, 3, 98. *n. this,* H4B IV, 1, 197. *we will hear, n. and believe,* H5 I, 2, 30. *first n. that he is near you in descent,* H6B III, 1, 21. *what need*

*you n. it?* H8 II, 4, 128. *n. this dangerous conception,* I, 2, 138. *mark him, n. him,* Troil. I, 2, 251. *n. me this,* Cor. I, 1, 131. *n. but this fool,* IV, 2, 17. *rather than pity n. how much,* V, 2, 93. *n. how she quotes the leaves,* Tit. IV, 1, 50. *do you n. me?* Rom. IV, 5, 121. *ever n., Lucilius,* Caes. IV, 2, 19. *you must n. beside that we have tried the utmost of our friends,* IV, 3, 213. *if much you n. him, you will offend him,* Mcb. III, 4, 56. *n., if your lady strain his entertainment,* Oth. III, 3, 250. *n. him, good Charmian,* Ant. I, 5, 53. *which worthily deserved —ing,* II, 2, 188. *a lower place, n. well, may make too great an act,* III, 1, 12. *lying, n. it, the woman's,* Cymb. II, 5, 22. *I would have you n., this is an honourable man,* Per. IV, 6, 54. c) to have in the eye, to look on with attention, to observe: *to n. the fighting conflict of her hue,* Ven. 345. *by —ing of the lady I have marked,* Ado IV, 1, 160. *do but n. a wild and wanton herd,* Merch. V, 71. *slink by, and n. him,* As III, 2, 267. *I did very well n. him,* Hml. III, 2, 301. *and n. the qualities of the people,* Ant. I, 1, 53. *we have —d it,* Cymb. III, 5, 34. d) to become aware of, to perceive, to see: *this solemn sympathy poor Venus —th,* Ven. 1057. *more flowers I —d,* Sonn. 99, 14. *they in thee a thousand errors n.* 141, 2. *didst thou n. the daughter of Signior Leonato?* Ado I, 1, 163. *that when I n. another man like him, I may avoid him,* V, 1, 269. *saw sighs reek from you, —d well your passion,* LLL IV, 3, 140. *heavens so shine, that they may fairly n. this act of mine,* Tw. IV, 3, 35 (lend a fair aspect to, regard with favour). *didst n. it?* Wint. I, 2, 214. *not —d is't but of the finer natures?* 225. *I have missingly —d, he is of late much retired from court,* IV, 2, 35. *what love I n. in the fair multitude of those her hairs,* John III, 4, 61. *a virtuous man whom I have often —d in thy company,* H4A II, 4, 460. *and never —d in him any study,* H5 I, 1, 57. *effeminate remorse, which we have —d in you to your kin,* R3 III, 7, 212. *this is —d, and generally,* H8 II, 1, 46. *do you n. how much her grace is altered?* IV, 2, 95. *which late I —d in tattered weeds,* Rom. V, 1, 38. *—ing this penury,* 49. *I have —d thee always wise,* Tim. III, 1, 33. *tell me what thou —st about the field,* Caes. V, 3, 22. *I have —d it well,* Lr. I, 4, 81. *he wears the rose of youth upon him, from which the world should n. something particular,* Ant. III, 13, 21. *I do n. that grief and patience mingle their spurs together,* Cymb. IV, 2, 56. *n. it not you?* Per. II, 3, 57.

5) to show; in a doubtful passage in Hml. I, 5, 178: *such ambiguous giving out, to n. that you know aught of me.* Ff *out to n.*

**Note-book,** a book in which memorandums are written: Wiv. I, 1, 147. H4B II, 4, 290. Caes. IV, 3, 98.

**Noted,** known: Sonn. 76, 6. LLL IV, 3, 88. Shr. III, 2, 14. John IV, 2, 21. H4A I, 2, 202. Troil. V, 2, 11 (quibbling). Tit. II, 3, 86. Hml. II, 1, 23.

**Notedly,** with good perception and remembrance, exactly: *do you remember what you said of the duke? Most n.* Meas. V, 335.

**Note-worthy,** worth seeing: Gent. I, 1, 13.

**Not-fearing,** fearless: Cymb. II, 4, 19.

**Nothing** (sometimes accented on the second syllable: R3 I, 2, 236. Tim. IV, 2, 2. Cymb. IV, 4, 15), not any thing, nought; Ven. 287. 288. 372. 418. 441. Sonn. 20, 12. 123, 3. Tp. I, 2, 16. 418. 457. II, 1, 170. 175. 313. III, 1, 94. III, 2, 23. 154. III, 3, 81.

85. Gent. I, 1, 103. 131. III, 2, 87. Wiv. IV, 1, 15. Meas. II, 2, 155. Err. II, 1, 16. III, 2, 105. Tw. V, 188 etc. etc. *I have n. with this answer*, Hml. III, 2, 101. *this peace is n. but to rust iron*, Cor. IV, 5, 234. *whose worth makes other worthies n.* Gent. II, 4, 166. *so surprised my sense that I was n.* Wint. III, 1, 11. *Edgar I n. am*, Lr. II, 3, 21. *'twill be n. yet*, Tw. III, 4, 432; cf. Ant. III, 5, 23. *we are undone and brought to n.* Shr. V, 1, 45. (the lion) *makes him n.* H8 III, 2, 208. *to make n. of*, Lr. III, 1, 9 (see *Make*). With *of: n. of him that doth fade*, Tp. I, 2, 399. *to have it added to the fault of mine, and n. of your answer*, Meas. II, 4, 73. *the gracious queen, part of his theme, but n. of his ill-ta'en suspicion*, Wint. I, 2, 459. *you are all in all in spleen, and n. of a man*, Oth. IV, 1, 90. *let this fellow be n. of our strife*, Ant. II, 2, 80 etc.

Substantively: *needy n. trimmed in jollity*, Sonn. 66, 3. *for n. hold me, so it please thee hold that n. me a something sweet to thee*, 136, 12. *gives to airy n. a local habitation*, Mids. V, 16. *speaks an infinite deal of n.* Merch. I, 1, 114. *thus he his special n. ever prologues*, All's II, 1, 95. *uses a known truth to pass a thousand —s with*, II, 5, 33. *nor n. have these —s*, Wint. I, 2, 295. *admiring the n. of it*, IV, 4, 626. *makes me with heavy n. faint*, R2 II, 2, 32. *grated to dusty n.* Troil. III, 2, 196. *to hear my —s monstered*, Cor. II, 2, 81. *this n. is more than matter*, Hml. IV, 5, 174. *that harsh, noble, simple n., that Cloten*, Cymb. III, 4, 135 etc.

Adverbially, = not at all: *my mistress' eyes are n. like the sun*, Sonn. 130, 1. *lawful mercy is n. kin to foul redemption*, Meas. II, 4, 113. *therein do men from children n. differ*, Ado V, 1, 33. *n. undervalued to Cato's daughter*, Merch. I, 1, 165. *n. acquainted with these businesses*, All's III, 7, 5. *it n. steads us*, 41. *she's n. allied to your disorders*, Tw. II, 3, 104. *delayed, but n. altered*, Wint. IV, 4, 475. *shall n. benefit your knowledge*, 514. *concerns him n.* 870. *Hermione was n. so aged*, V, 3, 28. *should n. privilege him*, R2 I, 1, 120. *would set my teeth n. on edge, n. so much as mincing poetry*, H4A III, 1, 133. *you were n. so strong and fortunate as I*, V, 1, 38. *n. so heavy*, H6B V, 2, 65. *being n. like the noble duke*, R3 III, 5, 92. *it will help me n.* H8 I, 1, 207. *I fear n., what can be said against me*, V, 1, 126. *they n. doubt prevailing*, Cor. I, 3, 111. *be to me n. so kind, but something pitiful*, Tit. II, 3, 156. *who n. hurt withal*, Rom. I, 1, 119. *I am n. slow*, IV, 1, 3. *n. doubting your present assistance*, Tim. III, 1, 20. *I am n. jealous*, Caes. I, 2, 162. *move only in command, n. in love*, Mcb. V, 2, 20. *we doubt it n.* V, 4, 2. Hml. I, 2, 41. *discomfort you it n. must*, III, 2, 176. *I have told you what I have seen and heard, but faintly, n. like the image and horror of it*, Lr. I, 2, 191. *to speak the truth shall n. wrong him*, Oth. II, 3, 224. *it n. ill becomes thee*, Ant. II, 6, 81. *I do n. doubt*, Cymb. I, 4, 106. *the vows of women of no more bondage be to where they are made than they are to their virtues, which is n.* II, 4, 112. *a doubt n. becoming you*, IV, 4, 15 etc.

**Nothing-gift**, a gift of no worth: *that n. of differing multitudes*, Cymb. III, 6, 86.

**Notice**, subst. 1) information, intelligence: *bring me just n. of the numbers dead*, H5 IV, 7, 122. *he hath carried n. to Escalus*, Meas. IV, 3, 135. *to give a p. n.:* Meas. IV, 4, 19. IV, 5, 7. H6A III, 2, 8. Lr. II, 1, 3. Cymb. III, 4, 127. *to give n. of:* Gent. II, 6, 36. Meas.

I, 4, 87. H6B III, 1, 370. R3 III, 1, 178. *to have n.* Ant. I, 2, 184. *I have no certain n.* H4B I, 3, 85. *to have n. of:* LLL II, 81. As I, 1, 145. H6B III, 1, 166. Tit. II, 3, 85 (M. Edd. *note*). Rom. V, 2, 27. Caes. III, 2, 275. *to take n.* = to be informed, to hear, to learn: *take n., lords, he has a loyal breast, for you have seen him open't*, H8 III, 2, 200. *that your wisdom yet, from one that so imperfectly conceits, would take no n.* Oth. III, 3, 150. *take n. that I am in Cambria*, Cymb. III, 2, 44.

2) observation: *to my poor unworthy n. he mocked us*, Cor. II, 3, 166 (as far as I observed him; as it appeared to me).

3) instruction, direction, order (cf. the German *zu wissen thun*): *and shall, at the least of thy sweet n., bring her to trial*. LLL I, 1, 279 (Armado's letter). *to give n. that no manner of person have recourse unto the princes*, R3 III, 5, 108 (Ff *order*). *gave n. he was from thence discharged*, H8 II, 4, 33.

4) attention, regard: *to no more will I give place or n.* Lr. II, 4, 252. *I have assailed her with music, but she vouchsafes no n.* Cymb. II, 3, 45. *and towards himself we must attend our n.* 65. *to take n.* = to mind, to care for: Ven. 341. H8 I, 1, 101. Cymb. I, 5, 70.

**Notify**, a word used by Mrs Quickly in the sense of to know, to learn: Wiv. II, 2, 85; and by the fool in Oth. III, 1, 31 in that of to give information.

**Notion**, intellectual power, sense, mind: *his own n. ... shall join to thrust the lie unto him*, Cor. V, 6, 107. *all things else that might to half a soul and to a n. crazed say 'This did Banquo,'* Mcb. III, 1, 83. *his n. weakens, his discernings are lethargied*, Lr. I, 4, 248.

**Notorious**, 1) manifest to the world, known to everybody; in a bad sense: *you have been a n. bawd*, Meas. IV, 2, 14. *a most n. pirate*, IV, 3, 75. *I would it were not n.* All's I, 1, 41. *Alençon, that n. Machiavel*, H6A V, 4, 74. *your goodness, since you provoke me, shall be most n.* H8 III, 2, 288.

2) notable, egregious: *thou foul abettor, thou n. bawd*, Lucr. 886. *bring in here two n. benefactors*, Meas. II, 1, 50. *to your n. shame*, Err. IV, 1, 84. *you n. villain*, Shr. V, 1, 54. *I know him a n. liar*, All's I, 1, 111. *you have done me wrong, n. wrong*, Tw. V, 337. *made the most n. geck and gull*, 351. *wherein I did not some n. ill*, Tit. V, 1, 127. *some base n. knave*, Oth. IV, 2, 140. *'tis a n. villain*, V, 2, 239.

**Notoriously**, egregiously, enormously: *there was never man so n. abused*, Tw. IV, 2, 94. *he hath been most n. abused*, V, 388.

**Not-pated**, according to some = having the hair close cut; to others, bull-headed, blockheaded: H4A II, 4, 78; cf. *knotty-pated*, 251.

**Notwithstanding**, adv. nevertheless, however: Tp. II, 1, 62. Wiv. I, 4, 97. 108. 155. Mids. III, 2, 394. Merch. I, 3, 26. III, 2, 322. V, 239. H4B IV, 4, 33. H6C II, 1, 37. Caes. II, 2, 117. Oth. II, 3, 5. Cymb. I, 4, 107.

**Notwithstanding**, prepos. in spite of: Gent. IV, 2, 12. Wiv. I, 4, 111. H5 V, 2, 240. H6B III, 2, 258. Tit. II, 4, 29. Placed after the noun: *he hath not money for these Irish wars, his burthenous taxations n.* R2 II, 1, 260. *which n. thou shalt be no less esteemed*, Tim. II, 2, 111.

= over and above, besides, abstractedly from: *so your hand and heart ... should, n. that your bond of duty, as 'twere in love's particular, be more to me, your friend, than any*, H8 III, 2, 188.

N

783

**Notwithstanding,** conj. though: *n. thy capacity receiveth as the sea, nought enters there ... but falls into abatement,* Tw. I, 1, 10. *n. she's your wife, be you assured I hate not you,* R3 I, 3, 22.

**Nought,** see *Naught.*

**Noun,** a substantive: Wiv. IV, 1, 22. H6B IV, 7, 43. *Od's —s* (an oath) Wiv. IV, 1, 25.

**Nourish,** vb. 1) intr. to be nutritious, to afford rich food: *—ing dishes,* Oth. III, 3, 78. *'tis age that —eth,* Shr. II, 341.

2) trans. to feed; in a proper and a figurative sense: Sonn. 73, 12. Gent. II, 1, 180. LLL IV, 2, 71. IV, 3, 353. Merch. III, 2, 65. Wint. II, 3, 36. H4A IV, 1, 112. H6C I, 1, 222. Cor. III, 1, 69. 117. Tit. V, 1, 60. 84. Rom. I, 1, 198. Tim. I, 1, 22. Ant. II, 7, 50. IV, 8, 21. = to support, to maintain: *whiles I in Ireland n. a mighty band,* H6B III, 1, 348.

**Nourish,** subst. nurse: *our isle be made a n. of salt tears,* H6A I, 1, 50 (some M. Edd. *marish*).*

**Nourisher,** that which nourishes: Mcb. II, 2, 40.

**Nourishment,** food, nutriment: LLL I, 1, 239. H8 V, 3, 44. Per. I, 2, 56. cf. *After-nourishment.*

**Nousle** or **Nouzle,** to nurse: *who, to n. up their babes, thought nought too curious,* Per. I, 4, 42. cf. *Nuzzle.*

**Novel,** new: *nothing n., nothing strange,* Sonn. 123, 3.

**Novelty,** newness, anything new and before unknown: *n. is only in request,* Meas. III, 2, 237. *it is a n. to the world,* All's II, 3, 22. *how n. may move,* Troil. IV, 4, 81 (Ff *—es*).

**No-verb,** a word which does not exist: *he gives me the proverbs and the —s,* Wiv. III, 1, 107 (the host's speech).

**Novice,** one new in a business or situation: *a n. of this place,* Meas. I, 4, 19 (= probationer). *you are —s,* Shr. II, 313. *Mars dote on you for his —s,* All's II, 1, 48. *Plantagenet, that princely n.* R3 I, 4, 228 (new to the world). *thou hast sold me to this n.* Ant. IV, 12, 14.

**Novum,** a game at dice, properly called *novem quinque,* from the two principal throws being nine and five: *abate throw at n.* LLL V, 2, 547.

**Now,** at this time, by this time: Ven. 45. 97. 181 etc. etc. = but now, Cor. I, 9, 79. Peculiar position: *punished for before-breach of the king's laws in n. the king's quarrel,* H5 IV, 1, 180. As for *but n., ere n., even n.,* see *But, Ere, Even.* Applied to a time past: *n. was she just before him,* Ven. 349. *that n. he was the ivy,* Tp. I, 2, 85. *I sprang not more in joy at first hearing he was a man-child than n. in first seeing he had probed himself a man,* Cor. I, 3, 18 etc. *n. and then* = at intervals, occasionally: Merch. II, 2, 200. As III, 5, 103. H5 III, 6, 71. Lr. IV, 3, 14. *n. ... n.* = at one time ... at another time: Ven. 224. 965. Tp. I, 2, 196. As III, 2, 436. Wint. IV, 4, 58. H6C II, 5, 5. H8 I, 1, 29. *n. ... and n.: n. she weeps, and n. she fain would speak, and n. her sobs do her intendments break,* Ven. 221. *n. he vows a league, and n. invasion,* Lucr. 287. *n. ... then,* in the same sense: *n. weep for him, then spit at him,* As III, 2, 437. *n. one the better, then another best,* H6C II, 5, 10.

= things being so, under these circumstances: *being mad before, how doth she n. for wits?* Ven. 249. *n. which way shall she turn?* 253. *what cares he n. for curb?* 285. *for pity n. she can no more detain him,* 577.

*for n. she knows it is no gentle chase,* 883. *n. would I give a thousand furlongs of sea for an acre of barren ground,* Tp. I, 1, 69. *how n. shall this be compassed?* III, 2, 66. Ven. 786. 953. 977. 991. 1077 etc. Hence forming a connection between the preceding and subsequent propositions: *n. for your answer ...,* Merch. IV, 1, 52. *n. in respect it is in the fields, it pleaseth me well,* As III, 2, 17. *thou swearest to me thou art honest: n., if thou wert a poet, I might have some hope thou didst feign,* III, 3, 26. *n. good or bad, 'tis but the chance of war,* Troil. Prol. 31. *n., to seem to affect the displeasure of the people is as bad as to flatter them,* Cor. II, 2, 23 etc. *n. that* = it being so that, since: *what may be wrought out of their discontent, n. that their souls are topful of offence?* John III, 4, 180. *n. that God and friends have shaken Edward from the regal seat, ... what are thy due fees?* H6C IV, 6, 1. Oftener *n.* alone, without *that,* in the same sense: *where shall I live n. Lucrece is unlived?* Lucr. 1754. *why should he live, n. Nature bankrupt is?* Sonn. 67, 9. *past cure I am, n. reason is past care,* 147, 9. *they are oppressed with travel, they will not use such vigilance,* Tp. III, 3, 15. Gent. I, 1, 123. I, 2, 1. III, 2, 2. Wiv. II, 1, 182. Meas. III, 1, 179. Ado I, 1, 303. LLL I, 1, 108. Mids. III, 2, 135. IV, 1, 67. As V, 4, 155. All's V, 3, 315. 335. John V, 2, 95. R2 V, 1, 99. H6A IV, 6, 29. IV, 7, 32. 96. V, 4, 4. 149. H6B I, 1, 216. III, 2, 55. IV, 4, 56. H6C II, 6, 6. 44. R3 I, 2, 170. Troil. V, 2, 90. Cor. II, 3, 180. Oth. IV, 2, 162 etc. Placed after: *her eye is sick on't, I observe her n.* All's I, 3, 142 (now that I observe her).

Hence added emphatically to wishes, prayers, obsecrations, and asseverations: *n. good angels preserve the king!* Tp. II, 1, 306. *n. all the blessings of a glad father compass thee about,* V, 179. *n. heaven send thee good fortune,* Wiv. III, 4, 105. *n. fair befall your mask!* LLL II, 124; cf. *n. fair befall thee,* R3 I, 3, 282; III, 5, 47. *n. justice on the doers,* All's V, 3, 154. *n. God in heaven forbid,* R2 II, 2, 51. *n. the Lord lighten thee,* H4B II, 1, 208. *n. heavens forbid such scarcity of youth,* Troil. I, 3, 302. *n. the gods keep you old enough,* Tim. III, 5, 104. *n. the red pestilence strike all trades in Rome,* Cor. IV, 1, 13. *n. the gods keep you,* IV, 6, 25. *n. the witch take me,* Ant. IV, 2, 37. *I pray n., keep below,* Tp. I, 1, 12. *I prithee n., lead the way,* II, 2, 177. *alas, n. pray you,* III, 1, 15. *pray n., rest yourself,* 20. *n., good my lord, let there be some more test made of my metal,* Meas. I, 1, 48. *sweet n., make haste,* Err. IV, 2, 29. *good n., hold thy tongue,* IV, 4, 22; Wint. V, 1, 19; Troil. III, 1, 122; Hml. I, 1, 70; Ant. I, 2, 25; I, 3, 78. *I prithee n.* As III, 2, 199. Troil. III, 1, 116. *pray you n.* Ant. III, 11, 22. Cymb. III, 1, 46. *lo n., lo!* Tp. II, 2, 14. John III, 4, 21. *n., by my modesty, a goodly broker!* Gent. I, 2, 41. *n. trust me, 'tis an office of great worth,* 44. II, 1, 115. Err. I, 1, 143. *that's meat and drink to me, n.* Wiv. I, 1, 306. *n., as I am a Christian, answer me,* Err. I, 2, 77. *n. by the faith of my love, I will,* As III, 2, 449. *in your conscience n.?* H5 IV, 1, 81. *n. for thy whore, Trojan! n. the sleeve,* Troil. V, 4, 25. *this is strange n.* Cor. II, 1, 24. *your serpent of Egypt is bred n. of your mud,* Ant. II, 7, 29.

Used to introduce an address, especially one expressive of surprise or curiosity: *n., blasphemy, not an oath on shore?* Tp. V, 218. *n., daughter Silvia, you are hard beset,* Gent. II, 4, 49. *n., Master Shallow, you'll complain of me to the king?* Wiv. I, 1, 112. *n., what's the matter, provost?* Meas. II, 2, 6. *n. in good time!* Wint. IV, 4, 163. *n., captain?* Tim. III, 5, 6. *n., thieves?* IV, 3, 415. *n., Cinna: n., Metellus,* Caes. II, 2, 120. *n., Lychorida!* Per. III, 1, 14. More frequently *how now* (sometimes = how do you do? at other times = what is the matter? or what are you doing here?): Tp. I, 2, 244. II, 1, 308. II, 2, 139. V, 285. Gent. I, 2, 16. 88. I, 3, 51. II, 1, 7. 147. III, 1, 279. III, 2, 11. IV, 2, 18. 54. IV, 4, 47. V, 2, 31. V, 4, 86. Wiv. I, 1, 198. I, 4, 142. II, 1, 152. Meas. I, 2, 58. 86. II, 1, 45. II, 4, 17. 30. IV, 2, 91. Err. II, 2, 7. IV, 1, 93. IV, 4, 9. Ado I, 2, 1. V, 1, 214. LLL IV, 3, 200. Mids. I, 1, 128. II, 1, 1. III, 2, 4. Merch. I, 2, 134. III, 1, 25. V, 288. Shr. IV, 1, 110. 113. Tw. III, 4, 118. Wint. III, 2, 148 *(how n. there!).* H6A IV, 4, 12. H6B I, 1, 53. Rom. III, 5, 150. Ant. I, 2, 134 (= ho!). Per. IV, 6, 22. *why how n.,* in the same sense: Wiv. III, 4, 72. Meas. I, 2, 128. Err. III, 2, 71. Ado III, 4, 41. Hml. III, 4, 13. *what n.,* in the same sense: Err. I, 2, 42. Troil. V, 3, 98.

**Now-a-days,** in the present age: Mids. III, 1, 148. Hml. V, 1, 181 (Qq om.). Per. II, 1, 73.

**Now-born** or **Now-borne?** now engendered? or now brought? All's II, 3, 186. See *Brief.*

**Nowhere,** not in any place: Compl. 27. Wiv. IV, 2, 166. As II, 7, 2. Hml. III, 1, 136.

**Nowl,** see *Nole.*

**Noyance,** injury: *to keep itself from n.* Hml. III, 3, 13.

**Numa,** the second king of Rome: Cor. II, 3, 247.

**Numb,** adj. torpid, chill: *these feet, whose strengthless stay is n.* H6A II, 5, 13. *the n. cold night,* R3 II, 1, 117. *cold and n.* Tit. III, 1, 259.

**Numb,** vb. (cf. *Benumb*) to make torpid: *—s each feeling part,* Ven. 892. *their —ed and mortified bare arms,* Lr. II, 3, 15.

**Number,** subst. 1) any particular aggregate of units: *n. there in love was slain,* Phoen. 28. *I thought there had been one n. more,* Wiv. IV, 1, 25. *good luck lies in odd — s,* V, 1, 3. *our compelled sins stand more for n. than for accompt,* Meas. II, 4, 58. *now is the n. even,* LLL IV, 3, 210. *may stand in n., though in reckoning none,* Rom. I, 2, 33.

2) a computed quantity; as many or few as are counted: *in n. more than ever woman spoke,* Mids. I, 1, 176. *you and those poor n. saved with you,* Tw. I, 2, 10. *add a royal n. to the dead,* John II, 347. *the little n. of your doubtful friends,* V, 1, 36. R2 I, 3, 210. II, 1, 177. III, 3, 123. H4B III, 2, 201. IV, 1, 21. V, 2, 61* H5 III, 6, 139. IV, 8, 79. R3 IV, 1, 45. V, 3, 9. Cor. I, 6, 80. Tit. I, 80. Rom. I, 2, 23. Caes. I, 2, 44. III, 1, 216. IV, 3, 208. Lr. II, 4, 64 (Qq *train*). 243. 256. Ant. III, 9, 3. Per. I, 4, 86. IV, 2, 100. Plur. *—s:* H4B IV, 1, 4. H5 IV Chor. 17. IV, 7, 122. V Chor. 4. Tim. III, 1, 54. Cymb. III, 7, 15.

3) a multitude, many: *among a n. one is reckoned none: then in the n. let me pass untold,* Sonn. 136, 8. 9. *you slew great n. of his people,* Tw. III, 3, 29. *we have a n. of shadows,* H4B III, 2, 145. H6B III, 1, 308. H8 II, 1, 9. III, 1, 34. Tim. I, 2, 40. Caes. III, 1, 68. Ant. III, 2, 65. Per. IV, 5, 43. Plur. *—s: such —s seek for thee,* Lucr. 896. *if the opposed —s pluck their hearts from them,* H5 IV, 1, 308. H6B II, 1, 40. H6C IV, 2, 2. Cor. III, 3, 72. Ant. I, 3, 52.

4) an assemblage of persons, company, troop,

band: *every of this happy n.* As V, 4, 178. *when you have drawn your n.* Cor. II, 3, 261. *mingling them with us, the honoured n.* III, 1, 72. *dissentious —s pestering streets,* IV, 6, 7. *go thou into the other street and part the —s,* Caes. III, 2, 3. Especially = host, army: *the n. of the king exceedeth ours,* H4A IV, 3, 28. Plur. *—s: when the achiever brings home full —s,* Ado I, 1, 9. *shall we do draw our —s and set on?* H4B I, 3, 109. II, 3, 43. III, 1, 98. H5 III, 5, 56. III, 6, 155. Troil. I, 3, 56. V, 5, 15. Cor. I, 5, 13. Mcb. I, 2, 51. V, 4, 6. Hml. IV, 4, 63. Cymb. IV, 2, 343.

5) Plur. *—s* = rhythmical cadence, metre: *here are only —s ratified,* LLL IV, 2, 125. *the —s true,* V, 2, 35. *the —s altered,* Tw. II, 5, 111. *I am ill at these —s; I have not art to reckon my groans,* Hml. II, 2, 120.

Hence = verse, poetry: *if I could in fresh —s number all your graces,* Sonn. 17, 6. *eternal —s to outlive long date,* 38, 12. *my gracious —s are decayed,* 79, 3. *redeem in gentle —s time so idly spent,* 100, 6. *these —s will I tear and write in prose,* LLL IV, 3, 57. *such fiery —s,* 322. *shall crown up the verse and sanctify the —s,* Troil. III, 2, 190. *the —s that Petrarch flowed in,* Rom. II, 4, 41.

6) the singular and plural in grammar: Wiv. IV, 1, 21. 72.

7) the fourth book of Moses: *in the book of —s it is writ,* H5 I, 2, 98.

**Number,** vb. 1) to enumerate: *in fresh numbers n. all your graces,* Sonn. 17, 6.

2) to count, to tell: *how many steps are —ed in the travel of one mile? we n. nothing that we spend for you,* LLL V, 2, 197. 198. *—ing sands,* R2 II, 2, 146. V, 5, 50. H5 IV, 8, 78. H6B I, 3, 59. H6C II, 1, 162. *the sands are —ed that make up my life,* I, 4, 25.

3) to be at the age of: *as when he —ed thirty,* All's IV, 5, 86. *when Viola from her birth had —ed thirteen years,* Tw. V, 252. cf. *a sibyl that had —ed in the world the sun to course two hundred compasses,* Oth. III, 4, 40.

4) to reckon, to account, to estimate: *henceforth be never —ed among men,* Mids. III, 2, 67. *were the —ing too* (true), *I were the fairest goddess on the ground,* LLL V, 2, 35.

5) to bring into verse: *scribes, bards, poets cannot ... write, sing, n. his love to Antony,* Ant. III, 2, 17.

**Numbered,** adj. rich in numbers, abundantly provided: *the twinned stones upon the n. beach,* Cymb. I, 6, 36 (Theobald *unnumbered*).

**Numberless,** innumerable: H8 II, 1, 84. Tim. IV, 3, 263.

**Numbness,** torpor: Wint. V, 3, 102.

**Nun,** a woman devoted to a religious life, and living in a cloister: Ven. 752. Compl. 232. 260. Meas. I, 4, 1. Mids. I, 1, 70.* As III, 4, 17. IV, 1, 102. All's II, 2, 28. R3 IV, 4, 201. Rom. V, 3, 157. Per. V, 3, 15.

**Nuncio,** messenger: *a n. of more grave aspect,* Tw. I, 4, 28.

**Nuncle,** the customary address of a licensed fool to his superiors (Nares): Lr. I, 4, 117. 130. 144. 170. 187. 195. 204. 234. 338. I, 5, 45. II, 4, 123. III, 2, 10. 12. III, 4, 39. III, 6, 10.

**Nunnery,** a cloister for females: Hml. III, 1, 122. 132. 142.

**Nuptial,** subst. wedding: Meas. III, 1, 122. V,

518. Ado IV, 1, 69. LLL IV, 1, 78. As V, 2, 47. Wint. IV, 4, 50. 406. Rom. I, 5, 37. Plur. —s, in the same sense: Per. V, 3, 80. In Oth. II, 2, 8 Ff n., Qq —s; in Tp. V, 308; Mids. I, 1, 125 and V, 75 the later Ff —s, the other O. Edd. n.

**Nuptial**, adj. pertaining to marriage: *our n. hour*, Mids. I, 1, 1. *day*, III, 2, 12. *ceremony*, V, 55. *rites*, Merch. II, 9, 6. *bed*, H6A V, 5, 58. *knot*, H6C III, 3, 55. *day*, Cor. I, 6, 31. *vow*, Tit. II, 3, 125. *breaches*, Lr. I, 2, 162.

**Nurse**, subst. 1) a woman that suckles or tends an infant: Ven. 974. Lucr. 813. 1162. Sonn. 22, 12. Gent. I, 2, 58. Meas. I, 3, 30. Ado III, 3, 70. 71. As II, 7, 144. Wint. II, 3, 187. R2 I, 3, 170. 307. II, 1, 51. V, 3, 113. R3 II, 4, 32. IV, 1, 102. Cor. II, 1, 222. V, 3, 110. V, 6, 97. Tit. II, 3, 28. IV, 2, 83. 86. 167. Rom. I, 3, 1. II, 4, 155. 182 etc. Ant. V, 2, 313. Per. III Prol. 43. IV Prol. 42. IV, 1, 53. V, 1, 161.

2) one who brings up, or takes a motherly care of another: *I will attend my husband, be his n.* Err. V, 98 (i. e. in his illness). *a loving n., a mother to his youth*, Tit. I, 332. *Euriphile, thou wast their n.* Cymb. III, 3, 104. V, 5, 340. *you have a n. of me*, Per. IV, 1, 25. —*s are not the fates*, IV, 3, 14. *put to n.* = entrusted to another's care, H6B IV, 2, 150. Misapplied by Evans: *his n., or his dry n.* Wiv. I, 2, 4.

3) Metaphorically, that which brings up, nourishes, or causes to grow: *what banquet wert thou to the taste, being n. and feeder of the other four*, Ven. 446. *night, desire's foul n.* 773. *night ... n. of blame*, Lucr. 767. *time is the n. and breeder of all good*, Gent. III, 1, 243. *pardon is still the n. of second woe*, Meas. II, 1, 298. *melancholy is the n. of frenzy*, Shr. Ind. 2, 135. *sleep, nature's soft n.* H4B III, 1, 6. *peace, dear n. of arts*, H5 V, 2, 35. *I am your sorrow's n.* R3 II, 2, 87. *Rome, the n. of judgement*, H8 II, 2, 94. *the dung, the beggar's n. and Caesar's*, Ant. V, 2, 8.

**Nurse**, vb. 1) to suckle, to tend in infancy: As IV, 1, 178. Wint. II, 1, 56. Rom. I, 3, 60. I, 5, 117.

2) to bring up: Sonn. 77, 11. Meas. III, 2, 126. Wint. II, 3, 183. Cymb. V, 5, 322. Per. III, 1, 81. V, 3, 8. With *up: here* —*d up and bred*, Meas. IV, 2, 134.

3) to tend, to take care of: *by* —*ing them* (the miseries of my father) Lr. V, 3, 181.

4) Metaphorically, to feed, to cherish, to foment: *the aim of all is but to n. the life with honour, wealth, and ease*, Lucr. 141. *thou* (time) —*st all and murderest all*, 929. —*th the disease*, Sonn. 147, 2. *all the*

*accommodations that thou bearest are* —*d by baseness*, Meas. III, 1, 15. *truth shall n. her*, H8 V, 5, 29. *they have* —*d this woe*, Tit. III, 1, 74.

**Nurse-like**, like a woman who attends to one's necessities: *never master had a page so kind, so duteous, diligent, so tender over his occasions, true, so feat, so n.* Cymb. V, 5, 88.

**Nurser**, one who brings up or causes to grow: *the bloody n. of his harms*, H6A IV, 7, 46.

**Nursery**, 1) the apartment where young children are nursed and brought up: *from their n. were stolen*, Cymb. I, 1, 59.

2) tender care and attendance: *I loved her most and thought to set my rest on her kind n.* Lr. I, 1, 126.

3) that which brings up or engenders something: *fair Padua, n. of arts*, Shr. I, 1, 2. *it well may serve a n. to our gentry*, All's I, 2, 16 (a school of war). *must or now be cropped, or, shedding, breed a n. of like evil*, Troil. I, 3, 319.

**Nurture**, good breeding, humanity: *a born devil, on whose nature n. can never stick*, Tp. IV, 189. *yet am I inland bred and know some n.* As II, 7, 97. cf. *Ill-nurtured.*

**Nut**, the fruit of the tree Corylus: Mids. IV, 1, 40. As III, 2, 115. 116. III, 4, 27. All's II, 5, 48. Troil. II, 1, 111. Rom. III, 1, 21. Used to denote a trifle: *a rush, a hair, a drop of blood, a pin, a n., a cherry-stone*, Err. IV, 3, 74.

**Nuthook**, contemptuous term for a catchpole: *if you run the* —*'s humour on me*, Wiv. I, 1, 171. *n., you lie*, H4B V, 4, 8.

**Nutmeg**, the fruit of Myristica moschata: Wint. IV, 3, 50. H5 III, 7, 20. A gilt n. a common gift at Christmas: LLL V, 2, 652.

**Nutriment**, that which nourishes: *why should it thrive and turn to n.* Tim. III, 1, 61.

**Nutshell**, the covering of the kernel of a nut: Tp. I, 1, 50. Hml. II, 2, 260.

**Nuzzle** (O. Edd. *nousle*), to thrust the nose in: *and* —*ing in his flank, the loving swine sheathed unaware the tusk in his soft groin*, Ven. 1115.

**Nym**, name in Wiv. I, 1, 129. II, 1, 128. 138. II, 2, 7. IV, 5, 33. H5 II, 1, 1. III, 2, 38 etc.

**Nymph**, 1) a goddess of the mountains, or woods, or waters: Ven. 9. 147. Sonn. 154, 3. Pilgr. 287. Tp. I, 2, 301. 402. IV, 66. 128. 132. 137. Mids. III, 2, 137. 226. H6C IV, 8, 21. Tit. I, 316. II, 1, 22.

2) a beautiful woman: Gent. V, 4, 12. Mids. II, 1, 245. IV, 1, 132. R3 I, 1, 17. Hml. III, 1, 89.

# O.

**O**, the fourth vowel: LLL V, 1, 60. Tw. II, 5, 118. 121. 132. 143.*151.

Substantively, = any thing circular: *O that your face were not so full of Oes*, LLL V, 2, 45 (marks of the small-pox). *all yon fiery oes*, Mids. III, 2, 188 (the stars). *may we cram within this wooden O the very casques that did affright the air at Agincourt?* H5 Prol. 13. *the little O, the earth*, Ant. V, 2, 81.

**O**, the arithmetical cipher: *thou art an O without a figure*, Lr. I, 4, 212.

**O**, interjection expressive of pain, of surprise or

of desire, or used to give the speech the character of earnestness: *O, how quick is love!* Ven. 38. *O, pity!* 95. *O, be not proud*, 113. *O, had thy mother borne so hard a mind*, 203. *O, what a sight it was*, 343. *O, what a war of looks*, 355. *O fairest mover on this mortal round*, 368. *O, give it me*, 375. *O, learn to love*, 407. *O, would thou hadst not*, 428. *but, O, what banquet wert thou*, 445. 493. 499. 506. 571. 615. 637. 721. 791. 860. 937. 939. 961. 985. 1015 etc. etc. *O me!* Sonn. 148, 1. LLL IV, 3, 165. Mids. III, 2, 282. Merch. I, 2, 24. John I, 220. IV, 3, 9. H4B IV, 4,

111. Cor. I, 6, 76. Rom. I, 1, 179. V, 3, 206. Hml. III, 4, 25. Oth. V, 1, 56. *O me, O me!* Rom. IV, 5, 19. *O me, the gods!* Cor. II, 3, 60.

Substantively: *why should you fall into so deep an O?* Rom. III, 3, 90 (= affliction. The nurse's speech).

Imitative of the voice of a beast: *like a full-acorned boar, a German one, cried O! and mounted,* Cymb. II, 5, 17.

**O',** abbreviation of the prepositions *of* and *on* (often substituted by M. Edd. for *a* of O. Edd.; cf. *A*); 1) = of (*o' the* making one syllable and mostly spelt *o' th',* even before consonants): *to think o' the teen,* Tp. I, 2, 64. *in lieu o' the premises,* 123. *the precursors o' the dreadful thunder-claps,* 202. *the rest o' the fleet,* 226. 232. *what is the time o'the day?* 239. *a nymph o' the sea,* 301. *showed thee all the qualities o'the isle,* 337. *some god o' the island,* 389. *all corners else o' the earth,* 491. *cat o' mountain,* IV, 262 (in Wiv. II, 2, 27 *cat a mountain*). *light o' love,* Gent. I, 2, 83 (in Ado III, 4, 44 *light a love*). *what time o' day,* As III, 2, 318. *she'll none o' the count,* Tw. I, 3, 115. *a fellow o' the strangest mind,* 120. *no more o' that,* I, 5, 32. *what kind o' man,* 159. *for the love o' God,* II, 3, 92. *out o' tune,* 122. *what o' that?* 196. *out o' favour,* II, 5, 9. *will you make an ass o' me?* III, 2, 14. *a jar o' the clock,* Wint. I, 2, 43. *o' the two,* 66. *to the blood o' the prince,* 330. *out o' door,* II, 3, 67. *rid o' the business,* III, 3, 14. *at the turning o' the tide,* H5 II, 3, 14. *a man o' the church,* H6B I, 1, 186. *the base o' the mount,* Tim. I, 1, 64. *the shores o' the haven,* Cymb. I, 3, 1 etc. etc.

2) = on: *a box o' the ear,* Meas. II, 1, 189. *clapped him o' the shoulder,* As IV, 1, 48. *he plays o' the viol-de-gamboys,* Tw. I, 3, 26. *till his brains turn o' the toe,* 44. *let him sit o' my coz,* I, 5, 143. *a blow o' the lips,* II, 5, 76. *set thy foot o' my neck,* 205. *o' the windy side of the law,* III, 4, 181. *her face o' fire with labour,* Wint. IV, 4, 60. *looked he o'the inside of the paper?* H8 III, 2, 78. *fare o' the trumpets' sound,* Tim. III, 6, 37. *o' both sides,* Lr. I, 4, 205. *o' the floor,* Cymb. IV, 2, 212 etc. *a pox o' your throat,* Tp. I, 1, 43. II, 1, 77. III, 2, 87. Meas. IV, 3, 26. *a plague o' this pickle-herring,* Tw. I, 5, 128. *o' my conscience,* H8 II, 1, 50. III, 1, 30. *o' my life,* Wiv. I, 1, 40. *o' my troth,* Tp. II, 2, 36. LLL IV, 1, 144 etc.

3) Used uncertain for what prepositions: *o' God's name,* R2 III, 3, 146. *o' nights,* H4B II, 1, 83. *o' mornings,* Cymb. II, 3, 13. *send o'the instant,* Tim. II, 2, 207. *to general filths convert o' the instant,* IV, 1, 7. *looked o' this fashion,* Hml. V, 1, 218 (Qq *a*). *it went o' the backside the town,* Cymb. I, 2, 14.

**Oak,** the tree Quercus: Lucr. 950. Pilgr. 60 and LLL IV, 2, 112. Tp. I, 2, 294. Wiv. IV, 4, 31. 40. 42. IV, 6, 19. V, 3, 15. 25. V, 5, 79. Meas. II, 2, 116. Ado II, 1, 247. Mids. I, 2, 113. As II, 1, 31. IV, 3, 105. H6C II, 1, 55. Troil. I, 3, 50. Cor. I, 1, 185. V, 2, 117. Tim. IV, 3, 264. 422. Caes. I, 3, 6. Oth. II, 1, 8. Cymb. IV, 2, 267. *rotten as ever o. or stone was sound,* Wint. II, 3, 90. *to seel her father's eyes up close as o.* Oth. III, 3, 210 (so as absolutely to hinder sight). *his brows bound with o.* Cor. I, 3, 16. *brow-bound with the o.* II, 2, 102 (a garland given in ancient Rome to one who had saved the life of a citizen; but according to our poet, bestowed for any deed of bravery). Sacred to Jove: Tp. V, 45.

**Oak-cleaving,** rending oaks: Lr. III, 2, 5.

**Oaken,** made of branches of oak: *the o. garland,* Cor. II, 1, 138.

**Oar,** subst. a pole with a broad end used to row boats: Gent. II, 3, 37. Ant II, 2, 199. Applied to the fins of a fish: Ado III, 1, 27.

**Oar,** vb. to row: *—ed himself with his good arms to the shore,* Tp. II, 1, 118.

**Oatcake,** name in Ado III, 3, 11.

**Oaten,** made of oats: *when shepherds pipe on o. straws,* LLL V, 2, 913.

**Oath,** a solemn asseveration or promise, corroborated by an appeal to God: Lucr. 569. Sonn. 152, 5. Compl. 279. Tp. IV, 52. Gent. II, 6, 16. II, 7, 69. IV, 4, 135. V, 4, 48. 101. Meas. IV, 2, 195. V, 156. 242. Err. I, 1, 144. V, 16. V, 106. Ado III, 3, 166. LLL I, 1, 23. V, 2, 356. Mids. I, 1, 243. II, 2, 49. III, 2, 93. 139. Merch. V, 155. Tw. III, 4, 326. John III, 1, 10. H6C V, 1, 89. R3 IV, 1, 28 etc. That which is sworn preceded by *for* or *of: taking an oath of them for her revenge,* Lucr. Arg. 20. *here is her o. for love,* Gent. I, 3, 47. *I have sworn deep —s of thy deep kindness, —s of thy love,* Sonn. 152, 9. *her —s of true love,* Pilgr. 92. *your o. of service to the pope,* John V, 1, 23. cf. Tw. III, 2, 16. *By o.: and him by o. they truly honoured,* Lucr. 410. *knights, by their —s, should right poor ladies' harms,* 1694. *affianced to her by o.* Meas. III, 1, 222. *enjoined by o.* Merch. II, 9, 9. Wint. III, 3, 53. *bound by o.* R3 IV, 1, 28. *to whom by o. he menaced revenge,* H8 I, 2, 137. *On o.: with the divine forfeit of his soul upon o.* All's III, 6, 34. *ask him upon his o.* V, 3, 185. *I will prove it legitimate upon the —s of judgment and reason,* Tw. III, 2, 16. *speak truly on thy knighthood and thy o.* R2 I, 3, 14. *to trust man on his o. or bond,* Tim. I, 2, 66. *to give an o.* = to administer an oath: *who can give an o.?* LLL IV, 3, 250; cf. *that power which gave me first my o.* Gent. II, 6, 4. *to take an o.* = a) to swear: *I'll take my o. on it,* Ado II, 3, 26. *has ta'en his o.* Merch. II, 9, 2. *I take the like unfeigned oath never to marry with her,* Shr. IV, 2, 32. *take your o. that you elect no other king,* H6A IV, 1, 3. H6C I, 1, 196. 201. I, 2, 15. Lr. III, 6, 49. b) to make swear: *—ing an oath of them for her revenge,* Lucr. Arg. 20. *we'll take your o., and all the peers', for surety of our leagues,* H5 V, 2, 399. *to have an o.* = to swear, or to have sworn: *I have an o. in heaven,* Merch. IV, 1, 228. *all men have the like —s,* All's IV, 2, 71. *to pass an o.* = to swear: *your —s are passed,* LLL I, 1, 19. 49. *to vow an o.* LLL V, 2, 356. *to swear an o.* Sonn. 152, 9. Pilgr. 92. LLL I, 1, 65. II, 97. V, 2, 451. Merch. III, 3, 5. As III, 4, 44. All's IV, 3, 252. H6A I, 1, 162. H6B III, 2, 158. Troil. III, 2, 44. V, 1, 47. Tit. V, 1, 80. Lr. III, 4, 90. *to keep one's o.* LLL I, 1, 161. II, 105. IV, 3, 362. Merch. II, 9, 77. Shr. IV, 2, 36. All's IV, 3, 282. Tw. III, 4, 341. R2 I, 3, 182. H5 IV, 7, 138. V, 2, 402. H6B V, 1, 183. Troil. V, 1, 47. Tit. V, 1, 80. Caes. V, 3, 40. *to break an o.* Pilgr. 42. LLL V, 2, 348. 440. 441. As I, 2, 23. III, 4, 45. Wint. IV, 4, 502. R2 II, 3, 151. H4A IV, 3, 101. H6C I, 2, 16. I, 4, 100. II, 2, 89. III, 1, 72. 79. 90. Cor. V, 6, 95. Lr. III, 4, 91. *to break an o. with:* Merch. V, 248. R3 IV, 4, 378 (Qq *by*). *to infringe an o.* Lucr. 1061. LLL IV, 3, 144. *to lose an o.* (to forget to keep, and hence = to break): LLL IV, 3, 73. 361. *to violate an o.* Lucr. 883.

Synonymous to swearing, cursing, curse: *not an*

*o. on shore?* Tp. V, 219. *your bold-beating —s,* Wiv. II, 2, 29. *with —s kept waking,* Shr. IV, 3, 10. *a terrible o.* Tw. III, 4, 197. *a lie with a slight o.* H4B V, 1, 92. *not an o.?* H6C II, 6, 77. *Cassio high in o.* Oth. II, 3, 235 (Q1 —*s*). *as if I borrowed mine —s of him,* Cymb. II, 1, 5.

**Oathable,** qualified to have an oath administered: Tim. IV, 3, 135.

**Oath-breaking,** perjury: H4A V, 2, 38.

**Oats,** the plant Avena sativa, or its seed: Tp. IV, 61. Mids. IV, 1, 36. Shr. III, 2, 207. H4A II, 1, 14. Lr. V, 3, 38.

**Ob,** abbreviation of *obolus,* = half-penny: H4A II, 4, 590.

**Obduracy,** hardness of heart, impenitence in wickedness: *as far in the devil's book as thou and Falstaff for o. and persistency,* H4B II, 2, 50.

**Obdúrate,** hard-hearted, inflexible: *o., flinty, hard as steel,* Ven. 199. *o. vassals fell exploits effecting,* Lucr. 429. *if your heart be so o.* Gent. IV, 2, 120. *he stands o.* Merch. IV, 1, 8. *if ... God should be so o. as yourselves,* H6B IV, 7, 122. *stern, o., flinty,* H6C I, 4, 142. *be o., do not hear him plead,* R3 I, 3, 347. *if she be o. to mild entreaties,* III, 1, 39. *be not o., open thy deaf ears,* Tit. II, 3, 160.

**Obedience,** 1) obsequiousness, submission to authority, compliance with command: Lucr. 1215. Tp. II, 1, 130. Meas. III, 1, 254. Mids. I, 1, 37. Shr. V, 2, 117. 153. John V, 1, 9. V, 4, 56. H4B IV, 2, 41. H5 I, 2, 187. H6A III, 1, 167. R3 II, 2, 108. H8 I, 2, 64. II, 4, 35. III, 1, 162. Troil. V, 3, 52. Cor. III, 1, 318. Tim. IV, 1, 4. Mcb. II, 4, 17. Oth. I, 3, 180. Ant. V, 2, 31. Cymb. I, 1, 136. II, 3, 117. III, 4, 68. 158. *one's o.* = a) the obsequiousness observed by one: *make them tame to their o.* John IV, 2, 262. *if you mind to hold your true o.* H6C IV, 1, 140. b) the obsequiousness paid to one: *from whose o. I forbid my soul,* John IV, 3, 64. *reclaimed to your o. fifty fortresses,* H6A III, 4, 6. *To give o.* = to be obedient: *to give o. where 'tis truly owed,* Mcb. V, 2, 26. With *to: the o. to a master,* Wint. I, 2, 354. *our o. to the king,* H5 IV, 1, 138. H6A I, 1, 164. Cor. III, 1, 166. With *of,* objectively: *drunkards, liars and adulterers by an enforced o. of planetary influence,* Lr. I, 2, 135.

2) dutifulness, reverence: *I am your wife in all o.* Shr. Ind. 2, 109. *commend my best o. to the queen,* Wint. II, 2, 36. *o. bids I should not bid again,* R2 I, 1, 163. *let me no more from this o. rise, which my most inward true and duteous spirit teacheth this prostrate and exterior bending,* H4B IV, 5, 147. *I do not know what kind of my o. I should tender,* H8 II, 3, 66. *to speak my thanks and my o.* 71. *zeal and o. he still bore your grace,* III, 1, 63. *all the fellowship I hold now with him is only my o.* 122. *one that in all o. makes the church the chief aim of his honour,* V, 3, 117. *honour, love, o., troops of friends,* Mcb. V, 3, 25. *who in her duty and o. hath given me this,* Hml. II, 2, 107. *you have o. scanted,* Lr. I, 1, 281. *shake in pieces the heart of his o.* I, 2, 92. *whose virtue and o. doth so much commend itself,* II, 1, 115. *if your sweet sway allow o.* II, 4, 194.

**Obedient,** 1) obsequious, submissive to command: Tp. II, 1, 283. Shr. I, 1, 217. IV, 1, 199. V, 2, 67. All's II, 3, 167 (*o. right* = right of obedience). II, 5, 77. Tw. II, 5, 64. V, 348. H4A V, 1, 17 (*o. orb* =

*orb of obedience).* H6A IV, 2, 7. R3 II, 2, 45. IV, 2, 68. H8 III, 2, 180. Tim. IV, 3, 296. Lr. I, 4, 255. Oth. III, 3, 89. IV, 1, 259. 266. Cymb. III, 4, 82. With *to:* Wiv. IV, 6, 33. Meas. I, 1, 26. Err. I, 1, 87. Shr. V, 2, 158. Wint. IV, 4, 494. Per. III Prol. 32.

2) reverent: *kisses the base ground with o. breast,* LLL IV, 3, 225. *your most o. counsellor,* Wint. II, 3, 55. *reproof, o. and in order,* Per. I, 2, 42.

**Obeisance,** reverence: *call him madam, do him o.* Shr. Ind. I, 108.

**Oberon,** the king of the fairies: Mids. II, 1, 20. 24. 44. 58. 61. 119. II, 2, 83. IV, 1, 81.

**Obey,** to submit, to be ruled by, to comply with; absol.: Ven. 61. 549. 563. Compl. 133. Tp. I, 2, 38. 372. 483. V, 2. Err. II, 1, 29. V, 231. Shr. V, 2, 164. Tw. III, 4, 366. H6B V, 1, 6. 108. 136. H6C III, 1, 93. R3 I, 1, 105. H8 I, 1, 210. III, 1, 139. Cor. II, 2, 110. III, 1, 176. Rom. III, 1, 145. V, 3, 57. Hml. I, 3, 137. II, 2, 29. III, 2, 345. Oth. I, 2, 87. III, 3, 468. Cymb. V, 1, 17. Transitively: Ven. 111. Lucr. 546. Compl. 229. Wiv. III, 3, 204 (*his dissolute disease will scarce o. this medicine,* = be weaker than, yield to). IV, 2, 112. 210. Meas. IV, 2, 110. Err. II, 2, 193. IV, 1, 70. 80. Ado III, 3, 193. LLL IV, 3, 216. Merch. III, 4, 36. Shr. III, 2, 225. All's I, 2, 41, II, 3, 165. II, 5, 62. Tw. III, 2, 82. V, 1, 36. Wint. I, 2, 427. IV, 2, 60. R2 III, 2, 210. H4B V, 2, 106. H6C III, 1, 99. III, 3, 96. IV, 1, 78. R3 IV, 4, 104. H8 I, 1, 216. III, 1, 130. V, 3, 24. Troil. IV, 5, 72. V, 1, 49. V, 5, 27. Cor. I, 3, 115. I, 6, 83. IV, 6, 125. V, 3, 35. Tit. IV, 4, 99. Tim. V, 1, 56. Caes. IV, 3, 227. Hml. I, 2, 120. I, 4, 88. II, 2, 68. III, 1, 37. V, 2, 227. Lr. I, 1, 100. III, 4, 82. 154. IV, 6, 163. 205. V, 3, 323. Oth. I, 3, 301. IV, 1, 270. V, 2, 196. Ant. II, 3, 33. III, 2, 47. III, 11, 69. III, 13, 88. V, 2, 116. 199. Cymb. I, 1, 2. II, 3, 56. Per. II, 1, 4. III, 3, 9. V, 1, 252.

With *to: to whose sound chaste wings o.* Phoen. 4. *his stubborn buckles, with these your white enchanting fingers touched, shall more o. than to the edge of steel or force of Greekish sinews,* Troil. III, 1, 165. With following: (this feather) *—ing with my wind when I do blow,* H6C III, 1, 86 (= obeying like my wind?). Misapplied by the watchman in Ado III, 3, 189.

**Obidicut,** name of an evil spirit in Lr. IV, 1, 62.

**Object,** subst. 1) that which is presented to the senses or the mind, a thing seen or thought of: *make me not o. to the tell-tale day,* Lucr. 806 (= make me not seen by the day). *no o. but her passion's strength renews,* 1103. *a thousand lamentable —s there art gave life,* 1373. *gilding the o. whereupon it gazeth,* Sonn. 20, 6. *of his* (the eye's) *quick —s hath the mind no part,* 113, 7. *as fast as —s to his beams assemble,* 114, 8. *the goodly —s which abroad they find of lands and mansions,* Compl. 137. *the heaven-hued sapphire and the opal blend with —s manifold,* 216. *when thou haply seest some rare note-worthy o. in thy travel,* Gent. I, 1, 13. *upon a homely o. love can wink,* Gent. II, 4, 98. *the remembrance of my former love is by a newer o. quite forgotten,* 195. *throwing it* (the eye) *on any other o.* Meas. V, 23. *never o. pleasing in thine eye,* Err. II, 2, 117. *every o. that the one* (his eye) *doth catch the other* (his wit) *turns to a mirth-moving jest,* LLL II, 70. *full of forms, figures, shapes, —s, ideas,* IV, 2, 69. *as the eye doth roll to every varied o.* V, 2, 775. *every o. that might make me fear misfortune,*

Merch. I, 1, 20. *compounded of many simples, extracted from many —s*, As IV, 1, 17. *sorrow's eye divides one thing entire to many —s*, R2 II, 2, 17. *how quickly nature falls into revolt when gold becomes her o.* H4B IV, 5, 67. *on this unworthy scaffold to bring forth so great an o.* H5 Prol. 11. (his contemplation) *fixed on spiritual o.* H8 III, 2, 132. *one that feeds on —s, arts and imitations ... out of use and staled by other men*, Caes. IV, 1, 37 (some M. Edd. unnecessarily *abjects, orts*). *of the truth herein this present o. made probation*, Hml. I, 1, 156 (= what we have seen even now). *countries different with variable —s shall expel this matter*, III, 1, 180. *men's natures wrangle with inferior things, though great ones are their o.* Oth. III, 4, 145 (thought of by them). *hitting each o. with a joy*, Cymb. V, 5, 396. *by those fearful —s to prepare this body*, Per. I, 1, 43.

Quite equivalent to sight, view: *mark what o. did present itself*, As IV, 3, 104. *extended or contracted all proportions to a most hideous o.* All's V, 3, 52. *could thought, without this o., form such another?* John IV, 3, 44. *doth not the o. cheer your heart?* H6C II, 2, 4. *the present eye praises the present o.* Troil. III, 3, 180. *the dismallest o. that ever eye with sight made heart lament*, Tit. II, 3, 204. *this o. kills me*, III, 1, 64. *dreadful —s so familiar*, Caes. III, 1, 266. *and with this horrible o. ... enforce their charity*, Lr. II, 3, 17. *seest thou this o., Kent?* V, 3, 238. *the o. poisons sight*, Oth. V, 2, 364. *this o. which takes prisoner the wild motion of mine eye*, Cymb. I, 6, 102. With *of: reason flies the o. of all harm*, Troil. II, 2, 41 (= the sight of). *the o. of our misery is as an inventory to particularize their abundance*, Cor. I, 1, 21.

2) any thing regarded with love or with dislike, inspiring sympathy or antipathy: *her o. will away*, Ven. 255 (her beloved Adonis). *so did the merciless and pitchy night fold in the o. that did feed her sight*, 822. *the o. and the pleasure of mine eye is only Helena*, Mids. IV, 1, 175. *have now the fatal o. in my eye where my poor young was limed*, H6C V, 6, 16. *his eye reviled me as his abject o.* H8 I, 1, 127. *Hector in his blaze of wrath subscribes to tender —s*, Troil. IV, 5, 106. *swear against —s*, Tim. IV, 3, 122 (let not any thing move you to pity). *fruitful o. be in eye of Imogen*, Cymb. V, 4, 55. *she, that even but now was your o.* Lr. I, 1, 217. cf. above: Gent. II, 4, 98. 195. Err. II, 2, 117. Cymb. I, 6, 102.

**Object**, vb. 1) to propose: *it is well —ed*, H6A II, 4, 43.

2) to oppose as an adverse reason or by way of accusation: Wiv. III, 4, 4. H6A III, 1, 7. H6C V, 1, 89. With *against:* R2 I, 1, 28. H6A II, 4, 116. With *to: the saying did not hold in him that did o. the same to thee*, R3 II, 4, 17.

**Objection**, criminal charge, accusation, reproach: *you do not well to bear with their perverse —s*, H6A IV, 1, 129. *your spiteful false —s*, H6B I, 3, 158. *I dare your worst —s*, H8 III, 2, 307. cf. the verb *object* in R2 I, 1, 28 and H6A III, 1, 7.

**Oblation**, offering, sacrifice: Sonn. 125, 10. Compl. 223. Per. V, 3, 70.

**Obligation**, 1) duty, the state of being bound by any regard: H8 II, 3, 96. Troil. IV, 5, 122. Hml. I, 2, 91. II, 2, 295. Lr. II, 4, 144.

2) bond, contract: *in any bill, warrant, quittance or o.* Wiv. I, 1, 11. *he can make —s*, H6B IV, 2, 100.

**Obliged**, bound in duty: *to keep o. faith unforfeited*, Merch. II, 6, 7.

**Oblique**, uneven, perverse, queer: *all is o.: there's nothing level in our cursed natures but direct villany*, Tim. IV, 3, 18 (O. Edd. *obliquie* or *obliquy*).

Scarcely intelligible in Troil. V, 1, 60: *the goodly transformation of Jupiter there, his brother, the bull, the primitive statue and o. memorial of cuckolds;* according to some, = indirect; to others, misprinted for *antique.*

**Oblivion**, 1) forgetfulness, in an active sense; cessation of remembering: *planting o., beating reason back*, Ven. 557. *second childishness and mere o.* As II, 7, 165. *thinking of nothing else, putting all affairs else in o.* H4B V, 5, 27. *whether it be bestial o. or some craven scruple*, Hml. IV, 4, 40. *my o. is a very Antony, and I am all forgotten*, Ant. I, 3, 90.

2) the state of being forgotten, of no more living in the memory of men: *to feed o. with decay of things*, Lucr. 947. *till each to razed o. yield his part*, Sonn. 122, 7. *a forted residence 'gainst the tooth of time and razure of oblivion*, Meas. V, 13. Shr. IV, 1, 85. All's II, 3, 147. V, 3, 24. H5 II, 4, 87. R3 III, 7, 129. Troil. III, 2, 194. III, 3, 146. IV, 5, 167. Tit. III, 1, 296.

**Oblivious**, causing forgetfulness: *with some sweet o. antidote cleanse the stuffed bosom*, Mcb. V, 3, 43. cf *All-oblivious.*

**Obloquy**, reproach, disgrace: *thou, the author of their o.* Lucr. 523. *which were the greatest o. in the world in me to lose*, All's IV, 2, 44. *which o. set bars before my tongue*, H6A II, 5, 49.

**Obscene**, offensive, abominable: *I did encounter that o. and most preposterous event*, LLL I, 1, 244. *so heinous, black, o. a deed*, R2 IV, 131. *thou whoreson, o., greasy tallow-catch*, H4A II, 4, 252.

**Obscenely**, misapplied by Costard and Bottom: *when it comes so smoothly off, so o. as it were, so fit*, LLL IV, 1, 145. *there we may rehearse most o. and courageously*, Mids. I, 2, 111.

**Obscure**, adj. (as for the accent, see Appendix I, 1) 1) dark, destitute of light: *brakes o. and rough*, Ven. 237. *to rib her cerecloth in the o. grave*, Merch. II, 7, 51. *wandered hither to an o. plot*, Tit. II, 3, 77. = living in the dark: *the o. bird clamoured the livelong night*, Mcb. II, 3, 64.

2) not obviously intelligible, not plain, abstruse: *to make plain some o. precedence that hath tofore been sain*, LLL III, 83. *some o. epistles of love*, Tw. II, 3, 168. *an index and o. prologue to the history of lust*, Oth. II, 1, 264.

3) humble, mean: *O base and o. vulgar*, LLL IV, 1, 69. *a little little grave, an o. grave*, R2 III, 3, 154. *o. and lowly swain*, H6B IV, 1, 50. *his means of death, his o. funeral — no trophy, sword, nor hatchment o'er his bones, no noble right nor formal ostentation*, Hml. IV, 5, 213.

**Obscure**, vb. 1) to make dark, to deprive of light: *Cynthia for shame —s her silver shine*, Ven. 728. *with —d lights*, Wiv. V, 3, 15. *what —d light the heavens did grant*, Err. I, 1, 67.

2) to keep in the dark, to hide, to prevent from being known: *why I —d myself*, Meas. V, 395. *'tis an office of discovery, and I should be —d*, Merch. II, 6, 44. *—s the show of evil*, III, 2, 77. *—ing and hiding from me all gentlemanlike qualities*, As I, 1, 73. *a great*

*magician, — d in the circle of this forest*, V, 4, 34. *the prince — d his contemplation under the veil of wildness,* H5 I, 1, 63. *what — d in this fair volume lies find written in the margent of his eyes,* Rom. I, 3, 85.

3) to make mean, to degrade: *your high self you have — d with a swain's wearing,* Wint. IV, 4, 8. *since then hath Richard been — d, deprived of honour and inheritance,* H6A II, 5, 26. *to o. my noble birth,* V, 4, 22. *informed of my — d course,* Lr. II, 2, 175.

**Obscúrely,** 1) in the dark, out of sight: *cavekeeping evils that o. sleep,* Lucr. 1250.

2) not plainly, indirectly: *wherein o. Caesar's ambition shall be glanced at,* Caes. I, 2, 323.

**Obscurity,** 1) darkness: *there's not a hollow cave or lurking-place, no vast o. or misty vale,* Tit. V, 2, 36.

2) state of being kept in the dark, of not coming to light: *if thou destroy them not in dark o.* Ven. 760.

**Obsequious,** 1) zealous, officious, devoted: *let me be o. in thy heart,* Sonn. 125, 9. *I see you are o. in your love, and I profess requital to a hair's breadth,* Wiv. IV, 2, 2. *and in o. fondness crowd to his presence,* Meas. II, 4, 28. *doting on his own o. bondage,* Oth. I, 1, 46.

2) Especially zealous with respect to what is due to the deceased; mourning (cf. subst. *Obsequy*): *how many a holy and o. tear hath dear religious love stolen from mine eye as interest of the dead,* Sonn. 31, 5. *to shed o. tears upon this trunk,* Tit. V, 3, 152. *for some term to do o. sorrow,* Hml. I, 2, 92. Applied to a person: *and so o. will thy father be as Priam was for all his valiant sons,* H6C II, 5, 118.

**Obsequiously,** in the character of a mourner: *whilst I awhile o. lament the untimely fall of virtuous Lancaster,* R3 I, 2, 3.

**Obsequy,** funeral ceremony: *keep the o. so strict,* Phoen. 12. Plur. *—ies* = 1) funeral rites: *at this tomb my tributary tears I render for my brethren's —ies,* Tit. I, 160. *her —ies have been as far enlarged as we have warrantise,* Hml. V, 1, 249. *we have done our —ies,* Cymb. IV, 2, 282.

2) love or piety shown to the deceased: *but all in vain are these mean —ies,* H6B III, 2, 146. *these tears are my sweet Rutland's —ies,* H6C I, 4, 147. *the— ies that I for thee will keep nightly shall be to strew thy grave and weep,* Rom. V, 3, 16. *to cross my —ies and true love's rite,* 20.

**Observance,** 1) observation, the act of perceiving a thing and gaining notions by it: *take a taste of my finding him, and relish it with good o.* As III, 2, 247. *I take my young lord to be a very melancholy man. By what o.?* All's III, 2, 5. *out of his scattering and unsure o.* Oth. III, 3, 151. *or I have no o.* Ant. III, 3, 25.

2) the act of keeping or adhering to in practice: *are there no other tokens between you 'greed concerning her o.?* Meas. IV, 1, 42. *to do o. to a morn of May,* Mids. I, 1, 167 (= to observe its rites, cf. IV, 1, 137). *use all the o. of civility,* Merch. II, 2, 204. *a custom more honoured in the breach than the o.* Hml. I, 4, 16. Hence = rule of practice: *there are other strict —s,* LLL I, 1, 36. *degrees, —s, customs and laws,* Tim. IV, 1, 19.

Denoting a strict adherence to truth and reality: *such sweet o. in this work was had, that one might see those far-off eyes look sad,* Lucr. 1385. *with this special o. that you o'erstep not the modesty of nature,* Hml. III, 2, 21.

3) reverential attention, homage: *followed her with a doting o.* Wiv. II, 2, 203. *all adoration, duty and o.* As V, 2, 102. 104. *and ever shall with true o. seek to eke out that wherein my homely stars have failed,* All's II, 5, 79. *nor of them look for such o. as fit the bridal,* Oth. III, 4, 149 (Qq —s; F1 *observancy*). With *of: with due o. of thy godlike seat,* Troil. I, 3, 31. *without o. or respect of any,* II, 3, 175. *to do o.* = to do homage: *do o. to my mercy,* H4B IV, 3, 16.

**Observancy,** homage: Oth. III, 4, 149 (the later Ff *observance,* Qq *observances*).

**Obsérvant,** adj. attentive, watchful: *know by measure of their o. toil the enemies' weight,* Troil. I, 3, 203. *this same strict and most o. watch,* Hml. I, 1, 71.

**Observant** (óbservant), obsequious attendant: *ducking —s that stretch their duties nicely,* Lr. II, 2, 109.

**Observation,** 1) the act of observing, of seeing, of taking notice: *what o. madest thou in this case of his heart's meteors tilting in his face?* Err. IV, 2, 5. *how hast thou purchased this experience? By my penny of o.* LLL III, 28.

2) knowledge gained by observing, experience: *if my o. deceive me not now,* LLL II, 228. *in his brain he hath strange places crammed with o.* As II, 7, 41. *he is but a bastard to the time that doth not smack of o.* John I, 208. *all forms, all pressures past, that youth and o. copied there,* Hml. I, 5, 101. *the o. we have made of it hath not been little,* Lr. I, 1, 292. Plur. *—s: trust not my reading nor my —s, which with experimental seal doth warrant the tenour of my book,* Ado IV, 1, 167 (some M. Edd. *o.*).

3) remark: *that's a foolish o.* H6C II, 6, 108.

4) act of keeping, of adhering to in practice: *our o. is performed,* Mids. IV, 1, 109 (i. e. of the rites of May; cf. I, 1, 167 and IV, 1, 137). Hence adherence to truth and reality, naturalness: *with good life and o. strange my meaner ministers their several kinds have done,* Tp. III, 3, 87.

**Observe,** 1) to look on with attention, to watch, to have in one's eye, to take notice; abs.: *I come to o.* Tim. I, 2, 33. *set on thy wife to o.* Oth. III, 3, 240. With a clause: *o. how Antony becomes his flaw,* Ant. III, 12, 34. Transitively: *o. his reports for me,* All's II, 1, 46. *o. his construction of it,* Tw. II, 3, 190. *o. him,* II, 5, 21. *he must o. their mood on whom he jests,* III, 1, 69. Compl. 60. All's I, 3, 142 (cf. *Now*). R2 I, 4, 24. H4B III, 1, 82. IV, 4, 36. 121. V, 1, 74. H5 III, 2, 29. H8 III, 2, 112. Cor. II, 3, 267. Caes. I, 2, 32. IV, 3, 45. 97. Mcb. V, 1, 23. Hml. II, 2, 625. III, 2, 85. Oth. III, 3, 197. IV, 1, 289.

2) to become aware of, to perceive: *hast thou —d that?* Gent. II, 1, 48. *I heard your guilty rhymes, — d your fashion,* LLL IV, 3, 139. *with honourable action, such as he hath —d in noble ladies,* Shr. Ind. 1, 111. *the wit which I can well o. to-day in our young lords,* All's I, 2, 32. *we did o.* R2 I, 4, 1. *will ye not o. the strangeness of his altered countenance?* H6B III, 1, 4. *o., he's moody,* H8 III, 2, 75. *I have —d thee always for a towardly prompt spirit,* Tim. III, 1, 36. *do you o. this?* III, 2, 70. *I'll show you how to o. a strange event,* III, 4, 17. *where they most breed and haunt, I have —d, the air is delicate,* Mcb. I, 6, 9. *which I —ing, took once a pliant hour,* Oth. I, 3, 150.

3) to reverence, to show respect to, to do homage: *he is gracious, if he be —d,* H4B IV, 4, 30. 49. *underwrite in an —ing kind his humorous predominance,*

Troil. II, 3, 137. *let his very breath, whom thou'lt o., blow off thy cap*, Tim. IV, 3, 212. *the —d of all observers*, Hml. III, 1, 162 (= looked up to).

4) to adhere to, to keep: *wait the season and o. the times*, LLL V, 2, 63. *to o. the rite of May*, Mids. IV, 1, 137. *I am enjoined by oath to o. three things*, Merch. II, 9, 9. *the premises —d, thy will by my performance shall be served*, All's II, 1, 204. *o. degree, priority and place*, Troil. I, 3, 86. *ceremonies which I have seen thee careful to o.* Tit. V, 1, 77. *o. his inclination in yourself*, Hml. II, 1, 71 (do yourself as he is inclined; be serviceable to him, whatever may be his disposition). *with us at sea it hath been still —d*, Per. III, 1, 52.

**Observer**, one who regards with attention: Meas. I, 1, 29. Caes. I, 2, 202. Hml. III, 1, 162.

**Observingly**, with close observation, attentively: H5 IV, 1, 5.

**Obstacle**, hinderance, obstruction: Tw. III, 4, 88. R3 I, 4, 143. III, 7, 156. Corrupted from *obstinate* by the shepherd in H6A V, 4, 17.

**Obstinacy**, stubbornness, unreasonable firmness: All's I, 3, 186. H6A V, 4, 155.

**Obstinate**, stubborn, not yielding to reason: Ado I, 1, 236. H6A III, 1, 113. H8 II, 4, 121. Cor. V, 3, 26. Hml. I, 2, 93.

**Obstinately**, stubbornly, in spite of reasons and arguments: *an esperance so o. strong*, Troil. V, 2, 121.

**Obstruct**, an idle conjecture of M. Edd. for *abstract* of O. Edd. in Ant. III, 6, 61.

**Obstruction**, 1) a state of being blocked up: *the clearstores toward the south north are as lustrous as ebony, and yet complainest thou of o.?* Tw. IV, 2, 43 (the clown's speech).

2) obstacle, difficulty: *there is no o. in this*, Tw. II, 5, 129.

3) stagnation of the blood: *to lie in cold o. and to rot*, Meas. III, 1, 119. *this does make some o. in the blood*, Tw. III, 4, 22. = that which causes a stagnation of the blood: *and purge the —s which begin to stop our very veins of life*, H4B IV, 1, 65.

**Obtain**, to get, to gain: *the sundry dangers of his will's —ing, yet ever to o. his will resolving*, Lucr. 128. 129. *to o. his lust*, 156. *I am desperate of —ing her*, Gent. III, 2, 5. *unless I be —ed by the manner of my father's will*, Merch. I, 2, 117. *the other, when she has —ed your eye, will have your tongue too*, Wint. V, 1, 105. *who hath —ed the glory of the day*, H6A IV, 7, 52. Especially = to impetrate, to gain by the concession or excited kindness of another: *where his suit may be —ed*, Lucr. 898. LLL V, 2, 749. Merch. II, 2, 153. 186. H4A I, 2, 80. 81 (quibbling). *to plead for that which I would not o.* Gent. IV, 4, 105. *having —ed her, give her to Count Claudio*, Ado I, 3, 65. II, 1, 311. III, 2, 129. *when (her love) is — ed*, Shr. II, 129. *having this (your leave) —ed*, All's II, 4, 53. *shall I o. it?* R2 IV, 304. *by fair words peace may be —ed*, H6A I, 1, 77. V, 4, 148. *ask mercy and o. no grace*, H6C II, 6, 69. *thou shalt o. and ask the empery*, Tit. I, 201. *let me o. my wish*, Per. V, 1, 35.

**Occasion**, subst. 1) anything occurring incidentally, accident, good or bad fortune: *every light o. of the wind upon his lips their silken parcels hurls*, Compl. 86. *I am courted now with a double o., gold and a means to do the prince my master good*, Wint. IV, 4, 864. *withhold thy speed, dreadful o.! O make a league*

*with me*, John IV, 2, 125. *enforced from our most quiet there by the rough torrent of o.* H4B IV, 1, 72. *like a gallant in the brow of youth repairs him with o.* H6B V, 3, 5 (or = cause? cf. John II, 82). *frame my face to all —s*, H6C III, 2, 185. *o. smiles upon a second leave*, Hml. I, 3, 54. *so much as from —s you may glean*, II, 2, 16 (Qq o.).

2) opportunity, favorable time: *the o. speaks thee*, Tp. II, 1, 207. *fee'd every slight o.* Wiv. II, 2, 204. *on the wing of all —s*, 210. *upon the mellowing of o.* LLL IV, 2, 72. *till I can find o. of revenge*, Shr. II, 36. *made mine own o. mellow*, Tw. I, 2, 43. *you may have very fit o. for it*, III, 4, 190. *as I may pick o.* H5 III, 2, 111. *as o. serves*, H6C III, 3, 236. *to meet the least o.* H8 III, 2, 7. *breed —s, that I may speak*, Lr. I, 3, 24. *a finder of —s*, Oth. II, 1, 246. Preceded by *on*: *I can gleek upon o.* Mids. III, 1, 150. *and so be mocked upon the next o. that we meet*, LLL V, 2, 143. Followed by an inf.: *have more o. to know one another*, Wiv. I, 1, 256. *you embrace the o. to depart*, Merch. I, 1, 64. *you took o. to be quickly wooed to gripe the general sway into your hand*, H4A V, 1, 56. *when you take —s to see leeks*, H5 V, 1, 58 (Fluellen's speech). *I'll sort o. to part the queen's proud kindred from the king*, R3 II, 2, 148. *to take the safest o. by the front to bring you in again*, Oth. III, 1, 52.

3) cause, motive: *he heartily prays some o. may detain us longer*, Ado I, 1, 151. *there is no measure in the o. that breeds (my sadness)* I, 3, 3. *that woman that cannot make her fault her husband's o., let her never nurse her child herself*, As IV, 1, 178 (= as caused by her husband). *nature, stronger than his just o.* IV, 3, 130. *what o. of import hath all so long detained you from your wife?* Shr. III, 2, 104. *goaded with most sharp —s*, All's V, 1, 14. *courage mounteth with o.* John II, 82 (cf. H6B V, 3, 5). *this most fair o., by the which we will untread the steps of damned flight*, V, 4, 51. *to behold the face of that o. that shall bring it on*, H4A I, 3, 276. *I well allow the o. of our arms*, H4B I, 3, 5. 86. *he cannot so precisely weed this land as his misdoubts present o.* IV, 1, 206. *there is —s and causes why and wherefore*, H5 V, 1, 3. *you have great reason to do Richard right, especially for those —s at Eltham place I told your majesty*, H6A III, 1, 155. *those —s were of force*, 157. *whate'er o. keeps him from us now*, H6B III, 1, 3. *I seek o. how to rise*, H6C I, 2, 45. *when I give o. of offence, then let me die*, I, 3, 44. *with what vehemency the o. shall instruct you*, H8 V, 1, 150. *when contention and o. meet*, Troil. IV, 1, 16. *a very little thief of o. will rob you of a great deal of patience*, Cor. II, 1, 32. *if I see o. in a good quarrel*, Rom. II, 4, 168. *an you will give me o.* III, 1, 45. *my master is awaked by great o. to call upon his own*, Tim. II, 2, 21. *he hath sent me an earnest inviting, which many my near —s did urge me to put off*, III, 6, 12 (almost = engagement, business. cf. Nares). *get on your nightgown, lest o. call us*, Mcb. II, 2, 70. *to visit you, my lord; no other o.* Hml. II, 2, 279. *how all —s do inform against me*, IV, 4, 32. *I shall recount the o. of my return*, IV, 7, 47. *—s of some poise*, Lr. II, 1, 122. *am I the o. of these tears?* Oth. IV, 2, 43 (Ff motive). *under a compelling o., let women die*, Ant. I, 2, 141. *brings the dire o. in his arms of what we blame him for*, Cymb. IV, 2, 196. *on an o.* = for a reason, from a motive: *on what o. break those tears from thee?* Lucr. 1270. *I am yet so near the manners*

*of my mother, that upon the least o. more mine eyes will tell tales of me,* Tw. II, 1, 42. *I sent for thee upon a sad o.* III, 4, 20. *to visit Bohemia on the like o.* Wint. I, 1, 2. *on what o. they have taken sanctuary,* R3 III, 1, 26. *I would on great o. speak with you,* Oth. IV, 1, 59. Followed by an inf.: *when you were gravelled for lack of matter, you might take o. to kiss,* As IV, 1, 75. *when he had o. to be seen,* H4A III, 2, 74. *as oft as he has o. to name himself,* H4B II, 2, 119. *having any o. to write,* H5 V, 2, 365. *to take o. from their mouths to raise a mutiny,* H6A IV, 1, 130. *had I so good o. to lie long,* Troil. IV, 1, 3. *find some o. to anger Cassio,* Oth. II, 1, 274. *what o. had Cadwal to give it motion?* Cymb. IV, 2, 187.

Passing into the sense of matter, theme, subject: *to minister o. to these gentlemen,* Tp. II, 1, 173 (a topic of jesting, food for laughter). *unless you laugh and minister o. to him, he is gagged,* Tw. I, 5, 94. *his eye begets o. for his wit,* LLL II, 69. *yet more quarrelling with o.* Merch. III, 5, 61 (= at odds with the matter in question; turning it into ridicule without reason). *that the time's enemies may not have this to grace —s,* John IV, 2, 62 (matters which they may urge against you).

4) need, want, necessity: *my purse, my person, my extremest means lie all unlocked to your —s,* Merch. I, 1, 139. *though lately we intended to keep in darkness what o. now reveals,* Tw. V, 156. *I am proud that my —s have found time to use 'em,* Tim. II, 2, 200. *I should ne'er have denied his o. so many talents,* III, 2, 26. *has only sent his present o. now,* 39. *if his o. were not virtuous,* 45. *his —s might have wooed me first,* III, 3, 15. *he married but his o. here,* Ant. II, 6, 140. *so tender over his —s,* Cymb. V, 5, 87. With an inf.: *if you have o. to use me for your own turn,* Meas. IV, 2, 60. *having great and instant o. to use fifty talents,* Tim. III, 1, 19.

**Occident,** the west: R2 III, 3, 67. Cymb. IV, 2, 372.

**Occidental,** western: All's II, 1, 166.

**Occulted,** committed in secret: *if his o. guilt do not itself unkennel,* Hml. III, 2, 85.

**Occupation,** 1) employment, business, work: *no o.; all men idle, all,* Tp. II, 1, 154. *Othello's o. is gone,* Oth. III, 3, 357.

2) trade, profession: *do you call your o. a mystery?* Meas. IV, 2, 35. 40. 41. *'tis my o.* Wint. IV, 4, 302. *'tis my o. to be plain,* Lr. II, 2, 98. *that thou couldst see my wars to-day and knewest the royal o.!* Ant. IV, 4, 17. Used in contempt: *the red pestilence strike all trades in Rome, and —s perish!* Cor. IV, 1, 14. *you that stood so much upon the voice of o. and the breath of garlic-eaters,* IV, 6, 97 (= low mechanics). *an I had been a man of any o., if I would not have taken him at a word, I would I might go to hell among the rogues,* Caes. I, 2, 269.

**Occupy,** a word formerly used in the sense of to practise, to busy one's self about, but having become indecent in the poet's time: *these villains will make the word as odious as the word o., which was an excellent good word before it was ill sorted,* H4B II, 4, 161. *I was come to the whole depth of my tale, and meant, indeed, to o. the argument no longer,* Rom. II, 4, 105 (very obscene quibbling).

**Occurrence,** that which happens, course of events: *all the o. of my fortune since hath been between this* lady and this lord, Tw. V, 264 (some M. Edd. *occurrents*). *all the —s, whatever chanced,* H5 V Chor. 40.

**Occurrents,** events, incidents: *so tell him, with the o., more and less,* Hml. V, 2, 368.

**Ocean,** the great sea, the main: Ven. 494. Lucr. 589. 655. 1231. Sonn. 56, 9. 64, 5. 80, 5. Compl. 256. Gent. II, 7, 32. 69. Wiv. II, 2, 143. Err. I, 2, 36. Merch. I, 1, 8. John II, 24. 340. IV, 3, 132. V, 4, 57. R2 II, 2, 146. H4B III, 1, 50. H5 Prol. 22. III, 1, 14. H6B III, 2, 143. H6C IV, 8, 20. R3 I, 1, 4. Tit. II, 1, 6. IV, 2, 101. 139. Caes. I, 3, 7. Mcb. II, 2, 60. Hml. IV, 5, 99. Ant. II, 6, 21. II, 7, 74. V, 2, 82. Cymb. I, 2, 22.

**Octavia,** the sister of Octavius Caesar: Ant. II, 2, 121 and passim.

**Octavius,** 1) Octavius Caesar, the grand-nephew and heir of Julius Caesar: Caes. III, 1, 276 and passim. Ant. I, 2, 29. 2) Marcus O., an officer of Antony's: Ant. III, 7, 73.

**Ocular,** depending on the eye, offered by sight: *give me the o. proof,* Oth. III, 3, 360.

**Od,** corruption of *God: od's blessed will,* Wiv. I, 1, 273. *od's me,* I, 4, 64 (Dr. Caius' speech). *od's heartlings,* III, 4, 59. *od's nouns,* IV, 1, 25. *od's my little life,* As III, 5, 43. *od's my will,* IV, 3, 17. *od's lifelings,* Tw. V, 187. *od's pity,* Oth. IV, 3, 75 (Ff *why*). *od's pittikins,* Cymb. IV, 2, 293.

**Odd,** 1) lonely, desert (German *oede*): *in an o. angle of the isle,* Tp. I, 2, 223.

2) single: *every man is o. No, Paris is not; for you know 'tis true, that you are o., and he is even with you,* Troil. IV, 5, 44.

3) unequalled, uncommon: *and to their hope they such o. action yield, that through their light joy seemed to appear ... a kind of heavy fear,* Lucr. 1433.

4) singular, peculiar: *her madness hath the —est frame of sense,* Meas. V, 61. *to be so o. and from all fashions,* Ado III, 1, 72. *he is too picked, too spruce, too affected, too o., as it were, too peregrinate, as I may call it,* LLL V, 1, 15.

5) strange, fantastical, whimsical: *some few o. lads,* Tp. V, 255. *over-eyeing of his o. behaviour,* Shr. Ind. 1, 95. *some o. humour pricks him to this fashion,* III, 2, 75. *you're an o. man,* Troil. IV, 5, 41. *but this is something o.* Cor. II, 3, 88. *how strange or o. soe'er I bear myself,* Hml. I, 5, 170. *'tis one of those o. tricks which sorrow shoots out of the mind,* Ant. IV, 2, 14. *the worm is an o. worm,* V, 2, 259.

6) applied to particular purposes, but with little propriety; commonplace in the worst sense: *I may chance have some o. quirks and remnants of wit broken on me,* Ado II, 3, 244. *according to Fates and Destinies and such o. sayings,* Merch. II, 2, 66. *with old o. ends stolen out of holy writ,* R3 I, 3, 337 (Ff *o. old*).

7) occasional, incidental: *I fear the trust Othello puts him in, on some o. time of his infirmity, will shake this island,* Oth. II, 3, 132.

8) not even, not divisible into two equal whole numbers: *good luck lies in o. numbers,* Wiv. V, 1, 3. Quibbling in Rom. I, 3, 16 and Troil. IV, 5, 41.

9) opposed to *even* in another sense: *the general state, I fear, can scarce entreat you to be o. with him,* Troil. IV, 5, 265 (to be on terms of enmity and contention with him).

10) indefinitely exceeding any number specified: *pound and o. shilling,* Wint. IV, 3, 34. *three hundred*

*and o. pounds*, H4A IV, 2, 15. *nine score and o. posts*, H4B IV, 3, 40. *a fortnight and o. days*, Rom. I, 3, 15. *I will win for him an I can; if not, I will gain nothing but my shame and the o. hits*, Hml. V, 2, 185 (i. e. the hits received into the bargain). Not preceded by *and*, = at least: *which doth amount to three o. ducats more than I stand debted to this gentleman*, Err. IV, 1, 30. *eighty o. years of sorrow have I seen*, R3 IV, 1, 96. *of wounds two dozen o.* Cor. II, 3, 135.

**Odd-conceited,** singularly devised: Gent. II, 7, 46.

**Odd-even**, according to Henley, the interval between twelve at night and one in the morning: *at this o. and dull watch o' the night*, Oth. I, 1, 124 (not hyphened in O. Edd. Steevens *odd steven*, Cartwright *odd hour*, Becket *even at this odd*).

**Oddly,** 1) strangely: Tp. V, 197. Merch. I, 2, 79. Rom. II, 5, 61.

2) not evenly, unequally: *our imputation shall be o. poised in this wild action*, Troil. I, 3, 339.

**Odds,** 1) uneven number: *were still at o., being but three*, LLL III, 86. 91 (quibbling). *and stayed the o. by adding four*, 93. 96. 99.

2) inequality: *yet death we fear, that makes these o. all even*, Meas. III, 1, 41. *five to one ... 'tis a fearful o.* H5 IV, 3, 5. *forsaketh yet the lists by reason of his adversary's o.: a poor earl's daughter is unequal o.* H6A V, 5, 33. 34. *five men to twenty! though the o. be great, I doubt not of our victory*, H6C I, 2, 72. *'twas o., belike, when valiant Warwick fled*, II, 1, 148. *this and my food are equals; there's no o.* Tim. I, 2, 61. *but now 'tis o. beyond arithmetic*, Cor. III, 1, 245. *I shall win at the o.* Hml. V, 2, 222 (viz of twelve to nine). *his quails ever beat mine at o.* Ant. II, 3, 38 (at disadvantage). *young boys and girls are level now with men, the o. is gone*, IV, 15, 66.

3) superiority, advantage: *Cupid's butt-shaft is too hard for Hercules' club, and therefore too much o. for a Spaniard's rapier*, LLL I, 2, 183. *there is such o. in the man*, As I, 2, 169. *I would allow him o.* R2 I, 1, 62. *and with that o. he weighs King Richard down*, III, 4, 89. *he shall take the o. of his great name and estimation*, H4A V, 1, 97. *yields up his life unto a world of o.* H6A IV, 4, 25. *that Iden took o. to combat a poor famished man*, H6B IV, 10, 47. *Hercules himself must yield to o.* H6C II, 1, 53. *advantageous care withdrew me from the o. of multitude*, Troil. V, 4, 23. *thou hast the o. of me*, Tit. V, 2, 19. *we have therefore o.* Hml. V, 2, 274. *he beats thee 'gainst the o.* Ant. II, 3, 27.

4) probability, likelihood: *then he shall have no o.* Shr. IV, 3, 155. *the stars will kiss the valleys first; the o. for high and low's alike*, Wint. V, 1, 207. *if that thy gentry, Britain, go before this lout as he exceeds our lords, the o. is that we scarce are men and you are gods*, Cymb. V, 2, 9.

*To lay o.* = to lay a wager: *I will lay o.* H4B V, 5, 111. *your grace hath laid the o. o' the weaker side*, Hml. V, 2, 272.

5) quarrel, contention, discord: *I desire nothing but o. with England*, H5 II, 4, 129. *that put'st o. among the rout of nations*, Tim. IV, 3, 42. *set them into confounding o.* 392. *I cannot speak any beginning to this peevish o.* Oth. II, 3, 185. *at o.* = at variance, quarrelling: Wiv. III, 1, 54. R3 II, 1, 70. Rom. I, 2, 5. Tim. III, 5, 116. Mcb. III, 4, 127. Lr. I, 3, 5.

**Ode,** a short poem, a panegyric in verse: LLL IV, 3, 99. As III, 2, 379.

**Odious,** hateful: Tp. III, 1, 5. Wiv. II, 1, 133. Mids. III, 1, 84. As III, 3, 52. All's II, 1, 175. H4B II, 4, 160. H6B IV, 4, 46. H8 III, 2, 331. Oth. V, 2, 180. Per. I, 4, 31.

**Odoriferous,** fragrant: LLL IV, 2, 128. John III, 4, 26.

**Odorous,** the same: Mids. II, 1, 110. Blunderingly for *odious:* Ado III, 5, 18; cf. Mids. III, 1, 84.

**Odour,** sweet scent, fragrance: Sonn. 54, 4. 12. 69, 13. 98, 6. Mids. III, 1, 85. Tw. I, 1, 7. III, 1, 96. 98. 101. Per. III, 2, 61.

**Oeillades** (O. Edd. *illiads, eliads, aliads*) amorous glances, ogles: *examined my parts with most judicious o.* Wiv. I, 3, 68. *she gave strange o. and most speaking looks to noble Edmund*, Lr. IV, 5, 25.

**O'er,** see *Over.*

**O'erbear** (cf. *Overbear*) to bear down, to overpower, to bring under: *oil and fire, too strong for reason's force, —s it and burns on*, All's V, 3, 8. *—ing interruption*, John III, 4, 9. *to command, to check, to o. such as are of better person than myself*, H6C III, 2, 166. *my desire all continent impediments would o.* Mcb. IV, 3, 64. Particularly used of waters overwhelming the land: Cor. III, 1, 249. IV, 5, 137 (O. Edd. *o'erbeat*). IV, 6, 78. Hml. IV, 5, 102. Oth. I, 3, 56. Cymb. V, 3, 48. Per. V, 1, 195.

**O'erbeat,** reading of O. Edd. in Cor. IV, 5, 137; M. Edd. rightly *o'erbear.*

**O'erblow,** to blow away, to disperse by wind: *whiles yet the cool and temperate wind of grace — s the filthy and contagious clouds*, H5 III, 3, 31.

**O'erboard,** from on board, out of the ship: Tp. II, 2, 127. V, 219. Per. IV, 2, 70.

**O'ercast,** darkened, clouded: *the sun's o. with blood*, John III, 1, 326. *how soon the day o.* R3 III, 2, 88.

**O'ercharge,** to load beyond the power of bearing: Sonn. 23, 8. Mids. V, 85. Wint. III, 2, 151. H6A I, 3, 64. H6C II, 5, 78. Per. III, 2, 54.

**O'ercloyed,** filled beyond satiety: R3 V, 3, 318.

**O'ercome,** 1) to spread over, to cover: *the trees ... o. with moss and mistletoe*, Tit. II, 3, 95.

2) to conquer; absol.: *in thirteen battles Salisbury o'ercame*, H6A I, 4, 78. Trans.: *Hamlet o'ercame Fortinbras*, Hml. V, 1, 156 (Qq *overcame*).

3) to subjugate, to rule, to domineer over: *Marcius was a worthy officer i' the war, but insolent, o. with pride*, Cor. IV, 6, 31. *to o. you with her show*, Cymb. V, 5, 54.

**O'ercount,** to outnumber: *at land, thou knowest how much we do o. thee. At land, indeed, thou dost o. me of my father's house*, Ant. II, 6, 26. 27. In the second place *of* = by; cf. *Of.*

**O'ercovered,** completely covered: *o. quite with dead men's rattling bones*, Rom. IV, 1, 82.

**O'ercrow,** to triumph over, to overpower: *the potent poison quite —s my spirit*, Hml. V, 2, 364.

**O'erdo,** to exaggerate: *I would have such a fellow whipped for —ing Termagant*, Hml. III, 2, 15.

**O'erdusted,** covered with dust: *give to dust that is a little gilt more laud than gilt o.* Troil. III, 3, 179.

**O'erdyed,** dyed over, bedaubed with another colour: *were they false as o. blacks*, Wint. I, 2, 132, i. e. black things painted with another colour, through which the ground will soon appear; cf. Tit. IV, 2, 100.

**O'ereaten,** eaten and begnawn on all sides: *the*

*fragments, scraps, the bits and greasy relics of her o. faith are bound to Dicmed*, Troil. V, 2, 160.

**O'ereye,** to see, to observe: *here sit I in the sky and wretched fools' secrets heedfully o.* LLL IV, 3, 80.

**O'erfed,** fed to excess: Per. III Prol. 3.

**O'erflourished,** varnished over: *the beauteous evil are empty trunks o. by the devil*, Tw. III, 4, 404.

**O'erflow,** vb. 1) intr. a) to swell and run over the banks: *the —ing Nilus*, Ant. I, 2, 49. Metaphorically, = to abound: *to make the coming hour o. with joy and pleasure drown the brim*, All's II, 4, 47.

b) to have too much water, to be drowned: *when heaven doth weep, doth not the earth o.?* Tit. III, 1, 222.

2) trans. a) to swell over, to overrun, to inundate, to drown: *who, being stopped, the bounding banks —s*, Lucr. 1119. *he that in this action contrives against his own nobility, in his proper stream —s himself*, All's IV, 3, 30. *this dotage —s the measure*, Ant. I, 1, 2. *the earth, fearing to be —ed*, Per. IV, 4, 40.

b) to stream with, to pour out in abundance: *such brooks are welcome to me, that o. such liquor*, Wiv. II, 2, 157.

**O'erfraught,** too heavily loaded: *the o. heart*, Mcb. IV, 3, 210.

**O'ergalled,** too much injured and worn away: *their eyes o. with recourse of tears*, Troil. V, 3, 55.

**O'erglance,** to look hastily over: *I have but with a cursorary eye —d the articles*, H5 V, 2, 78.

**O'ergo,** to walk or pass over: *of many weary miles you have —ne*, LLL V, 2, 196.

**O'ergreat,** too great: *the o. cardinal*, H8 I, 1, 222.

**O'ergreen,** to cover with verdure, to embellish: *so you o. my bad, my good allow*, Sonn. 112, 4.

**O'ergrow,** to cover with growth: *corn —n by weeds*, Lucr. 281. *—n with hair*, As IV, 3, 107. *they* (weeds) *will o. the garden*, H6B III, 1, 32. *yourself so out of thought, and thereto so —n, cannot be questioned*, Cymb. IV, 4, 33 (i. e. covered with hair; cf. As IV, 3, 107).

**O'ergrown,** having become too old: *like an o. lion in a cave, that goes not out to prey*, Meas. I, 3, 22. Perhaps also in Cymb. IV, 4, 33.

**O'ergrowth,** excessive growth: *by the o. of some complexion*, Hml. I, 4, 27.

**O'erhang,** to jut or hang over: *as doth a galled rock o. and jutty his confounded base*, H5 III, 1, 13. *this brave —ing firmament*, Hml. II, 2, 312 (Ff only *this brave —ing*).

**O'erhanging,** subst. that which hangs over like a canopy: *this brave o., this majestical roof fretted with golden fire*, Hml. II, 2, 312 (Qq *o. firmament*).

**O'erhasty,** too hasty: *our o. marriage*, Hml. II, 2, 57 (Qq *hasty*).

**O'erhear,** to hear without being addressed: LLL IV, 3, 130. As II, 2, 11. Hml. III, 3, 32. Lr. III, 6, 96.

**O'erjoyed,** transported with gladness: Cymb. V, 5, 401.

**O'erlaboured,** worn with labour, weary: Cymb. II, 2, 11.

**O'erleap,** to leap over, to clear by leaping: *a step on which I must fall down, or else, o.* Mcb. I, 4, 49. Metaphorically, = to omit: *let me o. that custom*, Cor. II, 2, 140.

*To o. one's self* = to exert one's self too much in leaping, to leap too far or too high: *vaulting ambition,*

*which —s itself and falls on the other* (side) Mcb. I, 7, 27.

**O'erleaven,** to leaven too much, to corrupt: *some habit that too much —s the form of plausive manners*, Hml. I, 4, 29.

**O'erlook,** 1) to inspect, to survey: *o. the walls*, R3 III, 5, 17. *o. what shipping and what lading's in our haven*, Per. I, 2, 48.

2) to peruse: Sonn. 82, 2. Gent. I, 2, 50. Mids. II, 2, 121. Lr. I, 2, 40. V, 1, 50.

3) to despise, to slight: *stoop low within those bounds we have —ed*, John V, 4, 55.

4) to subdue by the look, to confound, to unsettle: *vile worm, thou wast —ed even in thy birth*, Wiv. V, 5, 87. *beshrew your eyes, that have —ed me and divided me*, Merch. III, 2, 15.* cf. *overseen* in Lucr. 1206.

**O'ermaster,** 1) to have in one's power: *which owe the crown that thou —est*, John II, 109.

2) to subdue: *for your desire to know what is between us, o. it as you may*, Hml. I, 5, 140.

**O'ermatched,** oppressed by superior force: H6A IV, 4, 11. H6C I, 4, 64.

**O'ermount,** to rise above: *I could o. the lark*, H8 II, 3, 94.

**O'ernight,** during the night before something: (such rest) *as wretches have o. that wait for execution in the morn*, Gent. IV, 2, 133. *shame her with what he saw o.* Ado III, 3, 174. Substantively: *to cure thy —'s surfeit*, Tim. IV, 3, 227.

**O'er-office,** vb. to get the better of and lord over by virtue of an office: *it might be the pate of a politician, which this ass now —s*, Hml. V, 1, 87 (Qq *o'erreaches*).

**O'erparted,** having too difficult a part assigned: *he is a marvellous good neighbour and a very good bowler: but, for Alisander, — alas, you see how 'tis, — a little o.* LLL V, 2, 588.

**O'erpast,** passed by, gone: *in the time o.* R3 IV, 4, 388. 396.

**O'erpay,** to pay more than sufficiently: Lr. IV, 7, 4. Cymb. II, 4, 10.

**O'erpeer,** to overtop, to rise above: *too highly heaped for truth to o.* Cor. II, 3, 128.

**O'erperch,** to fly over: *with love's light wings did I o. these walls*, Rom. II, 2, 66.

**O'erpicture,** to be a better picture than: *—ing that Venus where we see the fancy outwork nature*, Ant. II, 2, 205.

**O'erpost,** to get quickly and easily over, to get clear of cheaply: *you may thank the unquiet time for your quiet —ing that action*, H4B I, 2, 171; cf. *posted over* in H6B III, 1, 255.

**O'erpower,** to conquer, to overcome: R2 V, 1, 31. Ant. II, 3, 22.

**O'erpressed,** oppressed by superior force, overwhelmed: *thy might is more than my o. defence can bide*, Sonn. 139, 8. *he bestrid an o. Roman*, Cor. II, 2, 97. *death may usurp on nature many hours, and yet the fire of life kindle again the o. spirits*, Per. III, 2, 84.

**O'erprize,** to exceed in value: *—d all popular rate*, Tp. I, 2, 92.

**O'errate,** to rate at too much: Cymb. I, 4, 41.

**O'erreach** (impf. and partic. *o'erraught*), 1) to overtake: *certain players we o'erraught on the way*, Hml. III, 1, 17.

2) to trick, to dupe: *so gross —ing as this*, Wiv

V, 5, 145. *the villain is o'erraught of all my money*, Err. I, 2, 96. *o. them in their own devices*, Tit. V, 2, 143. *the pate of a politician, which this ass now —es*, Hml. V, 1, 87 (Ff *o'er-offices*).

**O'erread,** to peruse: Sonn. 81, 10. H4B III, 1, 2. Caes. III, 1, 4. Lr. I, 2, 38.

**O'errule,** absol. to prevail: *then fate —s, that, one man holding troth, a million fail*, Mids. III, 2, 92. Trans., = to prevail with: *let me o. you now*, LLL V, 2, 516. *—d by prophecies*, H4A IV, 4, 18. *you shall o. my mind for once*, R3 III, 1, 57. With *to*: *so you will not o. me to a peace*, Hml. IV, 7, 61.

**O'errun,** 1) to tread under foot: *I will o. thee with policy*, As V, 1, 61. *o. and trampled on*, Troil. III, 3, 163.

2) to overflow: *till it o the stew*, Meas. V, 321. *the tears ... o. her lovely face*, Shr. Ind. 2, 67. *a chilling sweat —s my trembling joints*, Tit. II, 3, 212.

3) to look over, to review: *in thy thought o. my former time*, H6C I, 4, 45.

**O'erset,** to turn bottom upward, to overthrow: H4B I, 1, 185.

**O'ershade,** to make dark and gloomy: *fear —s me*, Wint. I, 2, 457. *dark cloudy death —s his beams of life*, H6C II, 6, 62. *black night o. thy day*, R3 I, 2, 131.

**O'ershine,** to outshine, to excel in lustre: H4B IV, 3, 57.

**O'ershoot;** 1) *to o. one's self* = to go too far, to say too much: *I have o'ershot myself to tell you of it*, Caes. III, 2, 155.

2) Partic. *o'ershot* = blundering, having the worse, put to shame: *are you not ashamed, nay, are you not, all three of you, to be thus much o'ershot?* LLL IV, 3, 160. cf. *Overshoot.*

**O'ershower,** to rain upon: *with sighs shot through, and biggest tears —ed*, Per. IV, 4, 26.

**O'ersized,** smeared as with glutinous matter: *o. with coagulate gore*, Hml. II, 2, 484.

**O'erskip,** to neglect, to treat with indifference: *then the mind much sufferance doth o, when grief hath mates*, Lr. III, 6, 113.

**O'erslip,** to pass unheeded: *when that hour —s me in the day wherein I sigh not*, Gent. II, 2, 9.

**O'ersnowed,** covered with snow: Sonn. 5, 8.

**O'erspread,** to cover: *the dragon wing of night —s the earth*, Troil. V, 8, 17. *with hostile forces he'll o. the land*, Per. I, 2, 24.

**O'erstare,** to look more fiercely than: *I would o. the sternest eyes that look*, Merch. II, 1, 27 (Q1 *outstare*).

**O'erstep,** to step over, to transgress: *that you o. not the modesty of nature*, Hml. III, 2, 21.

**O'erstink,** to drown a bad smell by one still worse, to stink more than: *the foul lake o'erstunk their feet*, Tp. IV, 184.

**O'erstrawed** = overstrewed (rhyming): *the top o. with sweets*, Ven. 1143.

**O'ersway,** 1) to control, to rule, to lord over: *so pertaunt-like would I o. his state, that he should be my fool and I his fate*, LLL V, 2, 67. *if he be so resolved, I can o. him*, Caes. II, 1, 203.

2) to surpass in power: *sad mortality —s their power*, Sonn. 65, 2. *great command —s the order*, Hml. V, 1, 251.

**O'erswell,** 1) intr. to rise above the banks: *let floods o.* H5 II, 1, 97 (Pistol's speech). 2) trans. to overflow: *o. thy shores*, John II, 337. *till the wine o. the cup*, Caes. IV, 3, 161.

**O'ertake** (partic. *o'ertook*) 1) to come upon, to take, to catch: *to let base clouds o. me in my way*, Sonn. 34, 3. *if the trial of the law o. ye*, H8 III, 1, 96. *o'ertook in's rouse*, Hml. II, 1, 58. *whom leprosy o.* Ant. III, 10, 11.

2) to come up with one going before: *his act did not o. his bad intent*, Meas. V, 456; cf. *the flighty purpose never is o'ertook unless the deed go with it*, Mcb. IV, 1, 145. *o. me, if thou canst*, H6A I, 5, 15. *if thou wilt o. us, hence a mile or twain*, Lr. IV, 1, 44. *I'll o. you*, V, 1, 39. *I will o. thee*, Ant. IV, 14, 44. *would I might never o. pursued success*, V, 2, 103. (Almost = to follow, in H6A I, 5, 15. Lr. V, 1, 39. Ant. IV, 14, 44).

**O'erteemed,** worn by bringing forth children: *her o. loins*, Hml. II, 2, 531.

**O'erthrow,** vb. to throw down, to defeat, to bring to nothing: Tp. Epil. 1. LLL V, 2, 153. Wint. IV, 1, 8. V, 1, 230. R2 III, 2, 72. H6A I, 1, 108. H6B III, 1, 181. Hml. III, 1, 158. Ant. IV, 15, 14. Cymb. III, 6, 20.

**O'ertop,** to rise above, to be higher than: H8 II, 4, 88. Troil. III, 3, 164. Hml. V, 1, 276.

**O'ertrip,** to trip over: *did Thisbe fearfully o. the dew*, Merch. V, 7.

**O'erturn,** to throw down: H4A IV, 1, 82. H5 IV, 2, 24.

**O'ervalue,** to be more worth than: *I dare pawn the moiety of my estate to your ring, which in my opinion —s it something*, Cymb. I, 4, 120.

**O'erwalk,** to go over, to cross: *to o. a current*, H4A I, 3, 192.

**O'erwatched,** worn out with watching: Caes. IV, 3, 241. Lr. II, 2, 177.

**O'erween,** to think arrogantly, to presume: *or I o. to think so*, Wint. IV, 2, 9. *a hot —ing cur*, H6B V, 1, 151. *my heart —s too much*, H6C III, 2, 144.

**O'erweigh,** to outweigh, to overbalance: Meas. II, 4, 170. Hml. III, 2, 31.

**O'erwhelm,** 1) to overspread and cover entirely: *foul deeds will rise, though all the earth o. them*, Hml. I, 2, 258. *humming water must o. thy corpse*, Per. III, 1, 64.

2) to hang down upon in a threatening manner: *his louring brows —ing his fair sight*, Ven. 183. *let the brow o. it as fearfully as doth a galled rock o'erhang his base*, H5 III, 1, 11.

3) to bear down, to crush, to overpower entirely: *to plant and o. custom*, Wint. IV, 1, 9. *like a sow that hath —ed all her litter but one*, H4B I, 2, 13 (crushed? or devoured? Q *overwhelmed*). *wrath —ed my pity*, Cor. I, 9, 86. *despite o. thee*, III, 1, 164. *with the hell-hated lie o. thy heart*, Lr. V, 3, 147. *—ed with your grief*, Oth. IV, 1, 77.

**O'erworn,** 1) worn out, spent, advanced in time: *musing the morning is so much o.* Ven. 866.

2) worn and spoiled by time: Ven. 135. Sonn. 63, 2. R3 I, 1, 81.

**O'erwrested** (O. Edd. *ore-rested*) strained: *such to be pitied and o. seeming he acts thy greatness in*, Troil. I, 3, 157.

**Of,** = from, in its different senses: *one that I brought up of a puppy*, Gent. IV, 4, 3. *being of so young* *days brought up with him*, Hml. II, 2, 11. *the imprison-ed absence of your liberty*, Sonn. 58, 6. *tear the stain-ed skin of my harlot brow*, Err. II, 2, 138 (M. Edd. off). *we John Cade, so termed of our supposed father*, H6B IV, 2, 33. *no more can you distinguish of a man than of his outward favour*, R3 III, 1, 10. *Lepidus of the triumvirate should be deposed*, Ant. III, 6, 28. *in the world's volume our Britain seems as of it*, *but not in it*, Cymb. III, 4, 141 (severed from it). *I take all my comfort of thy worth and truth*, Sonn. 37, 4. *of this book this learning mayst thou taste*, 77, 4. *of whom I have received a second life*, Tp. V, 194. *that cost me two shilling and two pence a piece of Yead Miller*, Wiv. I, 1, 160. *what he gets more of her than sharp words*, II, 1, 190. *where is the thousand marks thou hast of me?* Err. I, 2, 81. *he had of me a chain*, IV, 1, 10. V, 2. 256. *that I of him received the chain*, 228. *take of me my daughter*, Ado II, 1, 313. *where hadst thou it? Of Costard*, LLL IV, 3, 197. *there is the very remuneration I had of thy master*, V, 1, 76. *the Jew's bond which he hath of me*, Merch. II, 8, 41. *a ring that he had of your daughter for a monkey*, III, 1, 124. *which you received of me*, V, 185. *thou shalt have to pay for it of us*, As II, 4, 93. *take this of me*, Shr. II, 191. *would you take the letter of her*, All's III, 4, 1. *holding of the pope your sovereign greatness*, John V, 1, 3. *good wishes shall Suffolk ever have of Margaret*, H6A V, 3, 174. *you took bribes of France*, H6B III, 1, 104. *get a thousand crowns of the king*, H6B IV, 10, 29. *what he shall receive of us in duty*, Troil. III, 1, 169. *what wouldst thou of us?* III, 3, 17. *taking bribes of the Sardians*, Caes. IV, 3, 3. *to recover of us those lands*, Hml. I, 1, 102. *his majesty shall have tribute of me*, II, 2, 333. *the spurns that patient merit of the un-worthy takes*, III, 1, 74. *of whom he had this ring*, Cymb. V, 5, 136. *of your royal presence I'll adventure the borrow of a week*, Wint. I, 2, 38. *I of these* (winks, nods etc.) *will wrest an alphabet*, Tit. III, 2, 44. *there's a testril of me too*, Tw. II, 3, 34. *his cocks do win the battle still of mine*, Ant. II, 3, 36. *can get goal for goal of youth*, IV, 8, 22. *I would know that of your honour*, Meas. II, 1, 166. *if you will know of me what man I am*, As IV, 3, 96. *what shall I know of thee?* H5 III, 6, 122. *we desire to know of him of whence he is*, Per. II, 3, 73. *to help him of his blindness*, Gent. IV, 2, 47. *I discharge thee of thy prisoner*, Ado V, 1, 328. *rid the house of her*, Shr. I, 1, 150. *that which may unfur-nish me of reason*, Wint. V, 1, 123. *how I may be de-livered of these woes*, John III, 4, 55. *we'll deliver you of your great danger*, Cor. V, 6, 15. *heaven make thee free of it*, Hml. V, 2, 343. *my trust did beget of him a falsehood*, Tp. I, 2, 94. *if my lord get a boy of you*, Troil. III, 2, 113. *brawls bred of an airy word*, Rom. I, 1, 96. *I am descended of a gentler blood*, H6A V, 4, 8. H5 I, 2, 67. *had ta'en his last leave of the weeping morn*, Ven. 2. *I took my leave of Madam Silvia*, Gent. IV, 4, 38. cf. the verbs *to acquit, beg, bereave, beware, borrow, cheat, cleanse, clear, crave, cure, deliver, de-prive, discharge, ease, heal, purge, rob, wash* etc.; the adjectives *barren, clean, clear, devoid, free, short, void* etc.; the adverbs *forth, out, upward* etc.; the prepo-sition *within* etc. Hence = out of, in consequence of, by virtue of: *we were dead of sleep*, Tp. V, 230. *what shall become of this?* Ado IV, 1, 211. *bold of your worthiness*, LLL II, 28. *of thine own good will*, R2 IV, 177. *of no right, nor colour like to right, he doth fill*

*fields with harness*, H4A III, 2, 100. *which of a weak and niggardly projection doth like a miser spoil his coat with scanting a little cloth*, H5 II, 4, 46. *you have sub-orned this man, of purpose to obscure my noble birth*, H6A V, 4, 22. *camest thou here by chance or of devo-tion?* H6B II, 1, 88. *art thou a messenger, or come of pleasure?* V, 1, 16. *the king, of his own royal disposi-tion, .... makes him to send*, R3 I, 3, 63. *if great minds, of partial indulgence to their benumbed wills, resist the same*, Troil. II, 2, 178. *a madness, of which her life is in danger*, Cymb. IV, 3, 3. *and of that natural luck he beats thee 'gainst the odds*, Ant. II, 3, 26. *so, of his gentleness, he furnished me with volumes*, Tp. I, 2, 165. *I no question make to have it* (money) *of my trust*, Merch. I, 1, 185. *God of his mercy give you patience*, H5 II, 2, 179. *King Henry gives consent, of mere com-passion and of lenity*, H6A V, 4, 125. *accept the title thou usurpest, of benefit proceeding from our king, and not of any challenge of desert*, 152. *from Scotland am I stolen, even of pure love*, H6C III, 1, 13. *of his great grace and princely care foreseeing those fell mischiefs*, H8 V, 1, 48. Used in adjurations: *of charity, what kin are you to me?* Tw. V, 237. *speak, of all loves*, Mids. II, 2, 154; cf. Wiv. II, 2, 119 and Oth. III, 1, 13. And in adverbial phrases: *of force I must attempt you further*, Merch. IV, 1, 421. *I must of force*, H4A II, 3, 120. *some more audience than a mother ... should o'erhear the speech of vantage*, Hml. III, 3, 33 (i. e. besides, to boot). *though he speak of comfort*, Oth. II, 1, 31 (perhaps = comfortably). See besides the articles *Boast, Die, Repent, Relish, Smack, Taste, Weary* etc.

= by, after passive verbs: *be of thyself rejected*, Ven. 159. *I am expected of my friends*, 718. *O happi-ness enjoyed but of a few*, Lucr. 22. *to be admired of lewd eyes*, 392. *thou art beloved of many*, Sonn. 10, 3. *loved of more and less*, 96, 3. 150, 14. Ado I, 1, 126. LLL II, 57. Mids. I, 1, 104. As I, 1, 116. 174. Shr. I, 2, 176. All's I, 3, 203. H6B I, 2, 44. *too base of thee to be remembered*, Sonn. 74, 12. *to be praised of ages yet to be*, 101, 12. *of him, myself, and thee I am forsaken*, 133, 7. *when I forgot am of myself*, 149, 4. *of you well favoured*, Gent. II, 1, 57. *unseen of any*, V, 4, 4. *desired of such a person*, Meas. II, 4, 91. *to be disdain-ed of all*, Ado I, 3, 30. *taken up of these men's bills*, III, 3, 191. *excused of every hearer*, IV, 1, 219. *that a lady, of one man refused, should of another therefore be abused*, Mids. II, 2, 133. *hated most of those they did deceive*, 140. 142. *much marked of the melancholy Jaques*, As II, 1, 41. *abandoned of his friends*, 50. *un-claimed of any man*, II, 7, 87. *I have been told so of many*, III, 2, 361. *to be married of him*, III, 3, 92. *wooed of a snail*, IV, 1, 52. *discipled of the bravest*, All's I, 2, 28. *worse of worst extended*, II, 1, 176. *to be relin-quished of the artists*, II, 3, 10. *owed and worn of six ancestors*, V, 3, 196. *of many accounted beautiful*, Tw. II, 1, 27. *not noted but of the finer natures*, Wint. I, 2, 226. *pitied of thee*, III, 2, 235. *blessed of the King of kings*, H6A I, 1, 28. *assailed of none*, IV, 7, 10. *honoured of the people*, H6B I, 1, 198. *hated of God and man*, H6C I, 3, 9. *scorned of me*, R3 IV, 4, 102. *feared of all*, 103. *a night of groans endured of her*, 304. *tempted of the devil*, 418. *commanded of Aga-memnon*, Troil. II, 3, 69. *worshipped of that we hold an idol*, 199. *of Rome worse hated than of you*, Cor. I, 2, 13. *how you are censured, I mean of us*, II, 1, 25. *'tis thought of every one*, II, 2, 3. *we have been called so of many*, II, 3, 19. *highly honoured of your grace*, Tit. I, 245. *and is received of the most pious Edward*, Mcb. III, 6, 27. *seen of us*, Hml. I, 1, 25. *the observed of all observers*, III, 1, 162. *to be demanded of a sponge*, IV, 2, 12. *known of thee*, Lr. II, 2, 28. *that my charity be not of him perceived*, III, 3, 17. *to be but named of thee*, Cymb. II, 3, 138. *disdained of fortune*, III, 4, 20. *'tis no better reckoned but of those who worship dirty gods*, III, 6, 55. *I was taught of your daughter the difference*, V, 5, 194. Denoting a means, = with: *I am provided of a torch-bearer*, Merch. II, 4, 24. *you are not satisfied of these events at full*, V, 297. *whose self-same mettle, whereof thy proud child, arrogant man, is puffed*, Tim. IV, 3, 180. *Macdonald ... from the western isles of kerns and gallowglasses is supplied*, Mcb. I, 2, 13. Seldom after active verbs: *why of that loam might they not stop a beer-barrel?* Hml. V, 1, 233. *thou dost o'ercount me of my father's house*, Ant. II, 6, 27 (probably a play on the word: thou outnumberest me by my father's house; and: thou art too fond of my father's house; cf. *Count*). cf. Lr. II, 4, 161.

*Of one's self* = by one's self, in one's self, alone, if let alone, without the help or interference of anything else: *beauty itself doth of itself persuade the eyes of man without an orator*, Lucr. 29. *simple of itself; I'll no pullet-sperm in my brewage*, Wiv. III, 5, 32. *which they'll do fast enough of themselves*, IV, 1, 69. *better 'twere that both of us did fast, since of ourselves ourselves are choleric, than feed it with such overroasted flesh*, Shr. IV, 1, 177. *for then we wound our modesty and make foul the clearness of our deservings, when of ourselves we publish them*, All's I, 3, 7. *who of herself is a good lady*, V, 2, 33. *the world, who of itself is peised well*, John II, 575. *the iron of itself, though heat red-hot, approaching near these eyes, would drink my tears and quench his fiery indignation*, IV, 1, 61. *he being of age to govern of himself*, H6B I, 1, 166. *that of itself England is safe, if true within itself*, H6C IV, 1, 39. *it holds its estimate and dignity as well wherein 'tis precious of itself as in the prizer*, Troil. II, 2, 55. *nor doth he of himself know them* (his parts) *for aught till he behold them formed in the applause where they're extended*, III, 3, 118. *they* (the gates) *will open of themselves*, Cor. I, 4, 19. *had borne the action of yourself*, IV, 7, 15.

Used to denote any manner of proceeding from a cause or agent: *it was a mad fantastical trick of him*, Meas. III, 2, 98. *it was well done of you*, LLL II, 217. *this is a knavery of them*, Mids. III, 1, 116. *well aimed of such a young one*, Shr. II, 236. *who seeks for better of thee*, Tim. IV, 3, 24. *it was a brute part of him*, Hml. III, 2, 110. *what of this? what of that?* = what follows from this? Ven. 717. Wiv. IV, 4, 41; cf. *What.*

Denoting the material constituting a thing: *compact of fire*, Ven. 149. *I'll make a shadow for thee of my hairs*, 191. *a goal of snow*, 362. *a flock of sheep*, 685. *the choir of echoes*, 840. *my life, being made of four*, Sonn. 45, 7. *made such a sinner of his memory*, Tp. I, 2, 101. *make a vassal of him*, 374. *of his bones are coral made*, 397. *this bottle which I made of the bark of a tree*, II, 2, 128. *composed of harshness*, III, 1, 9. *created of every creature's best*, 48. *make a stock-fish of thee*, III, 2, 79. *a ladder made of cords*, Gent. III, 1, 117. *to make a virtue of necessity*, IV, 1, 62. *till he have made an oyster of me*, Ado II, 3, 27. *to make*

*a lamp of her*, Err. III, 2, 98. *to make her heavenly comforts of despair*, Meas. IV, 3, 114. *they make an ass of me*, Tw. V, 20. *he is composed and framed of treachery*, Ado V, 1, 257. *Henry is of a king become a banished man*, H6C III, 3, 25. *what would betide of me?* R3 I, 3, 6. *made peace of enmity, fair love of hate*, II, 1, 50 etc. etc. Hence the following expressions: *even such a husband hast thou of me*, Merch. III, 5, 89. *you shall find of the king a husband*, All's I, 1, 7. *you have won a wife of me*, IV, 2, 65. *we lost a jewel of her*, V, 3, 1. *you have an unspeakable comfort of your prince*, Wint. I, 1, 38. *that did but show thee of a fool inconstant and damnable ingrateful*, III, 2, 187. *they shall find dear deer of us*, H6A IV, 2, 54. *we should have found a bloody day of this*, IV, 7, 34. *thou shalt find — A fool of thee*, Tim. IV, 3, 232. *we shall find of him a shrewd contriver*, Caes. II, 1, 157. *you have a nurse of me*, Per. IV, 1, 25. cf. Cor. I, 9, 10.

Denoting the stuff or material filling a thing, as f. i. *a butt of sack*, Tp. II, 2, 126; *a glass of rhenish wine*, Merch. I, 2, 104. *an excellent head of hair*, Tw. I, 3, 101 etc. etc. cf. the adjectives *big*, *full*, *liberal* etc. Likewise that which affords matter to thought or language, = on, about: *so of concealed sorrow may be said*, Ven. 333. *to think but nobly of my grandmother*, Tp. I, 2, 119. *to hear thee speak of Naples*, 433. *you make me study of that*, II, 1, 82. *I wonder of their being here together*, Mids. IV, 1, 136. *I did dream of money-bags*, Merch. II, 5, 18. *mine own escape unfoldeth to my hope the like of him*, Tw. I, 2, 21. *who but to-day hammered of this design*, Wint. II, 2, 49. *inquire of him*, R2 III, 2, 186 (= about him). *having determined of the Volsces*, Cor. II, 2, 41. *to use as you think needful of the man*, Tit. V, 1, 39; cf. Mcb. III, 1, 101. *what it should be, I cannot dream of*, Hml. II, 2, 10. *I told him of myself*, Ant. II, 2, 78. *did you hear of a stranger*, Cymb. II, 1, 35. *must know of her departure*, IV, 3, 10 etc. etc. cf. *Acquaint, Brag, Despair, Doubt, Complain, Demand, Instruct, Read, Tell* etc.

Hence, in general, introducing the object of a verbal: *the expense of spirit*, Sonn. 129, 1. *thy neglect of truth*, 101, 2. *in care of thee*, Tp. I, 2, 16. *make not too rash a trial of him*, 467. *for fear of the storm*, II, 2, 116. *for love of you*, Gent. II, 4, 5. III, 1, 46. *'tis not in hate of you*, III, 1, 96. *'tis pity of him*, Meas. II, 3, 42. Mids. III, 1, 144. Ant. I, 4, 71. *make choice of which your highness will see first*, Mids. V, 43. *I have no mind of feasting forth*, Merch. II, 5, 37. *the borrow of a week*, Wint. I, 2, 39. *in haste whereof*, R2 I, 1, 150. *any challenge of desert*, H6A V, 4, 153. *the sight of me is odious in their eye*, H6B IV, 4, 46. *give us a prince of blood in change of him*, Troil. III, 3, 27. *of this my privacy I have strong reasons*, 190. *I have an eye of you*, Hml. II, 2, 301. *since of your lives you set so slight a valuation*, Cymb. IV, 4, 48 etc. etc. Remarkable passages: *you should not have the eminence of him*, Troil. II, 3, 266. *by the sovereign power you have of us*, Hml. II, 2, 27. *niggard of question, but of our demands most free in his reply*, III, 1, 13 (for *to our demands*). *by an enforced obedience of planetary influence*, Lr. I, 2, 135 (for *to planetary influence*). After adjectives: *ignorant of what thou art*, Tp. I, 2, 18. Meas. IV, 3, 113. *afeard of your four legs*, Tp. II, 2, 62. *what I am glad of*, III, 1, 74. *of so great a favour growing proud*, Gent. II, 4, 161 etc. (cf. *Ashamed, Capable,*

Certain, Enamoured, Fearful, Guilty, Fond, Innocent, Heedful, Joyful, Sensible, Sure etc.). Used after transitive verbs implying the idea of speaking or thinking, to express the particular import of the action: *accusing you of injury*, Sonn. 58, 8. *to appeal each other of high treason*, R2 I, 1, 27. *I am suspected of this murder*, Rom. V, 3, 224. *he shall never more be feared of doing harm*, Lr. I, 2, 113. *I shall desire you of more acquaintance*, Mids. III, 1, 185. *I humbly do desire your grace of pardon*, Merch. IV, 1, 402. *I desire you of the like*, As V, 4, 56. *whom of succours we entreated*, H5 III, 3, 45. *I humbly do beseech you of your pardon*, Oth. III, 3, 212. *till forging Nature be condemned of treason*, Ven. 729 etc. etc. After gerunds: *by telling of it*, Tp. I, 2, 100. *for kissing of their feet*, IV, 174. *by losing of your eyes*, LLL I, 1, 79. *by noting of the lady*, Ado IV, 1, 160. *by taking nor by giving of excess*, Merch. I, 3, 63. *the enjoying of my love*, III, 2, 29. *the praising of myself*, III, 4, 22. *this making of Christians*, III, 5, 25. *the getting up of the negro's belly*, 41. *the kissing of her batlet*, As II, 4, 49. *he professes not keeping of oaths*, All's IV, 3, 282. *for tainting of my love*, Tw. V, 141. *at knowing of thy choice*, Wint. IV, 4, 427. *by shaking of thy head*, John III, 1, 19. *with halloing and singing of anthems*, H4B I, 2, 213. *call you that backing of your friends?* H4A II, 4, 166. *with straining of my courage*, H6A I, 5, 10. *about relieving of the sentinels*, II, 1, 70. *by reputing of his high descent*, H6B III, 1, 48. *for stealing of sheep*, IV, 2, 67. *for giving up of Normandy*, IV, 7, 30. *threat you me with telling of the king?* R3 I, 3, 113. *for crowning of the king*, III, 4, 29. *in tempting of your patience*, H8 I, 2, 55. *by pronouncing of some doubtful phrase*, Hml. I, 5, 175. *for chiding of his fool*, Lr. I, 3, 1. *so find we profit by losing of our prayers*, Ant. II, 1, 6 (Instances of its omission see Tp. I, 2, 104. Lr. IV, 4, 9. Oth. III, 4, 22 according to the reading of Ff). In the same manner after participles of transitive verbs: *another licking of his wound*, Ven. 915. *fearing of time's tyranny*, Sonn. 115, 9. *so they mourn, becoming of their woe*, 127, 13. *tearing of papers*, Compl. 6. *whom I left cooling of the air with sighs*, Tp. I, 2, 222. *as willing as bondage e'er of freedom*, III, 1, 89. *while other sports are tasking of their minds*, Wiv. IV, 6, 30. *he's hearing of a cause*, Meas. II, 2, 1. *you granting of my suit*, II, 4, 70. *raising of more aid we came again*, Err. V, 153. *nature drawing of an antic*, Ado III, 1, 63. *valuing of her*, IV, 1, 141. *so I, admiring of his qualities*, Mids. I, 1, 231. *both warbling of one song*, III, 2, 206. *I am debating of my present store*, Merch I, 3, 54. *searching of thy wound*, As II, 4, 44. *here was he merry, hearing of a song*, II, 7, 4. *as she was writing of it*, IV, 3, 10. *overeyeing of his odd behaviour*, Shr. Ind. I, 95. *'tis by the seaside, browsing of ivy*, Wint. III, 3, 69. *their neighing courses daring of the spur*, H4B IV, 1, 119. *disgracing of these colours*, H6A III, 4, 29. *we took him setting of boys' copies*, H6B IV, 2, 95. *Warwick, backing of the Duke of York*, H6C II, 2, 69. *the shepherd, blowing of his nail*, II, 5, 3. *here ye lie baiting of bombards*, H8 V, 4, 85. *visiting of him*, Troil. II, 3, 87. *engaging and redeeming of himself*, V, 5, 39. *wanting of thy love*, Rom. II, 2, 78. *culling of simples*, V, 1, 40. *I was writing of my epitaph*, Tim. V, 1, 188. *saving of thy life*, Caes. V, 3, 38. *shaking of my arm*, Hml. II, 1, 92. *the ocean, overpeering of his list*, IV, 5, 99. *mumbling of wicked charms*, Lr. II, 1, 41. *is now

unloading of his mules*, Ant. IV, 6, 24. *honouring of Neptune's triumphs*, Per. V, 1, 17.

Partitive use: *certain of his friends*, Ven. 588. *by all of us*, Tp. II, 1, 129. *three inches of it*, 283. *here is more of us*, V, 216. *which of you know Ford*, Wiv. I, 3, 29. *all three of you*, LLL IV, 3, 160. *of enjoined penitents there's four or five at my house*, All's III, 5, 97. *both of you*, H6B III, 2, 182. Mcb. III, 1, 114. *worth five of Agamemnon*, H4B II, 4, 237 (cf. Cor. IV, 5, 174). *of those enough*, Ant. IV, 1, 13. *all of it*, Lr. I, 1, 202 (cf. *All* and *Both*). *'twas Aeneas' tale to Dido, and thereabout of it especially, where he speaks of Priam's slaughter*, Hml. II, 2, 468 etc. etc. Peculiar passages: *which, of he or Adrian, first begins to crow*, Tp. II, 1, 28 (a Gallicism). *whose right, of thine or mine, is most in Helena*, Mids. III, 2, 337. *he shall kill two of us*, Ado V, 1, 80 (= us both). *how many be there of them?* H4A II, 2, 66 (= how many are they?). *there be four of us here have ta'en a thousand pound*, II, 4, 175 (= we four here). *a hundred upon poor four of us*, 180. *four of which you please*, H4B III, 2, 259 (= which four you please). *some twenty of them fought in this black strife*, Rom. III, 1, 183 (there were some twenty who fought). *some dozen Romans of us*, Cymb. I, 6, 185 (cf. *on's* in Lr. III, 4, 110). *there's two of you; the devil make a third*, H6B III, 2, 303. The partitive particle dependent on the verb: *I have kept of them tame*, All's II, 5, 50 (= some of them). *you have of these pedlars*, Wint. IV, 4, 217. *my lord hath spent of Timon's wealth*, Tim. III, 4, 26. *when your false masters eat of my lord's meat*, 50. *I did want of what I was in the morning*, Ant. II, 2, 77; cf. *what hour now? I think it lacks of twelve*, Hml. I, 4, 3. *what should you need of more?* Lr. II, 4, 241.

By the omission of a superlative before the partitive *of*, the latter receives the sense of more than, above: *he whom next thyself of all the world I loved*, Tp. I, 2, 69. *he, of all the rest, hath never moved me*, Gent. I, 2, 27. *to see my friends in Padua, but of all my best beloved and approved friend Hortensio*, Shr. I, 2, 2. *but of all, the burst and the ear-deafening voice o' the oracle surprised my sense*, Wint. III, 1, 8. *York is most unmeet of any man*, H6B I, 3, 167. *I do not like the Tower of any place*, R3 III, 1, 68. *I would not be a Roman of all nations*, Cor. IV, 5, 185. *of all men else I have avoided thee*, Mcb. V, 8, 4. *of all the days in the year, I came to't that day*, Hml. V, 1, 155.

Used to denote a quality: *his art is of such power*, Tp. I, 2, 372. *be of comfort; my father's of a better nature*, 495. *it must needs be of subtle, tender and delicate temperance*, II, 1, 41. *who are of such sensible and nimble lungs*, 174. *are you of fourscore pound a year?* Meas. II, 1, 204. *I am not of many words*, Ado I, 1, 158. *his hair is of the dissembling colour*, As III, 4, 7. *now I find thy saw of might*, III, 5, 82. *shall my father's will be of no force?* John I, 130. *is not my arm of length?* R2 IV, 11. *are you of good or evil?* Oth. V, 1, 65 etc. After substantives: *the expense of spirit in a waste of shame is lust in action*, Sonn. 129, 1 (waste of shame = shameful waste). *two loves I have of comfort and despair*, 144, 1 (the one giving comfort, the other making me desperate). *god of power*, Tp. I, 2, 10 (= powerful god). *a prince of power*, 55. *the fire and cracks of sulphurous roaring*, 204. *gentlemen of brave mettle*, II, 1, 182. *this lord of weak remembrance*, 232. *men of sin*, III, 3, 53. *a gentleman of blood,*

Gent. III, 1, 121. *pageants of delight*, IV, 4, 164. *in a robe of white*, Wiv. IV, 4, 72. *our dance of custom*, V, 5, 79. *save that we do the denunciation lack of outward order*, Meas. I, 2, 152. *a man of stricture and firm abstinence*, I, 3, 12. *a dish of some three-pence*, II, 1, 95. *a man of fourscore pound*, 127. *a mind of honour*, II, 4, 179. *one all of luxury*, V, 506. *many such-like liberties of sin*, Err. I, 2, 102. *spots of grey*, Ado V, 3, 27. *an eye of favour*, V, 4, 22. *an eye of love*, 24. *yon fiery oes and eyes of light*, Mids. III, 2, 188. *your mind of love*, Merch. II, 8, 42, cf. 6, 43. *terms of zeal*, V, 205. *it was a passion of earnest*, As IV, 3, 172. *Kate of my consolation*, Shr. II, 191. *my similes of comfort*, All's V, 2, 26. *before I have got strength of limit*, Wint. III, 2, 107. *eyes of blood*, John IV, 2, 265. *an eye of death*, H4A I, 3, 143. *a man of falsehood*, II, 1, 71. *looks of favour*, V, 1, 31. *an adopted name of privilege*, V, 2, 18. *their eyes of fire*, II4B IV, 1, 121. *apes of idleness*, IV, 5, 123. *an enemy of craft and vantage*, H5 III, 6, 153. *a lad of life, an imp of fame*, IV, 1, 45. *we have consented to all terms of reason*, V, 2, 357. *planets of mishap*, H6A I, 1, 23. *why a king of years should be to be protected like a child*, H6B II, 3, 28. *this staff of honour*, 43. *a quicksand of deceit*, H6C V, 4, 26. *lump of deformity*, R3 I, 2, 57. *the king's name is a tower of strength*, V, 3, 12. *those suns of glory*, H8 I, 1, 6. *from a mouth of honour*, 137. *consequence of dread*, II, 4, 214. *you take a precipice for no leap of danger*, V, 1, 140. *this oracle of comfort*, V, 5, 67. *the thing of courage*, Troil. I, 3, 51. *to end a tale of length*, 136. *a proof of strength*, V, 2, 113. *the coal of fire*, Cor. I, 1, 177. *the man of my soul's hate*, I, 5, 11. *those maims of shame*, IV, 5, 93. *thou boy of tears*, V, 6, 101. *his fruit of bastardy*, Tit. V, 1, 48. *the parties of suspicion*, Rom. V, 3, 222. *no Rome of safety for Octavius yet*, Caes. III, 1, 289. *a fetch of wit*, Hml. II, 1, 38 (Ff *of warrant*). *we of wisdom and of reach*, 64. *they have dealt with me like thieves of mercy*, IV, 6, 21. *her brow of youth*, Lr. I, 4, 306. *a fixed figure for the time of scorn*, Oth. IV, 2, 54. *the Jove of power make me your reconciler*, Ant. III, 4, 29. *a thing of pity*, Cymb. V, 4, 47. *some marks of secret on her person*, V, 5, 206.

Joined to adjectives, = concerning, with respect to, in: *false of heart*, Sonn. 109, 1. Wint. IV, 3, 116. *slow of sail*, Err. I, 1, 117. *so shrewd of thy tongue*, Ado II, 1, 20. *black of hue*, Mids. III, 1, 128. *pale of cheer*, III, 2, 96. *quick of apprehension*, 178. *too rude and bold of voice*, Merch. II, 2, 190. *an honest woman of her word*, III, 1, 8. *hard of hearing*, Shr. II, 184. *true of heart*, Tw. II, 4, 109. *my nearest of kin*, Wint. III, 2, 54. *a tall fellow of thy hands*, V, 2, 177. *forward of her breeding*, IV, 4, 591. *full warm of blood*, John V, 2, 59 (M. Edd. *full of warm blood*). *so light of foot*, R2 III, 4, 92. *a proper fellow of my hands*, H4B II, 2, 72. *hard of heart*, H5 III, 3, 11. *of parents good, of fist most valiant*, IV, 1, 46. *he is the next of blood*, H6B I, 1, 151. *so weak of courage and in judgment*, H6C IV, 1, 12. *not ignoble of descent*, 70. *too late of our intents*, R3 III, 5, 69 (cf. *Short*). *of his own body he was ill*, H8 IV, 2, 43. *firm of word*, Troil. IV, 5, 97. *thin of substance*, Rom. I, 4, 99. *so senseless of expense*, Tim. II, 2, 1. *unshaked of motion*, Caes. III, 1, 70. *infirm of purpose*, Mcb. II, 2, 52. *sure of foot*, III, 1, 38. *false of heart, light of ear, bloody of hand*, Lr. III, 4, 95. *lame of sense*, Oth. I, 3, 63. *swift*

*of foot*, II, 3, 232. *free of speech*, III, 3, 185. *so loose of soul*, 416. *true of mind*, III, 4, 27. *dull of tongue*, Ant. III, 3, 19. *quenched of hope, not longing*, Cymb. V, 5, 196.

Supplying the place of the genitive case of other languages; in a possessive sense: *the heat of this descending sun*, Ven. 190. *the circuit of this ivory pale*, 230. *the engine of her thoughts*, 367. *the deadly bullet of a gun*, 461. *the sweetness of the spoil*, 553. *in the very lists of love*, 595. *the deep dark cabins of her head*, 1038. *the principal men of the army*, Lucr. Arg. 5. *at the tent of Sextus Tarquinius*, ib. *the virtues of his wife*, 6 etc. etc. Before personal pronouns: *heir to the lands of me*, Shr. V, 1, 89. *these curses turn the force of them upon thyself*, H6B III, 2, 332. *he rubs the vein of him*, Troil. II, 3, 210. Denoting the subject of an action: *barred the aidance of the tongue*, Ven. 330. *the conflict of her hue*, 345. *a war of looks*, 355. *the warm approach of sweet desire*, 386. *workmanship of nature*, 734 etc. etc. Peculiar expression: *the bringing home of bell and burial*, Hml. V, 1, 256. Before personal pronouns: *do not omit the heavy offer of it*, Tp. II, 1, 194. *it was the death of him*, H4A II, 1, 14. *not a man comes for redress of thee*, H6C III, 1, 20 (= that thou mayst redress). *miserable by the death of him*, R3 I, 2, 27. *grapples you to the heart and love of us*, Mcb. III, 1, 106. *to add the death of you*, IV, 3, 207. Joining things pertaining to each other in any manner: *the precedent of pith and livelihood*, Ven. 26. *god of war*, 98. *law of nature*, 171. *the sense of feeling*, 439. *the rights of time*, 759. *the manner of his dealing*, Lucr. Arg. 21. *the family of the Tarquins*, 22. *the king of Naples*, Tp. 1, 2, 112. *she was of Carthage*, II, 1, 82. *men of Ind*, II, 2, 61. *widows of this business' making*, II, 1, 133. *will thou be of our consort?* Gent. IV, 1, 64. *is nor of heaven nor earth*, V, 4, 80. *which of you know Ford of this town?* Wiv. I, 3, 29. *the old fantastical duke of dark corners*, Meas. IV, 3, 164. *two ships, of Corinth that, of Epidaurus this*, Err. I, 1, 94. *you are of Epidamnum*, I, 2, 1. *Kate of Kate-hall*, Shr. II, 189. *it is something of my negligence, nothing of my purpose*, Tw. III, 4, 280. *of whence are you? not of this country*, Meas. III, 2, 230. *Hector of Troy*, H4B II, 4, 237. *is she of the wicked?* 354. *of prisoners Hotspur took Mordake etc.* H4A I, 1, 70. *I had thought I had had men of some understanding and wisdom of my council*, H8 V, 3, 136 (cf. the words *City, Country, River, Town, Name* etc. etc.). Peculiar use: *the stillitory of thy face*, Ven. 443 (the face itself being the stillitory). *the closure of my breast*, 782. *written in the margent of his eyes*, Rom. I, 3, 86 (the eyes themselves being the margin of the face). *the division of the twentieth part*, Merch. IV, 1, 329. *the jewel of life*, John V, 1, 40. *this frail sepulchre of our flesh*, R2 I, 3, 196. *this Hydra son of war*, H4B IV, 2, 38 (i. e. war, this son of Hydra). *a very little thief of occasion*, Cor. II, 1, 32 (occasion itself being the thief).

In a temporal sense, = during, in: *not be seen to wink of all the day*, LLL I, 1, 43. *there sleeps Titania sometime of the night*, Mids. II, 1, 253. *did I never speak of all this time?* Shr. Ind. 2, 84. *did you not of late days hear*, H8 II, 1, 147. *as of late days our neighbours can dearly witness*, V, 3, 29. *my custom always of the afternoon*, Hml. I, 5, 60. Perhaps also *of her widowhood* = during her w. in Shr. II, 124. *Of late, of old* etc. see under *Late, Old* etc.

Confounded with on (cf. On): *pox of your love-letters*, Gent. III, 1, 390. *a plague of all drums*, All's IV, 3, 332. H4A II, 4, 127. *God's blessing of your good heart*, H4B II, 4, 329. *he came of an errand*, Wiv. I, 4, 80. *I go of message from the queen to France*, H6B IV, 1, 113. *what your name is else I know not, nor by what wonder you do hit of mine*, Err. III, 2, 30. *to bestow it all of your worship*, Ado III, 5, 24. All's III, 5, 103. Tw. III, 4, 2. Cor. II, 3, 215. *I hear as good exclamation on your worship as of any man*, Ado III, 5, 29. *ride of a horse*, 40. *we'll have dancing afterward. First, of my word*, V, 4, 123. Tit. IV, 3, 59. *therefore of all hands must we be forsworn*, LLL IV, 3, 219. *a box of the ear*, Merch. I, 2, 86. *turn of no hand*, II, 2, 45. *he had more hair of his tail than I have of my face*, 104. *both of one horse*, Shr. IV, 1, 71. *I'll venture so much of my hawk or hound, but twenty times so much upon my wife*, V, 2, 72. *I'll be revenged of her*, H4B II, 4, 167 (Ff on). *he cried out of sack*, H5 II, 3, 29. Cor. I, 1, 273. *of purpose*, H6A V, 4, 22. *a proper man, of mine honour*, H6B IV, 2, 103. *of the city's cost*, IV, 6, 3; cf. I, 1, 60. *his virtues, not virtuously of his own part beheld*, Troil. II, 3, 127 (Qq on). *they take vengeance of such kind of men*, Tit. V, 2, 63. *take it of my soul*, Tim. III, 4, 70. *how fares our cousin Hamlet? Of the chameleon's dish*, Hml. III, 2, 98. *to keep one's eyes of either side's nose*, Lr. I, 5, 22.

Omitted: *at either end the mast*, Err. I, 1, 86. *she is i the rear our birth*, Wint. IV, 4, 592. *upon this side the sea*, John II, 488. *on this side Tiber*, Caes. III, 2, 254. *of either side's nose*, Lr. I, 5, 22. *on each side her*, Ant. II, 2, 206. *o' the other side your monument*, IV, 15, 8. *it went o' the backside the town*, Cymb. I, 2, 14. *all the rest revolted faction*, R2 II, 2, 57 (only in Q1; the other O. Edd. *rest of the r.*). *on either hand thee there are squadrons pitched*, H6A IV, 2, 23. *south the city mills*, Cor. I, 10, 31. Cymb. II, 4, 81. *no manner person*, R3 III, 5, 108 (Qq *of person*). *what trade art thou?* Caes. I, 1, 5. *any moment leisure*, Hml. I, 3, 133. *many my near occasions*, Tim. III, 6, 11. *many our contriving friends in Rome*, Ant. I, 2, 189. *the Duke Alençon*, LLL II, 61. *the stout Earl Northumberland*, H8 IV, 2, 12. *the country Maine and Anjou*, H6A V, 3, 154. *in the famous ancient city Tours*, H6B I, 1, 5. I, 3, 53. Cor. I, 3, 111. V, 6, 93. *within the parish Saint Lawrence Poultney*, H8 I, 2, 152. *his surname Coriolanus*, Cor. V, 3, 170. *thy stolen name Coriolanus*, V, 6, 89.

Superfluous: *cousin of Hereford*, R2 I, 1, 28. H6B I, 1, 65. 167. 172. H6C IV, 8, 34. R3 III, 4, 37. III, 7, 227. IV, 2, 1. *uncle of Exeter*, H5 II, 2, 29. IV, 7, 191. H6B I, 1, 56. *brother of Gloster*, H6C III, 2, 1. IV, 5, 16. R3 I, 3, 62. *father of Warwick*, H6C V, 1, 81. *my son of York*, R3 II, 4, 6. Lr. I, 1, 42. 43. *aunt of Gloster*, R3 IV, 1, 2. — Used after many transitive verbs, originally perhaps in a partitive sense: see *Accept, Allow, Bear, Dislike, Distinguish, Hope, Like* etc. etc.

**Off** (sometimes confounded with *of* in O. Edd.), adv. 1) not near or by the side of a thing, but at a distance from it: *that our bloods stand off in differences so mighty*, All's II, 3, 127. *far off*, Ven. 697. 973. Tp. I, 2, 44. V, 316. Caes. III, 2, 171. Ant. II, 5, 11. Cymb. III, 3, 60. *far off from*, R2 III, 3, 45. *afar off*, Wiv. I, 1, 216. Ado III, 3, 160. *farther off*, Tp. III, 2, 92. *farther off from thee*, Sonn. 28, 8. *lie further off*, Mids.

II, 2, 44. *the farthest off you could have been to him*, Wint. IV, 4, 723. *three leagues off*, Gent. V, 1, 11. Ado I, 1, 4. Merch. III, 4, 31. H4B IV, 1, 19. H6C II, 1, 144. *six miles off from Ampthill*, H8 IV, 1, 27 etc. etc. Metaphorically: *stand no more off, but give thyself unto my sick desires*, All's IV, 2, 34. *he shall in strangeness stand no further off than in a politic distance*, Oth. III, 3, 12. *if you please to hold him off awhile*, 248. *that's off*, Cor. II, 2, 64 (not to the purpose).

2) to a distance, away from a place: *set her two courses off to sea again*, Tp. I, 1, 53 (away from the shore). *lay her off*, ib. *I'll go farther off*, Tp. III, 2, 81. *I will fetch off my bottle*, IV, 213. *go off; I discard you; go off*, Tw. III, 4, 99. *on mine own accord I'll off*, Wint. II, 3, 63. *he is settled, not to come off, in his displeasure*, H8 III, 2, 23. *alone he entered the mortal gate,... aidless came off*, Cor. II, 2, 116. *let me request you off*, Ant. II, 7, 127. *the soul and body rive not more in parting than greatness going off*, IV, 13, 6 etc.

3) denoting separation in general: *leave off* (discourse of disability), Gent. II, 4, 109 (cf. *Leave*). *inconstancy falls off ere it begins*, V, 4, 113 (cf. *Fall*). *hang off, thou cat*, Mids. III, 2, 260. *off with it while 'tis vendible*, All's I, 1, 168. *spin it* (your hair) *off*, Tw. I, 3, 110. *some must go off*, Mcb. V, 8, 36 (= be deducted). *my crown I should give off*, John V, 1, 27. *shake it off* (your heaviness), Tp. I, 2, 307. *shake off slumber*, II, 1, 304. *I will put off my hope*, III, 3, 7. *sit like a jackanapes, never off*, H5 V, 2, 148 (cf. *Break*). Used of a head cut from the body: Meas. IV, 3, 120. H6B IV, 1, 17. R3 IV, 5, 4. Caes. II, 1, 183. *off with his head*, Meas. IV, 2, 222. All's IV, 3, 342. H6C V, 5, 3. R3 III, 4, 78. V, 3, 344. Applied to articles of dress: Ven. 1089. Meas. V, 360. Mids. IV, 1, 85. Shr. IV, 1, 147. All's III, 2, 60. Wint. IV, 3, 55. 58. R2 I, 4, 31. H5 III, 7, 57. H6B II, 1, 150. Lr. III, 4, 113. Ant. II, 7, 63. IV, 14, 37. Cymb. II, 2, 33 etc. Peculiar passage: *since the wisdom of their choice is rather to have my hat than my heart, I will practise the insinuating nod and be off to them most counterfeitly*, Cor. II, 3, 107 (i. e. take off my hat, stand bareheaded; cf. R2 I, 4, 31. Ant. II, 7, 63). Followed by *of: a fall off of a tree*, H6B II, 1, 96. *Off and on* = to and fro: *I swam, ere I could recover the shore, five and thirty leagues off and on*, Tp. III, 2, 17.

4) modifying verbs by the idea of an easy and happy proceeding (almost = to the best advantage): *to bear off any weather*, Tp. II, 2, 19. *do not smile at me that I boast her off*, IV, 1, 9. *it came hardly off*, Gent. II, 1, 115. *this comes off well*, Meas. II, 1, 57. *it comes so smoothly off*, LLL IV, 1, 145 (cf. *Come*). *a fine volley of words, and quickly shot off*, Gent. II, 4, 34. *and speak off half a dozen dangerous words*, Ado V, 1, 97 (O. Edd. *of*). *she did print your royal father off, conceiving you*, Wint. V, 1, 125. *the truth of it stands off as gross as black and white*, H5 II, 2, 103 (striking the eye). *your skill shall, like a star i' the darkest night, stick fiery off indeed*, Hml. V, 2, 268. *to drink off* = to drink without hesitation: *drinks off candles' ends*, H4B II, 4, 267. *this distilled liquor drink thou off*, Rom. IV, 1, 94. *drink off this potion*, Hml. V, 2, 337.

5) *from off* = from: *from off a hill*, Compl. 1. *ere I take this charm from off her sight*, Mids. II, 1, 183. *take this transformed scalp from off the head*,

IV, 1, 70. *retire from off these fields*, H5 IV, 3, 87. *precipitation from off the rock Tarpeian*, Cor. III, 3, 103. *leap from off the battlements*, Rom. IV, 1, 78. *he was carried from off our coast*, Cymb. III, 1, 26. *put my brogues from off my feet*, IV, 2, 214.

**Off,** prepos. from, away from: *lead off this ground*, Tp. II, 1, 323. *fetch you a hair off the great Cham's beard*, Ado II, 1, 277. *speaks a little off the matter*, III, 5, 10 (O. Edd. *of*). *I could shake them off my coat*, As I, 3, 16. *to pluck him off me*, Shr. IV, 1, 80. *thou hast a son shall take this disgrace off me*, All's II, 3, 250. *this present enterprise set off his head*, H4A V, 1, 88. *to come off the breach*, H4B II, 4, 55. *her pinked porringer fell off her head*, H8 V, 4, 50. *to lay his fingers off it*, Caes. I, 2, 243. *pulling scarfs off Caesar's images*, 289. *brought off the field*, Mcb. V, 8, 44. *keep off them*, Ant. II, 7, 66. *our Britain seems as off it, but not in it*, Cymb. III, 4, 141 (O. Edd. *of*; cf. *Of*). *thou mayst cut a morsel off the spit*, Per. IV, 2, 142.

**Offal,** waste meat, the parts of a butchered animal not fit for use: *a barrow of butcher's o.* Wiv. III, 5, 5. Hence = refuse: *what trash is Rome, what rubbish and what o.* Caes. I, 3, 109. *I should have fatted all the region kites with this slave's o.* Hml. II, 2, 608 (i. e. with this slave, who is no more worth than offal).

**Offcap,** to take off the cap: *three great ones ... —ed to him*, Oth. I, 1, 10 (Qq *oft capt*).

**Offence,** 1) harm, hurt: *worm nor snail, do no o.* Mids. II, 2, 23. *faster than his tongue did make o. his eye did heal it up*, As III, 5, 117. *to do o. and scath in Christendom*, John II, 75. *and then our arms, like to a muzzled bear, ... hath all o. sealed up*, 250. *when I give occasion of o., then let me die*, H6C I, 3, 44. *you have some sick o. within your mind*, Caes. II, 1, 268 (*sick o.* = harmful disorder). *so shall he waste his means, weary his soldiers, doing himself o.* IV, 3, 201. *than it should do o. to Cassio*, Oth. II, 3, 222. *there is more o. in that than in reputation*, 268 (Ff *sense*).

2) any thing that wounds the feelings and causes displeasure, mortification, or even disgust, from the slightest mistake to the most grievous injury: *him that bears the strong —'s cross*, Sonn. 34, 12. *where their love must appear o.* Meas. II, 4, 30. Ado III, 3, 88. IV, 1, 99. All's II, 3, 270. H5 IV, 8, 49. H6A V, 5, 35. Cor. V, 1, 28. Hml. I, 5, 135. III, 2, 243. 245. Ant. IV, 15, 45 (*provoked by my o.*, i. e. the o. committed by me). Cymb. I, 5, 6. Per. II, 5, 52. With *to*: *what my o. to him is*, Tw. III, 4, 279. *no o. to the general*, Oth. II, 3, 109. *to commit o. to*: Cymb. II, 1, 32. *to do o. to*: Tw. III, 4, 249. Lr. I, 4, 231. Oth. IV, 2, 166. *to give o. to*: Lr. II, 2, 121. Cymb. II, 1, 29. *to take o. at*: H6C IV, 1, 13. Per. II, 5, 72. *take no o. that I would not offend you*, Ant. II, 5, 99.

3) displeasure, mortification: *every o. is not a hate at first*, Merch. IV, 1, 68. *a remorseful pardon, slowly carried, to the great sender turns a sour o.* All's V, 3, 59. *I am now so far in o. with my niece*, Tw. IV, 2, 75. *their souls are topful of o.* John III, 4, 180. *your looks are sad; hath the late overthrow wrought this o.?* H6A I, 2, 49. *banish all o.* V, 5, 96. *full of quarrel and o.* Oth. II, 3, 52. *sith love breeds such o.* III, 3, 380. *in his o. should my performance perish*, Ant. III, 1, 26. *to bar your o. herein*, Cymb. I, 4, 122.

4) any transgression, from the slightest fault to the greatest crime: Lucr. 613. 738. 749. 1071. 1483.

1702. Sonn. 51, 1 (*slow o.* = fault of slowness). 89, 2. 110, 4. Compl. 183. Gent. IV, 1, 25. V, 4, 75. Wiv. IV, 4, 12. V, 5, 238. Meas. I, 2, 90. 125. 139. II, 1, 27. 195. II, 2, 88. 102. II, 4, 85. III, 1, 100. IV, 2, 113. V, 540. Err. I, 1, 35. V, 127. Ado IV, 1, 284. V, 1, 216. 235. LLL I, 2, 151. V, 1, 147. As III, 2, 367. All's IV, 3, 271. V, 3, 23. Tw. III, 3, 30. Wint. IV, 4, 822. John I, 257. R2 III, 2, 134. IV, 230. H4A I, 2, 240. II, 3, 41. III, 2, 19. V, 2, 7. 20. H4B IV, 1, 69. 160. IV, 5, 103. H5 II, 2, 181. H6A IV, 1, 75. R3 I, 4, 187. II, 4, 45. H8 II, 1, 84. II, 2, 68. V, 1, 12. V, 3, 125. Troil. III, 1, 80. V, 2, 53. Cor. I, 1, 179. Tit. V, 3, 182. Rom. III, 1, 191. Tim. V, 1, 154. Caes. I, 3, 158. III, 2, 43. IV, 3, 8. Hml. I, 5, 137. III, 1, 127. III, 3, 36. 47. 58. IV, 3, 7. IV, 5, 218. Lr. I, 1, 221. I, 2, 127. II, 2, 95. II, 4, 199. IV, 2, 47. Oth. II, 3, 211. III, 4, 115. Cymb. I, 1, 106. III, 6, 64. V, 5, 334. Per. I, 2, 28. 92. II, 3, 68. II, 4, 5. II, 5, 52. With *to*: *his last —s to us*, Cor. V, 6, 127. *to do an o.*: Meas. II, 3, 14. Ado V, 1, 217. All's V, 3, 14. Tw. III, 4, 344. Wint. I, 2, 83. H6B III, 1, 59. R3 III, 7, 111. *to make an o.*: Meas. III, 2, 15. IV, 2, 200. H5 IV, 8, 59. Lr. II, 4, 61. Peculiar use: *may one be pardoned and retain the o.?* Hml. III, 3, 56 (i. e. the fruits of his crime).

**Offenceful,** criminal: *your most o. act was mutually committed*, Meas. II, 3, 26.

**Offenceless,** inoffensive, harmless: *beat his o. dog to affright a lion*, Oth. II, 3, 275.

**Offend,** 1) trans. a) to harm, to hurt, to injure: *dispersed those vapours that —ed us*, Err. I, 1, 90. *thou —est thy lungs to speak so loud*, Merch. IV, 1, 140. *the dust that did o. it* (my eye) All's V, 3, 55. *he shall not o. your majesty*, John III, 3, 65. *Hubert will not o. thee*, IV, 1, 132. *these rebels o. none but the virtuous*, H4A III, 3, 214. *she is pistol-proof; you shall hardly o. her*, H4B II, 4, 126. *this last surrender of his will but o. us*, Lr. I, 1, 310. Absol.: *a stone is silent and —eth not*, Tit. III, 1, 46.

b) to annoy, to pain, to molest: *if the true concord ... do o. thine ear*, Sonn. 8, 6. *the rankest compound of villanous smell that ever —ed nostril*, Wiv. III, 5, 94. *if bawdy talk o. you*, Meas. IV, 3, 188. *your silence most —s me*, Ado II, 1, 345. *himself being — ed*, Merch. IV, 1, 58. *the loathsomeness of them —s me*, Wint. IV, 3, 59. *we'll not o. one stomach*, H5 II Chor. 40. *they o. our sight*, IV, 7, 62. *buzz to o. thine ears*, H6C II, 6, 95. *such things as might o. the weakest spleen*, Troil. II, 2, 128. *what —s you, lady?* III, 2, 151. *no more of this; it does o. my heart*, Cor. II, 1, 185. *we but o. him*, Tim. IV, 3, 175. *it —s me to the soul to hear*, Hml. III, 2, 9. *a salt and sorry rheum —s me*, Oth. III, 4, 51. *I will not stay to o. you*, IV, 1, 258. *no more o. our hearing*, Cymb. V, 4, 94.

c) to sin against, to trespass on, to wrong: *he would give't thee, from this rank offence, so to o. him still*, Meas. III, 1, 101. *he hath —ed the law*, III, 2, 16. *who have you —ed, that you are thus bound*, Ado V, 1, 232. *never did I o. your highness*, As I, 3, 54. *if you o. him, I for him defy you*, Tw. III, 4, 345. *—ing charity*, John III, 4, 173. *to see a son of mine o. you*, H4B V, 2, 106. *to cut off those that have —ed him*, R3 I, 4, 225. *in what have I —ed you?* H8 II, 4, 19. *how loath you are to o. daylight*, Troil. III, 2, 51. *o. the stream of regular justice*, Tim. V, 4, 60. *wherein you may have —ed him*, Lr. I, 2, 175. *I never did o. you*, Oth. V, 2, 59. *I have —ed reputation*, Ant. III, 11, 49.

d) to displease, to mortify, to affront; absol.: *I shall o. in dedicating my lines to your lordship,* Ven. Dedic. 1. *to o., himself being —ed,* Merch. IV, 1, 58. *it is not that —s,* H6A III, 1, 35. *if this servile usage once o.* V, 3, 58. *O, pardon, I o.* Troil. IV, 5, 182. *this tongue had not —cd so,* Caes. V, 1, 46. *I cannot name it but I shall o.* Per. IV, 6, 75. With an obj.: Ado III, 3, 87. III, 4, 34. V, 1, 40. Mids. III, 2, 160. As I, 1, 84. Shr. Ind. 1, 98. Tw. V, 220. Wint. IV. 4, 711. H5 IV, 8, 51. H6A II, 3, 76. R3 I, 4, 182. 183. IV, 4, 178. Troil. V, 3, 4. Tit. II, 1, 100. II, 3, 161. Caes. III, 2, 32. 34. 36. 39. Mcb. III, 4, 57. Hml. I, 5, 134. III, 4, 9. 10. Lr. V, 3, 127. Oth. II, 3, 63. Ant. II, 5, 99. III, 1, 26. —*ed* = displeased, angry: *are you —ed too?* H6C IV, 1, 19. *it is —ed,* Hml. I, 1, 50. *devils, being —ed,* Oth. II, 1, 112. *if I should say myself —ed,* Ant. II, 2, 32. *the —ed king,* Cymb. I, 1, 75. *be not —ed,* LLL II, 204. All's I, 3, 202. Tw. IV, 1, 54. H6A V, 3, 54. Mcb. IV, 3, 37. Followed by *with*: *I am —ed with you,* Troil. V, 3, 77. *with no man here he is —ed,* R3 III, 4, 58. *I cannot be —ed with my trade,* Per. IV, 6, 76. By *in* (= by): *make me not —ed in your distrust,* Ant. III, 2, 33.

2) intr. to commit a fault or a crime, to sin, to trespass: Ven. 810. Meas. I, 2, 140. II, 1, 29. 251. II, 2, 4. V, 110. Ado III, 3, 43. LLL IV, 3, 126. 132. Mids. V, 108. 430. Merch. II, 9, 61. Shr. V, 1, 116. All's III, 4, 5. Wint. I, 2, 57. H4A I, 2, 240. H4B I, 1, 97. H5 I, 1, 29. IV, 3, 29. H6B II, 4, 59. IV, 7, 103. H6C V, 5, 54. Tim. V, 4, 35. 42. Lr. I, 2, 42. II, 4, 198. IV, 6, 172. Oth. I, 3, 80. IV, 1, 209. Cymb. I, 4, 50. Per. IV, 1, 80. IV, 2, 40.

**Offender,** 1) one that has wronged another: *the —'s sorrow lends but weak relief to him that bears the strong offence's cross,* Sonn. 34, 11.

2) one that has committed a sin or crime, a guilty person, a criminal: Lucr. 612. Sonn. 42, 5. Wiv. II, 2, 196. Meas. IV, 2, 116. Ado IV, 2, 7. V, 1, 314. Merch. IV, 1, 355. As IV, 1, 204. All's V, 3, 26. Wint. V, 1, 59. R2 I, 2, 8. H4A V, 5, 15. H4B IV, 1, 216. H5 III, 6, 113. H6A III, 1, 130. H6B I, 3, 136. II, 1, 203. III, 1, 122. 126. 176. R3 III, 4, 67. H8 V, 3, 121. Tit. V, 2, 40. Hml. IV, 3, 6. Lr. II, 1, 91. Cymb. V, 5, 300. With *to*: *as an o. to your father,* H4B V, 2, 81.

**Offendress,** the fem. of offender: *a desperate o. against nature,* All's I, 1, 153.

**Offensive,** 1) causing offence, stirring to anger, quarrelsome: *an o. wife that hath enraged him on to offer strokes,* H4B IV, 1, 210.

2) displeasing, disagreeable: *what most he should dislike seems pleasant to him; what like, o.* Lr. IV, 2, 11.

**Offer,** subst. a tender or proposal to be accepted or rejected: Pilgr. 54. Merch. IV, 1, 438. As Epil. 23. Shr. II, 388. Wint. II, 2, 48. H4A IV, 3, 30. V, 2, 2. V, 5, 4. H4B IV, 1, 147. 150. H5 I, 1, 82. III Chor. 32. Rom. II, 4, 190. Mcb. IV, 3, 43. Hml. I, 2, 46. Ant. II, 6, 40. III, 12, 29. *to accept an o.* R2 II, 3, 162. *to embrace an o.* Ado V, 1, 303. Tw. V, 328. John IV, 3, 13. V, 7, 84. Per. III, 3, 38. *to forsake an o.* (= to refuse): H6A IV, 2, 14. *to make an o.* LLL V, 2, 810. Merch. IV, 1, 81. 289. H5 I, 1, 75. Ant. II, 6, 34. *to omit an o.* (= to refuse): Tp. II, 1, 194. H8 III, 2, 4. *to pass an o.* (in the same sense): John II, 258. *to refuse an o.* R2 IV, 16. III, 2, 31. *to shake off an o.* (in the same sense): Ant. III, 7, 33. *to*

*take an o.* (= to accept): Gent. IV, 1, 70. Merch. IV, 1, 318. As III, 5, 61. IV, 3, 60. All's III, 5, 104. H4A V, 1, 106. Lr. III, 4, 161. Ant. II, 6, 31. 42.

**Offer,** vb. 1) to present for acceptance or rejection; absol.: *we o. fair,* H4A V, 1, 114. Governing an accus.: Tp. III, 1, 77. Gent. IV, 1, 69. Err. II, 2, 188. III, 2, 186. Merch. I, 3, 143. IV, 1, 293. Shr. II, 382. 383. R2 II, 1, 204. IV, 178. R3 II, 1, 77. H8 III, 1, 66. 113. Troil. I, 2, 309. Cor. V, 3, 13. Tim. V, 1, 48. 127. Hml. V, 2, 262. Lr. I, 1, 197. IV, 6, 270. Ant. II, 7, 89. Cymb. I, 3, 4.*With a dat. and accus.: Gent. IV, 4, 58. 61. Err. IV, 3, 6. Ado II, 1, 224. II, 2, 41. Merch. IV, 1, 227. Shr. Ind. 1, 78. I, 2, 132. All's IV, 3, 92. Wint. IV, 3, 87. John V, 1, 34. R2 II, 3, 32. H4B IV, 1, 75. H5 III Chor. 29. III, 5, 60. IV, 4, 21. H6A III, 1, 126. H6B IV, 8, 12. Tim. V, 1, 75. Caes. I, 2, 220. 221. 237. 241. 268. Hml. II, 2, 331. Lr. III, 1, 41.

2) to sacrifice: Lucr. 194. Wint. III, 1, 8. H4A IV, 1, 115. H6B II, 1, 92. H6C II, 2, 32. Troil. IV, 3, 9. Per. V, 3, 70. With *up*: H5 IV, 5, 18. H6A I, 1, 46. Rom. III, 2, 104. Mcb. IV, 3, 16. Metaphorically, = to bring in like a sacrifice, to dedicate: *she hath —ed to the doom a sea of melting pearl,* Gent. III, 1, 222. *thou —est fairly to thy brother's wedding: to one his lands etc.* As V, 4, 173. cf. Wint. IV, 4, 389.

3) to intend, to be ready, to attempt, (sometimes almost = to dare); with an inf.: *so —s he to give what she did crave,* Ven. 88. *if by strong hand you o. to break in,* Err. III, 1, 98. *man is but a patched fool, if he will o. to say what methought I had,* Mids. IV, 1, 216. *if he should o. to choose,* Merch. I, 2, 99. *my conscience is but a kind of hard conscience to o. to counsel me to stay with the Jew,* II, 2, 30. *o. to swear upon a book,* 167. *to o. to get your living by the copulation of cattle,* As III, 2, 84. *what are you that o. to beat my servants?* Shr. V, 1, 65. *if he do not o. to betray you,* All's III, 6, 31. *a ram-tender, to o. to have his daughter come into grace,* Wint. IV, 4, 805. *I had as lief they would put ratsbane in my mouth as o. to stop it with security,* H4B I, 2, 48. *Agamemnon is a fool to o. to command Achilles,* Troil. II, 3, 67. *I —ed to awaken his regard for his private friends,* Cor. V, 1, 23. *all that o. to defend him,* Lr. III, 6, 101. *he —ed to cut a caper at the proclamation, but he made a groan at it,* Per. IV, 2, 116.

With an accus., = to attempt, to prepare, to menace, to bring upon, to inflict: *when every grief is entertained that's —ed,* Tp. II, 1, 16. *I do not think the knight would o. it,* Wiv. II, 1, 180. *wit ... —ed by a child to an old man,* LLL V, 1, 65. *that women are so simple to o. war where they should kneel for peace,* Shr. V, 2, 162. *you o. him a wrong something unfilial,* Wint. IV, 4, 416. *that greatness should so grossly o. it* (foul play) John IV, 2, 94. *a mighty and a fearful head as ever —ed foul play in a state,* H4A III, 2, 169. *hath enraged him on to o. strokes,* H4B IV, 1, 211. *o. nothing here!* H5 II, 1, 41. *'tis as arrant a piece of knavery as can be —ed,* IV, 7, 4. *those bitter injuries which Somerset hath —ed to my house,* H6A II, 5, 125. *o. him no violence,* H6C I, 1, 33. *more miseries than my enemies dare o.* H8 III, 2, 390. *that time —ed sorrow; this, general joy,* IV, 1, 6. *it* (double dealing) *were an ill thing to be —ed to any gentlewoman,* Rom. II, 4, 180. *to o. it the show of violence,* Hml. I, 1, 144. *we scorn her most, when most she —s blows,* Ant. III, 11, 74.

Absol., = to menace, to act offensively: *we of the —ing side must keep aloof from strict arbitrement,* H4A IV, 1, 69. *his power, like to a fangless lion, may o., but not hold,* H4B IV, 1, 219.

**Offering,** oblation, sacrifice: Tw. V, 117. H4A I, 2, 141. Troil. V, 3, 17. Caes. II, 2, 39. Mcb. II, 1, 52.

**Office,** subst. 1) particular duty: *not only in the simple o. of love,* Wiv. IV, 2, 5. *you have forgot a husband's o.* Err. III, 2, 2. *I will attend my husband, for it is my o.* V, 99. *the ministration and required o. on my particular,* All's II, 1, 5, 65. *know the o. that belongs to such,* H6A III, 1, 55.

2) a charge conferred by public or private authority; a place: Lucr. 628. Tp. I, 2, 84. Wiv. V, 5, 44. Meas. I, 3, 40. II, 1, 276. IV, 2, 10. 119. V, 466. Err. III, 1, 44. Ado III, 3, 54. 59. Merch. II, 9, 41. 61. Shr. Ind. 2, 36. R2 II, 3, 27. H4A V, 1, 34. H4B IV, 5, 130. V, 3, 120. 128. H6A I, 1, 175. H6B I, 3, 138. R3 III, 7, 119. H8 I, 2, 16. 172. II, 4, 115. III, 2, 156. IV, 1, 15. V, 3, 33. Troil. I, 3, 88. 231. V, 6, 4. Cor. II, 1, 238. II, 3, 129. III, 3, 64. Tim. I, 2, 207. Caes. IV, 3, 11. Mcb. I, 7, 18. Lr. IV, 6, 163. Oth. I, 3, 118. II, 3, 218. III, 3, 375. IV, 2, 91. 132. Ant. II, 3, 1. IV, 6, 27. Per. II, 1, 97.

3) the duty and function imposed by virtue of a place conferred: *do thy o., Muse,* Sonn. 101, 13. Meas. II, 2, 13. IV, 2, 129. Tw. III, 4, 359. H4B II, 1, 43. H5 III, 6, 148. *speak your o.* Tw. I, 5, 223. *so much my o.* H5 III, 6, 145. *it is my o.* H6B II, 4, 102. 103. *take thy o. from thee,* R3 IV, 1, 26. *your o., sergeant; execute it,* H8 I, 1, 198. *what are your —s,* Cor. III, 1, 35. *bears that o.* Tim. I, 2, 125.

4) any particular function, agency, or employment: *they* (the eyes) *resign their o. and their light,* Ven. 1039. *time's o. is to fine the hate of foes,* Lucr. 936. *who so base would such an o. have as slanderous death's-man to so base a slave?* 1000. *these —s shall profit thee and much enrich thy book,* Sonn. 77, 13. Pilgr. 196. Tp. I, 1, 40. I, 2, 312. V, 156. Gent. I, 2, 44. III, 2, 40. 44. Meas. V, 369. 383. Ado II, 1, 183. 390. III, 1, 12. IV, 1, 268. V, 1, 27. V, 4, 14. LLL IV, 3, 332. V, 2, 350. Mids. II, 2, 8. Merch. II, 6, 43. II, 9, 61. As I, 2, 43. Shr. Ind. I, 73. IV, 1, 34. 37. V, 2, 36. All's IV, 3, 68. V, 2, 52. V, 3, 305. Wint. II, 2, 31. IV, 4, 582. V, 1, 77. John IV, 1, 119. V, 2, 177. V, 7, 71. R2 I, 3, 256. II, 1, 47. IV, 5, 177. H4A V, 1, 112. H4B Ind. 28. I, 1, 101. H5 II, 1, 88. H6B III, 2, 93. H6C I, 4, 109. V, 6, 19. R3 III, 5, 10. H8 II, 4, 190. Rom. IV, 5, 85. V, 1, 23. Tim. IV, 3, 237. Caes. V, 5, 29. Mcb. III, 3, 3. IV, 1, 68. Lr. III, 1, 42. V, 3, 248 *(who hath the o. = who is on duty).* Oth. I, 3, 394. III, 3, 410. Ant. I, 1, 5. II, 2, 216. III, 12, 10. Cymb. I, 6, 92. III, 5, 10. V, 5, 257.

5) an act of good will, a kind service: *I would I could do a good o. between you,* Wiv. I, 1, 102. III, 1, 49. *I will no more enforce mine o. on you,* All's II, 1, 129. *these thy —s, so rarely kind,* Wint. V, 1, 149. Merch. IV, 1, 33. All's IV, 4, 5. Tw. III, 4, 278. Wint. II, 3, 189. IV, 3, 81. R2 II, 2, 137. H4B IV, 4, 24. H5 II, 2, 33. V, 2, 29. Mcb. II, 3, 142. Lr. II, 1, 108. II, 4, 107. 181. Oth. III, 4, 113 (Q1 *duty*). Per. II, 5, 48.

6) an act of worship: *for holy —s I have a time,* H8 III, 2, 144. *bows you to a morning's holy o.* Cymb. III, 3, 4.

7) persons entrusted with public functions, officers: *the o. did distinctly his full function,* H8 I, 1, 44. *the insolence of o.* Hml. III, 1, 73.

8) a room or apartment intended for particular duties attached to the service of a house: *unpeopled —s,* R2 I, 2, 69. *draw anew the model in fewer —s,* H4B I, 3, 47. *through the cranks and —s of man,* Cor. I, 1, 141. *when all our —s have been oppressed with riotus feeders,* Tim. II, 2, 167. *sent forth great largess to your —s,* Mcb. II, 1, 14. *all —s are open,* Oth. II, 2, 9.

**Office,** vb. to perform a particular duty or function, to serve in a place: *although the air of paradise did fan the house and angels —d all,* All's III, 2, 129. With an accus. denoting the effect: *cannot o. me from my son Coriolanus,* Cor. V, 2, 68.*

**Office-badge,** sign or emblem of office: H6B I, 2, 25.

**Officed,** having a place or function: *so stands this squire o. with me,* Wint. I, 2, 172. *my speculative and o. instruments,* Oth. I, 3, 271 (Qq *active*).

**Officer,** 1) one who performs an office or service for another: *'tis an office of great worth, and you* (Lucetta) *an o. fit for the place,* Gent. I, 2, 45. *that's my office. Spoke like an o.* Shr. V, 2, 37 (like one who does her business). *a filthy o. he is in those suggestions for the young earl,* All's III, 5, 18. *your master, in his own change, or by ill —s, hath given me some worthy cause to wish things done undone,* Caes. IV, 2, 7. *soaks up the king's countenance, his rewards, his authorities; but such —s do the king best service in the end,* Hml. IV, 2, 18. *Caesar and Antonio have ever won more in their o. than person,* Ant. III, 1, 17. *the gods can have no mortal o. more like a god than you,* Per. V, 3, 62.

2) retainer, servant: *every o. his wedding garment on,* Shr. IV, 1, 50. *calling my —s about me,* Tw. II, 5, 53. *his spongy —s,* Mcb. I, 7, 71.

3) a public functionary: Tp. I, 2, 84. Meas. II, 2, 112. IV, 2, 93. LLL II, 162. As III, 1, 16. R2 I, 1, 204. I, 3, 44. H4B IV, 5, 118. H5 I, 2, 190. H6A I, 3, 72. I, 4, 44. H6C III, 1, 98. Cor. I, 5, 28. III, 1, 93. 330. III, 3, 45. 78. V, 2, 3. Hml. IV, 5, 102. Oth. I, 1, 183. Ant. III, 5, 19. Cymb. III, 1, 65 (cf. *Domestic*). Especially applied to constables or catchpolls: Wiv. III, 3, 114. Meas. I, 3, 198. II, 1, 58. 186. 194. III, 2, 32. V, 120. Err. IV, 1, 6. 61. 69. 76. IV, 3, 29. IV, 4, 117. V, 230. 233. Ado III, 5, 22. IV, 2, 73. 83. V, 1, 217. LLL I, 1, 271. Merch. III, 1, 131. Shr. V, 1, 94. 98. Tw. III, 4, 352. H4A II, 2, 114. H4B II, 1, 56. 117. 139. H6C I, 4, 43. V, 6, 12. Or to other servants of public justice: R3 V, 1, 28 (Ff *come lead me, —s, to the block of shame;* Qq *come, sirs, convey me to* etc.). Lr. V, 3, 1. Cymb. V, 4, 180 (= hangman).

4) one who has a military command under another: All's IV, 3, 226. 301. H5 IV, 1, 37. H6A III, 2, 127. Cor. IV, 6, 30. 126. Oth. I, 1, 17. I, 3, 281. II, 3, 198. 249. 280. IV, 1, 214. Ant. I, 2, 183.

**Official,** pertaining to an office or place: *in the o. marks invested,* Cor. II, 3, 148.

**Officious,** ready to do service, busy: *be every one o. to make this banquet,* Tit. V, 2, 202. In a bad sense, = obtruding one's service, meddling: Mids. III, 2, 330. Wint. II, 3, 159. IV, 4, 871. H8 III, 2, 237. Cor. I, 8, 14.

**Offspring,** issue of the body, child or children, descendants: Lucr. 1757. Merch. II, 5, 44. John II,

13. H6C IV, 4, 18. R3 V, 3, 136. Troil. II, 2, 207. Tit. IV, 2, 79.

**Oft,** frequently: Ven. 567. 1068. Lucr. 38. 70. 131. Sonn. 77, 13. 78, 1. 128, 1. 142, 7. Compl. 15. Pilgr. 339. Gent. II, 4, 103. II, 6, 15. V, 4, 103. Meas. I, 4, 78. II, 1, 280. 297. II, 4, 117. III, 1, 18. IV, 1, 14. IV, 2, 159. Err. I, 2, 19. V, 56. LLL V, 2, 556. Mids. III, 2, 389. Merch. I, 1, 144. III, 3, 22. As III, 4, 50. III, 5, 106. IV, 3, 135. V, 4, 87. All's I, 1, 115. II, 1, 140. Tw. III, 4, 3 *(more o.).* John IV, 2, 204. H6A I, 4, 3. H6B II, 4, 89. III, 2, 161. IV, 1, 134. IV, 4, 1. V, 2, 54. H6C I, 4, 11. 128. V, 2, 20. R3 III, 1, 55. Troil. III, 2, 78. III, 3, 20. Rom. V, 3, 88. Ant. III, 6, 18. Cymb. I, 5, 14 etc. etc. *many a time and o.* Merch. I, 3, 107; cf. *Many.*

As an adjective: *by o. predict that I in heaven find,* Sonn. 14, 8.

**Often,** frequently: Ven. 825. Lucr. 565. 1237. Sonn. 18, 6. 105, 13. Compl. 19. 20. Pilgr. 91. Tp. I, 2, 33. II, 1, 227. V, 193. Gent. I, 1, 74. II, 1, 171. III, 1, 90. 350. IV, 1, 35. IV, 2, 74. Wiv. IV, 2, 108. Meas. II, 4, 8. 13. Err. I, 1, 41. V, 66. LLL V, 2, 752. Mids. I, 1, 214. II, 1, 125. V, 161. 190. 192. Merch. II, 7, 66. As III, 2, 63. V, 4, 42. Wint. V, 1, 200. H6A II, 2, 56. V, 3, 193. H6B I, 1, 80. III, 1, 268. 367. III, 2, 114. IV, 1, 56. H6C I, 1, 127. III, 3, 131. Troil. III, 3, 20 etc. etc. *many a time and o.* Tim. III, 1, 25; cf. *Many.* Compar. *oftener:* Meas. IV, 2, 54. Mids. III, 2, 93. H6B II, 1, 90. Mcb. IV, 3, 110.

As an adjective: *in which my o. rumination wraps me in a most humorous sadness,* As IV, 1, 19.

**Oftentimes,** frequently: Ven. 845. Gent. III, 1, 26. Err. III, 1, 113. Shr. III, 2, 76. John IV, 2, 30. H4A III, 1, 27. 183. Mcb. I, 3, 123.

**Oft-subdued,** conquered many times: H6A I, 5, 32.

**Ofttimes,** often: Cymb. I, 6, 62.

**Oh,** exclamation expressive of pain or sorrow: Tp. II, 2, 58. 66. Wiv. V, 5, 93. R3 I, 3, 11 (Ff *ah*). II, 2, 27 and 34 (Ff *ah*). Troil. III, 1, 131 (O. Edd. *oh ho,* M. Edd. *oh oh*), Mcb. V, 1, 58. Hml. IV, 5, 33 (Qq *o ho,* Ff. om., M. Edd. *oh oh*) etc. Confounded with *O:* Gent. II, 3, 25. Err. III, 2, 137 etc. Imitative of the voice of beasts: Mids. V, 269. Cymb. II, 5, 17. *Oho,* see sub *Ho.*

**Oil,** unctuous substance used for various purposes, chiefly for nourishing the flame in lamps: Ven. 756. Tp. II, 1, 153. Wiv. II, 1, 65 (= train-oil). V, 5, 39. Err. IV, 1, 89. All's I, 2, 59. V, 3, 7. Wint. III, 2, 178 *(boiling in leads or —s;* Walker *in lead or o.).* H4A I, 3, 7. H6A II, 5, 8. H6B V, 2, 55. H8 IV, 1, 88 *(holy oil).* Troil. I, 1, 61. Tim. I, 2, 140. Lr. II, 2, 83.

**Oil-dried,** having consumed its oil: *my o. lamp,* R2 I, 3, 221.

**Oily,** 1) consisting of oil: *stain your own* (lip) *with o. painting,* Wint. V, 3, 83 (= oil-colour). 2) fat: *this o. rascal,* H4A II, 4, 575. 3) moist: *if an o. palm be not a fruitful prognostication,* Ant. I, 2, 53. 4) smooth: *I want that glib and o. art,* Lr. I, 1, 227.

**Old,** subst. wold, upland downs: *Saint With- old footed thrice the o.* Lr. III, 4, 125 (apparently from an old song).

**Old,** adj. (compar. *older:* Sonn. 110, 11. Rom. II, 4, 127. Caes. IV, 3, 31. Mcb. IV, 3, 191. In R3 III, 2, 62 Ff *—er,* Qq *elder.* Superl. *oldest:* H4B IV, 5, 127. Cor. IV, 6, 68. Lr. V, 3, 325. cf. *Elder* and

*Eldest).* 1) advanced in years, aged: Ven. 837. 1152. Compl. 128. Sonn. 68, 12. 97, 4. Tp. II, 1, 30. III, 3, 2. 4. IV, 159. V, 15. Gent. II, 4, 69. Wiv. II, 1, 118. II, 2, 134. 144. Meas. I, 1, 46. III, 1, 36. Err. I, 1, 97. IV, 2, 19. V, 317. Tw. I, 3, 126. R2 V, 2, 13. Troil. II, 2, 104 (Q *elders).* Cor. III, 1, 228 etc. etc. *this fair child of mine shall sum my count and make my o. ex- cuse,* Sonn. 2, 11 (= the excuse of my oldness). *I'll rack thee with o. cramps,* Tp. I, 2, 369 (such as old people are wont to suffer; cf. *Aged).* *he'll shape his o. course in a country new,* Lr. I, 1, 190 (the course of his old age).

2) of any specified age: *how o. are you?* As V, 1, 20. Lr. I, 4, 39. *three years o.* Tp. I, 2, 41. Wiv. I, 1, 55. Meas. III, 2, 214. LLL IV, 2, 36. As IV, 1, 95. V, 2, 66. Shr. V, 1, 86 etc. *at nine months o.* H6B IV, 9, 4. H6C III, 1, 76. R3 II, 3, 17. *at two hours o.* II, 4, 28. *at twelve year o.* Rom. I, 3, 2. Cymb. I, 1, 58. III, 3, 101. Peculiar phrases: *one that is a prisoner nine years o.* Meas. IV, 2, 135 (= a prisoner since nine years). *my absence was not six months o.* Err. I, 1, 45. *in Ephesus I am but two hours o.* II, 2, 150. *ere we were two days o. at sea,* Hml. IV, 6, 15. *changing still one vice, but of a minute o., for one not half so o. as that,* Cymb. II, 5, 31.

3) being of long continuance: *o. woes, not infant sorrows, bear them mild,* Lucr. 1096. *to try an —er friend,* Sonn. 110, 11. *the o. saying,* Gent. V, 2, 11. LLL IV, 1, 121 (cf. *o. ends* sub *End). the o. Windsor way,* Wiv. III, 1, 6. *'tis o. but true,* IV, 2, 109. *an o. tale,* IV, 4, 28. Ado I, 1, 218. *this news is o. enough,* Meas. III, 2, 243. 296. IV, 3, 4. V, 2. Ado III, 2, 41. IV, 1, 208. V, 2, 78. LLL III, 21. IV, 3, 78. Mids. I, 1, 4. Shr. III, 1, 80. 81. III, 2, 30. 42. Tw. II, 4, 3. John III, 4, 145. H4A V, 4, 102. R3 IV, 1, 73. Caes. IV, 3, 31. Oth. I, 1, 37. Cymb. III, 5, 54 etc. Hence = accustomed, practised, customary: *your o. vice still,* Gent. III, 1, 283. *an o. lovemonger,* LLL II, 254. *o. mocker,* V, 2, 552. *my o. ward,* H4A II, 4, 215. *is he so young a man and so o. a lifter?* Troil. I, 2, 128. *the seas and winds, o. wranglers,* II, 2, 75. *doth she not think me an o. murderer?* Rom. III, 3, 94. *o. Cassius still,* Caes. V, 1, 63. *the o. course of death,* Lr. III, 7, 101. = worn and decayed by time: *the text is o.* Ven. 806. *an o. coat,* Wiv. I, 1, 18. I, 3, 18. *o. ginger,* Meas. IV, 3, 6. *her o. gloves,* As IV, 3, 26. *the rest were ragged, o. and beggarly,* Shr. IV, 1, 140. *your fooling grows o.* Tw. I, 5, 119 etc. *Of o.* = since long: *I know you of o.* Ado I, 1, 146. H6A I, 2, 39.

4) having existed in former ages, ancient: *o. Adam,* Err. IV, 3, 13. R2 III, 4, 73. *of an o. father's mind,* LLL IV, 2, 33. *good o. Mantuan,* 97. *an o. Roman coin,* V, 2, 617. *o. Ninny's tomb,* Mids. V, 268. *like the o. Robin Hood,* As I, 1, 122. *the o. age,* Tw. II, 4, 49. *o. Troy,* R2 V, 1, 11. *since the o. days of goodman Adam,* H4A II, 4, 105. *wolves, thy o. inhabi- tants,* H4B IV, 5, 138. *the o. Assyrian slings,* H5 IV, 7, 65. *the nine sibyls of o. Rome,* H6A I, 2, 56. *o. Brutus' statue,* Caes. I, 3, 146. *this borrowed passion stands for true o. woe,* Per. IV, 4, 24. *Of o.* = ancient, an- ciently: *sad stories chanced in the times of o.* Tit. III, 2, 83. *the hearts of o. gave hands,* Oth. III, 4, 46.

5) former: *is in his o. lines again,* Wiv. IV, 2, 22. *his o. betrothed,* Meas. III, 2, 293. *the o. ornament of his cheek,* Ado III, 2, 46. *I have a trick of the o. rage,* LLL V, 2, 417. *thy o. master,* Merch. II, 2, 162. II, 4,

17. *the o. duke*, As I, 1, 104. *o. care done*, R2 IV, 196. *o. desire doth in his death-bed lie*, Rom. II Chor. 1. *thy o. groans ring yet in my ancient ears*, II, 3, 74. Of *o.* = former, formerly: *nor with such free and friendly conference as he hath used of o.* Caes. IV, 2, 18. *for that our love of o.* V, 5, 27. *for those of o. and the late dignities*, Mcb. I, 6, 18.

6) Used as a familiar term expressive of some cordiality: *go thy ways, o. lad*, Shr. V, 2, 181. Tw. III, 2, 9. H4A I, 2, 47. Tit. IV, 2, 121. *go thy ways, o. Jack*, H4A II, 4, 141. *God-a-mercy, o. heart*, H5 IV, 1, 34. *well said, o. mole*, Hml. I, 5, 162. *art thou mad, o. fellow?* Lr. II, 2, 91. cf. *the rotten carcass of o. Death*, John II, 456. *o. Time the clock-setter*, III, 1, 324. *o. father antic the law*, H4A I, 2, 69. *o. grub*, Rom. I, 4, 68. *from o. Verona.* Shr. I, 2, 49. *to o'ertop o. Pelion*, Hml. V, 1, 276. *where's my serpent of o. Nile?* Ant. I, 5, 25.

7) copius, plentiful, overmuch; in familiar language: *here will be an o. abusing of God's patience*, Wiv. I, 4, 5. *yonder's o. coil at home*, Ado V, 2, 98. *we shall have o. swearing*, Merch. IV, 2, 15. *news, o. news*, Shr. III, 2, 30. *here will be o. Utis*, H4B II, 4, 21. *he should have o. turning the key*, Mcb. II, 3, 2.

Used as an adverb: *a song that o. was sung*, Per. Prol. 1 (Gower's speech).

**Old-accustomed** (not hyphened in O. Edd.), customary from old times: Rom. I, 2, 20.

**Oldcastle,** the name originally given by the poet to Falstaff, but afterwards changed, as it was also that of the well-known martyred adherent of Wicleff: H4B V, 5, 148. cf. H4A I, 2, 47 and the Famous Victories of Henry V.

**Olden,** old: *i' the o. time*, Mcb. III, 4, 75.

**Old-faced,** looking old and venerable: *your o. walls*, John II, 259.

**Oldness,** old age: Lr. I, 2, 50.

**Olive,** the tree Olea: As III, 5, 75. Emblem of peace: Sonn. 107, 8. Tw. I, 5, 226. H4B IV, 4, 87. H6C IV, 6, 34. Tim. V, 4, 82. Ant. IV, 6, 7.

**Oliver,** 1) a famous knight of Charlemagne's Round Table: H6A I, 2, 30. 2) the elder brother of Orlando in As, never named in the dialogue. 3) Sir O. Martext: As III, 3, 43. 64. 100. V, 1, 5.

**Olive-tree,** the tree Olea: As IV, 3, 78.

**Olivia,** female name in Tw. I, 1, 19 etc.

**Olympian,** pertaining to Olympia in ancient Greece: *at the O. games*, H6C II, 3, 53. *an O. wrestling*, Troil. IV, 5, 194.

**Olympus,** the mountain which was the residence of the ancient gods: Troil. II, 3, 11. Proverbially high: Cor. V, 3, 30. Tit. II, 1, 1. Caes. III, 1, 74. IV, 3, 92. Hml. V, 1, 277.

**Olympus-high,** high as Olympus: Oth. II, 1, 190.

**'Oman,** Evans' pronunciation of *woman:* Wiv. I, 1, 234 and passim.

**Omen,** a fatal event portended by signs: *the like precursor of fierce events, as harbingers preceding still the fates and prologue to the o. coming on*, Hml. I, 1, 123 (not in Ff).

**Ominous,** 1) foreboding evil, portentous: *very o. endings*, Ado V, 2, 39. *he was furnished like a hunter. O, o.! he comes to kill my heart*, As III, 2, 260. *thou o. and fearful owl of death*, H6A IV, 2, 15. *Gloster's dukedom is too o.* H6C II, 6, 107. *my dreams will prove o. to the day*, Troil. V, 3, 6.

2) fatal, pernicious: *bloody prison, fatal and o. to noble peers*, R3 III, 3, 10. *thy mother's name is o. to children*, IV, 1, 41. *to tell thee that this day is o.* Troil. V, 3, 66. *the quarrel's most o. to us*, V, 7, 21. *when he lay couched in the o. horse*, Hml. II, 2, 476.

**Omission,** neglect: *o. to do what is necessary*, Troil. III, 3, 230.

**Omit,** 1) to pass by, to leave, to let go: *what if we do o. this reprobate, till he were well inclined*, Meas. IV, 3, 77 (= let him live, do not execute him). *do o. their mortal natures, letting go safely by the divine Desdemona*, Oth. II, 1, 71 (= lay aside, forget for a time).

2) to leave out, not to speak of: *and o. all the occurrences*, H5 Prol. 39. *his apparent open guilt —ed, he lived from all attainder of suspect*, R3 III, 5, 30. *o. we all their dole and woe*, Per. III Prol. 42. *no needful thing —ed*, V, 3, 68.

3) not to profit by, to neglect: *a star, whose influence if now I court not but o.* Tp. I, 2, 183. *do not o. the heavy offer of it*, II, 1, 194. *—ing the sweet benefit of time*, Gent. II, 4, 65. *no time shall be —ed*, LLL IV, 3, 381. *o. nothing may give us aid*, Wint. IV, 4, 637. *o. no happy hour that may give furtherance to our expedition*, H5 I, 2, 300. *if you o. the offer of this time*, H8 III, 2, 3. *I will o. no opportunity*, Rom. III, 5, 49. *still —est it* (the time) Tim. I, 1, 268. *there is a tide in the affairs of men, which .... —ed, all the voyage is bound in shallows*, Caes. IV, 3, 220. *the due of honour in no point o.* Cymb. III, 5, 11. *nothing we'll o. that bears recovery's name*, Per. V, 1, 53.

4) not to care for, to neglect, to leave unregarded: *therefore o. him not*, H4B IV, 4, 27. *wherefore grieve I at an hour's poor loss, —ing Suffolk's exile*, H6B III, 2, 382. *it must o. real necessities and give way the while to unstable slightness*, Cor. III, 1, 146.

**Omittance,** forbearance, neglect, omission: *o. is no quittance*, As III, 5, 133.*

**Omnipotent,** 1) almighty: Wiv. V, 5, 8. R2 III, 3, 85.

2) absolute, arrant: *this is the most o. villain that ever cried 'Stand' to a true man*, H4A I, 2, 121.

**On,** prepos. denoting the being in, or coming into, contact with the surface of a thing: *why not lips on lips?* Ven. 120. *dance on the sands*, 148. *on mountain or in dale*, 232. *graze on my lips*, 233. *a proud rider on so proud a back*, 300. *fairest mover on this mortal round*, 368. *on the grass she lies*, 473. *strikes her on the cheeks*, 475. *trodden on by many*, Ven. 707. *on just proof surmise accumulate*, Sonn. 117, 10. *to ride on the curled clouds*, Tp. I, 2, 192. *now on the beak*, 196. 199. *on their garments not a blemish*, 218. *sitting on a bank*, 389. *our search on land*, III, 3, 10. IV, 73. Gent. I, 1, 158. IV, 4, 35. Err. II, 2, 166. Mids. III, 2, 205. LLL V, 2, 9. Mcb. II, 1, 46. Oth. II, 3, 216 etc. *his falchion on a flint he smiteth*, Lucr. 176. *set a mark so bloody on the business*, Tp. I, 2, 142. *wicked dew drop on you both*, 323. *all the charms of Sycorax light on you*, 340. *to fall it* (your hand) *on Gonzalo*, II, 1, 296. *all the infections ... on Prosper fall*, II, 2. *to belch you on this island*, III, 3, 56. *mount on my swiftest horse*, H6A IV, 5, 9. *thou camest on earth to make the earth my hell*, R3 IV, 4, 166 etc. This primary sense traceable in the phrases *to play on an instrument* (f. i. *on a lute;* and hence also *on pipes of corn*, Mids. II, 1, 67), *on fire* (Ven. 388. H4A IV, 1,

117), *on high* (Ven. 854), *kiss on kiss, passion on passion,* and the like (Ven. 832. Shr. II, 310. H4A IV, 3, 101. H6B III, 1, 337); no less in curses or blessings called down over a person: *mercy on us!* Tp. I, 1, 64 (cf. *justice on the doers!* All's V, 3, 154). *heavens rain grace on that which breeds between 'em,* III, 1, 76. *a murrain on your monster,* III, 2, 88. *Juno sings her blessings on you,* IV, 109. *Ceres' blessing so is on you,* 117. *out on thy mistress,* Err. II, 1, 68. *so will you wish on me,* Lr. II, 4, 171. etc.

Denoting not only a contact with the upper surface, but with any part of sth.: *on his neck her arms she throws,* Ven. 592. *set this bateless edge on his keen appetite,* Lucr. 9. *as a nose on a man's face,* Gent. II, 1, 142. *a codpiece to stick pins on,* II, 7, 56. *lest he catch cold on's feet,* Err. III, 1, 37. *on either hand,* H6A IV, 2, 23 (cf. *Hand*). *with a palsy fumbling on his gorget,* Troil. I, 3, 174. *this found I on my tent,* R3 V, 3, 303 (attached to it) etc. Hence used of articles of dress covering the body or part of it, (f. i. *put my tires and mantles on him,* Ant. II, 5, 22), and metaphorically: *what do I see on thee!* Mids. III, 1, 118. *the king hath on him such a countenance,* Wint. I, 2, 368. *I have tremor cordis on me,* 110. *you that have so fair parts of woman on you,* H8 II, 3, 27. *signs of nobleness shall shine on all deservers,* Mcb. I, 4, 42. *some marks of secret on her person,* Cymb. V, 5, 206. cf. the verbs *Bestow, Confer, Estate, Cast, Throw away* etc.

Placed before that by which a thing is supported: *the bridle on a ragged bough she fastens,* Ven. 37. *leaning on their elbows,* 44. *stand on end,* 272 (*on foot,* see sub *Foot*). *hang not on my garments,* Tp. I, 2, 474. *tripping on his toe,* IV, 46. *hang them on this line,* 193. *the blossom that hangs on the bough,* V, 94. *any model to build mischief on,* Ado I, 3, 49. *down on your knees,* As III, 5, 57. *grovel on thy face,* H6B I, 2, 9. *hang him on this tree,* Tit. V, 1, 47. *on their knees and hands,* Tim. I, 1, 87 etc. Metaphorically: *as one relying on your lordship's will and not depending on his friendly wish,* Gent. I, 3, 61. *in these times you stand on distance,* Wiv. II, 1, 233. *I charge thee on thy duty,* Ado I, 1, 210. *I stay here on my bond,* Merch. IV, 1, 242. *and took it on his death that this my mother's son was none of his,* John I, 110. *it lies you on to speak,* Cor. III, 2, 52 (cf. the respective verbs). In asseverations and obsecrations: *on mine honour,* Tp. III, 2, 123. Meas. II, 4, 147. Ado V, 1, 104. *on your souls,* Ado IV, 1, 14. 148. John V, 1, 43. *on his blessing,* As I, 1, 4. *on my life,* I, 2, 294. *on height of our displeasure,* Tim. III, 5, 87. *on thine allegiance,* Lr. I, 1, 170. *on thy love,* Oth. II, 3, 178. Similarly in betting: *five shillings to one on't,* Ado III, 3, 84. *my soul and body on the action,* H6B V, 2, 26. *mine honour on my promise,* Tim. I, 1, 148. *I had put my estate on the approbation,* Cymb. I, 4, 134. Before *condition: let me know my fault: on what condition stands it?* R2 II, 3, 107; by which passage perhaps the following may be explained: *intended or committed was thy fault? if on the first,* V, 3, 34 (= if it stands on the first condition).

Hence denoting the ground or occasion of any thing done: *what following sorrow may on this arise,* Lucr. 186. *to be revenged on her death,* 1778. *on better judgment making,* Sonn. 87, 12. *to leave her on such slight conditions,* Gent. V, 4, 138. *he arrests him on it,* Meas. I, 4, 66. *shall you on your knowledge find this way?* IV, 1, 37. *he is your husband on a pre-contract,* 72. *was he arrested on a band?* Err. IV, 2, 49. *on this travail look for greater birth,* Ado IV, 1, 215. *on pain of losing her tongue,* LLL I, 1, 123. *she must lie here on mere necessity,* 149. *I shall do it on a full stomach,* I, 2, 154. *and not demands, on payment of a hundred thousand crowns, to have his title live in Aquitaine,* II, 145. *that on so little acquaintance you should like her,* As V, 2, 1. *not fearing the displeasure of your master, which on your just proceeding I'll keep off,* All's V, 3, 236. *on a moderate pace I have since arrived but hither,* Tw. II, 2, 3. *on her frights and griefs she is before her time delivered,* Wint. II, 2, 23. *on the sight of us ... the French vouchsafe a parle,* John II, 222. *killed on your suggestion,* IV, 2, 166. *on constraint,* V, 1, 28. *on ancient malice,* R2 I, 1, 9. *on some apparent danger seen in him,* 13. *find pardon on my true submission,* H4A III, 2, 28. *a thing to thank God on,* III, 3, 134. *little faults, proceeding on distemper,* H5 II, 2, 54. *my duty to you both, on equal love,* V, 2, 23. *on pure heart's love,* R3 IV, 1, 4. *my conscience received a scruple and prick on certain speeches,* H8 II, 4, 171. *and on a safer judgment all revoke your ignorant election,* Cor. II, 3, 226. *on safeguard he came to me,* III, 1, 9. *shall on a dissension of a doit break out to bitterest enmity,* IV, 4, 17. *hanged himself on the expectation of plenty,* Mcb. II, 3, 5. *lest more mischance, on plots and errors, happen,* Hml. II, 2, 406. *I'd shake it (your beard) on this quarrel,* Lr. III, 7, 77. *did on my free will,* Ant. III, 6, 57. *would obey it on all cause,* III, 11, 68. *he alone dealt on lieutenantry,* 39. *think what a chance thou changest on,* Cymb. I, 5, 68. *letting them thrive again on their abatement,* V, 4, 21. cf. the articles *Compulsion, Condition, Instinct, Necessity* (Lr. I, 2, 132), *Purpose* etc.

Hence the temporal use: *on the first view to swear, I love thee,* Mids. III, 1, 144. *the year growing ancient, not yet on summer's death, nor on the birth of trembling winter,* Wint. IV, 4, 80. *on thinking on no thought I think,* R2 II, 2, 31. *on the winking of authority to understand a law,* John IV, 2, 211. *we will answer on their charge,* Caes. V, 1, 24. *on a day,* Pilgr. 227. *one meal on every day,* LLL I, 1, 40. *on Saturday,* IV, 1, 6. Ado V, 1, 169. Mids. I, 2, 7. Merch. I, 3, 127. II, 5, 25. Wint. III, 3, 143. *how's the day? On the sixth hour,* Tp. V, 4. *ne'er may I look on day, nor sleep on night,* Err. V, 210. *on to-morrow,* H5 III, 6, 181. *on the moment,* Tim. I, 1, 79. *on the present,* 141. *on the instant,* Oth. I, 2, 38. *on a trice,* Tp. V, 238. *on the sudden,* Ven. 749. H8 IV, 2, 96 etc.

Used to indicate the direction given to an action (cf. *Frown, Gaze, Look, Smile* etc.): *blushing on her,* Lucr. 1339. *the eastern gate opening on Neptune with fair blessed beams,* Mids. III, 2, 392. *gives all gaze and bent of amorous view on the fair Cressid,* Troil. IV, 5, 283. *if Caesar nod on him,* Caes. I, 2, 118. *these are portents, but yet I hope, they do not point on me,* Oth. V, 2, 46. *my writ is on the life of Lear,* Lr. V, 3, 246; cf. *the star-gazers, having writ on death,* Ven. 509 etc. Often in a hostile sense: *on the lion he will venture,* Ven. 628. *rush on his host,* H5 III, 5, 50. *turn on the bloody hounds,* H6A IV, 2, 51. *flew on him,* Lr. IV, 2, 76. *I did draw on him,* Err. V, 43. Mids. III, 2, 411. Lr. II, 2, 131. *they are almost on him,* Caes. V, 3, 30. *do execution on the watch,* H6A III, 2, 35. *shuts the gate on us,* Err. V, 156. Tit. V, 3, 105. *exclaims on death,* Ven. 930. *I railed on thee,* 1002.

(cf. *Grow*). And generally denoting that with respect to which, or by means of which, something is done: *tires with her beak on feathers*, Ven. 56. *be wreaked on him*, 1004. *revenge it on him*, Tp. III, 2, 62. *the foul boar's conquest on her fair delight*, Ven. 1030. *on this sad shadow Lucrece spends her eyes*, Lucr. 1457. *that they may work all exercise on thee*, Tp. I, 2, 328. *hath made his meal on thee*, II, 1, 113; *we'll browze on that*, Cymb. III, 6, 38; *half dined on the gentleman*, Wint. III, 3, 108; *have we eaten on the insane root?* Mcb. I, 3, 84; *thou existest on many a thousand grains*, Meas. III, 1, 20; *to feed on such sweet honey*, Gent. I, 2, 106; II, 1, 179; *live on thy confusion*, Err. II, 2, 182; LLL V, 1, 41; *to prey on nothing*, As IV, 3, 119; *sip on a cup with the proudest*, Wiv. II, 2, 77; Hml. IV, 7, 161. *that you might kill your stomach on your meat*, Gent. I, 2, 68. *I'll have mine action of battery on thee*, Meas. II, 1, 188. *who can do good on him?* IV, 2, 71; Rom. IV, 2, 13. *I'll prove it on his body*, Ado V, 1, 74; *to prove on Mowbray that he is a traitor*, R2 I, 3, 38; *on him, on you, I will maintain my honour*, Lr. V, 3, 100. *I'll die on him that says so*, Gent. II, 4, 114. *this civil war of wits were much better used on Navarre*, LLL II, 227. *to perish on my sword*, Mids. II, 2, 107 (1,244); *to die on Brutus' sword*, Caes. V, 1, 58; *stain all your edges on me*, Cor. V, 6, 113; Mcb. V, 8, 2. *if hĕ do not mightily grace himself on thee*, As I, 1, 156. *have I commandment on the pulse of life?* John IV, 2, 92; *the power that I have on you is to spare you*, Cymb. V, 5, 418. *the scourge of greatness to be used on it*, H4A I, 3, 11. *I will redeem all this on Percy's head*, III, 2, 132. *blood will I draw on thee*, H6A I, 5, 6; *some blood drawn on me*, Lr. II, 1, 35. *on us thou canst not enter but by death*, H6A IV, 2, 18. *never attempt any thing on him*, H8 III, 2, 18. *the spoil got on the Antiates*, Cor. III, 3, 4. *given hostile strokes on the ministers of state*, 98. *let them satisfy their lust on thee*, Tit. II, 3, 180. *a deed of death done on the innocent*, III, 2, 56. *I begot him on the empress*, V, 1, 87. *do on them some violent death*, V, 2, 108. *on them shalt thou ease thy angry heart*, 119. *see justice done on Aaron*, V, 3, 201. *did violence on herself*, Rom. V, 3, 264. *hath done this deed on Caesar*, Caes. III, 1, 172. *by the verities on thee made good*, Mcb. III, 1, 8. *so will you wish on me*, Lr. II, 4, 172. Hml. IV, 7, 82. *what art thou that hast this fortune on me?* V, 3, 165. *hath seen a grievous wreck and sufferance on most part of their fleet*, Oth. II, 1, 24. *begot upon itself, born on itself*, III, 4, 162. *what his rage can do on me*, Cymb. I, 1, 88. *I will try the forces of thy compounds on such creatures*, I, 5, 19. *show thy spite on mortal flies*, V, 4, 31 (cf. *Attend, Call, Dote, Seize, Wait* etc. etc.).

Denoting the design or business in which a person is employed: *the message I am sent on*, Gent IV, 4, 117. *on what submissive message art thou sent?* H6A IV, 7, 53. *the daughter of the King of France, on serious business, craving quick dispatch, importunes personal conference*, LLL II, 31. *I shall raise you on business*, Caes. IV, 3, 248. *on a forgotten matter we can hardly make distinction of our hands*, Tw. II, 3, 174. *I'll hence to London on a serious matter*, H6C V, 5, 47. Lr. IV, 5, 8. *hither sent on the debating of a marriage*, H8 II, 4, 173. *my mind's not on't*, V, 1, 57. *when my fancy's on my play*, 60. *on whose employment I was sent to you*, Lr. II, 2, 136. *went to Jewry on affairs of Antony*, Ant. IV, 6, 12. Peculiar use: *on a love-book

*pray for my success*, Gent. I, 1, 19 (as love-books will be your reading instead of prayer-books). *read on this book*, Hml. III, 1, 44. *created both one flower, both on one sampler*, Mids. III, 2, 205. *here comes the townsmen on procession*, H6B II, 1, 68 (= engaged in making a procession). *to set on* = to cause to begin: *a bell, once set on ringing, with his own weight goes*, Lucr. 1494 (= set a ringing). *set the table on a roar*, Hml. V, 1, 211.

After expressions of thought and speech, = of, about: *haply I think on thee*, Sonn. 29, 10. 149, 3. Gent. I, 1, 12. H6B III, 1, 338. R3 IV, 2, 125. *dream on evil*, Lucr. 87. Gent. II, 4, 172. Ado IV, 1, 214. *complain on theft*, Ven. 160. 544. *censure thus on lovely gentlemen*, Gent. I, 2, 19. *say what the play treats on*, Mids. I, 2, 9. *as near as I could sift him on that argument*, R2 I, 1, 12. *your exposition on the holy text*, H4B IV, 2, 7. *I wonder on't*, Tim. III, 4, 10. *I am resolved on two points*, Tw. I, 5, 24 etc.

Confounded with *of*: *to take advantage on presented joy*, Ven. 405. *such stuff as dreams are made on*, Tp. IV, 157. *many thousand on's*, Wint. I, 2, 206. *to break the pate on thee*, H4A II, 1, 33 (Ff *of*). *the master-cord on's heart*, H8 III, 2, 106. *unless Apollo get his sinews to make catlings on*, Troil. III, 3, 306. *will he swagger himself out on's own eyes*, V, 2, 136. *one on's father's moods*, Cor. I, 3, 72. *at very root on's heart*, II, 1, 202. *one on's ears*, II, 2, 85. *worth six on him*, IV, 5, 174 (cf. H4B II, 4, 237). *he is so made on here*, 203. *be not jealous on me*, Caes. I, 2, 71. *i' the very throat on me*, Mcb. II, 3, 43. *all those his lands which he stood seized on*, Hml. I, 1, 88 (Qq *of*). *God ha' mercy on his soul, and of all Christian souls*, IV, 5, 199. *two on's daughters*, Lr. I, 4, 114. *stands i' the middle on's face*, I, 5, 20. *here's three on's are sophisticated*, III, 4, 110. *the rest on's body*, 118. *born on itself*, Oth. III, 4, 162. *that we have made so much on*, Cymb. V, 2, 198. *two on's*, V, 5, 311 (cf. *Fond, Amorous, Enamoured*). Very often *on't* for *of it*: Tp. I, 2, 87. 363. 456. II, 1, 127. 145. 156. IV, 248. V, 162. Wiv. III, 4, 24. V, 5, 191. Meas. II, 2, 132. Ado III, 4, 23. LLL V, 2, 460. All's I, 3, 142. Tw. V, 202. Wint. II, 1, 169. II, 2, 31. II, 3, 15. III, 1, 14. IV, 4, 5. H4B IV, 3, 53 (Ff *of it*). H8 II, 3, 102. V, 3, 109. Cor. I, 1, 229. III, 1, 152. Tim. I, 2, 33. III, 2, 19. Caes. I, 3, 137. Hml. V, 1, 133. Lr. IV, 1, 52. Cymb. IV, 2, 297. V, 2, 3 etc. etc.

**On**, adv. 1) denoting contact with the body, in speaking of clothes and the like: *put his bonnet on*, Ven. 1087. *my gloves are on*, Gent. II, 1, 1. As IV, 3, 26. *the Athenian garments he hath on*, Mids. II, 1, 264. III, 2, 349. H4A IV, 2, 44. Hml. I, 1, 60. Ant. IV, 4, 22. *goes off and on at pleasure*, All's IV, 3, 279. *get on your nightgown*, Mcb. II, 2, 70. *what makes that frontlet on?* Lr. I, 4, 208. *left this head on*, Cymb. IV, 2, 323; *while my fearful head is on*, R3 IV, 2, 126. *every officer his wedding-garment on*, Shr. IV, 1, 51. *on with your vizards*, H4A II, 2, 55. *with his beaver on*, IV, 1, 104. *with thy best apparel on*, Caes. I, 1, 8. *with your comb on*, Cymb. II, 1, 26. *with his best ruff on*, Per. IV, 2, 111. Metaphorically: *she puts on outward strangeness*, Ven. 310. *thy native semblance on*, Caes. II, 1, 83. *we put on a compelled valour*, Hml. IV, 6, 17. *when the rash mood is on*, Lr. II, 4, 172.

Denoting progression, = forward: *the path is smooth that leadeth on to danger*, Ven. 788. *marching *on with trembling paces*, Lucr. 1391. *sometimes they do extend their view right on*, Compl. 26. *it goes on, as my soul prompts it*, Tp. I, 2, 419. *say on*, II, 1, 228. *to hasten on this expedition*, Gent. I, 3, 77. *my duty pricks me on*, III, 1, 8. *on went he for a search*, Wiv. III, 5, 107. *money is a good soldier and will on*, II, 2, 176. *dares me on*, Mids. III, 2, 413. *travel you far on, or are you at the farthest?* Shr. IV, 2, 73. *in coming on he has the cramp*, All's IV, 3, 324. *come on, brave soldiers*, H6C IV, 7, 87. *when fitness calls them on*, Troil. I, 3, 202. *pride must tarre the mastiffs on*, 392. *shall we on and not depend on you*, Caes. III, 1, 217. *whose voice will draw on more*, Hml. V, 2, 403. *prologue to the omen coming on*, I, 1, 123. Without a verb, imperatively or exhortingly: *on, officer!* Err. IV, 1, 108. *on, gentlemen*, Merch. II, 6, 58. III, 3, 35. Tw. III, 4, 274. John III, 2, 9. III, 3, 73. H4A II, 2, 95. H5 III, 1, 17. III, 2, 1. H6A V, 2, 21. R3 V, 2, 14. Troil. IV, 1, 49. Rom. I, 4, 113. Oth. I, 1, 184. I, 3, 190. Ant. III, 1, 37. Cymb. V, 5, 134 etc. *off and on* = to and fro: *I swam thirty leagues off and on*, Tp. III, 2, 17. Sometimes joined to the imperatives of *to come* and *to go*, by way of making the demand more urgent: *come on, obey*, Tp. I, 2, 483. *come on then, down and swear*, II, 2, 157. *come on, Trinculo, let us sing*, III, 2, 129. *come on, Panthino*, Gent. I, 3, 76. *go on before*, II, 4, 186. *go on, out at the postern*, V, 1, 8 etc.

Denoting continuation, = without ceasing: *hate on*, Sonn. 149, 13. *he weeps on*, Gent. II, 3, 29. *read on*, III, 1, 329. *Benedick, love on*, Ado III, 1, 111. *if you go on thus*, V, 1, 1. *wonder on*, Mids. V, 129. *if the midnight bell did sound on into the drowsy race of night*, John III, 3, 39 (i. e. if it were striking twelve, and the strokes were continuing, as if they would never cease. Some M. Edd. *one*). cf. *still to strike on*, H6A I, 2, 42. *scoff on*, III, 2, 45. *speak on*, III, 3, 43. *read on*, H6B I, 1, 56. *gaze on*, I, 2, 9. *jest on*, H6C III, 2, 116. *say on*, R3 IV, 2, 11. *let him on*, H8 I, 2, 176. *hear me on*, Tim. I, 1, 77. Without a verb: *well, on*, Wiv. II, 2, 48. Wint. I, 2, 411. Hml. V, 2, 167. Ant. I, 2, 100. II, 2, 86 etc.

**Once**, subst. see *Ounce*.

**Once**, 1) one time, a single time: *three times with sighs she gives her sorrow fire, ere o. she can discharge one word of woe*, Lucr. 1604. *I must o. in a month recount*, Tp. I, 2, 262. *o. a day*, 490. Wiv. III, 5, 103. Err. III, 2, 177. LLL V, 2, 227. Ado II, 3, 47. Merch. IV, 1, 215. Tim. V, 1, 220. Hml. II, 2, 456. Cymb. II, 4, 143 etc. *o. again*,Tp. III, 2, 44. Gent. V, 4, 78. Err. V, 130 (cf. *Again*). *once more*, Gent. I, 1, 53 etc. (cf. *More*). *this o.* = this single time, on this occasion: *help me this o.* H6A V, 3, 12. *for this o.*, in the same sense: *put your grace in your pocket for this o.* Tw. V, 36. *for this o. I will be squared by this*, Wint. III, 3, 40. H6C IV, 1, 50. Rom. IV, 2, 43. *for o. in the same sense: I'll be so bold to break the seal for o.* Gent. III, 1, 139. H6C V, 4, 20. R3 III, 1, 57. *for o. for all*, R2 II, 2, 148. *at o.* = a) at the same time, together: *they all at o. began to cry*, Lucr. 1709. *their gazes lend to every place at o.* Compl. 27. *that the money and the matter may be both at o. delivered*, Gent. I, 1, 138. Ado III, 2, 35. Mids. III, 2, 118. All's III, 2, 123. V, 3, 34. Wint. I, 2, 303. R2 II, 2, 99. H6A I, 2, 109. H6B II, 3, 41. Tim. III, 4, 7; cf. H6C III, 3, 221. Mcb. I, 3, 44. *and all at o.* =

and all the rest, and every thing else (cf. *All*): *that you insult, exult, and all at o., over the wretched*, As III, 5, 36. *never Hydra-headed wilfulness so soon did lose his seat and all at o. as in this king*, H5 I, 1, 36. b) not gradually, not one thing after another, not in a lingering or hesitating manner, but on a sudden, in a breath, directly, promptly: *lingering perdition, worse than any death can be at o.* Tp. III, 3, 78. *let them from forth a sawpit rush at o.* Wiv. IV, 4, 53. *which they will at o. display to the night*, V, 3, 17. *better it were a brother died at o. than that a sister should die for ever*, Meas. II, 4, 106. *you speak all your part at o., cues and all*, Mids. III, 1, 102. *come at o.* Merch. II, 6, 46. *either too much at o., or none at all*, As III, 2, 212. *at o. uncase thee*, Shr. I, 1, 211. *fare ye well at o.* Tw. II, 1, 40. *farewell at o.* R2 II, 2, 148. *die at o.* R3 I, 2, 152. *break at o.* Rom. III, 2, 57. *do it at o.* Ant. IV, 14, 82. 88. Hence = without circumlocution, in a word, to the point: *say at o. if I maintained the truth*, H6A II, 4, 5. *my lords, at o., the care you have of us is worthy praise, but....*, H6B III, 1, 66. *my lords, at o., the cause why we are met is....*, R3 III, 4, 1 (Ff *now, noble peers*). *Once*, alone, = at once: *to be o. in doubt is o. to be resolved*, Oth. III, 3, 180.

2) Used (like the German *einmal*) to signify that the matter spoken of is a point of fact, for which there is no remedy, or which must be profited by as it is: *when the heart's attorney o. is mute, the client breaks*, Ven. 335. *the lesson is but plain, and o. made perfect, never lost again*, 408. *like soldiers, when their captain o. doth yield, they basely fly*, 893. *the heart, which o. corrupted takes the worser part*, Lucr. 294. *nor think the bitterness of absence sour when you have bid your servant o. adieu*, Sonn. 57, 8. *death o. dead, there's no more dying*, 146, 14. *being o. perfected how to grant suits*, Tp. I, 2, 79. *an you be a cursing hypocrite o., you must be looked to*, Ado V, 1, 212. *having o. this juice, I'll watch Titania*, Mids. II, 1, 176. *and will not .... o. remove the root of his opinion*, Wint. II, 3, 88 (German: *will einmal nicht*). *if this servile usage o. offend, go and be free again*, H6A V, 3, 58. *can you behold my sighs and tears and will not o. relent?* III, 1, 108 (cf. Wint. II, 3, 88). *what we oft do best, by sick interpreters. o. weak ones, is not ours, or not allowed*, H8 I, 2, 82 (German: *schwachköpfig wie sie einmal sind*). *an you begin to rail on society o., I am sworn not to give regard to you*, Tim. I, 2, 251. *have I o. lived to see two honest men?* V, 1, 59 (= have I lived indeed, and must I believe it?). *to be o. in doubt*, Oth. III, 3, 179. *if idle talk will o. be necessary, I'll not sleep neither*, Ant. V, 2, 50. *fight I will no more, but yield me to the veriest hind that shall o. touch my shoulder*, Cymb. V, 3, 78. Peculiar passages: *o. this, your long experience of her wisdom, her sober virtue, years and modesty, plead on her part some cause to you unknown*, Err. III, 1, 89 (= so much is certain). *'tis o., thou lovest*, Ado I, 1, 320 (it is a fact past help; German: *du liebst nun einmal*). *o. if he do require our voices, we ought not to deny him*, Cor. II, 3, 1 (German: *wenn er einmal* etc.).

3) Used in imperative sentences as an emphatical expletive: *I pray thee, o. to-night give my sweet Nan this ring*, Wiv. III, 4, 103. *let us o. lose our oaths to find ourselves*, LLL IV, 3, 361. *O, o. tell true, tell true, even for my sake*, Mids. III, 2, 68. Stephano says *speak o. in thy life*, Tp. III, 2, 24.

4) at a certain time, on a certain occasion, one day: *the little Love-god lying o. asleep,* Sonn. 154, 1. *o. did I see a fair sweet youth here,* Pilgr. 125. *where o. thou calledst me up,* Tp. I, 2, 227. II, 2, 29. Ado II, 1, 289. Mids. I, 1, 166. II, 1, 149. IV, 1, 117. John I, 74. H6C I, 1, 221. Cor. II, 3, 16 etc.

5) in past or future times, formerly, in future: *I no more can see what o. I was,* Lucr. 1764. *nativity, o. in the main of light,* Sonn. 60, 5. 120, 8. Tp. I, 2, 47. Meas. II, 2, 73. V, 208. Err. II, 2, 115. V, 342. Merch. IV, 1, 277. *what darest thou not when o. thou art a king?* Lucr. 606. *yet o. ere night I will embrace him with a soldier's arm,* H4A V, 2, 73. *I hope to see London o. ere I die,* H4B V, 3, 64. Caes. IV, 3, 191 etc.

6) at any time, ever: *no cloudy show of stormy blustering weather doth yet in his fair welkin o. appear,* Lucr. 116. *better o. than never,* Shr. V, 1, 155. *why have those banished and forbidden legs dared o. to touch a dust of England's ground?* R2 II, 3, 91. *we may not think the justness of each act such and no other than event doth form it, nor o. deject the courage of our minds, because Cassandra's mad,* Troil. II, 2, 121. *that so degenerate a strain as this should o. set footing in your generous bosoms,* 155. *where nothing, but who knows nothing, is o. seen to smile,* Mcb. IV, 3, 167. *would heart of man o. think it?* Hml. I, 5, 121. *more laughed at that I should o. name you derogately,* Ant. II, 2, 34. *nor o. be chastised with the sober eye of dull Octavia,* V, 2, 54.

**One** (probably sometimes pronounced *on:* Gent. II, 1, 1 and LLL IV, 2, 86; rhyming to *bone, alone, Scone, thrown:* Ven. 293. Sonn. 39, 6. Mcb. V, 8, 74. Cymb. V, 4, 61. cf. Walker's Critical Examination II, 90), 1) the first whole number consisting of a single unit: *one: tell,* Tp. II, 1, 15. *five for one,* III, 3, 48. *twenty to one,* Gent. I, 1, 72. *'twixt twelve and o.* Wiv. IV, 6, 19. V, 5, 78. Err. I, 2, 46. Ado IV, 1, 85. Tw. I, 3, 113. Hml. V, 2, 74 etc.

As an adjective: *ten kisses short as one, one long as twenty,* Ven. 22. *one sweet kiss,* 84. *not one wrinkle,* 139. 207. 209. 210. 371. 416. 746. 885. 1069. 1187 etc. *a thousand more mischances than this one,* Gent. V, 3, 3. *this one night,* Tp. V, 302. *if I could shake off but one seven years,* Cor. IV, 1, 55. *making the green one red,* Mcb. II, 2, 63; cf. *seemed all one mutual cry,* Mids. IV, 1, 122; *let one spirit of the first-born Cain reign,* H4B I, 2, 157; *make of your prayers one sweet sacrifice,* H8 II, 1, 77; *all with one consent,* Troil. III, 3, 176; *there is but one mind in all these men,* Caes. II, 3, 6. Cor. III, 1, 288. IV, 6, 137. Hml. I, 2, 4.

2) a single person or thing: *not one of them that yet looks on me,* Tp. V, 82. *I will make shift for one,* H6B IV, 8, 33. *by ones, by twos and by threes,* Cor. II, 3, 47. *there's never a one of you but trusts a knave,* Tim. V, 1, 96 (cf. *A*). *there's not one of them but in his house I keep a servant fee'd,* Mcb. III, 4, 131. *the censure of the which one,* Hml. III, 2, 30 etc. *why write I still all one, ever the same,* Sonn. 76, 5. *gleaning all the land's wealth into one,* H8 III, 2, 284. *as I have made ye one, lords, one remain,* V, 3, 181 (i. e. in concord, unanimous). *to be much at o.* H5 V, 2, 204 (= of the same value). *all one* = the same: *stand-under and understand is all one,* Gent. II, 5, 34. *that's all one,* Gent. III, 1, 263. Wiv. I, 1, 30. LLL V, 2, 530. Mids. I, 2, 51. As III, 5, 133. Shr. III, 2, 83. Tw. V, 201. H4A IV, 2, 52. *all is one,* Ado V,

1, 49. Oth. IV, 3, 23. *it's all one,* Tw. I, 5, 137. *all is one with her,* Wiv. II, 2, 79. *all's one to him,* All's IV, 3, 158. Wint. V, 2, 131. H6B I, 3, 105. *all's one for that* (= no matter for that, never mind): H4A II, 4, 172. R3 V, 3, 8. *'twere all o. that I should love a bright particular star,* All's I, 1, 96. *were't not all one an empty eagle were set to guard the chicken,* H6B III, 1, 248. *he doth resemble you. As much as an apple doth an oyster, and all one,* Shr. IV, 2, 101 (= and no matter what? any thing?).

3) a particular person (= a person, a man, somebody): *one on shore,* Ven. 817. *one that hath dropped a jewel,* 823. 878. *the one doth flatter thee,* 989. Tp. I, 2, 99. III, 1, 49. V, 265. Gent. I, 3, 61. II, 1, 22. 25. 179. IV, 3, 5. IV, 4, 22. Wiv. IV, 2, 152 *(there was one conveyed out of my house).* Meas. I, 1, 42. Tw. I, 5, 134 *(there's one at the gate).* II, 5, 30. Wint. IV, 4, 398 *(one being dead, I shall have more than you can dream of).* Caes. II, 1, 112 *(one by one)* etc. (For *one another* look sub *Another*). *be one of them* (= join their company), Gent. IV, 1, 39. *to make one* (= to be of a party): Wiv. II, 3, 48. LLL V, 1, 160. Tw. I, 5, 213. H4A I, 2, 113. 152. Caes. V, 5, 72. Per. II, 1, 118. Joined with adjectives: *one sore sick,* Ven. 702. *one full of despair,* 955. *as one with treasure laden,* 1022. *to one so dear,* Gent. II, 7, 12. III, 1, 12. Err. V, 217 *(one wiser).* Merch. II, 1, 37 *(one unworthier).* Shr. Ind. 1, 31. Wint. III, 2, 99. H6A III, 1, 44 etc. With substantives: *was reckoned one the wisest prince that there had reigned,* H8 II, 4, 48 (= one that was the wisest prince). *one mine ancient friend,* Tim. V, 2, 6. *a Frenchman, one an eminent monsieur,* Cymb. I, 6, 64. cf. *he is one the truest mannered,* 165. *or ever spake one the least word that might be to the prejudice of her present state,* H8 II, 4, 153.

Adjective (applied to things as well as to persons): *under one arm the lusty courser's rein,* Ven. 31. *with one fair hand,* 351. 1058. *she locks her lily fingers one in one,* 228. *pay them* (kisses) *one by one,* 518. *one midnight,* Tp. I, 2, 128. *taught thee each hour one thing or other,* 355. *one of his pockets,* II, 1, 64. *one of their kind,* V, 23. *you shall one day find it,* Wiv. III, 3, 88. *I will marry one day,* Err. II, 1, 42. *the one ... the other,* II, 2, 98. *one* (staff) *tipped with horn,* Ado V, 4, 125. *one of these days,* As I, 2, 91. *one night,* Tw. I, 3, 16. *one fire drives out one fire, one nail one nail,* Cor. IV, 7, 54 etc. = *any? it is not Caesar's natural vice to hate one great competitor,* Ant. I, 4, 3 (most M. Edd. *our*). cf. *'tis a great charge to come under one body's hand,* Wiv. I, 4, 105 (Simple's speech). Before names = a certain: *one Julia,* Gent. IV, 4, 124. *one Mistress Quickly,* Wiv. I, 2, 3. II, 2, 46. 150. III, 5, 85. IV, 5, 33. V, 5, 175. Meas. II, 4, 18. III, 2, 210. IV, 3, 10. 75. Err. IV, 4, 135. V, 237. Ado V, 1, 317. LLL III, 122. IV, 1, 53. Mids. V, 157. 226. Merch. II, 2, 48. 116. Shr. IV, 2, 96. All's II, 1, 43. IV, 3, 199. 241. Tw. V, 183. John V, 4, 40. H4A II, 4, 391. H8 II, 2, 122. Tit. IV, 2, 152. Rom. II, 4, 213. Hml. III, 2, 254. Oth. II, 1, 66. Ant. III, 7, 79. Supplying the place of a preceding substantive: *nor thought I had one* (a father) Tp. V, 191. *a witch and one so strong,* 269. *I would have one* (a dog) Gent. IV, 4, 13. *if there be a kind woman in Windsor, she is one,* Wiv. II, 2, 126 etc. Joined to adjectives by way of supplying a substantive: *so did this horse excel a common one,* Ven. 293. *our dear love lose name of single one,* Sonn. 39, 6. *my good one* (angel) 144, 14. *the fairest one* (daughter) *of three,* Pilgr. 211. *as if it had lungs and rotten ones,* Tp. II, 1, 47. 318. II, 2, 21. V, 273. 288. Err. II, 2, 92. 94. 96. Mids. V, 322. Merch. V, 20. Shr. I, 2, 171. Wint. IV, 4, 78. H8 I, 3, 63. Lr. II, 1, 8. IV, 6, 99 etc. Peculiar passage: *a hundred mark is a long one for a poor lone woman to bear,* H4B II, 1, 35 (perhaps *a long mark,* i. e. sign or character. Some M. Edd. *loan*). Imparting, in this manner, to adjectives the nature of substantives: *my dear one,* Tp. I, 2, 17. *great ones,* Meas. II, 2, 59. Tw. I, 2, 33. Wint. II, 1, 128. Hml. III, 1, 196. Lr. II, 4, 75 *(the great one that goes up the hill).* V, 3, 18. Oth. I, 1, 8. III, 3, 273. *such a young one,* Shr. II, 236. All's V, 3, 303. John II, 521. H6B III, 1, 215. H8 V, 3, 180. Tit. II, 3, 142. Mcb. IV, 2, 11. Cymb. IV, 2, 360. *fair one,* Meas. II, 3, 19. All's II, 1, 102. H5 V, 2, 120. H8 I, 4, 14. *a couple of quiet ones,* Shr. III, 2, 242. *good gentle one,* Tw. I, 5, 192. IV, 2, 37. *sweet one,* V, 221. *a forked one,* Wint. I, 2, 186. *come, little ones,* R2 V, 5, 15. H8 V, 5, 77. Mcb. IV, 2, 69. *the wicked ones,* H6B II, 1, 186. *their tender ones,* H6C II, 2, 28. *pretty ones,* R3 IV, 1, 101. Mcb. IV, 3, 216. *four throned ones,* H8 I, 1, 11. *the learned ones,* II, 2, 93. *a pair of strange ones,* Cor. II, 1, 89. *one good one,* II, 2, 83. Oth. II, 1, 212. *you married ones,* Cymb. V, 1, 2. *his dearest one,* V, 4, 61. *many a bold one,* V, 5, 71 etc. Similarly after pronouns: *no one,* Lucr. 792. Tw. II, 4, 58. R3 II, 1, 84. *every one,* Sonn. 53, 3. Tp. IV, 137. Wiv. V, 5, 255. Tit. V, 2, 202. *if that one be prodigal, bountiful they will him call,* Pilgr. 411. *each one,* Tp. IV, 46. Mcb. V, 8, 74. *such a one,* Wiv. III, 3, 122. Tw. I, 5, 252. *such an one,* Mcb. IV, 3, 66 etc. *every one* = *every single, every: every one fault seeming monstrous,* As III, 2, 372. *no one* = *not one: the owner of no one good quality,* All's III, 6, 12. *poor in no one fault,* Cor. II, 1, 20.

4) an indefinite person, = man, people (the speaker meaning especially himself): *one would swear he saw them quake,* Lucr. 1393. *one may enter at her window,* Gent. III, 1, 113. *one cannot climb it without danger of his life,* 115. *as one should say,* IV, 4, 12. *if I have horns to make one mad,* Wiv. III, 5, 154. *not as one would say healthy,* Meas. I, 2, 55. *one would think,* IV, 3, 2. *as good cause as one would desire,* As III, 4, 5. *how might one do to lose it to her own liking,* All's I, 1, 163. *might have drawn one to a longer voyage,* Tw. III, 3, 7. *while one would wink,* V, 93 etc. Gen. *one's: who should be trusted, when one's own right hand is perjured to the bosom?* Gent. V, 4, 67. *some devils ask but the parings of one's nail,* Err. IV, 3, 72.

**One-trunk-inheriting,** possessing not more than one trunk: Lr. II, 2, 20.

**Oneyers,** see *Great oneyers.***

**Onion,** the bulbous root of Allium cepa: Mids. IV, 2, 43. Causing tears: Shr. Ind. 1, 126. All's V, 3, 321. Ant. I, 2, 176.

**Onion-eyed,** ready to weep: Ant. IV, 2, 35.

**Only,** adj. 1) sole, one alone, being without another: *his o. heir,* Tp. I, 2, 58. *the o. means,* H6A V, 1, 8. Gent. III, 1, 339. Err. V, 309. Mids. I, 1, 160. H6B II, 2, 19. H6C I, 1, 225. Cor. I, 9, 36. Rom. I, 5, 139. Caes. I, 2, 157 etc.

2) principal, chief: *'gainst venomed sores the o.*

sovereign plaster, Ven. 916. *thou that art now the world's fresh ornament and o. herald to the gaudy spring,* Sonn. 1, 10. *best of dearest and mine o. care,* 48, 7. *we are the o. love-gods,* Ado II, 1, 402. *he is the o. man of Italy,* III, 1, 92. *it is the o. thing for a qualm,* III, 4, 75. *motley's the o. wear,* As II, 7, 34. *it is my o. suit,* 44. III, 4, 13. V, 3, 13. 20. V, 4, 108. All's II, 1, 110. H4A I, 3, 261. II, 4, 83. H5 II, 3, 54. H6A IV, 7, 77. Rom. I, 5, 140. Hml. II, 2, 421. III, 2, 131. IV, 3, 22.

**Only,** adv. 1) singly, with no other besides, alone: *o. Collatinus finds his wife,* Lucr. Arg. 9. *she was o. mine,* Lucr. 1798. *I never saw a woman, but o. Sycorax my dam and she,* Tp. III, 2, 109. Ado I, 1, 126. Mids. I, 1, 243. IV, 1, 176. Merch. IV, 1, 356. H6A I, 5, 8 etc. Transposed: *and o. must be wailed by Collatine,* Lucr. 1799 (= by Collatine only). *novelty is o. in request,* Meas. III, 2, 237 (= only novelty). *o. attended by Nerissa,* Merch. III, 4, 29. *judgement o. doth belong to thee,* H6B III, 2, 140 (= to thee only). *why o., Suffolk, mourn I not for thee?* 383.

2) merely, barely: *o. to flatter fools,* Lucr. 1559. *o. me for thee,* Sonn. 125, 12. *my foolish rival that her father likes o. for his possessions are so huge,* Gent. II, 4, 175. II, 7, 82. 88. III, 1, 276. Wiv. II, 1, 224. II, 2, 242. Meas. I, 2, 154. I, 3, 25. III, 1, 3. IV, 1, 43. Ado I, 3, 41. Mids. II, 1, 206. Merch. I, 1, 96. H4B IV, 5, 116 etc. Peculiar passages: *I know not how I shall offend in dedicating my unpolished lines to your lordship, nor how the world will censure me for choosing so strong a prop to support so weak a burden, only, if your honour seem but pleased, I account myself highly praised,* Ven. Dedic. 3 (i. e. only this I know). *Love no god, that would not extend his might, o. where qualities were level,* All's I, 3, 118 (used as if the sentence were not negative, but affirmative, = but). *Not o. ... but: not o. with what my revenue yielded, but what my power might else exact,* Tp. I, 2, 98. IV, 209. Wiv. II, 2, 206. 307. IV, 2, 4. Meas. III, 1, 245 etc. *but o.* = only, but: *as if I did but o. chew his name,* Meas. II, 4, 5. *I intend but o. to surprise him,* H6C IV, 2, 25. *o. but: discourse grow commendable in none o. but parrots,* Merch. III, 5, 51. *your son had o. but the corpse,* H4B I, 1, 192. *he o. lived but till he was a man,* Mcb. V, 8, 40. Transposed: *o. he hath an eye to gaze on beauty,* Lucr. 496 (= only to gaze). *this deed will make thee o. loved for fear,* 610 (loved for fear only). *their virtue o. is their show,* Sonn. 54, 9. *o. my plague thus far I count my gain,* 141, 13. *he's a spirit of persuasion, o. professes to persuade,* Tp. II, 1, 235. *I seek to heal it o. by his wealth,* Wiv. III, 4, 6 (= I only seek). *o. he hath made an assay of her virtue to practise his judgment,* Meas. III, 1, 163 (= only to practise). *he made trial of you o.* 202 (= he only made trial). *that o. wounds by hearsay,* Ado III, 1, 23 (only by hearsay). *men are o. turned into tongue,* IV, 1, 323 (into tongue only, mere tongue). *I o. swore to study with your grace,* LLL I, 1, 51 (swore only to study). *he o. loves the world for him,* Merch. II, 8, 50. *o. in the world I fill up a place,* As I, 2, 204. *wretched shall France be o. in my name,* H6A I, 4, 97 (in my mere name). *o. I yield to die.* Caes. V, 4, 12 (I yield only to die). *o. I say,* Mcb. III, 6, 2 (I only say).

**Onset,** beginning, setting about: *if thou wilt leave me, do not leave me last, when other petty griefs have* *done their spite, but in the o. come*, Sonn. 90, 11. *I have a sonnet that will serve the turn to give the o. to thy good advice*, Gent. III, 2, 94. *and for an o.*, *Titus, to advance thy name, Lavinia will I make my empress*, Tit. I, 238. = beginning of a combat: *swell in their pride, the o. still expecting*, Lucr. 432. *the o. and retire of both your armies*, John II, 326.

**Onward,** 1) forward, on: *o. to Troy he goes*, Lucr. 1504. Ado I, 1, 299. Cor. II, 3, 271.

2) on the way yet to be made; opposed to behind: *my grief lies o. and my joy behind*, Sonn. 50, 14.

**Onwards,** the same: *as thou goest o.* Sonn. 126, 6.

**Onyx,** a gem: Hml. V, 2, 283 (Ff *union*).

**Ooze,** subst. the soft mud at the bottom of water: Tp. I, 2, 252. III, 3, 100. H5 I, 2, 164. Ant. II, 7, 25. Cymb. IV, 2, 205. Per. III, 1, 61 (O. Edd. *oare*).

**Ooze,** vb. to flow gently: *as a gum, which —s from whence 'tis nourished*, Tim. I, 1, 21.

**Oozy,** muddy, slimy: Tp. V, 151.

**Opal,** a precious stone reflecting different colours: Compl. 215. Tw. II, 4, 77.

**Ope,** adj. open; never joined to a noun attributively: *the gates are o.* Cor. I, 4, 43. *to break o.* Lucr. 446. Err. III, 1, 73. Cor. III, 1, 138. Mcb. II, 3, 72. *to fling o.* John II, 449. *to pluck o.* Caes. I, 2, 267. *to set o.* H6B IV, 9, 13. *unlaid o.* Per. I, 2, 89.

**Ope,** vb. to open; 1) trans.: *o. the gate*, Ven. 424. John II, 536. H6C II, 1, 21. V, 1, 21. *a door*, Tit. V, 2, 10. *a window*, Cymb. V, 4, 81. *a tomb*, Rom. V, 3, 283. *a coffin*, Per. V, 3, 23. *her lap*, Rom. I, 1, 220. *arms*, Tit. V, 3, 108. Hml. IV, 5, 145. *jaws*, Troil. I, 3, 73. Hml. I, 4, 50. *mouth*, Tit. V, 3, 175. *lips*, Merch. I, 1, 94. Caes. III, 1, 260. Oth. V, 2, 305. *thine ear*, Tp. I, 2, 37. *eyes*, Ado IV, 1, 125. H6B III, 2, 35. Cymb. II, 3, 26. *a letter*, Merch. III, 2, 235. Lr. V, 1, 40. *a testament*, R2 III, 3, 93 (Qq *open*).

2) intr.; used of eyes: Lucr. 383. of gates, H6C II, 3, 40. Tim. V, 4, 47. of graves, Tp. V, 49. of the heavens, Cor. V, 3, 183.

**Open,** adj. 1) not shut, unclosed: *an o. ear*, Lucr. 283. Wint. IV, 4, 685. V, 2, 68. *eye*, Lucr. 520. Tp. II, 1, 214. Wiv. II, 1, 126. Mcb. V, 1, 28. *door*, Shr. III, 2, 212. H4B IV, 5, 56. Troil. IV, 2, 19. Mcb. II, 2, 5. *mouth*, John IV, 2, 195. *ports of slumber*, H4B IV, 5, 24. *gates*, H6C V, 1, 60. *the o. ulcer of my heart*, Troil. I, 1, 53. *the offices are o.* Oth. II, 2, 9. *purse*, Per. III, 2, 47. *to be secretly o.* Troil. V, 2, 24 (quibbling). *to break o.* Wiv. I, 1, 115. H6B IV, 3, 18. Tim. IV, 3, 450. *burst o.* H6A I, 3, 28. *how came the posterns o.?* Wint. II, 1, 53. *gape o.* R3 I, 2, 65. *keep o.* Sonn. 27, 7. 61, 1. *leave o.* Mids. III, 1, 58. *wrench o.* Per. III, 2, 53. *An o. hand* the emblem a) of unreserved and honest sentiments: *where a noble heart hath pawned an o. hand in sign of love*, H6C IV, 2, 9. b) of liberality: Tw. IV, 1, 22. H4B IV, 4, 32. Troil. IV, 5, 100. *your o. bounty*, Tim. V, 1, 61.

2) unenclosed, not obstructed, accessible: *if money goes before, all ways lie o.* Wiv. II, 2, 175. *lodge in o. field*, H6B I, 1, 80. *let me have o. means to come to them*, R3 IV, 2, 77. Metaphorically: *o. to incontinency*, Hml. II, 1, 30. Hence = exposed: *hath left me o. to all injuries*, H4B V, 2, 8. *I lie o. to the law*, H6B I, 3, 159. H8 III, 2, 334. *left me o., bare for every storm*, Tim. IV, 3, 265.

3) not covered, not sheltered: *the o. air*, Wint. III, 2, 106. John V, 7, 7. H6C III, 2, 177. R3 I, 1,

124. Lr. III, 6, 1. *the tyranny of the o. night*, Lr. III, 4, 2. Double meaning: *a hand o. as day*, H4B IV, 4, 32

4) public: *thy secret pleasure turns to o. shame*, Lucr. 890. Err. IV, 4, 70. H6B II, 4, 19. *an o. room*, Meas. II, 1, 135. **in the o. court*, Merch. IV, 1, 338. *as she hath been publicly accused, so shall she have a just and o. trial*, Wint. II, 3, 205. *sequestration from o. haunts and popularity*, H5 I, 1, 59. *to make o. proclamation*, H6A I, 3, 71. *in o. market-place*, I, 4, 40. *in the o. streets*, I, 6, 13. *three days' o. penance*, H6B II, 3, 11. *we are too o. here to argue this; let's think in private more*, H8 II, 1, 168. *all run, with o. outcry, toward our monument*, Rom. V, 3, 193. *in o.* = in public: *was viewed in o. as his queen*, H8 III, 2, 405.

Adverbially: *do not then walk too o.* Tw. III, 3, 37; cf. H8 II, 1, 168.

5) undisguised, free from dissimulation: *by o. war*, H6C I, 2, 19. *o. perils*, Caes. IV, 1, 47. *to show their o. banner*, Lr. III, 1, 34. *truth loves o. dealing*, H8 III, 1, 40. *the Moor is of a free and o. nature*, Oth. I, 3, 405.

6) apparent, evident, plain: *his thefts were too o.* Wiv. I, 3, 28. *what's o. made to justice, that justice seizes*, Meas. II, 1, 21. *this is o.* Tw. II, 5, 174. *gross as a mountain, o., palpable*, H4A II, 4, 250. *this o. and apparent shame*, 292. *their faults are o.* H5 II, 2, 142. *his apparent o. guilt*, R3 III, 5, 30. *to lay o.* = to show, to reveal: Lucr. 747. 1248. Wiv. II, 2, 191. Err. III, 2, 34. Wint. III, 2, 19. John IV, 3, 38. H4A II, 3, 34. R3 III, 7, 15. Cymb. III, 2, 29.

**Open,** vb. 1) trans. a) to unclose, to unlock, to unfold: *the gates*, Ven. 960. Tp. I, 2, 129. H6A I, 3, 4. 17. 18. IV, 2, 5. H6C IV, 7, 28. 29. *a door*, Lucr. 359. Err. III, 1, 38. *a casement*, All's II, 3, 226. *latches*, Wint. IV, 4, 449. *a purse*, Gent. I, 1, 137. *an oyster*, Wiv. II, 2, 3. *a letter*, Tw. V, 297. *a bearing-cloth*, Wint. III, 3, 120. *the mouth*, Ven. 248. Tp. II, 2, 85. 87. R3 I, 2, 56. *chaps*, Tp. II, 2, 89. *eyes*, Ven. 1051. Lucr. 105. H6B II, 1, 105. H8 II, 2, 42. Tim. V, 1, 25. *lips*, Meas. III, 1, 198. As I, 3, 84. V, 1, 37. 39. Tw. I, 5, 2. *arms*, Wint. IV, 4, 559. *hand*, Tw. II, 5, 159. Wint. I, 2, 103. *I feel my heart new —ed*, H8 III, 2, 366 (susceptible of new sentiments). Peculiar expression: *my hand has —ed bounty to you*, H8 III, 2, 184 (= has been open to do you good).

b) to disclose, to expand: *in whom I know all the particulars of vice so grafted that, when they shall be —ed,...* Mcb. IV, 3, 52.

c) to disclose, to reveal, to show: *o. the matter in brief*, Gent. I, 1, 135. *to o. thy affair*, Wint. IV, 4, 764. *which I have —ed to his grace*, H5 I, 1, 78. *—ing titles miscreate*, I, 2, 16. Hml. II, 2, 18. Cymb. V, 5, 42. 58. Per. I, 2, 87. IV, 3, 23. V, 1, 133.

2) intr. a) to unclose itself; used of locks, Lucr. 304. Mcb. IV, 1, 46. of gates, Ven. 451. Mids. III, 2, 392. Cor. I, 4, 19. of clouds, Tp. III, 2, 150. of lips, Ven. 48. of jaws, Rom. V, 3, 47. of eyes, Lucr. 399. Tp. II, 1, 319. *at the first —ing of the gorgeous east*, LLL IV, 3, 223; cf. Mids. III, 2, 393.

b) to bark on scent or view of the game: *if I cry out thus upon no trail, never trust me when I o. again*, Wiv. IV, 2, 209.

**Open-arse,** the vulgar name of the medlar; not spoken to the end, but broken off in the middle in Rom. II, 1, 38: *O, that she were an open, or thou a* *poperin pear!* (M. Edd. following the surreptitious Q1, *an open et cetera*).

**Opener**, one who reveals and interprets: *the very o. and intelligencer between the grace, the sanctities of heaven and our dull workings,* H4B IV, 2, 20.

**Open - eyed**, waking and watching: *while you here do snoring lie, o. conspiracy his time doth take,* Tp. II, 1, 301.

**Opening**, 1) unclosing: *a gate that makes his o. with this bigger key,* Meas. IV, 1, 31. 2) aperture, entrance: *the o. of his mouth,* As IV, 3, 111. *we saw him at the o. of his tent,* Troil. II, 3, 91.

**Openly**, 1) publicly: *proclaimed it o.* Shr. IV, 2, 85. *we so o. proceed in justice,* Wint. III, 2, 5. *my case so o. known,* H4B II, 1, 33. *be dishonoured o.* Tit. I, 432. *maintain such a quarrel o.* II, 1, 47.

2) without reserve or disguise, manifestly: *this chain which now you wear so o.* Err. V, 1, 17. *my love shall show itself more o.* H4B IV, 2, 76. *calls your grace usurper o.* H6B IV, 4, 30.

**Openness**, plainness, clearness: *deliver with more o. your answers to my demands,* Cymb. I, 6, 88.

**Operant**, operative, active: *sauce his palate with thy most o. poison,* Tim. IV, 3, 25. *my o. powers their functions leave to do,* Hml. III, 2, 184.

**Operate**, to be active: *the effect doth o. another way,* Troil. V, 3, 109. *mine Italian brain 'gan in your duller Britain o. most vilely,* Cymb. V, 5, 197.

**Operation**, agency, effect: *a good sherris-sack hath a twofold o. in it,* H4B IV, 3, 104. *hath an o. more divine,* Troil. III, 3, 203. Rom. III, 1, 8. Lr. I, 1, 113. Ant. II, 7, 30. IV, 15, 26. Used confusedly by Nym: *I have —s which be humours of revenge,* Wiv. I, 3, 98 (= disposition, sentiments).

**Operative**, effective: *that (sleep) to provoke in him, are many simples o.* Lr. IV, 4, 14.

**Ophelia**, name in Hml. I, 3, 33 etc.

**Opinion**, 1) judgment formed concerning any thing, persuasion: *errors by o. bred,* Lucr. 937. *I do now let loose my o.* Tp. II, 2, 36. *I cannot put off my o. so easily,* Wiv. II, 1, 243. Ado I, 1, 234. Merch. III, 5, 76. IV, 1, 157. As II, 7, 46. Tw. IV, 2, 54. 58. 60. 62. Wint. I, 2, 297. II, 1, 37. II, 3, 89. John IV, 2, 26. R2 III, 1, 26. H4A II, 4, 445. H5 III, 2, 105. H6A I, 4, 64. II, 4, 52. H6C IV, 1, 29. H8 Prol. 20. III, 1, 60. IV, 2, 37. V, 3, 17. Troil. II, 2, 188. Cor. I, 1, 169. I, 2, 1. Caes. V, 1, 78. Hml. I, 1, 68. II, 1, 115. V, 2, 201. Lr. I, 2, 80. Cymb. I, 4, 68. *in an opinion* = of a persuasion: *he shall yield the other in the right o.* H6A II, 4, 42. *he is returned in his —s,* H8 III, 2, 64; cf. Ado I, 1, 235. *in my o.* = to my thinking: Gent. I, 2, 6. Meas. II, 1, 245. All's IV, 2, 31. H6A V, 5, 61. H6B II, 1, 106. R3 II, 2, 131. III, 1, 52. III, 4, 45 (Ff *judgment*). Cymb. I, 4, 119. *with that o.* = thinking, supposing: *that thou neglect me not with that o. that I am touched with madness,* Meas. V, 50. *to hold an o.:* Ado II, 3, 224. Merch. IV, 1, 131. Caes. II, 1, 196; cf. I, 2, 322. Followed by *of* (= concerning, about): *ask my o. of that,* Merch. III, 5, 90. *what's your o. of your sister?* Shr. III, 2, 245. H4B I, 3, 3. H6B II, 2, 4. Caes. II, 1, 196. II, 2, 6.

2) the judgment or sentiments formed about persons and their qualities: *to bear a hard o. of his truth,* Gent. II, 7, 81. *in this mystery of ill —s,* Wiv. II, 1, 73. *bear a good o. of my knowledge,* As V, 2, 60. *sailed into the north of my lady's o.* Tw. III, 2, 28. *a most*

*hideous o. of his rage,* III, 4, 212. *killed with your hard —s,* H4B V, 5, 148. H8 II, 2, 125. II, 3, 61. III, 1, 36. Caes. I, 2, 322. Mcb. I, 7, 33. Oth. IV, 2, 209. Cymb. I, 4, 175. II, 4, 58. Peculiar passage: *that he might stick the smallest o. on my least misuse,* Oth. IV, 2, 109 (= ill opinion).

3) the favourable judgment which a person forms of himself; a) in a good sense, = self-confidence: *to steel a strong o. to themselves,* Troil. I, 3, 353. *let us rear the higher our o.* Ant. II, 1, 36. b) in a bad sense, = arrogance, conceitedness: *pride, haughtiness, o. and disdain,* H4A III, 1, 185. *learned without o.* LLL V, 1, 6. *a plague of o.* Troil. III, 3, 265.

4) reputation, credit, public opinion: *to be dressed in an o. of wisdom,* Merch. I, 1, 91. *this fool gudgeon, this o.* 102. *o. that did help me to the crown,* H4A III, 2, 42. *it lends a lustre and more great o. to our enterprise,* IV, 1, 77. *thou hast redeemed thy lost o.* V, 4, 48. *to thee it shall descend with better quiet, better o.* H4B IV, 5, 189. *to raze out rotten o. who hath writ me down after my seeming,* V, 2, 128. *o. shall be surgeon to my hurt,* H6A II, 4, 53. *Achilles, whom o. crowns the sinew and the forehead of our host,* Troil. I, 3, 142. 186. *in the trial much o. dwells,* 336. *we did our main o. crush in taint of our best man,* 373. *yet go we under our o. still that we have better men,* 383. *others fish with craft for great o.* IV, 4, 105. *policy grows into an ill o.* V, 4, 19. *o. that so sticks on Marcius,* Cor. I, 1, 275. *in o. and in honour wronged,* Tit. I, 416. *will purchase us a good o.* Caes. II, 1, 145. *false o. whose wrong thought defiles thee,* Lr. III, 6, 119. *o., a sovereign mistress of success,* Oth. I, 3, 225. *your rich o.* II, 3, 195. *o. 's but a fool,* Per. II, 2, 56. *begets you a good o.* IV, 2, 131.

**Opinioned**, Dogberry's blunder for *pinioned:* Ado IV, 2, 69.

**Opportune**, seasonable, convenient, fit: *the most o. place,* Tp. IV, 1, 26. *and most o. to our need I have a vessel,* Wint. IV, 4, 511.

**Opportunity**, convenient time, favourable circumstances, fit occasion: Lucr. 874. 876. 895. 903. 932. Wiv. III, 4, 20. Mids. II, 1, 217. Tw. III, 2, 27. H5 III, 2, 151. H6A II, 1, 13. V, 4, 158. Troil. IV, 5, 62. Tit. I, 1, 137. Rom. III, 5, 49. Oth. II, 1, 290. Cymb. I, 4, 116. 141. III, 1, 14. III, 2, 19. III, 4, 29. Plural: Wiv. II, 2, 203. III, 1, 15. Lr. IV, 6, 268.

**Oppose**, 1) to place in front or face to face, to set over against: *I do o. my patience to his fury,* Merch. IV, 1, 10. *o. thy steadfast-gazing eyes to mine, see if thou canst outface me,* H6B IV, 10, 48. *—ing freely the beauty of her person to the people,* H8 IV, 1, 67. *eye to eye —d salutes each other with each other's form,* Troil. III, 3, 107. *o. not Scythia to ambitious Rome,* Tit. I, 132. *was this a face to be —d against the warring winds?* Lr. IV, 7, 32 (Qq *exposed*). *sluttery to such neat excellence —d,* Cymb. I, 6, 44. = to set against, by way of hinderance or combat: *are my doors —d against my passage?* Tim. III, 4, 80. *to o. the bolt against my coming in,* Lr. II, 4, 179. *whom may you else o. that can from Hector bring his honour off?* Troil. I, 3, 333. *misprizing the knight — d,* IV, 5, 75. *they are —d already,* 94. *—d to hinder me,* V, 3, 57. *though Birnam wood be come to Dunsinane, and thou —d,* Mcb. V, 8, 31.

Partic. —d, adjectively, = a) opposite, contrary: *fashioning our humours even to the —d end of our in-*

*tents,* LLL V, 2, 768. *of —d natures,* Merch. II, 9, 62. *—d winds,* Wint. I, 1, 34. *the — d continent,* H4A III, 1, 110. b) adverse, hostile : *to give my hand —d against my heart unto a mad-brain rudesby,* Shr. III, 2, 9. *those —d eyes,* H4A I, 1, 9. *we stand —d,* V, 1, 67. *towards fronting peril and —d decay,* H4B IV, 4, 66. *the —d numbers,* H5 IV, 1, 308. *two such —d kings,* Rom. II, 3, 27. *though in general part we were —d,* Tim. V, 2, 7. *bear it that the —d may beware of thee,* Hml. I, 3, 67. *from one that's of a neutral heart, and not from one —d,* Lr. III, 7, 49.

Reflexively : *if you o. yourselves to match Lord Warwick,* H6B V, 1, 156. Hence = to resist, to defy, to offer resistance : *she —s her against my will,* Gent. III, 2, 26. *I alone do me o. against the pope,* John III, 1, 170. *I o. not myself against their will,* R2 III, 3, 18. *o. himself against a troop of kernes,* H6B III, 1, 361. *makes him o. himself against the king,* V, 1, 133.

2) to be set against, to be an adversary to, to face, to confront : *your resolution cannot hold, when 'tis —d by the power of the king,* Wint. IV, 4, 37. *they shall be well — d,* H4A IV, 4, 33. *too weak to o. your cunning,* H8 II, 4, 107. *you are potently —ed,* V, 1, 135. *to o. his hatred fully,* Cor. III, 1, 20. *—ing laws with strokes,* III, 3, 79. *he did o. his foe,* Tim. III, 5, 20. *o. my will,* Mcb IV, 3, 65. *if you —d them* (French scrimers) Hml. IV, 7, 103. Ant. III, 13, 169.

3) intr. a) to be placed over against each other : *when half to half the world —d,* Ant. III, 13, 9. *the four —ing coigns which the world together joins,* Per. III Prol. 17. b) to be adverse, to make opposition : *o. against their wills,* Wint. V, 1, 46. *and by —ing end them,* Hml. III, 1, 60. *whom most just and heavy causes make o.* Lr. V, 1, 27. *found no opposition but what he looked for should o.* Cymb. II, 5, 18. *against,* Lr. IV, 2, 74.

**Opposeless,** not to be opposed, irresistible : *your great o. wills,* Lr. IV, 6, 38.

**Opposer,** enemy : All's III, 1, 6. Cor. I, 5, 23. II, 2, 98. IV, 3, 36.

**Opposite,** subst. 1) adversary : Meas. III, 2, 175. Tw. III, 2, 68. III, 4, 253. 293. H4B I, 3, 55. IV, 1, 16. H6B V, 3, 22. R3 V, 4, 3. Cor. II, 2, 23. Hml. V, 2, 62. Lr. V, 3, 42. 153.

2) contrary : *just o. to what thou justly seemest,* Rom. III, 2, 78. *each o. that blanks the face of joy meet what I would have well and it destroy,* Hml. III, 2, 230 (or = contrariety?). *the present pleasure, by revolution lowering, does become the o. of itself,* Ant. I, 2, 130.

**Opposite,** adj. 1) adverse, repugnant, hostile : *free from a stubborn o. intent,* H6B III, 2, 251. *at their births good stars were o.* R3 IV, 4, 215. *be o. all planets of good luck to my proceedings,* 402. *he's o. to humanity,* Tim. I, 1, 284. *how o. I stood to his purpose,* Lr. II, 1, 51. *so o. to marriage,* Oth. I, 2, 67. Followed by *with: be o. with a kinsman,* Tw. II, 5, 162 (show him your aversion). *to be thus o. with heaven,* R3 II, 2, 94.

2) contrary : *cross him with their o. persuasion,* Lucr. 286. *what is o. to England's love,* John III, 1, 254. *thou art as o. to every good as the Antipodes are unto us,* H6C I, 4, 134. *the office o. to Saint Peter,* Oth. IV, 2, 91.

**Opposition,** 1) the act of setting against, of offering for combat : *the o. of your person in trial,* Hml. V, 2, 178.

2) that which is set against, by way of combat or comparison : *your whole plot too light for the counter-poise of so great an o.* H4A II, 3, 15. *alike conversant in general services, and more remarkable in single —s,* Cymb. IV, 1, 14 (i. e. when compared as to particular accomplishments. According to the usual interpretation, = single combats).

3) repugnance, resistance : *the liberal o. of our spirits,* LLL V, 2, 743. *the sin of disobedient o. to you and your behests,* Rom. IV, 2, 18. *why should we in our peevish o. take it to heart,* Hml. I, 2, 100. *found no o.* Cymb. II, 5, 17.

4) combat, encounter : *in single o., hand to hand,* H4A I, 3, 99. *tilting one at other's breast, in o. bloody,* Oth. II, 3, 184.

**Oppress,** 1) to press, to act upon by pressure : *the weak —ed, the impression of strange kinds is formed in them,* Lucr. 1242.

2) to press down, to depress, to overpower : *day's oppression is not eased by night, but day by night, and night by day, — ed,* Sonn. 28, 4. *my life sinks down to death, —ed with melancholy,* 45, 8. *they are —ed with travel,* Tp. III, 3, 15. *a young maid with travel much —ed,* As II, 4, 74. *— ed with two weak evils, age and hunger,* II, 7, 132. *—ed with wrongs,* John III, 1, 13. *fear —eth strength,* R2 III, 2, 180. *doleful dumps the mind o.* Rom. IV, 5, 129. *when nature, being —ed, commands the mind to suffer with the body,* Lr. II, 4, 109. *—ed nature sleeps,* III, 6, 104. *belief of it —es me already,* Oth. I, 1, 144.

3) to suppress : *the mutiny he there hastes to o.* Per. III Prol. 29.

4) to afflict, to distress, to harass, to bring to misery : *you ne'er —ed me with a mother's groan,* All's I, 3, 153. *this —ed boy,* John II, 177. 245 ( or = supplanted?). *nor much —ed them with great subsidies,* H6C IV, 8, 45. *by —ing and betraying me thou mightst have sooner got another service,* Tim. IV, 3, 510. *for thee, —ed king, am I cast down,* Lr. V, 3, 5. *be not with mortal accidents —ed,* Cymb. V, 4, 99.

5) to take all to one's self, to cover and encompass the whole of, to overwhelm : *did o. our nest,* H4A V, 1, 61. *when all our offices have been —ed with riotous feeders,* Tim. II, 2, 167. *why dost thou so o. me with thine eye?* Troil. IV, 5, 241 (examine every part with a devouring look). *thrice he walked by their —ed and fear-surprised eyes,* Hml. I, 2, 203.

**Oppression,** 1) pressure : *stoop with o. of their prodigal weight,* R2 III, 4, 31. *too great o. for a tender thing,* Rom. I, 4, 24.

2) tyranny against subjects or enemies : *you would have sold ... his subjects to o.* H5 II, 2, 172. *such as your o. feeds upon,* H6A IV, 1, 58. *free from o. or the stroke of war,* V, 3, 155. *I lack gall to make o. bitter,* Hml. II, 2, 606. *the o. of aged tyranny,* Lr. I, 2, 52. *the earth is thronged by man's o.* Per. I, 1, 102 (or perhaps = avidity taking all to itself; cf. *Oppress* sub 5).

3) embarrassment, difficulty ; affliction, distress, misery : *how under my o. I did reek,* H8 II, 4, 208. *our o. exceeds what we expected,* Ant. IV, 7, 2. *when day's o. is not eased by night,* Sonn. 28, 3. *day of shame, o., perjury,* John III, 1, 88 (or = tyranny?). *our o. hath made up this league,* 106. *to counterfeit o. of such grief,* R2 I, 4, 14. *at thy good heart's o.* Rom. I, 1, 190. *need and o. starveth in thine eyes,* V, 1, 70.

**Oppressor,** one who tramples on the rights of

another: *the orphan pines while the o. feeds*, Lucr. 905. *the —'s wrong*, Hml. III, 1, 71.

**Opprobriously**, injuriously, invectively: R3 III, 1, 153.

**Oppugnancy**, opposition, contention: *each thing meets in mere o.* Troil. I, 3, 111.

**Opulency**, affluence, riches: *the flatteries that follow youth and o.* Tim. V, 1, 38.

**Opulent**, rich, plenteous, ample: *to draw a third more o. than your sisters*, Lr. I, 1, 88. *I will piece her o. throne with kingdoms*, Ant. I, 5, 46.

**Or**, a particle marking, or only seeming to mark, an alternative; really disjunctive: *whether he run or fly they know not*, Ven. 304. *in earth or heaven?* 493. *do I delight to die or life desire?* 496. *high or low*, 1139. *fall to't, or we run ourselves aground*, Tp. I, 1, 4. *I have inly wept, or should have spoke ere this*, V, 201 etc. etc. Denoting indifference of choice: *foul or wrinkled-old*, Ven. 133. *would dissolve or seem to melt*, 144. *I will enchant thine ear, or trip upon the green*, 146. 206. 232. 285 etc. etc. *four or five*, Tp. I, 2, 47. *a turn or two*, IV, 162. *twice or thrice*, Gent. I, 2, 117. III, 1, 365. Wiv. III, 5, 103. IV, 4, 48. V, 5, 129. Meas. II, 1, 287. III, 1, 76. Ado III, 2, 74. Mids. IV, 1, 41. Merch. III, 2, 1. IV, 1, 147 etc. The same variety even in the use of *either ... or*, and of *or else*; cf. *Either* and *Else* (add to the instances quoted there: *but you are wise, or else you love not, for to be wise and love exceeds man's might*, Troil. III, 2, 163). Sometimes quite = and: *more white and red than doves or roses are*, Ven. 10. *if you suspect my husbandry or falsehood*, Tim. II, 2, 164 (a hendiadis, = my false husbandry, or my husbandry as false; cf. *And*). Placed only before the last of several parts of the sentence: *no grass, herb, leaf, or weed*, Ven. 1055. *either this is envy in you, folly, or mistaking*, Meas. III, 2, 149. *neither in time, matter, or other circumstance*, IV, 2, 108. *not to wear, handle, or use any sword, weapon, or dagger*, H6A I, 3, 78 etc. *or ... or* = either ... or; 1) disjunctively: *or gluttoning on all, or all away*, Sonn. 75, 14. *or I shall live your epitaph to make, or you survive*, 81, 1. 112, 8. Tp. IV, 1, 30. Merch. I, 1, 150. Wint. II, 1, 165. IV, 4, 42. H4A I, 3, 194. H5 I, 2, 12. 225. H8 II, 4, 192. Troil. I, 3, 318. Cor. I, 3, 40. III, 1, 208. IV, 1, 32. Caes. IV, 1, 11. V, 5, 3. Lr. IV, 7, 98. Ant. IV, 2, 5. Per. V, 1, 248. *or ... or else: illannexed opportunity or kills his life or else his quality*, Lucr. 875. *or you must fight or else be hanged*, H6B I, 3, 222. Cor. V, 3, 109. 2) indifferently: *without or yea or no*, Lucr. 1340. *without or grudge or grumblings*, Tp. I, 2, 249. *to leave unsought or that or any place*, Err. I, 1, 137. *would mad or man or beast*, V, 84. *will make or man or woman madly dote*, Mids. II, 1, 171. *am I or that or this for what he'll utter?* All's V, 3, 208. Meas. V, 368. Wint. I, 2, 428. R2 I, 1, 93. Troil. III, 3, 97. Caes. II, 1, 135. Cymb. I, 4, 90 (O. Edd. *or if there were*, most M. Edd. *if there were*) etc. *Or ... or* = whether ... or: *what hour is this? or morn or weary even?* Ven. 495. *or in the ocean drenched, or in the fire?* 494. *looked he or red or pale, or sad or merrily?* Err. IV, 2, 4. *where is fancy bred, or in the heart or in the head?* Merch. III, 2, 64. *thou art overthrown, or Charles or something weaker masters thee*, As I, 2, 272. H4A V, 2, 12. H6B I, 3, 105. Caes. V, 4, 24. Lr. III, 6, 69. Cymb. II, 4, 71. IV, 2, 356. *Or whether ... or whether* = whether ... or: *or whether*

*doth my mind drink up the monarchs' plague, this flattery, or whether shall I say ...?* Sonn. 114, 1. cf. *move these eyes? or whether ... seem they in motion?* Merch. III, 2, 118. *or whether his fall enraged him, or how 'twas*, Cor. I, 3, 69.

**Or**, before, sooner than: *would I had met my dearest foe in heaven or ever I had seen that day*, Hml. I, 2, 183 (Ff *ere I had ever seen*). *or I could make a prologue to my brains, they had begun the play*, V, 2, 30 (Ff *ere*). *I'll think he'll grant the tribute or look upon our Romans*, Cymb. II, 4, 14. Particularly *or ere* (or *e'er?*) used in this sense: Tp. I, 2, 11. V, 103. Shr. IV, 5, 8. John IV, 3, 20. V, 6, 44. Mcb. IV, 3, 173. Hml. I, 2, 147. Lr. II, 4, 289. Cymb. III, 2, 67. V, 3, 50 (cf. *Ere*).

**Oracle**, 1) the decision of a god respecting a question: Tp. IV, 1, 12. V, 244. Gent. II, 7, 75. LLL I, 1, 218. Wint. II, 1, 190. III, 1, 18. III, 2, 116. 119. 128. 141. 155. V, 1, 38. V, 2, 24. V, 3, 126. H6B I, 4, 74. H8 V, 5, 67. Troil. I, 3, 74. Cymb. V, 5, 450.

2) the place where, or the person of whom the determinations of heaven are inquired: Merch. I, 1, 93. Wint. II, 1, 185. II, 3, 194. III, 1, 9. R3 II, 2, 152. H8 III, 2, 104. Troil. I, 3, 192. IV, 5, 252. Tim. IV, 3, 120. V, 1, 222. Mcb. III, 1, 9.

**Orange**, the fruit of Citrus Aurantium: *civil as an o.* Ado II, 1, 305 (cf. *Civil*). *this rotten o.* IV, 1, 33.

**Orange-tawny**, dark-yellow: *your o. beard*, Mids. I, 2, 96. *the ousel cock with o. bill*, III, 1, 129.

**Orange-wife**, a woman that sells oranges: Cor. II, 1, 78.

**Oration**, a public speech, a harangue: Merch. III, 2, 180. Troil. I, 3, 166. II, 1, 19. Tit. IV, 3, 96. 98. 116. Caes. III, 1, 293.

**Orator**, a speaker by way of eminence, one who pleads a case with some eloquence: Ven. 806. Lucr. 30. 268. 815. Err. III, 2, 10. As IV, 1, 75. All's V, 3, 254. H6A IV, 1, 175. H6B III, 2, 274. H6C I, 2, 2. II, 2, 43. III, 1, 33. III, 2, 188. R3 III, 5, 95. IV, 2, 38. IV, 4, 129. Tit. III, 1, 26. IV, 1, 14. Caes. III, 2, 221.

**Oratory**, art of speaking, eloquence: Lucr. 564. 815. H6A II, 2, 49. R3 III, 1, 37. III, 7, 20. Tit. V, 3, 90.

**Orb**, 1) a circle: *you seem to me as Dian in her o.* Ado IV, 1, 58 (surrounded by her nymphs. Or perhaps = the moon in her sphere?). *to dew her —s upon the green*, Mids. II, 1, 9 (i. e. fairy-rings). *the moon that monthly changes in her circled o.* Rom. II, 2, 110.

2) any thing spherical: *the small o. of one particular tear*, Compl. 289.

3) the sphere in which a star moves: *my good stars have empty left their —s*, Ant. III, 13, 146. Metaphorically, = sphere of action: *move in that obedient o. again where you did give a fair and natural light*, H4A V, 1, 17. *blest pray you be, that after this strange starting from your —s you may reign in them now*, Cymb. V, 5, 371. *in our —s we'll live so round and safe*, Per. I, 2, 122.

4) a celestial body: *not the smallest o. which thou beholdest but in his motion like an angel sings*, Merch. V, 60. *below thy sister's o.* (the moon) *infect the air*, Tim. IV, 3, 2. *by all the operation of the —s*, Lr. I, 1, 113. *the fiery —s above*, Cymb. I, 6, 35.

5) the earth (German: *Erdkreis*): *foolery does walk about the o. like the sun,* Tw. III, 1, 43. *his fame folds in this o. o' the earth,* Cor. V, 6, 127. *the o. below as hush as death,* Hml. II, 2, 507. *when he meant to quail and shake the o.* Ant. V, 2, 85.

**Orbed,** circular, round: *their poor balls are tied to the o. earth,* Compl. 25. *that o. continent* (the sun) Tw. V, 278. *Tellus' o. ground,* Hml. III, 2, 166.

**Orchard,** a garden: Compl. 171. Ado I, 2, 10. II, 3, 4. III, 1, 5. III, 3, 161. V, 1, 244. As I, 1, 44. Shr. II, 112. Tw. III, 2, 8. III, 4, 194. 244. John V, 7, 10. H4B I, 1, 4. V, 3, 1. Troil. III, 2, 17. Rom. II, 1, 5. II, 2, 63. Caes. III, 2, 253. Hml. I, 5, 35.

**Ordain,** 1) to decree: *devise, o., impose some gentle order,* John III, 1, 250. Particularly used of the decrees of fate: *fate —ing he should be a cuckold,* Wiv. III, 5, 106. *a holy maid, —ed to raise this siege,* H6A I, 2, 53. *wast thou —ed to die in ruffian battle?* H6B V, 2, 45. *for this* (to kill thee) *was I —ed,* H6C V, 6, 58. *this shoulder was —ed so thick to heave,* V, 7, 23.

2) to institute, to establish, to found: *the cause why music was —ed,* Shr. III, 1, 10. *when first this order* (of the garter) *was —ed,* H6A IV, 1, 33. *Mulmutius —ed our laws,* Cymb. III, 1, 56.

3) to appoint, to prepare: *the feast is ready, which the careful Titus hath —ed to an honourable end,* Tit. V, 3, 22. *all things that we —ed festival, turn from their office to black funeral,* Rom. IV, 5, 84.

4) to set apart for an office, to appoint: *being —ed his special governor,* H6A I, 1, 171.

**Order,** subst. 1) regular disposition, proper state, settled mode of being or proceeding: *yourselves in o. set,* Wiv. V, 5, 81. *she is fast my wife, save that we do the denunciation lack of outward o.* Meas. I, 2, 153. *can you nominate in o. now the degrees of the lie?* As V, 4, 92. *to learn the o. of my fingering,* Shr. III, 1, 65 (= method). *every thing in o.* IV, 1, 53. *confine yourself within the limits of o.* Tw. I, 3, 9. *ere ancient'st o. was,* Wint. IV, 1, 10. *all form is formless, o. orderless,* John III, 1, 253. *such temperate o. in so fierce a cause,* III, 4, 12. *I live out of all o.* H4A III, 3, 22. *let o. die,* H4B I, 1, 154. *teach the act of o. to a peopled kingdom,* H5 I, 2, 189. *if any o. might be thought upon,* IV, 5, 21. *things are set in o.* H6A II, 2, 32. *they are all in o.* H6B IV, 2, 198. *but then are we in o. when we are most out of o.* 199. 200. *let's set our men in o.* H6C I, 2, 70. *o. gave each thing view,* H8 I, 1, 44. *in all line of o.* Troil. I, 3, 88. *stand not upon the o. of your going,* Mcb. III, 4, 119. *great command o'ersways the o.* Hml. V, 1, 251. *reproof, obedient and in o.* Per. I, 2, 42. *by o. of law* = legally, legitimately: *allowed by o. of law a furred gown,* Meas. III, 2, 8. *I have a son by o. of law,* Lr. I, 1, 19. Plur.: *there are pretty —s beginning: it is but heading and hanging,* Meas. II, 1, 249.

2) arrangement, determination made or to be made: *to whom the o. of the siege is given,* H5 III, 2, 70. *divided by any voice or o. of the field,* Troil. IV, 5, 70 (conditions to be settled concerning the combat). *consent upon the o. of their fight,* 90. *according to our o.* Mcb. V, 6, 6 (our plan of battle). *see high o. in this great solemnity,* Ant. V, 2, 369 (take care that it be arranged in a dignified manner). Hence even = stipulation, condition: *send fair-play —s and make compromise,* John V, 1, 67. *that, having our fair o. written down, both they and we, perusing o'er these*

notes, may know ..., V, 2, 4. *shall we divide our right according to our threefold o. ta'en?* H4A III, 1, 71 (= indentures tripartite in v. 80).

*To take o.* = to make the necessary dispositions, to take measures: *now will we take some o. in the town,* H6A III, 2, 126. Followed by *for: if your worship will take o. for the drabs and the knaves,* Meas. II, 1, 246. *to take o. for the wrongs that here and there his fury had committed,* Err. V, 146. *there is o. ta'en for you,* R2 V, 1, 53. *ere you can take due —s for a priest,* H6B III, 1, 274. *whiles I take o. for mine own affairs,* 320. *until the duke take o. for his burial,* R3 I, 4, 288 (Ff *give o.*). *I will take o. for her keeping close,* IV, 2, 53. *honest Iago hath ta'en o. for it,* Oth. V, 2, 72. By an inf.: *to take some privy o. to draw the brats of Clarence out of sight,* R3 III, 5, 106. By a dependent sentence: *therefore this o. hath Baptista ta'en, that none shall have access unto Bianca,* Shr. I, 2, 126. *I'll o. take my mother shall not hear,* All's IV, 2, 55. *I will take such o. that thy friends shall ring for thee,* H4B III, 2, 198. *some one take o. Buckingham be brought to Salisbury,* R3 IV, 4, 539.

3) the way and manner in which a thing has come or is coming to pass; course, process: *the manner and true o. of the fight this packet contains,* H4B IV, 4, 100. *until they hear the o. of his death,* H6B III, 2, 129. *will you go see the o. of the course?* Caes. I, 2, 25. *speak in the o. of his funeral,* III, 1, 230.

4) direction, mandate, command: *hadst thou not o.?* Meas. II, 2, 8. *there shall be o. for it,* Meas. II, 2, 25 (or = arrangement?). *that should by private o. else have died,* V, 471. *impose some gentle o.* John III, 1, 251. *thou shalt receive money and o. for their furniture,* H4A III, 3, 226. *the o. was reversed,* R3 II, 1, 86. *achievements, plots, —s, preventions,* Troil. I, 3, 181. *Cicero is dead, and by that o. of proscription,* Caes. IV, 3, 180. *they have already o. this night to play before him,* Hml. III, 1, 20. *to give o.* = a) to direct, to command: *give o. to my servants that ...,* Merch. V, 119. *Grumio gave o. how it should be done,* Shr. IV, 3, 118. 119. *the shrill whistle which doth o. give to sounds confused,* H5 III Chor. 9. *to give o. that no manner of person have recourse unto the princes,* R3 III, 5, 108 (Qq *notice*). *yours we have given o. to be next our own,* Per. II, 3, 111. b) to give directions, to prescribe the arrangement of a thing; usually with *for: I have given o. for our horses,* All's II, 5, 27. *give o. for my funeral,* H6A II, 5, 112. *until the duke give o. for his burial,* R3 I, 4, 288 (Qq *take o.*). *there's o. given for her coronation,* H8 III, 2, 46. *o. for sea is given,* Ant. IV, 10, 6. *give o. that these bodies high on a stage be placed to the view,* Hml. V, 2, 388.

5) a fraternity of religious persons or of knights: Wiv. V, 5, 65. Meas. I, 3, 44. II, 3, 3. III, 2, 232. IV, 2, 180. IV, 3, 152. Err. V, 107. Mids. II, 1, 123. Shr. IV, 1, 148. H6A IV, 1, 33. 41. IV, 7, 68. H8 IV, 1, 26. Rom. III, 3, 114. V, 2, 6.

**Order,** vb. to arrange, to regulate, to dispose: *strikes each in each by mutual —ing,* Sonn. 8, 10. *the direful spectacle of the wreck I have so safely —ed,* Tp. I, 2, 29. *'tis vile, unless it may be quaintly —ed,* Merch. II, 4, 6. *the —ing on't is ours,* Wint. II, 1, 159. *if thou hast the —ing of the mind too,* II, 3, 106. *for the —ing your affairs,* IV, 4, 139. *have thou the —ing of this present time,* John V, 1, 77. *o. the trial, mar-*

*shal*, R2 I, 3, 99. *how to o. these affairs*, II, 2, 109. *to o. peace between them*, H5 V Chor. 39. *thus my battle shall be —ed*, R3 V, 3, 292. *all this was —ed by the good discretion of the cardinal*, H8 I, 1, 50. *to o. well the state*, Tit. V, 3, 203. *within my tent his bones to-night shall lie, most like a soldier, —ed honourably*, Caes. V, 5, 79. *bear his courses to be —ed by Lady Fortune*, Per. IV, 4, 47. Peculiar passages: *help to o. several powers to Oxford*, R2 V, 3, 140 (i. e. to superintend and regulate their conveyance there). *our countrymen are men more —ed than when Julius Caesar smiled at their lack of skill*, Cymb. II, 4, 21 (better regulated and disciplined).

**Orderless,** disorderly, out of rule: John III, 1, 253.

**Orderly,** adj. such as a thing ought to be, according to rule, proper: *gave such o. and well-behaved reproof to all uncomeliness*, Wiv. II, 1, 59. *frame yourself to o. solicits*, Cymb. II, 3, 52.

**Orderly,** adv. according to rule, properly, duly: *how do you bear with me? Marry, sir, the letter, very o.* Gent. I, 1, 130. *these things being bought and o. bestowed*, Merch. II, 2, 179. *you are too blunt: go to it o.* Shr. II, 45. *you bid me make it o. and well, according to the fashion and the time*, IV, 3, 94. *and o. proceed to swear him*, Rich. I, 3, 9. *but o. to end where I begun*, Hml. III, 2, 220.

**Ordinance,** 1) established rule or custom, observance: *by custom and the o. of times*, H5 II, 4, 83. *why all these things change from their o. their natures*, Caes. I, 3, 66.

2) divine dispensation: *by God's just o.* R3 IV, 4, 183. V, 5, 31. *the superfluous and lust-dieted man, that slaves your o.* Lr. IV, 1, 71. *let o. come as the gods foresay it*, Cymb. IV, 2, 145.

3) order, rank: *when one but of my o. stood up*, Cor. III, 2, 12.

3) ordnance, cannon: John II, 218. H5 II, 4, 126.

**Ordinant,** ordaining, swaying: *even in that was heaven o.* Hml. V, 2, 48 (Ff *ordinate*).

**Ordinary,** adj. 1) usual, habitual, frequent: *these fits are with his highness very o.* H4B IV, 4, 115. *the lunacy is so o. that the whippers are in love too*, As III, 2, 423.

2) common, inferior: *I have no more wit than an o. man has*, Tw. I, 3, 90. *I saw him put down with an o. fool*, I, 5, 91. *my heart hath melted at a lady's tears, being an o. inundation*, John V, 2, 48. H8 V, 1, 174. Caes. I, 1, 78. I, 2, 73. III, 1, 37. Lr. I, 4, 36.

**Ordinary,** subst. 1) the mass; all that is common and insignificant: *I see no more in you than in the o. of nature's sale-work*, As III, 5, 42.

2) a meal, repast: *I did think thee, for two —es, to be a pretty wise fellow*, All's II, 3, 211. *goes to the feast, and for his o. pays his heart for what his eyes eat only*, Ant. II, 2, 230.

**Ordinate,** ordaining, swaying: *even in that was heaven o.* Hml. V, 2, 48 (Qq and M. Edd. *ordinant*).

**Ordnance** (cf. *Ordinance*) cannon: Shr. I, 2, 204. H5 III Chor. 26. H6A I, 4, 15. Hml. V, 2, 281.

**Ordure,** dung, filth: H5 II, 4, 39.

**Ore,** a vein of gold: *when beauty boasted blushes, in despite virtue would stain that o. with silver white*, Lucr. 56 (M. Edd. *o'er*).* *to what metal this counterfeit lump of o. will be melted*, All's III, 6, 40 (O. Edd. *ours*). *like some o. among a mineral of metals base*, Hml. IV, 1, 25.

**Organ,** 1) natural instrument: Wiv. V, 5, 55.

Ado IV, 1, 228. Merch. III, 1, 62. Tw. I, 4, 33. H5 IV, 1, 21. Troil. V, 2, 123. Hml. II, 2, 623. Lr. I, 4, 301. Ant. II, 7, 49.

2) any instrument: *and given his deputation all the —s of our own power*, Meas. I, 1, 21. *his powerful sound within an o. weak*, All's II, 1, 179. *there is much music in this little o.* Hml. III, 2, 385. *that I might be the o.* IV, 7, 71.

**Organ-pipe,** wind-pipe, throat (cf. *organ* in Tw. I, 4, 33): *this pale faint swan, who chants a doleful hymn to his own death, and from the o. of frailty sings his soul and body to their lasting rest*, John V, 7, 23. Hence = voice: *methought the billows spoke and told me of it; the winds did sing it to me, and the thunder, that deep and dreadful o., pronounced the name of Prosper*, Tp. III, 3, 98 (apparently not the pipe of a musical organ, which would have been unable to pronounce a name).

**Orgillous** (M. Edd. *orgulous*) proud, haughty: Troil. Prol. 2.

**Orient,** subst. the east: Sonn. 7, 1. H4B Ind. 3.

**Orient,** adj. bright, shining: *an o. drop* (a tear) Ven. 981. *bright o. pearl*, Pilgr. 133. Mids. IV, 1, 59. R3 IV, 4, 322. Ant. I, 5, 41.

**Orifex** (the later Ff *orifice*) opening, aperture: *and yet the spacious breadth of this division admits no o. for a point as subtle as Ariachne's broken woof to enter*, Troil. V, 2, 151.

**Origin,** first beginning, source of existence: Compl. 222. Hml. I, 4, 26. III, 1, 185. Lr. IV, 2, 32.

**Original,** subst. origin: *we are their parents and o.* Mids. II, 1, 117. *it hath its o. from much grief*, H4B I, 2, 131.

**Orisons,** prayers: H5 II, 2, 53. H6C I, 4, 110. Rom. IV, 3, 3. Hml. III, 1, 89. Cymb. I, 3, 32.

**Orlando,** name in As I, 1, 131 etc.

**Orleans** (O. Edd. *Orleance*; dissyll. and trisyll.) French town: H6A I, 1, 60. 111. 157. I, 2, 6. 125. 148. I, 4, 1. 59. I, 5, 14. 36. I, 6, 9. II, 2, 15. III, 3, 69. Cymb. I, 4, 36. *the Duke of O.* H5 II, 4, 5. III, 5, 41. III, 7, 7. IV, 2, 6. IV, 8, 81. H6B I, 1, 7. II8 II, 4, 174. *the Bastard of O.* H6A I, 1, 93. I, 2, 47. *O. the Bastard*, IV, 4, 26. *Bastard O.* IV, 6, 14. 42.

**Ornament,** subst. that which embellishes and adorns, decoration: Lucr. 322. Sonn. 1, 9. 21, 3. 54, 2. 68, 10. 70, 3. 142, 6. Compl. 115. Gent. II, 1, 4. Ado III, 2, 46. LLL II, 79. Merch. III, 2, 74. 80. 97. Shr. IV, 3, 61. Tw. III, 4, 417. Wint. I, 2, 158. H4A III, 1, 125. H6A IV, 1, 29. V, 1, 54. H6C III, 2, 149. R3 III, 7, 99. H8 III, 2, 126. Tit. I, 52. II, 4, 18. Rom. I, 1, 100. II, 6, 31.*III, 3, 130. IV, 2, 34. Mcb. I, 7, 42. Per. V, 3, 73.

**Orodes,** king of Parthia: Ant. III, 1, 4.

**Orphan,** subst. a child bereft of parents: Lucr. 905. Sonn. 97, 10.*H5 II, 4, 106. H6B V, 1, 187. H6C V, 6, 40. 42. R3 II, 2, 6. 78. H8 III, 2, 399. Mcb. IV, 3, 5. Cymb. V, 4, 40.

**Orphan,** adj. bereft of parents: *you o. heirs of fixed destiny*, Wiv. V, 5, 43 (i. e. the fairies).

**Orpheus,** the fabulous poet and musician: Lucr. 553. Gent. III, 2, 78. Merch. V, 80. H8 III, 1, 3. Alluded to, though not named: Tit. II, 4, 51.

**Orsino,** name in Tw. I, 2, 27. I, 5, 109 etc.

**Ort,** leaving, remnant, refuse: *a beggar's —s to crave*, Lucr. 985. *the fractions of her faith, —s of her* *love*, Troil. V, 2, 158. *where should he have this gold? it is some poor fragment, some slender o. of his remainder*, Tim. IV, 3, 400.

**Orthography,** correct spelling and speaking: *he was wont to speak plain and to the purpose, like an honest man and a soldier: and now is he turned o.; his words are a very fantastical banquet, just so many strange dishes*, Ado II, 3, 21 (abstr. pro concr. Some M. Edd. *orthographer*, others *orthographist*. cf. *sonnet* in LLL I, 2, 190). *such rackers of o., as to speak dout, sine B, when he should say doubt*, LLL V, 1, 22.

**Osier,** the water-willow: Pilgr. 60. 75. LLL IV, 2, 112. As IV, 3, 80. Rom. II, 3, 7.

**Osprey** (O. Edd. *aspray*), the fish-hawk, Pandion haliaetus, supposed to have the power of fascinating the fish: Cor. IV, 7, 34.

**Osrick,** name in Hml. V, 2, 204. 270. 317.

**Ossa,** mountain in Thessaly: Hml. V, 1, 306.

**Ostent,** external show: *well studied in a sad o.* Merch. II, 2, 205. *such fair —s of love*, II, 8, 44. *giving full trophy, signal and o. quite from himself to God*, H5 V Chor. 21 (all external signs of honour. cf. *ostentation* in Hml. IV, 5, 215). In Per. I, 2, 25 O. Edd. *the stint of war*, M. Edd. *the o. of war*.

**Ostentation,** 1) external show, display: *maintain a mourning o.* Ado IV, 1, 207. *all o. of sorrow*, H4B II, 2, 54. *make good this o., and you shall divide in all with us*, Cor. I, 6, 86. *no noble rite nor formal o.* Hml. IV, 5, 215 (cf. *ostent* in H5 V Chor. 21). *prevented the o. of our love*, Ant. III, 6, 52.

2) open show, exhibition: *frighting her villages with war and o. of despised arms*, R2 II, 3, 95.

3) spectacle: *present the princess with some delightful o., or show, or pageant, or antique, or firework*, LLL V, 1, 118 (Armado's speech).

4) ambitious display, boastful vanity: *these summer-flies have blown me full of maggot o.* LLL V, 2, 409.

**Ostler,** the person who has the care of horses at an inn: H4A II, 1, 4. 12 (Ff *Robin the o.*, Qq *Robin O.*). 24. 105. II, 2, 45. IV, 2, 31. Cor. III, 3, 32 (O. Edd. *hostler*).

**Ostridge** or **Ostrich,** the bird Struthio camelus: *eat iron like an o.* H6B IV, 10, 31.

**Oswald,** name in Lr. I, 4, 336. 350. 356.

**Ote-cake,** see *Oatcake.*

**Othello,** name in Oth. I, 3, 48 etc.

**Other** (*t' other* or *tother* for *the other*: H4B II, 4, 92. H6B I, 3, 87. Cor. I, 1, 246. In Hml. II, 1, 56 Ff *tother*, Qq *th' other*; in Lr III, 7, 71 and Oth. IV, 1, 137 Qq *tother*, Ff *the other*. cf. *The*), 1) the second of two: *under her o.* (arm) *was the tender boy*, Ven. 32. 352. 990. *thy o. mouth*, Tp. II, 2, 98. *the one so like the o.* Err. I, 1, 52. *one of these men is Genius to the o.* V, 332. *my o. self*, R3 II, 2, 151. *to take the one the o.* Cor. IV, 4, 20. *each wreathed in the —'s arms*, Tit. II, 3, 25. *thou o. gold-bound brow*, Mcb. IV, 1, 114. *throw between them all the food thou hast, they'll grind the o.* Ant. III, 5, 16 (= each of them will grind the o. Most M. Edd. *the one the o.*). Cor. I, 1, 246. Lr. III, 7, 71 etc. etc. The article omitted: *each day still better —'s happiness*, R2 I, 1, 22 (or: —*s' ?*). *both one and o. he denies me now*, Err. IV, 3, 86. *every letter he hath writ hath disvouched o.* Meas. IV, 4, 2 (= the others). *on one and o. side*, Troil. Prol. 21. *tilting one at —'s breast*, Oth. II, 3, 183. *every time gentler than o.* Caes. I, 2, 230. Particularly

after *each: that which each to o. hath' so strongly sworn*, LLL I, 1, 309. *wink each at o.* Mids. III, 2, 239. *gazed each on o.* R3 III, 7, 26. *men of heart looked wondering each at o.* Cor. V, 6, 100 (O. Edd. *others*). *make each to prescribe to o. as each —'s leech*, Tim. V, 4, 84. *her love to both would each to o. and all loves to both draw after her*, Ant. II, 2, 138 (cf. *Each*).

2) one except or besides that or those mentioned or understood: *his o. agents aim at like delight*, Ven. 400. *the o. four*, 446. *all o. eyes*, 952. *by any o. house or person*, Tp. I, 2, 42. *o. princess'*, 173. *there's o. business for thee*, 315. 367. *one thing or o.* 355. *there is no o. shelter*, II, 2, 40. *th' o. two*, III, 2, 7. *taught thee one thing or o.* I, 2, 355. *o. men put forth their sons*, Gent. I, 3, 6. *by some device or o.* Err. I, 2, 95. *some gentleman or o.* Ado I, 1, 135. *some man or o. must present wall*, Mids. III, 1, 69. *with some delight or o.* Merch. II, 8, 53. *some indirect means or o.* As I, 1, 159. *three parts disbursed I duly, …. the o. part reserved I*, R2 I, 1, 128. *and such o. gambol faculties 'a has*, H4B II, 4, 272. *one time or o.* IV, 3, 32. *ransoming him, or pitying, threatening the o.* Cor. I, 6, 36 (= another). *so much for this: now shall you see the o.* Hml. V, 2, 1 (= the rest). *one gross crime or o.* Lr. I, 3, 4. *and o. of his conquered kingdoms*, Ant.. III, 6, 36. *let's have one o. gaudy night*, III, 13, 183 (= one more) etc. *the o. day* = lately: Wiv. I, 1, 294. Ado V, 1, 161. Tw. I, 5, 91. H4A I, 2, 95. H4B II, 4, 92. V, 1, 26. H6B I, 3, 87. 202. Troil. I, 2, 100. Tim. I, 2, 217. Hml. II, 1, 56. Oth. IV, 1, 137. *this o. day*, in the same sense: All's IV, 3, 226. Wint. V, 2, 140. H4A III, 3, 152. Tim. III, 6, 3. 47. Lr. I, 2, 153. *the o. night:* H4A III, 3, 112. Before the possessive pronoun: *a thousand o. her defences*, Wiv. II, 2, 259. *with Poins and o. his continual followers*, H4B IV, 4, 53. *of o. your new pranks*, Lr. I, 4, 259. Substantively: *some o.* = somebody else: *knew of it by some o.* Ado II, 3, 161. *I will some o. be, some Florentine*, Shr. I, 1, 209. cf. *some say he is with the Emperor of Russia, o. some, he is in Rome*, Meas. III, 2, 94. *how happy some o'er o. some can be*, Mids. I, 1, 226. Plur. —*s:* Ven. 691. 843. Sonn. 142, 8. Err. II, 1, 111. John IV, 2, 164 (—*s more*) etc. Plural o. for —*s: may lend thee light, as thou dost lend to o.* Ven. 864. *some would sing, some o. in their bills would bring him mulberries*, 1102. *as I all o. in all worths surmount*, Sonn. 62, 8. *every letter has disvouched o.* Meas. IV, 4, 2. *there's o. of our friends will greet us here*, IV, 5, 12. *some o. give me thanks for kindnesses*, Err. IV, 3, 5. *suggestions are to o. as to me*, LLL I, 1, 159 (Ff Q2 —*s*). *awaking when the o. do*, Mids. IV, 1, 71. *and o. of such vinegar aspect*, Merch. I, 1, 54. *and her withholds from me and o. more*, Shr. I, 2, 121. *this matched with o.* H4A I, 1, 49. *and then come in the o.* II, 4, 202. *and o. of your highness' privy council*, H6B II, 1, 176. *many o. of noble fame*, R3 IV, 5, 13 (Qq *moe*). *sphered amidst the o.* Troil. I, 3, 91. *call Claudius and some o. of my men*, Caes. IV, 3, 242. *I myself have all the o.* Mcb. I, 3, 14. *o. of your insolent retinue do hourly carp*, Lr. I, 4, 221. *o. of them may have crooked noses*, Cymb. III, 1, 37. *civility not seen from o.* IV, 2, 179.

3) different: *thy heart in o. place*, Sonn. 93, 4. *I am for o. than for dancing measures*, As V, 4, 199. *o. gold, less fine in carat, is more precious*, H4B IV, 5,

162 etc. Remarkable passages: *they can be meek that have no o. cause*, Err. II, 1, 33. *free from o. misbegotten hate*, R2 I, 1, 33 (i. e. hate of a different nature and misbegotten). *all these are portable, with o. graces weighed*, Mcb. IV, 3, 90 (i. e. with other things, that are graces). *to preserve this vessel for my lord from any o. foul unlawful touch*, Oth. IV, 2, 84 (Qq *hated*). Mcb. I, 7, 28.*

Adverbially, = otherwise (German *anders*), and *no o.* = not otherwise: *were she o. than she is*, Ado I, 1, 176. *nor met with fortune o. than at feasts*, John V, 2, 58. *any that calls me o. than Lord Mortimer*, H6B IV, 6, 6. *he had a black mouth that said o. of him*, H8 I, 3, 58. *before you find it o.* Cor. IV, 6, 102. *who dares receive it o.* Mcb. I, 7, 77. *if you think o.* Oth. IV, 2, 13. *who can be o.* (than merry) *in this royal presence?* Per. II, 3, 49. *it is no o.* Meas. IV, 3, 122. *I believe no o.* V, 60. *being no o. but as she is*, Ado I, 1, 177. *can't no o., but, I your daughter, he must be my brother?* All's I, 3, 171. *he hopes it is no o.* Troil. II, 3, 119. *'tis no o.* Mcb. III, 4, 97. *I think it be no o. but e'en so*, Hml. I, 1, 108. *if 'twere no o.* Oth. IV, 2, 168. — Substantively, *o.* = any thing else, *no o.* = nothing else: *do the wise think them o.?* LLL III, 81. *he shall suppose no o. but that he is carried...*, All's III, 6, 27. *the duke knows him for no o. but a poor officer of mine*, IV, 3, 225. *if you say I am any o. than an honest man*, H4B I, 2, 98. *we hope no o. from your majesty*, V, 2, 62. *not to be o. than one thing*, Cor. IV, 7, 42. *we learn no o. but the confident tyrant keeps still in Dunsinane*, Mcb. V, 4, 8.

**Othergates,** in another manner: Tw. V, 198 (Sir Andrew's speech).

**Otherwhere,** in or to another place: Err. II, 1, 30. 104. H8 II, 2, 60. Rom. I, 1, 204.

**Otherwhiles,** at other times, sometimes: *o. the famished English faintly besiege us*, H6A I, 2, 7.

**Otherwise,** 1) in another manner besides that mentioned: *you were kneeled to and importuned o.* Tp. II, 1, 128. *my maiden's name seared o.* All's II, 1, 176.

2) in a different manner: *thou art a beast to say o.* H4A III, 3, 140. *we do no o. than we are willed*, H6A I, 3, 10. *and o. will Henry ne'er presume*, V, 5, 22. Cor. II, 2, 36. Caes. IV, 3, 251. Cymb. IV, 2, 364. Per. I, 1, 115. II, 5, 63. Used = not so, to supply a preceding adjective or another predicate: *I never knew him o.* Gent. II, 5, 45. *if she be o.* (than honest) Wiv. II, 1, 247. *God forbid it should be o.* Ado I, 1, 222. *seemed I ever o. to you?* IV, 1, 56. *you'll find it o.* Tw. III, 4, 251. H5 V, 1, 82. *if it prove she's o.* Wint. II, 1, 134. *it is o.* R2 II, 2, 29. *I would it were o.* H4B I, 2, 161. V, 2, 32. Troil. II, 3, 4. *when it proved o.* Hml. II, 2, 155. *if this be o.* 156. *I do beguile the thing I am, by seeming o.* Oth. II, 1, 124. *you not making it appear o.* Cymb. I, 4, 174.

3) but for this, without this, else: *I have sat in the stocks for puddings he hath stolen, o. he had been executed*, Gent. IV, 4, 34. *three of Master Ford's brothers watch the door,.... o. you might slip away*, Wiv. IV, 2, 54. 72. Ado III, 4, 37. Shr. Ind. I, 138. All's V, 3, 146. H6A I, 2, 97. Troil. II, 1, 140.

**Otter,** the animal Lutra: H4A III, 3, 142.

**Ottoman,** adj. or subst.? Turk or Turkish: *the general enemy O.* Oth. I, 3, 49.

**Ottomite,** Turk: Oth. I, 3, 33. 235. II, 3, 171.

**Ouches,** ornaments, jewels: *your brooches, pearls, and o.* (scrap of a song) H4B II, 4, 53.

**Ought,** pron. see *Aught.*

**Ought,** vb. 1) owed: *you o. him a thousand pound*, H4A III, 3, 152 (Mrs Quickly's speech).

2) to be bound in duty; should necessarily; followed by an inf. with *to:* Wiv. I, 1, 103. Meas. II, 1, 56. Ado II, 3, 202. III, 3, 87. Mids. III, 1, 30. 34. As II, 4, 7. Tw. V, 303. R2 V, 3, 110. H5 III, 2, 139. III, 6, 58. H6A IV, 1, 28. H6B IV, 7, 54. H6C IV, 7, 44. R3 II, 2, 131. Cor. II, 3, 2. Caes. II, 1, 270. Lr. V, 3, 324. *I o. so* (viz to answer) Cor. III, 3, 62. Inf. without *to: you o. not walk without the sign of your profession*, Caes. I, 1, 3.

**Ounce,** the animal Felis uncia: Mids. II, 2, 30.

**Ounce,** the sixteenth part of a pound: LLL III, 136. Tw. IV, 1, 47. Wint. IV, 4, 725. Troil. II, 2, 28. Cor. III, 1, 301. Lr. IV, 6, 132.

**Ouphes,** elves, goblins: *like urchins, o. and fairies*, Wiv. IV, 4, 49. *strow good luck, o., on every sacred room*, V, 5, 61.

**Our,** pertaining to us: Ven. 124. Tp. I, 1, 14. 29. 34. 35. 40. 56. 58. 59 etc. etc. *hence shall we see what our seemers be*, Meas. I, 3, 54. *the toe of the peasant comes so near the heel of our courtier*, Hml. V, 1, 153 (Qq *the courtier*). *at our more leisure*, Meas. I, 3, 49. *poor our sex*, Troil. V, 2, 109. = my, in the royal style: *our old and faithful friend, we are glad to see you*, Meas. V, 1, 2. *tongue-tied our queen*, Wint. I, 2, 27. *our very loving sister, well be-met*, Lr. V, 1, 20. *come, our queen*, Cymb. II, 3, 68. *by our* contracted to *by 'r (by'r lady):* Tp. III, 3, 1. Ado III, 3, 82. 89. III, 4, 82. R3 II, 3, 4 etc. (cf. *Lady*).

**Ours,** the absol. poss. pron. of the first pers. plur.: Lucr. 873. Meas. V, 428. Err. II, 1, 10. H4A IV, 3, 27. V, 4, 156. Cor. I, 4, 9. Cymb. I, 4, 70 etc. Without reference to a preceding substantive: *queen of us, of o., and our fair France*, Lr. I, 1, 260 (= our subjects). *whilst o. was blurted at and held a malkin*, Per. IV, 3, 34 (= our child). *of o.* = of us (cf. *His, Hers* etc.): *we are their offspring, and they none of o.* Lucr. 1757. *what says Lucentio to this shame of o.?* Shr. III, 2, 7. *this toil of o. should be a work of thine*, John II, 93. *the variation of each soil betwixt that Holmedon and this seat of o.* H4A I, 1, 65. *so much strength as will revenge these bitter woes of o.* Tit. III, 2, 3.

**Ourself** (two words in O. Edd.), = myself, in the regal style: Meas. I, 1, 44. H6A III, 1, 86. IV, 1, 169. H6B III, 1, 196. H6C II, 6, 104. Caes. III, 1, 8. Mcb. III, 1, 42. Hml. I, 2, 122 etc. Used by other persons in general maxims: *we cannot weigh our brother with o.* Meas. II, 2, 126. *learning is but an adjunct to o.* LLL IV, 3, 314.

**Ourselves,** 1) we or us in our own persons, not others: Gent. IV, 1, 76. Meas. II, 3, 32. Err. I, 1, 14. Shr. IV, 1, 177. H6A III, 1, 139 etc.

2) refl. pron. of the first pers. plur.: Tp. I, 1, 4. V, 212. Wiv. IV, 4, 63. Err. I, 1, 86. V, 292. II, 1, 37. LLL IV, 3, 316 etc.

3) Peculiar use: a) = ourself: *o. will hear the accuser and the accused*, R2 I, 1, 16. *we do abase o., to look so poorly and to speak so fair*, III, 3, 127 (Ff *ourself*). b) us mutually, each other: *we will then ... defy each other and pell-mell make work upon o.* John II, 407. *we two, that with so many thousand sighs did buy each other, must poorly sell o. with the rude bre-*

*vity and discharge of one*, Troil. IV, 4, 42. *as we walk, to our own selves bend we our needful talk*, 141. *to-morrow we'll hear o. again*, Mcb. III, 4, 32 (some M. Edd. *we'll hear, o., again*).

**Ousel**, the blackbird: Mids. III, 1, 128 (O. Edd. *woosel*). H4B III, 2, 9 (Qq *woosel*).

**Out**, adv. 1) without, on or to the outside, opposed to *in: from this fair throne to heave the owner out*, Lucr. 413. *till my bad angel fire my good one out*, Sonn. 144, 14. *made gape the pine and let thee out*, Tp. I, 2, 293. *scratched out your eyes*, Gent. IV, 4, 209. *search Windsor castle within and out*, Wiv. V, 5, 60 (*with* belonging to both *in* and *out*). *a lion that goes not out to prey*, Meas. I, 3, 23. *keepest me out from the house*, Err. III, 1, 42. *so turns she every man the wrong side out*, Ado III, 1, 68. *when the age is in, the wit is out*, III, 5, 37. *if my hand be out*, LLL IV, 1, 137 (quibbling). *keep him o.* All's I, 1, 125. *my shoulder-blade is out*, Wint. IV, 3, 77 (dislocated). *a' (the knave) will not out, he's true bred*, H4B V, 3, 71. *I would see his heart out*, H6A III, 1, 120. *his eye-balls further out than when he lived*, H6B III, 2, 169. *ye blaze to burn them out*, H6C V, 4, 71. *there were wit in this head, an' twould out*, Troil. III, 3, 256. *your wit will not so soon out*, Cor. II, 3, 30. *help me out from this hole*, Tit. II, 3, 209. *and bad'st me bury love. Not in a grave, to lay one in, another out to have*, Rom. II, 3, 84. *before I were forced out*, Tim. I, 2, 208. *stay thou out for earnest*, IV, 3, 47 (instead of being buried). *we must out and talk*, Caes. V, 1, 22 (step forth). *when the brains were out*, Mcb. III, 4, 79 (cf. *Knock*). *let in the maid, that out a maid never departed more*, Hml. IV, 5, 54 etc. Used of weapons, = drawn: *if I see a sword out*, Wiv. II, 3, 47. H4B II, 1, 17. Rom. I, 1, 39. Lr. II, 1, 40. IV, 6, 233 (cf. the indecent quibble in As IV, 1, 82—84). Applied to thoughts or actions, = uttered, disclosed, made public: *truth will out*, Merch. II, 2, 85. *your private grudge will out*, H6A IV, 1, 109. *rancour will out*, H6B I, 1, 142. *this will out*, R3 I, 4, 290. *and out they shall*, H8 III, 2, 304. *'twill out*, Oth. V, 2, 219 (cf. *Find, Seek, Single* etc.). Used imperatively without a verb: *out, out!* Wiv. IV, 2, 195. *out, sword!* Mids. V, 301. Cymb. IV, 1, 24. *out, tawny coats! out, scarlet hypocrite!* H6A I, 3, 56. *out, some light horse-men!* IV, 2, 43. *arm, arm, and out!* Mcb. V, 5, 46. Followed by *with: out with the dog!* Gent. IV, 4, 22. *out with it!* All's I, 1, 159. *out with it boldly*, R2 II, 1, 233. H8 III, 1, 39. *out with your knives*, Tim. IV, 1, 9 etc. (cf. *With*). Hence used as an interjection expressive of anger or abhorrence: *out, idle words!* Lucr. 1016. *out, out, Lucetta! that will be ill-favoured*, Gent. II, 7, 54. *out, dog! out, cur!* Mids. III, 2, 65. *out, tawny Tartar, out! out, loathed medicine, hated potion, hence!* 263. *out, fool!* As III, 2, 105. Shr. IV, 1, 150. Tw. II, 5, 82. IV, 2, 29. Wint. II, 3, 66. John II, 122. IV, 3, 87. H4A II, 2, 45. II, 3, 80. II, 4, 531. H4A V, 4, 10. R3 I, 3, 118. Troil. V, 1, 40. Rom. III, 5, 157. Hml. II, 2, 515. Lr. IV, 6, 249. Oth. V, 2, 77. Ant. I, 2, 40. With *on: out upon't! what have I forgot?* Wiv. I, 4, 179. *out upon you! how am I mistook in you!* III, 3, 110. *out on thy mistress!* Err. II, 1, 68. *out upon thee, kind!* III, 1, 77. *out on thee, villain!* IV, 4, 129. Ado IV, 1, 57. Merch. III, 1, 38. 125. All's V, 2, 51. Wint. IV, 3, 108. John I, 64. H4A I, 3, 208. R3 IV, 4, 509. H8 III, 1, 99.

Tit. III, 2, 54. Rom. II, 4, 120. III, 5, 169. Emphatically before *alack* and *alas: but out, alack! he was but one hour mine*, Sonn. 33, 11. *out, alas! here comes my master*, Wiv. I, 4, 37. *out, alas, sir! cozenage, mere cozenage*, IV, 5, 64. Wint. IV, 4, 110. H6C I, 4, 18. Rom. IV, 5, 24. *out, and alas!* Oth. V, 2, 119.

Followed by *of*, and thus receiving the force of a preposition; a) opposed to *in* or *into: out of our way!* Tp. I, 1, 29. *sucked my verdure out on't*, I, 2, 87. *extirpate me and mine out of the kingdom*, 126. *you would lift the moon out of her sphere*, II, 1, 183. *lead me out of my way*, II, 2, 7. *dropped out of the moon*, 141. *I'll turn my mercy out o' doors*, III, 2, 78. *I'll turn you out of my kingdom*, IV, 253. *guide us out of this fearful country*, V, 106. *will never out of my bones*, 283. *out of my door!* Wiv. IV, 2, 193. *he looks out of the window*, Shr. V, 1, 57. *his mother's milk were scarce out of him*, Tw. I, 5, 171. *sad tidings bring I to you out of France*, H6A I, 1, 58. *would have armour here out of the Tower*, I, 3, 67. *put out of office*, Tim. I, 2, 207 etc. *out of service*, Wiv. II, 1, 182. *time out of mind*, Meas. IV, 2, 17. *out of all eyes, tongues, minds and injuries*, Ado IV, 1, 245. *he would fight... out of his pavilion*, LLL V, 2, 660. *out of hearing? gone?* Mids. II, 2, 152. *were he out of Venice*, Merch. III, 1, 133. *not out of your apparel, and yet out of your suit*, As IV, 1, 88. *so I were out of prison*, John IV, 1, 17. *born out of your dominions*, H8 II, 4, 16. *never seek for aid out of himself*, I, 2, 114 (in others). *when did he regard the stamp of nobleness in any person o. of himself?* III, 2, 13. *what good sport is out of town to-day*, Troil. I, 1, 116. *there's livers out of Britain*, Cymb. III, 4, 143.

b) denoting distance, absence and separation: *I cannot live out of her company*, As I, 3, 88. *I cannot be out of the sight of Orlando*, IV, 1, 221. *buried in highways out of all sanctified limit*, All's I, 1, 152. *that question is out of my part*, Tw. I, 5, 191 (= not in). *that's out of my note*, Wint. IV, 3, 49. *would I were fairly out on't*, H8 V, 3, 109. Cor. I, 3, 28. *live out of the teeth of emulation*, Caes. II, 3, 14. *keep you out of the shot and danger of desire*, Hml. I, 3, 35. *Lord Hamlet is a prince, out of thy star*, Hml. II, 2, 141. Hence = beyond: *and out of all suspicion she is virtuous*, Ado II, 3, 166. *out of doubt*, Merch. I, 1, 21. Err. IV, 3, 82. *wonderful, out of all hooping*, As III, 2, 203. And = without, wanting: *I will never buy and sell out of this word*, LLL III, 143. *I am out of friends*, All's I, 3, 42. *his approach, so out of circumstance and sudden*, Wint. V, 1, 90. *to be out of the king's protection*, H8 III, 2, 344. *she should have been buried out o' Christian burial*, Hml. V, 1, 28. *I am now from home and out of that provision which shall be needful for your entertainment*, Lr. II, 4, 208. *arts inhibited and out of warrant*, Oth. I, 2, 79. *out of beef*, H5 III, 7, 163. *we were never so much out of creatures*, Per. IV, 2, 6. cf. the following phrases: *things out of hope*, Ven. 567. Tp. III, 3, 11. *I'm out of patience*, Tp. I, 1, 58. *out o' your wits and hearing too*, III, 2, 86. *out of all count*, Gent. II, 1, 62. *out of tune*, IV, 2, 60. *out of all nick*, 76. *out of love with thee*, IV, 4, 210. *these jests are out of season*, Err. I, 2, 68. *if I would think my heart out of thinking*, Ado III, 4, 85. *she would laugh me out of myself*, III, 1, 76. *out of heart*, LLL III, 45. *out of question*, IV, 1, 30. *fright the ladies out of their wits*, Mids. I, 2, 82. *out of breath,*

II, 2, 88. Cor. III, 1, 189. Rom. II, 5, 30. *be out of hope, of question, doubt*, III, 2, 279. *out of all reasonable match*, As III, 2, 87. *out of all cess*, H4A II, 1, 8. *I am out of fear of death*, IV, 1, 135. *I prattle out of fashion*, Oth. II, 1, 208. *I have wasted myself out of my means*, IV, 2, 188.

c) denoting the origin or source whence a thing or action proceeds: *thou speakest out of thy sleep*, Tp. II, 1, 212. *out of that 'no hope' what great hope have you!* 239. *but how out of this can she avail?* Meas. III, 1, 243. *and entreat, out of a new-sad soul*, LLL V, 2, 741. *my hounds are bred out of the Spartan kind*, Mids. IV, 1, 124. *out of this silence yet I picked a welcome*, V, 100. *it* (thy nose) *is a copy out of mine*, Wint. I, 2, 122; cf. *these eyes were moulded out of his*, John II, 100. *I learnt it out of women's faces*, Wint. II, 1, 12; *as fear may teach us out of late examples*, H5 II, 4, 12; *therefore this maxim out of love I teach*, Troil. I, 2, 318. *made himself much sport out of him*, All's IV, 5, 68; *I will devise matter enough out of this Shallow*, H4B V, 1, 87. *and speak out of my injury*, Tw. V, 319. *more is to be said and to be done than out of anger can be uttered*, H4A I, 1, 107 (in that angry disposition which would now suggest my words).* *what you have collected out of the Duke of Buckingham*, H8 I, 2, 131. *it is spoke freely out of many mouths*, Cor. IV, 6, 64. *out of thy long-experienced time give me some counsel*, Rom. IV, 1, 60. *out of your proof you speak*, Cymb. III, 3, 27. *I speak not out of weak surmises*, III, 4, 23. Hence = by means of: *wilt thou be made a man out of my vice?* Meas. III, 1, 138. *a barber shall never earn sixpence out of it*, H4B I, 2, 29. *abusing better men than they can be, out of a foreign wisdom*, H8 I, 3, 29. *found thee a way out of his wreck to rise in*, III, 2, 438. *thou hast forced me, out of thy honest truth, to play the woman*, 431. *he that will have a cake out of the wheat*, Troil. I, 1, 15. *nothing can be made out of nothing*, Lr. I, 4, 146. *even out of that will I cause these of Cyprus to mutiny*, Oth. II, 1, 281. *the wars must make examples out of their best*, III, 3, 66. *make yourself some comfort out of your best advice*, Cymb. I, 1, 156. *what your love will out of this advise you*, III, 2, 45. And = from, induced by, in consequence of: *he did believe he was indeed the duke, out o' the substitution* etc. Tp. I, 2, 103. *Gonzalo, out of his charity, did give us....*, 162. *which out of my neglect was never done*, Gent. V, 4, 89. *out of your favours vouchsafe*, LLL V, 2, 166. *out of my love to you, I came hither*, As I, 1, 137. *which his majesty, out of a self-gracious remembrance, did first propose*, All's IV, 5, 77. *out of my dear love I'll give thee more*, John II, 157. *out of your grace devise, ordain*, III, 1, 250. *I then, out of my grief and my impatience, answered neglectingly*, H4A I, 3, 51. *you speak it out of fear*, IV, 3, 7. *give their money out of hope they may believe*, H8 Prol. 8. *when the king once heard it, out of anger he sent command*, II, 1, 150. *have out of malice possessed him with a scruple*, 157. *been, out of fondness, superstitious to him*, III, 1, 131. *out of pity*, III, 2, 382. *your grace, out of the pain you suffered, gave no ear to it*, IV, 2, 8. *out of which frailty.... you have misdemeaned yourself*, V, 3, 12. *if we suffer, out of our easiness and childish pity,.... this sickness*, 25. *and out of his noble carelessness lets them plainly see*, Cor. II, 2, 16. *pride, which out of daily fortune ever taints the happy man*, IV, 7, 38. *Lucius, out of his free*

*love, hath presented to you...*, Tim. I, 2, 188. *I would not have your free and noble nature out of self-bounty be abused*, Oth. III, 3, 200.

Sometimes followed by the prepos. *at*, but only in a local sense, denoting a passage or outlet: *out at the postern*, Gent. V, 1, 9. *leans out at her mistress' window*, Ado III, 3, 156. IV, 1, 85. 311. Merch. II, 5, 41. As IV, 1 163. 164. 165. Shr. V, 1, 32. John V, 7, 29. *lest resolution drop out at mine eyes*, John IV, 1, 36. *see him out at gates*, Cor. III, 3, 138. 142. IV, 1, 47. *he goes out at the portal*, Hml. III, 4, 136.

2) abroad (in the Shakespearian sense of the word): *and seek preferment out*, Gent. I, 3, 7 (in foreign countries). *he hath been o. nine years*, Lr. I, 1, 33. *there ran a rumour of many worthy fellows that were out*, Mcb. IV, 3, 183 (= had taken the field). Hence = loudly, so as to be heard by others: *how I cried out then*, Tp. I, 2, 133 (cf. *Cry*). *volleys out his voice*, Ven. 921. *read out this*, Lr. V, 3, 109. *sound and be hanged, sound out*, Ant. II, 7, 140. cf. *ring out:* H6A I, 6, 11. IV, 2, 41. H8 II, 1, 32. Similarly: *shine out, fair sun*, R3 I, 2, 263 (do not suffer thy rays to be clouded, but let them fall everywhere; cf. *outshining* in I, 3, 268).

3) off, away: *out with it, and place it for her chief virtue*, Gent. III, 1, 339. 347. *O that that were out!* 375 (not written in the catalogue). *well, sit you out:* go home, Biron*, LLL I, 1, 110 (do not make one; stay away). *his own letter, the honourable board of council out, must fetch him in he papers*, H8 I, 1, 79 (= not consulted). *I am not so well as I should be, but I'll ne'er out*, Ant. II, 7, 36 (I will not stay behind, will not fail you). *but o., affection! all bond and privilege of nature break!* Cor. V, 3, 24. *out, damned spot!* Mcb. V, 1, 39. *when these* (tears) *are gone, the woman will be out*, Hml. IV, 7, 190. Joined to verbs, to indicate that something is made away with or eluded by the action: *tell him there is measure in every thing and so dance out the answer*, Ado II, 1, 75. *your grace hath sworn out house-keeping*, LLL II, 104 (= forsworn). *thinks with oaths to face the matter out*, Shr. II, 291. *sleeps out the afternoon*, All's V, 3, 66. cf. Lr. II, 2, 163. *and laughs it out*, Oth. IV, 1, 115. *dreading the curse that money may buy out*, John III, 1, 164.

4) at an end, or to the end; finished: *before the time be out*, Tp. I, 2, 246. *when the butt is out*, III, 2, 1. *on the catastrophe and heel of pastime, when it was out*, All's I, 2, 58. *their date is out*, H4A II, 4, 553. *the limit of your lives is out*, R3 III, 3, 8. *his spell in that is out*, H8 III, 2, 20. *my provision was out*, Tim. III, 6, 18. *do but blow them to their trial, the bubbles are out*, Hml. V, 2, 202. *our hour is fully out*, Ant. IV, 9, 33. Especially of fires and lights extinguished, and of eyes blinded: *the eye of heaven is out*, Lucr. 356. (mine eye) *seems seeing, but effectually is out*, Sonn. 113, 4. *till candles and starlight and moonshine be out*, Wiv. V, 5, 106. *his own* (eyes) *are out*, As IV, 1, 219. *my eyes are out with the fierce looks of these men*, John IV, 1, 73. *his fire is out*, H5 III, 6, 112. *your eyes, half out*, Troil. V, 10, 49. *their candles are all out*, Mcb. II, 1, 5. *out, out, brief candle*, V, 5, 23. *Gloster's eyes being out*, Lr. IV, 5, 9. *our lamp is spent, it's out*, Ant. IV, 15, 85. Joined to verbs: *their light blown out*, Ven. 826. *two lamps burnt out*, 1128. *burn out thy light*, Lucr. 190. *she burned out love as soon*

*us straw outburneth*, Pilgr. 98. *dashes the fire out*, Tp. I, 2, 5. *wear out thy youth with shapeless idleness*, Gent. I, 1, 8. *so you will sing it out*, I, 2, 89. *you that have worn your eyes almost out in the service*, Meas. I, 2, 113. *this will last out a night in Russia*, II, 1, 139. *rend apparel out*, Merch. II, 5, 5. *extreme gusts will blow out fire and all*, Shr. II, 1, 136. *I would repent out the remainder of nature*, All's IV, 3, 272. *we'll have this song out anon*, Wint. IV, 4, 315. *will weep my date of life out*, John IV, 3, 106. *play out the play*, H4A II, 4, 531. *as a candle, the better part burnt out*, H4B I, 2, 178. *we'll fight it out*, H6A I, 2, 128. *then out it goes* (the candle) H8 III, 2, 97. *your eyes weep out at Pandar's fall*, Troil. V, 10, 49. *night's candles are burnt out*, Rom. III, 5, 9. *drawing days out*, Caes. III, 1, 100. *burn out the sense and virtue of mine eye*, Hml. IV, 5, 155. *out went the candle*, Lr. I, 4, 237. *my snuff ... should burn out itself*, IV, 6, 40. *put out the light*, Oth. V, 2, 7. *he rides it out* (the tempest) Per. IV, 4, 31.

5) thoroughly, completely, fully: *thou wast not out three years old*, Tp. I, 2, 41. *and be a boy right out*, IV, 101. *the word is too good to paint out her wickedness*, Ado III, 2, 112; cf. *limning out a well-proportioned steed*, Ven. 290. *if thy qualities .... could speak thee out*, H8 II, 4, 140. *thou hast beat me out twelve several times*, Cor. IV, 5, 127.

6) Some peculiar significations: a) put beside one's part, having forgot what one has to say: *if he be out*, LLL V, 2, 152. 165. *they do not mark me, and that brings me out*, 172. *when they are out, they will spit*, As IV, 1, 76. *who could be out, being before his mistress?* 82. *I have forgot my part, and I am out*, Cor. V, 3, 41.

b) on the wrong scent, aiming or going a wrong way: *your hand is out*, LLL IV, 1, 135. *if I cannot recover your niece, I am a foul way out*, Tw. II, 3, 201. *these petty brands that calumny doth use, — O, I am out — that mercy does*, Wint. II, 1, 72. *bred out* = degenerated: H5 III, 5, 29. Tim. I, 1, 259.

c) at odds: *Launcelot and I are out*, Merch. III, 5, 34. *be not out with me*, Caes. I, 1, 18.

d) not in office: *who's in, who's out*, Lr. V, 3, 15. cf. Tim. I, 2, 208. cf. *to sit* and *to stand out.*

e) not in the hands of the owner: *they* (your possessions) *are out by lease*, Gent. V, 2, 29. *if I had a monopoly out, they would have part on't*, Lr. I, 4, 167 (granted, bestowed on me).

f) having torn clothes: *if you be out, I can mend you*, Caes. I, 1, 18. Followed by *at elbow* or *at heels*, by way of denoting very poor circumstances: *he's out at elbow*, Meas. II, 1, 61. *I am almost out at heels*, Wiv. I, 3, 34. *grow out at heels*, Lr. II, 2, 164.

**Out**, prepos. = out of: *those that bawl out the ruins of thy linen*, H4B II, 2, 27.* *when you have pushed out your gates the very defender of them*, Cor. V, 2, 41. In Tim. IV, 1, 38 *within and out that wall* is = within and without that wall; cf. Wiv. V, 5, 60.

Mostly preceded by *from*: *purchasing the semblance of my soul from out the state of hellish misery*, Merch. III, 4, 21. *to whip this dwarfish war from out the circle of his territories*, John V, 2, 136. R2 III, 3, 64. IV, 206. R3 I, 4, 186.

**Outbid**, to overpower by offering a higher price: *there is a good angel about him, but the devil —s him too*, H4B II, 4, 363.

**Outbrag**, to brag more than, to exceed in pride of beauty: *that termless skin whose bare —ed the web it seemed to wear*, Compl. 95.

**Outbrave**, 1) to surpass in beauty and worth: *if that flower with base infection meet, the basest weed —s his dignity*, Sonn. 94, 12.

2) to exceed in bravery: *I would o. the heart most daring on the earth*, Merch. II, 1, 28.

**Outbreak**, a bursting forth, eruption: *the flash and o. of a fiery mind*, Hml. II, 1, 33.

**Outbreathed**, adj. having spent one's breath, exhausted: *rendering faint quittance, wearied and o., to Harry Monmouth*, H4B I, 1, 108.

**Outburn**, to burn away, to be wholly consumed by fire: *as soon as straw —eth*, Pilgr. 98.

**Outcast**, a depraved wretch, one generally despised: *as Ovid be an o. quite abjured*, Shr. I, 1, 33. *o. of Naples*, H6B V, 1, 118. Adjectively: *I all alone beweep my o. state*, Sonn. 29, 2 (= my state of being an outcast).

**Outcrafty**, to be more crafty than, to overpower by cunning and guile: *that drug-damned Italy hath —ed him*, Cymb. III, 4, 15.

**Outcry**, loud cry: Lucr. 679. Rom. V, 3, 193. Plur. *—es:* Merch. II, 8, 4.

**Outdare**, 1) to exceed in daring bravery: *who sensibly —s his senseless sword*, Cor. I, 4, 53.

2) to brave, to defy: *or with pale beggar-fear impeach my height before this —d dastard?* R2 I, 1, 190. *and boldly did o. the dangers of the time*, H4A V, 1, 40.

**Outdo**, to surpass: *he hath outdone his former deeds*, Cor. II, 1, 150.

**Outdwell**, to stay beyond: *he —s his hour*, Merch. II, 6, 3.

**Outface**, 1) to brave, to put out of countenance, to bear down with looks: *with no face, as 'twere, —ing me*, Err. V, 244. *we have given thee faces. But you have —d them all*, LLL V, 2, 626. *we'll o. them and outswear them too*, Merch. IV, 2, 17. *o. the brow of bragging horror*, John V, 1, 49. *was at last —d by Bolingbroke*, R2 IV, 286. *see if thou canst o. me with thy looks*, H6B IV, 10, 49. *to o. me with leaping in her grave*, Hml. V, 1, 301. *o. the winds and persecutions of the sky*, Lr. II, 3, 11. With *from*, = to frighten away by looks: *—d you from your prize*, H4A II, 4, 283. Hence, without *from*, = to supplant, to put down by terror: *hast —d infant state and done a rape upon the maiden virtue of the crown*, John II, 97.

2) to face the matter out with looks, to gain one's point by a good appearance, to dissemble: *scambling, —ing, fashion-monging boys*, Ado V, 1, 94. With *it*: *cowards ... that do o. it with their semblances*, As I, 3, 124. Transitively, = to put a good face on, to seem blind to: *—ing faults in love with love's ill rest*, Pilgr. 8 (a verse remodelled by the poet in Sonn. 138, 8).

**Outfly**, to fly faster than, to escape by flying: *his evasion, winged thus swift with scorn, cannot o. our apprehensions*, Troil. II, 3, 124.

**Outfrown**, to frown down, to overbear by frowning: *o. false fortune's frown*, Lr. V, 3, 6.

**Outgo**, to go beyond, to leave behind: *so thou, thyself —ing in thy noon*, Sonn. 7, 13 (passing beyond thy highest pitch). *he would o. his father*, H8 I, 2, 207 (surpass). *he —es the very heart of kindness*, Tim. I, 1, 285. *the time shall not o. my thinking on you*, Ant. III, 2, 61 (life shall not last longer than my thinking of you). *the cutter outwent her* (nature) Cymb. II, 4, 84.

**Outgrow,** to surpass in growth, to grow taller than: R3 III, 1, 104.

**Out-herod,** to exceed in bombast and passionate grandiloquence: *it —s Herod,* Hml. III, 2, 15.

**Outjest,** to jest away, to make unfelt by jesting: *who labours to o. his heart-struck injuries,* Lr. III, 1, 16.

**Outlaw,** subst. 1) one excluded from the benefit and protection of the law, an exile: *a poor unminded o. sneaking home,* H4A IV, 3, 58.

2) a robber: H6A III, 1, 47. Cymb. IV, 2, 67. 138.

**Outlawed,** exiled, banished: *I had a son, now o. from my blood,* Lr. III, 4, 172.

**Outlawry,** the putting a man out of the protection of the law, proscription: *by proscription and bills of o.* Caes. IV, 3, 173.

**Outlive,** 1) to live longer than, to live beyond: Sonn. 38, 12. 55, 2. 101, 11. Merch. IV, 1, 269. H4A V, 2, 67. H4B II, 4, 284. H5 IV, 1, 194. IV, 3, 41. H6B I, 4, 34. R3 I, 3, 203. H8 IV, 2, 60. Troil. III, 2, 169. Tit. I, 167. Tim. IV, 3, 224. Caes. II, 1, 157. Hml. III, 2, 140. V, 1, 50. Oth. V, 2, 245. Ant. I, 2, 31. Per. V, 1, 15.

2) to live better, or to better purpose: *willing misery —s incertain pomp, is crowned before,* Tim. IV, 3, 243.

3) to remain in life, to survive: *let not this wasp o., us both to sting,* Tit. II, 3, 132.

**Outlook,** to look bigger than, to face down: *to o. conquest,* John V, 2, 115.

**Outlustre,** to excel in brightness: Cymb. I, 4, 79.

**Out-night,** to excel in mentioning memorable nights: Merch. V, 23.

**Out-paramour,** to exceed in the number of mistresses: Lr. III. 4, 94.

**Out-peer,** to surpass: Cymb. III, 6, 87.

**Out-pray,** to exceed in earnestness and efficiency of entreaty: *our prayers do o. his,* R2 V, 3, 109.

**Outprize,** to exceed in value: *— d by a trifle,* Cymb. I, 4, 88.

**Outrage,** subst. 1) rude violence, contempt shown to law and decency: Gent. V, 4, 17. R2 III, 2, 40. H6C V, 1, 24. Cor. V, 6, 125. Tit. IV, 2, 22. Rom. III, 1, 90. Tim. III, 5, 72. With *to: the rancorous o. of your duke to merchants,* Err. I, 1, 6. *to do such o.* Lucr. 605. Tit. V, 3, 52. *to do o. on:* Gent. IV, 1, 71. Lr. II, 4, 24. *to do o. to:* Err. IV, 4, 119. Ado II, 3, 159.

2) an outbreak of rage, fury: *I fear some o., and I'll follow her,* John III, 4, 106. *this immodest clamorous o.* H6A IV, 1. 126. *my charity is o.* R3 I, 3, 277. *preposterous and frantic o., end thy damned spleen,* II, 4, 64. *seal up the mouth of o. for a while,* Rom. V, 3, 216.

**Outrageous,** 1) violent, atrocious: Lucr. 607. Err. V, 139. Merch. II, 8, 13. H6A III, 1, 11. V, 4, 97. Hml. III, 1, 58. Oth. IV, 2, 139 (Ff *villanous*).

2) excessive, exorbitant: *when thy poor heart beats with o. beating,* Tit. III, 2, 13.

**Outride,** to ride faster than, to pass by riding: H4B I, 1, 36.

**Outright,** directly, without hesitation or uncertainty: *kill me o. with looks,* Sonn. 139, 14. *as the jest did glance away from me, 'tis ten to one it maimed you two o.* Shr. V, 2, 62. *the king is almost wounded*

*to the death, and in the fortune of my lord your son, Prince Harry slain o.* H4B I, 1, 16 (not only wounded). *this kills thy father's heart o.* H6A V, 4, 2. *then must I chide o.* H6B I, 2, 41.

**Outroar,** to roar louder than: Ant. III, 13, 127.

**Outrun,** to leave behind in running; sometimes to escape by running: Ven. 681. Lucr. 1668 (cf. *Sight-outrunning*). Gent. V, 3, 7. Wiv. I, 1, 92. All's IV, 3, 323. H5 IV, 1, 176. H6B V, 2, 73. H6C I, 2. 14. H8 I, 1, 141. Tim. II, 2, 93. Mcb. II, 3, 117. Oth. II, 3, 233.

**Outscold,** to exceed in scolding: John V, 2, 160.

**Outscorn,** to exceed in contempt: Lr. III, 1, 10.

**Outsell,** to exceed in value: *her pretty action did o. her gift, and yet enriched it too,* Cymb. II, 4, 102. *she, of all compounded, —s them all,* III, 5, 74.

**Out-shining,** shining in unclouded brightness: R3 I, 3, 268. cf. I, 2, 263.

**Outside,** 1) external part, surface: *the o. of his hand,* Wint. IV, 4, 834. *you look but on the o. of this work,* John V, 2, 109. 110. *make his wrongs his —s,* Tim. III, 5, 33 (not letting them enter the heart).

2) exterior, external appearance, person: Merch. I, 3, 103. II, 7, 68. As I, 3, 122. Tw. II, 2, 19. Wint. IV, 4, 646. H5 II, 4, 37. V, 2, 244. Tim. I, 1, 159. Lr. V, 3, 142. Per. II, 2, 50.

**Outsleep,** to sleep away: *we shall o. the coming morn,* Mids. V, 372.

**Outspeak,** to have a meaning beyond, to exceed: *it —s possession of a subject,* H8 III, 2, 127.

**Outsport,** to go beyond in sporting: *not to o. discretion,* Oth. II, 3, 3.

**Outstand,** to stay beyond: *I have outstood my time,* Cymb. I, 6, 207.

**Outstare,** to face down, to stare out of countenance: Merch. II, 1, 27 (Ff and later Qq *o'erstare*). H8 I, 1, 129. Ant. III, 13, 195.

**Outstay,** to stay beyond: *if you o. the time,* As I, 3, 90.

**Outstretch** (used only in the partic. —ed), 1) to stretch or measure to the end: *Timon is dead, who hath —ed his span,* Tim. V, 3, 3 (cf. As III, 2, 139).

2) to extend to the utmost: *raught at mountains with —ed arms,* H6C I, 4, 68. *and with his arms —ed, as he would fly, grasps in the comer,* Troil. III, 3, 167.

3) to strain to the utmost: *with an —ed throat I'll tell the world aloud what man thou art,* Meas. II, 4, 153 (cf. Troil. IV, 5, 10). *our monarchs and —ed heroes,* Hml. II, 2, 270 (strained, puffed up, hyperbolical).

**Outstrike,** to exceed in striking, to strike faster than: *if swift thought break it not, a swifter mean shall o. thought,* Ant. IV, 6, 36.

**Outstrip,** to leave behind: Ven. 324. Sonn. 32, 6. Tp. IV, 10. = to escape: *though they can o. men,* H5 IV, 1, 177. *o. death,* R3 IV, 1, 42.

**Outswear,** 1) to exceed in swearing: *we'll outface them and o. them too,* Merch. IV, 2, 17. 2) to conquer by swearing: *I think scorn to sigh: methinks I should o. Cupid,* LLL I, 2, 67 (Armado's speech).

**Outsweeten,** to surpass in sweetness: *the leaf of eglantine —ed not thy breath,* Cymb. IV, 2, 224.

**Outswell,** to exceed in swelling: *till thy cheek o. the colic of puffed Aquilon,* Troil. IV, 5, 9.

**Out-talk,** to get the better of, to bear down, by talking: *this gentleman will o. us all,* Shr. I, 2, 248.

**Out-tongue**, the same: *my services shall o. his complaints*, Oth. I, 2, 19.

**Outvenom**, to be more venomous than: *whose tongue —s all the worms of Nile*, Cymb. III, 4, 37.

**Out-vie**, to outbid, to exceed in offers: *Gremio is —d*, Shr. II, 387.

**Out-villain**, to exceed in villany: *he hath —ed villany*, All's IV, 3, 305.

**Out-voice**, to sound louder than: *whose shouts and claps o. the deep-mouthed sea*, H5 V Chor. 11.

**Out-wall**, outside, exterior: *I am much more than my o.* Lr. III, 1, 45 (cf. *wall* in Tw. I, 2, 48 and John III, 3, 20).

**Outward**, subst. external form, exterior: Sonn. 69, 5. 125, 2. Troil. III, 2, 169. Cymb. I, 1, 23. Plur. —*s: by nature's —s so commended*, Compl. 80.

**Outward**, adj. external: Ven. 310. 435. Lucr. 91. 1545. Sonn. 16, 11. 46, 13. 69, 5. 108, 14. 146, 4. Pilgr. 336. Tp. I, 2, 104. Meas. I, 2, 153. III, 2, 286. V, 15. Ado II, 3, 100. 190 (*a good o. happiness* = a happy exterior). IV, 1, 102. V, 1, 96. LLL IV, 1, 32 (cf. H5 IV, 3, 27). Merch. II, 9, 29. III, 2, 73. 82. Tw. I, 2, 51 (*thy fair and o. character*, = outwardly fair). John I, 211. II, 583. V, 7, 15. R2 IV, 240. V, 5, 52.*H4A I, 2, 202. H5 IV, 1, 8. 118. IV, 3, 27. H6A II, 3, 75. R3 I, 3, 66. I, 4, 79. 83. III, 1, 10. Cor. I, 6, 77. III, 1, 77 (= foreign). Caes. I, 2, 91. Mcb. V, 5, 1. Hml. II, 2, 91. V, 2, 198. Lr. IV, 4, 10. Oth. I, 1, 61. Ant. III, 13, 32. Cymb. I, 1, 9. Per. II, 2, 48. 57. II, 3, 25. Peculiar expression: *a common and an o. man*, All's III, 1, 11 (one having only an exoterical knowledge, not initiated in statesecrets).

**Outward**, adv. 1) externally: *they show well o.* Ado I, 2, 8. Hml. II, 2, 392 (Qq *outwards*).

2) out, to the outside: *how quickly the wrong side may be turned o.* Tw. III, 1, 14. Oth. II, 3, 54 (Ff *out*).

**Outwardly**, externally: Compl. 203. Wint. III, 2, 207. Troil. V, 2, 68. Mcb. I, 3, 54. Cymb. II, 2, 35.

**Outwards**, externally: Hml. II, 2, 392 (Ff *outward*).

**Outward-sainted** (not hyphened in O. Edd.) saint in external appearance: Meas. III, 1, 89.

**Outwear**, to pass, to spend, to waste (used only of time): *her song was tedious and outwore the night*, Ven. 841. *shows me a bare-boned death by time outworn*, Lucr. 1761. *the rich proud cost of outworn buried age*, Sonn. 64, 2. *thus is his cheek the map of days outworn*, 68, 1 (= times past). *till painful study shall o. three years*, LLL II, 23. *the sun is high, and we o. the day*, H5 IV, 2, 63.

**Outweigh**, to exceed in weight, to surpass: *which (cost) —s ability*, H4B I, 3, 45. *brave death —s bad life*, Cor. I, 6, 71.

**Outwork**, to work better than, to surpass: *where we see the fancy o. nature*, Ant. II, 2, 206.

**Outworth**, to exceed in value: *a beggar's book —s a noble's blood*, H8 I, 1, 123.

**Oven**, a construction of brick or stone work for baking: Ven. 331. Troil. I, 1, 24. Tit. II, 4, 36. Per. III Prol. 7.

**Over** or **O'er**, prepos. 1) from side to side along the surface, across, through: *pursue these fearful creatures o'er the downs*, Ven. 677. *over hill, over dale, over park, over pale*, Mids. II, 1, 2. 4. *I'll not over the threshold*, Cor. I, 3, 82. *a promised march over his kingdom*, Hml. IV, 4, 4. *come o'er the bourn*, Lr. III, 6, 27. *a conduct over land*, Cymb. III, 5, 8 etc. With the idea of a height surmounted: *climb o'er the house*, LLL I, 1, 109. *fell over the threshold*, III, 118. *in so high a style that no man living shall come over it*, Ado V, 2, 7. *o'er the hatch*, John I, 171. Implying motion on the surface without the thought of passing through: *he'll go along o'er the wide world with me*, As I, 3, 134. *gallop o'er the field*, H5 IV, 7, 89 etc. Metaphorically: *she did so course o'er my exteriors*, Wiv. I, 3, 72. *every man look o'er his part*, Mids. IV, 2, 38. Temporally: *o'er night*, Gent. IV, 2, 133. Ado III, 3, 174. *an we might have a good woman born but o'er every blazing star*, All's I, 3, 91 (M. Edd. *one*).

2) higher in place, = on or above, with the idea of resting or impending on what is below: *over one arm the lusty courser's rein*, Ven. 31. *over my altars hath he hung his lance*, 103. *over one shoulder doth she hang her head*, 1058. *the shore that o'er his basis bowed*, Tp. II, 1, 120. *hang o'er the altar*, Wiv. IV, 2, 217. *spread o'er the silver waves thy golden hairs*, Err. III, 2, 48. *no man come over me*, Ado V, 2, 9. *pluck it o'er your brows*, Wint. IV, 4, 665. *reproach and dissolution hangeth over him*, R2 II, 1, 258. *the heavens are o'er our heads*, III, 3, 17. *looks proudly o'er the crown*, R3 IV, 3, 42 (cf. H6C I, 3, 12. see *Look*. Ff and most M. Edd. *on*) etc. Metaphorically, denoting power or influence: *when I was certain o'er incertainty*, Sonn. 115, 11. *sovereign mistress over wreck*, 126, 5. *I strong o'er them, and you o'er me being strong*, Compl. 257. *o'er whom I give thee power*, Tp. IV, 38. *they strive to be lords o'er their lords*, LLL IV, 1, 38. *Dian's bud o'er Cupid's flower hath such force and blessed power*, Mids. IV, 1, 78. *queen o'er myself*, Merch. III, 2, 171. Lr. IV, 3, 16. *king o'er him and all that he enjoys*, John II, 240. *regent o'er the French*, H6B I, 3, 209. *o'er them Aufidius*, Cor. I, 6, 54. *mixtures powerful o'er the blood*, Oth. I, 3, 104 etc.

3) passing beyond: *though I be o'er ears for my labour*, Tp. IV, 214. *he was more than over shoes in love*, Gent. I, 1, 24. 25. *a man may go over shoes in the grime*, Err III, 2, 106. *o'er shoes in blood*, Mids. III, 2, 48. *o'er head and ears a forked one*, Wint. I, 2, 186 etc. *over and above* = besides: Wiv. V, 5, 177; cf. *over and beside*: Shr. I, 2, 149. Metaphorically, with the idea of surpassing or conquering: *come over it*, Ado V, 2, 7. *I came o'er his heart*, LLL V, 2, 278. *how happy some o'er other some can be*, Mids. I, 1, 126. *to triumph over*: H8 V, 1, 124. Tit. I, 178 etc.

4) Denoting a state of being engaged in, or attentive to, something: *as the grim lion fawneth o'er his prey*, Lucr. 421. *so looks the pent-up lion o'er the wretch*, H6C I, 3, 12 (cf. R3 IV, 3, 42). *utter your gravity o'er a gossip's bowl*, Rom. III, 5, 175. *over thy wounds now do I prophesy*, Caes. III, 1, 259. Hence indicating the cause or motive of an action as present and in sight: *the remainder mourning over them*, Tp. V, 13. *their father, making such pitiful dole over them*, As I, 2, 139. *that you insult, exult, and all at once, over the wretched*, III, 5, 37. *I will be more jealous of thee than a Barbary cock-pigeon over his hen*, IV, 1, 151. *you, that are thus so tender o'er his follies*, Wint. II, 3, 128. *seems to weep over his country's wrongs*, H4A IV, 3, 82. *weeps over them*, H6B I, 1, 226. *weeping and wailing over Tybalt's corse*, Rom. III, 2, 128. *o'er whom his very madness shows itself*

*pure*, Hml. IV, 1, 25. *so tender over his occasions,* Cymb. V, 5, 87. Thus sometimes almost = on occasion of, at: *when after execution judgement hath repented o'er his doom,* Meas. II, 2, 12. *I weep o'er my father's death anew,* All's I, 1, 3. *I do at this hour joy o'er myself, prevented from a damned enterprise,* H5 II, 2, 163. *if you are so fond over her iniquity,* Oth. IV, 1, 208.

**Over** or **O'er,** adv. 1) from one side to the other, especially from one shore to the other: *I'll send those powers o'er to your majesty,* John III, 3, 70. *I'll over then to England,* H6A V, 3, 167. H6B I, 1, 60. H6C III, 3, 224. 253. Lr. III, 6, 30 etc. In Wint. IV, 4, 668 read: *that you may (for I do fear eyes) over to shipboard get undescried.*

2) from one person to another: *see him delivered o'er,* LLL I, 1, 307. *I put you o'er to heaven and to my mother,* John I, 62. *dost thou now fall over to my foes?* III, 1, 127. *to give over* see sub *Give.*

3) from beginning to end: *I must each day say o'er the very same,* Sonn. 108, 6. *read it over,* Gent. II, 1, 136. V, 4, 46. Ado II, 3, 143. LLL IV, 3, 195. R2 IV, 243. H4B III, 1, 36. H6B IV, 4, 14. R3 III, 6, 3. H8 III, 2, 201. Troil. IV, 5, 239. Rom. I, 3, 81. *I'll fight their legions o'er,* Tp. III, 3, 103 (from the first to the last). *he did show me the way twice o'er,* Meas. IV, 1, 41. Cymb. IV, 2, 392. *all the story of the night told over,* Mids. V, 23. Cor. I, 9, 1. Tit. III, 2, 27. Oth. IV, 1, 117. *I have heard it over, and it is nothing,* Mids. V, 77. *we turned o'er many books together,* Merch. IV, 1, 156. *we'll whisper o'er a couplet or two of most sage saws,* Tw. III, 4, 412. *he sings 'em over,* Wint. IV, 4, 209. *perusing o'er these notes,* John V, 2, 5. *to write it over,* R3 III, 6, 5. *give me your hands all over, one by one,* Caes. II, 1, 112. *shall this our lofty scene be acted over,* III, 1, 112.

Hence almost = again, once more, (cf. above: Sonn. 108, 6): *I will cry it o'er again,* Tp. I, 2, 134. *and laugh this sport o'er at a country fire,* Wiv. V, 5, 256. *which I had rather seal with my death than repeat over to my shame,* Ado V, 1, 248. *I can but say their protestation over,* LLL I, 1, 33. *I will have that subject newly writ o'er,* I, 2, 120. *but saying o'er what I have said before,* Rom. I, 2, 7. *and shall make your lord that which he is new o'er,* Cymb. I, 6, 165. *over and over* = again and again: *fold it over and over, 'tis threefold too little,* Gent. I, 1, 115. *I ha' told them over and over,* Wiv. III, 3, 18. *o'er and o'er divides him 'twixt his unkindness and his kindness,* Wint. IV, 4, 562.

And = fully, completely; after numerical words: *which to do trebles thee o'er,* Tp. II, 1, 221. *to pay the petty debt twenty times over,* Merch. III, 2, 309. IV, 1, 211. *the fanned snow that's bolted by the northern blasts twice o'er,* Wint. IV, 4, 376. *barbered ten times o'er,* Ant. II, 2, 229. *over and over* = throughout: *they were never so truly turned over and over as my poor self in love,* Ado V, 2, 35. *I'll kill thee everywhere, yea, o'er and o'er,* Troil. IV, 5, 256.

4) on the surface, so as to cover it: *the desk that's covered o'er with Turkish tapestry,* Err. IV, 1, 104. *they are often tarred over with the surgery of our sheep,* As III, 2, 63. *strew me over with maiden flowers,* H8 IV, 2, 168. *boils and plagues plaster you o'er,* Cor. I, 4, 32. *our Italy shines o'er with civil swords,* Ant. I, 3, 45. Preceded by *all* or *quite:* Sonn. 12, 4. Tp. I,

2, 324. Err. III, 2, 137. John V, 2, 53. Troil. II, 1, 3. Tim. III, 6, 109. *over and over:* Wint. IV, 4, 129.

5) past, by, beyond: *his guilt should be but idly posted over,* H6B III, 1, 255. *so minutes, hours, days ...passed over to the end they were created,* H6C II, 5, 39. *you have shot over,* H5 III, 7, 133. Hence = besides: *and something over to remember me by,* H8 IV, 2, 151. *over and above:* Merch. IV, 1, 413.

6) *over and over* = tumbling head over heels, making a summerset in falling: *here o'er and o'er one falls,* Mids. III, 2, 25. *and over and over he comes, and up again,* Cor. I, 3, 68.

7) Peculiar passage: *swear his thought over by each particular star,* Wint. I, 2, 424 (= bear down, unsettle by swearing). *to fight o.* in Tp. III, 3, 103 = to outfight?

**Overawe,** to keep in complete subjection: H6A I, 1, 36.

**Overbear** (cf. *O'erbear*), to bear down, to overwhelm, to overrule, to subdue: *the ecstasy hath so much overborne her,* Ado II, 3, 157. *they* (the rivers) *have overborne their continents,* Mids. II, 1, 92. *I will o. your will,* IV, 1, 184. *it pleased your highness to o. it* (our counsel) John IV, 2, 37. —*s attaint with cheerful semblance,* H5 IV Chor. 39. *weak shoulders, overborne with burthening grief,* H6A II, 5, 10. *see the bishop be not overborne,* III, 1, 53. V, 1, 60. *an emperor in Rome thus overborne,* Tit. IV, 4, 2.

**Overblown** (cf. *O'erblow*), blown away, having spent the power of blowing: *is the storm o.?* Tp. II, 2, 114. Hence = past, gone: *to smile at scapes and perils o.* Shr. V, 2, 3. *this ague-fit of fear is o.* R2 III, 2, 190. *my choler being o.* H6B I, 3, 155. *domestic broils clean o.* R3 II, 4, 61.

**Overboard** (cf. *O'erboard*) from on board, out of the ship: H6C V, 4, 3. R3 I, 4, 19. Per. III, 1, 47. V, 3, 19.

**Overbold,** too bold: Mcb. III, 5, 3.

**Overboldly,** too boldly: LLL V, 2, 744.

**Overbulk,** to overtower, to overwhelm: *breed a nursery of like evil, to o. us all,* Troil. I, 3, 320.

**Overbuy,** to buy at too dear a rate: *—s me almost the sum he pays,* Cymb. I, 1, 146.

**Over-canopied,** covered as with a canopy: Mids. II, 1, 251.

**Over-careful,** too careful: H4B IV, 5, 68.

**Overcast** (cf. *O'ercast*) to cloud, to darken: *o. the night,* Mids. III, 2, 355.

**Overcharged** (cf. *O'ercharge*) loaded beyond the power of bearing: Gent. I, 1, 107. H6B III, 2, 376. Applied to guns: H6B III, 2, 331. Mcb. I, 2, 37.

**Overcloyed,** see *O'ercloyed.*

**Overcome** (cf. *O'ercome*) 1) to come or pass over: *can such things be and o. us like a summer's cloud,* Mcb. III, 4, 111.

2) to overpower, to conquer: Ven. 891. 955. LLL IV, 1, 74. As II, 3, 7. H4B V, 4, 27. H6B II, 3, 100. H6C I, 1, 187. Tim. III, 5, 71. Caes. III, 2, 177. V, 5, 56. Hml. III, 2, 72. V, 1, 156 (Ff *o'ercame*).

3) intr. to be victorious: LLL IV, 1, 70. 71. 73. As V, 2, 35. H4B IV, 3, 46. H6A I, 1, 107. Cymb. III, 1, 24. Per. I, 4, 70.

**Overcool,** to make excessively cold: *thin drink doth so o. their blood,* H4B IV, 3, 98.

**Overcount,** see *O'ercount.*

**Overcover,** see *O'ercover.*

**Over-credulous,** too credulous: Mcb. IV, 3, 120.

**Overcrow,** see *O'ercrow.*

**Over-daring,** too daring: H6A IV, 4, 5.

**Overdone** (cf. *O'erdo*) overacted, exaggerated: Hml. III, 2, 22. 28.

**Overdone,** name in Meas. II, 1, 85. 209. 212. IV, 3, 3.

**Overdusted,** see *O'erdusted.*

**Overdyed,** see *O'erdyed.*

**Over-earnest,** too earnest, ill humoured, severe: *when you are o. with your Brutus, he'll think your mother chides,* Caes. IV, 3, 122.

**Overeaten,** see *O'ereaten.*

**Overeye** ( cf. *O'ereye*) to observe, to witness: —*ing of his odd behaviour,* Shr. Ind. 1, 95.

**Overfar,** too far, going too great lengths: *though I could not with such estimable wonder o. believe that,* Tw. II, 1, 29, i. e. though I could not believe that like those admirers who estimated her at too high a rate; cf. *Estimable.*

**Overfed,** see *O'erfed.*

**Overflourished,** see *O'erflourished.*

**Overflow,** subst. (cf. *O'erflow*) such a quantity as runs over, exuberance: *a kind o. of kindness* (viz tears) Ado I, 1, 26. *thy o. of good converts to bad,* R2 V, 3, 64.

**Overflow,** vb. 1) to inundate, to cover with water: Ven. 72. Tit. III, 1, 230. Per. II, 4, 24.

2) to spread and moisten with any liquid: *I would be loath to have you —n with a honey-bag,* Mids. IV, 1, 17 (Bottom's speech).

**Overfly,** to overtake in flying: Ven. 324.

**Over-fond,** fond to excess: Wint. V, 2, 126.

**Overfraught,** see *O'erfraught.*

**Over-full,** too full: *o. of self-affairs,* Mids. I, 1, 113.

**Overgalled,** see *O'ergalled.*

**Overglance** (cf. *O'erglance*) to look hastily over: LLL IV, 2, 135.

**Overgo** (cf. *O'ergo*), to go beyond, to exceed: *a face that — es my blunt invention,* Sonn. 103, 7. *to o. thy plaints and drown thy cries,* R3 II, 2, 61.

**Overgone,** too much overpowered: *sad-hearted men, much o. with care,* H6C II, 5, 123 (cf. *Go*).

**Overgorged,** gorged to excess: H6B IV, 1, 84.

**Overgreat,** see *O'ergreat.*

**Overgreedy,** too greedy: H4B I, 3, 88.

**Overgreen,** see *O'ergreen.*

**Overgrown** (cf. *O'ergrow*) covered by growth: *o. with hair,* H5 V, 2, 43.

**Overgrowth,** see *O'ergrowth.*

**Over-handled,** handled too much, mentioned too often: *your idle o. theme,* Ven. 770.

**Overhang,** see *O'erhang.*

**Overhappy,** too happy: Hml. II, 2, 232.

**Overhasty,** see *O'erhasty.*

**Overhead,** above: *as she walked o.* LLL IV, 3, 281.

**Overhear** (cf. *O'erhear*) 1) to hear without being spoken to: Meas. III, 1, 161. Ado I, 2, 11. III, 1, 6. V, 1, 241. LLL V, 2, 95. Mids. II, 1, 187. As II, 3, 26. Wint. IV, 4, 639. Tit. IV, 4, 74. Rom. II, 2, 103.

2) to hear again, or to hear from beginning to end: *and —d what you shall o.* LLL V, 2, 95.

**Overhold,** to estimate at too dear a rate: *if he o. his price so much, we'll none of him,* Troil. II, 3, 142.

**Overjoy,** subst. excessive joy, transport: H6B I, 1, 31.

**Overjoyed** (cf. *O'erjoyed*) transported with gladness: Ado II, 1, 230. Shr. Ind. 1, 120. Per. V, 3, 21.

**Overkind,** too kind: *Sicilia cannot show himself o. to Bohemia,* Wint. I, 1, 23.

**Overkindness,** excessive kindness: Ado V, 1, 302.

**Overlaboured,** see *O'erlaboured.*

**Overleap,** see *O'erleap.*

**Overleather,** the upper part of a leathern shoe: Shr. Ind. 2, 12.

**Overleaven,** see *O'erleaven.*

**Overlive,** to outlive, to live longer than: *that your attempts may o. the hazard and fearful meeting of their opposite,* H4B IV, 1, 15.

**Over-long,** too long: H6A V, 3, 13.

**Overlook** (cf. *O'erlook*) 1) to view from a higher place: *Titan with burning eye did hotly o. them,* Ven. 178. *the earth this climate —s,* John II, 344. *so York may o. the town of York,* H6C I, 4, 180. *and —s the highest-peering hills,* Tit. II, 1, 8 (viz the sun).

2) to look down on, to be higher than: *shall our scions ... spirt up so suddenly into the clouds and o. their grafters?* H5 III, 5, 9.

3) to superintend, to take care of: *bequeathed to my —ing,* All's I, 1, 45.

4) to peruse: *o. this pedigree,* H5 II, 4, 90. *when thou shalt have —ed this,* Hml. IV, 6, 13.

**Over-lusty,** too lively and merry: *the confident and o. French do the low-rated English play at dice,* H5 IV Chor. 18. *when a man's o. at legs, then he wears wooden nether-stocks,* Lr. II, 4, 10.

**Overmaster** (cf. *O'ermaster*) to have in one's power, to rule: *to be —ed with a piece of valiant dust,* Ado II, 1, 64.

**Overmatching** (cf. *O'ermatched*), superior in power: *spend her strength with o. waves,* H6C I, 4, 21.

**Over-measure,** something given over the due measure: *enough, with o.* Cor. III, 1, 140.

**Over-merry,** too merry: Shr. Ind. 1, 137.

**Overmounting** (cf. *O'ermount*) rising too high: *and in that sea of blood my boy did drench his o. spirit,* H6A IV, 7, 15.

**Overmuch,** too much: *you tempt him o.* Wint. V, 1, 73. *and o. consumed his royal person,* R3 I, 1, 140.

**Overname,** to name in a series: Merch. I, 2, 39.

**Overnight** (cf. *O'ernight*) night before bed-time: *if I had given you this at o., she might have been o'erta'en,* All's III, 4, 23.

**Over-office,** see *O'er-office.*

**Over-parted,** see *O'er-parted.*

**Over-partial,** too partial: Sonn. 137, 5.

**Overpass** (cf. *O'erpast*) to pass away, to spend: *hast like a hermit —ed thy days,* H6A II, 5, 117.

**Overpay** (cf. *O'erpay*) to pay more than sufficiently: *which I will o. and pay again,* All's III, 7, 16.

**Overpeer** (cf. *O'erpeer*) to look down on, to rise above: *your argosies do o. the petty traffickers,* Merch. I, 1, 12. *wont through a secret grate of iron bars in yonder tower to o. the city and thence discover,* H6A I, 4, 11. *whose top-branch —ed Jove's spreading tree,* H6C V, 2, 14. *the ocean, —ing of his list,* Hml. IV, 5, 99.

**Overperch,** see *O'erperch.*

**Overpicture,** see *O'erpicture.*

**Overplus,** surplus, more than is enough or due: *and Will to boot, and Will in o.* Sonn. 135, 2. *our o.*

*of shipping will we burn*, Ant. III, 7, 51. *Antony hath after thee sent all thy treasure, with his bounty o.* IV, 6, 22.

**Overpost,** see *O'erpost.*

**Overpower,** see *O'erpower.*

**Overpress,** see *O'erpress.*

**Overprize,** see *O'erprize.*

**Overproud,** too proud: *lest, being o. in sap and blood, with too much riches it confound itself,* R2 III, 4, 59. *we think him o.* Troil. II, 3, 132.

**Overrate,** see *O'errate.*

**Overreach** (cf. *O'erreach*) to dupe: Shr. III, 2, 147.

**Overread** (cf. *O'erread*) to peruse: Meas. IV, 2, 212.

**Over-red,** to smear with red: *go prick thy face, and o. thy fear,* Mcb. V, 3, 14.

**Override,** to overtake and leave behind by riding: H4B I, 1, 30.

**Over-ripened,** grown too ripe: H6B I, 2, 1.

**Over-roasted,** too much roasted: Shr. IV, 1, 178. Cymb. V, 4, 154.

**Overrule** (cf. *O'errule*) to control, to sway; absol.: *thus he that —d I overswayed,* Ven. 109. *when a world of men could not prevail with all their oratory, yet hath a woman's kindness —d,* H6A II, 2, 50. Trans.: *whose mind and mine in that are one, not to be —d,* Lr. I, 3, 16.

**Overrun** (cf. *O'errun*) 1) to outrun, to leave behind by running: *we may outrun, by violent swiftness, that which we run at, and lose by —ing,* H8 I, 1, 143. 2) to invade and cover with troops: *an army, wherewith already France is o.* H6A I, 1, 102.

**Overscutched:** *o. huswives,* supposed to mean over-whipped strumpets: H4B III, 2, 340. According to Malone, and perhaps with more propriety, = *worn in the service.* cf. the Glossaries of Nares and Dyce. The derivation very uncertain.*

**Oversee,** to superintend: *thou, Collatine, shalt o. this will,* Lucr. 1205.

**Overseen,** confounded, disabled: *how was I o. that thou shalt see it,* Lucr. 1206. cf. *O'erlook.*

**Overset** (cf. *O'erset*) to subvert, to turn upside down: Rom. III, 5, 137.

**Overshade** (cf. *O'ershade*) to cover with shade: Tit. II, 3, 273.

**Overshine** (cf. *O'ershine*), 1) to shine upon, to illumine: *o. the earth,* H6C II, 1, 38. 2) to outshine, to excel in lustre: Troil. III, 1, 171. Tit. I, 317.

**Overshoot** (cf. *O'ershoot*) to fly beyond: *the poor wretch, to o. his troubles how he outruns the wind,* Ven. 680 (O. Edd. *ouershut*). Partic. *overshot,* properly exceeded in shooting, = blundering, put to shame: *so study evermore is overshot,* LLL I, 1, 143. *'tis not the first time you were overshot,* H5 III, 7, 134.

**Overshower,** see *O'ershower.*

**Oversight,** mistake, error: H4B II, 3, 47.

**Oversized,** see *O'ersized.*

**Overskip,** see *O'erskip.*

**Overslip** (cf. *O'erslip*) to pass unheeded, not to be minded by: *which all this time hath —ed her thought,* Lucr. 1576.

**Oversnowed,** see *O'ersnowed.*

**Overspread** (cf. *O'erspread*) grown over, covered: *o. with weeds,* H4B IV, 4, 56.

**Overstained,** stained over, quite discoloured:

*besmeared and o. with slaughter's pencil,* John III, 1, 236.

**Overstare,** see *O'erstare.*

**Overstep,** see *O'erstep.*

**Overstink,** see *O'erstink.*

**Overstrawed,** see *O'erstrawed.*

**Oversway** (cf. *O'ersway*) to rule, to lord over: *thus he that overruled I —ed,* Ven. 109.

**Overswear,** to swear again: *all those sayings will I o.* Tw. V, 276. cf. *swear over* in Wint. I, 2, 424 (= to swear down, to bear down with swearing).

**Overswell,** see *O'erswell.*

**Overt,** open to view, apparent: *without more certain and more o. test,* Oth. I, 3, 107 (Ff *over-Test*).

**Overtake** (cf. *O'ertake*) 1) to come up with, to catch: Gent. I, 1, 133. Wiv. I, 1, 55. Merch. IV, 1, 452. IV, 2, 5. All's III, 4, 24. R3 II, 4, 7. Cor. I, 9, 19. Mcb. I, 4, 18. Lr. III, 7, 66. 2) to meet or pass by on the way: *giving a gentle kiss to every sedge he —th in his pilgrimage,* Gent. II, 7, 30. *to break a jest upon the company you o.* Shr. IV, 5, 73. *as I came along, I met and overtook a dozen captains,* H4B II, 4, 387.

**Over-tedious,** too tedious: H6A III, 3, 43.

**Overteemed,** see *O'erteemed.*

**Overthrow,** subst. 1) ruin, perdition, death: *till mutual o. of mortal kind,* Ven. 1018. *give not a windy night a rainy morrow, to linger out a purposed o.* Sonn. 90, 8. *whose misadventured piteous —s ... bury their parents' strife,* Rom. Chor. 7. *expecting o.* Per. I, 4, 94. 2) defeat, fall: Ado I, 3, 69. Tw. V, 170. John V, 1, 16. R2 V, 6, 16. H5 IV, 3, 81. H6A I, 1, 24. I, 2, 49. III, 2, 111. H6C II, 6, 3. H8 IV, 2, 64. *to give the o.* = to defeat: Caes. V, 2, 5. *to have the o.* = to be defeated: H6A III, 2, 106.

**Overthrow,** vb. (cf. *O'erthrow*) 1) to ruin, to bring to nothing, to destroy: *you're shamed, you're —n, you're undone for ever,* Wiv. III, 3, 102. *and all the preparation —n,* Ado II, 2, 51. *you have —n Alisander the conqueror,* LLL V, 2, 577. *seeks to o. religion,* H6A I, 3, 65. *so many captains, gentlemen and soldiers, that in this quarrel have been —n,* V, 4, 105 (= killed). *though fortune's malice o. my state,* H6C IV, 3, 46. *by thee* (death) *quite —n,* Rom. IV, 5, 57. *treasons capital have —n him,* Mcb. I, 3, 116. *our devices still are —n,* Hml. III, 2, 222. 2) to defeat, to beat, to conquer: As I, 2, 266. 271. H4B IV, 4, 99. Caes. V, 3, 52. Oth. II, 3, 85.

**Overtop** (cf. *O'ertop*) intr. to rise too high: *who to trash for —ing,* Tp. I, 2, 81.*trans. to rise higher than: *that —ed them all,* Ant. IV, 12, 24.

**Overtrip,** see *O'ertrip.*

**Overture,** 1) disclosure, communication: *I wish you had only in your silent judgement tried it, without more o.* Wint. II, 1, 172. *it was he that made the o. of thy treasons to us,* Lr. III, 7, 89. 2) proposal, offer: *I hear there is an o. of peace,* All's IV, 3, 46. *I could not answer in that course of honour as she had made the o.* V, 3, 99. *I bring no o. of war,* Tw. I, 5, 225. Obscure passage: *when steel grows soft as the parasite's silk, let him be made an o. for the wars,* Cor. I, 9, 46 (most M. Edd. *coverture,* some *ovation,* others *nurture,* without making the sense plainer).

**Overturn** (cf. *O'erturn*), to throw down, to turn upside down, to destroy: *when wasteful war shall* *statues o.* Sonn. 55, 5. *I fear all will be —ed,* H4B V, 2, 19.

**Overvalue,** see *O'ervalue.*

**Overveil,** to veil, to cover: *night is fled, whose pitchy mantle —ed the earth,* H6A II, 2, 2.

**Overview,** inspection, observation: *are we betrayed thus to thy o.?* LLL IV, 3, 175.

**Overwalk,** see *O'erwalk.*

**Overwashed,** moistened over: *her fair cheeks o. with woe,* Lucr. 1225.

**Overwatch** (cf. *O'erwatched*) to pass in watching, to be up through: *I fear we shall outsleep the coming morn, as much as we this night have —ed,* Mids. V, 373.

**Overweathered,** battered by violence of weather, weather-beaten to excess: *with o. ribs and ragged sails,* Merch. II, 6, 18.

**Overween** (cf. *O'erween*) to think arrogantly: *you o. to take it so,* H4B IV, 1, 149. *thou dost o. in all,* Tit. II, 1, 29. *—ing* = arrogant, presumptuous: Gent. III, 1, 157. Tw. II, 5, 34. R2 I, 1, 147. H6B III, 1, 159. R3 V, 3, 328.

**Overweigh** (cf. *O'erweigh*), to outweigh, to overbalance: *my place ... will your accusation o.* Meas. II, 4, 157.

**Overwhelm** (cf. *O'erwhelm*) 1) to hang down, to overlook gloomily: *with —ing brows,* Rom. V, 1, 39.

2) to bear down, to crush, to destroy: *whose joy if her is —ed like mine,* Ado V, 1, 9. *a sow that hath —ed all her litter,* H4B I, 2, 13 (Ff *o'erwhelmed*). *thou seekest the greatness that will o. thee,* H4B IV, 5, 98. *his sorrows have so —ed his wits,* Tit. IV, 4, 10. *your house would sink and o. you,* Per. IV, 6, 128.

**Overworn** (cf. *O'erworn*) spoiled by too much use; stale: *the word is o.* Tw. III, 1, 66.

**Overwrested,** see *O'erwrested.*

**Ovid,** the Roman poet: As III, 3, 8. Shr. I, 1, 33. Tit. IV, 1, 42.

**Ovidius,** the same in the language of the learned Holofernes: LLL IV, 2, 127.

**Owch,** see *Ouch.*

**Owd,** Scotticism for *old: take thine o. cloak about thee,* Oth. II, 3, 99 (scrap of a song. The later Qq and Ff *auld*).

**Owe,** 1) to be the right owner of: *I —d her, and 'tis mine that she hath killed,* Lucr. 1803. *thou dost here usurp the name thou —st not,* Tp. I, 2, 454. *which o. the crown that thou o'ermasterest,* John II, 109. *to him that —s a (*duty*)* 248. *that blood which —d the breadth of all this isle,* IV, 2, 99. *the slaughter of the prince that —d that crown,* R3 IV, 4, 142.

2) to have, to possess: *I will not o. it (*love*)* Ven. 411. *that fair thou —st,* Sonn. 18, 10. *thou alone kingdoms of hearts shouldst o.* 70, 14. *the landlord which doth o. them,* Compl. 140. *no sound that the earth —s,* Tp. I, 2, 407. *the noblest grace she —d,* III, 1, 45. Gent. V, 2, 28. Meas. I, 4, 83. II, 4, 123. Err. III, 1, 42. LLL I, 2, 111. II, 6. Mids. II, 2, 79. All's II, 1, 9. II, 5, 84. III, 2, 122. V, 3, 297. Tw. I, 5, 329. Wint. III, 2, 39. John IV, 1, 123. R2 IV, 185. H4A V, 2, 68. H4B I, 2, 5. Troil. III, 3, 99. Cor. III, 2, 130 (the later Ff *own*). V, 2, 89. Rom. II, 2, 46. Mcb. I, 3, 76. I, 4, 10. III, 4, 113. Lr. I, 1, 205. I, 4, 133. Oth. I, 1, 66. III, 3, 333. Ant. IV, 8, 31. Cymb. III, 1, 38. Per. V, 1, 118. Passive: *all that borrowed motion seeming —d,* Compl. 327 (seeming to belong to him). *of six preceding ancestors hath it been —d*

*and worn,* All's V, 3, 198. With a dative and accusative: *to o. a person love* or *hate* = to bear love or hate: *if any love you o. me,* Ven. 523. *o. no man hate,* As III, 2, 78. *I could not have —d her a more rooted love,* All's IV, 5, 12. *between that love a woman can bear me and that I o. Olivia,* Tw. II, 4, 106. *what love women to men may o.* 108. Similarly: *the great danger which this man's life did o. you,* Cor. V, 6, 139 (had for you).

3) to be indebted, to be bound to pay; absol.: *he —s for every word,* Tim. I, 2, 204. With an accus.: *that praise which Collatine doth o.* Lucr. 82. *paying more slavish tribute than they o.* 299. *the debt he —s,* Err. IV, 4, 121. 136. Merch. I, 1, 134. All's II, 3, 168. IV, 3, 259. R2 I, 1, 167. H5 IV, 1, 146. Cor. III, 1, 242 (one time will o. another; i. e. time will bring the remedy). Tit. I, 251. Rom. III, 1, 188. Tim. III, 4, 22. 103. Mcb. I, 4, 22. V, 4, 18. Oth. I, 3, 180. Cymb. V, 5, 415. With an accus. and dat. (with or without *to*): Sonn. 79, 14. Meas. IV, 2, 62. Err. III, 2, 43. IV, 1, 7. 63. IV, 2, 58. Ado I, 1, 157. Mids. III, 2, 85. Merch. I, 1, 131. 146. 147. III, 2, 290. 299. As II, 5, 22. Shr. V, 2, 131. 155. 156. All's IV, 2, 13. Wint. I, 1, 8. John II, 247. III, 3, 20. R2 I, 3, 180. H4A I, 3, 185. III, 3, 75. 153. V, 1, 127. H4B II, 1, 91. 130. II, 4, 366. III, 2, 251. V, 5, 76. H5 I, 2, 34. V, 1, 68. H6A IV, 4, 34. H6C IV, 7, 19. V, 7, 28. R3 I, 3, 170. Troil. V, 6, 7. Cor. II, 2, 137. Tit. I, 414. Tim. II, 1, 2. III, 5, 83. Caes. V, 3, 101. Lr. III, 2, 18. IV, 1, 9. Ant. II, 6, 49. Cymb. II, 3, 117. Passive: *never may that state or fortune fall into my keeping, which is not —d to you,* Tim. I, 1, 151 (considered as due, as belonging to you). *to give obedience where 'tis truly —d,* Mcb. V, 2, 26. The gerund in a passive sense: *there is more —ing her than is paid,* All's I, 3, 108. Peculiar expression: *I will o. thee an answer for that,* Ado III, 3, 108. *for this I o. you,* V, 4, 52 (i. e. for this I remain in your debt, I will quit scores).

4) to be obliged for, to have to thank for: *since you —d no more to time,* Wint. V, 1, 219 (were at the same age). *all these three o. their estates unto him,* Tim. III, 3, 5. *thou —st the worm no silk,* Lr. III, 4, 108; cf. IV, 1, 9.

**Owen,** Christian name of Glendower: H4A I, 3, 117. III, 3, 27. II, 4, 375 etc. H6B II, 2, 41.

**Owl,** a bird of the genus Strix: Ven. 531. Tp. V, 90. LLL V, 2, 896. 927. 936. Mids. II, 2, 6. H6C V, 4, 56. Tit. II, 3, 97. Mcb. II, 2, 16. II, 4, 13. IV, 2, 11. Lr. II, 4, 213. Cymb. III, 6, 94. Its cries ominous and portending death: Lucr. 165. H6A IV, 2, 15. H6C V, 6, 44. R3 IV, 4, 509. Mcb. II, 2, 3. Accompanying evil spirits: *we walk with goblins, —s and sprites,* Err. II, 2, 192. Term of contempt: *good night, my good o.* LLL IV, 1, 141. *I bade the vile o. go learn me the tenour of the proclamation,* Troil. II, 1, 99. *to be a dog, a mule, a cat, a fitchew, a toad, a lizard, an o., a puttock,* Troil. V, 1, 68. Allusion to a legendary tale: *they say the o. was a baker's daughter,* Hml. IV, 5, 41 (a baker's daughter, who grudged bread to our Saviour, was transformed by him into an owl).

**Owlet,** see *Howlet.*

**Own,** vb. 1) to acknowledge as one's property, to claim: *two of these fellows you must know and o.* Tp. V, 275. *no father —ing it,* Wint. III, 2, 89. *a baboon, could he speak, would o. a name too dear,* Per. IV, 6, 190.

2) to possess: *move still, still so, and o. no other function*, Wint. IV, 4, 143. *not Afric —s a serpent I abhor more than thy fame and envy*, Cor. I, 8, 3.

3) to confess: *you will not o. it*, Wint. III, 2, 60.

**Own,** adj. proper, belonging to one's self; placed after poss. pronouns (and sometimes, as in Sonn. 20, 1 and Meas. IV, 3, 3, after Saxon genitives): Ven. Dedic. 7. Ven. 117. 157. 160. 216. 251. 776. Lucr. Arg. 1. 7. Lucr. 35. 241. 479 etc. Sonn. 87, 9. Tp. I, 1, 34. I, 2, 102. 167. 342. 347. 356. II, 1, 135. 163. 270. III, 1, 50. IV, 13. 32. 218. Epil. 2. Gent. I, 2, 120. I, 3, 82. II, 4, 156 etc. *of one's own*, following an indefinite subst.: *An fool's head of your own*, Wiv. I, 4, 134. *we have bucklers of our own*, Ado V, 2, 19. Mids. III, 1, 120. As IV, 1, 16. Shr. IV, 1, 102. Tw. V, 288. R3 III, 7, 34. Rom. I, 1, 192. Hml. III, 2, 223. Lr. I, 4, 361 etc. Superfluously joined to *proper*: *your own proper wisdom*: All's IV, 2, 49. H6B I, 1, 61. III, 1, 115. Caes. V, 3, 96. Sometimes not so much denoting property, as imparting to the expression a peculiar tenderness: *thine own true knight*, Wiv. II, 1, 15. *I'll not remember you of my own lord*, Wint. III, 2, 231. *tell me, mine own*, V, 3, 123. *your own Percy*, H4B II, 3, 12. *mine own lord*, Hml. IV, 1, 5 (Ff *my good lord*). *I am your own for ever*, Oth. III, 3, 479. Remarkable expressions: *when no man was his own*, Tp. V, 213 (= was master of himself, in his senses). *the boldness is mine own*, Shr. II, 89 (= it is I myself that am bold; German: die Dreistigkeit ist auf meiner Seite).

Substantive use; 1) as a plural: *her own shall bless her, her foes shake*, H8 V, 5, 31. *Rome must know the value of her own*, Cor. I, 9, 21. *that Rome should now eat up her own*, III, 1. 294. *you are darkened even by your own*, IV, 7, 6. Caes. V, 3, 2. *to entice his own to evil*, Per. Prol. 27. 2) as a sing., = property, or that which is due to one: *those same tongues that give thee so thine own*, Sonn. 69, 6. *every man should take his own*, Mids. III, 2, 459. *our just and lineal entrance to our own*, John II, 85. *his coming is but for his own*, R2 III, 3, 149. III, 2, 191. III, 3, 196. 197. H4A V, 5, 44. *I trust ere long to choke thee with thine own*, H6A III, 2, 46. *dare not touch his own*, H6B I, 1, 229. 239. *steel thy melting heart to hold thine own*

*and leave thine own with him*, H6C II, 2, 42. *seizeth but his own*, Tit. I, 281. *Scotland hath foisons to fill up your will of your mere own*, Mcb. IV, 3, 89. *he gives me so much of mine own*, Ant. V, 2, 20. *to hold one's own* = to play one's part well, to hold up: *hold your own in any case, with such austerity as 'longeth to a father*, Shr. IV, 4, 6. H4B III, 2, 218. Troil. IV, 5, 114.

**Owner,** rightful possessor, proprietor, master: Lucr. 27. 413. Sonn. 94, 7. 102, 4. Wiv. V, 5, 64. Err. IV, 1, 86. 92. Ado II, 1, 240. Mids. V, 426. Merch. III, 2, 19. As IV, 3, 90. All's III, 6, 12. John III, 1, 69. H4A IV, 3, 94. H6B I, 1, 225. IV, 10, 37. Troil. II, 2, 174. Tit. V, 1, 134. Tim. I, 1, 170. Hml. IV, 1, 21 (*the o. of a foul disease*).

**Ox,** the general name for black-cattle; particularly a castrated bull: Wiv. V, 5, 126. LLL V, 2, 250. Mids. II, 1, 93. As I, 1, 11. III, 3, 80. Shr. III, 2, 234. H4A II, 4, 498. H6B IV, 2, 28. Troil. V, 1, 65. 66. Plur. *oxen*: Shr. II, 360. Tw. III, 2, 64. H4A V, 2, 14. H6A I, 5, 31. V, 5, 54. H6B IV, 3, 5. V, 1, 27. Troil. II, 1, 116.

**Ox-beef,** the flesh of oxen used as food: Mids. III, 1, 197.

**Oxford,** English town: R2 V, 2, 52. 99. V, 3, 14. 141. V, 6, 13. 16. H4B III, 2, 12 (university); cf. H8 IV, 2, 59.

= Earl of Oxford: R2 V, 6, 8 (only in Qq). H6C III, 3, 88. 98. 109. 234. IV, 6, 96. IV, 8, 17. 30. V, 1, 1. 58. V, 3, 15. V, 4, 16. 58. V, 5, 2. R3 II, 1, 112. IV, 5, 11. V, 3, 27.

**Oxfordshire,** English county: H6C IV, 8, 18.

**Ox-head,** the head of an ox: John II, 292 (emblem of cuckoldom).

**Oxlip,** a sort of cowslip, Primula elatior: Mids. II, 1, 250. Wint. IV, 4, 125.•

**Oyes,** hear ye, give attention; the usual introduction to a proclamation of the public crier: Wiv. V, 5, 45. Troil. IV, 5, 143.

**Oyster,** the animal Ostrea: Wiv. II, 2, 2. Ado II, 3, 25. 27. Shr. IV, 2, 101. Lr. I, 5, 26. Supposed to contain a precious pearl in its shell: As V, 4, 64. Ant. I, 5, 44.

**Oyster-wench,** a woman that sells oysters: R2 I, 4, 31.

# P.

**P,** the fifteenth letter of the alphabet: Tw. II, 5, 97.

**Pace,** name in H8 II, 2, 122.

**Pace,** subst. 1) step, a movement made by the removal of the foot: *steal from his figure, and no p. perceived*, Sonn. 104, 10. *with the armed hoofs of hostile —s*, H4A I, 1, 9.

2) manner of walking: *in shape, in courage, colour, p. and bone*, Ven. 294. *with strengthless p.* Lucr. 709. *marching on with trembling —s*, 1391. *what p. is this that thy tongue keeps*, Ado III, 4, 93. *time travels in divers —s*, As III, 2, 327. *he has no p., but runs where he will*, All's IV, 5, 70 (= he observes no rule, pays no regard to form). *on a moderate p.* Tw. II, 2, 3. R2 V, 2, 10. H5 V Chor. 15. H8 I, 1, 132. IV, 1, 82. Cor. I, 10, 32. II, 3, 57. Mcb. II, 1, 54. V, 5, 20. Hml. II, 2, 354. III, 1, 149 (Qq *face*). Oth. III, 3, 457. Per.

V, 1, 112. *to hold a person pace* = to keep up, not to be left behind: *hold me p. in deep experiments*, H4A III, 1, 49. *to keep p. with*, in the same sense: Sonn. 51, 9. Mids. III, 2, 445.

3) a measure of two feet and a half: *two —s of the vilest earth*, H4A V, 4, 91. H5 II!, 7, 136. Ant. II, 2, 234.

4) step, degree of elevation: *that by a p. goes backward*, Troil. I, 3, 128. *every step, exampled by the first p. that is sick of his superior*, 132.

**Pace,** vb. 1) intr. to step, to walk, to go: *'gainst death ... shall you p. forth*, Sonn. 55, 10. *where is the horse that doth untread again his tedious measures with the unbated fire that he did p. them first*, Merch. II, 6, 12 (cf. trans.). *—ing through the forest*, As IV, 3, 101. *and with speed so p. to speak of Perdita*, Wint. IV, 1, 23. IV, 3, 121. R3 I, 4, 16. H8 I, 3, 12. IV, 1, 93.

2) trans. to teach (a horse) to move according to the will of the rider, to break in (cf. the intr. use in Merch. II, 6, 12 and H8 I, 3, 12): *those that tame wild horses p. 'em not in their hands to make 'em gentle, but stop their mouths with stubborn bits,* H8 V, 3, 22. *which with a snaffle you may p. easy,* Ant. II, 2, 64. Applied to men: *p. your wisdom in that good path that I would wish it go,* Meas. IV, 3, 137. *she's not —d yet: you must take some pains to work her to your manage,* Per. IV, 6, 68.

**Pacify**, to appease: Tw. III, 4, 309. H4A III, 3, 195. H4B II, 4, 87 (misapplied by Mrs. Quickly).

**Pack**, subst. 1) a bundle tied up, a bale: Wint. IV, 4, 289. 318. 611. H6B IV, 2, 51. Metaphorically: *a p. of sorrows,* Gent. III, 1, 20. *a p. of blessings,* Rom. III, 3, 141. *pour out the p. of matter to mine ear,* Ant. II, 5, 54.

2) a confederacy for a bad purpose: *a knot, a ging, a p., a conspiracy,* Wiv. IV, 2, 123. *confederate with a damned p.* Err. IV, 4, 105. *sorrow on thee and all the p. of you,* Shr. IV, 3, 33. Tw. V, 386. R3 III, 3, 5. *—s and sects of great ones,* Lr. V, 3, 18.

**Pack**, vb. 1) to place close together for some purpose: *the gifts she looks from me are —ed and locked up in my heart,* Wint. IV, 4, 369. *where the bones of all my buried ancestors are — ed,* Rom. IV, 3, 41. With *up: cushions, leaden spoons ... these slaves p. up,* Cor. I, 5, 9 (= tie up for the purpose of carrying them away).

2) to load (properly with goods tied up): *and yet our horse not — ed,* H4A II, 1, 3. *our thighs —ed with wax, our mouths with honey,* H4B IV, 5, 77.

3) to be in readiness for going, and hence to go off in a hurry; to be gone: *p. night, peep day,* Pilgr. 209. *seek shelter, p.!* Wiv. I, 3, 91. *'tis time, I think, to trudge, p. and be gone,* Err. III, 2, 158. *the most courageous fiend bids me p.* Merch. II, 2, 11. Shr. II, 178. *or p. to their old playfellows,* H8 I, 3, 33. *hence, p.!* Tim. V, 1, 115. *will p. when it begins to rain,* Lr. II, 4, 81. *—ed* = gone: *the night so —ed, I post unto my pretty,* Pilgr. 201. *he must not die till George be —ed with post-horse up to heaven,* R3 I, 1, 146. *to be --ing* = to go away: *be —ing, therefore, thou that wast a knight,* H6A IV, 1, 46. *are you —ing, sirrah?* come hither, Cymb. III, 5, 80. *and bid mine eyes be —ing with my heart,* H6B III, 2, 111. *to send —ing* = to send away: H4A II, 4, 328. H6B III, 1, 342. R3 III, 2, 63. *to set —ing* = to cause to go or be sent off in a hurry: *this man will set me —ing,* Hml. III, 4, 211.

4) to sort or shuffle in an unfair manner: *she has —ed cards with Caesar,* Ant. IV, 14, 19 (O. Edd. *Caesars*). Absol., = to practise deceitful collusion, to plot: *here's —ing, to deceive us all,* Shr. V, 1, 121. *go p. with him,* Tit. IV, 2, 155. *—ed* = confederate in a plot: *that goldsmith there, were he not —ed with her, could witness it,* Err. V, 219. *who was —ed in all this wrong,* Ado V, 1, 308.

**Packet**, subst. a bundle, parcel: Shr. II, 101. Especially a mail of letters: LLL II, 164. H4A II, 3, 68. H4B IV, 4, 101. H8 III, 2, 76. 129. 215. 286. V, 2, 32. Hml. V, 2, 15.

**Packhorse**, horse of burden; metaphorically = drudge: Lucr. 928. H4B II, 4, 177. R3 I, 3, 122.

**Packing**, plotting: *here's p.* Shr. V, 1, 121. *in snuffs and —s of the dukes,* Lr. III, 1, 26.

**Packsaddle**, a saddle on which burdens are laid: Cor. II, 1, 99.

**Packthread**, thread used in tying up parcels: Shr. III, 2, 64. Rom. V, 1, 47.

**Pacorus**, son of the Parthian King Orodes: Ant. III, 1, 4.

**Paction**, contract, agreement; conjecture of M. Edd. for *pation* or *passion* of O. Edd. in H5 V, 2, 393.

**Paddle**, to play, to finger, to handle, to feel amorously: *to be —ing palms and pinching fingers,* Wint. I, 2, 115. *—ing in your neck with his damned fingers,* Hml. III, 4, 185. *didst thou not see her p. with the palm of his hand,* Oth. II, 1, 259.

**Paddock**, a toad: Hml. III, 4, 190. = a familiar spirit, in the shape of a toad: *P. calls,* Mcb. I, 1, 9.

**Padua**, town in Italy: Gent. II, 5, 2 (M. Edd. *Milan*). Ado I, 1, 36. Merch. III, 4, 49. IV, 1, 109. 119. 403. V, 268. Shr. I, 1, 2. 22 and passim.

**Pagan**, subst. a heathen, one not believing in Christ: Merch. II, 3, 11. R2 IV, 95. H4A I, 1, 24. H4B II, 2, 168. Hml. III, 2, 36. Oth. I, 2, 99.

**Pagan**, adj. heathenish: John V, 2, 36. H4A II, 3, 31. H8 I, 3, 14.

**Page**, subst. a young boy attending on a person of distinction: Lucr. 910. Sonn. 108, 12. Gent. I, 2, 38. II, 7, 43. V, 4, 164. Wiv. I, 3, 93. II, 2, 119. LLL III, 82. IV, 1, 149. V, 1, 136. V, 2, 97. 336. Mids. II, 1, 185. Merch. II, 1, 35. II, 4, 33. As I, 3, 126. V, 3, 6. Shr. Ind. I, 105. Wint. I, 2, 135 (*sir p.* a term of endearment). H4A IV, 3, 72. H4B III, 2, 28. V, 3, 29. H8 I, 1, 22. II, 2, 48. V, 2, 25. Cor. I, 5, 24. V, 6, 99. Rom. III, 1, 97. V, 3, 279. Tim. II, 2, 75. Cymb. II, 1, 45. IV, 2, 355. V, 5, 86. 118. 228. Per. II, 3, 108.

**Page**, name in Wiv. I, 1, 45 etc.

**Page**, vb. to follow like a page: *will these trees p. thy heels?* Tim. IV, 3, 224.

**Pageant**, subst. show, spectacle, especially a theatrical exhibition: *this insubstantial p.* Tp. IV, 155. *when our —s of delight were played,* Gent. IV, 4, 164. *or show, or p., or antique, or firework,* LLL V, 1, 118. *shall we their fond p. see?* Mids. III, 2, 114. *as it were, the —s of the sea,* Merch. I, 1, 11. *this wide and universal theatre presents more woeful —s,* As II, 7, 138. *if you will see a p. truly played,* III, 4, 55. *a woeful p. have we here beheld,* R2 IV, 321. *to play my part in Fortune's p.* H6B I, 2, 67. *the flattering index of a direful p.* R3 IV, 4, 85. *shows, —s and sights of honour,* H8 IV, 1, 11. *in all Cupid's p. there is presented no monster,* Troil. III, 2, 81. *I will put on his presence ... you shall see the p. of Ajax,* III, 3, 273 (i. e. Ajax mimicked). *'tis a p., to keep us in false gaze,* Oth. I, 3, 18. *they are black vesper's —s,* Ant. IV, 14, 8.

**Pageant**, vb. to play, to mimic as in a theatre: *he —s us,* Troil. I, 3, 151.

**Pageantry**, theatrical spectacles: Per. V, 2, 6.

**Pah**, an exclamation of disgust: Hml. V, 1, 221 (Ff *puh*). Lr. IV, 6, 132.

**Pail**, a wooden vessel in which water or milk is carried: Err. V, 173. LLL V, 2, 925. *I have a hundred milch-kine to the p.* Shr. II, 359.

**Pailful**, the quantity that a pail will hold: *yond same cloud cannot choose but fall by — s,* Tp. II, 2, 24.

**Pain**, subst. 1) an afflicting sensation of the body, smart, ache, throe, torture: Ven. 1034. Wiv. V, 5,

90. Err. III, 1, 65. LLL IV, 3, 172. As III, 2, 340. R2 II, 1, 8. H6B III, 1, 377. III, 3, 4. R3 I, 4, 21. Tit. II, 3, 285. Rom. I, 2, 47. Lr. V, 3, 185. Oth. III, 3, 284. III, 4, 148. V, 2, 88. Ant. V, 2, 255. Per. V, 1, 193. Used of the throes of childbirth: H6C I, 1, 221. V, 6, 49. R3 IV, 4, 303. Tit. IV, 2, 47. of the tortures of hell: John IV, 3, 138. R2 III, 1, 34.

2) any heavy suffering: *this momentary joy breeds months of p.* Lucr. 690. *thrall to living death and p. perpetual,* 726. *perplexed in greater p.* 733. *so should I have co-partners in my p.* 789. 861. *looking with pretty ruth upon my p.* Sonn. 132, 4. 139, 14. 140, 4. 141, 14. Pilgr. 219. Err. II, 1, 36. LLL I, 1, 73. IV, 3, 122. Mids. I, 1, 250. H6C III, 3, 128. R3 I, 3, 168. H8 IV, 2, 8. Hml. V, 2, 359. Lr. III, 6, 115. Cymb. IV, 2, 290.

3) punishment; preceded by *on: accountant to the law upon that p.* Meas. II, 4, 86. *on p. of losing her tongue,* LLL I, 1, 124. *on p. to be found false,* R2 I, 3, 106. 111. *on p. of their perpetual displeasure,* Lr. III, 3, 4. *on p. of punishment,* Ant. I, 1, 39. *on p. of death,* R2 I, 3, 42. H4B V, 5, 67. H6A I, 3, 79. IV, 1, 47. R3 I, 3, 167. *on the p. of death,* H6B III, 2, 288. *upon p. of life,* R2 I, 3, 140. 153. *on p. of torture,* Rom. I, 1, 93. Preceded by *in: no man should disturb your rest in p. of your dislike or p. of death,* H6B III, 2, 257.

4) work, toil, effort: *since thou dost give me —s,* Tp. I, 2, 242 (work or task to perform). *to refresh the mind of man after his studies or his usual p.* Shr. III, 1, 12. *which I with more than with a common p. 'gainst all the world will rightfully maintain,* H4B IV, 5, 224. *my —s are quite forgot,* R3 I, 3, 117. *he is franked up for his —s,* 314. *your country's fat shall pay your —s the hire,* V, 3, 258. *so conversant with p.* Per. III, 2, 25. *your knowledge, personal p.* 46.

5) labour or trouble undergone for a certain purpose: *p. pays the income of each precious thing,* Lucr. 334. *the p. be mine, but thine shall be the praise,* Sonn. 38, 14. *in spite of physic, painting, p. and cost,* Pilgr. 180. *with p. purchased,* LLL I, 1, 73. *conned with cruel p.* Mids. V, 80. H6A V, 3, 138. R3 IV, 4, 303. Troil. III, 3, 30. IV, 1, 57. Mcb. II, 3, 55. Lr. III, 1, 53. Cymb. III, 3, 50. *to take p.* Merch. II, 2, 194. *hath ta'en much p.* H8 III, 2, 72. *take the p., but cannot pluck the pelf,* Pilgr. 192.

*Pains* (always used as a sing.: Gent. II, 1, 118. Ado II, 3, 270. Shr. IV, 3, 43. Tim. V, 1, 92. Ant. IV, 6, 15) in the same sense: Gent. II, 1, 118. Wiv. III, 4, 104. Meas. II, 1, 279. V, 246. Ado II, 3, 258. V, 1, 323. 326. V, 4, 18. Merch. II, 6, 33. IV, 1, 412. Shr. IV, 3, 43. All's I, 1, 240. R2 IV, 150. H6B I, 4, 47. Rom. II, 4, 194. Oth. I, 1, 184. IV, 2, 93. Ant. IV, 6, 15 etc. *to take —s:* Tp. I, 2, 354. IV, 189. Ado II, 3, 259. 260. 270. Mids. I, 2, 112. Merch. IV, 1, 7. V, 182. Tw. I, 5, 186. John I, 219. Troil. III, 2, 207. Tim. III, 5, 26. V, 1, 92 etc. *you have taken the —s to set it together,* Gent. I, 1, 123. Err. V, 393. John I, 78. V, 4, 15.

**Pain,** vb. 1) to put to bodily distress or torment: *that kills and —s not,* Ant. V, 2, 244. Partic. *—ed: give physic to the sick, ease to the —ed,* Lucr. 901. *to enforce the —ed impotent to smile,* LLL V, 2, 864. Superl. *—edst: the —edst fiend of hell,* Per. IV, 6, 173.

2) to put to labour and trouble: *that I have employed and —ed your unknown sovereignty,* Meas. V, 391.

**Painful,** 1) giving distress to the body, tormenting: *the aged man is plagued with cramps and gouts and p. fits,* Lucr. 856. *with most p. feeling of thy speech,* Meas. I, 2, 38.

2) laborious, toilsome: *the p. ~~rrior,* Sonn. 25, 9. *some sports are p.* Tp. III, 1, 1. *if it had been p. I would not have come,* Ado II, 3, 261. *p. study,* LLL II, 23. *p. labour both by sea and land,* Shr. V, 2, 149. *marching in the p. field,* H5 IV, 3, 111. *the p. service,* Cor. IV, 5, 74. *by many a dern and p. perch,* Per. III Prol. 15.

**Painfully,** 1) with distress of the body or mind: *within which rift thou didst p. remain a dozen years,* Tp. I, 2, 278. *thou hast p. discovered,* Tim. V, 2, 1 (so as to distress us by the result of thy discovery).

2) laboriously: *p. to pore upon a book,* LLL I, 1, 74. *who p. have brought a countercheck,* John II, 223.

**Paint** (cf. the subst. *Painting*) 1) to produce or to represent by delineation and colours: Ven. 212. 601. Lucr. 1466. 1492. 1541. 1577. Sonn. 47, 6. 53, 8. Tp. II, 2, 30. Wiv. IV, 5, 8. Meas. IV, 2, 38. Ado I, 1, 267. Mids. I, 1, 235. Shr. Ind. 2, 52. 58. R2 V, 2, 16. H5 III, 6, 32. 34. Tit. IV, 2, 98. Tim. I, 1, 156. 200. Mcb. II, 2, 55. V, 8, 26 (*—ed upon a pole,* i. e. on cloth suspended on a pole). Hml. II, 2, 502. Ant. II, 5, 116. Cymb. III, 4, 6. *—ed cloth,* i. e. cloth or canvas painted in oil and used for hangings in rooms (cf. *Cloth*): *who fears a sentence or an old man's saw shall by a —ed cloth be kept in awe,* Lucr. 245. *you will be scraped out of the —ed cloth,* LLL V, 2, 579. *I answer you right —ed cloth, from whence you have studied your questions,* As III, 2, 290. *as ragged as Lazarus in the —ed cloth,* H4A IV, 2, 28. *set this in your —ed cloths,* Troil. IV, 10, 46.

2) to colour, to dye: *with Nature's own hand —ed,* Sonn. 20, 1. *—ed Maypole,* Mids. III, 2, 296. *and p. your face,* Shr. I, 1, 65 (i. e. make it bloody). *where revenge did paint the fearful difference of incensed kings,* John III, 1, 237. *to gild refined gold, to p. the lily,* IV, 2, 11. *—ed with the crimson spots of blood,* 253. H5 III, 5, 49. H6A II, 4, 50. H6C I, 4, 12. Cor. II, 2, 115. Rom. I, 4, 5. Tim. IV, 3, 59. Especially used of colours laid on the face for embellishment; absol.: *why should false —ing imitate his cheek,* Sonn. 67, 5. *in spite of —ing,* Pilgr. 180. *your whores using —ing,* Meas. IV, 2, 40. *—ing and usurping hair,* LLL IV, 3, 259. 263. *does Bridget p. still?* Meas. III, 2, 83. *p. till a horse may mire upon your face,* Tim. IV, 3, 147. *let her p. an inch thick,* Hml. V, 1, 213. *you shall p.* Ant. I, 2, 18. trans.: *the one is —ed,* Gent. II, 1, 61. 64. *were I —ed,* Wint. IV, 4, 101. refl.: *to p. himself,* Ado III, 2, 58. *red —s itself black,* LLL IV, 3, 265.

3) to diversify with colours: *cuckoo-buds of yellow hue do p. the meadows with delight,* LLL V, 2, 907. *pluck the wings from —ed butterflies,* Mids. III, 1, 175. *the adder's —ed skin contents the eye,* Shr. IV, 3, 180. *from Cupid's shoulder pluck his —ed wings,* Troil. III, 2, 15. *the skies are —ed with unnumbered sparks,* Caes. III, 1, 63.

4) to colour, to adorn, to deck with artificial colours: *my sable ground of sin I will not p.* Lucr. 1074. *—ing my age with beauty of thy days,* Sonn. 62, 14. *their gross —ing,* Sonn. 82, 13. *I never saw that you did —ing need and therefore to your fair no —ing set,* 83, 1. *—ing thy outward walls so costly gay,* 146, 4.

*with colours fairer —ed their foul ends*, Tp. I, 2, 143.
*the —ed flourish of your praise*, LLL II, 14. *never p.
me now: where fair is not, praise cannot mend the brow*,
IV, 1, 16. *fie, —ed rhetoric*, IV, 3, 239. *gilded loam or
—ed clay*, R2 I, 1, 179. *Helen must needs be fair, when
with your blood you daily p. her thus*, Troil. I, 1, 94.
Hence —ed = artificial, counterfeit, unreal: *that
Muse stirred by a —ed beauty to his verse*, Sonn. 21,
2. *—ed pomp*, As II, 1, 3. *—ed peace*, John III, 1,
105. *poor —ed queen*, R3 I, 3, 241. IV, 4, 83. *your
—ed gloss*, H8 V, 3, 71. *and with that —ed hope braves
your mightiness*, Tit. II, 3, 126 (the later Ff *she
braves*). *to have his pomp and all what state compounds
but only —ed*, Tim. IV, 2, 36. *my most —ed word*,
Hml. III, 1, 53.

5) to describe, to represent: *the word is too good
to p. out her wickedness*, Ado III, 2, 112. *I p. him in
the character*, Cor. V, 4, 28.

**Painter**, one skilled in the art of representing
objects by colours: Ven. 289. Lucr. 1371. 1390. 1450.
Sonn. 24, 1. 4. 5. Gent. IV, 4, 192. LLL V, 2, 648.
Merch. III, 2, 121. Rom. I, 2, 41. Tim. I, 1, 202. IV,
3, 356. Lr. II, 2, 64.

**Painting** (cf. *Paint*) 1) the art or practice of a
painter: Tim. I, 1, 156. *this is the very p. of your
fear*, Mcb. III, 4, 61. *a piece of p.* Lucr. 1367. Tim.
I, 1, 155.

2) a picture: Lucr. 1499. Ado III, 3, 143. LLL
III, 21. Tim. I, 1, 90. 157. Hml. IV, 7, 109.

3) colour laid on: *you'll stain your lips with oily
p.* Wint. V, 3, 83. *this p. wherein you see me smeared*,
Cor. I, 6, 68.

4) the practice of laying colours on the face: *their
very labour was to them as a p.* H8 I, 1, 26. *I have
heard of your —s*, Hml. III, 1, 148 (Ff *prattlings*).
*whose mother was her p.* Cymb. III, 4, 52.

**Pair**, subst. 1) two things of the same kind used
together: *a p. of maiden worlds* (i. e. breasts) Lucr.
408. *of eyes*, 1680. John IV, 1, 99. *of anchoring hooks*,
Gent. III, 1, 118. *of horns*, Wiv. V, 1, 7. *of shears*,
Meas. I, 2, 28. *of stocks*, Err. III, 1, 60. Shr. Ind. 1,
2. *of lips*, As III, 4, 16. *of stairs*, V, 2, 41. *of breeches*,
Shr. III, 2, 44. *of boots*, 45. *of gloves*, Wint. IV, 4,
253. *of gallows*, H4A II, 1, 74. *of heels*, II, 4, 53. *of
sheets*, H4B II, 4, 243. *of legs*, H5 III, 6, 158. *of spectacles*, Troil. IV, 4, 14. *of chaps*, Ant. III, 5, 14. *of
bases*, Per. II, 1, 167. 169. Uninflected in the plural:
*twenty p. of eyes*, Gent. II, 4, 95. *how many p. of
stockings*, H4B II, 2, 17.

2) couple, brace: *a p. of honourable men*, Ado V,
1, 275. *a p. of these*, Tw. III, 1, 55. *of kings*, Wint.
V, 3, 146. *of carved saints*, R2 III, 3, 152. *of graves*,
167. *of knaves*, H6B I, 2, 103. *of bleeding hearts*, R3
IV, 4, 272. *of strange ones*, Cor. I, 1, 89. *of tribunes*,
V, 1, 16. *of hell-hounds*, Tit. V, 2, 144. *of maiden-
hoods*, Rom. III, 2, 13. *of kisses*, Hml. III, 4, 184. *of
indentures*, V, 1, 119. *of twins*, Ant. III, 10, 12. *of sons*,
Cymb. V, 5, 356. = two beings of different ꜰex joined
in love: As V, 4, 37. H6A II, 2, 30. Rom. Prol. 6.
Ant. I, 1, 37. V, 2, 363. Plur. *—s: the —s of faithful
lovers*, Mids. IV, 1, 96.

**Pair**, vb. 1) to couple: *so turtles p.* Wint IV, 4,
154. 2) to suit, to fit as a counterpart: *he* (our prince)
*had —ed well with this lord*, V, 1, 116.

**Pajock**, peacock: *and now reigns here a very,
very p.* Hml. III, 2, 295.*

**Palabras**, Ado III, 5, 18 and *paucas pallabris*,
Shr. Ind. I, 5, a mutilation and corruption of the
Spanish *pocas palabras*, i. e. few words.

**Palace**, a royal house: Tp. IV, 152. Meas. V,
544. Mids. I, 2, 104. IV, 2, 38. V, 425. Merch. I, 2,
15. Wint. IV, 4, 731 (*at p.*, in the speech of the
clown). 737. 789. R2 III, 3, 148. H6A V, 2, 7. V, 3,
170. H6B III, 2, 100. 246. IV, 1, 102. H6C I, 1, 25.
IV, 8, 33. V, 1, 45 (*at the bishop's p.*). Tit. I, 327. II,
1, 46. 127. Mcb. III, 1, 132. IV, 1, 57. Lr. I, 2, 117.
I, 4, 267. Ant. IV, 8, 32. Cymb. III, 3, 84. V, 4, 113.
Figuratively: *my soul's p. is become a prison*, H6C
II, 1, 74. *that deceit should dwell in such a gorgeous
p.* Rom. III, 2, 85. *this p. of dim night*, V, 3, 107.
*where's that p. whereinto foul things sometime intrude
not?* Oth. III, 3, 137. *thou seemest a p. for the crowned
truth to dwell in*, Per. V, 1, 122.

**Palace-gate:** H6C I, 1, 92. III, 2, 119. Tit. IV,
2, 35. Mcb. III, 1, 47. III, 3, 13.

**Palamedes**, name of a Greek in Troil. V, 5, 13.

**Palate**, subst. the roof of the mouth as an organ of taste: Sonn. 114, 12. 118, 2. Compl. 167.
Merch. IV, 1, 96. Tw. II, 4, 101. Troil. I, 3, 338. III,
2, 22. IV, 4, 7. Cor. II, 1, 61. Tim. IV, 3, 24. Oth. I,
3, 263. IV, 3, 96. Ant. I, 4, 63. Per. I, 4, 39.

**Palate**, vb. to perceive by the taste, to taste:
*not —ing the taste of her dishonour*, Troil. IV, 1, 59.
*you are plebeians, if they be senators: and they are no
less, when, both your voices blended, the greatest taste
most —s theirs*, Cor. III, 1, 104 (when the predominant taste of the compound is that of their voices).
*and never —s more the dung*, Ant. V, 2, 7.

**Palatine;** *count or county p.* = Palsgrave: Merch.
I, 2, 49. 64.

**Pale**, subst. 1) an enclosure (especially of a park):
*I have hemmed thee here within the circuit of this ivory
p.; I'll be a park, and thou shalt be my deer*, Ven. 230.
*too unruly deer, he breaks the p.* Err. II, 1, 100. *over
park, over p.* Mids. II, 1, 4. *why should we in the compass of a p. keep law*, R2 III, 4, 40. *parked and bounded in a p.* H6A IV, 2, 45. *which, like a bourn, a p.,
a shore, confines thy parts*, Troil. II, 3, 260. *breaking
down the —s and forts of reason*, Hml. I, 4, 28.
Doubtful passage: *I'll peck you o'er the —s else*, H8
V, 4, 94.

2) paleness; see Adj.

**Pale**, vb. 1) to enclose, to encompass: *the English beach —s in the flood with men*, H5 V Chor. 10.
*will you p. your head in Henry's glory* (i. e. the crown)
H6C I, 4, 103. *whate'er the ocean —s or sky enclips*,
Ant. II, 7, 74. *stands as Neptune's park, ribbed and
—d in with rocks*, Cymb. III, 1, 19.

2) to make pale: *the glow-worm shows the matin
to be near and 'gins to p. his uneffectual fire*, Hml. I,
5, 90.

**Pale**, adj. not fresh of colour, not red or ruddy;
wan: Ven. 21. 76. 347. 468. 739. 1123. 1169. Lucr.
441. 478. 1391. Sonn. 97, 14. Compl. 5. Gent. III,
1, 228. Err. IV, 2, 4. IV, 4, 96. V, 82. Ado I, 1, 250.
V, 1, 131. LLL I, 2, 107. IV, 3, 129. Mids. I, 1, 15.
As I, 1, 164 etc. *I am p. at mine heart to see thine eyes
so red*, Meas. IV, 3, 157 (cf. *Pale-hearted*). Used of
ashes: Lucr. 5. R3 I, 2, 6. Rom. III, 2, 55. Of things
wanting lustre and brightness; as of the moon: Gent.
IV, 2, 100. Mids. II, 1, 104. As III, 2, 3. Wint. IV,
3, 16. Rom. III, 5, 20. Tim. IV, 3, 441. of moonlight:

Merch. V, 125. of a dim sky: As I, 3, 106. H4A V, 1, 2. H5 III, 5, 17. H6C II, 1, 28. of lack-lustre eyes: *look, how thou diest! look, how thy eye turns p.* Troil. V, 3, 81 (cf. Hml. III, 4, 125). of lead: Rom. II, 5, 17. of silver: Merch. III, 2, 103. cf. *gilding p. streams with heavenly alchemy*, Sonn. 33, 4. Synonymous to white: *a lily p.* Pilgr. 89. *hands as p. as milk*, Mids. V, 345 (Thisbe's speech). *p. primroses*, Wint. IV, 4, 122. H6B III, 2, 63. Cymb. IV, 2, 221. *this p. and maiden blossom*, H4A II, 4, 47 (cf. *Maid-pale* and *Pale-visaged*). *that p., that white-faced shore*, John II, 23. H5 V, 2, 378. Compar. —r: Pilgr. 118. Merch. V, 125. As IV, 3, 178.

Substantively: *a sudden p. usurps her cheek*, Ven. 589. *nor ashy p.* (showed) *the fear*, Lucr. 1512. *the red blood reigns in the winter's p.* Wint. IV, 3, 4 (perhaps with a play on the word: *p.* = district, confine).

Adverbially: *so p. did shine the moon on Pyramus*, Tit. II, 3, 231. *how p. he glares*, Hml. III, 4, 125 (cf. Troil. V, 3, 81).

**Paled**, writing of M. Edd. in Compl. 198; O. Edd. *palyd* or *palid*; see *Pallid*.

**Pale-dead**, lack-lustre as in death: *their p. eyes*, H5 IV, 2, 48.

**Pale-dull** (O. Edd. not hyphened), wanting colour and life: *their p. mouths*, H5 IV, 2, 49.

**Pale-faced**: Ven. 569. R2 II, 3, 94. II, 4, 10. H4A I, 3, 202. H6B III, 1, 335.

**Pale-hearted**, wanting courage, cowardly: Mcb. IV, 1, 85. cf. Meas. IV, 3, 157.

**Paleness**, wanness: *swooning p.* Compl. 305. = want of lustre or colour: *thy* (lead's) *p. moves me more than eloquence*, Merch. III, 2, 106. *the p. of this flower*, H6A IV, 1, 106.

**Palestine**, the country of the Saviour: John II, 4. Oth. IV, 3, 39.

**Pale-visaged**: *your own ladies and p. maids*, John V, 2, 154 (cf. *Maid-pale*).

**Palfrey**, a noble horse: *to get my p. from the mare*, Ven. 384. 385. *it is the prince of* —s, H5 III, 7, 29. 35. *in Cheapside shall my p. go to grass*, H6B IV, 2, 75. *provide thee two proper* —s, *to hale thy vengeful waggon swift away*, Tit. V, 2, 50.

**Palisadoes**, stakes set in the ground by way of defence: H4A II, 3, 55.

**Pall**, to wrap up as in a cloak: *come, thick night, and p. thee in the dunnest smoke of hell*, Mcb. I, 5, 52.

**Pall**, to become vapid, to wane, to decay: *our indiscretion sometimes serves us well, when our deep plots do p.* Hml. V, 2, 9. *I'll never follow thy* —ed *fortunes more*, Ant. II, 7, 88.

**Pallas**, the goddess Minerva: Tit. IV, 1, 66. Name of a planet: IV, 3, 55. 64.

**Pallet**, a mean bed: *upon uneasy* —s *stretching thee*, H4B III, 1, 10 (Ff *pallads*).

**Palliament**, a robe: Tit. I, 182.

**Pallid** (O. Edd. *palyd* or *palid*), pale: *p. pearls and rubies red as blood*, Compl. 198.*

**Palm**, the inner part of the hand: Ven. 25. 144. Err. III, 2, 124. LLL V, 2, 816. As III, 5, 24. Wint. I, 2, 115. 126. John II, 590. III, 1, 244. H4B I, 2, 24. Troil. I, 1, 59. V, 1, 25. Cor. V, 2, 46. Rom. I, 5, 102. Caes. IV, 3, 10. Hml. I, 3, 64. Oth. II, 1, 168. 259. Ant. I, 2, 47. 53.

**Palm**, a tree of the order Palma; the emblem of glory and superiority: *must not so stale his p. nobly*

acquired, Troil. II, 3, 201. *gives us more p. in beauty than we have*, III, 1, 170. *bear the p. for having bravely shed thy wife and children's blood*, Cor. V, 3, 117. *you shall see him a p. in Athens again and flourish with the highest*, Tim. V, 1, 12 (cf. Psalms 92, 12). *bear the p. alone*, Caes. I, 2, 131. *as love between them like the p. might flourish*, Hml. V, 2, 40.

**Palmer**, a pilgrim: Lucr. 791. All's III, 5, 38. R2 III, 3, 151. H6B V, 1, 97. Rom. I, 5, 102.

**Palm-tree**, a tree of the order Palma: *what I found on a p.* As III, 2, 186.

**Palmy**, glorious: *in the most high and p. state of Rome*, Hml. I, 1, 113.

**Palpable**, such as might be touched and handled: *in form as p. as this* (dagger) *which now I draw*, Mcb. II, 1, 40. Hence = obvious, manifest: (lies) *gross as a mountain, open, p.* H4A II, 4, 250. *this p. device*, R3 III, 6, 11. *a very p. hit*, Hml. V, 2, 292. *'tis probable and p. to thinking*, Oth. I, 2, 76.

Adverbially: *this p. gross play*, Mids. V, 374, i. e. so gross, that it requires no judgment to perceive its grossness (some M. Edd. *palpable-gross*).

**Palsied**, affected with a palsy: Meas. III, 1, 36. Cor. V, 2, 46.

**Palsy**, paralysis, cessation of animal function: R2 II, 3, 104. H6B IV, 7, 98. Troil. I, 3, 174 (O. Edd. *p. fumbling*, M. Edd. *palsy-fumbling*). Plur. —ies: Troil. V, 1, 23.

**Palter**, to shift, to dodge, to shuffle, to equivocate: *a whoreson dog, that shall p. thus with us*, Troil. II, 3, 244. *you p.* V, 2, 48. *this* —ing *becomes not Rome*, Cor. III, 1, 58. *Romans that have spoke the word and will not p.* Caes. II, 1, 126. *these juggling fiends, that p. with us in a double sense*, Mcb. V, 8, 20. *I must dodge and p. in the shifts of lowness*, Ant. III, 11, 63.

**Paltry**, vile, contemptible, sorry: Wiv. II, 1, 164. Merch. V, 147. Shr. IV, 3, 81. Tw. III, 4, 420. John II, 54. H6A IV, 6, 45. H6B IV, 1, 105. V, 2, 67. R3 V, 3, 323. Troil. II, 3, 218. Ant. V, 2, 2.

**Paly**, pale: *p. flames*, H5 IV Chor. 8. *his p. lips*, H6B III, 2, 141. *p. ashes*, Rom. IV, 1, 100.

**Pamper**, to feed to the full: *those* —ed *animals that rage in savage sensuality*, Ado IV, 1, 61. *I am your sorrow's nurse, and I will p. it with lamentations*, R3 II, 2, 88. Used nonsensically by Pistol: *hollow* —ed *jades of Asia*, H4B II, 4, 178 (a parody of a passage in Marlowe's Tamburlaine: *holla, you* —ed *jades of Asia, what, can you draw but twenty miles a day?*).

**Pamphlet**, a written composition: *whereof this p., without beginning, is but a superfluous moiety*, Lucr. Dedic. 1. *with written* —s *studiously devised*, H6A III, 1, 2.

**Pancake**, a cake fried in a pan: As I, 2, 67. 69. 85. All's II, 2, 25.

**Pandar**, abbreviated from *Pandarus*: Troil. I, 1, 98. 106. I, 2, 311. V, 10, 49.

**Pandarus**, the archetype of pimps in Troil. I, 1, 48 etc. *shall I Sir P. of Troy become?* Wiv. I, 3, 83. *I would play Lord P. of Phrygia*, Tw. III, 1, 58. Alluded to in All's II, 1, 100.

**Pander** or **Pandar**, subst. a pimp, a procurer: Wiv. V, 5, 176. Ado V, 2, 31. Wint. II, 1, 46. H5 IV, 5, 14. Troil. III, 2, 210. 212. 220. V, 10, 48. Lr. II, 2, 23. Cymb. III, 4, 32. III, 5, 81.

**Pander,** vb. to pimp for, to procure for: *reason —s will,* Hml. III, 4, 88 (Qq *pardons*).

**Panderly,** adj. pimping: Wiv. IV, 2, 122.

**Pandion,** king of Athens and father of Philomela, who was transformed into a nightingale: Pilgr. 395.

**Pandulph,** name of the cardinal in John III, 1, 138. V, 7, 82.

**Panel,** a piece of board inserted into the groove of a thicker surrounding frame: As III, 3, 89. (cf. *Impanneled*).

**Pang,** subst. extreme pain, torment, agony: Compl. 272. Wiv. III, 5, 109. Meas. III, 1, 80. Tw. I, 5, 81. II, 4, 16. 93. III, 4, 262. John V, 4, 59. H4B IV, 4, 117. H6B III, 3, 24. H6C II, 3, 17. H8 II, 3, 1. III, 2, 370. V, 1, 69. Tim. V, 1, 203. Hml. III, 1, 72. Cymb. I, 1, 82. 136. Per. III, 1, 13.

**Pang,** vb. to afflict with great pain, to torment: *a sufferance —ing as soul and body's severing,* H8 II, 3, 15. *thy memory will then be —ed by me,* Cymb. III, 4, 98.

**Pannel,** subst. see *Panel.*

**Pannel,** vb. reading of O. Edd. in Ant. IV, 12, 21: *the hearts that pannelled me at heels.* Most M. Edd. *spaniel'd,* some *pantler'd,* others *paged.*

**Pannier,** a large basket carried on a horse: H4A II, 1, 30.

**Pannonian,** inhabitant of Pannonia: Cymb. III, 1, 74. III, 7, 3.

**Pansa,** name in Ant. I, 4, 58.

**Pansy,** the flower Viola tricolor: *there is —ies, that's for thoughts,* Hml. IV, 5, 176 (cf. the French *pensée*).

**Pant,** subst. palpitation of the heart: *make love's quick —s in Desdemona's arms,* Oth. II, 1, 80 (Qq *and swiftly come to D.). leap to my heart, and there ride on the —s triumphing,* Ant. IV, 8, 16.

**Pant,** vb. 1) to have the breast heaving and the heart palpitating: *—ing he lieth and breatheth in her face,* Ven. 62. *while in his hold-fast foot the weak mouse —eth,* Lucr. 555. *she like a wearied lamb lies —ing there,* 737. *and —s and looks pale,* Tw. III, 4, 323. *smothered it within my —ing bulk,* R3 I, 4, 40. *now breathless wrong shall sit and p. in your great chairs of state,* Tim. V, 4, 11. Sometimes the idea of palpitation, sometimes that of breathlessness prevalent: *my boding heart —s, beats and takes no rest,* Ven. 647. *the —ing sides of his poor jade,* H4B I, 1, 45. *half breathless, —ing forth from Goneril his mistress salutations,* Lr. II, 4, 31. *I p. for life,* V, 3, 243 (= I gasp for life). *having lost her breath, she spoke and —ed,* Ant. II, 2, 235.

2) to take breath after great exertion: *find we a time for frighted peace to p.* H4A I, 1, 2. *he never stood to ease his breast with —ing,* Cor. II, 2, 126.

**Pantaloon,** an old fool; a standing character of the Italian comedy: *the lean and slippered p., with spectacles on nose and pouch on side,* As II, 7, 158. *that we might beguile the old p.* Shr. III, 1, 37.

**Pantheon,** a temple at Rome dedicated to all the gods: Tit. I, 242 (Qq F1 *Pathan*). 333 (Qq and earlier Ff *Panthean*).

**Panther,** the animal Felis pardus: Tit. I, 493. II, 2, 21. II, 3, 194.

**Panthino,** name in Gent. I, 3, 1. 76.

**Pantingly,** as if gasping for breath: *she heaved the name of father p. forth,* Lr. IV, 3, 28.

**Pantler,** the servant who had charge of the pantry: Wint. IV, 4, 56. H4B II, 4, 258. 342. Cymb. II, 3, 129.

**Pantry,** a room in which provisions are kept: Rom. I, 3, 102.

**Panyn,** an unintelligible word (according to some = painim) used by Sir Toby in the state of intoxication: *a passy measures p.* Tw. V, 207. The later Ff and most M. Edd. *pavin.*

**Pap** (cf. *Milk-pap*) the nipple of males: *thou hast thumped him with thy bird-bolt under the left p.* LLL IV, 3, 25. *out, sword, and wound the p. of Pyramus,* Mids. V, 302. 303.

**Paper,** subst. 1) substance made to write on, and for other purposes: Lucr. 1289. 1297. Wiv. I, 4, 93. Meas. IV, 3, 6. Ado II, 3, 138. 249. LLL IV, 2, 26. V, 2, 7. Merch. II, 4, 13. III, 2, 255. R2 III, 2, 146. H5 II, 2, 74. R3 I, 3, 175. V, 3, 23. Rom. V, 1, 25 etc.

2) a piece of paper: *let the —s lie,* Gent. I, 2, 100 (the fragments of the torn letter). *each several p.* 108. *wrapped in a p.* All's I, 3, 94.

3) any thing written, as a letter, a document, a bond, a deed, a poem etc.: Compl. 6. Sonn. 17, 9. 38, 4. Gent. I, 2, 34. 46. 73. III, 1, 284. IV, 4, 128. Ado V, 4, 86. LLL I, 1, 116. IV, 2, 145. Merch. III, 2, 246. Shr. I, 2, 151. All's V, 1, 31. R2 I, 3, 250. H4A II, 4, 583. H6C III, 3, 176. H8 III, 2, 121. Tim. I, 2, 248. Lr. IV, 6, 266 etc. Criminals undergoing punishment usually wore papers on their backs containing their offence: *he comes in like a perjure, wearing —s,* LLL IV, 3, 47. *mailed up in shame, with —s on my back,* H6B II, 4, 31.

**Paper,** vb. to set down in a list, to note: *his own letter .... must fetch him in he —s,* H8 I, 1, 80 (Campbell *the papers,* Staunton *he paupers*).

**Paper-faced,** pale: H4B V, 4, 12; cf. H5 II, 2, 74.

**Paper-mill,** a mill in which paper is manufactured: H6B IV, 7, 41.

**Paphlagonia,** country in Asia Minor: Ant. III, 6, 71.

**Paphos,** town in Cyprus, sacred to Venus: Ven. 1193. Tp. IV, 93. Per. IV Prol. 32.

**Papist,** an adherent of the pope: All's I, 3, 56.

**Parable,** a word perversely used by Launce: *thou shalt never get such a secret from me but by a p.* Gent. II, 5, 41 (he means to say: indirectly).

**Paracelsus,** the famous reformer of medical science: All's II, 3, 12.

**Paradise,** 1) the garden of Eden, where Adam and Eve lived at first: *what largeness thinks in P. was sown,* Compl. 91. *not that Adam that kept the P.* Err. IV, 3, 16.

2) the blissful seat of sanctified souls: *make this place P.* Tp. IV, 124. *you would for P. break faith,* LLL IV, 3, 143. *the air of P. did fan the house,* All's III, 2, 128.

3) any place of bliss: *a p.* Pilgr. 42 and LLL IV, 3, 73. Meas. III, 1, 131. Mids. I, 1, 205. H5 I, 1, 30. *in mortal p. of such sweet flesh,* Rom. III, 2, 82. *if ye should lead her in a fool's p., as they say,* II, 4, 176, i. e. if you should disappoint, make an April fool of her.

**Paradox,** an absurdity: *no face is fair that is not full so black. O p.!* LLL IV, 3, 254. *success or loss,* *what is or is not, serves as stuff for these two to make —es*, Troil. I, 3, 184. *you undergo too strict a p., striving to make an ugly deed look fair*, Tim. III, 5, 24. *this was sometime a p., but now the time gives it proof*, Hml. III, 1, 115. *these are old fond —es to make fools laugh*, Oth. II, 1, 139.

**Paragon**, subst. a model, a pattern, something of supreme excellence: Tp. II, 1, 75. Gent. II, 4, 146. Mids. IV, 2, 13. Wint. V, 1, 153. Hml. II, 2, 320. Cymb. III, 6, 44. V, 5, 147. Per. IV, 1, 36. IV, 2, 152.

**Paragon**, vb. 1) to show off as a pattern: *before the primest creature that's —ed o' the world*, H8 II, 4, 230.

2) to serve as a pattern for, to excel: *a maid that —s description and wild fame*, Oth. II, 1, 62.

3) to compare as with a pattern: *I will give thee bloody teeth, if thou with Caesar p. again my man of men*, Ant. I, 5, 71.

**Parallel**, subst. 1) a line on the same plain and in the same direction as another: *delves the —s in beauty's brow*, Sonn. 60, 10. *that's done, as near as the extremest ends of —s*, Troil. I, 3, 168 (i. e. as the opposed extremities of two parallels).

2) equal: *without a p.* Tp. I, 2, 74. *this ring, whose high respect and rich validity did lack a p.* All's V, 3, 193. *where was he that could stand up his p.* Cymb. V, 4, 54.

**Parallel**, adj. conformable to the purpose: *to counsel Cassio to this p. course, directly to his good*, Oth. II, 3, 355.

**Parallel**, vb. 1) to keep in the same direction, to make conformable: *his life is —ed even with the stroke and line of his great justice*, Meas. IV, 2, 82.

2) to equal: *for rapes and ravishments he —s Nessus*, All's IV, 3, 281. *whom the world's large spaces cannot p.* Troil. II, 2, 162.

3) to allege or adduce as equal, to compare: *my young remembrance cannot p. a fellow to it*, Mcb. II, 3, 67.

**Paramour**, 1) mistress: Mids. IV, 2, 12. 13 (not understood by Quince). H6A V, 1, 23. V, 3, 82. Rom. V, 3, 105.

2) lover: *hag of all despite, encompassed with thy lustful —s*, H6A III, 2, 53.

**Parapet**, a breastwork: H4A II, 3, 55.

**Paraquito**, a little parrot: H4A II, 3, 88.

**Parasite**, a trencher friend, a mean and fawning flatterer: Ven. 848. Wint. I, 2, 168. R2 II, 2, 70. Cor. I, 9, 45. Tim. III, 6, 104.

**Parca**, one of the three goddesses who wove and cut the thread of human life: *fold up —'s fatal web*, H5 V, 1, 21 (Pistol's speech). Alluded to in Mids. V, 343 and Merch. II, 2, 66.

**Parcel**, subst. 1) a single constituent part, a particular, a piece, an article, an item: *every light occasion of the wind upon his lips their* (his curls') *silken —s hurls*, Compl. 87. *to your audit comes their distract —s in combined sums*, 231. *the lips is p. of the mouth*, Wiv. I, 1, 237 (Evans' speech). *it is a branch and p. of mine oath*, Err. V, 106. *had they marked him in —s as I did*, As III, 5, 125. *these main —s of dispatch*, All's IV, 3, 104. *his eloquence the p. of a reckoning*, H4A II, 4, 113. *ere break the smallest p. of this vow*, III, 2, 159. *I sent your grace the —s and particulars of our grief*, H4B IV, 2, 36. *many a thousand, which now mistrust no p. of my fear*, H6C

V, 6, 38. *the several —s of his plate*, H8 III, 2, 125. *some —s of their power are forth already*, Cor. I, 2, 32. *'tis as it were a p. of their feast*, IV, 5, 231. *here comes a p. of our hopeful booty*, Tit. II, 3, 49. *whereof by —s she had something heard*, Oth. I, 3, 154. *men's judgments are a p. of their fortunes*, Ant. III, 13, 32.

2) a bundle, a package: *I have about me many —s of charge*, Wint. IV, 4, 261 (or articles, items?). *that swollen p. of dropsies*, H4A II, 4, 496.

3) a number of persons, a party: *a holy p. of the fairest dames*, LLL V, 2, 160. *this p. of wooers*, Merch. I, 2, 119. *this youthful p. of noble bachelors*, All's II, 3, 58.

**Parcel**, vb. to enumerate by items, to specify: *that mine own servant should p. the sum of my disgraces by addition of his envy*, Ant. V, 2, 163 (cf. *Addition*). — Partic. *—ed* = particular: *their woes are —ed, mine are general*, R3 II, 2, 81.

**Parcel-bawd** and **Parcel-gilt**, words used by Elbow and Mrs Quickly, and explained by the commentators as meaning half bawd and half gilt; but not hyphened in O. Edd. and probably intended to have another sense (nearly = species): *a tapster, sir, parcel bawd, one that serves a bad woman*, Meas. II, 1, 63 (i. e. perhaps a tapster of that species whose particular business is procuring). *thou didst swear to me upon a parcel gilt goblet*, H4B II, 1, 94 (a goblet which was gilt, as must be specially stated).

**Parch**, 1) tr. to scorch, to dry: *—ing heat*, Lucr. 1145. H6A I, 2, 77. H6B I, 1, 81. *—ed lips*, John V, 7, 40. *hath thy fiery heart so — ed thine entrails*, H6C I, 4, 87. *impasted with the —ing streets*, Hml. II, 2, 481.

2) intr. to be scorched: *p. in Afric sun*, Troil. I, 3, 370.

**Parchment**, sheep-skin made fit for writing on: Err. III, 1, 13. Wint. I, 2, 360. John V, 7, 33. R2 II, 1, 64. H6B IV, 2, 87. Caes. III, 2, 133. Hml. V, 1, 123.

**Pard**, leopard: Tp. IV, 262. Mids. II, 2, 31. As II, 7, 150. Troil. III, 2, 201.

**Pardon**, subst. 1) forgiveness of any offence: *I p. crave of thee*, Pilgr. 141. *let me ask my sister p.* Meas. III, 1, 173. As III, 5, 6. Oth. V, 1, 93 etc. Not governed by a verb: *p., master!* Tp. I, 2, 296. Gent. I, 2, 17. Wiv. V, 5, 229. Mids. IV, 1, 146 etc. *p., I pray thee, for my mad mistaking*, Shr. IV, 5, 49. *p., my lord, for me and for my tidings*, All's II, 1, 63. *your honour's p.* = forgiveness granted by your honour: Meas. II, 2, 14. Mcb. I, 4, 6. *our p.* = forgiveness granted by us: All's V, 3, 22. H6C IV, 1, 87. H8 I, 2, 56 etc. But sometimes with the poss. pron. in the sense of forgiveness granted to a person: *has brought his p.* All's II, 1, 65. *I beg my p.* V, 3, 12. *beg thy p.* R2 V, 2, 113. *O, my p.!* Ant. III, 11, 61. *I will o'ertake thee and weep for my p.* IV, 14, 45; cf. Meas. IV, 2, 104. *to give p. or one's p.:* Meas. V, 390. H4B V, 3, 113. R3 II, 1, 103. Troil. I, 3, 357. Hml. V, 2, 237. Cymb. I, 6, 162. *to have p.* = to be pardoned: *as you look to have my p.* Tp. V, 293. Plur. *—s:* Wint. V, 3, 147. H4B V, 5, 119. H6B IV, 8, 23. Cor. III, 1, 65. III, 2, 88 (*they have —s* = they know to pardon).

Used as a form of courteous denial or contradiction: *no, p.* Meas. III, 2, 142. *I crave your p.* Err. I, 2, 26. *p., sir!* LLL V, 1, 137. *your p., sir!* Wint. IV,

4, 594. *by your p.* Caes. III, 1, 235. Ant. I, 5, 72. Cymb. I, 4, 46. *under your p.* Caes. IV, 3, 213. *under p.* Lr. I, 4, 365.

Sometimes almost = leave, permission: *p., guest-justice*, Wiv. II, 3, 59. *by your grace's p.* Ado II, 1, 354. *under p., sir, what are the contents?* LLL IV, 2, 103. *and bow them to your gracious leave and p.* Hml. I, 2, 56. *asking your p. thereunto*, IV, 7, 46. *whereon I begged his p. for return*, Ant. III, 6, 60.

2) forgiveness of a crime and remission of a penalty; mercy, grace: *p. is still the nurse of second woe*, Meas. II, 1, 298. *ignomy in ransom and free p. are of two houses*, II, 4, 111. *sign me a present p. for my brother*, 152. *you hope of p. from Lord Angelo*, III, 1, 1. IV, 2, 74. 104. 111. IV, 3, 112. H6B IV, 8, 9. 14. 23. R3 V, 5, 16. H8 IV, 2, 121. = absolution: *purchase corrupted p. of a man, who in that sale sells p. from himself*, John III, 1, 166.

**Pardon**, vb. 1) to forgive; absol.: *you must p.* Meas. V, 407. *if you p., we will mend*, Mids. V, 437. With an accus. a) noting the person who has offended: Compl. 246. Tp. Epil. 7. Gent. II, 4, 165. V, 4, 158. Wiv. III, 3, 240. 243. Ado V, 3, 12. Tw. V, 221. Shr. IV, 4, 38. H6C IV, 1, 89 etc. Passively: *you are —ed*, Meas. V, 392. R2 II, 1, 188. Rom. V, 3, 308. Hml. III, 3, 56. b) the offence committed: *p. the fault*, Gent. I, 2, 40. *p. it*, Meas. V, 89. *p. this fault*, Merch. V, 247. Wint. III, 2, 154. R2 IV, 214. H4A I, 3, 149 etc. Person and offence placed together: *p. me my wrongs*, Tp. V, 119. *p. love this wrong*, LLL IV, 2, 121. Tw. II, 1, 34. Wint. V, 2, 160. H6C V, 1, 24. V, 5, 70. R3 III, 7, 102. Troil. IV, 5, 257 etc. The person placed after with *to: my high-repented blames p. to me*, All's V, 3, 37. The offence with *from* or *of: to you it doth belong yourself to p. of self-doing crime*, Sonn. 58, 12. *as you from crimes would —ed be*, Tp. Epil. 19.

Used to express courteous denial or contradiction: *p. me*, Gent. IV, 4, 127. 131. Wiv. I, 1, 225. Meas. II, 4, 117. IV, 2, 194. LLL IV, 1, 13. V, 2, 710. Merch. IV, 1, 437. Ant. IV, 14, 80 etc. *all women shall p. me*, Ado I, 1, 244 (i. e. excuse me from doing so). *no, you shall p. me*, II, 1, 131. *I do entreat your grace to p. me*, Mids. I, 1, 58. *I p. you for that*, As III, 2, 395 (I do not ask you to do that). *let me entreat of you to p. me yet for a night or two*, Shr. Ind. 2, 121. *would you'ld p. me*, Tw. III, 3, 24. *your grace shall p. me*, John V, 2, 78. *p. me in that*, Tim. I, 2, 219.

= to give leave (of departure): *even now about it! I will p. you*, Gent. III, 2, 98.

2) to absolve, to release (from a penalty): *you might p. him*, Meas. II, 2, 49. II, 4, 43. V, 496. 504. 540. Err. I, 1, 98. LLL I, 2, 152 etc. The penalty the object: *take my life and all, p. not that*, Merch. IV, 1, 374. *I p. that man's life*, Lr. IV, 6, 111. *I p. thee thy life*, Merch. IV, 1, 369.

**Pardoner**, one who absolves an offender: Meas. IV, 2, 112.

**Pardonmees**, courteous persons who always say '*pardon me*': Rom. II, 4, 35 (Theob. *pardonnez-moy's;* Cambr. Ed. *perdona-mi's*).

**Pare**, to shorten by trimming and cutting: *let not him p. his nails*, Mids. IV, 2, 41. All's V, 2, 31. Tw. IV, 2, 140. H5 IV, 4, 76. *to have his princely paws —d all away*, Tit. II, 3, 152. *thou hast —d thy wit o' both sides*, Lr. I, 4, 204. Hence = to diminish in ge-

neral: *but —d my present havings, to bestow my bounties upon you*, H8 III, 2, 159.

**Parel**, for *apparel*, in the language of the old man in Lr. IV, 1, 51.

**Parent**, father or mother: Tp. I, 2, 94. Cor. V, 3, 56. Lr. I, 2, 158. Per. I, 1, 131. II, 3, 46. Plur. —*s* = father and mother: Err. I, 1, 57. V, 360. LLL IV, 2, 162. All's I, 3, 163. Wint. I, 2, 393. 442. H5 IV, 1, 46. H6C V, 6, 42. R3 IV, 4, 391. 393. H8 V, 5, 8. Rom. Prol. 8. 10. Tim. IV, 1, 8. Lr. III, 4, 83. Cymb. V, 4, 70. Metaphorically, = authors: *we are their* (evils') —*s and original*, Mids. II, 1, 117.

**Parentage**, extraction, birth: As III, 4, 39. Shr. II, 96. Tw. I, 5, 296. V, 238. H6A II, 5, 73. V, 4, 14. H6B IV, 2, 152. Rom. III, 5, 181. Per. II, 3, 74. V, 1, 93. 98. 100. 130. 190.

**Parfect**, Costard's blunder for *perform* in LLL V, 2, 503.

**Paring** (cf. *Cheese-paring*) that which is pared off: *virginity breeds mites much like a cheese; consumes itself to the very p.* All's I, 1, 155. Plur. —*s: some devils ask but the —s of one's nail*, Err. IV, 3, 72. *the very —s of our nails shall pitch a field*, H6A III, 1, 102. *here comes one of the —s*, Lr. I, 4, 206.

**Paring-knife**, a knife used to pare things off: *like a glover's p.* Wiv. I, 4, 21.

**Paris**, name of 1) the son of Priam who ravished Helen: Lucr. 1473. Shr. I, 2, 247. H6A V, 5, 104. Troil. Prol. 10. I, 1, 112 and passim. 2) Count P.: Rom. I, 2, 16 and passim. 3) the capital of France: All's I, 2, 22. I, 3, 225. 237. 239. H5 II, 5, 131 (*P. balls*). 132 (*P. Louvre*). H6A I, 1, 61. 65. III, 2, 128. IV, 1, 3. IV, 7, 95. V, 2, 4. H6B I, 1, 94. 215. I, 3, 175. R3 II, 3, 17. Hml. II, 1, 7.

**Paris-garden** (O. Edd. *Parish-garden*) a bear-garden on the Bankside in Southwark: H8 V, 4, 2.

**Parish**, the district belonging to a particular church: Meas. II, 1, 287. H6A V, 4, 11. H8 I, 2, 152 (*within the p. Saint Lawrence Poultney*). Cymb. IV, 2, 168. Per. II, 1, 38. 47. Adjectively: *the p. curate*, LLL V, 2, 538. *p. church*, As II, 7, 52. *the p. heifers*, H4B II, 2, 171.

**Parish-garden**, see *Paris-garden.*

**Parishioners**, the persons belonging to a parish: LLL IV, 2, 76. As III, 2, 164.

**Parish-top**, a large top kept for public exercise in a parish: *till his brains turn o' the toe like a p.* Tw. I, 3, 44.

**Parisians**, inhabitants of Paris: H6A V, 2, 2.

**Paris-ward**: *their powers are marching unto P.* H6A III, 3, 30, i. e. towards Paris; cf. *Bedward, Parkward;* Brooke has even to *himward.*

**Paritor**, apparitor, an officer of the Bishop's Court, who carries out citations: (Cupid) *sole imperator and great general of trotting —s*, LLL III, 188 ("as citations are most frequently issued for fornication, the p. is put under Cupid's government." Johnson). OEdd. *parrators.*

**Park**, a piece of ground enclosed and stored with beasts of chase: Ven. 231. 239. Wiv. I, 4, 115. III, 3, 240. IV, 4, 19. V, 1, 12. V, 3, 4. LLL I, 1, 210. 242. I, 2, 123. 136. III, 165. IV, 3, 374. Mids. II, 1, 4. Merch. III, 4, 83 (*p. gate*). Shr. V, 1, 133. R2 III, 1, 23. H4A II, 3, 75. H6C IV, 5, 3. 19 (*p. corner*). V, 2, 24. Tit. III, 1, 88. Cymb. III, 1, 19.

**Parked**, enclosed as in a park: *how are we p.*

*and bounded in a pale, a little herd of England's timo-rous deer,* H6A IV, 2, 45.

**Parkward**, towards the park: *the pittie-ward, the p., every way,* Wiv. III, 1, 5. cf. *Paris-ward.*

**Parle**, subst. parley, conversation, conference (with a view to come to an agreement): *the gentlemen that every day with p. encounter me,* Gent. I, 2, 5. Chiefly a conference with enemies tending to restore peace: *the nature of our quarrel yet never brooked p.* Shr. I, 1, 117. *our trumpet called you to this gentle p.* John II, 205. *vouchsafe a p.* 226. *sound so base a p.* R2 I, 1, 192. *send the breath of p. into his ruined ears,* III, 3, 33 (Qq *parlee*). *this is the latest p. we will admit,* H5 III, 3, 2. *sound a p.* H6C V, 1, 16. *break the p.* Tit. V, 3, 19. *in an angry p.* Hml. I, 1, 62.

**Parle**, vb. to speak, to converse with a view to come to an agreement: *she could pick no meaning from their —ing looks,* Lucr. 100. *their purpose is to p., to court and dance,* LLL V, 2, 122 (O. Edd. *parlee*).

**Parley**, subst. a conversation or conference tending to come to an agreement: *in such a p.* (of looks) *should I answer thee,* H4A III, 1, 204. *calls to p. the sleepers of the house,* Mcb. II, 3, 87. *what an eye she has! methinks it sounds a p. of provocation,* Oth. II, 3, 23 (Ff *a p. to provocation*). Chiefly a conference with enemies: Lucr. 471. John V, 1, 68. R2 III, 3, 33 (Qq *parlee,* Ff *parle*). H4B IV, 1, 159. H5 III, 2, 149. H6A III, 3, 35. 36. 37. V, 3, 130. H6B IV, 8, 5. H6C II, 2, 110. Tit. IV, 4, 101. V, 1, 159. Caes. V, 1, 21.

**Parley**, vb. to confer with a view to come to an understanding; absol.: *they are at hand, to p. or to fight,* John II, 78. *set your entreatments at a higher rate than a command to p.* Hml. I, 3, 123. With *to: therefore we p. to you: are you content to be our general?* Gent. IV, 1, 60. *this tongue hath —ed unto foreign kings for your behoof,* H6B IV, 7, 82. With *with: to p. with the sole inheritor,* LLL II, 5. *p. with sin,* John IV, 2, 238. *I will p. with Jack Cade,* H6B IV, 4, 13.

**Parliament**, the legislative council of the representatives of the nation: Wiv. II, 1, 29. R2 V, 2, 44. H4B IV, 2, 18. V, 2, 134. V, 5, 109. H6A II, 4, 117. II, 5, 127. III, 2, 60. H6B II, 4, 70. III, 1, 197. IV, 7, 17. V, 3, 25. H6C I, 1, 35. 39. 64. 249. I, 4, 71. II, 1, 118. 173. II, 2, 91.

**Parliament-house**, the house where the representatives of the nation meet: H6C I, 1, 71.

**Parlour**, the room in a house in which the family use to meet and receive company: Ado III, 1, 1. Shr. V, 2, 102. Oth. II, 1, 111.

**Parlous**, a popular corruption of *perilous,* = alarming, mischievous: *a p. fear,* Mids. III, 1, 14 (Snout's speech). *thou art in a p. state,* As III, 2, 45. *a p. boy,* R3 II, 4, 35. In R3 III, 1, 154 and Rom. I, 3, 54 most M. Edd. *parlous,* O. Edd. *perilous.*

**Parmaceti**, spermaceti: H4A I, 3, 58.*

**Parolles**, name in All's I, 1, 201 and passim.

**Parricide**, 1) the murder of a father: Mcb. III, 1, 32. 2) the murderer of his father: Lr. II, 1, 48.

**Parrot**, the bird Psittacus: Merch. I, 1, 53. III, 5, 51. As IV, 1, 152 (*more clamorous than a p. against rain*). H4A II, 4, 111. H4B II, 4, 282. Troil. V, 2, 193. Oth. II, 3, 281. *Mistress, respice finem, respect your end; or rather the prophecy like the p.,* '*beware the rope's end'*, Err. IV, 4, 45 (a quibble between *finem* and *funem,* end and rope. Warburton: the passage alludes to people's teaching parrots unlucky words,

*with which when any passenger was offended, it was the standing joke of the owner to say:* '*take heed, sir, my parrot prophesies'.* cf. the following verses from Butler's Hudibras: *could tell what subtlest parrots mean, what member 'tis of whom they talk, when they cry rope, and walk, knave, walk.*).

**Parrot-teacher**, one who teaches parrots to speak: Ado I, 1, 139.

**Parsley**, the plant Petroselinum sativum: *for p. to stuff a rabbit,* Shr. IV, 4, 101.

**Parson** (supposed to be derived from *persona;* cf. the quibble in LLL IV, 2, 84; in IV, 3, 194 O. Edd. *person*) the priest of a parish: Wiv. I, 1, 9. I, 4, 34. 81. II, 1, 218. II, 2, 317. III, 1, 36. 45. 50. 75. 106. LLL IV, 2, 84. IV, 3, 194. V, 2, 932. All's I, 3, 89. Tw. IV, 2, 13. 17. 18. 31. Rom. I, 4, 80.

**Part**, subst. 1) a piece or quantity taken from the whole: *her p.* (of the mast) Err. I, 1, 108. *in what p. of her body stands Ireland?* II, 2, 118. *the third p. of a minute,* Mids. II, 2, 2. *if every ducat were in six —s, and every p. a ducat,* Merch. IV, 1, 86. Ado III, 1, 31. IV, 1, 136. LLL II, 136. Merch. I, 3, 152. IV, 1, 329. As III, 2, 157. IV, 1, 45. 46. R2 I, 1, 128. H5 I, 1, 51. H6A IV, 5, 39 etc. etc. *a p.:* Lucr. 1328. Sonn. 37, 12. Pilgr. 428. Rom. I, 2, 17. Ant. III, 2, 24. *p.,* without the article: Lucr. Dedic. 4. Tp. V, 302. LLL IV, 3, 15. Wint. II, 3, 3. IV, 2, 51. R2 IV, 194. H6A IV, 5, 38. H8 III, 1, 24. Lr. III, 3, 13. Oth. II, 3, 187. Ant. III, 6, 35. *three —s =* three quarters: *three —s of that receipt,* R2 I, 1, 126. *where being three —s melted away, the fourth would return,* Cor. II, 3, 35. *three —s of him is ours already,* Caes. I, 3, 154. *a thought which, quartered, hath but one p. wisdom and ever three —s coward,* Hml. IV, 4, 43. *the half p. =* half: *he is the h. part of a blessed man,* John II, 437. *most p.:* H6A II, 1, 67. Oth. II, 1, 24. *for the most p.:* As III, 2, 435. Wint. IV, 2, 5. Hml. III, 2, 13. *the better p.* either = that which is most valuable in sth.: *thou art all the better p. of me,* Sonn. 39, 2. 74, 8. *Atalanta's better p.* As III, 2, 155. *mine own self's better p.* Err. III, 2, 61. *the better p. of valour is discretion,* H4A V, 4, 121. or = the greatest number or quantity: *thy dear self's better p.* Err. II, 2, 125. *the better p. of my affections would be abroad,* Merch. I, 1, 16. *were I not the better p. made mercy,* As III, 1, 2. *the better p. of us,* H4A IV, 3, 27. *the better p. burnt out,* H4B I, 2, 178. *the best p. of an hour,* H4A I, 3, 100. *great p. =* a great deal, much; *little p. =* little: *Imogen, the great p. of my comfort,* Cymb. IV, 3, 5. *that I should purchase the day before for a little p. and undo a great deal of honour,* Tim. III, 2, 53. *no p.:* All's II, 1, 135. H6B IV, 1, 47. *some p.:* As I, 1, 82. Caes. I, 2, 28. *in p.* = partly: Compl. 144. H4B IV, 1, 99. Tit. I, 236. Tim. V, 2, 13. Hml. I, 1, 165. II, 1, 15. Lr. I, 2, 43. Cymb. II, 5, 28. *in some p.* Shr. III, 2, 109. *p.,* alone, = partly: (mine eye) *doth p. his function and is partly blind,* Sonn. 113, 3. *and p. being prompted by your present trouble,* Tw. III, 4, 377. *this wretch hath p. confessed his villany,* Oth. V, 2, 296. *p. shame, p. spirit renewed,* Cymb. V, 3, 35.

2) any thing pertaining to and constituent in a whole: *when every p. a p. of woe doth bear,* Lucr. 1327. *all is semblative a woman's p.* Tw. I, 4, 34 (constituting a woman). *my lessons make no music in three —s,* Shr. III, 1, 60 (i. e. no trio). cf. *if thou'lt bear*

*a p., thou shalt hear; 'tis in three —s*, Wint. IV, 4, 299. *it is music in —s*, Troil. III, 1, 20. Particularly used of the component organs and powers of man: *when thou reviewest this* (i. e. my poems), *thou dost review the very p. was consecrate to thee*, Sonn. 74, 6 (i. e. my mind). *although in me each p. will be forgotten*, 81, 4 (body and soul). *I do betray my nobler p. to my gross body's treason*, 151, 6. *dispossessing all my other —s of necessary fitness*, Meas. II, 4, 22. *I profane my lips on thy foot, my eyes on thy picture, and my heart on thy every p.* LLL IV, 1, 87. *what is infirm from your sound —s shall fly*, All's II, 1, 170. *these weeds to each p. of you do give a life*, Wint. IV, 4, 1. *my reasonable p. produces reason*, John III, 4, 54. *the outward —s*, V, 7, 15. *every p. about you blasted with antiquity*, H4B I, 2, 207. *the immortal p. needs a physician*, II, 2, 112; cf. Rom. V, 1, 19 and Oth. II, 3, 264. *course from the inwards to the —s extreme*, H4B IV, 3, 116. *he gave his blessed p. to heaven*, H8 IV, 2, 30. *the mutinous —s*, Cor. I, 1, 115. *this, being smelt, with that p. cheers each p.* Rom. II, 3, 25. *every p. about me quivers*, II, 4, 171. *each p. stiff and cold*, IV, 1, 102. *it hath cowed my better p. of man*, Mcb. V, 8, 18. *in the secret —s of fortune*, Hml. II, 2, 239. *none our —s so poor*, Ant. I, 3, 36. *make a battery through his deafened —s*, Per. V, 1, 47. cf. besides: Ven. 436. 892. 1049. Sonn. 31, 3. 46, 13. 62, 2. LLL IV, 2, 28. 30. Merch. III, 2, 82. As I, 2, 261. John III, 1, 291. Troil. I, 3, 200. II, 3, 184.

3) a portion assigned, a share: *who all their —s of me to thee did give*, Sonn. 31, 11. *the clear eye's moiety and the dear heart's p.* 46, 12. *and in his thoughts of love doth share a p.* 47, 8. *in all external grace you have some p.* 53, 13. *of his quick objects hath the mind no p.* 113, 7. *till each to razed oblivion yield his p. of thee*, 122, 7. *my p. of this sport*, Tw. II, 5, 195. *Sir Robert might have eat up his p. in me*, John I, 234. *the p. I had in Woodstock's blood*, R2 I, 2, 1. *our p. therein we banish with yourselves*, I, 3, 181. H4A I, 2, 58. III, 1, 75. III, 3, 87. R3 I, 3, 308. V, 3, 268. Cor. V, 3, 168. Rom. IV, 5, 67. Ant. III, 6, 26. Hence = lot, fate: *my p. of death, no one so true did share it*, Tw. II, 4, 58. To take in good p. = to receive or judge with kindness: *take them* (my cates) *in good p.* Err. III, 1, 28. *in the duke's behalf I'll give my voice, which I presume, he'll take in gentle p.* R3 III, 4, 21.

4) that which is bestowed upon one, gift, endowment, quality; mostly in the plural: *thy outward —s*, Ven. 435. *shows not half your —s*, Sonn. 17, 4. *those —s of thee that the world's eye doth view*, 69, 1. *when in his fair —s she* (love) *did abide*, Compl. 83. *my —s had power to charm a sacred nun*, 260. *that I thy —s admire*, Pilgr. 66 and LLL IV, 2, 118. Wiv. I, 3, 67. II, 2, 110. Ado V, 2, 60. 65. LLL II, 44. Mids. III, 2, 153. Merch. I, 2, 46. II, 2, 191. As I, 1, 150. II, 2, 13. Shr. V, 2, 168. All's I, 2, 21. Tw. II, 4, 86. John I, 89. III, 4, 96. H4A III, 1, 188. H5 V, 2, 213. H8 II, 3, 27. II, 4, 139. Troil. III, 3, 117. Rom. III, 3, 2. III, 5, 183. Tim. II, 2, 23. III, 1, 40. Hml. IV, 7, 74. Lr. I, 4, 285. Oth. III, 3, 264. Seldomer in the sing.: *they will not admit any good p. to intermingle with them*, Ado V, 2, 64. *for fame's sake, for praise, an outward p.* LLL IV, 1, 32. *I'ld bid you mark her eye and tell me for what dull p. in't you chose her*, Wint. V, 1, 64. *your sum of —s did not together pluck*

*such envy from him as did that one. What p. is that?* Hml. IV, 7, 77. *the continent of what p. a gentleman would see*, V, 2, 115.

5) share of action, particular business, task: *every p. a p. of woe doth bear*, Lucr. 1327. *confounds in singleness the —s that thou shouldst bear*, Sonn. 8, 8. *whether beauty, birth, or wealth, or wit, ... entitled in their parts, do crowned sit*, Sonn. 37, 7 (M. Edd. *in thy parts*; cf. *Entitled).* *one that can my p. in him advertise*, Meas. I, 1, 42. *the general, subject to a well-wished king, quit their own p. and in obsequious fondness crowd to his presence*, II, 4, 28. *and never could maintain his p.* Ado I, 1, 238. *that is your grace's p.* 215. *you may do the p. of an honest man in it*, II, 1, 172. *the extreme —s of time extremely forms all causes to the purpose of his speed*, LLL V, 2, 750. *which you use in abject and in slavish —s*, Merch. IV, 1, 92. *is this your speeding? nay, then, good night our p.* Shr. II, 303. *ours be your patience then, and yours our —s*, All's V, 3, 339. *by all the —s of man which honour does acknowledge*, Wint. I, 2, 400. *I have done the p. of a careful friend*, H4B II, 4, 348. *Lord Hastings had pronounced your p., I mean your voice*, R3 III, 4, 28. *it is our p. and promise to the Athenians to speak with Timon*, Tim. V, 1, 123. *it is the p. of men to fear and tremble*, Caes. I, 3, 54. *your highness' p. is to receive our duties*, Mcb. I, 4, 23. *that p. thou must act for me*, Cymb. III, 4, 26. *the gods have done their p. in you*, Per. IV, 2, 74. cf. besides: Lucr. 278. 1135. 1830. H8 I, 2, 195. Cor. IV, 3, 55.

Particularly = the character appropriated in a play, and what is like it: Sonn. 23, 2. Wiv. V, 4, 2. Meas. IV, 6, 3. Ado I, 1, 323. III, 1, 18. LLL V, 2, 150. 336. Mids. I, 2, 20. 32. III, 1, 76. IV, 2, 38. V, 206. Shr. I, 1, 199. Tw. I, 5, 191. Cor. III, 2, 105 etc. *to play a p.:* Tp. I, 2, 107. Gent. IV, 4, 165. 171. Ado II, 1, 220. III, 2, 79. Wint. I, 2, 188 etc.

6) particular task done, characteristic action, merit or demerit: *this device ... upon some stubborn and uncourteous —s we had conceived against him*, Tw. V, 369. *this p. of his conjoins with my disease*, H4B IV, 5, 64. *if not for any —s in him — though his right arm might purchase his own time and be in debt to none — yet, more to move you, take my deserts to his*, Tim. III, 5, 77. *it was a brute p. of him to kill so capital a calf*, Hml. III, 2, 110. *my —s, my title, and my perfect soul shall manifest me rightly*, Oth. I, 2, 31. *his honours and his valiant —s*, I, 3, 254.

7) side: *from all —s they are coming*, H8 V, 4, 72. Particularly in the sense of interest, party: *with either —'s agreement*, Shr. IV, 4, 50. *to stand on either p.* All's I, 2, 15. *holy seems the quarrel upon your grace's p.* III, 1, 5. *brings in the champion Honour on my p.* IV, 2, 50. *let confusion of one p. confirm the other's peace*, John II, 359. *upon which better p. our prayers come in*, III, 1, 293. *of the p. of England*, V, 6, 2. *on his p. I'll empty all these veins*, H4A I, 3, 133 (Ff *in his behalf). those that are misled upon your cousin's p.* V, 1, 105. *the numbers dead on both our —s*, H5 IV, 7, 123. *banding themselves in contrary —s*, H6A III, 1, 81. *the frozen bosoms of our p.* H6B V, 2, 35. *uncurable discomfit reigns in the hearts of all our present —s*, 87 (p.?). *my father came on the p. of York*, H6C II, 5, 66. *our Trojan p.* Troil. IV, 5, 156. *the p. that is at mercy*, Cor. I, 10, 7. *fought on p. and p.* Rom. I, 1, 121. *who parted either p.* 122. *though in*

*general p. we were opposed*, Tim. V, 2, 7. *I'll fight against the p. I come with*, Cymb. V, 1, 25 etc. *to take p.* = to embrace one's side or party: *which* (heart) *once corrupted takes the worser p.* Lucr. 294. *with my nobler reason 'gainst my fury do I take p.* Tp. V, 27. *take my p.* Meas. V, 435. Mids. III, 2, 322. 333. As I, 2, 140. I, 3, 22. H4B V, 2, 96. H6A I, 1, 94. H6B I, 1, 240. IV, 2, 197. Rom. III, 3, 26. Lr. I, 4, 111 etc. Hence the phrase *for my p.*, *for your p.* = as for me, as far as concerns me etc.: Tp. III, 2, 15. Wiv. I, 1, 178. Ado V, 4, 110. Merch. III, 1, 29. III, 2, 229. V, 144. As I, 1, 7. All's III, 2, 46. H4B III, 2, 270. H6B I, 3, 104. R3 II, 4, 70. Caes. III, 1, 172 etc. *for mine own p.:* Wiv. III, 4, 65. Meas. II, 1, 219. Ado III, 5, 23. LLL V, 2, 502. 507. 732. Merch. II, 2, 109 etc. *for mine own poor p.* Hml. I, 5, 131.

*On one's p.* = a) on one's side, in or by one: (honour) *much deserved on his p.* Ado I, 1, 12. *that is too much presumption on thy p.* H6B V, 1, 38. *this interchange of love upon my p. shall be unviolable*, R3 II, 1, 27. *all his virtues, not virtuously on his own p. beheld*, Troil. II, 3, 127 (Ff *of his own p.*). *if on both —s this be not cherished*, Ant. III, 2, 32. b) in one's behalf: *to guard the lawful reasons on thy p.* Sonn. 49, 12. *upon thy p. I can set down a story*, 88, 6. *plead on her p. some cause to you unknown*, Err. III, 1, 91. *to speak on the p. of virginity*, All's I, 1, 148. *we do here pronounce upon the p. of the people*, Cor. III, 1, 210. Similarly in *one's p.: what in your own p. can you say to this?* Oth. I, 3, 74.

8) Plur. *—s* = quarters, regions, districts: *skilless in these —s*, Tw. III, 3, 9. *have in these —s from morn till even fought*, H5 III, 1, 20. *to be our regent in these —s of France*, H6A IV, 1, 163. H6B I, 1, 67. R3 IV, 2, 47. Cor. IV, 5, 148. Caes. III, 1, 264. Per. V, 1, 171. cf. Tw. III, 4, 294. H5 II, 4, 22.

**Part**, vb. 1) trans. a) to divide into pieces or into shares: *let's p. the word*, LLL V, 2, 249. *like to a double cherry, seeming —ed, but yet an union in partition*, Mids. III, 2, 209. *I see these things with —ed eye, when every thing seems double*, IV, 1, 194. *the old proverb is very well —ed between my master Shylock and you*, Merch. II, 2, 158. *we'll p. the time between's*, Wint. I, 2, 18. *to tug and scamble and to p. by the teeth the unowed interest of state*, John IV, 3, 146. *raught at mountains, yet —ed but the shadow with his hand*, H6C I, 4, 69 (i. e. cut it in two by extending his hand). *p. in just proportion our small strength*, R3 V, 3, 26. *I had thought they had —ed so much honesty among 'em*, H8 V, 2, 28. *—s bread with him*, Tim. I, 2, 48. *p. the numbers*, Caes. III, 2, 4. *to p. the glories of this happy day*, V, 5, 81. *this coronet p. betwixt you*, Lr. I, 1, 141. *have my heart —ed betwixt two friends*, Ant. III, 6, 77.

b) to separate: *the ocean which —s the shore*, Sonn. 56, 10. *to p. a fray*, Ado V, 1, 114. *how canst thou p. sadness and melancholy?* LLL I, 2, 7. *thou —est a fair fray*, V, 2, 484. *when we have chid the hasty-footed time for —ing us*, Mids. III, 2, 201. *for —ing my fair Pyramus and me*, V, 191. *the wall that —ed their fathers*, 359. *the narrow seas that p. the French and English*, Merch. II, 8, 28. *severed lips, —ed with sugar breath*, III, 2, 119. *thus misery doth p. the flux of company*, As II, 1, 51. V, 2, 45. V, 4, 137. Shr. I, 2, 23. All's III, 6, 113. Wint. IV, 4, 354. John II, 389. V, 5, 18. R2 V, 1, 76. H4B I, 2, 257.

H5 Prol. 22. H6B IV, 7, 140. R3 II, 2, 150. Troil. III, 2, 55. Rom. I, 1, 76. 122. Lr. V, 3, 22. Oth. II, 1, 93. Per. III, 2, 101.

c) to leave: *your souls must p. your bodies*, R2 III, 1, 3. *when we —ed Pentapolis*, Per. V, 3, 38. Sonn. 113, 3.*

2) intr. a) to divide, to go asunder: *the bushes, as fearful of him, p., through whom he rushes*, Ven. 630. *who* (the pillow) *therefore angry, seems to p. in sunder*, Lucr. 388. *if what —s can so remain*, Phoen. 48. *make thy knotted and combined locks to p. and each particular hair to stand on end*, Hml. I, 5, 18.

b) to be separated, to quit each other, to take farewell: *let us p.* Ven. 421. *summon us to p.* 534. *the honey fee of —ing*, 538. Gent. II, 2, 21. II, 3, 13. Err. V, 321. LLL V, 2, 57. 220. 821. Merch. II, 8, 36. 49. As I, 3, 100. V, 4, 91. Shr. III, 2, 181. All's II, 1, 36. Wint. IV, 4, 155. John V, 4, 47. R2 I, 4, 5. II, 1, 222. V, 1, 70. H4B II, 1, 207. H6B III, 2, 355. 403. H6C IV, 3, 30. V, 5, 7. Rom. I, 1, 71. Caes. V, 1, 119. 122. Ant. III, 2, 1 etc. Followed by *from:* Gent. IV, 4, 102. Wiv. II, 2, 274. Mids. III, 2, 80. Merch. III, 2, 174. 186. As IV, 3, 99. R2 II, 2, 13. H4A V, 4, 71. Troil. IV, 4, 63. Lr. I, 4, 44. By *with:* Gent. II, 5, 11. III, 1, 253. Err. V, 221. Mids. II, 1, 137. As III, 2, 235. Shr. II, 64. Wint. V, 1, 160. R2 I, 4, 10. II, 2, 2. III, 2, 8. H4A I, 2, 187. III, 1, 194. H6C II, 6, 4. R3 I, 4, 251. Rom. III, 3, 174. Cymb. V, 5, 386 etc. Sometimes = to give away: *to p. so slightly with your wife's first gift*, Merch. V, 167. 171. *I will not p. with a village of it*, H5 V, 2, 183. *you will p. but with light gifts*, R3 III, 1, 118. *you cannot take from me any thing that I will more willingly p. withal*, Hml. II, 2, 220. With *to: therefore I p. with him, and p. with him to one that I would have him help to waste his borrowed purse*, Merch. II, 5, 49. *a greater sum than ever the clergy yet did to his predecessors p. withal*, H5 I, 1, 81.

c) to depart, to go away: *from whence at pleasure thou mayst come and p.* Sonn. 48, 12. *at my —ing sweetly did she smile*, Pilgr. 187. *but now he —ed hence*, Gent. I, 1, 71. *the company —s*, IV, 2, 81. *we shall p. with neither*, Err. III, 1, 67. *thus losers p.* Merch. II, 7, 77. *procured his leave for present —ing*, All's II, 5, 61. *an thou let p. so*, Tw. I, 3, 65. *we will not p. from hence*, V, 394. *pay then when you p.* Wint. I, 2, 10. *let them have pay and p.* H4B IV, 2, 70. *if the trial of the law o'ertake ye, you'll p. away disgraced*, H8 III, 1, 97. *so she —ed*, IV, 1, 92. *after we p. from Agamemnon's tent*, Troil. IV, 5, 285. *when I —ed hence*, Cor. V, 6, 73. *I would not p. a bachelor from the priest*, Tit. I, 488. *we must all p. into this sea of air*, Tim. IV, 2, 21. *France in choler —ed*, Lr. I, 2, 23. *what thing was that which —ed from you?* IV, 6, 68. *was not that Cassio —ed from my wife?* Oth. III, 3, 37. *Octavia weeps to p. from Rome*, Ant. III, 2, 4. *and —ed with prayers for the provider*, Cymb. III, 6, 52. Euphemism for to die: *a' —ed between twelve and one*, H5 II, 3, 12. *now in peace my soul shall p. to heaven*, R3 II, 1, 5. *thy —ing soul*, H6A II, 5, 115. *he —ed well*, Mcb. V, 8, 52.

**Part**, adv. partly; see *Part* subst.

**Partake** (partic. *partaken:* All's IV, 5, 11) 1) to take another's party, to side: *canst thou say I love thee not, when I against myself with thee p.?* Sonn. 149, 2.

2) to have part, to share; with *in: not meaning to*

*p. with me in danger*, Tw. V, 90. *would not let him p. in the glory of the action*, Ant. III, 5, 9. With *of: if she had —n of my flesh*, All's IV, 5, 11 (i. e. had been my daughter). *you may p. of any thing we say*, R3 I, 1, 89 (= hear). Absol.: *what, what, what? let's p.* (= hear) Cor. IV, 5, 184. Trans.: *one may drink and yet p. no venom*, Wint. II, 1, 41. *thy bosom shall p. the secrets of my heart*, Caes. II, 1, 305.

3) to communicate: *your exultation p. to every one*, Wint. V, 3, 132. *our mind —s her private actions to your secrecy*, Per. I, 1, 153.

**Partaker,** 1) one who takes the party of another, confederate: *for your p. Pole and you yourself, I'll note you in my book of memory*, H6A II, 4, 100.

2) participator, sharer: *p. in thy happiness*, Gent. I, 1, 14. *—s of a little gain*, H6A II, 1, 52. *to let me be p.* Ant. I, 4, 83 (= to let me hear of it).

**Part-created,** half-made, half-accomplished: H4B I, 3, 60.

**Parted,** gifted, endowed: *how dearly ever p.* Troil. III, 3, 96.

**Parthia,** country in Asia, at war with Rome: Caes. V, 3, 37. Ant. II, 2, 15. II, 3, 32. III, 1, 1. 33. III, 6, 14.

**Parthian,** 1) subst. a native of Parthia: Ant. III, 1, 7. Cymb. I, 6, 20. 2) adj. pertaining to Parthia: Ant. I, 2, 104. III, 1, 6. IV, 14, 70.

**Partial,** inclined to favour one party more than the other: *and nothing come in p.* Meas. II, 1, 31 (let no body speak for me as you do for Claudio). *a p. slander sought I to avoid*, R2 I, 3, 241 (= reproach of partiality). H4B III, 1, 26. Troil. II, 2, 178. Hml. III, 3, 32. With *to:* Lr. I, 4, 334. With an inf.: Err. I, 1, 4. Unintelligible: Pilgr. 302.

**Partialize,** to make partial: R2 I, 1, 120.

**Partially,** with undue favour: Lucr. 634. Oth. II, 3, 218.

**Participate,** vb. to have in common with others: *that dimension which from the womb I did p.* Tw.V,245.

**Participate,** adj. acting in common: *and mutually p. did minister unto the appetite of the whole body*, Cor. I, 1, 106.

**Participation,** community, fellowship: *thou hast lost thy princely privilege with vile p.* H4A III, 2, 87. *their spirits are so married in conjunction with the p. of society that they flock together in consent, like so many wild geese*, H4B V, 1, 78.

**Particle,** any single part, particular, item: *it shall be inventoried, and every p. and utensil labelled to my will*, Tw. I, 5, 264. *if he do break the smallest p. of any promise*, Caes. II, 1, 139.

**Particular,** adj. 1) single: *what a hell of witchcraft lies in the small orb of one p. tear!* Compl. 289. *oft it chances in p. men*, Hml. I, 4, 23. *take corruption from that p. fault*, 36. *each p. hair to stand on end*, I, 5, 19. *come you more nearer than your p. demands will touch it*, II, 1, 12. cf. the jest of Cade: *where's our general? Here I am, thou p. fellow*, H6B IV, 2, 119.

2) special, one among many considered in itself: *the p. accidents gone by since I came to this isle*, Tp. V, 305. *thy oaths, though they would swear down each p. saint*, Meas. V, 243. *you shall recount their p. duties afterwards*, Ado IV, 1, 3. *thus did she transshape thy p. virtues*, V, 1, 172. *that I should love a bright p. star*, All's I, 1, 97. *in what p. action to try him*, III, 6, 18. *the p. confirmations, point from point*, IV, 3, 71. *swear*

*his thought over by each p. star in heaven*, Wint. I, 2, 425. *the king is not bound to answer the p. endings of his soldiers*, H5 IV, 1, 163. *whose tenours and p. effects you have enscheduled briefly in your hands*, V, 2, 72. *but what p. rarity?* Tim. I, 1, 4. *in what p. thought to work I know not*, Hml. I, 1, 67.

3) pertaining to a single person or thing: *I will have it in a p. ballad else*, H4B IV, 3, 52. *doth any name p. belong unto the lodging?* IV, 5, 233. *the prescript praise and perfection of a good and p. mistress*, H5 III, 7, 50. *hath robbed many beasts of their p. additions*, Troil. I, 2, 20. *the success although p., shall give a scantling of good or bad unto the general*, I, 3, 341. *value dwells not in p. will*, II, 2, 53. *yet is the kindness but p.; 'twere better she were kissed in general*, IV, 5, 20. *whereby he does receive p. addition*, Mcb. III, 1, 100. *why seems it so p. with thee?* Hml. I, 2, 75.

Hence = individual, private, personal: *that no p. scandal once can touch but it confounds the breather*, Meas. IV, 4, 30. *their profits, their own p. thrifts*, Wint. I, 2, 311. *upon my p. knowledge of his directions*, H5 III, 2, 84. *to lay apart their p. functions*, III, 7, 41. *make yourself mirth with your p. fancy, and leave me out on't*, H8 II, 3, 101. *but by p. consent proceeded under your hands and seals*, II, 4, 221. *thine own p. wrongs*, Cor. IV, 5, 92. *the glorious gods sit in hourly synod about thy p. prosperity*, V, 2, 74. *though in general part we were opposed, yet our old love made a p. force*, Tim. V, 2, 8. *as he in his p. act and place may give his saying deed*, Hml. I, 3, 26 (Ff *in his peculiar sect and force*). *inform her full of my p. fear*, Lr. I, 4, 360. *these domestic and p. broils*, V, 1, 30. *my p. grief*, Oth. I, 3, 55. *from which the world should note something p.* Ant. III, 13, 22 (some personal merit).

**Particular,** subst. 1) single person: *he's to make his request by —s, wherein every one of us has a single honour*, Cor. II, 3, 48. *I wish, sir — I mean, for your p. — you had not joined in commission with him*, IV, 7, 13. *though no man lesser fears the Greeks than I as far as toucheth my p.* Troil. II, 2, 9. *for his p., I'll receive him gladly, but not one follower*, Lr. II, 4, 295.

2) a single point, a single thing: *these — s* (glory, skill, wealth etc. ) *are not my measure*, Sonn. 91, 7. *give us —s of thy preservation*, Tp. V, 135. *to say ay and no to these —s is more than to answer in a catechism*, As III, 2, 240. *your doing, so singular in each p.* Wint. IV, 4, 144. *examine me upon the —s of my life*, H4A II, 4, 414. *I sent your grace the parcels and —s of our grief*, H4B IV, 2, 36. *a tapster's arithmetic may soon bring his —s therein to a total*, Troil. I, 2, 124. *in whom I know all the —s of vice so grafted*, Mcb. IV, 3, 51. *that all —s of duty know*, Lr. I, 4, 286. *your fortunes are alike. But how? give me —s*, Ant. I, 2, 57. *more —s must justify my knowledge*, Cymb. II, 4, 78.

3) private concern, personal relation: *my course, which holds not colour with the time, nor does the ministration and required office on my p.* All's II, 5, 66. *my brother general, the commonwealth, to brother born an household cruelty, I make my quarrel in p.* H4B IV, 1, 96. *every function of your power should, notwithstanding that your bond of duty, as 'twere in love's p., be more to me, than any*, H8 III, 2, 189. *who loved him in a most dear p.* Cor. V, 1, 3. *him that, his p. to foresee, smells from the general weal*, Tim.

IV, 3, 159. *my more p. is Fulvia's death,* Ant. I, 3, 54. *forgive me in thine own p., but let the world rank me in register a master-leaver,* IV, 9, 20.

4) minute detail of things singly enumerated: *let me answer to the p. of the inter'gatories: demand them singly,* All's IV, 3, 207. *with every course in his p.* H4B IV, 4, 90. *let me question more in p., what have you deserved at the hands of fortune,* Hml. II, 2, 244.

**Particularities,** single or private respects: *being as good a man as yourself, both in the disciplines of war, and in the derivation of my birth, and in other p.* H5 III, 2, 142 (Fluellen's speech). *now let the general trumpet blow his blast, p. and petty sounds to cease,* H6B V, 2, 44.

**Particularize,** to specify: *as an inventory to p. their abundance,* Cor. I, 1, 21.

**Particularly,** personally, privately: *who hath done to thee p. and to all the Volsces great hurt,* Cor. IV, 5, 72. *my free drift halts not p.* Tim. I, 1, 46 (does not stop at any single person).

**Partisan,** see *Partizan.*

**Partition,** 1) division: *like to a double cherry, seeming parted, but yet an union in p.* Mids. III, 2, 210.

2) distinction: *and good from bad find no p.* H4B IV, 1, 196. *and can we not p. make 'twixt fair and foul?* Cymb. I, 6, 37.

3) a party-wall: *it is the wittiest p. that ever I heard discourse,* Mids. V, 168.

**Partizan,** a kind of halbert: Rom. I, 1, 80. 101. Hml. I, 1, 140. Ant. II, 7, 14. Cymb. IV, 2, 399.

**Partlet,** the name of the hen in the story-book of Reynard the Fox: *thy dame P. here,* Wint. II, 3, 75. *how now, Dame P. the hen,* H4A III, 3, 60.[*]

**Partly,** in part, in some measure: Sonn. 113, 3. Gent. IV, 1, 55. Meas. II, 1, 231. V, 450. Ado V, 4, 96. Mids. III, 2, 243. Merch. III, 5, 11. As II, 4, 24. Tw. V, 125. Wint. III, 2, 19. V, 3, 142. H5 III, 6, 52. H6C III, 2, 66. R3 III, 7, 235. IV, 2, 41. Troil. III, 1, 19. Cor. I, 1, 40. II, 3, 270. Caes. V, 1, 79. 90. Oth. I, 1, 123. II, 1, 303. Ant. III, 13, 66. V, 2, 325. Cymb. IV, 2, 64. *p. .... p. .... and p.* H5 III, 2, 102. *p. ... but in chief,* Meas. V, 219. *p ... but chiefly,* Gent. IV, 4, 69. Rom. V, 3, 29. *p. .... p. .... but chiefly,* Ado III, 3, 166. H4A III, 4, 444.

**Partner,** subst. companion, associate; with *in: to be thy p. in this shameful doom,* Lucr. 672. Wint. IV, 2, 58. Ant. II, 2, 59. Cymb. I, 6, 184. With *of: wishing me with him, p. of his fortune,* Gent. I, 3, 59. Wint. IV, 4, 558. H6A III, 2, 92. Mcb. I, 5, 12. *my vows are equal —s with thy vows,* H6A III, 2, 85. = colleague: Meas. IV, 2, 19. Ado III, 3, 65. III, 5, 62. IV, 2, 4. Cor. V, 3, 2. V, 6, 39. Mcb. I, 3, 54. 142. Ant. I, 4, 8. II, 2, 22. = one who stands godfather with another: H8 V, 3, 168. V, 5, 6. = one who dances with another: H8 I, 4, 103. = accomplice: Meas. II, 3, 37.

**Partnered,** associated, consorted: *to be p. with tomboys,* Cymb. I, 6, 121.

**Partridge,** the bird Perdix cinerea: Ado II, 1, 155. H6B III, 2, 191.

**Party,** 1) part, side, cause, interest: *till she had kindled France and all the world upon the right and p. of her son,* John I, 34. *whose p. do the townsmen yet admit?* II, 361. *to brag and stamp and swear upon my p.* III, 1, 123. *your southern gentlemen in arms upon his p.* R2 III, 2, 203 (Ff *faction*). *which on thy royal p. granted once,* III, 3, 115. *maintain the p. of the truth,* H6A II, 4, 32. *will I upon thy p. wear this rose,* 123. *to find you forward upon his p.* R3 III, 2, 47. *they came from Buckingham upon his p.* IV, 4, 528. *factionary on the p. of your general,* Cor. V, 2, 30. *have you nothing said upon his p. 'gainst the Duke of Albany?* Lr. II, 1, 28.

2) one of two litigants: *thy adverse p. is thy advocate,* Sonn. 35, 10. *when the —es were met,* As V, 4, 104. *in witness whereof the —s,* Troil. II, 2, 61. *hearing a matter between p. and p.* Cor. II, 1, 82. *calling both the —es knaves,* 88.

3) one concerned or interested in any affair; with *in: I must be a p. in this alteration,* Wint. I, 2, 383. *are you a p. in this business?* IV, 4, 843. *I do suspect this trash to be a p. in this injury,* Oth. V, 1, 86. With *to: not a p. to the anger of the king,* Wint. II, 2, 61. Absol.: *where neither p. is nor true nor kind,* Compl. 186. *canst thou bring me to the p.?* Tp. III, 2, 67. *from the two —es,* Wiv. IV, 5, 107. *the —es themselves, the actors,* LLL V, 2, 500. *the p. is gone, she is gone,* 678. *the p. 'gainst the which he doth contrive,* Merch. IV, 1, 352. *the p. tried the daughter of a king,* Wint. III, 2, 2. *bring forth the —es of suspicion,* Rom. V, 3, 222. *the love of the —es,* Ant. II, 6, 127.

Hence = person in general: *and the three p. is mine host,* Wiv. I, 1, 142 (Evans' speech). *the p. writing,* LLL IV, 2, 138. *tax any private p.* As II, 7, 71. *the p. that owed it,* H4B I, 2, 4. *the people of Rome, for whom we stand a special p.* Tit. I, 21. *your p. in converse,* Hml. II, 1, 42. *I would not be the p. that should desire you to touch him,* Ant. V, 2, 246. *though it be allowed in meaner —es,* Cymb. II, 3, 121.

4) an association or confederacy formed in a community against others of a contrary opinion: *then both —es nobly are subdued, and neither p. loser,* H4B IV, 2, 90. 91. *to fight on Edward's p.* R3 I, 3, 138. IV, 4, 190. *making —es strong,* Cor. I, 1, 198. *lest —es break out,* III, 1, 315. *win the noble Brutus to our p.* Caes. I, 3, 141. *what p. I do follow,* Lr. IV, 5, 40.

5) one of two powers at war with each other; preceded by *on: three knights upon our p. slain,* H4A V, 5, 6. *which they upon the adverse p. want,* R3 V, 3, 13 (Ff *faction*). *there's not the meanest spirit on our p.* Troil. II, 2, 156. *and he upon my p.* Cor. I, 1, 238.

6) armed force, army: *our p. may well meet a prouder foe,* John V, 1, 79. *to fright our p.* H4B I, 1, 67. *from his metal was his p. steeled,* 116. *the English army, that divided was into two —es,* H6A V, 2, 12 (some M. Edd. *parts,* as indeed the metre requires). *I saw our p. to their trenches driven,* Cor. I, 6, 12. *'tis fit you make strong p.* III, 2, 94. *seek him out upon the British p.* Lr. IV, 6, 256. *to the king's p. there's no going,* Cymb. IV, 4, 9.

7) ally, confederate: *in himself too mighty, and in his —es, his alliance,* Wint. II, 3, 21. *these promises are fair, the —es sure,* H4A III, 1, 1. *wherein you wished us —es,* Cor. V, 6, 14. *which approved him an intelligent p. to the advantages of France,* Lr. III, 5, 12.

**Party-coated,** dressed in a coat of divers colours, like a fool: LLL V, 2, 776.

**Party-coloured,** having divers colours: Merch. I, 3, 89.

**Party-verdict,** a judgment given by a particular member of a court of justice: *whereto thy tongue a p. gave,* R2 I, 3, 234.[*]

**Pash,** subst. the head (Jamieson's Etym. Dict. of the Scot. Language): *thou wantest a rough p. and the shoots that I have, to be full like me,* Wint. l, 2, 128.

**Pash,** vb. to strike, to strike down: *with my armed fist I'll p. him o'er the face,* Troil. ll, 3, 213 (Q *push*). *stands ... upon the —ed corses of the kings,* V, 5, 10.

**Pass,** subst. 1) the act of going from one place to another, passage: *charming the narrow seas to give you gentle p.* H5 ll Chor. 39. *to give quiet p. through your dominions,* Hml. ll, 2, 77.

2) permission or right of going, license: *when evil deeds have their permissive p. and not the punishment,* Meas. I, 3, 38.

3) currency, estimation: *common speech gives him a worthy p.* All's ll, 5, 58.

4) act, proceeding, course: *your grace, like power divine, hath looked upon my —es,* Meas. V, 375. Perhaps also in Sonn. 103, 11: *to no other p. my verses tend than of your graces and your gifts to tell.*

5) a narrow passage, a defile: *the strait p. was dammed with dead men hurt behind,* Cymb. V, 3, 11.

6) an embarrassing situation, predicament, extremity: *being at that p., you would keep from my heels,* Err. III, 1, 17. *till I be brought to such a silly p.* Shr. V, 2, 124. *have his daughters brought him to this p.?* Lr. III, 4, 65.

7) As a term of fencing, a) a push, a thrust at the adversary: *'tis dangerous when the baser nature comes between the p. and fell incensed points of mighty opposites,* Hml. V, 2, 61. b) a course of fencing, till one of the combatants is hit: *in these times you stand on distance, your —es, stoccadoes,* Wiv. II, 1, 233. *I had a p. with him,* Tw. III, 4, 302. *in a dozen —es between yourself and him,* Hml. V, 2, 173.

Figuratively: *an excellent p. of pate,* Tp. IV, 244 (a sally of wit). *and in a p. of practice requite him for your father,* Hml. IV, 7, 139.

**Pass,** vb. 1) to make one's way, to proceed, to go, to come: *that o'er the green cornfield did p.* As V, 3, 19. *to think your father should p. this way,* Wint. IV, 4, 20. *your gallery have we —ed through,* V, 3, 11. *if we may p., we will,* H5 III, 6, 169. *— ing to and fro,* H6A ll, 1, 69. *if one of so mean condition may p. into the presence of a king,* H6B V, 1, 65. *Edward hath —ed in safety through the narrow seas,* H6C IV, 8, 3. *let the coffin p.* R3 I, 2, 38. *that I may see my shadow as I p.* 264. *his long trouble now is —ing out of this world,* H8 IV, 2, 162. *when they p. back from the christening,* V, 4, 78. *find a way out to let the troop p. fairly,* 89. *a most unspotted lily shall she p. to the ground,* V, 5, 62. *as they p. toward Ilium,* Troil. I, 2, 194. *p. no further,* Cor. III, 1, 24. *if you will p. to where you are bound,* 53. *I'll tell thee as we p.* Rom. II, 3, 63. *let me p. quietly,* Tim. III, 4, 54. *these words become your lips as they p. through them,* V, 1, 198. *any promise that hath —ed from him,* Caes. II, 1, 140. *—ing through nature to eternity,* Hml. I, 2, 73. *this trusty servant shall p. between us,* Lr. IV, 2, 19. *let poor folk p.* IV, 6, 243. *as my farthest band shall p. on thy approof,* Ant. III, 2, 27. *to p. along:* Gent. V, 4, 168. LLL ll, 245. As I, 3, 115. R2 V, 2, 21. H6C ll, 1, 195. R3 III, 1, 136. H8 V, 2, 11. Troil. III, 3, 51. Caes. II, 3, 11. Ant. III, 1, 37. *to p. away:* H8 I, 4, 33. LLL I, 1, 49 (= to avoid). *to p. by:* H6B II, 4, 48. III, 1, 16. IV, 8, 18. Troil. I, 2, 199. III, 3, 71. Rom. I, 1, 46. Tim. II, 1, 12. V,

4, 73. Caes. I, 2, 179. *to p. by sth.:* Sonn. 70, 9 (= to avoid). All's II, 3, 247. Troil. III, 3, 39. 142. Caes. IV, 3, 68. *to p. on:* Mids. II, 1, 163. H8 II, 4, 130. Caes. II, 4, 26. *to p.,* alone, = to go on: Caes. I, 2, 24. = to go away: *letting her p. so,* All's III, 4, 20. *I have no power to let her p.* H6A V, 3, 60. *what ransom must I pay before I p.?* 73. *till thou speak, thou shalt not p. from hence,* H6B I, 4, 30.

2) to go by; locally and temporally: *scorning it (the tear) should p.* Ven. 982. *in rage sent out, recalled in rage, being —ed,* Lucr. 1671. *when thou shalt strangely p. and scarcely greet me,* Sonn. 49, 5. *till the dregs of the storm be —ed,* Tp. II, 2, 43. *the best is —ed,* III, 3, 51. *kneel to the duke before he p. the abbey,* Err. V, 129. *till this company be —ed,* LLL I, 2, 131. *the troop is —ed,* All's III, 5, 96. *daffed the world aside and bid it p.* H4A IV, 1, 97 (as not caring for it; see below; and cf. Sly's *let the world slide,* Shr. Ind. 1, 6). *let's stay till he be —ed,* H6C III, 1, 12. *behold the Lady Anne pass from her coronation,* H8 IV, 1, 3. *flung gloves ... upon him as he —ed,* Cor. II, 1, 281. *ere three days p.* Shr. IV, 2, 38. *hath told the thievish minutes how they p.* All's II, 1, 169. *let never day nor night unhallowed p.* H6B II, 1, 85. *ere half an hour p.* Tit. III, 1, 192. *to let p.* = to disregard, to take no notice of: *did I let p. the abuse done to my niece?* H6C III, 3, 188. *let former grudges p.* 195. *let it,* or *let that p.* = make no more words about it: Wiv. I, 4, 15. LLL V, 1, 102. 106. 111. 115. R3 IV, 2, 88 (Ff *rest*). Per. II, 3, 35 (cf. H4A IV, 1, 97). see *Past.*

Transitively, = to neglect, to disregard, to omit: *he shall not p. you,* Meas. IV, 6, 12. *if you fondly p. our proffered offer,* John II, 258. *please you that I may p. this doing,* Cor. II, 2, 143. *and —ed him unelected,* II, 3, 207. cf. *to p. by* in All's II, 3, 247.

3) to go over, to go across, to go through: *he should not p. those grounds,* Pilgr. 124. *the ways are dangerous to p.* Gent. IV, 3, 24. *the Vapians —ing the equinoctial,* Tw. II, 3, 24. *—ing these flats,* John V, 6, 40. *he hath —ed the river Somme,* H5 III, 5, 1. *well have we —ed and now repassed the seas,* H6C IV, 7, 5. *curses never p. the lips of those that breathe them in the air,* R3 I, 3, 285. *who —ed the melancholy flood,* I, 4, 45. *to see great Pompey pass the streets of Rome,* Caes. I, 1, 47.

Used of time, = to spend, to live through: *you have —ed a hell of time,* Sonn. 120, 6. *I have —ed a miserable night,* R3 I, 4, 2. *p. the remainder of our hateful days,* Tit. III, 1, 132. *in our last conference, —ed in probation with you, how you were borne in hand,* Mcb. III, 1, 80.* Joined with adverbs: *years, —ed over to the end they were created,* H6C II, 5, 39. *have no delight to p. away the time,* R3 I, 1, 25.

Figuratively, = to see, to experience, to suffer: *were I alone to p. the difficulties,* Troil. II, 2, 139. *the battles, sieges, fortunes, that I have —ed,* Oth. I, 3, 131. *she loved me for the dangers I had —ed,* 167. *be quiet then as men should be, till he hath —ed necessity,* Per. II Prol. 6.

4) to go beyond: *—ing all conceit,* Pilgr. 110. *and so conclusions —ed the careires,* Wiv. I, 1, 184, i. e. carried the joke too far; cf. *he —es some humours and careers,* H5 II, 1, 132. *she —es praise,* LLL IV, 3, 241 (exceeds). *though it p. your patience and mine,* Shr. I, 1, 130. *as —es colouring,* Wint. II, 2, 20. *who*

—ed that —ing fair, Rom. I, 1, 242 (= surpassed). not a man shall p. his quarter, Tim. V, 4, 60. I have that within which —eth show, Hml. I, 2, 85. so far he —ed my thought, IV, 7, 89 (Qq topt).

Absolutely, = to exceed bounds, to beggar description: the women have so shrieked at it that it —ed, Wiv. I, 1, 310. this —es, Master Ford, IV, 2, 127. 143. all the rest so laughed that it —ed, Troil. I, 2, 182. he —es, Tim. I, 1, 12. cf. Passing.

5) to have the liberty of going and coming, to have free passage: you may not p., you must return, Cor. V, 2, 5. 23. 26. 34. my lord, you p. not here, Tit. I, 290. then thou canst not p. to Mantua, Rom. III, 3, 149. sweet marjoram. P. Lr. IV, 6, 94. let him not p., but kill him rather, Oth. V, 2, 241.

Transitively, = to allow to go: I know not what I shall incur to p. it, Wint. II, 2, 57. = to come into, to enter: no villanous bounty yet hath —ed my heart, Tim. II, 2, 182 (?).

Figuratively, = a) to be suffered, to be borne with: in the number let me p. untold, Sonn. 136, 9. will that humour p.? Wiv. I, 3, 57. that I may p. with a reproof the easier, sith you yourself know etc. Wiv. II, 2, 194. thou didst make tolerable vent of thy travel; it might p. All's II, 3, 213. let me p. the same I am, Wint. IV, 1, 9. and so agree the play may p. H8 Prol. 11. Transitively, = to suffer, and to make to be suffered or acknowledged: p. good humours, Wiv. I, 1. 169. we must have cracked crowns, and p. them current too, H4A II, 3, 97. some strange indignity, which patience could not p. Oth. II, 3, 246. uses a known truth to p. a thousand nothings with, All's II, 5, 32. b) to be enacted, to receive the sanction of the legislature: that bill had indeed against us —ed, H5 I, 1, 3. if it p. against us, 7. your request shall make me let it p. V, 2, 372. if your will p., I shall both find your lordship judge and juror, H8 V, 3, 59. to yield what —es here, Cor. II, 2, 58. And transitively, = to receive the sanction of: hath he not —ed the noble and the common? Cor. III, 1, 29. being —ed for consul with full voice, III, 3, 59. c) to be current, to be regarded or estimated: they may p. for excellent men, Mids. V, 219. let him p. for a man, Merch. I, 2, 61. p. for a wise man, Tw. I, 5, 38. to p. for honest, Wint. II, 3, 72.

6) to die: let him p. peaceably, H6B III, 3, 25. thus might he p. indeed, Lr. IV, 6, 47. let him p. V, 3, 313.

7) to happen, to proceed, to be done: what hath —ed between me and Ford's wife, Wiv. III, 5, 63. Meas. III, 1, 161. Ado V, 2, 48. Tw. V, 158. this practice hath most shrewdly —ed upon thee, 360. the injuries that have on both sides - ed, 376. thou seest what's —ed, H6C III, 3, 226. how —ed it? H8 II, 1, 10. nought hath —ed, but even with law, Tit. IV, 4, 7. to bring to p. = to effect: Wiv. IV, 2, 183. Merch. I, 3, 93. Shr. III, 2, 131. to come to p. = to happen: Meas. II, 1, 256. Mids. III, 2, 33. IV, 1, 83. As II, 5, 52. All's IV, 3, 371. Tw. III, 4, 196. H8 I, 2, 63. Hml. II, 2, 437. Ant. IV, 14, 121.

Transitively, = to perform, to effect, to do: to see thee p. thy punto, thy stock, thy reverse, Wiv. II, 3, 26. this swain shall p. Pompey the Great, LLL V, 1, 135. and p. my daughter a sufficient dower, Shr. IV, 4, 45. we'll p. the business privately and well, 57.

8) to utter, to pronounce: —ed sentence may not be recalled, Err. I, 1, 148. your oaths are —ed, LLL I, 1, 19. 49. my doom which I have —ed upon her, As

I, 3, 86. to p. assurance of a dower, Shr. IV, 2, 117. I'll add three thousand crowns to what is —ed already, All's III, 7, 36. he will not p. his word for two pence that you are no fool, Tw. I, 5, 86. remember thy promise —ed, R2 V, 3, 51. we will p. our accept and peremptory answer, H5 V, 2, 82. make thee beg pardon for thy —ed speech, H6B III, 2, 221. that (voice) not —ed me but by learned approbation of the judges, H8 I, 2, 70 (me dat. ethicus). I have —ed my word and promise to the emperor, Tit. I, 468.

Absol., = to pass sentence, to give judgment: the jury, —ing on the prisoner's life, Meas. II, 1, 19. thieves do p. on thieves, 23. we may not p. upon his life without the form of justice, Lr. III, 7, 24.

9) to thrust, to make a push in fencing: I pray you, p. with your best violence, Hml. V, 2, 309. Figuratively: an thou p. upon me, I'll no more with thee, Tw. III, 1, 48 (if thou makest sallies of wit on my score).

10) to care for: as for these silken-coated slaves, I p. not, H6B IV, 2, 136 (Cade's speech; the trans. use sub 2 misconceived).

**Passable,** 1) having free passage: the virtue of your name is not here p. Cor. V, 2, 13. 2) affording free passage: his body's a p. carcass, if he be not hurt, Cymb. I, 2, 10.

**Passado,** a motion forwards and thrust in fencing: the p. he (Cupid) respects not, LLL I, 2, 184. ah, the immortal passado. Rom. II, 4, 26. come, sir, your p. III, 1, 88.

**Passage,** 1) the act of passing or moving, motion, course, entrance or exit: the wind, imprisoned in the ground, struggling for p. Ven. 1047. to make more vent for p. of her breath, Lucr. 1040. my (time's) swift p. Wint. IV, 1, 5. whose p., vexed with thy impediment, shall leave his native channel, John II, 336. the mouth of p. (i. e. the gate) shall we fling wide ope, 449. the sullen p. of thy weary steps esteem as foil, R2 I, 3, 265. must I not serve a long apprenticehood to foreign —s, 272 (= a pilgrimage in foreign countries). his (the sun's) bright p. to the occident, III, 3, 67. to give sweet p. to my sinful soul, H6C II, 3, 41. and with bloody p. led your wars even to the gates of Rome, Cor. V, 6, 76. are my doors opposed against my p.? Tim. III, 4, 80. if such actions may have p. free, Oth. I, 2, 98.

2) a going to and fro of people: if by strong hand you offer to break in now in the stirring p. of the day, Err. III, 1, 99. no watch? no p.? Oth. V, 1, 37.

3) access, entry, avenue, way leading to and out of sth.: which to his speech did honey p. yield, Ven. 452. through the velvet leaves the wind gan p. find, Pilgr. 232 and LLL IV, 3, 106. Err. IV, 2, 38. Tw. I, 3, 41. R2 I, 1, 125. V, 3, 62. V, 5, 20. H5 II, 2, 16. H6A III, 2, 22. V, 4, 121. H6C I, 3, 22. IV, 3, 20. Cor. IV, 5, 215. Tit. I, 12. Mcb. I, 2, 19. I, 5, 45. Cymb. V, 3, 23. Figuratively: the several and unhidden —s of his true titles to some certain dukedoms, H5 I, 1, 86 (= open, manifest traces?).*

4) departure, death: would some part of my young years might but redeem the p. of your age, H6A II, 5, 108. when he is fit and seasoned for his p. Hml. III, 3, 86. and, for his p., the soldiers' music and the rites of war speak loudly for him, V, 2, 409. cf. H6C II, 3, 41.

5) occurrence, accident, incident: this young gentlewoman had a father — O, that had! how sad a p. 'tis! All's I, 1, 20. I see, in —s of proof, time qualifies the spark and fire of it (love) Hml. IV, 7,

113. *it is no act of common p., but a strain of rareness,* Cymb. III, 4, 94.

6) course, process: *our justice, in whose easiest p. look for no less than death,* Wint. III, 2, 91. *the fearful p. of their death-marked love,* Rom. Prol. 9. *as if the p. and whole carriage of this action rode on his tide,* Troil. II, 3, 140.

7) a single act tending to some purpose or expressive of sentiments: *no Christian can ever believe such impossible —s of grossness,* Tw. III, 2, 77.*thou dost in thy —s of life make me believe,* H4A III, 2, 8. *there is gallant and most brave —s,* H5 III, 6, 97 (Fluellen's speech). *but oft have hindered the —s made toward it* (this business), H8 II, 4, 165.

**Passant,** a term of heraldry, = walking: Wiv. I, 1, 20 (Evans' speech).

**Passenger,** a traveller on foot, a wayfarer: Ven. 91. Gent. IV, 1, 1. 72. V, 4, 15. R2 V, 3, 9. H6B III, 1, 129. 227.

**Passing,** 1) adj. egregious, excessive: *a p. shame,* Gent. I, 2, 17. *her p. deformity,* II, 1, 81. *O p. traitor,* H6C V, 1, 106.

2) adv. (used only before adjectives and adverbs) exceedingly: *p. strong,* Ven. 297. *p. fair,* Pilgr. 229 and LLL IV, 3, 103. Gent. IV, 4, 153. *p. shrewdly,* Ado II, 1, 84. Mids. II, 1, 20. As III, 5, 138. Shr. Ind. 1, 67. II, 113. 244. III, 2, 24. IV, 1, 193. IV, 3, 18. Wint. IV, 4, 294. H4B IV, 2, 85. H5 IV, 2, 42. R3 I, 1, 94. Cor. I, 1, 207. Tit. II, 3, 84. Rom. I, 1, 240. Hml. II, 2, 427. Oth. I, 3, 160.

**Passing-bell,** the bell that rings at the hour of death: Ven. 702.

**Passion,** subst. 1) any suffering: *any p. under heaven that does afflict our natures,* Hml. II, 1, 105. Emphatically, the last suffering of the Saviour; only in scurrilous exclamations: *Cock's p.* Shr. IV, 1, 121. *Cox my p.* All's V, 2, 43. Evans says: *Got's will, and his p. of my heart,* Wiv. III, 1, 62.

2) disorder, disease: *till this afternoon his p. ne'er brake into extremity of rage,* Err. V, 47. *our grandam earth, having this distemperature, in p. shook,* H4A III, 1, 35. *you shall offend him and extend his p.* Mcb. III, 4, 57.

3) any violent commotion of the mind: *variable —s throng her constant woe,* Ven. 967. 969. *such p. her assails,* Lucr. 1562. *your father's in some p. that works him strongly,* Tp. IV, 143. *what means this p. at his name?* Gent. I, 2, 16. *each one with ireful p.* Err. V, 151. Ado V, 1, 23. LLL IV, 3, 202. Mids. III, 2, 74. Merch. II, 8, 12. III, 1, 63. Tw. III, 4, 407. IV, 1, 56. Wint. II, 3, 28. IV, 4, 507. John III, 4, 39. IV, 2, 79. 263. H4B I, 1, 161. 165. IV, 4, 40. H5 I, 2, 242. H6A IV, 1, 183. H8 I, 1, 149. Troil. II, 2, 169. III, 2, 37. V, 2, 162. 181. Cor. IV, 4, 19. Tit. III, 1, 218. Tim. III, 1, 59. Mcb. IV, 3, 114. Hml. III, 2, 8. 11. 77. 204. III, 4, 107. V, 2, 80. Lr. II, 2, 181. II, 4, 237. Oth. II, 3, 206. III, 3, 124. 391. IV, 1, 78. 277. V, 2, 44. Ant. II, 2, 12. III, 10, 5.

Especially, = violent sorrow: *p. on p. deeply is redoubled,* Ven. 832. *no object but her —'s strength renews,* Lucr. 1103. *the life and feeling of her p. she hoards,* 1317. *my woe too sensible thy p. maketh more feeling-painful,* 1678. *his p. but an art of craft,* Compl. 295. *allaying both their fury and my p. with its sweet air,* Tp. I, 2, 392. *—'s solemn tears,* LLL V, 2, 118. *this p., and the death of a dear friend,* Mids. V, 293.

*her p. ends the play,* 321. *it was a p. of earnest,* As IV, 3, 172. *it did relieve my p. much,* Tw. II, 4, 4. *I must speak in p.* H4A II, 4, 425. *not in pleasure, but in p.* 458. *his p. moves me so,* H6C I, 4, 150. *that makes me bridle p.* IV, 4, 19. *a mother's tears in p. for her son,* Tit. I, 106. III, 2, 48. Hml. II, 2, 541. 578. 587. IV, 5, 188. Lr. IV, 3, 16. Oth. IV, 1, 268. Per. IV, 4, 24. Caes. III, 1, 283.

4) amorous desire: *love's strong p.* All's I, 3, 139. *unfold the p. of my love,* Tw. I, 4, 24. *the beating of so strong a p. as love doth give my heart,* II, 4, 97. *breed love's settled —s,* H6A V, 5, 4. *any p. of inflaming love,* 82. *plead my —s for Lavinia's love,* Tit. II, 1, 36. *my true love's p.* Rom. II, 2, 104. Absol., = ardent love: *trembling in her p.* Ven. 27. 218. *smothering his —s for the present,* Lucr. Arg. 13. *the master-mistress of my p.* Sonn. 20, 2. Ado I, 1, 221. II, 3, 110. 112. III, 1, 83. As II, 4, 41. 61. V, 2, 101. Shr. III, 1, 74. All's I, 3, 180. 196. Tw. II, 2, 23. III, 1, 164. III, 4, 226. H6C III, 3, 62. Rom. II Prol. 13. II, 1, 7. Tim. I, 1, 133.

5) any disposition or affection ruling the mind: *catching all —s in his craft of will,* Compl. 126. *they their —s likewise lent me of grief and blushes,* 199. *more merry tears the p. of loud laughter never shed,* Mids. V, 70. *how all the other —s fleet to air, as doubtful thoughts, and rash-embraced despair, and shuddering fear, and green-eyed jealousy,* Merch. III, 2, 108. *break into some merry p.* Shr. Ind. 1, 97. *a notable p. of wonder,* Wint. V, 2, 17. (merriment) *a p. hateful to my purposes,* John III, 3, 47. *free from gross p. or of mirth or anger,* H5 II, 2, 132. *of all base —s fear is most accursed,* H6A V, 2, 18. *vexed I am with —s of some difference,* Caes. I, 2, 40. *I have much mistook your p.* 48. *two extremes of p., joy and grief,* Lr. V, 3, 198. *whose every p. fully strives to make itself fair and admired,* Ant. I, 1, 50. LLL IV, 3, 140. Merch. IV, 1, 51. As I, 2, 269. III, 2, 433. Tim. III, 5, 21. Oth. IV, 1, 41. Ant. I, 2, 151. IV, 15, 74. V, 1, 63. Per. I, 2, 11.

**Passion,** vb. to feel pain and sorrow, to grieve: *dumbly she —s,* Ven. 1059. *shall not myself, that relish all as sharply, p. as they, be kindlier moved than thou art?* Tp. V, 24. *Ariadne —ing for Theseus' perjury,* Gent. IV, 4, 172. *I p. to say wherewith,* LLL I, 1, 264.

**Passionate,** adj. 1) expressing great commotion of mind: Mids. III, 2, 220. H6B I, 1, 104. Hml. II, 2, 452.

2) sorrowful: *poor forlorn Proteus, p. Proteus,* Gent. I, 2, 124. *warble, child; make p. my sense of hearing,* LLL III, 1 (Armado's speech; cf. Merch. V, 69). *she is sad and p.* John II, 544.

3) Misapplied for *compassionate: this p. humour of mine,* R3 I, 4, 121 (Qq *my holy humour*).

**Passionate,** vb. to express sorrowfully: *thy niece and I, poor creatures, want our hands and cannot p. our tenfold grief with folded arms,* Tit. III, 2, 6.

**Passive,** unresisting, yielding, obedient (?): *such as may the p. drugs of it* (the world) *freely command,* Tim. IV, 3, 254.

**Passport,** a written permission of passage: All's III, 2, 58. H5 IV, 3, 36. Per. III, 2, 66.

**Passy measure,** corrupted from *passamezzo,* the Italian name of a slow and stately dance: *he's a rogue and a —s panyn* (later Ff *pavin*) Tw. V, 206 (Malone: "Sir Toby means that the surgeon is a grave solemn coxcomb").

**Past,** adj. 1) gone by; done or accomplished in, and belonging to, a time previous to the present: *all sins p.* Lucr. 923. *what is p.* 1685. *things p.* Sonn. 30, 2. Tp. II, 1, 253. II, 2, 43. III, 3, 51. Meas. IV, 2, 151. John IV, 3, 51. H6A I, 2, 57. R3 IV, 4, 390. Troil. III, 3, 177. Tim. II, 1, 21 etc.

2) former, done before a time mentioned or understood: *my folly p.* Gent. I, 2, 65. *my riots p.* Wiv. III, 4, 8. *my p. endeavours,* All's I, 3, 5. *may token to the future our p. deeds,* IV, 2, 63. *our dear services p. and to come,* Wint. II, 3, 151. *my p. life,* III, 2, 34. *my service p.* Oth. III, 4, 116.

3) gone by, over, gone, existing no more, lost: *my day's delight is p.* Ven. 380. *your cue is p.* Mids. III, 1, 103. IV, 1, 144. Merch. II, 6, 2. H6C IV, 6, 98. R3 IV, 4, 364. H8 IV, 1, 95. Troil. V, 2, 97. Tim. III, 2, 7. Oth. I, 3, 204 etc. *for doing I am p.* All's II, 3, 246 (= I can no more do). *'tis p., and so am I,* Lr. V, 3, 164. *had he been where he thought, by this had thought been p.* IV, 6, 45. *when remedies are p.* Oth. I, 3, 202. *until some half hour p.* Lr. V, 3, 193 (half an hour ago).

**Past,** subst. the time previous to the present: Sonn. 123, 10. H4B I, 3, 108. Troil. III, 3, 164 (*in p.*).

**Past,** prepos. 1) beyond; temporally: *p. prime,* Sonn. 12, 3. *my days are p. the best,* 138, 6. *p. the mid season,* Tp. I, 2, 239. Wiv. II, 3, 4. III, 5, 134. Meas. III, 2, 193. V, 402. As IV, 3, 1. Shr. III, 1, 71. Wint. V, 2, 137. H4B I, 2, 110. III, 2, 269 etc. *'tis one o' clock and p.* H4B III, 1, 34.

2) beyond, further than; locally: *the enemy is p. the marsh,* R3 V, 3, 345. *I have tumbled p. the throw,* Cor. V, 2, 21.

3) more than: *not p. three quarters of a mile,* Wint. IV, 3, 85. *not p. three or four hairs,* Troil. I, 2, 121. *six weeks and p.* Tim. II, 2, 31. *not p. a pint,* Oth. II, 3, 68.

4) beyond, out of the reach of, not to be attained by: *p. the help of law,* Lucr. 1022. *p. reason's weak removing,* 243. *a limit p. my praise,* Sonn. 82, 6. *p. cure,* 147, 9. Tp. V, 141. Meas. II, 1. 115. Shr. III, 2, 54. All's II, 1, 161. John IV, 2, 86. Rom. IV, 1, 45. *p. thought,* Err. IV, 189. Ado II, 3, 106. Oth. I, 1, 167. *p. the endurance of a block,* Ado II, 1, 246. *thou drivest me p. the bounds of maiden's patience,* Mids. III, 2, 65. H8 II, 4, 130. *p. the wit of man,* Mids. IV, 1, 211. Rom. IV, 1, 47. *p. all saying nay,* Merch. III, 2, 232. *p. all expressing,* III, 5, 78. *our weakness p. compare,* Shr. V, 2, 174. *p. question,* Tw. I, 3, 104. *p. enduring,* Wint. II, 1, 2. *urged p. my defence,* John I, 258. *p. redress, p. care,* R2 II, 3, 171. *that's p. praying for,* H4A II, 4, 211. *p. recovery,* H6B I, 1, 116. *p. hiding, p. watching,* Troil. I, 2, 294. 295. *a joy p. joy,* Rom. III, 3, 173. *p. hope, p. cure, p. help,* IV, 1, 45. *p. depth,* Tim. III, 5, 12. *a sight p. speaking of,* Lr. IV, 6, 209. *p. the size of dreaming,* Ant. V, 2, 97 etc.

5) without: *p. reason hunted,* Sonn. 129, 6. *now reason is p. care,* 147, 9. *when help p. sense we deem,* All's II, 1, 127. *my art is not p. power,* 161. *a wreck p. hope he was,* Tw. V, 82. *that's p. doubt,* Wint. I, 2, 268. *p. all shame,* III, 2, 85. *p. all truth,* 86. *p. doubt,* Cor. II, 3, 265.

**Past-cure,** adj. incurable: *our p. malady,* All's II, 1, 124.

**Paste,** the pie-crust: Tit. V, 2, 188. 189. 201.

Lr. II, 4, 124. *that small model of the barren earth which serves as p. and cover to our bones,* R2 III, 2, 154.

**Pastern,** a horse's leg: *any that treads but on four —s,* H5 III, 7, 13 (F1 *postures*).

**Pastime,** amusement: Tp. V, 38. Gent. II, 7, 35. LLL IV, 3, 377. V, 2, 360. As V, 4, 201. Shr. Ind. 1, 67. I, 1, 68. All's I, 2, 57. Tw. III, 4, 151. Wint. I, 2, 152. II, 3, 24 (*make their p. at my sorrow*). Tit. II, 3, 26. Hml. III, 1, 15. IV, 7, 33. Lr. II, 4, 6. Cymb. III, 1, 79 (*make p. with us*).

**Pastor,** a minister of the gospel: Hml. I, 3, 47.

**Pastoral,** subst. a play representing the life and manners of shepherds: *methinks I play as I have seen them do in Whitsun —s,* Wint. IV, 4, 134. *the best actors in the world, either for tragedy, comedy, history, p.* Hml. II, 2, 416.

**Pastoral-comical,** combining the qualities of an idyl and of a comedy: Hml. II, 2, 416.

**Past-proportion** (not hyphened in O. Edd.) immensity: *will you with counters sum the p. of his infinite?* Troil. II, 2, 29.

**Pastry,** a room in which pies and the like are made: *they call for dates and quinces in the p.* Rom. IV, 4, 2.

**Past-saving,** abandoned, damned: *what a p. slave is this!* All's IV, 3, 158.

**Pasture,** 1) ground on which cattle or other beasts feed: Gent. I, 1, 105. LLL II, 221. As II, 4, 88. III, 2, 28. R2 III, 3, 100. H5 II Chor. 5. Ant. I, 4, 65. Cymb. V, 4, 2.

2) the food taken by grazing: As II, 1, 53. H5 III, 1, 27. Tim. IV, 3, 12.

**Pasty,** a pie baked in a crust: Wiv. I, 1, 202. All's IV, 3, 140. Tit. V, 2, 190.

**Pat,** quite to the purpose, fitly, exactly: *are we all met? p. p.* Mids. III, 1, 2. *it will fall p. as I told you,* V, 188. *nor could come p. betwixt too early and too late,* H8 II, 3, 84. *now might I do it p.* Hml. III, 3, 73. *and p. he comes,* Lr. I, 2, 146.

**Patay,** correction of M. Edd. in H6A IV, 1, 19; O. Edd. *Poictiers.*

**Patch,** subst. 1) a piece sewed on to cover a hole: *—es set upon a little breach,* John IV, 2, 32. *botch and bungle up damnation with —es, colours,* H5 II, 2, 116. *a king of shreds and —es,* Hml. III, 4, 102.

2) a piece of silk or velvet used to cover a defect on the face: *with a p. of velvet on's face,* All's IV, 5, 100. *—es will I get unto these cudgelled scars,* H5 V, 1, 93.

3) a plot of ground: *to gain a little p. of ground,* Hml. IV, 4, 18.

4) a paltry fellow: *what a pied ninny's this! thou scurvy p.* Tp. III, 2, 71. *coxcomb, idiot, p.* Err. III, 1, 32. *what p. is made our porter?* 36. *a p. set on learning,* LLL IV, 2, 32. *a crew of —es, rude mechanicals,* Mids. III, 2, 9. *the p. is kind enough, but a huge feeder,* Merch. II, 5, 46. *what soldiers, p.?* Mcb. V, 3, 15.

In the cited passages of Tp., Err. and Merch. the word is by most commentators interpreted as meaning a domestic fool, supposed to be called so from his parti-coloured dress. Douce proves that several fools in the sixteenth century bore the nickname of *Patch.*

**Patch,** vb. 1) to mend with a piece sewed on: Tw. I, 5, 52. John IV, 2, 34. Cor. III, 1, 252. *—ed* = paltry: *a —ed fool,* Mids. IV, 1, 215 (according to some, = parti-coloured).

2) to make up of pieces and shreds: *if you'll p. a quarrel, as matter whole you have not to make it with,* Ant. II, 2, 52. *you —ed up your excuses,* 56.

3) to repair with pieces of any kind: *that that earth, which kept the world in awe, should p. a wall,* Hml. V, 1, 239.

4) to mend or repair as well as may be: *p. grief with proverbs,* Ado V, 1, 17. *virtue that transgresses is but —ed with sin,* Tw. I, 5, 53. 54. *begin to p. up thine old body for heaven,* H4B II, 4, 252. cf. Cor. III, 1, 252.

5) to disfigure: *—ed with foul moles,* John III, 1, 47.

**Patch-breech,** name in Per. II, 1, 14.

**Patchery,** botchery intended to hide faults; gross and bungling hypocrisy: *here is such p., such juggling and such knavery,* Troil. II, 3, 77. *you hear him cog, see him dissemble, know his gross p.* Tim. V, 1, 99.

**Pate,** the head; used in contempt or in ridicule: Tp. IV, 244. Wiv. II, 1, 197. Err. I, 2, 65. 82. II, 1, 78. II, 2, 71. 220. III, 1, 74. LLL I, 1, 26. Shr. I, 2, 12. II, 155. All's II, 1, 68. Wint. I, 2, 223. John II, 568. H4A II, 1, 33. V, 3, 32. H5 IV, 1, 54. V, 1, 43. 62. V, 2, 169. H6A III, 1, 82. H6B V, 1, 135. Cor. IV, 6, 82. Rom. IV, 5, 120. Tim. IV, 3, 17. Hml. II, 2, 599. V, 1, 86. 116. 305. Oth. II, 1, 127. Cymb. II, 1, 8.

**Patent,** subst. a privilege: Sonn. 87, 8. Mids. I, 1, 80. All's IV, 5, 69. Oth. IV, 1, 209. *letters —s =* writings by which some rights are granted: R2 II, 1, 202. II, 3, 130. H8 III, 2, 250.

**Paternal,** fatherly: Lr. I, 1, 115.

**Path,** subst. a track, a way for foot-passengers: Ven. 908. Wiv. IV, 4, 59. Mids. V, 389. As I, 3, 15. R2 I, 3, 143. H5 II, 4, 52. R3 I, 1, 117. Troil. III, 3, 155. Rom. II, 3, 4. Cymb. III, 6, 18. Figuratively: Ven. 788. Meas. IV, 3, 138. John III, 4, 129. R3 III, 7, 157. Tit. II, 1, 111. Hml. I, 3, 50.

**Path,** vb. to walk, to go: *if thou p., thy native semblance on,* Caes. II, 1, 83 (Pope *march,* Dyce *put,* Grant White *hadst,* Anon. *pass* or *pace*).

**Pathetical,** a word used by the poet, as it seems, with intentional impropriety, in the sense of pleasing or displeasing in a high degree; striking, shocking: *sweet invocation of a child; most pretty and p.* LLL I, 2, 103 (Armado's speech). *it is a most p. nit,* IV, 1, 150 (Costard's speech). *the most p. break-promise,* As IV, 1, 196.

**Pathway,** path: R2 I, 2, 31. Rom. I, 1, 178. II, 3, 4 (reading of F1; the rest of O. Edd. *path*).

**Patience,** name of a gentlewoman of Queen Katharine: H8 IV, 2, 76. 82. 127.

**Patience,** 1) a calm temper in grief and suffering: *p. tame to sufferance,* Sonn. 58, 7. *do not press my tongue-tied p. with too much disdain,* 140, 2. Tp. V, 140. Ado IV, 1, 256. V, 1, 10. 19. 27. LLL I, 1, 197. Mids. I, 1, 152. III, 1, 197. As I, 3, 80. V, 2, 103. V, 4, 193. Shr. II, 297. Wint. III, 2, 33 etc. Personified as a fem.: Troil. I, 1, 28. Oth. IV, 2, 63. cf. Tp. V, 140. Err. II, 1, 32. As IV, 3, 13. Represented by statues placed on graves: *she sat like P. on a monument, smiling at grief,* Tw. II, 4, 117. *yet thou dost look like P. gazing on kings' graves and smiling extremity out of act,* Per. V, 1, 139.

2) quiet perseverance in waiting for sth.: *O, p.! the statue is but newly fixed,* Wint. V, 3, 46. *linger*

your p. on, H5 II Chor. 31. H6B I, 4, 18. H8 V, 2, 19.

3) calmness, composure; opposed to passionateness: *where thou with p. must my will abide,* Lucr. 486. 1158. 1268. 1505. *I'm out of p.* Tp. I, 1, 58. *have p.* Gent. II, 2, 1. V, 4, 27. Wiv. III, 1, 55. IV, 2, 28. Meas. IV, 3, 123. V, 116. 235. Err. II, 1, 32. 39. 41. III, 1, 85. 94. IV, 2, 16. V, 174. LLL IV, 3, 165. Mids. III, 2, 66. 161. As IV, 3, 13. Shr. I, 2, 45. III, 2, 21. All's III, 2, 50. Tw. II, 5, 83. Rom. I, 5, 91 (cf. *Perforce*). Hml. III, 4, 124. V, 1, 317. 322. Per. V, 1, 145 etc. *take p. =* have p. Lr. II, 4, 140. *take your p. to you,* Wint. III, 2, 232. *you must take your p. to you,* H8 V, 1, 106. *we will not wake your p.* Ado V, 1, 102; cf. *to wake our peace,* R2 I, 3, 132 (and the contrary: *peace shall go sleep,* IV, 139). *lest thou move our p.* R3 I, 3, 248; cf. Err. II, 1, 32; Meas. V, 235; Mids. III, 2, 161.

4) indulgence, forbearance, leniency: *my p., more than thy desert, is privilege for thy departure hence,* Gent. III, 1, 159. *I do entreat your p. to hear me speak the message,* IV, 4, 116. *an old abusing of God's p.* Wiv. I, 4, 5. *I know not how to pray your p.* Ado V, 1, 280. *begged my p.* Mids. IV, 1, 6.. *your p. for my long abode,* Merch. II, 6, 21. *ours be your p. then,* All's V, 3, 339. *your p. this allowing, I turn my glass,* Wint. IV, 1, 15 etc.

Hence = permission: *but only, with your p., that we may taste of your wine,* H6A II, 3, 78. *under your p.* Tit. II, 3, 66. *they stay upon your p.* Hml. III, 2, 112. *by your p. =* by your leave: Tp. III, 3, 3. As V, 4, 186. Tw. II, 1, 3. H5 III, 6, 31. R3 IV, 1, 15. Cor. I, 3, 81. I, 9, 55. Lr. V, 3, 59. *by your gracious p.* Oth. I, 3, 89.

Misapplied by Costard: LLL I, 2, 170.

**Patient,** adj. 1) bearing evils with calmness and fortitude: *for your sake am I this p. log-man,* Tp. III. 1, 67. *a p. sufferance,* Ado I, 3, 10. *still have I borne it with a p. shrug,* Merch. I, 3, 110. R2 I, 4, 29. II, 1, 163. 169. H4B I, 2, 145. H5 III, 7, 24. Troil. I, 3, 36. Hml. III, 1, 74.

2) quietly waiting: *I'll be as p. as a gentle stream,* Gent. II, 7, 34. *be p., lords, and give them leave to speak,* H6A IV, 1, 82. Caes. I, 1, 46. III, 2, 154. Lr. II, 4, 233.

3) calm, composed, not passionate: *playing p. sports in unconstrained gyves,* Compl. 242. *I will be p.* Wiv. II, 1, 130. *a wise and p. churchman,* II, 3, 57. *thou must be p.* Meas. III, 3, 159. *as p. as the midnight sleep,* Cor. III, 1, 85. *as p. as the female dove,* Hml. V, 1, 309 etc. *be p. =* compose yourself: Tp. I, 1, 16. IV, 205. Gent. V, 3, 2. Err. II, 1, 9. IV, 4, 19. V, 102. As I, 1, 66. Shr. II, 304. Tw. II, 3, 142. H5 III, 5, 66. H6B I, 3, 68. II, 4, 26. III, 2, 36. H6C I, 1, 214. 215. R3 I, 2, 82. I, 3, 157. III, 5, 21. IV, 4, 151. V, 1, 2 etc.

4) indulgent, conniving: *the which if you with p. ears attend, what here shall miss, our toil shall strive to mend,* Rom. Prol. 13.

**Patient,** subst. a person attended by a physician in illness: Lucr. 904. Sonn. 111, 9. Wiv. II, 3, 97. Err. V, 294. All's II, 1, 207. II. 3, 53. R2 II, 1, 97. H4B I, 2, 147. H8 III, 2, 41. Troil. II, 3, 224. V, 1, 12. Mcb. V, 3, 37. 45. Per. V, 1, 71.

**Patient,** vb. refl. to compose one's self: *p. yourself,* Tit. I, 121.

**Patiently,** 1) with calm endurance in suffering: Lucr. 1641. Gent. V, 3, 4. Meas. II, 3, 20. III, 2, 79. Err. I, 2, 86. Ado V, 1, 36. Merch. II, 9, 78. H4A V, 5, 12. H5 V, 2, 300. Cymb. III, 5, 118.

2) calmly, tranquilly: Mids. II, 1, 140. As II, 7, 61. H5 IV Chor. 24. R3 IV, 4, 156. Troil. V, 9, 7. Lr. IV, 6, 36.

3) with indulgence: *we beg your hearing p.* Hml. III, 2, 161. *good heavens, hear p. my purpose,* Cymb. V, 1, 22.

**Patines** (F1 Qq *pattens,* the later Ff *patterns*) plates of metal: *the floor of heaven is thick inlaid with p. of bright gold,* Merch. V, 59.*

**Patrician,** a nobleman in ancient Rome: Cor. I, 1, 16. 68. 75. I, 9, 4. II, 1, 51. 212. III, 1, 91. 186. IV, 3, 15. IV, 7, 30. V, 6, 82. Tit. I, 1. 204. 231. 445.

**Patrick,** name of a saint: Gent. IV, 3, 43. V, 1, 3. V, 2, 42. Hml. I, 5, 136.

**Patrimony,** heritage: Shr. IV, 4, 22. R2 II, 1, 237. H6B V, 1, 187. Lr. V, 3, 75.

**Patroclus,** name of the friend of Achilles: Troil. I, 3, 146 etc.

**Patron,** he on whom another depends, in whose protection or dominion he lives: *O thou clear god* (the sun) *and p. of all light,* Ven. 860. *twenty years have I* (the duke) *been p. to Antipholus,* Err. V, 327. *my body's fostering p.* (the king) LLL I, 1, 223. *I'll plead for you as for my p.* Shr. I, 2, 156. *and will repute you the p. of my life and liberty,* IV, 2, 113. *call Warwick p.* H6C V, 1, 27. *patricians, —s of my right,* Tit. I, 1. *Andronicus, p. of virtue,* 65. *the five best senses acknowledge thee their p.* Tim. I, 2, 130. *my great p.* Lr. I, 1, 144. *my worthy arch and p.* II, 1, 61.

**Patronage,** vb. to maintain, to make good: *as an outlaw in a castle keeps and useth it to p. his theft,* H6A III, 1, 48. *darest thou maintain the former words thou spakest? Yes, sir, as well as you dare p. the envious barking of your saucy tongue,* III, 4, 32.

**Patroness,** protectress: *the p. of heavenly harmony,* Shr. III, 1, 5. *behold our p.* Cor. V, 5, 1. *Lucina, divinest p. to those that cry by night,* Per. III, 1, 11.

**Pattern,** subst. 1) a model proposed for imitation: *figures of delight, drawn after you, you p. of all those,* Sonn. 98, 12. *by the p. of mine own thoughts I cut out the purity of his,* Wint. IV, 4, 393. *their memory shall as a p. or a measure live, by which his grace must mete the lives of others,* H4B IV, 4, 76.

Hence = a precedent: *so we could find some p. of our shame,* John III, 4, 16. *a p., precedent and lively warrant for me to perform the like,* Tit. V, 3, 44.

2) something of supreme excellence, fit to serve as a model or exemplar: *beauty's p. to succeeding men,* Sonn. 19, 12. *p. in himself to know,* Meas. III, 2, 277. *he is one of the —s of love,* As IV, 1, 100. *a p. to all princes,* H8 V, 5, 23. *I will be the p. of all patience,* Lr. III, 2, 37.

3) something made after a model, an example, an instance: *this p. of the worn-out age pawned honest looks,* Lucr. 1350. *knew the —s of his foul beguiling,* Compl. 170. *a p. of celestial peace,* H6A V, 5, 65. *the —s that by God and by French fathers had twenty years been made,* H5 II, 4, 61. Emphatically, a masterpiece: *behold this p. of thy butcheries,* R3 I, 2, 54. *thou cunningest p. of excelling nature,* Oth. V, 2, 11.

**Pattern,** vb. to be an example or precedent for:

*let mine own judgment p. out my death,* Meas. II, 1, 30. *which is more than history can p.* Wint. III, 2, 37. *—ed by thy fault, foul sin may say,* Lucr. 629. *such a place, —ed by that the poet here describes,* Tit. IV, 1, 57.

**Paul,** name of the thirteenth apostle: R3 I, 1, 138 (Ff *John*). I, 2, 36. 41. I, 3, 45. III, 4, 78. V, 3, 216. *Paul's* = Saint Paul's Church, the principal cathedral of London: H4A II, 4, 576. H4B I, 2, 58. R2 I, 2, 30. III, 6, 3. H8 V, 4, 16 (O. Edd. *Powles* or *Poules*). Nares: "St. Paul's church was a constant place of resort for business and amusement." Our poet mentions the custom of hiring servants there, with allusion to the proverb: *"who goes to Westminster for a wife, to St. Paul's for a man, and to Smithfield for a horse, may meet with a whore, a knave, and a jade."*

**Paulina,** the wife of Antigonus in Wint. III, 3, 36. V, 1, 49 etc.

**Paunch,** subst. the region of the guts, the belly: *fat —es have lean pates,* LLL I, 1, 26. *Sir John P.* H4A II, 2, 69. *ye fat p.* II, 4, 159.

**Paunch,** vb. to rip the belly, to eviscerate: *p. him with a stake,* Tp. III, 2, 98.

**Pause,** subst. 1) a temporary stop, an intermission of acting or speaking: *swelling passion doth provoke a p.* Ven. 218. *he rouseth up himself and makes a p.* Lucr. 541. R3 I, 2, 162. Hml. II, 2, 509. Oth. V, 2, 82.

2) a stop made and time taken for consideration: *without any p. or staggering,* Wiv. III, 3, 12. *hadst thou but shook thy head or made a p.* John IV, 2, 231. *a night is but small breath and little p. to answer matters of this consequence,* H5 II, 4, 145. *give me some breath, some little p.* R3 IV, 2, 24. *what dreams may come ... must give us p.* Hml. III, 1, 68. *steps in to Cassio and entreats his p.* Oth. II, 3, 229. *he mocks the —s that he makes,* Ant. V, 1, 3.

3) consideration, reflexion: *sad p. and deep regard beseem the sage,* Lucr. 277. *too long a p. for that which you find there,* Merch. II, 9, 53. *but yet I'll make a p.* H6C III, 2, 10. *justles roughly by all time of p.* Troil. IV, 4, 37. *like a man to double business bound, I stand in p. where I shall first begin,* Hml. III, 3, 42. *this sudden sending him away must seem deliberate p.* IV, 3, 9.

**Pause,** vb. 1) to make a stop, to intermit or discontinue acting or speaking: *p. a while, and let my counsel sway you in this case,* Ado IV, 1, 202. *p. a day or two before you hazard,* Merch. III, 2, 1. *while I p., serve in your harmony,* Shr. III, 1, 14. *we coldly p. for thee,* John II, 53 (to hear thy message). *p. or be more temperate,* 195. *stay and p. a while,* H4A I, 3, 129. *there did he p.* V, 2, 66. *p. and take thy breath,* H6A IV, 6, 4. *what seest thou in me? why dost thou p.?* H6B V, 2, 19. *I'll never p. again, never stand still,* H6C II, 3, 30. *good fortune bids us p.* II, 6, 31. *I have seen thee p. and take thy breath,* Troil. IV, 5, 192. *I p. for a reply,* Caes. III, 2, 36. *I must p. till it come back to me,* 112. *yet p. a while,* Per. II, 3, 53.

2) to take time for consideration, to consider before acting: *—ing for means to mourn some newer way,* Lucr. 1365. *patience unmoved, no marvel though she p.* Err. I, 1, 32. *take time to p.* Mids. I, 1, 83. *p. there, Morocco,* Merch. II, 7, 24. *but yet I'll p.* R2 II, 3, 168. *other offenders we will p. upon,* H4A V, 5, 15.

3) to hesitate, to hold back, to delay: *were I hard-*

*favoured.... then mightst thou p.* Ven. 137. *why doth the Jew p.? take thy forfeiture,* Merch. IV, 1, 335. *p. not,* John V, 1, 14. *do not p.* R3 I, 2, 180. *p., if thou wilt,* Troil. V, 6, 14.

4) Used reflexively, = to repose one's self: *only we want a little personal strength, and p. us, till these rebels come underneath the yoke of government,* H4B IV, 4, 9.

**Pauser,** one who deliberates much: *the p. reason,* Mcb. II, 3, 117.

**Pausingly,** deliberately: *with demure confidence this p. ensued,* H8 I, 2, 168.

**Paved,** laid over and floored as with stones: *his p. bed* (the grave) Meas. V, 440. *if the streets were p. with thine eyes,* LLL IV, 3, 278. *by p. fountain,* Mids. II, 1, 84 (= pebbly). *my way shall be p. with English faces,* H5 III, 7, 87. *when the way was made, and p. with gold,* H8 I, 1, 188.

**Pavement,** that which is laid over the way to make it passable: *lie there for p. to the abject rear,* Troil. III, 3, 162. *the marble p. closes,* Cymb. V, 4, 120, i. e. the sky, heaven; cf. *floor* in Merch. V, 58.

**Pavilion,** a tent: LLL II, 250. V, 1, 94. V, 2, 660. H5 IV, 1, 27. Troil. Prol. 15. I, 3, 305. Ant. II, 2, 204.

**Pavilioned,** tented, encamped: H5 I, 2, 129.

**Pavin,** a grave Spanish dance (French *pavane*): *a passy-measures p.* Tw. V, 207. F1 *panyn.*

**Paw,** the foot of a beast of prey: Sonn. 19, 1. John III, 1, 259. R2 V, 1, 29. H6B V, 1, 153. H6C I, 3, 13. Tit. II, 3, 152.

**Pawn,** subst. 1) something given as a security, a pledge: Gent. I, 3, 47. II, 4, 91. Wint. IV, 4, 853. John V, 2, 141. R2 I, 1, 74. IV, 55. 70. *to lay to p.:* Wiv. II, 2, 5. III, 1, 113. *to leave in p.:* Wint. IV, 4, 839.

2) a stake hazarded in a wager: *my life I held but as a p. to wage against thine enemies,* Lr. I, 1, 157.

3) the state of being pledged: *redeem from broking p. the blemished crown,* R2 II, 1, 293. *my honour is at p.* H4B II, 3, 7.

**Pawn,** vb. 1) to pledge: Lucr. 1351. Err. V, 389. H4B II, 1, 153. 167. 171. IV, 2, 112. H6C III, 3, 116. IV, 2, 9. R3 IV, 2, 92. Cor. V, 6, 21. Tim. I, 1, 147. Cymb. I, 6, 194. *to p. down:* Lr. I, 2, 92. With *to:* *till he hath —ed his horses to mine host,* Wiv. II, 1, 99. John III, 1, 98. H6C V, 7, 39. Tim. III, 5, 81.

2) to put to stake, to stake: *—ing his honour to obtain his lust,* Lucr. 156. *something else —ed with the other,* Merch. III, 5, 87. *I'll p. the little blood which I have left to save the innocent,* Wint. II, 3, 166. H6B V, 1, 113. Cor. III, 1, 15. Cymb. I, 4, 118. Almost = to lose, to forfeit: *the garter, blemished, —ed his knightly honour,* R3 IV, 4, 370. *p. their experience to their present pleasure,* Ant. I, 4, 32.

3) to secure by a pledge: *I'll p. this truth with my three drops of blood,* Troil. I, 3, 301 (Q prove).

**Pax,** the cover of the sacred chalice at mass: H5 III, 6, 42. 47.

**Pay,** subst. payment, the giving something in compensation or recompense for a service done: *when her lips were ready for his p.* Ven. 89. *such uncurrent p.* (viz thanks) Tw. III, 3, 16. *a noble shalt thou have and present p.* H5 II, 1, 112. *that you have ta'en these tenders for true p.* Hml. I, 3, 106. *thy sacred physic shall receive such p.* Per. V, 1, 74. Particularly, wages given to soldiers: H4B IV, 2, 70. H6B III, 1, 62. 105.

108. H6C II, 1, 134. IV, 7, 88. V, 5, 88. *to have in p.* R2 III, 2, 60; cf. H5 IV, 1, 315. *to fight against me under Percy's p.* H4A III, 2, 126.

**Pay,** vb. 1) to give as an equivalent or compensation or debt owed; without an object: *he shall p. for him,* Tp. II, 2, 81. *I'll make them p.* Wiv. IV, 3, 11. Meas. II, 1, 105. III, 2, 126. Tw. V, 40. Wint. I, 1, 18. H4A III, 3, 201 (—ing back). H5 II, 3, 51 (cf. *Pitch*) etc. With an accus.: *p. slavish tribute,* Lucr. 299. *what he owes thee thou thyself dost p.* Sonn. 79, 14. Tp. II, 1, 293. Merch. III, 2, 56. *till some certain shot be paid,* Gent. II, 5, 7. *I paid nothing for it,* Wiv. IV, 5, 62. V, 5, 118. Err. I, 2, 85. IV, 1, 72. 74. V, 131. 284. LLL V, 2, 334 (*p. him the due*). H4A II, 4, 599 and III, 3, 200 (*paid back again*). H6A II, 2, 7 (*I have paid my vow,* i. e. done what I vowed. Cymb. V, 4, 165 etc.

2) to satisfy, to quit by giving an equivalent; a) the debt to be quitted being the object: *one sweet kiss shall p. this countless debt,* Ven. 84. *pain —s the income of each precious thing,* Lucr. 334. *p. the willing loan,* Sonn. 6, 6. Tp. III, 2, 140. Wiv. II, 2, 123. Err. IV, 4, 124. Tw. II, 4, 71. 72 etc. b) the person satisfied as object: *so you're paid,* Tp. II, 1, 36. *I am paid,* Gent. V, 4, 77. *I was paid for my learning,* Wiv. IV, 5, 63. *to p. the saddler,* Err. I, 2, 56. Ado V, 1, 255. Merch. IV, 1, 415. Shr. IV, 3, 166. 168. H6B IV, 1, 30 etc. Dat. and accus.: *till every minute —s the hour his debt,* Lucr. 329. *pay a daily debt to their sovereign,* 649 etc.

3) to give, to offer, to render: *to which love's eyes p. tributary gazes,* Ven. 632. *the sad account of forebemoaned moan, which I new p. as if not paid before,* Sonn. 30, 12. *no bed-right shall be paid,* Tp. IV, 1, 96. *you have paid the heavens your function,* Meas. III, 2, 263. *not —ing me a welcome,* Mids. V, 99. *my honour's paid to him,* All's V, 3, 143. *to p. Bohemia the visitation which he justly owes him,* Wint. I, 1, 7. *paid down more penitence,* V, 1, 3. *to p. that duty,* John II, 247. *let us p. that mass of moan,* Troil. II, 2, 106. *I'll p. that doctrine, or else die in debt,* Rom. I, 1, 244. *—s homage to us,* Hml. IV, 3, 64. *thy cheek —s shame,* Ant. I, 1, 31. *he could not but p. me terms of honour,* III, 4, 7. *death of one person can be paid but once,* IV, 14, 27 etc.

4) absol., to have requital: *he shall p. for this,* Merch. II, 8, 26. *if this prove true, they'll p. for it,* Wint. II, 1, 146. *they shall p. for their presumption,* H6C IV, 1, 114. Trans. a) to suffer in requital, to fulfil as a punishment: *make us p. down for our offence by weight the words of heaven,* Meas. I, 2, 125. b) to give in requital: *more nor less to others —ing than by self-offences weighing,* III, 2, 279. c) to requite, to reward or punish: *I will p. thy graces home both in word and deed,* Tp. V, 70. *haste still —s haste,* Meas. V, 415. *p. with falsehood false exacting,* III, 2, 295. *here's that* (a rope) *will p. them all,* Err. IV, 4, 10. *all my services you have paid home,* Wint. V, 3, 4. *you p. him then,* H5 IV, 1, 209. *the service —s itself,* Mcb. I, 4, 23. *our duties did his welcome p.* IV, 1, 132. *he was paid for that,* Cymb. IV, 2, 246. *you are paid too much,* V, 4, 166.

5) to give it soundly, to quit scores with a person, to hit or kill in fighting: *on the answer he —s you as surely as your feet hit the ground,* Tw. III, 4, 305. *two I am sure I have paid,* H4A II, 4, 213. *with a*

*thought seven of the eleven I paid,* 242. V, 3, 48.

**Payment,** 1) the act of paying, of giving in compensation: *reward not hospitality with such black p.* Lucr. 576. *the p. of a hundred thousand crowns,* LLL II, 130. 145. H4A I, 3, 186. H6C I, 4, 32. Tim. II, 2, 28. Cymb. V, 4, 161.

2) that which is given in compensation: *fair p. for foul words,* LLL IV, 1, 19. *too little p. for so great a debt,* Shr. V, 2, 154. Tw. IV, 1, 21. H4B V, 5, 135. H8 V, 1, 174. Tim. V, 1, 116.

3) requital: *if he come to-morrow, I'll give him his p.* As I, 1, 166. H5 IV, 8, 15. Mcb. I, 4, 19.

**Pea,** only in the plur. *pease,* the fruit of Pisum sativum used as food: Tp. IV, 1, 61. LLL V, 2, 315. Mids. IV, 1, 42. H4A II, 1, 9.

**Peace,** 1) freedom from war with a foreign nation, cessation of hostilities: Lucr. 831. Gent. V, 2, 17. Meas. I, 2, 17. John II, 84. 586. III, 1, 1. 105. 110. 113. V, 7, 84. R2 II, 1, 174. H5 V, 2, 34. H6A I, 1, 77. Cymb. V, 1, 20 etc. etc. *to make p.* = a) to finish war: John V, 1, 63. Cor. V, 6, 79 etc. b) to effect a p.: *all the swords in Italy could not have made this p.* Cor. V, 3, 209 (cf. *Make*). *the cardinal cannot make your p.* John V, 1, 74. *to make up a p.* Cor. V, 3, 140. *to conclude p.* H6A V, 4, 107. *to contract a p.* H6B I, 1, 40.

2) public tranquillity, quiet and order: *to wake our p., which in our country's cradle draws the sweet infant breath of gentle sleep,* R2 I, 3, 132; cf. *p. shall go sleep with Turks and infidels,* IV, 139 (i. e. Turks etc. shall live in peace); *and there awake God's gentle sleeping p.* R3 I, 3, 288. *I am not here against your father's p.* H4B IV, 2, 31; cf. *the king's p.* H6A I, 3, 75. *the rod, and bird of p.* (the dove) H8 IV, 1, 89. *trouble not the p.* Cor. V, 6, 129; cf. 125. *uproar the universal p.* Mcb. IV, 3, 99 etc. etc. *to break the p.* H6A I, 3, 58. *to break p.* H4B IV, 1, 85. *to keep the p.* John IV, 3, 93. H4B II, 1, 67. H6A III, 1, 87. Tit. II, 1, 37. Rom. I, 1, 75. 1, 2, 3. *a justice of p.* Wiv. I, 1, 6. 226. H4B III, 2, 65. H6B IV, 7, 45. *now a man of p.* Wiv. II, 3, 45. *though I now be old and of the p.* 47 (i. e. an officer of the public peace); cf. *I am sworn of the p.* 55; *it well befits you should be of the p.* H4B III, 2, 99. *lads of p.* Wiv. III, 1, 113. *men of p.* LLL V, 1, 37. Represented as being under the protection of God: Meas. I, 2, 4. John II, 35. 88. H4B IV, 2, 29. H5 IV, 3, 31. H6A I, 3, 75. R3 I, 3, 288 etc.

3) a state of concord or reconciliation between persons or parties: *for the p. of you I hold such strife,* Sonn. 75, 3. *a' must keep p.* Ado II, 3, 202. *break the p.* ib. *the treason and you go in p. away together,* LLL IV, 3, 192. *p. and gentle visitation,* V, 2, 181. *all things shall be p.* Mids. III, 2, 377. Tw. I, 5, 227. V, 389. John IV, 2, 250. R2 III, 2, 127. H4A IV, 3, 62. H5 V, 2, 1. Mcb. I, 5, 47 (*keep p. between the effect and it =* prevent its execution) etc. *to be at p.* H6A III, 1, 117. IV, 1, 115. *to set at p.* R3 II, 1, 6 (Ff *made at p.*). *to take p. with =* to appease, to conciliate: H8 II, 1, 85. *to make one's p.:* Tw. III, 4, 296. R3 I, 2, 198. Caes. III, 1, 197. Ant. II, 5, 70.

4) quiet, content, secure tranquillity: *work the p. of the present,* Tp. I, 1, 24. *incensed the seas and shores against your p.* III, 3, 75. *p. be in this place,* Meas. I, 4, 6. 15. III, 1, 44. IV, 3, 110. *depart in p.* Ado III, 3, 73; cf. H6B II, 3, 26. *p. be to me and every*

*man that dares not fight,* LLL I, 1, 228. *encounters mounted are against your p.* V, 2, 83. *this uncivil and unjust extent against your p.* Tw. IV, 1, 58. *p. in this prison!* IV, 2, 21. *p. be with us,* H4B V, 2, 26. *nor heaven nor earth have been at p.* Caes. II, 2, 1. *the tyrant has not battered at their p.* Mcb. IV, 3, 178. *to put up in p. what I have suffered,* Oth. IV, 2, 181 etc. *p. be with you,* a kind wish at parting: Wiv. III, 5, 57. Meas. III, 2, 274. Ado V, 1, 196. Merch. IV, 1, 448. Rom. III, 1, 59. Lr. I, 1, 250.

Particularly denoting the internal quiet of the mind: *we wish your p.* Tp. IV, 163. *bless with sweet p.* Mids. V, 425. *that my soul may live at p.* Tw. IV, 3, 28. *put rancours in the vessel of my p.* Mcb. III, 1, 67. *to gain our p.* III, 2, 20 etc. Found in death: Meas. V, 401. H4B V, 2, 25. R3 II, 1, 5. H8 IV, 2, 156. Mcb. III, 2, 20. IV, 3, 179 etc.

5) silence: *to hold one's p.* = to be silent: Gent. V, 2, 18. Meas. V, 79. Tw. II, 3, 68. 74. Wint. I, 2, 28. R2 III, 4, 47. H6A III, 2, 58. H6B I, 3, 179. Rom. I, 3, 49. Hml. I, 2, 246. Lr. I, 4, 202. Oth. V, 2, 219 etc. *hold your —s,* Wint. II, 1, 139. *p., alone,* = be silent: Lucr. 1284. Tp. II, 1, 9. 127. Gent. II, 1, 99. IV, 1, 9. 41. IV, 2, 38. Wiv. I, 1, 138. Err. IV, 4, 61. V, 178. Ado IV, 2, 46. LLL I, 1, 228. V, 2, 483. Merch. V, 109. R2 V, 2, 80. H6A I, 3, 59. H6B I, 3, 178 etc. etc. *p. your tongue,* Wiv. I, 4, 85 (Dr. Caius' speech). *p. your tattlings,* IV, 1, 26 (Evans' speech). *p., foolish woman. I will not p.* R2 V, 2, 81. *p. thou!* H6C I, 1, 120. *when the thunder would not p. at my bidding,* Lr. IV, 6, 104. *hold your p. I p.!* Oth. V, 2, 219 (Qq *I hold my p.*).

Personified as a fem.: H4B I, 2, 233. H5 V, 2, 34.

**Peaceable,** peaceful, quiet: Ado III, 3, 61. Per. II, 1, 108.

**Peaceably,** quietly, in peace: Ado V, 2, 73. H6B III, 3, 25.

**Peaceful,** free from the excitement of war, quiet, undisturbed: Ven. 652. John II, 340. R2 II, 3, 93. III, 2, 125. H5 IV, 3, 86. V Chor. 33. H6A II, 2, 45. V, 4, 117. H6B I, 1, 122. H6C II, 6, 32. IV, 6, 71. Troil. I, 3, 105. Per. I, 2, 4. 35.

**Peace-maker,** one who composes differences: As V, 4, 108. H6B II, 1, 35. H8 III, 1, 167.

**Peace-parted,** having died in peace: *p. souls,* Hml. V, 1, 261.

**Peach,** vb. to impeach, to accuse, to denounce: *some four suits of peach-coloured satin, which now —es him a beggar,* Meas. IV, 3, 12. *if I be ta'en, I'll p. for this,* H4A II, 2, 47.

**Peach-coloured,** of the colour of a peach blossom: Meas. IV, 3, 12. H4B II, 2, 19.

**Peacock,** the bird Pavo: Tp. IV, 74. Err. IV, 3, 81. H5 IV, 1, 213. H6A III, 3, 6. Troil. III, 3, 252.

**Peak,** vb. 1) to grow lean, to fall away: *shall he dwindle, p. and pine,* Mcb. I, 3, 23.

2) to sneak, to play a contemptible part: *the —ing cornuto her husband,* Wiv. III, 5, 71. *yet I, a dull and muddy-mettled rascal, p., like John-a-dreams,* Hml. II, 2, 594.

**Peal,** a mighty sound: *the p. begins* (i. e. Armado's speech) LLL V, 1, 46. *whether those —s of praise be his,* Merch. III, 2, 146. *ring a hunter's p.* Tit. II, 2, 5. 13. *ere to black Hecate's summons the shard-borne beetle with his drowsy hums hath rung night's yawning p.* Mcb. III, 2, 43 (like a bell).

**Peal-meal**, see *Pell-mell*.

**Pear**, the fruit of Pyrus communis: *as crestfallen as a dried p.* Wiv. IV, 5, 103. *our French withered —s*, All's I, 1, 175. 176. 177. *thou a poperin p.* Rom. II, 1, 38.

**Pearl**, a white and shining body found in certain testaceous fish and worn as a jewel: Pilgr. 133. LLL IV, 2, 91. V, 2, 458. Mids. II, 1, 15. As V, 4, 63. Tw. IV, 3, 2. Troil. I, 1, 103. Hml. V, 2, 293. Oth. V, 2, 347. Ant. I, 5, 41. Plur. *—s:* Ven. 980. Compl. 198. Tp. I, 2, 398. Gent. V, 2, 11. Ado III, 4, 20. LLL V, 2, 53. Mids. IV, 1, 59. H4B II, 4, 53. Lr. IV, 3, 24. Ant. II, 5, 46. Plur. *p.:* Sonn. 34, 13. Gent. II, 4, 170. III, 1, 224. Wiv. V, 5, 75. Mids. I, 1, 211. Shr. Ind. 2, 44. II, 355. V, 1, 77. H5 IV, 1, 279. R3 I, 4, 26. IV, 4, 322. Tit. II, 1, 19. Used of tears: *wiped the brinish p. from her bright eyes*, Lucr. 1213. *those round clear —s of his*, 1553. *draws those —s from his eyes*, John II, 169 (cf. Ven. 980. Sonn. 34, 13. Gent. III, 1, 224. R3 IV, 4, 322. Lr. IV, 3, 24). Denoting any thing precious: *black men are —s in beauteous ladies' eyes*, Gent. V, 2, 12. *this is the p. that pleased your empress' eye*, Tit. V, 1, 42. *she is a p.* Troil. II, 2, 81. *I see thee compassed with thy kingdom's p., that speak my salutation in their minds*, Mcb. V, 8, 56 (i. e. the ornament, the élite, viz the high nobility).

**Pearly**, resembling pearls: *with p. sweat*, Lucr. 396.

**Peasant**, one whose business is rural labour, a hind: As I, 1, 73. H5 IV, 1, 301. IV, 2, 26. H6B IV, 4, 33. Caes. IV, 3, 74. Cymb. V, 1, 24. Adjectively: *through the p. towns*, H4B Ind. 33 (Ff *peasant-towns*).*
Mostly used as a term of reproach: Lucr. 1392. Gent. IV, 4, 47. V, 2, 35. Wiv. II, 2, 294. Err. II, 1, 81. V, 231. Shr. Ind. 1, 135. R2 IV, 252. H4B I, 1, 113. H5 IV, 4, 40. H6A V, 4, 21. V, 5, 53. H6B IV, 8, 21. R3 V, 3, 317. Tim. II, 2, 174. Hml. V, 1, 152. Lr. III, 7, 80. IV, 6, 235. Adjectively: *you p. swain*, Shr. IV, 1, 132. *their p. limbs*, H5 IV, 7, 80. *like p. foot-boys*, H6A III, 2, 69. *the p. boys of France*, IV, 6, 48. *what a rogue and p. slave am I*, Hml. II, 2, 576.

**Peasantry**, mean people: *how much low p. would then be gleaned from the true seed of honour*, Merch. II, 9, 46.

**Peasant-towns**, reading of Ff in H4B Ind. 33; see *Peasant*.

**Peascod**, the husk of peas: Mids. III, 1, 191. As II, 4, 52 (quibbling with *codpiece?* Green pease a favourite present of rustic lovers).* Tw. I, 5, 167. H4B II, 4, 413 (*come p. time*). Lr. I, 4, 219.

**Pease**, see *Pea*.

**Peaseblossom**, name of a fairy: Mids. III, 1, 165. 189. 192. IV, 1, 5. 7.

**Peat**, a pet, a darling: *a pretty p.* Shr. I, 1, 78.

**Pebble** (sometimes spelt *peeble* in O. Edd.; cf. *Pibble*) a small stone, such as may be found and picked up everywhere: Wiv. IV, 1, 35. Cor. V, 3, 58. Hml. V, 1, 254. Lr. IV, 6, 21. *a p. stone:* Gent. II, 3, 11. H6A III, 1, 80.

**Pebbled**, full of small stones: *the p. shore*, Sonn. 60, 1.

**Peck**, subst. the fourth part of a bushel: Wiv. III, 5, 113. Mids. IV, 1, 35.

**Peck**, name in H8 I, 1, 219. II, 1, 20.

**Peck**, vb. 1) to strike with the beak; trans.:

H6C I, 4, 41. Cor. III, 1, 139. Ant. III, 13, 197. Cymb. V, 3, 93. Absol.: *doves will p. in safeguard of their brood*, H6C II, 2, 18. With *at: for daws to p. at.* Oth. I, 1, 65.
2) to pick up food with the beak: *when beasts most graze, birds best p.* LLL I, 1, 239. Trans.: *this fellow —s up wit as pigeons pease*, V, 2, 315 (Ff Q² *picks*).
3) to strike? or to throw? *I'll p. you o'er the pales else*, H8 V, 4, 94 (most M. Edd. *pick;* the porter's speech).

**Peculiar**, belonging to one person only, not common, particular, private: *where mortal stars ... did him p. duties*, Lucr. 14. *groping for trouts in a p. river*, Meas. I, 2, 91. *in will p.* Troil. II, 3, 176. *in his p. sect and force*, Hml. I, 3, 26 (Qq *particular act and place*). *the single and p. life*, III, 3, 11. *for my p. end*, Oth. I, 1, 60. *to do a p. profit to your own person*, III, 3, 79. *beds which they dare swear p.* IV, 1, 70. *so much for my p. care*, Cymb. V, 5, 83.

**Pedant**, a schoolmaster: *a domineering p. o'er the boy*, LLL III, 179. *the p. presents Judas Maccabaeus*, V, 2, 539. 545. *wrangling p.* Shr. III, 1, 4. 48. 87. *a mercatante or a p.* IV, 2, 63. *a p. that keeps a school i' the church*, Tw. III, 2, 80.

**Pedantical**, becoming a schoolmaster, awkwardly ostentatious of learning: *figures p.* LLL V, 2, 408.

**Pedascule**, vocative of a supposed Latin word, = pedant, schoolmaster: Shr. III, 1, 50.

**Pede**, see *Bead* and *Bede*.

**Pedigree**, genealogy, register of a line of ancestors: H5 II, 4, 90. H6A II, 5, 77. H6C III, 3, 92. 99.

**Pedlar** or **Pedler**, one who carries about and sells small commodities: LLL V, 2, 317. Shr. Ind. 2, 20. Wint. IV, 4, 181. 217. 319. 328. 361. 734. H6B IV, 2, 48. R3 I, 3, 149.

**Pedro**, name of the prince in Ado I, 1, 13. 95. 204. II, 2, 34.

**Peel**, to decorticate, to strip off: *the bark —ed from the lofty pine*, Lucr. 1167. *—ed certain wands*, Merch. I, 3, 85.* *—ed priest*, H6A I, 3, 30 (= shaved).

**Peep**, subst. (the later Ff and M. Edd. *pip*), a spot on cards: *being perhaps two and thirty, a p. out*, Shr. I, 2, 33; supposed to allude to a game at cards called *One and thirty*, whose name was used to denote a person somewhat fuddled. N. L.

**Peep**, vb. (cf. *By-peep*) 1) intr. a) to look as through a crevice, or by stealth: *under whose brim the gaudy sun would p.* Ven. 1088. *who (her eyes) —ing forth this tumult to behold*, Lucr. 447. (the stars) *through night's black bosom should not p. again*, 788. *why pry'st thou through my window? leave thy —ing*, 1089; cf. Sonn. 24, 12. *nymphs back —ing fearfully*, Pilgr. 287. *p. through their eyes* (half closed in risibility) Merch. I, 1, 52. *he had made two holes in the alewife's new petticoat and so —ed through*, H4B II, 2, 89. *through a rusty beaver —s*, H5 IV, 2, 44. *durst not p. out*, H6B IV, 10, 4. Cor. IV, 6, 46. *nor heaven p. through the blanket of the dark*, Mcb. I, 5, 54.
Sometimes = to look, with a tinge of contempt: *when thou wakest, with thine own fool's eyes p.* Mids. IV, 1, 89. *and p. about to find ourselves dishonourable graves*, Caes. I, 2, 137. *treason can but p. to what it would, acts little of his will*, Hml. IV, 5, 124. *p. through thy marble mansion*, Cymb. V, 4, 87.
b) to be or become visible, to appear: *through*

*crystal walls each little mote will* p. Lucr. 1251. *some beauty —ed through lattice of seared age*, Compl. 14. *pack night, p. day*, Pilgr. 209. *an oak whose antique root —s out upon the brook*, As II, 1, 31. *the true blood which —eth fairly through it*, Wint. IV, 4, 148. *where thou darest not* p. H6B II, 1, 42. *I can see his pride* p. *through each part of him*, H8 I, 1, 69. *from this league —ed harms that menaced him*, 183. *forth at your eyes your spirits wildly* p. Hml. III, 4, 119. *no vessel can* p. *forth but 'tis ta'en*, Ant. I, 4, 53. *I'll force the wine* p. *through their scars*, III, 13, 191.

2) tr. to make visible, to let appear: *all his behaviours did make their retire to the court of his eye, —ing thorough desire*, LLL II, 235. *which* (an office done) *gratitude through flinty Tartar's bosom would* p. *forth*, All's IV, 4, 7. *there is not a dangerous action can* p. *out his head but I am thrust upon it*, H4B I, 2, 238.

**Peer,** subst. 1) an equal: *his —s have found him guilty of high treason*, H8 II, 1, 26. In Per.Pr. 21 O. Edd. *this king unto him took to* p.; M. Edd. *a fere.*

2) a nobleman: Lucr. 21. John IV, 2, 127. 179. 260. R2 I, 3, 93. III, 4, 88. H4B IV, 1, 90. V, 2, 144. H5 I, 2, 33. II, 2, 84. IV, 2, 14. V, 2, 8. 400. H6A III, 1, 70. 189. III, 4, 1. IV, 1, 146. V, 1, 57. V, 4, 103. H6B I, 1. 75. 98. 218. 253. I, 3, 77. 129. II, 1, 21. 28. 34. III, 2, 10. IV, 7, 127. H6C I, 1, 52. III, 3, 91. R3 II, 1, 2. 47. 51. II, 2, 112. III, 3, 10. III, 4, 1 (Qq *lords*). IV, 4, 95. H8 III, 2, 9. Troil. IV, 5, 271. Mcb. III, 4, 96. Per. I, 3, 11. II, 4, 58. *King Stephen was a worthy* p. Oth. II, 3, 92, a song alluded to in Tp. IV, 221.

**Peer,** vb. 1) to look narrowly, to pry: *—ing in maps for ports*, Merch. I, 1, 19.

2) to come in sight, to appear: *like a dive-dapper —ing through a wave*, Ven. 86. *p. out!* Wiv. IV, 2, 26. *honour —eth in the meanest habit*, Shr. IV, 3, 176. *when daffodils begin to* p. Wint. IV, 3, 1. *Flora —ing in April's front*, IV, 4, 3. *through the hollow eyes of death I spy life —ing*, R2 II, 1, 271. *how bloodily the sun begins to* p. *above yon bosky hill*, H4A V, 1, 1. *yet a many of your horsemen* p. *and gallop o'er the field*, H5 IV, 7, 88. *an hour before the sun —ed forth the golden window of the east*, Rom. I, 1, 126. *it shall as level to your judgment* p. Hml. IV, 5, 151 (Ff *pierce*). *to* p. *over* = to overpeer (q. v.): *a proud river —ing o'er his bounds*, John III, 1, 23. cf. *Highest-peering, Stillpeering.*

3) to bring into sight, to let appear: *who o'er the white sheet —s her whiter chin*, Lucr. 472.

**Peerless,** unequalled: Lucr. 21. Tp. III, 1, 47. Wint. V, 1, 94. V, 3, 14. H6A V, 5, 68. Mcb. I, 4, 58. Ant. I, 1, 40. Per. IV Prol. 40.

**Peesel,** corrupted from *Pistol:* H4B II, 4, 174.

**Peevish,** silly, childish, thoughtless: *this it is to be a* p. *girl that flies her fortune*, Gent. V, 2, 49. *he is something* p. *that way*, Wiv. I, 4, 14. *thou* p. *sheep, what ship of Epidamnum stays for me?* Err. IV, 1, 93. *what wilt thou do, thou* p. *officer?* IV, 4, 117. *'tis but a* p. *boy*, As III, 5, 110. *run after that same* p. *messenger*, Tw. I, 5, 319. *wronged by this* p. *town*, John II, 402. *a wretched and* p. *fellow*, H5 III, 7, 142. *I scorn thee*, p. *boy*, H6A II, 4, 76. *leave this* p. *broil*, III, 1, 92. *to send such* p. *tokens to a king*, V, 3, 186. *what a* p. *fool was that of Crete*, H6C V, 6, 18. *that* p. *brat*, R3 I, 3, 194. *what an indirect and* p. *course*, III, 1, 31. *when*

*Richmond was a little* p. *boy*, IV, 2, 100. *be not* p. *found in great designs*, IV, 4, 417 (Qq p. *fond*). *the gods are deaf to hot and* p. *vows*, Troil. V, 3, 16. *a* p. *school-boy*, Caes. V, 1, 61. *in our* p. *opposition*, Hml. I, 2, 100. *this* p. *odds*, Oth. II, 3, 185. p. *jealousies*, IV, 3, 90. *he is strange and* p. Cymb. I, 6, 54. Especially = childishly wayward, capricious: *she is* p., *sullen, froward*, Gent. III, 1, 68. *creep into the jaundice by being* p. Merch. I, 1, 86. *froward*, p., *sullen, sour*, Shr. V, 2, 157. *virginity is* p., *proud, idle, made of self-love*, Alls I, 1, 156. *a* p. *self-willed harlotry*, H4A III, 1, 198 and Rom. IV, 2, 14. *the* p. *baggage*, Per. IV, 6, 20. *your* p. *chastity*, 130.

**Peevish-fond,** wayward or silly and foolish: R3 IV, 4, 417 (Ff *peevish found*).

**Peevishly,** in a wayward and unbecoming manner: *you* p. *threw it to her*, Tw. II, 2, 14.

**Peg,** subst. *—s* = the pins of an instrument on which the strings are strained: Oth. II, 1, 202.

**Peg,** vb. to fasten with a peg, to wedge: *I will* p. *thee in his knotty entrails*, Tp. I, 2, 295.

**Peg-a-Ramsey,** the name of an old ballad now unknown, nonsensically applied to Malvolio by Sir Toby: Tw. II, 3, 81.

**Pegasus,** the winged horse of the ancient fable: H4A IV, 1, 109. H5 III, 7, 15. Name of an inn: Shr. IV, 4, 5.*

**Peize,** to poise: *'tis to* p. *the time, to eke it and to draw it out in length*, Merch. III, 2, 22 (to retard it by hanging weights on it). *the world who of itself is —d well*, John II, 575. With *down*, = to weigh down: *lest leaden slumber* p. *me down*, R3 V, 3, 105.

**Pelf,** riches, goods: *shadows like myself*, *as take the pain, but cannot pluck the* p. Pilgr. 192. *I crave no* p. Tim. I, 2, 63. *all perishen of man, of* p. Per. II Prol. 35.

**Pelican,** the bird Pelecanus, supposed to feed its young with its own blood: R2 II, 1, 126. Hml. IV, 5, 146. Lr. III, 4, 77.

**Pelicock,** reading of Qq in Lr. III, 4, 78; Ff *Pillicock*, q. v.

**Pelion,** mountain in Thessaly: Wiv. II, 1, 82. Hml. V, 1, 276.

**Pella,** name in Caes. IV, 3, 2.

**Pellet,** vb. to form into small balls: *the brine that seasoned woe had —ed in tears*, Compl. 18. *this —ed storm* (of hail) Ant. III, 13, 165.

**Pell-mell,** with confused violence, as in a scuffle where strokes are dealt at random: *upon them, lords!* p., *down with them*, LLL IV, 3, 368. *defy each other, and* p. *make work upon ourselves*, John II, 406. *let us to't* p. R3 V, 3, 312. *to't, luxury*, p. Lr. IV, 6, 119. Adjectively: p. *havock and confusion*, H4A V, 1, 82.

**Peloponnesus,** the ancient name of the Morea: Ant. III, 10, 31.

**Pelt,** to throw as with pellets; intr. *do* p. *so fast at one another's pate*, H6A III, 1, 82. *bide the —ing of this pitiless storm*, Lr. III, 4, 29. = to throw out words, to use abusive language, to curse: *another smothered seems to* p. *and swear*, Lucr. 1418. Trans.: *the chidden billow seems to* p. *the clouds*, Oth. II, 1, 12.

**Pelting,** paltry: *every* p. *petty officer*, Meas. II, 2, 112. *have every* p. *river made so proud*, Mids. II, 1, 91 (Ff *petty*). *a tenement or* p. *farm*, R2 II, 1, 60. *we* *have had p. wars*, Troil. IV, 5, 267. *poor p. villages*, Lr. II, 3, 18.

**Pembroke**, place in Wales: R3 IV, 5, 7. Earl of P.: John I, 30. H6C IV, 1, 130. IV, 3, 54. R3 IV, 5, 11. V, 3, 29. Marchioness of P.: H8 II, 3, 63. 94. III, 2, 90.

**Pen**, subst. a small enclosure, a coop: *stole two geese out of a p.* Wiv. III, 4, 41.

**Pen**, subst. a goose-quill used for writing (often = writer, or art of writing): Lucr. 1289. Sonn. 16, 10. 19, 10. 32, 6. 78, 3. 79, 6. 84, 5. 85, 8. 100, 8. 106, 7. Ado I, 1, 255. III, 5, 63. LLL I, 1, 245. I, 2, 191. IV, 2, 158. IV, 3, 346. Mids. V, 15. Merch. V, 237. All's II, 1, 80. Tw. III, 2, 53. IV, 2, 87. Wint. II, 1, 11. John V, 7, 32. H4B IV, 1, 51. H5 III, 3, 17. Epil. 1. H6A III, 1, 13. V, 3, 66. H6B IV, 2, 117. Troil. Prol. 24. III, 3, 204. Tit. IV, 1, 75. IV, 3, 106. Rom. I, 3, 82. Lr. III, 4, 100. Oth. II, 1, 63. Cymb. V, 4, 173. Per. IV Prol. 28.

**Pen**, vb. (partic. *pent*; impf. not found) to confine, to shut up: *he —s her piteous clamours in her head*, Lucr. 681. *a liquid prisoner —t in walls of glass*, Sonn. 5, 10. 133, 13. *my —t heart*, R3 IV, 1, 34. *—t from liberty*, I, 4, 267. *in his chamber —s himself*, Rom. I, 1, 144. *— t to linger but with a grain a day*, Cor. III, 3, 89. With *up:* Tp. I, 2, 326.\*LLL I, 2, 160. H6B II, 4, 24. H6C I, 3, 12. R3 IV, 3, 36. Lr. III, 2, 57. Cymb. I, 1, 153.

**Pen**, vb. (partic. *penned*) to commit to paper, to write with care: Compl. 47. LLL V, 2, 147. 305. 402. All's III, 6, 80 *(down).* Tw. I, 5, 185. H4A III, 1, 209. *mark but the —ing of it* (= the style) Lr. IV, 6, 142.

**Penalty**, punishment, forfeiture: Meas. I, 2, 170. IV, 2, 177. Err. I, 1, 23. LLL I, 1, 123. 125. 128. Merch. I, 3, 138. IV, 1, 22. 207. 248. 322. 410. As II, 1, 5. Rom. I, 2, 2.

**Penance**, infliction suffered for transgression, or as an expression of repentance: Sonn. 111, 12. Gent. I, 2, 64. V, 2, 38. V, 4, 170. Ado V, 1, 282. LLL I, 1, 115. V, 2, 717. Merch. IV, 1, 271. Shr. I, 1, 89. Tw. III, 4, 151. H6B II, 4, 75. H8 I, 4, 17. 32. V, 4, 45. *to do p.*: Gent. II, 4, 129. H6B II, 3, 11. II, 4, 20. 105. Misapplied by Dull in LLL I, 2, 134.

**Pencil**, the small brush used by painters to lay on colours: Sonn. 16, 10. 101, 7; cf. LLL V, 2, 43 (Q1 and F1 *pensals*). John III, 1, 237. Rom. I, 2, 41.

**Pencilled**, painted: Lucr. 1497. Tim. I, 1, 159.

**Pendent**, hanging: *with ribands p.* Wiv. IV, 6, 42. *blown with restless violence round about the p. world*, Meas. III, 1, 126 (the earth suspended in the universe). *this bird hath made his p. bed*, Mcb. I, 6, 8. *on the p. boughs*, Hml. IV, 7, 173. *a p. rock*, Ant. IV, 14, 4.

**Pendragon**, the father of King Arthur: H6A III, 2, 95.

**Pendulous**, impending: *all the plagues that in the p. air hang fated o'er men's faults*, Lr. III, 4, 69 (cf. the Birth of Merlin IV, 1: *knowest thou what p. mischief roofs thy head, how fatal, and how sudden?*).

**Penelope**, the wife of Ulysses: Cor. I, 3, 92.

**Penelophon**, the beggar maid loved by King Cophetua, called *Zenelophon* by Don Armado: LLL IV, 1, 67.

**Penetrable**, susceptible, impressible: *his heart granteth no p. entrance to her plaining*, Lucr. 559. *p.*

*to your kind entreats*, R3 III, 7, 225. *made of p. stuff*, Hml. III, 4, 36.

**Penetrate**, to make a deep impression, to touch; absol.: *they say it will p.* Cymb. II, 3, 14. *if this p.* 31. Trans.: *p. the breasts of ever angry bears*, Tp. I, 2, 288. *could p. her uncompassionate sire*, Gent. III, 1, 231. *if you can p. her with your fingering*, Cymb. II, 3, 15.

**Penetrative**, affecting the heart strongly: *his face subdued to p. shame*, Ant. IV, 14, 75.

**Penitence**, repentance: *by p. the Eternal's wrath's appeased*, Gent. V, 4, 81. *paid down more p. than done trespass*, Wint. V, 1, 4. *and try your p., if it be sound,* Meas. II, 3, 22. *fear, and not love, begets his p.* R2 V, 3, 56. *my p. comes after all*, H5 IV, 1, 321. *repent in bootless p.* H6C II, 6, 70.

**Penitent**, 1) repentant: Tp. V, 28. Meas. IV, 2, 53. V, 480. Wint. IV, 2, 7. 25. H6B III, 2, 4. H6C V, 1, 27. R3 I, 2, 221. Oth. III, 3, 63. Cymb. V, 4, 10. Substantively: *it was the desire of the p.* Meas. IV, 2, 188. *thy p. reformed*, Wint. I, 2, 239. *I'll play the p.* Ant. II, 2, 92.

2) doing penance: *we that know what 'tis to fast and pray are p. for your default to-day*, Err. I, 2, 52. Substantively: *of enjoined —s there's four or five, to great Saint Jaques bound*, All's III, 5, 97.

**Penitential**, enjoined as penance: *have punished me with bitter fasts, with p. groans*, Gent. II, 4, 131.

**Penitently**, with repentance: Meas. IV, 2, 147.

**Penker** (O. Edd. *Peuker, Reuker, Beuker*), name in R3 III, 5, 104.\*

**Penknife**, a knife used to cut pens: H4B III, 2, 286.

**Pennon**, wing, and small flag; both significations combined: *sweeps through our land with —s painted in the blood of Harfleur*, H5 III, 5, 49.\*

**Penny**, the twelfth part of a shilling: Wiv. II, 2, 1. 4. LLL III, 28. 140. V, 1, 74. As II, 5, 29. Shr. III, 2, 85. All's V, 2, 39. H4A I, 3, 91. H4B I, 2, 252. V, 1, 34 (proverb: *a friend i' the court is better than a penny in purse).* H5 III, 6, 50. H6B III, 1, 109. IV, 2, 71. H8 III, 2, 453. Troil. II, 1, 77. Rom. II, 4, 195. Cymb. II, 4, 20. V, 4, 170. Plur. *pence:* Gent. II, 5, 10. Wiv. I, 1, 160. II, 2, 14. Shr. Ind. 2, 24. Tw. I, 5, 87. IV, 1, 33. John I, 153. H4B I, 2, 263. H5 IV, 8, 68. H8 II, 3, 89. Cor. II, 1, 80.

= money in general: *her father is make her a petter p.* Wiv. I, 1, 62 (Evans' speech). *what p. hath Rome borne, what men provided, what munition sent, to underprop this action?* John V, 2, 97.

**Pennyworth**, as much as is bought for a penny, no great quantity, a trifle: Ado II, 3, 44.\*LLL III, 103. Merch. I, 2, 77. Wint IV, 4, 650 *(though the p. on his side be the worst*, i. e. though he have the worst of the bargain). H4A II, 4, 25. 65. III, 3, 180. H6B I, 1, 222. Rom. IV, 5, 4 (—s, viz of sleep).

**Pension**, an annuity: Tw. II, 5, 196. H4B I, 2, 276. Lr. II, 4, 217.

**Pensioners**, gentlemen in the personal service of the king or queen: Wiv. II, 2, 79. Mids. II, 1, 10.

**Pensive**, sorrowfully thoughtful: H6C IV, 1, 10. Rom. IV, 1, 39.

**Pensived**, sad, melancholy: *of p. and subdued desires the tender*, Compl. 219.

**Pensiveness**, sorrow: *so Lucrece sad tales doth tell to pencilled p.* Lucr. 1497.

**Pentapolis**, the kingdom of Simonides in Per. II, 1, 104. III Prol. 34. V, 3, 4. 38. 72.

**Pentecost**, Whitsuntide: Gent. IV, 4, 163. Err. IV, 1, 1. Rom. I, 5, 38.

**Penthesilea**, the queen of the Amazons killed by Achilles: Tw. II, 3, 193.

**Penthouse**, a shed hanging out aslope from the main building: Ado III, 3, 110. Merch. II, 6, 1. Used of the eyelid: *sleep shall neither night nor day hang upon his p. lid*, Mcb. I, 3, 20.

**Penthouse-like**, hanging over like the roof of a penthouse: LLL III, 17.

**Penurious**, suffering extreme want: *in my p. band*, Tim. IV, 3, 92.

**Penury**, extreme poverty and indigence: Sonn. 84, 5. Meas. III, 1, 130. As I, 1, 42. III, 2, 343. R2 V, 5, 34. Rom. V, 1, 49. Lr. II, 3, 8.

**Peonied**, writing of some M. Edd. for *pioned* of O. Edd. in Tp. IV, 64. See *Pioned*.

**People**, subst. 1) all the persons who compose a nation or any community (never plur. —*s*): Lucr. Arg. 3. 23. Tp. I, 2, 141. II, 1, 164. Meas. I, 1, 10. 68. I, 3, 35. 45. As I, 3, 81. John III, 4, 150. IV, 2, 144. V, 1, 9. H4A V, 1, 104. H5 III, 3, 28. III, 5, 24 (*a more frosty p.*). H6A V, 5, 93. H6B I, 1, 79. H6C III, 3, 117. Caes. IV, 3, 204. Hml. IV, 5, 81 etc.

2) the commonalty, in contradistinction to the nobility (*the common p.*: R2 I, 4, 24. H6B I, 1, 158. H6C II, 6, 8. IV, 2, 2 etc.): *our p. and our peers are both misled*, H6C III, 3, 35. *chief enemy to the p.* Cor. I, 1, 8. *always loved the p.* 53. *tribunes for the p.* 258. I, 2, 11. II, 1, 4 and passim in this tragedy.

3) persons, men indefinitely: *the world's poor p. are amazed at apparitions*, Ven. 925. *like a press of p.* Lucr. 1301. *these are p. of the island*, Tp. III, 3, 30. V, 184. *if these be good p.* Meas. II, 1, 42. Err. V, 38. 91. 258. Ado II, 1, 266. V, 1, 290. LLL V, 2, 832. IV, 2, 61. Merch. III, 2, 143. V, 295. As I, 2, 292. II, 3, 5. III, 2, 166. Tw. I, 5, 119. IV, 1, 29. V, 347. R2 V, 5, 10. 31. Tit. III, 1, 277. Mcb. I, 7, 33. IV, 3, 150. Ant. I, 1, 54 etc.

4) attendants, followers, troops: *you slew great number of his p.* Tw. III, 3, 29. *a thousand of his p. butchered*, H4A I, 1, 42. *my p. are with sickness much enfeebled*, H5 III, 6, 154. *fan our p. cold*, Mcb. I, 2, 50. *the tyrant's p. on both sides do fight*, V, 7, 25. Quite = servants: *mine own p.* Wiv. II, 2, 52. IV, 2, 14. As I, 1, 176. *my p.* Merch. III, 4, 37. Tw. I, 5, 112. II, 5, 64. III, 4, 69. Wint. I, 2, 450. Lr. I, 4, 277. 293. Oth. I, 1, 142. *your p.* Mids. IV, 1, 43. *his p.* Lr. II, 4, 291. IV, 7, 88.

**People**, vb. to stock with inhabitants: Tp. I, 2, 350. Gent. V, 4, 3. Ado II, 3, 251. As V, 4, 149. R2 V, 5, 9. H4B V, 5, 138. H5 I, 2, 189.

**Pepin**, the founder of the Carlovingian dynasty: H5 I, 2, 65. 87. Representative of ancient times: *when king P. of France was a little boy*, LLL IV, 1, 122. *powerful to araise king P.* All's II, 1, 79. *their very noses had been counsellors to P. or Clotharius*, H8 I, 3, 10.

**Pepper**, subst. the fruit of Piper nigrum: *there's vinegar and p. in it*, Tw. III, 4, 158.

**Pepper**, vb. to serve out, to finish, to make an end of: *I have —ed two of them*, H4A II, 4, 212. *I have led my ragamuffins where they are —ed*, V, 3, 37.

*I am —ed, I warrant, for this world*, Rom. III, 1, 102.

**Pepper-box**, a box holding pepper: Wiv. III, 5, 149.

**Peppercorn**, the berry of the pepper-plant: H4A III, 3, 9.

**Pepper-gingerbread**, spice gingerbread: H4A III, 1, 260.

**Peradventure**, perhaps: Wiv. I, 1, 44. 78 (Evans: —*s*). Meas. III, 1, 209. IV, 6, 5. Ado I, 2, 24. II, 1, 153. Mids. IV, 1, 224. As I, 2, 54. John V, 6, 31. H4B III, 2, 315. H5 III, 2, 137. IV, 1, 170. IV, 8, 4. Cor. II, 1, 102. Tim. IV, 3, 333. Oth. II, 1, 301.

**Perceive**, 1) to become aware of, to discover, to see with the eye of the body or the mind: Ven. 317. 727. Sonn. 15, 5. 73, 13. 104, 10. Tp. V, 153. Gent. I, 1, 127. 142. I, 3, 35. II, 1, 34. 35. 159. 163. III, 1, 33. IV, 2, 66. Wiv. II, 1, 55. III, 1, 118. V, 5, 124. Meas. II, 2, 125. V, 235. 374. 499. Err. IV, 2, 2. Mids. II, 2, 155. III, 2, 193. 267. 290. As III, 2, 350. Shr. II, 19. H6A II, 1, 2. III, 3, 27. IV, 1, 74. H6B II, 3, 104. R3 III, 1, 191. III, 4, 56. Caes. V, 3, 13. Oth. V, 1, 106. Ant. III, 6, 80. Per. V, 1, 128 etc. With a double accus.: *who —th our natural wits too dull*, As I, 2, 55. *when you p. his blood inclined to mirth*, H4B IV, 4, 38. *where you p. them thick*, Caes. I, 1, 76. *when you above p. me like a crow*, Cymb. III, 3, 12. With an inf. without *to*: *if I p. the love come from her*, Ado II, 3, 234. *you shall p. them make a mutual stand*, Merch. V, 77. *when he —d me shrink and on my knee*, H6A IV, 7, 5.

2) to see through: *you p. my mind?* H6A II, 2, 59. H6B III, 1, 374. H6C III, 2, 66. 67. *lest Hector or my father should p. me*, Troil. I, 1, 36. *O, I p. you*, IV, 5, 87. *the king in this —s him, how he coasts and hedges his own way*, H8 III, 2, 38.

3) to receive (only in quibbling): *I could p. nothing at all from her, no, not so much as a ducat*, Gent. I, 1, 144 (Speed's speech; cf. II, 1, 163).

**Perch**, subst. that on which birds sit: Meas. II, 1, 4. Figuratively: *by many a dern and painful p. of Pericles the careful search … is made*, Per. III Prol. 15; = resting-place? or is the measure of length meant?

**Perch**, vb. to sit or roost as a bird: R3 I, 3, 71. Caes. V, 1, 80. cf. *O'erperch*.

**Perchance**, perhaps: Lucr. 36. Tp. II, 2, 17. Gent. II, 1, 118. Meas. IV, 2, 216. V, 277. Err. I, 2, 86. IV, 1, 39. Ado III, 4, 81. LLL II, 199. Mids. II, 1, 139. V, 128. 224. Merch. V, 75. All's III, 5, 90. Tw. I, 2, 5. I, 5, 300. II, 5, 66. Wint. I, 2, 228. II, 1, 110. John IV, 1, 115. IV, 2, 213. V, 1, 74. Troil. I, 3, 360. II, 3, 88. III, 2, 160. Tit. III, 1, 114. Rom. II, 5, 3. Tim. II, 2, 138. Mcb. IV, 3, 11. 25. Hml. I, 2, 243. I, 5, 171. II, 1, 59. III, 1, 65. III, 4, 130. Lr. II, 2, 97. II, 4, 144. III, 1, 29. V, 3, 200. Oth. III, 3, 145. V, 2, 197. Ant. I, 1, 20. IV, 2, 27. Cymb. I, 5, 38. II, 5, 15. Followed by *that*: *p. that envy of so rich a thing did sting his thoughts*, Lucr. 39. Peculiar passage: *p. he is not drowned. It is p. that you yourself were saved*, Tw. I, 2, 6; i. e. by chance, by accident.

**Percussion**, the effect of sound on the ear: *the thunder-like p. of thy sounds*, Cor, I, 4, 59.

**Percy**, family name of the Earl of Northumberland: H4B II, 3, 4. H6A II, 5, 67. His son Henry called so by eminence: R2 II, 2, 53. II, 3, 21. 45. V, 6, 11. H4A I, 1, 53 etc. H4B I, 1, 42 etc.

**Perdie** or **Perdy,** by God, in sooth: Err. IV, 4, 74. Tw. IV, 2, 81. H5 II, 1, 52. Hml. III, 2, 305. Lr. II, 4, 86.

**Perdita,** female name in Wint. III, 3, 33. IV, 1, 24 etc.

**Perdition,** 1) destruction, ruin: *lingering p.... shall step by step attend you,* Tp. III, 3, 77. *commend them and condemn them to her service or to their own p.* Wint. IV, 4, 389. *where reason can revolt without p.* Troil. V, 2, 145. *importing the mere p. of the Turkish fleet,* Oth. II, 2, 3. *p. catch my soul,* III, 3, 90. *to lose't or give't away were such p. as nothing else could match,* III, 4, 67.

2) loss: *not so much p. as an hair betid to any creature,* Tp. I, 2, 30. *this shall end without the p. of souls,* Tw. III, 4, 318. *the p. of the adversary hath been great,* H5 III, 6, 103. *his definement suffers no p. in you,* Hml. V, 2, 117.

**Perdu,** a soldier sent on a forlorn hope: *to watch, poor p., with this thin helm,* Lr. IV, 7, 35.

**Pérdurable,** lasting: H5 IV, 5, 7. Oth. I, 3, 343.

**Pérdurably,** lastingly: Meas. III, 1, 115.

**Perdy,** see *Perdie.*

**Peregrinate,** adj. foreign; in the language of Holofernes: LLL V, 1, 15.

**Peremptorily,** positively: H4A II, 4, 472.

**Peremptory,** 1) absolute, positive, so as to cut off all further debate: Gent. I, 3, 71. LLL V, 1, 11. Shr. II, 132. H5 V, 2, 82. Cor. III, 1, 94. Per. II, 5, 73. With an inf., = firmly resolved: *we are p. to dispatch this viperous traitor,* Cor. III, 1, 286; cf. John II, 454.

2) unawed, regardless, bold: *what p. eagle-sighted eye dares look upon the heaven of her brow,* LLL IV, 3, 226. *not Death himself in mortal fury half so p.* John II, 454. *your presence is too bold and p.* H4A I, 3, 17.\**is your priesthood grown p.?* H6B II, 1, 23. *how proud, how p. and unlike himself,* III, 1, 8. *where p. Warwick now remains,* H6C IV, 8, 59.

**Perfect,** adj. (comp. —er: Cor. II, 1, 91. superl. —est: Sonn. 51, 10. Ado II, 1, 317. Mcb. I, 5, 2) 1) faultless, fully accomplished, not to be surpassed: *whose p. white,* Lucr. 394. *creating every bad a p. best,* Sonn. 114, 7. *so p. and so peerless,* Tp. III, 1, 47. Gent. IV, 2, 124. V, 4, 111. Mids. III, 2, 137. Wint. V, 1, 15. H8 V, 5, 38. Oth. V, 2, 145. Cymb. I, 6, 158. III, 3, 67.

2) complete, entire, unqualified: *forget to say the p. ceremony of love's rite,* Sonn. 23, 6. *desire, of —est love being made,* 51, 10. *his complexion is p. gallows,* Tp. I, 1, 32. *he cannot be a p. man, not being tried and tutored in the world,* Gent. I, 3, 20 (German: ein ganzer Mann). *her hair is auburn, mine is p. yellow,* IV, 4, 194. *silence is the —est herald of joy,* Ado II, 1, 317. *your p. yellow,* Mids. I, 2, 98 (Qq *perfit*). *so holy and so p. is my love,* As III, 5, 99; cf. Shr. IV, 3, 12; H6A V, 5, 50; R3 II, 1, 16; III, 7, 90. *I will return p. courtier,* All's I, 1, 219. *finds them p. Richard,* John I, 90. *law itself is p. wrong,* III, 1, 189. *the true and p. image of life,* H4A V, 4, 120. *three glorious suns, each one a p. sun,* H6C II, 1, 26. *can neither call it p. day nor night,* II, 5, 4. *to make the p. period of this peace,* R3 II, 1, 44. *the grief is fine, full, p., that I taste,* Troil. IV, 4, 3. *which (health) in his death were p.* Mcb. III,

1, 108. *is't not p. conscience, to quit him with this arm?* Hml. V, 2, 67. *let it look like p. honour,* Ant. I, 3, 80.

3) fully answering the purpose; a) right, correct: *thou hast a p. thought,* John V, 6, 6. *Richard might create a p. guess,* H4B III, 1, 88. *acquaint you with the p. spy o' the time,* Mcb. III, 1, 130 (see *Spy*).

b) sound, unimpaired: *he was not in his p. wits,* Err. V, 42. *I fear I am not in my p. mind,* Lr. IV, 7, 63.

c) full, ripe: *sons at p. age,* Lr. I, 2, 77.

d) having one's wish, satisfied, happy: *might we but have that happiness ... we should think ourselves for ever p.* Tim. I, 2, 90. *I had else been p., whole as the marble,* Mcb. III, 4, 21.

e) well informed, well knowing: *thou art p. then, our ship hath touched upon the deserts of Bohemia?* Wint. III, 3, 1. *I have learned by the —est report,* Mcb. I, 5, 2. *I am p. that the Pannonians are now in arms,* Cymb. III, 1, 73. *what hast thou done? I am p. what,* IV, 2, 118 (I know full well, I am fully aware).

f) knowing what to do or to say, well prepared for what may happen: *when you have a business for yourself, pray heaven you then be p.* Meas. V, 82. *my parts, my title and my p. soul shall manifest me rightly,* Oth. I, 2, 31.

g) not deficient, acting up to one's part: *take pains, be p.* Mids. I, 2, 112. *I hope I was p.* LLL V, 2, 562. *thou art p.* H4A II, 4, 39. Hence = expert, skilled: *the lesson is but plain, and once made p., never lost again,* Ven. 408. *a —er giber for the table than a necessary bencher in the Capitol,* Cor. II, 1, 91. With *in: that pretty Welsh I am too p. in,* H4A III, 1, 203. *thou art p. in lying down,* 229. H4B IV, 1, 155. H5 III, 6, 73. Tit. III, 2, 40. Mcb. IV, 2, 66. Per. V, 1, 208.

**Pérfect,** vb. 1) to bring to perfection, to complete: *experience is by industry achieved and —ed by the swift course of time,* Gent. I, 3, 23.

2) to effect, to perform: *ere I can p. mine intents,* All's IV, 4, 4. *we must needs admit the means how things are —ed,* H5 I, 1, 69.

3) to instruct fully: *being once —ed how to grant suits,* Tp. I, 2, 79. *her cause and yours I'll p. him withal,* Meas. IV, 3, 146. *Apollo, p. me in the characters,* Per. III, 2, 67.

**Perfection,** 1) the state of being perfect, supreme degree of development and excellence: *whose full p. all the world amazes,* Ven. 634. 736. *no p. is so absolute,* Lucr. 853. *every thing holds in p. but a little moment,* Sonn. 15, 2. Gent. II, 4, 66. 197. II, 7, 13. III, 1, 177. IV, 1, 57. Merch. V, 108. All's V, 3, 18. Tw. II, 4, 42. John II, 440. R3 IV, 4, 66. Rom. II, 2, 46. Abstr. for the concr.: *right p. wrongfully disgraced,* Sonn. 66, 7. *divine p. of a woman,* R3 I, 2, 75. *p. so could err,* Oth. I, 3, 100. *she is indeed p.* II, 3, 28.

2) an excellent quality or endowment: *to put a strange face on his own p.* Ado II, 3, 49. *would turn their own p. to abuse,* H4B II, 3, 27. *which (bearing well) is the prescript praise and p. of a good and particular mistress,* H5 III, 7, 50. *she did make defect p.* Ant. II, 2, 236. Plur. —s: Gent. II, 4, 211. LLL II, 6. Tw. I, 1, 39. 1, 5, 315. H6A V, 5, 12. H6C III, 2, 86. Hml. IV, 7, 29. Per. I, 1, 11. 79.

3) excellent manner, exemplariness: *I would with such p. govern,* Tp. II, 1, 167.

4) execution, performance: *my honey lost, and I, a drone-like bee, have no p. of my summer left,* Lucr. 837. *it will grow to a most prosperous p.* Meas. III, 1,

272. *vowing more than the p. of ten and discharging less than the tenth part of one,* Troil. III, 2, 94. *no p. in reversion shall have a praise in present,* 99. *you knot of mouth-friends! smoke and lukewarm water is your p.* Tim. III, 6, 100 ( cf. Troil. V, 1, 98. Tim. IV, 3, 72. V, 1, 24).

**Perfectly,** absolutely, completely: Wint. V, 2, 108. H5 III, 6, 79 (Ff *perfitly*). V, 2, 310. Troil. III, 3, 206.

**Perfectness,** 1) acquired skill and dexterity: *is this your p.? be gone, you rogue,* LLL V, 2, 173.
2) ripeness: *the prince will in the p. of time cast off his followers,* H4B IV, 4, 74.

**Perfidious,** faithless, treacherous: Tp. I, 2, 68. II, 2, 154. All's V, 3, 205. H8 I, 2, 156.

**Perfidiously,** treacherously: Cor. V, 6, 91.

**Perfit,** = perfect, reading of Qq in Mids. I, 2, 98. 112. Lr. I, 2, 77; of Ff H5 III, 6, 73. R3 III, 7, 90.

**Perfitly,** perfectly: H5 III, 6, 79 (the surreptitious Qq *perfectly*).

**Perforce,** 1) by force, by violence: *he rushed into my house and took p. my ring away,* Err. IV, 3, 95. *and take p. my husband from the abbess,* V, 117. *what he hath taken away from thy father p., I will render thee again in affection,* As I, 2, 21. John I, 268. R2 II, 3, 121. H6C I, 1, 34. 142. V, 5, 68. R3 III, 1, 30. 36. Tit. II, 3, 134. Rom. V, 3, 238. Lr. I, 4, 320. I, 5, 43. Cymb. III, 1, 72. *force p.,* in the same sense: *and force p. keep Stephen Langton from that holy see,* John III, 1, 142. *the king was force p. compelled to banish him,* H4B IV, 1, 116. *and force p. I'll make him yield the crown,* H6B I, 1, 258.
2) necessarily (joined to *must*): *of thy misprision must p. ensue some true love turned,* Mids. III, 2, 90. *which* (your health) *must p. decay,* H4B I, 1, 165. *these unseasoned hours p. must add unto your sickness,* III, 1, 105. *that light and weightless down p. must move,* IV, 5, 34. H5 V, 2, 161. Troil. I, 3, 123. Lr. IV, 2, 35. 49. *p. and needs* joined: *p. you must needs stay a time,* Tit. IV, 3, 41.
3) of necessity, yielding to necessity (German: nothgedrungen): *I, being pent in thee, p. am thine,* Sonn. 133, 14. *patience p.* Rom. I, 5, 91 (cf. R3 I, 1, 116. Proverb: *patience perforce is a medicine for a mad dog). when p. he could not but pay me terms of honour,* Ant. III, 4, 6. Joined to *must: with foul offenders thou p. must bear,* Lucr. 612. *which p. thou must restore,* Tp. V, 133. *p. I must confess I thought you lord of more true gentleness,* Mids. II, 2, 131. *p. a third must take up us,* H4B I, 3, 72. *I must p. compound with mistful eyes,* H5 IV, 6, 33. *how I am braved and must p. endure it,* H6A II, 4, 115. R3 I, 1, 116. H8 I, 2, 47. III, 2, 147. Tit. II, 1, 107. Oth. V, 2, 256. Ant. V, 1, 37.
4) at any rate (German: durchaus): *rain added to a river that is rank p. will force it overflow the bank,* Ven. 72. *p. against all checks I must advance the colours of my love,* Wiv. III, 4, 84. *but she p. withholds the boy,* Mids. II, 1, 26. *thy fair virtue's force p. doth move me to swear, I love thee,* III, 1, 143. *they must p. have melted,* R2 V, 2, 35. *this weaves itself p. into my business,* Lr. II, 1, 17. *force p.,* in the same sense: *venom of suggestion, as force p. the age will pour it in,* H4B IV, 4, 46.

**Perform,** 1) to execute, to act, to do, to accomplish, to effect; absol.: *they did p. beyond thought's compass,* H8 I, 1, 35. *though he p. to the utmost of a* man, Cor. I, 1, 271. *to act, to do, to p.* Hml. V, 1, 13. Trans.: *hast thou —ed the tempest?* Tp. I, 2, 194. *to p. an act,* II, 1, 252. *to p. it first,* Wint. III, 2, 58. V, 1, 130. *a piece —ed by Julio Romano,* V, 2, 105. *what good love may I p. for you?* John IV, 1, 49. H8 I, 1, 161. Cor. II, 2, 49. Tit. V, 1, 66. V, 3, 45. 188. Mcb. I, 7, 69. III, 4, 77. IV, 1, 130. Hml. I, 4. 21. Lr. IV, 2, 40. Ant. V, 2, 334. Cymb. V, 4, 76. Per. IV, 3, 39.
2) to carry into execution, to discharge: *thy charge exactly is —ed,* Tp. I, 2, 238. *must I p. much business,* III, 1, 95. *your last service you did worthily p.* IV, 36. *let this be duly —ed,* Meas. IV, 2, 127. *our observation is —ed,* Mids. IV, 1, 109. *to p. it* (the wrestling) As I, 2, 122. 155. Shr. III, 2, 143. All's II, 3, 187. Wint. II, 1, 115. 196. II, 3, 169. IV, 4, 852. V, 1, 1. R2 II, 2, 138. IV, 4. H6B I, 1, 9. 74. II, 2, 67. III, 1, 321. H6C III, 1, 100. III, 2, 54. R3 I, 1, 110. IV, 2, 19. H8 IV, 1, 90. Troil. III, 2, 93. Tit. I, 143. II, 1, 59. Rom. II, 2, 146. Tim. IV, 3, 72. Caes. I, 2, 10. Mcb. III, 1, 127. V, 8, 73. Hml. V, 2, 404. Oth. III, 3, 21. Ant. I, 1, 24. III, 12, 23. III, 13, 86. V, 2, 203. Cymb. III, 5, 113. IV, 3, 18. V, 4, 122. Per. II, 2, 16. II, 3, 99. V, 1, 248. V, 3, 1. = to act, to play, to represent: *bravely the figure of this harpy hast thou —ed,* Tp. III, 3, 84. *that will ask some tears in the true —ing of it,* Mids. I, 2, 27. Shr. Ind. 1, 87. Wint. V, 3, 154. Cor. III, 2, 109. Per. III Prol. 54.
3) to fulfil, to act up to: (a promise) *which is not yet —ed me,* Tp. I, 2, 244. H4A III, 2, 154. H4B IV, 2, 115. *p. an old contracting,* Meas. III, 2, 296. *to p. your father's will,* Merch. I, 2, 100. *a vow,* John III, 1, 266. 269. H4A IV, 3, 65. H6C I, 1, 201. *hath —ed her word,* H6A I, 6, 3. Absol.: *when he —s, astronomers foretell it,* Troil. V, 1, 99. *if thou dost p., confound thee,* Tim. IV, 3, 74.

**Performance,** 1) execution: All's II, 1, 205. H4B II, 4, 284. H6B I, 4, 2. H8 I, 2, 208. IV, 2, 42. Troil. II, 2, 196. III, 2, 91. V, 10, 39. Tim. V, 1, 26. 29. Caes. II, 1, 135. Mcb. II, 3, 33. Hml. IV, 7, 152. Oth. IV, 2, 185. Per. IV, 2, 67.
2) acting, exhibition: *eke out our p. with your mind,* H5 III Chor. 35. *a piece of your p.* Troil. III, 1, 55.
3) action: *besides her walking and other actual —s,* Mcb. V, 1, 13. *in his offence should my p. perish,* Ant. III, 1, 27.

**Performer,** doer: *the merit of service is seldom attributed to the true and exact p.* All's III, 6, 65. *—s of this deed,* Tit. V, 1, 80. *three —s are the file when all the rest do nothing,* Cymb. V, 3, 60.

**Pérfume** or **Perfúme,** subst. 1) sweet odour, fragrance: Sonn. 104, 7. Ado III, 4, 63. Shr. I, 2, 153. Tim. IV, 3, 302. Hml. I, 3, 9. III, 1, 99. Ant. II, 2, 217.
2) a substance emitting sweet odour: Sonn. 130, 7. Wint. IV, 4, 225. John IV, 2, 12. Mcb. V, 1, 57. Lr. III, 4, 110. Cymb. I, 5, 13. *their diseased —s,* Tim. IV, 3, 207, = perfumed mistresses.

**Perfúme** (*pérfumed* in H4B III, 1, 12) vb. to scent, to impregnate with sweet odour: Ven. 444. Sonn. 54, 6. Tp. II, 1, 48. As III, 2, 65. Shr. I, 1, 180. I, 2, 152. H4A I, 3, 36. H4B III, 1, 12. H6B I, 1, 255. Tit. I, 145. Oth. IV, 1, 150. Ant. II, 2, 198. Cymb. II, 2, 19. Misapplied by Mrs Quickly in H4B II, 4, 30.

**Perfumer**, one whose office is to perfume the chambers: Ado I, 3, 60.

**Perhaps**, maybe: Sonn. 71, 10. Gent. I, 1, 32. Meas. I, 2, 160. Err. II, 1, 4. V, 321. Ado IV, 1, 256. LLL V, 2, 279. Mids. III, 1, 82. III, 2, 303. Merch. II, 5, 52. Shr. I, 1, 171. I, 2, 110. Tw, II, 1, 5. II, 4, 92. III, 1, 175. John IV, 2, 178. R2 II, 1, 289. H5 III, 7, 53. H6A II, 4, 16. III, 2, 48. V, 3, 104. H6C II, 6, 64. V, 1, 89. R3 I, 3, 348. IV, 2, 101. Troil. III, 3, 226. Cor. V, 3, 157. Tit. IV, 1, 26. Rom. I, 2, 61. Caes. I, 2, 42. Hml. I, 3, 14. IV, 7, 10 etc.

**Periapts**, amulets: H6A V, 3, 2.

**Péricles** (*Perícles* in Per. II, 3, 81) name in Per. I, 1, 25 etc.

**Perigenia** (some M. Edd. *Perigune*), daughter of Sinnis, ravished by Theseus: Mids. II, 1, 78.

**Perigort**, name in LLL II, 41.

**Peril**, danger: Compl. 158. Meas. II, 4, 65. As II, 1, 4. Shr. V, 2, 3. All's IV, 1, 47. Tw. I, 2, 12. H4A I, 3, 191. H4B I, 1, 170. 184. III, 1, 55. IV, 4, 66. IV, 5, 197. H6B III, 1, 152. H6C II, 1, 191. R3 III, 5, 44. V, 3, 39. H8 III, 2, 194. Rom. II, 2, 71. Caes. IV, 1, 47. V, 1, 92. Oth. V, 1, 21. Ant. IV, 8, 35. Cymb. I, 1, 80. III, 4, 155. V, 1, 28. *p. of* = danger caused by: *without the p. of the Athenian law*, Mids. IV, 1, 158. *the p. of waters*, Merch. I, 3, 25. *the p. of our curses light on thee*, John III, 1, 295. = danger caused to: *to be in p. of my life*, Merch. II, 2, 173; cf. Meas. II, 4, 67. *My p.* = the danger in which I am: Wiv. III, 3, 130. As I, 2, 159. All's II, 1, 136. Troil. I, 3, 267. Tim. V, 1, 231. Preceded by *at, in, on,* and *to,* = at the hazard: *to do't at p. of your soul*, Meas. II, 4, 67. *you will answer it at your p.* IV, 2, 130. *to be so taken at thy p.* Merch. IV, 1, 344. Lr. III, 7, 52. Oth. I, 2, 81. *your physicians have expressly charged, in p. to incur your former malady, that I*... Shr. Ind. 2, 124. *banish him our city, in p. of precipitation from off the rock Tarpeian never more to enter our Rome gates*, Cor. III, 3, 102. *stay, on thy p.* Mids. II, 2, 87. *on your displeasure's p. and on mine*, Wint. II, 3, 45. 181. *on p. of a curse, let go the hand*, John III, 1, 191. *on my p.* R3 IV, 1, 26. Ant. V, 2, 143. Cymb. V, 4, 189. *lest to thy p. thou aby it dear*, Mids. III, 2, 175. Cor. III, 1, 326. Ant. V, 2, 146.

**Perilous**, dangerous: Meas. II, 4, 172. John IV, 3, 13. H4A IV, 1, 43. V, 2, 96. H5 Prol. 22. IV, 1, 209. R3 III, 1, 154 (Q7. 8 and many M.Edd. *parlous*). Troil. II, 2, 40. Rom. I, 3, 54 (most M. Edd. *parlous*). Caes. I, 3, 47. Mcb. V, 3, 44. Hml. I, 3, 102. Cymb. IV, 2, 145.

**Period**, subst. 1) limit, term, end to be attained: *this is the p. of my ambition,* Wiv. III, 3, 47. *there would be no p. to the jest, should he not be publicly shamed,* IV, 2, 237 (German: kein rechter Abschluss). *to make the perfect p. of this peace,* R3 II, 1, 44 (German: den Frieden zum vollständigen Abschluss zu bringen). *there's his p., to sheathe his knife in us,* H8 I, 2, 209. *my point and p. will be throughly wrought,* Lr. IV, 7, 97. *this would have seemed a p. to such as love not sorrow,* V, 3, 204.

2) conclusion, end: *then had they seen the p. of their ill,* Lucr. 380. *make —s in the midst of sentences,* Mids. V, 96 (= stop, make full stops). *my worldly business makes a p.* H4B IV, 5, 231. *the p. of thy tyranny approacheth,* H6A IV, 2, 17. *the p. of their tyranny,* H6B III, 1, 149. *now here a p. of tumultuous*

*broils,* H6C V, 5, 1. *let me make the p. to my curse,* R3 I, 3, 238. *O bloody p.* Oth. V, 2, 357. *may be it is the p. of your duty,* Ant. IV, 2, 25. *time is at his p.* IV, 14, 107.

3) a sentence, in a grammatical sense: *she puts the p. often from his place,* Lucr. 565. *a pretty p.* Gent. II, 1, 122. In both passages it may be = stop, end.

**Period**, vb. to put an end to: *which failing, —s his comfort,* Tim. I, 1, 99.

**Perish**, 1) intr. to come to nothing, to die, to be destroyed: Lucr. 1547. Sonn. 11, 10. Tp. I, 2, 9. 217. 237. Gent. I, 1, 157. Meas. III, 1, 225. V, 458. LLL V, 2, 521. Mids. II, 2, 107. V, 86. As V, 1, 56. Shr. I, 1, 160. II, 331. Wint. V, 1, 44. R2 II, 1, 266. H5 IV, 1, 182. H6A IV, 4, 28. H6B IV, 4, 11. R3 IV, 4, 185. H8 I, 1, 203. III, 1, 153. III, 2, 420. Troil. V, 5, 16. Cor. III, 2, 28. IV, 6, 105. Oth. IV, 1, 191. Ant. II, 6, 8. III, 1, 27. Cymb. III, 5, 101. IV, 2, 60. Per. I, 3, 29. Used as an imprecation: Meas. III, 1, 144. H5 IV, 3, 72. H6A III, 1, 175. 178. III, 2, 57. IV, 1, 124. Cor. IV, 1, 14.

2) to cause to perish, to destroy: *thy flinty heart might in thy palace p. Margaret,* H6B III, 2, 100.

**Perishen**, vb. to perish: Per. II Prol. 35 (Gower's speech).

**Periwig**, false hair worn: Gent. IV, 4, 196. Err. II, 2, 76.

**Periwig-pated**, wearing a periwig (probably = having much hair on the head): *a robustious p. fellow,* Hml. III, 2, 10.

**Perjure**, subst. a perjured person, perjurer: *he comes in like a p., wearing papers,* LLL IV, 3, 47 ("convicted perjurers, while undergoing punishment, wore a paper expressing their offence." Dyce. It was, indeed, a custom observed in all criminals exposed to public view).

**Perjure**, vb. to make perjured, to corrupt; *want will p. the ne'er-touched vestal,* Ant. III, 12, 30.

**Perjured**, having sworn falsely, forsworn: Lucr. 1521. Sonn. 129, 3. 152, 6. 13. Gent. IV, 2, 95. V, 4, 39. 68. Err. V, 212. 227. LLL II, 113. III, 196. IV, 3, 51. 125 (*a p. note* = a note of perjury). 157. V, 2, 346. 800. Mids. I, 1, 241. John III, 1, 107. 120. H5 IV, 7, 147. H6C II, 2, 81. V, 1, 106. V, 5, 34. R3 I, 4, 55. H8 V, 1, 137. Rom. III, 2, 86. Lr. III, 2, 54. Oth. V, 2, 63. Cymb. III, 4, 65.

**Perjury**, false oath, the crime of being forsworn: Lucr. 919. 1517. Pilgr. 31 and LLL IV, 3, 62. Gent. II, 6, 5. IV, 4, 173. V, 4, 49. 102. Ado IV, 1, 175. IV, 2, 44. LLL IV, 3, 289. V, 2, 394. 470. 829. Merch. IV, 1, 229. John III, 1, 88. H5 IV, 1, 172. H6C V, 5, 40. R3 I, 4, 50. V, 3, 196. Rom. II, 2, 92 (*—es*). III, 3, 128. Oth. V, 2, 51.

**Perked**, with *up,* = dressed up, adorned: *to be p. up in a glistering grief,* H8 III, 2, 21.

**Perkes**, name in H4B V, 1, 42.

**Permanent**, durable, lasting: Hml. I, 3, 8.

**Permission**, allowance, liberty granted: Caes. III, 1, 239. 247. III, 2, 64. Oth. I, 3, 340.

**Permissive**, granted, permitted: *when evil deeds have their p. pass,* Meas. I, 3, 38.

**Permit**, to grant leave, to allow, to suffer: Lucr. 775. Sonn. 33, 5. Meas. V, 121. John II, 84. R2 I, 3, 194. II, 2, 121. II, 3, 119. H4A I, 2, 222. H6A II, 5, 61. H8 I, 2, 161 (*to p. my chaplain a choice hour*). Cor. II, 3, 177. IV, 5, 81. Tit. II, 3, 218. Lr. I, 2, 3. Ant. III, 1, 36. Cymb. V, 1, 13.

**Pernicious**, mischievous, malicious, wicked: *most p. purpose*, Meas. II, 4, 150. *this p. caitiff deputy*, V, 88. *thou p. woman*, 241. *this p. slave*, Err. V, 241. *troubled with a p. suitor*, Ado I, 1, 130. *the p. and indubitate beggar Zenelophon*, LLL IV, 1, 66 (Armado's letter). *thy adverse p. enemy*, R2 I, 3, 82. *your p. lives*, III, 1, 4. *to rid the realm of this p. blot*, IV, 325. *you p. ass*, H4B II, 2, 80 (Q *virtuous*). *a most p. usurer*, H6A III, 1, 17. *your p. faction*, IV, 1, 59. *p. protector*, H6B II, 1, 21. *p. bloodsucker*, III, 2, 226. *may prove p.* H8 V, 3, 19. *your p. rage*, Rom. I, 1, 91. *this p. hour*, Mcb. IV, 1, 133. *with more p. root*, IV, 3, 85. *O most p. woman!* Hml. I, 5, 105. *two p. daughters*, Lr. III, 2, 22. *his p. soul*, Oth. V, 2, 155. *O the p. caitiff*, 318.

**Perniciously**, maliciously: *all the commons hate him p.* H8 II, 1, 50.

**Peroration**, harangue: *what means this p. with such circumstance?* H6B I, 1, 105.

**Perpend** (a word used only by Pistol, Polonius, and the clowns) to consider, to look to it: Wiv. II, 1, 119. As III, 2, 69. Tw. V, 307. Hml. II, 2, 105. Trans.: *p. my words*, H5 IV, 4, 8.

**Perpendicular**, vertical, forming a right angle with the ground: *runs up a hill p.* H4A II, 4, 378.

**Perpendicularly**, vertically, in a straight line down: Lr. IV, 6, 54.

**Perpetual**, never ceasing, everlasting, endless: Lucr. 726. 784. 1638. Sonn. 56, 8. 154, 10. Tp. II, 1, 285. Wiv. V, 5, 62. Meas. III, 1, 67. 77. All's IV, 3, 313. Wint. III, 2, 214. 239. John V, 7, 77. H4A III, 3, 46. H4B I, 2, 246. H6C V, 4, 51. R3 I, 4, 47. II, 2, 46 (Ff *ne'er changing night*). IV, 4, 12. V, 2, 15. Cor. II, 2, 124. Lr. III, 3, 5. Ant. II, 2, 127.
Adverbially: *you p. sober gods*, Tim. IV, 3, 503 (M. Edd. *perpetual-sober*). *to thine and Albany's issue be this p.* Lr. I, 1, 68.

**Perpetually**, continually: Lucr. 686. Shr. II, 142. All's IV, 3, 314. Per. I, 1, 74.

**Perpetual-sober:** Tim. IV, 3, 503; see *Perpetual.*

**Perpetuity**, endless time: Wint. I, 2, 5. H6A IV, 7, 20. Cymb. V, 4, 6.

**Perplex**, to confound, to bewilder: *will p. thee more*, John III, 1, 222. —*ed* = bewildered: Ven. 1043. Lucr. 733. John III, 1, 221. H6A V, 5, 95. Oth. V, 2, 346. Cymb. III, 4, 7. IV, 3, 41. V, 5, 108.

**Perplexity**, bewilderment: Gent. II, 3, 9. Wiv. IV, 5, 86. LLL V, 2, 298 (*avaunt, p.* = cease to speak riddles).

**Persecute**, to afflict, to harass; not very intelligibly used: *he hath abandoned his physicians, under whose practices he hath —d time with hope, and finds no other advantage in the process but only the losing of hope by time*, All's I, 1, 16; i. e. perhaps: he has, by the advice of his physicians, maltreated the present time (cf. *Time*) for the sake of hope, inflicted upon himself much pain as a cure for his disorder.

**Persecution**, ill treatment, hostility: Lr. II, 3, 12.

**Persecutor**, one who harasses and afflicts others: H6C V, 6, 31.

**Perseus**, the ancient hero who rode the winged horse Pegasus: H5 III, 7, 22. Tróil. I, 3, 42. IV, 5, 186.

**Perséver**, to persevere, to persist in what is begun: Gent. III, 2, 28. Err. II, 2, 217. Mids. III, 2, 237. As V, 2, 4. All's III, 7, 37. IV, 2, 37. John II, 421. Hml. I, 2, 92. Lr. III, 5, 23 (Qq *persevere*). Per. IV, 6, 113.

**Perséverance**, persistency, constancy: Troil. III, 3, 150. Mcb. IV, 3, 93.

**Persevere**, spelling of Qq in Lr. III, 5, 23; Ff *persever*, q. v.

**Persia**, country in Asia: Err. IV, 1, 4.

**Persian**, pertaining to Persia: Merch. II, 1, 25. Lr. III, 6, 85.

**Persist**, to continue steadily in an evil course: All's III, 7, 42. With *in*: Troil. II, 2, 186. *In* omitted: *to lament our most —ed deeds*, Ant. V, 1, 30, = our deeds most persisted in.

**Persistency**, steady pursuit of an evil course: *as far in the devil's book as thou and Falstaff for obduracy and p.* H4B II, 2, 50.

**Persistive**, steady in pursuit, persevering: *to find p. constancy in men*, Troil. I, 3, 21.

**Person**, 1) human being, individual: *by any other house or p.* Tp. I, 2, 42. *that very p.* Wiv. I, 1, 50. *some p.* III, 1, 53. Meas. II, 1, 173. II, 4, 91. V, 262. Ado III, 5, 50. LLL IV, 2, 139. As III, 2, 327. All's II, 3, 2. Tw. III, 3, 99. III, 1, 70. V, 223. R2 V, 5, 31. H6B II, 1, 167. H8 Prol. 26 etc.
2) the particular state and existence of a human being; used in a periphrastical way: *health to thy p.* = to thee, Lucr. 1305. *set thy p. forth to sell*, Pilgr. 310. *they saw the king's ship wrecked and his great p. perish*, Tp. I, 2, 237. *we will guard your p.* II, 1, 197. *do no stain to your own gracious p.* Meas. III, 1, 208. *you must change —s with me*, V, 339. *authentic in your place and p.* Wiv. II, 2, 236. *puts the world into her p.* Ado II, 1, 216. *to present the prince's own p.* III, 3, 79. *which is the duke's own p.?* LLL I, 1, 182. 184. III, 125. *to present the p. of Moonshine*, Mids. III, 1, 62. *my purse, my p.* Merch. I, 1, 138; cf. *both in purse and p.* H4B II, 1, 127. *as his p. is mighty*, Wint. I, 2, 453. II, 1, 194. III, 3, 29. IV, 4, 826. V, 1, 156. 171. John II, 189. 366. III, 1, 224. R2 III, 3, 38. V, 5, 110. H4B V, 2, 73. Mcb. III, 4, 41. 128 etc. *in the p. of* = in the place of, acting for: *did supply thee at thy garden-house in her imagined p.* Meas. V, 213. *in her p. I say I will not have you*, As IV, 1, 92. *as 'twere i' the father's p.* Wint. IV, 4, 561. *in mine own p.* = I myself: As IV, 1, 93. 97. H6B II, 1, 41. *in p.* = with bodily presence, not by representative: Err. V, 116. 119. 234. Wint. III, 2, 10. R2 I, 4, 42. II, 3, 82. H4A IV, 1, 91. H6C IV, 1, 133. H8 I, 1, 117. I, 2, 5. Troil. III, 1, 33. IV, 1, 2. Ant. III, 1, 17. III, 7, 6. 57 etc. Cor. I, 6, 70.(*)
3) external appearance: *thou mightst call him a goodly p.* Tp. I, 2, 416; cf. Tw. I, 5, 281 and Per. V, 1, 36. *she takes exceptions at your p.* Gent. V, 2, 3. *how I may formally in p. bear me like a true friar*, Meas. I, 3, 47. *he hath the best p. too*, Mids. IV, 2, 11. *such as are of better p. than myself*, H6C III, 2, 167. *by his p. more worthy this place*, H8 I, 4, 78. *the beauty of her p.* IV, 1, 68. *a proper man of p.* Troil. I, 2, 209. *how novelty may move, and parts with p.* IV, 4, 81. *honour would become such a p.* Cor. I, 3, 11. III, 2, 86. *if it assume my noble father's p.* Hml. I, 2, 244. *he hath a p. to be suspected*, Oth. I, 3, 403. *for her own p. Ant.* II, 2, 202. *some marks of secret on her p.* Cymb. V, 5, 206.
4) = parson (which is derived from *persona*): LLL IV, 2, 85. 3, 194. Q2 in Rom. I, 4, 80. (M. Edd. *parson*).

**Personage,** 1) person, man: *saucy with lords and honourable —s*, All's II, 3, 278.

2) appearance, figure: *with her p., her tall p.* Mids. III, 2, 292. *of what p. and years is he?* Tw. I, 5, 164.

**Personal,** 1) done or experienced in one's own person, not by a representative or other indirect means: *to remain in p. duty, following where he haunted,* Compl. 130. *importunes p. conference with his grace,* LLL II, 32. *their encounters, though not p.* Wint. I, 1, 29. *when he was p. in the Irish war,* H4A IV, 3, 88. *thy p. venture in the rebels' fight,* Mcb. I, 3, 91. *his p. return was most required,* Lr. IV, 3, 6. *in p. suit,* Oth. I, 1, 9. *with my p. eye will I look to't,* II, 3, 5. *dares me to p. combat,* Ant. IV, 1, 3. *your p. pain,* Per. III, 2, 46.

2) appertaining to an individual: *we want a little p. strength,* H4B IV, 4, 8. *no mightier than thyself or me in p. action,* Caes. I, 3, 77. *I know no p. cause to spurn at him,* II, 1, 11. *giving to you no further p. power,* Hml. I, 2, 36.

**Personally,** in person, not by a substitute, directly: *so vulgarly and p. accused,* Meas. V, 160. *therefore p. I lay my claim,* R2 II, 3, 135. *I could not p. deliver to her what you commanded me,* H8 V, 1, 62.

**Personate,** vb. to represent, to depaint: *he shall find himself most feelingly —d,* Tw. II, 3, 173. *one do I p. of Lord Timon's frame,* Tim. I, 1, 69. *it must be a —ing of himself,* V, 1, 35. *the lofty cedar —s thee,* Cymb. V, 5, 454.

**Pérspective,** a glass cut in such a manner as to produce an optical deception, when looked through: *mine eye hath played the painter and hath stelled thy beauty's form in table of my heart; my body is the frame wherein 'tis held, and p. it is best painter's art,* Sonn. 24, 4 (the painter himself, i. e. the eye, being the glass through which the form must be seen). *contempt his scornful p. did lend me, which warped the line of every other favour,* All's V, 3, 48. *a natural p., that is and is not,* Tw. V, 224 (simply = deception). *like —s, which rightly gazed upon show nothing but confusion, eyed awry distinguish form,* R2 II, 2, 18.*

**Perspectively,** as through a perspective: *you see them p., the cities turned into a maid,* H5 V, 2, 347.

**Perspicuous,** apparent, manifest: *the purpose is p.* Troil. I, 3, 324.

**Persuade,** 1) to prevail on by argument or entreaty; absol.: *well she can p.* Meas. I, 2, 191. *the silence often of pure innocence —s,* Wint. II, 2, 42. *fair-spoken and —ing,* H8 IV, 2, 52. *call my father to p.* Troil. V, 3, 30. With an accus.: *they should sooner p. Harry,* H5 V, 2, 304. H6A III, 2, 93. --d, H6C IV, 7, 30. Cor. I, 1, 205. *O be —d,* Troil. V, 3, 19. Accus. and *to: p. my heart to this false perjury,* Pilgr. 31 and LLL IV, 3, 62. *we shall soon p. him unto reason,* H6C IV, 7, 33. *p. me to the murder of your lordship,* Lr. II, 1, 46. With an inf. preceded by *to: whiles I p. this rude wretch willingly to die,* Meas. IV, 3, 85. *I —d them to wish him wrestle with affection,* Ado III, 1, 41. *if your love do not p. you to come,* Merch. III, 2, 324. Shr. III, 2, 127. H4A II, 4, 339. H4B II, 3, 15. H6A III, 1, 105. R3 III, 1, 33. Cor. V, 3, 120. Oth. V, 2, 16. Ant. IV, 6, 13. Inf. without *to: let me p. you take a better course,* H6A IV, 1, 132.

2) to convince, to bring to an opinion; absol.: *only professes to p.* Tp. II, 1, 236. *your discretions better can p. than I am able to instruct,* H6A IV, 1, 158. With an accus. and *to: my reason that —s me to any*

other trust, Tw. IV, 3, 14. With a clause: *my glass shall not p. me I am old,* Sonn. 22, 1. *hath almost —d the king his son's alive,* Tp. II, 1, 234. Gent. V, 4, 65. Wiv. III, 3, 74. As II, 1, 11. Shr. Ind. 1, 63. Tw. III, 4, 321. R2 II, 2, 29. V, 5, 35. H6B III, 2, 137. Lr. II, 4, 114. *to p. one's self* = to be of opinion: *do you p. yourself that I respect you?* Meas. IV, 1, 53. *I p. me, from her will fall some blessing to this land,* H8 III, 2, 50. *I p. myself, to speak the truth shall nothing wrong him,* Oth. II, 3, 223. —d = of opinion, convinced, confident: *we are well —d we carry not a heart with us ...,* H5 II, 2, 20. *are you now —d that Talbot is but shadow of himself?* H6A II, 3, 61. *I should be false —d I had daughters,* Lr. I, 4, 254. *she is —d I will marry her,* Oth. IV, 1, 132. With *of: one well —d of —,* Cymb. II, 4, 132. *the best —d of himself,* Tw. II, 3, 162 (having the best opinion of himself).

3) to advise, to counsel, to try to prevail on, to exhort: absol.: *cease to p.* Gent. I, 1, 1. With an accus. designating the person advised: *p. me not,* Wiv. I, 1, 1. *it —s him and disheartens him,* Mcb. II, 3, 37. Accus. and *to: weak-built hopes p. him to abstaining,* Lucr. 130. *by —ing me to it,* Tim. IV, 3, 455. Accus. and inf.: *rather p. him to hold his hands,* Err. IV, 4, 23. *—ing me not to kill the duke,* R3 I, 4, 150. Lr. II, 4, 219. With *from* (= to dissuade from): *that have so mightily —d him from a first,* As I, 2, 219. *— d him from any further act,* H6B V, 3, 10. With an accus. denoting that which a person is exhorted to do: *hadst thou thy wits and didst p. revenge,* Hml. IV, 5, 168. Dat. and accus.: *sends me a paper to p. me patience,* H6C III, 3, 176.

4) to do one's endeavour to influence or win the opinion of a person; absol.: *how I —d, how I prayed and kneeled,* Meas. V, 93. *the duke himself and the magnificoes of greatest port have all —d with him,* Merch. III, 2, 283. Trans. = to win, to reconcile: *he ran upon the boar with his sharp spear, who did not whet his teeth at him again, but by a kiss thought to p. him there,* Ven. 1114. *beauty itself doth of itself p. the eyes of men,* Lucr. 29. *nor am I yet —d to put up in peace what already I have foolishly suffered,* Oth. IV, 2, 180.

**Persuasion,** 1) the act or art of influencing the mind of another by arguments: *he's a spirit of p.* Tp. II, 1, 235. *with what p. did he tempt thy love?* Err. IV, 2, 13. Ado V, 4, 95. Tw. III, 4, 383. H4A I, 2, 170. III, 1, 199. V, 2, 79. H6A III, 3, 18. H8 V, 1, 148. Troil. II, 2, 171. With a subjective genitive: *I will not die to-day for any man's p.* Meas. IV, 3, 63. *it should not be, by the p. of his new feasting,* Tim. III, 6, 8 (as his new feasting induces us to believe). *the p. of his augurers,* Caes. II, 1, 200. With a possessive pronoun in a subjective sense: *cross him with their opposite p.* Lucr. 286. *where you may temper her by your p.* Gent. III, 2, 64. Meas. IV, 2, 205. Shr. V, 2, 120. John V, 5, 11.

2) opinion, belief: *whose p. is I come about my brother,* Meas. IV, 1, 47. *a good p.* Mids. I, 1, 156. *you are a great deal abused in too bold a p.* Cymb. I, 4, 125.

**Pert,** lively, alert: *this p. Berowne was out of countenance quite,* LLL V, 2, 272. *awake the p. and nimble spirit of mirth,* Mids. I, 1, 13.

**Pertain,** 1) to belong, to appertain: *intermission*

*no more —s to me than you*, Merch. III, 2, 202 (does not become me more than you. O. Edd. *intermission. No* etc.). *if she p. to life let her speak too*, Wint. V, 3, 113 (if she lives). *all honours that p. unto the crown of France*, H5 II, 4, 82. *all their honorable points of ignorance —ing thereunto*, H8 I, 3, 27.

2) to relate, to concern: *in aught —s to the state*, H8 I, 2, 42. *the main part —s to you alone*, Mcb. IV, 3, 199. *more than —s to feats of broil and battle*, Oth. I, 3, 87.

**Pertaunt-like** (Ff Q2) or **Perttaunt-like** (Q1) a word not yet explained nor satisfactorily amended in LLL V, 2, 67: *so p. would I o'ersway his state that he should be my fool and I his fate.* Theobald *pedantlike*, Hanmer *portent-like*, Singer *potent-like*, Collier M. C. *potently*, Grant White *persaunt-like.**

**Pertinent**, apposite, to the purpose: *'good' should be p., but it is not*, Wint. I, 2, 221. *my caution was more p. than the rebuke you give it*, Cor. II, 2, 67.

**Pertly**, promptly, on the alert: *appear, and p.* Tp. IV, 58. *yonder walls that p. front your town*, Troil. IV, 5, 219.

**Perturbation**, disturbance, disorder, disquiet: *horror and p. follows her*, Ado II, 1, 268. *p. of the brain*, H4B I, 2, 132. *O polished p., golden care*, IV, 5, 23. *fills thy sleep with —s*, R3 V, 3, 161. *a great p. in nature*, Mcb. V, 1, 10.

**Perturbed**, disquieted: *rest, p. spirit*, Hml. I, 5, 183. *the p. court for my being absent*, Cymb. III, 4, 108.

**Perusal**, 1) careful examination: *he falls to such p. of my face as he would draw it*, Hml. II, 1, 90.

2) the act of reading: Sonn. 38, 6.

**Peruse**, 1) to survey, to examine: *this picture she advisedly —d*, Lucr. 1527. *I'll view the manners of the town, p. the traders*, Err. I, 2, 13. *p. them well; not one of those but had a noble father*, All's II, 3, 67. *that from this castle's tattered battlements our fair appointments may be well —d*, R2 III, 3, 53. *that we may p. the men we should have coped withal*, H4B IV, 2, 94. *p. their wings*, H6A IV, 2, 43. *I have —d her well*, H8 II, 3, 75. *I have with exact view —d thee*, Troil. IV, 5, 232. *let me p. this face*, Rom. V, 3, 74. *will not p. the foils*, Hml. IV, 7, 137. *to p. him by items*, Cymb. I, 4, 7.

2) to read; trans.: Compl. 44. Gent. I, 2, 34. IV, 4, 126. Merch. II, 4, 39. Shr. I, 2, 145. Tw. V, 338. R2 V, 3, 49. H6A V, 1, 1. H8 III, 2, 121. Cor. V, 6, 62. Lr. I, 2, 39. II, 2, 172. Per. II, 5, 41. With *over: —ing o'er these notes*, John V, 2, 5.

**Perverse**, 1) uncharitable, unkind, litigious: *if I were covetous, ambitious or p., how am I so poor?* H6A III, 1, 29. *you do not well to bear with their p. objections*, IV, 1, 129.

2) averse to love, cold: *p. it* (love) *shall be where it shows most toward*, Ven. 1157. *if thou thinkest I am too quickly won, I'll frown and be p. and say thee nay*, Rom. II, 2, 96.

**Perversely**, unkindly, coldly: *p. she persevers so* (not to love Thurio) Gent. III, 2, 28.

**Perverseness**, unkindness, coldness: *still so constant, lord. What, to p.?* Tw. V, 115.

**Pervert**, 1) to turn another way, to avert: *let's follow him and p. the present wrath he hath against himself*, Cymb. II, 4, 151.

2) to lead astray, to corrupt, to seduce: *and new p. a reconciled maid*, Compl. 329. *trust not my holy*

*order, if I p. your course*, Meas. IV, 3, 153. *he hath —ed a young gentlewoman*, All's IV, 3, 17.

**Pester**, to annoy, to harass, to infest: *to be so —ed with a popinjay*, H4A I, 3, 50. *how the poor world is —ed with such waterflies*, Troil. V, 1, 38. *who rather had dissentious numbers —ing streets than see our tradesmen singing in their shops*, Cor. IV, 6, 7 (= infesting). *who shall blame his —ed senses to recoil*, Mcb. V, 2, 23. *to p. us with message*, Hml. I, 2, 22.

**Pestiferous**, venomous, malignant: *such p. reports*, All's IV, 3, 340. *thy lewd, p. and dissentious pranks*, H6A III, 1, 15.

**Pestilence**, plague, contagious disease: Ven. 740. Ado I, 1, 87. Tw. I, 1, 20. R2 I, 3, 284. III, 3, 87. H8 V, 1, 45. Rom. V, 2, 10. Oth. II, 3, 362. Ant. III, 10, 9. *to have the p.* Gent. II, 1, 22. *a p. on him!* Troil. IV, 2, 21. Hml. V, 1, 196. *the red p. strike all trades in Rome*, Cor. IV, 1, 13. *the most infectious p. upon thee!* Ant. II, 5, 61.

**Pestilent**, 1) producing, or relating to, the plague: *a foul and p. congregation of vapours*, Hml. II, 2, 315. *I'll make death love me, for I will contend even with his p. scythe*, Ant. III, 13, 194 (= the scythe of pestilence, the deaths occasioned by pestilence).

2) very disagreeable: *most p. to the hearing*, H8 I, 2, 49. *a p. knave*, Rom. IV, 5, 147. *to infect his ear with p. speeches of his father's death*, Hml. IV, 5, 91. *a p. gall to me*, Lr. I, 4, 127. *a p. complete knave*, Oth. II, 1, 252.

**Petar**, a case filled with explosive materials: *to have the enginer hoist with his own p.* Hml. III, 4, 207.

**Peter**, name of 1) the apostle P.: Ado II, 1, 50. Rom. III, 5, 115. 117. Oth. IV, 2, 91. 2) the prince of Arragon in Ado I, 1, 1. 10. 3) P. Simple in Wiv. I, 4, 15. 4) Friar P. in Meas. IV, 3, 142. IV, 6, 9. 5) P. Quince in Mids. I, 2, 8. 15. 45. 61. 64. III, 1, 7. IV, 1, 207. 6) P. Bullcalf in H4B III, 2, 183. 7) several servants and mean persons in Shr. Ind. 2, 96. IV, 1, 137. 182. John I, 186. H6B II, 3, 67 etc. Rom. II, 4, 110 etc. II, 5, 20. IV, 4, 16. 18.

**Petition**, subst. 1) request, entreaty: Meas. I, 4, 82. IV, 4, 11. Wint. V, 1, 228. John II, 478. H5 V, 2, 305. H6A IV, 1, 101. H8 I, 2, 17. IV, 2, 138. Troil. V, 3, 9. Cor. I, 1, 214. V, 3, 176. Caes. II, 1, 58. III, 1, 11. Hml. I, 2, 59. With *to: my p. to thee*, Troil. IV, 4, 124. Cor. V, 1, 20. *at your —s*, Wint. I, 2, 215. III, 2, 225. H5 V, 1, 25.

2) a single article of a prayer at church: *the p. that prays for peace*, Meas. I, 2, 16.

3) a written request from an inferior to a superior: All's V, 1, 19. V, 3, 130. H8 V, 1, 119. Tit. IV, 3, 14.

**Petition**, vb. 1) to pray, to supplicate: *you have —ed all the gods for my prosperity*, Cor. II, 1, 187.

2) to request, to demand: *the letters of our friends in Rome p. us at home*, Ant. I, 2, 190 (wish us at home, request us to come home).

**Petitionary**, supplicatory: *I prithee with most p. vehemence*, As III, 2, 199. *thy p. countrymen*, Cor V 2, 82.

**Petitioner**, supplicant: Ven. 356. LLL V, 2, 207. Shr. II, 72. H6B I, 3, 26. H6C V, 5, 80. R3 III, 7, 183.

**Peto**, name: H4A I, 2, 182 (O. Edd. *Rossill*). II, 2, 22. II, 4, 330. 521. 601 (most M. Edd. *Poins*). IV, 2, 9. H4B II, 4, 383.

**Petrarch**, the famous Italian poet: Rom. II, 4, 41.

**Petruchio**, name: Shr. I, 2, 21 etc. Rom. I, 5, 133.

**Petticoat**, an under garment worn by women: As I, 3, 15. II, 4, 7. III, 2, 354. Shr. II, 5. H4B II, 2, 89. III, 2, 166. H6C V, 5, 23. Oth. IV, 3, 74. Ant. I, 2, 176.

**Pettiness**, littleness, inconsiderableness: *which in weight to re-answer, his p. would bow under,* H5 III, 6, 136.

**Pettish**, capricious: *his p. lines,* Troil. II, 3, 139.

**Pettitoes**, feet; in contempt: Wint. IV, 4, 619 (originally the feet of pigs as food).

**Petty**, little, small, inconsiderable, trifling: Ven. 394. Lucr. 649. 656. Sonn. 41, 1. 90, 10. Gent. IV, 1, 52. Meas. II, 2, 112. Merch. I, 1, 12. III, 2, 309. Wint. II, 1, 71. IV. 4, 4 *(as a meeting of the p. gods).* H4B IV, 3, 119. H5 I, 2, 177. III Chor. 31. H6A I, 1, 91. H6B III, 1, 64. IV, 1, 22. V, 2, 44. R3 IV, 4, 332. Cor. I, 1, 122. II, 3, 186. Tit. II, 1, 62. Caes. I, 2, 136. Mcb. V, 5, 20. Hml. I, 4, 82. III, 3, 21. Oth. IV, 3, 74. Ant. I, 5, 45. II, 1, 34. 49. III, 12, 8. V, 2, 140. Cymb. I, 1, 111 *(such parting were too p.).* V, 4, 93. Per. IV, 3, 22.

**Pew**, a seat (in a church?): *that hath laid knives under his pillow, and halters in his p.* Lr. III, 4, 55.

**Pewfellow**, companion: *makes her p. with others' moan,* R3 IV, 4, 58.

**Pewter**, an artificial metal, consisting mainly of tin and lead: Shr. II, 357. H4A II, 4, 51.

**Pewterer**, one who works in pewter: H4B III, 2, 281.

**Phaethon** (O. Edd. *Phaeton*) the son of Helios who tried to drive the chariot of his father: Gent. III, 1, 153 (Merops' son). R2 III, 3, 178. H6C I, 4, 33. II, 6, 12. Rom. III, 2, 3.

**Phantasime** or **Phantasim** (the later Ff and some M. Edd. *phantasm*), a fantastic: *a p., a Monarcho,* LLL IV, 1, 101. *I abhor such fanatical — s,* V, 1, 20.

**Phantasma**, a vision, a day-dream: *all the interim is like a p., or a hideous dream,* Caes. II, 1, 65.

**Pharamond**, a king of the Franks: H5 I, 2, 37. 41. 58.

**Pharaoh**, the title of the ancient kings of Egypt: Ado III, 3, 142. H4A II, 4, 520.

**Pharsalia**, Pharsalus, place in Thessaly, where Caesar conquered Pompey: Ant. III, 7, 32.

**Pheasant**, the bird Phasianus: Wint. IV, 4, 768. 770.

**Phebe** (cf. *Phoebe*) name of the cruel shepherdess in As II, 4, 43. III, 5, 1. 27. IV, 3, 7 etc.

**Phebe**, vb. to treat in the manner of Phebe, viz cruelly: *she —s me,* As IV, 3, 39.

**Pheere**, see *Fere.*

**Pheezar**, a word of the mad host's making, derived from *pheeze* and rhyming to *Caesar: thou'rt an emperor, Caesar, Keisar, and P.* Wiv. I, 3, 10.

**Pheeze**, according to some commentators = to beat, to others = to drive; probably a verb signifying any kind of teazing and annoying: *I'll p. you, in faith,* Shr. Ind. 1, 1 (Sly's speech). *an a' be proud with me, I'll p. his pride,* Troil. II, 3, 215.

**Phial**, see *Vial.*

**Phibbus**, corrupted from *Phoebus* by Bottom: Mids. I, 2, 37.

**Philadelphos**, king of Paphlagonia: Ant. III, 6, 70.

**Philario** (O. Edd. *Filorio* or *Florio*), name in Cymb. I, 1, 97.

**Philarmonus**, name of the soothsayer in Cymb. V, 5, 433.

**Philemon**, 1) the kind and contented peasant who entertained Jove and Mercury: Ado II, 1, 99. 2) name of a servant in Per. III, 2, 1.

**Philip**, name of 1) the father of Alexander the Great: H5 IV, 7, 21. 2) King P. Augustus of France: John I, 7. II, 531. III, 1, 191. 3) the apostle, who has his feast with James on the first of May: *come P. and Jacob,* Meas. III, 2, 214.*nor yet Saint —'s daughters were like thee,* H6A I, 2, 143 (cf. the Acts of the Apostles XXI, 9: *"and the same man had four daughters, virgins, which did prophesy"*). 4) P. the Bastard in John I, 158. 161. 231. III, 2, 4. 5) a servant in Shr. IV, 1, 92. 125. 6) a familiar appellation for a sparrow: *P.! sparrow!* John I, 231.

**Philippan**, used in the battle of Philippi: *his sword P.* Ant. II, 5, 23.

**Philippe** (O. Edd. *Phillip* or *Philip*) daughter of Lionel of Clarence: H6B II, 2, 35. 49.

**Philippi**, the last battle-field of the Roman republicans: Caes. IV, 3, 170. 197 etc. Ant. II, 6, 13. III, 2, 56. III, 11, 35.

**Phillida**, name of a shepherdess: Mids. II, 1, 68.

**Philomel**, 1) the nightingale: Lucr. 1079. 1128. Sonn. 102, 7. Mids. II, 2, 13.

2) the daughter of Pandion, ravished by Tereus, who cut her tongue afterwards, to conceal his crime: Lucr. 1128. Tit. II, 3, 43. II, 4, 43. IV, 1, 47. V, 2, 195. Cymb. II, 2, 46.

**Philomela**, 1) the nightingale: Pilgr. 197. 2) the daughter of Pandion: Tit. II, 4, 38. IV, 1, 53.

**Philosopher**, one versed in moral and intellectual science: Wiv. I, 1, 236. Ado I, 3, 35. Merch. I, 2, 53 *(the weeping p.;* so Heraclitus of Ephesus was called, in opposition to the laugher Democritus). As III, 2, 33. V, 1, 36. Tim. I, 1, 221. II, 2, 131. Lr. III, 4, 159. 177. 181. *The —'s stone,* a preparation supposed to have the power of converting any metal into gold, mentioned in a quibbling manner (cf. *Stone*): *I will make him a —'s two stones to me,* H4B III, 2, 355. *sometime like a p., with two stones moe than's artificial one,* Tim. II, 2, 117.

**Philosophical**, skilled in philosophy: *we have our p. persons,* All's II, 3, 2.

**Philosophy**, the science of intellectual and moral truth: LLL I, 1, 32. As III, 2, 22. Shr. I, 1, 18. 28. III, 1, 13. John III, 4, 51. Troil. II, 2, 167. Rom. III, 3, 55. 57. Caes. IV, 3, 145. V, 1, 101. Hml. I, 5, 167.* II, 2, 385.

**Philostrate**, name in Mids. I, 1, 11. V, 38.

**Philoten**, the daughter of Cleon in Per. IV Prol. 18. 30. 36.

**Philotus**, name in Tim. III, 4, 6.

**Phisnomy**, see *Fisnomy.*

**Phlegmatic**, a word misapplied by Mrs Quickly in Wiv. I, 4, 79.

**Phoebe** (cf. *Phebe*) Diana as the goddess of the moon: LLL IV, 2, 39. Mids. I, 1, 209. Tit. I, 316.

**Phoebus**, Apollo: *the sweet melodious sound that —' lute, the queen of music, makes,* Pilgr. 112. Particularly as the god of the sun: Tp. IV, 30. Ado V.

3, 26. Mids. I, 2, 37 (corrupted to *Phibbus*). Merch. II, 1, 5. Wint. IV, 4, 124. H4A I, 2, 16.*H5 III Chor. 6.*IV, 1, 290. H6C II, 6, 11. Troil. I, 3, 230. Cor. II, 1, 234. Rom. III, 2, 2. Hml. III, 2, 165. Lr. II, 2, 114. Ant. I, 5, 28. IV, 8, 29. V, 2, 320. Cymb. II, 3, 22. V, 5, 190.

**Phoenicia,** country in Asia: Ant. III, 6, 16.

**Phoenician,** a native of Phoenicia: Ant. III, 7, 65.

**Phoenix,** the fabulous Arabian bird which existed single and rose again from its own ashes (used as a fem.: Phoen. 31. Sonn. 19, 4. H8 V, 5, 41): Sonn. 19, 4. Phoen. 23. 31. Tp. III, 3, 23. As IV, 3, 17. H6A IV, 7, 93. H6C I, 4, 35. H8 V, 5, 41. Tim. II, 1, 32. Not named, but alluded to in R3 IV, 4, 424. Denoting any thing rare and matchless: All's I, 1, 182. *his p. down,* Compl. 93 (= matchless).

Name of a house: Err. I, 2, 75. 88. II, 2, 11. Of a ship: Tw. V, 64.

**Phótinus,** name in Ant. III, 7, 15.

**Phrase,** subst. 1) an expression, a term: Wiv. I, 1, 151. I, 3, 33. II, 1, 13. II, 2, 28. Meas. V, 90. LLL I, 1, 166. V, 2, 406. All's IV, 3, 162. Tw. II, 5, 102. H4B III, 2, 76. 79. 81. 82 (not understood by Bardolph). H5 IV, 7, 19. Troil. III, 1, 45. Rom. I, 4, 37. Hml. I, 3, 108. I, 4, 19. I, 5, 175. II, 1, 47. II, 2, 111. 112. V, 2, 165.

2) style, manner of language: *precious p. by all the Muses filed,* Sonn. 85, 4. *write from it in hand or p.* Tw. V, 340. *this they con perfectly in the p. of war,* H5 III, 6, 79. *no sallets in the lines to make the matter savoury, nor no matter in the p. that might indict the author of affectation,* Hml. II, 2, 463. *whose p. of sorrow conjures the wandering stars,* V, 1, 278. *thou speakest in better p. and matter,* Lr. IV, 6, 8. *little blessed with the soft p. of peace,* Oth. I, 3, 82. *rail thou in Fulvia's p.* Ant. I, 2, 111.

**Phrase,** vb. to style, to call: *these suns, for so they p. 'em,* H8 I, 1, 34.

**Phraseless,** probably = indescribable, beggaring description: *advance of yours that p. hand,* Compl. 225 (see *Termless*). But cf. *his speechless hand* in Cor. V, 1, 67.

**Phrygia,** country in Asia Minor: Tw. III, 1, 58. Troil. Prol. 7. I, 2, 136 (supposed to be the country of the Trojans).

**Phrygian,** pertaining to Phrygia: Lucr. 1502. Wiv. I, 3, 97. Troil. IV, 5, 186. 223. V, 10, 24.

**Phrynia** (O. Edd. *Phrinica* or *Phrinia*) Phryne, a celebrated courtesan of ancient Athens: Tim. V, 1, 5.

**Phthisick,** see *Tisick.*

**Physic,** subst. 1) a remedy for a disease: Lucr. 901. Sonn. 34, 9. 147, 8. Pilgr. 180. Meas. IV, 6, 7. LLL I, 1, 235. As III, 2, 376. All's II, 1, 188. III, 1, 19. Tw. II, 3, 188. Wint. I, 2, 200. John V, 2, 21 *(for the health and p. of our right).* H4B I, 1, 137. IV, 5, 14. H6A III, 1, 147. H8 I, 3, 36. III, 2, 40. IV, 2, 122. V, 3, 27. Cor. III, 1, 154. III, 2, 33. Tit. IV, 2, 162. Tim. III, 6, 110. Mcb. V, 3, 47. Hml. III, 3, 96. Lr. III, 4, 33 *(take p.).* Per. I, 1, 72. IV, 6, 105.

2) the art of healing diseases: *doctor of p.* Wiv. III, 1, 4 (Evans' speech). *would that do it good? My p. says Ay,* LLL II, 188. *both our remedies within thy help and holy p. lies,* Rom. II, 3, 52. *thy sacred p. shall receive such pay,* Per. V, 1, 74. *I ever have stu-*

*died p.* III, 2, 32. Abstr. pro concr., = physicians: *the sceptre, learning, p., must all follow this and come to dust,* Cymb. IV, 2, 268.

**Physic,** vb. to work on as a remedy, to heal, to cure: *to p. your cold breast,* Compl. 259. *I will p. your rankness,* As I, 1, 92. *one that indeed —s the subject, makes old hearts fresh,* Wint. I, 1, 43. *that will p. the great Myrmidon,* Troil. I, 3, 378. *the labour we delight in —s pain,* Mcb. II, 3, 55. *some griefs are med'cinable; that is one of them, for it doth p. love,* Cymb. III, 2, 34 (preserves its health).

**Physical,** medicinal, wholesome: *the blood I drop is rather p. than dangerous to me,* Cor. I, 5, 19. *is it p. to walk unbraced and suck up the humours of the dank morning?* Caes. II, 1, 261.

**Physician,** one whose profession is to heal diseases: Lucr. 904. Sonn. 140, 8. 147, 5. Gent. II, 1, 42. Wiv. II, 3, 56. III, 1, 61. III, 4, 101. Shr. Ind. 2, 123. All's I, 1, 15. I, 2, 70. I, 3, 243. II, 3, 122. Wint. II, 3, 54. R2 I, 1, 154. I, 4, 59. II, 1, 99. H4A IV, 1, 24. H4B I, 2, 143. II, 2, 112. IV, 1, 60. R3 I, 1, 137. H8 V, 2, 11. Troil. II, 3, 223. Cor. II, 1, 127. Tim. III, 3, 11. IV, 3, 434. Mcb. V, 1, 82. Lr. I, 1, 166. Oth. I, 3, 311. Ant. V, 2, 357. Cymb. V, 4, 7. V, 5, 27. Per. I, 2, 67.

**Physiognomy** (cf. *Fisnomy*) the art of discerning the temper from the features of the face: *in Ajax and Ulysses, O, what art of p. might one behold,* Lucr. 1395.

**Pia mater,** the membrane which covers the brain; used for the brain itself: *nourished in the womb of p.* LLL IV, 2, 71 (O. Edd. *primater*). *one of thy kin has a most weak p.* Tw. I, 5, 123. *his p. is not worth the ninth part of a sparrow,* Troil. II, 1, 77.

**Pibbles,** pebbles (M. Edd. *pebbles*): *such a shower of p.* H8 V, 4, 60. Cor. V, 3, 58.

**Picardy,** French province: H6A II, 1, 10. H6B IV, 1, 88.

**Pick** (cf. *Peck*), 1) to prick, to stick, to strike with a pointed instrument: *p. out mine eyes with a ballad-maker's pen,* Ado I, 1, 254. *to p. one's teeth =* to cleanse them by means of a toothpick: All's III, 2, 8. Wint. IV, 4, 780. *I'll p. your teeth =* I'll curry you, Lr. IV, 6, 250.

2) to pluck, to gather, to take up: *we may p. a thousand salads,* All's IV, 5, 15. *p. a sallet,* H6B IV, 10, 9. *he could not stay to p. them in a pile of musty stuff,* Cor. V, 1, 25. Figuratively, = to cull, to gather, to find out: *could p. no meaning from their parling looks,* Lucr. 100. *at —ed leisure, which shall be shortly, single I'll resolve you,* Tp. V, 247. *what an unweighed behaviour hath this Flemish drunkard —ed out of my conversation,* Wiv. II, 1, 24. *out of this silence yet I —ed a welcome,* Mids. V, 100. *how much honour would be —ed from the chaff and ruin of the times,* Merch. II, 9, 48. *and p. strong matter of revolt and wrath out of the bloody fingers' ends of John,* John III, 4, 167. *now you p. a quarrel,* H4A III, 3, 76 (= seek; Mrs. Quickly's speech). *—ed from the wormholes of long-vanished days,* H5 II, 4, 86. *as I may p. occasion,* III, 2, 111 (Captain Jamy's speech). *to be honest is to be one man —ed out of ten thousand,* Hml. II, 2, 179. *not to p. bad from bad,* Oth. IV, 3, 106. *to p. out =* to find out: *hath —ed out an act,* Meas. I, 4, 64. *—ed out the dullest scent,* Shr. Ind. 1, 24. *the whole world again cannot p. out five such,* LLL V, 2, 548 (Ff Q2 prick).

*could the world p. thee out three such enemies*, H4A II, 4, 403. *what hotter hours you have luxuriously —ed out*, Ant. III, 13, 120. *to p. up* = to gather, to acquire, to make: *if in our youths we could p. up some pretty estate*, Per. IV, 2, 36.

Partic. *—ed*, adjectively, = refined: *he is too —ed, too spruce, too affected*, LLL V, 1, 14. *my —ed man of countries*, John I, 193. *the age is grown so —ed*, Hml. V, 1, 151. The gerund *—ing*, adjectively, = sought industriously: *the king is weary of dainty and such —ing grievances*, H4B IV, 1, 198 (German: *gesucht*).

3) to open (originally by a pointed instrument), and hence to steal from, to steal: *were beauty under twenty locks kept fast, yet love breaks through and —s them all at last*, Ven. 576. Cymb. II, 2, 41. *the penitent instrument to p. that bolt*, V, 4, 10. *—ing a kernel out of a pomegranate*, All's II, 3, 276. *to p. a purse*, Wiv. I, 1, 154. Wint. IV, 4, 627. H4A II, 1, 56. Tim. IV, 2, 12. *—ed my pocket*, H4A III, 3, 61. 70. 94. 113. 114. 176. 190.

4) to pitch, to throw: *as high as I could p. my lance*, Cor. I, 1, 204. In H8 V, 4, 94 O. Edd. *peck.*

**Pick-axe**, an axe not with an edge, but with a sharp point: Hml. V, 1, 102. Cymb. IV, 2, 389 (*these poor —s*, i. e. my hands).

**Pickbone**, name in H4B III, 2, 23.

**Pickers**, thieves: *so I do still, by these p. and stealers*, Hml. III, 2, 348 (i. e. my hands. "The phrase is taken from our church catechism, where the catechumen, in his duty to his neighbour, is taught to keep his hands from picking and stealing." Whalley).

**Pickle**, subst. a lye of salt liquor: *stewed in brine, smarting in lingering p.* Ant. II, 5, 66. Used jocularly of sad circumstances: *how camest thou in this p.?* (i. e. drunkenness). *I have been in such a p. since I saw you last that, I fear me, will never out of my bones: I shall not fear fly-blowing*, Tp. V, 281. 282 (Trinculo is speaking of his having been drenched in the pool).

**Pickle-herring**, a herring preserved in salt liquor: Tw. I, 5, 129 (Sir Toby seems to suffer from heart-burning).

**Pick-lock**, an instrument by which locks are opened without the key: *we have found upon him a strange p.* Meas. III, 2, 18 (probably one for Spanish padlocks).

**Pick-purse**, one that steals purses or from purses: Wiv. I, 1, 163. LLL IV, 3, 208. As III, 4, 24. H4A II, 1, 53 (*at hand, quoth p.*, a proverbial phrase).

**Pick-thanks**, persons studious to obtain thanks and gain favour, officious fellows: H4A III, 2, 25.*

**Pickt-hatch**, a quarter of London celebrated as a retreat of prostitutes and thieves: Wiv. II, 2, 19.

**Picture**, subst. 1) a piece of painting: Ven. 211 (cf. Hml. IV, 5, 86). Lucr. 1527. Wiv. II, 2, 90. As III, 2, 97. Shr. Ind. 1, 47. 2, 51. Tw. I, 5, 252; cf. Troil. III, 2, 50. Tim. I, 1, 26. 197. Mcb. II, 2, 54. Hml. III, 4, 53. IV, 5, 86 (cf. Ven. 211). Oth. II, 1, 110. Cymb. II, 2, 25. V, 5, 204. *the p. of We three*, Tw. II, 3, 17 (i. e. the heads of two fools with the inscription '*We three loggerheads be*'; the spectator making the third).

2) a portrait, likeness: Compl. 134. Sonn. 46, 3. 47, 5. 9. 13. Tp. III, 2, 136. Gent. II, 4, 209. IV, 2, 121. 122. IV, 4, 92. 120. 122. 189. Err. IV, 3, 13.

Ado II, 3, 273. LLL V, 2, 38. Merch. II, 7, 11. 48. Tw. I, 3, 136. III, 4, 228. Wint. V, 1, 74. V, 2, 187. H4B IV, 3, 53. H6A II, 3, 37. IV, 7, 83. Tit. III, 1, 103. Hml. II, 2, 383. Lr. II, 1, 83. Per. IV, 2, 101.

3) image: *presenteth to mine eye the p. of an angry chafing boar*, Ven. 662. *she, the p. of pure piety*, Lucr. 542. *I profane mine eyes on thy p.* LLL IV, 1, 87. *he is a proper man's p.* Merch. I, 2, 78. *I saw whose purse was best in p.* Wint. IV, 4, 615 (Autolycus is playing the amateur). *thou p. of what thou seemest*, Troil. V, 1, 6. *the p. of my youth*, Tit. IV, 2, 108. *hath altered that good p.* Cymb. IV, 2, 365. *he began his mistress' p.* V, 5, 175.

**Pictured**, painted, represented: *where your true image p. lies*, Sonn. 24, 6. *I have not seen him* (death) *so p.* (with eyes) Cymb. V, 4, 185.

**Picture-like**, like a painting: Cor. I, 3, 12.

**Pie**, 1) the bird Pica, magpie: *chattering —s in dismal discords sung*, H6C V, 6, 48.

2) paste baked with something in it: Shr. IV, 3, 82. All's I, 1, 173. Wint. IV, 3, 49. Troil. I, 2, 280. Tit. V, 3, 60. Rom. II, 4, 139. Proverbial expression: *no man's p. is freed from his ambitious finger*, H8 I, 1, 52.

3) the service-book of the Romish church, supposed to be meant in the oath *by cock and pie*: Wiv. I, 1, 316. H4B V, 1, 1.

**Piece**, subst. 1) a part, a fragment: *eat a p. of my sword*, H4A V, 4, 156. *on the —s of the broken wand*, H6B I, 2, 28. *a p. of him*, Hml. I, 1, 19. *this p. of your dead queen* (i. e. her new-born child) Per. III, 1, 17. *in —s* and *to —s* = asunder, into fragments, in two: *spurn in —s posts of adamant*, H6A I, 4, 52. *break thou in —s*, V, 4, 92. R3 II, 2, 52. Rom. II, 5, 50. Lr. I, 2, 92. *dashed all to —s*, Tp. I, 2, 8. Wiv. II, 1, 22. LLL V, 2, 399. Shr. IV, 3, 129. All's IV, 3, 193. Wint. V, 2, 68. John IV, 3, 93. R2 II, 2, 139. H4B IV, 1, 18. H5 I, 2, 225. H6A IV, 7, 47. R3 I, 3, 260. IV, 4, 234. Cor. V, 6, 112. 121. Caes. III, 3, 30. IV, 3, 82. Mcb. III, 2, 49. Lr. III, 2, 55. Oth. III, 3, 431. Cymb. III, 4, 55. IV, 1, 19. Per. IV, 2, 20. *torn a —s*, H8 V, 4, 80.

2) a part considered by itself and taken as a whole: *a p. of cheese*, Wiv. V, 5, 86. 147. *a three piled p.* (of velvet) Meas. I, 2, 33. *overmastered with a valiant p. of dust*, Ado II, 1, 64. *as pretty a p. of flesh as any*, IV, 2, 85. As III, 2, 68. Tw. I, 5, 30. *a p. of ice*, Shr. IV, 1, 14. *of beef*, IV, 3, 23. *the most peerless p. of earth*, Wint. V, 1, 94. cf. H5 V, 1, 14. R3 I, 3, 334. H8 III, 2, 280. IV, 1, 81. Rom. I, 1, 34. I, 5, 9. Caes. III, 1, 254. Lr. IV, 6, 90. Cymb. IV, 2, 127. V, 4, 140. V, 5, 437. Per. IV, 6, 153. *Of the same p.* = of the same kind: *just of the same p. is every flatterer's spirit*, Tim. III, 2, 71. *p. by p.* = one after another: *I'll murder all his wardrobe, p. by p.* H4A V, 3, 27.

Very often used in a periphrastical way: *a p. of skilful painting*, Lucr. 1366. *the most dangerous p. of lechery*, Ado III, 3, 180. *is this such a p. of study?* LLL I, 2, 53. *a very good p. of work*, Mids. I, 2, 14. Shr. I, 1, 258. *that p. of song*, Tw. II, 4, 2. *the prince is about a p. of iniquity*, Wint. IV, 4, 693. *it were a p. of honesty*, 695. *I knew by that p. of service*, H5 III, 2, 49. *there's not a p. of feather in our host*, IV, 3, 112. *a p. of knavery*, IV, 7, 3. cf. H6B I, 4, 47. V, 1, 155. R3 IV, 3, 5. H8 V, 2, 8. Tit. II, 3, 7. Tim. I, 1, 155. 202.

Caes. II, 1, 327. Mcb. II, 3, 134. Hml. II, 2, 315. III, 2, 51. 251. Oth. IV, 1, 156. Ant. I, 2, 160. Cymb. II, 4, 72. Per. IV, 3, 2.

Applied to persons, sometimes in contempt: *thou fresh p. of excellent witchcraft*, Wint. IV, 4, 433. *drink up the lees and dregs of a flat tamed p.* Troil. IV, 1, 62. *give that changing p. to him*, Tit. I, 309. Oftener to denote a person of supreme excellence: *thy mother was a p. of virtue*, Tp. I, 2, 56. *the p. of virtue, which is set betwixt us as the cement of our love*, Ant. III, 2, 28. *thou art a p. of virtue*, Per. IV, 6, 118. *their transformations were never for a p. of beauty rarer*, Wint. IV, 4, 32. *O ruined p. of nature*, Lr. IV, 6, 137. *nature's p. 'gainst fancy*, Ant. V, 2, 99. *I have gone through for this p.* Per. IV, 2, 48. *when nature framed this p.* 151. Difficult passage: *all princely graces, that mould up such a mighty p. as this is, shall still be doubled on her*, H8 V, 5, 27 (young Esizabeth cannot be meant by the mighty p., but what person else? King Henry VIII?).

3) a work of art, a painting or statue: *this well-painted p.* Lucr. 1443. *a p. many years in doing*, Wint. V, 2, 104. V, 3, 38. Tim. I, 1, 28. 255. V, 1, 21. = a song: Troil. III, 1, 55.

4) a coin: *a p. of silver*, Tp. II, 2, 31. *some p. of money*, Meas. II, 1, 284. *a p. of gold*, H4A II, 4, 540. Hml. II, 2, 447. Oth. III, 1, 26. Cymb. V, 5, 183. *that for the poorest p. will bear the knave by the volume*, Cor. III, 3, 32. *a thousand —s*, Tim. III, 6, 23. Per. IV, 2, 56. IV, 6, 124. *take —s for the figure's sake*, Cymb. V, 4, 25.

5) a weapon, offensive or defensive: *a' would manage you his p. thus*, H4B III, 2, 301 (= musket). *a p. of ordnance*, H6A I, 4, 15. *bruised —s, go*, Ant. IV, 14, 42. cf. *Murdering-piece.*

**Piece**, vb. 1) to make whole or mend by pieces joined together; to patch: *one girth six times — d*, Shr. III, 2, 61. *here and there —d with packthread*, 63.

2) to make full, to make up, to complete, to supply: *shall we thither and with our company p. the rejoicing?* Wint. V, 2, 117. With *out: p. out our imperfections with your thoughts*, H5 Prol. 23. *you shall p. it out with a piece of your performance*, Troil. III, 1, 55. *thus must I p. it out*, Caes. II, 1, 51. With *up: to take off so much grief from you as he will p. up in himself*, Wint. V, 3, 56 (hoard up, so as to have his fill).

3) to enlarge, to increase, to add to: *their purposed trim —d not his grace, but were all graced by him*, Compl. 119. *I twice five hundred and their friends to p. 'em*, Cor. II, 3, 220. *all of it, with our displeasure —d*, Lr. I, 1, 202. *I will p. her opulent throne with kingdoms*, Ant. I, 5, 45. With *out: he —s out his wife's inclination; he gives her folly motion and advantage*, Wiv. III, 2, 34. *and p. the way out with a heavy heart*, R2 V, 1, 92. *I will p. out the comfort with what addition I can*, Lr. III, 6, 2.

**Pie-corner**, a street-corner or place in London: *a' comes continuantly to P. — saving your manhoods — to buy a saddle*, H4B II, 1, 28 (Mrs. Quickly's speech).

**Pied**, variegated, particoloured: *a p. ninny*, Tp. III, 2, 71 (on account of his motley coat). *daisies p.* LLL V, 2, 904. *eanlings streaked and p.* Merch. I, 3, 80. cf. *Proud-pied.*

**Piedness**, variegation: Wint. IV, 4, 87.

**Pieled**, see *Peel.*

**Pier**, a mole projecting into the sea: Merch. I, 1, 19. H5 III Chor. 4.

**Pierce** (rhyming to *rehearse* in R2 V, 3, 127, and used in playing on the words *person* and *Percy:* LLL IV, 2, 86. H4A V, 3, 59) 1) to penetrate, to force a way into, to thrust into with a pointed instrument: *that the dribbling dart of love can p. a complete bosom*, Meas. I, 3, 3. *the princess —d a pricket*, LLL IV, 2, 58. Mids. II, 1, 160. III, 2, 59. R2 I, 1, 171. H4A V, 3, 59. H6C II, 1, 203. Cor. V, 4, 21. Tit. IV, 3, 12. Lr. IV, 6, 171. Ant. II, 5, 12. Absol.: *the air that sings with —ing*, All's III, 2, 114 (when pierced by bullets). *a thorn sharp and —ing*, H6A II, 4, 70. H6C I, 4, 41. Rom. III, 1, 164. Caes. V, 3, 76.

2) to broach: *an if one should be —d, which is the one? He that is likest to a hogshead*, LLL IV, 2, 86 (O. Edd. *perst*).

3) to penetrate, to enter in any manner; trans.: *a closet never —d with crystal eyes*, Sonn. 46, 6. *with sweetest touches p. your mistress' ear*, Merch. V, 67. *in high and boastful neighs —ing the night's dull ear*, H5 IV Chor. 11. *can curses p. the clouds and enter heaven?* R3 I, 3, 195. *that the appalled air may p. the head* (= the ear) *of the great combatant*, Troil. IV, 5, 5. *there is Aufidius, —ing our Romans*, Cor. I, 5, 12 (breaking through). *the din of war gan p. his ready sense*, II, 2, 119. *it was the nightingale that —d the fearful hollow of thine ear*, Rom. III, 5, 3. *whose proof nor yells of mothers nor sight of priests shall p.* Tim. IV, 3, 126. *the woundings of a father's curse p. every sense about thee*, Lr. I, 4, 323. *that the bruised heart was —d through the ear*, Oth. I, 3, 219. *whose solid virtue the shot of accident could neither graze nor p.* IV, 1, 279. Absol.: *brand not my forehead with thy —ing light*, Lucr. 1091. *ambition cannot p. a wink beyond*, Tp. II, 1, 242. *thus most invectively he —th through the body of the country*, As II, 1, 58. *eyes as —ing as the midday sun, to search the secret treasons of the world*, H6C V, 2, 17. *let some graver eye p. into that*, H8 I, 1, 68. *it shall as level to your judgment p. as day does to your eye*, Hml. IV, 5, 151 (Qq pear). *how far your eyes may p. I cannot tell*, Lr. I, 4, 368. *the air is quick, and it —s and sharpens the stomach*, Per. IV, 1, 29.

4) to affect, to touch, to move deeply; trans.: *plain words best p. the ear of grief*, LLL V, 2, 763. *can no prayers p. thee?* Merch. IV, 1, 126. *whose loss hath —d him deep*, Tit. IV, 4, 31. *did your letters p. the queen to any demonstration of grief?* Lr. IV, 3, 11. *it —d me thorough*, Per. IV, 3, 35. Absol.: *prayer, which —s so that it assaults mercy itself*, Tp. Epil. 17. *she uttereth —ing eloquence*, Shr. II, 177. *as it is now —ing to my soul*, Wint. V, 3, 34. *hearing how our plaints and prayers do p.* R2 V, 3, 127. *her tears will p. into a marble heart*, H6C III, 1, 38. *thy woes will make them* (thy words) *p. like mine*, R3 IV, 4, 125. *provide more —ing statutes daily, to chain up and restrain the poor*, Cor. I, 1, 86 (mortifying, revolting the feelings? or = sweeping; entering and affecting all the interests of the people?).

**Pierce**, name: *Sir P. of Exton*, R2 V, 5, 100.

**Piety**, duty and reverence to those who are entitled to it: *if to fight for king and commonweal were piety in thine, it is in these*, Tit. I, 115. *O cruel, irreligious p.* 130. *p. and fear, religion to the gods*, Tim. IV, 1, 15. Used with some latitude, = virtue in general: *while she, the picture of pure p., like a white hind under the gripe's sharp claws*, Lucr. 542. *how his p. does my deeds make the blacker*, Wint. III, 2, 172. *bungle up damnation with forms being fetched from glistering semblances of p.* H5 II, 2, 117. Misapplied by Dogberry in Ado IV, 2, 81.

**Pig**, a young swine: Err. I, 2, 44. II, 1, 66. Merch. IV, 1, 47. 54. Tit. IV, 2, 146.

**Pigeon**, the bird Columba: LLL V, 2, 315. Merch. II, 6, 5 (*Venus' —s*). As I, 2, 99. III, 3, 82. H4B V, 1, 18. 27. Tit. IV, 3, 87. 92. 97. 103. IV, 4, 44.

**Pigeon-egg**, used by Costard to denote smallness: *thou p. of discretion*, LLL V, 1, 77.

**Pigeon-livered**, of too mild a temper: *I am p. and lack gall*, Hml. II, 2, 605.

**Pight**, pitched, fixed: *tents thus proudly p. upon our Phrygian plains*, Troil. V, 10, 24 (Q *pitch*). = settled, firmly resolved: *found him p. to do it*, Lr. II, 1, 67. cf. *Straight-pight*.

**Pigmy**, a dwarf, and adj. dwarfish: *these p. arms*, John V, 2, 135. *a —'s straw*, Lr. IV, 6, 171. *The —es*, a fabulous nation of antiquity: *any embassage to the —es*, Ado II, 1, 278.

**Pig-nuts**, earth-nuts: Tp. II, 2, 172.*

**Pigrogromitus**, a name known only to Sir Andrew: Tw. II, 3, 23.

**Pike**, a sort of lance: Ven. 620. Tp. II, 1, 161. H4B II, 4, 55. H5 III, 3, 38. IV, 1, 40. H6A I, 1, 116. H6C I, 1, 244. Cor. I, 1, 23. V, 6, 152. Cymb. IV, 2, 399. V, 3, 39. *you must put in the —s with a vice*, Ado V, 2, 21, i. e. central spikes sometimes used in targets, to which they were affixed by means of a screw.

**Pike**, the fish Esox lucius: H4B III, 2, 356.

**Pilate**, the governor who washed his hands to show that he was innocent of the blood of Christ: R2 IV, 239. 240. R3 I, 4, 279.

**Pilch**, name in Per. II, 1, 12. O. Edd. *what, to pelch?*

**Pilcher**, a fish of the genus Clupea, much resembling the herring: Tw. III, 1, 39 (most M. Edd. *pilchards*).

**Pilcher**, a scabbard; in contempt: Rom. III, 1, 84.

**Pile**, subst. things heaped high together: *what —s of wealth hath he accumulated*, H8 III, 2, 107. *in heaps and —s of ruin*, Cor. III, 1, 207. *to pick them in a p. of musty chaff*, V, 1, 25. Particularly used of wood: Tp. III, 1, 25. Tit. I, 97. 128.

**Pile**, subst. a hair, a fiber of wool: *his left cheek is a cheek of two p. and a half*, All's IV, 5, 103, i. e. covered with a patch of velvet; cf. *Three-piled*.

**Pile**, to heap up high: Tp. III, 1, 17. Wint. I, 2, 430. Cor. III, 2, 3. Hml. V, 1, 274. With *up*: Tp. III, 1, 10. H4B IV, 5, 71.

**Piled**, "a quibble between *piled* = peeled, stripped of hair, bald (from the French disease), and *piled* as applied to velvet, three-piled velvet meaning the finest and costliest kind of velvet" (Dyce): *I had as lief be a list of an English kersey as be p., as thou art p., for a French velvet*, Meas. I, 2, 35.

**Pilfer**, to steal: H5 I, 2, 142.

**Pilferings**, thefts: Lr. II, 2, 151.

**Pilgrim**, one who travels to a holy place: Gent. II, 7, 9. All's III, 4, 4. III, 5, 33. 35. 42. 47. 96. H4A I, 2, 140. Rom. I, 5, 97. 99. 101. 104.

**Pilgrimage**, 1) a travel undertaken for purposes of devotion: Lucr. 791. All's IV, 3, 57. R2 I, 3, 49.

2) any long and weary journey: Lucr. 960. Sonn. 7, 8. 27, 6. Gent. II, 7, 30. Merch. I, 1, 120. R2 I, 3, 230. 264. Rom. IV, 5, 45. Used of human life: Meas. II, 1, 36. Mids. I, 1, 75. As III, 2, 138. R2 II, 1, 154. H6A II, 5, 116. Lr. V, 3, 196. Oth. I, 3, 153.

**Pill**, subst. a medicine in the form of a small ball: Gent. II, 4, 149. Wiv. III, 5, 24.

**Pill**, vb. to pillage, to rob, to plunder: *the commons hath he —ed with grievous taxes*, R2 II, 1, 246. *that which you have —ed from me*, R3 I, 3, 159. *p. by law*, Tim. IV, 1, 12.

**Pillage**, subst. 1) spoil, plunder, booty: *slaves for p. fighting*, Lucr. 428. *which p. they with merry march bring home*, H5 I, 2, 195. *to be the p. of a giglot wench*, H6A IV, 7, 41. *make cheap pennyworths of their p.* H6B I, 1, 222.

2) the act of spoiling or plundering: *p. and robbery*, H5 IV, 1, 174. *thy sons make p. of her chastity*, Tit. II, 3, 44.

**Pillar**, a column, a supporter: Tp. V, 208. Merch. IV, 1, 239. H6B I, 1, 75. H6C II, 3, 51. H8 III, 2, 382. Troil. IV, 5, 212. Ant. I, 1, 12.

**Pillicock** (Qq *Pelicock*) a term of endearment, with a lascivious double-meaning: Lr. III, 4, 78 (alluding to an old rhyme: *Pillicock, Pillicock sat on a hill: if he's not gone, he sits there still*).

**Pillory**, a frame of wood with movable boards and holes, through which were put the head and hands of a criminal for punishment: *I have stood on the p.* Gent. IV, 4, 35. *there I stood as on a p., looking through the lute*, Shr. II, 157.

**Pillow**, a cushion laid under the head to sleep on: Lucr. 387. 1620. Mids. II, 2, 41. As II, 4, 27. Shr. IV, 1, 204. H4B IV, 5, 5. 21. 58. H5 IV, 1, 14. H6B III, 2, 375. R3 IV, 3, 14. Troil. III, 1, 49. Tit. II, 3, 130. V, 3, 163. Tim. IV, 3, 32. Mcb. II, 3, 109. V, 1, 81. Lr. III, 4, 55. Ant. III, 13, 106. Cymb. III, 6, 35. IV, 2, 363. Per. III, 1, 69. V, 1, 237.

**Pilot**, one who steers a ship: Lucr. 279. All's II, 1, 168. Wint. I, 2, 448. H6C IV, 6. 20. Troil. II, 2, 64. Rom. II, 2, 82. V, 3, 117. Mcb. I, 3, 28. Oth. II, 1, 48. III, 2, 1. Per. IV, 4, 18.

**Pimpernell**, name in Shr. Ind 2, 96.

**Pin**, subst. 1) a small pointed instrument chiefly used to fasten clothes: Gent. II, 7, 56. As III, 5, 21. Wint. IV, 4, 228. R2 III, 2, 169. H4B III, 2, 156. H6B IV, 10, 32. Lr. II, 3, 16. IV, 7, 56. *—s' heads:* H4A IV, 2, 24. H4B IV, 3, 58.

Used to denote an insignificant trifle: Gent. I, 1, 115. II, 7, 55. Meas. II, 1, 99. II, 2, 45. III, 1, 106. Err. IV, 3, 73. LLL IV, 3, 19. H4B II, 4, 189. Hml. I, 4, 65. *my wretchedness unto a row of —s*, R2 III, 4, 26. Sometimes used to cut short any futile evasion: *you have beaten my men, killed my deer, and broke open my lodge. But not kissed your keeper's daughter? Tut a p.! this shall be answered*, Wiv. I, 1, 117. *I'll tell you what, — Foh, foh! come, tell a p., you are forsworn*, Troil. V, 2, 22.

2) the middle point of the butt, the centre: *then will she get the upshoot by cleaving the p.* LLL IV, 1, 138. *the very p. of his heart cleft with the blind bow-boy's buttshaft*, Rom. II, 4, 15.

3) an induration of the membranes of the eye, cataract: *all eyes blind with the p. and web*, Wint. I, 2, 291. *he gives the web and the p.* Lr. III, 4, 122.

**Pin**, vb. 1) to fasten with pins: LLL V, 2, 321. Cor. II, 1, 225.

2) to fasten, to fix in general: *and so locks her in embracing, as if she would p. her to her heart,* Wint. V, 2, 84. *our gates we have but —ed with rushes,* Cor. I, 4, 18.

**Pin-buttock,** a buttock thin and pointed like a pin: All's II, 2, 18.

**Pinch**, subst. 1) a squeeze with the fingers: Tp. I, 2, 329. IV, 233. Ant. I, 5, 28. V, 2, 298.

2) seizure with the teeth, bite: *not rascal-like to fall down with a p.* H6A IV, 2, 49 (cf. the verb in H6C II, 1, 16).

3) pain, pang: *inward —es,* Tp. V, 77 (remorse). *necessity's sharp p.* Lr. II, 4, 214 (cf. *belly-pinched*). *there cannot be a p. in death more sharp than this is,* Cymb. I, 1, 130.

**Pinch,** name in Err. IV, 4, 50. V, 237. 294.

**Pinch**, vb. 1) to squeeze with the fingers: Tp. I, 2, 328. II, 2, 4. V, 276. Wiv. IV, 4, 57. 61. IV, 6, 44. V, 5, 49. 58. 96. 103—105. Err. II, 2, 194. All's IV, 3, 140. Wint I, 2, 115. IV, 4, 622. Strange expression: *let the bloat king tempt you again to bed, p. wanton on your cheek, call you his mouse,* Hml. III, 4, 183. Should it be *pinch-wanton* (dally with pinches)? or *pinch, wanton on your cheek?*

2) to gripe and bite: *as a bear, encompassed round with dogs, who having —ed a few and made them cry,* H6C II, 1, 16 (cf. the subst. in H6A IV, 2, 49).

3) to discolour as by squeezing: *the air hath —ed the lily tincture of her face,* Gent. IV, 4, 160 (cf. *with Phoebus' amorous —es black,* Ant. I, 5, 28).

4) to pain, to afflict: *the earth is with a kind of colic —ed and vexed,* H4A III, 1, 29. Cor. II, 1, 82. *the pox —es the other,* H4B I, 2, 258. *in this our —ing cave,* Cymb. III, 3, 38 (very cold). *O majesty! when thou dost p. thy bearer,* H4B IV, 5, 29 (meaning the crown pressing the head). *here's the pang that —es,* H8 II, 3, 1. *to gall and p. this Bolingbroke,* H4A I, 3, 229. *thou art —ed for it now,* Tp. V, 74.

5) to make ridiculous, to serve a trick: *have I —ed you, Signior Gremio?* Shr. II, 373. *I remain a —ed thing,* Wint. II, 1, 51. *as they p. one another by the disposition,* Ant. II, 7, 7.

**Pinch-spotted,** spotted by pinches: Tp. IV, 261.

**Pindarus**, name in Caes. IV, 2, 4. V, 3, 20 etc.

**Pine,** subst. the tree Pinus: Lucr. 1167. Tp. I, 2, 277. 293. V, 48. Merch. IV, 1, 75. Wint. II, 1, 34. R2 III, 2, 42. H6B II, 3, 45. Troil. I, 3, 8. Ant. IV, 12, 1. 23. Cymb. IV, 2, 175 (masc.).

**Pine,** vb. 1) intr. a) to want food, to starve: *the orphan —s while the oppressor feeds,* Lucr. 905. *like still —ing Tantalus he sits,* 858. *he ten times —s that —s beholding food,* 1115. *thus do I p. and surfeit day by day,* Sonn. 75, 13. *why doest thou p. within and suffer dearth,* 146, 3. 10. *the dearth that I have —d in,* Gent. II, 7, 16. *the mind shall banquet, though the body p.* LLL I, 1, 25. *to love, to wealth, to pomp, I p. and die,* 31. With *for,* = to hunger for: *cloyed with much, he —th still for more,* Lucr. 98.

b) to wear away, to languish: *I alone must sit and p.* Lucr. 795. *hanging her pale and —d cheek beside,* Compl. 32. *now all these hearts... with bleeding groans they p.* 275. Shr. I, 1, 160. Tw. II, 4, 115. H5 II, 4, 107. IV Chor. 41. H6A II, 5, 57. III, 3, 49. Mcb. I, 3, 23. Per. I, 2, 31. *to p. away:* R2 III, 2, 209. Lr.

I, 4, 80. With *for,* = to languish for: *for whom, and not for Tybalt, Juliet —d,* Rom. V, 3, 236. *all which we p. for now,* Mcb. III, 6, 37.

2) trans. a) to starve: *poor birds, deceived with painted grapes, do surfeit by the eye and p. the maw,* Ven. 602. b) to wear out, to afflict: *where shivering cold and sickness —s the clime,* R2 V, 1, 77.

**Pinfold,** a place in which beasts are confined, a pound: Gent. I, 1, 114. Lr. II, 2, 9.

**Pinion,** subst. a feather: *so poor a p. of his wing,* Ant. III, 12, 4.

**Pinion,** vb. to make defenceless by binding the elbows behind together: Wiv. IV, 2, 129. Ado IV, 2, 69 (Dogberry says *opinioned*). Lr. III, 7, 23. Ant. V, 2, 53.

**Pinioned,** winged, in *Nimble-pinioned,* q. v.

**Pink,** subst. 1) a nonpareil, a nonesuch: *I am the very p. of courtesy,* Rom. II, 4, 61.

2) the flower Dianthus: *p. for flower,* Rom. II, 4, 62.

**Pink,** adj. winking, half-shut: *plumpy Bacchus with p. eyne,* Ant. II, 7, 121.

**Pinked,** pierced in small holes, reticulated: *railed upon me till her p. porringer fell off her head,* H8 V, 4, 50. cf. *Unpinked* in Shr. IV, 1, 136.

**Pinnace,** a kind of small and light vessel: Wiv. I, 3, 89. H6B IV, 1, 9. 107.

**Pint,** half a quart: H4A II, 4, 29. Oth. II, 3, 68. cf. *Half-pint.*

**Pint-pot,** a pot containing a pint: H4A II, 4, 438.

**Pioned,** overgrown with marsh-marigold: *thy banks with p. and twilled brims,* Tp. IV, 64 ("the marsh-marigold is even at present called *peony* in the neighbourhood of Stratford.". Edinb. Rev. 1872, Oct. p. 363).*

**Pioner,** pioneer, one whose business is to level the roads, throw up works, or form mines: Lucr. 1380 (rhyming to *appear*). H5 III, 2, 92. Hml. I, 5, 163. Oth. III, 3, 346 (the later Ff *pioneers*).

**Pious,** godly, religious: Meas. I, 3, 16. H8 II, 2, 37. II, 4, 140. Tim. IV, 3, 140. Mcb. III, 6, 12. 27. Hml. I, 3, 130. II, 2, 438. III, 1, 48. Cymb. III, 3, 72. Per. IV, 3, 17 (Qq *impious*).

**Pip,** a spot on cards: *being, perhaps, for aught I see, two and thirty, a p. out,* Shr. I, 2, 33 (the earlier Ff and Q *peep*. "An expression derived from the game of Bone-ace or One-and-thirty: *to be two and thirty, a p. out,* was an old cant phrase applied to a person who was intoxicated." Halliwell).

**Pipe,** subst. 1) a tube: *your statue spouting blood in many —s,* Caes. II, 2, 85. Applied to the veins of the body: Lucr. 1455. Cor. V, 1, 54.

2) throat, windpipe: *Philomel stops her p.* Sonn. 102, 8 (ceases to sing). Hence = voice: *thy small pipe is as the maiden's organ,* Tw. I, 4, 32. Cor. III, 2, 113.

3) a tubular wind instrument: *rumour is a p. blown by surmises,* H4B Ind. 15. *the p. of Hermes,* H5 III, 7, 18. *split thy brazen p.* (= trumpet) Troil. IV, 5, 7. *they are not a p. for fortune's finger,* Hml. III, 2, 75. *will you play upon this p.?* (a recorder) 366. 387. Especially used by shepherds and other peaceful musicians: Pilgr. 271. Mids. II, 1, 67. Rom. IV, 5, 96. Oth. III, 1, 20. *the tabor and the p.* (opposed to the drum and the fife) Ado II, 3, 15. Wint. IV, 4, 183. cf. *Piping* in R3 I, 1, 24.

**Pipe**, vb. 1) to play on a pipe: *when shepherds p. on oaten straws*, LLL V, 2, 913. *in this weak —ing time of peace*, R3 I, 1, 24 (when the pipe is sounding instead of the fife; or, perhaps, when no manly martial voice is heard, but only that of women and children).

2) to whistle, to have a shrill sound: *the winds, —ing to us in vain*, Mids. II, 1, 88. *his big manly voice, turning again toward childish treble, —s and whistles in his sound*, As II, 7, 162. *to p. for* = to whistle for, to give up for lost (German: *nachpfeifen*): *and then we may go p. for justice*, Tit. IV, 3, 24.

**Piper**, one who plays on a pipe: Ado V, 4, 131.

**Pipe-wine**, wine not from the bottle, but from the pipe or cask: *I shall drink in p. first with him; I'll make him dance*, Wiv. III, 2, 90. The jest consists in the double sense of *pipe* as the instrument after which people used to dance. cf. the preceding *canary*.

**Pippin**, a kind of apple: Wiv. I, 2, 13. H4B V, 3, 2.

**Pirate**, a sea-robber: Lucr. 335. Meas. I, 2, 8. IV, 3, 75. Merch. I, 3, 25. Tw. V, 72. 77. H6B I, 1, 222. IV, 1, 108. 138. IV, 9, 33. R3 I, 3, 158. Hml. IV, 6, 15. Ant. I, 4, 48. II, 6, 36. Per. IV, 1, 97. IV, 2, 69. V, 1, 176.

**Pisa**, town in Italy: Shr. I, 1, 10. 21. 210. II, 104. III, 1, 33. IV, 2, 93. 94. IV, 4, 71. IV, 5, 55. V, 1, 29. Adjectively: *within rich P. walls*, II, 369.

**Pisanio**, name in Cymb. I, 3, 22 and passim.

**Pish**, an interjection expressing contempt or even disgust: H5 II, 1, 43. 44. Oth. II, 1, 270. IV, 1, 42.

**Pismire**, the ant, emmet: *nettled and stung with —s*, H4A I, 3, 240.

**Piss**, subst. urine, in *Horse-piss*, q. v.

**Piss**, vb. to eject as urine: *to p. my tallow*, Wiv. V, 5, 16 (a hunters' term, used of deer becoming lean in rut-time). *a —ing while* = a short time, such as is sufficient to make water: Gent. IV, 4, 21. *the —ing conduit*, a conduit near the Royal Exchange ("so called from its running with a small stream," Nares) H6B IV, 6, 3.

**Pistol**, subst. a small fire-arm: Wiv. IV, 2, 53. H4A II, 4, 380. V, 3, 53. Per. I, 1, 168. Quibbling: H4B II, 4, 120. H5 II, 1, 55.

**Pistol**, name in Wiv. I, 1, 129. 149 etc. H4B II, 4, 74 etc. H5 II, 1, 3 etc.

**Pistol**, vb. to shoot with a pistol: Tw. II, 5, 42.

**Pistol-proof**, impenetrable to a pistol-shot: H4B II, 4, 125.

**Pit**, a cavity, a hole: *these round enchanting —s* (i. e. dimples) Ven. 247. *brine —s* (salt springs) Tp. I, 2, 338. *a saw-p.* Wiv. IV, 4, 53. V, 3, 14. V, 4, 3. *fallen into a p. of ink*, Ado IV, 1, 142. *an earthy p.* (a grave) R2 IV, 219. *they'll fill a p.* H4A IV, 2, 72. *this abhorred p.* Tit. II, 3, 98. 176. 193. 224. 230. 240. 273. 277. 283. 286. *our enemies have beat us to the p.* Caes. V, 5, 23 (like beasts of the chase). *at the pit of Acheron*, Mcb. III, 5, 15. *conscience and grace, to the profoundest p.* Hml. IV, 5, 132. *a p. of clay* (a grave) V, 1, 104. *the sulphurous p.* (hell) Lr. IV, 6, 130.

**Pitch**, subst. a thick black substance obtained by boiling down tar: Tp. I, 2, 3. II, 2, 54. H6A V, 4, 57. Proverbially defiling: Ado III, 3, 60. LLL IV, 3, 3. H4A II, 4, 455. H6B II, 1, 196. Emblem of moral pollution: *so will I turn her virtue into p.* Oth. II, 3, 366.

**Pitch**, subst. height: *when from highmost p. he*

(the sun) *reeleth*, Sonn. 7, 9. *to write above a mortal p.* 86, 6. *of what validity and p. soe'er*, Tw. I, 1, 12. *it* (the frame) *is of such a spacious lofty p.* H6A II, 3, 55. *the p. and height of all his thoughts*, R3 III, 7, 188. *and mount her p.* Tit. II, 1, 14. *I cannot bound a p. above dull woe*, Rom. I, 4, 21. *enterprises of great p. and moment*, Hml. III, 1, 86 (Ff *pith*). Used of the height to which a falcon soars: *which flies the higher p.* H6A II, 4, 11. *what a p. she flew*, H6B II, 1, 6. *bears his thoughts above his falcon's p.* 12. Figuratively: *how high a p. his resolution soars*, R2 I, 1, 109. *fly an ordinary p.* Caes. I, 1, 78. Uncertain which of the two homonyms is meant: *this imperious man will work us all from princes into pages: all men's honours lie like one lump before him, to be fashioned into what p. he please*, H8 II, 2, 50 (height? or baseness? Hanmer *pinch*, Theobald *batch*).

**Pitch**, vb. 1) to throw, to thrust: *p. me i' the mire*, Tp. II, 2, 5. *p. and pay* = pay down at once, pay ready money: *the word is P. and pay*, H5 II, 3, 51 (Pistol's speech. Perhaps = throw down your money and pay; or derived from the custom of pitching goods at markets).

2) to plant, to set: *shall we desire to raze the sanctuary and p. our evils there?* Meas. II, 2, 172. *they have —ed a toil*, LLL IV, 3, 2. *here p. our tents*, R3 V, 3, 1. *the Greeks do p. their brave pavilions*, Troil. Prol. 14. V, 10, 24 (Ff *pight*). *sharp stakes they —ed in the ground*, H6A I, 1, 118. From the custom of planting sharp stakes in the ground against the hostile horse came the signification of marshalling, arranging in a military sense: *a —ed battle*, Shr. I, 2, 206. H6C IV, 4, 4. *here p. our battle*, V, 4, 66. *the very parings of our nails shall p. a field*, H6A III, 1, 103. *all the land thou hast lie in a —ed field*, Tim. I, 2, 231. *on either hand thee there are squadrons —ed*, H6A IV, 2, 23.

3) to fix: *whose vulture thought doth p. the price so high*, Ven. 551 (or = raise? cf. *High-pitched*).

**Pitch-balls**, balls of pitch: LLL III, 199.

**Pitcher**, a jug; used only in the proverbial phrase *—s have ears* = there may be listeners overhearing us: Shr. IV, 4, 52. R3 II, 4, 37.

**Pitchy**, very dark: *p. night*, Ven. 821. All's IV, 4, 24. H6A II, 2, 2. *p. vapours*, Lucr. 550. *a p. day*, H6C V, 6, 85.

**Piteous**, 1) compassionate: *these eyes, but for thy p. lips, no more had seen*, Ven. 504. *a wretched image, that p. looks to Phrygian shepherds lent*, Lucr. 1502. *tell your p. heart*, Tp. I, 2, 14. *in thy p. heart plant thou thine ear*, R2 V, 3, 126.

2) exciting compassion: *he pens her p. clamours in her head*, Lucr. 681. *p. plainings of the pretty babes*, Err. I, 1, 73. As II, 1, 40. Wint. III, 3, 91. H6C I, 4, 163. II, 5, 73. R3 I, 2, 158. IV, 3, 2. Rom. I Chor. 7. III, 2, 54. III, 3, 86. V, 3, 180. Caes. III, 2, 202. Hml. II, 1, 82. 94. III, 4, 128. Lr. V, 3, 214.

3) miserable, wretched, pitiful: *in an act of this importance 'twere most p. to be wild*, Wint. II, 1, 182. *or p. they will look, like drowned mice*, H6A I, 2, 12. *his p. and unpitied end*, R3 IV, 4, 74.

**Piteously**, so as to excite compassion: *villanies ruthful to hear, yet p. performed*, Tit. V, 1, 66 (cf. *pitifully* in Wiv. IV, 2, 212). *say that the last I spoke was 'Antony', and word it, prithee, p.* Ant. IV, 13, 9.

**Pitfall**, a pit intended to catch beasts: *poor bird,*

*thou'ldst never fear the net nor lime, the p. nor the gin,* Mcb. IV, 2, 35.

**Pith,** 1) marrow: *let it feed even on the p. of life,* Hml. IV, 1, 23.

2) strength, force: *the precedent of p. and livelihood,* Ven. 26. *not arrived to p. and puissance,* H5 III Chor. 21. *since these arms of mine had seven years' p.* Oth. I, 3, 83. *enterprises of great p. and moment,* Hml. III, 1, 86 (at first undertaken with great energy. Qq *pitch*).

3) chief part, quintessence: *that's my p. of business,* Meas. I, 4, 70. *you marked not what's the p. of all,* Shr. I, 1, 171. *it takes from our achievements the p. and marrow of our attribute,* Hml. I, 4, 22.

**Pithless,** strengthless: *p. arms,* H6A II, 5, 11.

**Pithy,** forcible, impressive: *to teach you gamut in a briefer sort, more pleasant, p. and effectual,* Shr. III, 1, 68.

**Pitiful,** 1) compassionate: *that p. rumour may report my flight,* All's III, 2, 130. *good ground, be p. and hurt me not,* John IV, 3, 2. R2 V, 2, 103. H6A III, 1, 109. H6C I, 4, 141. III, 2, 32. R3 I, 3, 141. H8 IV, 2, 40. Tit. II, 3, 156. Caes. III, 1, 169. With *to: be p. to my sons,* Tit. III, 1, 8.

2) moving compassion: *p. mischances,* Lucr. 976. *such p. dole,* As I, 2, 139. *the ballad is very p.* Wint. IV, 4, 286. 845. H6A IV, 1, 57. Rom. IV, 5, 99. V, 3, 174. Mcb. III, 2, 47. Lr. IV, 6, 208. Oth. I, 3, 161. V, 2, 210. Per. II, 1, 22. With *to: p. to the eye,* Mcb. IV, 3, 151.

3) miserable, wretched, contemptible: *p. thrivers, in their gazing spent,* Sonn. 125, 8. *I should be a p. lady,* Wiv. III, 3, 56. *a p. bald crown,* H4A II, 4, 420. IV, 2, 70. Troil. III, 2, 208. Hml. III, 2, 49.

Adverbially: *how p. I deserve,* Ado V, 2, 29.

**Pitiful-hearted,** compassionate: H4A II, 4, 134.

**Pitifully,** 1) compassionately: *be p. good,* Tim. III, 5, 52.

2) so as to excite compassion: *he beat him most p.* Wiv. IV, 2, 212.

3) wretchedly, contemptibly: *which p. disaster the cheeks,* Ant. II, 7, 18. *they are so p. sodden,* Per. IV, 2, 21.

**Pitiless,** destitute of compassion: Err. IV, 2, 35. As III, 5, 40. Tit. II, 3, 162. Lr. III, 4, 29.

**Pittance,** portion of food, diet: *at so slender warning, you are like to have a thin and slender p.* Shr. IV, 4, 61 (cf. 70).

**Pittie-ward,** towards Pitty, which seems to have been the name of some place at Windsor: Wiv. III, 1, 5.

**Pittikins:** *'ods p.,* an exclamation corrupted from God's pity: Cymb. IV, 2, 293.

**Pity,** subst. 1) compassion: Ven. 95. 257. 1000. Lucr. 468. 595. 1553. Sonn. 111, 14. 112, 1. 142, 11. Tp. I, 2, 150. 446. Gent. II, 1, 12. Meas. II, 2, 99. III, 2, 223. Err. I, 1, 10. Merch. IV, 1, 5. As II, 7, 123. H6B III, 1, 125. 225. V, 2, 56. H6C II, 6, 26. Caes. III, 1, 171 etc. Plur. —*es:* Wint. II, 1, 110. *the one has my p.* (= I pity him) Meas. IV, 2, 64. *this is full of p.* H8 II, 1, 137 (= moves compassion). *an eye of p.* = a compassionate eye, Merch. IV, 1, 27. Wint. III, 2, 124. *a thing of p.* = to be pitied, Cymb. V, 4, 47. *for p.* = out of compassion: Ven. 577. Ado V, 4, 93. Wint. III, 3, 78. Cor. I, 3, 96. Tit. III, 1, 2. *in p.,* in the same sense: R2 V, 1, 9. *in p. of:* Ven. 1091. As I, 2, 170. H6A II, 5, 87. H6C II, 2, 161.

Tim. V, 1, 179. Lr. IV, 5, 12. *out of p.* H8 III, 2, 382. *to give p.* All's I, 3, 219. *to have p.* Compl. 178. Tp. I, 2, 474. Mids. III, 2, 241. All's II, 3, 254. H8 IV, 2, 139. *to take p.* Pilgr. 392. Meas. I, 2, 112. Err. IV, 3, 26. Ado II, 3, 271. H5 III, 3, 28. With *of:* Ven. 1091. Compl. 178. Ado II, 3, 271. As I, 2, 170. All's II, 3, 254. H5 III, 3, 28. H6A II, 5, 87. H6C II, 2, 161. Tit. III, 1, 2. Lr. IV, 5, 12. Per. I, 2, 29. With *on:* Pilgr. 392. Meas. I, 2, 112. Err. IV, 3, 26 (in these three passages *to take p. on*). *have some p. upon my women,* H8 IV, 2, 139. With *to: I myself find in myself no p. to myself,* R3 V, 3, 203. *out of our easiness and childish p. to one man's honour,* H8 V, 3, 25. *p. to the general wrong of Rome,* Caes. III, 1, 170.

*For p.,* an exclamation not only of distress, but of regretful surprise (cf. the German *dass sich Gott erbarm'!*): *alack, for p.! I, not remembering how I cried out then, will cry it o'er again,* Tp. I, 2, 132. *ay me, for p.!* Mids. II, 2, 147. *where — O for p.! — we shall much disgrace the name of Agincourt,* H5 IV Chor. 49. *O p., sir, where is the patience now,* Lr. III, 6, 61.

2) a ground or subject of compassion: *and there sung the dolefullest ditty, that to hear it was great p.* Pilgr. 384. *it were p. you should get your living by reckoning,* LLL V, 2, 497. *though it be p. so see such a sight, it well becomes the ground,* As III, 2, 255. *which though it be great p., yet it is necessary,* Wint. IV, 4, 804. *were it not p. that this goodly boy should lose his birthright?* H6C II, 2, 34. III, 2, 31. *it is a p. would move a monster,* H8 II, 3, 10. *their story is no less in p. than his glory,* Ant. V, 2, 365. *it is p.* = it is to be regretted: *that were p.* Merch. II, 2, 209. followed by an indicative: *'tis p. he is not honest,* All's III, 5, 85. Wint. II, 1, 68. *'tis p. that thou livest to walk,* Err. V, 27. *'tis p. she lacks instructions,* Wint. IV, 4, 592. by the impf. subj.: *'tis p. — What's p.? That wishing well had not a body in't,* All's I, 1, 193. *what p. is it that he had not so dressed his land,* R2 III, 4, 55. by *should: 'tis p. love should be so contrary,* Gent. IV, 4, 88. *'twere p. two such friends should be long foes,* V, 4, 118. John II, 507. H4A I, 3, 59 (*great p.*). R3 I, 1, 132. Tit. II, 3, 71. Oth. II, 3, 143 (*great p.*). Cymb. I, 4, 43 etc. by *but,* = that not: *p. but he were a king,* Pilgr. 414; cf. Verges' confused speech in Ado III, 3, 2. by an inf.: *'twere p. to sunder them,* H6C IV, 1, 22. Ant. I, 2, 142. by *of: it is p. of her life,* Meas. II, 1, 77. II, 3, 42. Mids. III, 1, 44. V, 229 (*on* = of). Tw. II, 5, 14. Oth. II, 3, 130. Ant. I, 4, 71. *and yet the p. of it,* Oth. IV, 1, 206. *the more p.* As I, 2, 92. *the more the p.* Mids. III, 1, 148. H4A II, 4, 514.

**Pity,** vb. to feel sympathy, to compassionate; absol.: *what 'tis to p.* As II, 7, 117. H6C II, 6, 25. H8 Prol. 5. Troil. IV, 3, 11. Trans.: Lucr. 977. 1747. Sonn. I, 13. 111, 8. 132, 1. 142, 12. Pilgr. 400. Tp. I, 2, 353. Gent. II, 7, 16. IV, 3, 37. IV, 4, 83. 98. V, 2, 26. Wiv. II, 1, 13. Meas. II, 2, 101. Err. I, 1, 98. Ado II, 3, 231. Mids. III, 2, 235. V, 1, 52. V, 295. As I, 2, 293. I, 3, 81. II, 4, 75. II, 7, 117. III, 5, 33. All's V, 3, 161. H6A III, 1, 77. H6B I, 3, 218. H6C II, 5, 88. II, 6, 74. III, 1, 36. R3 I, 3, 274. IV, 1, 88. Hml. IV, 5, 3 etc. After the passive the agent preceded by *of,* not by *by:* Ado IV, 1, 218. Wint. III, 2, 235. Mcb. III, 6, 4. Ant. V, 2, 33.

**Pity-pleading,** imploring compassion: Lucr. 561.

**Pity-wanting,** unpitied: Sonn. 140, 4.

**Pius,** surname of Andronicus: Tit. I, 23.

**Pix,** needless emendation of some M. Edd. in H5 III, 6, 42; O. Edd. *pax,* q. v.

**Pizzle,** the part in beasts official to the discharge of urine: *you bull's p.* H4A II, 4, 271.

**Place,** subst. 1) a portion of space occupied or to be occupied: *the most opportune p.* Tp. IV, 26. *makes this p. Paradise,* 124. *never welcome to a p.* Gent. II, 5, 6. *hath appointed them contrary —s,* Wiv. II, 1, 217. *in other —s she enlargeth her mirth,* II, 2, 231. *though you change your p., you need not change your trade,* Meas. I, 2, 110. *peace be in this p.* I, 4, 6. *a novice of this p.* 19. *had time cohered with p. or p. with wishing,* II, 1, 11. *at that p. call upon me,* III, 1, 278. *knows the p. where he abides,* V, 252. *that or any p. that harbours men,* Err. I, 1, 137. *in what safe p. you have bestowed my money,* I, 2, 78. *I'll meet you at that p.* III, 1, 122. *here's no p. for you maids,* Ado II, 1, 48. *thy own wish wish I thee in every p.* LLL II, 179. *to that p. the sharp Athenian law cannot pursue us,* Mids. I, 1, 162. *in that same p. will I meet with thee,* 177. *if I be lapsed in this p.* Tw. III, 3, 36. *each circumstance of p., time,* V, 259. *the rector of the p.* All's IV, 3, 69. *a crooked figure may attest in little p. a million,* H5 Prol. 16. *France were no p. for Henry's warriors,* H6A III, 3, 22. *Kent is termed the civillest p. of all this isle,* H6B IV, 7, 66. *it is p. which lessens and sets off,* Cymb. III, 3, 13 etc. etc. Synonymous to spot: *the cry remaineth in one p.* Ven. 885. *she falleth in the p. she stood,* 1121. *burn in many —s,* Tp. I, 2, 199. *barren p. and fertile,* 338. *that we quit this p.* II, 1, 322. *bring the rabble here to this p.* IV, 38. *here on this grass-plot, in this very p.* 73. V, 100. *all that are assembled in this p.* Err. V, 396. *to meet me in this p. of the forest,* As III, 3, 45. *hurt him in eleven —s,* Tw. III, 2, 37. *conscience! O, 'tis a tender p.* H8 II, 2, 144 (cf. the German: *ein wunder Fleck*) etc. *in p. =* present: *here's one in p. I cannot pardon,* Meas. V, 504. *as firmly as yourself were still in p.* Shr. I, 2, 157. *she was there in p.* H6C IV, 1, 103. *choosing me when Clarence is in p.* IV, 6, 31. *an I had thee in p. where thou shouldst know it,* Shr. IV, 3, 151 (i. e. if I had thee present there where I should teach you to know it. M. Edd. unintelligibly, at least to us: *an I had thee in p. where, thou* etc.).

2) a portion of space as allotted or belonging to a particular person or thing: *she puts the period often from his p.* Lucr. 565. *why should my heart think that a several plot which my heart knows the wide world's common p.?* Sonn. 137, 10. *we'll borrow p. of him,* Meas. V, 367. *what worser p. can I beg in your love than to be used as you use your dog?* Mids. II, 1, 208. *to hold a rival p. with one of them,* Merch. I, 1, 174. *bars me the p. of a brother,* As I, 1, 20. *in his brain he hath strange —s crammed with observation,* II, 7, 40. *you shall supply the bridegroom's p.* Shr. III, 2, 251. *I fill a p.* All's I, 2, 69. *my true p. in your favour,* Tw. V, 126. *standing in rich p.* Wint. I, 2, 7; cf. H5 Prol. 16. *might have known my p.* Tim. III, 3, 14; cf. Tw. II, 5, 60 etc. *in one's p. =* in one's stead: Meas. III, 1, 261. Err. III, 1, 46. Merch. III, 4, 39. H6A I, 2, 61. IV, 3, 25. H8 III, 2, 394. Tit. IV, 2, 159. Caes. III, 2, 116. *upon his p. =* in his p. Meas. I, 4, 55. *to keep p. together =* to be in accordance: *they do no more adhere and keep p. together than the Hundredth*

*Psalm to the tune of Green Sleeves,* Wiv. II, 1, 63; cf. *keeps p. with thought,* Troil. III, 3, 199. *to take one's p. =* to sit down, or to take one's stand: Mids. V, 84. Merch. IV, 1, 170. H6A II, 1, 1. H6B III, 2, 19. Tit. V, 3, 24. Lr. III, 6, 38. *take p. by us,* H8 I, 2, 10 (= sit down at our side). *to take p. =* to come to pass: H8 III, 2, 34.

3) station in life, position in society: *authentic in your p. and person,* Wiv. II, 2, 236. Tw. II, 5, 60. *a man of his p., gravity and learning, so wide of his own respect,* III, 1, 57. *whose own great p.* Meas. II, 4, 92. *many fools that stand in better p.* Merch. III, 5, 73. *who were below him he used as creatures of another p.* All's I, 2, 42 (= of another sphere). *from lowest p. when virtuous things proceed,* II, 3, 132. *a creature of thy p.* Wint. II, 1, 83. *thy —s shall still neighbour mine,* I, 2, 448. *when yet you were in p. and in account nothing so strong and fortunate as I,* H4A V, 1, 37. *a woman of less p.* H8 II, 2, 112. *poison which attends in p. of greater state,* Cymb. III, 3, 78 etc. etc. Peculiar expression: *these fixed evils sit so fit in him, that they take p., when virtue's steely bones look bleak i' the cold wind,* All's I, 1, 114 (= that they are received as equals in high society).

Hence = office, official station: Gent. I, 2, 45. Meas. I, 1, 79. I, 2, 167. I, 3, 13. II, 1, 273. II, 2, 13. II, 4, 12. 156. IV, 1, 60. V, 294. 537. Ado IV, 2, 76. H4A III, 2, 32. H4B IV, 2, 23. V, 2, 77. H5 IV, 1, 263. IV, 3, 78. H6B I, 3, 124. H8 I, 1, 161. V, 3, 40. Troil. II, 3, 89. III, 3, 82. Cor. II, 1, 165. II, 3, 255. Lr. III, 6, 58 *(corruption in the p.).* Ant. III, 1, 18 etc.

4) seat, residence, mansion: *love lacked a dwelling and made him her p.* Compl. 82. *this is no p.; this house is but a butchery,* As II, 3, 27. *in our native p.* (= home) Troil. II, 2, 96. *due reference of p. and exhibition,* Oth. I, 3, 238. cf. *Crosby p., Eltham p. =* Crosby house etc. *did Julius Caesar build that p.* (the Tower)? R3 III, 1, 69.

5) room, way, space afforded; with the verb *to give: bids Lucretius give his sorrow p.* Lucr. 1773. *my sick Muse doth give another p.* Sonn. 79, 4. *nor gives to necessary wrinkles p.* 108, 11. *all vows and consecrations giving p.* Compl. 263. *the unexperient gave the tempter p.* 318. *most rude melancholy, valour gives thee p.* LLL III, 69. *give us the p. alone,* Tw. I, 5, 235 (= leave us alone). *let all the rest give p.* (= withdraw) II, 4, 82. *my love can give no p., bide no denay,* 127. *fellow, give p., here is no longer stay,* R2 V, 5, 95. *will it* (the fever) *give p. to flexure?* H5 IV, 1, 272. *give p.; by heaven, thou shalt rule no more,* H6B V, 1, 104. *sirrah, give p.* Caes. III, 1, 10. *if you give p. to accidental evils,* IV, 3, 146. *good reasons must give p. to better,* 203.

6) pitch, the highest elevation of the hawk: *a falcon towering in her pride of p.* Mcb. II, 4, 12.

7) Periphrastically: *thy black is fairest in my judgment's p.* Sonn. 131, 12. *bears his head in such a rein, in full as proud a p. as broad Achilles,* Troil. I, 3, 189. *to attain in suit the p. of's bed,* Cymb. V, 5, 185. Peculiar passages: *yond's that same knave that leads him to these —s,* All's III, 5, 86. *have you forgot all p. of sense and duty?* Oth. II, 3, 167 (M. Edd. *sense of p.*).

**Place,** vb. 1) to put, to set, to lay: *in thy dead arms do I mean to p. him,* Lucr. 517. *like stones of worth they thinly —d are,* Sonn. 52, 7. *and p. my* *merit in the eye of scorn,* 88, 2. *p. your hands below your husband's foot,* Shr. V, 2, 177. *a piece of ordnance 'gainst it I have —d,* H6A I, 4, 15. *p. barrels of pitch upon the fatal stake,* V, 4, 57. *on the pieces of the broken wand were —d the heads,* H6B I, 2, 29. *your father's head which Clifford —d there,* H6C II, 6, 53. *two women —d together makes cold weather,* H8 I, 4, 22. *upon my head they — d a fruitless crown,* Mcb. III, 1, 61. *that these bodies high on a stage be —d to the view,* Hml. V, 2, 389. *p. him here by me,* Lr. I, 4, 156. *I'll p. it upon this fairest prisoner,* Cymb. I, 1, 122. *briefly die their joys that p. them on the truth of girls and boys,* V, 5, 107. *to p. upon the volume of your deeds ... your worth in arms,* Per. II, 3, 3. *though fortune have —d me in this sty,* IV, 6, 104. Reflexively: *p. you that side,* H8 I, 4, 20 (= take your seat).

2) to station, to assign a place or post to: *now in London p. him,* H5 V Chor. 35. *here we her p.* Per. V Prol. 11. *the prince, Claudio and my master, planted and —d and possessed by my master Don John,* Ado III, 3, 159. *—d behind,* H6A I, 1, 132. *—ing therein some expert officers,* III, 2, 127. *and — d a quire of such enticing birds,* H6B I, 3, 92. *our archers shall be —d in the midst,* R3 V, 3, 295. *on which side they have —d their men of trust,* Cor. I, 6, 52. *I'll be —d in the ear of all their conference,* Hml. III, 1, 192. *subscribed it, —d it safely,* V, 2, 52. *I will p. you where you shall hear us,* Lr. I, 2, 98. *the while I'll p. you,* Ant. II, 7, 116. Used of words, = to arrange, to choose: *be wary how you p. your words,* H6A III, 2, 3. *words sweetly —d and modestly directed,* V, 3, 179. *well —d,* H5 III, 7, 128 (= put in, alleged).

3) to establish (in an office), to appoint: *who is, if every owner were well —d, indeed his king,* H4A IV, 3, 94. *thou shalt be —d as viceroy under him,* H6A V, 4, 131. *as p. Duke Humphrey for the king's protector,* H6B III, 1, 250. *this yellow slave will p. thieves and give them title,* Tim. IV, 3, 35. *if I can p. thee, I will,* Per. IV, 6, 204. *how she came —d here in the temple,* V, 3, 67. Reflexively: *to take their rooms, ere I can p. myself,* H6C III, 2, 132 (i. e. become king).

3) to fix, to establish firmly: *where her faith was firmly fixed in love, there a nay is —d without remove,* Pilgr. 256. *my resolution is —d,* Ant. V, 2, 238.

4) to set, to repose: *doubt and suspect are —d too late,* Tim. IV, 3, 519. cf. Cymb. V, 5, 107.

5) to bestow, to dispose of: *which since I know they virtuously are —d,* Gent. IV, 3, 38. *if half thine outward graces had been —d about thy thoughts,* Ado IV, 1, 102. *she being down, I have the —ing of the British crown,* Cymb. III, 5, 65.

6) to hold, to estimate: *p. it for her chief virtue,* Gent. III, 1, 339. *and therefore, like herself, wise, fair and true, shall she be —d in my constant soul,* Merch. II, 6, 57. *let your fervour, like my master's, be — d in contempt,* Tw. I, 5, 307. *the ram they p. before his hand that made the engine,* Troil. I, 3, 208. *those she —th highest,* Cor. I, 5, 25.

**Placentio,** name in Rom. I, 2, 69.

**Placket,** probably a stomacher (according to some a petticoat, or the opening in it): *dread prince of —s,* LLL III, 186. *will they wear their —s where they should bear their faces?* Wint. IV, 4, 245 (the clown's speech; = will they openly show to strangers what they ought to keep for their friends?). *you might have pinched a p., it was senseless,* 622. *those that war for*

*a p.* Troil. II, 3, 22.*keep thy hand out of —s,* Lr. III, 4, 100.

**Plague,** subst. 1) vexation, torment, calamity: *why should the private pleasure of some one become the public p. of many moe?* Lucr. 1479. *drink up the monarchs' p., this flattery,* Sonn. 114, 2. *in things right true my heart and eyes have erred, and to this false p. are they now transferred,* 137, 14 (= this p. of falsity, of being false). *my p. thus far I count my gain,* 141, 13. *a most unholy match, which heaven and fortune still rewards with – s,* Gent. IV, 3, 31. *I had as lief have heard the night-raven, come what p. could have come after it,* Ado II, 3, 85. *O p. right well prevented!* III, 2, 136. *'twas pretty, though a p., to see him every hour,* All's I, 1, 103. *too well I feel the different p. of each calamity,* John III, 4, 60. R2 V, 3, 3. H6C V, 5, 28. Troil. I, 3, 96. V, 10, 8. Tim. IV, 3, 357. V, 1, 56. 192. Hml. III, 1, 140 (or = curse?). IV, 7, 13. Lr. I, 2, 3.*IV, 1, 48. 67. Oth. III, 3, 146. 273. 276. IV, 1, 97.

2) punishment: *it is a p. that Cupid will impose,* LLL III, 203. *light wenches may prove —s to men forsworn,* IV, 3, 385. *thus pour the stars down – s for perjury,* V, 2, 394. *God hath made her sin and her the p. on this removed issue,* John II, 185. 187. *if heaven have any grievous p. in store,* R3 I, 3, 217. *the p. that needs must light on this ingratitude,* Caes. I, 1, 59. *all the —s of hell,* Cymb. I, 6, 111.

3) pestilence: *the p. is banished by thy breath,* Ven. 510. *of —s, of dearths,* Sonn. 14, 4. *they have the p.* LLL V, 2, 421. Tw. I, 5, 314. H5 IV, 3, 103. Tim. IV, 1, 21. IV, 3, 108. V, 1, 140. 224. Oftenest used in cursing: *the red p. rid you!* Tp. I, 2, 364. *the p. of Greece upon thee!* Troil. II, 1, 13. *a p. break thy neck,* V, 4, 34. *biles and —s plaster you o'er,* Cor. I, 4, 31. *the hoarded p. o'the gods requite your love,* IV, 2, 11. *a p. consume you,* Tim. V, 4, 71. *all the —s ... light on thy daughters,* Lr. III, 4, 69. *O p. and madness,* Troil. V, 2, 35. *the common file — a p.!* Cor. I, 6, 43. *more man? p., p.!* Tim. IV, 3, 197. *vengeance! p.! death!* Lr. II, 4, 96. *p. on't!* Tw. III, 4, 311. Cor. II, 3, 56. *a p. upon this howling,* Tp. I, 1, 39. II, 2, 166. All's IV, 3, 134. John II, 190. H4A I, 3, 243. II, 1, 31. II, 2, 21. 29. 31. II, 4, 166. 546. III, 1, 5. H6A IV, 3, 9. H6B III, 2, 309. R3 I, 3, 58. Troil. IV, 2, 78. Tim. II, 2, 50. IV, 3, 365. Lr. II, 2, 87. V, 3, 269. Per. II, 1, 28. *a p. of all drums,* All's IV, 3, 331. *a p. of all cowards,* H4A II, 4, 127. 131. 148. 365. H8 III, 2, 259. Troil. III, 3, 265. *a p. o' these pickle-herring,* Tw. I, 5, 128. *a p. a both your houses,* Rom. III, 1, 94. *what a p. =* what the devil: *what a p. means my niece,* Tw. I, 3, 1. *what a p. have I to do with a buff jerkin,* H4A I, 2, 51. II, 2, 39. II, 4, 373.

Hence it almost seems that, in some expressions, the word has quite passed into the sense of curse: *I'll give thee this p. for thy dowry,* Hml. III, 1, 140. *it is my nature's p. to spy into abuses,* Oth. III, 3, 146. 273. 276. *'tis the strumpets' p. to beguile many and be beguiled by one,* IV, 1, 97.

**Plague,** vb. 1) to afflict, to torment; absol.: *a —ing mischief light on Charles,* H6A V, 3, 39. trans.: *the aged man is —d with cramps,* Lucr. 856. *I will p. them all, even to roaring,* Tp. IV, 192. Merch. III, 1, 121. H6A V, 4, 154. Troil. I, 1, 97. Tim. IV, 3, 162. Oth. I, 1, 71.

2) to punish: *for one's offence why should so many*

*fall, to p. a private sin in general?* Lucr. 1484. *the ambition in my love thus —s itself,* All's I, 1, 101. *he is —d for her sin,* John II, 184. 186. *p. injustice with the pains of hell,* R2 III, 1, 34. *to p. thee for thy foul misleading me,* H6C V, 1, 97. *I'll p.thee for that word,* V, 5, 27. *God hath —d thy bloody deed,* R3 I, 3, 181. Troil. V, 2, 105. Cor. V, 3, 166. Rom. I, 4, 75. Tim. IV, 3, 73. Mcb. I, 7, 10. Lr. V, 3, 171. Cymb. II, 5, 35.

**Plague-sore,** a plague-spot, a pestilent boil: Lr. II, 4, 227.

**Plaguy,** used adverbially, = pestilently: *he is so p. proud that the death-tokens of it cry 'No recovery',* Troil. II, 3, 187.

**Plain,** subst. level ground: Ven. 236. Lucr. 1247. H8 V, 5, 55. Tit. II, 2, 24. Having *on* or *upon* (never *in*) before it: Pilgr. 290. R2 III, 3, 50. H4A I, 1, 70. H6B I, 4, 39. 71. Troil. Prol. 13. I, 3, 80. V, 10, 24. Lr. II, 2, 89. = battle-field: John II, 295. H5 IV, 6, 8. R3 V, 3, 291.

**Plain,** adj. 1) even, level, smooth: *the p. bald pate of father Time,* Err. II, 2, 71; i. e. not hairy; cf. *we are but p. fellows. A lie; you are rough and hairy,* Wint. IV, 4, 743. *follow me then to —er ground,* Mids. III, 2, 404. *p. as way to parish church,* As II, 7, 52. *on the p. masonry,* All's II, 1, 31. *this sandy plot is p.* Tit. IV, 1, 69. cf. Merch. III, 1, 13.

2) open, clear, easily understood, evident: *all this dumb play had his acts made p. with tears,* Ven. 359. *that my love may appear p. and free,* Gent. V, 4, 82. *a rule as p.* Err. II, 2, 70. LLL III, 82. IV, 3, 121. Mids. V, 129. As II, 7, 52. All's V, 3, 318. H6A III, 1, 200. H6B II, 2, 53. Troil. IV, 4, 31. Tit. II, 3, 301. Oth. II, 1, 321.

3) simple: *in true p. words,* Sonn. 82, 12. *the lesson is but p.* Ven. 407. *a p. kerchief,* Wiv. III, 3, 62. *'tis a p. case,* Err. IV, 3, 22. *I meant p. holy-thistle,* Ado III, 4, 80. *the p. form of marriage,* IV, 1, 2. *plantain, a p. plantain,* LLL III, 74. *that some p. man recount their purposes,* V, 2, 176. *p. statute-caps,* 281. *honest p. words best pierce the ear of grief,* 763. *the p. highway of talk,* Merch. III, 1, 13. *as you would say in p. terms,* II, 2, 68. *understand a p. man in his p. meaning,* III, 5, 63. *with all brief and p. conveniency,* IV, 1, 82. *thus in p. terms,* Shr. II, 271. *the p. single vow that is vowed true,* All's IV, 2, 22. *it* (the song) *is old and p.* Tw. II, 4, 44. *honest p. men,* Wint. IV, 4, 824. *we are but p. fellows,* 743. *p. old form,* John IV, 2, 22. *how a p. tale shall put you down,* H4A II, 4, 281. *of so easy and so p. a stop,* H4B Ind. 17. *in p. shock and even play of battle,* H5 IV, 8, 114. *such a p. king,* V, 2, 128. *I speak to thee p. soldier,* 156. *take a fellow of p. and uncoined constancy,* 161. *p. proceeding* H6B II, 2, 53. *cannot a p. man live and think no harm,* R3 I, 3, 51. *in p. terms tell her my loving tale,* R3 IV, 3, 359 (Ff *plainly to her*). *p. and not honest is too harsh a style,* 360. *that's the p. truth,* H8 V, 3, 71. *be p., good son, and homely in thy drift,* Rom. II, 3, 55. *and, but in the —er and simpler kind of people, the deed of saying is quite out of use,* Tim. V, 1, 27. *a p. blunt man,* Caes. III, 2, 222. *in p. terms,* Hml. I, 3, 132. *deliver a p. message bluntly,* Lr. I, 4, 35.

4) artless, without disguise, frank, honest: *such signs of truth in his p. face she spied,* Lucr. 1532. *p. and holy innocence,* Tp. III, 1, 82. *in p. dealing, I shall*

*have you whipt,* Meas. II, 1, 263. *do I not in —est truth tell you, I do not love you?* Mids. II, 1, 200. *I was always p. with you,* Merch. III, 5, 4. V, 166. Wint. I, 2, 265. IV, 4, 174. *p. well-meaning soul,* R2 II, 1, 128. *p. and right must my possession be,* H4B IV, 5, 223. *to be p.* H6B I, 2, 96. H6C III, 3, 19. *simple p. Clarence,* R3 I, 1, 118. *the —est harmless creature,* III, 5, 25. *shall I be p.?* I wish the bastards dead, IV, 2, 18. *the moral of my wit is 'p. and true',* Troil. IV, 4, 110. *laid falsely in the p. way of his merit,* Cor. III, 1, 61. *there are no tricks in p. and simple faith,* Caes. IV, 2, 22. *'tis my occupation to be p.* Lr. II, 2, 98. 105. 106. 117. *chill be p. with you,* IV, 6, 248.

5) mere, bare, nothing else but: *one of them is a p. fish,* Tp. V, 266. *Judas Maccabaeus clipt is p. Judas,* LLL V, 2, 603. *he speaks p. cannon fire,* John II, 462. *it is p. pocketing up of wrongs,* H5 III, 2, 54. *the p. devil and dissembling looks,* R3 I, 2, 237. *a p. knave,* Lr. II, 2, 118.

**Plain,** adv. clearly, so as to leave no doubt: *to be received p., I'll speak more gross,* Meas. II, 4, 82. *to tell you p., I'll find a fairer face not washed to-day,* LLL IV, 3, 272. *to confirm it p., you gave me this,* V, 2, 452. *my scutcheon p. declares that I am Alisander,* 567. *to tell thee p., I aim to lie with thee,* H6C III, 2, 69. 70. *heaven guide thy pen to print thy sorrows p.* Tit. IV, 1, 75.

2) distinctly: *sometime 'Tarquin' was pronounced p.* Lucr. 1786. *spake you not these words p. 'knock me here,'* Shr. I, 2, 40. *as p. as I see you now,* Tw. III, 2, 11.

3) simply, downrightly: *he was wont to speak p. and to the purpose,* Ado II, 3, 19. *I'll tell her p. she sings as sweetly as a nightingale,* Shr. II, 171. *you are called p. Kate* (not Katharine) 186. *no more but, p. and bluntly, 'To the king,'* H6A IV, 1, 51.

**Plain,** vb. to explain: *what's dumb in show I'll p. with speech,* Per. III Prol. 14 (Gower's speech).

**Plain,** vb. to complain: *of how unnatural and bemadding sorrow the king hath cause to p.* Lr. III, 1, 39. The gerund substantively: *his heart granteth no penetrable entrance to her —ing,* Lucr. 559. *the piteous —ings of the pretty babes,* Err. I, 1, 73. *after our sentence —ing comes too late,* R2 I, 3, 175.

**Plain-dealers,** simpletons: *thou didst conclude hairy men —s without wit,* Err. II, 2, 88. Compar. *plainer dealer,* 89.

**Plain-dealing,** subst. openness, undisguised honesty: LLL IV, 3, 370. Tim. I, 1, 216. cf. Meas. II, 1, 263.

**Plain-dealing,** adj. undisguised, open, honest: Ado I, 3, 33. H6B IV, 2, 119.

**Plaining,** see *Plain,* vb.

**Plainly,** 1) clearly, distinctly: *p. conceive, I love you,* Meas. II, 4, 141. *spake he so doubtfully? Nay, he struck so p.* Err. II, 1, 52. *I must tell thee p., Claudio undergoes my challenge,* Ado V, 2, 57. *who mayst see as p. as heaven sees earth,* Wint. I, 2, 315. *do p. give you out an unstained shepherd,* IV, 4, 149. *tongues of heaven p. denouncing vengeance,* John III, 4, 159. *hear me more p.* H4B IV, 1, 66. *which p. signified that I should snarl and bite,* H6C V, 6, 76. *lets them p. see it,* Cor. II, 2, 16. *then p. know,* Rom. II, 3, 57.

2) without disguise, openly, honestly, sincerely: *p. say thou lovest her well,* Pilgr. 309. *tell them p. he is Snug the joiner,* Mids. III, 1, 47. *my foes tell me p.*

*I am an ass*, Tw. V, 20. *and tell him p., the selfsame sun....*, Wint. IV, 4, 454. H4B I, 3, 3. H5 III, 5, 28. H6C IV, 1, 8. Cor. V, 3, 3. Lr. IV, 7, 62 *(to deal p.).*
3) simply, without ornament: *an honest tale speeds best being p. told,* R3 IV, 4, 358.

**Plainness,** 1) clearness, evidentness: *for the truth and p. of the case I pluck this pale and maiden blossom here,* H6A II, 4, 46.
2) openness, frankness, sincerity: Shr. I, 1, 157. IV, 4, 39. H5 I, 2, 244. H6B I, 1, 191. Troil. IV, 4, 108. Lr. I, 1, 131. 150. II, 2, 107. Oth. I, 1, 97. Ant. II, 6, 80.

**Plain-song,** simple notes: *the p. cuckoo,* Mids. III, 1, 134.* *an honest country lord may bring his p. and have an hour of hearing,* H8 I, 3, 45. = the simple melody as the fundamental part of variegated music: *the humour of it is too hot, that is the very p. of it. The p. is most just,* H5 III, 2, 6. 7 (Nym and Pistol speaking).

**Plaint,** subst. see *Plaints.*

**Plaintful,** complaining, expressing sorrow: Compl. 2.

**Plaintiff,** one who accuses another before a judge: Tw. V, 362. Misapplied by Dogberry in Ado V, 1, 261. 314.

**Plaints,** complaints, lamentations: Lucr. 1364. R2 V, 3, 127. H6C II, 6, 23. III, 1, 41. R3 II, 2, 61 (Ff *woes*).

**Plaister,** see *Plaster.*

**Plait,** a fold: *hiding base sin in —s of majesty,* Lucr. 93 (O. Edd. *pleats*).

**Plaited,** folded: *time shall unfold what p. cunning hides,* Lr. I, 1, 183 (Qq *pleated,* Ff *plighted*).

**Planched,** made of planks or boards: *a p. gate,* Meas. IV, 1, 30.

**Planet,** a star as influencing the fate of men: *I was not born under a rhyming p.* Ado V, 2, 41. *it is a bawdy p. that will strike,* Wint. I, 2, 201. *some ill p. reigns,* II, 1, 105. *the —s of mishap,* H6A I, 1, 23. *combat with adverse —s,* 54. *ruled like a wandering p. over me,* H6B IV, 4, 16. *all —s of good luck,* R3 IV, 4, 402. *the —s and this centre observe degree,* Troil. I, 3, 85. *the glorious p. Sol, whose medicinable eye corrects the ill aspects of —s evil,* 89. 92. *but when the —s to disorder wander, what plagues and what portents!* 94. *struck Corioli like a p.* Cor. II, 2, 118. *some p. strike me down,* Tit. II, 4, 14. *then no —s strike,* Hml. I, 1, 162. *as if some p. had unwitted men,* Oth. II, 3, 182. *now the fleeting moon no p. is of mine,* Ant. V, 2, 241. *the senate-house of —s all did sit, to knit in her their best perfections,* Per. I, 1, 10.

**Planetary,** pertaining to, or produced by, planets: *a p. plague,* Tim. IV, 3, 108. *p. influence,* Lr. I, 2, 135.

**Planks,** boards, timbers: John V, 2, 140. Ant. III, 7, 63.

**Plant,** subst. 1) a vegetable, particularly one bearing edible fruit: *sappy —s (are made) to bear,* Ven. 165. *when I perceive that men as —s increase,* Sonn. 15, 5. *his —s in others' orchards grew,* Compl. 171. *green —s bring not forth their dye,* Pilgr. 283. *trees did grow, and —s did spring,* 378. *—s with goodly burthen bowing,* Tp. IV, 113. *such barren —s are set before us,* LLL IV, 2, 29. *abuses our young —s with carving Rosalind on their barks,* As III, 2, 378. *the —s thou graft'st may never grow,* R2 III, 4, 101.

*amongst a grove the very straightest p.* H4A I, 1, 82. *his love was an eternal p. whereof the root was fixed in virtue's ground,* H6C III, 3, 124. *how sweet a p. have you untimely cropped,* V, 5, 62. *her royal stock graft with ignoble —s,* R3 III, 7, 127. *old withered —s,* IV, 4, 394. *to his music —s and flowers ever sprung,* H8 III, 1, 6. *he watered his new —s with dews of flattery,* Cor. V, 6, 23. *the grace that lies in herbs, —s, stones,* Rom. II, 3, 16. *the canker death eats up that p.* 30. *how dare the —s look up to heaven,* Per. I, 2, 55.
2) the sole of the foot: *some o' their —s are ill-rooted already,* Ant. II, 7, 2 (quibbling).

**Plant,** vb. 1) to put in the ground for growth: *and p. this thorn, this canker Bolingbroke,* H4A I, 3, 176. *every man shall eat in safety what he —s,* H8 V, 5, 35. *p. nettles,* Oth. I, 3, 325. Figuratively, = to give rise, to call into existence: *it is in us to p. thine honour where we please to have it grow,* All's II, 3, 163. *to p. and o'erwhelm custom,* Wint. IV, 1, 9. *he hath so —ed his honours in their eyes,* Cor. II, 2, 32. *I have begun to p. thee,* Mcb. I, 4, 28. *what's more to do, which would be —ed newly with the time,* V, 8, 65. *at the first I saw the treasons —ed,* Ant. I, 3, 26.
Hence = to engender: *—ing oblivion, beating reason back,* Ven. 557. *thou —est scandal and displacest laud,* Lucr. 887. *and p. in tyrants mild humility,* LLL IV, 3, 349. *it engenders choler, —eth anger,* Shr. IV, 1, 175. *p. neighbourhood and Christian-like accord in their sweet bosoms,* H5 V, 2, 381. *this may p. courage in their quailing breasts,* H6C II, 3, 54. *p. love among us,* Cor. III, 3, 35. *a faith that reason without miracle could never p. in me,* Lr. I, 1, 226.
2) to install, to instate, to invest: *anointed, crowned, —ed many years,* R2 IV, 127. *to p. unrightful kings,* 163. *they laboured to p. the rightful heir,* H6A II, 5, 80. *I'll p. Plantagenet, root him up who dares,* H6C I, 1, 48. *we will p. some other in the throne,* R3 III, 7, 216. *you are but newly —ed in your throne,* Tit. I, 444. cf. H4A I, 3, 176. cf. *Replant.* Jocularly: *a man in all the world's new fashion —ed,* LLL I, 1, 165.
3) to place: *—ed and placed and possessed by my master,* Ado III, 3, 159. *the fool hath —ed in his memory an army of good words,* Merch. III, 5, 71. *I will p. you two,* Tw. II, 3, 188. *in thy piteous heart p. thou thine ear,* R2 V, 3, 126. *and p. our joys in living Edward's throne,* R3 II, 2, 100. *I will advise you where to p. yourselves,* Mcb. III, 1, 129. *p. those that have revolted in the van,* Ant. IV, 6, 9. cf. *Sky-planted.*
4) to furnish as with plants: *thy temples should be —ed with horns,* Tit. II, 3, 62.

**Plantage,** anything planted: *as true as steel, as p. to the moon,* Troil. III, 2, 184 ('plants were supposed to improve as the moon increases'. Nares).

**Plantagenet,** name of the royal dynasty which reigned over England from 1154 to 1485: John I, 9. 162. 167. II, 238. V, 6, 11. H4A I, 1, 89. H5 V, 2, 259. H6A I, 4, 95. II, 4, 36. 64. II, 5, 18. III, 1, 61. 150 etc. H6B IV, 2, 44. H6C I, 1, 40. 48. 121 etc. R3 I, 2, 118. III, 7, 100 etc.

**Plantain,** the herb Plantago; supposed to have great efficacy in healing wounds: LLL III, 74. Rom. I, 2, 52.

**Plantation,** a first planting, a first etablishment, a first founding of laws and manners: *had I p. of this isle,* Tp. II, 1, 143.

**Plash,** a collection of water, a pool: *as he that leaves a shallow p. to plunge him in the deep,* Shr. I, 1, 23.

**Plashy,** place in Essex: R2 I, 2, 66. II, 2, 90. 120.

**Plaster,** subst. (O. Edd. *plaister* or *plaster*) 1) composition of lime, water and sand, used to overlay walls: Mids. III, 1, 70.

2) a salve applied to sores: Ven. 916. Tp. II, 1, 139. John V, 2, 13.

**Plaster,** vb. (O. Edd. *plaister*) to overlay, to cover: *biles and plagues p. you o'er,* Cor. I, 4, 32 (?).= to cover with a view to conceal defects: *the harlot's cheek, beautied with —ing art,* Hml. III, 1, 51.

**Plasterer** (O. Edd. *playsterer*), a bricklayer; in contempt: *thy father was a p.* H6B IV, 2, 140.

**Plat,** subst. braid of hair: *her hair, nor loose nor tied in formal p.* Compl. 29.

**Plat,** vb. to braid, to plait: *this is that very Mab that —s the manes of horses,* Rom. I, 4, 89. *a —ed hive of straw,* Compl. 8.

**Plate,** subst. 1) any flat piece of metal; hence a piece of money: *realms and islands were as —s dropped from his pocket,* Ant. V, 2, 92.

2) silver wrought into articles of household furniture: Shr. II, 349. R2 II, 1, 161. 210. H4B II, 1, 153. H8 III, 2, 125. Rom. I, 5, 8. Tim. III, 2, 23. Ant. V, 2, 138. Cymb. I, 6, 189.

3) armour, in *Breastplate,* q. v.

**Plate,** vb. to clothe in armour: *—d in habiliments of war,* R2 I, 3, 28. *p. sin with gold, and the strong lance of justice hurtless breaks,* Lr. IV, 6, 169 (O. Edd. *place*). *like —d Mars,* Ant. I, 1, 4.

**Platform,** 1) a terrace, an esplanade: Hml. I, 2, 213. 252. Oth. II, 3, 124.

2) plan, scheme: *lay new —s to endamage them,* H6A II, 1, 77.

**Plausible,** pleased, contented, willing, ready: *answer his requiring with a p. obedience,* Meas. III, 1, 253.

**Plausibly,** contentedly, willingly, readily: *the Romans p. did give consent to Tarquin's everlasting banishment,* Lucr. 1854.

**Plausive,** pleasing, specious, plausible: *his p. words he scattered not in ears, but grafted them,* All's I, 2, 53. *it must be a very p. invention that carries it,* IV, 1, 29. *some habit that too much o'erleavens the form of p. manners,* Hml. I, 4, 30.

**Plautus,** the celebrated Roman comedy-writer: Hml. II, 2, 420.

**Play,** subst. 1) any exercise or action intended for pleasure; opposed to work: *he from forage will incline to p.* LLL IV, 1, 93. *all hid; an old infant p.* IV, 3, 78. *death should have p. for lack of work,* All's I, 1, 23 (cf. the verb in Ant. V, 2, 232 and 322). *primo, secundo, tertio, is a good p.* Tw. V, 39.

2) game for amusement or for a prize: *with whom thou wast at p.* Tp. V, 185. *the p. so lies,* Wint. IV, 4, 669 (quibbling). *if I make my p.* H8 I, 4, 46. V, 1, 60. *shall hold ye p. these two months,* V, 4, 90. Figuratively: *in plain shock and even p. of battle,* H5 IV, 8, 114. Used of a match of fence: *before you fall to p.* Hml. V, 2, 217 (or verb?).

3) a dramatic composition or representation; in a proper and a metaphorical sense: Ven. 359. Mids. I, 2, 9. 67. III, 1, 53 (*we p. our p.*). III, 2, 11 (*to rehearse a p.*). IV, 1, 223. As Epil. 4. Shr. Ind. 2, 136.

All's V, 3, 335. H4A II, 4, 531 (*p. out the p.*). H4B V, 5, 125. H5 Prol. 34. Troil. Prol. 26. 29. Hml. II, 2, 460. 618 (*sitting at a p.*). III, 2, 95 (*coming to the p.*). V, 2, 31 etc. etc.

4) practice, manner of acting; with the adjectives *fair* and *foul: fair p.* Tp. V, 175. John V, 2, 118. H8 IV, 2, 36. Troil. V, 3, 43. *foul p.:* Tp. I, 2, 62. John IV, 2, 93. H4A III, 2, 169. Hml. I, 2, 256. Per. IV, 3, 19. *what foul p. had we?* Tp. I, 2, 60. *played foul p. with our oaths,* LLL V, 2, 766. *do me no foul p.* Lr. III, 7, 31.

**Play,** vb. 1) to sport, to do anything not as a task, but for pleasure: *my curtal dog, that wont to have —ed, —s not at all,* Pilgr. 273. *he will shoot no more, but p. with sparrows,* Tp. IV, 100. *let the boys leave to p.* Wiv. IV, 1, 12. 81. LLL V, 2, 235. As I, 3, 76. Wint. I, 2, 187. H4A I, 2, 228. Hml. III, 2, 283. Oth. II, 1, 116. Ant. V, 2, 232. 322. Per. II, 1, 34 etc. Applied to fencing: *—ing at sword and dagger,* Wiv. I, 1, 294. *to p. with him,* Hml. IV, 7, 106. V, 2, 206. 217.

2) to toy, to dally: *be bold to p., our sport is not in sight,* Ven. 124. *the wind would p. with his locks,* 1090. *her hair —ed with her breath,* Lucr. 400. *the canker-blooms p. as wantonly,* Sonn. 54, 7. *as with your shadow I with these did p.* 98, 14. *a blossom —ing in the wanton air,* Pilgr. 230 and LLL IV, 3, 104. *when she will p. with reason and discourse,* Meas. I, 2, 190. *as the waving sedges p. with wind,* Shr. Ind. 2, 55. *lust doth p. with what it loathes,* All's IV, 4, 24. *p. with some rich jewel,* Tw. II, 5, 66. *a bank for love to lie and p. on,* Wint. IV, 4, 130. *—s fondly with her tears and smiles,* R2 III, 2, 9. *p. with flowers,* H5 II, 3, 15. *my master rather —ed than fought,* Cymb. I, 1, 162 etc.

3) to make sport, to practise merriment or illusion: *a very trick for them to p. at will,* Wint. II, 1, 52. With *on* or *upon: how every fool can p. upon the word,* Merch. III, 5, 48. *the most notorious geck and gull that e'er invention —ed on,* Tw. V, 352. *I'ld p. incessantly upon these jades,* John II, 385 (i. e. fire upon them). *is it fantasy that —s upon our eyesight?* H4A V, 4, 138. *whom both the waters and the wind, in that vast tennis-court, have made the ball for them to p. upon,* Per. II, 1, 65. cf. Hml. III, 2, 380. 389. Followed by *with: p. with all virgins so,* Meas. I, 4, 33. *so p. the foolish throngs with one that swoons,* II, 4, 24. *can sick men p. so nicely with their names?* R2 II, 1, 84. *p. with your fancies, and behold ....,* H5 III Prol. 7. *p. and trifle with your reverence,* John I, 1, 133. *who with half the bulk o' the world —ed as I pleased,* Ant. III, 11, 64. *do not p. with that which is so serious,* Cymb. IV, 2, 230 etc.

4) to move irregularly, to wanton, to dangle, to hover (cf. Sonn. 54, 7. Pilgr. 230): *fortune p. upon thy prosperous helm, as thy auspicious mistress,* All's III, 3, 7; cf. *victory, with little loss, doth p. upon the dancing banners of the French,* John II, 307. *whiles warm life —s in that infant's veins,* III, 4, 132. *and bid you p. it off,* H4A II, 4, 18 (= toss it off). *as —s the sun upon the glassy streams,* H6A V, 3, 62. *the cap —s in the right hand, thus,* Tim. II, 1, 19. *those happy smilets that —ed on her ripe lip,* Lr. IV, 3, 22.

5) to perform on an instrument of music, to make music: *Pluto winks while Orpheus —s,* Lucr. 553. *he —s false. How, out of tune?* Gent. IV, 2, 59. *p., music,*

Ado V, 4, 123. LLL V, 2, 211. 216. As V, 4, 184. Shr. III, 1, 22. III, 2, 185. Tw. I, 1, 1 etc. *I will p. on the tabor*, LLL V, 1, 160. Mids. II, 1, 67. V, 122. Tw. I, 3, 26. H4B Ind. 20. H6A I, 4, 96. Hml. III, 2, 366. 380. 389. Per. I, 1, 84 etc. Transitively: *when thou music —est*, Sonn. 128, 1. *the tune of our catch, —ed by the picture of Nobody*, Tp. III, 2, 135. Gent. IV, 2, 70. As IV, 3, 68. Caes. IV, 3, 269 etc.

6) to contend in a game, for pleasure or for gain: *you p. me false*, Tp. V, 172. *p. with Mardian* (at billiards) Ant. II, 5, 4. Followed by *at: Nestor play at push-pin with the boys*, LLL IV, 3, 169. *when he —s at tables*, V, 2, 326. *if Hercules and Lichas p. at dice*, Merch. II, 1, 32. Tw. II, 5, 207. III, 4, 129. R2 III, 4, 3. H4B II, 4, 266. H5 IV Chor. 19. IV, 5, 8. Troil. IV, 4, 89. Tim. I, 2, 12. Hml. V, 1, 100. Ant. II, 3, 25 etc. With *for: when lenity and cruelty p. for a kingdom*, H5 III, 6, 119. IV, 5, 8. Rom. III, 2, 13. Transitively; a) the game being the object: *p. some heavenly match*, Merch. III, 5, 84. *a game —ed home*, Wint. I, 2, 248. *play fast and loose with faith*, John III, 1, 242. *you have —ed your prize*, Tit. I, 399. *a match*, Rom. III, 2, 13. Hml. V, 2, 264. 295. b) The gain or prize the object: *we'll p. with them the first boy for a thousand ducats*, Merch. III, 2, 216. *shall I p. my freedom at tray-trip?* Tw. II, 5, 207. *the French do the low-rated English p. at dice*, H5 IV Chor. 19. *and false — ed my glory unto an enemy's triumph*, Ant. IV, 14, 19.

Metaphorically, = to act: *you p. me false*, Tp. V, 172. *he —s false*, Gent. IV, 2, 59. *my mother —ed my father fair*, Meas. III, 1, 141. *if thou p. false*, Err. II, 2, 144. Merch. I, 2, 48. John I, 118. H6B III, 1, 184. Mcb. I, 5, 22. *thou —'dst most foully for it*, III, 1, 3. Transitively: *—ed some tricks of desperation*, Tp. I, 2, 209. *—s such fantastic tricks*, Meas. II, 2, 121. *—ed foul play with our oaths*, LLL V, 2, 766.

7) to act on the stage: *fit to p. in our interlude*, Mids. I, 2, 5. As II, 7, 139. Hml. II, 2, 104. Transitively: *p. the mother's part*, Sonn. 143, 12. *this part he —ed*, Tp. I, 2, 107. *when all our pageants were —ed*, Gent. IV, 4, 164. 165. LLL V, 1, 150. Mids. I, 2, 31. 93. III, 1, 53. IV, 2, 22. H4A II, 4, 531 (*p. out the play*). Hml. III, 2, 93. Per. IV, 4, 48 etc.

Hence = to act, to represent in general, to be, to prove: *those hours .... will p. the tyrants to the very same*, Sonn. 5, 3. *mine eye hath —ed the painter*, 24, 1. *to p. the watchman*, 61, 12. *p. the men*, Tp. I, 1, 11.* *your fairy has —ed the Jack with us*, IV, 197. *I have —ed the sheep in losing him*, Gent. I, 1, 73. IV, 2, 72. IV, 4, 1. Wiv. V, 1, 27. Meas. III, 2, 207. Err. II, 2, 213. LLL II, 74. Merch. II, 3, 12. III, 2, 121. Tw. I, 5, 196. III, 1, 67. John II, 135. H4A V, 1, 4. R3 IV, 2, 8 etc. etc.

**Player,** 1) one who plays in a game: *you base foot-ball p.* Lr. I, 4, 96.

2) an idler, trifler: *—s in your housewifery*, Oth. II, 1, 113.

3) a dramatic performer, actor: Mids. I, 2, 42. V, 65. 364. As II, 7, 140. Shr. Ind. 1, 77. 2, 131. H4A II, 4, 437. Troil. I, 3, 153. Caes. I, 2, 263. Mcb. V, 5, 24. Hml. II, 2, 329. 339. 365. 373. 386. 391. 406. 547. 577. 623. III, 1, 16. III, 2, 3. 32. 54. 111. 152. 289.

**Playfellow,** a companion in amusement: Mids. I, 1, 220. Wint. I, 2, 80. II, 1, 3. H6B III, 2, 302.

R3 IV, 1, 102. IV, 4, 385 (Ff *bed-fellows*). H8 I, 3, 33. Ant. III, 13, 125. Cymb. I, 1, 145. Per. Prol. 34.

**Playhouse,** a theatre: H5 II Chor. 36. H8 V, 4, 64.

**Playing-day,** not a school-day, a holiday: Wiv. IV, 1, 9.

**Plea,** 1) that which is alledged by a party in support of a demand: *no rightful p. might plead for justice there*, Lucr. 1649. *the defendant doth that p. deny*, Sonn. 46, 7. *what p. so tainted and corrupt but, being seasoned with a gracious voice, obscures the show of evil?* Merch. III, 2, 75. *that is my brother's p.* John I, 67.

2) that which is demanded in court or by any kind of pleading: *the p. of no less weight than Aquitaine*, LLL II, 7. *none can drive him from the envious p. of forfeiture, of justice and his bond*, Merch. III, 2, 284. *though justice be thy p., consider this*, IV, 1, 198. *to mitigate the justice of thy p., which if thou follow ....*, 203.

3) a law-suit: *and 'gainst myself a lawful p. commence*, Sonn. 35, 11. *how with this rage shall beauty hold a p., whose action is no stronger than a flower?* 65, 3.

**Pleached,** intertwined, interwoven: *steal into the p. bower*, Ado III, 1, 7. *with p. arms*, Ant. IV, 14, 73 (folded). cf. *Even-pleached, Impleached, Thick-pleached.*

**Plead,** 1) intr. to argue, to speak by way of persuasion (often very nearly = to speak): *impatience chokes her —ing tongue*, Ven. 217. *that love-sick Love by —ing may be blest*, 328. *her —ing hath deserved a greater fee*, 609. *all orators are dumb when beauty —eth*, Lucr. 268. *while she —s to the rough beast that knows no gentle right*, 544. *there —ing might you see grave Nestor stand*, 1401. *I will so p. that you shall say my cunning drift excels*, Gent IV, 2, 82. *p. no more*, Err. I, 1, 3. *p. you to me?* II, 2, 149. *that he did p. in earnest*, IV, 2, 3. *if he were mad, he would not p. so coldly*, V, 272. *—s he in earnest?* R2 V, 3, 100. *—ing so wisely in excuse of it*, H4B IV, 5, 181. *it fitteth not a prelate so to p.* H6A III, 1, 57 (quite = speak). *do not hear him p.* R3 I, 3, 347. *the golden fee for which I p.* III, 5, 96. *if you p. as well for them* (= in their place) *as I can say nay for myself*, III, 7, 52. *in that name doth nature p.* Tit. I, 370. *go successantly and p. to him*, IV, 4, 113. *I will be deaf to —ing and excuses*, Rom. III, 1, 197. With *against: I will p. against it with my life*, Meas. IV, 2, 192. *his virtues will p. against the deep damnation of his taking off*, Mcb. I, 7, 19. With *for* (= in favour of, or in order to obtain): *the colour in thy face shall p. for me*, Lucr. 480. *no rightful plea might p. for justice there*, 1649. *who p. for love*, Sonn. 23, 11. Gent. I, 2, 48. IV, 4, 105. Meas. II, 2, 31. 32. Err. IV, 2, 11. Mids. III, 2, 113. Shr. I, 2, 155. II, 1, 15. All's I, 2, 10. John IV, 1, 99. V, 2, 165. H6B III, 2, 289. 291. IV, 1, 122. IV, 7, 113. R3 I, 3, 87. II, 1, 130 (Ff *beg*). Tit. I, 356. 381. III, 1, 30. Oth. II, 3, 361 (*to*).

2) tr. a) to speak for, to defend: *to p. Hortensio's passion*, Shr. III, 1, 74. *p. his love-suit to her gentle heart*, H5 V, 2, 101. *our swords shall p. it in the field*, H6C I, 1, 103. *assembled to p. your cause*, H8 II, 4, 61. *the lustre in your eye —s your fair usage*, Troil. IV, 4, 121. *p. my successive title with your swords*, Tit. I, 4. *and p. my passions for Lavinia's love*, II,

1, 36. *that he may never more false title p.* Tim. IV, 3, 154.

b) to allege in support or favour of something: *I here p. a new state in thy unrivalled merit,* Gent. V, 4, 144. *he cannot p. his estimation with you; he hath been a bawd,* Meas. IV, 2, 27. *her sober virtue, years and modesty p. on her part some cause to you unknown,* Err. III, 1, 91. All's IV, 5, 95. H8 I, 1, 208. Tit. I, 45. 424. With a subordinate clause: *my heart doth p. that thou in him dost lie,* Sonn. 46, 5. *p. what I will be, not what I have been,* R3 IV, 4, 414.

c) to expose, to declare as in a law-suit: *in such a presence here to p. my thoughts,* Mids. I, 1, 61. *if he suppose that I have —ed truth,* H6A II, 4, 29. *where to his accusations he —ed still not guilty,* H8 II, 1, 13.

d) to demand as in a court of justice: *when good will is showed, the actor may p. pardon,* Ant. II, 5, 9.

**Pleader,** one who speaks in favour of another: *silenced their —s,* Cor. II, 1, 263. *if you would be your country's p.* V, 1, 36.

**Pleasance,** gaiety, merriment: *youth is full of p., age is full of care,* Pilgr. 158. *that we should with joy, p., revel and applause transform ourselves into beasts,* Oth. II, 3, 293.

**Pleasant,** 1) delightful: *stray lower, where the p. fountains lie,* Ven. 234. *the summer is less p. now,* Sonn. 102, 9. *sitting in a p. shade,* Pilgr. 375. *to make thy riches p.* Meas. III, 1, 38. Ado III, 1, 26 (—*est*). Shr. I, 1, 4. III, 1, 68. Wint. III, 1, 13. R2 IV, 98. H6B III, 2, 390. Tit. II, 3, 255. Rom. IV, 1, 106. Tim. I, 1, 63. Mcb. I, 6, 1. Hml. II, 2, 39. Lr. IV, 2, 10. V, 3, 170.

2) merry, facetious: *in that p. humour they all posted to Rome,* Lucr. Arg. 8. *you are p. and speak apace,* Meas. III, 2, 120. *as p. as ever he was,* Ado I, 1, 37. LLL IV, 1, 131. V, 1, 4. V, 2, 360. 790. Shr. Ind. 2, 132. I, 2, 47. II, 247. IV, 5, 72. Wint. IV, 4, 190. H4B V, 3, 147. H5 I, 2, 281. H8 I, 4, 90. Cymb. I, 6, 59. *to be p. with* = to be facetious with, to play upon: *that I have been thus p. with you both,* Shr. III, 1, 58. H5 I, 2, 259. Troil. III, 1, 67.

**Pleasantly,** sportively, merrily: *thinkest thou to catch my life so p.* Troil. IV, 5, 249.

**Pleasant-spirited,** merry: *a p. lady,* Ado II, 1, 355.

**Please,** 1) to gratify, to be to the taste of a person; absol.: *my project was to p.* Tp. Epil. 13. *that sport best —s,* LLL V, 2, 517. Mids. III, 1, 10. As Epil. 18. Wint. IV, 4, 338. Oth. IV, 1, 222 etc. Transitively: *a nurse's song ne'er — d her babe so well,* Ven. 974. *if my slight Muse do p. these curious days,* Sonn. 38, 13. 147, 4. Tp. I, 2, 85. Gent. II, 1, 137. 138. 139. Wiv. III, 3, 189. Meas. II, 4, 32. IV, 1, 13. Err. II, 1, 56. Mids. III, 2, 120. As I, 2, 240. III, 5, 112. V, 2, 127. Shr. IV, 4, 39. Tw. III, 4, 23. 25. V, 417. H4B V, 5, 114. Ant. IV, 10, 2 etc. Passively: *if your honour seem but —d,* Ven. Dedic. 3. *if —d themselves, others they think delight in such-like circumstance,* Ven. 843.

2) to gratify, to give pleasure, to content, to amuse: *to p. him* (the day) *thou art bright,* Sonn. 28, 9. *how many tales to p. me hath she coined,* Pilgr. 93. *you may .... much p. the absent duke, if peradventure he shall ever return to have hearing of this business,* Meas. III, 1, 209. *go home with it and p. your wife withal,* Err. III, 2, 178. *and I will p. you what you will de-*

mand, IV, 4, 52. *he both —s men and angers them,* Ado II, 1, 146. *how to p. the eye indeed by fixing it upon a fairer eye,* LLL I, 1, 80. *my voice is ragged: I know I cannot p. you,* As II, 5, 16. *more at your request than to p. myself,* 23. *he cut it to p. himself,* IV, 4, 78. *till I have —d my discontented peers,* John IV, 2, 126 (= appeased, reconciled). *dost p. thyself in it* (a villain's office)? Tim. IV, 3, 238. *do not p. sharp fate to grace it with your sorrows,* Ant. IV, 14, 135. *p. your thoughts in feeding them with those my former fortunes,* IV, 15, 52. *perhaps they will but p. themselves upon her,* Per. IV, 1, 101 (= satisfy their desire). —*d* = gratified, contented, happy: *grief best is —d with grief's society,* Lucr. 1111. *who in despite of view is —d to dote,* Sonn. 141, 4. *she would be best —d to be so angered with another letter,* Gent. I, 2, 102. *he will scarce be —d withal,* II, 7, 67. *these* (heaven and earth) *are —d,* V, 4, 80. *I am best —d with that,* LLL V, 2, 229. Merch. III, 2, 136. *the buzzing —d multitude,* 182. *so you stand —d withal,* 211. *I thank you for your wish and am well —d to wish it back on you,* III, 4, 43. As II, 5, 43. Shr. II, 305. IV, 4, 107. Wint. IV, 4, 495. John II, 531. IV, 1, 86. R2 II, 1, 187. IV, 217. V, 5, 40. H6B I, 1, 218. IV, 10, 25. Troil. IV, 1, 64 etc. = in good humour, not angry: *be not angry; I am —d again,* H6B I, 2, 55. *Herod of Jewry dare not look upon you but when you are well —d,* Ant. III, 3, 4.

3) Used as a word of ceremony, = to like, to vouchsafe, to allow; a) in the passive: *wilt thou be —d to hearken to the suit?* Tp. III, 2, 44. *if you be —d, retire into my cell,* IV, 161. *an the heavens were so —d that thou wert my bastard,* LLL V, 1, 79. *if I be —d to give ten thousand ducats to have it baned,* Merch. IV, 1, 45. *if the heavens had been —d, would we had so ended,* Tw. II, 1, 21. *be —d that I shake off these names,* V, 76. *be —d then to pay that duty,* John II, 246. *if heaven be —d that you must use me ill,* IV, 1, 55. *which if He be —d I shall perform,* H4A III, 2, 154. *the king is —d you shall to the Tower,* H8 I, 1, 213. *you may be —d to catch at mine intent by what did here befall me,* Ant. II, 2, 41. *be —d to tell us,* II, 6, 29. *be —d awhile,* Cymb. V, 5, 356 (= vouchsafe to listen to what I have to say) etc. The participle adjectively: —*d Fortune does of Marcus Crassus' death make me revenger,* Ant. III, 1, 2 (= it is the pleasure of Fortune to make me etc.).

b) in the active voice (the third person of the present *please* or *pleases,* indiscriminately): 1) used personally: *it rested in your grace to unloose this tied-up justice when you —d,* Meas. I, 3, 32. *let me say no, my liege, an if you p.* LLL I, 1, 50. *if you p. to shoot another arrow,* Merch. I, 1, 147. *if you had — d to have defended it,* V, 204. *as I p.* Shr. IV, 3, 80. *if he p., my hand is ready,* V, 2, 178. *where we p. to have it grow,* All's II, 3, 164. *if she —d,* III, 5, 71. *when he p. again to be himself,* H4A I, 2, 224. *when he p. to make commotion,* H6B III, 1, 29. *command in Anjou what your honour —s,* H6A V, 3, 147. Gent. IV, 4, 46. Meas. III, 1, 51. Ado II, 1, 95. 96. Merch. II, 6, 23. Shr. III, 1, 20. III, 2, 211. 214. IV, 4, 32. As I, 1, 70. II, 7, 49. V, 2, 65. All's II, 3, 64. 90. Wint. IV, 4, 532. John IV, 2, 3. H4B V, 2, 77. H6A III, 2, 110. V, 1, 24. V, 4, 173. R3 I, 2, 176. III, 2, 99 (Ff *your lordship p. to ask;* Qq *it please your l.*). H8 I, 1, 170. II, 2, 50. Tit. IV, 2, 168. Hml. III, 2, 76. Ant. III,

11, 64. V, 1, 9. V, 2, 18 etc. Partic. —*ing* = willing: *relish your nimble notes to* —*ing ears*, Lucr. 1126. (such as will hear them). Peculiar passage: *heaven hath* —*d it so, to punish me with this*, Hml. III, 4, 173.

2) impersonally (*to* before a following infinitive inserted or omitted indiscriminately): *will't p. you taste of what is here?* Tp. III, 3, 42. *will't p. you go?* Gent. I, 2, 140. *to-morrow, may it p. you, Don Alphonso with other gentlemen ... are journeying*, I, 3, 39. 52. *will't p. your worship to come in?* Wiv. I, 1, 275. *the better that it* —*s your worship to ask*, I, 4, 144. Meas. III, 2, 209. IV, 1, 59. *I had rather it would p. you I might be whipt*, V, 511. *p. it your grace lead on*, Ado I, 1, 160. *her hair shall be of what colour it p. God*, II, 3, 37. *father, as it p. you*, II, 1, 56. 59. *it* —*s your worship to say so*, III, 5, 21. *p. it your majesty command me any service?* LLL V, 2, 311. *it* —*th his greatness to impart*, V, 1, 112. *it* —*s him to call you so*, As IV, 1, 66. *howe'er it* —*s you to take it so*, All's V, 3, 88. *it* —*d your highness to overbear it*, John IV, 2, 36. *it* —*d your majesty to turn your looks from us*, H4A V, 1, 30. *one it* —*s me to call my friend*, H4B II, 2, 44. *as long as it* —*s his grace*, H5 IV, 7, 114. Mids. V, 359. Shr. Ind. 2, 2. III, 2, 20. IV, 4, 1. All's III, 6, 117. Tw. II, 3, 107. V, 119. Wint. IV, 4, 457. H4B IV, 1, 2. H6A I, 2, 74. H6B II, 4, 80. R3 I, 2, 211. III, 1, 136. III, 2, 99. H8 II, 4, 114. Ant. II, 5, 41. *what p. yourself*, Err. III, 2, 175. *in what part of your body* —*th me*, Merch. I, 3, 152. *to like as much of this play as p. you*, As Epil. 14. *may direct his course as p. himself*, R3 II, 2, 129 etc. Conditionally; with *an: not so, an 't p. your worship*, Wiv. II, 2, 37. *yes, an't p. you, sir*, Meas. II, 1, 205. Merch. II, 2, 61. H6A V, 4, 10. H6B II, 4, 76. With *if: where, if it p. you, you may intercept him*, Gent. III, 1, 43. Meas. II, 1, 47. 53. V, 449. Ado III, 2, 87. Merch. I, 3, 33. As I, 2, 120 etc. Oftenest with *so: so it p. thee hold that nothing me a something sweet to thee*, Sonn. 136, 11. *on a trice, so p. you, were we divided from them*, Tp. V, 238. *so p. you, this friar hath been with him*, Meas. III, 2, 224. LLL II, 164. Mids. V, 106. Merch. IV, 1, 2. 380. As I, 1, 97. I, 2, 166. Shr. Ind. 1, 82. I, 2, 276. Tw. V, 324. H5 V, 2, 352. H6B I, 1, 39. II, 3, 51. II, 4, 17. III, 1, 315. V, 1, 76. H6C II, 6, 98. Tim. V, 1, 162. Caes. III, 1, 140. Lr. IV, 7, 17. Cymb. IV, 2, 394 etc. The conjunction omitted: *p. you, farther*, Tp. I, 2, 65. *p. you, sir, do not omit the heavy offer of it*, II, 1, 193. V, 318. Gent. I, 2, 7. I, 3, 73. II, 1, 120. 135. IV, 4, 126. V, 4, 168. Meas. II, 4, 64. Err. I, 2, 27. Wint. II, 1, 131. V, 1, 180. H6C III, 2, 78. Cymb. III, 4, 18. *p. but your honour hear me*, Meas. II, 2, 28. *p. your lordship, here is the wine*, Tim. III, 1, 32. *p. it you, as much in private*, LLL V, 2, 240. H4B IV, 4, 101. *p. it your grace, there is a messenger*, Gent. III, 1, 52. *p. it this matron to eat with us*, All's III, 5, 100. H6B I, 3, 184. IV, 9, 23. Cor. V, 6, 140. —*d you to do't at peril of your soul*, Meas. II, 4, 67. Sometimes the form of the indicative employed: —*th you walk with me down to his house, I will discharge my bond*, Err. IV, 1, 12. —*th your lordship to meet his grace*, H4B IV, 1, 225. —*th your grace to answer them directly*, IV, 2, 52. —*th your grace to appoint...., we will....*, H5 V, 2, 78. —*th your majesty to give me leave, I'll muster up my friends*, R3 IV, 4, 488 (Qq *please it*). —*th your highness, ay*,

Cymb. I, 5, 5. *P. you* or *so p. you*, sometimes a courteous answer in the affirmative: *will you hear the letter? So p. you*, As IV, 3, 37. *who's there? my woman Helen?* P. *you, madam*, Cymb. II, 2, 1. *darest thou resolve to kill a friend of mine?* P. *you, but I had rather kill two enemies*, R3 IV, 2, 71 (Qq *ay, my lord*). cf. Ado III, 2, 87 and H5 V, 2, 352. Similarly: *is it yourself? If you shall p. so, pilgrim*, All's III, 5, 47.

**Please-man**, a pickthank: LLL V, 2, 463.

**Pleasing**, subst. pleasure, arbitrary will, command: *he capers to the lascivious p. of a lute*, R3 I, 1, 13.

**Pleasing**, adj. agreeable, delightful, pretty: *who all in one, one p. note do sing*, Sonn. 8, 12. *music hath a far more p. sound*, 130, 10. *the p. punishment that women bear*, Err. I, 1, 47. *never object p. in thine eye*, II, 2, 117. *a pretty p. pricket*, LLL IV, 2, 57. *more p. stuff*, Shr. Ind. 2, 142. *a gown more quaint, more p.* IV, 3, 102. *a p. eye*, H4A II, 4, 465. *p. heaviness*, III, 1, 218. *to whom I would be p.* H6C IV, 1, 73. *a passing p. tongue*, R3 I, 1, 94. *a p. cordial*, II, 1, 41. *seem p. to her tender years*, IV, 4, 342. *upon a p. treaty*, Cor. II, 2, 59. *p. smiles*, Tit. II, 3, 267. *such p. eloquence*, III, 1, 83. *some p. tale*, II, 2, 47. V, 1, 119. *a very p. night to honest men*, Caes. I, 3, 43. *a p. shape*, Hml. II, 2, 629. *p. harmony*, Per. II, 5, 28.

**Pleasure**, subst. 1) delight, gratification, enjoyment, amusement; objectively and subjectively: Ven. 1140. Lucr. 860. 890. 1478. Sonn. 8, 4. 52, 4. 97, 2. 121, 3. 126, 9. Tp. III, 1, 7. III, 2, 125. Meas. III, 2, 248. Mids. IV, 1, 175. As I, 2, 7. V, 4, 198. Shr. II, 251. All's II, 4, 37. V, 3, 326. Tw. II, 4, 71. 72. III, 3, 2. III, 4, 151. John III, 3, 35. IV, 3, 68. R2 I, 3, 262. H4A II, 4, 458. H6B I, 2, 45. H6C II, 2, 53. R3 I, 1, 31. Troil. I, 3, 178. III, 1, 25. Cor. II, 1, 35. Caes. III, 2, 255. *Mcb. II, 1, 13 (*in unusual p.*). IV, 3, 71. Lr. I, 1, 83. IV, 6, 123. Oth. I, 3, 376 (*thou dost thyself a p.*) etc. etc. *to take p.* = to be delighted, to find amusement: Ven. 1101. Shr. I, 1, 39. *pray 'em take their* —*s*, H8 I, 4, 74. With *in*: Ado II, 3, 262. Tw. II, 4, 69. Ant. I, 5, 9.

2) will, choice, command: Tp. I, 2, 190. IV, 165. Gent. II, 4, 117. IV, 3, 10. Meas. I, 1, 27. II, 1, 192. II, 2, 3. II, 4, 31. V, 240. 527. LLL I, 2, 132. II, 27. V, 1, 92. Merch. III, 2, 323 (*use your p.*). As I, 3, 72. All's III, 1, 16. Tw. III, 4, 65. John III, 1, 252 (*to do your p.*). H4A V, 5, 28. H4B III, 2, 65. H6A III, 1, 158. V, 4, 164. H6B I, 1, 138. I, 2, 56. II, 1, 73. IV, 1, 140. R3 IV, 2, 21 (*do*). H8 I, 2, 68. I, 4, 64. Rom. I, 2, 37. Tim. I, 2, 126. Caes. II, 1, 286 (*dwell I but in the suburbs of your good p.?* i. e. are you tied to me by no duty? and can you do, with regard to me, as you please?). Hml. II, 2, 28. Lr. III, 2, 19. Ant. I, 5, 8. Cymb. II, 3, 85 etc. etc. *at p.:* Sonn. 48, 12. All's V, 3, 279. H6A I, 2, 6. Tit. IV, 4, 86. *at one's p.:* Meas. IV, 2, 213. LLL V, 1, 90. Mids. IV, 1, 62. Shr. I, 1, 54. H4A I, 2, 191. H6B I, 3, 124. I, 4, 82. H6C IV, 2, 17. Troil. III, 1, 25. Cor. II, 1, 34. Oth. IV, 2, 244. Ant. V, 2, 182. Cymb. II, 1, 6 etc. *for one's p.* H4B II, 4, 129. Rom. III, 1, 58. *of p.* = of one's own accord, voluntarily: *art thou a messenger, or come of p.?* H6B V, 1, 16. *to speak one's p.* = to say too much, to go too far: *you speak your* —*s*, H8 III, 2, 13 (i. e. take care what you say; it is not without danger to speak one's mind). *you speak your fair p., sweet queen*, Troil. III, 1, 51

(you are too kind). *your lordship speaks your p.* Tim. III, 1, 35.

**Pleasure**, vb. to gratify, to fulfil the wish of: *what I do is to p. you*, Wiv. I, 1, 251. *draw, to p. us*, Ado V, 1, 129. *may you stead me? will you p. me?* Merch. I, 3, 7. *what pleases him shall p. you*, H6C III, 2, 22. *I count it one of my greatest afflictions, that I cannot p. such an honourable gentleman*, Tim.III,2,63.

**Pleat**, see *Plait*.

**Plebeians**, the common people of ancient Rome: H5 V Chor. 27. Cor. I, 9, 7. II, 1, 10. 106. III, 1, 101. V, 4, 39. Tit. I, 231. Ant. IV, 12, 34.

**Plebeii**, the same: Cor. II, 3, 192.

**Plebs**; *tribunal p.*, the clown's blunder for *tribunus plebis:* Tit. IV, 3, 93.

**Pledge**, subst. 1) a pawn, a gage: *there is my p.* H6A IV, 1, 120. *this jewel, p. of my affection*, V, 1, 47. *what p. have we of thy firm loyalty?* H6C III, 3, 239. *now the p.* Troil. V, 2, 65. 77. *there is my p.* Lr. V, 3, 94. *that recognizance and p. of love*, Oth. V, 2, 214.

2) surety, bail: *1 am Grumio's p.* Shr. I, 2, 45. *I am in parliament p. for his truth*, R2 V, 2, 44. *all my sons, as —s of my fealty*, H6B V, 1, 50. *he leaves his —s dearer than his life*, Tit. III, 1, 292. *bid him demand what p. will please him best*, IV, 4, 106. *let the emperor give his —s*, V, 1, 163.

3) a drinking to the health of another: *my heart is thirsty for that noble p.* Caes. IV, 3, 160. *our duties, and the p.* Mcb. III, 4, 92. *bray out the triumph of his p.* Hml. I, 4, 12.

**Pledge**, vb. 1) to secure by a pledge: *to p. my vow, I give my hand*, H6C III, 3, 250.

2) to answer in drinking to the health of a person: *I p. your grace*, H4B IV, 2, 73. V, 3, 57. *I'll p. you all*, H6B II, 3, 66. *here's to your ladyship, and p. it, madam*, H8 I, 4, 47. *—s the breath of him in a divided draught*, Tim. I, 2, 48. *this health to Lepidus! I'll p. it for him*, Ant. II, 7, 91. *and p. him freely*, Per. II, 3, 78.

**Plenitude**, plenty, abundance: *in him a p. of subtle matter, applied to cautels, all strange forms receives*, Compl. 302.

**Plenteous**, copious, exuberant, abundant: *her p. womb expresseth his full tilth*, Meas. I, 4, 43. *a most p. crop*, As III, 5, 101. *Ceres' p. load*, H6B I, 2, 2. *p. tears*, R3 II, 2, 70. *honour and p. safety*, H8 I, 1, 104. *to gratulate thy p. bosom*, Tim. I, 2, 131. *made p. wounds*, III, 5, 66. *from forth thy p. bosom*, IV, 3, 186. *my p. joys*, Mcb. I, 4, 33. *with p. rivers*, Lr. I, 1, 66. *of so high and p. wit*, Oth. IV, 1, 201.

**Plenteously**, copiously: H4B IV, 5, 40.

**Plentiful**, copious, abundant: *so p. an excrement*, Err. II, 2, 79. *if reasons were as p. as blackberries*, H4A II, 4, 265 (Ff and the later Qq *plenty*). *they have a p. lack of wit*, Hml. II, 2, 202. *having work more p. than tools to do't*, Cymb. V, 3, 9.

**Plentifully**, copiously: LLL V, 2, 2. As I, 1, 17. Wint. IV, 4, 338.

**Plenty**, abundance: Ven. 20. 545. Lucr. 557. As III, 2, 21. Tw. II, 3, 51. R3 V, 5, 34. H8 V, 5, 48. Tim. III, 5, 67. Mcb. II, 3, 6. IV, 3, 71. Cymb. III, 6, 21. V, 4, 145. V, 5, 458. Per. I, 4, 22 and 52 (fem.). Plur. *—es: peace, dear nurse of arts, —es and joyful births*, H5 V, 2, 35.

Adjectively: *earth's increase, foison p.* Tp. IV,

110. *if reasons were as p. as blackberries*, H4A II, 4, 265 (Q1 *plentiful*).

**Pleurisy**, see *Plurisy*.

**Pliant**, fit, convenient: *took once a p. hour*, Oth. I, 3, 151.

**Plight**, subst. 1) state, condition: *Lucrece, in this lamentable p.* Lucr.Arg. 17. *how can I return in happy p.* Sonn. 28, 1. *my doleful p.* Pilgr. 277. *in better p. for a lender than you*, Wiv. II, 2, 172. Wint. II, 1, 118. H6C III, 3, 37. Troil. III, 2, 168 (*to keep her constancy in p. and youth outliving beauty's outward*). Tit. III, 1, 103. IV, 4, 32. Mcb. I, 2, 2. Ant. V, 2, 33.

2) pledge, assurance given: *that lord whose hand must take my p. shall carry half my love with him*, Lr. I, 1, 103.

**Plight**, vb. to pledge; with *faith:* Lucr. 1690. LLL V, 2, 283. Tw. IV, 3, 26. H6A V, 3, 162. With *troth:* Lr. III, 4, 128. Cymb. I, 1, 96.

**Plighted**, folded: *time shall unfold what p. cunning hides*, Lr. I, 1, 283 (Qq *pleated*).

**Plighter**, that which pledges or engages: *your hand, this kingly seal and p. of high hearts*, Ant. III, 13, 126.

**Plod**, 1) to walk heavily and laboriously: *the beast that bears me —s dully on*, Sonn. 50, 6. *trudge, p. away o' the hoof*, Wiv. I, 3, 91. *barefoot p. I the cold ground upon*, All's III, 4, 6. *though patience be a tired mare, yet she will p.* H5 II, 1, 26. *—ed by my foot-cloth mule*, H6B IV, 1, 54. Transitively: *if one of mean affairs may p. it* (the way) *in a week*, Cymb. III, 2, 53.

2) to toil, to drudge: *universal —ing poisons up the nimble spirits*, LLL IV, 3, 305. *I have laid by my majesty and —ed like a man for working-days*, H5 I, 2, 277.

**Plodder**, a toiler, a drudge: *small have continual —s ever won save base authority from others' books*, LLL I, 1, 86.

**Plot**, subst. 1) a spot of ground: *why should my heart think that a several p. which my heart knows the wide world's common place?* Sonn. 137, 9. *this green p. shall be our stage*, Mids. III, 1, 3. *to cull the —s of best advantages*, John II, 40. *this blessed p., this earth*, R2 II, 1, 50. *we first survey the p.* H4B I, 3, 42. *the p. of situation*, 51. *I'll maintain my words on any p. of ground*, H6A II, 4, 89. *in this private p. be we the first*, H6B II, 2, 60 (= sequestered spot). *were there but this single p. to lose, this mould of Marcius*, Cor. III, 2, 102 (O. Edd. *single p.*, to *loose this* etc.). *many unfrequented —s*, Tit. II, 1, 115. *to an obscure p.* II, 3, 77. *this sandy p. is plain*, IV, 1, 69. *fight for a p. whereon the numbers cannot try the cause*, Hml. IV, 4, 62. *the prettiest daisied p.* Cymb. IV, 2, 398. Quibbling in H6B I, 4, 59.

2) a scheme: Tp. III, 2, 117. IV, 141. Gent. III, 1, 12. Wiv. IV, 4, 13. 45. IV, 6, 32. Meas. IV, 5, 2. Merch. I, 1, 133. All's III, 7, 44. IV, 3, 360. Tw. II, 5, 84. Wint. II, 1, 47. R2 IV, 324. H4A I, 3, 279. II, 3, 14. 19. 20. 23. H6B I, 4, 59. R3 III, 4, 62. H8 I, 1, 220. III, 2, 60. Troil. I, 3, 181. Cor. III, 1, 38. 41. IV, 4, 19. Tit. V, 2, 6. Hml. V, 2, 9. 406. Lr. II, 1, 75. III, 6, 96 (*upon*). IV, 6, 279 (*upon*). Ant. IV, 12, 49. Cymb. II, 1, 64. *to lay a p.:* Lucr. 1212. Wiv. III, 2, 39. III, 3, 202. John III, 4, 146. R2 IV, 334. H4A II, 1, 57. II, 3, 18. H6A II, 3, 4. R3 I, 1, 32.

**Plot**, vb. to scheme, to contrive; absol.: *then she*

—s, *then she ruminates,* Wiv. II, 2, 320. Trans.: Lucr. 879. Tp. IV, 88. Gent. II, 4, 183. II, 6, 43. Shr. I, 1, 193. R2 I, 1, 100. I, 3, 189. IV, 10. V, 5, 18. H4A I, 3, 274. H6A I, 1, 24. IV, 4, 3. H6B III, 1, 153. Tit. II, 1, 78. III, 1, 134. V, 1, 129. With an inf.: *had* —ed *with them to take my life,* Tp. V, 273. —ed *to murder me,* R3 III, 5, 38.

**Plot-proof,** not to be hurt by plots: Wint. II, 3, 6.
**Plotter,** contriver: Tit. V, 3, 122.
**Plough,** subst. instrument with which furrows are cut in the ground: *to hold the p.* (= to be a ploughman) LLL V, 2, 893.

**Plough,** vb. to turn up the ground in order to sow seed: Cor. III, 1, 71. Metaphorically: *wounds* —ed *up with neighbours' sword,* R2 I, 3, 128. *yoke you like draught-oxen and make you p. up the wars,* Troil. II, 1, 117. *let the Volsces p. Rome and harrow Italy,* Cor. V, 3, 34. *this sword shall p. thy bowels up,* Tit. IV, 2, 87. —est *the foam,* Tim. V, 1, 53. *he* —ed *her, and she cropped,* Ant. II, 2, 233. *let Octavia p. thy visage up with her nails,* IV, 12, 38. *she shall be* —ed, Per. IV, 6, 154.

**Plough-iron,** the coulter: H4B V, 1, 20.
**Ploughman,** one that uses the plough: Lucr. 958. Mids. II, 1, 94. V, 380. LLL V, 2, 914. Troil. I, 1, 59.
**Plough-torn,** turned up by the plough: *p. leas,* Tim. IV, 3, 193.

**Pluck,** 1) to pull off, to gather, to pick; applied to flowers or fruits: Ven. 416. 528. 574. 946. Sonn. 98, 8. Pilgr. 131. 238. 240 and LLL IV, 3, 112. 114. Tp. II, 2, 164. Merch. I, 1, 18 (—ing *the grass, to know where sits the wind*). R2 III, 2, 19. H4A II, 3, 10. H6A II, 4, 30. 33. 36. 37. 39. 47. 49. 129. Oth. V, 2, 13. Per. IV, 6, 46. *to p. up* = to tear up by the root: *and by the spurs* —ed *up the pine and cedar,* Tp. V, 47. *the weeds ... are* —ed *up root and all by Bolingbroke,* R2 III, 4, 52 (Ff *pulled*). *such withered herbs are meet for* —ing *up,* Tit. III, 1, 179. *as if he* —ed *up kisses by the roots that grew upon my lips,* Oth. III, 3, 423.

2) to pull, to tug, to tear; absol.: —ing *to unfix an enemy,* H4B IV, 1, 208. Transitively: *liberty* —s *justice by the nose,* Meas. I, 3, 29. V, 343. —s *dead lions by the beard,* John II, 138. Lr. III, 7, 36. *p. him by the elbow,* H4B I, 2, 81. *by the sleeve,* Caes. I, 2, 179. With adverbs or prepositional expressions denoting an effect: *p. them asunder,* Hml. V, 1, 287. *as he* —ed *his cursed steel away,* Caes. III, 2, 181. *you p. my foot awry,* Shr. IV, 1, 150. *whose overweening arm I have* —ed *back,* H6B III, 1, 159. —s *it back again,* Rom. II, 2, 181. *to p. down* = a) to pull or throw down: *let's p. him down* (from the throne) H6C I, 1, 59. *p. Aufidius down by the hair,* Cor. I, 3, 33. cf. *p. down my officers, break my decrees,* H4B IV, 5, 118. *to p. down justice from your awful bench,* V, 2, 86. b) to demolish, to overthrow: *p. down the rich,* Ven. 1150. *all houses must be* —ed *down,* Meas. I, 2, 99. II, 1, 65. *your cares set up do not p. my cares down,* R2 IV, 195. *to p. a kingdom down and set another up,* H4B I, 3, 49. *who set thee up and* —ed *thee down,* H6C V, 1, 26. *Ajax employed* —s *down Achilles plumes,* Troil. I, 3, 386. *do one p. down another,* III, 3, 86. *p. down benches, forms,* Caes. III, 2, 263. 264. — —ing *the entrails of an offering forth,* Caes. II, 2, 39. *p. off the bull's horns,* Ado I, 1, 265. —s *off my beard,* Hml. II, 2, 600. *pursue him to his*

*house and p. him thence,* Cor. III, 1, 309. *his guilty hand* —ed *up the latch,* Lucr. 358. *and p. up drowned honour by the locks,* H4A I, 3, 205. *to p. out: p. me out all the linen,* Wiv. IV, 2, 155. *p. out his eyes,* Meas. IV, 3, 124. Err. IV, 4, 107. Mcb. II, 2, 59. Lr. I, 4, 324. III, 7, 5. *to p. it out* (the sting) Shr. II, 212. *p. out the multitudinous tongue,* Cor. III, 1, 155. *p. it* (a hair) *out,* Troil. I, 2, 179. *you would p. out the heart of my mystery,* Hml. III, 2, 382. *it* —s *out brains and all,* Oth. II, 1, 128. — *to p. him from his horse,* Ven. 30. *to p. the quills from ancient ravens' wings,* Lucr 949. —ed *the knife from Lucrece' side,* 1807. *p. the keen teeth from the fierce tiger's jaws,* Sonn. 19, 3. *a team of horse shall not p. that from me,* Gent. III, 1, 266. *to p. this crawling serpent from my breast,* Mids. II, 2, 146. *p. the wings from painted butterflies,* III, 1, 175. *p. the young cubs from the she-bear,* Merch. II, 1, 29. *my rights and royalties* —ed *from my arms perforce,* R2 II, 3, 121. *to p. him headlong from the throne,* V, 1, 65. *to p. bright honour from the pale-faced moon,* H4A I, 3, 202. *I* —ed *this glove from his helm,* H5 IV, 7, 162. *p. the crown from Henry's head,* H6B V, 1, 2. H6C III, 1, 153. —ed *two crutches from my feeble limbs,* R3 II, 2, 58. *and from her jealous arms p. him perforce,* III, 1, 36. *from Cupid's shoulder p. his painted wings,* Troil. III, 2, 15. *p. the mangled Tybalt from his shroud,* Rom. IV, 3, 52. *p. the grave senate from the bench,* Tim. IV, 1, 5. *p. the lined crutch from thy old limping sire,* 14. *p. stout men's pillows from below their heads,* IV, 3, 32 (to make them die). *these growing feathers* —ed *from Caesar's wing,* Caes. I, 1, 77. *I would have* —ed *my nipple from his boneless gums,* Mcb. I, 7, 57. *p. from the memory a rooted sorrow,* V, 3, 41. *I may be* —ed *into the swallowing womb of this deep pit,* Tit. II, 3, 239. *to p. him off me,* Shr. IV, 1, 80. *stakes* —ed *out of hedges,* H6A I, 1, 117. *will you p. your sword out of his pilcher by the ears?* Rom. III, 1, 83. *p. but his name out of his heart,* Caes. III, 3, 38. *to p. a dainty doe to ground,* Tit. II, 2, 26. *I have no strength to p. thee to the brink,* II, 3, 241. *may all the building in my fancy p. upon my hateful life,* Lr. IV, 2, 85.

Used of garments or ornaments put on or taken off with some force: *p. my magic garment from me,* Tp. I, 2, 24. *p. the borrowed veil of modesty from the so seeming Mistress Page,* Wiv. III, 2, 41. *nor p. it* (the ring) *from his finger,* Merch. V, 173. *we must have your doublet and hose* —ed *over your head,* As IV, 1, 207. *mend the* —ing *off the other* (boot) Shr. IV, 1, 151. *p. but off these rags,* Wint. IV, 3, 55. *p. it o'er your brows* (i. e. a hat) IV, 4, 665. *that high royalty* (i. e. the crown; cf. R3 V, 5, 6) *was ne'er* —ed *off,* John IV, 2, 5. *the cloak of night being* —ed *off from their backs,* R2 III, 2, 45. *from the commonest creature p. a glove,* R2 V, 3, 17. *the fifth Harry from curbed licence* —s *the muzzle of restraint,* H4B IV, 5, 131. *they will p. the gay new coats o'er the French soldiers' heads,* H5 IV, 3, 118. *this long-usurped royalty from the dead temples of this bloody wretch have I* —ed *off,* R3 V, 5, 6. *he* —ed *me ope his doublet,* Caes. I, 2, 267. *their hats are* —ed *about their ears,* II, 1, 73. *off, p. off!* Ant. IV, 14, 37. *she* —ed *it off to send it me,* Cymb. II, 4, 104.

3) to strip of feathers: *since I* —ed *geese,* Wiv. V, 1, 26. *we'll p. a crow together,* Err. III, 1, 83 (a proverbial expression, = we have to settle accounts).

*an argument that he is —ed, when hither he sends so poor a pinion of his wing,* Ant. III, 12, 3.

4) to draw (without the idea of force or violence): *I here could p. his highness' frown upon you,* Tp. V, 127. *to p. his indignation on thy head,* All's III, 2, 32. *the angle that —s our son thither,* Wint. IV, 2, 52. *they will p. away his natural cause and call them meteors,* John III, 4, 156. *you p. a thousand dangers on your head,* R2 II, 1, 205. *when youth with comeliness —ed all gaze his way,* Cor. I, 3, 8. *to p. proud Lucius from the warlike Goths,* Tit. IV, 4, 110. *modest wisdom —s me from over-credulous haste,* Mcb. IV, 3, 119. *that stroke, which since hath —ed him after,* Lr. IV, 2, 78. *to p. the common bosom on his side,* V, 3, 49. *how she —ed him to my chamber,* Oth. IV, 1, 145. *that our stirring can from the lap of Egypt's widow p.* Antony, Ant. II, 1, 37. With *back: if Nature, as thou goest onwards, still will p. thee back,* Sonn. 126, 6 (= will not let thee become old). *more straining on for —ing back,* Wint. IV, 4, 476. *one that will either push on or p. back thy business there,* 762. *the hand could p. her back that shoved her on,* Ant. I, 2, 131. With *on,* = to excite, to cause: *to p. on others,* Meas. II, 4, 147. *may rather p. on laughter than revenge,* Tw. V, 374. *hath —ed on France to tread down fair respect,* John III, 1, 57. *sin will p. on sin,* R3 IV, 2, 65.

With *from,* = to derive, to receive, to obtain: *not from the stars do I my judgment p.* Sonn. 14, 1. *and p. commiseration of his state from brassy bosoms,* Merch.IV, 1,30. *I did p. allegiance from men's hearts,* H4A III, 2, 52. *—s comfort from his looks,* H5 IV Chor. 42. *would p. reproof and rebuke from every ear that heard it,* Cor. II, 2, 37. *thus to have said, ... had from him —ed either his gracious promise,* II, 3, 200. *did not p. such envy from him,* Hml. IV, 7, 75. *I would not thy good deeds should from my lips p. a hard sentence,* Cymb. V, 5, 289. *cf. his speech sticks in my heart. Mine ear must p. it thence,* Ant. I, 5, 42.

5) Even without *from,* = to get, to obtain, to win: *a word for shadows like myself, as take the pain, but cannot p. the pelf,* Pilgr. 192. *a man may draw his heart out, ere a' p. one* (a good woman in a lottery) All's I, 3, 93. With *down: what my prayers p. down,* All's I, 1, 78. *can I do this, and cannot get a crown? tut, were it farther off, I'll p. it down,* H6C III, 2, 195.

6) to take away: *to p. all fears out of you,* Meas. IV, 2, 206. *thy sad aspect hath from the number of thy banished years —ed four away,* R2 I, 3, 211. *thou canst p. nights from me, but not lend a morrow,* 228. *wilt thou p. my fair son from my age?* V, 2, 92. *if the opposed numbers p. their hearts from them,* H5 IV, 1, 309. *and from the cross-row —s the letter G,* R3 I, 1, 55. *all this from my remembrance brutish wrath sinfully —ed,* II, 1, 119. *p. off a little,* H8 II, 3, 40 (= let us descend still lower). *to p. from them their tribunes for ever,* Cor. IV, 3, 25. *such a deed as from the body of contraction —s the very soul,* Hml. III, 4, 46. *to p. away* = to make away with: *the caterpillars of the commonwealth, which I have sworn to weed and p. away,* R2 II, 3, 167. *seeking means to p. away their power,* Cor. III, 3, 96.

7) *p. up thy spirits* = raise thy spirits, take courage: *p. up thy spirits; look cheerfully upon me,* Shr. IV, 3, 38. Intr. *p. up* = collect thyself: *p. up, my heart, and be sad,* Ado V, 1, 207.

**Plucker-down,** overthrower: *thou setter up and p. of kings,* H6C II, 3, 37.

**Plum,** the fruit of the tree Prunus domestica Ven. 527. Pilgr. 135. John II, 162. H6B II, 1, 101

**Plume,** subst. feathers which serve to adorn, particularly a tuft of feathers worn as an ornament: *he* (the horse) *vails his tail that, like a falling p., cool shadow to his melting buttock lent,* Ven. 314. *as diminish one dowle that's in my p.* Tp. III, 3, 65 (= wing? or is Ariel supposed to wear a plumage on his head? O. Edd. *plumbe*). *my gravity could I with boot change for an idle p.* Meas. II, 4, 11. *he; that with the p.* All's III, 5, 81. *how he jets under his advanced —s,* Tw. II, 5, 37 (= a turkey-cock). *no p. in any English crest,* John II, 317. *shame sits mocking in our —s,* H5 IV, 5, 5. *with nodding of their —s,* Cor. III, 3, 126. Emblem of pride: *we'll pull his —s,* H6A III, 3, 7. *Ajax employed plucks down Achilles' —s,* Troil. I, 3, 386. *what p. of feathers is he that indicted this letter? what vane? what weathercock?* LLL IV, 1, 96.

**Plume,** vb., with *up,* = to trick up, to make proud, to make to triumph: *to get his place and to p. up my will in double knavery,* Oth. I, 3, 399.

**Plumed,** wearing plumes: H4A IV, 1, 98. H6A V, 3, 25. Lr. IV, 2, 57. Oth. III, 3, 349.

**Plume-plucked,** humbled, brought down: R2 IV, 108.

**Plummet,** a plumb-line, by which the depth of water is sounded: Tp. III, 3, 101. V, 56. *ignorance itself is a p. o'er me,* Wiv. V, 5, 173 (Tyrwhitt: ignorance itself is not so low as I am, by the length of a plummet line. Grant White: ignorance itself points out my deviations from rectitude. Perhaps: ignorance itself sounds my depth and searches my bottom. Johnson: *has a plume o' me.* Farmer: *is a planet o'er me*).

**Plump,** full, round, fleshy: *my flesh is soft and p.* Ven. 142. *banish p. Jack,* H4A II, 4, 527.

**Plumpy,** the same: *p. Bacchus,* Ant. II, 7, 121.

**Plum-tree,** the tree Prunus domestica: H6B II, 1, 97. Hml. II, 2, 201.

**Plunge,** vb. 1) tr. to put under water, to immerse: Shr. I, 1, 23. Figuratively: *do not p. thyself too far in anger,* All's II, 3, 222. *thou wouldst have —d thyself in riot,* Tim. IV, 3, 255. *would p. him into far more choler,* Hml. III, 2, 318.

2) intr. a) to dive, to rush into water: Tp. I, 2, 211. Mids. III, 2, 48. Tim. III, 5, 13. Caes. I, 2, 105.

b) to pitch, to thrust out one's limbs in water· *like an unpractised swimmer —ing still,* Lucr. 1098.

**Plural,** more than one: *better have none than p.* faith, Gent. V, 4, 52. Term of grammar: *genitive case p.* Wiv. IV, 1, 59.

**Plurisy,** a plethora, redundancy of blood: *goodness, growing to a p., dies in his own too much,* Hml. IV, 7, 118.

**Pluto,** the god of the infernal regions: Lucr. 553. H4B II, 4, 169. Troil. IV, 4, 129. V, 2, 102. 153. Cor. I, 4, 36. Tit. IV, 3, 13. 37.

**Plutus,** the god of gold and riches: All's V, 3, 101. Troil. III, 3, 197 (Q *everything*). Tim. I, 1, 287. Caes. IV, 3, 102.

**Ply,** 1) to urge, to importune, to press hard: *he —es the duke at morning and at night,* Merch. III, 2, 279. *p. her hard,* As III, 5, 76. H6C III, 2, 50. *canst thou not guess wherefore she —es thee thus?* Tit. IV, 1, 15. *—es Desdemona to repair his fortunes,* Oth. II,

3, 360. IV, 1, 107. *he —ed them both with excellent praises*, Ant. III, 2, 14.

2) to apply to, to practise: *p. his book*, Shr. I, 1, 201. *go p. thy needle*, II, 25. *I must p. my theme*, Tit. V, 2, 80. *let him p. his music*, Hml. II, 1, 73.

**Po**, river in Italy: John I, 203.

**Pocket**, subst. a bag inserted in a garment: Tp. II, 1, 65. 91. Wiv. I, 4, 56. Meas. III, 2, 50. Ado V, 4, 89. LLL III, 20. Merch. II, 2, 201. All's IV, 3, 228. Tw. V, 35. H4A II, 4, 580. III, 3, 61. 70. 93. 113. 114. 176. 178. 181. 190. H5 III, 2, 51. 54. V, 1, 65. H6A III, 1, 80. H6B IV, 2, 97. Cor. II, 1, 135. Caes. IV, 3, 253. Hml. III, 4, 101. Lr. I, 2, 33. IV, 6, 261. Oth. V, 2, 309. Ant. V, 2, 92. Cymb. III, 1, 44. V, 5, 280.

**Pocket**, vb., with *up*, = to put in the pocket: *let me p. up my pedlar's excrement*, Wint. IV, 4, 734. Metaphorically, = to take no notice of: *or very falsely p. up his report*, Tp. II, 1, 67. *you did p. up my letters*, Ant. II, 2, 73. *to p. up wrong* = to suffer wrong without resenting it: John III, 1, 200. H4A III, 3, 183 and H5 III, 2, 54 (quibbling).

**Pocky**, infected with syphilis: *p. corses*, Hml. V, 1, 181.

**Poem**, poetical composition: *scene individable, or p. unlimited*, Hml. II, 2, 419.

**Poesy**, 1) the art of a poet: *much is the force of heaven-bred p.* Gent. III, 2, 72. *our p. is as a gum*, Tim. I, 1, 21.

2) poetical compositions: *and under thee their p. disperse*, Sonn. 78, 4. *the elegancy, facility, and golden cadence of p.* LLL IV, 2, 126. *music and p. use to quicken you*, Shr. I, 1, 36.

**Poet**, an author of fiction, a writer of metrical compositions: Sonn. 17, 7. 11. 32, 13. 79, 7. 83, 4. 14. Pilgr. 115. Gent. III, 2, 78. LLL IV, 3, 346. Mids. V, 7. 12. 15. Merch. V, 79. As III, 3, 8. 26. H5 III, 6, 39. H6C I, 2, 31. R3 I, 4, 46. Tit. II, 4, 51. IV, 1, 57. Tim. I, 1, 220. 226. IV, 3, 356. Caes. III, 3, 32. Hml. II, 2, 372. Ant. III, 2, 16.

**Poetical**, possessing the sense or the peculiar qualities of poetry: *I would the gods had made thee p.* As III, 3, 16. 17. 24. *'tis p.* Tw. I, 5, 207.

**Poetry**, 1) the art of a poet: *if music and sweet p. agree*, Pilgr. 103. *neither savouring of p., wit, nor invention*, LLL IV, 2, 165.

2) poetical compositions, verse: *like cutler's p.* Merch. V, 149. *the truest p. is the most feigning*, As III, 3, 19. 20. 21. Shr. I, 1, 93. I, 2, 170. H4A III, 1, 134. Tit. IV, 1, 14.

**Poictiers**, town and province (Poitou) in France: John I, 11. II, 487. H6A I, 1, 61. IV, 1, 19 (M. Edd. *Patay*). IV, 3, 45.

**Poins**, name: Wiv. III, 2, 74. H4A I, 2, 118 etc. H4B II, 2, 35 etc,

**Point**, subst. 1) the sharp end of an instrument: *with javelin's p.* Ven. 616. *thy spear's p.* 626. Wiv. III, 5, 113. Ado II, 3, 264. IV, 1, 110. Wint. III, 3, 87. R2 I, 3, 74. IV, 40. V, 5, 53 *(a dial's p.); cf.* H4A V, 2, 84. H5 II Chor. 9. IV, 4, 9. H6B IV, 10, 74. H6C I, 3, 37. I, 4, 80. II, 3, 16. V, 6, 27. R3 I, 2, 96. V, 1, 24. Troil. V, 2, 151 (cf. Wint. III, 3, 87). Tit. IV, 2, 71. 85. V, 3, 63. Rom. IV, 3, 57. Caes. III, 1, 173. Hml. V, 2, 332. *I saw him hold Lord Percy at the p.* H4A IV, 4, 21 (cf. Holinshed: *kept him at the sword's p.*). Pars pro toto, = sword: *turn face*

*to face and bloody p. to p.* John II, 390; Rom. III, 1, 165. *thus I bore my p.* H4A II, 4, 216. 224. 238. *p. against p. rebellious*, Mcb. I, 2, 56. *the enemy's p.* Tit. V, 3, 111. *beats down their fatal —s*, Rom. III, 1, 171. *I'll touch my p. with this contagion*, Hml. IV, 7, 147. *between the pass and fell incensed —s of mighty opposites*, V, 2, 61. Figuratively: *blunting the fine p. of seldom pleasure*, Sonn. 52, 4. *how sharp the p. of this remembrance is*, Tp. I, 2, 138. *the thorny p. of bare distress*, As II, 7, 94. *the sharp thorny —s of my alleged reasons*, H8 II, 4, 224.

2) a tagged lace, used to tie parts of the dress, especially the breeches: *with two broken —s*, Shr. III, 2, 49. *mingle eyes with one that ties his —s*, Ant. III, 13, 157. Worn for ornament: *for a silken p. I'll give my barony*, H4B I, 1, 53. *God's light, with two —s on your shoulder?* II, 4, 142 (perhaps a mark of his commission). Quibbling: *I am resolved on two —s. That, if one break, the other will hold*, Tw. I, 5, 25. *their —s being broken — Down fell their hose*, H4A II, 4, 238. cf. Wint. IV, 4, 206.

3) the pommel of a saddle: *beat Cut's saddle, put a few flocks in the p.* H4A II, 1, 7.

4) a stop in writing: *come we to full —s here, and are etceteras nothing?* H4A II, 4, 198 (quibbling).

5) an exactly defined part of space or time: *swim to yonder p.* Caes. I, 2, 104. *arrive the p. proposed*, 110. *I have touched the highest p. of all my greatness*, H8 III, 2, 223. *thou wert dignified enough, even to the p. of envy, to be styled the under-hangman of his kingdom*, Cymb. II, 3, 133. *which makes her story true, even to the p. of her death*, All's IV, 3, 67. *to prove it on thee to the extremest p. of mortal breathing*, R2 IV, 47. *vows obedience till the p. of death*, H6A III, 1, 168. *when men are at the p. of death*, Rom. V, 3, 88. *at p.* = on the point, about, going: *you are at p. to lose your liberties*, Cor. III, 1, 194. *almost at p. to enter*, V, 4, 64. *and are at p. to show their open banner*, Lr. III, 1, 33. *who was once at p. to master Caesar's sword*, Cymb. III, 1, 30. *at p. to sink for food*, III, 6, 17. *at p. of death*, Tw. V, 121. H6B III, 2, 369.

6) highest elevation, summit: *touching now the p. of human skill*, Mids. II, 2, 119. *what a p. your falcon made*, H6B II, 1, 5 (= how high she soared). Hence used to denote a state of perfection and readiness: *say what the play treats on, then read the names of the actors, and so grow to a p.* Mids. I, 2, 10. *come we to full —s here*, H4B II, 4, 198 (quibbling). *armed at all —s*, R2 I, 3, 2. Hml. I, 2, 200 (Qq *at p.*). *I do enjoy at ample p. all that I did possess*, Troil. III, 3, 89. *at a p.* or *at p.* = completely, in full preparation for any emergency: *old Siward, with ten thousand warlike men, already at a p., was setting forth*, Mcb. IV, 3, 135. *armed at p. exactly, cap-a-pe*, Hml. I, 2, 200 (Ff. *at all points*). *to let him keep at p. a hundred knights*, Lr. I, 4, 347. cf. *Appointed*.

7) a division of the mariner's compass: *to all the —s o' the compass*, Cor. II, 3, 25. = direction, side in general: *let your best love draw to that p. which seeks best to preserve it*, Ant. III, 4, 21.

8) state, situation, predicament: *the state of Normandy stands on a tickle p.* H6B I, 1, 216. *Rome and her rats are at the p. of battle*, Cor. I, 1, 166. *at such a p., when half to half the world opposed*, Ant. III, 13, 8. *he's at some hard p.* Cymb. III, 4, 16.

9) subject, matter, question: *touching that p.* Meas.

I, 1, 84. *errea in this p.* II, 1, 15. *one of the —s in which women still give the lie to their consciences,* As III, 2, 409. *I am resolved on two —s,* Tw. I, 5, 25. *—s more than all the lawyers can handle,* Wint. IV, 4, 206 (quibbling). *the p. of my petition,* H8 I, 2, 16. *to this p. hast thou heard him at any time speak aught?* 145. *I speak my good lord cardinal to this p.* II, 4, 166. *in such a p. of weight,* III, 1, 71. *in this p. all his tricks founder,* III, 2, 39. *the main p. of this our after-meeting,* Cor. II, 2, 43. *there's a fearful p.* Rom. IV, 3, 32. *I took your hands, but was indeed swayed from the p. by looking down on Caesar,* Caes. III, 1, 219. *which is now our p. of second meeting,* Mcb. III, 1, 86. *to this p. I stand,... only I'll be revenged,* Hml. IV, 5, 133. *stand aloof from the entire p.* Lr. I, 1, 243. *my p. and period will be throughly wrought, as this day's battle's fought,* IV, 7, 96. *touch you the sourest —s with sweetest terms,* Ant. II, 2, 24. *make my senses credit thy relation to —s that seem impossible,* Per. V, 1, 125.

10) the main question, the precise thing to be considered: *this is the p.* Meas. I, 4, 49. H5 III, 2, 108. *but to the p.* (= to the purpose) Meas. II, 1, 100. H4A IV, 3, 89. *that's not to the p.* Wint. III, 3, 91. *ay, there's the p.* Wiv. I, 1, 229. H4B I, 3, 18. Oth. III, 3, 228. Ant. II, 6, 31. Cymb. III, 4, 156. *here lies the p.* H4A II, 4, 448. Hml. V, 1, 10. *let me know the p.* Meas. III, 1, 73.

11) single thing or subject, article, particular: *do all —s of my command,* Tp. I, 2, 500. *examine him upon that p.* Ado V, 1, 322. *that I did suit me all —s like a man,* As I, 3, 118. *he does obey every p. of the letter,* Tw. III, 2, 83. *the fail of any p. in it,* Wint. II, 3, 171. *this dangerous conception in this p.* H8 I, 2, 139. *with all their honourable —s of ignorance,* I, 3, 26. *in this p. charge him home,* Cor. III, 3, 1. *all our service in every p. twice done,* Mcb. I, 6, 15. *the due of honour in no p. omit,* Cymb. III, 5, 11. *from p. to p.* All's III, 1, 1. V, 3, 325. *p. from p.* IV, 3, 72. *p. by p.* H6C II, 5, 24. H8 I, 2, 7. Per. V, 1, 227. *to p. or to the p.* = in every article, exactly: *hast thou performed to p. the tempest?* Tp. I, 2, 194. *agree with his demands to the p.* Meas. III, 1, 254.

12) punctilio, nice respect: *this fellow doth not stand upon —s,* Mids. V, 118 (is not over-scrupulous). *wherefore stand you on nice —s?* H6C IV, 7, 58. Hence nearly = respect in general: *he takes on the p. of honour to support so dissolute a crew,* R2 V, 3, 11. *'tis a p. of friendship,* H4A V, 1, 122. *it is a p. of wisdom,* R3 I, 4, 99.*and in that p. I will conclude to hate her,* Cymb. III, 5, 77 (= in that respect, therefore).

13) a signal given by the blast of a trumpet: *to a loud trumpet and a p. of war,* H4B IV, 1, 52. Hence = direction, command: *Aufidius obeys his —s as if he were his officer,* Cor. IV, 6, 125.

14) *no p.,* in imitation of the French *non point,* = not at all, by no means; for the sake of quibbling: LLL II, 190. V, 2, 277.

**Point,** vb. 1) to sharpen, to make as thin and small as a point: *till the diminution of space had —ed him sharp as my needle,* Cymb. I, 3, 19.

2) to direct towards an object, to aim: *here, as I p. my sword,* Caes. II, 1, 106. *a figure for the time of scorn to p. his finger at,* Oth. IV, 2, 55.

3) to direct the finger, to note as with the finger; absol.: *how the giddy multitude do p.* H6B II, 4, 21. With *at: the dial —s at five,* Err. V, 118. *now must*

*the world p. at poor Katharine,* Shr. III, 2, 18. *whence they gape and p. at your industrious scenes and acts of death,* John II, 375. *why art thou so —ed at?* H4A II, 4, 449. *—s at them for his,* Mcb. IV, 1, 124. = to call attention to, to mention: *our then dictator, whom with all praise I p. at,* Cor. II, 2, 94. = to aim at, to menace: *in a time when fearful wars p. at me,* Cymb. IV, 3, 7. With *on,* = a) to be directed to (to send rays on): *whatsoever star —s on me graciously with fair aspect,* Sonn. 26, 10. *his golden beams to you here lent shall p. on me and gild my banishment,* R2 I, 3 147. b) to aim at: *find Hector's purpose —ing on him,* Troil. I, 3, 331. *these are portents, but yet I hope, they do not p. on me,* Oth. V, 2, 46. *they are portentous things unto the climate that they p. upon,* Caes. I, 3, 32. With *to,* = a) to point at: *whereto my finger is —ing still,* R2 V, 5, 54. *and —ed to this brace,* Per. II, 1, 133. b) to tend to, to be destined for: *most poor matters p. to rich ends,* Tp. III, 1, 4. *they* (mine ends) *—ed to the good of your person,* H8 III, 2, 172. *who would not wish to be from wealth exempt, since riches p. to misery and contempt?* Tim. IV, 2, 32. *for any benefit that —s to me,* IV, 3, 526.

4) to show as with the finger: *as we p. the way,* Caes. IV, 1, 23. With *forth: the which shall p. you forth at every sitting what you must say,* Wint. IV, 4, 572. *thy lopped branches p. thy two sons forth,* Cymb. V, 5, 454. With *out: day seems to p. her out where she sits weeping,* Lucr. 1087. *doth p. out thee as his triumphant prize,* Sonn. 151, 9. *will these mossed trees page thy heels and skip where thou —est out?* Tim. IV, 3, 225. Hence = to direct: *who, tendering their own worth from where they were glassed, did p. you to buy them,* LLL II, 245 (Ff p. out to). *I'll p. you where you shall have such receiving as shall become your highness,* Wint. IV, 4, 537. *as your business and desire shall p. you,* Hml. I, 5, 129.

5) to appoint (spelt *'point,* in this sense, by M. Edd.): *whoever plots the sin, thou —est the season,* Lucr. 879. *nor can I fortune to brief minutes tell, —ing to each his thunder, rain and wind,* Sonn. 14, 6. *I'll not be tied to hours nor —ed times,* Shr. III, 1, 19. *this is the —ed day,* III, 2, 1. *p. the day of marriage,* 15.

**Point-blank,** with a certain aim, so as not to miss: *as easy as a cannon will shoot p. twelve score,* Wiv. III, 2, 34. Substantively: *now art thou within p. of our jurisdiction regal,* H6B IV, 7, 28 (Cade's speech).

**Point-device** or **Point-devise,** affectedly nice, finical: *such insociable and p. companions,* LLL V, 1, 21. *you are rather p. in your accoutrements,* As III, 2, 401. Adverbially, = exactly: *I will be p. the very man,* Tw. II, 5, 176.

**Pointing-stock,** a butt, a laughing-stock: H6B II, 4, 46.

**Poise,** subst. weight: *equal p. of sin and charity,* Meas. II, 4, 68. *so is the equal p. of this fell war,* H6C II, 5, 13. *the great swing and rudeness of his p.* Troil. I, 3, 207. *occasions of some p.* Lr. II, 1, 122 (O. Edd. prize). *full of p. and difficult weight,* Oth. III, 3, 82.

**Poise,** vb. 1) to weigh: *we, —ing us in her defective scale, shall weigh thee to the beam,* All's II, 3, 161. *p. the cause in justice' equal scales,* H6B II, 1, 204. *our imputation shall be oddly —d,* Troil. I, 3, 339. *both merits —d,* IV, 1, 65. *herself —d with herself,* Rom. I, 2, 100.

2) to counterbalance: *if the balance of our lives*

*had not one scale of reason to p. another of sensuality,* Oth. I, 3, 331.

**Poison**, subst. that which artificially, and by means not obvious to the sight, destroys or injures life: Ven. 1143. Tp. III, 3, 105. Wiv. I, 3, 110. Err. II, 2, 145. V, 70. Ado II, 2, 21. V, 1, 253. As I, 1, 157. V, 1, 60. Tw. II, 5, 123. Wint. I, 2, 321. John I, 213. V, 7, 9. 46. R2 I, 1, 173. V, 6, 38. H4A II, 2, 49. H4B I, 1, 137. H6B III, 2, 45. 321. III, 3, 18. R3 I, 2, 146. 147. III, 1, 14. IV, 1, 62 (Ff *venom*). H8 III, 2, 283. Cor. III, 1, 87. 157. Rom. I, 2, 51. II, 3, 24. III, 3, 44. III, 5, 98. IV, 3, 24. V, 1, 50. 60. 80. 83. 85. V, 3, 162. 165. 288. Tim. III, 1, 62. IV, 1, 32. IV, 3, 25. 109. 296. 435. Mcb. III, 2, 24. Hml. IV, 5, 76. V, 2, 339. 364. Lr. IV, 7, 72. V, 3, 96 (Ff *medicine*). Oth. III, 3, 325. 389. IV, 1, 216. 220. Ant. I, 2, 201 (*a serpent's p.*). I, 5, 27. V, 2, 348. Cymb. I, 1, 128. I, 5, 34. III, 3, 77. V, 5, 47. 213. 238. 250. Per. I, 1, 133 (in serpents). 139. 155.

**Poison**, vb. to infect, injure, or kill with poison; absol.: H6C I, 4, 112. Cor. III, 1, 88. Rom. III, 2, 46. Hml. III, 2, 244. Lr. III, 6, 70 (*tooth that —s*). Transitively: Lucr. 1072. 1659. 1707. Sonn. 114, 13. 118, 14. Compl. 301. Merch. III, 1, 68. All's III, 5, 87. Wint. III, 2, 161. John V, 6, 23. V, 7, 35. R2 III, 2, 159. H4A I, 3, 233. H5 IV, 1, 268. Tit. III, 2, 73. Mcb. I, 7, 11. IV, 1, 5. Hml. III, 2, 272. IV, 1, 43. V, 2, 303. 321. 330. Lr. I, 3, 227. 240. Ant. III, 13, 160. V, 2, 343. Cymb. I, 6, 126. V, 5, 156. 243. Per. IV, 4, 10. Metaphorically, = to taint, to corrupt: *thou wouldst have —ed good Camillo's honour*, Wint. III, 2, 189. *my valour's —ed*, Cor. I, 10, 17. *whose welcome had —ed mine*, Lr. II, 4, 39. *p. his delight*, Oth. I, 1, 68. *p. this young maid's affections*, I, 3, 112. *—ed hours*, Ant. II, 2, 90. = to destroy: *plodding —s up the nimble spirits in the arteries*, LLL IV, 3, 305 (most M. Edd. *prisons*). *boiling choler chokes the hollow passage of my —ed voice*, H6A V, 4, 121. *that we have been familiar, ingrate forgetfulness shall p.* Cor. V, 2, 92. *that bare vowel I shall p. more than the death-darting eye of cockatrice*, Rom. III, 2, 46. *the object —s sight*, Oth. V, 2, 364. cf. *Empoison.*

**Poisoner**, one who poisons: Wint. I, 2, 352.

**Poisonous**, having the qualities of poison, injurious to life: Lucr. 530. 777 (*clouds*). H4A V, 4, 56. H6B III, 2, 77 (*adder*). R3 I, 3, 246 (*toad*). Cor. III, 1, 221. Tim. I, 2, 144. Ant. IV, 9, 13. Cymb. I, 5, 8. = virulent: *thou p. slave*, Tp. I, 2, 319. With *of*, = destructive: *you might condemn us, as p. of your honour*, Cor. V, 3, 135.

**Poisonous-tongued:** *what false Italian, as p. as handed*, Cymb. III, 2, 5.

**Poitiers**, see *Poictiers.*

**Poke**, pocket: As II, 7, 20.

**Poking-stick**, a small iron stick used for setting the plaits of ruffs: Wint. IV, 4, 228.

**Polack**, a native of Poland: Hml. II, 2, 63. 75. IV, 4, 23. Adjectively: *the P. wars*, V, 2, 387. Dubious passage: *so frowned he once, when in an angry parle he smote the sledded —s on the ice*, Hml. I, 1, 63. O. Edd. *pollax* or *Pollax*, q. v.

**Poland**, country to the east of Germany: Meas. I, 3, 14. Hml. IV, 4, 12. V, 2, 361. Adjectively: *a P. winter* (i. e. a very long winter) Err. III, 2, 100.

**Pole**, 1) the extremity of the axis of the earth: *by the north p.* LLL V, 2, 699.

2) the pole-star: Hml. I, 1, 36. Oth. II, 1, 15. = loadstar: *the soldier's p. is fallen*, Ant. IV, 15, 65.

**Pole**, a long, slender piece of wood: LLL V, 2, 700. H6B IV, 1, 127. IV, 7, 101. 119. Mcb. V, 8, 26.*

**Pole**, = Polander: Hml. IV, 4, 21.

**Pole**; *De la P.*, name (of the Earl of Suffolk; cf. *Poole*): H6A V, 3, 67. H6B I, 1, 44. I, 2, 30. IV, 1, 45.

**Pole-axe**, an axe fixed on a pole: LLL V, 2, 580. Writing of some M. Edd. in Hml. I, 1, 63: *he smote the sledded p. on the ice.* O. Edd. *pollax;* most M. Edd. *Polacks.* cf. *Smite* and *Sledded.*

**Polecat**, the fitchew: Wiv. IV, 1, 29. Term of reproach: *you baggage, you p., you ronyon*, IV, 2, 195.

**Pole-clipt**, hedged in with poles: *thy p. vineyard*, Tp. IV, 68 (Dyce: a vineyard in which the poles are clipt, i. e. embraced, by the vines).

**Polemon**, name in Ant. III, 6, 74.

**Policy**, 1) the frame of civil government in a state: *this p. and reverence of age makes the world bitter to the best of our times*, Lr. I, 2, 48.

2) the art of managing public affairs: *turn him to any cause of p.* H5 I, 1, 45. *our nation lose the name of hardiness and p.* I, 2, 220. *and with pale p. seek to divert the English purposes*, II Chor. 14. H6B I, 1, 84. Troil. I, 3, 197. V, 4, 10. 14. 18. Cor. IV, 6, 127. Hml. II, 2, 47. Ant. II, 2, 69. II, 6, 126. Used as a fem.: H4A I, 3, 108.

3) prudent wisdom in the management of public or private concerns: *a little harm done to a great good end for lawful p. remains enacted*, Lucr. 529. *that shallow habit, wherein deep p. did him disguise*, 1815. *thus p. in love, to anticipate the ills that were not, grew to faults assured*, Sonn. 118, 9. 124, 9. Ado IV, 1, 200. LLL V, 2, 513. As V, 1, 62. Shr. II, 294. Tw. III, 2, 31. 33. R2 V, 1, 84. H4B IV, 1, 148. H6A V, 4, 159. H6B III, 1, 23. 235. 238. 293. IV, 1, 83. H6C I, 2, 58. V, 4, 62. H8 III, 2, 259. Tit. II, 1, 104. IV, 2, 148. Tim. III, 2, 94. Oth. II, 3, 274. III, 3, 14. With the def. art.: *smacks it not something of the p.?* John II, 396 (i. e. of that which you call policy?).

4) cunning, stratagem: *is there no military p., how virgins might blow up men?* All's I, 1, 132. *the gates of Rouen, through which our p. must make a breach*, H6A III, 2, 2. *'tis but his p. to counterfeit*, H6C II, 6, 65. *I'll play the hunter for thy life with all my force, pursuit and p.* Troil. IV, 1, 17. *honour and p. i' the war do grow together*, Cor. III, 2, 42. 48. Plur. *—es* = stratagems: *search out thy wit for secret —es*, H6A III, 3, 12.

**Polished**, glossy: *in p. form of well-refined pen*, Sonn. 85, 8. *O p. perturbation!* (the crown) H4B IV, 5, 23.

**Politic**, 1) relating to politics as the science of government: *I will read p. authors*, Tw. II, 5, 174.

2) versed in public affairs: *this land was famously enriched with p. grave counsel*, R3 II, 3, 20. *a certain convocation of p. worms are e'en at him*, Hml. IV, 3, 21 (Ff *convocation of worms*).

3) prudent, wise, artful, cunning: *stands hugely p.* Sonn. 124, 11. *am I p.? am I subtle?* Wiv. III, 1, 103. *which maintained so p. a state of evil that they will not admit any good part to intermingle with them*, Ado V, 2, 63. *the lawyer's melancholy, which is p.* As IV, 1, 14. *I have been p. with my friend, smooth with mine enemy*, V, 4, 46. *it is not p. in the commonwealth of nature to preserve virginity*, All's I, 1, 137. *you*

*must seem very p.* IV, 1, 24. *with silence be thou p.* H6A II, 5, 101. *bites his lip with a p. regard,* Troil. III, 3, 254. *the devil knew not what he did when he made man p.* Tim. III, 3, 29. *of such a nature is his p. love,* 35. *'tis p. and safe to let him keep at point a hundred knights,* Lr. I, 4, 346. *he shall stand no further off than in a p. distance,* Oth. III, 3, 13.

**Politician,** one versed in politics, or at least in the habit to talk of them: Tw. II, 3, 80.*III, 2, 34.* H4A I, 3, 241.*Hml. V, 1, 86.*Lr. IV, 6, 175.*

**Politicly,** prudently, wisely: Shr. IV, 1, 191. H6B III, 1, 341.

**Polixenes,** name: Wint. I, 2, 353 and passim. Troil. V, 5, 11.

**Poll,** subst. (O. Edd. mostly *Pole*) 1) head: *hath his p. clawed like a parrot,* H4B II, 4, 282. *all flaxen was his p.* Hml. IV, 5, 196.

2) a register of heads, a list of persons: *the muster-file amounts not to fifteen thousand p.* All's IV, 3, 190. *we are the greater p.* Cor. III, 1, 134. *all the voices that we have procured set down by the p.* III, 3, 10.

**Poll-ax,** see *Pole-axe.*

**Polled** (O. Edd. *pouled*) stripped, plundered: *he will mow all down before him and leave his passage p.* Cor. IV, 5, 215 (the servant's speech).

**Pollusion,** Dull's blunder for *allusion:* LLL IV, 2, 46.

**Pollute,** to soil, to stain, to defile: Lucr. 854. 1063. 1726. H6A V, 4, 43. Troil. V, 3, 17.

**Pollution,** defilement: Lucr. 1157. Meas. II, 4, 183. Tw. I, 2, 49.

**Polonius,** name: Hml. I, 2, 57. IV, 1, 34. IV, 3, 17. IV, 5, 83.

**Poltroon,** coward: *patience is for —s,* H6C I, 1, 62.

**Polydamas** (Ff *Polidamus,* Q *Polidamas*), name in Troil. V, 5, 6.

**Polydore,** name in Cymb. III, 3, 86 and passim.

**Polymnestor,** king of Thrace, not named, but alluded to in Tit. I, 138.

**Polyxena,** daughter of Priam: Troil. III, 3, 208.

**Polyxenes,** see *Polixenes.*

**Pomander,** a ball composed of perfumes: Wint. IV, 4, 609.

**Pomegranate,** the fruit of Pomus granatum: All's II, 3, 276. *p. tree,* Rom. III, 5, 4. cf. *Pomgarnet.*

**Pomewater,** a kind of apple: LLL IV, 2, 4.

**Pomfret,** place in England: John IV, 2, 148. R2 V, 1, 52. V, 4, 10. H4B I, 1, 205. H6B II, 2, 26. R3 II, 4, 42. III, 1, 183 *( P. castle ).* III, 2, 50. 85. III, 3, 9. III, 4, 92. V, 3, 140.

**Pomgarnet,** the waiter's pronunciation of *Pome-granate* (name of a room): H4A II, 4, 42 (M. Edd. *Pomegranate*).

**Pommel,** see *Pummel.*

**Pomp,** 1) magnificence, splendour: LLL I, 1, 31. Mids. I, 1, 19. As II, 1, 3. Wint. IV, 4, 499. R2 III, 2, 163. IV, 211. V, 1, 78. H5 IV, 1, 281. H6A I, 1, 142. H6C V, 2, 27. H8 I, 1, 15. 163. II, 3, 7. III, 2, 365. Tim. I, 2, 140. IV, 2, 35. IV, 3, 243. Lr. III, 4, 33. Oth. III, 3, 354.

2) a festival procession; a feast: *the pale companion is not for our p.* Mids. I, 1, 15. *go we, as well as haste will suffer us, to this unlooked for unprepared p.* John II, 560. *shall braying trumpets and loud churlish drums be measures to our p.?* III, 1, 304. *when adverse fo-*

*reigners affright my towns with dreadful p. of stout invasion,* IV, 2, 173. *safer triumph is this funeral p.* Tit. I, 176. *what need these feasts, —s and vain-glories?* Tim. I, 2, 249.

3) greatness, power: *it (my love) suffers not in smiling p., nor falls under the blow of thralled discontent,* Sonn. 124, 6 (*smiling p.* = the favour of greatness). *the house with the narrow gate, which I take to be too little for p. to enter,* All's IV, 5, 54. *to be possessed with double p.* John IV, 2, 9. *vast confusion waits the imminent decay of wrested p.* IV, 3, 154. *to think upon my p. shall be my hell,* H6B II, 4, 41. *much better she ne'er had known p.* H8 II, 3, 13. *let the candied tongue lick absurd p.* Hml. III, 2, 65. *how p. is followed!* Ant. V, 2, 151. cf. also Wint. IV, 4, 499. R2 IV, 211. H6C V, 2, 27.

**Pompeius,** the Latin form of *Pompey: Sextus P.* Ant. I, 2, 190. I, 3, 45. III, 6, 25.

**Pompey,** 1) Cneius P. the Great: Meas. II, 1, 230. LLL V, 1, 136. V, 2, 538. 550 etc. H5 IV, 1, 70. 72. H6B IV, 1, 138. Caes. I, 1, 42. 47. 56.*I, 3, 126. 152. III, 1, 115. III, 2, 192. V, 1, 75. Ant. I, 2, 195. I, 5, 31. III, 13, 118. 2) Sextus P., his son: Ant. I, 3, 49 and passim. 3) P. Bum, the clown in Meas. II, 1, 224 etc.

**Pompion,** Costard's blunder for *Pompey:* LLL V, 2, 503. 507.

**Pompous,** magnificent, splendid: As V, 4, 188. R2 IV, 250. Per. III Prol. 4.

**Pond,** a small basin of standing water: Meas. III, 1, 94. Merch. I, 1, 89. Wint. I, 2, 195. H4B I, 1, 200. Cymb. I, 4, 98.

**Ponder,** to muse, to meditate; with *on: to p. on things would hurt me more,* Lr. III, 4, 24.

**Ponderous,** 1) very heavy: *to draw with idle spiders' strings most p. and substantial things,* Meas. III, 2, 290. *why the sepulchre hath oped his p. and marble jaws,* Hml. I, 4, 50.

2) forcible, strongly impulsive: *if your more p. and settled project may suffer alteration,* Wint. IV, 4, 535. *my love's more p. than my tongue,* Lr. I, 1, 80 (Qq *richer*).

**Poniard,** subst. a dagger: Ado II, 1, 255 (cf. Hml. III, 2, 414). All's IV, 1, 83. H6C II, 1, 98. Tit. II, 3, 120. Hml. V, 2, 157.

**Pont,** the kingdom of Pontus in Asia Minor: Ant. III, 6, 72.

**Pontic:** *the P. sea,* = the Euxine or Black Sea, Oth. III, 3, 453.

**Pontifical,** belonging to a high priest: *my presence, like a robe p., ne'er seen but wondered at,* H4A III, 2, 56.

**Ponton,** French name in H6A I, 4, 28.

**Pooh** (O. Edd. *puh*) interj. expressive of contempt or disgust: Hml. I, 3, 101. V, 1, 221 (Qq *pah*).

**Pool,** a collection of stagnant water: Tp. IV, 182. 208. H6B IV, 1, 70. Lr. III, 4, 139. Cymb. III, 4, 142.

**Poole** or **Pole,** name of the Earl of Suffolk: H6A II, 4, 78. 80. 100. 114. 122. H6B I, 1, 44. I, 2, 30. I, 3, 53. IV, 1, 70.

**Poop,** subst. the hindmost part of a ship: H4A III, 3, 29. Ant. II, 2, 197.

**Poop,** vb. to strike in a fatal manner, to sink like a ship: *she quickly —ed him; she made him roast-meat for worms,* Per. IV, 2, 25 (Boult's speech).

**Poor,** 1) destitute of riches or even of any property, indigent, needy: Lucr. 693. Tp. I, 2, 20. V, 212. Gent. IV, 1, 72. Wiv. I, 3, 95. II, 1, 117. II, 2, 283. V, 5, 164. Meas. III, 1, 25. Err. I, 1, 57. Ado III, 3, 121. All's I, 3, 201. H5 IV, 1, 315. H8 IV, 2, 148 etc. etc. With *in: p. in worth,* Troil. III, 3, 130. Cor. II, 1, 18. Hml. II, 2, 280. With *of: I am p. of thanks,* Cymb. II, 3, 94.

2) of a bad quality, mean, beggarly: *most p. matters point to rich ends,* Tp. III, 1, 3. *p. descent,* Gent. III, 2, 32. *these p. habiliments,* IV, 1, 13. *I'll put myself in p. and mean attire,* As I, 3, 113. Shr. III, 2, 121. IV, 3, 173. 182. H4B V, 5, 13. *while his blood was p.* H4A IV, 3, 76. *mean and right p. blood,* H6A IV, 6, 23.

3) little, insignificant, worthless: *what were thy lips the worse for one p. kiss?* Ven. 207. *p. wretches have remorse in p. abuses,* Lucr. 269. *that p. retention could not so much hold,* Sonn. 122, 9. *stones whose rates are either rich or p.* Meas. II, 2, 150. *I have a p. pennyworth in the English,* Merch. I, 2, 76. *the twentieth part of one p. scruple,* IV, 1, 330. *p. a thousand crowns,* As I, 1, 2. *give me the p. allottery my father left me,* 77. *the —est service is repaid with thanks,* Shr. IV, 3, 45. *in their p. praise he humbled,* All's I, 2, 45. *and my p. doing eternal,* II, 3, 246. *your oaths are words and p. conditions,* IV, 2, 30. *his qualities being at this p. price,* IV, 3, 308. *those p. number saved with you,* Tw. I, 2, 10. *p. trespasses, more monstrous standing by,* Wint. III, 2, 190. *one p. pennyworth of sugarcandy,* H4A III, 3, 180. *wherefore grieve I at an hour's p. loss?* H6B III, 2, 381. *communication of a most p. issue,* H8 I, 1, 87. *for one p. grain or two,* Cor. V, 1, 27. *this is a p. epitome of yours,* V, 3, 68. *one p. root,* Tim. IV, 3, 186. *some p. fragment,* 400. *give me one p. request,* Hml. I, 5, 142. *our basest beggars are in the —est thing superfluous,* Lr. II, 4, 268. *one (life) is too p., too weak for my revenge,* Oth. III, 3, 443. *I have seen her die twenty times upon far —er moment,* Ant. I, 2, 146. *none our parts so p., but was a race of heaven,* I, 3, 36. *I had thought to have held it* (my birthday) *p.* III, 13, 186 (not to have celebrated it). *my p. self,* Cymb. I, 1, 119 etc.

4) weak, impotent: *feeble desire, all recreant, p. and meek,* Lucr. 710. *her blood, in p. revenge, held it in chase,* 1736. *in my p. and old motion,* H4B IV, 3, 37. *our p. malice remains in danger,* Mcb. III, 2, 14. *I have very p. and unhappy brains for drinking,* Oth. II, 3, 35. *as deep as these p. pickaxes can dig,* Cymb. IV, 2, 389.

5) paltry, contemptible: *a most p. credulous monster,* Tp. II, 2, 149. 170. *fear the soft and tender fork of a p. worm,* Meas. III, 1, 17. *such p., such bare, such lewd, such mean attempts,* H4A III, 2, 13. *fickle changelings and p. discontents,* V, 1, 76. *yon p. and starved band,* H5 IV, 2, 16. *rubbing the p. itch of your opinion,* Cor. I, 1, 169. *a p. unmanly melancholy,* Tim. IV, 3, 203. *thy father, that p. rag,* 271. *with what p. judgment,* Lr. I, 1, 294. *these thin habits and p. likelihoods,* Oth. I, 3, 108. *this p. trash of Venice,* II, 1, 312. *so p. a pinion of his wing,* Ant. III, 12, 4. *be shown for —est diminutives,* IV, 12, 37.

6) used as a term of compassion, = moving pity: Ven. 251. 316. 502. 578. 601. 604. 680. 697. 925. 1057. 1075. 1177 etc. etc. (the most frequent use).

7) A term of tenderness: *p. ape, how thou sweatest,*

H4B II, 4, 233. *God help thee, p. monkey,* Mcb. IV, 2, 59. Often joined to *fool;* cf. *Fool.*

8) A term of modesty, used in speaking of things pertaining to one's self: *I invite you to my p. cell,* Tp. V, 301. *in my p. opinion,* Meas. II, 1, 245. *to lean upon my p. shoulder,* LLL V, 1, 108. *under my p. instructions,* All's IV, 4, 27. *to give this p. petition to the king,* V, 1, 19. *to visit her p. castle,* H6A II, 2, 41. *my next p. petition,* H8 IV, 2, 138. *to my p. unworthy notice,* Cor. II, 3, 166. *for my own p. part,* Hml. I, 5, 131. *there's a p. piece of gold for thee,* Oth. III, 1, 26. *you o'errate my p. kindness,* Cymb. I, 4, 41.

**Poor John,** a coarse kind of fish (called also hake) salted and dried: *a very ancient and fish-like smell; a kind of not of the newest P.* Tp. II, 2, 28. *'tis well thou art not fish; if thou hadst, thou hadst been P.* Rom. I, 1, 37.

**Poorly,** 1) in indigence: *but, p. rich, so wanteth in his store, that, cloyed with much, he pineth still for more,* Lucr. 97.

2) in a mean and beggarly manner: *the counterfeit is p. imitated after you,* Sonn. 53, 6. *their ragged curtains p. are let loose,* H5 IV, 2, 41. *we two, that with so many thousand sighs did buy each other, must p. sell ourselves with the rude brevity and discharge of one,* Troil. IV, 4, 42. *my father p. led,* Lr. IV, 1, 10.

3) insignificantly: *I'll rob none but myself; and let me die, stealing so p.* Cymb. IV, 2, 16.

4) without spirit, dejectedly: *to look so p. and to speak so fair,* R2 III, 3, 128. *be not lost so p. in your thoughts,* Mcb. II, 2, 72 (cf. *poor* in Lucr. 710).

**Poor-rich** (not hyphened in O. Edd.) seemingly rich, but indeed poor: *they prove bankrupt in this p. gain,* Lucr. 140.

**Pop,** 1) to thrust suddenly and unexpectedly, to jerk: *a' —s me out from five hundred pound,* John I, 68. *for thus —ed Paris in his hardiment,* Troil. IV, 5, 28.

2) intr. to enter suddenly and unexpectedly: *he that ... —ed in between the election and my hopes,* Hml. V, 2, 65.

**Pope,** the head of the Roman catholic church: John III, 1, 135. 139. 151. 159. 171. V, 1, 3. 18. 23. 62. H6A I, 3, 50. 52. V, 1, 1. H6B I, 3, 65. H8 II, 2, 56. II, 4, 119. III, 2, 30. 220. 287.

**Popedom,** the papal dignity: H8 III, 2, 212.

**Poperin,** see *Poprin.*

**Popilius,** name in Caes. III, 1, 14. 15.

**Popinjay,** a parrot: H4A I, 3, 50.

**Popish,** bigoted: *hast a thing within thee called conscience, with twenty p. tricks and ceremonies,* Tit. V, 1, 76.

**Poppy,** the plant Papaver somniferum: Oth. III, 3, 330.

**Poprin,** a kind of pear: *O, that she were an open et caetera, thou a p. pear,* Rom. II, 1, 38. *

**Popular,** vulgar, plebeian: *that which, but by being so retired, o'erprized all p. rate,* Tp. I, 2, 92. *art thou officer? or art thou base, common and p.?* H5 IV, 1, 38. *seld-shown flamens do press among the p. throngs and puff to win a vulgar station,* Cor. II, 1, 230. *I will counterfeit the bewitchment of some p. man and give it bountiful to the desirers,* II, 3, 109. *who puts his Shall, his p. Shall, against a graver bench than ever frowned in Greece,* III, 1, 106. *and in a violent p. ignorance, given your enemy your shield,* V, 2, 43.

**Popularity,** vulgarity: *grew a companion to the common streets, enfeoffed himself to p.* H4A III, 2, 69. *any retirement, any sequestration from open haunts and p.* H5 I, 1, 59.

**Populous,** well peopled: R2 V, 5, 3. H6B III, 2, 360. Oth. I, 1, 77. IV, 1, 64. Per. IV, 6, 197. = composed of many people, numerous: *the dust ... raised by your p. troops,* Ant. III, 6, 50.

**Porch,** a vestibule, entrance: Wiv. I, 4, 63. Cor. III, 1, 240. Figuratively: *in the —es of my ears,* Hml. I, 5, 63. = portico: *in Pompey's p.* Caes. I, 3, 126.*

**Porcupine,** see *Porpentine.*

**Pore,** to look intently and closely: *painfully to p. upon a book,* LLL I, 1, 74. *dream and p. and thereon look,* IV, 3, 298. *creeping murmur and the —ing dark fills the wide vessel of the universe,* H5 IV Chor. 2, i. e. straining its eyes and yet seeing only the nearest things, purblind (i. e. *pore-blind*).*

**Pork,** flesh of swine used for food: Merch. I, 3, 34. III, 5, 39.

**Pork-eater,** one who feeds on swine's flesh: Merch. III, 5, 27.

**Porpentine** (most M. Edd. *porcupine*), the animal Hystrix cristata, now called porcupine: H6B III, 1, 363. Troil. II, 1, 27 (applied to Thersites as a term of reproach, probably on account of the prevailing opinion that the porcupine could dart its quills). Hml. I, 5, 20. Name of an inn: Err. III, 1, 116. III, 2, 172. IV, 1, 49. V, 222. 275.

**Porpus,** the animal Delphinus phocaena: Per. II, 1, 26.

**Porridge,** broth, soup: Tp. II, 1, 10. Wiv. III, 1, 64. Err. II, 2, 100. LLL I, 1, 305. All's I, 1, 173. H6A I, 2, 9. Troil. I, 2, 263. Lr. III, 4, 56.

**Porringer,** a vessel in which broth is eaten: *this* (cap) *was moulded on a p.* Shr. IV, 3, 64. *till her pinked p. fell off her head,* H8 V, 4, 50; i. e. a cap looking like a porringer.

**Port,** 1) a safe station for ships, a harbour: Merch. I, 1, 19. R2 I, 3, 276. Troil. Prol. 3. II, 2, 76. Tit. IV, 4, 38. Mcb. I, 3, 15. Lr. II, 1, 82. II, 3, 3. III, 1, 33. Ant. I, 3, 46. I, 4, 38.

2) a gate: All's III, 5, 39. Troil. IV, 4, 113. 138. Cor. I. 7, 1. V, 6, 6. Tim. V, 4, 55. Ant. IV, 4, 23. Metaphorically: *golden care that keepest the —s of slumber open wide,* H4B IV, 5, 24.

3) carriage, bearing, deportment; used only of a stately, portly appearance: *assume the p. of Mars,* H5 Prol. 6. *bear the name and p. of gentlemen,* H6B IV, 1, 19. *and with our sprightly p. make the ghosts gaze,* Ant. IV, 14, 52. Hence = state, splendid manner of living: *a more swelling p. than my faint means would grant continuance,* Merch. I, 1, 124. *the magnificoes of greatest p.* III, 2, 283. *keep house and p. and servants, as I should,* Shr. I, 1, 208. *my man Tranio, bearing my p.* III, 1, 36.

**Portable,** 1) such as may be carried from place to place: *like an engine not p.* Troil. II, 3, 144.

2) sufferable: *all these are p., with other graces weighed,* Mcb. IV, 3, 89. *how light and p. my pain seems now,* Lr. III, 6, 115.

**Portage,** 1) port-hole: *let it* (the eye) *pry through the p. of the head like the brass cannon,* H5 III, 1, 10.*

2) arrival in port (?): *thy loss is more than can thy p. quit, with all thou canst find here,* Per. III, 1, 35.*

**Portal,** door, gate: Ven. 451. Lucr. 309. R2 III, 3, 64. Hml. III, 4, 136.

**Portance,** conduct, deportment: *your loves took from you the apprehension of his present p.* Cor. II, 3, 232. *of my redemption thence and p. in my travels' history,* Oth. I, 3, 139.

**Portcullised,** shut up as with a portcullis: R2 I, 3, 167.

**Portend,** 1) to signify: *what should that alphabetical position p.?* Tw. II, 5, 130.

2) to foreshow; as a bad omen: H4A II, 4, 354. Lr. I, 2, 113. 149. Ant. III, 13, 154. Cymb. IV, 2, 182. As a good omen: Cymb. IV, 2, 350.

**Portent,** omen of ill: H4A II, 3, 65. V, 1, 20. Troil. I, 3, 96. Caes. II, 2, 80. Oth. V, 2, 45.

**Portentous,** ominous: Rom. I, 1, 147. Caes. I, 3, 31. Hml. I, 1, 109.

**Porter,** 1) one that carries burdens: Wiv. II, 2, 181. LLL I, 2, 75. H5 I, 2, 200. Troil. I, 2, 270. cf. the name *Tale-porter* (i. e. talebearer) in Wint. IV, 4, 273.

2) a doorkeeper: Err. II, 2, 213. 219. III, 1, 36. 43. H6A II, 3, 1. H8 V, 4, 4. 73. Cor. IV, 5, 13. 213. Rom. I, 5, 10. Tim. II, 1, 10. Mcb. II, 3, 2. 23. Lr. III, 7, 64.

**Portia,** 1) the wife of Brutus: Merch. I, 1, 166. Caes. II, 1, 234 and passim.

2) name in Merch. I, 1, 165 and passim.

**Portion,** 1) a part assigned, a share: *and have no p. in the choice myself,* H6A V, 3, 125. *what piles of wealth hath he accumulated to his own p.* H8 III, 2, 108.

2) inheritance settled on a person: *the p. and sinew of her fortune, her marriage-dowry,* Meas. III, 1, 230. *what prodigal p. have I spent,* As I, 1, 41. *make her p. equal his,* Wint. IV, 4, 397. *give but that p. which yourself proposed,* Lr. I, 1, 245. Hence = possession, estate in general: *I have a hundred milchkine to the pail, sixscore fat oxen standing in my stalls, and all things answerable to this p.* Shr. II, 361.

**Port le Blanc,** port in Britany: R2 II, 1, 277.

**Portly,** 1) good-looking, of a stately appearance, imposing: *my p. belly,* Wiv. I, 3, 69. *with p. sail,* Merch. I, 1, 9. *that same greatness which our own hands have holp to make so p.* H4A I, 3, 13. *a goodly p. man, and a corpulent,* II, 4, 464. *his large and p. size,* Troil. IV, 5, 162. *a p. sail of ships,* Per. I, 4, 61.

2) of a good deportment, well-behaved, well-bred: *he bears him like a p. gentleman,* Rom. I, 5, 68.

**Portrait,** picture of a person: *the p. of a blinking idiot,* Merch. II, 9, 54.

**Portraiture,** image: *by the image of my cause I see the p. of his,* Hml. V, 2, 78.

**Portugal,** country in Europe: *my affection hath an unknown bottom, like the bay of P.* As IV, 1, 213.*

**Pose,** to puzzle, to gravel, to set by questions: *say you so? then I shall p. you quickly,* Meas. II, 4, 51.

**Posied,** bearing an inscription: *cracked many a ring of p. gold and bone,* Compl. 45.

**Position,** 1) manner of being placed: *what should that alphabetical p. portend?* Tw. II, 5, 130.

2) advanced opinion, assertion: *I do not strain at the p.* Troil. III, 3, 112. *it is a most pregnant and unforced p.* Oth. II, 1, 240. *I do not in p. distinctly speak of her,* III, 3, 234.

**Positive,** certain, unquestionable: *it is as p. as*

the earth is firm, Wiv. III, 2, 49. 'tis p. 'gainst all exceptions, H5 IV, 2, 25. Patroclus is a fool p. Troil. II, 3, 70 (= unconditional).

**Positively,** without dubitation: before I p. speak herein, R3 IV, 2, 25. that I have p. said: 'tis so, Hml. II, 2, 154.

**Possess,** 1) to hold, to have, to enjoy: happiness .... if —ed, as soon decayed, Lucr. 23. that which they p. they scatter, 135. till manly shame bids him p. his breath and live, 1777. neither may p. the claim they lay, 1794. —ing or pursuing no delight, Sonn. 75, 11. thou art too dear for my —ing, 87, 1. if aught p. thee from me, it is dross, Err. II, 2, 179 (i. e. so as to deprive me of thee; cf. From). still her cheeks p. the same, LLL I, 2, 110. I am yours, and all that I p. V, 2, 383. 'tis in reversion that I do p. R2 II, 2, 38. the present benefit which I p. II, 3, 14. and that we now —ed the utmost man of expectation, H4B I, 3, 64. nor did the French p. the Salique land, H5 I, 2, 56. certain and —ed conveniences, Troil. III, 3, 7. so shall you share all that he doth p. Rom. I, 3, 93. how sweet is love itself —ed, V, 1, 10. all other joys, which the most precious square of sense —es, Lr. I, 1, 76 (Ff professes). be a child o' the time. P. it, I'll make answer, Ant. II, 7, 107 (= be master of it).

2) to become master of, to take possession of, to gain, to occupy, to get: the old bees die, the young p. their hive, Lucr. 1769. remember first to p. his books, Tp. III, 2, 100. now tell me how long you would have her after you have —ed her, As IV, 1, 144. would make her sainted spirit again p. her corpse, Wint. V, 1, 58. this the regal seat: p. it, York, H6C I, 1, 26. the which you promised I should p. R3 IV, 2, 94. away, my disposition, and p. me some harlot's spirit, Cor. III, 2, 111. we may, our pastimes done, p. a golden slumber, Tit. II, 3, 26 (= begin to enjoy). I have bought the mansion of a love, but not —ed it, Rom. III, 2, 27.

3) to fill, to take up entirely: sin of self-love —eth all mine eye, Sonn. 62, 1. what a strange drowsiness —es them, Tp. II, 1, 199. my ears are stopt and cannot hear good news, so much of bad already hath —ed them, Gent. III, 1, 206. weakness —eth me, John V, 3, 17. good thoughts p. thee, R3 IV, 1, 94. I am most joyful, such good dreams p. your fancy, H8 IV, 2, 94. things rank and gross in nature p. it (the world) merely, Hml. I, 2, 137. with a sudden vigour it doth p. and curd the thin and wholesome blood, Hml. I, 5, 68 (Ff and M. Edd. posset). Followed by with, = to fill, to affect: thou art so —ed with murderous hate, Sonn. 10, 5. thy conscience is so —ed with guilt, Tp. I, 2, 471. I will p. him with yellowness, Wiv. I, 3, 110. that spirit's —ed with haste, Meas. IV, 2, 91. I am —ed with an adulterate blot, Err. II, 2, 142. —ed with the glanders, Shr. III, 2, 50. and thou —ed with a thousand wrongs, John III, 3, 41. I find the people —ed with rumours, IV, 2, 145. why seekest thou to p. me with these fears? 203. the thieves are scattered and —ed with fear, H4A II, 2, 112. no man should p. him with any appearance of fear, lest he, by showing it, should dishearten his army, H5 IV, 1, 115. p. them not with fear, 307. —ed him with a scruple, H8 II, 1, 158. which (my tongue) shall p. them (your ears) with the heaviest sound that ever yet they heard, Mcb. IV, 3, 202. Used of evil spirits and other dark influences ruling the mind of man: an she were not —ed with a Fury, Ado I, 1, 193. if Legion himself —ed him, Tw.

III, 4, 95. —ed with devilish spirits, H6B IV, 7, 80. Flibbertigibbet, who —es chambermaids, Lr. IV, 1, 65. both man and master is —ed (= mad) Err. IV, 4, 95. V, 245. Tw. III, 4, 9. —ed he is with greatness, Troil. II, 3, 180 (German: er leidet an Groessenwahnsinn). unless some fit or frenzy do p. her, Tit. IV, 1, 17. Cor. III, 2, 111. placed and —ed by my master, Ado III, 3, 159. partly by his oaths, which first —ed them, 167 (made them mad). Absolutely: dost thou think in time she will not quench and let instructions enter where folly now —es? Cymb. I, 5, 48.

4) to make master of, to give possession or command of: I will p. you of that ship and treasure, Ant. III, 11, 21. Refl.: had —ed himself of the kingdom, Lucr. Arg. 3. Partic. —ed: I am as well derived, as well —ed, Mids. I, 1, 100 (as rich). deposing thee before thou wert —ed, which art —ed now to depose thyself, R2 II, 1, 107. 108*(quibbling). —ed of: of all he dies —ed, Merch. IV, 1, 389; cf. of all he dies —ed of, V, 293. the movables whereof our uncle Gaunt did stand —ed, R2 II, 1, 162. R3 III, 1, 196. I am —ed of that is mine, Tit. I, 408. Hml. III, 3, 53. Ant. V, 2, 139. —ed with: like him with friends —ed, Sonn. 29, 6. —ed with such a grace, Err. III, 2, 165. to be —ed with double pomp, John IV, 2, 9. —ed with more than half the Gallian territories, H6A V, 4, 138. H6C II, 5, 57.

5) to communicate to, to inform: I have —ed him my most stay can be but brief, Meas. IV, 1, 44. p. the people in Messina here how innocent she died, Ado V, 1, 290. is he yet —ed how much ye would? Merch. I, 3, 65. p. us, tell us, something of him, Tw. II, 3, 149. by the way I'll p. thee what she is, Troil. IV, 4, 114. With of: I have —ed your grace of what I purpose, Merch. IV, 1, 35. the king is certainly —ed of all our purposes, H4A IV, 1, 40. is the senate —ed of this? Cor. II, 1, 145. With with: some reasons of this double coronation I have —ed you with, John IV, 2, 41.

**Possession,** 1) the having, holding, or enjoying sth.: Lucr. 18. 803. Sonn. 18, 10. 129, 9. Err. IV, 4, 58. John I, 39. 40. R2 III, 1, 13. IV, 110. H4A III, 2, 43 (opinion had still kept loyal to p.; abstr. pro concr., = to the actual occupant of the crown). H4B IV, 5, 223. H5 III, 6, 98. H6C II, 2, 53. Troil. II, 2, 152. Hml. V, 2, 90. Oth. V, 2, 278. Ant. V, 2, 318. Cymb. III, 5, 126. in p., opposed to in reversion: after my death the one half of my lands, and in p. twenty thousand crowns, Shr. II, 123. now to London, to see these honours in p. H6C II, 6, 110. to bear p. John II, 366. to get p. Meas. I, 2, 150. Err. III, 1, 106. to take p. Gent. V, 4, 130. All's II, 5, 28. John IV, 1, 32. H6C I, 1, 44.

2) things owned, property: the virtue that p. would not show us whiles it was ours, Ado IV, 1, 223. stalk in blood to our p. John II, 266. we lose the better half of our p. H5 I, 1, 8. it outspeaks p. of a subject, H8 III, 2, 128. I have abandoned Troy, left my p. Troil. III, 3, 5. Plur. —s: Gent. II, 4, 175. III, 1, 79. V, 2, 25. Meas. V, 427. Shr. Ind. 2, 16.

3) frenzy, madness: how long hath this p. held the man? Err. V, 44. cf. IV, 4, 58.

**Possessor,** occupant, owner: Merch. I, 3, 75. H6C III, 3, 24.

**Posset,** subst. a drink composed of hot milk, curdled by some strong infusion, and used to be taken before going to bed: Wiv. I, 4, 8. V, 5, 180 (eat a p.). Mcb. II, 2, 6.

**Posset,** vb. to curdle: *it doth p. and curd, like eager droppings into milk, the thin and wholesome blood,* Hml. I, 5, 68 (Qq *possess*).

**Possibility,** that which may be done or happen: *seven hundred pounds and —es,* Wiv. I, 1, 65 (i. e. prospects of inheritance; Evans' speech). *I know thou'rt valiant, and, to the p. of thy soldiership, will subscribe for thee,* All's III, 6, 88 (i. e. as far as the matter depends on what thy soldiership may possibly accomplish). *I have speeded hither with the very extremest inch of p.* H4B IV, 3, 39. *I'll rather keep that which I have than, coveting for more, be cast from p. of all,* H6A V, 4, 146 (perhaps with intended ambiguity. Charles was evidently going to say: than, by seeking to have the possibility or chance of gaining all, possibly lose all). *O brother, speak with —es,* Tit. III, 1, 215.

**Possible,** such as may be done or happen: Gent. I, 2, 82. Meas. III, 2, 132. Ado I, 1, 74. II, 3, 102. 186. IV, 1, 272. Mids. IV, 2, 7. Merch. I, 3, 122. As III, 2, 198. Shr. I, 1, 154. 199. III, 2, 191. IV, 2, 1. All's IV, 3, 203. Tw. III, 4, 139. Wint. I, 2, 139. II, 3, 167. John V, 4, 21. H4B V, 5, 136. H6A I, 2, 87. R3 V, 3, 39. H8 I, 1, 37. Troil. IV, 2, 76. IV, 4, 34. Cor. IV, 6, 56. V, 4, 4. 9. Caes. IV, 3, 38. Hml. II, 2, 374. V, 2, 25. 131. Oth. I, 3, 9. II, 1, 222. II, 3, 288. III, 3, 358. III, 4, 68. IV, 1, 43. IV, 2, 87. Cymb. IV, 2, 160. *can it be p.* As II, 2, 1. *may it be p.* H5 II, 2, 100. *be it p. =* if it is p. Shr. III, 2, 127. *it is not p.,* followed by *should:* H4A V, 2, 4. Likewise *is it p.:* Ado I, 1, 121. III, 3, 117. As I, 3, 27. V, 2, 1. Shr. I, 1, 151. All's IV, 1, 48. H5 V, 2, 178. H8 I, 3, 1. Tim. III, 1, 49. Hml. IV, 5, 159.

**Possibly,** in any way that may be granted: Gent. II, 2, 3. LLL I, 1, 133. Tw. III, 4, 294. Per. V, 3, 57.

**Possitable,** Evans' blunder for *positively:* Wiv. I, 1, 244.

**Post,** subst. 1) a piece of timber set upright: Ado II, 1, 207 (quibbling). As IV, 1, 9. H5 III, 2, 44. H6A I, 4, 52. Used to keep the score by chalk or notches: *I shall be p. indeed, for she will score your fault upon my pate,* Err. I, 2, 64 (quibbling). And to fix proclamations on: *myself on every p. proclaimed a strumpet,* Wint. III, 2, 102. *he'll stand at your door like a sheriff's p.* Tw. I, 5, 157 (cf. *Sheriff*).

2) a messenger: Lucr. 926. 1333. Tp. II, 1, 248. Merch. II, 9, 100. V, 46 (with a horn). Tw. I, 5, 303. Wint. II, 3, 193. R2 II, 2, 103. H4A I, 1, 37. H4B Ind. 37. I, 1, 214. II, 4, 385. H6B I, 4, 81. H6C II, 1, 109. III, 3, 162. V, 1, 1. 5. H8 V, 2, 32. Cor. V, 6, 50. Tit. IV, 3, 77. Mcb. I, 3, 98. Lr. II, 4, 30. III, 7, 11. IV, 6, 281. Ant. I, 5, 61. Gent. I, 1, 161.

3) a post-horse, relay-horse: *I have foundered nine score and odd —s,* H4B IV, 3, 40. *and presently took p. to tell you,* Rom. V, 1, 21.

4) *in p. =* in haste: Err. I, 2, 63. Wint. II, 1, 182. R2 II, 1, 296. H6C III, 3, 222. Rom. V, 3, 273. *all in p.* Lucr. 1. H6C V, 5, 84. *in all p.* R3 III, 5, 73. *in such p.* H6C I, 2, 48.

*P.* alone, adverbially, in the same sense: All's IV, 5, 85. R2 V, 2, 112. H4B II, 4, 408. Per. IV Prol. 48.

**Post,** vb. 1) intr. to go with speed, to hasten: Lucr. Arg. 8. Lucr. 220. Sonn. 51, 4. Pilgr. 201. 205. Gent. II, 3, 37. Err. III, 2, 152. LLL IV, 3, 188. All's V, 1, 1. John V, 7, 94. R2 I, 1, 56. III, 4, 90. V, 5, 59. H4A V, 1, 35. H6A V, 5, 87. H6C I, 2, 55.

II, 5, 128. R3 II, 2, 142. III, 2, 17. IV, 4, 440. 443. 455. Troil. I, 3, 93. Caes. III, 1, 287. Hml. I, 2, 156. Lr. III, 7, 1. Oth. I, 3, 46 (Q1 *wish him p. post-haste;* the rest of O. Edd. *post post haste dispatch*). Cymb. III, 4, 38. V, 5, 192. 283. Conjugated with *to be: and is —ed,* H8 III, 2, 59. Lr. IV, 5, 8.

2) trans. a) to convey rapidly: *the swiftest harts have —ed you by land,* Cymb. II, 4, 27.

b) with *over, =* to hurry over, to get over with too much ease and negligence: *his guilt should be but idly —ed over,* H6B III, 1, 255 (cf. *O'erpost*). With *off, =* to put off carelessly: *nor —ed off their suits with slow delays,* H6C IV, 8, 40.

**Poster,** speedy traveller: *—s of the sea and land,* Mcb. I, 3, 33.

**Posterior,** latter part; an expression used by Armado, admired and adopted by Holofernes: *in the —s of this day,* LLL V, 1, 94. *the p. of the day,* 96. 126.

**Posterity,** 1) descendants: Ven. 758. Lucr. 208. Sonn. 3, 8. 6, 12. Phoen. 59. Mids. IV, 1, 95 (Q2 Ff *prosperity*). Wint. IV, 4, 420. John II, 6. 96. Cor. IV, 2, 26. Mcb. III, 1, 4.

2) succeeding generations, future times: Sonn. 55, 11. H6A I, 4, 48. R3 III, 1, 77. Rom. I, 1, 226.

**Postern,** a small gate: Gent. V, 1, 9. Meas. IV, 2, 92. Wint. I, 2, 438. 464. II, 1, 52. R2 V, 5, 17 (*to thread the p. of a needle's eye*).

**Post-haste,** very great haste: *Norfolk and myself in haste, p., are come,* H6C II, 1, 139. *the chief head of this p. and romage in the land,* Hml. I, 1, 107. Adjectively: *requires your haste, p. appearance,* Oth. I, 2, 37 (M. Edd. *haste-post-haste*).

Adverbially, *=* very hastily: *and hath sent p. to entreat your majesty,* R2 I, 4, 55. *write from us to him, wish him post p.* Oth. I, 3, 46 (Q2 Ff *post post haste dispatch*).

**Post-horse,** a horse stationed for the rapid conveyance of persons; emblem of swiftness: *making the wind my p.* H4B Ind. 4. *till George be packed with p. up to heaven,* R3 I, 1, 146. *hire —s,* Rom. V, 1, 26.

**Posthumus** (accented on the second syllable), name in Cymb. I, 1, 41. 74. 144. III, 4. 90. III, 5, 56. 62. IV, 2, 308. V, 4, 45 etc.

**Postmaster,** one who has the direction of a post-office: Wiv. V, 5, 199. 211.

**Post-post-haste,** superlative haste; adjectively: *p. dispatch,* Oth. I, 3, 46 (Q1 *wish him post post-haste*).

**Postscript,** a paragraph added to the end of a letter: Tw. II, 5, 187. Hml. IV, 7, 53.

**Posture,** attitude: *her natural p.* Wint. V, 3, 23. *in most strange —s we have seen him set himself,* H8 III, 2, 118. *gave him graceful p.* Cor. II, 1, 237. *i' the p. of a whore,* Ant. V, 2, 221. *puts himself in p. that acts my words,* Cymb. III, 3, 94. Almost *=* appearance, shape, form: *laming the shrine of Venus or straight-pight Minerva, —s beyond brief nature,* Cymb. V, 5, 165.

Very strange use: *Antony, the p. of your blows are yet unknown,* Caes. V, 1, 33 (Singer *puncture,* a word unknown to Sh.).*

**Posy,** 1) a motto inscribed on a ring: *a ring whose p. was like cutler's poetry,* Merch. V, 148. 151. *the p. of a ring,* Hml. III, 2, 162.

2) a nosegay: *a thousand fragrant —es,* Pilgr. 362 and Wiv. III, 1, 20 (not Shakespearian).

**Pot**, a vessel more deep than broad, used for several purposes: LLL V, 2, 930. 939. Shr. Ind. 2, 1. 77. IV, 1, 6 (*a little p. and soon hot*). H4A I, 3, 233. H5 III, 2, 13. H6B II, 3, 64. IV, 2, 72. IV, 10, 16. Troil. I, 2, 161. Rom. V, 1, 46. Mcb. IV, 1, 9. *they have shut him in. To the p., I warrant him*, Cor. I, 4, 47 (i. e. to destruction, to certain death; cf. the German: *in die Pfanne gehauen werden*).

**Potable**, drinkable: H4B IV, 5, 163.

**Potation**, 1) drink, beverage: *to forswear thin —s*, H4B IV, 3, 135.
2) a draught: *caroused —s pottle-deep*, Oth. II, 3, 56.

**Potato**, the root of Solanum tuberosum; regarded as a strong provocative: *let the sky rain —es*, Wiv. V, 5, 21. *how the devil Luxury, with his fat rump and p. finger, tickles these together*, Troil. V, 2, 56.

**Potch** (some M. Edd. *poach*) to thrust: *I'll p. at him some way*, Cor. I, 10, 15.

**Potency**, power: *I would to heaven I had your p.* Meas. II, 2, 67. *read the cardinal's malice and his p. together*, H8 I, 1, 105. *when we will tempt the frailty of our powers, presuming on their changeful p.* Troil. IV, 4, 99. *arriving at place of p. and sway o' the state*, Cor. II, 3, 190. *or throw him* (the devil) *out with wondrous p.* Hml. III, 4, 170. *our p. made good, take thy reward*, Lr. I, 1, 175.

**Potent**, powerful; used of things as well as of persons: Tp. I, 2, 275. IV, 1, 34. V, 50. Wiv. IV, 4, 89. As V, 4, 175. Tw. III, 4, 224 (*a headstrong p. fault*). Wint. I, 2, 51. H4A IV, 1, 11. H8 II, 4, 76. Troil. III, 2, 25. III, 3, 192. Tim. IV, 1, 22. Mcb. IV, 1, 76. Hml. II, 2, 631. V, 2, 364. Oth. I, 3, 76. II, 3, 79 (*most p. in potting*). Ant. III, 6, 95. Cymb. V, 4, 84. Per. III, 2, 63.
Substantively, = one powerful: *back to the stained field, you equal —s*, John II, 358.

**Potentate**, a person of high rank: *this gentleman is come to me, with commendation from great —s*, Gent. II, 4, 79. *dost thou infamonize me among —s*, LLL V, 2, 684. *kings and mightiest —s must die*, H6A III, 2, 136.

**Potential**, powerful: Compl. 264. Lr. II, 1, 78. Oth. I, 2, 13.

**Potently**, powerfully: *you are p. opposed*, H8 V, 1, 135. *all which though I most powerjully and p. believe*, Hml. II, 2, 204.

**Pothecary**, apothecary: Rom. V, 3, 289. Per. III, 2, 9.

**Pother**, turmoil: *such a p., as if that whatsoever god who leads him were slily crept into his human powers*, Cor. II, 1, 234 (O. Edd. *poother*). *the great gods, that keep this dreadful p. o'er our heads*, Lr. III, 2, 50 (Ff *pudder*, Q1.3 *thundring*, Q2 *powther*).

**Potion**, a drink administered, either medicinal or poisonous: Sonn. 111, 10. 119, 1. Wiv. III, 1, 105. Mids. III, 2, 264 (Ff Q2 *poison*). Wint. I, 2, 319. H4A V, 4, 56. H4B I, 1, 197. I, 2, 145. Rom. V, 3, 244. 249. Hml. V, 2, 337. Per. I, 2, 68.

**Potpan**, name in Rom. I, 5, 1. 11.

**Pots**, name in Meas. IV, 3, 19.

**Potter**, one who makes earthen vessels: *my thoughts are whirled like a —'s wheel*, H6A I, 5, 19.

**Potting**, drinking: *most potent in p.* Oth. II, 3, 79.

**Pottle**, a large tankard (originally a measure of two quarts): Wiv. II, 1, 223. III, 5, 30. Oth. II, 3, 87.

**Pottle-deep**, to the bottom of the tankard: *potations p.* Oth. II, 3, 56.

**Pottle-pot**, a tankard containing two quarts: H4B II, 2, 83. V, 3, 68.

**Pouch**, a bag, a purse: *tester I'll have in p. when thou shalt lack*, Wiv. I, 3, 96. *the lean and slippered pantaloon, with spectacles on nose and p. on side*, As II, 7, 159.

**Poulter**, poulterer, one who deals in game and fowls: H4A II, 4, 480.

**Poultice**, a cataplasm: Rom. II, 5, 65.

**Poultney**: *the parish Saint Lawrence P.* H8 I, 2, 153.

**Pouncet-box**, a box perforated with small holes, for carrying perfumes: H4A I, 3, 38.

**Pound**, subst. 1) a weight of sixteen ounces: Merch. I, 3, 150. 166. III, 3, 33. IV, 1, 23. 99. 326. *will too late tie leaden —s to's heels*, Cor. III, 1, 314. With a numeral, plur. *p.*: Wint. IV, 3, 40. 51. Troil. I, 2, 126.
2) the sum of twenty shillings: Gent. I, 1, 111. 115. Wint. IV, 3, 34 (*p. and odd shilling*). H6B III, 1, 115. IV, 7, 25. *for any suit of —s*, H8 II, 3, 85. With a numeral, plur. a) *p.*: Wiv. I, 1, 60. III, 3, 131. IV, 6, 5. Meas. II, 1, 127. Err. IV, 1, 21. Ado I, 1, 90. III, 5, 27. Shr. Ind. I, 21. V, 1, 22. Tw. V, 181. John I, 69. R2 II, 2, 91. H4A II, 4, 69. 163. 176. III, 3, 86. 117. 152. 154. 155. H4B I, 2, 251. II, 1, 160. III, 2, 261. V, 5, 12. 77. H6B III, 3, 13. H8 II, 3, 64. Hml. III, 2, 298. Cymb. II, 1, 3. b) *—s*: Wiv. I, 1, 52. I, 3, 8. 41. 4, 33. 50. V, 5, 117. Meas. II, 1, 204. IV, 3, 7. Shr. V, 1, 23. H4A IV, 2, 15. H4B III, 2, 57. H5 I, 1, 19. H8 II, 3, 95. Cymb. III, 1, 9.

**Pound**, subst. a pinfold: Gent. I, 1, 113.

**Pound**, vb. to shut up as in a pinfold: *'twere best p. you*, Gent. I, 1, 110. *we'll break our walls, rather than they shall p. us up*, Cor. I, 4, 17. cf. Impound.

**Pour**, 1) trans. to send or to throw streaming, as a fluid or like one: *mine* (fountain) *I p. your ocean all among*, Compl. 256. *I will p. some* (wine) *in thy other mouth*, Tp. II, 2, 98. *let me p. in some sack to the Thames water*, Wiv. III, 5, 22. Mids. II, 1, 50. As III, 2, 210. IV, 1, 215. V, 1, 46. All's I, 3, 209. II, 3, 126. Wint. V, 3, 122. H4B IV, 4, 46. R3 II, 2, 87. Tit. II, 3, 163. Mcb. IV, 1, 64. IV, 3, 98. Hml. I, 5, 63. V, 1, 197. Oth. IV, 3, 89. Ant. II, 5, 34. Used of balms applied to wounds: *in these windows I p. the helpless balm of my poor eyes*, R3 I, 2, 13. *—est in the open ulcer of my heart her eyes, her hairs* etc. Troil. I, 1, 53. *is this the balsam that the usuring senate —s into captains' wounds*, Tim. III, 5, 111. cf. *meet we the medicine of the sickly weal, and with him p. we in our country's purge each drop of us*, Mcb. V, 2, 28 (or = shed?). Of rain and what comes down like it: *the sky would p. down stinking pitch*, Tp. I, 2, 3. *thus p. the stars down plagues*, LLL V, 2, 394. *some airy devil —s down mischief*, John III, 2, 3. *that pretty Welsh which thou —est down from these swelling heavens*, H4A III, 1, 202. *p. on; I will endure*, Lr. III, 4, 18 (= rain on). Of the promiscuous contents of packets: *I would have ransacked the pedlar's silken treasury and have —ed it to her acceptance*, Wint. IV, 4, 361. *p. out the pack of matter to mine ear*, Ant. II, 5, 54.
Figurative use: *thou that —est into my verse thine own sweet argument*, Sonn. 38, 2. *I would into thy bo-*

*som p. my thoughts*, John III, 3, 53. *p. down thy weather*, IV, 2, 109 (= tell thy bad news). *how London doth p. out her citizens*, H5 V Chor. 24. *force him with praises; p. in, p. in; his ambition is dry*, Troil. II, 3, 233. *—ing war into the bowels of ungrateful Rome*, Cor. IV, 5, 135 (like a flood). *he outgoes the very heart of kindness. He —s it out*, Tim. I, 1, 287. *and —ed them* (thy praises) *down before him*, Mcb. I, 3, 100. *that I may p. my spirits in thine ear*, I, 5, 27. *I'll p. this pestilence into his ear*, Oth. II, 3, 362. *your honour has through Ephesus —ed forth your charity*, Per. III, 2, 43. *who p. their bounty on her*, V Prol. 16.

2) intr. to flow, to rush in a stream: *the Scot on his unfurnished kingdom came —ing, like the tide into a breach*, H5 I, 2, 149.

**Pout**, to look sullen: *who blushed and —ed in a dull disdain*, Ven. 33. *then we p. upon the morning*, Cor. V, 1, 52. *thou —est upon thy fortune and thy love*, Rom. III, 3, 144.

**Poverty**, want of riches, indigence: Tp. II, 1, 150. Meas. I, 2, 85. LLL V, 2, 269. 380. Merch. IV, 1, 271. As III, 5, 100. V, 2, 7. Wint. IV, 4, 647. H4A IV, 2, 76. H4B I, 2, 146. I, 3, 75. II, 1, 116. H6B I, 3, 84. R3 III, 7, 159. H8 IV, 2, 149. Rom. V, 1, 75. 76. Tim. IV, 2, 14. Oth. IV, 2, 50. Per. I, 4, 30. Abstr. pro concr., = 1) one poor, or poor persons: *to think my p. is treacherous*, As I, 3, 67 (= poor I). *you houseless p.* Lr. III, 4, 26. 2) a little paltry stock of goods: *although thou steal thee all my p.* Sonn. 40, 10. *what p. my Muse brings forth*, 103, 1.

**Pow**, = pooh, an exclamation of contempt: Cor. II, 1, 157.

**Powder**, subst. 1) any substance comminuted, dust: Tit. V, 2, 199. Ant. IV, 9, 17.

2) gunpowder: John II, 448. H4A IV, 2, 72. Rom. II, 6, 10. III, 3, 132. V, 1, 64.

**Powder**, vb. to salt: *if thou embowel me to-day, I'll give you leave to p. me and eat me too*, H4A V, 4, 112. Applied to the customary cure of the lues venerea by sweating in a heated tub: *ever your fresh whore and your —ed bawd*, Meas. III, 2, 62. *from the —ing tub of infamy fetch forth the lazar kite of Cressid's kind*, H5 II, 1, 79.

**Power** (sometimes dissyll.; f. i. Merch. IV, 1, 241. H4B IV, 1, 177. R3 IV, 4, 480. Rom. V, 3, 93), 1) force, strength, ability, whether bodily or intellectual, physical or moral: *thy* (death's) *p. had lost his p.* Ven. 944. *when more is felt than one hath p. to tell*, Lucr. 1288. *he hath no p. to ask her how she fares*, 1594. *brass, nor stone, nor earth .... but sad mortality o'ersways their p.* Sonn. 65, 2. *darkening thy p. to give base subjects light*, 100, 4. *use p. with p. and slay me not by art*, 139, 4 (cf. Cor. II, 3, 4). *had I been any god of p.* Tp. I, 2, 10. *his art is of such p.* 372. *till mine enemy has more p.* 466. *and deal in her* (the moon's) *command without her p.* V, 271 (without being subject to the pernicious influence of the moon). *assay the p. you have*, Meas. I, 4, 76. *devices, which shall then have no p. to stand against us*, IV, 4, 15. *to your p. I'll yield*, Err. III, 2, 40. *whose edge hath p. to cut*, LLL II, 50. *all the p. thereof it doth apply to prove*, V, 2, 77. *ere a man hath p. to say Behold*, Mids. I, 1, 147. *your p. to draw*, II, 1, 197. *all the p. this charm doth owe*, II, 2, 79. *Dian's bud o'er Cupid's flower hath such force and blessed p.* IV, 1, 79. *there is no p. in the tongue of man to alter me*, Merch. IV, 1,

241. *the sweet p. of music*, V, 79. *the p. of fancy*, As III, 5, 29. *be able for thine enemy rather in p. than use*, All's I, 1, 75. (a medicine) *chief in p.* II, 1, 115. *I will prove so to my p.* Wint. V, 2, 182 (to the best of my ability); cf. Cor. II, 1, 262. *to bear above our p.* John V, 6, 38. *beyond his p. to build it*, H4B I, 3, 59. *knit our —s to the arm of peace*, IV, 1, 177. *I have no p. to let her pass*, H6A V, 3, 60. *the eternal God, whose name and p. thou tremblest at*, H6B I, 4, 28. *I have not the p. to muzzle him*, H8 I, 1, 121. *wisdom o'ertopping woman's p.* II, 4, 88. *entered me with a splitting p.* 183. *we have p. in ourselves to do it, but it is a p. that we have no p. to do*, Cor. II, 3, 4 (we are legally authorized to do it, but it would be immoral to make use of our authority). *what a mental p. this eye shoots forth*, Tim. I, 1, 31. *be of any p. to expel sickness*, III, 1, 65. *his whole action grows not in the p. on't*, Ant. III, 7, 70 (does not rest on that which makes its strength) etc. etc.

2) authority, dominion, sway, influence: *a prince of p.* Tp. I, 2, 55. *what my p. might else exact*, 99. *and given his deputation all the organs of our p.* Meas. I, 1, 22. *a p. I have, but of what strength and nature I am not yet instructed*, 80. *my absolute p. and place here in Vienna*, I, 3, 13. *if p. change purpose*, 54. *which he spurs on his p. to qualify in others*, IV, 2, 85. *there to give up their p.* IV, 3, 137. *advance their pride against that p. that bred it*, Ado III, 1, 11. *if law, authority and p. deny not*, Merch. III, 2, 291. *upon my p. I may dismiss this court*, IV, 1, 104. *his sceptre shows the force of temporal p.* 190. *earthly p. doth then show likest God's*, 196. *there is no p. in Venice can alter a decree*, 218. *I must produce my p.* All's II, 3, 157. *what his hatred would effect wants not a minister in his p.* H8 I, 1, 108. *by commission and main p.* II, 2, 7. *my p. rained honour on you*, III, 2, 185. *every thing includes itself in p., p. into will*, Troil. I, 3, 119. *our office may during his p. go sleep*, Cor. II, 1, 239. *seeking means to pluck away their* (the people's) *p.* III, 3, 96. *in the name o' the people, and in the p. of us the tribunes, we banish him*, 100. *ere thou hadst p.* Tim. V, 4, 15. *I could with barefaced p. sweep him from my sight*, Mcb. III, 1, 119. *giving to you no further personal p. to business with the king*, Hml. I, 2, 36. *my powers are crescent, and my auguring hope says it will come to the full*, Ant. II, 1, 10 etc. etc. With *in:* *by that fatherly and kindly p. that you have in her*, Ado IV, 1, 75. *you have p. in me as in a kinsman*, R3 III, 1, 109. With *of:* *by the sovereign p. you have of us*, Hml. II, 2, 27. *my mother, having p. of his testiness*, Cymb. IV, 1, 22. With *on:* *unless the next word have some malignant p. upon my life*, Gent. III, 1, 238. *death hath had no p. yet upon thy beauty*, Rom. V, 3, 93. *no man shall e'er have p. upon thee*, Mcb. V, 3, 7. *I have no p. upon you*, Ant. I, 3, 23. *the p. that I have on you is to spare you*, Cymb. V, 5, 418. With *over:* *not age, but sorrow, over me hath p.* Compl. 74. *the rabble, o'er whom I give thee p.* Tp. IV, 1, 38. *thou hadst but p. over his mortal body*, R3 I, 2, 47 (cf. Mids. IV, 1, 79). With *unto:* *his p. unto Octavia*, Ant. II, 2, 146 (cf. Hml. I, 2, 36). in *or within the p. of* = at the discretion or disposal of: Sonn. 126, 1. Tp. I, 2, 450. III, 3, 90. LLL II, 51. Mids. I, 1, 50. Merch. I, 3, 93. All's II, 1, 197. III, 6, 33. Wint. II, 3, 26. H6A I, 4, 37. Mcb. IV, 3, 119 etc.

3) a supernatural agent having dominion over

man: *having solicited the eternal p. that his foul thoughts might compass his fair fair*, Lucr. 345. *from what p. hast thou this powerful might*, Sonn. 150, 1. *for which foul deeds the — s have incensed the seas*, Tp. III, 3, 73. *some heavenly p. guide us*, V, 105. Gent. II, 6, 4. Meas. V, 374. Err. IV, 3, 44. Mids. I, 1, 59. IV, 1, 169. Merch. IV, 1, 292. John V, 7, 75. H6C IV, 6, 68. Tit. III, 1, 209. Caes. V, 1, 107. Mcb. IV, 1, 69. IV, 3, 238. Lr. I, 1, 210. Oth. II, 1, 197. Ant. II, 1, 6 etc. etc.⸪

4) vital organ, physical or intellectual function: *and therein heartens up his servile — s*, Lucr. 295. *these rebel — s that thee (the soul) array*, Sonn. 146, 2. *the sudden surprise of my — s*, Wiv. V, 5, 131. *courses as swift as thought in every p.*, and gives to every p. a double p. LLL IV, 3, 330. 331. *to flatter up these — s of mine with rest*, V, 2, 824. *all my — s, address your love and might to honour Helen*, Mids. II, 2, 143. *there is such confusion in my — s*, Merch. III, 2, 179. *thy conceit is nearer death than thy — s*, As II, 6, 9. *sorrow and grief have vanquished all my — s*, H6B II, 1, 183. *whose dismal tune bereft my vital — s*, III, 2, 41. *your brain and every function of your p.* H8 III, 2, 187. *too sharp in sweetness for the capacity of my ruder — s*, Troil. III, 2, 26. *my — s do their bestowing lose*, 39. *when we will tempt the frailty of our — s*, IV, 4, 98. *as if a god were slily crept into his human — s and gave him graceful posture*, Cor. II, 1, 236. *my operant — s their functions leave to do*, Hml. III, 2, 184. *what his every action speaks in every p. that moves*, Ant. III, 12, 36 etc.

5) armed force: *the p. of Greece*, Lucr. 1368. *shall we knit our — s*, John II, 398. *never such a p. was levied*, IV, 2, 110. V, 5, 18. V, 6, 39. R2 II, 2, 124. III, 2, 63. H4A IV, 1, 132. H4B IV, 4, 5. H6A I, 4, 103. II, 2, 33. III, 3, 83. IV, 2, 8. IV, 3, 4. H6B IV, 4, 40. H6C V, 2, 31. R3 IV, 3, 48. IV, 4, 449. 480. V, 3, 10. Cor. I, 2, 32. Tit. IV, 4, 63. Mcb. IV, 3, 236. Ant. III, 7, 58 etc. etc. The plur. form in the sense of the sing.: *I'll send those — s o'er to your majesty*, John III, 3, 70. *those — s of France*, IV, 2, 129. *the Dauphin and his — s*, V, 1, 32. R2 V, 3, 140. H4A I, 3, 262. H6A III, 3, 30. V, 2, 5. H6B IV, 9, 10. V, 1, 44. Tim. V, 4, 52. Hml. IV, 4, 9. Cymb. III, 5, 24 etc.

Seemingly abstr. pro concr.: *most p. to do most harm, least knowing ill*, LLL II, 58 (= a man most able?). *and now are mounted where — s are your retainers*, H8 II, 4, 113 (persons of the highest authority?).

**Powerful**, 1) strong, mighty, forcible: *this p. rhyme*, Sonn. 55, 2. *this p. might*, 150, 1. *O p. love*, Wiv. V, 5, 4. *p. to araise King Pepin*, All's II, 1, 79. *his p. sound*, 179. *'tis p.* (the planet) Wint. I, 2, 202. *you're p. at it*, II, 1, 28 (you are a master in it). *gallows and knock are too p. on the highway*, IV, 3, 29. *p. policy*, H6C I, 2, 58. *winter's p. wind*, V, 2, 15. *with a broad and p. fan*, Troil. I, 3, 27. *p. grace*, Rom. II, 3, 15. *a charm of p. trouble*, Mcb. IV, 1, 18. *drawn by the p. sun*, Lr. II, 4, 169. *mixtures p. o'er the blood*, Oth. I, 3, 104. *thy p. breath*, II, 1, 78.

2) having great authority or command: *some p. spirit*, Wint. II, 3, 186. *all their p. friends*, R2 II, 2, 55. *the p. regions under earth*, H6A V, 3, 11. *his p. arm*, R3 I, 4, 223. *his p. mandate*, Ant. I, 1, 22.

**Powerfully**, strongly: *all which though I most p. and potently believe*, Hml. II, 2, 203.

**Powerless**, weak, impotent: *I give you welcome with a p. hand*, John II, 15.

**Powle**, see *Paul.*

**Pox**, the venereal disease: *a man can no more separate age and covetousness than a' can part young limbs and lechery: but the gout galls the one, and the p. pinches the other*, H4B I, 2, 258. *a p. of this gout! or a gout of this p.! for the one or the other plays the rogue with my great toe*, 273. *the p. upon her green-sickness for me! Faith, there's no way to be rid on't but by the way to the p.* Per. IV, 6, 17.

Mostly used as a slight curse (and supposed, in this case, to mean the smallpox; cf. LLL V, 2, 46): *the p. of such fantasticoes!* Rom. II, 4, 29. *the p. upon her green-sickness*, Per. IV, 6, 14. *a p. of that jest*, LLL V, 2, 46. H4B I, 2, 272. H5 III, 7, 130. Tim. IV, 3, 148. Oth. I, 3, 365. *a p. on him*, All's IV, 3, 307. *a p. upon him for me*, 295. *a p. on't*, All's III, 6, 48. Cymb. II, 1, 20. *a p. o' your throat*, Tp. I, 1, 43. II, 1, 77. III, 2, 87. Meas. IV, 3, 26. *p. of your love-letters*, Gent. III, 1, 390. *p. on't*, Tw. III, 4, 308. *p., leave thy damnable faces*, Hml. III, 2, 263. *show your knave's visage, with a p. to you*, Meas. V, 359. *what a p. have I to do with my hostess*, H4A I, 2, 53.

**Poysam**, name: *old P. the papist*, All's I, 3, 56 (called so from *poison?*).

**Practic**, practical, opposed to theoretical: *so that the art and p. part of life must be the mistress to this theoric*, H5 I, 1, 51.

**Practice**, subst. 1) doing, proceeding, action: *we detest such vile base — s* (as to do outrages on women) Gent. IV, 1, 73. *courage and hope both teaching him the p.* Tw. I, 2, 13. *than ... he be approved in p. culpable*, H6B III, 2, 22. *heavens make our presence and our — s pleasant and helpful to him*, Hml. II, 2, 38. *these blushes of hers must be quenched with some present p.* Per. IV, 2, 136. With *of,* = performance: *paid me richly for the p. of it*, Ado V, 1, 255. *to put in p.* = to carry into execution: Pilgr. 217. Gent. III, 2, 89. Ado I, 1, 330. II, 2, 53. LLL I, 1, 308.

2) habitual doing, frequent use, exercise: *this is a p. as full of labour as a wise man's art*, Tw. III, 1, 72. *and by still p. learn to know thy meaning*, Tit. III, 2, 45. *I have been in continual p.* Hml. V, 2, 221. *your highness shall from this p. but make hard your heart*, Cymb. I, 5, 24.

3) exercises made for instruction: *proceed in p. with my younger daughter*, Shr. II, 165.

4) exercise of a profession: *he hath abandoned his physicians, under whose — s he hath persecuted time with hope*, All's I, 1, 16.

5) experience, skill acquired by experience (opposed to theory): *as art and p. hath enriched any*, Meas. I, 1, 13. *despite his nice fence and his active p.* Ado V, 1, 75. *one (receipt) as the dearest issue of his p.* All's II, 1, 109. *had the whole theoric of war in the knot of his scarf, and the p. in the chape of his dagger*, IV, 3, 163. *older in p.* Caes. IV, 3, 31. *this disease is beyond my p.* Mcb. V, 1, 65. *mere prattle, without p.* Oth. I, 1, 26. *and no p. had in the brave squares of war*, Ant. III, 11, 39. *together with my p.* Per. III, 2, 34.

6) artifice, stratagem, insidious device: *lest she some subtle p. smell*, Pilgr. 307. *suborned in hateful p.* Meas. V, 107. *this needs must be a p.* 123. *to find this p. out*, 239. *the p. of it lives in John the Bastard,*

Ado IV, 1, 190. *I overheard him and his —s*, As II, 3, 26. *this p. hath most shrewdly passed upon thee*, Tw. V, 360. *unclasped my p.* Wint. III, 2, 168. *it is the p. and the purpose of the king*, John IV, 3, 63. *sworn unto the —s of France, to kill us here*, H5 II, 2, 90. *God acquit them of their —s*, 144. H6A IV, 1, 7. H6B III, 1, 46. H8 I, 1, 204. I, 2, 127. III, 2, 29. V, 1, 129. Cor. IV, 1, 33. Tit. V, 2, 77. Hml. IV, 7, 68. 139 (*a pass of p.;* according to some, = a pass in which Laertes was well practised). V, 2, 328. Lr. I, 2, 198. II, 1, 75. 109. II, 4, 116. V, 3, 151. Oth. I, 3, 102. III, 4, 141. V, 2, 292. Cymb. V, 5, 199. Unintelligible: *making p. on the times*, Meas. III, 2, 288.

**Practisans**, performers of a stratagem: *here entered Pucelle and her p.* H6A III, 2, 20.*

**Practise**, vb. 1) to execute: *aught but Talbot's shadow whereon to p. your severity*, H6A II, 3, 47. *till you p. them* (your infirmities) *on me*, Caes. IV, 3, 88 (German: *auslassen*).

2) to do habitually, to apply to, to use for instruction or as a profession: *there shall he p. tilts and tournaments*, Gent. I, 3, 30. *a thousand tricks .... which I will p.* Merch. III, 4, 78. *p. rhetoric in your common talk*, Shr. I, 1, 35. *which though I will not p. to deceive, yet, to avoid deceit, I mean to learn*, John I, 214. *canst thou catch any fishes? I never —ed it*, Per. II, 1, 71. *he appears to have —ed more the whipstock than the lance*, II, 2, 51. *those that p. them* (measures) II, 3, 105.

3) to exercise one's self; a) intr. *on them* (books and instruments) *to look and p. by myself*, Shr. I, 1, 83. b) with an inf.: *my true eyes have never —d how to cloak offences with a cunning brow*, Lucr. 748. *even I learn love, I'll p. to obey*, Err. II, 1, 29. *shall sweet Bianca p. how to bride it?* Shr. III, 2, 253. c) with an accus., = 1) to make one's self master of, to study (German: *einüben, einstudiren*): *throttle their —d accent in their fears*, Mids. V, 97. *making —d smiles*, Wint. I, 2, 116. *p. an answer*, H4A III, 4, 412. *he had no legs that —d not his gait*, H4B II, 3, 23. *I will p. the insinuating nod*, Cor. II, 3, 106. With *to*, = to teach by much exercise: *—ing behaviour to his own shadow*, Tw. II, 5, 20. 2) to exercise, to drill, to instruct: *the children must be —d well to this*, Wiv. IV, 4, 65. *to p. his judgement with the disposition of natures*, Meas. III, 1, 164. *cry, Trojans, cry! p. your eyes with tears*, Troil. II, 2, 108 (= study the art of weeping, learn to weep).

4) to use stratagems, to contrive, to plot; intr.: *I will so p. on Benedick that he shall fall in love with Beatrice*, Ado II, 1, 398. *he will p. against thee by poison*, As I, 1, 156. *I will p. on this drunken man*, Shr. Ind. 1, 36. *you have —d upon the easy yielding spirit of this woman*, H4B II, 1, 125. *wouldst thou have —d on me for thy use*, H5 II, 2, 99. *let them p. and converse with spirits*, H6A II, 1, 25. *have —d dangerously against your state*, H6B II, 1, 171. *hast —d on man's life*, Lr. III, 2, 57. *thou hast —d on her with foul charms*, Oth. I, 2, 73. *—ing upon his peace and quiet*, Oth. II, 1, 319. *if you there did p. on my state*, Ant. II, 2, 39. 40. With an inf.: *for —ing to steal away a lady*, Gent. IV, 1, 48. With an accus.: *my uncle —s more harm to me*, John IV, 1, 20. *that heaven should p. stratagems upon so soft a subject*, Rom. III, 5, 211.

**Practiser**, practitioner, one engaged in the exer-

cise or profession of an art: *other arts ... finding barren —s*, LLL IV, 3, 325. *sweet p., thy physic I will try*, All's II, 1, 188 (= physician). *a p. of arts inhibited*, Oth. I, 2, 78.

**Praemunire**, a writ issued against one who has committed the offence of introducing a foreign authority or power into England: H8 III, 2, 340.

**Praetor**, title of the judicial officers of ancient Rome: Caes. I, 3, 143. II, 4, 35.

**Prague**, capital of Bohemia: *as the old hermit of P. said to a niece of King Gorboduc*, Tw. IV, 2, 15 (Douce: "not the celebrated heresiarch Jerome of Prague, but another of that name born likewise at Prague, and called the hermit of Camaldoli in Tuscany." Douce must, indeed, have been mightily imposed on by the learning which the clown displays on other occasions; cf. II, 3, 23—29).

**Praise**, subst. 1) commendation bestowed, high approbation: Sonn. 2, 8. 39, 3. 59, 14. 69, 5. 70, 11. 84, 2. 14. 85, 2. 95, 7. 101, 9. Compl. 226. Pilgr. 70. 325. Tp. IV, 10. Gent. II, 4, 196. Ado I, 1, 174. LLL II, 14. IV, 1, 17. 37. IV, 3, 240 (*to things of sale a seller's p. belongs*). 241. V, 2, 40. Merch. I, 2, 133. III, 2, 127. As II, 4, 38. Alls I, 1, 56. H4A V, 1, 87. H6A I, 6, 20. IV, 2, 33. H6B III, 1, 68. H8 I, 1, 31 (*him in eye, still him in p.*) etc. etc. Plur. —s: Lucr. 108. Sonn. 105, 3. 106, 9. Gent. II, 4, 72. 148. As II, 3, 22. All's II, 1, 106. Wint. I, 2, 94. IV, 4, 147. R2 II, 1, 18. H4A V, 2, 57. Mcb. I, 3, 92. 99 etc. *in p. of* = in commendation of: Sonn. 106, 4. Ado V, 2, 5. LLL I, 2, 26. 27. V, 2, 896. Tw. I, 5, 202. H5 III, 7, 42. *to give p.* Wiv. III, 4, 62. LLL V, 2, 366. Cymb. II, 4, 92. *to have p.* All's IV, 5, 10. John III, 4, 15. Troil. III, 2, 100.

2) glorification, thanks, tribute of gratitude: *I give heaven p.* Wiv. III, 4, 62. *my vows of thanks and p.* H6B IV, 9, 14. *to sin's rebuke and my Creator's p.* H6C IV, 6, 44. cf. H6A V, 3, 173.

3) fame, renown: *if my slight Muse do please these curious days, the pain be mine, but thine shall be the p.* Sonn. 38, 14. *your p. shall still find room even in the eyes of all posterity*, 55, 10. *your p. is come too swiftly home before you*, As II, 3, 9. *the most virtuous gentlewoman that ever nature had p. for creating*, All's IV, 5, 10.

4) that which deserves to be extolled; desert, virtue: *praise, which makes your —s worse*, Sonn. 84, 14. *how many things by season seasoned are to their right p. and true perfection*, Merch. V, 108. *which is the prescript p. and perfection of a good mistress*, H5 III, 7, 49. *so to be valiant is no p. at all*, Troil. II, 2, 145. *her face the book of —s*, Per. I, 1, 15.

**Praise**, vb. 1) to commend, to applaud, to extol; absol.: *p. in departing*, Tp. III, 3, 39 (proverbial expression). *I will not p.* Sonn. 21, 14. Trans.: Ven. Ded. 3. Lucr. 11. 79. Sonn. 39, 4. 60, 14. 101, 12. Compl. 315. Gent. III, 1, 102. 354. III, 2, 54. IV, 4, 107. Wiv. II, 1, 58. III, 2, 48. Err. IV, 2, 15. Ado II, 1, 394. III, 1, 19. LLL I, 2, 28. IV, 1, 14. Merch. II, 9, 98. III, 4, 22. All's II, 3, 179 (*she is now the —d of the king*). Tw. II, 4, 33. H4A III, 3, 215. Troil. IV, 2, 113 (*scratch my —d cheeks*). Per. III, 2, 102 (*the diamonds of a most —d water*) etc. etc.

2) to recommend, to cry up: *I will not p. that purpose not to sell*, Sonn. 21, 14. *she will often p. her liquor*, Gent. III, 1, 350 (probably by setting the ex-

ample of drinking). *the soothsayer that you —d so to the queen*, Ant. I, 2, 3. cf. Alls II, 3, 179.

3) to glorify, to thank: *I p. heaven for it*, Wiv. I, 4, 150. *I p. God for you*, Ado V, 1, 325. LLL IV, 2, 75. V, 1, 2. All's V, 2, 59. *p. God for the merry year*, H4B V, 3, 19. *p. my Maker*, H8 V, 5, 69. *God be —d*, Wiv. II, 2, 324. As III, 3, 40. Tw. II, 5, 187. Wint. III, 2, 138. H5 III, 6, 10. IV, 7, 119. H6B II, 1, 96 etc. etc.

4) to appraise, to estimate: *were you sent hither to p. me?* Tw. I, 5, 268. *p. us as we are tasted, allow us as we prove*, Troil. III, 2, 97. Perhaps also in Per. III, 2, 102 (*the diamonds of a most —d water*).

**Praiseful**, laudable; writing of some M. Edd. in LLL IV, 2, 58; Qq F1 *prayful*, F2 *praysful*, F3.4 *preyful*.

**Praiseworthy**, deserving commendation: Ado V, 2, 90.

**Prance**, to bound, to move in a sprightly and showy manner: *trimmed like a younker —ing to his love*, H6C II, 1, 24.

**Prank**, vb. to deck, to dress up, to adorn: *'tis that miracle and queen of gems that nature — s her in attracts my soul*, Tw. II, 4, 89. *and me, poor lowly maid, most goddess-like —ed up*, Wint. IV, 4, 10. *they do p. them in authority*, Cor. III, 1, 23.

**Pranks**, licentious or mischievous tricks: Err. II, 2, 210. Tw. IV, 1, 59. Wint. IV, 4, 718. H6A III, 1, 15. Hml. III, 4, 2. Lr. I, 4, 259. Oth. II, 1, 143 (*does foul p.*). III, 3, 202.

**Prat**, name of an old woman, from which Ford derives a verb: *come, mother P., come, give me your hand. I'll p. her*, Wiv. IV, 2, 191. 193.

**Prate**, subst. tattle: *with his innocent p. he will awake my mercy*, John IV, 1, 25. *and perish ye, with your audacious p.* H6A IV, 1, 124.

**Prate**, vb. to tattle, to talk idly, particularly in a bragging manner: Tp. II, 1, 263. Wiv. I, 4, 128. III, 3, 51. Err. I, 2, 101. II, 1, 81. II, 2, 195. Merch. V, 164. Shr. IV, 3, 114. Wint. III, 2, 42. IV, 4, 349. H4B III, 2, 327. H5 IV, 1, 79. R3 I, 3, 351. III, 1, 151. Cor. I, 1, 49. III, 3, 83. IV, 5, 54. V, 3, 48. 159. Rom. II, 4, 212. IV, 5, 135. 138 (the surreptitious Q1 *pretty*, Q2 *prates*, the rest of O. Edd. *pratest*). Mcb. II, 1, 58. Hml. III, 4, 215. V, 1, 303. Oth. I, 2, 6. II, 1, 227. II, 3, 153.

**Prater**, a twaddler: *a speaker is but a p.* H5 V, 2, 166.

**Prattle**, subst. empty talk, tattle: *thinking his p. to be tedious*, R2 V, 2, 26. *mere p. without practice*, Oth. I, 1, 26.

**Prattle**, vb. to tattle: Tp. III, 1, 57. Wiv. V, 1, 1. Meas. V, 182. Tw. I, 2, 33. H6A III, 1, 16. Cor. II, 1, 222. Oth. II, 1, 208. With an accus. denoting the effect: *if you p. me into these perils*, All's IV, 1, 46.

**Prattler**, tattler: Mcb. IV, 2, 64.

**Prattlings**, idle talk: *I have heard of your p. too*, Hml. III, 1, 148 (Qq and M. Edd. *paintings*).

**Prawn**, the animal Palaemon serratus: *a good dish of —s*, H4B II, 1, 104.

**Pray**, 1) to ask earnestly, to entreat; absol.: *I p. now, keep below*, Tp. I, 1, 12. *pardon the fault, I p.* Gent. I, 2, 40. *give us leave, I p., a while*, III, 1, 1. *how I —ed and kneeled*, Meas. V, 93. *tell me this, I p.* Err. I, 2, 53 etc. etc. With *for: the guilty rebel for remission —s*, Lucr. 714. *a conqueror that will p. in aid*

*for kindness, where he for grace is kneeled to*, Ant. V, 2, 27 (*to p. in aid*, a law-term, = to call in for help one who has interest in the cause). With a clause: *and —s that you will hie you home*, Err. I, 2, 90 etc. *I* often omitted before it: *p., set it down*, Tp. III, 1, 18. *p., tell me that*, Gent. III, 1, 123. Elliptically: *to what, I p.?* Meas. I, 2, 48 (i. e. I p. you to tell me). *I p., sir, why am I beaten?* Err. II, 2, 39. *what are you, I p., but ...* H6A III, 1, 43. *what, I p., is Margaret more than that?* V, 5, 36 etc. Transitively: *I p. you, hence*, Ven. 382. *I p. thee, mark me*, Tp. I, 2, 67. 88. 175. III, 3, 109. Gent. I, 3, 89. III, 1, 239. Meas. IV, 1, 16. Shr. IV, 4, 21 etc. *I* omitted: *no, p. thee*, Tp. I, 2, 371. III, 1, 15. IV, 194. V, 167. Meas. II, 2, 2 etc. Elliptically: *I p. you, sir, of what disposition was the duke?* Meas. III, 2, 244. *I p. you, is Signor Mountanto returned?* Ado I, 1, 30. *I p. you, how many hath he killed?* 42. *but, I p. you, who is his companion?* 81. *p. you, where lies Sir Proteus?* Gent. IV, 2, 137. *p. you, how goes the world*, Tim. II, 2, 35. *she is now the wife of Marcus Antonius. P. ye, sir?* 'Tis true, Ant. II, 6, 120 (i. e. tell me if you are in earnest) etc. A clause following: *the poor fool —s her that he may depart*, Ven. 578. An inf. following; a) with *to: I will p., Pompey, to increase your bondage*, Meas. III, 2, 78. *and so I p. you all to think yourselves*, Shr. II, 114. Tw. III, 4, 103. H5 I, 2, 9. IV, 4, 47. IV, 8, 68. V Chor. 3. H8 III, 1, 18 etc. b) without *to: your father —s you leave your books*, Shr. III, 1, 82. *in that I p. you use her well*, H6B II, 4, 81. *p. 'em take their pleasures*, H8 I, 4, 74. *to p. Achilles see us at our tent*, Troil. V, 9, 8. With an accus. and *to: and p. her to a fault for which I chid her*, Gent. I, 2, 52. *I p. you home to dinner with me*, Meas. II, 1, 292. With an accus. denoting the thing asked: *I know not how to p. your patience*, Ado V, 1, 280. H4B V, 5, 125. H5 Prol. 33. *p. your mother's blessing*, Wint. V, 3, 120. All's I, 3, 260. *he humbly —s your speedy payment*, Tim. II, 2, 28. *—ed me oft forbearance*, Cymb. II, 5, 10.

2) to make petitions to heaven; absol.: *for his prey to p. he doth begin*, Lucr. 342. *on a love-book p. for my success*, Gent. I, 1, 19. *you must p.* Wiv. IV, 2, 162. *to p. against thy foes*, H6A I, 1, 43. Meas. I, 2, 16. IV, 3, 55. Err. I, 2, 51. IV, 2, 28. LLL I, 1, 304. Merch. I, 3, 39. V, 31. H4A II, 1, 87. H6A I, 1, 33 etc. With a clause (almost = to wish): *so will I p. that thou mayst have thy will*, Sonn. 143, 13. *I p. she may* (persuade) Meas. I, 2, 192. *he heartily —s some occasion may detain us longer*, Ado I, 1, 151. *I am not fair, and therefore I p. the gods make me honest*, As III, 3, 34; cf. R2 V, 3, 146. *let wives with child p. that their burthens may not fall this day*, John III, 1, 90. *I cannot p. that thou mayst win*, 331. 332. *and —s the Moor be safe*, Oth. II, 1, 33. 34. *to p. they have their will*, Cymb. II, 5, 34. *I* omitted: *p. heartily he be at palace*, Wint. IV, 4, 731. *blest p. you be*, Cymb. V, 5, 370. With *to: the powers to whom I p.* Lucr. 349. *I think and p. to several subjects*, Meas. II, 4, 1. H4A II, 1, 88. John III, 1, 310. Tit. IV, 2, 48. Caes. I, 1, 59 etc. With an accus.: *I p. the gods she may*, Shr. IV, 4, 67. *God, I p. him*, R3 I, 3, 212. *I p. God, amen!* H8 II, 3, 56 etc. *I* omitted: *p. heaven he prove so*, Gent. II, 7, 79. *p. heaven she win him*, Meas. II, 2, 125. *p. heaven his wisdom be not tainted*, IV, 4, 4. As I, 2, 109. Oth. II, 1, 34. *p. God our cheer may answer my good will*, Err. III, 1, 19. R2 I,

4, 64 etc. The word *prayer* as object: *I'll p. a thousand prayers for thy death*, Meas. III, 1, 146.

**Prayer** (monosyll. or dissyll. indiscriminately), 1) entreaty, supplication: *but she with vehement —s urgeth still under what colour he commits this ill*, Lucr. 475. *his ear her —s admits*, 558. *by your fair p. to soften Angelo*, Meas. I, 4, 69. *until my tears and —s have won his grace*, Err. V, 115. Mids. III, 2, 250. Merch. III, 3, 20. IV, 1, 126 (*to make*). As IV, 3, 55. R2 V, 3, 97. 101. 107. 109. 110. 127. H6B IV, 7, 73. H6C IV, 6, 7. Hml. I, 2, 118. Oth. I, 3, 152.

2) petition to heaven: Lucr. 344. Sonn. 108, 5. Phoen. 67. Tp. I, 1, 55. 57. I, 2, 422. III, 1, 35. Epil. 16. Gent. I, 1, 17. Wiv. II, 2, 102. Meas. II, 2, 151. II, 4, 71. IV, 3, 44. Err. IV, 4, 58. V, 104. Mids. I, 1, 197. II, 2, 62. Merch. III, 1, 23. Wint. V, 3, 141. H6A I, 1, 32. R3 I, 3, 21. V, 3, 241 etc. etc. With *to*: *my —s to heaven for you*, H8 III, 2, 177. Cor. V, 3, 105. Ant. II, 3, 3. *a book of p.* R3 III, 7, 98. *a book of —s*, IV, 3, 14. *at —s*, Tp. I, 1, 57. *at his —s*, All's II, 5, 46. *fall to thy —s*, H4B V, 5, 51. *forgot my —s*, H8 III, 1, 132. *when you make your —s*, H6B IV, 7, 121. *I'll pray a thousand —s for thy death*, Meas. III, 1, 146. *said many a p.* Wint. V, 3, 141. *while I say one p.* Oth. V, 2, 83. *said a century of —s*, Cymb. IV, 2, 391. *to say my —s*, Wiv. IV, 5, 105. *has thrice her —s said*, V, 5, 54. Ado II, 1, 108. All's I, 1, 228. Tw. III, 4, 131. H4A V, 1, 124. H5 III, 2, 40. IV, 2, 56. Troil. II, 3, 23. Mcb. II, 2, 25. Per. IV, 1, 66. IV, 6, 149. Passing into the sense of kind wishes: *you had my —s*, All's II, 4, 17. *concludes in hearty —s that your attempts may overlive the hazard*, H4B IV, 1, 14. *shall have my —s*, H8 III, 1, 180. *madam, my thanks and —s*, Per. III, 3, 34.

3) the act of addressing the Supreme Being: *he is given to p.* Wiv. I, 4, 13. *the more my p., the lesser is my grace*, Mids. II, 2, 89. *to live in p. and contemplation*, Merch. III, 4, 28. *he is famed for mildness, peace and p.* H6C II, 1, 156. *wast thou in p.?* Troil. II, 3, 39.

**Prayer-book**, a book containing prayers or the forms of devotion: Merch. II, 2, 201. R3 III, 7, 47.

**Preach**, to pronounce a sermon, to speak exhortatively on religious and moral subjects: *harms that p. in our behoof*, Compl. 165. *I have heard you p. that malice was a sin*, H6A III, 1, 127. *his form and cause conjoined, —ing to stones*, Hml. III, 4, 126. Lr. IV, 6, 184. Transitively, = to inculcate as by a sermon, to teach earnestly: *he —ed pure maid*, Compl. 315 (i. e. chastity). *my master —es patience to him*, Err. V, 174. *where manners ne'er were —ed*, Tw. IV, 1, 53. *p. some philosophy to make me mad*, John III, 4, 51. *to have divinity —ed there*, Per. IV, 5, 4.

**Preacher**, one who inculcates religious and moral truth: H5 IV, 1, 9.

**Preachment**, a sermon, a highflown discourse: *made a p. of your high descent*, H6C I, 4, 72.

**Preambulate**, premised, introductory to the main subject: LLL V, 1, 85 (Armado's speech. Most M. Edd. *praeambula*`.

**Precede**, to go before in the order of time: *six —ing ancestors*, All's V, 3, 196. *harbingers —ing still the fates*, Hml. I, 1, 122.

**Precedence** (*precédence*) something going (said) before: *to make plain some obscure p. that hath before been sain*, LLL III, 83. *I do not like 'But yet', it does allay the good p.* Ant. II, 5, 51.

**Precedent** (*precédent*), adj. former: *our own p. passions do instruct us what levity's in youth*, Tim. I, 1, 133. *your p. lord*, Hml. III, 4, 98. *thy p. services*, Ant. IV, 14, 83.

**Precedent** (*précedent*) subst. 1) original copy of a writing: *return the p. to these lords again*, John V, 2, 3. *the p. was full as long a doing*, R3 III, 6, 7.

2) presage, sign: *she seizes on his sweating palm, the p. of pith and livelihood*, Ven. 26.

3) example: *the p. whereof in Lucrece view*, Lucr. 1261. *who ever shunned by p. the destined ill she must herself assay?* Compl. 155. *thy case shall be my p.* Tp. II, 1, 291. *that I may example my digression by some mighty p.* LLL I, 2, 122. *'twill be recorded for a p.* Merch. IV, 1, 220. *lest barbarism, making me the p.* Wint. II, 1, 84. R2 II, 1, 130. H4A II, 4, 37. H6C II, 2, 33. H8 I, 2, 91. II, 2, 86. Tit. V, 3, 44. Hml. V, 2, 260. Lr. II, 3, 13. Cymb. III, 1, 75.

**Precept**, 1) *précept*, instruction, lesson: *what are —s worth of stale example?* Compl. 267. *my father's —s I therein forget*, Tp. III, 1, 58. *in action all of p.* Meas. IV, 1, 40. *I will bestow some —s of this virgin*, All's III, 5, 103. *to load me with —s*, Cor. IV, 1, 10. *never learned the icy —s of respect*, Tim. IV, 3, 258. *these few —s*, Hml. I, 3, 58. *then I —s gave her*, II, 2, 142 (Qq *prescripts*).

2) *précept*, mandate, summons: *those —s cannot be served*, H4B V, 1, 14. *send —s to the leviathan to come ashore*, H5 III, 3, 26.

**Preceptial**, instructive: *would give p. medicine to rage*, Ado V, 1, 24, i. e. the medicine of precepts, of instructions.

**Precinct** (*precínct*), district, quarter: *within her quarter and mine own p. I was employed in passing to and fro*, H6A II, 1, 68.

**Precious**, 1) of great price, valuable: Ven. 824. Lucr. 334. Sonn. 57, 3. 77, 2. 86, 2. 131, 4. Gent. II, 6, 24. Ado IV, 1, 29. 229. Merch. II, 8, 20. III, 1, 91. As I, 3, 4. II, 1, 14. John V, 2, 161. R2 I, 1, 32. I, 2, 19. I, 3, 267. II, 1, 46. III, 3, 90. H4A II, 4, 420. H4B III, 4, 391. H6A I, 6, 24. V, 3, 119. R3 III, 2, 23. V, 3, 250. Troil. II, 2, 55. Cor. II, 2, 129. Tit. I, 72. II, 3, 227. Rom. V, 3, 31. Tim. IV, 3, 26. Hml. III, 4, 100. Lr. III, 2, 71. V, 3, 190. Cymb. I, 4, 81. III, 4, 192.

2) exquisite, rare, of great worth: Ven. 543. Lucr. 870. Sonn. 30, 6. 85, 4. Tp. III, 1, 25. Wiv. V, 5, 66. LLL II, 4. IV, 3, 333. V, 2, 445. Mids. III, 2, 227. As III, 3, 64. Shr. IV, 3, 177. Wint. I, 2, 79. 452. IV, 2, 27. V, 1, 222. 223. V, 3, 131.* John III, 1, 79. IV, 1, 94. IV, 3, 40. H4B IV, 5, 162. R3 II, 1, 123. Troil. IV, 4, 10. Rom. I, 1, 239. I, 3, 87. Tim. I, 2, 108. Mcb. IV, 3, 27. 223. Hml. IV, 5, 162. Lr. I, 1, 76.* 262. Oth. III, 4, 66. Ant. I, 3, 73. Cymb. I, 6, 37. II, 3, 127. III, 5, 59. IV, 2, 326. V, 5, 9. 242.

Ironically: *p. villain*, Oth. V, 2, 235. *you p. pandar*, Cymb. III, 5, 81. *thou p. varlet*, IV, 2, 83.

**Precious-dear**, not hyphened in Q and the earlier Ff: Troil. V, 3, 28.

**Precious-juiced** (not hyphened in O. Edd.) of an exquisite sap: *p. flowers*, Rom. II, 3, 8.

**Preciously**, valuably: *the time must by us both be spent most p.* Tp. I, 2, 241 (in business of great importance).

**Precipice**, a headlong steep: H8 V, 1, 140.

**Precipitate**, to fall headlong: *so many fathom down —ing*, Lr. IV, 6, 50.

**Precipitation**, the throwing or being thrown headlong: *pile ten hills on the Tarpeian rock, that the p. might down stretch below the beam of sight*, Cor. III, 2, 4. *in peril of p. from off the rock Tarpeian*, III, 3, 102.

**Precise**, exact, nice, punctilious: *to keep the terms of my honour p.* Wiv. II, 2, 23. *he was ever p. in promise-keeping*, Meas. I, 2, 76. *Lord Angelo is p., stands at a guard with envy*, I, 3, 50. *taffeta phrases, silken terms p.* LLL V, 2, 406. *to hold your honour more p. and nice with others than with him*, H4B II, 3, 40. In the language of Elbow, = decided, doubtless: *I know not well what they are, but p. villains they are*, Meas. II, 1, 54.

**Precisely**, 1) exactly, expressly: *I have taught him, even as one would say p., 'thus I would teach a dog'*, Gent. IV, 4, 6 (Launce's speech). *therefore, p., can you carry your good will to the maid?* Wiv. I, 1, 237 (Evans' speech). *tell me p. of what complexion*, LLL I, 2, 85 (Armado's speech). *such a fellow, to say p., were not for the court*, All's II, 2, 12 (the clown's speech).

2) accurately, nicely, scrupulously: *he cannot so p. weed this land as his misdoubts present occasion*, H4B IV, 1, 205. *some craven scruple of thinking too p. on the event*, Hml. IV, 4, 41.

**Preciseness**, nicety, scrupulousness: *is all your strict p. come to this?* H6A V, 4, 67.

**Precisian**, perhaps = one who stands upon punctilios: *though Love use Reason for his p., he admits him not for his counsellor*, Wiv. II, 1, 5, i. e. though Love may calculate the exact proportion of age, temper etc. in making his choice (as Falstaff does in what follows) yet, after all, he is not to be controlled by the advice of reason. Most M. Edd., referring to Sonn. 147, 5, *physician*, but the two passages have nothing in common.

**Pre-contract** (*pre-contráct*), a betrothment previous to another: Meas. IV, 1, 72.

**Precurrer**, forerunner: Phoen. 6.

**Precurse**, subst. forerunning: *the like p. of fierce events*, Hml. I, 1, 121 (only in Qq).

**Precursor**, forerunner: Tp. I, 2, 201.

**Predecease**, to die before: *if children p. progenitors*, Lucr. 1756. —*d* = deceased in ancient times, of old: *worn as a memorable trophy of p. valour*, H5 V, 1, 76.

**Predecessor**, 1) one who was in an office before another: H5 I, 1, 81. Cor. II, 2, 147.

2) ancestor: H5 I, 2, 248. Cor. II, 1, 101. Mcb. II, 4, 34.

**Predestinate**, decreed by fate: *a p. scratched face*, Ado I, 1, 136.

**Predicament**, category, condition, situation: *the offender's life lies in the mercy of the duke only, ... in which p. thou standest*, Merch. IV, 1, 357. *that I descend so low, to show the line and the p. wherein you range*, H4A I, 3, 168. *piteous p.! even so lies she*, Rom. III, 3, 86.

**Predict**, prediction, prophecy: *by oft p. that I in heaven find*, Sonn. 14, 8.

**Prediction**, presage; prophecy: *these —s are to the world in general as to Caesar*, Caes. II, 2, 28. *my partner you greet with great p. of noble having*, Mcb. I, 3, 55. Lr. I, 2, 119. 152.

**Predominance**, superior power and influence:

*underwrite his humorous p.* Troil. II, 3, 138. *is't night's p. or the day's shame*, Mcb. II, 4, 8. *knaves, thieves and treachers by spherical p.* Lr. I, 2, 134.

**Predominant**, prevalent, supreme in influence; used of planets: All's I, 1, 211. Wint. I, 2, 202. Of bad qualities: H6B III, 1, 145. Rom. II, 3, 29. Mcb. III, 1, 87.

**Predominate**, to prevail, to oversway; with *over: I will p. over the peasant*, Wiv. II, 2, 294 (like a meteor or planet). Transitively: *let your close fire p. his smoke*, Tim. IV, 3, 142.

**Pre-eminence**, superiority in rank and power: Err. II, 1, 23. Lr. I, 1, 133.

**Pre-employ**, to employ before another: *that villain whom I employed was —ed by him*, Wint. II, 1, 49.

**Preface**, subst. introduction by preliminary remarks: *this superficial tale is but a p. of her worthy praise*, H6A V, 5, 11.

**Prefer**, 1) to like better than, to choose before another: *have I not reason to p. mine own?* Gent. II, 4, 156. *in our opinions she should be —ed*, H6A V, 5, 61. *why Somerset should be —ed*, H6B I, 3, 117. *thou —est thy life before thine honour*, H6C I, 1, 246. *p. a noble life before a long*, Cor. III, 1, 152. *this before all the world do I p.* Tit. IV, 2, 109. —*ing you before her father*, Oth. I, 3, 187. *you must not so far p. her fore ours of Italy*, Cymb. I, 4, 70. Refl.: *our haste from hence is of so quick condition that it —s itself and leaves unquestioned matters of needful value*, Meas. I, 1, 55 (= that it —s itself before the most important matters, which it leaves unquestioned).

2) to present, to lay before, to show: *that strong-bonded oath that shall p. and undertake my troth*, Compl. 280. *our play is —ed*, Mids. IV, 2, 39 (given in among others for the duke's option). *although in writing I —ed the manner of thy vile outrageous crimes*, H6A III, 1, 10. *why then —ed you not your sums and bills, when your false masters eat of my lord's meat?* Tim. III, 4, 49. *and ne'er p. his injuries to his heart*, III, 5, 34. *let him go and presently p. his suit to Caesar*, Caes. III, 1, 28. *I'll have —ed him a chalice for the nonce*, Hml. IV, 7, 160 (Ff *prepared*). *without more wider and more overt test than these thin habits and poor likelihoods of modern seeming do p. against him*, Oth. I, 3, 109. *who is the first that doth p. himself?* Per. II, 2, 17.

3) to address, to direct: *if you know any such, p. them hither*, Shr. I, 1, 97. *fellow, wilt thou bestow thy time with me? Ay, if Messala will p. me to you. Do so, good Messala*, Caes. V, 5, 62.* *stood I within his grace, I would p. him to a better place*, Lr. I, 1, 277.

4) to recommend: *to call her bad, whose sovereignty so oft thou hast —ed with twenty thousand soul-confirming oaths*, Gent. II, 6, 15. *Shylock hath —ed thee*, Merch. II, 2, 155. *who —eth peace more than I do?* H6A III, 1, 33. 110. *my book —ed me to the king*, H6B IV, 7, 77. *who lets go by no vantages that may p. you to his daughter*, Cymb. II, 3, 51. *the emperor's letters should not sooner than thine own worth p. thee*, IV, 2, 386. *he is —ed by thee to us*, 400.

5) to promote, to advance: *I will help thee to p. her too*, Gent. II, 4, 157. *under the colour of commending him I have access my own love to p.* IV, 2, 4. *I will love thee and p. thee too*, R3 IV, 2, 82. (a bishop) *newly —ed from the king's secretary*, H8 IV, 1, 102.

*so shall you have a shorter journey to your desires by the means I shall then have to p. them*, Oth. II, 1, 286. *to be styled the under-hangman of his kingdom and hated for being — ed so well*, Cymb. II, 3, 136. *ere I arise, I will p. my sons*, V, 5, 326.

**Preferment,** 1) preference given, precedence granted: *nor is your firm resolve unknown to me, in the p. of the eldest sister*, Shr. II, 94.

2) advancement, promotion: *these do labour for their own p.* H6B I, 1, 181. *help you to many fair —s*, R3 I, 3, 95. H8 V, 1, 36. Oth. I, 1, 36. Synonymous to good fortune: *to seek p. out*, Gent. I, 3, 7. *if it be p. to leave a rich Jew's service, to become the follower of so poor a gentleman*, Merch. II, 2, 155. *had I not the dash of my former life in me, would p. drop on my head*, Wint. V, 2, 123. Lr. IV, 5, 38. Cymb. I, 5, 71. III, 5, 116. 159. V, 4, 215.

**Prefigure,** to form or shape in anticipation: *all their praises are but prophecies of this our time, all you — ing*, Sonn. 106, 10.

**Prefixed,** appointed beforehand: Meas. IV, 3, 83. Wint. I, 2, 42. Troil. IV, 3, 1. Rom. V, 3, 253.

**Preformed,** formed in the beginning, original: *why all these things change their natures and p. faculties to monstrous quality*, Caes. I, 3, 67.

**Pregnancy,** cleverness: *p. is made a tapster, and hath his quick wit wasted in giving reckonings*, H4B I, 2, 192.

**Pregnant,** 1) expert, clever, ingenious, artful: *the terms of common justice you are as p. in as ... any*, Meas. I, 1, 12. *wherein the p. enemy does want*, Tw. II, 2, 29. *to your own most p. and vouchsafed ear*, III, 1, 100. *how p. sometimes his replies are*, Hml. II, 2, 212.

2) disposed, prompt, ready: *crook the p. hinges of the knee*, Hml. III, 2, 66. *the profits of my death were very p. and potential spurs to make thee seek it*, Lr. II, 1, 78. *cursed Dionyza hath the p. instrument of wrath prest for this blow*, Per. IV Prol. 44. With *to: fair virtues all, to which the Grecians are most prompt and p.* Troil. IV, 4, 90. *who, by the art of known and feeling sorrows, am p. to good pity*, Lr. IV, 6, 227.

3) probable in the highest degree, clear, evident: *'tis very p.* Meas. II, 1, 23. Cymb. IV, 2, 325. *most true, if ever truth were p. by circumstance*, Wint. V, 2, 34. *it is a most p. and unforced position*, Oth. II, 1, 239. *were't not that we stand up against them all, 'twere p. they should square between themselves*, Ant. II, 1, 45.

**Pregnantly,** clearly, evidently: *a thousand moral paintings I can show that shall demonstrate these quick blows of Fortune's more p. than words*, Tim. I, 1, 92.

**Prejudicate,** to judge or determine beforehand to disadvantage: *wherein our dearest friend —s the business and would seem to have us make denial*, All's I, 2, 8.

**Prejudice,** subst. detriment, injury: H8 I, 1, 182. II, 4, 154.

**Prejudice,** vb. to injure: H6A III, 3, 91.

**Prejudicial,** detrimental, tending to impair: H6C I, 1, 144.

**Prelate,** a dignitary of the church: H4A I, 3, 267. V, 5, 37. H5 I, 1, 40. H6A I, 3, 23. III, 1, 14. 46. 57. H6B I, 1, 142. R3 IV, 4, 502.

**Premeditate,** to revolve in the mind beforehand, to contrive or design previously: *he doth p. the dan-*

*gers*, Lucr. 183. *—d welcomes*, Mids. V, 94. *—d murder*, H5 IV, 1, 170. *deep —d lines*, H6A III, 1, 1.

**Premeditation,** previous deliberation: *a cold p. for my purpose*, H6C III, 2, 133.

**Premised** (*premised*) sent before the time: *let the vile world end, and the p. flames of the last day knit earth and heaven together*, H6B V, 2, 41.

**Premises** (*prémises*) conditions, suppositions: *that he, in lieu o' the p. of homage ..., should presently extirpate me*, Tp. I, 2, 123. *the p. observed, thy will by my performance shall be served*, All's II, 1, 204. *'t has done, upon the p., but justice*, H8 II, 1, 63.

**Prenominate,** to forename, foretell: *to p. in nice conjecture where thou wilt hit me dead*, Troil. IV, 5, 250. Partic. *p.* = aforesaid: *the p. crimes*, Hml. II, 1, 43.

**Prentice,** apprentice: All's IV, 3, 211. H4B I., 2, 194. H6B I, 3, 201. II, 3, 71.

**Prenzie** or **Prenzy,** probably = too nice, precise, demure, prim: *the p. Angelo*, Meas. III, 1, 94. *the damned'st body to invest and cover in p. guards*, 97. cf. Burns' Halloween: *poor Willie, wi' his bowkail runt, was brunt wi' primsie Mallie.* cf. also the modern *prim*, and the ancient Scotch *prunse*.

**Pre-occupied,** prepossessed: *your minds, p. with what you rather must do than what you should*, Cor. II, 3, 240.

**Pre-ordinance,** a rule previously established: *turn p. and first decree into the law of children*, Caes. III, 1, 38.

**Preparation,** 1) the act of making fit, of putting in readiness: *you make grand p. for a duke de Jamany*, Wiv. IV, 5, 88. *and have all charitable p.* Meas. III, 2, 222. Ado I, 1, 280. II, 2, 50. Merch. II, 4, 4. All's III, 6, 82. H5 IV, 1, 192. Mcb. I, 5, 34. Ant. V, 2, 225. Particularly the act of putting one's self in readiness for combat: Tw. III, 4, 245. John II, 213. IV, 2, 111. H5 II Chor. 13. II, 4, 18. IV Chor. 14. H6A I, 1, 166. Cor. IV, 3, 18. Mcb. V, 3, 57. Hml. I, 1, 105 (*—s*). II, 2, 63. Lr. III, 7, 10. Ant. III, 4, 26 (*I'll raise the p. of a war*). IV, 10, 1 (*their p. is today by sea*).

2) the state of looking forward to sth., notice given: *I make bold to press with so little p. upon you*, Wiv. II, 2, 162 (so unexpectedly and with so little ceremony).

3) a force ready for combat, an army or navy: *the king is set forth with strong and mighty p.* H4A IV, 1, 93. *these three lead on this p.* Cor. I, 2, 15. *our p. stands in expectation of them*, Lr. IV, 4, 22. *the Turkish p. makes for Rhodes*, Oth. I, 3, 14. 221. *your p. can affront no less*, Cymb. IV, 3, 29.

4) accomplishment, qualification: *your many warlike, court-like, and learned —s*, Wiv. II, 2, 237.

**Prepare,** subst. preparation, armaments: *make p. for war*, H6C IV, 1, 131.

**Prepare,** vb. 1) trans. a) to make fit, to make ready: Sonn. 114, 12. Tp. I, 2, 145. Meas. II, 2, 84. III, 1, 4. III, 2, 254. Ado I, 2, 23. Merch. III, 5, 56. IV, 1, 245. 264. As II, 5, 65. All's II, 5, 66. IV, 4, 34. Tw. II, 4, 57. Wint. IV, 4, 512. H5 I, 2, 234. V Chor. 13. H6B II, 4, 15. R3 V, 3, 88. H8 III, 2, 328. IV, 1, 64. Cor. V, 2, 77. Tit. IV, 2, 146. V, 2, 197. Rom. I, 1, 116 (cf. Lr. II, 1, 53. Ant. IV, 12, 39). Caes. III, 1, 253. Lr. I, 4, 280. II, 1, 53 (cf. Rom. I, 1, 116). Ant. III, 3, 41. IV, 12, 39. Per. I, 1, 43. = to make ready for combat: John II, 83. **V, 2, 130. 134.** R2 I, 3, 5. H4A II, 3, 37. H4B Ind. 12. Cor. III, 2, 139. IV, 5, 140. Ant. III, 7, 41. Reflexively: *p. yourself to death*, Meas. III, 1, 169. IV, 2, 72. IV, 3, 57. Merch. II, 4, 23. IV, 1, 324. Wint. II, 3, 201. John IV, 1, 90. R2 IV, 320. V, 1, 37 (*p. thee hence for France*). H6C V, 4, 60. Caes. V, 1, 12. Hml. III, 3, 2. IV, 3, 45.

b) to make to expect, to give notice to: *bring him his confessor, let him be — d*, Meas. II, 1, 35. *go you and p. Aliena*, As V, 2, 17. *mine ear is open and my heart — d*, R2 III, 2, 93. *p. her ears to hear a wooer's tale*, R3 IV, 4, 327. *p. thy brow to frown*, Cor. IV, 5, 69. *p. thy aged eyes to weep*, Tit. III, 1, 59. *p. her against this wedding day*, Rom. III, 4, 32. *to p. him up against to-morrow*, IV, 2, 45 (Qq *up* him).

Partic. *—d* = ready: *I am — d, here is my sword*, H6A I, 2, 98. *for that I am —d and full resolved*, Tit. II, 1, 57. *be —d to hear*, Caes. I, 2, 66. *an you will not, come when you are next —d for*, Oth. IV, 1, 168. *be —d to know*, Ant. I, 3, 66. *I came here a man —d to take this offer*, II, 6, 41. = deliberate: *with a leavened and —d choice*, Meas. I, 1, 52.

c) to provide: *let us p. some welcome for the mistress*, Merch. V, 37. *have —d great store of wedding cheer*, Shr. III, 2, 188. *p. thy grave*, Tim. IV, 3, 378. *Cleon's wife a present murderer does p. for good Marina*, Per. IV Prol. 38.

2) intr. a) to make every thing ready, to put things in order: *Boyet, p., I will away to-night*, LLL V, 2, 737. *p. for dinner*, Merch. III, 5, 52 (purposely misinterpreted by Launcelot). Lr. I, 3, 26. *p. there, the duke is coming*, H8 II, 1, 97. Caes. IV, 3, 140.

b) to make one's self ready: *to bid the wind a base he now —s*, Ven. 303. *p. to carry it*, Lucr. 1294. 1296. 1607. Tp. IV, 166. Meas. IV, 3, 136. LLL V, 2, 81. 510. Merch. IV, 1, 304. H5 IV, 1, 196. H6B I, 2, 57. R3 I, 4, 185. Cor. V, 2, 51. Rom. I, 5, 123. III, 3, 162. IV, 5, 92. Caes. II, 2, 118. With *against*: Sonn. 13, 3. With *for*: H5 V, 2, 398. Per. II, 3, 7. = to make one's self ready for combat: John II, 78. IV, 2, 114. H4A V, 2, 90. Cor. I, 2, 30. Mcb. III, 6, 39. Ant. III, 6, 58. *the Dauphin is —ing hitherward*, John V, 7, 59; cf. R2 V, 1, 37 and Cor. IV, 5, 140.

c) to look forward to, to expect, to keep one's self ready for what is to happen: *upon that day either p. to die or else to wed Demetrius*, Mids. I, 1, 86. *p. to see the life as lively mocked as ever ...*, Wint. V, 3, 18. *bid him p., for I will cut his throat*, H5 IV, 4, 34. *you must p. to fight without Achilles*, Troil. II, 3, 238. *in, and p.; ours is the fall, I fear*, Tim. V, 2, 16. *if you have tears, p. to shed them now*, Caes. III, 2, 173.

**Preparedly**, in a state of readiness for what is to happen: *that she p. may frame herself to the way she's forced to*, Ant. V, 1, 55.

**Preposterous**, perverse, running counter to common sense and nature: H6C V, 6, 5. R3 II, 4, 63. Troil. V, 1, 27. Oth. I, 3, 333. Applied to persons: *p. ass*, Shr. III, 1, 9 (because he would invert the natural order of things). Used with impropriety by Armado, LLL I, 1, 244, and blunderingly for *prosperous* by the clown in Wint. V, 2, 159.

**Preposterously**, perversely, against the natural order of things: *that it* (my nature) *could so p. be stained, to leave for nothing all thy sum of good*, Sonn. 109, 11. *methinks you prescribe to yourself very p.*

Wiv. II, 2, 250. *those things do best please me that befal p.* Mids. III, 2, 121. *whatsoever cunning fiend it was that wrought upon thee so p.* H5 II, 2, 112. *for nature so p. to err*, Oth. I, 3, 62.

**Prerogative**, 1) preeminence, precedence, first rank: *executing the outward face of royalty with all p.* Tp. I, 2, 105. *then give me leave to have p.* Shr. III, 1, 6. *a very serious business calls on him. The great p. and right of love, which as your due time claims, he does acknowledge*, All's II, 4, 42. *our p. calls not your counsels*, Wint. II, 1, 163. *shall I detract so much from that p., as to be called but viceroy of the whole?* H6A V, 4, 142.

2) privilege: *my fortunes ... give me this p. of speech*, Tw. II, 5, 78. *p. of age, crown, sceptres, laurels*, Troil. I, 3, 107. *insisting on the old p. and power*, Cor. III, 3, 17. Misapplied by Fluellen for rule, statute: H5 IV, 1, 67.

**Prerogatived**, privileged, exempt from certain evils: *p. are they less than the base*, Oth. III, 3, 274.

**Presage**, subst. (*présage* or *preságe*), 1) prognostic: Ven. 457. Tw. III, 2, 69. John I, 28. III, 4, 158.

2) foreboding, presentiment: *the sad augurs mock their own p.* Sonn. 107, 6. *if heart's p. be not vain*, R2 II, 2, 142.

**Presage**, vb. (*preságe*), 1) to foreshow, to indicate prophetically: Merch. III, 2, 175. H6A IV, 1, 191. Rom. V, 1, 2. Caes. V, 1, 79. Lr. IV, 6, 121. Ant. I, 2, 47. 49.

2) to have a presentiment, to foresee prophetically: Merch. I, 1, 175. H6C IV, 6, 92. V, 1, 71.

**Presager**, one who, or that which, indicates something: *let my books be then the eloquence and dumb —s of my speaking breast*, Sonn. 23, 10.

**Prescience** (*préscience* or *prescience*) foreknowledge; foresight: *which in her p. she controlled still*, Lucr. 727. *by my p. I find my zenith doth depend upon a most auspicious star*, Tp. I, 2, 180. *count wisdom as no member of the war, forestall p. and esteem no act but that of hand*, Troil. I, 3, 199. *vex not his p.* Ant. I, 2, 20 (jestingly used as a title belonging to the soothsayer).

**Prescribe**, to set down authoritatively for direction: *p. not us our duties*, Lr. I, 1, 279. Used of the directions given by a physician: Wiv. II, 2, 249. R2 I, 1, 154. Tim. V, 4, 84. In Lr. I, 2, 24 Ff *—d*, Qq and most M. Edd. *subscribed*.

**Prescript**, subst. direction, order: *and then I —s gave her*, Hml. II, 2, 142 (Ff *precepts*). *do not exceed the p. of this scroll*, Ant. III, 8, 5.

**Prescript**, adj. set down as a rule, according to the canon (or = prescriptive, immemorial?): *your mistress bears well. Me well; which is the p. praise and perfection of a good and particular mistress*, H5 III, 7, 49.

**Prescription**, 1) direction: *I'll go along by your p.* H8 I, 1, 151. Particularly a medical direction, a recipe: Sonn. 147, 6. All's I, 3, 227. H4B I, 2, 147. Cor. II, 1, 127. Oth. I, 3, 310.

2) a right derived from immemorial custom: *a pedigree of threescore and two years, a silly time to make p. for a kingdom's worth*, H6C III, 3, 94.

**Presence**, 1) the state of being in a certain place or company: *we fairies that do run from the p. of the sun*, Mids. V, 392. *my p. may well abate the over-merry* *spleen,* Shr. Ind. 1, 136. *his p. must be the whip of the other,* All's IV, 3, 42. *what p. must not know, from where you do remain, let paper show,* R2 I, 3, 249 (= what cannot be uttered here where we are together). John II, 542. IV, 3, 22. H4A III, 2, 39. 84. H6A III, 1, 181. H6B I, 1, 141. III, 2, 219. R3 I, 2, 58. III, 4, 26. H8 I, 1, 30. V, 5, 72. Tit. V, 3, 42. Mcb. III, 1, 15. III, 6, 22. Oth. III, 3, 281. Ant. III, 7, 11. Per. II, 3, 21. *in the p. of:* Meas. I, 4, 11. H4A III, 2, 54. Cor. III, 3, 97. Caes. III, 1, 199. *in p. of:* H6B I, 1, 6. R3 I, 3, 115. *in your p.* Merch. III, 4, 1. Tw. II, 5, 191. H6B III, 2, 238. H8 V, 3, 124. Lr. IV, 3, 13. *in p.* = present, not absent: *you were in p. then,* R2 IV, 62. H4B IV, 4, 17. H5 I, 2, 2. II, 4, 111. *when he approacheth to your p.* Gent. V, 4, 32 (= when he approaches you). H6C III, 3, 44. *crowd to his p.* Meas. II, 4, 29 (= round him). *if you come in her p.* Ado I, 1, 124. H8 I, 2, 197. *to come into his p.* All's V, 1, 21. H6B V, 1, 65. H8 I, 4, 59. *tender your persons to his p.* Wint. IV, 4, 827. *desires access to your high p.* V, 1, 88. *call them to our p.* R2 I, 1, 15. H6B III, 2, 15. R3 I, 3, 39. *admitted to your p.* Tit. V, 1, 153. *will not be denied your highness' p.* Ant. V, 2, 234. *take him from our p.* Cymb. V, 5, 301.

Often = company: *wherefore with infection should he live and with his p. grace impiety?* Sonn. 67, 2. *repair me with thy p.* Gent. V, 4, 11. *I promised your p. and the chain,* Err. IV, 1, 23. *no marvel though Demetrius do fly my p.* Mids. II, 2, 97. *from his p. I am barred,* Wint. III, 2, 98. *be somewhat scanter of your maiden p.* Hml. I, 3, 121. *heavens make our p. and our practices pleasant and helpful to him,* II, 2, 38. Mids. III, 2, 80. Wint. I, 2, 38. R2 II, 3, 63. V, 3, 40. Troil. III, 3, 28. Lr. I, 2, 176.

2) Abstr. pro concr., = persons of rank assembled in a place, noble company: *p. majestical would put him out,* LLL V, 2, 102 (i. e. the princess being present). *here is like to be a good p. of Worthies,* 536. *in such a p. here to plead my thoughts,* Mids. I, 1, 61. *it ill beseems this p. to cry aim,* John II, 196. *come I appellant to this princely p.* R2 I, 1, 34. *the best in all this p.* IV, 32. 115. 117. H6A I, 1, 21. H6B I, 3, 114. II, 3, 101. III, 2, 228. R3 I, 3, 54. II, 1, 58. 78. 84. III, 4, 66. H8 IV, 2, 37 (*i' the p. he would say untruths,* i. e. before the king and his court). Hml. V, 2, 239 (*this p. knows*). Ant. II, 2, 111. Per. II, 3, 49. cf. Cade's speech in H6B IV, 7, 32: *be it known unto thee by these p.;* cf. As I, 2, 132.

3) personal appearance, air, mien, port: *be as thy p. is, gracious and kind,* Sonn. 10, 11. *bear a fair p., though your heart be tainted,* Err. III, 2, 13. *of such enchanting p. and discourse,* 166. *which parti-coloured p. of loose love put on by us,* LLL V, 2, 776. *now he goes, with no less p., but with much more love, than young Alcides,* Merch. III, 2, 54. *of excellent growth and p.* As I, 2, 130. *how should I behold the sternness of his p.* Wint. IV, 4, 24. *your p. is too bold and peremptory,* H4A I, 3, 17. *I will put on his p.* Troil. III, 3, 272. *show a fair p. and put off these frowns,* Rom. I, 5, 75. *nature this dowry gave, to glad her p.* Per. I, 1, 9. *is't not a goodly p.?* V, 1, 66 (German: *eine schöne Erscheinung*).

4) person, personality, the whole of the personal qualities of an individual: *lord of thy p. and no land beside,* John I, 137. *lord of our p., Angiers, and of you,* II, 367. *your royal —s be ruled by me,* 377. *how dare thy joints forget to pay their awful duty to our p.?* R2 III, 3, 76. *my p., like a robe pontifical, ne'er seen but wondered at,* H4A III, 2, 56; cf. 39. 84; and Verges' blunder in Ado III, 5, 34.

5) presence-chamber, state-room: *suppose the grass whereon thou treadest the p. strewed,* R2 I, 3, 289. *the two great cardinals wait in the p.* H8 III, 1, 17. *her beauty makes this vault a feasting p. full of light,* Rom. V, 3, 86.

**Present,** adj. 1) being in a certain place, not absent: Lucr. 1696. Sonn. 47, 10. Tp. III, 3, 35. As III, 1, 4. Wint. IV, 4, 274. R2 I, 3, 259. IV, 129. H6B V, 2, 87. R3 I, 3, 187. H8 I, 1, 8. II, 4, 95. Troil. III, 3, 180. Tim. I, 1, 71. III, 6, 92. Mcb. III, 4, 41. Cymb. IV, 2, 343. V, 5, 36. With *at:* All's III, 6, 29. Wint. II, 2, 17. V, 2, 1.

2) being at this time, not past or future: Ven. 970. Lucr. 632. Sonn. 106, 13. Tp. I, 2, 136. IV, 122. Gent. II, 1, 81. Meas. IV, 2, 151. Err. I, 2, 29. IV, 3, 88. V, 401. Ado I, 2, 15. LLL I, 1, 5. Merch. I, 1, 44. I, 3, 54. 141. IV, 1, 172. As V, 3, 31. Shr. Ind. 2, 22. All's II, 3, 306. IV, 3, 183. Tw. II, 3, 49. III, 4, 377. V, 365. Wint. IV, 4, 145. V, 1, 32. 96. John V, 1, 14. 77. R2 II, 1, 132. II, 3, 14. H4A II, 4, 106. IV, 1, 44. V, 1, 66. 88. H4B I, 1, 211. I, 3, 10. 16. 36. 108. IV, 1, 83. 108. IV, 2, 74. IV, 5, 153. H5 IV, 1, 18. R3 I, 1, 69. V, 1, 8. H8 I, 1, 206. II, 4, 154. 219. III, 2, 159. Troil. II, 2, 201. Cor. I, 1, 262. 283. II, 2, 47. II, 3, 232. 257. IV, 6, 2. Rom. IV, 1, 118. Caes. III, 1, 166. Mcb. I, 3, 55. 137. II, 1, 59. Hml. I, 1, 156. Lr. II, 1, 103. V, 3, 121. 318. Oth. I, 1, 156. I, 3, 235. II, 2, 10. III, 4, 116. Ant. I, 2, 128. I, 3, 52. I, 4, 32. 79. II, 2, 101. 140 (= momentary). Cymb. II, 4, 5. 151. IV, 3, 43. V, 4, 214. V, 5, 256. Per. V, 3, 40. Adverbially, = at present: *wherefore we are now p. here together,* H8 II, 4, 202. *you may salve so, not what is dangerous p., but the loss of what is past,* Cor. III, 2, 71.

3) done or used on the spot, instant, immediate. *hindering their p. fall by this dividing,* Lucr. 551. *with circumstances strong of p. death,* 1263. *to afford some p. speed,* 1307. *do I not spend revenge upon myself with p. moan,* Sonn. 149, 8. *I'll make a p. recompense,* Wiv. IV, 6, 55. *sign me a p. pardon,* Meas. II, 4, 152. *a p. and a dangerous courtesy,* IV, 2, 171. *I will give him a p. shrift,* 223. *make p. satisfaction,* Err. IV, 1, 5. *I am not furnished with the p. money,* 34 (= I have not the money about me, to pay you here at this instant; cf. Merch. I, 1, 179 and III, 2, 276). *send some p. help,* V, 176. *a p. remedy,* Ado I, 3, 9. *neither have I money nor commodity to raise a p. sum,* Merch. I, 1, 179 (= to be immediately paid). cf. III, 2, 276. *beggars upon entreaty have a p. alms,* Shr. IV, 3, 5. 14. All's II, 2, 67. II, 5, 61. Wint. I, 2, 281. II, 3, 184. III, 3, 4. IV, 2, 57. H4B IV, 1, 174. IV, 3, 80. H5 II, 1, 112. II, 4, 67. H6A III, 4, 39. H6B V, 3, 25. R3 IV, 5, 5. H8 I, 2, 211. Cor. III, 1, 212. III, 3, 21. IV, 3, 53. Tit. II, 3, 173. Rom. IV, 1, 61. V, 1, 51. Tim. I, 1, 71. II, 2, 154 (*p. debts* = instantly to be paid, due). 157. III, 1, 21. III, 2, 39 (*his p. occasion,* i. e. urgent). IV, 3, 527. V, 2, 4. Caes. II, 2, 5. Mcb. I, 2, 64. Hml. IV, 3, 67. V, 1, 318. Lr. I, 1, 195. Oth. I, 2, 90. III, 3, 47. Cymb. II, 4, 137. Per. IV Prol. 38. IV, 3, 136. V, 1, 193.

**Present,** subst. 1) a gift, a donative: Tp. II, 2, 72. Gent. III, 1, 92. IV, 2, 80. IV, 4, 7. 54. Wiv. II,

2, 206. Merch. II, 2, 108. 112. 114. H5 I, 2, 260. R3 I, 1, 120. Tit. IV, 1, 116. IV, 3, 75. Tim. I, 2, 190. II, 2, 145. Ant. I, 5, 45. Cymb. I, 6, 187. 208.

2) the present time: *smothering his passions for the p.* Lucr. Arg. 13. Mcb. III, 4, 31. *crowning the p., doubting of the rest,* Sonn. 115, 12. 123, 10. Tp. I, 1, 25. *such a one I was this p.* Tw. I, 5, 253 (= this moment). *many a man there is even at this p.* Wint. I, 2, 192. *make stale the glistering of this p.* IV, 1, 14. *I'm very sorry to sit here at this p.* H8 V, 3, 9. *no perfection in reversion shall have a praise in p.* Troil. III, 2, 100. *what they do in p., though less than yours in past,* III, 3, 163. *three talents on the p., in future all,* Tim. I, 1, 141. *for this p., I would not be any further moved,* Caes. I, 2, 165. *thy letters have transported me beyond this ignorant p.* Mcb. I, 5, 58. *her son gone, so needful for this p.* Cymb. IV, 3, 48.

3) an affair in hand, a question under consideration: *use him for the p. and dismiss him,* Meas. IV, 2, 27 (i. e. for the present occasion). *and that you not delay the p., but we prove this very hour,* Cor. I, 6, 60. *shall I be charged no further than this p.? must all determine here?* III, 3, 42. *this is from the p.* Ant. II, 6, 30 (not to the purpose).

4) the money which a person has about him: *I'll make division of my p. with you,* Tw. III, 4, 380.

5) a mandate, a writing: *what p. hast thou there?* LLL IV, 3, 189. *be it known unto all men by these —s,* As I, 2, 132; cf. Cade's blunder in H6B IV, 7, 32.

**Present,** vb. 1) to introduce: *let's p. him to the duke like a Roman conqueror,* As IV, 2, 3. *thou shalt p. me as an eunuch to him,* Tw. I, 2, 56. *and there p. yourself and your fair princess fore Leontes,* Wint. IV, 4, 555. 873. H6B V, 1, 59. H8 II, 2, 98. Lr. V, 3, 294. Cymb. III, 4, 176.

2) to offer: *to take advantage on —ed joy,* Ven. 405. *a remedy —s itself,* Meas. III, 1, 204. *a blinking idiot —ing me a schedule,* Merch. II, 9, 55. *this theatre —s more woeful pageants,* As II, 7, 138. *we shall p. our services to a fine new prince,* Wint. II, 1, 17. *p. your hand,* V, 3, 107. *the vilest stroke that ever staring rage —ed to the tears of soft remorse,* John IV, 3, 50. *within this coffin I p. thy buried fear,* R2 V, 6, 30. *he —s no mark to the enemy,* H4B III, 2, 284. IV, 1, 206. H6B V, 1, 66. R3 IV, 4, 274. Cor. IV, 5, 101. V, 6, 31. Caes. I, 3, 51. III, 2, 101. Mcb. III, 2, 31. Lr. II, 3, 11. Oth. I, 3, 124 (= to lay before). *to p. sth. to a person* = to make a person a present of sth.: *p. the fair steed to my lady Cressid,* Troil. V, 5, 2. *hath —ed to you four horses,* Tim. I, 2, 188. V, 1, 19.

3) to show: *jealousy —eth to mine eye the picture of a chafing boar,* Ven. 661. *this huge stage —eth nought but shows,* Sonn. 15, 3. *my soul's imaginary sight —s thy shadow to my sightless view,* 27, 10. *thou —est a pure unstained prime,* 70, 8. *I will discase me and myself p. as I was sometime Milan,* Tp. V, 85. *the folly of my soul dares not p. itself,* Wiv. II, 2, 253. *the truth being known, we'll all p. ourselves,* IV, 4, 63. *to what end their shallow shows should be —ed at our tent to us,* LLL V, 2, 307. As IV, 3, 104. Wint. II, 1, 42. IV, 4, 67. John IV, 2, 266. H4A III, 1, 183. H5 IV Chor. 27. H8 I, 1, 30. Troil. III, 2, 81. Cor. III, 2, 1. Tim. IV, 3, 192. 476. Caes. II, 1, 110. Oth. II, 1, 249. Per. I, 3, 30. II, 2, 3. 23.

4) to represent; a) to supply the place of: *you are to p. the prince's own person,* Ado III, 3, 79. *the image*

*of the king whom I —ed,* H4B V, 2, 79. *the other (colour of our house) his pale cheek — eth,* H6C II, 5 100. b) to act, to perform: *when I —ed Ceres,* Tp. IV, 167. *must my sweet Nan p. the Fairy Queen,* Wiv. IV, 6, 20. *you shall p. the Nine Worthies,* LLL V, 1, 124. 130. 132. 140. V, 2, 519. 537. 542. 592. Mids. III, 1, 62. 69. III, 2, 14. V, 132. 137. 157. 243. H5 V Chor. 6. H8 Prol. 5. Ant. V, 2, 217.

5) *to p. a person with sth.* = to present sth. to a person: *the king would have me p. the princess with some delightful ostentation,* LLL V, 1, 117. *I do p. you with a man of mine, cunning in music and the mathematics,* Shr. II, 55. *I did p. him with the Paris balls,* H5 II, 4, 131. *where I hope to be — ed by your victories with Charles, Alençon, and that traitorous rout,* H6A IV, 1, 172. *here comes the townsmen on procession, to p. your highness with the man,* H6B II, 1, 69. *and with his gifts p. your lordships,* Tit. IV, 2, 14.

6) to accuse, to bring an action against: *you would p. her at the leet, because she brought stone jugs and no sealed quarts,* Shr. Ind. 2, 89.

**Present-absent,** present and at the same time absent, being at the same time at different places: Sonn. 45, 4.

**Presentation,** show, (deceptive) semblance: *he uses his folly like a stalking-horse and under the p. of that he shoots his wit,* As V, 4, 112. *I called thee then poor shadow, painted queen, the p. of but what I was,* R3 IV, 4, 84.

**Presently,** immediately, on the spot: *who in their pride do p. abuse it,* Lucr. 864. *the moon being clouded p. is missed,* 1007. *should p. extirpate me and mine,* Tp. I, 2, 125. *p.? Ay, with a twink,* IV, 42. *enforce them to this place, and p., I prithee,* V, 101. *when you fasted, it was p. after dinner,* Gent. II, 1, 30. *I will send him hither to you p.* II, 4, 86. *and then I'll p. attend you,* 189. II, 5, 9. II, 6, 36. II, 7, 83. 89. III, 1, 42. III, 2, 91. IV, 2, 94. IV, 4, 45. 76. V, 2, 45. Wiv. III, 3, 95. IV, 2, 99. Meas. III, 1, 276. IV, 3, 82. 86. Err. III, 2, 152. IV, 1, 32. V, 31. Ado I, 1, 88. 308. 330. II, 2, 57. III, 1, 14. III, 3, 30. IV, 1, 253. V, 2, 102. V, 4, 71. Merch. I, 1, 183. II, 9, 3. IV, 1, 281 (Ff Q2.3.4 *instantly*). 387. 404. 455. As III, 2, 152. Shr. III, 1, 108. IV, 4, 59. All's II, 3, 166. II, 4, 53. II, 5, 69. III, 6, 80. Tw. III, 4, 217. V, 176. Wint. II, 2, 47. V, 3, 86. John II, 538. V, 7, 86. R2 I, 4, 52. II, 2, 91. III, 1, 3. III, 2, 179. H4A V, 2, 39. H4B II, 1, 190. II, 4, 401. H5 III, 2, 58. V, 2, 79. H6A I, 2, 149. II, 3, 60. III, 2, 34. V, 1, 40. V, 2, 13. 15. H6B I, 1, 171. I, 2, 60. I, 3, 38. II, 1, 139. III, 2, 18. IV, 2, 128. IV, 7, 116. 137. H6C I, 2, 36. II, 2, 59. V, 1, 110. R3 I, 2, 213. III, 1, 34. III, 2, 16. H8 I, 2, 157. III, 2, 78. 229. V, 2, 10. V, 4, 29. Troil. II, 3, 148. IV, 3, 6. Cor. II, 3, 261. III, 3, 12. IV, 5, 229. V, 2, 72. V, 6, 122. Tit. II, 3, 62. IV, 2, 166. IV, 4, 45. V, 1, 146. V, 3, 59. Rom. IV, 1, 54. 95. V, 1, 21. Tim. III, 5, 103. III, 6, 38. IV, 3, 378. Caes. III, 1, 28. 142. IV, 1, 45. IV, 3, 197. Mcb. IV, 3, 145. Hml. II, 2, 170. 620. III, 2, 63. 392. V, 2, 404. Lr. I, 2, 109. I, 4, 159. II, 4, 34. 118. V, 1, 33. Oth. III, 1, 38. V, 2, 52. Ant. II, 2, 161. III, 4, 15. III, 5, 22. Cymb. II, 3, 143. III, 2, 77. IV, 2, 166. Per. III, 1, 82. IV, 2, 58.

The following passages may be taken in the modern sense of shortly, soon: Pilgr. 172. Gent. I, 2, 59. Wiv. IV, 1, 3. Mids. IV, 2, 37. Merch. I, 3, 177.

II, 6, 65. As II, 6, 11. R2 II, 2, 119. H4A III, 2, 3. IV, 3, 74. H5 II, 1, 93. Oth. II, 1, 215. II, 3, 310. Ant. III, 5, 8.

**Presentment,** 1) presentation, the act of offering as a testimony of respect: *when comes your book forth? Upon the heels of my p.* Tim. I, 1, 27.

2) representation, picture: *the counterfeit p. of two brothers,* Hml. III, 4, 54.

**Preservation,** 1) the act of preserving, of keeping from injury or destruction: *in their dear care and p. of our person,* H5 II, 2, 59. *by great p. we live to tell it you,* R3 III, 5, 36 (by the care of Providence). *nature does require her times of p.* H8 III, 2, 147. *those* (faces) *for p. cased,* Cymb. V, 3, 22.

2) the state of being preserved, escape from danger, safety: *our p.* Tp. II, 1, 7. *give us particulars of thy p.* V, 135.

**Preservative,** a means of preserving life and health: Cor. II, 1, 129.

**Preserve,** 1) to keep in the same state, to defend from injury or destruction, to save; absol.: *a choking gall and a —ing sweet,* Rom. I, 1, 200. Transitively: *feeding on that which doth p. the ill,* Sonn. 147, 3. *a cherubin that did p. me,* Tp. I, 2, 153. *prayers from —d souls,* Meas. II, 2, 153 (kept pure). *to p. virginity,* All's I, 1, 138. Tw. V, 263. Wint. I, 2, 328. V, 3, 124. 127. H4B II, 2, 103. IV, 5, 163. H6A IV, 5, 33. B III, 1, 301. R3 II, 2, 119. Tit. III, 2, 2. V, 3, 110. Lr. II, 3, 6. IV, 6, 74. Oth. I, 3, 206. Ant. III, 4, 22. Cymb. V, 3, 58. Per. II, 2, 16. IV, 3, 15. V, 3, 57. With *from: to p. my sovereign from his foe,* H6B III, 1, 271. Oth. IV, 2, 84. Cymb. I, 4, 148. Per. V, 3, 89 (O. Edd. *preferred*). Optatively: *good angels p. the king,* Tp. II, 1, 307. *Jesu p. thee,* R2 V, 2, 17. H4B II, 4, 315. H5 IV, 7, 113. H6B I, 1, 162. I, 2, 70. R3 I, 3, 59. Cor. III, 3, 143. IV, 6, 20. Tim. I, 1, 162. Mcb. IV, 2, 72. Ant. V, 1, 60. Per. IV, 6, 114. V, 1, 14.

2) to condite, to pickle: *to make perfumes, distil, p.* Cymb. I, 5, 13.

**Preserver,** saver: Tp. V, 69. All's II, 3, 53. Wint. IV, 4, 597. Cymb. V, 5, 2.

**President,** chief, head, sovereign: *and as the p. of my kingdom, will appear there for a man,* Ant. III, 7, 18.

**Press,** subst. 1) crowd, throng: Lucr. 1301. 1408. Joh V, 7, 19 (= thronging). H8 IV, 1, 78. V, 4, 88. Caes. I, 2, 15. Cymb. II, 4, 72.

2) the machine for printing books: *he cares not what he puts into the p.* Wiv. II, 1, 80 (quibble between printing and squeezing).

3) a closet for the safe-keeping of clothes or other things: Wiv. III, 3, 226. IV, 2, 62.

4) a commission to force men into military service: *I have misused the king's p. damnably,* H4A IV, 2, 13.

**Press,** vb. 1) trans. a) to act on by weight, to be heavy on: *now —ed with bearing,* Ven. 430. *he with her plenty —ed,* 545. *with half that wish the wisher's eyes be —ed,* Mids. II, 2, 65. *while thou on —ed flowers doest sleep,* III, 1, 162. *on his —ed bed lolling,* Troil. I, 3, 162. (Ff *prest-bed*). *p. one heavy bier,* Rom. III, 2, 60. *the hag that —es them,* I, 4, 93. *Tarquin thus did softly p. the rushes,* Cymb. II, 2, 13. *her breast, worthy the —ing,* II, 4, 135. Allusions to an ancient kind of torture (*peine forte et dure*): *—ing to death,* Meas. V, 528. *she would p. me to death with*

wit, Ado III, 1, 76. *I am —ed to death through want of speaking,* R2 III, 4, 72. *p. it* (the bed) *to death,* Troil. III, 2, 217. Metaphorically: *do not p. my tongue-tied patience with too much disdain,* Sonn. 140, 1. *griefs of mine own lie heavy in my breast, which thou wilt propagate, to have it —ed with more of thine,* Rom. I, 1, 193. *as if it —ed her breast,* Lr. IV, 3, 28. *I have this while with leaden thoughts been —ed,* Oth. III, 4, 177. With *down: a pack of sorrows which would p. you down ... to your timeless grave,* Gent. III, 1, 20. *I am —ed down with conceit,* Err. IV, 2, 65. *enow to p. a royal merchant down,* Merch. IV, 1, 29.

b) to urge, to ply hard, to constrain: *why should he stay, whom love doth p. to go?* Mids. III, 2, 184. *you p. me far, and therefore I will yield,* Merch. IV, 1, 425. *p. me not, beseech you,* Wint. I, 2, 19. *p. not a falling man too far,* H8 III, 2, 333. With *from,* = to drive from, to keep from: *what love could p. Lysander from my side?* Mids. III, 2, 185. *that humour that —s him from sleep,* Wint. II, 3, 39.

c) to force into military service: R2 III, 2, 58. H4A IV, 2, 16. 22. 40. H6C II, 5, 64 (*forth*). 66. Cor. I, 2, 9. III, 1, 122.

2) intr. a) to crowd, to throng: *no humble suitors p. to speak for right,* H6C III, 1, 19. *many mazed considerings did throng and —ed in with this caution,* H8 II, 4, 186. *it —es to my memory, like damned guilty deeds to sinners' minds,* Rom. III, 2, 110. *great men shall p. for tinctures,* Caes. II, 2, 88. *what suitors p. to him,* II, 4, 15. *p. near and second him,* III, 1, 29. *p. not so upon me,* III, 2, 171.

b) to urge forward with force or importunity, to strain and strive eagerly: *unless thy lady prove unjust, p. never thou to choose anew,* Pilgr. 332. *to p. with so little preparation upon you,* Wiv. II, 2, 162. *I p. in here amongst the rest,* As V, 4, 57. *flamens do p. among the throngs,* Cor. II, 1, 230. *to p. to heaven in my young days,* Tit. IV, 3, 90. *to p. before thy father to a grave,* Rom. V, 3, 215.

**Press-money,** money given to one taken into military service: Lr. IV, 6, 87.

**Pressure,** impression, stamp, character impressed: *I'll wipe away ... all saws of books, all forms, all —s past,* Hml. I, 5, 100. *to show ... the very age and body of the time his form and p.* III, 2, 27.

**Prest,** prompt, ready: *I am p. unto it,* Merch. I, 1, 160. *Dionyza hath the pregnant instrument of wrath p. for this blow,* Per. IV Prol. 45. *Prest-bed,* see *Press* vb.

**Prester,** priest: *P. John,* Ado II, 1, 276; the title of a fabulous monarch supposed to have a great empire in the East.*

**Presume,** 1) to suppose, to imagine: *this gentleman is happily arrived, my mind —s, for his own good and ours,* Shr. I, 2, 214. *I p., sir, that you are not fallen from the report,* All's V, 1, 12. *p. not that I am the thing I was,* H4B V, 5, 60. *O that I thought it could be in a woman, as, if I can, I will p. in you,* Troil. III, 2, 166. *I p.* or *I dare p.* = I dare say: All's V, 1, 32. R3 III, 4, 21. H8 III, 2, 183. Troil. II, 2, 203. 213. H6A IV, 1, 179. Oth. III, 3, 125 (Q1 *I dare p.*, the rest of O. Edd. *I dare be sworn*).

2) to be overconfident, to venture beyond license, to be insolent: *p. not,* Shr. III, 1, 44. *otherwise will Henry ne'er p.* H6A V, 5, 22. *hadst thou been killed when first thou didst p.* H6C V, 6, 35. With an inf. = to be so bold: Gent. I, 2, 42. Merch. II, 9, 39.

Shr. IV, 1, 96. H6A I, 1, 140. IV, 1, 44. V, 3, 185. H6C III, 3, 178. Cor. I, 1, 195. Per. I, 1, 33. With *on* before the ground of confidence: —*ing on an ague's privilege*, R2 II, 1, 116. Troil. IV, 4, 99. Caes. IV, 3, 63. Peculiar expression: *p. not on thy heart when mine is slain; thou gavest me thine, not to give back again*, Sonn. 22, 13 (evidently = do not lay claim to thy heart).

**Presumption,** arrogance, insolence: All's II, 1, 154. H6A II, 3, 70. H6B I, 2, 34. V, 1, 38. H6C IV, 1, 114. V, 6, 34.

**Presumptuous,** arrogant, insolent: All's I, 3, 204. H6A III, 1, 8. IV, 1, 125. H6B I, 2, 42. H6C I, 1, 157.

**Presupposed,** supposed or required as a previous condition: *then camest in smiling, and in such forms which here were p. upon thee in the letter*, Tw. V, 358.

**Presurmise,** thought or suspicion previously formed: *it was your p. that in the dole of blows your son might drop*, H4B I, 1, 168.

**Pretence,** 1) pretext: *her p. is a pilgrimage to Saint Jaques*, All's IV, 3, 57. *under p. to see the queen his aunt*, H8 I, 1, 177. *the p. for this is named your wars in France*, I, 2, 59. *why hast thou abused so many miles with a p.* Cymb. III, 4, 106. *make p. of wrong that I have done him*, Per. I, 2, 91.

2) intention, purpose, design: *hath made me publisher of this p.* Gent. III, 1, 47. *the p. whereof being laid open*, Wint. III, 2, 18. *to keep your great —s veiled*, Cor. I, 2, 20. *against the undivulged p. I fight of treasonous malice*, Mcb. II, 3, 137. *he hath wrote this .... to no further p. of danger*, Lr. I, 2, 95. *which I have rather blamed as mine own jealous curiosity than as a very p. and purpose of unkindness*, I, 4, 75.

**Pretend,** 1) to assert: *why shall we fight, if you p. no title?* H6C IV, 7, 57. *whom you p. to honour and adore*, Tit. I, 42.

2) to alledge falsely, to use as a pretext: —*ing in her discoveries of dishonour*, Meas. III, 1, 236. *the contract you p. with that base wretch*, Cymb. II, 3, 118. *importuned me to temper poisons for her, still —ing the satisfaction of her knowledge*, V, 5, 250.

3) to intend, to mean: *reward not hospitality with such black payment as thou hast —ed*, Lucr. 576. *their —ed flight*, Gent. II, 6, 37. *such as shall p. malicious practices against his state*, H6A IV, 1, 16. *doth this churlish superscription p. some alteration in good will?* 54 (= mean). *what good could they p.?* Mcb. II, 4, 24.

**Pretext** (*pretéxt*) motive assigned: *my p. to strike at him admits a good construction*, Cor. V, 6, 20.

**Prettily,** in a pleasing manner, neatly: Ven. 73. Gent. I, 2, 126. Mids. II, 2, 53. Wint. IV, 4, 377. H6A IV, 1, 175. R3 III, 1, 134.

**Prettiness,** a pleasing form and manner: Hml. IV, 5, 189.

**Pretty,** adj. pleasing, neat, fine: Ven. 74. 242. Lucr. 1233. Sonn. 41, 1 (some M. Edd. *petty;* but cf. Merch. II, 6, 37). 132, 4. 139, 10. Gent. II, 1, 122. Wiv. I, 1, 46. I, 4, 146. 148. III, 2, 18. Err. III, 1, 110. Ado II, 3, 141. IV, 1, 99. IV, 2, 85 (cf. Rom. I, 1, 34). LLL I, 2, 19. 22. V, 2, 97. Mids. II, 1, 130. IV, 1, 60. Merch. II, 6, 37 (cf. Sonn. 41, 1). III, 4, 64 (cf. Wint. I, 2, 62). V, 21. As II, 4, 50. Shr. II, 188. All's I, 1, 103 (*'twas p., to see him every hour*). Wint. I, 2, 62. IV, 4, 156. 193. V, 2, 89. John III, 4, 95. R2 III, 3, 165. H6C IV, 6, 70. R3 I, 1, 93. Rom. I, 1, 34 (cf.

Ado IV, 2, 85). I, 3, 60. Cymb. III, 4, 150.\*IV, 2, 398 etc. etc. = moderately great: *a p. while*, Lucr. 1233. *my daughter's of a p. age*, Rom. I, 3, 10. Used as a term of endearment and supplying the place of diminutives: *why, my p. youth?* Gent. IV, 2, 58. *O p. Isabella*, Meas. IV, 3, 157. *piteous plainings of the p. babes*, Err. I, 1, 73; cf. R3 IV, 1, 101 and Mcb. IV, 3, 216. *p. soul*, Mids. II, 2, 76. *my —est Perdita*, Wint. IV, 4, 595. *p. traps to catch the petty thieves*, H5 I, 2, 177. *my p. cousins*, R3 II, 2, 8. *my p. York*, II, 4, 26 (Ff *young*). 31. *O p., p. pledge*, Troil. V, 2, 77. *what hast thou there under thy cloak, p. Flaminius?* Tim. III, 1, 15. *how now, my p. knave*, Lr. I, 4, 107. *the p. worm of Nilus*, Ant. V, 2, 243 etc. Ironically: *that's a p. jest indeed*, Wiv. III, 4, 59. *there are p. orders beginning*, Meas. II, 1, 249. *I can tell thee p. tales of the duke*, IV, 3, 175. *'tis p., sure, and very probable*, As III, 5, 11. *I thank your p. sweet wit for it*, H4B I, 2, 231. *a p. plot, well chosen to build upon*, H6B I, 4, 59. Substantively: *I post unto my p.* Pilgr. 201. *may breed thee, p.* Wint. III, 3, 48.

**Pretty,** adv. in some degree, tolerably: *I did think thee a p. wise fellow*, All's II, 3, 212 (or adj.?).

**Pretty-vaulting** (not hyphened in O. Edd.) bounding in an agreeable manner: *the p. sea refused to drown me*, H6B III, 2, 94.

**Prevail,** to have the upperhand, to carry the victory, to gain one's object, to overrule: *a sin —ing much in youthful men*, Err. V, 52. *God forbid any malice should p.* H6B III, 2, 23. *they shall no more p. than we give way*, H8 V, 1, 144. *my practise so —ed, that I returned with simular proof enough*, Cymb. V, 5, 199. Used of reasons, entreaties and the like, having effect: *you have —ed*, Gent. III, 2, 46 (= I will be ruled by you). V, 4, 158. Err. III, 1, 107. *no love-broker can more p. than report of valour*, Tw. III, 2, 40. *his authority, which often hath no less —ed than so*, Wint. II, 1, 54. *if word nor oath p. not, go and see*, III, 2, 205. *I shall so p. to force him after*, IV, 4, 678. *since my office hath so far —ed, that ... you have congreeted*, H5 V, 2, 29. *when a world of men could not p. with all their oratory*, H6A II, 2, 49. *I would p., if prayers might p., to join your hearts*, III, 1, 67. *thus Suffolk hath —ed*, V, 5, 103. H6B IV, 2, 184. H6C IV, 6, 7. Cor. V, 4, 43. Tit. I, 459. III, 1, 26. Caes. II, 2, 54. Ant. IV, 5, 2. Cymb. III, 3, 66. Per. V, 1, 262. *it* (philosophy) *helps not, it —s not*, Rom. III, 3, 60 (= has no effect). *if wishes would p. with me*, H5 III, 2, 16 (= if wishes, in my case, were of any avail; Pistol's poetry). cf. *Unprevailing.* = to conquer an enemy, to be victorious: *if we p., their heads shall pay for it*, R2 III, 2, 126. *can you suffer hell so to p.?* H6A I, 5, 9. *sleeping or waking, must I still p.?* II, 1, 56. *the Dauphin hath —ed beyond the seas*, H6B I, 3, 128. *whose* (justice's) *rightful cause —s*, II, 1, 205. *thou hast —ed in right*, II, 3, 101. *sometime the flood —s, and then the wind*, H6C II, 5, 9. *they nothing doubt —ing*, Cor. I, 3, 111. *but how —ed you?* I, 6, 45. *whose ministers would p. under the service of a child*, Ant. III, 13, 23. Used of success in love: *when a woman woos, what woman's son will sourly leave her till she have —ed?* Sonn. 41, 8. *how he did p. I shame to speak*, John I, 104. *'twas Reignier, king of Naples, that —ed*, H6A V, 4, 78. *to understand you have —ed*, Cymb. I, 4, 171.

With *against*, = to be victorious over: *the spite of man —eth against me*, H6B I, 3, 218. With *on,* =

to work upon efficaciously, to influence, to overcome: *they that were your enemies are his, and have —ed as much on him as you*, R3 I, 1, 131. *have —ed upon my body with their hellish charms*, III, 4, 63. *could it work so much upon your shape as it hath much —ed on your condition, I should not know you*, Caes. II, 1, 254. *what false Italian hath —ed on thy too ready hearing?* Cymb. III, 2, 5. With *with*, = to win, to gain the favour or assent of: *with her personage, her height, forsooth, she hath —ed with him*, Mids. III, 2, 293. *thy grave admonishments p. with me*, H6A II, 5, 98. *with whom an upright zeal to right —s more than the nature of a brother's love*, H6C V, 1, 78. *did York's dread curse p. so much with heaven*, R3 I, 3, 191. *he (the devil) cannot p. with me*, I, 4, 155. *the rabble should have first unroofed the city, ere so —ed with me*, Cor. I, 1, 223. *most dangerously you have with him —ed*, V, 3, 188. *the ladies of Rome may p. with him*, V, 4, 6. cf. Tw. III, 2, 40.

**Prevailment**, prevalence, superior influence: *messengers of strong p. in unhardened youth*, Mids. I, 1, 35.

**Prevent**, 1) to come before, to anticipate, to be beforehand with: *I would have stayed till I had made you merry, if worthier friends had not —ed me*, Merch. I, 1, 61. *I will answer you with gait and entrance. But we are —ed*, Tw. III, 1, 94; cf. Per. V, 1, 64. *but that I am —ed, I should have begged I might have been employed*, H6A IV, 1, 71. *I must p. thee, Cimber*, Caes. III, 1, 35. *I do find it cowardly and vile, so to p. the time of life*, V, 1, 105. *so shall my anticipation p. your discovery*, Hml. II, 2, 305.
2) to frustrate, to disappoint, to avoid, to escape: *I could p. this storm and shun thy wrack*, Lucr. 966. *give my love fame faster than time wastes life; so thou —est his scythe and crooked knife*, Sonn. 100, 14. *to p. our maladies unseen, we sicken to shun sickness when we purge*, 118, 3. *I would p. the loose encounters of lascivious men*, Gent. II, 7, 40. *that it wants matter to p. so gross o'erreaching*, Wiv. V, 5, 144. *he comes armed in his fortune and —s the slander of his wife*, As IV, 1, 61. *she hath —ed me*, Shr. V, 2, 49 (got out of my way, escaped me). *I could have well diverted her intents, which thus she hath —ed*, All's III, 4, 22. *a disaster of war that Caesar himself could not have —ed*, III, 6, 56. *many a good hanging —s a bad marriage*, Tw. I, 5, 20. *which way to be —ed*, Wint. I, 2, 405. *p. the ways to wail*, R2 III, 2, 179 (avoid). *so both the degrees p. my curses*, H4B I, 2, 259 (escape). *to p. the tyrant's violence, I'll hence forthwith unto the sanctuary*, H6C IV, 4, 29. *for I, too fond, might have —ed this*, R3 III, 4, 83. *how shall this be —ed?* Rom. III, 5, 206. IV, 1, 51. 70. *I'll teach them to p. wild Alcibiades' wrath*, Tim. V, 1, 206. *to p. the fiend and to kill vermin*, Lr. III, 4, 164. *you are come a market-maid to Rome and have —ed the ostentation of our love*, Ant. III, 6, 51.
3) to hinder by something done before, to obviate: *which cunning love did wittily p.* Ven. 471. *this vile purpose to p.* Lucr. 220. *thou didst p. me*, Tp. I, 2, 350. Wiv. II, 1, 121. II, 2, 325. Ado III, 2, 136. John I, 35. R2 IV, 148. V, 2, 55. H4A IV, 4, 35. H6C IV, 6, 96. R3 II, 2, 131. II, 3, 26. III, 5, 55. Troil. IV, 4, 38. Cor. IV, 6, 36. Caes. II, 1, 28 *(then, lest he may, p.)*. 160. Hml. III, 1, 175. Lr. I, 1, 46. Lr. III, 7, 83 *(lest it see more, p. it)*. Ant. IV, 12, 42. Cymb. V, 5,

46. Per. Prol. 35. With *from:* —*ed from a damned enterprise*, H5 II, 2, 164.

**Prevention,** 1) something done before an emergency, precaution: *achievements, plots, orders, —s*, Troil. I, 3, 181.
2) hinderance by something done before: R2 II, 1, 167. H5 I, 1, 21. II, 2, 158. H6B II, 4, 57. Caes. II, 1, 85. III, 1, 19.

**Prey**, subst. 1) spoil, booty: *rich —s make true men thieves*, Ven. 724. *the p. of every vulgar thief*, Sonn. 48, 8. *reft the fishers of their p.* Err. I, 1, 116. *the French might have a good p. of us*, H5 IV, 4, 81. *the rascal people, thirsting after p.* H6B IV, 4, 51. Particularly that which carnivorous animals seize and feed on: Ven. 58. 63. 547. 1097. Lucr. 421. 677. 697. Sonn. 74, 10. LLL IV, 1, 91. Merch. II, 1, 30. Tw. III, 1, 139. H6A I, 2, 28. H6B V, 2, 11. H6C I, 3, 14. R3 IV, 4, 386. Tit. III, 1, 55. Caes. V, 1, 87. Ant. III, 13, 167.
2) one, or something, given up to another; a victim: *for his p. to pray he doth begin*, Lucr. 342. *the tenderness of her nature became as a p. to her grief*, All's IV, 3, 61. *give her as a p. to law and shame*, H6B II, 1, 198. H6C I, 1, 185. II, 3, 39. R3 IV, 4, 106. Tit. IV, 2, 96.
3) the act of preying, of catching and devouring other creatures: *an o'ergrown lion that goes not out to p.* Meas. I, 3, 23. *methought a serpent eat my heart away, and you sat smiling at his cruel p.* Mids. II, 2, 150. *the eagle England being in p.* H5 I, 2, 169. *night's black agents to their —s do rouse*, Mcb. III, 2, 53. *dog in madness, lion in p.* Lr. III, 4, 97. *subtle as the fox for p.* Cymb. III, 3, 40. *to make p.* R3 I, 3, 71 (the later Qq *may p.*). III, 5, 84 (Ff *make a p.*, Qq *make his p.*). Troil. I, 3, 123. *birds of p.* Meas. II, 1, 2. *creatures of p.* Wint. III, 3, 13. *beasts and birds of p.* Tit. V, 3, 198.

**Prey,** vb. to chase and feed on animals: Ado V, 3, 25. R3 I, 1, 133. I, 3, 71 (the later Qq *may p.*; the earlier Qq and Ff *make p.*). Tit. III, 1, 55. Oth. III, 3, 263. With *on:* As IV, 3, 119. John V, 7, 15. R2 II, 1, 39. H4A II, 1, 90. R3 IV, 4, 57. Hml. I, 5, 57. Lr. IV, 2, 49. Ant. III, 13, 199 (O. Edd. *in reason*).

**Preyful,** rich in prey, killing much game: LLL IV, 2, 58 (Qq F1 *prayfull*, F2 *praysfull*).

**Priam,** the old king of Troy: Lucr. 1367. 1448. 1485. 1490. All's I, 3, 77. H4B I, 1, 72. 74. H6C II, 5, 120. Troil. Prol. 15. I, 1, 29 etc. Tit. I, 80. V, 3, 84. Hml. II, 2, 469. 486. 494. 501. 514.

**Priamus,** the same: Troil. II, 2, 207. V, 3, 54.

**Priapus,** an ancient god the characteristic of whose statues was an erected yard: *to freeze the god P.* Per. IV, 6, 4.

**Pribbles,** a word of Evans' making: *p. and prabbles* = idle prattle and quarrelling, Wiv. I, 1, 56. V, 5, 168.

**Price,** 1) the sum paid for a thing, or at which it is valued: Ven. 551. Ado III, 3, 122. LLL III, 139. Merch. III, 5, 26. H4A II, 1, 14. H5 II, 2, 154. III, 6, 47. Cor. II, 3, 79. 81. Rom. III, 1, 188. Oth. IV, 3, 69. Per. IV, 2, 54. *At* before it: *we can afford no more at such a p.* LLL V, 2, 223. All's IV, 3, 309. V, 3, 190. Tw. III, 4, 252. Cor. I, 1, 11. III, 3, 91. Tit. III, 1, 199.
2) worth, value: *happy news of p.* H4B V, 3, 100 (Pistol's speech). *a pearl, whose p. hath launched above*

*a thousand ships*, Troil. II, 2, 82. *if he overhold his p.* II, 3, 142. Rom. IV, 1, 27. Lr. I, 1, 200. Oth. I, 1, 11. Cymb. I, 1, 51.

3) estimation: *held in idle p. to haunt assemblies*, Meas. I, 3, 9. *our rash faults make trivial p. of serious things we have*, All's V, 3, 61. *falls into abatement and low p.* Tw. I, 1, 13.

**Priceless,** inestimable: Lucr. 17.

**Prick,** subst. 1) a prickle: *hedgehogs mount their —s*, Tp. II, 2, 12. *he that sweetest rose will find must find love's p. and Rosalind*, As III, 2, 118 (obscene quibbling). *pins, wooden —s, nails*, Lr. II, 3, 16.

2) an impression or hurt made by a prickle, a sting, stitch: *she is too hard for you at —s*, LLL IV, 1, 140. *live honestly by the p. of their needles*, H5 II, 1, 36. *my conscience first received a tenderness, scruple, and p.* H8 II, 4, 171. *I feel this pin p.* Lr. IV, 7, 56 (or verb?).

3) a mark: *ere he arrive his weary noontide p.* Lucr. 781. *made an evening at the noontide p.* H6C I, 4, 34. *the bawdy hand of the dial is now upon the p. of noon*, Rom. II, 4, 119. = the point in the centre of the butts: *let the mark have a p. in't*, LLL IV, 1, 134.

4) a small roll: *in such indexes, although small —s to their subsequent volumes*, Troil. I, 3, 343.

5) By way of quibbling, = the privy member: LLL IV, 1, 134. 140. As III, 2, 118. Rom. II, 4, 119. Perhaps also in H5 II, 1, 36.

**Prick,** vb. 1) to pierce or wound as with a prickle, to sting: *the —ing spur*, Ven. 285. *the needle his finger —s*, Lucr. 319. Tp. IV, 180. Ado III, 4, 76. LLL II, 189. IV, 2, 58. Merch. III, 1, 67. All's IV, 2, 19. John V, 7, 17. H4B II, 2, 121. III, 2, 186. 190. H5 II, 1, 61. H6A II, 4, 49. H6C I, 4, 55. V, 5, 13. Cor. I, 3, 96. Rom. I, 4, 26. 28. Mcb. V, 3, 14. Hml. I, 5, 88. Lr. IV, 7, 56 (or subst.?). Cymb. I, 1, 168. *if honour p. me off*, H4A V, 1, 132 (= stab me, kill me; quibbling). *a little worm —ed from the lazy finger of a maid*, Rom. I, 4, 66 (= picked with a needle. The surreptitious Q1 and some M. Edd. *picked*). *by the —ing of my thumbs, something wicked this way comes*, Mcb. IV, 1, 44 (= a pricking sensation, an itching).

2) to goad, to spur, to incite: *some odd humour —s him to this fashion*, Shr. III, 2, 75. *and p. my tender patience to these thoughts*, R2 II, 1, 207. Caes. II, 1, 124. Mcb. I, 7, 26. Oth. III, 3, 412. With *on*: *my duty —s me on to utter that*, Gent. III, 1, 8. LLL I, 1, 269. R2 II, 3, 78. H4A V, 1, 131. H6A III, 2, 78. Hml. I, 1, 83.

3) to erect, to point: *they —ed their ears*, Tp. IV, 176.

4) to stick by means of a pin: *the humour of forty fancies —ed in it for a feather*, Shr. III, 2, 70.

5) to designate by a puncture, to choose, to mark: *she —ed thee out for women's pleasure*, Sonn. 20, 13. *the whole world again cannot p. out five such*, LLL V, 2, 548 (Q1 *pick*). *the fiend hath —ed down Bardolph irrecoverable*, H4B II, 4, 359. *p. him*, III, 2, 121. 125. 144. 153 *(down)*. 156. 162. 171. 186. 190. *will you be —ed in number of our friends?* Caes. III, 1, 216. *their names are —ed*, IV, 1, 1. *p. him down*, 3. *who should be —ed to die*, 16.

6) to dress up, to trim: *I was —ed well enough before*, H4B III, 2, 122. *p. him no more*, 156. *if he had been a man's tailor, he'ld ha' —ed you*, 164.

**Prick-eared,** having pointed ears: *p. cur of Iceland*, H5 II, 1, 44.

**Pricket,** a buck in his second year: LLL IV, 2, 12. 22. 48. 53. 58. 61.

**Prickle,** the thorn of a rose: Ven. 574.

**Prick-song,** music sung from notes: Rom. II, 4, 21 (*he fights as you sing p.*; German: *nach Noten*).

**Pride,** 1) splendid show, beauty displayed, ornament: *began to clothe his wit in state and p.* Lucr. 1809. *in themselves their p. lies buried*, Sonn. 25, 7. *new unfolding his imprisoned p.* 52, 12. *why is my verse so barren of new p.?* 76, 1. *he of tall building and of goodly p.* 80, 12. *the purple p. that on thy* (the violet's) *soft cheek dwells*, 99, 3. *having such a scope to show her p.* 103, 2. *three winters cold have from the forests shook three summers' p.* 104, 4. *her hair, nor loose nor tied in formal plat, proclaimed in her a careless hand of p.* Compl. 30 (= a hand careless of ornament). *livery falseness in a p. of truth*, 105. *the madams did almost sweat to bear the p. upon them*, H8 I, 1, 25. *let two more summers wither in their p.* Rom. I, 2, 10. *'tis much p. for fair without the fair within to hide*, I, 3, 89 (it is a great ornament of external beauty, to enclose internal excellence'.

2) state of being at the highest pitch: *while lust is in his p.* Lucr. 705. *in the very heat and p. of their contention*, H4A I, 1, 60. *a falcon towering in her p. of place*, Mcb. II, 4, 12. Hence = prime, glory: *thou loathed in their shame, they in thy p.* Lucr. 662. *in p. of all his growth a vengeful canker eat him up to death*, Sonn. 99, 12. *having thee, of all men's p. I boast*, 91, 12. *O short-lived p.! not fair?* LLL IV, 1, 15. *let's die in p.* H6A IV, 6, 57. *there died my Icarus, my blossom, in his p.* IV, 7, 16. *I cannot flatter thee in p.* H6B I, 3, 169 (cf. Oth. III, 3, 404). *thus Eleanor's p. dies in her youngest days*, H6B II, 3, 46. *mowed down in tops of all their p.* H6C V, 7, 4. *Richard falls in height of all his p.* R3 V, 3, 176. *my high-blown p. at length broke under me*, H8 III, 2, 361. *whose easy-borrowed p. dwells in the fickle grace of her he follows*, Lr. II, 4, 188. *p., pomp and circumstance of glorious war*, Oth. III, 3, 354.

= exuberance of animal spirits, mettle, fire: *the colt that's backed and burdened being young loseth his p. and never waxeth strong*, Ven. 420. *their* (the horses') *p. and mettle is asleep*, H4A IV, 3, 22. *as their captain, so their p. doth grow*, Lucr. 298. 432. *the tide.... boundeth in his p.* 1669. *wert thou the unicorn, p. and wrath would confound thee*, Tim. IV, 3, 339. Hence = lust, eager sexual desire: *his hand, smoking with p.* Lucr. 438. *wooing his purity with her foul p.* Sonn. 144, 8. *proud of this p. he is contented thy poor drudge to be, to stand in thy affairs, fall by thy side*, 151, 10 (the words *stand* and *fall* cannot be understood too literally). *his heart, like an agate, with your print impressed, proud with his form, in his eye p. expressed*, LLL II, 237. *as salt as wolves in p.* Oth. III, 3, 404.

= wantonness, extravagance: *leaves it* (his gold) *to be mastered by his young, who in their p. do presently abuse it*, Lucr. 864. *now much beshrew my manners and my p., if Hermia meant to say Lysander lied*, Mids. II, 2, 54. *ambitions, covetings, change of —s, disdain*, Cymb. II, 5, 25 (= one excess changed for another). Hence = impertinence, impudence: *advance their p. against that power that bred it*, Ado III,

1, 10. *to abide thy kingly doom and sentence of his p.* R2 V, 6, 23. *such is thy audacious wickedness, thy lewd, pestiferous and dissentious pranks, as very infants prattle of thy p.* H6A III, 1, 16. *chastised with arms our enemies' p.* Tit. I, 33. *with strained p. to come between our sentence and our power,* Lr. I, 1, 172. = force strained to the utmost, full power: *could entertain with half their forces the full p. of France,* H5 I, 2, 112. *hardly we escaped the p. of France,* H6A III, 2, 40. *and from the p. of Gallia rescued thee,* IV, 6, 15.

3) self-esteem, mostly in a bad sense, haughtiness, arrogance: Ven. 278. Err. IV, 3, 81. LLL II, 36. As I, 2, 264. II, 7, 70. III, 5, 114. All's I, 2, 37. R2 I, 3, 129. III, 2, 81. IV, 206. V, 5, 22. 88. H4A I, 1, 92. III, 1, 185. H4B IV, 5, 171. H5 V Chor. 20. H6B I, 1, 172. 180. 201. I, 3, 179. II, 2, 71. IV, 1, 60. H6C II, 2, 159. H8 I, 1, 68. II, 2, 82. II, 4, 110. Troil. I, 3, 316. 371. 391. II, 3, 95. 162. 165. 181. 215. 228. III, 3, 45. 47. 136. IV, 5, 79. 82. Cor. II, 1, 22. 28. 42. II, 3, 227. III, 2, 126. IV, 6, 31. IV, 7, 37. V, 3, 170. Tit. IV, 3, 62. Tim. IV, 3, 240. Hml. I, 1, 83. Oth. I, 1, 12. II, 3, 98. Cymb. II, 4, 72. Per. I, 4, 30. *to take p.* = to be proud, to glory in sth.: *my gravity, wherein I take p.* Meas. II, 4, 10. *men of all sorts take a p. to gird at me,* H4B I, 2, 7. *took some p. to do myself this wrong,* Cor. V, 6, 37. = the thing of which men are proud: As III, 2, 81. H4A I, 1, 83.

4) cold selfishness, unkindness: *in thy p. so fair a hope is slain,* Ven. 762. *this p. of hers,* Gent. III, 1, 72. *stand I condemned for p. and scorn so much?* Ado III, 1, 108. 109. *maugre all thy p., nor wit nor reason can my passion hide,* Tw. III, 1, 163. *let p., which she calls plainness, marry her,* Lr. I, 1, 131. *fall and blast her p.* II, 4, 170. cf. also As III, 5, 114.

**Priest,** one who officiates at the altar of any deity; a clergyman: Phoen. 13. Wiv. I, 4, 116. 123. II, 1, 149. 209. II, 3, 32. 65. III, 1, 106. IV, 6, 31. 53. Ado III, 3, 144. As III, 2, 337. III, 3, 86. IV, 1, 124. 140. V, 1, 3. Shr. III, 2, 5. 160. 163. 166. IV, 4, 88. 94. 103. V, 1, 1. All's III, 3, 286. Tw. III, 4, 298. V, 350. Wint. III, 2, 129. IV, 4, 469. John III, 1, 153. 163. R2 IV, 173. H5 IV, 1, 318. H6A I, 3, 30. 47. I, 6, 19. III, 1, 8. 45. 120. V, 4, 23. H6B II, 1, 51. II, 4, 53. III, 1, 272. 274. V, 2, 71. R3 III, 2, 114. III, 4, 89. H8 II, 2, 21. 82. 97. III, 2, 252. 276. Troil. I, 2, 245. II, 2, 37. IV, 3, 9. Cor. I, 10, 21. II, 1, 93. Tit. I, 323. 488. Tim. IV, 3, 31. 125. Caes. II, 1, 129. II, 2, 5. Hml. V, 1, 263. Lr. III, 2, 81. Cymb. IV, 2, 242. Per. IV, 6, 13.

Fem., = priestess: *live, like Diana's p., between cold sheets,* Cymb. I, 6, 133. *my maiden —s,* Per. V, 1, 243. **Priesthood,** the character of a priest: H6B II, 1, 23. H6C I, 3, 3.

**Priest-like,** 1) adj.: *our p. fasts,* Cor. V, 1, 56. 2) adv.: *wherein p. thou hast cleansed my bosom,* Wint. I, 2, 237.

**Priestly,** sacerdotal: *whiles I say a p. farewell to her,* Per. III, 1, 70.

**Prig,** a thief: Wint. IV, 3, 108.

**Primal,** first: *it hath the p. eldest curse upon't,* Hml. III, 3, 37. *it hath been taught us from the p. state,* Ant. I, 4, 41.

**Primater** for *pia mater,* q. v.; reading of O. Edd. in LLL IV, 2, 71.

**Prime,** adj. 1) first (in time or excellence): *Pros-*

*pero the p. duke,* Tp. I, 2, 72. *my p. request,* 425. *from the p. creation,* R3 IV, 3, 19. *the p. man of the state,* H8 III, 2, 162. *to such proceeding who ever but his approbation added, though not his p. consent,* Per. IV, 3, 27. Comp. and Superl.: *there is no —r business,* H8 I, 2, 67 (more important). *the —st creature,* II, 4, 229.

2) ruttish (like beasts in spring-time): *were they as p. as goats, as hot as monkeys,* Oth. III, 3, 403.

**Prime,** subst. 1) height of perfection, flower of life: *flowers that are not gathered in their p.* Ven. 131. *they wither in their p.* 418. *sith in his p. Death doth my love destroy,* 1163. *the lovely April of her p.* Sonn. 3, 10. *past p.* 12, 3. *a pure unstained p.* 70, 8. *losing this verdure even in the p.* Gent. I, 1, 49. *love is crowned with the p. in spring time,* As V, 3, 33. *all that happiness and p. can happy call,* All's II, 1, 185. *come to p.* R2 V, 2, 51. *the p. of youth,* H6C II, 1, 23. *cropped the golden p. of this sweet prince,* R3 I, 2, 248. *thy p. of manhood,* IV, 4, 170. *in my p. of youth,* V, 3, 119.

2) the spring of the year: *to add a more rejoicing to the p.* Lucr. 332. *bearing the wanton burden of the p.* Sonn. 97, 7.

**Primero,** a game at cards now unknown: Wiv. IV, 5, 104. H8 V, 1, 7.

**Primitive,** original, archetypal: *the p. statue of cuckolds,* Troil. V, 1, 60.

**Primogenitive,** the right of primogeniture: *the p. and due of birth,* Troil. I, 3, 106 (Q *primogenitie*).

**Primrose,** the flower Primula: Wint. IV, 4, 122. H6B III, 2, 63. Cymb. I, 5, 83. IV, 2, 221. Adjectively: *this p. bank,* Ven. 151. *p. beds,* Mids. I, 1, 215. *go the p. way to the everlasting bonfire,* Mcb. II, 3, 21. *the p. path of dalliance,* Hml. I, 3, 50.

**Primy,** being in its prime, flourishing: *a violet in the youth of p. nature,* Hml. I, 3, 7.

**Prince,** subst. 1) a ruler of a state, a sovereign: Lucr. 615. Sonn. 25, 5. Tp. I, 2, 55. V, 108. Gent. III, 1, 10. Meas. I, 3, 45. V, 22. 48. 57. 224. 375. 387. 530. Err. I, 1, 145. V, 162 etc. etc. *the black p., alias the p. of darkness,* All's IV, 5, 44. *P. Lucifer,* John IV, 3, 122. *the p. of fiends,* H5 III, 3, 16. *p. of plackets,* LLL III, 186. *p. of cats,* Rom. II, 4, 19. *the p. of palfreys,* H5 III, 7, 29. *the p. of chivalry,* Troil. I, 2, 249.

2) a male member of a royal family: Tp. I, 1, 57. III, 1, 60. Wiv. III, 2, 74. Ado IV, 1, 154. 165. Wint. I, 2, 164. 330. II, 1, 17. III, 2, 41. 145. IV, 2, 29 *(the P. Florizel)* etc. etc. *P. of Wales:* R2 II, 1, 172. H4A II, 4, 10. R3 I, 3, 199. *the Black P.* (eldest son of Edward III): R2 II, 3, 101. H5 I, 2, 105. H6B II, 2, 11. *— s* = lords: Ado V, 1, 277. John V, 7, 97. 115. H5 IV, 1, 25. H8 II, 2, 48.

Plur. *— s* including both sexes: *these two —s, if you marry them,* John II, 445. *young —s, close your hands,* 533. Therefore we ought perhaps to read in Tp. I, 2, 173: *made thee more profit than other —s can;* O. Edd. *princesse;* most M. Edd. *princesses* against the metre. (*Prince* sometimes fem. with the contemporaries of Sh.; f. i. in Greene's Pandosto, ed. Collier, p. 15: *alas, Bellaria, better thou hadst been born a beggar than a prince.* p. 20: *seeing she was a prince she ought to be tried by her peers*).

**Prince,** vb., with *it,* = to play the prince: *nature prompts them in simple and low things to p. it much beyond the trick of others,* Cymb. III, 3, 85.

**Prince-like**, becoming a prince: *the wrongs he did me were nothing p.* Cymb. V, 5, 293.

**Princely**, 1) pertaining to, or coming from, a prince: *woundest his p. name,* Lucr. 599. *thy p. office,* 628. *hid my p. trunk,* Tp. I, 2, 86. *his p. feet before,* LLL IV, 1, 92. *your p. knee,* R2 III, 3, 190. *p. favour,* V, 6, 42. H4A III, 2, 17. 86. H4B IV, 2, 66. H5 I, 2, 171. H6A V, 3, 143. 176. H6B V, 1, 98. R3 II, 2, 51. H8 IV, 2, 118. Cymb. III, 3, 93.

2) of the rank of princes (and hence = high, august, royal): *her p. guest,* Lucr. 90. *these p. suitors,* Merch. I, 2, 38. *thy p. son,* John II, 484. IV, 3, 35. R2 I, 1, 34. H4B II, 2, 58. IV, 1, 141. H5 V, 2, 4. H6A II, 2, 34. III, 1, 173. III, 3, 38. IV, 1, 18. IV, 3, 17. V, 3, 152. H6B I, 1, 72. IV, 1, 91. H6C I, 1, 166. II, 1, 1. II, 6, 51. V, 7, 27. R3 I, 3, 280. I, 4, 228. 241. II, 1, 29. 41. 47. 53. III, 1, 34. III, 2, 70. III, 3, 20. III, 5, 88. IV, 4, 405. IV, 5, 6. Troil. IV, 5, 174. Tit. I, 429. Cymb. III, 4, 93. IV, 2, 171. 249. V, 5, 360. 473. Per. I, 3, 33.

3) becoming a prince: *a p. testimony!* Ado IV, 1, 317. *his p. exercises,* Wint. IV, 2, 37. *p. liberty,* H6A V, 3, 140. *p. care,* H8 V, 1, 49. V, 5, 26. Tit. I, 266. 272. Per. I, 2, 100. III, 3, 16.

4) high-minded, noble: *his p. heart,* John I, 267. *that young and p. gentleman,* R2 II, 1, 175. *trimmed up your praises with a p. tongue,* H4A V, 2, 57. *as full of valour as of kindness, p. in both,* H5 IV, 3, 16. *he was most p.* H8 IV, 2, 57. H6C II, 1, 91. V, 2, 12. Troil. IV, 5, 279, Ant. V, 2, 22.

5) magnificent, majestic: *her p. gait,* Shr. II, 261. *too precious p. for a grave,* John IV, 3, 40. *beauty's p. majesty is such,* H6A V, 3, 70. *most p. gifts,* Cor. I, 9, 80.

Adverbially: *my appetite was not p. got,* H4B II, 2, 12.

**Princess** (O. Edd. *princesse*), 1) a female sovereign, or the consort of a sovereign: Lucr. 721. H8 V, 5, 58. Lr. IV, 7, 29. Ant. V, 2, 329.

2) the daughter of a sovereign, or the consort of his son: Tp. I, 2, 59. LLL I, 1, 141. II, 90. 150. 172. V, 1, 93 etc. As I, 2, 175. II, 2, 10. Wint. II, 3, 78 (used of a babe, and neuter). IV, 4, 555. 562. V, 1, 86. H6A V, 3, 110. H8 III, 2, 70; IV, 1, 23 *(p. dowager).* V, 4, 91. Cymb. V, 2, 3 etc. *let me kiss this p. of pure white* (your hand), *this seal of bliss,* Mids. III, 2, 144 (cf. *prince,* and Ant. III, 13, 125). Used in flattery as a familiar compellation: Tw. III, 1, 108. V, 307.

Seemingly not inflected in the plural: Tp. I, 2, 173, but cf. *prince.* In As I, 2, 175 some M. Edd. *the princess' call for you,* but O. Edd. *the princesse cals for you.*

**Principal**, adj. chief: Lucr. Arg. 5. As III, 2, 369. 371. H6C III, 1, 4.

**Principal**, subst. 1) a capital sum lent on interest: Merch. IV, 1, 26. 336. 342. All's I, 1, 161.

2) abettor, accomplice: *what she should shame to know herself but with her most vile p.* Wint. II, 1, 92.

3) employer: *hath your p. made known unto you who I am?* Per. IV, 6, 89. 91.

4) a corner-post of a house: *the very —s did seem to rend,* Per. III, 2, 16.

**Principality**, 1) a country ruled by a prince: *he will fill thy wishes to the brim with —es,* Ant. III, 13, 19.

2) a person of the highest dignity, superior to other men: *if not divine, yet let her be a p., sovereign to all the creatures on the earth,* Gent. II, 4, 152 (according to some commentators, = an angel of the first order).

**Principle**, a truth, a rule: *these warlike —s do not throw from you,* All's II, 1, 1. *that need must needs infer this p. that faith would live again by death of need,* John III, 1, 213. *if I had a thousand sons, the first humane p. I would teach them should be, to forswear thin potations,* H4B IV, 3, 133.

**Princox**, a pert boy, an impertinent: *you are a p., go,* Rom. I, 5, 88.

**Print**, subst. 1) any mark made by impression: *his tenderer cheek receives her soft hand's p.* Ven. 353. *which any p. of goodness wilt not take,* Tp. I, 2, 352. Meas. II, 4, 130. Ado I, 1, 203. LLL II, 236. John IV, 3, 26. Cymb. II, 3, 48.

2) typographical writing: *we quarrel in p., by the book,* As V, 4, 94. *although the p. be little,* Wint. II, 3, 98. *I love a ballad in p.* IV, 4, 264. *in p.* = to the letter, accurately: *all this I speak in p., for in p. I found it,* Gent. II, 1, 175. *I will do it, sir, in p.* LLL III, 173.

**Print**, vb. 1) to form by impression, to stamp: *the story that is —ed in her blood,* Ado IV, 1, 124 (with the stain of which her blood is polluted).* — *ing their hoofs in the earth,* H5 Prol. 27. *could this kiss be —ed in thy hand,* H6B III, 2, 343. *heaven guide thy pen to p. thy sorrows plain,* Tit. IV, 1, 75.

2) to make books by means of the press; intr.: *thou hast caused —ing to be used,* H6B IV, 7, 39. Trans.: *thou shouldst p. more, not let that copy die,* Sonn. 11, 14. *he will p. them,* Wiv. II, 1, 79. *she did p. your royal father off, conceiving you,* Wint. V, 1, 125 (cf. II, 3, 98).

**Printless**, leaving no trace: Tp. V, 34.

**Prioress**, a female superior of a convent of nuns: Meas. I, 4, 11.

**Priority**, precedence, superior rank: Troil. I, 3, 86. Cor. I, 1, 251.

**Priory**, a convent under the superintendence of a prior or prioress: Err. V, 37. John I, 48.

**Priscian**, name of a Latin grammarian: LLL V, 1, 31.

**Priser**, see *Prizer.*

**Prison**, subst. a place of confinement: Lucr. 119. 379. 1726. Tp. I, 2, 362. 490. 493. Gent. III, 1, 235 *(close p.).* Meas. II, 3, 5. III, 2, 74. IV, 2, 9. 156. IV, 3, 73. V, 135 and 331 *(at the p.).* 470. Err. IV, 3, 17. Mids. I, 2, 36. Tw. IV, 2, 21. Wint. II, 2, 1. John III, 4, 19. IV, 3, 34. V, 2, 143. R2 V, 5, 2. 21. H4B V, 5, 36. H5 I, 2, 243. H6A IV, 7, 58. H6B II, 4, 110. H6C II, 1, 74. R3 III, 3, 9. Tit. I, 99. II, 3, 283. III, 2, 10. Tim. IV, 3, 537. Hml. II, 2, 249. Lr. V, 3, 18. 253. Ant. V, 2, 185 *(make not your thoughts your —s).* Cymb. III, 3, 34. Without the article, = state of imprisonment: *has deserved p.* Wint. II, 1, 120. *I had the most of them out of p.* H4A IV, 2, 45. H6B IV, 9, 42. Tim. III, 3, 4. *in p.:* Meas. I, 4, 25. IV, 2, 148. Wint. II, 2, 4. H6A II, 5, 116. H6C I, 3, 43. III, 2, 70. Hml. III, 2, 229. *cast in p.* Cymb. III, 2, 38. *put in p.* H6B IV, 7, 48. Cor. IV, 6, 38. *shut up in p.* Rom. I, 2, 56. *out of p.:* John IV, 1, 17. H8 I, 2, 201. *to p.:* Meas. I, 2, 61. 66. 118. 121. III, 2, 32. 64. 201. 218. V, 121. 326. Err. IV, 1, 108. LLL I, 2, 163. Shr. V, 1,

98. 100. All's V, 3, 283. Wint. II, 1, 103. H4B V, 2, 70. H6B I, 3, 223. II, 3, 5. Rom. III, 2, 58. Hml. II, 2, 246. Lr. V, 3, 8. 27. Oth. I, 2, 85.

**Prison,** vb. to confine, to restrain from liberty: *a lily —ed in a gaol of snow,* Ven. 362. *her tears ... being —ed in her eye like pearls in glass,* 980. *his true respect will p. false desire,* Lucr. 642. *p. my heart in thy steel bosom's ward,* Sonn. 133, 9. *universal plodding —s up the nimble spirits in the arteries,* LLL IV, 3, 305 (O. Edd. *poisons*). *the —ed bird,* Cymb. III, 3, 43.

**Prisoner,** 1) one confined, whether by legal arrest, or as taken by an enemy: Ven. 110. Sonn. 5, 10. Tp. V, 9. Gent. II, 4, 92. Meas. III, 2, 264. 272. IV, 2, 135. IV, 3, 70. V, 492. Err. IV, 4, 113. 115. Ado V, 1, 328. LLL I, 2, 168. As III, 2, 390. Wint. I, 2, 55. 57. II, 2, 28. John III, 4, 75. 123. H4A I, 1, 92. I, 3, 29. 48 etc. II, 3, 57. V, 3, 10. H5 I, 2, 162 (*p. kings*). III, 5, 55. III, 7, 94. IV, 6, 37. V, 2, 43. H6A I, 4, 24. 27 etc. etc. The person in whose custody a prisoner is kept, as well as the place in which he is confined, following with *to:* *—s to her womanly persuasion,* Shr. V, 2, 120. *p. to her womb,* Wint. II, 2, 59. *p. to the palsy,* R2 II, 3, 104. *to whose flint bosom ... doomed a p.* V, 1, 4. *p. to your son,* H4B I, 1, 20. *p.! to whom?* H6A II, 3, 33. *thy daughter p.! To whom? To me!* V, 3, 131. *our king is p. to the bishop here,* H6C IV, 5, 5. *Henry is p. to the foe,* V, 4, 77. *now are you p. to an emperor,* Tit. I, 258. *To hold p.* Gent. II, 4, 92. Tit. II, 1, 15. *to keep p.* Wint. I, 2, 52. H6A V, 3, 57. *to take p.* Lucr. 1608. Ado I, 1, 326. LLL I, 2, 65. John III, 4, 7. H4A I, 1, 70. I, 3, 23. H4B I, 1, 126. H5 IV, 8, 80. H6A I, 1, 145. IV, 1, 26. IV, 7, 56. H6C IV, 4, 7. Tim. III, 5, 69. Caes. V, 3, 37. Mcb. I, 3, 85. Hml. II, 2, 499. Cymb. I, 6, 103.

2) one tried in a court of justice: *when the judge is robbed the p. dies,* Lucr. 1652. *the jury passing on the —'s life,* Meas. II, 1, 19. *what 'twere to be a judge, and what a p.* II, 2, 70. *produce the p.* Wint. III, 2, 8.

**Prison-house,** prison, gaol: *forbid to tell the secrets of my p.* Hml. I, 5, 14.

**Prisonment,** imprisonment, confinement: John III, 4, 161.

**Pristine,** ancient: *the p. wars of the Romans,* H5 III, 2, 87 (Fluellen's speech). *purge it to a sound and p. health,* Mcb. V, 3, 52.

**Prithee,** a corruption of *pray thee;* with *I:* Tp. I, 2, 246. II, 1, 25. II, 2, 153. 171. 177. III, 2, 38. V, 101. Meas. I, 2, 181. I, 3, 45. III, 2, 141. Err. II, 1, 55. As I, 2, 28. II, 4, 71. II, 5, 9. 14. III, 2, 193. 199 (*I p. now with most petitionary vehemence*). III, 4, 2. H6A V, 2, 10. H6B II, 1, 33. R3 II, 4, 31 (Qq *I pray thee*). IV, 4, 179. Cymb. IV, 2, 163 etc. Without *I:* Tp. II, 1, 9. 127. 170. 228. II, 2, 74. 118. III, 2, 91. IV, 215. Wiv. IV, 1, 75. V, 1, 1. Merch. I, 2, 39 (Ff and later Qq *I pray thee*). II, 2, 194 and III, 5, 93 (Ff and later Qq *pray thee*). As I, 2, 86. I, 3, 96. Wint. II, 2, 18. H8 I, 4, 91 etc.

**Privacy,** 1) secrecy: *fie! p.? fie!* Wiv. IV, 5, 24. 2) retirement: *of this my p. I have strong reasons,* Troil. III, 3, 190. 191.

**Private,** adj. 1) being by one's self, lonely, solitary: *in respect that it* (a shepherd's life) *is solitary, I like it very well; but in respect that it is p., it is a very vile life,* As III, 2, 17 (Touchstone's speech). *how is*

*the king employed? I left him p., full of sad thoughts and troubles,* H8 II, 2, 15. *how dare you thrust yourselves into my p. meditations?* 66. *and p. in his chamber pens himself,* Rom. I, 1, 144.

2) particular (opposed to general): *when every p. widow may keep her husband's shape in mind,* Sonn. 9, 7 (whereas thy widow is the world at large). *who cries on pride, that can therein tax any p. party?* As II, 7, 71.

3) personal, respecting particular individuals (opp. to public): *thy secret pleasure turns to open shame, thy p. feasting to a public fast,* Lucr. 891. *why should the p. pleasure of some one become the public plague of many moe?* 1478. *to plague a p. sin in general,* 1484. *the p. wound is deepest,* Gent. V, 4, 71. *had you a special warrant for the deed? No, my good lord, it was by p. message,* Meas. V, 465. *one in the prison, that should by p. order else have died,* 471. *for p. quarrel 'twixt your duke and him,* Shr. IV, 2, 84. *he is a devil in p. brawl,* Tw. III, 4, 259. *in p. brabble did we apprehend him,* V, 68. *with some few p. friends,* R2 III, 3, 4. *a poor and p. displeasure,* H5 IV, 1, 210. *let not your p. discord keep away your levied succours,* H6A IV, 4, 22. *the state takes notice of the p. difference betwixt you and the cardinal,* H8 I, 1, 101. *how innocent I was from any p. malice in his end,* III, 2, 268. *both in his p. conscience and his place,* V, 3, 40. *for my p. part,* Troil. II, 2, 125. *one that knows the youth even to his inches, and with p. soul did in great Ilion thus translate him to me,* IV, 5, 111 (unbosoming to me his personal opinion, not speaking in a public capacity). *his regard for's p. friends,* Cor. V, 1, 24. V, 3, 18. *that these great towers should fall for p. faults in them,* Tim. V, 4, 26. *for your p. satisfaction,* Caes. II, 2, 73. *what p. griefs they have,* III, 2, 217. *to manage p. and domestic quarrel,* Oth. II, 3, 215.

4) belonging to a particular person: *his p. arbours,* Caes. III, 2, 253. cf. *in this p. plot,* H6B II, 2, 60.

5) not known or not open to everybody, but only to one person or to a few: *in this p. plot,* H6B II, 2, 60 (retired from the public view, as belonging to a private man). *may it please you to withdraw into your p. chamber,* H8 III, 1, 28 (the queen having received the cardinals in the midst of her court-ladies). *saucy controller of our p. steps,* Tit. II, 3, 60 (where we would be alone). *we talk here in the public haunt of men: either withdraw unto some p. place,* Rom. III, 1, 54. *bring me to some p. place,* Per. IV, 6, 98. *a p. conference etc. = a conversation between two persons, not overheard by others* (German: *unter vier Augen*): Mids. I, 1, 116. All's II, 5, 62. H4A III, 2, 2. R3 I, 1, 86. H8 II, 2, 81. Cor. V, 3, 7. Per. II, 4, 17.

Hence = secret: *O unfelt sore! crest-wounding p. scar,* Lucr. 828. *your p. grudge will out, though ne'er so cunningly you smother it,* H6A IV, 1, 109. *our mind partakes her p. actions to your secrecy,* Per. I, 1, 153. *by public war or p. treason,* I, 2, 104.

6) not invested with a public function, or not done in an official capacity: *a p. man,* H5 IV, 1, 254. H6A V, 4, 136. H8 V, 3, 55. Tit. IV, 4, 75. Ant. III, 12, 15. *a p. life,* H6C IV, 6, 42. *England's p. wrongs,* R2 II, 1, 166 (= wrongs committed against private men, against quiet citizens). *he hath very oft given p. time to you,* Hml. I, 3, 92 (time spared from public

duties, leisure-time). *not almost a fault to incur a p. check*, Oth. III, 3, 67 (a reproach made by a personal friend, much less a degradation from office). *'tis not a time for p. stomaching*, Ant. II, 2, 9 (for personal grudge, in the midst of threatening public dangers).

7) *a p. soldier* = a common soldier, not an officer: H4B III, 2, 177.

**Private,** subst. 1) privacy, retirement: *let me enjoy my p.* Tw. III, 4, 100. *I shall be sent for in p. to him,* H4B V, 5, 83 (when he is alone; though he may think fit to disavow me in public). *we are too open here to argue this; let's think in p.* more, H8 II, 1, 169. *in p.* = the French *entre quatre yeux (unter vier Augen):* Err. V, 60. Ado III, 2, 86. LLL V, 2, 229. 241. 254. H6A I, 2, 69. H8 II, 4, 206. Cor. II, 3, 84. 174. V, 3, 93. Lr. III, 4, 165. Oth. IV, 1, 2. Cymb. V, 5, 115.

2) personal, not official, communication: *whose p. with me of the Dauphin's love is much more general than these lines import,* John IV, 3, 16.

3) one not invested with a public office: *what have kings, that —s have not too?* H5 IV, 1, 255.

4) a common soldier: *her* (Fortune's) *—s we,* Hml. II, 2, 238 (purposely misunderstood by Hamlet).

**Privately,** 1) alone, by one's self, without the attendance of others: *she hath p. twice or thrice a day, ever since the death of Hermione, visited that removed house,* Wint. V, 2, 114.

2) not officially, but in the character of a private man, personally: *be it as you shall p. determine, either for her stay or going,* Oth. I, 3, 276.

3) not before others, but only in the presence of the persons concerned *(entre quatre yeux):* *if you handled her p., she would sooner confess,* Meas. V, 277. *speak it p.* Merch. II, 4, 21. *we'll pass the business p. and well,* Shr. IV, 4, 57. *he hears nought p. that comes from Troy,* Troil. I, 3, 249.

**Privilege,** subst. 1) a particular right or immunity: Mids. III, 2, 79 (cf. II, 1, 220). All's II, 3, 220. IV, 5, 96. Wint. III, 2, 104. John IV, 3, 32. R2 II, 1, 116. H4A III, 2, 86. V, 2, 18. H6A V, 4, 61. R3 III, 1, 41. 54. Troil. III, 2, 136. Cor. I, 10, 23. V, 3, 25. Tit. IV, 4, 57. Lr. II, 2, 76. V, 3, 129. *on one's p.* = confiding or presuming on a particular right: LLL IV, 2, 162. H6A II, 4, 86. *under p.*, in the same sense, Ado V, 1, 60. *to bear a p.* John I, 261. Tit. IV, 2, 116.

2) advantage, favourable circumstance: *take heed of this large p.* Sonn. 95, 13. *think my patience, more than thy desert, is p. for thy departure hence,* Gent. III, 1, 160. *your virtue is my p.* Mids. II, 1, 220 (or = your virtue is my immunity from the common laws of decency?). *compassion on the king commands me stoop, or I would see his heart out, ere the priest should ever get that p. of me,* H6A III, 1, 121.

3) right in general: *have you nuns no farther —s?* Meas. I, 4, 1. *I beg the ancient p. of Athens, as she is mine, I may dispose of her,* Mids. I, 1, 41. *where no venom else but only they they hath p. to live,* R2 II, 1, 158. *retain but p. of a private man,* H6A V, 4, 136.

**Privilege,** vb. 1) to invest with a particular right or immunity: *such neighbour nearness to our blood should nothing p. him,* R2 I, 1, 120. Partic. *—d:* Compl. 62. H6A I, 3, 46. H6C II, 2, 120. H8 I, 4, 52. Troil. II, 3, 61. IV, 4, 132. With *from: it shall p. him from your hands,* Err. V, 95 (exempt him from the danger of falling into your hands).

2) to authorize, to license: *to p. dishonour in thy name,* Lucr. 621. *you yourself may p. your time to what you will,* Sonn. 58, 10.

**Privily,** under hand, without much noise, secretly: *whence he shortly after p. withdrew himself,* Lucr. Arg. 14. *I'll p. away,* Meas. I, 1, 68. *tell him p. of our intent,* H6C I, 2, 39. *he p. deals with our cardinal,* H8 I, 1, 183. *I will p. relieve him,* Lr. III, 3, 15.

**Privity,** joint knowledge, concurrence: *without the p. o' the king,* H8 I, 1, 74.

**Privy,** 1) not destined for general use, but for particular accommodation: *his face is Lucifer's p. kitchen,* H4B II, 4, 360. *is the banquet ready in the p. chamber?* H8 I, 4, 99 (not a reception-room).

2) not seen openly, secret: *what p. marks I had about me,* Err. III, 2, 146. *the p. maidens' groans,* H5 II, 4, 107 (= the secret groans of maidens. The surreptitious Qq and M. Edd. *pining*). *to take some p. order, to draw the brats of Clarence out of sight,* R3 III, 5, 106.

3) assigned to secret uses: *the other half comes to the p. coffer of the state,* Merch. IV, 1, 354; cf. 371.

4) with *to,* = being in the secret of: Gent. III, 1, 12. Wint. II, 1, 94. H6B III, 1, 47. H6C I, 2, 46. Rom. V, 3, 266. Hml. I, 1, 133. Ant. I, 2, 42.

5) admitted to secrets of state: *your highness' p. council,* H6B II, 1, 176. H8 IV, 1, 112.

**Prize,** subst. 1) anything taken and seized as booty: *truth proves thievish for a p. so dear,* Sonn. 48, 14. *a p.! a p.!* Gent. V, 4, 121. *give fire: she is my p.* Wiv. II, 2, 143. Tp. IV, 205. Wint. IV, 3, 31. H4A I, 1, 75. II, 4, 283. H4B III, 1, 101. H6A V, 3, 33. H6B IV, 1, 8. 25. IV, 7, 22. Troil. II, 2, 86. V, 6, 10. Caes. V, 4, 27. Lr. IV, 6, 230. Oth. I, 2, 51. *to make p. of* = to gain: R3 III, 7, 187.

2) anything gained as the reward of exertion or contest: *desire my pilot is, beauty my p.* Lucr. 279. *the proud full sail of his great verse, bound for the p. of all too precious you,* Sonn. 86, 2. *doth point out thee as his triumphant p.* 151, 10. *lest too light winning make the p. light,* Tp. I, 2, 452. Merch. II, 9, 60. As I, 1, 168. Shr. II, 344. Hml. III, 3, 59.

3) a contest for a reward: *two contending in a p.* Merch. III, 2, 142. *you have played your p.* Tit. I, 399.

4) any gain or advantage, privilege: *it is war's p. to take all vantages,* H6C I, 4, 59. *'tis p. enough to be his son,* II, 1, 20. *place, riches, favour, —s of accident as oft as merit,* Troil. III, 3, 83.

**Prize,** subst. estimation: *Caesar's no merchant, to make p. with you of things that merchants sold,* Ant. V, 2, 183. *then had my p. been less, and so more equal ballasting to thee,* Cymb. III, 6, 77. Lr. II, 1, 122 (Edd. *poise*).

**Prize,** vb. 1) to estimate, to rate: *volumes that I p. above my dukedom,* Tp. I, 2, 168. *so swift and excellent a wit as she is —d to have,* Ado III, 1, 90. *what we have we p. not to the worth,* IV, 1, 220; cf. Troil. IV, 4, 136. *p. you yourselves: what buys your company?* LLL V, 2, 224. As III, 2, 160. Wint. III, 2, 43. 111. H6A I, 3, 22. Troil. I, 2, 315. II, 2, 91. Cor. III, 3, 121. Tim. I, 1, 171 (*things are —d by their masters,* i. e. according to the merit of their owners). Oth. IV, 1, 186. Ant. I, 1, 56. *to p. at* = to rate at, to esteem worth: *if you —d my lady's favour at any thing more than contempt,* Tw. II, 3, 130. *slight regard, contempt ... doth he p. you at,* H5 II, 4, 119. *p. their hours at a cracked drachm,* Cor. I, 5, 5. *a* *kinder value than he hath hereto —d them at*, II, 2, 64. *I do p. it at my love*, Tim. V, 1, 184 (think it worth my love). *p. me at her worth*, Lr. I, 1, 72.

2) to value highly, to esteem: *I do love, p., honour you*, Tp. III, 1, 73. *his good nature — s the virtue that appears in Cassio, and looks not on his evils*, Oth. II, 3, 139 (Qq *praises*). *she —d it once*, Cymb. II, 4, 104. *not to p.* = to make no account of: *not —ing her poor infant's discontent*, Sonn. 143, 8. *my love —s not quantity of dirty lands*, Tw. II, 4, 85. Wint. IV, 4, 368. 386.

**Prizer,** 1) a prize-fighter: *the bonny p. of the humorous duke*, As II, 3, 8.

2) one that sets the value of a thing: *it holds his estimate and dignity as well wherein 'tis precious of itself as in the p.* Troil. II, 2, 56.

**Probable,** 1) likely, having more evidence than the contrary: As III, 5, 11. All's III, 6, 107. Oth. I, 2, 76. Ant. V, 2, 356. Cymb. II, 4, 115. IV, 2, 141.

2) calculated to bias the judgment, satisfactory: *single I'll resolve you, which to you shall seem p., of every these happened accidents*, Tp. V, 249. *strenghtened with what apology you think may make it p. need*, All's II, 4, 52. *the least of all these signs were p.* H6B III, 2, 178. *it is spoke freely out of many mouths, — how p. I do not know*, Cor. IV, 6, 65.*

**Probal,** calculated to bias the judgment, satisfactory: *this advice is free I give and honest, p. to thinking*, Oth. II, 3, 344.

**Probation,** 1) proof: *what he with his oath and all p. will make up full clear*, Meas. V, 157. *passed in p. with you, how you were borne in hand*, Mcb. III, 1, 80. *of the truth herein this present object made p.* Hml. I, 1, 156. *that the p. bear no hinge nor loop to hang a doubt on*, Oth. III, 3, 365. *which for more p. I can with ease produce*, Cymb. V, 5, 362.

2) examination, trial: *I, in p. of a sisterhood*, Meas. V, 72 (= the year of noviciate). *that suffers under p.* Tw. II, 5, 142.

**Proceed,** 1) to go forth, to issue, to come from: *his eye drops fire, no water thence —s*, Lucr. 1552. *such childish humour from weak minds — s*, 1825. *showing their birth and where they did p.* Sonn. 76, 8. *and thence this slander —s*, 131, 14. *from lowest place when virtuous things p.* All's II, 3, 132. H4B IV, 1, 148. H6A V, 4, 152. R3 I, 3, 28. H8 II, 3, 78. Cor. I, 1, 157. Tit. IV, 4, 52. Mcb. II, 1, 39. Hence = to arise, to be caused: *little faults, —ing on distemper*, H5 II, 2, 54. *I pray his absence p. by swallowing that*, Cymb. III, 5, 58.

2) to advance, to go on, to take one's course: *and doth so far p., that what is vile shows like a virtuous deed*, Lucr. 251. *might but my bending down reprieve thee from thy fate, it should p.* Meas. III, 1, 145. *if thou p. as high as word, my deed shall match thy meed*, All's II, 1, 212. *—ed further, cut me off the heads ...*, H4A IV, 3, 85. H6B IV, 4, 35. H8 II, 4, 90. Cor. I, 1, 1. Mcb. I, 7, 31. Cymb. I, 5, 15. Singular passage: *hadst thou like us ... —ed the sweet degrees*, Tim. IV, 3, 252 (*the sweet degrees* not an object governed by *—ed*, but an accus. denoting the way made).

3) to go forward, to pass, to be done: *what in time —s may token to the future our past deeds*, All's IV, 2, 62. *where nothing can p. whereof I shall not have intelligence*, R3 III, 2, 23. *he will tell you what hath —ed*, Caes. I, 2, 181.

4) to go on, to continue: Tp. III, 2, 59. 94. Gent. III, 1, 360. Wiv. II, 2, 197. Meas. V, 87. LLL IV, 3, 23. V, 2, 570. Mids. I, 2, 21. 59. V, 260. As III, 2, 252. Shr. IV, 3, 139. Wint. III, 2, 109. 142. H8 I, 2, 17. 188. II, 4, 66. Troil. II, 3, 61. Caes. III, 3, 21. Hml. II, 2, 487. Cymb. II, 4, 66. V, 5, 42. With *in: p. in practice with my younger daughter*, Shr. II, 165. *if thou p. in this thy insolence*, H6A I, 3, 37. V, 4, 162. Oth. IV, 1, 267.

5) to go to work, to act: *muse not that I thus suddenly p.* Gent. I, 3, 64. *when you have seen more, p. accordingly*, Ado III, 2, 125. *—ed well, to stop all good —ing*, LLL I, 1, 95. *O, some authority how to p.* IV, 3, 287. *p., p.* As III, 3, 72. V, 4, 203. Wint. V, 3, 97. *the Venetian law cannot impugn you as you do p.* Merch. IV, 1, 179. All's V, 3, 236. Wint. III, 2, 6. R2 IV, 156. H5 I, 2, 9. H6B I, 3, 152. R3 III, 5, 48. H8 II, 4, 5. 221. V, 1, 108. Cor. I, 2, 3. II, 2, 85. III, 1, 314. 333. V, 6, 16. Caes. III, 1, 183. Hml. V, 2, 27. Lr. IV, 7, 19. Ant. III, 9, 4. V, 1, 75. Cymb. II, 4, 55. *to p. against* = to take measures, to go to work against: H6B III, 2, 20. Cor. I, 1, 26. Hml. IV, 7, 6. Lr. I, 2, 89. *with* in the same sense: *from thence, by cold gradation and weal-balanced form, we shall p. with Angelo*, Meas. IV, 3, 105. *to p. in* = to set about: *which I was much unwilling to p. in*, Gent. II, 1, 112. *that I may p. in my speech*, Tw. I, 5, 193. With an inf.: *p. to procure my fall*, Err. I, 1, 1. *orderly p. to swear him*, R2 I, 3, 9. *that thus you should p. to put me off*, H8 II, 4, 21. With *to: we have with a leavened and prepared choice —ed to you*, Meas. I, 1, 53 (= chosen you). *p. to judgment*, Merch. IV, 1, 240. *p. thus rashly to the villain's death*, R3 III, 5, 43. Cor. III, 1, 219. Oth. I, 3, 220. V, 2, 138. Per. I, 1, 113.

**Proceeder,** one who goes on and makes a progress: *quick —s*, Shr. IV, 2, 11.

**Proceeding,** subst. 1) doing, action, course taken: *his —s teach thee*, Ven. 406. *like the —s of a drunken brain*, 910. *I'll cross Thurio's dull p.* Gent. II, 6, 41. *and here an engine fit for my p.* III, 1, 138. *determine our —s*, III, 2, 97. *to these violent —s all my neighbours shall cry aim*, Wiv. III, 2, 44. *the straitness of his p.* Meas. III, 2, 270. *unpregnant and dull to all —s*, IV, 4, 24. Merch. IV, 1, 358. All's II, 4, 50. Wint. II, 1, 179. John II, 214. III, 1, 97. IV, 1, 114. IV, 2, 133. V, 2, 11. H4A II, 3, 34. IV, 1, 65. H4B IV, 2, 110. V, 5, 103. H6C IV, 2, 11. R3 III, 5, 66. IV, 4, 403. H8 I, 2, 108. II, 4, 18. III, 2, 26. Troil. V, 7, 7. Cor. II, 2, 163. Tit. V, 3, 8. Caes. II, 2, 103. Hml. V, 1, 322. Lr. I, 4, 233. V, 1, 32. Oth. I, 3, 65. 93. Per. IV, 3, 25.

2) process, course: *what plain p. is more plain than this?* H6B II, 2, 53. *I have an interest in your hate's p.* Rom. I, 1, 193.

**Process,** 1) course, the act of going on and passing by (of time): *in p. of the seasons*, Sonn. 104, 6. (time) *often at his very loose decides that which long p. could not arbitrate*, LLL V, 2, 753. *beguiled the tediousness and p. of my travel*, R2 II, 3, 12. *ere the glass finish the p. of his sandy hour*, H6A IV, 2, 36. *lest that the p. of thy kindness last longer telling than thy kindness' date*, R3 IV, 4, 253 (the p. of telling thy kindness). *in the course and p. of this time*, H8 II, 4, 38.

2) a series of actions or events: *and finds no other advantage in the p. but only the losing of hope by time,*

All's I, 1, 18. *after this p. to give her the avaunt*, H8 II, 3, 9.

3) the way and order in which something goes forward or happens: *to set the needless p. by*, Meas. V, 92. *tell her the p. of Antonio's end*, Merch. IV, 1, 274. *by law and p. of great nature freed*, Wint. II, 2, 60. *tell the p. of their death*, R3 IV, 3, 32. *witness the p. of your speech*, Troil. IV, 1, 8. Hml. I, 5, 37. III, 3, 29. Oth. I, 3, 142.

4) regular proceeding, course of law: *proceed by p.* Cor. III, 1, 314.

5) a mandate: *thou mayst not coldly set our sovereign p.* Hml. IV, 3, 65: *where's Fulvia's p.?* Ant. I, 1, 28.

**Procession**, a train marching with ceremonious solemnity: *in p.* H5 IV, 8, 118. H6A I, 6, 20. *on p.* H6B II, 1, 68.

**Process-server**, probably one who carries and delivers mandates or summons: Wint. IV, 3, 102 (Autolycus' speech).

**Proclaim**, to declare or announce openly, either by words or in another way: *peace —s olives of endless age*, Sonn. 107, 8. *her hair —ed in her a careless hand of pride*, Compl. 30. *the setting of thine eye and cheek p. a matter from thee*, Tp. II, 1, 229. *I will p. myself what I am*, Wiv. III, 5, 146. *as those cheek-roses p. you are no less* (than a virgin) Meas. I, 4, 17. *these black masks p. an enshield beauty*, II, 4, 80. *I will p. thee*, 151 (tell every body what thou art). *outward courtesies would fain p. favours that keep within*, V, 15. *the world's large tongue —s you for a man replete with mocks*, LLL V, 2, 853. *I am not an impostor that p. myself against the level of mine aim*, All's II, 1, 158. *this satisfaction the by-gone day —ed*, Wint. I, 2, 32. *whom I p. a man of truth*, III, 2, 158. *the hottest day prognostication — s*, IV, 4, 818. *whose daughter his tears —ed his*, V, 1, 160. *many other evidences p. her to be the king's daughter*, V, 2, 42. H4A I, 3, 145. 156. H5 II, 2, 168. H6A II, 4, 26. H6C V, 1, 94. H8 I, 1, 138. Troil. V, 4, 18 *(the Grecians begin to p. barbarism*, i. e. announce it to be their cause). Tim. IV, 3, 503 *(I do p. one honest man)*. Hml. I, 3, 72. II, 2, 621. III, 4, 85. IV, 5, 117. V, 2, 243. Lr. III, 6, 56. V, 3, 95. Ant. III, 11, 19. III, 13, 129. IV, 14, 126. Cymb. I, 1, 52. Per. I, 4, 15. IV, 6, 83. Intr. = to make one's declaration openly and publicly: *her tender shame will not p. against her maiden loss*, Meas. IV, 4, 27.

Particularly = to make known to the public by criers or by advertisements: Meas. IV, 4, 9. 17. V, 514. Err. V, 130. LLL I, 1, 121. 262. 289. 293. Shr. III, 2, 16 *(p. the banns)*. IV, 2, 85. 87. Wint. III, 2, 103. John II, 310. R2 II, 2, 56. II, 3, 30. H4A V, 1, 73. H5 IV, 3, 34. IV, 8, 119. H6A I, 1, 169. V, 4, 117. H6B II, 1, 60. IV, 1, 43. IV, 2, 187. IV, 4, 28. IV, 9, 28. H6C II, 1, 194. II, 2, 71. IV, 7, 54. 63. 69. IV, 8, 53. R3 IV, 4, 517 *(Qq given out)*. V, 5, 16. Troil. II, 1, 26. 133. Tit. I, 275. Caes. III, 1, 79. V, 4, 3. Lr. II, 1, 62. II, 3, 1. IV, 6, 230. Oth. I, 1, 69. II, 2, 9. Ant. III, 6, 13. Per. I, 2, 44. IV, 6, 194.

**Proclamation**, open declaration, manifestation: *invention is ashamed, against the p. of thy passion, to say thou dost not* (love my son) All's I, 3, 180. *the very stream of his life and the business he hath helmed must upon a warranted need give him a better p.* Meas.

III, 2, 152 (i. e. proclaim or manifest him to be a better man).

Especially = publication, notice given to the public: Gent. III, 1, 216. III, 2, 12. Meas. I, 2, 81. LLL I, 1, 286. Merch. IV, 1, 436. Wint. III, 1, 15. H4A I, 3, 147. H8 I, 3, 17. Troil. II, 1, 22. 25. 34. 100. Tit. I, 190. Lr. V, 3, 183. Per. IV, 2, 117. *to make p.* H6A I, 3, 71. H6C IV, 7, 70. V, 5, 9. R3 IV, 4, 519.

**Procne**, see *Progne*.

**Proconsul**, a Roman officer who was charged with the government of a province: Cymb. III, 7, 8.

**Procrastinate**, to delay to the morrow: Err. I, 1, 159.

**Procreant**, generating, begetting young: *this bird hath made his pendent bed and p. cradle*, Mcb. I, 6, 8.

**Procreants**, two persons engaged in cohabitation: *leave p. alone and shut the door*, Oth. IV, 2, 28.

**Procreation**, the act of begetting, generation: *whose p., residence and birth scarce is dividant*, Tim. IV, 3, 4.

**Procris** (misnamed *Procrus* in the play of Pyramus and Thisbe) daughter of Erechtheus and wife to Cephalus: Mids. V, 200. 201.

**Proculeius**, name in Ant. IV, 15, 48. V, 1, 61. 70. V, 2, 12.

**Procurator**, one who transacts affairs for another, a substitute: H6B I, 1, 3.

**Procure**, 1) to bring about, to effect, to cause: *I am sorry that such sorrow I p.* Meas. V, 479. *to p. my fall*, Err. I, 1, 1. *all these could not p. me any scathe*, H6B II, 4, 62. *the injuries that they themselves p.* Lr. II, 4, 306. *what cause —s her hither?* Rom. III, 5, 68 (= causes her to come hither). With an inf.: *p. the vicar to stay for me*, Wiv. IV, 6, 48. *one that I'll p. to come to thee*, Rom. II, 2, 145. With a clause: *p. that Lady Margaret do vouchsafe to come*, H6A V, 5, 88.

2) to obtain, to contrive to have, to gain, to get: *not to be tempted, would she be immured, and now, to tempt, all liberty —d*, Compl. 252. *have —d his leave for present parting*, All's II, 5, 60. Wint. IV, 4, 634. R2 IV, 159. H6C II, 1, 180. H8 V, 1, 133. Troil. III, 3, 276. Cor. III, 3, 9. Cymb. V, 4, 162. With a dat. and accus.: *p. me music ready*, Shr. Ind. 1, 50. *you should p. him better assurance*, H4B I, 2, 35. Wiv. II, 3, 95. H4A II, 4, 597. III, 3, 208. H6A I, 4, 7. Oth. III, 1, 38.

3) to contrive: (my dog) *with sighs so deep —s to weep in howling wise*, Pilgr. 276 (some M. Edd. *my sighs … p. to weep*).

4) to pimp: *—s she still?* Meas. III, 2, 58.

**Prodigal**, 1) lavish, profuse: Ven. 755. Pilgr. 411. Merch. I, 1, 129. II, 5, 15. Wint. IV, 3, 103 *(the P. Son;* cf. *the prodigious son*, in Launce's language, Gent. II, 3, 4). R2 I, 3, 256. H8 V, 5, 13. Tim. III, 4, 12. Hml. I, 3, 36. With *of: p. of all dear grace*, LLL II, 9. Adverbially: *how p. the soul lends the tongue vows*, Hml. I, 3, 116.

Substantively: *the niggard p. that praised her so*, Lucr. 79. *a p.* Merch. II, 6, 14. III, 1, 47. Tw. I, 3, 25. Troil. V, 1, 37. Tim. IV, 3, 278. *the P.*, the spendthrift of S. Luke ch. 15: Wiv. IV, 5, 8. Err. IV, 3, 19. Merch. II, 6, 17. H4A IV, 2, 37. H4B II, 1, 157.

2) ample, abundant: *spend his p. wits*, LLL V, 2, 64. *what p. portion have I spent*, As I, 1, 41. *with*

*oppression of their p. weight*, R2 III, 4, 31. *p. bits*, Tim. II, 2, 174.

**Prodigality**, excessive liberality, profusion: R3 I, 2, 244.

**Prodigally**, lavishly, profusely: LLL II, 12.

**Prodigious**, portentous: *nor mark p., such as are despised in nativity*, Mids. V, 419. *crooked, swart, p., patched with foul moles*, John III, 1, 46. *if ever he have child, abortive be it, p. and untimely brought to light*, R3 I, 2, 22. *when he performs, astronomers foretell it; it is p., there will come some change*, Troil. V, 1, 100. *p. birth of love it is to me*, Rom. I, 5, 142. *yet p. grown and fearful, as these strange eruptions are*, Caes. I, 3, 77. Misapplied by Launce for *prodigal:* Gent. II, 3, 4.

**Prodigiously**, portentously: *pray that their burthens may not fall this day, lest that their hopes p. be crossed*, John III, 1, 91 (viz by monstrous births).

**Prodigy**, portent, ominous apparition: *the people are amazed at apparitions, signs and —es*, Ven. 926. *as if they saw some wondrous monument, some comet or unusual p.* Shr. III, 2, 98. *call them meteors, —es and signs*, John III, 4, 157. *now hath my soul brought forth her p.* R2 II, 2, 64 (her monstrous birth). *a p. of fear and a portent of mischief*, H4A V, 1, 20. *where's that valiant crook-back p.?* H6C I, 4, 75. *disturbed with —es*, Tit. I, 101. *when these —es do so conjointly meet*, Caes. I, 3, 28. *these apparent —es*, II, 1, 198.

**Proditor**, traitor: *usurping p., and not protector, of the king and realm*, H6A I, 3, 31.

**Produce**, 1) to bring forward, to offer to view: All's IV, 1, 6. John I, 46. H6A I, 4, 40. Caes. III, 1, 228 (*p. his body to the market-place*). Lr. V, 1, 43. V, 3, 230. Especially = to place before a court of justice; either as a defendant: *p. the prisoner*, Wint. III, 2, 8. *—ing forth the cruel ministers of this dead butcher*, Mcb. V, 8, 68. Or as an evidence: *to p. so bad an instrument*, All's V, 3, 201. *to be —d against the Moor*, Oth. I, 3, 147 (Ff produced). Used of things, = to exhibit: *I must p. my power*, All's II, 3, 157. Particularly to exhibit in proof of sth.: LLL II, 161. Merch. I, 3, 100. Wint. II, 3, 118. John II, 191. H5 I, 2, 37. H8 II, 4, 68. III, 2, 293. Lr. II, 1, 73. Cymb. V, 5, 363.

2) to bring forth, to bear: Tp. II, 1, 159. Wint. II, 1, 150. John III, 4, 54.

**Producted**, = produced; reading of Ff in Oth. I, 1, 147; Qq and M. Edd. *produced.*

**Proface**, much good may it do you (cf. *Prosit* in German): H4B V, 3, 30.

**Profanation**, the act of violating holy things, irreverence: Meas. II, 2, 128. Tw. I, 5, 233. Misapplied by Elbow in Meas. II, 1, 55.

**Profane**, adj. 1) not sacred, not holy: *in shape p.* Wiv. IV, 4, 60. *our p. hours*, R2 V, 1, 25.

2) irreverent: *lest I, too much p., should do it wrong*, Sonn. 89, 11. *p. coxcomb*, LLL IV, 3, 84. *that word grace in an ungracious mouth is but p.* R2 II, 3, 89. = gross in language, coarse-tongued: *so old and so p.* H4B V, 5, 54. *what p. wretch art thou?* Oth. I, 1, 115. *a most p. and liberal counsellor*, II, 1, 165. *p. fellow*, Cymb. II, 3, 129.

**Profane**, vb. to desecrate, to pollute; absol.: *no hand can gripe our sceptre unless he do p., steal, or usurp*, R2 III, 3, 81. Transitively: Lucr. 847. Sonn. 127, 8. 142, 6. Gent. IV, 4, 141. LLL IV, 1, 86. R2

I, 3, 59. I, 4, 13. H4A III, 2, 64. H4B II, 4, 391. V, 2, 93. H6A IV, 1, 41. R3 IV, 4, 367. 369. Cor. I, 9, 41. Rom. I, 5, 95. Hml. V, 1, 259. Oth. I, 3, 390.

**Profanely**, grossly: *not to speak it p.* Hml. III, 2, 34.

**Profaneness**, irreverence: *my great p. 'gainst thine oracle*, Wint. III, 2, 155.

**Profaner**, polluter, defiler: *—s of this neighbour-stained steel*, Rom. I, 1, 89.

**Profess**, 1) to declare openly and earnestly, to assure, to avow: *crown what I p. with kind event if I speak true*, Tp. III, 1, 69. *he —es to have received no sinister measure*, Meas. III, 2, 256. *Angelo hath to the public ear —ed the contrary*, IV, 2, 103. *since you do p. to be a suitor*, Shr. I, 2, 272. *let me hear what you p.* Wint. IV, 4, 380. *I do p. you speak not like yourself*, H8 II, 4, 84. *think us those we p., peace-makers, friends*, III, 1, 167. *I p. you have it* (your wish) III, 2, 44. *I do p. that for your highness' good I ever laboured more than mine own*, 190. *hear me p. sincerely*, Cor. I, 3, 24. *to your —ed bosoms I commit him*, Lr. I, 1, 275 (your declared, avowed sentiments). *so much* (duty) *I challenge that I may p. due to the Moor*, Oth. I, 3, 188. *where, I confess, I slept not, but p. had that was well worth watching*, Cymb. II, 4, 67. Refl. = to declare, to pretend to be: *whether dost thou p. thyself, a knave or a fool?* All's IV, 5, 23. *who p. myself your loyal servant*, Wint. II, 3, 53. *the day almost itself —es yours*, Mcb. V, 7, 27. *I p. myself an enemy to all other joys*, Lr. I, 1, 74. cf. 76. *such a one do I p. myself*, Oth. I, 1, 55. *I have —ed me thy friend*, I, 3, 342. *I p. myself her adorer*, Cymb. I, 4, 73. *I now p. myself the winner of her honour*, II, 4, 53. Partic. *—ed* = declared, avowed: *a —ed tyrant to their sex*, Ado I, 1, 170. *my friend —ed*, Rom. III, 3, 50. *thieves —ed*, Tim. IV, 3, 429.

2) to avow, to acknowledge, to declare adherence to the dictates (of a person or a duty): *I p. requital*, Wiv. IV, 2, 3 (declare it to be my duty). *by the saint whom I p.* Meas. IV, 2, 192. Refl. = to own to be: *so we p. ourselves the slaves of chance*, Wint. IV, 4, 550. *that I p. myself in banqueting to all the rout*, Caes. I, 2, 77 (perhaps = unbosom myself to all the rout by constantly saying: I p. myself such or such a one)

Hence absol.: = to declare friendship: *dishonoured by a man which ever —ed to him*, Wint. I, 2, 456.

3) to set up for, to make it one's business or trade: *she —es a hot-house*, Meas. II, 1, 66 (Elbow's speech). *how long have you —ed apprehension?* Ado III, 4, 68. *I p. curing it* (love) *by counsel*, As III, 2, 425. Shr. IV, 2, 8. All's II, 1, 105. IV, 3, 282. H4A V, 2, 92. Troil. III, 3, 270. Mcb. IV, 1, 50. Lr. I, 4, 12. Per. IV, 6, 189. With an inf.: *he only —es to persuade*, Tp. II, 1, 236. *rather rejoicing to see another merry, than merry at any thing which —ed to make him rejoice*, Meas. III, 2, 250. *I do p. to be no less than I seem*, Lr. I, 4, 14.

**Profession**, 1) that which a person declares to be or to be able to do: *one that in her sex, her years, p., wisdom and constancy, hath amazed me*, All's II, 1, 86. *I must not yield to any rites of love, for my p. 's sacred from above*, H6A I, 2, 114. *it is the privilege of mine honours, my oath, and my p.* Lr. V, 3, 130.

2) business, calling, trade: Wiv. II, 3, 42. IV, 2, 184. Meas. IV, 3, 2. Shr. Ind. 2, 22. All's I, 1, 29. I, 3, 250 (cf. *Great*). Wint. IV, 3, 105. IV, 4, 698. H4A

II, 1, 78. H6A III, 1, 20. H8 II, 4, 117. III, 1, 157. Tim. IV, 3, 431. 455. Caes. I, 1, 5. Mcb. II, 3, 21. Hml. V, 1, 35. Cymb. V, 2, 6. Per. IV, 2, 42 *(neither is our p. any trade; it's no calling).* IV, 6, 7. 78. 144.

**Professor,** one who makes declaration of his sentiments: *woe upon ye and all such false —s,* H8 III, 1, 115. Particularly one who makes avowal of a religious belief: *this is a creature, would she begin a sect, might quench the zeal of all —s else,* Wint. V, 1, 108. *—s of one faith,* H6A V, 1, 14.

**Proffer,** subst. offer: Pilgr. 52. All's II, 1, 150. H6A V, 1, 41. V, 4, 137. Per. II, 3, 68.

**Proffer,** vb. 1) to offer, to propose for acceptance: John II, 258 *(our —ed offer ).* R2 III, 2, 32. H4A I, 3, 252. IV, 3, 71. H6A IV, 2, 9. V, 1, 19. R3 III, 7, 196. 202. Cymb. III, 5, 49.

2) to offer, to attempt to do sth.: *when time shall serve, be thou not slack to p., though she put thee back,* Pilgr. 334.

**Profferer,** offerer: Gent. I, 2, 56.

**Proficient,** one who has made progress: *I am so good a p. in one quarter of an hour, that I can drink with any tinker in his own language,* H4A II, 4, 19.

**Profit,** subst. 1) any gain or advantage: *the p. of excess is but to surfeit,* Lucr. 138. *my p. on't is, I know how to curse,* Tp. I, 2, 363. *have no more p. of their shining lights,* LLL I, 1, 90. *snail-slow in p.* Merch. II, 5, 47. *the trade and p. of the city consisteth of all nations,* III, 3, 30. *if you like upon report the soil, the p., and this kind of life,* As II, 4, 98 (= produce). Wint. I, 2, 310. IV, 2, 21. R2 III, 4, 38. IV, 225. H5 II, 1, 117. H6A III, 3, 63. H6B I, 1, 204. 206. H8 III, 1, 83. III, 2, 158. 174. Tim. V, 1, 45. Mcb. V, 3, 62. Hml. II, 2, 24. 344. IV, 4, 19. Lr. II, 1, 77. Oth. I, 3, 392. II, 3, 10. III, 3, 79 *(to do a peculiar p. to your own person);* cf. IV, 2, 238. Ant. II, 1, 7. II, 7, 82. Cymb. IV, 2, 163. V, 4, 214. Per. IV, 1, 4. 81. IV, 2, 128. 132.

2) proficiency, improvement: *doth blunt his natural edge with —s of the mind, study and fast,* Meas. I, 4, 61. *report speaks goldenly of his p.* (at school) As I, 1, 7. *no p. grows where is no pleasure ta'en,* Shr. I, 1, 39. *I thank you for this p.* Oth. III, 3, 379 (= this good lesson); cf. *to apprehend thus, draws us a p. from all things we see,* Cymb. III, 3, 18.

**Profit,** vb. 1) tr. to be of use to, to benefit, to advantage: *these offices shall p. thee,* Sonn. 77, 14. Tp. I, 2, 313. *this nor hurts him nor —s you,* Meas. IV, 3, 128. *ill blows the wind that —s nobody,* H6C II, 5, 55.

2) intr. to be proficient, to make progress, to improve; ·intellectually or morally: *here have I made thee more p. than other princess can,* Tp. I, 2, 172. *my son —s nothing in the world at his book,* Wiv. IV, 1, 15. *correction and instruction must both work, ere this rude beast will p.* Meas. III, 2, 34. *their daughters p. very greatly under you,* LLL IV, 2, 77. *p. you in what you read?* Shr. IV, 2, 6. *by my foes I p. in the knowledge of myself,* Tw. V, 21. *God give him the ears of —ing,* H4A I, 2, 171. *well read and —ed in strange concealments,* III, 1, 166. *has not the boy —ed?* H4B II, 2, 90. *to p. by =* to be instructed by, to learn from: *men their creation mar in —ing by them,* Meas. II, 4, 128 (men spoil women by that which these learn from them). *if that an eye may p. by a tongue, then should I know you by description,* As IV, 3, 84. *I p. not by thy talk,* Troil. V, 1, 16.

**Profitable,** gainful, useful: LLL V, 2, 760. Merch. I, 3, 167. All's II, 4, 36. H5 IV, 1, 294.

**Profitably,** 1) advantageously: *the impediment most p. removed,* Oth. II, 1, 286. 2) in a manner fit to instruct and improve: *would I had a rod in my mouth, that I might answer thee p.* Tim. II, 2, 80.

**Profitless,** void of gain or advantage: *p. usurer,* Sonn. 4, 7. *thy counsel, which falls into mine ears as p.* Ado V, 1, 4. *wage a danger p.* Oth. I, 3, 30.

**Profound,** 1) deep: *in so p. abysm I throw all care,* Sonn. 112, 9. *the p. sea,* Wint. IV, 4, 501. *to the —est pit,* Hml. IV, 5, 132.

2) deep-fetched, coming from the depth of the soul, hearty: *with such a zealous laughter, so p.* LLL V, 2, 116. *a sigh so piteous and p.* Hml. II, 1, 94. *these sighs, these p. heaves,* IV, 1, 1. Hence = heartfelt, touching to the core: *when such p. respects do pull you on,* John III, 1, 318. *with a respect more tender, more holy and p.* Cor. III, 3, 113.

3) intellectually deep, very wise, sage: *to see ... p. Solomon to tune a jig,* LLL IV, 3, 168. *an opinion of wisdom, gravity, p. conceit,* Merch. I, 1, 92. *a magician most p. in his art,* As V, 2, 67. *no, my p. heart,* Tw. I, 5, 195. Hence = full of meaning and import: *upon the corner of the moon there hangs a vaporous drop p.* Mcb. III, 5, 24.*

4) thorough, complete: *which of your hips has the most p. sciatica?* Meas. I, 2, 59. *in most p. earnest,* Ado V, 1, 198. *p. simplicity,* LLL V, 2, 52.

**Profoundly,** deeply, heartily: *why sigh you so p.?* Troil. IV, 2, 83.

**Progenitors,** 1) parents: *if children predecease p.* Lucr. 1756. 2) ancestors: H5 I, 2, 95. H6A IV, 1, 166. V, 4, 110.

**Progeny,** 1) offspring: *though the mourning brow of p. forbid the smiling courtesy of love the holy suit,* LLL V, 2, 754 (i. e. a daughter who has lost her father). *this same p. of evils comes from our debate,* Mids. II, 1, 115.

2) descent: *doubting thy birth and lawful p.* H6A III, 3, 61.

3) race, ancestry: *issued from the p. of kings,* H6A V, 4, 38. *the Hector that was the whip of your bragged p.* Cor. I, 8, 12.

**Progne** (some M. Edd. *Procne*) daughter of Pandion and wife to Tereus, to whom she in revenge gave his slaughtered son Itys to eat: Tit. V, 2, 196.

**Prognosticate,** to foretell, to prophesy: Sonn. 14, 13.

**Prognostication,** 1) the art of knowing the future: *in the hottest day p. proclaims,* Wint. IV, 4, 817 (there are almanacs of the poet's time extant with the title: *An Almanack and Prognostication made for the year* etc.).

2) foretoken, sign: *if an oily palm be not a fruitful p.* Ant. I, 2, 54.

**Progress,** subst. 1) a going forward, advance, course: *time's thievish p. to eternity,* Sonn. 77, 8. *future evils ... new-conceived, and so in p. to be hatched and born,* Meas. II, 2, 97. *of that and all the p., more or less, more leisure shall express,* All's V, 3, 331. *keep a peaceful p. to the ocean,* John II, 340. *before* (the sun) *begins his golden p. in the east,* H4A III, 1, 222. *the happiest youth, viewing his p. through,* H4B III, 1, 54. *in the p. of this business he did require a respite,* H8 II, 4, 175. *in all the p. of my life and office,* V, 3,

*32. no pulse shall keep his native p.* Rom. IV, 1, 97. *I cannot by the p. of the stars give guess how near to day,* Caes. II, 1, 2.

2) a journey made by a sovereign through his own country: *the king is now in p. towards Saint Albans,* H6B I, 4, 76. *how a king may go a p. through the guts of a beggar,* Hml. IV, 3, 33.

**Progress,** vb. to move, to proceed, to pass: *this honourable dew, that silverly doth p. on thy cheeks,* John V, 2, 46.

**Progression,** a word not very distinctly used by Holofernes: *a letter which accidentally, or by the way of p., hath miscarried,* LLL IV, 2, 144 (perhaps = by going from stage to stage, from hand to hand).

**Prohibit,** used in a wrong sense by Dogberry: Ado V, 1, 335.

**Prohibition,** forbiddance, interdiction: Cymb. III, 4, 79.

**Project,** subst. 1) a chalking out, a forming in the mind, an idea: *she cannot love, nor take no shape nor p. of affection, she is so self-endeared,* Ado III, 1, 55. *flattering himself in p. of a power much smaller than the smallest of his thoughts,* H4B I, 3, 29 (Ff with *p.*).

2) a scheme, design: Tp. II, 1, 299. IV, 175. V, 1. Epil. 12. All's I, 1, 243. Wint. IV, 4, 535. Troil. I, 3, 385. II, 2, 134. Cor. V, 6, 34. Hml. IV, 7, 153.

**Project,** vb. *(próject)* to chalk out, to form, to shape: *I cannot p. mine own cause so well to make it clear,* Ant. V, 2, 121.

**Projection,** outline, plan, calculation: *which of a weak and niggardly p. doth like a miser spoil his coat with scanting a little cloth,* H5 II, 4, 46.

**Prolixious,** tiresome and superfluous: *lay by all nicety and p. blushes,* Meas. II, 4, 162.

**Prolixity,** tiresome length, tediousness: Merch. III, 1, 13. Rom I, 4, 3.

**Prologue,** subst. introduction to a discourse or performance: Tp. II, 1, 253. Wiv. III, 5, 75. LLL V, 2, 305. Mids. III, 1, 18. 24. 35. V, 106. 119. 122. As V, 3, 13. Epil. 3. H4A I, 2, 23. H6B III, 1, 151. Troil. Prol. 23. Rom. I, 4, 7 (only in Q1). Mcb. I, 3, 128. Hml. I, 1, 123. III, 2, 162. IV, 5, 18. V, 2, 30. Oth. II, 1, 264. II, 3, 134.

**Prologue,** vb. to introduce, to preface: *thus he his special nothing ever —s,* All's II, 1, 95.

**Prologue-like,** like a prologue: H5 Prol. 33.

**Prolong,** 1) to lengthen, to draw out in time: Err. I, 1, 120. H6C I, 4, 52. Tim. III, 1, 66. Hml. III, 3, 96. Cymb. V, 5, 29.

2) to defer, to put off: *this wedding-day perhaps is but —ed,* Ado IV, 1, 256. *I am not so well provided as else I would be, were the day —ed,* R3 III, 4, 47.

**Promethean,** given to men by Prometheus: *the true P. fire,* LLL IV, 3, 304. 351. Oth. V, 2, 12.

**Prometheus,** the demigod who stole fire from heaven: *P. tied to Caucasus,* Tit. II, 1, 17.

**Promise,** subst. 1) a declaration by which a person binds himself to do something: Ven. 85. Tp. IV, 41. Wiv. III, 5, 43. Mids. V, 174. Merch. II, 7, 6. III, 2, 207 *(if p. last).* As IV, 1, 43. IV, 3, 100. H4A III, 1, 1. H4B I, 3, 28. H6A I, 6, 6. H6B I, 4, 2. R3 IV, 2, 91. Cymb. I, 6, 202 etc. etc. With *for* (= concerning): *the p. for her heavenly picture,* Gent. IV, 4, 92. *your p. for the earldom,* R3 IV, 2, 105. With *of* (objectively): Wiv. II, 2, 217. Meas. III, 1, 275. III,

2, 260. All's III, 6, 30. H4B I, 3, 28. H6C II, 1, 134. III, 1, 51 etc. With *to: your breach of p. to the Porpentine,* Err. IV, 1, 49 (= to come to the P.). *it is our part and p. to the Athenians,* Tim. V, 1, 123 (= made to). With an infinitive: Meas. IV, 1, 34. Merch. III, 2, 208. Cymb. I, 6, 202. *to break p.* As IV, 1, 44. 194. IV, 3, 155. Tw. II, 3, 137 *(with).* Mcb. V, 8, 22. *to claim a p.* (= to request its fulfilment) Gent. IV, 4, 92. R3 III, 1, 197. *to give p.* Meas. III, 1, 275. *to hold p.* H5 II Prol. 29. *to keep p.* Mids. I, 1, 179. Merch. II, 3, 20. As I, 2, 255. IV, 1, 200. Tw. V, 106 *(with).* H4A III, 2, 168. Mcb. V, 8, 21. *to make p.* Wiv. IV, 6, 34. Meas. IV, 1, 34. Cor. III, 3, 86. Caes. II, 1, 56. Hml. I, 3, 119. *to pass one's p.* Tit. I, 469. cf. Caes. II, 1, 140.

2) expectation raised: *he hath borne himself beyond the p. of his age,* Ado I, 1, 14. *you have exceeded all p.* As I, 2, 256. *nothing of that wonderful p.* Tw. III, 4, 290. *a gentleman of the greatest p.* Wint. I, 1, 39. *the p. of his greener days,* H5 II, 4, 58. *make gallant show and p. of their mettle,* Caes. IV, 2, 24.

**Promise,** vb. 1) to declare to be willing to do or give something; absol.: *knows at what time to p.* H4A IV, 3, 53. *to p. is most courtly,* Tim. V, 1, 29. With an accus.: *p. more speed,* Lucr. 1349. *to p. aid,* 1696. Sonn. 34, 1. Compl. 70. Tp. I, 2, 243. Meas. V, 219. Err. IV, 1, 23. IV, 3, 70. H6A I, 2, 82. IV, 3, 10. Tit. I, 298. Caes. I, 2, 293 *(I am —d forth* = I have accepted an invitation) etc. With a dative: *p. you infinitely,* H4B V, 5, 132. Accus. and dative; a dat. with *to: she is —d by her friends unto a gentleman,* Gent. III, 1, 106. *will not p. her to any man,* Shr. I, 2, 262. *to whom I p. a counterpoise,* All's II, 3, 181. *could p. to himself a thought of added honour,* Troil. IV, 5, 144. H5 II Chor. 11. H6C II, 2, 58. b) without *to: and p. you calm seas,* Tp. V, 314. Wiv. III, 3, 239. Meas. III, 2, 212. Err. II, 1, 106. IV, 3, 47. 85. Merch. III, 2, 34. All's II, 1, 193. Wint. IV, 4, 239. H4B V, 5, 126. H6C II, 3, 52 etc. The dative subject in the passive: *I was —d them* (gloves) Wint. IV, 4, 237. *shalt be what thou art —d,* Mcb. I, 5, 17. *he is —d to be wived to fair Marina,* Per. V, 2, 10. With an inf.: *thou didst p. to bate me a full year,* Tp. I, 2, 249. Wiv. II, 3, 5. Meas. I, 2, 75. IV, 1, 18. Err. V, 222. Ado I, 1, 44. V, 4, 13. LLL I, 2, 37. Merch. I, 1, 121. As III, 3, 44. H6B I, 2, 78 etc. With a clause: Meas. III, 1, 181. H4B V, 5, 129 etc. cf. Wiv. III, 4, 112.

2) to afford reason to hope or to expect; absol.: *where most it* (expectation) *—s,* All's II, 1, 146. *we lay our best love and credence upon thy —ing fortune,* III, 3, 3. *a cause more —ing than ...,* Wint. IV, 4, 576. Ant. II, 7, 24. Transitively: *my mind —s with my habit no loss shall touch her,* Meas. III, 1, 181. *thou meagre lead, which rather threatenest than dost p. aught,* Merch. III, 2, 105. *those hopes of her good that her education —s,* All's I, 1, 46. *his image, which did p. most venerable worth,* Tw. III, 4, 396. *his expedition —s present approach,* Tim. V, 2, 3. H6C II, 2, 40. H8 I, 1, 48. II, 3, 97. V, 1, 168. Ant. III, 7, 47. IV, 8, 35 etc.

3) *I p. you* = let me tell you: *not by my consent, I p. you,* Wiv. III, 2, 72. *I do not like thy look, I p. thee,* Ado IV, 2, 47. *I fear it, I p. you,* Mids. III, 1, 29. *I p. you, your kindred hath made my eyes water ere now,* 199. *therefore, I p. ye, I fear you,* Merch. III, 5, 3. *the first time that ever I heard .... Or I, I p. thee,*

As I, 2, 148. Shr. II, 144. 287. III, 1, 54. H6A IV, 1, 174. R3 I, 4, 65 (Ff *methinks*). II, 3, 2. V, 3, 232. Tit. II, 3, 196. Rom. III, 4, 6. Tim. I, 2, 118. Lr. I, 2, 156.

**Promise-breach**, violation of promise: Meas. V, 410.

**Promise-breaker**, violator of promises: All's III, 6, 12. Cor. I, 8, 2.

**Promise-crammed**, stuffed with promises: Hml. III, 2, 99.

**Promise-keeping**, fulfilling one's promise: Meas. I, 2, 77.

**Promontory**, a high headland: Tp. V, 46. Mids. II, 1, 149. H6C III, 2, 135. Tit. II, 2, 22. Hml. II, 2, 311. Ant. IV, 14, 5.

**Promotion**, exaltation in rank, preferment: As II, 3, 60. Wint. I, 2, 357. John II, 492. R3 I, 3, 80. IV, 4, 314. H8 V, 2, 23. Rom. IV, 5, 71.

**Prompt**, adj. full of alacrity, brisk and clever: *all replication p. and reason strong*, Compl. 122. *fair virtues all, to which the Grecians are most p. and pregnant*, Troil. IV, 4, 90. *I have observed thee always for a towardly p. spirit*, Tim. III, 1, 37. *a natural and p. alacrity*, Oth. I, 3, 233. *I am p. to lay my crown at's feet*, Ant. III, 13, 75 (ready without hesitation).

**Prompt**, vb. 1) to make willing and ready, to move, to incite: *p. us to have mercy on him*, Tw. III, 4, 152. *—ed by your present trouble*, 377. *the advantage of the time —s me aloud to call for recompense*, Troil. III, 3, 2. *my —ed sword falling on Diomed*, V, 2, 175 (= eager). *ready, when time shall p. them, to make road upon us*, Cor. III, 1, 5. *love, who first did p. me to inquire*, Rom. II, 2, 80. *—ed to my revenge by heaven and hell*, Hml. II, 2, 613. *nature —s them to prince it*, Cymb. III, 3, 84.

2) to suggest words and thoughts; absol.: *the —ing eyes of beauty's tutors*, LLL IV, 3, 322 (= inspiring). With an object, denoting a) the thought suggested: *it goes on as my heart —s it*, Tp. I, 2, 420. b) the person instructed or inspired: *p. me, plain and holy innocence*, Tp. III, 1, 82. *desires, all —ing me how fair young Hero is*, Ado I, 1, 306. *my voice shall sound as you do p. mine ear*, H4B V, 2, 119. *vouchsafe to those that have not read the story, that I may p. them*, H5 V Chor. 2. *my proud heart sues and —s my tongue to speak*, R3 I, 2, 171. *we'll p. you*, Cor. III, 2, 106. *some devil p. me*, Tit. V, 3, 12. Double accus., or dat. and acc.: *nor by the matter which your heart —s you*, Cor. III, 2, 54. *to p. in* = to instruct about, to make fully acquainted with: *I did endure no slight checks, when I have —ed you in the ebb of your estate and your great flow of debts*, Tim. II, 2, 150.

**Prompter**, one who suggests the words to be spoken: Rom. I, 4, 8 (only in Q1). Oth I, 2, 84.

**Prompture**, instigation: *though he hath fallen by p. of the blood*, Meas. II, 4, 178.

**Promulgate** (Q1 *provulgate*) to make known, to publish: Oth. I, 2, 21.

**Prone**, eagerly ready: *that p. lust should stain so pure a bed*, Lucr. 684. *unless a man would marry a gallows and beget young gibbets, I never saw one so p.* Cymb. V, 4, 208. With *to*: *nor tender feeling, to base touches p.* Sonn. 141, 6. *I am not p. to weeping*, Wint. II, 1, 108. *as p. to mischief as able to perform 't*, H8 I, 1, 160. Peculiar passage: *in her youth there is a p. and speechless dialect, such as move men*, Meas. I, 2,

188 (Nares: prompt, ready; Malone: significant, expressive. The words *p. and speechless* must be considered as a hendiadis, = speechlessly prone, prone even without speaking, speaking fervently and eagerly without words).

**Pronoun**, a word used instead of a noun: Wiv. IV, 1, 41. 77.

**Pronounce**, 1) to speak, to utter solemnly or officially: *and do p. by me: lingering perdition shall attend you*, Tp. III, 3, 76. *that Edward be —d a traitor*, H6C IV, 6, 54. *whom the oracle hath doubtfully —d thy throat shall cut*, Tim. IV, 3, 121. *the spirits that know all mortal consequences have —d me thus*, Mcb. V, 3, 5 (cf. H8 I, 1, 196). *that I am to p. Caesar thine enemy*, Cymb. III, 1, 63. Especially applied to the decisions of a judge: *we do here p., Marcius is worthy of death*, Cor. III, 1, 209. *let them p. the steep Tarpeian death*, III, 3, 88. *p. his present death*, Mcb. I, 2, 64. *whose condemnation is —d*, H5 III, 6, 144. *to p. a doom*, R2 I, 3, 149. Tit. III, 1, 50. *pardon*, Merch. IV, 1, 392. H6B IV, 8, 9. *a sentence*, Meas. II, 4, 62. LLL I, 1, 302. As I, 3, 87. R3 I, 4, 190. cf. Rom. II, 3, 79.

2) to deliver, to recite: *good sentences and well —d*, Merch. I, 2, 11. *after your way his tale —d shall bury his reasons with his body*, Cor. V, 6, 58. *speak the speech as I —d it to you*, Hml. III, 2, 2. *I am tame, sir; p.* 322.

3) to articulate by the organs of speech: *det, when he should p. debt*, LLL V, 1, 23.

4) to declare, to express in words: *I hate thee, p. thee a gross lout*, Wint. I, 2, 301. *this sessions, to our great grief we p., even pushes 'gainst our heart*, III, 2, 1. *—ing that the paleness of this flower bewrayed the faintness of my master's heart*, H6A IV, 1, 106. *I do p. him in that very shape he shall appear in proof*, H8 I, 1, 196 (cf. Mcb. V, 3, 5). *as 't please yourself p. their office*, II, 4, 115. *if thou dost love, p. it faithfully*, Rom. II, 2, 94. *I do here p. . . . . I care not for you*, Cymb. II, 3, 112.

5) to speak out, to give utterance to: *sometime 'Tarquin' was —d plain, but through his teeth*, Lucr. 1786. *my prime request, which I do last p.* Tp. I, 2, 426. *the thunder —d the name of Prosper*, III, 3, 98. *for that name, which till this time my tongue did ne'er p.* John III, 1, 307. *is now leased out, I die —ing it*, R2 II, 1, 59. *slanders . . . . the which in every language I p.* H4B Ind. 7. *Lord Hastings had —d your part, I mean your voice*, R3 III, 4, 28. *no tongue could ever p. dishonour of her*, H8 II, 3, 4. *if what I now p. you have found true*, III, 2, 163. *p. but love and dove*, Rom. II, 1, 10. *wherefore could not I p. Amen*, Mcb. II, 2, 31. *p. it* (welcome) *for me to all our friends*, III, 4, 7. *the devil could not p. a title more hateful*, V, 7, 8. *by —ing of some doubtful phrase*, Hml. I, 5, 175. *'gainst fortune's state would treason have —d*, II, 2, 534. *not I . . . p. the beggary of his change*, Cymb. I, 6, 114.

**Proof**, subst. 1) trial, experiment, test: *mine appetite I never more will grind on newer p.* Sonn. 110, 11. *if you, in your own p., have vanquished the resistance of her youth*, Ado IV, 1, 46. *you have seen cruel p. of this man's strength*, As I, 2, 184. *a terrible oath . . . gives manhood more approbation than ever p. itself could have earned him*, Tw. III, 4, 199. *as you are like to find him in the p. of his valour*, 292. *we leave that to the p.* H4A II, 2, 72. *gentle exercise and p. of arms*,

V, 2, 55. *only this p. I'll of thy valour make*, H6A I, 2, 94. *in the reproof of chance lies the true p. of men*, Troil. I, 3, 34. *Troilus will stand to the p.* I, 2, 142. *set me on the p.* Tim. II, 2, 166 (let me be tried, examined). *I have made strong p. of my constancy*, Caes. II, 1, 299. *that might hold, if this should blast in p.* Hml. IV, 7, 155. *I'll put it in p.* Lr. IV, 6, 189. *of whom his eyes had seen the p.* Oth. I, 1, 28. *I will make p. of thine* (coat) V, 1, 26. *let p. speak*, Cymb. III, 1, 77.

2) a state of having been tried and having stood the test: *all my pains is sorted to no p.* Shr. IV, 3, 43 (= proves to be to no purpose). *there's never none of these demure boys come to any p.* H4B IV, 3, 98 (= has proved to be of any worth). *I have chastised the amorous Trojan and am her knight by p.* Troil. V, 5, 5. *when false opinion ... in thy just p. repeals and reconciles thee*, Lr. III, 6, 120 (= in thy proving to be just). cf. Sonn. 110, 11. Hml. III, 1, 115. Oth. I, 1, 28. Particularly applied to defensive arms tried and found impenetrable: *his brawny sides ... are better p. than thy spear's point can enter*, Ven. 626. *be thou armed for some unhappy words. Ay, to the p.* Shr. II, 141. *add p. unto mine armour with thy prayers*, R2 I, 3, 73. *his coat is of p.* H6B IV, 2, 65 (quibbling). *ten thousand soldiers armed in p.* R3 V, 3, 219. *in strong p. of chastity well armed*, Rom. I, 1, 216. *put armour on thine ears ... whose p. nor yells of mothers ... nor sight of priests ... shall pierce*, Tim. IV, 3, 124. *lapped in p.* Mcb. I, 2, 54. *Mars's armour forged for p. eterne*, Hml. II, 2, 512. *leap thou through p. of harness to my heart*, Ant. IV, 8, 15. *whose naked breast stepped before targets of p.* Cymb. V, 5, 5.

3) experience; a) the state of experiencing, of trying and seeing something: *a bliss in p., and proved, a very woe*, Sonn. 129, 11. *I do pronounce him in that very shape he shall appear in p.* H8 I, 1, 197. *p. is called impossibility*, Troil. V, 5, 29. *that love, so gentle in his view, should be so tyrannous and rough in p.* Rom. I, 1, 176. b) truth or knowledge gathered by experience: *we must curb it* (our blood) *upon others' p.* Compl. 163. *this is an accident of hourly p.* Ado II, 1, 188. *we have ten —s to one that blood hath the victory*, II, 3, 171. *I urge this childhood p.* Merch. I, 1, 144. *'tis a vulgar p. that very oft we pity enemies*, Tw. III, 1, 135. *as by p. we see the waters swell before a storm*, R3 II, 3, 43. *'tis a common p. that lowliness is young ambition's ladder*, Caes. II, 1, 21. *what my love is, p. hath made you know*, Hml. III, 2, 179. *I see in passages of p., time qualifies the spark and fire of it* (love) IV, 7, 113. *the country gives me p. and precedent of Bedlam beggars*, Lr. II, 3, 13. *who knows by history, report, or his own p.* Cymb. I, 6, 70. *out of your p. you speak*, III, 3, 27.

4) a convincing token or argument: Compl. 153. Sonn. 117, 10. Gent. I, 1, 97. Wiv. IV, 2, 106. V, 5, 126. Meas. III, 2, 31. IV, 2, 45. 143. Ado II, 2, 27. V, 1, 105. All's V, 3, 121. 199. Tw. I, 5, 67 *(make)*. 71. Wint. III, 2, 113. V, 1, 180. V, 2, 36. R2 IV, 70. H4A I, 2, 37. H6A III, 3, 68. V, 1, 46. V, 3, 8. H8 I, 1, 154. II, 1, 16. Troil. V, 2, 113 (*a p. of strength* = a strong proof). Caes. V, 1, 49. Oth. I, 3, 106. III, 3, 191. 196. 324. 360. 386. 430. 441. Cymb. III, 4, 24. V, 5, 200.

Used nonsensically by Mrs Quickly: H4B II, 4, 127.

**Proof**, adj. able to resist, impenetrable: *I am p. against that title*, Wint. IV, 4, 872. *fight with hearts more p. than shields*, Cor. I, 4, 25. *I am p. against their enmity*, Rom. II, 2, 73. *it* (your heart) *is p. and bulwark against sense*, Hml. III, 4, 38. cf. *Ague-proof, High-proof, Pistol-proof, Plot-proof, Shame-proof.*

**Prop**, subst. a support, a stay: Ven. Dedic. 2. Merch. II, 2, 70. 72. IV, 1, 375. H6C II, 1, 68. R3 III, 7, 96. Hml. IV, 5, 105.

**Prop**, vb. to support: H8 I, 1, 59. Cymb. I, 5, 60. Per. IV, 6, 127.

**Propagate**, 1) to beget: *from whence an issue I might p.* Per. I, 2, 73.

2) to promote, to improve, to increase: *my low and humble name to p. with any branch or image of thy state*, All's II, 1, 200. *griefs of mine own lie heavy in my breast, which thou wilt p., to have it prest with more of thine*, Rom. I, 1, 193. *all kind of natures, that labour on the bosom of this sphere to p. their states*, Tim. I, 1, 67.

**Propagation**, augmentation, increase: *this we came not to, only for p. of a dower remaining in the coffer of her friends, from whom we thought it meet to hide our love till time had made them for us*, Meas. I, 2, 154; i. e. to receive a richer dower than she was likely to have under the existing circumstances. Malone *prorogation*, Jackson *procuration*, Grant White *preservation*.

**Propend**, to incline: *I p. to you in resolution to keep Helen*, Troil. II, 2, 190.

**Propension**, inclination, bent of mind: *your full consent gave wings to my p.* Troil. II, 2, 133.

**Proper**, 1) peculiar, belonging to a particular person or state: *thyself and thy belongings are not thine own so p. as to waste thyself upon thy virtues*, Meas. I, 1, 31; cf. *what better or —er can we call our own than the riches of our friends?* Tim. I, 2, 106. *it imports no reason that with such vehemency he should pursue faults p. to himself*, Meas. V, 110. *with great imagination p. to madmen*, H4B I, 3, 32. *which cannot in their huge and p. life be here presented*, H5 V Chor. 5. *conceptions only p. to myself*, Caes. I, 2, 41. *it is as p. to our age to cast beyond ourselves in our opinions*, Hml. II, 1, 114.

2) (one's) own: *men hang and drown their p. selves*, Tp. III, 3, 60. *like rats that ravin down their p. bane*, Meas. I, 2, 133. *the mere effusion of thy p. loins*, III, 1, 30. *in the witness of his p. ear to call him villain*, V, 310. *from his p. tongue*, 413. All's IV, 3, 29. Tw. V, 327. Wint. II, 3, 139. H4B V, 2, 109. Troil. II, 2, 89. Cor. I, 9, 57. Hml. V, 2, 66. III, 3, 69. 265. Cymb. IV, 2, 97. Combined with *own: your own p. wisdom brings in the champion Honour on my part*, All's IV, 2, 49. *of the king of England's own p. cost*, H6B I, 1, 61. III, 1, 115. Caes. V, 3, 96.

3) conformable, adapted, suitable, becoming: *to cover with excuse that which appears in p. nakedness*, Ado IV, 1, 177. *that the comparison may stand more p.* Merch. III, 2, 46. *why not the swift foot of time? had not that been as p.?* As III, 2, 325. *if damned commotion so appeared, in his true, native and most p. shape*, H4B IV, 1, 37. *this noble isle doth want her p. limbs*, R3 III, 7, 125. *provide thee two p. palfreys, black as jet*, Tit. V, 2, 50. *p. deformity seems not in the fiend so horrid as in woman*, Lr. IV, 2, 60 (deformity conformable to the character). *'tis p. I obey him, but not now*, Oth. V, 2, 196.

4) honest, respectable (used of women): *that is

*an* advertisement to a p. maid in Florence, to take heed ...., All's IV, 3, 240. what pagan may that be? A p. gentlewoman, and a kinswoman of my master's, H4B II, 2, 169.

5) fine, nice, pretty (used of men): as p. a man, as ever went on four legs, Tp. II, 2, 63. he's a p. man, Gent. IV, 1, 10. Ado II, 3, 189. V, 1, 174. Mids. I, 2, 88. Merch. I, 2, 77. As I, 2, 129. III, 5, 51. 55. 115. Tw. III, 1, 144. John I, 250. H6A V, 3, 37. H6B IV, 2, 102. R3 I, 2, 255. Troil. I, 2, 209 (a p. man of person). Rom. II, 4, 217. Caes. I, 1, 28. Oth. I, 3, 398. IV, 3, 35. Ant. III, 3, 41. Cymb. III, 4, 64 (quite = handsome). a p. squire, Ado I, 3, 54. a p. stripling, Shr. I, 2, 144. a p. fellow of my hands, H4B II, 2, 72 (cf. Hand). the issue being of it so p. Lr. I, 1, 18.

Applied to things with irony: a p. saying, Ado IV, 1, 312. a p. jest, H6B I, 1, 132. a p. title of a peace, H8 I, 1, 98. O p. stuff, Mcb. III, 4, 60.

**Proper-false** (not hyphened in O. Edd.) well-looking and deceitful: Tw. II, 2, 30.

**Properly**, 1) peculiarly, as belonging to a particular person: we need no more of your advice; the matter, the loss, the gain, the ordering on't, is all p. ours, Wint. II, 1, 170. though I owe my revenge p., my remission lies in Volscian breasts, Cor. V, 2, 90.

2) conformably to the matter, suitably: he keeps me rustically at home, or, to speak more p., stays me here at home unkept, As I, 1, 8. or if you will, to speak more p., I will enforce it easily to my love, John II, 514.

**Property**, 1) particularity, individuality: p. was thus appalled, that the self was not the same, Phoen. 37.

2) particular quality: it (the diamond) was beautiful and hard, whereto his invised —es did tend, Compl. 212. of government the —es to unfold, Meas. I, 1, 3. whose liquor hath this virtuous p. Mids. III, 2, 367. the p. of rain is to wet, As III, 2, 27. if I break time, or flinch in p. of what I spoke, All's II, 1, 190. the p. by what it is should go, not by the title, II, 3, 137. R2 III, 2, 135. H4B III, 3, 111. Hml. II, 1, 103. III, 2, 270. V, 1, 75. Oth. I, 1, 173. Ant. I, 1, 58.

3) ownership: here I disclaim all my paternal care, propinquity and p. of blood, Lr. I, 1, 116.

4) a thing owned, possession: a king, upon whose p. and most dear life a damned defeat was made, Hml. II, 2, 597.

5) a thing wanted for a particular purpose, a tool, implement: 'tis a thing impossible I should love thee but as a p. Wiv. III, 4, 10 (as a means to get rid of my debts). do not talk of him but as a p. Caes. IV, 1, 40. Plur. —es = stage requisites: get us —es and tricking for our fairies, Wiv. IV, 4, 78. I will draw a bill of —es, such as our play wants, Mids. I, 2, 108.

**Property**, vb. 1) to make a property or tool of: they have here —ed me, keep me in darkness, Tw. IV, 2, 99 (they have done with me as with a thing having no will of its own). I am too high-born to be —ed, to be a secondary at control, John V, 2, 79. his large fortune ... subdues and —es to his love and tendance all sorts of hearts, Tim. I, 1, 57.

2) partic., or rather adj., —ed, = endowed with qualities: his voice was —ed as all the tuned spheres, Ant. V, 2, 83.*

**Prophecy**, subst. prediction, vaticination: Ven. 928. Sonn. 106, 9. Meas. II, 1, 259. Err. IV, 4, 44. Wint. IV, 4, 662. H4A III, 1, 150. IV, 4, 18. H4B III, 1, 69. V, 2, 127. H6A I, 2, 55. III, 1, 195. H6C

IV, 6, 92. V, 6, 86. R3 I, 1, 33. 39. 54. H8 I, 1, 92. I, 2, 147. II, 1, 23. Troil. IV, 5, 218. Mcb. IV, 3, 157. Lr. III, 2, 80. 95.

**Prophesier**, prophet: All's IV, 3, 115.

**Prophesy**, vb. to foretell future events, to predict; tr. and intr.: Ven. 671. 1135. Tp. V, 217. Wint IV, 1, 26. John IV, 2, 186. R2 IV, 136. H4A V, 4, 83. H4B III, 1, 82. IV, 5, 237. H6A II, 4, 124. V, 1, 31. H6B I, 1, 146. II, 2, 76. III, 2, 283. H6C V, 6, 37. R3 I, 3, 186. III, 4, 106. IV, 2, 99. IV, 4, 79. V, 3, 129. Caes. III, 1, 259. Mcb. II, 3, 62. Hml. II, 2, 405. V, 2, 366. Lr. V, 3, 175. Ant. II, 6, 125. IV, 14, 120.

**Prophet**, one who foretells future events: Meas. II, 2, 94. Merch. I, 3, 35 (your p. the Nazarite). All's I, 3, 62. John IV, 2, 147. V, 1, 25. R2 II, 1, 31. 104. II, 4, 11. H6A I, 2, 150. III, 2, 32 (a p. to the fall of all our foes). H6B I, 3, 60. H6C V, 6, 57. R3 II, 2, 152. IV, 2, 103. Troil. I, 2, 10. III, 2, 190. V, 3, 65. Lr. V, 3, 71.

**Prophetess**, a female prophet: H6A I, 4, 102. I, 6, 8. R3 I, 3, 301. V, 1, 27.

**Prophetic**, foretelling future events, divinatory: Sonn. 107, 1. John III, 4, 126. Troil. II, 2, 102. Mcb. I, 3, 78. Hml. I, 5, 40. Oth. III, 4, 72 (in her p. fury).

**Prophetically**, with a divining soul: H4A III, 2, 38. Troil. III, 3, 248.

**Prophet-like**, like a prophet: Mcb. III, 1, 59.

**Propinquity**, nearness of blood, kindred: p. and property of blood, Lr. I, 1, 116.

**Propontic**, the Sea of Marmora: Oth. III, 3, 456.

**Proportion**, subst. 1) comparative relation: the realms of England, France and Ireland bear that p. to my flesh and blood as did the fatal brand .... unto the prince's heart of Calydon, H6B I, 1, 233. and part in just p. our small strength, R3 V, 3, 26. your enemies are many and not small; their practices must bear the same p. H8 V, 1, 130. would thou hadst less deserved, that the p. both of thanks and payment might have been mine, Mcb. I, 4, 19 (= that it had been in my power to reward thee in proportion).

2) due relation, symmetry, order: you would have married her most shamefully, where there was no p. held in love, Wiv. V, 5, 235. why should we in the compass of a pale keep form and law and due p. R2 III, 4, 41. when time is broke and no p. kept, V, 5, 43. but thou, 'gainst all p., didst bring in wonder to wait on treason and on murder, H5 II, 2, 109. whom to disobey were against all p. of subjection, IV, 1, 153. the planets and this centre observe degree, priority and place, insisture, course, p., season, form, Troil. I, 3, 87. keeps time, distance and p. Rom. II, 4, 22.

3) measure: a second Hector for his grim aspect and large p. of his strong-knit limbs, H6A II, 3, 21. what you see is but the smallest part and least p. of humanity, 53. dost thou not usurp the just p. of my sorrow? R3 IV, 4, 110. will you with counters sum the past p. of his infinite? Troil. II, 2, 29 (the greatness beyond measure). Even = metre, cadence: what? in metre? In any p. or in any language, Meas. I, 2, 23; cf. R2 V, 5, 43.

4) form, shape: there must be needs a like p. of lineaments, of manners and of spirit, Merch. III, 4, 14. extended or contracted all —s to a most hideous object, All's V, 3, 51. I thought King Henry had resembled thee in courage, courtship and p. H6B I, 3, 57. I that

*am curtailed of this fair p.* R3 I, 1, 18. *well mayst thou know her by thine own p., for up and down she doth resemble thee,* Tit. V, 2, 106.

5) calculation: *whose power was in the first p.* H4A IV, 4, 15. *the just p. that we gave them out,* H4B IV, 1, 23. *lay down our —s to defend against the Scot,* H5 I, 2, 137. *let our —s for these wars be soon collected,* 304. *so the —s of defence are filled,* II, 4, 45. *the levies, the lists and full —s are all made out of his subject,* Hml, I, 2, 32 (estimation of supplies).

6) portion, allotment, fortune: *I have received my p.* Gent. II, 3, 3. *her promised —s came short of composition,* Meas. V, 219. *three or four thousand chequins were as pretty a p. to live quietly,* Per. IV, 2, 29.

**Proportion,** vb. to be adjusted, to correspond to: *which* (ransom) *must p. the losses we have borne,* H5 III, 6, 134. —*ed,* partic. or adj., = 1) adjusted, made equal: *our size of sorrow, —ed to our cause, must be as great as that which makes it,* Ant. IV, 15, 5. 2) regular, orderly: *make war against —ed course of time,* Lucr. 774. 3) formed, shaped: *—ed as one's thought would wish a man,* Rom. III, 5, 184. cf. *Disproportioned, Unproportioned, Well-proportioned.*

**Proportionable,** having a due comparative relation, corresponding, equal: *for us to levy power p. to the enemy is all unpossible,* R2 II, 2, 125.

**Propose,** subst. conversation: *to listen our p.* Ado III, 1, 12 (Ff *purpose*).

**Propose,** vb. 1) to offer for consideration or acceptance: *the wager which we will p.* Shr. V, 2, 69. *which his majesty did first p.* All's IV, 5, 78. *the king hath granted every article .... according to their firm —d natures,* H5 V, 2, 362. *you would not hear me at many leisures I —d,* Tim. II, 2, 137. *that portion which yourself —d,* Lr. I, 1, 245. *many —d matches,* Oth. III, 3, 229.

2) to place before, to point out as a goal to be reached, to promise as a reward to be obtained: *when great treasure is the meed —d,* Lucr. 132. *a joy —d,* Sonn. 129, 12. *so* (for advantage) *is running away, when fear —s the safety,* All's I, 1, 216. *the gain —d,* H4B I, 1, 183. *now thy beauty is —d my fee,* R3 I, 2, 170. *the lily-beds —d for the deserver,* Troil. III, 2, 14. *ere we could arrive the point —d,* Caes. I, 2, 110. *what to ourselves in passion we p., the passion ending, doth the purpose lose,* Hml. III, 2, 204.

2) to call before the eye of the mind, to image: *be now the father and p. a son,* H4B V, 2, 92. *I p. not merely to myself the pleasures such a beauty brings with it,* Troil. II, 2, 146. Hence = to look forward to, to be ready to meet: *a thousand deaths would I p. to achieve her,* Tit. II, 1, 80.

4) to speak: *my cousin Beatrice —ing with the prince and Claudio,* Ado III, 1, 3. *whilst I p. the self-same words to thee which thou wouldst have me answer to,* H6C V, 5, 20. *p. the oath, my lord,* Hml. I, 5, 152. *wherein the toged consuls can p. as masterly as he,* Oth. I, 1, 25.

**Proposer,** speaker, orator: *and by what more dear a better p. could charge you withal,* Hml. II, 2, 297.

**Proposition,** 1) reward or success offered to sight; promise: *the ample p. that hope makes in all designs begun . on earth below fails in the promised largeness,* Troil. I, 3, 3.

2) a question asked: *it is as easy to count atomies as to resolve the —s of a lover,* As III, 2, 246.

**Propound,** to propose, to ask: *such questions as by your grace shall be —ed him,* H6B I, 2, 81.

**Propriety,** individuality, proper and particular state: *it is the baseness of thy fear that makes thee strangle thy p.* Tw. V, 150 (= makes thee disavow thyself). *it frights the isle from her p.* Oth. II, 3, 176 (i. e. out of herself).

**Propugnation,** means of combat, defence: *what p. is in one man's valour, to stand the push and enmity of those this quarrel would excite?* Troil. II, 2, 136.

**Prorogue,** 1) to delay: *death —d,* Rom. II, 2, 78. *nothing may p. it,* IV, 1, 48.

2) to draw out, to linger out, to keep in a languishing state: *that sleep and feeding may p. his honour even till a Lethe'd dullness,* Ant. II, 1, 26. *nor taken sustenance but to p. his grief,* Per. V, 1, 26.

**Proscription,** the act of dooming to death without legal proceeding: Caes. IV, 1, 17. IV, 3, 173. 178. 180.

**Prose,** language unconfined to poetical measure: LLL IV, 3, 57. Tw. II, 5, 154.

**Prosecute,** 1) to pursue with a view to reach or accomplish: *why should not I then p. my right?* Mids. I, 1, 105. *that we will p. mortal revenge upon these traitorous Goths,* Tit. IV, 1, 92.

2) to pursue by law: *what they will inform 'gainst any of us all, that will the king severely p. 'gainst us, our lives* etc. R2 II, 1, 244. *rather comfort his distressed plight than p. the meanest or the best for these contempts,* Tit. IV, 4, 33.

**Prosecution,** pursuit: *when I should see behind me the inevitable p. of disgrace and horror,* Ant. IV, 14, 65.

**Proselyte,** a convert: Wint. V, 1, 108.

**Proserpina,** the daughter of Ceres and wife of Pluto: Wint. IV, 4, 116. Troil. II, 1, 37.

**Prospect,** subst. sight, view: *shall come ... into the eye and p. of his soul,* Ado IV, 1, 231. *nothing that can be can come between me and the full p. of my hopes,* Tw. III, 4, 90. *these flags of France, that are advanced here before the eye and p. of your town,* John II, 208. *their chiefest p. murdering basilisks,* H6B III, 2, 324. *to be king stands not within the p. of belief,* Mcb. I, 3, 74. *it were a tedious difficulty, to bring them to that p.* Oth. III, 3, 398.

**Prosper,** abbreviation of Prospero: Tp. II, 2, 2. 83. III, 3, 99.

**Prosper,** vb. 1) tr. to render successful, to make happy: Wiv. III, 1, 30. V, 2, 14. Mids. I, 1, 172. H4B III, 2, 313. H6A I, 1, 53. IV, 2, 56. Lr. III, 7, 92. IV, 6, 30.

2) intr. to succeed, to thrive, to be fortunate: Tp. II, 1, 72. Wiv. IV, 5, 103. Merch. III, 2, 189. Tw. I, 4, 38. Wint. IV, 3, 126. IV, 4, 70. R2 V, 3, 84. H6A V, 5, 106. H6C II, 5, 18. R3 II, 1, 16. IV, 4, 397. H8 I, 2, 169. Lr. I, 1, 285. I, 2, 21. Per. IV, 2, 13.

**Prosperity,** good fortune, success: Meas. I, 4, 15. LLL V, 2, 871 (*a jest's p.*). Mids. II, 1, 73. IV, 1, 95 (Q2 Ff *posterity*). Wint. IV, 4, 584. John III, 4, 28. V, 2, 61. R2 IV, 280. R3 IV, 4, 1. Cor. I, 5, 24. II, 1, 188. V, 2, 75. Tim. IV, 3, 77 (*when I had p.*). V, 1, 36. Oth. II, 1, 288. Plur. —*es: plenty's cup and her —es,* Per. I, 4, 53. Misapplied by Costard in LLL I, 1, 316.

**Prospero,** name in Tp. I, 2, 20. 72. II, 1, 271. 326. III, 2, 155. III, 3, 70. V, 107. 119. 134. 159. 211.

**Prosperous,** 1) successful, fortunate; of persons: Tp. IV, 104. Wint. II, 3, 189. R2 I, 3, 78. H6A I, 1, 32. Rom. IV, 1, 122. V, 3, 42. Mcb. I, 3, 73. Per. I, 1, 59 *(of all say'd yet may'st thou prove p.).* V, 1, 80. Of things: Meas. I, 2, 189. III, 1, 271. III, 2, 253. Err. I, 1, 41. All's III, 3, 7. H4A III, 1, 2. H5 V, 2, 402. H6A II, 5, 114. R3 V, 5, 34. H8 V, 5, 2. Cor. II, 1, 114. Mcb. III, 1, 22. Ant. IV, 6, 6. Per. V, 1, 72.

2) favourable: *a p. south-wind,* Wint. V, 1, 161. *I leave you to the protection of the p. gods,* Tim. V, 1, 186. *to my unfolding lend your p. ear,* Oth. I, 3, 245 (Qq *a gracious ear*).

**Prosperously,** successfully: Cor. V, 6, 75. Hml. II, 2, 214 (cf. *prosperity* in LLL V, 2, 871).

**Prostitute,** vb. to abandon, to expose, to give up: *to p. our past-cure malady to empirics,* All's II, 1, 124. *p. me to the basest groom,* Per. IV, 6, 201.

**Prostrate,** adj. lying at one's length: *mother Jourdain, be you p. and grovel on the earth,* H6B I, 4, 13. = in a posture of extreme humility: *this p. and exterior bending,* H4B IV, 5, 149. *look gracious on thy p. thrall,* H6A I, 2, 117. *being p.* Caes. III, 1, 125. *I will fall p. at his feet,* Err. V, 114. Rom. IV, 2, 20.

**Protect,** 1) to guard, to defend, to shield: Tw. II, 4, 75. H6A I, 3, 9. H6B I, 3, 5. 40. II, 1, 54. H8 III, 2, 276. V, 1, 142. V, 4, 11. Lr. I, 4, 227. Cymb. I, 1, 128. IV, 2, 126. Per. I, 4, 97. With *from:* R3 IV, 1, 20. Per. II, 1, 135.

2) to guard, to superintend, to tend: *must you p. my lady here?* H6B II, 4, 79. *despite the bearward that —s the bear,* V, 1, 210.

3) to be protector, to be regent for: *why should he then p. our sovereign,* H6B I, 1, 165. *why a king of years should be to be —ed like a child,* II, 3, 29. *the king had virtuous uncles to p. his grace,* R3 II, 3, 21.

**Protection,** defence, shelter from evil: Merch. V, 235. Tw. I, 2, 38. Wint. II, 3, 178. John II, 236. H6B III, 2, 180 *(had him in p.).* H6C II, 2, 28. H8 III, 1, 93. III, 2, 344. Tim. V, 1, 186. Lr. III, 6, 99. Cymb. I, 1, 41 *(he takes the babe to his p.).* I, 6, 193 *(to take them in p.).* II, 2, 8.

**Protector,** 1) one who favours and defends: *whom we have left —s of the king,* H6C I, 2, 57. *thou p. of this damned strumpet,* R3 III, 4, 76. *under the covering of a careful night, who seemed my good p.* Per. I, 2, 82.

2) a regent: H6A I, 1, 37. I, 3, 8. 12. 32. 66. III, 1, 45. 60. 112. IV, 1, 48. V, 1, 48. V, 5, 23. H6B I, 1, 39. 147. 164. 177. I, 2, 44. 56. I, 3, 2. 14. 15. 41. 71. 79. 122. 123. I, 4, 79. II, 1, 10. 54. II, 3, 24. III, 1, 250. IV, 2, 167. H6C I, 1, 240. I, 2, 57. IV, 6, 37. 41. R3 I, 3, 14. III, 1, 141 etc.

**Protectorship,** the office of protector or regent: H6B II, 1, 30 ( O. Edd. *an't like your lordly lord's p.,* M. Edd. *lordly lord-protectorship*). III, 1, 60. 121.

**Protectress,** a female guardian or keeper: *she is p. of her honour too,* Oth. IV, 1, 14.

**Protest,** subst. (*protést*) asseveration: *leave 'in sooth' and such p. of pepper-gingerbread,* H4A III, 1, 260. *full of p., of oath and big compare,* Troil. III, 2, 182.

**Protest,** vb. 1) to declare with solemnity, to asseverate; absol.: *after we had embraced, kissed and —ed,* Wiv. III, 5, 75 (i. e. declared our love). *none is left to p.* Ado IV, 1, 289. With *against* (= to contra-

dict solemnly): *but then you'll think — which I p. against — I am assisted by wicked powers,* Wint. V, 3, 90. With an accus. denoting the thing averred: *do me right, or I'll p. your cowardice,* Ado V, 1, 149. *that, on mine honour, here I do p.* Tit. I, 477. *the lady —s too much,* Hml. III, 2, 240. *said nothing but what I p. intendment of doing,* Oth. IV, 2, 205. Double accus.: *p. me the baby of a girl,* Mcb. III, 4, 105 (= to be the b.). Accus. denoting the effect: *—ing oath on oath,* Shr. II, 311. The person with *to: I p. to you,* Wiv. II, 2, 201. IV, 2, 33. Rom. II, 4, 183. Per. IV, 6, 95. Dat. and accus.: *when I p. true loyalty to her,* Gent. IV, 2, 7. With an inf.: *whom I p. to love,* All's IV, 2, 28. Oftenest with a subordinate clause: *the which* (her heart) *by Cupid's bow she doth p. he carries thence,* Ven. 581. *I do p. that I have wept,* Gent. IV, 4, 149. Wiv. II, 1, 75. 222. Meas. V, 344. Err. III, 1, 112. V, 2. Ado IV, 1, 282. 286. LLL I, 1, 176. II, 158. V, 2, 352. 410. 531. Merch. IV, 1, 290. As IV, 1, 110. IV, 3, 21. All's II, 3, 73. IV, 3, 246. Tw. I, 5, 94. III, 4, 330. V, 173. John II, 501. R2 II, 3, 11. V, 6, 45. H4A V, 1, 25. H6A IV, 2, 19. H6C III, 3, 181. R3 I, 1, 52. II, 1, 26. III, 2, 81. Troil. II, 2, 138. Rom. III, 1, 71. Tim. III, 2, 86. Caes. III, 1, 238. Lr. V, 3, 130. Oth. II, 3, 333. III, 1, 50. IV, 2, 211. Per. II, 5, 27.

2) to promise solemnly, to vow: *on Diana's altars, to p. for aye austerity and single life,* Mids. I, 1, 89. *do villany, do, since you p. to do't, like workmen,* Tim. IV, 3, 437. cf. LLL V, 2, 410. Peculiar passage: *many unrough youths that even now p. their first of manhood,* Mcb. V, 2, 11 (vow to try. According to Johnson, it means here to prove, to give evidence of).

Not understood by the nurse in Rom. II, 4, 189.

**Protestation,** 1) a solemn declaration: *here is a coil with p.* Gent. I, 2, 99. (letters) *stuffed with —s,* IV, 4, 133. *but to your p.; let me hear what you profess,* Wint. IV, 4, 379. *I have no cunning in p.* H5 V, 2, 150.

2) a solemn promise, a vow: *each present lord began to promise aid; but she ... the p. stops,* Lucr. 1700. *and to his p. urged the rest, who, wondering at him, did his words allow,* 1844. *I can but say their p. over,* LLL I, 1, 33. *upon his many —s to marry me ... he won me,* All's V, 3, 139. *be thus true, say I, to fashion in my sequent p.* Troil. IV, 4, 68.

**Protester,** one who utters a solemn declaration: *to stale with ordinary oaths my love to every new p.* Caes. I, 2, 74.

**Protestings,** solemn declarations, vows: Pilgr. 95.

**Proteus** (dissyll. and trisyll. indiscriminately), 1) a marine god who had the faculty of assuming whatever shape he pleased: H6C III, 2, 192.

2) (O. Edd. *Protheus*) name of the inconstant lover in Gent. I, 1, 1. 12. 56. 70. I, 2, 14. 20. 38. 97. 113. 117. 124. I, 3, 3. 12. 43. 88 etc. etc.

**Protract,** 1) to draw out, to prolong: *he shrives this woman to her smock; else ne'er could he so long p. his speech,* H6A I, 2, 120.

2) to delay: *let us bury him and not p. with admiration what is now due debt,* Cymb. IV, 2, 232.

**Protractive,** dilatory: *the p. trials of great Jove to find persistive constancy in men,* Troil. I, 3, 20.

**Proud,** adj. 1) gorgeous: *which the conceited painter drew so p. as heaven, it seemed, to kiss the turrets bowed,* Lucr. 1371. *thy youth's p. livery,* Sonn.

2, 3. *from their p. lap pluck them where they grew,* 98, 8. *rich scarf to my p. earth,* Tp. IV, 82. *why should p. summer boast,* LLL I, 1, 102. *the p. day is all too wanton and too full of gawds,* John III, 3, 34. *report of fashions in p. Italy,* R2 II, 1, 21. *set not thy sweet heart on p. array,* Lr. III, 4, 85. Adverbially: *his crest that —er than blue Iris bends,* Troil. I, 3, 380.

2) lofty; full of vigour, mettle or beauty: *rein his p. head to the saddle-bow,* Ven. 14. *a breeding jennet, lusty, young and p.* 260. *nothing else with his p. sight agrees,* 288. *a p. rider on so p. a back,* 300. *the blunt boar, rough bear, or lion p.* 884. *clapping their p. tails to the ground below,* 923. *this p. issue of a king,* Lucr. 37. *the flesh being p., desire doth fight with grace,* 712. *to ruinate p. buildings,* 944. *a complement of p. compare,* Sonn. 21, 5. *p. tilles,* 25, 2. *the p. full sail of his verse,* 86, 1. *the —est of them shall well hear of it,* Ado IV, 1, 194. *have every pelting river made so p.* Mids. II, 1, 91. *I'll bring mine action on the —est he,* Shr. III, 2, 236. *our purses shall be p., our garments poor,* IV, 3, 173. *our party may well meet a —er foe,* John V, 1, 79. *with p. desire of bold-faced victory,* H6A IV, 6, 11. *it would amaze the —est of you all,* IV, 7, 84. *at such p. rate,* H8 III, 2, 127. *will rouse the —est panther in the chase,* Tit. II, 2, 21 etc. etc.

3) full of self-esteem, elated, haughty: Sonn. 75, 5. 80, 6. Wiv. II, 2, 77. Meas. II, 2, 117. Ado III, 1, 10. H6A I, 2, 138; cf. H6C II, 1, 168 and II, 2, 84. H6A IV, 3, 24. H6B I, 3, 143. Ant. III, 13, 142. Cymb. III, 3, 9 etc. etc. With *of:* Lucr. 437. Sonn. 67, 12. 78, 9. Compl. 108. Gent. II, 4, 161. Err. I, 1, 59. LLL II, 35. Merch. III, 4, 8. All's I, 2, 44. H5 III, 3, 4. IV Chor. 17. H6B IV, 10, 77. Troil. III, 3, 248. Rom. III, 5, 148. Tit. I, 254. Cymb. IV, 4, 135. *p. of this pride,* Sonn. 151, 10 (proud of being so full of mettle? or simply = so proud?). With *on: mine that I was p. on,* Ado IV, 1, 139. With *with,* = a) by: *p. with his form,* LLL II, 237. *O death, made p. with pure and princely beauty,* John IV, 3, 35. *to make the base earth p. with kissing it,* R2 III, 3, 191. V, 5, 86. b) to, against: *an a' be p. with me,* Troil. II, 3, 215. Followed by an inf.: *p. to see him woo her,* Ven. 309. LLL II, 17. V, 2, 66. As I, 2, 245. Troil. III, 3, 37. Cor. I, 1, 240. II, 1, 247. Ant. IV, 15, 88. By a clause: *so p. that Bolingbroke was on his back,* R2 V, 5, 84. Rom. III, 5, 147. Tim. II, 2, 199.

4) selfish, cold, unkind: *O, be not p.* Ven. 113. *thy p. heart's slave,* Sonn. 141, 12. *p., disobedient, stubborn,* Gent. III, 1, 69. *she is p. Out with that too; it was Eve's legacy and cannot be ta'en from her,* 341. *I must not seem p.* Ado II, 3, 237. *never framed a woman's heart of — er stuff,* III, 1, 50. *p. Titania,* Mids. II, 1, 60. *peevish, p., idle, made of self-love,* All's I, 1, 156; cf. As III, 2, 431. *is she not p.?* Rom. III, 5, 144.

**Proud,** a verb of Capulet's making, = to speak of being proud: *thank me no thankings, nor p. me no prouds,* Rom. III, 5, 153 (don't speak of being thankful or proud).

**Proud-hearted,** haughty: H6C V, 1, 98.

**Proudly,** 1) in a showy manner, gaudily: *bearing their birthrights p. on their backs,* John II, 70.

2) with full force: *the tide of blood in me hath p. flowed in vanity till now,* H4B V, 2, 130.

3) in a lofty or a haughty manner: Sonn. 131, 2. Ado II, 3, 234. R2 V, 5, 83. H5 IV, 3, 108. H6A I, 2,

62. IV, 7, 43. R3 IV, 3, 42. Troil. IV, 5, 74. V, 10, 24. Comp. —*er: he bears himself more —er,* Cor. IV, 7, 8.

**Proud-minded,** arrogant, obstinate: Shr. II, 132.

**Proud-pied,** gorgeously variegated: *p. April dressed in all his trim,* Sonn. 98, 2.

**Proud-swelling** (not hyphened in O.Edd.) lofty, majestical: *the unowed interest of p. state,* John IV, 3, 147.

**Provand,** provender, food: Cor. II, 1, 267.

**Prove,** 1) trans. a) to try, to bring to the test *to tie the rider she begins to p.* Ven. 40. *she hath assayed as much as may be —d,* 608. *not show my head where thou mayst p. me,* Sonn. 26, 14. *to p. the constancy and virtue of your love,* 117, 13. *how Falstaff ... his dove will p.* Wiv. I, 3, 107. *shall we go p. what's to be done?* Ado I, 3, 75. *to p. whose blood is reddest,* Merch. II, 1, 7. *which if you seek to p.,* I dare not stand by, Wint. I, 2, 443. *I mean to p. this lady's courtesy,* H6A II, 2, 58. *p. me, my gracious sovereign,* R3 IV, 2, 69. *we p. this very hour,* Cor. I, 6, 62. *to p. more fortunes thou'rt tired,* IV, 5, 99. *I'll p. him, speed how it will,* V, 1, 60. *'tis a question left us yet to p., whether love lead fortune, or else fortune love,* Hml. III, 2, 212. *I'll see before I doubt; when I doubt, p.* Oth. III, 3, 190. *which first she'll p. on cats and dogs,* Cymb. I, 5, 38. Partic. —*d* = approved, tried: *prescriptions of rare and —d effects,* All's I, 3, 228. *by nature —d an enemy to the flock,* H6B III, 1, 258. cf. Hml. III, 1, 47.

b) to make for trial or by trying: *thou art a murderer. Do not p. me so,* John IV, 3, 90. *my brain I'll p. the female to my soul,* R2 V, 5, 6. *Troilus will stand to the proof, if you'll p. it so,* Troil. I, 2, 143.

c) to find by trying, to ascertain, to find: *when they in thee the like offences p.* Lucr. 613. *you in me can nothing worthy p.* Sonn. 72, 4. *a seething bath, which yet men p. against strange maladies a sovereign cure,* 153, 7. *I am an ass, indeed; you may p. it by my long ears,* Err. IV, 4, 29. *to p. my saying true,* John III, 1, 28. *that e'er I —d thee false,* H6B III, 1, 205. *if I do p. her haggard,* Oth. III, 3, 260. *as you shall p. us, praise us,* V, 1, 66.

d) to experience, to taste, to see, to feel: *all is imaginary she doth p.* Ven. 597. *a bliss in proof, and —d, a very woe,* Sonn. 129, 11. *in things of great receipt with ease we p. among a number one is reckoned none,* 136, 7. *this by that I p., love's fire heats water, water cools not love,* 154, 13. *we will all the pleasures p.* Pilgr. 354. *'tis too much —d, that with devotion's visage we do sugar o'er the devil himself,* Hml. III, 1, 47. *you have seen and —d a fairer former fortune than that which is to approach,* Ant. I, 2, 33. *p. you that or p. that* = if you hear that, if: *p. that ever I lose more blood with love than I will get again with drinking, pick out mine eyes,* Ado I, 1, 252. *p. you that any man with me conversed ... refuse me, hate me,* IV, 1, 183. *p. that ever I dress myself handsome till thy return,* H4B II, 4, 302. *p. that I cannot, take me home again,* Per. IV, 6, 200.

e) to evince, to show: *to p. by wit worth in simplicity,* LLL V, 2, 78. *doth not the crown of England p. the king?* John II, 273. With a double accus., = to show to be: *—ing his beauty by succession thine,* Sonn. 2, 12. *and p. thee virtuous,* 88, 4. *—d thee my best of love,* 110, 8. *this —s me still a sheep,* Gent. I, 1, 82. *rather —d the sliding of your brother a merri-*

*ment*, Meas. II, 4, 115. IV, 2, 40. LLL I, 2, 59. IV, 3, 274. Mids. III, 2, 127. 253. Tw. I, 5, 64. John IV, 3, 55. H6C III, 3, 71. R3 I, 3, 146 etc. Reflexively: *mercy to thee would p. itself a bawd*, Meas. III, 1, 150. *true she is, as she hath —d herself*, Merch. II, 6, 55. *in first seeing he had —d himself a man*, Cor. I, 3, 18.

f) to evince or establish as a truth, to demonstrate: *—ing their right*, Lucr. 67. *I'll p. it*, Gent. I, 1, 86. III, 1, 369. Meas. II, 1, 88. III, 2, 30. LLL II, 159. III, 39. Mids. III, 2, 255. Shr. I, 2, 177. 178. Tw. III, 1, 29. John I, 68. H6B I, 3, 159. H6C I, 1, 131. Tim. III, 5, 23 etc. With *against: I'll p. mine honour against thee presently*, Err. V, 30. *if it be —d against an alien that he seek the life of any citizen*, Merch. IV, 1, 349. With *on*, in the same sense: *if this be error and upon me —d*, Sonn. 116, 13. *as shall be —d upon thee by good witness*, Ado IV, 2, 82. *I'll p. it on his body*, V, 1, 74. Shr. IV, 3, 148. R2 I, 3, 37. IV, 47. H6A II, 4, 98. Cor. III, 3, 47. Lr. IV, 6, 91. V, 3, 93. With a double accus.: *be sure thou p. my love a whore*, Oth. III, 3, 359. *his description —d us unspeaking sots*, Cymb. V, 5, 178. With a clause: Pilgr. 33. Gent. III, 1, 297. Err. II, 2, 101. Ado IV, 2, 23. V, 2, 98. Troil. I, 2, 140 etc.

2) intr. to be found, to be ascertained, to fall out: *they wither in their prime, p. nothing worth*, Ven. 418. *since men p. beasts, let beasts bear gentle minds*, Lucr. 1148. Sonn. 151, 4. Tp. V, 175. Gent. I, 1, 37. Wiv. IV, 2, 119. Mids. V, 317. John II, 270. *that my revengeful services p. as benefits to thee*, Cor. IV, 5, 95. *p. this a prosperous day*, Ant. IV, 6, 6 (if this p. a prosperous day). *if it should p. that thou art so inhuman*, All's V, 3, 115. *O, if it p., tempests are kind*, Tw. III, 4, 418. *if it p. she's otherwise*, Wint. II, 1, 133. *allow us as we p.* Troil. III, 2, 98 etc. With an adverb: *hasty marriage seldom —th well*, H6C IV, 1, 18. *he was likely to have —d most royally*, Hml. V, 2, 409 (Qq *royal*). *my purpose would p. well*, Cymb. III, 4, 122 (cf. *well found* in All's II, 1, 105). *pray heaven he p. so*, Gent. II, 7, 79. *if it p. so*, Err. I, 2, 103. Ado III, 1, 105. Merch. III, 2, 20. All's V, 3, 116. Caes. V, 1, 4.

Often quite = to become, to be: *they p. bankrupt in this poor rich gain*, Lucr. 140. *since he died and poets better p.* Sonn. 32, 13. *truth —s thievish for a prize so dear*, 48, 14. *now, jerkin, you are like to lose your hair and p. a bald jerkin*, Tp. IV, 238. *I cannot now p. constant to myself, without some treachery used to Valentine*, Gent. II, 6, 31. *with a prayer they* (his events) *may prosperous p.* Meas. III, 2, 253. *this may p. worse than hanging*, V, 365. *lest I should p. the mother of fools*, Ado II, 1, 295. *how art thou —d Judas?* LLL V, 2, 604. *the world will p. a cockney*, Tw. IV, 1, 15. *in hope he'll p. a widower shortly*, H6C III, 3, 227. Ven. Dedic. 5. Sonn. 8, 14. 10, 12. 39, 9. 125, 4. Pilgr. 59. Tp. III, 2, 40. 153. Gent. I, 1, 147. III, 2, 20. IV, 4, 110. Meas. II, 4, 169. III, 2, 32. Ado III, 3, 190. LLL III, 40. V, 2, 563. Mids. II, 1, 265. III, 2, 350. Merch. I, 2, 53. III, 4, 64. As III, 3, 89. R2 III, 2, 25 etc. etc.

**Provender,** dry food for beasts: Mids. IV, 1, 35. H5 IV, 2, 58. H6A I, 2, 11. Caes. IV, 1, 30. Oth. I, 1, 48.

**Prover,** one who tries: *why am I a fool? Make that demand of the p.* Troil. II, 3, 72 (Ff *to the creator*).

**Proverb,** a current phrase or a maxim of wisdom, an adage: Gent. III, 1, 305. Wiv. III, 1, 107. III, 5,

154. Err. III, 1, 51. Ado V, 1, 17. Mids. III, 2, 458. Merch. II, 2, 158. II, 5, 55. Wint. II, 3, 96. John II, 137. H4A I, 2, 132. H5 III, 7, 72. 124. 129. 131. H6B III, 1, 170. Cor. I, 1, 209. Hml. III, 2, 359.

**Proverbed,** provided with a proverb: *I am p. with a grandsire phrase*, Rom. I, 4, 37.*

**Provide,** 1) to procure beforehand, to prepare in careful foresight: *a small spare mast, such as seafaring men p. for storms*, Err. I, 1, 81. *to p. a salve for any sore that may betide*, H6C IV, 6, 87. *according to our law immediately —d in that case*, Mids. I, 1, 45; cf. *p. more piercing statutes daily*, Cor. I, 1, 86. *to hold what distance his wisdom can p.* Mcb. III, 6, 45. Used of a heavenly dispensation (cf. *Providence*): *'tis an accident that heaven —s*, Meas. IV, 3, 81. *he was —d to do us good*, Wint. IV, 4, 860. *the gods themselves have —d that I shall have much help from you*, Tim. I, 2, 92.

*—d*, or *—d that*, followed by the subjunctive, = on condition: Gent. IV, 1, 71. Merch. III, 2, 209. As II, 7, 45. Shr. I, 2, 217. Wint. I, 2, 335. R2 III, 3, 40. Hml. V, 2, 210. Cymb. I, 4, 166. Per. V, 1, 77. *two things —d more, that... he become a Christian*, Merch. IV, 1, 386.

2) to take care; absol.: *we must to horse again; go, go p.* All's V, 1, 38. *my cook and I'll p.* Tim. III, 4, 119. *we'll p.* Per. II, 1, 168. With an infinitive: *you must p. to bottom it* (her love) *on me*, Gent. III, 2, 53. *let us p. to see her coronation be performed*, H6B I, 1, 73. With *for* = to take care of, to do what is necessary for: *Fortune that did not better for my life p. than public means*, Sonn. 111, 3. *I have —d for you*, Meas. II, 3, 17. *take this mercy to p. for better times to come*, V, 489. *his wonted followers shall all be very well —d for*, H4B V, 5, 105. *we will presently p. for them*, H6A V, 2, 15 (i. e. arm). *p. for thine own future safety*, H8 III, 2, 421. *he that's coming must be —d for*, Mcb. I, 5, 68.

Transitively; with an accus. of the person, = to furnish, to supply with what is necessary: *p. yourself*, As I, 3, 89. *I will p. thee*, H6C IV, 1, 60. *we will ourselves p.* Hml. III, 3, 7. Partic. *—d: I cannot be so soon —d*, Gent. I, 3, 72. *it* (danger) *will seek me in another place and find me worse —d*, H4B III, 3, 50. *with a sharp —d wit*, R3 III, 1, 132. *you shall know many dare accuse you boldly, more than, I fear, you are —d for*, H8 V, 3, 57. H6B I, 4, 3. R3 III, 4, 46. Tim. I, 2, 185. Lr. II, 4, 235. With *of: I am —d of a torch-bearer*, Merch. II, 4, 24. *you are as well —d of both*, H5 III, 7, 9.

With an accus. of the thing, = to procure, to prepare: *p. your block and your axe to-morrow*, Meas. IV, 2, 55. *hath he —d this music?* Ado I, 2, 2. Shr. II, 318. All's III, 4, 40. John V, 2, 98. R2 II, 2, 106. H6B III, 1, 276. Troil. III, 2, 220. Rom. III, 5, 180. Tim. I, 2, 198. V, 1, 35. Mcb. III, 5, 18. Oth. I, 3, 378. Ant. III, 4, 36 (*p. your going*). V, 2, 195. Dat. and accus.: *I'll p. you a chain*, Wiv. V, 1, 6. H4A I, 2, 214. H4B III, 2, 102. H6B III, 1, 319. Cymb. III, 2, 77.

**Providence,** 1) foresight, timely care: *the p. that's in a watchful state*, Troil. III, 3, 196. *it will be laid to us, whose p. should have ... restrained this mad young man*, Hml. IV, 1, 17.

2) the care of God, divine dispensation: Tp. I, 2, 159. V, 189. Caes. V, 1, 107. Hml. V, 2, 231.

**Provident,** forecasting, prudent in preparing for future exigencies: Tw. I, 2, 12. H5 II, 4, 11.

**Providently,** providentially: *He that ... p. caters for the sparrow,* As II, 3, 44.

**Provider,** one who procures what is wanted: *parted with prayers for the p.* Cymb. III, 6, 53.

**Province,** a country which makes part of an empire: Meas. III, 2, 185. Wint. I, 2, 369. John II, 528. III, 1, 3. H6A III, 3, 24. H6B I, 1, 120. HCC I, 1, 109. Ant. II, 5, 68. III, 10, 8. Per. V, 1, 61.

**Provincial,** belonging to an ecclesiastical province and subject to its jurisdiction: *his subject am I not, nor here p.* Meas. V, 318.

**Provincial,** coming from Provins in France: *would not this and a forest of feathers, with two P. roses on my razed shoes, get me a fellowship in a cry of players?* Hml. III, 2, 288 (meaning ornamental shoe-ties called roses, which Hamlet intends to have particularly conspicuous).*

**Provision,** 1) provident care, preparation, measures taken beforehand: *with such p. in mine art,* Tp. I, 2, 28. *herself had made p. for her following me,* Err. I, 1, 48. *for p. to shield thee from diseases of the world,* Lr. I, 1, 176.

2) stores of any kind necessary for an exigency: *we shall be short in our p.* Rom. IV, 2, 38. *I am now from home, and out of that p. which shall be needful for your entertainment,* Lr. II, 4, 208. *follow me, that will to some p. give thee quick conduct,* III, 6, 103. = store of money: *that my p. was out,* Tim. III, 6, 18. = victuals: *that for our gold we may p. have,* Per. V, 1, 56. 258.

**Proviso,** condition: *he doth deny his prisoners, but with p. and exception,* H4A I, 3, 78.

**Provocation,** stimulation to lust: *let there come a tempest of p.* Wiv. V, 5, 23. *what an eye she has! methinks it sounds a parley of p.* Oth. II, 3, 23.

**Provoke,** 1) to call forth, to rouse, to cause: *swelling passion doth p. a pause,* Ven. 218. *dost thou drink tears, that thou —st such weeping?* 949. *my tale —s that question,* Tp. I, 2, 140. *thy best of rest is sleep, and that you oft —st,* Meas. III, 1, 18. *rebuke me not for that which you p.* LLL V, 2, 347. *let my presumption not p. thy wrath,* H6A II, 3, 70. *the palsy, and not fear, —s me* (to quiver) H6B IV, 7, 98. *thy deed —s this deluge,* R3 I, 2, 61. *in this rage, —d by him, you cannot,* Cor. V, 6, 138. *our gentle flame —s itself,* Tim. I, 1, 24. *what three things does drink especially p.?* Mcb. II, 3, 30. 32. 33. *the need we have to use you did p. our hasty sending,* Hml. II, 2, 3. *that* (sleep) *to p. in him,* Lr. IV, 4, 13. *p. not battle,* Ant. III, 8, 3. *one sin another doth p.* Per. I, 1, 137.

2) to incite, to impel, to instigate; absol.: *no further enemy to you than the constraint of hospitable zeal ... religiously —s,* John II, 246. *a —ing merit,* Lr. III, 5, 8 (cf. *Merit*). Transitively: *—d with raging ire,* Err. V, 216. *beauty —th thieves sooner than gold,* As I, 3, 112. *did you not p. me?* John IV, 2, 207. *like as rigour of tempestuous gusts —s the mightiest hulk against the tide,* H6A V, 5, 6. *thou wast —d by thy bloody mind,* R3 I, 2, 99. *'twas thy beauty that —d me,* 181. *not —d by any suitor,* I, 3, 64. *the king, —d by the queen, devised impeachments,* II, 2, 21. *With to: what this ecstasy may now p. them to,* Tp. III, 3, 109. *even that power —s me to this perjury,* Gent. II, 6, 5. Wiv. II, 3, 73. Meas. IV, 1, 15. LLL III, 78.

R2 II, 2, 101. H6A IV, 1, 141. Per. Prol. 26. With an inf.: *so full of him, that thou —st thyself to cast him up,* H4B I, 3, 96. With *hither* and *thither: thither —d and instigated by his distemper,* Wiv. III, 5, 77. *p. us hither now to slaughter thee,* R3 I, 4, 231. With *on: the bloody spur cannot p. him on,* Sonn. 50, 9.

3) to rouse to anger, to incense: Ven. 1003. H6A III, 1, 34. IV, 1, 104. R3 I, 2, 97. H8 III, 2, 288. Troil. IV, 5, 99. Rom. V, 3, 70. Oth. I, 2, 7. II, 1, 280. Ant. IV, 15, 45. Cymb. I, 4, 72. V, 5, 293.

**Provoker,** that which excites or causes: *drink is a great p. of three things,* Mcb. II, 3, 27.

**Provost,** the keeper of a prison, a gaoler: Meas. I, 2, 118. I, 4, 73. II, 1, 32. II, 2, 6. II, 3, 1. III, 1, 177 and passim in this play.

**Provulgate,** to make public: Oth. I, 2, 21 (only in Q1; the rest of O. Edd. *promulgate*).

**Prowess,** bravery: H6B V, 2, 22. H6C III, 3, 86. Mcb. V, 8, 41.

**Prudence,** wisdom; used with irony: *this Sir P.* Tp. II, 1, 286. *hold your tongue, good p.* Rom. III, 5, 172.

**Prudent,** wise: *'tis thought among the p.* Tw. I, 3, 34. *O p. discipline!* John II, 413. *your father was reputed for a prince most p.* H8 II, 4, 46. *those cold ways, that seem like p. helps,* Cor. III, 1, 221.

**Prune,** subst. a dried plum: Wint. IV, 3, 51. *stewed —s* a favourite dish in bawdy-houses: Wiv. I, 1, 296. Meas. II, 1, 93. 103. 111. H4A III, 3, 128. H4B II, 4, 159.

**Prune,** vb. to trim; applied to trees, = to lop superfluous branches: Err. II, 2, 181. As II, 3, 63. To persons, = to dress up: *or spend a minute's time in —ing me,* LLL IV, 3, 183. To birds, = to pick out damaged feathers and arrange the plumage with the bill: *which makes him p. himself and bristle up the crest of youth,* H4A I, 1, 98. *his royal bird —s the immortal wing,* Cymb. V, 4, 118.

**Pry,** to look with scrutinizing curiosity: *why —est thou through my window?* Lucr. 1089. *into my deeds to p.* Sonn. 61, 6. *which —es not to the interior,* Merch. II, 9, 28. *I have cause to p. into this pedant,* Shr. III, 1, 87. *the eye of reason may p. in upon us,* H4A IV, 1, 72. *to p. into his title,* IV, 3, 103. *let it p. through the portage of the head,* H5 III, 1, 10. *to p. into the secrets of the state,* H6B I, 1, 250. *p. on every side,* R3 III, 5, 6. *I —ed me through the crevice,* Tit. V, 1, 114. *to p. in what I further shall intend to do,* Rom. V, 3, 33. cf. *Narrow-prying.*

**Psalm,** a holy song: Wiv. II, 1, 63 (O. Edd. *the hundred —s,* M. Edd. *the hundredth p.*). Wint. IV, 3, 47. H4A II, 4, 147 (Ff *all manner of songs*).

**Psalmist,** the author of the Psalms: *death, as the P. saith, is certain to all,* H4B III, 2, 41.

**Psalteries,** stringed instruments of music: Cor. V, 4, 52.*

**Ptolemy,** name of the Macedonian dynasty in Egypt: Ant. I, 4, 6. 17. III, 6, 15. Plur. *—es:* II, 7, 39. III, 12, 18.

**Public,** adj. 1) pertaining to the state: *the body p.* Meas. I, 2, 163. *the p. body,* Tim. V, 1, 148. *p. weal,* H6A I, 1, 177. Cor. III, 1, 176. *pricked on by p. wrongs,* H6A III, 2, 78. *for the p. good,* H6B I, 1, 199. *treasury,* I, 3, 134. *peace,* H8 V, 3, 41. *benefit,* Cor. I, 1, 156. *power,* III, 1, 269. *laws,* Tim. V, 4, 62. *reasons,* Caes. III, 2, 7. *p. leave to speak,* 224 (= official). *chair*, 68. *a p. minister of justice*, Ant. V, 1, 20. *by p. war*, Per. I, 2, 104.

2) general, common, open to all, or done in the sight of the people: *a p. fast*, Lucr. 891. *the p. plague of many*, 1479. *p. honour*, Sonn. 25, 2. *with p. kindness*, 36, 11. *p. means*, 111, 4. *sport*, Wiv. IV, 4, 14. *the p. ear*, Meas. IV, 2, 102. Ant. III. 4, 5. *in the p. eye*, III, 6, 11. *thanks*, Meas. V, 7. *p. accusation*, Ado IV, 1, 307; cf. Hml. IV, 7, 17. *shame*, LLL I, 1, 132. *street*, Merch. II, 5, 32. Ant. II, 2, 234. *our p. court*, As I, 3, 46. *haunt*, II, 1, 15. Rom. III, 1, 53. *spectacle*, H6A I, 4, 41. *commoner*, Oth. IV, 2, 73. = vulgar: *p. means which p. manners breeds*, Sonn. 111, 4. *in p.* = in open view, not in private or secretly: Wint. II, 1, 197. Cymb. I, 4, 59.

**Publican,** a collector of toll: Merch. I, 3, 42.

**Publication,** notification to the world, proclamation: Troil. I, 3, 326.

**Publicly,** in open view, in public: Wiv. IV, 2, 236. Meas. IV, 3, 101. V, 278. Err. V, 127. 130. Wint. II, 3, 204. R3 I, 4, 222. H8 II, 4, 3. Ant. III, 6, 5.

**Publicola,** Roman name: Cor. V, 3, 64. Ant. III, 7, 74.

**Publish,** 1) to make generally known: Lucr. 1852. Sonn. 102, 4. Ado IV, 1, 206. Shr. IV, 2, 85. H4B I, 3, 86. H6B III, 2, 17. H8 III, 2, 68. Lr. I, 1, 44. IV, 6, 236 (*a —ed traitor*). Cymb. V, 5, 478.

2) to bring to light, to show, to utter, to express in words: *whose trial shall better p. his commendation*, Merch. IV, 1, 165. *then we wound our modesty and make foul the clearness of our deservings, when of ourselves we p. them*, All's I, 3, 7. *thus far I will boldly p. her, she bore a mind that envy could not but call fair*, Tw. II, 1, 30.* *how will this grieve you, when you shall come to clearer knowledge, that you thus have —ed me*, Wint. II, 1, 98. *a proof of strength she could not p. more*, Troil. V, 2, 113. *if I tell how these two did coact, shall I not lie in —ing a truth?* 119.

**Publisher,** one who shows, who brings to light: *why is Collatine the p. of that rich jewel he should keep unknown from thievish ears*, Lucr. 33. *love of you, not hate unto my friend, hath made me p. of this pretence*, Gent. III, 1, 47.

**Publius,** Roman praenomen: Lucr. Arg. 19. Cor. II, 3, 249. Tit. IV, 3, 10. 25. V, 2, 161 etc. Caes. III, 1, 53. 57. Incorrectly used as a family name in Caes. II, 2, 108. III, 1, 85. 89. 91. IV, 1, 4.

**Pucelle** (O. Edd. *Puzel, Puzell,* and *Pucell*), the usual name of Joan of Arc, the maid of Orleans: H6A I, 2, 110. I, 4, 101 (O. Edd. *Joan de Puzel*). 107 (O. Edd. *Puzel* or *Pussel*). I, 5, 36. I, 6, 3 (O. Edd. *Joane de Puzel*). II, 1, 20. III, 2, 20. 38. 58. 121. III, 3, 40. 88.

**Puck,** the goblin styled also Robin Goodfellow: Mids. II, 1, 40. 148. IV, 1, 69. V, 438. 442.

**Pudder,** see *Pother*.

**Pudding,** a kind of food generally made of meal, milk and eggs: Gent. IV, 4, 34. Wiv. II, 1, 32. All's II, 2, 29. H4A II, 4, 498. H5 II, 1, 92. Oth. II, 1, 258. Per. II, 1, 86. Name in Meas. III, 3, 17.

**Puddle,** subst. a muddy plash: Lucr. 657. 658. H6B IV, 1, 71. Ant. I, 4, 62.

**Puddle,** vb. to make muddy: Err. V, 173. Oth. III, 4, 143.

**Pudency,** modesty: *did it with a p. so rosy*, Cymb. II, 5, 11.

**Puff,** name in H4B V, 3, 94.

**Puff,** vb. 1) to blow with a quick blast: *his hot heart ... —s forth another wind that fires the torch*, Lucr. 315. *tapers they are, with your sweet breaths —ed out*, LLL V, 2, 267. *like foggy south —ing with wind and rain*, As III, 5, 50. *the sea —ed up with winds*, Shr. I, 2, 202. *distinction, with a broad and powerful fan — ing at all*, Troil. I, 3, 28. *—s away from thence*, Rom. I, 4, 102. *when it* (the cannon) *hath from his very arm — ed his own brother*, Oth. III, 4, 137.

2) to breathe with vehemence, as after violent exertion: *and p. to win a vulgar station*, Cor. II, 1, 230.

3) to blow up, to inflate: *a —ed man*, Wiv. V, 5, 160. *till thy cheek outswell the colic of —ed Aquilon*, Troil. IV, 5, 9. *whose selfsame mettle, whereof arrogant man is —ed*, Tim. IV, 3, 180. *a —ed and reckless libertine*, Hml. I, 3, 49. *spirit with divine ambition —ed*, IV, 4, 49. With *up: the heart, who, great and —ed up with this retinue*, H4B IV, 3, 121. cf. *Lazy-puffing*.

**Pugging,** thievish: *set my p. tooth on edge*, Wint. IV, 3, 7.*

**Puh,** see *Pooh*.

**Puisny** (cf. *Puny*) petty, having but the skill of a novice: *as a p. tilter breaks his staff like a noble goose*, As III, 4, 46.

**Puissance** (dissyll. or trisyll.) 1) strength: *not arrived to pith and p.* H5 III Chor. 21. *thereby is England mained and fain to go with a staff, but that my p. holds it up*, H6B IV, 2, 173.

2) armed force: *draw our p. together*, John III, 1, 339. *to look with forehead bold and big enough upon the power and p. of the king*, H4B I, 3, 9. *come against us in full p.* 77. *till that the nobles and the armed commons have of their p. made a little taste*, II, 3, 52. *make imaginary p.* H5 Prol. 25. *let us deliver our p. into the hand of God*, II, 2, 190. *in the main battle, whose p. shall be well winged with our chiefest horse*, R3 V, 3, 299.

**Puissant,** mighty, powerful: *with your p. arm renew their feats*, H5 I, 2, 116. *my thrice p. liege*, 119. *trailest thou the p. pike?* IV, 1, 40 (Pistol's speech). *with a p. and a mighty power*, H6B IV, 9, 25. *with a p. host*, H6C II, 1, 207. V, 1, 6. V, 2, 31. *a p. navy*, R3 IV, 4, 434. *most high, most mighty, and most p. Caesar*, Caes. III, 1, 33. *his grief grew p.* Lr. V, 3, 216.

**Puke,** to spew, to vomit: *the infant mewling and —ing in the nurse's arms*, As II, 7, 144.

**Puke-stocking,** probably = dark-coloured stocking: H4A II, 4, 78.*

**Puling,** whining, whimpering: Gent. II, 1, 26. Troil. IV, 1, 61. Cor. IV, 2, 52. Rom. III, 5, 185.

**Pull,** subst. a pluck, a shake, a jerk: *two —s at once, his lady banished, and a limb lopped off*, H6B II, 3, 41.

**Pull,** vb. to draw, to tug, to pluck; absol.: *thou hast to p. at a smack o' the contrary*, All's II, 3, 237 (at a taste of folly, as at a vessel. cf. *Smack*). Trans.: *I'll p. thee by the lesser legs*, Tp. II, 2, 108. *—ed the law upon you*, Meas. II, 1, 16. *we'll p. his plumes*, H6A III, 3, 7. *let them p. all about mine ears*, Cor. III, 2, 1. *p. her out of Acheron*, Tit. IV, 3, 44. *you —ed me by the cloak*, Caes. I, 2, 215. *ne'er p. your hat upon your brows*, Mcb. IV, 3, 208. *her garments ... —ed the poor wretch ... to muddy death*, Hml. IV, 7, 183. *hales and*

*—s me,* Oth. IV, 1, 144. With adverbs: *doth backward p. our slow designs,* All's I, 1, 233. *shall all our houses be —ed down,* Meas. I, 2, 105. *p. down the Savoy,* H6B IV, 7, 1. *hath —ed fair England down,* I, 1, 259 (brought down, brought low). *the weight that —ed me down,* H8 III, 2, 408. *'tis pride that —s the country down,* Oth. II, 3, 98. *I p. in resolution,* Mcb. V, 5, 42 (= lose confidence).* *to p. off* = to take off (ornaments or articles of dress): Shr. II, 4. Caes. I, 2, 289. Mcb. V, 3, 54. Lr. IV, 6, 177. *profound respects do p. you on,* John III, 1, 318. *unless his teeth be —ed out,* H6B IV, 7, 19. *—ed out thy tongue,* As I, 1, 64. *the weeds .... are —ed up root and all by Bolingbroke,* R2 III, 4, 52 (Qq *plucked*).

**Puller-down,** one who subverts or deposes: *setter-up and p. of kings,* H6C III, 3, 157.

**Pullet-sperm,** treadle: Wiv. III, 5, 32.

**Pulpit,** the rostra of ancient Rome: Caes. III, 1, 80. 84. 229. 236. 250.

**Pulpiter,** preacher; conjectured by M. Edd. in As III, 2, 163; O. Edd. *Jupiter.*

**Pulse,** the throbbing of the arteries as the blood is driven through them: Ven. 476. Tp. V, 103. 113. Err. IV, 4, 55. V, 243. All's I, 3, 175. John IV, 2, 92. Troil. III, 2, 38. Rom. IV, 1, 96. Hml. III, 4, 140. Per. V, 1, 155.

**Pulsidge,** Mrs Quickly's form of the word *pulse:* H4B II, 4, 25.

**Pummel** (M. Edd. *Pommel*) the knob on the hilt of a sword: LLL V, 2, 618.

**Pump,** a light shoe (often worn with ribbons formed into the shape of flowers): *new ribbons to your —s,* Mids. IV, 2, 37. *Gabriel's —s were all unpinked i' the heel,* Shr. IV, 1, 136. *then is my p. well flowered,* Rom. II, 4, 64. *till thou hast worn out thy p.* 66.

**Pumpion,** a gourd, Cucurbita Pepo: Wiv. III, 3, 43.

**Pun,** vb. to pound as in a mortar, to dash to pieces: *he would p. thee into shivers with his fist, as a sailor breaks a biscuit,* Troil. II, 1, 42.

**Punch,** vb. to bore, to perforate: *—ed full of deadly holes,* R3 V, 3, 125.

**Punish,** 1) to afflict with a penalty, to chastise, to correct: Gent. II, 4, 130. Wiv. IV, 4, 25. Meas. V, 31. 240. LLL I, 2, 155. Tw. V, 141. Wint. I, 2, 59. III, 2, 226. IV, 4, 712. John II, 189. III, 1, 11. H4A III, 2, 11. V, 2, 7. H4B I, 2, 141. H5 II, 2, 45. 48. 60. H6B II, 4, 7. R3 II, 1, 34. H8 II, 4, 75. Cor. III, 1, 81. IV, 6, 52. V, 1, 21. Rom. V, 3, 295. 308. Hml. III, 4, 174. Lr. II, 2, 152. III, 4, 16. IV, 2, 54. Ant. II, 5, 100. Cymb. III, 2, 7. Per. I, 2, 28. 32. V, 3, 100.

2) to afflict with pain and suffering: *if I have too austerely —ed you, your compensation makes amends,* Tp. IV, 1, 1. *p. me not with your hard thoughts,* As I, 2, 195. *the reason why they are not so —ed and cured,* III, 2, 423. *whose very naming —es me with the remembrance of that penitent king,* Wint. IV, 2, 24. *that the people may not be —ed with my thwarting stars,* H6C IV, 6, 22. *how I am —ed with sore distraction,* Hml. V, 2, 240. *bid that welcome which comes to p. us, and we p. it seeming to bear it lightly,* Ant. IV, 14, 137.

**Punishment,** 1) penalty, chastisement, correction: Pilgr. 32 and LLL IV, 3, 63. Wiv. III, 3, 208. Meas. I, 3, 39. I, 4, 28. Ado III, 3, 4. V, 1, 31ა. V,

4, 130. LLL I, 1, 270. H5 IV, 1, 176. H6B III, 1, 130 *(to give).* R3 II, 1, 105. H8 III, 2, 183. Tit. V, 3, 145. Lr. III, 4, 76. IV, 2, 94. Oth. II, 3, 274. Ant. I, 1, 39 *(on pain of p.).* Cymb. I, 4, 129. III, 6, 11. V, 5, 334. 343.

2) affliction, suffering: *the pleasing p. that women bear,* Err. I, 1, 47 (but cf. Genesis III, 16).

**Punk,** a strumpet: Wiv. II, 2, 141. Meas. V, 179. 528. All's II, 2, 24.

**Punto,** a thrust or stroke in fencing: *to see thee pass thy p.* Wiv. II, 3, 26. *the p. reverso* = a backhanded stroke or cut: Rom. II, 4, 27.

**Puny** (cf. *Puisny*) little, petty: *p. lies,* Merch. III, 4, 74. *a p. subject strikes at thy great glory,* R2 III, 2, 86. *my p. drawer,* H4A II, 4, 33. *his p. sword,* H6A IV, 7, 36. *that thy wives with spits and boys with stones in p. battle slay me,* Cor. IV, 4, 6. *every p. whipster gets my sword,* Oth. V, 2, 244.

**Pupil,** 1) one under the care of a tutor: Gent. II, 1, 144. LLL IV, 2, 160. 163. Shr. II, 108. R2 I, 3, 171. H4A III, 1, 46. Rom. II, 3, 82. Cymb. I, 5, 12. Per. V Prol. 9.

2) one under the care of a guardian, a ward: H6B I, 3, 49. Adjectively, = not of age, unripe: *my p. pen,* Sonn. 16, 10. *to the p. age of this present twelve o' clock,* H4A IV, 1, 4, 106. *his p. age man-entered thus,* Cor. II, 2, 102.

**Pupil-like,** like a child instructed by a tutor: R2 V, 1, 31.

**Puppet,** a small human figure made to play with, a doll: Gent. II, 1, 101. Mids. III, 2, 288. 289. Shr. I, 2, 79, IV, 3, 103. 104. 106. Lr. II, 2, 39. Ant. V, 2, 208. *I could interpret between you and your love, if I could see the —s dallying,* Hml. III, 2, 257; meaning, according to some commentators, the babies, or miniature reflections, in the eyes, but more probably alluding to a puppet-show, in which Ophelia and her lover were to play a part.

**Puppy,** a young dog, a whelp: Gent. IV, 4, 3. Wiv. III, 5, 11. H8 I, 1, 175. Oth. I, 3, 341. Adjectively: *a p. dog* = a new-born dog, John II, 460. H5 III, 2, 78. *a p. greyhound,* H4B II, 4, 107. Term of contempt, implying stupidity: Wint. IV, 4, 726. H8 V, 4, 30. Cymb. I, 2, 22.

**Puppy-headed,** stupid: *this p. monster,* Tp. II, 2, 159.

**Pur,** the low murmuring sound of a cat: *here is a p. of fortune's, sir, or of fortune's cat,* All's V, 2, 20. *p., the cat is gray,* Lr. III, 6, 47.

**Purblind,** 1) quite blind: *this whimpled, whining, p., wayward boy,* LLL III, 181. *lower messes perchance are to this business p.* Wint. I, 2, 228. *p. Argus, all eyes and no sight,* Troil. I, 2, 31 (Ff *purblinded*). *her p. son* (Cupid) Rom. II, 1, 12.

2) half-blind, short-sighted: *the p. hare,* Ven. 679. *any p. eye may find it out,* H6A II, 4, 21.

**Purblinded,** = purblind; reading of Ff in Troil. I, 2, 31; Q *purblind.*

**Purchase,** subst. acquisition of any kind and by any means: *the difference is p. of a heavy curse from Rome, or the light loss of England for a friend,* John III, 1, 205. *the p. made, the fruits are to ensue,* Oth. II, 3, 9. *the p. is to make men glorious,* Per. Prol. 9 (= gain, profit). *I sought the p. of a glorious beauty,* I, 2, 72. = acquisition by money, buying, bargain: *which p. if thou make,* Ven. 515. *these wise men that* *give fools money get themselves a good report after fourteen years' p.* Tw. IV, 1, 24 (after having paid for it a pretty long time). **there's no p. in money,* H4A III, 3, 45. *will his vouchers vouch him no more of his —s,* Hml. V, 1, 117. *if there were wealth enough for the p.* Cymb. I, 4, 91. = booty: *thou shalt have a share in our p.* H4A II, 1, 101 (Ff *purpose*). *they will steal any thing and call it p.* H5 III, 2, 45. *made prize and p. of his lustful eye,* R3 III, 7, 187.

**Purchase,** vb. to acquire, to obtain, to gain (a profit), or to draw on one's self (an evil) in any manner; absol.: *there's wondrous things spoke of him. Wondrous! ay, I warrant you, and not without his true —ing,* Cor. II, 1, 155 (desert earned by exertion). Transitively: *as my gift and thine own acquisition worthily —d take my daughter,* Tp. IV, 1, 14. *I have —d as many diseases under her roof,* Meas. I, 2, 46. *his pardon, —d by such sin,* IV, 2, 111. *and never gives to truth and virtue that which simpleness and merit —th,* Ado III, 1, 70 (= deserves; cf. above). *which with pain —d doth inherit pain,* LLL I, 1, 73. *how hast thou —d this experience?* III, 27. *that clear honour were —d by the merit of the bearer,* Merch. II, 9, 43. *your accent is something finer than you could p. in so removed a dwelling,* As III, 2, 360. *with die and drab I —d this caparison,* Wint. IV, 3, 27. *p. the sight again of dear Sicilia,* IV, 4, 522. *I sent thee forth to p. honour,* R2 I, 3, 282. *how can tyrants safely govern home, unless abroad they p. great alliance,* H6C III, 3, 70. *true peace, which I will p. with my duteous service,* R3 II, 1, 63. *which (peace) she shall p. with still lasting war,* IV, 4, 344. *do this and p. us thy lasting friends,* Tit. II, 3, 275. *though his right arm might p. his own time,* Tim. III, 5, 78. *—ing but trouble,* Cymb. II, 3, 93. Dat. and accus., = to bring in, to gain sth. to a person: *one poor retiring minute in an age would p. thee a thousand friends,* Lucr. 963. *lest it make you choleric and p. me another dry basting,* Err. II, 2, 63. *the glove may haply p. him a box o' the ear,* H5 IV, 7, 181. *his silver hairs will p. us a good opinion,* Caes. II, 1, 145. Partic. — d, opposed to hereditary: *what in me was —d* (viz the crown) *falls upon thee in a more fairer sort,* H4B IV, 5, 200. *his faults ... hereditary rather than —d,* Ant. I, 4, 14.

= to acquire by paying an equivalent, to buy: Wiv. II, 2, 213. LLL V, 2, 59. Merch. III, 2, 89. III, 4, 20. IV, 1, 90. Tw. III, 3, 45. Wint. IV, 3, 127. John III, 1, 166 (*of*). H6B I, 1, 223. III, 3, 3. H6C III, 2, 73. H8 I, 1, 98. Tit. III, 1, 199. Ant. V, 2, 148. *to p. out* = to buy out (q. v.), to redeem: *nor tears nor prayers shall p. out abuses,* Rom. III, 1, 198. Absol., = to make a bargain: *that I should p. the day before for a little part,* Tim. III, 2, 52.

**Pure,** 1) free from mixture, unalloyed: *p. gold,* Gent. II, 4, 171. Rom. V, 3, 299. *he is p. air and fire,* H5 III, 7, 22. Hence figuratively, = pure, sheer: *a halting sonnet of his own p. brain,* Ado V, 4, 87. *p. idolatry,* LLL IV, 3, 75. *dry-beaten with p. scoff,* V, 2, 263. *what follows is p. innocence,* Merch. I, 1, 145. *with safety of a p. blush,* As I, 2, 30 (a blush and nothing else). *who after me hath many a weary step limped in p. love,* II, 7, 131. IV, 3, 3. All's III, 4, 38. *p. fear,* H4B II, 4, 352. *blush for p. shame,* H6A II, 4, 66. *of p. devotion,* H6B II, 1, 89. *we did it for p. need,* 157. H6C III, 1, 13. R3 IV, 1, 4. H8 II, 3, 95.

Caes. II, 2, 78. Lr. II, 4, 127. Oth. V, 2, 205. Per. III, 2, 17.

b) absolute, perfect, not impaired or adulterated in any manner: *to mingle p. perfection with impure defeature,* Ven. 736. *welcome, p. wit,* LLL V, 2, 484. *death, made proud with p. and princely beauty,* John IV, 3, 35. *the —st treasure mortal times afford,* R2 I, 1, 177. *in p. truth,* H5 I, 2, 73. *with p. heart's love,* R3 IV, 4, 403 (= sincere, true). *that praise, sole p., transcends,* Troil. I, 3, 244. *the eye itself, that most p. spirit of sense,* III, 3, 106. *let desert in p. election shine,* Tit. I, 16 (not influenced by any other considerations). *to turn your households' rancour to p. love,* Rom. II, 3, 92. *the finest part of p. love,* Ant. I, 2, 152.

2) unsullied, unspotted, undisturbed, clean, clear: *that p. congealed white, high Taurus' snow,* Mids. III, 2, 141. 144. *in p. white robes,* Wint. III, 3, 22. *the —st spring is not so free from mud,* H6B III, 1, 101. *—st snow,* Cor. V, 3, 66. *the meanest bird that flies in the —r air,* Per. IV, 6, 109. *his p. brain ... doth by the idle comments that it makes foretell the ending of mortality,* John V, 7, 2; cf. *ingrateful man with liquorish draughts greases his p. mind,* Tim. IV, 3, 195 (i. e. naturally clear and undisturbed). *o'er whom his very madness ... shows itself p.* Hml. IV, 1, 27 (i. e. as having a clear perception of what has happened). Hence in a moral sense, = a) stainless, blameless: *our p. honours,* John IV, 3, 25. *in my p. and immaculate valour,* H4B IV, 3, 41. *that p. blood,* H6A IV, 6, 23. *virtues as p. as grace,* Hml. I, 4, 33. *p. honour,* Cymb. II, 4, 59.

b) innocent, guiltless, chaste: Ven. 69. 511. 558. Lucr. 14. 73. 167. 194. 531 (*a p. compound,* i. e. not poisonous). 542. 684. 826 (*p. to Collatine*). 1078. 1704. Sonn. 66, 4. 110, 14. Compl. 315. Pilgr. 95. Tp. II, 1, 155. Gent. II, 7, 77. III, 1, 144. 229. IV, 2, 88. IV, 3, 21. Err. III, 2, 37. Ado IV, 1, 105. LLL V, 2, 351. Wint. II, 2, 41. John II, 429. R2 IV, 99. H5 I, 2, 32. III, 3, 20. H6A II, 1, 20. V, 3, 182. V, 4, 83. H8 V, 5, 26. Rom. III, 3, 38. Tim. IV, 3, 366. 384. Mcb. IV, 3, 53. Hml. III, 1, 141. Oth. I, 1, 107. III, 3, 138. IV, 2, 18. Per. V, 3, 69.

Adverbially: *p. for his love,* Tw. V, 86 (= merely). *live the —r with the other half,* Hml. III, 4, 158 (the more chastely, virtuously).

**Purely,** without alloy: *faith and troth, strained p. from all hollow bias-drawing,* Troil. IV, 5, 169.

**Purgation,** 1) the act of cleansing the body by evacuation: *to put him to his p.* Hml. III, 2, 318.

2) clearing from the imputation of guilt, exculpation: As I, 3, 55. Wint. III, 2, 7. H8 V, 3, 152. Misapplied by Costard in LLL III, 128, and used with purposed impropriety by Touchstone in As V, 4, 45.

**Purgative,** adj. having the power to cause evacuation: *p. drug,* Mcb. V, 3, 55.

**Purgatory,** the place where departed souls are purged by fire from carnal impurity: Rom. III, 3, 18. Oth. IV, 3, 77.

**Purge,** subst. cure, restoration to health: *meet we the medicine of the sickly weal, and with him pour we in our country's p. each drop of us,* Mcb. V, 2, 28.

**Purge,** vb. 1) to purify, to cleanse; absol.: *slight air and —ing fire,* Sonn. 45, 1. Trans.: *mine eyes ... shall gush pure streams to p. my impure tale,* Lucr. 1078. *you must be —d too,* LLL V, 2, 828. *I will p. thy mortal grossness so that thou shalt like an airy* *spirit go*, Mids. III, 1, 163. *and but in —d judgment trusting neither*, H5 II, 2, 136. *love is ... being —d, a fire sparkling in lovers' eyes*, Rom. I, 1, 197 (cleaned from smoke). *ere human statute —d the gentle weal*, Mcb. III, 4, 76. *to take him in the —ing of his soul*, Hml. III, 3, 85. With *from: my heart is —d from grudging hate*, R3 II, 1, 9. With *of: she —d the air of pestilence*, Tw. I, 1, 20. *to p. him of that humour*, Wint. II, 3, 38. *these hands, so lately —d of blood*, John III, 1, 239. *p. you of your scum*, H4B IV, 5, 124. *to p. this field of such a hilding foe*, H5 IV, 2, 29. *we would p. the land of these drones*, Per. II, 1, 50.

2) to evacuate the body by a cathartic; absol.: *we sicken to shun sickness when we p.* Sonn. 118, 4. *I'll p. and leave sack*, H4A V, 4, 168. Trans.: *and p. it* (my land) *to a sound and pristine health*, Mcb. V, 3, 52.

3) to clear from crime; always reflexively: *you cannot with such freedom p. yourself*, H8 V, 1, 103. *hoping to p. himself with words*, Cor. V, 6, 8. *to impeach and p. myself*, Rom. V, 3, 226. With *of: I can p. myself of many* (offences) H4A III, 2, 20. *whereof you cannot easily p. yourself*, H6B III, 1, 135.

4) to remove, to expel, to sweep away, to void; with *from: the blessed gods p. all infection from our air*, Wint. V, 1, 169. *from his bosom p. this black despair*, H6B III, 3, 23. *thus from my lips, by yours, my sin is —d*, Rom. I, 5, 109. With a simple accus.: *he is gone aboard a new ship to p. melancholy and air himself*, Wint. IV, 4, 790. *until our fears be —d and deposed*, John II, 372. *let's p. this choler without letting blood*, R2 I, 1, 153. *and p. the obstructions which begin to stop our very veins of life*, H4B IV, 1, 65. *to p. his fear, I'll be thy death*, H6C V, 6, 88. *till the foul crimes done in my days of nature are burnt and —d away*, Hml. I, 5, 13. *their eyes —ing thick amber*, II, 2, 200 (= secreting). *when she saw that your rage would not be —d*, Ant. IV, 14, 124.

5) intr. to be cured, to be restored to health (cf. the transitive use in Wint. IV, 4, 790. R2 I, 1, 153. H6C V, 6, 88. Mcb. V, 3, 52): *quietness, grown sick of rest, would p. by any desperate change*, Ant. I, 3, 53.

**Purger**, one who cures and restores to health by clearing away noxious matter: *we shall be called —s, not murderers*, Caes. II, 1, 180.

**Purify**, to make pure, to clear of evil or reproach: *his venom in effect is —ed*, Lucr. 532. *the spots whereof could weeping p.* 685. *falsehood thus —es itself and turns to grace*, LLL V, 2, 786. *which is a —ing o' the song*, All's I, 3, 87.

**Puritan**, an adherent of the sect which intended to restore the church to the pure form of the apostolic time; disliked and ridiculed by the poet: All's I, 3, 56. 98. Tw. II, 3, 152. 155. 159. Wint. IV, 3, 46. Per. IV, 6, 9.

**Purity**, freedom from any stain or foreign admixture (cf. *Pure*): Lucr. 780. Sonn. 144, 8. Wiv. II, 2, 258. Ado IV, 1, 105. As V, 2, 104. Wint. I, 2, 327. IV, 4, 394. John IV, 3, 53. Troil. III, 2, 174. IV, 4, 26. Tim. IV, 3, 14.

**Purl**, to curl, to run in circles: *from his lips did fly thin winding breath, which —ed up to the sky*, Lucr. 1407.

**Purlieus**, the grounds on the borders of a forest: *in the p. of this forest*, As IV, 3, 77.

**Purloin**, to steal: *his scarlet lust came evidence*

*to swear that my poor beauty had —ed his eyes*, Lucr. 1651.

**Purple**, subst. 1) a purple dress: *I never see thy face but I think upon hell-fire and Dives that lived in p., for there he is in his robes*, H4A III, 3, 36.
2) the flower Orchis mascula: Hml. IV, 7, 171.

**Purple**, adj. 1) of the colour of the violet: *the p. pride which on thy* (the violet's) *soft cheek for complexion dwells*, Sonn. 99, 3. *the p. violets*, Per. IV, 1, 16. *before milk-white, now p. with love's wound* (the viola tricolor) Mids. II, 1, 167. III, 2, 102. *p. grapes*, III, 1, 170. *p. the sails*, Ant. II, 2, 198. cf. Wiv. V, 5, 74. Ven. 1168.
2) red; used of blood: *p. tears that his wound wept*, Ven. 1054. *the p. fountain* (of her wound) Lucr. 1734. R2 III, 3, 94. H6C I, 4, 12. II, 5, 99. V, 6, 64. R3 IV, 4, 277. Rom. I, 1, 92.

**Purple-coloured**, red: *as the sun with p. face had ta'en his last leave of the weeping morn*, Ven. 1.

**Purpled**, red with blood: John II, 322. Caes. III, 1, 158.

**Purple-hued**, in *Mustachio-purple-hued*, q. v.

**Purple-in-grain**, see *Grain*.

**Purport**, subst. (*purpórt*) meaning, expression: *with a look so piteous in p.* Hml. II, 1, 82.

**Purpose**, subst. 1) that which a person intends to do, design, plan, project: *far from the p. of his coming hither, he makes excuses*, Lucr. 113. *this vile p. to prevent*, 220. *one midnight fated to the p.* Tp. I, 2, 129. *the ministers for the p.* 131. *forego the p.* III, 3, 12. *the sole drift of my p.* V, 29. Gent. II, 6, 42. Wiv. II, 2, 233. IV, 4, 77. IV, 6, 3. 21. V, 5, 214. Meas. I, 1, 74. I, 3, 4. IV, 5, 2. V, 314. LLL II, 109. V, 2, 122. Merch. I, 1, 133. III, 2, 230. As I, 1, 145. Tw. II, 3, 181. III, 4, 280. Wint. V, 1, 36. John II, 28. III, 1, 274. H4A I, 1, 28. II, 3, 7 (*undertake*). H4B II, 2, 195. IV, 2, 56. V, 2, 5. H6B III, 1, 256. R3 III, 1, 171. H8 I, 2, 209. III, 2, 168. Cor. III, 1, 148. Tim. V, 1, 17. Hml. III, 2, 23. Lr. II, 1, 113 (*make your own p., how in my strength you please*; cf. *Make*). Oth. I, 1, 12. I, 3, 39. Ant. I, 3, 67 (*bear*). II, 6, 126. IV, 3, 12 (*'tis a brave army, and full of p.*). V, 2, 131 etc. *to have a p.* John V, 1, 76. H4B IV, 5, 210. Mcb. I, 6, 21. *to have p.* Wint. IV, 4, 152. Cor. IV, 5, 125. *to have the p.* Meas. III, 1, 163. *this their p. hither to this wood*, Mids. IV, 1, 166. *our holy p. to Jerusalem*, H4A I, 1, 102. *we recommend to you, tribunes of the people, our p. to them*, Cor. II, 2, 156. *my p. was for Tharsus*, Per. V, 1, 253. *by advised p.* R2 I, 3, 188. *for the selfsame p.* Lucr. 1047. *for the p.* Gent. III, 1, 152. Meas. II, 1, 155. LLL V, 1, 143. Merch. I, 3, 99. As IV, 2, 7. R3 V, 3, 274. Rom. II, 2, 130. Cymb. III, 4, 30. *that more for praise than p. meant to kill*, LLL IV, 1, 29 (a kind of zeugma, = more for praise than on purpose). *of p.* = with a design: *of p. to obscure my noble birth*, H6A V, 4, 22. *this is of p. laid by some that hate me to quench mine honour*, H8 V, 2, 14. *of p. to have him spend less*, Tim. III, 1, 26 (later Ff on p.). *on p.* = designedly, intentionally, expressly: *a swallowed bait on p. laid to make the taker mad*, Sonn. 129, 8. *belike his wife, acquainted with his fits, on p. shut the doors against his way*, Err IV, 3, 92. *people sin upon p., because they would go thither* (to hell) Ado II, 1, 267. *as hushed on p. to grace harmony*, II, 3, 41. *the lustful bed on p. trimmed up for Semiramis*, Shr. Ind. 2, 41. *she sends him on* *p. that I may appear stubborn to him*, Tw. III, 4, 74. H4B II, 4, 334. Lr. IV, 2, 94. Cymb. I, 6, 202. II, 3, 61 *(on angry p.).* Per. II, 2, 54 *(on set p.).* *to this p.* Sonn. 126, 7. Wiv. II, 2, 227. Meas. IV, 6, 4 *(to vailful p.; some M. Edd. to veil full p.).* Err. IV, 1, 97. R2 I, 3, 253. Cymb. IV, 1, 25 *(to a sore p.).* *with a p.* Troil. I, 3, 128. *with p.* Merch. I, 1, 91. John V, 7, 86. H6A I, 1, 133.

2) that which a person pursues and wishes to obtain, aim, object, and hence = bent of mind: *adding one thing to my p. nothing*, Sonn. 20, 12. *you are so strongly in my p. bred that all the world besides methinks are dead*, 112, 13. *if power change p.* Meas. I, 3, 54. *that the resolute acting of your blood could have attained the effect of your own p.* II, 1, 13. *but the next morn betimes, his p. surfeiting, he sends a warrant for my poor brother's head*, V, 102 (having satisfied his desire to excess). *am the tongue of these to sound the —s of all their hearts*, John IV, 2, 48. *it is the shameful work of Hubert's hand, the practice and the p. of the king*, IV, 3, 63. *this shall make our p. necessary and not envious*, Caes. II, 1, 178. *be a soldier to thy p.* Per. IV, 1, 8. *ask him his —s, why he appears upon this call o' the trumpet*, Lr. V, 3, 118.

3) that which a person demands; request, proposal: *in the morning early shall my uncle bring him our —s*, H4A IV, 3, 111. *your p. is both good and reasonable*, H6A V, 1, 36. *we'll execute your p. and put on a form of strangeness as we pass along*, Troil. III, 3, 50. *may I never to this good p. dream of impediment*, Ant. II, 2, 147. *therefore have we our written —s before us sent*, II, 6, 4. *our p. to them*, Cor. II, 2, 156.

4) that which a person or thing means to say or express, sense, meaning, purport: *I endowed thy —s with words*, Tp. I, 2, 357. *how you the p. cherish*, II, 1, 224. *my words express my p.* Meas. II, 4, 148. 150. *if they do speak our language, 'tis our will that some plain man recount their —s*, LLL V, 2, 176. *the intent and p. of the law hath full relation to the penalty*, Merch. IV, 1, 247. *solicits her in the unlawful p.* All's III, 5, 73. *a passion hateful to my —s*, John III, 3, 47. *you start away and lend no ear unto my —s*, H4A I, 3, 217. *this challenge relates in p. only to Achilles*, Troil. I, 3, 323. *men may construe things after their fashion, clean from the p. of the things themselves.* Caes. I, 3, 35. *you bear a graver p., I hope*, Cymb. I, 4, 151. Lr. I, 4, 260. With *to: have you importuned her to such a p.?* Wiv. II, 2, 221 (= in such a sense; with respect to this). *the speech we had to such a p.* Meas. I, 2, 79. *I will think nothing to any p. that the world can say against it*, Ado V, 4, 107 (of any meaning, i. e. of any importance). *now I speak to some p.* As V, 2, 58. *thou never spokest to better p.* Wint. I, 2, 89. *he bade me take a trumpet and to this p. speak*, Troil. I, 3, 264. *they have pardons as free as words to little p.* Cor. III, 2, 89. *speakest with every tongue to every p.* Tim. IV, 3, 390.

5) something spoken of or to be done, matter, question, subject: *to listen our p.* Ado III, 1, 12 (Qq *propose*). *the extreme parts of time extremely forms all causes to the p. of his speed*, LLL V, 2, 751 (i. e. the haste and shortness of time, which is then the chief subject of consideration). *any such proverb so little kin to the p.* H5 III, 7, 72. *haste her to the p.* Troil. IV, 3, 5. *what have you dreamed of late of this war's p.?* Cymb. IV, 2, 345 (i. e. concerning this war).

*to the p.* = a) come to the matter in question: Gent. IV, 1, 53. Meas. II, 1, 120. All's V, 3, 241. H4B V, 5, 122. Lr. II, 4, 184. Cymb. V, 5, 178. b) conformably to the subject or object in view, well, rightly: *he was wont to speak plain and to the p.* Ado II, 3, 20. Tw. I, 3, 21. Wint. I, 2, 100. 106. Cor. II, 1, 95. Rom. II, 4, 46. Caes. III, 1, 146. Hml. II, 2, 287. V, 1, 44. *to p.*, in the same sense: *nothing is done to p.* Cor. III, 1, 149.

**Purpose**, vb. 1) to intend, to design; absol.: *yet did I p. as they do entreat*, H6B III, 2, 282. *to-morrow, as he —s*, Mcb. I, 5, 61. *to speak and p. not*, Lr. I, 1, 228. *he —th to Athens*, Ant. III, 1, 35 (= to go to A.). With an inf.: Lucr. 514. Sonn. 21, 14. Tp. II, 1, 20. Gent. III, 1, 26. Ado V, 4, 106. LLL V, 2, 343. Mids. V, 93. As IV, 3, 128. John IV, 1, 124. R2 V, 2, 55. H6A III, 1, 7. IV, 6, 25. Cor. V, 3, 119. Cymb. V, 5, 52. With an accus.: LLL II, 142. V, 2, 759. Merch. II, 2, 212. Wint. IV, 4, 480. 483. H4A V, 1, 43. H4B IV, 5, 155. H5 IV, 1, 165. H8 II, 1, 164. V, 3, 149. Caes. II, 2, 27. Ant. I, 2, 184. Cymb. III, 4, 110. IV, 3, 15. Per. III, 4, 12. *—d* = intended, designed: Sonn. 90, 8.; Compl. 118. LLL V, 2, 91. Mids. IV, 1, 188. Cor. III, 1, 38. Hml. IV, 4, 11. V, 2, 252. Lr. II, 2, 149. Oth. III, 4, 117. Dat. and accus.: *does p. honour to you*, H8 II, 3, 62. *we p. her no shame*, Ant. V, 1, 62. *his daughter whom he —d to his wife's sole son*, Cymb. I, 1, 5.

2) to mean, to wish: *I have possessed your grace of what I p.* Merch. IV, 1, 35. *when I spake darkly what I —d*, John IV, 2, 232. *or do you p. a victor shall be known?* Troil. IV, 5, 66.

**Purpose-changer,** one who makes people change their intentions: John II, 567.

**Purposed**, having a purpose, resolved: *so am I p.* Lr. II, 4, 296.

**Purposely**, designedly, intentionally, expressly: *which were on foot p. to take his brother here*, As V, 4, 163. *put quarrels p. on others to taste their valour*, Tw. III, 4, 267. *p. therefore left I the court*, H6B II, 3, 52. *come hither p. to poison me*, Tit. III, 2, 73.

**Purr,** see *Pur.*

**Purse**, subst. a small money-bag carried in the pocket: Gent. I, 1, 134. III, 1, 357. IV, 4, 181. Wiv. I, 3, 59. II, 1, 198. II, 2, 138. Err. IV, 1, 105 *(a p. of ducats).* IV, 2, 29. IV, 4, 90 *(a p. of ducats).* Ado II, 1, 16. Merch. I, 1, 138. II, 5, 51. As II, 4, 14. Shr. I, 2, 57. IV, 3, 173. All's III, 7, 14 *(this p. of gold).* IV, 5, 46. Tw. I, 5, 303. Wint. IV, 3, 127 *(your p. is not hot enough).* John V, 2, 61. H4A I, 2, 142 *(fat —s).* II, 4, 355 *(cold —s).* H4B V, 1, 34 *(a friend i' the court is better than a penny in p.).* H5 II, 2, 10. IV, 3, 37. H6A I, 3, 64. H6B I, 1, 112. R3 I, 4, 131. 144. IV, 4, 516 etc. etc. *she bears the p.* Wiv. I, 3, 76; cf. *hast had my p.* Oth. I, 1, 2. *nor will he know his p.* Tim. I, 2, 200 (the state of his finances). *a halfpenny p.* Wiv. III, 5, 149. *thou halfpenny p. of wit*, LLL V, 1, 77.

**Purse**, vb. 1) to put in a purse: *I will go and p. the ducats*, Merch. I, 3, 175. With *up: she —d up his heart*, Ant. II, 2, 192 (German: *sie hatte sein Herz in der Tasche*).

2) to contract into wrinkles, to knit: *didst contract and p. thy brow together*, Oth. III, 3, 113.

**Purse-bearer,** one who bears the purse of another: Tw. III, 3, 47.

**Pursent,** Costard's corruption from *present:* LLL V, 2, 488.

**Purse-taking,** stealing: H4A I, 2, 115.

**Pursue,** 1) to follow, to attend: *your sense —s not mine,* Meas. II, 4, 74. *p. him and entreat him to a peace,* Tw. V, 389. *your love —s a banished traitor,* R2 II, 3, 59. *where* (to his bed) *eagerly his sickness —d him still,* H8 IV, 2, 25. *p. we him on knees,* Troil. V, 3, 10. *ignomy and shame p. thy life,* V, 10, 34. *—d my humour not —ing his,* Rom. I, 1, 135. *p. me lasting strife,* Hml. III, 2, 232. *Fortune p. thee!* Ant. III, 12, 25.

2) to proceed in, to carry on, to follow up, to continue: *I pray thee, p. sentence,* Merch. IV, 1, 298. *I will p. the amity,* All's II, 5, 15. *I cannot p. this sport to the upshot,* Tw. IV, 2, 76. *had we —d that life,* Wint. I, 2, 71. *thus far our bending author hath —d the story,* H5 Epil. 2. *a speedier course must we p.* Tit. II, 1, 111. *can vengeance be —d further than death?* Rom. V, 3, 55. *howsoever thou —st this act,* Hml. I, 5, 84. *will they p. the quality no longer than they can sing?* Hml. II, 2, 363. *she hath —d conclusions infinite of easy ways to die,* Ant. V, 2, 358.

3) to follow with a view to overtake, to chase; absol.: *clap on more sails, p.* Wiv. II, 2, 142. *when cowardice —s,* Mids. II, 1, 234. H6C I, 4, 22. R3 III, 2, 28. Transitively: *p. these fearful creatures,* Ven. 677. 699. Err. V, 155. Mids. I, 1, 163. 248. II, 1, 188. 232. Shr. V, 2, 47. Tw. I, 1, 23. III, 4, 144. H4B IV, 2, 120. H6B V, 3, 26. H6C I, 1, 2. I, 4, 5. II, 6, 33. Cor. III, 1, 309. IV, 6, 94. Lr. II, 1, 45. 91. 111. Oth. II, 3, 230. Cymb. III, 5, 100. 166. IV, 2, 157.

4) to persecute, to treat with hostility, to seek to injure: *p. him with any further revenge,* Wiv. IV, 2, 221. *that with such vehemency he should p. faults proper to himself,* Meas. V, 109. *will you the knights shall to the edge of all extremity p. each other, or shall be divided by any voice or order of the field?* Troil.IV,5,69.

5) to follow with a desire to obtain, to strive to gain: *they fright him, but he still —s his fear,* Lucr. 308. *possessing or —ing no delight,* Sonn. 75, 11. *I have —d her as love hath —d me,* Wiv. II, 2, 208. 215. 216. *our natures do p. a thirsty evil,* Meas. I, 2, 132. *she shall p. it with the soul of love,* Mids. II, 1, 182. *he —d my life,* Hml. IV, 7, 5. *if I knew what hoop should hold us stanch, from edge to edge o' the world I would p. it,* Ant. II, 2, 118. *would I might never o'ertake —d success,* V, 2, 103. Absol.: *emulation hath a thousand sons that one by one p.* Troil. III, 3, 157.

In R3 II, 3, 43 Ff *men's minds mistrust —ing dangers,* Qq *ensuing dangers.*

**Pursuers,** such as follow in hostility: Ven. 688. H4A V, 5, 22.

**Pursuit,** 1) the act of following and seeking: *my willing love set forth in your p.* Tw. III, 3, 13.

2) the act of following with a view to overtake; mostly in a hostile sense: Lucr. 1691. Mids. IV, 1, 128. All's III, 4, 25. H4B IV, 3, 77. H5 II, 4, 69. H6A II, 2, 3. H6C II, 1, 3. 149. II, 3. *to make p.* Lucr. 696. As I, 3, 138. R3 III, 2, 30. *death doth hold us in p.* H6C II, 5, 127. *in p. of:* Sonn. 143, 4.

3) endeavour to gain: *mad in p. and in possession so,* Sonn. 129, 9. *Paris should ne'er retract what he hath done, nor faint in the p.* Troil. II, 2, 142. *I'll play the hunter for thy life with all my force, p. and policy,* IV, 1, 18.

**Pursuivant,** an officer at arms, of a lower rank than heralds: *these grey locks, the —s of death,* H6A II, 5, 5 (as forerunning and announcing death). *send for his master with a p.* H6B I, 3, 37. *I told the p.* R3 III, 4, 90. *send out a p. at arms,* V, 3, 59. *— s, pages and footboys,* H8 V, 2, 24.

**Pursy,** fat and short-winded: *and p. insolence shall break his wind with fear and horrid flight,* Tim. V, 4, 12. *in the fatness of these p. times virtue itself of vice must pardon beg,* Hml. III, 4, 153.

**Purveyor,** one who goes before to make provision for the table: *we coursed him at the heels and had a purpose to be his p.* Mcb. I, 6, 22.

**Push,** interj. pshaw, pish: *made a p. at chance and sufferance,* Ado V, 1, 38. *p.! did you see my cap?* Tim. III, 6, 119.

**Push,** subst. a thrust, calculated either to overturn something, or to set it in motion; hence 1) attack, onset: *sudden p. gives them the overthrow,* Caes. V, 2, 5. *this p. will cheer me ever, or disseat me now,* Mcb. V, 3, 20. *to stand the p. of* = to expose one's self to, to face: *stand the p. of every beardless vain comparative,* H4A III, 2, 66. *I stand the p. of your one thing that you will tell,* H4B II, 2, 40. *to stand the p. and enmity of those this quarrel would excite,* Troil.II,2,137.

2) an impulse given, a setting in motion: *lest they desire upon this p. to trouble your joys with like relation,* Wint. V, 3, 129. *we'll put the matter to the present p.* Hml. V, 1, 318 (= let us push on the matter immediately, let us immediately go to work).*

**Push,** vb. to thrust; absol. = to make a thrust: *this sessions ... —es 'gainst our heart,* Wint. III, 2, 2. *make a head to p. against a kingdom,* H4A IV, 1, 81. *p. home,* H5 II, 1, 103. *we may as well p. against Paul's,* H8 V, 4, 16. Transitively, = to thrust, to drive, to press by force: *backward she —ed him,* Ven. 41. *to p. grief on, and back the same grief draw,* Lucr. 1673. *p. him out of doors,* As III, 1, 15. *will you not put her out?* Wint. II, 3, 73. *do not p. me,* 125. John V, 7, 77. H5 I, 1, 5. Cor. V, 2, 41. Rom. I, 1, 21. Caes. V, 5, 25. Mcb. III, 4, 82. Per. V, 1, 127. With *on,* = to urge on, to promote: *doth p. on this proceeding,* Wint. II, 1, 179. *one that will either p. on or pluck back thy business,* IV, 4, 762.

In Troil. II, 3, 213 Qq *I'll p. him o'er the face,* Ff *pash.*

**Push-pin,** a child's play in which pins are pushed alternately: LLL IV, 3, 169.

**Pusillanimity,** want of courage: *the liver white and pale, which is the badge of p. and cowardice,* H4B IV, 3, 114.

**Put,** I. trans. 1) to place, to set, to lay; expressing, in the most general manner, the causing of a change or effect in local position: *she —s the period often from his place,* Lucr. 565. *what eyes hath Love p. in my head,* Sonn. 148, 1. *p. some lime upon your fingers,* Tp. IV, 246. *I'll never p. my finger in the fire,* Wiv. I, 4, 91. *what he —s into the press,* II, 1, 80. *p. a toast in it,* III, 5, 3. *p. him into the basket,* IV, 2, 48. *to p. metal in restrained means,* Meas. II, 4, 48. *—ing the hand in the pocket,* III, 2, 49. *to p. a ducat in her clack-dish,* 134. *p. them in secret holds,* IV, 3, 91. *to p. the finger in the eye,* Err. II, 2, 206. *a case to p. it into,* Ado I, 1, 184. *you must p. in the pikes with a* vice, V, 2, 21. *p. together*, LLL I, 1, 210. *how easy it is to p. years to the word three*, I, 2, 55. *I'll p. a girdle round about the earth*, Mids. II, 1, 175. *your vows, p. into two scales*, III, 2, 132. *the man should be p. into the lanthorn*, V, 251. *he p. his hand behind him*, Merch. II, 8, 47. *p. bars between the owners and their rights*, III, 2, 19. *so you may p. a man in your belly*, As III, 2, 215. *to p. a good meat into an unclean dish*, III, 3, 36. *he p. it into his mouth*, V, 1, 38. *p. finger in the eye*, Shr. I, 1, 79. *p. me in thy books*, II, 225. *p. you in the catalogue of those*, All's I, 3, 149. *tongue, I must p. you into a butter-woman's mouth*, IV, 1, 44. *p. your grace in your pocket*, Tw. V, 35. *p. me into darkness*, 312. *to p. him i' the ground* (= to bury him) Wint. III, 3, 140. *the rogue that p. me into this apparel*, IV, 3, 111. *my name p. in the book of virtue*, 131. *I'll not p. the dibble in earth*, IV, 4, 99. *and p. the same* (sword) *into young Arthur's hand*, John I, 14. *p. my eyeballs in thy brows*, III, 4, 30. *p. a little water in a spoon*, IV, 3, 131. *p. a few flocks in the point*, H4A II, 1, 7. *p. ratsbane in my mouth*, H4B I, 2, 48. *he hath p. all my substance into that belly of his*, II, 1, 81. *p. me a caliver into Wart's hand*, III, 2, 289. *has p. us in these ill-beseeming arms*, IV, 1, 84. *p. thy face between his sheets*, H5 II, 1, 87. *I p. my hand into the bed*, II, 3, 24. *to p. into mine* (pocket) III, 2, 54. *our scions, p. in wild and savage stock*, III, 5, 7. *crowns ... p. into his purse*, IV, 3, 37. *to p. a golden sceptre in thy hand*, H6A V, 3, 118. *you p. sharp weapons in a madman's hands*, H6B III, 1, 347. *p. them in prison*, IV, 7, 48. *p. in their hands thy bruising irons of wrath*, R3 V, 3, 110. *would have p. his knife into him*, H8 I, 2, 199. *p. my cause into his hands*, III, 1, 118. *a noble spirit, as yours was p. into you*, 170. *there p. unwittingly*, III, 2, 123. *some spirit p. this paper in the packet*, 129. 215. *—s me her hand to his chin*, Troil. I, 2, 131. *and in my vantbrace p. this withered brawn*, I, 3, 297. *we'll p. you i' the fills*, III, 2, 48. *wherein he —s alms for oblivion*, III, 3, 146. *p. your shields before your hearts*, Cor. I, 4, 24. *we'll p. you in manacles*, I, 9, 56. *to p. our tongues into those wounds*, II, 3, 7. *p. not your worthy rage into your tongue*, III, 1, 241. *p. in prison*, IV, 6, 38. *if he were —ing to my house the brand*, 115. *a case to p. my visage in*, Rom. I, 4, 29. *p. this in any liquid thing*, V, 1, 77. *has no house to p. his head in*, Tim. III, 4, 64. *we p. a sting in him*, Caes. II, 1, 16. *p. a tongue in every wound*, III, 2, 232. *I p. it in the pocket*, IV, 3, 253. *p. on my brows this wreath of victory*, V, 3, 82. *p. a barren sceptre in my gripe*, Mcb. III, 1, 62. *p. rancours in the vessel of my peace*, 67. *enchanting all that you p. in*, IV, 1, 43. *we will fetters p. upon this fear*, Hml. III, 3, 25. *p. it in his pocket*, III, 4, 101. *to p. his head in*, Lr. I, 5, 32. *p. in his legs*, II, 2, 157. *she p. 'em i' the paste*, II, 4, 124. *who p. my man i' the stocks*, 185. *a house to p. his head in*, III, 2, 25. *p. money in thy purse*, Oth. I, 3, 345. 347. 349. *she —s her tongue in her heart*, II, 1, 107. *to p. you in your place again*, II, 3, 324. *p. in every honest hand a whip*, IV, 2, 142. *p. it* (your rapier) *home*, V, 1, 2 (do not miss your adversary). *p. garlands on thy head*, Ant. III, 1, 11. *not what you reserved ... p. we i' the roll of conquest*, V, 2, 181. *you should have been p. together with so mortal a purpose*, Cymb. I, 4, 43. *p. the moon in his pocket*, III, 1, 44. *did p. the yoke upon's*, 52. *p. his brows within a golden crown*, 60.

Reflexively: *hast p. thyself upon this island as a spy*, Tp. I, 2, 454. *have p. themselves into voluntary exile*, As I, 1, 106. *I'll p. myself in poor and mean attire*, I, 3, 113. *p. you in your best array*, V, 2, 78. *I p. myself into thy file*, All's III, 3, 9. *p. myself into my mortal preparation* III, 6, 81. *England hath p. himself in arms*, John II, 57. Ant. II, 2, 168. *p. yourself under his shroud*, III, 13, 71. *—s himself in posture*, Cymb. III, 3, 94. III, 4, 8.

Figurative use: *that same groan doth p. this in my mind*, Sonn. 50, 13. *and in it* (his picture) *p. their mind*, Compl. 135 (cf. Cymb. V, 5, 176). *the strangeness of your story p. heaviness in me*, Tp. I, 2, 306. *and p. your trial in the villain's mouth*, Meas. V, 304. *—s the world into her person*, Ado II, 1, 215. *to p. a strange face on his own perfection*, II, 3, 49. *had p. such difference betwixt their two estates*, All's I, 3, 116. *would not p. my reputation now in any staining act*, III, 7, 6. *to p. fire in your heart*, Tw. III, 2, 21. *could p. breath into his work*, Wint. V, 2, 107. *that e'er I p. between your holy looks my ill suspicion*, V, 3, 148. *p. spirit in the French*, John V, 4, 2. *now p. it, God, in the physician's mind*, R2 I, 4, 59. *p. the world's whole strength into one giant arm*, H4B IV, 5, 44. *God p. it in thy mind*, 179. *let me p. in your minds*, R3 I, 3, 131. II, 1, 120. *p. meekness in thy mind*, II, 2, 107. *p. in her tender heart the aspiring flame*, IV, 4, 328. *p. your main cause into the king's protection*, H8 III, 1, 93. *—s his Shall against a graver bench*, Cor. III, 1, 105. *—'st odds amongst the rout of nations*, Tim. IV, 3, 42. *I will p. that business in your bosoms*, Mcb. III, 1, 104. *—s toys of desperation into every brain*, Hml. I, 4, 75. *with more offences at my beck than I have thoughts to p. them in*, III, 1, 128. *p. your discourse into some frame*, III, 2, 320. *you must p. me in your heart for friend*, IV, 7, 2. *if any wretch have p. this in your head*, Oth. IV, 2, 15. *p. colour in thy cheek*, Ant. IV, 14, 69. *would I had p. my estate on the approbation of what I have spoke*, Cymb. I, 4, 133 (= laid, betted). *p. them into mine hand*, V, 1, 25. *p. the strength of the Leonati in me*, V, 1, 31. *and then a mind p. in it* (the picture) V, 5, 176. *those arts they have as I could p. into them*, 339. *in your supposing once more p. your sight of heavy Pericles*, Per. V Prol. 21 (but Ff *on heavy Pericles*).

Used of articles of dress or ornament taken on or off the body: *—s apparel on my tattered loving*, Sonn. 26, 11. *rings p. upon his fingers*, Shr. Ind. 1, 38. *on your finger I'll p. another ring*, All's IV, 2, 61. *she would never p. it from her finger*, V, 3, 109. *I p. it* (the crown) *on my head*, H4B IV, 5, 166. *never would he ... on him p. the vesture of humility*, Cor. II, 1, 249. *p. armour on thine ears*, Tim. IV, 3, 123. *we p. fresh garments on him*, Lr. IV, 7, 22. *p. my tires and mantles on him*, Ant. II, 5, 22. *p. my brogues from off my feet*, Cymb. IV, 2, 214. With adverbs: *—'st down thine own breeches*, Lr. I, 4, 189. *p. off that gown*, Tp. IV, 226. *—ing off his hat*, H4B II, 4, 7. All's II, 2, 9. 10. Lr. IV, 7, 8. Ant. IV, 15, 56. *p. his bonnet on*, Ven. 1087. *when we p. them* (our garments) *on*, Tp. II, 1, 69. *your rye-straw hats p. on*, IV, 136. *to p. on your hose*, Gent. II, 1, 84. Wiv. IV, 2, 73. 85. Ado V, 3, 30. Merch. IV, 1, 442. Shr. I, 1, 234. III, 2, 115. 128. Tw. II, 5, 186. IV, 2, 1. 5. V, 346. John IV, 2, 27. R2 V, 6, 48. H4B II, 2, 189. H6C II, 2, 130. III, 3, 230. R3 II, 3, 32. Cor. II, 2, 141. III, 2, 34.

Tit. I, 185. Caes. I, 1, 53. III, 2, 175. Mcb. IV, 3, 154. V, 1, 68. V, 3, 34. Oth. I, 1, 86. Ant. IV, 4, 10. Per. II, 1, 83. IV, 4, 29. Peculiar use: *some hangman must p. on my shroud*, Wint. IV, 4, 468 (i. e. for me; = some hangman must put my shroud on me). *that the bleak air will p. thy shirt on warm*, Tim. IV, 3, 223. *p. mine armour on*, Mcb. V, 3, 48 (for me). *p. thine iron on*, Ant. IV, 4, 3 (i. e. put on me the iron which thou hast in thy hand. Some M. Edd. *mine iron*).

Figurative use: *she —s on outward strangeness*, Ven. 310. *hast thou p. on this shape*, Lucr. 597. *each hand hath p. on nature's power*, Sonn. 127, 5 (in imitating nature by painting). *have p. on black*, 132, 3. *to p. fair truth upon so foul a face*, 137, 12. (penitence) *hollowly p. on*, Meas. II, 3, 23. *—ing on the destined livery*, II, 4, 138. *which parti-coated presence of loose love p. on by us*, LLL V, 2, 777. *if I do not p. on a sober habit*, Merch. II, 2, 199. *to p. on your boldest suit of mirth*, 210. *the seeming truth which cunning times p. on*, III, 2, 100. *therefore p. I on the countenance of stern commandment*, As II, 7, 108. *the duke hath p. on a religious life*, V, 4, 187. *the semblance I p. on*, Tw. V, 315. *may a free face p. on*, Wint. I, 2, 112. *—s on his pretty looks*, John III, 4, 95. *p. on the dauntless spirit of resolution*, V, 1, 52. *happily may your sweet self p. on the lineal state and glory of the land*, V, 7, 101. *death p. on his ugliest mask*, H4B I, 1, 66. *p. not you on the visage of the times*, II, 3, 3. *p. the fashion on*, V, 2, 52. *p. off your maiden blushes*, H5 V, 2, 253. *p. on some other shape*, R3 IV, 4, 286. *whose figure this cloud —s on*, H8 I, 1, 225. *thy topless deputation he —s on*, Troil. I, 3, 152. *the savage strangeness he —s on*, II, 3, 135. III, 3, 50. *I will p. on his presence*, 272. *I would have had you p. your power well on*, Cor. III, 2, 17. *p. off these frowns*, Rom. I, 5, 75. *p. on a most importunate aspect*, Tim. II, 1, 28. *—ing on the cunning of a sharper*, IV, 3, 209. *didst p. this sour-cold habit on*, 239. *—s on this tardy form*, Caes. I, 2, 303. *and p. on fear*, I, 3, 60. *let not our looks p. on our purposes*, II, 1, 225. *let's p. on manly readiness*, Mcb. II, 3, 139. *p. we on industrious soldiership*, V, 4, 15. *we p. on a compelled valour*, Hml. IV, 6, 17. *to p. an antic disposition on*, I, 5, 172. *p. on a livery*, III, 4, 165. *p. on weary negligence*, Lr. I, 3, 12. *p. upon him such a deal of man*, II, 2, 127. *—ing on the mere form of civil seeming*, Oth. II, 1, 243.

2) to bestow, to confer, to impose, to inflict, to charge; with the prepos. *on* or *upon: do you p. tricks upon's?* Tp. II, 2, 60. *—s the neglected act freshly on me*, Meas. I, 2, 174. *if I p. any tricks upon 'em*, All's IV, 5, 63. *dost thou p. upon me the office of God?* V, 2, 51. *p. quarrels purposely on others*, Tw. III, 4, 266. *that forced baseness which he has p. upon't*, Wint. II, 3, 79. *this business, p. on thee by my lord*, III, 3, 35. *p. not another sin upon my head*, Rom. V, 3, 62. *what cannot you and I ... p. upon his spongy officers?* Mcb. I, 7, 70. *which —s upon them suspicion of the deed*, II, 4, 26. *when first they p. the name of king upon me*, III, 1, 58. *p. on him what forgeries you please*, Hml. II, 1, 19. *you must not p. another scandal on him*, 29. *yet must not we p. the strong law on him*, IV, 3, 3. *or p. upon you what restraint and grievance the law ... will give him cable*, Oth. I, 2, 15. *you shall think yourself bound to p. it* (death) *on him*, IV, 2, 248. *honour, if p. upon you*, Per. IV, 6, 100. *p. your sight on heavy Pericles*, V Prol. 21 (Qq *of*). Inverted relation: *they do you wrong to p. you so oft upon't* (the office of constable) Meas. II, 1, 280 (= to p. it so often on you).

Sometimes = to impart, to communicate, to tell: *why do you p. these sayings upon me?* Meas. II, 2, 133. *news ... which he will p. on us, as pigeons feed their young*, As I, 2, 99. *p. strange speech upon me*, Tw. V, 70. *if it be so, as so 'tis p. on me*, Hml. I, 3, 94. Without *on*, = to tell, to pretend: *am not one that rejoices in the common wreck, as common bruit doth p. it*, Tim. V, 1, 196. cf. Oth. III, 3, 392.

3) to place in a state or condition: *is p. besides his part*, Sonn. 23, 2. *to p. him beside his patience*, H4A III, 1, 179. *p. Armado's page out of his part*, LLL V, 2, 336. 478. *I will not p. him out of countenance*, 611. 624. *this will p. them out of fear*, Mids. III, 1, 23. *p. out of office*, Tim. I, 2, 207. *when we first p. this dangerous stone a rolling*, H8 V, 3, 104. With *from*, = to deprive of, to deliver from, to take from: *such a deal of skimble-skamble stuff as —s me from my faith*, H4A III, 1, 155. *p. the king from these sad thoughts*, H8 II, 2, 57. *did I p. Henry from his native right*, H6C III, 3, 190. *to p. thee from thy heaviness*, Rom. III, 5, 109. *which* (sorrow) *may be p. from her by society*, IV, 1, 14. *they have e'en p. my breath from me*, Tim. III, 4, 104. *that thus hath p. him so much from the understanding of himself*, Hml. II, 2, 8. *—s him from fashion of himself*, III, 1, 182. *hath p. himself from rest, and must needs taste his folly*, Lr. II, 4, 293. *this is a trick to p. me from my suit*, Oth. III, 4, 87. With *into* or *in: to p. in practice*, Pilgr. 217. Gent. III, 2, 89. Ado I, 1, 330. II, 2, 53. LLL I, 1, 308. *you have p. the wild waters in this roar*, Tp. I, 2, 2. *to p. me into everlasting liberty*, Wiv. III, 3, 31. *p. not yourself into amazement*, Meas. IV, 2, 219. *I could p. thee in comfort*, LLL IV, 3, 52. *we have p. thee in countenance*, V, 2, 623. *—s the wretch in remembrance of a shroud*, Mids. V, 384. *we could p. us in readiness*, Shr. I, 1, 43. *this has p. me in heart*, IV, 5, 77. *p. me into good fooling*, Tw. I, 5, 35. *you should p. your lord into a desperate assurance*, II, 2, 8. *p. thyself into the trick of singularity*, II, 5, 164. *thou hast p. him in such a dream*, 210. *may p. you in mind*, V, 42. *—s some of us in distemper*, Wint. I, 2, 385. *the prince p. thee into my service*, H4B I, 2, 14. *—ing all affairs else in oblivion*, V, 5, 27. *government ... p. into parts*, H5 I, 2, 181. *—ing it in expedition*, II, 2, 191. *to p. your grace in mind*, R3 IV, 2, 113. *he hath into monstrous habits p. the graces that once were his*, H8 I, 2, 122. *the queen is p. in anger*, II, 4, 161. *to p. it in execution*, Cor. II, 1, 256. *this mutiny were better p. in hazard*, II, 3, 264. *will you be p. in mind of his blind fortune*, V, 6, 118. Rom. I, 1, 237. *I would have p. my wealth into donation*, Tim. III, 2, 90. *you shall p. this night's great business into my despatch*, Mcb. I, 5, 68. *p. me into a towering passion*, Hml. V, 2, 79. *will p. me in trust*, Lr. I, 4, 15. *I'll p. it in proof*, IV, 6, 189. *I would not my free condition p. into circumscription*, Oth. I, 2, 27. *to p. my father in impatient thoughts*, I, 3, 243. *I p. the Moor into a jealousy*, II, 1, 309. *every man p. himself into triumph*, II, 2, 4. *to p. our Cassio in some action*, II, 3, 62. *the trust Othello —s him in*, 131. *the general were p. in mind of it*, 137. *p. into courage*, Cymb. II, 3, 8. *p. into contempt the suits*, III, 4, 92. *to p. those powers in motion*, IV, 3, 31. *you have p. me into rhyme*, V, 3, 63.

With *to*; a) followed by an inf., = to make: *I*

*am p. to know that your own science exceeds* ..., Meas. I, 1, 5. *had I first been p. to speak my mind*, H6B III, 1, 43. *you p. me to forget a lady's manners*, Cymb. II, 3, 110. b) by a noun, = 1) to bring to, to cause to come to; whether to acting or to suffering: *or my affection p. to the smallest teen*, Compl. 192. *'twould p. me to my slipper*, Tp. II, 1, 277. *to the perpetual wink might p. this ancient morsel*, 285. *some defect ... p. it* (her grace) *to the foil*, III, 1, 46. *to rise and be p. to death*, Meas. IV, 3, 29. R2 V, 3, 73. R3 III, 2, 105. III, 5, 76. Rom. III, 5, 17. Caes. IV, 3, 175. Hml. V, 2, 46. *p. me to this shame and trouble*, Err. V, 14. *p. the liveries to making*, Merch. II, 2, 123. *then she —s you to entreaty*, As IV, 1, 80. *let him p. me to my purgation*, V, 4, 44. *p. him to the sword*, 164. H6B III, 1, 284. *I shall now p. you to the height of your breeding*, All's II, 2, 1. *I p. you to the use of your own virtues*, V, 1, 15. *p. them* (your legs) *to motion*, Tw. III, 1, 87. *as mine honesty —s it to utterance*, Wint. I, 1, 21. *to p. you to it* (fear), IV, 4, 153. *to p. to torment*, John IV, 1, 84. *I p. thee now to thy book-oath: deny it, if thou canst*, H4B II, 1, 111. *p. him to execution*, H5 III, 6, 58. *if you would p. me to verses or to dance*, V, 2, 137. *our soldiers p. to flight*, H6C III, 3, 36. *it should be p. to no apparent likelihood of breach*, R3 II, 2, 135. *there's in him stuff that —s him to these ends*, H8 I, 1, 58. *while it is hot, I'll p. it to the issue*, V, 1, 178. *—ing him to rage*, Cor. II, 3, 205. *shall it be p. to that?* III, 1, 233. *you have p. me now to such a part which never I shall discharge to the life*, III, 2, 105. *p. him to choler*, III, 3, 25. *we need not p. new matter to his charge*, 76 (or = lay?). *—s us to our shifts*, Tit. IV, 2, 176. *nature —s me to a heavy task*, V, 3, 150. *his land's p. to their books*, Tim. I, 2, 206. *are p. to silence*, Caes. I, 2, 290. *p. your dread pleasures more into* (= unto) *command than to entreaty*, Hml. II, 2, 28 (cf. As IV, 1, 80). *to p. him to his purgation*, III, 2, 318. *we'll p. the matter to the present push*, V, 1, 318. *to p. him to ill thinking*, Oth. III, 4, 29. *p. me to some impatience*, Ant. II, 6, 43. *you shall p. your children to that destruction*, V, 2, 131. *go p. it to the haste*, 196. *and p. us to our answer*, Cymb. IV, 2, 161. *—s himself unto the shipman's toil*, Per. I, 3, 24. *p. me to present pain*, V, 1, 193. *to p. to it* = to try hard, to drive to straits: *he —s transgression to't*, Meas. III, 2, 101. *nay, p. me to't*, All's II, 2, 50. *p. him to't, let him have his way*, III, 6, 1. *we are tougher than you can p. us to't*, Wint. I, 2, 16. *they have a leader that will p. you to it*, Cor. I, 1, 233. *p. them not to't*, II, 2, 145. *do not p. me to't, for I am nothing, if not critical*, Oth. II, 1, 119. *and will upon the instant p. thee to't*, III, 3, 471 (try thee? or require thy activity?). 2) to leave, to give up, to confide to: *and to him p. the manage of my state*, Tp. I, 2, 69. *p. it to fortuna della guerra*, LLL V, 2, 533. *I'll p. my fortunes to your service*, Wint. I, 2, 440. *and p. his cause and quarrel to the disposing of the cardinal*, John V, 7, 91. *p. we our quarrel to the will of heaven*, R2 I, 2, 6. *being p. to nurse*, H6B IV, 2, 150. *his minority is p. unto the trust of Richard Gloster*, R3 I, 3, 12. *p. thy fortune to the arbitrement of bloody strokes*, V, 3, 89. *I p. it to your care*, H8 I, 2, 102. *'tis p. to lottery*, Troil. II, 1, 140. *which else would p. you to your fortune and the hazard of much blood*, Cor. III, 2, 60. *I p. myself to thy direction*, Mcb. IV, 3, 122. *to be p. to the arbitrement of swords*, Cymb. I, 4, 52. 3) to apply,

to employ: *gold that's p. to use*, Ven. 768. *thou usurer that —'st forth all to use*, Sonn. 134, 10. *what use to p. her to*, Err. III, 2, 97. Tw. III, 1, 56. *happy are they that hear their detractions and can p. them to mending*, Ado II, 3, 238. *I cannot p. him to a private soldier*, H4B III, 2, 177. 4) to impart: *—s fear to valour, courage to the coward*, Ven. 1158. *if their daughters be capable, I will p. it to them*, LLL IV, 2, 82. *who in spite p. stuff to some she beggar and compounded thee*, Tim. IV, 3, 272. *p. strength enough to it* (your sword) Lr. IV, 6, 235. *I do repent me that I p. it to you*, Oth. III, 3, 392. *—s to him all the learnings*, Cymb. I, 1, 43.

With *upon*, = to move, to incite to: *when his soaring insolence shall touch the people, which time shall not want, if he be p. upon it*, Cor. II, 1, 272. *'tis they have p. him on the old man's death*, Lr. II, 1, 101.

Joined with adverbs; a) *to p. apart* and *to p. away* = to send off, to remove: *to p. apart these your attendants*, Wint. II, 2, 14. *Henry p. apart, the next for me*, H6B III, 1, 383. *and twice desire that which with scorn she p. away*, Pilgr. 316. *two may keep counsel, —ing one away*, Rom. II, 4, 209. *p. away these dispositions*, Lr. I, 4, 241.

b) *to p. back* = to refuse, to say nay to, not to admit: *coming from thee, I could not p. him back*, Lucr. 843. *though she p. thee back*, Pilgr. 334. *petitioners for blood thou ne'er —'st back*, H6C V, 5, 80. *injury of chance —s back leave-taking*, Troil. IV, 4, 36. *when my indisposition p. you back*, Tim. II, 2, 139.

c) *to p. by* = 1) to push aside: *he p. it by with the back of his hand*, Caes. I, 2, 221. 229. 231. 2) to desist from, to abandon, to leave: *these both* (Lady Lucy and Bona) *p. by, a poor petitioner ... made prize and purchase of his lustful eye*, R3 III, 7, 183. *p. by this barbarous brawl*, Oth. II, 3, 172.

d) *to p. down* = to overthrow, to confound, to repress, to abolish, to baffle: *I'll exhibit a bill in the parliament for the —ing down of men*, Wiv. II, 1, 30. *the merriest* (usury) *was p. down*, Meas. III, 2, 7. *till eating and drinking be p. down*, 111. *you have p. him down*, Ado II, 1, 292 (with a quibble; cf. Shr. V, 2, 36 and Tw. I, 3, 88). *how the ladies and I have p. him down*, LLL IV, 1, 143. *my Kate does p. her down*, Shr. V, 2, 35. *when did I see thee p. so down?* Tw. I, 3, 86. *I saw him p. down with an ordinary fool*, II, 5, 90. *we'll p. thee down, 'gainst whom these arms we bear*, John II, 346. *to p. down Richard, that sweet lovely rose*, H4A I, 3, 175. *how a plain tale shall p. you down*, II, 4, 281. *—ing down kings and princes*, H6B IV, 2, 38. *until a power be raised to p. them down*, IV, 4, 40. *to p. me down and reign thyself*, H6C I, 1, 200. *to p. a tyrant down*, R3 V, 3, 255.

e) *to p. forth* = 1) to extend: *to p. forth my rightful hand in a well-hallowed cause*, H5 I, 2, 292. *p. forth thy hand*, H6B I, 2, 11. 2) to send out: *p. forth their sons to seek preferment out*, Gent. I, 3, 7. 3) to lay out: *—'st forth all to use*, Sonn. 134, 10. 4) to shoot out, to emit as a sprout: *peace —s forth her olive everywhere*, H4B IV, 4, 87. *her hedges p. forth disordered twigs*, H5 V, 2, 44. *to-day he —s forth the tender leaves of hopes*, H8 III, 2, 352. Wint. I, 2, 14.*

f) *to p. in* = a) to instate, to install in an office: *to blot out me and p. his own son in*, H6C II, 2, 92. b) to give in, to offer, to present: *I'll p. in bail*, All's V, 3, 286. *p. in now*, Titus, Tim. III, 4, 85 (i. e. your claim).

g) *to p. off* = 1) to lay aside, to dismiss, to discard: *I will p. off my hope,* Tp. III, 3, 7. *I cannot p. off my opinion so easily,* Wiv. II, 1, 243. *when you p. off that* (the court) *with such contempt,* All's II, 2, 6. *the clothiers have p. off the spinsters,* H8 I, 2, 32. *to p. me off,* II, 4, 21. 2) to turn away, to elude, to baffle: *finely p. off,* LLL IV, 1, 112. *there's a simple —ing off,* All's II, 2, 43. *you p. me off with limber vows,* Wint. I, 2, 47. *—s him off, slights him,* IV, 4, 200. *to p. off the shame,* Per. I, 1, 140. 3) to refuse: *your steward —s me off,* Tim. II, 2, 31. *which* (invitation) *my near occasions did urge me to p. off,* III, 6, 12. 4) to defer, to delay (by referring to): *—s it off to a compelled restraint,* All's II, 4, 44. *he hath p. me off to the succession of new days this month,* Tim. II, 2, 19.

h) *to p. on* = 1) to lay on (as a blow): *finely p. on,* LLL IV, 1, 115. 118. 2) to set to work: *the powers above p. on their instruments,* Mcb. IV, 3, 239. *we'll p. on those shall praise your excellence,* Hml. IV, 7, 132. *he was likely, had he been p. on, to have proved most royally,* V, 2, 408 (= had he become king). *one that in the authority of her merit did justly p. on the vouch of very malice itself,* Oth. II, 1, 147. 3) to incite, to instigate, to cause by instigating: *awakens me with this unwonted —ing on,* Meas. IV, 2, 120. *you ne'er had done it, but by our —ing on,* Cor. II, 3, 260. *why he —s on this confusion,* Hml. III, 1, 2. *deaths p. on by cunning and forced cause,* V, 2, 394. *you protect this course and p. it on by your allowance,* Lr. I, 4, 227. *if this poor trash of Venice stand the —ing on,* Oth. II, 1, 313. *when devils will the blackest sins p. on,* II, 3, 357. *I never had lived to p. on this,* Cymb. V, 1, 9.

i) *to p. out* = 1) to extend, to show: *p. out all your hands,* Tim. IV, 2, 28. *p. out your wit,* Rom. IV, 5, 124. 2) to make to forget one's part, to embarrass, to puzzle: *presence majestical would p. him out,* LLL V, 2, 102. *I have p. you out,* Wint. IV, 4, 378. 3) to extinguish, to blind: Compl. 250. Gent. V, 2, 13. Ado V, 3, 24. John IV, 1, 56. 69. Rom. V, 3, 2. Lr. IV, 2, 71. Oth. V, 2, 7. 10.

k) *to p. over* = to refer: *I p. you o'er to heaven and to my mother,* John I, 62.

l) *to p. up,* = 1) to hold up, to raise: *why Peace should not p. up her lovely visage,* H5 V, 2, 37. *why then do I p. up that womanly defence, to say I have done no harm?* Mcb. IV, 2, 78. 2) to hide in a place where a thing is kept when not used: *p. thy sword up* (in the scabbard) Tp. I, 2, 469. Tw. III, 4, 343. IV, 1, 42. John IV, 3, 79. 98. H4B II, 4, 222. H5 II, 1, 46. 109. R3 I, 2, 197. Cor. V, 6, 136. Tit. II, 1, 53. Rom. I, 1, 72. III, 1, 87. IV, 5, 123. 126. *p. up this* (letter) LLL IV, 1, 109 (in the pocket). All's IV, 3, 243. Lr. I, 2, 28. *had not your man p. up the fowl so suddenly,* H6B II, 1, 45 (called it back from pursuit). *we may p. up our pipes,* Rom. IV, 5, 96. Oth. III, 1, 20. *p. up thy gold,* Tim. IV, 3, 107. Hence 3) = not to resent, to pocket: *be dishonoured openly and basely p. it up without revenge,* Tit. I, 433. *nor am I yet persuaded to p. up in peace what already I have foolishly suffered,* Oth. IV, 2, 181.

4) to propose: *I'll p. another question to thee,* Hml. V, 1, 43 (the clown's speech).

II. intr. 1) to go or come by water, to sail: *who p. unluckily into this bay,* Err. V, 125. *the bark —s from her native bay,* Merch. II, 6, 15. *to p. to sea,* Err. V, 21. Tw. II, 4, 78. Wint. IV, 4, 509. *to p. forth,* Meas. I, 2, 14. Err. III, 2, 155. IV, 3, 35. H4B I, 1, 186. Troil. Prol. 7. Per. II Prol. 27. Ant. IV, 10, 7. *p. in,* Oth. II, 1, 25. 65. *p. off,* Ant. II, 7, 78. Per. V, 1, 3. *p. out,* Tp. V, 225. Err. III, 2, 190.

2) with *forth,* = to shoot out, to bud: *before one leaf p. forth,* Ven. 416. *to make us say: this is p. forth too truly,* Wint. I, 2, 14. *his negligence, his folly, fear ... sometimes —s forth,* 254. *hewing Rutland when his leaves p. forth,* H6C II, 6, 48. *your valour —s well forth,* Cor. I, 1, 255.

3) with *in,* = to intercede: *a wise burgher p. in for them,* Meas. I, 2, 103.

4) with *to,* = to go to it: *as any flax-wench that —s to before her troth-plight,* Wint. I, 2, 277.

**Putrify,** to corrupt: *blood untainted still doth red abide, blushing at that which is so —ed,* Lucr. 1750. *they would but stink and p. the air,* H6A IV, 7, 90. *most —ed core, so fair without,* Troil. V, 8, 1.

**Putter-on,** 1) author: *they vent reproaches most bitterly on you as p. of these exactions,* H8 I, 2, 24. 2) instigator: *you are abused and by some p.* Wint. II, 1, 141.

**Putter-out,** one who goes abroad (by sea), a voyager: *which now we find each p. of five for one will bring us good warrant of,* Tp. III, 3, 48 (a traveller of the class of five for one, i. e. one who puts to sea on purpose to see wonders, and therefore, on setting out on his voyage, places out a sum of money, on condition of receiving five for one at his return. The interpretation generally received is: one who lays out money; but abstractedly from the verb *to put out* not being used by Sh. in this sense, the context would then require: *each p. of one for five,* as Dyce and others are indeed bold enough to write).

**Puttock,** a kite: *who finds the partridge in the —'s nest,* H6B III, 2, 191. *a toad, a lizard, an owl, a p.* Troil. V, 1, 68. *I chose an eagle, and did avoid a p.* Cymb. I, 1, 140.

**Puzzel,** a hussy: H6A I, 4, 107; cf. *Pucelle.*

**Puzzle,** to perplex, to embarrass: *in which* (ignorance) *thou art more —d than the Egyptians in their fog,* Tw. IV, 2, 48. *the dread of something after death —s the will,* Hml. III, 1, 80. *your presence needs must p. Antony,* Ant. III, 7, 11.

**Pygmalion,** an ancient artist who fell in love with a female statue which he had made, and prevailed on the gods to give it life: Meas III, 2, 48.

**Pyramid,** one of the celebrated structures of ancient Egypt: Sonn. 123, 2.* Mcb. IV, 1, 57. Ant. II, 7, 21.

**Pyramis,** the same: H6A I, 6, 21. Pl. *pyramises:* Ant. II, 7, 40. *pyramides:* V, 2, 61.

**Pyramus,** the lover of Thisbe: Mids. I, 2, 12. 24 etc. Tit. II, 3, 231.

**Pyrenean,** the range of mountains between France and Spain: John I, 203.

**Pyrrhus,** the son of Achilles: Lucr. 1449. 1467. Troil. III, 3, 209. Hml. II, 2, 472. 485. 494. 499. 502. 509. 513. 536.

**Pythagoras,** the famous Greek philosopher, supposed to have professed the doctrine of the migration of souls: Merch. IV, 1, 131. As III, 2, 187. Tw. IV, 2, 54. 62.

# Q.

**Q,** writing of Ff for *cue* in R3 III, 4, 27.

**Quadrangle,** the inner square or court of a large building: H6B I, 3, 156.

**Quaff,** to drink freely and copiously: *this —ing and drinking,* Tw. I, 3, 14. With an accus.: Shr. I, 2, 277. H4B IV, 5, 86. With *off:* Shr. III, 2, 174.

**Quagmire,** a bog: *and make a q. of your mingled brains,* H6A I, 4, 109. *o'er bog and q.* Lr. III, 4, 54.

**Quail,** subst. the bird Perdix coturnix; trained to fighting by the ancients (as cocks at present): Ant. II, 3, 37. Cant term for a loose woman: Troil. V, 1, 57.

**Quail,** vb. 1) tr. to quell, to crush, to overawe: *q., crush, conclude and quell,* Mids. V, 292 (Pyramus' speech). *when he meant to q. and shake the orb,* Ant. V, 2, 85.

2) intr. to shrink, to faint, to slacken: *let not search and inquisition q.* As II, 2, 20. *there is no —ing now, because the king is certainly possessed of all our purposes,* H4A IV, 1, 39. *this may plant courage in their —ing breasts,* H6C II, 3, 54. *my false spirits q. to remember,* Cymb. V, 5, 149.

**Quaint,** fine, neat, pretty, pleasant: *my q. Ariel,* Tp. I, 2, 317. *q. in green she shall be loose enrobed,* Wiv. IV, 6, 41. *a fine, q., graceful and excellent fashion,* Ado III, 4, 22. *the q. mazes in the wanton green,* Mids. II, 1, 99. *the owl wonders at our q. spirits,* II, 2, 7. *tell q. lies,* Merch. III, 4, 69. *the q. musician, amorous Licio,* Shr. III, 2, 149. *a gown more q., more pleasing,* IV, 3, 102. *with forged q. conceit,* H6A IV, 1, 102. *to show how q. an orator you are,* H6B III, 2, 274.

**Quaintly,** finely, neatly, pleasantly: *the lines are very q. writ,* Gent. II, 1, 128. *a ladder q. made of cords,* III, 1, 117. *'tis vile, unless it may be q. ordered,* Merch. II, 4, 6. *to carve out dials q.* H6C II, 5, 24. *breathe his faults so q. that they may seem the taints of liberty,* Hml. II, 1, 31. *and time ... with your fine fancies q. eche,* Per. III Prol. 13.

**Quake,** to tremble; mostly with fear: Ven. 899. 1045. Lucr. 1393. 1556 *(with cold).* Wiv. III, 5, 104. Meas. III, 1, 74. Ado I, 1, 274 *(thou wilt q. for this shortly).* Mids. II, 2, 148. V, 224. Wint. V, 1, 199. John III, 1, 18. H6A I, 1, 156. H6B IV, 8, 17. R3 I, 3, 162. III, 5, 1. Tit. V, 2, 40. Hml. III, 2, 410. Lr. IV, 6, 110. Cymb. II, 4, 5 *(q. in the present winter's state).* Per. III, 2, 15 *(as the earth did q.).*

**Quaked** = affected with quakes, quaking: *where ladies shall be frighted, and, gladly quaked, hear more,* Cor. I, 9, 6.

**Qualification,** appeasement, abatement: *even out of that will I cause these of Cyprus to mutiny, whose q. shall come into no true taste again but by the displanting of Cassio,* Oth. II, 1, 282.

**Qualified,** 1) of a quality, of a kind: *she is so q. as may beseem the spouse of any noble gentleman,* Shr. IV, 5, 66. *with thoughts so q. as your charities shall best instruct you, measure me,* Wint. II, 1, 113.

2) having a qualification, endowed, fit: *that which ordinary men are fit for, I am q. in,* Lr. I, 4, 37. *more fair, virtuous, wise, chaste, constant, q.* Cymb. I, 4, 65 (some M. Edd. *constant-qualified).*

**Qualify,** to temper, to moderate, to abate, to soften: *his rage of lust by gazing —ed, slacked, not suppressed,* Lucr. 424. *absence seemed my flame to q.* Sonn. 109, 2. *the fire's rage,* Gent. II, 7, 22. *to enforce or q. the laws,* Meas. I, 1, 66. *he doth with holy abstinence subdue that in himself which he spurs on his power to q. in others,* IV, 2, 86. *all this amazement can I q.* Ado V, 4, 67. *to q. his rigorous course,* Merch. IV, 1, 7. *your discontenting father strive to q.* Wint. IV, 4, 543. *this inundation of mistempered humour rests by you only to be —ed,* John V, 1, 13. *is your blood so madly hot that no discourse of reason can q. the same?* Troil. II, 2, 118. *my love admits no —ing dross,* IV, 4, 9. *time —es the spark and fire of it,* Hml. IV, 7, 114. *till some little time hath —ed the heat of his displeasure,* Lr. I, 2, 176. *one cup, and that was craftily —ed too,* Oth. II, 3, 41 (mixed with water).

**Quality,** 1) any thing which can be predicated as characteristic of a thing or person; a natural or adventitious property or adjunct: *favour, savour, hue and —es, whereat the impartial gazer late did wonder,* Ven. 747. *of plagues, or dearths, or seasons' q.* Sonn. 14, 4. *full of virtue, bounty, worth and —es beseeming such a wife,* Gent. III, 1, 65. *endued with worthy —es,* V, 4, 153. *of what q. was your love, then?* Wiv. II, 2, 223. *I have many ill —es,* Ado II, 1, 106. *owner of no one good q.* All's III, 6, 12. *his —es being at this poor price,* IV, 3, 308. *fruit of baser q.* H5 I, 1, 62. (peace) *bless us with her former —es,* V, 2, 67 (the state of things described in what precedes). *—es are so weighed,* Lr. I, 1, 5 (Qq *equalities). all the —es that man loves woman for,* Cymb. V, 5, 166.

2) nature, character, particular condition (German: *Wesen, Art): may know her grief, but not her grief's true q.* Lucr. 1313. *we have no good that we can say is ours, but ill-annexed opportunity or kills his life or else his q.* 875. *what is the q. of mine offence, being constrained with dreadful circumstance?* 1702. *it is the q. of the climate,* Tp. II, 1, 200. *the q. of mercy is not strained,* Merch. IV, 1, 184. *he must observe the q. of persons,* Tw. III, 1, 70. *the q. of the time and quarrel might well have given us bloody argument,* III, 3, 31. *the q. and hair of our attempt brooks no division,* H4A IV, 1, 61. *this present q. of war,* H4B I, 3, 36. *to establish here a peace indeed, concurring both in name and q.* IV, 1, 87. *you must now speak Sir John Falstaff fair, which swims against your stream of q.* V, 2, 34. *what worst, as oft, hitting a grosser q., is cried up for our best act,* H8 I, 2, 84. *of grave and austere q.* Tim. I, 1, 54. *the flamen that scolds against the q. of flesh,* IV, 3, 156. *why birds and beasts from q. and kind,* Caes. I, 3, 64. *change their faculties to monstrous q.* 68. *such rebel blood that will be thawed from the true q. with that which melteth fools,* III, 1, 41. *whose true-fixed and resting q.* 61. *I hold ambition of so airy and light a q. that it is but a shadow's shadow,* Hml. II, 2, 268. *take more composition and fierce q.* Lr. I, 2, 12. *the q. of nothing hath not such need to hide itself,* 33. *you know the fiery q. of the duke,* II, 4, 93. 97. *my heart's subdued even to the very q. of my lord,* Oth. I, 3, 252. *knows*

all *—es of human dealings*, III, 3, 259 (Ff Q2. 3 *quantities*). *all q., pride, pomp and circumstance of glorious war*, 353. *note the —es of people*, Ant. I, 1, 54. *whose q., going on, the sides o' the world may danger*, I, 2, 198. *things outward do draw the inward q. after them, to suffer all alike*, III, 13, 33. *give her what comforts the q. of her passion shall require*, V, 1, 63.

3) virtue, power, efficacy (of things); accomplishment, faculty (of persons): *each stone's dear nature, worth and q.* Compl. 210. *showed thee all the —es of the isle*, Tp. I, 2, 337. *in your fine frame hath love no q.?* All's IV, 2, 4. *allay the burning q. of that fell poison*, John V, 7, 8. *the venom of such looks, we fairly hope, have lost their q.* H5 V, 2, 19. *their (the herbs', stones' etc.) true —es*, Rom. II, 3, 16. *his —es were beauteous as his form*, Compl. 99. *to thy strong bidding task Ariel and all his q.* Tp. I, 2, 193. *she has more —es than a water-spaniel*, Gent. III, 1, 271. *admiring of his —es*, Mids. I, 1, 231. *in fortunes, in graces, and in —es of breeding*, Merch. II, 7, 33. *hiding from me all gentleman-like —es*, As I, 1, 74. *her wondrous —es and mild behaviour*, Shr. II, 50. *where an unclean mind carries virtuous —es*, All's I, 1, 49. *we will, according to your strengths and — es, give you advancement*, H4B V, 5, 73. *thy rare —es*, H8 II, 4, 137. Troil. I, 2, 94. *the Grecian youths are full of q.* Troil. IV, 4, 78 (= are highly accomplished). *I have bred her in —es of the best*, Tim. I, 1, 125. *give us a taste of your q.* Hml. II, 2, 452. *a q. wherein you shine*, IV, 7, 73. *taking a beggar without less q.* Cymb. I, 4, 24.* *the adornment of my —es*, III, 5, 141. *has she any —es?* Per. IV, 2, 50. 53.

4) profession: *a man of such perfection as we do in our q. much want*, Gent. IV, 1, 58. *attend your office and your q.* Wiv. V, 5, 44. *what q. are they of?* Meas. II, 1, 59. *what is thy name? I know thy q.* H5 III, 6, 146. *will they pursue the q. no longer than they can sing?* Hml. II, 2, 363;*cf. 452. Peculiar passage: *because you are not of our q., but stand against us like an enemy*, H4A IV, 3, 36 (do not follow the same cause, are not of our party). Plur. *—es* = arts, tricks: *she hath lived too long, to fill the world with vicious —es*, H6A V, 4, 35. cf. Gent. III, 1, 271.

5) rank: *Love no god, that would not extend his might, only where —es were level*, All's I, 3, 118. *with such powers as might hold sortance with his q.* H4B IV, 1, 11. *your name? your q.?* Lr. V, 3, 120. *he shall our commission bring to you, with such things else of q. and respect as doth import you*, Oth. I, 3, 283. = high rank: *gentlemen of blood and q.* H5 IV, 8, 95. *any man of q. or degree*, Lr. V, 3, 111. Oth. II, 3, 110. *a stranger of his q.* Cymb. I, 4, 30.

6) a state of affairs producing certain effects; occasion, cause: *give him note of our approach, with the whole q. wherefore*, Troil. IV, 1, 44. *know you the q. of Lord Timon's fury?* Tim. III, 6, 117.

7) manner: *hate counsels not in such a q.* Merch. IV, 2, 6. *with how depraved a q.* Lr. II, 4, 139 (Qq of how deprived *a q.*).

**Qualm**, a fit of sickness, nausea: Ado III, 4, 75. LLL V, 2, 279. H4B II, 4, 40 (the hostess pronounces calm). H6B I, 1, 54.

**Qualmish**, affected with nausea: H5 V, 1, 22.

**Quandary**, perplexity; the word supposed to be meant by canary in Mrs Quickly's language: Wiv. II, 2, 61. 64.

**Quantity**, 1) measure, mass, extent, number, size: *he is not q. enough for that Worthy's thumb*, LLL V, 1, 137 (Armado's speech). *my love prizes not q. of dirty lands*, Tw. II, 4, 85. *my moiety in q. equals not one of yours*, H4A III, 1, 97. *he enriched poor straggling soldiers with great q.* (of gold) Tim. V, 1, 7. *with loves above their (thy griefs') q.* V, 4, 18. *to set on some q. of barren spectators to laugh too*, Hml. III, 2, 45. *it reserved some q. of choice*, III, 4, 75. *with all their q. of love*, V, 1, 293. *how much the q., the weight as much, as I do love my father*, Cymb. IV, 2, 17.

2) correspondent degree, proportion: *things base and vile, holding no q., love can transpose to form and dignity*, Mids. I, 1, 232 (bearing no proportion to what they are estimated at by love). *women's love and fear holds q.; in neither aught, or in extremity*, Hml. III, 2, 177 (have the same proportion).

3) a small portion, any thing very little and diminutive: *thou rag, thou q., thou remnant*, Shr. IV, 3, 112. *retaining but a q. of life*, John V, 4, 23. *if I were sawed into —es, I should make four dozen of such*, H4B V, 1, 70.

In Oth. III, 3, 259 Ff and later Qq *quantities*, Q1 and M. Edd. *qualities*.

**Quarrel**, subst. any dispute or contest that cannot be settled by words; a private difference as well as a dissension and combat for a public cause and on a larger scale: a) *in the managing of —s he is wise*, Ado II, 3, 197. *enter into a q.* 203. *in a false q. there is no true valour*, V, 1, 120. *a q. already!* Merch. V, 146. 238. As II, 7, 151. V, 4, 48. 51. 70. Shr. I, 1, 116. 236. I, 2, 27. IV, 2, 84. Tw. III, 4, 266. 327. V, 364. R2 I, 2, 6. 37. II, 1, 248. H4B IV, 5, 195. H5 IV, 1, 219. 225. IV, 8, 69. H6A II, 4, 134. IV, 1, 118. 136. H6B II, 1, 28. II, 3, 53. H6C I, 2, 5. 6. R3 I, 4, 223. H8 I, 3, 20. Tit. I, 293. 465. II, 1, 47. 67. II, 3, 54. V, 3, 20. Rom. I, 1, 23. 111. II, 4, 168. III, 1, 24. 159. Mcb. IV, 3, 83. Hml. I, 3, 66. Lr. II, 1, 56. II, 2, 66. III, 7, 77. IV, 6, 38. Oth. II, 3, 52. 215. 290. Ant. II, 2, 52. Cymb. I, 4, 51. *to pick a q.* H4A III, 3, 76. *to take up a q.* (= to compose it): As V, 4, 104. Tw. III, 4, 320. *to have a q. to* = to have a difference, to be at odds with: Ado II, 1, 243. Tw. III, 4, 248. Cor. IV, 5, 133. b) *holy seems the q. upon your grace's part*, All's III, 1, 4. *the quality of the time and q. might well have given us bloody argument*, Tw. III, 3, 31. *put his cause and q. to the disposing of the cardinal*, John V, 7, 91. *O, would the q. lay upon our heads*, H4A V, 2, 48. *derives from heaven his q. and his cause*, H4B I, 1, 206. *I make my q. in particular*, IV, 1, 96. *hold this q. up*, IV, 2, 48. *foreign —s*, IV, 5, 215. H5 II, 4, 17. V, 1, 133. 240. V, 2, 20. H6A V, 4, 105. H6C II, 2, 65. II, 5, 91. III, 3, 216. Troil. Prol. 10. II, 2, 123. 138. II, 3, 79. 217. V, 7, 21. Cor. IV, 5, 133. Tit. V, 3, 102. Mcb. I, 2, 14 (O. Edd. *quarry*). *in q.* or *in the q. of* = in the cause of: *in the king's q.* H5 IV, 1, 180. *in q. of the house of York the worthy gentleman did lose his life*, H6C III, 2, 6. *to fight in q. of the house of Lancaster*, R3 I, 4, 209. *my blood in Rome's great q. shed*, Tit. III, 1, 4.

Often = cause, occasion and motive of dispute: *what's thy q.?* R2 I, 3, 33. *the q. of a true inheritor*, H4B IV, 5, 169. *it is a q. most unnatural, to be revenged on him that loveth you*, R3 I, 2, 134. 136. *since the q. will bear no colour for the thing he is*, Caes. II,

1, 28. H6B III, 2, 233. Hml. IV, 4, 55. Mcb. IV, 3, 137. Lr. V, 3, 56.

In H8 II, 3, 14: *if that q. fortune do divorce it* (pomp) *from the bearer, 'tis a sufferance panging* etc., some commentators suppose the word to be used in the sense of dart, arrow; but it may well be abstr. pro concr., = quarreller.

**Quarrel**, vb. to wrangle, to seek occasion of a fray, to pick a quarrel (German: *Händel suchen*): Ado V, 1, 51. As V, 4, 94. Tw. I, 3, 33. Rom. I, 1, 39. 59. III, 1, 26. 32. 34. Tim. III, 5, 27. Hml. II, 1, 25. Lr. I, 4, 222. Ant. I, 3, 66. With *at:* Wiv. I, 1, 303. Troil. II, 3, 182. With *with:* Ado V, 1, 50. Rom. III, 1, 18. 20. 26. *to q. with* = to be in contrast with, to be contrary to: *some defect in her did q. with the noblest grace she owed,* Tp. III, 1, 45. *yet more —ing with occasion,* Merch. III, 5, 61 (contrary to, and seeking to elude, the matter in question; cavilling). *our people q. with obedience,* John V, 1, 9.

**Quarreller**, one who picks quarrels: Tw. I, 3, 31.

**Quarrellous**, disposed to quarrel: Cymb. III, 4, 162.

**Quarrelsome**, the same: As V, 4, 85. 99. Shr. I, 2, 13.

**Quarry**, 1) a place where stones are taken from rocks: Oth. I, 3, 141.

2) a heap of slaughtered game (Fr. *curée*): *I'ld make a q. with thousands of these slaves,* Cor. I, 1, 202. *fortune, on his damned q. smiling,* Mcb. I, 2, 14 (M. Edd. *quarrel*). *on the q. of these murdered deer,* IV, 3, 206. *this q. cries on havoc,* Hml. V, 2, 375.

**Quart**, a vessel containing the fourth part of a gallon: Wiv. III, 5, 3. Shr. Ind. 2, 90. Wint. IV, 3, 8. H4B V, 3, 66. *a q. pot,* H6B IV, 10, 16.

**Quart d'écu**, see *Cardecue.*

**Quarter**, subst. 1) a fourth part: Wiv. I, 1, 28. IV, 4, 5. Meas. III, 2, 213. Err. III, 2, 112. Ado V, 2, 85. Shr. IV, 3, 109. Wint. IV, 3, 85. IV, 4, 814. H4A II, 4, 19. III, 3, 20. H5 I, 2, 215. Rom. III, 1, 36. Mcb. V, 1, 34. = the fourth part of a year: *once or twice in a q.* H4B V, 1, 53.

2) a region in the hemisphere: *all the —s that they know i' the shipman's card,* Mcb. I, 3, 16.

3) the place where troops are lodged: All's III, 6, 70. John V, 5, 20. H6A II, 1, 63. 68. Tim. V, 4, 60. Ant. IV, 3, 22.

4) peace, friendship, concord: *keep fair q. with his bed,* Err. II, 1, 108 (cf. John V, 5, 20). *in q. and in terms like bride and groom,* Oth. II, 3, 180.

**Quarter**, vb. 1) to divide into four parts: *a thought which, —ed, hath but one part wisdom and ever three parts coward,* Hml. IV, 4, 42. = to execute by cutting or tearing into four parts: John II, 506. 508.

2) to divide in general: *I that with my sword —ed the world,* Ant. IV, 14, 58.

3) to cut to pieces, to slaughter: *—ing steel and climbing fire,* H6A IV, 2, 11. *make a quarry with thousands of these —ed slaves,* Cor. I, 1, 203. *their infants —ed,* Caes. III, 1, 268.

4) to place the arms of another family in the compartments of a shield: Wiv. I, 1, 24. 26.

5) Partic. —ed = lodged, stationed: R3 V, 3, 34. H8 V, 4, 56. Caes. IV, 2, 28. *behold their —ed fires,* Cymb. IV, 4, 18 (burning in the quarters of their army).

**Quat**, a pustule, a pimple: *I have rubbed this young q. almost to the sense,* Oth. V, 1, 11 (Q1 *gnat*).

**Quatch-buttock**, a squat or flat backside: All's II, 2, 18.

**Quean**, a contemptible wench, a hussy: *a witch, a q., an old cozening q.* Wiv. IV, 2, 180. *as a scolding q. to a wrangling knave,* All's II, 2, 27. *throw the q. in the channel,* H4B II, 1, 51. cf. *Cotquean.*

**Queasiness**, nausea, disgust: *they did fight with q., as men drink potions,* H4B I, 1, 196.

**Queasy**, 1) inclined to nausea, squeamish, fastidious: *in despite of his quick wit and his q. stomach he shall fall in love with Beatrice,* Ado II, 1, 399. *q. with* = disgusted with: *q. with his insolence,* Ant. III, 6, 20.

2) ticklish, nice: *I have one thing of q. question, which I must act,* Lr. II, 1, 19.*

**Queen**, subst. a female sovereign, or the consort of a king: Sonn. 96, 5. Tp. I, 2, 449. II, 1, 75. 246. III, 2, 115. V, 150. LLL II, 8. IV, 1, 125. Mids. I, 1, 173. H6A V, 3, 111. H6B I, 1, 12 etc. etc. *q. of love,* Ven. 251; cf. 175. *beauty's q.* Pilgr. 3, 12. *the q. o'the sky,* Tp. IV, 70. 82. *q. of night,* Gent. IV, 2, 100. As III, 2, 2. *the fairy q.* Wiv. IV, 4, 71. IV, 6, 20. V, 5, 50. Mids. II, 1, 8 etc. *Dian no q. of virgins,* All's I, 3, 119. *Juno, that is q. of marriage,* Per. II, 3, 30. *Phoebus' lute, the q. of music,* Pilgr. 112. *that miracle and q. of gems,* Tw. II, 4, 88. *she is the q. of curds and cream,* Wint. IV, 4, 161. *q. o' the feast,* Per. II, 3, 17. *O q. of —s,* LLL IV, 3, 41. H8 IV, 1, 141. III, 2, 95. *all your acts are —s,* Wint. IV, 4, 146. *Henry's q.* H6A V, 3, 117 (= his royal consort). H6C IV, 1, 102. *Menelaus' q.* Troil. Prol. 9. *the q. of Ptolemy,* Ant. I, 4, 6. *q. to the worthy Leontes,* Wint. III, 2, 12. *the turtle and his q.* Phoen. 31. *my q.* Mids. III, 2, 375. IV, 1, 80. Wint. I, 2, 27. H6A V, 5, 51. H6C II, 6, 90. III, 2, 88. 89. H8 III, 2, 405. V, 1, 168. Hml. I, 2, 8. Per. III Prol. 40 etc. Used as a flattering compellation to other women: Merch. II, 1, 12. All's I, 1, 116. Cymb. I, 1, 92. I, 3, 5. = mistress: *these mine eyes, true leaders to their q.* Ven. 503. *of either's colour was the other q.* Lucr. 66. *his fancy's q.* Tw. V, 397. *but now I was q. o'er myself,* Merch. III, 2, 171. *she was a q. over her passion,* Lr. IV, 3, 15.

Adjectively: *his q. mother* = his royal mother, Hml. III, 1, 190.

**Queen**, vb., with *it,* = to play the queen: *I'll q. it no inch farther,* Wint. IV, 4, 460. *a three-pence bowed would hire me to q. it,* H8 II, 3, 37.

**Quell**, subst. euphemistically = murder: *who shall bear the guilt of our great q.* Mcb. I, 7, 72.

**Quell**, vb. to crush, to destroy: Gent. IV, 2, 13. Mids. V, 292. H6A I, 1, 163. H6B V, 1, 212. Tim. IV, 3, 163.

**Queller**, in *Boy-queller, Man-queller, Woman-queller,* q. v.

**Quench**, 1) tr. a) to put out, to extinguish (a fire or light): Ven. 192. Lucr. 47. 1231. 1468. Sonn. 154, 9. Gent. II, 7, 20. Err. V, 173. Mids. II, 1, 162. All's II, 1, 167. Wint. IV, 4, 61. John III, 1, 345. IV, 1, 63. H4B Ind. 26. H6C II, 1, 80. IV, 8, 8. H8 I, 1, 148. II, 4, 80. Cor. III, 1, 197. V, 2, 78. Tit. V, 1, 134. Rom. I, 1, 91. I, 5, 30. Lr. III, 7, 61. Oth. II, 1, 15. V, 2, 8. Per. I, 4, 4. III, 1, 5. Figuratively; of blushes: Ven. 50. Wint. IV, 4, 67. Per. IV, 2, 135. of love: Meas. III, 1, 250. of thirst: Shr. I, 1, 24.

b) to suppress, to stifle, to check: *the supposition*

*of the lady's death will q. the wonder of her infamy*, Ado IV, 1, 241. *—ing my familiar smile with an austere regard of control*, Tw. II, 5, 72. *might q. the zeal of all professors else*, Wint. V, 1, 107. *to q. mine honour*, H8 V, 2, 16. *what hath —ed them hath given me fire*, Mcb. II, 2, 2. *—ed of hope, not longing*, Cymb. V, 5, 195 (checked, disappointed in my hope).

2) intr. a) to be extinguished, to go out: *in never —ing fire*, R2 V, 5, 109.

b) to lose zeal, to become cool: *dost thou think in time she will not q. and let instructions enter where folly now possesses?* Cymb. I, 5, 47.

**Quenchless**, inextinguishable: Lucr. 1554. H6C I, 4, 28.

**Quern**, a handmill: *skim milk, and sometimes labour in the q.* Mids. II, 1, 36.

**Quest**, 1) search: *with all due diligence that horse and sail and high expense can stead the q.* Per. III Prol. 21. *in q.* or *in the q. of* = in search of: Err. I, 1, 130. I, 2, 40. = a body of searchers: *the senate hath sent about three several —s to search you out*, Oth. I, 2, 46 (cf. *search* in I, 1, 159).

2) pursuit, suit: *cease your q. of love*, Lr. I, 1, 196. *had, having, and in q. to have, extreme*, Sonn. 129, 10. *many Jasons come in q. of her*, Merch. I, 1, 172. *go in q. of beauty*, John II, 426.

3) inquiry: *volumes of report run with these false and most contrarious —s upon thy doings*, Meas. IV, 1, 62.

4) inquest, jury: *to cide this title is impanneled a q. of thoughts*, Sonn. 46, 10. *what lawful q. have given their verdict up*, R3 I, 4, 189. *crowner's q. law*, Hml. V, 1, 24.

**Questant**, seeker, aspirant: *when the bravest q. shrinks, find what you seek, that fame may cry you loud*, All's II, 1, 16.

**Question**, subst. 1) the act of asking, and the thing asked: Tp. I, 2, 140. 184. Ado V, 2, 84. LLL II, 119. Merch. III, 4, 79. As III, 2, 291. All's II, 2, 16. 20. 31. 41 (*I will be a fool in q.*). II, 5, 42 (*suffer q. for your residence*). Tw. I, 5, 191. John I, 195. 199. H6B I, 2, 80. 82. H8 II, 4, 212. Troil. I, 2, 173. IV, 5, 248. Hml. II, 1, 10. III, 1, 56. III, 2, 212. Lr. II, 4, 66. *to ask a p. a q.:* Wiv. IV, 1, 16. LLL II, 117. All's I, 1, 123. III, 2, 7. H4A II, 3, 89. II, 4, 451. 452. H6A I, 2, 87. Cor. IV, 5, 205. Tim. II, 2, 61. Hml. V, 1, 65. Cymb. I, 5, 11. *to make a q.* H4B IV, 1, 167. Oth. III, 4, 17. *let me but move one q. to your daughter*, Ado IV, 1, 74. *I'll put another q. to thee*, Hml. V, 1, 43 (the clown's speech). *the q. standeth thus*, H4B I, 3, 15. IV, 1, 53. *in q.* = in demand: *a commodity in q.* Ado III, 3, 192 (quibbling).

2) a thing disputed, a subject of debate: *a certain q. in the law*, H6A IV, 1, 95. *not ever the justice and the truth o' the q. carries the due o' the verdict with it*, H8 V, 1, 131. *the q. of his death is enrolled in the Capitol*, Caes. III, 2, 41. *debate the q. of this straw*, Hml. IV, 4, 26.

3) judicial trial: *a commodity in q.* Ado III, 3, 192 (quibbling). *who now has these poor men in q.* Wint. V, 1, 198. *he that was in q. for the robbery*, H4B I, 2, 68.

Hence also a trial and decision by the force of arms, as the ultima ratio regum: *so may he* (the Turk) *with more facile q. bear it* (Cyprus) Oth. I, 3, 23.

4) controversy, doubt: *controversy hence a q. takes, whether ... or ...*, Compl. 110. *that is a q.: how shall*

*we try it?* Err. V, 421. *breed a kind of q. in our cause*, H4A IV, 1, 68. *ay, there's the q.* H6B IV, 2, 149. *how that might change his nature, there's the q.* Caes. II, 1, 13. *to call in q.* = to doubt of: Tw. I, 4, 6. Troil. IV, 4, 86. *to make q.* = to doubt: *I fell; and yet do q. make, what I should do again for such a sake*, Compl. 321. *you do me now more wrong in making q. of my uttermost*, Merch. I, 1, 156. *I no q. make to have it*, 184. *make that thy q. and go rot*, Wint. I, 2, 324. Troil. I, 2, 174. Cor. II, 1, 246. *no q.* = no doubt: *wise! why, no q. but he was*, Meas. III, 2, 146. *no q.* Tw. I, 3, 92. *no q. of that*, H6B IV, 2, 61. Troil. II, 3, 155. Oth. IV, 3, 63. *out of q.* = out of doubt: Ado II, 1, 346. V, 4, 117. LLL IV, 1, 30. Mids. III, 2, 279. Tw. V, 355. H5 V, 1, 48. *past q., sans q.*, and *in contempt of q.*, in the same sense: Tw. I, 3, 104. LLL V, 1, 91. Tw. II, 5, 98.

5) subject, matter, cause: *that is not the q.* Wiv. I, 1, 227. *as it appears in the true course of all the q.* Ado V, 4, 6. *since the first sword was drawn about this q.* Troil. II, 2, 18. *the cause and q. now in hand*, 164. *I'll decline the whole q.* II, 3, 55. *we dare not move the q. of our place*, 89. *the king that was and is the q. of these wars*, Hml. I, 1, 111. *little eyases that cry out on the top of q.* II, 2, 356 (above the subject, more and louder than the occasion requires).*there was no money bid for argument, unless the poet and the player went to cuffs in the q.* 373 (obscure passage). *though some necessary q. of the play be then to be considered*, III, 2, 47. *so jump upon this bloody q.* V, 2, 386. *these domestic and particular brawls are not the q. here*, Lr. V, 1, 31. *the q. of Cordelia and her father requires a fitter place*, V, 3, 58. *if you there did practise on my state, your being in Egypt might be my q.* Ant. II, 2, 40. *he being the mered q.* III, 13, 10.

6) discussion, disquisition, consideration: *then of thy beauty do I q. make, that thou among the wastes of time must go*, Sonn. 12, 9. *all kind of arguments and q. deep*, Compl. 121. *Escalus, though first in q., is thy secondary*, Meas. I, 1, 47 (= first in consideration). *I subscribe not that, nor any other, but in the loss of q.* II, 4, 90 (cf. *Loss*). *the difference that holds this present q. in the court*, Merch. IV, 1, 172. *make the trial of it in any constant q.* Tw. IV, 2, 53. *this haste was hot in q.* H4A I, 1, 34. *the unquiet time did push it out of farther q.* H5 I, 1, 5. *though war nor no known quarrel were in q.* II, 4, 17. *laid any scruple in your way, which might induce you to the q. on't*, H8 II, 4, 151. *I'ld have it come to q.* Lr. I, 3, 13. *one thing of a queasy q.* II, 1, 19 (to be discussed, or treated, with nicety). *thy great employment will not bear q.* V, 3, 33. *if we contend, out of our q. wipe him*, Ant. II, 2, 81. *this gentleman in q.* Cymb. I, 1, 34. *to call in q.* = to take into consideration, to inquire into, to examine: *neither call the giddiness of it in q., nor ...*, As V, 2, 6. *'tis the way to call hers* (beauty) *in q. more*, Rom. I, 1, 235. *and call in q. our necessities*, Caes. IV, 3, 165. *I must call't in q.* Hml. IV, 5, 217. *she'll bereave you o' the deeds too, if she call your activity in q.* Troil. III, 2, 60 (= if she examines it by trying).

7) conversation, speech, talk: *I will not stay thy —s; let me go*, Mids. II, 1, 235. *you may as well use q. with the wolf why he hath made the ewe bleat for the lamb*, Merch. IV, 1, 73. *I'll stay no longer q.* 346. *I met the duke yesterday and had much q. with him*, As III, 4, 39. *where meeting with an old religious man,*

after some *q. with him, was converted,* V, 4, 167. *where we will have some q. with the shepherd,* Wint. IV, 2, 55. *staying no longer q.* H4B I, 1, 48 (German: *Rede stehen*). *health to you during all q. of the gentle truce,* Troil. IV, 1, 11. *speak not ...; q. enrages him,* Mcb. III, 4, 118. *niggard of q., but, of our demands, most free in his reply,* Hml. III, 1, 13. *made she no verbal q.?* Lr. IV, 3, 26 (= did she not speak?). *came it by request and such fair q. as soul to soul affordeth,* Oth. I, 3, 113.

**Question,** vb. 1) to ask; absol.: *let me q. more in particular,* Hml. II, 2, 244. *you q. with a wicked tongue,* III, 4, 12. With a clause: *than q. how 'tis born,* Wint. I, 2, 433. V, 3, 139. With an accus. a) indicating the person asked: *my daughter will I q. how she loves you,* Wiv. III, 4, 94. *do you q. me for my simple true judgment?* Ado I, 1, 167. *q. him yourself,* I, 2, 20. As II, 4, 64. II, 7, 172. All's II, 1, 208. III, 5, 35. H4A II, 3, 106. II, 4, 33. H4B I, 3, 53. H5 II, 4, 31. V, 2, 211. Troil. III, 3, 42. Tit. II, 3, 48. Mcb. I, 5, 4. b) indicating the thing asked after: *to q. our delay,* H5 II, 4, 142. *— ed me the story of my life,* Oth. I, 3, 129. The thing asked after with *of: I am —ed by my fears of what may chance or breed upon our absence,* Wint. I, 2, 11. *I'll q. you of my lord's tricks,* 60. *go we to the man that took him, q. of his apprehension,* H6C III, 2, 122. *now will I q. Cassio of Bianca,* Oth. IV, 1, 94. *to q. me of your king's departure,* Per. I, 3, 12.

2) to examine, to inquire into by interrogatory: *give me leave to q.* Meas. V, 272. *q. your desires,* Mids. I, 1, 67. *q. your royal thoughts,* H4B V, 2, 91. *q. her proudly,* H6A I, 2, 62. *to every county where this is —ed send our letters,* H8 I, 2, 99. *and q. this most bloody piece of work,* Mcb. II, 3, 134. *I would thou grewest unto the shores o' the haven and, q. with my jealous thought where you may be,* Sonn. 57, 9. *let your reason with your choler q. what 'tis you go about,* H8 I, 1, 130. With *of: q. no further of the case, how or which way,* H6A II, 1, 72.

3) to doubt of: *it is not to be —ed that they had gathered a wise council to them,* H8 II, 4, 50.

4) to discuss, to consider, to reason: *nor dare I q. with my jealous thought where you may be,* Sonn. 57, 9. *let your reason with your choler q. what 'tis you go about,* H8 I, 1, 130. With *of: q. no further of the case, how or which way,* H6A II, 1, 72.

5) to talk, to converse: *after supper long he —ed with modest Lucrece,* Lucr. 122. *disarm them, and let them q.* Wiv. III, 1, 78. *think you q. with the Jew,* Merch. IV, 1, 70. *feed yourselves with —ing,* As V, 4, 144. *stay not to q., for the watch is coming,* Rom. V, 3, 158. *had I not brought the knowledge of your mistress home, I grant we were to q. further,* Cymb. II, 4, 52 (i. e. to fight a duel). Transitively, = to speak to: *with many holiday and lady terms he —ed me,* H4A I, 3, 47. *live you? or are you aught that man may q.?* Mcb. I, 3, 43. *it would be spoke to; q. it,* Hml. I, 1, 45 (Qq *speak to it*).

**Questionable,** propitious to conversation, affable: *thou comest in such a q. shape that I will speak to thee,* Hml. I, 4, 43. cf. *Unquestionable.**

**Questionless,** adj. doubtless: Merch. I, 1, 176. Per. V, 1, 45.

**Questrist,** one going in quest of another: *some thirty of his knights, hot —s after him, met him at gate,* Lr. III, 7, 17 (Qq *questrits*).

**Queubus,** name of a place in Sir Andrew's geography: Tw. II, 3, 25.

**Quick,** adj. 1) living, alive: *I had rather be set q. i' the earth and bowled to death with turnips,* Wiv. III, 4, 90. *one that's dead is q.* All's V, 3, 304. *not to be buried, but q. and in mine arms,* Wint. IV, 4, 132. *the mercy that was q. in us ... by your own counsel is suppressed and killed,* H5 II, 2, 79. *O earth, gape open wide and eat him q.* R3 I, 2, 65. *thou'rt q., but yet I'll bury thee,* Tim. IV, 3, 44. *'tis for the dead, not for the q.* Hml. V, 1, 137. 274. 302. cf. the quibbles in LLL V, 2, 687 and R3 IV, 4, 361. *to the q.* = to the living flesh, so as to cause a keen sensation: *with their high wrongs I am struck to the q.* Tp. V, 25. Err. II, 2, 122. Tit. IV, 2, 28. IV, 4, 36. cf. *I'll tent him to the q.* Hml. II, 2, 626. *but to the q. of the ulcer: Hamlet comes back,* IV, 7, 124.

2) lively, sprightly, nimble: *mine eyes are gray and bright and q. in turning,* Ven. 140. *now q. desire hath caught the yielding prey,* 547. *in youth q. bearing and dexterity,* Lucr. 1389. *my verse, so far from variation or q. change,* Sonn. 76, 2. *you have a q. wit,* Gent. I, 1, 132. *dumb jewels ... more than q. words do move a woman's mind,* III, 1, 91. *his q. wit,* Ado II, 1, 399. V, 2, 11. *is there no q. recreation granted?* LLL I, 1, 162. *therefore apt, because q.* I, 2, 25. 31. *a q. venue of wit,* V, 1, 62. *q. Biron hath plighted faith to me,* V, 2, 283. *I long to see q. Cupid's post,* Merch. II, 9, 100. *sudden and q. in quarrel,* As II, 7, 151. *if the q. fire of youth light not your mind,* All's IV, 2, 5. *O spirit of love, how q. and fresh art thou,* Tw. I, 1, 9. *thy assailant is q., skilful and deadly,* III, 4, 245. *his q. wit,* H4B I, 2, 193. *apprehensive, q., forgetive,* IV, 3, 107. *shall our q. blood, spirited with wine, seem frosty?* H5 III, 5, 21. *cheer his grace with q. and merry words,* R3 I, 3, 5. *give way, dull clouds, to my q. curses,* 196. *bold, q., ingenious,* III, 1, 155. *a woman of q. sense,* Troil. IV, 5, 54. *an eagle hath not so green, so q., so fair an eye,* Rom. III, 5, 222. *that q. spirit that is in Antony,* Caes. I, 2, 29. *he was q. mettle when he went to school,* 300. *his q. hunting,* Oth. II, 1, 313. *the q. comedians will stage us,* Ant. V, 2, 216.

3) fresh: *where the q. freshes are,* Tp. III, 2, 75. *when our q. winds lie still,* Ant. I, 2, 114 (some M. Edd. *q. minds*). *the air is q. there, and it pierces and sharpens the stomach,* Per. IV, 1, 28.

4) sensitive, perceptive in a high degree: *you have a q. ear,* Gent. V, 2, 63. *night ... the ear more q. of apprehension makes,* Mids. III, 2, 178. *to have an open ear, a q. eye,* Wint. IV, 4, 685. *q. is mine ear to hear of good towards him,* R2 II, 1, 234. *my eye's too q., my heart o'erweens too much,* H6C III, 2, 144. *have a q. eye to see,* Oth. I, 3, 293 (Ff and later Qq *if thes hast eyes to see*). *the gods are q. of ear,* Per. IV, 1, 70 (hear also a short prayer).

5) swift, speedy: Ven. 38. Sonn. 45, 5. 55, 7. 113, 7. Tp. I, 2, 366. IV, 39. Meas. I, 1, 54. IV, 2, 113. LLL I, 2, 30. II, 31. Mids. III, 2, 342. Shr. IV, 2, 11. All's V, 3, 40. H4A II, 4, 286. H5 V Chor. 23. V, 1, 91. H6A V, 3, 8. H6B III, 1, 288. R3 IV, 4, 283. H8 I, 2, 66. Cor. I, 4, 10. Rom. V, 3, 120. Tim. I, 1, 91. Hml. III, 1, 176. V, 1, 139. V, 2, 120. Lr. III, 6, 104. IV, 7, 35. Oth. II, 1, 80. Ant. I, 2, 203. III, 1, 19. = rash: *you must not be so q.* LLL II, 118. *your reasons are too shallow and too q.* R3 IV, 4, 361.

6) pregnant, with child; in the language of Costard: *she's q.; the child brags in her belly already,* LLL V, 2, 682. *Jaquenetta that is q. by him,* 687.

**Quick**, adv. speedily, rapidly: Tp. V, 304. Wiv. IV, 2, 84. IV, 5, 3. 44. Meas. IV, 1, 7. IV, 3, 96. LLL V, 1, 63. Mids. I, 1, 149. III, 2, 256. Merch. II, 9, 1. H4A III, 1, 230. Oth. V, 1, 3. Ant. I, 3, 5. IV, 15, 31. V, 2, 39. 286.

**Quick-answered**, furnished with, or having, nimble and brisk answers: Cymb. III, 4, 161.

**Quick-conceiving**, readily and easily understanding: H4A I, 3, 189.

**Quicken**, 1) tr. a) to make alive: —*s what's dead*, Tp. III, 1, 6. *to breathe life into a stone, q. a rock*, All's II, 1, 77. R3 IV, 4, 297. Tim. IV, 3, 184. Ant. I, 3, 69.

b) to cheer, to refresh: *q. his embraced heaviness with some delight*, Merch. II, 8, 52. *music and poesy use to q. you*, Shr. I, 1, 36. H5 IV, 1, 20. H6A IV, 6, 13. R3 IV, 4, 124.

2) intr. to receive life: *I see a* —*ing in his eye*, Meas. V, 500. *these hairs will q. and accuse thee*, Lr. III, 7, 39. *this forked plague is fated to us when we do q.* Oth. III, 3, 277. *summer flies that q. even with blowing*, IV, 2, 67. *q. with kissing*, Ant. IV, 15, 39.

**Quickly**, (compar. —*er*, All's I, 1, 135) speedily; without delay, soon: Ven. 87. 520. 990. 1192. Sonn. 153, 3. Compl. 113. Pilgr. 416. Tp. V, 86. Gent. II, 4, 34. II, 6, 40. IV, 2, 89. Wiv. III, 3, 2. 155. 157. III, 5, 48. IV, 2, 112. IV, 4, 83. V, 3, 4. Meas. II, 4, 51. III, 1, 151. 279. IV, 3, 33. Ado IV, 1, 126. LLL V, 2, 244. 899. Mids. I, 1, 7. As II, 6, 15. III, 2, 208. IV, 3, 132. Shr. III, 2, 243. All's I, 2, 66. II, 4, 12. Tw. I, 5, 314. III, 1, 14. John V, 6, 1. R2 I, 3, 260. H5 V, 2, 145. H6A I, 3, 28. V, 6, 19. H6B I, 1, 169. I, 3, 140. II, 1, 151. II, 4, 69. III, 1, 133. 171. V, 1, 84. H6C I, 1, 69. I, 4, 174. IV, 1, 132. IV, 8, 7. V, 1, 65. R3 IV, 4, 313. Mcb. I, 7, 2. Ant. III, 7, 23. Cymb. V, 3, 62 etc. etc.

**Quickly**, name of the hostess and procuress of Falstaff: Wiv. I, 2, 3 etc. H4A III, 3, 106. H4B II, 1, 49 etc. H5 II, 1, 20. 82.

**Quickness**, speed: Hml. IV, 3, 45.

**Quick-raised**, swiftly levied: H4A IV, 4, 12.

**Quicksand**, moving sand affording an unsolid footing: *a q. of deceit*, H6C V, 4, 26. —*s*, Ant. II, 7, 65.

**Quick-shifting**, rapidly changing: *q. antics, ugly in her eyes*, Lucr. 459.

**Quicksilver**, mercury; emblem of swiftness: *the rogue fled from me like q.* H4B II, 4, 248. *swift as q. it courses through the natural gates and alleys of the body*, Hml. I, 5, 66.

**Quick-witted**, having a ready and sprightly wit: Shr. V, 2, 38.

**Quiddities**, equivocations, subtilties, cavils: H4A I, 2, 51. Hml. V, 1, 107 (Ff *quiddits*).

**Quiddits**, the same: Hml. V, 1, 107 (Qq *quiddities*).

**Quid for quo**, measure for measure, tit for tat: *I cry you mercy, 'tis but Q.* H6A V, 3, 109.

**Quiet**, subst. 1) freedom from disturbance or alarm, tranquillity, peace, repose: *her house is sacked, her q. interrupted*, Lucr. 1170. *my limbs ..., my mind ... no q. find*, Sonn. 27, 14. *q. in the match*, Shr. II, 332. *thought to fill his grave in q.* Wint. IV, 4, 465. *to thee it shall descend with better q.* H4B IV, 5, 188. IV, 1, 71. H6C I, 1, 173. R3 III, 1, 142. H8 II, 2, 75. Rom. I, 1, 98. III, 5, 100. Mcb. II, 3, 18 (*at q.*).

Hml. III, 1, 3. V, 1, 321. Oth. I, 1, 101. II, 1, 319. III, 3, 152. Per. I, 2, 5.

2) freedom from passion or emotion of the mind, peace of the soul, patience, calmness: *the staring ruffian shall it keep in q.* Ven. 1149. *I will depart in q.* Err. III, 1, 107. *she is much out of q.* Tw. II, 3, 144. *thy greatest help is q.* H6B II, 4, 67. *for your own q.* H8 II, 4, 63.

**Quiet**, adj. (comp. —*er* in Tw. III, 4, 147) 1) free from disturbance or alarm, at rest, still, tranquil, peaceful: *the q. closure of my breast*, Ven. 782. *mustering to the q. cabinet* (the heart) Lucr. 442. *q. days*, Tp. IV, 24. *Jove would ne'er be q.* Meas. II, 2, 111. *he hath got a q. catch*, Shr. II, 333. *q. life*, V, 2, 108. *the house will be the* —*er*, Tw. III, 4, 147. John III, 4, 134. R2 I, 3, 96. 137. IV, 69. H4A II, 4, 117. V, 1, 25. H4B I, 2, 171. II, 4, 199. H5 I, 2, 79. H6A II, 1, 6. III, 2, 110. H6B IV, 10, 19. H6C II, 5, 40. R3 I, 3, 60. V, 3, 43. 149. 160. H8 III, 2, 380. V, 1 77. Hml. I, 1, 10. II, 2, 77. Oth. I, 3, 95. IV, 1, 54. Cymb. III, 3, 30. IV, 2, 280. Per. III, 1, 29. 42.

2) free from emotion, calm, patient, contented: *be q.* Tp. IV, 215. 235. Err. V, 38. 112. Shr. III, 2, 219. H4B II, 4, 174. H6B I, 3, 146. Cor. V, 6, 135. Rom. I, 5, 89. Hml. V, 1, 288. Per. II. Prol. 5. *I am glad he is so q.* Wiv. I, 4, 95. *a wretched soul ... we bid be q.* Err. II, 1, 35. *I can be q.* LLL I, 2, 171. *translate the stubbornness of fortune into so q. and so sweet a style*, As II, 1, 20. *a couple of q. ones*, Shr. III, 2, 242. *a killing tongue and a q. sword*, H5 III, 2, 36.

Misapplied by Dogberry in Ado III, 3, 42.

Adverbially: *a man may live as q. in hell*, Ado II, 1, 266. *let me q. go*, Mids. III, 2, 314. John IV, 1, 80. H8 IV, 2, 81 (= still, without motion).

**Quiet**, vb. to calm, to appease: *q. thy cudgel*, H5 V, 1, 54 (Pistol's speech). *q. yourselves*, H6A IV, 1, 115.

**Quietly**, 1) still, without motion: *lie q.* Ven. 709.

2) without disturbance or alarm, peaceably: *so shall you q. enjoy your hope*, Shr. III, 2, 138. H6A V, 3, 153. 159. H6C I, 2, 15. Tim. III, 4, 54. III, 5, 44. Hml. I, 4, 49. Per. IV, 2, 29.

3) calmly: *these quarrels must be q. debated*, Tit. V, 3, 20.

**Quietness**, 1) tranquillity, peace: H6A V, 1, 10. H6C IV, 3, 16. Troil. II, 1, 90. Cor. IV, 6, 3. Ant. I, 3, 53.

2) calmness: Merch. IV, 1, 12. Ant. IV, 15, 68.

**Quietus**, final settlement of an account, audit: *her audit, though delayed, answered must be, and her q. is to render thee*, Sonn. 126, 12. *when he himself might his q. make with a bare bodkin*, Hml. III, 1, 75.

**Quill**, 1) the prickle of a porcupine: Hml. I, 5, 20.

2) the strong feather of the wing of a bird: *to pluck the* —*s from ancient ravens' wings*, Lucr. 949. *the wren with little q.* Mids. III, 1, 131 (Bottom's song). Hence = pen: Lucr. 1297. Sonn. 83, 7. 85, 3. cf. *Goose-quill.*

Obscure passage: *then we may deliver our supplications in the q.* H6B I, 3, 4 (Steevens: written, penned; Nares: in form and order, like a quilled ruff; Singer: *in the coil;* Halliwell: all together).♦

**Quilled**, in *Sharp-quilled*, q. v.

**Quillets**, sly tricks in argument, subtleties, cavilling, chicanery: *some tricks, some q., how to cheat the* *devil*, LLL IV, 3, 288. *these nice sharp q. of the law*, H6A II, 4, 17. *do not stand on q. how to slay him*, H6B III, 1, 261. *crack the lawyer's voice, that he may never more ... sound his q. shrilly*, Tim. IV, 3, 155. *his quiddities, his q.* Hml. V, 1, 108. *keep up thy q.* Oth. III, 1, 25.

**Quilt**, a cover made by putting wool or cotton between two cloths; Falstaff called so: H4A IV, 2, 54.

**Quinapalus**, an apocryphal philosopher mentioned by the clown in Tw. I, 5, 39.

**Quince**, the fruit of Pyrus Cydonia: Rom. IV, 4, 2. Name in Mids. I, 2, 8. 15 etc.

**Quintain**, a post or figure set up for beginners in tilting to run at: *my better parts are all thrown down, and that which here stands up is but a q., a mere lifeless block*, As I, 2, 263.

**Quintessence**, *(quíntessence)* an extract from a thing, containing its virtues in a small quantity; and hence the best and purest part of a thing: *the q. of every sprite heaven would in little show*, As III, 2, 147.* *what is this q. of dust?* Hml. II, 2, 321.

**Quintus**, Roman name in Cor. II, 3, 249.

**Quip**, a sharp jest, a sarcasm: *her sudden —s, the least whereof would quell a lover's hope*, Gent. IV, 2, 12. *no —s now, Pistol*, Wiv. I, 3, 45. *—s and sentences and these paper bullets of the brain*, Ado II, 3, 249. *this is called the Q. Modest*, As V, 4, 79. *in thy —s and thy quiddities*, H4A I, 2, 51.

**Quire**, subst. 1) company: *the whole q. hold their hips and laugh*, Mids. II, 1, 55.

2) a company of singers, a chorus: *placed a q. of such enticing birds*, H6B I, 3, 92.

3) a place for singers: *our cage we make a q., as doth the prisoned bird*, Cymb. III, 3, 43.

**Quire**, vb. to sing in concert and be tuned accordingly: *the smallest orb ... like an angel sings, still —ing to the young-eyed cherubins*, Merch. V, 62. *my throat of war which —d with my drum*, Cor. III, 2, 113.

**Quirk**, 1) humour, caprice: *I have felt so many —s of joy and grief, that the first face of neither, on the start, can woman me unto't*, All's III, 2, 51. *belike this is a man of that q.* Tw. III, 4, 268.* *she has me her —s, her reasons*, Per. IV, 6, 8.

2) a shallow conceit: *I may chance have some odd —s and remnants of wit broken on me*, Ado II, 3, 245. *one that excels the —s of blazoning pens*, Oth. II, 1, 63.

**Quit**, (impf. and partic. *quit*; partic. *—ed* only in Wint. V, 1, 192) 1) to leave: *time had not scythed all that youth begun, nor youth all q.* Compl. 13. *the rats had q. it*, Tp. I, 2, 148. *q. the vessel*, 211. *that we q. this place*, II, 1, 322. Meas. II, 4, 28. Wint. V, 1, 192. III, 2, 168. V, 3, 86. H5 III, 2, 92. III, 5, 3. V Chor. 33. Mcb. III, 4, 93 *(q. my sight)*. Lr. IV, 2, 94. Ant. III, 13, 65. Cymb. I, 1, 38 *(he q. being)*. V, 5, 397. Per. III, 2, 18.

2) to set at liberty, to free, to deliver: *your master —s you*, Tw. V, 329. With *of: for your great seats now q. you of great shames*, H5 III, 5, 47. *—ing thee thereby of ten thousand shames*, H6B III, 2, 218. *God safely q. her of her burthen*, H8 V, 1, 70. *q. = free, safe, rid: he that dies this year is q. for the next*, H4B III, 2, 255. *so I would he were* (up to the neck in Thames) *and I by him, so we were q. here*, H5 IV, 1, 122. *I am q.* Tim. IV, 3, 397. *of this contradiction you shall now be q.* Cymb. V, 4, 169. cf. the pun in H4B II, 4, 371.

3) to clear, to excuse, to absolve, to acquit: *till*

*thou canst q. thee by thy brother's mouth of what we think against thee*, As III, 1, 11. *here I q. him*, All's V, 3, 300. *I would I could q. all offences with as clear excuse*, H4A III, 2, 19. *I think thou art q. for that*, H4B II, 4, 371. *God q. you in his mercy*, H5 II, 2, 166.

4) to remit, to release from: *unless a thousand marks be levied, to q. the penalty*, Err. I, 1, 23. *those earthly faults, I q. them all*, Meas. V, 488. *to q. the fine for one half of his goods*, Merch. IV, 1, 381.

5) to requite, to repay, to pay for: *like doth q. like, and measure still for measure*, Meas. V, 416. *your evil —s you well*, 501 (you receive good for evil). *to q. their grief, tell thou the lamentable tale of me*, R2 V, 1, 43 (to pay them for their sad stories. Qq *quite*). *I shall q. you*, H5 III, 2, 110 (tell you also interesting things). *unless the Lady Bona q. his pain*, H6C III, 3, 128 (= reward). *Plantagenet doth q. Plantagenet*, R3 IV, 4, 20. 64. *your children's children q. it in your age*, V, 3, 262. *to q. the bloody wrongs upon her foes*, Tit. I, 141. *I'll q. thy pains*, Rom. II, 4, 204 (O. Edd. *quite*). *is't not perfect conscience, to q. him with this arm?* Hml. V, 2, 68. *if Hamlet give the first or second hit, or q. in answer of the third exchange*, 280. *enkindle all the sparks of nature, to q. this horrid act*, Lr. III, 7, 87. *God q. you!* Ant. III, 13, 124. *whom he may at pleasure whip ... to q. me*, 151. *thy loss is more than can thy portage q.* Per. III, 1, 35. *to q. oneself of* = to be even with: *to q. me of them thoroughly*, Ado IV, 1, 202. *q. of*, and *q. with*, = even with: *to be full q. of those my banishers*, Cor. IV, 5, 89. *Hortensio will be q. with thee*, Shr. III, 1, 92.

6) to q. oneself = to acquit oneself: *now q. you well*, Lr. II, 1, 32.

**Quite**, vb. = quit; reading of Qq in R2 V, 1, 43; of Ff in Rom. II, 4, 204; of Qq in Per. III, 2, 18 (Ff *leave*, M. Edd. *quit*).

**Quite**, adv. completely: Ven. 783. Lucr. 1563. Sonn. 5, 7. 25, 11. 62, 11. 72, 3. 103, 7. Pilgr. 253. Tp. IV, 190. Gent. II, 4, 195. Meas. I, 3, 30. II, 2, 186. III, 2, 110. IV, 4, 23. Err. III, 2, 1. LLL I, 1, 70. 142. V, 2, 150. Mids. II, 1, 32. 251. III, 2, 88. Merch. V, 251. As III, 4, 45. All's II, 3, 127. Tw. III, 1, 75. John IV, 3, 4. H5 V Chor. 22. H6A I, 1, 90. III, 1, 25. IV, 1, 43. H6C IV, 3, 6. Hml. III, 1, 162. Ant. V, 2, 100 etc.

**Quittal**, requital: *as in revenge or q. of such strife*, Lucr. 236.

**Quittance**, subst. 1) discharge from a debt, acquittance: *in any bill, warrant, q. or obligation*, Wiv. I, 1, 10. *omittance is no q.* As III, 5, 133.

2) payment, return, requital: *rendering faint q. to Harry Monmouth*, H4B I, 1, 108. *shall forget the office of our hand sooner than q. of desert*, H5 II, 2, 34. *no gift to him, but breeds the giver a return exceeding all use of q.* Tim. I, 1, 291.

**Quittance**, vb. to requite, to retaliate: *to q. their deceit*, H6A II, 1, 14.

**Quiver**, subst. a case for arrows: Ado I, 1, 274.

**Quiver**, adj. nimble, active: H4B III, 2, 301.

**Quiver**, vb. to tremble, to shake: Lucr. 1030. H6B IV, 7, 97. Tit. II, 3, 14. Rom II, 1, 19. II, 4, 171.

**Quoif**, a cap or hood: Wint. IV, 4, 226. H4B I, 1, 147.*

**Quoint**, name in R2 II, 1, 284.

**Quoit**, subst. something thrown at a fixed object in play: *a' plays at —s well*, H4B II, 4, 266.

**Quoit**, vb. to throw: *q. him down like a shove-groat shilling*, H4B II, 4, 206.

**Quondam**, that was; former: *these q. carpet-mongers*, Ado V, 2, 32. *I did converse this q. day with a companion of the king's*, LLL V, 1, 7 (Sir Nathaniel's speech). *hold the q. Quickly for the only she*, H5 II, 1, 82. *this is the q. king*, H6C III, 1, 23. III, 3, 153. Troil. IV, 5, 179.

**Quote**, (sometimes written *cote* or *coate*, and probably pronounced so; cf. Gent. IV, 2, 18. 19) 1) to note, to observe, to examine: *I have perused thee, and —d joint by joint*, Troil. IV, 5, 233. *note how she —s the leaves*, Tit. IV, 1, 50. *I am sorry that with better heed and judgment I had not —d him*, Hml. II, 1, 112.

2) to construe, to interpret: *our letters showed much more than jest. So did our looks. We did not q. them so*, LLL V, 2, 796. cf. *Misquote*.

3) to perceive, to read: *the illiterate will q. my loathsome trespass in my looks*, Lucr. 812. *how q. you my folly? I q. it in your jerkin*, Gent. II, 4, 18. 19. *what curious eye doth q. deformities*, Rom. I, 4, 31.

4) to note, to set down, as in writing: *his face's own margent did q. such amazes*, LLL IV, 3, 246 (like marginal notes). *her amber hair for foul hath amber —d*, IV, 3, 87. *he's —d for a most perfidious slave*, All's V, 3, 205. *a fellow by the hand of nature marked, —d and signed to do a deed of shame*, John IV, 2, 222.

**Quoth**, say, says, said: 1) pres. say, says; used only to repeat in jest or irony what another has said before: *did they, q. you?* LLL IV, 3, 221. *veal, q. the Dutchman*, V, 2, 247. *at hand, q. pickpurse*, H4A II,

1, 53. 54. *I do, q. he, perceive my king is tangled in affection*, H8 III, 2, 34 (quotation from a letter). *q. he*, Tp. III, 2, 36. H4A II, 1, 44 (Ff *q. a*). *q. a*, Wiv. II, 1, 142. All's I, 3, 90. H4A II, 1, 44 (Qq *q. he*). H4B V, 3, 17. Troil. V, 1, 82. Rom. II, 4, 124. Per. II, 1, 82 (O. Edd. *ke-tha*).

2) impf. said; sometimes placed before the speech: *q. he: she took me kindly by the hand*, Lucr. 253. *q. he. I must deflower*, 348. *q. she: reward not hospitality*, 575. *q. she: here's but two*, Troil. I, 2, 171. *q. she: before you tumbled me*, Hml. IV, 5, 62. Oftener inserted in the speech: *q. Venus*, Ven. 187. *q. Adon*, 769. *q. Lucrece*, Lucr. 1284. *q. Lucretius*, 1800. *q. who?* Gent. II, 1, 69. *q. my master*, 70. *q. the king*, LLL V, 2, 103. *q. Jaques*, As II, 1, 54. *q. my uncle*, R3 II, 4, 12. *q. Dighton*, IV, 3, 9. *q. the dove-house*, Rom. I, 3, 33. *q. my husband*, 55. *q. I*: Gent. IV, 4, 27. 29. Err. II, 1, 62. 63. 64. 66. 67. LLL V, 2, 277. As II, 7, 18. H5 II, 3, 18. R3 III, 7, 38. IV, 1, 72. Mcb. I, 3, 5. *q. he*: Ven. 409. 523. 715. 718. Lucr. 330. 512. 645. 667. Pilgr. 235. Gent. IV, 4, 28. Err. II, 1, 62. 63. 64. 66. 71. LLL IV, 3, 109. As II, 1, 47. 51. II, 7, 18. 23. Shr. I, 1, 219. III, 2, 162. All's I, 2, 58. R2 V, 4, 4. H8 I, 2, 193. Troil. I, 2, 175. 179. Cor. I, 1, 134. Rom. I, 3, 41. 48. Ant. I, 5, 42. *q. she*: Ven. 427. 493. 537. 589. 613. 717. 720. 997. 1015. 1070. 1133. 1177. Lucr. 652. Pilgr. 84. 125. 147. 185. Shr. II, 153. All's I, 3, 74. R3 V, 1, 26. Troil. I, 2, 177.

**Quotidian**, a fever whose paroxysms return every day: *he seems to have the q. of love upon him*, As III, 2, 383. Mrs Quickly knows *a burning q. tertian*, H5 II, 1, 124.

# R.

**R**, the eighteenth letter of the alphabet: *both (begin) with an R. Ah, mocker! that's the dog's name*, Rom. II, 4, 222 (cf. *Dog*).

**Rabato** (O. Edd. *rebato*) a kind of ruff: Ado III, 4, 6.

**Rabbit**, the animal Lepus cuniculus: LLL III, 19. Shr. IV, 4, 101. H4B II, 2, 91.

**Rabbit-sucker**, a sucking rabbit: H4A II, 4, 480.

**Rabble**, 1) a crowd: *bring the r., o'er whom I give thee power, here to this place*, Tp. IV, 37. *at his heels a r. of his companions*, Wiv. III, 5, 76. *we met my wife, her sisters, and a r. more of vile confederates*, Err. V, 236. *followed with a r. that rejoice to see my tears*, H6B II, 4, 32. *there's a trim r. let in*, H8 V, 4, 75. *your disordered r. make servants of their betters*, Lr. I, 4, 277.

2) the mean people, populace: *the r. should have first unroofed the city*, Cor. I, 1, 222. *make the r. call our cares fears*, III, 1, 136. IV, 2, 33. Mcb. V, 8, 29. Hml. IV, 5, 102.

**Rabblement**, rabble: Caes. I, 2, 245.

**Race**, 1) a root: *a r. or two of ginger*, Wint. IV, 3, 50 (cf. *Raze*).

2) lineage, generation (of men); breed (of animals or plants): *a wanton herd or r. of youthful and unhandled colts*, Merch. V, 72. *make conceive a bark of baser kind by bud of nobler r.* Wint. IV, 4, 95. *of the Nevils' noble r.* H6B III, 2, 215. *a happy r. of kings*, R3 V, 3, 157. *the whole r. of mankind*, Tim. IV, 1, 40.

*Duncan's horses, the minions of their r.* Mcb. II, 4, 15. *the getting of a lawful r.* Ant. III, 13, 107. *a valiant r.* Cymb. V, 4, 83. *pupils of noble r.* Per. V Prol. 9. Peculiar passage: *none our parts so poor but was a r. of heaven*, Ant. I, 3, 37 (= a breed of heaven, of heavenly origin. Warburton: had a smack or flavour of heaven).

3) natural disposition: *thy vile r., though thou didst learn, had that in't which good natures could not abide to be with*, Tp. I, 2, 358. *now I give my sensual r. the rein*, Meas. II, 4, 160.

**Race**, running, course: Sonn. 51, 11. John III, 3, 39. H6C II, 3, 1.

**Rack**, subst. floating vapour, a cloud: *permit the basest clouds to ride with ugly r. on his celestial face*, Sonn. 33, 6. *and like this insubstantial pageant faded, leave not a r. behind*, Tp. IV, 156. *as we often see ... the r. stand still*, Hml. II, 2, 506. *the r. dislimns*, Ant. IV, 14, 10.

**Rack**, subst. an engine of torture: Meas. V, 313. Merch. III, 2, 25. 26. 32. Wint. III, 2, 177. H4A II, 4, 262. H6A II, 5, 3. Troil. I, 2, 152. Lr. V, 3, 314 (O. Edd. *wrack*). Oth. III, 3, 335.

**Rack**, vb. to move as clouds; to fleet: *three suns ... not separated with the —ing clouds*, H6C II, 1, 27.

**Rack**, vb. 1) to extend, to stretch, to strain; a) trans.: *being lacked and lost, why, then we r. the value*, Ado IV, 1, 222. *that (my credit) shall be —ed, even* to the uttermost, Merch. I, 1, 181. thousand escapes of wit make thee the father of their idle dreams and r. thee in their fancies, Meas. IV, 1, 65 (form strained and unnatural conceptions of thee, disfigure thee; cf. Racker). b) intr. = to strain, to make violent efforts: a pair of tribunes that have – ed for Rome, to make coals cheap, Cor. V, 1, 16 (O. Edd. wracked).

2) to torture by stretching the limbs: Meas. V, 317. H6B III, 1, 376.

3) to put to pain, to torment, to harass: I'll r. thee with old cramps, Tp. I, 2, 369. how have the hours —ed and tortured me, Tw. V, 226. the commons hast thou —ed, H6B I, 3, 131 (i. e. by exaction).

In LLL V, 2, 828 O. Edd. —ed, M. Edd. rank.

**Racker**, one who disfigures by forcing into an unnatural form (or simply = tormentor?): such —s of orthography, as to speak dout, when he should say doubt, LLL V, 1, 21.

**Racket**, the instrument with which players at tennis strike the ball: H4B II, 2, 23. H5 I, 2, 261.

**Raddock** (some M. Edd. ruddock) the redbreast: Cymb. IV, 2, 224.

**Radiance**, brightness shooting in rays or beams: All's I, 1, 99. Lr. I, 1, 111. Used of eyes: weak sights their sickly r. do amend, Compl. 214.

**Radiant**, beaming, bright: Wiv. V, 5, 50. Mids. III, 1, 95. Tw. I, 5, 181. Hml. I, 5, 55. Lr. II, 2, 113. Cymb. I, 6, 86. V, 4, 121. V, 5, 475.

**Radish**, the root of Raphanus: H4B III, 2, 334. Not inflected in the plural: a bunch of r. H4A II, 4, 206.

**Raft**, a float: Err. V, 348.

**Rag**, 1) a piece torn off, a tatter: not a r. of money, Err. IV, 4, 89. tear a passion to tatters, to very —s, Hml. III, 2, 11.

2) a shabby beggarly person: you witch, you r., you baggage, Wiv. IV, 2, 194 (the later Ff and some M. Edd. hag). thou r., thou quantity, thou remnant, Shr. IV, 3, 112. thou r. of honour, R3 I, 3, 233. these over-weening —s of France, V, 3, 328. thy father, that poor r. Tim. IV, 3, 271 (cf. Tag-rag).

3) Plur. —s, = worn out clothes, mean dress: Wiv. II, 2, 27. Err. III, 2, 99. LLL IV, 1, 84. Wint. IV, 3, 56. 58. John II, 457. H6B IV, 1, 46. Tim. IV, 3, 303. Lr. II, 4, 48. IV, 6, 171. Cymb. V, 5, 4.

**Ragamuffins** (O. Edd. rag of Muffins) paltry fellows: H4A V, 3, 36.

**Rage**, subst. 1) violent anger, fury: Lucr. 1419. Sonn. 23, 3. Compl. 55. Tp. I, 2, 276. LLL IV, 1, 95. Mids. V, 49. 225. Merch. IV, 1, 13. Tw. III, 4, 213. IV, 2, 137. John III, 1, 329. 341. 344. IV, 2, 261. 264. IV, 3, 49. 85. R2 I, 1, 19. 173. III, 3, 59. V, 1, 30. H5 III, 2, 24. IV, 7, 82. H6A IV, 7, 11. H6B III, 1, 174. IV, 1, 112. H6C I, 1, 265. 1, 4, 28. R3 I, 2, 188. I, 3, 278. I, 4, 229. II, 1, 56. H8 III, 1, 101. Troil. I, 3, 52. V, 10, 6. Cor. II, 3, 205. III, 1, 241. 248. 312. V, 6, 137. 148. Tit. IV, 2, 114. Rom. Prol. 10. I, 1, 91. III, 1, 66. Tim. V, 4, 39. Caes. II, 1, 176. III, 2, 127. Mcb. III, 6, 12. Hml. III, 3, 89. IV, 7, 93. Lr. I, 2, 182. IV, 4, 19. Oth. II, 3, 173. Ant. II, 5, 70. IV, 12, 44. IV, 14, 123. Cymb. I, 1, 77. 88. Per. I, 2, 107. V, 3, 97. Plur. —s: H5 IV, 7, 37 (Fluellen's speech). Cor. V, 3, 85. to be in r. Lr. II, 4, 299. to fall in r. Cor. II, 3, 266. took it in r. Per. II, 1, 138. in r. = furious: Lucr. 1671. Err. IV, 4, 79. 140. H4A IV, 3, 100. H6A IV, 7, 80. H6B V, 3, 2. Tim. IV, 2, 45. Hml. II, 2, 494. Oth. II, 3,

243. a r. = r.: it moved her. Not to a r. Lr. IV, 3, 18. in a r. H6B I, 1, 147. in a desperate r. Lucr. 219.

2) extreme violence, wild impetuosity, furious fighting: in fell battle's r. Lucr. 145. murder's —s, 909. against the stormy gusts of winter's day and bar-ren r. of death's eternal cold, Sonn. 13, 12. when some-time lofty towers I see down-razed, and brass eternal slave to mortal r. 64, 4 (mortal r. = r. of mortality). how with this r. shall beauty hold a plea, 65, 3. spite of heaven's fell r. some beauty peeped through lattice of seared age, Compl. 13. shall we give the signal to our r. John II, 265. to enjoy by r. and war, R2 II, 4, 14. dry with r. and extreme toil, H4A I, 3, 31. the king be-fore the Douglas' r. stooped his anointed head, H4B Ind. 31. disguise fair nature with hard-favoured r. H5 III, 1, 8. left us to the r. of France his sword, H6A IV, 6, 3. quickened with youthful spleen and warlike r. 13. if I die not with Frenchmen's r. 34. commence rough deeds of r. IV, 7, 8.

Used of the elements: a river ... swelleth with more r. Ven. 332. qualify the fire's extreme r. Gent. II, 7, 22. so high above his limits swells the r. of Boling-broke, R2 III, 2, 109 (like a river). when the r. allays, the rain begins, H6C I, 4, 146. the blasts, with eyeless r. Lr. III, 1, 8. the furious winter's —s, Cymb. IV, 2, 259.

3) headlong passion, vehement desire: his r. of lust by gazing qualified, Lucr. 424. this moves in him more r. 468. when r. and hot blood are his counsellors, H4B IV, 4, 63.

4) raving madness: this present instance of his r. Err. IV, 3, 88. felt the vigour of his r. IV, 4, 81. till this afternoon his passion ne'er brake into extremity of r. V, 48. bearing thence rings, jewels, any thing his r. did like, 144. in this r. Rom. IV, 3, 53. the great r. is killed in him, Lr. IV. 7, 78.

Applied, in contempt, to poetical inspiration: termed a poet's r. Sonn. 17, 11.

5) vehement sensation of pain: would give pre-ceptial medicine to r. Ado V, 1, 24. I have a trick of the old r.; bear with me, I am sick, LLL V, 2, 417. send succours, lords, and stop the r. betime, before the wound do grow uncurable, H6B III, 1, 285. to give thy —s balm, Tim. V, 4, 16.

6) savageness: in Ajax' eyes blunt r. and rigour rolled, Lucr. 1398. nought so stockish, hard and full of r., but music for the time doth change his nature, Merch. V, 81. kiss the rod and fawn on r. R2 V, 1, 33. harsh r., defect of manners, H4A III, 1, 183. mi-sery could beguile the tyrant's r. Lr. IV, 6, 63.

**Rage**, vb. 1) intr. a) to be furious with anger or any wild excitement: Err. V, 216. R2 II, 1, 70. H4B V, 5, 34. H6C I, 4, 143. Troil. II, 3, 185. Lr. I, 2, 178. III, 4, 137. Cymb. III, 5, 67. Per. III, 3, 10. Used of the elements: Gent. I, 2, 122. II, 7, 26. Err. V, 75. Shr. I, 2, 203. II, 133. Wint. III, 3, 90. H6B III, 1, 302. 351. H6C I, 4, 145. Troil. I, 3, 97. Tit. III, 1, 223. Rom. III, 5, 136. Caes. I, 3, 7. Lr. III, 2, 1. III, 4, 10. Per. IV, 4, 43.

b) to ravage, to act with mischievous impetuosity: Mids. I, 2, 33 (the —ing rocks; Bottom's poetry). Shr. V, 2, 2. John V, 7, 80. H6A IV, 1, 185. H6C II, 3, 26. II, 5, 126. Cor. IV, 6, 76.

c) to be driven headlong by desire and passion: when we r., advice is often seen to make our wits more keen, Compl. 160. those pampered animals that r. in *savage sensuality,* Ado IV, 1, 62. *where his —ing eye listed to make his prey,* R3 III, 5, 83 (Qq *lustful*). *those —ing appetites,* Troil. II, 2, 181. *to cool our —ing motions,* Oth. I, 3, 334.

d) to rave: *doth he still r.?* John V, 7, 11. *still in motion of —ing waste,* Tim. II, 1, 4. *when one so great begins to r.* Ant. IV, 1, 7.

e) to cause extreme pain: *like the hectic in my blood he —s,* Hml. IV, 3, 68. *troubled with a —ing tooth,* Oth. III, 3, 414.

2) tr. to enrage, to chafe: *young hot colts being —d do rage the more,* R2 II, 1, 70. *in war was never lion —d more fierce,* 173.

**Ragged,** 1) rent or worn into tatters: *r. sails,* Merch. II, 6, 18. *more r. than an old faced ancient,* H4A IV, 2, 33. *r. curtains,* H5 IV, 2, 41.

2) wearing tattered clothes, and hence = beggarly, wretched: *thy smoothing titles* (turn) *to a r. name,* Lucr. 892. *a wretched r. man,* As IV, 3, 107. *the rest were r.,* old and beggarly, Shr. IV, 1, 140. *as r. as Lazarus,* H4A IV, 2, 27. *thou art a very r.* Wart, H4B III, 2, 152. *a r. appearance,* 279. *a r. and forestalled remission,* V, 2, 38. *four or five most vile and r. foils,* H5 IV Chor. 50. *the r. soldiers,* H6B IV, 1, 90. *a r. multitude,* IV, 4, 32.

3) rugged, uneven: *a r. bough,* Ven. 37. *a r. fearful hanging rock,* Gent. I, 2, 121. *r. horns,* Wiv. IV, 4, 31. *my r. prison walls,* R2 V, 5, 21. *hold of r. stone,* H4B Ind. 35. *their* (the rocks') *r. sides,* H6B III, 2, 98. *the r. staff,* V, 1, 203. *a r. rock,* H6C V, 4, 27. *rude r. nurse* (the Tower) R3 IV, 1, 102. *the r. entrails of the pit,* Tit. II, 3, 230. *on the r. stones,* V, 3, 133. Metaphorically, = rough: *winter's r. hand,* Sonn. 6, 1. *my voice is r.* As II, 5, 15. *the —st hour that time and spite dare bring,* H4B I, 1, 151.

**Raggedness,** state of being dressed in tatters: Lr. III, 4, 31.

**Raging-mad,** raving: Ven. 1151. H6B III, 2, 394.

**Raging-wood,** the same (cf. *Wood*): H6A IV, 7, 35.

**Ragozine,** name in Meas. IV, 3, 75. 80. V, 539.

**Rah tah tah,** an exclamation expressive of nimbleness: *r. would a' say; bounce would a' say,* H6B III, 2, 303.

**Raied,** see *Rayed.*

**Rail,** subst. a cross-beam forming part of a balustrade: H8 V, 4, 93.

**Rail,** vb. intr. to use reproachful language, to scold in opprobrious terms: Err. IV, 4, 77. V, 71. Mids. III, 2, 362. As IV, 3, 42. 43. 46. Shr. I, 2, 112. II, 171. IV, 1, 187. 209. Tw. I, 5, 102. John II, 593. H4A III, 1, 160. H6A III, 2, 64. H6B III, 1, 172. Troil. II, 3, 26. V, 4, 30. Lr. II, 2, 126. Oth. IV, 1, 170. Ant. I, 2, 111. IV, 15, 43. With *against:* Wiv. IV, 2, 23. Ado II, 3, 246. As II, 5, 63. III, 2, 295. H5 II, 2, 41. Tim. III, 4, 65. With *at:* Lucr. 1023. Gent. III, 2, 4. Ado II, 3, 147. H6C II, 6, 81. Troil. II, 3, 3. 5. Tit. II, 4, 35. Cymb. IV, 2, 56. With *on* or *upon:* Ven. 1002. Lucr. 1467. Merch. I, 3, 49. As I, 1, 65. II, 7, 16. Shr. Ind. 2, 88. John II, 587. 592. R2 V, 5, 90. R3 IV, 4, 150. H8 V, 4, 50. Troil. I, 3, 191. II, 1, 35. 100. Rom. III, 3, 119. Tim. I, 2, 245. 250. Lr. II, 2, 28. IV, 6, 155. With an accus. to denote the effect: *till thou canst r. the seal from off my bond,* Merch. IV, 1, 139. *I shall sooner r. thee into wit,* Troil. II, 1, 17.

**Railer,** a scold: H6C V, 5, 38.

**Raiment,** vesture, dress: Sonn. 22, 6. Gent. V, 4, 106. Shr. Ind. 2, 4. 8. II, 5. Cor. V, 3, 94. Tim. III, 5, 33. Lr. II, 4, 158.

**Rain,** subst. water falling in drops from the clouds: Ven. 71. 200. 238. 799. 965. Lucr. 1788. Sonn. 14, 6. 34, 6. 135, 9. Meas. III, 2, 52. Ado III, 3, 111. LLL IV, 3, 270. Mids. I, 1, 130. Merch. IV, 1, 185. As III, 2, 27. III, 5, 50. IV, 1, 152. Tw. V, 399. 401. John II, 128. H4B IV, 5, 9. H6A II, 1, 7. III, 2, 59. H6B III, 2, 341. C III, 2, 50 (*much r. wears the marble;* cf. Ven. 200. Tit. II, 3, 141. Lucr. 560). R3 I, 2, 164. Cor. IV, 5, 226. Tit. II, 3, 141. Mcb. I, 1, 2. III, 3, 16. Hml. III, 3, 45. Lr. III, 1, 11. III, 2, 14. 47. 75. 77. IV, 3, 20. IV, 6, 102. Cymb. III, 3, 37. Per. II, 1, 2. Used of tears: Ven. 959. Compl. 7. H6C I, 4, 146. Tit. III, 1, 16. Ant. I, 2, 156. cf. Lucr. 1788. Mids. I, 1, 130. As III, 5, 50. H4B IV, 5, 9.

**Rain,** vb. 1) iutr. to fall in drops: *the rain it —eth,* Tw. V, 401. Lr. III, 2, 77. *dissolve, thick cloud, and r.* Ant. V, 2, 302. Impersonally: *it —s,* Ven. 458. Lucr. 1790. Rom. III, 5, 129. *it begins to r.* Lr. II, 4, 81. *though marble wear with —ing,* Lucr. 560. 1677. Metaphorically, of tears: *her tears, which long have —ed,* Ven. 83. Lucr. 1271. H4B II, 3, 59. Troil. IV, 4, 55. Hml. IV, 5, 166.

2) tr. to shower down like rain: *on the earth I r. my waters,* R2 III, 3, 59. Used of any thing poured down in great plenty (therefore in Merch. III, 2, 113 read *rein*): *heavens r. grace on that,* Tp. III, 1, 75. *let the sky r. potatoes,* Wiv. V, 5, 21. *the heavens r. odours on you,* Tw. III, 1, 96. *r. their drift of bullets,* John II, 412. *r. hot vengeance,* R2 I, 2, 8. *with showers of blood —ed from the wounds,* III, 3, 44. *it —ed down fortune on your head,* H4A V, 1, 47. *my power —ed honour on you,* H8 III, 2, 185. *r. sacrificial whisperings in his ear,* Tim. I, 1, 81. *—ed all kinds of shames on my head,* Oth. IV, 2, 48. *as it —ed kisses,* Ant. III, 13, 85. Of tears: Ven. 360. LLL V, 2, 819. Shr. Ind. 1, 125.

**Rainbow,** the iris: Lucr. 1587 (cf. All's I, 3, 157). Wiv. IV, 5, 119. Wint. IV, 4, 206. John IV, 2, 14.

**Rainold** (Ff *Rainald*), name: R2 II, 1, 279.

**Rain-water,** water falling from the clouds: Lr. III, 2, 11.

**Rainy,** 1) attended with rain: *a r. morrow,* Sonn. 90, 7. *besmirched with r. marching,* H5 IV, 3, 111.

2) raining, weeping: *r. eyes,* R2 III, 2, 146. Tit. V, 1, 117.

**Raise,** 1) to lift, to put in a higher place: *did he r. his chin,* Ven. 85. *r. aloft the milk-white rose,* H6B I, 1, 254. *when the morning sun shall r. his car,* H6C IV, 7, 80. *to r. the waters* = to set all wheels a-going, to do one's best: Merch. II, 2, 51 (Launcelot's speech). Refl.: *let me r. me from my knees,* Meas. V, 231.

Metaphorically, = a) to enhance, to increase: *r. the price of hogs,* Merch. III, 5, 26. b) to exalt, to advance: *to advance or r. myself,* H6A III, 1, 32. *he would r. his issue,* H6C II, 2, 22. *one —d in blood,* R3 V, 3, 247. *whose hand has —d me,* H8 II, 2, 120. *I —d him,* Cor. V, 6, 21. *my estate deserves an heir more —d,* Tim. I, 1, 119. *r. me this beggar,* V3, 3, 9. *to r. my fortunes,* Lr. IV, 6, 232. With *to:* *I —d him to the crown,* H6C III, 3, 262. IV, 1, 68. R3 I, 3, 83.

2) to erect, to build up: *he hath —d the wall,* Tp.

II, 1, 87. *those twins of learning that he —d in you,* *Ipswich and Oxford,* H8 IV, 2, 58. *I will r. her statue* *in pure gold,* Rom. V, 3, 299. *the stones whereof it* (the house) *is —d,* Lr. III, 2, 64.

3) to heave, to force from the breast: *sighs that* *burning lungs did r.* Compl. 228. *he —d a sigh so* *piteous and profound,* Hml. II, 1, 94.

4) to rouse, to stir up, to awake, to make to rise: *thy unworthiness —d love in me,* Sonn. 150, 13. *which* *—d in me an undergoing stomach,* Tp. I, 2, 156. *—ing* *this sea-storm,* 177. *I —d the tempest,* V, 6. *I'll r. all* *Windsor,* Wiv. V, 5, 223. *—d with it* (beating) *when* *I sit,* Err. IV, 4, 35. *the villain Jew with outcries —d* *the duke,* Merch. II, 8, 4. *to r. such love in mine* (eyes) As IV, 3, 51. *she has —d me from my sickly bed,* All's II, 3, 118. 120. *this business will r. us all. To laughter,* Wint. II, 1, 198. *if you r. this house against this house,* R2 IV, 145 (German: *empören*). *r. the power of France* *upon his head,* John III, 1, 193. *to r. a mutiny,* H6A IV, 1, 131. *the county's page, that —d the watch,* Rom. V, 3, 279. *I shall r. you by and by on business,* Caes. IV, 3, 247. *he —d the house with loud cries,* Lr. II, 4, 43. *the —d search,* Oth. I, 1, 159. 168. 183. I, 2, 29. 43. I, 3, 54. *it —s the greater war between him* *and his discretion,* Ant. II, 7, 10. *dust —d by your* *troops,* III, 6, 50. With *up: r. up the organs of her* *fantasy,* Wiv. V, 5, 55. *r. up such a storm,* Shr. I, 1, 177. *r. up the Montagues,* Rom. V, 3, 178. *if my* *gentle love be not —d up,* Oth. II, 3, 250.

5) to call up (a spirit) from below, to conjure: H4A III, 1, 60. H6B I, 2, 79. I, 4, 24. Troil. II, 3, 6. Rom. II, 1, 24. Mcb. III, 5, 27. With *up:* H6B II, 1, 174. Rom. II, 1, 29.

6) to levy, to collect; used of troops: Err. V, 153. H4A I, 3, 284. V, 1, 66. H6B IV, 4, 40. V, 1, 21. H6C V, 3, 8. H8 II, 1, 108. Tit. III, 1, 286. 300. Ant. III, 4, 26. Of money: Merch. I, 1, 179. H5 I, 2, 133. Caes. IV, 3, 71. With *up:* Merch. I, 3, 56.

7) to bring into being, to beget: *from her blood* *r. up issue to me,* H5 V, 2, 376. Of news, = to invent, to originate: *his —ing; nothing but his report,* Cor. IV, 6, 60. *—d only, that the weaker sort may* *wish good Marcius home again,* 69.

8) *to r. a siege* = to relieve a besieged place by dislodging the enemy: H5 III, 3, 47. H6A I, 2, 13. 53. 130. 146. I, 4, 103.

**Raisin,** dried grape: *—s o' the sun,* Wint. IV, 3, 52 (dried in the sun).

**Rake,** subst. 1) an instrument with teeth used in gathering up things from the ground; 2) a dissolute man; with a pun: *let us revenge this with our pikes,* *ere we become —s,* Cor. I, 1, 24 (alluding to the proverb: *as lean as a rake*).

**Rake,** vb. to scrape, to gather as with a rake; with *from,* = to bring to light from under the covering earth: *let me r. it from the earth,* Gent. IV, 2, 116. *from the dust of old oblivion —d,* H5 IV, 1, 87. With *for,* = to search for: *even in your hearts, there will* *he r. for it,* H5 II, 4, 98. With *together,* = to scrape together: *how does he r. this together,* H8 III, 2, 110. With *up,* = to cover up with earth, to bury: *here in* *the sands thee I'll r. up,* Lr. IV, 6, 281.

**Raker,** in *Foot-land-raker,* q. v.

**Ralph,** name: Shr. IV, 1, 139. H4A II, 4, 42. H4B III, 2, 109.

**Ram,** subst. 1) a male sheep: Pilgr. 247. Merch.

I, 3, 82. 96. As III, 2, 83. 87. V, 2, 34. Wint. IV, 4, 29. Oth. I, 1, 88.

2) the Aries of the zodiac: Tit. IV, 3, 72.

3) a battering-ram: Lucr. 464. H8 IV, 1, 77. Troil. I, 3, 206. Ant. III, 2, 30.

**Ram,** vb. 1) to thrust or drive with violence: *r.* *thou thy fruitful tidings in mine ears,* Ant. II, 5, 24 (cf. *to thrust* in Caes. V, 3, 74. 75).

2) to stuff, to cram tightly: *—ed me in with foul* *shirts,* Wiv. III, 5, 90. *till that time have we —ed up* *our gates,* John II, 272 (German: *verrammeln*).

**Rambures,** French name: H5 III, 5, 43. IV, 8, 99.

**Ramp,** subst. a leap: *whiles he is vaulting va-* *riable —s, in your despite, upon your purse,* Cymb. I, 6, 134 (according to others, = prostitutes).

**Ramp,** vb., used only in the partic. *—ing,* = 1) rampant, springing up: *a couching lion and a —ing* *cat,* H4A III, 1, 153. 2) knowing no restraint: *what* *a fool art thou, a —ing fool,* John III, 1, 122. *under* *whose shade the —ing lion slept,* H6C V, 2, 13.

**Rampallian,** a term of low abuse for a woman. *you scullion, you r.* H4B II, 1, 65.

**Rampant,** standing on the hind legs (term of heraldry): *the r. bear chained to the ragged staff,* H6B V, 1, 203.

**Rampired,** barred, barricaded, rammed: *set but* *thy foot against our r. gates, and they shall ope,* Tim. V, 4, 47 (cf. Lodge's Rosalynd, ed. Collier, p. 48: *Rosader rampierd up the house).*

**Ramston,** name in R2 II, 1, 283.

**Ram-tender,** one who tends rams, a shepherd: Wint. IV, 4, 805.

**Rancorous,** malignant: Err. I, 1, 6. H6A IV, 1, 185. H6B III, 1, 24. III, 2, 199. R3 I, 3, 50.

**Rancour,** malice, hatred: Ado IV, 1, 308. R2 I, 1, 143. H6B I, 1, 142. III, 1, 144. R3 II, 2, 117. III, 2, 89. Rom. II, 3, 92. *put —s in the vessel of my* *peace,* Mcb. III, 1, 67 (made myself live in discord with myself).

**Random;** *at r.* = without a settled aim or purpose, without care, at hap-hazard: Ven. 940.*Sonn. 147, 12. Gent. II, 1, 117. Err. I, 1, 43. H6A V, 3, 85.

**Range,** subst. rank: *that great face of war, whose* *several —s frighted each other,* Ant. III, 13, 5.

**Range,** vb. 1) tr. to dispose in order: *the wide* *arch of the —d empire fall,* Ant. I, 1, 34 (Ffraing'd).

2) intr. to be ranked: *whatsoever comes athwart* *his affection —s evenly with mine,* Ado II, 2, 7. *the* *line and the predicament wherein you r. under this* *subtle king,* H4A I, 3, 169. *r. with humble livers in* *content,* H8 II, 3, 20. *bury all, which yet distinctly —s,* *in heaps and piles of ruin,* Cor. III, 1, 206.

**Range,** vb. 1) intr. to roam, to rove at large: As I, 3, 70. R2 III, 2, 39. H4B I, 1, 174. H5 III, 3, 12. H6C II, 1, 11. Caes. II, 1, 118. III, 1, 270. Hml. III, 3, 2. Metaphorically, = to be inconstant: *if I have* *—d, like him that travels I return again,* Sonn. 109, 5. *if once I find thee —ing, Hortensio will be quit with* *thee by changing,* Shr. III, 1, 91.

2) tr. to roam, to rove through: *he did r. the town* *to seek me out,* Tw. IV, 3, 7.

**Ranger,** one who tends the game of a forest: *'tis gold which makes Diana's —s false themselves,* *yield up their deer to the stand o' the stealer,* Cymb. II, 3, 74 (= makes Diana's nymphs yield up their chastity?).

**Rank,** subst. 1) a row, a line: *the r. of osiers...* *brings you to the place,* As IV, 3, 80. *on the brow o' the sea stand —s of people,* Oth. II, 1, 54. Doubtful passage: *it is the right butterwomen's r. to market,* As III, 2, 103 (= file? Some M. Edd. *rate*).*Plur. —s = lines of troops:* Lucr. 73. 440. 783. 1439. John IV, 2, 244. V, 2, 29. R2 II, 3, 102. H4A I, 1, 14. H5 IV, 5, 6. H6C II, 3, 10. Troil. IV, 5, 185. Tim. V, 4, 39. Caes. II, 2, 20. Mcb. I, 3, 95. Lr. IV, 2, 25. Oth. III, 4, 135. Ant. III, 1, 32. Singular: *a gallant horse fallen in first r.* Troil. III, 3, 161.

2) degree of dignity: *to march in —s of better equipage,* Sonn. 32, 12. *holds his r. before,* 85, 12. *which shall above that idle r. remain,* 122, 3. *if I keep not my r.* As I, 2, 113. *bowed his eminent top to their low —s,* All's I, 2, 43. *go in equal r. with the best governed nation,* H4B V, 2, 137. *holds on his r.* Caes. III, 1, 69. *not in the worst r. of manhood,* Mcb. III, 1, 103. *of the best r. and station,* Hml. I, 3, 73. *stands in some r. of praise,* Lr. II, 4, 261. *one of my r.* Cymb. II, 1, 17.

3) = rankness, by way of punning: *if I keep not my r. — Thou losest thy old smell,* As I, 2, 113. *would he had been one of my r.! To have smelt like a fool,* Cymb. II, 1, 17.

**Rank,** adj. 1) too luxuriant, exuberant, grown to immoderate height: *rain added to a river that is r. perforce will force it overflow the bank,* Ven. 71 (= brimful). *weed your better judgments of all opinion that grows r. in them that I am wise,* As II, 7, 46 (like a weed). *I should think my honesty —er than my wit,* IV, 1, 85 (= greater). *wanting the scythe, all uncorrected, r.* H5 V, 2, 50. *r. fumitory,* V, 2, 45. cf. Lr. IV, 4, 3. *the seeded pride that hath to this maturity blown up in r. Achilles must be cropped,* Troil. I, 3, 318 (= insolent). *do not spread the compost on the weeds, to make them —er,* Hml. III, 4, 152 (Ff r.). *nor would it yield to Norway or the Pole a —er rate,* IV, 4, 22 (= greater).

Adverbially, = overmuch, abundantly: *while other jests are something r. on foot,* Wiv.IV, 6, 22. *to weaken and discredit our exposure, how r. soever rounded in with danger,* Troil. I, 3, 196.

2) lustful: *the ewes, being r., turned to the rams,* Merch. I, 3, 81. *abuse him to the Moor in the r. garb,* Oth. II, 1, 315 (Ff *right*). *lust and r. thoughts,* Cymb. II, 5, 24.

3) sick (of hypertrophy), corrupted, morbid: *brought to medicine a healthful state which, r. of goodness, would by ill be cured,* Sonn. 118, 12 (cf. v. 7: *sick of welfare*). *what r. diseases grow,* H4B III, 1, 39. *to diet r. minds sick of happiness,* IV, 1, 64. *the r. poison of the old (infection) will die,* Rom. I, 2, 51. *who else must be let blood, who else is r.* Caes. III, 1, 152. *r. corruption, mining all within, infects unseen,* Hml. III, 4, 148. *one may smell in such a will most r.* Oth. III, 3, 232. Troil. IV, 5, 132.

4) virulent, noisome, foul, disgusting, gross: *to thy fair flower add the r. smell of weeds,* Sonn. 69, 12. *by their r. thoughts my deeds must not be shown,* 121, 12. *to blush at speeches r.* Compl. 307. *I do forgive thy —est fault,* Tp. V, 132. *the —est compound of villanous smell,* Wiv. III, 5, 93. *he would give't thee, from this r. offence, so to offend him still,* Meas. III, 1, 100. *deserves a name as r. as any flax-wench,* Wint. I, 2, 277. *ha! what, so r.?* H8 I, 2, 186. *he's a r. weed,* V, 1, 52.

*when r. Thersites opes his mastic jaws,* Troil. I, 3, 73. *things r. and gross in nature possess it merely,* Hml. I, 2, 136. *none (forgery) so r. as may dishonour him,* II, 1, 20. *thou mixture r., of midnight weeds collected,* III, 2, 268. *my offence is r., it smells to heaven,* III, 3, 36. *to live in the r. sweat of an enseamed bed,* III, 4, 92. *r. and not-to-be endured riots,* Lr. I, 4, 223. *their thick breaths, r. of gross diets,* Ant. V, 2, 212.

5) strong-scented, rancid: *Sowter will cry upon it for all this, though it be as r. as a fox,* Tw. II, 5, 136. cf. Hml. III, 3, 36.

**Rank,** vb. 1) tr. a) to place with respect to degree and dignity: *my fortunes (are) as fairly —ed as Demetrius',* Mids. I, 1, 101. *I will not r. me with the barbarous multitudes,* Merch. II, 9, 33. *he was a man of an unbounded stomach, ever —ing himself with princes,* H8 IV, 2, 34. *let the world r. me in register a master-leaver,* Ant. IV, 9, 21. b) to match, to couple: *to r. our chosen truth with such a show as fool and fight is,* H8 Prol. 18. *if sour woe delights in fellowship and needly will be —ed with other griefs,* Rom. III, 2, 117.

2) intr. to be coupled, to go together: *let that one article r. with the rest,* H5 V, 2, 374.

**Ranked,** 1) placed in lines: *embattailed and r.* John IV, 2, 200. 2) disposed of and occupied with respect to degree and dignity: *the base o' the mount is r. with all deserts, all kind of natures,* Tim. I, 1, 65 ("covered with ranks of all kinds of men". Johnson).

**Rankle,** to breed corruption, to poison: *fell sorrow's tooth doth never r. more than when he bites, but lanceth not the sore,* R2 I, 3, 302. *when he bites, his venom tooth will r. to the death,* R3 I, 3, 291 (Qq *r. thee to death*).

**Rankly,** grossly, foully: *the whole ear of Denmark is by a forged process of my death r. abused,* Hml. I, 5, 38.

**Rankness,** exuberance: *like a bated and retired flood, leaving our r. and irregular course, stoop low within those bounds we have o'erlooked,* John V, 4, 54. *I am stifled with the mere r. of their joy,* H8 IV, 1, 59. Hence = insolence: *I will physic your r.* As I, 1, 92.

**Rank-scented,** having a bad smell: *the mutable r. many,* Cor. III, 1, 66.

**Ransack,** 1) to pillage, to plunder: *and I, a drone-like bee, have no perfection of my summer left, but robbed and —ed by injurious theft,* Lucr. 838. *my coffers —ed,* Wiv. II, 2, 306. *I would have —ed the pedlar's silken treasury,* Wint. IV, 4, 360. *—ing the church,* John III, 4, 172. *to r. Troy,* Troil. Prol. 8.

2) to ravish: *the —ed queen,* Troil. II, 2, 150.

**Ransom,** subst. 1) price paid for the redemption of a prisoner; in a proper and a metaphorical sense: Ven. 550. Meas. II, 4, 111. IV, 4, 33. All's I, 3, 121. IV, 1, 74 (*O r., r.!*). R2 II, 1, 56 (*the world's r.,* blessed Mary's son; cf. Wint. V, 2, 16). H4A I, 3, 141. 260. II, 3, 57. IV, 3, 96. H5 III, 5, 60. 63. III, 6, 133. 163. IV, 3, 80. 120. 122. 128. IV, 4, 11. 48. IV, 5, 9. IV, 7, 72. 73. H6A I, 1, 148. 150. III, 3, 72. V, 3, 73. 77. 80. 157. H6B III, 2, 297. V, 1, 10 (*make their r.,* = pay). 15. 28. 139. H6C V, 7, 40. Tim. I, 1, 105 (= a sum paid to deliver a prisoner for debt). Caes. III, 2, 94 (*—s*). Lr. IV, 6, 196.

2) atonement, expiation: *if hearty sorrow be a sufficient r. for offence,* Gent. V, 4, 75. *lowly words were r. for their fault,* H6B III, 1, 127. R3 V, 3, 265 Tit. III, 1, 156. Cymb. V, 3, 80. V, 5, 80.

**Ransom**, vb. 1) to redeem from captivity: Err. I, 1, 23. H4A I, 3, 79. 92 (*to r. home*). 219. H5 IV, 1, 127. 203. 206. H6A I, 4, 29. Ant. III, 13, 180. Cymb. V, 5, 85.

2) to set at liberty, to release: —*ing him, or pitying*, Cor. I, 6, 36. With *to: I would take Desire prisoner and r. him to any French courtier for a new-devised courtesy*, LLL I, 2, 65 (Armado's speech).

3) to deliver: *labouring art can never r. nature from her inaidible estate*, All's II, 1, 121. *to r. my two nephews from their death*, Tit. III, 1, 173. = to redeem, in a religious sense: *a world —ed, or one destroyed*, Wint. V, 2, 16 (cf. R2 II, 1, 56). With *into*, = to restore to: *that nor my service past nor present sorrows can r. me into his love again*, Oth. III, 4, 118.

4) to atone for: *they* (tears) *r. all ill deeds*, Sonn. 34, 14. *your trespass now becomes a fee; mine —s yours, and yours must r. me*, 120, 14.

**Ransomless**, without ransom: H4A V, 5, 28. Tit. I, 274.

**Rant**, vb. to speak bombast, to bluster: *my —ing host*, Wiv. II, 1, 196. *an thou'lt mouth, I 'll r. as well as thou*, Hml. V, 1, 307.

**Rap**, 1) to strike with a quick blow, to knock: *knock me at this gate and r. me well*, Shr. I, 2, 12. 31. *she —ed 'em o' the coxcombs with a stick*, Lr. II, 4, 125 (Ff *knapped*).

2) to affect with ecstasy, to transport: *what, dear sir, thus —s you?* Cymb. I, 6, 51. Partic. *rapt* = a) enraptured, transported: *more dances my r. heart than when I first my wedded mistress saw bestride my threshold*, Cor. IV, 5, 122. *of royal hope that he seems r. withal*, Mcb. I, 3, 57. *how our partner's r.* 142. *whiles I stood r. in the wonder of it* I, 5, 6. b) beside one's self: *I am r. and cannot cover the monstrous bulk of this ingratitude with any size of words*, Tim. V, 1, 67. c) quite absorbed, engrossed; with *in: transported and r. in secret studies*, Tp. I, 2, 77. *I was much r. in this*, Troil. III, 3, 123. *you are r., sir, in some work*, Tim. I, 1, 19. (cf. *Enrapt*).

**Rape**, ravishment: Lucr. 909. 1369 (*Helen's r.*). All's IV, 3, 281. John II, 97. Troil. II, 2, 148. Tit. I, 404. II, 1, 116. IV, 1, 49. 58. 91. IV, 2, 9. V, 1, 63. V, 2, 37. 45. 94. 157.

**Rapier**, a small sword used in thrusting: Tp. V, 84. Wiv. I, 4, 61. 72. II, 3, 13. LLL I, 2, 183. 187. Tw. III, 4, 258. 303. R2 IV, 40. H4B II, 4, 215. H5 II, 1, 60. H6C I, 3, 37. I, 4, 80. Tit. II, 1, 54. IV, 2, 85. Rom. I, 5, 57. III, 1, 87. IV, 3, 57. Hml. II, 2, 359. IV, 1, 10. Oth. V, 1, 2. *the Frenchman hath good skill in his r.* Wiv. II, 1, 231. *I do excel thee in my r.* LLL I, 2, 78. *gave you such a masterly report for your r.* Hml. IV, 7, 99. *the r. and dagger man*, Meas. IV, 3, 15. *what's his weapon? R. and dagger*, Hml. V, 2, 152. *six French —s and poniards*, 156 (cf. *Dagger*).

**Rapine**, rape, ravishment: Tit. V, 2, 59. 62. 83. 103.

**Rapt**, see *Rap*.

**Rapture**, 1) transport, delirium: *her brain-sick —s cannot distaste the goodness of a quarrel*, Troil. II, 2, 122. *in this r. I shall surely speak the thing I shall repent*, III, 2, 138.

2) a syncope, a trance: *your prattling nurse into a r. lets her baby cry*, Cor. II, 1, 223 (*rupture* proposed by some men for emendation. But cf. the German: lässt es schreien, dass es wegbleibt).*

3) violent seizure (?): *spite of all the r. of the sea*,

*this jewel holds his building on my arm*, Per. II, 1, 161 (O. Edd. *rupture*).

**Rare**, 1) uncommon, not often seen: *were man as r. as phoenix*, As IV, 3, 17. *nothing pleaseth but r. accidents*, H4A I, 2, 231. *we'll have thee, as our —r monsters are, painted upon a pole*, Mcb. V, 8, 25. *lived in court — which r. it is to do — most praised*, Cymb. I, 1, 47.

2) extraordinary; mostly in the sense of excellent, very praiseworthy: *all things r. that heaven's air in this huge rondure hems*, Sonn. 21, 7. *therefore are feasts so solemn and so r., since, seldom coming,* ... 52, 5. *makes summer's welcome thrice more wished, more r.* 56, 14. *I think my love as r. as any she*, 130, 13. *whose —st havings made the blossoms dote*, Compl. 235. *the —st* (queen) *that e'er came there*, Tp. II, 1, 99. *two most r. affections*, III, 1, 75. *so r. a wondered father*, IV, 123. *the —r action is in virtue*, V, 27. Gent. I, 1, 13. V, 4, 161. Ado I, 1, 139. 187. III, 1, 91. III, 4, 15. V, 1, 260. LLL IV, 2, 64. V, 2, 689. Mids. III, 2, 226. IV, 1, 210. Merch. II, 2, 116. 118. As V, 4, 109. All's I, 3, 228. II, 3, 7. Tw. II, 5, 35. III, 1, 97. III, 2, 60. Wint. I, 1, 14. I, 2, 367 (*what is the news i' the court? None r.*). 452. III, 1, 13. 20. IV, 2, 48. IV, 4, 32. V, 1, 112. V, 2, 105. H4A I, 2, 72. 76. II, 4, 436 (Ff *O r.*, Qq *O Jesu*). III, 3, 229. H6A II, 3, 10. IV, 7, 62. V, 5, 1. H8 I, 2, 111. II, 4, 137. Troil. II, 3, 8. Cor. II, 2, 108. IV, 5, 169. Hml. IV, 7, 144. Lr. I, 1, 58. I, 4, 285. Ant. I, 4, 22. II, 2, 210. 223. V, 1, 31. Cymb. I, 1, 135. I, 4, 66. I, 6, 16. 175. 189. III, 4, 163. III, 5, 77. IV, 2, 208. V, 4, 133. V, 5, 160. 381. Per. III, 2, 105. 107. IV Prol. 37. V, 1, 163. 233.

**Rarely**, extraordinarily, excellently: *r. featured*, Ado III, 1, 60. *doth not my wit become me r.?* III, 4, 70. *I could play Ercles r.* Mids. I, 2, 31. *these thy offices, so r. kind*, Wint. V, 1, 150. *how r. does it meet with this time's guise, when man was wished to love his enemies!* Tim. IV, 3, 472. *is not this buckled well? R., r.* Ant. IV, 4, 11. *slave, soulless villain, dog! O r. base!* V, 2, 158. *so r. and exactly wrought*, Cymb. II, 4, 75. *I'ld wish no better choice and think me r. wed*, Per. V, 1, 69.

**Rareness**, 1) state of happening seldom: *and won by r. such solemnity*, H4A III, 2, 59. *it is no act of common passage, but a strain of r.* Cymb. III, 4, 95.

2) excellence: *his infusion of such dearth and r.* Hml. V, 2, 123.

**Rarity**, 1) excellence: *beauty, truth, and r.* Phoen. 53. *but here o. of it is*, Tp. II, 1, 58. *he hath out-villained villany so far, that the r. redeems him*, All's IV, 3, 306.

2) something excellent: *feeds on the —es of nature's truth*, Sonn. 60, 11. *beyond credit, as many vouched —es are*, Tp. II, 1, 60. *but what particular r.?* Tim. I, 1, 4. *sorrow would be a r. most beloved, if all could so become it*, Lr. IV, 3, 20.

**Rascal**, subst. 1) a mean sorry wretch, a scoundrel: Tp. I, 1, 60. Wiv. I, 1, 128. II, 2, 300. III, 3, 196. IV, 2, 122. Meas. V, 284. 306. 357. Shr. I, 2, 37. II, 158 (O. Edd. *r., fiddler*; M. Edd. *r. fiddler*). IV, 1, 142. All's III, 5, 87. Tw. I, 5, 90. III, 1, 24. V, 383. Wint. IV, 4, 197. 821. H4A II, 2, 5. 11. 19. II, 3, 24. 31. II, 4, 383. 385. 575. III, 3, 177. IV, 2, 70. H4B II, 4, 43. 76. 137. 140. 203. 224. 230. 232. V, 4, 10. H5 III, 2, 134. III, 6, 64. IV, 7, 6. 130. H6A I, 2, 35. H6B III, 1, 381. R3 V, 3, 316. H8 V, 4, 1. 11. Troil. II, 3, 59. V, 4, 11. 30. Cor. I, 6. 45. IV,

5, 182. Tim. III, 4, 114. IV, 3, 217. Hml. II, 2, 594.* Lr. I, 4, 92. II, 2, 15. 38. 42. 59. Oth. II, 3, 150. IV, 2, 143. Cymb. I, 5, 27. II, 1, 42. IV, 2, 81.

2) a lean deer not fit to hunt or kill: *the noblest deer hath them* (horns) *as huge as the r.* As III, 3, 58. Quibbling in H4B II, 4, 45. V, 4, 34. H6A I, 2, 35. Cor. I, 1, 163.

**Rascal**, adj. mean, base; good for nothing; always before a subst.: *some r. groom,* Lucr. 671. *these r. knaves,* Shr. IV, 1, 134. 165. H4B II, 4, 247. H6B II, 4, 47. IV, 4, 51. Tim. IV, 3, 431. V, 1, 118. Caes. IV, 3, 80. Lr. IV, 6, 164. Superl. *—est: the most comparative, —est sweet young prince,* H4A I, 2, 90 (Q1. 2 *rascalliest*).

**Rascal-like**, like lean and worthless deer: *if we be English deer, be then in blood; not r. to fall down with a pinch,* H6A IV, 2, 49.

**Rascally**, adj. base; good for nothing: Wiv. II, 2, 276. As IV, 1, 218. All's V, 2, 25. Tw. II, 5, 6. H4B I, 2, 41. II, 2, 93. II, 4, 133. 240. H5 IV, 8, 36. V, 1, 5. Troil. V, 3, 101. Superl. *—est:* H4A I, 2, 90 (Ff Q3. 4 *rascallest*).

**Rase**, see *Raze.*

**Rash**, adj. (used only in the positive) 1) quick, hasty, sudden: *the reason of this r. alarm to know,* Lucr. 473. *you may marvel why I would not rather make r. remonstrance of my hidden power than let him so be lost,* Meas. V, 397. *with no r. potion, but with a lingering dram,* Wint. I, 2, 319. *his r. fierce blaze of riot cannot last,* R2 II, 1, 33. *r. bavin wits, soon kindled and soon burnt,* H4A III, 2, 61. *r. gunpowder,* H4B IV, 4, 48. *I scarce have leisure to salute you, my matter is so r.* Troil. IV, 2, 62. *was it well done of r. Virginius to slay his daughter?* Tit. V, 3, 36. *I have no joy of this contract to-night: it is too r., too unadvised, too sudden,* Rom. II, 2, 118. Adverbially: *why do you speak so startingly and r.?* Oth. III, 4, 79 (cf. Appendix).

2) overhasty, precipitate, inconsiderate: *her r. suspect she doth extenuate,* Ven. 1010. *O r. false heat,* Lucr. 48. *seducing lust, thy r. relier,* 639. 706. Tp. I, 2, 467. Meas. II, 2, 9. Mids. II, 1, 63. All's III, 2, 30. V, 3, 60. John II, 49. 67. H6B IV, 1, 28. Cor. I, 1, 133. IV, 7, 32. Caes. IV, 3, 39. 120. Hml. III, 4, 27. 31. V, 1, 284. Lr. I, 1, 299. II, 4, 172. Oth. II, 1, 279. V, 2, 134. 283. Cymb. IV, 2, 272.

**Rash**, name in Meas. IV, 3, 5.

**Rash**, vb. to strike (as a boar does): *I would not see ... thy sister in his anointed flesh r. boarish fangs,* Lr. III, 7, 58 (Ff and M. Edd. *stick*). cf. Nares' Glossary.

**Rash-embraced**, too readily harboured: *r. despair,* Merch. III, 2, 109.

**Rasher**, a slice of bacon: Merch. III, 5, 28.

**Rash-levied**, hastily collected: R3 IV, 3, 50.

**Rashly**, 1) hastily: *that we would against the form of law proceed thus r. to the villain's death,* R3 III, 5, 43. *r ... in the dark groped I to find out them,* Hml. V, 2, 6.

2) inconsiderately: H6A IV, 4, 3. R3 V, 5, 25.

**Rashness**, 1) quickness, haste: *rashly, and praised be r. for it, let us know, our indiscretion sometimes serves us well,* Hml. V, 2, 7 (the two significations joined).

2) inconsiderate haste, thoughtlessness: Gent. III, 1, 30. Wint. III, 2, 222. H5 III, 6, 127. R3 II, 1, 134. Tim. III, 5, 53. IV, 3, 502. Lr. I, 1, 153. Ant. II, 2, 124. III, 11, 14.

**Rat**, the animal Mus rattus: Tp. I, 2, 147. Wiv. II, 1, 237. Meas. I, 2, 133. Merch. IV, 1, 44. As III, 2, 188 (*Irish —s,* rhymed to death, cf. Nares' Glossary). R3 V, 3, 331. Cor. I, 1, 166. 253. Rom. III, 1, 104. Mcb. I, 3, 9. Hml. III, 4, 24. IV, 1, 10. Lr. II, 2, 80. III, 4, 138. 144. V, 3, 306. Cymb. V, 5, 248.

**Rat-catcher**, one who catches rats: Rom. III, 1, 78.

**Ratcliff**, name in R3 II, 1, 45 (not in Qq). III, 3, 2. III, 4, 80 etc.

**Rate**, subst. 1) estimate: *which o'erprized all popular r.* Tp. I, 2, 92. *my son is lost, and in my r. she too,* II, 1, 109. *stones whose —s* (O. Edd. *r.*) *are either rich or poor as fancy values them,* Meas. II, 2, 150. *I am a spirit of no common r.* Mids. III, 1, 157 (worth). *she reckoned it at her life's r.* All's V, 3, 91. *I judge their number upon or near the r. of thirty thousand,* H4B IV, 1, 22.

2) price: *reckoning his fortune at such high-proud r.* Lucr. 19. *a jewel that I have purchased at an infinite r.* Wiv. II, 2, 213. *thy substance, valued at the highest r.* Err. I, 1, 24. IV, 4, 14. All's V, 3, 217. H6A III, 2, 43. H6C II, 2, 51. H8 I, 1, 99. III, 2, 127. Cor. I, 1, 193. Rom. V, 3, 301. Hml. I, 3, 122. IV, 4, 22.

3) degree in which a thing is done: *to be abridged from such a noble r.* Merch. I, 1, 127 (style of living). *brings down the r. of usance,* I, 3, 46. 105.

**Rate**, vb. 1) to estimate, to value: *if thou be'st —d by thy estimation,* Merch. II, 7, 26. *all that life can r. worth name of life,* All's II, 1, 182. *paying the fine of —d treachery even with a treacherous fine of all your lives,* John V, 4, 37 (= appraised). *who was a —d sinew too,* H4A IV, 4, 17 (taken into account, reckoned upon). *then must we r. the cost of the erection,* H4B I, 3, 44. Tim. I, 1, 168. II, 2, 135. Cymb. I, 4, 83. *we had not —d him his part o' the isle,* Ant. III, 6, 25 (= computed, calculated, and assigned in consequence). With *at:* LLL V, 2, 789. Merch. III, 2, 260. H6B IV, 1, 30. Peculiar passage: *one of them* (thy tears) *—s all that is won and lost,* Ant. III, 11, 69 (estimates, expresses the value of, is worth).

2) to chide (cf. *Tax*); absol.: Shr. IV, 1, 187. trans.: Ven. 906. Lucr. 304. Merch. I, 3, 108. H4A I, 2, 95. H4B III, 1, 68. V, 2, 70. H6B III, 2, 56. H6C II, 2, 84. Troil. II, 2, 89. Tit. II, 3, 81. V, 1, 33. Rom. III, 5, 170. Caes. II, 1, 216. Ant. I, 4, 31. Cymb. V, 4, 34. With an accus. and a prepositional phrase indicating the effect: *affection is not —d from the heart,* Shr. I, 1, 165. *—d mine uncle from the council-board,* H4A IV, 3, 99. With *at:* upbraided, chid and *—d at,* H6B III, 1, 175.

**Rather**, (monosyll. in H6C I, 1, 224) 1) sooner, preferably, before, more: *and r. make them born to our desire than think that we before have heard them told,* Sonn. 123, 7. *r. like a dream than an assurance,* Tp. I, 2, 45. *r. new-dyed than stained,* II, 1, 63. *I r. will suspect the sun with cold,* Wiv. IV, 4, 7. *r. rejoicing to see another merry than merry at any thing,* Meas. III, 2, 249. *this you should pity r. than despise,* Mids. III, 2, 235. *I will from henceforth r. be myself than my condition,* H4A I, 3, 5. *r. with their teeth the walls they'll tear down than forsake the siege,* H6A I, 2, 39 etc. *the r.* = the more: *the r. will I spare my praises,* All's II, 1, 106. *the r. by these arguments of fear,* Tw. III, 3, 12. *he will the r. do it when he sees,* John V, 7, 87. *and I the r. wean me from despair for love of Edward's* *offspring*, H6C IV, 4, 17. *the r. for* = the more so because, especially because: *let me ask, the r. for I now must make you know*, Meas. I, 4, 22. *the r. for I have some sport in hand*, Shr. Ind. 1, 91. *the r. for I think I know your hostess*, All's III, 5, 45. *the r. for I earnestly beseech*, Ant. II, 2, 23. *the r. for 'tis said a woman's fitness comes by fits*, Cymb. IV, 1, 5. *the r. because*, and *the r. that*, in the same sense: *the r. because I love thee cruelly*, H5 V, 2, 215. *the r. that you give his offspring life*, John II, 13.

2) more properly, more correctly speaking: *I have followed it, or it hath drawn me r.* Tp. I, 2, 394. *thou let'st thy fortune sleep, die r.* II, 1, 216. *like bulls, or r. lions*, 312. *where you found it. Or stole it r.* V, 299. *returned so soon! r. approached too late*, Err. I, 2, 43. *r. persuade him to hold his hands*, IV, 4, 23. *I would my father looked but with my eyes. R. your eyes must with his judgment look*, Mids. I, 1, 57. *did scare away, or r. did affright*, V, 142. *lend it r. to thine enemy*, Merch. I, 3, 136. *mend nature, change it r.* Wint. IV, 4, 96. *neglected r.* Ant. II, 2, 89. *dead or sleeping? But r. dead*, Cymb. IV, 2, 356 etc.

3) on the contrary: *and yet not cloy thy lips ... but r. famish them*, Ven. 20. *patience says it is past her cure. I r. think you have not sought her help*, Tp. V, 141. *I r. would entreat thy company*, Gent. I, 1, 5. *'tis not in hate of you, but r. to beget more love in you*, III, 1, 97. *I speak not as desiring more, but r. wishing a more strict restraint*, Meas. I, 4, 4. *but r. tell me*, II, 1, 28. *do I speak you fair? or r. do I not in plainest truth tell you I cannot love you?* Mids. II, 1, 200 etc.

4) more willingly, with better liking: *I r. chose to cross my friend*, Gent. III, 1, 17. *why not death r. than living torment?* 170. *any extremity r. than a mischief*, Wiv. IV, 2, 76. *thou r. with thy sharp and sulphurous bolt split'st the oak than the myrtle*, Meas. II, 2, 115. Followed by *than* and an inf., with or without *to*: *bring a corollary r. than want a spirit*, Tp. IV, 58. *let us be keen and r. cut a little than fall and bruise to death*, Meas. II, 1, 5. *he r. means to lodge you in the field than seek a dispensation for his oath*, LLL II, 85. *leap all civil bounds r. than make unprofited return*, Tw. I, 4, 22. *would thou wert shipped to hell, r. than rob me of the people's hearts*, Tit. I, 207. *bid me leap, r. than marry Paris, from off the battlements*, Rom. IV, 1, 77. *if, r. than to marry County Paris, thou hast the strength of will to slay thyself*, 71. *I will r.* = I like better: *I will r. trust a Fleming with my butter*, Wiv. II, 2, 316. *she will die r. than she will bate ...*, Ado II, 3, 183. Merch. I, 3, 156. H6A V, 4, 144. Caes. V, 5, 7 etc. *I would r.: would let him go r. than triumph in so false a foe*, Lucr. 77. *would not bless our Europe with your daughter, but r. lose her to an African*, Tp. II, 1, 125. *I would have been a breakfast to the beast r. than have false Proteus rescue me*, Gent. V, 4, 35. *would not r. make rash remonstrance of my hidden power than let him so be lost*, Meas. V, 396. *I r. would have lost my life than bring a burthen of dishonour home*, H6B III, 1, 297. *thou wouldst have left thy dearest heart-blood there r. than have made that savage duke thine heir*, H6C I, 1, 224. *I would r. hide me from my greatness*, R3 III, 7, 161 (Qq *I had r.*). *he would miss it r. than carry it but by the suit of the gentry*, Cor. II, 1, 253 etc. *I had r.* = I should like better: *I had r. than forty shillings I had my book of songs here*, Wiv. I, 1, 205. *I had r. than a thousand*

*pound he were out of the house*, III, 3, 130. 134. *which had you r., that the law took your brother's life, or give up your body*, Meas. II, 4, 52. *I had r. it would please you*, V, 511. *I had r. he should shrive me than wive me*, Merch. I, 2, 144. *I had r. than forty shillings I had such a leg*, Tw. II, 3, 20. *I had r. you would have bid me argue like a father*, R2 I, 3, 237. *me* (= I) *r. had my heart might feel your love*, III, 3, 192. *Troilus had r. Troy were borne to Greece*, Troil. IV, 1, 46. *I'd r. than the worth of thrice the sum, had sent to me first*, Tim. III, 3, 22 (O. Edd. *I'de*, M. Edd. *I'ld*). *had you r. Caesar were living and die all slaves, than that Caesar were dead?* Caes. III, 2, 24. *which I had r. you felt than make't my boast*, Cymb. II, 3, 115. *I had r. thou shouldst live*, V, 5, 151. With an inf. following; a) with *to*, = it would have been better: *I had r. to adopt a child than get it*, Oth. I, 3, 191. b) oftener without *to*, = I should like better: *I had r. walk here*, Wiv. I, 1, 293. *I had r. be a giantess*, II, 1, 81. 239. III, 4, 90. Meas. II, 4, 56. Err. II, 2, 36. Ado I, 1, 132. I, 3, 28. II, 1, 33. LLL I, 1, 304. Mids. III, 2, 64. IV, 1, 41. Merch. I, 2, 55. As III, 5, 65. H4A III, 1, 129. H5 III, 7, 62. H6C III, 2, 70. R3 I, 3, 107. IV, 2, 72. H8 III, 2, 309. Ant. I, 2, 23. Cymb. II, 1, 20 etc. *now had he r. hear the tabor*, Ado II, 3, 15. *whether she had r. stay or go to bed now*, Merch. V, 302. *which we much r. had depart withal*, LLL II, 147. *whether had you r. lead mine eyes or eye your master's heels?* Wiv. III, 2, 3. *you had r. be at a breakfast*, Tim. I, 2, 78. Acc. and inf.: *I had r. my brother die*, Meas. III, 1, 195. *I had r. had eleven die*, Cor. I, 3, 26. The second inf. with *to*: *Brutus had r. be a villager than to repute himself a son of Rome*, Caes. I, 2, 172. *I had r. drop my blood ... than to wring ...*, IV, 3, 72. Without *to*: *I had r. wink than look on thee*, Gent. V, 2, 14. Ado V, 1, 247. As II, 4, 11. H6C V, 1, 50. Cor. IV, 6, 5. Ant. V, 2, 146. Cymb. IV, 2, 198 etc. *Than followed by should*: *I had r. crack my sinews than you should such dishonour undergo*, Tp. III, 1, 26. *I had r. my brother die than my son should be unlawfully born*, Meas. III, 1, 195. *I had r. have this tongue cut from my mouth than it should do offence to Cassio*, Oth. II, 3, 221. cf. *r. than it shall, I will be free*, Shr. IV, 3, 79. *I myself, r. than bloody war shall cut them short, will parley with Jack Cade*, H6B IV, 4, 12. *r. than I'll shame my mother's womb*, H6A IV, 5, 35. *Than followed by an accus. governed by had*: *that you had r. refuse the offer of an hundred thousand crowns than Bolingbroke's return*, R2 V, 15.

**Ratherest**, most properly speaking; a superlative very ungrammatically formed by the grammarian Holofernes: *untrained, or rather unlettered, or ratherest unconfirmed fashion*, LLL IV, 2, 19.

**Ratifier**, that which sanctions: *as the world were now but to begin, antiquity forgot, custom not known, the —s and props of every word*, Hml. IV, 5, 105.

**Ratify**, to confirm, to sanction, to make valid: *here, afore Heaven, I r. this my rich gift*, Tp. IV, 1, 8. *as doubtful whether what I see be true, until confirmed, signed, —ed by you*, Merch. III, 2, 149. *free power to r., augment, or alter ... any thing*, H5 V, 2, 86. *the articles ... were —ed as he cried 'Thus let be'*, H8 I, 1, 170. *with Him above to r. the work*, Mcb. III, 6, 33. *a sealed compact, well —ed by law and heraldry*, Hml. I, 1, 87. *in the temple of great Jupiter our peace we'll r.* Cymb. V, 5, 483.

Peculiarly used by Holofernes: *here are only num-*
*bers —ed*, LLL IV, 2, 125 (perhaps = sanctioned and
acknowledged in their excellence by careful observation; as the Alexandrine verse, in which the poem
in question is written, shows the good schooling of
its author).

**Rational,** 1) endowed with reason: *the r. hind
Costard,* LLL I, 2, 123 (i. e. the human hind; as *hind*
may also signify an animal. Armado's speech).

2) wise, judicious: *loss of virginity is r. increase,*
All's I, 1, 139 (Hanmer *national,* but this is no Shakespearian word).

**Ratolorum,** Slender's blunder for *Rotulorum:*
Wiv. I, 1, 8.

**Ratsbane,** poison for rats: H4B I, 2, 48. H6A
V, 4, 29. Lr. III, 4, 55.

**Rattle,** subst. an instrument with which a clattering sound is made: Wiv. IV, 4, 51.

**Rattle,** vb. 1) intr. to make a clattering sound:
*dead men's —ing bones,* Rom. IV, 1, 82. *our —ing
tabourines,* Ant. IV, 8, 37. Used of a clattering tongue:
*the —ing tongue of saucy and audacious eloquence,*
Mids. V, 102. Of the thunder: *the dread —ing thunder,*
Tp. V, 44. *he was as —ing thunder,* Ant. V, 2, 86.

2) to berattle, to stun with noise: *another* (drum)
*shall as loud as thine r. the welkin's ear,* John V, 2, 172.

**Raught,** see *Reach.*

**Rave,** to be delirious, to talk or act like a mad-
man: Lucr. 982. Tw. III, 4, 10. H6C I, 4, 91. Troil.
III, 3, 249. Tit. V, 3, 180. Hml. II, 2, 150. Cymb.
IV, 2, 135.

**Ravel,** 1) tr. to entangle: *the —ed sleave of care,*
Mcb. II, 2, 37. *to r. out* = to disentangle: *must I r.
out my weaved-up folly?* R2 IV, 228. *to r. all this
matter out,* Hml. III, 4, 186.

2) intr. to become entangled: *as you unwind her
love from him, lest it should r., you must provide to
bottom it on me,* Gent. III, 2, 52.

**Raven,** subst. the bird Corvus corax: Tp. I, 2,
322. Wiv. I, 3, 38. Mids. II, 2, 114. As II, 3, 43.
Wint. II, 3, 186. John IV, 3, 153. H4A III, 1, 152.
Tit. II, 3, 149. Caes. V, 1, 85. Cymb. II, 2, 49. Living
to a great age: Lucr. 949. Proverbial for blackness:
Sonn. 127, 9. LLL IV, 3, 88. Troil. II, 3, 221. Rom.
III, 2, 19. Ominous: H6B III, 2, 40. H6C V, 6, 47.
Troil. V, 2, 191. Tit. II, 3, 97. III, 1, 158. Mcb. I,
5, 39. Hml. III, 2, 264. Oth. IV, 1, 21. Destitute of
any kind affections: Tw. V, 134. H6B III, 1, 76. Rom.
III, 2, 76. Feeding forsaken children: Tit. II, 3, 153;
cf. Wint. II, 3, 186.

**Raven,** vb. see *Ravin.*

**Raven-coloured,** black: Tit. II, 3, 83.

**Ravenous,** furiously voracious: Merch. IV, 1,
138. R2 III, 2, 13. H6A V, 4, 31. H6B III, 1, 78.
H8 I, 1, 159. I, 2, 79. Tit. V, 3, 5.

**Ravenspurgh,** name of a sea-port in Yorkshire:
R2 II, 1, 296. II, 2, 51. II, 3, 9. 31. H4A I, 3, 248.
III, 2, 95. IV, 3, 77. H6C IV, 7, 8.

**Ravin,** adj. ravenous: *the r. lion,* All's III, 2, 120.

**Ravin,** vb. to devour greedily: *like rats that r.
down their proper bane,* Meas. I, 2, 133. *thriftless ambition that wilt r. up thine own life's means,* Mcb. II,
4, 28. *—ing the lamb,* Cymb. I, 6, 49. cf. *Wolvish-
ravening.*

**Ravined,** adj. ravenous: *the r. salt-sea shark,*
Mcb. IV, 1, 24.

**Ravish,** 1) to rob, to carry away by force: *the
—ed Helen,* Troil. Prol. 9. *these hairs which thou dost
r. from my chin,* Lr. III, 7, 38.

2) to deflower by violence; absol.: *with Tarquin's
—ing strides,* Mcb. II, 1, 55. Trans.: Lucr. Arg. 16.
Mids. II, 1, 78. H6B IV, 8, 31. R3 V, 3, 337. Cor.
IV, 6, 81. Tit. II, 4, 2. IV, 1, 53. V, 1, 92. 129. V,
3, 53. 57. 99. Cymb. III, 5, 142. Per. IV, 1, 103.
IV, 6, 5. 11. Metaphorically, = to pollute (?): *with
rotten damps r. the morning air,* Lucr. 778.

3) to enchant, to transport; absol.: H4A III, 1,
211. H6B I, 1, 32. Trans.: Pilgr. 108. Ado II, 3, 60.
LLL I, 1, 168. II, 75. IV, 3, 260. 348. H6A V, 5, 15.
H8 I, 2, 120.

**Ravisher,** one who deflowers by violence: Lucr.
770. 888. Cor. IV, 5, 243. Tit. V, 2, 103.

**Ravishment,** violation of chastity: Lucr. 430.
1128. All's IV, 3, 281.

**Raw,** 1) not covered with the skin, showing the
naked flesh: *r. as he is* (having been flayed alive)
Wint. IV, 4, 816. *since yet thy cicatrice looks r. and
red,* Hml. IV, 3, 62. Hence the following expressions:
*her eyes, though sod in tears, looked red and r.* Lucr.
1592. *Marian's nose looks red and r.* LLL V, 2, 934.
*r. eyes* = inflamed eyes, Troil. V, 1, 23.

2) unripe, untutored: *a thousand r. tricks of these
bragging Jacks,* Merch. III, 4, 77. *thou art r.* As III,
2, 76. (my service) *being tender, r. and young,* R2 II,
3, 42. *why do we wrap the gentleman in our more —er
breath?* Hml. V, 2, 129. *that she may not be r. in her
entertainment,* Per. IV, 2, 60.

3) inclement, bleak, chilly: *this r. rheumatic day,*
Wiv. III, 1, 47. *is not their climate foggy, r. and dull,*
H5 III, 5, 16. *the air* (Ff *dew*) *is r. and cold,* R3 V,
3, 46. *a r. and gusty day,* Caes. I, 2, 100. *the r. cold
morning,* II, 1, 236.

**Raw-boned,** having no flesh on the bones: *lean
r. rascals,* H6A I, 2, 35.

**Rawly,** without due preparation and provision:
*their children r. left,* H5 IV, 1, 147.

**Rawness,** want of due preparation and provision:
*why in that r. left you wife and child,* Mcb. IV, 3, 26.

**Ray,** a beam of light: LLL IV, 3, 28. H6A I, 2,
85. H8 I, 1, 56. Troil. I, 3, 47. Tit. I, 226. Caes.
V, 3, 61.

**Rayed** (O. Edd. *raied* or *raide*) defiled, dirtied:
*r. with the yellows,* Shr. III, 2, 54. *was ever man so
beaten? was ever man so r.? was ever man so weary?*
IV, 1, 3.

**Raze,** subst. = race (root)? or = package? *I
have a gammon of bacon and two —s of ginger,* H4A
II, 1, 27 (Nares: it is not necessary to suppose the
carriers quite accurate in their expression).

**Raze,** vb. 1) to strike on the surface: *the boar
had —d his helm,* R3 III, 2, 11 (Ff *rased off*). III, 4,
84 (Qq *race,* Ff *rowse*).

2) to level with the ground, to subvert: *to r. the
sanctuary,* Meas. II, 2, 171. *—th your cities,* H6A II, 3, 65.

3) to destroy, to make away with: *to massacre
them all and r. their faction,* Tit. I, 451. *that* (the tribute) *the Britons have —d out,* Cymb. V, 5, 70 (O.
Edd. *raced*).

4) to erase, to blot out: *from the book of honour
—d quite,* Sonn. 25, 11. *that was —d,* Meas. I, 2, 11.
*—ing the characters of your renown,* H6B I, 1, 101.
*I —d my likeness,* Lr. I, 4, 4. *as from thence sorrow*

*were ever —d*, Per. I, 1, 17. With *out:* R2 II, 3, 75. III, 1, 25. H4B V, 2, 127. Mcb. V, 3, 42. *Razed,* adjectively, = leaving no trace behind: *till each to —d oblivion yield his part*, Sonn. 122, 7.

**Razed** (Ff *raced*), = slashed or streaked in patterns: *with two Provincial roses on my r. shoes*, Hml. III, 2, 288.

**Razor,** a knife used in shaving: LLL V, 2, 257. Per. V, 3, 75. *these words are —s to my wounded heart,* Tit. I, 314.

**Razorable,** fit to be shaved: *till new-born chins be rough and r.* Tp. II, 1, 250.

**Razure,** erasure, obliteration: *r. of oblivion,* Meas. V, 13.

**Re,** note in the musical scale: *ut, re, sol, la, mi, fa,* LLL IV, 2, 102. Shr. III, 1, 74. 77. Used as a verb: *I'll re you, I'll fa you,* Rom. IV, 5, 121.

**Reach,** subst. 1) the sphere to which an agency or a power is limited: *the moral of my wit is 'plain and true'; there's all the r. of it,* Troil. IV, 4, 110. *not to strain my speech to grosser issues nor to larger r. than to suspicion,* Oth. III, 3, 219. Preceded by *above, beyond, from,* out *of: above the r. and compass of thy thought,* H6B I, 2, 46. *advanced above pale envy's threatening r.* Tit. II, 1, 4. *beyond the infinite and boundless r. of mercy art thou damned,* John IV, 3, 117. *to shake our disposition with thoughts beyond the —es of our souls,* Hml. I, 4, 56. *from forth thy r. he would have laid thy shame,* R2 II, 1, 106. *from the r. of hell,* R3 IV, 1, 43. *from the r. of these my hands,* Rom. III, 5, 86. *out of his envy's r.* Merch. IV, 1, 10.

2) power or means of attainment or contrivance, ability: *we of wisdom and of r.* Hml. II, 1, 64.

**Reach,** vb. (impf. *raught:* LLL IV, 2, 41. H5 IV, 6, 21. H6C I, 4, 68. Partic. *raught:* H6B II, 3, 43. Ant. IV, 9, 30. *reached:* Oth. I, 2, 24) 1) trans. a) to attain, to touch, to arrive at: *wilt thou r. stars, because they shine on thee?* Gent. III, 1, 156. *if my royal fox could r. them* (grapes) All's II, 1, 75. *they should not laugh if I could r. them,* Wint. II, 3, 25. *this staff of honour raught,* H6B II, 3, 43. *what envy* (can) *r. you?* H8 II, 2, 89. *as proud a fortune as this that I have —ed,* Oth. I, 2, 24. *the hand of death hath raught him,* Ant. IV, 9, 30. *which, without desert, because thine eye presumes to r.* Per. I, 1, 33. *when canst thou r. it* (Tyre)? III, 1, 76.

b) to extend, to stretch out, to hand: *raught me his hand,* H5 IV, 6, 21. Tit. II, 3, 237. *he shall r. his branches to all the plains about him,* H8 V, 5, 54. *r. a chair,* IV, 2, 3.

2) intr. a) to stretch out the hand in order to touch or attain a thing: *one may r. deep enough and yet find little,* Tim. III, 4, 15. With *at:* to *r. at victory above my head,* R2 I, 3, 72. *r. at the glorious gold,* H6B I, 2, 11. *—es at the moon,* III, 1, 158. *raught at mountains,* H6C I, 4, 68. *a black Ethiope —ing at the sun,* Per. II, 2, 20.

b) to be extended enough, to have the power of touching or attaining a thing: *great men have —ing hands,* H6B IV, 7, 86. *I cannot r. so high,* Gent. I, 2, 87 (double meaning). *my arm —eth from the English court as far as Calais,* R2 IV, 12. *it* (his sword) *—es far,* H8 I, 1, 111. With *to,* = to extend to, to attain to, to amount to: *raught not to five weeks,* LLL IV, 2, 41. *my nails can r. unto thine eyes,* Mids. III, 2, 298. *what may the king's whole battle r. unto?* H4A IV, 1,

129. *another close intent which I must r. unto,* R3 I, 1, 159. *to me you cannot r.* H8 V, 3, 126.

**Read** or **Rede,** subst. speech, counsel, advice: *recks not his own r.* Hml. I, 3, 51.

**Read,** vb. (impf. and partic. *read*) 1) to utter or pronounce written words after seeing them in writing: Mids. I, 2, 9. All's IV, 3, 131. Tw. V, 297. 302. Wint. III, 2, 132. H4A V, 1, 73 etc. With a dative: *r. me this letter,* LLL IV, 2, 92. *shall I r. it to you,* All's IV, 3, 234. H4A I, 3, 190. Tim. II, 2, 81. Ant. III, 4, 4 etc. With *over: r. it over,* LLL IV, 3, 195. *that it may be r. over in Paul's,* R3 III, 6, 3. *to r. out* = to r. aloud: Lr. V, 3, 109 (cf. *Out*).

2) to peruse; absol.: Lucr. 616. Gent. III, 1, 291. 329. Wiv. II, 1, 54. Ado III, 3, 12. 16. LLL I, 2, 88. Tw. III, 4, 161. V, 305. 307. John IV, 1, 33. H6B IV, 2, 93. Tim. II, 2, 84. Hml. III, 1, 44 (*r. on this book,* cf. *On*) etc. Transitively: Lucr. 618. Gent. I, 3, 51. III, 1, 289. Meas. II, 4, 8. LLL II, 109. Mids. I, 1, 132. Shr. III, 1, 72. Tw. I, 5, 246. II, 5, 174. III, 4, 157. Wint. III, 2, 131. Tim. V, 1, 158 (*write in thee the figures of their love, ever to r. them thine*). Mcb. I, 3, 152 etc. A clause following: H6A III, 2, 94. H6B I, 1, 128 etc. With *over:* Gent. II, 1, 136. Ado II, 3, 142. R2 IV, 242. H4B III, 1, 36. H6B IV, 4, 14. H8 III, 2, 201. Troil. IV, 5, 239.

Metaphorically, = to gather the meaning of, to perceive, to discover, to guess, to understand, to learn: *how Tarquin must be used, r. it in me,* Lucr. 1195. *mine own self-love quite contrary I r.* Sonn. 62, 11. *I r. your fortune in your eye,* Gent. II, 4, 143. *r. over Julia's heart,* Gent. V, 4, 46. *if I r. it not truly, my ancient skill beguiles me,* Meas. IV, 2, 164. *let not my sister r. it in your eye,* Err. III, 2, 9. 18. *in the modesty of fearful duty I r. as much,* Mids. V, 102. *to r. him by his form,* Tw. III, 4, 291. *I can r. waiting gentlewoman in the scape,* Wint. III, 3, 73. *he'll stand and r. as 'twere my daughter's eyes,* IV, 4, 173. *do you not r. some tokens of my son in the large composition of this man?* John I, 87. *therein should we r. the very bottom and the soul of hope,* H4A IV, 1, 49. *that you shall r. in your own losses,* H5 II, 4, 138. *r. the cardinal's malice and his potency together,* H8 I, 1, 104. *I r. in his looks matter against me,* 125. *like a book of sport thou'lt r. me over,* Troil. IV, 5, 239. *r. o'er the volume of young Paris' face,* Rom. I, 3, 81. *r. not my blemishes in the world's report,* Ant. II, 3, 5. *by her election may be truly r. what kind of man he is,* Cymb. I, 1, 53. *a precedent which not to r. would show the Britons cold,* III, 1, 76. *this story the world may r. in me,* III, 3, 56. *who is't can r. a woman?* V, 5, 48.

3) to gather instruction by means of books, to study: *never r. so far to know the cause why music was ordained,* Shr. III, 1, 9. *profit you in what you r.?* IV, 2, 6. cf. H6B II, 2, 40. Caes. I, 2, 201. Hence = to learn: *those about her from her shall r. the perfect ways of honour,* H8 V, 5, 38 (Mcb. I, 3, 90?). *—ing* = learning: *trust not my —ing nor my observations, which with experimental seal doth warrant the tenour of my book,* Ado IV, 1, 167. *to reason against —ing,* LLL I, 1, 94. *such as his —ing and manifest experience had collected,* All's I, 3, 228. *that you should fashion, wrest or bow your —ing,* H5 I, 2, 14. *read* = learned: *how well he's r., to reason against —ing,* LLL I, 1, 94. *well r. in poetry and other books,* Shr. I, 2, 170.

*exceedingly well* r. H4A III, 1, 166. *thou art deeper* r. *and better skilled*, Tit. IV, 1, 33.

4) to give lessons about, to teach: *what will you* r. *to her?* Shr. I, 2, 154. 155. *give me leave to* r. *philosophy*, III, 1, 13. *what, master,* r. *you?* IV, 2, 7. *I* r. *that I profess, the art to love*, 8. *calls me pupil or hath* r. *to me*, H4A III, 1, 46. *to* r. *lectures:* Shr. I, 2, 148. R2 IV, 232. Cor. II, 3, 243 (cf. *Lecture*).

5) to guess, to divine (German: *rathen*)? *this proves that thou canst not* r. Gent. III, 1, 298 (punning).

**Reader,** one who peruses any thing written: *unclasp the tables of their thoughts to every ticklish* r. Troil. IV, 5, 61.

**Readily,** promptly, easily: *one encompassed with a winding maze, that cannot tread the way out* r. Lucr. 1152. *where this breach now in our fortunes made may* r. *be stopped*, H6B V, 2, 83.

**Readiness,** 1) a state of due preparation for what is to be done: *I am joyful to hear of their* r. Cor. IV, 3, 51. *let's briefly put on manly* r. Mcb. II, 3, 139 (i. e. dress ourselves; cf. *Ready*). *the* r. *is all*, Hml. V, 2, 234. *in* r. = ready, prepared: Gent. I, 3, 70. Merch. II, 4, 33. Shr. I, 1, 43. H6A III, 1, 186. H6C II, 2, 67. V, 4, 64. R3 V, 3, 52. Tit. I, 325. Tim. I, 2, 172. Cymb. III, 5, 23. IV, 2, 336.

2) facility, ease: *I thought, by your* r. *in the office, you had continued in it some time*, Meas. II, 1, 275.

**Reading,** subst. see *Read* vb.

**Readins,** Evans' blunder for *Reading* (town in Berkshire): Wiv. IV, 5, 80.

**Ready** (superl. —*est;* compar. not used), 1) quick, prompt, not hesitating, not backward: *what a* r. *tongue suspicion hath*, H4B I, 1, 84. *the answer is as* r. *as a borrowed cap*, II, 2, 124. *bid the cheek be* r. *with a blush*, Troil. I, 3, 228. *the din of war gan pierce his* r. *sense*, Cor. II, 2, 120. *Rome's —est champions*, Tit. I, 151. r. *in gibes, quick-answered*, Cymb. III, 4, 161. Sir Andrew says: *I'll get 'em all three all* r. Tw. III, 1, 102 (= I will keep them in mind and make prompt use of them).

2) easy, opportune, commodious: *which is the —est way to the house of Baptista?* Shr. I, 2, 220. *the —est way to make the wench amends*, R3 I, 1, 155. *which I could with a* r. *guess declare*, H5 I, 1, 96.

3) apt, willing, disposed: *it makes me almost* r. *to wrangle with mine own honesty*, Wiv. II, 1, 88. *me shall you find* r. *and willing to have her so bestowed*, Shr. IV, 4, 34. *I am* r. *to distrust mine eyes*, Tw. IV, 3, 13. r. *to catch each other by the throat*, R3 I, 3, 189. *more* r. *to cry out 'Who knows what follows'?* Troil. II, 2, 13. *the —est man to kill him*, Tim. I, 2, 49. *prevailed on thy too* r. *hearing*, Cymb. III, 2, 6 (cf. the quibble in II, 3, 86).

4) being at the point, near, about: *riches* r. *to drop upon me*, Tp. III, 2, 151. *my heart is* r. *to crack*, Wiv. II, 2, 301. r. *to leap out of himself for joy*, Wint. V, 2, 54. *if my heart be not* r. *to burst*, H4B IV, 4, 409. r. *to starve*, H6B I, 1, 229. IV, 10, 2. r., *with every nod, to tumble down*, R3 III, 4, 102. *the fire your city is* r. *to flame in*, Cor. V, 2, 49. *we are* r. *to decline*, Caes. III, 3, 217. r. *to give up the ghost*, V, 1, 89. *I am almost* r. *to dissolve*, Lr. V, 3, 203.

5) prepared, sufficiently fit for a purpose: *when her lips were* r. *for his pay*, Ven. 89. *one of my husband's men bid thou be* r. *to bear a letter*, Lucr. 1292. *make yourself* r. *for the mischance of the hour*, Tp. I,

1, 27. *I am* r. *now*, I, 2, 187. *dinner is* r. Gent. I, 2, 131. *it* (the rapier) *is* r. *here in the porch*, Wiv. I, 4, 63. *be* r. *here hard by*, III, 3, 10. *be* r. *for your death*, Meas. III, 1, 107. *who hath a story* r. *for your ear*, IV, 1, 56. *is the axe upon the block? Very* r., *sir*, IV, 3, 40. Ado II, 3, 218. III, 4, 53. III, 5, 61. V, 4, 39. Mids. III, 2, 402. Merch. II, 2, 122. IV, 1, 15. 256. 337. As I, 2, 155. Shr. Ind. 1, 50. IV, 1, 41. Tw. II, 4, 50. John II, 211 (r. *mounted);* cf. V, 2, 169. H6A II, 4, 104. H6B III, 3, 49. H6C IV, 1, 105. Troil. III, 2, 31. Ant. III, 3, 40. V, 1, 72. Cymb. II, 3, 86 (= dressed; cf. the stage-direction in H6A II, 1, 39: *half* r. *and half unready*). V, 4, 152. 154. Per. III, 1, 72 etc. etc. *make* r. *breakfast*, H4A III, 3, 192. *make you* r. *your stiff bats*, Cor. I, 1, 165. *to make* r. = to make things ready, to be prepared: *go to your knees and make* r. Meas. III, 1, 172. *let us make* r. *straight*, Troil. IV, 4, 146.

6) in place, here, at hand (in answering to a call): *Nick Bottom! R.* Mids. I, 2, 20. III, 1, 166. *where's Peaseblossom? R.* IV, 1, 6. 9. 19. *is Antonio here? R.* Merch. IV, 1, 2. *where is this young gallant? R.* As I, 2, 214. Rom. I, 5, 12.

7) present in hand, in cash: *he made five marks* r. *money*, Meas. IV, 3, 7.

**Reak,** see *Reck.*

**Real,** 1) actually being, true, not imaginary: *is't* r. *that I see?* All's V, 3, 307. *it must omit* r. *necessities*, Cor. III, 1, 147.

2) genuine, not artificial or factitious: *his* r. *habitude gave life and grace to appertainings and to ornament*, Compl. 114.

**Really,** in truth, indeed: *is't not possible to understand in another tongue? you will do't, sir,* r. Hml. V, 2, 132.

**Realm,** kingdom: Wiv. V, 5, 153. John IV, 3, 144. R2 I, 3, 198. I, 4, 45. II, 1, 50. 256. IV, 325. V, 1, 60. H4A III, 2, 101. IV, 3, 66. H4B V, 3, 92. H5 I, 2, 41. V, 2, 388. H6A I, 1, 38. 53. I, 3, 12. 32. 66. I, 6, 19. II, 2, 36. III, 1, 114. III, 4, 2. IV, 1, 147. IV, 7, 71. V, 1, 6. V, 4, 112. V, 5, 108. H6B I, 1, 89. 182. 232. I, 2, 43. I, 3, 123. 129. 164. II, 2, 24. II, 3, 30 (*England's* r.). 31. III, 1, 61. IV, 1, 74. IV, 2, 74. IV, 7, 16. 36. 75. 127. H6C I, 1, 126. 240. II, 6, 18. V, 4, 78. R3 III, 2, 40. H8 II, 4, 52. 197. V, 3, 16. Tim. III, 3, 34. Hml. III, 2, 293. Lr. III, 2, 91. V, 3, 320. Ant. V, 2, 91.

**Re-answer,** to compensate, to repay, to make amends for: *which in weight to* r. *his pettiness would bow under*, H5 III, 6, 136.

**Reap,** to cut down and gather (corn at harvest); absol.: As III, 2, 113. Ant. V, 2, 88. Trans.: Meas. IV, 1, 76. LLL IV, 3, 383. H4A I, 3, 34 (*his chin new —ed*, i. e. shorn). *to* r. *a harvest:* Sonn. 128, 7. As III, 5, 103. H6B III, 1, 381. R3 II, 2, 116. V, 2, 15. Metaphorically, = to gather, to obtain, to earn: r. *thanks*, All's II, 1, 150. *when wit and youth is come to harvest, your wife is like to* r. *a proper man*, Tw. III, 1, 144. *little vantage shall I* r. R2 I, 3, 218. *such comfort as now I* r. *at thy too cruel hand*, H6C I, 4, 166. *of our labours thou shalt* r. *the gain*, V, 7, 20. *the benefit which thou shalt thereby* r. Cor. V, 3, 143. *to* r. *the fame*, V, 6, 36. *this is a thing which you might from relation likewise* r. Cymb. II, 4, 86 (= hear, learn). In a bad sense: *what sudden anger's this? how have I —ed it?* H8 III, 2, 204.

**Reaper,** one that cuts corn, an agricultural labourer: Ant. III, 7, 36.

**Rear,** subst. the hinder part of an army: *lie there for pavement to the abject r.* Troil. III, 3, 162. *in the r. of* = behind: *keep you in the r. of your affection,* Hml. I, 3, 34. *Of* omitted: *she is i' the r. our birth,* Wint. IV, 4, 592 (cf. *Of*).

**Rear,** vb. 1) tr. a) to raise: *when I r. my hand,* Tp. II, 1, 295. *you are the first that —s your hand,* Caes. III, 1, 30. *his —ed arm crested the world,* Ant. V, 2, 82. *r. up his body,* H6B III, 2, 34. *—ed aloft the bloody battle-axe,* Tit. III, 1, 169. *had our weak spirits ne'er been higher —ed,* Wint. I, 2, 72. *whom I from meaner form have benched and —ed to worship,* 314. *checks and disasters grow in the veins of actions highest —ed,* Troil. I, 3, 6. *let us r. the higher our opinion,* Ant. II, 1, 35.

b) to erect (cf. *High-reared* in R3 V, 3, 242): *a statelier pyramis to her I'll r.* H6A I, 6, 21. *of the paste a coffin I will r.* Tit. V, 2, 189. *some beast —ed this,* Tim V, 3, 4 (O. Edd. *reade*).

c) to place high: *r. it* (his head) *in the place your father's stands,* H6C II, 6, 86.

d) to rouse, to stir up: *if you r. this house against this house,* R2 IV, 145 (Qq *raise*).

e) to breed, to bring up: *I'll not r. another's issue,* Wint. II, 3, 192. *shall thy old dugs once more a traitor r.?* R2 V, 3, 90. *from their ashes shall be —ed a phoenix,* H6A IV, 7, 92. With *up: for her sake do I r. up her boy,* Mids. II, 1, 136.

2) intr. to rise up on the hind legs: *he —s upright, curvets and leaps,* Ven. 279.

**Rear-mice** (O. Edd. *reremise*), leather-winged bats: Mids. II, 2, 4.

**Rearward,** subst. the last troop, rearguard: H6A III, 3, 33. Figuratively: *do not come in the r. of a conquered woe,* Sonn. 90, 6 (viz to attack and afflict me anew). *myself would, on the r. of reproaches, strike at thy life,* Ado IV, 1, 128 (would come after them to finish what they had only done by halves). *came ever in the r. of the fashion,* H4B III, 2, 339. *with a r. following Tybalt's death, Romeo is banished,* Rom. III, 2, 121.

**Reason,** subst. 1) the rational faculty, the power of the mind by which it distinguishes truth from falsehood, or good from bad, and forms correct ideas of things: *beating r. back,* Ven. 557. *when r. is the bawd to lust's abuse,* 792. *my will is strong, past —'s weak removing,* Lucr. 243. *past r. hunted,* Sonn. 129, 6. *my r., the physician to my love,* 147, 5. Pilgr. 301. Phoen. 47. Tp. I, 2, 208. V, 26. 68. 155. Gent. II, 4, 210. II, 7, 23. Wiv. II, 1, 5. Meas. IV, 4, 28. V, 64. 65. Err. V, 189. Mids. II, 2, 115. 116. V, 6. Shr. V, 2, 171. Tw. I, 5, 212. III, 1, 164. III, 2, 16. H4B IV, 1, 157. Rom. IV, 5, 83. Cymb. IV, 2, 22 etc. *rhyme and r.* joined: *in despite of the teeth of all rhyme and r.* Wiv. V, 5, 133. *in the why and the wherefore is neither rhyme nor r.* Err. II, 2, 49. *in r. nothing. Something then in rhyme,* LLL I, 1, 99. *a dangerous rhyme against the r. of white and red,* I, 2, 112. *neither rhyme nor r. can express how much,* As III, 2, 418. cf. Gent. II, 1, 149 and H5 V, 2, 165. *in r.* = in justice, with rational ground: *his unjust unkindness, that in all r. should have quenched her love,* Meas. III, 1, 250. *keeping such vile company as thou art hath in r. taken from me all ostentation of sorrow,* H4B II, 2, 53. *yet in r. no man should possess him with any appearance of fear,* H5 IV, 1, 115. *his trespass, in our common r., is*

*not almost a fault,* Oth. III, 3, 64. *in all safe r. he must have some attendants,* Cymb. IV, 2, 131.

Abstr. pro concr., = any thing conformable to the principles of the rational faculty: *I shall do that that is r.* Wiv. I, 1, 218. *as it shall become one that would do r.* 242. *I will do a greater thing than that in any r.* 249 (Slender's speeches). *you should hear r.* Ado I, 3, 6. *thou speakest r.* V, 1, 41. *his —s are as two grains of wheat hid in two bushels of chaff,* Merch. I, 1, 116. *an you will not be answered with r., I must die,* As II, 7, 100. *I am loath to prove r. with them* (words) Tw. III, 1, 29. *my reasonable part produces r. how I may be delivered of these woes,* John III, 4, 54. *more than r.* = beyond measure: *do not you love me? Why, no; no more than r.* Ado V, 4, 74. 77. *it is much that the Moor should be more than r.* (i. e. with child) Merch. III, 5, 45.

2) equity, fairness, justice: *but yet in courtesy, in all r., we must stay the time,* Mids. V, 259. *in r. we should never come to heaven,* Merch. III, 5, 83. *r. my son should choose himself a wife, but as good r. the father ... should hold some counsel in such a business,* Wint. IV, 4, 417. 418. *we have consented to all terms of r.* H5 V, 2, 358. *'tis but r. that I be released from giving aid,* H6C III, 3, 147. *to have r.* = to be in the right: *you have no r. to withhold me so,* Ven. 612. *love hath r., r. none,* Phoen. 47. *have I not r. to prefer mine own?* Gent. II, 4, 156. cf. Err. IV, 2, 62.

3) argumentation, discourse, speech: *flesh stays no farther r.* Sonn. 151, 8. *when she will play with r. and discourse,* Meas. I, 2, 190. *your —s at dinner have been sharp and sententious,* LLL V, 1, 2. *lame me with —s,* As I, 3, 6. *feed yourselves with questioning, that r. wonder may diminish how thus we met,* V, 4, 145. *your —s are too shallow and too quick,* R3 IV, 4, 361. 362. *those fell mischiefs our —s laid before him,* H8 V, 1, 50. *perhaps thy childishness will move him more than can our —s,* Cor. V, 3, 158. 6, 59.

4) satisfaction; *to do r.* = Fr. *faire raison: at thy request I will do r., any r.* Tp. III, 2, 128 (*je vous ferai raison*). *resolved withal to do myself this r. and this right,* Tit. I, 279 (*à me faire raison moi-même*).

5) cause, ground, motive: Sonn. 49, 8. 115, 3. Gent. I, 2, 23. II, 1, 149. II, 4, 206. Wiv. II, 1, 4. III, 1, 48. Meas. IV, 4, 13. Err. II, 2, 91. 105. III, 1, 97. IV, 2, 62. IV, 3, 87. Ado IV, 1, 260. V, 1, 211 (punning, according to some commentators, upon *reasons* and *raisins;* reference being made to H4A II, 4, 264). LLL I, 2, 92. Mids. III, 1, 146. Merch. III, 1, 60. As V, 2, 39. All's III, 1, 2. 12. Tw. II, 5, 178. H5 IV, 1, 113. H6B I, 3, 116. 166. H8 II, 2, 7. Cymb. IV, 2, 22 etc. *by r. of* = on account of: As II, 4, 85. H6A V, 5, 33. *to give —s* = a) to give cause: *he loves me well, and I have given him —s,* Caes. II, 1, 219. b) to tell one's motive or occasion: *so can I give no r.* Merch. IV, 1, 59. *I'll give him —s for't,* Tw. I, 5, 325. III, 2, 3. H4A II, 4, 264. *to render —s,* in the same sense: Meas. I, 3, 48. Merch. IV, 1, 53. *there is no r. but* = it is necessary, it cannot be helped: *there is no r. but I shall be blind,* Gent. II, 4, 212. cf. *I see no r. but supposed Lucentio must get a father, called supposed Vincentio,* Shr. II, 409. Elliptical expressions: *r.* = there is good reason for it: *r., you rogues, r.* Wiv. II, 2, 15. *r.: because they then less need one another,* Cor. IV, 5, 247. *he is prepared, and r. too he should:* John V, 2, 130. *and r. too: who*

*should succeed the father but the son?* H6C II, 2, 93. *great r.*, in the same sense: *great r., for past cure is still past care*, LLL V, 2, 28. *then fly … great r. why: lest I revenge*, R3 V, 3, 185. *and being intercepted in your sport, great r. that my noble lord be rated for sauciness*, Tit. II, 3, 81. *the r.?* = tell me your reason: H4B II, 2, 55. *your r.?* in the same sense: Tp. I, 2, 176. Gent. I, 2, 22. Err. II, 2, 62. LLL II, 233. As III, 2, 40. Tw. II, 3, 156. III, 1, 26. H4A II, 4, 260.

**Reason,** vb. 1) to argue, to debate: *that makes me reasonless to r. thus*, Gent. II, 4, 198. *r. thus with life*, Meas. III, 1, 6. *rightly —ed*, Ado V, 1, 229. *to r. against reading*, LLL I, 1, 94. *this — ing is not in the fashion to choose me a husband*, Merch. I, 2, 23. *teach thy necessity to r.* thus, R2 I, 3, 277. *I must not have you henceforth question me whither I go, nor r. whereabout*, H4A II, 3, 107. *hear him but r. in divinity*, H5 I, 1, 38. *I will not r. what is meant hereby*, R3 I, 4, 94. *let's r. with the worst that may befall*, Caes. V, 1, 97. *I cannot r.* Hml. II, 2, 272. *why is this —ed?* Lr. V, 1, 28. With an accus. denoting the effect: *these fellows of infinite tongue, that can rhyme themselves into ladies' favours, they do always r. themselves out again*, H5 V, 2, 165. Transitively: *though the wisdom of nature can r. it thus and thus*, Lr. I, 2, 114. *r. not the need*, II, 4, 267.

2) to speak: *what are you —ing with yourself?* Gent. II, 1, 147. *are you mad, that you do r. so?* Err. III, 2, 53. *how fondly dost thou r.* IV, 2, 57. *I —ed with a Frenchman yesterday, who told me …*, Merch. II, 8, 27. *too dull to r. of such goddesses*, As I, 2, 56. *our griefs, and not our manners, r. now*, John IV, 3, 29. *'tis a subject for a sovereign to r. on*, H5 III, 7, 38. *let's r. with him*, R3 I, 4, 165. *you cannot r. almost with any man that looks not heavily*, II, 3, 39. *with what a sharp-provided wit he —s*, III, 1, 132. *while we r. here, a royal battle might be won and lost*, IV, 4, 537. *we'll put you in manacles, then r. safely with you*, Cor. I, 9, 58. *r. with the fellow, where he heard this*, IV, 6, 51. *and r. coldly of your grievances*, Rom. III, 1, 55. *I am not very sick, since I can r. of it*, Cymb. IV, 2, 14. *my commission is not to r. of the deed, but do it*, Per. IV, 1, 84. Transitively: *this boy, that cannot tell what he would have, but kneels and holds up hands for fellowship, does r. our petition with more strength than thou hast to deny it*, Cor. V, 3, 176.

**Reasonable,** 1) endued with, or conformable to, reason: *their understanding begins to swell, and the approaching tide will shortly fill the r. shore*, Tp. V, 81 (= the shore of reason? or, by a prolepsis, the shore which is thus restored to reason?). *my jealousy is r.* Wiv. IV, 2, 155 (cf. 147). *a r. creature*, Ado I, 1, 71. Merch. I, 2, 119. *out of all r. match*, As III, 2, 87. *incapable of r. affairs*, Wint. IV, 4, 409. *a r. man*, 617. *my r. part produces reason*, John III, 4, 54. *all things thought upon that may with r. swiftness add more feathers to our wings*, H5 I, 2, 306 (a wise, considerate swiftness). *your purpose is both good and r.* H6A V, 1, 36.

2) equitable: *you shall find me r.* Wiv. I, 1, 217. *upon any r. demands*, 233. *my pension shall seem the more r.* H4B I, 2, 276. *it is a quarrel just and r.* R3 I, 2, 136.

3) tolerable, not immoderate: *if he be of any r. stature*, Wiv. III, 3, 138. *out of all r. compass*, H4A III, 3, 26. *a r. measure*, H5 V, 2, 141. Used adver-

bially by Bottom and Fluellen: Mids. IV, 1, 31. H5 III, 6, 104.

**Reasonably,** equitably: *whate'er Lord Harry Percy then had said … may r. die*, H4A I, 3, 74.

**Reasonless,** void of reason: Gent. II, 4, 198. H6A V, 4, 137.

**Reave** (impf. and partic. *reft*) 1) to bereave, to deprive; with *of:* —*s his son of life*, Ven. 766. *would have reft the fishers of their prey*, Err. I, 1, 116. 129. Ado IV, 1, 198. All's V, 3, 86. H6B V, 1, 187. R3 IV, 4, 233. Cymb. III, 3, 103 (O. Edd. *refts*, M. Edd. *reft'st*). Per. II, 3, 84.

2) to take away: *since he himself is reft from her by death*, Ven. 1174.

**Rebate,** to blunt, to disedge: *doth r. and blunt his natural edge*, Meas. I, 4, 60.

**Rebato,** see *Rabato.*

**Rebeck** (a three-stringed fiddle) name in Rom. IV, 5, 135.

**Rebel,** subst. one who revolts from lawful authority: Lucr. 714. Shr. V, 2, 159. R2 I, 4, 38. II, 3, 147. III, 2, 7. V, 6, 2. H4A III, 2, 160. 165. III, 3, 214. V, 2, 40. V, 4, 14. 62. H4B Ind. 27. I, 2, 86. IV, 2, 9. 116. IV, 3, 69. IV, 4, 9. 86. H6B I, 1, 283. IV, 4, 8. 27. 42. IV, 5, 6. 9. IV, 8, 13. V, 1, 62. 212. H6C I, 1, 50. R3 I, 3, 162. IV, 4, 332. 483. 532. Mcb. I, 2, 10. 15. I, 3, 91. 112. With *to* (= against): *a very r. to my will*, Ant. IV, 9, 14. *a r. to her state*, Per. II, 5, 62.

Adjectively: *thy r. will*, Lucr. 625. *r. powers*, Sonn. 146, 2. *any r. or vain spirit*, H4B IV, 5, 172. *such r. blood*, Caes. III, 1, 40.

**Rebel,** vb. to 'rise in violent opposition against lawful authority, to revolt: Merch. III, 1, 37. 38. R2 III, 2, 119. H6A IV, 1, 142. Tim. IV, 3, 391. Lr. II, 2, 82. Oth. III, 4, 43. Cymb. V, 4, 96. With *against:* H4B II, 4, 379. Cor. I, 1, 100. With *to*, in the same sense: H8 I, 1, 43. Hml. I, 3, 44. Ant. I, 4, 33.

**Rebel-like,** like a rebel: Lr. IV, 3, 16.

**Rebellion,** insurrection against lawful authority, revolt: Meas. III, 2, 122. All's IV, 3, 23. V, 3, 6 (*natural r.* = r. of nature). John III, 1, 298. V, 4, 11. R2 II, 3, 109. 147. III, 2, 26. H4A V, 1, 28. 74. V, 5, 1. 41. H4B Ind. 26. I, 1, 41. 194. I, 2, 90. IV, 1, 32. 92. IV, 2, 117. H5 V Chor. 32. H6C I, 1, 133 (four syllables in the middle of the verse). H8 I, 2, 29. Cor. I, 1, 162. III, 1, 70. 167. Hml. IV, 5, 121. Followed by *to* (= against): *r. to thyself*, John III, 1, 289. By *with: in r. with himself*, Wint. I, 2, 355.

**Rebellious,** revolted, or apt to revolt: As II, 3, 49 (*hot and r. liquors*). R2 V, 1, 5. H6A II, 3, 64. H6B IV, 2, 130. Rom. I, 1, 88. Mcb. I, 2, 56. IV, 1, 97. Hml. III, 4, 82. With *to:* H6A V, 4, 171. Hml. II, 2, 492.

**Rebound,** subst. resilience, reverberation: *I do feel, by the r. of yours, a grief that smites my very heart at root*, Ant. V, 2, 104.

**Rebreathe,** to reanimate: *that need to be revived and breathed in me*, H4B IV, 1, 114 (the prefix *re* belonging to both verbs).

**Rebukable,** reprehensible, disgraceful: Ant. IV, 4, 30.

**Rebuke,** subst. 1) check, restraint, correction, chastisement: *not Gaunt's —s, nor England's private wrongs*, R2 II, 1, 166. *r. and dread correction wait on us*, H4A V, 1, 111. *thus ever did rebellion find r.* V,

5, 1. *to sin's r.* H6C IV, 6, 44. *for living murmurers there's places of r.* H8 II, 2, 132. *receives r. from Norway,* Hml. II, 2, 69. *the best of you shall sink in my r.* Oth. II, 3, 209. *so tender of —s that words are strokes and strokes death to her,* Cymb. III, 5, 40.

2) reproof, reproach: *against all checks, —s and manners,* Wiv. III, 4, 84. *why bear you these —s and answer not?* Err. V, 89. *I never knew yet but r. and check was the reward of valour,* H4B IV, 3, 34. *this dear and deep r.* IV, 5, 141. *would pluck reproof and r. from every ear,* Cor. II, 2, 38. *my caution was more pertinent than the r. you give it,* 68. *we have your wrong r.* Oth. I, 1, 131. *a good r.* Ant. III, 7, 26.

**Rebuke,** vb. 1) to check, to restrain, to quell: *to r. the usurpation of thy uncle,* John II, 9. *we could have —d him at Harfleur,* H5 III, 6, 128. *under him my Genius is —d,* Mcb. III, 1, 56. *thou god of this great vast, r. these surges,* Per. III, 1, 1.

2) to chastise: *so I return —d to my content,* Sonn. 119, 13. *the gods r. me, but it is tidings to wash the eyes of kings,* Ant. V, 1, 27.

3) to reprove, to chide: *r. me not for that which you provoke,* LLL V, 2, 347. *why r. you him that loves you so?* Mids. III, 2, 43. *does not the stone r. me for being more stone than it?* Wint. V, 3, 37. *rate, r. and roughly send to prison the heir of England,* H4B V, 2, 70.

**Rebuse,** Grumio's blunder for *abuse* or *rebuke:* Shr. I, 2, 7.

**Recall,** 1) to call back: *in rage sent out, —ed in rage,* Lucr. 1671. *— ed from their exile,* Gent. V, 4, 155. Wint. III, 2, 157. *—ed to life again,* H6A I, 1, 66. *r. his life,* H6B III, 2, 61.

2) to revoke, to annul by a subsequent act: *passed sentence may not be —ed,* Err. I, 1, 148. *r. not what we give,* Per. III, 1, 25.

**Recant,** to retract, to contradict or unsay what one has said: Merch. IV, 1, 391. R2 I, 1, 193. Tim. I, 2, 17.

**Recantation,** retraction, declaration contradictory to a former one: All's II, 3, 195.

**Recanter,** one that recants: Tim. V, 1, 149.

**Receipt,** 1) the act of receiving, of taking a thing given or sent: *thou didst deny the gold's r.* Err. II, 2, 17. *disburse the sum on the r. thereof* (a chain) IV, 1, 38. *to confess r. of that which hath so faithfully been paid,* LLL II, 156. *at the r. of your letter,* Merch. IV, 1, 151. Applied to things taken as food or medicine: *Romeo should, upon r. thereof* (a poison) *soon sleep in quiet,* Rom. III, 5, 99.

2) the thing received; used of a sum of money: *three parts of that r. I had for Calais disbursed I duly,* R2 I, 1, 126. Of meat and drink: *drunken desire must vomit his r.* Lucr. 703. *the mutinous parts that envied his* (the stomach's) *r.* Cor. I, 1, 116.

3) capacity, power of receiving and containing: *in things of great r. with ease we prove among a number one is reckoned none,* Sonn. 136, 7.

4) reception, admission of entrance for holding and containing: *the most convenient place that I can think of for such r. of learning is Blackfriars,* H8 II, 2, 139.

5) receptacle, place receiving and containing: *the r. of reason a limbeck only,* Mcb. I, 7, 66.

6) a recipe, medical prescription: *his good r. shall for my legacy be sanctified by the luckiest stars in*

heaven, All's I, 3, 250. *many —s he gave me,* II, 1, 108. *we have the r. of fern-seed,* H4A II, 1, 96.

**Receive,** 1) to get; to take or obtain or suffer as a thing offered or sent (whether good or evil): *—ing nought by elements so slow but heavy tears,* Sonn. 44, 13. *my name —s a brand,* 111, 5. *not to be —s reproach of being,* 121, 2. *of whom I have —d a second life,* Tp. V, 195. *—ing them from such a worthless post,* Gent. I, 1, 161. *what maintenance he from his friends —s,* I, 3, 68. *I have —d my proportion,* II, 3, 3. *she hath —d your letter,* Wiv. II, 2, 83. *meed I have —d none,* 212. *no promise,* 217. *I shall not only r. this villanous wrong,* 308. *having —d wrong by some person,* III, 1, 53. *r. her approbation,* Meas. I, 2, 183. *he should r. his punishment in thanks,* I, 4, 28. *that gracious denial which he is most glad to r.* III, 1, 167. *to have —d no sinister measure from his judge,* III, 2, 256. *to r. some instruction from my fellow partner,* IV, 2, 18. *he —s letters,* 215. *—ing a dishonoured life with ransom of such shame,* IV, 4, 34. Err. II, 2, 9. IV, 1, 11. IV, 4, 101. V, 228. Ado IV, 2, 49. LLL I, 1, 269. II, 134. V, 2, 787. Merch. I, 1, 164. III, 2, 141. IV, 1, 41. V, 185. All's II, 1, 4. IV, 3, 362 (*women that had —d so much shame*). Wint. III, 2, 179 (*torture*). 224 (*affliction*). H4A I, 3, 111 (*wounds*). H6A V, 1, 51. V, 5, 47. H6B I, 1, 87. II, 1, 64. II, 3, 3 (cf. Per. I, 1, 90). 36. Troil. III, 1, 169. Cor. II, 3, 113. Tim. III, 5, 85. Lr. I, 1, 299. II, 1, 110. III, 7, 95. Oth. III, 3, 196 etc.

2) to take into one's hand as a thing due or serving a certain purpose (German: in Empfang nehmen): *—s the scroll without or yea or no,* Lucr. 1340. *did in your name r. it,* Gent. I, 2, 40. *I'll visit you and then r. my money for the chain,* Err. III, 2, 180. *r. the money now,* 181. *r. it so,* Tw. II, 2, 12. *follow me and r. it* (your commission) Ant. II, 3, 42.

3) to accept, not to refuse: *she —d my dog?* Gent. IV, 4, 55. *keep you your word, O duke, to give your daughter; you yours, Orlando, to r. his daughter,* As V, 4, 20. *think you, if you should tender your supposed aid, he would r. it?* All's I, 3, 243. *would never r. the ring again,* V, 3, 101. *thou shalt be fortunate, if thou r. me for thy warlike mate,* H6A I, 2, 92. *admit no messengers, r. no tokens,* Hml. II, 2, 144.

4) to welcome, to grant admittance to: *the fairest queen that ever king —d,* H6B I, 1, 16. *r. 'em nobly,* H8 I, 4, 58. *did he r. you well?* Hml. III, 1, 10. *we must r. him according to the honour of his sender,* Cymb. II, 3, 62. Wint. IV, 4, 537 (*—ing = reception*). H4B II, 4, 97. 101. H5 V, 2, 396. Tit. I, 421. IV, 2, 158. Caes. III, 1, 175 (*r. you in*). Mcb. III, 6, 26. Lr. II, 4, 295. Oth. III, 4, 88. Cymb. IV, 4, 5.

5) to take as into a vessel or on a surface, in order to hold and contain: absol.: *thy capacity —th as the sea,* Tw. I, 1, 11. *printing their proud hoofs i' the —ing earth,* H5 Prol. 27. Trans.: *the sea, all water, yet —s rain still,* Sonn. 135, 9. *which gifts ... the capacity of your soft cheveril conscience would r.* H8 II, 3, 32. *the basin that —s your guilty blood,* Tit. V, 2, 184. *Lavinia, r. the blood,* 198. *his cheek —s her soft hand's print,* Ven. 353. *to trust those tables* (viz brain and heart) *that r. thee more,* Sonn. 122, 12.

6) to take in a moral sense, to embrace: *why lovest thou that which thou —st not gladly?* Sonn. 8, 3. *he —s comfort like cold porridge,* Tp. II, 1, 10. *our hearts r. your warnings,* All's II, 1, 22. *if they will patiently r. my medicine,* As II, 7, 61. *which* (truth) *I r. much*

*better than to be pitied of thee*, Wint. III, 2, 234. *how did this offer seem —d?* H5 I, 1, 82. *how hath she —d his love?* Hml. II, 2, 129. *my sister may r. it much more worse*, Lr. II, 2, 155. *how mine* (death) *—d shall be*, Ant. I, 3, 65.

7) to entertain, to feel: *the queen —s much comfort in 't*, Wint. II, 2, 27. *my conscience first —d a tenderness, scruple and prick*, H8 II, 4, 170. *r. what cheer you may*, Mcb. IV, 3, 239.

8) to embrace intellectually, to acknowledge, to believe: *once again I do r. thee honest*, Gent. V, 4, 78. *drove the grossness of the foppery into a – d belief*, Wiv. V, 5, 132. *so I have strewed it in the common ear, and so it is —d*, Meas. I, 3, 16. *move under the influence of the most —d star*, All's II, 1, 57. *his youth will aptly r. it*, Tw. III, 4, 212. *mine integrity being counted falsehood, shall, as I express it, be so —d*, Wint. III, 2, 29. *let me pass the same I am, ere ancient'st order was, or what is now —d*, IV, 1, 11. *will it not be —d that they have done it?* Mcb. I, 7, 74. *who dares r. it other*, 77. *it was, as I —d it, an excellent play*, Hml. II, 2, 458.

9) to become aware of, to perceive by the senses, to see, to hear, to smell: *—d and did deliver to our age this tale*, Wiv. IV, 4, 37. *we here r. it a certainty*, All's I, 2, 4. *—s not thy nose court-odour from me?* Wint. IV, 4, 757. *the fixed sentinels almost r. the secret whispers of each other's watch*, H5 IV Chor. 6. *this from a dying man r. as certain*, H8 II, 1, 125. *—ing the bad air*, Caes. I, 2, 252. *the most piteous tale that ever ear —d*, Lr. V, 3, 215. *r. it from me then*, Cymb. III, 1, 66 (cf. Oth. III, 3, 196). *you have at large —d the danger of the task*, Per. I, 1, 1. cf. H6B II, 3, 3 and Per. I, 1, 90.

10) to conceive, to understand: *to be —d plain, I'll speak more gross*, Meas. II, 4, 82. *to one of your —ing enough is shown*, Tw. III, 1, 131.

11) Quite synonymous to take: *if for my love thou my love — st*, Sonn. 40, 5. *in him a plenitude of subtle matter all strange forms – s*, Compl. 303. *ere I last —d the holy sacrament*, R2 I, 1, 139. *thou didst r. the holy sacrament, to fight in quarrel of the house of Lancaster*, R3 I, 4, 208; cf. R2 IV, 328. *the nobles r. so to heart the banishment of Coriolanus*, Cor. IV, 3, 22.

**Receiver,** one to whom a thing is given: *puts to him all the learnings that his time could make him the r. of*, Cymb. I, 1, 44.

**Receptacle** (*réceptacle*), a place destined to receive what life secerns from itself; used of graves and sewers: *O sacred r. of my joys*, Tit. I, 92. *this fell devouring r.* II, 3, 235. *in a vault, an ancient r.* Rom. IV, 3, 39. *empty old —s, or common shores, of filth*, Per. IV, 6, 186.

**Recheat,** (O. Edd. *rechate*) a hunting term for a certain set of notes, sounded on the horn, to call the dogs off: *but that I will have a r. winded in my forehead, ... all women shall pardon me*, Ado I, 1, 242 (= supply horns for such a purpose. Nares).

**Reciprocal,** mutual: Lr. IV, 6, 267.

**Reciprocally,** mutually: H8 I, 1, 162..

**Recite,** to expose, to relate, to tell: *to r. what merit lived in me*, Sonn. 72, 1 (cf. *Fore-recited*).

**Reck** (O. Edd. *reak* or *wreak*), to care for, to mind: *what —eth he his rider's angry stir*, Ven. 283. *—ing as little what betideth me*, Gent. IV, 3, 40. *and little —s to find the way to heaven by doing deeds of*

*hospitality*, As II, 4, 81. *I r. not though I end my life to-day*, Troil. V, 6, 26. *—s not his own rede*, Hml. I, 3, 51. *that's all I r.* Cymb. IV, 2, 154.

**Reckless** (O. Edd. *reckless* or *wreakless*), careless, thoughtless: *the love of r. Silvia*, Gent. V, 2, 52. *careless, r.* Meas. IV, 2, 150. *so flies the r. shepherd from the wolf*, H6C V, 6, 7. *you grave but r. senators*, Cor. III, 1, 92. *I am r. what I do*, Mcb. III, 1, 110. *a puffed and r. libertine*, Hml. I, 3, 49.

**Reckon,** 1) to cast account, to compute, to calculate; intr.: *truth is truth to the end of —ing*, Meas. V, 46. *I am ill at —ing*, LLL I, 2, 42. V, 2, 498. *until the twelve celestial signs have brought about the annual —ing*, 808. *by this —ing he is more shrew than she*, Shr. IV, 1, 87. *thou hast called her to a —ing many a time and oft*, H4A I, 2, 55. *a trim —ing*, V, 1, 137. *take from them the sense of— ing*, H5 IV, 1, 308. *if you could tell how to r.* 241. *may stand in number, though in —ing none*, Rom. I, 2, 33. *how goes our —ing?* Tim. II, 2, 159. *I have no more to r., he to spend*, III, 4, 56. *—ing*, substantively, = the money charged by a host: As III, 3, 15 (cf. *Bill*). III, 4, 35. H4A II, 4, 113. III, 3, 179. H4B I, 2, 194. Troil. III, 3, 254. Cymb. V, 4, 159.

2) to settle an account, in a moral sense: *to call young Claudio to a —ing for it*, Ado V, 4, 9. *here comes other —ings*, 52. *I will tear the —ing from his heart*, H4A III, 2, 152. *the king hath a heavy —ing to make*, H5 IV, 1, 141. *before we r. with your several loves*, Mcb. V, 8, 61. *no —ing made*, Hml. I, 5, 78.

3) to count, to compute, to number; trans.: *I have not art to r. my groans*, Hml. II, 2, 121. *O weary —ing*, Oth. III, 4, 176. *there's beggary in the love that can be —ed*, Ant. I, 1, 15. With *up*: *they that level at my abuses r. up their own*, Sonn. 121, 10. *you know no house, nor no such men as you have —ed up*, Shr. Ind. 2, 94. *in —ing up the several devils' names*, H4A III, 1, 157. *to r. of* = to number among: *more monstrous trespasses, whereof I r. the casting forth to crows thy baby-daughter*, Wint. III, 2, 191.

4) to take account of: *but —ing time, ... why, fearing of time's tyranny*, Sonn. 115, 5.

5) to esteem, to think, to hold: *among a number one is – ed none*, Sonn. 136, 8. *I r. this always that a man is never undone till he be hanged*, Gent. II, 5, 4 (Launce's speech). *the pig, or the great, or the mighty ... are all one —ings*, H5 IV, 7, 18 (Fluellen's speech). *my father was —ed one the wisest prince*, H8 II, 4, 48. *of honourable — ing are you both*, Rom. I, 2, 4 (= estimation). *a warlike people, whom we r. ourselves to be*, Cymb. III, 1, 53. *all gold and silver rather turn to dirt! and' tis no better —ed, but of those who worship dirty gods*, III, 6, 55. With *at*, = to estimate at: *—ing his fortune at such high-proud rate*, Lucr. 19. *she —ed it at her life's rate*, All's V, 3, 90.

**Reckoning,** subst. see *Reckon*.

**Reclaim,** to subdue, to tame, to make gentle: *this arm that hath — ed to your obedience fifty fortresses*, H6A III, 4, 5. *beauty that the tyrant oft — s shall to my flaming wrath be oil and flax*, H6B V, 2, 54. *since this same wayward girl is so —ed*, Rom. IV, 2, 47. cf. *Unreclaimed* in Hml. II, 1, 34.

**Reclusive,** retired from society: *in some r. and religious life*, Ado IV, 1, 244.

**Recognizance,** 1) badge, token: *that r. and pledge of love which I first gave her*, Oth. V, 2, 214.

2) acknowledgment of a debt: *his statutes, his —s,* Hml. V, 1, 113.*

**Recoil,** 1) to rebound: *the very thought of my revenges that way r. upon me,* Wint. II, 3, 20. *these dread curses, like the sun 'gainst glass, or like an overcharged gun, r. and turn the force of them upon thyself,* H6B III, 2, 331.

2) to go back: *methoughts I did r. twenty three years,* Wint. I, 2, 154. *her will, —ing to her better judgement, may fall to match you with her country forms and happily repent,* Oth. III, 3, 236.

3) to fall off, to degenerate: *a good and virtuous nature may r. in an imperial charge,* Mcb. IV, 3, 19. *you r. from your great stock,* Cymb. I, 6, 128.

4) to shrink: *who then shall blame his pestered senses to r. and start,* Mcb. V, 2, 23.

**Recollect,** to gather, to pick up: *these fishers ... from their watery empire r. all that may men approve or men detect,* Per. II, 1, 54. *light airs and —ed terms of these most brisk and giddy-paced times,* Tw. II, 4, 5 (= picked, refined? or trivial?)

**Recomfiture** (cf. *Discomfit*), see *Recomforture*.

**Recomforted,** comforted again: *ne'er through an arch so hurried the blown tide as the r. through the gates,* Cor. V, 4, 51.

**Recomforture,** (Qq *recomfiture*) new comfort: *they shall breed selves of themselves, to your r.* R3 IV, 4, 425.

**Recommend,** to deliver and commit in kindness: *mine own purse which I had —ed to his use,* Tw. V, 94. *we r. to you our purpose to them,* Cor. II, 2, 155. Hence = to inform, to send word in courtesy: *Signior Montano with his free duty —s you thus, and prays you to believe him,* Oth. I, 3, 41. Refl., = to be agreeable: *the air nimbly and sweetly —s itself unto our gentle senses,* Mcb. I, 6, 2.

**Recompense,** subst. 1) compensation, amends: *if the encounter acknowledge itself hereafter, it may compel him to her r.* Meas. III, 1, 263. *wherein it doth impair the seeing sense, it pays the hearing double r.* Mids. III, 2, 180. *with a r. more fruitful than their offence can weigh down,* Tim. V, 1, 153.

2) requital, reward: Sonn. 23, 11. Wiv. IV, 6, 55 *(make).* LLL I, 1, 58. As III, 5, 97. Tw. I, 5, 304. II, 1, 7. Wint. II, 3, 150. R2 II, 3, 49. 62. H6A I, 2, 116. V, 3, 19 *(pay).* Troil. III, 3, 3. Cor. III, 1, 121. Tim. I, 1, 15. Mcb. I, 4, 17. Cymb. II, 3, 97. Per. III, 4, 17. *in r.* = in return: Ado V, 4, 83. Tw. V, 7. 372.

**Recompense,** vb. 1) to make amends for: *so shall his father's wrongs be —d,* H6A III, 1, 161.

2) to requite, to reward: Meas. V, 522. As II, 3, 75. All's IV, 4, 18. Tw. I, 5, 272. Wint. IV, 4, 531. John V, 4, 15. Tim. III, 6, 35.

**Reconcile,** 1) to make to like again, to restore to friendship: Compl. 329. All's V, 3, 21. Wint. IV, 2, 25. R2 I, 3, 186. H6C I, 1, 204. 273. Cor. V, 3, 136. Tit. I, 467. Rom. III, 3, 151. With *to:* Ado I, 1, 156. H6B IV, 8, 72. R3 I, 4, 184. Refl.: *I'll r. me to Polixenes,* Wint. III, 2, 156. *hath —d himself to Rome,* John V, 2, 69. *to r. me to his friendly peace,* R3 II, 1, 59. Figuratively, to bring to agreement, to make consistent: *such welcome and unwelcome things at once 'tis hard to r.* Mcb. IV, 3, 139. *—d my thoughts to thy good truth and honour,* 116. *—s them to his entreaty, and himself to the drink,* Ant. II, 7, 8. *your ears unto your eyes I'll r.* Per. IV, 4, 22.

2) to make to be liked again: *when false opinion ... repeals and —s thee,* Lr. III, 6, 120.

**Reconcilement,** reconciliation, renewal of friendship: Hml. V, 2, 258.

**Reconciler,** one who restores to friendship: Ant. III, 4, 30.

**Reconciliation,** restoration to favour: *his present r. take,* Oth. III, 3, 47 (according to others, = atonement, expiation).

**Record,** subst. (*recórd* and *récord* indiscriminately) 1) memory, remembrance: *that r. is lively in my soul,* Tw. V, 253. *every action whereof we have r.* Troil. I, 3, 14. *we have r. that very well it can,* Cor. IV, 6, 49. *the r. of what injuries you did us, though written in our flesh, we shall remember as things but done by chance,* Ant. V, 2, 117. Especially memory preserved by history: *so should my shame still rest upon r.* Lucr. 1643. *O that r. could with a backward look show me your image in some antique book,* Sonn. 59, 5. *thy r. never can be missed,* 122, 8. *and on r. left them the heirs of shame,* R3 V, 3, 335 (Q1.2 *in r.*). *what strange, which manifold r. not matches?* Tim. I, 1, 5. *when men revolted shall upon r. bear hateful memory,* Ant. IV, 9, 8. *have got upon me a nobleness in r.* IV, 14, 99.

2) that which preserves memory; a memorial: *nor Mars his sword nor war's quick fire shall burn the living r. of your memory,* Sonn. 55, 8. *thy* (time's) *—s and what we see doth lie,* 123, 11. *brief abstract and r. of tedious days,* R3 IV, 4, 28.

3) something set down in writing for the purpose of preserving its memory: *burn all the —s of the realm,* H6B IV, 7, 16. *from the table of my memory I'll wipe away all trivial fond —s,* Hml. I, 5, 99. *hath as oft a slanderous epitaph as r. of fair act,* Cymb. III, 3, 53. *in r.,* and *upon r.* = set down, registered: *to fine the faults whose fine stands in r.* Meas. II, 2, 40. *my villany they have upon r.* Ado V, 1, 247. *if thy offences were upon r.* R2 IV, 230. *is it upon r.?* R3 III, 1, 72.

4) witness: *heaven be the r. to my speech,* R2 I, 1, 30.

**Record,** vb. 1) to set down in writing, to register: *I, now the voice of the —ed law,* Meas. II, 4, 61. *r. it with your high and worthy deeds,* Ado V, 1, 278. *those statutes that are —ed in this schedule,* LLL I, 1, 18. *'twill be —ed for a precedent,* Merch. IV, 1, 220. *that he do r. a gift, here in the court, of all he dies possessed,* 388. *Froissart —s, England all Olivers and Rowlands bred,* H6A I, 2, 29. *made him my book wherein my soul —ed the history of all her secret thoughts,* R3 III, 5, 27. *to the last syllable of —ed time,* Mcb. V, 5, 21. *and have our two wagers —ed,* Cymb. I, 4, 181.

2) to witness: *how proud I am of thee and of thy gifts, Rome shall r.* Tit. I, 255. *let me be —ed by the righteous gods, I am as poor as you,* Tim. IV, 2, 4 (= I take the gods to witness).

3) to sing; used of the nightingale: *here can I to the nightingale's complaining notes tune my distresses and r. my woes,* Gent. V, 4, 6. *made the night-bird mute, that still —s with moan,* Per. IV Prol. 27.

**Recordation,** remembrance, recollection: *that it* (remembrance) *may grow and sprout as high as heaven, for r. to my noble husband,* H4B II, 3, 61. *to make a r. to my soul of every syllable that here was spoke,* Troil. V, 2, 116 (= to recall to mind).

**Recorder,** 1) the keeper of the rolls in a city: R3 III, 7, 30.

2) a kind of flute or flageolet: Mids. V, 123.*Hml. III, 2, 303. 360.

**Recount,** to detail; to tell: Sonn. 45, 12. Tp. I, 2, 262. Ado IV, 1, 2. LLL V, 1, 111. V, 2, 176. Mids. IV, 1, 204. As III, 2, 375. H6C II, 1, 96. III, 3, 132. H8 I, 2, 126. Tit. III, 1, 29. Caes. I, 2, 165. II, 2, 16. Hml. IV, 7, 46. Lr. V, 3, 215. Per. V, 1, 63. 142.

**Recountment,** relation, tale: As IV, 3, 141.

**Recourse,** 1) repeated course, frequent flowing: *their eyes o'ergalled with r. of tears,* Troil. V, 3, 55.

2) access, admission: *no man hath r. to her by night,* Gent. III, 1, 112. *to give me r. to him,* Wiv. II, 1, 223. *that no manner of person at any time have r. unto the princes,* R3 III, 5, 109.

**Recover,** 1) trans. a) to get again, to regain, to reconquer: Err. II, 2, 73. All's III, 6, 60. 61. 63. IV, 1, 67. R2 V, 3, 47 *(r. breath).* H6A I, 6, 9. II, 5, 32. III, 2, 115. III, 3, 2. H6B IV, 7, 71. IV, 8, 27. H6C IV, 7, 52. V, 2, 30. R3 I, 3, 2. Hml. V, 1, 166. With *of:* to r. of us those lands, Hml. I, 1, 102.

b) to reconcile: *to r. the general again,* Oth. II, 3, 273.

c) to restore from illness or from a swoon: Tp. II, 2, 71. 79. 97. As IV, 3, 151. All's III, 2, 22. Wint. IV, 4, 815. Caes. I, 1, 28 (punning). Per. III, 2, 9. 86. V, 3, 24.

d) to save from danger: *kill him whom you have —ed,* Tw. II, 1, 39.

e) to cover again, to sole or cobble: *when they are in great danger, I r. them,* Caes. I, 1, 28 (punning).

f) to get, to gain, to reach: *I swam, ere I could r. the shore, five and thirty leagues,* Tp. III, 2, 16 (Stephano's speech). *if we r. that* (the forest) *we are sure enough,* Gent. V, 1, 12. *r. the lost hair of another man,* Err. II, 2, 77 (Dromio's speech). *if I cannot r. your niece,* Tw. II, 3, 200 (Sir Andrew's speech). With *from: this weapon which I have here —ed from the Moor,* Oth. V, 2, 240 (= taken from). With *of: why do you go about to r. the wind of me, as if you would drive me into a toil?* Hml. III, 2, 361 (a term borrowed from hunting, = to get the animal pursued to run with the wind. Singer).*

2) intr. to grow well again, to be restored from illness or swooning: Mids. V, 317. As IV, 3, 161. Wint. III, 2, 151. John V, 6, 31. H4B IV, 4, 129. IV, 5, 13. Oth. IV, 1, 58. Ant. IV, 9, 34. V, 2, 248. Per. V, 3, 28. = to grow sober after intoxication: *how came you thus —ed?* Oth. II, 3, 296.

Confounded with *discover* by the watch in Ado III, 3, 179.

**Recoverable,** possible to be brought back to a better condition: *a prodigal course is like the sun's, but not, like his, r.* Tim. III, 4, 13.

**Recovery,** 1) the act of gaining or conquering again: *the r. of this drum,* All's IV, 1, 38. *they* (the counties) *are past r.* H6B I, 1, 116. *fine and r.,* a term of law: Wiv. IV, 2, 225.* Err. II, 2, 75. Hml. V, 1, 114. 115. cf. *Fine.*

2) restoration from illness or swooning: Err. V, 41. All's II, 3, 42. H6C V, 5, 45. Troil. II, 3, 188. Per. V, 1, 54. 76.

**Recreant,** adj. originally = retracting one's errors (recredens) and crying for mercy: *feeble desire, all r., poor and meek,* Lucr. 710. *a caitiff r. to my*

cousin *Hereford,* R2 I, 2, 53. Hence = cowardly, faithless: *hang a calf's-skin on those r. limbs,* John III, 1, 129. 131. 133. *a r. and most degenerate traitor,* R2 I, 1, 144. *to be found false and r.* I, 3, 106. *puff in thy teeth, most r. coward base,* H4B V, 3, 96.

**Recreant,** subst. a cowardly and faithless wretch: *come, r.; come, thou child,* Mids. III, 2, 409. *distrustful —s, fight till the last gasp,* H6A I, 2, 126. *you are all —s and dastards,* H6B IV, 8, 28. *may that soldier a mere r. prove, that means not, hath not, or is not in love,* Troil. I, 3, 287. *must as a foreign r. be led with manacles through our streets,* Cor. V, 3, 114. *O vassal, r.!* Lr. I, 1, 163 (Ff *miscreant). hear me, r.* 169.

**Recreate,** vb. refl. to divert one's self: *to r. himself when he hath sung,* Ven. 1095. *to walk abroad and r. yourselves,* Caes. III, 2, 256.

**Recreation,** 1) refreshment: *we will to our r.* (i. e. to dinner) LLL IV, 2, 173 (Holofernes' speech).

2) diversion, amusement: *sweet r. barred, what doth ensue but moody and dull melancholy,* Err. V, 78. *is there no quick r. granted?* LLL I, 1, 162. *make him a common r.* Tw. II, 3, 146. *tears shed there shall be my r.* Wint. III, 2, 241. *the true prince may, for r. sake, prove a false thief,* H4A I, 2, 173. *most fit for your best health and r.* R3 III, 1, 67. *it is a r. to be by and hear him mock the Frenchman,* Cymb. I, 6, 75.

**Rectify,** to set right: *some oracle must r. our knowledge,* Tp. V, 245. *to r. what is unsettled in the king,* H8 II, 4, 63. *to r. my conscience,* 203.

**Rector,** the chief of a religious house: All's IV, 3, 69.

**Rectorship,** government, guidance: *had you tongues to cry against the r. of judgment?* Cor. II, 3, 213.

**Recure,** to restore to health or soundness, to heal: *a smile —s the wounding of a frown,* Ven. 465. *until life's composition be —d,* Sonn. 45, 9. *which to r., we heartily solicit your gracious self to take on you the charge,* R3 III, 7, 130. cf. *Unrecuring.*

**Red,** adj. (compar. —er: Caes. V, 1, 49. Superl. —est: Merch. II, 1, 7); of the colour similar to blood: Ven. 10. 21. 35. 36. 77. 107. 116. 219. 453. 468. 1073. Lucr. 258. 1353. Sonn. 130, 2. Wiv. I, 1, 173. Meas. IV, 3, 158. Err. IV, 2, 4. LLL I, 2, 96. 104. IV, 3, 264. V, 2, 44. 934. Mids. III, 1, 96. Merch. II, 1, 7. III, 1, 43. As III, 4, 57. III, 5, 121. Shr. III, 2, 69. Tw. I, 5, 266. Wint. IV, 3, 4. IV, 4, 54. John IV, 2, 163. H4A II, 4, 423. H4B V, 1, 17. H5 III, 6, 111. 170. H6A II, 4, 33. 37. 50. 126. H6B II, 1, 110. III, 1, 154. IV, 2, 97. IV, 7, 92. H6C II, 5, 97. III, 2, 51. R3 II, 1, 85. IV, 3, 12. V, 5, 19. H8 I, 4, 43. Troil. V, 2, 164. Cor. I, 4, 37. V, 1, 64. Tit. II, 4, 31. Caes. III, 1, 100. III, 2, 120. V, 1, 49. V, 3, 61. Hml. I, 2, 233. IV, 3, 62. Lr. III, 6, 16. Per. IV, 6, 37. *the r. plague rid you,* Tp. I, 2, 364. *a r. murrain o' thy jade's tricks,* Troil. II, 1, 20. *the r. pestilence strike all trades in Rome,* Cor. IV, 1, 13 (three different kinds of the plague-sore being mentioned by the physicians of the time: the red, the yellow, and the black).

Substantively: Ven. 346. 901. Lucr. 11. 59. 63. 65. 1511. Sonn. 130, 2. LLL IV, 3, 264. As III, 5, 123. Shr. IV, 5, 30. Tw. I, 5, 257. H6A II, 4, 61. Mcb. II, 2, 63.

**Redbreast,** the robin: *to relish a love-song like a robin r.* Gent. II, 1, 21. *r. teacher,* H4A III, 1, 265.

**Rede,** see *Read.*

**Redeem,** 1) to ransom, to purchase back, to deliver from forfeiture or captivity by paying a price: *to r. him, give up your body*, Meas. II, 4, 53. 107. 163. *wanting guilders to r. their lives*, Err. I, 1, 8. *I sent you money to r. you*, IV, 4, 86. *shall our coffers be emptied to r. a traitor home?* H4A I, 3, 86. *you may r. your banished honours*, 180. *my honour is at stake, and, but my going, nothing can r. it*, H4B II, 3, 8. *thou hast —ed thy lost opinion*, H4A V, 4, 48. *—ed I was as I desired*, H6A I, 4, 34. *would some part of my young years might but r. the passage of your age*, II, 5, 108. *this day have you —ed your lives*, H6B IV, 9, 15. In a religious sense: *all seals and symbols of — ed sin*, Oth. II, 3, 350. With *from: r. your brother from the angry law*, Meas. III, 1, 207. *if you will take it on you to assist him, it shall r. you from your gyves*, IV, 2, 11. *let me r. my brothers both from death*, Tit. III, 1, 181. *whom he —ed from prison*, Tim. III, 3, 4.

2) to deliver, to set free, to save in any manner: *when he did r. the virgin tribute paid by Troy*, Merch. III, 2, 55 (= delivered the virgin offered as a tribute). *O that these hands could so r. my son*, John III, 4, 71. *weening to r. and have installed me in the diadem*, H6A II, 5, 88. *engaging and —ing of himself*, Troil. V, 5, 39. *before the time that Romeo come to r. me*, Rom. IV, 3, 32. With *from: that boy ... from the rude sea's enraged and foamy mouth did I r.* Tw. V, 82. *bequeath to death your numbness, for from him dear life —s you*, Wint. V, 3, 103. *r. from broking pawn the blemished crown*, R2 II, 1, 293. *—s nature from the general curse*, Lr. IV, 6, 210. *hath the king five times —ed from death*, Cymb. I, 5, 63. cf. *so he that doth r. her* (honour) *thence* (from the deep) H4A I, 3, 206. *I expect an embassage from my Redeemer to r. me hence*, R3 II, 1, 4.

3) to absolve, to acquit: *he hath outvillained villany so far, that the rarity —s him*, All's IV, 3, 306. *how fain would I have hated all mankind! and thou —est thyself*, Tim. IV, 3, 507.

4) to atone for, to make compensation or amends for: *in gentle numbers time so idly spent*, Sonn. 100, 5; cf. *—ing time*, H4A I, 2, 241. *unless you do r. it by some laudable attempt of valour*, Tw. III, 2, 30. *no fault could you make which you have not —ed*, Wint. V, 1, 3. *I will r. all this on Percy's head*, H4A III, 2, 132. *a chance which does r. all sorrows*, Lr. V, 3, 266.

**Redeemer,** Saviour: R3 II, 1, 4. 123.

**Re-deliver,** 1) to give back: *remembrances that I have longed long to r.* Hml. III, 1, 94. In Meas. IV, 4, 6 F1 reliver, F2.3.4 deliver, M. Edd. redeliver.

2) to report: *shall I r. you e'en so?* Hml. V, 2, 186 (Qq deliver, q. v.).

**Redemption,** 1) ransom, release: *lawful mercy is nothing kin to foul r.* Meas. II, 4, 113. *will you send him, mistress, r., the money in his desk?* Err. IV, 2, 46. *my r. hence*, Oth. I, 3, 138.

2) salvation: *you bid me seek r. of the devil*, Meas. V, 29. *damned without r.* R2 III, 2, 129. *the year of our r.* H5 I, 2, 60. *held thee dearly as his soul's r.* H6C II, 1, 102. *as you hope to have r.* R3 I, 4, 194. Misapplied by Dogberry in Ado IV, 2, 59.

**Red-faced,** having a red face: H5 III, 2, 34.

**Red-hipped,** having red hips: *a r. humble-bee*, Mids. IV, 1, 12.

**Red-hot,** heated to redness: Tp. IV, 171. John IV, 1, 61. R3 IV, 1, 61.

**Red-lattice,** a lattice window painted red, the customary distinction of an alehouse: *your r. phrases*,

Wiv. II, 2, 28 (= alehouse language). cf. H4B II, 2, 86.

**Red-looked,** looking red: *r. anger*, Wint. II,2,34.

**Redness,** red colour: As III, 5, 120.

**Red-nose,** having a red nose: *the r. innkeeper*, H4A IV, 2, 51.

**Redouble,** to repeat often; to multiply: *passion on passion deeply is —d*, Ven. 832. *thy blows, doubly —d*, R2 I, 3, 80. *on my head my shames —d*, H4A III, 2, 144. *they doubly —d strokes upon the foe*, Mcb. I, 2, 38.

**Redoubted,** formidable: *assume but valour's excrement to render them r.* Merch. III, 2, 88. Before names and other designations of persons, = dread: *my most r. lord*, R2 III, 3, 198. *my most r. father*, H5 II, 4, 14. *r. Burgundy*, H6A II, 1, 8. *r. Pembroke*, R3 IV, 5, 11.

**Redound,** to conduce, to turn out, to result: *as all things shall r. unto your good*, H6B IV, 9, 47.

**Redress,** subst. 1) amendment, remedy, deliverance from wrong: *tell thy grief, that we may give r.* Lucr. 1603. *r. of injustice*, Meas. IV, 4, 10. *wring r. from you*, V, 32. *good night to your r.* 301. *things past r. are with me past care*, R2 II, 3, 171. *for these foolish officers, I beseech you I may have r. against them*, H4B II, 1, 118 (satisfaction? or help?). *there is no need of any such r.* IV, 1, 97. *I take your princely word for these —es*, IV, 2, 66. *I promised you r. of these same grievances*, 113. *not a man comes for r. of thee*, H6C III, 1, 20 (r. to be made by thee). *he writes to heaven for his r.* Tit. IV, 4, 13. *use the wars as thy r.* Tim. V, 4, 51. *r. of all these griefs*, Caes. I, 3, 118. *if the r. will follow*, II, 1, 57. *to prick us to r.* 124. *to have found a safe r.* Lr. I, 4, 225. *nor the —es sleep*, 229.

2) help, succour, safety: *I defy all counsel, all r., but that which ends all counsel, true r., death*, John III, 4, 23. 24. *the proffered means of succour and r.* R2 III, 2, 32. *no way canst thou turn thee for r.* H6A IV, 2, 25. *no hope to have r.* V, 3, 18. *then music with her silver sound with speedy help doth lend r.* Rom. IV, 5, 146. Perhaps also in H4B II, 1, 118.

**Redress,** vb. to set right, to remedy, to relieve from: *broken glass no cement can r.* Pilgr. 178. *if it be confessed, it is not —ed*, Wiv. I, 1, 107. *each article herein —ed*, H4B IV, 1, 170. IV, 2, 59. *with honour to r.* (wrongs) H6A II, 5, 126. *to r. their harms*, H6C V, 4, 2. *what you would thus violently r.* Cor. III, 1, 220. *speak, strike, r.* Caes. II, 1, 47. *that Caesar must r.* III, 1, 32. *what I can r.* Mcb. IV, 3, 9.

**Red-rose,** (not hyphened in O. Edd.): *in a r. chain*, Ven. 110.

**Red-tailed,** having a red tail: All's IV, 5, 7.

**Reduce,** 1) to bring back: *which to r. into our former favour*, H5 V, 2, 63. *that would r. these bloody days again*, R3 V, 5, 36.

2) to bring, to convey: *all springs r. their currents to mine eyes*, R3 II, 2, 68.

**Reechy,** probably = smoky, and hence squalid, filthy, stinking: *Pharaoh's soldiers in the r. painting*, Ado III, 3, 143. *her r. neck*, Cor. II, 1, 225. *r. kisses*, Hml. III, 4, 184.

**Reed,** the hollow stem of several aquatic plants: Tp. I, 2, 213. V, 17 (*eaves of —s*). H4A I, 3, 105. Ant. II, 7, 13. Cymb. IV, 2, 267. Musical pipes made of it: *speak between the change of man and boy, with a r. voice*, Merch. III, 4, 67.

**Re-edify,** to continue and finish building: *he did begin that place; which since succeeding ages have —ed,* R3 III, 1, 71. *this monument five hundred years hath stood, which I have sumptuously —ed,* Tit.1,351.

**Reedy,** abounding with reeds: *Simois' r. banks,* Lucr. 1437.

**Reek,** subst. smoke, vapour: *the r. of a lime-kiln,* Wiv. III, 3, 86. *r. o' the rotten fens,* Cor. III, 3, 121.

**Reek,** vb. to emit vapour, to steam: *her face doth r. and smoke,* Ven. 555. *the red blood —ed,* Lucr. 1377. *the breath that from my mistress —s,* Sonn. 130, 8. *saw sighs r. from you,* LLL IV, 3, 140. *draw their honours —ing up to heaven,* H5 IV, 3, 101. *how under my oppression I did r.* H8 II, 4, 208. *where he did run —ing o'er the lives of men,* Cor. II, 2, 123. *sprinkles in your faces your —ing villany,* Tim. III, 6, 103 (cf. v. 99: *smoke and luke-warm water is your perfection). whilst your purpled hands do r. and smoke,* Caes. III, 1, 158. *to bathe in —ing wounds,* Mcb. I, 2, 39. *a —ing post,* Lr. II, 4, 30. *the violence of action hath made you r.* Cymb. I, 2, 2.

**Reeky,** smoky, squalid and stinking: *with r. shanks and yellow chapless skulls,* Rom. IV, 1, 83 (Ff *recky*). In Ado III, 3, 143 O. Edd. *rechie,* some M. Edd. *reeky.*

**Reel,** vb. to stagger as one drunk: *when from highmost pitch, with weary car, like feeble age, he* (the sun) *—eth from the day,* Sonn. 7, 10; cf. *fleckled darkness like a drunkard —s from forth day's path,* Rom. II, 3, 3. *Trinculo is —ing ripe,* Tp. V, 279. *it is a —ing world,* R3 III, 2, 38 (v. 37: *our tottering state). would shake the press and make 'em r. before 'em,* H8 IV, 1, 79. *I will make my very house r. to-night,* Cor. II, 1, 121. *depart —ing with too much drink,* Cymb. V, 4, 164. With an accus.: *keeps wassail and the swaggering up-spring —s,* Hml. I, 4, 9. *to r. the streets at noon,* Ant. I, 4, 20.

**Reels,** motions like those of drunken men; used in this sense for the rhyme's sake: *the third part, then, is drunk: would it were all, that it might go on wheels. Drink thou, increase the r.* Ant. II, 7, 100.

**Refel,** to refute: *how he —ed me, and how I replied,* Meas. V, 94.

**Refer,** to direct as to one who is to decide the question: *these weird sisters saluted me and —ed me to the coming on of time,* Mcb. I, 5, 9. Refl., = to appeal: *I do r. me to the oracle,* Wint. III, 2, 116. *I'll r. me to all things of sense,* Oth. I, 2, 64. And = to have recourse, to betake one's self to, to claim: *only r. yourself to this advantage, first, that your stay with him may not be long,* Meas. III, 1, 255. Euphuism: *his daughter ... hath —ed herself unto a poor but worthy gentleman,* Cymb. I, 1, 6 (explained by the speaker in the following words: *she's wedded;* cf. v. 17 and 18).

**Reference,** 1) assignment, appointment: *I crave fit disposition for my wife, due r. of place and exhibition,* Oth. I, 3, 238. *to have r. to* = be appointed and destined for, to belong to: *all that he is hath r. to your highness,* All's V, 3, 29. *many things, having full r. to one consent, may work contrariously,* H5 I, 2, 205.

2) relation, respect: *what will you be called? Something that hath a r. to my state,* As I, 3, 129.

3) appeal: *make your full r. freely to my lord,* Ant. V, 2, 23.

**Refigure,** to show the figure of, to represent as

in a copy: *if ten of thine ten times —d thee,* Sonn. 6, 10.

**Refined,** 1) purified: *r. gold,* John IV, 2, 11. *souls r.* R2 IV, 130 (freed from guilt and redeemed by Christ).

2) polished: *a r. traveller of Spain,* LLL I, 1, 164.

**Reflect,** 1) to throw back light: *two glasses ... and now no more r.* Ven. 1130.

2) to shine: *whether it is that she —s so bright,* Lucr. 376. *there were crept, as 'twere in scorn of eyes, —ing gems,* R3 I, 4, 31. *whose virtues will r. on Rome as Titan's rays on earth,* Tit. I, 226. Nearly = to look: *he is one to whose kindnesses I am most infinitely tied. R. upon him accordingly,* Cymb. I, 6, 24. Transitively: *r. I not on thy baseness court-contempt?* Wint. IV, 4, 758.

**Reflection,** 1) the act of throwing back: Troil. III, 3, 99. Caes. I, 2, 53. 68. Cymb. I, 2, 35.

2) the act of shining: *as whence the sun 'gins his r. shipwrecking storms and direful thunders break,* Mcb. I, 2, 25. *she's a good sign, but I have seen small r. of her wit,* Cymb. I, 2, 33.

**Reflex,** subst. reflected light (or light, shine in general?): *'tis but the pale r. of Cynthia's brow,* Rom. III, 5, 20.

**Reflex,** vb. to let shine, to send, to dart (as rays): *may never glorious sun r. his beams upon the country where you make abode,* H6A V, 4, 87.

**Reform,** vb. 1) to change from worse to better: *they are —ed, civil, full of good,* Gent. V, 4, 156. *thy penitent —ed,* Wint. I, 2, 239. *what you would have —ed,* John IV, 2, 44. *as we hear you do r. yourselves,* H4B V, 5, 72.

2) to abolish, to redress, to remedy: *takes on him to r. some certain edicts,* H4A IV, 3, 78. *which are heresies, and, not —ed, may prove pernicious,* H8 V, 3, 19. *I hope we have —ed that indifferently with us, sir. O, r. it altogether,* Hml. III, 2, 40. 42.

Misapplied for to inform by Dogberry: Ado V, 1, 262.

**Reformation,** 1) amendment of manners and sentiments: LLL V, 2, 879. H4A I, 2, 237. H5 I, 1, 33. H8 I, 3, 19.

2) redress of abuses: *your captain is brave and vows r.* H6B IV, 2, 70. *which r. must be sudden too,* H8 V, 3, 20.

**Refractory,** contumacious: Troil II, 2, 182.

**Refrain,** to forbear, to abstain: Mcb. II, 3, 122. Hml. III, 4, 165. With *from:* Pilgr. 388. John II, 525. Oth. IV, 1, 99. Transitively: *scarce I can r. the execution of my big-swoln heart,* H6C II, 2, 110.

**Refresh,** to make fresh again, to recreate, to revive: Pilgr. 176. Tp. III, 1, 14. IV, 79. Shr. III, 1, 11. Wint. IV, 4, 343 (= to amuse, divert). H5 II, 2, 37. Caes. IV, 3, 209. Per. V, 1, 257.

**Refuge,** subst. 1) protection from danger, expedient in distress: R2 II, 2, 135. H6A II, 2, 25. V, 4, 69. Tim. III, 3, 11. Cor. V, 3, 11.

2) specious excuse, subterfuge: *at the least this r. let me find,* Lucr. 1654.

**Refuge,** vb. to make a specious excuse for, to palliate: *who sitting in the stocks r. their shame, that many have and others must sit there,* R2 V, 5, 26.

**Refusal,** denial of any thing demanded: Cor. II, 3, 267.

**Refuse,** subst. that which is thrown away as

worthless and noisome: *whence hast thou this becoming of things ill, that in the very r. of thy deeds there is such strength and warrantise of skill that in my mind thy worst all best exceeds?* Sonn. 150, 6.

**Refuse,** vb. 1) to decline to do: —*ing her grand hests,* Tp. I, 2, 274. *if thou r. and wilt encounter with my wrath,* Wint. II, 3, 137. With an inf.: *he* —*d to take her figured proffer,* Pilgr. 52. Err. III, 1, 120. Mids. I, 1, 64. Merch. I, 2, 100. 101. As V, 4, 13. H6B III, 2, 94. Tit. III, 1, 22.

2) to decline to grant: *if you r. your aid,* Cor. V, 1, 33. Per. II, 1, 80.

3) to decline to take, to disdain, to reject: Sonn. 40, 8. Pilgr. 219. Gent. IV, 4, 106. Err. III, 2, 186. Ado III, 1, 90. IV, 2, 65. Mids. II, 2, 133. Merch. I, 2, 25. 28. IV, 1, 338. V, 211. As V, 4, 22. 24. All's II, 3, 76. Tw. III, 4, 229. John I, 127. R2 III, 2, 31. IV, 15. H6B V, 1, 121. R3 III, 7, 202. 208. H8 II, 4, 82 and 118 (*I r. you for my judge*). Cor. I, 9, 38. 80. V, 3, 14. Caes. I, 2, 245. 266. III, 2, 102. Cymb. I, 2, 28. Per. IV, 2, 53.

4) to disavow: to disown: *r. me, hate me, torture me to death,* Ado IV, 1, 186. *since you* —*d the Grecians' cause,* Troil. IV, 5, 267. *deny thy father and r. thy name,* Rom. II, 2, 34. *that in wholesome wisdom he might not but r. you,* Oth. III, 1, 50.

5) to say no to: *no disgrace shall fall you for* —*ing him at sea,* Ant. III, 7, 40.

**Regal,** kingly, royal: *the r. throne,* R2 IV, 113. *thoughts,* 163. *dignity,* H6A V, 4, 132. *jurisdiction,* H6B IV, 7, 29. *seat,* H6C I, 1, 26. *title,* III, 3, 28. *crown,* 189. *throne,* IV, 3, 64. *seat,* IV, 6, 2. *throne,* 74. *crown,* IV, 7, 4. *crownets,* Troil. Prol. 6.

**Regan,** second daughter of Lear: Lr. I, 1, 69 etc.

**Regard,** subst. 1) look: *vail your r. upon a wronged maid,* Meas. V, 20. *after a demure travel of r.* Tw. II, 5, 59. *quenching my familiar smile with an austere r. of control,* 73. *you throw a strange r. upon me,* V, 219. *I have looked on thousands, who have sped the better by my r.* Wint. I, 2, 390. *lay negligent and loose r. upon him,* Troil. III, 3, 41. *bites his lip with a politic r.* 255. *in my r.* = in my eyes, see below.

2) view, sight: *the deep-green emerald, in whose fresh r. weak sights their sickly radiance do amend,* Compl. 213. *till we make the main and the aerial blue an indistinct r.* Oth. II, 1, 40.

3) view of the mind, estimation: *your worth is very dear in my r.* Merch. I, 1, 62. *sick in the world's r.* H4A IV, 3, 57. *virtue is of so little r.* H4B I, 2, 191. *slight r., contempt,* H5 II, 4, 117. *a toy, a thing of no r.* H6A IV, 1, 145. *nature, what things there are most abject in r. and dear in use,* Troil. III, 3, 128. *and that, in my r., of the unworthiest siege,* Hml. IV, 7, 76.

4) attention bestowed, care, interest: *full many a lady I have eyed with best r.* Tp. III, 1, 40. *a son that well deserves the honour and r. of such a father,* Gent. II, 4, 60. *you have showed a tender fatherly r.* Shr. II, 288. *no attendance? no r.? no duty?* IV, 1, 129. *that in r. of me he shortens four years,* R2 I, 3, 216. *the king is full of grace and fair r.* H5 I, 1, 22. *your loss is great, so your r. should be,* H6A IV, 5, 22.*I offered to awaken his r. for's private friends,* Cor. V, 1, 23. *an you begin to rail on society once, I am sworn not to give r. to you,* Tim. I, 2, 251. *things without all remedy should be without r.* Mcb. III, 2, 12. *and in the most exact r.*

*support the worships of their name,* Lr. I, 4, 287 (= with the greatest care).

5) consideration, deliberation, thought: *sad pause and deep r. beseem the sage,* Lucr. 277. *which drives the creeping thief to some r.* 305. *the mild glance that sly Ulysses lent showed deep r.* 1400. *where will doth mutiny with wit's r.* R2 II, 1, 28. *our reasons are so full of good r.* Caes. III, 1, 224. *full of r. and honour,* IV, 2, 12 (= wise and honourable).

6) consideration, respect, account: *enterprises of great pith with this r. their currents turn awry,* Hml. III, 1, 87. *love's not love when it is mingled with* —*s that stand aloof from the entire point,* Lr. I, 1, 242 (Qq *respects*). *in r.* = in consideration: *in r. of causes now in hand,* H5 I, 1, 77. *in r. King Henry gives consent,* H6A V, 4, 124. *in which r ... I must show out a flag and sign of love,* Oth. I, 1, 154. *on such* —*s* = on such conditions: *that it might please you to give quiet pass through your dominions for this enterprise, on such* —*s of safety and allowance as therein are set down,* Hml. II, 2, 79.*

**Regard,** vb. 1) to look on, to observe, to notice: *your niece* —*s me with an eye of favour,* Ado V, 4, 22. *r. him well,* Troil. II, 1, 67. *let them r. me as I do not flatter, and therein behold themselves,* Cor. III, 1, 67. *r. Titinius, and tell me what thou notest about the field,* Caes. V, 3, 21. *feed and r. him not,* Mcb. III, 4, 58.

2) to consider: *neither* —*ing that she is my child, nor fearing me,* Gent. III, 1, 70. *r. thy danger,* Err. V, 1, 93.

3) to show attention to, to take care of: *ere we go, r. this dying prince,* H6A III, 2, 86. *let him be* —*ed as the most noble corse that ever herald did follow,* Cor. V, 6, 144. *see how I* —*ed Caius Cassius,* Caes. V, 3, 88.

4) to care for, to mind: *love's deep groans I never shall r.* Ven. 377. *how and which way I may bestow myself to be* —*ed in her sun-bright eye,* Gent. III, 1, 88. *the duello he* —*s not,* LLL I, 2, 185. H4A I, 2, 97. 100. III, 2, 76. H6A I, 3, 60. H6B III, 1, 18. IV, 2, 11. H6C I, 1, 189. H8 III, 2, 11. Tit. V, 2, 130. Cymb. II, 3, 98.

**Regardance,** in *Non-regardance,* q. v.

**Regardfully,** respectfully: *whom the world voiced so r.* Tim. IV, 3, 81.

**Regenerate,** born anew: *whose youthful spirit, in me r.* R2 I, 3, 70.

**Regent,** 1) governor, ruler: *r. of love-rhymes,* LLL III, 183. *wert thou r. of the world,* R2 II, 1, 109. *here is the r. of Mytilene,* Per. V, 1, 188. V, 2, 8.

2) one invested with vicarious royalty: H6A I, 1, 84. II, 1, 8. IV, 1, 163. IV, 6, 2. V, 3, 1. V, 4, 94. H6B I, 1, 66. 197. I, 3, 109. 164. 209. III, 1, 290. 294. 305. R2 II, 3, 77.

**Regentship,** vicarious royalty: H6B I, 3, 107.

**Regiment,** 1) rule, sway: *gives his potent r. to a trull,* Ant. III, 6, 95.

2) a certain body of soldiers: All's II, 1, 42. IV, 1, 76. John II, 296. R3 V, 3, 29. 37. 60. 103.

**Region,** tract of land or space, country, parts: *'twixt which* —*s there is some space,* Tp. II, 1, 256. *she is a r. in Guiana,* Wiv. I, 3, 76. *to reside in thrilling r. of thick-ribbed ice,* Meas. III, 1, 123. *every r. near seemed all one mutual cry,* Mids. IV, 1, 121. *to other* —*s France is a stable,* All's II, 3, 300. *as he had lost some province and a r. loved as he loves him-*

*self*, Wint. I, 2, 369. *to the English court assemble now from every r.* H4B IV, 5, 123. *the —s of Artois, Wallon and Picardy,* H6A II, 1, 9. *out of the powerful —s under earth,* V, 3, 11. *all the —s do smilingly revolt,* Cor. IV, 6, 102. *when you come to Pluto's r.* Tit. IV, 3, 13. *keep the hills and upper —s,* Caes. V, 1, 3. *to seek through the —s of the earth for one his like,* Cymb. I, 1, 20. *y-ravished the —s round,* Per. III Prol. 35. *from r. to r.* IV, 4, 4.

Applied to the upper air: *the r. cloud hath masked him from me now,* Sonn. 33, 12; cf. *fatted all the r. kites,* Hml. II, 2, 607. *her eyes in heaven would through the airy r. stream so bright,* Rom. II, 2, 21. *the dreadful thunder doth rend the r.* Hml. II, 2, 509.

Used of parts of the body: *made to tremble the r. of my breast,* H8 II, 4, 184. *though the fork invade the r. of my heart,* Lr. I, 1, 147. *scorns that dwell in every r. of his face,* Oth. IV, 1, 84.

= place, rank: *he is of too high a r.* Wiv. III, 2, 75. *you petty spirits of r. low,* Cymb. V, 4, 93.

**Register,** subst. account regularly kept, record: *O night, dim r. and notary of shame,* Lucr. 765. *thy* (time's) *—s and thee I both defy,* Sonn. 123, 9. *r. of lies,* Compl. 52. *as you hear them* (my follies) *unfolded, turn another* (eye) *into the r. of your own,* Wiv. II, 2, 194. *let the world rank me in r. a master-leaver,* Ant. IV, 9, 21.

**Register,** vb. to record: *what's new to speak, what new to r.* Sonn. 108, 3. *let fame live —ed upon our brazen tombs,* LLL I, 1, 2. *but say it were not —ed,* R3 III, 1, 75. *those many —ed in promise,* Troil. III, 3, 15. *your pains are — ed where every day I turn the leaf to read them,* Mcb. I, 3, 151.

**Regreet,** subst. greeting: *from whom he bringeth sensible —s, to wit, besides commends and courteous breath, gifts of rich value,* Merch. II, 9, 89. *shall these hands, so lately purged of blood, so newly joined in love, unyoke this seizure and this kind r.?* John III, 1, 241.

**Regreet,** vb. 1) to greet again, to resalute: *shall not r. our fair dominions,* R2 I, 3, 142.

2) to greet, to address, to meet: *as at English feasts, so I r. the daintiest last,* R2 I, 3, 67. *nor never write, r., nor reconcile ...,* 186.

**Regress,** passage back: *thou shalt have egress and r.* Wiv. II, 1, 226 (the host's speech).

**Reguerdon,** subst. reward: *in r. of that duty done,* H6A III, 1, 170.

**Reguerdon,** vb. to reward: *—ed with so much as thanks,* H6A III, 4, 23.

**Regular,** conformable to laws and rules: *offend the stream of r. justice,* Tim. V, 4, 61.

**Rehearsal,** 1) narration, recital: *I'll requite it with sweet r. of my morning's dream,* H6B I, 2, 24.

2) recital of a piece previous to public exhibition: Mids. III, 1, 3.

**Rehearse,** 1) to recite, to tell, to mention: *who heaven itself for ornament doth use and every fair with his fair doth r.* Sonn. 21, 4. *too excellent for every vulgar paper to r.* 38, 4. *do not so much as my poor name r.* 71, 11. *tongues to be your being shall r.* 81, 11. *r. that once more,* Gent. III, 1, 366. *that which now torments me to r.* IV, 1, 26. *r. your song by rote,* Mids. V, 404. *thou hast incurred the danger formerly by me —d,* Merch. IV, 1, 362. *those defects I have before —d,* Shr. I, 2, 124. *like an old tale which will have matter to r.* Wint. V, 2, 67. *pity may move thee 'par-*

*don' to r.* R2 V, 3, 128 (= to pronounce; for the sake of the rhyme). *verbatim to r. the method of my pen,* H6A III, 1, 13.

2) to recite previously to public exhibition: Mids. I, 2, 105. 110. III, 1, 75. III, 2, 11. V, 68.

**Reign,** subst. 1) exercise of royal authority, sovereignty: Wint. V, 2, 61. John III, 4, 152. H4A V, 4, 66. H4B IV, 5, 198. H5 I, 1, 2. H6B IV, 6, 5. IV, 9, 49. H6C V, 2, 27. R3 III, 7, 170. Per. II, 1, 108. *during whose r.* H6A II, 5, 67. *in the r. of Bolingbroke,* H6B II, 2, 39. Used of any dominion: *thus have I politicly begun my r.* Shr. IV, 1, 191. *Timon hath done his r.* Tim. V, 1, 226 (rhyming).

2) prevalence, exercise of power: *all the faults which in thy* (night's) *r. are made,* Lucr. 804. *grim care's r.* 1451. *each* (viz day and night) *though enemies to either's r.* Sonn. 28, 5.

**Reign,** vb. 1) to have royal power, to be king: Tp. III, 3, 24. John III, 1, 157. R2 IV, 164. H6A I, 2, 31. II, 5, 23. H6B II, 2, 20. 32. 56. IV, 2, 138 *(over):* 167. H6C I, 1, 53. 146. 171. 173. 200. 234. I, 2, 15. 17. R3 I, 1, 161. II, 3, 10. III, 7, 215. H8 II, 4, 49. Mcb. IV, 1, 103. IV, 3, 66. Hml. III, 2, 294. Per. II, 4, 38. V, 3, 82.

2) to be predominant, to prevail: *where love —s,* Ven. 649. Sonn. 31, 3. *though in my nature —ed all frailties,* 109, 9. *he did in the general bosom r.* Compl. 127. 196. *what folly —s in us,* Gent. I, 2, 15. *a fever she —s in my blood,* LLL IV, 3, 96. *happy star r. now,* Wint. I, 2, 363. II, 1, 105. *the freshest things now — ing,* V, 1, 13. *the red blood —s in the winter's pale,* IV, 3, 4. *civil tumult —s,* John IV, 2, 247. *let one spirit of the first-born Cain r. in all bosoms,* H4B I, 1, 158. *honour's thought —s solely in the breast of every man,* H5 II Chor. 4. *that such bloody strife should r. among professors of one faith,* H6A V, 1, 14. *discomfit —s in the hearts,* H6B V, 2, 87. *the spavin or springhalt —ed among 'em,* H8 I, 3, 13. *twenty of the dog-days now r. in his nose,* V, 4, 43. *there golden sleep doth r.* Rom. II, 3, 38. *a house where the infectious pestilence did r.* V, 2, 10. *in his royalty of nature —s that which would be feared,* Mcb. III, 1, 51. *our Jovial star —ed at his birth,* Cymb. V, 4, 105. *till Lucina —ed,* Per. I, 1, 8. *to r. in =* a) to be master of: *Fortune —s in gifts of the world, not in the lineaments of nature,* As I, 2, 43. *blest pray you be, that after this strange starting from your orbs you may r. in them now,* Cymb. V, 5, 372. *I'll show you those in troubles r.* Per. II Prol. 7. b) to exult in, to be made happy by: *all men are bad, and in their badness r.* Sonn. 121, 14. *—s in galled eyes of weeping souls,* R3 IV, 4, 53.

**Reignier** (O. Edd. *Reignier, Reignard, Reynard, Reynold*)duke of Anjou and titular king of Naples: H6A I, 1, 94. I, 2, 61. 65. IV, 4, 27. V, 3, 131. 148. 163. 169. V, 4, 78. V, 5, 47. H6B I, 1, 47. 111. H6C V, 7, 38.

**Rein,** subst. bridle: Ven. 31. 264. 392. H5 III, 3, 22. *to give the r.* = to leave without restraint: Tp. IV, 1, 52. Meas. II, 4, 160. LLL IV, 2, 663. Cor. II, 1, 33. *giving — s and spurs to my free speech,* R2 I, 1, 55. *to take the r.* = to go on without restraint: Wint. II, 3, 51. *where every horse bears his commanding r. and may direct his course as please himself,* R3 II, 2, 128 (*as please himself* relating to both verbs). *bears his head in such a r.* Troil. I, 3, 189 (= bridles up). *the hard r. which both of them have borne against the old kind king,* Lr. III, 1, 27.

**Rein,** vb. to govern by a bridle, to restrain: Lucr. 706. LLL V, 2, 662. Merch. III, 2, 113 (O. Edd. *rain*). With *from: spur them to ruthful work, r. them from ruth,* Troil. V, 3, 48. With *to: r. his proud head to the saddle-bow,* Ven. 14. *he cannot be —ed again to temperance,* Cor. III, 3, 28.

Intr. = to be governed by the bridle: *he will bear you easily and —s well,* Tw. III, 4, 358.

**Reinforce,** to strengthen with additional troops, to come in for rescue; absol.: *betimes let's r. or fly,* Cymb. V, 2, 18. Trans.: *the French have —d their scattered men,* H5 IV, 6, 36.

**Reinforcement,** fresh assistance: *haste we to r.* Troil. V, 5, 16. *with a sudden r. struck Corioli like a planet,* Cor. II, 2, 117.

**Reins,** the kidneys: Wiv. III, 5, 24.

**Reiterate,** to repeat: *you never spoke what did become you less than this, which to r. were sin,* Wint. I, 2, 283.

**Reject,** to refuse with contempt: *woo thyself, be of thyself —ed,* Ven. 159. *you will r. her,* LLL V, 2, 438.

**Rejoice,** 1) intr. to be joyful, to exult: Ven. 977. Tp. V, 206. Err. V, 413. John II, 312. H5 III, 6, 54. Caes. I, 1, 37. With *at:* Wiv. V, 3, 8. Ado V, 4, 45. LLL V, 2, 761. H4B IV, 4, 109. H5 II, 2, 161. III, 3, 56. Caes. III, 2, 27. With *in:* Gent. III, 1, 394. As I, 2, 17. R3 IV, 2, 6. Cor. I, 3, 3. Rom. I, 2, 106. IV, 5, 47. Tim. V, 1, 195. Caes. I, 1, 35. With an inf.: Tp. V, 39. Meas. III, 2, 249. H6B II, 4, 32. With a subordinate clause: Wint. V, 1, 30. Cor. V, 6, 139. The gerund substantively: *to add a more —ing to the prime,* Lucr. 332. *my —ing at nothing can be more,* Tp. III, 1, 93. *piece the —ing,* Wint. V, 2, 117. *the dues of —ing,* Mcb. I, 5, 13. *—ing fires,* Cymb. III, 1, 32.

2) tr. a) to make joyful, to gladden: *it —th my intellect,* LLL V, 1, 63. *it —s me,* All's IV, 5, 89.

b) to be joyful at: *which I in sufferance heartily will r.* H5 II, 2, 159. *ne'er mother —d deliverance more,* Cymb. V, 5, 370.

**Rejoicing,** subst. see *Rejoice.*

**Rejoicingly,** with joy or exultation: *she hath despised me r., and I'll be merry in my revenge,* Cymb. III, 5, 149.

**Rejoindure,** the act of joining again: *beguiles our lips of all r.* Troil. IV, 4, 38 (i. e. kisses).

**Rejourn,** to adjourn, to put off: *and then r. the controversy to a second day of audience,* Cor. II, 1, 79.

**Relapse,** subst. *(relápse* and *rélapse),* 1) a falling back into a disease: Per. III, 2, 110.

2) a springing back, rebounding: *killing in r. of mortality,* H5 IV, 3, 107 (= by a rebound of death or deadliness).*

**Relate,** 1) tr. to tell, to narrate, to report: Meas. V, 26. LLL I, 1, 172. H6C IV, 1, 88. H8 I, 2, 8. 129. Mcb. IV, 3, 205. V, 4, 19. Oth. V, 2, 341. 371. Per. I, 4, 2. III Prol. 55.

2) intr. to have reference: *this challenge —s in purpose only to Achilles,* Troil. I, 3, 323.

**Relation,** 1) account, report: Tp. V, 164. Wint. V, 2, 2. 92. V, 3, 130. Troil. III, 3, 201. Mcb. IV, 3, 173. Cymb. II, 4, 86. Per. V, 1, 124.

2) reference, connexion: *the intent and purpose of*

the law hath full r. to the penalty, Merch. IV, 1, 248 (= has full bearing on the p.). *augures and understood —s have by magot-pies and choughs and rooks brought forth the secret'st man of blood,* Mcb. III, 4, 124 (incidents which were perceived to have reference to the question).

**Relative,** having reference to, and bearing on, the question; to the purpose, conclusive: *I'll have grounds more r. than this,* Hml. II, 2, 633.

**Release,** subst. dismission from confinement: *they cannot budge till your r.* Tp. V, 11 (the later Ff *till you r.*).

**Release,** vb. 1) to set free from confinement, obligation, or servitude: *and from her twining arms doth urge —ing,* Ven. 256. *the charter of thy worth gives thee —ing,* Sonn. 87, 3. *r. them,* Tp. V, 30. *r. me from my bands,* Epil. 9. *he hath —d him from the world,* Meas. IV, 3, 119. *he would not r. my brother,* V, 99. *I will her charmed eye r. from monster's view,* Mids. III, 2, 376. *I will r. the fairy queen,* IV, 1, 75. *by what means got'st thou to be —d?* H6A I, 4, 25. *'tis but reason that I be —d from giving aid,* H6C III, 3, 147.

2) to quit, to let go, to remit, to give up: *with mine own breath r. all duty's rites,* R2 IV, 210 (Ff *r. all duteous oaths*). *that the duchy of Anjou shall be —d and delivered to the king her father,* H6B I, 1, 51.

**Relent,** 1) to soften, to grow less hard, in a physical sense: *stone at rain —eth,* Ven. 200 (cf. *unrelenting* in Tit. II, 3, 141). *he, a marble to her tears, is washed with them, but —s not,* Meas. III, 1, 239.

2) to give way, to yield, to comply: *you will not do it, you? I do r.* Wiv. II, 2, 31. *r., sweet Hermia,* Mids. I, 1, 91. *can you behold my (the king's) sighs and tears and will not once r.?* H6A III, 1, 108. 132. *will ye r. and yield to mercy?* H6B IV, 8, 11. Especially = to become tender and compassionate: Meas. II, 2, 3. 124. Merch. III, 3, 15. H6A III, 3, 59. H6B IV, 4, 17. IV, 7, 124. R3 I, 4, 263. 264. 265. Tit. II, 3, 165. IV, 1, 124. *—ing,* adjectively, = too easily moved, given to weakness: *do not steep thy heart in such —ing dew of lamentations,* Lucr. 1829. *as the mournful crocodile with sorrow snares —ing passengers,* H6B III, 1, 227. *—ing fool,* R3 IV, 4, 431.

**Reliance,** trust, confidence: *my —s on his fracted dates have smit my credit,* Tim. II, 1, 22.

**Relics,** see *Reliques.*

**Relief,** 1) alleviation of pain or distress, remedy, comfort: *within this limit is r. enough,* Ven. 235. *the offender's sorrow lends but weak r. to him that bears the strong offence's cross,* Sonn. 34, 11. *I will give him some r.* Tp. II, 2, 70. *wherever sorrow is, r. would be,* As III, 5, 86. *it (thy grief) shall be eased, if France can yield r.* H6C III, 3, 20. *my r. must be to loathe her,* Oth. III, 3, 267.

2) assistance, support: *how true a gentleman you send r.* Merch. III, 4, 6. *in the r. of this oppressed child,* John II, 245. *to r. of lazars and weak age,* H5 I, 1, 15. *away, for your r.!* H6B V, 2, 88 (= to save yourselves). *to beg r. among Rome's enemies,* Tit. V, 3, 106. *immediate are my needs, and my r. must not be tossed and turned to me in words,* Tim. II, 1, 25. *my means for thy r.* Cymb. III, 5, 115.

3) release of a sentinel from duty: *for this r. much thanks,* Hml. I, 1, 8.

**Relier,** one too confident: *to thee, to thee my*

*heaved-up hands appeal, not to seducing lust, thy rash r.* Lucr. 639 (i. e. lust which confides too rashly in thy present disposition and does not foresee its necessary change *j.*

**Relieve,** 1) to help in distress, to free from want, pain, grief, or danger: *he* (the sun) *cheers the morn and all the world — th,* Ven. 484. *misery ... never —d by any,* 708. *stooping to r. him,* Tp. II, 1, 121. *will not give a doit to r. a lame beggar,* II, 2, 33. *—d by prayer,* Epil. 16. Err. II, 1, 39. As II, 4, 77. All's V, 3, 86. Tw. II, 4, 4. III, 4, 395. John V, 7, 45. Cor. I, 1, 17. 19. Tit. V, 3, 181. Tim. IV, 3, 536. Hml. IV, 3, 10. Lr. I, 1, 121. Lr. III, 3, 15. 20. Ant. V, 2, 41. Cymb. III, 6, 8. V, 5, 400. Per. I, 2, 99. III, 3, 22. V, 2, 4. With *of: to r. them of their heavy load,* Per. I, 4, 91.

2) to release from duty; applied to troops: *placed behind with purpose to r. and follow them,* H6A I, 1, 133. To sentinels: H6A II, 1, 70. Hml. I, 1, 17. Ant. IV, 9, 1.

**Religion,** 1) the sense of any holy obligation; duty and awe paid to things held sacred; conscience: *keep your promise. With no less r. than if thou wert indeed my Rosalind,* As IV, 1, 201. *when the devout r. of mine eye maintains such falsehood,* Rom. I, 2, 93. *piety and fear, r. to the gods,* Tim. IV, 1, 16. *your command, which my love makes r. to obey,* Ant. V, 2, 199. *I see you have some r. in you, that you fear,* Cymb. I, 4, 149.

- 2) the form and practice of divine faith and worship: Compl. 250. Meas. I, 2, 24. LLL IV, 3, 363. Merch. III, 2, 77. All's I, 3, 57. John III, 1, 279. 280. H4B I, 1, 201. H6A I, 1, 41. I, 3, 65. Tim. III, 2, 83. IV, 3, 34. Hml. III, 4, 47.

**Religious,** 1) devoted to any holy obligation, conscientious: *how many a holy and obsequious tear hath dear r. love stolen from mine eye,* Sonn. 31, 6. *r. love put out religion's eye,* Compl. 250. *as thou lovest her, thy love's to me r.; else, does err,* All's II, 3, 190. *a coward, a most devout coward, r. in it,* Tw. III, 4, 424. *with all r. strength of sacred vows,* John III, 1, 229. *with thy r. truth and modesty,* H8 IV, 2, 74. *most holy and r. fear it is,* Hml. III, 3, 8.

2) belonging to the form and practice of divine faith and worship: *in some r. house,* R2 V, 1, 23. *r. canons,* Tim. IV, 3, 60.

3) godly, pious: Ado IV, 1, 244. As III, 2, 362. V, 4, 166. 187. All's I, 3, 211. H5 II, 2, 130. H6A I, 1, 40. III, 1, 54. R3 III, 7, 92. H8 V, 1, 28. V, 3, 116. Tit. V, 1, 74.

**Religiously,** 1) with respect to any holy obligation, conscientiously: *being no further enemy to you than the constraint of hospitable zeal in the relief of this oppressed child r. provokes,* John II, 246. *our souls r. confirm thy words,* IV, 3, 73. *justly and r. unfold,* H5 I, 2, 10.

2) according to the precepts of divine law: *you have done this in the fear of God, very r.* LLL IV, 2, 153. *a nun of winter's sisterhood kisses not more r.* As III, 4, 18. *do in his* (the pope's) *name r. demand,* John III, 1, 140. *r. they ask a sacrifice,* Tit. I, 124.

**Relinquish,** to give up, to despair of: *to be —ed of the artists,* All's II, 3, 10.

**Reliques,** 1) remnants: *the fragments, scraps, the bits and greasy r. of her o'ereaten faith,* Troil. V, 2, 159.

2) things which keep alive the memory of persons gone or times past: *now he's gone, and my idolatrous fancy must sanctify his r.* All's I, 1, 109. *the nature of his great offence is dead, and deeper than oblivion we do bury the incensing r. of it,* V, 3, 25. *shall we go see the r. of this town?* Tw. III, 3, 19 (= monuments). *press for tinctures, stains, r. and cognizance,* Caes. II, 2, 89.

**Relish,** subst. 1) a pleasing taste: *what r. is in this?* Tw. IV, 1, 64. *the imaginary r. is so sweet,* Troil. III, 2, 20. *some crab-trees that will not be grafted to your r.* Cor. II, 1, 206 (O. Edd. *rallish*).

2) an admixture just perceptible, a tincture: *some smack of age, some r. of the saltness of time,* H4B I, 2, 111. *the king-becoming graces ... I have no r. of them,* Mcb. IV, 3, 95. *some act that has no r. of salvation in it,* Hml. III, 3, 92.

3) quality, sort: *his fears ... be of the same r. as ours are,* H5 IV, 1, 114.

**Relish,** vb. 1) intr. a) to have a pleasing taste: *it would not have —ed among my other discredits,* Wint. V, 2, 132.

b) with *of,* = to have a taste or flavour: *virtue cannot so inoculate our old stock but we shall r. of it,* Hml. III, 1, 120. *let what is here contained r. of love,* Cymb. III, 2, 30. *my thoughts, that never —ed of a base descent,* Per. II, 5, 60.

2) trans. a) to taste, and hence to feel, to perceive: *one of their kind, that r. all as sharply,* Tp. V, 23. *take a taste of my finding him, and r. it with good observance,* As III, 2, 247. *which if you ... cannot or will not r. a truth like us,* Wint. II, 1, 167.

b) to like, to be pleased with: *r. your nimble notes to pleasing ears,* Lucr. 1126 (take pleasure in singing where others like to hear you. Or = serve up as a relish?). *to r. a love-song,* Gent. II, 1, 20. *I do not r. well their loud applause,* Meas. I, 1, 70. I, 2, 16. Troil. I, 3, 388. Lr. I, 2, 51. Oth. II, 1, 166.

**Relive,** to live again: *how this dead queen —s,* Per. V, 3, 64.

**Reliver,** to give back: *and r. our authorities there,* Meas. IV, 4, 6 (the later Ff *deliver,* M. Edd. *redeliver*).

**Relume,** to rekindle, to light again: *that Promethean heat that can thy light r.* Oth. V, 2, 13 (Q1 *return,* Q2.3 *relumine*).

**Rely,** with *on,* = to lean, to rest on, to depend on: *as one —ing on your lordship's will, and not depending on his friendly wish,* Gent. I, 3, 61. *if thou hast* (wit or impudence), *r. upon it till my tale be heard, and hold no longer out,* Meas. V, 370. *for I, thy resolved patient, on thee still r.* All's II, 1, 207. *bade me r. on him as on my father,* R3 II, 2, 25. *he doth r. on none* (excuse) Troil. II, 3, 173. *that destruction which I'll guard them from, if thereon* (my good purposes) *you r.* Ant. V, 2, 133.

**Remain,** subst. 1) stay: *let's fetch him off, or make r. alike,* Cor. I, 4, 62 (cf. *Here-remain*). 2) that which is left to be done: *all the r. is 'Welcome',* Cymb. III, 1, 87.

Plur. *—s* = that which is left: *of five and twenty valiant sons behold the poor —s, alive and dead,* Tit. I, 81. *poor —s of friends,* Caes. V, 5, 1.

**Remain,** vb. 1) to stay behind after others have withdrawn: *if what parts can so r.* Phoen. 48 (and consequently continue to be together). *trouble being gone, comfort should r.* Ado I, 1, 101. *the ladies follow* *her and but one visor —s,* II, 1, 164. *I r. a pinched thing,* Wint. II, 1, 51. *if she r., whom they have ravished must by me be slain,* Per. IV, 1, 102. Hence = to be left as a trace: *the scar that will despite of cure r.* Lucr. 732. *those blots that do with me r.* Sonn. 36, 3. *scratch thee but with a pin, and there —s some scar of it,* As III, 5, 21. cf. *proofs new-bleeding, which —ed the foil of this false jewel,* Compl. 153. *I hope it —s not unkindly with your lordship, that I returned you an empty messenger,* Tim. III, 6, 39.

2) to be left out of a greater number or quantity: *what face —s alive that's worth the viewing?* Ven. 1076. *of what she was no semblance did r.* Lucr. 1453. *there —s unpaid a hundred thousand more,* LLL II,134. *where now —s a sweet reversion,* H4A IV, 1, 53. *for me nothing —s,* H6A I, 1, 174. I, 2, 15. H6C V, 6, 66. Cor. IV, 5, 79. Rom. II, 4, 67. Tim. II, 2, 156. IV, 2, 2. Oth. II, 3, 264. = to be left to be done: *then no more —s,* Meas. I, 1, 7. *nothing —s but that I kindle the boy thither,* As I, 1, 179. *nought —s but so,* Shr. I, 1, 166. R2 IV, 222. H4A V, 5, 34. H6C IV, 3, 60. IV, 7, 7. Cor. II, 2, 42. 138. Tit. I, 146 (*—eth nought*). Mcb. V, 6, 5. Hml. II, 2, 104. III, 4, 179. Oth. V, 2, 368. *—s that you anon do meet the senate,* Cor. II, 3, 147. *and now —s that we find out the cause,* Hml. II, 2, 100.

= to be reserved: *for thee —s a heavier doom,* R2 I,3, 148. *to thee and thine r. this ample third,* Lr.I,1,82.

3) to rest or abide in a place, not to go away, not to remove: *the cry —eth in one place,* Ven. 885. *his hand, that yet —s upon her breast,* Lucr. 463. *a dower —ing in the coffer of her friends,* Meas. I, 2, 155. *where would you had —ed until this time,* Err. IV, 4, 69. Mids. III, 1, 156. III, 2, 83. 173. All's IV, 2, 58. IV, 5, 52. 91. Tw. IV, 2, 61. Wint. IV, 4, 853. H5 III, 3, 52. III, 5, 66. Cor. III, 1, 87. 88. III, 3, 124. Hml. I, 2, 115. III, 3, 97. Ant. I, 3, 44. 104. Cymb. IV, 2, 1. cf. Ant. II, 6, 29. Cymb. I, 1, 117.

4) to stay, to be in a place: *by praising him here who doth hence r.* Sonn. 39, 14. *while here you do r.* Mids. V, 152. *from where you do r. let paper show,* R2 I, 3, 250. *where Warwick now —s,* H6C IV, 8, 59. *where she —s now sick,* H8 IV, 1, 35. *there to r. till the king's further pleasure be known unto us,* V, 3, 90. *—ing now in Gallia,* Cymb. III, 7, 12. *I nothing know where —s,* IV, 3, 14.

Hence = to dwell: *in men r. cave-keeping evils,* Lucr. 1249. *one knight loves both, and both in thee r.* Pilgr. 116. *I see inconstancy more in women than in men r.* 262. *if you r. upon this island,* Tp. I, 2, 423. *where —s he?* As III, 2, 235. *by his authority he —s here,* All's IV, 5, 69. *in this country, where we now r.* H6C III, 1, 75. *that only like a gulf it did r. i' the midst o' the body,* Cor. I, 1, 101. *r. in it* (my father's house) Ant. II, 6, 29. *r. thou* (a ring) *here, while sense can keep it on,* Cymb. I, 1, 117.

And even simply = to be: *but there —s a scruple in that too,* H6A V, 3, 93. *wouldst thou r. a beast with the beasts?* Tim. IV, 3, 326. *r. assured,* V, 1, 100. cf. Lucr. 529.

5) to last, not to perish, not to cease: *both* (night and morrow) *she thinks too long with her —ing,* Lucr. 1572. *and this with thee —s,* Sonn. 74, 14. *which shall above that idle rank r. beyond all date,* 122, 3. *aye —ing lamps,* Per. III, 1, 63. = to be preserved, not to be killed: *if Cassio do r.* Oth. V, 1, 18.

6) to continue in a state or quality. *doth always fresh r.* Ven. 801. *thy husband shall r. the scornful mark of every eye,* Lucr. 519. *a little harm done to a great good end for lawful policy —s enacted,* 529 (= is always). *to have their unseen sin r. untold,* 753. *some of her blood still pure and red —ed,* 1742. *to dwell with him in thoughts, or to r. in personal duty,* Compl. 129. *imprisoned thou didst painfully r.* Tp. I, 2, 278. *this mystery —ed undiscovered,* Wint. V, 2, 130. *I do r. as neuter,* R2 II, 3, 159. *there* (on the gates of York) *it* (York's head) *doth r.* H6C II, 1, 66 (= is still). *thou shalt still r. the duke of York,* V, 1, 28. H8 V, 3, 181. Cor. II, 3, 191. III, 1, 202. IV, 1, 51. V, 3, 147. V, 6, 17. Caes. I, 3, 18. III, 1, 73. Mcb. III, 2, 15. Lr. I, 1, 160. II, 1, 59. V, 1, 59. Ant. II, 2, 115. V, 2, 189. 205. Cymb. I, 1, 175. I, 4, 173. II, 4, 3. II, 2, 47. IV, 4, 42. Per. III, 3, 29. *let her r.* = let her alone: Cymb. II, 3, 17 (German: *lass sie bleiben*).

**Remainder,** 1) that which is left, the rest: *abide all three distracted, and the r. mourning over them,* Tp. V, 13 (= the others). *I would repent out the r. of nature,* All's IV, 3, 272. *my sovereign liege was in my debt upon r. of a dear account,* R2 I, 1, 130. *as much as one sound cudgel of four foot — you see the poor r. — could distribute,* H8 V, 4, 20. *the r. of our hateful days,* Tit. III, 1, 132. *the poor r. of Andronici,* V, 3, 131. *some slender ort of his r.* Tim. IV, 3, 401 (of the rest of his fortune). *thus it remains, and the r. thus,* Hml. II, 2, 104. *and the r. to be such men,* Lr. I, 4, 271 (Ff *—s*). *the gods protect you and bless the good —s of the court,* Cymb. I, 1, 129 (viz the court which now gets rid of my 'unworthiness').

Adjectively: *as dry as the r. biscuit after a voyage,* As II, 7, 39. *the r. viands we do not throw in unrespective sieve, because we now are full,* Troil. II, 2, 70.

2) an eventual inheritance or possession: *cut the entail from all —s,* All's IV, 3, 313.*

**Remains,** subst. see *Remain* subst.

**Remarkable,** worthy of note, conspicuous, distinguished: *there is nothing left r. beneath the visiting moon,* Ant. IV, 15, 67. *more r. in single oppositions,* Cymb. IV, 1, 14.

**Remarked,** the same: *you speak of two the most r. i' the kingdom,* H8 V, 1, 33.

**Remediate,** remedial, medicinal: *be aidant and r. in the good man's distress,* Lr. IV, 4, 17.

**Remedy,** subst. 1) a medicine, physic: Sonn. 154, 11. Mids. III, 2, 452. As III, 2, 386. All's I, 3, 234. Wint. III, 2, 154. H4B I, 2, 264. Troil. I, 3, 141. Rom. II, 3, 51. *you set up your rest 'gainst r.* All's II, 1, 138 (= against being cured).

2) a cure for any evil, help, redress: *the r. indeed to do me good is to let forth my foul defiled blood,* Lucr. 1028. *for this sin there is no r.* Sonn. 62, 3. Meas. II, 2, 75. III, 1, 204. Ado I, 1, 321. I, 3, 9. Mids. III, 2, 109. As I, 1, 29. Shr. Ind. I, 11. II, 212. All's I, 1, 231. V, 3, 164 (*without your r.* = without your help). R2 III, 3, 203 (*tears show their love, but want their —es,* = do not avail). H6A V, 3, 135. H8 II, 4, 201. V, 1, 151 (*render*). Cor. IV, 6, 2 (*his —es are tame;* i. e. his means of redress). Tit. IV, 3, 30. Rom. III, 5, 241. IV, 1, 67. 76 (*give*). Mcb. III, 2, 11. Hml. II, 2, 18. Lr. I, 4, 268. II, 2, 177 (*give*). Oth. I, 3, 202. Cymb. I, 6, 97. 98. *there's no r.* = it cannot be helped: Wiv. I, 3, 36. Meas. II, 1, 295. 299. III,

1, 61. 62. III, 2, 1. All's IV, 3, 337. Tw. III, 4, 325. John IV, 1, 91. H6A II, 2, 57. Cor. III, 2, 26. Oth. I, 1, 35. *no r.:* Wiv. II, 2, 127. Meas. II, 2, 48. Mids. V, 210. Wint. IV, 4, 670. V, 1, 77. Troil. IV, 4, 57. Cymb. III, 4, 165. *where is no r.* Gent. II, 2, 2. *here is no r.* Wiv. V, 5, 244. *what r.?* = what is to be done? Wiv. V, 5, 250. Tw. I, 5, 56. H6A V, 3, 132.

**Remedy,** vb. to redress, to repair: *my own fault, which death or absence soon shall r.* Mids. III, 2, 244. *Rome shall r. this,* H6A III, 1, 51. *things that are not to be —ed,* III, 3, 4. *I will r. this gear ere long,* H6B III, 1, 91. *not a man shall pass his quarter, or offend the stream of regular justice, but shall be —ed to your public laws at heaviest answer,* Tim. V, 4, 62 (= it shall be redressed according to your laws. M. Edd. *rendered*).

**Remember,** 1) to bear in mind, to call to mind, to recollect: Sonn. 3, 13. 71, 5. 74, 12. Tp. I, 2, 38. 51. 133. II, 1, 270. III, 1, 49. III, 3, 68. V, 255. Gent. IV, 4, 37. 103. Wiv. I, 1, 174. I, 4, 29. Meas. I, 1, 14. V, 330. Err. V, 291. Ado II, 3, 141. III, 3, 135. LLL I, 1, 258. IV, 1, 98. IV, 3, 96. Mids. II, 1, 154. Merch. I, 2, 123. As I, 1, 1. II, 4, 34. III, 2, 188. V, 4, 26. Wint. IV, 1, 21. V, 1, 6. 67. H4B IV, 1, 112. H6B II, 1, 86. IV, 1, 59. H6C I, 1, 93. H8 IV, 2, 151. Caes. IV, 3, 18. Cymb. V, 5, 149 etc. With a double accus.: *I r. him worthy of thy praise,* Merch. I, 2, 132. cf. *—ed tolling a departing friend,* H4B I, 1, 103. Followed by *since: thou —est since once I sat,* Mids. II, 1, 148. *r. since you owed no more to time,* Wint. V, 1, 219. *do you r. since we lay all night in the windmill,* H4B III, 2, 206.

Intr. with of: *I r. of such a time,* H8 I, 2, 190. *I r. me* = I remember: Tw. V, 286. H4A II, 4, 468. R3 IV, 2, 98 (Qq as *I r.*). *I have —ed me, thou's hear our counsel,* Rom. I, 3, 9 (= on second thoughts).

2) to think of; to consider: *thy sweet love —ed such wealth brings,* Sonn. 29, 13. *to keep an adjunct to r. thee,* 122, 13. *r. whom thou hast aboard,* Tp. I, 1, 20. *r. I have done thee worthy service,* I, 2, 247. *r. first to possess his books,* III, 2, 99. *I r. the story,* III, 2, 156. *I will forget that Julia is alive, —ing that my love to her is dead,* Gent. II, 6, 28. *r. you your cue,* Wiv. III, 3, 38. *r. my daughter,* V, 2, 2. V, 4, 1. *r. now my brother,* Meas. IV, 1, 70. *much deserved on his part, and equally —ed by Don Pedro,* Ado I, 1, 13. *marry, well —ed,* Merch. II, 8, 26. *unless you could teach me to forget a banished father, you must not learn me how to r. any extraordinary pleasure,* As I, 2, 7. *if ever I r. to be holy,* John III, 3, 15. *my humble duty —ed,* H4B II, 1, 137. *whom we met here both to thank and to r. with honours like himself,* Cor. II, 2, 51. *if he r. a kinder value of the people,* 62. *r. thy swashing blow,* Rom. I, 1, 69. *must I r.? why, she would hang on him,* Hml. I, 2, 143. Ado II, 1, 69. IV, 2, 79. V, 1, 315. R2 III, 2, 82. H6A I, 1, 162. 165. I, 4, 94. Tim. II, 2, 237 etc. *r. the porter,* Mcb. II, 3, 23 (i. e. give him a present). *r. thy courtesy,* LLL V, 1, 103 (i. e. put on thy hat; cf. Hml. V, 2, 108, and see *Courtesy*). *briefly thyself r.* Lr. IV, 6, 233 (think of thy sins; cf. Err. V, 292).

3) to mention: *the ditty does r. my drowned father,* Tp. I, 2, 405. *nat —ed in thy epitaph,* H4A V, 4, 101. *we will accite, as I before —ed, all our state,* H4B V, 2, 142. *r. me in all humility unto his highness,* H8 IV, 2, 160 (= commend me).

4) to remind: *O that our night of woe might have —ed my deepest sense, how hard true sorrow hits,* Sonn. 120, 9. *let me r. thee what thou hast promised,* Tp. I, 2, 243. *I'll not r. you of my own lord,* Wint. III, 2, 231. *—s me of all his gracious parts,* John III, 4, 96. *every stride will but r. me what a deal of world I wander,* R2 I, 3, 269. *it doth r. me the more of sorrow,* III, 4, 14. *I must r. you,* H4A V, 1, 32. *—ing you 'tis past,* H5 V Chor. 43. *thou but —est me of mine own conception,* Lr. I, 4, 72.

**Remembered,** having memory: *thy sting is not so sharp as friend r. not,* As II, 7, 189. *to be r.* = 1) to recollect: *if you be —ed,* Meas. II, 1, 110. 114. *and now I am r., scorned at me,* As III, 5, 131. *if you be r., I did not bid you mar it,* Shr. IV, 3, 96. *if your majesties is r. of it,* H5 IV, 7, 102 (Fluellen's speech). 2) to think of, to consider: *O be r., no outrageous thing from vassal actors can be wiped away,* Lucr. 607. *if I had been r., I could have given my uncle's grace a flout,* R3 II, 4, 23. *be you r., Marcus, she's gone,* Tit. IV, 3, 5.

**Remembrance** (sometimes quadrisyll., not only at the end of the line, as in Tw. I, 1, 32 and John V, 2, 2, but in the middle: Wint. IV, 4, 76. Tim. III, 5, 92. Mcb. III, 2, 30) 1) memory; a) the faculty of recollecting: *this lord of weak r.* Tp. II, 1, 232. *from the time of his r. to this very instant disaster,* All's IV, 3, 126. *unkind r.!* John V, 6, 12. *lest my r. suffer ill report,* Ant. II, 2, 159. *praise be given to your r.* Cymb. II, 4, 93.

b) recollection, retention in mind, or calling to mind: *nor it nor no r. what it was,* Sonn. 5, 12. *I summon up r. of things past,* 30, 2. *hath kept with thy r.* Tp. I, 2, 44. 46. *which is from my r.* 65. *how sharp the point of this r. is,* V, 138. *let us not burthen our r. with a heaviness that's gone,* 199. *the r. of my former love,* Gent. II, 4, 194. Wiv. IV, 1, 48. IV, 2, 63. LLL V, 2, 820. Mids. IV, 1, 172. V, 385. As I, 1, 67. All's I, 1, 56. 91. I, 3, 140. V, 2, 20. Tw. I, 1, 32. II, 1, 33. III, 4, 248. V, 289. Wint. IV, 2, 24. V, 3, 40. John V, 2, 2. R2 II, 1, 14. III, 4, 107. H4B IV, 1, 204. H5 I, 2, 115. 129. R3 II, 1, 118. IV, 4, 251. 421. V, 3, 233. H8 III, 2, 8 (*give*). Tit. III, 1, 241. Tim. III, 5, 92. III, 6, 52. Mcb. III, 3, 67. V, 1, 37. Hml. II, 2, 26. Cymb. II, 3, 48. II, 4, 14. III, 1, 2. IV, 4, 24. Per. V, 3, 12. The rosemary its emblem: Wint. IV, 4, 76. Hml. IV, 5, 175. 179. cf. R2 III, 4, 107. H4B II, 3, 59.

c) the being kept in mind, memory preserved: *his good r.* All's I, 2, 48. *you pity not the state, nor the r. of his most sovereign name,* Wint. V, 1, 25. cf. Cymb. II, 3, 48. II, 4, 14. III, 1, 2.

2) a token by which one is kept in memory, a keepsake: *keep this r. for thy Julia's sake,* Gent. II, 2, 5. *take some r. of us,* Merch. IV, 1, 422. *I have —s of yours,* Hml. III, 1, 93. *this was her first r. from the Moor,* Oth. III, 3, 291. *this is from some mistress, some r.* III, 4, 186. cf. H5 I, 2, 229: *tombless, with no r. over them.*

3) thought, regard, consideration, a state of being mindful: *his majesty, out of a self-gracious r., did first propose,* All's IV, 5, 78. *with this r., that you use the same with the like just spirit,* H4B V, 2, 115 (or = admonition?). *one thus descended ... we did commend to your —s,* Cor. II, 3, 256. *let your r. apply to Banquo,* Mcb. III, 2, 30. *together with r. of ourselves,*

Hml. I, 2, 7. *his r. lay in Egypt with his joy,* Ant. I, 5, 57.

Misapplied by Evans in Wiv. III, 3, 255.

**Remembrancer,** one who reminds: *sweet r.* Mcb. III, 4, 37. *the agent for his master and the r. of her to hold the hand-fast to her lord,* Cymb. I, 5, 77.*

**Remiss** (seemingly *rémiss* in H6A IV, 3, 29) slack, negligent, careless: Meas. IV, 2, 119. R2 III, 2, 33. H6A IV, 3, 29. Troil. IV, 4, 143. Hml. IV, 7, 135.

**Remission,** forgiveness, pardon: Lucr. 714. Gent. I, 2, 65. Meas. V, 503 (*an apt r.* = an inclination to pardon). H4B V, 2, 38. Cor. V, 2, 90.

**Remissness,** slackness, want of energy: Meas. II, 2, 96.

**Remit,** 1) to leave unpunished, to pardon: Meas. II, 4, 44. V, 526. Tit. I, 484.

2) to give up, to resign: *will you have me, or your pearl again? Neither of either; I r. both twain,* LLL V, 2, 459.

**Remnant,** that which is left, the rest: *the r. of mine age,* Gent. III, 1, 74. *where I may think the r. of my thoughts in peace,* John V, 4, 46. *to you the r. northward,* H4A III, 1, 79. *bloodless r. of that royal blood,* R3 I, 2, 7. *—s of packthread,* Rom. V, 1, 47. Used in contempt, = scrap, fragment: *some odd quirks and —s of wit broken on me,* Ado II, 3, 245. *thou rag, thou quantity, thou r.* Shr. IV, 3, 112. *they must leave those —s of fool and feather,* H8 I, 3, 24.

**Remonstrance,** demonstration, manifestation: *would not rather make rash r. of my hidden power than let him so be lost,* Meas. V, 397.

**Remorse,** 1) compunction of conscience: *poor wretches have r. in poor abuses,* Lucr. 269. *what says Monsieur R.?* H4A I, 2, 125. *thy words move rage and not r. in me,* H6B IV, 1, 112. R3 I, 4, 110. IV, 3, 20. Troil. II, 2, 115. Caes. II, 1, 19. Oth. III, 3, 369. 468 (*to obey shall be in me r.*).

2) pity, tenderness of heart: *pity, she cries, some favour, some r.* Ven. 257. *expelled r. and nature,* Tp. V, 76. *slighted me into the river with as little r.* Wiv. III, 5, 10. *if so your heart were touched with that r. as mine is to him,* Meas. II, 2, 54. *my sisterly r. confutes mine honour,* V, 100. *shall change slander to r.* Ado IV, 1, 213. *thou'lt show thy mercy and r.* Merch. IV, 1, 20. *it was your pleasure and your own r.* As I, 3, 72. *without any mitigation or r. of voice,* Tw. II, 3, 98. *pity and r.* John II, 478. *the tears of soft r.* IV, 3, 50. *rivers of r. and innocency,* 110. H6B IV, 7, 111. H6C III, 1, 40. V, 5, 64. R3 III, 7, 211. Tim. IV, 3, 122. Mcb. I, 5, 45. Hml. II, 2, 513. Lr. IV, 2, 73. With *of: moved with r. of these outrageous broils,* H6A V, 4, 97.

**Remorseful,** tender-hearted, compassionate: Gent. IV, 3, 13. All's V, 3, 58. H6B IV, 1, 1. R3 I, 2, 156.

**Remorseless,** pitiless: Lucr. 562. H6B III, 1, 213. H6C I, 4, 142. Hml. II, 2, 609.

**Remote,** 1) distant: Sonn. 44, 4. Phoen. 29. John V, 2, 31. H4A I, 1, 4. Cor. IV, 5, 148. With *from: from Athens is her house r. seven leagues,* Mids. I, 1, 159 (Ff removed). *r. from all the pleasures of the world,* LLL V, 2, 806.

2) solitary, desert: *bear it to some r. and desert place,* Wint. II, 3, 176. *places r. enough are in Bohemia,* III, 3, 31.

**Remotion,** the act of keeping aloof, nonappearance: *all thy safety were r.,* Tim. IV, 3,

346. *this r. of the duke and her is practice only,* Lr. II, 4, 115.

**Remove,** subst. 1) change of place, departure, absence: *there a nay is placed without r.* Pilgr. 256 (= irremovably). *in our r. be thou at full ourself,* Meas. I, 1, 44. *so shall your loves woo contrary, deceived by these —s,* LLL V, 2, 135 (viz of love-tokens interchanged). *author of his own just r.* Hml. IV, 5, 81. *there was no purpose in them of this r.* Lr. II, 4, 4. *our pleasure requires our quick r. from hence,* Ant. I, 2, 203.

2) the raising of a siege: *if they set down before us, for the r. bring up your army,* Cor. I, 2, 28. cf. the verb in Ven. 423 and Rom. V, 3, 237.

3) a post-stage: *here's a petition from a Florentine, who hath for four or five —s come short to tender it herself,* All's V, 3, 131 (by failing to overtake the king in his journey).

**Remove,** vb. 1) trans. a) to put away, to cause to be no longer in a place; in a proper and figurative sense: *r. your siege from my unyielding breast,* Ven. 423. *my will is strong, past reason's weak —ing,* Lucr. 2.3. *thy will r.* 614. *love and am beloved where I may not r. nor be —d,* Sonn. 25, 14. *it will go near to r. his fit,* Tp. II, 2, 79. *to shine, those clouds —d, upon our watery eyne,* LLL V, 2, 206. *mountains may be —d with earth-quakes,* As III, 2, 195. *let him that moved you hither r. you hence,* Shr. III, 197. I, 2, 72. All's III, 6, 42. Wint. I, 2, 428. II, 3, 88. John II, 318. III, 1, 218. H4A II, 2, 1. H6A II, 5, 103. H6B I, 2, 64. IV, 9, 29. V, 1, 36. R3 I, 3, 69. H8 II, 4, 102. Rom. Prol. 11. I, 1, 148. I, 5, 7. V, 3, 237. Mcb. IV, 3, 162. V, 1, 84. Oth. II, 1, 287. IV, 2, 14. V, 2, 55. Cymb. IV, 2, 257. —d = 1) distant, remote: *although my foot did stand upon the farthest earth —d from thee,* Sonn. 44, 6. *this time —d,* 97, 5 (= time of absence; cf. Absent). *who is so far from Italy —d,* Tp. II, 1, 110. *grew a twenty years —d thing,* Tw. V, 92 (as if he had not seen me for twenty years). Used of steps in the scale of gradation: *a lie seven times —d,* As V, 4, 71. *those that are germane to him, though —d fifty times,* Wint. IV, 4, 802. *being but the second generation —d from thy sin-conceiving womb,* John II, 182. *on this —d issue,* 186. *blood —d but little from her own,* Rom. III, 3, 96. *nor did he think it meet to lay so dear a trust on any soul —d but his own,* H4A IV, 1, 35 (who was a stranger to him in any degree). 2) retired, sequestered: *I have ever loved the life —d,* Meas. I, 3, 8. *your accent is something finer than you could purchase in so —d a dwelling,* As III, 2, 360. *visited that —d house,* Wint. V, 2, 116. *it waves you to a more —d ground,* Hml. I, 4, 61.

b) to bring to another place: *I must r. some thousands of these logs,* Tp. III, 1, 9. *see you the fornicatress be —d,* Meas. II, 2, 23. *she was —d to Kimbolton,* H8 IV, 1, 34. Partic. *—d: as interest of the dead, which now appear but things —d that hidden in thee lie,* Sonn. 31, 8 (as having only changed their place). *Lysander! what, —d?* Mids. II, 2, 151 (gone away).

c) to make away with, to cut off: *when he's —d, your highness will take again your queen as yours,* Wint. I, 2, 335. *King Richard thus —d,* H6A II, 5, 71. *who —d, Earl Surrey was sent thither,* H8 II, 1, 42. *none can be so determinate as the —ing of Cassio,* Oth. IV, 2, 232. 234. cf. H6B I, 2, 64.

2) intr. a) to go away, to depart: *from his soft*

*bosom never to r.* Ven. 81. *I must r.* 186. *love and am beloved where I may not r. nor be* —*d*, Sonn. 25, 14. *did thence r.* Compl. 237. *he hence* —*d last night*, All's V, 1, 23. *now thy uncle is* —*ing hence* (i. e. dying) H6A II, 5, 104.

b) to change place, to go elsewhere: *love is not love which alters when it alteration finds, or bends with the remover to r.* Sonn. 116, 4 (to seek another love). *let us r.* As III, 4, 59 (= go there). *O nation, that thou couldst r.* John V, 2, 33. *as I upon advantage did r.* V, 7, 62. *till Birnam wood r. to Dunsinane*, Mcb. V, 3, 2. *once more r., good friends*, Hml. I, 5, 163.

**Removedness,** retirement: *I have eyes under my service which look upon his r.* Wint. IV, 2, 41.

**Remover,** one who changes his place, one inconstant: *bends with the r. to remove*, Sonn. 116, 4.

**Remunerate,** to reward: Tit. I, 398.

**Remuneration,** reward, requital: LLL III, 133. 137. 139. 141. 147. 148. V, 1, 76. Troil. III, 3, 170.

**Rend,** (sometimes substituted by M. Edd. for rent, q. v. Partic. *rent*, impf. not used) 1) trans. to tear asunder, to split: *I will r. an oak*, Tp. I, 2, 294. *thou didst r. thy faith into a thousand oaths*, Gent. V, 4, 47. *these rent lines*, LLL IV, 3, 220. *r. apparel out*, Merch. II, 5, 5. *lean, rent and beggared by the strumpet wind*, II, 6, 19. *to r. our own soldiers*, All's III, 6, 53 (to break their lines, to scatter them). *I could r. bars of steel*, H6A I, 4, 51. *France should have torn and rent my very heart*, H6B I, 1, 126. *he* (the lion) *comes to r. his limbs asunder*, H6C I, 3, 15. *whose rage doth r. like interrupted waters and o'erbear what they are used to bear*, Cor. III, 1, 248. *the thunder doth r. the region*, Hml. II, 2, 509. *let not a leaner action r. us*, Ant. II, 2, 19. With *from*, = to tear from: *from thy burgonet I'll r. thy bear*, H6B V, 1, 208. *these nails should r. that beauty from my cheeks*, R3 I, 2, 126 (Ff *rent*). *r. and deracinate the unity and married calm of states quite from their fixure*, Troil. I, 3, 99. *we must not r. our subjects from our laws and stick them in our will*, H8 I, 2, 93.

2) intr. to split, to part asunder: *the very principals did seem to r.* Per. III, 2, 16.

**Render,** subst. 1) a surrender, a giving up: *but mutual r., only me for thee*, Sonn. 125, 12. *take no stricter r. of me than my all*, Cymb. V, 4, 17.

2) account, statement: *and send forth us, to make their sorrowed r.* Tim. V, 1, 152 (or = the offer of their sorrow?)\. *may drive us to a r. where we have lived*, Cymb. IV, 4, 11.

**Render,** vb. 1) to give back; to give in return: *to r. it unto the gentleman*, Merch. IV, 1, 383. *I have given him a penny, and he* —*s me the beggarly thanks*, As II, 5, 29 (cf. sub 3 Lucr. 943. LLL V, 2, 147. Merch. IV, 1, 88. 201)\. *it shall r. vengeance and revenge*, R2 IV, 67. —*ing faint acquittance to Harry Monmouth*, H4B I, 1, 108. *if my father r. fair return, it is against my will*, H5 II, 4, 127. —*s good for bad*, R3 I, 2, 69. *for your great graces ... I can nothing r. but allegiant thanks*, H8 III, 2, 176. *all dues be* —*ed to their owners*, Troil. II, 2, 174. *there to r. him the fair Cressid*, IV, 1, 37. *he seeks their hate with greater devotion than they can r. it him*, Cor. II, 2, 22. *that thou wilt never r..to me more*, Tit. I, 95.

2) to give: *Claudio shall r. me a dear account*, Ado IV, 1, 337. *what is mine my love shall r. him*, Mids. I, 1, 96. *see thou r. this into my cousin's hand*,

Merch. III, 4, 49. *the dearest grace it* —*s you*, H4A III, 1, 182. *in kissing, do you r. or receive? Both take and give*, Troil. IV, 5, 36. *of all the treasure ... we r. you the tenth*, Cor. I, 9, 34. *let each man r. me his bloody hand*, Caes. III, 1, 184. With *again*: Ado IV, 1, 30. As I, 2, 21. With *back*: Troil. III, 3, 122. Tim. IV, 1, 9.

3) to afford, to grant, to offer, to do: *to wrong the wronger till he r. right*, Lucr. 943. *some entertainment, some show ... to be* —*ed by our assistants*, LLL V, 1, 127. *to their penned speech r. we no grace*, V, 2, 147. *how shalt thou hope for mercy,* —*ing none?* Merch. IV, 1, 88. *to r. the deeds of mercy*, 201. 378. *which shall r. you no blame*, All's V, 1, 32. *slept in his face and* —*ed such aspect as cloudy men use*, H4A III, 2, 82. *if entreaties will r. you no remedy*, H8 V, 1, 151. *at this tomb my tributary tears I r. for my brethren's obsequies*, Tit. I, 160; cf. *this, for whom we* —*ed up this woe*, Ado V, 3, 33.

4) to surrender, to give up, to yield: *her quietus is to r. thee*, Sonn. 126, 12. *yield them up where I myself must r.* Compl. 221. *the castle's gently* —*ed*, Mcb. V, 7, 24. *to Caesar will I r. my legions and my horse*, Ant. III, 10, 33. *she* —*ed life*, IV, 14, 33. With *up*: *I'll make her r. up her page to me*, Mids. II, 1, 185. *he shall r. every glory up*, H4A III, 2, 150. *to r. up the great seal into our hands*, H8 III, 2, 229. *when I to sulphurous and tormenting flames must r. up myself*, Hml. I, 5, 4. In Tim. V, 4, 62 M. Edd. —*ed*, O. Edd. *remedied*.

5) to report, to state, to tell, to show (cf. *Deliver*): *more reasons for this action at our more leisure shall I r. you*, Meas. I, 3, 49; cf. Merch. IV, 1, 53. Tim. II, 2, 109. Caes. III, 2, 7. 10. *he did r. him the most unnatural that lived amongst men*, As IV, 3, 123. *the languishings whereof the king is* —*ed lost*, All's I, 3, 236. *that freely* —*ed me these news for true*, H4B I, 1, 27. *the word of peace is* —*ed: hark, how they shout*, IV, 2, 87 (= spoken along, going from mouth to mouth). *list his discourse of war, and you shall hear a fearful battle* —*ed you in music*, H5 I, 1, 44. *to give us leave freely to r. what we have in charge*, I, 2, 238. *it were a mock apt to be, for some one to say*, Caes. II, 2, 97. *r. to me some corporal sign about her*, Cymb. II, 4, 119. *report should r. him hourly to your ear as truly as he moves*, III, 4, 153. *that this gentleman may r. of whom he had this ring*, V, 5, 135.

6) to cause to be, to make: *to r. them redoubted*, Merch. III, 2, 88. *r. me worthy of this noble wife*, Caes. II, 1, 303.

**Rendezvous,** 1) meeting-place: *you know the r.* Hml. IV, 4, 4.

2) refuge: *a r., a home to fly unto*, H4A IV, 1, 57. *that is my rest, that is the r. of it*, H5 II, 1, 18 (Nym's speech). *there my r. is quite cut off*, V, 1, 88 (Pistol's speech).

**Renegado** (O. Edd. *Renegatho*) an apostate: Tw. III, 2, 74.

**Renege** (apparently pronounced *renegue*) to act in the manner of a renegade; to deny; to disown: *r., affirm*, Lr. II, 2, 84. *his captain's heart ... —s all temper*, Ant. I, 1, 8. cf. *Reny*.

**Renew,** 1) trans. a) to make new, to give new life and force to, to revive: *no object but her passion's strength* —*s*, Lucr. 1103. *sweet love, r. thy force*, Sonn. 56, 1. *wish I were* —*ed*, 111, 8. *herbs that did r. old Aeson*, Merch. V, 14. *I'll r. me in his fall*, Cor.

V, 6, 49. *r. his sorrows*, Tit. V, 3, 42. *—ed fire*, Oth. II, 1, 81. *r. me with your eyes*, Cymb. III, 2, 43. *spirit —ed*, V, 3, 35. *r. thy strength*, V, 5, 150.

b) to make or cause once more, to begin again, to repeat: *whose fresh repair if now thou not —est*, Sonn. 3, 3. *let our old acquaintance be —ed*, H4B III, 2, 315. *r. their feats*, H5 I, 2, 116. *r. the fight*, H6A I, 5, 27. *r. his glories*, H6C V, 4, 54.

2) intr. a) to begin again, not to desist: *r., r.!* Troil. V, 5, 6 (i. e. the fight).

b) to become new: *a mind that doth r. swifter than blood decays*, Troil. III, 2, 170. *r. I could not like the moon*, Tim. IV, 3, 68.

**Renounce,** to disown, to disclaim, to forswear: H6A I, 2, 97. I, 5, 29. H6C III, 3, 194. H8 I, 3, 29. Lr. IV, 6, 35. Oth. II, 3, 349.

**Renouncement,** the act of renouncing the world: *by your r. an immortal spirit*, Meas. I, 4, 35.

**Renown,** subst. 1) reputation: *a young gentlewoman of a most chaste r.* All's IV, 3, 19. *that dignifies the r. of a bawd*, Per. IV, 6, 42.

2) fame, glory: John V, 2, 115. H4A III, 2, 139. H4B IV, 5, 146. H6A II, 2, 39. IV, 5, 40. H6B I, 1, 101. H6C I, 4, 8. II, 1, 199. Cor. I, 3, 13. Oth. II, 3, 96. Ant. III, 1, 19. Per. III, 2, 48.

3) praise: *if Fortune once do frown, then farewell his great r.* Pilgr. 420. *of whom so often I have heard r.* Tp. V, 193. *high honour and r. to Hymen*, As V, 4, 151. *so am I driven by breath of her r. either to suffer shipwreck or arrive ...*, H6A V, 5, 7. *she is a theme of honour and r.* Troil. II, 2, 199. *the king of every virtue gives r. to men*, Per. I, 1, 14. Sometimes = that which deserves praise; praiseworthy quality (cf. *Glory*): *whate'er the course, the end is the r.* All's IV, 4, 36. *r. and grace is dead*, Mcb. II, 3, 99. *by wounding his belief in her r. with tokens thus and thus*, Cymb. V, 5, 202. *as jewels lose their glory if neglected, so princes their —s if not respected*, Per. II, 2, 13.

**Renown,** vb. to make famous: *the things of fame that do r. this city*, Tw. III, 3, 24. *the blood and courage that —ed them*, H5 I, 2, 118. *—ed* = famous, illustrious: Wiv. III, 1, 61. Meas. III, 1, 228. Err. V, 368. 393. Ado II, 2, 24. LLL V, 2, 690. Mids. I, 2, 20. Merch. I, 1, 169. II, 1, 20. Shr. I, 1, 10. I, 2, 100. IV, 2, 95. John IV, 3, 101. V, 2, 54. R2 II, 1, 53. H4A III, 2, 107. H4B IV, 5, 164. H6A IV, 3, 12. IV, 4, 24. IV, 5, 41. H6B V, 1, 176. H6C II, 1, 88. III, 3, 88. 214. V, 7, 5. R3 I, 4, 49. IV, 5, 9. Troil. III, 3, 132. Cor. II, 1, 183. III, 1, 291. Tit. I, 373. V, 1, 20. Rom. III, 5, 62. Ant. III, 7, 46. III, 13, 53. Cymb. IV, 2, 281. Per. II, 2, 18.

**Rent,** subst. that which is paid for anything held of another: Sonn. 125, 6. 142, 8. R2 IV, 212. H5 IV, 1, 260. Lr. I, 4, 148.

**Rent,** subst. fissure, breach: *see what a r. the envious Casca made*, Caes. III, 2, 179.

**Rent,** vb. to rend, to tear, to split: *in top of rage the lines asunder —s*, Compl. 55. *will you r. our ancient love asunder*, Mids. III, 2, 215. *—s the thorns and is rent with the thorns*, H6C III, 2, 175. *these nails should r. that beauty from my cheeks*, R3 I, 2, 126 (Qq *rend*). *r. off thy silver hair*, Tit. III, 1, 261. *groans and shrieks that r. the air*, Mcb. IV, 3, 168.

**Rent,** vb. to hold by lease: *I'll r. the fairest house after three-pence a bay*, Meas. II, 1, 254.

**Reny,** to disown, to become a renegade: *love's*

denying, faith's defying, heart's *—ing*, Pilgr. 250. cf. *Renege.*

**Repair,** subst. restoration, renovation: *whose fresh r. if now thou not renewest*, Sonn. 3, 3. *what holier than, for royalty's r., to bless the bed of majesty again with a sweet fellow*, Wint. V, 1, 31. *even in the instant of r. and health*, John III, 4, 113. *whose (our laws') r. and franchise shall be our good deed*, Cymb. III, 1, 57.

**Repair,** subst. a resorting to a place, a coming: *a r. i' the dark*, Meas. IV, 1, 43. *all sense to that sense did make their r.* LLL II, 240. *that we could hear no news of his r.* H6C V, 1, 20 (= coming, arrival). *I will forestal their r. hither*, Hml. V, 2, 228.

**Repair,** vb. to restore after decay: *seeking that beauteous roof to ruinate which to r. should be thy chief desire*, Sonn. 10, 8; cf. Gent. V, 4, 11; Err. II, 1, 99; Merch. IV, 1, 141; R3 IV, 4, 319. *so should the lines of life that life r.* Sonn. 16, 9. *like a German clock, still a —ing*, LLL III, 193. *burst and now —ed with knots*, Shr. III, 2, 60. *could I r.* (like clothes) *what she will wear in me*, 120. *it much —s me to talk of your good father*, All's I, 2, 30. *to line and new r. our towns of war with men of courage and with means defendant*, H5 II, 4, 7. *like a gallant in the brow of youth, —s him* (= himself) *with occasion*, H6B V, 3, 5. *to r. my honour lost for him*, H6C III, 3, 193. *times to r. our nature*, H8 V, 1, 3. *I'll r. the misery thou dost bear with something rich about me*, Lr. IV, 1, 79. *let this kiss r. those violent harms*, IV, 7, 28. *to r. his fortunes*, Oth. II, 3, 360. *shouldst r. my youth*, Cymb. I, 1, 132. *man's sense —s itself by rest*, II, 2, 12. *thou givest me somewhat to r. myself*, Per. II, 1, 128. *here he does but r. it* (his disease) IV, 2, 120. The gerund intr.: *opposites of such —ing nature*, H6B V, 3, 22 (i. e. easily recovering themselves from a defeat).

**Repair,** vb. to betake one's self, to go, to come; with *to*: Phoen. 65. Gent. IV, 2, 46. Ado I, 1, 278. Mids. IV, 1, 72. John II, 554. R2 II, 1, 216. II, 3, 35. H6A I, 3, 77. H6C IV, 7, 15. R3 I, 2, 213. I, 3, 345. Troil. I, 3, 82. Cor. II, 3, 156. 262. V, 6, 3. Tit. V, 2, 124. V, 3, 2. Tim. II, 2, 25. Caes. I, 3, 147. 152. Hml. IV, 6, 23. Oth. III, 2, 4. Ant. I, 4, 39. Without *to*, = to come: *when they r., blow like sweet roses*, LLL V, 2, 292. *if I might beseech you to r. some other hour*, Tim. III, 4, 69.

**Repass,** to pass back, to cross again: *well have we passed and now —ed the seas*, H6C IV, 7, 5.

**Repast,** past, gone: *by times ill-used r.* R3 IV, 4, 396 (Qq *by time misused o'erpast*).

**Repast,** subst. a meal: LLL IV, 2, 160. Shr. IV, 3, 15. Cymb. V, 4, 157.

**Repast,** vb. to feed, to nourish: *r. them with my blood*, Hml. IV, 5, 147.

**Repasture,** food: *food for his rage, r. for his den*, LLL IV, 1, 95 (Armado's poetry).

**Repay,** to pay back; to requite: Sonn. 117, 2. Wiv. V, 5, 178. LLL II, 143. 159 (*back*). Merch. I, 3, 147. Shr. IV, 3, 45. Tw. III, 3, 33. H6C II, 3, 3. R3 I, 3, 313. II, 2, 92. IV, 2, 123 (Qq *rewards*). Tit. III, 1, 235. Tim. I, 1, 288. Ant. III, 11, 71.

**Repeal,** subst. recall from exile: *I sue for exiled majesty's r.* Lucr. 640. *when she for thy r. was suppliant*, Gent. III, 1, 234. *a cause for thy r.* Cor. IV, 1, 41. *as rash in the r.* IV, 7, 32. *have an immediate freedom of r.* Caes. III, 1, 54 (cf. *Freedom*).

**Repeal,** vb. 1) to recall from exile: *r. thee home again,* Gent. V, 4, 143. *whose banished sense thou hast —ed,* All's II, 3, 55. *the banished Bolingbroke —s himself,* R2 II, 2, 49. *if he may be —ed,* IV, 85. 87. H6B III, 2, 349. Cor. V, 5, 5. Caes. III, 1, 51.

2) to restore to honour or place: *when false opinion ... —s and reconciles thee,* Lr. III, 6, 120. *that she —s him for her body's lust,* Oth. II, 3, 363.

3) to revoke, to abrogate: *my banishment —ed,* R2 III, 3, 40. *until that act of parliament be —ed,* H6C I, 1, 249. *r. daily any wholesome act,* Cor. I, 1, 84.

**Repeat,** 1) to speak or tell again: Tp. III, 2, 46. John IV, 2, 19. H4B IV, 1, 203. With *again:* Lucr. 1848. R3 IV, 1, 78. With *over:* Ado V, 1, 248.

2) to recite, to mention, to tell: *r. their names,* Gent. I, 2, 7. *the third of the five vowels, if you r. them,* LLL V, 1, 57. 58. *for I the ballad will r.* All's I, 3, 64. *she is too mean to have her name —ed,* III, 5, 64. *r. your will and take it,* H8 I, 2, 13. *sorry to r. what follows,* V, 1, 97. *these evils thou —est upon thyself,* Mcb. IV, 3, 112. *those —ed vexations of it,* Cymb. I, 6, 4. *vice —ed is like the wandering wind,* Per. I, 1, 96. *'twould be too tedious to r.* V, 1, 28. Absol., = to talk: *thou speakest like him's untutored to r.* Per. I, 4, 74 (placed in the rhyme).

3) to call before the eye of the mind, to represent or figure to one's self: *what I have I need not to r.* R2 III, 4, 17. *grief puts on his pretty looks, —s his words,* John III, 4, 95. *r. their semblance often on the seas,* H6A V, 3, 193.

**Repel,** to turn away (from a love-suit): *foul words and frowns must not r. a lover,* Ven. 573. *I did r. his letters,* Hml. II, 1, 109. *and he, —ed, fell into a sadness,* II, 2, 146 (Ff repulsed).

**Repent,** 1) to feel or express regret and self-reproach; a) absol.: Sonn. 34, 10. Pilgr. 313. Wiv. IV, 5, 105. Meas. II, 3, 30. Ado II, 1, 76. Merch. III, 4, 72. All's I, 3, 39. II, 5, 13. John III, 1, 196. IV, 2, 103. H4A III, 3, 5. 8. H4B I, 2, 221. H5 III, 6, 161. H6C II, 6, 70. R3 IV, 4, 397. Tim. I, 1, 184. Hml. III, 3, 66. III, 4, 173. Lr. I, 4, 279. Oth. III, 3, 238. Ant. IV, 9, 10. Cymb. V, 1, 10. V, 4, 13. b) with an inf.: *that I must r. to be just,* Lr. III, 5, 11. c) with a clause: Merch. IV, 1, 278. R3 III, 4, 90. Oth. III, 3, 392. Ant. II, 7, 83. d) with prepositions: *r. at idle times,* H4B II, 2, 140. *I never did r. for doing good,* Merch. III, 4, 10. *all r. in their election,* Cor. II, 3, 263. *r. you of the sin?* Meas. II, 3, 19. *hath —ed o'er his doom,* II, 2, 12 (cf. *Over*). e) trans.: Gent. IV, 1, 27. 30. Meas. II, 3, 29. Mids. II, 2, 111. All's III, 7, 28. Wint. III, 2, 209. 221. John II, 48. H5 II, 2, 152. III, 6, 131. R3 I, 3, 307. IV, 4, 293. Troil. III, 2, 139. Cor. III, 2, 37. Tit. I, 404. V, 3, 186. 190. Rom. III, 1, 196. IV, 2, 17. Hml. III, 4, 150. Oth. IV, 2, 202. Per. IV, 1, 37. With an accus. denoting the effect: *I would r. out the remainder of nature,* All's IV, 3, 272. f) refl.: *I do r. me,* Meas. II, 3, 35. V, 469. R2 V, 3, 52. R3 I, 4, 285. Oth. III, 3, 392. V, 2, 10. Ant. III, 3, 42. *I do r. me of my fury,* Mcb. II, 3, 112. *that you should here r. you,* Mids. V, 115.

2) to feel any sorrow: *r. but you that you shall lose your friend, and he —s not that he pays your debt,* Merch. IV, 1, 278. *I r. my fault more than my death,* H5 II, 2, 152. *let him r. thou wast not made his daughter,* Ant. III, 13, 134. *—ed the evils she hatched were not effected,* Cymb. V, 5, 59.

**Repentance,** regret and self-reproach, penitence, contrition: Gent. V, 4. 79. Ado II, 1, 81. H4B II, 1, 132. H5 IV, 3, 85. H8 IV, 2, 27. Mcb. I, 4, 7. Hml. III, 3, 65. With *of:* H5 II, 2, 180.

**Repentant,** adj. penitent: Lucr. 48. 502. John IV, 1, 111. R3 I, 2, 216.

**Repetition,** 1) the act of speaking again; used of the echo: *the neighbour caves make verbal r. of her moans,* Ven. 831. *make her airy tongue more hoarse than mine with r. of my Romeo's name,* Rom. II, 2, 164.

2) utterance, recital, mention: *if it should be told, the r. cannot make it less,* Lucr. 1285. *to cry aim to these ill-tuned —s,* John II, 197. *what makest thou in my sight? But r. of what thou hast marred,* R3 I, 3, 165. *he hath faults, with surplus, to tire in r.* Cor. I, 1, 47. *a name whose r. will be dogged with curses,* V, 3, 144. *the r., in a woman's ear, would murder as it fell,* Mcb. II, 3, 90. *give them r. to the life,* Per. V, 1, 247.

3) a calling to mind, remembrance: *we are reconciled, and the first view shall kill all r.* All's V, 3, 22.

**Repine,** subst. vexation, mortification: *had not his (eyes) clouded with his brow's r.* Ven. 490.

**Repine,** vb. to be mortified, to murmur in discontent: H6A V, 2, 20. Troil. I, 3, 243. Cor. III, 1, 43.

**Replant,** to reinstate: *and r. Henry in his former state,* H6C III, 3, 198.

**Replenish,** 1) to fill: *the more she saw the blood his cheeks r.* Lucr. 1357.

2) to accomplish, to perfect: *his intellect is not —ed,* LLL IV, 2, 27. *—ed = complete, consummate: the most —ed villain in the world,* Wint. II, 1, 79. *the most —ed sweet work of nature,* R3 IV, 3, 18.

**Replete,** filled, full: *a counterpoise, if not to thy estate a balance more r.* All's II, 3, 183. Followed by *with: r. with too much rage,* Sonn. 23, 3. *incapable of more, r. with you,* 113, 13. *a man r. with mocks,* LLL V, 2, 853. H6A I, 1, 12. I, 6, 15. V, 5, 17 (*full r.;* M. Edd. *full-r.*). H6B I, 1, 20. H6C III, 2, 84.

**Replication,** 1) reverberation, echo: *Tiber trembled underneath her banks, to hear the r. of your sounds made in her concave shores,* Caes. I, 1, 51.

2) reply, repartee: *all kind of arguments and question deep, all r. prompt, and reason strong,* Compl. 122. *facere as it were r., or rather ostentare, to show, as it were, his inclination,* LLL IV, 2, 15. *to be demanded of a sponge! what r. should be made by the son of a king?* Hml. IV, 2, 13.

**Reply,** subst. answer: Meas. III, 2, 51. LLL IV, 1, 86. As V, 4, 80. 98. Wint. IV, 4, 366. H4A V, 1, 113. H4B II, 1, 134. R3 I, 3, 237. Tim. III, 3, 25. Caes. III, 2, 37. Hml. I, 2, 121. II, 2, 212. III, 1, 14. *to make r.* John III, 3, 49. *nor make —es of loathness,* Ant. III, 11, 18. *before I make r. to aught you say,* R2 II, 3, 73.

**Reply,** vb. to make answer: Ven. 385. 695. 918. Lucr. 477. 1277. 1796. Gent. II, 1, 172. Meas. V, 94. LLL V, 2, 105. Mids. V, 1, 151. Merch. III, 2, 66. Shr. V, 2, 21. All's II, 3, 87. H6C IV, 8, 23. R3 III, 7, 145. H8 I, 2, 155. Troil. I, 1, 50. III, 3, 262. Cor. V, 1, 19. Rom. II, 5, 61. III, 5, 164. Lr. II, 1, 68. Oth. III, 1, 47. Ant. II, 2, 225. III, 7, 6. With *to:* H4B V, 5, 59. Cor. I, 1, 114. Tit. II, 3, 18. Trans.: *what I shall r.* H6A III, 1, 28.

**Report,** subst. 1) a telling or speaking of something: *therefore have I slept in your r.* Sonn. 83 **5**

(= omitted to speak of you). *which lames r. to follow it*, Wint. V, 2, 62. *which may suffer the r.* Cymb. I, 4, 60 (= may be told).

2) that which a person says or tells; assertion, statement, account, tale: *naming thy name blesses an ill r.* Sonn. 95, 8 (thy mere name changes blame to praise). *would it not say he lies? Ay, or very falsely pocket up his r.* Tp. II, 1, 67. *you shall stifle in your own r.* Meas. II, 4, 158. *the duke is marvellous little beholding to your —s*, IV, 3, 167 (to what you say of him). *you must change persons with me, ere you make that my r.* V, 340. *they have committed false r.* Ado V, 1, 220 (Dogberry's speech). *much too little of that good I saw is my r. to his great worthiness*, LLL II, 63. *observe his —s for me*, All's II, 1, 46 (= what he says concerning me). *not daring the —s of my tongue*, IV, 1, 34. *I'll fill these dogged spies with false —s*, John IV, 1, 129. *throw this r. on their incensed rage*, IV, 2, 261. *let not his r. come current*, H4A I, 3, 67. *stand my good lord in your good r.* H4B IV, 3, 89 (speak in my favour). *whether it be through force of your r.* H6A V, 5, 79. *flatter my sorrows with r. of it*, R3 IV, 4, 245. *I am free of your r.* H8 II, 4, 99 (innocent of what you say against me). *nothing but his r.* Cor. IV, 6, 61. *my scars can witness that my r. is just*, Tit. V, 3, 115. *thou wrongest it more than tears with that r.* Rom. IV, 1, 32 (with these words). *thrusting this r. into his ears*, Caes. V, 3, 74. *I have learned by the perfectest r.* Mcb. I, 5, 2 (from the best authority). *can perceive no truth in your r.* V, 1, 2. *truster of your own r. against yourself*, Hml. I, 2, 172. *you were better have a bad epitaph than their ill r.* II, 2, 550. *this r. of his did Hamlet so envenom*, IV, 7, 103. *all my —s go with the modest truth*, Lr. IV, 7, 5. *if you do find me foul in her r.* Oth. I, 3, 117. *your —s have set the murder on*, V, 2, 187. *men's —s give him much wronged*, Ant. I, 4, 39. *read not my blemishes in the world's r.* II, 3, 5. *a thing too bad for bad r.* Cymb. I, 1, 17 (worse than can be expressed in words). *I honour him even out of your r.* 55. *charms this r. out*, I, 6, 117. *who is as far from my r.* 146. *to try your taking of a false r.* 173. *sell me your good r.* II, 3, 88 (speak well of me for money). *son to the queen, after his own r.* IV, 2, 119. *thou hast the harvest out of thy own r.* Per. IV, 2, 153. *to give good r.* = to speak well of a p.: *to give me your good r. to the prince*, Wint. V, 2, 162. *to give him good r. for it*, Cor. I, 1, 33. *gave you such a masterly r. for art and exercise*, Hml. IV, 7, 97 (spoke of you as being a master). *to make r.* = to speak, to tell: *made such pestiferous —s of men*, All's IV, 3, 340. *his clothes made a false r. of him*, Cor. IV, 5, 157. *making just r.* Lr. III, 1, 37. *I made no such r.* Ant. II, 5, 57. *she makes a very good r. o'the worm*, V, 2, 256. *by the r. of* = according to what a person says: *by your own r. a linguist*, Gent. IV, 1, 56. *not better than he, by her own r.* Meas. V, 274. *to seek me out by computation and mine host's r.* Err. II, 2, 4. *one three of them, by their own r., hath danced before the king*, Wint. IV, 4, 345. *upon r.* = on or from information, by having been told: *we know on Valentine's r.* Gent. III, 2, 57 (by having been told by V.). *if you like upon r. the soil*, As II, 4, 97. *I have it upon his own r.* Wint. IV, 4, 170. *if she be accused on true r.* R3 I, 3, 27 (Qq *in true r.*).

Used of official statements or accounts returned: *else had I half an hour since brought my r.* Cor. I, 6,

21. *the slave's r. is seconded*, IV, 6, 62. *are his files as full as thy r.?* Tim. V, 2, 2. *bring me no more —s*, Mcb. V, 3, 1. *make discovery err in r. of us*, V, 4, 7. *every hour shalt thou have r. how 'tis abroad*, Ant. I, 4, 35. *and have my learning from some true —s, that drew their swords with you*, II, 2, 47 (for: such that drew etc., elliptically; or abstr. pro concr., *r. for reporter*). *who worse than a physician would this r. become?* Cymb. V, 5, 28.

3) that which people say or tell: *the r. 'goes she has all the rule*, Wiv. I, 3, 58. *volumes of r. run with these false and most contrarious quests upon thy doings*, Meas. IV, 1, 61. *my gossip r.* Merch. III, 1, 7. *r. speaks goldenly of his profit*, As I, 1, 6. *to make mine eye the witness of that r. which I so oft have heard*, Shr. II, 53. *by r. I know him well*, 105. *I find r. a very liar*, 246. *for the good r. I hear of you*, IV, 4, 28. *know it before the r. come*, All's III, 2, 25. *let's return again and suffice ourselves with the r. of it*, III, 5, 11. *the r. that goes upon your goodness*, V, 1, 13. *r. of fashions in proud Italy*, R2 II, 1, 21. *stuffing the ears of men with false —s*, H4B Ind. 8. *to give their censure of these rare —s*, H6A II, 3, 10. *r. is fabulous and false*, 18. *whether 'twas r. of her success*, H6C II, 1, 125. *let him, like an engine not portable, lie under this r.* Troil. II, 3, 144. *of no better r. than a horsedrench*, Cor. II, 1, 129 (not better spoken of, of no better estimation). *if it be a just and true r. that goes of his having*, Tim. V, 1, 18. *this r. hath so exasperate the king*, Mcb. III, 6, 37. *I would not take this from r.* Lr. IV, 6, 144. *r. is changeable*, IV, 7, 92. *can you inquire him out and be edified by r.?* Oth. III, 4, 15. *if r. be square to her*, Ant. II, 2, 189. *knows by history, r., or his own proof*, Cymb. I, 6, 70. *r. should render him hourly to your ear as truly*, III, 4, 153. *our courtiers say all's savage but at court: experience, O, thou disprovest r.* IV, 2, 34. *drawn by r.* Per. I, 1, 35. *when he shall come and find our paragon to all —s thus blasted*, IV, 1, 36.

Hence = reputation, fame: *thou being mine, mine is thy good r.* Sonn. 36, 14 and 96, 14. *hath blistered her r.* Meas. II, 3, 12. *goes foremost in r. through Italy*, Ado III, 1, 97. Tw. III, 2, 41. III, 4, 210. IV, 1, 24. Wint. IV, 2, 48. H6A II, 2, 43. Cor. I, 3, 22. I, 6, 70. I, 9, 54. II, 2, 32. Ant. II, 2, 159. Cymb. II, 3, 88 (quibbling). III, 3, 57. Per. IV, 6, 43.

4) noise: *with the clamorous r. of war*, R3 IV, 4, 152. Especially the sound of fire-arms: *rising and cawing at the gun's r.* Mids. III, 2, 22. *such as fear the r. of a caliver*, H4A IV, 2, 20.

**Report,** vb. 1) to tell: *as thou —est thyself*, Tp. I, 2, 271. *if in Naples I should r. this now*, III, 3, 28. *some r. a sea-maid spawned him*, Meas. III, 2, 115. *that is false thou doest r. to us*, Err. V, 179. *his tongue (is not able) to conceive, nor his heart to r. what my dream was*, Mids. IV, 1, 219 (Bottom's speech). *why does the world r. that Kate doth limp?* Shr. II, 254. *so 'tis —ed*, All's I, 2, 3. *I shall r. it so*, II, 4, 56. *that pitiful rumour may r. my flight*, III, 2, 130. *it is —ed that he has taken...*, III, 5, 5. *unless it be to r. your lord's taking of it*, Tw. II, 2, 11. *I shall be hated to r. it*, Wint. III, 2, 144. *though I r. it*, IV, 4, 177. *nor concern me the —ing*, 515. V, 1, 179. John I, 25. R2 II, 2, 95. H4A I, 1, 51 (Qq *import*). II, 4, 456. H4B I, 1, 75. 97. H6B III, 2, 122. V, 3, 1 (*who can r. of him?*). H6C IV, 3, 8. R3 I, 3, 185. II, 4, 39 (Qq *unfold*). III, 1, 72. IV, 4, 459 (Ff *but well may it be —ed*, Qq *but* *it may well be told*). H8 II, 4, 38. Cor. I, 9, 2. II, 2, 48. IV, 6, 39. V, 3, 3. Tim. IV, 3, 198. V, 1, 5. Mcb. I, 2, 1. 36. I, 4, 4. V, 1, 16. V, 3, 31. V, 5, 31. Oth. I, 3, 15. II, 3, 240. V, 2, 128. Ant. I, 2, 155. I, 3, 4. I, 4, 67. III, 6, 19. V, 2, 25. 32. Cymb. II, 3, 89. V, 3, 87. V, 4, 39. V, 5, 16. 26. 34. Per. IV, 2, 149. V, 1, 120. 130.

2) to describe, to represent: *he shall know you better, if I may live to r. you*, Meas. III, 2, 172. *nor a temporary meddler, as he's —ed by this gentleman*, V, 146. *is she so hot a shrew as she's —ed?* Shr. IV, 1, 22. *if you r. him truly*, Cor. V, 4, 27. *r. me and my cause aright to the unsatisfied*, Hml. V, 2, 350. *bid him r. the feature of Octavia*, Ant. II, 5, 112. *I must r. ye my master's enemy*, Cymb. III, 5, 3. *never saw I figures so likely to r. themselves*, II, 4, 83 (= to give information about themselves, to speak themselves; cf. *how this grace speaks his own standing*, Tim. I, 1, 31). With an accus. and inf.: *a notable lubber, as thou —est him to be*, Gent. II, 5, 47. *a coward, as you then —ed him to be*, Meas. V, 338. As V, 4, 33. H6B I, 4, 8.

3) to speak of with praise: *I shall r., for most it caught me, the celestial habits*, Wint. III, 1, 3.

4) to speak, to say: *there is a gentleman —s but coarsely of her*, All's III, 5, 60. *let this my sword r. what speech forbears*, H6B IV, 10, 57. *that man who shall r. he has a better wife*, H8 II, 4, 134. *to r. otherwise were a malice*, Cor. II, 2, 36. *where the aim —s*, Oth. I, 3, 6.

**Reporter,** one that tells or gives an account: *there she appeared indeed, or my r. devised well for her*, Ant. II, 2, 193.

**Reportingly,** on hearsay: *others say thou dost deserve, and I believe it better than r.* Ado III, 1, 116.

**Reposal** (Qq *reposure*), the act of reposing, ascribing, attributing: *would the r. of any trust, virtue, or worth in thee make thy words faithed?* Lr. II, 1, 70.

**Repose,** subst. rest, especially in sleep: Lucr. 757. Sonn. 27, 2. 50, 3. Tp. II, 1, 213. 310. H4B III, 1, 26. H5 IV, 1, 275. H8 V, 1, 4. Rom. II, 2, 123. Caes. IV, 3, 233. Mcb. II, 1, 9. 29. Hml. III, 2, 227. Lr. IV, 4, 12. Ant. IV, 4, 13. Per. III, 2, 23.

**Repose,** vb. 1) tr. to place: *the king —th all his confidence in thee*, R2 II, 4, 6.

2) refl. a) to take rest (the refl. pronoun in the form of the personal): *means to r. him here*, Shr. Ind. 1, 76. R2 II, 3, 161. H6B II, 1, 200. R3 III, 1, 65. Cor. I, 9, 74. Tit. I, 151. Lr. III, 2, 63. b) to lean on, to confide: *on thy fortune I r. myself*, H6C IV, 6, 47. 3) intr. a) to lie in rest: *and so r., sweet gold, for their unrest*, Tit. II, 3, 8. *his right cheek —ing on a cushion*, Cymb. IV, 2, 212. b) to rest, to sleep: Lucr. 382. 933. Tp. IV, 162. R3 I, 4, 76. Tit. I, 353. c) to confide: *upon whose faith and honour I r.* Gent. IV, 3, 26. *—ing too far in his virtue*, All's III, 6, 15.

**Repossess,** to obtain again possession of: H6C III, 2, 4. IV, 5, 29. IV, 9, 99. V, 7, 19.

**Reposure,** see *Reposal*.

**Reprehend,** to reprove, to blame: Ven. 470. 1065. Err. V, 57. 87. Mids. V, 436. R3 III, 7, 27. 113. Tit. III, 2, 69. Confounded with *represent* by Dull in LLL I, 1, 184.

**Represent,** to fill the place of, to personate: H6A IV, 1, 93. H6B I, 1, 14. Tit. V, 2, 89.

**Reprieve,** subst. respite after condemnation: *three —s for you and your coach-fellow Nym*, Wiv. II,

2, 6. *that in his r. he may be so fitted*, Meas. II, 4, 39. *some pardon or r. for Claudio*, IV, 2, 74. *wrought —s for him*, 140. *out of r. and pardon*, Cor. V, 2, 53. *thy token of r.* Lr. V, 3, 249.

**Reprieve,** vb. to release, to acquit, to set free: *unless her prayers r. him from the wrath of greatest justice*, All's III, 4, 28. *might but my bending down r. thee from thy fate*, Meas. III, 1, 145.

**Reprisal,** prize: *I am on fire to hear this rich r. is so nigh and yet not ours*, H4A IV, 1, 118.

**Reproach,** subst. 1) opprobrious censure: Sonn. 121, 2. Ado IV, 1, 82. 128. H6A IV, 1, 98. R3 III, 7, 231. H8 I, 2, 23.

2) disgrace, infamy: *r., disdain and deadly enmity*, Lucr. 503. *thou backest r. against long-living laud*, 622. *will couple my r. to Tarquin's shame*, 816. *undeserved r.* 824. *r. is stamped in Collatinus' face*, 829. *when life is shamed, and death —'s debtor*, 1155. *how much of me their r. contains*, Compl. 189. *r. and dissolution hangeth over him*, R2 II, 1, 258. H5 III, 6, 50. IV, 5, 4. H6A I, 1, 97. III, 2, 76. V, 5, 29. H6B II, 4, 64. 96. III, 2, 69. IV, 1, 101. Troil. I, 1, 57. Tit. IV, 1, 94. Oth. IV, 1, 48.

Misapplied for *approach* by Launcelot: Merch. II, 5, 20.

**Reproach,** vb. to disgrace: *else imputation, for that he knew you, might r. your life*, Meas. V, 426.

**Reproachful,** bringing reproach, disgraceful: *what r. words are these?* Tit. I, 308. II, 1, 55.

**Reproachfully,** disgracefully: *shall I then be used r.* H6B II, 4, 97.

**Reprobance** (Qq *reprobation*) perdition, eternal damnation: *curse his better angel from his side and fall to r.* Oth. V, 2, 209.

**Reprobate,** subst. one abandoned to sin and lost to virtue: Meas. IV, 3, 78.

**Reprobate,** adj. abandoned to sin: Lucr. 300. LLL I, 2, 64.

**Reprobation,** see *Reprobance*.

**Reproof,** 1) confutation, refutation: *in the r. of this lies the jest*, H4A I, 2, 213. *in r. of many tales devised*, III, 2, 23. *in the r. of chance lies the true proof of men*, Troil. I, 3, 33. *would pluck r. and rebuke from every ear*, Cor. II, 2, 37.

2) contradiction: *r. and reason beat it dead*, Lucr. 489. *your r. is something too round*, H5 IV, 1, 216. *r., obedient and in order, fits kings*, Per. I, 2, 42.

3) check, reprimand: *the R. Valiant*, As V, 4, 82. 98. *that man is not alive might so have tempted him without the taste of danger and r.* H4A III, 1, 175. Even = punishment: *whom you yourselves shall set out for r.* Tim. V, 4, 57.

4) reproach, blame: Wiv. II, 1, 59. II, 2, 195. Meas. III, 1, 269. Err. V, 90. Tw. III, 4, 225. R3 III, 7, 142. IV, 4, 158. Ant. II, 2, 123 (*your r. were well deserved of rashness*, i. e. you would deserve the reproach of rashness. O. Edd. *proof*). Per. II, 4, 19.

**Reprove,** 1) to disprove, to confute: *what have you urged that I cannot r.?* Ven. 787. *'tis so, I cannot r. it*, Ado II, 3, 241. *r. my allegation, if you can*, H6B III, 1, 40.

2) to reprehend, to blame: Lucr. 242. Sonn. 142, 4. LLL IV, 3, 153. Tw. I, 5, 104. III, 4, 223. R3 III, 7, 148. H8 I, 2, 189. Ant. III, 11, 14. Per. I, 2, 95.

**Reproveable,** blamable: Lr. III, 5, 9.

**Repugn,** to oppose: *when stubbornly he did r. the truth,* H6A IV, 1, 94.

**Repugnancy,** opposition, resistance: *let the foes quietly cut their throats, without r.* Tim. III, 5, 45.

**Repugnant,** opposite, refractory: *r. to command,* Hml. II, 2, 493.

**Repulse,** subst. 1) a beating back (of an enemy): *in the r. of Tarquin,* Cor. II, 1, 166.

2) refusal, denial: Gent. III, 1, 100. H6A III, 1, 113. Cymb. I, 4, 128.

3) failure, disappointment: *do not for one r. forego the purpose,* Tp. III, 3, 12.

**Repulse,** vb. to refuse, to reject: Hml. II, 2, 146 (Qq *repelled*).

**Repurchased,** bought again, regained: *r. with the blood of enemies,* H6C V, 7, 2.

**Repured,** purified, refined: *love's thrice r. nectar,* Troil. III, 2, 23 (Ff *reputed*).

**Reputation,** 1) character by report, whether good or bad: Lucr. 623. 820. Gent. I, 3, 6. II, 7, 87. Wiv. II, 2, 258. 307. III, 3, 126. Meas. V, 221. Err. III, 1, 86. IV, 1, 71. V, 5. Ado II, 2, 38. IV, 1, 243. LLL II, 155. As I, 2, 191. All's III, 7, 6. IV, 3, 154. 201. 223. V, 3, 176. Wint. I, 2, 420. R2 I, 1, 178. II, 1, 58. 96. H4B II, 1, 142.•H5 IV, 7, 148. R3 I, 4, 157. Troil. III, 3, 187. 227. Rom. III, 1, 116. Tim. III, 5, 19. Hml. II, 2, 344. Oth. II, 3, 194. 262. 268. 271. Cymb. I, 4, 121. Per. IV, 6, 174.

2) a good name, honour, credit: *I will keep the haviour of r.* Wiv. I, 3, 86. *seeking the bubble r. even in the cannon's mouth,* As II, 7, 152. *I have offended r.* Ant. III, 11, 49. *to lose one's r.* LLL V, 2, 709. Oth. II, 3, 263. I, 3, 275 (Ff *estimation*).

**Repute,** subst. estimation, reputation: *here the Trojans taste our dearest r. with their finest palate,* Troil. I, 3, 337. *a man of good r.* = of good reputation, in the language of Armado: LLL I, 1, 271. I, 2, 72.

**Repute,** vb. 1) to estimate, to value, to prize: *how will the world r. me?* Gent. II, 7, 59. *by —ing of his high descent,* H6B III, 1, 48 (=valuing at a high rate; cf. *Of*). *well —d* = of good esteem: Gent. II, 4, 57. Caes. II, 1, 295. In Troil. III, 2, 23 Ff *—d,* Qq *repured.*

2) to think, to account, to hold: Tp. I, 2, 72. Ado II, 1, 214. LLL III, 65. Merch. I, 1, 96. Shr. IV, 2, 112. All's IV, 3, 322. H4A V, 1, 54. H4B IV, 1, 131. H6B V, 1, 177. Tit. I, 366. 448. Caes. I, 2, 173. Oth. II, 3, 271. *the —d son of Cordelion,* John I, 136 (supposed). With *for*: *your father was —d for a prince most prudent,* H8 II, 4, 45.

**Reputeless,** obscure, inglorious: *left me in r. banishment,* H4A III, 2, 44.

**Request,** subst. 1) question: *my prime r. is ... if you be maid or no,* Tp. I, 2, 425. *how do you, Malvolio? At your r.!* Tw. III, 4, 38.

2) petition, whether entreaty or demand: Lucr. 1695. Gent. IV, 2, 101. Meas. II, 4, 186. LLL II, 150. Merch. IV, 1, 161. Tw. V, 4. Wint. I, 2, 22. III, 2, 117. John IV, 2, 46. H5 V, 2, 372. H6C III, 2, 79. R3 III, 7, 50. 101. 155. IV, 2, 87 and 97 (Qq *demand*). H8 IV, 2, 116. Troil. II, 3, 179. Cor. II, 3, 150. V, 1, 57. V, 3, 90. 132. 164. Tim. III, 2, 201. Hml. I, 5, 142. Oth. I, 3, 113. Ant. III, 12, 13. 20. Cymb. I, 6, 181. V, 5, 89. *to make a r.:* Caes. V, 5, 11. *to make one's —s:* Cor. II, 3, 48. Tim. I, 1, 279. *at one's r.:* Tp. III, 2, 128. Gent. II, 1, 132. Wiv. I, 1,

253. Merch. III, 3, 10. As II, 5, 23. Wint. I, 2, 87. V, 1, 221. John V, 6, 35. H4B V, 1, 49. H5 V, 1, 24. H6C III, 3, 110. IV, 3, 51. Troil. II, 3, 191. III, 1, 31. Oth. III, 3, 474 (Ff *at your r.,* Qq *as you r.*). *upon one's r.:* Wiv. I, 1, 249. Meas. V, 152. Troil. II, 3, 177.

3) state of being demanded and asked for: *novelty is only in r.* Meas. III, 2, 237. *ginger was not much in r.* IV, 3, 9. *answer the time of r.* All's I, 1, 169. Wint. IV, 4, 297. Cor. III, 1, 251. III, 2, 51. IV, 3, 37.

**Request,** vb. to ask, to beg, to demand: Oth. III, 3, 474 (Qq *as you r.,* Ff *at your r.*). Ant. III, 4, 24. With an inf.: *she would r. to know your heaviness,* Lucr. 1283. Shr. IV, 3, 122. With an accus. indicating the person asked, and an inf.: *did r. me to importune you,* Gent. I, 3, 13. Mids. I, 2, 102. III, 1, 41. Cor. I, 9, 86. Tim. III, 2, 40. *to do more than she is —ed,* Oth. II, 3, 327. *let me r. you off,* Ant. II, 7, 127. With an accus. indicating the thing demanded: *—s your company,* Wiv. III, 3, 25. LLL V, 2, 208. Shr. II, 95. John IV, 2, 51. IV, 3, 22. Cor. II, 2, 56. 161. III, 1, 133. Rom. II, 2, 128. Mcb. III, 1, 15. *what he —s of us,* Troil. III, 3, 32. *—s a parley of Lucius,* Tit. IV, 4, 101.

**Requicken,** to revive, to reanimate: *his doubled spirit —ed what in flesh was fatigate,* Cor. II, 2, 121.

**Requiem,** a hymn sung for the dead: Phoen. 16. Hml. V, 1, 260.

**Require,** 1) to ask, to beg, to demand: Sonn. 57, 4. Tp. II, 2, 186. Meas. III, 1, 253. H5 II, 4, 101. H8 III, 2, 122. With an inf.: *—s to live in Egypt,* Ant. III, 12, 12. With an accus. indicating the person asked: *to desire and r. her to solicit ...,* Wiv. I, 2, 10 (Evans' speech). *I r. your highness that it shall please you to declare,* H8 II, 4, 144. *he will r. them, as if he did contemn what he requested should be in them to give,* Cor. II, 2, 160. The accus. indicating the thing asked for: Lucr. Arg. 3. Tp. V, 51. Meas. III, 1, 156. All's I, 3, 30. H5 III, 2, 151 (misapplied by Fluellen). R3 II, 2, 95. H8 II, 4, 177. Cor. II, 3, 1. Tim. III, 6, 77. Mcb. III, 4, 6. Lr. I, 1, 195. Oth. I, 2, 37. Ant. II, 2, 88. III, 12, 28. With *of*: *my dukedom of thee,* Tp. V, 132. Err. IV, 4, 121. All's IV, 3, 108. Tit. III, 1, 77. Lr. V, 3, 43. Ant. III, 13, 66.

2) to render necessary, to need, to want: *my plight —s it,* Wint. II, 1, 118. *—s nothing but secrecy,* III, 3, 130. H6C III, 3, 150. IV, 5, 18. H8 I, 1, 125. 132. II, 1, 144. III, 2, 146. V, 1, 105. Cor. III, 2, 63. V, 3, 130. Tit. V, 3, 168. Tim. V, 1, 231. Mcb. III, 1, 133. Lr. V, 3, 59. Oth. III, 4, 39. Ant. I, 2, 202. V, 1, 63. Per. IV, 1, 68. *—d* = requisite, necessary: *it is —d you do awake your faith,* Wint. V, 3, 94. I, 2, 245. All's II, 5, 65. Lr. IV, 3, 6. Oth. II, 1, 234.

Passing into the sense of to deserve: *be prosperous in more than this deed does r.* Wint. II, 3, 190. *I loved him as in honour he —d,* III, 2, 64.

**Requisite,** adj. needful, necessary: *a good nose is r. also,* Wint. IV, 4, 687.

**Requisites,** necessary things: *hath all those r. in him,* Oth. II, 1, 251.

**Requit,** to retribute: *exposed unto the sea, which hath r. it, him and his innocent child,* Tp. III, 3, 71. *let heaven r. it with the serpent's curse,* Oth. IV, 2, 16 (thus F1; the rest of O. Edd. *requite*). *the gods r. his charity,* Per. III, 2, 75 (reading of Q1; the rest of O. Edd. *requite*). Cor. IV, 2, 12. 5, 76 (*requitted*).

**Requital,** retribution, reward: Wiv. IV, 2, 3.

Meas. V, 8. All's V, 1, 5. John II, 34. Cor. II, 2, 54. *in r. of:* Gent. I, 1, 153. Meas. II, 1, 258.

**Requite,** to repay, in a good or bad sense; to reward, to retaliate; the person rewarded or punished as object: Tp. V, 169. Ado III, 1, 111. V, 4, 24. Merch. I, 2, 70. All's III, 5, 102. H5 III, 6, 51. H6A II, 5, 50. R3 I, 4, 68. Troil. V, 10, 38. Tim. IV, 3, 529. V, 1, 76. Mcb. II, 3, 44. Hml. IV, 7, 140. The deed rewarded or revenged as object: Gent. III, 1, 23. Ado II, 3, 232. As I, 1, 144. Tw. IV, 2, 128. H6B I, 2, 23. H6C IV, 5, 23. IV, 6, 10. IV, 7, 78. H8 II, 1, 46. III, 2, 168. Cor. IV, 2, 12. (cf. *requit*). Tit. I, 237. III, 1, 297. V, 1, 12. Tim. III, 3, 19. Hml. I, 2, 251. Oth. IV, 2, 16 (F1 *requit*). Per. III, 2, 75 (Q1 *requit*).

**Rere-mice,** see *Rear-mice.*

**Re-salute,** to greet again, to see again: Tit. I, 75. 326.

**Rescue,** subst. deliverance by main force: *without r. in the first assault,* All's I,3,120. *where honourable r. and defence cries out upon the name of Salisbury,* John V, 2, 18. *this fair r. thou hast brought to me,* H4A V, 4, 50. *a r.!* H4B II, 1, 61 (not understood by Mrs Quickly). *spur to the r. of the noble Talbot,* H6A IV, 3, 19. *looks for r.* IV, 4, 19. *too late comes r.* 42. *came in strong r.* IV, 6, 26. *brought r. in,* IV, 7, 33. *r., my lord,* R3 V, 4, 1. *in the r. of Lavinia,* Tit. I, 417. *no r.?* Lr. IV, 6, 194. *to make a r.* = to deliver forcibly from the custody of an officer: Err. IV, 4, 114. Cor. III, 1, 277. cf. *death will seize her, but your comfort makes the r.* Ant. III, 11, 48.

**Rescue,** vb. 1) to deliver by main force: Gent. V, 4, 35. As III, 3, 134. Shr. III, 2, 239. Tw. V, 53. John III, 2, 7. H6A V, 3, 104. H6B III, 1, 364. H6C I, 4, 2. R3 II, 1, 112. Per. V, 1, 176. With *from:* Gent. V, 4, 21. H6A I, 6, 2. IV, 6, 5. 15. H6C IV, 6, 84. Tit. III, 1, 49. —*d the Black Prince from forth the ranks of many thousand French,* R2 II, 3, 101.

2) to save in any manner: *r. those breathing lives to die in beds,* John II, 419. With *from: how well this yielding* —*s thee from shame,* LLL I, 1, 118. *wouldst have me r. thee from this reproach,* H6B II, 4, 64. *unless thou r. him from foul despair,* H6C III, 3, 215.

**Resemblance,** 1) likeness, similitude: *the majesty of the creature in r. of the mother,* Wint. V, 2, 39. *and his r., being not like the duke,* R3 III, 7, 11 (or = semblance?).

2) likelihood, probability: *but what likelihood is in that? Not a r., but a certainty,* Meas. IV, 2, 203.

**Resemble,** to be like, to have likeness to: Ven. 848. 1169. Lucr. 396. 1392. Sonn. 7, 6. 8, 11. 114, 6. Gent. I, 3, 84 (—*th* quadrisyll.). LLL IV, 3, 257. Merch. III, 1, 70. Shr. IV, 2, 100. Tw. II, 1, 27. II, 5, 131. John III, 1, 100. H6B I, 3, 56. III, 1, 373. H6C II, 1,23. II, 5, 99. Tit. V, 2, 107. Tim. I, 2, 102. Mcb. II, 2, 13. Hml. II, 2, 7. 475. Cymb. V, 5, 121.

**Re-send,** to send back: All's III, 6, 123.

**Reservation,** the act of keeping, preserving and guarding something for one's self: *that he willed me in heedfullest r. to bestow them,* Alls I, 3, 231 (not to give them away). *I most unfeignedly beseech your lordship to make some r. of your wrongs,* II, 3, 260 (= to keep your affronts to yourself). *have the power still to banish your defenders, till at length your ignorance (which finds not till it feels) making but r. of yourselves (still your own foes) deliver you as most abated captives to some nation,* Cor. III, 3, 130 (preserving, guarding 'only yourselves, and banishing those who would be able to protect you. M. Edd. erroneously: *making not r. of yourselves). with r. of an hundred knights,* Lr. I, 1, 135. *but kept a r. to be followed with such a number,* II, 4, 255.

**Reserve,** vb. 1) to keep to one's self and withhold from others: —*d the stalk and gave him all my flower,* Compl. 147. *r. them (your jests) till a merrier hour,* Err. I, 2, 69. *what is yours to bestow is not yours to r.* Tw. I, 5, 201. *the other part* —*d I by consent,* R2 I, 1, 128. *all lovers swear more performance than they are able and yet r. an ability that they never perform,* Troil. III, 2, 92. *r. still to give,* Tim. III, 6, 81. *if he covetously r. it, how shall's get it,* IV, 3, 408. *the table is full. Here is a place* —*d,* Mcb. III, 4, 46 (not occupied by others). *take each man's censure, but r. thy judgment,* Hml. I, 3, 69. *r. thy state,* Lr. I, 1, 151 (Qq *reverse thy doom*). *he* —*d a blanket,* III, 4, 67. *I have* —*d to myself nothing,* Ant. V, 2, 143. *that I some lady trifles have* —*d,* 165. 180.

2) to except from the conditions of an agreement: *shall our condition stand? It shall: only* —*d, you claim no interest in any of our towns of garrison,* H6A V, 4, 167.

3) to guard, to keep safe, to preserve: *r. them for my love, not for their rhyme,* Sonn. 32, 7. *one in the prison I have* —*d alive,* Meas. V, 472. *all her deserving is a* —*d honesty, and that I have not heard examined,* All's III, 5, 65 (cf. Cymb. I, 4, 143). *Richard yet lives, hell's black intelligencer, only* —*d their factor,* R3 IV, 4, 72. *Kind Rome, that hast thus lovingly* —*d the cordial of mine age,* Tit. I, 165. *sense to ecstasy was ne'er so thralled but it* —*d some quantity of choice,* Hml. III, 4, 75. *she* —*s it evermore about her,* Oth. III, 3, 295. *but nothing* — *always* —*d my holy duty* — *what his rage can do on me,* Cymb. I, 1, 87. *I will bring from thence that honour of hers which you imagine so* —*d,* I, 4, 143. *no reason I, since of your lives you set so slight a valuation, should r. my cracked one to more care,* IV, 4, 49. *r. that excellent complexion,* Per. IV, 1, 40.

Probably corrupt: *while comments of your praise, richly compiled, r. their character with golden quill and precious phrase,* Sonn. 85, 3 (Anon. *rehearse*).

**Reside,** to dwell: Tp. III, 1, 65. Meas. III, 1, 122. 277. All's IV, 3, 60. Wint. I, 2, 272. Troil. I, 1, 104. I, 3, 117. III, 2, 155. Tim. V, 1, 113. Oth. I, 3, 242. Ant. I, 3, 103. II, 2, 37.

**Residence,** 1) act of dwelling in a place: *out of it (my displeasure) you'll run again, rather than suffer question for your r.* All's II, 5, 42. *how chances it they travel? their r. was better,* Hml. II, 2, 343.

2) dwelling, habitation: Meas. V, 12. John II, 284. R2 II, 1, 119. Rom. II, 3, 24. Tim. IV, 3, 4. Cymb. I, 1, 97. III, 4, 151.

**Resident,** living, dwelling: *hath so long been r. in France,* H6A III, 4, 14. *this word 'love' be r. in men like one another,* H6C V, 6, 82.

**Residue,** what remains, the rest: *the r. of your fortune, go to my cave and tell me,* As II, 7, 196.

**Resign,** to give up, to surrender an office or possession; absol.: *willing to r.* R2 IV, 190. With an accus.: Tp. V, 118. John II, 154. R2 I, 1, 176. II, 2, 59. IV, 200. H5 II, 4, 93. H6B I, 3, 124. II, 3, 33. H6C V, 5, 19. Tit. I, 191 (*r. my life*). With *to*, = to yield one's place or state to another: *I r. to thee*, R2 IV, 202. *vile earth, to earth r.* Rom. III, 2, 59 (turn to dust, die). With accus. and *to*, = to yield or commit to: *they r. their office to the disposing of her brain*, Ven. 1039. *what thou art r. to death*, H6B III, 1, 334. *—ed the crown to Henry*, H6C I, 1, 139. IV, 6, 24. R3 I, 4, 98. II, 4, 70. III, 7, 117. Lr. V, 3, 298.

**Resignation**, cession: *the r. of thy state and crown to Henry Bolingbroke*, R2 IV, 179.

**Resist**, 1) to withstand, to oppose, to strive against; absol.: Ven. 563. Meas. V, 355. Shr. III, 2, 223. John II, 38. Cor. IV, 6, 103. Oth. I, 2, 80. Cymb. V, 3, 50. Per. I, 2, 27. I, 4, 84. Trans.: Tp. I, 2, 465. R2 IV, 148. H5 I, 1, 6. H6C II, 5, 79. IV, 3, 59. Troil. II, 2, 179. Cor. III, 1, 267. 319. Ant. I, 4, 55. Cymb. III, 1, 68. Per. I, 1, 40.

2) to be distasteful to: *these cates r. me*, Per. II, 3, 29.

**Resistance**, the act of resisting, opposition: Ven. 69. Lucr. 1265. Ado IV, 1, 47. All's I, 1, 128. H4B II, 4, 109.

**Resolute**, having a fixed purpose, determined, full of bold decision: Meas. II, 1, 12. LLL V, 2, 705. As I, 1, 147. Tw. I, 5, 23. H6A III, 1, 91. IV, 1, 38. H6B III, 1, 267. IV, 4, 60. H6C I, 1, 43. V, 4, 61. R3 I, 4, 115. Mcb. IV, 1, 79.

Substantively: *a list of lawless —s*, Hml. I, 1, 98 (= desperadoes).

**Resolutely**, with bold determination: Wiv. I, 1, 263. H4A I, 2, 38. H6B III, 1, 266.

**Resolution**, 1) fixed purpose, determination: *think you I can a r. fetch from flowery tenderness?* Meas. III, 1, 82. *so I take my leave, in r. as I swore before*, Shr. IV, 2, 43. *your r. cannot hold*, Wint. IV, 4, 36. *in this r. I defy thee*, H6C II, 2, 170. V, 1, 95. R3 III, 7, 218. H8 II, 4, 176. Troil. II, 2, 191. Cor. V, 6, 95. Rom. IV, 1, 53. Caes. II, 1, 113. Ant. V, 2, 238.

2) firmness, resoluteness, undaunted courage: *my will is backed with r.* Lucr. 352. *my r., love, shall be thy boast*, 1193. 1200. Meas. III, 1, 170. John IV, 1, 35. V, 1, 53. R2 I, 1, 109. H4A I, 2, 67.** H5 II, 4, 35. H6B III, 1, 332. IV, 8, 65. H6C II, 2, 77. Tit. III, 1, 239. Mcb. V, 5, 42. Hml. III, 1, 84. Oth. V, 1, 5. Ant. IV, 15, 49. 91. Cymb. III, 6, 4.

3) satisfactory information, freedom from doubt, certainty: *I would unstate myself, to be in a due r.* Lr. I, 2, 108.

**Resolve**, subst. 1) settled purpose, fixed determination: *continue your r. to suck the sweets of sweet philosophy*, Shr. I, 1, 27. II, 93. H6C III, 3, 129. Rom. IV, 1, 123.

2) firmness of mind: *a lady of so high r.* H6A V, 5, 75.

**Resolve**, vb. 1) to dissolve, to melt; a) trans.: *his passion —d my reason into tears*, Compl. 296. *the sea's a thief, whose liquid surge —s the moon into salt tears*, Tim. IV, 3, 442. *thaw and r. itself into a dew*, Hml. I, 2, 130. b) intr.: *as a form of wax —th from his figure 'gainst the fire*, John V, 4, 25.

2) to solve, to explain: *as you will live, r. it you* (viz the riddle) Per. I, 1, 71.

3) to free from doubt or perplexity and bring to a determination: *this shall absolutely r. you*, Meas. IV, 2, 225. *until our fears, —d, be by some certain king purged and deposed*, John II, 371. *r. my doubt*, H6C IV, 1, 135. Refl.: *r. thee, Richard*, H6C I, 1, 49.

*r. yourselves apart*, Mcb. III, 1, 138. *I have myself —d upon a course*, Ant. III, 11, 9.

Partic. *—d* = a) fixed in a determination: Gent. II, 6, 12. LLL I, 1, 24. Shr. I, 1, 49. 90. II, 395. All's II, 1, 207. R2 II, 3, 29. H5 I, 2, 222. Caes. II, 1, 202. Mcb. III, 1, 139. Oth. III, 3, 180. Per. IV, 1, 12. 13. With a subordinate clause: *I am —d that thou shalt spend some time with Valentinus*, Gent. I, 3, 66. *I firmly am —d you shall have aid*, H6C III, 3, 219. With an inf.: *she is —d no longer to restrain him*, Ven. 579. Gent. III, 1, 76. All's III, 7, 19 (O. Edd. *r.*). H6A V, 1, 37. H6B V, 1, 198. Cor. I, 1, 4. II, 3, 40. Tit. I, 278. Caes. V, 1, 91. With *for*: *—d for flight*, Wint. IV, 4, 519. *I am —d for death or dignity*, H6B V, 1, 194. *for that I am prepared and full —d*, Tit. II, 1, 57. With *on*: *I am —d on two points*, Tw. I, 5, 24 (*on* = concerning). b) resolute, constant in purpose: *a —d villain*, John V, 6, 29. *that thy father had been so —d*, H6C V, 5, 22. *my hardy, stout —d mates*, R3 I, 3, 340.

4) to free from uncertainty or ignorance, to satisfy, to inform: *I cannot joy, until I be —d where our father is become*, H6C II, 1, 9. *that Antony may safely come to him and be —d how Caesar hath deserved to lie in death*, Caes. III, 1, 131. *to be —d if Brutus so unkindly knocked*, III, 2, 183. *how he received you, let me be —d*, IV, 2, 14. *r. me, which way thou mightst deserve this usage*, Lr. II, 4, 25. *r. your angry father, if my tongue did e'er solicit ...*, Per. II, 5, 68. *he can r. you*, V, 1, 1. II, 4, 31. V, 3, 61. With *of*: *single I'll r. you ... of every these happened accidents*, Tp. V, 248. *we would be —d of some things of weight*, H5 I, 2, 4. *these letters will r. him of my mind*, R3 IV, 5, 19.

Hence almost = to answer (German: *Bescheid geben*): *I am now going to r. him*, Meas. III, 1, 194. *r. me in my suit*, LLL II, 110. *it is as easy to count atomies as to r. the propositions of a lover*, As III, 2, 245. *what, master, read you? first r. me that*, Shr. IV, 2, 7. *may it please your highness to r. me now*, H6C III, 2, 19. *I will r. your grace immediately*, R3 IV, 2, 26. *r. me whether you will or no*, 120. *r. me this: was it well done of rash Virginius*, Tit. V, 3, 35.

*—d* = satisfied, convinced: *long since we were —d of your truth, your faithful service and your toil in war*, H6A III, 4, 20. *I am —d that Clifford's manhood lies upon his tongue*, H6C II, 2, 124.

5) to make ready in mind, to prepare (German: *gefasst machen*): *quit presently the chapel or r. you for more amazement*, Wint. V, 3, 86. *and now he is —d to die*, Meas. III, 2, 262. *stand —d, but hope withal*, Tit. I, 135.

6) to determine, to decree, to resolve on; only in the partic. *—d: a —d and honourable war*, John II, 585. *holds his infant up and hangs —d correction in the arm*, H4B IV, 1, 213.

7) to make up one's mind, to determine: *how yet —s the governor of the town?* H5 III, 3, 1. *and so must you r., that what you cannot as you would achieve, you must perforce accomplish as you may*, Tit. II, 1, 105. With an inf.: *to obtain his will —ing*, Lucr. 129. Tp. III, 3, 13. LLL IV, 3, 371. H6A II, 1, 27. R3 IV, 2, 70. With *for*: *I will r. for Scotland*, H4B II, 3, 67 (= to go to Scotland). With *on*: *r. on this, thou shalt be fortunate, if thou receive me for thy warlike mate*, H6A I, 2, 91 (i. e. come to a resolution on this supposition, that thou shalt be fortunate etc).

**Resolvedly**, so that doubts and uncertainties are removed, satisfactorily, clearly: *of that and all the progress more or less, r. more leisure shall express*, All's V, 3, 332 (O. Edd. *resolduedly*).

**Resort**, subst. visits paid by way of intercourse and converse: *kept severely from r. of men*, Gent. III, 1, 108. *our houses of r.* Meas. I, 2, 104, i. e. our brothels; cf. Per. IV, 6, 86. *the cause of my son's r. thither*, Wint. IV, 2, 57. *forbid him her r.* Tim. I, 1, 127. *what men to-night have had r. to you*, Caes. II, 1, 276. *she should lock herself from his r.* Hml. II, 2, 143. Peculiar passage: *of all the fair r. of gentlemen that every day with parle encounter me, in thy opinion which is worthiest love?* Gent. I, 2, 4 (cf. the German *Besuch* for *Besucher*).

**Resort**, vb. to betake one's self, to repair by way of intercourse and connexion: *merry fools to mock at him r.* Lucr. 989. *thou makest faults graces that to thee r.* Sonn. 96, 4. *I would r. to her by night*, Gent. III, 1, 110. *doth this Sir Proteus often r. unto this gentlewoman?* IV, 2, 74. *to walk where any honest men r.* Err. V, 28. *men of great worth —ed to this forest*, As V, 4, 161. *what men of name r. to him?* R3 IV, 5, 8. *where at some hours in the night spirits r.* Rom. IV, 3, 44.

**Resorter**, one that frequents: *that your —s stand upon sound legs*, Per. IV, 6, 27.

**Resound**, vb. to send back sound, to reverberate: Ven. 268. Mcb. IV, 3, 6. = to be echoed back: *how sighs r. through heartless ground*, Pilgr. 278.

**Respeak**, to repeat, to echo: *—ing earthly thunder*, Hml. I, 2, 128.

**Respect**, subst. 1) the act of seeing, contemplation, view; *in my r.* = in my eyes: *you in my r. are all the world*, Mids. II, 1, 224. *his meanest garment is dearer in my r. than all the hairs above thee*, Cymb. II, 3, 140.

2) deliberation, reflection, thought in reference to something: *full of —s, yet nought at all respecting*, Ven. 911. *r. and reason, wait on wrinkled age*, Lucr. 275; cf. *reason* and *r. make livers pale*, Troil. II, 2, 49. *in our two loves there is but one r., though in our lives a separable spite*, Sonn. 36, 5. *what poor duty cannot do, noble r. takes it in might, not merit*, Mids. V, 91. *more devout than this in our —s have we not been*, LLL V, 2, 792. *when perchance it frowns more upon humour than advised r.* John IV, 2, 214. *on both sides more r.* Cor. III, 1, 181. *never learned the icy precepts of r.* Tim. IV, 3, 258. With *of* or *on*: *you hold too heinous a r. of grief*, John III, 4, 90 (= you heinously think too much of your grief). *you have too much r. upon the world*, Merch. I, 1, 74.

3) consideration, reason or motive in reference to something: *called to that audit by advised —s*, Sonn. 49, 4. *if it were not for one trifling r., I could come to such honour*, Wiv. II, 1, 45. *I would have daffed all other —s and made her half my self*, Ado II, 3, 176. *my —s are better than they seem*, All's II, 5, 71. *when such profound —s do pull you on*, John III, 1, 318. *what a noble combat hast thou fought between compulsion and a brave r.* V, 2, 44. *the love of him, and this r. besides, for that my grandsire was an Englishman, awakes my conscience*, V, 4, 41. *the gain proposed choked the r. of likely peril feared*, H4B I, 1, 184. *an ancient tradition, begun upon an honourable r.* H5 V, 1, 75. *this argues conscience in your grace, but the —s thereof are nice and trivial*, R3 III, 7, 175.

*in one r. I'll thy assistant be*, Rom. II, 3, 90 (= for one consideration). *there's the r. that makes calamity of so long life*, Hml. III, 1, 68. *the instances that second marriage move are base —s of thrift*, III, 2, 193. *mingled with —s that stand aloof from the entire point*, Lr. I, 1, 242 (Ff *regards*). *—s of fortune are his love*, 251. *in r.* = in consideration: *she is not to be kissed fasting, in r. of her breath*, Gent. III, 1, 327. *in r. that it is a shepherd's life, it is naught*, As III, 2, 14. *I could be well contented to be there, in r. of the love I bear your house*, H4A II, 3, 2. *minister the potion of imprisonment to me in r. of poverty*, H4B I, 2, 146. *in that r., then, like a loving child, shed yet some small drops*, Tit. V, 3, 166. *and yet but yaw neither, in r. of his quick sail*, Hml. V, 2, 120. *in r. of that I would fain think it were not*, Lr. I, 2, 69. *our general's wife is now the general: I may say so in this r., for that he hath devoted and given up himself to the contemplation of her parts*, Oth. II, 3, 321.

4) relation, regard, point of view; *in r. of* = a) with regard to, as to: *that in some —s makes a beast a man*, Wiv. V, 5, 5. *misgraffed in r. of years*, Mids. I, 1, 137. *in r. of itself it is a good life*, As III, 2, 13. *I speak in r. —*, All's II, 3, 32. *my uncle's will in this r. is mine*, John II, 510. *in some —s I grant I cannot go*, H4B I, 2, 189. *she will be ruled in all —s by me*, Rom. III, 4, 14. *nature's above art in that r.* Lr. IV, 6, 86. b) in comparison with; to: *but a night-gown in r. of yours*, Ado III, 4, 19. *Hector was but a Troyan in r. of this*, LLL V, 2, 639. *thou worms-meat in r. of a good piece of flesh*, As III, 2, 68. *he was a man, this in r. a child*, H6C V, 5, 56. *he does deny him, in r. of his, what charitable men afford to beggars*, Tim. III, 2, 81. *in r. of a fine workman I am but a cobbler*, Caes. I, 1, 10.

5) attention, notice, care: *to show me worthy of thy sweet r.* Sonn. 26, 12. *shall we serve heaven with less r. than we do minister to our gross selves?* Meas. II, 2, 86. *he is not for your lordship's r.* All's III, 6, 109. *is there no r. of place, persons, nor time in you?* Tw. II, 3, 98. *so it be new, there's no r. how vile*, R2 II, 1, 25 (= he cares not). *if you vouchsafe me hearing and r.* H4A IV, 3, 31. *without observance or r. of any*, Troil. II, 3, 175. *I do love my country's good with a r. more tender than mine own life*, Cor. III, 3, 112. *have r. to mine honour, that you may believe*, Caes. III, 2, 15 (take care of, look to, my honour). *the malevolence of fortune nothing takes from his high r.* Mcb. III, 6, 29. *you shall do small r., show too bold malice against .... my master*, Lr. II, 2, 137 (Ff —s). *returned me expectations and comforts of sudden r. and acquaintance*, Oth. IV, 2, 192. *she held the very garment of Posthumus in more r. than my person*, Cymb. III, 5, 139. *not a man hath r. with him but he*, Per. II, 4, 18. *who (my child) should not be more dear to my r. than yours*, III, 3, 33. cf. Sonn. 36, 5 and Mids. V, 91 sub def. 2; and Merch. V, 99: *nothing is good, I see, without r.*, i. e. without notice taken and attention bestowed; according to others, = without consideration of circumstances.

6) esteem, regard, reverence: *r. to your great place!* Meas. V, 294. *a place of high r. with me*, Mids. II, 1, 209. *I attend them with all r. and duty*, As I, 2, 177. *if your lordship find him not a hilding, hold me no more in your r.* All's III, 6, 4. *she uses me with a more exalted r.* Tw. II, 5, 31. *to tread down fair r. of*

*sovereignty*, John III, 1, 58. *what good r. I have of thee*, III, 3, 28. *throw away r.* R2 III, 2, 172. *that title of r. which the proud soul ne'er pays but to the proud*, H4A I, 3, 8. *he holds your temper in a high r.* III, 1, 170. *out of the great r. they bear to beauty*, H8 I, 4, 69. *a thousand pounds a year for pure r.* II, 3, 95. *should find r. for what they have been*, V, 3, 75. *out of dear r.* 119. *you know me dutiful; therefore, dear sir, let me not shame r.*, *but give me leave to take that course*, Troil. V, 3, 73. *with courtesy and with r. enough*, Caes. IV, 2, 15. *with all r. and rites of burial*, V, 5, 77. *that from their coldest neglect my love should kindle to inflamed r.* Lr. I, 1, 258. *to do upon r. such violent outrage*, II, 4, 24. *his worthiness does challenge much r.*, Oth. II, 1, 213.

7) state of deserving or being treated with regard; honour, respectability (of persons); high value, importance (of things): *true valour still a true r. should have*, Lucr. 201. *his true r. will prison false desire*, 642. *such offers of our peace as we with honour and r. may take*, John V, 7, 85. *many of the best r. in Rome*, Caes. I, 2, 59. *thou art a fellow of a good r.* V, 5, 45. *this ring, whose high r. and rich validity did lack a parallel*, All's V, 3, 192. *he shall our commission bring to you, with such things else of quality and r. as doth import you*, Oth. I, 3, 283.

8) modest and becoming deportment, decency: *such harmless creatures have a true r. to talk in deeds*, Lucr. 1347. *I never heard a man of his place, gravity and learning, so wide of his own r.* Wiv. III, 1, 58. *if I do not put on a sober habit, talk with r. and swear but now and then*, Merch. II, 2, 200. *there's a letter for you. Delivered with good r.* H4B II, 2, 109.

**Respect,** vb. 1) to consider: *respice finem, r. your end*, Err. IV, 4, 43. —*ing* = considering: *there is none worthy —ing her that's gone*, Wint. V, 1, 35 (cf. *in r. of* in *Respect*, subst. 4. b). —*ing what a rancorous mind he bears*, H6B III, 1, 24. *whether our daughter were legitimate, —ing this our marriage with the dowager*, H8 II, 4, 180. With *as: she —s me as her only son*, Mids. I, 1, 160. *I do r. thee as my soul*, H4A V, 4, 20. With *for: the service of the foot, being once gangrened, is not then —ed for what before it was*, Cor. III, 1, 307.

2) to care for, to take notice of: *like the proceedings of a drunken brain, full of respects, yet nought at all —ing*, Ven. 911 (cf. *well —ed* in H4A IV, 3, 10). *nor children's tears, nor mothers' groans —ing*, Lucr. 431. *then others for the breath of words r.* Sonn. 85, 13. *what merit do I in myself r.* 149, 9. *if you r. them* (the papers) *best to take them up*, Gent. I, 2, 134. *win her with gifts, if she r. not words*, III, 1, 89. *though you r. not aught your servant doth*, V, 4, 20. *in love who —s friend?* 54. *since she —s my mistress' love so much*, IV, 4, 187. *what should it be that he —s in her*, 199. *and six or seven winters more r. than a perpetual honour*, Meas. III, 1, 76. *do you persuade yourself that I r. you?* IV, 1, 53 (= am interested for you). *the passado he —s not*, LLL I, 2, 185. *that more than all the world I did r. her*, V, 2, 437. *I am mean indeed, —ing you*, Shr. V, 2, 32. *thou —est not spilling Edward's blood*, R2 II, 1, 131 (doest not care to spill, i. e. spillest without remorse). *what doth she say? Nothing that I r.* R3 I, 3, 296. *spoke like a tall fellow that —s his reputation*, I, 4, 157. *as you r. the common good*, H8 III, 2, 290. *only their ends you have —ed,*

Cor. V, 3, 5. *when we banished him, we —ed not them* (the gods), *and he returning to break our necks, they r. not us*, V, 4, 35. 37. *it is my will, the which if thou r., show a fair presence*, Rom. I, 5, 74. *they pass by me as the idle wind, which I r. not*, Caes. IV, 3, 69. *he hath a court he little cares for and a daughter who he not —s at all*, Cymb. I, 6, 155. *as jewels lose their glory if neglected, so princes their renowns if not —ed*, Per. II, 2, 13.

3) to regard with reverence: *well, well, my lords, r. him*, H8 V, 3, 153. *learn me how to r. you*, Oth. I, 3, 184.

4) Misapplied by Elbow and Pompey: *the house is a —ed house, this is a —ed fellow, and his mistress is a —ed woman*, Meas. II, 1, 169—172. *the time is yet to come that she was ever —ed with man, woman, or child*, 176. *she was —ed with him before he married with her*, 177. 183. 184 (for ill reputed).

**Respective,** 1) caring for, regardful: *you should have been r. and have kept it*, Merch. V, 156. *'tis too r. and too sociable for your conversion*, John I, 188. *away to heaven, r. lenity*, Rom. III, 1, 128.

2) worthy of being cared for: *what should it be that he respects in her but I can make r. in myself*, Gent. IV, 4, 200. cf. *Unrespective.*

**Respectively,** regardfully, with careful notice taken: *you are very r. welcome*, Tim. III, 1, 8.

**Respite,** subst. delay, time granted: *to make you understand this, I crave but four days' r.* Meas. IV, 2, 170. *ourself ... after some r. will return to Calais*, H6A IV, 1, 170. *this All-Souls' day to my fearful soul is the determined r. of my wrongs*, R3 V, 1, 19 (= term; cf. the German *frist*).* *the bishop did require a r.* H8 II, 4, 177. 181.

**Respite,** vb. to grant delay for a limited time: *injurious love, that —s me a life*, Meas. II, 3, 41. *forty days longer we do r. you*, Per. I, 1, 116.

**Responsive,** correspondent, suited: *r. to the hilts*, Hml. V, 2, 159.

**Rest,** subst. 1) cessation from motion or disturbance, repose: Lucr. 757 *(repose and r.).* Meas. III, 1, 17. LLL V, 2, 824. Merch. III, 2, 329. John IV, 2, 55. H4B I, 2, 243. IV, 5, 212. Troil. V, 6, 17. Tit. IV, 2, 64 *(God give her good r).* Rom. II, 3, 43. Caes. II, 1, 86. V, 5, 80. Hml. II, 2, 84 *(go to your r.).* Ant. I, 3, 53. *full of r.* = refreshed by rest: H4A IV, 3, 27. Caes. IV, 3, 202. *to take r.:* Ven. 647. 1185. Tp. V, 301. *here will I set up my everlasting r.* Rom. V, 3, 110. *thought to set my r. on her kind nursery*, Lr. I, 1, 125 (an expression probably originating in the use of the other word of the same form. cf. Lodge's Rosalind, ed. Collier, p. 45: *Aliena resolved there to set up her r.*).

= sleep: Ven. 784. 853. Lucr. 125. 974. Sonn. 28, 2. 61, 11. 73, 8. Pilgr. 195. Err. V, 83. LLL V, 2, 91. H5 IV, 1, 287. H6B III, 2, 256. R3 I, 2, 112. IV, 1, 82 (Qq *sleep*). IV, 4, 401. Rom. I, 5, 129. V, 3, 189. Caes. IV, 3, 228. 262. Lr. III, 6, 105. Cymb. II, 2, 12. Per. II, 3, 115. *at r.* = abed: Mcb. II, 1, 12; cf. John V, 7, 82. *one that thinks a man always going to bed and says: God give you good r.* Err. IV, 3, 33. R3 I, 4, 75. V, 3, 43. cf. Mids. II, 2, 64. *to take r. or one's r.:* Tp. II, 1, 197. Wint. II, 3, 10. H6C I, 5, 32. IV, 3, 5. *good r.* (as a kind wish): Pilgr. 181. 182. Gent. IV, 2, 133. = the repose of death: John I, 7, 24. H6C II. 1, 76. R3 II, 2, 46

(Qq *perpetual r.*, Ff *ne'er-changing night*). Tit. I, 133. Hml. V, 1, 260. V, 2, 371.

= quiet, ease, peace of the mind: Meas. II, 4, 187. Merch. II, 5, 17. Wint. II, 1, 191. II, 3, 1. 8. John III, 4, 134. R3 IV, 1, 95. IV, 2, 74. Rom. II, 2, 123 (*repose and r.*). Mcb. V, 3, 39. Lr. II, 4, 293. *set your heart at r.* Mids. II, 1, 121 (= do not trouble yourself about it). *and I ... to do you r.*, *a thousand deaths would die,* Tw. V, 136.

2) stay, abode: *vouchsafe your r. here in our court some little time,* Hml. II, 2, 13. *that in Tarsus was not best longer for him to make his r.* Per. II Prol. 26.

3) a pause in music: *my restless discord loves no stops nor —s,* Lucr. 1124. *to steal at a minute's r.* Wiv. I, 3, 31. *he rests his minum r.* Rom. II, 4, 23.

**Rest,** subst. 1) that which is left, the remainder: Sonn. 115, 12. Tp. I, 2, 226. 232. 344. IV, 247. Meas. II, 1, 105. LLL I, 1, 53. 132. Mids. I, 1, 191. V, 150. Merch. III, 1, 70. Shr. I, 1, 169. All's II, 3, 83. 155. Tw. III, 2, 67. V, 246. H6A V, 4, 141. H6B I, 4, 66. II, 2, 43. H6C III, 3, 92 (*for the r.* = moreover, German *übrigens*). Cymb. I, 6, 28 etc. etc. *above the r.* = above all: *wherein it finds a joy above the r.* Sonn. 91, 6. *therefore, above the r., we parley to you,* Gent. IV, 1, 60. *above the r. be gone,* Lr. IV, 1, 50. *to set up one's r.* (a phrase taken from gaming) = to have fully made up one's mind, to be resolved: *he that sets up his r. to do more exploits with his mace than a morris-pike,* Err. IV, 3, 27. *I have set up my r. to run away,* Merch. II, 2, 110. *since you set up your r. 'gainst remedy,* All's II, 1, 138. *the County Paris hath set up his r. that you shall rest but little,* Rom. IV, 5, 6.* cf. *that is my r., that is the rendezvous of it,* H5 II, 1, 17;* and see in the preceding article Rom. V, 3, 110 and Lr. I, 1, 125.

2) the others: Lucr. 1844. Arg. 13. Tp. II, 1, 287. V, 256. Gent. I, 2, 20. 27. 28. Wiv. IV, 2, 34. Meas. I, 2, 13. LLL II, 55. V, 1, 149. Mids. I, 2, 30. V, 250. Merch. II, 2, 214. II, 6, 62. III, 2, 42. As V, 4, 57. H6A II, 5, 90. III, 2, 65 etc. etc. *above the r.* = above all others: H6B II, 1, 6. Troil. I, 2, 200. *Of* omitted after it: *all the r. revolted faction,* R2 II, 2, 57 (Ff and the later Qq *all the r. of the revolted faction*).

Passage not understood: *outfacing faults in love with love's ill r.* Pilgr. 8; cf. Sonn. 138, 8.

**Rest,** vb. 1) intr. a) to cease from labour, to indulge in repose: Tp. III, 3, 6. Gent. II, 7, 37. LLL V, 2, 831. Mids. II, 2, 8. Merch. II, 2, 111. R2 V, 1, 5. 6. H6C I, 2, 32. II, 3, 5. IV, 8, 33. H8 IV, 1, 66. Troil. V, 8, 4. Caes. IV, 5, 1. Hml. I, 5, 182. Cymb. IV, 2, 43. V, 4, 97. = to sleep: Mids. V, 427. H8 I, 4, 12. Rom. II, 2, 188. IV, 3, 13. IV, 5, 7. Lr. III, 6, 36. 87. Per. V, 1, 236. to repose in death: Phoen. 58. H6C V, 2, 48. H8 IV, 2, 31. Tit. I, 150. 349. Caes. V, 5, 41. Lr. V, 3, 150. Per. II, 4, 30. = to enjoy quiet, not to be disturbed: *you should not r. between the elements of air and earth,* Tw. I, 5, 293. *my lord shall never r.* Oth. III, 3, 22.

b) to lie, to stay, to abide: *what nobleman is that that with the king here —eth in his tent?* H6C IV, 3, 10. *at Northampton they do r. to-night,* R3 II, 4, 1 (Qq *they lay at N.*). *devise with thee where thou shalt r.* Cor. IV, 1, 39.

c) to make a pause, to cease: *there r. in your foolery,* Err. IV, 3, 34. *you have too courtly a wit for me:*

*I'll r.* As III, 2, 73. *—s his minum rest,* Rom. II, 4, 22. *and not —ing here, accuses him of letters,* Ant. III, 5, 10.

d) to lie, to be in the power of; with *in: it —ed in your grace to unloose this tied-up justice,* Meas. I, 3, 31. *to strive for that which —eth in my choice,* Shr. III, 1, 17. *what service wilt thou do me? What you command, that —s in me to do,* H6C III, 2, 45. *never hopes more heaven than —s in thee,* Tit. II, 3, 41. Similarly: *the Mortimers, in whom the title —ed,* H6A II, 5, 92. Without *in: this inundation of mistempered humour —s by you only to be qualified,* John V, 1, 13 (= it rests, lies in you to qualify).

e) to lean, to depend: *r. on my word,* Tit. I, 267. *that spirit upon whose weal depend and r. the lives of many,* Hml. III, 3, 14.

f) to pass, to be no longer spoken of; in the phrase *let it r.: but let it r.* Shr. III, 1, 56. *let the mustard r.* IV, 3, 26. *let that r.* H6A II, 5, 119. IV, 1, 180. *let her r.* H6B I, 3, 95. R3 III, 1, 157. IV, 2, 88 (Qq *pass*). *let her r. in her unrest awhile,* Tit. IV, 2, 31.

2) trans. to place at rest, to give repose to: *to r. thy weary head,* Lucr. 1621. Mids. II, 2, 40. H4A III, 1, 215. *the man that, when gentlemen are tired, gives them a sob and —s them,* Err. IV, 3, 25 (punning). *r. your minds in peace,* H6A I, 1, 44. *r. thy unrest on England's lawful earth,* R3 IV, 4, 29. *then would I hide my bones, not r. them here,* 33. Refl.: *set it down and r. you,* Tp. III, 1, 18. *r. yourself,* 20. *I needs must r. me,* III, 3, 4. *my herald thoughts in thy pure bosom r. them,* Gent. III, 1, 144. *we'll r. us,* Mids. II, 2, 37. III, 2, 418. 446. As II, 4, 73. H6A II, 5, 2. R3 I, 2, 32. Lr. IV, 6, 260. Per. I, 4, 1.

Used in kind wishes for departed souls: *is my boy, God r. his soul! alive or dead?* Merch. II, 2, 75. *God r. all Christian souls!* Rom. I, 3, 18. *heaven r. them now!* Mcb. IV, 3, 227. *r. her soul,* Hml. V, 1, 147. For a salutation in meeting, and oftener in parting (the word *God* mostly omitted): *God r. you merry,* As V, 1, 65. *r. you well,* Meas. IV, 3, 186. *r. you fair, good signior,* Merch. I, 3, 60. *ye say honestly: r. you merry,* Rom. I, 2, 65. 86. *r. you happy,* Ant. I, 1, 62.

**Rest,** vb. to remain; 1) to be left: *nought —s for me but to make open proclamation,* H6A I, 3, 70. *there —s no other shift but this,* II, 1, 75. 2) to continue to be: *I r. thy secret friend,* Lucr. 526. *so should my shame still r. upon record,* 1643. *there r.* Meas. II, 3, 36 (= continue in this mind). *r. debtor for the first,* Merch. I, 1, 152. *wilt thou r. damned?* As III, 2, 74. *to whom we all r. generally beholding,* Shr. I, 2, 274. *may both breed thee and still r. thine,* Wint. III, 3, 49. *to r. without a spot for evermore,* John V, 7, 107. *if England to itself do r. but true,* 118. *these differences shall all r. under gage,* R2 IV, 86. *this festered joint cut off, the rest r. sound,* V, 3, 85. *let it r. where it began at first,* H6A IV, 1, 121. *till you do return, I r. perplexed,* V, 5, 95. *I hold it cowardice to r. mistrustful,* H6C IV, 2, 8. *there shall I r. secure from force,* IV, 4, 33. *my sovereign shall r. in London,* IV, 8, 22. *—ing* = not subject to motion or change: *the northern star, whose true-fixed and —ing quality,* Caes. III, 1, 61. 3) to be to be done: *and here it —s that you'll procure the vicar,* Wiv. IV, 6, 48. *one thing more —s,* Shr. I, 1, 250. *what —eth more, but that I seek occasion how to rise?* H6C I, 2, 44. *and now what —s but ...,* IV, 2, 13. V, 7, 42. *what then? what —s?* Hml. III, 3, 64. 4) Used almost as a mere copula, = to be, of whose soft grace for the like loss I have her sovereign aid and r. myself content, Tp. V, 144. which with ourselves all r. at thy dispose, Gent. IV, 1, 76. now, thus it —s, Wiv. IV, 6, 34 (thus it is, thus matters stand). I r. much bounden to you, As I, 2, 298. but r. unquestioned welcome and undoubted blest, All's II, 1, 210. I r. your servant, H8 V, 1, 55. —ing well assured they ne'er did service for it, Cor. III, 1, 121. that I may r. assured whether yond troops are friend or enemy, Caes. V, 3, 17. the affairs of men r. still incertain, V, 1, 96. we r. your hermits, Mcb. I, 6, 20. you shall close prisoner r. Oth. V, 2, 335. till then r. your debtor, Per. II, 1, 149.

**Rest,** vb. = arrest (M. Edd. 'rest): Err. IV, 2, 42. 45. IV, 3, 25. IV, 4, 3.

**Re-stem,** to force back, to retrace: now they do r. their backward course, Oth. I, 3, 37.

**Restful,** quiet, peaceful: Sonn. 66, 1. R2 IV, 12.

**Restitution,** reparation, indemnification: Wiv. V, 5, 33 (he makes r.). H6B III, 1, 118. Cor. III, 1, 16. Oth. V, 1, 15.

**Restive,** writing of some M. Edd. for resty, q. v., of O. Edd. in Sonn. 100, 9.

**Restless,** never resting: Lucr. 974. 1124. Meas. III, 1, 125. H5 III, 6, 30. R3 I, 4, 81. Mcb. III, 2, 22.

**Restoration,** recovery, convalescence: Lr. IV, 7, 26.

**Restorative,** an efficacious medicine: Rom. V, 3, 166. Per. Prol. 8 (read it for —s).

**Restore,** 1) to give back to the owner: myself I'll forfeit, so that other mine thou wilt r. Sonn. 134, 4. Tp. V, 134. LLL II, 138. R2 III, 3, 41. R3 I, 4, 144. With to: r. them to the owner, Ado II, 1, 240. As V, 4, 170. Tit. I, 210. 296.

Hence = to make amends for, to compensate: all losses are —d, Sonn. 30, 14. And even: Robin shall r. amends, Mids. V, 445.

2) to bring back, to renew: our —d love and amity, H4B IV, 2, 65. I can again thy former light r. Oth. V, 2, 9.

3) to bring back to a former and better state; a) from dishonour or degradation: she that you wronged, look you r. Meas. V, 531. till thou be —d, thou art a yeoman, H6A II, 4, 95. With to: —d again to all his lands, R3 IV, 88. H4B IV, 1, 110. —d to my blood, H6A II, 5, 128. III, 1, 159. —d me to my honours, H8 II, 1, 114. With into: r. yourselves into the good thoughts of the world again, H4A I, 3, 181.

b) to recover from disease, to cure, to heal: his (tears) poisoned me, and mine did him r. Compl. 301. their senses I'll r. Tp. V, 31. to see your wit —d, Shr. Ind. 2, 79. All's II, 3, 154. Tw. III, 4, 51. IV, 2, 104. H6B II, 1, 76. H8 II, 2, 30. Hml. III, 1, 147. Lr. IV, 4, 9. Ant. III, 13, 199. Cymb. I, 1, 148. Per. III, 2, 45. With to: God r. you to health, Ado V, 1, 333. Shr. Ind. 1, 121. All's II, 3, 70. which to his former strength may be —d, H4B III, 1, 42. could r. this cripple to his legs again, H6B II, 1, 133.

**Restrain,** 1) to strain, to draw tight: a headstall of sheep's leather which, being —ed to keep him from stumbling, hath been often burst, Shr. III, 2, 59.

2) to check, to hinder from motion, to confine: she is resolved no longer to r. him, Ven. 579. immured, —ed, captivated, bound, LLL III, 126. you have —ed yourself within the list of too cold an adieu, All's II, 1, 52. none of this could r. the stiff-borne action, H4B

I, 1, 176. my little stomach to the war and your great love to me —s you thus, Troil. III, 3, 221. should have kept short, —ed and out of haunt, this mad young man, Hml. IV, 1, 18. should have him thus —ed, Lr. II, 2, 154. With from: hoxes honesty behind, —ing from course required, Wint. I, 2, 244. With of: me of my lawful pleasure she —ed, Cymb. II, 5, 9.

3) to suppress, to repress, to oppress: his eye, which late this mutiny —s, Lucr. 426. when men r. their breath on some great sudden hest, H4A II, 3, 64. to chain up and r. the poor, Cor. I, 1, 87. if they should by the cormorant belly be —ed, 125. r. in me the cursed thoughts, Mcb. II, 1, 8. if she have —ed the riots of your followers, Lr. II, 4, 145.

4) to keep back, to withhold: they would r. the one (your lands), distain the other, R3 V, 3, 322 (withhold them from you and keep them to themselves. cf. restraint in Err. III, 1, 97). With from: —est from me the duty which to a mother's part belongs, Cor. V, 3, 167. With to: —ing aid to Timon, Tim. V, 1, 151. —ed = prohibited: to put metal in —ed means, Meas. II, 4, 48.

**Restraint,** 1) the keeping a check on a p.: wishing a more strict r. upon the sisterhood, Meas. I, 4, 4. from curbed license plucks the muzzle of r. H4B IV, 5, 132. put upon you what r. and grievance the law will give me cable, Oth. I, 2, 15. throwing r. on us, IV, 3, 91.

2) confinement, detention: whence comes this r.? Meas. I, 2, 128. 132. a r. to a determined scope, III, 1, 68. whose r. John IV, 2, 52. lock up your r. Cymb. I, 1, 74.

3) the act of withholding, of keeping back: to know the reason of this strange r. Err. III, 1, 97 (of shutting out the master of the house; cf. restrain in R3 V, 3, 322). Hence = abstinence, reserve: puts it off to a compelled r. All's II, 4, 44. madding my eagerness with her r. V, 3, 213. my love, without retention or r. Tw. II, 4, 84.

**Resty,** stiff with too much rest, torpid (cf. Restystiff in Edward 3 III, 3): rise, r. Muse, Sonn. 100, 9 (some M. Edd. restive).* who in this dull and long-continued truce is r. grown, Troil. I, 3, 263 (Ff and M. Edd. rusty). when r. sloth finds the down pillow hard, Cymb. III, 6, 34.

**Resume,** 1) to take again, to take back: Cor. IV, 1, 16. Lr. I, 4, 331. Cymb. III, 1, 15. V, 3, 75.

2) to take: nor —s no care of what is to continue, Tim. II, 2, 4 (O. Edd. r. no care). cf. rebate for bate, redeliver for deliver, regreet for greet, repast for past, reprisal for prize etc.

**Resurrection,** revival from death: Wiv. I, 1, 54 (Evans' speech).

**Resurvey,** to read and examine again: Sonn 32, 3. H5 V, 2, 81.

**Retail,** 1) to tell: he is furnished with no certainties more than he haply may r. from me, H4B I, 1, 32. the truth should live from age to age, as 'twere —ed to all posterity, R3 III, 1, 77. to whom I will r. my conquest won, IV, 4, 335.

2) to sell at second hand and in small quantities: he is wit's pedlar and —s his wares at wakes and wassails, LLL V, 2, 317.

**Retain,** 1) to keep, not to lose or lay aside: Tp. IV, 185. Err. I, 1, 66. 129. John V, 4, 23. H6A V, 4, 136. Rom. II, 2, 46. Hml. III, 3, 56. Lr. I, 1, 137. III, 6, 62.

2) to take into service, to hire: *being my sworn servant, the duke —ed him his*, H8 I, 2, 192.

**Retainers**, attendants, servants: *mounted where powers are your r.* H8 II, 4, 113.

**Retell**, to tell again: Oth. I, 3, 372. Partic. *retold:* H4A I, 1, 46. I, 3, 73.

**Retention**, the power of keeping or confining, as well as that which keeps or confines; 1) the power or means of preserving impressions: *that poor r.* (viz a table-book) *could not so much hold*, Sonn. 122, 9. *no woman's heart so big to hold so much; they lack r.* Tw. II, 4, 99. 2) reserve, restraint: *my love, without r. or restraint*, Tw. V, 84. 3) confinement, custody: *to send the king to some r. and appointed guard*, Lr. V, 3, 47.

**Retentive**, confining, restraining: *must my house be my r. enemy, my gaol?* Tim. III, 4, 82. *nor strong links of iron can be r. to the strength of spirit*, Caes. I, 3, 95.

**Retinue**, persons attending a prince: H4B IV, 3, 121. Lr. I, 4, 221.

**Retire**, subst. 1) retreat in war: Lucr. 174. John II, 326. V, 5, 4. H4A II, 3, 54. H5 IV, 3, 86 *(make)*. H6C II, 1, 150. Troil. V, 3, 53. V, 4, 21. V, 8, 15 (Ff *retreat*). Cor. I, 6, 3. Cymb. V, 3, 40.

2) return: *that to his borrowed bed he make r.* Lucr. 573. *with a blessed and unvexed r. we will bear home that lusty blood again*, John II, 253.

3) repair: *all his behaviours did make their r. to the court of his eye*, LLL II, 234.

**Retire**, vb. 1) trans. to draw back, to lead back: *each* (lock), *by him enforced, —d his ward*, Lucr. 303. *that he might have —d his power*, R2 II, 2, 46.

2) refl. a) to withdraw from a public to a more private place: *and thence r. me to my Milan, where every third thought shall be my grave*, Tp. V, 310. *you must r. yourself into some covert*, Wint. IV, 4, 663. R2 IV, 96. Cor. I, 3, 30. Tim. II, 2, 171. Oth. II, 3, 386.

b) to retreat from battle: *the French fight coldly and r. themselves*, John V, 3, 13.

3) intr. (forming its perfect with *to be*) a) to withdraw from action, or from a public to a more private place: Tp. IV, 161. Wint. IV, 2, 36. H4B IV, 1, 13. H5 III, 3, 56. Cor. III, 1, 11. Rom. III, 1, 1. Tim. V, 1, 62. Mcb. II, 2, 66. Lr. I, 2, 183. Ant. IV, 4, 35. *—d* = withdrawn from society, living in private: Tp. I, 2, 91. Wint. IV, 4, 62. Cymb. III, 5, 36. cf. Wint. IV, 2, 36 and Tim. V, 1, 62.

b) to retreat from battle or danger: Lucr. 641. 1441. Wiv. III, 4, 86. John V, 4, 53. H5 III, 6, 99. H6A I, 1, 111. I, 5, 2. 33. IV, 2, 21. H6B IV, 4, 39. IV, 9, 9. H6C I, 4, 14. II, 1, 188. II, 5, 8. Cor. I, 4, 28. I, 6, 50. Oth. V, 2, 271. Ant. IV, 7, 1. 8.

c) to return: *this way she runs, and now she will no further, but back —s*, Ven. 906. *one poor —ing minute in an age would purchase thee a thousand friends*, Lucr. 962. *he'll say in Troy when he —s, the Grecian dames are sunburnt*, Troil. I, 3, 281. *whose icy current and compulsive course ne'er feels —ing ebb*, Oth. III, 3, 455. = to return, even in the sense of to answer (?): *with an accent tuned in selfsame key —s to chiding fortune*, Troil. I, 3, 54 (M. Edd. *retorts*, or *returns*).

**Retirement**, 1) the act of withdrawing from company or from action: *certain words he spake against your grace in your r.* Meas. V, 130 (= during

your absence). *make up, lest your r. do amaze your friends*, H4A V, 4, 6 (your absence from the battle). *the king is in his r. marvellous distempered*, Hml. III, 2, 312.

2) a private way of life: H5 I, 1, 58.

3) retreat, refuge: *a comfort of r. lives in this*, H4A IV, 1, 56.*

**Retort**, subst. reply to an incivility: *this is called the r. courteous*, As V, 4, 76. 96.

**Retort**, vb. to throw back: *the duke's unjust, thus to r. your manifest appeal*, Meas. V, 303 (= to reject, not to accept). *I do r. the solus in thy bowels*, H5 II, 1, 54. *his virtues shining upon others heat them, and they r. that heat again to the first giver*, Troil. III, 3, 101. *with one hand beats cold death aside, and with the other sends it back to Tybalt, whose dexterity —s it*, Rom. III, 1, 169. In Troil. I, 3, 54 some M. Edd. *—s*, O. Edd. *retires;* in Wiv. II, 2, 4 some M. Edd., after the surreptitious Qq: *I will r. the sum in equipage.* Ff. om.

**Retract**, to disavow, to wish undone: *Paris should ne'er r. what he hath done*, Troil. II, 2, 141.

**Retraite**, retreat, flight: *and for a, r.; how swiftly will this Feeble run off!* H4B III, 2, 286 (the later Ff and M. Edd. *retreat*).

**Retreat**, subst. the act of retiring in war: All's IV, 3, 323. H4B III, 2, 286 (the earlier O. Edd. *retraite*). H6C I, 1, 5. Troil. V, 8, 15 (Q *retire*). *to make r.* As III, 2, 170. H4B IV, 3, 78. *to sound r.* H4A V, 4, 163. H5 III, 2, 94. H6A II, 2, 3. H6B IV, 8, 4.,

**Retrograde**, moving backward, retreating; and (in astronomy) seeming to move contrary to the succession of the signs: *born under Mars. When he was predominant. When he was r., I think, rather*, All's I, 1, 212. With *to*, = contrary, counteracting: *it is most r. to our desire*, Hml, I, 2, 114.

**Return**, subst. 1) the act of coming or going back: Sonn. 56, 12. Tp. II, 1, 73. Meas. IV, 2, 211. IV, 3, 143. V, 3. Merch. II, 8, 38. III, 4, 26. All's IV, 5, 75 *(was upon his r. home).* Tw. III, 4, 282. John III, 1, 321. R2 IV, 17. H4A IV, 3, 109 *(again).* H4B II, 4, 303. H5 III, 6, 72. H8 II, 1, 45. Tit. I, 76. Hml. III, 2, 329. IV, 7, 48. Lr. I, 4, 363. IV, 3, 6. Ant. III, 6, 60. Cymb. I, 4, 155. II, 4, 31. IV, 2, 66. III, 4, 110. IV, 2, 186. IV, 3, 15. Per. II, 4, 52. *our home r.* Err. I, 1, 60. R2 I, 3, 267. *to make r.* Gent. II, 7, 14. Meas. IV, 3, 107. Tw. I, 4, 22. H6B I, 2, 83. H6C IV, 1, 5. Lr. II, 4, 153.

2) repayment, requital: *no gift to him but breeds the giver a r. exceeding all use of quittance*, Tim. I, 1, 290. *I'll pawn my honours to you upon his good —s*, III, 5, 82. *as rich men deal gifts, expecting in r. twenty for one*, IV, 3, 517. *I have been bold to them to use your signet and your name; but they do shake their heads, and I am here no richer in r.* II, 2, 212 (= for it? or no richer in returning than in going?). *most fair r. of greetings and desires*, Hml. II, 2, 60. Hence = answer: *if my father render fair r.* H5 II, 4, 127.

3) reimbursement: *a month before this bond expires, I do expect r. of thrice three times the value*, Merch. I, 3, 159.

**Return**, vb. 1) intr. a) to come or go back: Ven. 704. Lucr. 321. 641. 961. 1359. Sonn. 28, 1. 45, 10. 51, 4. Tp. IV, 99. V, 102. Gent. II, 2, 3. IV, 4, 65. Meas. III, 1, 198. III, 2, 164. 174. 183. 189. Err. I, 2, 14. 42. 64. II, 1, 1. III, 2, 156. IV, 1, 44. IV, 4,

17. Ado I, 1, 30. 37. 205. 303. LLL III, 70. Mids. III, 2, 172. Merch. I, 2, 111. II, 5, 52. II, 6, 17. V, 34. 116. 272. As II, 7, 134. V, 4, 180 (*our —ed fortune*). Shr. IV, 1, 85. All's I, 2, 34. Tw. III, 4, 63. H6A I, 4, 23. H8 III, 2, 64. Cor. III, 2, 135. V, 1, 42. Tit. I, 33. Mcb. I, 7, 9. Lr. II, 4, 160. 210. 214. Oth. IV, 3, 8 (*I will be — ed forthwith*) etc. etc. *to r. again:* Meas. III, 2, 183. Mids. II, 1, 133. As IV, 3, 100. Tw. III, 4, 264 etc. *to r. back again:* R2 I, 3, 120.

b) to speak again of a subject lost out of sight: *but to r. to the verses,* LLL IV, 2, 156. *but now r. we to the false Duke Humphrey,* H6B III, 1, 322.

c) to come back to a former, and usually a better state: *r., forgetful Muse, and straight redeem in gentle numbers time so idly spent,* Sonn. 100, 5. *if I have ranged, like him that travels I r. again,* 109, 6. *so I r. rebuked to my content,* 119, 13. *r., r., and make thy love amends,* Gent. IV, 2, 99. *r. thee therefore with a flood of tears,* H6A III, 3, 56 (*thee* for *thou*). *come, come, r., r., thou wandering lord,* 76. *the worst —s to laughter,* Lr. IV, 1, 6. In a bad sense: *to what base uses we may r.* Hml. V, 1, 223. *Alexander —eth into dust,* 232.

d) to fall to, to become the share of: *had his necessity made use of me, I would have put my wealth into donation, and the best half should have —ed to him,* Tim. III, 2, 91. *which had —ed to the inheritance of Fortinbras, had he been vanquisher,* Hml. I, 1, 91. *your servants ever have theirs, themselves and what is theirs, in compt, to make their audit at your highness' pleasure, still to r. your own,* Mcb. I, 6, 28.

2) trans. a) to send back: *she —s this ring to you,* Tw. II, 2, 5. *say that Marcius r. me unheard,* Cor. V, 1, 42. *that I —ed you an empty messenger,* Tim. III, 6, 40.

b) to bring back: *r. him here again,* Meas. V, 384. *and this thou didst r. from him, that he did buffet thee,* Err. II, 2, 159. *I might not be admitted, but from her handmaid do r. this answer,* Tw. I, 1, 25. *shall I r. this answer to the king?* H4A IV, 3, 106. *—ed my letter back,* Rom. V, 3, 252.

c) to give back: *see it be —ed,* Gent. I, 2, 46. *send for your ring, I will r. it home,* All's V, 3, 223. *it should be so —ed,* Tw. II, 2, 15. *r. the precedent to these lords again,* John V, 2, 3. *r. an injury,* H5 IV, 7, 189. *these moral laws speak aloud to have her back —ed,* Troil. II, 2, 186. *till all these mischiefs be —ed again even in their throats,* Tit. III, 1, 274. *I do r. those talents,* Tim. I, 2, 6. *if she will r. me my jewels,* Oth. IV, 2, 201. *if you borrow one another's love for the instant, you may r. it again,* Ant. II, 2, 105.

d) to give in reply or in recompense or retribution: *until it had —ed these terms of treason doubled down his throat,* R2 I, 1, 56. *that thou —est no greeting to thy friends,* I, 3, 254. *caves shall r. your mock in second accent of his ordnance,* H5 II, 4, 125. *tell her I r. great thanks,* H6A II, 2, 51. *answer was —ed that he will come,* II, 5, 20. *who — ed her thanks,* H8 V, 1, 64. *I r. the lie,* Per. II, 5, 57. *which never —s us thanks,* All's I, 1, 200 (= yields, brings in). *prayers and wishes are all I can r.* H8 II, 3, 70. *when for some trifling present you have bid me r. so much,* Tim. II, 2, 146. *she hath received them and —ed me expectations and comforts,* Oth. IV, 2, 191. *I r. those duties back as are right fit,* Lr. I, 1, 99.

e) to answer: *say thus the king —s,* R2 III, 3, 121. *the Dauphin —s us that his powers are yet not ready,* H5 III, 3, 46.

f) to announce, to make known to: *while we r. these dukes what we decree,* R2 I, 3, 122. *r. them we are ready,* Per. II, 2, 4.

**Reunited,** joined again: *by the which marriage the line of Charles the Great was r. to the crown of France,* H5 I, 2, 85.

**Reveal,** to disclose, to discover, to lay open: Lucr. Arg. 20. Lucr. 1086. Tw. V, 157. H6A V, 3, 100. H6B II, 3, 105. Tit. IV, 1, 36. Hml. I, 5, 119. Per. V, 1, 245. Refl.: *r. yourself to him,* Meas. V, 28 (expound your case to him). *we still see them r. themselves,* All's IV, 3, 27 (betray themselves). *in complete glory she — ed herself,* H6A I, 2, 83. *never —ed myself unto him,* Lr. V, 3, 192.

**Revel,** subst. festivity, merry-making: Wiv. IV, 4, 58. John V, 2, 132. Hml. I, 4, 17. Oth. II, 3, 293. Ant. I, 4, 5. Plur. *—s:* Ven. 123 (keep). Tp. IV, 148. LLL IV, 3, 379. Mids. II, 1, 18 (keep). 141. V, 36. 377. Tw. I, 3, 121. 145. H8 I, 4, 72. Rom. I, 4, 109. Oth. II, 2, 6. II, 3, 45. Ant. V, 2, 218. Per. II, 3, 93.

**Revel,** vb. 1) to feast, to make merry: Lucr. 11. Ado I, 1, 322. Mids. I, 1, 19. Shr. III, 2, 226. H4B IV, 5, 126. H5 I, 2, 253. Rom. III, 4, 26. Caes. II, 2, 116. With a superfluous *it: r. and feast it at my house,* Err. IV, 4, 65. *and r. it as bravely as the best,* Shr. IV, 3, 54. H6C III, 3, 225. IV, 1, 95.

2) to indulge one's inclination or caprice, to wanton, to do at pleasure: *there it* (desire) *—s,* Lucr. 713. *who all this while hath —ed in the night,* R2 III, 2, 48. *—ing like lords till all be gone,* H6B I, 1, 224. *—ed in our parliament,* H6C I, 4, 71. *his father — ed in the heart of France,* II, 2, 150. *to r. in the entrails of my lambs,* R3 IV, 4, 228. *and r. all with him,* Cor. IV, 5, 227. *and r. in Lavinia's treasury,* Tit. II, 1, 131. *where joy most —s,* Hml. III, 2, 208.

**Reveller,** one who feasts and makes merry: Wiv. V, 5, 42. Ado II, 1, 87. Caes. V, 1, 62. Cymb. I, 6, 61.

**Revelry,** a merry-making: As V, 4, 183.

**Revenge,** subst. return of an injury, retaliation, vengeance: Lucr. 1823. Wiv. I, 3, 99. IV, 2, 222. Ado V, 1, 281. 301. Merch. III, 1, 56. 72. 74. 98. As III, 1, 4. IV, 3, 129. Tw. V, 374. Wint. III, 2, 124. John IV, 3, 38. H6A III, 2, 31. H6B IV, 1, 41. H6C I, 1, 190. I, 3, 26. II, 1, 86. R3 V, 1, 9. Tit. III, 1, 271. Cymb. IV, 2, 157 etc. *in r.* = by way of retaliation: Lucr. 236. 1736. Gent. I, 2, 110. II, 4, 133. Mids. II, 1, 89. H6A II, 2, 11; cf. I, 5, 35. H6B III, 2, 127. H6C I, 3, 41. *his r.* sometimes = the act of revenging him: Lucr. Arg. 20. H6A I, 5, 35. H6B III, 2, 127. cf. *my death's r.* H6A IV, 6, 39. With *for: prophesied r. for it,* R3 I, 3, 186. With *on:* Lucr. 1180. Sonn. 149, 8. John II, 172. H6C I, 1, 55. III, 3, 265. H8 I, 2, 138. Tit. I, 137. III, 1, 117. Tim. V, 4, 37. Plur. *—s,* in the same sense: Meas. IV, 3, 140. All's V, 3, 10. Tw. V, 385. Wint. I, 2, 456. II, 3, 19. Cor. IV, 5, 143. V, 2, 44. V, 3, 85. Tim. V, 4, 32. 37. Mcb. V, 2, 3. Lr. III, 7, 7. Cymb. II, 5, 24. IV, 2, 159. *to have one's r. or —s:* Lr. II, 4, 282. III, 5, 1. *to render vengeance and r.* R2 IV, 67 (cf. *Render*). *to take r. or —s:* Meas. IV, 4, 33. Tit. III, 1, 117. Tim. V, 4, 37. Lr. III, 7, 7.

**Revenge,** vb. to take vengeance; absol.: Wiv.

I, 3, 100. Merch. III, 1, 69. H5 V, 1, 49. H6B IV, 1, 97. H6C II, 3, 19. Tit. IV, 1, 128. Mcb. III, 3, 18. Lr. II, 1, 47. With *for: r., ye heavens, for old Andronicus,* Tit. IV, 1, 129. cf. Lucr. 1683. Shr. V, 1, 139. Hml. IV, 5, 135. With *upon: a bird that will r. upon you all,* H6C I, 4, 36.

Trans., the injury or injured person being the object: Lucr. 1841. Mids. III, 2, 420. R2 I, 2, 40. I, 3, 58. H4A I, 3, 183. V, 3, 12. H6A III, 2, 49. IV, 5, 18. IV, 6, 30. H6B IV, 1, 26. 146. H6C I, 1, 100. II, 3, 19. Cymb. I, 6, 135. V, 4, 34 etc. With *on: r. it on him,* Tp. III, 2, 62. Per. III, 3, 24. Refl.: *lest I r. What, myself upon myself?* R3 V, 3, 186. H8 II, 1, 162. Caes. IV, 3, 94. Passively; a) the injury as subject: *these injuries will be —d home,* Lr. III, 3, 13. *'twill be —d,* Cymb. IV, 2, 154. b) the injured person as subject; *to be —d* = to take vengeance: Lucr. 1194. Ado II, 1, 217. Shr. II, 29. H6A I, 4, 58. 105. H6C III, 3, 212. Tit. V, 2, 196. Caes. III, 2, 207. Hml. III, 3, 75. IV, 5, 135. Cymb. I, 6, 126. 129. 132. II, 3, 160. With *on:* Lucr. 1683. Gent. V, 2, 51. Wiv. II, 1, 30. 31. 66. 96. II, 2, 326. III, 1, 122. V, 1, 30. Tw. V, 386. H4A I, 3, 291. H6C I, 1, 57. 266. I, 3, 20. R3 I, 2, 133. 135. I, 3, 333. H8 III, 2, 9. Tit. III, 1, 301. V, 2, 95. Ant. IV, 12, 16. Cymb. III, 5, 79. *Of* for *on: I'll be —d of her,* H4B II, 4, 167 (Pistol's speech. Ff *on*). *On* for *for: live to be —d on her death,* Lucr. 1778.

**Revengeful,** vindictive: Lucr. 1693. R2 IV, 50. V, 3, 42. H6C II, 1, 164. R3 I, 2, 174. H8 I, 1, 109. Cor. IV, 5, 95. Tit. IV, 3, 32. Hml. III, 1, 126.

**Revengement,** vengeance, punishment: *out of my blood He'll breed r. and a scourge for me,* H4A III, 2, 7.

**Revenger,** one who takes vengeance: Ant. II, 6, 11. III, 1, 3.

**Revengingly,** vindictively: Cymb. V, 2, 4.

**Revenue** (*révenue* or *revénue*), income: Tp. I, 2, 98. Mids. I, 1, 6. 158. As III, 2, 397. V, 2, 12. Wint. IV, 3, 28. John III, 1, 169. R2 I, 4, 46. II, 1, 226. R3 III, 7, 158.*Troil. II, 2, 206. II, 3, 31. Hml. III, 2, 63. Lr. I, 1, 139. I, 2, 56. 79. Ant. III, 6, 30. Cymb. II, 3, 148. Plur. —*s:* Sonn. 142, 8. As I, 1, 107. R2 II, 1, 161. IV, 212. H6B I, 3, 83. Lr. II, 1, 102.

**Reverb,** to reverberate, to resound: *whose low sound —s no hollowness,* Lr. I, 1, 156.

**Reverberate,** to resound; trans. and intr.: *a drum is ready braced that shall r. all as loud as thine,* John V, 2, 170. *who, like an arch, —s the voice again,* Troil. III, 3, 120.

**Reverberate,** adj. reverberant, resounding: *halloo your name to the r. hills,* Tw. I, 5, 291.

**Reverence,** subst. 1) high respect, veneration: R2 I, 4, 27. III, 2, 172. H4B IV, 2, 6. H6A II, 3, 71. H6B III, 2, 207. H8 IV, 2, 101. Troil. I, 3, 227. Caes. III, 1, 176. Lr. II, 2, 75. Cymb. IV, 2, 247. With *of: the fair r. of your highness curbs me,* R2 I, 1, 54. *this policy and r. of age makes the world bitter,* Lr. I, 2, 48. *in the due r. of a sacred vow,* Oth. III, 3, 461. With *to: all r. set apart to him,* John III, 1, 159. *for r. to some alive,* R3 III, 7, 193. *r. to your calling makes me modest,* H8 V, 3, 69. *to do a p. r.:* Merch. I, 1, 13. Caes. III, 2, 125. *to have in r.:* Tit. V, 1, 83.

2) a character entitled to particular regard: *I have as much of my father in me as you, albeit your coming before me is nearer to his r.* As I, 1, 54 (i. e. your

being older than I gives you a nearer claim to the respect which was due to him). *settlest admired r. in a slave,* Tim. V, 1, 54. *that I thus would play and trifle with your r.* Oth. I, 1, 133. Applied to venerable age: *knavery cannot hide himself in such r.* Ado II, 3, 125. *I am forced to lay my r. by,* V, 1, 64 (i. e. the privilege of my age). *in thy r. and thy chair-days,* H6B V, 2, 48. *a gracious aged man, whose r. even the head-lugged bear would lick,* Lr. IV, 2, 42. *those violent harms that my two sisters have in thy r. made,* IV, 7, 29. To clerical persons: *trust not my age, my r.* Ado IV, 1, 170. *I charge thee* (the priest) *by thy r.* Tw. V, 154. *the r. of the grave wearers,* Wint. III, 1, 5. *a clergyman of holy r.* R2 III, 3, 29. *you misuse the r. of your place,* H4B IV, 2, 23. *what your r. shall incite us to,* H5 I, 2, 20.

*Saving your r.,* a phrase used to introduce an offensive or indecent expression: Meas. II, 1, 92. Ado III, 4, 32. Merch. II, 2, 27. 139. H4A II, 4, 515. *the rather — saving r. of the word — for 'tis said a woman's fitness comes by fits,* Cymb. IV, 1, 5. *save your r.,* in the same sense: *we'll draw you from the mire or, save your r., love,* Rom. I, 4, 42. Corrupted to *sir r.: a very reverent body, ay, such a one as a man may not speak of without he say Sir r.* Err. III, 2, 93. In Rom. I, 4, 42 the surreptitious Q1 and M. Edd. *from the mire of this sir r. love.*

3) bow, obeisance: *and with a low submissive r. say,* Shr. Ind. 1, 53. cf. *to do r.* in Merch. I, 1, 13 and Caes. III, 2, 125.

**Reverence,** vb. to regard with high respect and veneration: H6A III, 3, 15. V, 4, 140. Cymb. IV, 2, 95. Per. II, 3, 40.

**Reverend** or **Reverent** (the two forms used indiscriminately in O. Edd.) 1) entitled to high respect, venerable; a) *reverend:* Compl. 57. Wiv. III, 1, 52. Err. V, 134. Ado V, 1, 325. V, 4, 125. Merch. IV, 1, 226. Shr. IV, 5, 48. 60. Tw. III, 4, 80. Wint. IV, 4, 73. H4B III, 2, 181. H5 III, 3, 37. Troil. I, 3, 61. IV, 5, 204. Cor. II, 1, 66. II, 2, 46. Tim. III, 5, 80. V, 1, 132. 185 (*reverends,* i. e. reverend'st). Oth. I, 1, 93. I, 3, 33. 76. Per. V, 1, 14. V, 3, 18. 61. 93. b) *reverent:* Err. III, 2, 91. V, 5. R3 IV, 4, 35. Tit. II, 3, 296 (M. Edd. *reverend*). III, 1, 23 (M. Edd. *reverend*). V, 3, 137 (M. Edd. *reverend*). c) Different spelling in O. Edd.; Ff *reverend,* Qq *reverent:* R2 V, 6, 25. H4A II, 4, 499. R3 IV, 1, 31. Hml. II, 2, 501. Ff *reverent,* Qq *reverend:* H4A III, 2, 104. The earlier Ff *reverent,* the later *reverend:* Err. V, 124. H6A III, 1, 49. H8 III, 1, 26.

Applied to ecclesiastics and religious institutions: John III, 1, 224. R2 V, 6, 25 (*some r. room*). H4A III, 2, 104. H4B IV, 1, 38. H6B I, 1, 8. R3 III, 5, 100. III, 7, 61. H8 I, 1, 51. 100. II, 2, 77. II, 4, 58. 205. 220. III, 1, 26. 103. 181. IV, 1, 26. 99. IV, 2, 18. Rom. IV, 2, 31.

Nearly equivalent to old: *as you are old and r., you should be wise,* Lr. I, 4, 261. *you r. braggart,* II, 2, 133 (Qq *unreverent,* Ff *reverent,* M. Edd. *reverend*).

2) testifying veneration, humble; a) *reverend:* Lucr. 90. Merch. IV, 1, 163. Shr. IV, 1, 207. H4B I, 2, 113. H6A V, 3, 47. b) *reverent:* LLL IV, 2, 1. H6B III, 1, 34.

**Reverently,** with respectful regard, with veneration: H4B IV, 4, 37. H6A I, 2, 145. H6C II, 2, 109 (*I hold thee r.*).

**Reverse**, subst. a back-handed stroke in fencing (cf. *Punto reverso*): *thy punto, thy stock, thy r.* Wiv. II, 3, 27.

**Reverse**, vb. to repeal, to annul: R3 II, 1, 86. Tit. III, 1, 24. Rom. III, 3, 59. Lr. I, 1, 151 (Qq. *r. thy doom*, Ff *reserve thy state*). cf. *Unreversed*.

**Reversion**, right or hope of future possession or enjoyment: *as were our England in r. his*, R2 I,4,35. II, 2, 38. *now remains a sweet r.* H4A IV, 1, 53. *no perfection in r. shall have a praise in present*, Troil. III, 2, 100.

**Reverso**, see *Punto* and *Reverse* subst.

**Revert**, to turn back: (France) *armed and —ed, making war against her heir*, Err. III, 2,126 (perhaps, with a pun, = fallen to, devolved on, another proprietor). *my arrow would have —ed to my bow again*, Hml. IV, 7, 23.

**Review**, vb. to see again, to see: *when thou —est this, thou dost r. the very part was consecrate to thee*, Sonn. 74, 5. *I shall r. Sicilia*, Wint. IV, 4, 680.

**Revile**, to vilify, to treat with contumely: *did not she r. me there?* Err. IV, 4, 75. 76. *his eye —d me as his abject object*, H8 I, 1, 126.

**Revisit**, to visit again: Hml. I, 4, 53.

**Revive**, 1) intr. to return to life: Ven. 338. 464. Meas. II, 4, 26. H6A I, 1, 18. H6B III, 2, 36. Rom. IV, 5, 20. V, 1, 9. Lr. IV, 6, 47. Cymb. I, 5, 42. V, 4, 142. V, 5, 456.
2) tr. to bring again to life, to reanimate: Ven. 977. All's IV, 4, 34 (*time —s us;* viz as summer does briars, cf. v. 32). John IV, 1, 112. H4B IV, 1, 114. 200. H6A III, 2, 97. IV, 5, 3. H6C I, 1, 163. III, 3, 21. Rom. III,3,165. Caes. II, 2, 88. Cymb. V, 5, 120.

**Revoke**, to repeal, to reverse: H6C II, 6, 46. Cor. II, 3, 226. 258. Lr. I, 1, 167. 182.

**Revokement**, repeal, revocation: H8 I, 2, 106.

**Revolt**, subst. 1) rebellion: Wiv. I, 3,111. John III, 4, 167. IV, 2, 6. H4B IV, 5, 66. Troil. V, 2,146. Cor. III, 1, 126. Tim. IV, 3, 91 (*make r.* = cause rebellion). Mcb. I, 2, 2.
2) desertion, going over to the enemy: *to corrupt him to a r.* All's IV, 3, 204. *let not him be slandered with r.* H4A I, 3, 112. *seek a plaster by contemned r.* John V, 2, 13. *more and less have given him the r.* Mcb. V, 4, 12. V, 2, 18. Ant. IV, 9, 19. With *to: gravity's r. to wantonness*, LLL V, 2, 74 (= falling into wantonness).
3) gross departure from duty: *this r. of thine is like another fall of man*, H5 II, 2, 141. *images of r. and flying off*, Lr. II, 4, 91. *your daughter hath made a gross r.* Oth. I, 1, 135. Especially faithlessness in love, inconstancy: *my life on thy r. doth lie*, Sonn. 92, 10. *their love may be called appetite, no motion of the liver, but the palate, that suffer surfeit, cloyment and r.* Tw. II,4,102. *O foul r. of French inconstancy*, John III, 1, 322. *ere my true heart with treacherous r. turn to another*, Rom. IV, 1, 58. *the smallest fear or doubt of her r.* Oth. III, 3, 188. *that all the plagues of hell should at one time encounter such r.* Cymb. I, 6, 112. *thy r.* III, 4, 57.
4) deserter: *you degenerate, you ingrate —s*, John V, 2, 151. *lead me to the —s of England here*, V, 4, 7. *receive us for barbarous and unnatural —s*, Cymb. IV, 4, 6.

**Revolt**, vb. 1) to rebel: John III, 1, 257. V, 1, 8. R2 II, 2, 57. III, 2, 100. III, 3, 163. H6A I, 1, 4.

H6B III, 1, 63. IV, 1, 87. Troil. V, 2, 144. Ant. I, 4, 52.
2) to desert, to fall off, to go over to the enemy: *if gold will corrupt him to r.* All's IV,3,310. *the commons will r. on Hereford's side*, R2 II, 2, 89 (= go over to Hereford). *—ed Mortimer*, H4A I, 3, 92. 93. *doth my uncle Burgundy r.?* H6A IV, 1,64. *the stout Parisians do r. and turn again unto the warlike French*, V, 2, 2. *the king is merciful, if you r.* H6B IV, 2, 133 (i. e. if you fall off from Cade). *thou wilt r. and fly to him*, R3 IV,4,478. IV,5,4. *were he upon my party, I'ld r.* Cor. I, 1, 238. *all the regions do smilingly r.* IV, 6, 103. *the kings that have —ed*, Ant. IV, 5, 4. *plant those that have —ed in the van*, IV, 6, 9. 12. IV, 9, 8. *now my thoughts r.* Per. I, 1, 78 (fall off). *—ed tapsters*, H4A IV, 2, 31 (having left their masters without leave-taking). With *from: doth r. from his allegiance*, John III, 1, 174. *r. from him*, III, 4, 165. *France is —ed from the English*, H6A I, 1, 90. H6C I, 1, 151. Tit. IV, 4, 80. Rom. II, 3, 20.
3) to be faithless: *you are love's firm votary and cannot soon r.* Gent. III, 2, 59. *—ed wives*, Wiv. III, 2, 40. Wint. I, 2, 199. *—ed fair*, Troil. V, 2, 186.

**Revolution**, change produced by time: *that I might see what the old world could say to this composed wonder of your frame; whether we are mended, or whether better they, or whether r. be the same*, Sonn. 59, 12 (whether change be identity, i. e. no change). *see the r. of the times make mountains level*, H4B III, 1, 46. *here's fine r., an we had the trick to see't*, Hml. V, 1, 98. *the present pleasure, by r. lowering, does become the opposite of itself*, Ant. I, 2,129. Apparently = any change: *full of forms, figures, shapes, objects, ideas, apprehensions, motions, —s*, LLL IV, 2, 70 (Holofernes' speech).

**Revolve**, to consider deeply, to meditate; absol.: Tw. II, 5, 155. Trans.: Lucr. 127. H6A V, 5, 101. R3 IV,4,123. Troil. II,3,198. With a clause: Cymb. III, 3, 14. cf. *Deep-revolving*.

**Reward**, subst. recompense: As I, 1, 87. All's II, 1, 150. Wint. III, 2, 165. H4A V, 4, 166 (*I'll follow, as they say, for r.*). H4B IV, 3, 35. H6A III, 4, 22. H6B I, 2, 85. I, 4, 81. II, 3, 108 (*follow us for thy r.*). IV, 8, 70. V, 1, 79. H6C II, 1, 134. II, 3, 52. III, 3, 233. V, 5, 10. R3 I, 4, 126. 129. 133. IV, 4, 518. H8 III, 2, 245. Tit. II, 3, 271. IV, 3, 112. Tim. I, 2, 197. Hml. III, 2, 72. IV, 2, 17. Ant. III, 13, 123. Cymb. V, 5, 13. As a vox media, = punishment: *I desire nothing but the r. of a villain*, Ado V, 1, 250. *take thy r.* Lr. I, 1, 175. *sin had his r.* Per. II,4,15. *of monstrous lust the due and just r.* V,3,86.

**Reward**, vb. to recompense, to requite; in a good as well as a bad sense: *r. not hospitality with such black payment*, Lucr. 575. *which heaven and fortune still —s with plagues*, Gent. IV,3,31. *they are but lightly —ed*, LLL I, 2, 157. *—ing my dependents*, III, 134. H4A III, 3, 54. V, 4, 153. 167. H6B III, 2, 9. IV, 3, 7. R3 I, 4, 236. IV, 2, 123 (Ff *repays*). H8 III, 1, 133. Cor. I, 9, 26. II, 2, 131. Tit. I, 82. Tim. I, 1, 130. Lr. III, 6, 5. Oth. II, 1, 317. Ant. IV, 7, 14.

**Rewarder**, one who recompenses: R3 I, 3, 124.

**Re-word**, 1) to repeat in the same words: *bring me to the test, and I the matter will r.* Hml. III, 4,143.
2) to re-echo: *a hill whose concave womb —ed a plaintful story*, Compl. 1.

**Reynaldo** (Ff *Reynoldo*) name in Hml. II,1.3.15.

**Reynold,** writing of O. Edd. in H6A I, 1, 94; M. Edd. *Reignier.*

**Rhapsody,** a cento: *such a deed as from the body of contraction plucks the very soul, and sweet religion makes a r. of words,* Hml. III, 4, 48.

**Rheims** (O. Edd. *Rheimes* or *Rhemes*) French town: Shr. II, 81. H6A I, 1, 60. 92.

**Rhenish,** adj. pertaining to the town of Rheims? or to the river Rhine? Probably the latter: *a deep glass of R. wine,* Merch. I, 2, 104. *more difference between your bloods than there is between red wine and R.* III, 1, 44. Substantively: *his draughts of R.* Hml. I, 4, 10. *a flagon of R.* V, 1, 197.

**Rhesus,** a Thracian king who came to the assistance of Troy, but was slaughtered at night by Ulysses and Diomedes: H6C IV, 2, 20.

**Rhetoric,** the science of oratory, the art of speaking: Sonn. 82, 10. Pilgr. 29. LLL II, 229. III, 64. IV, 3, 60. 239. As V, 1, 45. Shr. I, 1, 35.

**Rheum,** 1) rheumatism, morbid defluxion of humours: *curse the gout, serpigo, and the r.* Meas. III, 1, 31. *is he not stupid with age and altering —s?* Wint. IV, 4, 410. *I have a r. in mine eyes,* Troil. V, 3, 105. *that year he was troubled with a r.* Ant. III, 2, 57.

2) humid matter secreted from the eyes, mouth, or nose; a) tears: *an hour in clamour and a quarter in r.* Ado V, 2, 85. *why holds thine eye that lamentable r.* John III, 1, 22. *how now, foolish r.* IV, 1, 33. *villany is not without such r.* IV, 3, 108. *the north-east wind awaked the sleeping r. and so by chance did grace our hollow parting with a tear,* R2 I, 4, 8. *a few drops of women's r.* Cor. V, 6, 46. *threatening the flames with bisson r.* Hml. II, 2, 529. b) saliva: *you that did void your r. upon my beard,* Merch. I, 3, 118. cf. *the valleys whose low vassal seat the Alps doth spit and void his r. upon,* H5 III, 5, 52. c) moisture from the nose: *I guess it stood in her chin, by the salt r. that ran between France and it,* Err. III, 2, 131. *I have a salt and sorry r. offends me,* Oth. III, 4, 51.

**Rheumatic,** affected with rheumatism, causing rheumatism, or pertaining to it: *o'erworn, despised, r. and cold,* Ven. 135. *this raw r. day,* Wiv. III, 1, 47. *that r. diseases do abound,* Mids. II, 1, 105.* Misapplied by Mrs Quickly: *you are both as r. as two dry toasts,* H4B II, 4, 62. *but then he was r. and talked of the whore of Babylon,* H5 II, 3, 40.*

**Rheumy,** causing rheumatism: *tempt the r. and unpurged air to add unto his sickness,* Caes. II, 1, 266.

**Rhinoceros,** the animal Rhinoceros: Mcb. III, 4, 101.

**Rhodes,** the island of Rhodus: Oth. I, 1, 29. I, 3, 14. 22. 26. 34.

**Rhodope,** a famous courtezan, who is said to have acquired riches enough by her trade to build one of the most beautiful Egyptian pyramids: H6A I, 6, 22.

**Rhubarb,** the plant Rheum, used as a purgative: Mcb. V, 3, 55.

**Rhyme,** subst. 1) correspondence of sound in the terminating words of verses: Ado V, 2, 37. 38. 39. Rom. II, 1, 9. Cymb. V, 3, 63. *r. and reason* (originally = number and sense) joined: *in despite of the teeth of all r. and reason,* Wiv. V, 5, 133 (i. e. quite absurdly). Err. II, 2, 49. *neither r. nor reason can express how much,* As III, 2, 418. cf. Gent. II, 1, 149. LLL. I, 1, 99. I, 2, 112. H5 V, 2, 164.

2) verses, poetry: Lucr. 524. Sonn. 16, 4. 17, 14. 32, 7. 55, 2. 106, 3. 107, 11. Gent. I, 2, 79. III, 2, 69. Wiv. V, 5, 95. LLL I, 2, 190. IV, 3, 15. 58. 139. 181. V, 2, 6. 64. 405. Mids. I, 1, 28. As III, 2, 417. All's IV, 3, 263. John IV, 2, 150. H5 V, 2, 167. Troil. III, 2, 181. IV, 4, 22. Rom. I, 5, 144. Per. Prol. 12. IV Prol. 48.

**Rhyme,** vb. 1) to use words corresponding in sound: Ado V, 2, 40. As III, 2, 101. Caes. IV, 3, 133. Hml. III, 2, 296. Cymb. V, 3, 55.

2) to make verses: Gent. II, 1, 149. LLL IV, 3, 14. H5 V, 2, 164.

**Rhymer,** a poetaster: *those old nine which —s invocate,* Sonn. 38, 10. *scald —s ballad us out o' tune,* Ant. V, 2, 215.

**Rialto,** that part of Venice where the exchange was: *upon the R.* Merch. I, 3, 20. 39. III, 1, 1. 48. *in the R.* I, 3, 108.

**Rib,** subst. 1) a bone forming part of the frame of the thorax: LLL I, 1, 27 (*dainty bits make rich the —s*). Merch. II, 2, 114. As I, 2, 136. 147. John III, 3, 9 (*the fat —s of peace*). H4A IV, 2, 80 (*three fingers on the —s,* i. e. very fat). Troil. I, 3, 177. Mcb. I, 3, 136. Oth. I, 2, 5. Falstaff called —s by the prince, i. e. a fat rib-piece: H4A II, 4, 125; cf. the similar names *goodman Bones, Chops, Fatguts, Jackanapes, Pots, Thicklips* etc.

2) the timber which forms and strengthens the side of a ship: Merch. I, 1, 28. II, 6, 18. Oth. II, 1, 8.

3) Figuratively, that which encloses and protects or sustains a thing: *that is stronger made which was before barred up with —s of iron,* Ado IV, 1, 153. *the flinty —s of this contemptuous city,* John II, 384. *go to the rude —s of that ancient castle,* R2 III, 3, 32. V, 5, 20. *join you with them like a r. of steel,* H4B II, 3, 54. cf. *Thick-ribbed.*

**Rib,** vb. to enclose and protect from injury: *it* (lead) *were too gross to r. her cerecloth in the obscure grave,* Merch. II, 7, 51. *as Neptune's park, —ed and paled in with rocks,* Cymb. III, 1, 19.

**Ribald:** *but that the busy day, waked by the lark, hath roused the r. crows,* Troil. IV, 2, 9 (base, rudely obstreperous, in contradistinction to the lark?).

**Riband,** (cf. *Ribbon*) a long and narrow web of silk, worn for ornament: Wiv. IV, 6, 42. Rom. III, 1, 32. Hml. IV, 7, 79.

**Ribaudred,** lewd, profligate: *yon r. nag of Egypt,* Ant. III, 10, 10 (some M. Edd. *ribald nag, ribald hag* etc.).

**Ribbon,** riband (q. v.): LLL III, 146. Mids. IV, 2, 37. Wint. IV, 4, 205. 236. 609.

**Rib-breaking,** breaking of ribs: As I, 2, 151.

**Ribs,** see *Rib* subst.

**Rice,** the seed of Oryza sativa: Wint. IV, 3, 41. 42.

**Rice ap Thomas,** name in R3 IV, 5, 12.

**Rich,** adj. 1) opulent, wealthy: Ven. 1150. Sonn. 52, 1. 91, 10. Tp. IV, 75. Gent. I, 2, 12. III, 1, 64. Wiv. I, 3, 95. II, 1, 117. Meas. III, 1, 25. 36. III, 2, 10. Ado II, 3, 32. III, 3, 120. 121. IV, 2, 86. LLL V, 2, 1. Merch. I, 1, 10. II, 2, 130. Wint. III, 2, 171 etc. etc. Used of eyes, = having seen much: *to have seen much and to have nothing, is to have r. eyes and poor hands,* As IV, 1, 24. *a wife whose beauty did astonish the survey of —est eyes,* All's V, 3, 17. With *in,* = a) enriched by: *I as rich in having such a jewel,* Gent. II, 4, 169. *most r. in Timon's nod,* Tim.

I, 1, 62. *r. in his father's honour*, Ant. I, 3, 50. b) having in plenty: *sets you most r. in youth before my sight*, Sonn. 15, 10. *more r. in hope*, 29, 5. *r. in will*, 135, 11. *make your garden r. in gillyvors*, Wint. IV, 4, 98. V, 1, 214. John II, 491. Troil. I, 3, 30. Rom. I, 1, 221. II, 6, 30. V, 1, 11. Tim. III, 5, 109. IV, 2, 29. Cymb. V, 5, 384. With *with*, = a) enriched by: *her womb then r. with my young squire*, Mids. II, 1, 131. b) having in plenty: *r. with merchandise*, 134. *make her chronicle as r. with praise as is the bottom of the sea with sunken wreck*, H5 I, 2, 163.

2) abundant, plentiful; copious, luxuriant, fruitful: *this r. praise, that you alone are you*, Sonn. 84, 2. *thy r. leas*, Tp. IV, 60. *dainty bits make r. the ribs, but bankrupt quite the wits*, LLL I, 1, 27. *our duty is so r., so infinite*, V, 2, 199. *in your r. wisdom*, 742. *your love, so r. within his soul*, Mids. III, 2, 229. *a ship of r. lading*, Merch. III, 1, 3. *r. honesty dwells in a poor house*, As V, 4, 62. *a goodly dwelling and a r.* H4B V, 3, 7. *our r. fields*, H5 III, 5, 25. *the r. stream of lords and ladies*, H8 IV, 1, 62. *something not worth in me such r. beholding as they have often given*, Troil. III, 3, 91. *r. conceit taught thee to make vast Neptune weep*, Tim. V, 4, 77. *your wisdom should show itself more —er*, Hml. III, 2, 317. *the r. crop of sea and land*, Cymb. I, 6, 33.

3) precious: *r. caparisons*, Ven. 286. *his lips' r. treasure*, 552. *r. preys make true men thieves*, 724. *r. gems*, Sonn. 21, 6. *those tears are pearl which thy love sheds, and they are r. and ransom all ill deeds*, 34, 14. *the r. proud cost of outworn buried age*, 64, 2. *that love is merchandized whose r. esteeming the owner's tongue doth publish every where*, 102, 3. *within be fed, without be r. no more*, 146, 12. *spirits of —est coat*, Compl. 236. *r. garments*, Tp. I, 2, 164. *something r. and strange*, 401. *most poor matters point to r. ends*, III, 1, 4. *my r. gift*, IV, 1, 8. *r. scarf*, 82. *r. embroidery*, Wiv. V, 5, 75. *stones whose rates are either r. or poor*, Meas. II, 2, 150. *this r. and precious gift*, Ado IV, 1, 29. *the r. worth of your virginity*, Mids. II, 1, 219. *love's stories written in love's —est book*, II, 2, 122. *two r. and precious stones*, Merch. II, 8, 20. *gifts of r. value*, II, 9, 91. *'tis the mind that makes the body r.* Shr. IV, 3, 174 (i. e. not ornaments). *this ring he holds in most r. choice*, All's III, 7, 26. *the r. golden shaft*, Tw. I, 1, 35. *r. jewel*, II, 5, 67. *a cipher standing in r. place*, Wint. I, 2, 7. *when the r. blood of kings is set on fire*, John II, 351. *whose veins bound —er blood than Lady Blanch?* 431. *the r. advantage of good exercise*, IV, 2, 60. *so r. advantage of a promised glory*, Troil. II, 2, 204. *her —est lockram*, Cor. II, 1, 225. *your r. opinion*, Oth. II, 3, 195 (good fame). *with admirable r. words*, Cymb. II, 3, 19. *I am —er than to hang by the walls* (like a garment) Hml. IV, 4, 54. *with r. and constant pen*, Per. IV Prol. 28 etc.

4) delightful: *love-thoughts lie r. when canopied with bowers*, Tw. I, 1, 41 (cf. All's I, 2, 49 and Rom. V, 3, 303). *doth think it r. to hear the wooden dialogue and sound 'twixt his stretched footing and the scaffoldage*, Troil. I, 3, 154. *let r. music's tongue unfold the happiness*, Rom. II, 6, 27.

**Richard**, name of 1) King R. I. Coeur de Lion: John I, 90. 253. 274. II, 3. 2) King R. II: R2 I, 3, 32 etc. V, 6, 33 (*R. of Bordeaux*). H4A I, 3, 146 etc. III, 2, 94. H4B I, 1, 205. I, 3, 98. 101 etc. H5 IV, 1, 312, 319. H6A II, 5, 71. H6B II, 2, 19. 27. R3

III, 3, 12. 3) King R. III: H6B V, 3, 16. H6C I, 1, 17 etc. R3 I, 1, 52 etc. H8 I, 2, 196. II, 1, 108. 4) R. Earl of Cambridge, son of Edmund of York, executed under Henry V: H5 II Chor. 23. H6A II, 4, 90. II, 5, 84. H6B II, 2, 45. 5) R. Plantagenet, his son, afterwards Duke of York: H6A II, 4, 114. II, 5, 18. 26. III, 1, 150 etc. H6B I, 3, 186 etc. H6C I, 1, 83 etc. 6) the second son of Edward IV: R3 III, 1, 96 etc. 7) Sir R. Plantagenet, bastard of Richard I: John I, 162. 185 etc. 8) Sir R. Vernon: H4A V, 2, 1. 9) Sir R. Ketly: H5 IV, 8, 109. 10) Sir R. Grey: H6C III, 2, 2.*11) Sir R. Ratcliff: R3 II, 1, 45 (not in Qq). III, 3, 2. 12) Imaginary persons: *R. Conqueror*, Shr. Ind. 1, 4 (for *William*. Sly's speech). *R. du Champ*, Cymb. IV, 2, 377.

**Rich-built**, built in a magnificent style: *r. Ilion*, Lucr. 1524.

**Riched**, enriched: *with shadowy forests and with champains r.* Lr. I, 1, 65.

**Rich-embroidered**, adorned with rich embroidery: H6C II, 5, 44 (O. Edd. without hyphen).

**Riches**, wealth, great store, opulence (from the Fr. *richesse*): Sonn. 94, 6. Tp. II, 1, 150. III, 2, 150. IV, 106. Gent. IV, 1, 13. Wiv. III, 4, 17. Meas. III, 1, 27. 38. Shr. II, 16. H6B IV, 7, 67. R3 IV, 4, 319. H8 II, 3, 35. Troil. III, 3, 82. Tim. I, 2, 107. Per. III, 2, 28. As a plural noun: *since r. point to misery and contempt*, Tim. IV, 2, 32. *my r. to the earth, from whence they came*, Per. I, 1, 52. Often as a singular: *for that r. where is my deserving?* Sonn. 87, 6. *with too much r. it confounds itself*, R2 III, 4, 60. *that's all the r. I got in his service*, H5 II, 3, 46. *the r. of the ship is come on shore*, Oth. II, 1, 83. *r. fineless is as poor as winter*, III, 3, 173. *thy master is not there, who was indeed the r. of it*, Cymb. III, 4, 73. Personified as a fem.: *r. strewed herself even in the streets*, Per. I, 4, 23.

**Rich-jewelled**, adorned with precious jewels: H6A I, 6, 25.

**Rich-left**, inheriting great wealth: Cymb. IV, 2, 226.

**Richly**, 1) with riches, wealthily: *a lady r. left*, Merch. I, 1, 161 (= *rich-left* in Cymb. IV, 2, 226). *three of your argosies are r. come to harbour*, V, 277. *a vessel r. fraught*, II, 8, 30.

2) in a costly manner, splendidly: *comments of your praise, r. compiled*, Sonn. 85, 2. *r. suited*, All's I, 1, 170. *cased as r.* Per. V, 1, 112.

3) abundantly, copiously, amply: *paid me r.* Ado V, 1, 255. Ant. IV, 14, 37. Cymb. I, 5, 74. *r. furnished with plate*, Shr. II, 349. *whose worth and honesty is r. noted*, Wint. V, 3, 145. *r. in both*, R2 II, 1, 227. *see away their shilling r. in two hours*, H8 Prol. 13. *the poor soldier that so r. fought*, Cymb. V, 5, 3.

**Richmond**, name of an English earldom: John II, 552. *Henry Earl of R.*, afterwards King Henry VII: H6C IV, 6, 67. 93. 100. R3 IV, 1, 43 etc. His mother, the Countess R., married to Lord Stanley: R3 I, 3, 20.

**Rid**, vb. (partic. *rid*, impf. not used), 1) to make away with, to dispatch, to destroy: *kill me outright with looks and r. my pain*, Sonn. 139, 14. *the red plague r. you*, Tp. I, 2, 364. *I am the king's friend and will r. his foe*, R2 V, 4, 11. *willingness —s way*, H6C V, 3, 21 (= annihilates). *as you have r. this prince*, V, 5, 67.

2) With *from* or *of*, = to free, to clear, to deliver

*to r. us from the fear*, H6B III, 1, 234. R3 IV, 2, 78. *to r. her from this second marriage*, Rom. V, 3, 241. *r. me these villains from your companies*, Tim. V, 1, 104. *to r. me of this shame*, Lucr. 1031. *r. the house of her*, Shr. I, 1, 150. *till the father r. his hands of her*, 186. R2 IV, 325. V, 4, 2. H4B I, 2, 226. Ant. II, 6, 36. V, 2, 42.

Partic. *rid*, adjectively, with *of*, = clear of, free from, having a thing or person off one's hands: Meas. III, 1, 174. Ado III, 3, 31. Shr. IV, 2, 49. Tw. IV, 2, 73. Wint. III, 3, 15. R2 III, 2, 96. H6A IV, 7, 94. R3 IV, 1, 87. Troil. IV, 5, 164. Tim. IV, 3, 323. Caes. III, 2, 75. Lr. V, 1, 64. Per. IV, 6, 5. *r. on't*, Mcb. III, 1, 114. Per. IV, 6, 16. *Of* omitted: *this Gloster should be quickly r. the world*, H6B III, 1, 233.

**Riddance,** a getting rid of, deliverance, disencumbrance: *a gentle r.* Merch. II, 7, 78. *a good r.* Troil. II, 1, 132.

**Riddle,** subst. an enigma: Wiv. I, 1, 209 *(the Book of —s)*. Meas. III, 2, 242. LLL III, 72. All's V, 3, 304. Tw. II, 5, 119. H6C V, 5, 26. R3 IV, 4, 460. Mcb. III, 5, 5. Lr, V, 1, 37. *to tell a r.* = to solve it: Per. Prol. 38.

**Riddle,** vb. to speak enigmatically: Mids. II, 2, 53. H6A II, 3, 57. Rom. II, 3, 56.

**Riddle-like,** like an enigma: All's I, 3, 223.

**Ride,** (impf. *rode;* partic. *rid:* Mids. V, 119. Caes. III, 2, 274. *rode:* H4B V, 3, 98. H5 IV, 3, 2. *ridden:* Wiv. V, 5, 145. H8 II, 2, 3. *Rid* and *rode* used in the active, *ridden* in the passive voice) 1) intr. a) to sit on a horse and manage it; to go on horseback: Compl. 106. Meas. I, 2, 164. Ado III, 5, 40. Shr. Ind. 2, 43. Shr. IV, 1, 69. Tw. I, 3, 94. John I, 217. R2 I, 3, 251. V, 2, 22. 115. V, 5, 78. 81. H4A I, 2, 141. 179. II, 3, 103. II, 4, 379. III, 3, 222. IV, 1, 125. H4B I, 1, 55. 58. V, 3, 98. 137. V, 5, 21. H5 III, 7, 39. 56. 60. IV, 3, 2. IV, 7, 60. H6A IV, 1, 9. H6B I, 2, 57. 59. IV, 7, 51. 144. R3 III, 2, 85. V, 3, 340. Troil. IV, 4, 144. Rom. V, 3, 77. Tim. I, 2, 218. V, 2, 9. Caes. III, 2, 274. V, 2, 1. 6. Mcb. I, 6, 22. III, 1, 19. 24. Lr. I, 4, 34. 134. III, 4, 57. 142. Cymb. I, 1, 110. III, 2, 69. 72. 73. 78.

b) to be mounted on any thing, to sit astraddle: *to r. on the curled clouds*, Tp. I, 2, 191. *r. upon their* (the surges') *backs*, II, 1, 115. *the devil —s upon a fiddlestick*, H4A II, 4, 534. *the air whereon they r.* Mcb. IV, 1, 138.

c) to drive (in a carriage): *thou shinest in every tear that I do weep: no drop but as a coach doth carry thee; so —st thou triumphing in my woe*, LLL IV, 3, 35. *that erst did follow thy proud chariot-wheels, when thou didst r. in triumph through the streets*, H6B III, 4, 14.

d) to be borne along in any manner: *you leaden messengers that r. upon the violent speed of fire*, All's III, 2, 112. *upon my tongues continual slanders r.* H4B Ind. 6. *the venomed vengeance r. upon our swords*, Troil. V, 3, 47. *whose* (slanders') *breath —s on the posting winds*, Cymb. III, 4, 38. Especially = to be borne, or to drive, on the sea: *whilst he upon your soundless deep doth r.* Sonn. 80, 10. *anchored in the bay where all men r.* 137, 6. *a vessel —s fast by*, Wint. IV, 4, 512. *on the western coast —th a puissant navy*, R3 IV, 4, 434. *as if the passage and whole carriage of this action rode on his tide*, Troil. II, 3, 141. *seeing this goodly vessel r. before us*, Per. V, 1, 18. *'gainst whose shore —ing*, V, 3, 11. *he —s it* (a tempest) *out*,

IV, 4, 31, = he maintains himself against it, is not driven off by it.

e) to be supported, to lean, to rest, to depend in moving: *if life did r. upon a dial's point*, H4A V, 2, 84. *the axletree on which heaven —s*, Troil. I, 3, 67; cf. II, 3, 141.

f) to move or drive in a triumphant manner: *permit the basest clouds to r. with ugly rack on his celestial face*, Sonn. 33, 5. *disdain and scorn r. sparkling in her eyes*, Ado III, 1, 51. *move these eyes? or whether, —ing on the balls of mine, seem they in motion?* Merch. III, 2, 118. *let thy dauntless mind still r. in triumph over all mischance*, H6C III, 3, 18. *and there r. on the pants triumphing*, Ant. IV, 8, 16. cf. Sonn. 80, 10 and LLL IV, 3, 35.

g) to have free play, to practise at will: *they r. up and down on her* (the commonwealth) H4A II, 1, 90. *on whose foolish honesty my practices r. easy*, Lr. I, 2, 198.

2) trans. a) to sit on, to mount and manage: *you may r. us with one soft kiss a thousand furlongs ere with spur we heat an acre*, Wint. I, 2, 94. *I will r. thee o' nights like the mare*, H4B II, 1, 83. *—s the wild-mare with the boys*, II, 4, 268 (= plays at see-saw). cf. the quibbling expressions in Err. II, 2, 202; Mids. V, 119 and Tw. III, 4, 319. = to break in (a horse): *the horses I saw well chosen, ridden and furnished*, H8 II, 2, 3. = to be supported by, to be mounted on: *her levelled eyes their carriage r., as they did battery to the spheres intend*, Compl. 22.

b) to treat at will, to tease, to make a fool of: *am I ridden with a Welsh goat too?* Wiv. V, 5, 145 (with = by). *she —s me* (like an ass) *and I long for grass*, Err. II, 2, 202. *he hath rid his prologue like a rough colt*, Mids. V, 119. *I'll r. your horse as well as I r. you*, Tw. III, 4, 319.

**Rider,** one who rides: Ven. 40. 283. 300. Sonn. 50, 8. Compl. 107. LLL II, 121 (with a pun; cf. *Ride* 2b). IV, 2, 131. R2 I, 2, 52. V, 2, 9. H5 III, 7, 24. Cymb. IV, 4, 39. = one who breaks in horses: *they are taught their manage, and to that end —s dearly hired*, As I, 1, 14.

**Ridge,** the top of a long and narrow elevation: *the wild waves, whose —s with the meeting clouds contend*, Ven. 820. Lucr. 1439 (cf. *Enridged*). *the frozen —s of the Alps*, R2 I, 1, 64. *in as high a flow as the r. of the gallows*, H4A I, 2, 43. *leads filled and —s* (of roofs) *horsed*, Cor. II, 1, 227.

**Ridiculous,** 1) worthy of being laughed at: Ven. 988. Tp. II, 2, 169. LLL V, 1, 13. V, 2, 306. 769. As II, 4, 30. III, 2, 47. Tw. III, 4, 40. John III, 1, 150. IV, 2, 16. H5 IV Chor. 51. H8 I, 3, 3. Troil. I, 3, 149. Cor. II, 1, 94.

2) risible, inclined to laughter: *the heaving of my lungs provokes me to r. smiling*, LLL III, 78 (Armado's speech). *in this spleen r. appears, to check their folly, passion's solemn tears*, V, 2, 117.

**Riding-robe,** a robe to ride in: John I, 217.

**Riding-rod,** a switch: John I, 140.

**Riding-suit,** a suit to ride in: Cymb. III, 2, 78.

**Rife,** prevailing, in fashion(?): *there is a brief how many sports are r.* Mids. V, 42 (Q1 *ripe*).

**Rifle,** vb. to rob, to strip: Gent. IV, 1, 4. With *of:* Lucr. 692. 1050.

**Rift,** subst. a fissure, a rent: Tp. I, 2, 277. Ant. III, 4, 32.

**Rift,** vb. 1) tr. to cleave, to split: *and —ed Jove's stout oak with his own bolt,* Tp. V, 45.

2) intr. to burst, to be split: *I'ld shriek, that even your ears should r. to hear me,* Wint. V, 1, 66.

**Rig,** to fit with tackling: Tp. I, 2, 146. V, 224. Tim. V, 1, 53. Ant. II, 6, 20. III, 5, 20.

**Riggish,** wanton, lewd, unchaste: *the holy priests bless her when she is r.* Ant. II, 2, 245.

**Right,** subst. 1) that which is conformable to justice and natural or human law: *the rough beast that knows no gentle r.* Lucr. 545. *heaven prosper the r.* Wiv. III, 1, 30; cf. *God defend the r.* LLL I, 1, 216. R2 I, 3, 101. H6B II, 3, 55. Lr. V, 2, 2. *hooking both r. and wrong to the appetite,* Meas. II, 4, 176. *whom r. and wrong have chose as umpire,* LLL I, 1, 169. *to do a great r., do a little wrong,* Merch. IV, 1, 216. *I should have been a woman by r.* As IV, 3, 177. *something about, a little from the r.* John I, 170. *on our actions set the name of r.* V, 2, 67. *heaven still guards the r.* R2 III, 2, 62. *of no r., nor colour like to r., he doth fill fields,* H4A III, 2, 100. *may I with r. and conscience make this claim?* H5 I, 2, 96. *he held the r.* H6A II, 4, 38. *which they hold by force and not by r.* H6B II, 2, 30. *thou hast prevailed in r.* II, 3, 102. *draw thy sword in r.* H6C II, 2, 62. *did ever fence the r.* III, 3, 98. *the sorrow that I have by r. is yours,* R3 I, 3, 172 etc. etc. = law: *by all our country's —s in Rome maintained,* Lucr. 1838.

2) title, just claim: *that posterity which by the —s of time thou needs must have,* Ven. 759. *thou art the next of blood, and 'tis thy r.* 1184. *proving their r.* Lucr. 67. *your true —s be termed a poet's rage,* Sonn. 17, 11. *my heart (would bar) mine eye the freedom of that r.* 46, 4. 14. *your own dear-purchased r.* 117, 6. *the r. of sepulchres,* 68, 6. Phoen. 34. Mids. I, 1, 92. 105. Merch. II, 1, 16. III, 2, 19. John I, 39. 40. II, 105. V, 2, 21. H5 I, 2, 16. H6A II, 1, 35. IV, 2, 55. H6B I, 1, 244. V, 1, 1. R3 I, 3, 206 etc. With *in: you had in him no r.* Err. IV, 2, 7. LLL II, 140. Mids. III, 2, 336. John II, 22. Hml. V, 2, 400. With *of,* in the same sense: *all my r. of her I do estate unto Demetrius,* Mids. I, 1, 97. *my treasures and my —s of thee,* H4A II, 3, 48. *in r. of* or *in the r. of* = in support of the claim of: John II, 153. 268. 548. III, 4, 142. H5 I, 2, 247. H6A III, 1, 150. Cor. III, 3, 14. In the same sense: *upon the r. and party of her son,* John I, 34. *upon the r. of him it holds,* II, 237.

3) that which is due to a person or thing: *to wrong the wronger till he render r.* Lucr. 943 (make satisfaction). *for thy r. myself will bear all wrong,* Sonn. 88, 14. *lest the requiem lack his r.* Phoen. 16. *it is the r. of it, it must be so,* Meas. III, 2, 61. *'tis his r.* 71. *give her the r. you should have given her cousin,* Ado V, 1, 300. *to see like r. bereft,* Err. II, 1, 40. *lamentation is the r. of the dead,* All's I, 1, 64. *if justice had her r.* R2 II, 1, 227. *shall we divide our r. according to our threefold order ta'en?* H4A III, 1, 70. *let me have r., and let desert mount,* H4B IV, 3, 60. *r. for r. hath dimmed your infant morn to aged night,* R3 IV, 4, 15 etc. *to do a person r.* = to give him his due, to do him justice, to satisfy him: *this helpless smoke of words doth me no r.* Lucr. 1027. *do him r.* Meas. II, 2, 103. *do me the common r. to let me see them,* II, 3, 5. Err. IV, 2, 8. Ado I, 1, 246. As II, 7, 84. All's II, 3, 167. IV, 2, 17. Tw. V, 317. John II, 18. III, 1, 185. R2 II, 3, 138. H6A III, 1, 154. H6C

I, 1, 166. IV, 1, 69. Tit. I, 203 etc. *do me r.* (= satisfaction by combat) Ado V, 1, 149. *now you have done me r.* (by drinking after me, pledging me) H4B V, 3, 76. 77.

4) that which is conformable to reason and truth: *Nym, thou hast spoke the r.* H5 II, 1, 129 (Pistol's speech). *to be in the r.* = not to be wrong: Meas. II, 1, 100. 167. Shr. IV, 3, 157. Tw. II, 3, 128. R3 V, 3, 275. Hml. I, 5, 126. II, 2, 429. Ant. III, 7, 68. Sometimes = to take the right way: *thou'rt i' the r., girl; more o' that,* Meas. II, 2, 129 (= well done!). *I will beseech the virtuous Desdemona to undertake for me.... You are in the r.* Oth. II, 3, 339.

**Right,** adj. 1) accordant to the standard of truth or to that of justice: *it may be r.* Meas. V, 86. *a r. description,* LLL V, 2, 522. *'tis r.* 572. Cor. II, 1, 252. *'tis r.; thus misery doth part the flux of company,* As II, 1, 51. *as thy cause is r.* R2 I, 3, 55. *our most just and r. desires,* H4B IV, 2, 40. *plain and r. must my possession be,* IV, 5, 223. *shall yield the other in the r. opinion,* H6A II, 4, 42. *be thy title r. or wrong,* H6C I, 1, 159. *I am glad your grace has made that r. use of it,* H8 III, 2, 386. *when every case in law is r.* Lr. III, 2, 85. *you might quickly make it r.* Oth. IV, 3, 83.

2) not erring, not mistaken: *none else to me, nor I to none alive, that my steeled sense or changes r. or wrong,* Sonn. 112, 8 (that may make an impression on me, whether I be guided by truth or misled by error). *the base is r.* Shr. III, 1, 47. *you are r.* H4B V, 2, 102. *you are not r.* Cor. II, 3, 54.

3) true, real, not spurious, not only pretended or supposed: *who hath got the r.* Anne? Wiv. V, 5, 225. *call up the r. master constable,* Ado III, 3, 178. *an it be the r. husband and the r. wife,* III, 4, 36. *thou hast frighted the word out of his r. sense,* V, 2, 56. *choose the r. casket,* Merch. I, 2, 100. II, 7, 10. II, 9, 12. *my r. Rosalind,* As IV, 1, 109. *the r. Vincentio,* Shr. IV, 2, 70. IV, 4, 12. V, 1, 118. *read i' thy r. wits. So I do, but to read his r. wits is to read thus,* Tw. V, 305. 306. *its r. father,* Wint. III, 3, 46. *you stars that move in your r. spheres,* John V, 7, 74. *being in his r. wits,* H5 IV, 7, 49. *'tis the r. ring,* H8 V, 3, 103. *I will make thee do thy r. nature,* Tim. IV, 3, 44. *this courtesy is not of the r. breed,* Hml. III, 2, 327. *put your bonnet to his r. use,* V, 2, 95.

4) truly deserving the name, being exactly what the word implies: *and r. perfection wrongfully disgraced,* Sonn. 66, 7. *thou hast the r. arched beauty of the brow that becomes the ship-tire,* Wiv. III, 3, 59. *they sparkle still the r. Promethean fire,* LLL IV, 3, 351. *I am a r. maid for my cowardice,* Mids. III, 2, 302. *how many things by season seasoned are to their r. praise and true perfection,* Merch. V, 108. *it is the r. butterwomen's rank to market,* As III, 2, 103. *that's the r. virtue of the medlar,* 127. *I answer you r. painted cloth,* 290. *awful rule and r. supremacy,* Shr. V, 2, 109. *this is the r. fencing grace,* H4B II, 1, 206. *being the r. idea of your father,* R3 III, 7, 13. *like a r. gipsy,* Ant. IV, 12, 28.

5) not left, but on the other side: *r. hand,* Ven. 158. Gent. V, 4, 67. Ado I, 3, 51. Merch. II, 2, 42. As IV, 3, 81. Wint. IV, 4, 856. John II, 236. H6C II, 1, 152. II, 6, 80. Caes. V, 1, 18 etc. *this the cranny is, r. and sinister,* Mids. V, 164. *his r. cheek,* All's IV, 5, 103. Cymb. IV, 2, 211. *on his r. side,* H6C III, 1, 44. *his r. arm,* Tim. III, 5, 78

**Right,** adv. 1) in a straight line, directly: *sometimes they do extend their view r. on,* Compl. 26. *it* (your nose) *stands too r.* LLL V, 2, 568 (Alexander used to hold his head inclined to the left side). *I only speak r. on,* Caes. III, 2, 227.

2) truly, correctly, not erroneously: *you say not r., old man,* Ado V, 1, 73. *I could teach you how to choose r.* Merch. III, 2, 11. *then think you r.: I am not what I am,* Tw. III, 1, 153. *he is not his craft's master, he doth not do it r.* H4B III, 2, 298. *'tis r.* Cor. II, 1, 252. *you say r., sir,* Hml. II, 2, 406. *thou hast spoken r.* Lr. V, 3, 173. Elliptically: *r., sir,* Err. III, 1, 39. Meas. V, 85. Ado V, 1, 163. As III, 3, 54. Shr. V, 2, 31. All's II, 3, 15. R2 II, 1, 145. Tit. IV, 2, 24. Rom. II, 4, 63. Tim. I, 1, 195. Hml. I, 5, 126 etc.

3) not wrongly, not with a false aim, in order and to the purpose: *when once our grace we have forgot, nothing goes r.* Meas. IV, 4, 37. *that-it* (a clock) *may still go r.* LLL III, 195. *I then do most go r.* Wint. IV, 3, 18. *if all things fall out r.* H6A II, 3, 4. *I know a way, if it take r., in spite of fortune will bring me off again,* H8 III, 2, 219. *ever r.* Cor. II, 1, 208 (= ever the nail hit on the head). *I hit it r.* Rom. II, 3, 41. *this hits r.* Tim. III, 1, 6. *that ever I was born to set it r.* Hml. I, 5, 189. *it falls r.* IV, 7, 71.

4) exactly, just: *here begins his morning story r.* Err. V, 356. *I will tell you every thing, r. as it fell out,* Mids. IV, 2, 31. *came he r. now to sing a raven's note,* H6B III, 2, 40. *he is kind. R. as snow in harvest,* R3 I, 4, 248. *'tis Nestor r.* Troil. I, 3, 170.

5) in a manner deserving the name: *I'll smoke your skin-coat, an I catch you r.* John II, 139 (according to my wish; so that I would call it catching indeed). *there is no tongue hath power to curse him r.* III, 1, 183. *I do see the cruel pangs of death r. in thine eye,* V, 4, 60 (German: *ich sehe recht die Todesqual in deinem Auge*). *if thou tellest the heavy story r., the hearers will shed tears,* H6C I, 4, 160. With *out: and be a boy r. out,* Tp. IV, 101.

6) Before adjectives and adverbs, = highly, very, most: *to the r. honorable,* Ven. Ded. Lucr. Ded. *shall will in others seem r. gracious,* Sonn. 135, 7. *in things r. true my heart and eyes have erred,* 137, 13. *the better angel is a man r. fair,* 144, 3. *I am r. glad that he's so out of hope,* Tp. III, 3, 11. *O plague r. well prevented,* Ado III, 2, 136. *and buy it with your gold r. suddenly,* As II, 4, 100. Ado I, 1, 84. LLL V, 2, 879. Merch. II, 5, 16. As II, 7, 198. Shr. IV, 4, 40. Tw. V, 271. John I, 15. R2 II, 1, 120. H5 IV Chor. 51. V, 2, 9. H6A IV, 6, 23. H6C II, 1, 10. II, 5, 99. III, 2, 18. R3 I, 2, 245. III, 7, 61. 103. IV, 1, 15. Troil. III, 3, 21. V, 2, 39. Rom. I, 1, 124. 212. Mcb. III, 6, 5 (M. Edd. *right-valiant*). Lr. I, 1, 99. Oth. II, 3, 25. Cymb. II, 4, 135 etc.

**Right,** vb. (used only in the inf.) to do justice to, to vindicate, to avenge: *being judge in love, she cannot r. her cause,* Ven. 220. *knights, by their oaths, should r. poor ladies' harms,* Lucr. 1694. *how much might the man deserve of me that would r. her,* Ado IV, 1, 264. *if he could r. himself with quarrelling,* V, 1, 51. *I will r. myself like a soldier,* LLL V, 2, 734. *you scarce can r. me throughly then to say you did mistake,* Wint. II, 1, 99. *whom the king hath wronged, whom conscience and my kindred bids to r.* R2 II, 2, 115. *here's to r. our gentle-hearted king,* H6C I, 4, 176. *so just is God, to r. the innocent,* R3 I, 3, 182. *your mother's hand shall*

*r. your mother's wrong,* Tit. II, 3, 121. *swear unto my soul to r. your wrongs,* III, 1, 279. *to join with him and r. his heinous wrongs,* V, 2, 4.

**Right-drawn,** drawn in a just cause: *what my tongue speaks my r. sword may prove,* R2 I, 1, 46.

**Righteous,** 1) just: *this shall ye do, so help you r. God,* H6A IV, 1, 8. *Rome and the r. heavens be my judge,* Tit. I, 426. *let me be recorded by the r. gods,* Tim. IV, 2, 4.

2) lawful, loyal, upright: *I love your daughter in such a r. fashion,* Wiv. III, 4, 83. *they should be good men, their affairs as r.* H8 III, 1, 22. *seal with a r. kiss a dateless bargain,* Rom. V, 3, 114.

**Righteously,** uprightly, honestly, genuinely: *if the truth of thy love to me were so r. tempered as mine is to thee,* As I, 2, 14.

**Rightful,** 1) just: *no r. plea might plead for justice there,* Lucr. 1649. *most r. judge,* Merch. IV, 1, 301. *whose r. cause prevails,* H6B II, 1, 205.

2) lawful, legitimate: *for the deposing of a r. king,* R2 V, 1, 50. *to put forth my r. hand in a well-hallowed cause,* H5 I, 2, 293. *to plant the r. heir,* H6A II, 5, 80. IV, 1, 60. H6B I, 3, 30. 187. II, 2, 24. 61. IV, 2, 139. V, 1, 178.

**Rightfully,** lawfully, legitimately: *which I'gainst all the world will r. maintain,* H4B IV, 5, 225.

**Right-hand file,** the Tory party, the aristocrats: Cor. II, 1, 26.

**Rightly,** 1) straightly, directly, in front: *perspectives, which r. gazed upon show nothing but confusion,* R2 II, 2, 18.

2) correctly, fitly, not erroneously: *the hardest voice of her behaviour, to be Englished r.* Wiv. I, 3, 52. *r. reasoned,* Ado V, 1, 229. *will never be chosen by any r.* Merch. I, 2, 35. *if I heard you r.* As V, 4, 186. *no Christian soul that means to be saved by believing r.* Tw. III, 2, 76. *choler, my lord, if r. taken,* H4A II, 4, 356. 357. *I am assured, if I be measured r., your majesty hath no just cause to hate me,* H4B V, 2, 65. *thy name is Gaultier, being r. sounded,* H6B IV, 1, 37. *few men r. temper with the stars,* H6C IV, 6, 29. *he tells you r.* H8 III, 1, 97. *that justly thinkest and hast most r. said,* Lr. I, 1, 186. *my parts, my title and my perfect soul shall manifest me r.* Oth. I, 2, 32.

3) truly, really: *they r. do inherit heaven's graces,* Sonn. 94, 5. *he it was that might r. say, Veni, vidi, vici,* LLL IV, 1, 68. *one who shall r. love,* Merch. I, 2, 36. *this thorn doth to our rose of youth r. belong,* All's I, 3, 136. *you may be r. just, whatever I shall think,* Mcb. IV, 3, 30. *r. to be great,* Hml. IV, 4, 53. *transform you from what you r. are,* Lr. I, 4, 243. *thou hast been r. honest,* Ant. IV, 2, 11.

4) exactly: *digest things r. touching the weal o' the common,* Cor. I, 1, 154. *if you consider r. of the matter,* Caes. III, 2, 114. *to-morrow I shall be furnished to inform you r.* Ant. I, 4, 77. *that I was shipped at sea, I well remember, but whether there delivered, I cannot r. say,* Per. III, 4, 8.

**Rigol,** a circle: *about the mourning and congealed face of that black blood a watery r. goes,* Lucr. 1745. *this golden r.* (the crown) H4B IV, 5, 36.

**Rigorous,** relentless: Err. I, 1, 9. Merch. IV, 1, 8. Cor. III, 1, 267.

**Rigorously,** relentlessly: H6A V, 4, 52.

**Rigour,** relentless severity, hard-heartedness, cruelty: *her best work is ruined with thy r.* Ven. 954.

*in Ajax' eyes blunt rage and r. rolled*, Lucr. 1398. *thou canst not then use r. in my gaol*, Sonn. 133, 12. *follows close the r. of the statute*, Meas. I, 4, 67. *'tis r. and not law*, Wint. III, 2, 115. *r. of tempestuous gusts*, H6A V, 5, 5. *let him have all the r. of the law*, H6B I, 3, 199. *fear of Clifford's r. who thunders to his captives blood and death*, H6C II, 1, 126. *let my life be sacrificed unto the r. of severest law*, Rom. V, 3, 269. *whom the r. of our state forced to cry out*, Lr. V, 1, 22.

**Rim**, the abdomen: *I will fetch thy r. out at thy throat*, H5 IV, 4, 15 (Pistol's speech. O. Edd. *rymme*).

**Rinaldo**, name in All's III, 4, 19. 29.

**Rind**, the skin of vegetables, bark, husk· As III, 2, 115. Rom. II, 3, 23.

**Ring**, subst. a circle: *like to the Garter's compass*, *in a r.* Wiv. V, 5, 70. *I'll fear no other thing so sore as keeping safe Nerissa's r.* Merch. V, 307 (quibbling). *ere twice the horses of the sun shall bring their fiery torcher his diurnal r.* All's II, 1, 165. *when that a r. of Greeks have hemmed thee in*, Troil. IV, 5, 193. *make a r. about the corpse*, Caes. III, 2, 162. 168. *like elves and fairies in a r.* Mcb. IV, 1, 42. *my father with his bleeding —s (the sockets of the eyes), their precious stones new lost*, Lr. V, 3, 189. *pray God, your voice, like a piece of uncurrent gold, be not cracked within the r.* Hml. II, 2, 448.\*

Especially the gold ornament worn on the fingers: Compl. 6. 45. Gent. IV, 4, 76. 90. 102. 136. 141. V, 4, 89. Wiv. III, 4, 104. Err. IV, 3, 69. 84. 96 etc. LLL V, 2, 616. Mids. I, 1, 33. Merch. III, 1, 123. III, 2, 173. 185. IV, 1, 427 etc. As III, 2, 289.\* Shr. Ind. 1, 38. II, 325. IV, 3, 55. All's III, 2, 59 etc. Tw. I, 5, 320 etc. Wint. V, 2, 71. R2 II, 2, 92. H4A III, 3, 162. R3 I, 2, 202. 204. H8 V, 1, 151 etc. Tit. II, 3, 227. Rom. III, 2, 142 etc. Hml. III, 2, 162. Lr. III, 1, 47. Cymb. I, 4, 98 etc. Per. V, 3, 39. Proverb: *he that runs fastest gets the r.* Shr. I, 1, 145 (a ring being one of the prizes given in running and wrestling matches).

**Ring**, vb. to encircle (cf. *Enring*): *and r. these fingers with thy household worms*, John III, 4, 31. *—ed about with bold adversity*, H6A IV, 4, 14.

**Ring**, vb. (impf. and partic. *rung*), 1) intr. to sound: *this dismal cry —s sadly in her ear*, Ven. 889. *thy old groans r. yet in mine ancient ears*, Rom. II, 3, 74. Used especially of the sound of metal, and more especially of bells: Lucr. 1494. Pilgr. 326. Meas. IV, 2, 78. Err. IV, 2, 51. Ado V, 2, 51. H4B IV, 5, 112. H6A I, 6, 11 (*r. out*). H6B V, 1, 3. Rom. IV, 4, 4. 2) trans. to cause to sound: *r. a hunter's peal*, Tit. II, 2, 5. 14. Especially applied to bells; absol.: *with —ing in the king's affairs upon his coronation-day*, H4B III, 2, 194. *thy friends shall r. for thee*, 198. With a superfluous *it*: *I'll r. it*, Shr. I, 2, 16 (punning upon *wring*). With an accus., denoting a) the bell set in motion: John II, 312. H6A III, 2, 16. Mcb. II, 3, 79. 85. V, 5, 51. Oth. II, 3, 160. b) the sound produced: *then little strength —s out the doleful knell*, Lucr. 1495. *my wether's bell —s doleful knell*, Pilgr. 272. Tp. I, 2, 402. Merch. III, 2, 70. H8 II, 1, 32. *hath rung night's yawning peal*, Mcb. III, 2, 43. c) the cause of sounding: *the Dauphin's drum, a warning bell, sings heavy music, and mine shall r. thy dire departure out*, H6A IV, 2, 41. *no mournful bell shall r. her burial*, Tit. V, 3, 197.

**Ring-carrier**, a go-between: All's III, 5, 95.

**Ringer**, writing of O. Edd. in Wiv. I, 2, 5 (Evans' speech); M. Edd. *wringer*.

**Ringleader**, the head of a factious body: H6B II, 1, 170.

**Ringlets**, small circles: Tp. V, 37. Mids. II, 1, 86.

**Ring-time**, the time of exchanging rings, of making love: *in the spring time, the only pretty r.* As V, 3, 20 (O. Edd. *rang time*).

**Ringwood**, name of a dog: *like Sir Actaeon he, with R. at thy heels*, Wiv. II, 1, 122.

**Rinse**, to cleanse with water: *like a glass did break i' the —ing*, H8 I, 1, 167 (O. Edd. *wrenching*).

**Riot**, 1) tumultuous disturbance of the peace: *the council shall hear it, it is a r.* Wiv. I, 1, 35. 36. 37. 39. *on the marriage-bed of smiling peace to march a bloody host and make a r. on the gentle brow of true sincerity*, John III, 1, 247. *my care could not withhold thy —s*, H4B IV, 5, 135. *breaking forth in rank and not to be endured —s*, Lr. I, 4, 223. II, 4, 145. 2) revel, wild and loose feasting, dissoluteness: Ven. 1147. Sonn. 41, 11. Wiv. III, 4, 8. Mids. V, 48. R2 II, 1, 33. H4A I, 1, 85. H4B IV, 4, 62. IV, 5, 136. V, 5, 66. H5 I, 1, 56. Tim. II, 2, 3. IV, 1, 28. IV, 3, 256. Per. I, 4, 54.

**Rioter**, one given to excessive feasting, a reveller: Tim. III, 5, 68.

**Rioting**, revelling: Ant. II, 2, 72.

**Riotous**, 1) tumultuous, seditious: *his r. youth, with dangerous sense, might have ta'en revenge*, Meas. IV, 4, 32. *shall it charm thy r. tongue*, H6B IV, 1, 64. *slew a r. gentleman*, R3 II, 1, 100. *Laertes, in a r. head, o'erbears your officers*, Hml. IV, 5, 101. *his knights grow r.* Lr. I, 3, 6. 2) dissolute: Tim. II, 2, 168. Lr. I, 4, 265. II, 1, 96. 3) excessive, knowing no restraint: *goes to it with a more r. appetite*, Lr. IV, 6, 125. *r. madness, to be entangled with those mouth-made vows*, Ant. I, 3, 29.

**Rip**, to cut open: *to know our enemies' minds, we'ld r. their hearts*, Lr. IV, 6, 265. *I must be —ed (like a garment)* Cymb. III, 4, 55. *I'll r. thy heart to find it*, III, 5, 86. With *up: —ing up the womb of your dear mother England*, John V, 2, 152. 2) to take out by cutting: *Macduff was from his mother's womb untimely —ed*, Mcb. V, 8, 16. Cymb. V, 4, 45.

**Ripe**, adj. brought to perfection in growth, mature: Sonn. I, 3. LLL IV, 2, 4. Mids. II, 2, 117. As III, 2, 127. IV, 3, 88. R2 II, 1, 153. H5 III, 6, 130. Cor. III, 2, 79. V, 4, 18. Oth. II, 3, 383. Used of lips (= full and red): Mids. III, 2, 139. As III, 5, 121. Lr. IV, 3, 22. Figurative use: Sonn. 86, 3. 102, 8. Tp. V, 279 (*reeling r.* = in a state of intoxication sufficiently advanced for reeling). Gent. II, 4, 70. Wiv. IV, 6, 43. Mids. V, 42 (*how many sports are r.*, i. e. in due preparation; Q2 Ff *rife*). Merch. I, 3, 64 (*the r. wants of my friend*, i. e. arrived at a point where they must be supplied). As V, 1, 22. Tw. V, 132 (*my thoughts are r. in mischief*). 157. Wint. I, 2, 332 (*without r. moving to it*). John IV, 2, 79. R2 I, 2, 7. II, 2, 10. H4A I, 3, 294. H4B IV, 5, 97. H5 I, 2, 121. R3 I, 3, 219. III, 7, 158 (*as my r. revenue and due of birth*). H8 IV, 2, 51. Troil. V, 5, 24. Cor. IV, 3, 23. Rom. I, 2, 11. Tim. IV, 1, 23. Caes. IV, 3, 215. Mcb. IV, 3, 238. Hml. IV, 7, 65. Per. Prol. 12. IV Prol. 17. cf. *Sinking-ripe*.

**Ripe,** vb. 1) tr. to make ripe, to mature: *no sun to r. the bloom,* John II, 472. *to r. his growing fortunes,* H4B IV, 1, 13.

2) to grow ripe, to be matured: *so I, being young, till now r. not to reason,* Mids. II, 2, 118. *stay the very —ing of the time,* Merch. II, 8, 40. *we r. and r.* As II, 7, 26.

**Ripely,** pressingly, urgently (the time being fully ripe): *it fits us therefore r. our chariots and our horsemen be in readiness,* Cymb. III, 5, 22.

**Ripen,** 1) trans. to make ripe, to mature; absol.: *summer's —ing breath,* Rom. II, 2, 121. With an obj.: R2 II, 3, 43. Tit. I, 227. Partic. *—ed:* Meas. V, 116. Ado III, 1, 8. H6A II, 4, 99. R3 II, 3, 14.

2) intr. to grow ripe, to be matured: R2 II, 3, 48. H4B IV, 2, 12. H5 I, 1, 61. H8 III, 2, 357. Ant. II, 7, 103.

**Ripeness,** maturity: H8 V, 5, 21. *r. is all,* Lr. V, 2, 11 (cf. *the readiness is all,* Hml. V, 2, 234).

**Ripe-red,** ripe and red: Ven. 1103.

**Rise,** subst. the appearance of the sun in the morning, the beginning of day: *the morning r. doth cite each moving sense from idle rest,* Pilgr. 194. *from the r. to set,* H5 IV, 1, 289.

**Rise,** vb. (impf. *rose;* partic. *risen*) 1) to ascend, to mount from a lower to a higher place: *round —ing hillocks,* Ven. 237; cf. *meet with me upon the —ing of the mountain-foot,* Gent. V, 2, 46. *flesh, —ing at thy name,* Sonn. 151, 9. (choughs) *—ing and cawing at the gun's report,* Mids. III, 2, 22. *r. from the ground like feathered Mercury,* H4A IV, 1, 106. *I will r. there with so full a glory* (like the sun) H5 I, 2, 278. *from the —ing of the lark to the lodging of the lamb,* III, 7, 34. *he —s on the toe* (in walking) Troil. IV, 5, 15. *a river of warm blood doth r. and fall between thy rosed lips,* Tit. II, 4, 24. *—s like the issue of a king,* Mcb. IV, 1, 87. *foul deeds will r., though all the earth o'erwhelm them, to men's eyes,* Hml. I, 2, 257. *like to groves, being topped, they higher r.* Per. I, 4, 9. Applied to the blood and sighs ascending, as it were, from the inner parts of the body: *how her fear did make her colour r.* Lucr. 257; cf. *the red wine first must r. in their fair cheeks,* H8 I, 4, 43. *with a —ing sigh,* H4A III, 1, 10. *stop the —ing of blood-sucking sighs,* H6C IV, 4, 22. Similarly: *my —ing heart,* Lr. II, 4, 122; cf. Lucr. 466. *my gorge —s at it,* Hml. V, 1, 207 (I am like to vomit).

2) to get up; from sitting: Pilgr. 56. Merch. II, 6, 8. R3 III, 4, 81. H8 IV, 1, 82. Cor. IV, 5, 250. Tim. I, 2, 132. Mcb. III, 4, 52. Hml. III, 2, 276. Ant. II, 7, 62. From kneeling: Err. V, 115. John I, 161. R2 V, 3, 32. 105. H4B IV, 5, 147. H6A III, 1, 172. 173. H6C II, 3, 35. R3 II, 1, 97. IV, 2, 80. Troil. V, 3, 42. Cor. V, 1, 66. Tit. I, 383. Lr. II, 4, 29. Oth. III, 3, 462. Ant. V, 2, 114. Cymb. V, 4, 106. Per. I, 2, 59. V, 1, 215. *to r. up:* R2 V, 2, 116. V, 3, 92. H6B IV, 2, 128. V, 1, 78. From lying: Ven. 480. 710. Lucr. 1281. Wiv. II, 2, 124. Meas. IV, 3, 23. 29. Ado III, 4, 2. As I, 3, 76. Shr. I, 2, 27. Wint. IV, 4, 106. H4A V, 4, 125. 128. 150. H5 IV, 1, 292. R3 III, 2, 31. Rom. III, 3, 89. Caes. II, 1, 234. Mcb. V, 1, 5. Hml. V, 2, 330. Oth. II, 1, 116. II, 3, 161. Ant. IV, 4, 20. *to r. up:* Lucr. 466. Mids. IV, 1, 137. Mcb. II, 3, 84. Hml. IV, 5, 52. From the dead: John III, 4, 86. H4A I, 3, 74. H6A I, 1, 64. Mcb. III, 4, 80. cf. H8 V, 5, 47 and Mcb. II, 3, 84. From any state of rest: *r., resty Muse,* Sonn. 100, 9.

*a holy prophetess new —n up,* H6A I, 4, 102. *early to-morrow will we r., and hence,* Caes. IV, 3, 230. *till the wood of Birnam r.* Mcb. IV, 1, 98. Applied to a beginning tempest: *now begins a second storm to r.* H6C III, 3, 47. To the sun appearing above the horizon: Wint. IV, 4, 105. Troil. I, 2, 8. V, 10, 25. Tit. V, 2, 56. Figuratively: *their —ing senses begin to chase the ignorant fumes* (as the sun does vapours) Tp. V, 66. *shall see us —ing in our throne, the east,* R2 III, 2, 50. cf. H5 I, 2, 278.

3) to increase: *the humour —s,* Wiv. I, 3, 63. *since the price of oats rose,* H4A II, 1, 14. *our griefs are —n to the top,* Per. II, 4, 23.

4) to thrive, to be promoted, to become great: *some r. by sin,* Meas. II, 1, 38. *it shall strew the footsteps of my —ing,* John I, 216. *that r. thus nimbly by a true king's fall,* R2 IV, 318. *fearing he would r.* H8 II, 2, 128. *found thee a way to r. in,* III, 2, 438. (the university of Oxford) *so excellent in art and still so —ing,* IV, 2, 62. *who's like to r.* Cor. I, 1, 196. *the younger —s, when the old doth fall,* Lr. III, 3, 26. *whose fortunes shall r. higher,* Ant. II, 3, 16. *this day I'll r.* Per. II, 1, 172.

5) to get up for action, to be ready for combat: *that, if it chance the one of us do fail, the other yet may r. against their force,* H6A II, 1, 32. *the scattered foe that hopes to r. again,* H6C II, 6, 93. Especially = to rebel: H4B I, 1, 204. H6B III, 1, 240. H6C I, 1, 141. I, 2, 41. 45. Cor. I, 1, 48. Caes. III, 2, 21. 234. Mcb. IV, 1, 97. With *up:* H6B IV, 1, 93.

**Rite,** solemn observance, ceremony: Tp. IV, 1, 17. Ado II, 1, 373. V, 4, 68. Mids. IV, 1, 138 (O. Edd. *right*). Merch. II, 9, 6. As V, 4, 203. Shr. III, 2, 6. John II, 539. R2 I, 1, 75. IV, 210 (Qq *duty's —s,* Ff *duteous oaths*). Tit. I, 78. 143. 337. V, 3, 196. Rom. V, 3, 20. Caes. III, 1, 241. V, 5, 77. Hml. IV, 5, 215. V, 1, 242. 255 (Qq *crants*). V, 2, 410. *to do a r.:* Ado IV, 1, 209. V, 3, 23. H4A V, 4, 98. H5 IV, 8, 127. Rom. III, 2, 8. *to perform the r.* Rom. II, 2, 146. Applied to the duties in the intercourse of love: *forget to say the perfect ceremony of love's r.* Sonn. 23, 6. *the great prerogative and r. of love,* All's II, 4, 42. *I must not yield to any —s of love,* H6A I, 2, 113 (O. Edd. *rights*). *God give us leisure for these —s of love,* R3 V, 3, 101. *to do their amorous —s,* Rom. III, 2, 8. *the —s for which I love him are bereft me,* Oth. I, 3, 258.

**Rivage,** the shore: *think you stand upon the r. and behold a city on the inconstant billows dancing,* H5 III Chor. 14.

**Rival,** subst. 1) competitor: Gent. II, 4, 174. IV, 4, 203 (fem.). Mids. III, 2, 155. 358. Shr. I, 1, 119. I, 2, 122. 142. Tim. I, 1, 72. Lr. I, 1, 47. Adjectively: *you are two r. enemies,* Mids. IV, 1, 147. *to hold a r. place with one of them,* Merch. I, 1, 174.

2) associate, companion: *and now both —s to mock Helena,* Mids. III, 2, 156. *Horatio and Marcellus, the —s of my watch,* Hml. I, 1, 13. cf. *Corrival* and *Rivality.*

**Rival,** vb. intr. to be competitor: *who with this king hath —ed for our daughter,* Lr. I, 1, 194.

**Rival-hating,** hating any competitor, jealous: *r. envy,* R2 I, 3, 131.

**Rivality,** copartnership, equality: *Caesar, having made use of him in the wars 'gainst Pompey, presently denied him r.* Ant. III, 5, 8.

**Rive,** 1) tr. to split, to cleave, to rend: *blunt wed-*

*ges r. hard knots*, Troil. I, 3, 316. *a bolt that should but r. an oak*, Cor. V, 3, 153. *when the scolding winds have —d the knotty oaks*, Caes. I, 3, 6. *Brutus hath —d my heart*, IV, 3, 85. *close pent-up guilts, r. your concealing continents*, Lr. III, 2, 58.

Hence applied to heavy discharges of artillery, which seem to burst the cannon: *to r. their dangerous artillery upon no Christian soul but English Talbot*, H6A IV, 2, 29.

2) intr. to be split: *when my heart, as wedged with a sigh, would r. in twain*, Troil. I, 1, 35. *the soul and body r. not more in parting than greatness going off*, Ant. IV, 13, 5.

**Rivelled**, corrugated, wrinkled: *the r. fee-simple of the tetter*, Troil. V, 1, 26.

**River**, a considerable land current of water: Ven. 71. 331. Compl. 38. Gent. II, 3, 58. Wiv. III, 1, 17. III, 5, 10. IV, 4, 22. Meas. I, 2, 91. Mids. II, 1, 91. John III, 1, 23. V, 7, 38. R2 III, 2, 107. H4A III, 1, 98. H4B IV, 4, 125. H5 III, 6, 180. IV, 7, 28. 29. 31. H6C IV, 8, 8. H8 III, 2, 198. Troil. III, 2, 56. Cor. I, 1, 139. Lr. I, 1, 66. Ant. II, 5, 10. Cymb. IV, 2, 36. With a name: *the r. Po*, John I, 203. *the r. Sala*, H5 I, 2, 63. *the r. Somme*, III, 5, 1. *the r. Styx*, Troil. V, 4, 20. With *of*: *upon the r. of Cydnus*, Ant. II, 2, 192. Used of streams of blood: Lucr. 1738. Tit. II, 4, 22. Of tears: *each cheek a r.* Compl. 283. *like —s of remorse*, John IV, 3, 110. *drewest —s from his eyes*, R3 I, 3, 176. *the fruitful r. in the eye*, Hml. I, 2, 80.

**Rivers**, name of the brother of Lady Grey: H6C IV, 4, 2. R3 I, 3, 93. 129. 210. 333. II, 1, 66 etc.

**Rivet**, subst. a pin of iron driven through a hole, to keep different pieces of armour together: *the armourers, with busy hammers closing —s up*, H5 IV Chor. 13. *with a palsy-fumbling at his gorget, shake in and out the r.* Troil. I, 3, 175. *I'll frush it and unlock the —s all*, V, 6, 29.

**Rivet**, vb. to fasten with rivets: *a thousand have on their —ed trim*, Ant. IV, 4, 22 (their armours). Metaphorically, = to fasten strongly: *—ed with faith unto your flesh*, Merch. V, 169. *I mine eyes will r. to his face*, Hml. III, 2, 90. *that's — ed, screwed to my memory*, Cymb. II, 2, 43.

**Rivo**, an exclamation used in Bacchanalian revelry (of uncertain origin): *r., says the drunkard*, H4A II, 4, 124.

**Road**, 1) a highway: Ado V, 2, 33. Merch. II, 9, 30. As II, 3, 33. H4A II, 1, 16. Cor. V, 1, 59. Per. IV, 5, 9. *this Doll Tearsheet should be some r. I warrant you, as common as the way between Saint Albans and London*, H4B II, 2, 183.

2) a roadstead; or rather a port, haven: *my father at the r. expects my coming*, Gent. I, 1, 53. *I must unto the r., to disembark some necessaries*, II, 4, 187.*post to the r.* Err. III, 2, 152. *peering in maps for ports and piers and —s*, Merch. I, 1, 19. *my ships are safely come to r.* V, 288. *an argosy that now is lying in Marseilles r.* Shr. II, 377.

3) a journey: *at last, with easy —s, he came to Leicester*, H8 IV, 2, 17.

4) inroad, incursion: *the Scot who will make r. upon us*, H5 I, 2, 138. *ready to make r. upon's again*, Cor. III, 1, 5.

**Road-way**, common highway: H4B II, 2, 63.

**Roam**, to wander without a certain direction, to

ramble, to rove: Err. I, 1, 134. Shr. Ind. 2, 59. Tw, II, 3, 40. H4B V, 3, 21. H6A III, 1, 51. With *on:* *shall the current of our right r. on? whose passage, vexed with thy impediment, shall leave his native channel*, John II, 335 (i. e. shall the current continue to overswell its banks, instead of remaining in its channel? The later Ff and some M. Edd. *run on*). With a superfluous *it: not to crack the wind of the poor phrase, —ing it thus*, Hml. I, 3, 109 (Qq *wrong it thus;* some M. Edd. *wronging*, others *wringing, ranging*, most *running*).*

**Roan**, ancient spelling of *Rouen*, q. v.

**Roan**, a dark dappled bay horse: H4A II, 3, 72. 73. *r. Barbary*, R2 V, 5, 78. *my r. horse*, H4A II, 4, 120.

**Roar**, subst. the full sound of a mighty deep voice: *put the wild waters in this r.* Tp. I, 2, 2. *the r. of a whole herd of lions*, II, 1, 315. *to set the table on a r.* (of laughter) Hml. V, 1, 211.

**Roar**, vb. to utter a deep mighty voice; used of lions: LLL IV, 1, 90. Mids. I, 2, 71. 72. 74. 75. 84. 85. V, 225. 270. 378. Merch. II, 1, 30 *(for prey)*. Shr. I, 2, 201. All's III, 2, 120. John II, 294. 459. H4A III, 3, 167. H6B III, 1, 19. Caes. I, 3, 74. Of bears: Mids. III, 1, 113. Wint III, 3, 103. H6C V, 7, 12. Rom. IV, 1, 80. Of bulls: H4B III, 2, 187. 189. Of cannon: H6A III, 3, 79. Of fire: Tp. I, 2, 204. Of tempests: John III, 4, 1. Lr. III, 2, 47; cf. H4B II, 4, 182 (*let the welkin r.;* Pistol's speech). Of the noise of waters, particularly the sea: Lucr. 1667. Tp. I, 2, 149 (*—ed to us*). V, 44. Merch. I, 1, 34. Wint. III, 3, 103. John II, 24. H4A I, 3, 192. H4B V, 5, 42. Rom. V, 3, 39. Caes. I, 2, 107. Hml. I, 4, 78. Lr. III, 4, 10 (Ff —*ing*, Qq *raging*). Cymb. III, 1, 20. V, 5, 295 (*r. to me*). Per. III, 3, 10. Of any thing frightful: *he had not apprehension of —ing terrors*, Cymb. IV, 2, 111. Of men, particularly in distress: Tp. I, 2, 370. IV, 193. 262. V, 233. Wint. III, 3, 101. 102. 103. H4A II, 2, 118. II, 4, 286 *(for mercy).* H8 V, 4, 7. Troil. V, 3, 83. V, 5, 37 (*—ing for Troilus*). Cor. II, 1, 85 *(for a chamber-pot).* II, 3, 59. Caes. I, 3, 74. Mcb. I, 7, 78. Lr. II, 3, 14. Oth. V, 2, 198. Ant. III, 2, 55. Per. III, 3, 10. Of devils: H4A I, 3, 125 *(for).* H5 IV, 4, 75. R3 IV, 4, 75. cf. —*ing Typhon*, Troil. I, 3, 160. *this torture should be —ed in dismal hell*, Rom. III, 2, 44 (i. e. proclaimed by the voice of devils). *what act, that —s so loud and thunders in the index?* Hml. III, 4, 52 (cries with the voice of hell).

Transitively: *r. these accusations forth*, H6A III, 1, 40; cf. above Rom. III, 2, 44. With an accus. denoting the effect: *he whined and —ed away your victory*, Cor. V, 6, 98. *they'll r. him in again*, IV, 6, 124.

**Roarer**, one that roars, a blusterer: Tp. I, 1, 18.

**Roast**, subst. in the phrase *to rule the r.* = to have the lead, to domineer: H6B I, 1, 109.

**Roast**, vb. to dress or cook by exposure to the fire: LLL V, 2, 935. Mids. II, 1, 48. H4A II, 4, 498. H4B II, 4, 361. Mcb. II, 3, 17. Oth. V, 2, 279. Ant. II, 2, 183. (Pyrrhus) *baked and impasted with the parching streets, ... —ed in wrath and fire*, Hml. II, 2, 483.

**Roast-meat**, roasted meat: Per. IV, 2, 26.

**Rob**, 1) to take away unlawfully; absol.: *I r.?* H4A I, 2, 153. *to r. in that thief's company*, II, 2, 10. 23. H4B IV, 5, 125. Troil. V, 3, 22. Oth. I, 1, 105. With *from: that sweet thief which sourly —s from me*, Sonn. 35, 14. Trans.: *he'll r. his bottle*, Tp. II, 2, 155. *the jewel of life was —ed*, John V, 1, 41. *conceit may* *r. the treasury of life*, Lr. IV, 6, 42. With *from: to r. love from any*, Ado I, 3, 31.

2) to take from, to strip unlawfully; absol.: *to watch like one that fears —ing*, Gent. II, 1, 26 (i. e. being robbed; cf. Ven. 321; Wiv. III, 3, 206; All's IV, 3, 127; H4A V, 1, 64 etc.). Trans.: *when the judge is —ed the prisoner dies*, Lucr. 1652. 838. Sonn. 68, 12. Tp. V, 272. Wiv. IV, 5, 17. Wint. IV, 3, 64. 90. John IV, 3, 78. R2 V, 3, 9. H4A I, 2, 182. 185. II, 2, 68. 99. II, 4, 77. 570. III, 3, 205. H5 III, 6, 106. H6B IV, 1, 109. IV, 10, 36. V, 1, 185. H8 II, 4, 146. Tim. IV, 3, 436. 440. 448. Caes. V, 1, 34. Oth. I, 1, 86. I, 3, 208. 209. III, 3, 342. Cymb. IV, 2, 15. *by the —ing of the banished duke*, R2 II, 1, 261. H6B IV, 8, 42 (cf. *Of*). With *from*, = to deprive of: *which —s my tongue from breathing native breath*, R2 I, 3, 173. With *of: to r. thee of a kiss*, Ven. 723. 1086. 1132. Sonn. 79, 8. 142, 8. Merch. II, 3, 3 (*didst r. it of some taste of tediousness*). As I, 3, 82. All's III, 2, 69. John I, 268. II, 3. R2 V, 2, 93. H4A III, 1, 105. V, 4, 77. H6B III, 1, 108. III, 2, 104. 217. H6C I, 4, 104. II, 1, 124. II, 3, 4. H8 III, 2, 255. Troil. I, 2, 19. IV, 1, 5. Cor. I, 1, 276. II, 1, 32. Tit. I, 207. II, 3, 179. V, 1, 41. Oth. III, 3, 160. Ant. IV, 14, 23. V, 1, 25. Cymb. IV, 2, 159. Per. II, 1, 51. IV, 1, 14. IV, 6, 122.

**Robber**, one who steals or plunders: R2 III, 2, 39. H5 IV, 1, 160. H6C I, 4, 64. II, 6, 22. Troil. IV, 4, 44. Tim. IV, 1, 11. Caes. IV, 3, 23. Lr. III, 7, 40. Cymb. IV, 2, 74.

**Robbery**, the act of robbing or pillaging: Sonn. 40, 9. 99, 11. Meas. II, 2, 176. H4A II, 4, 569. III, 3, 197. H4B I, 2, 69. H5 IV, 1, 175. Cor. V, 6, 89. Cymb. III, 3, 62.

**Robe**, any garment: *in these unreverent —s*, Shr. III, 2, 114. *that lion's r.* John II, 141. 142. *is not a buff jerkin a most sweet r. of durance?* H4A I, 2, 49. *our easy —s of peace*, V, 1, 12. *they* (our soldiers) *will be in fresher —s*, H5 IV, 3, 117. *a child that hath new —s*, Rom. III, 2, 30. *lest our old —s sit easier than our new*, Mcb. II, 4, 38. *like a giant's robe upon a dwarfish thief*, V, 2, 21. *when old —s are worn out*, Ant. I, 2, 171

= a splendid female gown: Wiv. IV, 4, 72. LLL IV, 1, 84. Wint. III, 3, 22. IV, 4, 134. John I, 217. H6B II, 4, 108. Rom. IV, 1, 110. Hml. II, 2, 530.

= a gown of state, a dress of dignity: Sonn. 52, 10. Meas. II, 2, 61. Shr. I, 2, 132. Wint. V, 2, 143. John IV, 2, 27. H4A III, 2, 56. III, 3, 37. H5 IV, 1, 279. H6A I, 1, 86. I, 3, 42. H8 III, 2, 453. Tit. I, 189. Caes. II, 2, 107. Mcb. I, 3, 109. Lr. IV, 6, 169. Ant. V, 2, 283. Per. V, 1, 224.

**Robed**, dressed in a gown of dignity: *thou r. man of justice*, Lr. III, 6, 38.

**Robert**, Christian name of 1) R. Faulconbridge in John I, 52. 80. 82. 139. 159 etc. 2) Sir R. Waterton: R2 II, 1, 284. 3) Sir R. Brakenbury: R3 V, 5, 14. 4) Justice Shallow: Wiv. I, 1, 4. 110. H4B III, 2, 63. IV, 3, 139. V, 1, 3. 67. V, 3, 128. V, 5, 5. 5) a servant of Mrs Ford's: Wiv. III, 3, 1. 10.

**Robin**, diminutive of *Robert*; name of 1) R. Hood, the celebrated outlaw: Gent. IV, 1, 36. As I, 1, 122. H4B V, 3, 107. 2) R. Goodfellow, alias Puck: Mids. II, 1, 34. III, 2, 355. IV, 1, 51. 85. V, 445. 3) of an imaginary person in love-songs: *hey, R., jolly R., tell me how thy lady does*, Tw. IV, 2, 78. *for bonny sweet*

*R. is all my joy*, Hml. IV, 5, 187. 4) of R. Starveling, the tailor: Mids. I, 2, 60. 62. 5) of the little page of Falstaff: Wiv. III, 3, 21. 6) of a servant of Mr Ford's: Wiv. III, 3, 4. 7) of some other persons: *since R. Ostler died*, H4A II, 1, 12. *had R. Nightwork by old Nightwork*, H4B III, 2, 222. *here, R., an if I die, I give thee my apron*, H6B II, 3, 74.

**Robin-redbreast**, the bird Sylvia rubecula: *to relish a love-song like a r.* Gent. II, 1, 21.

**Robustious**, stout, sturdy: *the men do sympathize with the mastiffs in r. and rough coming on*, H5 III, 7, 159. *to see a r. periwig-pated fellow tear a passion to tatters*, Hml. III, 2, 10.

**Rochester**, English town: H4A I, 2, 144.

**Rochford**, name in H8 I, 4, 93.*

**Rock**, subst. a large mass of stone: Lucr. 335. Sonn. 65, 7. Pilgr. 357. Tp. I, 2, 343. 361. II, 2, 138. 176. Gent. I, 2, 121. II, 4, 171. Err. I, 1, 102. Ado III, 1, 36. Mids. I, 2, 33. Merch. I, 1, 31. I, 3, 26. III, 2, 274. All's II, 1, 77. John II, 452. 458. H5 III, 1, 12. H6B III, 2, 91. 97. V, 1, 24. H6C II, 2, 5. V, 4, 10. 23. 27. 31. 36. H8 I, 1, 113. 158. Troil. III, 2, 84 (*eat —s*). Cor. III, 1, 213. 223. 266. III, 2, 3. III, 3, 75. 103. V, 2, 117. Tit. III, 1, 93. Rom. V, 3, 118. Caes. V, 5, 1. Mcb. III, 4, 22. Oth. I, 3, 141. II, 1, 69. Ant. IV, 14, 4. Cymb. III, 1, 20. 29. III, 3, 8. 70. IV, 2, 152. 163. V, 5, 262. Per. II, 1, 5.

**Rock**, vb. 1) tr. to move to and fro as in a cradle, to lull asleep: *my throbbing heart shall r. thee day and night*, Ven. 1186. *take hands with me and r. the ground whereon these sleepers be*, Mids. IV, 1, 91. *death r. me asleep*, H4B II, 4, 211. *r. his brains in cradle of the rude imperious surge*, III, 1, 19. *sleep r. thy brain*, Hml. III, 2, 237. *if drink r. not his cradle*, Oth. II, 3, 136.

2) intr. to shake, to tremble: *and then it* (her hand) *faster —ed*, Lucr. 262.

**Rocky**, consisting of rocks: *r. shore*, R2 II, 1, 62. *as firm as r. mountains*, H4B IV, 1, 188. Metaphorically, = hard, unfeeling: *thy r. and wreck-threatening heart*, Lucr. 590. Compl. 291. R3 IV, 4, 234.

**Rocky-hard**, = rocky: *thy sea-marge, sterile and r.* Tp. IV, 69 (in the rhyme).

**Rod**, (cf. *Riding-rod*), 1) the instrument of chastisement for children (or men compared with children): Meas. I, 3, 26. Ado II, 1, 227. 234. 236. Mids. III, 2, 410. H4A I, 3, 239. H4B IV, 1, 215. Cor. II, 3, 98. Tim. II, 2, 79. Lr. I, 4, 189. Ant. IV, 1, 3. *the r. of heaven*, H4A III, 2, 10. *to kiss the r.* = to show submission after chastisement: Gent. I, 2, 59. R2 V, 1, 32.

2) a kind of sceptre: *the Earl of Surrey with the r.* H8 IV, 1, 39. *the r. and bird of peace*, 89.

**Roderigo**, (O. Edd. *Rodorigo*), Italian name: Tw. II, 1, 17. Oth. I, 1, 57 and passim.

**Roe**, the animal Cervus capreolus: Ven. 561. 676. LLL V, 2, 309. Shr. Ind. 2, 50.

**Roe**, the spawn of fishes: Troil. V, 1, 68. Rom. II, 4, 39.

**Roger**, name of 1) R. Earl of March: H6B II, 2, 37. 38. H6C I, 1, 106. 2) R. Bolingbroke, the conjurer: H6B I, 2, 76.

**Rogero**, name in Wint. V, 2, 23.

**Rogue**, a term of reproach, = rascal, knave: Wiv. I, 3, 90. 93. II, 1, 146. 182. II, 2, 15. 26. 286. 290. III, 5, 9. Meas. IV, 3, 30. 46. LLL V, 2, 167. 173. Shr. Ind. 1, 2. 3. I, 1, 226. IV, 1, 147. V, 1, 49.

All's IV, 3, 153. 176. 179. 251. Tw. I, 5, 32. II, 5, 34. III, 4, 179. H4A I, 2, 210. II, 2, 16. II, 4, 137. H5 III, 6, 70. Cor. I, 1, 168. Rom. III, 1, 105. Caes. I, 2, 271. Oth. IV, 2, 131. Ant. II, 5, 73 etc. etc. Used in pity and tenderness: *you sweet little r.* H4B II, 4, 233. 235. *hear poor —s talk of court news,* Lr. V, 3, 13. In this case even a fem.: *alas, poor r., I think she loves me,* Oth. IV, 1, 112.

Perhaps = vagabond (which has been supposed by some etymologists to be the original signification): *having flown over many knavish professions, he settled only in r.* Wint. IV, 3, 106. *to hovel thee with swine and —s forlorn,* Lr. IV, 7, 39. cf. *Roguing.*

**Roguery,** knavery: H4A II, 4, 138. Troil. V, 2, 19.

**Roguing,** vagrant, roaming: *these r. thieves serve the great pirate Valdes,* Per. IV, 1, 97.

**Roguish,** the same: *get the Bedlam to lead him where he would; his r. madness allows itself to any thing,* Lr. III, 7, 104.

**Roisting,** bullying, blustering: *I have a r. challenge sent,* Troil. II, 2, 208.

**Roll,** subst. register, catalogue: H4A III, 1, 43. H4B III, 2, 106. Ant. V, 2, 181. *master o' the —s,* H8 V, 1, 35 (keeper of the patents that pass the great seal).

**Roll,** vb. 1) tr. a) to move in a circle, to turn round: *—ing his greedy eyeballs in his head,* Lucr. 368. b) to wrap round on itself, to form into a circular body: *the snake —ed in a flowering bank,* H6B III, 1, 228. Tit. II, 3, 13.

2) intr. a) to move circularly, by turning round on its axis: *stands upon the —ing restless stone,* H5 III, 6, 30. 38. *put this stone a —ing,* H8 V, 3, 104. Used of eyes: *the poet's eye, in a fine frenzy —ing,* Mids. V, 12. *makes fearful action with wrinkled brows, with nods, with —ing eyes,* John IV, 2, 192. *when your eyes r. so,* Oth. V, 2, 38.

b) to move in general; used of volumes of water: *deep woes r. forward like a gentle flood,* Lucr. 1118. And of eyes, = to look about: *in Ajax' eyes blunt rage and rigour —ed,* Lucr. 1398. *an eye more bright than theirs, less false in —ing,* Sonn. 20, 5. *varying in subjects as the eye doth r. to every varied object in his glance,* LLL V, 2, 774. *make his eyeballs r. with wonted sight,* Mids. III, 2, 369.

**Romage,** bustle, turmoil: *this post-haste and r. in the land,* Hml. I, 1, 107.

**Roman,** subst. a native of Rome: Lucr. 1811. 1828. 1854. H4B II, 2, 135. H5 III, 2, 87. Cor. I, 2, 14 etc. Tit. I, 9 etc. Caes. I, 2, 125 etc. Hml. V, 2, 352. Oth. IV, 1, 121. Ant. I, 5, 43 etc. Cymb. I, 1, 30 etc.

**Roman,** adj. pertaining to Rome: Lucr. Arg. 2. Lucr. 3. 51. 505. 1628. 1831. LLL V, 2, 617. Merch. III, 2, 297. As IV, 2, 4. Shr. II, 298. Tw. III, 4, 31 (*we do know the sweet R. hand;* i. e. Latin letters; cf. Tit. V, 1, 139). H5 III, 4, 37. III, 2, 77. H6B IV, 1, 135. Cor. I, 1, 71 etc. Tit. I, 22 etc. Caes. II, 1, 226 etc. Mcb. V, 8, 1. Hml. I, 1, 116. Ant. I, 2, 87 (*a R. thought,* i. e. a thought of Rome) etc. Cymb. III, 3, 57. IV, 2, 348 etc.

**Romano;** *Julio R.,* the celebrated Italian painter (and statuary?): Wint. V, 2, 106.*

**Rome,** (rhyming to *doom:* Lucr. 715; to *groom:* 1644; pronounced like *room:* John III, 1, 180. Caes. I, 2, 156. But cf. H6A III, 1, 51) the famous town in Italy: Lucr. Arg. 4. Lucr. 715. 1644. 1833 (fem.).

Meas. III, 2, 94. LLL V, 2, 719. Merch. IV, 1, 154. Shr. IV, 2, 75. John III, 1, 180. 194. 205. 207. V, 2, 70. 72. 92. 96. 97. H4B IV, 3, 45. H5 V Chor. 26. H6A I, 2, 56. III, 1, 51. H6B I, 3, 65. H8 II, 2, 94. 105. III, 2, 57. 90. 213. 313. 328. Cor. I, 1, 166. III, 3, 104 (*our R. gates; cf. Verona streets, Carthage queen, Tiber banks, Britain court* etc.). 110 (fem.) etc. Tit. I, 6 etc. Caes. I, 1, 38 etc. Hml. I, 1, 113. II, 2, 410. Ant. I, 1, 18 etc. Cymb. I, 1, 96 etc.

**Romeo,** name in Rom. I, 1, 123 etc.

**Romish,** Roman (in contempt): *as in a R. stew,* Cymb. I, 6, 152.

**Rondure** (cf. *Roundure*) circle: *all things rare that heaven's air in his huge r. hems,* Sonn. 21, 8.

**Ronyon,** a mangy creature: *you baggage, you polecat, you r.* Wiv. IV, 2, 195. *the rump-fed r.* Mcb. I, 3, 6.

**Rood,** the holy cross, crucifix: *by the r.!* H4B III, 2, 3. Rom. I, 3, 36. Hml. III, 4, 14. *by the holy r.* R3 III, 2, 77. IV, 4, 165.

**Roof,** 1) the upper part and cover of a house: Meas. I, 2, 47 (*under her r.*). Ado II, 1, 99. LLL II, 92. Tw. IV, 3, 25. R2 IV, 282. H5 I, 2, 198. H6A II, 3, 56. Cor. III, 1, 205. Lr. II, 4, 211. Cymb. III, 3, 2. 84. Per. II, 4, 36. = the skull, the head, in contempt: *thatch your poor thin —s with burthens of the dead,* Tim. IV, 3, 144.

2) the ceiling: *the r. o' the chamber,* Cymb. II, 4, 87; cf. III, 3, 2.

3) Pars pro toto, = the house: *seeking that beauteous r. to ruinate which to repair should be thy chief desire,* Sonn. 10, 7. *within this r. the enemy of all your graces lives,* As II, 3, 17.

4) the vault of heaven, the firmament: *this majestical r. fretted with golden fire,* Hml. II, 2, 313. *to the r. of heaven,* Ant. III, 6, 49. *he is entered his radiant r.* Cymb. V, 4, 121. cf. LLL II, 92.

5) the palate: *swearing till my very r. was dry,* Merch. III, 2, 206. *my tongue might freeze to the r. of my mouth,* Shr. IV, 1, 7. R2 V, 3, 31.

**Roofed,** being within a house: *here had we now our country's honour r.* Mcb. III, 4, 40.

**Rook,** subst. a kind of crow, Corvus frugilegus: LLL V, 2, 915. Mcb. III, 4, 125.

**Rook,** vb. to ruck, to cower: *the raven —ed her on the chimney's top,* H6C V, 6, 47 (= perched, roosted).

**Rooky,** full of crows: *the crow makes wing to the r. wood,* Mcb. III, 2, 51 (or = misty, gloomy?).

**Room,** 1) space, any measure of extent affording opportunity of being or moving in it: *if r. enough,* Tp. I, 1, 9.* H4A V, 4, 92. Caes. I, 2, 156. *there's no r. for faith in this bosom,* H4A III, 3, 174. H5 Epil. 3. H8 V, 4, 77. Ant. IV, 7, 10. *to give r.* All's I, 2, 67. Rom. I, 5, 28. Caes. IV, 3, 39. *to make r.* Ado II, 1, 88. Merch. IV, 1, 16. John I, 255. Elliptically: *r. for the incensed worthies,* LLL V, 2, 703. Mids. II, 1, 58. Caes. III, 2, 170. 172. V, 4, 16. *lawful let it be that I have r. with Rome to curse awhile,* John III, 1, 180 (= opportunity, liberty).

2) a confined space, apartment, chamber: Wiv. V, 5, 61. Meas. II, 1, 135. 219. Err. IV, 4, 97. Ado I, 3, 61. As III, 3, 15. Tw. III, 4, 148. Wint. II, 2, 47. R2 V, 6, 25. H4A II, 4, 2. H4B II, 4, 14. IV, 5, 4. 17. 83. H6C V, 6, 92. R3 I, 4, 161. Rom. I, 5, 30. Tim. II, 2, 169. Hml. III, 4, 212. V, 2, 16. Oth. V, 2, 330.

3) place occupied or to be occupied: *your praise shall still find r. even in the eyes of all posterity*, Sonn. 55, 10 (= shall find a place, shall dwell). *in their —s come delicate desires*, Ado I, 1, 304. *let Bianca take her sister's r.* Shr. III, 2, 252. *grief fills the r. up of my absent child*, John III, 4, 93. *fill another r. in hell*, R2 V, 5, 108. *to fill up the —s of them*, H4A IV, 2, 35. *let this supply the r.* H6C II, 6, 54. *to take their —s, ere I can place myself*, III, 2, 132.

**Roost**, in *Unroosted*, q. v.

**Root**, subst. that part of a plant by which it is supported and nourished: Lucr. 665. 823. As II, 1, 31. R2 I, 2, 13. 18. III, 4, 52. H5 II, 4, 39. H6C III, 3, 125. R3 II, 2, 41. H8 I, 2, 97. III, 2, 357. Mcb. IV, 1, 25. 95. Oth. III, 3, 423. Cymb. IV, 2, 60. Per. I, 2, 30. *to take r.* = to become planted and fixed: *we should take r. here where we sit, or sit state-statues only*, H8 I, 2, 87. = to grow and thrive: Lucr. 870. Ado I, 3, 25. *to pluck* or *hew up by the r.* H6C V, 4, 69; cf. Troil. IV, 4, 56 and Oth. III, 3, 423. *—s used for food*: Tp. I, 2, 463. Wiv. IV, 1, 56. Tit. IV, 2, 177. Tim. I, 2, 72. 140. IV, 3, 23. 186. 192. 420. V, 1, 77. Mcb. I, 3, 84 (cf. *Insane*). Cymb. IV, 2, 48. Per. IV, 6, 93. Metaphorical use: *to the r. o' the tongue*, Tim. V, 1, 136. *how oft hast thou with perjury cleft the r.*, Gent. V, 4, 103 (of the heart). *my heart will be blown up by the r.* Troil. IV, 4, 56. *a curse begin at very r. on's heart*, Cor. II, 1, 202. *a grief that smites my very heart at r.* Ant. V, 2, 105. *spring crestless yeomen from so deep a r.?* H6A II, 4, 85. *the r. and father of many kings*, Mcb. III, 1, 5. *I cannot delve him to the r.* Cymb. I, 1, 28. *we set the axe to thy usurping r.* H6C II, 2, 165. II, 6, 49. *grows with more pernicious r. than lust*, Mcb. IV, 3, 85. *remove the r. of his opinion*, Wint. II, 3, 89. *hath weeded from my heart a r. of ancient envy*, Cor. IV, 5, 109. *rape was the r. of thine annoy*, Tit. IV, 1, 49.

**Root**, vb. 1) intr. to take root, to grow: *there —ed betwixt them such an affection*, Wint. I, 1, 25. *which should not find a ground to r. upon*, H4B III, 1, 91. *her fallow leas the darnel ... doth r. upon*, H5 V, 2, 46. *the grove of sycamore that westward —eth from the city's side*, Rom. I, 1, 129.

2) trans. a) to plant, to make to grow: *r. pity in thy heart*, Sonn. 142, 11. *lest the base earth ... disdain to r. the summer-swelling flower*, Gent. II, 4, 162. Refl. = to grow: *the fat weed that —s itself in ease on Lethe wharf*, Hml. I, 5, 33 (Ff *rots*). Partic. *—ed* = planted deeply, fixed in the heart: *a more —ed love*, All's IV, 5, 13. *thy truth and thy integrity are —ed in us*, H8 V, 1, 115. *a —ed sorrow*, Mcb. V, 3, 41. *if your affiance were deeply —ed*, Cymb. I, 6, 164. *grief and patience, —ed in him both, mingle their spurs together*, IV, 2, 57.

b) to turn up the ground, to dig as swine do: *would r. these beauties as he —s the mead*, Ven. 636. *—ing hog*, R3 I, 3, 228. With *away*, *out*, and *up*, — to unroot, to extirpate, to exterminate: *I will go r. away the noisome weeds*, R2 III, 4, 37. *to r. out the whole hated family*, Lucr. Arg. 22. *broils r. out the work of masonry*, Sonn. 55, 6. H6C I, 3, 32. H8 V, 1, 53. Per. V, 1, 93. *I'll plant Plantagenet, r. him up who dares*, H6C I, 1, 48. *who, like a boar, doth r. up his country's peace*, Tim. V, 1, 168.

**Rootedly**, fixedly, inveterately, from the heart: *they all do hate him as r. as I*, Tp. III, 2, 103.

**Rope**, cord, halter, cable: *we will not hand a r. more*, Tp. I, 1, 25. *the r. of his destiny*, 33 (= halter). *buy a —'s end* Err. IV, 1, 16 (for flogging). 20. 21. 96. 98. IV, 4, 12. 16. 45. 94. H6A I, 3, 53. Rom. III, 2, 132. Per. IV, 1, 55. Unintelligible: *I see that men make —s in such a scarre that we'll forsake ourselves*, All's IV, 2, 38.

**Rope-maker**, one who makes cordage: Err. IV, 4, 93.

**Ropery**, the nurse's word for *roguery*, perhaps unintentionally alluding to the halter: Rom. II, 4, 154.

**Rope-tricks**, tricks deserving the halter; Grumio's word for *rhetoric*: Shr. I, 2, 112.

**Roping**, running down and concreting, hanging down (cf. *Down-roping*): *let us not hang like r. icicles upon our houses' thatch*, H5 III, 5, 23.

**Rosalind**, female name in As I, 1, 110 etc.

**Rosalinda**, the same: As III, 2, 145 (in a verse).

**Rosaline**, female name in LLL II, 210. III, 168. IV, 1, 53. 107. IV, 3, 221. V, 2, 30. 130. 442. Rom. I, 2, 72. 88. II, 1, 17. II, 3, 44 etc.

**Roscius**, the most celebrated actor of ancient Rome: *what scene of death hath R. now to act?* H6C V, 6, 10. *when R. was an actor in Rome*, Hml. II, 2, 410.

**Rose**, the flower Rosa: Ven. 10. 574. 590. 936. Lucr. 71. 258. 479. 492. Sonn. 35, 2. 54, 3. 6. 11. 95, 2. 98, 10. 130, 5. Pilgr. 131. Wiv. III, 1, 19. Ado I, 3, 29. LLL I, 1, 105. IV, 3, 27. V, 2, 293. 295. 297. Mids. I, 1, 76. II, 1, 108. III, 1, 96. As III, 2, 117. Shr. II, 174. All's IV, 2, 18. Tw. II, 4, 39. III, 1, 161. Wint. IV, 4, 222. John III, 1, 54. R2 V, 1, 8. H4A I, 3, 175. H4B II, 4, 28. R3 IV, 3, 12. Rom. II, 2, 43. Oth. V, 2, 13. Ant. III, 13, 39. Per. IV, 6, 38. V Prol. 7. Worn in the ears: John I, 142 (cf. *Three-farthings*). on the shoes: Hml. III, 2, 288. *cakes of —s*: Rom. V, 1, 47. A red and a white r. the badges of the houses of Lancaster and York: H6A II, 4, 30. 33 etc. IV, 1, 91. 152. H6B I, 1, 254. H6C I, 2, 33. II, 5, 97. 101. R3 V, 5, 19. Denoting a florid complexion, red cheeks: *why should poor beauty indirectly seek —s of shadow* (i. e. painting), *since his r. is true*, Sonn. 67, 8. 130, 6. Compl. 286. Gent. IV, 4, 159. Meas. I, 4, 16. Mids. I, 1, 129. Rom. IV, 1, 99. Symbol of youth and beauty: *that beauty's r. might never die*, Sonn. 1, 2. *our r. of youth*, All's I, 3, 136. *the expectancy and r. of the fair state*, Hml. III, 1, 160. *takes off the r. from the fair forehead of an innocent love*, III, 4, 42. *he wears the r. of youth upon him*, Ant. III, 13, 20 (cf. Wint. IV, 4, 115). Fond compellation: *save thou, my r.* Sonn. 109, 14. *my sweet R., my dear R.* As I, 2, 24. *O r. of May, dear maid*, Hml. IV, 5, 157. cf. R2 V, 1, 8 and H4A I, 3, 175.

Name of a house: *the duke being at the R., within the parish Saint Lawrence Poultney*, H8 I, 2, 152.*

**Rose-cheeked**, having red cheeks: Ven. 3. Tim. IV, 3, 86.

**Rosed**, crimsoned, red: *a maid yet r. over with the virgin crimson of modesty*, H5 V, 2, 323. *thy r. lips*, Tit. II, 4, 24.

**Rose-lipped**, having red lips: Oth. IV, 2, 63.

**Rosemary**, the plant Rosmarinus: Lr. II, 3, 16. *my dish of chastity with r. and bays*, Per. IV, 6, 160 ("Anciently many dishes were served up with this garniture, during the season of Christmas". Steevens). Symbol of remembrance, particularly used at weddings and funerals: *for you there's r. and rue, ... grace and* *remembrance be to you both*, Wint. IV, 4, 74. *doth not r. and Romeo begin both with a letter?* Rom. II, 4, 219. *she hath the prettiest sententious of it, of you and r.* 226. *stick your r. on this fair corse*, IV, 5, 79. *there's r., that's for remembrance*, Hml. IV, 5, 175.

**Rosencrantz,** (Ff *Rosincrance* or *Rosincrane*, Qq *Rosencraus*), name in Hml. II, 2, 1. 33. 34. 229. IV, 6, 28. V, 2, 56. 382.

**Rose-water,** water distilled from roses: Shr. Ind. 1, 56.

**Rosse,** name: R2 II, 2, 54. II, 3, 10. Mcb. I, 2, 45.

**Rossill,** name in H4A I, 2, 182; M. Edd. *Peto.*

**Rosy,** resembling a rose, blooming, red: Lucr. 386. Sonn. 116, 9. Cymb. II, 5, 11. V, 5, 121.

**Rot,** subst. putrefaction: *I will not kiss thee; then the r. returns to thine own lips again,* Tim. IV, 3, 64.

**Rot,** vb. (impf. not used; partic. — *ed:* Lucr. 823. Mids. II, 1, 95. Tit. IV, 4, 93. ordinarily *rotten*) 1) tr. to make putrid, to bring to corruption: *I would my tongue could r. them* (your hands) *off,* Tim. IV, 3, 370. Refl. = to become putrid: *the fat weed that — s itself in ease on Lethe wharf,* Hml. I, 5, 33 (Qq *roots*). *like to a vagabond flag upon a stream, goes to and back to r. itself with motion,* Ant. I, 4, 47. = to confound, to destroy in general: *the other* (a sheep) *—ed with delicious food* (honey-stalks) Tit. IV, 4, 93. *vengeance r. you all,* Tit. V, 1, 58. *the south-fog r. him,* Cymb. II, 3, 136.

Partic. —*en* = a) putrid, corrupted, decayed: —*en death,* Lucr. 1767. *when I in earth am —en,* Sonn. 81, 2. *a —en carcass of a butt,* Tp. I, 2, 146. —*en lungs,* II, 1, 47. *a jealous —en bell-wether,* Wiv. III, 5, 111. Meas. IV, 3, 184. Ado IV, 1, 33. LLL V, 2, 666. Merch. I, 3, 102. As III, 2, 126. Shr. I, 1, 139. All's IV, 3, 189. Wint. II, 3, 89. III, 3, 82. John II, 456. H5 III, 7, 155. H6C I, 3, 28. R3 IV, 4, 2. Troil. V, 1, 21. Rom. V, 3, 47. Cor. V, 6, 96 (—*en silk*). Hml. V, 1, 180. Lr. V, 3, 285. Ant. III, 7, 63. Per. IV, 2, 9. Used of unwholesome vapours: —*en damps,* Lucr. 778. *their —en smoke,* Sonn. 34, 4. —*en dews,* Cor. II, 3, 35. *reek o' the —en fens,* III, 3, 121. —*en humidity,* Tim. IV, 3, 2. b) unsound, corrupt, perverse: —*en parchment bonds,* R2 II, 1, 64. *base and —en policy,* H4A I, 3, 108. *a —en case abides no handling,* H4B IV, 1, 161. *the unguided days and —en times that you shall look upon,* IV, 4, 60. *to raze out —en opinion who hath writ me down after my seeming,* V, 2, 128. *their —en privilege and custom,* Cor. I, 10, 23. *hence, —en thing,* III, 1, 179. *something is —en in the state of Denmark,* Hml. I, 4, 90.

2) intr. to be decomposed and corrupted, to putrify: *to lie in cold obstruction and to r.* Meas. III, 1, 119. *the green corn hath —ed ere his youth attained a beard,* Mids. II, 1, 95. *festered members r. but by degrees,* H6A III, 1, 192. Troil. II, 3, 130. Hml. V, 1, 179. Lr. V, 2, 8. Cymb. IV, 2, 246. Used in cursing: *go r.* Wint. I, 2, 324. *may my hands r. off,* R2 IV, 49. *thy lips r. off,* Tim. IV, 3, 63. *let her r. and perish,* Oth. IV, 1, 191. *may his pernicious soul r. half a grain a day,* V, 2, 156. *their tongues r.* Ant. III, 7, 16.

Applied to plants, = to fade, to wither: *flowers r. and consume themselves in little time,* Ven. 132. *the branches of another root are —ed,* Lucr. 823. *shall thy love-springs r.?* Err. III, 2, 3. *thou prunest a —en tree,* As II, 3, 63. *from hour to hour we ripe and ripe, and then, from hour to hour, we r. and r.* II, 7, 27.

**Rote;** *by r.* = by heart, by memory, without book: *rehearse your song by r.* Mids. V, 404. *they will learn you by r. where services were done,* H5 III, 6, 75. *thy love did read by r. and could not spell,* Rom. II, 3, 88 (consisted of phrases learned by heart, but knew nothing of the true characters of love). *conned by r.* Caes. IV, 3, 98.

**Roted,** learned by heart, not coming from the heart: *nor by the matter which your heart prompts you, but with such words that are but r. in your tongue,* Cor. III, 2, 55 (O. Edd. *roated,* some M. Edd. *rooted*).

**Rother,** an ox; only by conjecture in Tim. IV, 3, 12; O. Edd. *brother's.*

**Rotten,** see *Rot.*

**Rottenness,** putrefaction: John III, 4, 26. Cymb. I, 6, 125.

**Rotundity,** roundness, spherical form: Lr. III, 2, 7.

**Rouen** (O. Edd. *Roan*), town in Normandy: H5 III, 5, 54. 64. H6A I, 1, 65. III, 2, 1. 11. 17. 19. 27. 91. 124 (fem.). 133. III, 3, 2.

**Rougemont,** name of the castle of Exeter: R3 IV, 2, 108.

**Rough,** 1) rugged, not smooth: *r. uneven ways,* R2 II, 3, 4. *r. cradle,* R3 IV, 1, 101. *r. quarries,* Oth. I, 3, 141. = thorny: *brakes obscure and r.* Ven. 237. *r. thistles,* H5 V, 2, 52. *the r. brake that virtue must go through,* H8 I, 2, 75. = hairy, shaggy: *till new-born chins be r.* Tp. II, 1, 250. *thou wantest a r. pash,* Wint. I, 2, 128. *you are r. and hairy,* IV, 4, 744. *his beard made r. and rugged,* H6B III, 2, 175. Figuratively: *beauty's princely majesty is such, confounds the tongue and makes the senses r.* H6A V, 3, 71 (disturbs them like a troubled water, ruffles them).

2) harsh and grating to the senses: *r. winter,* Lucr. 1255. *r. winds do shake the buds of May,* Sonn. 18, 3. *make r. winter,* Gent. II, 4, 163. *r. weather,* As II, 5, 8. *a lullaby too r.* Wint. III, 3, 55. *we shall be winnowed with so r. a wind,* H4B IV, 1, 194. H6C V, 4, 22. *that r. touch,* Rom. I, 5, 98. *time and the hour runs through the —est day,* Mcb. I, 3, 147. *'twas a r. night,* II, 3, 66. *the tyranny of the open night's too r. for nature to endure,* Lr. III, 4, 2. *the r. seams of the waters,* Per. II, 1, 155. = grating to the taste, sour, bitter: *thy palate then did deign the —est berry,* Ant. I, 4, 64. *to the ear: the r. and woeful music that we have, cause it to sound,* Per. III, 2, 88 (?).

3) harsh, not soft and gentle, but rugged of temper and manners: *this r. magic I here abjure,* Tp. V, 50. *ill-favoured r. things,* Wiv. I, 1, 311. *she's too r. for me,* Shr. I, 1, 55. I, 2, 73. *I am r. and woo not like a babe,* II, 138. 245. *in these parts, which to a stranger often prove r. and unhospitable,* Tw. III, 3, 11. *the grappling vigour and r. frown of war,* John III, 1, 104. *what need you be so boisterous r.* IV, 1, 76. *r. chastisement,* R2 I, 1, 106. *so r. a course to come by her own,* H4B II, 1, 89. *in robustious and r. coming on,* H5 III, 7, 159. *our tongue is r.* V, 2, 313. *Suffolk's imperial tongue is stern and r.* H6B IV, 1, 121. *be not too r. in terms,* IV, 9, 44. *you have been too r.* Cor. III, 2, 25. *his nature, never known before but to be r., unswayable and free,* V, 6, 26. *do not take his —er accents for malicious sounds,* III, 3, 55. *my so r. usage,* Cymb. IV, 1, 22. Adverbially: *so I did* (reprehend him). *Ay, but not r. enough,* Err. V, 58.

4) not mild and peaceful, but stern and requiring

energy and severity: *had a —er task in hand*, Ado I, 1, 301. *give even way unto my r. affairs*, H4B II, 3, 2. *enforced by the r. torrent of occasion*, IV, 1, 72.

5) hard, unfeeling, cruel: *the r. beast that knows no gentle right*, Lucr. 545. *a fiend, a fury, pitiless and r.* Err. IV, 2, 35. *brassy bosoms and r. hearts of flint*, Merch. IV, 1, 31. *the fleshed soldier, r. and hard of heart*, H5 III, 3, 11. *r. deeds of rage*, H6A IV, 7, 8. *stern, obdurate, flinty, r., remorseless*, H6C I, 4, 142. Ven. 884. Mids. V, 225. As I, 2, 253. All's V, 3, 107. Tw. III, 4, 124. R2 III, 2, 54. H6C I, 4, 27. II, 1, 63. Rom. I, 1, 176. I, 4, 25. 27. Tim. IV, 3, 446. Lr. I, 2, 142. Per. II, 1, 137. II, 3, 84. III, 2, 79.

6) unpolished, rude, gross, coarse: *their r. carriage so ridiculous*, LLL V, 2, 306. *if it be not too r. for some*, Wint. IV, 4, 337. *those r. rug-headed kerns*, R2 II, 1, 156. *with r. and all unable pen*, H5 Epil. 1. *I have, in this r. work, shaped out a man*, Tim. I, 1, 44.

7) wild, boisterous: *he hath rid his prologue like a r. colt*, Mids. V, 119. *as r., their royal blood enchafed, as the rudest wind*, Cymb. IV, 2, 173.

**Rough-cast,** a kind of plaster mixed with pebbles: Mids. III, 1, 71. V, 132. 162.

**Rough-grown,** grown so as to have a surface rough and full of inequalities: *in men, as in a r. grove, remain cave-keeping evils that obscurely sleep*, Lucr. 1249.

**Rough-hew,** to give the first rude form to: *there's a divinity that shapes our ends, r. them how we will*, Hml. V, 2, 11.

**Roughly,** harshly, rudely: Err. V, 59. 88 (*r., rude and wildly;* the suffix *ly* belonging to all the three words). Tw. III, 4, 124. H4B V, 2, 70. Troil. IV, 4, 36. Hml. I, 2, 142. V, 2, 243.

**Roughness,** harshness, asperity: *doth affect a saucy r.* Lr. II, 2, 103.

**Round,** adj. 1) circular: *r. enchanting pits*, Ven. 247. *a great r. beard*, Wiv. I, 4, 20. *at the r. table*, H4B II, 1, 95. *the r. nave*, Hml. II, 2, 518. *her face ... is't long or r.?* Ant. III, 3, 32. 33.

2) spherical: *r. rising hillocks* (the breasts) Ven. 237; cf. Lucr. 441. *these six dry, r., old, withered knights* (viz apple-johns) H4B II, 4, 8. *a r. little worm*, Rom. I, 4, 65. *the r. world*, Ant. V, 1, 15. Used of tears, drops of blood, and pearls: Ven. 1170. Lucr. 1553. Mids. IV, 1, 59. As II, 1, 38.

3) big, bulky (of things); corpulent, fleshy, plump (of men and animals): *a r. hose*, Gent. II, 7, 55. *he bought his r. hose in France*, Merch. I, 2, 80 (round swelling breeches, trunk hose). *I'll wear a boot, to make it* (my leg) *somewhat —er*, Gent. V, 2, 6. *their r. haunches*, As II, 1, 25. *the justice, in fair r. belly*, II, 7, 154. H4B I, 2, 212. *you whoreson r. man*, H4A II, 4, 155 (Qq round-man).

4) full, large: *'tis a good r. sum*, Merch. I, 3, 104. *I'll on your heads clap r. fines*, H8 V, 4, 84.

5) plain, fair, honest: *I will a r. unvarnished tale deliver*, Oth. I, 3, 90. *but in our orbs we'll live so r. and safe*, Per. I, 2, 122 (*teres atque rotundus*). Particularly = plain-spoken, unceremonious: *your reproof is something too r.* H5 IV, 1, 216. *to be round with =* to speak freely with: *am I so r. with you as you with me, that like a foot-ball you do spurn me thus*, Err. II, 1, 82. *I must be r. with you*, Tw. II, 3, 102. Tim. II, 2, 8. Hml. III, 1, 191. III, 4, 5. *he answered me in the —est manner he would not*, Lr. I, 4, 58.

**Round,** subst. 1) a circle: *fairest mover on this mortal r.* Ven. 368. *turn the giddy r. of Fortune's wheel*, Lucr. 952. *with —s of waxen tapers on their heads*, Wiv. IV, 4, 50. *the golden r.* (the crown) Mcb. I, 5, 29. *wears upon his baby-brow the r. and top of sovereignty*, IV, 1, 88.

2) performance in a circle: *I'll lead you about a r.* Mids. III, 1, 109. = a dance in a circle: *if you will patiently dance in our r.* Mids. II, 1, 140. *while you perform your antic r.* Mcb. IV, 1, 130. Used of a curveting horse: *what —s, what bounds, what course, what stop he makes*, Compl. 109.

3) the step of a ladder: *when he once attains the upmost r.* Caes. II, 1, 24.

**Round,** adv. 1) circularly; a) turning on the axis: *he that is giddy thinks the world turns r.* Shr. V, 2, 20. *I am giddy, expectation whirls me r.* Troil. III, 2, 19. *cup us till the world go r.* Ant. II, 7, 124. *does the world go r.?* Cymb. V, 5, 232. b) standing or moving in an orb: *nineteen zodiacs have gone r.* Meas. I, 2, 172. *a health! let it go r.* H8 I, 4, 97. Tim. I, 2, 54. *time is come r.* Caes. V, 3, 23. Followed by *about*: Lucr. 1586. Wiv. IV, 4, 31. V, 5, 79. 83. Meas. III, 1, 125. Ado V, 3, 15. Mids. II, 1, 175. Tit. III, 1, 123. Mcb. IV, 1, 4.

2) on every side, or in every direction: *r. underborne with a bluish tinsel*, Ado III, 4, 21. *hang it r. with all my wanton pictures*, Shr. Ind. 1, 47. *r. encompassed*, H6A I, 1, 114. *r. engirt with misery*, H6B III, 1, 200. V, 1, 99. H6C II, 1, 15. III, 2, 171. Caes. III, 2, 168. Hml. V, 2, 239. Oth. II, 1, 87. Per. III Prol. 35 (*the regions r.*). *r. about: empale him with your weapons r. about*, Troil. V, 7, 5. Caes. V, 3, 28. Oth. III, 3, 464. *the noise is r. about us*, Cymb. IV, 4, 1.

3) in every part, everywhere within a certain locality: *she throws her eyes about the painting r.* Lucr. 1499. *water once a day her chamber r. with eye-offending brine*, Tw. I, 1, 29. Followed by *about*: *the gentle day ... r. about dapples the drowsy east with spots of grey*, Ado V, 3, 26. *a scroll, and written r. about*, Tit. IV, 2, 18. *proclaim it r. about the city*, Meas. V, 514. *look r. about the wicked streets of Rome*, Tit. V, 2, 98.

4) roundly, straightforwardly and without much ceremony: *I went r. to work*, Hml. II, 2, 139.

**Round,** prepos. circularly about: *gone r. Neptune's salt wash and Tellus' orbed ground*, Hml. III, 2, 165. Following its noun: *we'll drink a measure the table r.* Mcb. III, 4, 12. = on every side, about: *skirr the country r.* Mcb. V, 3, 35.

**Round,** vb. 1) tr. to surround, to encompass: *she his hairy temples then had —ed with coronet of fresh and fragrant flowers*, Mids. IV, 1, 56. *the may-coloured Iris —s thine eye*, All's I, 3, 158. *the hollow crown that —s the mortal temples of a king*, R2 III, 2, 161. R3 IV, 1, 60. *—ed in with danger*, Troil. I, 3, 196. Peculiar passage: *we are such stuff as dreams are made on, and our little life is —ed with a sleep*, Tp. IV, 158 (the whole round or course of life has its beginning and end in a sleep, is nothing but a sleep. cf. Caes. V, 3, 23).

2) intr. to become round, to grow big: *the queen —s apace*, Wint. II, 1, 16.

**Round,** vb. to whisper: *to r. me i' the ear*, Pilgr. 349. *whispering, —ing 'Sicilia is a so-forth'*, Wint. I, 2, 217. *France, —ed in the ear with that same purpose-changer*, John II, 566.

**Roundel,** a dance in a circle: *now a r. and a fairy song,* Mids. II, 2, 1.

**Round-hoofed,** having round hoofs: Ven. 295.

**Roundly,** straightforwardly, without much ceremony: *shall we clap into't r., without hawking or spitting or saying we are hoarse?* As V, 3, 11. *shall I then come r. to thee and wish thee to a shrewd ill-favoured wife?* Shr. I, 2, 59. *that take it on you at the first so r.* III, 2, 216. *I'll r. go about her,* IV, 4, 108. *r. replied,* V, 2, 21. *this tongue that runs so r. in thy head,* R2 II, 1, 122. *come, r., r.* H4A I, 2, 24. *I would have done any thing indeed too, and r. too,* H4B III, 2, 21. *and fell so r. to a large confession, to angle for your thoughts,* Troil. III, 2, 161.

**Round-man,** a corpulent man; writing of Qq in H4A II, 4, 155; Ff and M. Edd. without the hyphen.

**Roundure** (cf. *Rondure*) round, circle: *'tis not the r. of your old-faced walls can hide you from our messengers of war,* John III, 259.

**Round-wombed,** big, with child: Lr. I, 1, 14.

**Rouse,** subst. free and copious drinking, a full measure of liquor: *the king's r. the heavens shall bruit again,* Hml. I, 2, 127. *the king doth wake to-night and takes his r.* I, 4, 8. *there was a' gaming, there o'ertook in's r.* II, 1, 58. *they have given me a r. already,* Oth. II, 3, 66.

**Rouse,** vb. 1) tr. a) to raise, to erect, to rear: *being mounted and both —d in their seats,* H4B IV, 1, 118. Refl., = to rise, to raise one's self to one's full height: *when I do r. me in my throne of France,* H5 I, 2, 275. *will stand a tip-toe when this day is named, and r. him at the name of Crispian,* IV, 3, 43. *I see him r. himself to praise my noble act,* Ant. V, 2, 287. With *up*: *he —th up himself and makes a pause,* Lucr. 541.

b) to wake from sleep or repose: *shall we r. the night-owl in a catch?* Tw. II, 3, 60. *r. from sleep that fell anatomy,* John III, 4, 40. H6A II, 2, 23. Troil. IV, 5, 143. IV, 2, 9. Tit. II, 2, 5. Rom. IV, 1, 42. 108. Oth. I, 1, 68. With *up*: *—d up with boisterous drums,* R2 I, 3, 134.

c) to drive (a beast) from his lair: *no dog shall r. thee,* Ven. 240. *to r. a lion,* H4A I, 3, 198. Tit. II, 2, 21. Cymb. III, 3, 98. Figuratively: *to r. his wrongs and chase them to the bay,* R2 II, 3, 128. Applied to men: *we'll quickly r. the traitors,* H6C V, 1, 65. cf. H6A II, 2, 23.

e) to excite to action: *to r. our Roman gods with invocations,* Lncr. 1831. *r. thy vaunting veins,* H5 II, 3, 4. *as —d with rage,* Troil. I, 3, 52. 279. V, 5, 32. Hml. II, 2, 510 (O. Edd. *a roused vengeance,* M. Edd. *aroused v.*). Lr. II, 1, 56. With *up*: *r. up a brave mind and run,* Merch. II, 2, 12. *r. up thy youthful blood,* R2 I, 3, 83. H4B IV, 3, 15. V, 5, 39. Refl.: *expect that you should r. yourself,* H5 I, 2, 123. Troil. III, 3, 222. *r. thee, man,* Rom. III, 3, 135.

2) intr. a) to stand erect, to stand on end: *my fell of hair would at a dismal treatise r.* Mcb. V, 5, 12.

b) to rise, to get up: *night's black agents to their preys do r.* Mcb. III, 2, 53.

**Rousillon** (O. Edd. *Rosignoll, Rosilion, Rossilion*) name in All's I, 2, 18. I, 3, 161. II, 3, 200. III, 2, 104. 123 etc.

**Roussi,** French name: H5 III, 5, 44. IV, 8, 104.

**Rout,** subst. 1) the mass, the multitude: *a vulgar comment will be made of it, and that supposed by the* common *r.* Err. III, 1, 101. *and after me, I know, the r. is coming,* Shr. III, 2, 183. *that put'st odds among the r. of nations,* Tim. IV, 3, 43. *that I profess myself in banqueting to all the r.* Caes. I, 2, 78. *now sleep yslaked hath the r.* Per. III Prol. 1 (= evening party?).

2) a gang, a set: *if that rebellion came like itself, in base and abject —s,* H4B IV, 1, 33. *cheering a r. of rebels with your drum,* IV, 2, 9. *Charles, Alençon and that traitorous r.* H6A IV, 1, 173. *the ringleader and head of all this r.* H6B II, 1, 170.

3) uproar, brawl: *how this foul r. began,* Oth. II, 3, 210.

4) disordered flight: *all is on the r.* H6B V, 2, 31. *a retire, anon a r., confusion thick,* Cymb. V, 3, 41.

**Rout,** vb. to defeat and put to flight in disorder: Ant. III, 1, 9. Cymb. V, 2, 12.

**Rove,** to wander at random, to ramble: *to go r. with one that's yet unbruised,* Cor. IV, 1, 46.

**Rover,** a fly-away, a rogue, a scapegrace: *next to thyself and my young r. he's apparent to my heart,* Wint. I, 2, 176.

**Row,** a line: *a r. of pins,* R2 III, 4, 26. *the first r. of the pious chanson,* Hml. II, 2, 438. *a-r.* = in a line, one after another: *beaten the maids a r.* Err. V, 170.

**Rowel,** the wheel-shaped points of a spur: Cymb. IV, 4, 39.

**Rowel-head,** the axis on which the rowel turns: *struck his armed heels against the panting sides of his poor jade up to the r.* H4B I, 1, 46.

**Rowland,** name of 1) the most famous of Charlemagne's peers: H6A I, 2, 30. Lr. III, 4, 187. 2) Sir R. de Boys, the father of Oliver and Orlando in As I, 1, 60. I, 2, 235. 245. 248. I, 3, 28. II, 3, 4. II, 7, 191. V, 2, 13. V, 4, 158. 3) a person mentioned in Meas. IV, 5, 8.

**Roy:** *Harry le R.,* name assumed by King Henry in H5 IV, 1, 49.

**Royal,** subst. a gold coin of the value of ten shillings; not expressly mentioned, but alluded to by way of punning: *hail, r. prince! Thanks, noble peer; the cheapest of us is ten groats too dear,* R2 V, 5, 67 (cf. *Noble*). *thou camest not of the blood r., if thou darest not stand for ten shillings,* H4A I, 2, 157. *there is a nobleman of the court at door would speak with you. Give him as much as will make him a r. man,* II, 4, 321. *he may keep it still at a face r., for a barber shall never earn sixpence out of it,* H4B I, 2, 28. Perhaps also in All's II, 1, 75.

**Royal,** adj. 1) pertaining or allied to a king, kingly, regal: *into the r. hand of the king,* LLL IV, 2, 146. *with his r. finger,* V, 1, 109. V, 2, 891. *thy r. sweet breath,* 524 (Armado's speeches). *in your r. speech,* All's V, 3, 51. *the r. blood of France,* II, 1, 199. R2 I, 2, 18. V, 5, 114. H4A I, 2, 157. R3 I, 2, 7. *your r. thoughts,* All's II, 1, 130. *their r. necessities,* Wint. I, 1, 28. *your r. presence,* I, 2, 38. *your r. birth,* H6A III, 1, 95. *in Henry's r. name,* V, 3, 160. *my seat's right r. majesty,* R2 II, 1, 120. *England's r. seat,* H6B V, 1, 178. H6C V, 7, 1. *our r. fleet,* H6C III, 3, 253. *your r. preparation,* Mcb. V, 3, 57 etc. etc. Applied to persons: *r. sir,* and *most r. sir,* All's V, 3, 296. Wint. I, 2, 366. V, 1, 159. Mcb. III, 4, 19. *my r. fox,* All's II, 1, 73. 75. *a r. husband,* Wint. I, 2, 107. *the r. fool thou copest with,* IV, 4, 435. *r. kings,* R2 II, 1, 51. III, 1, 8. *your most r. image,* H4B V, 2, 89. *r. Charles of*

*France*, H6A V, 2, 4. *England's r. king*, V, 3, 115. V, 5, 24. H6C II, 6, 88. R3 III, 7, 22. *your r. majesty*, H6B I, 3, 198. 215. *your most r. person*, H6B III, 2, 254. *r. commanders*, H6C II, 2, 67. *the king, my ever r. master*, H8 III, 2, 273. *the emperor, my r. nephew*, IV, 2, 110. *r. Priam*, Troil. V, 3, 75. *Rome's r. empress*, Tit. II, 3, 55. V, 3, 141. *r. Lear*, Lr. I, 1, 141. *most r. majesty*, 196. *I am a king ... a r. one*, IV, 6, 205. *r. queen*, Ant. V, 2, 37. *O r. Pericles*, Per. V, 3, 14 etc. Applied to countries: *our r. realm*, R2 I, 4, 45. *r. Rome*, Tit. I, 11.

Peculiar use: *O r. piece*, Wint. V, 3, 38 (representing a queen). *add a r. number to the dead*, John II, 347 (by the fall of kings). *to clap this r. bargain up of peace*, III, 1, 235 (made between kings). *so be thy fortune in this r. fight*, R2 I, 3, 56 (in the presence of the king). *that r. field of Shrewsbury*, H4B Ind. 34 (battle fought by kings). *were our r. faiths martyrs in love*, H4B IV, 1, 193 (fidelity to the king). *unto this bar and r. interview*, H5 V, 2, 27 (meeting of kings); cf. *this r. view*, 32. *when is the r. day?* R3 III, 4, 3. 4 (the day of the coronation). *a r. battle might be won or lost*, IV, 4, 538 (one deciding the fate of kings). *here I'll make my r. choice*, H8 I, 4, 86 (choice of a king). *it's fit this r. session do proceed*, II, 4, 66. *the citizens have shown at full their r. minds*, IV, 1, 8 (their devotion to the king). *r. hope*, Mcb. I, 3, 56 (hope of becoming king). *O r. knavery*, Hml. V, 2, 19 (knavery of a king).

Applied to princes of less high dignity: *attends the emperor* (i. e. the duke) *in his r. court*, Gent. I, 3, 27. III, 1, 165. *your* (the duke's) *r. grace*, Meas. V, 3. *O r. Duke*, 20. 57. 137. 139. *in your r. walks*, Mids. V, 31. *a r. prince*, R2 II, 1, 239. *your* (the Duke of York's) *r. excellence*, H6B I, 1, 161.

2) fit to be king; becoming a king: *young, valiant, wise, and, no doubt, right r.* R3 I, 2, 245. *go on: right r.* Ant. III, 13, 55.

3) noble, generous; dignified: *how doth that r. merchant, good Antonio?* Merch. III, 2, 242. *enow to press a r. merchant down*, IV, 1, 29. *the r. disposition of that beast*, As IV, 3, 118. *here was a r. fellowship of death*, H5 IV, 8, 106. *how r. 'twas to pardon*, Cor. V, 1, 18. *noble, worthy, r.* Timon, Tim. II, 2, 177. *mighty, bold, r. and loving*, Caes. III, 1, 127. III, 2, 249. *did prophesy a r. nobleness*, Lr. V, 3, 176. *r. wench!* Ant. II, 2, 231.

4) magnificent: *our r., good and gallant ship*, Tp. V, 237. 316. *sport r.* Tw. II, 3, 187. *all was r.* H8 I, 1, 42. *a r. train*, IV, 1, 37. *a most r. one* (army) Cor. IV, 3, 47. *r. cheer*, Tim. III, 6, 56. *the r. banner*, Oth. III, 3, 353. *which promises r. peril*, Ant. IV, 8, 35. *golden Phoebus never be beheld of eyes again so r.* V, 2, 321.

**Royalise**, to make royal: *to r. his blood I spilt mine own*, R3 I, 3, 125.

**Royally**, 1) in a manner becoming a king: *their encounters, though not personal, have been r. attorneyed with interchange of gifts*, Wint. I, 1, 30. *to have you r. appointed*, IV, 4, 603. *sorrow so r. in you appears*, H4B V, 2, 51. *to answer r. in our defences*, H5 II, 4, 3. *to have proved most r.* Hml. V, 2, 409 (Qq *royal*).

2) magnificently: *r. entertained and lodged*, Lucr. Arg. 14. Ado I, 3, 45. *the castle r. is manned*, R2 III, 3, 21. 23 (with a quibble: manned by the king in person). *let us banquet r.* H6A I, 6, 30.

**Royalty**, 1) the office and dignity of a king: *for —'s repair*, Wint. V, 1, 31. *is this the government of Britain's isle, and this the r. of Albion's king?* H6B I, 3, 48. *lose the r. of England's throne*, R3 III, 4, 42. *married your r., was wife to your place*, Cymb. V, 5, 39. Used of the office of a duke: Tp. I, 2, 104.

2) a title of kings, = majesty: *sweet r.* LLL V, 2, 670. *I have stayed to tire your r.* Wint. I, 2, 15. *this morsel of dead r.* John IV, 3, 143. *swearing allegiance to stranger blood, to foreign r.* V, 1, 11. *thus his r. doth speak in me*, V, 2, 129. *mingled his r. with capering fools*, H4A III, 2, 63. *have seen the well-appointed king embark his r.* H5 III Chor. 5. *whose health and r. I pray for*, H8 II, 3, 73. *take vanity the puppet's part against the r. of her father*, Lr. II, 2, 40. *your r. holds idleness your subject*, Ant, I, 3, 91.

3) a deportment becoming a king: *that an invisible instinct should frame them to r. unlearned*, Cymb. IV, 2, 178. And in general, = nobleness: *in his r. of nature reigns that which would be feared*, Mcb. III, 1, 50.

4) royal birth, high extraction: *setting aside his high blood's r.* R2 I, 1, 58. *by the —es of both your bloods*, III, 3, 107. Abstr. pro concr. = persons of royal birth or rank; kings: *a branch and member of this r.* H5 V, 2, 5. *to the succeeding r. he leaves the healing benediction*, Mcb. IV, 3, 155 (= to the succeeding kings).

5) emblem of kingly dignity: *that high r.* (i. e. the crown) *was ne'er plucked off*, John IV, 2, 5. *did give him that same r. he wears*, H4A IV, 3, 55. *this long usurped r. from the dead temples of this bloody wretch have I plucked off*, R3 V, 5, 4 (Ff and later Qq —es). Plur. —es = regalia, and then feudal rights in general: *of temporal —es he thinks me now incapable*, Tp. I, 2, 110. *the dominations, —es and rights of this oppressed boy*, John II, 176. *the —es and rights of banished Hereford*, R2 II, 1, 190. *my rights and —es plucked from my arms*, II, 3, 120. *his coming hither hath no further scope than for his lineal —es*, III, 3, 113. In R3 V, 5, 4 Ff and later Qq —es, Q1 r.

**Roynish**, a term of extreme contempt (cf. *Ronyon*); paltry, mean: *the r. clown, at whom so oft your grace was wont to laugh, is also missing*, As II, 2, 8.

**Rub**, subst. 1) that which causes friction; unevenness, inequality: *to leave no —s nor botches in the work*, Mcb. III, 1, 134 (= to make all smooth).

2) obstacle, impediment, contrariety, cross-purpose: *shall blow each dust, each straw, each little r., out of the path*, John III, 4, 128. *'twill make me think the world is full of —s*, R2 III, 4, 4 (cf. the verb). *every r. is smoothed on our way*, H5 II, 2, 188. *what r. or what impediment there is*, V, 2, 33. *when they once perceive the least r. in your fortunes*, H8 II, 1, 129. *nor has Coriolanus deserved this so dishonoured r. laid falsely i' the plain way of his merit*, Cor. III, 1, 60. *there's the r.* Hml. III, 1, 65.

**Rub**, vb. 1) to perfricate, to touch or handle by moving the hand to and fro: *vaded gloss no —ing will refresh*, Pilgr. 176. *r. your chain with crumbs*, Tw. II, 3, 128. *a' —s himself with civet*, Ado III, 2, 50. *she —s her hands*, Mcb. V, 1, 31. *r. thy brows*, Hml. V, 2, 299. *r. him about the temples*, Oth. IV, 1, 53. *you r. the sore, when you should bring the plaster*, Tp. II, 1, 138. *he —s the vein of him*, Troil. II, 3, 210. *that, —ing the poor itch of your opinion, make yourselves scabs*, Cor. I, 1, 169. *I have —ed this young* *quat almost to the sense*, Oth. V, 1, 11. *to r. the elbow, a gesture of exultation:* LLL V, 2, 109. H4A V, 1, 77. Used as a technical term in the game of bowls, (a bowl being said to rub, when it was diverted from its course by an impediment): *challenge her to bowl. I fear too much —ing*, LLL IV, 1, 141; cf. the subst. in R2 III, 4, 4. *r. on, and kiss the mistress*, Troil. III, 2, 52.

2) to hinder, to cross: *whose disposition will not be —ed nor stopped*, Lr. II, 2, 161. cf. the subst.

**Rubbish,** waste matter, refuse, sweepings: R2 V, 2, 6. Caes. I, 3, 109.

**Rubied,** red like a ruby: *the r. cherry*, Per. V Prol. 8.

**Rubious,** the same: *Diana's lip is not more smooth and r.* Tw. I, 4, 32.

**Ruby,** a precious stone of a lively red colour: *—es red as blood*, Compl. 198. *the impression of keen whips I'ld wear as —es*, Meas. II, 4, 101. *her nose, all o'er embellished with —es*, Err. III, 2, 138. *those be —es, fairy favours*, Mids. II, 1, 12. *the natural r. of your cheeks*, Mcb. III, 4, 115. *—es unparagoned* (Imogen's lips) Cymb. II, 2, 17. Adjectively: *ope their r. lips*, Caes. III, 1, 260.

**Ruby-coloured,** red: Ven. 451.

**Rudder,** the instrument at the stern of a vessel, by which it is steered: Ant. III, 10, 3. III, 11, 57.

**Ruddiness,** red colour: *the r. upon her lip is wet*, Wint. V, 3, 81.

**Ruddock,** see *Raddock*.

**Ruddy,** red: *as dear to me as are the r. drops that visit my sad heart*, Caes. II, 1, 289.

**Rude,** 1) raw, crude, unformed: *you are born to set a form upon that indigest which he hath left so shapeless and so r.* John V, 7, 27 (with obvious allusion to the *rudis indigestaque moles* of Ovid).

2) harsh, rough, unpleasing to the sense: *let those whom nature hath not made for store, harsh, featureless and r., barrenly perish*, Sonn. 11, 10. *if it see the —st or gentlest sight*, 113, 9. *the r. sea grew civil*, Mids. II, 1, 152; cf. Tw. V, 81; R2 III, 2, 54; H4B III, 1, 20. *why are you grown so r.* Mids. III, 2, 262. *the poor r. world hath not her fellow*, Merch. III, 5, 87. *although thy* (the winter wind's) *breath be r.* As II, 7, 179; cf. H4B III, 1, 27; Lr. IV, 2, 30; Cymb. IV, 2, 174. *their* (the walls') *r. circumference*, John II, 262; R2 III, 3, 32; R3 IV, 1, 102. *howsoever r. exteriorly*, John IV, 2, 257. *peace, r. sounds*, Troil. I, 1, 92. *make blessed my r. hand*, Rom. I, 5, 53. *r. throats* (of cannon) Oth. III, 3, 355 (Qq *wide*). *the roughest berry on the —st hedge*, Ant. I, 4, 64.

3) raw, unrefined, uncivilized: *these poor r. lines of thy deceased lover*, Sonn. 32, 4. *my r. ignorance*, 78, 14. *like a r. and savage man of Inde*, LLL IV, 3, 222. *which the r. multitude call the afternoon*, V, 1, 95. *r. mechanicals*, Mids. III, 2, 9. *she deserves a lord that twenty such r. boys might tend upon*, All's III, 2, 84. *in r. harsh-sounding rhymes*, John IV, 2, 150. *unlettered, r. and shallow*, H5 I, 1, 55. *to salute my king with —r terms*, H6B I, 1, 30. *one so r. and of so mean condition*, V, 1, 64. *r., in sooth; in good sooth, very r.* Troil. III, 1, 59. *too subtle-potent for the capacity of my —r powers*, III, 2, 26. *r. am I in my speech*, Oth. I, 3, 81. *nor measure our good minds by this r. place we live in*, Cymb. III, 6, 66 (= barbarous, savage).

4) ill-mannered, uncivil, coarse: *let go that r. un-*

*civil touch*, Gent. V, 4, 60. *our r. transgression*, LLL V, 2, 431. *too wild, too r. and bold of voice*, Merch. II, 2, 190. *a r. despiser of good manners*, As II, 7, 92. *out on thee, r. man*, John I, 64. *how dares thy harsh r. tongue sound this unpleasing news?* R2 III, 4, 74. *r. misgoverned hands*, V, 2, 5. *barren pleasures, r. society*, H4A III, 2, 14. *he gave it like a r. prince*, H4B I, 2, 219. *in confutation of which r. reproach*, H6A IV, 1, 98. *stay with the r. multitude till I return*, H6B III, 2, 135. *r. unpolished hinds*, 271. IV, 10, 33. *to use so r. behaviour*, H8 IV, 2, 103. *ye r. slaves*, V, 4, 2. 11. Hml. V, 1, 109.

5) destitute of delicacy of feeling, brutal: *beaten away by brain-sick r. desire*, Lucr. 175. *r. ram, to batter such an ivory wall*, 464. *savage, extreme, r., cruel*, Sonn. 129, 4. *ere this r. beast will profit*, Meas. III, 2, 34. IV, 3, 85. *r. fishermen of Corinth*, Err. V, 351. *thy r. hand to act the deed*, John IV, 2, 240. *was by the r. hands of that Welshman taken*, H4A I, 1, 41. *r. and merciless*, H6B IV, 4, 33. *the r. son should strike his father dead*, Troil. I, 3, 115. *with the r. brevity and discharge of one* (sigh) IV, 4, 43. *grace and r. will*, Rom. II, 3, 28. *your r. brawls*, III, 1, 194. *O r. unthankfulness*, III, 3, 24. *who is here so r. that would not be a Roman?* Caes. III, 2, 33. *that thou darest wag thy tongue in noise so r. against me*, Hml. III, 4, 40.

6) violent, wild, boisterous: *most r. melancholy, valour gives thee place*, LLL III, 69 (Armado's speech). *what means death in this r. assault?* R2 V, 5, 106. *that the r. scene may end*, H4B I, 1, 159. *what means this scene of r. impatience?* R3 II, 2, 38. *to the mercy of a r. stream*, H8 III, 2, 364. *too rough, too r., too boisterous*, Rom. I, 4, 26. cf. *the rude sea* in the passages cited above. As for the *r. eye of rebellion*, in John V, 4, 11, see *Unthread*.

**Rude-growing,** rough: *r. briers*, Tit. II, 3, 199.

**Rudely,** 1) harshly, roughly: *I that am r. stamped*, R3 I, 1, 16. *r. beguiles our lips of all rejoindure*, Troil. IV, 4, 37. *or r. visit them in parts remote*, Cor. IV, 5, 148. *thou art the —est welcome to this world that ever was prince's child*, Per. III, 1, 30.

2) uncivilly: *he demeaned himself rough, rude and wildly*, Err. V, 88 (the suffix *by* belonging to *rough* and *rude* as well as to *wildly*). *you began r.* Tw. I, 5, 228.

3) brutally, coarsely: *enforced hate shall r. tear thee*, Lucr. 669. *maiden virtue r. strumpeted*, Sonn. 66, 6. *thy place in council thou hast r. lost*, H4A III, 2, 32.

4) violently, wildly: *throwing his mantle r. o'er his arm*, Lucr. 170.

**Rudeness,** 1) want of good manners, incivility, rusticity: *the r. that hath appeared in me have I learned from my entertainment*, Tw. I, 5, 230. *this r. is a sauce to his good wit*, Caes. I, 2, 304.

2) brutality; abstr. pro concr.: *do, r.; do, camel*, Troil. II, 1, 58.

3) coarseness, want of fineness, clumsiness: *put my clouted brogues from off my feet, whose r. answered my steps too loud*, Cymb. IV, 2, 214.

4) rough violence: *his r. so with his authorized youth did livery falseness in a pride of truth*, Compl. 104. *for the great swing and r. of his* (the ram's) *poise*, Troil. I, 3, 207.

**Rudesby,** a coarse fellow, a brute: Shr. III, 2, 10. Tw. IV, 1, 55.

**Rudiments,** first principles, elements: As V, 4, 31. Shr. III, 1, 66.

**Rue,** subst. the plant Ruta graveolens, called also *herb of grace,* and used, on account of its name (cf. verb) as a symbol of sorry remembrance: *reverend sirs, for you there's rosemary and r.* Wint. IV, 4, 74. *I'll set a bank of r., sour herb of grace: r., even for ruth, here shortly shall be seen, in the remembrance of a weeping queen,* R2 III, 4, 105. *there's r. for you, and here's some for me: we may call it herb-grace o' Sundays: O, you must wear your r. with a difference,* Hml. IV, 5, 181 (*with a difference,* because you are old, and I am young. Perhaps a passage from Cogan's Haven of Health serves to illustrate Ophelia's speech: *The second property is that rue abateth carnal lust, which is also confirmed by Galen. Yet schola Salerni in this point maketh a difference between men and women, for they say: ruta viris coitum minuit, mulieribus auget*).

**Rue,** vb. 1) to grieve for, to regret, to lament: absol.: John III, 1, 325. V, 7, 117. R3 III, 2, 14. Transitively: John III, 1, 323. R2 I, 3, 205. H6A III, 2, 36. H6B II, 4, 24. H6C I, 1, 94. II, 5, 109. V, 6, 43. R3 III, 7, 222. Tit. V, 1, 109. Mcb. III, 6, 42.

2) to pity: *r. the tears I shed,* Tit. I, 105. cf. *Ruth.*

**Ruff,** a neck-ornament made of plaited linen; worn by both sexes: Shr. IV, 3, 56. All's III, 2, 7. H4B II, 4, 145. 157. Per. IV, 2, 111.

**Ruffian,** a brutal, boisterous, mischievous fellow: Ven. 1149. Gent. V, 4, 60. Ado IV, 1, 92. Shr. II, 290. Tw. IV, 1, 60. John III, 1, 200. R2 II, 4, 12. H4A II, 4, 500. H4B IV, 5, 125. H6B I, 1, 188. V, 1, 164. Troil. I, 3, 38. Tim. IV, 3, 160. Lr. II, 2, 67. Oth. I, 1, 111. Ant. IV, 1, 4.

Adjectively: *r. lust,* Err. II, 2, 135. *the r. billows,* H4B III, 1, 22. *to die in r. battle,* H6B V, 2, 49.

**Ruffian,** vb. to play the ruffian, to be boisterous, to rage: *if it* (the wind) *had —ed so upon the sea,* Oth. II, 1, 7. cf. H4B III, 1, 22 and Troil. I, 3, 38.

**Ruffle,** subst. agitation, stir, bustle: *sometime a blusterer, that the r. knew of court, of city,* Compl. 58 (*a ruffler,* in contemporary writers, = a rake).

**Ruffle,** vb. 1) tr. a) to disorder by disturbing a smooth surface: *with robbers' hands my hospitable favours you should not r. thus,* Lr. III, 7, 41.

b) with *up,* = to stir up: *would r. up your spirits,* Caes. III, 2, 232.

2) intr. to be noisy; a) to rustle: *to deck thy body with his —ing treasure,* Shr. IV, 3, 60. b) to be turbulent and boisterous: *one fit to bandy with thy lawless sons, to r. in the commonwealth of Rome,* Tit. I, 313. *the bleak winds do sorely r.* Lr. II, 4, 304 (Qq *russel*).

**Rugby,** name of a servant in Wiv. I, 4, 1. 41 etc.

**Rugged,** rough, bristling, shaggy: *his well proportioned beard made rough and r.* H6B III, 2, 175. *the r. Russian bear,* Mcb. III, 4, 100. *the r. Pyrrhus, like the Hyrcanian beast* (cf. what follows) Hml. II, 2, 472. 474. Used of looks: *sleek o'er your r. looks,* Mcb. III, 2, 27 (= disturbed, uneasy).

**Rug-headed,** having shaggy hair: *those rough r. kerns,* R2 II, 1, 156. cf. H6B III, 1, 367.

**Ruin,** subst. 1) decay: *r. hath taught me thus to ruminate,* Sonn. 64, 11. *let it presage the r. of your love,* Merch. III, 2, 175. *repair thy wit, or it will fall to cureless r.* IV, 1, 142. *buildings fall to r.* Per. II, 4, 37. *time's r.* = the decay caused by time: Lucr. 1451. cf. *the chaff and r. of the times,* Merch. II, 9, 48.

2) fall, overthrow, destruction, perdition: *by your r.* Wint. IV, 4, 541. *cry woe, destruction, r. and decay,* R2 III, 2, 102. *whose r. you have sought,* H5 II, 2, 176. *what r. happened in revenge of him,* H6A II, 2, 11. *there comes the r., there begins confusion,* IV, 1, 194. *when my angry guardant stood alone, tendering my r.* IV, 7, 10. *r. combat with their palaces,* V, 2, 7. *to thy foul disgrace and utter r. of the house of York,* H6C I, 1, 254. *our ranks are broke, and r. follows us,* II, 3, 10. *seek their r. that usurped our right,* V, 6, 73. *I see the r. of our house,* R3 II, 4, 49 (Qq *downfall*). *death, desolation, r. and decay,* IV, 4, 409. *weigh thee down to r.* V, 3, 153. *my r.* H8 III, 1, 98. *as if r. leaped from his eyes,* III, 2, 205. *may bring my r.* 242. Troil. V, 3, 58. *fed the r. of the state,* Cor. III, 1, 118. *bury all in heaps and piles of r.* 207. *come all to r.* III, 2, 125. *for —'s wasteful entrance,* Mcb. II, 3, 120. *each small annexment attends the boisterous r.* Hml. III, 3, 22.

Followed by *of* in an active or subjective sense: *see the cities and the towns defaced by wasting r. of the cruel foe,* H6A III, 3, 46 ( = the destructions which the enemy makes); cf. above: *time's r.* Lucr. 1451. Hence similarly with the possessive pronoun: *there is betwixt that smile we would aspire to, that sweet aspect of princes, and their r., more pangs and fears than wars or women have,* H8 III, 2, 369 ( = the ruin which they cause).

3) any thing decayed, destroyed, or demolished; especially decayed buildings; sing.: *kneeling before this r. of sweet life,* John IV, 3, 65. *thou new r. of old Clifford's house,* H6B V, 2, 61. *what's past and what's to come is strewed with husks and formless r. of oblivion,* Troil. IV, 5, 167. *triumphantly tread on thy country's r.* Cor. V, 3, 116. *bow this feeble r. to the earth,* Tit. III, 1, 208. *the r. speaks that sometime it was a worthy building,* Cymb. IV, 2, 354. With *of,* to note the cause of the decay: *the noble r. of her magic,* Ant. III, 10, 19; cf. Merch. II, 9, 48. Plur. *—s: his soul's fair temple is defaced, to whose weak —s muster troops of cares,* Lucr. 720. *what —s are in me ... by him not —ed?* Err. II, 1, 96. *the —s of thy linen,* H4B II, 2, 27. *all the —s of distressful times repaired,* R3 IV, 4, 318. *and out of —s, made my name once more noble,* H8 II, 1, 114. *thou art the —s of the noblest man,* Caes. III, 1, 256.

**Ruin,** vb. to demolish, to destroy, to subvert; absol.: Sonn. 125, 4 (*—ing* = ruin). H8 IV, 2, 40. Trans.: Ven. 954. Sonn. 73, 4. 119, 11. R2 III, 4, 45. H4A III, 2, 37. H5 IV Chor. 29. H8 II, 1, 54. III, 2, 382. 440. Cor. III, 2, 69. Tim. IV, 2, 16. Lr. IV, 6, 137. Ant. V, 2, 51. *—ed* = ruinous: *send the breath of parley into his —ed ears,* R2 III, 3, 34. Peculiar expression: *what ruins are in me that can be found, by him not —ed?* Err. II, 1, 97 (cf. *worth the want that you have wanted,* Lr. I, 1, 282. *our love, which, left unshown, is often left unloved,* Ant. III, 6, 52. *to mend the hurt that his unkindness marred,* Ven. 478. cf. *honoured* (Ff) in Troil. III, 3, 81).

**Ruinate,** vb. to ruin, to bring to decay, to demolish: *to r. proud buildings with thy hours,* Lucr. 944. *seeking that beauteous roof to r. which to repair should be thy chief desire,* Sonn. 10, 7. *I will not r. my father's house,* H6C V, 1, 83. *to order well the state, that like events may ne'er it r.* Tit. V, 3, 204. Partic. *r.:* Err. III, 2, 4; M. Edd. for the sake of the rhyme *ruinous.*

**Ruined** = ruinous: R2 III, 3, 34; see *Ruin*, vb.

**Ruinous**, 1) decayed: Gent. V, 4, 9. Err. III, 2, 4 (O. Edd. *ruinate*). Troil. V, 1, 32. Tit. V, 1, 21. *yond despised and r. man ... full of decay and failing*, Tim. IV, 3, 465.

2) pernicious: *machinations, hollowness, treachery, and all r. disorders*, Lr. I, 2, 123.

**Rule**, subst. 1) an instrument by which straight lines are drawn, a ruler (or a square?): *where is thy leather apron and thy r.?* Caes. I, 1, 7. Ant. V, 2, 210. Hence = standard: *so long as out of limit and true r. you stand against anointed majesty*, H4A IV, 3, 39. *to square the general sex by Cressid's r.* Troil. V, 2, 133. *I have not kept my square, but that to come shall all be done by the r.* Ant. II, 3, 7.

2) canon, principle, maxim: *I durst have denied that. By what r.?* Err. II, 2, 69. 70. *to change true —s for old inventions*, Shr. III, 1, 81. *in military —s*, H4B II, 3, 30. *if your own r. be true*, H4B IV, 2, 86. H5 IV, 1, 157. R3 II, 4, 20. Caes. V, 1, 101. Lr. V, 3, 145. Hence = law, precept: *'gainst r., 'gainst sense, 'gainst shame*, Compl. 271. *'tis against the r. of nature*, All's I, 1, 148. *creatures that by a r. in nature teach the act of order to a peopled kingdom*, H5 I, 2, 188. *you know no —s of charity*, R3 I, 2, 68. *if there be r. in unity itself*, Troil. V, 2, 141. *against all —s of nature*, Oth. I, 3, 101.

3) course of proceeding, line of conduct: *of a strange nature is the suit you follow, yet in such r. that the Venetian law cannot impugn you*, Merch. IV, 1, 178. *you would not give means for this uncivil r.* Tw. II, 3, 132. cf. *Night-rule*.

4) dominion, sway: Shr. V, 2, 109. 163. H6B I, 1, 259. H6C III, 3, 76 (*sway the r.*). V, 2, 27. H8 II, 1, 92. Troil. I, 3, 78. Tit. I, 19. 191. Mcb. V, 2, 16. Hml. III, 4, 99. Lr. I, 1, 50. Per. I, 2, 109. With *of*: Wiv. I, 3, 59. With *over*: Tw. V, 313.

**Rule**, vb. 1) intr. a) to have command, to exercise supreme authority: H6A IV, 1, 111. H6B II, 4, 44. V, 1, 6. R3 II, 3, 29. Cor. III, 1, 40. Lr. V, 3, 320. Oth. V, 2, 332. Per. II, 4, 38. With *over*: H5 I, 2, 226. H6B IV, 4, 16. V, 1, 104.

b) to prevail, to decide, to give the casting vote: *let senses r.* H5 II, 3, 51. *away with scrupulous wit! now arms must r.* H6C IV, 7, 61. *if Cassius might have —d*, Caes. V, 1, 47.

2) tr. a) to command, to govern, to have dominion over: *there be that can r. Naples as well as he*, Tp. II, 1, 262. *we'll do thee homage and be —d by thee*, Gent. V, 1, 66. Merch. II, 2, 23. 26. H6A V, 5, 107. 108. H6B I, 1, 109 (cf. *Roast*). V, 1, 94. R3 I, 1, 62. II, 3, 29. Caes. II, 1, 147. Lr. II, 4, 150. Oth. II, 3, 205.

b) to control, to bridle, to restrain: *never woman yet could r. them* (tongues) *both*, Ven. 1008. *let reason r. things worthy blame*, Pilgr. 301. *canst not r. her*, Wint. II, 3, 46. 50. *canst not r. a traitor*, H6B V, 1, 95. *an army cannot r. 'em*, H8 V, 4, 81. *you being their mouths, why r. you not their teeth?* Cor. III, 1, 36. 41. *close delations working from the heart that passion cannot r.* Oth. III, 3, 124.

c) to prevail on, to persuade; used only passively; *to be —d* = to follow another's advice: *I trust you will be —d by your father*, Ado II, 1, 54. *would thou'ldst be —d by me*, Tw. IV, 1, 68. *had they been —d by me*, H4B IV, 3, 72. H6A III, 3, 8. H6C III, 2, 30. Rom. III, 4, 13. Hml. IV, 7, 60. 69. Oftenest in the impe-

rative: *be —d by me*, Ven. 673. Wiv. I, 1, 72. Meas. IV, 6, 4. Err. III, 1, 94. John II, 377. R2 I, 1, 152. H6A I, 4, 5. Troil. II, 3, 268. Cor. III, 2, 90. Tit. I, 442. Rom. I, 1, 231. Hml. I, 4, 81. Oth. II, 1, 270. Per. II, 5, 83.

**Ruler**, one that has the supreme command and power: H6A V, 5, 30. H6B III, 1, 291. V, 1, 105. With *of*: H6B I, 1, 189. II, 4, 43. III, 2, 296. With *over*: H6A III, 2, 11.

**Rumble**, to make a low and heavy sound: *r. thy bellyful* (viz the thunder) Lr. III, 2, 14.

**Ruminate**, 1) intr. to muse, to meditate, to ponder: Gent. I, 2, 49. Wiv. II, 2, 321. Troil. III, 3, 252. Oth. III, 3, 132. With *on*: H8 I, 2, 180. With a subordinate clause: Sonn. 64, 11.

2) tr. to muse on, to meditate over and over again: H4A I, 3, 274. H5 IV Chor. 24. H6A V, 5, 101. Troil. II, 3, 198. Tit. V, 2, 6. Ant. II, 2, 141.

**Rumination**, meditation: As IV, 1, 19.

**Rummage**, spelling of some M. Edd. for *romage*, q. v.

**Rumour**, subst. 1) popular report: All's III, 2, 130. Wint. I, 2, 270. John IV, 2, 123. 145. H4B Ind. 2. 11. 15. 22. 39. III, 1, 97. R3 I, 3, 46. H8 II, 1, 152. Cor. III, 3, 125. Tim. III, 2, 6. V, 1, 4. Mcb. IV, 2, 19. IV, 3, 182. Ant. IV, 3, 5.

2) fame: *great is the r. of this dreadful knight,* H6A II, 3, 7.

3) a confused and indistinct noise: *bear me hence from forth the noise and r. of the field*, John V, 4, 45. *I heard a bustling r., like a fray*, Caes. II, 4, 18.

**Rumour**, vb. to spread abroad, to tell among the people: *this have I —ed through the peasant towns*, H4B Ind. 33. *r. it abroad*, R3 IV, 2, 51. *it is —ed*, Cor. I, 2, 11.

**Rumourer**, a spreader of reports: *see this r. whipped*, Cor. IV, 6, 47.

**Rump**, the buttocks: *how the devil Luxury, with his fat r. and potato-finger, tickles these together*, Troil. V, 2, 56.

**Rump-fed**, according to Steevens, = fed on offals (flaps, kidneys, rumps, and other scraps, having been among the low perquisites of the kitchen given away to the poor); more probably, according to Nares, = fat-bottomed, fed or fattened in the rump: *aroint thee, witch! the r. ronyon cries*, Mcb. I, 3, 6.*

**Run**, subst. a distance passed over, a passage from one place to another: *thou mayst slide from my shoulder to my heel with no greater a r. but my head and my neck*, Shr. IV, 1, 16 (as if the distance were no greater than from my head to my neck).

**Run**, vb. (impf. usually *ran*; sometimes *run*: Pilgr. 156; Shr. Ind. 2, 67; Mcb. II, 3, 117; in H4A II, 4, 287 Ff *ran*, Qq *run*. Partic. *run*; the perf. sometimes formed with *to be*, where *to have* would have been expected, as in H8 I, 2, 110 and Caes. V, 3, 25; cf. *Be*), 1) intr. a) to move by leaps or quick steps: Ven. 304. 685. 813. 871. 905. Sonn. 51, 14. 143, 1. Gent. III, 1, 188. 387. Meas. III, 1, 13. Err. III, 2, 72. IV, 2, 30. Ado III, 1, 1. Mids. V, 271. Merch. II, 2, 9. As III, 2, 9. Shr. I, 1, 145. V, 2, 53. H4A II, 4, 287. III, 3, 43. H5 IV, 4, 71. H6A I, 4, 19. Rom. II, 1, 5. III, 1, 142 etc. etc. *to r. away*: Pilgr. 156. Wiv. IV, 5, 67. Merch. II, 2, 6. V, 9. All's III, 2, 25. 42 etc. *he ran in here*, Wiv. I, 4, 38. Err. V, 257. *to r. on*, R2 V, 2, 59 etc. = to flee: Lucr. 742. Tp. III, 2, 21.

John III, 4, 5. Troil. II, 1, 6. *to r. away*, in the same sense: All's III, 2, 42. H4A II, 4, 349. *to r. from =* to make haste to get away from: Err. III, 2, 98. 149. IV, 4, 152. Mids. II, 1, 227. Merch. II, 2, 2. *= to flee from: as from a bear a man would r. for life*, Err. III, 2, 159. *r. from the presence of the sun*, Mids. V, 390. *sheep r. from the wolf*, H6A I, 5, 30. Cor. I, 4, 35. II, 3, 59. Lr. IV, 6, 161. *to r. before =* to flee before: *thou —est before me*, Mids. III, 2, 423. Used as a term of huntsmen: *he ran upon the boar*, Ven. 1112. *when night-dogs r., all sorts of deer are chased*, Wiv. V, 5, 252. *a hound that —s counter*, Err. IV, 2, 39.

Metaphorical use: *lovers ever r. before the clock*, Merch. II, 6, 4 (are before their hour). *a woman's thought —s before her actions*, As IV, 1, 141. *those (thoughts) to God that r. before our business*, H5 I, 2, 303. *my desires r. not before mine honour*, Wint. IV, 4, 34. *I r. before my horse to market*, R3 I, 1, 160. *use and liberty, which have for long r. by the hideous law, as mice by lions*, Meas. I, 4, 63. *a woman would r. through fire and water for such a kind heart*, Wiv. III, 4, 107. *and r. through fire I will for thy sweet sake*, Mids. II, 2, 103. *time and the hour —s through the roughest day*, Mcb. I, 3, 147; cf. Cymb. V, 5, 128. *this tongue that —s so roundly in thy head*, R2 II, 1, 122; cf. LLL V, 2, 664. *a —ing banquet =* a hasty refreshment: *some of these should find a —ing banquet, ere they rested*, H8 I, 4, 12. *besides the —ing banquet of two beadles*, V, 4, 69 (cf. *Banquet*).

b) to flow, to move as a fluid: *in Simois' reedy banks the red blood ran*, Lucr. 1437. *a river —ing from a fount*, Compl. 283. *his tears r. down his beard*, Tp. V, 16. *the salt rheum that ran between France and it*, Err. III, 2, 131. *the course of true love never did r. smooth*, Mids. I, 1, 134. *all the wealth I had ran in my veins*, Merch. III, 2, 258. *the —ing brooks*, As II, 1, 16. Shr. Ind. 2, 52. *as fast as you pour affection in, it —s out*, As IV, 1, 215. *what relish is in this? how —s the stream?* Tw. IV, 1, 64. *shall the current of our right r. on?* John II, 335 (F1 *rome*). *which (blood) else —s tickling up and down the veins*, III, 3, 44. *calmly r. on to our ocean*, V, 4, 56. *who (Severn) ran fearfully among the trembling reeds*, H4A I, 3, 105. *the silver Trent shall r. in a new channel*, III, 1, 102. 108. 114. H4B IV, 1, 70. *the blood... —s in your veins*, H5 I, 2, 119. *smooth —s the water where the brook is deep*, H6B III, 1, 53. *till it* (the liquor) *r. o'er*, H8 I, 1, 144. *her eyes ran o'er*, Troil. I, 2, 157. 161. *those boils did r.* II, 1, 5. *my mother's blood —s on the dexter cheek*, IV, 5, 128. *all the tears may r. into that sink*, Tit. III, 2, 19. *through all thy veins shall r. cold and drowsy humour*, Rom. IV, 1, 95. *it* (grief) *—s over at his eyes*, Caes. V, 5, 14. *from the which my current —s*, Oth. IV, 2, 59. *the fresh streams ran by her*, IV, 3, 45. *that tub both filled and —ing*, Cymb. I, 6, 49. *it would have r. all out*, II, 1, 10. Figuratively: *whose names r. smoothly in the even road of a blank verse*, Ado V, 2, 33.

Applied to the sand in an hour-glass: *I should not see the sandy hour-glass r.* Merch. I, 1, 25. *the —ing of one glass*, Wint. I, 2, 306. *the glass that now begins to r.* H6A IV, 2, 35. *our sands are almost r.* Per. V, 2, 1. Hence: *to see the minutes how they r.* H6C II, 5, 25.

c) Used of any kind of quick motion; *=* to ride: *to r. upon the sharp wind of the north*, Tp. I, 2, 254;

cf. H4A II, 4, 377. H4B I, 1, 47. *=* to turn, to roll: *well run, dice!* LLL V, 2, 233. *thus the bowl should r.* Shr. IV, 5, 24. *the world, made to r. even*, John II, 576. *my fortune —s against the bias*, R2 III, 4, 5. *when a great wheel —s down a hill*, Lr. II, 4, 73. Figuratively: *much upon this riddle —s the wisdom of the world*, Meas. III, 2, 242 (= turns). *=* to rush, to fall: *whilst I r. on it* (the sword) Caes. V, 5, 28. 48. 65.

d) Equivalent to to pass, to go: *lest the deceiving harmony should r. into the quiet closure of my breast*, Ven. 781. *ebbing men most often do so near the bottom r.* Tp. II, 1, 227. *makes him r. through all the sins*, Gent. V, 4, 112. *—s not this speech like iron through your blood?* Ado V, 1, 252; cf. *in this place ran Cassius' dagger through*, Caes. III, 2, 178 and V, 3, 42. *I must rather give it* (my tongue) *the rein, for it —s against Hector*, LLL V, 2, 664; cf. R2 II, 1, 122. *the prettiest lass that ever ran on the greensward*, Wint. IV, 4, 157. *even so must I r. on, and even so stop*, John V, 7, 67. *where he did r. reeking o'er the lives of men*, Cor. II, 2, 123. *where the flight so —s against all reason*, Mcb. IV, 2, 14. *our wills and fates do so contrary r.* Hml. III, 2, 221. *so —s the world away*, 285. *let the time r. on to good or bad*, Cymb. V, 5, 128. *to r. through =* to go through, to pursue in thought: *I ran it through*, Oth. I, 3, 132. *to r. over =* to think over, to call to mind: *which you now were —ing o'er*, H8 III, 2, 139.

e) With *into* or *to, =* to come or get into a state: *r. into no further danger*, Tp. III, 2, 76. *such disgrace as he shall r. into*, As I, 1, 141. *the slightest folly that ever love did make thee r. into*, II, 4, 35. *lovers r. into strange capers*, 55. *to r. into my lord's displeasure*, All's II, 5, 37. *have I r. into this danger*, IV, 3, 334. *the commonwealth hath daily r. to wreck*, H6B I, 3, 127. *would r. to these and these extremities*, Caes. II, 1, 31. In for *into: is r. in your displeasure*, H8 I, 2, 110.

*to r. mad =* to become mad: Lucr. 997. Ado I, 1, 88. 93. Tw. II, 5, 212. Wint. III, 2, 184. H4A III, 1, 145. 212. H8 II, 2, 130. Troil. V, 1, 54. Tit. IV, 1, 21. Rom. II, 4, 5. IV, 3, 48. IV, 5, 76. Oth. III, 3, 317.

f) to be reported, to be spread, to go: *volumes of report r. with these false and most contrarious quests upon thy doings*, Meas. IV, 1, 62. *there ran a rumour*, Mcb. IV, 3, 182.

g) to have a tenor or purport: *thus —s the bill*, H5 I, 1, 19. *so r. the conditions*, H8 I, 3, 24.

2) trans. a) to drive: *we r. ourselves aground*, Tp. I, 1, 4. *you r. this humour out of breath*, Er. IV, 1, 57. *beggars mounted r. their horse to death*, H6C I, 4, 127. *r. on the dashing rocks thy weary bark*, Rom. V, 3, 117.

b) to let flow, to emit: *the pissing-conduit r. nothing but claret wine*, H6B IV, 6, 4. *which ... did r. pure blood*, Caes. II, 2, 78. III, 2, 193.

c) to strike, to pierce, to stab: *I'll r. him up to the hilts*, H5 II, 1, 68 (Bardolph's speech). *r. through the ear with a love-song*, Rom. II, 4, 14 (the surreptitious Q1 and most M. Edd. *shot*).

d) to bring to a state, to make, to get: *this tongue that —s so roundly in thy head, should r. thy head from thy irreverent shoulders*, R2 II, 1, 123.

e) to take, to pursue (a course), to perform: *this course which you are —ing here*, H8 II, 4, 217. *when he has r. his course and sleeps in blessings*, III, 2, 398. *when he doth r. his course*, Caes. I, 2, 4. *you shall r.*

*a certain course*, Lr. I, 2, 88. *full merrily hath this brave manage, this career, been r.* LLL V, 2, 482. *r. a tilt at death*, H6A III, 2, 51. *thou ran'st a tilt in honour of my love*, H6B I, 3, 54. *r. the wild-goose chase*, Rom. II, 4, 75. *lads more like to r. the country base*, Cymb. V, 3, 19. *how brief the life of man —s his erring pilgrimage*, As III, 2, 138. *my life is r. his compass*, Caes. V, 3, 25. In the language of Nym, *to r. humours* = what he else calls *to pass humours:* Wiv. I, 1, 171. I, 3, 85. H5 II, 1, 127. Ven. 871.*

**Runagate,** a vagabond: *Richmond is on the seas. White-livered r., what doth he there?* R3 IV, 4, 465* *where that same banished r. doth live*, Rom. III, 5, 90. *I cannot find those —s*, Cymb. IV, 2, 62. With *to: that r. to your bed*, Cymb. I, 6, 137, = *bed-swerver*, q. v.

**Runaway,** 1) one that runs away or flies: *thou r., thou coward, art thou fled?* Mids. III, 2, 405. *the close night doth play the r.* Merch. II, 6, 47 (will quickly pass). *to bring again these foolish —s*, As II, 2, 21. *we are most lofty —s*, H5 III, 5, 35.

2) one who runs a-ways, i. e. in the ways, one who roves and rambles about, a vagabond: *a sort of vaga-bonds, rascals and —s*, R3 V, 3, 316. *spread thy close curtain, love-performing night, that runaways' eyes may wink, and Romeo leap to these arms, untalked of and unseen*, Rom. III, 2, 6 (eavesdroppers rambling about the streets at night, to spy out the doings of others).*

**Runner,** 1) a racer: *forspent with toil, as —s with a race*, H6C II, 3, 1. 2) a fugitive: *'tis sport to maul a r.* Ant. IV, 7, 14.

**Rupture,** 1) a breach, a gap, an injury: *it is a r. that you may easily heal*, Meas. III, 1, 244. 2) break-ing (of the sea): *spite of all the r. of the sea, this jewel holds his building on my arm*, Per. II, 1, 161. 3) hernia: *the guts-griping —s*, Troil. V, 1, 22. Substituted for *rapture* by M. Edd. in Cor. II, 1, 223.

**Rural,** existing or living in the country, rustic: *if ever henceforth thou these r. latches to his entrance open*, Wint. IV, 4, 449. *here is a r. fellow*, Ant. V, 2, 233.

**Rush,** subst. a plant of the genus Juncus; used, before the introduction of carpets, to strow the floors of apartments: *he takes it from the —es where it lies*, Lucr. 318. *—es strewed*, Shr. IV, 1, 48. *on the wanton —es lay you down*, H4A III, 1, 214. *more —es*, H4B V, 5, 1 (to be scattered on the pavement for the pro-cession of the king). *tickle the senseless —es with their heels*, Rom. I, 4, 36. *our Tarquin thus did softly press the —es*, Cymb. II, 2, 13. Used to make rings as pro-visional emblems of marriage: *as fit as Tib's r. for Tom's forefinger*, All's II, 2, 24. Proverbial for a trifle: *a r., a hair, a drop of blood, a pin*, Err. IV, 3, 73. *spurns the r. that lies before him*, Ant. III, 5, 18. Symbol of weakness and inefficiency: *in which cage of —es* (love) *I am sure you are not prisoner*, As III, 2, 389. *lean but upon a r., the cicatrice thy palm some moment keeps*, III, 5, 22. *a r. will be a beam to hang thee on*, John IV, 3, 129. *hews down oaks with —es*, Cor. I, 1, 185. *our gates we have but pinned with —es*, I, 4, 18. *man but a r. against Othello's breast, and he retires*, Oth. V, 2, 270 (cf. *Straw*).

**Rush,** vb. to move with suddenness and eager impetuosity: Ven. 630. Lucr. 373. Wiv. IV, 4, 53. Err. IV, 3, 95. V, 143. H6A I, 1, 129. IV, 7, 42. Rom. III, 1, 172. Caes. III, 2, 183. Mcb. II, 3, 128. Ant. IV, 15, 81. *to r. by*, Troil. III, 3, 159. *to r. forth*,

Ven. 262. John IV, 1, 3. *to r. in*, Shr. III, 2, 93. *to r. on* = to attack: *to r. upon your peace*, John II, 221. *what a tide of woe comes —ing on this woeful land*, R2 II, 2, 99. *the king should so with civil and uncivil arms be —ed upon*, III, 3, 103. H5 III, 5, 50. H6A I, 2, 18. 28. Tit. V, 1, 37. Caes. III, 1, 93. = to bear upon, to overwhelm: *this great sea of joys —ing upon me*, Per. V, 1, 194. *to r. to pieces* = to be shattered by the violence of the motion and the ensuing shock: *and I, like a poor bark, r. all to pieces on thy rocky bosom*, R3 IV, 4, 234. Metaphorically: *many an error ... will r. into the state*, Merch. IV, 1, 222. *something rare even then will r. to knowledge*, Wint. III, 1, 21. *the prince hath —ed aside the law*, Rom. III, 3, 26 (has openly and with partial eagerness eluded the law; cf. *have run by the hideous law*, Meas. I, 4, 63).

**Rush-candle,** a candle made of a rush dipped in tallow: Shr. IV, 5, 14.

**Rushle,** Mrs. Quickly's word for *rustle:* so *—ing in silk and gold*, Wiv. II, 2, 68.

**Rushy,** full of rushes: *by r. brook*, Mids. II, 1, 84.

**Russet,** 1) red, reddish: *the morn, in r. mantle clad*, Hml. I, 1, 166. 2) coarse, homespun: *in r. yeas and honest kersey noes*, LLL V, 2, 413.

**Russet-pated,** having reddish heads: *r. choughs*, Mids. III, 2, 21.

**Russia,** the country in the East of Europe: *this will last out a night in R.* Meas. II, 1, 139. *the Emperor of R.* III, 2, 94. Wint. III, 2, 120.

**Russian,** subst. a native of Russia: LLL V, 2, 121. 361. 443.

**Russian,** adj. pertaining to Russia: LLL V, 2, 368 (F1 *Russia*). 401. H5 III, 7, 154. Mcb. III, 4, 100.

**Rust,** subst. the oxyd forming a rough coat on the surface of metals: *foul cankering r. the hidden treasure frets*, Ven. 767. John IV, 1, 65. R2 III, 3, 116. H4B I, 2, 246 (O. Edd. *with a r.*, most M. Edd. *with r.*). Figuratively: *how he glisters thorough my r.* Wint. III, 2, 172.

**Rust,** vb. 1) intr. to gather rust: LLL I, 2, 187. All's IV, 3, 373. H5 V, 2, 46. H6B III, 2, 198. H6C I, 3, 51 (*this thy son's blood shall r. upon my weapon*). Rom. V, 3, 170. Per. II, 2, 54.

2) tr. to make rusty: *this peace is nothing, but to r. iron*, Cor. IV, 5, 234. *the dew will r. them*, Oth. I, 2, 59.

**Rustic,** adj. rural; existing or practised in the country: *fall into our r. revelry*, As V, 4, 183. *of that kind our r. garden's barren*, Wint. IV, 4, 84. Used with contempt, = boorish: *yield, r. mountaineer*, Cymb. IV, 2, 100.

**Rustic,** subst. peasant: *how now, —s!* Wint. IV, 4, 735 (Autolycus' speech).

**Rustically,** in a manner becoming a peasant: *he keeps me r. at home*, As I, 1, 7.

**Rustle,** to make a noise like the rubbing of silk or straw: Meas. IV, 3, 38. Lr. III, 4, 98. Cymb. III, 3, 24. In Lr. II, 4, 304 Qq *the winds do sorely russel*, Ff *ruffle*. In Wiv. II, 2, 68 Mrs. Quickly *rushle*.

**Rusty,** covered with rust: Pilgr. 88. Shr. III, 2, 46. R2 III, 2, 118. H4A I, 2, 68. H5 IV, 2, 44. Troil. I, 3, 263 (Q *resty*). III, 3, 152. Hml. II, 2, 352. Per. II, 1, 125. II, 2, 50.

**Rut,** see *Rutting.*

**Ruth,** pity: *looking with pretty r. upon my pain*, Sonn. 132, 4. *a spectacle of r.* Pilgr. 127. *rue, even* *for r., here shortly shall be seen*, R2 III, 4, 106. *spur them to ruthful work, rein them from r.* Troil. V, 3, 48. *would the nobility lay aside their r. and let me use my sword*, Cor. I, 1, 201.

**Ruthful**, piteous: *that my death would stay these r. deeds*, H6C II, 5, 95. *this r. piece of butchery*, R3 IV, 3, 5 (Qq *ruthless*). *spur them to r. work*, Troil. V, 3, 48. *villanies r. to hear*, Tit. V, 1, 66.

**Ruthless**, pitiless, cruel: Pilgr. 394. Meas. III, 2, 121. H6A V, 4, 161. H6B II, 4, 34. H6C I, 4, 31. 156. II, 1, 61. V, 4, 25. 36. R3 IV, 3, 5 (Ff *ruthful*). Tit. II, 1, 128. IV, 1, 53.

**Rutland**, 1) the earldom granted to Edward Au-merle, after he was deprived of his dukedom: R2 V, 2, 43. V, 3, 96. 2) son of Richard Duke of York, slain by Clifford: H6C I, 4, 78. 88. 147. II, 1, 63 etc. R3 I, 2, 158. I, 3, 178. IV, 4, 45. 275.

**Rut-time**, the time of the copulation of deer: Wiv. V, 5, 15.

**Rutting**, copulating, lusting like deer: Per. IV, 5, 9.

**Ruttish**, lustful, lecherous: All's IV, 3, 243.

**Rye**, the plant Secale cereale: Tp. IV, 1, 61. As V, 3, 23.

**Rye-straw**, made of rye-stalks: *your r. hats put on*, Tp. IV, 136.

# S.

**S**, the nineteenth letter of the alphabet; abbreviation of *shilling*: H4A II, 4, 585. 587. 589. of *Saint*: All's III, 4, 4. III, 5, 39. H6A IV, 2, 55. IV, 7, 68. H6B I, 2, 57 etc.

**Sa**, (four times reiterated) an exclamation inciting to swift running: Lr. IV, 6, 207.

**Saba**, the queen of Sheba: *S. was never more covetous of wisdom*, H8 V, 5, 24 (cf. 2 Chronicles, Chap. IX).

**Sabbath**, the seventh day of the week, as kept holy by the Jews: Merch. IV, 1, 36. R3 III, 2, 113.

**Sable**, adj. black, dark: *till s. night, mother of dread and fear, upon the world dim darkness doth display*, Lucr. 117. *my s. ground of sin I will not paint*, 1074. *s. curls all silvered o'er with white*, Sonn. 12, 4. *thou treble-dated crow, that thy s. gender makest with the breath thou givest and takest*, Phoen. 18. *whose s. arms, black as his purpose, did the night resemble*, Hml. II, 2, 474. *his banners s.* Per. V Prol. 19.

Substantively: *a s. silvered*, Hml. I, 2, 242. Plur. —*s* (cf. *Blacks*): *let the devil wear black, for I'll have a suit of —s*, III, 2, 137 (with a pun; cf. *Sables*).

**Sable-coloured**, black: *s. melancholy*, LLL I, 1, 233 (Armado's letter).

**Sables**, the fur of Mustela zibellina: *for youth no less becomes the light and careless livery that it wears than settled age his s. and his weeds*, Hml. IV, 7, 81. Quibbling in III, 2, 137.

**Sack**, subst. the generic name of Spanish and Canary wines: Tp. II, 2, 126. III, 2, 15. 31. 88. Wiv. II, 1, 9. II, 2, 153. III, 5, 3. 22. V, 5, 167. Shr. Ind. 2, 2. 6. H4A I, 2, 8. II, 2, 49. II, 4, 129. 132. 137. 140. 345. 497. 501. 587. 592. III, 3, 50. IV, 2, 2. V, 4, 169. H4B II, 2, 147. II, 4, 121. 194. 196. IV, 3, 124. 135. V, 3, 15. H5 II, 3, 29. H6B II, 3, 60. *Sherris s.* H4B IV, 3, 104. *old s.* H4A I, 2, 3. H4B I, 2, 222. *s. and sugar*, H4A I, 2, 125. II, 4, 516. *burnt s.* Wiv. II, 1, 223. III, 1, 112. Tw. II, 3, 206. *brew me a pottle of s.* Wiv. III, 5, 30.

**Sack**, subst. a large bag: LLL IV, 3, 81 (*more —s to the mill!*). H4B V, 1, 25. H6A III, 2, 10.

**Sack**, subst. storm and plunder of a town: *the s. of Orleans*, H6A II, 2, 15.

**Sack**, vb. to storm, destroy and pillage: Lucr. 1170. 1740. All's I, 3, 75. H4A V, 3, 56. H6A III, 2, 10. V, 1, 62. Cor. III, 1, 316. Rom. III, 3, 107. Tim. V, 1, 174.

**Sackbut**, the trombone, a kind of trumpet: Cor. V, 4, 52.

**Sack-cloth**, coarse cloth worn in mourning and mortification: H4B I, 2, 222. Per. IV, 4, 29. cf. Esther IV, 1.

**Sackerson**, name of a large bear at Paris-garden: Wiv. I, 1, 307.

**Sacrament**, the Eucharist: *ere I last received the s. I did confess it*, R2 I, 1, 139. Vows made and oaths taken on the sacrament; hence *to receive the s.* = to take an oath: *thou didst receive the holy s. to fight in quarrel of the house of Lancaster*, R3 I, 4, 208. *to take the s.*: All's IV, 3, 156. John V, 2, 6. R2 IV, 328. V, 2, 97. H6A IV, 2, 28. R3 V, 5, 18.

**Sacred**, such as must be kept holy, entitled to awe and veneration: Lucr. 1172. Compl. 260. Wiv. IV, 4, 59. V, 5, 61. Meas. IV, 3, 149. V, 410. Merch. I, 3, 49. As II, 7, 123. Wint. II, 1, 183. II, 3, 84. III, 3, 7. V, 3, 122. John III, 1, 229. H6A I, 2, 114. IV, 1, 40. H6B I, 3, 61. Tit. I, 92. 242. II, 1, 120 (*our empress with her s. wit to villany and vengeance consecrate*; Aaron's speech). Tim. I. 1, 82. Caes. III, 2, 138. Mcb. II, 4, 34. Hml. III, 2, 170. Lr. I, 1, 111. Oth. III, 3, 461. Ant. I, 3, 63. II, 2, 85. Per. V, 1, 74. Epithet of royalty: *serving with looks his* (the sun's) *s. majesty*, Sonn. 7, 4. *justice, most s. duke*, Err. V, 133. *O my most s. lady*, Wint. I, 2, 76. *whose person, so s. as it is*, V, 1, 172. *a s. king*, John III, 1, 148. *our s. blood*, R2 I, 1, 119. I, 2, 17. III, 3, 9. IV, 209. V, 2, 30. V, 6, 6. H5 I, 2, 7. H8 II, 4, 41. III, 2, 173. V, 5, 46. Troil. IV, 5, 134 (*thy mother, my s. aunt*). Per. I, 2, 33. Applied by enthusiastic lovers to the objects of their affection: *tan s. beauty*, Sonn. 115, 7. *no Valentine for s. Silvia*, Gent. III, 1, 211. *s. and sweet was all I saw in her*, Shr. I, 1, 181.

**Sacrifice**, subst. 1) the act of offering any thing to God: Wint. III, 1, 6. Troil. IV, 2, 66. Cor. I, 10, 21. Tit. II, 3, 164. Oth. V, 2, 65. Cymb. V, 5, 398. *to do s.* Caes. II, 2, 5. Per. V, 1, 242. V, 2, 12. *give you thankful s.* Cor. I, 6, 9. Ant. I, 2, 167.

2) that which is offered or immolated: Merch. III, 2, 57. John II, 420. H4A IV, 1, 113. H5 IV Chor. 23. H8 II, 1, 77. Troil. I, 2, 308. V, 3, 18. Tit. I, 124. Lr. V, 3, 20. Cymb. I, 2, 3.

3) that which is destroyed for the sake of something else: *the back is s. to the load*, H8 I, 2, 50. *poor —s of our enmity*, Rom. V, 3, 304.

**Sacrifice,** vb. 1) to offer up to heaven (or to what is compared with it): Gent. III, 2, 74. R2 I, 1, 104. H6C V, 1, 91. Tit. I, 98. 144 *(the —ing fire =* the fire of sacrifice).

2) to destroy or give up for the sake of something else: Merch. IV, 1, 286. Tw. V, 133. Rom. V, 3, 268.

**Sacrificer,** one that bring an offering to the gods: Caes. II, 1, 166.

**Sacrificial,** made as to a god in sacrificing, full of devotion: *rain s. whisperings in his ear*, Tim. I, 1, 81.

**Sacrilegious,** violating sacred things: Mcb. II, 3, 72. Cymb. V, 5, 220.

**Sacring bell,** the little bell rung at mass to give notice that the elements are consecrated: H8 III, 2, 295.*

**Sad,** (comp. *—er:* Gent. IV, 2, 54. Ado III, 2, 16. Shr. III, 2, 101. Superl. *—est:* Mids. II, 1, 51. H6C II, 1, 67) 1) sorry, sorrowful, melancholy; used of things as well as persons: Ven. 929. Lucr. 262. 556. 1386. 1591. Sonn. 153, 12. Tp. I, 2, 224. Gent. II, 4, 8. III, 1, 230. IV, 2, 54. IV, 4, 94. Meas. III, 2, 54. Err. I, 1, 121. IV, 2, 4. V, 45. Ado I, 3, 2. III, 2, 20. V, 1, 292. LLL I, 2, 3. Mids. II, 1, 51. Merch. I, 1, 1. 22. 37. 40. 45. 47. 79. As IV, 1, 8. Shr. III, 2, 100. 101. John II, 544. H6A I, 2, 48. H6C II, 1, 8. 67. Ant. I, 3, 3 etc. etc.

2) grave, serious: *s. pause and deep regard beseem the sage,* Lucr. 277. *what s. talk was that,* Gent. I, 3, 1. *you're s.* Err. III, 1, 19. *speak you this with a s. brow?* Ado I, 1, 185. *in s. conference,* I, 3, 62. *she is never s. but when she sleeps,* II, 1, 358. *you are — er,* III, 2, 16. *counterfeit s. looks, make mouths upon me when I turn my back,* Mids. III, 2, 237. *then, my queen, in silence s. trip we after the night's shade,* IV, 1, 100. *well studied in a s. ostent to please his grandam,* Merch. II, 2, 205. *s. Lucretia's modesty,* As III, 2, 156. *s. brow and true maid,* 227. *he is s. and civil,* Tw. III, 4, 5. *I sent for thee upon a s. occasion,* 20. 21. *a s. face, a reverend carriage,* 80. *in s. talk,* Wint. IV, 4, 316. *a jest with a s. brow,* H4B V, 1, 92. *the s. and solemn priests,* H5 IV, 1, 318. *the widow likes it not, for she looks very s.,* H6C III, 2, 110. = surly: *that s. dog that brings me food,* R2 V, 5, 70.

**Sad-attending,** (not hyph. in O. Edd.) sadly listening: Tit. V, 3, 82.

**Sad-beholding,** looking sad? (cf. Per. V, 1, 224): *which when her s. husband saw,* Lucr. 1590.

**Saddle,** subst. the seat put on a horse's back for the rider: Shr. III, 2, 49. IV, 1, 59. H4A II, 1, 6. H4B II, 1, 29. H5 V, 2, 143.

**Saddle,** vb. to put a saddle on, to cover with a saddle: R2 V, 2, 74. H4B V, 3, 127. R3 V, 3, 64. Lr. I, 4, 274.

**Saddle-bow,** the crooked pieces of wood which form the skeleton of a saddle: Ven. 14.

**Saddler,** one whose trade is to make saddles: Err. I, 2, 56.

**Sad-eyed,** grave-looking: H5 I, 2, 202.

**Sad-faced,** looking sad: Tit. V, 3, 67.

**Sad-hearted,** sad, full of grief: H6C II, 5, 123.

**Sadly,** 1) sorrowfully, mournfully: Ven. 889. 917. Lucr. 561. 736. 1212. Sonn. 8, 1. Compl. 47. Tp. I, 2, 235. Gent. II, 1, 31. All's III, 5, 70. John III, 1, 20. R2 V, 6, 51. H6C V, 5, 7. R3 V, 3, 287. Tim. II, 2, 106. Hml. II, 2, 168. Oth. II, 1, 32. Cymb. V, 5, 23. 160. *sad or merrily* for *sadly or merrily:* Err.

IV, 2, 4. H4A V, 2, 12 (the suffix *ly* belonging to both words).

2) gravely, seriously, in earnest: *this can be no trick; the conference was s. borne,* Ado II, 3, 229. *my father is gone wild into his grave, for in his tomb lie my affections, and with his spirit s. I survive, to mock the expectation of the world,* H4B V, 2, 125. *but s. tell me who,* Rom. I, 1, 207.

**Sadness,** 1) sorrow, grief, dejection of mind: Ado I, 3, 4. LLL I, 2, 4. 7. Merch. I, 1, 6. I, 2, 54. As I, 1, 5. IV, 1, 20. Shr. Ind. 2, 34. John II, 546. H4B V, 2, 46. Troil. I, 1, 40. Rom. I, 1, 169. Hml. II, 2, 147. Cymb. I, 6, 62. V, 4, 162.

2) seriousness: *this merry inclination accords not with the s. of my suit,* H6C III, 2, 77. *in s.* or *in good s. =* in earnest: *therefore, in s., now I will away,* Ven. 807. *in good s., I am sorry that for my sake you have suffered all this,* Wiv. III, 5, 125. *ay, in good s., is he,* IV, 2, 93. *now, in good s., son Petruchio, I think thou hast the veriest shrew of all,* Shr. V, 2, 63. *in good s., I do not know,* All's IV, 3, 230. *tell me in s. who is that you love,* Rom. I, 1, 205.

**Sad-set,** writing of M. Edd. in Lucr. 1662; not hyphened in O. Edd.; see *Set.*

**Sad-tuned,** of a sad sound and purport: *to list the s. tale,* Compl. 4.

**Safe,** adj. and adv. 1) sound, right, good: *nor do I think the man of s. discretion,* Meas. I, 1, 72. *on a —r judgment all revoke your ignorant election,* Cor. II, 3, 226. *a trade that I may use with a s. conscience,* Caes. I, 1, 14. *the —r sense will ne'er accommodate his master thus,* Lr. IV, 6, 81. *what s. and nicely I might well delay,* V, 3, 144. *my blood begins my —r guides to rule,* Oth. II, 3, 205. *are his wits s.?* IV, 1, 280. *in all s. reason he must have some attendants,* Cymb. IV, 2, 131. *in our orbs we'll live so round and s., that time of both this truth shall ne'er convince, thou showedst a subject's shine, I a true prince,* Per. I, 2, 122.

2) in good condition, without damage, unhurt, uninjured: *are they s.? Not a hair perished,* Tp. I, 2, 217. *heaven keep your honour s.* Meas. II, 2, 157. *and soon and s. arrived,* Err. I, 1, 49. IV, 4, 125. 154 *(s. and sound).* R2 II, 2, 50. H4A IV, 3, 109. H5 II Chor. 37. III, 6, 5. IV, 3, 21. R3 V, 3, 320. Troil. I, 3, 381. Tit. I, 176. 221. Mcb. III, 2, 6. V, 8, 35. Lr. III, 6, 121. Oth. II, 1, 33. Ant. IV, 14, 36. Cymb. III, 5, 105. Per. II Chor. 32.

3) free from danger: *Angelo perceives he's s.* Meas. V, 499. *my money is not s.* Err. I, 2, 105. *thou liest warm at home, secure and s.* Shr. V, 2, 151. *live —st in shame,* All's IV, 3, 374. *nor shall you be —r,* Wint. I, 2, 444. *thou mayst hold a fasting tiger —r by the tooth,* John III, 1, 260. III, 4, 161. R2 III, 2, 80. H5 IV, 1, 182. H6A IV, 3, 169. H6B I, 4, 39. 71. H6C I, 1, 241. IV, 1, 40. 41. R3 I, 1, 70. III, 2, 68. IV, 4, 213. V, 5, 10. Troil. III, 2, 77. IV, 4, 117. Cor. IV, 6, 37. Tit. II, 1, 2. IV, 2, 131. Caes. V, 4, 20. Mcb. V, 4, 2. Lr. V, 3, 144 (cf. *Safely*). Ant. IV, 15, 26. Cymb. I, 4, 138. *to keep s. =* a) to protect, to secure from danger: H6A III, 2, 100. H6C IV, 1, 81. Cor. I, 2, 37. Tit. IV, 2, 110. Caes. V, 4, 27. Mcb. II, 3, 145. Hml. III, 3, 9. b) to guard well: *the doors be locked and keys kept s.* Gent. III, 1, 111. *that you keep Costard s.* LLL I, 2, 133. *keeping s. Nerissa's ring,* Merch. V, 307. *let this be copied out and keep it s.* John V, 2, 2. *I'll keep this door s.* Tit. I, 288. *it*

*shall s. be kept*, Cymb. I, 6, 209. Similarly: *the gold is laid up s. at the Centaur*, Err. II, 2, 2. *one he bade me store up, as a triple eye, —r than mine own two*, All's II, 1, 112. *my horse is tied up s.* Cymb. IV, 1, 24.

4) affording security and safety: *with —st distance I mine honour shielded*, Compl. 151. *in what s. place you have bestowed my money*, Err. I, 2, 78. *dispatch you with your —st haste and get you from our court*, As I, 3, 43 (i. e. with haste, which is the best means ⁺o save yourself). *devise the fittest time and —st way to hide us*, 137. *'tis —r to avoid what's grown*, Wint. I, 2, 432. *convey them with s. conduct*, H5 I, 2, 297; cf. Troil. III, 3, 277. 288. *where is the best and —st passage in*, H6A III, 2, 22. *by what s. means the crown may be recovered*, H6C IV, 7, 52. *a sure and s. one* (way) H8 III, 2, 439. *their mother's bedchamber should not be s. for these bad bondmen*, Tit. IV, 1, 108. *if Aaron now be wise, then is all s.* IV, 4, 38. *good for their meat, and —r for their lives*, Tim. I, 2, 46. *which do but what they should by doing every thing s. toward your love and honour*, Mcb. I, 4, 27 (every thing that is sure to show you love and honour? Or every thing consistent with the love and honour we bear you? An expression undoubtedly strained and obscure on purpose). *our —st way is to avoid the aim*, II, 3, 148. *nor stands it s. with us to let his madness range*, Hml. III, 3, 1. *to have found a s. redress*, Lr. I, 4, 225. *'tis politic and s. to let him keep a hundred knights*, 346. *—r than trust too far*, 351. *opinion throws a more —r voice on you*, Oth. I, 3, 226. *to take the —st occasion by the front*, III, 1, 52. *to be direct and honest is not s.* III, 3, 378. *to have them in s. stowage*, Cymb. I, 6, 192.

5) no longer dangerous, not able to do harm: *he's s. for these three hours*, Tp. III, 1, 21. *Baptista is s., talking with the deceiving father of a deceitful son*, Shr IV, 4, 82. *villain, I'll make thee s.* R2 V, 3, 41. *see him s. i'the Tower*, H8 V, 3, 97. *but Banquo's s.? Ay, my good lord, s. in a ditch he bides*, Mcb. III, 4, 25.

**Safe,** vb. 1) to render safe, to conduct safely: *best you —d the bringer out of the host*, Ant. IV, 6, 26. 2) to justify: *that which most with you should s. my going, is Fulvia's death*, Ant. I, 3, 55.

**Safe-conduct** (not hyphened in O. Edd.) a warrant of security, or a guard through an enemy's territory: H5 I, 2, 297. Troil. III, 3, 277. 288.

**Safe-conducting,** attending and conducting by way of protection: *s. the rebels from their ships*, R3 IV, 4, 483.

**Safeguard,** subst. 1) defence, protection: *to the s. of your honour*, Meas. V, 424. *doves will peck in s. of their brood*, H6C II, 2, 18. *fight in s. of your wives*, R3 V, 3, 259. *for the inheritance of their loves and s. of what that want might ruin*, Cor. III, 2, 68.

2) safe-conduct: *on s. he came to me*, Cor. III, 1, 9.

**Safeguard,** vb. to guard, to protect, to secure: *to s. thine own life*, R2 I, 2, 35. *we have locks to s. necessaries*, H5 I, 2, 176.

**Safely,** 1) without injury, fortunately, happily: *s. in harbour is the king's ship*, Tp. I, 2, 226. *we have s. found our king and company*, V, 221. *my ships are s. come to road*, Merch. V, 288. *God, and not we, hath s. fought*, H4B IV, 2, 121 (without any bloodshed). *see them guarded and s. brought to Dover*, H6A V, 1, 49. H6B IV, 1, 114. *God s. quit her of her burthen*, H8 V, 1, 70. *that my teaching and the strong course of my authority might go one way, and s.* V, 3, 36 (both

undamaged). *has clucked thee to the war, and s. home,* Cor. V, 3, 163. *letting go s. by the divine Desdemona,* Oth. II, 1, 72. *that the gods would s. deliver me from this place,* Per. IV, 6, 191.

2) without danger; or rather without fear of danger or offence, securely (German: *ruhig*): *go s. on to seek thy son,* Tp. II, 1, 327. *running out, that was s. within,* Caes. III, 1, 131. *to be s. thus,* Mcb. III, 1, 49. *go s. on,* Hml. IV, 4, 8 (German: *marschirt nur ruhig vorwärts.* Qq *softly*). *what safe and nicely I might well delay,* Lr. V, 3, 144 (the suffix *ly* belonging to both words). *can we with manners ask what was the difference? S., I think,* Cymb. I, 4, 58. *and might so s.* (have staked the ring) *had it been all the worth ...,* V, 5, 190.

3) so as to prevent danger or escape, carefully, closely: *I have with such provision in mine art so s. ordered,* Tp. I, 2, 29. *I'll keep him dark and s. locked,* All's IV, 1, 104. *to keep him s. till his day of trial,* R2 IV, 153. *had all your quarters been as s. kept,* H6A II, 1, 63. *s. stowed,* Hml. IV, 2, 1. *placed it s.* V, 2, 52.

In both words, *safe* and *safely,* the line of demarcation between adjective and adverb scarcely discernible; see f. i. Tp. V, 221. LLL III, 117. Cor. V, 3, 163. Oth. II, 1, 72. cf. Appendix.

**Safety** (trisyll. in Hml. I, 3, 21; Ff *sanctity*); 1) state of being unhurt or uninjured: *as this is true, let me in s. raise me from my knees,* Meas. V, 231. *nor* (love no man) *further in sport neither than with s. of a pure blush thou mayst in honour come off again,* As I, 2, 30 (with no other hurt than a mere blush). *my arrival and my wife's in s.* Wint. V, 1, 167. *hath passed in s. through the narrow seas,* H6C IV, 8, 3. *the worthy Leonatus is in s. and greets your highness dearly,* Cymb. I, 6, 12 (= is well).

Hence sometimes = welfare, good fortune, success: *the gods give s. to your purposes,* Meas. I, 1, 74. *I will pray for your fair s.* John III, 3, 16. *your s., for the which myself and them bend their best studies,* IV, 2, 50. *tendering the precious s. of my prince,* R2 I, 1, 32. *for his s. there I'll best devise,* H6A I, 1, 172. *wishes towards you honour and plenteous s.* H8 I, 1, 104. *provide for thine own future s.* III, 2, 422. *the gods with s. stand about thee,* Troil. V, 3, 94.

2) freedom from danger: Tp. II, 1, 198. Meas. IV, 3, 94. Err. I, 1, 77. Mids. V, 427. As I, 2, 189. All's I, 1, 217. Tw. III, 4, 273. IV, 2, 76. V, 218. Wint. III, 2, 21. John III, 1, 120. III, 2, 8. III, 4, 147. 148. IV, 3, 12. V, 2, 142. H4A II, 3, 11. III, 2, 117. IV, 3, 103. V, 1, 65. V, 5, 11. H4B Ind. 10. I, 1, 124. 213. IV, 2, 35. IV, 5, 31.*V, 2, 88. H5 II, 2, 175. III, 2, 14. IV, 7, 85. H6B III, 1, 277. V, 3, 23. H6C I, 1, 241. III, 3, 211. IV, 1, 46. IV, 7, 18. R3 I, 1, 44. III, 5, 45. IV, 4, 214. H8 V, 5, 34. Cor. III, 3, 34. Tit. IV, 2, 134. IV, 4, 105. Tim. II, 1, 13. IV, 3, 345. Caes. III, 1, 289. Mcb. III, 1, 54. IV, 3, 30 (*—es*). Hml. I, 3, 21 (Ff *sanctity*). 43. II, 2, 79. IV, 3, 42. IV, 7, 8. Lr. I, 1, 159. V, 3, 44. Oth. I, 1, 150. II, 3, 216. Ant. II, 6, 96. IV, 15, 46. Cymb. I, 6, 194.

3) custody, ward: *deliver him to s.* John IV, 2, 158 *hold him in s.* Rom. V, 3, 183.

**Saffron,** the plant Crocus sativus; used to colour paste: *whose villanous s. would have made all the unbaked and doughy youth of a nation in his colour,* All's IV, 5, 2 (perhaps with an allusion to the fashionable custom of wearing yellow). *I must have s. to colour the warden pies,* Wint. IV, 3, 48.

Adjectively, = deep yellow: *with thy* (Iris') *s. wings,* Tp. IV, 78. *this companion with the s. face,* Err. IV, 4, 64.

**Sag,** to sink, to droop, to flag: *shall never s. with doubt nor shake with fear,* Mcb. V, 3, 10.

**Sage,** grave and wise: Lucr. 222. 277. Tw. III, 4, 413. H4B IV, 5, 121. R3 III, 7, 227. Per. IV, 6, 102. In Hml. V, 1, 260 Ff *s. requiem,* Qq *a requiem.*

**Sagittary,** 1) a Centaur who came to the assistance of the Trojans: Troil. V, 5, 14. 2) a public building in Venice: Oth. I, 1, 159.\*I, 3, 115.

**Sail,** subst. 1) the sheet which catches the wind and carries the vessel on: Tp. I, 2, 147. V, 315. Err. I, 1, 117. Merch. I, 1, 9. John IV, 2, 23. H6C II, 6, 35. Hml. I, 3, 56. IV, 6, 17. V, 2, 120. Oth. II, 1, 78. *under s.* = sailing: LLL V, 2, 549. Mids. I, 1, 174. Merch. II, 6, 68. II, 8, 1. 6. Cor. II, 2, 110. *to hoist s.* = to draw up and set the sail: Sonn. 117, 7. Err. V, 21. Tw. I, 5, 215. R3 IV, 4, 529. Ant. III, 10, 15. *to strike s.,* i. e. to lower the sail, = to humble one's self: H4B V, 2, 18. H6C III, 3, 5. *bear so low a s., to strike to thee,* V, 1, 52. Metaphorically: *the proud full s. of his great verse,* Sonn. 86, 1. *be like a king and show my s. of greatness,* H5 I, 2, 274. Plur. —*s:* Tp. Epil. 11. Wiv. II, 2, 142. Mids. II, 1, 128. Merch. II, 6, 18. R2 II, 1, 265. H5 III Chor. 10. R3 IV, 4, 233. Troil. II, 2, 74. Rom. I, 4, 113. Ant. II, 2, 198. III, 11, 55. IV, 12, 4. Cymb. II, 4, 28. Per. V, 1, 256. V, 2, 15.

Pars pro toto, *s.* = a ship: Sonn. 80, 6. Rom. II, 4, 108. Oth. II, 1, 4. 51. 54. 93. Cymb. I, 3, 2. Per. III Prol. 20. Plur. —*s:* Ant. II, 6, 24. III, 7, 50. Plur. *s.:* John III, 4, 2. Oth. I, 3, 37.

2) voyage by sea, sailing: *my butt and very seamark of my utmost s.* Oth. V, 2, 268.

3) fleet, squadron: *we have descried a portly s. of ships make hitherward,* Per. I, 4, 61.

**Sail,** vb. 1) intr. to be conveyed in a vessel, to pass by water: Wiv. I, 3, 89. Err. I, 1, 63. Ado III, 4, 58. Mids. II, 1, 132. Tw. III, 2, 28. John V, 7, 53. H6C V, 1, 53. Troil. I, 1, 106. I, 3, 35. II, 3, 277. Rom. II, 2, 32. III, 5, 135. Mcb. I, 3, 8. Oth. II, 3, 65. Cymb. I, 3, 13.

2) to pass through in a vessel: *s. seas in cockles,* Per. IV, 4, 2.

**Sail-maker,** one whose trade is to make sails: Shr. V, 1, 80.

**Sailor,** a common mariner: Tp. I, 2, 270. II, 1, 4. II, 2, 53. 127. Err. I, 1, 77. Merch. I, 3, 23. III, 1, 109. Tw. I, 2, 5. III, 2, 18. H6C III, 2, 186. V, 4, 5. R3 III, 4, 101. Troil. II, 1, 43. Mcb. I, 3, 4. Hml. IV, 6, 2. IV, 7, 39. Cymb. IV, 2, 56. Per. IV, 1, 54.

**Sain,** = said; used by Armado for the sake of the rhyme: LLL III, 83. cf. *Say.*

**Saint,** subst. a person sanctified and canonized, or deserving to be so: Lucr. 85. Sonn. 144, 7. Gent. II, 4, 145. Meas. I, 4, 37. II, 2, 127. 180. IV, 2, 192. V, 243. Err. III, 2, 14. IV, 4, 60. Merch. I, 2, 143. II, 7, 40. Shr. III, 2, 28. All's V, 3, 108. John III, 1, 177. R2 III, 3, 152. H4A I, 2, 102. II, 1, 88. H6A

I, 6, 29. III, 3, 15. H6B I, 3, 63. R3 I, 2, 49. I, 3. 338. IV, 1, 70. IV, 4, 75. V, 3, 241. H8 V, 5, 61. Rom. I, 5, 101. 103. 105. 107. II, 2, 55. 61. III, 2, 79. Tim. V, 1, 55. Oth. II, 1, 112. Before names: *S. Anne,* Tw. II, 3, 126. *Alban,* H6B I, 2, 57. *Bennet,* Tw. V, 42. *Charity,* Hml. IV, 5, 58. *Clare,* Meas. I, 4, 5. *Colme,* Mcb. I, 2, 61. *Davy,* H5 IV, 1, 55. *Dennis,* LLL V, 2, 87. H6A I, 6, 28. III, 2, 18. *Edmundsbury,* John IV, 3, 11. *George,* LLL V, 2, 620. John II, 288. H6A I, 1, 154. IV, 2, 55. IV, 7, 68. *Gregory,* Gent. IV, 2, 84. *Jaques,* All's III, 4, 4. IV, 3, 58. *Jamy,* Shr. III, 2, 84. *Katharine,* H6A I, 2, 100. *Lambert,* R2 I, 1, 199. *Luke,* Meas. III, 1, 276. *Magnus,* H6B IV, 8, 1. *Martin,* H6A I, 2, 131. *Mary,* John II, 538. *Michael,* H6A IV, 7, 69. *Nicholas,* Gent. III, 1, 300. H4A II, 1, 67. *Paul,* R3 I, 1, 138. *Peter,* Ado II, 1, 50. Oth. IV, 2, 91. *Philip,* H6A I, 2, 143. *Valentine,* Mids. IV, 1, 144. Hml. IV, 5, 48. cf. the resp. names. Jocularly: *S. Cupid,* LLL IV, 3, 366. V, 2, 87.

**Saint,** vb. to play the saint: *think women still to strive with men, to sin and never for to s.* Pilgr. 342.

**Sainted,** sanctified, holy: Meas. I, 4, 34. III, 1, 89 (M. Edd. *outward-sainted*). All's III, 4, 7. Wint. V, 1, 57. Mcb. IV, 3, 109.

**Saint-like,** like a saint: Lucr. 1519. Wint. V, 1, 2. H8 II, 4, 138. IV, 1, 83.

**Saint-seducing,** seducing a saint: Rom. I, 1, 220.

**Sake,** cause, interest; always preceded by *for* (by *from* only in Evans' language: Wiv. III, 1, 42), = in behalf, on account: *what I should do again for such a s.* Compl. 322. With *of: for the s. of them thou sorrowest for,* Err. I, 1, 122. *for the s. of merit,* Ant. II, 7, 61. *for the s. of it,* Per. III, 1, 21. Usually with an Anglosaxon genitive: Lucr. 533. Pilgr. 120. Gent. II, 2, 5. III, 1, 17. III, 2, 63. IV, 4, 182. 207. V, 4, 149. Meas. V, 408. Err. I, 2, 93. II, 1, 77. II, 2, 24. III, 2, 6. LLL IV, 1, 32. IV, 3, 357. 358. 359. 360. Merch. II, 4, 35. IV, 1, 379. As I, 2, 293. Shr. Ind. 2, 1. All's I, 1, 24. I, 3, 43. Tw. III, 3, 34. 4, 336. H6A II, 5, 51. R3 I, 4, 216 etc. Proverbial phrases: *can you tell for whose s.?* Err. III, 1, 57. *are now 'for the Lord's s'.* Meas. IV, 3, 21. *will lend nothing for God's s.* Ado V, 1, 322. The *s* of the genitive omitted; after sibilants: *for praise s.* LLL IV, 1, 37. *for alliance s.* H6A II, 5, 53. *for goodness s.* H8 Prol. 23. *for their poor mistress s.* III, 1, 47. *for Venus s.* Troil. IV, 5, 49. *for conscience s.* Cor. II, 3, 36. *for Brutus s.* Caes. III, 2, 70. *for justice s.* IV, 3, 19. After other letters: *for fashion s.* As III, 2, 271. *for's oath s.* Tw. III, 4, 326. *for heaven s.* John IV, 1, 78. *for recreation s.* H4A I, 2, 174. *for sport s.* II, 1, 78. *for their own credit s.* 80. *for safety s.* V, 1, 65. *for your health and your digestion s.* Troil. II, 3, 120. With personal pronouns: *for my s.* Ven. 105. Sonn. 42, 7. 111, 1. Gent. II, 1, 136. Wiv. III, 5, 126. Ado IV, 1, 321. V, 2, 70. Merch. I, 1, 185 etc. *for thy s.* Gent. II, 2, 10. V, 4, 70. All's II, 3, 245. H6A V, 4, 19. 29. R3 I, 2, 146 etc. *for his s.* Meas. III, 1, 238. V, 495. Ado IV, 1, 320. Mids. II, 2, 29. All's I, 1, 110. Tw. V, 85 etc. *for her s.* Sonn. 145, 3. LLL IV, 3, 134. Mids. II, 1, 136. 137. As II, 4, 76 etc. *for your s.* Tp. III, 1, 66. Gent. IV, 2, 23. Wiv. I, 1, 268. Merch. IV, 1, 426 etc. *for their s.* H5 Epil. 13 (rhyming). With an adjective before it: *for whose dear s.* Gent. V, 4, 47. Rom. III, 3, 136. *for your lovely s.* Meas. V, 496. *for your own s.* Ado II, 1, 105. As I, 2, 189. All's II, 3, 96. cf. Gent. IV,

2, 24. *for thy sweet s.* Mids. II, 2, 103. *for your good s.* Shr. II, 61. *for your worthy s.* All's III, 3, 5. Plur. —*s: for their* —*s,* Wiv. IV, 5, 110. *for your fair* —*s,* LLL V, 2, 765. *for both our* —*s,* Shr. V, 2, 15.

**Sala,** name of a German river: H5 I, 2, 45. 52. 63.

**Salad,** see *Sallad* and *Sallet.*

**Salamander,** an animal supposed to be able to live in fire: H4A III, 3, 53.

**Salary,** recompense, hire: *this is hire and s., not revenge,* Hml. III, 3, 79 (Qq *base and silly*).

**Sale,** 1) the act of selling: *not uttered by base s. of chapmen's tongues,* LLL II, 16. *who in that s. sells pardon from himself,* John III, 1, 167. *this s. of offices,* H6B I, 3, 138. *whose s. is present death,* Rom. V, 1, 51.

2) state of being venal or vendible: *to things of s. a seller's praise belongs,* LLL IV, 3, 240. *are now on s.* As II, 4, 84. *such a house of s., videlicet a brothel,* Hml. II, 1, 60. *is not a thing for s.* Cymb. I, 4, 92. *a creature of s.* Per. IV, 6, 84.

**Salerio,** name in Merch. III, 2, 222. 223. 231. 241. 269 (some M. Edd. *Salanio*).

**Sale-work,** things made for general sale, and hence wrought with no particular care: *I see no more in you than in the ordinary of nature's s.* As III, 5, 43.

**Salique,** pertaining to the Salic tribe of the Franks: *the law S.* H5 I, 2, 11. 54 (a law excluding females from succession). *S. land,* 39. 40. 44. 51. 52. 56.

**Salisbury,** 1) name of an English town: R3 IV, 4, 443. 450. 537. 540. H8 I, 2, 196. 2) of several earls famous in English history: John IV, 2, 96. 162. IV, 3, 81. 95. V, 2, 19. 54. R2 II, 4, 1. III, 3, 2. 27. V, 6, 8. H5 IV, 3, 11. 54. H6A I, 1, 159. I, 2, 15. 25. I, 4, 73 etc. I, 5, 17. 34. 38. II, 1, 35. II, 2, 4. H6B I, 1, 70. 86. I, 3, 77 etc.

**Sallad** or **Salad** or **Sallet,** raw herbs dressed for food with salt and other ingredients: All's IV, 5, 15. 18. H6B IV, 10, 9. 11. 16. Lr. III, 4, 137. *there were no* —*s in the lines to make the matter savoury,* Hml. II, 2, 462 (nothing that gave a relish to the lines as salads do to meat). Adjectively: *my s. days,* Ant. I, 5, 73 (= green, unripe age).

**Sallet,** a close-fitting headpiece: H6B IV, 10, 12.

**Sallow,** sickly pale, yellow: *s. cheeks,* Rom. II, 3, 70.

**Sally,** subst. an issue of troops from a besieged place: H4A II, 3, 54. H6A IV, 4, 4. Troil. V, 3, 14.

**Sally,** vb. to rush, to pounce: *when you s. upon him,* All's IV, 1, 2.

**Salmon,** the fish Salmo salar: H5 IV, 7, 32. Oth. II, 1, 156.

**Salomon,** orthography of the earlier O. Edd. for *Solomon:* LLL I, 2, 180. IV, 3, 168 (F3.4 *Solomon*).

**Salt,** subst. the substance generally used for seasoning food: Gent. III, 1, 369 (according to some, = salt-cellar). Ado IV, 1, 144. H5 V, 1, 9. Figuratively: *the spice and s. that season a man,* Troil. I, 2, 277. *we have some s. of our youth in us,* Wiv. II, 3, 50. Applied to tears: *the salt in them* (your tears) *is hot,* John V, 7, 45. *the s. of most unrighteous tears,* Hml. I, 2, 154. *for certain drops of s.* Cor. V, 6, 93. *this would make a man a man of s.* Lr. IV, 6, 199.

**Salt,** adj. seasoned or impregnated with salt: *the s. fish,* Wiv. I, 1, 22 (= a fish from salt water, a sea-fish?).*Ant. II, 5, 17. Used of the sea: *their s. sove-*

*reign,* Lucr. 650. *the s. deep,* Tp. I, 2, 253. *stained with s. water,* II, 1, 64. LLL V, 1, 61. Mids. III, 2, 393. Tw. II, 1, 32. III, 4, 419. H5 I, 2, 209. Tim. V, 1, 219. Hml. III, 2, 166. Of tears: *my s. tears,* Ven. 1071. *drops full s.* Tp. I, 2, 155. Mids. II, 2, 92. All's I, 3, 178. Tw. II, 1, 32. R2 IV, 245. H6A I, 1, 50. H6B III, 2, 96. 143. Cor. IV, 1, 22 (—*er*). Rom. II, 3, 71. III, 5, 135. Tim. IV, 3, 443. Hml. IV, 5, 154. Oth. IV, 3, 47. R3 I, 2, 154. Of other defluxions: *s. rheum,* Err. III, 2, 131. Oth. III, 4, 51.

Figuratively, = 1) bitter, pungent: *the pride and s. scorn of his eyes,* Troil. I, 3, 371. 2) lecherous: *whose s. imagination hath wronged your honour,* Meas. V, 406. *make use of thy s. hours: season the slaves for tubs and baths,* Tim. IV, 3, 85. *his s. and most hidden loose affection,* Oth. II, 1, 244. *as s. as wolves in pride,* III, 3, 404. *s. Cleopatra,* Ant. II, 1, 21.

**Salt-butter,** butter seasoned with salt: *mechanical s. rogue,* Wiv. II, 2, 290 (i. e. a huckster).

**Saltiers,** the servant's blunder for *Satyrs* in Wint. IV, 4, 334.

**Saltness,** taste of salt: *some relish of the s. of time,* H4B I, 2, 112 (opposed to the freshness of youth).

**Salt-petre,** nitre: H4A I, 3, 60.

**Salt-sea** (cf. *Salt* adj.): *the s. shark,* Mcb. IV, 1, 24.

**Salt-water,** sea-water; adjectively: *thou s. thief,* Tw. V, 72 (= pirate). *our s. girdle,* Cymb. III, 1, 81 (cf. Tp. II, 1, 64. Tw. II, 1, 32. R2 IV, 245. Rom. II, 3, 71).

**Salt-waved:** *who in a s. ocean quench their light,* Lucr. 1231 (i. e. in tears).

**Salutation,** a greeting: LLL V, 1, 38. As V, 4, 39. H4A III, 2, 53. Rom. II, 4, 47. Mcb. V, 8, 57. Lr. II, 4, 32. *to do s.* R3 V, 3, 210. Caes. IV, 2, 5. *why should others' false adulterate eyes give s. to my sportive blood?* Sonn. 121, 6 (= affect in any manner, gratify or mortify. cf. the verb *salute,* and *greet* in Per. IV, 3, 38).

**Salute,** 1) to greet, to take courteous notice of in meeting: Err. IV, 3, 1. LLL IV, 2, 83. R2 III, 2, 6. H5 V, 2, 7. 22. H8 I, 4, 2. Troil. IV, 2, 61. Tit. II, 1, 5. Rom. II, 3, 32.

2) to greet each other: *you s. not at the court, but you kiss your hands,* As III, 2, 50. *saw them s. on horseback,* H8 I, 1, 8.

3) to show respect, to pay homage to: *to s. the emperor,* Gent. I, 3, 41. *if the prince do live, let us s. him,* Per. II, 4, 27.

4) to address with the purpose of showing courtesy or paying homage: *Venus* —*s him with this fair good-morrow,* Ven. 859. *s. thee for her king,* John II, 30. *to s. my king with ruder terms,* H6B I, 1, 29. *be we the first that shall s. our rightful sovereign with honour of his birthright,* II, 2, 61. *then I s. you with this kingly title,* R3 III, 7, 239. *I'll s. your grace as mother of two queens,* IV, 1, 30. *eye to eye opposed* —*s each other with each other's form,* Troil. III, 3, 108. *our general doth s. you with a kiss,* IV, 5, 19. *by wich title these sisters* —*d me,* Mcb. I, 5, 9. *lord of his fortunes he* —*s thee,* Ant. III, 12, 11.

5) to touch, to affect: *when his fair angels would s. my palm,* John II, 590. *if this s. my blood a jot,* H8 II, 3, 103. cf. *Salutation* and *Greet.*

**Salvation,** redemption, reception to the bliss of heaven: Merch. IV, 1, 200. All's IV, 3, 312. H4A II,

4, 10 (Ff *confidence*). Hml. III, 3, 92. V, 1, 2. Mis-applied by Verges in Ado III, 3, 3.

**Salve**, subst. medicinal substance applied to wounds and sores: Ven. 28. Lucr. 1116. Sonn. 34, 7. 120, 12. LLL III, 73. 75. 79. 80. 81. IV, 3, 289. H6C IV, 6, 88.

**Salve**, vb. to remedy; to palliate: *myself corrupting, —ing thy amiss*, Sonn. 35, 7. *lest my liking might too sudden seem, I would have —d it with a longer treatise*, Ado I, 1, 317. *your majesty may s. the long-grown wounds of my intemperance*, H4A III, 2, 155. *you may s. so, not what is dangerous present, but the loss of what is past*, Cor. III, 2, 70.

**Same**, 1) identical, not another; f. i.: *she would be best pleased to be so angered with another letter. No, would I were so angered with the s.* *this is the very s.* Wiv. II, 1, 84. *the very s. man*, IV, 5, 37. *the s. Aegeon*, Err. V, 344. *the s. Aemilia*, 345. *the s. Athenian*, Mids. III, 2, 41. *Owen, the s.* H4A II, 4, 375. *this s. very day*, R3 III, 2, 49.

2) that, the one: *what lady is the s. to whom you swore a secret pilgrimage?* Merch. I, 1, 119. Alls V, 3, 226. *to seem the same you are not*, Cor. III, 2, 47 (= to seem what you are not). Added to demonstrative pronouns, not to denote identity, but to lay stress on them: *call that s. Isabel here once again*, Meas. V, 270. *in that s. place thou hast appointed me*, Mids. I, 1, 177. *get thee to yond s. sovereign cruelty*, Tw. II, 4, 83. *you shall secretly into the bosom creep of that s. noble prelate, well beloved, the archbishop*, H4A I, 3, 267. *this s. Cranmer's a worthy fellow*, H8 III, 2, 71. *for all this s. I'll hide me hereabout*, Rom. V, 3, 43. *but let this s. be presently performed*, Hml. V, 2, 404. *when shall we come to the top of that s. hill?* Lr. IV, 6, 1. *how far it is to this s. blessed Milford*, Cymb. III, 2, 61. Hence used to point at a person or thing, = yonder: *yond s. black cloud looks like a foul bombard*, Tp. II, 2, 20. 24. *what is this s.?* III, 2, 134. *what letter is this s.?* Gent. III, 1, 137. *this s. is she*, Ado V, 4, 54. *what lady is that s.?* LLL II, 194. *this s. shall go*, IV, 3, 59. *there are some shrewd contents in yon s. paper*, Merch. III, 2, 246. 253. *take this s. letter*, III, 4, 47. *a pound of that s. merchant's flesh is thine*, IV, 1, 299. *what cracker is this s.* John II, 147. *if this s. were a churchyard where we stand*, III, 3, 40. *this s. half-faced fellow, give me this man*, H4B III, 2, 283. *this s. (commission) is yours*, H5 II, 2, 68. *what new alarum is this s.?* IV, 6, 35. *whip him till he leap over that s. stool*, H6B II, 1, 149. *what Trojan is that s. that looks so heavy?* Troil. IV, 5, 95. *this s. should be the voice of Friar John*, Rom. V, 2, 2. *when yond s. star that's westward from the pole had made his course*, Hml. I, 1, 36. *for this s. lord, I do repent*, III, 4, 172. *I'll talk a word with this s. learned Theban*, Lr. III, 4, 162. *what did you mean by that s. handkerchief you gave me even now?* Oth. IV, 1, 154. *what trumpet is that s.?* 226 etc.

Hence used to express contempt or vexation: *that s. Biron I'll torture ere I go*, LLL V, 2, 60. *this s. progeny of evils comes from our debate*, Mids. II, 1, 115. *that s. cowardly giant-like ox-beef hath devoured many a gentleman of your house*, Mids. III, 1, 197. *I must be one of these s. dumb wise men*, Merch. I, 1, 106. *that s. wicked bastard of Venus, let him be judge*, As IV, 1, 216. *yond's that s. knave that leads him to these places*, All's III, 5, 85. *run after that s. peevish*

messenger, Tw. I, 5, 319. *my brother Robert, that s. mighty man*, John I, 225. *this s. fat rogue*, H4A I, 2, 209 (Ff *this fat rogue*). *that s. sword and buckler prince of Wales*, I, 3, 230. *that s. mad fellow of the north*, II, 4, 369. *these s. metre ballad mongers*, III, 1, 130. *that s. word rebellion*, H4B I, 1, 194. *fallen into this s. whoreson apoplexy*, I, 2, 123. *this s. young soberblooded boy*, IV, 3, 94. *that s. Diomed is a false-hearted rogue*, Troil. V, 1, 95. *that s. scurvy young knave*, V, 4, 3. *that s. pale hard-hearted wench*, Rom. II, 4, 4. *where that s. banished runagate doth live*, III, 5, 90. *this s. wayward girl*, IV, 2, 47. *what a pestilent knave is this s.* IV, 5, 147. *Caesar was ne'er so much your enemy as that s. ague which hath made you lean*, Caes. II, 2, 113. *these s. crosses spoil me*, Lr. V, 3, 278. *these s. whoreson devils*, Ant. V, 2, 277 etc.

3) Used for the third pers. pron., = it: *he had of me a chain: at five o' clock I shall receive the money for the s.* Err. IV, 1, 11. *a ring he hath of mine worth forty ducats, and for the s. he promised me a chain*, IV, 3, 85. *give me the paper, let me read the s.* LLL I, 1, 116. *desiring thee to lay aside the sword and put the s. into young Arthur's hand*, John I, 14. *will not you maintain the thing you teach, but prove a chief offender in the s.?* H6A III, 1, 130. H6B I, 2, 10. II, 3, 33. IV, 4, 18. H6C II, 1, 66. V, 1, 65. R3 II, 4, 17. III, 4, 79. III, 5, 59. Troil. II, 2, 118. 179. Tit. III, 1, 154 etc.

**Samingo**, probably a blunder of Mr. Silence for *San Domingo*, the patron saint of topers: H4B V, 3, 79.

**Samphire** (O. Edd. *sampire*), sea-fennel: Lr. IV, 6, 15.

**Sample**, example, model: *a s. to the youngest*, Cymb. I, 1, 48.

**Sampler**, a piece of needle-work made by young girls for improvement: Mids. III, 2, 205. Tit. II, 4, 39.

**Sampson**, name in H4B III, 2, 35.

**Samson** or **Sampson**, the hero of the Old Testament: LLL I, 2, 73. 77. 78. 80. 91. 179. H6A I, 2, 33. H8 V, 4, 22.

**Sanctify**, to make holy, to consecrate: *my idolatrous fancy must s. his reliques*, All's I, 1, 109. *his good receipt shall for my legacy be —ed by the luckiest stars in heaven*, I, 3, 251. *whilst I from far his name with zealous fervour s.* III, 4, 11. *drops of balm to s. thy head*, H4B IV, 5, 115. *'as true as Troilus' shall crown up the verse and s. the numbers*, Troil. III, 2, 190. *—es himself with's hand*, Cor. IV, 5, 208. *—ed* = holy, consecrated, sacred: *a nun, or sister —ed*, Compl. 233. *your virtues are —ed and holy traitors to you*, As II, 3, 13. *buried in highways out of all —ed limit*, All's I, 1, 152. *and draw no swords but what are —ed*, H4B IV, 4, 4. *—ed and pious bonds*, Hml. I, 3, 130. *so help me every spirit —ed*, Oth. III, 4, 126.

**Sanctimonious**, bespeaking or expressing sanctity: *all s. ceremonies*, Tp. IV, 16. Hence = outwardly holy, hypocritical: *like the s. pirate, that went to sea with the ten commandments*, Meas. I, 2, 7.

**Sanctimony**, that which implies the idea of sanctity: *if vows be —es*, Troil. V, 2, 139. Hence piety and devoutness shown: *which holy undertaking with most austere s. she accomplished*, All's IV, 3, 59. *if s. be the gods' delight*, Troil. V, 2, 140. And = outward sanctity, hypocrisy: *if s. and a frail vow betwixt an erring barbarian and a supersubtle Venetian be not too hard for my wits*, Oth. I, 3, 362.

**Sanctity,** holiness: *his kissing is as full of s. as the touch of holy bread,* As III, 4, 14. *which way is he, in the name of s.?* Tw. III, 4, 94 (Sir Toby's speech). *with such s. of love,* 395. *in pure white robes, like very s.* Wint. III, 3, 23. *the very opener and intelligencer between the grace, the —es of heaven and our dull workings,* H4B IV, 2, 21. *such s. hath heaven given his hand,* Mcb. IV, 3, 144. *my s. will to my sense bend no licentious ear,* Per. V, 3, 29. In Hml. I, 3, 21 Ff *the s. and health of the whole state,* Qq *the safety.* Theobald conj. *sanity;* cf. II, 2, 214, where also the writing of Qq is *sanctity.*

**Sanctuarize,** to be a sanctuary to, to protect from punishment: *no place should murder s.* Hml. IV, 7, 128.

**Sanctuary,** a sacred place: Meas. II, 2, 171. Ado II, 1, 266. Cor. I, 10, 19. Especially a sacred asylum affording protection from any persecution: H6C IV, 4, 31.*R3 II, 4, 66. 73. III, 1, 42. IV, 1, 94. *to take s.* = to take refuge in such a place: Err. V, 94. R3 III, 1, 28. *to break s.* = to violate it: R3 III, 1, 47. *s. men,* 55. *s. children,* 56.

**Sand,** a fine dust-like particle of stone, a grain of sand: *one s. another not more resembles,* Cymb. V, 5, 120. Collectively, = a mass of such grains: *whose hearts are all as false as stairs of s.* Merch. III, 2, 84. Particularly those covering the shores of the sea and forming shelves in it: *twenty seas, if all their s. were pearl,* Gent. II, 4, 170. *my wealthy Andrew docked in s.* Merch. I, 1, 27. *wrecked upon a s.* H5 IV, 1, 100. *make their ransom on the s.* H6B IV, 1, 10. *tread on the s.* H6C V, 4, 30. Plur. —*s,* = 1) grains of sand: *numbering —s,* R2 II, 2, 146. *turn the —s into eloquent tongues, and my horse is argument for them all,* H5 III, 7, 36. *the northern wind will blow these —s abroad,* Tit. IV, 1, 105. cf. H6C I, 4, 25. 2) the mass of such grains covering the shore of the sea, or forming shelves: Ven. 148. Tp. I, 2, 376. V, 34. Gent. III, 2, 81. IV, 3, 33. Mids. II, 1, 126. Lr. IV, 6, 280. Lucr. 335. John V, 3, 11. V, 5, 13. H6B III, 2, 97. C V, 4, 36. Oth. II, 1, 69. Cymb. III, 1, 21. 3) the contents of hour glasses: *the —s are numbered that make up my life,* H6C I, 4, 25. *horses have been nimbler than the — s,* Cymb. III, 2, 74. *our —s are almost run,* Per. V, 2, 1.

**Sandal,** name of the castle of the duke of York, near Wakefield: H6C I, 2, 63.

**Sandal shoon,** shoes consisting only of soles tied to the feet: Hml. IV, 5, 26.

**Sand-blind,** purblind: Merch. II, 2, 37. 77.

**Sanded,** of a sandy colour: Mids. IV, 1, 125.

**Sands,** name in H8 I, 3, 47. I, 4, 23. 40.*

**Sandy,** 1) covered with sand: *the s. plains,* H6B I, 4, 39. *this s. plot is plain,* Tit. IV, 1, 69.

2) consisting of sand: *as false as air, as water, wind, or s. earth,* Troil. III, 2, 199. Applied to the hourglass: *I should not see the s. hour-glass run,* Merch. I, 1, 25. *ere the glass finish the process of his s. hour,* H6A IV, 2, 36.

**Sandy-bottomed,** having a sandy channel: *s. Severn,* H4A III, 1, 66.

**Sanguine,** having the colour of blood, red: *this s. coward,* H4A II, 4, 268 (red-faced with much drinking). *the s. colour of the leaves* (of the rose) H6A IV, 1, 92. *ye s. shallow-hearted boys, ye white-limed walls, ye ale-house painted signs, coal-black is better than another hue,* Tit. IV, 2, 97. *had upon his neck a mole, a s. star,* Cymb. V, 5, 364.

**Sanity,** a sound state: *a happiness that often madness hits on, which reason and s. could not so prosperously be delivered of,* Hml. II, 2, 214 (Qq *sanctity*). In I, 3, 21 Ff *the sanctity and health of the whole state;* probably a misprint for *sanity.* Similarly *insanie* in LLL V, 1, 28 was changed by the compositors to *infamie.*

**Sans,** without: *a confidence s. bound,* Tp. I, 2, 97. *s. fable,* Err. IV, 4, 76. *s. question,* LLL V, 1, 91. *s. crack or flaw. S. sans, I pray you,* V, 2, 415. 416. *s. intermission,* As II, 7, 32. *s. teeth, s. eyes, s. taste, s. every thing,* 166. *s. compliment,* John V, 6, 16. *s. check,* Troil. I, 3, 94. *s. remorse,* Tim. IV, 3, 122. *s. all,* Hml. III, 4, 79. *s. witchcraft,* Oth. I, 3, 64.

**Santrailles** (O. Edd. *Santrayle* or *Santraile*) French name in H6A I, 4, 28.

**Sap,** the vital juice of plants: Ven. 1176. Lucr. 950. 1168. Sonn. 5, 7. 15, 7. Err. II, 2, 182. R2 III, 4, 59. R3 II, 2, 42. H8 I, 2, 98. Troil. I, 3, 7. Lr. IV, 2, 35. Used of blood: *did drain the purple s. from her sweet brother's body,* R3 IV, 4, 277. Metaphorically: *there is some s. in this,* Wint. IV, 4, 576 (there is life in it; it bids fair). Ant. III, 13, 192. *if with the s. of reason you would quench or but allay the fire of passion,* H8 I, 1, 148.

**Sap-consuming,** wasting the vital juice: Err. V, 312.

**Sapient,** sage: *thou, s. sir, sit here,* Lr. III, 6, 24.

**Sapless,** wanting sap: H6A II, 5, 12. IV, 5, 4.

**Sapling,** a young tree: R3 III, 4, 71. Used of young persons: Tit. III, 2, 50. Per. IV, 2, 93.

**Sapphire,** a precious blue stone: Compl. 215. Wiv. V, 5, 75 (O. Edd. *saphire-pearl*). Err. III, 2, 138.

**Sappy,** full of sap: Ven. 165.

**Saracen,** an Arabian, a Moor: *black pagans, Turks and —s,* R2 IV, 95.

**Sarcenet,** fine woven silk: *givest such s. surety for thy oaths,* H4A III, 1, 256 (such as becomes a mercer's wife). *thou green s. flap for a sore eye,* Troil. V, 1, 36.

**Sardians,** the inhabitants of the town of Sardis: Caes. IV, 3, 3.

**Sardinia,** island in the Mediterranean: Ant. II, 6, 35.

**Sardis,** the capital of Lydia: Caes. IV, 2, 28. V, 1, 80. V, 5, 18.

**Sarpego,** see *Serpigo.*

**Sarum plain,** Salisbury plain: Lr. II, 2, 89.

**Satan,** the prince of hell: Wiv. V, 5, 163. Err. IV, 3, 48. 49. IV, 4, 57. All's V, 3, 261. Tw. III, 4, 130. IV, 2, 35. H4A II, 4, 509.

**Satchel,** a bag used by schoolboys to carry their books and papers in: As II, 7, 145.

**Sate,** to feed beyond the limit of natural desire: *lust will s. itself in a celestial bed and prey on garbage,* Hml. I, 5, 56. *when she is —d with his body,* Oth. I, 3, 356.

**Satiate,** fed to the full, glutted: *the cloyed will, that s. yet unsatisfied desire,* Cymb. I, 6, 48.

**Satiety** (O. Edd. *society,* except in Oth.) 1) full gratification: *and with s. seeks to quench his thirst,* Shr. I, 1, 24.

2) excess of gratification, state of being glutted: Ven. 19. Tim. I, 1, 166. Oth. II, 1, 231.

**Satin,** soft and glossy silk: Meas. IV, 3, 12. H4B I, 2, 34. 50. Per. III, 1, 68.

**Satire,** a poem in which wickedness or folly is censured: *be a s. to decay,* Sonn. 100, 11 (the poet's Muse addressed). Ado V, 4, 103. Mids. V, 54. Tim. V, 1, 36.

**Satirical,** full of bitter mockery: Hml. II, 2, 198.

**Satisfaction,** 1) gratification: *nor gives it s. to our blood, that we must curb it upon others' proof,* Compl. 162. *have you received no promise of s. at her hands?* Wiv. II, 2, 217. Meas. III, 1, 156. 275. Wint. I, 2, 31. Rom. II, 2, 126. Oth. I, 3, 265.

2) payment: *make present s.* Err. IV, 1, 5. *a good conscience will make any possible s.* H4B V, 5, 137. cf. Oth IV, 2, 203.

3) amends, atonement: Merch. III, 1, 98. Tw. III, 4, 261. H5 III, 6, 141. H6A II, 3, 77. Troil. II, 3, 4. Hml. IV, 5, 209. Oth. IV, 2, 203. *to give s.* Err. V, 252. Cymb. II, 1, 16. *to make s.* Err. V, 399. H5 IV, 8, 48. H6C V, 5, 14. Tit. V, 1, 8.

4) full information, release from uncertainty and suspense, conviction: *we may soon our s. have touching that point,* Meas. I, 1, 83. *for my better s. let me have Claudio's head sent me,* IV, 2, 125. *she ceased in heavy s.* All's V, 3, 100 (sadly acquiescing in what she acknowledged to be necessary). *King Lewis his s.* H5 I, 2, 88. *for the s. of my mind,* III, 2, 106. *for your private s.* Caes. II, 2, 73. *and by an auricular assurance have your s.* Lr. I, 2, 99. *for a s. of my thought,* Oth. III, 3, 97. *where's s.?* 401. *will give you s.* 408. *pretending the s. of her knowledge only,* Cymb. V, 5, 251.

**Satisfy,** 1) to feed to the full: *which, having all, all could not s.* Lucr. 96. *sharp hunger by the conquest —ed,* 422. *let us s. our eyes with the things of fame that do renown this city,* Tw. III, 3, 22. *my fancy may be —ed,* H6A V, 3, 91. *whose thirst York and young Rutland could not s.* H6C II, 6, 84. *she makes hungry where most she —es,* Ant. II, 2, 243. cf. the quibble in II, 7, 56.

2) to give satisfaction; to content; to gratify: Gent. V, 4, 79. Wiv. II, 1, 195. IV, 2, 172. Meas. II, 2, 104. III, 1, 170 (*do not s. your resolution with hopes that are fallible*; i. e. do not set yourself at ease, do not gratify yourself, who were just now resolved to die, with false hopes). IV, 3, 79. Ado V, 1, 285. LLL II, 153. Merch. IV, 1, 415. 416. As V, 2, 124. Shr. III, 2, 111. All's II, 3, 206. Wint. I, 2, 232. 233. 234. IV, 4, 635. John II, 557. R2 IV, 272. 273. H4B II, 1, 143. H6A II, 5, 21. H6C II, 2, 99. II, 5, 104. 106. 108. III, 2, 20. R3 III, 3, 21. V, 3, 72. H8 II, 4, 148. Troil. II, 3, 149. Tit. II, 3, 180. Rom. II, 1, 9. III, 1, 75. III, 5, 93. 94. Caes. II, 2, 72. III, 1, 48 (*Caesar does not wrong, nor without cause will he be —ed*; i. e. not base flattery, but a real cause, a reasonable motive, can alone content him and induce him to grant a pardon). 141. 226. IV, 2, 10.* Hml. V, 2, 255. Oth. I, 2, 88. V, 2, 318. Ant. II, 7, 56. III, 13, 167. Cymb. IV, 4, 16. V, 4, 15 (= to give satisfaction, to make amends). Per. IV, 1, 72.

3) to free from doubt and uncertainty, to inform fully, to convince: *s. me so,* LLL II, 163. *to s. you in what I have said,* Shr. IV, 2, 4. *though I am —ed and need no more than what I know,* Wint. II, 1, 189. *I will be —ed, let me see the writing,* R2 V, 2, 59. *would be better —ed how in our means we should advance ourselves,* H4B I, 3, 6. *—ed that Queen Isabel was lineal of the Lady Ermengare,* H5 I, 2, 80. *to s. my opinion,* H5 III, 2, 105 (Fluellen's speech). *to s. myself, in craving your opinion,* H6B II, 2, 3. *how far*

*you —ed me,* H8 II, 4, 211. *he is returned in his opinions, which have —ed the king for his divorce,* III, 2, 65. *let me be —ed, is't good or bad?* Rom. II, 5, 37. *we will be —ed,* Caes. III, 2, 1. *I will be —ed,* Mcb. IV, 1, 104. *to s. my remembrance the more strongly,* V, 1, 37. *s. yourself,* Oth. I, 1, 138. *would I were —ed,* III, 3, 390. 393. 394. *you shall be —ed,* IV, 2, 252. *he hath given me —ing reasons,* V, 1, 9. *if you seek for further —ing,* Cymb. II, 4, 134. *s. me home what is become of her,* III, 5, 92. *if further yet you will be —ed,* Per. I, 3, 16. With *of,* = to give full information about: *you are not —ed of these events at full,* Merch. V, 296. *of this my letters before did s. you,* Ant. II, 2, 52.

**Saturday,** the seventh day of the week: LLL IV, 1, 6. As IV, 1, 116.

**Saturn,** the god who reigned before Jupiter; supposed to be of a melancholy and morose temper: *hath put a spirit of youth in every thing, that heavy S. laughed and leaped with him,* Sonn. 98, 4. *a pudency so rosy the sweet view on't might well have warmed old S.* Cymb. II, 5, 12. The planet of the same name causing hate, melancholy and moroseness: *born under S.* Ado I, 3, 12. *S. and Venus this year in conjunction,* H4B II, 4, 286. *though Venus govern your desires, S. is dominator over mine,* Tit. II, 3, 31. *to S., Caius, not to Saturnine,* IV, 3, 56 (O. Edd. *to Saturnine, Caius, not to Saturnine*).

**Saturnine,** name of the emperor in Tit. I, 208. 225. 233 etc.

**Saturninus,** the same: Tit. I, 203. 205. 232. II, 1, 90. IV, 4, 24.

**Satyr,** a sylvan god, part man and part goat: Hml. I, 2, 140.

**Sauce,** subst. a mixture eaten with food to improve its relish and provoke the appetite: Sonn. 118, 6. Ado IV, 1, 281. As III, 3, 31. H4A II, 4, 586. H5 V, 1, 36. 52. Rom. II, 4, 84. Caes. I, 2, 304. Mcb. III, 4, 36. IV, 3, 81. Ant. II, 1, 25.

**Sauce,** vb. 1) to accompany with a sauce, to give a relish to: *his meat was —d with thy upbraidings,* Err. V, 73. *his folly —d with discretion,* Troil. I, 2, 24. *praises —d with lies,* Cor. I, 9, 53. *to s. thy dishes* (with poison) Tim. IV, 3, 299. *—d our broths, as Juno had been sick and he her dieter,* Cymb. IV, 2, 50.

2) to gratify, to tickle: *s. his palate with thy most operant poison,* Tim. IV, 3, 24.* Ironically, = to pepper: *I'll make them pay, I'll s. them,* Wiv. IV, 3, 11. 13. *I'll s. her with bitter words,* As III, 5, 69.

**Saucer,** a small pan or platter: LLL IV, 3, 98.

**Saucily,** with impertinent boldness: *while others s. promise more speed, but do it leisurely,* Lucr. 1348. *this knave came something s. into the world before he was sent for,* Lr. I, 1, 22. *displayed so s. against your highness,* II, 4, 41.

**Sauciness,** impertinent boldness, impudence: Err. II, 2, 28. All's IV, 5, 70. John V, 2, 133. H4B II, 1, 123. 135. Tit. II, 3, 82.

**Saucy,** 1) pungent, full of salt: *there's vinegar and pepper in it* (the letter). *Is't so s.?* Tw. III, 4, 159 (punning).

2) petulant, wanton, lascivious: *to remit their s. sweetness that do coin heaven's image in stamps that are forbid,* Meas. II, 4, 45. *O strange men, that can such sweet use make of what they hate, when s. trusting of the cozened thoughts defiles the pitchy night,* All's

IV, 4, 23. But in both passages the word may be understood in its third and stronger sense.

3) impudent, insolent: Sonn 80, 7. 128, 13. Gent. I, 2, 92. Meas. V, 135. LLL I, 1, 85. Mids. V, 103. As III, 2, 314. Tw. I, 5, 209. John II, 404. H4B II, 4, 139. H6A III, 1, 45. III, 4, 33. H6B IV, 10, 38. H8 IV, 2, 100. Troil. I, 3, 42. Tit. II, 3, 60. Rom. I, 5, 85. II, 4, 153. Caes. I, 1, 21. IV, 3, 134. Mcb. III, 4, 25 (*bound in to s. doubts and fears;* i. e. unbounded, extravagant; a very expressive oxymoron)* III, 5, 3. Oth. I, 1, 129. Ant. IV, 14, 25. V, 2, 214. Cymb. I, 6, 151. III, 4, 161. V, 5, 325. Followed by *with: s. with lords,* All's II, 3, 278. *the world, too s. with the gods,* Caes. I, 3, 12. *so s. with the hand of she here,* Ant. III, 13, 138.

**Saunder,** Christian name of Simpcox (Alexander?): H6B II, 1, 124. 125.

**Savage,** adj. 1) wild, untamed: *in time the s. bull doth bear the yoke,* Ado I, 1, 263. V, 1, 183. V, 4, 43. *their* (colts') *s. eyes turned to a modest gaze,* Merch. V, 78. *any thing s.* As II, 6, 7 (= game). *a s. clamour,* Wint. III, 3, 56 (as of wild beasts chased).

2) beastly, brutal: *these pampered animals that rage in s. sensuality,* Ado IV, 1, 62. *his lustful eye or s. heart,* R3 III, 5, 83. *breaks out to s. madness,* Oth. IV, 1, 56. *I have s. cause,* Ant. III, 13, 128 (= cause to act like a wild beast). Substantively: *when thou didst not, s., know thine own meaning,* Tp. I, 2, 355.

3) wild, uncultivated: *our scions, put in wild and s. stock,* H5 III, 5, 7. Particularly applied to people in the uncivilized state of nature: *like a rude and s. man of Inde,* LLL IV, 3, 222. *s. islanders* (stabbed) *Pompey,* H6B IV, 1, 137. *some s. hold,* Cymb. III, 6, 18. In this sense it becomes quite a subst., forming a regular plural: *with —s and men of Ind,* Tp. II, 2, 60 (O. Edd. *salvages*). LLL V, 2, 202. H5 V, 2, 59. Ant. I, 4, 61.

4) rude, unpolished, uncivil: *I thought that all things had been s. here,* As II, 7, 107; cf. *our courtiers say all's s. but at court,* Cymb. IV, 2, 33. III, 6, 23. *the s. strangeness he puts on,* Troil. II, 3, 135. *to fright you thus, methinks, I am too s.* Mcb. IV, 2, 70.

5) ferocious, barbarous, atrocious: *bloody, full of blame, s., extreme, rude, cruel,* Sonn 129, 4. *his lines would ravish s. ears and plant in tyrants mild humility,* LLL IV, 3, 348. *a s. jealousy,* Tw. V, 122. *the s. spirit of wild war,* John V, 2, 74. H5 II, 2, 95. H6C I, 1, 224. R3 I, 4, 265. Tim. V, 1, 168. Caes. III, 1, 223. Lr. III, 3, 7. Per. V, 1, 218. Troil. V, 3, 49.

**Savagely,** atrociously: Mcb. IV, 3, 205.

**Savageness,** 1) wild ferocity: *wolves and bears, casting their s. aside, have done like offices of pity,* Wint. II, 3, 187. *she will sing the s. out of a bear,* Oth. IV, 1, 200.

2) licentiousness, unruliness, proneness to excess: *the flash and outbreak of a fiery mind, a s. in unreclaimed blood of general assault,* Hml. II, 1, 34.

**Savagery,** 1) wild growth: *the coulter rusts that should deracinate such s.* H5 V, 2, 47.

2) atrocity: *the bloodiest shame, the wildest s.* John IV, 3, 48.

**Savage-wild** (not hyphened in O. Edd.) cruel, ferocious: *the time and my intents are s.* Rom. V, 3, 37.

**Save,** vb. 1) to preserve, to rescue, to release, to guard: Wiv. II, 3, 6. Meas. II, 1, 7. II, 4, 64. 88. 95. III, 1, 62. 134. 147. 264. V, 396. 492. Err. I, 1, 114.

V, 168. 193. 283. Ado II, 1, 155. All's II, 1, 181. Wint. II, 3, 161. John IV, 1, 73. H6A I, 2, 147. III, 2, 105. IV, 3, 26. Cor. V, 3, 75. Hml. III, 4, 103. Cymb. II, 4, 94 etc. With *from: to s. your ship from wreck,* Gent. I, 1, 156. IV, 4, 3. Meas. II, 2, 161. IV, 3, 89. Wint. IV, 4, 521. H6A V, 4, 160. H6B II, 1, 143. Tit. II, 3, 164. Hml. IV, 7, 146. Lr. V, 3, 191 etc. *God s. =* God may preserve or guard: Meas. II, 2, 25. Ado III, 2, 82. V, 1, 327. LLL IV, 2, 149. V, 2, 310. As V, 2, 20. Shr. I, 2, 219. R2 II, 2, 41. H6A IV, 1, 2. R3 III, 7, 22. H8 III, 1, 1 etc. (As for *God s. the mark,* see *Mark*). God omitted: *s. his majesty,* Tp. II, 1, 168 (M. Edd. *God s. his majesty*). *s. our graces,* III, 2, 115. Particularly as a kind wish in meeting or parting: *Sir Proteus, s. you,* Gent. I, 1, 70. *s. your honour,* Meas. II, 2, 161. Wiv. II, 3, 19. III, 1, 41. All's I, 1, 117. III, 2, 47. Tw. III, 1, 1. 76. Tim. IV, 3, 414. Lr. II, 1, 1 etc. *s. your reverence,* in the same sense as *saving your reverence* (see *Saving*): Rom. I, 4, 42 (the surreptitious Q1 and M. Edd. *this sir reverence*).

2) to preserve from eternal death: *my beauty will be —d by merit,* LLL IV, 1, 21. *I shall be —d by my husband,* Merch. III, 5, 21 (cf. 1 Corinthians VII, 14: *the unbelieving wife is sanctified by the husband*). *to be —d by believing,* Tw. III, 2, 75. *if men were to be —d by merit,* H4A I, 2, 119. *so Christ s. me,* H5 III, 2, 97. *I have a —ing faith within me,* V, 2, 217. *there be souls must be —d,* Oth. II, 3, 106. 107. 111. 114. *no, as I shall be —d,* IV, 2, 86. *he that will believe all that they say, shall never be —d by half that they do,* Ant. V, 2, 257.

3) to keep undamaged or untouched: *his youthful hose, well —d,* As II, 7, 160. *that honour —d may upon asking give,* Tw. III, 4, 232. *to s. unscratched your city's threatened cheeks,* John II, 225. *s. me a piece of marchpane,* Rom. I, 5, 9. *couldst thou s. nothing? didst thou give them all?* Lr. III, 4, 66. Absol.: *he is gone to s. far off, whilst others come to make him lose at home,* R2 II, 2, 80.

4) to lay up, to gather: *the thrifty hire I —d under your father,* As II, 3, 39.

5) to keep to one's self, not to spend, to spare: *to s. the money that he spends in trimming,* Err. II, 2, 98. *to s. their gifts,* Merch. IV, 1, 444. *to s. both* (charge and trouble) Wint. I, 2, 26. *to s. the blood on either side,* H4A V, 1, 99. *s. that labour,* Lucr. 1290. Err. IV, 1, 14. As II, 7, 8. Troil. III, 3, 241. Cor. I, 3, 90. Oth. V, 1, 101. *s. your word,* All's V, 2, 40. *s. your thanks,* Wint. I, 2, 54. Troil. IV, 4, 119. *I may s. speech,* Oth. IV, 1, 291 etc.

6) to hinder from spending or being spent, from using or being used, to make superfluous: *you might have —d me my pains,* Tw. II, 2, 6. *a thousand sighs to s.* II, 4, 64. *thou hast —d me a thousand marks in links,* H4A III, 3, 48. *and —d the treacherous labour of your son,* V, 4, 57. *—s me so much talking,* H8 I, 4, 40. *I'll s. you that labour,* II, 1, 3. *and —d your husband so much sweat,* Cor. IV, 1, 18. *—d me a day's journey,* IV, 3, 12. *you have —d my longing, and I feed most hungerly on your sight,* Tim. I, 1, 261.

7) to spare, to treat with pity, not to destroy: *relent and s. my life,* H6B IV, 7, 124. *—ing of thy life,* Caes. V, 3, 38. *s. him,* Lr. V, 3, 151. *makes the true man killed and —s the thief,* Cymb. II, 3, 76.

**Save,** adv. (not prepos., as it is followed by the case required by the verb: Sonn. 109, 14. Tw. III, 1,

172. Tim. IV, 3, 507. Caes. III, 2, 66. V, 5, 69) except: Ven. 300. Lucr. 95. 126. 409. 1426. Sonn. 12, 14. 48, 10. 57, 12. 75, 12. 109, 14. 131, 13. Pilgr. 380. Tp. II, 1, 50. III, 1, 50. Ado II, 1, 183. V, 1, 71. LLL I, 1, 87. Merch. III, 2, 184. All's II, 3, 129. Tw. II, 4, 19. III, 1, 172. John II, 250. R2 I, 3, 207. H6B IV, 1, 126. Troil. II, 3, 197. Tim. IV, 3, 507. Caes. I, 3, 88. III, 2, 66. V, 5, 69 etc. *s. for* = but for: *then was this island, s. for the son that she did litter here, not honoured with a human shape,* Tp. I, 2, 282. *of all one pain, s. for a night of groans,* R3 IV, 4, 303. *s. that* = were it not that: *looking on darkness, s. that my soul's imaginary sight presents thy shadow,* Sonn. 27, 9. *from these would I be gone, s. that, to die, I leave my love alone,* 66, 14. Meas. I, 2, 152. IV, 4, 32. Mids. III, 2, 309. All's III, 2, 2. H5 I, 1, 84. R3 III, 7, 193. Oth. III, 3, 65. Cymb. IV, 2, 238. *s. for save that,* in the language of Evans: Wiv. I, 1, 261.

**Saving,** 1) except: *ere answer knows what question would, s. in dialogue of compliment,* John I, 201.

2) all due respect shown to, no offence to: *s. your merry humour, here's the note,* Err. IV, 1, 27. *s. your tale, Petruchio, I pray, let us speak too,* Shr. II, 71. *which gifts, s. your mincing, the capacity of your cheveril conscience would receive,* H8 II, 3, 31. Especially used to apologize for the boldness or impropriety of an expression: *s. your reverence, a husband,* Ado III, 4, 32. *and longing, s. your honour's reverence, for stewed prunes,* Meas. II, 1, 92. Merch. II, 2, 27. 138. H4A II, 4, 515. = *reverence of the word,* Cymb. IV, 1, 5. *s. your manhoods,* H4B II, 1, 29. H5 IV, 8, 35.

**Saviour,** the Redeemer: Hml. I, 1, 159.

**Savory,** the plant Satureja hortensis: Wint. IV, 4, 104.

**Savour,** subst. smell; in a proper and a figurative sense: *both favour, s., hue and qualities ... are on the sudden wasted,* Ven. 747. *for compound sweet foregoing simple s.* Sonn. 125, 7. *she loved not the s. of tar nor of pitch,* Tp. II, 2, 54. *in those freckles live their* (the cowslips') *—s,* Mids. II, 1, 13. *the flowers of odious —s sweet,* III, 1, 84. *I smell sweet —s,* Shr. Ind. 2, 73. *a s. that may strike the dullest nostril,* Wint. I, 2, 421. *keep seeming and s. all the winter long,* IV, 4, 75. *the uncleanly —s of a slaughter-house,* John IV, 3, 112. *this admiration is much o'the s. of other your new pranks,* Lr. I, 4, 258 (Q3 and some M. Edd. *favour*); cf. the verb.

**Savour,** vb. 1) intr. to have a particular smell: *to me the very doors and windows s. vilely,* Per. IV, 6, 117. Metaphorically, = to be of a particular nature: *a savage jealousy that sometime —s nobly,* Tw. V, 123. With *of: neither —ing of poetry, wit, nor invention,* LLL IV, 2, 165. *this —s not much of distraction,* Tw. V, 322. *—s of tyranny,* Wint. II, 3, 119. *you s. too much of your youth,* H5 I, 2, 250. *his jest will s. but of shallow wit,* 295.

2) trans. to like: *filths s. but themselves,* Lr. IV, 2, 39.

**Savoury,** pleasing to the taste: *there were no sallets in the lines to make the matter s.* Hml. II, 2, 463. *our stomachs will make what's homely s.* Cymb. III, 6, 33.

**Savoy,** name of a palace in London: H6B IV, 7, 2.

**Saw,** subst. a moral saying, a maxim, a sentence: *who fears a sentence or an old man's s.* Lucr. 244.

*coughing drowns the parson's s.* LLL V, 2, 932. *full of wise —s and modern instances,* As II, 7, 156. *now I find thy s. of might,* III, 5, 82. *we'll whisper o'er a couplet or two of most sage —s,* Tw. III, 4, 413. *his weapons holy saws of sacred writ,* H6B I, 3, 61. *all —s of books,* Hml. I, 5, 100. *that must approve the common s.* Lr. II, 2, 167.

**Saw,** subst. (cf. *Handsaw*) a cutting instrument with a dentated edge: *his sighs, his sorrows, make a s., to push grief on, and back the same grief draw,* Lucr. 1672.

**Saw,** vb. (partic. *sawed*) to cut with a saw: H4B V, 1, 70. *do not s. the air too much with your hand,* Hml. III, 2, 5.

**Sawn,** = sown (or, according to others, = seen): Compl. 91.

**Saw-pit,** a pit over which timber is sawed: Wiv. IV, 4, 53.

**Saxons,** name of a German people: H5 I, 2, 46. 62.

**Saxony,** a German country: Merch. I, 2, 91.

**Say,** subst. a kind of silk: *thou s., thou serge, nay, thou buckram lord,* H6B IV, 7, 27.

**Say,** subst. assay, taste, relish: *thy tongue some s. of breeding breathes,* Lr. V, 3, 143.

**Say,** name in H6B IV, 2, 170. 174. IV, 4, 19. IV, 7, 23.

**Say,** vb. to assay: *of all —ed yet, mayst thou prove prosperous! of all —ed yet, I wish thee happiness,* Per. I, 1, 59.

**Say,** vb. (impf. and partic. *said;* partic. *sain* used by Armado in rhyming) 1) to utter, to express, declare or pronounce in words: Ven. 12. 53. 217. 229. 253. 329. 373. 374. 510. 535 (*s. Good night*). 537 (*s. Adieu*). 583. 611. 805. 851. 852. 865. 1173. Lucr. 320 (*as who should say;* cf. Ven. 280; see *Should*). 358. 505 etc. etc. *to say farewell,* R3 I, 2, 225. Ant. IV, 14, 90. The passive personally: *thou art said to have a stubborn soul,* Meas. V, 485. Ado I, 3, 32. Mids. I, 1, 238. Tw. IV, 2, 10. Cor. IV, 5, 243. Mcb. II, 3, 34. With *of* = concerning, about: *so of collected sorrow may be said,* Ven. 333. *what you said of the duke,* Meas. V, 334. As IV, 1, 47 etc. The addressed person preceded by *to:* Gent. IV, 3, 35. Tw. I, 5, 153. IV, 2, 16 etc. *To* omitted after *to say nay* = to refuse, when the dative is placed between *say* and *nay: said him nay,* John I, 275. *you'll say a beggar nay,* R3 III, 1, 119. Rom. II, 2, 96. *I can say nay to thee,* R3 III, 7, 53. Having *to* before the person or thing spoken of, in the sense of to think, to judge of: *what the old world could say to this composed wonder of your frame,* Sonn. 59, 9. *what say you to a letter from your friends of much good news,* Gent. II, 4, 51. *what says she to my little jewel?* IV, 4, 51. *what says Silvia to my suit?* V, 2, 1. 8. *what says she to me?* Wiv. II, 2, 81. *what say you to young Master Fenton?* III, 2, 67. Meas. IV, 2, 131. Merch. I, 2, 71. Shr. IV, 3, 17. 20 (*how say you to a fat tripe?*). Tw. I, 5, 88 (*how say you to that?*). John IV, 2, 132. R2 III, 2, 177. H4A V, 1, 15. H4B I, 2, 1. H6C IV, 1, 107. Rom. III, 3, 97. Lr. I, 1, 241. IV, 6, 100. Oth. I, 3, 74. V, 2, 293. Similarly: *how say you by the French lord?* Merch. I, 2, 58. *how sayest thou that my master is become a notable lover?* Gent. II, 5, 43. Mcb. III, 4, 128.

*To say so:* Ven. 536. Tp. II, 2, 65. III, 1, 37. Meas. III, 2, 195. Ado II, 1, 136. LLL IV, 3, 5 etc. etc. *no, sayst me so, friend?* Shr. I, 2, 190. *sayst thou me so?* H6B II, 1, 109 (*me* a dativus ethicus).

*I say,* inserted emphatically: *how would, I say, mine eyes be blessed made,* Sonn. 43, 9. *O, if, I say, you look upon this verse,* 71, 9. *new created the creatures that were mine, I say, or changed them,* Tp. I, 2, 82. *what, I say, my foot my tutor?* 468. Especially in commanding, or calling to, a person: *stand, I say,* Ven. 284. *out of our way, I say,* Tp. I, 1, 29. *what, Robin, I say,* Wiv. III, 3, 4. *Bardolph, I say,* III, 5, 1. Tp. I, 2, 315. Gent. IV, 4, 66. V, 4, 122. Wiv. IV, 2, 125. Meas. I, 1, 16. V, 460. Ado III, 3, 104. Merch. II, 5, 6. H4B IV, 1, 2. H8 II, 4, 241. Cor. IV, 3, 40. Rom. I, 3, 58. IV, 2, 30. Tim. II, 1, 14. Caes. II, 1, 3. Mcb. V, 3, 20. Lr. I, 4, 350. II, 1, 21 etc. *avoid the gallery; ha! I have said, be gone,* H8 V, 1, 86. *I have said* = yes, as I said: Mcb. IV, 3, 213. Ant. I, 2, 58.

*Say you?* = what do you say? *not better than he, by her own report. Say you?* Meas. V, 275. *what imports this song? Say you?* nay, pray you, mark, Hml. IV, 5, 28. *heaven bless us. Say you?* Oth. III, 4, 82. *you are cock and capon too. Sayest thou?* Cymb. II, 1, 27. *say you, sir? Thy name. Fidele,* IV, 2, 379. cf. *how say you? O, I should remember him,* Wiv. I, 4, 29.

2) to tell: *the mariners say how thou hast disposed,* Tp. I, 2, 225. *say what thou seest yond,* 409. *say how thou camest here,* V, 181. *say how you came hither,* 228. *say, Lucetta, wouldst thou counsel me to fall in love?* Gent. I, 2, 1. *say, from whom?* 35. *say, who gave it thee?* 37. *and may I say to thee, this pride of hers hath drawn my love from her,* III, 1, 72. *the duke, I say to thee again, would eat mutton on Fridays,* Meas. III, 2, 192. *say in brief the cause,* Err. I, 1, 29. *say to me, when sawest thou the Prince Florizel?* Wint. IV, 2, 28. *canst thou say all this and never blush,* Tit. V, 1, 121. *say to the king the knowledge of the broil as thou didst leave it,* Mcb. I, 2, 6. *the lady shall say her mind freely,* Hml. II, 2, 338. *say to me, whose fortunes shall rise higher,* Ant. II, 3, 15. *say to Ventidius I would speak with him,* 31. *shall I say to Caesar what you require of him?* III, 13, 65. *say his name,* Cymb. IV, 2, 376 etc.

3) to mention: *the said Henry shall espouse the Lady Margaret,* H6B I, 1, 46.

4) to speak: *to say grace,* Meas. I, 2, 20. Merch. II, 2, 202. Tit. IV, 3, 100. *to say one's prayers:* Wiv. V, 5, 54. Ado II, 1, 108. All's I, 1, 227. Wint. V, 3, 140. H5 IV, 2, 56. Troil. II, 3, 22. Cymb. IV, 2, 391 etc. Absol.: *you say honestly,* Ado II, 1, 242. *you say not right, old man,* V, 1, 73. *say on,* As III, 2, 264. *I have to say with you,* John IV, 1, 8. *first hear me speak. Well, say,* Cor. III, 3, 41. *answer to us. Say then,* 62. *say, what, is Horatio here?* Hml. I, 1, 18. *ye say honestly,* Rom. I, 2, 65. *hast most rightly said,* Lr. I, 1, 186. *say in mine ear,* Ant. II, 7, 42. *say boldly,* III, 13, 47. *go to, say no more,* Oth. IV, 1, 177 (enough of it; agreed). *I have said,* Ant. III, 2, 34 (= I have no more to say). *you have said but whether wisely or no, let the forest judge,* As III, 2, 129. *you have said =. well said, quite right:* Gent. II, 4, 29. Tw. III, 1, 12. Oth. IV, 2, 204. Ant. II, 6, 113. *there thou sayest,* Hml. V, 1, 29 (= speakest to the purpose; the clown's speech). *to say well* = 1) to speak well and to the purpose: Wint. I, 2, 90. H8 III, 2, 149. 152. 153. Troil. II, 2, 163. 2) to be right: *thou hast said well, for some of you there present are worse than devils,*

Tp. III, 3, 35. *said I well?* Wiv. I, 3, 11. *ha, Sir John, said I well?* H4B III, 2, 227. *ill will never said well,* H5 III, 7, 123. *you say well,* Rom. II, 4, 130. *well said* = 1) spoken well and to the purpose: Wiv. IV, 2, 141. Meas. II, 2, 89. Ado III, 5, 38. LLL V, 2, 552. Merch. II, 9, 37. As I, 2, 112. Shr. I, 1, 73. Tw. IV, 2, 31. H4A I, 2, 161. H4B III, 2, 169. H6B II, 1, 111. Troil. III, 1, 61. V, 1, 14. V, 2, 75. Cor. III, 2, 31. Rom. II, 4, 65. IV, 4, 19. Hml. II, 1, 6. 2) well done: As II, 6, 14. H4A IV, 1, 1. V, 4, 75. H4B III, 2, 295. V, 3, 10. H6B I, 4, 16. H8 I, 4, 30. Tit. IV, 3, 63. Rom. I, 5, 88. Hml. I, 5, 162. Oth. II, 1, 169. IV, 1, 117. V, 1, 98. Ant. II, 5, 46. IV, 4, 28. Per. III, 2, 87.

5) The imperative *say* = suppose; followed by the subjunctive: *say that the sense of feeling were bereft me, yet would my love to thee be still as much,* Ven. 439. *say, for non-payment that the debt should double, is twenty hundred kisses such a trouble?* 521. *say, this were death,* Tp. II, 1, 260. *but say this weed her love from Valentine, it follows not that she will love Sir Thurio,* Gent. III, 2, 49. *say that she be,* IV, 2, 109. *say that she rail: why then I'll tell her plain she sings as sweetly as a nightingale,* Shr. II, 171. *'tis most dangerous. Say it be, 'tis true,* Wint. I, 2, 298. *say that she were gone, a moiety of my rest might come to me again,* II, 3, 7. *say there be,* IV, 4, 88. *say he be taken, I know no pain will make him say I moved him to those arms,* H6B III, 1, 376. *say that he thrive,* 379. *say that King Edward take thee for his queen,* H6C III, 2, 89. *but say it were not registered,* R3 III, 1, 75. *say that Marcius return me unheard, what then?* Cor. V, 1, 41. Followed by an indicative: *well, say I am,* LLL I, 1, 102. *but say it is my humour: is it answered?* Merch. IV, 1, 43. *say that some lady, as perhaps there is, hath for your love as great a pang of heart,* Tw. II, 4, 92. *well, say there is no kingdom then for Richard, what other pleasure can the world afford?* H6C III, 2, 146. *say they are vile and false,* Oth. III, 3, 136. Uncertain, whether indic. or subjunctive: LLL II, 133. Shr. Ind. 2, 42. 49. Tw. I, 4, 23. H6C V, 4, 29. R3 I, 2, 89. IV, 4, 288. Oth. IV, 3, 88. 91. Ant. V, 2, 164. 167. *say so* = suppose it to be the case; if so: Troil. II, 1, 5. cf. *and by a sleep to say we end the heart-ache and the thousand natural shocks that flesh is heir to, 'tis a consummation devoutly to be wished,* Hml. III, 1, 61.

**Saying,** subst. 1) that which is or has been said by a person: *what mean you by that s.?* Gent. V, 4, 167. *you say he dined at home; the goldsmith here denies that s.* Err. V, 274. *if their singing answer your s.* Ado II, 1, 241. *talk with a man out at a window; a proper s.!* IV, 1, 312. *I pretty, and my s. apt,* LLL I, 2, 21. *the priest was good enough, for all the old gentleman's s.* As V, 1, 4. *all those —s will I overswear,* Tw. V, 276. *you would believe my s.* Wint. II, 1, 63. *'tis a s. not due to me,* III, 2, 59. *to prove my s. true,* John III, 1, 28. *you'll never trust his word after! come, 'tis a foolish s.* H5 IV, 1, 215. *the deed of s. is quite out of use,* Tim. V, 1, 28 (= the performance of what one has said or promised). *there is much reason in his —s,* Caes. III, 2, 113. *thou hast proved Lucilius' s. true,* V, 5, 59. *my father is not dead for all your s.* Mcb. IV, 2, 37. *give his s. deed,* Hml. I, 3, 27.

2) a phrase: *Fates and Destinies, and such odd —s,* Merch. II, 2, 66. *where that s. was born of I fear*

*no colours*, Tw. I, 5, 10. *blush like a black dog, as the s. is*, Tit. V, 1, 122.

3) a sentence, a proverb, a saw: Gent. V, 2, 11. Meas. II, 2, 133. LLL IV, 1, 121. Merch. II, 7, 36. II, 9, 82. As III, 2, 136. V, 1, 34. Tw. V, 40. H5 I, 2, 166. IV, 4, 73. R3 II, 4, 16. Troil. IV, 4, 15.

**'Sblood,** abbreviated from *God's blood;* a curse apparently thought indecent, and therefore usually omitted or replaced by other words in Ff.: H4A I, 2, 82. I, 3, 247. II, 2, 37. II, 4, 270 (Ff *away*). 488 (Ff *i' faith*). III, 3, 56. 100. V, 4, 113. Hml. II, 2, 384. III, 2, 386 (Ff *why*). Oth. I, 1, 4. Found also in Ff: H5 IV, 8, 10.

**Scab,** the incrustation formed over sores by dried matter; applied to persons as a term of extreme contempt and disgust: *my elbow itched: I thought there would a s. follow*, Ado III, 3, 107. *out, s.* Tw. II, 5, 82. *well said, i' faith, Wart; thou'rt a good s.* H4B III, 2, 296. *the loathsomest s. in Greece*, Troil. II, 1, 31. *that, rubbing the poor itch of your opinion, make yourselves —s*, Cor. I, 1, 169.

**Scabbard,** the sheath of a sword: Ado V, 1, 125. Tw. III, 4, 303. H6A II, 4, 60. Cymb. III, 4, 82.

**Scaffold,** 1) a stage: H5 Prol. 10. 2) a structure erected for the execution of malefactors: R3 IV, 4, 242.

**Scaffoldage** (O. Edd. *scaffolage*), the timberwork of the stage: *to hear the wooden dialogue and sound twixt his stretched footing and the s.* Troil. I, 3, 156.

**Scald,** adj. scabby, scurvy: *the rascally, s., beggarly, lousy, bragging knave*, H5 V, 1, 5. 31. 33. *and s. rhymers ballad us out o' tune* Ant. V, 2, 215. Corrupted to *scall* by Evans: Wiv. III, 1, 123.

**Scald,** vb. to burn with (or as with) hot liquor: *I am —d with my violent motion*, John V, 7, 49. *a rich armour worn in heat of day, that —s with safety*, H4B IV, 5, 31. *in summer's —ing heat*, H6C V, 7, 18. *she's e'en setting on water to s. such chickens as you are*, Tim. II, 2, 71 (it being anciently the practice to scald off the feathers of poultry instead of plucking them. But here, of course, the powdering-tub is meant). *may these add to the number that may s. thee*, Tim. III, 1, 54 (viz in hell). *there's hell, ... there's burning, —ing*, Lr. IV, 6, 131. *a wheel of fire, that mine own tears do s. like molten lead*, IV, 7, 48.

**Scale,** subst. 1) the dish of a balance: Compl. 226. Mids. III, 2, 132. All's II, 3, 161. R2 III, 4, 85. H6B II, 1, 204. Troil. II, 2, 27. Mcb. II, 3, 10. Hml. I, 2, 13. Oth. I, 3, 331. *till our s. turn the beam*, Hml. IV, 5, 157 (weigh the other down). *a feather will turn the s.* Meas. IV, 2, 32. *turn the —s*, H4B II, 4, 276. *if the s. do turn but in the estimation of a hair*, Merch. IV, 1, 330. *—s, =* balance, used as a singular: *in that crystal —s* (the two eyes) *let here be weighed your lady's love against some other maid*, Rom. I, 2, 101.

2) a shell: *s. of dragon*, Mcb. IV, 1, 22.

3) a step, or anything used for measuring: *they take the flow o' the Nile by certain —s in the pyramid*, Ant. II, 7, 21.

**Scale,** vb. 1) to weigh, to measure: *the corrupt deputy —d*, Meas. III, 1, 266 (weighed. According to others, = stripped as of scales, unmasked). *—ing his present bearing with his past*, Cor. II, 3, 257.

2) to climb as with a ladder; absol.: Lucr. 440. Transitively: Lucr. 481. Gent. III, 1, 119. H6A II, 1, 27.

Doubtful passage: *since it* (a tale) *serves my purpose, I will venture to s. it a little more*, Cor. I, 1, 95; some M. Edd. *stale. =* to unscale it?

**Scaled,** covered with scales or shells: Troil. V, 5, 22 (Q *scaling*). Ant. II, 5, 95.

**Scales,** name: H6A I, 1, 146. H6C IV, 1, 52. R3 II, 1, 67 (omitted in Qq and M. Edd.).

**Scaling,** reading of Q in Troil. V, 5, 22; Ff and M. Edd. *scaled*.

**Scall,** Evans' word for *scald:* Wiv. III, 1, 123.

**Scalp,** the skull, the head: *the —s of many, almost hid behind, to jump up higher seemed*, Lucr. 1413. *by the bare s. of Robin Hood's fat friar*, Gent. IV, 1, 36. *take this transformed s. from off the head of this Athenian swain*, Mids. IV, 1, 69 (viz the ass-head). *their thin and hairless —s*, R2 III, 2, 112.

**Scaly,** covered with scales: *a s. gauntlet*, H4B I, 1, 146.

**Scamble,** to scramble, to struggle: *—ing, outfacing, fashion-monging boys*, Ado V, 1, 94. *England now is left to tug and s. and to part by the teeth the unowed interest of proud-swelling state*, John IV, 3, 146. *the —ing and unquiet time*, H5 I, 1, 4. *I get thee with —ing, and thou must therefore needs prove a good soldier-breeder*, V, 2, 218.

**Scamels,** a word not yet satisfactorily explained or amended: *I'll get thee young s. from the rock*, Tp. II, 2, 176. Theobald conj. *shamois, seamalls, staniels* (a kind of hawks building in rocks).*

**Scan,** to weigh in the mind, to consider with care: *every word by all my wit being —ed*, Err. II, 2, 152. *which must be acted ere they may be —ed*, Mcb. III, 4, 140. *that would be —ed*, Hml. III, 3, 75. *I might entreat your honour to s. this thing no further*, Oth. III, 3, 245. *opinion's but a fool, that makes us s. the outward habit by the inward man*, Per. II, 2, 56 (to examine, judge of, and explain the outward appearance by taking into account the qualities of the mind, with which it may perhaps have nothing to do).

**Scandal,** subst. opprobrium, reproach, shame, disgrace: *though I die, the s. will survive*, Lucr. 204. *thou plantest s. and displacest laud*, 887. *greatest s. waits on greatest state*, 1006. *the impression which vulgar s. stamped upon my brow*, Sonn. 112, 2. *no particular s. once can touch but it confounds the breather*, Meas. IV, 4, 30. *not without some s. to yourself*, Err. V, 15. *in a tomb where never s. slept*, Ado V, 1, 70. *your wrongs do set a s. on my sex*, Mids. II, 1, 240. *give s. to the blood o' the prince my son*, Wint. I, 2, 330. *would the s. vanish with my life*, R2 II, 1, 67. *what a s. is it to our crown, that two such noble peers as you should jar*, H6A III, 1, 69. *thy s. were not wiped away*, H6B II, 4, 65. *his s. of retire*, H6C II, 1, 150. 151. *if black s. or foul-faced reproach attend the sequel of your imposition*, R3 III, 7, 231. *to his own s.* Hml. I, 4, 38. *you must not put another s. on him*, II, 1, 29.

**Scandal,** vb. to defame, to bring into disgrace *—ed the suppliants for the people, called them timepleasers*, Cor. III, 1, 44. *hug them hard and after s. them*, Caes. I, 2, 76. *Sinon's weeping did s. many a holy tear*, Cymb. III, 4, 62. Partic. *—ed =* scandalous, disgraceful: *her and her blind boy's —ed company*, Tp. IV, 90.

**Scandalized,** defamed, disgraced: *it will make me s.* Gent. II, 7, 61. *s. and foully spoken of*, H4A I, 3, 154.

**Scandalous,** 1) opprobrious, defamatory: *a blasting and a s. breath to fall on him so near us,* Meas. V, 122.

2) disgraced, infamous: *will ignoble make you, yea, s. to the world,* Wint. II, 3, 121.

**Scant,** adj. scanty, not copious: *if store of crowns be s., no man will supply thy want,* Pilgr. 409. With *of,* = 1) sparing of: *be somewhat —er of your maiden presence,* Hml. I, 3, 121. 2) deficient in: *he's fat and s. of breath,* V, 2, 298.

**Scant,** adv. scarcely, hardly: *she shall s. show well that now shows best,* Rom. I, 2, 104.

**Scant,** vb. 1) to straiten, to limit, to shorten: *if my father had not —ed me and hedged me by his wit,* Merch. II, 1, 17. *s. this excess,* III, 2, 113. *I s. this breathing courtesy,* V, 141. *and —s us with a single famished kiss,* Troil. IV, 4, 49. *to s. my sizes,* Lr. II, 4, 178. *you think I will your serious and great business s.* Oth. I, 3, 268 (be deficient in, neglect). *s. our former having,* IV, 3, 92. *s. not my cups,* Ant. IV, 2, 21.

2) to afford sparingly and with reluctance, to grudge: *I have —ed all wherein I should your great deserts repay,* Sonn. 117, 1. *what he hath —ed men in hair he hath given them in wit,* Err. II, 2, 81. *spoil his coat with — ing a little cloth,* H5 II, 4, 47. *you have obedience —ed,* Lr. I, 1, 281. *to s. her duty,* II, 4, 142. *force their —ed courtesy,* III, 2, 67.

**Scantle,** a piece: *cuts me from the best of all my land ... a monstrous s. out,* H4A III, 1, 100 (Ff *cantle*).

**Scantling,** a pattern, a sample: *the success, although particular, shall give a s. of good or bad unto the general,* Troil. I, 3, 341.

**Scantly,** niggardly, grudgingly: *spoke s. of me,* Ant. III, 4, 6.

**Scape,** subst. = escape (q. v.) 1) a getting safe out of danger: Shr. V, 2, 3. Oth. I, 3, 136.

2) a transgression, impropriety of conduct: *day night's —s doth open lay,* Lucr. 747. *simple —s,* Merch. II, 2, 174. *some s.* Wint. III, 3, 73. Substituted for *escape* by M. Edd.: Meas. IV, 1, 63. for *scope:* John III, 4, 154.

**Scape,** vb. (cf. *Escape*) 1) intr. to get out of danger: Tp. II, 2, 117. 124. Gent. V, 3, 11. As III, 2, 90. Shr. II, 242. H4A II, 4, 184. V, 3, 30. H4B II, 1, 28. H6A II, 1, 40. H6B V, 2, 79. H6C II, 1, 1. 6. Mcb. III, 4, 20. IV, 3, 234. Lr. II, 1, 82. II, 3, 5. III, 6, 59. 121. Oth. V, 1, 113. With *from:* H4A II, 2, 64. H6C II, 1, 2. Rom. IV, 1, 75.

2) trans.: a) to be saved from, to avoid, to shun: Sonn. 90, 5. Compl. 244. 310. Tp. II, 1, 146. II, 2, 61. Wiv. II, 1, 1. III, 5, 119. 147. Meas. III, 2, 197. Ado I, 1, 135. Mids. IV, 2, 21 (*he could not have —d sixpence a day*, i. e. he must necessarily have earned so much). V, 439. Merch. II, 2, 172. III, 2, 273. H4A II, 2, 15. III, 1, 69. H6A IV, 7, 22. H6B IV, 9, 32. H6C I, 3, 1. II, 2, 15. Troil. I, 3, 372. Cor. I, 8, 13. Rom. III, 1, 3. Tim. IV, 3, 434. Caes. IV, 3, 150. Hml. I, 3, 38. II, 2, 556. III, 2, 94. Lr. I, 4, 229. Ant. II, 5, 77. Per. I, 3, 29. II, 1, 93. IV, 2, 80. V Prol. 1.

b) to pass unnoticed, not to be perceived or recognized by: *that any accent breaking from thy tongue should s. the true acquaintance of mine ear,* John V, 6, 15.

**Scar,** subst. 1) a cicatrice: H5 IV, 3, 47. H6B III, 1, 300. Cor. II, 2, 152. Tit. V, 3, 114. Ant. III, 13, 191. IV, 5, 2. Doubtful, whether a cicatrice or a fresh wound: All's III, 2, 124. H4B I, 1, 173 (*wounds and —s*). Cor. III, 3, 52. Cymb. V, 5, 305.

2) a hurt, a wound: *bearing away the wound that nothing healeth,* the *s. that will despite of cure remain,* Lucr. 732. *O unfelt sore, crest-wounding private s.* 828. *the —s of battle scapeth,* Compl. 244. *I bestrit thee in the wars and took deep — s to save thy life,* Err. V, 193. *scratch thee but with a pin, and there remains some s. of it,* As III, 5, 22. *whether there be a s. under it* (the patch of velvet) All's IV, 5, 101. *patches will I get unto these cudgelled —s,* H5 V, 1, 93. *received deep —s,* H6B I, 1, 87. *let Paris bleed, 'tis but a s. to scorn,* Troil. I, 1, 114. *to such as boasting show their —s a mock is due,* IV, 5, 290. *hath more —s of sorrow in his heart,* Tit. IV, 1, 126. *he jests at —s that never felt a wound,* Rom. II, 2, 1.

3) any defacing mark, a blemish: *never mole, hare-lip, nor s. shall upon their children be,* Mids. V, 418. *her face defaced with —s of infamy,* R3 III, 7, 126. *the —s upon your honour he does pity,* Ant. III, 13, 58.

**Scar,** vb. to wound, to hurt: *England hath long been mad and —ed herself,* R3 V, 5, 23. *and —ed the moon with splinters,* Cor. IV, 5, 115 (Rowe *scared;* cf. R3 V, 3, 341. According to Nares, *to scar* was sometimes equivalent to *scare.* cf. *Scar-crow*). *whose loss hath pierced him deep and —ed his heart,* Tit. IV, 4, 31. *I'll not shed her blood, nor s. that skin of hers,* Oth. V, 2, 4. cf. *Unscarred.*

**Scarce,** adj. scanty, not plentiful: *where words are s., they are seldom spent in vain,* R2 II, 1, 7. *so abundant s.* Troil. II, 3, 17.

**Scarce,** adv. hardly, scantily: Lucr. 857. 1360. Pilgr. 71. 72. 388. Tp. V, 155. Gent. II, 7, 67. III, 1, 388. Wiv. III, 3, 204. Meas. I, 3, 51. III, 2, 240. Err. II, 1, 49. 54. III, 1, 23. Ado I, 1, 197. LLL IV, 3, 231. 326. V, 2, 617. Merch. II, 1, 5. II, 2, 139. III, 1, 47. As II, 7, 170. IV, 1, 37. All's II, 3, 219. II, 5, 88. IV, 1, 64. Tw. I, 5, 171. III, 3, 28. III, 4, 310. 328. Wint. II, 1, 99. III, 2, 26. IV, 4, 296. V, 3, 51. H4A II, 4, 170. H5 IV, 2, 20. H6A IV, 3, 50. H6B II, 3, 40. V, 1, 23. H6C II, 1, 80. II, 2, 110. R3 I, 1, 21. I, 3, 60. 82. 256. IV, 1, 68. H8 III, 2, 139. 292. Troil. IV, 2, 61. IV, 5, 265. Cor. V, 2, 109. Rom. III, 5, 165. Tim. I, 2, 186. IV, 3, 5. Mcb. IV, 3, 171. Hml. II, 2, 360. V, 1, 182. Lr. II, 2, 57. II, 4, 138. 305. III, 4, 9. IV, 1, 37. IV, 6, 14. IV, 7, 51. Oth. III, 3, 327. V, 2, 201. Ant. I, 1, 21. III, 1, 29. Cymb. II, 3, 95. III, 5, 155. III, 6, 12. IV, 2, 109. IV, 4, 36. V, 2, 10. V, 5, 469. Per. I, 4, 49. II, 1, 23. *full s.* H6A I, 1, 112 (cf. *Full*).

= seldom? *those that she makes fair she s. makes honest,* As I, 2, 40.

**Scarce-bearded,** reading of O. Edd. in Ant. I, 1, 21.

**Scarce-cold,** reading of O. Edd. in H6A IV, 3, 50 and Cymb. V, 5, 469 (*scarce-cold-battle*).

**Scarcely,** adv. = scarce: Sonn. 49, 6. Ado II, 2, 41. H4B IV, 1, 19. H5 II, 2, 104. R3 I, 3, 21. I, 4, 180. II, 3, 2 (Ff *hardly*). Cor. III, 2, 35. Mcb. I, 5, 37. IV, 3, 127. Hml. I, 2, 29. Lr. I, 2, 179. II, 4, 273. III, 6, 110. V, 3, 148. Cymb. III, 6, 26. Per. III, 1, 16.

**Scarcity,** scantiness, the contrary to plenty: Ven. 753. Tp. IV, 116. Troil. I, 3, 302. Tim. II, 2, 234.

**Scar-crow,** see *Scare-crow.*

**Scare,** (O. Edd. often *scarre*) to frighten: H6A II, 2, 28. H6C III, 1, 7. Rom. I, 4, 6. *to s. away:* Mids. V, 142. Wint. III, 3, 66. *thy jealous fits have —d thy husband from the use of wits,* Err. V, 86. *—d my choughs from the chaff,* Wint. IV, 4, 630. Rom. V, 3, 261. *the spirit of wantonness is —d out of him,* Wiv. IV, 2, 224. *s. Troy out of itself,* Troil. V, 10, 21. *—d out of his wits,* Lr. IV, 1, 59.

**Scare-crow** (O. Edd. *scar-crow*), a figure set up to frighten the birds from the field; or what resembles it: Meas. II, 1, 1. H4A IV, 2, 41. H6A I, 4, 43.

**Scarf,** subst. a silken ornament hung loosely on the shoulders or any part of the dress: *rich s. to my proud earth* (viz the rainbow) Tp. IV, 82. *under your arm, like a lieutenant's s.* Ado II, 1, 198. *the beauteous s. veiling an Indian beauty,* Merch. III, 2, 98. *to see thee wear thy heart in a s. It is my arm,* As V, 2, 23. *with —s and fans and double change of bravery,* Shr. IV, 3, 57. *the —s and the bannerets about thee,* All's II, 3, 214. *bound in thy s.* 238. *that jackanapes with —s,* III, 5, 88. *had the whole theoric of war in the knot of his s.* IV, 3, 163. *you are undone, all but your s.* 359. *matrons flung gloves, ladies and maids their —s and handkerchers upon him,* Cor. II, 1, 280. *Cupid hoodwinked with a s.* Rom. I, 4, 4. *pulling —s off Caesar's images,* Caes. I, 2, 289.

**Scarf,** vb. to put on loosely like a scarf: *my seagown —ed about me,* Hml. V, 2, 13. With *up,* = to cover as with a scarf, to blindfold (cf. Rom. I, 4, 4): *seeling night, s. up the tender eye of pitiful day,* Mcb. III, 2, 47.

**Scarfed,** furnished, adorned with flags: *the s. bark,* Merch. II, 6, 15.

**Scarlet,** bright-red: *their* (the lips') *s. ornaments,* Sonn. 142, 6. *a s. cloak,* Shr. V, 1, 69. R2 III, 3, 99. H4A II, 4, 17. H6A I, 3, 42. Rom. II, 1, 18. Tim. IV, 3, 422. = dressed in red robes: *his s. lust came evidence to swear,* Lucr. 1650. *s. hypocrite,* H6A I, 3, 56 (alluding to the red soutaine of the cardinal). *thou s. sin,* H8 III, 2, 255; cf. H6A I, 3, 42 and H8 III, 2, 280. Substantively: *jaded by a piece of s.* H8 III, 2, 280. *they* (thy cheeks) *will be in s. straight,* Rom. II, 5, 73. Name of one of Robin Hood's companions: *Robin Hood, S. and John,* H4B V, 3, 107. Bardolph called *S. and John* on account of his red face: Wiv. I, 1, 177.

**Scarre,** a broken precipice; a word used in an unintelligible and probably corrupt passage: *I see that men make ropes in such a s. that we'll forsake ourselves,* All's IV, 2, 38.

**Scathe,** subst. injury, damage: *to do offence and s. in Christendom,* John II, 75. *all these could not procure me any s.* H6B II, 4, 62. *to pray for them that have done s. to us,* R3 I, 3, 317. *wherein Rome hath done you any s.* Tit. V, 1, 7.

**Scathe,** vb. to injure: *this trick may chance to s. you,* Rom. I, 5, 86.

**Scathful,** doing damage, pernicious: *with which such s. grapple did he make,* Tw. V, 59.

**Scatter,** 1) tr. a) to disperse: Lucr. 136. Merch. I, 1, 33. Shr. I, 2, 50. John II, 304. III, 4, 3. H4A II, 2, 112. H4B IV, 2, 120. H5 IV, 6, 36. H6C II, 6, 93. R3 I, 4, 28. 33. H8 V, 4, 14. Tit. V, 3, 69. 71. Per. IV, 2, 121. *—ed and dispersed,* H6A II, 1, 76. *to s. and disperse the giddy Goths,* Tit. V, 2, 78. *dispersed and —ed,* R3 IV, 4, 513.

b) to spread or set thinly: *loose now and then a —ed smile,* As III, 5, 104 (like the single ears left for the gleaners). *the troops are all —ed,* All's IV, 3, 152. *old cakes of roses were thinly —ed,* Rom. V, 1, 48.

c) to strew: *his plausive words he —ed not in ears, but grafted them,* All's I, 2, 54. *he dives into the king's soul and there —s dangers, doubts,* H8 II, 2, 27. *the cockle of rebellion, which we ourselves have ploughed for, sowed and —ed,* Cor. III, 1, 71. *the seedsman upon the slime and ooze —s his grain,* Ant. II, 7, 25.

d) to disunite, to distract: *from France there comes a power into this —ed kingdom,* Lr. III, 1, 31.

2) intr. to go dispersedly, to straggle; and hence to go at random and without a certain aim: *the commons, like an angry hive of bees that want their leader, s. up and down and care not who they sting in his revenge,* H6B III, 2, 126. *nor build yourself a trouble out of his —ing and unsure observance,* Oth. III, 3, 151.

**Scene,** 1) a stage, a theatre; or the place represented by the stage: *forsook his s. and entered in a brake,* Mids. III, 2, 15. *the s. is now transported to Southampton; there is the playhouse now,* H5 II Prol. 34. 42. *woe's s.* R3 IV, 4, 27 (so the duchess of York calls herself). *a queen in jest, only to fill the s.* 91. *in Troy there lies the s.* Troil. Prol. 1. *when he might act the woman in the s.* Cor. II, 2, 100. *where we lay our s.* Rom. I Prol. 2.

2) part of an act; so much of a play as passes between the same persons in the same place: *last s. of all is second childishness,* As II, 7, 163. *they gape and point at your industrious —s and acts of death,* John II, 376. *a breath, a little s.* R2 III, 2, 164. H6C V, 6, 10. R3 II, 2, 38. Hml. II, 2, 460. III, 2, 81. Ant. I, 3, 78.

3) an action exhibited to spectators, a play, a spectacle: *as Chorus to their tragic s.* Phoen. 52. *fat Falstaff hath a great s.* Wiv. IV, 6, 17. *that's the s. that I would see,* Ado II, 3, 225. *what a s. of foolery have I seen,* LLL IV, 3, 163. *the s. begins to cloud,* V, 2, 730. *a tedious brief s. of young Pyramus,* Mids. V, 56. *more woeful pageants than the s. wherein we play in,* As II, 7, 138. Wint. IV, 1, 16. IV, 4, 604. R2 V, 3, 79. H4B I, 1, 159. V, 5, 198. H5 I Chor. 4. III Chor. 1. IV Chor. 48. H8 Prol. 4. Troil. I, 3, 173. Cor. V, 3, 184. Rom. IV, 3, 19. Caes. III, 1, 112. Hml. II, 2, 418. 619. Per. IV Prol. 6. IV, 4, 7.

**Scent,** subst. the smell of game: *picked out the dullest s.* Shr. Ind. I, 24. *at a cold s.* Tw. II, 5, 134 (i. e. at fault; cf. *Cold*).

**Scent,** vb. to smell, to perceive by the nose: *I s. the morning air,* Hml. I, 5, 58.

**Scented,** in *Rank-scented,* q. v.

**Scent-snuffing,** perceiving by the nose the track of the game: *s. hounds,* Ven. 692.

**Sceptre,** the staff borne as an ensign of royalty: Lucr. 217. Merch. IV, 1, 190. All's II, 1, 195. Wint. IV, 4, 430. V, 1, 146. John III, 4, 135. R2 I, 1, 118. II, 1, 294. III, 3, 80. 151. IV, 109. 205. H4A II, 4, 416. III, 2, 97. H5 II, 4, 27. IV, 1, 277. H6A IV, 1, 192. V, 3, 118. H6B I, 1, 245. V, 1, 9. 10. 98. 102. H6C I, 4, 17. II, 1, 154. III, 1, 16. IV, 6, 73. H8 I, 2, 135. IV, 1, 38. Troil. I, 3, 107. Tit. I, 199. Mcb. III, 1, 62. IV, 1, 121. Ant. III, 6, 76. IV, 15, 76. Cymb. IV, 2, 268.

**Sceptred,** bearing a sceptre, royal: *this s. sway,*

Merch. IV, 1, 193. *this s. isle*, R2 II, 1, 40. *the s. office of your ancestors*, R3 III, 7, 119.

**Schedule,** (O. Edd. mostly *Scedule*) a piece of paper written on: Lucr. 1312 (a letter). Compl. 43. LLL I, 1, 18. Merch. II, 9, 55. Tw. I, 5, 263 (= inventory). H4B IV, 1, 168. Caes. III, 1, 3. cf. *Enscheduled.*

**Scholar,** 1) a schoolboy: *I am no breeching s. in the schools*, Shr. III, 1, 18.

2) one who learns of a teacher, a pupil, disciple: *he is a better s. than I thought*, Wiv. IV, 1, 82. *my cousin William is become a good s.* H4B III, 2, 11. *thy master dies thy s.* Ant. IV, 14, 102. Per. II, 3, 17. II, 5, 31. 39. IV, 6, 198.

3) a man of letters: Wiv. II, 2, 186. Meas. III, 2, 154. LLL IV, 2, 9. Merch. I, 2, 124. As IV, 1, 10. Shr. I, 2, 159. II, 79. Tw. II, 3, 13. IV, 2, 12. H5 I, 1, 32. H6B IV, 4, 36. H8 II, 2, 113. IV, 2, 51. Hml. I, 5, 141. III, 1, 159. Oth. II, 1, 167. *I would to God some s. would conjure her*, Ado II, 1, 264. *thou art a s., speak to it*, Hml. I, 1, 42 (Latin being the language of conjurers and exorcists).

**Scholarly,** like a man of letters and learning: *speak s. and wisely*, Wiv. I, 3, 2.

**School,** subst. 1) an establishment for the instruction of youth: Lucr. 615. 617. 1018. Ado V, 2, 39. LLL IV, 2, 32. Shr. III, 1, 18. Tw. III, 2, 81. H4B IV, 2, 104. IV, 3, 20 (*I have a whole s. of tongues in this belly of mine*). H6B IV, 7, 37 (*a grammar s.*). Troil. I, 3, 104. Tim. V, 4, 25. Oth. III, 3, 24. In Mcb. I, 7, 6 O. Edd. *upon this bank and s. of time;* M. Edd. *shoal.* cf. *Bank.*

2) the instruction given in such a place: *no s. to day?* Wiv. IV, 1, 10. *I have discontinued s. above a twelvemonth*, Merch. III, 4, 75. *at s.* As I, 1, 6. *from s.* Shr. III, 2, 152. *to s.* Wiv. IV, 1, 8. Mids. III, 2, 324. As II, 7, 147. Caes. I, 2, 300. V, 5, 26. Hml. I, 2, 113. *toward s.* Rom. II, 2, 158. *to set to s.* = to teach, to instruct: Lucr. 1820. H6C III, 2, 193. *we'll set thee to s. to an ant*, Lr. II, 4, 68 (= we'll give thee an ant for thy teacher).

3) learning: *hath wisdom's warrant and the help of s.* LLL V, 2, 71.

4) a sect adhering to a system of doctrine: *the —s, embowelled of their doctrine, have left off the danger to itself*, All's I, 3, 246. Perhaps corrupt in the following passage: *black is the badge of hell, the hue of dungeons and the s. of night*, LLL IV, 3, 255 (cf. *Night.* Theobald *scowl*, Hanmer *stole*, Thirlby *soul*, Dyce *soil*, Cambr. Edd. *suit*).

**School,** vb. 1) to teach, to instruct, to train: *never —ed and yet learned*, As I, 1, 173. *here comes your boy; 'twere good he were —ed*, Shr. IV, 4, 9. *ill —ed in bolted language*, Cor. III, 1, 321.

2) to set to rights, to reprimand: *I have some private —ing for you both*, Mids. I, 1, 116. *well, I am —ed*, H4A III, 1, 190. *I pray you, s. yourself*, Mcb. IV, 2, 15.

**Schoolboy,** a boy that is in his rudiments at school: Gent. II, 1, 22. Ado II, 1, 229. LLL V, 2, 403. As II, 7, 145. Wint. II, 1, 103. H6A I, 1, 36. Cor. III, 2, 116. Rom. II, 2, 156. Caes. V, 1, 61.

**School-days,** the age in which youth are sent to school; boyhood, girlhood: Mids. III, 2, 202. Merch. I, 1, 140. R3 IV, 4, 169.

**Schooled,** see *School*, vb.

**Schoolfellow,** one bred at the same school: Hml. III, 4, 202.

**Schooling,** see *School*, vb.

**School-maids,** girls at school: Meas. I, 4, 47.

**Schoolmaster,** 1) one who presides and teaches in a public school: LLL IV, 2, 87. V, 2, 531.

2) a private teacher: *here have I, thy s., made thee more profit*, Tp. I, 2, 172. *—s will I keep within my house*, Shr. I, 1, 94. *to get her cunning —s*, 192. *you will be s. and undertake the teaching of the maid*, 196. *a s. well seen in music*, I, 2, 133. 167. III, 2, 140. Cor. I, 3, 61. Lr. I, 4, 195. II, 4, 307 (*the injuries that they themselves procure must be their —s*). Ant. III, 11, 71. III, 12, 2. Per. II, 5, 40.

**Sciatica,** a painful affection of the hip; considered as a symptom of syphilis: Meas. I, 2, 59. Troil. V, 1, 25. Tim. IV, 1, 23 (*cold s.*).

**Science,** 1) knowledge, learning: *your own s. exceeds the lists of all advice*, Meas. I, 1, 5. *Plutus himself hath not in nature's mystery more s.* All's V, 3, 103.

2) an object of study, a branch of knowledge: *to instruct her fully in those —s*, Shr. II, 57. *do not learn the —s that should become our country*, H5 V, 2, 58.

**Scimitar,** a sword: Merch. II, 1, 24. Troil. V, 1, 2. *he dies upon my —'s sharp point*, Tit. IV, 2, 91 (consequently not a sabre with a convex edge).

**Scion,** a small twig taken from one tree and ingrafted in another: Wint. IV, 4, 93. H5 III, 5, 7. Oth. I, 3, 337.

**Scissars,** an instrument consisting of two cutting blades; used for cutting the hair: Err. V, 175. cf. *Unscissared.*

**Scoff,** subst. raillery, mockery, ridicule: LLL V, 2, 263. H6A I, 4, 39. III, 2, 113. R3 I, 3, 104.

**Scoff,** vb. to mock, to ridicule; trans.: *—ing his state*, R2 III, 2, 163. absol.: *s. on, vile fiend*, H6A III, 2, 45.

**Scoffer,** a mocker: As III, 5, 62.

**Scogan,** see *Skogan.*

**Scold,** subst. a wrangling foul-mouthed woman: Shr. I, 2, 188. John II, 191. H6C V, 5, 29.

**Scold,** vb. intr. to wrangle, to brawl, to be clamorous: Wiv. II, 1, 240. Ado II, 1, 249 (*s. with her*). Shr. I, 1, 177. I, 2, 100. 109. 254. All's II, 2, 27. H6C V, 5, 30. Cor. V, 6, 106. Tim. IV, 3, 156 (*—s against the quality of flesh*). Caes. I, 3, 5 (*the —ing winds*). Ant. I, 1, 32. With an accus. denoting the effect: *I will have more, or s. it out of him*, H8 V, 1, 175.

**Sconce,** subst. 1) a fortification, bulwark: *at such a s., at such a breach*, H5 III, 6, 76. Applied in jest to a covering for the head: *an you use these blows long, I must get a s. for my head*, Err. II, 2, 37.

2) the head; in contempt: *I shall break that merry s. of yours*, Err. I, 2, 79. II, 2, 34. 35. *must I go show them my unbarbed s.?* Cor. III, 2, 99. *to knock him about the s. with a dirty shovel*, Hml. V, 1, 110.

**Sconce,** vb. = ensconce; only by conjecture in Hml. III, 4, 4; O. Edd. *silence.*

**Scone,** the place where the Scottish kings were crowned: Mcb. II, 4, 31. 35. V, 8, 75.

**Scope,** 1) aim, intention, drift: *whose worthiness gives s., being had, to triumph, being lacked, to hope*, Sonn. 52, 13. *to find out shames and idle hours in me, the s. and tenour of thy jealousy*, 61, 8. *his coming hither hath no further s. than for his lineal royalties,*

R2 III, 3, 112. *curbs himself even of his natural s.* H4A III, 1, 171. *'tis conceived to s.* Tim. I, 1, 72 (= to the purpose).

2) the space within which one's aims and intentions are bounded: *a restraint, though all the world's vastidity you had, to a determined s.* Meas. III, 1, 70. *an she agree, within her s. of choice lies my consent,* Rom. I, 2, 18. *making your wills the s. of justice,* Tim. V, 4, 5. *an anchor's cheer in prison be my s.* Hml. III, 2, 229.

3) room to move in, free play, vent: *(my Muse) have such a s. to show her pride,* Sonn. 103, 2. *three themes in one, which wondrous s. affords,* 105, 12. *now give me the s. of justice,* Meas. V, 234. *the fated sky gives us free s.* All's I, 1, 233. *no natural exhalation in the sky, no s. of nature, no distempered day, no common wind, no customed event, but they will pluck away his natural cause,* John III, 4, 154 (no effect produced within the regular limits of nature. Most M. Edd. preposterously *scape*). *and as you answer, I do know the s. and warrant limited unto my tongue,* V, 2, 122. *I'll give thee (the heart) s. to beat, since foes have s. to beat both thee and me,* R2 III, 3, 140. 141. *being moody, give him line and s.* H4B IV, 4, 39. *and the offender granted s. of speech,* H6B III, 1, 176. *that my pent heart may have some s. to beat,* R3 IV, 1, 35. *let them (words) have s.* IV, 4, 130. *be angry when you will, it shall have s.* Caes. IV, 3, 108. *in what particular thought to work I know not, but in the gross and s. of my opinion this bodes some strange eruption to our state,* Hml. I, 1, 68. *giving to you no further personal power more than the s. of these delated articles allow,* I, 2, 37. *let his disposition have that s. that dotage gives it,* Lr. I, 4, 314.

4) power: *desiring this man's art and that man's s.* Sonn. 29, 7. *your s. is as mine own, so to enforce or qualify the laws as to your soul seems good,* Meas. I, 1, 65.

5) liberty, license: *as surfeit is the father of much fast, so every s. by the immoderate use turns to restraint,* Meas. I, 2, 131. *'twas my fault to give the people s.* I, 3, 35.

**Scorch,** to burn on the surface, to parch: *his hot heart, which fond desire doth s.* Lucr. 314. *the appetite of her eye did seem to s. me up like a burning-glass,* Wiv. I, 3, 74. *to s. your face,* Err. V, 183. *within the —ed veins of one new-burned,* John III, 1, 278. *thy burning car never had —ed the earth,* H6C II, 6, 13. In Mcb. III, 2, 13 O. Edd. *—ed,* M. Edd. *scotched.*

**Score,** subst. 1) a notch made on a tally: *our forefathers had no other books than the s. and the tally,* H6A IV, 7, 38.

2) an account kept by notches, and hence account or reckoning generally: *I am not fourteen pence on the s.* Shr. Ind. 2, 25. *he's an infinitive thing upon my s.* H4B II, 1, 26. *eat and drink on my s.* H6B IV, 2, 80. *he never pays the s.* All's IV, 3, 253. *strikes some —s away from the great compt,* V, 3, 56. *he parted well and paid his s.* Mcb. V, 8, 52. *strike off this s. of absence,* Oth. III, 4, 179.

3) (cf. *Threescore, Fourscore* etc.) a number of twenty: Rom. II, 4, 145. Lr. I, 4, 140. Cymb. III, 2, 70. *eight s.* Oth. III, 4, 174. 175. *as easy as a cannon will shoot point-blank twelve s.* (viz yards) Wiv. III, 2, 34. *his death will be a march of twelve s.* H4A II, 4, 598. *a would have clapped i' the clout at twelve s.*

H4B III, 2, 52. Followed by *of:* Tp. V, 174. H4B III, 2, 55. 56. R3 I, 2, 257. Tim. III, 6, 87. Cymb. III, 2, 69. *Of* omitted: Shr. I, 2, 111. II, 360. H4A II, 4, 5.

**Score,** vb. 1) to notch, to cut, to chip: *let us s. their backs,* Ant. IV, 7, 12.

2) to mark or set down for an account; absol.: *after he —s, he never pays the s.* All's IV, 3, 253. *here's no —ing but upon the pate,* H4A V, 3, 31. trans.: *nor need I tallies thy dear love to s.* Sonn. 122, 10. *she will s. your fault upon my pate,* Err. I, 2, 65. *s. me up for the lyingest knave in Christendom,* Shr. Ind. 2, 25. *s. a pint of bastard,* H4A II, 4, 29. *have you —d me?* Oth. IV, 1, 130 (i. e. made my reckoning. Q1 *stored*).

**Scorn,** subst. 1) contempt, disdain: *to love a cheek that smiles at thee in s.* Ven. 252. *in my death I murder shameful s.* Lucr. 1189. *place my merit in the eye of s.* Sonn. 88, 2. *twice desire, ere it be day, that which with s. she put away,* Pilgr. 316. *to be in love, where s. is bought with groans,* Gent. I, 1, 29. *s. at first makes after-love the more,* III, 1, 95. *the red glow of s. and proud disdain,* As III, 4, 57. *if the s. of your bright eyne have power to raise such love in mine,* IV, 3, 50. H4B IV, 2, 37. H5 II, 4, 117. H6A IV, 4, 77 (*—s*). IV, 7, 39. R3 I, 2, 172. Troil. I, 3, 371. Rom. III, 1, 166. Hml. III, 1, 70 (*—s*). Oth. IV, 3, 52. *to take s. and to think s.* = to disdain: *take thou no s. to wear the horn,* As IV, 2, 14. *and take foul s. to fawn on him,* H6A IV, 4, 35. *your majesty takes no s. to wear the leek,* H5 IV, 7, 107. *I think s. to sigh,* LLL I, 2, 66. *by moonshine did these lovers think no s. to meet at Ninus' tomb,* Mids. V, 138. *the nobility think s. to go in leather aprons,* H6B IV, 2, 13. *their blood thinks s. till it fly out and show them princes born,* Cymb. IV, 4, 53 (despises and disdains every other respect, sets all at nought).

2) mockery, scoff, derision: *at my parting did she smile, in s. or friendship, nill I construe whether,* Pilgr. 188. *become the argument of his own s. by falling in love,* Ado II, 3, 12. *have so oft encountered him with s.* 133. III, 1, 51. 108. V, 2, 38. *bruise me with s.* LLL V, 2, 397. *if sickly ears will hear your idle —s,* 875. *when at your hands did I deserve this s.?* Mids. II, 2, 124. *why should you think that I should woo in s.? S. and derision never come in tears,* III, 2, 122. 123. 126. 222. All's I, 2, 34. Tw. I, 5, 187. III, 1, 157. John I, 243. H4A III, 2, 64. H5 I, 2, 288. H6A I, 4, 39. H6C II, 1, 64. IV, 1, 24. R3 I, 3, 176. III, 1, 133 (*give*). Troil. II, 3, 123. IV, 5, 30. Cor. II, 3, 175. Tit. III, 1, 238. Rom. I, 1, 119. Oth. IV, 1, 83. IV, 2, 54 (see *Time*). Cymb. V, 2, 7 (cf. *Of*). V, 4, 125 (but, *O s.! = O* mockery!). *a-scorn* = in scorn (?): *I have, as when the sun doth light a-s., buried this sigh in wrinkle of a smile,* Troil. I, 1, 37 (F1.2 and Qq *a s.,* M. Edd. *a storm*). *in s. of* = in defiance of, vying with: *a thousand lamentable objects there, in s. of nature, art gave lifeless life,* Lucr. 1374. *in those holes where eyes did once inhabit, there were crept, as 'twere in s. of eyes, reflecting gems,* R3 I, 4, 31. *to laugh to s. =* to deride, to make a mock of: Ven. 4. Err. II, 2, 207. As IV, 2, 19. H6A IV, 7, 18. Mcb. IV, 1, 79. V, 5, 3. V, 7, 12. Similarly: *let Paris bleed: 'tis but a scar to s.* Troil. I, 1, 114 (cf. *To*).

3) an object of derision: *to make a loathsome abject s. of me,* Err. IV, 4, 106. *these oaths and laws will prove an idle s.* LLL I, 1, 311. *that is honour's s., which challenges itself as honour's born and is not like the sire,*

All's II, 3, 140. *to be shame's s. and subject of mischance*, H6A IV, 6, 49. *thou comest not to be made a s. in Rome*, Tit. I, 265. *to become the geck and s. o' th' other's villany*, Cymb. V, 4, 67.

Peculiar expression: *to show virtue her own feature, s. her own image*, Hml. III, 2, 26 (mockery, satire? or disdain, pride?).

**Scorn,** vb. 1) trans. a) to disdain, to refuse or lay aside with contempt: —*ing his churlish drum*, Ven. 107. *spurns at his love and* —*s the heat he feels*, 311. *the sun doth s. you and the wind doth hiss you*, 1084. *she did s. a present that I sent her*, Gent. III, 1, 92. *a woman sometime* —*s what best contents her*, 93. *if thou s. our courtesy, thou diest*, IV, 1, 68. Ado IV, 1, 304. Mids. III, 2, 331. As II, 4, 22. All's V, 3, 50. John III, 4, 42. H5 II, 1, 32. H6A I, 4, 32. R3 I, 2, 165. Rom. III, 1, 123. Tim. I, 2, 38. Cymb. V, 5, 106. Per. I, 1, 56. *I s. that with my heels*, Ado III, 4, 50. *s. running with thy heels*, Merch. II, 2, 9 (cf. Ven. 312). Dat. and accus. following: *law shall s. him further trial*, Cor. III, 1, 268. With an inf.: *I s. to change my state with kings*, Sonn. 29, 14. Shr. IV, 2, 18. All's V, 3, 18. R2 IV, 9. H5 III, 2, 40. R3 III, 4, 85. Tit. IV, 2, 100. With a clause: *yet sometimes falls an orient drop beside, which her cheek melts, as* —*ing it should pass, to wash the foul face of the sluttish ground*, Ven. 982. *all those eyes adored them ere their fall s. now their hand should give them burial*, Per. II, 4, 12.

b) to despise: *so should my papers be* —*ed like old men of less truth than tongue*, Sonn. 17, 10. *I s. you, scurvy companion*, H4B II, 4, 132. 322. *I s. thy strength*, H6A I, 5, 15. *I s. thee and thy fashion*, II, 4, 76. *our nobility will s. the match*, V, 3, 96. *in her heart she* —*s our poverty*, H6B I, 3, 84. H6C I, 1, 101. I, 4, 38. R3 I, 3, 297. Tim. IV, 3, 6. V, 4, 76. Caes. II, 1, 26. Per. I, 4, 30.

c) to scoff, to make a mock of, to laugh at: *so mild, that patience seemed to s. his woes*, Lucr. 1505. *all fears s. I*, Pilgr. 264. *if he should s. me so apparently*, Err. IV, 1, 78. *did not her kitchen-maid rail, taunt and s. me?* IV, 4, 77. 78. *he'll s. it* (her love), *for the man hath a contemptible spirit*, Ado II, 3, 186. *to join with men in* —*ing your poor friend*, Mids. III, 2, 216. 221. 247. *mocked at my gains,* —*ed my nation*, Merch. III, 1, 58. *do not s. me*, As III, 5, 1. *dare he presume to s. us in this manner*, H6C III, 3, 178. *to be thus taunted,* —*ed and baited at*, R3 I, 3, 109. *dallies with the wind and* —*s the sun*, 265. *to s. his corse*, II, 1, 80. *to taunt and s. you thus opprobriously*, III, 1, 153. *laughed at,* —*ed*, H8 III, 1, 107. *this Troyan* —*s us*, Troil. I, 3, 233. *does the cuckold s. me?* III, 3, 64. *how in his suit he* —*ed you*, Cor. II, 3, 230. *as if he mocked himself and* —*ed his spirit*, Caes. I, 2, 206. *spurn fate, s. death*, Mcb. III, 5, 30. *Fortune knows we s. her most when most she offers blows*, Ant. III, 11, 74.

2) intr. to mock, to scoff: *how will he s.! how will he spend his wit*, LLL IV, 3, 147. *you s.* Per. V, 1, 168. With *at:* —*ed at me*, As III, 5, 131. *why* —*est thou at Sir Robert?* John I, 228. *one that* —*ed at me*, R3 IV, 4, 102. *to fleer and s. at our solemnity*, Rom. I, 5, 59. 65.

**Scornful,** 1) disdainful: Ven. 501. Shr. V, 2, 137. All's II, 3, 158. V, 3, 48. Lr. II, 4, 168.

2) derisive, mocking, jeering: *sing a s. rhyme*, Wiv. V, 5, 95. *s. Lysander*, Mids. I, 1, 95. *thou s. page, there lie thy part*, Cymb. V, 5, 228.

3) causing contempt and derision, disgraceful: *thy surviving husband shall remain the s. mark of every open eye*, Lucr. 520.

**Scornfully,** disdainfully, contemptuously: Ven. 275. Lucr. 187. H5 IV, 2, 42. Cor. II, 3, 171.

**Scorpion,** the animal Scorpio; proverbial for its venomous sting: *seek not a* —*s' nest*, H6B III, 2, 86. *full of* —*s is my mind*, Mcb. III, 2, 36. *your daughter was as a s. to her sight*, Cymb. V, 5, 45.

**Scot,** a native of Scotland: H4A I, 1, 54. 68. I, 3, 212. 214. 215. II, 4, 116. 377. IV, 1, 1. IV, 3, 12. V, 3, 11. 15. V, 4, 39. 114. V, 5, 17. H4B I, 1, 126. IV, 4, 98. H5 I, 2, 138. 144. 148. 161. 170. H6A IV, 1, 157.

**Scot and lot,** taxes, contributions: *or that hot termagant Scot had paid me scot and lot too*, H4A V, 4, 115.

**Scotch,** subst. slight cut, shallow incision: *I have yet room for six* — *es more*, Ant. IV, 7, 10.

**Scotch,** vb. to cut with shallow incisions: *he* —*ed him and notched him like a carbonado*, Cor. IV, 5, 198. *we have* —*ed the snake*, Mcb. III, 2, 13 (O. Edd. *scorched*).

**Scotch,** adj. pertaining to Scotland: *a S. jig*, Ado II, 1, 77.

**Scotland,** the country to the north of England: *where S.? I found it by the barrenness*, Err. III, 2, 122. H4A I, 3, 262. 265. 280. III, 1, 45. III, 2, 164. IV, 1, 85. H4B II, 3, 50. 67. IV, 1, 14. H5 I, 2, 168. H6C III, 1, 13. III, 3, 26. 34. 151. R3 III, 7, 15. Mcb. I, 2, 28. IV, 3, 7. 88. 100. 113. 164. 186. 233. V, 8, 59. 63.

**Scots** = Scotch, native of Scotland: *the S. captain*, H5 III, 2, 79.

**Scottish,** pertaining to Scotland: Merch. I, 2, 83 (Ff *other*). H4A I, 3, 259. III, 1, 85.

**Scoundrel,** a rascal, a villain: *they are* —*s and substractors that say so of him*, Tw. I, 3, 36.

**Scour,** 1) to rub hard: *the chairs of order s. with juice of balm*, Wiv. V, 5, 65. *to be* —*ed to nothing with perpetual motion*, H4B I, 2, 246.

2) to rub for the purpose of cleaning, to cleanse; absol.: *she can wash and s.* Gent. III, 1, 313. Wiv. I, 4, 101. trans.: Gent. III, 1, 315. H5 II, 1, 60. H6B I, 3, 195. III, 2, 199. Per. II, 2, 55.

3) to remove for the purpose of cleaning, to sweep away, to purge: *which* (blood), *washed away, shall s. my shame with it*, H4A III, 2, 137. *never came reformation in a flood, with such a heady currance,* —*ing faults*, H5 I, 1, 34. *what rhubarb would s. these English hence?* Mcb. V, 3, 56.

**Scour,** to run swiftly, to scamper: *never saw I men s. so on their way*, Wint. II, 1, 35. *fearful* —*ing doth choke the air with dust*, Tim. V, 2, 15.

**Scourge,** subst. a whip, a lash; used as the symbol of punishment and vindictive affliction: H4A I, 3, 11. III, 2, 7. H6A I, 2, 129. II, 3, 15. IV, 2, 16. IV, 7, 77. H6B V, 1, 118. R3 I, 4, 50. Cor. II, 3, 97. Rom. V, 3, 292. Hml. III, 4, 175. IV, 3, 6.

**Scourge,** vb. to whip, to lash: *I am whipped and* —*d with rods*, H4A I, 3, 239. *with them* (tresses) *s. the bad revolting stars*, H6A I, 1, 4. = to chastise, to afflict: H4A V, 2, 40. H6A II, 4, 102. Lr. I, 2, 115. V, 3, 171 (Ff *plague*). Ant. II, 6, 22.

**Scout,** subst. one sent to reconnoitre the enemy: LLL V, 2, 88. H6A IV, 3, 1. V, 2, 10. H6C II, 1, 116. IV, 2, 18. V, 1, 19.

S 1013

**Scout,** vb. to be on the look-out: *s. me for him at the corner of the orchard like a bum-baily,* Tw. III, 4, 193.

**Scout,** vb. to sneer at: *flout 'em and s. 'em and s. 'em and flout 'em,* Tp. III, 2, 130 (Stephano's song).

**Scowl,** to look sullen: *another sadly —ing,* Ven. 917. *he —s and hates himself for his offence,* Lucr. 738. *men's eyes did s. on gentle Richard,* R2 V, 2, 28. *how with signs and tokens she can s.* Tit. II, 4, 5 (Qq *scrowl*). *glad at the thing they s. at,* Cymb. I, 1, 15.

**Scrap,** used only in the plur. *—s,* = pieces of food, fragments and relics of a banquet: *disdain to him disdained —s to give,* Lucr. 987. *they have been at a great feast of languages and stolen the —s,* LLL V, 1, 40. *those —s are good deeds past,* Troil. III, 3, 148. *the fragments, —s, the bits and greasy relics,* V, 2, 159. *one bred of alms and fostered with cold dishes, with —s o' the court,* Cymb. II, 3, 120.

**Scrape,** vb. 1) to clean by rubbing with something hard: *nor s. trencher,* Tp. II, 2, 187 (Caliban's song). *he s. a trencher?* Rom. I, 5, 2 (the servant's speech).

2) with *from* or *out of,* = to take away by rubbing hard; to erase: *the blood of King Richard, —d from Pomfret stones,* H4B I, 1, 205. *to s. the figures out of your husband's brains,* Wiv. IV, 2, 231. *—d one* (commandment) *out of the table,* Meas. I, 2, 9. *you will be —d out of the painted cloth,* LLL V, 2, 579.

3) to gather riches by small gains and savings: *their —ing fathers,* R2 V, 3, 69.

**Scratch,** subst. a slight incision in the surface made with something sharp: H4A V, 4, 11. Cor. III, 3, 51. Rom. III, 1, 96.

**Scratch,** vb. to rub, or wound slightly, with something sharp: Ven. 705. 924. Lucr. 1035. Tp. II, 2, 55. Gent. I, 2, 58. Ado I, 1, 136. 137. LLL V, 1, 32 (*Priscian a little —ed,* i. e. offended by so gross a mistake).*Mids. IV, 1, 7. 25. 28. As III, 5, 21. Shr. Ind. 2, 60. All's V, 2, 29. 33. Wint. IV, 4, 436. 728. H8 V, 4, 9. Troil. II, 1, 30. IV, 2, 113. Cor. II, 2, 79. Hml. III, 1, 104. Caes. II, 1, 243. Hml. IV, 7, 147. Ant. I, 2, 54. *to s. out* = to tear out with the nails: *s. out the angry eyes,* Lucr. 1469. Gent. IV, 4, 209.

**Scream,** subst. a shrill cry, a shriek: *strange —s of death,* Mcb. II, 3, 61.

**Scream,** vb. to utter a shrill cry, to shriek: *I heard the owl s.* Mcb. II, 2, 16.

**Screech** (Ff Q2 *scritch*), to cry as a night-owl: *whilst the screech-owl, —ing loud,* Mids. V, 383.

**Screech-owl,** an owl hooting at night, and supposed to be ominous of evil: Mids. V, 383 (Ff Q2 *scritch-owl*). H6B I, 4, 21. III, 2, 327. H6C II, 6, 56. Troil. V, 10, 16.

**Screen,** subst. anything that separates or conceals: *to have no s. between this part he played and him he played it for,* Tp. I, 2, 107. *your leafy —s throw down,* Mcb. V, 6, 1.

**Screen,** vb. (cf. *Bescreen*) to protect by being between: *that your grace hath —ed and stood between much heat and him,* Hml. III, 4, 3.

**Screw,** vb. 1) to fasten as with a screw: *that's riveted, —ed to my memory,* Cymb. II, 2, 44.

2) to wrest, to wrench, to force: *the instrument that —s me from my true place in your favour,* Tw. V, 126. *s. your courage to the sticking-place,* Mcb. I, 7, 60.

**Scribble,** to write without skill or care, to scrawl: *I am a —d form, drawn with a pen upon a parchment, John V, 7, 32. *that parchment, being —d o'er, should undo a man,* H6B IV, 2, 88.

**Scribe,** one writing, one penning down something: *that my master, being s., to himself should write the letter,* Gent. II, 1, 146. *if thy stumps will let thee play the s.* Tit. II, 4, 4. *hearts, tongues, figures, —s, bards, poets, cannot think, speak, cast, write, sing, number his love to Antony,* Ant. III, 2, 16.

**Scrimer,** a fencer: Hml. IV, 7, 101.

**Scrip,** a small writing, a schedule: *to call them generally, man by man, according to the s.* Mids. I, 2, 3.

**Scrip,** a small bag, a wallet: *with s. and scrippage,* As III, 2, 171.

**Scrippage,** the contents of a scrip: As III, 2, 171.

**Scripture,** 1) any writing: *the —s of the loyal Leonatus, all turned to heresy,* Cymb. III, 4, 83.

2) sacred writing, the bible: Merch. I, 3, 99. R3 I, 3, 334. Hml. V, 1, 41.

**Scrivener,** one who draws contracts: Shr. IV, 4, 59.

**Scroll,** a paper written on, a schedule, a letter, a list: *receives the s.* Lucr. 1340 (a letter). *here is the s. of every man's name,* Mids. I, 2, 4. 16. *within whose empty eye there is a written s.* Merch. II, 7, 64. *here's the s., the continent and summary of my fortune,* III, 2, 130. 140. *the s. that tells of this war's loss,* John II, 348. *do you set down your name in the s. of youth,* H4B I, 2, 202. *accept this s. which in the right of Richard Plantagenet we do exhibit to your majesty,* H6A III, 1, 149. *give him from me this most needful s.* R3 V, 3, 41 (Ff note). *give the king this fatal-plotted s.* Tit. II, 3, 47. *a s., and written round about,* IV, 2, 18. IV, 4, 16. *do not exceed the prescript of this s.* Ant. III, 8, 5.

**Scroop,** name: R2 III, 2, 192. III, 3, 28. H4A I, 3, 271. IV, 4, 3. V, 5, 37. H4B IV, 4, 84. H5 II Chor. 24. II, 2, 58. 67. 94.

**Scrowl,** unintelligible reading of Qq in Tit. II, 4, 5; Ff *scowl.*

**Scroyles,** scabby fellows, rascals: John II, 373.

**Scrubbed,** paltry: *a little s. boy, no higher than thyself,* Merch. V, 162. 261 (Coles, Lat. and Engl. Dictionary: *a scrub,* homo misellus, and *scrubbed,* squalidus).*

**Scruple,** subst. 1) the third part of a dram; proverbially a very small quantity: Meas. I, 1, 38. Ado V, 1, 93. Merch. IV, 1, 330. All's II, 3, 234. Tw. II, 5, 2. Tw. III, 4, 87 (punning). Troil. IV, 1, 70.

2) doubt: *no dram of a s., no s. of a s.* Tw. III, 4, 87. 88. *how I should be your patient to follow your prescriptions, the wise may make some dram of a s., or indeed a s. itself,* H4B I, 2, 149. *made s. of his praise,* Cymb. V, 5, 182.

3) doubtful perplexity, cause of indetermination: Wiv. V, 5, 157. Meas. I, 1, 65. John II, 370. IV, 1, 7. R2 V, 5, 13. H6A V, 3, 93. H8 II, I, 158. II, 2, 88. II, 4, 150. 171. IV, 1, 31. Troil. IV, 1, 56 (*not making any s. of her soilure* = taking no offence at her soilure). Mcb. II, 3, 135. IV, 3, 116. Hml. IV, 4, 40.

**Scrupulous,** full of doubt and perplexity, too nice in determinations of conscience: *away with s. wit! now arms must rule,* H6C IV, 7, 61. *equality of two domestic powers breed s. faction,* Ant. I, 3, 48 (prying too nicely into the merits of either cause).

**Scud,** to run swiftly: *sometime he —s far off and there he stares,* Ven. 301.

**Scuffle,** a close fight hand to hand: *in the —s of great fights,* Ant. I, 1, 7.

**Scull,** the cranium, see *Skull.*

**Scull,** a shoal, a multitude of fish: *like scaled —s before the belching whale,* Troil. V, 5, 22.

**Scullion,** the lowest domestic servant, that washes the kettles and dishes in the kitchen; used as a term of contempt: H4B II, 1, 65. Hml. II, 2, 616.

**Sculp,** in *Insculped,* q. v.

**Scum,** the impurities rising to the surface of liquors in boiling; and hence the dross, refuse: Wiv. I, 1, 167. H4B IV, 5, 124. H6B IV, 2, 130. R3 V, 3, 317.

**Scurrile,** grossly jocose, becoming a buffoon: *breaks s. jests,* Troil. I, 3, 148.

**Scurrility,** mean buffoonery, broad jokes: LLL IV, 2, 55. V, 1, 4.

**Scurrilous,** the same as scurrile: Wint. IV, 4, 215.

**Scurvy,** scabby, vile, contemptible: Tp. II, 2, 46. 57. 159. III, 2, 71. Wiv. I, 4, 115. II, 3, 65. III, 1, 123. Meas. V, 136. All's II, 3, 250. V, 3, 324. Tw. III, 4, 163. H4B II, 4, 132. 296. H5 V, 1, 19. 23. Troil. II, 1, 49. 56. V, 4, 4. 30. Rom. II, 4, 161. Lr. IV, 6, 175. Oth. I, 2, 7. IV, 2, 140. 196.

**'Scuse,** subst. excuse: Merch. IV, 1, 444. Oth. IV, 1, 80.

**Scut,** the tail of a deer: *my doe with the black s.* Wiv. V, 5, 20.

**Scutcheon,** a shield with armorial ensigns: LLL V, 2, 567. H4A V, 1, 143. Ant. V, 2, 135.

**Scylla,** a rock in the straits of Sicily dangerous to seamen: Merch. III, 5, 19 (alluding to the well-known verse: *Incidis in Scyllam cupiens vitare Charybdim*).

**Scythe,** subst. the instrument used to mow grass and corn: H5 V, 2, 50. Attribute of time and death: Sonn. 12, 13. 60, 12. 100, 14. 123, 14. LLL I, 1, 6. Ant. III, 13, 194.

**Scythe,** vb. to cut off as with a scythe: *time had not —d all that youth begun,* Compl. 12.

**Scythia,** a country in the east of Europe, part of the present Russia: *was ever S. half so barbarous?* Tit. I, 131. 132.

**Scythian,** a native of Scythia: H6A II, 3, 6. *the barbarous S.* Lr. I, 1, 118.

**'Sdeath,** corrupted from *God's death;* an exclamation expressive of impatience: Cor. I, 1, 221.

**Sea,** the ocean, or a branch of it (used as a fem. in Troil. I, 3, 34): Ven. 389. Lucr. 652. Sonn. 113, 11. Tp. I, 1, 17. I, 2, 4. 11. 149. 155. 301. II, 1, 62. 92. III, 2, 15. III, 3, 9. 71. 74. V, 43. Gent. I, 2, 122. IV, 3, 33. Mids. II, 1, 152. R2 I, 1, 19. H5 IV, 1, 156. V Chor. 9. H6A IV, 1, 89. H6C II, 6, 89. 97. R3 IV, 2, 47. Hml. IV, 1, 7. Oth. II, 1, 7. V, 2, 362. Ant. III, 10, 25 etc. etc. Metaphorically: *hulling in the wild sea of my conscience,* H8 II, 4, 200. *I have ventured in a s. of glory, but far beyond my depth,* III, 2, 360. *float upon a wild and violent s.* Mcb. IV, 2, 21. Symbol of insatiable avidity: *the never surfeited s.* Tp. III, 3, 55. *thy capacity receiveth as the s.* Tw. I, 1, 11. *as hungry as the s.* II, 4, 103. Denoting any great quantity: *drenched in a s. of care,* Lucr. 1100. *a s. of melting pearl* (i. e. tears) Gent. III, 1, 224. *in that s. of blood,* H6A IV, 7, 14. *shed —s of tears,* H6C II, 5, 106. *to weep —s,* Troil. III, 2, 84. *in a*

*wide s. of wax,* Tim. I, 1, 47 (cf. *Wax*). *we must all part into this s. of air,* IV, 2, 22. *to take arms against a s. of troubles,* Hml. III, 1, 59. *lest this great s. of joy o'erbear the shores of my mortality,* Per. V, 1, 194. Proverbially rich: Gent. II, 4, 170. Wint. IV, 4, 501. H5 I, 2, 164. R3 I, 4, 28. Troil. II, 2, 92. Oth. I, 2, 28. Cymb. I, 6, 34. Representing the element of water in general: *thus have I shunned the fire and drenched me in the s.* Gent. I, 3, 79. *in earth, in s.,* *in sky,* Err. II, 1, 17. *whether in s. or fire, in earth or air, the extravagant and erring spirit hies to his confine,* Hml. I, 1, 153. *earth, s. and air,* Per. I, 4, 34.

Used without the article, in general contradistinction to the land: *a thousand furlongs of s.* Tp. I, 1, 70. *by wreck of s.* Err. V, 49. *one foot in s. and one on shore,* Ado II, 3, 66. *Publicola and Caelius are for s.* Ant. III, 7, 74 (= are to fight at sea). *order for s. is given,* IV, 10, 6. *at s.:* Gent. III, 1, 282. Meas. III, 1, 218. 225. Err. V, 359. Merch. I, 1, 24. 177. III, 1, 45. H6A III, 4, 28. H8 IV, 1, 72. Hml. IV, 6, 15. Oth. II, 1, 1. 28. Ant. I, 4, 36. II, 6, 25. 87. III, 7, 40. III, 8, 4. Cymb. III, 4, 192. Per. III, 1, 51. III, 3, 13. III, 4, 5. IV, 6, 49. V, 1, 158. 198. 245. V, 3, 5. *by s.:* Ant. II, 2, 165. II, 6, 96. III, 7, 29. 41. 62. IV, 10, 1. *by s. and land:* Shr. V, 2, 149. Wint. III, 3, 84. Caes. I, 3, 87. Ant. I, 4, 78. III, 6, 54. IV, 2, 5. *to s.:* Tp. I, 1, 53. I, 2, 145. II, 2, 44. 56. Wiv. II, 1, 96. Meas. I, 2, 8. Err. IV, 1, 33. H5 II, 2, 192. Per. III Prol. 44. IV, 4, 29. *put to s.:* Err. V, 21. Tw. II, 4, 78. Wint. IV, 4, 509.

*At the s.* instead of *at s.* only in Per. I, 3, 29 and V, 3, 47. *to —s* for *to s.* only in Per. II Prol. 27 (rhyming).

Plur. *—s* for the sing.: *though the —s threaten, they are merciful,* Tp. V, 178. *promise you calm —s,* 314. *the —s waxed calm,* Err. I, 1, 92. *lords of the wide world and wide watery —s,* II, 1, 21. *in the narrow —s that part the French and English,* Merch. II, 8, 28. III, 1, 4. *the swelling Adriatic —s,* Shr. I, 2, 74. II, 331. R2 III, 2, 3. H5 II Chor. 38. H6A III, 1, 180. V, 3, 193. V, 5, 90. H6B I, 3, 128. IV, 8, 45. H6C I, 1, 239. III, 3, 235. IV, 7, 5. IV, 8, 3. R3 IV, 1, 42. IV, 1, 463. 464. 474 (Qq *sea*). Cymb. I, 6, 202 etc.

**Sea-bank,** coast: Merch. V, 11. Oth. IV, 1, 138.

**Sea-boy,** a ship-boy: H4B III, 1, 27.

**Sea-cap,** a cap worn at sea: Tw. III, 4, 364.

**Sea-change,** a change wrought by the sea: Tp. I, 2, 400.

**Sea-coal,** pit-coal: *a s. fire,* Wiv. I, 4, 9. H4B II, 1, 95. Name in Ado III, 3, 12. 13. III, 5, 63.

**Sea-farer,** a traveller by sea: Per. III, 1, 41.

**Sea-faring,** following the business of seamen: *s. men,* Err. I, 1, 81. Hml. IV, 6, 2 (Ff *sailors*).

**Sea-fight,** a battle at sea: Tw. III, 3, 26. Hml. V, 2, 54.

**Sea-gown,** a garment worn at sea: Hml. V, 2, 13.

**Seal,** subst. 1) a stamp engraved with some device or inscription, to be imprinted on wax: R3 II, 4, 71. H8 III, 2, 245. Hml. V, 2, 50. *the great s.* (the principal seal of the kingdom): H8 III, 2, 229. 319. 347. Figuratively: *pure lips, sweet —s in my soft lips imprinted,* Ven. 511. *set thy s. manual on my wax-red lips,* 516. *Nature carved thee for her s. and meant thereby thou shouldst print more,* Sonn. 11, 13. *although my s. be stamped in his face,* Tit. IV, 2, 127.

2) the impression thus made in wax and used as a testimony: Meas. IV, 2, 208. Merch. IV, 1, 139. Tw. V, 341. R2 V, 2, 56. Cor. V, 6, 83. Caes. III, 2, 133. *here is your hand and s. for what I did,* John IV, 2, 215. *proceeded under your hands and —s,* H8 II, 4, 222. *here is the will, and under Caesar's s.* Caes. III, 2, 245. *to break the s.* (= to open a sealed letter): Gent. III, 1, 139. Wint. III, 2, 130. 132. Figuratively: *the empress sends it* (the child) *thee, thy stamp, thy s.* Tit. IV, 2, 70. *O, could this kiss be printed in thy hand, that thou mightst think upon these by the s.* H6B III, 2, 344.

3) token, proof, testimony: *to stamp the s. of time in aged things,* Lucr. 941. *it is the show and s. of nature's truth,* All's I, 3, 138. *there is my gage, the manual s. of death, that marks thee out for hell,* R2 IV, 25. *a form indeed, where every god did seem to set his s.* Hml. III, 4, 61. *all —s and symbols of redeemed sin,* Oth. II, 3, 350.

4) ratification, confirmation, sanction, pledge: *my kisses, —s of love,* Meas. IV, 1, 6. *my observations, which with experimental s. doth warrant the tenour of my book,* Ado IV, 1, 168. *let me kiss* (your hand) *this princess of pure white, this s. of bliss,* Mids. III, 2, 144. *this zealous kiss, as a s. to this indenture of my love,* John II, 20. *that you should seal this lawless bloody book of forged rebellion with a s. divine,* H4B IV, 1, 92. *beguiling virgins with the broken —s of perjury,* H5 IV, 1, 172. *whom after under the confession's s. he solemnly had sworn that what he spoke my chaplain to no creature living should utter,* H8 I, 2, 164. *to shame the s. of my petition to you in praising her,* Troil. IV, 4, 124 (= to disgrace your granting what I ask by praising her and thus showing that it is not my request but other motives that cause your complaisance. Most M. Edd. preposterously *zeal*). *how in my words soever she be shent, to give them —s never, my soul, consent,* Hml. III, 2, 417 (i. e. performance). *this kingly s. and plighter of high hearts* (Cleopatra's hand) Ant. III, 13, 125.

**Seal,** vb. 1) to imprint as with a stamp; figuratively: *seals of love, but —ed in vain,* Meas. IV, 1, 6. *upon his will I —ed my hard consent,* Hml. I, 2, 60.

2) to mark with a stamp, either by way of evidence and testimony, or in order to shut and close (as letters, bags of money); absol.: *he was fain to s. on Cupid's name,* LLL V, 2, 9. *the Frenchman became his surety and —ed under for another,* Merch. I, 2, 89. *her Lucrece, with which she uses to s.* Tw. II, 5, 104. H4A III, 1, 270. H4B IV, 3, 142. Ant. III, 2, 3. Figuratively: Ven. 512. With *to: I'll s. to such a bond,* Merch. I, 3, 153. 155. 172. *I did but s. once to a thing,* H6B IV, 2, 90. Transitively: *her letter now is —ed,* Lucr. 1331. *a —ed compact,* Hml. I, 1, 86. Compl. 49. Wiv. III, 4, 16. Merch. I, 3, 145. II, 6, 6. II, 8, 18. Shr. Ind. 2, 90 (—ed *quarts,* i. e. quart-measures officially stamped to show that they held the proper quantity). H4A III, 1, 81. IV, 4, 1. Mcb. V, 1, 8. Hml. III, 4, 202. V, 2, 47. Ant. II, 6, 60. Per. I, 3, 13. With *up,* = to close with a seal: *this —ed up counsel,* LLL III, 170. *the oracle, thus by Apollo's great divine —ed up,* Wint. III, 1, 19. *this —ed up oracle,* III, 2, 128. *this paper, thus —ed up,* Caes. II, 1, 37.

3) to close, to shut (cf. *seel,* with which it is sometimes confounded): *for —ing the injury of tongues,*

Wint. I, 2, 337. *who have power to s. the accuser's lip* Lr. IV, 6, 174. *I had rather s. my lips,* Ant. V, 2, 146 With *up: black night that —s up all in rest,* Sonn. 73, 8. *our arms, like to a muzzled bear, hath all offence —ed up,* John II, 250. *s. up the ship-boy's eyes,* H4B III, 1, 19. *s. up your lips,* H6B I, 2, 89. *the searchers of the town —ed up the doors and would not let us forth,* Rom. V, 2, 11. *s. up the mouth of outrage for awhile,* V, 3, 216. *to s. her father's eyes up close as oak,* Oth. III, 3, 210 (Ff *seel*).

4) to complete, to finish, to make up; absol.: *the —ing day betwixt my love and me,* Mids. I, 1, 84 (bringing to a close what has been begun; or the day on which we are to sign our contract). *s. then, and all is done,* Ant. IV, 14, 49 (= make an end). trans.: *till we have —ed thy full desire,* Tim. V, 4, 54. *every thing is —ed and done,* Hml. IV, 3, 58. With *up: and by him s. up thy mind, whether that thy youth and kind will the faithful offer take,* As IV, 3, 58 (= make up, bring to a determination). *here had the conquest fully been —ed up,* H6A I, 1, 130.

5) to confirm, to ratify, to sanction, to attest: (those lips) *—ed false bonds of love,* Sonn. 142, 7. *to s. our happiness with their consents,* Gent. I, 3, 49. *s. the bargain with a holy kiss,* II, 2, 7. *his worth and credit that's —ed in approbation,* Meas. V, 245. *have —ed his rigorous statutes with their bloods,* Err. I, 1, 9. *which I had rather s. with my death,* Ado V, 1, 247. *and s. the title with a lovely kiss,* Shr. III, 2, 125. *all the ceremony of this compact —ed in my function, by my testimony,* Tw. V, 164. *my hand thus —s it* (the covenant) R2 II, 3, 50. *that you should s. this lawless bloody book of forged rebellion with a seal divine,* H4B IV, 1, 91. *with blood he —ed a testament of noble-ending love,* H5 IV, 6, 26. *now thou art —ed the son of chivalry,* H6A IV, 6, 29. *the match is made, she —s it with a curtsy,* H6C III, 2, 57. *thus* (with kissing the king's hand) *I s. my truth,* IV, 8, 29. *the duty that I owe unto your majesty I s. upon the lips of this sweet babe,* V, 7, 29. *—ed in thy nativity the slave of nature,* R3 I, 3, 229. *with my hand I s. my true heart's love,* II, 1, 10. *s. thou this league with thy embracements,* 29. *I now s. it* (the truth) H8 II, 1, 105. *a bargain made, s. it,* Troil. III, 2, 204. *omission to do what is necessary —s a commission to a blank of danger,* III, 3, 231. *you have received many wounds. I will not s. your knowledge with showing them,* Cor. II, 3, 115. *what may be sworn by, both divine and human, s. what I end withal,* III, 1, 142. *this hand, by thee to Romeo —ed,* Rom. IV, 1, 56. *s. with a righteous kiss a dateless bargain,* V, 3, 114. *her election hath —ed thee for herself,* Hml. III, 2, 70. *now must your conscience my acquittance s.* IV, 7, 1. *had the virtue which their own conscience —ed them,* Cymb. III, 6, 85. *s. it* (our peace) *with feasts,* V, 5, 483. *your hands and lips must s. it too,* Per. II, 5, 85. With *up,* = to confirm fully: *thou hast —ed up my expectation,* H4B IV, 5, 104.

**Sealed-up,** see *Seal,* vb.

**Sea-like,** likely to keep the sea: *our severed navy too have knit again and fleet, threatening most s.* Ant. III, 13, 171.

**Sealing-day,** see *Seal,* vb.

**Seal-manual,** see *Seal* and *Manual.*

**Seal-ring,** a ring containing a seal: H4A III, 3, 94. 117.

**Seam,** subst. grease, lard: *the proud lord that*

*bastes his arrogance with his own s.* Troil. II, 3, 195 (cf. *Enseamed*).

**Seam,** subst. suture: *'twas we that made up this garment through the rough —s of the waters,* Per. II, 1, 156 (the fisherman's speech).

**Sea-maid,** mermaid, siren: Meas. III, 2, 115. Mids. II, 1, 154 (v. 150 *mermaid*).

**Seaman,** a mariner: Ven. 454. John III, 1, 92. Per. III, 1, 8. IV, 1, 54.

**Sea-marge,** shore: Tp. IV, 1, 69.

**Sea-mark,** an object serving for a direction to mariners: *stick i' the wars like a great s.* Cor. V, 3, 74. *here is my butt and very s. of my utmost sail,* Oth. V, 2, 268.

**Sea-monster,** a huge and terrible animal living in the sea: Merch. III, 2, 57. *ingratitude, more hideous when thou showest thee in a child than the s.* Lr. I, 4, 283 (almost generally, though not the less absurdly, supposed to mean the hippopotamus, which lives in rivers.*cf. Lr. IV, 2, 50. Cymb. IV, 2, 35).

**Seamy,** having and showing the sutures: *that turned your wit the s. side without,* Oth. IV, 2, 146 (i.e. inside out).

**Sea-nymph,** a nymph or goddess of the sea: Tp. I, 2, 402.

**Sear,** subst. the state of being dry and withered: *my way of life is fallen into the s., the yellow leaf,* Mcb. V, 3, 23. cf. *Sere.*

**Sear,** adj. see *Sere.*

**Sear,** vb. 1) to burn, to scorch: *the sun that —ed the wings of my sweet boy,* H6C V, 6, 23. *were red-hot steel, to s. me to the brain,* R3 IV, 1, 61. *thy crown does s. mine eye-balls,* Mcb. IV, 1, 113.

2) to dry up, to wither: *some beauty peeped through lattice of —ed age,* Compl. 14.

3) to brand: *my maiden's name —ed otherwise,* All's II, 1, 176. *calumny will s. virtue itself,* Wint. II, 1, 73.

4) With *up,* = to dry up, to deprive of vitality? *and s. up my embracements from a next with bonds of death,* Cymb. I, 1, 116 (Grant White *cere,* Singer *seal).**
*—ed* substituted for *feared* by M. Edd.: Meas. II, 4, 9 and Cymb. II, 4, 6 (cf. *Fear*).

**Search,** subst. 1) the act of seeking: *our frustrate s. on land,* Tp. III, 3, 10. *see the issue of his s.* Wiv. III, 3, 186. III, 5, 107. *not worth the s.* Merch. I, 1, 118. *what's spent in the s.* III, 1, 96. As II, 2, 20. All's II, 4, 35. Hml. V, 2, 374. Cymb. I, 1, 64. Per. II, 4, 51. With *for: let's make further s. for my poor son,* Tp. II, 1, 323. With *of;* subjectively: *infold me from the s. of eyes,* Rom. III, 3, 73. Objectively: *of Pericles the careful s.* Per. III Prol. 16.

2) quest, pursuit: *it is a thing of his own s. and altogether against my will,* As I, 1, 142. *seeks not to find that her s. implies,* All's I, 3, 222. *go in s. of virtue,* John II, 428. *a pain that only seems to seek out danger i' the name of fame and honour, which dies i' the s.* Cymb. III, 3, 51.

3) a body of seekers: *lead to the Sagittary the raised s.* Oth. I, 1, 159 (cf. *quest* in I, 2, 46).

**Search,** vb. 1) to seek; absol.: *the clock gives me my cue, and my assurance bids me s.* Wiv. III, 2, 47. *s., seek, find out,* III, 3, 173. *once more s. with me,* IV, 2, 172. *we'll s.* All's IV, 3, 229. H4A III, 3, 64. Rom. V, 3, 172. 178. Cymb. II, 3, 154. Per. II, 4, 50. With *for: to s. for a gentleman,* Wiv. III, 3, 115. 122. III,

5, 82. IV, 2, 32. Cymb. II, 3, 146. With a clause: *you and my brother s. what companies are near,* Cymb. IV, 2, 68. Transitively: *to s. you out,* Oth. I, 2, 47. *he hath been —ed among the dead and living,* Cymb. V, 5, 11. Doubtful passage: Per. II, 1, 58.*

2) to look through and examine for the purpose of finding something: *would have —ed it* (the basket) Wiv. III, 5, 105. *I will s. impossible places,* 151. IV, 2, 167. V, 5, 60. Merch. II, 8, 5. III, 2, 86. H4A II, 4, 537. 580. Lr. IV, 4, 7. Per. IV, 2, 3. Acc. and *for: to s. his house for his wife's love,* Wiv. III, 5, 78. IV, 2, 171. Caes. II, 1, 36. *s. out thy wit for secret policies,* H6A III, 3, 12.

3) to probe, to tent, to sound: *thus I s. it* (the wound) *with a sovereign kiss,* Gent. I, 2, 116. *—ing of thy wound,* As II, 4, 44. *the tent that —es to the bottom of the worst,* Troil. II, 2, 16. *now to the bottom dost thou s. my wound,* Tit. II, 3, 262. *with this good sword s. this bosom,* Caes. V, 3, 42.

4) to penetrate, to pass into and affect the interior: *mirth doth s. the bottom of annoy,* Lucr. 1109 (causes the deepest sensation of annoy). *the heaven's glorious sun that will not be deep —ed with saucy looks,* LLL I, 1, 85. *when the —ing eye of heaven is hid,* R2 III, 2, 37; cf. *these eyes, as piercing as the midday sun, to s. the secret treasons of the world,* H6C V, 2, 18; *for Achilles, mine own —ing eyes shall find him by his large and portly size,* Troil. IV, 5, 161. *that's a marvellous —ing wine,* H4B II, 4, 30 (affecting and stirring the blood). *bitter —ing terms,* H6B III, 2, 311 (cutting to the heart).

**Searchers,** officers trusted with the sanitary police during a pestilence: Rom. V, 2, 8.

**Sea-room,** sufficient distance from land, or shoals, or rocks; open sea: Per. III, 1, 45.

**Sea-salt,** briny: *s. tears,* Tit. III, 2, 20.

**Sea-sick,** 1) affected with nausea from the pitching of a vessel: LLL V, 2, 393. Wint. V, 2, 128.

2) weary of travelling by sea: *run on the dashing rocks thy s. weary bark,* Rom. V, 3, 118.

**Sea-side,** the edge of the sea, the shore: *by the s.* Tp. I, 2, 138. Wint. III, 3, 68. *to the s.* IV, 4, 682. 856. John V, 7, 91. Oth. II, 1, 36. Ant. III, 11, 20.

**Season,** subst. 1) time generally: *now the happy s. once more fits,* Ven. 327. *now serves the s. that they may surprise the silly lambs,* Lucr. 166. *make glad and sorry —s,* Sonn. 19, 5. *what is the time o' the day? Past the mid s.* Tp. I, 2, 239. *so it would have done at the same s., if your mother's cat had but kittened,* H4A III, 1, 19. *not a soldier of this —'s stamp should go so general current through the world,* IV, 1, 4. *you wish me health in very happy s.* H4B IV, 2, 79 (= in good time). *I trembling waked and for a s. after could not believe but that I was in hell,* R3 I, 4, 61. *in brief, — for so the s. bids us be,* V, 3, 87. *he is wise and best knows the fits o' the s.* Mcb. IV, 2, 17. *that s. wherein our Saviour's birth is celebrated,* Hml. I, 1, 158. *it draws near the s. wherein the spirit held his wont to walk,* I, 4, 5. *confederate s.* III, 2, 267. *I will tell you at some meeter s.* Ant. V, 1, 49. *be friended with aptness of the s.* Cymb. II, 3, 53. *youth of such a s.* III, 4, 175 (= age). *we'll slip you for a s.* IV, 3, 22. *you did relieve me to see this gracious season,* V, 5, 401.

2) one of the four divisions of the year: Sonn. 14, 4. 104, 6. Mids. II, 1, 107. II, 2, 117. As II, 1, 6. Wint. IV, 4, 81. H4B IV, 4, 123. H6B II, 4, 4.

Tim. III, 6, 58. Caes. II, 1, 108. Almost = weather: *defend you from —s such as these,* Lr. III, 4, 32. Metaphorically: *it is I that, lying by the violet in the sun, do as the carrion does, not as the flower, corrupt with virtuous s.* Meas. II, 2, 168 (with the benign influence of summer-weather and sunshine). *I am not a day of s., for thou mayst see a sunshine and a hail in me at once,* All's V, 3, 32 (not such a day as one would expect in the present time of the year; cf. *Unseasonable* in R2 III, 2, 106).

3) fit and convenient time: *whoever plots the sin, thou 'point'st the s.* Lucr. 879. *I warrant you, buck, and of the s. too,* Wiv. III, 3, 169 (cf. *unseasonable* in Lucr. 581). *even for our kitchens we kill the fowl of s.* Meas. II, 2, 85 (duly matured, prepared and fattened). *these jests are out of s.* Err. I, 2, 68. II, 2, 48. *time is a very bankrupt and owes more than he's worth to s.* IV, 2, 58 (is seldom so convenient and opportune as one would wish). Ado I, 3, 26. LLL I, 1, 107. V, 2, 63. Merch. V, 107. R3 I, 4, 76. Troil. I, 3, 87. Lr. II, 1, 121.

4) that which keeps fresh and tasteful; seasoning: *salt too little which may s. give to her foul-tainted flesh,* Ado IV, 1, 144. *the s. of all natures, sleep,* Mcb. III, 4, 141.*

**Season**, vb. 1) to spice, to give a relish to, to make fresh and tasteful: *the spice and salt that s. a man,* Troil. I, 2, 278. *have their honest wills, which —s comfort,* Cymb. I, 6, 9 (gives happiness its proper relish). Applied to tears as resembling rain, and having, besides, a salt-flavour: *—ing the earth with showers of silver brine,* Lucr. 796. *'tis the best brine a maiden can s. her praise in,* All's I, 1, 55. *all this to s. a brother's dead love, which she would keep fresh,* Tw. I, 1, 30. *how much salt water thrown away in waste, to s. love,* Rom. II, 3, 72. cf. Compl. 18.

2) to render more agreeable, to recommend and set off by some admixture: *what plea so tainted and corrupt but, being —ed with a gracious voice, obscures the show of evil,* Merch. III, 2, 76. *how many things by season —ed are to their right praise and true perfection,* V, 107. *this suit of yours, so —ed with your faithful love to me,* R3 III, 7, 149.

3) to qualify, to temper: *so are you to my thoughts as food to life, or as sweet —ed showers are to the ground,* Sonn. 75, 2. *earthly power doth then show likest God's, when mercy —s justice,* Merch. IV, 1, 197. *to take from Rome all —ed office and to wind yourself into a power tyrannical,* Cor. III, 3, 64.* s. *your admiration for a while with an attent ear,* Hml. I, 2, 192. *you may s. it in the charge,* II, 1, 28.

4) to mature, to ripen, to prepare: *s. the slaves for tubs and baths,* Tim. IV, 3, 85. *my blessing s. this in thee,* Hml. I, 3, 81. *who in want a hollow friend doth try, directly —s him his enemy,* III, 2, 219. *when he is fit and —ed for his passage,* III, 3, 86.

5) to gratify the taste of: *let their palates be —ed with such viands,* Merch. IV, 1, 97.

**Seasonable**, in *Unseasonable,* q. v.

**Sea-sorrow**, grief suffered at sea: Tp. I, 2, 170.

**Sea-storm**, a tempest on the sea: Tp. I, 2, 177.

**Sea-swallowed**, drowned in the sea: Tp. II, 1, 251.

**Seat**, subst. 1) that on which one may sit; as a chair: *give us some —s,* Meas. V, 165. *I must take like s. unto my fortune, and to my humble s. conform myself,* H6C III, 3, 10. 11. R3 IV, 4, 32. *keep s.* Mcb. III, 4, 54. *forsake thy s.* Ant. II, 7, 43. *the wheeled s. of Caesar,* IV, 14, 75 (= triumphal car). A saddle: *newly in the s.* Meas. I, 2, 165. *vaulted with such ease into his* H4A IV, 1, 107. H4B IV, 1, 118. Hml. IV, 7, 86. Oth. II, 1, 305. A chair of office: *struck me in my very s. of judgment,* H4B V, 2, 80. *we'll hoise Duke Humphrey from his s.* H6B I, 1, 169. Cor. III, 1, 136. Caes. III, 1, 34. Particularly the throne: *by my —'s right royal majesty,* R2 II, 1, 120. *manage rusty bills against thy s.* III, 2, 119. IV, 218. *the crown and s. of France,* H5 I, 1, 88. I, 2, 269. H6B I, 2, 36. V, 1, 178. H6C I, 1, 26. II, 6, 100. III, 3, 28. 206. IV, 6, 2. V, 7, 13. R3 I, 3, 112. III, 1, 164. III, 7, 118. 169. Troil. I, 3, 31. Tit. I, 14. Cymb. I, 1, 142.

2) place of residence, abode, place possessed as a property: *oft they interchange each other's s.* Lucr. 70. *within his thought her heavenly image sits, and in the selfsame s. sits Collatine,* 289. *thou mightst my s. forbear,* Sonn. 41, 9. *which three till now never kept s. in one,* 105, 14. *let love forbid sleep his s. on thy eyelid,* Mids. II, 2, 81. *it gives a very echo to the s. where love is throned,* Tw. II, 4, 21. *this earth of majesty, this s. of Mars,* R2 II, 1, 41. IV, 140. V, 5, 112. H4A I, 1, 65. H5 I, 1, 36. III, 5, 51. R3 III, 3, 13. Cor. I, 1, 140. Tim. IV, 2, 45. Hml. I, 5, 96 *(hold a s.)*. Cymb. V, 4, 69. Per. Prol. 18.

3) estate, landed property: *her s. of Belmont,* Merch. I, 1, 171. *the s. of Gaunt, dukedom of Lancaster,* H4A V, 1, 45. *for your great —s now quit you of great shames,* H5 III, 5, 47. *thrown from Leonati s.* Cymb. V, 4, 60.

4) situation, site: *this castle hath a pleasant s.* Mcb. I, 6, 1.

**Seat**, vb. 1) to settle: *did s. the French beyond the river Sala,* H5 I, 2, 62.

2) to fix, to set firm: *let Caesar s. him sure,* Caes. I, 2, 325. *make my —ed heart knock at my ribs,* Mcb. I, 3, 136.

**Seated**, 1) sitting: *now you are fairly s.* H8 I, 4, 31. *when he was s. in a chariot,* Per. II, 4, 7. Particularly = sitting, placed on a throne: *if he were s. as King Edward is,* H6C III, 1, 96. *being s., the conquerors make war upon themselves,* R3 II, 4, 60. H6C I, 1, 22. IV, 3, 64. V, 7, 35. R3 IV, 2, 4.

2) placed: *it is no mean happiness to be s. in the mean,* Merch. I, 2, 8. *see what a grace was s. on this brow,* Hml. III, 4, 55.

3) situated: *some dark deep desert, s. from the way,* Lucr. 1144.

**Sea-tost**, tossed by the sea: Per. III, Prol. 60.

**Sea-walled**, fenced by the sea: *our s. garden,* R2 III, 4, 43.

**Sea-water**, water of the sea: Tp. I, 2, 462. LLL I, 2, 86.

**Sea-wing**, a sail: Ant. III, 10, 20.

**Sebastian**, name: Tp. II, 1, 136. 205. 215. 260. V, 74. 76. Gent. IV, 4, 48. All's IV, 3, 184. Tw. II, 1, 17. 18. III, 4, 400. 414. V, 228. 231. 239. 240.

**Second**, adj. the ordinal of two; 1) the next in order to the first: Wiv. II, 1, 78. LLL I, 2, 183. Merch. II, 7, 6. As I, 2, 137. V, 4, 97. 158. All's V, 3, 70. Tw. I, 5, 141. Wint. II, 1, 145. III, 2, 97. R3 III, 3, 12 *(Richard the s.).* V, 3, 31 etc.

2) not the first: *a s. brother,* H4B II, 2, 71. With *to,* = inferior to: *s. to none,* Err. V, 7. H4B II, 3, 34.

3) inferior only to one: *art thou not s. woman in the realm?* H6B I, 2, 43. *Tullus Aufidius, the s. name of men,* Cor. IV, 6, 125. *great nature's s. course,* Mcb. II, 2, 39.

4) another, one more: *struck dead at first, what needs a s. striking?* Ven. 250. *a s. fear through all her sinews spread,* 903. *bear amiss the s. burden of a former child,* Sonn. 59, 4. *to live a s. life on s. head,* 68, 7. *death's s. self,* 73, 8. Tp. V, 195. Meas. II, 1, 298. Merch. III, 2, 95. IV, 1, 333. 340. As I, 2, 218. II, 7, 165. Shr. II, 297. All's I, 1, 2. R2 III, 4, 76. H5 II, 4, 126. H6A III, 3, 20 etc. *a s. time* and *the s. time* = once more: All's II, 3, 55. H4A V, 2, 101. Hml. III, 2, 194. Per. V, 3, 44. Err. II, 2, 47. Troil. IV, 5, 237. Hml. II, 2, 402.

5) secondary, acting by deputation and in subordination: *the agents, or base s. means,* H4A I, 3, 165. *mock your workings in a s. body,* H4B V, 2, 90. *in s. voice we'll not be satisfied; we come to speak with him,* Troil. II, 3, 149.

6) helpful, lending assistance: *good my lords, be s. to me,* Wint. II, 3, 27.

**Second,** subst. 1) one next in order to another: *where each second stood heir to the first,* Oth. I, 1, 37. *such a place as is his own s.* II, 3, 144.

2) one who, or that which, assists and supports: *I'll be thy s.* Tp. III, 3, 103. *now prove good —s,* Cor. I, 4, 43. *you have shamed me in your condemned —s,* I, 8, 15.*this project should have a back or s., that might hold, if this should blast in proof,* Hml. IV, 7, 154. *no —s? all myself?* Lr. IV, 6, 198. *if —s had answered him,* Cymb. V, 3, 90.

3) Plur. —s, a provincial term for the second kind of flour, collected after the smaller bran is sifted: *my oblation which is not mixed with —s,* Sonn. 125, 11 (= not mixed with baser matter).*

**Second,** vb. 1) to follow up: *you some permit to s. ills with ills,* Cymb. V, 1, 14.

2) to assist, to support, to back: Wiv. I, 3, 114. Ado V, 1, 2. As III, 3, 13. John IV, 3, 102. H4B IV, 2, 45. 46. H6B IV, 9, 35. H8 III, 2, 60. Troil. I, 3, 122. Cor. IV, 6, 62. V, 6, 57. Caes. III, 1, 29. Oth. IV, 2, 244. Ant. V, 1, 70. Per. II, 4, 20.

**Secondarily** = secondly, in the language of Dogberry: Ado V, 1, 221.

**Secondary,** one subordinate to another: *old Escalus, though first in question, is thy s.* Meas. I, 1, 47. *to be a s. at control,* John V, 2, 80.

**Secrecy,** 1) state of being hidden, privacy, concealment: *thus breathes she forth her spite against the unseen s. of night,* Lucr. 763. *sealed to curious s.* Compl. 49. *in nature's infinite book of s. a little I can read,* Ant. I, 2, 9. *in s.* = in secret: *whom the king hath in s. long married,* H8 III, 2, 404. *this to me in dreadful s. impart they did,* Hml. I, 2, 207.

2) a secret, that which is kept concealed: *nor read the subtle-shining —es writ in the glassy margents of such books,* Lucr. 101.

3) habit of keeping secrets, discretion: *this s. of thine shall be a tailor to thee,* Wiv. III, 3, 33. *thanks for thy care and s.* Meas. V, 536. LLL V, 1, 116. Wint. III, 3, 130. H4A II, 3, 112. H6B I, 2, 90. II, 2, 68. Troil. I, 2, 286. Hml. II, 2, 305. III, 4, 192. Per. I, 1, 153.

**Secret,** subst. 1) something studiously concealed: *a thousand honey —s shalt thou know,* Ven. 16. *to*

hear her —s so bewrayed, Pilgr. 352. Gent. II, 5, 40. III, 1, 2. 394. Meas. III, 2, 142. Ado I, 1, 206. LLL I, 1, 232. IV, 3, 25. 80. All's IV, 1, 93. IV, 3, 339. Wint. III, 2, 131. IV, 4, 248. 307. 783. V, 2, 132. H6A V, 3, 100. H6B I, 1, 250. III, 2, 376. R3 I, 4, 35. H8 II, 1, 144. II, 3, 51. III, 2, 215. V, 1, 17. Tit. IV, 2, 170. Caes. II, 1, 281. 291. 302. 306. Mcb. V, 1, 81. Hml. I, 5, 14. Oth. IV, 2, 22. Cymb. II, 2, 40. III, 5, 86. Per. I, 1, 117. I, 3, 7. *some marks of s.* = some secret marks: Cymb. V, 5, 206 (cf. *Of*).

2) privacy, state or place not seen: *the —s of the grave this viperous slander enters,* Cymb. III, 4, 40. *in s.* = privately, secretly: Ado IV, 1, 95. LLL V, 2, 236. Rom. I, 3, 8. Hml. IV, 5, 88.

3) a thing not yet discovered or explained, a mystery: *the —s of nature have no more gift in taciturnity,* Troil. IV, 2, 74 (Q *the —s of neighbour Pandar*). *all blest —s, all you unpublished virtues of the earth, spring with my tears,* Lr. IV, 4, 15.

**Secret,** adj. 1) hidden, concealed, unseen and unknown: *and therein so ensconced his s. evil,* Lucr. 1515. *those s. things,* Wint. IV, 4, 714. *their s. purposes,* V, 1, 36. *some s. place, some reverend room,* R2 V, 6, 25. *that in his s. doom out of my blood he'll breed revengement,* H4A III, 2, 6. *live alone as s. as I may,* H6B IV, 4, 48. *drag her husband to some s. hole,* Tit. II, 3, 129. *the —'st man of blood,* Mcb. III, 4, 126. *have s. feet in some of our best ports,* Lr. III, 1, 32. *to rush into the s. house of death,* Ant. IV, 15, 81.

2) private, confined to the knowledge of one's self: *nor shall he smile at thee in s. thought,* Lucr.1065. *I have toward heaven breathed a s. vow,* Merch. III, 4, 27. *I have unclasped to thee the book even of my s. soul,* Tw. I, 4, 14. *as s. as maidenhead,* I, 5, 232. *another s. close intent,* R3 I, 1, 158. *the history of all her s. thoughts,* III, 5, 28. *in the s. parts of fortune,* Hml. II, 2, 239.

3) kept from observation, not observed, acting or done underhand: *their s. and sudden arrival,* Lucr. Arg. 8. *birds never limed no s. bushes fear,* Lucr. 88. *thy s.pleasure turns to open shame,* 890. *the s. nameless friend of yours,* Gent. II, 1, 111. *to give me s. harbour,* Meas. I, 3, 4. *put them in s. holds,* IV, 3, 91. *to whom you swore a s. pilgrimage,* Merch. I, 1, 120. *a s. and villanous contriver against me,* As I, 1, 150. *by any s. course,* John I, 1, 178. *unclasp a s. book,* H4A I, 3, 188. *the s. whispers of each other's watch,* H5 IV Chor. 7. H6A I, 4, 10. V, 4, 147. H6B III, 1, 174. III, 2, 31. H6C IV, 5, 9. IV, 6, 83. V, 2, 18. R3 I, 3, 325. Rom. II, 4, 203. Mcb. V, 2, 17.

4) mysterious, occult: *shows whereon the stars in s. influence comment,* Sonn. 15, 4. *rapt in s. studies,* Tp. I, 2, 77. *search out thy wit for s. policies,* H6A III, 3, 12. *if s. powers suggest but truth to my divining thoughts,* H6C IV, 6, 68. *you s., black and midnight hags,* Mcb. IV, 1, 48. *I ever have studied physic, through which s. art … I have made familiar to me the blest infusions,* Per. III, 2, 32.

5) discreet, not apt to blab: *if thou yield, I rest thy s. friend,* Lucr. 526. *wherein thou must be s.* Gent. III, 1, 60. *I can be s. as a dumb man,* Ado I, 1, 212. R2 II, 1, 298. Rom. II, 4, 208. Caes. II, 1, 125. Hml. I, 5, 122. III, 4, 214. With *to,* = keeping the secrets of: *confess to thee that art to me as s. and as dear as Anna to the queen of Carthage was,* Shr. I, 1, 158. *to himself so s. and so close,* Rom. I, 1, 155.

**Secretary**, one who writes orders, letters etc. for another: H8 II, 2, 116. IV, 1, 102. V, 1, 35. V, 3, 1. 77.

**Secret-false,** faithless in secret: Err. III, 2, 15.

**Secretly,** privily, not openly, underhand: Wiv. IV, 3, 6. Ado IV, 1, 205. 250. IV, 2, 63. Mids. V, 161. Merch. II, 3, 7. As I, 1, 130. II, 2, 11. H4A I, 3, 266. R3 I, 1, 100. Troil. V, 2, 24. Tit. IV, 2, 174.

**Sect,** 1) a body of people united in some settled tenets: Wint. V, 1, 107. H8 V, 3, 81.

2) party, faction: *when —s and factions were newly born,* Tim. III, 5, 30. *packs and —s of great ones,* Lr. V, 3, 18.

3) class, order, rank: *all —s, all ages smack of this vice,* Meas. II, 2, 5. *as he in his particular s. and force may give his saying deed,* Hml. I, 3, 26 (Qq *act and place*).

4) a cutting, a scion: *whereof I take this that you call love to be a s. or scion,* Oth. I, 3, 336.

5) sex: *so is all her s.; an they be once in a calm, they are sick,* H4B II, 4, 41 (or = class?).

**Sectary,** 1) one who belongs to a sect, a dissenter: H8 V, 3, 70.

2) a follower, disciple: *how long have you been a s. astronomical?* Lr. I, 2, 164.

**Secure,** adj. (as for the accent, see Appendix I, 1, Chang. A.) 1) free from apprehension, careless, unsuspecting, confident: *though Page be a s. fool,* Wiv. II, 1, 241. II, 2, 315. III, 2, 43. *sleep doubtless and s. that Hubert for the wealth of all the world will not offend thee,* John IV, 1, 130. *s. foolhardy king,* R2 V, 3, 43. *proud of their numbers and s. in soul,* H5 IV Chor. 17. *this happy night the Frenchmen are s., having all day caroused,* H6A II, 1, 11. *the wound of peace is surety, surety s.* Troil. II, 2, 15. *upon my s. hour thy uncle stole,* Hml. I, 5, 61. *not jealous nor s.* Oth. III, 3, 198. *to lip a wanton in a s. couch,* IV, 1, 72. Adverbially: *we may do it as s. as sleep,* H4A I, 2, 145. *all which s. and sweetly he enjoys,* H6C II, 5, 50 (the suffix *ly* belonging to both adverbs).

2) free from danger, safe: *there is scarce truth enough alive to make societies s.* Meas. III, 2, 240. *while thou liest warm at home, s. and safe,* Shr. V, 2, 151. *mine (quarter) was s.* H6A II, 1, 66. *once again we'll sleep s. in Rouen,* III, 2, 19. *no man is s.* R3 I, 1, 71. III, 2, 83. III, 4, 93. Per. I, 1, 95. With *from:* John II, 27. H6C IV, 4, 33. Tit. I, 152. With *of: s. of thunder's crack or lightning flash,* Tit. II, 1, 3.

3) prevented from doing harm: *in iron walls they deemed me not s.* H6A I, 4, 49.

**Secure,** vb. 1) to make careless and confident: *to think I shall lack friends? s. thy heart,* Tim. II, 2, 185. *our means s. us, and our mere defects prove our commodities,* Lr. IV, 1, 22. *I do not so s. me in the error,* Oth. I, 3, 10.

2) to make safe, to guard from danger: *whiles we stood here —ing your repose,* Tp. II, 1, 310. *to give the enemy way and to s. us by what we can, which can no more but fly,* H6B V, 2, 76. *heaven s. him!* Hml. I, 5, 113. *we'll higher to the mountains, there s. us,* Cymb. IV, 4, 8.

**Securely,** carelessly, confidently: *she s. gives good cheer and reverend welcome to her princely guest,* Lucr. 89. *she dwells so s. on the excellency of her honour,* Wiv. II, 2, 252. *stand s. on their battlements,* John II, 374. *s. I espy virtue with valour couched in thine eye,* R2 I, 3, 97. *and yet we strike not, but s. perish,* II, 1, 266. *'tis done like Hector, but s. done, a little proudly, and great deal misprizing the knight opposed,* Troil. IV, 5, 73. *whose youth was spent in dangerous wars, whilst you s. slept,* Tit. III, 1, 3.

**Security,** 1) carelessness, want of caution, confidence: *Bolingbroke through our s. grows strong,* R2 III, 2, 34. *that's mercy, but too much s.* H5 II, 2, 44. *s. gives way to conspiracy,* Caes. II, 3, 8. *s. is mortal's chiefest enemy,* Mcb. III, 5, 32.

2) safety from danger: *thus have we swept suspicion from our seat and made our footstool of s.* H6C V, 7, 14. *and give up yourself merely to chance and hazard, from firm s.* Ant. III, 7, 49.

3) suretyship: *but s. enough to make fellowships accurst,* Meas. III, 2, 241 (cf. Proverbs XI, 15).* *he liked not the s.* (of Bardolph) H4B I, 2, 38. 43. 47. 49. 51. 52. *fair leave and large s.* Troil. I, 3, 223. *this is no time to lend money without s.* Tim. III, 1, 46. III, 5, 81.

**Sedge,** a narrow flag, a reed: Gent. II, 7, 29. Ado II, 1, 210. Shr. Ind. 2, 53. 55.

**Sedged,** made of sedges: *your s. crowns,* Tp. IV, 129.

**Sedgy,** overgrown with sedge: *on the gentle Severn's s. bank,* H4A I, 3, 98.

**Sedition,** factious commotion: H6A IV, 3, 47. H6C II, 2, 158. Cor. III, 1, 70.

**Seditious,** factious, rebellious: *since the mortal and intestine jars 'twixt thy s. countrymen and us,* Err. I, 1, 12. *s. to his grace and to the state,* H6B V, 1, 37.

**Seduce,** to mislead, to corrupt, to deprave: Lucr. 639. Gent. IV, 2, 97. LLL I, 2, 180. All's III, 5, 22. John I, 254. H5 II, 2, 155. H6B III, 1, 356. H6C IV, 8, 37. V, 1, 19. R3 III, 7, 188. Cor. V, 6, 24. Caes. I, 2, 316. Hml. I, 5, 45. cf. *Saint-seducing* in Rom. I, 1, 220.

**Seducer,** one that seduces: All's V, 3, 146.

**See,** subst. the seat of the pope or of an archbishop: Meas. III, 2, 232. John III, 1, 144. V, 2, 72. H4B IV, 1, 42.

**See,** vb. (impf. *saw,* partic. *seen; sawn* in Compl. 91 perhaps = sown. *—ing* sometimes monosyll.: Shr. Ind. 2, 34. III, 2, 182. H6C I, 1, 218. 247. Hml. III, 1, 33. Oth. I, 3, 203 etc.) 1) to perceive by the eye; absol.: *to hear nor s.* Ven. 437. *I could not s.* 440. *these mine eyes, but for thy piteous lips, no more had —n,* 504. 720. 939. 952. Sonn. 18, 13. 113, 4. Ado I, 1, 191. LLL IV, 3, 333. V, 2, 375. Mids. III, 2, 179. IV, 1, 77. H5 V, 2, 325. H8 IV, 1, 61. Hml. III, 1, 33. Cymb. III, 2, 80 etc. With an accus. denoting the effect: *s. away their shilling,* H8 Prol. 12. Transitively: *her help she —s,* Ven. 93. *what —st thou in the ground?* 118. *thou canst not s. one wrinkle in my brow,* 139. 148. 287. 337. 357. 393. 397. 492. 604. 644. 667. 703. 819. 938. 962. 1031. 1093. 1107. 1109. 1194 etc. With an accus. and inf.: *those that I saw suffer,* Tp. I, 2, 6. *which thou sawest sink,* 32. *I saw him beat the surges,* II, 1, 114 etc. Inf. with *to: I saw her coral lips to move,* Shr. I, 1, 179; cf. Sonn. 64, 9 and 119, 4. Double accus.: *to s. him buried,* R3 II, 1, 90. *to s. thy Antony making his peace,* Caes. III, 1, 197. *to s. my best friend ta'en,* V, 3, 35. *let me see thee a steward still,* Tw. II, 5, 169 etc. cf. *it is not the fashion to s. the lady the epilogue,* As Epil. 1. *you see it lawful then,* All's III, 7, 30. *where death's approach* *is seen so terrible*, H6B III, 3, 6. H8 III, 2, 335. Cor. III, 1, 225. Lr. III, 6, 14. *I shall s. some squeaking Cleopatra-boy my greatness*, Ant. V, 2, 220.

= to see each other, to meet: *since last we saw in France*, H8 I, 1, 2. *when shall we see again?* Cymb. I, 1, 124 (cf. *greet, kiss, know* etc.).

2) to perceive mentally, to discover, to understand, to observe: *I s. you have a month's mind to them*, Gent. I, 2, 137. *I s. things too*, 139. *now I s. you'll be a courtier*, Wiv. III, 2, 8. Tp. I, 2, 49. II, 1, 208. Gent. I, 2, 15. Wiv. II, 2, 305. III, 3, 69. III, 4, 1. IV, 2, 2. IV, 6, 36. V, 3, 2. V, 5, 135. Err. I, 1, 72. Ado III, 5, 38. All's III, 7, 30. Tw. I, 5, 269. Wint. II, 3, 12. H6B III, 3, 6. R3 III, 6, 14. Troil. III, 2, 131. V, 10, 41 (*let me s.* = this it is, here I have it; cf. Hml. II, 2, 471. IV, 7, 155). Rom. I, 3, 45. Hml. V, 2, 1 (*so much for this, sir: now let me s. the other*, = now let me consider, let me speak of the other; cf. *let's s. your song*, Gent. I, 2, 88. Qq *now shall you see*). Lr. I, 2, 198 (*I s. the business* = I see how it will be) etc. etc.

—*ing* = in consideration, since, as: *so your doctors hold it very meet*, —*ing too much sadness hath congealed your blood*, Shr. Ind. 2, 134. —*ing thou fallest on me so luckily, I will assay thee*, H4A V, 4, 33. —*ing the deed is meritorious*, H6B III, 1, 270. —*ing gentle words will not prevail, assail them with the army of the king*, IV, 2, 184. —*ing ignorance is the curse of God, you cannot but forbear to murder me*, IV, 7, 78. —*ing thou hast proved so unnatural a father*, H6C I, 1, 218. —*ing thou dost* (prefer thy life before thine honour) *I here divorce myself*, 247. —*ing 'twas he that made you to depose, your oath is vain*, I, 2, 26. —*ing that death will come when it will come*, Caes. II, 2, 36.

3) to visit, to call on: Wiv. I, 1, 67. III, 2, 11. R3 V, 3, 32. H8 I, 1, 177. Troil. IV, 5, 229. V, 9, 8. Caes. I, 3, 154 etc.

4) to witness, to become acquainted with: *when I have seen such interchange of state*, Sonn. 64, 9. *will you walk in to s. their gossiping?* Err. V, 419. *mean to s. the Tuscan service*, All's I, 2, 13. *the hermit that never saw pen and ink*, Tw. IV, 2, 15. cf. such expressions as Gent. II, 1, 72. Wiv. II, 1, 103 etc. *civility not* —*n from other*, Cymb. IV, 2, 179 (= not learned by observing others; German: *nicht andern abgesehen*).

*Well seen* = well skilled, versed: *a schoolmaster well seen in music*, Shr. I, 2, 134.

5) to experience, to know, to have, to suffer, to enjoy: *still losing when I saw myself to win*, Sonn. 119, 4. *I have* —*n when judgement hath repented o'er his doom*, Meas. II, 2, 10. *and not be* —*n to wink of all the day*, LLL I, 1, 43. *some shall s.* I, 2, 165 (Costard's speech). *is there any else longs to s. this broken music in his sides?* As I, 2, 149. *fourteen they shall not s.* Wint. II, 1, 147. *had our prince* —*n this hour*, V, 1, 116. *who ever saw the like?* H6A I, 2, 22. *we have many goodly days to s.* R3 IV, 4, 320. *he ne'er saw three and twenty*, Troil. I, 2, 255. *shall never s. his pardon*, Lr. V, 1, 68. *I have* —*n the day*, V, 3, 276. *the griefs are ended by* —*ing the worst*, Oth. I, 3, 203 etc. *to live to see*, see *Live*.

6) to take care, to look to, to be attentive: *see further*, Cymb. V, 5, 124. 127. Per. IV, 1, 100. With *for*, = to look out for, to inquire after: *let's s. for means*, Rom. V, 1, 35. *s. for the news*, Oth. II, 1, 95.

With *to*, = to look to: *s. to my house*, Merch. I, 3, 176. *s. to't well, protect yourself*, H6B II, 1, 54. With an accus., = to take care of, to provide for: *s. that at any hand*, Shr. I, 2, 147. *to s. this business*, R2 II, 1, 217. *to s. my gelding in the stable*, H4A II, 1, 38 (Gadshill's speech). *s. high order in this great solemnity*, Ant. V, 2, 368. With a double accus.: *I myself will s. his burial better than his life*, H6A II, 5, 121 (= will take care that his burial be better than his life). *s. the lists and all things fit*, H6B II, 3, 54. *s. him safe i' the Tower*, H8 V, 3, 97. *I'll play the cook and s. them ready 'gainst their mother comes*, Tit. V, 2, 206. cf. *to s. these honours in possession*, H6C II, 6, 110. *s. him out at gates*, Cor. III, 3, 138. *I'll s. the church o' your back*, Shr. V, 1, 5 (will help you to get beyond the church). The second accus. a participle: *there to s. me shipped*, Gent. I, 1, 54 (to take care of my embarking). *s. our pleasure herein executed*, Meas. V, 527. *s. him presently discharged*, Err. IV, 1, 32. *s. him safe conveyed home*, IV, 4, 125. *s. him delivered o'er*, LLL I, 1, 307. *s. these letters delivered*, Merch. II, 2, 123. *s. it done*, 164. Shr. Ind. 1, 106. 129. IV, 3, 166. Tw. V, 323. Wint. II, 3, 134. R2 III, 1, 29. H6A I, 3, 89. III, 2, 133. V, 1, 48. H6B I, 2, 84. I, 3, 225. I, 4, 49. III, 1, 321. 330. H6C IV, 3, 64. H8 II, 2, 141. Tim. II, 2, 45. Cor. IV, 6, 47. Mcb. I, 2, 66. Followed by a subjunctive: *s. it be returned*, Gent. I, 2, 46. *s. that Claudio be executed*, Meas. II, 1, 33. *s. you the fornicatress be removed*, II, 2, 23. *s. this be done*, IV, 3, 83. *s. thou do it*, Err. II, 2, 141. *s. thou do commend*, LLL III, 169. *s. thou bring her here*, Mids. III, 2, 98. Merch. III, 4, 49. Shr. I, 2, 148. II, 9. John III, 3, 7. H4B IV, 3, 81. H6A III, 1, 53. H6B I, 1, 74. II, 3, 85. H6C III, 2, 120. Tit. II, 3, 299. Rom. V, 3, 24. Hml. I, 3, 59 (Qq *look*).

7) With *into*, = to penetrate, to look through: *well hath your highness* —*n into this duke*, H6B III, 1, 42. *I s. into thy end*, Cymb. III, 4, 169.

**Seed**, that from wich plants spring: Ven. 167. Tp. II, 1, 144. Meas. I, 2, 102. All's I, 3, 152. Wint. IV, 4, 490. Rom. V, 1, 46. Hml. I, 2, 136 (*an unweeded garden that grows to s.*). Metaphorical use: H4B III, 1, 84. 90. Mcb. I, 3, 58. Per. IV, 6, 93. = offspring: Merch. II, 9, 47. Troil. IV, 5, 121. = son, descendant: *saw his heroical s., and smiled to see him*, H5 II, 4, 59. *to make them kings, the* —*s of Banquo kings*, Mcb. III, 1, 70 (M. Edd. *seed*).

**Seeded**, running to seed, matured, full-grown: *how will thy shame be s. in thine age, when thus thy vices bud before thy spring*, Lucr. 603. *the s. pride that hath to this maturity blown up*, Troil. I, 3, 316.

**Seedness**, the state of being sown: *as blossoming time that from the s. the bare fallow brings to teeming foison*, Meas. I, 4, 42.

**Seedsman**, a sower: Ant. II, 7, 24.

**Seek** (impf. and partic. *sought*), 1) to take pains to find, to go in search or quest of, to look for something; absol.: *search, s., find out*, Wiv. III, 3, 173. Rom. V, 3, 198. Caes. III, 2, 208. *he will s. there*, Wiv. IV, 2, 61. *I'll not s. far*, Wint. V, 3, 141. *let us s.* John V, 7, 79. *without* —*ing find*, Cymb. V, 4, 139. *s. through this grove*, Mids. II, 1, 259. *your nobles s. through your camp to find you*, H5 IV, 1, 303. cf. Cymb. I, 1, 20. With *for*: *he's not here I s. for*, Wiv. IV, 2, 165. *the four strangers s. for you*, Merch. I, 2, 135 (Ff s. *you*). II, 6, 66. As III, 2, 303. H6C V, 2,

3. R3 V, 4, 5. Caes. IV, 3, 252. V, 3, 79. Hml. I, 2, 71. Oth. I, 2, 54. Cymb. I, 1, 20. With *into: that you would have me s. into myself for that which is not in me*, Caes. I, 2, 64 (= to search, sound, examine myself). With *to*, = to apply to: *that eye which him beholds, as more divine, unto a view so false will not incline, but with a pure appeal — s to the heart*, Lucr. 293.

Transitively: *s. a knife*, Lucr. 1047. *to s. anew some fresher stamp*, Sonn. 82, 7. *to s. thy son*, Tp. II, 1, 327. III, 3, 101. Gent. I, 1, 88. 89. IV, 2, 78. Wiv. I, 3, 91. IV, 2, 168. Err. I, 2, 36. 104. II, 1, 2. V, 225. Mids. I, 1, 219. Tw. I, 5, 142. H5 III, 6, 149. John V, 7, 79. Ant. II, 2, 161. Cymb. IV, 2, 160 (cf. *Through*) etc. With *out*, in the same sense: *to s. out you*, Gent. II, 4, 94. *s. him out*, III, 1, 188. Wiv. II, 1, 144. Err. II, 2, 3. As III, 2, 108. Tw. II, 4, 14. IV, 3, 7. H6B V, 2, 14. H6C I, 4, 178. II, 1, 166. H8 III, 1, 38. Rom. IV, 3, 56. Hml. V, 2, 323. Ant. II, 2, 162 etc.

2) to try to gain, to strive, to pursue, to solicit, to aim at; absol.: *how I would make him fawn and beg and s.* LLL V, 2, 62. *what's their —ing?* Cor. I, 1, 192 (their petition). With *for: how comes it then, vile opportunity, being so bad, such numbers s. for thee*, Lucr. 896. *s. for grace*, Tp. V, 295. *the sailors sought for safety by our boat*, Err. I, 1, 77. *s. for rule*, Shr. V, 2, 163. *and s. for sorrow with thy spectacles*, H6B V, 1, 165. *unless they s. for hatred at my hands*, H6C IV, 1, 80. H8 I, 2, 114. Lr. II, 4, 79. Cymb. II, 4, 133. IV, 2, 162 etc. With *after: how men of merit are sought after*, H4B II, 4, 405. *that's more than we know. Ay, or more than we should s. after*, H5 IV, 1, 136 (= than we should inquire into; the soldier's speech). With an infinitive: *to fan and blow them dry again she —s*, Ven. 52. *the warm effects she —s to kindle*, 606. 477. 525. 964. Lucr. 488. 655. 998. 1438. Sonn. 10, 7. Tp. I, 2, 347. III, 1, 80. Gent. II, 7, 20. III, 1, 61. Wiv. III, 4, 6. Meas. III, 1, 42. R2 I, 3, 241 etc. With a subordinate clause: *and s. how we may prejudice the foe*, H6A III, 3, 91. *but cheerly s. how to redress their harms*, H6C V, 4, 2.

Transitively: *what win I if I gain the thing I s.?* Lucr. 211. *barred him from the blessed thing he sought*, 340. Sonn. 30, 3. *what I s., my weary travel's end*, 50, 2. *against the thing he sought he would exclaim*, Compl. 313. *she was sought by spirits of richest coat*, 236; cf. Wiv. III, 4, 19; LLL III, 191; Mids. II, 1, 246; Merch. III, 4, 70; Tw. I, 2, 34; III, 1, 168; Rom. I, 3, 74; Per. Prol. 33. *you have not sought her help*, Tp. V, 142; Err. I, 1, 152 (M. Edd. *life*). *to s. preferment out*, Gent. I, 3, 7 (*out* = abroad). *doth he so s. his life?* Meas. I, 4, 72; Merch. III, 3, 21; IV, 1, 351; Lr. III, 4, 172; Per. IV, 1, 90. *and —ing death, find life*, Meas. III, 1, 43. *forced me to s. delays for them and me*, Err. I, 1, 75. *s. a dispensation for his oath*, LLL II, 87. *many their fortunes s.* As II, 3, 73; Shr. I, 2, 51; Troil. V, 6, 19. *that sought at Oxford thy dire overthrow*, R2 V, 6, 16. *we would not s. a battle*, H5 III, 6, 173. *s. prevention of thy foes*, H6B II, 4, 57. *s. my death*, IV, 7, 107; Lr. III, 4, 168; III, 5, 7. *the business that —s dispatch by day*, H8 V, 1, 16. *I never sought their malice*, V, 2, 15. *men's prayers then would s. you, not their fears*, V, 3, 83 (= would attend you). *s. not my name*, Tim. V, 4, 71 etc. Dat. and accus.: *I s. you a better husband*, Wiv. III, 4, 88. With *of*, = to try to obtain, to beg, to request of: *you bid me s. redemption of the devil*, Meas. V, 29. *come you to s. the lamb here of the fox?* 300. *let him not s. it* (mercy) *of us*, H8 I, 2, 213. *I will s. satisfaction of you*, Oth. IV, 2, 203. *of Caesar s. your honour with your safety*, Ant. IV, 15, 46. *which* (honour) *he to s. of me again, behoves me keep at utterance*, Cymb. III, 1, 72 (to demand back again, to reclaim). cf. *who —s for better of thee, sauce his palate with thy most operant poison*, Tim. IV, 3, 24. With *out*: *drove us to s. out this head of safety*, H4A IV, 3, 102. *in cruelty will I s. out my fame*, H6B V, 2, 60. *they are sheep and calves which s. out assurance in that*, Hml. V, 1, 125.

3) to search: *have I sought every country far and near, and, now it is my chance to find thee out, must I behold thy timeless cruel death?* H6A V, 4, 3 (or *every country* = in every country? the shepherd's speech). cf. *unsought* in Err. I, 1, 136.

**Seel,** to close up the eyes, to blind (originally a term of falconry): *come, —ing night, scarf up the tender eye of pitiful day*, Mcb. III, 2, 46. *when light-winged toys of feathered Cupid s. with wanton dullness my speculative and officed instruments*, Oth. I, 3, 270 (Qq *foyles*). *to s. her father's eyes up close as oak*, III, 3, 210 (Qq *seal*).* *the wise gods s. our eyes*, Ant. III, 13, 112. cf. *Seal*.

**Seely,** name in R2 V, 6, 14.

**Seely,** adj. see *Silly*.

**Seem,** 1) to look like, to have the appearance of being: *a summer's day will s. an hour but short*, Ven. 23. *so shall the day s. night*, 122. *—s unkind*, 310. 540. 830. 842. 858. 970. 984. 1064. 1067. 1156 etc. With an inf.: *would s. to melt*, Ven. 144. *—ing to bury that posterity*, 758. *how strange it —s not to believe*, 985. *—ed with him to bleed*, 1056. *the fire and cracks the mighty Neptune s. to besiege*, Tp. I, 2, 205. II, 1, 36. 258 etc. With a clause: *the sky, it — s, would pour down pitch*, Tp. I, 2, 3. Gent. IV, 4, 79. Err. II, 1, 56 etc. *it should s.* = it seems: *who, it should s., hath sometime loved*, Wint. IV, 4, 372. R2 III, 2, 7 (Ff *appears*). Troil. III, 1, 39. Tim. III, 4, 30. Followed by *as*: Err. I, 1, 108. Mids. I, 1, 205. IV, 1, 171. As IV, 3, 119. All's III, 7, 31 etc. by *like*: *makes it s. like rivers of remorse*, John IV, 3, 109. Cor. III, 1, 221. With *to*: *which to you shall seem probable*, Tp. V, 249. Wiv. II, 2, 284. Ado IV, 1, 58. Mids. IV, 1, 171. 198. Shr. Ind. 1, 43. H4B V, 5, 83 etc. *me —eth* = it seems to me: *me —eth then it is no policy*, H6B III, 1, 23. *me —eth good*, R3 II, 2, 120.

*—ing*, adjectively, = being in appearance: *he entertained a show so —ing just*, Lucr. 1514. *love's best habit is in —ing trust*, Sonn. 138, 11. *we have very oft awaked him, as if to carry him to execution, and showed him a —ing warrant for it*, Meas. IV, 2, 160. *there shall appear such —ing truth of Hero's disloyalty*, Ado II, 2, 49. *with two —ing bodies, but one heart*, Mids. III, 2, 212. *the —ing truth*, Merch. III, 2, 100. *the father of this —ing lady*, Wint. V, 1, 191. *this —ing brow of justice*, H4A IV, 3, 83. *the —ing sufferances that you had borne*, V, 1, 51. *there is no —ing mercy in the king*, V, 2, 35. *I dare swear you borrow not that face of —ing sorrow, it is sure your own*, H4B V, 2, 29. *sorrow that is couched in —ing gladness*, Troil. I, 1, 39. *unseemly woman in a —ing man*, Rom. III, 3, 112. *a —ing mermaid*, Ant. II, 2, 214.

*—ing*, substantively, = appearance, show, exterior: *my love is strengthened, though more weak in*

—*ing*, Sonn. 102, 1. *tie the wiser souls to thy false —ing*, Meas. II, 4, 15. *these keep —ing and savour all the winter long*, Wint. IV, 4, 75. *dismantle you and, as you can, disliken the truth of your own —ing*, 667. *rotten opinion, who hath writ me down after my —ing*, H4B V, 2, 129. *you sign your place and calling, in full —ing, with meekness and humility*, H8 II, 4, 108. *such to-be-pitied and o'erwrested —ing he acts thy greatness in*, Troil. I, 3, 157. *we will both our judgments join in censure of his —ing*, Hml. III, 2, 92. *that under covert and convenient —ing hast practised on man's life*, Lr. III, 2, 56. *these thin habits and poor likelihoods of modern —ing*, Oth. I, 3, 109. *putting on the mere form of civil and humane —ing*, II, 1, 244. *more than a mortal —ing*, Cymb. I, 6, 171. *all good —ing shall be thought put on for villany*, III, 4, 56. *thought her like her —ing*, V, 5, 65.

2) to be only in appearance and not really: *truth may s., but cannot be*, Phoen. 62. *s. you that you are not?* Gent. II, 4, 10. *what s. I that I am not?* 14. *that we were all, as some would s. to be*, Meas. III, 2, 40. *either you are ignorant or s. so craftily*, II, 4, 75. Shr. IV, 2, 17. 70. All's II, 5, 71. IV, 3, 332. H4A V, 4, 140. H4B V, 5, 83. R3 I, 3, 338. Troil. V, 1, 6. Cor. III, 1, 218. Tim. III, 6, 6 etc. Mcb. I, 3, 51; V, 1, 33.* —*ing*, substantively, = false appearance, hypocrisy: —*ing, —ing!* Meas. II, 4, 150. *faults from —ing free*, III, 2, 41. *out on thee, —ing!* Ado IV, 1, 57. *she that, so young, could give out such a —ing*, Oth. III, 3, 209.

3) to appear, to be seen, to show oneself or itself: *the man doth fear God, howsoever it —s not in him by some large jests he will make*, Ado II, 3, 205. *there did s. in him a kind of joy to hear of it*, Hml. III, 1, 18. Hence = to assume an air, to pretend to be: *'tis my familiar sin with maids to s. the lapwing and to jest, tongue far from heart*, Meas. I, 4, 32. *it is my study to s. despiteful and ungentle to you*, As V, 2, 86. *nothing she does or —s but smacks of something greater than herself*, Wint. IV, 4, 157. With an inf.: *is not this a strange fellow, that so confidently —s to undertake this business, which he knows is not to be done*, All's III, 6, 94. *so should he look that —s to speak things strange*, Mcb. I, 2, 47. *the golden round, which fate and metaphysical aid doth s. to have thee crowned withal*, I, 5, 30. *how courtesy would s. to cover sin*, Per. I, 1, 121 (but cf. *to make the truth appear where it —s hid*, Meas. V, 66. *love that would s. hid*, Tw. III, 1, 160; in which passages the word is almost periphrastical. Similarly: *let the prologue s. to say, we will do no harm*, Mids. III, 1, 19. *an it shall please you to break up this, it shall s. to signify*, Merch. II, 4, 11; Bottom's and Launcelot's speeches).

4) to have a specious appearance; only in the partic. and gerund: *the so —ing Mistress Page*, Wiv. III, 2, 42. *that little —ing substance*, Lr. I, 1, 201. cf. *ill-seeming* in Shr. V, 2, 143. *this hath some —ing*, Cymb. V, 5, 452 (seems very well founded). Adverbially: *bear your body more —ing*, As V, 4, 72 (Touchstone's speech).

**Seemer**, one who makes a show of sth.: *hence shall we see, if power change purpose, what our —s be*, Meas. I, 3, 54.

**Seeming**, subst. and adj. see *Seem.*

**Seemingly**, in appearance: Wiv. IV, 6, 33.

**Seeming-virtuous**, virtuous in appearance, dissembling: Hml. I, 5, 46.

**Seemly**, specious, showy: *all that beauty that doth cover thee is but the s. raiment of my heart*, Sonn. 22, 6. *lacking wit to make a s. answer to such persons*, H8 III, 1, 178.

**Seethe** (partic. *sod* or *sodden*), to boil; 1) trans.: *her eyes, though sod in tears, looked red and raw*, Lucr. 1592. *sodden water*, H5 III, 5, 18. *till the high fever s. your blood to froth*, Tim. IV, 3, 433. Allusions to the cure of the powdering-tub: *my business —s. Sodden business! there's a stewed phrase indeed*, Troil. III, 1, 44. *the stuff we have, a strong wind will blow it to pieces, they are so pitifully sodden*, Per. IV, 2, 21. The partic. applied to the highest degree of dulness (as it were, a decoction and quintessence of stupidity): *twice sod simplicity, bis coctus!* LLL IV, 2, 23. *sodden-witted lord*, Troil. II, 1, 47.

2) intr.: *a —ing bath*, Sonn. 153, 7. —*ing brains*, Mids. V, 4. *my business —es*, Troil. III, 1, 43.

**Segregation**, dispersion: *what shall we hear of this? A s. of the Turkish fleet*, Oth. II, 1, 10.

**Seize**, 1) to rush and lay hold on, to gripe, to grasp, to catch; trans.: Lucr. 677. 882. Gent. V, 4, 33. John III, 4, 131. R2 III, 4, 55. H6B IV, 10, 27. H6C IV, 2, 24. R3 II, 4, 50. III, 1, 47. Cor. III, 1, 183. 214. Tim. IV, 3, 343. Mcb. II, 3, 128. Oth. IV, 2, 37. Ant. III, 5, 12. III, 11, 47. Cymb. V, 5, 30. Per. IV, 1, 98. IV, 3, 48.

With *on*: *let vultures vile s. on his lungs also*, H4B V, 3, 145. *let's s. upon him*, H6C III, 1, 23. *s. on the shame-faced Henry, bear him hence*, IV, 8, 52. *s. on him, Furies*, R3 I, 4, 57.

2) to take, or get possession of by force; trans.: *having first —d his books*, Tp. III, 2, 97. *what's open made to justice, that justice —s*, Meas. II, 1, 22. *shall s. one half his goods*, Merch. IV, 1, 353 (Q1 *on half*). *I'll s. thy life, with what thou else callest thine*, Wint. II, 3, 137. *if you do wrongfully s. Hereford's rights*, R2 II, 1, 201. *our treasure —d*, H6C III, 3, 36. Followed by prepositional expressions: *thy lands and all things ... do we s. into our hands*, As III, 1, 10. R2 II, 1, 189. 209. *we do s. to us the plate*, 160. *nor the god of war shall s. this prey out of his father's hands*, Tit. IV, 2, 96.

With *on*: *shall s. on half his goods*, Merch. IV, 1, 353 (Ff Q2 *one half*). *Bolingbroke —d on the realm*, H6B II, 2, 24. —*d upon their towns and provinces*, H6C I, 1, 109. *his lands then —d on by the conqueror*, III, 2, 3. *s. upon Fife*, Mcb. IV, 1, 151.

3) to fall on, to attack, to overpower: *say this were death that now hath —d them*, Tp. II, 1, 261 (cf. Ant. III, 11, 47. Cymb. V, 5, 30). *infirmity ... hath something —d his wished ability*, Wint. V, 1, 142. *sleep hath —d me wholly*, Cymb. II, 2, 7. *despair hath —d her*, III, 5, 60.

4) to take, to get possession of in any manner: *s. thee that list*, Shr. III, 1, 91. *s. it* (the glove) *if thou darest*, R2 IV, 48. *here, cousin, s. the crown*, 181. *this prince in justice —th but his own*, Tit. I, 281. 405.

With *on*: *with this she —th on his sweating palm*, Ven. 25. *even thus he —d on my lips*, Pilgr. 151. *another ship had —d on us*, Err. I, 1, 113 (had taken us on board). *which is the lady I must s. upon?* Ado V, 4, 53. *they may s. on the white wonder of dear Juliet's hand*, Rom. III, 3, 35. *thee and thy virtues I here s. upon*, Lr. I, 1, 255. *natures of such deep trust we shall much need: you we first s. on*, II, 1, 118. *s.*

*upon the fortunes of the Moor*, Oth. V, 2, 366. *to s. love* = to conceive love? *can thy right hand s. love upon thy left?* Ven. 158 (the earlier Qq *ceaze*).

**Seized,** with *of*, = possessed of: *all those his lands which he stood s. of*, Hml. I, 1, 89. Ff. *s. on.*

**Seizure,** 1) the act of seizing, grasp, clasp: *and with her lips on his did act the s.* Pilgr. 152. *shall these hands, so newly joined in love, unyoke this s.?* John III, 1, 241. *her hand, to whose soft s. the cygnet's down is harsh*, Troil. I, 1, 57.

2) the act of taking possession by force: *all things that thou dost call thine worth s.* As III, 1, 10.

**Seld,** adv. seldom: *goods lost are s. or never found*, Pilgr. 175. *as s. I have the chance*, Troil. IV, 5, 150. cf. *seld-shown.*

**Seldom,** adj. rare, not frequent: *the fine point of s. pleasure*, Sonn. 52, 4. *my state, s. but sumptuous, showed like a feast*, H4A III, 2, 58.

**Seldom,** adv. rarely, not often: Lucr. 87. 633. 1574. Sonn. 52, 6. Tp. II, 1, 195. Wiv. II, 2, 105. LLL II, 228. All's II, 1, 100. III, 6, 64. IV, 5, 88. Wint. IV, 2, 43. V, 1, 20. R2 II, 1, 7. H4A I, 2, 230. III, 2, 46. 80. H6B III, 1, 268. 301. H6C III, 1, 65. IV, 1, 18. R3 II, 3, 4 (*s. comes the better*). III, 1, 11. Tim. I, 2, 228. II, 2, 149. 225. V, 1, 148. Caes. I, 2, 205. Ant. V, 2, 248. Per. II Prol. 28. *s. when* = rarely: *s. when the steeled gaoler is the friend of men*, Meas. IV, 2, 89. *'tis s. when the bee doth leave her comb in the dead carrion*, H4B IV, 4, 79. *s. but* = usually: *to weep that you live as ye do makes pity in your lovers: s. but that pity begets you a good opinion, and that opinion a mere profit*, Per. IV, 2, 130.

**Seld-shown,** seldom exhibited to public view: *s. flamens do press among the popular throngs*, Cor. II, 1, 229.

**Select,** adj. choice, excellent: *are of a most s. and generous chief in that*, Hml. I, 3, 74.

**Select,** vb. to choose, to pick out: Cor. I, 6, 81.

**Seleucus,** name in Ant. V, 2, 140. 144. 153. 175.

**Self** (plur. *selves*) subst., one's own person, the identical individual: *make thee another s.* Sonn. 10, 13 (i. e. a child). *s. so self-loving were iniquity*, 62, 12. *banished from her is s. from s.* Gent. III, 1, 173. *blood against blood, s. against s.* R3 II, 4, 63. *in that nest of spicery they shall breed selves of themselves*, IV, 4, 425 (cf. Sonn. 10, 13). *I have a kind of s. resides with you, but an unkind s.* Troil. III, 2, 155. With an Anglosaxon genitive: *death's second s.* Sonn. 73, 8. *which action's s. was tongue to*, H8 I, 1, 42. *Tarquin's s. he met*, Cor. II, 2, 98. Oftenest with possessive pronouns: *mine enemy was strong, my poor s. weak*, Lucr. 1646. *my unsounded s.* 1819. *mine own s.* Sonn. 39, 3. *my next s. thou harder hast engrossed*, 133, 6. *my woeful s.* Compl. 143. *my poor s.* Meas. IV, 3, 148. *mine own —'s better part*, Err. III, 2, 61. Ado V, 2, 35. *my woeful s.* LLL V, 2, 818. *my worthless s.* Merch. II, 9, 18. *my former s.* H4B V, 5, 62. *my wretched s.* R3 I, 3, 203. *my other s.* II, 2, 151. *my weary s.* Rom. I, 1, 135 (reading of the authentic texts). *for my single s.* Caes. I, 2, 94. *to thy sweet s. too cruel*, Sonn. 1, 8. *thou of thyself thy sweet s. dost deceive*, 4, 10. *as thy sweet s. growest*, 126, 4. 151, 4. *me and thy crying s.* Tp. I, 2, 132. *better than thy dear —'s better part*, Err. II, 2, 125. *thy cursed s.* R3 I, 2, 80. *thy gracious s.* Rom. II, 2, 113. *to thine own s. be true*, Hml. I, 3, 78. *to see him so little of his great s.* H8 III, 2, 336. *his

*royal s.* V, 3, 120. *his poor s.* Tim. IV, 2, 12. *her humble s.* Gent. III, 1, 226. *in her naked seeing s.* H5 V, 2, 325. *woman it pretty s.* Cymb. III, 4, 160 (cf. *It*). *our great s.* All's II, 1, 126. *our innocent s.* Mcb. III, 1, 79. *our gross —ves*, Meas. II, 2, 87. *our royal —ves*, John III, 1, 232. *to our own —ves bend we our needful talk*, Troil. IV, 4, 141 (i. e. to each other). *your sweet s.* Sonn. 114, 6. *your perfect s.* Gent. IV, 2, 124. *your fair s.* LLL II, 151. *your sweet s.* V, 1, 120. *your double s.* Merch. V, 245. *when your sweet s. was got*, All's IV, 2, 10. *your precious s.* Wint. I, 2, 79. *your high s.* IV, 4, 7. *your gracious s.* 534. *your sweet s.* John V, 7, 101. *your royal s.* R3 III, 1, 63. *your gracious s.* III, 7, 131. 195. *your noble s.* H8 II, 2, 95. Oth. I, 2, 92. *make an interior survey of your good —ves*, Cor. II, 1, 44. *hang their proper —ves*, Tp. III, 3, 60. The verb following in the third person, f. i. All's IV, 2, 10 and Oth. I, 2, 92; except in Sonn. 126, 4, where an irregularity is caused by the exigency of the rhyme. It must be observed that the reflexive pronouns, except *himself* and *themselves*, are written in two words in O. Edd., and this would be the only rational spelling in such passages as: *'tis thee, my s., that for myself I praise*, Sonn. 62, 13 (German: *mein zweites Ich*). *thy s. I call it, ... that am better than thy dear —'s better part*, Err. II, 2, 123. III, 2, 61. *'even so my s. bewails good Gloster's case*, H6B III, 1, 217. *your s. is not exempt from this*, R3 II, 1, 18 (Qq *your s. are*). *thy s. is self-misused*, IV, 4, 376 (Qq *thy self thy self misusest*). *in hope thy s. should govern Rome and me*, Tit. IV, 4, 60. *my s. hath often overheard them say*, 74. *unfold to me, your s., your half*, Caes. II, 1, 274.

**Self,** pronominal adjective, 1) = one's self: *ere it be s. killed*, Sonn. 6, 4 (M. Edd. *self-killed*). *if I had s. applied love to myself and to no love beside*, Compl. 76 (M. Edd. *self-applied*). *a common and an outward man, that the great figure of a council frames by s. unable motion*, All's III, 1, 13 (i. e. a motion, which is itself unable. M. Edd. *self-unable*).

2) pertaining to one's self: *which his majesty, out of a s. gracious remembrance, did first propose*, All's IV, 5, 78 (= out of his own gracious remembrance. Most M. Edd. *self-gracious*). *infusing him with s. and vain conceit*, R2 III, 2, 166 (= a vain self-conceit). *who by s. and violent hands took off her life*, Mcb. V, 8, 70. *my strange and s. abuse is the initiate fear*, III, 4, 142.

3) same; *the s.* = the same: *property was thus appalled, that the s. was not the same*, Phoen. 38. *this s. and that s.* = this same, that same: *that s. chain about his neck, which he forswore to have*, Err. V, 10. *do not curst wives hold that s. sovereignty only for praise sake*, LLL IV, 1, 36 (O. and M. Edd. *self-sovereignty*). *to shoot another arrow that s. way which you did shoot the first*, Merch. I, 1, 148. *that metal, that s. mould that fashioned thee made him a man*, R2 I, 2, 23. *that s. bill is urged which in the eleventh year of the last king's reign was like ... to pass*, H5 I, 1, 1. *what befel me on a day in this s. place where now we mean to stand*, H6C III, 1, 11. *fed of that s. blood that first gave life to you*, Tit. IV, 2, 123. *I am made of that s. metal that my sister is*, Lr. I, 1, 71 (Qq *of the selfsame*). *that s. hand which writ his honour in the acts he did, hath ... splitted the heart*, Ant. V, 1, 21. *tomboys hired with that s. exhibition which your own

*coffers yield*, Cymb. I, 6, 122. *one s.* = one and the same: *when liver, brain and heart are all supplied, and filled her sweet perfections with one s. king*, Tw. I, 1, 39 (the later Ff *selfsame*). *it is in my* (time's) *power to o'erthrow law and in one s. born hour to plant and o'erwhelm custom*, Wint. IV, 1, 8 (O. and M. Edd. *one self-born*, quite unintelligibly). *else one s. mate and mate could not beget such different issues*, Lr. IV, 3, 36.

**Self-abuse**, self-deception, illusion: Mcb. III, 4, 142; cf. *Self* and *And.*

**Self-admission**, commonly explained as self-approbation, but perhaps = particular and personal choice (cf. *Admit* 3): *carries on the stream of his dispose without observance or respect of any, in will peculiar and in s.* Troil. II, 3, 176.

**Self-affairs**, one's own business: Mids. I, 1, 113.

**Self-affected**, self-loving: Troil. II, 3, 250.

**Self-affrighted**, frightened at one's self: R2 III, 2, 53.

**Self-applied**, see *Self* pron.

**Self-assumption**, one's own conception, conceit: *in s. greater than in the note of judgement*, Troil. II, 3, 133.

**Self-born**, see *Self* pron.

**Self-borne**, borne for one's self (not for the king): *to take advantage of the absent time* (= the time of the king's absence) *and fright our native peace with s. arms*, R2 II, 3, 80. Some M. Edd. *self-born*, i. e. begot of one's self.

**Self-bounty**, inherent kindness and benevolence: *I would not have your free and noble nature, out of s., be abused*, Oth. III, 3, 200.

**Self-breath**, one's own words: *a pride that quarrels at s.* Troil. II, 3, 182.

**Self-charity**, charity shown to one's self, charity beginning at home: Oth. II, 3, 202.

**Self-comparison**, the act of comparing or measuring one's self with another personally: *till that Bellona's bridegroom, lapped in proof, confronted him with —s, point against point rebellious, arm 'gainst arm*, Mcb. I, 2, 55.

**Self-covered**, clothed, dressed in one's native semblance (cf. *Cover*): *thou changed and s. thing, for shame, bemonster not thy feature*, Lr. IV, 2, 62 (Goneril must be supposed to have, by changing countenance, betrayed all her wickedness).

**Self-danger**, personal danger: Cymb. III, 4, 149.

**Self-doing**, committed by one's self: *yourself to pardon of s. crime*, Sonn. 58, 12.

**Self-drawing**, made by drawing out of one's self: *spider-like, out of his s. web*, H8 I, 1, 63.

**Self-endeared**, self-loving: Ado III, 1, 56.

**Self-example**, one's own precedent: *by s. mayst thou be denied*, Sonn. 142, 14.

**Self-explication**, a giving account of one's self: *a thing perplexed beyond s.* Cymb. III, 4, 8.

**Self-figured**, conceived and planned by one's self: *to knit their souls in s. knot*, Cymb. II, 3, 124.

**Self-glorious**, glorifying one's self, boastful: *vainness and s. pride*, H5 V Chor. 20.

**Self-gracious**, see *Self*, pron. 2.

**Self-harming**, injuring one's self: Err. II, 1, 102. R2 II, 2, 3 (Qq *life-harming*).

**Self-killed**, killed by one's self: Sonn. 6, 4 (O. Edd. *self killed*, i. e. killed itself).

**Self-love**, love of one's self: Lucr. 266. Sonn.

3, 8. 62, 1. 11. All's I, 1, 157. Tw. I, 5, 97. H5 II, 4, 74. H6B V, 2, 38.

**Self-loving**, loving one's self: Ven. 752. Sonn. 62, 12. Cor. IV, 6, 32.

**Self-mettle**, one's own fiery temper: *a full-hot horse, who being allowed his way, s. tires him*, H8 I, 1, 134.

**Self-misused**, misemployed by one's self: *thy self is s.* R3 IV, 4, 376 (Qq *thy self thy self misusest*).

**Self-mould**, see *Self* pron.

**Self-neglecting**, a neglecting of one's self: H5 II, 4, 75.

**Self-offences**, one's own offences: Meas. III, 2, 280.

**Self-place**, see *Self*, pron.

**Self-reproving**, a disproving of one's own proceedings: *he's full of alteration and s.* Lr. V, 1, 4.

**Selfsame**, identical, the very same; with the def. art.: Lucr. 289. 1047. Sonn. 15, 6. Err. I, 1, 54. Merch. I, 1, 141. 142. Wint. IV, 4, 455. H6C II, 5, 7. V, 5, 20. R3 I, 2, 11. 143. V, 3, 286. Tit. I, 136. Tim. IV, 3, 179 (*whose s. mettle*). Caes. IV, 3, 171. Mcb. I, 3, 88. 94. Lr. I, 1, 70 (Qq *the s. metal*, Ff *that self metal*). II, 2, 145. *one and the s.* Meas. II, 4, 173. LLL I, 2, 4. Without article: *in s. manner*, Meas. V, 196. *with s. kindness*, Shr. V, 2, 5. *s. wind*, H6C II, 1, 82. *of s. feather*, III, 3, 161. *in s. key*, Troil. I, 3, 53.

**Self-slaughter**, suicide: Hml. I, 2, 132. Cymb. III, 4, 78.

**Self-slaughtered**, killed by one's self: Lucr. 1733.

**Self-sovereignty**, writing of O. and M. Edd. for *self sovereignty*, i. e. the same sovereignty, in LLL IV, 1, 36.

**Self-subdued**, subdued, conquered by one's self: Lr. II, 2, 129.

**Self-substantial**, consisting of one's own substance: *feedest thy life's flame with s. fuel*, Sonn. I, 6.

**Self-trust**, self-reliance, faith kept to one's self: *where is truth, if there be no s.?* Lucr. 158.

**Self-unable**, writing of most M. Edd. for *self unable*, in All's III, 1, 13; see *Self*, pron.

**Self-will**, one's own will and desire: *till like a jade s. himself doth tire*, Lucr. 707.

**Self-willed**, governed by one's own will and desires: Sonn. 6, 13. H4A III, 1, 198. Troil. I, 3, 188. Rom. IV, 2, 14.

**Self-wrong**, injury done to one's self: Err. III, 2, 168.

**Sell** (impf. and partic. *sold*) 1) tr. to give for an equivalent, to vend; absol.: *I will not praise that purpose not to s.* Sonn. 21, 14 (cf. Troil. IV, 1, 78. LLL II, 16. IV, 3, 240). *set thy person forth to s.* Pilgr. 310. LLL V, 2, 319. As III, 5, 60. Tim. I, 1, 169. *to buy and s.*: LLL III, 143. Merch. I, 3, 36. Wint. IV, 4, 138. Cor. III, 2, 10. Mcb. IV, 2, 41. With an object: Ven. 513. Lucr. 214. Meas. III, 2, 2 (*buy and s.*). Ado II, 1, 202. Merch. IV, 1, 443. As II, 4, 96. IV, 1, 22. All's IV, 3, 311. Wint. IV, 4, 608. John I, 153. II, 69. R2 II, 3, 131. H4A I, 2, 127. H4B IV, 3, 74. H5 II Prol. 5. III, 2, 46. III, 5, 12. IV, 3, 91. 93. V, 2, 129. H6A III, 2, 15. H6B I, 1, 231. IV, 1, 41. 86. IV, 2, 49. 71. 170. IV, 7, 23. 70. Troil. IV, 1, 78. IV, 4, 42. Cor. I, 4, 6. Rom. III, 2, 27. V, 1, 52. 54. 83. Tim. II, 1, 7. II, 2, 154. Caes.

IV, 3, 11. 25. Mcb. III, 4, 33. Hml. IV, 4, 22. Oth. I, 3, 138 (*sold to slavery*). 388. IV, 1, 95. V, 2, 146. Ant. V, 2, 184. Cymb. I, 4, 90. II, 3, 88. Per. IV, 6, 105. Figuratively: *Lucrece to their sight must s. her joy, her life,* Lucr. 385. *sold cheap what is most dear,* Sonn. 110, 3. *buy terms divine in —ing hours of dross,* 146, 11. *wives are sold by fate,* Wiv. V, 5, 246. *s. my title for a glorious grave,* H6B III, 1, 92. *to s. a bargain,* LLL III, 102. 104 (cf. *Bargain*). *to s. one's life* = *to meet death:* Merch. II, 7, 67. H6A IV, 2, 53. H6C V, 1, 74 (*have sold their lives unto the house of York,* = have sold their lives in fighting against the house of York). *sold their bodies,* H6A V, 4, 106. With *from: who in that sale —s pardon from himself,* John III, 1, 167. *for a day of kings' entreaties a mother should not s. him an hour from her beholding,* Cor. I, 3, 9. Often = to betray: *sold his sovereign's life to death and treachery,* H5 II, 2, 10. 170. Cor. V, 6, 47. Ant. IV, 12, 14. 48. *to buy and s.,* in the same sense: *the cardinal does buy and s. his honour,* H8 I, 1, 192. *bought and sold* = betrayed: Err. III, 1, 72. John V, 4, 10. H6A IV, 4, 13. R3 V, 3, 305. Troil. II, 1, 51.

2) intr. to find purchasers: *let us like merchants show our foulest wares and think perchance they'll s.* Troil. I, 3, 360.

**Seller,** one who sells, a vender: LLL IV, 3, 240.

**Semblable,** resembling, similar, like, equal: *it is a wonderful thing to see the s. coherence of his men's spirits and his,* H4B V, 1, 72. *his s., yea, himself, Timon disdains,* Tim. IV, 3, 22. *to make true diction of him, his s. is his mirror,* Hml. V, 2, 124. *that and thousands more of s. import,* Ant. III, 4, 3.

**Semblably,** similarly: *s. furnished like the king himself,* H4A V, 3, 21.

**Semblance** (trisyll. at the end of the verse in Err. V, 358 and Per. I, 4, 71) 1) appearance, show, exterior, form: *under whose* (love's) *simple s. he* (lust) *hath fed upon fresh beauty,* Ven. 795. *true sorrow then is feelingly suffised when with like s. it is sympathised,* Lucr. 1113. *if you go out in your own s., you die,* Wiv. IV, 2, 67. *another fault in the s. of a fowl,* V, 5, 11. *these two Dromios, one in s.* Err. V, 358. *cozened with the s. of a maid,* Ado II, 2, 39. *she's but the sign and s. of her honour,* IV, 1, 34. *now thy image doth appear in the rare s. that I loved it first,* V, 1, 260. *many other mannish cowards that do outface it with their —s,* As I, 3, 124. *your own letter that induced me to the s. I put on,* Tw. V, 315. *this ship-boy's s. hath disguised me quite,* John IV, 3, 4. *forms being fetched from glistering —s of piety,* H5 II, 2, 117. *overbears attaint with cheerful s.* IV Chor. 40. *of ashy s.* H6B III, 2, 162. *as he made s. of his duty, would have put his knife into him,* H8 I, 2, 198. *put off these frowns, an ill-beseeming s. for a feast,* Rom. I, 5, 76. *if thou path, thy native s. on,* Caes. II, 1, 83. *to assume a s. that very dogs disdained,* Lr. V, 3, 187. *let there be no honour, where there is beauty; truth, where s.* Cymb. II, 4, 109. *with speechless tongue and s. pale,* Per. I, 1, 36. *by the s. of their white flags they bring us peace,* I, 4, 71.

2) likeness, image: *no more than wax shall be accounted evil wherein is stamped the s. of a devil,* Lucr. 1246. *of what she was no s. did remain,* 1453. *poor broken glass, I often did behold in thy sweet s. my old age new born,* 1759. *your sweet s. to some other give,* Sonn. 13, 4. *purchasing the s. of my soul from out the state of hellish misery,* Merch. III, 4, 20. *repeat their*

*s. often on the seas,* H6A V, 3, 193. *two mirrors of his princely s. are cracked in pieces,* R3 II, 2, 51.

**Semblative,** appearing, seeming: *all is s. a woman's part,* Tw. I, 4, 34.

**Semicircle,** a half round: Wint. II, 1, 10.

**Semicircled,** half round: *a s. farthingale,* Wiv. III, 3, 68.

**Semiramis,** queen of Assyria, proverbial for her voluptuousness and cruelty: Shr. Ind. 2, 41. Tit. II, 1, 22. II, 3, 118.

**Sempronius,** name in Tit. IV, 3, 10 and Tim. II, 2, 198. III, 4, 112.

**Senate,** the common council of ancient Rome; and hence similar assemblies in other towns: Cor. I, 1, 59. 190. II, 1, 145. 148. II, 2, 136. II, 3, 149. III, 1, 69. 132. 138. IV, 6, 74. V, 6, 83. 141. Tit. I, 27. 41. IV, 4, 17. Tim. I, 2, 180. III, 5, 5. 100. 110. IV, 1, 5. V, 1, 132. Caes. II, 2, 72. 93. 98. III, 1, 32. Oth. I, 2, 46. III, 2, 2. IV, 1, 275. Cymb. IV, 2, 337. IV, 3, 26.

**Senate-house,** the house in which a senate meets: Cor. II, 3, 153. 156. IV, 6, 58. Caes. II, 2, 52. 59. II, 4, 1. Per. I, 1, 10.

**Senator,** a member of a senate: H5 V Chor. 26. Cor. I, 1, 117. 152. I, 3, 106. I, 9, 3. III, 1, 92. 102. III, 2, 65. III, 3, 7. IV, 3, 14. IV, 5, 138. 206. IV, 7, 30. V, 4, 56. Tim. I, 1, 39. II, 1, 205. III, 6, 90. IV, 1, 24. IV, 3, 10. V, 1, 139. 143. 161. Caes. I, 2, 188. I, 3, 85. II, 2, 61. II, 4, 35. III, 1, 82. IV, 3, 175. 177. Oth. I, 1, 119. I, 3, 230. IV, 1, 231. Ant. II, 6, 9.

**Send** (impf. and partic. *sent*), 1) to emit, to throw or drive forth, to let fly: *as from a furnace, vapours doth he s.* Ven. 274. *will s. destruction into this city's bosom,* John II, 409. *trumpet, s. thy brass voice through all these lazy tents,* Troil. I, 3, 257. *to s. their smiles before them to Achilles,* III, 3, 72. cf. *s. forth thine eye,* All's II, 3, 58.

2) to cause to go on an errand or message or any purpose; absol.: *sent to me in the morning,* Gent. IV, 2, 132. *my wife hath sent to him,* Wiv. II, 2, 303. *Master Slender sent to her, to know,* IV, 5, 31. *s. to Falstaff straight,* IV, 4, 75. 83. *s. after the duke and appeal to him,* Meas. I, 2, 178. *let him s. no more,* Tw. I, 5, 299. *he —s to know your pleasure,* R3 III, 2, 15. Mcb. V, 3, 49. Cymb. V, 5, 214 etc. etc. Passively: *I was sent to by my brother,* Meas. V, 73. With *for: I would s. for certain of my creditors,* Meas. I, 2, 136. *let him be sent for to-morrow,* IV, 3, 209. *she sent for you by Dromio home to dinner,* Err. II, 2, 156 (= she sent Dromio for you). *why am I sent for to a king?* R2 IV, 162; Troil. IV, 1, 35; Cor. II, 1, 276. *am I sent for hither,* R2 IV, 176; Hml. III, 1, 29. cf. Meas. V, 249. Merch. IV, 1, 106. H4B V, 5, 82. H6C IV, 6, 61. Cymb. V, 5, 214 (*s. out*) etc. etc.

Transitively: Tp. Epil. 5. Gent. I, 1, 159. I, 3, 24. 29. II, 4, 86. II, 7, 77. Wiv. II, 2, 118. 127. III, 3, 206. Meas. IV, 5, 10. Err. II, 1, 77. II, 2, 6. IV, 1, 56. Ado II, 1, 274. II, 3, 227 etc. etc. With *for:* Gent. IV, 4, 120. Err. IV, 4, 9. V, 231 etc. Joined with adverbs: *—s me forth,* Tp. II, 1, 298. Err. V, 158. All's III, 4, 13. R2 I, 3, 282. H4B III, 1, 100. IV, 1, 3. 5. Tim. V, 1, 152. Lr. IV, 4, 6. *Fortune sent in this fool,* As I, 2, 49. *I have sent twenty out,* Mcb. II, 6, 66. Mcb. V, 3, 35 etc. *to s. packing* = to send away, to dispatch: H4A II, 4, 328. H6B III, 1, 342. R3 III, 2, 63. cf. *slaves they* (my thoughts) *are to me that s. them flying,* Gent. III, 1, 141.

3) to cause to be conveyed or transmitted; absol.: *he's ever —ing* (i. e. presents) Tim. III, 2, 36. Trans.: Gent. I, 2, 38. I, 3, 53. III, 1, 92. 94. IV, 2, 132. IV, 4, 136. 137. V, 4, 95. Wiv. III, 3, 141. IV, 2, 126 (*forth*). IV, 4, 3. Meas. V, 102. Err. IV, 1, 56. IV, 2, 46. V, 145. Merch. IV, 1, 396. V, 216. R2 III, 3, 33. Tim. III, 2, 35. Mcb. II, 1, 14 (*forth*) etc. etc. *to s. word* = to tell or declare by message: Wiv. III, 5, 59 (*he sent me word to stay at home*). IV, 4, 18. Meas. I, 4, 89 (*I'll s. him certain word of my success*). As V, 4, 74. 76. 77. Shr. V, 2, 80. John V, 3, 7. H4A I, 1, 94. H6B III, 2, 243. R3 III, 2, 10. Tit. III, 1, 151 (*—s thee this word*) etc. cf. *s. fair-play orders to arms invasive*, John V, 1, 67. *—s allegiance to his royal person*, R3 III, 3, 37. *s. defiance to the traitor*, 129. *has only sent his present occasion now*, Tim. III, 2, 39. *shall Caesar s. a lie?* Caes. II, 2, 65. *I s. him the greatness he has got*, Ant. V, 2, 29 (= acknowledge by message).

4) to grant, to bestow: *heaven s. Anne Page no worse fortune*, Wiv. I, 4, 33. III, 4, 105. *s. me a cool rut-time, Jove*, V, 5, 15. *I shall lessen God's —ing that way*, Ado II, 1, 24. *God —s a curst cow short horns*, 25. 26. 27. 29. III, 4, 60. Shr. II, 321. V, 1, 43. All's I, 1, 190 (*God s. him well*). Tw. III, 1, 51. Wint. II, 3, 126. R2 IV, 221. H4B I, 2, 223. 225. II, 2, 152. Tit. IV, 2, 63 etc.

**Sender**, one that sends: All's V, 3, 59. H5 I, 2, 299. II, 4, 119. Cymb. II, 3, 63.

**Seneca**, the Roman tragic poet: Hml. II, 2, 419.

**Senior** (O. Edd. *signior, signeor signeur*) one older than another: *we'll draw cuts for the s.* Err. V, 422. *my tough s.* LLL I, 2, 10 (reply to: *my tender juvenal*).

**Senior-junior**, old and young at once: *this s. giant-dwarf, Dan Cupid*, LLL III, 182 (O. Edd. *signior Junios.* Some M. Edd. *Signior Julio's*, i. e. Julio Romano's; whom, however, Sh. very well knew not to be of the rank of a signior; cf. Wint. V, 2, 106).

**Seniory** (O. Edd. *signorie* and *signeurie*), seniority, eldership: *if ancient sorrow be most reverend, give mine the benefit of s.* R3 IV, 4, 36.

**Senna**, the plant Cassia senna, used as a cathartic; writing of F4 and M. Edd. in Mcb. V, 3, 55; the earlier Ff *cyme.*

**Se'nnight**, a week: As III, 2, 333. Mcb. I, 3, 22 (O. Edd. *sev'nights*). Oth. II, 1, 77.

**Senoys**, = Siennese, the people of Sienna: *the Florentines and S. are by the ears*, All's I, 2, 1.

**Sense**, (sometimes not inflected in the plural: Sonn. 112, 10. Mcb. V, 1, 29. Oth. IV, 3, 95). 1) one of the five organs by which external objects are perceived: *say that the s. of feeling were bereft me*, Ven. 439. *my adder's s. to critic and to flatterer stopped are*, Sonn. 112, 10. *my five wits nor my five —s can dissuade one foolish heart from serving thee*, 141, 9. Tp. I, 2, 412. Wiv. I, 1, 181. LLL I, 1, 64. II, 240. 242. III, 2. V, 2, 259. 670. Mids. III, 2, 179. IV, 1, 87. Merch. III, 1, 62. All's I, 3, 114. Wint. II, 1, 151. IV, 4, 621. 688. John IV, 1, 94. R2 III, 2, 13. H5 IV, 1, 308 (*take from them now the s. of reckoning*). H6A V, 3, 71. Troil. I, 3, 252. Cor. II, 2, 120. Tim. I, 2, 129. Mcb. II, 1, 44. Hml. III, 4, 80. Lr. III, 4, 13. IV, 6, 5. Oth. IV, 2, 69. 154. IV, 3, 95. Ant. II, 2, 217. Cymb. III, 2, 60. *spirit of s.* = the most delicate faculty of perception: *to whose soft seizure the cygnet's*

down *is harsh and spirit of s. hard as the palm of ploughman*, Troil. I, 1, 58. *nor doth the eye itself, that most pure spirit of s., behold itself*, III, 3, 105.

2) perception by those organs: *above the s. of s.* LLL V, 2, 259 (above the perception of the eye). *the s. of death is most in apprehension*, Meas. III, 1, 78. *this healthful hand, whose banished s. thou hast repealed*, All's II, 3, 54. *though my soul disputes well with my s., that this may be some error*, Tw. IV, 3, 9. *all his —s have but human conditions*, H5 IV, 1, 108. *every fool, whose s. no more can feel but his own wringing*, 252. *dost thou think I have no s., thou strikest me thus*, Troil. II, 1, 23. *they must take it in s. that feel it*, Rom. I, 1, 32. *her eyes are open; but their s. are shut*, Mcb. V, 1, 29 (M. Edd. *is shut*). *s., sure, you have, else could you not have motion, but sure, that s. is apoplexed, for madness would not err, nor s. to ecstasy was ne'er so thralled*, Hml. III, 4, 71. *burn out the s. and virtue of mine eye*, IV, 5, 155. *the hand of little employment hath the daintier s.* V, 1, 78. *all other joys which the most precious square of s. possesses*, Lr. I, 1, 76. *a father's curse pierce every s. about thee*, I, 4, 323. *not deficient, blind, or lame of s.* Oth. I, 3, 63. *there is more s. in that* (a wound) *than in reputation*, II, 3, 268. *I have rubbed this young quat almost to the s.* V, 1, 11 (= to the quick). *that s. of pain*, III, 4, 147. *remain thou here, while s. can keep it on*, Cymb. I, 1, 118. *be her s. but as a monument*, II, 2, 32. *it smells most sweetly in my s.* Per. III, 2, 60.

3) perception by the mind, apprehension, feeling: *impossible be strange attempts to those that weigh their pains in s.* All's I, 1, 240 (in thought). *now to all s. 'tis gross you love my son*, I, 3, 178. *which of them both is dearest to me, I have no skill in s. to make distinction*, III, 4, 39. *lacked the s. to know her estimation home*, V, 3, 3. *that monster custom, who all s. doth eat*, Hml. III, 4, 161. *if 'tis not gross in s. that thou hast practised on her with foul charms*, Oth. I, 2, 72. *in my s. 'tis happiness to die*, V, 2, 290 (in my state of feeling). With *of:* *to suck in the s. of fear*, Troil. II, 2, 12. *hath s. of its own fail*, Tim. V, 1, 151. *if my love thou holdest at aught, as my great power thereof may give thee s.* Hml. IV, 3, 61. *do not believe that, from the s. of all civility, I thus would trifle with your reverence*, Oth. I, 1, 132. *having s. of beauty*, II, 1, 71. *have you forgot all s. of place and duty*, II, 3, 166. *what s. had I of her stolen hours of lust?* III, 3, 338. *hast such noble s. of thy friend's wrong*, V, 1, 32.

4) sensuality: *one who never feels the wanton stings and motions of the s.* Meas. I, 4, 59. *modesty may more betray our s. than woman's lightness*, II, 2, 169. *if he be none of mine, my sanctity will to my s. bend no licentious ear, but curb it spite of seeing*, Per. V, 3, 30.

5) understanding, power of sound reasoning: *she speaks this in the infirmity of s.* Meas. V, 47. *men... indued with intellectual s. and souls*, Err. II, 1, 22. *establish him in his true s. again*, IV, 4, 51. *things hid and barred from common s.* LLL I, 1, 57. *their s. thus weak lost with their fears thus strong*, Mids. III, 2, 27. *I spake unto this crown as having s.* H4B IV, 5, 158. *a woman of quick s.* Troil. IV, 5, 54. *as common as any the most vulgar thing to s.* Hml. I, 2, 99. *restoring his bereaved s.* Lr. IV, 4, 9. *the safer s. will ne'er accommodate his master thus*, IV, 6, 81. *I'll refer me to all things of s.* Oth. I, 2, 64. *a speaking such as s. cannot untie*, Cymb. V, 4, 149. Lr. I, 1, 76?

6) rational meaning, reason: *to thy sensual fault I bring in s.* Sonn. 35,9. *'gainst rule, 'gainst s., 'gainst shame,* Compl. 271. *were there s. in his idolatry, my substance would be statue in thy stead,* Gent. IV, 4, 205. *he speaks s.* Wiv. II, 1, 129. *she speaks, and 'tis such s.* Meas. II, 2, 142. *her madness hath the oddest frame of s.* V, 61. *as there is s. in truth,* 226. *against all s. you do importune her,* 438. *when help past s. we deem,* All's II, 1, 127. *what impossibility would slay in common s., s. saves another way,* 181. *the time disordered doth in common s. crowd us and crush us to this monstrous form, to hold our safety up,* H4B IV, 2, 33. *let —s rule, the word is Pitch and Pay,* H5 II, 3, 51 (Pistol's speech). *our project's life this shape of s. assumes,* Troil. I, 3, 385. *I see no s. for't, but his occasions might have wooed me first,* Tim. III, 3, 14. *proof and bulwark against s.* Hml. III, 4, 38. *in despite of s. and secrecy,* 192.

7) meaning, import, signification: *and with good thoughts makes dispensation, urging the worser s. for vantage still,* Lucr. 249 (i. e. always interpreting them in a bad sense; giving them a bad turn). *he in the worst s. construes their denial,* 324. *'It cannot be' she in that s. forsook,* 1538. *an act, under whose heavy s. your brother's life falls into forfeit,* Meas. I, 4, 65. II, 1, 229. II, 4, 74. Ado V, 2, 56. Mids. II, 2, 45. Shr. I, 1, 220. V, 2, 18. Tw. I, 5, 285. H6B III, 1, 186. H6C III, 2, 60. Rom. I, 1, 31. III, 1, 62. Mcb. V, 8, 20. Hml. IV, 5, 7. Oth. I, 3, 12. 69. Ant. IV, 2, 39. Cymb. V, 5, 431.

Hence *in all s.* = in every respect: *you should in all s. be much bound to him,* Merch. V, 136. *in no s.* = in no respect, in no manner: *it blots thy beauty ... and in no s. is meet or amiable,* Shr. V, 2, 141. cf. *the grief is fine, full, perfect, that I taste, and violenteth in a s. as strong as that which causes it,* Troil. IV, 4, 4 (Ff *and no less in a s. as strong*).

8) mental power, faculty of thinking and feeling, spirit, mind: *none else to me, nor I to none alive, that my steeled s. or changes right or wrong,* Sonn. 112, 8. *O, that our night of woe might have remembered my deepest s. how hard true sorrow hits,* 120, 10. *ravish human s.* Pilgr. 108. *the morning rise doth cite each moving s.* 195. *you cram these words into mine ears against the stomach of my s.* Tp. II, 1, 107. *my s. breeds with it,* Meas. II, 2, 142. *your s. pursues not mine,* II, 4, 74 (you do not understand my meaning). *his riotous youth, with dangerous s., might in the times to come have ta'en revenge,* IV, 4, 32. *let fancy still my s. in Lethe steep,* Tw. IV, 1, 66. *surprised my s.* Wint. III, 1, 10. *it enchants my s.* Troil. III, 2, 21. *how stiff is my vile s., that I stand up and have ingenious feeling of my huge sorrows,* Lr. IV, 6, 286. *have you a soul or s.* Oth. III, 3, 374. *steeped our s. in soft and delicate Lethe,* Ant. II, 7, 113. *stupify and dull the s. awhile,* Cymb. I, 5, 37. *men's o'erlaboured s. repairs itself by rest,* II, 2, 11. *you are a fair viol, and your s. the strings,* Per. I, 1, 81.

Plur. *—s: the timorous yelping of the hounds appals her —s and her spirit confounds,* Ven. 882. *cheering up her —s all dismayed,* 896. *their —s I'll restore, and they shall be themselves,* Tp. V, 31. *to work mine end upon their —s,* 53. *their rising —s begin to chase the ignorant fumes,* 66. *howsoe'er you have been justled from your —s,* 158. *call all your —s to you,* Wiv. III, 3, 126. *younger spirits, whose apprehensive —s all but new things disdain,* All's

I, 2, 60. *yet have I the benefit of my —s as well as your ladyship,* Tw. V, 314. *your —s, unintelligent of our insufficience,* Wint. I, 1, 15. *if not, my —s, better pleased with madness, do bid it welcome,* IV, 4, 495. *no settled —s of the world can match the pleasure of that madness,* V, 3, 72. *steep my —s in forgetfulness,* H4B III, 1, 8. (sleep) *give as soft attachment to thy —s as infants empty of all thought,* Troil. IV, 2, 5. *being tasted, slays all —s with the heart,* Rom. II, 3, 26. *awake your —s, that you may the better judge,* Caes. III, 2, 17. *the air nimbly and sweetly recommends itself unto our gentle —s,* Mcb. I, 6, 3. *who then shall blame his pestered —s to recoil,* V, 2, 23. *my —s would have cooled to hear a night-shriek,* V, 5, 10. *this rest might yet have balmed thy broken —s,* Lr. III, 6, 105. *the untuned and jarring —s, O, wind up of this child-changed father,* IV, 7, 16. *put thyself into a haviour of less fear, ere wildness vanquish my staider —s,* Cymb. III, 4, 10. *found it murderous to the —s,* IV, 2, 328. *and make my —s credit thy relation,* Per. V, 1, 124.

**Senseless,** 1) having no organ of perception: *that you in all obey her, save when command to your dismission tends, and therein you are s.* Cymb. II, 3, 58 (= have no ear).

2) not feeling, insensible: *cold and s. stone,* Ven. 211. *she tears the s. Sinon with her nails,* Lucr. 1564. *s. trees they cannot hear thee,* Pilgr. 393. Gent. III, 1, 143. IV, 4, 203. Err. IV, 4, 25. Mids. III, 2, 28. Wint. IV, 4, 622. R2 V, 1, 46. H6B IV, 1, 77. Cor. I, 4, 53. Rom. I, 4, 36. Caes. I, 1, 40. Hml. II, 2, 496. V, 2, 380. Cymb. I, 3, 7. III, 2, 20. With *of: to seem s. of the bob,* As II, 7, 55. *I am s. of your wrath,* Cymb. I, 1, 135.

3) unfelt: *let my good name, that s. reputation, for Collatine's dear love be kept unspotted,* Lucr. 820; cf. 828. *mock not my s. conjuration,* R2 III, 2, 23 (perhaps = conjuration of insensible things).

4) unreasonable: *s. villain,* Err. IV, 4, 24. Shr. I, 2, 36. *to esteem a s. help when help past sense we deem,* All's II, 1, 127. Tw. III, 4, 174. *so s. of expense,* Tim. II, 2, 1 (= so unreasonably expensive; cf. *Of*). Misapplied by Dogberry in Ado III, 3, 23 (for *sensible*).

5) void of sense, unmeaning: *or s. speaking or a speaking such as sense cannot untie,* Cymb. V, 4, 148.

**Senseless-obstinate,** unreasonably obstinate: R3 III, 1, 44 (not hyph. in O. Edd.).

**Sensible,** 1) having a sensation, perceiving, feeling: *I might not this believe without the s. and true avouch of mine own eyes,* Hml. I, 1, 57. With *of: being not mad, but s. of grief,* John III, 4, 53 (= feeling grief, grieved). *if thou wert s. of courtesy,* H4A V, 4, 94. *his hand, not s. of fire, remained unscorched,* Caes. I, 3, 18 (feeling no heat).

In a moral sense, = feeling: *my woe too s. thy passion maketh more feeling-painful,* Lucr. 1678. *with affection wondrous s. he wrung Bassanio's hand,* Merch. II, 8, 48. *that I am guiltless of your father's death, and am most s. in grief for it,* Hml. IV, 5, 150 (Qq *sensibly*).

2) capable of perception, endowed with feeling: *thy outward parts would move each part in me that were but s.* Ven. 436. *who are of such s. and nimble lungs that they always use to laugh at nothing,* Tp. II, 1, 174. *this s. warm motion,* Meas. III, 1, 120. *thou art s. in nothing but blows,* Err. IV, 4, 27. *only s. in the duller parts,* LLL IV, 2, 28. *love's feeling is more*

*soft and s.* IV, 3, 337. *the wall, being s., should curse again,* Mids. V, 183. *I would your cambric were s. as your finger,* Cor. I, 3, 95.

3) perceptible, tangible: *from whom he bringeth s. regreets, to wit, besides commends and courteous breath, gifts of rich value,* Merch. II, 9, 89. *art thou not, fatal vision, s. to feeling as to sight,* Mcb. II, 1, 36. Punning in Shr. IV, 1, 66.

4) full of good sense, judicious: *'twas a good s. fellow,* Wiv. II, 1, 151. *if ever the s. Benedick bear it,* Ado I, 1, 265. V, 1, 184. *above the sense of sense, so s. seemeth their conference,* LLL V, 2, 259. *a s. tale,* Shr. IV, 1, 66. *you are very s., aud yet you miss my sense,* V, 2, 18. *you took it like a s. lord,* H4B I, 2, 220. *to be now a s. man, and presently a beast,* Oth. II, 3, 309.

**Sensibly,** 1) feelingly: *how was there a costard broken in the shin? I will tell you s.* LLL III, 114. *and am most s. in grief for it,* Hml. IV, 5, 150 (Ff *sensible*).

2) in a state of being sensible, of having feeling: *who s. outdares his senseless sword,* Cor. I, 4, 53. *he is your brother, lords, s. fed of that self blood that first gave life to you,* Tit. IV, 2, 122 (= as a sensible creature, endowed with the same feeling as you).

**Sensual,** devoted to the gratification of the senses, carnal: *to thy s. fault I bring in sense,* Sonn. 35, 9. *invited to any s. feast,* 141, 8. *I give my s. race the rein,* Meas. II, 4, 160. *a libertine, as s. as the brutish sting itself,* As II, 7, 66.

**Sensuality,** carnal appetite: Ado IV, 1, 62. Oth. I, 3, 331.

**Sentence,** subst. 1) a maxim, an axiom: Lucr. 244. Ado II, 3, 249. Merch. I, 2, 11. Tw. III, 1, 13. H5 I, 1, 50. Oth. I, 3, 199. 212. 214. 216.

2) a period in writing or speaking: Lucr. 566. Mids. V, 96. As III, 2, 144. H6C V, 1, 56.

3) a judgment, judicial decision: Meas. II, 4, 37 (*under your s.*). 109. V, 378. Merch. IV, 1, 304. All's III, 2, 64. R2 I, 3, 154. 172. 175. 242. III, 3, 134. V, 6, 23. H5 II, 2, 166. H6B II, 3, 3. Rom. I, 1, 95. Caes. IV, 1, 17. Lr. I, 1, 173. Oth. I, 3, 119. Cymb. I, 1, 78. V, 5, 289. Per. I, 1, 90. *to give s.:* Meas. II, 2, 106. Merch. IV, 1, 205. All's I, 3, 80. R2 IV, 121. Tit. V, 3, 177. *to pass s.* Err. I, 1, 148. *to pronounce a s.:* Meas. II, 4, 62. LLL I, 1, 302. As I, 3, 87. R3 I, 4, 191. Rom. II, 3, 79. *pursue s.* Merch. IV, 1, 298.

Misapplied for *sense* by Bardolph: Wiv. I, 1, 179.

**Sentence,** vb. 1) to pass judgment on, to condemn: Meas. II, 2, 55. II, 3, 13. III, 2, 271. IV, 2, 168. H4B V, 2, 98. Cor. III, 3, 109. V, 4, 8.

2) to pronounce as judgment: *what we chance to s.* Cor. III, 3, 22.

**Sententious,** abounding with sentences, rich in judicious observations: *your reasons have been sharp and s.* LLL V, 1, 3. *he is very swift and s.* As V, 4, 66. Misapplied by the nurse in Rom. II, 4, 225.

**Sentinel,** subst. one who watches or keeps guard to prevent surprise: Ven. 650. Mids. II, 2, 26 (*stand s.*). H5 IV Chor. 6. H6A II, 1, 70. R3 V, 3, 54. Troil. IV, 4, 74. Mcb. II, 1, 53.

**Sentinel,** vb. to watch, to guard: *time's glory is ... to wake the morn and s. the night,* Lucr. 942.

**Separable,** separating, parting: *in our two loves there is but one respect, though in our lives a s. spite,* Sonn. 36, 6 (= a spite of separation, a spiteful separation).

**Separate,** to sever, to disjoin: Err. V, 111. Tw. II, 3, 105. H4B I, 2, 256. H6C II, 1, 27. R3 III, 2, 20. Troil. V, 8, 18. Rom. IV, 5, 27. Mcb. II, 3, 144.

**Separation,** act of separating, or state of being separated: Sonn. 39, 7. Mids. II, 2, 58. Wint. I, 1, 28 (*made s. of their society*). H8 II, 1, 148 (= divorce). Ant. I, 3, 102.

**Septentrion,** the north: H6C I, 4, 136.

**Sepulchre,** subst. (ordinarily *sépulchre,* but *sepúlchre* in R2 I, 3, 196. Not used in prose, except by the ranting Sir Toby in Tw. III, 4, 262), a grave, a tomb: Ven. 622. Sonn. 68, 6. Compl. 46. Merch. III, 2, 96. Tw. III, 4, 262. R2 I, 3, 196. II, 1, 55. H4A I, 1, 19. H6C I, 1, 236. I, 4, 17. II, 5, 115. V, 2, 20. Rom. V, 3, 141. 207. Hml. I, 4, 48.

**Sepulchre,** vb. (*sepúlchre*), to bury: Lucr. 805. Gent. IV, 2, 118. Lr. II, 4, 134.

**Sequel,** that which follows: *I guess the s.* Gent. II, 1, 122. *mark the s.* Wiv. III, 5, 109. *gather the s. by what went before,* Err. I, 1, 96. *when you have seen the s.* Ado III, 2, 137. *Moth, follow. Like the s. I,* LLL III, 135 (i. e. like the continuation of a story). *there is no consonancy in the s.* Tw. II, 5, 142. *his daughter first, and then in s. all,* H5 V, 2, 361. *mark how well the s. hangs together,* R3 III, 6, 4. *if black scandal attend the s. of your imposition,* III, 7, 232. *is there no s. at the heels of this mother's admiration?* Hml. III, 2, 341.

**Sequence,** succession: *cut off the s. of posterity,* John II, 96. *how art thou a king but by fair s. and succession?* R2 II, 1, 199. *why lifts she up her arms in s. thus?* Tit. IV, 1, 37 (= one after the other, alternately; cf. *sequent* in Oth. I, 2, 41). *tell Athens, in the s. of degree from high to low throughout,* Tim. V, 1, 211.

**Sequent,** adj. following, successive, consequent: *each (minute) changing place with that which goes before, in s. toil all forwards do contend,* Sonn. 60, 4. *immediate sentence then and s. death,* Meas. V, 378. *your 'O Lord, sir' is very s. to your whipping,* All's II, 2, 56. *conferred by testament to the s. issue,* V, 3, 197. *to fashion in my s. protestation,* Troil. IV, 4, 68. *what to this was s. thou knowest already,* Hml. V, 2, 54. *nature finds itself scourged by the s. effects,* Lr. I, 2, 115. *the galleys have sent a dozen s. messengers at one another's heels,* Oth. I, 2, 41.

**Sequent,** subst. a follower, attendant: *a letter to a s. of the stranger queen's,* LLL IV, 2, 142 (Holofernes' speech).

**Sequester,** subst. sequestration, separation, seclusion: *this hand of yours requires a s. from liberty,* Oth. III, 4, 40.

**Sequester,** vb. to separate: *a poor —ed stag,* As II, 1, 33. *—ing from me all that time, acquaintance, custom and condition made tame and most familiar to my nature,* Troil. III, 3, 8. *why are you —ed from all your train,* Tit. II, 3, 75 (*séquestered?* cf. the subst. in Oth. III, 4, 40).

**Sequestration,** separation, seclusion: *any retirement, any s. from open haunts and popularity,* H5 I, 1, 58. *this loathsome s. have I had,* H6A II, 5, 25. *it was a violent commencement, and thou shalt see an answerable s.* Oth. I, 3, 351 (division, rupture, divorce).

**Sere,** (cf. *Sear*), subst.: *the clown shall make those laugh whose lungs are tickled o' the s.* Hml. II, 2, 337 (*sear* or *sere* = the catch in a gunlock, which keeps the hammer on half or full cock and is released by the trigger. A gun which explodes with the least touch on the sere, was said to be *tickle of the sere.* Wright).

**Sere**, adj. (cf. *Sear*) dry, withered: *deformed, crooked, old and s.* Err. IV, 2, 19.

**Serge**, a kind of woollen cloth: *thou say, thou s., nay, thou buckram lord,* H6B IV, 7, 27.

**Sergeant**, 1) a sheriff's officer, a bailiff: *if any hour meet a s., a' turns back for very fear,* Err. IV, 2, 56. 61. *the s. of the band, he that brings any man to answer it that breaks his band,* IV, 3, 30. 40. *your office, s.* H8 I, 1, 198. *this fell s. death is strict in his arrest,* Hml. V, 2, 347.

2) a non-commissioned officer in the army: H6A II, 1, 5. Mcb. I, 2, 3.

**Serious**, 1) not jesting, being or meant in earnest, grave, solemn: *I am more s. than my custom,* Tp. II, 1, 219. *make a common of my s. hours,* Err. II, 2, 29. *if thou beest capable of things s.* Wint. IV, 4, 791. *our scene is altered from a s. thing,* R2 V, 3, 79. *a weighty and a s. brow,* H8 Prol. 2. *he did it with a s. mind,* III, 2, 80. *not worth his s. considering,* 135. *O heavy lightness, s. vanity,* Rom. I, 1, 184. *lend thy s. hearing,* Hml. I, 5, 5. *what s. contemplation are you in,* Lr. I, 2, 150. *with a s. industry,* Cymb. III, 5, 111. *play with that which is so s.* IV, 2, 231. *for more s. wooing,* Per. IV, 6, 95.

2) weighty, important, not trifling: *on s. business,* LLL II, 31. All's II, 4, 41. Oth. I, 3, 268. *important and most s. designs,* LLL V, 1, 105. *our rash faults make trivial price of s. things we have,* All's V, 3, 61. *a servant grafted in my s. trust,* Wint. I, 2, 246. *I'll hence to London on a s. matter,* H6C V, 5, 47. Tim. II, 2, 219. Lr. IV, 5, 8. *there's nothing s. in mortality, all is but toys,* Mcb. II, 3, 98. *what else more s. importeth thee to know,* Ant. I, 2, 124.

**Seriously**, gravely, in earnest, not in jest: *Juno and Ceres whisper s.* Tp. IV, 125. *if s. I may convey my thoughts in this my light deliverance,* All's II, 1, 84. *this that s. he does address himself unto,* III, 6, 103. *dost thou speak s.?* Tim. III, 2, 47. *this to hear would Desdemona s. incline,* Oth. I, 3, 146.

**Sermon**, subst. a discourse pronounced by a divine for the edification of the people: As II, 1, 17. Shr. IV, 1, 185 (*making a s. of continency to her*).

**Sermon**, vb. to lecture, to lesson: *s. me no further,* Tim. II, 2, 181.

**Serpent**, a reptile of the genus Ophidii: Ven. 17. Lucr. 362. Ado V, 1, 90. LLL V, 2, 595. Mids. II, 2, 146. 149. III, 2, 73. 261. V, 440 (*to scape the —'s tongue* = not to be hissed). Merch. IV, 1, 69. All's I, 3, 147. John III, 1, 258. III, 3, 61. R2 III, 4, 75. V, 3, 58. H6B III, 2, 47. 259. 266. 326. H6C II, 2, 15 (fem.). Troil. V, 1, 97 (masc.). Cor. I, 8, 3. Rom. III, 2, 73. IV, 1, 80. Caes. II, 1, 32. Mcb. I, 5, 67. III, 4, 29. Hml. I, 5, 36. 39. Lr. I, 4, 310. V, 3, 84. Oth. IV, 2, 16. Ant. I, 2, 201. I, 5, 25. II, 5, 79. II, 7, 27. 29. 54. IV, 15, 25. Per. I, 1, 132.

**Serpentine**, pertaining to a serpent: *Mercury, lose all the s. craft of thy caduceus,* Troil. II, 3, 13 (Mercury's rod being wound with snakes).

**Serpent-like**, like a serpent: Lr. II, 4, 163.

**Serpigo**, (Ff *sapego* and *suppeago,* the later Ff *sarpego* and *serpego*), a kind of tetter, or dry eruption on the skin: Meas. III, 1, 31. Troil. II, 3, 81.

**Servant**, one whose office is to obey the commands of another; masc. and fem.: Lucr. 932. Sonn. 57, 8. 146, 9. Tp. I, 2, 187. 271. II, 1, 273. III, 1, 85. IV, 33. Gent. III, 1, 147. IV, 4, 1. 32. 109. Wiv. I, 4, 11. II, 2, 54 (*God bless them and make them his —s*). Meas. IV, 1, 46. Err. II, 2, 189. Mids. II, 1, 268. Merch. III, 2, 170. As II, 3, 46. All's II, 5, 77. Wint. II, 3, 54. H4A III, 3, 66. H4B I, 1, 28. H6A III, 1, 167. IV, 1, 80. IV, 2, 4 (*s. in arms to Harry King of England*). H8 II, 2, 106. II, 4, 238. Cor. II, 3, 186 (*a petty s. to the state*). Ant. I, 3, 69 etc. *I shall be glad to be your s.* Wiv. II, 2, 185 (= to be at your service; to serve you). *being unprepared, our will became the s. to defect,* Mcb. II, 1, 18 (was obliged to conform to deficiency). *s. to* = at the service of, waiting on the pleasure of: *idle words, —s to shallow fools,* Lucr. 1016. *all these* (oaths, tears) *are —s to deceitful men,* Gent. II, 7, 72. *the best wishes that can be forged in your thoughts be —s to you,* All's I, 1, 85. Adjectively: *the moody frontier of a s. brow,* H4A I, 3, 19.

Used as a word of civility between equals: *who calls? Your s. and your friend,* Gent. IV, 3, 4. *Cesario is your —'s name,* Tw. III, 1, 108. cf. LLL V, 2, 574. H6A V, 3, 178. H8 V, 1, 55. Especially applied, as a term of gallantry, to gentlemen conversing with ladies, not only by themselves, but by the ladies to whom they make their court: Gent. II, 1, 106. 114. 140. II, 4, 1. 8. 36. 106. 107. 110. 113. IV, 2, 91. V, 4, 20. LLL V, 2, 277. R3 I, 2, 207 (Qq *suppliant*). cf. the verb *to serve* in Pilgr. 329. LLL V, 2, 841. All's IV, 2, 17.

**Servanted**, subjected: *my affairs are s. to others,* Cor. V, 2, 89.

**Servant-maid**, a maid-servant: R3 I, 3, 107.

**Servant-monster**, a monster in one's service: Tp. III, 2, 3. 4. 9.

**Serve**, 1) to be in the employment and under the command of another person or of any authority; absol.: *s. always with assured trust,* Pilgr. 329 (as a lover). *—d without or grudge or grumblings,* Tp. I, 2, 248. *—s in offices that profit us,* 312 (the later Ff *—s offices*). *—s for wages,* Gent. III, 1, 270. Merch. I, 3, 92. Shr. V, 2, 164. All's V, 3, 18. H4A II, 4, 45. H6C III, 3, 5. Tim. IV, 2, 19. Lr. I, 4, 5. II, 4, 79. Used of military duty performed: *beware of being captives before you s.* All's II, 1, 22. *to s. bravely is to come halting off,* H4B II, 4, 54. *under what captain s. you?* H5 IV, 1, 95. IV, 7, 154. *Danger —s among them,* H8 I, 2, 37. Mcb. V, 4, 13. Ant. III, 7, 8.

Transitively: *—ing with looks his sacred majesty,* Sonn. 7, 4. *dissuade one foolish heart from —ing thee,* 141, 10. *the tyrant that I s.* Tp. II, 2, 166. III, 1, 6. III, 2, 27. 65. Meas. II, 1, 64. IV, 2, 52. Err. II, 1, 116 (*s. mad jealousy*). IV, 4, 30. V, 161. LLL V, 2, 841 (used of a lover). Mids. II, 1, 8. Merch. II, 2, 117. 120. 151. All's IV, 2, 17 (as a lover). Tw. I, 2, 41. 55. II, 5, 127. V, 263. Tim. III, 4, 59 etc. *s. heaven,* Wiv. IV, 5, 130. Meas. II, 2, 85. *s. God,* Wiv. V, 5, 136. Ado IV, 2, 18. V, 2, 95. LLL V, 2, 526 etc. Applied to public duties: Cor. V, 3, 134. *are there not men in your ward sufficient to s. it?* Meas. II, 1, 281 (sc. your office); cf. *must I not s. a long apprenticehood,* R2 I, 3, 271. *I s. you* = I am at your service: Lr. II, 1, 130.

With *to*: *s. by indenture to the common hangman* Per. IV, 6, 187.

2) to perform at table the office of a menial attendant; absol.: *break up this capon. I am bound to s.* LLL IV, 1, 56. *s. with thy trencher,* Cor. IV, 5, 54. Trans. = to bring and place on the table: *how durst you bring it from the dresser and s. it thus to me that love it not,* Shr. IV, 1, 167. With adverbs: *s. in the meat,* Merch. III, 5, 65. *the table shall be — d in,* 67. *while I pause, s. in your harmony,* Shr. III, 1, 14. *why hast thou not —d thyself in to my table so many meals?* Troil. II, 3, 45. *is it* (a sharp sauce) *not well —d in to a sweet goose?* Rom. II, 4, 85. *to s. in meat to villains,* Tim. IV, 3, 485. *supper — d up,* Rom. I, 3, 101.

3) to attend: *health, at your bidding, s. your majesty,* All's II, 1, 18. *thou* (mischance) *thinkest to s. me last,* R2 III, 4, 95. *shame —s thy life and doth thy death attend,* R3 IV, 4, 195. cf. above Sonn. 7, 4.

4) to be employed: *let it s. for table-talk,* Merch. III, 5, 93. *— s as paste and cover to our bones,* R2 III, 2, 154. *our bridal flowers s. for a buried corse,* Rom. IV, 5, 89. *would you in their* (the clothes') *—ing 'fore noble Lucius present yourself,* Cymb. III, 4, 173.

5) to be of use, to be good, to be fit, to avail, to suffice, to do: *what will s. is fit,* Ado I, 1, 320. *it* (the ballad of the king and the beggar) *would neither s. for the writing nor the tune,* LLL I, 2, 119 (*for* = with respect to). *Priscian a little scratched, 'twill s.* V, 1, 32. *things may s. long, but not s. ever,* All's II, 2, 60. *there it —s well again,* 64. *hardly s.* IV, 1, 59. *if this syllogism will s., so,* Tw. I, 5, 55. *it* (my answer) *shall s. among wits of no higher breeding than thine,* H4B II, 2, 38. *Shadow will s. for summer,* III, 2, 144. *no excuse shall s.* V, 1, 7. *moy shall not s.* H5 IV, 4, 14. *a subtle knave! but yet it shall not s.* H6B II, 1, 104. *if our words will s.* V, 1, 139. *if all this will not s., I'll drown you in the malmsey-butt,* R3 I, 4, 276 (Ff *do*). *your grace's word shall s.* III, 5, 62. *a little help will s.* Cor. II, 3, 16. *it* (fair speech) *will s.* III, 2, 96. *'tis enough, 'twill s.* Rom. III, 1, 101. *this answer will not s.* Tim. III, 4, 57. 58. *some quantity of choice, to s. in such a difference,* Hml. III, 4, 76. *she would s. after a long voyage,* Per. IV, 6, 48. The aim and purpose expressed; by an inf.: *would s. to scale another Hero's tower,* Gent. III, 1, 119. *let your reason s. to make the truth appear,* Meas. V, 65. *the smallest thread will s. to strangle thee,* John IV, 3, 129. H4A I, 2, 23. H6C II, 1, 80. Hml. III, 3, 46 etc. By *as* or *for: will it s. for any model to build mischief on?* Ado I, 3, 48. *one turf shall s. as pillow for us both,* Mids. II, 2, 41. Tw. I, 2, 20. H6A III, 1, 138. Cor. I, 7, 3. Rom. I, 1, 241. III, 5, 52. Ant. III, 7, 33 etc.

Transitively: *that 'scuse —s many men to save their gifts,* Merch. IV, 1, 444. *their graces s. them but as enemies,* As II, 3, 11. *I have an answer will s. all men,* All's II, 2, 14. *which —s it in the office of a wall,* R2 II, 1, 47. *the powers of us may s. so great a day,* H4A IV, 1, 132 (= answer, be enough for). *the cry of Talbot —s me for a sword,* H6A II, 1, 79. *it —s you well, my lord, to say so much,* H6B III, 1, 119. *our indiscretion sometimes —s us well,* Hml. V, 2, 8. Used of garments, = to fit: *it will s. him,* Wiv. IV, 2, 79. *Julia's gown, which —d me as fit,* Gent. IV, 4, 167. *will your answer s. fit to all questions?* All's II, 2, 20. *how fit his garments s. me,* Cymb. IV, 1, 3. *to s. the turn* = to answer the purpose, to do: *a cloak as long as thine will s. the turn,* Gent. III, 1, 131. 134. 388. III, 2, 93. Shr. IV, 2, 62. All's IV, 1, 51. Tit. II, 1,

96. III, 1, 165. *will none but Herne the hunter s. your turn?* Wiv. V, 5, 108. *this maid will not s. your turn,* LLL I, 1, 300. 301. I, 2, 184. Mids. III, 1, 154. As V, 2, 53. Wint. IV, 4, 520. R2 III, 2, 90. Troil. III, 1, 81. Cor. IV, 5, 94. Tit. II, 1, 96. Tim. II, 1, 20 *(I must s. my turn out of mine own).* Hml. III, 3, 52. Oth. I, 1, 42.

6) to be favourable, to be at one's disposal; especially used of time; absol.: *now —s the season that they may surprise the silly lambs,* Lucr. 166. *debate where leisure —s with dull debaters,* 1019. *when time shall s., be thou not slack to proffer,* Pilgr. 333. *the time now —s not to expostulate,* Gent. III, 1, 251. *if your leisure —d, I would speak with you,* Ado III, 2, 84 (= if you had time). *when time and place shall s.* V, 1, 264. *let him be, until a time may s.* Wint. II, 3, 22. H4A I, 3, 180. H4B IV, 1, 74. H5 II, 1, 6. H6B I, 1, 248. Cor. I, 6, 46. IV, 3, 32. Tim. I, 1, 267 (*that time —s still* = there is always time for that). Mcb. II, 1, 22. Lr. V, 1, 48. Ant. II, 2, 10. Similarly: *break it* (the compact) *when your pleasure —s,* H6A V, 4, 164 (= when you please). *as occasion —s,* H6C III, 3, 236. *when the day —s, before black-cornered night, find what thou wantest,* Tim. V, 1, 47 (= by day-light). *we must take the current when it —s,* Caes. IV, 3, 223.

Transitively, = to favour, not to fail, to be ready to do work for: *if fortune s. me, I'll requite this kindness,* H6C IV, 7, 78. *my conscience will s. me to run from this Jew,* Merch. II, 2, 1 (= will say nothing against it, but, on the contrary, exhort me to it). *fall to them as you find your stomach —s you,* Shr. I, 1, 38 (as you have appetite). *soldiers' stomachs always s. them well,* H6A II, 3, 80. *I am sorry that your leisure —s you not,* Merch. IV, 1, 405 (that you are in such haste). *my leisure —s me now,* Rom. IV, 1, 39.

7) to satisfy, to content, to act up to, to fulfil: *did his picture get, to s. their eyes,* Compl. 135. *less than a pound shall s. me for carrying your letter,* Gent. I, 1, 111. *till necessity be —d,* As II, 7, 89. *to s. all hopes conceived,* Shr. I, 1, 15. *thy will by my performance shall be —d,* All's II, 1, 205. *those precepts cannot be —d,* H4B V, 1, 15. *s. your lusts,* Tit. II, 1, 130. IV, 2, 42. *what touches us ourself shall be last —d,* Caes. III, 1, 8.

8) to do with, to treat: *s. thou false Tarquin so,* Lucr. 1197. *shall we tell our husbands how we have —d him?* Wiv. IV, 2, 229. *when I s. him so, he takes it ill,* Err. II, 1, 12. *the prince would have —d him thus,* Ado II, 1, 203. *so he —d the second, and so the third,* As I, 2, 137. *would God would s. the world so all the year,* All's I, 3, 88. *were you well —d, you would be taught your duty,* R3 I, 3, 250. 251. 253. *he is justly —d,* Hml. V, 2, 338. *she is —d as I would s. a rat,* Cymb. V, 5, 247.

9) to offer, to present for acceptance, to afford: *I'll s. you five hundred at the rate,* Err. IV, 4, 14. *it* (the Tuscan service) *well may s. a nursery to our gentry,* All's I, 2, 15 (or *as* omitted?). *—ing of becks and jutting-out of bums,* Tim. I, 2, 237. Hence = to cause, to produce: *the deep vexation of his inward soul had —d a dumb arrest upon his tongue,* Lucr. 1780. *to s. a trick* = to play a trick: *the trick you —d me,* Gent. IV, 4, 38. *if I be —d such another trick,* Wiv. III, 5, 6. *an you s. me such another trick,* As IV, 1, 40.

**Service,** 1) place and office of a servant: *whom now I keep in s.* Tp. I, 2, 286. *use of s. none,* II, 1,

151. *lose thy* s. Gent. II, 3, 49. 57. *if I last in this s.*, *you must case me in leather*, Err. II, 1, 85. *I cannot get a* s. Merch. II, 2, 165. *famished in his* s. 113. *to leave a rich Jew's* s. 156. *lost my teeth in your* s. As I, 1, 88. *to leave his* s. Shr. I, 2, 30. *s. is no heritage*, All's I, 3, 25 (a proverb, meaning that a servant is a wretched creature). *she that would alter —s with thee*, Tw. II, 5, 172. *your oath of* s. *to the pope*, John V, 1, 23. *have got another* s. Tim. IV, 3, 511. *what wouldst thou?* s. Lr. I, 4, 25. *out of* s. Wiv. II, 1, 183. Wint. IV, 3, 14. *to turn out of s.* As I, 3, 26 (metaphorically). H5 IV, 3, 119 etc.

2) the attendance and duty of a servant: *love will creep in* s. *where it cannot go*, Gent. IV, 2, 20. *I'll lend you all my life to do you* s. Meas. V, 437. *when s. should in my old limbs lie lame*, As II, 3, 41. *the constant* s. *of the antique world, when s. sweat for duty*, 57. 58. *choke their* s. *up even with the having*, 61. *s. shall with steeled sinews toil*, H5 II, 2, 36. *both fell by our servants, a most unnatural and faithless* s. H8 II, 1, 123. *what* s. *is here! I think our masters are a-sleep*, Cor. IV, 5, 1 etc. *one's* s., either subjectively, = the attendance performed by one: *to commend their* s. *to his will*, Gent. I, 3, 42. *have nothing for my* s. *but blows*, Err. IV, 4, 32. Mids. V, 86. As II, 3, 54. All's II, 3, 110. Tw. V, 329. H8 III, 1, 52 etc. Or objectively, = the attendance due to one: *thy* s. *to despise*, Sonn. 149, 10. *worth his* s. Tw. I, 2, 59. *I have eyes under my* s. *which look upon his removedness*, Wint. IV, 2, 41. *I'll put my fortunes to your* s. I, 2, 440. *you at your sick s. had a prince*, John IV, 1, 52. *you bind me to your highness'* s. H6C III, 2, 43 etc. *at a person's* s.: Gent. II, 5, 63. Meas. V, 390. All's IV, 5, 25. Tw. I, 5, 318. John I, 198. R3 III, 5, 9 etc.

Used as a term of mere courtesy: *to do you* s. Mids. V, 81. *indebted in love and s. to you*, Merch. IV, 1, 414. *my duty and most humble* s. Tw. III, 1, 105. H5 IV, 6, 23. H8 III, 1, 179. IV, 2, 115. Troil. V, 5, 3. Tim. I, 1, 55. Lr. I, 1, 29 etc. Especially, in the language of gallantry, = the homage paid by a lover: *did my heart fly to your* s. Tp. III, 1, 65. *nor to his* (love's) s. *no such joy on earth*, Gent. II, 4, 139; cf. IV, 2, 20. *and shape his* s. *wholly to my hests*, LLL V, 2, 65. *Dumain was at my* s. 276. *Longaville was for my s. born*, 284. *all made of faith and s.* As V, 2, 95. *will for ever do thee all rights of* s. All's IV, 2, 17. *to her* s. Wint. IV, 4, 388.

3) business done by a servant (often as a term of courtesy): *nor —s to do, till you require*, Sonn. 57, 4. *I have done thee worthy* s. Tp. I, 2, 247. *thou and thy fellows your last s. did worthily perform*, V, 35. *what s. is it your pleasure to command me in*, Gent. IV, 3, 9. *impose some s. on me*, LLL V, 2, 850. *'tis my limited s.* Mcb. II, 3, 57. Tp. IV, 267. V, 225. Gent. IV, 4, 45. V, 4, 19. Meas. I, 2, 181. Ado II, 1, 271. LLL V, 2, 312. Mids. III, 2, 331. Wint. I, 1, 3. II, 1, 17. II, 3, 150. IV, 2, 12. 18. IV, 4, 527. V, 3, 3. John V, 7, 104. H5 II, 2, 38. Cymb. III, 2, 14 etc.

And hence, generally, work, business done for another: *it* (the cudgel) *hath done meritorious* s. Wiv. IV, 2, 218. *do his* (the husband's) s. All's IV, 5, 29. 33. *accept his* (the schoolmaster's) s. Shr. II, 84. *the poorest* s. *is repaid with thanks*, IV, 3, 45. *his counsel now might do me golden* s. Tw. IV, 3, 8; cf. Oth. I, 2, 4 and Ant. II, 7, 14. *I am for other* s. *first*, Per. V, 1, 255.

4) religious worship or ceremony: *earnest in the* s. *of my God*, R3 III, 7, 106. *'tis mad idolatry to make the* s. *greater than the god*, Troil. II, 2, 57. *we should profane the* s. *of the dead to sing a requiem*, Hml. V, 1, 259. = an action concerning religious duty: *whether God will have it so, for some displeasing* s. *I have done*, H4A III, 2, 5.

5) military duty, or achievement in war: *he hath done good* s. *in these wars*, Ado I, 1, 48. *to see the Tuscan* s. All's I, 2, 14. *he did look far into the* s. *of the time and was discipled of the bravest*, 27. *that was not to be blamed in the command of the* s. III, 6, 55. *the merit of* s. *is seldom attributed to the true performer*, 64. III, 5, 4. 51. Tw. III, 3, 27. H4A IV, 2, 24. H4B I, 2, 167. H5 IV, 2, 8. H6C II, 2, 104. V, 1, 33. Oth. I, 1, 35. Ant. II, 6, 98. III, 13, 24 (*under the* s. *of a child*). Cymb. IV, 1, 14. V, 3, 93 etc. Used with irony, and applied to other kinds of business: *have worn your eyes almost out in the* s. Meas. I, 2, 114 (i. e. as a bawd); cf. *he knew the* s. III, 2, 127. *it* (the coat) *hath seen hot* s. Wint. IV, 3, 71. *I knew by that piece of s.* (viz stealing instead of fighting) *the men would carry coals*, H5 III, 2, 49. *such a piece of s. will you do* (run away) H6B V, 1, 155. cf. *the land* s., in the language of the clown: Wint. III, 3, 96.

6) course, order of dishes at table: *your fat king and your lean beggar is but variable s., two dishes, but to one table*, Hml. IV, 3, 25.

**Serviceable**, officious; in a good as well as a bad sense: *whose composed rhymes should be full fraught with s. vows*, Gent. II, 2, 70. *be s. to my son*, Shr. I, 1, 219. *wherein Olivia may seem s.* Tw. V, 105. *a s. villain, as duteous to the vices of thy mistress as badness would desire*, Lr. IV, 6, 257. *if it be so to do good service, never let me be counted s.* Cymb. III, 2, 15.

**Servile**, slavish: Lucr. 295. R2 III, 2, 185. H6A V, 3, 58. H6B IV, 1, 105. Tit. II, 1, 18 (Ff *idle*). V, 2, 55. Caes. I, 1, 80. Lr. III, 2, 21. With *to*, = meanly subject: *s. to my coy disdain*, Ven. 112. *subject and s. to all discontents*, 1161. *s. to all the skyey influences*, Meas. III, 1, 9.

**Servilely**, slavishly, meanly: Ven. 392.

**Servility**, slavery: *to be a queen in bondage is more vile than is a slave in base s.* H6A V, 3, 113.

**Servilius**, name in Tim. II, 2, 194. III, 2, 30. 47. 67. III, 4, 66. 79.

**Serving-creature** (not hyphened in O. Edd.) a servant; in contempt: Rom. IV, 5, 117. 119.

**Serving-man**, a servant: Wiv. I, 3, 19. III, 1, 2. Shr. IV, 1, 49. Tw. III, 2, 7. John V, 2, 81. H4A IV, 2, 30. H4B V, 1, 76. V, 3, 12. Term of gallantry (cf. *Servant*): *a s. proud in heart and mind, that curled my hair*, Lr. III, 4, 87 (*cavaliere servente?*).

**Servitor**, servant: *as —s to the unjust*, Lucr. 285. *thus are poor —s ... constrained to watch in darkness*, H6A II, 1, 5. *henceforth I am thy true* s. H6C III, 3, 196. *fearful commenting is leaden s. to dull delay*, R3 IV, 3, 52. *here none but soldiers and Rome's —s repose in fame*, Tit. I, 352. *your trusty and most valiant* s. Oth. I, 3, 40.

**Servitude**, slavery: Err. II, 1, 26. As I, 1, 25. H5 II, 2, 171. Per. V, 1, 95.

**Servius Tullius**, the Roman king dethroned by Tarquinius Superbus: Lucr. Arg. 2.

**Sessa**, probably a cry used by way of exhorting to swift running (cf. the German *sasa*): *let the world* slide, *s.* Shr. Ind. 1, 6. *Dolphin my boy, s.! let him trot by,* Lr. III, 4, 104. *dogs leap the hatch, and all are fled. Do de de de. S.! come march to wakes,* III, 6, 77.

**Session,** the sitting of a council, particularly of a court of justice: *when to the —s of sweet silent thought I summon up remembrance of things past,* Sonn. 30, 1. *from this s. interdict every fowl of tyrant wing,* Phoen. 9. *summon a s. that we may arraign our most disloyal lady,* Wint. II, 3, 202. *every shop, church, s., hanging, yields a careful man work,* IV, 4, 702. H8 II, 4, 66. Oth. I, 2, 86. III, 3, 140 (Ff —s). *to hold s.:* Meas. V, 376. Lr. V, 3, 54. —s, in the same sense: *this —s even pushes gainst our heart,* Wint. III, 2, 1. *the —s shall proceed,* 142. *in —s sit,* Oth. III, 3, 140 (Qq s.). cf. Sonn. 30, 1.

**Sestos,** Thracian town on the Hellespont, where Hero lived: As IV, 1, 106.

**Set,** subst. 1) a number of things suited to each other and making a whole: *take you the lute, and you the s. of books,* Shr. II, 107. *a s. of beads,* R2 III, 3, 147. *he'll watch the horologe a double s.* Oth. II, 3, 135 (twice through the twelve hours).

2) a game, a match, a bout: *a s. of wit well played,* LLL V, 2, 29. *shall I now give o'er the yielded s.?* John V, 2, 107. *we will in France play a s. shall strike his father's crown into the hazard,* H5 I, 2, 262. *as sure a card as ever won the s.* Tit. V, 1, 100.

3) the descent of the sun below the horizon: *from the rise to s.* H5 IV, 1, 289. *the sun hath made a golden s.* R3 V, 3, 19. *ere the s. of sun,* Mcb. I, 1, 5.

**Set,** vb. (impf. and partic. set) I) trans. 1) to make to sit or stand (not lie): *sets you before my sight,* Sonn. 15, 10. *sets down her babe,* 143, 3. *I had rather be set quick i' the earth,* Wiv. III, 4, 90. *set me i' the stocks,* IV, 5, 123; All's IV, 3, 127; Lr. II, 4, 13; 65; 202. *to set her before your eyes,* As V, 2, 73. *whoever shoots at him, I set him there,* All's III, 2, 115. *have you not set mine honour at the stake* (like a bear) Tw. III, 1, 129. *set on the head of a wasps' nest,* Wint. IV, 4, 813. *set against a brick-wall,* 818. *set before my face the Lord Aumerle,* R2 IV, 6. *set me lower,* H8 IV, 2, 76. *set me against Aufidius,* Cor. I, 6, 59. *to be set high in place,* II, 3, 255. *and set them upright at their dear friends' doors,* Tit. V, 1, 136. *set him breast-deep in earth,* V, 3, 179. *you will set cock a-hoop,* Rom. I, 5, 83 (cf. *Cock-a-hoop*). *set him before me,* Caes. I, 2, 20. *within my sword's length set him,* Mcb. IV, 3, 234. *I am set naked on your kingdom,* Hml. IV, 7, 44. *where may we set our horses?* Lr. II, 2, 4. *that their great stars throned and set high,* III, 1, 23. *set me where you stand,* IV, 6, 24. *thou hast set me on the rack,* Oth. III, 3, 335. *I'll set thee in a shower of gold,* Ant. II, 5, 45. *Antony shall set thee on triumphant chariots,* III, 1, 10. *the piece of virtue* (Octavia) *which is set betwixt us,* III, 2, 28. *set thee by Jove's side,* IV, 15, 36. *To be set* = to sit: *being set, I'll smother thee with kisses,* Ven. 18. *upon whose weeping margent she was set,* Compl. 39. *I would you were set,* Gent. II, 1, 91. *here I am set,* H4A II, 4, 482. *I was set at work among my maids,* H8 III, 1, 74. *set at upper end o' the table,* Cor. IV, 5, 204. Refl., = a) to sit down: *set thee down, sorrow,* LLL IV, 3, 4 (in I, 1, 317 *sit thee down*). *the king by this is set him down to sleep,* H6C IV, 3, 2 (viz in a chair. The watch's speech). b) to posture one's self: *in most strange postures we have seen him set himself,* H8 III, 2, 119.

Used of things, = to place in a standing, or any proper and natural posture: *set thy seal manual on my lips,* Ven. 516; Hml. III, 4, 61; cf. *in women's waxen hearts to set their forms,* Tw. II, 2, 31 (= to imprint). *against my heart he sets his sword,* Lucr. 1640. *he sets his foot upon the light,* 673; Shr. II, 404; Tw. II, 5, 205; R2 I, 1, 66; H4A III, 2, 95; H6C II, 2, 16; Tim. V, 4, 46; Caes. I, 3, 119; II, 1, 331 (*set on your foot* = go forward); Lr. III, 7, 68; Cymb. III, 3, 92. *to set footing:* R2 II, 2, 48. H6A III, 3, 64. H6B III, 2, 87. H8 III, 1, 183. Troil. II, 2, 155. *set her two courses off to sea again,* Tp. I, 1, 52. *set it down and rest you,* III, 1, 18; Wiv. III, 3, 6; IV, 2, 112; 120; As II, 7, 167; H4B II, 4, 11; R3 I, 2, 1; 33; 36; V, 3, 75; Per. III, 2, 51. *then may I set the world on wheels,* Gent. III, 1, 317. *love set on thy horns,* Wiv. V, 5, 4; Ado I, 1, 266; V, 1, 183. *shall I set in my staff?* Err. III, 1, 51. *such barren plants are set before us,* LLL IV, 2, 29. *on Hyems' crown a chaplet is set,* Mids. II, 1, 111. *set a glass of wine on the contrary casket,* Merch. I, 2, 104. *patches set upon a little breach,* John IV, 2, 32; cf. *set a new nap upon it,* H6B IV, 2, 7. *you that set the crown upon the head of this man,* H4A I, 3, 160; H6A IV, 1, 1; V, 3, 119; H6B I, 2, 40; I, 3, 66; H6C I, 1, 115; I, 4, 95; II, 2, 82; IV, 4, 27; Per. III Prol. 27. *the prince set a dish of apple-johns before him,* H4B II, 4, 5. *set me the crown upon my pillow here,* IV, 5, 5. *he wanted pikes to set before his archers,* H6A I, 1, 116. *set your knee against my foot,* III, 1, 169. *to set a head on headless Rome,* Tit. I, 186. *set me the stoups of wine upon that table,* Hml. V, 2, 278. *set it by,* 295. *when such a spacious mirror's set before him,* Ant. V, 1, 34. With *up:* as one would *set up a top,* Cor. IV, 5, 161. *till I set you up a glass,* Hml. III, 4, 19 (i. e. a mirror). With *on:* *she's e'en setting on water to scald such chickens,* Tim. II, 2, 71 (placing water over a fire to heat it).*

2) to plant: *I'll not put the dibble in earth to set one slip of them,* Wint. IV, 4, 100. *in this place I'll set a bank of rue,* R2 III, 4, 105. *set hyssop and weed up thyme,* Oth. I, 3, 325. *she that —s seeds and roots of shame and iniquity,* Per. IV, 6, 92. cf. LLL IV, 2, 29.

3) to erect, to raise: *there is no sure foundation set on blood,* John IV, 2, 104. *we'll set thy statue in some holy place,* H6A III, 3, 14. *hath he set bounds betwixt their love and me?* R3 IV, 1, 21. *set up the bloody flag against all patience,* Cor. II, 1, 84; cf. *setting it up* (a scarecrow) *to fear the birds of prey,* Meas. II, 1, 2. *to set up,* especially used of persons or states raised to power: *to pluck a kingdom down and set another up,* H4B I, 3, 50. *can set the duke up in despite of me,* H6C I, 1, 158. *who set thee up and plucked thee down,* V, 1, 26. *set up Lancaster,* 85. *may they not be my oracles as well and set me up in hope?* Mcb. III, 1, 10. Figuratively: *your cares set up do not pluck my cares down,* R2 IV, 195. *set up your fame for ever,* Per. III, 2, 97.

4) to place with a certain purpose, to fix, to arrange, to regulate: *set spurs* = clapped spurs to their horses, Wiv. IV, 5, 70. *thou art come to set mine eye,* John V, 7, 51 (to close it). *to set the teeth* = to press them close together: H5 III, 1, 15. Cor. I, 3, 70. Ant. III, 13, 181. *set your countenance* = look grave, Shr. IV, 4, 18. *to s. in order:* Wiv. V, 5, 81. H6A II, 2, 32. H6C I, 2, 70. Used of troops drawn up, and what is like them: *on his bow-back he hath a battle set of bristly*

*pikes*, Ven. 619. *set we our squadrons on yond side o' the hill*, Ant. III, 9, 1. *the French are bravely in their battles set*, H5 IV, 3, 69. *that never set a squadron in the field*, Oth. I, 1, 22. *we will before the walls of Rome to-morrow set down our host*, Cor. V, 3, 2. *where we'll set forth in best appointment all our regiments*, John II, 295. *bid him set on his powers*, Caes. IV, 3, 308. *set our battles on*, V, 3, 108. Used of lime-twigs placed to catch birds: *lime-twigs set to catch my winged soul*, H6B III, 3, 16. *poor birds they are not set for*, Mcb. IV, 2, 36. Of gems placed on a ground of less worth: *feasts ... in the long year set like stones of worth*, Sonn. 52, 6. *never so rich a gem was set in worse than gold*, Merch. II, 7, 55. *wherein so curiously he had set this counterfeit*, All's IV, 3, 39. *as foil wherein thou art to set the precious jewel of thy home-return*, R2 I, 3, 266. *this precious stone set in the silver sea*, II, 1, 46. *I will set you neither in gold nor silver*, H4B I, 2, 19 (Qq *inset*). *set this diamond safe in golden palaces*, H6A V, 3, 169. *a base foul stone, made precious by the foil of England's chair, where he is falsely set*, R3 V, 3, 251. (hence probably the signification of *to set off* sub 17). *set with* = studded with: Ado III, 4, 20. In music, = to compose, to tune, to fit to music: *set all hearts to what tune pleased his ear*, Tp. I, 2, 84. *give me a note: your ladyship can set*, Gent. I, 2, 81. In mechanics, = to regulate, to contrive: *their arms are set like clocks, still to strike on*, H6A I, 2, 42. In writing, = to copy fair: *we took him setting of boys' copies*, H6B IV, 2, 95. *which in a set hand fairly is engrossed*, R3 III, 6, 2. Partic. *set*, used of words, = well-placed, terse, elegant: *in good set terms*, As II, 7, 17. *the set phrase of peace*, Oth. I, 3, 82 (Ff *soft*).

5) to appoint, to station, to post: *thou set'st the wolf where he the lamb may get*, Lucr. 878. *crow so at these set kind of fools*, Tw. I, 5, 95 (appointed, customarily kept). *the heaven sets spies upon us*, Wint. V, 1, 203. *like heralds 'twixt two dreadful battles set*, John IV, 2, 78. *set to dress this garden*, R2 III, 4, 73. *an empty eagle were set to guard the chicken*, H6B III, 1, 248. *they are set here for examples*, H8 I, 3, 62. *stay not till the watch be set*, Rom. III, 3, 148. *set some watch over your son*, Hml. V, 1, 319. *my father hath set guard to take my brother*, Lr. II, 1, 18. *let's set the watch*, Oth. II, 3, 125. *set on thy wife to observe*, III, 3, 240.

6) to fix, to determine, to appoint: *now shall we know if Gadshill have set a match*, H4A I, 2, 119 (= made an appointment). *these whose ransom we have set*, H6B IV, 1, 139. *I'll set a bourn how far to be beloved*, Ant. I, 1, 16. *on set purpose*, Per. II, 2, 54. With *down*: *'tis set down so in heaven, but not in earth*, Meas. II, 4, 50. *you are set down for Pyramus*, Mids. I, 2, 22. *sets down the manner how*, Tw. III, 4, 79. *as I mine own course have set down*, Wint. I, 2, 340. *on Wednesday next we solemnly set down our coronation*, R2 IV, 319. *many limits of the charge set down*, H4A I, 1, 35. *ruminated, plotted and set down*, I, 3, 274. *we have not yet set down this day of triumph*, R3 III, 4, 44. *to set down her reckoning*, Troil. III, 3, 254. *keep your duties, as I have set them down*, Cor. I, 7, 2. *set down thine own ways*, IV, 5, 144. *I have in quick determination thus set it down*, Hml. III, 1, 177.

7) to stake at play: *who sets me else? by heaven, I'll throw at all*, R2 IV, 57.* *to set all at one cast*, H4A IV, 1, 46. *I have set my life upon a cast*, R3 V, 4, 9.

*expectation —s all on hazard*, Troil. Prol. 22. *to set upon one battle all our liberties*, Caes. V, 1, 75. *I would set my life on any chance*, Mcb. III, 1, 113. *set less than thou throwest*, Lr. I, 4, 136. With *up*, in the phrase *to set up one's rest* = to take a firm resolution: Err. IV, 3, 27. Merch. II, 2, 110. All's II, 1, 138. Rom. IV, 5, 6.

8) to put in a condition, to make or cause to be; with a double accus.: *the villanies of man will set him* (the devil) *clear*, Tim. III, 3, 31. *I'll set thee free*, Tp. I, 2, 442. V, 252. Epil. 20. Shr. I, 1, 142. I, 2, 268. All's III, 4, 17. H6A III, 3, 72. H6C IV, 5, 13. IV, 6, 16. Tit. I, 274. Per. IV, 6, 107. *set ope thy everlasting gates*, H6B IV, 9, 13. *set it right*, Hml. I, 5, 189. With prepositions: *hast set thy mercy and thy honour at difference in thee*, Cor. V, 3, 200. *set mine eyes at flow*, Tim. II, 2, 172. *setting thee at liberty*, LLL III, 124. John III, 3, 9. *sets us all at odds*, Lr. I, 3, 5. *I have set my friends at peace*, R3 II, 1, 6 (Ff *made*). *set your heart at rest*, Mids. II, 1, 121. *set thee from durance*, LLL III, 129. *sack sets it* (learning) *in act and use*, H4B IV, 3, 126. *shall set them in present action*, Cor. IV, 3, 52. *setting endeavour in continual motion*, H5 I, 2, 185. *set my brother and the king in deadly hate*, R3 I, 1, 34. *set them into confounding odds*, Tim. V, 3, 392. *let my unsounded self now set thy wit to school*, Lucr. 1820. *set the murderous Machiavel to school*, H6C III, 2, 193. *we'll set thee to school to an ant*, Lr. II, 4, 68. Oftenest with *on*: *a bell once set on ringing*, Lucr. 1494. *to set his sense on the attentive bent*, Troil. I, 3, 252. *to set on edge*, Wint. IV, 3, 7. H4A III, 1, 133. *to set on fire* (= to kindle, to inflame): Ven. 388. Wiv. V, 5, 39. John II, 351. H6B I, 4, 20. IV, 6, 16. Rom. III, 3, 133. Tim. III, 3, 34. *set me on the proof*, Tim. II, 2, 166. *to set the table on a roar*, Hml. V, 1, 210. On corrupted to *a*: *sets every joint a shaking*, Lucr. 452. *thou'lt set me a weeping*, H4B II, 4, 301. *set a work*: Lucr. 1496. H4B IV, 3, 124. Troil. V, 10, 38. Hml. II, 2, 510. Lr. III, 5, 8. omitted: *this man shall set me packing*, Hml. III, 4, 211.

Hence *set on* = intent on: *a patch set on learning*, LLL IV, 2, 32. *each heart being set on bloody courses*, H4B I, 1, 158. *my heart's on mischief set*, H6B V, 2, 84. And *to set on* = to make intent on, to determine to any thing with settled purpose: *set not thy sweet heart on proud array*, Lr. III, 4, 84. *to set my rest on her kind nursery*, Lr. I, 1, 125. cf. below: Rom. II, 3, 57. with *up*: *here will I set up my everlasting rest*, Rom. V, 3, 110.

9) to incite, to instigate: *for every trifle are they set upon me*, Tp. II, 2, 8. *one fruitful meal would set me to it*, Meas. IV, 3, 161. *have you not set Lysander to follow me*, Mids. III, 2, 222. *I set him every day to woo me*, As III, 2, 428. *envy and base opinion set against them*, H8 III, 1, 36. *sets Thersites to match us in comparisons with dirt*, Troil. I, 3, 192. *to set dogs on sheep*, Cor. II, 1, 273. *set the dogs o' the street to bay me*, Cymb. V, 5, 222. With *up*: *thou didst set up my disobedience 'gainst the king*, Cymb. III, 4, 90. Oftener with *on*: *some one hath set you on*, Meas. V, 112. 132. 238. 248. 251. *did my brother set thee on to this?* Ado V, 1, 254. Mids. III, 2, 231. Tw. V, 189. Wint. II, 3, 131. 141. R2 I, 3, 131. H4B II, 1, 165. H5 II, 2, 42. H6A IV, 4, 8. 29. R3 I, 2, 183. I, 4, 261. Cor. III, 1, 37. Mcb. II, 3, 36. Hml. III, 2, 45. Oth. II, 3, 390. V, 2, 329. Cymb. I, 5, 73.

10) to cause, to produce, to contrive; in a bad sense: *set dissension 'twixt the son and sire*, Ven. 1160. *twixt the green sea and the azured vault set roaring war*, Tp. V, 44. *myself and Toby set this device against Malvolio*, Tw. V, 368. *set armed discord 'twixt these perjured kings*, John III, 1, 111. *and set abroad new business for you all*, Tit. I, 192. *set deadly enmity between two friends*, V, 1, 131. With *on: who set it on* (the rout) Oth. II, 3, 210. *your reports have set the murder on*, V, 2, 187. *to set abroach* (cf. *Abroach*): H4B IV, 2, 14. R3 I, 3, 325. Rom. I, 1, 111.

11) to place in estimation, to value: *I have letters sent me that set him high in fame*, All's V, 3, 31 (but cf. Cor. II, 3, 255 and Lr. III, 1, 23 sub 1). *to set me light*, Sonn. 88, 1. R2 I, 3, 293. *thou mayst not coldly set our sovereign process*, Hml. IV, 3, 64. With *at: set the world at nought*, Gent. I, 1, 68. H4B V, 2, 85. Cor. III, 1, 270. *there shall no figure at such rate be set*, Rom. V, 3, 301. Hml. I, 3, 122. *I do not set my life at a pin's fee*, I, 4, 65. The construction inverted: *since of your lives you set so slight a valuation*, Cymb. IV, 4, 48. *set little by such toys*, Gent. I, 2, 82 (= make little account of). *you set nothing by a bloody coxcomb*, Tw. V, 194.

12) to direct, to cast, to fix (the eye): *with sad set eyes*, Lucr. 1662 (M. Edd. *sad-set*). *the setting of thine eye and cheek proclaim a matter from thee*, Tp. II, 1, 229. *to set eye on* = to see, to perceive: *King Cophetua set eye upon the beggar Zenelophon*, LLL IV, 1, 66. *no single soul can we set eye on*, Cymb. IV, 2, 131.

13) to oppose: *who would set his wit to so foolish a bird?* Mids. III, 1, 137. *and like a civil war set'st oath to oath, thy tongue against thy tongue*, John III, 1, 264. *sets the word itself against the word*, R2 V, 3, 122. V, 5, 13. *will you set your wit to a fool's?* Troil. II, 1, 94. *set limb to limb, and thou art far the lesser*, H6B IV, 10, 50. *I'll set those to you that can speak*, Hml. III, 4, 17. With *up: if knowledge could be set up against mortality*, All's I, 1, 35. *O madness of discourse that cause sets up with and against itself*, Troil. V, 2, 143. *they set me up, in policy, that mongrel cur Ajax against that dog Achilles*, V, 4, 13.

14) to write, to note down: *that it* (the day) *in golden letters should be set among the high tides in the calendar*, John III, 1, 85. *I'ld set my ten commandments in your face*, H6B I, 3, 145. *set quarrelling upon the head of valour*, Tim. III, 5, 27. *his faults observed, set in a note-book*, Caes. IV, 3, 98. Usually with *down:* Lucr. 1299. Sonn. 88, 6. Tp. V, 207. Gent. III, 1, 337. Ado III, 5, 68. Shr. III, 2, 63. All's I, 3, 234. III, 4, 33. IV, 3, 155. Tw. III, 2, 51. IV, 2, 118. Wint. III, 2, 140. IV, 4, 189. R2 V, 3, 54. V, 2, 98. H4B I, 2, 201. R3 III, 1, 86. Troil. IV, 5, 61 (cf. *Write*). Cor. III, 3, 10. Tit. V, 2, 14. Tim. IV, 3, 118 (cf. Troil. IV, 5, 61 and *Write*). Mcb. V, 1, 36. Hml. I, 5, 107. II, 2, 80. 205. 460. 567. III, 2, 43. Lr. III, 7, 47. V, 3, 37. Oth. V, 2, 343. 351. Cymb. I, 4, 178.

15) With *to*, = a) to apply to: *we set the axe to thy usurping root*, H6C II, 2, 165. *set his knife unto the root*, II, 6, 49. *he is set so only to himself*, Tim. V, 1, 120 (wrapt up in self-contemplation). b) to add to, to attach, to join with, to impart: *set smell to the violet*, Ven. 935. *I never saw that you did painting need and therefore to your fair no painting set*, Sonn. 83, 2. *I would set an oxhead to your lion's hide*, John II, 292. *set feathers to thy heels*, IV, 2, 174. *till I have*

*set a glory to this hand*, IV, 3, 71. *if he do set the very wings of reason to his heels*, Troil. II, 2, 43. With the adverb *to: can honour set to a leg?* H4A V, 1, 133 (restore a leg cut off).

16) With the prepos. *on*, = to bestow on, to affect with, to impart: *his breath and beauty set gloss on the rose*, Ven. 935. *set this bateless edge on his keen appetite*, Lucr. 9. *on Helen's cheek all art of beauty set*, Sonn. 53, 7. *time doth transfix the flourish set on youth*, 60, 9. *set a mark so bloody on the business*, Tp. I, 2, 141. *your wrongs do set a scandal on my sex*, Mids. II, 1, 240. *set upon Aguecheek a notable report of valour*, Tw. III, 4, 209. *and on our actions set the name of right with holy breath*, John V, 2, 67. *to set a form upon that indigest*, V, 7, 26. *time hath set a blot upon my pride*, R2 III, 2, 81. *all their prayers and love are set on Hereford*, H4B IV, 1, 138. *to set a gloss upon his bold intent*, H6A IV, 1, 103; cf. Tim. I, 2, 16. *sin, death and hell have set their marks upon him*, R3 I, 3, 293. *what grief hath set the jaundice on your cheeks?* Troil. I, 3, 2. *set fire on barns and haystacks*, Tit. V, 1, 133 (never *to set fire to*). *my heart's dear love is set on the fair daughter of rich Capulet*, Rom. II, 3, 57. 59. *set a fair fashion on our entertainment*, Tim. I, 2, 152. *set a double varnish on the fame the Frenchman gave you*, Hml. IV, 7, 133.

17) Equivalent to the verbs *to place* or *to put:* *fools that in the imagination set the goodly objects*, Compl. 136. *that I might set it in my prayers*, Tp. III, 1, 35. *where should they* (the eyes) *be set else?* III, 2, 11. 12. *thou wert best set thy lower part where thy nose stands*, All's II, 3, 267. *thine eye begins to speak: set thy tongue there*, R2 V, 3, 125. *this present enterprise set off his head*, H4A V, 1, 88 (not charged to his account). *set bars before my tongue*, H6A II, 5, 49. *set it* (the head) *on York gates*, H6C I, 4, 179. Cymb. IV, 2, 99. 123. *set this in your painted cloths*, Troil. V, 10, 46. *set honour in one eye*, Caes. I, 2, 86. *set a huge mountain 'tween my heart and tongue*, II, 4, 7. *and sets a blister there*, Hml. III, 4, 44. *sets ratsbane by his porridge*, Lr. III, 4, 55. *I'll set down the pegs that make this music*, Oth. II, 1, 202 (let down, lower). *that parting kiss which I had set betwixt two charming 'words*, Cymb. I, 3, 34. *I set it at your will*, IV, 3, 13.

With adverbs; *to set apart* = to cast off, to neglect: *all reverence set apart to him and his usurped authority*, John III, 1, 159. *to set aside* (cf. *Aside*): Wiv. II, 2, 109. Mids. IV, 1, 188. Shr. II, 270. R2 I, 1, 58. H4A III, 3, 137. 139. H4B I, 2, 93. 95. H6A III, 1, 93. H6C III, 3, 119. IV, 1, 24. Tim. III, 5, 14. *to set by* = to pass over, not to dwell on: *to set the needless process by*, Meas. V, 92. *to set forth* = a) to show: *set forth a deep repentance*, Mcb. I, 4, 6. b) to recommend, to praise: *to set forth that which is so singular*, Lucr. 32. *set thy person forth to sell*, Pilgr. 310. *I'll set you forth*, Merch. III, 5, 95. *to set off* = a) to remove: *every thing set off that might so much as think you enemies*, H4B IV, 1, 145 (cf. H4A V, 1, 88). b) to show to the best advantage: *their labour delight in them sets off*, Tp. III, 1, 2. *hath no foil to set it off*, H4A I, 2, 239. *to set me off*, H4B I, 2, 15. *he hath a kind of honour sets him off*, Cymb. I, 6, 170. *it is place which lessens and sets off*, III, 3, 13. *to set out* = to choose, to pick out: *those enemies of Timon's and mine own whom you yourselves shall set out for reproof fall and no more*, Tim. V, 4, 57. *to set up* = to placard: *he set up his bill here*, Ado I, 1, 39. *set this up with wax upon old Brutus' statue*, Caes. I, 3, 145. *to set together* = to join, to compound, to connect: Gent. I, 1, 122. H8 I, 1, 46.

II) intr. 1) to go down, to descend below the horizon: Lucr. 784. 1226. 1230. Tp. III, 1, 22. Err. I, 2, 7. Shr. Ind. 2, 122. John V, 5, 1. R2 II, 1, 12. II, 4, 21. R3 II, 3, 34. H8 III, 2, 225. 416. Troil. V, 8, 5. Rom. III, 5, 127. Tim. I, 2, 150. Caes. V, 3, 60. 62. 63. Applied to eyes: *thy eyes are almost set in thy head*, Tp. III, 2, 10 (extinguished, dimmed). *his eyes were set at eight in the morning*, Tw. V, 205.

2) *to set about* = to fall to, to begin: *shall we set about some revels?* Tw. I, 3, 145.

3) to fall on, to make an attack; followed by *against*: *you all are bent to set against me for your merriment*, Mids. III, 2, 146. By *on*: *we'll set upon them*, H4A I, 2, 194. II, 4, 193. 200. 279. V, 1, 119. H6A I, 1, 114. III, 2, 103. H6B III, 2, 241. H6C V, 1, 61. R3 V, 3, 348. Cor. V, 1, 58. With the adverb *on*: *Percy and set on!* H4A V, 2, 97. *let them set on at once*, Caes. V, 2, 3. *Cassio hath here been set on by Roderigo*, Oth. V, 1, 112.

4) to begin a march or journey or walk: *the king is set from London*, H5 II Chor. 34. With *forth*: *it is meet I presently set forth*, Merch. IV, 1, 404. V, 271. Tw. III, 3, 13. R2 V, 1, 78. H4A I, 2, 187. 189. I, 3, 149. II, 3, 119. III, 1, 84. III, 2, 170. IV, 1, 91. H6A IV, 4, 11. Mcb. IV, 3, 135. Lr. IV, 5, 1. 16. With *forward*: John IV, 3, 19. H4A II, 3, 30. 38. III, 2, 173. With *on*: Meas. III, 1, 61. Wint. IV, 4, 682. John V, 3, 16. R2 III, 3, 208. H4B I, 3, 109. H5 V Chor. 14. With *out*: *ready to set out for London*, H8 II, 2, 5. *set forward* and *set on* = go on: R2 I, 3, 109. 117. H4B IV, 1, 227. Cymb. V, 5, 479. H4B V, 5, 76. H8 II, 4, 241. Cor. III, 1, 58. Caes. I, 2, 11. Cymb. V, 5, 484.

5) With *down*, = to sit down, to pitch a camp, to begin a siege: *man, setting down before you, will undermine you*, All's I, 1, 129 (M. Edd. *sitting*). *if they set down before us*, Cor. I, 2, 28. I, 3, 110. Tim. V, 3, 9. Mcb. V, 4, 10. Ant. III, 13, 168 (M. Edd. *sits*).

**Setebos**, the god of Sycorax (said to have been the supreme God of the Patagons): Tp. I, 2, 373. V, 261.*

**Setter**, a pointer, or one who makes appointments and watches opportunities: H4A II, 2, 53.

**Setter-up**, one who appoints and raises to power and dignity: H6C II, 3, 37. III, 3, 157.

**Settle**, 1) trans. a) to place: (love) *never —d equally, but high or low*, Ven. 1139. *—st admired reverence in a slave*, Tim. V, 1, 54.

b) to fix, to establish, to make permanent in a place or condition: *left behind and —d certain French*, H5 I,2,47. *if beauty, wisdom, modesty, can s. the heart of Antony*, Ant. II, 2, 246. Partic. *—d* = α) fixed, permanent, not to be removed: *we'll light upon some —d low content*, As II, 3, 68. *if your more ponderous and —d project may suffer alteration*, Wint. IV,4,535. *your —d hate*, R2 I, 1, 201. *cloyed with long continuance in a —d place*, H6A II, 5, 106. *breed love's —d passions in my heart*, V, 5, 4. *he's —d, not to come off, in his displeasure*, H8 III, 2, 22. *this something —d matter in his heart*, Hml. III, 1, 181. *imagine Pericles arrived at Tyre, welcomed and —d to his own desire*,

Per. IV Prol. 2 (no more wandering abroad). Used of blood, = stagnant, stagnated: *the blood which, before cold and —d, left the liver white and pale*, H4B IV, 3, 112. *how the blood is —d in his face*, H6B III, 2, 160. *her blood is —d, and her joints are stiff*, Rom. IV, 5, 26.

β) firmly resolved: *I am —d*, Mcb. I, 7, 79.

γ) composed, calm, sober, grave: *shall reasons find of —d gravity*, Sonn. 49, 8. *whose —d visage and deliberate word nips youth i' the head*, Meas. III, 1, 90. *no —d senses of the world can match the pleasure of that madness*, Wint. V, 3, 72. *—d age*, Hml. IV, 7, 81.

2) intr. a) to be placed, to find a place: *all the honours that can fly from us shall on them s.* All's III, 1, 21.

b) to become stationary after change: *having flown over many knavish professions, he —d only in rogue*, Wint. IV, 3, 106.

c) to become calm: *till the fury of his highness s.* Wint. IV, 4, 482. *trouble him no more till further —ing*, Lr. IV, 7, 82.

**Seven**, one more than six: Gent. III, 1, 126. Wiv. I, 1, 51. 59. 158. II, 3, 37. Meas. II, 1, 274. 277. 287. Err. V, 309. 320. Ado III, 3, 134. Mids. I, 1, 159. As II, 7, 143. III, 2, 184. 335. V, 4, 71. 103. Shr. Ind. 1, 122. IV, 3, 189. 193. Tw. I, 1, 26. II, 5, 64. Wint. IV, 3, 50. R2 I, 2, 11. H4A II, 4, 115. 199. 224. 225. 229. 242. III, 3, 18. IV, 1, 87. H4B I, 2, 263. H6A III, 4, 7. H6B I, 1, 8. II, 2, 10. IV, 2, 71. R3 V, 3, 10. Troil. I, 3, 12. III, 3, 278. Cor. II, 1, 166. Tim. III, 4, 10. Caes. II, 1, 277. III, 1, 286. Mcb. III, 1, 42. Oth. I, 3, 3. 83. III, 4, 173. Per. IV, 6, 81. *the s. stars*: H4A I, 2, 16. H4B II, 4, 201. Lr. I, 5, 38. *the deadly s. sins*: Meas. III, 1, 111 (pride, envy, wrath, sloth, covetousness, gluttony, lechery). *all is uneven, and every thing is left at six and s.* R2 II, 2, 122 (= in disorder). *s. years*, proverbially, = a pretty considerable time: *there shall not at your father's house these s. years be born another such*, Wint. IV, 4, 589. *I did that I did not this s. year before*, H4A II, 4, 343. *this s. years did not Talbot see his son*, H6A IV, 3, 37. *I saw not better sport these s. years' day*, H6B II, 1, 2. *it gives me an estate of s. years' health*, Cor. II, 1, 126. *if I could shake off but one s. years*, IV, 1, 55. *for s. long year*, Lr. III, 4, 145. *where a man may serve s. years for the loss of a leg*, Per. IV, 6, 182; cf. also Meas. II, 1, 274. III, 1, 76. Ado III, 3, 134. As III, 2, 235. Shr. Ind. 1, 122. Tw. I, 1, 26. Oth. I, 3, 313. Similarly: *the fire s. times tried this: s. times tried that judgement is*, Merch. II, 9, 63. *tears s. times salt*, Hml. IV, 5, 154. cf. Troil. III, 3, 278.

**Sevenfold**, 1) adj. having seven layers: *the s. shield of Ajax*, Ant. IV, 14, 38. 2) adv. in a proportion of seven to one: Tim. I, 1, 289.

**Sevennight**, a week: Ado II, 1, 375. Wint. I, 2, 17. cf. *Sennight*.

**Seventeen**, seven and ten: Wiv. I, 1, 55. Meas IV, 3, 6. As II, 3, 71. 73. All's IV, 1, 83. Cor. II 2, 104.

**Seventh**, the ordinal of seven: LLL V, 2, 234. As V, 4, 52. 101. H6B II, 2, 17. H8 II, 1, 112. Mcb. IV, 1, 118.

**Seventy**, seven times ten: Cor. IV, 5, 135. Caes. III, 2, 247. IV, 3, 177.

**Sever,** 1) trans. to separate: Tp. V, 187. Merch. III, 2, 118. All's I, 3, 57. H4B I, 2, 227. H6C II, 1, 28. IV, 1, 21. Tit. V, 3, 68. Ant. III, 13, 170. With *from:* Err. I, 1, 119. LLL IV, 3, 365. Tw. V, 279. H6A IV, 5, 48. Lr. IV, 6, 289. Refl.: *s. themselves,* Mids. III, 2, 23.

2) intr. to be separated, to part: *soul and body's —ing,* H8 II, 3, 16. *the —ing clouds,* Rom. III, 5, 8.

**Several,** adj. 1) separate, different, distinct: *all jointly listening, but with s. graces,* Lucr. 1410. *for s. virtues have I liked s. women,* Tp. III, 1, 42. *I suffered the pangs of three s. deaths,* Wiv. III, 5, 110. *I think and pray to s. subjects,* Meas. II, 4, 2. *which they'll know by favours s.* LLL V, 2, 125. Wint. I, 2, 438. H5 I, 2, 207. H6A II, 1, 30. R3 III, 2, 78 (cf. v. 20 and III, 1, 179). V, 3, 193. 194. 198. Cor. IV, 5, 128. IV, 6, 39. Tim. IV, 3, 5. Caes. I, 2, 320. 321. V, 5, 18. Oth. I, 2, 46. Ant. I, 5, 62. 77. III, 13, 5. *each s. and every s.* = every single, every particular: *each s. limb is doubled,* Ven. 1067. *each s. stone, with wit well blazoned, smiled or made some moan,* Compl. 216. *I'll kiss each s. paper,* Gent. I, 2, 108. Mids. V, 424. H4B IV, 1, 170. Mcb. IV, 3, 96. Per. IV, 4, 6. *with every s. pleasure in the world,* H6B III, 2, 363. Rom. I, 3, 83 (Q2 *married).* Caes. III, 2, 247.

2) particular, private: *why should my heart think that a s. plot which my heart knows the wide world's common place?* Sonn. 137, 9. *my lips are no common, though s. they be,* LLL II, 223 (fields that were enclosed were called severals, in opposition to commons, the former belonging to individuals, the others to the inhabitants generally. Halliwell).

3) particular, respective: *my meaner ministers their s. kinds have done,* Tp. III, 3, 88. *each fair instalment, coat and s. crest,* Wiv. V, 5, 67. *each his s. way,* Ado V, 3, 29. *every one his love-feat will advance unto his s. mistress,* LLL V, 2, 124. *their s. counsels they unbosom shall to loves mistook,* 141. *let us take farewell of our s. friends,* R2 I, 3, 51. *discharge your powers unto their s. counties,* H4B IV, 2, 61. H6A I, 3, 77. V, 1, 34. H6B IV, 9, 21. R3 V, 3, 25. Troil. II, 2, 124. 193. Tim. I, 2, 224. Caes. II, 1, 138. Mcb. V, 8, 61. Lr. I, 1, 45. II, 1, 126. Cymb. I, 5, 23. Per. II, 3, 110.

4) different, divers, more than one: *dancing and revelling, or in s. disports,* Lucr. Arg. 11. *these talents of their hair ... I have received from many a s. fair,* Compl. 206 (cf. Hml. V, 2, 20). *with strange and s. noises of roaring, shrieking, howling,* Tp. V, 232. *I have wept a hundred s. times,* Gent. IV, 4, 150. *the s. chairs of order,* Wiv. V, 5, 65. *discover the s. caskets,* Merch. II, 7, 2. *where s. worthies make one dignity,* LLL IV, 3, 236. *the rest have worn me out with s. applications,* All's I, 2, 74. *he sings s. tunes,* Wint. IV, 4, 184. John I, 13. R2 V, 3, 140. H4A III, 1, 157. H4B I, 3, 76. H6A I, 1, 71. H6B II, 1, 128. H8 III, 2, 125. Cor. I, 1, 189. Tim. III, 6, 7. Hml. V, 2, 20 (cf. Compl. 206). Per. I, 4, 18.

**Several,** subst. (used only in the plural) 1) individual, a single person: *not noted but by some —s of head-piece extraordinary,* Wint. I, 2, 226.

2) that which concerns a particular person or question: *the —s and unhidden passages of his true titles,* H5 I, 1, 86. *—s and generals of grace,* Troil. I, 3, 180.

**Severally,** 1) every one in his particular way

and manner: *compare their reasons, when s. we hear them rendered,* Caes. III, 2, 10. *I will dispatch you s.* Tim. II, 2, 196. *hitting each object with a joy: the counterchange is s. in all;* Cymb. V, 5, 397.

2) particularly, singly, every one for himself: *there in the full convive we: afterwards s. entreat him,* Troil. IV, 5, 274.

**Severe,** rigid, hard, merciless: *the boar, that bloody beast, which knows no pity, but is still s.* Ven. 1000 (rhyming). *it shall be merciful and too s.* 1155. *Lord Angelo is s.* Meas. II, 1, 296. *O just but s. law,* II, 2, 41. III, 2, 267. *he who the sword of heaven will bear should be as holy as s.* 276. *with eyes s. and beard of formal cut,* As II, 7, 155. *such strict and s. covenants,* H6A V, 4, 114. *the rigour of —st law,* Rom. V, 3, 269. *you are too s. a moraler,* Oth. II, 3, 301.

**Severely,** rigorously: *kept s. from resort of men,* Gent. III, 1, 108. *that will the king s. prosecute 'gainst us,* R2 II, 1, 244.

**Severity,** rigor, mercilessness: *it is too general a vice, and s. must cure it,* Meas. III, 2, 106. *whereon to practise your s.* H6A II, 3, 47. *law shall scorn him further trial than the s. of the public power,* Cor. III, 1, 269. *beauty starved with her s.* Rom. I, 1, 225.

**Severn,** river in England: H4A I, 3, 98 (*on the gentle —'s sedgy bank).* 103. III, 1, 66 (*sandy-bottomed).* 74. 76. Cymb. III, 5, 17.

**Sew,** subst. see *Sieve.*

**Sew** or **Sow,** vb. to work with a needle and thread; absol.: Gent. III, 1, 307. Tit. II, 4, 43. Hml. II, 1, 77. Per. IV, 6, 194. Trans.: H4A II, 4, 130. Cor. I, 3, 55. Oth. III, 4, 72. With *up: the sleeves should be cut out and —ed up again,* Shr. IV, 3, 148. With an accus. denoting the effect: *s. me in the skirts of it and beat me to death with a bottom of brown thread,* Shr. IV, 3, 137. *and in a tedious sampler —ed her mind,* Per. II, 4, 39.

**Sewer** (O. Edd. *sure* or *shore*) a drain to convey off water and filth: Troil. V, 1, 83. Per. IV, 6, 186. Perhaps also in Troil. II, 2, 71 (O. Edd. *sieve).*

**Sex,** in the plur. = both men and women: *and —es both enchanted,* Compl. 128. In the sing. = womankind, womanhood; once with the article: *to square the general s. by Cressid's rule,* Troil. V, 2, 132. Ordinarily with a possessive pronoun: *their gentle s. to weep are often willing,* Lucr. 1237. *one of my s.* Tp. III, 1, 49. *this testimony of your own s.* Meas. II, 4, 131. Ado I, 1, 170. Mids. II, 1, 240. III, 2, 218. As III, 2, 368. IV, 1, 205. All's II, 1, 86. Tw. V, 330. Wint. II, 1, 108. H6A I, 2, 90. H6C I, 4, 113. Caes. II, 1, 296. Ant. IV, 12, 36. V, 2, 124. Cymb. III, 6, 88. *poor our s.* Troil. V, 2, 109.

**Sexton,** an under officer of the church: Ado IV, 2, 2. 72. V, 1, 262. 267. Shr. III, 2, 175. John III, 1, 324 (*that bald s. Time).* Hml. V, 1, 98. 177. Per. II, 1, 41.

**Sextus,** Roman name: *S. Tarquinius,* Lucr. Arg. 5. 12. *S. Pompeius,* Ant. I, 2, 190. III, 6, 25.

**Seymour,** name in R2 II, 3, 55.

**Seyton,** name in Mcb. V, 3, 19. 20. 29.

**Seyward,** see *Siward.*

**'Sfoot,** corrupted from *God's foot;* an oath used by Thersites: Troil. II, 3, 6.

**Shackle,** to chain, to fetter: *which —s accidents and bolts up change,* Ant. V, 2, 6. *dost in vile misprision s. up my love and her desert,* All's II, 3, 159.

**Shackles,** fetters: *bolts and s.* Tw. II, 5, 62.

**Shade,** subst. 1) the figure of a body produced on the ground by the interception of light: *every one hath one s.* Sonn. 53, 3 (rhyming).

2) the fainter light (implying coolness) produced by the interception of the sunbeams: *coucheth the fowl with his wing's s.* Lucr. 507. *gone to the hedge for s.* Pilgr. 72. *toward that s.* LLL V, 2, 92. *their sweetest s. a grove of cypress trees,* H6B III, 2, 323. H6C II, 5, 42. *let us seek out some desolate s.* Mcb. IV, 3, 1. *to some s.* Cymb. III, 4, 194. Preceded by *in:* Pilgr. 375. Mids. V, 149. By *under:* Pilgr. 144. LLL V, 2, 89. As II, 7, 111. IV, 3, 114. H6C II, 5, 49. V, 2, 13. Tit. II, 3, 16. *fled under s.* Troil. I, 3, 51. Metaphorically: *under the sweet s. of your government,* H5 II, 2, 28.

3) darkness: *the snail shrinks backward in his shelly cave and there in s. doth sit,* Ven. 1035. *sepulchred in thy* (night's) *s.* Lucr. 805. *nor shall death brag thou wanderest in his s.* Sonn. 18, 11. Mids. IV, 1, 101. H4A I, 2, 29. H6A V, 4, 89. H6B III, 2,54. R3 I, 3, 266. 267. Plur. *—s: to dwell in solemn —s of endless night,* R2 I, 3, 177. V, 6, 43.

4) a faint imaginary semblance, opposed to substance: *when to unseeing eyes thy s. shines so,* Sonn. 43, 8. 11.

5) a spirit, a supernatural being: *you moonshine revellers and —s of night,* Wiv. V, 5, 42.

**Shade,** vb. 1) to darken: *bright orient pearl, alack, too timely —d,* Pilgr. 133.

2) to shelter: *good angels fly o'er thy royal head and s. thy person under their blessed wings,* H8 V, 1,162. *ere in our own house I do s. my head,* Cor. II, 1, 211.

3) to hide: *sweet leaves, s. folly,* LLL IV, 3, 44.

**Shadow,** subst. 1) the figure of a body projected on the ground by the interception of the light: *each s. makes him stop,* Ven. 706. *at his own s. let the thief run mad,* Lucr. 997. *love like a s. flies when substance love pursues,* Wiv. II, 2, 215. *he will fence with his own s.* Merch. I, 2, 66. V, 8. Tw. II, 5, 21. R3 I, 1, 26. I, 2, 264. Cor. I, 1, 264. Tim. II, 2, 52. Caes. V, 1, 87. Lr. III, 4, 58. Oth. II, 3, 282. *I am your s., I follow you,* H4B II, 2, 174. *we'll yoke together, like a double s., to Henry's body,* H6C IV, 6, 49 (cf. below).

2) shade; the fainter light and coolness caused by the interception of the sun-beams: *where they lay the s. had forsook them,* Ven. 176. *I'll make a s. for thee of my hairs,* 191. *that cool s. to his melting buttock lent,* 315. *I'll go find a s.* As IV, 1, 222. Tp. IV, 67. R2 III, 4, 25. Tit. II, 3, 15. II, 4, 19. IV, 4, 85. Lr. V, 2, 1. Metaphorically (= shelter): *what mischiefs might be set abroach in s. of such greatness,* H4B IV, 2, 15. *slept within the s. of your power,* Tim. V, 4, 6. *he will come in our s.* Per. IV, 2, 121. Symbol of swiftness: *swift as a s., short as any dream,* Mids. I, 1, 144, which passage is illustrated by the following: *ten times faster than the sun's beams, driving back —s over louring hills,* Rom. II, 5, 6. cf. Wiv. II, 2, 215.

3) darkness: *whose s. —s doth make bright,* Sonn. 43, 5. *that the time may have all s. and silence in it,* Meas. III, 1, 257.

4) the reflected image in a looking-glass or in water: *died to kiss his s. in the brook,* Ven. 162. 1099. *the s. of myself formed in her eye,* John II, 498. 499. *the s. of your face,* R2 IV, 293. *no such mirrors ... that you might see your s.* Caes. I, 2, 58.

5) any image or portrait: *on this sad s.* (Hecuba's image) *Lucrece spends her eyes,* Lucr. 1457. *what is your substance, whereof are you made, that millions of strange —s on you tend? since every one hath, every one, one shade, and you, but one, can every s. lend. Describe Adonis, and the counterfeit is poorly imitated after you;... speak of the spring and foison of the year; the one doth s. of your beauty show, the other as your bounty doth appear,* Sonn. 53, 2. 4. 10. *you away, as with your s., I with these did play,* 98, 14. *to your s.* (Sylvia's picture) *will I make true love,* Gent. IV, 2, 126. *would better fit his chamber than this s.* IV, 4, 125. 202. *how far the substance of my praise doth wrong this s.* (Portia's portrait) *in underprizing it, so far this s. doth limp behind the substance,* Merch. III, 2, 127. *so many of his —s thou hast met and not the very king,* H4A V, 4, 30. *long time thy s. hath been thrall to me, for in my gallery thy picture hangs,* H6A II, 3, 36. Hence = one representing the person of another: *that are the substance of that great s. I did represent,* H6B I, 1, 14. *we'll yoke together, like a double s., to Henry's body and supply his place,* H6C IV, 6, 49.

6) an image produced by the imagination: *such —s are the weak brain's forgeries,* Lucr. 460. *let ghastly —s his lewd eyes affright,* 971. *my soul's imaginary sight presents thy s. to my sightless view,* Sonn. 27, 10. *whilst that this s. doth such substance give that I in thy abundance am sufficed,* 37, 10. *whose s. —s doth make bright,* 43, 5. *dost thou desire my slumbers should be broken, while —s like to thee do mock my sight,* 61, 4. *and feed upon the s. of perfection,* Gent. III, 1, 177. *this is the silliest stuff that ever I heard. The best in this kind are but —s, and the worst are no worse, if imagination amend them,* Mids. V, 213. *—s to-night have struck terror to the soul of Richard,* R3 V, 3, 216. *he takes false —s for true substances,* Tit. III, 2, 80. *when but love's —s are so rich in joy,* Rom. V, 1, 11. *come like —s, so depart,* Mcb. IV, 1, 111. *nature's piece 'gainst fancy, condemning —s quite,* Ant. V, 2, 100. *like motes and —s see them move awhile,* Per. IV, 4, 21.

7) any thing unsubstantial or unreal, though having the deceptious appearance of reality: *love thrives not in the heart that —s dreadeth,* Lucr. 270. *why should poor beauty indirectly seek roses of s.* (i. e. painting) *since his rose is true?* Sonn. 67, 8. *to worship —s and adore false shapes,* Gent. IV, 2, 131. *some there be that —s kiss; such have but a —'s bliss,* Merch. II, 9, 66. *'tis but the s. of a wife you see, the name and not the thing,* All's V, 3, 308. *each substance of a grief hath twenty —s,* R2 II, 2, 14. *nought but —s of what it is not,* 23. *the s. of your sorrow,* IV, 292. 294. 297. *your son had only but the corpse, but —s and the shows of men, to fight,* H4B I, 1, 193. *thy mother's son, like enough, and thy father's s.* H4B III, 2, 140. 141 (not really thy father's son. Mark the quibble between *son* and *sun*). *that you have aught but Talbot's s.* H6A II, 3, 46. *I am but s. of myself,* 50. 62. V, 4, 133. *raught at mountains with outstretched arms, but parted but the s. with his hand,* H6C I, 4, 69. *and be true king indeed, thou but the s.* IV, 3, 50. *poor s., painted queen,* R3 IV, 4, 83. *be not afraid of —s,* V, 3, 215. *I am the s. of poor Buckingham,* H8 I, 1, 224. *hence, horrible s., unreal mockery,* Mcb. III, 4, 106. *life's but a walking s.* V, 5, 24. *the very substance of the ambitious is mere-*

*ly the s. of a dream*, Hml. II, 2, 265. 266. 268. *our monarchs and outstretched heroes the beggars' —s*, 271. *Lear's s.* Lr. I, 4, 251. *haply you shall not see me more, or if, a mangled s.* Ant. IV, 2, 27.

Applied to persons by way of expressing that they have a life scarcely worth the name: *'wander', a word for —s like myself, as take the pain, but cannot pluck the pelf*, Pilgr. 191. *since the substance of your perfect self is else devoted, I am but a s.* Gent. IV, 2, 125. *come, s., come and take this s. up*, IV, 4, 202. *such as you, that creep like —s by him and do sigh at each his needless heavings*, Wint. II, 3, 34. *thou the s. of succession*, H4A III, 2, 99. *which being but the s. of your son, becomes a sun and makes your son a s.* John II, 499. 500.

8) a departed spirit: *then came wandering by a s. like an angel*, R3 I, 4, 53. *that so the —s be not unappeased*, Tit. I, 100. 126. *poor —s of Elysium*, Cymb. V, 4, 97. cf. Pilgr. 191 (quibble). = corpse? Ant. IV, 2, 27 (cf. *Ghost*).

9) any spirit: *gentle s.* (Death) Ven. 1001. *believe me, king of —s* (the fairies) Mids. III, 2, 347. *if we —s have offended*, V, 430 (cf. Mcb. IV, 1, 111. Per. IV, 4, 21).

**Shadow**, name in H4B III, 2, 132. 135. 137. 144. 267. 283.

**Shadow**, vb. 1) to hide: *coal-black clouds that s. heaven's light*, Ven. 533. *his nose being —ed by his neighbour's ear*, Lucr. 1416. *there serve your lust, —ed from heaven's eye*, Tit. II, 1, 130. *thereby shall we s. the numbers of our host and make discovery err in report of us*, Mcb. V, 4, 5.

2) to shelter, to protect: *—ing their right under your wings of war*, John II, 14.

**Shadowed**, adj. shady, dark: *the s. livery of the burnished sun*, Merch. II, 1, 2.

**Shadowing**, full of shapes and images of things: *nature would not invest herself in such s. passion without some instruction. It is not words that shake me thus. Pish! noses, ears and lips*, Oth. IV, 1, 41.

**Shadowy**, full of shade: Gent. V, 4, 2. Lr. I, 1, 65.

**Shady**, dark: Lucr. 881. Mids. I, 1, 71. Rom. I, 1, 142. *thy dial's s. stealth*, Sonn. 77, 7, = the stealthy progress of the shade of the dial.

**Shafalus**, blunderingly for *Cephalus:* Mids. V, 200.

**Shaft**, an arrow: Wiv. III, 4, 24 (*I'll make a s. or a bolt on't*, a proverbial expression, = I will take the risk come what may). Mids. II, 1, 161. Merch. I, 1, 140. Tw. I, 1, 35. H4B III, 2, 52. Troil. III, 1, 128. Tit. IV, 3, 61. Rom. I, 4, 19. Mcb. II, 3, 147. Lr. I, 1, 145. Per. II, 4, 15. III, 3, 6.

**Shag**, shaggy, hairy: *fetlocks s. and long*, Ven. 295.

**Shag-eared**, having hairy ears: *thou s. villain*, Mcb. IV, 2, 83 (M. Edd. *shag-haired*).

**Shag-haired**, having rough and shaggy hair: *a s. crafty kern*, H6B III, 1, 367 (cf. R2 II, 1, 156). Writing of M. Edd. in Mcb. IV, 2, 83; O. Edd. *shag-eared*.

**Shake**, vb. (impf. and partic. usually *shook;* impf. *shaked:* Tp. II, 1, 319. H4A III, 1, 17. part. *shaked:* H5 II, 1, 124. Troil. I, 3, 101. Cymb. I, 5, 76. cf. *love-shaked, unshaked, wind-shaked. shaken:* Sonn. 116, 6. 120, 5. H4A I, 1, 1. H6C IV, 6, 2. Tit. IV, 3, 17). I. trans. 1) to put into a vibrating motion, to cause

to tremble or totter or shiver; abs.: *Macbeth is ripe for —ing*, Mcb. IV, 3, 238 (like fruit). Trans.: *—ing her wings*, Ven. 57. *—s thee on my breast*, 648. *—ing their scratched ears*, 924. *when the wind earth's foundation —s*, 1047. *winds s. the buds of May*, Sonn. 18, 3. *I —d you*, Tp. II, 1, 319. Gent. II, 5, 37. Shr. V, 2, 140. Tw. I, 5, 82. Wint. I, 2, 428. John III, 3, 7. H4A III, 1, 32. H5 II, 1, 124. III, 7, 52. IV, 2, 42. H6B III, 1, 366. H6C I, 1, 20. 47. R3 I, 3, 259. H8 IV, 1, 78. Mcb. III, 4, 50. Hml. II, 1, 92. Oth. II, 1, 6. V, 2, 44. *to s. the beard of a p.* (an act of contemptuous defiance): Hml. IV, 7, 32. Lr. III, 7, 77. *to s. a chain* (to make it jingle): Wiv. IV, 4, 33. Err. IV, 3, 77. H6B V, 1, 145. *to s. one's ears* (a sign of impotent displeasure): Tw. II, 3, 134. Caes. IV, 1, 26. *to s. hands* (cf. *Hand*): Sonn. 28, 6. As V, 4, 107. Wint. I, 1, 32. H6C I, 4, 102 (*s. hands with death* = die). Mcb. I, 2, 21.\*Hml. I, 5, 128. Ant. IV, 12, 20. *let me s. thy hand*, Ant. II, 6, 75. *—s his parting guest by the hand*, Troil. III, 3, 166. *—ing the bloody fingers of thy foes*, Caes. III, 1, 198. *first, Marcus Brutus, will I s. with you*, 185 (viz hands). *to s. the head* (in sorrow, or disapprobation, or denial; cf. *Head*): Ven. 223. Ado II, 1, 377. Merch. III, 3, 15. John III, 1, 19. IV, 2, 188. 231. H6B I, 1, 227. R3 II, 2, 5. Tim. II, 2, 146. 211. IV, 2, 25. Lr. IV, 6, 122. = to nod: H6B IV, 1, 55.

Followed by adverbs or prepositional expressions, to denote an effect: *three winters have from the forests shook three summers' pride*, Sonn. 104, 4. *I will s. thee from me like a serpent*, Mids. III, 2, 261. *I could s. them* (burs) *off my coat*, As I, 3, 16. *dare not s. the snow from off their cassocks, lest they s. themselves to pieces*, All's IV, 3, 191. *—s the rotten carcase of old death out of his rags*, John II, 456. *which* (dust) *with such gentle sorrow he shook off*, R2 V, 2, 31. *hardly to be shook off*, H5 V, 2, 191. *I'll s. thy bulwarks to the ground*, H6A III, 2, 17. *tempest shook down trees*, H6C V, 6, 46. *s. in and out the rivet*, Troil. I, 3, 175. *that thou mayst s. the superflux to them*, Lr. III, 4, 35. H6C IV, 6, 2. Troil. III, 3, 225. Cor. III, 1, 179. IV, 6, 98. 100. Rom. V, 3, 111. Lr. I, 1, 40. IV, 3, 31. Ant. V, 1, 16. Cymb. I, 3, 37. III, 3, 63. With *up*, = to treat with rude violence: *thou shalt hear how he will s. me up*, As I, 1, 30. With *out*, = to blab: *many a man's tongue —s out his master's undoing*, All's II, 4, 24 (suspected passage).

Oftenest with *off*, metaphorically, = a) to lay aside, to discontinue: *shook off my sober guards and civil fears*, Compl. 298. *before I have shook off the regal thoughts*, R2 IV, 163. Used of sleep: Tp. I, 2, 307. II, 1, 304. Mcb. II, 3, 81. Per. III, 2, 23. b) to rid one's self of, to get free from (cf. *to s. from one's self* in Rom. V, 3, 111 and Lr. I, 1, 40): *s. off fifty years*, LLL IV, 3, 243; Cor. IV, 1, 55. *as you s. off one* (misery) *to take another*, Wint. IV, 4, 580. *thou shalt not s. them* (our curses) *off*, John III, 1, 296. *if we shall s. off our slavish yoke*, R2 II, 1, 291. *s. off their sterile curse*, Caes. I, 2, 9. I, 3, 100. Lr. IV, 6, 36. Cymb. III, 1, 52. c) to abandon, to discard, to cast off: *—ing off so good a wife*, All's IV, 3, 8. *discarded and shook off by him*, H4A I, 3, 178. *to s. my friend when he must need me*, Tim. I, 1, 100. *though he do s. me off to beggarly divorcement*, Oth. IV, 2, 157. d) to deny, to refuse: *that I s. off these names*, Tw. V, 76. *these offers he —s off*, Ant. III, 7, 34.

2) to brandish: *he —s aloft his Roman blade*, Lucr. 505. *whilst I can s. my sword*, All's II, 5, 96. *s. he his weapon at us and pass by*, H6B IV, 8, 18. *Clifford shook his sword at him*, R3 I, 2, 159. *—s his threatening sword against the walls of Athens*, Tim. V, 1, 169. *hath ... his conquering banner shook from Syria to Lydia*, Ant. I, 2, 106.

3) to unsettle in any manner, as to cause to waver, to trouble, to frighten, to provoke: *looks on tempests and is never —n*, Sonn. 116, 6. *if you were by my unkindness —n*, 120, 5. *this will s. your —ing*, Tp. II, 2, 87. *faults may s. our frames*, Meas. II, 4, 133. *with a passion would I s. the world*, John III, 4, 39. *so —n as we are*, H4A I, 1, 1. *s. the peace and safety of our throne*, III, 2, 117. *unfasten so and s. a friend*, H4B IV, 1, 209. *this respite shook the bosom of my conscience*, H8 II, 4, 181. *when degree is —d*, Troil. I, 3, 101. *which shall s. him more than if not looked on*, III, 3, 53. *let every rumour s. your hearts*, Cor. III, 3, 125. *—n with sorrows in ungrateful Rome*, Tit. IV, 3, 17. Caes. I, 2, 326. Mcb. I, 3, 140. I, 5, 47. II, 3, 135. III, 2, 19. Hml. I, 4, 55. Lr. I, 2, 91. I, 4, 319. Oth. II, 3, 133. IV, 1, 42. 277. Ant. I, 3, 28 (cf. Tim. IV, 3, 136). III, 13, 81. V, 2, 85. Cymb. I, 5, 76.

II. intr. to tremble violently: *doth make him s. and shudder*, Ven. 880. *my frail joints s.* Lucr. 227. 452. 467. *those boughs which s. against the cold*, Sonn. 73, 3. Tp. I, 2, 206. II, 2, 87. V, 47. Shr. II, 142. III, 2, 169. Wint. IV, 4, 641. John II, 228. V, 2, 143. H4A III, 1, 17. 21. 23. 25. 35. H4B II, 4, 114. H5 I, 2, 154. 216. II Chor. 14. II, 4, 132. H8 V, 5, 32. Troil. I, 3, 97. V, 2, 50. Cor. I, 4, 60. V, 3, 100. Tit. I, 188. Caes. I, 2, 121. I, 3, 4. Mcb. II, 3, 66. V, 3, 10. Oth. III, 3, 207. V, 1, 118. 119. Ant. III, 13, 139. Per. III, 2, 15. *caitiff, to pieces s.* Lr. III, 2, 55. *their vessel —s on Neptune's billow*, Per. III Prol. 44. Used as an interjection: *s., quoth the dove-house*, Rom. I, 3, 33.

**Shakespeare**, name of the poet: Ven. Ded. 10. Lucr. Ded. 8.

**Shale**, shell, husk: *leaving them but the —s and husks of men*, H5 IV, 2, 18.

**Shall** (corrupted to 's: *thou's hear our counsel*, Rom. I, 3, 9. *ise try*, Lr. IV, 6, 246. cf. Cor. I, 1, 130. *I shall* etc. as monosyllables: Tw. IV, 1, 21. John III, 4, 78. H4A IV, 2, 83) 1) denoting an obligation or compulsion, under a necessity imposed by a particular will: *if thou wilt chide, thy lips shall never open*, Ven. 48 (i. e. as far as it lies in my power to prevent them). *thou shalt be my deer*, 231. *no dog shall rouse thee*, 240. *which way shall she turn? what shall she say?* 253 (= what would you have her say?). *thou shalt not rise*, 710. *within her bosom it shall dwell*, 1173. 1186. 1187. *shall we give o'er and drown?* Tp. I, 1, 41 (= is it your wish that etc.). *what shall I do?* I, 2, 300. *seawater shalt thou drink, thy food shall be the fresh-brook muscles*, 462. *hark what thou else shalt do me*, 495. *shall I put him into the basket again?* Wiv. IV, 2, 48. 56. Merch. II, 4, 40. H5 V, 2, 269. Caes. I, 3, 87 etc. etc.

The impf. *should*, as suggesting the idea of a previous determination, used of subjective as well as absolute obligation, = ought to: *beauty within itself should not be wasted*, Ven. 130. *what a horse should have*, 299. *upon the earth's increase why shouldst thou feed*, 169. *thy palfrey, as he should, welcomes the warm approach of sweet desire*, 385. *if I love thee, I thy death*

*should fear*, 660. *what should I do?* 667. *love's golden arrow at him should have fled*, 947. 1066. 1154. *against this coming end you should prepare*, Sonn. 13, 3. *heaven did decree that in thy face sweet love should ever dwell*, 93, 10. 12. *that he should extirpate me*, Tp. I, 2, 125. *you rub the sore when you should bring the plaster*, II, 1, 139. 150. 207. III, 2, 11. Gent. I, 1, 41. II, 6, 18 II, 1, 156. Wiv. IV, 2, 47. Meas. III, 2, 276. IV, 4, 11. Err. II, 1, 10. III, 1, 17. V, 57. Mids. I, 1, 47. II, 1, 242. All's V, 3, 27. Merch. II, 6, 44. H4B IV, 4, 109. Mcb. V, 5, 31. Ant. I, 4, 40. III, 3, 45 etc. etc. cf. *what should I think?* and *what should I say?* in Lucr. 1291. Meas. III, 1, 140. H6A I, 1, 15. Troil. II, 3, 186. Hml. II, 2, 286. Cymb. V, 5, 158.

2) denoting a futurity thought inevitable and answered for by the speaker: *a thousand honey secrets shalt thou know*, Ven. 16. *one sweet kiss shall pay this countless debt*, 84. *which thou unasked shalt have*, 102. *the kiss shall be thine own as well as mine*, 117. *thou shalt have it*, 374. 536. *sorrow on love hereafter shall attend*, 1136. 1137. 1140. 1141. 1144. 1145. 1147. *this fair child of mine shall sum my count*, Sonn. 2, 11. *for this to-night thou shalt have cramps, side-stitches that shall pen thy breath up*, Tp. I, 2, 325. *it shall be done*, 318. *beasts shall tremble at thy din*, 371. *one word more shall make me chide thee*, 476. II, 1, 233. 291. 293. 294. II, 2, 77. Gent. I, 2, 115. II, 5, 40. Meas. II, 2, 14 etc. etc. In subordinate clauses: *they watch the door, that none shall issue out*, Wiv. IV, 2, 53 (those who are watching being supposed to say: none shall issue out). *to humour your cousin, that she shall fall in love with Benedick*, Ado II, 1, 396. *that thou shalt see the difference of our spirits, I pardon thee thy life*, Merch. IV, 1, 368. *that you shall surely find him, lead to the Sagittary the raised search*, Oth. I, 1, 158. Similarly *should: his art with nature's workmanship at strife, as if the dead the living should exceed*, Ven. 292. *this day my sister should the cloister enter*, Meas. I, 2, 182. *why should we proclaim it?* IV, 4, 9. *would make such fearful cries as any mortal body hearing it should straight fall mad*, Tit. II, 3, 104. *thou knewest too well my heart was to thy rudder tied, and thou shouldst tow me after*, Ant. III, 11, 58 etc.

Inevitability and indispensableness implied also in the following expressions: *it shall go hard but I'll prove it by another*, Gent. I, 1, 86. *he that escapes me without some broken limb shall acquit him well*, As I, 1, 134. *he that parts us shall bring a brand from heaven and fire us hence like foxes*, Lr. V, 3, 22 (else his labour will be lost). *then shalt thou see the dew-bedabbled wretch turn and return*, Ven. 703. *if they but hear perchance a trumpet sound, you shall perceive them make a mutual stand*, Merch. V, 77. *you shall mark many a duteous knave*, Oth. I, 1, 44. cf. *a proper man as one shall see in a summer's day*, Mids. I, 2, 89. *your grace shall understand that ... I am very sick*, Merch. IV, 1, 150.

3) denoting futurity in general, the notion of certainty and inevitability being, perhaps, theoretically traceable, but hardly prevalent in the speaker's mind; not only in the first, but in the 2nd and 3d persons: *love's deep groans I never shall regard*, Ven. 377. *going I shall fall*, 719. 1074. Sonn. 93, 1. Tp. II, 2, 45. John III, 4, 78. 87 etc. (*I shall* often used in replying to the orders of superiors: Meas. IV, 4, 21. All's V, 3, 27. H5 IV, 1, 28. 305. IV, 3, 126. Ant. III, 12, 36.

IV, 6, 4. V, 1, 3. 68). *more gentle-kind than of our human generation you shall find many*, Tp. III, 3, 33. *most welcome shall you be*, As II, 4, 87. *if much you note him, you shall offend him*, Mcb. III, 4, 57. *you shall find there a man who is the abstract of all faults*, Ant. I, 4, 8. *wink again, and I will wink; so shall the day seem night*, Ven. 122. *I'll sigh celestial breath, whose gentle wind shall cool the heat*, 190. *if thou survive my well-contented day, when that churl Death my bones with dust shall cover, and shalt by fortune once more re-survey these lines, compare them ...*, Sonn. 32, 1. *this lord of weak remembrance, who shall be of as little memory when he is earthed*, Tp. II, 1, 233. *which I'll waste with such discourse as shall make it go quick away*, V, 301. *there shall he practise tilts and tournaments*, Gent. I, 3, 30. *they are fairies; he who speaks to them shall die*, Wiv. V, 5, 51. *men shall deal unadvisedly sometimes*, R3 IV, 4, 292 (quite = will, expressing frequent occurrence and what is to be expected). Gent. II, 7, 11. III, 2, 10. Meas. I, 1, 57. II, 1, 268. III, 1, 6. 200. 210. Err. III, 1, 123. Ado IV, 1, 226. 229. 232. Mids. I, 1, 10. II, 1, 268. Merch. II, 8, 26. Tw. III, 3, 44. John III, 4, 165. H5 II, 2, 2. IV, 3, 120. R3 V, 3, 201. Mcb. IV, 3, 47. Hml. III, 4, 166. Ant. II, 1, 1. 39. IV, 8, 3. Cymb. IV, 3, 18 etc. Especially after *when: what excuse can my invention make, when thou shalt charge me with so black a deed?* Lucr. 226. *when forty winters shall besiege thy brow, thy youth's proud livery will be a tattered weed*, Sonn. 2, 1. *against that time when thou shalt strangely pass*, 49, 5. Gent. IV, 4, 1. Ado IV, 1, 225. John III, 4, 162. H5 III, 5, 58. H6A I, 6, 16. IV, 1, 113 (cf. R3 IV, 4, 292). 144. H6B I, 1, 239. H6C IV, 7, 80. H8 I, 2, 115 (cf. H6A IV, 1, 113 and R3 IV, 4, 292). Cor. III, 1, 5. Mcb. IV, 3, 45. *when time shall serve:* Pilgr. 333. Ado V, 1, 264. Lr. V, 1, 48.

*Should* in subordinate clauses: *you have taken it wiselier than I meant you should*, Tp. II, 1, 22. *to bear up against what should ensue*, I, 2, 158. *with cat-like watch, when that the sleeping man should stir*, As IV, 3, 117. *told me Hubert should put out mine eyes*, John IV, 1, 69. *to whom he sung that your highness should deliver up your crown*, IV, 2, 152. *I looked a' should have sent me two and twenty yards of satin*, H4B I, 2, 49. *I thought I should have seen some Hercules*, H6A II, 3, 19. *she replied it should be better he became her guest*, Ant. II, 2, 226. *which, being took, should feed on life*, Cymb. V, 5, 51 etc. Once in a principal sentence, quite = would, in the sense of *used: pity was all the fault that was in me, for I should melt at an offender's tears*, H6B III, 1, 126 (cf. *shall* in Wiv. V, 5, 51. H6A IV, 1, 113. R3 IV, 4, 292. H8 I, 2, 115). Oftenest used to form the conditional tense, in all the three persons: Ven. 438. Sonn. 11, 7. 13, 5. 16, 9. 17, 9. Tp. I, 2, 118. LLL IV, 1, 50. IV, 3, 281. Merch. I, 2, 100. As I, 2, 240. All's I, 1, 23. Wint. I, 2, 57. John II, 427. IV, 1, 69. Troil. I, 3, 112. 114. 115. 116. Cor. I, 3, 22. Hml. V, 1, 27. Ant. III, 1, 27. Cymb. III, 4, 153 etc.

4) denoting not so much futurity, as destination, = to be going to, to be to: *how shall that Claribel measure us back to Naples?* Tp. II, 1, 258. *what is he that shall buy his flock*, As II, 4, 88. *if then we shall shake off our slavish yoke, away with me*, R2 II, 2, 291. *this day my sister should the cloister enter*, Meas. I, 2, 182. *when the priest should ask, if Katharine should be his wife*, Shr. III, 2, 161. *his son, that should have married a shepherd's daughter*, Wint. IV, 4, 794. *all so soon as the all-cheering sun should in the forthest east begin to draw the shady curtains from Aurora's bed, away from light steals home my heavy son*, Rom. I, 1, 141. *they all strain courtesy who shall cope him first*, Ven. 888. *striving who should best become her grief*, 968. *would strive who first should dry his tears*, 1092. *they throng who should buy first*, Wint. IV, 4, 612. cf. *who should find them but the empress' villain?* Tit. IV, 3, 73. Especially *as who should say* = as if to say: *anon he rears upright, as who should say 'Lo, thus my strength is tried'*, Ven. 280. *the needle his finger pricks, as who should say 'This glove to wanton tricks is not inured'*, Lucr. 320. *do a wilful stillness entertain, as who should say 'I am Sir Oracle'*, Merch. I, 1, 93. *he doth nothing but frown, as who should say 'If you will not have, choose'*, I, 2, 51. Shr. IV, 3, 13. R2 V, 4, 8. H6A I, 4, 93. IV, 7, 27. H6B IV, 7, 99. Troil. III, 3, 255. Tit. IV, 2, 121. Mcb. III, 6, 42.

5) In an interrogative sentence *shall* equivalent to let me, let us etc. in an imperative sentence: *shall we meet to-morrow? say, shall we, shall we?* Ven. 585 (= let us meet. German: *wollen wir uns morgen wieder treffen?*). *where shall we dine?* Rom. I, 1, 179 (*wo wollen wir essen?*). *shall I entreat a word?* Caes. II, 1, 100 (= let me entreat). *shall we to the court?* Hml. II, 2, 271. *shall we see it?* Oth. III, 2, 5. cf. *do you consent we shall acquaint him with it*, Hml. I, 1, 172.

6) *should* used to express doubt, uncertainty, and even perplexity (as that which ought to be is often contrary to what is indeed): *I should know that voice: it should be —*, Tp. II, 2, 90 (= if I am not mistaken, I know that voice). *how say you?* O, *I should remember him*, Wiv. I, 4, 29. *so should a murderer look, so dead, so grim*, Mids. III, 2, 57 (German: *so mag wol ein Mörder aussehen*); cf. *so should he look that seems to speak things strange*, Mcb. I, 2, 46. *I should believe you*, All's III, 7, 12. *this Doll Tearsheet should be some road*, H4B II, 2, 182 (German: *ist wol eine Strassendirne*). *a man at least, for less I should not be*, H6C III, 1, 57 (*bin ich doch wol nicht*). *there should be one amongst 'em, by his person, more worthy this place than myself*, H8 I, 4, 78. *that should be the Duke of Suffolk?* IV, 1, 40. *if my sight fail not, you should be lord ambassador from the emperor*, IV, 2, 109. *I fear it is, and yet methinks it should not, for he hath still been tried a holy man*, Rom. IV, 3, 28 (*ist doch wol nicht*). *as I remember, this should be the house*, V, 1, 55. *this same should be the voice of Friar John*, V, 2, 2. *it should not be, by the persuasion of his new feasting. I should think so*, Tim. III, 6, 8. 10. *you should be women*, Mcb. I, 3, 45. *there thou shouldst be*, V, 7, 20. *what it should be, I cannot dream of*, Hml. II, 2, 7. *thou shouldst be honest*, Oth. III, 3, 381. *by heaven, that should be my handkerchief*, IV, 1, 164. *may you suspect who they should be that have thus mangled you?* V, 1, 79. *it should appear, it should seem:* Merch. II, 2, 102. III, 2, 275. Wint. IV, 4, 372. Likewise in questions (followed by the inf. of the present even in speaking of things past): *where should this music be?* Tp. I, 2, 387. *where the devil should he learn our language?* II, 2, 69. *where should they find this liquor?* V, 279. *how should this grow?* Wint. I, 2, 431. *how or which way should they first break in?* H6A II, 1, 71. *why should you sigh?* H6C I, 1, 191. *where should I lose that handkerchief?*

Oth. III, 4, 23. *how should she be murdered?* V, 2, 126. Tp. V, 119. Gent. IV, 4, 83. 199. Wiv. V, 5, 36. Ado III, 2, 42. As II, 7, 90. H4B I, 1, 55. IV, 4, 102. H8 III, 2, 203. Tit. IV, 1, 59. Rom. II, 4, 1. V, 3, 190. Tim. IV, 3, 399. Caes. I, 2, 142. Ant. IV, 3, 15. Cymb. IV, 2, 323.

7) *should* with the inf., periphrastically, for the simple verb in subordinate clauses: *may it be that thou shouldst think it heavy unto thee?* Ven. 156. *what am I that thou shouldst contemn me this?* 205. *it cannot be ... thou shouldst strike at it,* 938. *it cannot be that John should entertain one quiet breath of rest,* John III, 4, 133. *say that the debt should double,* Ven. 521. *why should you think that I should woo in scorn?* Mids. III, 2, 122. *I would have sunk the sea within the earth or ere it should the good ship so have swallowed,* Tp. I, 2, 12. *I had rather crack my sinews than you should such dishonour undergo,* III, 1, 27. *'tis time I should inform thee farther,* I, 2, 23. *to know ... why thou ... should raise so great a power,* H6B V, 1, 21. *I have been content you should lay my countenance to pawn,* Wiv. II, 2, 5. *I am not glad that such a sore of time should seek a plaster by contemned revolt,* John V, 2, 13. *'tis not well that you and I should meet upon such terms,* H4A V, 1, 10. *it is no policy that he should come about your royal person,* H6B III, 1, 26. *that he should die is worthy policy,* 235. *a proper jest that Suffolk should demand a whole fifteenth,* I, 1, 133. *who is it like should lead his forces,* H4B I, 3, 81. *scorning it should pass,* Ven. 982. *this is my spite, that, thou being dead, the day should yet be light,* 1134. *'tis not good that children should know any wickedness,* Wiv. II, 2, 134. *that I should be attached in Ephesus, 'twill sound harshly in her ears,* Err. IV, 4, 6. *what a scandal is it that two such noble peers should jar,* H6A III, 1, 70. *it ill befits thy state that thou shouldst stand,* H6C III, 3, 3. *which we disdain should tetter us,* Cor. III, 1, 79. *did sting his high-pitched thoughts that meaner men should vaunt that golden hap,* Lucr. 41. *'tis a passing shame that I should censure thus on lovely gentlemen,* Gent. I, 2, 19. *lest jealousy should disturb the feast,* Ven. 450. 726. 781. *for fear thou shouldst lose thy tongue,* Gent. II, 3, 52. *it mourns that painting should ravish doters,* LLL IV, 3, 260. *to grieve it should be,* Wint. II, 1, 77. *alack the heavy day when such a sacred king should hide his head,* R2 III, 3, 9. *alack, for woe, that any harm should stain so fair a show,* 71. *I melt with woe that winter should cut off our spring-time so,* H6C II, 3, 47. *'twill grieve your grace my sons should call you father,* III, 2, 100. *put not yourself into amazement how these things should be,* Meas. IV, 2, 220. *this I wonder at, that he should be in debt,* Err. IV, 2, 48. *wonder to what end their shallow shows should be presented to us,* LLL V, 2, 307. *didst thou hear without wondering how thy name should be hanged and carved upon these trees?* As III, 2, 182. *which is a wonder how his grace should glean it,* H5 I, 1, 53. *'tis strange that death should sing,* John V, 7, 20. *is it not strange that desire should outlive performance?* H4B II, 4, 283. *it seems to me most strange that men should fear,* Caes. II, 2, 35 etc. etc. Very often after *if: if it should thunder, I know not where to hide my head,* Tp. II, 2, 22. IV, 202. Gent. IV, 1, 14. Err. IV, 1, 78. Ado II, 3, 81. Merch. I, 2, 99. Shr. IV, 3, 13. John IV, 1, 68. Cymb. V, 1, 8. *if* omitted: *should she thus be stolen away from you, it would be much vexation to your age,*

Gent. III, 1, 15. A principal sentence for one with *if: for a store of kingdoms you should wrangle, and I would call it fair play,* Tp. V, 174. *I should knock you first, and then I know after who comes by the worst,* Shr. I, 2, 13.

Elliptical expression by omission of the principal sentence: *that a brother should be so perfidious!* Tp. I, 2, 67. *that a monster should be such a natural!* III, 2, 37. *'mongst all foes that a friend should be the worst!* Gent. V, 4, 72. *O, that a lady, of one man refused, should of another therefore be abused!* Mids. II, 2, 134. H4B V, 4, 27. H6A I, 3, 58. 90. R3 II, 2, 27. Rom. I, 1, 176. 178. Tim. IV, 3, 177. Cymb. II, 1, 58.

8) *shall* and *should*, directly joined with adverbs or prepositional expressions, = shall go, should go: *I shall no more to sea,* Tp. II, 2, 44. *thou shalt to prison,* LLL I, 2, 163. *thou shalt not from this grove,* Mids. II, 1, 146. *you shall hence upon your wedding-day,* Merch. III, 2, 313. *back you shall not to the lady,* Tw. III, 4, 271. II, 4, 125. H4B V, 1, 1. H6B I, 4, 54. V, 3, 27. H6C I, 2, 36. 38. 40. IV, 5, 20. IV, 6, 100. R3 I, 4, 157. III, 2, 91. H8 III, 2, 304. Tim. III, 6, 37. Caes. II, 2, 10. Hml. II, 2, 271. III, 3, 4. Ant. II, 3, 32. *if the bottom were as deep as hell, I should down,* Wiv. III, 5, 14. *if I had a thunderbolt in mine eye, I can tell who should down,* As I, 2, 227. *I should to Plashy too,* R2 II, 2, 120. *that we should on,* H4A IV, 1, 37.

**Shall,** used as a subst.: *mark you his absolute Shall?* Cor. III, 1, 90. 94.

**Shallow,** adj. 1) not deep; used of water: *s. fords,* Lucr. 1329. Sonn. 80, 9 *(—est).* Wiv. III, 1, 17. III, 5, 15. Shr. I, 1, 23. of vessels: *for s. draught and bulk unprizable,* Tw. V, 58. *s. bauble boats,* Troil. I, 3, 35. of wounds: *a s. scratch,* H4A V, 4, 11.

2) superficial, empty, trifling: *that her husband's s. tongue in that high task had done her beauty wrong,* Lucr. 78. *idle words, servants to s. fools,* 1016. *apish, s., inconstant,* As III, 2, 432. H4A III, 2, 61. H4B IV, 2, 50. H5 I, 1, 55. II, 4, 28. H6A II, 4, 16. R3 IV, 4, 361. With *in: you're s. in great friends,* All's I, 3, 45 (you are a superficial judge of the character of great friends. Most M. Edd. *e'en great friends*).

3) silly, stupid: *he throws that s. habit by,* Lucr. 1814. *a very s. monster,* Tp. II, 2, 147. *some s. story of deep love,* Gent. I, 1, 21. *so s., so conceitless, to be seduced by thy flattery,* IV, 2, 96. *the —est thick-skin of that barren sort,* Mids. III, 2, 13. Gent. I, 2, 8. Err. III, 2, 35. Ado II, 3, 10. V, 1, 240. LLL I, 1, 256. V, 2, 305. 870. Merch. II, 5, 35. As III, 2, 58. 62. 67. Tw. III, 4, 137. H4A II, 3, 16. H4B II, 4, 257. H5 I, 2, 295. H6C IV, 1, 62. R3 II, 2, 18. III, 2, 25. IV, 4, 431 *(s. changing* hyphened in Ff). V, 3, 219. Lr. II, 2, 16.

**Shallow,** name in Wiv. I, 1, 4. 77. 110 etc. and H4B III, 2, 5 etc.

**Shallow-hearted,** superficial, trifling: *ye sanguine, s. boys! ye white-limed walls, ye alehouse painted signs,* Tit. IV, 2, 97.

**Shallowly,** sillily, stupidly: *most s. did you these arms commence, fondly brought here and foolishly sent hence,* H4B IV, 2, 118.

**Shallow-rooted,** having no deep root: H6B III, 1, 31.

**Shallows,** subst. flats, sandbanks: Merch. I, 1, 26. Caes. IV, 3, 221.

**Shambles,** a butchery: H6C I, 1, 71. Oth. IV, 2, 66.

**Shame,** subst. 1) the state of being ashamed, the sensation which makes to blush: *red for s.* Ven. 36. *he burns with bashful s.* 49. 69. 76. 558. 728. 808. Lucr. 54. Sonn. 34, 9. Gent. V, 4, 73. Meas. IV, 4, 26. V, 96. LLL V, 2, 583. Mids. III, 2, 285. Merch. V, 217. John V, 2, 153. H5 II, 2, 81. H6A II, 4, 66. R3 I, 3, 143. 273. 274. Troil. III, 2, 43. V, 5, 18. Tim. V, 4, 28. Hml. IV, 7, 189. Ant. I, 1, 31. Cymb. V, 3, 22 etc. Plur. *—s: a thousand innocent —s in angel whiteness beat away those blushes,* Ado IV, 1, 162. *let his —s quickly drive him to Rome,* Ant. I, 4, 72. *With of: glow with s. of your proceedings,* John IV, 1, 114. *for s.! =* blush for yourself, be ashamed: Ven. 379. Sonn. 10, 1. Wiv. III, 3, 133. IV, 1, 66. Mids. II, 1, 74. As III, 5, 18. Shr. II, 26. John III, 1, 128. H6A III, 1, 132. H6B V, 1, 173. 213. V, 2, 72. H6C I, 1, 77. II, 2, 33. III, 3, 100. H8 III, 1, 105. Rom. IV, 5, 22. 65 etc. *for godly s.* Troil. II, 2, 32. *for Christian s.* Oth. II, 3, 172.

2) that of which one ought to be ashamed, cause of reproach, opprobrium: *'tis a passing s. that I should censure thus on lovely gentlemen,* Gent. I, 2, 17. *it were a s. to call her back again,* 51. *the more s. for him that he sends it me,* IV, 4, 138. *why give you me this s.?* Meas. III, 1, 81 (= why do you cast this reproach on me?). *be not thy tongue thy own —'s orator,* Err. III, 2, 10. *s. hath a bastard fame, well managed,* 19. *is't good to soothe him in these contraries? It is no s.* IV, 4, 83. *to desire that were a s.* LLL II, 200. *yield to such inevitable s. as to offend, himself being offended,* Merch. IV, 1, 57. *that argues but the s. of your offence,* H4B IV, 1, 160 (= that your offence is a shameful one). *to tell thee whence thou camest were s. enough to shame thee,* H6C I, 4, 120. *sisters, s. of ladies, sisters!* Lr. IV, 3, 29. *what a wounding s. is this,* Ant. V, 2, 159. Plur. *—s: to find out —s and idle hours in me,* Sonn. 61, 7. *to know my —s and praises from your tongue,* 112, 6. *satisfaction for these deep —s and great indignities,* Err. V, 253. *thy spirits were stronger than thy —s,* Ado IV, 1, 127. *lest day should look their —s upon,* Mids. III, 2, 385. *I would forget the —s that you have stained me with,* Merch. I, 3, 140. *must I hold a candle to my —s?* II, 6, 41. *his grandam's wrongs and not his mother's —s draws those pearls from his eyes,* John II, 168. H4A I, 3, 179. III, 2, 144. H5 III, 5, 47. H6B III, 2, 218. Troil. I, 3, 19. Cor. I, 4, 31. Oth. IV, 2, 49.

3) dishonour, disgrace: Lucr. 223. 1188. 1190. 1202. Sonn. 95, 1. Gent. IV, 4, 67 *(turns me to s.).* V, 4, 106. Wiv. III, 3, 130. IV, 2, 46. Meas. II, 3, 20. 31. III, 1, 140. IV, 4, 35. V, 376. Err. IV, 4, 70. V, 14 *(put me to this s.).* 18. Ado IV, 1, 117. V, 3, 7. LLL I, 1, 118. 132. V, 2, 606. As IV, 3, 96. All's IV, 3, 363 *(received so much s.).* R2 II, 1, 110. 112. H6A I, 4, 46. III, 2, 57. IV, 4, 8. IV, 5, 39. 46. H6B III, 1, 307 *(a s. take all!).* 308. Mcb. III, 4, 66 *(s. itself!)* etc. Followed by an indicative: *'tis s. such wrongs are borne in him,* R2 II, 1, 238. *by should:* John IV, 2, 93. H6B IV, 8, 43. *by to: s. to knighthood,* Lucr. 197. Meas. III, 2, 281. H6A IV, 1, 13. H6B V, 1, 162 etc. *by on or upon: s. on Angelo,* Meas. III, 2, 283. Ado IV, 1, 123. John II, 167. R3 I, 3, 249. *shall it for s. be spoken,* H4A I, 3, 170. *in more s.* 177. *the gods do this in s. of cowardice,* Caes. II, 2, 41. *to*

*your notorious s.* Err. IV, 1, 84. Ado V, 1, 248. LLL V, 2, 358. H4A V, 1, 93. *to do s.* = to disgrace: *to do him s.* Lucr. 597. Sonn. 36, 10. Err. II, 1, 113. LLL IV, 3, 204. Tw. III, 4, 400. V, 317. John IV, 3, 97. V, 6, 13 (= put to the blush). *think no s. of me,* Lucr. 1204.

**Shame,** vb. 1) trans. a) to expose to contempt or reproach, to make ashamed, to put to the blush: *to s. the sun by day and her by night,* Ven. 732. *now shall the devil be —d,* Wiv. V, 2, 124 (cf. H4A III, 1, 57). *my cunning shall not s. me,* Ado II, 2, 56. *they will s. us,* LLL V, 2, 512. *I will not s. myself to give you this,* Merch. IV, 1, 431. *wherein our entertainment shall s. us,* Wint. I, 1, 9. *his mother —s him so, poor boy, he weeps,* John II, 166 (= he is so ashamed of his mother). *would it not s. thee to read a lecture of them,* R2 IV, 231. H4A III, 1, 57. 58. 62 (cf. Wiv. IV, 2, 124). 61 *(to s. him hence).* H6C I, 4, 120. Troil. II, 1, 96. V, 3, 73. Cor. V, 3, 169. Rom. II, 2, 19. Tim. IV, 3, 208. Lr. III, 4, 68. Cymb. IV, 2, 225. V, 1, 32. V, 5, 4.

b) to disgrace: *my posterity, —d with the note,* Lucr. 208. *to s. his hope with deeds degenerate,* 1003. *when life is —d,* 1155. *my name live no more to s. nor me nor you; for I am —d by that which I bring forth,* Sonn. 72, 12. 13. Wiv. III, 3, 102. IV, 2, 43. 236. 238. Meas. III, 1, 117. Ado III, 2, 128. III, 3, 173. As I, 2, 200. Wint. IV, 4, 242. John I, 64. III, 1, 114. R2 II, 1, 112. V, 3, 71. H6A IV, 5, 35. H6B V, 1, 170. R3 I, 2, 155. Troil. IV, 4, 124 (cf. *Seal).* Cor. I, 8, 14. Tit. IV, 2, 112. Rom. II, 5, 23. III, 3, 122. Caes. I, 2, 150. Oth. II, 3, 162 (Ff *ashamed).* Ant. V, 2, 124.

2) intr. to be ashamed, to blush: *Lucrece —s herself to see,* Lucr. 1084. *as —ing any eye should thee behold,* 1143. *thou —st to acknowledge me in misery,* Err. V, 322. *I do not s. to tell you what I was,* As IV, 3, 136. Wint. II, 1, 91. Tit. III, 1, 15. John I, 104. H6C I, 1, 231. II, 2, 142. H8 V, 2, 16. Cor. II, 2, 71. Caes. II, 1, 78. Mcb. II, 2, 64. Hml. III, 2, 155. Per. IV, 3, 23.

**Shame-faced,** bashful: H6C IV, 8, 52. R3 I, 4, 142 (Qq *shamefast,* the usual spelling of the time).

**Shameful,** such as to make ashamed, disgraceful, scandalous: Lucr. 239. 672. 832. 1189. Err. IV, 108. All's V, 3, 66 (O. Edd. *s. hate).* Tw. III, 1, 127. John IV, 3, 62. R2 II, 1, 66. H6B I, 1, 98. II, 4, 37. IV, 1, 95. R3 I, 3, 88. Troil. V, 10, 5. Tit. V, 2, 190. V, 3, 76. Hml. I, 5, 45. Lr. II, 2, 179. Ant. IV, 4, 31.

**Shamefully,** in a manner that may cause shame or disgrace: Sonn. 66, 5. Wiv. V, 5, 234. H6A II, 1, 65. H6B III, 2, 269. R3 I, 3, 276.

**Shameless,** wanting shame, insensible to disgrace, impudent: H4A I, 1, 44. H6A III, 2, 45. H6C I, 4, 120. II, 2, 145. III, 3, 156. Adverbially: *the wrong that she hath s. thrown on me,* Err. V, 202. *grew s. desperate,* Cymb. V, 5, 58 (M. Edd. *shameless-desperate).*

**Shame-proof,** impenetrable to shame: LLL V, 2, 513.

**Shank,** the part of the leg from the knee to the ankle: As II, 7, 161. Plur. *—s:* Rom. IV, 1, 83. Lr II, 2, 41. Cymb. V, 4, 9.

**Shape,** subst. 1) form, figure, outline: *success will fashion the event in better s.* Ado IV, 1, 237. *in every lineament, branch, s. and form,* V, 1, 14. *the s.*

*of love's Tyburn* (the gallows) LLL IV, 3, 54. *the s. of his leg*, Tw. II, 3, 170. Cymb. IV, 2, 309. *s. of likelihood*, H4A I, 1, 58. *the front of heaven was full of fiery —s*, III, 1, 14. *that gave it* (action) *surmised s.* Troil. I, 3, 17. 313. 385. *what convenience both of time and means may fit us to our s.* Hml. IV, 7, 151 (for our form of proceeding).*I'll move the king to any s. of thy preferment*, Cymb. I, 5, 71. *nature's own s. of bud, bird* etc. Per. V Prol. 6.

Used of the form of living beings, especially of men: Ven. 294. Lucr. 597. 1529. Sonn. 24, 10. 62, 6. 113, 6. Tp. I, 2, 284. 303. 478. III, 1, 56. III, 3, 31. 37. IV, 185. V, 291. Gent. IV, 1, 56. V, 4, 109. Wiv. IV, 4, 60. Meas. II, 1, 3. Err. II, 2, 199. Ado III, 1, 96. LLL II, 59. 60. V, 2, 288. Mids. II, 1, 32. 66. III, 1, 142. Merch. III, 2, 278. As V, 4, 126. All's I, 1, 71. Tw. I, 5, 280. Wint. IV, 4, 27. John I, 138. 144. R2 V, 1, 26. H6A II, 3, 69. V, 3, 35. 36. 38. H6B V, 1, 158. H6C III, 2, 192. R3 IV, 4, 286. Troil. I, 2, 275. I, 3, 179. Cor. I, 4, 35. Rom. I, 4, 55. III, 3, 122. 125. 126. 130. Caes. II, 1, 253. Mcb. III, 4, 102. Hml. III, 2, 394. Lr. I, 2, 8. IV, 2, 67. Ant. IV, 8, 26. IV, 14, 14. *to worship shadows and adore false —s*, Gent. IV, 2, 131.

2) external appearance, semblance: *you in every blessed s. we know*, Sonn. 53, 12. *I would my husband would meet him in this s.* Wiv. IV, 2, 87. IV, 4, 44. V, 1, 22. *she cannot love, nor take no s. nor project of affection*, Ado III, 1, 55. *in the s. of two countries at once*, III, 2, 34. *if commotion appeared in his true s.* H4B IV, 1, 37. H5 IV, 8, 56. H6B III, 1, 79. R3 II, 2, 27. H8 I, 1, 196. Tim. II, 2, 119. III, 2, 80. IV, 3, 430. Hml. I, 4, 43. I, 5, 54. II, 2, 629. Lr. I, 4, 331. II, 3, 7.

3) any thing bodied forth by the imagination: *full of forms, figures, —s*, LLL IV, 2, 69. V, 2, 773. *the poet's pen turns them to —s*, Mids. V, 16. *so full of —s is fancy*, Tw.I,1,14. *find —s of grief, more than himself, to wail*, R2 II, 2, 22. *full of nimble fiery and delectable —s*, H4B IV, 3, 108. *—s and forms of slaughter*, Troil. V, 3, 12. *imagination to give them s.* Hml. III, 1, 129. *in forgery of —s and tricks*, IV, 7, 90.

**Shape**, vb. (impf. and partic. —*d*), 1) trans. a) to mould, to form; absol.: *let time s.* H4B III, 2, 358. With an accus.: *to the forge with it, s. it*, Wiv. IV, 2, 240. *some pastime, such as the shortness of the time can s.* LLL IV, 3, 378. *all the other gifts appertinent to man, as the malice of this age —s them*, H4B I, 2, 195. *to s. my legs of an unequal size*, H6C III, 2, 159. V, 6, 78. R3 I, 1, 14. *that —s man better*, Cor. IV, 6, 92. *nor age nor honour shall s. privilege*, Tit. IV, 4, 57. *a divinity that —s our ends*, Hml. V, 2, 10. *he'll s. his old course in a country new*, Lr. I, 1, 190. *it is —d like itself*, Ant. II, 7, 47. With *to*, = to adjust, to make conformable: *—s her sorrow to the beldam's woes*, Lucr. 1458. *it —s them to your feature*, Sonn. 113, 10. *and s. his service wholly to my hests*, LLL V, 2, 65. *s. thou thy silence to my wit*, Tw. I, 2, 61. b) to image, to body forth; absol.: *such —ing fantasies*, Mids. V, 5. With an accus.: *when I do s. in forms imaginary the unguided days*, H4B IV, 4, 58. *it is the weakness of mine eyes that —s this monstrous apparition*, Caes. IV, 3, 277. *my hopes do s. him for the governor*, Oth. II, 1, 55. *my jealousy —s faults that are not*, III, 3, 148. With a double accus.: *s. every*

*bush a devil*, Lucr. 973. With *out: I have —d out a man*, Tim. I, 1, 43.

2) intr.; with *to*, = to be conformable, to square, to suit: *their dear loss, the more of you 'twas felt, the more it —d unto my end of stealing them*, Cymb. V, 5, 346.

**Shapeless**, 1) not shaped into a regular form, formless: *who wears a garment s. and unfinished?* Ven. 415. *wear out thy youth with s. idleness*, Gent. I, 1, 8 (like a stone unwrought).*to set a form upon that indigest which he hath left so s. and so rude*, John V, 7, 27.

2) deformed, ugly: *a hideous s. devil*, Lucr. 973. *ill faced, worse bodied, s. everywhere*, Err. IV, 2, 20. *disguised like Muscovites, in s. gear*, LLL V, 2, 303. cf. *Featureless* and *Sightless*.

**Shard-borne**, borne through the air by scaly wings or rather wing-cases: *the s. beetle*, Mcb. III, 2, 42.

**Sharded**, the same: *the s. beetle*, Cymb. III, 3, 20.

**Shards**, 1) fragments of pottery, potsherds: *s., flints and pebbles should be thrown on her*, Hml. V, 1, 254.

2) the scaly wing-cases of beetles: *they are his s. and he their beetle*, Ant. III, 2, 20.

**Share**, subst. portion allotted to one in a company: Pilgr. 181. H6B IV, 1, 14. Troil. II, 3, 230. Hml. III, 2, 290. With *in: I shall have s. in this most happy wreck*, Tw. V, 273. H4A II, 1, 101. With *of:* Shr. V, 1, 146. H5 IV, 3, 22. H6C I, 4, 129.

**Share**, vb. 1) to divide in portions: *let us s.* H4A II, 2, 104. II, 4, 199. *while all is —d and all is borne away*, H6B I, 1, 228. R3 I, 3, 159. *the latest of my wealth I'll s. amongst you*, Tim. IV, 2, 23.

2) to partake of, to enjoy or suffer in common with others; absol.: *didst not thou s.?* Wiv. II, 2, 14. Trans.: Sonn. 47, 8. Wiv. III, 2, 40. Mids. III, 2, 198. As V, 4, 180. All's II, 1, 3. R2 II, 1, 273. Rom. I, 3, 93. Tim. I, 1, 263 (*we'll s. a bounteous time in pleasures*). Caes. IV, 1, 15. Mcb. IV, 3, 198. *to s. with* = to enjoy or suffer in common with: *such gifts that heaven shall s. with you*, Meas. II, 2, 147. Troil. I, 3, 368. II, 3, 178. Oth. III, 4, 95. Intr., with *in: every one shall s. in the gains*, Mcb. IV, 1, 40. *there is an art which in their piedness —s with great creating nature*, Wint. IV, 4, 87 (which contributes as much as nature to make them pied).

3) to receive as one's portion, to experience, to enjoy or suffer: *many Trojan mothers, —ing joy to see their youthful sons bright weapons wield*, Lucr. 1431. *my part of death, no one so true did s. it*, Tw. II, 4, 59. *the least of you shall s. his part thereof*, R3 V, 3, 268. *that book in many's eyes doth s. the glory, that in gold clasps locks in the golden story*, Rom. I, 3, 91. With *from*, = to receive from, to gain from or at the expense of: *I would not lose so great an honour as one man more would s. from me*, H5 IV, 3, 32. *what glory our Achilles —s from Hector*, Troil. I, 3, 367. Absol., with *with*, = to go even with, to be as great as, to equal: *and thy goodness s. with thy birthright*, All's I, 1, 73. *think not to s. with me in glory any more*, H4A V, 4, 64. cf. Wint. IV, 4, 87.

**Shark**, subst. the fish Squalus: Mcb. IV, 1, 24.

**Shark**, vb., with *up*, = to pick up, to collect in a dishonest and illegal manner: *young Fortinbras hath in the skirts of Norway here and there —ed up a list of lawless resolutes*, Hml. I, 1, 98.

**Sharp**, adj. 1) keen, having a very thin edge or fine point: Ven. 663. 1112. Lucr. 543. 1138. Pilgr. 134. Tp. IV, 180. V, 138. Meas. II, 2, 115. All's III, 4, 18. IV, 4, 33. Wint. II, 3, 86 (cf. Cymb. III, 4, 36). John IV, 3, 82. R2 I, 2, 9. H6A I, 1, 117. II, 4, 70. H6B III, 1, 347. H8 I, 1, 110. II, 4, 224. Tit. IV, 2, 91. Lr. II, 1, 40. Ant. V, 2, 307. Cymb. III, 4, 36 (cf. Wint. II, 3, 86). Per. IV Prol. 23. IV, 2, 159.

2) very thin, lean: *his nose was as s. as a pen*, H5 II, 3, 17. *strike their s. shins and mar men's spurring*, Tim. IV, 3, 152. *till the diminution of space had pointed him s. as my needle*, Cymb. I, 3, 19.

3) pinching, biting, rough: *s. air*, Ven. 1085. *the s. wind of the north*, Tp. I, 2, 254. *thy (the sky's) sting is not so s.* As II, 7, 188.

4) acrid, acid, bitter: *it is a most s. sauce*, Rom. II, 4, 84. *s. physic is the last*, Per. I, 1, 72. cf. *some joy too fine, tuned too s. in sweetness*, Troil. III, 2, 25.

5) keen, pungent, sarcastic, acrimonious: *what he gets more of her than is s. words*, Wiv. II, 1, 191. *these s. mocks*, LLL V, 2, 251. *thrust thy s. wit quite through my ignorance*, 398. *s. Buckingham unburthens with his tongue the envious load that lies upon his heart*, H6B III, 1, 156. *thy woes will make them (thy words) s.* R3 IV, 4, 125.

6) harsh, severe, afflicting, painful: *to keep thy s. woes waking*, Lucr. 1136. *in sorrow's s. sustaining*, 1573. *a groan, more s. to me than spurring to his side*, Sonn. 50, 12. *to that place the s. Athenian law cannot pursue us*, Mids. I, 1, 162. *the —est death*, Wint. IV, 4, 809. *bend your —est deeds of malice on this town*, John II, 380. *shall feel this day as s. to them as thorn*, R2 IV, 323. *I feel such s. dissension in my breast*, H6A V, 5, 84. *this one bloody trial of s. war*, R3 V, 2, 16. *give me up to the —est kind of justice*, H8 II, 4, 44. *whet his anger at him; s. enough*, III, 2, 92. *you are a little too s.* V, 3, 74. *our s. wars are ended*, Troil. V, 9, 10. *opportunity of s. revenge*, Tit. I, 137. *we'll be as s. with you*, 410. *s. misery had worn him to the bones*, Rom. V, 1, 41. *—er than a serpent's tooth it is to have a thankless child*, Lr. I, 4, 310. *necessity's s. pinch*, II, 4, 214. *do not please s. fate to grace it with your sorrows*, Ant. IV, 14, 135. *there cannot be a pinch in death more s.* Cymb. I, 1, 131. *you that have a —er* (life) *known*, III, 3, 31. *forbear s. speeches to her*, III, 5, 39. *we'll enforce it from thee by a s. torture*, IV, 3, 12. *I wait the —est blow*, Per. I, 1, 55.

7) eager, keen: *an empty eagle, s. by fast*, Ven. 55. *s. hunger by the conquest satisfied*, Lucr. 422. *blunt the —est intents*, Sonn. 115, 7. *you are not s. enough*, Gent. III, 2, 67. *fit thy consent to my s. appetite*, Meas. II, 4, 161. *how fiery and how s. he looks*, Err. IV, 4, 53. *thy s. envy*, Merch. IV, 1, 126. *my falcon now is s. and passing empty*, Shr. IV, 1, 193. *roared with s. constraint of hunger*, All's III, 2, 121. *goaded with most s. occasions*, V, 1, 14. *my desire, more s. than filed steel*, Tw. III, 3, 5. *with spirit of honour edged more —er than your swords*, H5 III, 5, 39. *let him greet England with our s. defiance*, 37. *though you bite so s. at reasons*, Troil. II, 2, 33. *his great love, s. as his spur*, Mcb. I, 6, 23. *though inclination be as s. as will*, Hml. III, 3, 39. *so s. are hunger's teeth*, Per. I, 4, 45.

8) subtle, witty, nice, acute: *voluble and s. discourse*, Err. II, 1, 92. *a good s. fellow*, Ado I, 2, 19. *a s. wit matched with too blunt a will*, LLL II, 49 (cf.

V, 2, 398). *your reasons have been s. and sententious,* LLL V, 1, 3. *these nice s. quillets of the law*, H6A II, 4, 17. *alleged many s. reasons*, H8 II, 1, 14.

9) shrill: *it* (this tune) *is too s.* Gent. I, 2, 91. cf. Troil. III, 2, 25.

Adverbially: Err. IV, 4, 53. H5 III, 5, 39. H8 III, 2, 92. Troil. II, 2, 33. see above.

**Sharp**, subst. an acute and shrill sound: *the lark, straining harsh discords and unpleasing —s*, Rom. III, 5, 28.

**Sharpen**, to make more keen and eager: (appetite) *—ed in his former might*, Sonn. 56, 4. *now she —s: well said, whetstone!* Troil. V, 2, 75. *s. with cloyless sauce his appetite*, Ant. II, 1, 25. *it pierces and —s the stomach*, Per. IV, 1, 29.

**Sharp-ground**, whetted: Rom. III, 3, 44.

**Sharp-looking**, emaciated, lean (?) or looking hungry (?): *a needy, hollow-eyed, s. wretch, a living deadman*, Err. V, 240.

**Sharply**, 1) keenly, pungently: *for s. he did think to reprehend her*, Ven. 470. *relish all as s., passion as they*, Tp. V, 23. *my greatest grief, though little he do feel it, set down s.* All's III, 4, 33. *feel the treason s.* Cymb. III, 4, 88.

2) in a quick and cutting manner: *a terrible oath, with a swaggering accent s. twanged off*, Tw. III, 4, 198.

**Sharpness**, severity, harshness: *contempt nor bitterness were in his pride or s.* All's I, 2, 37. *the best quarrels are cursed by those that feel their s.* Lr. V, 3, 57. *thou must not take my former s. ill*, Ant. III, 3, 38.

**Sharp-pointed**, having a sharp point: R3 I, 2, 175.

**Sharp-provided** (not hyphened in O. Edd.), see *Provide*.

**Sharp-quilled**, having sharp quills: H6B III, 1, 363.

**Sharp-toothed**, having sharp teeth: *s. unkindness*, Lr. II, 4, 137.

**Shatter**, to crack, to split, to break into pieces: *a sigh so piteous and profound that it did seem to s. all his bulk and end his being*, Hml. II, 1, 95.

**Shave** (partic. *—d*; attributively *—n*), 1) to strip of the hair or beard: *s. the head*, Meas. IV, 2, 187. *the —n Hercules*, Ado III, 3, 145. *Bardolph was —d*, H4A III, 3, 168. *I'll s. your crown*, H6B II, 1, 51.

2) to cut off with a razor: *were I the wearer of Antonius' beard, I would not s. it*, Ant. II, 2, 8.

**Shaw**, name of a clergyman in R3 III, 5, 103.

**She** (apostrophized in John III, 1, 56: *sh' adulterates hourly*; M. Edd. *she adulterates*), fem. pers. pron.; obj. case *her*: Ven. 7. 25. 35. 38. 40. 41 etc. 29. 53. 264. 307 etc. *poor she*, Lucr. 1674. Demonstratively: *mastering her that foiled the god of fight*, Ven. 114. *where is she so fair whose womb disdains thy husbandry?* Sonn. 3, 5. *she that you gaze on so*, Gent. II, 1, 46. *she that hath love's wings to fly*, II, 7, 11. *I come to her in white*, Wiv. V, 2, 6. V, 5, 209. *fetch forth the lazar kite of Cressid's kind, Doll Tearsheet she by name*, H5 II, 1, 81. *cast from her his dearest one*, Cymb. V, 4, 61 etc. Reflexively: *my Muse holds her still*, Sonn. 85, 1. *she opposes her against my will*, Gent. III, 2, 26. *there will she hide her*, Ado III, 1, 11. *bid Bianca make her ready*, Shr. IV, 4, 63. *arms her with the boldness of a wife*, Wint. I, 2, 184. *bowed her to the people*, H8 IV, 1, 85. *doth she not count her blest*, Rom. III, 5, 144 etc. *she for her: for* *she that was thy Lucrece*, Lucr. 1682. Tp. III, 2, 109. *detest myself also as well as she*, Meas. II, 1, 76 (Elbow's speech). *she should this Angelo have married*, III, 1, 221. *but she I can hook to me*, Wint. II, 3, 6. *for she that scorned at me, now scorned of me*, R3 IV, 4, 102 (Qq one). *praise him that got thee, she that gave thee suck*, Troil. II, 3, 252. *the earth hath swallowed all my hopes but she*, Rom. I, 2, 14. *you have seen Cassio and she together*, Oth. IV, 2, 3. *so saucy with the hand of she here*, Ant. III, 13, 98. *her for she? her I love now doth grace for grace and love for love allow*, Rom. II, 3, 85 (but perhaps *who* omitted before *doth*).

Substantively, = 1) woman: *I think my love as rare as any she belied with false compare*, Sonn. 130, 14. *you are the cruellest she alive*, Tw. I, 5, 259. *if I spared any that had a head to hit, either young or old, he or she, cuckold or cuckold-maker*, H8 V, 4, 25. *that she beloved knows nought that knows not this*, Troil. I, 2, 314. *that she was never yet that ever knew love got so sweet as when desire did sue*, 316. *the shes of Italy should not betray mine interest*, Cymb. I, 3, 29. *apes and monkeys 'twixt two such shes would chatter this way*, I, 6, 40. *Doctor She*, All's II, 1, 82. *I love thee not a jar o'the clock behind what lady she her lord*, Wint. I, 2, 44 (i. e. a woman that is a lady). 2) mistress: *the ladies did change favours, and then we, following the signs, wooed but the sign of she*, LLL V, 2, 469. *the fair, the chaste and unexpressive she*, As III, 2, 10. *I was wont to load my she with knacks*, Wint. IV, 4, 360. *I have and I will hold the quondam Quickly for the only she*, H5 II, 1, 83.

Adjectively, = female: *a she angel*, Wint. IV, 4, 211. *the she bear*, Merch. II, 1, 29. *put stuff to some she beggar*, Tim. IV, 3, 273. *you she foxes*, Lr. III, 6, 24. *a she lamb*, As III, 2, 86. *my good she Mercury*, Wiv. II, 2, 82. *you she knight errant*, H4B V, 4, 25. *she wolf of France*, H6C I, 4, 111.

**Sheaf**, subst. a bundle of stalks of corn bound together: Tit. V, 3, 71. Plur. *sheaves*: Sonn. 12, 7.

**Sheaf**, vb. to bind up stalks of corn in a bundle: *they that reap must s. and bind*, As III, 2, 113.

**Shealed**, shelled: *that's a s. peascod*, Lr. I, 4, 219.

**She-angel**, a female angel: Wint. IV, 4, 211.

**Shear** (impf. *shore*, partic. *shorn*. Partic. *shore* used by Thisbe, for the sake of the rhyme, in Mids. V, 347) to cut with shears or scissors: *before the golden tresses were shorn away*, Sonn. 68, 6. *have shore with shears his thread of silk*, Mids. V, 347. *pure grief shore his old thread in twain*, Oth. V, 2, 206. Used for the cutting of wool from sheep: As II, 4, 79. Wint. IV, 3, 35. H6C II, 5, 37. *—ing*, substantively: Wint. IV, 4, 77.

**Shearer**, one that cuts wool from sheep: Wint. IV, 3, 44. 130.

**Shearing**, = sheep-shearing: Wint. IV, 4, 77.

**Shearman**, one whose occupation is to shear cloth: H6B IV, 2, 141.

**Shears**, a cutting instrument consisting of two blades: *there went but a pair of s. between us*, Meas. I, 2, 29 (i. e. we are both of the same piece). Mids. V, 348. *the s. of destiny*, John IV, 2, 91. 196.

**Sheath**, a scabbard: H4A II, 4, 273. H6B IV, 10, 61. Tit. II, 1, 41. Rom. V, 3, 170.

**Sheathe**, 1) to put in a scabbard: H5 III, 1, 21. IV, 2, 23. Tit. I, 85. 204. Caes. IV, 3, 107. Mcb. V, 7, 20. Hence = to cover, to hide as in a case, to put

up in general: *whose tushes never —d he whetteth still*, Ven. 617. *her eyes had —d their light*, Lucr. 397. *s. thy impatience*, Wiv. II, 3, 88 (the host's speech). Especially applied to weapons plunged into a person's body: *—d the tusk in his groin*, Ven. 1116. *she —d in her breast a knife*, Lucr. 1723. John. IV, 3, 80. H6C V, 5, 70. H8 I, 2, 210. Tit. II, 1, 54. V, 3, 112. 2) to furnish with a scabbard: *Walter's dagger was not come from —ing*, Shr. IV, 1, 138.

**Sheaved**, made of straw: *her s. hat*, Compl. 31.

**Sheba**, see *Saba*.

**She-bear**, female bear: Merch. II, 1, 29.

**She-beggar**, female beggar: Tim. IV, 3, 273.

**Shed**, vb. (impf. and part. *shed*) 1) to let fall, to scatter, to cast: *the seeded pride must or now be cropped, or, —ing, breed a nursery of like evil*, Troil. I, 3, 319.

2) to suffer or cause to flow out, to pour: *a bombard that would s. his liquor*, Tp. II, 2, 22. *a wench that s. her milk*, All's IV, 3, 124. Oftenest used of blood and tears; of blood: Ven. 665. Merch. IV, 1, 309. 325. John II, 49. R2 I, 3, 57. H4A I, 3, 134. H5 IV, 3, 61. H6A IV, 6, 19. H6B I, 1, 118. III, 2, 227. IV, 1, 52. H6C V, 5, 53. R3 I, 4, 195. V, 5, 25. Cor. I, 6, 57. III, 1, 76. IV, 5, 76. V, 3, 117. Tit. III, 1, 4. Rom. III, 1, 154. III, 2, 71. Caes. III, 1, 258. Mcb. III, 4, 75. Oth. V, 2, 3. Per. I, 2, 88. Of tears: Lucr. 683. 1376. 1549. Sonn. 34, 13. Gent. II, 3, 10. 34. III, 1, 230. Mids. V, 70. Merch. III, 1, 101. Shr. Ind. 1, 120. 2, 66. All's I, 1, 92. Wint. III, 2, 194. 240. V, 2, 156. 157. R2 I, 4, 5. III, 3, 165. H4A III, 1, 94. H6A IV, 4, 19. H6B I, 1, 118. H6C I, 4, 161. 162. II, 5, 106. V, 6, 64. R3 I, 2, 156. IV, 4, 321. H8 III, 2, 429. Tit. I, 105. 162. 389. II, 3, 289. III, 1, 267. V, 3, 152. 167. Caes. III, 2, 173.

**Sheen**, shine, brightness, splendour: *they never meet in grove or green, by fountain clear, or spangled starlight s., but they do square*, Mids. II, 1, 29. *thirty dozen moons with borrowed s.* Hml. III, 2, 167. In both passages rhyming.

**Sheep**, the animal Ovis: Gent. I, 1, 74. 76. 81. 82. 88. 89. 91. 92. 93. 96. LLL II, 220. 221. IV, 3, 8. H6C V, 6, 8. Troil. III, 3, 315. Lr. III, 4, 109. Unchanged in the plural: Ven. 532. 685. Tp. IV, 1, 62. LLL IV, 3, 7. Merch. I, 3, 72. As III, 2, 29. 64. Wint. III, 3, 66. 131. John IV, 1, 17. H6A I, 5, 29. V, 5, 54. H6B IV, 2, 68. IV, 3, 4. V, 1, 27. H6C II, 5, 43. Cor. II, 1, 273. Tit. IV, 4, 91. Lr. III, 6, 44. *to wash your liver as clean as a sound —'s heart*, As III, 2, 444. *—'s guts*, Ado II, 3, 61. *—'s leather*, Shr. III, 2, 58. Symbol of harmlessness: H6A I, 3, 55. of stupidity: Gent. I, 1, 74 etc. Err. IV, 1, 93. LLL IV, 3, 8. V, 1, 53. 59. Wint. IV, 3, 130. Hml. V, 1, 125. of cowardice: H6A I, 5, 29. Caes. I, 3, 105. Quibbling with sheep: Gent. I, 1, 73. Err. IV, 1, 93. LLL II, 219.

**Sheep-biter**, evidently = a morose, surly and malicious fellow: *wouldst thou not be glad to have the niggardly rascally s.* (i. e. Malvolio) *come by some notable shame?* Tw. II, 5, 6 (Dyce: "a cant term for a thief").

**Sheep-biting**, morose, surly, malicious: *show your s. face*, Meas. V, 359.*

**Sheep-cote**, the cottage of a shepherd: As II, 4, 84. IV, 3, 78. Wint. IV, 4, 808. Lr. II, 3, 18.

**Sheep-hook**, a hook fastened to a pole used by shepherds: Wint. IV, 4, 431.

**Sheep-shearing**, a feast made on the occasion of shearing sheep: Wint. IV, 3, 125. 128. IV, 4, 3. 69. *our s. feast*, IV, 3, 39.

**Sheep-skin**, the skin of sheep: Hml. V, 1, 123.

**Sheep-whistling**, whistling after sheep, tending sheep: Wint. IV, 4, 805.

**Sheer**, clear, pure: *thou s., immaculate and silver fountain*, R2 V, 3, 61. *if she say I am not fourteen pence on the score for s. ale*, Shr. Ind. 2, 25 (= unmixed? or ale alone, nothing but ale?).

**Sheet**, subst. 1) any thing expanded: *such — s of fire*, Lr. III, 2, 46.

2) a large piece of linen: Wint. IV, 3, 5. 23. H6B II, 4, 105. 107. Used to shroud the dead: Rom. V, 3, 97. Hml. V, 1, 103. as a part of bed-furniture: Lucr. 472. plur. —*s:* Ven. 398. Shr. IV, 1, 205. Wint. I, 2, 327. H4B II, 4, 244 (*a pair of —s*). H5 II, 1, 88. II, 3, 15. H6B III, 2, 174. Hml. I, 2, 157. Lr. IV, 6, 118. Oth. I, 3, 393. II, 3, 29. IV, 2, 105. IV, 3, 22. 25. Ant. I, 2, 41. Cymb. I, 6, 133. II, 2, 16.

3) a broad piece of paper, as it comes from the manufacturer: *a s. of paper*, Ado II, 3, 138. 140. LLL V, 2, 7. Tw. III, 2, 50.

Punning: Ado II, 3, 144. Tw. III, 2, 50.

**Sheet**, vb. to shroud: *the —ed dead*, Hml. I, 1, 115. *when snow the pasture —s*, Ant. I, 4, 65.

**Sheffield:** *Lord Furnival of S.*, one of Talbot's titles: H6A IV, 7, 66.

**She-fox**, a female fox: Lr. III, 6, 24.

**Shekels**, writing of M. Edd. for *sickles* of O. Edd. q. v.

**She-knight-errant**, a female knight errant: H4B V, 4, 25.

**She-lamb**, a female lamb: As III, 2, 86.

**Shelf**, 1) a board fixed against a supporter to place things on: Hml. III, 4, 100. Plur. *shelves:* Rom. V, 1, 44.

2) Plur. *shelves* = sandbanks: Lucr. 335. H6C V, 4, 23.

**Shell**, (cf. *Walnut-shell*) 1) the covering of testaceous animals: Lr. I, 5, 27. Per. II, 1, 65.

2) the covering of eggs: Troil. I, 2, 148. Caes. II, 1, 34. Hml. V, 2, 193.

**Shelly**, testaceous: *his* (the snail's) *s. cave*, Ven. 1034.

**Shelter**, subst. 1) a covered place affording safety: Tp. II, 2, 40. Wiv. I, 3, 91. As II, 6, 17. R2 II, 1, 264. H6C V, 2, 12. Ant. III, 1, 8. Per. V, 1, 51.

2) protection: *you will ensconce your rags under the s. of your honour*, Wiv. II, 2, 29. *thou shalt prove a s. to thy friends*, H4B IV, 4, 42. *his feigned ecstasies shall be no s. to these outrages*, Tit. IV, 4, 22. *the gods to their dear s. take thee*, Lr. I, 1, 185 (Qq *protection*).

**Shelter**, vb. 1) tr. a) to cover and protect: *to s. thee from tempest*, Ven. 238. R2 III, 4, 50.

b) to cover and disguise: *he was the covert'st —ed traitor*, R3 III, 5, 33.

2) refl. to betake one's self to a safe place: *let there come a tempest of provocation, I will s. me here*, Wiv. V, 5, 24.

3) intr. to take shelter, to seek a safe place: *come, s.* H4A II, 2, 1.

**Shelving**, projecting like a shelf: *her chamber is aloft, far from the ground, and built so s. that one cannot climb it without apparent hazard of his life*, Gent. III, 1, 115.

**Shelvy**, consisting of a sandbank, shallow: *I had been drowned, but that the shore was s. and shallow*, Wiv. III, 5, 15.

**She-Mercury**, female Mercury: Wiv. II, 2. 82.

**Shent**, put to the blush, blamed, reproached, reviled (partic.): *here comes my master; we shall all be s.* Wiv. I, 4, 38. *I am s. for speaking to you*, Tw. IV, 2, 112. *do you hear how we are s. for keeping your greatness back?* Cor. V, 2, 104. *how in my words soever she be s., to give them seals never my soul consent*, Hml. III, 2, 416. In Troil. II, 3, 86 Q *he sate our messengers*, Ff *he sent* etc. Some M. Edd. *shent;* but there is no authorized instance of the impf.

**Shepherd**, one who tends sheep: Ven. 455. Lucr. 1502. Pilgr. 167. 271. Gent. I, 1, 75. 76. 83. 88. 89. 92. 93. IV, 4, 97. Meas. IV, 2, 219. LLL V, 2, 913. 923. Mids. I, 1, 184. Merch. I, 3, 85. As II, 4, 44. 61. 71. 78. III, 2, 11. 23. 34. 45. 52. 71. 89. 167. 169. III, 4, 51. III, 5, 49. 63. 76. 82. IV, 3, 19. 40. 65. 156. V, 2, 14. 87. 89. V, 4, 14. 22. 26. Wint. I, 2, 2. IV, 1, 27. IV, 2, 43 etc. H6A I, 2, 72. V, 4, 37 (*a s. swain*). H6B II, 2, 73. III, 1, 191. H6C II, 5, 3. 43. 46. V, 6, 7. Cor. I, 6, 25. IV, 6, 111. Tim. V, 4, 42. Hml. IV, 7, 171. Lr. III, 6, 43. Cymb. I, 1, 150.

**Shepherdess**, a woman that tends sheep: As III, 2, 353. III, 4, 53. III, 5, 77. Wint. IV, 4, 2. 77.

**Sheriff** (cf. *Shrieve*) an officer to whom the execution of the laws in a county is entrusted: H4A II, 3, 70. II, 4, 529. 545. 554. 555. 563. H4B IV, 4, 99 (Q *shrieve*). H6B II, 4, 17. 74. 100. *he'll stand at your door like a —'s post*, Tw. I, 5, 157 (at the doors of sheriffs usually posts were set up, on which proclamations were fixed).

**Sherris**, a Spanish wine, so called from the town of Xeres: H4B IV, 3, 111. 114. 122. 131.

**Sherris-sack**, the same: H4B IV, 3, 104.

**She-wolf**, a female wolf: H6C I, 4, 111.

**Shield**, subst. a buckler: Ven. 104. Lucr. 61. LLL V, 2, 556. H5 III, 2, 9. R3 IV, 3, 56. Cor. I, 4, 24. I, 6, 80. V, 2, 44. Tit. IV, 1, 127. Mcb. V, 8, 33. Ant. IV, 13, 2. IV, 14, 38. Per. II, 1, 132. II, 2, 19.

**Shield**, vb. 1) to guard, to protect: *with safest distance I mine honour —ed*, Compl. 151. *a woman's shape doth s. thee*, Lr. IV, 2, 67. With *from: to s. thee from diseases of the world*, Lr. I, 1, 177. — *ed him from this smart*, Cymb. V, 4, 41. Optatively: *God s. us!* Mids. III, 1, 31. *heavens s. Lysander*, III, 2, 447. *Jove s. thee well for this*, V, 179. With *from:* *heaven s. your grace from woe*, Meas. V, 118. H8 I, 2, 26. Tit. II, 3, 70. *God* omitted: *s. thee from Warwick's frown*, H6C IV, 5, 28.

2) to forefend, to forbid, to avert (optatively): *heaven s. my mother played my father fair*, Meas. III, 1, 141 (i. e. God grant that thou wert not my father's son). *God s. you mean it not*, All's I, 3, 174. *God s. I should disturb devotion*, Rom. IV, 1, 41.

**Shift**, subst. 1) change: *when Fortune in her s. and change of mood spurns down her late beloved*, Tim. I, 1, 84.

2) expedient, resource, contrivance, stratagem, trick: *danger deviseth —s, wit waits on fear*, Ven. 690. *a man here needs not live by —s, when in the streets he meets such golden gifts*, Err. III, 2, 187. *the cleanliest s. is to kiss*, As IV, 1, 78. *I'll find a thousand —s to get away*, John IV, 3, 7. *now there rests no*

*other s. but this*, H6A II, 1, 75. *cursed be that heart that forced us to this s.* Tit. IV, 1, 72. *it is you that puts us to our* —*s*, IV, 2, 176. *dodge and palter in the* —*s of lowness*, Ant. III, 11, 63. In a bad sense, without any apposition: *guilty of treason, forgery and* —*s*, Lucr. 920. *For s. or for a s.* = to serve a turn: *thou singest well enough for a s.* Ado II, 3, 80. *an onion will do well for such a s.* Shr. Ind. 1, 126. *when he was made a shriver, 'twas for s.* H6C III, 2, 108.* *to make s. or to make a s.* = to contrive, to devise: *I hope I shall make s. to go without him*, Merch. I, 2, 97. *you have made s. to run into it* (my displeasure) All's II, 5, 39. *I'll make other s.* H4B II, 1, 169. *the rest of thy low countries have made a s. to eat up thy holland*, II, 2, 25. *I will make s. for one*, H6B IV, 8, 33. *I made a s. to cast him*, Mcb. II, 3, 46.

**Shift**, vb. 1) to change; a) trans.: *what an unthrift in the world doth spend* —*s but his place*, Sonn. 9, 10. *thou runnest before me,* —*ing every place*, Mids. III, 2, 423. *I mean to s. my bush*, Shr. V, 2, 46. *like a* —*ed wind*, John IV, 2, 23. *not to have patience to s. me*, H4B V, 5, 23 (to put on fresh clothes). *unto Southampton do we s. our scene*, H5 II Chor. 42. *my shame will not be* —*ed with my sheet*, H6B II, 4, 107. *he s. a trencher! he scrape a trencher!* Rom. I, 5, 2. *we'll s. our ground*, Hml. I, 5, 156. *should we s. estates*, Ant. V, 2, 152 (= exchange). *to s. a shirt*, Cymb. I, 2, 1. 6. *to s. his being is to exchange one misery with another*, I, 5, 54.

b) intr. = to change, to transform, to metamorphose one's self; to get or come to be by change: *not acquainted with* —*ing change*, Sonn. 20, 4. *thy complexion* —*s to strange effects, after the moon*, Meas. III, 1, 24. *the sixt age* —*s into the lean and slippered pantaloon*, As II, 7, 157. *taught me to s. into a madman's rags*, Lr. V, 3, 186. Hence absol., = to pass by, to fade away: *no object but her passion's strength renews, and as one* —*s, another straight ensues*, Lucr. 1104.

2) to contrive, to devise, to practise; absol.: *injurious,* —*ing time*, Lucr. 930 (cf. 920). *every man s. for all the rest*, Tp. V, 256. *I must cony-catch, I must s.* Wiv. I, 3, 37. *s. and save yourself*, Err. V, 168. With the notion of change: *thou hast* —*ed out of thy tale into telling me of the fashion*, Ado III, 3, 151 (= contrived to get). *let us not be dainty of leave-taking, but s. away*, Mcb. II, 3, 151 (contrive to get away). cf. Lr. V, 3, 186. With an accus. denoting the effect: *I* —*ed him away*, Oth. IV, 1, 79 (contrived to get him away). — In All's II, 1, 147 O. Edd. —*s* unintelligibly, M. Edd. *fits.*

**Shilling**, English coin, the twentieth part of a pound: H4B II, 4, 207. H5 IV, 8, 76. H6B IV, 7, 25. H8 Prol. 12. Plur. —*s*: Wiv. I, 1, 205. Ado III, 3, 84. Tw. II, 3, 20. H4A I, 2, 158. II, 4, 27. III, 3, 83. H4B II, 1, 111. III, 2, 236. H5 II, 1, 98. Plur. *s.*: Wiv. I, 1, 160 (Slender's speech). Wint. IV, 3, 34 (the clown's speech).

**Shin**, the fore part of the leg: Tp. IV, 181. Wiv. I, 1, 294. V, 5, 58. LLL III, 71. 107. 113. 118. 120. As II, 4, 60. Rom. I, 2, 53. Tim. IV, 3, 152.

**Shine**, subst. (cf. *Sheen*) the light emitted by a celestial body; in a proper and a metaphorical sense: *as the bright sun glorifies the sky, so is her face illumined with her eye, whose beams upon his hairless face are fixed, as if from thence they borrowed all their s.*

Ven. 488. *Cynthia for shame obscures her silver s.* 728. *if after two days' s. Athens contain thee*, Tim. III, 5, 101. *in our orbs we'll live so round and safe, that time of both this truth shall ne'er convince, thou showedst a subject's s., I a true prince*, Per. I, 2, 124.

**Shine**, vb. (imperf. and part. *shone*) 1) to give light by emitting rays; used of celestial bodies: Ven. 193. 492. 861. Lucr. 786. Pilgr. 208. Err. II, 2, 30. LLL I, 1, 90. IV, 3, 30. 91. Mids. I, 2, 38. III, 1, 52. 56. 59. III, 2, 380. 432. V, 272. 278. Merch. V, 92. Tw. IV, 3, 34. Wint. IV, 3, 16. H6A III, 2, 31. H6B IV, 1, 98. H6C II, 1, 28. 40. R3 II, 2, 102. V, 3, 278. 285. H8 V, 5, 51. Tit. II, 3, 96. 231. Caes. III, 1, 64. Lr. II, 2, 34. Cymb. III, 4, 139. IV, 4, 34. V, 5, 476. *to s. on sth.:* Sonn. 33, 9. Pilgr. 38. Gent. III, 1, 156. Wiv. I, 3, 70. LLL IV, 3, 69. V, 2, 205. Wint. IV, 4, 455. V, 1, 95. R2 I, 3, 145. H6A I, 2, 3. Tim. IV, 3, 184. *my stars s. darkly over me*, Tw. II, 1, 3. *to s. bright:* Merch. V, 1. Shr. IV, 5, 2. 4. 5. Wint. V, 1, 95. H5 V, 2, 172. *to s. brightly:* Tit. IV, 2, 90. *to s. fair:* H4A III, 1, 142. *to s. hot:* Sonn. 18, 5. H6C IV, 8, 60. *to s. warm:* Ven. 193. *to s. out*, R3 I, 2, 263 (cf. *Out* and *Outshining*).

Metaphorical use: *thou* —*st in every tear*, LLL IV, 3, 33. *when his love he doth espy, let her s. as gloriously as the Venus of the sky*, Mids. III, 2, 106. *so* —*s a good deed in a naughty world*, Merch. V, 91. *foolery* —*s everywhere*, Tw. III, 1, 44. Merch. V, 94. R2 IV, 287. H4A III, 2, 80. H6A I, 2, 75. H6C II, 6, 10. H8 I, 1, 20 (*the French shone down the English*). I, 4, 60. Troil. III, 3, 100. Tim. III, 4, 10. Ant. I, 5, 55. II, 3, 28. Cymb. I, 2, 34.

2) to be bright, to glitter: *his eyes like glow-worms s. when he doth fret*, Ven. 621. —*ing arms*, Lucr. 197. *the* —*ing glory of Ilion*, 1523. *with* —*ing falchion*, 1626. *when to unseeing eyes thy shade* —*s so*, Sonn. 43, 8. 55, 3. 65, 14. Pilgr. 170. Phoen. 33. LLL IV, 3, 246. As II, 7, 146. H4A I, 3, 54. H6A II, 4, 23. H6B III, 1, 229. Tit. II, 1, 19. II, 3, 229. Rom. I, 2, 103. Ant. I, 3, 45. Cymb. V, 4, 89.

3) to be conspicuous: *let it* (desert) *s.* H4B IV, 3, 63. 64. *let desert in pure election s.* Tit. I, 16. *signs of nobleness, like stars, shall s. on all deservers*, Mcb. I, 4, 41. *as upon thee their speeches s.* III, 1, 7. *a quality wherein, they say, you s.* Hml. IV, 7, 74.

4) to be visible: *the subtle* —*ing secrecies writ in the glassy margents of such books*, Lucr. 101. *shall will in others seem right gracious, and in my will no fair acceptance s.?* Sonn. 135, 8 (rhyming); cf. Phoen. 33. With *through*: *these follies are within you and s. through you like the water in an urinal*, Gent. II, 1, 40. *the lightness of his wife* —*s through it*, H4B I, 2, 53. *your spirits s. through you*, Mcb. III, 1, 128.

**Shiny**, bright: *the night is s.* Ant. IV, 9, 3.

**Ship**, subst. a large vessel made to pass over the sea with sails: Tp. I, 1, 50. I, 2, 196. 224. 236. V, 97. 222. 307. Gent. I, 1, 156. Err. I, 1, 78. 93. 101. 104. 113. III, 2, 190. IV, 1, 94. IV, 3, 35. Merch. I, 3, 22. 182. II, 8, 3. 6. 11. III, 1, 3. 6. 19. III, 2, 317. V, 287. Shr. IV, 2, 83. Tw. I, 2, 9. Wint. I, 2, 451. II, 1, 36. III, 3, 1. 93. 99. 112. IV, 4, 790. R2 II, 1, 286. H6A I, 2, 138. III, 1, 186. H6B IV, 9, 32. H6C I, 4, 4. V, 4, 10. R3 IV, 4, 483. Troil. Prol. 3. II, 2, 81. Hml. IV, 6, 19. Oth. II, 1, 22. 25. 79. 83. Ant. III, 7, 36. 39. 60. III, 9, 3. III, 11, 4. 21. III, 13, 22. IV, 14, 59. Cymb. I, 3, 14. IV, 2, 335. Per. I, 4, 61.

86. 92. 100. II Prol. 31. II, 3, 84. III Prol. 50. III, 1, 49. IV, 4, 17. V Prol. 18. Fem.: Tp. I, 2, 12. 227. V, 237. Err. IV, 1, 90. LLL V, 2, 549. Neut.: Gent. III, 1, 281. *to take s.* = to embark: H5 II Chor. 30. Punning upon *ship* and *sheep*: Gent. I, 1, 73. LLL II, 219.

**Ship,** vb. 1) to put on board of a ship, to embark: *to see me —ed,* Gent. I, 1, 54. 72. II, 3, 37. *and —ed, from thence to Flanders,* H6C IV, 5, 21 (F1 *shipt;* M. Edd. *ship*). *that I was —ed at sea, I well remember,* Per. III, 4, 5. With *for: the king is not yet —ed for Ireland,* R2 II, 2, 42. *there I'll s. them all for Ireland,* H6B III, 1, 329.

2) to transport in a ship: *would thou wert —ed to hell,* Tit. I, 206. *may have —ed her hence,* IV, 3, 23. *we will s. him hence,* Hml. IV, 1, 30. *hath —ed me intil the land,* V, 1, 81.

In Oth. II, 1, 47 *—ed,* adjectively, = furnished with a ship, having a ship: *is he well —ed?*

**Shipboard,** preceded by prepositions, = the ship: *shall I fetch your stuff from s.?* Err. V, 408. *to s. get undescried,* Wint. IV, 4, 668.

**Shipboy,** a boy that serves in a ship: John IV, 3, 4. H4B III, 1, 19. H5 III Chor. 8.

**Shipman,** a mariner: Troil. V, 2, 172. Mcb. I, 3, 17. Per. I, 3, 24.

**Shipped,** see *Ship* vb.

**Shipping,** 1) ships, vessels: *he lent me some s.* Ant. III, 6, 27. *our overplus of s.* III, 7, 51. *his s., poor ignorant baubles,* Cymb. III, 1, 26. *what s. and what lading's in our haven,* Per. I, 2, 49. *to take s.* = to take ship, to embark: H6A V, 5, 87.

2) navigation: *God send 'em good s.* Shr. V, 1, 43.

**Ship-side;** *by the s.* = by the side of the ship: Wint. III, 3, 112 (the clown's speech).

**Ship-tire,** a peculiar head-dress, perhaps resembling a ship: Wiv. III, 3, 60.

**Shipwreck,** subst. (O. Edd. *shipwrack;* cf. *Wreck*) the destruction of a ship by rocks or shelves: H6A V, 5, 8. Tit. II, 1, 24. Per. II, 1, 139. II, 3, 85.

**Shipwreck,** vb. (O. Edd. *shipwrack*) to throw destructively on rocks or shelves: *their — ed guests,* Err. I, 1, 115. *—ed upon a kingdom, where no pity,* H8 III, 1, 149. *—ing storms,* Mcb. I, 2, 26.

**Shipwright,** a builder of ships: Hml. I, 1, 75. V, 1, 47.

**Shire,** county: H8 I, 2, 103.

**Shirley,** name in H4A V, 4, 41.*

**Shirt,** a garment worn by men next the body: Wiv. III, 5, 91 (*—s and smocks*). LLL V, 2, 704. 711. 717. H4A III, 3, 77. IV, 2, 46. 47. 49. H4B I, 2, 234. II, 2, 20. H6B IV, 7, 57. Rom. II, 4, 109 (*a s. and a smock* = a man and a woman). Tim. IV, 3, 223. Hml. II, 1, 81. Lr. III, 4, 142. Oth. V, 1, 47. 73. Ant. IV, 12, 43. Cymb. I, 2, 2. 6.

**Shive,** a slice: *easy it is of a cut loaf to steal a s.* Tit. II, 1, 87 (proverb).

**Shiver,** vb. 1) tr. to break into splinters, to dash to pieces: *—ed all the beauty of my glass,* Lucr. 1763. *—ing shocks,* Mids. I, 2, 34.

2) intr. a) to fall into pieces: *thou'dst —ed like an egg,* Lr. IV, 6, 51.

b) to quake, to tremble: *I have seen them s. and look pale,* Mids. V, 95. *—ing cold,* R2 V, 1, 77.

**Shivers,** small fragments, splinters: *cracked in a hundred s.* R2 IV, 289. *he would pun thee into s. with his fist,* Troil. II, 1, 42.

**Shoal,** a shallow: *sounded all the depths and —s of honour,* H8 III, 2, 437. In Mcb. I, 7, 6 M. Edd. *upon this bank and s. of time;* O. Edd. *school.*

**Shock,** subst. a violent collision, a conflict, encounter: *and sweetens … the aloes of all forces, —s and fears,* Compl. 273. *shivering —s,* Mids. I, 2, 34. *with grating s. of wrathful iron arms,* R2 I, 3, 136. *when their thundering s. at meeting tears the cloudy cheeks of heaven,* III, 3, 56. *the intestine s. and furious close of civil butchery,* H4A I, 1, 12. *in plain s. and even play of battle,* H5 IV, 8, 114. *in this doubtful s. of arms,* R3 V, 3, 93. *the thousand natural —s tha flesh is heir to,* Hml. III, 1, 62.

**Shock,** vb. to meet with force, to encounter, to face: *come the three corners of the world in arms, and we shall s. them,* John V, 7, 117.

**Shoe,** subst. (plur. *shoes; shoon* in a popular rhyme, Hml. IV, 5, 26; and in the language of Cade, H6B IV, 2, 195), a covering for the foot: Tp. III, 2, 26. Gent. II, 1, 86. II, 3, 16. 17. 19. 27. Err. IV, 2, 104. LLL I, 2, 173. As III, 2, 399. Shr. Ind. 2, 10. All's II, 1, 31. John II, 144 (*great Alcides' —s upon an ass;* cf. in Gosson's School of Abuse: *Hercules' shoes on a child's feet.* Most M. Edd. *shows*). H4B I, 2, 44. H5 IV, 1, 47. IV, 7, 149. IV, 8, 74. 75. Cor. I, 1, 200. Rom. I, 4, 14. III, 1, 31. Caes. I, 1, 27. 33. Hml. I, 2, 147. II, 2, 234. III, 2, 288. Lr. III, 4, 98. *over —s* = deeply; deep enough, though not knee-deep: *more than over —s in love,* Gent. I, 1, 24. *a man may go over —s in the grime,* Err. III, 2, 106. *over —s in blood,* Mids. III, 2, 48. *over —s in snow,* R3 V, 3, 326.

**Shoe,** vb. to furnish with a horseshoe: Merch. I, 2, 47. H4B V, 1, 20. Lr. IV, 6, 188.

**Shoeing-horn,** a horn used to facilitate the entrance of the foot into a narrow shoe; emblem of one who is a subservient tool to the caprices of another: *a thrifty s. in a chain, hanging at his brother's leg,* Troil. V, 1, 61 (alluding, at the same time, to the cuckoldom of Menelaus).

**Shoemaker,** one whose occupation is to make shoes and boots: Rom. I, 2, 39.

**Shoe-tie,** a riband with which women fasten their shoes: Wint. IV, 4, 611.

**Shog,** Nym's word for *jog,* = to move off, to go: *will you s. off? I would have you solus,* H5 II, 1, 47. *shall we s.? the king will be gone from Southampton,* II, 3, 47.

**Shoon,** see *Shoe.*

**Shoot,** vb. (impf. and partic. *shot;* but see *Shotten, Shoulder-shotten* and *Nook-shotten*) 1) tr. a) to let fly, to discharge, to dart; absol.: *he will s. no more,* Tp. IV, 100. LLL IV, 1, 11. IV, 2, 59. Shr. V, 2, 51. John V, 6, 1. H6C III, 1, 5. Tit. IV, 3, 70. Rom. II, 1, 13. Hml. V, 2, 414. *s. point-blank twelve score,* Wiv. III, 2, 34. *—ing well,* LLL IV, 1, 25. John I, 174. *must s. nearer,* LLL IV, 1, 136. *s. in each other's mouth,* John II, 414. *you have shot over,* H5 III, 7, 133. *to s. against the wind,* Tit. IV, 3, 57. With cf.: Sonn. 117, 12. Ado I, 1, 260. II, 1, 254. III, 2, 12. All's III, 2, 110. 115. H6A I, 4, 3. With an object: *a fine volley of words, and quickly shot off,* Gent. II, 4, 34. *to s. an arrow,* Merch. I, 1, 141. 148. As V, 4, 112. John II, 229. H5 III, 7, 132 (*a fool's bolt is soon shot*). Tit. IV, 3, 61. Rom. III, 3, 103. Hml. V, 2, 254. Mcb. II, 3, 147. Per. I, 1, 163. Accus. and

S 1049

*at: they join and s. their foam at Simois' banks,* Lucr. 1442. LLL III, 66. H6A IV, 7, 80. Cymb. IV, 2, 300. Acc. of the effect: *he shot a fine shoot,* H4B III, 2, 49. *thou hast shot off one of Taurus' horns,* Tit. IV, 3, 69.

Metaphorical use: *my revenges were high bent upon him and watched the time to s.* All's V, 3, 11. *to s. forth thunder upon these drudges,* H6B IV, 1, 104; cf. Lr. II, 4, 230. *what a mental power his eye —s forth,* Tim. I, 1, 32. *my good stars have shot their fires into the abysm of hell,* Ant. III, 13, 146.

b) to hit, strike or kill with any missile: *a mark marvellous well shot,* LLL IV, 1, 132. *shot, by heaven!* IV, 3, 23. *who was shot,* H5 III, 6, 77. *to s. me to the heart,* H6A I, 4, 56. *love's bow —s buck and doe,* Troil. III, 1, 127. *with sighs shot through,* Per. IV, 4, 26. cf. *Grief-shot.*

c) to send out, to push forth: *'tis one of those odd tricks which sorrow —s out of the mind,* Ant.IV,2,14.

2) intr. a) to move with velocity; used of falling stars: Ven. 815. Lucr. 1525. Mids. II, 1, 153. R2 II, 4, 19.

b) to germinate, to bud, to sprout: *the rarest argument of wonder that hath shot out in our latter times,* All's II, 3, 8.

**Shoot,** subst. 1) the discharge of a missile: *end thy ill aim before thy s. be ended,* Lucr. 579. *where you may make the fairest s.* LLL IV, 1, 10. 12. 26. H4B III, 2, 49. H6C III, 1, 7. *at a s.* = at one s. Hml. V, 2, 377 (Qq *shot*).

2) a young branch: *thou wantest a rough pash and the —s I have,* Wint. I, 2, 128.

**Shooter,** one who shoots: LLL IV,1,116 (quibbling on *suitor* v. 110).

**Shootie** (perhaps *Shoe-tie*) name in Meas. IV, 3, 18 *(Master S. the great traveller).*

**Shop,** a room where any thing is sold or made for sale, or to which customers of any kind resort: *which (your image) in my bosom's s. is hanging still,* Sonn. 24, 7. *a barber's s.* Meas. V,323. *at your (the goldsmith's) s.* Err. III, 1, 3. IV, 1, 82. IV, 3, 7. LLL III, 18 *(with your hat penthouse-like o'er the s. of your eyes).* Shr. IV, 3, 91. Wint. IV, 4, 701. H6A III, 1, 85. Cor. I, 1, 137. IV, 6, 8. Rom. V, 1, 42. 56. Tim. IV, 3, 450. Caes. I, 1, 31. Cymb. V, 5, 166 *(a s. of all the qualities that man loves woman for).*

**Shore,** subst. 1) the coast of the sea: Sonn. 56, 10. 60, 1. 64, 6. Tp. I, 2, 180. II, 1, 120. III, 2, 16. III, 3, 74. V, 137. 161. Wiv. I, 3, 89. Merch. III, 2, 97. Wint. III, 3, 90. IV, 4, 578. V, 1, 164. John II, 23. 338. V, 2, 36. R2 II, 1, 62. 288. H4A IV, 3, 59. 77. H5 V, 2, 378. H6B III, 2, 87. 90. 102. IV, 1, 11. H6C III, 2, 136. R3 IV, 4, 434. 482. 525. Troil. I, 3, 105. 112. II, 2, 64. II, 3, 260. Rom. II, 2, 83. Oth. II, 1, 11. Ant. II, 7, 133. Cymb. I, 3, 1. Per. I, 4, 60. II, 1, 6. 111. II, 3, 85. 89. III, 2, 50. III, 3, 35. IV, 4, 43. V, 1, 104. 257. V, 3, 23. Without the article: *and make my vouch as strong as s. of rock,* H8 I, 1, 158 (as a rock standing the rage of the waves). Especially after prepositions, = land: *if the wind blow from s.* Err. III, 2, 153. *was not this nigh s.?* Tp. I, 2, 216. *to drown in ken of s.* Lucr. 1114. *on s.:* Ven. 817. Tp. V, 219. Gent. I, 1, 158. Ado II, 3, 66. Tw. V, 281. Wint. IV, 4, 510. H6B III, 2, 95. Oth. II, 1, 28. 83. Ant. II, 7, 137. Per. V, 1, 17. Similarly: *large lengths of seas and —s,* John I, 105 (= land). *the tide of*

*pomp that beats upon the high s. of this world,* H5 IV, 1, 282 (i. e. the most exalted stations). *darkling stand the varying s. of the world,* Ant. IV, 15, 11 (i. e. the world itself, that part of the universe in which we live). Metaphorical use: *the approaching tide will shortly fill the reasonable s.* Tp. V, 81. *I have laboured to the extremest s. of my modesty,* Meas. III, 2, 266.

2) the bank of a river: Lucr. 1440. Wiv. III, 5, 15. John II, 443. R2 III, 2, 107. H4A III, 1, 76. Tit. I, 88. Caes. I, 1, 52. 65. I, 2, 101.

**Shore,** subst. see *Sewer.*

**Shore;** *Mrs S.,* name of the mistress of Edward IV, and, after his death, of Lord Hastings: R3 I, 1, 73. 93. 98. III, 1, 185. III, 4, 73. III, 5, 31. 51.

**Shore,** vb. to set on land: *if he think it fit to s. them again,* Wint. IV, 4, 869.

**Short,** adj. 1) not long in space or extent: Ven. 297. 627. Wiv. II, 2, 18. Ado II, 1, 25. LLL III, 57. R2 II, 3, 17. V, 1, 91. V, 3, 117. H4B I, 2, 34. H6B I, 2, 12. H8 I, 3, 31. Lr. I, 5, 55. IV, 7, 40. Oth. II, 1, 284. Ant. II, 4, 7. Per. IV, 4, 1. Opposed to tall: Ado I, 1, 216. H4B V, 3, 36.

2) not long in time: Ven. 22. 842. Lucr. 791. 991. 1573. Sonn. 18, 4. 125, 4. 146, 5. Meas. II, 4, 40. Err. V, 309. LLL I, 1, 181. V, 2, 798. Mids. I, 1, 144. Wint. I, 2, 169. R2 I, 4, 17. II, 1, 35. 223. V, 1, 80. H4A I, 3, 301. III, 1, 91. V, 2, 82. H5 IV, 5, 23. R3 III, 1, 94. III, 4, 97. IV, 1, 79. H8 Prol. 13. Cor. I, 7, 4. V, 4, 9. Rom. I, 1, 170. II, 6, 5. IV, 1, 1. V, 3, 229. Tim. III, 4, 11. Lr. IV, 7, 2. *in s. time,* H4A IV, 3, 90. Cymb. V, 5, 256. *in s. space,* H4A V, 1, 46. *s. breath,* H4A V, 2, 49. H4B I, 2, 206. *fetches her wind so s.* Troil. III, 2, 33. 36. Used, for the sake of the rhyme, as a relative term of duration, = long: *a summer's day will seem an hour but s.* Ven. 23. Peculiar passage: *it must be shortly known to him from England what is the issue of the business there. It will be s.* Hml. V, 2, 73 (= shortly? or = a short time? cf. *three years is but s.* LLL I, 1, 181).

3) brief, not prolix, not tedious, not over-ceremonious: *this s. schedule,* Lucr. 1312. *s. answer,* Ado I, 1, 215. *s. letter,* LLL V, 2, 56. *we will make s. work,* Rom. II, 6, 35. *a s. farewell,* Cymb. III, 4, 188. *brief, s., quick, snap,* Wiv. IV, 5, 2. *to be s.* Shr. V, 2, 110. H8 IV, 1, 30. *s. tale to make,* H6C II, 1, 120. *a s. tale to make,* Hml. II, 2, 146 (cf. the quibbling in Rom. II, 4, 104). *to be s. with* = not to make much ceremony with: *I will be bitter with him and passing s.* As III, 5, 138. H8 V, 3, 52. Tit. I, 409. Substantively: *the s. and the long* (= the whole in few words), a phrase used by Mrs. Quickly and her equals: Wiv. II, 1, 137. II, 2, 60. Mids. IV, 2, 39. Merch. II, 2, 135.

4) deficient, inadequate: *praise too s. doth blot,* LLL IV, 3, 241. *we shall be s. in our provision,* Rom. IV, 2, 38. *his means most s.* Tim. I, 1, 96. *whose aim seems far too s. to hit me here,* Per. I, 2, 8. *to come s.* = to fail, to be insufficient: *how far a modern quill doth come too s.* Sonn. 83, 7. *who hath for four or five removes come s. to tender it herself,* All's V, 3, 131. *your reputation comes too s. for my daughter,* 176. R2 I, 4, 47. Lr. I, 1, 74. II, 1, 90. Ant. II, 5, 8. *with of: her proportions came too s. of composition,* Meas. V, 220 (did not equal the composition). *he comes too s. of you,* Ado III, 5, 45. LLL V, 2, 748. H8 III, 2, 170. Troil. I, 3, 11. Hml. IV, 7, 91. Ant. I, 1, 58. Similarly: *striking too s. at Greeks,* Hml. II, 2, 491.

5) Adverbially, = so as to restrain or put a stop: take up the English s. H5 II, 4, 72. *should have kept s., restrained and out of haunt this mad young man,* Hml. IV, 1, 18. *to cut s.* = to make away with: *cutting s. that fraudful man,* H6B III, 1, 81. *bloody war shall cut them s.* IV, 4, 12. *cut s. all intermission,* Mcb. IV, 3, 232.

**Short,** vb. 1) to shorten, to abridge: *s., night, to-night, and length thyself to-morrow,* Pilgr. 210.

2) to take from, to impair, to infringe (antithetically): *I shall s. my word by lengthening my return,* Cymb. I, 6, 200.

**Short-armed,** having short arms, not reaching far: *s. ignorance,* Troil. II, 3, 15.

**Shortcake,** name in Wiv. I, 1, 211.

**Shorten,** 1) to make short in measure, extent or time: Ado III, 2, 106. R2 I, 3, 227. H6A V, 4, 58. Hml. V, 1, 22. The measure by which something is diminished expressed by an accus.: *I can but s. thy life one week,* Wint. IV, 4, 433. *to s. you your whole head's length,* R2 III, 3, 13. *God s. Harry's happy life one day,* H4B V, 2, 145. *the —ing of my life one day,* H6A IV, 6, 37. Hence = to deduct, to strike off: *he —s four years of my son's exile,* R2 I, 3, 217. With *up* = to cramp together (so that free motion is hindered): *s. up their sinews with aged cramps,* Tp. IV, 260.

2) to make to fall short, to make to fail, to prejudice: *by the discovery we shall be —ed in our aim,* Cor. I, 2, 23. *to be known —s my made intent,* Lr. IV, 7, 9.

**Short-grassed,** covered with short grass: Tp. IV, 83.

**Short-jointed,** having short pasterns: Ven. 295.

**Short-legged,** having short legs: *s. hens,* H4B V, 1, 28.

**Short-lived,** early dying: LLL II, 54. IV, 1, 15.

**Shortly,** in a little time, soon; used of future time: Tp. IV, 265. V, 81. 248. Meas. II, 2, 21. Ado I, 1, 221. 274. IV, 2, 25. V, 2, 58. Merch. III, 5, 27. 31. 49. As II, 7, 6. Tw. II, 1, 47. R2 II, 1, 288. III, 4, 106. H4A III, 3, 7. H4B III, 2, 14. IV, 3, 141. H6A I, 3, 26. H6B II, 4, 50. H6C III, 3, 227. IV, 1, 64. R3 I, 1, 119. III, 4, 109. IV, 1, 87. IV, 4, 428 *(very s.).* H8 III, 2, 67. Cor. IV, 7, 57. Rom. III, 1, 17. Tim. I, 2, 248. IV, 3, 395. V, 1, 210. Hml. III, 2, 183. IV, 7, 33. V, 1, 321 (Qq *thereby*). V, 2, 71. Lr. I, 4, 113. V, 3, 321. Oth. I, 3, 355. II, 1, 90. III, 3, 56. Ant. II, 7, 26. Of past time: *he s. after withdrew himself,* Lucr. Arg. 14. *who s. also died,* Tw. I, 2, 39. *he did return to be s. murdered,* H4A I, 3, 152. *died s. after this world had aired them,* H8 II, 4, 192.

**Shortness,** 1) little duration: LLL IV, 3, 378. H4A V, 2, 83. Cymb. II, 4, 44.

2) fewness of words, straightforwardness: *your plainness and your s. please me well,* Shr. IV, 4, 39.

**Short-numbered** (not hyphened in O. Edd.), few in number: *on leases of s. hours,* Sonn. 124, 10.

**Short-winded,** short-breathed, panting, asthmatic: H4A I, 1, 3. H4B II, 2, 136.

**Shot,** 1) the act of shooting, discharge of missile weapons: *with a volley of our needless s.* John V, 5, 5. *I fear the s. here,* H4A V, 3, 31 (punning). *a perilous s. out of an elder-gun,* H5 IV, 1, 210. *vex us with s. or with assault,* H6A I, 4, 13. *I abide your s.* H6C I, 4, 29. *the aim of every dangerous s.* R3 IV, 4,

90. *transports his poisoned s.* Hml. IV, 1, 43. *discharge their s. of courtesy,* Oth. II, 1, 56. Figuratively: *safe out of Fortune's s.* Tit. II, 1, 2. *out of the s. and danger of desire,* Hml. I, 3, 35. *at a s.* V, 2, 377 (Ff *shoot*). *the s. of accident,* Oth. IV, 1, 278. *abide the hourly s. of angry eyes,* Cymb. I, 1, 89.

2) a marksman: *a little, lean, old, chopt, bald s.* H4B III, 2, 295. As a collective noun, = marksmen, shooters: *a guard of chosen s.* H6A I, 4, 53. *a file of boys behind 'em, loose s.* H8 V, 4, 59.

**Shot,** a tavern-reckoning: Gent. II, 5, 7. 10. Cymb. V, 4, 158. Punning in H4A V, 3, 31.

**Shot-free,** free from charge, not obliged to pay the reckoning: H4A V, 3, 30.

**Shotten,** having spent the roe: *a s. herring,* H4A II, 4, 143.

**Shough,** a kind of shaggy dog: Mcb. III, 1, 94.

**Should,** see *Shall.*

**Shoulder,** subst. 1) the projection formed by the bones called Scapulae: Ven. 1058. Wiv. III, 3, 13. III, 5, 102. IV, 2, 111. V, 5, 58. Err. III, 2, 147. LLL IV, 3, 90. V, 1, 108. Shr. IV, 1, 15. Wint. IV, 4, 60. John I, 245; cf. R2 I, 1, 79. H4A II, 4, 164. H4B II, 4, 143. 231. V, 4, 3. H6A I, 5, 11. H6C V, 7, 23. Troil. III, 2, 15. Cor. II, 1, 163. Hml. II, 1, 97. Cymb. V, 3, 78 (cf. *Shoulder-clapper*). *to clap on the s.,* in sign of approval and kindness: Ado I, 1, 261. LLL V, 2, 107. Troil. III, 3, 139. or in sign of arrestation: As IV, 1, 48 (cf. *shoulder-clapper*). *thrust virtue out of our hearts by the head and —s,* Wiv. V, 5, 156. The place on which the head stands: Meas. I, 2, 177. Ado I, 1, 115. R2 II, 1, 123. H4A I, 2, 186. H5 IV, 1, 244. H6B IV, 7, 128. R3 III, 2, 43. Lr. II, 2, 100. Cymb. IV, 1, 17. *men whose heads do grow beneath their —s,* Oth. I, 3, 145 (instead of standing on them). Emblem of supporting strength: *weak —s, overborne with burthening grief,* H6A II, 5, 10. *on thy s. will I lean,* H6C II, 1, 189. *in thy s. do I build my seat,* II, 6, 100. And in general, the part of the body designed to bear burdens: *so bear I thee upon my manly —s,* H6B V, 2, 63. R3 III, 1, 131. *laid their guilt upon my guilt-less —s,* I, 2, 98. *from these —s taken a load,* H8 III, 2, 381. *did from the flames of Troy upon his s. the old Anchises bear,* Caes. I, 2, 113. Hence

2) back: *the wind sits in the s. of your sail,* Hml. I, 3, 56. Plur. *—s: my mistress' marks upon my —s,* Err. I, 2, 83. II, 1, 73. II, 2, 39. IV, 4, 38. *no ill luck stirring but what lights on my —s,* Merch. III, 1, 99. *the city-woman bears the cost of princes on unworthy —s,* As II, 7, 76. *lay on that shall make your —s crack,* John II, 146. *thrown over the —s like an herald's coat without sleeves,* H4A IV, 2, 48. *never had the ache in his —s,* H4B V, 1, 94. *to run and show their —s,* Ant. III, 1, 164.

3) the upper joint of the fore leg of edible animals: Wiv. V, 5, 29.

**Shoulder,** vb. to push with violence and with a view of supplanting: *this —ing of each other in the court,* H6A IV, 1, 189. *her royal stock graft with ignoble plants, and almost —ed in the swallowing gulf of blind forgetfulness,* R3 III, 7, 128.

**Shoulder-blade,** the scapula: Wint. IV, 3, 77.

**Shoulder-bone,** the same: Wint. III, 3, 97,

**Shoulder-clapper,** one that shows cordial favour and applause; and one who claps on the shoulder by way of arrestation; quibblingly: *a back-friend, a* *s.* Err. IV, 2, 37 (cf. for one signification: LLL V, 2, 107; Ado I, 1, 261 and Troil. III, 3, 139; for the other: As IV, 1, 48 and Cymb. V, 3, 78).

**Shoulder - shotten**, sprained in the shoulder: Shr. III, 2, 56.

**Shout**, subst. loud outcry of a multitude of men, expressing exultation: Merch. III, 2, 144. H4A III, 2, 53. H5 V Chor. 11. H6C IV, 8, 51. R3 III, 7, 39. Troil. V, 9, 1. Cor. I, 1, 47. II, 1, 283. V, 3, 19. Caes. I, 1, 49 *(make).* I, 2, 132. III, 2, 58. V, 3, 83.

**Shout**, vb. to cry in exultation: H4B IV, 2, 87. Cor. V, 4, 53. Caes. I, 2, 79. 223. 226. 231. V, 3, 32. Ant. IV, 12, 34. V, 2, 56. With *out:* John V, 2, 103. With an accus. of the effect: —*ing their emulation,* Cor. I, 1, 218 (showing by shouts). *you s. me forth in acclamations hyperbolical,* I, 9, 50 (O. Edd. *shooting* and *shoot* in the two last passages). cf. *Unshout.*

**Shove**, to push or drive by main force: *the particulars of our grief, ... with scorn —d from the court,* H4B IV, 2, 37. *offence's gilded hand may s. by justice,* Hml. III, 3, 58. *the hand could pluck her back that —d her on,* Ant. I, 2, 131.

**Shove-groat**, a game wich consisted in pushing pieces of money on a board, to reach certain marks: *quoit him down like a s. shilling,* H4B II, 4, 206.

**Shovel**, subst. an instrument with a broad blade used especially for throwing earth: Hml. V, 1, 110.

**Shovel**, vb. to throw with a shovel: Wint. IV, 4, 469.

**Shovel-board**, the same as *shove-groat* (q. v.): *two Edward —s, that cost me two shilling and two pence a-piece,* Wiv. I, 1, 159 (Edward the Sixth's shillings were then for the most part used at shove-groat or shovel-board).

**Show**, subst. 1) the act of showing, of exhibiting to the view: *no cloudy s. of stormy weather doth yet appear,* Lucr. 115. *I love not less, though less the s. appear,* Sonn. 102, 2 (= though I show it less). *small s. of man was yet upon his chin,* Compl. 92. *neither singly can be manifested, without the s. of both,* Wiv. IV, 6, 16. *you must not make the full s. of this,* Ado I, 3, 21. *if thou dost intend never so little s. of love to her,* Mids. III, 2, 334. *what plea so tainted and corrupt but, being seasoned with a gracious voice, obscures the s. of evil?* Merch. III, 2, 77. *it is the s. and seal of nature's truth,* All's I, 3, 138. *I should not make so dear a s. of zeal,* H4A V, 4, 95. *if her feathers turn back in any s. of resistance,* H4B II, 4, 109. *he is not the man that he would gladly make s. to the world he is,* H5 III, 6, 88. *make a s. of love to proud Duke Humphrey,* H6B I, 1, 241. *that gentleness and s. of love,* Caes. I, 2, 34. 47. *thus much s. of fire,* 177. *to offer it the s. of violence,* Hml. I, 1, 144. —*s of grief,* I, 2, 82 (Qq *shapes).* *I have that within which passeth s.* 85. *'tis my breeding that gives me this bold s. of courtesy,* Oth. II, 1, 100.

2) display, parade, ostentation: *who makest a s., but darest not strike,* Tp. I, 2, 470. *have not the grace to grace it with such s.* LLL V, 2, 320. *the little foolery that wise men have makes a great s.* As I, 2, 97. *if these —s be not outward, which of you but is four Volsces,* Cor. I, 6, 77. *to make up a s.* Rom. V, 1, 48. *make gallant s. and promise of their mettle,* Caes. IV, 2, 24. *the enemy comes on in gallant s.* V, 1, 13. *our army shall in solemn s. attend this funeral,* Ant. V, 2, 367. *who makes the fairest s. means most deceit,* Per.

I, 4, 75. *as if the entertainment had not a s. might countervail his worth,* II, 3, 56.

3) appearance, whether false or true: *flattered by their leader's jocund s.* Lucr. 296. *he entertained a s. so seeming just,* 1514. *burying in Lucrece' wound his folly's s.* 1810. *flowers distilled leese but their s.* Sonn. 5, 14. *their virtue only is their s.* 54, 9. *thy odour matcheth not thy s.* 69, 13. *if some suspect of ill masked not thy s.* 70, 13. 93, 14. *dissembled with an outward s.* Pilgr. 336. Tp. V, 63. Wiv. II, 1, 98. Err. III, 2, 8. Ado IV, 1, 36. 41. Mids. III, 2, 139. 151. Merch. II, 9, 26. III, 2, 73. As II, 7, 95. All's II, 1, 153. Tw. II, 4, 120. III, 4, 317. John V, 2, 77. H4B I, 1, 193. V, 5, 14. H5 I, 2, 72. II, 4, 23. IV, 2, 17. H6B III, 1, 54. 225. R3 III, 1, 10. III, 5, 29. Troil. I, 3, 46. Rom. III, 2, 77. Mcb. I, 7, 81. Hml. III, 1, 45. Oth. I, 1, 52. II, 3, 358. Cymb. I, 5, 40. V, 5, 54. Per. II, 2, 48. II, 3, 6. IV, 4, 23.

4) any thing presented to the view, an object attracting notice, an aspect, an external sign: *and give the harmless s. an humble gait,* Lucr. 1507 (viz the painted figure of Sinon). *losing her woes in —s of discontent,* 1580 (viz pictures). *how would thy shadow's form form happy s.* Sonn. 43, 6. *fright me with urchin —s,* Tp. II, 2, 5. *a snow in May's new-fangled —s,* LLL I, 1, 106 (M. Edd. *mirth,* for the sake of the rhyme). *a golden mind stoops not to —s of dross,* Merch. II, 7, 20. *that any harm should stain so fair a s.* R2 III, 3, 71. *throng our large temples with the —s of peace,* Cor. III, 3, 36. *live to be the s. and gaze o' the time,* Mcb. V, 8, 24. *leaving free things and happy —s behind,* Lr. III, 6, 112. *with other spritely —s of mine own kindred,* Cymb. V, 5, 428.

5) a spectacle, a play: *this huge stage presenteth nought but —s,* Sonn. 15, 3. *swoon at tragic —s,* Compl. 308. *or s. or pageant,* LLL V, 1, 118. 126. V, 2, 305. 514. 541. 543. Mids. V, 116. 128. Shr. I, 1, 47. H4B III, 2, 300. H6C V, 7, 43. H8 Prol. 10. 18. Hml. III, 2, 149. 153. Ant. III, 13, 30. IV, 15, 23. Per. V, 2, 271. *a dumb s.* = a pantomime: Ado II, 3, 226. Merch. I, 2, 79. Tit. III, 1, 131. Hml. III, 2, 14. cf. *Per. III* Prol. 14.

**Show** (impf. *showed,* partic. *showed* or *shown),* 1) trans. a) to exhibit to view; absol.: *be not ashamed to s.* Hml. III, 2, 155. With objects: Tp. I, 2, 337. II, 2, 144. 152. 164. 173. III, 2, 74. 150. Gent. I, 2, 31. I, 3, 80. 86. II, 3, 15. III, 2, 18. Meas. I, 2, 120. IV, 2, 160. LLL V, 2, 296. Mids. II, 1, 169. Merch. IV, 2, 11. As III, 5, 20. Wint. V, 3, 59. H6B III, 1, 15. Cor. II, 3, 171. III, 2, 22. Rom. I, 2, 103. Hml. III, 2, 154. Ant. II, 5, 8. V, 2, 227. Cymb. V, 5, 432 etc. etc. With *to* before the dative: Troil. III, 3, 79. Ant. IV, 14, 112. V, 1, 38. The dative subject of the passive: *no such sight to be —n,* Rom. I, 2, 105 (= to see). With a refl. pronoun: Tp. III, 2, 137. Wiv. II, 1, 22. Ado III, 2, 133. Shr. II, 51. All's II, 5, 73. H4A II, 4, 105. Cor. I, 2, 21. Tim. III, 2, 51 etc. With *off*: *I like your silence, it the more —s off your wonder,* Wint. V, 3, 21. With *out: I must s. out a flag and sign of love,* Oth. I, 1, 157.

b) to let be seen, not to conceal, to betray: *this visitation —s it,* Tp. III, 1, 32. *the more it seeks to hide itself, the bigger bulk it —s,* III, 1, 81. *see it so grossly —n in thy behaviours,* All's I, 3, 184. *to one of your receiving enough is —n,* Tw. III, 1, 132. *I have —ed too much the rashness of a woman,* Wint. III, 2, 221.

*s. me an iron heart*, Tim. III, 4, 84. *to s. one's head:* Sonn. 26, 14. Merch. III, 1, 47. R2 V, 6, 44. Troil. V, 6, 1. *to s. one's face:* Troil. V, 5, 45. Mcb. V, 7, 14. *to s. thy dangerous brow*, Caes. II, 1, 78.

c) to discover, to reveal, to communicate, to teach: *I'll s. my mind*, Gent. I, 2, 7 (= tell my opinion). *s. no colour for my extremity*, Wiv. IV, 2, 168. *he —s his reason for that*, Meas. IV, 4, 13. *where we'll s. what's yet behind*, V, 544. *s. me briefly how*, Ado II, 2, 11. *all the secrets of our camp I'll s.* All's IV, 1, 93 (a strange passage in All's II, 3, 25—27). *I will s. thee no reason*, Tw. III, 4, 166. *where you do remain let paper s.* R2 I, 3, 250. *s. some reason why Somerset should be preferred*, H6B I, 3, 116. 166. *I'll s. thee wondrous things*, Tit. V, 1, 55. *I'll s. you how to observe a strange event*, Tim. III, 4, 17. *to you they have —ed some truth*, Mcb. II, 1, 21. *with an entreaty, herein further —n*, Hml. II, 2, 76. *this hath my daughter —n me*, 125. *let his queen mother all alone entreat him to s. his grief*, III, 1, 191. *s. me thy thought*, Oth. III, 3, 116.

d) to prove: *his eye —s his hot courage*, Ven. 276. *by their rank thoughts my deeds must not be —n*, Sonn. 121, 12. *that the contents will s.* Gent. I, 2, 36. *I have to s. to the contrary*, Wiv. III, 1, 38. 41. *the country proverb known in your waking shall be —n*, Mids. III, 2, 460. *—ing we would not spare heaven*, Meas. II, 3, 33. *hast —ed thou makest some tender of my life*, H4A V, 4, 49. *there was very little honour —ed in this*, Tim. III, 2, 21. *s. us to be watchers*, Mcb. II, 2, 71. *when I have —ed the unfitness*, Lr. I, 4, 356 etc. With a double accus.: *—s thee unripe*, Ven. 128. *Silvia —s Julia but a swarthy Ethiope*, Gent. II, 6, 26. I, 2, 29. Wiv. II, 3, 56. 57. Shr. V, 1, 76 etc.

e) to offer, to condescend, to do, to bestow: *s. some pity*, Meas. II, 2, 99. *s. justice*, 100. *you have —ed me that which well approves you're great in fortune*, All's III, 7, 13. *the fair kindness you have —ed me here*, Tw. III, 4, 376. *that souls refined should s. so heinous a deed*, R2 IV, 131. *you s. great mercy*, H5 II, 2, 50. IV, 4, 68. H8 I, 1, 223. Cor. I, 3, 5. V, 3, 55. 137. 161. Tit. II, 3, 147. Tim. IV, 3, 534. Hml. I, 2, 40. 53. Lr. II, 1, 107. Cymb. V, 4, 30 etc.

f) to point out the way to, to guide: *will you s. me to this house?* Merch. IV, 2, 19.

2) intr. a) to appear, to become visible: *fire in a flint, which will not s. without knocking*, Troil. III, 3, 258. *the fire i' the flint —s not till it be struck*, Tim. I, 1, 23. *s., s., s.!* Mcb. IV, 1, 107. With a dative without *to*: *s. his eyes, and grieve his heart*, Mcb. IV, 1, 110.

b) to appear, to look, to have appearance, to be in appearance (joined with substantives, or adjectives, or adverbs): *this beauteous combat —ed like two silver doves*, Ven. 366. *perverse it shall be where it —s most toward*, 1157. *my duty would s. greater*, Lucr. Ded. 5. *what is vile —s like a virtuous deed*, Lucr. 252. *whose perfect white —ed like an April daisy*, 395. *in whom all ill well —s*, Sonn. 40, 13. *the one doth shadow of your beauty s.* 53, 10. *to make him seem long hence as he —s now*, 101, 14. 105, 2. Compl. 96. Gent. II, 7, 48. Meas. IV, 4, 4. Err. III, 2, 31. Ado I, 2, 8. Merch. II, 2, 193. IV, 1, 196. As I, 3, 83. All's III, 5, 24. Wint. IV, 4, 636. John III, 4, 115. R2 II, 2, 15. H4A I, 2, 238. I, 3, 35. III, 2, 58. V, 2, 51. H4B II, 2, 7. IV, 1, 63. IV, 2, 4. IV, 3, 55. 58. H5 II, 2, 127. H6B

V, 1, 205. H8 I, 1, 22. Troil. I, 3, 84. Cor. III, 3, 50. IV, 5, 68. IV, 6, 114. V, 3, 13. Rom. I, 2, 104. I, 5, 50. 51. Tim. III, 4, 21. V, 1, 15. Mcb. I, 3, 54. V, 6, 2. Hml. II, 2, 391. V, 2, 113 (*of very soft society and great —ing;* = distinguished appearance; Osrick's euphuism). Lr. I, 4, 265. 289. IV, 6, 14. Oth. V, 2, 203. Ant. II, 2, 147. III, 3, 23. IV, 8, 7. Per. IV, 1, 89. Perhaps followed by an inf., at least one understood: *they that have power to hurt, and will do none, that do not do the thing they most do s.* Sonn. 94, 2 (= they most s. to do? But it may be explained otherwise).

**Shower,** subst. a short fall of rain: Ven. 66. Sonn. 75, 2. 124, 12. Tp. IV, 79. Wiv. III, 2, 38. R2 II, 1, 35. H6B III, 1, 337. H6C II, 2, 156. H8 III, 1, 7. Tit. III, 1, 18. Tim. II, 2, 180. Ant. I, 2, 156 (*a s. of rain*). Used of any thing falling fast and thick; of tears: Lucr. 796. Shr. Ind. 1, 125. John V, 2, 50. H6C I, 4, 145. II, 5, 85. Tit. V, 3, 161. Hml. IV, 5, 39. Ant. III, 2, 44. of blood: R2 III, 3, 43. of pebbles: H8 V, 4, 60. *a s. of gold*, Ant. II, 5, 45. *in the great s. of your gifts*, Tim. V, 1, 73. *made a s. and thunder with their caps and shouts*, Cor. II, 1, 283. *—s of oaths*, Mids. I, 1, 245.

**Shower,** vb. to rain: *evermore —ing?* (i. e. weeping) Rom. III, 5, 131. = to fall down plenteously: *it rained down fortune —ing on your head*, H4A V, 1, 47. Trans. = to pour down plenteously: *I s. a welcome on you; welcome all*, H8 I, 4, 63. *your royal graces —ed on me daily*, III, 2, 167.

**Show-place:** *the common s. where they exercise,* Ant. III, 6, 12; North's translation, adopted by the poet, of the Greek word γυμνάσιον in Plut. Ant. LIV.

**Shreds,** fragments, patches: *with these s. they vented their complainings*, Cor. I, 1, 212. *a king of s. and patches*, Hml. III, 4, 102.

**Shrew,** subst. (often spelt *shrow* in O. Edd. and always pronounced so; cf. the rhymes in LLL V, 2, 46. Shr. IV, 1, 213. V, 2, 28. 188) a vixen, a scold: Err. IV, 1, 51. LLL V, 2, 46. Merch. V, 21. Shr. II, 315. III, 2, 29. IV, 1, 22. 87 (*he is more s. than she*). 213. IV, 2, 58. V, 2, 28. 64. 188. Tw. I, 3, 50. H4B V, 3, 36.

**Shrew,** vb. = beshrew (q. v.): *s. my heart, you never spoke what did become you less*, Wint. I, 2, 281. *s. me, if I would lose it for a revenue of any king's*, Cymb. II, 3, 147.

**Shrewd,** 1) bad, evil, mischievous (German: *boese, arg*): *thy eyes' s. tutor, that hard heart of thine, hath taught them scornful tricks*, Ven. 500. *there is s. construction made of her*, Wiv. II, 2, 232. *prove a s. Caesar to you*, Meas. II, 1, 263. *so s. of thy tongue*, Ado II, 1, 20. *when she's angry, she is keen and s.* Mids. III, 2, 323. *there are some s. contents in yon same paper*, Merch. III, 2, 246. *endured s. days and nights*, As V, 4, 179. *her eldest sister is so curst and s.* Shr. I, 1, 185. I, 2, 60. 70. 90. *this young maid might do her a s. turn*, All's III, 5, 71. *foul s. news*, John V, 5, 14. *to lift s. steel against our golden crown*, R2 III, 2, 59. *made a s. thrust at your belly*, H4B II, 4, 228. *bears so s. a maim*, H6B II, 3, 41. *you are too s.* R3 II, 4, 35. *do my Lord of Canterbury a s. turn, and he is your friend for ever*, H8 V, 3, 178. *we shall find of him a s. contriver*, Caes. II, 1, 158. *'tis a s. doubt*, Oth. III, 3, 429. *this last day was a s. one to us*, Ant. IV, 9, 5.

2) sly, cunning, artful, arch: *a s. unhappy gallows* (Cupid) LLL V, 2, 12. *that s. and knavish sprite,* Mids. II, 1, 33. *a s. knave and an unhappy,* All's IV, 5, 66. *these women are s. tempters with their tongues,* H6A I, 2, 123. *a fit or two o' the face, but they are s. ones,* H8 I, 3, 7. *he has a s. wit,* Troil. I, 2, 206.

**Shrewdly,** in a high and mischievous degree (quite = the German adverb *arg*): *you apprehend passing s.* Ado II, 1, 84. *he is s. vexed at something,* All's III, 5, 91. *you boggle s.* V, 3, 232. *this practice hath most s. passed upon thee,* Tw.V, 360. *'tis s. ebbed,* Wint. V, 1, 102. *your mistress s. shook your back,* H5 III, 7, 52. *these English are s. out of beef,* 163. *my fame is s. gored,* Troil. III, 3, 228. *my misgiving still falls s. to the purpose,* Caes. III, 1, 146. *the air bites s.* Hml. I, 4, 1.

**Shrewdness,** cunning: Ant. II, 2, 69.

**Shrewish,** quarrelsome, vixenly: Err. III, 1, 2.

**Shrewishly,** tartly: Tw. I, 5, 170.

**Shrewishness,** quarrelsomeness: Mids. III, 2, 301.

**Shrewsbury,** English town: H4A III, 1, 86. III, 2, 166. IV, 2, 58. IV, 4, 10. V, 4, 151. H4B Ind. 24. I, 1, 12. 24. 40. 64. 65. I, 2, 71. 116. 167. I, 3, 26. *Earl of S.* (Talbot): H6A III, 4, 26. IV, 7, 61.

**Shriek,** subst. a sharp outcry, a scream: Wint. III, 3, 36. Troil. II, 2, 97. Rom. IV, 3, 47. Mcb. IV, 3, 168. cf. *Night-shriek.*

**Shriek,** vb. to scream: Lucr. 307. Tp. V, 233. Wiv. I, 1, 309. Mids. I, 2, 78. Wint. V, 1, 65. Rom. V, 3, 190. Caes. II, 2, 24. Per. III Prol. 51. Used of the cry of the owl: Ven. 531. Phoen. 5. R2 III, 3, 183. H6C V, 6, 44. Caes. I, 3, 28. Mcb. II, 2, 3. With *out:* R3 I, 4, 54 (Qq *squeaked*). Transitively: *—ing undistinguished woe,* Compl. 20.

**Shrieve,** sheriff: All's IV, 3, 213. H4B IV, 4, 99 (Ff *sheriff*).

**Shrift,** confession made to a priest, and the absolution consequent upon it: *I will give him a present s.* Meas. IV, 2, 223 (hear his confession and absolve him). *The ghostly father now hath done his s.* H6C III, 2, 107. *make a short s.* R3 III, 4, 97. *to hear true s.* Rom. I, 1, 165. *riddling confession finds but riddling s.* II,3,56. *to come to s.* II, 4, 192. *to go to s.* II,5,68. *she comes from s.* IV, 2,15. *his bed shall seem a school, his board a s.* Oth. III, 3, 24.

**Shrill,** 1) resounding, loud, clangorous: *thy hounds shall make the welkin answer them and fetch s. echoes from the hollow earth,* Shr. Ind. 2, 48. *with this s. addition, 'anon, anon, sir',* H4A II, 4, 29. *a tongue —er than all the music,* Caes. I, 2, 16. *the s. trump,* Oth. III, 3, 351.

2) of a high tone, not low: *thy small pipe is as the maiden's organ, s. and sound,* Tw. I, 4, 33. *hear the s. whistle,* H5 III Chor. 9.

**Shrill,** vb., with *forth,* = to utter loudly: *Andromache —s her dolours forth,* Troil. V, 3, 84.

**Shrill-gorged,** singing in a high tone: *the s. lark,* Lr. IV, 6, 58.

**Shrill-shrieking,** screaming in a high voice: H5 III, 3, 35.

**Shrill-sounding,** loud: *the cock ... with his lofty and s. throat,* Hml. I, 1, 151.

**Shrill-tongued,** 1) having a loud and resounding voice: *s. tapsters,* Ven. 849. *when s. Fulvia scolds,* Ant. I, 1, 32.

2) speaking in a high tone: *is she s. or low?* Ant. III, 3, 15.

**Shrill-voiced,** speaking loudly, clamorous: *what s. suppliant makes this eager cry?* R2 V, 3, 75.

**Shrilly,** loudly: *the echo ... replying s. to the well-tuned horns,* Tit. II, 3, 18. *nor sound his quillets s.* Tim. IV, 3, 155.

**Shrimp,** a dwarfish person, a mannikin: LLL V, 2, 594. H6A II, 3, 23.

**Shrine,** 1) altar, or rather the place where the image of a saint is deposited: *at Saint Alban's s.* H6B II, 1, 63. 88. 92.

2) the image of a saint: *offer pure incense to so pure a s.* (i. e. Lucrece) Lucr. 194. *from the four corners of the earth they come, to kiss this s., this mortal-breathing saint,* Merch. II, 7, 40. *if I profane with my unworthiest hand this holy s.* Rom. I, 5, 96. *laming the s. of Venus or straight-pight Minerva,* Cymb. V, 5, 164.

**Shrink** (impf. and partic. *shrunk*) 1) to contract itself, to shrivel, to dry up: *wanting the spring that those shrunk pipes* (the veins) *had fed,* Lucr. 1455. *his shrunk shank,* As II, 7, 161. *a shrunk panel,* III, 3, 89. *against this fire do I s. up,* John V, 7, 34. *ill-weaved ambition, how much art thou shrunk,* H4A V, 4, 88. *in this borrowed likeness of shrunk death,* Rom.IV, 1, 104. *Timon is shrunk indeed,* Tim. III, 2, 68 (= brought low). *are all thy conquests ... shrunk to this little measure?* Caes. III, 1, 150. cf. *Custom-shrunk.*

Transitively, = to wither: *to s. mine arm up like a withered shrub,* H6C III, 2, 156.

2) to shiver with cold; to shudder, to quake with fear: *till I s. with cold,* As II, 1, 9. *to be still hot summer's tanlings and the —ing slaves of winter,* Cymb. IV, 4, 30. *makes me with heavy nothing faint and s.* R2 II, 2, 32. *he shall s. under my courtesy,* H4A V, 2, 75. *not fearing death, nor —ing for distress,* H6A IV, 1, 37. *when he perceived me s. and on my knee,* IV, 7, 5. *as if his foot were on brave Hector's breast, and great Troy —ing,* Troil. III, 3, 141 (Q *shriking,* some M. Edd. *shrieking*). *the ground —s before his treading,* Cor. V, 4, 20.

3) to recoil, to fall back with fear: *the snail, whose tender horns being hit, —s backward,* Ven. 1034. *if there be ten, s. not,* Gent. IV, 1, 2. *when the bravest questant —s, find what you seek,* All's II, 1, 16. *if the first hour I s. and run away,* H6A IV, 5, 31. *at the sound it shrunk in haste away,* Hml. I, 2, 219. Without *away,* in the same sense as in Hml.: *that this sight should make so deep a wound, and yet detested life not s. thereat,* Tit. III, 1, 248.

4) With *from,* = to forsake, to leave in distress: *friends for fear, which in his greatest need will s. from him,* R3 V, 2, 21 (Ff *fly*). *if any mean to s. from me,* V, 3, 222. *will find a friend will not s. from him,* H8 IV, 1, 107. *his estate —s from him,* Tim. III, 2, 7.

**Shrive,** to hear at confession and absolve: *I had rather he should s. me than wive me,* Merch. I, 2, 144. *he —s this woman to her smock,* H6A I, 2, 119. *your honour hath no —ing work in hand,* R3 III, 2, 116. *there she shall be —d and married,* Rom. II, 4, 194. *not —ing time allowed,* Hml. V, 2, 47. With *of,* = to hear the confession and absolve of: *I'll s. you of a thousand idle pranks,* Err. II, 2, 210.

**Shrivel,** with *up,* = to dry up and contract into wrinkles: Per. II, 4, 9.

**Shriver,** a confessor: H6C III, 2, 108.

**Shroud**, subst. 1) shelter, cover, protection: *put yourself under his s.* Ant. III, 13, 71.

2) a winding-sheet: LLL V, 2, 479. Mids. V, 385. Tw. II, 4, 56. Wint. IV, 4, 468. Rom. IV, 1, 85. IV, 3, 43. 52. Hml. IV, 5, 35.

3) Plur. —*s*, = sail-ropes: John V, 7, 53. H6C V, 4, 18. H8 IV, 1, 72.

**Shroud**, vb. 1) to shelter, to cover, to conceal: *I have been closely —ed in this bush*, LLL IV, 3, 137. *under this brake we'll s. ourselves*, H6C III, 1, 1. *to s. yourselves from enemies*, IV, 3, 40.

2) to dress for the grave: R3 I, 2, 2. Troil. II, 3, 36. Hml. V, 1, 103. Oth. IV, 3, 24. Per. III, 2, 65.

3) intr. to take shelter: *I will here s. till the dregs of the storm be past*, Tp. II, 2, 42 (Trinculo's speech).

**Shrove-tide**, the day before Lent: H4B V, 3, 38.

**Shrove-tuesday**, the same: All's II, 2, 25.

**Shrow**, see *Shrew*.

**Shrub**, a woody plant of a size less than a tree, a bush: Lucr. 664. Tp. II, 2, 18. H6C III, 2, 156. V, 2, 15. Tit. IV, 3, 45.

**Shrug**, subst. a drawing up of the shoulders, expressive of slight contempt: Merch. I, 3, 110. Wint. II, 1, 71. 74.

**Shrug**, vb. to draw up the shoulders in contempt: Tp. I, 2, 367. Cor. I, 9, 4.

**Shrupt**, unintelligible reading of Q in Troil. IV, 5, 193: *when that a ring of Greeks have shrupt thee in.* Ff and M. Edd. *hemmed.*

**Shudder**, subst. a shaking with horror: Tim. IV, 3, 137.

**Shudder**, vb. to shake with horror: Ven. 880. Merch. III, 2, 110.

**Shuffle**, to practise shifts, to play tricks: *I am fain to s., to hedge and to lurch*, Wiv. II, 2, 25. *'tis like the forced gait of a —ing nag*, H4A III, 1, 135 (viz the gait of 'mincing poetry'). *'tis not so above; there is no —ing*, Hml. III, 3, 61. *with a little – ing you may choose a sword unbated*, IV, 7, 138. *your life must s. for itself*, Cymb. V, 5, 105. With an accus. denoting the effect: *he shall likewise s. her away*, Wiv. IV, 6, 29. *oft good turns are —d off with such uncurrent pay* (thanks) Tw. III, 3, 16 (= are eluded, got rid of). *when we have —d off this mortal coil*, Hml. III, 1, 67 (have got rid, in any way, of this troublesome life).

**Shun**, 1) to avoid, to keep far from, not to approach, to endeavour to escape: Lucr. 966. 1322. Sonn. 118, 4. 129, 14. Compl. 155. 234. Tp. IV, 116. Gent. I, 3, 78. III, 1, 30. Wiv. V, 5, 241. Meas. III, 1, 12. Mids. II, 1, 142. Merch. III, 5, 18. As II, 5, 40. Shr. Ind. 2, 30. All's II, 3, 79. Wint. I, 2, 422. V, 3, 105. H5 III, 6, 174. H6C I, 4, 24. R3 III, 2, 18. III, 7, 155. H8 I, 1, 114. Cor. I, 3, 34. I, 6, 44. Rom. I, 1, 136. Lr. III, 4, 9. 21. V, 3, 210. Oth. I, 2, 67. Cymb. I, 4, 47. V, 3, 27. Per. I, 1, 136. 142. I, 2, 6. 121. H6B I, 4, 38. 70.

2) to escape: *weak we are and cannot s. pursuit*, H6C II, 3, 13. *you cannot s. yourself*, Troil. III, 2, 152.

**Shunless**, inevitable: *s. destiny*, Cor. II, 2, 116.

**Shut** (impf. and partic. *shut*) 1) to close so as to hinder ingress or egress; used of doors, gates and windows: As IV, 1, 164. Tw. III, 1, 103. V, 404. H4B II, 4, 82. H6C IV, 7, 18. 35. Troil. II, 2, 47. Cor. I, 4, 17. Rom. IV, 1, 44. Oth. IV, 2, 28. of shops: H6A III, 1, 85. Rom. V, 1, 56. of the spring of a trunk: Cymb. II, 2, 47. of books: H4B III, 1, 56. Per. I, 1,

95. of eyes: Rom. III, 2, 49. Mcb. V, 1, 29. of the mouth: Lr. V, 3, 154 (Qq *stop*). of a purse: Gent. III, 1, 358. Followed by *after*: *s. the door after you*, Merch. II, 5, 53 (i. e. when you are in the house). by *against* (= to the exclusion of): *his own doors being s. against his entrance*, Err. IV, 3, 90. 92. *s. his bosom against our prayers*, All's III, 1, 8. Tim. I, 2, 150. Mcb. I, 7, 15. by *on* or *upon*, = a) so as to hinder egress: *let the doors be s. upon him, that he may play the fool nowhere but in's own house*, Hml III, 1, 135. b) so as to hinder ingress: Err. IV, 4, 66. V, 156. 204. As III, 5, 13. H8 II, 4, 43. Tit. V, 3, 105. c) so as to part with: *s. the gates upon one wooer*, Merch. I, 2, 147. *s. your gates upon's*, Cor. I, 7, 6.

With *in* and *out* (denoting the effect): *they have s. him in*, Cor. I, 4, 47. *were not my doors locked up and I s. out?* Err. IV, 4, 73. *fears which I would fain s. out*, All's V, 3, 115. H6A I, 3, 26. 30. Lr. III, 4, 18. Similarly with *from*: *the chamber-door that —s him from the heaven of his thought*, Lucr. 338. With *up*: *I wish mine eyes would, with themselves, s. up my thoughts*, Tp. II, 1, 192. *sleep, that sometimes —s up sorrow's eye*, Mids. III, 2, 435. *the gates of mercy shall be all s. up*, H5 III, 3, 10. *our halberds did s. up his passage*, H6C IV, 3, 20. —*s up his windows*, Rom. I, 1, 145. *thy eyes' windows fall, like death, when he —s up the day of life*, IV, 1, 101. *s. up your doors*, Lr. II, 4, 307. 311. Rom. I, 2, 56.

2) to inclose, to confine: *is all thy comfort s. in Gloster's tomb?* H6B III, 2, 78. *s. me nightly in a charnel-house*, Rom. IV, 1, 81. With *up*: LLL I, 2, 158. V, 2, 817. Wint. IV, 1, 19. Rom. I, 2, 56. Tim. I, 1, 98. Oth. III, 3, 114. Figurative use: *that we whose baser stars do s. us up in wishes, might with effects of them follow our friends*, All's I, 1, 197 (= confine). *in whom the tempers and the minds of all should be s. up*, Troil. I, 3, 58. *were all the wealth I have s. up in thee, I'ld give thee leave to hang it*, Tim. IV, 3, 279 (= inclosed, summed up). *and s. up in measureless content*, Mcb. II, 1, 16 (summed up all that he had to say, in expressing his measureless content). *and s. myself up in some other course to fortune's alms*, Oth. III, 4, 121 (make up my mind by confining myself. A passage much controverted. Q1 *shoot*).

**Shuttle**, the instrument with which the weaver shoots the cross threads: *life is a s.* Wiv. V, 1, 25 (Job VII, 6: *my days are swifter than a weaver's shuttle, and are spent without hope*).

**Shy**, keeping at a distance, reserved, demure: *a s. fellow was the duke, and I believe I know the cause of his withdrawing*, Meas. III, 2, 138. *as s., as grave, as just, as absolute as Angelo*, V, 54.

**Shylock**, name of the Jew in Merch. I, 3, 53 etc.

**Sibyl**, one of a number of prophetesses renowned in the history of ancient Rome: *exceeding the nine —s of old Rome*, H6A I, 2, 56. *blow these sands like —s' leaves abroad*, Tit. IV, 1, 105. *as old as S.* Shr. I, 2, 70. = prophetess, sorceress in general: *a s. that had numbered the sun to course two hundred compasses*, Oth. III, 4, 70.

**Sibylla**, the same: *if I live to be as old as S.* Merch. I, 2, 116. cf. Shr. I, 2, 70.

**Sicil**, the kingdom of Sicily: H6B I, 1, 6. *both the —s*, H6C I, 4, 122 (i. e. Naples and Sicily). *the —s*, V, 7, 39.

**Sicilia,** 1) the island to the south of Italy: Wint. I, 1, 5. III, 2, 13. IV, 2, 23. 59. IV, 4, 522. 554. 600 (the later Ff *Sicily*). 680. V, 1, 139. H6B I, 1, 48. 2) the king of it: Wint. I, 1, 23. I, 2, 146. 218.

**Sicilian,** pertaining to Sicily: Wint. V, 1, 164.

**Sicilius,** name of the father of Posthumus in Cymb. I, 1, 29. V, 4, 51.

**Sicily,** the island to the south of Italy: Wint. I, 2, 175. IV, 4, 600 (F1 *Sicilia*). Tit. III, 1, 242. Ant. II, 6, 7. 35. 46. III, 6, 24.

**Sicinius,** name of a tribune in Cor. I, 1, 221.

**Sick,** adj. (compar. *—er:* R2 II, 1, 91) 1) diseased, not in health, ill: Ven. 702. Lucr. 901. Sonn. 140, 7. 153, 11. Ado II, 1, 301. 303. III, 4, 72. V, 1, 131. LLL I, 1, 139. V, 2, 832. 861. Merch. III, 2, 237. IV, 1, 151. Tw. I, 5, 117. 148. John IV, 1, 28. 52 (*at your s. service* = to attend you in illness). IV, 2, 88. V, 4, 6. R2 I, 3, 65. I, 4, 54. II, 1, 84. V, 3, 133 (*s. for fear*). H4A IV, 1, 16. 17. 28. H4B I, 1, 138. I, 2, 108. II, 2, 34. 52. II, 4, 42. IV, 3, 83. IV, 4, 102. IV, 5, 13. H5 II, 1, 86. III, 5, 57. IV, 1, 188. 268. H6A III, 2, 95. R3 IV, 2, 52. H8 IV, 1, 35. V, 5, 75. Troil. II, 3, 92. III, 1, 98. Cor. I, 1, 182. I, 10, 20. Rom. I, 1, 186. 208. IV, 4, 7. V, 2, 7. Tim. III, 4, 74. IV, 3, 110. Caes. I, 2, 128. II, 1, 261. 263. 310. 315. 316. 327. 328. II, 2, 65. Mcb. V, 3, 37. Hml. III, 2, 173. Lr. I, 3, 8. II, 4, 89. V, 3, 95. Ant. I, 3, 5. 13. Cymb. I, 6, 119. III, 6, 3. IV, 2, 5. 7. 8. 13. 37. 44. 50. Per. I, 1, 47. *to fall s :* Sonn. 118, 14. Merch. III, 4, 71. H8 IV, 2, 15. *s. to death:* Pilgr. 233; LLL IV, 3, 107. H8 IV, 2, 1. Tim. III, 1, 64. With *of* before the name of the disease: Meas. V, 151. All's I, 3, 142 (*on't* = of it). Troil. I, 3, 139. Cymb. V, 4, 5. *s. with* = ill in consequence of: Gent. I, 1, 69. H6A V, 5, 86. H6B III, 2, 62. Troil. III, 3, 238. *s. and green* = chlorotic, Rom. II, 2, 8 (cf. *Green-sickness*). *my heart is s.* = I feel faint, John V, 3, 4. *my s. heart,* H6C V, 2, 8. *'tis bitter cold, and I am s. at heart,* Hml. I, 1, 9.

Applied to indispositions of the mind: *you have some s. offence within your mind,* Caes. II, 1, 268. Especially to the state of being in love: Ven. 584. Pilgr. 233 and LLL IV, 3, 107. Gent. I, 1, 69. II, 4, 149. Ado III, 1, 21 (*sick in love*). III, 4, 42. LLL II, 185 (*s. at the heart*). V, 2, 417. As III, 2, 377. All's IV, 2, 35. Oth. II, 3, 53.

2) affected with nausea: *I am s. when I do look on thee,* Mids. II, 1, 212. 213. *s. of a calm,* H4B II, 4, 40. *I am s. at heart, when I behold —,* Mcb. V, 3, 19. *s. at sea,* Cymb. III, 4, 192. Hence = disgusted, weary: *eyes s. and blunted with community,* H4A III, 2, 77. with *of: the commonwealth is s. of their own choice,* H4B I, 3, 87. *I am s. of this false world,* Tim. IV, 3, 376.

3) Used of any irregular, distempered and corrupted state: *after many accents and delays, untimely breathings, s. and short assays,* Lucr. 1720. *now my gracious numbers are decayed and my s. Muse doth give another place,* Sonn. 79, 4. *they are as s. that surfeit with too much as they that starve with nothing,* Merch. I, 2, 6. *makes sound opinion s. and truth suspected,* John IV, 2, 26. *the present time's so s.* V, 1, 14. *now comes the s. hour that his surfeit made,* R2 II, 2, 84. *though that* (his immortal part) *be s.* H4B II, 2, 114. *poor kingdom, s. with civil blows,* IV, 5, 134. *to view the s. and feeble parts of France,* H5 II, 4, 22.

*what we oft do best, by s. interpreters, once weak ones, is not ours, or not allowed,* H8 I, 2, 82. *this priest has no pride in him? Not to speak of: I would not be so s. though for his place,* II, 2, 83. *put my s. cause into his hands that hates me,* III, 1, 118. *my conscience, which I then did feel full s.* II, 4, 204. *the enterprise is s.* Troil. I, 3, 103. 139. *to my s. soul each toy seems prologue to some great amiss,* Hml. IV, 5, 17. Used of a dim and pale light: *let their breaths make s. the life of purity, the supreme fair,* Lucr. 779. *this night methinks is but the daylight s.; it looks a little paler,* Merch. V, 124. *the moon ... s. and pale with grief,* Rom. II, 2, 5; cf. 8. *the moist star was s. almost to doomsday with eclipse,* Hml. I, 1, 120.

With *for,* = pining for: *as to a bed that longing have been s. for,* Meas. II, 4, 103. *almost s. for me,* Ado V, 4, 80. *s. for breathing and exploit,* All's I, 2, 16. *s. for one* (beard) Tw. III, 1, 53. *the young king is s. for me,* H4B V, 3, 141. cf. *I am s. till I see her,* Wiv. III, 2, 28. With *in,* = a) in a bad state with respect to: *wherein thou liest in reputation s.* R2 II, 1, 96. *s. in the world's regard, wretched and low,* H4A IV, 3, 57. *when we are s. in fortune,* Lr. I, 2, 129. b) morbidly affected, distempered by: *I am s. in displeasure to him,* Ado II, 2, 5. With *of,* = afflicted, tainted, or corrupted by: *I was not s. of any fear from thence,* Sonn. 86, 12. *and s. of welfare, found a kind of meetness to be diseased,* 118, 7. *drugs poison him that so fell s. of you,* 14. *you are s. of self-love,* Tw. I, 5, 97. *I am s. and capable of fears,* John III, 1, 12. *rank minds s. of happiness,* H4B IV, 1, 64. *exampled by the first pace that is s. of his superior,* Troil. I, 3, 132 (= envious of). *s. of proud heart,* II, 3, 93. *I am s. of that grief too,* Tim. III, 6, 19. *I am s. of shame,* 46. *that nature, being s. of man's unkindness, should yet be hungry,* IV, 3, 176. *I am s. of many griefs,* Caes. IV, 3, 144. *quietness, grown s. of rest, would purge by any desperate change,* Ant. I, 3, 53.

**Sick,** vb. to sicken, to fall ill: *Edward—ed and died,* H4B IV, 4, 128.

**Sicken,** 1) intr. a) to grow sick, to fall ill: Sonn. 118, 4. As III, 2, 25. Mcb. IV, 3, 173. In a moral sense: *that his soul s. not,* Meas. II, 4, 41. *when love begins to s. and decay,* Caes. IV, 2, 20. *mine eyes did s. at the sight,* Ant. III, 10, 17.

b) to feel disgust, to become weary: *whose nature —s but to speak a truth,* All's V, 3, 207. *that, surfeiting, the appetite may s. and so die,* Tw. I, 1, 3. *though the treasure of nature's germens tumble all together, even till destruction s.* Mcb. IV, 1, 60.

2) tr. to impair: *have by this so —ed their estates,* H8 I, 1, 82.

**Sick-fallen,** sick, diseased: *confusion waits, as doth a raven on a s. beast,* John IV, 3, 153 (cf. Caes. V, 1, 87).

**Sickle,** a reaping-hook; attribute of Time: Sonn. 116, 10. 126, 2.

**Sickle,** an ancient coin among the Jews: *with fond —s of the tested gold,* Meas. II, 2, 149 (M. Edd. *shekels*).

**Sicklemen,** reapers: Tp. IV, 134.

**Sicklied o'er,** tainted and overspread in a sickly manner: *the native hue of resolution is s. with the pale cast of thought,* Hml. III, 1, 85.

**Sickliness,** illness: *impute his words to wayward s. and age in him,* R2 II, 1, 142.

**Sickly,** adj. diseased, not in health (quite = *sick,* but usually joined to a subst., whereas *sick* is oftener in the predicate): *the uncertain s. appetite to please,* Sonn. 147, 4. *I am not such a s. creature,* Wiv. III, 4, 61 (to make my will). *if s. ears will hear your idle scorns,* LLL V, 2, 873. *she has raised me from my s. bed,* All's II, 3, 118. *hence, thou s. quoif,* H4B I, 1, 147. H5 III, 6, 164. IV, 2, 20. R3 I, 1, 136. II, 1, 42. Caes. II, 4, 14. V, 1, 87 (cf. John IV, 3, 153). Hml. III, 3, 96. III, 4, 80. Lr. II, 4, 112. = disordered in general: *this s. land might solace as before,* R3 II, 3, 30. *the s. weal,* Mcb. V, 2, 27. = dim: *in whose fresh regard weak sights their s. radiance do amend,* Compl. 214.

**Sickly,** adv. 1) ill, not in health: *who wear our health but s. in his life,* Mcb. III, 1, 107.
2) with disgust, reluctantly: *cold and s. he vented them,* Ant. III, 4, 7.

**Sickness,** 1) disease, illness: Ven. 741. Sonn. 118, 4. Err. V, 99. Ado I, 1, 251. Mids. I, 1, 142. 186. IV, 1, 178. Shr. IV, 3, 14. All's I, 2, 74. II, 1, 171. Wint. I, 2, 384. 398. II, 3, 11. IV, 2, 2. John IV, 2, 86. V, 7, 13. R2 II, 1, 132 *(the present s. that I have).* V, 1, 77. H4A IV, 1, 26. 28. 31. 42. IV, 4, 14. H4B III, 1, 106. IV, 5, 82. H5 III, 3, 55. III, 6, 154. H6A III, 2, 89. H6B III, 2, 370. IV, 7, 94. R3 I, 3, 29. II, 2, 9. H8 I, 2, 184. IV, 2, 24. V, 3, 26. Troil. I, 3, 140. Tim. III, 1, 66. V, 1, 189 *(my long s. of health and living).* Caes. II, 1, 267. 321. IV, 3, 152. Hml. II, 2, 66. Lr. V, 3, 105. Ant. I, 2, 124. II, 2, 173. Cymb. III, 2, 76. IV, 2, 148. *it warms the very s. in my heart, that I shall live and tell him to his teeth,* Hml. IV, 7, 56 (= faintness, depressed spirits).
2) nausea, squeamishness: LLL V, 2, 280.
3) any disordered state: *a great s. in his judgement,* Tim. V, 1, 31.

**Sick-thoughted,** full of love-thoughts: *s. Venus makes amain to him,* Ven. 5.

**Sicyon,** town in ancient Greece: Ant. I, 2, 117. 118. 123.

**Side,** subst. 1) the part of an animal body fortified by the ribs, between the back and the belly: *his brawny —s, with hairy bristles armed,* Ven. 625. *plucked the knife from Lucrece' s.* Lucr. 1807. *more sharp to me than spurring to his s.* Sonn. 50, 12. *backs, shoulders, —s,* Wiv. V, 5, 58. As III, 4, 47. H4B I, 1, 45. H6A V, 3, 49. Mcb. I, 7, 26. *and by my s. wear steel,* Wiv. I, 3, 84. Ado V, 1, 126. Tit. II, 1, 39. Hml. V, 2, 166. Cymb. I, 4, 6. *draw this metal from my s.* John V, 2, 16. *spectacles on nose and pouch on s.* As II, 7, 159.

Used to denote immediate nearness and proximity: *whose messengers are here about my s.* Oth. I, 2, 89. *tempteth my better angel from my s.* Sonn. 144, 6. Mids. III, 2, 185. R2 III, 2, 80. H6A IV, 5, 48. IV, 7, 12. H6B III, 1, 191. Tim. IV, 3, 31. Oth. V, 2, 208. *oft came Edward to my s.* H6C I, 4, 11. Oftenest preceded by *by: by Venus' s.* Ven. 180. *the boy that by her s. lay killed,* 1165. *by Lucrece' s.* Lucr. 381. 425. Sonn. 151, 12. 154, 2. Compl. 65. Mids. II, 1, 125. II, 2, 51. III, 2, 39. Merch. III, 2, 307. All's II, 3, 53. Shr. Ind. 2, 146. Tw. V, 80. R2 I, 3, 252. H5 IV, 6, 8. H6A IV, 6, 56. H6C III, 3, 16. Tit. V, 1, 48. V, 2, 45. Caes. III, 1, 271. Lr. III, 6, 40. Oth. IV, 1, 195. V, 2, 237. Ant. II, 3, 18. IV, 15, 36. Cymb. V, 5, 1. *s. by s.* H6A IV, 5, 54. Pre-

ceded by *on: she, on his left s., craving aid,* H6C III, 1, 43. *on his right,* 44. *went on each s. of the queen,* H8 IV, 1, 100. *Of* omitted after it: *on each s. her stood pretty boys,* Ant. II, 2, 206.
2) Plur. *—s* = frame of the body; in a proper and metaphorical sense: *this broken music in his —s,* As I, 2, 150. *let nature crush the —s o' the earth together,* Wint. IV, 4, 489. *breaks the —s of loyalty,* H8 I, 2, 28. *whose quality the —s o' the world may danger,* Ant. I, 2, 199. *Caesar's ambition which swelled so much that it did almost stretch the —s o' the world,* Cymb. III, 1, 51. Especially = the breast, as containing the heart or the lungs: *both on one sampler, ... both warbling of one song, as if our hands, our —s, voices and minds, had been incorporate,* Mids. III, 2, 207. *Taurus, that's —s and heart,* Tw. I, 3, 148. *there's no woman's —s can bide the beating of so strong a passion,* II, 4, 96. *he cracks his gorge, his —s, with violent hefts,* Wint. II, 1, 44. *hacked one another in the —s of Caesar,* Caes. V, 1, 40. *O —s, you are too tough,* Lr. II, 4, 200. *the —s of nature will not sustain it,* Ant. I, 3, 16. *as loud as his strong —s can volley,* II, 7, 118. *cleave, my —s,* IV, 14, 39. *can my —s hold,* Cymb. I, 6, 69. Considered as the part principally fed by nourishment: *it is the pasture lards the brother's —s,* Tim. IV, 3, 12. *your houseless heads and unfed —s,* Lr. III, 4, 30. As the seat of carnal desire: *I will keep my —s to myself,* Wiv. V, 5, 28. *with Tarquin's ravishing —s,* Mcb. II, 1, 55 (most M. Edd. *strides*).
3) Applied, after the analogy of the animal body, to other things having two principal parts or surfaces opposed to each other: (the pillow) *swelling on either s.* (of the hand) *to want his bliss,* Lucr. 389. *angel on the outward s.* Meas. III, 2, 286. *on the windy s. of care,* Ado II, 1, 327; cf. *still you keep o' the windy s. of the law,* Tw. III, 4, 181. *my vessel's s.* Merch. I, 1, 32. *damned like an ill-roasted egg, all on one s.* As III, 2, 39. *our cake is dough on both —s,* Shr. I, 1, 110. *her head on one s.* Wint. III, 3, 20; cf. *hang my head at one s.* Oth. IV, 3, 32. *on this s. my hand, and on that s. yours,* R2 IV, 183. V, 2, 18. H4A III, 1, 109. 111. 113. H6A I, 2, 99. H6B III, 2, 98. R3 V, 3, 299. H8 I, 4, 20; cf. Mcb. III, 4, 10. Troil. I, 3, 43. Cor. I, 1, 48. I, 6, 51. Caes. V, 2, 2. Hml. I, 1, 85. Lr. I, 4, 205. III, 7, 71. Ant. III, 9, 1. *to turn the wrong s. out* = to pervert, to distort, to derange: *so turns she every man the wrong s. out,* Ado III, 1, 68. *how quickly the wrong s. may be turned outward,* Tw. III, 1, 14. Lr. IV, 2, 9. Oth. II, 3, 54. cf. *that turned your wit the seamy s. without,* IV, 2, 146. *Of* after s. omitted: *writ o' both —s the leaf,* LLL V, 2, 8. *upon this s. the sea,* John II, 488. *on this s. Tiber,* Caes. III, 2, 254. *to keep one's eyes of either s. 's nose,* Lr. I, 5, 22 (= on either side his nose; cf. *Of*). *look out o' the other s. your monument,* Ant. IV, 15, 8. cf. II, 2, 206.

Hence, generally, one of two parts, or directions, or respects, placed in contradistinction to each other: *this s. is Hiems, winter, this Ver,* LLL V, 2, 901. *Armado o'th' one s., and his page o' t' other,* IV, 1, 146. 149. *then, on the other s., I checked my friends,* R3 III, 7, 150. *my back o' t' other s.* Rom. II, 5, 51. = line of descent, as only from one of the two parents: *brother by the mother's s.* John I, 163. Tit. IV, 2, 126. Ant. II, 2, 120. Oftenest = party, opposed interest, one of two at war: *Fortune shall cull forth out of one s. her happy minion*, John II, 392. *which is the s. that I must go withal?* III, 1, 327. *we of the offering s.* H4A IV, 1, 69. *both —s fiercely fought*, H6C II, 1, 121. *there is expectance here from both the —s*, Troil. IV, 5, 146. *the one s. must have bale*, Cor. I, 1, 167. *these are a s. that would be glad to have this true*, IV, 6, 151. *which s. should win*, V, 3, 113. *each in either s. give the all-hail to thee*, 138. *damnable both-sides rogue*, All's IV, 3, 251. *hardly shall I carry out my s.* Lr. V, 1, 61 (= be a winner in the game). Preceded by *on: upon thy s. against myself I'll fight*, Sonn. 88, 3. *on both —s thus is simple truth suppressed*, 138, 8. Compl. 113. Meas. IV, 6, 6. LLL IV, 1, 76. 77. 78. IV, 3, 8. Tw. V, 69. 376. Wint. II, 3, 191. IV, 4, 650. John III, 1, 117. 124. 335. V, 2, 8. R2 II, 2, 89. 147. H4A II, 4, 348. V, 1, 99. H4B I, 1, 198. I, 2, 88. H6A I, 2, 3. II, 4, 20. 22. 40. 48. 51. 54. 64. V, 1, 10. H6B IV, 8, 54. R3 I, 4, 272. III, 2, 53. V, 3, 94. 175. 240. V, 5, 12. H8 II, 4, 54 *(on all —s)*. Troil. Prol. 21. I, 1, 93. V, 4, 10. Cor. III, 1, 181. Rom. II, 4, 169. Caes. II, 4, 6. IV, 3, 4. Mcb. V, 7, 25. Hml. II, 2, 370. V, 2, 272. 315. Lr. V, 3, 49. Oth. I, 3, 217. Ant. III, 10, 9. Cymb. V, 3, 81. *of for on: let us take the law of our —s*, Rom. I, 1, 44. 54 (the servant's speech). Preceded by *to: to train ten thousand English to their s.* John III, 4, 175. *flieth to his s.* H6A I, 1, 95.

4) any external part in respect to its direction or situation: *the blood circles her body in on every s.* Lucr. 1739. *whose western s. is with a vineyard backed*, Meas. IV, 1, 29. *on the east s. of the grove*, H6B II, 1, 43. 48. *pry on every s.* R3 III, 5, 6. *upon the north s. of this pleasant chase*, Tit. II, 3, 255. *puffs away from thence, turning his s. to the dew-dropping south*, Rom. I, 4, 103 (= turning to the side of the dew-dropping south. The surreptitious Q1 and M. Edd. *face*). *as he was coming from this churchyard s.* V, 3, 186.

5) margin, verge, border: *close by the Thames s.* Wiv. III, 3, 16. *I would you had been by the ship s.* Wint. III, 3, 112. *thy cheek's s. struck off*, H6A I, 4, 75. *on our long-boat's s. strike off his head*, H6B IV, 1, 68. *on the forest s.* H6C IV, 6, 83. *to the water s. I must conduct your grace*, H8 II, 1, 95. *that westward rooteth from the city's s.* Rom. I, 1, 129. *abuts against the island's s.* Per. V, 1, 52.

**Side,** vb. 1) intr. to take one's party in a quarrel: *the nobility are vexed, whom we see have —d in his behalf*, Cor. IV, 2, 2. 2) trans. to take the party of, to join: *s. factions*, Cor. I, 1, 197. In Sonn. 46, 9 O. Edd. *s.*, M. Edd. *'cide*.

**Side-piercing,** heart-rending: *O thou s. sight*, Lr. IV, 6, 85.

**Side-sleeves,** hanging sleeves: Ado III, 4, 21.
**Side-stitches,** stitches in the side: Tp. I, 2, 326.
**Siege,** 1) the act of besetting a fortified place: Lucr. Arg. 5. John II, 54. 213. R2 II, 1, 62. H5 I, 2, 152. III Chor. 25. III, 2, 70. H6A I, 1, 111. IV, 3, 11. Troil. I, 3, 12. Mcb. V, 5, 3. IV, 3, 130. *forsake the s.* H6A I, 2, 40. *to raise the s.* (= to dislodge the besiegers): H5 III, 3, 47. H6A I, 2, 13. 53. 130. I, 4, 103. Metaphorically, = strong endeavours to gain entrance, assaults, attacks in general: *the wreckful s. of battering days*, Sonn. 65, 6. *war, death, or sickness did lay s. to it*, Mids. I, 1, 142. *his* (death's)

*s. is now against the mind*, John V, 7, 16. *the busy fiend that lays strong s. unto this wretch's soul*, H6B III, 3, 22. *to remove that s. of grief from her*, Rom. V, 3, 237. *to whom all sores lay s.* Tim. IV, 3, 7. Used of an assiduous love-suit: *remove your s. from my unyielding heart*, Ven. 423. *this s. that hath engirt his marriage*, Lucr. 221. *to lay an amiable s. to the honesty of this Ford's wife*, Wiv. II, 2, 243. *lays down his wanton s. before her beauty*, All's III, 7, 18. *she will not stay the s. of loving terms*, Rom. I, 1, 218. cf. *whose love-suit hath been to me as fearful as a s.* Cymb. III, 4, 137.

2) seat: *upon the very s. of justice*, Meas. IV, 2, 101.

3) place, rank: *your sum of parts did not together pluck such envy from him as did that one, and that, in my regard, of the unworthiest s.* Hml. IV, 7, 77. *I fetch my life and being from men of royal s.* Oth. I, 2, 22 (Qq *height*).

3) stool, excrement, fecal matter: *how camest thou to be the s. of this moon-calf?* Tp. II, 2, 110.

**Sienna,** see *Syenna*.

**Sieve,** a utensil by which the fine parts of a pulverized substance are separated from the coarse: Ado V, 1, 5. All's I, 3, 208. Mcb. I, 3, 8. In Troil. II, 2, 71 Q *the remainder viands we do not throw in unrespective siue;* F1 *same;* the later Ff *place;* Johnson *sieve*, others *sew* or *sure*, i. e. sewer.

**Sift,** to examine minutely, to scrutinize, to sound: All's V, 3, 124. R2 I, 1, 12. H6A III, 1, 24. Hml. II, 2, 58.

**Sigh,** subst. a deep respiration indicative of grief: Ven. 1071. Lucr. 563. 586. 1319. 1004. Tp. I, 2, 222. Gent. II, 3, 60. III, 1, 230. H4A III, 1, 10. H4B I, 1, 80. Tit. III, 1, 228. Cymb. III, 4, 5 etc. especially caused by love: Ven. 51. 376. 964. 966. Sonn. 47, 4. Gent. I, 1, 30. II, 4, 132. III, 2, 74. Ado V, 1, 173. LLL III, 177. 184. IV, 3, 164. 347. Mids. I, 1, 154. As V, 2, 90. All's II, 3, 82. Tw. I, 5, 275. II, 4, 64. 68. Wint. I, 2, 287 etc. *to breathe a s.* Merch. III, 1, 100. Tw. II, 2, 40. H6B III, 2, 345. *to raise a s.* Compl. 228. Hml. II, 1, 94. Sighs forming clouds (cf. R2 III, 1, 20): *saw —s reek from you*, LLL IV, 3, 140. *with our —s we'll breathe the welkin dim and stain the sun with fog*, Tit. III, 1, 212. *adding to clouds more clouds with his deep —s*, Rom. I, 1, 139. *love is a smoke raised with the fume of —s*, 196. *the sun not yet thy —s from heaven clears*, II, 3, 73 (cf. III, 3, 72). *he furnaces the thick —s from him*, Cymb. I, 6, 67. Wasting life by costing every one a drop of blood: *consume away in —s*, Ado III, 1, 78. *sighs of love, that costs the fresh blood dear*, Mids. III, 2, 97. *blood-consuming —s*, H6B III, 2, 61. *blood-drinking —s*, 63. *blood-sucking —s*, H6C IV, 4, 22. *like a spendthrift s. that hurts by easing*, Hml. IV, 7, 123. cf. Ado III, 1, 78.

**Sigh,** vb. to suffer a deep single respiration, as in grief: Compl. 44. Pilgr. 204. Tp. I, 2, 150. Ado III, 2, 26. V, 3, 17. Merch. II, 2, 203. III, 3, 15. Shr. V, 2, 123. Wint. II, 3, 34 etc. especially in pangs of love: Gent. II, 1, 22. II, 2, 10. Ado II, 3, 64. LLL I, 2, 67. III, 68. 206. As IV, 1, 222. Wint. I, 2, 117 etc. *to s. for* = to be in love with: Tp. I, 2, 446. LLL III, 202. Tw. II, 5, 165. *to s. to* = to tell one's grief, to complain to: *to s. to the winds*, Tp. I, 2, 149. *te that I'll s. and weep*, Gent. IV, 2, 123.

Transitively, 1) with an adverb or prepositional expression, to denote an effect: *may s. it off* (your head) Meas. I, 2, 178. *s. away Sundays*, Ado I, 1, 204. *—ed his soul toward the Grecian tents*, Merch. V, 5. 2) = to convey or express in sighs: *for these dead birds s. a prayer*, Phoen. 67. *s. a note and sing a note*, LLL III, 13. *—ed forth proverbs*, Cor. I, 1, 209. 3) to emit, to exhale in sighs: *I'll s. celestial breath*, Ven. 189. *draws up her breath and —ing it again, exclaims on death*, 930. *—ed my English breath in foreign clouds*, R2 III, 1, 20. *never man —ed truer breath*, Cor. IV, 5, 121. 4) to lament, to mourn: *I s. the lack of many a thing*, Sonn. 30, 3.

**Sight,** 1) the sense of seeing, faculty of vision: *her s. dazzling makes the wound seem three*, Ven. 1064. *sweets that shall the truest s. beguile*, 1144. *the sun bereaves our s.* Lucr. 373. *my soul's imaginary s. presents thy shadow to my sightless view*, Sonn. 27, 9. 148, 2. 150, 3. Tp. I, 2, 302. Err. III, 2, 57. Mids. III, 2, 369. As V, 4, 124. 125. 126. H4B III, 2, 336 *(thick s.).* IV, 4, 110. H5 IV, 7, 62. H6B I, 2, 6. II, 1, 64. 71. 129. R3 IV, 4, 26. H8 IV, 2, 108. Troil. I, 2, 31. Cor. III, 2, 5. Tit. II, 3, 195 *(dull).* III, 2, 84 *(thy s. is young).* Rom. I, 5, 54. Caes. V, 3, 21 *(thick).* Mcb. II, 1, 37. II, 3, 76. Hml. III, 4, 78. Lr. IV, 6, 20. 23. V, 3, 282 *(dull).* Oth. V, 2, 364. Perhaps = insight, knowledge, skill, in Troil. III, 3, 4; but the passage seems to be corrupt.

2) the eyes: *his louring brows o'erwhelming his fair s.* Ven. 183. *the object that did feed her s.* 822. *nor could she moralize his wanton s.* Lucr. 104. *it beguiled attention, charmed the s.* 1404. *sets you most rich in youth before my s.* Sonn. 15, 10. *if aught in me worthy perusal stand against thy s.* 38, 6. *shadows like to thee do mock my s.* 61, 4. *to every place at once, and nowhere fixed, the mind and s. distractedly commixed*, Compl. 28. *weak —s their sickly radiance do amend*, 214. *the turtle saw his right flaming in the Phoenix' s.* Phoen. 35. *we must starve our s. from lover's food*, Mids. I, 1, 222. *take this charm from off her s.* II, 1, 183. *laid the love-juice on some true-love's s.* III, 2, 89. *never more abase our s. so low as to vouchsafe one glance unto the ground*, H6B I, 2, 15. *in s. of God and us your guilt is great*, II, 3, 2. *kill the innocent gazer with thy s.* III, 2, 53. *to rob my s. of thy land's view*, 105. *to greet mine own land with my wishful s.* H6C III, 1, 14. *if I be so disgracious in your s.* R3 IV, 4, 177 (Ff *eye*). *the bleared —s are spectacled to see him*, Cor. II, 1, 221. *schoolboys' tears take up the glasses of my s.* III, 2, 117. *amazed my s.* Mcb. V, 1, 86. *looked upon this love with idle s.* Hml. II, 2, 138. *strike the s. of the duke*, Lr. IV, 6, 283. *a scorpion to her s.* Cymb. V, 5, 45. *why cloud they not their —s*, Per. I, 1, 74. *to glad the s.* I, 4, 28.

Hence, as eyes, = presence: *quit my s.* Mcb. III, 4, 93. *avoid my s.* Lr. I, 1, 126. *should transport me farthest from your s.* Sonn. 117, 8. *banished from her s.* Gent. III, 2, 2. R2 IV, 315. H6B II, 3, 103. III, 2, 394. Tit. III, 1, 284. Mcb. III, 1, 119. Hml. I, 2, 220. Lr. II, 4, 190. Cymb. I, 1, 125. V, 5, 237. *in my s. forbear to glance thine eye aside*, Sonn. 139, 5. *never come in my s. more*, As IV, 1, 41. 52. Shr. II, 30. Tw. III, 2, 20. III, 4, 171. R2 I, 1, 188. I, 2, 38. V, 2, 86. H4B IV, 1, 179. H6B I, 1, 11. IV, 2, 189. III, 2, 389. H6C III, 3, 181. R3 I, 3, 164. V, 3, 96. Tit. I, 246. III, 1, 67. Rom. II, 6, 5. Lr. IV, 6, 35. 115. *return no more into my s.* Gent. I, 2, 47. IV, 4, 65. Mcb. I, 3, 102. *durst not come near your s.* H4A V, 1,

63. *God keep him out of my s.* Ado II, 1, 113. *out of my s.!* Tw. IV, 1, 53. As IV, 1, 221. John IV, 2, 242. H4A V, 1, 66. H6B III, 2, 48. R3 I, 2, 149. Lr. I, 1, 159. Oth. IV, 1, 258. *bring me to the s. of Isabella*, Meas. I, 4, 18. *you shall not be admitted to his s.* IV, 3, 125. Shr. Ind. 2, 76. R3 IV, 1, 25. *come not within his s.* Mids. II, 1, 19.

3) the act of seeing, look, view: *his eyes, whose —s till then were levelled on my face*, Compl. 282. *at the first s. they have changed eyes*, Tp. I, 2, 440. *at first s.* As III, 5, 82. Troil. V, 2, 9.

4) the manner of seeing: *nothing else with his proud s. agrees*, Ven. 288. *the s. whereof* (your eye) *I think you had from me*, Ado V, 4, 25. *none could be so abused in s. as he*, As III, 5, 80.

5) the perceiving or being perceived by the eye, view, Lat. conspectus: *our sport is not in s.* Ven. 124 (cannot be seen). *wear the favours most in s.* LLL V, 2, 136. *vanished out of s.* Sonn. 63, 7. R3 III, 5, 107. *lacked s. only*, Wint. II, 1, 177. *the dismallest object that ever eye with s. made heart lament*, Tit. II, 3, 205. *you know him well by s.* Caes. I, 3, 15. Relatively: *he fed them with his s., they him with berries*, Ven. 1104. *melted like a vapour from her s.* 1166. *each under eye doth homage to his new-appearing s.* Sonn. 7, 3. *to divide the conquest of thy s.* 46, 2. *feasting on your s.* 75, 9. *heart hath his hope, and eyes their wished s.* Pilgr. 202. *every slight occasion that could give me s. of her*, Wiv. II, 2, 205. *upon their s. we two will fly*, IV, 4, 54. *to stick it* (the rod) *in their children's s.* Meas. I, 3, 25. *in our s. they three were taken up*, Err. I, 1, 111. *to-morrow you shall have a s. of them* (papers) LLL II, 166. *to have his s.* Mids. I, 1, 251. *at his s. away his fellows fly*, III, 2, 24. *takest true delight in the s. of thy former lady's eye*, 456. *I trust to take of truest Thisbe s.* V, 280. *good wrestling, which you have lost the s. of*, As I, 2, 117. *the s. of lovers feedeth those in love*, III, 4, 60. III, 5, 4. Shr. Ind. 2, 61. I, 1, 225. Tw. I, 2, 41. Wint. II, 2, 40. III, 3, 139. IV, 4, 481. 522. 680. V, 3, 57. John II, 222. III, 1, 36. IV, 2, 219. R2 II, 3, 18. III, 2, 52. H4A III, 2, 88. IV, 5, 230. H6A I, 1, 30. V, 3, 69. V, 4, 122. H6B I, 1, 32. IV, 4, 46. V, 1, 90. V, 2, 49. H6C I, 3, 30. II, 5, 130 *(having the flying hare in s.).* Cor. V, 3, 98. Tit. V, 1, 4. Rom. III, 2, 56. Tim. I, 1, 255 *(joyful of your —s).* 262. IV, 3, 125. Ant. III, 10, 17. Per. V Prol. 21. V, 1, 33.

6) things seen or to be seen, show, spectacle, vision: *what a s. it was*, Ven. 343. *doth view the s. which makes supposed terror true*, Lucr. 455. *daunts them with more dreadful —s*, 462. *to see sad —s moves more than hear them told*, 1324. *moan the expense of many a vanished s.* Sonn. 30, 8. *if we see the rudest or gentlest s.* 113, 9. *but dressings of a former s.* 123, 4. *here's a goodly s.* Tp. V, 260. *you may say what —s you see; I see things too*, Gent. I, 2, 138. Mids. IV, 1, 51. As III, 2, 255. All's III, 5, 2. Wint. III, 3, 107. 118. IV, 4, 849 *(we must show our strange —s,* i. e. things worth seeing; the clown's speech). V, 2, 46. H6A I, 4, 62. H6C II, 2, 6. R3 I, 4, 3. 23. H8 IV, 1, 11. V, 2, 20. Tit. II, 3, 216. II, 4, 53. III, 1, 247. 257. 262. V, 1, 52. Rom. I, 2, 105. IV, 5, 42. V, 3, 174. 206. Caes. I, 3, 138. II, 2, 16. III, 2, 206. V, 3, 78. Mcb. II, 2, 21. III, 4, 114. IV, 1, 122. 155. Hml. I, 1, 25. I, 2, 247. IV, 7, 100. V, 2, 373. 378. 412. Lr. IV, 6, 85. 208. Oth. V, 2, 207. 278. Ant. IV, 15, 40.

7) aperture for the eyes in a helmet: *their eyes of fire sparkling through —s of steel*, H4B IV, 1, 121.

**Sighted,** having eyes: *s. like the basilisk*, Wint. I, 2, 388. cf. *Thick-sighted*.

**Sight-hole,** a chink through which one may look, a peeping-hole: *stop all —s, every loop from whence the eye of reason may pry in upon us*, H4A IV, 1, 71.

**Sightless,** 1) not seeing, blind, dark: *poor grooms are s. night, kings glorious day*, Lucr. 1013. *my soul's imaginary sight presents thy shadow to my s. view*, Sonn. 27, 10. *when in dead night thy shade on s. eyes doth stay*, 43, 12.

2) not seen, invisible: *wherever in your s. substances you wait on nature's mischief*, Mcb. I, 5, 50. *the s. couriers of the air*, I, 7, 23.

3) offensive to the eye, unsightly: *full of unpleasing blots and s. stains*, John III, 1, 45. cf. *Featureless* and *Shapeless*.

**Sightly,** pleasing to the eye: John II, 143.

**Sight-outrunning,** swifter than sight: Tp. I, 2, 203. cf. Lucr. 1668.

**Sign,** subst. 1) a distinguishing mark: *we, following the —s, wooed but the s. of she*, LLL V, 2, 469. *though he does bear some —s of me, yet you have too much blood in him*, Wint. II, 1, 57. *leaving me no s. to show the world I am a gentleman*, R2 III, 1, 25. *the s. of your profession*, Caes. I, 1, 4. *—s of nobleness, like stars, shall shine on all deservers*, Mcb. I, 4, 41. *render to me some corporal s. about her*, Cymb. II, 4, 119. Especially a figure distinguishing a house (the custom of numbering houses being of a recent date): Ado I, 1, 256. 269. H4A I, 2, 9. H4B II, 4, 271. H6B III, 2, 81. V, 2, 67. R3 III, 5, 79. Tit. IV, 2, 98. Per. IV, 2, 124. Figuratively = something of a deceptive semblance, not answering the promise: *before these bastard —s of fair were born*, Sonn. 68, 3. *she's but the s. and semblance of her honour*, Ado IV, 1, 34. *wooed but the s. of she*, LLL V, 2, 469. *a s. of dignity, a garish flag*, R3 IV, 4, 89. *which is indeed but s.* Oth. I, 1, 158. *she's a good s.* Cymb. I, 2, 33.

2) that by which something is shown or perceived; a) an external proof or evidence: *sawest thou not —s of fear lurk in mine eye?* Ven. 644. *such —s of rage they bear*, Lucr. 1419. 1532. Pilgr. 429. Gent. III, 2, 18. Ado II, 3, 236. III, 2, 41. Shr. V, 2, 117. Wint. V, 2, 95. John III, 1, 24. R2 V, 5, 65. H6A V, 4, 82. H6B I, 1, 18. III, 2, 178. 314. III, 3, 5. IV, 2, 22. H8 III, 1, 66. Cor. I, 9, 26 *(in s. of what you are)*. IV, 6, 153. Tit. V, 3, 77. Cymb. III, 4, 128. b) a symbol: *in s. whereof... we may quaff carouses*, Shr. I, 2, 275. *in sign whereof I pluck a white rose*, H6A II, 4, 58. III, 4, 5. V, 3, 162. H6C IV, 2, 9. IV, 8, 26. R3 I, 3, 281. Ant. V, 2, 135. Hence *—s of war* = ensigns: H5 II, 2, 192. Caes. V, 1, 14. cf. Oth. I, 1, 157. *with —s of war about his aged neck*, R2 II, 2, 74*(= in armour). c) a prognostic: *apparitions, — s and prodigies*, Ven. 926. *she at these sad —s draws up her breath*, 929. LLL I, 2, 1. 3. John III, 4, 157. R2 II, 4, 15. H4A III, 1, 41. H6A V, 3, 4. H6C V, 6, 44. Tit. II, 3, 37. Mcb. IV, 2, 62. Ant. IV, 14, 7. d) a nod, a gesture, any motion to intimate one's meaning: Shr. IV, 4, 80. John IV, 2, 237. Tit. II, 4, 5. III, 1, 143. III, 2, 12. 36. IV, 1, 8. *give —s*, 61. *gave s. for me to leave you*, Caes. II, 1, 247. *make a s.* H6B III, 3, 29. Tit. III, 1, 121. III, 2, 43. e) a signal: H6A II, 1, 3. III, 2, 8.

3) a constellation in the zodiac: *the twelve celestial —s*, LLL V, 2, 807.

**Sign,** vb. 1) to mark, to make distinguishable, to set a stamp on: *by the hand of nature marked, quoted and —ed to do a deed of shame*, John IV, 2, 222. *you s. your place and calling, in full seeming, with meekness and humility*, H8 II, 4, 108. *here thy hunters stand, —ed in thy spoil*, Caes. III, 1, 206.

2) to ratify by underwriting one's name: Meas. II, 4, 152. Merch. III, 2, 149. IV, 1, 397. IV, 2, 2.

3) to be a prognostic or omen: *it —s well, does it not?* Ant. IV, 3, 14.

**Signal,** subst. 1) sign, token: *in s. of my love to thee will I wear this rose*, H6A II, 4, 121. *hold up thy hand, make s. of thy hope*, H6B III, 3, 28. *the sun... gives s. of a goodly day to-morrow*, R3 V, 3, 21 (cf. *Sign 2c*). *giving full trophy, s. and ostent quite from himself to God*, H5 V Chor. 21 (= the symbol of victory. cf. *Sign 2b*).

2) notice given by a sign at a distance, especially in war: John II, 265. R2 I, 3, 116. H6C II, 2, 100. V, 4, 72. 82. Rom. V, 3, 8. Caes. V, 1, 26.

**Signet,** seal manual: Meas. IV, 2, 209. Tim. II, 2, 210. Hml. V, 2, 49.

**Significant,** subst. something intimating one's meaning, a sign, a symbol: *in dumb —s proclaim your thoughts*, H6A II, 4, 26. Armado calls a letter so: *bear this s. to the country maid Jaquenetta*, LLL III, 131; cf. *to signify* in Gent. III, 1, 56 and Merch. II, 4, 11.

**Signify,** 1) to mean, to purport, to have a certain sense: Wiv. I, 1, 21. Meas. III, 2, 10. Mids. III, 1, 71. H5 III, 6, 33. H6C V, 6, 54. 76. Tit. II, 3, 32. Caes. II, 2, 87. 90. Mcb. V, 5, 28.

2) to give notice, to announce, to impart (German: *melden*): *the tenour of them doth but s. my health and happy being at your court*, Gent. III, 1, 56. *s. so much*, LLL II, 33. *to s. the approaching of his lord*, Merch. II, 9, 88. *s. within the house, your mistress is at hand*, V, 51. *to s. their coming*, 118. *to s. my success in Libya*, Wint. V, 1, 165. R2 III, 3, 49. H6B III, 1, 283. III, 2, 368. R3 I, 4, 97 (Ff *s. to him*, Qq *certify his grace*). III, 5, 59. III, 7, 70 (Ff *I'll s. so much unto him*, Qq *I'll tell him what you say*). Troil. IV, 5, 155. Tit. V, 1, 3. Rom. III, 3, 170. Tim. I, 2, 125. III, 4, 37. Hml. II, 2, 317. V, 2, 105. Ant. III, 1, 30. Absol.: *it (a letter) shall seem to s.* Merch. II, 4, 11 (Launcelot's speech). *in such great letters as they write "Here is good horse to hire" let them s. under my sign "Here you may see Benedick the married man,"* Ado I, 1, 268.

**Signior,** a title of respect among the Italians: Gent. III, 1, 279. Ado I, 1, 30. II, 3, 2. 265. III, 2, 73. V, 1, 111. 113. V, 2, 44. 103. V, 4, 19. 21. Merch. I, 1, 66. 73. I, 3, 41. 60. 98. Shr. I, 1, 85. Rom. I, 2, 67. II, 4, 46. Oth. I, 1, 78. 84. 93. I, 2, 57. 60. 91. I, 3, 50. 76. 289. IV, 1, 234. Cymb. I, 4, 111 etc. Applied to people of other countries: Meas. I, 2, 64. III, 1, 49. V, 261. Err. III, 1, 1. 19. IV, 1, 36. LLL I, 1, 188. III, 135. Mids. IV, 1, 17. Tw. II, 5, 1. H5 IV, 4, 67. H6A III, 2, 67. Per. I, 2, 44 etc. Used as an appellative: *like —s and rich burghers on the flood*, Merch. I, 1, 10.

**Signory,** 1) principality: *through all the —es it was the first*, Tp. I, 2, 71.

2) estate, landed property of a lord; manor: *you*

*have fed upon my —es*, R2 III, 1, 22. *restored to all his lands and —es*, IV, 89. H4B IV, 1, 111.

3) the aristocracy, or the grand council of Venice: *my services which I have done the s.* Oth. I, 2, 18.

4) spelling of *seniory* (q. v.) in O. Edd.

**Silence**, subst. 1) stillness, absence of sound or noise: Gent. III, 2, 85 *(dead s.).* Meas. III, 1, 257. Mids. II, 2, 70. Merch. V, 25. 101. Tit. I, 155. Hml. II, 2, 506.

2) forbearance of speech: Sonn. 83, 9. 86, 11. 101, 10. Tp. I, 1, 23 *(command these elements to s.).* Gent. III, 1, 207. Meas. V, 190. Ado II, 1, 317. 345. Mids. V, 100. Merch. I, 1, 111. III, 5, 50. As I, 3, 80. Shr. I, 1, 70. II, 29. All's I, 1, 76. Tw. II, 5, 70. Wint. II, 2, 41. V, 3, 21. H6A II, 4, 1. H6B IV, 2, 39 *(command s.).* R3 III, 7, 28. H8 I, 4, 45. II, 4, 2 *(let s. be commanded).* Troil. II, 3, 211. III, 2, 139. Tit. II, 3, 33. Tim. II, 2, 222. Caes. I, 2, 290 *(put to s.).* Hml. V, 1, 311. V, 2, 369. Cymb. III, 5, 97. *s.,* alone, imperatively: Tp. I, 1, 19. I, 2, 475. IV, 124. Wiv. V, 5, 46. Mids. IV, 1, 85. V, 170. 266. Wint. III, 2, 10. John I, 1, 6. IV, 1, 133. H6B IV, 2, 40. H6C III, 2, 15. Caes. III, 2, 11. 59. *in s.* = without words, not speaking: Mids. IV, 1, 100. Merch. II, 8, 32. H6A II, 4, 44. R3 III, 7, 141. Troil. IV, 1, 78. Tit. I, 90. Cymb. V, 4, 29. *with s.,* in the same sense: *it* (my heart) *must break with s.* R2 II, 1, 228. *the grief that swells with s. in the tortured soul,* IV, 298. H6A II, 5, 101. V, 3, 13. Abstr. pro concr.: *my gracious s.* Cor. II, 1, 192.

3) secrecy: Tw. I, 2, 61. II, 5, 116. H4B II, 2, 178. Hml. I, 2, 248. Per. I, 2, 19.

**Silence**, name in H4B III, 2, 4. V, 3, 4 etc.

**Silence**, vb. to put to silence; 1) to oblige to hold the peace, to restrain from speaking: Meas. V, 181. As I, 2, 95. H8 III, 2, 447. Cor. I, 9, 23. II, 1, 263. Tim. II, 1, 17. Mcb. I, 3, 93. Refl.: *I'll s. me even here,* Hml. III, 4, 4 (= I'll say no more about it, though I could say much. Polonius' last words. Most M. Edd. *sconce*). 2) to stop in sounding: *s. that bell,* Oth. II, 3, 175. 3) to appease: *s. those whom this vile brawl distracted,* Oth. II, 3, 256. 4) to put under restraint, to restrain from liberty (euphemistically): *in your power soft —ing your son,* H4B V, 2, 97. *the ambassador is —d;* H8 I, 1, 97. cf. *put to s.* in Caes. I, 2, 290.

**Silent**, adj. 1) still, having no noise: LLL II, 24. R3 IV, 4, 330. V, 3, 85. Oth. V, 1, 64.

2) not speaking, dumb: Lucr. 71. 84. Sonn. 23, 13. 30, 1. Gent. III, 1, 90. Ado III, 1, 67. Wint. II, 1, 171. R2 IV, 290. H6B I, 2, 90. II, 2, 68. H6C IV, 2, 28. Tit. II, 4, 8. Tim. I, 2, 37. *to be s.:* Tp. IV, 1, 59. Ado IV, 1, 158. LLL I, 2, 169. Wint. IV, 4, 178. H6C I, 1, 122. Troil. II, 3, 241. V, 1, 16. Cor. II, 2, 34. V, 3, 94. Tit III, 1, 46. Caes. III, 2, 14. Mcb. IV, 3, 137. Lr. I, 1, 63. I, 4, 70. Ant. II, 2, 109. Cymb. II, 3, 99. V, 5, 127.

**Silent**, subst. = silence, stillness: *the s. of the night,* H6B I, 4, 19.

**Silently**, without speaking: Mids. III, 1, 206.

**Silius**, name in Ant. III, 1, 11. 13.

**Silk**, cloth made of the thread of Bombyx mori: Compl. 48. Wiv. II, 2, 68. IV, 4, 73. LLL III, 150. Mids. V, 348. Wint. IV, 4, 325. H4B I, 2, 222. Troil. V, 1, 35. Cor. I, 9, 45. V, 6, 96. Tim. IV, 3, 206. Lr. III, 4, 108. Oth. III, 4, 73. Cymb. II, 4, 69. III, 3, 24. Per. IV Prol. 21. V Prol. 8. Plur. *—s:* Err. IV, 3, 8.

Merch. I, 1, 34. Troil. II, 2, 69. Lr. III, 4, 98. Adjectively: *s. hair,* As III, 5, 46. *s. stockings,* H4B II, 2, 17. *s. thread,* Rom. II, 2, 181. *a s. button,* H4B IV, 2, 7.

**Silken**, 1) made of silk: Compl. 17. Gent. II, 7, 45. Ado V, 1, 25. Shr. IV, 3, 55. 82. V, 1, 68. Wint. IV, 4, 361. H4B I, 1, 53. H5 III Chor. 6. Tit. II, 4, 46. Ant. II, 2, 214. Per. III, 2, 41. Used of hair: Compl. 87.

2) smooth, soft, effeminate: *taffeta phrases, s. terms precise,* LLL V, 2, 406. *shall a beardless boy, a cockered s. wanton, brave our fields,* John V, 1, 70. *s. dalliance in the wardrobe lies,* H5 II Chor. 2. *abused by s., sly, insinuating Jacks,* R3 I, 3, 53.

**Silken-coated**, wearing coats of silk: H6B IV, 2, 136.

**Silkman**, a dealer in silks: H4B II, 1, 31.

**Silliness**, simplicity, folly: *it is s. to live when to live is torment,* Oth. I, 3, 309.

**Silly** (spelt *seely* in Lucr. 1812; in R2 V, 5, 25 Ff *silly,* Qq *seely*), 1) harmless, innocent, helpless: *fright the s. lamb,* Ven. 1098. *it shall be raging mad and s. mild,* 1151 (M. Edd. *silly-mild*). *surprise the s. lambs,* Lucr. 167. *do no outrages on s. women,* Gent. IV, 1, 72. *which am a s. woman,* H6C I, 1, 243. *shepherds looking on their s. sheep,* II, 5, 43.

2) plain, simple: *s. groom! God wot, it was defect of spirit,* Lucr. 1345. *it is s. sooth,* Tw. II, 4, 47. *my revenue is the s. cheat,* Wint. IV, 3, 28 (= petty thievery). *here is a s. stately style indeed,* H6A IV, 7, 72. *there was a fourth man, in a s. habit, that gave the affront with them,* Cymb. V, 3, 86.

3) poor; a) as a term of pity: esteemed *so as s. jeering idiots are with kings,* Lucr. 1812. *she, s. queen, forbade the boy he should not pass,* Pilgr. 123. *it was a spite unto the s. damsel,* 218. *one s. cross wrought all my loss,* 257. *s. beggars who sitting in the stocks refuge their shame,* R2 V, 5, 25. *the s. owner of the goods weeps over them,* H6B I, 1, 225. *s. ducking observants that stretch their duties nicely,* Lr. II, 2, 109. b) as a term of contempt, = poor, petty: *a child, a s. dwarf,* H6A II, 3, 22. *a s. time to make prescription,* H6C III, 3, 93. or = simple, witless, foolish: *the s. boy claps her pale cheek,* Ven. 467. *of such a weak and s. mind,* 1016. *a s. answer, and fitting well a sheep,* Gent. I, 1, 81. *thy s. thought* (enforces) *my spleen,* LLL III, 77. *most s. sheep with a horn,* V, 1, 53. *this is the —est stuff that ever I heard,* Mids. V, 212. *till I be brought to such a s. pass,* Shr. V, 2, 124. *thou s. gentleman,* Oth. I, 3, 308.

**Silver**, the metal Argentum: Tp. II, 2, 31. Wiv. I, 1, 52. Ado III, 4, 20. Merch. I, 2, 33. I, 3, 96. II, 7, 6. 52. II, 9, 20. John III, 3, 13. H4B I, 2, 20. Troil. I, 3, 65. Cor. I, 5, 4. Rom. I, 2, 108. Tim. I, 2, 189. III, 2, 78. Ant. II, 2, 199. Cymb. II, 4, 69. 90. III, 6, 54. Used as a fem.: *what says the s. with her virgin hue?* Merch. II, 7, 22.

Adjectively: Merch. II, 9, 34. Shr. Ind. 1, 55. Tim. III, 1, 7. Denoting bright and pure whiteness: *s. doves,* Ven. 366. 1190. *s. white,* Lucr. 56. *s. cheeks,* 61. *s. down,* 1012. *s. skin,* Mcb. II, 3, 118. *whose beard the s. hand of peace had touched,* H4B IV, 1, 43. *s. beards,* H5 III, 3, 36. Troil. I, 3, 296. *s. hair,* H6B V, 1, 162. *the s. livery of advised age,* V, 2, 47. Tit. III, 1, 261. Caes. II, 1, 144. Applied to the pale lustre of the moon: Ven. 728. Lucr. 371. 786. LLL IV, 3, 30. Mids. I, 1, 9. 210. Per. V, 1, 249. V, 3, 7. cf. *the morning, from whose s. breast the sun ariseth,* Ven. 855. To the sea, to rivers and any limpid liquids: Ven. 959 *(tears); cf.* Lucr. 796; John III, 4, 63. Sonn. 35, 2. *the morning's s. melting dew,* Lucr. 24. *s. waves,* Err. III, 2, 48. Ado III, 1, 27. John II, 339. 441. R2 II, 1, 46. III, 2, 107. V, 3, 61. H4A III, 1, 102. H6B IV, 1, 72. To soft and clear sounds: Rom. IV, 5, 130. 131. 136. 142. 145 (taken from a popular rhyme and curiously commented on by Peter and the musicians).

**Silver,** a name of dogs: Tp. IV, 257. Shr. Ind. 1, 19.

**Silver-bright,** bright as silver: John II, 315.

**Silvered,** 1) covered with silver: Merch. II, 9, 69. Ant. III, 6, 3.

2) tinged with grey, hoary: *sable curls, all s. o'er with white,* Sonn. 12, 4. *a sable s.* Hml. I, 2, 242.

**Silverly,** bright as silver: *this honourable dew, that s. doth progress on thy cheeks,* John V, 2, 46.

**Silver-shedding,** an evident misprint of O. Edd., as it ought to be written in two words: *sad sighs, deep groans, nor silver shedding tears, could penetrate her uncompassionate sire,* Gent. III, 1, 230 (i. e. a silvery flow of tears; cf. *silver melting* in Lucr. 24).

**Silver-sweet,** having a delightful sound like silver bells: *how s. sound lovers' tongues by night,* Rom. II, 2, 166.

**Silver-voiced,** having a soft and clear voice: Per. V, 1, 111.

**Silver-white,** white as silver: *his beard, all s.* Lucr. 1405. *lady-smocks all s.* LLL V, 2, 905.

**Silvia,** female name in Gent. II, 1, 5. 45 etc.

**Silvius,** name in As III, 5, 83 etc. and Ant. II, 1, 18.

**Similation,** see *Simulation.*

**Simile,** a comparison (as a term of rhetoric): As II, 1, 45. Shr. V, 2, 54. H4A I, 2, 89 (Qq F1 *smiles*). Troil. III, 2, 183. *take all these —s to your command,* Compl. 227 (i. e. symbolical love-tokens). In All's V, 2, 26 some M. Edd. —s, O. Edd. *smiles.*

**Simois,** a Trojan river: Lucr. 1437. Shr. III, 1, 42.

**Simon,** Christian name of subordinate persons in H4B III, 2, 132 and Rom. IV, 5, 132. In H6B II, 1, 91 F1.2 *Symon,* F3.4 *Simon,* some M. Edd. *Saunder,* others *Simpcox.*

**Simonides,** name of the king of Pentapolis in Per. II, 1, 48. 49. 104. 105. II, 3, 20. II, 5, 1. 24. III Prol. 23.

**Simony,** sale of church-offices: H8 IV, 2, 36.

**Simpcox,** name in H6B II, 1, 124. In v. 91 O. Edd. *Symon* or *Simon,* some M. Edd. *Simpcox.*

**Simpering,** smiling in an affected manner: *I perceive by your s. none of you hates them,* As Epil. 16. *yond s. dame,* Lr. IV, 6, 120.

**Simple,** adj. 1) consisting of one thing only, uncompounded: *for compound sweet forgoing s. savour,* Sonn. 125, 7. *s. were so well compounded,* Phoen. 44. *with eggs, sir? S. of itself,* Wiv. III, 5, 32.

2) mere, pure, being no more and no less than, nothing else but: *she tells to your highness s. truth,* Err. V, 211. *here's a s. line of life,* Merch. II, 2, 169. *nine maids is a s. coming-in for one man,* 171. *here are s. scapes,* 174. *that is another s. sin in you, to bring the ewes and rams together,* As III, 2, 82. *whose s. touch is powerful to araise King Pepin,* All's II, 1, 78.

*Salisbury and Warwick are no s. peers,* H6B I, 3, 77. *attended by a s. guard,* H6C IV, 2, 16. *lying with s. shells,* Per. III, 1, 65.

3) plain, not distinguished by any excellence, of an average quality, common: *my shallow s. skill,* Gent. I, 2, 8; Wiv. I, 1, 30; Ado I, 1, 168; Mids. V, 110. *he's a justice of peace, s. though I stand here,* Wiv. I, 1, 226. *not only in the s. office of love,* IV, 2, 4. *you have s. wits,* LLL V, 2, 264. *doth my s. feature content you?* As III, 3, 3. *toward the education of your daughters I here bestow a s. instrument,* Shr. II, 100. *great floods have flown from s. sources,* All's II, 1, 143. *there's a s. putting off,* II, 2, 43. *I am a s. maid,* II, 3, 72. *this s. syllogism,* Tw. I, 5, 55. *it* (mine iron) *is a s. one,* H5 II, 1, 8. *no s. man that sees this jarring discord,* H6A IV, 1, 187. *our s. supper ended,* H6B II, 2, 2. *I am a s. woman,* H8 II, 4, 106. *nature prompts them in s. and low things to prince it,* Cymb. III, 3, 85. Almost = mean, of low rank: *this s. peasant,* Shr. Ind. 1, 135. *we that are not s. men,* Wint. IV, 4, 772. *a s. countryman,* Ant. V, 2, 342.

4) plain, artless, harmless, unaffected, sincere: *he might be buried in a tomb so s.* (as Adonis' dimples) Ven. 244. *under whose* (love's) *s. semblance he* (lust) *hath fed upon fresh beauty,* 795. *s. truth miscalled simplicity,* Sonn. 66, 11. 138, 8. *who, young and s., would not be so lovered?* Compl. 320. *to witness s. virtue,* Ado IV, 1, 39. *this is a gift that I have, s., s.* LLL IV, 2, 67. *in his s. show he harbours treason.* H6B III, 1, 54. *his s. truth must be abused,* R3 I, 3, 52. *and —r than the infancy of truth,* Troil. III, 2, 177. *think true love acted s. modesty,* Rom. III, 2, 16. *there are no tricks in plain and s. truth,* Caes. IV, 2, 22. *in s. and pure soul I come to you,* Oth. I, 1, 107.

5) silly, witless, weak in intellect: Gent. II, 1, 38. Wiv. IV, 2, 182. Err. III, 2, 16. LLL IV, 1, 142. Mids. III, 2, 317. Merch. III, 2, 81. Shr. V, 2, 161. Wint. IV, 4, 355. 607. H6B IV, 4, 10. H6C I, 2, 59. III, 1, 83. R3 I, 1, 118. I, 3, 328. III, 2, 26 (Qq *fond*). Rom. II, 5, 38. III, 1, 37. Tim. V, 1, 27 *(—r).* Hml. I, 2, 97. Lr. IV, 6, 155. Oth. IV, 2, 20. Ant. V, 2, 273. Cymb. III, 4, 135.

**Simple,** subst. a single ingredient in a compound, especially in a compounded medicine: *the poisonous s. sometimes is compacted in a pure compound,* Lucr. 530. *a melancholy of mine own, compounded of many —s,* As IV, 1, 16. *collected from all —s that have virtue,* Hml. IV, 7, 145. Hence = medicinal herb: *dere is some —s in my closet,* Wiv. I, 4, 65. *smell like Bucklersbury in s. time,* III, 3, 79.* *culling of —s,* Rom. V, 1, 40. *that to provoke in him, are many —s operative,* Lr. IV, 4, 14.

**Simple,** name in Wiv. I, 1, 136. 207. I, 4, 15. III, 1, 2.

**Simple-answered,** making a simple answer: *be s.* Lr. III, 7, 43 (Qq *simple answerer*).

**Simpleness,** 1) plainness, unrefined nativeness, innocence: *and never gives to truth and virtue that which s. and merit purchaseth,* Ado III, 1, 70. *never anything can be amiss, when s. and duty tender it,* Mids. V, 83. *in her they are the better for their s.* All's I, 1, 51. *let me find a charter in your voice, to assist my s.* Oth. I, 3, 247.

2) silliness, folly: *what s. is this!* Rom. III, 3, 77.

**Simplicity,** 1) plainness, naturalness, absence of everything that seems extraordinary: *grace in all s.*

Phoen. 54. *whiles others fish with craft for great opinion, I with great truth catch mere s.* Troil. IV, 4, 106.

2) plainness, artlessness, innocence: *by the s. of Venus' doves,* Mids. I, 1, 171. *love and tongue-tied s. in least speak most,* V, 104. *I am as true as truth's s.* Troil. III, 2, 176.

3) silliness, folly: *simple truth miscalled s.* Sonn. 66, 11. *twice-sod s.* LLL IV, 2, 23. *Love's Tyburn that hangs up s.* IV, 3, 54. *profound s.* V, 2, 52. 78. Merch. I, 3, 44. Wint. IV, 2, 55. Used with impropriety by Costard in LLL I, 1, 219, and confounded with *simple* by Evans in Wiv. IV, 1, 31.

**Simply,** 1) without addition, of itself, alone: *if he take her, let him take her s.* Wiv. III, 2, 78 (without her fortune). *s. the thing I am shall make me live,* All's IV, 3, 369. *not a man, for being s. man, hath any honour,* Troil. III, 3, 80.

2) without adding a word, without restriction, unconditionally, absolutely: *s. I credit her false-speaking tongue,* Sonn. 138, 7. *he hath s. the best wit of any handicraft man,* Mids. IV, 2, 9. *for s. your having in beard is a younger brother's revenue,* As III, 2, 396. *you have s. misused our sex,* IV, 1, 205. *I am a simple maid and therein wealthiest, that I protest I s. am a maid,* All's II, 3, 73. *I have the back-trick s. as strong as any man in Illyria,* Tw. I, 3, 132. *I were s. the most active fellow in Europe,* H4B IV, 3, 24. *he is s. the most active gentleman in France,* H5 III, 7, 105. *he is s. the rarest man i' the world,* Cor. IV, 5, 169.

**Simular,** subst. simulator, hypocritical pretender: *s. of virtue,* Lr. III, 2, 54 (Qq *simular man*).

**Simular,** adj. counterfeited, false: *s. man of virtue,* Lr. III, 2, 54 (Ff *simular of virtue*).*I returned with s. proof enough,* Cymb. V, 5, 200.

**Simulation,** counterfeiting, disguise: *this s. is not as the former,* Tw. II, 5, 151 (Capell: *similation*).

**Sin,** subst. transgression of the divine law: Lucr. 93. Sonn. 62, 1. 142, 1. Tp. III, 2, 139. III, 3, 53. Gent. V, 4, 112. Wiv. III, 3, 226. V, 5, 35. 57. Meas. I, 4, 31. II, 1, 38. II, 3, 19. 28. 31. II, 4, 57. 63. 66. 68. 69. 71. III, 1, 149. III, 2, 31. IV, 1, 73. IV, 2, 111. Err. I, 2, 102. III, 2, 14. V, 52. Ado II, 1, 67. IV, 1, 37. 51. 175. 182. V, 1, 283. LLL II, 105 etc. etc. *the seven deadly —s,* Meas. III, 1, 111 (pride, envy, wrath, sloth, covetousness, gluttony, lechery). *to do a s.* Meas. III, 1, 134. Wint. V, 1, 172 (*against*). *to leave you in your madness, 'twere my s.* Cymb. II, 3, 104 (= 'twere sin in me). Personified as a masc.: Lucr. 629. 882. 913. Abstr. pro concr.: *cardinal —s and hollow hearts I fear ye,* H8 III, 1, 104. *thou scarlet s.* III, 2, 255.

**Sin,** vb. to offend against the divine law: Lucr. 630. Sonn. 141, 14. Pilgr. 342. Tp. I, 2, 118. Gent. II, 6, 7. Wiv. III, 3, 51. Meas. II, 2, 163. 183. Ado II, 1, 266. V, 1, 283. All's III, 7, 47. Wint. I, 2, 84. H4A I, 1, 78. H4B I, 1, 98. H6A I, 3, 35. Troil. II, 3, 131. Cor. I, 1, 234. Tit. IV, 1, 64. Tim. I, 2, 72. 246. Per. I, 1, 146. I, 3, 22. With *against:* All's II, 5, 10. Cymb. II, 3, 116. *a man more —ed against than —ing,* Lr. III, 2, 60.

**Sin-absolver,** one who pronounces sin to be remitted: Rom. III, 3, 50.

**Since,** prepos., adv. and conj.; 1) ever from the time of, after; f. i.: *not s. widow Dido's time,* Tp. II, 1, 76. *s. his exile she hath despised me most,* Gent. III, 2, 3. *s. the mortal and intestine jars,* Err. I, 1, 11. *s.*

*Pentecost the sum is due,* IV, 1, 1. *never s. the middle summer's spring met we on hill,* Mids. II, 1, 83. *s. death of my dearest mother it did not speak before,* Cymb. IV, 2, 190. Peculiar passage: *s. night you loved me, yet s. night you left me,* Mids. III, 2, 275 (= it is no longer than last night that you loved me; or transposed: *a night since,* i. e. a night ago).

2) from the time when; f. i.: *love to heaven is fled, s. sweating lust on earth usurped his name,* Ven. 794. *nature cares not for thy vigour, s. her best work is ruined,* 954. *which I made with mine own hands, s. I was cast ashore,* Tp. II, 2, 129. *s. they did plot the means ... her company I have forsworn,* IV, 88. *s. I saw thee, the affliction of my mind amends,* V, 114. *all this service have I done s. I went,* 226. *I have been in such a pickle s. I saw you last,* 282. *s. she did neglect her looking-glass, the air hath starved the roses in her cheeks,* Gent. IV, 4, 157. *I never prospered s. I forswore myself at primero,* Wiv. IV, 5, 103. *I could not speak with Dromio s. at first I sent him from the mart,* Err. II, 2, 5. 15. *how long is it s. the physician died,* All's I, 2, 70. *s. the youth of the count's was to-day with my lady, she is much out of quiet,* Tw. II, 3, 143. *I was not angry s. I came to France until this instant,* H5 IV, 7, 58. With another conjunction: *they have been grand-jurymen s. before Noah was a sailor,* Tw. III, 2, 18. *s. that* = since: *the jealous o'erworn widow and herself, s. that our brother dubbed them gentlewomen, are mighty gossips in this monarchy,* R3 I, 1, 82.

3) as, seeing that; f. i.: *s. I have hemmed thee here ... I'll be a park,* Ven. 229. *why not lips on lips, s. eyes in eyes?* 120. 239. *s. thou art dead, lo, here I prophesy,* 1135. 1174. *s. thou dost give me pains, let me remember thee what thou hast promised,* Tp. I, 2, 242. *no matter, s. they have left their viands behind,* III, 3, 40. 50. V, 168. Epil. 6. Gent. I, 1, 9. I, 2, 55. II, 1, 129. IV, 2, 124. 130. Meas. I, 1, 5. Err. III, 1, 120. *s. that,* in the same sense (cf. *That*): *I force not argument a straw, s. that my case is past the help of law,* Lucr. 1022. *thou canst not vex me with inconstant mind, s. that my life on thy revolt doth lie,* Sonn. 92, 10. *s. that my beauty cannot please his eye, I'll weep what's left away,* Err. II, 1, 114. Merch. III, 3, 30. As III, 5, 94. H5 IV, 1, 321. R3 V, 3, 202. Cor. III, 2, 50. V, 3, 98. Mcb. IV, 3, 106. Lr. I, 1, 251.

4) after that time, from then till now; f. i.: *stuffs and necessaries, which s. have steaded much,* Tp. I, 2, 165. *mine eyes, never s. at ebb,* 435. *I cannot abide the smell of hot meat s.* Wiv. I, 1, 297. *and s. I have not much importuned you,* Err. IV, 1, 2. *my bones bear witness, that s. have felt the vigour of his rage,* IV, 4, 81. *my desires e'er s. pursue me,* Tw. I, 1, 23. *Saint George, that swinged the dragon, and e'er s. sits on his horse,* John II, 288. *who s. I heard to be discomfited,* H6B V, 1, 63. *is fled, as he hears s., to Burgundy,* H6C IV, 6, 79. *and s., methinks, I would not grow so fast,* R3 II, 4, 14. *which s. succeeding ages have reedified,* III, 1, 71. *and s. too, murders have been performed,* Mcb. III, 4, 77. *brought up with him, and s. so neighboured to his youth,* Hml. II, 2, 12 (Qq *sith*). *I did not see him s.* Ant. I, 3, 1.

5) ago (transitional use: *it is but eight years s. this Percy was the man nearest my soul,* H4B III, 1, 60. *how long is it s. the physician died?* All's I, 2, 70); f. i.: *twelve year s. thy father was the duke of Milan,* Tp. I, 2, 53. *how thou hast met us here, who three hours s.*

*were wrecked upon this shore*, V, 136. *our ship which, but three glasses s., we gave out split*, 223. *he promised to meet me two hours s.* Meas. I, 2, 76. *five years s. there was some speech of marriage*, V, 217. *not half an hour s.* Err. II, 2, 14. *I gave it you half an hour s.* IV, 1, 65. IV, 3, 38. *but seven years s. thou knowest we parted*, V, 320. *I told your lordship a year s.* Ado II, 2, 12. *the world was very guilty of such a ballad some three ages s.* LLL I, 2, 117. *some six months s.* All's I, 2, 71. *his wife some two months s. fled from his house*, IV, 3, 57. *a count that died some twelvemonth s.* Tw. I, 2, 37. *posts are come an hour s.* Wint. II, 3, 195. *who half an hour s. came from the Dauphin*, John V, 7, 83. *who two hours s. I met in travel*, H6A IV, 3, 35. *whom I some three months s. stabbed*, R3 I, 2, 241. *else had I half an hour s. brought my report*, Cor. I, 6, 21. *how long is 't s.?* I, 6, 14. *how long is that s.?* Hml. V, 1, 158. *long s.* = a) long ago: *long s. thy husband served me in my wars*, Err. V, 161. *for the service that long s. I did thee, now grant me justice*, 191. Joined to substantives, = long past: *what canst thou boast of things long s.* Ven. 1078. *what wealth she had in days long s.* Sonn. 67, 14. b) since a long time, already a long time: *and weep afresh love's long s. cancelled woe*, Sonn. 30, 7. *she and I, long s. contracted, are now so sure*, Wiv. V, 5, 236. *long s. we were resolved of your truth, yet never have you tasted our reward*, H6A III, 4, 20.

6) when (after verbs denoting recollection): *thou rememberest s. once I sat upon a promontory, and heard a mermaid on a dolphin's back*, Mids. II, 1, 149. *this fellow I remember, s. once he played a farmer's eldest son*, Shr. Ind. 1, 84. *remember s. you owed no more to time than I do now*, Wint. V, 1, 219. *do you remember s. we lay all night in the windmill in Saint George's field?* H4B III, 2, 206. *we know the time s. he was mild and affable*, H6B III, 1, 9.

**Sincere** (as for the accent, see Appendix I, 1) undissembling, honest, upright: Gent. II, 7, 76. H4B I, 1, 202. H8 I, 1, 153. Lr. II, 2, 111.

**Sincerely**, unfeignedly, from one's heart: Ado V, 1, 201. H8 II, 3, 59. Cor. I, 3, 24.

**Sincerity**, freedom from hypocrisy, honesty of intention, earnestness: Meas. I, 4, 36. V, 451. Ado IV, 1, 55. John III, 1, 248. H4A III, 3, 32. Oth. II, 3, 333.

**Sin-concealing**, hiding sins: Lucr. 767.

**Sin-conceiving**, conceiving and bringing forth sins: *thy s. womb*, John II, 182.

**Sinel**, name of Macbeth's father: Mcb. I, 3, 71.

**Sinew**, subst. tendon: Tp. III, 1, 26. IV, 260. H5 III, 1, 7. H6A III, 1, 193. Troil. IV, 5, 126. V, 3, 33. Hml. I, 5, 94. III, 3, 71. *Orpheus' lute was strung with poets' —s*, Gent. III, 2, 78; cf. *unless the fiddler Apollo get his —s to make catlings on*, Troil. III, 3, 305. Considered as the seat of strength, and hence = strength: *the portion and s. of her fortune, her marriage-dowry*, Meas. III, 1, 230. *we break the —s of our plot*, Tw. II, 5, 83. *knit your —s to the strength of mine*, John V, 2, 63. *who with them was a rated s. too*, H4A IV, 4, 17. H5 I, 2, 223. II, 2, 36. H6A II, 3, 63. H6C II, 3, 4. Troil. I, 3, 136. 143. II, 1, 109. III, 1, 166. V, 8, 12. Cor. V, 6, 45. Caes. I, 2, 108.

Confounded with nerve: *a second fear through all her —s spread*, Ven. 903. *this rest might yet have balmed thy broken —s*, Lr. III, 6, 105 (but perhaps = strength. M. Edd. *senses*) O. Edd. often *sinnow*.

**Sinew**, vb., with *together*, = to knit in strength: *so shalt thou s. both these lands together*, H6C II, 6, 91. cf. *Insinewed*. O. Edd. *sinow*.

**Sinewed**, having sinews, armed with strength: *when he sees ourselves well s. to our defence*, John V, 7, 88.

**Sinewy**, well braced with sinews, strong: Ven. 99. LLL IV, 3, 308. As II, 2, 14. All's II, 1, 62. Troil. II, 3, 259. O. Edd. *sinnowy*.

**Sinful**, tainted with sin, unholy, wicked: Sonn. 103, 9. 142, 2. 146, 1, Wiv. V, 5, 97. Merch. II, 7, 54. All's III, 7, 47. R2 III, 1, 11. H4B II, 4, 309. H6B V, 1, 183. H6C III, 3, 41. Mcb. IV, 3, 224. Per. Prol. 31. 1, 2, 77.

**Sinfully**, 1) in a sinful manner: R3 II, 1, 119. 2) in a sinful state: *if a son that is by his father sent about merchandise do s. miscarry upon the sea*, H5 IV, 1, 155.

**Sing** (impf. and partic. *sung;* impf. *sang* only in Sonn. 73, 4 for the sake of the rhyme) 1) to utter melodious sounds; absol.: Ven. 1095. 1102. Sonn. 73, 4. 97, 13. Tp. III, 2, 129. Wiv. V, 5, 69. Err. III, 2, 47. Ado II, 1, 239. II, 3, 50. 51. LLL I, 1, 103. Mids. III, 1, 126. Tw. I, 2, 57. II, 3, 21. 42. John V, 7, 12. H4B V, 5, 113. Lr. I, 4, 192. Ant. I, 5, 73 etc. *when to the lute she sung*, Per. IV Prol. 26. With *of:* —*est of ravishment*, Lucr. 1128. with *to:* *then to Silvia let us s.* Gent. IV, 2, 49. John IV, 2, 150. Indicating joy: *I have decreed not to s. in my cage*, Ado I, 3, 36. *now she —s in heaven*, All's IV, 3, 63. *I could s., would weeping do me good*, R2 III, 4, 22. *that I may s. and dance*, H6C I, 4, 91. cf. Cor. I, 3, 1. IV, 6, 8. H5 III, 7, 17. Used of birds of any kind, even of the owl: LLL V, 2, 927 (cf. H6C II, 6, 57). of the cuckoo: Wiv. II, 1, 127. LLL V, 2, 909. of pies: H6C V, 6, 48. of the crow: Merch. V, 102. of the raven: Tit. III, 1, 158. of crickets: Cymb. II, 2, 11. Per. III Prol. 7. of the bagpipe: Merch. IV, 1, 49.

Hence applied to the whistling of the wind: *through his mane and tail the high wind —s*, Ven. 305. *the winds did s. it to me*, Tp. III, 3, 97. *move the still-peering air, that —s with piercing*, All's III, 2, 114. Such a sound supposed to announce a tempest: *I hear it* (the storm) *s. in the wind*, Tp. II, 2, 20. *a man may hear this shower s. in the wind*, Wiv. III, 2, 38. *we hear this fearful tempest s.* R2 II, 1, 263.

With an accus. denoting an effect: *s. me now asleep*, Mids. II, 2, 7. Tit. V, 3, 163. *s. him home*, As IV, 2, 13. *who had even tuned his bounty to s. happiness to him*, All's IV, 3, 12. *flights of angels s. thee to thy rest*, Hml. V, 2, 371. *she will s. the savageness out of a bear*, Oth. IV, 1, 200. *let us s. him to the ground*, Cymb. IV, 2, 236.

2) trans.; a) to utter or recite melodiously: —*s a woeful ditty*, Ven. 836. *thy trespass sung by children*, Lucr. 525. Pilgr. 383. Tp. II, 2, 46. IV, 109. Gent. I, 2, 80 (*s. it to a tune*). 83. 86. 89 (*s. it out*). Wiv. III, 1, 18. V, 5, 95. Ado V, 1, 294 (*s. it to her bones*). LLL III, 1, 14. 15. Mids. I, 1, 30. V, 44 (*to the harp*). Tw. I, 5, 290. Wint. IV, 4, 190. 282. H4A II, 2, 48 (*sung to filthy tunes*). III, 1, 210. H4B III, 2, 340 (*to*). H5 IV, 8, 128. H6A I, 6, 20. H6C II, 6, 57. H8 IV, 1, 92. Tit. III, 1, 85. Per. Prol. 5 etc. *to s. a song:* As III, 2, 261. Wint. IV, 4, 58. H4A III, 1, 216. III, 3, 15. H8 V, 5, 35. Per. Prol. 1.

b) to celebrate, to give praises to in verse: *that*

*happy verse which aptly —s the good*, Tim. I, 1, 17. *s. our bondage*, Cymb. III, 3, 44. Dubious passage: *she will s. any man at first sight. And any man may s. her, if he can take her cliff*, Troil. V, 2, 9. 10 (Ff *avy man may find her, if he can take her life*. Some M. Edd. *s. to any man*, and *s. to her*. N. L.).

**Singe,** to scorch, to burn slightly or superficially: Err. V, 171 *(off)*. Merch. II, 9, 79. H8 I, 1, 141. Hml. V, 1, 305. Lr. III, 2, 6.

**Singer,** one that sings: Wiv. I, 3, 29. Ado II, 3, 78. Mids. V, 49. Rom. IV, 5, 141.

**Singing-man,** a man whose business is to sing: *liking his father to a s. of Windsor*, H4B II, 1, 98.

**Single,** adj. 1) only one in number, not more than one: *even for this let us divided live, and our dear love lose name of s.* one, Sonn. 39, 6. *s. nature's double name neither two nor one was called*, Phoen. 39. *a double heart for his s.* one, Ado II, 1, 289 (quibbling). *two bosoms and a s. troth*, Mids. II, 2, 50. *'tis not the many oaths that makes the truth, but the plain s. oath that is vowed true*, All's IV, 2, 22. *to hear me one s. word*, V, 2, 38. *you beg a s. penny more*, 39. *I have no further gone in this than by a s. voice*, H8 I, 2, 70. *scants us with a s. famished kiss*, Troil. IV, 4, 49. *to seek a s. man*, Cor. IV, 1, 42. *when the s. sole of it is worn*, Rom. II, 4, 66. *with his own s. hand he'ld take us in*, Cymb. IV, 2, 121. *no s. soul can we set eye on*, 130. *a princess to equal any s. crown o' the earth*, Per. IV, 3, 8.

2) separate, alone, by one's self: *at picked leisure s. I'll resolve you of every these happened accidents*, Tp. V, 248 (i. e. of every accident singly). *what can these my s. arms?* Troil. II, 2, 135. *the glory of our Troy doth this day lie on his fair worth and s. chivalry*, IV, 4, 150. *thou standest s., thou art not on him yet*, Tim. II, 2, 58. *some s. vantages you took*, 138. *each man apart, all s. and alone*, V, 1, 110. *the s. and peculiar life is bound to keep itself from noyance*, Hml. III, 3, 11. *when sorrows come, they come not s. spies, but in battalions*, IV, 5, 78. *a s. combat* = a combat in which only one man is opposed to another: H6A I, 2, 95. H6B I, 3, 212. *a s. fight:* H4A V, 1, 100. V, 2, 47. H6C IV, 7, 75. Ant. III, 7, 31. IV, 4, 37. *in s. opposition:* H4A I, 3, 99. Cymb. IV, 1, 14. Often = living alone, unmarried: *die s., and thine image dies with thee*, Sonn. 3, 14. *thou s. wilt prove none*, 8, 14. *s. life*, 9, 2. Ado V, 4, 116. *in s. blessedness*, Mids. I, 1, 78. 90. 121. *is the s. man therefore blessed?* As III, 3, 58. *I'll to the wars, she to her s. sorrow*, All's II, 3, 313. *till this time pomp was s., but now married to one above itself*, H8 I, 1, 15.

3) concerning only one, particular, individual: *I know but of a s. part in aught pertains to the state*, H8 I, 2, 41. *wherein every one of us has a s. honour in giving him our own voices*, Cor. II, 3, 49. *were there but this s. plot to lose, this mould of Marcius*, III, 2, 102. *for my s. self, I had as lief not be*, Caes. I, 2, 94. *shakes so my s. state of man*, Mcb. I, 3, 140. *all our service in every point twice done were poor and s. business to contend against those honours deep and broad*, I, 6, 16. *a fee-grief due to some s. breast*, IV, 3, 197. *trust to thy s. virtue*, Lr. V, 3, 103. *the death of Antony is not a s. doom*, Ant. V, 1, 18.

4) no more than, mere, only: *he thought to steal the s. ten*, H6C V, 1, 43. *seal me there your s. bond*, Merch. I, 3, 146.* cf. *what wert thou, if the king of*

*Naples heard thee? A s. thing, as I am now*, Tp. I, 2, 432.

5) simple, silly (only in quibbling): *your chin double, your wit s.* H4B I, 2, 207. *your helps are many, or else your actions would grow wondrous s.* Cor. II, 1, 40. cf. Ado II, 1, 289.

6) not double-minded, sincere: *I speak it with a s. heart*, H8 V, 3, 38. cf. All's IV, 2, 22.

**Single,** vb. 1) to isolate, to separate: *we will be —d from the barbarous*, LLL V, 1, 85 (Q1 *singuled*). *s. you thither then this dainty doe*, Tit. II, 1, 117 (bring her thither unattended).*

2) to select from among a number: *we s. you as our solicitor*, LLL II, 28. *I have —d thee alone*, H6C II, 4, 1. With *forth:* H6C II, 1, 12. Tit. II, 3, 69. with *out:* Ven. 693. H6C II, 4, 12.

**Singleness,** 1) unmarried state: Sonn. 8, 8. 2) simplicity (quibbling): Rom. II, 4, 70.

**Single-soled,** with a quibble on *sole* and *soul*, = having but one sole, and silly, contemptible: Rom. II, 4, 69 (Cotgrave's French and English Dictionary, sub *Relief: Gentilhomme de bas relief, a threadbare or single-soled gentleman, a gentleman of low degree).*

**Singly,** 1) taking but one: *the man I speak of cannot in the world be s. counterpoised*, Cor. II, 2, 91.

2) separately: *neither can be s. manifested, without the show of both*, Wiv. IV, 6, 15. *demand them s.* All's IV, 3, 208. *he must fight s. with Hector*, Troil. III, 3, 247 (in single fight).

3) alone, only: *thou s. honest man*, Tim. IV, 3, 530.

**Singular,** alone in its kind, unparalleled, rare, eminent: *what needeth then apologies be made, to set forth that which is so s.?* Lucr. 32. *a most s. and choice epithet*, LLL V, 1, 17. *so s. in each particular*, Wint. IV, 4, 144. *men of s. integrity and learning*, H8 II, 4, 59. *the jest may remain after the wearing sole s.* Rom. II, 4, 68. 69. *some villain, ay, and s. in his art*, Cymb. III, 4, 124. Adverbially: *very s. good*, H4B III, 2, 119.

**Singularity,** the quality of being alone in one's kind, peculiarity: *put thyself into the trick of s.* Tw. II, 5, 164. *let's hear in what fashion, more than his s., he goes upon this present action*, Cor. I, 1, 282 (independently from his peculiar private character). Used of things, = rarity, curiosity: *your gallery have we passed through, not without much content in many —es*, Wint. V, 3, 12.

**Singule,** to separate: *we will be —d from the barbarous*, LLL V, 1, 85 (lection of Q1; Q2 Ff *singled*).

**Sinister,** *(sinister)* 1) left, not right: *this the cranny is, right and s.* Mids. V, 164. *on his s. cheek*, All's II, 1, 44. *my mother's blood runs on the dexter cheek, and this s. bounds in my father's*, Troil. IV, 5, 128.

2) unfair, wrong: *he professes to have received no s. measure from his judge*, Meas. III, 2, 256. *I am very comptible, even to the least s. usage*, Tw. I, 5, 188. *'tis no s. nor no awkward claim*, H5 II, 4, 85.

**Sink,** subst. a drain to carry off filthy water, a jakes: H5 III, 5, 59. H6B IV, 1, 71. Troil. V, 1, 83. Cor. I, 1, 126. Tit. III, 2, 19.

**Sink,** vb. (impf. not used; partic. *sunk*, and, when joined to a noun, *sunken:* Sonn. 2, 7. As III, 2, 393. H5 I, 2, 165) 1) intr. a) to go down, to go to the bottom (in water or sands): *who fears —ing where such treasure lies?* Lucr. 280. *have you a mind to s.?* Tp. I, 1, 42. 67. I, 2, 32. Wiv. III, 5, 13. Err. III, 2,

52. John V, 5, 13. H4A I, 3, 194. H5 I, 2, 165. H6C V, 4, 30. R3 IV, 4, 464. Caes. I, 2, 111. Ant. II, 7, 66. III, 10, 26. III, 13, 64.

b) to go down, to descend; opposed to rise: *love is a spirit all compact of fire, not gross to s., but light, and will aspire,* Ven. 150. *see the brave day sunk in hideous night,* Sonn. 12, 2. *my life —s down to death,* 45, 8. *till he s. into his grave,* Ado II, 1, 83. *s. in apple of his eye,* Mids. III, 2, 104. *the splitting rocks cowered in the —ing sands,* H6B III, 2, 97. *will the aspiring blood of Lancaster s. in the ground?* H6C V, 6, 62. *s., my knee, i' the earth,* Cor. V, 3, 50. *to s. in it,* Rom. I, 4, 23. *as in thy red rays thou dost s. to night,* Caes. V, 3, 61 (some M. Edd. *s. to-night*). *why —s that cauldron?* Mcb. IV, 1, 106. *sunken eyes =* hollow eyes: Sonn. 2, 7. As III, 2, 393.

c) to fall slowly to the ground: Ven. 593. Ado IV, 1, 111 (*down*). R2 V, 5, 113 (*downward*). Cymb. III, 6, 17 (*at point to s. for food;* cf. *For*). *here many s.* Per. I, 4, 48 (die of hunger). Hence = to decay: *ne'er speak or think that Timon's fortunes 'mong his friends can s.* Tim. II, 2, 240. Ant. III, 10, 26.

d) to be pressed down, not to bear up against a weight: (camels) *—ing under them* (burdens) Cor. II, 1, 269. *under love's heavy burden do I s.* Rom. I, 4, 22. Caes. IV, 2, 24. Mcb. IV, 3, 39.

e) to fall, to perish: *for every false drop in her bawdy veins a Grecian's life hath sunk,* Troil. IV, 1, 70. *the best of you shall s. in my rebuke,* Oth. II, 3, 209. *now, Troy, s. down,* Troil. V, 8, 11. *s. Athens!* Tim. III, 6, 114. *s. Rome!* Ant. III, 7, 16. *your house would s. and overwhelm you,* Per. IV, 6, 128.

2) trans. a) to make to go down, to submerge: *I would have sunk the sea within the earth,* Tp. I, 2, 11. *where they mean to s. ye,* H8 II, 1, 131. *a load would s. a navy,* III, 2, 383.

b) to make to fall: *why doth it not then our eyelids s.?* Tp. II, 1, 201. *my heavy conscience —s my knee,* Cymb. V, 5, 413.

c) to make to perish, to ruin: *lay a more noble thought upon mine honour than for to think that I would s. it here,* All's V, 3, 181. *if I have a conscience, let it s. me, even as the axe falls, if I be not faithful,* H8 II, 1, 60.

**Sink-a-pace,** spelling of Ff for *cinque-pace* (q. v.) in Tw. I, 3, 139.

**Sinking-ripe,** near sinking: *the ship, then s.* Err. I, 1, 78.

**Sinner,** one who commits or has committed sin: Tp. I, 2, 101. Err. II, 2, 190. Tw. V, 37. H6A I, 4, 70. H6B III, 3, 31. Rom. III, 2, 111. Tim. I, 2, 59. Hml. III, 1, 123.

**Sinon,** name of the Greek who persuaded the Trojans to carry the wooden horse into Troy: Lucr. 1521. 1529. H6C III, 2, 190. Tit. V, 3, 85. Cymb. III, 4, 61.

**Sip,** to drink a small quantity and as if only with the lips: Shr. V, 2, 145. With *on: s. on a cup,* Wiv. II, 2, 77. *whereon but —ing,* Hml. IV, 7, 161. With *to: she would to each one s.* Wint. IV, 4, 62.

**Sir,** 1) used as a noun appellative, = a) sovereign, lord, master: *sole s. o' the world,* Ant. V, 2, 120. b) gentleman: *a loyal s. to him thou followest,* Tp. V, 69. *in the habit of some s. of note,* Tw. III, 4, 81. *hear me breathe my life before this ancient s.* Wint. IV, 4, 372. *the worthiest s.* Cymb. I, 6, 160. *a s. so*

*rare,* 175. *a nobler s. ne'er lived,* V, 5, 145. Used with irony: *Camillo, this great s. will yet stay longer,* Wint I, 2, 212. *no hearing, no feeling, but my —'s song,* IV, 4, 625. *that s. which serves and seeks for gain,* Lr. II, 4, 79. *it had been better you had not kissed your three fingers so oft, which now again you are most apt to play the s. in,* Oth. II, 1, 176 (i. e. a gentleman of good breeding). *to draw upon an exile! O brave s.!* Cymb. I, 1, 166.

2) a general form of address, used to men of any station: Tp. I, 2, 41. 55. 78. 256. 259. 268. II, 1, 1. 14. 83. 96. 102. 113. 193. Gent. I, 1, 101. 129. 139. II, 1, 9. 14 etc. etc. *s., my liege,* Tp. V, 245. Wint. V, 1, 224. Cymb. III, 1, 16. *s., my lord,* Wint. I, 2, 318. *s., my gracious lord,* IV, 4, 5. Preceded by adjectives: *most absolute s.* Cor. IV, 5, 142. *fair s.* Merch. I, 3, 127. As II, 4, 75. Shr. IV, 5, 53. *most generous s.* LLL V, 1, 96. *gentle s.* As II, 4, 70. *good s.* Tp. I, 2, 88. 442. II, 1, 8. Meas. I, 4, 90. Err. IV, 1, 60. As I, 2, 273. Wint. II, 1, 26. H8 IV, 1, 61. Lr. IV, 6, 32. *grave s.* Tp. I, 2, 189. *great s.* Wint. V, 1, 180. *holy s.* John III, 1, 248. *lordly s.* H6A III, 1, 43. *mighty s.* Cymb. V, 5, 327. *most military s.* LLL V, 1, 38. *old s.* Wint. IV, 4, 367. *pious s.* Meas. I, 3, 16. *sovereign s.* Wint. V, 3, 2. *most wicked s.* Tp. V, 130. *worthy s.* Cor. I, 5, 15. *young s.* As I, 2, 191 etc. *how fares my gracious s.?* Tp. V, 253. *my holy s.* Meas. I, 3, 7. *my grave s.* Wint. IV, 4, 422. Before titles and compellations of various kinds: *s. king,* Tp. V, 106. *s. knight,* H5 II, 2, 67. *away, s. Corporal Nym,* Wiv. II, 1, 128. *s. knave,* Err. I, 2, 72. 92. III, 1, 64. All's I, 3, 94. H6B I, 3, 25. *s. boy,* Ado V, 1, 83. Tit. IV, 3, 2. *s. page,* Wint. I, 2, 135. Ironically before abstracts used concretely: *this S. Prudence,* Tp. II, 1, 286. *I am S. Oracle,* Merch. I, 1, 93. *S. Smile, his neighbour,* Wint. I, 2, 196. *at this sport S. Valour dies,* Troil. I, 3, 176. *such a one as a man may not speak of without he say Sir-reverence,* Err. III, 2, 93 (corrupted from *save your reverence.* In Rom. I, 4, 42 the surreptitious Q1 and M. Edd. *this sir-reverence,* the authentic O. Edd. *or save your reverence*).

Plur. *—s* mostly used in addressing persons below the degree of the speaker, or persons of low rank: Gent. IV, 1, 38. Wiv. I, 3, 34. IV, 2, 110. As II, 5, 32. Shr. Ind. I, 36. IV, 3, 195. Wint. IV, 4, 73 (*reverend —s*). H4A II, 2, 62. II, 4, 192. H6A II, 1, 1. V, 2, 14. V, 4, 55. H6B II, 4, 5. III, 1, 188. III, 2, 242. IV, 7, 1. R3 I, 2, 226. I, 4, 261. Troil. V, 7, 7. Tit. III, 3, 278. 283. III, 1, 178. IV, 3, 6. V, 3, 15. Caes. IV, 3, 246. 250 (*good —s*). Hml. IV, 5, 112 etc. The original meaning so obliterated, that even women are addressed with *— s:* LLL IV, 3, 211. Ant. IV, 15, 85. cf. *sirrah* in V, 2, 229 and *now sir* in R2 V, 5, 55. Often a whole thought implied in the simple word: *Jack Rugby! Sir?* Wiv. II, 3, 2 (= what is your pleasure?). *Fulvia is dead. Sir!* Ant. I, 2, 163 (= you don't say so!) etc.

3) Before the Christian names of knights or baronets, and of priests: Wiv. I, 1, 3. II, 1, 115. John I, 80. 82. 139. 185. R2 III, 3, 28. H4A I, 1, 63. 69. IV, 4, 1 etc. (jestingly: *Sir Alice Ford,* Wiv. II, 1, 51). Wiv. I, 1, 1. 216. I, 4, 114. II, 1, 209. LLL IV, 2, 11. 50. 140. As III, 3, 43. V, 1, 5. Tw. IV, 2, 2. H6B I, 2, 68. 88. R3 III, 2, 111. IV, 5, 1 etc. *had rather go with sir priest than sir knight,* Tw. III, 4, 298.

Applied to names of foreigners belonging to the

gentry: Gent. I, 1, 70. I, 2, 9. 38. I, 3, 88. II, 1, 78. 106. II, 4, 3. 50. 67. II, 7, 13. IV, 3, 6. Shr. IV, 2, 105. H5 IV, 8, 100. Troil. IV, 4, 111. Rom. III, 4, 12. IV, 5, 92. Tim. III, 4, 6. *Sir Pandarus*, Wiv. I, 3, 83. *Sir Actaeon*, II, 1, 122.

**Sire**, subst. father (only in verse, and never as an address): Ven. 1160. 1178. Lucr. 232. 1477. Sonn. 8, 11. Gent. III, 1, 231. Meas. III, 1, 29. Shr. II, 413. All's II, 3, 142 (dissyll.). Wint. III, 2, 198. R2 III, 4, 30. H5 II, 4, 57. H6A IV, 6, 54. H6C II, 2, 22. 135. 155. II, 4, 9. R3 V, 5, 26. Tit. V, 1, 50. Tim. IV, 1, 14. IV, 3, 383.

**Sire**, vb. to be father to (cf. *Father*, vb.): *cowards father cowards and base things s. base*, Cymb. IV, 2, 26.

**Siren**, a mermaid, a female charmer: *what potions have I drunk of S. tears*, Sonn. 119, 1. *sing, s., for thyself and I will dote*, Err. III, 2, 47. *this nymph, this s., that will charm Rome's Saturnine*, Tit. II, 1, 23.

**Sirrah** (never plur.) a compellation used in addressing comparatively inferior persons: Tp. V, 287. 291. Gent. II, 1, 7. III, 1, 204. 259. Wiv. I, 1, 281. I, 3, 88. III, 2, 21. IV, 1, 19. Meas. III, 2, 20. IV, 2, 1. 23. IV, 3, 22. V, 214. 505. Err. II, 2, 211. V, 274. LLL I, 1, 283. V, 1, 36. Merch. I, 2, 146. II, 5, 38. III, 5, 51. As III, 2, 168. Shr. Ind. I, 74. I, 1, 226. 231. 246. I, 2, 16. II, 109. III, 1, 15. IV, 1, 153. All's I, 3, 72. 85. II, 3, 208. 257. II, 4, 57. V, 2, 55. V, 3, 234. Tw. V, 148. John I, 90. 116. R2 II, 2, 90. H4A II, 4, 6. III, 3, 153. 173. IV, 2, 80. H4B I, 2, 1. II, 1, 6. II, 2, 176. II, 4, 403. H5 IV, 7, 151. H6A I, 4, 1. III, 1, 62. III, 4, 35. H6B I, 3, 222. II, 1, 117. 140. II, 3, 81. IV, 2, 104. V, 1, 111. H6C V, 6, 6. R3 III, 2, 98. H8 V, 4, 30. Troil. III, 2, 7. Cor. V, 2, 55. V, 3, 75. Tit. III, 2, 75. IV, 3, 78. IV, 4, 47. Rom. I, 2, 34. IV, 2, 2. IV, 4, 15. V, 3, 280. Tim. III, 1, 41. Caes. III, 1, 10. IV, 3, 134. V, 3, 25. 36. Mcb. III, 1, 45. IV, 2, 30. Hml. V, 1, 127. Lr. I, 2, 83. I, 4, 48. 123. 186. 197. II, 2, 74. III, 4, 184. IV, 1, 53. Oth. III, 4, 1. Ant. II, 3, 10. Cymb. III, 5, 80. 106. 109. Resented by one who thinks himself a gentleman: *yours, s.? I am a gentleman, sir, and my name is Conrade*, Ado IV, 2, 14. Used between equals of low degree: Gent. II, 5, 11. Err. III, 1, 83. H4A II, 1, 67. H4B II, 4, 16. Lr. I, 4, 109. Implying disrespect when used to persons of note: Wiv. IV, 2, 142. Err. IV, 1, 81. John II, 140. H4A I, 3, 118. V, 4, 130. or at least an unbecoming familiarity: *and, s., I have cases of buckram*, H4A I, 2, 200. Followed by a noun proper or appellative: *s. Costard*, LLL III, 121. *s. Grumio*, Shr. I, 2, 5. V, 2, 95. *s. villain*, I, 2, 19. *s. young gamester*, II, 402. *s. Biondello*, IV, 4, 10. V, 2, 86. *s. carrier*, H4A II, 1, 46. *s. Jack*, II, 2, 73. *s. beadle*, H6B II, 1, 148. *s. Claudius*, Caes. IV, 3, 300. Used as an address to a woman: *s. Iras, go*, Ant. V, 2, 229.

Sometimes forming part of a soliloquy and addressed to an imaginary person or rather to the speaker himself (always preceded by *ah*): *ah, s., a body would think this was well counterfeited*, As IV, 3, 166. *ah, s., quoth-a, we shall do nothing but eat and make good cheer*, H4B V, 3, 17. *ah, s., this unlooked-for sport comes well*, Rom. I, 5, 31. *ah, s., by my fay, it waxes late*, 128.

**Sir-reverence**, see *Sir*.

**Sirup**, see *Syrup*.

**Sister**, subst. 1) a female born of the same parents: Pilgr. 104. Tp. IV, 103. Gent. II, 3, 7. IV, 4, 5. Meas. I, 2, 182. I, 4, 19. 23. Err. I, 2, 76. II, 1, 6. III, 2, 46. LLL V, 2, 13. As IV, 3, 88 etc. etc. == sister-in-law: Err. V, 416. As V, 2, 21. Shr. V, 2, 6. Tw. V, 325. 393. R2 I, 2, 56. II, 2, 90. 105. R3 I, 1, 109. II, 2, 101 (Qq *madam*). IV, 1, 7. Hml. I, 2, 8. Lr. III, 7, 7. Term of endearment: *our —s' vows*, Mids. III, 2, 199.

2) a female of the same kind or order: *the —s three* == the Parcae: Mids. V, 343. Merch. II, 2, 66. H4B II, 4, 213. *the weird —s*: Mcb. I, 3, 32. I, 5, 9. II, 1, 20. III, 1, 57. III, 4, 133. IV, 1, 136. cf. I, 3, 1. IV, 1, 127. *brethren and —s of the household trade*, Troil. V, 10, 52. == a nun: Compl. 233. Meas. II, 4, 18. III, 1, 152. Mids. I, 1, 72. The French queen addressed so by the English king: H5 V, 2, 2. 90.

**Sister**, vb. 1) to be akin, to resemble closely: *her art —s the natural roses*, Per. V Prol. 7. 2) to be near: *from a —ing vale*, Compl. 2.

**Sisterhood**, an order or convent of nuns: Meas. I, 4, 5. II, 2, 21. V, 72. As III, 4, 17. Rom. V, 3, 157.

**Sisterly**, pertaining to or becoming a sister: *my s. remorse confutes mine honour*, Meas. V, 100.

**Sisture**, in *Insisture*, q. v.

**Sit** (impf. and partic. *sat*) 1) to be in a position of rest (on the buttocks, as animals, or on the feet, as birds): Ven. 349. 366. Pilgr. 143. Tp. I, 2, 223. 389. III, 1, 28. Gent. V, 4, 4. Wiv. III, 1, 24. Meas. II, 1, 66. 126. 132. Err. IV, 4, 36. Ado II, 1, 332. LLL IV, 3, 165. Mids. II, 1, 149. II, 2, 150. As II, 4, 37. Tw. II, 4, 117. H5 II, 2, 27. H6B I, 2, 36. H6C I, 1, 50. 84. 125. Caes. I, 1, 45. Ant. II, 2, 196 etc. *s. you fast*, H6C IV, 1, 119. *s. fast*, V, 2, 3. *s. still*, Tp. I, 2, 170. Mcb. III, 4, 108. *s. at dinner*, Err. I, 2, 62. Ant. II, 1, 12. *at supper*, Gent. II, 1, 46. R3 II, 4, 10. *at any good man's feast*, As II, 7, 115. *at a play*, Hml. II, 2, 618. *he does s. in gold*, Cor. V, 1, 63; cf. V, 4, 22. *stalk on, the fowl —s* (and may, therefore, easily be caught) Ado II, 3, 96. *birds s. brooding in the snow*, LLL V, 2, 933. *o'er which his melancholy —s on brood*, Hml. III, 1, 173. *to s. in the stocks*, Gent. IV, 4, 33. All's IV, 3, 116. R2 V, 5, 26. 27. Lr. II, 2, 141. II, 4, 114. Denoting any state of rest and inactivity: *stand, ... if not, we'll make you s. and rifle you*, Gent. IV, 1, 4. *York must s. and fret and bite his tongue*, H6B I, 1, 230. *I have sat too long*, Cor. V, 3, 131 (but cf. *Sitting*). *till then s. still, my soul*, Hml. I, 2, 257.

*To s. out* == not to take part: LLL I, 1, 110 (an expression taken from the card-table).

2) to set one's self down, to take a seat: Ven. 17. Compl. 65. 66 (*being sat*). Tp. IV, 1, 32. Wiv. I, 1, 289. Merch. V, 58. As V, 3, 8. H4B IV, 5, 182. H6C III, 3, 16 (*s. thee by our side; thee* nom. or accus.?) etc. With *down*: Ven. 325. Tp. I, 2, 32. III, 1, 23. III, 3, 6. Err. III, 1, 33. LLL I, 1, 239. Mids. III, 1, 75. Merch. II, 6, 9. H6C III, 3, 2. H8 IV, 1, 65. IV, 2, 81. Tit. IV, 2, 132. Hml. I, 1, 30. Ant. III, 11, 28 etc. *s. you down*, Meas. V, 366. As II, 7, 124. *s. thee down*, LLL I, 1, 317. Mids. IV, 1, 1. Caes. V, 5, 4 (*you* and *thee* nom. or accus.?).

3) to hold a session, to be engaged in public business: *s. with my cousin*, Meas. V, 246. *let the crowner s. o' my coz*, Tw. I, 5, 143. Hml. V, 1, 4. *to s. with us once more*, H5 V, 2, 80. *sat in the council-house*,

H6B I, 1, 90. *long —ing to determine poor men's causes*, IV, 7,93. *to s. about the coronation*, R3 III, 1, 173. *the gods s. in hourly synod about thy particular prosperity*, Cor. V, 2, 74. 3, 131. *s. in council*, Caes. IV, 1, 45. *le's s. together*, Lr. I, 1, 308 (Qq *hit*). *and in session s. with meditations lawful*, Oth. III, 3, 140. *the senate-house of planets all did s. to knit in her their best perfections*, Per. I, 1, 10. *we s. too long on trifles*, II, 3, 92.

4) to be or stay or remain in a place: *and there (*the snail*) all smothered up, in shade doth s.* Ven. 1035. *in the Bunch of Grapes, where you have a delight to s.* Meas. II, 1, 134. *I have sat here all day*, IV, 1, 20. *he shows me where the bachelors s.* Ado II, 1, 51. *the god of love that —s above*, V, 2, 27. *here upon thy cheek the stain doth s. of an old tear*, Rom. II, 3, 75. = to be about a sick person: John IV, 1, 30. H4B IV, 5, 20. 53. cf. R3 I, 4, 73 (Ff *s. by me*, Qq *stay by me*). *to s. up* = not to go to bed: Rom. IV, 3, 10.

5) to have a seat, to be placed, to dwell: *whether beauty, birth, or wealth or wit ... entitled in their parts do crowned s.* Sonn. 37, 7; cf. *that cruel eye where he —s crowned*, Tw. V, 131; *upon thy eye-balls murderous tyranny —s in grim majesty*, H6B III, 2, 50. *no love toward others in that bosom —s*, Sonn. 9, 13; *as if allegiance in their bosoms sat*, H5 II, 2, 4. *much more than in my verse can s. your own glass shows you*, Sonn. 103, 13. *the attribute to awe and majesty, wherein doth s. the dread and fear of kings*, Merch. IV, 1, 192. *my mother told me just how he would woo, as if she sat in his heart*, All's IV, 2, 70. *O, s. my husband's wrongs on Hereford's spear*, R2 I, 2, 47. *his treasons will s. blushing in his face*, III, 2, 51. *every honour —ing on his helm*, H4A III, 2, 142; *everlasting shame —s mocking in our plumes*, H5 IV, 5, 5; *fortune and victory s. on thy helm*, R3 V, 3, 79; *victory —s on our helms*, 351; *upon your sword s. laurel victory*, Ant. I, 3, 100. *now —s Expectation in the air*, H5 II Prol. 8. *to make an envious mountain on my back, where —s deformity to mock my body*, H6C III, 2, 158. *within thine eye sat twenty thousand deaths*, Cor. III, 3, 70. *take our good meaning, for our judgment —s five times in that ere once in our five wits*, Rom. I, 4, 46. *is there no pity —ing in the clouds*, III, 5, 198. *policy —s above conscience*, Tim. III, 2, 94 (has a higher place, is above c.). *he —s high in all the people's hearts*, Caes. I, 3, 157.

6) to be in a situation or condition: *I s. at twenty pounds a week*, Wiv. I, 3, 8. *under your hard construction must I s.* Tw. III, 1, 126. *Rome —s safe and still without him*, Cor. IV, 6, 37.

7) to lie, to bear on, to be felt: *your brother's death —s at your heart*, Meas. V, 394. *woe doth the heavier s., where it perceives it is but faintly borne*, R2 I, 3, 280. *let me s. heavy on thy soul to-morrow*, R3 V, 3, 118. 131. 139. *amazement on thy mother —s*, Hml. III, 4, 112. Peculiar expression: *this accord of Hamlet —s smiling to my heart*, Hml. I, 2, 124 (cf. *unclog my heart of what lies heavy to't*, Cor. IV, 2, 48). In All's II, 1, 147 O. Edd. *oft it hits where hope is coldest and despair most —s; M. Edd. fits.*

8) With *down*, = to begin a siege: *all places yield to him ere he —s down*, Cor. IV, 7, 28. In All's I, 1, 129 and Ant. III, 13, 168 O. Edd. *set*, most M. Edd. *sit.*

9) Used of clothes or ornaments worn: *here it (*the crown*) —s*, H4B IV, 5, 43. 187. The sense modified by adverbs and adjectives: *how well my garments s. upon me*, Tp. II, 1, 272. *O majesty, when thou dost pinch thy bearer, thou dost s. like a rich armour worn in heat of day*, H4B IV, 5, 29. *our old robes s. easier than our new*, Mcb. II, 4, 38. Metaphorically: *these fixed evils s. so fit in him*, All's I, 1, 113 (*in* = on). *this new and gorgeous garment majesty —s not so easy on me as you think*, H4B V, 2, 45.

10) Used of the wind, = to have a direction: *—s the wind in that corner?* Ado II, 3, 102. *to know where —s the wind*, Merch. I, 1, 18. *we see the wind s. sore upon our sails*, R2 II, 1, 265. *the wind —s fair for news to go to Ireland*, II, 2, 123. H5 II, 2, 12. *the wind —s in the shoulder of your sail*, Hml. I, 3, 56. *an thou canst not smile as the wind —s*, Lr. I, 4, 113. *though my reason —s in the wind against me*, Ant. III, 10, 37.

11) Refl., with *down*, = set: *would shut the book and s. him down and die*, H4B III, 1, 56. *here will I s. me down*, H6C II, 5, 14. *I sat me down*, Hml. V, 2, 31 (in Meas. V. 366. LLL I, 1, 110. 317. Mids. IV, 1, 1. As II, 7, 124. H6C III, 3, 16. IV, 1, 119. Caes. V, 5, 4 *thee* and *you* may be nominatives).

12) Transitively, = to keep the seat on: *he could not s. his mule*, H8 V, 2, 16.

**Sith,** 1) adv. since that time: *being of so young days brought up with him, and s. so neighboured to his youth and haviour*, Hml. II, 2, 12 (Ff *since*).

2) conj. since, as, seeing that: *the world will hold thee in disdain, s. in thy pride so fair a hope is slain*, Ven. 762. *s. in his prime death doth my love destroy, they that love best their loves shall not enjoy*, 1163. *I will not, s. so prettily he couples it to his complaining names*, Gent. I, 2, 126. Wiv. II, 2, 195. Meas. I, 3, 35. Shr. I, 1, 216. H6C I, 1, 110. 1, 3, 41. Troil. I, 3, 13. V, 2, 120. Tit. I, 271. 323. IV, 3, 49. Hml. II, 2, 6 (Ff *since*). IV, 4, 45. IV, 7, 3. Lr. I, 1, 183. Oth. III, 3, 380 (Qq *since*). 411. *s. that*, in the same sense: Meas. IV, 1, 74. Lr. II, 4, 242.

3) prepos. since, after: *I come to tell you things s. then befallen*, H6C II, 1, 106.

**Sithence,** 1) adv. since or after that time: *have you informed them s.?* Cor. III, 1, 47.

2) conj. since, as: *which I held my duty speedily to acquaint you withal, s. in the loss that may happen it concerns you to know it*, All's I, 3, 124.

**Sitting,** a being together, a meeting, a being in company: *fourscore ducats at a s.* Merch. III, 1, 117. *the which shall point you forth at every s. what you must say*, Wint. IV, 4, 572. cf. Cor. V, 3, 131.

**Situate,** placed, lying: *there's nothing s. under heaven's eye but hath his bound*, Err. II, 1, 16. *I know where it is s.* LLL I, 2, 142.

**Situation,** 1) position, site: *survey the plot of s. and the model*, H4B I, 3, 51. *the —s, look you, is both alike*, H5 IV, 7, 27.

2) state, condition: *they would change their state and s. with those dancing chips*, Sonn. 128, 10.

**Siward** (O. Edd. *Seyward*) name in Mcb. III, 6, 31. IV, 3, 134. V, 2, 2. 9.

**Six,** twice three: Tp. I, 2, 240. Wiv. II, 3, 37. Meas. II, 1, 287. III, 1, 76. Err. I, 1, 45. Merch. II, 5, 25. III, 2, 301. IV, 1, 84. 85. 86. As IV, 1, 95. Shr. II, 360. III, 2, 61. All's I, 2, 71. IV, 3, 151 170. V, 3, 196. Wint. IV, 4, 273. R2 I, 3, 211. 219.

# S

248. 260. H4A II, 4, 115. 199. IV, 3, 56. H4B II, 4, 8. V, 1, 89. H5 I, 1, 14. H6A I, 1, 112. IV, 1, 20. IV, 4, 41. H6C II, 1, 144. III, 3, 96. R3 V, 3, 10. V, 4, 11 H8 IV, 1, 27. Troil. III, 3, 278. Cor. II, 3, 135. IV, 1, 18. IV, 5, 174. V, 6, 130. Tim. II, 2, 30. IV, 3. 143. Caes. II, 1, 277. Hml. V, 2, 155. 157. 168. Lr. III, 4, 142. III, 7, 16. Ant. III, 10, 34. IV, 7, 10 Cymb. IV, 2, 293. Per. III Prol. 31. *written in eight and s.* Mids. III, 1, 25 (in verses of eight and six feet, like the popular ballads). *every thing is left at s. and seven,* R2 II, 2, 122 (= in disorder. *Six* and *seven* often combined: Meas. II, 1, 287. Wiv. II, 3, 37. H4A II, 4, 115. 199. Caes. II, 1, 277. *s. or seven times honoured,* Troil. III, 3, 278).

**Six-gated,** having six gates: Troil. Prol. 15.

**Sixpence,** half a shilling: Err. I, 2, 55. Ado II, 1, 42. Mids. IV, 2, 20. 21. Tw. II, 3, 26. 32. H4A II, 4, 28. H4B I, 2, 29. II, 2, 102. Oth. II, 3, 94. cf. *Mill-sixpence.*

**Sixpenny,** the same: *s. strikers,* H4A II, 1, 82.

**Six-score,** one hundred and twenty: Shr. II, 360.

**Sixteen,** six and ten: Gent. IV, 1, 21. All's IV, 3, 98. Wint. IV, 1, 6. V, 3, 31. H4A II, 4, 194. H5 IV, 8, 93. H8 II, 3, 82. Cor. II, 2, 91. Tim. IV, 1, 13. Hml. II, 2, 567. Cymb. IV, 2, 199.

**Sixt** (O. Edd.) or **Sixth** (M. Edd.), the ordinal of six: Tp. V, 4. Ado I, 1, 285. V, 1, 221 *(s. and lastly).* LLL I, 1, 238. As II, 7, 157. IV, 4, 100. H5 Epil. 9. H6A IV, 1, 2. IV, 7, 70. H6B II, 2, 16. H6C III, 3, 89. R3 III, 3, 16. IV, 2, 98. V, 3, 127. H8 I, 2, 58. 94. Lr. I, 1, 178. Cymb. I, 3, 31. V, 4, 20 *(a s.* = the sixth part). Per. II, 2, 40.

**Sixtly** or **Sixthly,** in the sixth place: *sixt and lastly,* Ado V, 1, 221 (the suffix *ly* belonging to both words).

**Sixty,** ten times six: Troil. Prol. 5. Ant. III, 7, 50. III, 10, 3. Cymb. IV, 2, 199.

**Size,** 1) settled portion, allowance: *to scant my —s,* Lr. II, 4, 178.

2) proportion, dimension, shape: *you may know by my s. that I have a kind of alacrity in sinking,* Wiv. III, 5, 12. *a word too great for any mouth of this age's s.* As III, 2, 240. *to shape my legs of an unequal s.* H6C III, 2, 159. *his large and portly s.* Troil. IV, 5, 162. *framed of the Cyclops' s.* Tit. IV, 3, 46. Figuratively, = measure, shape: *a malice of as great s.* H8 V, 1, 136. *I have ever verified my friends with all the s. that verity would without lapsing suffer,* Cor. V, 2, 18. *cannot cover the monstrous bulk of this ingratitude with any s. of words,* Tim. V, 1, 69. *our s. of sorrow, proportioned to our cause, must be as great as that which makes it,* Ant. IV, 15, 4. *it's past the s. of dreaming,* V, 2, 97.

3) shape, form: *in clamours of all s., both high and low,* Compl. 21. *it must be an answer of most monstrous s. that must fit all demands,* All's II, 2, 35. *he hath songs for man and woman, of all —s,* Wint. IV, 4, 192.

**Size,** a kind of glue, in *O'ersized,* q. v.

**Sized,** having a particular magnitude: *as my love is s., my fear is so,* Hml. III, 2, 180. cf. *Great-sized.*

**Skains-mate** (originally = brother in arms, from *skean* or *skein* = sword, dagger; cf. the German *Spiessgeselle*) a messmate, companion: *I am none of his flirt-gills, I am none of his —s,* Rom. II, 4, 162 (the nurse's speech. According to Staunton, *skain* is a Kentish provincialism for scape-grace).

**Skein,** a knot (of thread or silk): Shr. IV, 3, 111. Troil. V, 1, 35.

**Skilful,** 1) cunning, judicious: *the s. shepherd peeled me certain wands,* Merch. I, 3, 85.

2) well versed in an art, expert, dexterous: Lucr. 1367. All's I, 1, 34. Tw. III, 4, 245. 293. H6C V, 4, 20. Troil. I, 1, 7. Oth. III, 4, 74.

**Skilfully,** expertly: *thou art an old love-monger and speakest s.* LLL II, 254.

**Skill,** 1) discernment, sagacity, mental power, wit, cunning: *which (her beauty) far exceeds his barren s. to show,* Lucr. 81. *the impression of strange kinds is formed in them by force, by fraud, or s.* 1243. *in the very refuse of thy deeds there is such strength and warrantise of s. that, in my mind, thy worst all best exceeds,* Sonn. 150, 7. *I'll show my mind according to my shallow simple s.* Gent. I, 2, 8. *to compass her, I'll use my s.* II, 4, 214. *if I read it not truly* (viz your brow) *my ancient s. beguiles me,* Meas. IV, 2, 164. *dart thy s. at me,* LLL V, 2, 396. *touching now the point of human s., reason becomes the marshal to my will,* Mids. II, 2, 119. *which of them both is dearest to me, I have no s. in sense to make distinction,* All's III, 4, 39 (I cannot judge by what I feel). *or stupified or seeming so in s.* Wint. II, 1, 166 (= cunning). *I'll so offend, to make offence a s.* H4A I, 2, 240 (wisdom, good policy). *had I sufficient s. to utter them,* H6A V, 5, 13. *this vile deed we must with all our majesty and s. both countenance and excuse,* Hml. IV, 1, 31. *all the s. I have remembers not these garments,* Lr. IV, 7, 66. *'tis greater s. in a true hate, to pray they have their will,* Cymb. II, 5, 33.

2) familiar knowledge of any art or science, shown by readiness and dexterity in its application to practical purposes: Lucr. 1099. 1134. 1506. 1528. Sonn. 16, 14. 24, 5. 66, 10. 91, 1. 100, 8. 106, 12. 126, 7. Compl. 125. Ado I, 2, 28. LLL IV, 1, 28. Mids. I, 1, 195. V, 110. As III, 3, 63. All's I, 1, 21. I, 3, 249. II, 1, 187. Tw. III, 4, 213. 254. John IV, 2, 29. R2 III, 4, 103. H6A I, 2, 60. 63. Troil. I, 1, 8. V, 2, 170. Tit. II, 1, 43. Rom. II, 6, 25. Hml. III, 2, 378. V, 2, 267. Cymb. II, 4, 22. V, 5, 433. Per. IV, Prol. 30. V, 1, 76. Followed by *in: hath good s. in his rapier,* Wiv. II, 1, 231. All's IV, 5, 22. H4A V, 1, 135. H4B IV, 3, 123. Tim. V, 3, 7.

3) reason, motive (or rather a thought caused by consideration and judgment): *you have as little s. to fear as I have purpose to put you to't,* Wint. IV, 4, 152.

**Skill,** vb., in the phrase *it skills not greatly,* or *it skills not much,* = it makes no difference, it matters not greatly: Shr. III, 2, 134. Tw. V, 295. H6B III, 1, 281.

**Skill-contending,** rivalling in skill: Lucr. 1018.

**Skilled,** expert, versed: Tit. IV, 1, 33. With *in:* Gent. III, 2, 92. R3 IV, 4, 116.

**Skilless** or **Skilless,** inexpert, ignorant: Troil. I, 1, 12. Rom. III, 3, 132. With *in: being s. in these parts,* Tw. III, 3, 9 (unacquainted with this country). With *of: how features are abroad, I am s. of,* Tp. III, 1, 53.

**Skillet,** a boiler, a kettle: Oth. I, 3, 273.

**Skim,** vb. to take the cream off from: *s. milk,* Mids. II, 1, 36. *such a dish of —ed milk,* H4A II, 3, 36 (Qq skim milk).

**Skimble-skamble,** wandering, wild, confused: *such a deal of s. stuff,* H4A III, 1, 154.

**Skim-milk**, milk from which the cream has been taken: H4A II, 3, 36 (Ff *skim'd milk*).

**Skin**, subst. the natural covering of the flesh: Lucr. 419. Compl. 94. Tp. IV, 233. Wiv. III, 1, 111. Err. II, 2, 138. III, 1, 13. IV, 3, 18. Ado III, 5, 13 (*honest as the s. between his brows;* Dogberry's speech). Mids. II, 1, 255. As IV, 2, 12. Shr. IV, 3, 180. John IV, 3, 80. H4A III, 3, 3. H5 IV, 3, 93. H6B III, 1, 77. 300. IV, 2, 25. 86. H6C III, 1, 22. Tit. V, 1, 138. Rom. V, 1, 43. Mcb. II, 3, 118. Lr. III, 4, 7. Oth. V, 2, 4.

Applied to other things, = crust, bark, coat: *as fit as the pudding to his s.* All's II, 2, 29. *the s. of our fruit-trees*, R2 III, 4, 58. *the s.* (of leek) *is good for your broken coxcomb*, H5 V, 1, 56.

**Skin**, vb. to cover with skin: *authority, though it err like others, hath yet a kind of medicine in itself, that —s the vice o' the top*, Meas. II, 2, 136. *it will but s. and film the ulcerous place, whilst rank corruption, mining all within, infects unseen*, Hml. III, 4, 147.

**Skin-coat**, a (lion's) skin used as a coat: John II, 139.

**Skinker**, in *Under-skinker*, q. v.

**Skinny**, consisting of skin only, wanting flesh: *her s. lips*, Mcb. I, 3, 45.

**Skip**, 1) intr. to fetch quick bounds, to leap, to hop: Pilgr. 153. Wiv. II, 1, 237. Mids. II, 1, 61. Merch. I, 2, 21. Tim. IV, 3, 225. Lr. V, 3, 277. Cymb. IV, 2, 199. Per. IV, 1, 63. —*ing*, metaphorically, = thoughtless, flighty, wanton: *all wanton as a child, —ing and vain*, LLL V, 2, 771. *allay with some cold drops of modesty thy —ing spirit*, Merch. II, 2, 196. *to make one in so —ing a dialogue*, Tw. I, 5, 214. *the —ing king he ambled up and down*, H4A III, 2, 60. *compelled these —ing kerns to trust their heels*, Mcb. I, 2, 30.

2) tr. to leap over, to miss, to pass: *let not thy sword s. one*, Tim. IV, 3, 110.

**Skipper**, a thoughtless and flighty fellow: *s., stand back: 'tis age that nourisheth*, Shr. II, 341.

**Skirmish**, subst. a slight fight: Ado I, 1, 64. H6A I, 2, 34 (or verb?). I, 4, 69.

**Skirr**, to move rapidly, to scour: *make them s. away*, H5 IV, 7, 64. *s. the country round*, Mcb. V, 3, 35 (= round the country).

**Skirt**, 1) the edge of a garment: Wiv. I, 1, 29. Ado III, 4, 21. Shr. IV, 3, 137. cf. *Foreskirt*.

2) edge, margin, border: As III, 2, 354. V, 4, 165. Hml. I, 1, 97.

**Skirted**, wearing a coat with (laced?) skirts: *myself and s. page*, Wiv. I, 3, 93.

**Skittish**, volatile, fickle: *unstaid and s. in all motions else, save in the constant image of the creature that is beloved*, Tw. II, 4, 18. *now expectation, tickling s. spirits*, Troil. Prol. 20. *how some men creep in s. fortune's hall*, III, 3, 134.

**Skogan** (Qq *Skoggin*, Ff *Scoggan* or *Schoggan*) name (subject to much controversy, two notorious persons of the 14th and 15th centuries, one a poet and the other a jester, being called so): H4B III, 2, 33.

**Skulk**, to withdraw into a close place for concealment: —*ing in corners*, Wint. I, 2, 289.

**Skull**, the bone that encloses the head: Tp. III, 2, 98. V, 60. Merch. III, 2, 96. Tw. I, 5, 121. R2 IV, 69. 144. R3 I, 4, 29. Cor. II, 3, 23. Rom. IV, 1, 83. V, 3, 126. Hml. V, 1, 83. 107. 189. 190. 198.

**Sky**, the aërial region which surrounds the earth:
Ven. 153. 184. 348. 485. 815. Lucr. 12. 1587. Tp. I, 2, 3. IV, 70. Gent. V, 1, 1. Wiv. V, 5, 21. Err. II, 1, 17 (*in earth, in sea, in s.*). LLL IV, 2, 5. IV, 3, 79. Mids. III, 2, 23. 107. As II, 7, 184. IV, 1, 149. Wint. I, 2, 180. 294. III, 3, 86. John II, 397. III, 2, 2. III, 4, 153. IV, 2, 108. R2 I, 1, 41. III, 2, 194. H4B IV, 3, 56. H5 III, 7, 78. H6A I, 1, 3. IV, 7, 21. H6B III, 2, 104. H6C II, 1, 28. R3 V, 3, 283. Troil. V, 2, 149. Tit. I, 145. IV, 2, 89. Caes. I, 3, 39. Mcb. I, 2, 49. Lr. II, 3, 12. Ant. II, 7, 74. Cymb. V, 5, 146. Plur. *skies*, in the same sense: Ven. 696. 1191. Lucr. 506. 1524. Mids. IV, 1, 121. Shr. I, 2, 205. Wint. III, 3, 3. Caes. III, 1, 63. Lr. III, 2, 43. III, 4, 107. Oth. II, 1, 92.

Used in the sense of heaven: *the fated s. gives us free scope*, All's I, 1, 232 (rhyming). Considered as the region to which the souls of the departed rise: *my soul and body to the —es and ground*, Lucr. 1199. *my soul is in the s.* Mids. V, 308. H6A IV, 7, 21. cf. *they (curses) ascend the s. and there awake God's gentle-sleeping peace*, R3 I, 3, 287.

**Sky-aspiring**, high-aspiring, very ambitious: *s. thoughts*, R2 I, 3, 130.

**Skyey**, pertaining to the sky (as the cause of the weather): *servile to all the s. influences*, Meas. III, 1, 9.

**Skyish**, being in the skies, very high: *the s. head of blue Olympus*, Hml. V, 1, 276.

**Sky-planted**, placed in the skies: *the thunderer, whose bolt s. batters all rebelling coasts*, Cymb. V, 4, 96.

**Slab**, slabby, glutinous: *make the gruel thick and s.* Mcb. IV, 1, 32.

**Slack**, adj. remiss, backward, not eager: *be thou not s. to proffer, though she put thee back*, Pilgr. 333. *I shall not be s.* Shr. I, 2, 275. *if thou be s., I'll fight it out*, H6A I, 1, 99. *I will not be s. to play my part in Fortune's pageant*, H6B I, 2, 66. *the duke shall know how s. thou art*, R3 I, 4, 282. *so s., so slow*, Per. IV, 2, 68. *to come s. of* = to be remiss in: *if you come s. of former services*, Lr. I, 3, 9.

**Slack**, vb. 1) tr. a) to make less tight, to loosen: *s. the bolins there*, Per. III, 1, 43.

b) to make more slow: *his rage of lust by gazing qualified, —ed, not suppressed*, Lucr. 425. *I am nothing slow to s. his haste*, Rom. IV, 1, 3.

c) to neglect, to be remiss in: *what a beast am I to s. it*, Wiv. III, 4, 115. *if then they chanced to s. you, we could control them*, Lr. II, 4, 248. *they s. their duties*, Oth. IV, 3, 88.

2) intr. to languish, to flag: *their negotiations all must s., wanting his manage*, Troil. III, 3, 24.

**Slackly**, loosely; negligently: *her hair ... s. braided in loose negligence*, Compl. 35. *so s. guarded*, Cymb. I, 1, 64.

**Slackness**, remissness, negligence: Wint. V, 1, 151. Ant. III, 7, 28.

**Slake**, to abate, to decrease; 1) tr.: *it could not s. mine ire*, H6C I, 3, 29. cf. *Yslake*.

2) intr.: *no flood by raining —th*, Lucr. 1677.

**Slander**, subst. 1) defamation, calumny: Sonn. 70, 2. 131, 14. Gent. III, 2, 43. Meas. V, 525. Ado II, 1, 144. III, 1, 84. III, 3, 169 (*make*). IV, 1, 307. V, 1, 68. V, 4, 66. R2 I, 1, 171. H4B Ind. 6. H6B III, 2, 68. R3 I, 3, 26. Troil. I, 3, 193. Rom. IV, 1, 33 Hml. II, 2, 198. Lr. III, 2, 87. Oth. IV, 2, 133. Cymb. II, 5, 26. III, 4, 35. 41. IV, 2, 272. Misapplied for *slanderer* by Dogberry: Ado V, 1, 221.

2) ill report, disreputation: *and yet my nature never in the fight, to do in s.* Meas. I, 3, 43 (perhaps = to act in danger of being misjudged. A passage variously emended by the commentators). *s. lives upon succession,* Err. III, 1, 105. *change s. to remorse,* Ado IV, 1, 213 (i. e. ill report to pity). *that s. is found a truth now,* H8 II, 1, 153. *you shall not find me, after the s. of most stepmothers, evil-eyed unto you,* Cymb. I, 1, 71.

3) reproach, disgrace, scandal: *to clear this spot by death, at least I give a badge of fame to —'s livery,* Lucr. 1054. *my blood shall wash the s. of mine ill,* 1207. *free from these —s and this open shame,* Err. IV, 4, 70. *prevents the s. of his wife,* As IV, 1, 61. *he the sacred honour of himself ... betrays to s.* Wint. II, 3, 85. *a partial s. sought I to avoid,* R2 I, 3, 241 (= reproach of partiality). *thou hast wrought a deed of s. upon my head,* V, 6, 35. *every word you speak in his behalf is s. to your royal dignity,* H6B III, 2, 209. *for more s. to thy dismal seat,* R3 III, 3, 13. *the purest of their wives is foul as s.* Oth. IV, 2, 19. Abstr. pro concr.: *till I have told this s. of his blood,* R2 I, 1, 113 (this disgracer of his race). *learn to know such —s of the age,* H5 III, 6, 84. *thou s. of thy mother's heavy womb,* R3 I, 3, 231.

4) injury, offence done by words: *I did but act, he's author of thy s.* Ven. 1006 (= the insult committed against thee). *action of s.* Meas. II, 1, 190 (opposed to an *action of battery*). *s. to the state,* V, 325. *there is no s. in an allowed fool, though he do nothing but rail,* Tw. I, 5, 101. *you speak it out of fear and cold heart. Do me no s.,* Douglas, H4A IV, 3, 8. *my reputation stained with Tybalt's s.* Rom. III, 1, 117. *there is never a fair woman has a true face. No s., they steal hearts,* Ant. II, 6, 106 (= no offence).

**Slander,** vb. 1) to defame, to calumniate; abs.: Ado V, 1, 95. With an object: Gent. III, 2, 38. Meas. V, 290. 530. Ado IV, 1, 304. 315. V, 1, 88. 243. Merch. V, 22. John IV, 2, 256. H4A III, 3, 150. R3 I, 4, 247. IV, 4, 207. Cor. I, 1, 78. Rom. IV, 1, 35. Oth. III, 3, 368. *to s. with* = to reproach with: *to s. Valentine with falsehood,* Gent. III, 2, 31. *he —ed me with bastardy,* John I, 74. *let not him be —ed with revolt,* H4A I, 3, 112. *—s me with murder's crimson badge,* H6B III, 2, 200. *thy tongue that —s him with cowardice,* H6C I, 4, 47.

2) to disgrace: *now is black beauty's successive heir, and beauty —ed with a bastard shame,* Sonn. 127, 4. *—ing creation with a false esteem,* 12. *tax not so bad a voice to s. music any more than once,* Ado II, 3, 47. *I would not have you so s. any moment leisure as to give words or talk with the Lord Hamlet,* Hml. I, 3, 133. *disdaining me ... —s so her judgment that what's else rare is choked,* Cymb. III, 5, 76.

3) to detract from, to disparage: *the sentence that you have —ed so,* Meas. II, 4, 110. *the leaf of eglantine, whom not to s., out-sweetened not thy breath,* Cymb. IV, 2, 223.

**Slanderer,** calumniator: Sonn. 140, 12. Meas. V, 259. John II, 173. 175. Troil. I, 3, 150. Oth. II, 1, 114.

**Slanderous,** 1) calumnious: Lucr. 161. Wiv. V, 5, 163. Meas. III, 2, 199. Ado V, 3, 3. Shr. II, 255. R2 I, 1, 61. IV, 24. R3 I, 2, 97. Cymb. III, 3, 52.

2) disgraceful, scandalous: *who so base would such an office have as s. death's-man to so base a slave?*

Lucr. 1001. *ugly and s. to thy mother's womb,* John III, 1, 44. *though we lay these honours on this man, to ease ourselves of divers s. loads,* Caes. IV, 1, 20 (or = loads of calumny?).

**Slash,** to strike and cut with a sharp weapon: *I'll s., I'll do't by the sword,* LLL V, 2, 701. Substantively: *here's snip and nip and cut and slish and s.* Shr. IV, 3, 90.

**Slaughter,** subst. 1) the act of slaying or killing: Lucr. 955. Merch. IV, 1, 134. H5 II, 2, 170. R3 IV, 4, 209. Caes. V, 1, 55. Mcb. IV, 3, 227. Hml. V, 2, 393. Lr. I, 4, 342 *(should sure to the s., if my cap would buy a halter).* Per. IV Prol. 40. IV, 3, 2. With an objective genitive: *Priam's s.* Hml. II, 2, 469. *for s. of my son,* H6C II, 5, 105. R3 IV, 4, 142. Cymb. V, 5, 72. *to do s.:* R3 I, 2, 88 *(upon).* II, 1, 122. IV, 4, 139. *made the s.* H6B III, 2, 190. Per. IV, 4, 37 *(on).*

2) great destruction of life, massacre: John II, 349. III, 1, 237. H6A I, 1, 59. V, 4, 161. H6C V, 6, 59. Troil. V, 3, 12. Cymb. V, 3, 20 *(to commit).* With *of*: John II, 323. H6A V, 4, 103. *ha' done this s.* H5 IV, 7, 7. *great the s. is here made by the Roman,* Cymb. V, 3, 78.

**Slaughter,** vb. 1) to slay, to kill, to murder; absol.: *some direful —ing death,* Tit. V, 3, 144. Trans.: Lucr. 1376. 1634. R2 I, 2, 30. H6B III, 2, 197. H6C II, 1, 57. IV, 2, 24. R3 I, 2, 10. I, 4, 231. 250. IV, 4, 200 (Qq *murder*). V, 5, 25. Tit. II, 3, 223. Rom. III, 2, 65. III, 5, 80. 103. V, 3, 84. 199. Metaphorically: *still —ed lust,* Lucr. 188. *one good deed dying tongueless —s a thousand waiting upon that,* Wint. I, 2, 93.

2) to kill in masses, to massacre; absol.: *your —ing hands,* H6A III, 1, 87. *lolling the tongue with —ing,* Cymb. V, 3, 8. Trans.: John III, 1, 302. R2 III, 3, 44. H5 IV, 8, 79. H6A I, 1, 147. III, 1, 101. H6C V, 4, 15. R3 IV, 4, 391. V, 3, 249. Tit. I, 112. Mcb. III, 3, 205.

**Slaughterer,** slayer: H6A II, 5, 109.

**Slaughter-house,** butchery, shambles: Lucr. 1039. John IV, 3, 112. H6B III, 1, 212. IV, 3, 6. H6C V, 4, 78. R3 III, 4, 88. IV, 1, 44.

**Slaughterman,** slayer, destroyer: H5 III, 3, 41. H6A III, 3, 75. H6C I, 4, 169. Tit. IV, 4, 58. Cymb. V, 3, 49.

**Slaughterous,** bent on killing, murderous: *my s. thoughts,* Mcb. V, 5, 14.

**Slave,** subst. 1) a person who is absolutely subject to the will of another: Ven. 101. Lucr. 515. Sonn. 57, 1. 141, 12. Tp. I, 2, 270. 308. 313. 319. 344. 351. 375. Err. II, 1, 1. II, 2, 2. 171. Merch. IV, 1, 90. 98. As III, 2, 162. Shr. I, 1, 224. II, 2. John V, 2, 97. R2 IV, 251. H6A I, 5, 32. V, 3, 113. Tim. I, 1, 71. IV, 3, 391. Caes. I, 3, 15. III, 2, 25. IV, 3, 43. Lr. II, 4, 219. III, 2, 19. V, 3, 221. Oth. III, 3, 135. 158 etc. Metaphorically; with a genitive: *soft fancy's s.* Lucr. 200. *the gross world's baser —s,* LLL I, 1, 30. *a king, woe's s.* R2 III, 2, 210. *fortune's —s,* V, 5, 24. *passion's s.* Hml. III, 2, 77. *the —s of chance,* Wint. IV, 4, 551. *thought's the s. of life,* H4A V, 4, 81 (depends on life). *the —s of drink and thralls of sleep,* Mcb. III, 6, 13. *hot summer's tanlings and the shrinking —s of winter,* Cymb. IV, 4, 30. With *to*: *eater of youth, false s. to false delight,* Lucr. 927. *brass eternal s. to mortal rage,* Sonn. 64, 4 (i. e. subject to). *s. to slavery my sweetest friend must be,* 133, 4. Tp. III, 1, 66. Gent. III, 1, 141. H8 I, 2, 64. Troil. III, 2, 90. Rom. V, 3, 221. Hml. III, 2, 198.

2) an abject person, a wretch: *like straggling — s for pillage fighting,* Lucr. 428. *let him have time to live a loathed s.* 984. *death's-man to so base a s.* 1001. *base intruder, overweening s.* Gent. III, 1, 157. *an unmannerly s., that will thrust himself into secrets,* 393. *a s. that still an end turns me to shame,* IV, 4, 67. *hang 'em, —s,* Wiv. II, 1, 179. Err. I, 2, 87. 104. II, 1, 75. 78. IV, 1, 96. V, 241. Ado V, 1, 272. LLL I, 2, 159. Shr. IV, 1, 169. IV, 3, 31. All's II, 3, 144. IV, 3, 159. V, 3, 205. John I, 222. III, 1, 123. H4A II, 4, 288. IV, 2, 19. 26. H6A I, 2, 37. IV, 5, 15. H6B IV, 1, 67. R3 I, 2, 90. IV, 4, 144. V, 4, 9. H8 V, 4, 3. Rom. I, 1, 17. Tim. II, 2, 174. III, 1, 59 (cf. *Unto*). IV, 3, 33. Mcb. I, 2, 20. Lr. I, 4, 89. Oth. IV, 2, 132. V, 2, 292. Cymb. IV, 2, 72. 74 etc. *thou wast sealed in thy nativity the s. of nature and the son of hell,* R3 I, 3, 230 (i. e. thou wast marked and destined to be mean and contemptible by nature. cf. Cymb. V, 2, 5. see *Nature*).
Sometimes used (like wretch) with some tenderness: *stay, s., I must employ thee,* LLL III, 152. 164. *O —s, I can tell you news,* Cor. IV, 5, 181. *how the black s. smiles upon the father,* Tit. IV, 2, 120. *come on, you thick-lipped s.* 175. *peace, tawny s.* V, 1, 27. cf. Err. II, 2, 2.

**Slave,** vb. to make subject and subservient to one's self: *let the superfluous and lust-dieted man, that —s your ordinance, feel your power quickly,* Lr. IV, 1, 71 (Qq *stands*).*

**Slave-like,** becoming a slave: *this s. habit,* Tim. IV, 3, 205.

**Slaver,** to be smeared with spittle (i. e. to bear the traces of disgustful kisses): *should I s. then with lips* (= by lips) *as common as the stairs that mount the Capitol,* Cymb. I, 6, 105.

**Slavery,** servitude, bondage: Sonn. 133, 4. Tp. III, 1, 62. H6B IV, 8, 29. H8 II, 2, 44. Oth. I, 3, 138.

**Slavish,** servile; mean: Lucr. 299. 537. Merch. IV, 1, 92. R2 I, 1, 193. II, 1, 291. Tit. II, 1, 18. Cymb. IV, 2, 73.

**Slay** (impf. *slew,* partic. *slain*) to kill, to put to death: Ven. 243. 473. 624. 762. 1019. 1111. Lucr. 515. 518. 955. 1046. 1522. Sonn. 139, 4. 13. Gent. IV, 1, 28. Ado V, 3. Mids. II, 1, 190. III, 2, 47. 66. V, 146. Merch. II, 1, 25. All's III, 5, 7. Tw. IV, 4, 55. III, 3, 29. John III, 4, 7. V, 5, 10. R2 I, 1, 133. I, 2, 25. III, 2, 157. 183 etc. etc. *ta'en or slain:* R2 V, 6, 4. H6A IV, 4, 42. Troil. V, 5, 13. Caes. V, 5, 3. *to s. one's self:* Ven. 765. H6A I, 1, 141. Rom. III, 2, 45. III, 3, 116. IV, 1, 72. Caes. III, 1, 22. Ant. IV, 13, 7. Metaphorically, = to annihilate, to destroy, to ruin: *sad souls are slain in merry company,* Lucr. 1110. *number there in love was slain,* Phoen. 28. *what impossibility would s. in common sense, sense saves another way,* All's II, 1, 180. *to save a paltry life and s. bright fame,* H6A IV, 6, 45. *a man by his own alms empoisoned and with his charity slain,* Cor. V, 6, 12. *this, being tasted, —s all senses with the heart,* Rom. II, 3, 26.

**Slayer,** one that slays, a killer: *with plumed helm thy s. begins threats,* Lr. IV, 2, 57 (lection of Q1.3; Q2 *thy state begins thereat,* and hence some M. Edd. *thy state begins to threat.* Ff om.).

**Sleave** or **Sleave-silk,** soft floss silk used for

weaving: *sleep that knits up the ravelled sleave of care,* Mcb. II, 2, 37. *thou idle immaterial skein of sleave-silk,* Troil. V, 1, 35 (Ff *sleyd silk*).

**Sledded,** probably = having a sled or sledge, i. e. a heavy hammer, to it, or similar to a heavy hammer: *such was the very armour he had on when he the ambitious Norway combated; so frowned he once, when in an angry parle he smote the s. pollax* (or *pole-axe*) *on the ice,* Hml. I, 1, 63 (Qq *sleaded.* Hamlet, provoked to anger in a conference with the king of Norway, struck the ice with his pole-axe as with a mighty hammer.* Almost all M. Edd. *the sledded Polacks,* i. e. Polanders conveyed on sledges, whom Hamlet is supposed to have fought and defeated on a field of ice. But the whole scene is evidently taken from a war against Norway, where ice-fields may be expected; besides, *he smote the Polacks* cannot well be = he beat or defeated the Polacks, but only = he struck them).

**Sleek,** adj. smooth and glossy: *thy s. smooth head,* Mids. IV, 1, 3. In a moral sense: *how s. and wanton ye appear in every thing may bring my ruin,* H8 III, 2, 241.

**Sleek,** vb. to make smooth: *s. o'er your rugged looks,* Mcb. III, 2, 27.

**Sleek-headed,** having the hair well combed: *let me have ... s. men,* Caes. I, 2, 193.

**Sleekly,** smoothly, nicely: *let their heads be s. combed,* Shr. IV, 1, 93.

**Sleep,** subst. slumber, rest taken by a suspension of the voluntary exercise of the bodily and mental powers: Lucr. 163. Sonn. 87, 14. Tp. I, 2, 185. II, 1, 202. 212. 267. III, 2, 148. IV, 158. Gent. II, 4, 134. Meas. III, 1, 17. 33. IV, 2, 69. Mids. II, 2, 64. III, 2, 364 etc. etc. *dead of s.* Tp. V, 230. *in a most fast s.* Mcb. V, 1, 9. *a sound s.* H4B IV, 5, 35. With the poss. pron.: Gent. III, 1, 333. Mids. III, 2, 47. All's IV, 3, 286. H4A II, 3, 44. 60. H4B IV, 5, 62. H6B II, 1, 90. R3 I, 2, 122. V, 3, 130. Cor. IV, 4, 19. IV, 5, 130 etc. Plur.: *his —s were hindered,* Err. V, 71. *have broke their —s with thoughts,* H4B IV, 5, 69 (Ff s.). *break not your —s for that,* Hml. IV, 7, 30. *that in their —s will mutter their affairs,* Oth. III, 3, 417. Used of death: Tit. I, 155. II, 4, 15. Hml. III, 1, 66 etc.

**Sleep,** vb. (impf. and partic. *slept*) to take rest by a suspension of the voluntary exercise of the bodily and mental powers: Ven. 786. Sonn. 154, 8. Tp. I, 2, 305. 412. II, 1, 190. 238. 263. III, 2, 96. 149. Gent. I, 1, 80. II, 4, 141. III, 1, 334. Wiv. III, 5, 142. V, 5, 54. Meas. IV, 3, 35. Err. I, 2, 14. II, 2, 185. 215. V, 63. Mids. IV, 1, 152 (*half s., half waking;* the suffix *ing* belonging to both words). etc. etc. *to s. fast,* Lucr. 360. *to s. sound,* 363. Wiv. V, 5, 56. Meas. IV, 3, 50. Mids. II, 2, 74. III, 2, 449. H4B IV, 5, 26. Caes. II, 1, 233 etc. *to s. soundly:* Shr. Ind. 1, 33. H5 IV, 1, 285. *—ing hour,* Mids. III, 2, 8. As III, 2, 102. Troil. I, 3, 254. *a —ing potion,* Rom. V, 3, 244. *to s. on sth.* = a) to pass in sleep: *ne'er may I look on day nor s. on night,* Err. V, 210. b) to neglect, to be inattentive to: *heaven will one day open the king's eyes, that so long have slept upon this bold bad man,* H8 II, 2, 43. *why do fond men expose themselves to battle and not endure all threats? s. upon 't and let the foes quietly cut their throats?* Tim. III, 5, 43. With an accus. denoting the effect: *we did s. day out of counte-*

nance, Ant. II, 2, 181. *to s. out* = to pass and forget in sleep: All's V, 3, 66. Wint. III, 3, 61. IV, 3, 31. Lr. II, 2, 163. Ant. I, 5, 5. With an accus. of time: *never slept a quiet hour,* R3 V, 3, 160. H8 Epil. 3. *s. thou a quiet sleep,* R3 V, 3, 164 (cf. Cymb. V, 4, 178). *I have not slept one wink,* Cymb. III, 4, 103.

Used of death: Ven. 951. Ado V, 1, 70. H4A V, 4, 100. H4B IV, 4, 61. R3 IV, 3, 38. H8 III, 2, 398. 434. V, 1, 32. V, 5, 40. Rom. V, 1, 18. Mcb. III, 2, 23. Ant. V, 2, 7 etc.

Denoting any state of entire repose and quiet, or of idleness and inefficacy: *therefore have I slept in your report,* Sonn. 83, 5. *let'st thy fortune s.* Tp. II, 1, 216. *hath he any eyes? hath he any thinking? sure, they s.* Wiv. III, 2, 31. *the law hath not been dead, though it hath slept,* Meas. II, 2, 90. *why should a man s. when he wakes,* Merch. I, 1, 85. *how sweet the moonlight —s upon this bank,* V, 54 (lies still and silent). *all proofs —ing else but what your jealousies awake,* Wint. III, 2, 113. *those —ing stones,* John II, 216. *where hath it* (our intelligence) *slept,* IV, 2, 117. *awaked the — ing rheum,* R2 I, 4, 8. *peace shall go s. with Turks and infidels,* IV, 139. *a kind of —ing in the blood,* H4B I, 2, 128. *awake our — ing sword of war,* H5 I, 2, 22. *we die, while remiss traitors s.* H6A IV, 3, 29. *— ing neglection,* 49. *our title still had slept,* H6C II, 2, 160. *where slept our scouts?* V, 1, 19. *when didst thou* (God) *s. when such a deed was done?* R3 IV, 4, 24. *you have ever wished the —ing of this business,* H8 II, 4, 163. *our office may during his power go s.* Cor. II, 1, 239. *hath it* (hope) *slept since?* Mcb. I, 7, 36. *do not s., but let me hear from you,* Hml. I, 3, 3. *a knavish speech —s in a foolish ear,* IV, 2, 25. *have a father killed, a mother stained, excitements of my reason and my blood, and let all s.* IV, 4, 59. *nor the redresses s.* Lr. I, 4, 229. *truth can never be confirmed enough, though doubts did ever s.* Per. V, 1, 204.

**Sleeper,** one who sleeps: Tp. V, 49 *(graves at my command have waked their —s).* Mids. IV, 1, 91. R3 III, 4, 24. Mcb. II, 3, 88. Ant. IV, 9, 31.

**Sleepy,** 1) drowsy, inclined to sleep: *I am s.* Meas. IV, 3, 31. *this is a s. tune,* Caes. IV, 3, 267.

2) sleeping, not awake: *it is a s. language,* Tp. II, 1, 211 (= you speak as if in sleep). *when we have marked with blood those s. two,* Mcb. I, 7, 75. II, 2, 50.

3) causing sleep, soporiferous: *we will give you s. drinks,* Wint. I, 1, 15.

4) lazy, indolent, inactive: *ere twice in murk and occidental damp moist Hesperus hath quenched his s. lamp,* All's II, 1, 167 (inefficacious, not awakening to life and activity, but only attending on sleep). *in the mildness of your s. thoughts, which here we waken to our country's good,* R3 III, 7, 123. *peace is ... mulled, deaf, s., insensible,* Cor. IV, 5, 239. *'tis not s. business,* Cymb. III, 5, 26.

**Sleeve,** that part of a garment that covers the arm: Err. II, 2, 175. III, 2, 23. Ado III, 4, 20 *( down —s, side —s).* LLL V, 2, 321 *(this gallant pins the wenches on his s.)* 455. Mids. III, 2, 30. As III, 2, 398. Shr. IV, 3, 88. 142 *(a trunk s.).* 143. 147. All's II, 3, 266. H4A IV, 2, 49. H5 IV, 3, 47. Caes. I, 2, 179. Oth. I, 1, 64. Worn as a favour: Troil. IV, 4, 72. V, 2, 66. 69. 169. V, 3, 96. V, 4, 4. 8. 19. 26. *the tune of Green —s* (a lascivious song) Wiv. II, 1, 64. V, 5, 22.

**Sleeve-hand,** the cuff attached to a sleeve: Wint. IV, 4, 211.

**Sleeveless,** unprofitable, bootless: *of a s. errand,* Troil. V, 4, 9.

**Sleid** or **Sleided silk,** raw, untwisted silk: *letters ... with sleided silk enswathed,* Compl. 48. *skein of sleid silk,* Troil. V, 1, 35 (Q *sleave silk*). *she weaved the sleided silk,* Per. IV Prol. 21.

**Sleight,** trick, artifice, stratagem: *as Ulysses and' stout Diomede with s. and manhood stole to Rhesus' tents,* H6C IV, 2, 20. *distilled by magic —s,* Mcb. III, 5, 26 (O. Edd. *slights*).

**Slender,** 1) thin, slim, not thick or gross: LLL IV, 1, 49. As III, 2, 112. Shr. II, 256. H4B I, 2, 162 *(—er).* Tit. III, 2, 61.

2) small, inconsiderable, insufficient: *of s. reputation,* Gent. I, 3, 6. *s. wit,* LLL IV, 1, 49. *at so s. warning,* Shr. IV, 4, 60. *a thin and s. pittance,* 61. *means,* H4B I, 2, 159. *some s. ort of his remainder,* Tim. IV, 3, 400. *on s. accident,* Hml. III, 2, 209.

**Slender,** name in Wiv. I, 1, 7 etc.

**Slenderly,** indifferently, insufficiently: *he hath ever but s. known himself,* Lr. I, 1, 297.

**Slice,** a thin piece cut off: *s., I say, pauca, pauca: s.!* Wiv. I, 1, 134 (a term applied to Mr. Slender by Nym).

**'Slid,** a mean oath, used by such persons as Mr. Slender and Sir Andrew, corrupted from *God's lid:* Wiv. III, 4, 24. Tw. III, 4, 427. cf. Troil. I, 2, 228.

**Slide,** 1) to move without stepping, to slip, to glide: *thou mayst s. from my shoulder to my heel,* Shr. IV, 1, 15. *the fool —s o'er the ice,* Troil. III, 3, 215.

2) to pass swiftly or inadvertently: *these present absent* (thought and desire) *with swift motion s.* Sonn. 45, 4. *so —s he down upon his grained bat,* Compl. 64. *let the world s.* Shr. Ind. 1, 6 (Sly's speech. cf. *daff'd the world aside and bid it pass,* H4A IV, 1, 96; and Shr. Ind. 2, 146: *let the world slip).* *I s. o'er sixteen years,* Wint. IV, 1, 5. *let the famished flesh s. from the bone,* Tim. IV, 3, 535.

3) to slip, to fall, to offend: *the —ing of your brother,* Meas. II, 4, 115.

**Slight,** adj. 1) trifling, inconsiderable: *leave her on such s. conditions,* Gent. V, 4, 138. *fee'd every s. occasion that could but niggardly give me sight of her,* Wiv. II, 2, 204. *I will go on the —est errand now to the Antipodes,* Ado II, 1, 272. *in some s. measure,* Mids. III, 2, 86. As I, 1, 155. II, 4, 34. All's IV, 1, 41. H4A III, 2, 151. H4B II, 1, 156. IV, 1, 190. V, 1, 92 *(a lie with a s. oath).* H6A IV, 1, 112. H6C I, 2, 6. Cor. V, 3, 62. Tim. II, 2, 149. Hml. II, 1, 39. Cymb. I, 4, 45. 51. *s. regard =*'contempt, H5 II, 4, 117. *so s. a valuation,* Cymb. IV, 4, 49.

2) insignificant, worthless, frivolous: *if my s. Muse do please these curious days,* Sonn. 38, 13. *some please-man, some s. zany,* LLL V, 2, 463. *a name so s., unworthy and ridiculous,* John III, 1, 150. *I muse you make so s. a question,* H4B IV, 1, 167. *ye 're so s.* Cor. V, 2, 110. *a s. unmeritable man,* Caes. IV, 1, 12. *away, s. man,* IV, 3, 37. *so s., so drunken, and so indiscreet an officer,* Oth. II, 3, 279 (Qq *light*). *is Caesar with Antonius prized so s.?* Ant. I, 1, 56. *s. thing of Italy,* Cymb. V, 4, 64.

3) taking any thing light, careless, negligent: *be not ceased with s. denial,* Tim. II, 1, 17. *we have been too s. in sufferance,* Cymb III, 5, 35.

4) being made out of nothing, insubstantial, light: *s. air and purging fire,* Sonn. 45, 1.

**Slight**, vb. to treat as insignificant, to put off with contempt: *puts him off*, —*s him*, Wint. IV, 4, 200. *your most dreadful laws so loosely* —*ed*, H4B V, 2, 94. *my letters were* —*ed off*, Caes. IV, 3, 5. *the rogues* —*ed me into the river with as little remorse as they would have drowned a blind bitch's puppies*, Wiv. III, 5, 9 (= threw me heedlessly).

**'Slight**, Sir Andrew's oath, corrupted from *God's light* (cf. *'Sblood, 'Slid* etc.): Tw. II, 5, 38. III, 2, 14.

**Slightly**, 1) inconsiderably: *if I gall him s.* Hml. IV, 7, 148. *some s. touched*, Cymb. V, 3, 10.

2) carelessly, negligently: *the guards are but s. basted on neither*, Ado I, 1, 289. *to part so s. with your wife's first gift*, Merch. V, 167. *untouched or s. handled*, R3 III, 7, 19. *you have gone s. o'er low steps*, H8 II, 4, 112 (as if you were born for the highest place). *a host that s. shakes his parting guest by the hand*, Troil. III, 3, 166. *my arrows, too s. timbered*, Hml. IV, 7, 22 (cf. the adj. *slight* in Sonn. 45, 1.). *so s. valued in his messenger*, Lr. II, 2, 153.

**Slightness**, trifling, frivolousness: *it must omit real necessities, and give way the while to unstable s.* Cor. III, 1, 148.

**Slily**, see *Slyly.*

**Slime**, viscous mire; any glutinous substance: Tit. III, 1, 126. Ant. I, 3, 69. II, 7, 25. V, 2, 355. *hates the s. that sticks on filthy deeds*, Oth. V, 2, 148.

**Slimy**, overspread with slime: *the s. bottom of the deep*, R3 I, 4, 32. *their* (fishes') *s. jaws*, Ant. II, 5, 13.

**Sling**, a missive weapon with which stones are thrown: H5 IV, 7, 65. Hml. III, 1, 58.

**Slink** (impf. *slunk*) to move stealthily, to creep: *we will s. away in supper-time*, Merch. II, 4, 1. *s. by and note him*, As III, 2, 267. *or slunk not Saturnine, as Tarquin erst, that left the camp to sin in Lucrece' bed?* Tit. IV, 1, 63. *his familiars to his buried fortunes s. all away*, Tim. IV, 2, 11.

**Slip**, subst. 1) escape, desertion: *what counterfeit did I give you? The s.* Rom. II, 4, 51 (quibbling; see sub 4).

2) a false step, fault, offence: *for fear of* —*s*, Ven. 515 (quibbling; see sub 4). *without any* —*s of prolixity*, Merch. III, 1, 12. *these* —*s have made him noted long*, Tit. II, 3, 86. *wanton, wild and usual* —*s*, Hml. II, 1, 22. *'tis a venial s.* Oth. IV, 1, 9.

3) a noose in which greyhounds were held, before they were suffered to start for the game: *you stand like greyhounds in the* —*s*, H5 III, 1, 31.

4) a piece of false money: *for fear of* —*s set thy seal manual on my wax-red lips*, Ven. 515. Rom. II, 4, 51 (cf. sub 1).

5) a twig separated from the main stock, a scion: Meas. III, 1, 142. All's I, 3, 152. Wint. IV, 4, 85. 100. H6B II, 2, 58. III, 2, 214. Tit. V, 1, 9. Mcb. IV, 1, 27.

**Slip**, vb. 1) intr. a) to glide, to pass imperceptibly: *let the world s.* Shr. Ind. 2, 146 (cf. *let the world slide*, 1, 6; and H4A IV, 3, 96). Especially = to pass unnoticed: *let not advantage s.* Ven. 129. *laws ... which for these nineteen years we have let s.* Meas. I, 3, 21. *let him let the matter s.* Tw. III, 4, 314. With *away: you might s. away ere he came*, Wiv. IV, 2, 54. *to s. away with Slender*, IV, 6, 23. *the snake did s. away into a bush*, As IV, 3, 113. With *from* or *out of: then s. I from her bum*, Mids. II, 1, 53. *if I could have remembered*

a gilt counterfeit, thou wouldst not have —*ed out of my contemplation*, Troil. II, 3, 28. *a thing* —*ed idly from me*, Tim. I, 1, 22. *that from it* (the mind) *all consideration* —*s*, IV, 3, 196.

b) to start for the game; a coursing term used of greyhounds, but only in the phrase *to let s.: before the game is afoot, thou still let'st s.* H4A I, 3, 278. *holding Corioli in the name of Rome, even like a fawning greyhound in the leash, to let him s. at will*, Cor. I, 6, 39. *let s. the dogs of war*, Caes. III, 1, 273. (*"We let s. a greyhound, and we cast off a hound".* Art of Venerie).

c) to commit an offence: *you would have* —*ed like him*, Meas. II, 2, 65. *one so wise should s. so grossly*, V, 477. *that you* —*ed noth with any but with us*, Wint. I, 2, 85.

2) trans. a) to let pass unnoticed, not to be observant of, to neglect: *we had* —*ed our claim until another age*, H6C II, 2, 162. *I have almost* —*ed the hour*, Mcb. II, 3, 52. *the bonds of heaven are* —*ed, dissolved and loosed*, Troil. V, 2, 156.

b) to make or let loose: *from which* (yoke) *even here I s. my weary neck*, R3 IV, 4, 112. *we'll s. you for a season*, Cymb. IV, 3, 22. Used of greyhounds allowed to start for the game: *Lucentio* —*ed me like his greyhound*, Shr. V, 2, 52.

**Slipper**, subst. a light shoe worn in undress: Tp. II, 1, 277. LLL V, 2, 672. Shr. IV, 1, 156. John IV, 2, 197.

**Slipper**, adj. slippery: *a s. and subtle knave*, Oth. II, 1, 246 (the later Ff *slippery and subtle*, Qq *subtle slippery*).

**Slippered**, wearing slippers: *the lean and s. pantaloon*, As II, 7, 158.

**Slippery**, 1) smooth, glib: *as s. as the Gordian knot was hard*, Cymb. II, 2, 34. Metaphorically: *all minds, as well of glib and s. creatures as of grave and austere quality*, Tim. I, 1, 53. *a s. and subtle knave*, Oth. II, 1, 246 (F1 *slipper*).

2) not affording firm footing: *he that stands upon a s. place*, John III, 4, 137. *hanging them* (the billows) *in the s. clouds*, H4B III, 1, 24. *my credit now stands on such s. ground*, Caes. III, 1, 191. *whose top is so s.* Cymb. III, 3, 48.

3) not standing firm: *s. standers*, Troil. III, 3, 84. Hence = inconstant, unstable, fickle: *the love that leaned on them as s. too*, Troil. III, 3, 85. *O world, thy s. turns!* Cor. IV, 4, 12. *our s. people*, Ant. I, 2, 192. Even = unchaste, wanton: *my wife is s.* Wint. I, 2, 273.

**Slipshod**, wearing slippers: Lr. I, 5, 12.

**Slish and slash**, much cutting: *here's snip and nip and cut and s.* Shr. IV, 3, 90.

**Slit**, to cut lengthwise: *I'll s. the villain's nose*, Shr. V, 1, 134.

**Sliver**, subst. a small branch (broken off): *an envious s. broke*, Hml. IV, 7, 174.

**Sliver**, vb. to break or tear off (a branch): *slips of yew* —*ed in the moon's eclipse*, Mcb. IV, 1, 28. *she that herself will s. and disbranch from her material sap*, Lr. IV, 2, 34.

**Slobbery**, wet and foul: *to buy a s. and a dirty farm in that nook-shotten isle of Albion*, H5 III, 5, 13.

**Slop**, large loose trowsers: *a German from the waist downward, all* —*s*, Ado III, 2, 36. *my short cloak and my* —*s*, H4B I, 2, 34. *a French salutation* *to your French s.* Rom. II, 4, 47. In LLL IV, 3, 59 O. Edd. *shop,* some M. Edd. *slop.*

**Slope,** to bend down: *though palaces and pyramids do s. their heads to their foundations,* Mcb. IV, 1, 57.

**Sloth,** slowness, sluggishness, laziness: Tp. II, 1, 223. 228. H6A I, 1, 79. H8 II, 4, 237. Lr. III, 4, 96. Cymb. III, 6, 34.

**Slothful,** lazy: H6A III, 2, 7.

**Slough,** 1) a place of deep mud or mire: *in a s. of mire,* Wiv. IV, 5, 69.

2) the skin of a snake: *cast thy humble s.* Tw. II, 5, 161. III, 4, 76. *with casted s.* H5 IV, 1, 23. *with shining checkered s.* H6B III, 1, 229.

**Slovenly,** wanting neatness: *to bring a s. unhandsome corse betwixt the wind and his nobility,* H4A I, 3, 44.

**Slovenry,** want of neatness: *time hath worn us into s.* H5 IV, 3, 114.

**Slow,** not swift, not quick: Lucr. 696. 1081. 1220 *(with soft s. tongue).* 1336. 1738. Sonn. 44, 13. 51, 1 *(the s. offence = the offence of slowness).* Tp. II, 1, 249. Gent. I, 1, 133. II, 1, 13. III, 1, 336. 338. Meas. V, 400. LLL III, 60. 62. 63. Mids. IV, 1, 128. Shr. II, 248. IV, 1, 34. All's I, 1, 234. Tw. III, 4, 81. R2 V, 2, 10. H4A III, 1, 268. H6B IV, 1, 5. V, 2, 72. H6C IV, 8, 40. R3 I, 2, 116. II, 4, 15. H8 I, 1, 132. Troil. I, 2, 21. Rom. II, 5, 17. II, 6, 15. IV, 1, 3. Mcb. I, 4, 17. III, 1, 96. Hml. I, 2, 58. Oth. IV, 2, 55. Ant. V, 2, 324. Cymb. I, 1, 64. I, 5, 10. III, 4, 100. Per. IV, 2, 68. *s. of =* s. concerning sth.: *s. of tongue,* Gent. III, 1, 357 *(= slowly speaking). s. of sail,* Err. I, 1, 117. Hml. IV, 6, 17. *s. of study,* Mids. I, 2, 69. With *to: to temptation s.* Sonn. 94, 4 *(= slowly tempted).*

= dull, heavy: *it makes me have a s. heart,* Gent. IV, 2, 65. *other s. arts entirely keep the brain,* LLL IV, 3, 324.

Adverbially: *how s. time goes,* Lucr. 990. *how s. it creeps,* 1575. *how s. this old moon wanes,* Mids. I, 1, 3. *creep time ne'er so s.* John III, 3, 31. *thou strikest as s. as another,* Troil. II, 1, 33. *wisely and s.* Rom. II, 3, 94. *goes s. and stately by them,* Hml. I, 2, 202. *till the speed of his rage goes —er,* Lr. I, 2, 183. *how s. his soul sailed on,* Cymb. I, 3, 13. *could never go so s.* III, 2, 73.

**Slowed,** retarded: *I would I knew not why it should be s.* Rom. IV, 1, 16.

**Slow-gaited,** going slowly: LLL III, 56.

**Slowly,** not quickly, tardily: Tp. II, 2, 16. As IV, 1, 55. All's V, 3, 58. Wint. V, 1, 211. John IV, 2, 269.

**Slowness,** want of speed or of readiness: *the complaints I have heard of you I do not all believe: 'tis my s. that I do not,* All's I, 3, 10. *this fool's speed be crossed with s.* Cymb. III, 5, 168.

**Slow-winged,** flying slowly: Shr. II, 208.

**Slubber,** 1) to sully, to soil: *you must be content to s. the gloss of your new fortunes with this more stubborn and boisterous expedition,* Oth. I, 3, 227. cf. *Beslubber.*

2) to do carelessly and negligently, to slur over: *s. not business for my sake,* Merch. II, 8, 39.

**Slug,** a kind of snail; used as the symbol of slowness and laziness: *thou drone, thou snail, thou s.* Err. II, 2, 196. *what a s. is Hastings,* R3 III, 1, 22. *fie, you s. a-bed,* Rom. IV, 5, 2.

**Sluggard,** subst. a lazy fellow: R3 V, 3, 225.

**Sluggard,** adj. lazy: Lucr. 1278. R2 III, 2, 84 (Qq *coward*).

**Sluggardized,** made lazy and dronish: Gent. I, 1, 7.

**Sluggish,** slow, inert, indolent: Cymb. IV, 2, 205.

**Sluice,** subst. a floodgate, a vent for water: Ven. 956. Lucr. 1076.

**Sluice,** vb. to emit, to make to flow as by a floodgate: *she has been —d in his absence and his pond fished,* Wint. I, 2, 194. *—d out his innocent soul through streams of blood,* R2 I, 1, 103.

**Slumber,** subst. sleep: Lucr. 124 ( cf. R3 V, 3, 105). Sonn. 61, 3. Tp. II, 1, 304. As IV, 3, 133. Wint. III, 3, 39. H4A II, 3, 50. H4B III, 1, 11. IV, 5, 24. H5 III, 2, 123. H6B III, 2, 262. 390. R3 III, 2, 27. V, 3, 105 (cf. Lucr. 124). H8 I, 1, 122. Troil. II, 2, 37. Tit. II, 3, 26. III, 1, 253. Caes. II, 1, 230. IV, 3, 267. Oth. III, 3, 258. Cymb. V, 2, 210. Per. III, 2, 23 *(the golden s. of repose).* V, 1, 235.

**Slumber,** vb. to sleep: Mids. V, 432. Tit. II, 4, 15. III, 1, 255. Metaphorically, = to be inactive: *you must not now s. in it,* All's III, 6, 78. *if heaven s. while their creatures want,* Per. I, 4, 16.

**Slumbry,** sleeping, taking place in sleep: *in this s. agitation,* Mcb. V, 1, 12.

**Slut,** a slovenly and ungracious woman: Wiv. V, 5, 50. As III, 3, 36. 38. Tim. IV, 3, 134.

**Sluttery,** the qualities and practice of a slut: Wiv. V, 5, 50. Cymb. I, 6, 44.

**Sluttish,** unclean, nasty: Ven. 983. Sonn. 55, 4. All's V, 2, 7. Rom. I, 4, 90. In a moral sense: *s. spoils of opportunity,* Troil. IV, 5, 62 (cf. Tim. IV, 3, 134).

**Sluttishness,** the qualities and practice of a slut: As III, 3, 41.

**Sly,** name in Shr. Ind. 1, 3 etc.*

**Sly,** adj. 1) artful, cunning, insidious: Lucr. 1399. Gent. II, 6, 41. John II, 567. H6C III, 3, 160. R3 I, 3, 53. IV, 4, 171 (Ff *s. and bloody,* Qq *bloody, treacherous*). H8 I, 3, 39. Tit. IV, 4, 59 ( cf. *crafty*). Cymb. I, 5, 75.

2) secret, imperceptible: *the s. slow hours shall not determine the dateless limit of thy dear exile,* R2 I, 3, 150 (F2 and some M. Edd. *fly-slow*).

**Slyly** or **Slily,** 1) cunningly: *deceive more s. than Ulysses did,* H6C III, 2, 189.

2) secretly, imperceptibly, underhand: *a serpent that s. glided towards your majesty,* H6B III, 2, 260. *he s. stole away,* H6C I, 1, 3. *the king was s. fingered from the deck,* V, 1, 44. *here in these confines s. have I lurked,* R3 IV, 4, 3. *as if that god ... were s. crept into his human powers,* Cor. II, 1, 236.

**Smack,** subst. a loud kiss: Shr. III, 2, 180.

**Smack,** subst. 1) taste, savor, tincture: *thou hast to pull at a s. o'the contrary,* All's II, 3, 237 (with a pun? meaning also a small vessel, a sloop?). *some s. of age,* H4B I, 2, 111.

2) smattering: *he hath a s. of all neighbouring languages,* All's IV, 1, 18.

**Smack,** vb. to have a taste or tincture: *my father did something s., he had a kind of taste,* Merch. II, 2, 18. *whether I s. or no,* John I, 209. With *of: all sects, all ages s. of this vice,* Meas. II, 2, 5. *nothing she does or seems but —s of something greater than herself,* Wint. IV, 4, 158. John I, 208. II, 396. Mcb. I, 2, 44. IV, 3, 59.

**Small,** adj. 1) thin, fine: *as s. as a wand,* Gent. ll, 3, 23. *the —est twine may lead me,* Ado IV, 1, 252. *a —er hair than may be seen,* LLL V, 2, 258. *the —est thread that ever spider twisted,* John IV, 3, 127. *the —est spider's web,* Rom. I, 4, 61. *with fingers long, s., white as milk,* Per. IV Prol. 22. *s. showers* = soft and gentle showers: R2 II, 1, 35. *grind their bones to powder s.* Tit. V, 2, 199 (= fine). Peculiar expression: *these things seem s. and undistinguishable, like far-off mountains turned into clouds,* Mids. IV, 1, 192 (not gross and palpable, but thin and fading into indistinctness).

2) fine, of a clear and high sound: *thy s. pipe is as the maiden's organ,* Tw. I, 4, 32. *a pipe s. as an eunuch,* Cor. III, 2, 114.

Adverbially: *speaks s. like a woman,* Wiv. I, 1, 49. *you may speak as s. as you will,* Mids. I, 2, 52.

3) of minute dimensions, not large: *s. head,* Ven. 296. *s. lights,* Lucr. 647. *in the s. orb of one particular tear,* Compl. 289. *too s. a pasture,* Gent. I, 1, 105. Err. I, 1, 80. Mids. II, 2, 5. V, 223. Merch. V, 60. Shr. II, 101. IV, 3, 140. John IV, 1, 95. R2 II, 1, 102. III, 2, 153. H4A V, 4, 90. H6A II, 3, 52. IV, 6, 33. H6B III, 1, 18. IV, 10, 20. H6C II, 2, 17. IV, 8, 54. R3 II, 4, 13. Troil. I, 3, 343. Cor. I, 1, 142. Tit. V, 3, 167. Rom. I, 4, 64. Hml. III, 3, 21. Lr. III, 4, 117. 144. IV, 6, 20. 114. Cymb. IV, 2, 304.

4) short (in a temporal sense): *after some s. space,* As IV, 3, 152. *a night is but s. breath and little pause,* H5 II, 4, 145. *s. time,* Epil. 5. *within so s. a time,* R3 IV, 1, 79 (Qq *in so short a space*).

5) little, inconsiderable, not great: *of s. worth held,* Sonn. 2, 4. *some s. glory,* 84, 6. *s. show of man,* Compl. 92. *the —est teen,* 192. *shows his love but s.* Gent. I, 2, 29. *so s. a fault,* IV, 1, 31. *a —er boon,* V, 4, 24. *the —est scruple of her excellence,* Meas. I, 1, 38. *the —est article,* IV, 2, 107. *s. cheer and great welcome,* Err. III, 1, 26. *that violates the —est branch,* LLL I, 1, 21. *had s. reason for it,* I, 2, 92. *his s. light of discretion,* Mids. V, 257. *a s. trifle of wives,* Merch. II, 2, 169. *the s. acquaintance,* As V, 2, 7. *there's s. choice in rotten apples,* Shr. I, 1, 138. *s. experience,* I, 2, 52. *none so s. advantage,* John III, 4, 151. *of s. consequence,* R2 V, 2, 61. *the —est parcel of this vow,* H4A III, 2, 159. *our s. conjunction,* IV, 1, 37. *a power much —er than the —est of his thoughts,* H4B I, 3, 30. *s. offences,* H6B III, 1, 59. *s. things make base men proud,* IV, 1, 106. *thy share thereof* (beauty) *is s.* H6C I, 4, 129. *of s. defence,* V, 1, 64. *s. joy,* R3 I, 3, 110. *our s. strength,* V, 3, 26. *your enemies are many and not s.* H8 V, 1, 129. *of s. wit,* V, 4, 49. *s. thanks,* Troil. I, 1, 72. *things s. as nothing,* II, 3, 179. *a s. patience,* Cor. I, 1, 129. *a s. thing would make it flame,* IV, 3, 21. *the tears have got s. victory by that,* Rom. IV, 1, 30. *s. love,* Tim. I, 1, 258. *some s. kindnesses,* III, 2, 22. *the —est particle of any promise,* Caes. II, 1, 139. *s. fault,* Lr. I, 4, 288. *s. respect,* II, 2, 137. *s. train,* II, 4, 64. *s. vices,* IV, 6, 168. Oth. IV, 3, 70. *s. hurt,* II, 3, 381. *the —est fear,* III, 3, 188. *the —est opinion,* IV, 2, 109. *s. to greater matter must give way,* Ant. II, 2, 11. *s. reflection of her wit,* Cymb. I, 2, 33. *a s. request,* I, 6, 181. *though the gift s.* Per. III, 4, 18.

Adverbially: *it s. avails my mood,* Lucr. 1273.

Substantively: *to cross this in the —est,* Meas. IV, 2, 179. *s. have continual plodders ever won,* LLL I, 1, 86 *that unlettered s. knowing soul,* 253 (Armado's

letter. M. Edd. *small-knowing*). *I play the torturer, by s. and s. to lengthen out the worst,* R2 III, 2, 198.

6) Used of beverages, = weak: *s. ale,* Shr. Ind. 2, 1. 77. *s. beer,* H4B II, 2, 8. 13. H6B IV, 2, 73. Oth. II, 1, 161.

**Small,** subst. the part of the leg below the calf: *he is best indued in the s.* LLL V, 2, 646.

**Smallness,** minute dimension: *the s. of a gnat,* Cymb. I, 3, 21.

**Smalus,** name in Wint. V, 1, 157.

**Smart,** subst. (used, with one exception, only in rhyming): keen pain: Lucr. 1238. H8 II, 1, 166. Troil. IV, 4, 20. Cymb. V, 4, 42.

**Smart,** adj. painful, pungent: *their softest touch as s. as lizards' stings,* H6B III, 2, 325. *how s. a lash that speech doth give my conscience,* Hml. III, 1, 50.

**Smart,** vb. to feel a pungent pain: *some of us will s. for it,* Ado V, 1, 109. *although he s.* As II, 7, 54. H4A I, 3, 49. H6A IV, 6, 42. Ant. II, 5, 66. = to cause pain: *I have some wounds upon me, and they s.* Cor. I, 9, 28.

**Smartly,** briskly, vigorously: *and loosed his love-shaft s. from his bow, as it should pierce a hundred thousand hearts,* Mids. II, 1, 159 (or is it = in a manner calculated to inflict the most painful wounds?).

**Smatch,** smack, taste, tincture: *thy life hath had some s. of honour in it,* Caes. V, 5, 46.

**Smatter,** to chatter, to prattle: *s. with your gossips,* Rom. III, 5, 172.

**Smear,** to daub, to soil, to stain: *s. with dust their glittering golden towers,* Lucr. 945. 1381. *—ed thus and mired with infamy,* Ado IV, 1, 135 (Q *smirched*). *triumphant death, —ed with captivity,* H6A IV, 7, 3. *my glory —ed in dust and blood,* H6C V, 2, 23. *this painting wherein you see me —ed,* Cor. I, 6, 69. *s. the sleepy grooms with blood,* Mcb. II, 2, 49. *—ed with heraldry more dismal,* Hml. II, 2, 477. cf. *Besmear.*

**Smell,** subst. 1) the sense of which the nose is the organ: Ven. 441. Sonn. 141, 7. Tim. I, 2, 132.

2) odor, the manner of affecting the olfactory organ: Ven. 165. 936. Sonn. 69, 12. 98, 5. Tp. II, 2, 27. Gent. IV, 4, 25. Wiv. I, 1, 297. III, 5, 94. As I, 2, 114 (*if I keep not my rank, — Thou losest thy old s.;* see Rank subst. 3). John IV, 3, 113. H5 IV, 3, 103. V, 1, 22. H6B I, 1, 255. Rom. IV, 3, 46 (—s). Mcb. V, 1, 56. = scent: Ven. 686. 691. Lucr. 695.

**Smell,** vb. (impf. and partic. *smelt*) 1) to perceive by the nose; absol.: Ven. 444. Ado III, 4, 64. Tim. IV, 3, 160 (—s *from the common weal;* cf. *From*). Hml. III, 4, 79. Oth. IV, 3, 95. With an object: Ven. 1171. Tp. IV, 178. Wiv. V, 5, 84. LLL III, 17. Merch. I, 3, 34. Shr. Ind. 2, 73. All's V, 3, 321. H4B I, 2, 175. Cor. V, 1, 31. Rom. II, 3, 25. Lr. II, 4, 72. III, 4, 189. IV, 6, 183. Oth. V, 2, 16. Cymb. V, 4, 115. *to s. out* = to find out by the nose: LLL IV, 2, 128. Wint. IV, 4, 687. Lr. I, 5, 23. *to s.* = to smell out: *let him s. his way to Dover,* Lr. III, 7, 93.

Metaphorically, = to perceive, to guess at, to find out by mental sagacity: *lest she some subtle practice s.* Pilgr. 307. *I s. some l'envoy,* LLL III, 122. *I s. false Latin,* V, 1, 83. *I s. some device,* Tw. II, 3, 176. Wint. II, 1, 151. IV, 4, 657. H4A I, 3, 277. Lr. I, 1, 16. Oth. III, 3, 232. V, 2, 191. With *out: can you s. him out by that?* Ado III, 2, 51. *—ing out a suit,* Rom. I, 4, 78. *there I smelt 'em out,* Lr. IV, 6, 105.

2) to affect the olfactory nerves, to have a particular odor; absol.: Sonn. 99, 2. Tp. II, 2, 26. Wiv. III, 3, 79. H5 IV, 1, 106. Caes. III, 1, 274. Hml. III, 3, 36. V, 1, 221. Cymb. II, 1, 18. *to s. strong,* All's V, 2, 5. *strongly,* 8. *sweet,* H4A I, 3, 54. Rom. II, 2, 44. Oth. IV, 2, 68. *sweetly,* Wiv. II, 2, 67. Per. III, 2, 60. *tender —ing,* LLL V, 2, 569. *to s. well,* Cor. IV, 5, 5. *worse,* Sonn. 94, 14. *wooingly,* Mcb. I, 6, 6. With *of: it —s of mortality,* Lr. IV, 6, 136. *knaves that s. of sweat,* Ant. I, 4, 21. Metaphorically, = to have a smack or tincture of: *s. of calumny,* Meas. II, 4, 159. *s. of her strong displeasure,* All's V, 2, 5. *thy counsel —s of no cowardice,* Tit. II, 1, 132.

Trans.: *I do s. all horse-piss,* Tp. IV, 199 (= I smell or stink of nothing but horse-piss). *all the chamber smelt him,* Gent. IV, 4, 22 (= smelt like him, was filled with his scent). *he —s April and May,* Wiv. III, 2, 69. *she smelt brown bread and garlick,* Meas. III, 2, 194. *your nose —s no in this,* LLL V, 2, 569.

**Smile,** subst. a kind of slight laugh without utterance of a sound; a look expressive of pleasure or kindness or slight scorn: Ven. 465. Merch. I, 1, 55. As III, 5, 104. Tw. II, 5, 73. H4B Ind. 10. H5 IV Chor. 33. H6B V, 1, 100. H8 III, 2, 368. Troil. I, 1, 38. Cor. I, 1, 111. Tim. V, 4, 45. Cymb. IV, 2, 53. Plur. —*s:* Gent. III, 1, 158. Mids. I, 1, 195. As III, 2, 433. All's V, 2, 26 (M.Edd. *similes*). Tw. II, 5, 190. Wint. I, 2, 116. II, 3, 102. R2 I, 4, 28. III, 2, 9. V, 2, 32. H4A I, 3, 246. H5 II, 1, 6. R3 III, 5, 9. H8 III, 2, 413. Troil. III, 3, 72 etc. Metaphorically, = favour: *methought I stood not in the s. of heaven,* H8 II, 4, 187. *our stars that frown lend us a s.* Per. I, 4, 108.

**Smile,** name in As II, 4, 49 and Wint. I, 2, 196.

**Smile,** vb. to laugh without uttering a sound, to have a look of joy or kindness or slight scorn; absol.: Ven. 106. Lucr. 1400. Compl. 172. 217. Pilgr. 187. Tp. I, 2, 153. Gent. I, 2, 63. V, 4, 163. Meas. II, 2, 187. V, 233. Ado V, 1, 15. LLL III, 78. V, 2, 864. Mids. II, 1, 44. Merch. 1, 2, 52. As II, 1, 9. Shr. Ind. 1, 99. Tw. II, 5, 190. 193. III, 1, 137. H6A IV, 3, 32. IV, 7, 27. H6C V, 2, 22. R3 IV, 4, 115. Troil. III, 3, 168. Caes. I, 2, 205. Cymb. IV, 2, 52 etc. Followed by *at,* to denote the occasion or cause of smiling; by *on,* to denote the person or object to which it is directed and addressed: *at this Adonis —s,* Ven. 241. 252. *whereat she —d with so sweet a cheer,* Lucr. 264. *nor shall he s. at thee,* 1065. Tp. IV, 1, 9. Meas. V, 163. Mids. II, 2, 150. Ado I, 3, 15. Shr. V, 2, 3. Tw. II, 4, 118. IV, 1, 61. Wint. IV, 4, 822. John V, 2, 134. H6A IV, 7, 4. H6B IV, 1, 76. H6C III, 3, 91. 168. R3 III, 4, 109. Troil. V, 10, 7. Caes. I, 2, 207. Mcb. V, 7, 12. Lr. IV, 2, 5. Cymb. II, 4, 22. *the flower that —s on every one,* LLL V, 2, 331. *he will s. upon her,* Tw. II, 5, 220. *—s upon his fingers' ends,* H5 II, 3, 15. H6A I, 4, 92. Tit. IV, 2, 120. Rom. II, 3, 1. Mcb. IV, 1, 123. Oth. II, 1, 170. *at for on: —d at one another and shook their heads,* Caes. I, 2, 286. *on for at: —st upon the stroke that murders me,* Rom. III, 3, 23. *to s. in a p.'s face* = to smile on a p.: *he —d me in the face,* H5 IV, 6, 21. *s. in men's faces,* R3 I, 3, 48. *while it was —ing in my face,* Mcb. I, 7, 56. *s. to't* = s. in telling it: *if it be summer news, s. to't before,* Cymb. III, 4, 13. With an accus. denoting an effect: *he does s. his face into more lines than is in the new map,* Tw. III, 2, 84. —*ing extremity out of act,*

Per. V, 1, 139. *some Dick that —s his cheek in years,* LLL V, 2, 465 (i. e., as it is usually explained, who smiles so much that his cheek seems to be in years, i. e. old).

Trans. in a doubtful passage: *s. you my speeches, as I were a fool?* Lr. II, 2, 88 (lection of F4; the rest of O. Edd. *smoile*).

Metaphorically, = 1) to look gay and joyous: *affliction may one day s. again,* LLL I, 1, 316. —*ing plenty and fair prosperous days,* R3 V, 5, 34. *so rich advantage of a promised glory as —s upon the forehead of this action,* Troil. II, 2, 205. 2) to be propitious or favourable: *it (my love) suffers not in —ing pomp,* Sonn. 124, 6 (the favour of greatness). *s., gentle heaven,* H6C II, 3, 6. *Fortune, s. once more,* Lr. II, 2, 180. *with on: good fortune and the favour of the king s. upon this contract,* All's II, 3, 185. *who knows on whom fortune would then have —d,* H4B IV, 1, 133. *upon us he (Mars) —s,* H6A I, 2, 4. R3 V, 5, 20. Rom. II, 6, 1. IV, 3, 4. Mcb. I, 2, 14. Hml. I, 3, 54.

**Smilet,** diminutive of *smile:* Lr. IV, 3, 21.

**Smilingly,** with a look of pleasure or slight scorn: Lucr. 1567. Cor. IV, 6, 103. Lr. V, 3, 199.

**Smirch,** to smear, to daub, to soil: Ado III, 3, 145. IV, 1, 135 (Ff *smeared*). As I, 3, 114. H5 III, 3, 17. cf. *Besmirch, Unsmirched.*

**Smite** (impf. *smote;* partic. *smit* in Tim. II, 1, 23; *smote* or, in the spelling of O.Edd., *smot,* in LLL IV, 3, 28 and Cor. III, 1, 319) 1) to strike, to reach with a stroke or throw: *they smote the air,* Tp. IV, 172. *I will s. his noddles,* Wiv. III, 1, 128 (Evans' speech). *when their fresh rays have smote the night of dew,* LLL IV, 3, 28. *our aediles smote,* Cor. III, 1, 319. *my reliances ... have smit my credit,* Tim. II, 1, 23. *and smote him thus,* Oth. V, 2, 356. *the next Caesarion s.* Ant. III, 13, 162. *a grief that —s my very heart at root,* V, 2, 104 (O. Edd. *suits*). With an accus. denoting an effect: *s. flat the thick rotundity o' the world,* Lr. III, 2, 7 (Ff *strike*). *it —s me beneath the fall I have,* Ant. V, 2, 171.

2) to strike, to drive, to make to come down: *his falchion on a flint he softly —th,* Lucr. 176. *he smote the sledded pole-axe on the ice,* Hml. I, 1, 63 (cf. *Sledded*).

**Smith,** one who forges with the hammer: Merch. I, 2, 48. John IV, 2, 193. H4B V, 1, 19.

**Smith,** name in H6B IV, 2, 30.

**Smithfield,** a market-place in London (cf. *Paul*): H4B I, 2, 56. 59. H6B II, 3, 7. IV, 5, 10. IV, 6, 14.

**Smock,** the under garment of a woman, a shift: Wiv. III, 5, 91. Ado II, 3, 137. LLL V, 2, 479. 916. Wint. IV, 4, 210. H6A I, 2, 119. Oth. V, 2, 273. Used for a woman: All's II, 1, 30. Rom. II, 4, 109. Ant. I, 2, 175.

**Smoke,** subst. 1) the sooty exhalation from burning things: Lucr. 312. 1042. As IV, 1, 165. Tw. V, 56. John II, 462. H6A I, 5, 23. Tit. I, 145. Rom. I, 1, 186. Cymb. V, 5, 477. Per. I, 1, 138. Proverbial expression: *thus must I from the s. into the smother,* As I, 2, 299.

2) any vapour: *O night, thou furnace of foul-reeking s.* Lucr. 799. *their (the clouds') rotten s.* Sonn. 34, 4. *for s. and dusky vapours of the night,* H6A II, 2, 27. *in the dunnest s. of hell,* Mcb. I, 5, 52.

3) Metaphorically, = phrases, idle words: *this*

*helpless s. of words doth me no right*, Lucr. 1027 (cf. 1042). *sweet s. of rhetoric*, LLL III, 64 (Armado's speech). *they shoot but calm words folded up in s.* John II, 229; cf. 462. *love is a s. made* (Q1 and M. Edd. *raised*) *with the fume of sighs*, Rom. I, 1, 196. *s. and luke-warm water is your perfection*, Tim. III, 6, 99. *let your close fire predominate his s.* IV, 3, 142; cf. 140.

**Smoke**, vb. 1) intr. a) to emit vapour, to steam: *her face doth reek and s.* Ven. 555. *his hand* ... —*ing with pride*, Lucr. 438. *this night, whose black contagious breath already* —*s about the burning crest of the old sun*, John V, 4, 34. *his* —*ing blood*, H6C II, 3, 21; *thy falchion* —*ing in his blood*, R3 I, 2, 94; Cor. I, 4, 11; Caes. III, 1, 158; Mcb. I, 2, 18; Lr. V, 3, 223.

b) to suffer, to be in a sad pickle: *some of you shall s. for it in Rome*, Tit. IV, 2, 111.

2) tr. a) to scent by smoke: *I was* —*ing a musty room*, Ado I, 3, 61. *s. the temple with our sacrifices*, Cymb. V, 5, 398.

b) to smell out, to find out: *he was first* —*d by the old lord Lafeu*, All's III, 6, 111. *they begin to s. me*, IV, 1, 30.

c) to curry: *I'll s. your skin-coat, an I catch you right*, John II, 139.

**Smoky**, emitting smoke; filled with smoke; tarnished with smoke: Lucr. 783. All's III, 2, 111. H4A III, 1, 161. IV, 1, 114. H4B III, 1, 9. Cymb. I, 6, 109.

**Smolkin**, see *Smulkin*.

**Smooth**, adj. 1) having an even surface; opposed to rough: *my s. moist hand*, Ven. 143. *thy sleek s. head*, Mids. IV, 1, 3. *why are our bodies soft and weak and s.* Shr. V, 2, 165. *Diana's lip is not more s.* Tw. I, 4, 32. *wears his boots very s.* H4B II, 4, 270. *my s. body*, Hml. I, 5, 73. *s. as alablaster*, Oth. V, 2, 5.

2) level: *the path is s. that leadeth on to danger*, Ven. 788. Used of waters, = gently flowing, not ruffled: *the sea being s.* Troil. I, 3, 34.

Adverbially: *the course of true love never did run s.* Mids. I, 1, 134. *s. runs the water where the brook is deep*, H6B III, 1, 53. Metaphorically: *with such a s., discreet and stable bearing*, Tw. IV, 3, 19. *how s. and even they do bear themselves*, H5 II, 2, 3. *to bear all s. and even*, Hml. IV, 3, 7.

3) bland, mild, gentle, insinuative: *hath ta'en from me the show of s. civility*, As II, 7, 96. *I have been politic with my friend, s. with mine enemy*, V, 4, 47. *my condition, which hath been s. as oil*, H4A I, 3, 7. *s. tongue*, II, 4, 79. *my condition not s.* H5 V, 2, 314. *s. Duke Humphrey*, H6B III, 1, 65. *in this s. discourse*, H6C III, 3, 88. *most smiling, s., detested parasites*, Tim. III, 6, 104. *he hath a person and a s. dispose to be suspected*, Oth. I, 3, 403.

Adverbially: *looks cheerfully and s. to-day*, R3 III, 4, 50. *so s. he daubed his vice with show of virtue*, III, 5, 29.

4) easy and elegant, free from anything displeasing or indecent: *thy verse swells with stuff so fine and s.* Tim. V, 1, 87.

5) perfectly agreeable and acceptable, not alloyed with any painful sensation or difficulty: *s. and welcome news*, H4A I, 1, 66. *they bring s. comforts false*, H4B Ind. 40. *s. success be strewed before your feet*, Ant. I, 3, 100.

**Smooth**, name in H4B II, 1, 31.

**Smooth**, vb. 1) to make smooth or even: *to s. the ice*, John IV, 2, 13. *every rub is* —*ed on our way*,

H5 II, 2, 188. *I would remove these stumbling-stocks and s. my way upon their headless necks*, H6B I, 2, 65 *his* —*ed brows*, H6A III, 1, 124; H6C II, 6, 32; R3 I, 1, 9.

2) to make bland and insinuative: *s. not thy tongue with filed talk*, Pilgr. 306.

3) to soften, to palliate, to colour: *to s. his fault I should have been more mild*, R2 I, 3, 240. *Warwick tells his title,* —*s the wrong*, H6C III, 1, 48. *to s. that rough touch with a tender kiss*, Rom. I, 5, 98. *what tongue shall s. thy name, when I have mangled it?* III, 2, 98. *s. every passion that in the natures of their lords rebel*, Lr. II, 2, 81.

4) to soften with blandishments, to flatter, to humour; absol.: *thy* —*ing titles* (turn) *to a ragged name*, Lucr. 892. *let not his* —*ing words bewitch your hearts*, H6B I, 1, 156. *sweet* —*ing words*, R3 I, 2, 169 (Qq *soothing*). *s., deceive and cog*, I, 3, 48. *I can s. and fill his ear with golden promises*, Tit. IV, 4, 96. *s. and speak him fair*, V, 2, 140. *the sinful father seemed not to strike, but s.* Per. I, 2, 78. With a superfluous *it: dangerous peer, that* —*est it so with king and commonweal*, H6B II, 1, 22. Trans.: *every grise of fortune is* —*ed by that below*, Tim. IV, 3, 17.

**Smooth-faced**, having a bland and winning look: LLL V, 2, 838. John II, 573. R3 V, 5, 33.

**Smoothly**, with easy elegance: *whose names yet run s. in the even road of a blank verse*, Ado V, 2, 33. *when it comes so s. off*, LLL IV, 1, 145.

**Smoothness**, freedom from roughness, gentleness: *their* (women's) *s., like a goodly champaign plain, lays open all the little worms that creep*, Lucr. 1247. *her s., her very silence and her patience speak to the people*, As I, 3, 79. *in the very whirlwind of passion you must acquire and beget a temperance that may give it s.* Hml. III, 2, 9.

**Smooth-pate**, one having a sleek head (and bland manners): H4B I, 2, 43.

**Smother**, vb. to suffocate, to stifle: Ven. 18. Lucr. 783. 1418. R3 I, 4, 40. III, 7, 164. IV, 3, 17. IV, 4, 70. 134. V, 3, 151. Cymb. III, 2, 60. With *up: and there* (the snail) *all* —*ed up, in shade doth sit*, Ven. 1035. *stalls, bulks, windows, are* —*ed up*, Cor. II, 1, 227 (filled to stifling). *to s. up his* (the sun's) *beauty from the world*, H4A I, 2, 223.

Metaphorically, = to suppress; to crush; to destroy: —*ing his passions for the present*, Lucr. Arg. 13. *their own transgressions partially they s.* Lucr. 634. *thou* —*est honesty, thou murderest truth*, 885. *heart in love with sighs himself doth s.* Sonn. 47, 4. *since that our faults in love thus* —*ed be*, Pilgr. 14. *my earthy-gross conceit,* —*ed in errors*, Err. III, 2, 35. *your private grudge will out, though ne'er so cunningly you s. it*, H6A IV, 1, 110. *in the breath of bitter words let's s. my damned son*, R3 IV, 4, 133. *function is* —*ed in surmise*, Mcb. I, 3, 141. *it is fit, what being more known grows worse, to s. it*, Per. I, 1, 106. With *up: these things, come thus to light, s. her spirits up*, Ado IV, 1, 113 (cf. Ven. 1035). *enow to s. up the English in our throngs*, H5 IV, 5, 20.

**Smother**, subst. thick and suffocating smoke: *thus must I from the smoke into the s.* As I, 2, 299.

**Smug**, neat, trim, spruce: *used to come so s. upon the mart*, Merch. III, 1, 49. *the s. and silver Trent*, H4A III, 1, 102. *I will die bravely, like a s. bridegroom*, Lr. IV, 6, 202 (Qq *like a bridegroom*).

**Smulkin** (Qq *snulbug*, most M. Edd. *Smolkin*) name of a fiend: Lr. III, 4, 146.*

**Smutch**, to stain, to smirch: *hast —ed thy nose*, Wint. I, 2, 121.

**Snaffle**, a bridle which crosses the nose: Ant. II, 2, 63.

**Snail**, animal of the genus Cochlea or Limax: Ven. 1033. Mids. II, 2, 23. LLL IV, 3, 338. Lr. I, 5, 29. Emblem of slowness: Err. II, 2, 196. As II, 7, 146. IV, 1, 52.

**Snail-paced**, slow: R3 IV, 3, 53. Troil. V, 5, 18.

**Snail-slow**, slow, lazy: Merch. II, 5, 47.

**Snake**, a serpent: LLL V, 1, 142. 146. Mids. II, 1, 255 (fem.). II, 2, 9. As IV, 3, 71. 109. R2 III, 2, 131. H4B V, 5, 39. H6B III, 1, 228. 343. Tit. II, 3, 13. 100. III, 1, 252. Mcb. III, 2, 13 (fem.). IV, 1, 12. Ant. II, 5, 40. 95.

**Snaky**, serpentine, winding: *crisped s. golden locks*, Merch. III, 2, 92.

**Snap**, a kind of interjection, expressive of quickness: *brief, short, quick, s.* Wiv. IV, 5, 3. *snip, s., quick and home*, LLL V, 1, 63.

**Snap**, vb. 1) tr. to bite suddenly: *to have had our two noses —ed off with two old men without teeth*, Ado V, 1, 116. 2) intr., with *at*, = to aim at with the teeth: *I may s. at him*, H4B III, 2, 357.

**Snapper-up**, one who snatches up: *a s. of unconsidered trifles*, Wint. IV, 3, 26.

**Snare**, subst. a gin, a noose: Lucr. 928. H6A IV, 2, 22. H6B III, 1, 262. 340. Tim. V, 2, 17 (cf. H6A IV, 2, 22 and Ant. IV, 8, 18). Mcb. V, 8, 67. Ant. IV, 8, 18.

Name of a sheriff's officer: H4B II, 1, 6. 7. 10. 27. 44.

**Snare**, vb. to ensnare, to entrap: Tp. II, 2, 174. H6B II, 2, 73. II, 4, 56. III, 1, 227.

**Snarl**, to growl, to gnarl as an angry dog: John IV, 3, 150. H6C V, 6, 77. R3 I, 3, 188.

**Snatch**, subst. 1) a hasty catch: *some certain s. or so would serve your turns*, Tit. II, 1, 95.

2) any thing broken or interrupted: *the —es in his voice, and burst of speaking, were as his*, Cymb. IV, 2, 105 (his abrupt manner of speaking). Hence = scrap, fragment: *leave me your —es*, Meas. IV, 2, 6 (your scraps of wit). *she chanted —es of old tunes*, Hml. IV, 7, 178.

**Snatch**, vb. 1) tr. to seize suddenly: *a sceptre —ed with an unruly hand*, John III, 4, 135. *a purse of gold most resolutely — ed*, H4A I, 2, 38. *an honour —ed with boisterous hand*, H4A IV, 5, 192. *s. 'em up, as we take hares behind*, Ant. IV, 7, 13. *you s. some hence for little faults*, Cymb. V, 1, 12. *s. them* (gifts) *straight away*, Per. III, 1, 24. With *out of* or *from*, = to take or tear suddenly from: *from my finger —ed that ring*, Err. V, 276. *to s. words from my tongue*, LLL V, 2, 382. John III, 1, 244. R3 II, 2, 57. Troil. V, 2, 81. Tim. IV, 3, 441. *this youth I —ed one half out of the jaws of death*, Tw. III, 4, 394. Hence = to take away, to rob: *the life of Helen was foully —ed*, All's V, 3, 154.

2) intr. to catch eagerly at something; absol.: *they 'll be —ing*, Lr. I, 4, 169. With *at: briers and thorns at their apparel s.* Mids. III, 2, 29. *and like a dog s. at his master*, John IV, 1, 117. *fiends will s. at it* (my soul) Oth. V, 2, 275.

**Snatchers**, pilferers: H5 I, 2, 143.

**Sneak**, vb. to creep stealthily and meanly: *s. not away*, Meas. V, 363. *a poor unminded outlaw —ing home*, H4A IV, 3, 58. *the weasel Scot comes —ing and so sucks her princely eggs*, H5 I, 2, 171. *what —ing fellow comes yonder?* Troil. I, 2, 246. *s. away so guilty-like*, Oth. III, 3, 39 (Ff *steal*).

**Sneak**, name in H4B II, 4, 12. 23.

**Sneak-cup**, one who sneaks from his cup? or a sneak-up, one who creeps up to people in a mean and insidious manner? in any case a paltry fellow: *the prince is a Jack, a s.* H4A III, 3, 99.*

**Sneap**, subst. a reprimand, a snubbing: *I will not undergo this s. without reply*, H4B II, 1, 133.

**Sneap**, vb. to check, to pinch, to nip: *to add a more rejoicing to the prime and give the —ed birds more cause to sing*, Lucr. 333. *an envious —ing frost that bites the first-born infants of the spring*, LLL I, 1, 100. *that may blow no —ing winds at home*, Wint. I, 2, 13.

**Sneck up**, an exclamation of contempt used by Sir Toby to Malvolio, = go and be hanged: Tw. II, 3, 101 (cf. Nares' Glossary).

**Snip**, a quick cut with scissors, as well as that which is cut off, a small shred: *keep not too long in one tune, but a s. and away*, LLL III, 22. *s., snap, quick and home*, V, 1, 63. *here's s. and nip and cut and slish and slash*, Shr. IV, 3, 90.

**Snipe**, a simpleton: Oth. 1, 3, 391.

**Snipt**, cut off at once, consisting of a small shred: *your son was misled with a s. taffeta fellow there*, All's IV, 5, 2 (a fellow who wore a patch or rag of taffeta. M. Edd. *snipt-taffeta*).

**Snore**, vb. to breathe hard and noisily in sleep: Tp. II, 1, 217. 300. Mids. V, 380. Merch. II, 5, 5. H4B IV, 5, 28 *(out)*. Cymb. III, 6, 34.

**Snores**, subst. hard and noisy breathing in sleep: Tp. II, 1, 218. Mcb. II, 2, 6. Per. III Prol. 2.

**Snort**, to blow through the nose as a high-spirited horse: Ven. 262.

2) to snore: H4A II, 4, 578. Oth. I, 1, 90.

**Snout**, the nose of a swine: Ven. 622.

Name in Mids. I, 2, 63. IV, 1, 208. V, 157.

**Snow**, subst. water congealed into soft white flakes: Ven. 354. 362. 750. Lucr. 1218. Sonn. 130, 3. Gent. II, 7, 19. LLL I, 1, 106. V, 2, 933. Mids. III, 2, 141. IV, 1, 171. V, 59. Merch. III, 2, 31. All's IV, 3, 191. Wint. IV, 4, 220. 375. John III, 4, 176. R2 I, 3, 298. IV, 260. H5 III, 5, 50. H6B III, 1, 223. R3 I, 4, 249. V, 3, 326. Tit. III, 1, 20. Rom. III, 2, 19. Mcb. IV, 3, 53. Hml. III, 3, 46. IV, 5, 35. 195. Lr. II, 2, 83. Oth. V, 2, 4. Ant. I, 4, 65. Emblem of chastity: *the white cold virgin s. upon my heart*, Tp. IV, 55. *chaste as the icicle that's curdied by the frost from purest s.* Cor. V, 3, 66. *the consecrated s. that lies on Dian's lap*, Tim. IV, 3, 386. *as chaste as ice, as pure as s.* Hml. III, 1, 141. *whose face between her forks presages s.* Lr. IV, 6, 121. *as chaste as unsunned s.* Cymb. II, 5, 13. Of hoary age: *sap-consuming winter's drizzled s.* Err. V, 312.

**Snow**, vb. to fall as snow: *let it s. eringoes*, Wiv. V, 5, 22.

**Snow-ball**, a round lump of snow: Wiv. III, 5, 24. Per. IV, 6, 149.

**Snow-broth**, snow and water mixed: Meas. I, 4, 58.

**Snow-white**, white like snow: Lucr. 196. 420. 1011. LLL I, 1, 245. IV, 2, 136. Tit. II, 3, 76.

**Snowy,** white like snow: *a s. dove*, Rom. I, 5, 50.

**Snuff,** subst. 1) the burning wick of a candle, as darkening the flame or remaining after it: *there lives within the very flame of love a kind of wick or s. that will abate it*, Hml. IV, 7, 116. *to hide me from the radiant sun and solace i' the dungeon by a s.* Cymb. I, 6, 87. Denoting, metaphorically, weak and spiritless old age: *my s. and loathed part of nature should burn itself out*, Lr. IV, 6, 39. *let me not live, after my flame lacks oil, to be the s. of younger spirits*, All's I, 2, 59 (i. e. to be called a snuff by younger spirits). Quibbling in LLL V, 2, 22 and Mids. V, 254.

2) a huff expressed by a snuffing of the nose, resentment, offence-taking: *what hath been seen, either in —s and packings of the dukes*, Lr. III, 1, 26.* *to be in s.*, and *to take it in s.* = to take offence: *it is already in s.* Mids. V, 254. *you'll mar the light by taking it in s.* LLL V, 2, 22. *who* (the nose) *therewith angry ... took it in s.* H4A I, 3, 41.

**Snuff,** vb. 1) to inhale, to scent: *as if you —ed up love by smelling love*, LLL III, 16 (cf. *Scent-snuffing*).

2) to crop (a wick): *I must s. it*, H8 III, 2, 96.

**Snug,** name in Mids. I, 2, 66. III, 1, 47. V, 226.

**So,** 1) in such a degree; joined to verbs as well as to adjectives and adverbs: *being so enraged*, Ven. 29. *though mine be not so fair*, 116. *is love so light*, 155. *young and so unkind*, 187. *a tomb so simple*, 244. *blessed bankrupt, that by love so thriveth*, 466. *for having so offended*, 810. *give thanks you have lived so long*, Tp.I, 1, 27. 2, 29. 30. 68. 112. 142. 207. 419. 471. Gent. II, 1, 38. *I'll venture so much of my hawk*, Shr. V, 2, 72. As I, 3, 53. HCB IV, 1, 17. Mcb. I, 7, 51. *so out of hope*, Tp. III, 3, 11. *so out of love with life*, Meas. III, 1, 174. *he is so above me*, All's I, 1, 98. *Ceres' blessing so is on you*, Tp.IV,117. *so I charmed their ears that calf-like they my lowing followed*, 178. *prayer which pierces so that it assaults mercy itself*, Epil. 17. *she that you gaze on so*, Gent. II, 1, 46. *hath so humbled me as I confess there is no woe to his correction*, II, 4, 137. *chafed him so ... that ...*, III, 1, 233. *if so your heart were touched as mine is*, Meas. II, 2, 54. *my place ... will so your accusation overweigh, that you shall stifle ...*, II, 4, 157. *doth he so seek his life?* I, 4, 72. *hast thou so cracked my tongue that here my son knows not my feeble key*, Err. V, 308 etc. etc. Before an adj. followed by the ind. art.: *so hard a mind*, Ven. 203. *on so proud a back*, 300. *so white a friend*, 364. *so brave a lass*, Tp.III,2,111. *so high a servant*, Gent. II, 4, 106. *so great a favour*, 161 etc. etc. The article omitted: *in so profound abysm I throw all care*, Sonn. 112, 9. *with so full soul*, Tp. III, 1, 44. *of so quick condition*, Meas. I, 1, 54. *call him to so strict account*, H4A III,2,149. *of so floodgate and o'erbearing nature*, Oth. I, 3, 56.

Followed (without *as*) by an infinitive denoting the effect: *that is so proud thy service to despise*, Sonn. 149, 10 (= as thy service to despise; proud enough to despise thy service). *you must be so good to rise*, Meas. IV, 3, 29. *that thou art so fond to come abroad with him*, Merch. III, 3, 9. *no woman's heart so big to hold so much*, Tw.II,4,99. *he would have been so brief with you to shorten you*, R2 III, 3, 12. *shall I so much dishonour my fair stars, on equal terms to give him chastisement*, IV,21. *I wonder he is so fond to trust the mockery of unquiet slumbers*, R3 III, 2, 26. *I would thou wert so happy by thy stay, to hear true shrift*, Rom.

I,1,164. *this alliance may so happy prove, to turn your households' rancour to pure love*, II,3,91. *I'll make so bold to call*, Mcb. II, 3, 56. *As for to: I'll be so bold as stay*, Wiv. IV, 5, 13 (Simple's speech). *can you so stead me as bring me to the sight of Isabella*, Meas. I, 4, 17. *will you be so good as eat it*, H5 V, 1, 31 (Fluellen's speech). Omitted: Caes. III, 1, 39.

Followed by a relative: *no perfection is so absolute, that some impurity doth not pollute*, Lucr. 853. *a witch, and one so strong that could control the moon*, Tp. V, 269. *sail so expeditious that shall catch your royal fleet*, 315. *who's so gross that sees not this palpable device?* R3 III, 6, 10. *who so firm that cannot be seduced?* Caes. I, 2, 316. III, 2, 31. *a jealousy so strong that judgement cannot cure*, Oth. II, 1, 310. *the search so slow that could not trace them*, Cymb. I, 1, 64. Hence almost = ever so, however, by the omission of the relative in negative and interrogative sentences: *what king so strong can tie the gall up in the slanderous tongue?* Meas. III, 2, 198. *none so dry or thirsty will deign to sip*, Shr. V, 2, 144. *no cataplasm so rare can save the thing from death*, Hml. IV, 7, 144.

2) in the same degree; as: *so soon was she along as he was down*, Ven. 43. *Spurio, a hundred and fifty; Sebastian, so many*, All's IV, 3, 184. *to speak so much more French*, H5 V, 2, 196. *which sixteen winters cannot blow away, so many summers dry*, Wint. V, 3, 51. *as my love is sized, my fear is so*, Hml. III, 2, 180. *all of her that is out of door most rich! if she be furnished with a mind so rare*, Cymb. I, 6, 16. *so long as, so much as, so soon as* etc. = as long as etc.: *so long as men can breathe or eyes can see*, Sonn. 18,13. *so long as youth and thou are of one date*, 22,2. *so oft as thou wilt look*, 77, 13. *so long as brain and heart have faculty to subsist*, 122, 5. *had women been so strong as men*, Pilgr. 321. *so glad of this as they I cannot be*, Tp. III, 1, 92. *was there ever man a coward that hath drunk so much sack as I*, III, 2, 31. *so soon as I came beyond Eton, they threw me off*, Wiv. IV, 5, 67. *just so much as you may take upon a knife's point*, Ado II, 3, 263. *if the truth of thy love were so righteously tempered as mine*, As I,2,14. *so near our public court as twenty miles*, I, 3, 46. *he shall need none, so long as I live*, Shr. V, 1, 25. *twenty times so much*, V, 2, 73. *so long as I could see*, Tw. I, 2, 17. *so soon as ever thou seest him, draw*, III, 4, 194. *so sure as this beard's grey*, Wint. II, 3, 162. *so long as nature will bear up*, III, 2, 241. *so soon as you arrive*, IV, 4, 633. *the day shall not be up so soon as I*, John V, 5, 21. *how went he under him? So proudly as if he disdained the ground*, R2 V, 5, 83. *so far as my coin would stretch*, H4A I, 2, 61. *so long as out of limit and true rule you stand against anointed majesty*, IV, 3, 39. *I will live so long as I may*, H5 II, 1, 15. *ten times so much*, H6A II, 1, 53. *had I twenty times so many foes*, H6B II, 4, 60. *what sorrow can befall thee, so long as Edward is thy friend*, H6C IV, 1, 77. *look I so pale as the rest?* R3 II, 1, 83. *so long as heaven and nature lengthens it*, IV, 4, 353. *even so most fitly as you malign our senators*, Cor. I, 1, 116. *so far as thou hast power*, III, 2, 85. *all so soon as the sun should ... begin to draw the shady curtains*, Rom. I, 1, 140. *so soon as dinner's done, we'll forth again*, Tim. II, 2, 14. *so oft as that shall be, so often shall the knot of us be called ...*, Caes. III, 1, 116. *so well thy words become thee as thy wounds*, Mcb. I, 2, 43. *to devour so many as will to*

greatness dedicate themselves, IV, 3, 74. *with a look so piteous as if he had been loosed out of hell*, Hml. II, 1, 82. *so much as from occasion you may glean*, II, 2, 16. *provided I be so able as now*, V, 2, 211. *twice so many*, Lr. II, 4, 265. *that I might do you service so good as you have done*, Ant. IV, 2, 19. *follow the noise so far as we have quarter*, IV, 3, 22. *so soon as I can win the offended king*, Cymb. I, 1, 75. *to prove so worthy as since he hath been allowed the name of*, I, 4, 3. *so soon as I had made my meal*, III, 6, 51. V, 4, 126. V, 5, 323. *so sure as you your father's* (issue) 332 etc. Of course also in negative sentences: As I, 3, 53. H6B II, 4, 63 etc. etc.

Introducing an optative sentence, after or before asseverations: *I never saw the chain, so help me Heaven*, Err. V, 267. *never, Paulina; so be blest my spirit!* Wint. V, 1, 71. *speak like a true knight, so defend thee Heaven*, R2 I, 3, 34. *as my duty springs, so perish they*, H6A III, 1, 175. *so thrive I, as I truly swear the like*, R3 II, 1, 11. *so prosper I, as I swear perfect love*, 16. *so thrive I in my dangerous attempt*, IV, 4, 398. *so help me every spirit sanctified*, Oth. III, 4, 126 etc.

3) in such a manner, thus: *even so she kissed his brow*, Ven. 59. *how a bird lies tangled in a net, so fastened in her arms Adonis lies*, 68. *like a divedapper ... so offers he to give*, 88. *so shall the day seem night*, 122. *Narcissus so himself forsook*, 161. *and so thou dost survive*, 173. *even so she languisheth*, 603. *to withhold me so*, 612. *as their captain, so their pride doth grow*, Lucr. 298. *if it so hap*, Tp. I, 1, 28. *by being so retired*, I, 2, 91. *ere it should the good ship so have swallowed*, 12. *the visitor will not give him o'er so*, II, 1, 11 (cf. Meas. II, 2, 43). *as his body uglier grows, so his mind cankers*, IV, 192. *as the morning steals upon the night, so their rising senses begin to chase the fumes*, V, 66 (cf. Gent. I, 1, 43. Meas. I, 2, 131. I, 3, 27). *were I so minded*, V, 126. *he that is so yoked by a fool*, Gent. I, 1, 40. *you are so without these follies that these follies are within you*, II, 1, 39. *and so by many winding nooks he strays*, II, 7, 31. *my jealous aim might err and so unworthily disgrace the man*, III, 1, 29. *she persevers so*, III, 2, 28. *ne'er repent, if it were done so*, IV, 1, 30. *when it jars so*, IV, 2, 67. *I will so plead that you shall say my cunning drift excels*, 82. *so to enforce or qualify the laws as to your soul seems good*, Meas. I, 1, 66. I, 3, 15. II, 1, 27. 29. 229. II, 4, 24. Err. I, 1, 97. I, 2, 39. II, 1, 12. 14. 38. IV, 3, 83. H8 V, 3, 182. Troil. II, 3, 265 (*were your days as green as Ajax' and your mind so tempered;* i. e. thus tempered, tempered in that manner which we perceive in you). Rom. IV, 2, 47. Hml. I, 1, 104. II, 2, 14. Ant. III, 6, 19. V, 2, 186 etc. etc.

Hence = the case being such, accordingly: *so you're paid*, Tp. II, 1, 36. *so you may continue and laugh at nothing still*, 178. *so, king, go safely on*, 327. *I'll bring you to your ship and so to Naples*, V, 307. *so by your circumstance you call me fool*, Gent. I, 1, 36. *and so I'll commend you to my master*, 154. *and so farewell*, 62. *and so good morrow*, II, 1, 140. *and so good rest*, IV, 2, 133. *so fare you well*, Meas. I, 1, 59. *so you must be the first that gives this sentence*, II, 2, 106. *so then it seems your act was mutually committed*, II, 3, 26. *these knights will hack, and so thou shouldst not alter the article of thy gentry*, Wiv. II, 1, 52. *so let me hear you speak*, Tw. III, 1, 133 etc. Used (quite as in German) to introduce the principal sentence after a subordinate clause: *as you love strokes, so jest with me again*, Err. II, 2, 8. *if this were so, so were it uttered*, Ado I, 1, 217. *when this hail some heat from Hermia felt, so he dissolved*, Mids. I, 1, 245. *if thou canst serve where thou dost stand condemned, so may it come thy master shall find thee full of labours*, Lr. I, 4, 6. cf. *I would you were set, so your affection would cease*, Gent. II, 1, 91.

4) in the same manner; also: *now let me say Good night, and so say you*, Ven. 535. *mad in pursuit, and in possession so*, Sonn. 129, 9. *therefore my mistress' brows are raven black, her eyes so suited*, 127, 10. *my brother's daughter is queen of Tunis; so is she heir of Naples*, Tp. II, 1, 256 (cf. I, 2, 165). *so, with good life and observation strange, my meaner ministers their several kinds have done*, III, 3, 86. *'tis so with me*, Meas. I, 1, 82. *one of these men is genius to the other, and so of these*, Err. V, 333. *so won, so lost*, LLL I, 1, 147. *so he served the second, and so the third*, As I, 2, 136. *thou dost overween in all, and so in this*, Tit. II, 1, 30. *good morrow, Antony. So to most noble Caesar*, Caes. II, 2, 118.

5) Implying the sense of a word or sentence going before or following; = as I said, such, this, that: *hearing you praised, I say 'Tis so, tis true*, Sonn. 85, 9. Gent. II, 3, 18. III, 1, 152. Err. II, 2, 203. V, 10. LLL I, 1, 225. *can this be so?* Meas. III, 1, 233. *be it so! amen!* Tp. V, 215. *my friends — That's not so, we are your enemies*, Gent. IV, 1, 8. Meas. II, 1, 87. Err. III, 1, 85. 324. *too low a mistress for so high a servant. Not so, sweet lady*, Gent. II, 4, 107. IV, 2, 61. 140. IV, 4, 80. LLL V, 2, 359. *if so, the world will hold thee in disdain*, Ven. 761. *no more, unless the next word that thou speakest have some malignant power upon my life; if so, I pray thee, breathe it in mine ear*, Gent. III, 1, 239. *when they see time they'll go or come; if so, be patient*, Err. II, 1, 9. *and more than so, presenteth to mine eye the picture of an angry chafing boar*, Ven. 661. *it is worse for me than so*, Shr. IV, 2, 88. *so (a loyal wife) am I now*, Lucr. 1049. *though not to love, yet to tell me so*, Sonn. 140, 6. *being so (the prime duke) reputed*, Tp. I, 2, 72. *where was she born? In Argier. O, was she so?* 261. *I will do my spiriting gently. Do so*, 298. *cursed be I that did so*, 339. II, 1, 193. 222. *we would so (lift the moon out of her sphere)* 185. *dost thou think so?* V, 19. *thou liest. Do I so?* III, 2, 84. *you must be so too (more serious)* II, 1, 220. *I would, not so (a king)* III, 1, 61. *so (a fool) I fear you'll prove*, Gent. I, 1, 37. *I think him so (best)* I, 2, 24. *I seem so (sad)* II, 4, 9. *if you think so*, II, 7, 62. *pray heaven he prove so*, 79. *so I believe*, III, 2, 16. *I'll use thee kindly for thy mistress' sake, that used me so*, IV, 4, 208. *I will visit her: tell her so*, Wiv. III, 5, 50. *so you do (deserve it)* III, 3, 90. *I have done so (sent after the duke)* Meas. I, 2, 180. *say Pompey told you so*, II, 1, 257. *hail to you, provost! so I think you are*, II, 3, 1. *let me excuse me, and believe me so, my mirth it much displeased, but pleased my woe*, IV, 1, 12. *had the gods done so*, Err. I, 1, 99. III, 1, 123. V, 58. 206. *if it prove so*, I, 2, 103. *and so tell your master*, III, 1, 50. *brave conquerors, for so you are*, LLL I, 1, 8. *will they so (know their mistresses)?* V, 2, 126. *if love have touched you, nought remains but so, Redime te captum quam queas minimo*, Shr. I, 1, 166 (= but this. cf. above: Meas. IV, 1, 12). *how came the posterns so easily open? By his great authority, which often hath*

*no less prevailed than so*, Wint. II, 1, 54. *I say good queen, and would by combat make her good so, were I a man*, II, 3, 60 (M. Edd. preposterously: *good, so were I a man*). *cousin, farewell; and, uncle, bid him so*, R2 I, 3, 247. *I will after straight and tell him so*, H4A I, 3, 127. Troil. I, 3, 256. *aged custom, but by your voices, will not so permit me* (to be consul) Cor. II, 3, 177. *you so remain* (the people's magistrates) III, 1, 202. *tell them there I have gold; look, so I have*, Tim. IV, 3, 289. *the perfume and suppliance of a minute ... No more but so?* Hml. I, 3, 10. *but to know so must be my benefit*, Oth. III, 4, 119. *so to them both*, Ant. III, 12, 24. *yet is't not probable to come alone, either he so undertaking* (i. e. to come alone) *or they so suffering*, Cymb. IV, 2, 142 etc. Sometimes omitted, where modern usage would require it: *I think*, Meas. I, 2, 24. Cor. I, 6, 46. *which if, Lord have mercy on thee*, All's II, 3, 223. *O, if it prove, tempests are kind*, Tw. III, 4, 418. *not like a corse, or if, not to be buried*, Wint. IV, 4, 131. *haply you shall not see me more; or if, a mangled shadow*, Ant. IV, 2, 26. Inserted, on the contrary, where modern usage would omit it: *repair to the Capital. We will so*, Cor. II, 3, 262. cf. above: Tp. I, 2, 261. III, 2, 84. LLL V, 2, 126.

Emphatical inversion of the subject (*so am I* = so am I too): *let me say Good night, and so say you*, Ven. 535. *rich preys make true men thieves; so do thy lips make modest Dian cloudy*, 724. *you have cause, so have we all, of joy*, Tp. II, 1, 2. *the fault's your own. So is the dearest o' the loss*, 135. *I will stand, and so shall Trinculo*, III, 2, 47. *my nose is in great indignation. So is mine*, IV, 201. *she is fair, and so is Julia*, Gent. II, 4, 199. *and so suppose am I*, IV, 2, 114. IV, 4, 197. *I'll keep him above deck. So will I*, Wiv. II, 1, 95. *keep in your weapon. So do you*, III, 1, 77. *you shall go; so shall you*, III, 2, 83. *as I find her, so am I affected*, III, 4, 95. *so say I too*, IV, 2, 134. *so think I too*, IV, 4, 26. Err. II, 2, 198. IV, 3, 42. V, 372. Ado III, 2, 16. III, 5, 31. V, 4, 2. Mids. I, 1, 53. III, 1, 142. III, 2, 265. Merch. II, 4, 26. IV, 1, 98. As I, 2, 13. H4A III, 2, 163. H6A II, 4, 131. Ant. II, 6, 1 etc.

As for *how so* and *why so* = why, see *How* and *Why.*

6) provided that, if it be so that (cf. Mids. I, 1, 39), on condition that, if (followed by the subjunctive or an auxiliary verb): *wishing her cheeks were gardens full of flowers, so they were dewed with such distilling showers*, Ven. 66. 180. *she will never rise, so he will kiss her*, 480. *to sell myself I can be well contented, so thou wilt buy*, 514. *so thou be good, slander doth but approve thy worth the greater*, 70, 5. *what care I who calls me well or ill, so you o'ergreen my bad*, 112, 4. *myself I'll forfeit, so that other mine thou wilt restore*, 134, 3. *for nothing hold me, so it please thee hold that nothing me a something sweet to thee*, 136, 11. Gent. I, 2, 3. 89. II, 1, 119. III, 1, 120. 334. Wiv. II, 2, 149. Err. II, 1, 108. II, 2, 35. Ado II, 1, 91. V, 1, 152. LLL II, 127. 222. IV, 1, 124. Mids. III, 2, 314. Merch. III, 2, 197. 211. IV, 1, 291. As I, 2, 11. II, 3, 30. IV, 2, 10. Shr. II, 227. IV, 3, 16. All's IV, 3, 274. John III, 4, 16. IV, 1, 17. R2 II, 2, 101. H4A I, 3, 76. H6A IV, 7, 94. V, 3, 17. H6B III, 1, 264. III, 2, 361. H6C IV, 7, 32. R3 I, 2, 124. IV, 4, 209. 250. Troil. V, 1, 72. Rom. II, 2, 97. Caes. I, 2, 166. Ant. III, 13, 15 etc. *So please* = if it please: *on a trice, so please you, were we divided from them*, Tp. V, 238. *so please my lord*

*to quit the fine, I am content*, Merch. IV, 1, 380. *do you intend to stay with me to-night? So please your lordship to accept our duty*, Shr. Ind. 1, 82. *so please you, one day shall crown the alliance*, Tw. V, 324. *ready are the appellant and defendant, so please your highness to behold the fight*, H6B II, 3, 51. *I'll cross the sea, so it please my lord*, H6C II, 6, 98. *tell him, so please him come unto this place, he shall be satisfied*, Caes. III, 1, 140. *I will follow you, so please you entertain me*, Cymb. IV, 2, 394 (cf. *Please*).

Exceptions from the general rule: 1) *so* followed by the indicative: *nothing comes amiss, so money comes withal*, Shr. I, 2, 82 (Grumio's speech). 2) = though: *should I lie, madam? O, I would thou didst, so half my Egypt were submerged*, Ant. II, 5, 94.

*If so*, and *so that*, = if: *might you do't ... if so your heart were touched with that remorse*, Meas. II, 2, 54. *if so you'll not o'errule me to a peace*, Hml. IV, 7, 61 (Qq *so you will not*). *so that you had her wrinkles and I her money, I would she did as you say*, All's II, 4, 20. *so that thy state might be no worse, I would my skill were subject to thy curse*, R2 III, 4, 102. *So as*, in the same sense: *so as thou livest in peace, die free from strife*, R2 V, 6, 27.

7) Used with reference to a manner or degree or quantity not expressly mentioned, but only hinted at and left to guessing: *applying this to that, and so to so*, Ven. 713. *when for some trifling present you have bid me return so much*, Tim. II, 2, 146 (German: *so und so viel*). *to borrow so many talents*, III, 2, 13. 26. 41. *addicted so and so*, Hml. II, 1, 19. *this service is not service, so being done, but being so allowed*, Cymb. III, 3, 16. *Or so* = or anything like this, somewhere about this; often used as a mere expletive: *for an eternal moment or so*, Wiv. II, 1, 50. *is she wedded, or no? To her will, sir, or so*, LLL II, 212. *I'll make one in a dance or so*, V, 1, 160. *she may perhaps call him half a score knaves or so*, Shr. I, 2, 111. *some two thousand strong or so*, Tw. III, 2, 59. *score a pint of bastard in the Half-moon or so*, H4A II, 4, 30. *some half an hour or so*, H8 IV, 1, 66. *some certain snatch or so would serve your turns*, Tit. II, 1, 95. *Thisbe a grey eye or so, but not to the purpose*, Rom. II, 4, 45. *good sir, or so, or friend, or gentleman*, Hml. II, 1, 46. *girdle, hangers, or so*, V, 2, 158 (Qq *and so*).

8) Expressing acquiescence or approbation, = well: *so; lie there, my art*, Tp. I, 2, 24. *so, slave; hence*, 375. *are you of fourscore pounds a year? Yes, an't please you, sir. So; what trade are you of?* Meas. II, 1, 206. *your brother is to die. So*, II, 4, 84. *reach a chair: so; now, methinks, I feel a little ease*, H8 IV, 2, 4. *your grace must wait till you be called for. So*, V, 2, 7. *so: thou wilt not hear me now*, Tim. I, 2, 253. *have you wisdom? so*, Lr. I, 4, 102. *give me your arm; up, so*, IV, 6, 65. *lend me a garter; so*, Oth. V, 1, 82. *whose he is we are, and that is Caesar's. So*, Ant. III, 13, 52. *our crows shall fare the better for you, and there's an end. So, sir*, Cymb. III, 1, 85. *why, so* = well, well: Shr. IV, 3, 198. R2 II, 2, 87. R3 II, 1, 1 (Qq *so, now have I done*). Cor. V, 1, 15. Mcb. III, 4, 107. As for *even so*, see *Even*.

Supplying the place of a principal sentence, = it is well, it is good: *if it please you, so; if not, why, so*, Gent. II, 1, 137. *if it be my luck, so*, Wiv. III, 4, 67. *on whom it will, it will; on whom it will not, so*, Meas. I, 2, 127. *if he will take it, so*, Merch. I, 3, 170. *if that this simple syllogism will serve*, *so*, Tw. I, 5, 55. *if you will deny the sheriff*, *so*, H4A II, 4, 545. *if he do come in my way*, *so*, V, 3, 60. V, 1, 122. V, 3, 64. V, 4, 144. H4B III, 2, 252. Lr. II, 2, 106. Cymb. II, 3, 16.

*So, so,* = a) well, well (like the simple *so*): *so, so, quoth he, these lets attend the time*, Lucr. 330. *before you can breathe twice and cry so*, *so*, Tp. IV, 45. *the dog is me and I am myself; ay, so, so*, Gent. II, 3, 26. *so, so: farewell; we are gone*, Wint. II, 3, 130. *so, so; these are the limbs o' the plot*, H8 I, 1, 219. *so, so; rub on*, Troil. III, 2, 52. *so, so, we draw together*, V, 5, 44. *so, so; now sit*, Tit. III, 2, 1. *most welcome, sir. So, so, there!* Tim. I, 1, 256. *I would not have thee linger in thy pain: so, so*, Oth. V, 2, 89. *so, so; come, give me that*, Ant. IV, 4, 28. *so, so: well done*, Cymb. I, 5, 82. *so, so, so* (expressive of satisfaction): Tp. V, 96. Lr. III, 6, 90. 91. cf. Oth. IV, 1, 126. b) indifferent, not worth much, somewhat amiss (adjectively as well as adverbially): *what thinkest thou of the rich Mercatio? Well of his wealth, but of himself so so*, Gent. I, 2, 13. *his leg is but so so*, As III, 5, 119. *art rich? Faith, sir, so so*, V, 1, 28. *so so is good, very good, very excellent good; and yet it is not; it is but so so*, 29. *thou counterfeitest most lively. So so, my lord*, Tim. V, 1, 85. Costard uses the simple *so* in the same sense: *he is, in telling true, but so*, LLL I, 1, 227.

9) *so as* = such as: *so am I as the rich*, Sonn. 52, 1. *thou art as tyrannous, so as thou art, as those whose beauties proudly make them cruel*, 131, 1 (= though thou art such; cf. *against whose person, so sacred as it is, I have done sin*, Wint. V, 1, 172, = sacred as it is; though it is sacred).

**Soader,** see *Solder*.

**Soak,** 1) to draw in by the pores, to imbibe: *thy conceit is* —*ing, will draw in more than the common blocks*, Wint. I, 2, 224. *a sponge ... that* —*s up the king's countenance* etc. Hml. IV, 2, 16.

2) to steep in a fluid till the substance has imbibed what it can contain, to drench: *many princes ... lie drowned and soaked in mercenary blood*, H5 IV, 7, 79.

3) to enter by the pores or any interstices: *all the tears ... may run into that sink, and* —*ing in drown the lamenting fool*, Tit. III, 2, 19.

**Soar,** to fly aloft, to tower, to rise high: Shr. Ind. 2, 45. R2 I, 1, 109. H5 III, 7, 16. H6B II, 1, 14. III, 2, 193. Cor. II, 1, 270. Rom. I, 4, 18. 20. Caes. I, 1, 79. Cymb. V, 5, 471. cf. *High-soaring.*

**Sob,** subt. a convulsive sigh: Ven. 222. Err. IV, 3, 25 (most M. Edd. *fob*). R3 I, 4, 252. Troil. IV, 2, 114.

**Sob,** vb. to sigh with tears: Lucr. 1088. Ado II, 3, 153. As II, 1, 66. R3 I, 2, 162. Tit. III, 1, 137.

**Sober,** 1) not intoxicated: Ado III, 3, 49. Merch. I, 2, 93.

2) calm, serene, not rash: *with s. speed*, H4B IV, 3, 86. *with such s. and unnoted passion*, Tim. III, 5, 21. *forgive my general and exceptless rashness, you perpetual s. gods*, IV, 3, 503 (M. Edd. *perpetual-sober*). *this s. form of yours hides wrongs*, Caes. IV, 2, 40.

3) serious, earnest: *speak in s. judgement*, Ado I, 1, 171. *speakest thou in s. meanings*, As V, 2, 76.

4) grave, dignified, decent: *making such s. action with his hand*, Lucr. 1403. *as subtle Sinon here is painted, so s. sad*, 1542 (M. Edd. *sober-sad*). *nor that full star ... doth half that glory to the s. west*, Sonn.

132, 8. *if I do not put on a s. habit*, Merch. II, 2, 199. *let not the sound of shallow foppery enter my s. house*, II, 5, 36. *what damned error, but some s. brow will bless it*, III, 2, 78. *disguised in s. robes*, Shr. I, 2, 132. *a s. ancient gentleman*, V, 1, 75. Applied to women, = modest, demure, chaste: *shook off my s. guards and civil fears*, Compl. 298. *her wisdom, her s. virtue*, Err. III, 1, 90. *a queen, fair, s., wise*, Hml. III, 4, 189. *chastised with the s. eye of dull Octavia*, Ant. V, 2, 54.

**Sober-blooded,** calm, cool, considerate: H4B IV, 3, 94.

**Soberly,** with dignity: Ant. I, 5, 48.

**Sober-sad,** see *Sober.*

**Sober-suited,** decently dressed: Rom. III, 2, 11.

**Sobriety,** modesty, decency: *maid's mild behaviour and s.* Shr. I, 1, 71. H5 IV, 1, 74 (Fluellen's speech).

**Soccard** (Ff *Surecard*) name in H4B III, 2, 95.

**Sociable,** companionable: *'tis too respective and too s.* John I, 188. *to that drop ten thousand wiry friends do glue themselves in s. grief*, III, 4, 65. *can he not be s.?* Troil. II, 3, 220. *now art thou s.* Rom. II, 4, 93. *society is no comfort to one not s.* Cymb. IV, 2, 13. With *to*: *mine eyes, even s. to the show of thine, fall fellowly drops*, Tp. V, 63.

**Society,** company: *grief best is pleased with grief's s.* Lucr. 1111. *that sin should lace itself with his s.* Sonn. 67, 4. *of her s. be not afraid*, Tp. IV, 91. *my riots past, my wild* —*es*, Wiv. III, 4, 8. *there is scarce truth enough alive to make* —*es secure*, Meas. III, 2, 240. *I beseech your s.* LLL IV, 2, 166. *s. is the happiness of life*, 167. *thou makest the triumviry, the corner-cap of s.* IV, 3, 53. *that in love's grief desirest s.* 128. *to abjure the s. of men*, Mids. I, 1, 66. *I thank you for your s.* As III, 2, 272 (cf. 268). *s., which in the boorish is company*, V, 1, 53. 56. *made separation of their s.* Wint. I, 1, 29. *the s. of your father*, V, 1, 135. *this is worshipful s.* John I, 205. H4A III, 2, 14. H4B V, 1, 78. R3 IV, 4, 38. H8 I, 4, 14. Rom. IV, 1, 14. Tim. I, 2, 250. III, 6, 79. IV, 1, 31. IV, 3, 21. Mcb. III, 1, 42. III, 4, 3. Hml. V, 2, 112. Lr. V, 3, 210. Cymb. I, 6, 167. IV, 2, 12.

**Sock,** a short stocking covering only the foot: Wiv. III, 5, 91.

**Socrates,** the celebrated philosopher: Shr. I, 2, 71.

**Sod, Sodden,** and **Sodden-witted,** see *Seethe.*

**Soder,** see *Solder.*

**Soe'er,** adv. separated from *how, what,* or *who,* with which words it is usually compounded in *howsoe'er* or *howsoever,* etc.: Tw. I, 1, 12. John IV, 3, 91. Tit. V, 1, 82. Hml. I, 5, 170. Cymb. I, 6, 8. III, 5, 112.

**Soever,** the same: Wiv. IV, 2, 25. LLL I, 1, 194. R3 I, 1, 87. IV, 4, 224. Troil. I, 3, 196. Hml. III, 2, 416 (Ff and earlier Qq *somever*). Oth. III, 3, 469 (Qq *what bloody work s.*, Ff *what bloody business ever*).

**So-forth** (cf. *Forth*) et cetera: *Sicilia is a s.* Wint. I, 2, 218 (= what decency forbids to name).

**Soft,** 1) not hard or rough, but easily yielding to pressure and smooth to the touch: Ven. 81. 142. 353. 511. 633. 1053. 1116. Sonn. 99, 4. Pilgr. 88. Wiv. I, 3, 108. Meas. II, 2, 117. III, 1, 16. LLL IV, 3, 337. Merch. IV, 1, 96. As III, 5, 12. Shr. Ind. 2, 40. 73. V, 2, 165. Wint. IV, 4, 374. H5 II, 3, 61. IV, 1, 14. H6B III, 2, 325. Cor. I, 9, 45. V, 3, 53. Tit. III, 1, 45. Tim. V, 4, 68. Hml. III, 3, 71. Ant. II, 6, 51. Cymb. V, 3, 71.

2) affecting the senses in a bland and delicate manner: *with s. slow tongue*, Lucr. 1220 (= in a low voice). *touches so s. still conquer chastity*, Pilgr. 50. H6B III, 2, 325. *s. stillness*, Merch. V, 56. *with s. low tongue*, Shr. Ind. 1, 114. Lr. V, 3, 272. *that death is too s. for him*, Wint. IV, 4, 807. *whose* (her hands') *s. seizure*, Troil. I, 1, 56. *sleep give as s. attachment to thy senses*, IV, 2, 5. *like —est music*, Rom. II, 2, 167. *as sweet as balm, as s. as air*, Ant. V, 2, 314. *in s. and delicate Lethe*, II, 7, 114.

3) mild, gentle, delicate, tender: Ven. 376. Lucr. 200. Tp. V, 142. Meas. II, 4, 129. Ado I, 1, 305. Shr. II, 253. V, 2, 167. Tw. V, 331. Wint. I, 2, 95. John II, 478. H4A I, 3, 7. H4B III, 1, 6. H6C III, 2, 154. H8 II, 3, 32. Troil. I, 3, 25. II, 2, 11. 105. Cor. III, 2, 82. Rom. III, 5, 212. Hml. V, 2, 112. Oth. I, 3, 82. III, 3, 264. Ant. I, 1, 44. II, 2, 3. Per. IV, 4, 45. = tender-hearted, pitiful: Lucr. 595. Compl. 278. Merch. III, 3, 14. John IV, 3, 50. H5 III, 3, 48. H6C I, 4, 141. II, 2, 57. R3 I, 3, 141. Tit. III, 1, 45. Tim. IV, 3, 115.

Used adverbially: *little have you to say ... but s. and low, Remember now my brother*, Meas. IV, 1, 69. *and sleep as s. as captain shall*, All's IV, 3, 368. *and in your power s. silencing your son*, H4B V, 2, 97. *drink wine, lie s.* Tim. IV, 3, 206. Imperatively: = hold, stop: Pilgr. 347. Tp. I, 2, 449. Err. II, 2, 111. III, 1, 30. III, 2, 69. IV, 1, 19. LLL IV, 3, 186. V, 2, 418. Mids. IV, 1, 132. Merch. I, 3, 59. IV, 1, 320. As III, 2, 265. Shr. IV, 4, 23. Tw. I, 5, 312. Wint. IV, 4, 402. R2 V, 1, 7. H4A I, 3, 155. II, 1, 40. V, 4, 134. H6B II, 4, 15. R3 I, 3, 339. V, 3, 178. Tit. IV, 2, 51. Ant. II, 2, 83. Cymb. IV, 2, 295. 353 etc. *s. and fair*, Ado V, 4, 72 (= festina lente). *s. you:* Ado V, 1, 207. Hml. III, 1, 88. Oth. V, 2, 338.

**Soft-conscienced**, having a tender conscience: Cor. I, 1, 37.

**Soften**, 1) tr. to make soft: Lucr. 591. Gent. III, 2, 79. Meas. I, 4, 70. Merch. IV, 1, 79. H6B IV, 4, 1. Rom. III, 1, 120. Oth. IV, 3, 47. Ant. II, 1, 21.

2) intr. to become soft or tender: *how he may s. at the sight o' the child*, Wint. II, 2, 40.

**Soft-hearted**, tender-hearted (in a bad sense), weak: H6B III, 2, 307. H6C II, 3, 25.

**Softly**, 1) gently, quietly, without violence: *his falchion on a flint he s. smiteth*, Lucr. 176. *s., my masters*, Shr. I, 2, 238. Tw. II, 5, 132. Wint. IV, 3, 76. H4B IV, 4, 132. *speak your griefs s.* Caes. IV, 2, 42.

2) low, not loudly: Lucr. 1628. Tp. IV, 194. 206. Err. V, 9. LLL V, 2, 255. Shr. V, 1, 1. Wint. II, 1, 30. H6A I, 1, 63. H8 IV, 2, 82. Ant. V, 2, 323. Cymb. II, 2, 13.

3) slowly, leisurely: Ado II, 1, 91. As III, 2, 346. Wint. IV, 3, 121. Caes. V, 1, 16. Hml. IV, 4, 8 (Ff safely). Per. IV, 1, 49.

**Softly-sprighted**, a word used by Mrs Quickly, perhaps in the sense of gentle: Wiv. I, 4, 25.

**Softness**, vicious delicacy, effeminacy: *a satire against the s. of prosperity*, Tim. V, 1, 36.

**Soft-slow**, see *Soft*.

**Soho**, a cry of sportsmen, when the hare was found in her form: Gent. III, 1, 189. Rom. II, 4, 136.

**Soil**, subst. 1) ground, land, earth: *I have seen ... the firm s. win of the watery main*, Sonn. 64, 7. *on the face of terra, the s., the land, the earth*, LLL IV, 2, 7.

2) country: *flesh his spirit in a warlike soil*, John V, 1, 71. *England's ground, farewell; sweet s., adieu*, R2 I, 3, 306. *no more the thirsty entrance of this s shall daub her lips with her own children's blood*, H4A I, 1, 5. *renounce your s., give sheep in lions' stead*, H6A I, 5, 29. *I had hope of France, even as I have of fertile England's s.* H6B I, 1, 238. *leads discontented steps in foreign s.* R3 IV, 4, 312.

3) a field, a landed estate: *if you like the s., the profit and this kind of life*, As II, 4, 98. *here's the lord of the s.* H6B IV, 10, 26.

4) the ground with respect to its quality and fertility: *such the —'s fertility*, R2 III, 4, 39. *stained with the variation of each s. betwixt Holmedon and this seat*, H4A I, 1, 64. *most subject is the fattest s. to weeds*, H4B IV, 4, 54.

**Soil**, subst. stain, tarnish, blemish: Meas. V, 141. Ado III, 2, 5. LLL II, 47. 48. H4B IV, 5, 190. H8 I, 2, 26. Troil. II, 2, 148. IV, 1, 56 (Ff *soilure*). Caes. I, 2, 42. Hml. I, 3, 15. In Ant. I, 4, 24 some M. Edd. —*s* (a plural not used by Sh.), O. Edd. *foils*.

**Soil**, vb. to stain, to sully: R2 I, 3, 125. IV, 23. Troil. II, 2, 70 (Ff *spoiled*). V, 2, 134 (Q *spoil*). Tim. III, 5, 16. Hml. I, 4, 20. II, 1, 40. In Cymb. II, 3, 126 some M. Edd. *s.*, O. Edd. *foil*.

**Soiled**, high fed with green food (from the Fr. *soûl*): *the fitchew, nor the s. horse, goes to't with a more riotous appetite*, Lr. IV, 6, 124.

**Soilure**, stain, defilement: *not making any scruple of her s.* Troil. IV, 1, 56 (Q *soil*).

**Sojourn**, subst. (*sójourn*) stay, temporary residence: *in our court have made their amorous s.* Lr. I, 1, 48.

**Sojourn**, vb. (*sójourn* and *sojoúrn*) to stay, to dwell for a time: Gent. IV, 1, 20. Mids. III, 2, 171 (*my heart to her but as guest-wise sojourned; to her* the dat. commodi). John I, 103. R3 III, 1, 62. Rom. III, 3, 169. Lr. II, 1, 105. II, 4, 206. Cymb. I, 4, 24.

**Sojourner**, a temporary dweller: *report what a s. we have*, Per. IV, 2, 149.

**Sol**, the sun, in the language of astrologers: *therefore is the glorious planet S. in noble eminence enthroned and sphered amidst the other*, Troil. I, 3, 89.

**Sol**, a note in the gamut: *ut, re, sol, la, mi, fa*, LLL IV, 2, 102. Shr. I, 2, 17. III, 1, 76. Lr. I, 2, 149.

**Sola**, a cry to attract notice: LLL IV, 1, 151.

**Sola**, a cry to attract notice: Merch. V, 39. 41. 42. 44.

**Solace**, subst. 1) comfort: *sorrow would s. and mine age would ease*, H6B II, 3, 21.

2) delight, happiness: *sorrow changed to s.* Pilgr. 203. *with his soul fled all my worldly s.* H6B III, 2, 151. *my hazards still have been your s.* Cor. IV, 1, 28.

**Solace**, vb. 1) tr. to delight, to amuse: *we will with some strange pastime s. them*, LLL IV, 3, 377.

2) to be happy, to take delight: *this sickly land might s. as before*, R3 II, 3, 30. *one thing to rejoice and s. in*, Rom. IV, 5, 47. *to hide me from the radiant sun and s. i' the dungeon by a snuff*, Cymb. I, 6, 86.

**Solder**, to unite and make solid (as metallic substances): *that —est close impossibilities and makest them kiss*, Tim. IV, 3, 388. *as if the world should cleave, and that slain men should s. up the rift*, Ant. III, 4, 32 (O. Edd. *soader* or *sodder*).

**Soldier** (trisyll. at the end of the line in Cor. I, 1, 120 and V, 6, 71) a military man, a warrior: Gent. V, 4, 57. Wiv. II, 1, 12. II, 2, 10. 176. Meas. I, 2, 15.

18. Ado I, 1, 53. 300. II, 3, 20. III, 3, 143. LLL I, 2, 61. IV, 3, 366. V, 1, 113. V, 2, 710. 735. As II, 7, 149. IV, 1, 13. John I, 150. H4A III, 1, 195. H6A I, 1, 70. II, 1, 2. III, 2, 66. IV, 7, 31. H6B I, 1, 186. III, 1, 105. IV, 1, 8. Troil. I, 3, 286. Tim. IV, 3, 416. Ant. II, 2, 108. III, 7, 69. IV, 2, 4 etc. etc. Opposed to captain: Ven. 893. Meas. II, 2, 131. common —s, H6C I, 1, 9. *a private s.* H4B III, 2, 177. Emphatically: Meas. III, 1, 217. III, 2, 155. Merch. I, 2, 124. Hml. III, 1, 159 etc. *sworn my s.* John III, 1, 125. Cor. III, 2, 81. Ant. I, 3, 70. *as God's own s.* John II, 566. H4A I, 1, 20. Mcb. V, 8, 47. *s. to* == firmly and constantly devoted to: *this attempt I am s. to, and will abide it with a prince's courage,* Cymb. III, 4, 186. *nor let pity melt thee, but be a s. to thy purpose,* Per. IV, 1, 8.

**Soldier-breeder,** a woman that brings forth soldiers: H5 V, 2, 219.

**Soldier-like,** fit for a soldier: *a s. phrase,* Wiv. II, 1, 13. H4B III, 2, 83.

**Soldiership,** military character: All's I, 2, 26. III, 6, 89. IV, 3, 300. H4B I, 2, 93. Mcb. V, 4, 16. Oth. I, 1, 27. Ant. II, 1, 34. III, 7, 42.

**Sole,** subst. 1) the bottom of the foot: Ado III, 2, 10.

2) the bottom of a shoe: Gent. II, 3, 19. Merch. IV, 1, 123. Rom. I, 4, 15. II, 4, 68. Caes. I, 1, 15. Hml. II, 2, 234.

**Sole,** adj. 1) alone in its kind, unique: *on the s. Arabian tree,* Phoen. 2. *though it alter not love's s. effect,* Sonn. 36, 7. *the s. inheritor of all perfections that a man may owe, matchless Navarre,* LLL II, 5. *this murder, so s. and so unmatchable,* John IV, 3, 52. *s. singular,* Rom. II, 4, 68 (Ff *sole-singular*). *affecting one s. throne, without assistance,* Cor. IV, 6, 32.

2) alone, with no others beside: *that praise, s. pure, transcends,* Troil. I, 3, 244.

3) only: *the s. drift of my purpose doth extend not a frown further,* Tp. V, 29. *my s. earth's heaven,* Err. III, 2, 64. *s. dominator of Navarre,* LLL I, 1, 222. *s. imperator of trotting 'paritors,* III, 187. *s. possessor of my love,* H6C III, 3, 24. *she shall be s. victress,* R3 IV, 4, 336. *s. monarch of the earth,* Rom. III, 2, 94. *s. sir o' the world,* Ant. V, 2, 120. *his s. child,* All's I, 1, 44. H5 I, 2, 70. H6B II, 2, 50. Hml. III, 3, 77 (Ff *foul*). Cymb. I, 1, 5. 56. 138. Per. IV, 3, 39.

4) alone, without any addition, in itself, mere: *whose s. name blisters our tongues,* Mcb. IV, 3, 12.

**Solely** (O. Edd. sometimes *solie* or *soly*) adj. and adv. 1) alone in one's kind, having no equal, unique: *I think him a great way fool, s. a coward,* All's I, 1, 112. *s. singular,* Rom. II, 4, 69. *which shall to all our nights and days to come give s. sovereign sway and masterdom,* Mcb. I, 5, 71.

2) alone: *leave me s.* Wint. II, 3, 17. *to him had left it s.* Cor. IV, 7, 16. *honour's thought reigns s. in the breast of every man,* H5 II Chor. 4. *not s.* == not alone, not only: *I am not s. led by nice direction of a maiden's eyes,* Merch. II, 1, 13.

3) only: *left s. heir to all his lands,* Shr. II, 118.

**Solemn,** 1) religiously grave and venerable, attended with religious rites, and hence awful, ceremonious, formal in general: *therefore are feasts so s. and so rare,* Sonn. 52, 5. *the s. temples,* Tp. IV, 153. *sing your s. hymn,* Ado V, 3, 11. *our s. festival,* Shr. III, 2, 103. *the s. feast,* All's II, 3, 187. *before the s. priest I have sworn,* 286. *a s. combination of our souls,*

Tw. V, 392. *how ceremonious, s. and unearthly,* Wint. III, 1, 7. *the sad and s. priests,* H5 IV, 1, 318. *our s. hymns,* Rom. IV, 5, 88. *a s. air,* Tp. V, 58. *it hath in s. synods been decreed,* Err. I, 1, 13. *of whom he hath taken a s. leave,* All's IV, 3, 90. *mock not flesh and blood with s. reverence,* R2 III, 2, 172. *here we entertain a s. peace,* H6A V, 4, 175. *a s. vow,* H6B V, 1, 184. 190. H6C I, 4, 100. IV, 3, 4. *a dreadful oath, sworn with a s. tongue,* H6B III, 2, 158. Tit. V, 3, 81. *at thy s. feast,* V, 2, 115. Mcb. III, 1, 14. *a s. hunting is in hand,* Tit. II, 1, 112 (arranged and executed by the emperor and his court). *we'll make a s. wager,* Hml. IV, 7, 156. *with s. march,* I, 2, 201. *in s. show,* Ant. V, 2, 367.

2) grave, serious: *in s. talk,* As II, 4, 21. *with a s. earnestness,* Oth. V, 2, 227.

3) sad, melancholy, sullen: *this s. sympathy poor Venus noteth,* Ven. 1057. *s. night with slow sad gait descended to ugly hell,* Lucr. 1081. *rejoice to hear the s. curfew,* Tp. V, 40. *passion's s. tears,* LLL V, 2, 118. *why do you bend such s. brows on me?* John IV, 2, 90. *in s. shades of endless night,* R2 I, 3, 177. *suits of s. black,* Hml. I, 2, 78. *all s. things should answer s. accidents,* Cymb. IV, 2, 191.

**Solemness,** see *Solemnness.*

**Solemnity,** 1) ceremony performed (especially the celebration of nuptials; cf. *solemn* in Shr. III, 2, 103. All's II, 3, 187. Tw. V, 392. Rom. IV, 5, 88); and hence, festivity: Gent. V, 4, 161. Meas. III, 1, 224. Mids. I, 1, 11. IV, 1, 139. 190. V, 376. John II, 555. Rom. I, 5, 59. 65. IV, 5, 61. Ant. V, 2, 369.

2) awful grandeur, stateliness, dignity: *my state, seldom but sumptuous, showed like a feast and won by rareness such s.* H4A III, 2, 59.

**Solemnize,** to celebrate (a marriage): Tp. V, 309. LLL II, 42. Merch. II, 9, 6. III, 2, 194. As III, 2, 333. John II, 539. III, 1, 77. H6A V, 3, 168.

**Solemnly,** gravely, ceremoniously, formally: Mids. IV, 1, 93. R2 IV, 319. H4A I, 3, 228. H5 V Chor. 14. R3 I, 2, 214. H8 I, 2, 165.

**Solemnness,** gravity, sadness: *turn thy s. out o' door,* Cor. I, 3, 120.

**Solicit,** subst. solicitation: *frame yourself to orderly —s,* Cymb. II, 3, 52 (F1 *solicity;* some M. Edd. *soliciting*).

**Solicit,** vb. 1) to move, to rouse, to stir: *the part I had in Woodstock's blood doth more s. me than your exclaims, to stir against the butchers of his life,* R2 I, 2, 2. *s. Henry with her wondrous praise,* H6A V, 3, 190. *I am —ed, not by a few, that your subjects are in great grievance,* H8 I, 2, 18. *this supernatural —ing cannot be ill,* Mcb. I, 3, 130. *how he —s heaven, himself best knows,* IV, 3, 149. *with the occurrents, more and less, which have —ed,* Hml. V, 2, 369.

2) to make petition; absol.: *a still —ing eye,* Lr. I, 1, 234. *if my tongue did e'er s.* Per. II, 5, 69. *if you bethink yourself of any crime, ... s. for it straight,* Oth. V, 2, 28. Trans. == a) to apply to, to ask: *having —ed the eternal power that his foul thoughts might compass his fair fair,* Lucr. 345. *we heartily s. your gracious self to take on you the charge,* R3 III, 7, 130. Cor. II, 3, 208. Tit. IV, 3, 50. Oth. II, 3, 393. *to s. him for mercy,* Cor. V, 1, 72. Used of making love for lewd purposes: *s. me no more,* Gent. V, 4, 40. *if the prince do s. you in that kind, you know your answer,* Ado II, 1, 70. *how you have been —ed by a gentleman,* All's

III, 5, 16. *the amorous count —s her in the unlawful purpose*, 72. *—est here a lady*, Cymb. I, 6, 147. cf. Per. II, 5, 69.

b) to seek by petition, to ask for: *I had rather hear you to s. that*, Tw. III, 1, 120.

Misapplied by Evans in Wiv. I, 2, 10.

**Solicitation**, illicit courtship: *repent my unlawful s.* Oth. IV, 2, 202.

**Soliciting**, the same: *has his —s all given to mine ear*, Hml. II, 2, 126 (Ff *s.*). cf. Mcb. I, 3, 130 sub *Solicit.*

**Solicitor**, one who petitions for another, attorney, advocate: LLL II, 29. Oth. III, 3, 27.

**Solid**, firm: H4B III, 1, 48. Troil. I, 3, 113. Hml. I, 2, 129. Oth. IV, 1, 277.

**Solidare**, a small piece of money: Tim. III, 1, 46.

**Solidity**, firmness; abstr. pro concr.: *this s. and compound mass*, Hml. III, 4, 49.

**Solinus**, name of the duke in Err. I, 1, 1.

**Solitary**, lonely, destitute of company: Gent. IV, 4, 94. As III, 2, 16.

**Solomon**, see *Salomon.*

**Solon**, the sage who said that no man could be called happy before his death: Tit. I, 177.

**Solus**, Latin for alone, a word which causes much misunderstanding between Nym and Pistol: H5 II, 1, 48. 49. 50. 51. 54.

**Solve**, solution: *why thy odour matcheth not thy show, the s. is this, that thou dost common grow*, Sonn. 69, 14 (O. Edd. *solye*).*

**Soly**, see *Solely.*

**Solyman**, name of a sultan: Merch. II, 1, 26.

**Some**, indef. pron. used to note an indeterminate kind or quantity or number; 1) kind (often almost equivalent to the indef. article): *their light blown out in s. mistrustful wood*, Ven. 826. *her fawn hid in s. brake*, 876. *she hears s. huntsman hollo*, 973. *behind s. hedge*, 1094. *saying, s. shape in Sinon's was abused*, Lucr. 1529. *not a soul ... but played s. tricks of desperation*, Tp. I, 2, 210. *s. god o' the island*, 389. *s. sailor's wife*, II, 1, 4. 5. *this is s. monster of the isle*, II, 2, 67. *s. defect in her*, III, 1, 44. *s. vanity of mine art*, IV, 41. *your father's in s. passion that works him strongly*, 143. *when thou seest s. rare object*, Gent. I, 1, 13. *s. love of yours hath writ to you*, I, 2, 79. *such weeds as may beseem s. well-reputed page*, II, 7, 43. *s. merchant hath invited him*, Err. II, 1, 4. *s. such strange bull*, Ado V, 4, 49. *speak their mind in s. other sort*, LLL V, 2, 589. *I will s. other be, s. Florentine*, Shr. I, 1, 209 etc. etc. (*S. certain*, see *Certain*). With *one: why should the private pleasure of s. one become the public plague of many moe?* Lucr. 1478. *s. one with child by him*, Meas. I, 4, 45. *s. one hath set you on*, V, 112. *s. one among us*, All's IV, 1, 5. *if case s. one of you would fly from us*, H6C V, 4, 34. *s. one take order*, R3 IV, 4, 539. *for s. one to say, Break up the senate*, Caes. II, 2, 97 etc. Alone, substantively, = one, some one: *go s. of you and fetch a looking-glass*, R2 IV, 268. Lr. III, 1, 37. *for reverence to s. alive* (i. e. the mother of Richard), *I give a sparing limit to my tongue*, R3 III, 7, 193. *s. of* = something of, a sample of: *what must we understand by this? S. of my shame*, As IV, 3, 96. *s. of your function, mistress*, Oth. IV, 2, 27. — *S. other where* = somewhere else: Err. II, 1, 30. Rom. I, 1, 204.

2) Quantity: *s. favour, s. remorse*, Ven. 257. *s.*

food, Tp. I, 2, 160. *that you will s. good instruction give*, 424. *you have done yourself s. wrong*, 443. *lack s. gentleness*, II, 1, 137. *'twixt which regions there is s. space*, 257. *I will give him s. relief*, II, 2, 70. *put s. lime upon your fingers*, IV, 246. *s. more test of my metal*, Meas. I, 1, 49. *that is s. good*, Ado IV, 1, 213. *keep s. state in thy exit*, LLL V, 2, 598. *he would make s. speed of his return*, Merch. II, 8, 37. *intend s. fear*, R3 III, 7, 45 etc. etc. Without a subst.: *s. of her blood still red remained, and s. looked black*, Lucr. 1742. *get you s. of this distilled Carduus Benedictus*, Ado III, 4, 73. *take thou s. of it*, Mids. II, 1, 259. Referring to a subst.: *I will pour s.* (wine) *in thy other mouth*, Tp. II, 2, 98. *'tis all engaged, s.* (land) *forfeited and gone*, Tim. II, 2, 155 etc. Substantively, = something: *let not bounty fall where want cries s., but where excess begs all*, Compl. 42. cf. Lr. I, 4, 218. *let me see s. more*, H4A II, 3, 7. *bate me s. and I will pay you s.* H4B V, 5, 131. *you shall hear s.* Cor. IV, 2, 14. *take s.; nay, put out all your hands*, Tim. IV, 2, 27. *how's this? s. more; be sage*, Per. IV, 6, 102.

3) Number; in the sing. = many a: *who had, no doubt, s. noble creature in her*, Tp. I, 2, 7. *and undergoes such assaults as would take in s. virtue*, Cymb. III, 2, 9. Oftener plur.: *bore us s. leagues to sea*, Tp. I, 2, 145. *s. thousands of these logs*, III, 1, 10 etc. *as s. my equals did*, Compl. 148. *I have said to s. my standers by*, Troil. IV, 5, 190 (Ff *unto my standers by*). Without a subst.: Ven. 872. 1102. Tp. II, 1, 251. Err. IV, 3, 4. Ado V, 1, 109. Mids. I, 1, 226 (*other s.*). Wint. III, 3, 20 etc. etc. Before numerals, = about: *s. sixteen months*, Gent. IV, 1, 21. *a dish of s. three pence*, Meas. II, 1, 95. *s. six or seven*, 287. IV, 3, 11. LLL I, 2, 117: V, 2, 50. Mids. V, 61. Merch. IV, 1, 147. Shr. IV, 3, 189 (*s. seven o' clock*). All's I, 2, 71. III, 7, 24. III, 3, 56. Tw. III, 2, 48. Wint. II, 1, 145. H4A II, 2, 67. III, 3, 119. H6C II, 1, 144. V, 1, 10. R3 I, 2, 241. 257 (*s. score or two*). III, 7, 36. Rom. I, 5, 39. III, 4, 27. Lr. I, 2, 5. III, 7, 16. Oth. I, 3, 84 etc. Even before singular substantives of time, = about one, about a: *s. hour hence*, Err. III, 1, 122. Merch. II, 4, 27. *s. half an hour*, LLL V, 2, 90. H8 IV, 1, 66. *s. month or two*, Merch. III, 2, 9. *s. twelvemonth since*, Tw. I, 2, 37. *s. hour before you took me*, II, 1, 22. *s. day or two*, R3 III, 1, 64. *s. minute ere the time of her awaking*, Rom. V, 3, 257. *s. year elder*, Lr. I, 1, 20. V, 3, 193.

**Somebody**, a person undetermined: Wiv. IV, 2, 121. Ado III, 3, 137. Shr. V, 1, 40. H4B V, 4, 14. R3 I, 3, 311. V, 3, 280. Troil. I, 1, 45. Caes. II, 1, 60.

**Somerset**; John and Edmund Beaufort Dukes of S., descendants of John of Gaunt, and famous partisans of Henry VI during the wars of the Roses: H6A II, 4, 6. 37. 68. II, 5, 46. III, 4, 34. IV, 1, 108. IV, 3, 9. 24 etc. H6B I, 1, 69. 167. I, 2, 29 (*Edmund Duke of S.*) etc. H6C I, 1, 18. IV, 1, 27 etc.*

**Somerville**, name in H6C V, 1, 7.

**Something** (*sómething* and *somethíng*). 1) indef. pron.; a certain thing, or a certain quantity: *to the most of praise add s. more*, Sonn. 85, 10. *hold that nothing me a s. sweet to thee*, 136, 12. *s. rich and strange*, Tp. I, 2, 401. III, 3, 94. IV, 126. Wiv. III, 3, 75. IV, 2, 75. Meas. IV, 2, 99. Err II, 2, 52. 55. III, 1, 69. LLL I, 1, 99. IV, 3, 121. Mids. I, 1, 126. V, 26. Merch. III, 2, 4. 183 (*every s.*). III, 5, 86. IV, 1, 305. As I, 1, 18. I, 3, 129. III, 2, 433. All's III, 5,

92 etc. etc. *nothing hath begot my s. grief*, R2 II, 2, 36 (i. e. existing, but of uncertain nature); cf. *this s. settled matter in his heart*, Hml. III, 1, 181 (M. Edd. *something-settled*).

2) adv. in some measure, somewhat, rather, a little: *s. stained*, Tp. I, 2, 414. *I prattle s. too wildly*, III, 1, 58. *my will is s. sorted with his wish*, Gent. I, 3, 63. *s. peevish*, Wiv. I, 4, 14. *hath s. emboldened me*, II, 2, 173. IV, 6, 22. Meas. I, 1, 62. I, 2, 78. II, 4, 119. III, 2, 104. Ado II, 1, 305. LLL IV, 2, 56. Mids. III, 2, 304. IV, 1, 187. Merch. I, 1, 124. 129. II, 2, 18. 194. II, 3, 14 (Ff *somewhat*). As II, 4, 63. III, 2, 359. III, 4, 9. Shr. II, 184. V, 2, 54. All's I, 3, 125. Wint. I, 2, 147. II, 2, 25. 55. IV, 4, 417. V, 1, 142. John II, 396. H4B I, 2, 212 (*with a white head and s. a round belly;* cf. Merch. I, 1, 124 and R3 I, 2, 116). IV, 2, 80. H5 IV, 1, 216. V, 1, 91. H6C II, 2, 166. R3 I, 2, 116 (Qq *somewhat*). Cor. II, 1, 54. Tit. II, 3, 156. Tim. IV, 3, 55. Mcb. III, 1, 132. Hml. I, 3, 121 (Ff *somewhat*). Lr. I, 1, 21. Ant. IV, 8, 20 etc.

**Something-settled,** see *Something* sub 1.

**Sometime** (*sómetime* and *sometíme*) 1) from time to time, now and then (cf. *at some time* in Caes. I, 2, 139): Lucr. 95. 331. 1786. Sonn. 41, 2. 102, 13. Compl. 10. Tp. I, 2, 198. II, 2, 9. 12. III, 2, 147. Meas. II, 1, 14. V, 295. Ado I, 1, 288. II, 3, 158. LLL V, 1, 108. Mids. II, 1, 38. 47. 52. 253 (*there sleeps Titania s. of the night;* M. Edd. *some time*). II, 2, 435 (Qq *sometimes*). Shr. Ind. 2, 11. Tw. V, 123. Wint. I, 2, 254. H4A III, 1, 148. H6B II, 4, 42. IV, 1, 48. Troil. I, 3, 151. Cor. III, 1, 115. Tit. III, 1, 213. Rom. I, 4, 77. 79. Tim. II, 2, 131. Caes. II, 1, 251. Mcb. I, 6, 11. II, 3, 46. IV, 2, 76. Lr. IV, 3, 41. Oth. II, 3, 202 (Ff *sometimes*). Ant. IV, 14, 2. 3. Cymb. II, 3, 77. *s. ... s.* = now ... now: *that s. true news, s. false doth bring*, Ven. 658. Lucr. 1105. LLL III, 14. H6B III, 2, 373. Lr. II, 3, 19. *s... s... s.:* Mids. III, 1, 111. Tim. II, 2, 115. *s... and s.:* Mids. III, 2, 360. Ven. 685.—*s ... s ... s.:* Ado III, 3, 143. *s... anon:* Ven. 277. 301. Compl. 24. *s. all full, and by and by clean starved*, Sonn. 75, 9. *s. too hot the eye of heaven shines, and often is his gold complexion dimmed*, 18, 5. *s. the flood prevails, and then the wind*, H6C II, 5, 9.

2) once: *Herne the hunter, s. a keeper here*, Wiv. IV, 4, 29. *a gentleman which I have s. known*, All's III, 2, 87. *a fond creature, whom s. I have laughed with*, V, 3, 179. *this ancient sir, who ... hath s. loved*, Wint. IV, 4, 373. *Henry the Fifth did s. prophesy, ... he'll make his cap co-equal to the crown*, H6A V, 1, 31. *present to her, as s. Margaret did to thy father, a handkerchief*, R3 IV, 4, 274. *I s. lay here in Corioli*, Cor. I, 9, 82. V, 1, 2. *Belarius whom you s. banished*, Cymb. V, 5, 333. *it was s. target to a king*, Per. II, 1, 143.

3) formerly: *s. lofty towers I see down-razed*, Sonn. 64, 3. *s. a blusterer*, Compl. 58. *I will myself present as I was s. Milan*, Tp. V, 86. *did they not s. cry All hail to me*, R2 IV, 169. *which was s. his general*, Cor. V, 1, 2. *this was s. a paradox, but now the time gives it proof*, Hml. III, 1, 114. *the ruin speaks that s. it was a worthy building*, Cymb. IV, 2, 354. Adjectively, = that was, former, late, whilom: *good s. queen*, R2 V, 1, 37. *my s. general*, Cor. IV, 1, 23. *our s. sister, now our queen*, Hml. I, 2, 8 (Ff *sometimes*). *thou my s. daughter*, Lr. I, 1, 122.

4) at other times, on other occasions (German *sonst*): *that same dew which s. on the buds was wont to swell like round and orient pearls, stood now ... like tears*, Mids. IV, 1, 58. *even with those wings, which s. they have used with fearful flight, make war*, H6C II, 2, 30.

**Sometimes** (*sómetimes* and *sometímes*) 1) from time to time, now and then: Ven. 225. 981. Lucr. 530. Sonn. 50, 10. Tp. II, 2, 175. III, 2, 146. Gent. III, 1, 93. Wiv. I, 1, 283. II, 2, 23. Meas. IV, 5, 5. Err. II, 2, 26. LLL II, 198. IV, 1, 30. Mids. II, 1, 36. III, 2, 435 (Ff *sometime*). Shr. Ind. 2, 91. II, 187. All's IV, 3, 76. V, 1, 11. Tw. I, 3, 88. 121. II, 3, 151. Wint. I, 2, 151. III, 3, 92. IV, 4, 733. R2 V, 5, 32. H4A III, 1, 181. H6B II, 4, 1. R3 IV, 4, 292. H8 IV, 1, 55. Troil. IV, 4, 97. Cor. V, 2, 19. Rom. II, 3, 22. II, 4, 216. Caes. II, 1, 285. Hml. II, 2, 160. 212. V, 2, 8. Lr. I, 4, 202. Oth. I, 2, 4. II, 3, 241. III, 3, 138. 434. Ant. I, 1, 57. II, 3, 1. Cymb. IV, 2, 302. *s... s.* = now ... now: Wiv. I, 3, 68. *s... and s.:* As V, 4, 3. H5 III, 6, 110. *s... sometime:* Compl. 22. Ado III, 3, 142. *s... and then:* Ven. 223. *s. her head on one side, some another*, Wint. III, 3, 20.

2) once: *s. from her eyes I did receive fair speechless messages*, Merch. I, 1, 163.

3) formerly: *the dowager, s. our brother's wife*, H8 II, 4, 181. *in which the majesty of buried Denmark did s. march*, Hml. I, 1, 49. Adjectively: *thy s. brother's wife*, R2 I, 2, 54. *my s. royal master*, V, 5, 75. *our s. sister*, Hml. I, 2, 8 (Qq *sometime*). *yon s. famous princes*, Per. I, 1, 34.

**Somever,** soever: Hml. III, 2, 416 (Q6 and M. Edd. *soever*).

**Somewhat,** 1) pron. something: *here is a letter will say s.* Wiv. IV, 5, 128. *this gentleman told s. of my tale*, Meas. V, 84 (later Ff *something*). *s. we must do*, R2 II, 2, 116. *an old man can do s.* H4B V, 3, 83. *s. we will do*, R3 III, 1, 193 (Ff *something*). *s. doth she mean*, Tit. IV, 1, 9. *thou givest me s. to repair myself*, Per. II, 1, 128.

2) adv. in some measure, rather, a little: Gent. V, 2, 6. Meas. V, 89. Merch. II, 3, 14 (Qq *something*). Shr. IV, 2, 100. All's V, 2, 2. R2 I, 4, 44. H6A V, 2, 14. R3 I, 2, 116 and III, 5, 55 (Ff *something*). H8 III, 2, 394. V, 4, 41. Troil. I, 1, 41. Tit. II, 2, 15. Hml. I, 3, 121 (Qq *something*).

**Somewhere,** 1) in some place or other: *s. else*, Tw. IV, 1, 10 and Tit. IV, 3, 40. Severed: *some other where*, Err. II, 1, 30. Rom. I, 1, 204.

2) to some place or other: *he's s. gone to dinner*, Err. II, 1, 5.

**Somewhither,** to some place or other: Tit. IV, 1, 11.

**Somme,** a river in France: H5 III, 5, 1.

**Son,** male child: Ven. 201. 754. 766. 863. 1160. Tp. I, 2, 120. 212. 221. 282. 284. 438. II, 1, 91 etc. etc. *s. to:* As I, 2, 236. Shr. II, 104. V, 1, 118. Wint. V, 3, 150. H4A II, 4, 448. H6A II, 4, 84. V, 5, 73 etc. *the s. to Lewis*, H5 I, 2, 75. H6A II, 5, 75. *my s. of York* (= my son York) R3 II, 4, 6. IV, 1, 14. *my s. of Gloster*, H4B IV, 4, 12. *our s. of Cornwall*, Lr. I, 1, 42. 43. *like my lady's eldest son, evermore tattling*, Ado II, 1, 11. *that would hang us, every mother's s.* Mids. I, 2, 80 (cf. *there lives a s. that sucked an earthly mother*, Ven. 863). *mothers' —s*, R2 III, 3, 96. *should have fewer words than a parrot, and yet the s. of a* *woman*, H4A II, 4, 111. *we are the —s of women* (i. e. frail men) Wiv. II, 3, 51. *by my mother's s., and that's myself*, Shr. IV, 5, 6. = son in law: Wiv. III, 4, 79. V, 2, 3. V, 5, 188. Ado II, 1, 374. IV, 1, 27. Shr. V, 2, 13 etc. = descendant, or issue of any kind: *Adam's —s are my brethren*, Ado II, 1, 66. *the —s and children of this isle*, John V, 2, 25. *the —s of Troy*, Troil. Prol. 19. *—s of Rome*, Tit. V, 3, 67. Caes. I, 2, 173. *all thy* (earth's) *human —s*, Tim. IV, 3, 185. *they are villains and the —s of darkness*, H4A II, 4, 191. III, 3, 42. *this Hydra s. of war*, H4B IV, 2, 38 (i. e. war, the son of Hydra; cf. *Of*). *thou art sealed the s. of chivalry*, H6A IV, 6, 29. *O war, thou s. of hell*, H6B V, 2, 33. R3 I, 3, 230. *like the eldest s. of fortune*, H8 II, 2, 21. *emulation hath a thousand —s*, Troil. III, 3, 156. *all you have done hath been but for a wayward s.* Mcb. III, 5, 11 (i. e. a son of hell). Used as a tender appellation given to a younger man: Meas. III, 1, 161. Cor. V, 2, 68 etc. Quibbling on *sun:* Ven. 863. LLL V, 2, 168. 171. John II, 499. H4A II, 4, 135. 451. H4B III, 2, 139. H6C II, 1, 40. R3 I, 3, 267. Rom. III, 5, 127.

**Sonance**, sound, tune: *let the trumpets sound the tucket s.* H5 IV, 2, 35.

**Song,** 1) music made by modulations of the voice: Sonn. 8, 13. Gent. I, 2, 95. Wiv. IV, 4, 54. Ado I, 1, 188. Wint. IV, 3, 11.

2) a lay, a strain, a poem sung or to be sung: Ven. 777. 841. 974. Sonn. 17, 12. 100, 3. 102, 14. 105, 3. Pilgr. 226. Gent. I, 2, 88. Wiv. I, 1, 206. Meas. IV, 1, 7. Err. III, 2, 169. Ado II, 3, 45. 77. V, 3, 14. LLL V, 2, 405. 941. Mids. II, 1, 152. II, 2, 1. III, 2, 206. V, 404. As I, 5, 13. 32. II, 7, 4. III, 2, 261. IV, 2, 6. V, 3, 9. 41. All's I, 3, 85. 87. III, 2, 10. III, 7, 40. Tw. II, 3, 31. 33. 36 (*a s. of good life*). II, 4, 2. 3. 43. Wint. IV, 4, 58. 191. 315. 618. 625. H4A III, 1, 216. 250. III, 3, 16. H4B II, 4, 299. R3 IV, 4, 509 (*nothing but —s of death*). H8 I, 3, 41. V, 5, 36. Troil. III, 1, 115. 119. Tit. II, 3, 28. Hml. I, 3, 30. IV, 5, 27. V, 1, 209. Lr. I, 4, 186. Oth. II, 3, 77. 101. IV, 3, 28. 30. V, 2, 246. Cymb. IV, 2, 254 (*we'll say our s. the whilst*). Per. Prol. 1.

**Song-men,** singers: *three-man s.*, Wint. IV, 3, 45 (singers of songs in three parts. The clown's speech).

**Son-in-law,** a man married to one's daughter: Ado V, 1, 296. Shr. III, 2, 3. All's V, 3, 148. Wint. V, 2, 57. V, 3, 149. H4A II, 4, 375. H6B IV, 7, 117. H8 I, 2, 136. Tit. I, 311. Rom. IV, 5, 38. Lr. IV, 6, 190. Oth. I, 3, 291. Cymb. V, 5, 421.

**Sonnet,** a short poem made in praise of somebody or of something: *deep-brained —s that did amplify each stone's dear nature*, Compl. 209. *to tangle her desires by wailful —s, whose composed rhymes should be full-fraught with serviceable vows*, Gent. III, 2, 69. *I have a s. that will serve the turn*, 93. *my book of songs and —s*, Wiv. I, 1, 206. *will you then write me a s. in praise of my beauty?* Ado V, 2, 4. *a halting s. ... fashioned to Beatrice*, V, 4, 87. *she hath one of my —s already*, LLL IV, 3, 16. *did never s. for her sake compile*, 134. *the s. you writ to Diana in behalf of the Count Rousillon*, All's IV, 3, 355. *it is with me as the very true s. is, Please one, and please all*, Tw. III, 4, 25. *I once writ a s. in his praise*, H5 III, 7, 42. *I have heard a s. begin so to one's mistress*, 44. The Spaniard Armado, feeling disposed to fill '*whole volumes in folio*' with hymns of praise on his mistress, says: *I am sure I shall turn s.* LLL I, 2, 190 (all love and poetry from top to toe. M. Edd. *sonneteer, sonnetist, sonnetmaker;* but cf. *now is he turned orthography*, Ado II, 3, 21).

**Sonneting**, composing of sonnets: LLL IV, 3, 158.

**Sonties:** *by God's s.*, old Gobbo's oath in Merch. II, 2, 47, a corruption probably from *santé* or sanctity.

**Soon,** 1) shortly, early, quickly, before long: *s. she stops his lips*, Ven. 46. *which the hot tyrant stains and s. bereaves*, 797. Lucr. 23. Sonn. 120, 11. Pilgr. 205. Tp. II, 1, 191. Gent. I, 3, 72. II, 2, 4. III, 1, 390. Wiv. II, 2, 327. Meas. III, 1, 32. Err. I, 1, 49. 61. I, 2, 103. II, 1, 99. LLL II, 112. Merch. I, 2, 9. Tw. III, 1, 159 (*more s.*, in rhyming). H6A V, 1, 15. H6B I, 4, 17 (*the —er the better*). Troil. II, 1, 18. Rom. V, 1, 60 (M. Edd. *soon-speeding*) etc. *no —er ... but:* Sonn. 129, 5. Gent. IV, 4, 9. As V, 2, 36. H4A I, 2, 193. H5 I, 1, 25 (*but that*). V, 2, 257. H6B IV, 9, 3. Mcb. I, 2, 29. V, 8, 41. Hml. IV, 1, 29 etc. *so s. as:* Wiv. IV, 5, 68. Tw. III, 4, 195 (cf. *So*). *so s. was she along as he was down*, Ven. 43. *all so s. as:* Rom. I, 1, 140.

2) easily, readily, likely: *small lights are s. blown out*, Lucr. 647. *thou wouldst as s. go kindle fire with snow as seek to quench the fire of love with words*, Gent. II, 7, 19. *you are already love's firm votary and cannot s. revolt*, III, 2, 59. *if any man may, you may as s. as any*, Wiv. II, 2, 246. *let us withdraw together, and we may s. our satisfaction have touching that point*, Meas. I, 1, 83. *if you handled her privately, she would —er confess*, V, 277. *lest that your goods too s. be confiscate*, Err. I, 2, 2. *the plainer dealer, the —er lost*, II, 2, 89. *you sent me for a rope's end as s.* IV, 1, 98. *devils —est tempt, resembling spirits of light*, LLL IV, 3, 257. Mids. III, 2, 52. As I, 3, 112. III, 2, 61. Shr. II, 146. All's I, 3, 40. R2 I, 1, 101 (M. Edd. *soon-believing*). H5 II, 2, 34. H6A V, 5, 47. H6B IV, 1, 127. H6C IV, 7, 62. R3 III, 4, 9. Troil. II, 1, 17. 18. Rom. I, 1, 213. Caes. I, 2, 201. Hml. III, 1, 112. Ant. III, 13, 24. Cymb. IV, 2, 385. Per. IV, 1, 3 etc.

3) *s. at night* = this very night, so early as to-day in the evening: *we'll have a posset for 't s. at night*, Wiv. I, 4, 8. *come to me s. at night*, II, 2, 295. 298. *s. at night I'll send him certain word of my success*, Meas. I, 4, 88. *I shall be sent for s. at night*, H4B V, 5, 96. *you shall bear the burden s. at night*, Rom. II, 5, 78. *say if I shall see you s. at night*, Oth. III, 4, 198. Similarly: *s. at five o' clock I'll meet with you*, Err. I, 2, 26. *and s. at supper-time I'll visit you*, III, 2, 179. *s. at supper shalt thou see Lorenzo*, Merch. II, 3, 5. *come to me s. at after supper*, R3 IV, 3, 31 (Ff s., *and after supper*).

Superl. *—est* adjectively: *the gentler gamester is the —est winner*, H5 III, 6, 120. *make your —est haste*, Ant. III, 4, 27.

**Soon-believing** and **Soon-speeding**, see sub *Soon.*

**Soopstake**, see *Swoopstake.*

**Sooth,** 1) truth: *understand you this of me in s.* Shr. I, 2, 259. *it is silly s.* Tw. II, 4, 47. *he looks like s.* Wint. IV, 4, 171. *if I say s.* Mcb. I, 2, 36. *if thy speech be s.* V, 5, 40. *to say the s.* H5 III, 6, 151. *to say s.* H8 II, 3, 30. *s. to say*, Err. IV, 4, 72. Shr. IV, 2, 99. Oftenest used in asseverations: *in s.:* Wiv. III, 4, 110. LLL V, 2, 586 (Qq *faith*). Merch. I, 1, 1. Shr. II, 242. All's V, 2, 47 (*was I, in s.?* = indeed).

Tw. II, 3, 22. John I, 123. IV, 1, 29. H4A II, 3, 82 (Qq *in faith*). III, 1, 259. Troil. III, 1, 59. Oth. III, 4, 97. *in good s.:* Tp. II, 2, 151. Meas. III, 2, 108. As III, 2, 410. John IV, 1, 106. H4A III, 1, 251. 252. 254. Troil. III, 1, 59. Lr. II, 2, 111 (Qq). *s., without in:* Mids. III, 2, 265. Tw. II, 1, 11. II, 4, 91. Wint. IV, 4, 357. Caes. II, 4, 20. Oth. III, 3, 52. Ant. IV, 4, 8. *good s.:* Mids. II, 2, 129. Merch. II, 6, 42. Shr. III, 2, 118. Wint. IV, 4, 160. H4B II, 4, 40 (Q *faith*). Troil. II, 1, 119. Per. I, 1, 86. IV, 1, 89. *very s.:* Wint. I, 2, 17.

2) saying Yes to what another says, officious assentation, cajoling: *O God! that e'er this tongue of mine, that laid the sentence of dread banishment on yon proud man, should take it off again with words of s.* R2 III, 3, 136. *when Signior S. here does proclaim a peace, he flatters you,* Per. I, 2, 44.

**Soothe,** 1) to humour (properly to say Yes to what another says): *shrill-tongued tapsters answering every call, —ing the humour of fantastic wits,* Ven. 850. *is't good to s. him in these contraries? It is no shame: the fellow finds his vein and yielding to him humours well his frenzy,* Err. IV, 4, 82. *has your king married the Lady Grey? and now, to s. your forgery and his, sends me a paper to persuade me patience?* H6C III, 3, 175 (to enter into the humour of, to act in conformity with, your forgery).* *what doth she say, my Lord of Buckingham? Nothing that I respect, my gracious lord. What, dost thou scorn me for my gentle counsel, and s. the devil that I warn thee from?* R3 I, 3, 298. *I say again, in —ing them, we nourish 'gainst our senate the cockle of rebellion,* Cor. III, 1, 69. *good my Lord, s. him; let him take the fellow,* Lr. III, 4, 182.

2) to cajole, to flatter: *love's best habit is a —ing tongue,* Pilgr. 11. *thou art perjured too, and —st up greatness,* John III, 1, 121. *my tongue could never learn sweet —ing words,* R3 I, 2, 169 (Ff *smoothing*). *let courts and cities be made all of false-faced —ing,* Cor. I, 9, 44. *you —ed not, therefore hurt not,* II, 2, 77.

**Soother,** flatterer: *I do defy the tongues of —s,* H4A IV, 1, 7.

**Soothsay,** to foretell, to predict: Ant. I, 2, 52.

**Soothsayer,** one who foretells future events: Caes. I, 2, 19. Ant. I, 2, 3. 6. Cymb. V, 5, 426.

**Sooty,** black like soot: *to the s. bosom of such a thing as thou,* Oth. I, 2, 70.

**Sop,** any thing steeped and softened in liquor: *quaffed off the muscadel and threw the —s all in the sexton's face,* Shr. III, 2, 175. 178 ("at weddings, cakes, wafers, and the like, were blessed, and put into the sweet wine, which was always presented to the bride oh those occasions". Nares). *we will chop him in the malmsey-butt. O excellent device! make a s. of him,* R3 I, 4, 162. *the waters should lift their bosoms higher than the shores and make a s. of all this solid globe,* Troil. I, 3, 113. *I'll make a s. o' the moonshine of you,* Lr. II, 2, 35 (an allusion to the old dish of eggs in moonshine. Douce).

**Sophister,** a captious and fallacious reasoner, a prevaricator: *a subtle traitor needs no s.* H6B V, 1, 191.

**Sophisticated,** adulterated: *here's three on's are s.* Lr. III, 4, 110.

**Sophy,** the Shah of Persia: Merch. II, 1, 25. Tw. II, 5, 197. III, 4, 307.

**Sorcerer,** magician: Tp. III, 2, 49. Err. I, 2, 99. IV, 3, 11 (*Lapland —s*). H6A I, 1, 26.

**Sorceress,** a female magician: Err. IV, 3. 67. H6A III, 2, 38. V, 4, 1.

**Sorcery,** magic, witchcraft: Tp. III, 2, 60. H6A II, 1, 15. Plur. —*es:* Tp. I, 2, 264.

**Sore,** subst. any thing painful in the surface of the body, a wound as well as an ulcer: *'gainst venomed —s the only sovereign plaster,* Ven. 916 (= wounds). *O unfelt s.! crest-wounding private scar,* Lucr. 828. *here was the s.* Pilgr. 128 (= wound). *you rub the s.,* *when you should bring the plaster,* Tp. II, 1, 138. *to strange —s strangely they strain the cure,* Ado IV, 1, 254. As II, 7, 67. John V, 2, 12. R2 I, 3, 303. H4A IV, 2, 29. H6C IV, 6, 88. Troil. III, 1, 130. Cor. III, 1, 235. Tim. IV, 3, 7. 39. Oth. IV, 2, 49. cf. *Plaguesore.*

**Sore,** subst. a buck of the fourth year: LLL IV, 2, 59. 60.

**Sore,** adj. 1) feeling or causing pain: *his wounds will not be s.* Lucr. 1568. *now made s. with shooting,* LLL IV, 2, 59. *a s. eye,* Troil. V, 1, 36. *my arm is s.* Ant. II, 5, 4. *the s. eyes see clear,* Per. I, 1, 99 (blinded by dust). Quibbling: Tp. V, 288. Err. III, 1, 65. H6B IV, 7, 9.

2) grievous, heavy, evil: *upon a s. injunction,* Tp. III, 1, 11. *you'ld be king o' the isle, sirrah? I should have been a s. one then,* V, 288. *if you went in pain, master, this 'knave' would go s.* Err. III, 1, 65. *a woe, a s. complaint against him,* H5 I, 2, 26. *'twill be s. law,* H6B IV, 7, 9 (quibbling). *this s. agony,* R3 I, 4, 42. *s. blows,* Cor. II, 1, 268. *s. labour's bath,* Mcb. II, 2, 38. *this s. night,* II, 4, 3. *s. task,* Hml. I, 1, 75. *your water is a s. decayer of your whoreson dead body,* V, 1, 188. *punished with s. distraction,* V, 2, 241. *though the conflict be s.* Lr. III, 5, 24. *to lapse in fulness is —r than to lie for need,* Cymb. III, 6, 13. *out, sword, and to a s. purpose,* IV, 1, 25. *the s. terms we stand upon with the gods,* Per. IV, 2, 37.

**Sore,** adv. grievously, violently: *one s. sick,* Ven. 702. John V, 4, 6. H4B IV, 3, 83. *her senses s. dismayed,* Ven. 896 (the earlier Qq *all dismayed*). *I'll fear no other thing so s.* Merch. V, 307. *your sorrow was too s. laid on,* Wint. V, 3, 49. *we see the wind sit s. upon our sails,* R2 II, 1, 265. *his soul shall stand s. charged,* H5 I, 2, 283. *s. hurt and bruised,* Troil. V, 5, 14. *so s. enpierced with his shaft,* Rom. I, 4, 19. *O bill, s. shaming those rich-left heirs,* Cymb. IV, 2, 225.

**Sorel,** a buck of the third year: LLL IV, 2, 60 sq.

**Sorely,** grievously, violently: *this drum sticks s. in your disposition,* All's III, 6, 47. *thou strikest me s., to say I did,* Wint. V, 1, 18. *as a man s. tainted,* H8 IV, 2, 14. *the heart is s. charged,* Mcb. V, 1, 60. *the bleak winds do s. ruffle,* Lr. II, 4, 304. *I do accuse myself so s.* Ant. IV, 6, 19.

**Sorrow,** subst. sadness, grief: Ven. 455. 481. 583. 671. 963. 964. 970. Lucr. 186. 991. 1221. 1458. Compl. 7. Tp. II, 1, 9. 195. V, 14. 214. Gent. IV, 4, 152. 177. Meas. II, 3, 32 (*towards*). Err. I, 1, 36. Ado I, 1, 102. V, 1, 16. LLL I, 1, 317. IV, 3, 4. Mids. III, 2, 84. 435. Wint. V, 1, 2 (*performed a saint-like s.*). H6B I, 1, 183. H6C I, 1, 128. I, 4, 171. Tit. III, 1, 119 (*to make*). Hml. I, 2, 92 (*to do*) etc. etc. Plur. —*s:* Gent. III, 1, 20. IV, 3, 33. Err. V, 54. As I, 3, 106. John IV, 2, 102. H6C III, 3, 22. R3 I, 2, 166. Ant. IV, 14, 136 etc. Used of the torments of love (cf. Ven. 1136): Ven. 333. Gent. II, 4, 135. = a state of being sorry, of repenting or pitying sth.: *if hearty* *s. be a sufficient ransom for offence*, Gent. V, 4, 74. *your s. hath eaten up my sufferance*, Wiv. IV, 2, 1. *I am sorry ... I am sorry that such s. I procure*, Meas. V, 479. *I am sorry for thee, gentle Silvius. Wherever s. is, relief would be*, As III, 5, 87. 88. *that nor my service past, nor present —s ... can ransom me*, Oth. III, 4, 116. In Cymb. V, 5, 297 Fl *I am s. for thee*, the later Ff and M. Edd. *sorry*, but cf. Abbott's Shakespearian Grammar p. 153.

**Sorrow**, vb. to be sad, to grieve: Pilgr. 398. 425. Wint. V, 2, 99. Per. IV, 1, 24. With *at:* As III, 5, 87 (= to be sorry for). Ant. IV, 15, 52. With *for:* Err. I, 1, 107. 122. H6A II, 5, 111.

**Sorrowed**, adj. sorrowful, regretful: *to make their s. render*, Tim. V, 1, 152.

**Sorrowful**, sad, full of grief: Tit. III, 1, 147. IV, 2, 67. V, 3, 142. 154. Ant. I, 3, 64.

**Sorrow-wreathen**, folded in grief: *unknit that s. knot*, Tit. III, 2, 4 (arms folded in grief).

**Sorry**, 1) sore, painful: *a salt and s. rheum*, Oth. III, 4, 51 (Qq *sullen*).

2) sorrowful, sad: *burnt the shining glory of Ilion, that the skies were s.* Lucr. 1524. *make glad and s. seasons as thou fleets*, Sonn. 19, 5. *the place of death and s. execution*, Err. V, 121. *I never wished to see you s.* Wint. II, 1, 123. *I am but s., not afeard*, IV, 4, 474. *a s. breakfast for my lord protector*, H6B I, 4, 79. *glad or s. as I saw it inclined*, H8 II, 4, 26. *this is a s. sight*, Mcb. II, 2, 21. *of —est fancies your companions making*, III, 2, 9. *is't enough I am s.?* Cymb. V, 4, 11.

3) Used as an expression of any regret: H4B V, 2, 32 (*—er*). Tim. I, 2, 17. Oth. V, 2, 289. With *for: I am s. for her*, Ado II, 3, 172. 206. *I am s. for thy much misgovernment*, IV, 1, 100. *I am s. for my cousin*, 275. V, 1, 103. Merch. IV, 1, 3. As III, 5, 86. Lr. II, 2, 159. Cymb. V, 5, 297 (Fl *sorrow*). *are s. for our pains*, All's III, 2, 66. *I am so s. for my trespass made*, H6C V, 1, 92. Tit. V, 1, 123. Tim. V, 1, 142. Caes. IV, 3, 64. 65. Oth. III, 1, 44. *I am s. for't*, Wint. III, 2, 219. H6B IV, 2, 102. H8 II, 1, 9. Oth. I, 3, 73. Cymb. IV, 2, 93. V, 5, 270 etc. Followed by an inf.: *s. I am to hear what I have heard*, H6B II, 1, 193. H8 I, 1, 193. 204. Oth. III, 3, 344. V, 1, 81. Ant. I, 3, 14. III, 13, 135 etc. By a clause; in the indic.: Tp. III, 2, 119. Gent. V, 4, 69. Wiv. III, 5, 125. Meas. V, 479. Err. V, 1. 43. Ado IV, 1, 89. LLL V, 2, 726. Merch. II, 3, 1. IV, 1, 405. H5 III, 5, 56. H6A II, 3, 71. H8 I, 2, 109. Tim. III, 6, 17 etc. With *should: I am s. one so learned should slip so grossly*, Meas. V, 475. H4B I, 1, 105. R3 III, 7, 88. H8 III, 1, 51. *who I would be s. should be thus foolishly lost*, Meas. I, 2, 195. *I would be s. but the fool should be as oft with your master*, Tw. III, 1, 45. *I would be s. but it should be thus*, H4B IV, 3, 33 (= if it were not thus). With *if: he is much s., if any thing more than your pleasure did move your greatness to call upon him*, Troil. II, 3, 116.

**Sort**, subst. 1) kind, species: *all —s of deer are chased*, Wiv. V, 5, 252. *none of noble s. would so offend a virgin*, Mids. III, 2, 159. *we are spirits of another s.* 388. *there are a s. of men whose visages do cream ...*, Merch. I, 1, 88. *with musics of all —s*, All's III, 7, 40. *I can sing and speak to him in many —s of music*, Tw. I, 2, 58. *men of all —s take a pride to gird at me*, H4B I, 2, 7. *spirits of vile s.* V, 2, 18. *they have a king and officers of —s*, H5 I, 2, 190 (= of different

kinds; cf. what follows). *subdues all —s of hearts*, Tim. I, 1, 58. *I have bought golden opinions from all —s of people*, Mcb. I, 7, 33. *larded with many several —s of reasons*, Hml. V, 2, 20.

2) order, class of people: *of all —s enchantingly beloved*, As I, 1, 174. *the better s., as thoughts of things divine*, R2 V, 5, 11. *choked with ambition of the meaner s.* H6A II, 5, 123. *talk like the vulgar s. of market men*, III, 2, 4. *discharge the common s. with pay and thanks*, H6C V, 5, 87. *that the weaker s. may wish good Marcius home again*, Cor. IV, 6, 69. *with voices and applause of every s., Patricians and Plebeians*, Tit. I, 230. *assemble all the poor men of your s.* Caes. I, 1, 62. *it is common for the younger s. to lack discretion*, Hml. II, 1, 116. *other —s offend as well as we*, Per. IV, 2, 40. *the people, especially of the younger s.* 105.

3) rank, quality: *give notice to such men of s. and suit as are to meet him*, Meas. IV, 4, 19. *few of any s., and none of name*, Ado I, 1, 7. *there was none such in the army of any s.* 33. *a gentleman of great s.* H5 IV, 7, 142. *what prisoners of good s. are taken?* IV, 8, 80.

4) set, company (in a bad sense): *the shallowest thick-skin of that barren s.* Mids. III, 2, 13. *a s. of traitors*, R2 IV, 246. *a s. of naughty persons*, H6B II, 1, 167. *sent from a s. of tinkers to the king*, III, 2, 277. *any he the proudest of thy s.* H6C II, 2, 97. *a s. of vagabonds*, R3 V, 3, 316. Peculiar expression: *russet-pated choughs, many in s.* Mids. III, 2, 21 (= many consorted or assembled).

5) manner, way (always preceded by prepositions; Tp. II, 1, 104 no exception; usually *in*, once *by*): *I love thee in such s. as ... mine is thy good report*, Sonn. 36, 13 and 96, 13. *you do look in a moved s.* Tp. IV, 146. *I defy all angels, in any such s., as they say, but in the way of honesty*, Wiv. II, 2, 74. *will speak their mind in some other s.* LLL V, 2, 590. *unless you may be won by some other s. than your father's imposition*, Merch. I, 2, 113. *to teach you gamut in a briefer s.* Shr. III, 1, 67. *in a more fairer s.* H4B IV, 5, 201. *the mayor and all his brethren, in best s.* H5 V Chor. 25. *not furnished in his s.* H6A IV, 1, 39. *let's on our way in silent s.* H6C IV, 2, 28. *love in such a s.* Troil. IV, 1, 23. *in beastly s.* V, 10, 5. *express yourself in a more comfortable s.* Cor. I, 3, 2. *I'll deceive you in another s.* Tit. III, 1, 191. *smiles in such a s.* Caes. I, 2, 205. *am I yourself but, as it were, in s. or limitation?* II, 1, 283 (in a certain manner and with restrictions). *in some s.:* Wiv. I, 1, 106. Meas. III, 2, 29. Wint. IV, 4, 844. H4A I, 2, 77. H5 II, 3, 39. Cor. IV, 5, 242. Tit. III, 1, 39. Tim. II, 2, 190. IV, 3, 76. *in a s.:* Tp. II, 1, 103. Troil. V, 4, 37.

**Sort**, subst. lot: *let Ajax draw the s. to fight with Hector*, Troil. I, 3, 376.

**Sort**, vb. 1) trans. a) to order and put together or asunder with respect to kind and quality: *to s. our nobles from our common men*, H5 IV, 7, 77. Hence = to join, to associate: *—ed and consorted ... with a wench*, LLL I, 1, 261. *'occupy', which was an excellent good word before it was ill —ed*, H4B II, 4, 162. *I will not s. you with the rest of my servants*, Hml. II, 2, 274.

b) to choose with respect to fitness: *to s. some gentlemen well skilled in music*, Gent. III, 2, 92. *I'll s. some other time to visit you*, H6A II, 3, 27. *to help me s. such needful ornaments as you think fit to furnish me to-morrow,* Rom. IV, 2, 34.

c) to find out, to contrive: *when wilt thou s. an hour great strifes to end?* Lucr. 899. *all my pains is —ed to no proof,* Shr. IV, 3, 43. *I will s. a pitchy day for thee,* H6C V, 6, 85. *I'll s. occasion to part the queen's kindred from the king,* R3 II, 2, 148. With *out: hath —ed out a sudden day of joy,* Rom. III, 5, 110.

d) to ordain, to dispose: *but God s. all!* Merch. V, 132. *all may be well; but, if God s. it so, 'tis more than we deserve,* R3 II, 3, 36.

e) to adapt, to fit, to make conformable; with *to: and —s a sad look to her lady's sorrow,* Lucr. 1221. *s. thy heart to patience,* H6B II, 4, 68. With *with: my will is something —ed with his wish,* Gent. I, 3, 63.

2) intr. a) to associate, to consort: *and sometime —eth with a herd of deer,* Ven. 689.

b) to be fit: *why then it —s, brave warriors, let's away,* H6C II, 1, 209. *this woman's answer —s,* Troil. I, 1, 109. *to s. with* = to be in accordance with: *not —ing with a nuptial ceremony,* Mids. V, 55. *it —s well with your fiercenesss,* H5 IV, 1, 63. *his currish riddles s. not with this place,* H6C V, 5, 26.

c) to fall out, to have an issue: *if it s. not well, you may conceal her,* Ado IV, 1, 242. *I am glad that all things s. so well,* V, 4, 7. *so far am I glad it so did s.* Mids. III, 2, 352. *s. how it will, I shall have gold for all,* H6B I, 2, 107. *well may it s. that this portentous figure comes armed through our watch,* Hml. I, 1, 109 (or = it may be in accordance with your supposition?).

**Sortance,** suitableness, agreement: *with such powers as might hold s. with his quality,* H4B IV, 1, 11.

**Sossius,** name in Ant. III, 1, 17.

**Sot,** dolt, blockhead: Tp. III, 2, 101. Wiv. III, 1, 119. Err. II, 2, 196. Tw. I, 5, 129. V, 202. Lr. IV, 2, 8. Cymb. V, 5, 178. cf. *Besotted.*

**Soto,** name in Shr. Ind. 1, 88.

**Sottish,** stupid: Ant. IV, 15, 79.

**Soud,** a word imitative of a noise made by a person heated and fatigued: Shr. IV, 1, 145.

**Soul*** (sometimes fem.: Lucr. 719. 1169. John III, 3, 21. R2 II, 2, 64. H6C II, 1, 74. II, 6, 42. R3 III, 5, 27. Hml. II, 2, 579. III, 2, 68. cf. on the other hand: R2 V, 5, 6) the immaterial part of man (and of beasts, when considered as governed by human affections: Merch. IV, 1, 132. 135), the immortal spirit which inhabits the body and is the cause of life and sense: *a knife, that thence her s. unsheathed,* Lucr. 1724. *poor s., the centre of my sinful earth,* Sonn. 146, 1. 9. *body and s.* Ado III, 3, 3. IV, 1, 250. *within this wall of flesh there is a s. counts thee her creditor,* John III, 3, 21. *sluiced out his innocent s.* R2 I, 1, 103. *my —'s palace is become a prison: ah, would she break from hence,* H6C II, 1, 74. *whose s. is that which takes her heavy leave?* II, 6, 42. *if thy s. check thee that I come so near,* Sonn. 136, 1. *lending credent s. to that strong-bonded oath,* Compl 279. *the prophetic s. of the wide world dreaming on things to come,* Sonn. 107, 1. *it goes on, as my s. prompts it,* Tp. I, 2, 420. *his looks are my —'s food,* Gent. II, 7, 15. *to qualify the laws, as to your s. seems good,* Meas. I, 1, 67. *men indued with intellectual sense and —s,* Err. II, 1, 22. *now is his s. ravished! is it not strange that sheeps' guts should hale —s out of men's bodies,* Ado II, 3, 60. 62 (cf. Tw. II, 3, 61). *will you with free and unconstrained s. give me this maid?* IV, 1, 25. *come into the eye and prospect*

*of his s.* 231. *as sure as I have a thought or a s.* 334. *my soul doth tell me Hero is belied,* V, 1, 42. *entreat out of a new-sad s.* LLL V, 2, 741. *whose yoke my s. consents not to give sovereignity,* Mids. I, 1, 82. *made love to Helena and won her s.* 108. *by that which knitteth —s,* 172. *you must join in —s to mock me too,* III, 2, 150 (cf. *do in consent shake hands to torture me,* Sonn. 28, 6). *deny your love, so rich within his s.* 229. *shall she be placed in my constant s.* Merch. II, 6, 57. *with an unquiet s.* III, 2, 308. *not on thy sole, but on thy s. thou makest thy knife keen,* Merch. IV, 1, 123 (the same quibble in II, 4, 68 and Caes. I, 1, 15). *and all those swearings keep as true in s.* Tw. V, 277. *now hath my s. brought forth her prodigy,* R2 II, 2, 64. *that all have torn their —s by turning them from me,* III, 3, 83. *I'll prove the female to my s.* V, 5, 6. *never did young man fancy with so eternal and so fixed a s.* Troil. V, 2, 166. *this is the world's s., and just of the same piece is every flatterer's spirit,* Tim. III, 2, 71. *could force his s. so to his own conceit,* Hml. II, 2, 579. *it offends me to the s. to hear ...,* III, 2, 10. *I am glad at s.* Oth. I, 3, 196 etc. etc. Figuratively: *dear father, s. and substance of us all,* Tit. I, 374. *s. of Rome!* Caes. II, 1, 321. With emphasis: *if none of them have s. in such a kind,* Troil. I, 3, 285. *of no more s. nor fitness for the world than camels in the war,* Cor. II, 1, 266. *that might to half a s. and to a notion crazed say 'Thus did Banquo',* Mcb. III, 1, 83. *these fellows have some s.* Oth. I, 1, 54. Used in swearing: *sir, as I have a s., she is an angel,* H8 IV, 1, 44. *so thrive my s.* Rom. II, 2, 153. *by my s.!* Ado V, 1, 284. 309. LLL IV, 1, 142. H4A IV, 1, 86. H6A II, 4, 107. *I charge you, on your —s,* Ado IV, 1, 14. *on my s.!* 148. John V, 1, 43. H4A I, 3, 81. Oth. V, 2, 181 etc. Represented as the seat of real, not only professed, sentiments: *I have debated, even in my s., what sorrow I shall breed,* Lucr. 498. *hear my s. speak,* Tp. III, 1, 63. *whom my very s. abhors,* Gent. IV, 3, 17. Err. III, 2, 163. (I liked) *never any with so full s.* Tp. III, 1, 44. *we have with special s. elected him,* Meas. I, 1, 18. *were it not against our laws, my s. should sue as advocate for thee,* Err. I, 1, 146. *against my —'s pure truth why labour you to make it wander in an unknown field?* III, 2, 37. *think you in your s. the Count Claudio hath wronged Hero?* Ado IV, 1, 331. *there is some s. of goodness in things evil,* H5 IV, 1, 4 (= something really good). *speak it from your —s,* H6B III, 1, 247. *wherein my s. recorded the history of all her secret thoughts,* R3 III, 5, 27. *from my s. I mourn for yours,* IV, 1, 89. *from my s. I love your daughter,* IV, 4, 255. 262. *tell me true, even in the s. of sound good fellowship,* Troil. IV, 1, 52. *that I may swear unto my s. to right your wrongs,* Tit. III, 1, 279. Oth. I, 1, 251.

In a religious sense, 1) the moral agent liable to sin: *his —'s fair temple is defaced,* Lucr. 719. *sits Sin, to seize the —s that wander by him,* 882. 1169. *thinkest thou I'll endanger my s. gratis?* Wiv. II, 2, 16. II, 3, 40. Meas. II, 2, 73. 153. II, 4, 41. 56. 65. 187. V, 485 etc. 2) a departed spirit: Gent II, 7, 38. Mids. V, 308. Tw. I, 5, 74. John V, 7, 72. Ant. IV, 14, 51 etc.

Periphrastical use: *the folly of my s. dares not present itself,* Wiv. II, 2, 253 (= my folly). *bless my s.* III, 1, 11 (= bless me). *our s. cannot but yield you forth to public thanks,* Meas. V, 6 (= we cannot). *so befall my s. as this is false,* Err. V, 208. *to knit my s.*

to an approved wanton, Ado IV, 1, 45. *my father loved Sir Rowland as his* s. As I, 2, 247 (= as himself); cf. Gent. V, 4, 37, H4A V, 4, 20 and Tit. I, 373. *for mine* (demerits) *fell slaughter on their —s*, Mcb. IV, 3, 227. *since my dear* s. *was mistress of her choice*, Hml. III, 2, 68. *heaven defend your good —s that you think*, Oth. I, 3, 267. cf. Tp. I, 2, 420. Gent. II, 7, 15. Meas. I, 1, 67. Ado IV, 1, 25. Mids. I, 1, 82. 108. III, 2, 229. Hml. II, 2, 579 etc.

Similarly, often, = person, creature: *so o'er this sleeping* s. *doth Tarquin stay*, Lucr. 423. *free that* s. *which wretchedness hath chained*, 900. *guiltless —s*, 1482. *leave the faltering feeble —s alive*, 1768. *all ignorant that* s. *that sees thee without wonder*, Pilgr. 65. *no* s. Tp. I, 2, 29. *not a* s. *but felt a fever*, 208. *the fraughting souls within her*, 13. *the fair* s. *herself*, II, 1, 129. *tie the wiser —s to thy false seeming*, Meas. II, 4, 14. *a wretched* s., *bruised with adversity*, Err. II, 1, 34. *an honest* s. Ado III, 5, 41. *that unlettered small-knowing* s. LLL I, 1, 254. *mirth cannot move a* s. *in agony*, V, 2, 867. *pretty* s. Mids. II, 2, 76. *an evil* s. *producing holy witness*, Merch. I, 3, 100. *sweet* s., *let's in*, V, 49. *a gracious innocent* s. Wint. II, 3, 29. *to lay so dear a trust on any* s. *removed*, H4A IV, 1, 35. *there is no English* s. H8 I, 1, 146. *O this false* s. *of Egypt*, Ant. IV, 12, 25. *no single* s. *can we set eye on*, Cymb. IV, 2, 130. *poor* s., a term of pity: Tp. I, 2, 9. Meas. V, 46. 299. Err. I, 1, 108. IV, 2, 40. IV, 4, 62. 132. LLL IV, 1, 94. Mids. III, 2, 161. V, 134. H6B II, 1, 84. R3 II, 1, 87. 109. IV, 1, 64. 91 etc.

Denoting the chief part and quintessence of a thing: *grace, being the* s. *of your complexion*, Meas. III, 1, 187. *she shall pursue it with the* s. *of love*, Mids. II, 1, 182. *therein should we read the very bottom and the* s. *of hope*, H4A IV, 1, 50. *what is thy* s. *of adoration?* H5 IV, 1, 262. *the mortal Venus, the heart-blood of beauty, love's invisible* s. Troil. III, 1, 35. *my very* s. *of counsel*, III, 2, 141. *he's the very* s. *of bounty*, Tim. I, 2, 215. *brevity is the* s. *of wit*, Hml. II, 2, 90. *from the body of contraction plucks the very* s. 4, 47. *my* s., a term of endearment applied by lovers to their mistresses: Mids. III, 2, 246. Tw. I, 5, 288. Rom. II, 2, 165. III, 5, 25. Cymb. V, 5, 263. cf. LLL IV, 2, 104.

**Soul-confirming**, confirming, ratifying the sentiments of the soul: *with twenty thousand* s. *oaths*, Gent. II, 6, 16.

**Soul-curer**, a physician of the soul: Wiv. III, 1, 100.

**Soul-fearing**, terrifying the soul, appalling: *till their* (cannon's) s. *clamours have brawled down the flinty ribs*, John II, 383.

**Soul-killing**, killing the soul: Err. I, 2, 100.

**Soulless**, mean, base: *slave, s. villain, dog! O rarely base!* Ant. V, 2, 157.

**Soul-vexed**, irritated, made angry: Wint. V, 1, 59.

**Sound**, subst. a narrow passage of water: *deep —s make lesser noise than shallow fords*, Lucr. 1329.

**Sound**, subst. 1) any thing perceived by the ear, whether a voice, or a voice, or music: Ven. 780. 848. 976. Sonn. 8, 5. 130, 10. Pilgr. 111. Phoen. 4. Tp. I, 2, 406. III, 2, 145. 157. III, 3, 37. V, 234. LLL IV, 3, 335. Mids. I, 1, 143. V, 123. Merch. II, 5, 35. III, 2, 51. V, 55. 84. Shr. Ind. 1, 51. John III, 1, 230 (*gave the* s. *of words*). III, 3, 51. R2 II, 1, 17. 19. V, 5, 55. H4B II, 3, 37. III, 1, 14. H5 III Prol. 10. IV,

4, 74. H6A III, 3, 29. H6B III, 2, 44. IV, 1, 33. V, 2, 44. H6C II, 6, 58. V, 7, 9. Troil. I, 1, 92. I, 3, 155. Rom. IV, 5, 130. Tim. I, 2, 103. III, 6, 37. Mcb. IV, 1, 129 (*to give a* s., i. e. to make music). V, 5, 27. Hml. I, 2, 219. Lr. IV, 6, 215. V, 3, 115. Ant. IV, 8, 38. Per. II, 3, 63. V, 1, 233.

2) a particular manner of striking the ear: *I remember you by the* s. *of your voice*, Meas. V, 330. Merch. I, 1, 109. Cor. I, 6, 26. Rom. II, 2, 59. *that bears a frosty* s. H4A IV, 1, 128. *I'll have five hundred voices of that* s. Cor. II, 3, 219. *harsh in* s. IV, 5, 65.

3) something said or uttered, words, cries: *idle words, unprofitable —s*, Lucr. 1017. cf. 1464. *breathed forth the* s. *that said 'I hate'*, Sonn. 145, 2. *O heaven, O earth, bear witness to this* s. Tp. III, 1, 68. *converting all your —s of woe into Hey nonny nonny*, Ado II, 3, 70. *no* s., *no word?* Mids. II, 2, 152. *mine ear brought me to thy* s. III, 2, 182. *his voice pipes and whistles in his* s. As II, 7, 163 (in speaking). *in thee some blessed spirit doth speak his powerful* s. All's II, 1, 179. *it came o'er my ear like the sweet* s. *that breathes upon a bank of violets, stealing and giving odour*, Tw. I, 1, 5 (like the sweet talk of lovers upon a bank of violets, perfuming the air and perfumed by it. Some M. Edd. *south;* cf. *South*). *the thunder-like percussion of your —s*, Cor. I, 4, 59. *do not take his rougher accents for malicious —s*, III, 3, 55. *brief —s determine of my weal or woe*, Rom. III, 2, 51. *to hear the replication of your —s*, Caes. I, 1, 51. *shall possess them* (your ears) *with the heaviest* s. *that ever yet they heard*, Mcb. IV, 3, 202. *if thou hast any* s., *or use of words*, Hml. I, 1, 128.

**Sound**, adj. 1) healthy: Meas. I, 2, 54. 56. Ado III, 2, 13. As III, 2, 443 (*as clean as a* s. *sheep's heart*). All's II, 1, 170. IV, 3, 189. Wint. II, 3, 90 (*rotten as ever oak or stone was* s.). John III, 4, 26. R2 V, 3, 85. H5 III, 6, 26. Troil. I, 3, 8. Cor. I, 6, 30. Tim. I, 2, 240. Mcb. V, 3, 52. Lr. II, 4, 113. Per. IV, 6, 27.

2) not defective, whole, undecayed: *look that my staves be* s. R3 V, 3, 65. cf. Per. IV Prol. 24.

3) unhurt, safe: *safe and* s. *aboard*, Err. IV, 4, 154. *bleedest not, speakest, art* s. Lr. IV, 6, 52.

4) valid, solid, right, just: s. *advice*, Lucr. 1409. *try your penitence, if it be* s. Meas. II, 3, 22. s. *reasons*, Err. II, 2, 92. *my love to thee is* s., *sans crack or flaw*, LLL V, 2, 415. *your exposition hath been most* s. Merch. IV, 1, 238. *a more —er instance*, As III, 2, 62. *thy counsel's* s. Shr. I, 1, 169. *a* s. *affection*, Wint. IV, 4, 390. *makes* s. *opinion sick*, John IV, 2, 26. *men of* s. *direction*, R3 V, 3, 16. *one of the —est judgements*, Troil. I, 2, 208. *in the soul of* s. *good fellowship*, IV, 1, 52. *here's no* s. *jest*, Tit. IV, 2, 26. *the best and —est of his time hath been but rash*, Lr. I, 1, 298.

5) honest, virtuous, blameless: *dare mate a —er man than Surrey can be*, H8 III, 2, 274. *you are not* s. V, 3, 81.

6) strong, stout: *one* s. *cudgel of four foot*, H8 V, 4, 19.

7) profound, unbroken: *this sleep is* s. *indeed*, H4B IV, 5, 35.

8) clear, shrill: *thy small pipe is as the maiden's organ, shrill and* s. Tw. I, 4, 33. Quibbling: *so* s. *as things that are hollow*, Meas. I, 2, 56. *he hath a heart as* s. *as a bell*, Ado III, 2, 13.

Adverbial use: 1) *let the fairies pinch him* s. Wiv. IV, 4, 61. 2) *to sleep* s.: Lucr. 363. Wiv. V, 5, 56.

Meas. IV, 3, 50. Mids. II, 2, 74. III, 2, 449. H4B IV, 5, 26. Rom. IV, 5, 8 *(s. asleep)*. Caes. II, 1, 233.

**Sound**, vb. ancient orthography for *Swound* or *Swoon*, q. v.

**Sound**, vb. to search with a plummet, to try, to examine: Tp. III, 3, 101. V, 56. Wiv. II, 1, 246. As IV, 1, 211. Shr. V, 1, 141. R2 I, 1, 8. H4B IV, 2, 51. H6A I, 2, 63. R3 III, 1, 170. III, 4, 17. 38. IV, 2, 87. H8 III, 2, 437. V, 2, 13.\*Tit. IV, 3, 7. Rom. I, 1, 156. Caes. II, 1, 141. Hml. II, 1, 42. III, 1, 7. Lr. I, 2, 74. Cymb. IV, 2, 204. Quibbling in Hml. III, 2, 383.

**Sound**, vb. 1) intr. a) to make a noise, to utter a voice, to strike the ear in any manner: Sonn. 128, 2. Pilgr. 271. Tp. I, 2, 388. Meas. IV, 6, 12. Ado V, 3, 11. LLL V, 2, 157. Mids. IV, 1, 90. Merch. III, 2, 43. V, 75. Shr. Ind. 1, 74. R2 V, 5, 61. H4B I, 3, 74. V, 5, 2. 42. H5 IV Chor. 5. IV, 2, 34. H6A I, 4, 80. H8 IV, 1, 36. V, 4, 86. Troil. V, 3, 13. Cor. I, 9, 42. Lr. V, 1, 41. V, 3, 107. 217. Ant. II, 7, 140. Cymb. IV, 2, 187. Per. III, 2, 89. With *on: if the midnight bell did ... s. on into the drowsy race of night,* John III, 3, 39 (as if it would never cease). With *out: s. out,* Ant. II, 7, 140. = to make music: *musicians s. for silver,* Rom. IV, 5, 137. *have no gold for —ing,* 143.

b) to strike the ear in a particular manner: *how oddly will it s. that I must ask my child forgiveness,* Tp. V, 197. *Amaimon —s well,* Wiv. II, 2, 311. Err. IV, 4, 7. Merch. V, 100. H4B I, 1, 102. H6C V, 2, 44. Rom. II, 2, 166. Caes. III, 1, 50. Mcb. I, 3, 52.

2) trans. a) to cause to make a noise or utter a voice or make music: *s. but another* (drum) John V, 2, 171. *I have —ed the very base-string of humility,* H4A II, 4, 6. *s. all the lofty instruments of war,* V, 2, 98. *when fame shall in our islands s. her trump,* Troil. III, 3, 210. *they are not a pipe for fortune's finger to s. what stop she please,* Hml. III, 2, 76. *you would s. me from my lowest note to the top of my compass,* 383 (quibbling). *s. trumpet,* H6C IV, 7, 69. Lr. V, 3, 110. *s. trumpets,* R2 I, 3, 117. H6C II, 2, 173. *s. the trumpets,* H6C II, 1, 200. *s. thy trumpet,* Cor. I, 5, 27. *s. drums and trumpets,* H6B V, 3, 32. H6C I, 1, 118. V, 7, 45. R3 V, 3, 269. Absol.: *s.!* Lr. V, 3, 116.

b) to order or proclaim by a musical sound: *to s. a parley,* Lucr. 471. R2 I, 1, 192. H5 III, 2, 149. H6C V, 1, 16. Oth. II, 3, 23. *the trumpet —s retreat,* H4A V, 4, 163. H5 III, 2, 94. H6A II, 2, 3. H6B IV, 8, 4. Troil. V, 8, 16. *s. alarum,* R2 I, 2, 18. H6B II, 3, 95. V, 2, 3. *trumpet, s. the general doom,* Rom. III, 2, 67. *s. to this town our terrible approach,* Tim. V, 4, 1.

c) to make audible by the voice, to speak, to cry; absol.: *my voice shall s. as you do prompt mine ear,* H4B V, 2, 119. *every one with claps can s.: Our heir apparent is a king!* Per. III Prol. 36. With an object, = to pronounce, to express, to utter, to speak of: *now against himself he —s this doom,* Lucr. 717. *let it* (your heart) *not s. a thought upon your tongue against my brother's life,* Meas. II, 2, 140. *hearing thy beauty —ed,* Shr. II, 193. *as one that am the tongue of these to s. the purposes of all their hearts,* John IV, 2, 48. *how dares thy harsh rude tongue s. this unpleasing news?* R2 III, 4, 74. *thy name is Gaultier, being rightly —ed,* H6B IV, 1, 37. *crack my clear voice with sobs and break my heart with —ing Troilus,* Troil. IV, 2, 115. *no words can that woe s.* Rom. III, 2, 126. *no reason can s. his state in safety,* Tim. II, 1, 13 (can

proclaim, declare openly his state to be safe; or, can safely speak of his state? Most M. Edd. *found*). *that he may never s. ... his quillets shrilly,* IV, 3, 155. *what should that name be —ed more than yours?* Caes. I, 2, 143. *s. them, it doth become the mouth as well,* 145. *when to s. your name it not concerned me,* Ant. II, 2, 34. *our tongues and sorrows do s. deep our woes into the air,* Per. I, 4, 13.

**Soundless**, 1) unfathomable: Sonn. 80, 10. 2) devoid of sound, dumb: Caes. V, 1, 36.

**Soundly**, 1) well, satisfactorily: *effect this business s.* R3 III, 1, 186.

2) fast, closely, so as not to be easily awakened: *to sleep s.* Ven. 786. Shr. Ind. 1, 33. H5 IV, 1, 285. Caes. II, 1, 4. *when Duncan is asleep, whereto the rather shall his day's hard journey s. invite him,* Mcb. I, 7, 63.

3) truly, heartily: *if you will love me s. with your French heart,* H5 V, 2, 105. *suspects, yet s. loves,* Oth. III, 3, 170 (Qq *strongly*).

4) stoutly, strongly, smartly: *he shall pay for him, and that s.* Tp. II, 2, 81. *this will shake your shaking, and that s.* 88. *let them be hunted s.* IV, 263. *I had swinged him s.* Meas. V, 130. *knock me here s.* Shr. I, 2, 8. 31. 42. V, 2, 104. Tw. III, 4, 428. H4B V, 4, 21. H5 IV, 7, 136. H6A I, 3, 48. Cor. II, 1, 139. Rom. III, 1, 113. IV, 5, 113. Ant. III, 13, 132.

**Soundness**, health: All's I, 2, 24.

**Soundpost**, name of a musician in Rom. IV, 5, 138.

**Sour**, adj. 1) having a pungent taste, acid, tart: Ven. 528. Tp. V, 37. As III, 2, 115. R2 I, 3, 236. *s. breath,* Gent. III, 1, 331.

Substantively: *the sweets we wish for turn to loathed —s,* Lucr. 867. *palates both for sweet and s.* Oth. IV, 3, 96.

2) crabbed, morose, sullen: *jealousy, that s. unwelcome guest,* Ven. 449. 655. *he hath been heavy, s., sad,* Err. V, 45 (dissyll.). *you must not look so s.* Shr. II, 229. 231. *peevish, sullen, s.* V, 2, 157. *sweet love turns to the —est hate,* R2 III, 2, 136. *my s. husband, my hard-hearted lord,* V, 3, 121. *that s. ferryman,* R3 I, 4, 46 (Qq *grim*). *lofty and s. to them that loved him with H8 IV, 2, 53. nor with s. looks afflict his gentle heart,* Tit. I, 441. *so s. a face,* Rom. II, 5, 24. *this s. cold habit,* Tim. IV, 3, 239. *after his s. fashion,* Caes. I, 2, 180.

3) bitter, hateful, distasteful in any manner: *thy s. leisure gave sweet leave to entertain the time with thoughts of love,* Sonn. 39, 10. *nor think the bitterness of absence s.* 57, 7. *sweetest things turn —est by their deeds,* 94, 13. *the s. cup of prosperity,* LLL I, 1, 315 (Costard's speech). *a s. offence,* All's V, 3, 59. *how s. sweet music is, when time is broke,* R2 V, 5, 42. *to make a sweet lady sad is a s. offence,* Troil. III, 1, 80. *lips, let s. words go by,* Tim. V, 2, 223. *touch the —est points with sweetest terms,* Ant. II, 2, 24.

4) gloomy, sad: *speak sweetly, although thy looks be s.* R2 III, 2, 193. *a bank of rue, s. herb of grace,* III, 4, 105. *my s. cross,* IV, 241. *s. melancholy,* V, 6, 20. *heart's discontent and s. affliction,* H6B III, 2, 301. *s. adversity,* H6C III, 1, 24. *s. annoy,* H6C V, 7, 45. *s. woe,* Rom. II, 2, 116. *such s. company* (as sorrow) III, 3, 7. *s. misfortune,* V, 3, 82.

**Sour**, subst. see *Sour* adj.

**Sour**, vb. 1) trans. to make acid: *the tartness of*

*his face —s ripe grapes*, Cor. V, 4, 18. Figuratively, = a) to embitter: *to s. your happiness*, Cymb. V, 5, 26. b) *to s. one's cheek* = to look gloomy: *and now Adonis ... —ing his cheeks cries 'Fie, no more of love'*, Ven. 185. *have ever made me s. my patient cheek*, R2 II, 1, 169. Peculiar expression: *three crabbed months had —ed themselves to death*, Wint. I, 2, 102 (had gone by in bitter tediousness).

2) intr. to become acid: *his taste delicious, in digestion —ing*, Lucr. 699.

**Source**, spring, origin, first cause: *great floods have flown from simple —s*, All's II, 1, 143. *blow it (the cloud) to the s. from whence it came*, H6C V, 3, 11. *quell the s. of all erection*, Tim. IV, 3, 164. Mcb. II, 3, 104. Hml. I, 1, 106. II, 2, 55. Ant. III, 13, 160. In Per. IV, 3, 28 M. Edd. —s, O. Edd. *courses*.

**Sour-cold**, writing of M. Edd. in Tim. IV, 3, 239; O. Edd. not hyphened.

**Sourest-natured**, most harsh-tempered: Gent. II, 3, 6.

**Sour-eyed**, looking crabbed and sullen: *s. disdain*, Tp. IV, 20.

**Sour-faced**, looking sad: Lucr. 1334.

**Sourly**, 1) morosely, sullenly: *when a woman woos, what woman's son will s. leave her till she have prevailed?* Sonn. 41, 8. *though I showed s. to him*, Cor. V, 3, 13.

2) in a bitter and mortifying manner: *that sweet thief which s. robs from me*, Sonn. 35, 14.

**Souse**, to pounce upon: *and like an eagle o'er his aery towers, to s. annoyance that comes near his nest*, John V, 2, 150.

**Soused**, pickled: *a s. gurnet*, H4A IV, 2, 13.

**South**, 1) the part where the sun is at noon: *the s.* John II, 411. H6C I, 4, 136. Caes. II, 1, 107. *the rotten diseases of the s.* Troil. V, 1, 21. *all the contagion of the s.* Cor. I, 4, 30. *the dew-dropping s.* Rom. I, 4, 103. *the spongy s.* Cymb. IV, 2, 349. Without the article: *by east, west, north and s.* LLL V, 2, 566. *by s. and east*, H4A III, 1, 75. *from east, west, north and s.* Wint. I, 2, 203. *from north to s.* John II, 413. *from the north to s.* H4A I, 3, 196. *from s. to west*, Cymb. V, 5, 471. *s. =* to the south: *they take their courses east, west, north, s.* H4B IV, 2, 104 and Cor. II, 3, 24. *half a mile s. from the power of the king*, R3 V, 3, 38. *'tis s. the city mills*, Cor. I, 10, 31. *the chimney is s. the chamber*, Cymb. II, 4, 81.

Adjectively: *in the s. suburbs*, Tw. III, 3, 39. *s. wind*, Wint. V, 1, 161. *at the s. entry*, Mcb. II, 2, 66.

2) the wind that blows from the south: *like foggy s. puffing with wind and rain*, As III, 5, 50. *tempest of commotion, like the s. borne with black vapour*, H4B II, 4, 392. cf. the similar epithets sub 1, and besides, H4A V, 1, 3; H6B III, 2, 384 and Cor. II, 3, 32; therefore *the sweet s.* for *sound* in Tw. I, 1, 5 a more than improbable conjecture of M. Edd.

**Southam**, place in England: H6C V, 1, 9. 12.*

**Southampton**, place in England: H5 II Chor. 30. 35. 42. II, 3, 48. *Earl of S.:* Ven. Ded. and Lucr. Ded.

**Southerly**, coming from the south: *the wind is s.* Hml. II, 2, 397.

**Southern**, being in or coming from the south: R2 III, 2, 202. H4A V, 1, 3. H6B III, 2, 384. H6C I, 1, 155.

**South-fog**, a fog coming from the south: Cymb. II, 3, 136.

**South-north**, an impossible quarter devised by the clown in Tw. IV, 2, 42.

**South-sea**, the sea of the south, the Pacific; a sea very imperfectly known at the time of the poet: *one inch of delay more is a S. of discovery*, As III, 2, 207.

**Southward**, 1) adj. southern: *the sun looking with a s. eye upon him*, Wint. IV, 4, 819. 2) adv. towards the south: Cor. II, 3, 32.

**Southwark**, the southern part of London: H6B IV, 4, 27. IV, 8, 25.

**Southwell**, name in H6B I, 4, 14.

**South-west**, a wind coming from between south and west: *a s. blow on ye and blister you all o'er*, Tp. I, 2, 323. Per. IV, 1, 51.

**South-wind**: Wint. V, 1, 161.

**Sovereign**, subst. prince, king: Lucr. 650. Sonn. 57, 6. LLL III, 184. As I, 3, 68. Shr. V, 2, 147. All's V, 3, 37. 87. John I, 15. R2 I, 1, 21. 45. 111. I, 3, 46. H6A I, 2, 111. I, 3, 24. III, 1, 25. 149. III, 4, 4. IV, 1, 52. H6B I, 1, 28. II, 2, 61. R3 III, 1, 2. Rom. V, 3, 195 etc. etc. Applied to women, = queen: All's I, 1, 183. H6C III, 2, 92. Ant. I, 5, 34. IV, 15, 69.

**Sovereign**, adj. 1) princely, royal: *thou art a sea, a s. king*, Lucr. 652. *flatter the mountain tops with s. eye*, Sonn. 33, 2. *nature, s. mistress over wrack*, 126, 5. *with her s. grace to come and sport*, Tp. IV, 72. *s. power*, All's II, 3, 60. *liver, brain and heart, these s. thrones*, Tw. I, 1, 38. *my s. mistress*, Wint. I, 2, 280. *our s. lord the king*, III, 2, 17. *the remembrance of his most s. name*, V, 1, 26. *holding of the pope your s. greatness*, John V, 1, 4. V, 2, 82. R2 II, 3, 157. H5 V, 2, 386 *(my s. queen).* H6B III, 1, 161. 178. Tim. I, 1, 68. Mcb. I, 5, 71. V, 2, 30. Hml. II, 2, 27. IV, 3, 65. Ant. I, 3, 60. IV, 9, 12. V, 2, 81. *my s. liege*, R2 I, 1, 129. I, 3, 154. H4A I, 3, 10. H6C IV, 1, 86. R3 II, 1, 52. 75. IV, 3, 23. *my s. lord*, H4B IV, 4, 113. H5 IV, 3, 68. *my s. king*, R3 II, 1, 46. H8 I, 1, 202. *s. sir*, Wint. V, 3, 2.

2) supreme, paramount, excellent: *such a gentle s. grace*, Err. III, 2, 165. *a man of s. parts*, LLL II, 44. *yond same s. cruelty*, Tw. II, 4, 83. *thou shalt have charge and s. trust herein*, H4A III, 2, 161. *thy parts s. and pious else*, H8 II, 4, 140. *that noble and most s. reason*, Hml. III, 1, 165. *a s. shame so elbows him*, Lr. IV, 3, 44. *opinion, a s. mistress of effects*, Oth. I, 3, 225. *let me lament with tears as s. as the blood of hearts*, Ant. V, 1, 41. With *to*, = paramount to, superior to: *let her be a principality, s. to all the creatures on the earth*, Gent. II, 4, 153.

3) supremely medicinal and efficacious: *calls it balm, earth's s. salve*, Ven. 28. *'gainst venomed sores the only s. plaster*, 916. *against strange maladies a s. cure*, Sonn. 153, 8. *of whose (patience's) soft grace I have her s. aid*, Tp. V, 143. *thus I search it with a s. kiss*, Gent. I, 2, 116. *the —'st thing on earth was parmaceti for an inward bruise*, H4A I, 3, 57. *the most s. prescription in Galen is but empiricutic*, Cor. II, 1, 127.

**Sovereignly**, supremely: *so s. being honourable*, Wint. I, 2, 323.

**Sovereignty**, 1) royalty, royal dignity: *no s.* Tp. II, 1, 156. *employed your unknown s.* Meas. V, 392. John III, 1, 58. R2 IV, 251. H4B V, 2, 101.

H6B I, 3, 130. H6C III, 2, 86. 134. R3 III, 7, 79 (Ff *the s. thereof,* Qq *the s. thereon*). 146. IV, 4, 329. 356. H8 I, 2, 150. II, 3, 29. Mcb. II, 4, 30. IV, 1, 89. Lr. I, 4, 253. Cymb. III, 5, 6 (*to show less s. than they*).

2) any sway or predominant power: *the s. of either being so great,* Lucr. 69.* *whose yoke my soul consents not to give s.* Mids. I, 1, 82. *as is the osprey to the fish, who takes it by s. of nature,* Cor. IV, 7, 35. *might deprive your s. of reason,* Hml. I, 4, 73.

3) supreme excellence: *his boast of Lucrece' s.* Lucr. 36. *to call her bad, whose s. so oft thou hast preferred,* Gent. II, 6, 15. *of all complexions the culled s.* LLL IV, 3, 234.

4) highly efficacious medicinal quality: *prescriptions ... such as his reading and manifest experience had collected for general s.* All's I, 3, 230.

**Sow,** subst. a female swine: H4B I, 2, 13. H5 III, 7, 67. Mcb. IV, 1, 64.

**Sow,** vb. (cf. *Sew.* Impf. and partic. —*ed*) 1) to scatter on the ground for the purpose of growth: Tp. II, 1, 92. Meas. IV, 1, 76. LLL IV, 3, 383. H6B III, 1, 381. Cor. III, 1, 71. Oth. I, 3, 325. Cymb. IV, 2, 181. Figuratively: *when time hath —ed a grizzle on thy case,* Tw. V, 168. *we are to cure such sorrows, not to s. 'em,* H8 III, 1, 158. *consumptions s. in hollow bones of man,* Tim. IV, 3, 151.

2) to scatter over, to stock with seed: *he'ld s. it with nettle-seed,* Tp. II, 1, 144. H4B V, 1, 15. Figuratively: Tim. IV, 1, 29.

*Sawn,* in a very problematical passage (Compl. 91), explained by some as the partic. of the verb.

**Sowl** (O. Edd. *sole*) to pull by the ears: *he'll go and s. the porter of Rome gates by the ears,* Cor. IV, 5, 213.

**Sow-skin,** made of hog-leather: *the s. budget,* Wint. IV, 3, 20.

**Sowter,** name of a hound: Tw. II, 5, 135.

**Space,** 1) room, extent: *despite of s. I would be brought where thou dost stay,* Sonn. 44, 3. *vow, bond, nor s., in thee hath neither sting, knot, nor confine,* Compl. 264. *distance and no s. was seen 'twixt the turtle and his queen,* Phoen. 30. *s. enough have I in such a prison,* Tp. I, 2, 492. II, 1, 257. *with blank s. for different names,* Wiv. II, 1, 77. *the mightiest s. in fortune nature brings to join like likes,* All's I, 1, 237 (= the mightiest distance; cf. above: Phoen. 30). *for her whom, we know well, the world's large —s cannot parallel,* Troil. II, 2, 162. *no s. of earth shall sunder our two hates,* V, 10, 27. *sell the mighty s. of our large honours for so much trash as may be grasped thus,* Caes. IV, 3, 25. *for the whole s. that's in the tyrant's grasp, and the rich East to boot,* Mcb. IV, 3, 36. *a king of infinite s.* Hml. II, 2, 261. *dearer than eyesight, s. and liberty,* Lr. I, 1, 57. *no less in s.* 83. *O undistinguished s. of woman's will,* IV, 6, 278. *here is my s.* Ant. I, 1, 34. *make s. enough between you,* II, 3, 23. *the diminution of s.* Cymb. I, 3, 19.

2) time: *counterfeits to die with her a s.* Lucr. 1776 (= some time). *within which s. she died,* Tp. I, 2, 279. All's II, 1, 162. H4A III, 1, 89. *for three years' s.* LLL I, 1, 52. 151. H6B III, 2, 295. *after some small s. he sent me hither,* As IV, 3, 152. *the solemn feast shall more attend upon the coming s.* All's II, 3, 188. *thou art granted s.* IV, 1, 98. *in short s.* H4A V, 1, 46. *in so short a s.* R3 IV, 1, 79 (Ff *so small a time*). *to-*

*morrow, or at further s.* Lr. V, 3, 53. *'tis a s. for further travel,* Ant. II, 1, 31. *if you require a little s. for prayer,* Per. IV, 1, 68.

**Spacious,** wide, large, extensive: Sonn. 135, 5. All's II, 1, 51. H6A II, 3, 55. R3 I, 2, 246. Troil. II, 3, 261. V, 2, 150. Cor. IV, 6, 67. Tit. II, 1, 114. Tim. III, 5, 97. Mcb. IV, 3, 71. Hml. V, 2, 90 (*s. in the possession of dirt*). Ant. V, 1, 34. Per. IV, 3, 5.

**Spade,** an instrument for digging: Tit. IV, 3, 11. Rom. V, 3, 185. Tim. IV, 3, 204. Hml. V, 1, 33. 98. 102.

**Spain,** the country to the south-west of France: Err. III, 2, 133. 139. LLL I, 1, 164. 174 (*tawny S.*). John II, 64. 423. H5 III, 6, 62 (*the fig of S.*). H6C III, 3, 82. H8 II, 4, 48. 55. Caes. I, 2, 119. Oth. V, 2, 253 (*a sword of S.*).

**Span,** the space from the end of the thumb to the end of the little finger extended: Troil. II, 2, 31. Used of a short time, especially the duration of human life: As III, 2, 139. H8 III, 2, 140. Tim. V, 3, 3. Oth. II, 3, 74.

**Span,** vb. to measure, to fix the term of: *my life is —ed already,* H8 I, 1, 223.

**Span-counter,** a puerile game, in which one throws a counter, which the other wins, if he can throw another so as to hit it, or lie within a span of it (Nares): *in whose time boys went to s. for French crowns,* H6B IV, 2, 166.

**Spangle,** to sprinkle with spangles or small brilliant bodies: —*d starlight sheen,* Mids. II, 1, 29. *what stars do s. heaven with such beauty,* Shr. IV, 5, 31. *stuck and —d with your flatteries,* Tim. III, 6, 101 (O. Edd. —*d you with flatteries*).

**Spaniard,** a native of Spain: Ado III, 2, 36. LLL I, 2, 183. IV, 1, 100. H4B V, 3, 124. H8 II, 2, 90. Per. IV, 2, 108.

**Spaniel,** subst. a kind of dog: Shr. IV, 1, 153. Mcb. III, 1, 93. Lr. III, 6, 72. Per. IV, 6, 133 (*let me be gelded like a s.*). Emblem of fawning submissiveness: Mids. II, 1, 203. 205. H8 V, 3, 126. Caes. III, 1, 43.

**Spaniel,** vb. to follow like a spaniel: *the hearts that —ed me at heels,* Ant. IV, 12, 21 (O. Edd. *pannell'd*).

**Spaniel-like,** like a spaniel: Gent. IV, 2, 14.

**Spanish,** pertaining to Spain: *my S. word,* All's IV, 1, 52. *S. pouch,* H4A II, 4, 79.* *S. blades,* Rom. I, 4, 84. Substantively, = the language of Spain: *in S.* Per. II, 2, 27.

**Spare,** subst. parsimony, frugal use: *as much as one sound cudgel of four foot could distribute, I made no s.* H8 V, 4, 21 (the servant's speech).

**Spare,** adj. 1) parsimonious, frugal: *as it is a s. life, it fits my humour well,* As III, 2, 20. *s. in diet,* H5 II, 2, 131.

2) thin, lean: *give me the s. men, and spare me the great ones,* H4B III, 2, 288. *that s. Cassius,* Caes. I, 2, 201.

3) not wanted in ordinary circumstances, held in reserve for any emergency: *a small s. mast, such as seafaring men provide for storms,* Err. I, 1, 80.

**Spare,** vb. 1) to be parsimonious; a) intr.: *it shall be —ing and too full of riot,* Ven. 1147. *a niggardly host and more —ing guest,* Err. III, 1, 27. *in him —ing would show a worse sin than ill doctrine,* H8 I, 3, 60. *in that —ing makes huge waste,* Rom. I, 1, 224. With *for: we will s. for no wit,* Ado III, 5, 66 (Dogberry's speech). *s. for no faggots*, H6A V, 4, 56. *s. not for cost*, Rom. IV, 4, 6.

b) trans. = to use frugally, not to waste, to husband: *the rather will I s. my praises towards him*, All's II, 1, 106. *s. your threats*, Wint. III, 2, 92. *you may, then, s. that time*, H8 II, 4, 5. *you'ld s. your spoons*, V, 3, 167. *s. your oaths*, Tim. IV, 3, 138. *s. speech*, Lr. IV, 2, 21. Oth. II, 3, 199. *which (oath) you'll give me leave to s.* Cymb. II, 4, 65. *s. your arithmetic*, 142.

2) to forbear; absol.: *I prithee, s.* Tp. II, 1, 25. *shall I bid him go, and s. not?* Tw. II, 3, 120. *tell him, and s. not*, R3 I, 3, 114. With an inf.: *s. not to spend*, Pilgr. 324. *s. not to tell him that he hath wronged his honour*, Ado II, 2, 22. *being moved, he will not s. to gird the gods*, Cor. I, 1, 260. With an accus.: *shun me, and I will s. your haunts*, Mids. II, 1, 142. *give me the spare men, and s. me the great ones*, H4B III, 2, 289.

3) to do without, to dispense with: *you shall well be —d*, Meas. II, 2, 14. *I prize it as I weigh grief, which I would s.* Wint. III, 2, 44. *with other princes that may best be —d*, John V, 7, 97. *I could have better —d a better man*, H4A V, 4, 104. *such aid as I can s. you shall command*, H6B IV, 5, 7. *your presence must … take from his heart … what should not then be —d*, Ant. III, 7, 13.

4) to hold in reserve for the use of another, to grant, to allow: *I shall hardly s. a pound of flesh tomorrow to my bloody creditor*, Merch. III, 3, 33. *when Clifford cannot spare his friends an oath*, H6C II, 6, 78. *my youth can better s. my blood than you*, Tit. III, 1, 166. *I am poor of thanks and scarce can s. them*, Cymb. II, 3, 95.

5) to forbear to afflict or destroy, to use tenderly, to treat with mercy: Lucr. 582. 1687. Meas. II, 2, 83. Err. I, 1, 77. LLL II, 51. Shr. IV, 3, 153. All's I, 3, 47. II, 2, 47. 53. 55. IV, 1, 89. John IV, 1, 102. R2 II, 1, 124. H4B II, 1, 18. H6B IV, 1, 23. IV, 2, 195. IV, 8, 52. V, 2, 51. R3 I, 4, 72. III, 7, 194. H8 II, 4, 54. V, 4, 23. Cor. II, 3, 243. Tit. I, 120. III, 1, 184. Tim. I, 1, 177. IV, 3, 118. V, 4, 40. Lr. II, 2, 68. 72. Cymb. II, 3, 100. V, 5, 92. 327. 418. Per. I, 2, 93. II, 1, 137.

Doubtful passage: *we would not s. heaven as we love it, but as we stand in fear*, Meas. II, 3, 33 (Malone: = not spare to offend heaven).

**Sparingly**, in a forbearing manner, with management: *or shall we s. show you far off the Dauphin's meaning?* H5 I, 2, 239. *but touch this s., as 'twere far off*, R3 III, 5, 93.

**Spark**, 1) a small particle of fire emitted from burning bodies: Lucr. 177. H6B III, 1, 302. H8 II, 4, 73. Caes. IV, 3, 112. Lr. III, 4, 118. Per. I, 2, 40. Used of the stars: *the skies are painted with unnumbered —s*, Caes. III, 1, 63. Figuratively, = a small portion of any thing vivid and active: *some —s that are like wit*, Ado II, 3, 193. *some —s of better hope*, R2 V, 3, 21. *high —s of honour*, V, 6, 29. H6C I, 1, 184. *one s. of evil*, H5 II, 2, 101. *one s. of fire*, Troil. I, 3, 294. *s. of life*, H6C V, 6, 66. Caes. I, 3, 57. *the s. and fire of it* (love) Hml. IV, 7, 114. *enkindle all the —s of nature*, Lr. III, 7, 86. *how hard it is to hide the —s of nature*, Cymb. III, 3, 79.

2) a brisk and showy young man: *'tis not his fault, the s.* All's II, 1, 25. *good —s and lustrous*, 41.

**Sparkle**, 1) to emit sparks, to let sparks fly: *it*

(the fire) *will s. in your eyes*, John IV, 1, 115 (i. e. hurt your eyes by sparks). *a fire —ing in lovers' eyes*, Rom. I, 1, 197.

2) to shine, to glitter, to glisten: *—ing stars*, Sonn. 28, 12. *give a favour from you to s. in the spirits of my daughter*, All's V, 3, 75. *his viands —ing in a golden cup*, H6C II, 5, 52. *—s this stone as it was wont?* Cymb. II, 4, 40. Used of eyes (glowing with anger or excitement): Ado III, 1, 51. H4B IV, 1, 121. H6A I, 1, 12. H6B III, 1, 154. III, 2, 317. H6C II, 5, 131. Trans., = to shoot forth: *they* (ladies' eyes) *s. still the right Promethean fire*, LLL IV, 3, 351.

**Sparrow**, the bird Fringilla domestica or montana: Lucr. 849. Tp. IV, 100. Meas. III, 2, 185 (lecherous). Mids. III, 1, 133. As II, 3, 44. John I, 231 (cf. Philip). H4A II, 4, 380. 382. V, 1, 61. Troil. II, 1, 77. III, 2, 36. V, 7, 11. Mcb. I, 2, 35. Hml. V, 2, 231. Lr. I, 4, 235 (*hedge-s.*).

**Sparta**, town in ancient Greece: Troil. II, 2, 183. Per. II, 2, 18. *hounds of S.* Mids. IV, 1, 119. 131.

**Spartan**, native of Sparta: *hounds … of the S. kind*, Mids. IV, 1, 124. *O S. dog*, Oth. V, 2, 361.

**Spavin**, a disease of horses consisting in a swelling of some joints, by which lameness is produced: H8 I, 3, 12. *—s:* Shr. III, 2, 53.

**Spawn**, subst. a fry: *your multiplying s. how can he flatter*, Cor. II, 2, 82.

**Spawn**, vb. to bring forth as fishes do eggs: *a sea-maid —ed him*, Meas. III, 2, 115.

**Spay**, to castrate: *to geld and s. all the youth of the city*, Meas. II, 1, 243 (O. Edd. *splay*).

**Speak** (impf. *spake* or *spoke*; partic. *spoke* or *spoken; spake* in H8 II, 4, 153 to be explained by an anacoluthon); 1) to use language, to express one's thoughts by words: Ven. 208. 221. 943. 1097. 1146. Tp. I, 2, 260. 314. 354. 444. III, 1, 63. III, 3, 96. IV, 1, 31. V, 201. Gent. I, 2, 29. II, 1, 26. IV, 2, 87. Wiv. I, 3, 14. Meas. III, 1, 86. Err. II, 1, 50. Ado II, 1, 201. As IV, 1, 72. Shr. V, 2, 37. All's V, 2, 12. Wint. I, 2, 88. 106. John III, 1, 124. IV, 2, 177. V, 2, 64 (*even there, methinks, an angel spake*). R2 V, 2, 12. H4B I, 1, 59. IV, 5, 142. H6B III, 1, 266. H6C I, 1, 66. 257. 258. II, 2, 66. R3 I, 4, 156. Oth. III, 1, 4 (*they s. i' the nose.* cf. *Nose*). Ant. II, 2, 102 etc. etc. Used of the contents of writings: *or senseless —ing or a —ing such as sense cannot untie*, Cymb. V, 4, 148. cf. Caes. IV, 3, 177. *to stand and s.* = to be in life: Ant. V, 1, 7. V, 2, 344; cf. Tp. II, 1, 214. *to s. together* = to be together, to meet: R2 II, 3, 29. Tim. I, 1, 62. Caes. V, 1, 99. Mcb. III, 1, 74. *to s. on* = to continue to speak: H8 III, 2, 306. *you spake in Latin*, Wiv. I, 1, 185. *s. in English*, H8 III, 1, 46. *so far*, Lr. V, 3, 63. *too far*, Cymb. V, 5, 309. *s. true*, Tp. II, 1, 20. As V, 4, 82. H6B III, 1, 183. *truly*, Meas. V, 37. John IV, 3, 92. H4A I, 2, 105. (*to s. fair, false, big, low, small, thick*, see in the resp. articles). *to s. with a p.* = to talk, to converse with a p.: Gent. II, 4, 116. IV, 4, 114. Wiv. II, 2, 32. 151. III, 3, 95. IV, 5, 35. 40. V, 2, 4. Meas. I, 4, 10. V, 223. 271. Err. II, 1, 47. II, 2, 5. 167. Mids. I, 1, 112. Merch. I, 3, 31. II, 2, 154. III, 1, 78. IV, 2, 12. Shr. V, 1, 20. All's II, 1, 85. II, 5, 60. III, 4, 20. Wint. V, 1, 197. H4B I, 1, 25. R3 III, 7, 46. 57. Lr. I, 2, 169. IV, 5, 4. Cymb. I, 1, 177 etc. etc.

*to s. to* = to say sth. to, to address, to apply to by words: Ven. 918. Tp. II, 2, 105. Wiv. V, 5, 51.

Meas. III, 1, 198. V, 286. Err. II, 2, 120. 183. V, 12. As I, 3, 81. III, 5, 105. Tw. V, 190. H4B IV, 5, 158. R3 III, 4, 89. III, 7, 30. Hml. I, 1, 45. Ant. IV, 2, 40 etc. Sometimes = to apply to, to call upon, to address one's self to in any manner: *s. to the mariners*, Tp. I, 1, 3 (exhort them, bid them do their best). *s. to Mistress Page*, Wiv. III, 4, 81. *it is the manner of a man to s. to a woman*, LLL I, 1, 212. *never to s. to lady afterward in way of marriage*, Merch. II, 1, 41. *I was spoke to, with Sir Henry Guildford, this night to be comptrollers*, H8 I, 3, 66. *say thou No, this sword, this arm, and my best spirits, are bent to prove upon thy heart, whereto I s., thou liest*, Lr. V, 3, 140 (which I call up to bear evidence). *my demerits may s. unbonneted to as proud a fortune as this*, Oth. I, 2, 23 (= may apply to, may claim). *more urgent touches do strongly s. to us*, Ant. I, 2, 188.

*to s. of*, usually = to talk about: Wiv. IV, 4, 17. Meas. I, 2, 140. I, 3, 6. V, 284. 306. 340. Mids. I, 1, 112. Shr. II, 193. All's III, 6, 119. Tw. II, 3, 23. H4A I, 1, 46. III, 1, 12. R3 II, 1, 108. Oth. II, 1, 31 (but cf. *Comfort*) etc. etc. *to s. ill of*, Tw. III, 4, 111. *to s. well of*, Sonn. 34, 7. Wiv. IV, 5, 65. H4B II, 2, 69 (*on*). R3 V, 3, 192. Tim. IV, 3, 173. *better*, All's II, 5, 51. *foully*, H4A I, 3, 154. *admiringly*, All's I, 1, 33. *scantly*, Ant. III, 4, 6 etc. Peculiar passage: *we have not spoke us yet of torch-bearers*, Merch. II, 4, 5 (*us* evidently the dativus commodi; = we have not yet spoken of torch-bearers as necessary to our purpose, i. e. we have not yet bespoken torch-bearers). Sometimes *to s. of* = to express in words (in negative sentences): *I would not break with her for more money than I'll s. of*, Wiv. III, 2, 57. *they are not to be named, not to be spoke of*, Ado IV, 1, 97 (Ff *spoken of*). *then have you lost a sight, which was to be seen, cannot be spoken of*, Wint. V, 2, 47. *this priest has no pride in him? Not to s. of*, H8 II, 2, 82. *a sight past —ing of in a king*, Lr. IV, 6, 209.

*To s.*, abs., = to confer about sth. by way of coming to an agreement: *what says he to your daughter? have you spoke?* All's V, 3, 28. *we will s. further*, Mcb. I, 5, 72. *I have spoke already, and it is provided*, Ant. V, 2, 195.

Sometimes, in a kind of euphemism, = to exchange blows, to fight: *they lie in view, but have not spoke as yet*, Cor. I, 4, 4. *would we had spoke together*, Ant. II, 2, 167. *we'll s. with thee at sea*, II, 6, 25.

2) to be expressive, to have a meaning: *her foot —s*, Troil. IV, 5, 56. *she —s, yet she says nothing*, Rom. II, 2, 12. *most —ing looks*, Lr. IV, 5, 25. Trans., = to be expressive of, to show, to prove: *whose fury not dissembled —s his griefs*, Tit. I, 438. *how this grace —s his own standing*, Tim. I, 1, 31. *sundry blessings hang about his throne, that s. him full of grace*, Mcb. IV, 3, 159. *whose virtue and whose graces s. that which none else can utter*, Ant. II, 2, 132. *what his very action —s in every power that moves*, III, 12, 35. With a clause: *are you so much in love as your rhymes s.?* As III, 2, 417. *whose love had spoke, even since it could s., freely that it was yours*, Wint. III, 2, 70. *the ruin —s that sometime it was a worthy building*, Cymb. IV, 2, 354. *his sealed commission doth s. sufficiently he's gone*, Per. I, 3, 14. Absol.: *let proof s.* Cymb. III, 1, 77.

3) to utter with the mouth, to pronounce. to utter articulately· *s. fair words, or else be mute*, Ven. 208.

*spoke the prologue of our comedy*, Wiv. III, 5, 75. *are these things spoken, or do I but dream?* Ado IV, 1, 67. 68. *s. off half a dozen dangerous words*, V, 1, 97. *'then' is spoken*. V, 2, 46. *one that hath spoke most villanous speeches*, Meas. V, 265; LLL V, 2, 110; 148; Mids. III, 1, 77; Rom. I, 4, 1; Hml. II, 2, 454. *thou hast spoken no word all this while*, LLL V, 1, 156; Meas. V, 129; Err. II, 2, 13; As I, 1, 89; Shr. I, 2, 39; R2 V, 4, 1; H6A III, 4, 31; H6B I, 3, 200; R3 III, 7, 24; H8 II, 4, 153; Tit. I, 359; Caes. IV, 2, 33; Lr. III, 4, 91. *to s. dout, when he should say doubt*, LLL V, 1, 22. *vows in number more than ever women spoke*, Mids. I, 1, 176. *after some oration fairly spoke by a beloved prince*, Merch. III, 2, 180. *s. your office*, Tw. I, 5, 223. *but spoke the harm that is by others done*, John III, 1, 39. *God s. this Amen*, H5 V, 2, 396. *now we three have spoke it, it skills not greatly who impugns our doom*, H6B III, 1, 280. *and more he would have said, and more he spoke, ... that mought not be distinguished*, H6C V, 2, 43. *every syllable that here was spoke*, Troil. V, 2, 117. *s. out the rest*, Hml. II, 2, 545. *s. out thy sorrows*, Per. I, 4, 58 etc. = to recite, as opposed to singing: *we'll s. it, then*, Cymb. IV, 2, 242. Peculiar expressions: *he —s holiday*, Wiv. III, 2, 69 (festival terms). *she —s poniards*, Ado II, 1, 255; cf. *I will s. daggers to her, but use none*, Hml. III, 2, 414. *to s. all mirth and no matter*, Ado II, 1, 343. *s. sad brow and true maid*, As III, 2, 226 (= what becomes a grave and honest maid. Some M. Edd. *s., sad brow*. cf. Ado I, 1, 185). *he —s nothing but madman*, Tw. I, 5, 115. *he —s plain cannon fire*, John II, 462. *s. treason*, R2 V, 3, 44. R3 I, 1, 90. *I s. to thee plain soldier*, H5 V, 2, 156. *there's no leprosy but what thou —est*, Tim. IV, 3, 367. *s. parrot*, Oth. II, 3, 281.

4) to talk or converse in, to use or to be able to use as one's language: *the best of them that s. this speech*, Tp. I, 2, 429. 430. *s. the former language*, Meas. II, 4, 140. *—s three languages*, Tw. I, 3, 27. Wint. III, 2, 81. H4A II, 4, 26. H5 II, 1, 49. 121. H5 V, 2, 196. H6B IV, 7, 63. H8 I, 4, 57. 65 etc.

5) to convey in words, to express, to talk of: *if you s. love*, Ado II, 1, 103. *men can counsel and s. comfort to that grief which they not feel*, V, 1, 21. *to s. patience*, 27. *there thou —est reason*, 41; cf. Wiv. II, 1, 129. *it is my father's music to s. your deeds*, Wint. IV, 4, 530. *spoke your deservings like a chronicle*, H4A V, 2, 58. *may it please your highness to hear me s. his good now?* H8 IV, 2, 47. *Christendom shall ever s. his virtue*, 63. *not to s. it profanely*, Hml. III, 2, 34. *if thy rare qualities ... could s. thee out*, H8 II, 4, 140. *let me s. myself*, III, 1, 125. *thus far give me leave to s. him, and yet with charity*, IV, 2, 32. *I s. my good lord cardinal to this point, and thus far clear him*, II, 4, 166. *I cannot s. him home*, Cor. II, 2, 107. *you s. him far*, Cymb. I, 1, 24.

6) to say: *the truth you s. doth lack some gentleness*, Tp. II, 1, 137. *'twere false, if I should s. it*, Gent. IV, 2, 107. *it is spoke in hate*, III, 2, 34. *it must with circumstance be spoken*, 36. *s. the truth by her*, II, 4, 151 (cf. *By*). *I'll s. it before the best lord*, Wiv. III, 3, 53. *if it be honest you have spoke*, Meas. III, 2, 166. *what you have spoke I pardon*, V, 366. *I spoke it but according to the trick*, 509. *you s. this to fetch me in*, Ado I, 1, 225. 226. *I have for barbarism spoke more*, LLL I, 1, 112. *vice (not virtue) you should have spoke*, V,

2, 349. *thou —est it well*, Merch. II, 2, 161 (= well said). *I have spoke thus much*, IV, 1, 202. *you never spoke what did become you less*, Wint. I, 2, 282. V, 1, 21. *to lengthen out the worst that must be spoken*, R2 III, 2, 199. *I heard thee say, and vauntingly thou spakest it*, IV, 36. *under the correction of bragging be it spoken*, H5 V, 2, 144. *things are often spoke and seldom meant*, H6B III, 1, 268. *who spake aloud: what scourge for perjury ...*, R3 I, 4, 50 (Qq *cried*). *but nothing spake in warrant from himself*, III, 7, 33 (Ff *spoke*). *this is about that which the bishop spake*, H8 V, 1, 84. *repent what you have spoke*, Cor. III, 2, 37. *what I spake, I spake it to my face*, Rom. IV, 1, 34. *what he spake was not like madness*, Hml. III, 1, 171. *I dare s. it to myself*, Cymb. IV, 1, 7 etc. *I s. my thought*, Ado I, 1, 226. 227. 229. *I will s. my conscience*, H5 IV, 1, 123. H6B III, 1, 68. *s. his very heart*, Wint. IV, 4, 575. Mcb. I, 3, 154. *to s. your bosom freely*, Oth. III, 1, 58. *dare not s. their knowledge*, Ant. IV, 12, 6. (cf. *Mind*). *your lordship —s your pleasure*, Tim. III, 1, 35 (German: *es beliebt Euer Gnaden so zu sagen.* cf. *Pleasure*). *'tis dangerous to be spoken*, Lr. III, 3, 11.

7) to tell, to report, to communicate: *to s. my griefs unspeakable*, Err. I, 1, 33. *they have spoken untruths*, Ado V, 1, 220. *s. it privately*, Merch. II, 4, 21. *I have spoke the truth*, All's V, 3, 230. *if she be so abandoned to her sorrow as it is spoke*, Tw. I, 4, 20. *when I spake darkly what I purposed*, John IV, 2, 232. *whoever spoke it, it is true*, V, 5, 19. *s. plainly your opinions*, H4B I, 3, 3. *who hath not heard it spoken how deep you were within the books of God*, IV, 2, 16. *s. it to us*, H8 IV, 1, 61. *I heard a senator s. it*, Cor. I, 3, 107. *there's wondrous things spoke of him*, II, 1, 152. *and 'tis spoken, to the succeeding royalty he leaves the healing benediction*, Mcb. IV, 3, 154. *s. your griefs* Caes. IV, 2, 42. 3, 281. *I cannot s. any beginning to this peevish odds*, Oth. II, 3, 184. *did I but s. thy deeds*, IV, 2, 76. *even but now he spake, after long seeming dead. Iago hurt him*, V, 2, 327. *from what cause, he will by no means s.* Hml. III, 1, 6. *so far as thou wilt s. it* (thy story) Cymb. III, 6, 93 etc.

8) to make itself felt and call up to action: *therein you can never be too noble, but when extremities s.* Cor. III, 2, 41. *if his fitness —s, mine is ready*, Hml. V, 2, 209. *the shame itself doth s. for instant remedy*, Lr. I, 4, 267. *such time that —s as loud as his own state and ours*, Ant. I, 4, 29. *the present need —s to atone you*, II, 2, 102. With an obj. (accus. or dative?): *the occasion —s thee*, Tp. II, 1, 207 (summons thee, calls thee up).

9) to give sound: *beat thou the drum, that it s. mournfully*, Cor. V, 6, 151. *make all our trumpets s.* Mcb. V, 6, 9. *let the kettle to the trumpet s.* etc. Hml. V, 2, 286. *trumpets, s.!* Lr. V, 3, 150. *the wind hath spoke aloud at land*, Oth. II, 1, 5. *since death of my dearest mother it* (the instrument) *did not s. before*, Cymb. IV, 2, 191. cf. *I can sing and s. to him in many sorts of music*, Tw. I, 2, 58.

*Spoken*, adjectively, = speaking, having a language: *methinks you're better spoken*, Lr. IV, 6, 10. cf. *Foul-spoken, Well-spoken*.

**Speaker**, 1) one speaking: *that contempt will kill the —'s heart*, LLL V, 2, 149. *let me be privileged by my place and message, to be a s. free*, Troil. IV, 4, 133. *stay, you imperfect —s, tell me more*, Mcb. I, 3, 70. *what's the newest grief? That of an hour's age doth hiss*

*the s.* IV, 3, 175. *never say hereafter but I am truest s.* Cymb. V, 5, 376. *With of: after my death I wish no other herald, no other s. of my living actions, but such an honest chronicler as Griffith*, H8 IV, 2, 70.

2) an orator: *a s. is but a prater*, H5 V, 2, 166. *a most rare s.* H8 I, 2, 111.

3) the president of the parliament: *to us the s. in his parliament*, H4B IV, 2, 18. H6A III, 2, 60.

**Spear**, a lance: Ven. 626. 1112. Lucr. 1424. R2 I, 1, 171. I, 2, 48. I, 3, 60. 119. H4A I, 3, 193. H6A I, 1, 138. H6B IV, 7, 10. V, 1, 100.

**Spear-grass**, a long stiff grass: H4A II, 4, 340.*

**Special**, 1) particular, peculiar: Sonn. 52, 11. Gent. II, 1, 18. Wiv. III, 3, 200. Meas. I, 1, 18. I, 2, 123. III, 2, 233. IV, 3, 60. 119. H4A I, 3, 193. V, 5, 4. V, 464. LLL I, 1, 153. II, 162. Merch. V, 292. Shr. II, 11. 129. All's II, 2, 6 (*what place make you s.*, = specify in H6A III, 2, 21). H6A I, 1, 171. III, 1, 66. H6C IV, 1, 87. Rom. II, 3, 18. Hml. III, 2, 20. IV, 7, 9. V, 2, 231. Lr. IV, 6, 219. Oth. I, 1, 183. I, 3, 72. V, 2, 322.

2) particular, uncommon, select, choice: *to make some s. moment s. blest*, Sonn. 52, 11 (adverbially). *confirm his welcome with some s. favour*, Gent. II, 4, 101. *a s. virtue*, III, 1, 314. *you have ta'en a s. stand to strike at me*, Wiv. V, 5, 248. *some certain s. honours it pleaseth his greatness to impart to Armado*, LLL V, 1, 112. *thus he his s. nothing ever prologues*, All's II, 1, 95. *have a s. care of him*, Tw. III, 4, 69. R2 III, 1, 39. *the king hath drawn the s. head of all the land together*, H4A IV, 4, 28. *'tis my s. hope that you will clear yourself*, H6B III, 1, 139. *the people of Rome, for whom we stand a s. party*, Tit. I, 21. *thought on s. dignities*, Tim. V, 1, 145. *without our s. wonder*, Mcb. III, 4, 112.

**Special-blest**, see *Special*, 2.

**Specially**, particularly, especially, above all: Shr. I, 1, 20. 121.

**Specialty**, 1) particular nature: *the s. of rule hath been neglected*, Troil. I, 3, 78.

2) Plur. —es = special terms or articles of a contract: *the packet where that and other —es are bound*, LLL II, 165. *let —es be therefore drawn between us*, Shr. II, 127.

**Specify**, to indicate particularly, to point out: *how will she s. where is the best and safest passage in?* H6A III, 2, 21. cf. Dogberry's speech in Ado V, 1, 264.*Launcelot uses it in the sense of to tell, to expose: *as my father shall s.* Merch. II, 2, 131. 137.

**Speciously**, in the language of Mrs. Quickly, = especially: Wiv. III, 4, 113. IV, 5, 114.

**Spectacle**, 1) show, sight: Lucr. 631. Pilgr. 127. Tp. I, 2, 26. As II, 1, 44. John IV, 3, 56. H6A I, 4, 41. H6B IV, 1, 144. H6C II, 1, 67. II, 5, 73. Troil. IV, 4, 14 (*a pair of —s*; Pandarus' speech). Cor. IV, 1, 25. Caes. III, 1, 223. III, 2, 202.

2) Plur. —s, = a) glasses to assist the sight: Ado I, 1, 191. As II, 7, 159. H6B V, 1, 165. Lr. I, 2, 36.

b) organs of vision: *and bid mine eyes be packing with my heart and called them blind and dusky —s, for losing ken of Albion's wished coast*, H6B III, 2, 112. *hath nature given them eyes ..., and can we not partition make with —s so precious 'twixt fair and foul?* Cymb. I, 6, 37.

**Spectacled**, furnished with spectacles: *the bleared sights are s. to see him*, Cor. II, 1, 222.

**Spectator**, one who beholds a play or spectacle:

Wint. III, 2, 38. IV, 1, 20. Hml. III, 2, 46. Cymb. V, 4, 158.

**Spectatorship,** the act of beholding: *some death more long in s. and crueller in suffering,* Cor. V, 2, 71.

**Speculation,** 1) the act of looking on: *though we upon this mountain's basis by took stand for idle s.* H5 IV, 2, 31.

2) vision, power of sight: *s. turns not to itself, till it hath travelled and is married there where it may see itself,* Troil. III, 3, 109. *thou hast no s. in those eyes,* Mcb. III, 4, 95. Abstr. pro concr.: *servants ... which are to France the spies and —s intelligent of our state,* Lr. III, 1, 24 ( = speculators, observers, watchers).

**Speculative,** seeing, watching, prying: *thoughts s. their unsure hopes relate, but certain issue strokes must arbitrate,* Mcb. V, 4, 19 (i. e. the visions of the mind. Perhaps in the modern sense, = notional, theoretical). *when light-winged toys of feathered Cupid seel with wanton dulness my s. and officed instruments,* Oth. I, 3, 271 (i. e. my eye. Qq *speculative and active instruments*).

**Speech,** 1) speaking: *in s. his beard wagged up and down,* Lucr. 1405. *my father's of a better nature than he appears by s.* Tp. I, 2, 497. *to affect s. and discourse,* Meas. I, 1, 4. *there was some s. of marriage betwixt myself and her,* V, 217. *first he did praise my beauty, then my s.* Err. IV, 2, 15. *without more s.* Merch. II, 9, 7. *slow in s.* Shr. II, 248. *be checked for silence, but never taxed for s.* All's I, 1, 77. *common s. gives him a worthy pass,* II, 5, 57. *which deserves high s.* Wint. II, 1, 70. *pardon should be the first word of thy s.* R2 V, 3, 114. *in s., in gait, in diet,* H4B II, 3, 28. *my lungs are wasted so that strength of s. is utterly denied me,* IV, 5, 218. *his deeds exceed all s.* H6A I, 1, 15. *though thy s. doth fail,* I, 4, 82. *her grace in s.* H6B I, 1, 32. *granted scope of s.* III, 1, 176. *in face, in gait, in s.* 373. *what was the s. among the Londoners concerning the French journey,* H8 I, 2, 154. *'tis his kind of s.* Cor. II, 3, 169. *only fair s.* III, 2, 96. *be not a niggard of your s.* Mcb. IV, 3, 180. *she has no s.* Oth. II, 1, 103. *while I spare s., which something now offends me,* II, 3, 199. *to entreat your captain to soft and gentle s.* Ant. II, 2, 3 etc.

2) any thing said or spoken: *which to his s. did honey passage yield,* Ven. 452. *to blush at —es rank,* Compl. 307. *to utter foul —es,* Tp. II, 2, 96. *I do bend my s. to one,* Meas. I, 1, 41. *with most painful feeling of thy s.* I, 2, 38. *spoke most villanous — es of the duke,* V, 265. 343. *runs not this s. like iron through your blood?* Ado V, 1, 252. LLL V, 2, 110. 147. 341. 402. As II, 7, 82. Tw. I, 2, 20. V, 70. Wint. III, 2, 219. V, 1, 121. R2 I, 1, 30. H4B IV, 1, 32. H6A III, 1, 6. H6B I, 1, 140. I, 3, 197. III, 2, 221. H6C IV, 1, 47. Troil. IV, 1, 8. Tit. II, 1, 55. Mcb. III, 1, 7. 76. Hml. IV, 2, 25. IV, 5, 91. Ant. III, 13, 148. Cymb. III, 5, 39 etc. = oration: Caes. III, 1, 245. 251. III, 2, 62 *(make).* = a piece of poetry or any thing else recited: Mids. III, 1, 77. V, 125. H4A II, 4, 428. H4B Epil. 2. Rom. I, 4, 1. Hml. II, 2, 451. 454. III, 2, 1. Lr. I, 4, 128.

3) the act of speaking with another, conversation, interview: *to have free s. with you,* Meas. I, 1, 78. *the s. we had to such a purpose,* I, 2, 79. *I would have some s. with you,* III, 1, 155. *helping me to the s. of Beatrice,* Ado V, 2, 3. *he desires some private s. with you,* All's II, 5, 62. *if I may come to the s. of him,* Wint. IV, 4, 786. *protract his s.* H6A I, 2, 120. *o'erhear*

*the s.* Hml. III, 3, 33. Lr. V, 1, 38. Oth II, 3, S. 225 III, 1, 29.

4) language, tongue: *the best of them that speak this s.* Tp. I, 2, 429.

**Speechless,** not speaking, wanting language, silent, dumb: Lucr. 1674. Sonn. 8, 13 (*s. song,* i. e. without words). 107, 12. Meas. I, 2, 188. LLL V, 2, 246. 861. Merch. I, 1, 164. John V, 6, 24. R2 I, 3, 172. Cor. V, 1, 67. Tit. III, 2, 39. Caes. I, 2, 255. Hml. II, 2, 507 (*the bold winds s.,* cf. *Speak 9*). Cymb. I, 5, 52. Per. I, 1, 36.

**Speed,** subst. 1) swiftness, celerity: *s. more than s. but dull and slow she deems,* Lucr. 1336. *in winged s. no motion shall I know,* Sonn. 51, 8. *with more s.* Err. I, 1, 110. *the s. of your tongue,* Ado I, 1, 142. *ride upon the violent s. of fire,* All's III, 2, 112. *their s. hath been beyond account,* Wint. II, 3, 197. 199. *this action of swift s.* John IV, 233. III, 4, 11. IV, 2, 113. *rides at high s.* H4A II, 4, 379. *with great s. of judgement, ay, with celerity,* Troil. I, 3, 329. *this s. of Caesar's,* Ant. III, 7, 75. = impetuosity, headlong violence: *stop the headlong fury of his* (affection's) *s.* Lucr. 501. *withhold thy s., dreadful occasion,* John IV, 2, 125. *till the s. of his rage goes slower,* Lr. I, 2, 182.

2) haste: Lucr. 44. 745. 1307. LLL V, 2, 751. Merch. III, 4, 49. Wint. IV, 4, 683. V, 1, 210. John IV, 2, 176. V, 7, 50. H4A III, 2, 162. H4B I, 1, 37. Rom. V, 2, 12. Caes. I, 2, 6. Hml. I, 2, 156. Oth. I, 3, 278. *with s.:* Lucr. 1294. Meas. II, 2, 17. III, 1, 60. LLL V, 2, 804. Wint. IV, 1, 23. John IV, 3, 157. H4A I, 1, 105. V, 2, 76. H4B I, 1, 214. IV, 2, 59. H5 IV, 3, 68. H6C IV, 6, 61. Troil. V, 10, 6. Rom. IV, 1, 123. Caes. III, 1, 287. Hml. III, 1, 177. IV, 3, 56. *with all s.:* H4A III, 3, 48. H5 II, 4, 141. H6B I, 1, 73. H6C IV, 6, 64. R3 III, 2, 17. III, 5, 103. *with all convenient s.* Merch. III, 4, 56. *with all good s.* R2 I, 2, 66. *with what good s.* All's V, 1, 34. *with greatest s.* H4B I, 1, 120. *with sober s.* H4B IV, 3, 86. *with all swift s.* R2 V, 1, 54. *with imagined s.* Merch. III, 4, 52 (= with the s. of imagination). *with swiftest wing of s.* All's III, 2, 76. *with your dearest s.* H4A V, 5, 36. *to make s.: his rider loved not s. being made from thee,* Sonn. 50, 8. *make s. from hence,* Gent. III, 1, 169. *makes s.* Mids. II, 1, 233. H6C II, 5, 135. *I'll make all s.* Meas. IV, 3, 109. *make good s.* H4B III, 1, 3. *to make your s. to Dover,* Lr. III, 1, 36. *he would make some s. of his return,* Merch. II, 8, 37. *one of my fellows had the s. of him,* Mcb. I, 5, 36 (= was swifter than he, was in advance of him, had the start of him). cf. *whose footing here anticipates our thoughts a se'nnight's s.* Oth. II, 1, 77.

3) fortune, success: *happy be thy s.* Shr. II, 139. *with mere conceit and fear of the queen's s.* Wint. III, 2, 146 (= fear, that the queen might not succeed). *this fool's s. be crossed with slowness,* Cymb. III, 5, 167 (quibbling).

4) a protecting and assisting power: *Saint Nicholas be thy s.* Gent. III, 1, 301. *Hercules be thy s.* As I, 2, 222. *good manners be your s.* H4A III, 1, 190. *Saint Dennis be my s.* H5 V, 2, 194. *Saint Francis be my s.* Rom. V, 3, 121. *has had most favourable and happy s.* Oth. II, 1, 67 (i. e. Desdemona has been his guardian angel).

**Speed,** vb. (impf. and partic. *sped;* partic. *speeded* = hastened in Meas. IV, 5, 10 and H4B IV, 3, 38)
1) intr. a) to make haste: *and early in the morning*

*— eth away*, Lucr. Arg. 16. *your wit's too hot, it — s too fast*, LLL II, 120. *— s from me*, Wint. I, 2, 373. *we must s. for France*, John I, 178. II, 297. H4A I, 3, 283. IV, 4, 35. H4B IV, 3, 38. *s. thee straight*, Cor. IV, 5, 93 (*thee* = thou). = to go, to travel in general: *thus can my love excuse the slow offence of my dull bearer when from thee I s.* Sonn. 51, 2. *not long before your highness sped to France*, H8 I, 2, 151.

b) to fare, to have any fortune, good or bad: *O cruel — ing!* Pilgr. 269. *you shall know how I s.* Wiv. II, 2, 278. III, 5, 137. *how s. you with my daughter?* Shr. II, 283. *it were impossible I should s. amiss*, 285. *how I have sped among the clergymen*, John IV, 2, 141. *I marvel how he sped*, H6A II, 1, 48. Troil. III, 1, 155. *how you shall s. in your journey's end*, Cymb. V, 4, 190. Of things, = to fall out: *I'll prove him, s. how it will*, Cor. V, 1, 61.

c) to succeed; 1) applied to things: *which (plot) if it s., is wicked meaning in a lawful deed*, All's III!, 7, 44. *an honest tale —s best being plainly told*, R3 IV, 4, 358. *have got a —ing trick to lay down ladies*, H8 I, 3, 40. *if this letter s., Edmund the base shall top the legitimate*, Lr. I, 2, 19. 2) to persons: *my rams s. not*, Pilgr. 247 (do not thrive). *I would not have him s.* Gent. IV, 4, 112. *and sped you, sir?* Wiv. III, 5, 67. Merch. V, 115. Shr. I, 2, 247. II, 303. All's III, 6, 72. Wint. I, 2, 389. III, 3, 46 (*thee* = thou). H6C IV, 1, 58. R3 V, 3, 102. Tit. I, 372. II, 1, 101. Tim. III, 2, 69. Lr. IV, 6, 212. Oth. IV, 1, 109. Ant. II, 3, 35. Per. II, 3, 116.

2) trans. a) to hasten, to dispatch: *she will s. her foot again*, All's III, 4, 37. *it shall be —ed well*, Meas. IV, 5, 10. *where is Montjoy the herald? s. him hence*, H5 III, 5, 36.

Partic. *sped* = dispatched, undone (German: *abgethan*): *so be gone: you are sped*, Merch. II, 9, 72. *sped with spavins*, Shr. III, 2, 53. *we three are married, but you two are sped*, V, 2, 185. *I am sped*, Rom. III, 1, 94.

b) to assist, to guard, to favour; used only in expressing wishes; absol.: *God s.* R3 II, 3, 6 (only in Ff). With an object: *heaven so s. me in my time to come*, Wiv. III, 4, 12. *Hymen now with luckier issue s. us*, Ado V, 3, 32. *God s. fair Helena!* Mids. I, 1, 180. *Fortune s. us*, Wint. IV, 4, 681. R2 I, 4, 32. H6A III, 2, 60. H8 I, 1, 52. Caes. I, 2, 88. II, 4, 41. Lr. IV, 6, 212.

**Speedily**, quickly, with haste: Meas. I, 4, 84. III, 1, 274. All's I, 3, 124. V, 3, 152. H4A III, 1, 197. IV, 1, 92. 133. H6C IV, 6, 102. H8 III, 2, 89. Lr. III, 7, 1. IV, 2, 80. Cymb. III, 5, 27.

**Speediness**, quickness, haste: Cymb. II, 4, 31.

**Speedy**, 1) quick, hasty: Lucr. 695. 1853. Gent. I, 3, 37. All's I, 2, 7. Wint. III, 1, 13. John II, 554. H4A I, 3, 120. V, 4, 55. H6A IV, 3, 1. V, 3, 5. 8. R3 III, 1, 60. Tit. II, 1, 110. Rom. IV, 5, 146. Tim. II, 2, 28. Hml. IV, 6, 33 (*—er adverbially*). Lr. I, 5, 4. IV, 2, 82. IV, 6, 217. V, 1, 65. Ant. V, 1, 67 (*with your —est bring us what she says*; cf. *with your earliest*, Oth. II, 3, 7).

2) soon to be expected, quickly approaching, near: *God send you a s. infirmity*, Tw. I, 5, 84. *hath sent out a s. power to encounter you*, H4B I, 1, 133. *craves your company for s. counsel*, H6C II, 1, 208. *I will wish her s. strength*, Cor. I, 3, 87. *arm you to this s. voyage*, Hml. III, 3, 24.

**Speken**, obsol. for *speak*, substituted by M. Edd. for *spoken* of O. Edd. in Per. II Prol. 12.

**Spell**, subst. charm, magic: Tp. IV, 127. V, 253. Epil. 8. Wiv. IV, 2, 185 (*by charms, by —s*). Mids. II, 2, 17 (*nor s. nor charm*). Wint. V, 3, 105. H6A V, 3, 2. H8 I, 3, 1. III, 2, 20. Cor. V, 2, 102. Mcb. III, 5, 18. Oth. I, 3, 61. Ant. IV, 12, 30 (*ah, thou s.! avaunt!*).

**Spell**, vb. 1) to read by telling letters singly: *she would s. him backward*, Ado III, 1, 61 (turn the wrong side out, misconstrue his qualities). *a, b, spelt backward*, LLL V, 1, 50. *thy love did read by rote and could not s.* Rom. II, 3, 88 (you knew only some phrases of love, but not its true nature).

2) to charm: *with —ing charms*, H6A V, 3, 31 (in v. 2 *charming spells*).

**Spell-stopped**, spell-bound, locked up by a charm: Tp. V, 61.

**Spencer**, name in R2 V, 6, 8 (Ff *Salisbury, Spencer, Blunt*; Qq *Oxford, Salisbury, Blunt*).

**Spend**, (impf. and partic. *spent*) 1) to afford, to bestow, to lend, to employ (German: *spenden*): *which (blood) by him tainted shall for him be spent, and as his due writ in my testament*, Lucr. 1182. *on this sad shadow Lucrece —s her eyes*, 1457 (i. e. she looks on it). *why doest thou s. upon thyself thy beauty's legacy?* Sonn. 4, 1. *I have no precious time at all to s., nor services to do, till you require*, 57, 3. *and in the praise thereof —s all his might*, 80, 3. *all my best is dressing old words new, —ing again what is already spent*, 76, 12. *—est thou (my Muse) thy fury on some worthless song*, 100, 3. *in this change is my invention spent*, 105, 11. *why so large cost doest thou upon thy fading mansion s.* 146, 6. *the time 'twixt six and now must by us both be spent most preciously*, Tp. I, 2, 241. *suit ill spent and labour ill bestowed*, Ado III, 2, 103. *—ing your wit in the praise of mine*, LLL II, 19. *how will he s. his wit*, IV, 3, 147. *s. his prodigal wits in bootless rhymes*, V, 2, 64. *we number nothing that we s. for you*, 198. *thou —est such high-day wit in praising him*, Merch. II, 9, 98. *that we with thee may s. our wonder too*, All's II, 1, 92. *this man may help me to his majesty's ear, if he would s. his power*, V, 1, 8. *s. a fawn upon 'em*, Cor. III, 2, 67. *and s. our flatteries, to drink those men ...*, Tim. I, 2, 142. *this night I'll s. unto a fatal end*, Mcb. III, 5, 20. *I wore my life to s. upon his haters*, Ant. V, 1, 9. *his comforts thrive, his trials well are spent*, Cymb. V, 4, 104. *in your search s. your adventurous worth*, Per. II, 4, 51.

*To s. one's mouth*, used of dogs, = to bark: *then do they s. their mouths; Echo replies*, Ven. 695. *coward dogs most s. their mouths*, H5 II, 4, 70. *he will s. his mouth and promise, like Brabbler the hound*, Troil. V, 1, 98. cf. above: *—s her eyes*, Lucr. 1457.

Applied to words, = to utter, to speak: *where words are scarce, they're seldom spent in vain*, R2 II, 1, 7. *I will but s. a word here in the house*, Oth. I, 2, 48. cf. *we may as bootless s. our vain command upon the enraged soldiers*, H5 III, 3, 24. *and in his bosom s. my latter gasp*, H6A II, 5, 38. *as if I borrowed mine oaths of him and might not s. them at my pleasure*, Cymb. II, 1, 6.

Applied to notions of passion, = to indulge, to vent: *he did behave his anger ere 'twas spent*, Tim. III, 5, 22. *the fury spent*, Wint. III, 3, 26. *on sheep or oxen could I s. my fury*, H6B V, 1, 27. *men ne'er s. their fury on a child*, H6C V, 5, 57. *thy fury spent*, Tim. IV, 3, 127. *to s. his fury upon himself*, Ant. IV, 6, 10.

cf. Sonn. 100, 3. *he may well in fretting s. his gall,* H6A I, 2, 16. *our cannon's malice vainly shall be spent,* John II, 251. *what I think I utter, and s. my malice in my breath,* Cor. II, 1, 58. *the life and feeling of her passion she hoards, to s. when he is by to hear her,* Lucr. 1318. *you s. your passion on a misprised mood,* Mids. III, 2, 74. *do I not s. revenge upon myself with present moan?* Sonn. 149, 7. *he's worth more sorrow, and that I'll s. for him,* Mcb. V, 8, 51. cf. *he robs himself that —s a bootless grief,* Oth. I, 3, 209.

2) to part with, to give away, to lose: *and gain by ill thrice more than I have spent,* Sonn. 119, 14. *this arm shall do it, or this life be spent,* R2 I, 1, 108. *words, life and all, old Lancaster hath spent,* R2 II, 1, 150. *nought's had, all's spent, where our desire is got without content,* Mcb. III, 2, 4. *s. your rich opinion for the name of a night-brawler,* Oth. II, 3, 195. *on either side I come to s. my breath,* Cymb. V, 3, 81 (= to lose my life).

3) to consume, to use up: *Mouldy, it is time you were spent,* H4B III, 2, 128. *stale and hoar ere it be spent,* Rom. II, 4, 140. 146.

4) to consume, to waste, to exhaust, to destroy, to finish: *s. the dowry of a lawful bed,* Lucr. 938. *what spite hath thy fair colour spent?* 1600. *pitiful thrivers, in their gazing spent,* Sonn. 125, 8. *if Cupid have not spent all his quiver in Venice,* Ado I, 1, 273. *you s. but time,* Merch. I, 1, 153. *—ing his manly marrow in her arms,* All's II, 3, 298. *my son and my servant s. all,* Shr. V, 1, 72. *not to s. it* (blood) *so unneighbourly,* John V, 2, 39. *he shall s. mine honour with his shame,* R2 V, 3, 68. *did my brother s. his youth, his valour, coin and people, in the wars?* H6B I, 1, 78. *s. her strength with overmatching waves,* H6C I, 4, 21. *though we have spent our harvest of this king,* R3 II, 2, 115. *after so many hours, lives, speeches spent,* Troil. II, 2, 1. Partic. *spent* = exhausted: *two spent swimmers,* Mcb. I, 2, 8. *almost spent with hunger,* Cymb. III, 6, 63. cf. H6A II, 5, 8. Ant. IV, 15, 85. = gone, passed: *foretell new storms to those already spent,* Lucr. 1589. *when tyrant's crests and tombs of brass are spent,* Sonn. 107, 14. *a beauty spent and done,* Compl. 11. *the time is spent,* Ven. 255. *the night is spent,* 717. R2 I, 3, 211. II, 1, 154. H6B III, 1, 325. R3 III, 2, 91.

5) to lay out, to expend: *spare not to s.* Pilgr. 324. *thou hast wherewith to s.* 408. H4A IV, 1, 54. With an object: Sonn. 9, 9. Gent. II, 4, 39. 41. Wiv. II, 2, 166. 241. Err. II, 2, 99. Merch. III, 1, 96. Tw. I, 5, 302. R2 II, 1, 180. Tim. III, 4, 26 (cf. *Of.*) Mcb. V, 8, 60. Hml. V, 2, 137. Ant. V, 2, 305 etc.

6) to pass (time): Ven. 847. Lucr. 1577. Sonn. 100, 6. Gent. I, 3, 5. 14. 66. II, 4, 63. 80. IV, 2, 104. Err. I, 1, 133. LLL II, 68. IV, 3, 182. V, 2, 831. Mids. II, 2, 112. R2 I, 3, 219. H4A I, 1, 56. V, 2, 83. H6A II, 5, 116. H6C V, 7, 42. R3 I, 4, 5. Mcb. II, 1, 23 etc.

**Spendthrift,** a prodigal: *a s. of his tongue,* Tp. II, 1, 24. Adjectively: *a s. sigh,* Hml. IV, 7, 123.

**Spenser,** the celebrated English poet: Pilgr. 109.

**Spermaceti,** see *Parmaceti.*

**Sperr,** to shut; Theobald's emendation generally received by M. Edd. in Troil. Prol. 19 (O. Edd. *stirre*).

**Spet,** see *Spit* vb.

**Sphere,** the orbit in which a star moves: Tp. II, 1, 183. Mids. II, 1, 7. 153. III, 2, 61. As III, 2, 3. All's I, 1, 100. John V, 7, 74. H4A V, 4, 65. Rom. II, 2, 17. Hml. IV, 7, 15. Ant. IV, 15, 10. *as they did battery to the —s intend,* Compl. 23 (i. e. to the stars).

*all kind of natures that labour on the bosom of this s.* Tim. I, 1, 66 (the earth). The stars supposed to produce an unearthly music by their motion: *discord in the — s,* As II, 7, 6. *music from the —s,* Tw. III, 1, 121. Ant. V, 2, 84. Per. V, 1, 231. — Figurative use: *how have mine eyes out of their —s be fitted,* Sonn. 119, 7. *make thy two eyes, like stars, start from their —s,* Hml. I, 5, 17. *to be called into a huge s., and not to be seen to move in't,* Ant. II, 7, 16.

**Sphered,** 1) placed in a sphere: *therefore is the glorious planet Sol in noble eminence enthroned and s.* Troil. I, 3, 90. — 2) round: *blow, till thy s. bias cheek outswell the colic of puffed Aquilon,* Troil. IV, 5, 8.

**Spherical,** 1) planetary: *knaves, thieves, and treachers, by s. predominance,* Lr. I, 2, 134.

2) globular, round: *she is s. like a globe,* Err. III, 2, 116. *her foot is fixed upon a s. stone,* H5 III, 6, 37.

**Sphery,** star-like, celestial: *Hermia's s. eyne,* Mids. II, 2, 99.

**Sphinx,** the monster of ancient fable, that proposed riddles to the passers-by: *subtle as S.* LLL IV, 3, 342.

**Spial,** spy: writing of some M. Edd. in H6A I, 4, 8; O. Edd. *espials.*

**Spice,** subst. an aromatic vegetable substance used for seasoning: Wint. IV, 3, 128. Plur. *—s:* Merch. I, 1, 33. Wint. IV, 3, 125. Rom. IV, 4, 1. Per. III, 1, 66. III, 2, 66. Figuratively: *thy by-gone fooleries were but —s of it,* Wint. III, 2, 185 (served only to season it, to give it a zest). *for all this s. of your hypocrisy,* H8 II, 3, 26 (taste, tincture). *the s. and salt that season a man,* Troil. I, 2, 277. *he hath —s of them all, not all,* Cor. IV, 7, 46.

**Spice,** vb. to season with spice, to make aromatic: Mids. II, 1, 124. Tim. IV, 3, 40.

**Spicery,** spices, aromatic substances: *in that nest of s.* R3 IV, 4, 424.

**Spider,** the insect Aranea: Meas. III, 2, 289. Mids. II, 2, 20. Merch. III, 2, 121. Wint. II, 1, 40. 45. John IV, 3, 128. R2 III, 2, 14 *(thy —s, that suck up thy venom).* H6B III, 1, 339. R3 I, 2, 19. I, 3, 242. IV, 4, 81. Troil. II, 3, 18. Rom. I, 4, 61. Cymb. IV, 2, 90.

**Spider-like,** like a spider: H8 I, 1, 62.

**Spigot,** a peg put into the faucet to keep in the liquor: *wilt thou the s. wield?* Wiv. I, 3, 24.

**Spill** (impf. and partic. *spilled* or *spilt*) 1) to shed; once used of tears: Lucr. 1236. Usually of blood: Ven. 1167. Lucr. 999. 1801. LLL IV, 1, 35. John III, 1, 102. R2 I, 2, 19. II, 1, 131. V, 5, 115. H4B II, 2, 122. H6A IV, 6, 22. R3 I, 3, 125 (Ff *spent*). III, 3, 22. Rom. III, 1, 152. Tim. III, 5, 88. Ant. IV, 8, 3.

2) to destroy: *so full of artless jealousy is guilt, it —s itself in fearing to be spilt,* Hml. IV, 5, 20. *crack nature's moulds, all germens s. at once,* Lr. III, 2, 8. cf. Lucr. 1801 and R2 V, 5, 115.

**Spilth,** effusion: *our vaults have wept with drunken s. of wine,* Tim. II, 2, 169.

**Spin** (impf. and partic. *spun*) 1) tr. and intr. to draw out into threads; to work at drawing threads: Lucr. Arg. 10. Gent. III, 1, 316. Tw. I, 3, 110. H6B IV, 2, 31. Cor. I, 3, 93.

2) to issue in a thread or small current: *make incision in their hides, that their hot blood may s. in English eyes,* H5 IV, 2, 10.

**Spinii,** name in All's II, 1, 43: *in the regiment of the S.*

**Spinner,** a spider with long legs: Mids. II, 2, 21. Rom. I, 4, 59.

**Spinster,** one whose occupation is to spin: Tw. II, 4, 45. H8 I, 2, 33. Oth. I, 1, 24.

**Spire,** top, summit: *to silence that, which, to the s. and top of praises vouched, would seem but modest,* Cor. I, 9, 24.

**Spirit** (dissyll. and monosyll.) 1) vital power, life: *the expense of s. in a waste of shame is lust in action,* Sonn. 129, 1. *the breath of heaven hath blown his* (the coal's) *s. out,* John IV, 1, 110. *now my s. is going; I can no more,* Ant. IV, 15, 58. Plur. *—s: my —s, as in a dream, are all bound up,* Tp. I, 2, 486. *my —s are nimble,* II, 1, 202. *weariness, to the dulling of my —s,* III, 3, 6. *these things smother her —s up,* Ado IV, 1, 113. *thought I thy —s were stronger than thy shames,* 127. LLL IV, 3, 306. As II, 4, 1. All's V, 1, 2. Wint. V, 3, 41. John II, 232. Cymb. I, 5, 41 etc. Cf. Loening, Shakespeare-Jahrb. XXXI, 13.
2) vivacity, mettle, fire, courage: *defect of s., life and bold audacity,* Lucr. 1346. *I do applaud thy s.* Gent. V, 4, 140. *I have s. to do any thing,* Meas. III, 1, 213. *all things are with more s. chased than enjoyed,* Merch. II, 6, 13. *woo her with some s.* Shr. II, 170. *let thy blood and s. embrace them,* Tw. II, 5, 160. *threw off his s., his appetite, his sleep,* Wint. II, 3, 16. John V, 4, 2. H4A IV, 1, 101. H6B III, 2, 308. H6C I, 2, 43. R3 III, 4, 52. Cor. I, 5, 14. Cymb. V, 3, 35 etc. Plur. *—s: summon up your dearest —s,* LLL II, 1. *pluck up thy —s,* Shr. IV, 3, 38. *you do draw my —s from me with new lamenting ancient oversights,* H4B II, 3, 46. H5 II, 1, 72. H6A V, 2, 1. H6C II, 2, 56. Ant. III, 13, 69. V, 2, 173 etc.
3) temper, disposition, sentiments: *I measure him by my own s., for I should flout him,* Ado II, 3, 149. *the man hath a contemptible s.* 188. *his jesting s.* III, 2, 60. *a man of great s.* LLL I, 2, 2. *it* (reckoning) *fitteth the s. of a tapster,* 43. *of such a merry, nimble, stirring s.* V, 2, 16. *that's the way to choke a gibing s.* 868. *allay with some cold drops of modesty thy skipping s.* Merch. II, 2, 196. *thou shalt see the difference of our s.* IV, 1, 368 (Q1 — s). III, 2, 165. III, 4, 15. IV, 1, 133. As I, 1, 23. 74. Tw. I, 5, 311. John I, 167. IV, 2, 176. IV, 3, 9. V, 1, 53. H5 III, 5, 38. R3 IV, 4, 196. Rom. V, 1, 4. Cymb. I, 5, 34 etc. Plur. *—s: my —s to attend this double voice accorded,* Compl. 3. *these well express in thee thy latter —s,* Tim. V, 4, 74. *that I may pour my —s in thine ear,* Mcb. I, 5, 27. *your —s shine through you,* III, 1, 128. *that no revenue hast but thy good —s,* Hml. III, 2, 63 etc.
4) mental power, vigor of intellect: *was it his s. ... that struck me dead?* Sonn. 86, 5. *a foolish extravagant s., full of forms,* LLL IV, 2, 68. *I have perhaps some shallow s. of judgment,* H6A II, 4, 16. *so much is my poverty of s.* R3 III, 7, 159.
5) that which pervades and tempers the whole mind, or the whole state and nature of a thing (often used periphrastically, when followed by *of*): *April hath put a s. of youth in every thing,* Sonn. 98, 3. *do not kill the s. of love with a perpetual dulness,* 56, 8. *if the gentle s. of moving words can no way change you,* Gent. V, 4, 55. *the s. of wantonness is scared out of him,* Wiv. IV, 2, 223. *awake the pert and nimble s. of mirth,* Mids. I, 1, 13. *O s. of love, how quick and fresh art thou,* Tw. I, 1, 9. *the s. of humours intimate reading aloud to him,* II, 5, 93. *God give thee the s. of*

*persuasion,* H4A I, 2, 170. *as if he mastered there a double s. of teaching and of learning,* V, 2, 64. *the dove and very blessed s. of peace,* H4B IV, 1, 46. *conjure up the s. of love in her,* H5 V, 2, 316. *the s. of deep prophecy she hath,* H6A I, 2, 55. *O thou invisible s. of wine,* Oth. II, 3, 283. *to whose soft seizure the cygnet's down is harsh and s. of sense hard as the palm of ploughman,* Troil. I, 1, 58 (i. e. sense or sensibility itself). *the eye itself, that most pure s. of sense,* III, 3, 106 (i. e. which is sense itself, the very emblem of perceptivity). *Without of: love is a s. all compact of fire,* Ven. 149. *that surly s., melancholy,* John III, 3, 42. *death, that dark s., in's nervy arm doth lie,* Cor. II, 1, 177.
6) mind, soul: *appals her senses and her s. confounds,* Ven. 882. *my s. is thine, the better part of me,* Sonn. 74, 8. *their guilt now 'gins to bite the —s,* Tp. III, 3, 106. *—s are not finely touched but to fine issues,* Meas. I, 1, 36. *anything that appears not foul in the truth of my s.* III, 1, 214. *the delighted s. to bathe in fiery floods,* 121. *my s. grows heavy in love,* LLL I, 2, 127. *the liberal opposition of our —s,* V, 2, 743. *tempt not too much the hatred of my s.* Mids. II, 1, 211. *giddy in s.* Merch. III, 2, 145. *quietness of s.* IV, 1, 12. *the motions of his s. are dull as night,* V, 86. *had our weak —s ne'er been higher reared,* Wint. I, 2, 72. *so be blest my s.!* V, 1, 71. *holding the eternal s., against her will, in the vile prison of afflicted breath,* John III, 4, 18. *his s. is come in,* V, 2, 70. *hear me speak with a prophetic s.* III, 4, 126. *when that this body did contain a s.* H4A V, 4, 89. *your s. is too true, your fears too certain,* H4B I, 1, 92 (cf. *True*). *whisper the —s of thine enemies,* R3 IV, 4, 192. *can thy s. wonder a great man should decline?* H8 III, 2, 374. *of s. so still and quiet,* Oth. I, 3, 95. *with a learned s.* III, 3, 259. *puddled his clear s.* III, 4, 143 etc. Plur. *—s: heaven give your —s comfort,* Meas. IV, 2, 73. *her —s are as coy and wild as haggards of the rock,* Ado III, 1, 35. *John the bastard, whose —s toil in frame of villanies,* IV, 1, 191. *your —s are attentive,* Merch. V, 70. *your —s are too bold for your years,* As I, 2, 183. *entame my —s to your worship,* III, 5, 48. *give a favour from you to sparkle in the —s of my daughter,* All's V, 3, 75. *with my vexed —s I cannot take a truce,* John III, 1, 17. *her wanton —s look out at every joint,* Troil. IV, 5, 56. *forth at your eyes your —s wildly peep,* Hml. III, 4, 119. *his —s should hunt after new fancies,* Oth. III, 4, 62. *make thy —s all of comfort,* Ant. III, 2, 41. *his —s fly out into my story,* Cymb. III, 3, 90 etc.
7) a human being, a person with respect to his kind or sphere of activity: *a better s. doth use your name,* Sonn. 80, 2. *every hymn that able s. affords,* 85, 7. *she was sought by —s of richest coat,* Compl. 236. *he's a s. of persuasion,* Tp. II, 1, 235 (cf. def. 5). *the afflicted —s here in the prison,* Meas. II, 3, 4. *that s. is possessed with haste that wounds the unsisting postern with these strokes,* IV, 2, 91. *is no bar to stop the foreign —s,* Merch. II, 7, 46. *I will not jump with common —s,* II, 9, 32. *the best conditioned and unwearied s. in doing courtesies,* III, 2, 295. *to be the snuff of younger —s,* All's I, 2, 60. *a braver choice of dauntless —s,* John II, 72. *these fiery —s,* V, 2, 114. *inland petty —s,* H4B IV, 3, 119. *the flat unraised —s,* H5 Prol. 9. *the choice and master —s of this age,* Caes. III, 1, 163. *that s. upon whose weal depend and*

*rest the lives of many*, Hml. III, 3, 14. *noble swelling* —*s*, Oth. II, 3, 57. *there's a great s. gone*, Ant. I, 2, 126. *that huge s.* IV, 15, 89.

8) any supernatural being, an angel, a ghost, a demon, a fairy etc.: Sonn. 61, 5. 86, 5. 144, 2. Tp. I, 2, 193. 206. 215. 272. 409. 411. 420. 458. II, 2, 3. 15. 66. III, 2, 102. IV, 1, 58. 120. 149. 165. V, 2. 251. 261. Epil. 14. Gent. III, 1, 195. Wiv. III, 3, 230. IV, 4, 35. 63. V, 2, 13. V, 5, 33. Meas. I, 4, 35. IV, 2, 76. Err. V, 334. LLL IV, 3, 257. Mids. II, 1, 1. 16. II, 2, 7. III, 1, 157. III, 2, 382. 388. Tw. V, 242. H4A II, 4, 405. H6A II, 1, 25. V, 3, 10. H6B I, 2, 79. H8 III, 2, 129. Caes. I, 2, 147. IV, 3, 282. Mcb. IV, 1, 112. Hml. I, 1, 171. I, 4, 6. Lr. IV, 2, 46. Oth. III, 4, 126. Ant. II, 3, 19. Cymb. V, 4, 93 etc. In Lr. II, 1, 78 Qq *spurs.*

**Spirited,** inspirited, enlivened, animated: *our quick blood, s. with wine,* H5 III, 5, 21.

**Spiriting,** writing of some M. Edd. for *sprighting,* q. v.; O. Edd. *spryting.*

**Spiritless,** wanting life and animation: *so faint, so s., so dull, so dead in look,* H4B I, 1, 70.

**Spirit-stirring,** exciting the spirit: Oth. III, 3, 352.

**Spiritual,** not temporal, relating to sacred things, ecclesiastical, religious: Wint. II, 1, 186. H5 I, 1, 76. H6A III, 1, 50. H8 II, 4, 117. III, 2, 132. 140. In Lr. I, 2, 134 Qq *knaves, thieves, and treachers, by s. predominance;* Ff *spherical.*

**Spiritualty,** ecclesiastical body, clergy: *we of the s.* H5 I, 2, 132.

**Spirt,** to sprout, to shoot, to grow fast: *shall our scions, put in wild and savage stock, s. up so suddenly into the clouds,* H5 III, 5, 8.

**Spit,** subst. an iron prong on which meat is roasted: Err. I, 2, 44. Ado II, 1, 261 (*turned s.*). LLL III, 20. Cor. IV, 4, 5. Tit. IV, 2, 146. Lr. III, 6, 16. Per. IV, 2, 142.

**Spit,** vb. (partic. —*ed*) to put as on a spit: *infants —ed upon pikes,* H5 III, 3, 38. *did s. his body upon a rapier's point,* Rom. IV, 3, 56.

**Spit,** vb. (in Merch. *spet.* Impf. and partic. *spit*) 1) absol. to throw out saliva: *orators, when they are out, they will s.* As IV, 1, 76; cf. V, 3, 12 and Troil. I, 3, 173. *s. in the hole, man, and tune again,* Shr. III, 1, 40 (= fall to it with fresh courage). *if it be a hot day, and I brandish any thing but a bottle, I would I might never s. white again,* H4B I, 2, 237 (Nares adduces some passages from contemporary writers to prove that to spit white was thought to be the consequence of intemperance in drinking; but he has forgotten to ascertain the colour of other people's spittle)* *to s. at* or *on a p.,* a mark of extreme contempt and disgust: Err. II, 2, 36. As III, 2, 438. Wint. IV, 3, 113. R2 I, 1, 60. R3 I, 2, 145. Merch. I, 3, 113. 127. 132. R2 IV, 75. Tim. IV, 3, 364. Cymb. V, 5, 222. *she s. in his face,* Meas. II, 1, 86. H4A II, 4, 214.

2) tr. to throw out from the mouth: *a mouth that —s forth death and mountains,* John II, 458. *s. it in Mowbray's face,* R2 I, 1, 194. *tongues s. their duties out,* H8 I, 2, 61 (utter disrespectful language).

Applied, metaphorically, to other things ejecting fluids or fire: Merch. II, 7, 45. John II, 211. H5 III, 5, 52. Cor. I, 3, 45. Lr. III, 2, 14. Per. III, 1, 8.

**Spital,** an hospital (in contempt): H5 II, 1, 78. V, 1, 86.

**Spital-house,** the same: Tim. IV, 3, 39.

**Spite,** subst. 1) malice, ill-will: *made lame by fortune's dearest s.* Sonn. 37, 3. *join with the s. of fortune,* 90, 3. *when other petty griefs have done their s.* 10. *the ragged'st hour that time and s. can bring,* H4B I, 1, 151. *speak not in s.* H6B V, 1, 213. *let him do his s.* Oth. I, 2, 17. H6A IV, 1, 185. H6B I, 3, 218. H6C IV, 6, 19. Cor. IV, 5, 88. Tim. I, 2, 144. IV, 3, 228. Cymb. V, 4, 31.

2) any disposition to thwart and disappoint the wishes of another, as well as that which is done to mortify others: *what s. hath thy fair colour spent?* Lucr. 1600 (*what has happened to vex thee and make thee so pale?*). *in our two loves there is but one respect, though in our lives a separable s.* Sonn. 36, 6 (= a s. of separation). *kill me with —s, yet we must not be foes,* 40, 14 (however you may break my heart by doing what makes me unhappy). *I'll find Demetrius and revenge this s.* Mids. III, 2, 420. *the more my wrong, the more his s. appears,* Shr. IV, 3, 2. *where he sits crowned in his master's s.* Tw. V, 131. *a villain that is hither come in s.* Rom. I, 5, 64 (only to defy and provoke us). *who in s. put stuff to some she beggar,* Tim. IV, 3, 272 (against her will, notwithstanding her reluctance). *the tears have got small victory by that, for it* (the face) *was bad enough before their s.* Rom. IV, 1, 31.

*In s. of* = a) to the mortification of: *to fashion this false sport in s. of me,* Mids. III, 2, 194. *these my friends in s. of thee shall wear,* H6A II, 4, 106. *flourishes his blade in s. of me,* Rom. I, 1, 85. b) notwithstanding: Ven. 173. Pilgr. 180. Ado V, 2, 69 (quibbling). R2 III, 2, 28. H6A I, 3, 50. I, 5, 37. III, 3, 73. H6B IV, 10, 37. V, 1, 206. H8 III, 2, 219. Troil. V, 5, 41 (*in very s. of cunning*). Mcb. IV, 1, 86. Oth. I, 3, 96. *s. of* = in spite of, notwithstanding: Sonn. 107, 11. Compl. 13. LLL I, 1, 4. John III, 4, 9. Lr. II, 4, 33. Per. II, 1, 161. V, 3, 31. *in s. of s.,* or *s. of s.* = come the worst that may, notwithstanding any thing that may happen: *that misbegotten devil, Faulconbridge, in s. of s., alone upholds the day,* John V, 4, 5. *and s. of s. needs must I rest awhile,* H6C III, 3, 5.*

3) vexation, mortification: *this is my s., that, thou being dead, the day should yet be light,* Ven. 1133. *thus breathes she forth her s.* Lucr. 762. *to put in practice either, alas, it was a s. unto the silly damsel,* Pilgr. 217. *that change is the s.* Gent. IV, 2, 69. *O s. of —s! we talk with goblins,* Err. II, 2, 191. *the more my s.* IV, 2, 8. *O s.! too old to be engaged to young,* Mids. I, 1, 138. III, 2, 145. V, 281. *this is the deadly s. that angers me,* H4A III, 1, 192. *O unbid s.! is sportful Edward come?* H6C V, 1, 18. *that were some s.* Rom. II, 1, 27. *O cursed s., that ever I was born to set it right,* Hml. I, 5, 188. *'tis the s. of hell,* Oth. IV, 1, 71.

**Spite,** vb. to thwart malignantly, to mortify: *to s. me now, each minute seems a moon,* Pilgr. 207. *to s. my wife,* Err. III, 1, 118. *if you s. it* (your heart) *for my sake, I will s. it for yours,* Ado V, 2, 70. *that which —s me more than all these wants,* Shr. IV, 3, 11. *to s. a raven's heart,* Tw. V, 134. *beguiled, divorced, wronged, —d, slain,* Rom. IV, 5, 55. *I am reckless what I do to s. the world,* Mcb. III, 1, 111.

**Spiteful,** 1) malignant: H6B I, 3, 158. Troil. II, 3, 7. 2) disposed to thwart the expectations of others: *all you have done hath been but for a wayward*

-ton, s. and wrathful, who, as others do, loves for his own ends, not for you, Mcb. III, 5, 12.

**Splay**, lection of O. Edd. in Meas. II, 1, 243; M. Edd. spay, q. v.

**Spleen**, 1) fire, heat, impetuosity, eagerness: *a brook where Adon used to cool his s.* Pilgr. 76. *with ladies' faces and fierce dragons' —s*, John II, 68. *at this match, with swifter s. than powder can enforce, the mouth of passage shall we fling wide ope*, 448. *or teach thy hasty s. to do me shame*, IV, 3, 97. *scalded with my violent motion, and s. of speed*, V, 7, 50. *leaden age, quickened with youthful s. and warlike rage*, H6A IV, 6, 13. *robbed my soldiers of their heated s.* H6C II, 1, 124. *inspire us with the s. of fiery dragons*, R3 V, 3, 350. *Jove forbid there should be done amongst us such things as might offend the weakest s. to fight for and maintain*, Troil. II, 2, 128 (the dullest and coldest heart). *could not take truce with the unruly s. of Tybalt*, Rom. III, 1, 162.

2) hate, malice: *O preposterous and frantic outrage, end thy damned s.* R3 II, 4, 64. *take good heed you charge not in your s. a noble person*, H8 I, 2, 174. *I have no s. against you*, II, 4, 89 (cf. v. 83). *your heart is crammed with arrogancy, s. and pride*, 110. *I will fight against my cankered country with the s. of all the under fiends*, Cor. IV, 5, 97. *it is a cause worthy my s. and fury*, Tim. III, 5, 113. *create her child of s.* Lr. I, 4, 304.

3) a sudden motion, a fit: *the lightning, that, in a s., unfolds both heaven and earth*, Mids. I, 1, 146. Hence = any sudden impulse or fit beyond the control of reason; a) a fit of laughter: *who, with our —s, would all themselves laugh mortal*, Meas. II, 2, 122. *thy silly thought enforces my s.* LLL III, 77. *in this s. ridiculous appears, to check their folly, passion's solemn tears*, V, 2, 117. *abate their over-merry s.* Shr. Ind. 1, 137. *if you desire the s., and will laugh yourselves into stitches*, Tw. III, 2, 72 (or rather here = a splenetic disease). *I shall split all in pleasure of my s.* Troil. I, 3, 178.

b) a fit of passion: *a hair-brained Hotspur, governed by a s.* H4A V, 2, 19. *you shall digest the venom of your s.* Caes. IV, 3, 47. *marry, patience: or I shall say you are all in all in s., and nothing of a man*, Oth. IV, 1, 89.

c) a caprice; a disposition acting by fits and starts: *a thousand —s bear her a thousand ways*, Ven. 907. (love) *begot of thought, conceived of s. and born of madness*, As IV, 1, 217. *a mad-brain rudesby full of s.* Shr. III, 2, 10. *a weasel hath not such a deal of s. as you are tossed with*, H4A II, 3, 81. *like enough, through vassal fear, base inclination and the start of s., to fight against me*, III, 2, 125. *the performance of our heaving —s*, Troil. II, 2, 196.

**Spleenative** or **Spleenitive**, hot, passionate, impetuous: *though I am not s. and rash*, Hml. V, 1, 284. M. Edd. splenitive.

**Spleenful**, hot, eager: *myself have calmed their s. mutiny, until they hear the order of his death*, H6B III, 2, 128. *let my s. sons this trull deflower*, Tit. II, 3, 191.

**Spleeny**, eager, headstrong: *I know her for a s. Lutheran*, H8 III, 2, 99.

**Splendour**, great brightness, brilliant lustre: Lucr. 25. Sonn. 33, 10. John III, 1, 79. Rom. I, 2, 106.

**Splenitive**, see *Spleenative*.

**Splint**, see *Splinter, vb.*

**Splinter**, subst. a piece of wood broken off: Troil. I, 3, 283. Cor. IV, 5, 115.

**Splinter**, vb. to join again and secure by splints: *the broken rancour of your hearts, but lately —ed, knit and joined together*, R3 II, 2, 118 (Q2 and some M. Edd. splinted). *this broken joint between you and her husband entreat her to s.* Oth. II, 3, 329.

**Split**, 1) trans. (partic. splitted: Err. I, 1, 104. V, 308. H6B III, 2, 411. Ant. V, 1, 24. Impf. not found) to rive, to cleave, to burst: *thou rather —'st the gnarled oak*, Meas. II, 2, 116. *thou —'st thine own (heart)* Wint. I, 2, 349. *I stabbed your fathers' bosoms, s. my breast*, H6C II, 6, 30. *when he shall s. thy very heart with sorrow*, R3 I, 3, 300. V, 1, 26. *entered me with a —ing power*, H8 II, 4, 183. *when the —ing wind makes flexible the knees of knotted oaks*, Troil. I, 3, 49. *crack thy lungs, and s. thy brazen pipe*, IV, 5, 7. *—ing the air with noise*, Cor. V, 6, 52. *though it do s. you*, Caes. IV, 3, 48. *tear a passion to tatters, to very rags, to s. the ears of the groundlings*, Hml. III, 2, 12 (to fill them to bursting). *let sorrow s. my heart*, Lr. V, 3, 177. *hath —ed the heart*, Ant. V, 1, 24. *blow and s. thyself*, Per. III, 1, 44 (cf. Tp. I, 1, 8: blow till thou burst thy wind).

= to break on a rock: *our ship was —ed in the midst*, Err. I, 1, 104. *the —ing rocks cowered in the sands*, H6B III, 2, 97 (cf. the —ing wind, Troil. I, 3, 49). *a —ed bark*, 411.

Applied to the manner of speaking, = to mutilate, to make inarticulate: *mine own tongue —s what it speaks*, Ant. II, 7, 131. *hast thou so cracked and —ed my poor tongue*, Err. V, 308.

2) intr. (partic. split: Tp. V, 223. Per. II Prol. 32. Impf. not found) to burst, to part asunder: *give me ribs of steel! I shall s. all in pleasure of my spleen*, Troil. I, 3, 177 (burst with laughter). Quibbling: *a part to tear a cat in, to make all s.* Mids. I, 2, 32 ('to make all split, a phrase expressing violence of action.' Nares). = to be broken on a rock, to be wrecked: Tp. I, 1, 65. 66. V, 223. Tw. I, 2, 9. H6C V, 4, 10. Per. II Prol. 32.

**Spoil**, subst. 1) that which is taken from the enemy and carried home in triumph, the Latin spolia: *laden with honour's —s*, Tit. I, 36. *all thy conquests, glories, triumphs, —s*, Caes. III, 1, 149. *thou doest shame that bloody s. (the lion's skin)* John III, 1, 115. *is not this an honourable s.? a gallant prize?* H4A I, 1, 74.

2) booty: *having felt the sweetness of the s.* Ven. 553. *the s. got on the Antiates was ne'er distributed*, Cor. III, 3, 4. *we looked for no less s. than glory*, V, 6, 44. *a power of high-resolved men, bent to the s.* Tit. IV, 4, 64. Plur. *—s: I have loaden me with many —s*, H6A II, 1, 80. *our —s he kicked at*, Cor. II, 2, 128. *our —s we have brought home*, V, 6, 77.

3) the act of plundering or ransacking: *the enraged soldiers in their s.* H5 III, 3, 25. *heady murder, s. and villany*, 32. *defer the s. of the city until night*, H6B IV, 7, 142. *to live but by the s., by robbing of your friends*, IV, 8, 41. *his soldiers fell to s.* Caes. V, 3, 7.

4) ravage, destruction, havoc: *make time's —s despised everywhere*, Sonn. 100, 2. *the foil of this false jewel, and his amorous s.* Compl. 154. *fit for treasons, stratagems and —s*, Merch. V, 85. *old age can do no*

*more s. upon my face*, H5 V, 2, 249. *death doth front thee with apparent s.* H6A IV, 2, 26. *yonder is the wolf that makes this s.* H6C V, 4, 80. *having bought love with such a bloody s.* R3 IV, 4, 290. *commit their cheeks to the s. of Phoebus' burning kisses*, Cor. II, 1, 233. *where he did run reeking o'er the lives of men, as if 'twere a perpetual s.* II, 2, 124. *here thy hunters stand, signed in thy s. and crimsoned in thy lethe*, Caes. III, 1, 206. Followed by *of*, objectively, = waste, corruption, perdition: *who his* (time's) *s. of beauty can forbid?* Sonn. 65, 12. *he fleshes his will in the s. of her honour*, All's IV, 3, 20. *villanous company hath been the s. of me*, H4A III, 3, 11. *to have the waste and s. of his revenues*, Lr. II, 1, 102 (Ff *the expense and waste*).

5) prey: *leaving his s.* (i. e. Lucrece) *perplexed in greater pain*, Lucr. 733. *set them down for sluttish —s of opportunity and daughters of the game*, Troil. IV, 5, 62.

**Spoil**, vb. 1) to plunder; to strip by violence: *to s. the city and your royal court*, H6B IV, 4, 53. *having in Sicily Sextus Pompeius —ed, we had not rated him his part o'the isle*, Ant. III, 6, 25.

2) to seize by violence; to rob: *not his that —s her young before her face*, H6C II, 2, 14.

3) to corrupt; to damage; to mar; to destroy; to ruin: *to s. antiquities of hammered steel*, Lucr. 951. *her sacred temple spotted, —ed, corrupted*, 1172. *in, or we are —ed*, Err. V, 37. *—ed with the staggers*, Shr. III, 2, 55. *we are —ed*, V, 1, 113. *bitter shame hath —ed the sweet world's taste*, John III, 4, 110. *s. his coat with scanting a little cloth*, H5 II, 4, 47. *disorder, that hath —ed us*, IV, 5, 17. *the boar that —ed your summer fields*, R3 V, 2, 8. *and s. your nobler soul*, H8 I, 2, 175. *we turn not back the silks upon the merchant, when we have —ed them*, Troil. II, 2, 70 (Q *soiled*). *what hath she done, prince, that can s. our mothers?* V, 2, 134 (Ff better: *soil*). *it —s the pleasure of the time*, Mcb. III, 4, 98. *these same crosses s. me*, Lr. V, 3, 278. *I am —ed, undone by villains*, Oth. V, 1, 54.

**Spoken**, see *Speken*.

**Spokes** (cf. *Waggon-spokes*) the rays of a wheel serving to support the felly: Hml. II, 2, 517. III, 3, 19.

**Spokesman**, one who speaks for another: *to be a s. for Madam Silvia. To whom? To yourself: why, she wooes you by a figure*, Gent. II, 1, 152.

**Sponge**, a soft porous substance imbibing fluids: Merch. I, 2, 108. Hml. IV, 2, 12. 15. 22.

**Spongy**, 1) imbibing like a sponge: *more s. to suck in the sense of fear*, Troil. II, 2, 12. = drenched, soaked: *his s. officers*, Mcb. I, 7, 71.

2) soft, porous and pliable like a sponge: *that sad breath his s. lungs bestowed*, Compl. 326.

3) wet, rainy: *s. April*, Tp. IV, 65. *the s. south*, Cymb. IV, 2, 349. cf. *Dispunge*.

**Spoon**, a domestic utensil used in eating liquids: *I will leave him; I have no long s.* Tp. II, 2, 103. *bespeak a long s. Why, Dromio? Marry, he must have a long s. that must eat with the devil*, Err. IV, 3, 62. 64 (proverb). John IV, 3, 131. *you'd spare your —s*, H8 V, 3, 168 (spoons being at that time, as to this day in Germany, the common present made by sponsors at a christening). V, 4, 40. Cor. I, 5, 6.

**Spoon-meat**, food that must be taken with a spoon: Err. IV, 3, 61.

**Sport**, subst. 1) diversion; pastime; amusement; pleasure: *such time-beguiling s.* Ven. 24. *others delight in such-like circumstance, with such-like s.* 844. *his time of folly and his time of s.* Lucr. 992. *making lascivious comments on thy s.* Sonn. 95, 6. *some say thy grace is youth and gentle s.* 96, 2. *youth is full of s.* Pilgr. 161. *all our evening s. from us is fled*, 291. *there be some —s are painful*, Tp. III, 1, 1. *he strays with willing s. to the wild ocean*, Gent. II, 7, 32. *we have s. in hand*, Wiv. II, 1, 204. 219. III, 2, 82. III, 3, 180. IV, 6, 30. V, 2, 14. V, 5, 256. Err. V, 77. 83. Ado II, 3, 223. LLL I, 1, 180. V, 2, 153. Mids. II, 1, 87. III, 2, 119. 353. V, 79. 90. As I, 2, 26. 32. 106. 107. 142. 147. Shr. Ind. 1, 91. Tw. II, 1, 49. II, 3, 187. II, 5, 2. 195. 217. IV, 2, 76. John V, 2, 175. R2 III, 4, 1. 9. H4A II, 1, 78. II, 4, 430. H5 I, 1, 56 (*—s*). H6B III, 2, 338. Troil. II, 3, 117. Cor. II, 2, 109. Tit. III, 1, 239 (*—s*). IV, 3, 70. V, 1, 96. 118. Rom. I, 5, 31. 121. Tim. II, 2, 48. Caes. II, 1, 189 (*—s*). Hml. III, 2, 227. III, 4, 206. Lr. I, 1, 23. IV, 1, 39. Oth. I, 3, 376. 392. II, 2, 6. IV, 3, 98. 102. Ant. I, 1, 47. I, 4, 29. IV, 7, 14. IV, 15, 32. Cymb. IV, 2, 31 (*I wish ye s.*). Per. V, 3, 41. *to make s. to* = to amuse: *to make us public s.* Wiv. IV, 4, 14. *one that makes s. to the prince*, LLL IV, 1, 101. *my lord made himself much s. out of him*, All's IV, 5, 68. *we'll make you some s. with the fox*, III, 6, 110. *thou wouldst be fee'd, I see, to make me s.* H6C I, 4, 92. *to make s.* = to amuse one's self; to take pleasure; to play: *let foolish gnats make s.* Err. II, 2, 30. *I with the morning's love have oft made s.* Mids. III, 2, 389. *wait on me home, I'll make s. with thee*, All's V, 3, 323. *misery makes s. to mock itself*, R2 II, 1, 85. *when she saw Pyrrhus make malicious s. in mincing her husband's limbs*, Hml. II, 2, 536.

Special significations: a) a play, or theatrical performance: *to our s., away!* LLL V, 1, 162. *might not you foretell our s.* V, 2, 473. 517. 522. *have made our s. a comedy*, 886. *in their s. forsook his scene*, Mids. III, 2, 14. *this s., well carried, shall be chronicled*, 240. *if our s. had gone forward*, IV, 2, 17. V, 42. *mark the moral of this s.* R2 IV, 290. *our wars will turn unto a peaceful comic*, H6A II, 2, 45. *who set the body and the limbs of this great s. together?* H8 I, 1, 47. *at this s. Sir Valour dies*, Troil. I, 3, 175. *how many times shall Caesar bleed in s.* Caes. III, 1, 114. cf. Compl. 242 (?).

b) out of door diversions, especially the chase: Wiv. IV, 2, 35. LLL IV, 2, 1. H6B II, 1, 2. 46. Troil. IV, 5, 239 (*a book of s.*). Tit. II, 2, 19. II, 3, 197. Cymb. III, 3, 10. Used of bear-baiting: Wiv. I, 1, 302. Of war and fighting: *sheathe for lack of s.* H5 IV, 2, 23. *till fields and blows and groans applaud our s.* H4A I, 3, 302. *hark, what good s. is out of town today*, Troil. I, 1, 116. 118.

c) a game of hazard: *we shall never win at that s., and stake down*, Merch. III, 2, 219. *in our —s my better cunning faints under his chance*, Ant. II, 3, 34.

d) amorous dallying; sensual enjoyment of love: *our s. is not in sight*, Ven. 124. *he had some feeling of the s.* Meas. III, 2, 127. *intercepted in your s.* Tit. II, 3, 80. *when the blood is made dull with the act of s.* Oth. II, 1, 230. *she is s. for Jove*, III, 3, 17. cf. Tit. V, 1, 96. 118. Lr. I, 1, 23; and *sportful* in Shr. II, 263.

2) jest, as opposed to earnest: *'tis holy s. to be a little vain, when the sweet breath of flattery conquers*

*strife*, Err. III, 2, 27; cf. *of the same piece is every flatterer's s.* Tim. III, 2, 72 (M. Edd. *spirit, port* etc.). *in a merry s. let the forfeit be nominated for an equal pound of your fair flesh*, Merch. I, 3, 146. *what is this? s.?* Wint. II, 1, 58. *name not your loss your s.* Cymb. II, 4, 48. *in s.* = in jest: Ado I, 1, 179. As I, 2, 30. IV, 3, 157. Lr. II, 1, 37.

= contemptuous jesting, mockery: *you shall buy this s. as dear*, Err. IV, 1, 81. *would behold in me this shameful s.* IV, 4, 108. *to fashion this false s.* Mids. III, 2, 194. *all to make you s.* 161. *he would make but a s. of it*, Ado II, 3, 163. *to make s. at*, or *with*, = to mock at: *make s. at me*, Wiv. III, 3, 160. *lest she make s. at it*, Ado III, 1, 58. *to make s. withal*, As I, 2, 28.

**Sport**, vb. to amuse one's self, to make merry, to play; 1) intr.: *hath learned to s. and dance*, Ven. 105. *advice is —ing while infection breeds*, Lucr. 907. *bids thee ... to come and s.* Tp. IV, 1, 74. *to s. would be as tedious as to work*, H4A I, 2, 229.

2) refl.: *where I list to s. me*, Ven. 154. *to feast and s. us*, Shr. IV, 3, 185. *let her s. herself with that she's big with*, Wint. II, 1, 60. *must I s. myself*, H6C II, 5, 34.

**Sportful**, 1) merry, frolicsome: *how with a s. malice it was followed*, Tw. V, 373. *is s. Edward come?* H6C V, 1, 18.*

2) amorous, wanton (cf. *Sport*, subst. 1. d): *let Kate be chaste and Dian s.* Shr. II, 263.

3) done in jest: *though it be a s. combat*, Troil. I, 3, 335.

**Sporting-place**, play-ground: *like a school broke up, each hurries toward his home and s.* H4B IV, 2, 105.

**Sportive**, 1) giving or taking pleasure, merry, playful: *for s. words*, Lucr. 1813. *in a s. humour*, Err. I, 2, 58. *drive thee from the s. court*, All's III, 2, 109.

2) amorous, wanton: *why should others' false adulterate eyes give salutation to my s. blood?* Sonn. 121, 6. *I, that am not shaped for s. tricks*, R3 I, 1, 14.

**Spot**, subst. 1) a speck, a blot, a mark: Ado V, 3, 27. Mids. II, 1, 11. Caes. I, 2, 183. IV, 1, 6. Mcb. V, 1, 35. 39.

2) a small extent of space: *you cannot see a white s. about her*, Wiv. IV, 5, 116.

3) a stain, a disgrace: Lucr. 685. 1053. All's V, 3, 206. John V, 2, 30. V, 7, 107. H6A III, 3, 57. Hml. III, 4, 90. Ant. IV, 12, 35.

Quibbling: *there shall not be one s. of love in't*, As III, 2, 444. *not painted with the crimson —s of blood*, John IV, 2, 253. *lions make leopards tame. Yea, but not change his —s*, R2 I, 1, 175 (cf. Jeremiah XIII, 23). *wert thou a leopard, the —s of thy kindred were jurors on thy life*, Tim. IV, 3, 344. *his faults in him seem as the —s of heaven, more fiery by night's blackness*, Ant. I, 4, 12.

4) a figure in needle-work (?): *what are you sewing here? a fine s.* Cor. I, 3, 56*(cf. *spotted* in Oth. III, 3, 435).

**Spot**, vb. 1) to mark with a colour different from the ground; only in the partic. *—ed: —ed snakes*, Mids. II, 2, 9. *—ed livers*, Troil. V, 3, 18. *the —ed die*, Tim. V, 4, 34. *a handkerchief —ed with strawberries*, Oth. III, 3, 435.*

2) to stain, to taint: Lucr. 196. 721. 1172. Sonn. 95, 3. Wint. I, 2, 328. R3 I, 3, 283. Oth. V, 1, 36. *—ed* = polluted, guilty: *this —ed and inconstant man*,

Mids. I, 1, 110. *their —ed souls*, R2 III, 2, 134. *—ed, detested and abominable*, Tit. II, 3, 74. *let die the —ed*, Tim. V, 4, 35. cf. *Toad-spotted.*

**Spotless**, 1) free from spots or discoloration: *this palliament of white and s. hue*, Tit. I, 182.

2) untainted, immaculate: Lucr. 1656. Wint. II, 1, 131. R2 I, 1, 178. H5 IV, 1, 168. H6B V, 1, 186. H8 III, 2, 301. Tit. V, 2, 177.

**Spousal**, marriage, nuptials: H5 V, 2, 390. *s. rites*, Tit. I, 337.

**Spouse**, wife: Err. I, 1, 44. Shr. IV, 5, 67. H5 II, 1, 77. Lr. III, 4, 84.

**Spout**, subst. 1) a pipe out of which water is poured: Wint. III, 3, 26. Tit. II, 4, 30. Caes. II, 2, 77.

2) a violent discharge of water raised in a column at sea; a water-spout: *not the dreadful s. which shipmen do the hurricano call*, Troil. V, 2, 171.

**Spout**, vb. to pour, to throw out as from a spout: John II, 256. Troil. IV, 5, 10. Caes. II, 2, 85. Lr. III, 2, 2. 14.

**Sprack**, pronounced *sprag* by Sir Hugh, = quick, alert: *he is a good s. memory*, Wiv. IV, 1, 84.

**Sprat**, the fish Clupea sprattus: *tell me what a s. you shall find him*, All's III, 6, 113.

**Sprawl**, to struggle in the convulsions of death: H6C V, 5, 39. Tit. V, 1, 51.

**Spray**, a shoot, a branch, a twig: R2 III, 4, 34. H5 III, 5, 5. H6B II, 3, 45. H6C II, 6, 50.

**Spread** (impf. and partic. *spread*) 1) trans. a) to expand, to display: *lawn being s. upon the blushing rose*, Ven. 590. *the fishes s. on it their golden gills*, 1100. *great princes' favourites their fair leaves s.* Sonn. 25, 5; Rom. I, 1, 158. *s. o'er the silver waves thy golden hairs*, Err. III, 2, 48. *let there be the same net s. for her*, Ado II, 3, 221. *with one hand on his dagger, another s. on's breast*, H8 I, 2, 205. *s. thy close curtain, night*, Rom. III, 2, 5. *do not s. the compost on the weeds*, Hml. III, 4, 151. *with thy banners s.* Tim. V, 4, 30. Lr. IV, 2, 56. *to s. his colours*, John II, 8. V, 1, 72. H6A III, 3, 31. H6C I, 1, 91. 252. 253. Refl.: *masters, s. yourselves*, Mids. I, 2, 16 (place yourselves in a row. Bottom's speech).

b) to diffuse; to propagate; to divulge: *whose frothy mouth ... a second fear through all her sinews s.* Ven. 903. *I s. my conquering might*, LLL V, 2, 566. *so great fear of my name 'mongst them was s.* H6A I, 4, 50. *there's an ill opinion s. of yourself*, H8 II, 2, 125. *this challenge ... however it is s. in general name*, Troil. I, 3, 322. *when fame had s. their cursed deed*, Per. V, 3, 96. Refl.: *vice repeated is like the wandering wind, blows dust in others' eyes, to s. itself*, Per. I, 1, 97.

c) absol. to lay the cloth and serve up: *s. for dinner*, Err. II, 2, 189. *s., Davy*, H4B V, 3, 9.

2) intr. a) to expand or display itself: *I might as yet have been a —ing flower*, Compl. 75. *she is s. of late into a goodly bulk*, Wint. II, 1, 19. *his arms s. wider than a dragon's wings*, H6A I, 1, 11. *till by broad —ing it* (a circle) *disperse to nought*, 1, 2, 135. *Jove's —ing tree*, H6C V, 2, 14. *her clothes s. wide*, Hml. IV, 7, 176.

b) to be propagated from one place to others: *dying fear through all her body s.* Lucr. 1266. *lest his infection s. further*, Cor. III, 1, 311.

**Sprig**, a small shoot, a spray: Lr. II, 3, 16.

**Spright** or **Sprite**, = spirit; 1) mood, occasional state of the mind: *with a lazy s.* Ven. 181.

*intending weariness with heavy s.* Lucr. 121. *cheer we up his —s,* Mcb. IV, 1, 127.

2) mind, soul: *her winged s.* Lucr. 1728. *the quintessence of every s. heaven would in little show,* As III, 2, 147. Troil. I, 3, 56 (Ff *spirit*).

3) any supernatural being: Tp. I, 2, 381. II, 2, 121. Err. II, 2, 192. Mids. II, 1, 33. V, 400. Wint. II, 1, 26. 28. Mcb. III, 5, 27. = ghost: Lucr. 451. Mids. V, 388. Troil. III, 2, 34 (Q *spirit*). Mcb. II, 3, 84.

**Sprighted**, haunted: *I am s. with a fool,* Cymb. II, 3, 144.

**Sprightful**, or **Spriteful**, full of spirit: *a s. noble gentleman,* John IV, 2, 177.

**Sprightfully**, with great spirit: R2 I, 3, 3.

**Sprighting**, playing the spirit; the service done by a spirit: *and do my s. gently,* Tp. I, 2, 298.

**Sprightly** or **Spritely**, 1) lively, brisk, in good spirits: *dance canary with s. fire and motion,* All's II, 1, 78. *that s. Scot of Scots,* H4A II, 4, 377. *my s. brethren,* Troil. II, 2, 190. *thy s. comfort,* Ant. IV, 7, 15. *we'll ... with our s. port make the ghosts gaze,* IV, 14, 52. *be s., for you fall 'mongst friends,* Cymb. III, 6, 75.

Adverbially: *address yourself to entertain them s.* Wint. IV, 4, 53. *it* (war) *is s. walking, audible, and full of vent,* Cor. IV, 5, 237 ("the expression refers to the more lively and definite advance of a hound, arising from the discovery of good vent, i. e. scent, as compared with the dissatisfied snuffings and uncertain progress when nothing is in view." Edinb. Rev. Oct. '72, p. 342. Most M. Edd. *sprightly, waking*).

2) having the quality of a spirit: *Jupiter appeared to me, with other s. shows of mine own kindred,* Cymb. V, 5, 428.

**Spring**, subst. 1) fountain; source; in a proper and in a metaphorical sense: Lucr. 1455. Tp. I, 2, 338. II, 2, 164. R2 I, 1, 97. H4A V, 2, 23. H6B III, 1, 101. IV, 1, 72. H6C IV, 8, 55. R3 II, 2, 68. Tit. V, 2, 171. V, 3, 167. Rom. III, 2, 102. V, 3, 218. Tim. IV, 3, 421. Mcb. I, 2, 27. II, 3, 103. Hml. IV, 7, 20. Cymb. II, 3, 23.

2) the vernal season (only once without the article: Tp. IV, 114): Ven. 141. Lucr. 331. 869. Sonn. 1, 10. 53, 9. 98, 1. 104, 5. Pilgr. 132. Tp. IV, 114. LLL I, 1, 97. 101. V, 2, 901. Mids. II, 1, 111. As V, 3, 22. Tw. III, 1, 161. Wint. IV, 4, 113. V, 1, 152. R2 I, 3, 214. III, 4, 48. V, 2, 47. H4B I, 3, 38. H6B III, 1, 31. H6C II, 2, 163. R3 III, 1, 94. H8 III, 1, 8. Hml. I, 3, 39. Per. I, 1, 12. Emblematic of youth: *the tender s. upon thy tempting lip,* Ven. 127. *thy vices bud before thy s.* Lucr. 604. *stealing away the treasure of his s.* Sonn. 63, 8. *farewell, the latter s.* H4A I, 2, 177 (end of the spring; i. e. a man old in years and young in desires). *in's s. became a harvest,* Cymb. I, 1, 46. *who withered in her s. of year,* Per. IV, 4, 35.

Hence = the beginning, the first and freshest part of any state or time: *love's gentle s. doth always fresh remain,* Ven. 801. *thy hasty s. still blasts,* Lucr. 49. *our love was new and then but in the s.* Sonn. 102, 5. *how this s. of love resembleth the uncertain glory of an April day,* Gent. I, 3, 84. *in the s. of love,* Err. III, 2, 3. *the April's in her eyes: it is love's s.* Ant. III, 2, 43. *in this new s. of time,* R2 V, 2, 50. Even: *since the middle summer's s.* Mids. II, 1, 82. *as sudden as flaws congealed in the s. of day,* H4B IV, 4, 35.

3) a young shoot, a sprig: *this canker that eats up love's tender s.* Ven. 656. *to dry the old oak's sap and*

*cherish —s,* Lucr. 950 (perhaps also in 869). *shall in the s. of love thy love-springs rot?* Err. III, 2, 3.

4) an elastic body used in locks; a spring-lock: *to the trunk again, and shut the s. of it,* Cymb. II, 2, 47.

**Spring**, vb. (impf. *sprang:* H6C V, 7, 31. Cor. I, 3, 17. *sprung:* Ven. 1168. Err. I, 1, 6. H4B I, 1, 111. H8 III, 1, 7. Tim. I, 2, 116. Hml. III, 1, 186. Partic. *sprung*) 1) to leap, to bound: *away he —s,* Ven. 258. *from whence with life he never more sprung up,* H4B I, 1, 111. *straight —s out into fast gait,* H8 III, 2, 116. Metaphorically, = to exult: *I sprang not more in joy at first hearing he was a man-child,* Cor. I, 3, 17. cf. *joy ... at that instant like a babe sprung up,* Tim. I, 2, 116 (quibbling: exulted; and flowed forth as from a fountain).

2) to rise out of the ground and grow by vegetative power: Ven. 167. 417. Pilgr. 378. R2 I, 2, 13. H5 II, 4, 40. H6C II, 6, 50. H8 III, 1, 7. Tit. V, 1, 9. Hml. V, 1, 263. Lr. IV, 4, 17. With *up:* Ven. 1168. Troil. I, 2, 190. Used of any manner of growing and rising or thriving: *as my duty —s, so perish they,* H6A III, 1, 175. *they never then had sprung like summer-flies,* H6C II, 6, 17. *there is sprung up an heretic,* H8 III, 2, 101. cf. *Gallant-springing*.

Hence = to issue, to proceed, to originate; with *from:* Err. I, 1, 6. III, 2, 55. LLL IV, 3, 304. H6A II, 4, 85. III, 1, 166. H6C III, 2, 126. III, 3, 67. V, 7, 31. Rom. I, 5, 140. Tim. IV, 3, 203. Hml. III, 1, 186. IV, 5, 76. Lr. I, 1, 188. I, 4, 302. Per. V, 1, 29. With *of: what stock he —s of,* Cor. II, 3, 245. With the adv. *whence: whence —s this deep despair?* H6C III, 3, 12 (*from whence:* LLL IV, 3, 304. H6A III, 1, 166. H6C V, 7, 31).

3) to issue as from a fountain: *clear wells s. not,* Pilgr. 281. *currents that s. from one most gracious head,* R2 III, 3, 108.

**Springe**, a gin, a noose for catching birds: Wint. IV, 3, 36. Hml. I, 3, 115. V, 2, 317.

**Spring-halt**, a kind of lameness in which a horse suddenly twitches up his legs: H8 I, 3, 13.*

**Spring-time**, the vernal season: As V, 3, 20. 26. Shr. II, 248. H6B III, 1, 337. H6C II, 3, 47. Tit. III, 1, 21.

**Sprinkle**, 1) to scatter in drops: *—s in your faces your reeking villany,* Tim. III, 6, 102. *upon the heat and flame of thy distemper s. cool patience,* Hml. III, 4, 124.

2) to scatter on in drops, to besprinkle: *that blood should s. me to make me grow,* R2 V, 6, 46. *s. our society with thankfulness,* Tim. III, 6, 79.

**Sprite, Spriteful, Spritely,** see *Spright* etc.

**Sprout**, vb. to grow fast and high: *that it may grow and s. as high as heaven,* H4B II, 3, 60.

**Spruce**, 1) trim (in a bad sense); affected: *too picked, too s., too affected, too odd,* LLL V, 1, 14. *three-piled hyperboles, s. affectation,* V, 2, 407.

2) brisk, dashing: *now, my s. companions,* Shr. IV, 1, 116.

**Spunge** and **Spungy**, see *Sponge* and *Spongy*.

**Spur**, subst. 1) the instrument worn on horsemen's heels to prick the horses: Ven. 285. Sonn. 50, 9. Meas. I, 2, 166. All's II, 5, 40. Wint. I, 2, 96. H4B I, 1, 42. 49. IV, 1, 119. Rom. II, 4, 73. Caes. IV, 2, 25. V, 3, 15. Mcb. I, 6, 23. *set —s,* Wiv. IV, 5, 70. *usurping his —s too long,* All's IV, 3, 119 (in the ceremonial degradation of a knight his spurs were hacked off from

his legs). *giving reins and —s to my free speech*, R2
I, 1, 55. *from helmet to the s.* H5 IV, 6, 6. *horsemen
that make to him on the s.* Caes. V, 3, 29.

Figuratively, = incitement, instigation: *finds
brotherhood in thee no sharper s.?* R2 I, 2, 9. H6B I,
3, 153. Tim. III, 6, 73. Caes. II, 1, 123. Mcb. I, 7,
25. Per. III, 3, 23. With *to: which is another s. to my
departure*, Wint. IV, 2, 10. Troil. II, 2, 200. Lr. II,
1, 78 (Ff *spirits*).

2) a shoot of the root of a tree: *by the —s plucked
up the pine and cedar*, Tp. V, 47. *grief and patience,
rooted in him both, mingle their —s together*, Cymb. IV,
2, 58.

**Spur**, vb. to prick and drive with the spur; trans.:
LLL IV, 1, 1. As III, 4, 47. R2 IV, 72. H6C V, 7, 9.
R3 V, 3, 340. H8 V, 3, 23. Troil. IV, 5, 186. Absol.:
Sonn. 50, 12. 51, 7. R2 II, 3, 58. Tim. IV, 3, 153.
= to ride fast, to travel with great expedition: R2
II, 1, 36. V, 2, 112. H4B I, 1, 36. H6A IV, 3, 19.
Caes. V, 3, 30 (*he —s on*). Mcb. III, 3, 6. Ant. III,
1, 7.

Figuratively, = 1) to incite, to impel: *love will
not be —ed to what it loathes*, Gent. V, 2, 7. LLL II,
119. Troil. V, 3, 48. Hml. IV, 4, 33. With *forth: my
desire did s. me forth*, Tw. III, 3, 5. with *on:* Meas.
IV, 2, 85. R2 IV, 53. 2) to hasten: *so much they s.
their expedition*, Gent. V, 1, 6. *that to the pace of it I
may s. on my journey*, Cor. I, 10, 33. Opposed to stop
in both senses: *whose spiritual counsel shall stop or s.
me*, Wint. II, 1, 187. *discover to me what both you s.
and stop*, Cymb. I, 6, 99.

**Spur-galled**, wounded with the spur: *s. and tired
by jauncing Bolingbroke*, R2 V, 5, 94 (Qq *spurr'd,
galled*).

**Spurio**, name in All's II, 1, 43. IV, 3, 184.

**Spurn**, subst. 1) a thrust, a stroke, a hurt: *that
which gives my soul the greatest s., is dear Lavinia*,
Tit. III, 1, 101. *who dies that bears not one s. to their
graves of their friends' gift?* Tim. I, 2, 146.

2) a kick, an insult: *the —s that patient merit of
the unworthy takes*, Hml. III, 1, 73.

**Spurn**, vb. 1) to strike with the foot, to kick;
trans.: *that like a football you do s. me thus? you s. me
hence, and he will s. me hither*, Err. II, 1, 83. *and s.
in pieces posts of adamant*, H6A I, 4, 52. Usually expressive of disdain and contempt, or of anger: *spaniel-
like, the more she —s my love, the more it fawneth on
her*, Gent. IV, 2, 14. Mids. II, 1, 205. III, 2, 225. 313.
Merch. I, 3, 119. 128. 132. John II, 24. H6C I, 4,
58. Cor. V, 3, 165. Tim. I, 1, 85. 281. Caes. III, 1, 46.
Ant. II, 5, 63. III, 5, 17. Cymb. IV, 1, 20. V, 5, 294.

Intr.; with *against: why thou against the church,
our holy mother, so wilfully dost s.* John III, 1, 142
(cf. *to kick against the pricks*, Acts IX, 5). With *at:
—s at his love, ... beating his kind embracements with
her heels*, Ven. 311. *wouldst thou not spit at me and s.
at me*, Err. II, 2, 136. *—s enviously at straws*, Hml.
IV, 5, 6. With *upon: I'll strike thee to my foot, and s.
upon thee*, R3 I, 2, 42.

2) to treat with contempt, to scorn; trans.: *he shall
s. fate, scorn death*, Mcb. III, 5, 30. *what safe and
nicely I might well delay ... I disdain and s.* Lr. V, 3,
145. Intr., with *at: thou that —est at right, at law, at
reason*, Lucr. 880. *in vain I s. at my confirmed despite*,
1026. *to s. at your most royal image*, H4B V, 2, 89.
*wilt thou s. at his edict and fulfil a man's?* R3 I, 4,

203. = to be angry with: *I know no personal cause
to s. at him*, Caes. II, 1, 11.

**Spy**, subst. 1) seer, perceiver, observer: *if these
be true —es which I wear in my head, here's a goodly
sight*, Tp. V, 259.

2) one watching, or sent to watch, the movements
of others: Ven. 655. Tp. I, 2, 455. Gent. V, 1, 10.
John IV, 1, 129. Cor. I, 6, 18. Lr. III, 1, 24. V, 3, 17.
Ant. III, 7, 78. With *on: or on my frailties why are
frailer —es*, Sonn. 121, 7. *the heaven sets —es upon
us*, Wint. V, 1, 203.

3) an advanced guard, Fr. *éclaireur*, Germ. *Plänk-
ler: when sorrows come, they come not single —es, but
in battalions*, Hml. IV, 5, 78. *within this hour at most
I will advise you where to plant yourselves; acquaint
you with the perfect s. o' the time, the moment on't*, Mcb.
III, 1, 130 (i. e. that which will precede the time of
the deed, and indicate that it is at hand). Perhaps
also in Cor. I, 6, 18.

**Spy**, vb. 1) intr. to look, to pry: *revealing day
through every cranny —es*, Lucr. 1086. *now will I to
the chink, to s. an I can hear my Thisby's face*, Mids.
V, 195. *I s. You s.! what do you s.?* Troil. III, 1, 102
("the usual exclamation at a childish game called *Hie,
spy, hie*". Steevens). With *into: what a man cannot
smell out, he may s. into*, Lr. I, 5, 24. *it is my nature's
plague to s. into abuses*, Oth. III, 3, 147.

2) tr. to perceive, to see: *like one that —es an
adder*, Ven. 878. *she —ed the hunted boar*, 900. *—es
the foul boar's conquest*, 1029. *he —es Lucretia's glove*,
Lucr. 316. *in thy shady cell, where none may s. him,
sits Sin*, 881. *he —ed in her some blemish*, 1358. *such
signs of truth in his plain face she —ed*, 1532. *he, —ing
her, bounced in*, Pilgr. 83. *Love ... —ed a blossom*,
229 and LLL IV, 3, 103. *what is in Silvia's face, but
I may s. more fresh in Julia's*, Gent. V, 4, 114. *I s.
entertainment in her*, Wiv. I, 3, 48. IV, 2, 204. IV, 6,
43. Meas. III, 2, 44. Ado II, 3, 254. Mids. III, 2, 19.
V, 187. 328. Shr. IV, 2, 60. All's III, 5, 93. R2 II, 1,
271. H4B II, 2, 87. H6A I, 1, 127. I, 4, 19. 22. H6B
I, 1, 242. H6C III, 2, 136. IV, 6, 28. V, 3, 4. R3 I,
1, 26 (Ff *see*). I, 4, 270. Troil. I, 2, 153. 165. Rom.
IV, 1, 68. Tim. I, 2, 52. Lr. II, 4, 250. Oth. I, 1, 77.
*to s. out* (= to look out in Tim. III, 2, 67): *what eye
but such an eye would s. out such a quarrel?* Rom. III,
1, 23.

**Squabble**, to quarrel, to brawl: Oth. II, 3, 281.

**Squadron**, part of an army; a troop: H6A IV, 2,
23. Caes. II, 2, 20. Oth. I, 1, 22. Ant. III, 9, 1.

**Squander**, 1) tr. to scatter: *and other ventures he
hath, —ed abroad*, Merch. I, 3, 22.

2) intr. to go at random and without a certain aim
(cf. *Scatter*, intr.): *the wise man's folly is anatomized
even by the —ing glances of the fool*, As II, 7, 57.

**Square**, subst. 1) rule, regularity, just proportion:
*I have not kept my s., but that to come shall all be done
by the rule*, Ant. II, 3, 6. *all other joys, which the most
precious s. of sense professes*, Lr. I, 1, 76 (= which
the soundest sense acknowledges as joys. Qq *possesses*
for *professes*; see below).

2) squadron, troop: *our —s of battle*, H5 IV, 2, 28.
*no practice in the brave —s of war*, Ant. III, 11, 40.

3) equal extent on all sides; compass, range (?):
*all other joys, which the most precious s. of sense
possesses*, Lr. I, 1, 76 (Ff *professes* for *possesses*).

4) the embroidery on the bosom part of a shift

(Nares and Tollet): *you would think a smock were a she-angel, he so chants to the sleeve-hand and the work about the s. on't*, Wint. IV, 4, 212.

**Square,** adj. 1) having four equal sides: *my queen's s. brows*, Per. V, 1, 109 (a forehead as high as it is broad, consequently a high forehead).

2) suitable: *for those that were, it is not s. to take on those that are, revenges*, Tim. V, 4, 36. With *to*: *if report be s. to her*, Ant. II, 2, 190 (= if she is such as the report goes).

**Square,** vb. 1) to adjust, to regulate, to shape: *thou art said to have a stubborn soul, that apprehends no further than this world, and —st thy life according*, Meas. V, 487. *with us that s. our guess by shows*, All's II, 1, 153. *I will be —d by this* (dream) Wint. III, 3, 41. *O, that ever I had —d me to thy counsel!* V, 1, 52. *to s. the general sex by Cressid's rule*, Troil. V, 2, 132 (= to judge). *how franticly I s. my talk*, Tit. III, 2, 31.

2) to quarrel: *they never meet ... but they do s.* Mids. II, 1, 30. *are you such fools to s. for this?* Tit. II, 1, 100. 124. *'twere pregnant they should s. between themselves*, Ant. II, 1, 45. *mine honesty and I begin to s.* III, 13, 41.

**Squarer,** quarreller: *is there no young s. now that will make a voyage with him to the devil*, Ado I, 1, 82.

**Squash,** an unripe peascod: *Mistress S., your* (Peaseblossom's) *mother*, Mids. III, 1, 191. *as a s. is before 'tis a peascod*, Tw. I, 5, 166. *this kernel, this s., this gentleman*, Wint. I, 2, 160.

**Squeak,** to cry with a shrill acute tone: Merch. II, 5, 30 (Ff Q2.3.4 *squealing*). Tw. II, 3, 97. R3 I, 4, 54 (Ff *shrieked*). Hml. I, 1, 116. Ant. V, 2, 220.

**Squeal,** to cry with a shrill voice: *the vile —ing of the wry-necked fife*, Merch. II, 5, 30 (Q1 *squeaking*). *ghosts did shriek and s.* Caes. II, 2, 24.

**Squeeze,** to press closely with the fingers: Hml. IV, 2, 22.

**Squele,** name in H4B III, 2, 23.

**Squier** or **Squire,** a square, a rule, a measure: *do not you know my lady's foot by the s.?* LLL V, 2, 474. *twelve foot and a half by the s.* Wint. IV, 4, 348. *four foot by the s.* H4A II, 2, 13.

**Squint,** to turn (the eye) to an oblique position: *—s the eye*, Lr. III, 4, 122. cf. *Asquint.*

**Squiny,** to look asquint: *dost thou s. at me?* Lr. IV, 6, 140 (Q3 *squint*).

**Squire,** see *Squier.*

**Squire,** 1) a gentleman next in rank to a knight: *come cut and long-tail, under the degree of a s.* Wiv. III, 4, 48. *a bearing-cloth for a —'s child*, Wint. III, 3, 119. *a landless knight makes thee a landed s.* John I, 177. *now is this Vice's dagger become a s.* H4B III, 2, 344. *knights and —s*, H5 IV, 8, 83. 94. *I will make you a s. of low degree*, V, 1, 38 (allusion to a popular romance entitled 'The Squire of low degree'). *a hundred knights and —s*, Lr. I, 4, 262. *no s. in debt*, III, 2, 86. *a —'s cloth*, Cymb. III, 3, 128.

2) an attendant on a noble warrior or on a royal person: *us that are —s of the night's body*, H4A I, 2, 27. *my queen's a s. more tight at this than thou*, Ant. IV, 4, 14. cf. H5 IV, 8, 83. 94. Lr. I, 4, 262.

3) a familiar title, given sometimes in tenderness, and sometimes in contempt; almost = fellow: *a proper s.!* Ado I, 3, 54. *her womb then rich with my young s.* Mids. II, 1, 131. *so stands this s. officed with me,*

Wint. I, 2, 171. *like to a trusty s. did run away*, H6A IV, 1, 23. *some such s. he was that turned your wit the seamy side without*, Oth. IV, 2, 145.

**Squire-like,** like an attendant: *to knee his throne and s. pension beg*, Lr. II, 4, 217.

**Squirrel,** the animal Sciurus: Gent. IV, 4, 59. Mids. IV, 1, 40. Rom. I, 4, 68.

**Stab,** subst. a thrust with the sharp point of a weapon: Tp. III, 3, 63. Mcb. II, 3, 119. In a moral sense: *this sudden s. of rancour*, R3 III, 2, 89.

**Stab,** vb. 1) to thrust or to kill with the point of a weapon: Lucr. Arg. 21. Gent. IV, 1, 51. Meas. IV, 3, 19. Wint. I, 2, 138. H4A II, 4, 160. H5 IV, 5, 7. H6B IV, 1, 65. 137. H6C II, 4, 6. II, 6, 30. V, 5, 53. R3 I, 2, 11. 182. 242. I, 3, 212. I, 4, 56. 101. 108. III, 3, 16. IV, 4, 63. Tit. V, 2, 47. 100. 103. Rom. II, 4, 14. Tim. V, 1, 105. Caes. III, 2, 157. *I am —ed with laughter*, LLL V, 2, 80 (= I have side-stitches). Obscene double-meaning: *he —ed me in mine own house*, H4B II, 1, 15. *if Caesar had —ed their mothers*, Caes. I, 2, 277. cf. Wint. I, 2, 138(?).

2) absol. to make or offer a thrust with the point of a weapon: *—ing steel*, Wint. IV, 4, 748. *he will s.* H4B II, 1, 13. Caes. III, 2, 180. 188. IV, 3, 20. With *at*: *to s. at half an hour of my life*, H4B IV, 5, 109. In a moral sense, = to mortify, to be extremely cutting: *she speaks poniards, and every word —s*, Ado II, 1, 255. *to say a soldier lies, is —ing*, Oth. III, 4, 6. cf. *first let my words s. him*, H6B IV, 1, 66; and see H6C II, 1, 98.

3) to drive, to plunge, to thrust (the weapon as object): *s. poniards in our flesh*, H6C II, 1, 98.

**Stable,** subst. a house for horses: All's II, 3, 301. John V, 2, 140. R2 III, 3, 117. V, 5, 72. H4A II, 1, 39. 106. *if your husband have —s enough, you'll see he shall lack no barns*, Ado III, 4, 48. *I'll keep my —s where I lodge my wife*, Wint. II, 1, 134 (Ingleby: *to keep one's —s* meant to keep personal watch over one's wife's chastity. The common interpretation, according to which Antigonus would be hinting at some unnatural propensity of Semiramis recorded by Pliny, presupposes in the poet's audience too much scholarship and too strong nerves).

**Stable,** adj. steady, constant: *a smooth, discreet and s. bearing*, Tw. IV, 3, 19.

**Stableness,** constancy: Mcb. IV, 3, 92.

**Stablish,** to establish: *and s. quietness on every side*, H6A V, 1, 10.

**Stablishment,** settled inheritance: *unto her he gave the s. of Egypt*, Ant. III, 6, 9 (cf. *Establish*).

**Stack,** in *Hay-stack*, q. v.

**Staff** (plur. *staves;* the same form as Anglos. genitive in Tw. V, 292) 1) a stick carried for support, or used as a weapon: Gent. II, 3, 21. II, 5, 28. 31. III, 1, 246. Ado V, 4, 126. Merch. II, 2, 72. H6B IV, 2, 172. H8 V, 4, 8. Cor. I, 1, 70. Tit. I, 198. *by Jacob's s.* Merch. II, 5, 36. *hermits' staves*, H4B V, 1, 71. *a palmer's s.* H6B V, 1, 97. Hml. IV, 5, 25. *he holds Belzebub at the staves end*, Tw. V, 292 (stands at bay and keeps him off). *the s. of my age*, Merch. II, 2, 70. *we have no s., no stay*, H6C II, 1, 69. *of his fortunes you should make a s. to lean upon*, Ant. III, 13, 68. Proverbs: *a s. is quickly found to beat a dog*, H6B III, 1, 171. *have at you with a proverb — Shall I set in my s.?* Err. III, 1, 51 (is here a lance meant? And does the expression receive some light from Ado V, 2, 20: *you must put in the pike with a vice?*).

2) a pole, a stake: *the rampant bear chained to the ragged s.* H6B V, 1, 203.

3) an ensign of office, a badge of authority: R2 II, 2, 59. II, 3, 27. H4A V, 1, 34. H4B IV, 1, 126. H6B I, 2, 25. II, 3, 23. 32. 43. = magic wand: Tp. V, 54.

4) the shaft of a lance; and the lance itself: John II, 318. H4B IV, 1, 120. R3 V, 3, 65. Mcb. V, 3, 48. V, 7, 18. *to break a s.* = to tilt, to combat with a lance: Ado V, 1, 138. As III, 4, 47. R3 V, 3, 341. Per. II, 3, 35 (cf. the German *Lanzenbrechen*).

5) a strophe, a stanza: *let me hear a s. , a stanze, a verse*, LLL IV, 2, 107.

**Stafford,** name: H4A V, 3, 7. 13. V, 4, 41.*H4B I, 1, 18. H6B I, 4, 55. IV, 2, 120. IV, 4, 34. H6C I, 1, 7. 10. IV, 1, 130. H8 I, 1, 200.

**Staffordshire,** English county: H4B III, 2, 22.

**Stag,** the male red deer: Wiv. V, 5, 14. As II, 1, 33. Shr. Ind. 2, 50. H6A IV, 2, 50. Tit. II, 3, 71. Ant. I, 4, 65.

**Stage,** subst. 1) a temporary structure, a scaffold: *that these bodies high on a s. be placed to the view*, Hml. V, 2, 389. 407.

2) the floor on which theatrical performances are exhibited (often in a figurative sense): Lucr. 278. 766. Sonn. 15, 3. 23, 1. Mids. III, 1, 4. Merch. I, 1, 78. As II, 7, 139. Tw. III, 1, 140. Wint. V, 1, 58. R2 V, 2, 24. H4B I, 1, 155. H5 Prol. 3. Epil. 13. Rom. Prol. 12. Mcb. II, 4, 6. V, 5, 25. Hml. II, 2, 358. 588. Lr. IV, 6, 187. Per. III Prol. 59.

3) a single step of gradual process: *supplying every s. with an augmented greeting*, Ant. III, 6, 54. *to learn of me the —s of our story*, Per. IV, 4, 9.

**Stage,** vb. to exhibit publicly, as in a theatre: *I do not like to s. me to their eyes*, Meas. I, 1, 69. *be —d to the show against a sworder*, Ant. III, 13, 30. *the quick comedians will s. us*, V, 2, 217.

**Stagger,** 1) tr. a) to make to reel, to fell down: *that hand shall burn in never-quenching fire that —s thus my person*, R2 V, 5, 110.

b) to cause to hesitate, to bewilder: *the question did at first so s. me*, H8 II, 4, 212.

2) intr. to waver, to hesitate: *without any pause or —ing take this basket*, Wiv. III, 3, 12. *whether the tyranny be in his place, or in his eminence, I s. in*, Meas. I, 2, 169. *a man may s. in this attempt*, As III, 3, 49.

**Staggers,** 1) a sensation which makes to reel; giddiness, vertigo: *does the world go round? How come these s. on me?* Cymb. V, 5, 233.

2) perplexity, bewilderment: *I will throw thee from my care for ever into the s. and the careless lapse of youth and ignorance*, All's II, 3, 170.

3) a disease of horses indicated by staggering and falling down: *spoiled with the s.* Shr. III, 2, 55.

**Staid,** composed, calm: *put thyself into a haviour of less fear, ere wildness vanquish my —er senses*, Cymb. III, 4, 10.

**Stain,** subst. 1) any spot different from the colour of the ground: *the s. upon his silver down will stay*, Lucr. 1012. *scarce blood enough to give each curtle-axe a s.* H5 IV, 2, 21. *upon thy cheek the s. doth sit of an old tear*, Rom. II, 3, 75. *press for tinctures, —s,* Caes. II, 2, 89. = a natural mole: *full of unpleasing*

blots and sightless —s, John III, 1, 45. *you do remember this s. upon her*, Cymb. II, 4, 139.

2) tincture, tinge: *you have some s. of soldier in you*, All's I, 1, 122. *there is no man hath a virtue that he hath not a glimpse of, nor any man an attaint but he carries some s. of it*, Troil. I, 2, 26.

3) a taint of disgrace: Lucr. 1701. 1708. Sonn. 109, 8. Meas. III, 1, 208 (*do no s. to your person*). Wint. II, 2, 19. John II, 114. H4A III, 1, 187. H6A IV, 5, 42. R3 III, 7, 234. Cor. I, 10, 18 (*suffering s. by him*). Tim. V, 1, 176 (*giving our virgins to the s. ... of beastly war*). Cymb. II, 4, 140. *s. to all nymphs*, Ven. 9 (by eclipsing them). *s. to thy countrymen*, H6A IV, 1, 45.

**Stain,** vb. 1) tr. a) to dye, to tinge with a different colour: *beauty would s. that ore with silver white*, Lucr. 56.

b) to discolour, to spot, to maculate; absol.: *as the berry breaks before it —eth*, Ven. 460. With an object: Ven. 664. 1122. Tp. II, 1, 64. Mids. V, 144. 288. As IV, 3, 98. Wint. V, 3, 82. John II, 45. 357. R2 IV, 29. V, 5, 111. H4A I, 1, 64. III, 2, 136. V, 2, 94. V, 4, 13. H4B V, 5, 25. H6A V, 4, 44. H6B II, 2, 65. III, 1, 259. IV, 1, 11. H6C I, 4, 79. 153. II, 3, 21. Cor. V, 6, 113. Tit. I, 116. III, 1, 125. 213. V, 2, 171. Rom. III, 3, 95. V, 3, 140. Lr. II, 4, 281. Ant. V, 1, 25.

c) to darken, to dim: *through their light joy seemed to appear, like bright things —ed, a kind of heavy fear*, Lucr. 1435. *clouds and eclipses s. both moon and sun*, Sonn. 35, 3. *to s. the track of his bright passage*, R2 III, 3, 66. *if that her breath will mist or s. the stone*, Lr. V, 3, 262. In a moral sense, = to eclipse: *I'll raise the preparation of a war shall s. your brother*, Ant. III, 4, 27.

d) to disfigure, to deface: *which (beauty) the hot tyrant (lust) —s and soon bereaves*, Ven. 797. *he's something —ed with grief*, Tp. I, 2, 414. *—ed the beauty of a fair queen's cheeks with tears*, R2 III, 1, 14. *that any harm should s. so fair a show*, III, 3, 71. *I'll corrupt her manners, s. her beauty*, R3 IV, 4, 206.

e) to soil, to taint, to disgrace; absol.: *lust and murder wake to s. and kill*, Lucr. 168. *would not put my reputation in any —ing act*, All's III, 7, 7. With an object: Lucr. 196. 655. 684. 1181. 1655. 1743. 1836. Meas. II, 4, 55. Err. II, 2, 138. Ado III, 1, 85. Merch. I, 3, 140. John IV, 2, 6. H4A I, 1, 85. H6A IV, 5, 26. Troil. V, 2, 179. Tit. V, 3, 38. Rom. III, 1, 116. Tim. I, 1, 16. Caes. II, 1, 132. Hml. IV, 4, 57.

f) to pervert, to corrupt: *that it (my nature) could so preposterously be —ed, to leave for nothing all thy sum of good*, Sonn. 109, 11. *we must not so s. our judgment, to prostitute our malady to empirics*, All's II, 1, 123.

2) intr. to grow dim, to be obscured, to be soiled: *suns of the world may s. when heaven's sun —eth*, Sonn. 33, 14. *if virtue's gloss will s. with any soil*, LLL II, 48.

**Stained,** adj. (see Appendix) caused by a stain or concerning a stain; full of disgrace: *thou shalt not know the s. taste of violated troth*, Lucr. 1059. *ere she with blood hath stained her s. excuse*, 1316. *wash away thy country's s. spots*, H6A III, 3, 57.

**Staines,** place in England: H5 II, 3, 2.*

**Stainless,** immaculate: Tw. I, 5, 278. Rom. III, 2, 13.

**Stair,** 1) steps made for the purpose of ascending: *cords made like a tackled s.* Rom. II, 4, 201.

2) a single step leading up; but used only in the plural: *the —s, as he treads on them, kiss his feet,* LLL V, 2, 330. *as false as —s of sand,* Merch. III, 2, 84. *in these degrees have they made a pair of —s to marriage,* As V, 2, 41. *as common as the —s that mount the Capitol,* Cymb. I, 6, 105. Hence —s = the whole order of steps by which the upper part of a building is arrived at: *as you go up the —s,* Hml. IV, 3, 39. *keep below —s,* Ado V, 2, 10 (in the servants' room). *up —s and down —s,* H4A II, 4, 112. *gone down —s,* H4B II, 1, 107. 202.

**Stair-work,** work made on a staircase: Wint. III, 3, 75.

**Stake,** subst. 1) a strong stick or a post fixed in the ground: Tp. III, 2, 98. H6A I, 1, 117. Especially a) the post to which one condemned to die by fire is fastened: *I will die in it at the s.* Ado I, 1, 235. *when thou comest to the s.* H6A V, 3, 44. Hence = pyre: *place barrels of pitch upon the fatal s.* H6A V, 4, 57. And = judgment, execution in general: *bringing the murderous coward to the s.* Lr. II, 1, 64. b) the post to which a bear is tied to be baited: *have you not set mine honour at the s. and baited it,* Tw. III, 1, 129. *call hither to the s. my two brave bears,* H6B V, 1, 144. Caes. IV, 1, 48. Mcb. V, 7, 1. Lr. III, 7, 54. Used in a lascivious sense by way of punning: Merch. III, 2, 220.

2) that which is pledged or wagered: *the rich s. drawn,* Wint. I, 2, 248.

3) the state of being laid and pledged as a wager; always preceded by *at: at s.* Troil. III, 3, 227. Cor. III, 2, 63. Oth. IV, 2, 13. *at the s.* All's II, 3, 156. Hml. IV, 4, 56.

**Stake,** vb. 1) to set and plant like a stake: *I have a soul of lead so —s me to the ground I cannot move,* Rom. I, 4, 16.

2) to wager, to put to hazard: Cymb. V, 5, 188. *s. down,* Merch. III, 2, 218.

**Stale,** subst. 1) a decoy, a bait: *the trumpery in my house, go bring it hither, for s. to catch these thieves,* Tp. IV, 187. *to cast thy wandering eyes on every s.* Shr. III, 1, 90. Explained by some in this sense in Err. II, 1, 101 and H6C III, 3, 260.

2) a laughing-stock, a dupe: *but, too unruly deer, he breaks the pale and feeds from home; poor I am but his s.* Err. II, 1, 101 (perhaps with a quibble: he is my dear, but I his s., i. e. one of whom he is weary). *to make a s. of me amongst these mates,* Shr. I, 1, 58 (perhaps a quibbling allusion to the expression *stalemate* at chess). *had he none else to make a s. but me?* H6C III, 3, 260. *was there none else in Rome to make a s., but Saturnine?* Tit. I, 304.

3) that which has become vapid und tasteless, or is worn out by use (Err. II, 1, 101?); hence almost equivalent to a prostitute: *marrying the renowned Claudio to a contaminated s.* Ado II, 2, 26. *to link my dear friend to a common s.* IV, 1, 66.

4) the urine of horses: *thou didst drink the s. of horses,* Ant. I, 4, 62. The host calls Dr. Caius *bully s.* in Wiv. II, 3, 30; cf. *Castalion King Urinal,* v. 34.

**Stale,** adj. worse for age, vapid and tasteless, worn out by use: Lucr. 1362. Compl. 268. Merch. II, 5, 55. As II, 4, 63. Wint. IV, 1, 13. R2 V, 5, 104. H4A III, 2, 41. H4B II, 4, 141. Troil. II, 2, 79. V,

4, 11. Rom. II, 4, 139. Hml. I, 2, 133. Lr. I, 2, 13. Cymb. III, 4, 53.

**Stale,** vb. to render stale, to make common and worthless: *must not so s. his palm nobly acquired,* Troil. II, 3, 201 (O. Edd. staul). *to s. it* (an old story) *a little more,* Cor. I, 1, 95 (O. Edd. scale). *to s. with ordinary oaths my love to every new protester,* Caes. I, 2, 73. *out of use and —d by other men,* IV, 1, 38. *age cannot wither her, nor custom s. her infinite variety,* Ant. II, 2, 240.

**Staleness,** the state of being corrupted by time: Per. V, 1, 58.

**Stalk,** subst. the stem of a plant: Ven. 1175. Compl. 147. R3 IV, 3, 12. Per. IV, 6, 46.

**Stalk,** subst. a stately walk: *with martial s.* Hml. I, 1, 66.

**Stalk,** vb. 1) to walk with a stately step: *it —s away,* Hml. I, 1, 50. Used with some dislike or irony: *shall we give the signal to our rage and s. in blood to our possession?* John II, 266. *I s. about her door,* Troil. III, 2, 9. *he —s up and down like a peacock,* III, 3, 251.

2) to walk like a fowler behind a stalking-horse: *into the chamber wickedly he —s,* Lucr. 365. *s. on; the fowl sits,* Ado II, 3, 95.

**Stalking-horse,** a real or artificial horse, behind which the fowler conceals himself: *he uses his folly like a s. and under the presentation of that he shoots his wit,* As V, 4, 111.

**Stall,** subst. 1) the part of a stable in which a horse or an ox is kept: Shr. II, 360. H4A V, 2, 14 (*feed like oxen at a s.*). Mcb. II, 4, 16.

2) a small shed in which an occupation is carried on: *work for bread upon Athenian —s,* Mids. III, 2, 10. *—s, bulks, windows, are smothered up,* Cor. II, 1, 226.

**Stall,** vb. 1) to keep in a stall or stable: *differs not from the —ing of an ox,* As I, 1, 11.

2) to place as in a stall; to fix or fasten so as to prevent escape; to secure: *the steed is —ed up,* Ven. 39. *and —ed the deer that thou shouldst strike,* Pilgr. 300. Metaphorically, = to keep close: *s. this in your bosom,* All's I, 3, 131.

3) to install, to invest: *decked in thy rights, as thou art —ed in mine,* R3 I, 3, 206.

4) to dwell, to live as in a common stall: *we could not s. together in the whole world,* Ant. V, 1, 39.

**Stallion,** lection of O. Edd. in Tw. II, 5, 124 (M. Edd. staniel), and of Qq in Hml. II, 2, 616 (Ff and M. Edd. scullion).

**Stamford,** place in England: H4B III, 2, 43.

**Stammer,** to stutter: As III, 2, 209.

**Stamp,** subst. 1) the act of striking the foot forcibly downward: *at our s. here o'er and o'er one falls,* Mids. III, 2, 25.

2) an instrument by which an impression is made: *to seek anew some fresher s. of the time-bettering days,* Sonn. 82, 8. *coin heaven's image in —s that are forbid,* Meas. II, 4, 46. *his sword, death's s., where it did mark, it took,* Cor. II, 2, 111.

3) a mark imprinted, an impression: *hath upon him still that natural s.* (a mole) Cymb. V, 5, 366. Figuratively, = visible character: *without the s. of merit,* Merch. II, 9, 39. *not a soldier of this season's s. should go so general current,* H4A IV, 1, 4. *your fire-new s. of honour is scarce current,* R3 I, 3, 256. *the s. of nobleness,* H8 III, 2, 12. *he has the s. of*

*Marcius*, Cor. I, 6, 23. *carrying the s. of one defect,* Hml. I, 4, 31. *change the s. of nature,* III, 4, 168.

4) that which is marked with an impression: *the empress sends it thee, thy s., thy seal,* Tit. IV, 2, 70 (i. e. a child. cf. the verb in Cymb. II, 5, 5.). Especially = coin: *—s in gold or sums in sealed bags,* Wiv. III, 4, 16. *hanging a golden s. about their necks,* Mcb. IV, 3, 153 (the coin called *angel*). *'tween man and man they weigh not every s.* Cymb. V, 4, 24.

**Stamp,** vb. 1) to strike with the foot forcibly downward: Ven. 316. Shr. III, 2, 169. 230. John III, 1, 122. H6C I, 4, 91. III, 3, 169. Cor. I, 3, 35. Tim. I, 2, 149 *( s. upon me ).* Caes. II, 1, 244. With an accus. expressing an effect: *under my feet I s. thy cardinal's hat,* H6A I, 3, 49. *your hearts I'll s. out,* I, 4, 108.

2) to impress, to imprint: *wax … wherein is —ed the semblance of a devil,* Lucr. 1246. *reproach is —ed in Collatinus' face,* 829. 941. Sonn. 112, 2. Meas. I, 1, 51. Merch. II, 7, 57. H8 III, 2, 325. Tit. IV, 2, 127. Lr. I, 4, 306.

3) to mark with an impression: *as the event —s them,* Ado I, 2, 7. *—ed coin,* Wint. IV, 4, 747. *I that am rudely —ed,* R3 I, 1, 16. *when I was —ed,* Cymb. II, 5, 5 (cf. the subst. in Tit. IV, 2, 70).

4) to make valid and current (by marking with an impression): *and in his praise have almost —ed the leasing,* Cor. V, 2, 22. *has an eye can s. and counterfeit advantages,* Oth. II, 1, 247.

**Stanch,** adj. strong and tight, firm, steady: *what hoop should hold us s.* Ant. II, 2, 117.

**Stanch,** vb. to satiate: *let my tears s. the earth's dry appetite,* Tit. III, 1, 14. cf. *Unstanched.*

**Stanchless,** insatiate: *s. avarice:* Mcb. IV, 3, 78.

**Stand,** subst. 1) a stop, a halt: *make a mutual s.* Merch. V, 77. *all and every part of what we would doth make a s. at what your highness will,* John IV, 2, 39. *a stride and a s.* Troil. III, 3, 252. *the measure done, I'll watch her place of s.* Rom. I, 5, 52.

2) opposition, resistance: *neither foolish in our —s, nor cowardly in retire,* Cor. I, 6, 2. *where they made the s.* Cymb. V, 3, 1.

3) place where one stands, mostly for the purpose of waiting or watching; station: *I have found you out a s. most fit,* Meas. IV, 6, 10. *a s. where you may make the fairest shoot,* LLL IV, 1, 10. *to make one's s.* Lucr. 438. H6C III, 1, 3. *to make s.* Merch. II, 6, 2 (Ff *a s.*). *to take one's s.* Pilgr. 121. H6C IV, 3, 1. H8 IV, 1, 2. Caes. II, 4, 25. Oth. V, 1, 7. Cymb. III, 4, 111. *to take s.* H5 IV, 2, 31. *to take a special s.* Wiv. V, 5, 248. Particularly applied to the station of huntsmen waiting for game (Wiv. V, 5, 248. LLL IV, 1, 10. H6C III, 1, 3. Cymb. III, 4, 111): *yield up their deer to the s. of the stealer,* Cymb. II, 3, 75.

**Stand,** vb. (impf. and partic. *stood*) I. intr. 1) to be on the feet, in the upright posture between motion and rest; neither to walk or run, nor to sit or kneel or lie: *the fair breeder that is —ing by,* Ven. 282. *how like a jade he stood,* 391. *poor Wat … —s on his hinder legs,* 698. *thus —s she in a trembling ecstasy,* 895. 1121. Lucr. 1401. 1431. Gent. IV, 4, 35 *( I have stood on the pillory ).* V, 4, 129. Wiv. I, 1, 226. Err. III, 1, 68. 71. V, 185. Ado III, 3, 110. IV, 1, 70. V, 1, 275. LLL IV, 1, 8. Mids. II, 2, 26 *(one aloof s. sentinel; cf. as I did s. my watch upon the hill,* Mcb. V, 5, 33). Shr. IV, 1, 188. H4B V, 5, 5. H6C I, 1, 84. Mcb. IV, 1, 126. Ant. I, 5, 19 etc.

Emphatically: *had Narcissus seen her as she stood,* Lucr. 265 (German: *wie sie dastand*). *the poor frighted deer that —s at gaze,* 1149. *why s. you in this strange stare?* Tp. III, 3, 94. *I s. for judgment,* Merch. IV, 1, 103. 142 ( cf. below). *how many then should cover that s. bare,* II, 9, 44. *—est thou aloof upon comparison?* H6A V, 4, 150. *s. fair, I pray thee; let me look on thee,* Troil. IV, 5, 235. *I s. in pause where I shall first begin,* Hml. III, 3, 42.

Opposed to verbs of motion: *—ing lakes,* Tp. V, 33. *a —ing pond,* Merch. I, 1, 89. *the —ing pool,* Lr. III, 4, 139. *I am —ing water,* Tp. II, 1, 221 (between ebb and flood). *'tis with him in —ing water, between boy and man,* Tw. I, 5, 168. cf. *the swan's feather, that —s upon the swell at full of tide, and neither way inclines,* Ant. III, 2, 49. *my deadly —ing eye,* Tit. II, 3, 32 (fixed, staring). *never s. 'you had rather',* Wiv. III, 3, 133 (i. e. do not lose time with saying 'you had rather', but look to what you have to do). *s. not to discourse,* Gent. V, 2, 44. *—ing to prate and talk,* Wint. III, 2, 41. *take leave and s. not to reply,* H6C IV, 8, 23. *we will not s. to prate,* R3 I, 3, 351. *s. not to answer: here, take thou the hilts,* Caes. V, 3, 43. *he stood by, whilst I was made a wonder,* H6B II, 4, 45 (and did nothing to prevent it). *grace to s., and virtue go,* Meas. III, 2, 278 (probably = grace in rest, and virtue in action). *s., I say,* Ven. 284 (= stop). Gent. IV, 1, 3. Ado III, 2, 27. 32. 177. Caes. IV, 2, 1. Cor. V, 2, 1. Hml. I, 1, 14. Cymb. V, 3, 88 etc. *there s., for you are spell-stopped,* Tp. V, 60. *if thou darest s.* Err. V, 31 (i. e. remain here). cf. *which if you seek to prove, I dar not s. by,* Wint. I, 2, 444 (I am resolved to fly). *let it* (the dish) *s.* Shr. IV, 3, 44 (don't take it away). *s. again,* Troil. IV, 5, 248. *he —s still,* As III, 2, 329. Wint. IV, 3, 95. John IV, 1, 77. *s. fast,* in the same sense: Gent. IV, 1, 1. Caes. V, 1, 22. *darest not s.* Mids. III, 2, 424 (viz to fight with me). *to be valiant is to s.* Rom. I, 1, 12. *if thou darest not s. for ten shillings,* H4A I, 2, 157 (quibbling; see below). *s. fast* = do your best, do not flinch: John III, 1, 208. H4A II, 2, 75. Troil. II, 3, 273. V, 2, 187. Cor. I, 4, 41 etc. (cf. *Fast*). *I'll fight with him alone; s., Diomed,* Troil. V, 6, 9 (= forbear; let him alone). *s., Aufidius, and trouble not the peace,* Cor. V, 6, 128.

Opposed to sitting, or kneeling or lying: *—ing, speaking, moving,* Tp. II, 1, 214 (not lying and sleeping). *whiles we stood here securing your repose,* 310. *kneel and repeat it; I will s.* III, 2, 47. *here's a man —s,* All's II, 1, 65. *canst s.* Wint. IV, 3, 78. *that thou shouldst s. while Lewis doth sit,* H6C III, 3, 3. *s., rise and s.* Rom. III, 3, 88. *we will s. and watch your pleasure,* Caes. IV, 3, 249 (= be up). *she stood and spoke,* Ant. V, 2, 344 etc. *s. on end,* Ven. 272. R3 I, 3, 304 etc. (cf. *End*). *it —s upright,* H6B III, 3, 15. R3 III, 2, 38. Applied, in a quibbling way, to the erected yard: Sonn. 151, 12. Gent. II, 1, 90. 91. II, 5, 23. All's III, 2, 43. Shr. Ind. 2, 127. Rom. I, 1, 34. II, 1, 25. Mcb. II, 3, 38. *to s. up,* see below.

2) to remain upright, not to fall, not to be lost, not to perish: *to times in hope my verse shall s.* Sonn. 60, 13. *to s. in thy affairs, fall by thy side,* Sonn. 151, 12. *now doth thy honour s … as firm as faith,* Wiv. IV, 4, 8. *that it may s. till the perpetual doom,* V, 5, 62. *they shall s. for seed,* Meas. I, 2, 102. *that John may s., then Arthur needs must fall,* John III, 4, 139. *if it* (this day) *must s. still* (in the calendar) III, 1, 89.

*no conditions of our peace can s.* H4B IV, 1, 184. *our peace shall s. as firm as rocky mountains*, 188. *while England —s*, H6B IV, 10, 45. *the cardinal cannot s. under them* (your complaints) H8 III, 2, 3. *Troy walls s.* Troil. I, 3, 12. *Troy in our weakness —s, not in her strength*, 137 (Ff *lives*). *the commonwealth doth s.* Cor. IV, 6, 14. *it should not s. in thy posterity*, Mcb. III, 1, 4. *that thou mayst s., to enjoy thy banished lord and this great land*, Cymb. II, 1, 69. *when peers thus knit, a kingdom ever —s*, Per. II, 4, 58.

Hence = to be valid: *whose will —s but mine?* H6A I, 3, 11. *shall our condition s.?* V, 4, 165.

3) to be placed in any manner, to have a position or situation: *my heart —s armed in mine ear*, Ven. '779. *the blood which in round drops upon their whiteness stood*, 1170. *twenty consciences that s. 'twixt me and Milan*, Tp. II, 1, 279. *whose heads stood in their breasts*, III, 3, 47. *thy head —s so tickle on thy shoulders*, Meas. I, 2, 176. *two prunes ... stood, as it were, in a fruit-dish*, II, 1, 94 (Pompey's ideas are associated in a peculiar manner). *in what part of her body —s Ireland?* Err. III, 2, 118. *England stood in her chin*, 131. 142. *it* (your nose) *—s too right*, LLL V, 2, 568. *there s. the caskets*, Merch. II, 9, 4. *where ... —s a sheep-cote*, As IV, 3, 77. *where thy nose —s*, All's II, 3, 268. *my house doth s. by the church*, Tw. III, 1, 7. *if thy tabor s. by the church*, 9. *I will s. betwixt you and danger*, Wint. II, 2, 66. *there —s the castle*, R2 II, 3, 53. *the tomb that —s upon your grandsire's bones*, III, 3, 106. *where old Troy did s.* V, 1, 11. *the burning torch in yonder turret —s*, H6A III, 2, 30. *where castles mounted s.* H6B I, 4, 40. *this staff of honour raught, there let it s. where it best fits to be, in Henry's hand*, II, 3, 43. *his head will s. steadier on a pole*, IV, 7, 101. *in the place your father's* (head) *—s*, H6C II, 6, 86. *yonder —s the thorny wood*, V, 4, 67. *cold fearful drops s. on my trembling flesh*, R3 V, 3, 181. *how many Grecian tents do s. hollow upon this plain*, Troil. I, 3, 79. *let all untruths s. by thy stained name, and they'll seem glorious*, V, 2, 179. *the high east —s directly here*, Caes. II, 1, 111. *seeing those beads of sorrow s. in thine* (eyes) III, 1, 284. *—s Scotland where it did?* Mcb. IV, 3, 164. *behold where —s the usurper's cursed head*, V, 8, 54. *where late the diadem stood*, Hml. II, 2, 530. *why one's nose —s i' the middle on's face*, Lr. I, 5, 19. *nature in you —s on the very verge of her confine*, II, 4, 149. *a more unhappy lady, if this division chance, ne'er stood between*, Ant. III, 4, 13. *where yond pine does s.* IV, 12, 1. *your isle, which —s as Neptune's park*, Cymb. III, 1, 18 etc.

4) to be written: *if aught in me worthy perusal s. against thy sight*, Sonn. 38, 6. *whose fine —s in record*, Meas. II, 2, 40. *the strong statutes s. like the forfeits in a barber's shop*, V, 323. *it —s as an edict in destiny*, Mids. I, 1, 151. *if it* (this day) *must s. still* (in the calendar) John III, 1, 89. *s. aye accursed in the calendar*, Mcb. IV, 1, 134.

5) to exist; to make one's appearance: *nothing —s but for his scythe to mow*, Sonn. 60, 12. *the blots of nature's hand shall not in their issue s.* Mids. V, 417. *poor trespasses, more monstrous —ing by*, Wint. III, 2, 191. *every man that stood showed like a mine*, H8 I, 1, 21.

6) to be in a state or condition: *how —s the matter with them?* Gent. II, 5, 21. *when it —s well with him, it —s well with her*, 23. *thus —s it with me*, Meas. I,

2, 149. *as the matter now —s*, III, 1, 201. *so —s the comparison*, LLL IV, 1, 80. *you stood as fair as any comer for my affection*, Merch. II, 1, 20 (cf. H4A V, 3, 29). *to s. high in your account*, III, 2, 157. *many fools that s. in better place*, III, 5, 73. *it —s so that I may hardly tarry so long*, Shr. Ind. 2, 127. *thus it —s, I, 1, 184. *thus it —s with me*, I, 2, 53. *our soldiers s. full fairly for the day*, H4A V, 3, 29 (cf. Merch. II, 1, 20). *the question —eth thus*, H4B I, 3, 15. IV, 1, 53. *as the state stood then*, 115. *the state of Normandy —s on a tickle point*, H6B I, 1, 216. *so it —s*, I, 2, 104. *for my wife, I know not how it —s*, II, 1, 192. *in justice' equal scales, whose beam —s sure*, 205. *if Warwick knew in what estate he —s*, H6C IV, 3, 18. *thus —s the case*, IV, 5, 4. *they that s. high*, R3 I, 3, 259. *so stood the state when Henry the Sixth was crowned*, II, 3, 16. 18. *s. in authentic place*, Troil. I, 3, 108. *if e'er thou s. at mercy of my sword*, IV, 4, 116. *the Volsces s. but as at first, ready to make road*, Cor. III, 1, 4. *they s. in their ancient strength*, IV, 2, 7. *here —s all your state*, Rom. III, 3, 166. *how —s your disposition to be married?* I, 3, 65. *since the case so —s*, III, 5, 218. *doubtful it stood*, Mcb. I, 2, 7. *nor —s it safe with us, to let his madness range*, Hml. III, 3, 1. *how his audit —s*, 82. *how s. I then, that have a father killed, a mother stained, and let all sleep?* IV, 4, 56. *wherefore should I s. in the plague of custom*, Lr. I, 2, 3. *as the condition of this country —s*, Oth. II, 3, 303. *not to consider in what case thou —est*, Ant. III, 13, 54. *darkling s. the varying shore o' the world*, IV, 15, 10. *how the case —s with her*, Cymb. I, 5, 67. *Tyrus —s in a litigious peace*, Per. III, 3, 2 etc.

Hence almost equivalent to the auxiliary verb to be; with participles: *the truest issue of thy throne by his own interdiction —s accursed*, Mcb. IV, 3, 107 (cf. IV, 1, 134). *how s. you affected to his wish?* Gent. I, 3, 60. II, 1, 90. R3 III, 1, 171. *it —s agreed*, H8 V, 3, 87. *s. not amazed*, Wiv. V, 5, 244. *why s. these royal fronts amazed thus?* John II, 356. *s. you so assured*, Shr. I, 2, 156. *—est not thou attainted*, H6A II, 4, 92. *his soul shall s. sore charged*, H5 I, 2, 283. *s. I condemned for pride so much*, Ado III, 1, 108. R2 II, 2, 132. II, 3, 119. Troil. III, 3, 219. Lr. I, 4, 5. *thou shalt s. cursed*, John III, 1, 173. *more than I s. debted to this gentleman*, Err. IV, 1, 31. *through the length of times he —s disgraced*, Lucr. 718. 1833. *I s. dishonoured*, Ado IV, 1, 65. *I stood engaged*, All's V, 3, 96. Troil. V, 3, 68. *s. excommunicate*, John III, 1, 223. *s. excused*, IV, 3, 51. R3 I, 2, 86. *s. indebted to you*, Merch. IV, 1, 413. *how s. you minded*, H8 III, 1, 58. *if her fortunes ever stood necessitied to help*, All's V, 3, 84. *so —s this squire officed with me*, Wint. I, 2, 171. *whereby we s. opposed*, H4A V, 1, 67. *whereof our uncle did s. possessed*, R2 II, 1, 162. R3 III, 1, 196. *so you s. pleased withal*, Merch. III, 2, 211. *s. resolved*, Tit. I, 135. *lands which he stood seized of*, Hml. I, 1, 89. *things —ing thus unknown*, V, 2, 356. *and s. unshaken yours*, H8 III, 2, 199.

With adjectives: *I s. accountant for as great a sin*, Oth. II, 1, 302. *they would s. auspicious to the hour*, Lucr. 347. Wint. IV, 4, 52. *—s chief in power*, All's II, 1, 115. *the fold —s empty*, Mids. II, 1, 96. H8 V, 3, 10. *ancestors who stood equivalent with mighty kings*, Per. V, 1, 92. *s. forfeit*, LLL V, 2, 427. *the gods to-day s. friendly*, Caes. V, 1, 94. *s. gracious to the rites*, Tit. I, 78. *he —s obdurate*, Merch. IV, 1, 8. *of many mine being one may s. in number, though in reckoning none, Rom. I, 2, 33 (cf. Meas. II, 4, 58). he should s. one of the three to share it, Caes. IV, 1, 14. how loathly opposite I stood, Lr. II, 1, 51. but all alone —s hugely politic, Sonn. 124, 11. that the comparison may s. more proper, Merch. III, 2, 46.

With substantives: s. my friend, H4B III, 2, 235. 245. H8 IV, 2, 157. s. good father to me now, Shr. IV, 4, 21. where each second stood heir to the first, Oth. I, 1, 38. s. my good lord, H4B IV, 3, 89. —ing your friendly lord, Cor. II, 3, 198. to s. auspicious mistress, Lr. II, 1, 42.

With adverbs or prepositional expressions: the Cyprus wars, which even now s. in act, Oth. I, 1, 152. though our proper son stood in your action, I, 3, 70. s. under the adoption of abominable terms, Wiv. II, 2, 308. the people do s. but in a forced affection, Caes. IV, 3, 205. regards that s. aloof from the entire point, Lr. I, 1, 242. he that breaks them —s in attainder of eternal shame, LLL I, 1, 158. s. at my bestowing, All's II, 3, 59. his integrity —s without blemish, Meas. V, 108. what case s. I in? Wint. I, 2, 352. on what condition —s it (my fault) and wherein? R2 II, 3, 107. a true soul when most impeached —s least in thy control, Sonn. 125, 14. s. in hard cure, Lr. III, 6, 107. my hopes s. in bold cure, Oth. II, 1, 51. you s. within his danger, Merch. IV, 1, 180. s. in your own defence, LLL V, 2, 85. nice affections wavering stood in doubt, Compl. 97. to be worst, —s still in esperance, Lr. IV, 1, 4. you s. in coldest expectation, H4B V, 2, 31. our preparation —s in expectation of them, Lr. IV, 4, 22. if it s. within the eye of honour, Merch. I, 1, 136. as we s. in fear, Meas. II, 3, 34. H6B IV, 2, 66. I s. on fire: come to the matter, Cymb. V, 5, 168. the doom —s in effectual force, Gent. III, 1, 223. LLL I, 1, 111. my woeful self, that did in freedom s. Compl. 143. 'tis best we s. upon our guard, Tp. II, 1, 321. —s at a guard with envy, Meas. I, 3, 51. in the great hand of God I s. Mcb. II, 3, 136. one would speak to her and s. in hope of answer, Wint. V, 2, 110. Tit. II, 1, 119. which else would s. under grievous imposition, Meas. I, 2, 194. my life —s in the level of your dreams, Wint. III, 2, 82. such as s. not in their liking, Cor. I, 1, 199. s. in assured loss, Lr. III, 6, 102. many lives s. between me and home, H6C III, 2, 173. a note of what I s. in need of, Gent. II, 7, 84. what dangerous action, stood it next to death, V, 4, 41. freely have they leave to s. on either part, All's I, 2, 15. in which predicament thou —est, Merch. IV, 1, 357. to be king —s not within the prospect of belief, Mcb. I, 3, 74. not being the worst —s in some rank of praise, Lr. II, 4, 261. s. in readiness, Tit. I, 325. whose fine —s in record, Meas. II, 2, 40 (cf. sub 4). to both it —s in like request, Cor. III, 2, 51. if thou —est not in the state of hanging, V, 2, 70. the help of one —s me in little stead, H6A IV, 6, 31. have I lived to s. at the taunt of one, Wiv. V, 5, 151. but O, the thorns we s. upon, Wint. IV, 4, 596. none —s under more calumnious tongues, H8 V, 1, 113. Cor. IV, 2, 7.

7) Followed by prepositions; a) to s. against = to oppose; to offer resistance: devices ... which shall then have no power to s. against us, Meas. IV, 4, 16. s. against us like an enemy, H4A IV, 3, 37. H4B IV, 4, 95. manhood is called foolery, when it —s against a falling fabric, Cor. III, 1, 246. Caes. III, 2, 124. Lr. II, 1, 70. IV, 7, 33.

b) to s. by = to maintain, to support, to assist:

will you s. by us? H6C IV, 1, 145. to s. firm by honour, Troil. II, 2, 68. s. by our Ajax, IV, 5, 89 (as his second).

c) to s. for = 1) to be for, to side with, to support, to fight for: I s. wholly for you, Wiv. III, 2, 62. I will s. for it (virginity) a little, All's I, 1, 145. s. for your own, H5 I, 2, 101. I'll s. to-day for thee and me and Troy, Troil. V, 3, 36. that hath thus stood for his country, Cor. II, 2, 45. when Marcius stood for Rome, IV, 6, 45. —est so for Posthumus, Cymb. III, 5, 56. cf. Merch. IV, 1, 103. 142. Wint. III, 2, 46. 2) to be in the place of, to represent: for Achilles' image stood his spear, Lucr. 1424. a face, a leg, a head, stood for the whole, 1428. craft, being richer than innocency, —s for the facing, Meas. III, 2, 11. I am to s. for him, LLL V, 2, 508. I s. for sacrifice, Merch. III, 2, 57. thanks which ... —s for my bounty, R2 II, 3, 67. if thou darest not s. for ten shillings, H4A I, 2, 157 (quibbling). do thou s. for my father, II, 4, 413. 477. I s. here for him, H5 II, 4, 116. there —s your friend for the devil, III, 7, 128. my will shall s. for law, H6C IV, 1, 50. the commoners, for whom we s. Cor. II, 1, 243. the people of Rome, for whom we s. a special party, Tit. I, 20. must thou needs s. for a villain in thine own work? Tim. V, 1, 39. do thou for him s. Lr. I, 4, 157. this borrowed passion —s for true old woe, Per. IV, 4, 24. (cf. s. thou as Dauphin in my place, H6A I, 2, 61). 3) to be as good as; to be reckoned: a woman's nay doth s. for nought, Pilgr. 340. I hope this reason —s for my excuse, Shr. Ind. 2, 126. cf. our compelled sins s. more for number than for accompt, Meas. II, 4, 58 (compare Rom. I, 2, 33). 4) to offer one's self as a candidate (in the fashion of ancient Rome): when he shall s. for his place, Cor. II, 1, 165. were he to s. for consul, 248. II, 2, 2. II, 3, 195. V, 6, 28.

d) to s. in = to insist on; lection of O. Edd. in Tit. IV, 4, 105: if she s. in hostage for his safety. M. Edd. s. on hostage; but cf. R2 II, 3, 107.

e) to s. on = 1) to insist on: if that thy valour s. on sympathy, R2 IV, 33. and then s. upon security, H4B I, 2, 42. when articles too nicely urged be stood on, H5 V, 2, 94. and s. upon my common part, Cor. I, 9, 39. do not s. upon it, II, 2, 154. 2) to make much of, to attach a high value to: in these times you s. on distance, Wiv. II, 1, 233. you s. upon your honour! II, 2, 20. this fellow doth not s. upon points, Mids. V, 118. we s. upon our manners, Wint. IV, 4, 164. let him that is a true-born gentleman and —s upon the honour of his birth, H6A II, 4, 28. do not s. on quillets how to slay him, H6B III, 1, 261. wherefore s. you on nice points, H6C IV, 7, 58. your franchises, whereon you stood, Cor. IV, 6, 86. you that stood so much upon the voice of occupation, 96. this minion stood upon her chastity, Tit. II, 3, 124. who s. so much on the new form, Rom. II, 4, 35. I never stood on ceremonies, Caes. II, 2, 13. s. not upon the order of your going, Mcb. III, 4, 119. to s. on more mechanic compliment, Ant. IV, 4, 31. 3) to depend on (to rely on as well as to be in a state of dependance from): —s so firmly on his wife's frailty, Wiv. II, 1, 242. the good I s. on is my truth and honesty, H8 V, 1, 123. it stood upon the choice of friends, Mids. I, 1, 139. your fortune stood upon the casket there, Merch. III, 2, 203. upon whose influence Neptune's empire —s, Hml. I, 1, 119. 4) to concern, to be of importance to: consider how it —s upon my credit, Err. IV, 1, 68. my state —s on me to defend, not to debate, Lr. V, 1, 69. The preposition

transposed: *it —s your grace upon to do him right*, R2
II, 3, 138 (= it is your office, your duty). *it —s me
much upon to stop all hopes*, R3 IV, 2, 59. *does it not
s. me now upon, ... is't not perfect conscience, to quit
him with this arm?* Hml. V, 2, 63. *it only —s our lives
upon to use our strongest hands*, Ant. II, 1, 50. 5) to
have to do with; to concern one's self about: *—s on
tricks when I am indisposed*, Err. I, 2, 80. *I s. on sudden
haste*, Rom. II, 3, 93. *'tis but the time and drawing days
out that men s. upon*, Caes. III, 1, 100. 6) to be on:
*what terms the enemy stood on*, H5 III, 6, 78 (= what
were the terms of the enemy; cf. *Term*). *the sore terms
we s. upon with the gods*, Per. IV, 2, 38. *to determine
of what conditions we shall s. upon*, H4B IV, 1, 165
(= what shall be our conditions). *the main descry
—s on the hourly thought*, Lr. IV, 6, 218 (= is to be
expected every hour).

f) *to s. to* = 1) to side with, to assist, to support;
to maintain, to guard, to be firm in the cause of: *s.
to me*, H4B II, 1, 70. *call them pillars that will s. to
us*, H6C II, 3, 51. *s. to me in this cause*, Cor. V, 3, 199.
*who ever yet have stood to charity, and displayed the
effects of disposition gentle*, H8 II, 4, 86. *or let us s.
to our authority, or let us lose it*, Cor. III, 1, 208. 2) to
abide by, to persist in: *s. fast, good Fate, to his hanging*,
Tp. I, 1, 32. *now I'll s. to't, the pancakes were naught*,
As I, 2, 69. *Sir John —s to his word*, H4A I, 2, 130.
*and yet you will s. to it; you will not pocket up wrong*,
III, 3, 183. *will speak more in a minute than he will
s. to in a month*, Rom. II, 4, 157. *to this point I s....
that both the worlds I give to negligence, ... only I'll
be revenged*, Hml. IV, 5, 133. 3) to go through, to
maintain one's ground in: *Troilus will s. to the proof*,
Troil. I, 2, 142 (= stand the test). *to s. to it* = to
be brave and stout-hearted; not to flinch; to do one's
best: *an thy mind s. to it, boy, steal away bravely*, All's
II, 1, 29. *the danger is in —ing to it*, III, 2, 43 (quibbling). *is't a lusty yeoman? will a s. to't?* H4B II, 1, 5.
*we stood to't in good time*, Cor. IV, 6, 10. *'tis he. S. to
it*, Mcb. III, 3, 15..

g) *to s. with* = 1) to join, to make common cause
with: *I think he will s. very strong with us*, Caes. II, 1,
142. *then s. with us*, Mcb. III, 3, 4. 2) to agree; to be
consistent with: *your good will may s. with ours, this
day to be conjoined*, Ado V, 4, 29. *if it s. with honesty*,
As II, 4, 91. *such assurance ta'en as shall with either
part's agreement s.* Shr. IV, 4, 50. *if with thy will it
—s*, H6C II, 3, 38. *if it may s. with the tune of your
voices that I may be consul*, Cor. II, 3, 91.

8) with adverbs; a) *to s. off*, = 1) to keep at a
distance: *our bloods ... s. off in differences so mighty*,
All's II, 3, 127. *s. no more off*, IV, 2, 34. 2) to have
relief, to appear prominent: *the truth of it —s off as
gross as black and white*, H5 II, 2, 103.

b) *to s. out* = 1) not to take part, to keep off:
*repaying what we took from them, ... only myself stood
out*, Tw. III, 3, 35. *what, art thou stiff? —est out?*
Cor. I, 1, 245. 2) to be in arms, to rebel: *you have of
late stood out against your brother*, Ado I, 3, 22. *his
spirit is come in, that so stood out against the church*,
John V, 2, 71. *the rebels which s. out in Ireland*, R2 I, 4, 38.

c) *to s. to* = to fall to work: *I will s. to and feed*,
Tp. III, 3, 49. *makes him s. to and not s. to*, Mcb. II,
3, 38 (cf. All's II, 1, 29).

d) *to s. up* = 1) to be on the feet, to remain
upright: *that which here —s up is but a quintain*, As

I, 2, 262. *s. close up*, H8 V, 4, 92. *who sensibly out-
dares his senseless sword, and, when it bows, —s up*,
Cor. I, 4, 54. *how stiff is my vile sense, that I s. up*,
Lr. IV, 6, 287. *I have an absolute hope our landmen
will s. up*, Ant. IV, 3, 11. *whilst he stood up and spoke*,
V, 1, 7. 2) to ascend a higher place: *shall we s. up
here and see them?* Troil. I, 2, 193. 3) to rise: Meas.
V, 460. Mids. IV, 1, 146. Merch. II, 2, 86. All's II, 1,
64. 67. R2 V, 3, 111. H6A III, 4, 25. H8 V, 1, 114.
Cor. III, 2, 12. V, 3, 52. Tit. I, 485. Rom. III, 3, 75.
88. IV, 2, 28 etc. In a moral sense, = to rise in arms;
to fight; to rebel: *he that tempered thee bade thee s. up*,
*gave thee no instance why thou shouldst do treason*, H5
II, 2, 118. *we stood up about the corn*, Cor. II, 3, 16.
*we all s. up against the spirit of Caesar*, Caes. II, 1,
167. *gods, s. up for bastards*, Lr. I, 2, 22. *a peasant
s. up thus!* III, 7, 80. *were't not that we s. up against
them all*, Ant. II, 1, 44. = to rise in order to make a
declaration or put in a claim: *nature might s. up and
say to all the world*, Caes. V, 5, 74. *the which immediacy
may well s. up and call itself your brother*, Lr. V, 3, 65.
*to weet we s. up peerless*, Ant. I, 1, 40. *—s up for the
main soldier*, I, 2, 197. *where was he that could s. up
his parallel?* Cymb. V, 4, 54.

e) As with *up*, similarly with many other adverbs
it receives the sense of motion, or rather of a state
caused by previous motion, and becomes equivalent
to to step, to go, to come: *how coldly those impediments
s. forth of wealth, of filial fear*, Compl. 269. *that my
accusers ... may s. forth face to face*, H8 V, 3, 47.
Mostly in the imperative: *s. all aloof*, Merch. III, 2,
42. *s. apart*, Err. V, 364. R2 III, 3, 187. *s. aside*,
Gent. IV, 2, 81. Ado IV, 2, 32. LLL IV, 1, 55. As
III, 2, 132. H6C III, 3, 110. *s. away*, H5 IV, 8, 14.
All's V, 2, 17. *s. back*, Shr. II, 341. John IV, 3, 81.
H6A I, 2, 70. I, 3, 33. 38. R3 I, 2, 38. Caes. III, 2,
172. *s. by*, Ado IV, 1, 24. Shr. I, 2, 143. John IV, 3,
94 (= step aside, withdraw). H6B II, 1, 72 (= approach, come up). Ant. III, 11, 41. *s. forth*, Mids. I,
1, 24. III, 1, 83. Merch. I, 1, 175. R2 IV, 7. H8 I,
2, 129. *s. off*, Tp. III, 2, 92. 94. Caes. III, 2, 171. In
the same manner with the prepos. *from: s. from him*,
H4B II, 1, 74. IV, 4, 116. *s. from the hearse*, Caes.
III, 2, 169.

II. trans. 1) to resist: *an she s. him but a little, he
will throw a figure in her face*, Shr. I, 2, 113. *none
durst s. him*, H6A I, 1, 123. *a great sea-mark —ing
every flaw*, Cor. V, 3, 74. *the lust-dieted man, that —s
your ordinance*, Lr. IV, 1, 71 (Ff *slaves*). *the villain
would not s. me*, Cymb. I, 2, 15. *who dares not s. his
foe*, V, 3, 60.

2) to go through, to abide, to sustain: *thou hast
strangely stood the test*, Tp. IV, 7. *and s. the push of
every vain comparative*, H4A III, 2, 66. H4B II, 2, 40.
Troil. II, 2, 137. *I will s. the hazard of the die*, R3 V,
4, 10. Tim. V, 2, 5. *if this poor trash of Venice s. the
putting on*, Oth. II, 1, 313. *I must s. the course*, Lr. III,
7, 54. *his love, which —s an honourable trial*, Ant. I,
3, 74. *to s. the buffet with knaves*, I, 4, 20.

3) With an accus. of time: *you have stood your
limitation*, Cor. II, 3, 146 (your limited or prescribed
time). *as I did s. my watch*, Mcb. V, 5, 33 (cf. *s.
sentinel*, Mids. II, 2, 26).

**Standard,** 1) an ensign of war, a banner: LLL
IV, 3, 367. H6A II, 1, 23. H6B I, 1, 256. R3 V, 3, 22.
264. 348.

2) a standard-bearer: Tp. III, 2, 18 (Stephano's speech). 20 (quibbling between *s.* and *stander*).

**Stander**, one who stands: *being slippery —s*, Troil. III, 3, 84.

**Stander-by**, one present, a bystander: Wint. I, 2, 279. R3 I, 2, 163. I, 3, 210. Troil. IV, 5, 190. Cymb. II, 1, 12.

**Standing**, subst. 1) time of existence: *will continue the s. of his body*, Wint. I, 2, 431.

2) station: *how this grace speaks his own s.* Tim. I, 1, 31 (how exactly this grace expresses the place due to its owner. Steevens: 'how the graceful attitude of this figure proclaims that it stands firm on its centre, or gives evidence in favour of its own fixure'.

**Standing-bed**, a bed supported by legs (distinguished from a truckle-bed, q. v.): Wiv. IV, 5, 7.

**Standing-bowl** (not hyph. in O. Edd.) a bowl resting on a foot: Per. II, 3, 65.

**Standing-tuck** (not hyph. in O. Edd.) a rapier placed upright: H4B II, 4, 274.

**Stand-under**, a word coined by Launce by way of quibbling: Gent. II, 5, 33.

**Staniel**, a species of hawk; a word substituted by M. Edd. for *stallion* of O. Edd. in Tw. II, 5, 124; and proposed by some for *scamels* in Tp. II, 2, 176.

**Stanley**, name of 1) Sir John S. H6B II, 3, 13. II, 4, 77. 91. 104. 2) Sir William S. H6C IV, 5, 1. 23. R3 IV, 5, 10. 3) Lord S. (cf. *Derby*): R3 I, 3, 17. III, 1, 167. III, 2, 3. III, 4, 84. IV, 2, 90 etc. 4) his son George S. R3 IV, 4, 497. IV, 5, 3. V, 3, 346. V, 5, 9.

**Stannyel**, see *Staniel*.

**Stanze** (the later Ff and some M. Edd. *stanza*) a strophe: LLL IV, 2, 107.

**Stanzo** (some M. Edd. *stanza*) the same: As II, 5, 18. 19.

**Staple**, 1) a loop of iron made to receive a bolt: *with massy —s and corresponsive and fulfilling bolts*, Troil. Prol. 17.

2) thread, pile: *he draweth out the thread of his verbosity finer than the s. of his argument*, LLL V, 1, 19.

**Star** (masc. in Ven. 861) a celestial body shining in the night: Ven. 861. 1032. Lucr. 164. 1008. Sonn. 132, 7. Gent. II, 6, 9. III, 1, 156. Wiv. I, 3, 101. Meas. IV, 2, 219. LLL IV, 3, 231. V, 2, 205. Mids. III, 2, 407. Shr. IV, 5, 7. 31. All's I, 1, 97. Wint. I, 2, 48. 425. V, 1, 206. Ant. III, 13, 95 etc. *the seven —s*, H4A I, 2, 16. H4B II, 4, 201. Lr. I, 5, 38. *fixed s.* LLL I, 1, 89. *the north s.* Ado II, 1, 258. *the northern s.* Caes. III, 1, 60. *the watery s.* (the moon) Wint. I, 2, 1; *the moist s.* Hml. I, 1, 118. *a blazing s.* All's I, 3, 91. *a falling s.* H8 IV, 1, 55; cf. Ant. IV, 14, 106. *a shooting s.* R2 II, 4, 19; cf. Ven. 815; Lucr. 1525; Mids. II, 1, 153; Hml. I, 5, 17. Brilliant things called *—s*; especially bright eyes: Lucr. 13. Sonn. 14, 10. Wint. V, 1, 67. Or persons of brilliant qualities: Phoen. 51. H5 Epil. 6. H6A I, 2, 144. R3 II, 2, 102. H8 IV, 1, 54. Rom. I, 2, 25. Ant. IV, 14, 106. V, 2, 311. Eminent persons made *—s* after their death: H6A I, 1, 55. Cymb. V, 5, 352. Per. V, 3, 79. cf. Rom. III, 2, 22.

Influencing human fortune: Sonn. 14, 1. 25, 1. 26, 9. Tp. I, 2, 182. Gent. II, 7, 74. Ado II, 1, 349. LLL III, 79. V, 2, 394. Shr. IV, 5, 40. All's I, 1, 197. 205. I, 3, 252. II, 5, 80. Tw. I, 3, 142. II, 1, 3. II, 5, 156. 184. Wint. I, 2, 363. John III, 1, 126. R2 IV, 21. H6A I, 1, 4. IV, 5, 6. H6B III, 1, 206. H6C IV, 6, 22. R3 III, 7, 172. IV, 4, 215. Rom. I, 4, 107. V, 1, 24. V,

3, 111. Caes. I, 2, 140. Hml. I, 4, 32. Lr. IV, 3, 35. Ant. III, 13, 145. Cymb. V, 4, 105 *(Jovial s.)* etc. *Lord Hamlet is a prince, out of thy s.* Hml. II, 2, 141 (above thee in fortune).

= loadstar: *it* (love) *is the s. to every wandering bark*, Sonn. 116, 7. *there's no more sailing by the s.* Ado III, 4, 58. cf. Sonn. 26, 9 and All's II, 1, 57.

= a mark or figure resembling a star: *a mole, a sanguine s.* Cymb. V, 5, 364.

**Star-blasting**, pernicious influence of the stars (cf. *Blast*): Lr. III, 4, 60.

**Star-chamber**, a court of criminal jurisdiction: Wiv. I, 1, 2.

**Star-crossed**, not favoured by the stars, unfortunate: Rom. Prol. 6.

**Stare**, subst. a fixed look with eyes wide open: *why stand you in this strange s.?* Tp. III, 3, 95.

**Stare**, vb. 1) to be stiff, to stand on end: *makest ... my hair to s.* Caes. IV, 3, 280.

2) to look with fixed eyes wide open: Ven. 301. 1149. Wiv. V, 5, 168 (*—ings*, in Evans' speech). LLL V, 2, 927. 936. Shr. III, 2, 230. John IV, 3, 49. R2 V, 3, 24. H6B III, 2, 170. 371. Caes. I, 3, 2. III, 1, 97. IV, 3, 40. Mcb. II, 3, 110. Lr. IV, 6, 110. Oth. V, 1, 107 (Qq *stir*). V, 2, 188. Cymb. III, 4, 5. With *on*: Lucr. 1448. Wint. V, 2, 13. R3 III, 7, 26 (Qq *gazed*). Caes. II, 1, 242. *in her sad face he —s*, Lucr. 1591. With an accus. expressing the effect: *I will s. him out of his wits*, Wiv. II, 2, 291.

**Star-gazer**, astrologer: Ven. 509.

**Stark**, adj. stiff (used only in speaking of a dead body): *lies s. and stiff*, H4A V, 3, 42. *stiff and s. and cold*, Rom. IV, 1, 103. *how found you him? S., as you see*, Cymb. IV, 2, 209.

**Stark**, adv. absolutely, quite: *s. mad*, Err. II, 1, 59. V, 281. Shr. I, 1, 69. Wint. III, 2, 184. *s. naked*, Pilgr. 80. Tw. III, 4, 274. Ant. V, 2, 59. *s. spoiled*, Shr. III, 2, 55.

**Starkly**, stiffly (as in a dead body): *as fast locked up in sleep as guiltless labour when it lies s. in the traveller's bones*, Meas. IV, 2, 70.

**Starlight**, the light of the stars: Wiv. V, 5, 106. Mids. II, 1, 29. V, 320.

**Star-like**, resembling or like a star: H8 V, 5, 47. Tim. V, 1, 66.

**Starling**, the bird Sturnus vulgaris: H4A I, 3, 224.

**Starred**, fortuned, fated: *s. most unluckily*, Wint. III, 2, 100.

**Starry**, adorned with stars: *the s. welkin*, Mids. III, 2, 356.

**Start**, subst. 1) a sudden and involuntary motion of the body: *these flaws and —s ... would well become a woman's story*, Mcb. III, 4, 63.

2) a hasty fit, a sudden and capricious impulse; a sudden appearance: *the first face of neither* (joy or grief), *on the s., can woman me unto't*, All's III, 2, 52 (when it comes suddenly and unawares). *base inclination and the s. of spleen*, H4A III, 2, 125. *such unconstant —s are we like to have from him*, Lr. I, 1, 304. *by —s, his fretted fortunes give him hope and fear*, Ant. IV, 12, 7. *by —s* and *in —s* = by fits, by snatches, incoherently: *mangling by —s the full course of their glory*, H5 Epil. 4 (by a desultory and fragmentary representation; cf. the verb in Troil. Prol. 28). *she did speak in —s distractedly*, Tw. II, 2, 22.

3) a sudden setting out, a breaking forth: *take the*

*s.*, *run away*, Merch. II, 2, 6. *seven of my people, with an obedient s.*, *make out for him*, Tw. II, 5, 65. *you stand like greyhounds in the slips, straining upon the s.* H5 III, 1, 32. *the French ... should make a s. o'er seas and vanquish you*, H6B IV, 8, 45. *this will give it* (his rage) *s. again*, Hml. IV, 7, 194. *to get the s. of* = to leave behind: *should so get the s. of the majestic world*, Caes. I, 2, 130. *to have the s. of* = to have the advantage of: *you have the s. of me*, Wiv. V, 5, 171.

**Start,** vb. 1) intr. a) to make a sudden and involuntary motion of the body, as if by a twitch: Lucr. 348. Wiv. V, 5, 90. Wint. V, 3, 104. H4A II, 3, 46. H6B II, 4, 35. IV, 1, 32. R3 III, 4, 87 (Qq *startled*). H8 III, 2, 113. Mcb. I, 3, 51. V, 1, 50. V, 2, 23. Hml. I, 1, 148. With *at*: Ven. 302. 878. All's I, 3, 148. R3 III, 5, 7. IV, 2, 108. Rom. I, 4, 86.

b) to move suddenly, to rise or go away abruptly: *from her betumbled couch she —eth*, Lucr. 1037. *I did begin to s. and cry*, 1639. *by this, —s Collatine as from a dream*, 1772. *blushing apparitions to s. into her face*, Ado IV, 1, 162. *you s. away and lend no ear unto my purposes*, H4A I, 3, 216. *and —ing so he seemed in running to devour the way*, H4B I, 1, 46. *made him from my side to s.* H6A IV, 7, 12. *beginning in the middle, —ing thence away to what may be digested in a play*, Troil. Prol. 28. *with —ing courage give thy trumpet a loud note to Troy*, IV, 5, 2. *each chance that —s i' the way before thee*, Cor. IV, 1, 37. *s., eyes!* Mcb. IV, 1, 116 (i. e. from your sockets). *make thy two eyes, like stars, s. from their spheres*, Hml. I, 5, 17. *s. not so wildly from my affair*, III, 2, 321. *then away she —ed*, Lr. IV, 3, 33. *kings would s. forth*, Ant. III, 13, 91. *after this strange —ing from your orbs*, Cymb. V, 5, 371. The place mentioned, not from which, but for which, one suddenly sets out: *how if your husband s. some other where?* Err. II, 1, 30. With *up*: *and then —s up* (from her bed) Rom. III, 3, 100. *your bedded hair —s up*, Hml. III, 4, 122.

2) trans. a) to startle, to alarm suddenly: *every feather —s you*, All's V, 3, 232. *it straight —s you*, Troil. V, 2, 101. *direness ... cannot once s. me*, Mcb. V, 5, 15.

b) to rouse: *he —ed one poor heart of mine in thee*, Tw. IV, 1, 63 (play upon the words *heart* and *hart*). *do but s. an echo with the clamour of thy drum*, John V, 2, 167. *to s. a hare*, H4A I, 3, 198. *s. a spirit*, Caes. I, 2, 147. *to s. my quiet*, Oth. I, 1, 101.

**Starting-hole,** evasion, subterfuge: *what trick, what device, what s. canst thou now find out to hide thee from this open and apparent shame?* H4A II, 4, 290.

**Startingly,** by starts, abruptly: *why do you speak so s. and rash?* Oth. III, 4, 79.

**Startle,** 1) intr. to move in a sudden alarm; to be frighted or shocked: *patience herself would s. at this letter*, As IV, 3, 13. *my horse ... —d, when he looked upon the Tower*, R3 III, 4, 87 (Ff *started*). *what fear is this which —s in our ears?* Rom. V, 3, 194.

2) tr. to alarm, to rouse, to shock: *—s and frights consideration*, John IV, 2, 25. *—s mine eyes*, V, 2, 51. H8 III, 2, 294. Per. V, 1, 147.

**Start-up,** one newly come into notice; an upstart: Ado I, 3, 69.

**Starve** or **Sterve** (the latter form in Merch. IV, 1, 138. Cor. IV, 2, 51. Rom. I, 1, 225. Tim. I, 1, 257. Cymb. I, 4, 180. rhyming to *deserve* in Cor. II, 3, 120) 1) intr. a) to perish, to die: *I'll s. ere I'll rob a foot further*, H4A II, 2, 22. *he had better s. than but once*

*think this place becomes thee not*, H8 V, 3, 132. *better it is to die, better to s., than crave the hire which first we do deserve*, Cor. II, 3, 120. *we'll see 'em s. first*, Lr. V, 3, 25.

b) to be benumbed with cold: *you but warm the —d snake*, H6B III, 1, 343. *comfortless as frozen water to a —d snake*, Tit. III, 1, 252. *lest the bargain should catch cold and s.* Cymb. I, 4, 180.

c) to perish with hunger: H4A I, 3, 89. 159. II, 1, 30. H6A III, 2, 48. H6B I, 1, 135. 229. Cor. IV, 2, 51. Rom. III, 5, 194. Per. II, 1, 72.

d) to suffer hunger or want: Merch. I, 2, 7. V, 295. H5 IV, 2, 16. Rom. V, 1, 70. With *for* (cf. *Die*) = to be hungry for, extremely desirous of: *clean —d for a look*, Sonn. 75, 10. *I s. for a merry look*, Err. II, 1, 88. *am —ed for meat*, Shr. IV, 3, 9. *—ing for a time of pell-mell havoc*, H4A V, 1, 81. Partic. *—d* = 1) hungry, ravenous: *thy desires are wolvish, bloody, —d and ravenous*, Merch. IV, 1, 138. 2) famished, lean (cf. *Starveling*): *this same —d justice*, H4B III, 2, 327. *you —d bloodhound*, V, 4, 31.

2) trans. a) to paralyze, to disable: *aches contract and s. your supple joints*, Tim. I, 1, 257. *they* (their mouths) *are now —d for want of exercise*, Per. I, 4, 38. Peculiar expressions: *it is too —d a subject for my sword*, Troil. I, 1, 96 (too powerless, too inconsiderable). *never go home; here s. we out the night*, V, 10, 2 (let us here see the night come to an end).

b) to destroy with cold, to nip: *the air hath —d the roses in her cheeks*, Gent. IV, 4, 159.

c) to afflict with want or hunger: *when she* (nature) *did s. the general world beside and prodigally gave them* (graces) *all to you*, LLL II, 11. *beauty —d with her severity*, Rom. I, 1, 225. *give them life whom hunger —d half dead*, Per. I, 4, 96. *who —s the ears she feeds, and makes them hungry*, V, 1, 113. With *from*: *we must s. our sight from lovers' food till morrow*, Mids. I, 1, 222.

**Starve-lackey,** name: *S. the rapier and dagger man*, Meas. IV, 3, 15.

**Starveling,** a hunger-starved and extremely lean person: H4A II, 1, 76. II, 4, 270.

Name in Mids. I, 2, 60. 62. IV, 1, 208.

**State,** subst. 1) mode of standing: *a face, an eye, a gait, a s.* LLL IV, 3, 185.

2) condition, situation, circumstances of nature or fortune: *unlock the treasure of his happy s.* Lucr. 16. *thou shalt see thy s. and pity mine*, 644. *nor laugh with his companions at thy s.* 1066. *I all alone beweep my outcast s.* Sonn. 29, 2. 10. 14. *such interchange of s.* 64, 9. *a better s. to me belongs*, 92, 7. *brought to medicine a healthful s.* 118, 11. 128, 9. 142, 3. 145, 4. 150, 12. Gent. V, 4, 144. Wiv. V, 5, 63. Meas. I, 2, 184. Err. II, 2, 177. Ado V, 2, 63. V, 4, 30. Merch. III, 4, 21. IV, 1, 30. As I, 3, 129. III, 2, 45. All's I, 3, 196. 220. II, 5, 12. Tw. I, 5, 297. 309. II, 2, 38. V, 67. R2 III, 2, 195. IV, 225. H4A III, 3, 186. H4B I, 1, 107. H5 I, 2, 184. H6B I, 1, 215. III, 2, 154. H6C I, 4, 85. IV, 6, 3. R3 III, 2, 83. 86. IV, 4, 416. H8 II, 4, 228. V, 1, 128. Cor. V, 2, 70. Rom. III, 3, 166. Mcb. I, 2, 3. Hml. III, 1, 10. III, 3, 67. V, 2, 86. Ant. II, 5, 56 etc.

Equivalent to fortune: *my s. being galled with my expense*, Wiv. III, 4, 5. *when I told you my s. was nothing*, Merch. III, 2, 262. *shall share the good of our returned fortune, according to the measure of their —s*, As V, 4, 181. *were my s. far worser than it is, I would not wed her for a mine of gold*, Shr. I, 2, 91. *to set the exact wealth of all our —s all at one cast*, H4A IV, 1, 46.

3) station, place, rank: *the greatest scandal waits on greatest s.* Lucr. 1006. *made me exchange my s. with Tranio*, Shr. V,1,128. *thy beauty ... more homely than thy s.* Wint. IV, 4, 437. *and, as you are a king, speak in your s. what I have done that misbecame my place*, H4B V, 2, 99. *tell the Dauphin I will keep my s., be like a king*, H5 I, 2, 273. *when his holy s. is touched so near*, H6A III,1,58. *that* (the triple crown) *were a s. fit for his holiness*, H6B I, 3, 67. *there to be used according to your s.* II, 4, 95. 99. *sufficeth that I have maintains my s.* IV, 10, 24. *had he matched according to his s.* H6C II, 2, 152. *by my s. I swear to thee*, III, 2, 93. *it ill befits thy s. and birth that thou shouldst stand*, III, 3, 2. *replant Henry in his former s.* 198. *his s. usurped*, V, 4, 77. *thy honour s. and seat is due to me*, R3 I, 3, 112. *your s. of fortune and your due of birth*, III, 7, 120. *more honourable s., more courtship lives in carrion-flies than Romeo*, Rom. III, 3, 34. *I am not to you known, though in your s. of honour I am perfect*, Mcb. IV, 2, 66. *my s. stands on me to defend*, Lr. V, 1, 68 etc.

4) all that concerns and composes the life and existence of man: *this huge s. presenteth nought but shows*, Sonn. 15, 3 (= this vast world in which man lives. M. Edd. *stage*). *in love the heavens themselves do guide the s.* Wiv. V, 5, 245 (= the affairs of men). *the s. of man, like to a little kingdom, suffers then the nature of an insurrection*, Caes. II,1,67. *shakes so my single s. of man*, Mcb. I, 3, 140.

Hence used periphrastically: *how many gazers mightst thou lead away, if thou wouldst use the strength of all thy s.* Sonn. 96,12 (= all thy strength); cf. 150, 12. *thy thoughts, low vassals to thy s.* Lucr. 666 (= thy low vassals). *so perttaunt-like would I o'ersway his s. that he should be my fool and I his fate*, LLL V, 2, 67. *our —s are forfeit*, 425 (= we are forfeit). *praises of his s.* R2 II, 1, 18 (personal flatteries. Qq *praises, of whose taste* etc.). *my s., seldom but sumptuous, showed like a feast*, H4A III, 2, 57. *thus stands my s., 'twixt Cade and York distressed*, H6B IV,9,31. *to raise my s. to title of a queen*, H6C IV, 1, 68. *death on my s.! wherefore should he sit here?* Lr. II, 4, 113. *the question did at first so stagger me, bearing a s. of mighty moment in't*, H8 II, 4, 213 (= being of great consequence).

4) high place; power; greatness; majesty: *his honour, his affairs, his friends, his s., neglected all*, Lucr. 45. *the government I cast upon my brother and to my s. grew stranger*, Tp. I, 2, 76. *highest queen of s., great Juno comes*, IV, 101. *in s. as wholesome as in s. 'tis fit*, Wiv. V,5,63. *flat treason 'gainst the kingly s. of youth*, LLL IV, 3, 293. *my low and humble name to propagate with any branch or image of thy s.* All's II, 1, 201. *outfaced infant s.* John II, 97 (= infant majesty, i. e. the child that was the legitimate king). *my s. is braved, even at my gates, with ranks of foreign powers*, IV,2,243. *the unowed interest of proud-swelling s.* IV,3,147. *to be an instrument to any sovereign s.* V, 2, 82. *happily may your sweet self put on the lineal s. and glory of the land*, V, 7, 102. *bend their bows of yew against thy s.* R2 III, 2, 117. *scoffing his s. and grinning at his pomp*, 163. *proud majesty a subject, s. a peasant*, IV, 252. 192. 209. *whose s. and honour I for aye allow*, V, 2, 40. *to thy sacred s. wish I all happiness*, V, 6, 6. *carded his s., mingled his royalty with capering fools*, H4A III, 2, 62. *down, royal s.!* H4B IV, 5, 121. *look too near unto my s.* 213. *where it* (my blood) *shall mingle with the s. of floods and flow henceforth in formal majesty*, V, 2, 132 ('with the majestic dignity of the ocean'. Malone). *practised dangerously against your s.* H6B II,1,171. *false allegations to o'erthrow his s.* III,1,181. *mischance unto my s.* III, 2, 284. *I am unfit for s. and majesty*, R3 III, 7, 205. *reserve thy s.* Lr. I, 1, 151 (Qq *reverse thy doom*). *bending to your s.* Oth. I, 3, 236. *I came unto your court for honour's sake, and not to be a rebel to her s.* Per. II, 5, 62 etc.

5) appearance of greatness; a) dignity of deportment: *began to clothe his wit in s. and pride*, Lucr.1809. *a measure, full of s. and ancientry*, Ado II, 1, 80. *keep some s. in thy exit, and vanish*, LLL V, 2, 598. *an affectioned ass, that cons s. without book*, Tw. II,3,161. *to have the humour of s.* II, 5, 58. *let thy tongue tang arguments of s.* 164. *with what great s. he heard their embassy*, H5 II, 4, 32. *sad, high, and working, full of s. and woe*, H8 Prol. 3. *they keep s. so*, I, 3, 10.

b) pomp, splendour: *wear their brave s. out of memory*, Sonn. 15, 8. *s. itself confounded to decay*, 64, 10. *if my dear love were but the child of s.* 124, 1. *do their gay vestments his affections bait? that's not my fault; he's master of my s.* Err. II, 1, 95. *trim gallants, full of courtship and of s.* LLL V, 2, 363. *then his s. empties itself into the main of waters*, Merch. V, 95. *under the canopies of costly s.* H4B III, 1, 13. *with the same full s. paced back again*, H8 IV, 1, 93. *in this s. she gallops night by night*, Rom. I, 4, 70. *such necessaries as are behoveful for our s. to-morrow*, IV, 3, 8. *in place of greater s.* Cymb. III, 3, 78. *shrouded in cloth of s.* Per. III, 2, 65.

*A chair of s.* = a seat of dignity, a canopied chair: H6C I,1, 51. 168. H8 IV,1, 67. *s.*, alone, in the same sense: *sitting in my s.* Tw. II, 5, 50. *this chair shall be my s.* H4A II, 4, 416. 418. *he sits in his s. as a thing made for Alexander*, Cor. V, 4, 22. *our hostess keeps her s.* Mcb. III, 4, 5.

6) that which surrounds, as well as those who attend on, a great person; a court, a household: *to thy s. of darkness hie thee*, Err. IV,4,59. *the summer still doth tend upon my s.* Mids. III, 1, 158. *to me and to the s. of my great grief let kings assemble*, John III, 1, 70. *his grace of Canterbury, who holds his s. at door, 'mongst pursuivants*, H8 V, 2, 24. *would have brooked the eternal devil to keep his s. in Rome*, Caes. I, 2, 160.

7) persons representing a body politic, or entrusted with its highest functions: *how like you this wild counsel, mighty —s?* John II, 395 (= princes). *did move your greatness and this noble s. to call upon him*, Troil. II, 3, 118 (this retinue of princes). *hail, all you s. of Greece*, IV, 5, 65. *the general s., I fear, can scarce entreat you to be odd with him*, 264. *we will accite all our s.* H4B V, 2, 142 (the parliament). *without the king's will or the —'s allowance*, H8 III, 2, 322. *rails on our s. of war*, Troil. I, 3, 191 (council of war). *to call together all his s. of war*, II, 3, 271. *is it so concluded? By Priam and the general s. of Troy*, IV, 2, 69. *the s. hath another* (letter) Cor. II, 1, 118 (the senate). *I have a note from the Volscian s.* IV, 3, 11. *our s. thinks not so*, 17. *the s. cannot with safety cast*

*him*, Oth. I, 1, 148. *any of my brothers of the s.* I, 2, 96. *so was I bid report here to the s.* I, 3, 15 etc.

8) the body politic, community; the people united under one government as well as the government itself: Lucr. Arg. 25. Tp. I, 2, 70. 84. III, 2, 8. Meas. II, 4, 7. 156. III, 2, 99. V, 318. 325. Merch. III, 2, 280. III, 3, 29. IV, 1, 222. 312. 365. 367. 371. 373. All's III, 1, 10. R2 II, 1, 114.*H4A III, 2, 98. 169. H6A I, 1, 2. I, 6, 10. V, 4, 96. H6B I, 1, 75. V, 1, 37. R3 II, 3, 16. 18. III, 2, 37. Mcb. IV, 3, 53. Hml. I, 1, 101. Lr. V, 1, 22 etc. Without the article: *those that know the very nerves of s.* Meas. I, 4, 53. *they'll talk of s.* R2 III, 4, 27. *that trick of s. was a deep envious one,* H8 II, 1, 44. *papers of s. he sent me to peruse,* III, 2, 121. *an old man broken with the storms of s.* IV, 2, 21. *love the fundamental part of s.* Cor. III, 1, 151. *I am an officer of s.* V, 2, 3. *we shall have cause of s. craving us jointly,* Mcb. III, 1, 34. *divisions in s.* Lr. I, 2, 159. *something, sure, of s. ... hath puddled his clear spirit,* Oth. III, 4, 140.

**State-affairs**, public affairs: Oth. I, 3, 72. 190.

**Stately**, adj. lofty, majestic, dignified: Lucr. 946. R2 V, 2, 10. H6A I, 1, 21. I, 6, 21 *(—er).* IV, 2, 13. IV, 7, 72. H6C V, 7, 43. Tit. I, 316. IV, 2, 60. Cymb. V, 4, 140.

**Stately**, adv.: *goes slow and s. by them,* Hml. I, 2, 202.

**State-matters**, public affairs: Oth. III, 4, 155.

**Statesman**, one employed in public affairs and versed in the arts of government: Meas. III, 2, 155. Wint. I, 2, 168. Oth. I, 2, 99.

**State-statues**, not statesmen, but mere images resembling them: *or sit s. only,* H8 I, 2, 88.

**Statilius**, name in Caes. V, 5, 2.

**Station**, 1) act or mode of standing: *in the unshrinking s. where he fought,* Mcb. V, 8, 42. *a s. like the herald Mercury,* Hml. III, 4, 58. *her motion and her s. are as one,* Ant. III, 3, 22.

2) a place to stand in: *puff to win a vulgar s.* Cor. II, 1, 231. *take up some other s.* IV, 5, 33.

3) position: *if you have a s. in the file, not i' the worst rank of manhood,* Mcb. III, 1, 102. *they in France of the best rank and s.* Hml. I, 3, 73.

**Statist**, a statesman, a politician: *I do believe, s. though I am none, that this will prove a war,* Cymb. II, 4, 16. *I once did hold it, as our —s do, a baseness to write fair,* Hml. V, 2, 33.

**Statua**, writing of M. Edd. for *statue,* as often as this word is trisyllabic.

**Statue** (trisyll., and to be written *statuë,* in H6B III, 2, 80. R3 III, 7, 25. Caes. II, 2, 76. III, 2, 192) an image shaped by a sculptor: Ven. 213. 1013. Sonn. 55, 5. Gent. IV, 4, 206. Wint. V, 2, 103. V, 3, 10. 47. 88. H6A III, 3, 14. H6B III, 2, 80. R3 III, 7, 25. H8 I, 2, 88. Troil. V, 1, 60. V, 10, 20. Cor. II, 1, 282. Rom. V, 3, 299. Caes. I, 3, 146. II, 2, 76. 85. III, 2, 55. 192. Ant. III, 3, 24. Per. II Prol. 14.

Blunder of Dogberry for *statutes:* Ado III, 3, 85 (Q and the later Ff *statutes*).

**Stature**, size: Gent. IV, 4, 163. Wiv. III, 3, 138. Mids. III, 2, 291. As III, 2, 285. H4B III, 2, 277. Per. V, 1, 110.

**Statute**, 1) an edict, a law: Meas. I, 3, 19. I, 4, 67. V, 322. Err. I, 1, 9. I, 2, 6. V, 126. Ado III, 3, 85 (F1 *statues*). LLL I, 1, 17. R2 IV, 213. H6B IV, 7, 19. H6C V, 4, 79. Cor. I, 1, 86. Mcb. III, 4, 76.

2) a bond; a mortgage: *the s. of thy beauty thou wilt take, thou usurer, that put'st forth all to use,* Sonn. 134, 9. *a great buyer of land, with his —s, his recognizances,* Hml. V, 1, 113. .

**Statute-caps**, woollen caps, which, by Act of Parliament in 1571, the citizens were enjoined to wear on holydays: *better wits have worn plain s.* LLL V, 2, 281 (= better wits may be found among the citizens).

**Staunch**, see *Stanch.*

**Staves**, see *Staff.*

**Stay**, subst. 1) continuance in a place; forbearance of departure: Lucr. 328. *my s. must be stolen out of other affairs,* Meas. III, 1, 158. *your s. with him may not be long,* 256. IV, 1, 44. Wint. I, 2, 16. 25. 97. R2 II, 1, 223. V, 5, 95. H5 V Chor. 37. H6A IV, 6, 40. Rom. I, 1, 164. Oth. I, 3, 277. *I make some s.* Mids. III, 2, 87.

2) continuance in a state: *this inconstant s.* Sonn. 15, 9 (= transitoriness).

3) delay, tarrying: *no more of s.; to-morrow thou must go,* Gent. I, 3, 75. *no bed shall e'er be guilty of my s.* Merch. III, 2, 328. *our dinner will not recompense this long s.* Tim. III, 6, 35. *make no s.* Mids. V, 428. *let's make no s.* Tim. III, 6, 128.

4) prop, support: *what hope, what s.* John V, 7, 68. *these feet, whose strengthless s. is numb,* H6A II, 5, 13. H6B II, 3, 25. H6C II, 1, 69. R3 II, 2, 74. 75. 76. Troil. V, 3, 60.

5) The imperative of the verb used substantively: *here's a s. that shakes the rotten carcass of old death out of his rags,* John II, 455 (i. e. a word of command: *stay!* = stand! hold! stop! German: *ein Halt*).

**Stay**, vb. 1) intr. a) to stand: *so o'er this sleeping soul doth Tarquin s.* Lucr. 423. *who —s it* (time) *still withal?* As III, 2, 348. *I'll s. above the hill,* H6C III, 1, 5. *to s. on* = to stand on, to insist on: *I s. here on my bond,* Merch. IV, 1, 242. *to s.* = to make a stand, not to flee: *give them leave to fly that will not s.* H6C II, 3, 50. *not that I fear to s.* II, 5, 138. *an he had —ed by him,* Cor. II, 1, 143 (= opposed him). *s. by me, my lords,* H6C I, 1, 31 (= assist me). *s. thou by thy lord,* Caes. V, 5, 44. *you —ed well by't in Egypt,* Ant. II, 2, 179 (= you have stood your ground).

b) to stand still, to stop: *each shadow makes him stop, each murmur s.* Ven. 706. *to make her s:* 873. *there she —ed,* Lucr. 1275 (stopped, paused). *in pursuit of the thing she would have s.* Sonn. 143, 4. *and never —s to greet him,* As II, 1, 54. *the glorious sun —s in his course,* John III, 1, 78. *s. and breathe awhile,* H4A V, 4, 47. Oftenest in the imperative: Wiv. V, 5, 84. Meas. V, 354. Err. V, 364. Mids. II, 2, 84. 87. V, 281. H4A II, 2, 85 (Qq stand). H6A III, 1, 103. H6C IV, 3, 27. R3 I, 2, 33. Cor. V, 2, 1. Rom. IV, 3, 57. Hml. I, 1, 51. 127 etc. etc.

Hence = to cease, to have an end: *here my commission —s,* H6B II, 4, 76.

c) to be in a place: *when ... thy shade ... on sightless eyes doth s.* Sonn. 43, 12. *I would be brought where thou dost s.* 44, 4. *tell him where I s.* Meas. IV, 5, 7. *and s. here in your court for three years,* LLL I, 1, 52. *how long within this wood intend you s.?* Mids. II, 1, 138. *the chamber where we —ed,* H4B IV, 5, 57. *if he s. in France,* H5 II, 4, 139. Distinguished from to abide: *they cherish it* (virtue) *to make it s. there, and yet it will no more but abide,* Wint. IV, 3, 98 (the clown's speech).

d) to continue in a place or state, to remain: *she —s, exclaiming on the direful night*, Lucr. 741. *the stain upon his silver down will s.* 1012. *that to my use it might unused s. from hands of falsehood*, Sonn. 48, 3. *then s. at home and go not*, Gent. II, 7, 62. *s. with me awhile*, III, 1, 58. 244. IV, 1, 21. Wiv. I, 4, 40. III, 5, 59. Meas. II, 2, 26. Err. I, 2, 10. IV, 1, 86. IV, 4, 155. V, 336. LLL I, 1, 111. Mids. II, 1, 145. Tw. I, 3, 119. Wint. I, 2, 15. R2 I, 2, 57. H6A IV, 5, 20. 50. H6C III, 2, 58. Cor. II, 3, 45 (*we are not to s. all together*). Tim. IV, 3, 47 (*s. thou out for earnest*, = remain without) etc. etc. *to s. behind* = not to join a person or an enterprise: John III, 3, 1. V, 7, 70. R3 II, 2, 154. Lr. III, 6, 108. Ant. III, 7, 20. *not to s. behind* a person or an enterprise: As I, 1, 115. All's II, 1, 24. Tw. III, 3, 4. Troil. I, 1, 83. Cor. I, 1, 247.

e) to delay, to tarry, to be long: *thou —est too long*, Pilgr. 168. *thou hast —ed so long that going will scarce serve the turn*, Gent. III, 1, 388. *—est thou to vex me here?* IV, 4, 66. *we s. too long*, Wiv. IV, 1, 87. *no longer —ing but to give the mother notice*, Meas. I, 4, 86. *I s. too long from her*, Shr. III, 2, 112. Err. III, 2, 173. Err. IV, 1, 33. 91. V, 20. H6B III, 1, 94. IV, 8, 62 etc. *s. not to expostulate*, H6C II, 5, 135 (lose no time with expostulating; cf. *Stand*). *s. not to talk with them*, Tit. II, 3, 306. Cor. IV, 2, 43. Rom. V, 3, 158. cf. H6B II, 4, 86.

f) to wait: *but, like a sad slave, s. and think of nought*, Sonn. 57, 11. *s.: not yet*, Tp. I, 2, 36. *dinner is ready, and your father —s*, Gent. I, 2, 131. III, 1, 53. Wiv. IV, 5, 13. Meas. II, 3, 17. Err. III, 1, 36. LLL V, 2, 845. Merch. V, 302. H4A II, 4, 63. V, 3, 29. H6B IV, 10, 7. H6C IV, 1, 5 etc. With *for*: *not —ing for the people's suffrages*, Lucr. Arg. 3. *you are —ed for*, Gent. II, 2, 19. III, 1, 382. 385. Wiv. I, 1, 213. 314. IV, 6, 49. Err. I, 2, 76. III, 2, 189. IV, 1, 91. Mids. I, 1, 168. Merch. II, 6, 48. III, 4, 82. John II, 44. R2 I, 3, 5. Tim. I, 1, 179 etc.

With *on*, = 1) to attend on, to wait on: *I thank you, and will s. upon your leisure*, All's III, 5, 48. *thine eye hath —ed upon some favour that it loves*, Tw. II, 4, 24. *my house and welcome on their pleasure s.* Rom. I, 2, 37. *worthy Macbeth, we s. upon your leisure*, Mcb. I, 3, 148. *they* (the players) *s. upon your patience*, Hml. III, 2, 112. *he —s upon your will*, Ant. I, 2, 119. 2) to wait for: *I have a servant comes with me along, that —s upon me*, Meas. IV, 1, 47. *our throats are sentenced and s. upon execution*, Cor. V, 4, 8. cf. Err. V, 20.

2) trans. a) to help to stand upright, to keep from falling, to support, to prop: *makes nice of no vile hold to s. him up*, John III, 4, 138. *struck me, that thought to s. him, overboard*, R3 I, 4, 19. *two props … to s. him from the fall of vanity*, III, 7, 97.

b) to make to stand, to keep from proceeding on its way, to stop: *a river — ed swelleth with more rage*, Ven. 331. *all these poor forbiddings could not s. him*, Lucr. 323. *she her plaints a little while doth s.* 1364. *if you meet the prince, you may s. him*, Ado III, 3, 81. 85. 88. IV, 1, 285. Wint. II, 3, 110. H6A I, 5, 2. Rom. V, 2, 12.

c) to keep back; to restrain: *he was — ed by thee*, Lucr. 917. *your ships are —ed at Venice*, Shr. IV, 2, 83. *s. your thanks awhile*, Wint. I, 2, 9. *s. thy revengeful hand*, R2 V, 3, 42. H6A I, 2, 104. *s. my thoughts, that labour to persuade my soul*, H6B III, 2, 136. III,

1, 105. Caes. IV, 3, 127. Hml. IV, 5, 136. With *from*: *to s. you from election*, Merch. III, 2, 24. *you might s. him from his intendment*, As I, 1, 139. *how my men will s. themselves from laughter*, Shr. Ind. 1, 134. III, 2, 23. H4B IV, 1, 123.

d) to cease, to finish: *the goose came out of door, and —ed the odds by adding four*, LLL III, 93. 99. *retreat is made and execution —ed*, H4B IV, 3, 78. *O that my death would s. these ruthful deeds*, H6C II, 5, 95. *s. your strife*, Tit. III, 1, 193.

e) to put off, to retard: *to s. him not too long, I am content … to have him matched*, Shr. IV, 4, 30. *did entreat his holiness to s. the judgement o' the divorce*, H8 III, 2, 33. *we do our longing s. to hear the rest untold*, Per. V, 3, 83.

f) to make to remain, to detain: *that tide will s. me longer than I should*, Gent. II, 2, 15. *—s me here at home unkept*, As I, 1, 8. *if they* (anchors) *can but s. you where you'll be loath to be*, Wint. IV, 4, 582. *my heart hath one poor string to s. it by*, John V, 7, 55. H8 I, 1, 5. Tit. II, 3, 181. Rom. V, 3, 187. Caes. II, 2, 75. = to suffer to remain: *we —ed her for your sake*, As I, 3, 69.

g) to wait for: *flesh —s no farther reason*, Sonn. 151, 8. *my father —s my coming*, Gent. II, 2, 13. *we must s. the time*, Mids. V, 259. *s. the very riping of the time*, Merch. II, 8, 40. *let me s. the growth of his beard*, As III, 2, 221. R2 I, 3, 4. Troil. I, 1, 25. Rom. II, 5, 36. Mcb. IV, 3, 142. Hml. V, 2, 24. Oth. IV, 2, 170. Ant. III, 13, 155. *to s. one's leisure:* Sonn. 58, 4. Shr. III, 2, 219. IV, 3, 59. John II, 58. H4A I, 3, 258.

h) to remain for the purpose of: *I cannot s. thanksgiving*, LLL II, 193 (= I have no time for thanking you). *s. not thy compliment*, IV, 2, 147 (= lose no time with thy courtesy, but go). *I s. dinner there*, R3 III, 2, 122. Rom. IV, 5, 150. *to s. question* (German: *Rede stehen*): *I will not s. thy questions*, Mids. II, 1, 235. *I'll s. no longer question*, Merch. IV, 1, 346. *—ing no longer question*, H4B I, 1, 48.

i) to abide, to undergo, to meet, to stand: *they basely fly and dare not s. the field*, Ven. 894. *she will not s. the siege of loving terms*, Rom. I, 1, 218. *arming myself with patience to s. the providence of some high powers*, Caes. V, 1, 107.

**Stead**, subst. 1) place which another had or might have; preceded by *in*: Gent. IV, 4, 206. Merch. IV, 1, 161. Shr. I, 1, 207. H6A I, 5, 29. Cor. V, 3, 192 (*were you in my s.*). Tim. IV, 1, 6 (*—s*). Caes. V, 1, 85 (*—s*). Mcb. V, 3, 26.

2) use, help: *the help of one stands me in little s.* H6A IV, 6, 31.

**Stead**, vb. 1) to supply, to replace: *with up: we shall advise this wronged maid to s. up your appointment, go in your place*, Meas. III, 1, 260.

2) to be of use to, to benefit, to help: *necessaries which since have —ed much*, Tp. I, 2, 165. *so it s. you, I will write*, Gent. II, 1, 119. *can you so s. me as bring me to the sight of Isabella?* Meas. I, 4, 17. *may you s. me?* Merch. I, 3, 7. Shr. I, 2, 266. All's III, 7, 41. V, 3, 87. Rom. II, 3, 54. Oth. I, 3, 344. Per. III Prol. 21. IV Prol. 41. cf. *Bested*.

**Steadfast**, fixed, not turned aside: *and with a s. eye receives the scroll*, Lucr. 1339. *oppose thy s. gazing eyes to mine*, H6B IV, 10, 48.

**Steadfastly**, with fixed eyes: *upon this hurt she looks so s.* Ven. 1063.

**Steady,** firm, fixed, not tottering: *if his head will stand —er on a pole,* H6B IV, 7, 101.

**Steal** (impf. *stole;* partic. *stolen; stole* Mcb. II, 3, 73. Caes. II, 1, 238). 1) tr. a) to take clandestinely and without right; absol.: Tp. IV, 239. Wiv. I, 3, 30. 32. Meas. I, 2, 10. 14. II, 2, 177. H5 V, 1, 92 etc. With an object: Ven. 160. 934. 1056. Sonn. 48, 13. 75, 6. Tp. V, 299. Gent. IV, 4, 10. 34. Wiv. III, 4, 40. Meas. III, 1, 159. Err. III, 1, 44. Ado II, 1, 206. 231. III, 3, 44. LLL V, 1, 40. Merch. I, 3, 91. All's II, 5, 86. John IV, 3, 136. H6B III, 1, 55. H6C IV, 5, 17. V, 1, 43 etc. With *away:* Lucr. 1056. Sonn. 63, 8. With *from:* Lucr. 1068. 1555. Sonn. 36, 8. 79, 9. 99, 2. 15. Gent. IV, 4, 59. Meas. II, 4, 43. Ado V, 4, 89. Mids. III, 1, 171. III, 2, 284. 436. Merch. II, 8, 19. III, 2, 247. Wint. IV, 4, 646. H6C V, 5, 24. H8 III, 2, 140. Oth. I, 3, 208. III, 3, 310. Cymb. II, 4, 117 etc. With *of: s. dead seeing of his living hue,* Sonn. 67, 6. *had stolen of both,* 99, 10. *of a cut loaf to s. a shive,* Tit. II, 1, 87. Refl.: *but do thy worst to s. thyself away, for term of life thou art assured mine,* Sonn. 92, 1. *there's warrant in that theft which —s itself, when there's no mercy left,* Mcb. II, 3, 152 (in both passages quibbling). With a dat. comm.: *although thou s. thee all my poverty,* Sonn. 40, 10.

Applied to the act of running away with a girl or of ravishing children: Mids. II, 1, 22. H6B IV, 2, 151. Gent. III, 1, 11 *(away).* 15. IV, 1, 48 *(away).* Wiv. IV, 4, 74 *(away).* Merch. IV, 1, 385. Hml. IV, 5, 173. Oth. I, 3, 60. cf. As I, 3, 131.

Used in a good sense, in speaking of things taken or gained in a bland and imperceptible manner: *to s. a kiss,* Ven. 726. Gent. II, 4, 160. *how many a tear hath love stolen from mine eye,* Sonn. 31, 6. *I stole all courtesy from heaven,* H4A III, 2, 50. *which —s men's eyes,* Sonn. 20, 8. Merch. III, 2, 125. Per. IV, 1, 41. *stolest away the ladies' hearts,* H6B I, 3, 55. Caes. III, 2, 220. Ant. II, 6, 106. cf. Mids. III, 2, 284. *thou hast stolen the impression of her fantasy,* Mids. I, 1, 32. *—ing her soul,* Merch. V, 19. *to s. your thoughts,* II, 1, 12.

b) to assume hypocritically: *who cannot s. a shape that means deceit?* H6B III, 1, 79. *that deceit should s. such gentle shapes,* R3 II, 2, 27.

c) to conceal; to perform secretly: *'twere good to s. our marriage,* Shr. III, 2, 142. *stolen* = secret: *their stolen marriage day,* Rom. V, 3, 233. *her stolen hours of lust,* Oth. III, 3, 338.

2) refl. to creep, to slink furtively: *he will s. himself into a man's favour,* All's III, 6, 98. *he is wise, and hath stolen him home to bed,* Rom. II, 1, 4. cf. Sonn. 92, 1 and Mcb. II, 3, 152.

3) intr. to go or come furtively: *she came —ing to the wayward boy,* Ven. 344. *lest jealousy should by his —ing in disturb the feast,* 450. *he —eth into her chamber,* Lucr. Arg. 15. *away he —s,* Lucr. 283. *through the dark night he —eth,* 729. Sonn. 33, 8. 104, 10. Meas. III, 2, 99. Ado III, 1, 7. III, 3, 63. IV, 2, 64. LLL V, 2, 94. Mids. I, 1, 164. 213. II, 1, 65. 191. III, 2, 51. IV, 1, 161. 209. Merch. V, 15. As II, 1, 30. All's II, 1, 29. III, 2, 132. III, 5, 55. H4A II, 4, 392. H5 V, 1, 92. H6C I, 1, 3. 212. III, 1, 13. IV, 2, 20. R3 III, 7, 168. H8 III, 2, 57. Rom. I, 1, 132. Caes. II, 1, 238. Mcb. II, 4, 26. Hml. III, 4, 134. Oth. III, 3, 39 etc. With the adv. *on: the hour —s on,* Err. IV, 1, 52. IV, 2, 60. R3 V, 3, 85. With

the prep. *on* or *upon: now stole upon the time the dead of night,* Lucr. 162. *as the morning —s upon the night,* Tp. V, 65. *on us both did haggish age s. on,* All's I, 2, 29. *'tis strange he thus should s. upon us,* Wint. I, 1, 115. All's V, 3, 42. H4B II, 2, 172. Hml. I, 5, 61. Lr. IV, 6, 190. Ant. III, 6, 42.

**Stealer,** one who steals, a thief: Ado II, 1, 233. Hml. III, 2, 349. Cymb. II, 3, 75.

**Stealth,** 1) the act of stealing, theft: Tim. III, 4, 27. Lr. III, 4, 96.

2) clandestine practice: *the s. of our most mutual entertainment,* Meas. I, 2, 158. Lr. I, 2, 11. *by s. =* clandestinely: Err. III, 2, 7. Rom. III, 5, 217.

3) clandestine motion; a going secretly: *thy dial's shady s.* Sonn. 77, 7. *your s. unto this wood,* Mids. III, 2, 310. IV, 1, 165. *I feel this youth's perfections with an invisible and subtle s. to creep in at mine eyes,* Tw. I, 5, 316.

**Stealthy,** done clandestinely: *with his s. pace,* Mcb. II, 1, 54.

**Steam,** vapour: *she feedeth on the s.* (of Adonis' breath) Ven. 63.

**Steed,** a horse for state or war: Ven. 13. 39. 263. 290. Compl. 112. Tp. IV, 30. Shr. I, 2, 207. All's II, 3, 300. R2 III, 3, 117. V, 2, 8. 19. H4A II, 3, 52. H5 IV Chor. 10. IV, 2, 8. IV, 7, 81. H6B V, 2, 9. H6C II, 1, 183. II, 3, 20. II, 6, 12. IV, 2, 21. R3 I, 1, 10. Troil. IV, 5, 186. V, 5, 2. Cor. I, 1, 121. I, 9, 12. 61. 71. Tit. II, 3, 76. Rom. III, 2, 1. Oth. III, 3, 351. Ant. I, 5, 48. Cymb. II, 3, 23.

**Steel,** subst. refined and hardened iron: Wint. IV, 4, 228. H4B I, 1, 146. H6C II, 1, 160. R3 IV, 1, 61. Troil. III, 3, 121 *(a gate of s.; cf. Sonn. 65, 8).* Tit. IV, 1, 103. *true as s.:* Mids. II, 1, 197. Troil. III, 2, 184. Rom. II, 4, 210. Emblem of hardness: Ven. 111. 199. Lucr. 755. 951. Sonn. 65, 8. 120, 4. Gent. I, 1, 149. III, 2, 79. Err. III, 2, 150. IV, 2, 34. R2 III, 2, 111. H4B II, 3, 54. H6A I, 4, 51. IV, 2, 51. H6C II, 1, 201. Troil. I, 3, 177. Tit. IV, 3, 47. V, 3, 88. Rom. III, 1, 120. Hml. I, 3, 63. III, 3, 70. Ant. IV, 4, 33.

Denoting weapons or armour: Tp. II, 1, 283. Wiv. I, 3, 84. 102. As V, 1, 60. Tw. III, 3, 5. Wint. IV, 4, 748. John II, 352. R2 III, 2, 59. 111. IV, 50. H4A V, 1, 13. H4B IV, 1, 121. H5 III, 7, 161. H6A IV, 2, 11. H6B III, 2, 234. IV, 10, 59. H6C I, 1, 58. II, 5, 132. H8 II, 1, 76. Troil. III, 1, 165. IV, 5, 195. Cor. I, 9, 45. Tit. V, 3, 112. Rom. I, 1, 89. III, 1, 164. Caes. III, 2, 181. V, 3, 76. Mcb. I, 2, 17. III, 2, 24. Hml. I, 4, 52. Cymb. I, 2, 12. Per. II, 1, 160.

Adjectively: *thy s. bosom,* Sonn. 133, 9. *s. pikes,* Cor. V, 6, 152. *the flinty and s. couch of war,* Oth. I, 3, 231.

**Steel,** vb. to make hard: *s. my lance's point,* R2 I, 3, 74. Figuratively, = 1) to harden, to make insensible: *lest thy hard heart do s. it,* Ven. 375. 376. *my —ed sense,* Sonn. 112, 8. *the —ed gaoler,* Meas. IV, 2, 90. *had not God —ed the hearts of men,* R2 V, 2, 34. 2) to make firm and strong: *from his metal was his party —ed,* H4B I, 1, 116. *service shall with —ed sinews toil,* H5 II, 2, 36. *s. my soldiers' hearts,* IV, 1, 306. H6B III, 1, 331. H6C II, 2, 41. R3 I, 1, 148. Troil. I, 3, 353. Caes. II, 1, 121.

**Steeled,** adj. made of steel: *my s. coat,* H6A I, 1, 85. Ven. 377. Lucr. 1444*. Sonn. XXIV, 1.

**Steely,** made of steel: *the s. point of Clifford's*

*lance*, H6C II, 3, 16. Figuratively, = hard, firm, unbending: *but these fixed evils* (lying, folly, cowardice) *sit so fit in him, that they take place, when virtue's s. bones look bleak i' the cold wind*, All's I, 1, 114 (= steel-boned, unyielding and uncomplying virtue).

**Steep**, subst. rock, mountain (?): *come from the farthest s. of India*, Mids. II, 1, 69 (Q1 *steppe*).

**Steep**, adj. precipitous: LLL IV, 1, 2. H8 I, 1, 131. Cor. III, 3, 88. Hml. I, 3, 48. Lr. IV, 6, 3.

**Steep**, vb. to dip and soak in a liquid: *and his love-kindling fire did quickly s. in a cold fountain*, Sonn. 153, 3. *there may be in the cup a spider —ed*, Wint. II, 1, 40. *—s his safety in true blood*, John III, 4, 147. H4B II, 2, 147. H6C II, 1, 62. R3 I, 3, 178. IV, 4, 275. Rom. V, 3, 145. Mcb. II, 3, 121. Figuratively, = to imbue: *do not s. thy heart in such relenting dew of lamentations*, Lucr. 1828. *four days will quickly s. themselves in night*, Mids. I, 1, 7. *let fancy still my sense in Lethe s.* Tw. IV, 1, 66. *s. my senses in forgetfulness*, H4B III, 1, 8. *have —ed their galls in honey*, H5 II, 2, 30. *with tongue in venom —ed*, Hml. II, 2, 533. *—ed me in poverty to the very lips*, Oth. IV, 2, 50. *—ed our sense in Lethe*, Ant. II, 7, 113. *are —ed in favours*, Cymb. V, 4, 131.

**Steep-down**, precipitous: *wash me in s. gulfs of liquid fire*, Oth. V, 2, 280.

**Steeple**, turret of a church, spire: Gent. II, 1, 142. H4A III, 1, 33. Lr. III, 2, 3. Per. II, 1, 38.

**Steep-up**, high and precipitous: *having climbed the s. heavenly hill*, Sonn. 7, 5. *her stand she takes upon a s. hill*, Pilgr. 121.

**Steepy**, having a precipitous declivity: *when his youthful morn hath travelled on to age's s. night*, Sonn. 63, 5 (cf. 7, 5). *bowing his head against the s. mount to climb his happiness*, Tim. I, 1, 74.

**Steer**, subst. the male of the bovine kind; a bull as well as an ox: *the s., the heifer and the calf are all called neat*, Wint. I, 2, 124. *like youthful —s unyoked*, H4B IV, 2, 103.

**Steer**, vb. 1) tr. to direct, to govern (the course of a ship); abs.: *at the helm a seeming mermaid —s*, Ant. II, 2, 214. With an object: *you shall s. the happy helm*, H6B I, 3, 103. *a rarer spirit never did s. humanity*, Ant. V, 1, 32. *boats that are not —ed*, Cymb. IV, 3, 46.

2) intr. to direct one's course at sea; to sail: *thus hulling in the wild sea of my conscience, I did s. toward this remedy*, H8 II, 4, 200. *—ing with due course towards the isle of Rhodes*, Oth. I, 3, 34.

**Steerage**, the act of directing at sea: Rom. I, 4, 112. Per. IV, 4, 19.

**Stell**, to place, to fix: *to find a face where all distress is —ed*, Lucr. 1444.* *mine eye hath played the painter and hath —ed thy beauty's form in table of my heart*, Sonn. 24, 1. *quenched the —ed fires*, Lr. III, 7, 61 (the fixed stars. According to others, = stellated, starry).

**Stem**, subst. 1) stalk; branch: *two lovely berries moulded on one s.* Mids. III, 2, 211. *this is a s. of that victorious stock*, H5 II, 4, 62. *sweet s. from York's great stock*, H6A II, 5, 41.

2) the forepart of a ship: *fell below his s.* Cor. II, 2, 111. *they skip from s. to stern*, Per. IV, 1, 64.

**Stem**, vb. to oppose (a current), to press forward through: *to s. the waves*, H6C II, 6, 36. *—ing it*, Caes. I, 2, 109. cf. *Re-stem.*

**Stench**, a disgusting smell: John III, 4, 26. H6A I, 5, 23. Lr. IV, 6, 131.

**Step**, subst. 1) pace; progression by one advance of the foot: *as if he told the —s*, Ven. 277. *perdition shall attend you s. by s.* Tp. III, 3, 78. *to measure kingdoms with his feeble —s*, Gent. II, 7, 10. *make a pastime of each weary s.* 35. 36. LLL V, 2, 194. 195. As II, 7, 130. R2 I, 3, 265. *turn two mincing —s into a manly stride*, Merch. III, 4, 67. Wint. I, 2, 173. R2 I, 3, 290. III, 2, 17. 125. V, 1, 91. H8 I, 2, 43 (*front but in that file where others tell —s with me*). Troil. II, 3, 193 (*make*). Mcb. II, 1, 57. Hml. V, 1, 79. Cymb. IV, 2, 215. Per. II, 1, 164.

2) one remove in climbing, a stair, a degree: *they are as children but one s. below*, R3 IV, 4, 301. *you have gone slightly o'er low —s*, H8 II, 4, 112. *the general's disdained by him one s. below*, Troil. I, 3, 130. 131. *that is a s. on which I must fall down, or else o'erleap*, Mcb. I, 4, 48. *one s. I have advanced thee*, Lr. V, 3, 28. *as a grise or s.* Oth. I, 3, 200.

3) measure, proceeding, action: *no unchaste action or dishonoured s.* Lr. I, 1, 231. *doth watch Bianca's —s so narrowly*, Shr. III, 2, 141. Plur. *—s* = path, way (in a moral sense): *fears which attend the —s of wrong*, John IV, 2, 57. *we will untread the —s of damned flight*, V, 4, 52. *vengeance tend upon your —s*, H6B III, 2, 304. *leads discontented —s in foreign soil*, R3 IV, 4, 312. *controller of our private —s*, Tit. II, 3, 60. *followed your sad —s*, Lr. V, 3, 289.

**Step**, vb. 1) to tread: *as your feet hit the ground they s. on*, Tw. III, 4, 306.

2) to make some steps; to go a little distance and with a limited purpose: *who sees the lurking serpent —s aside*, Lucr. 362. *he —s me to her trencher*, Gent. IV, 4, 9. *s. into the chamber*, Wiv. IV, 2, 11. *now s. I forth to whip hypocrisy*, LLL IV, 3, 151. *deadly divorce s. between me and you*, All's I, 3, 319. *s. forth mine advocate*, Wint. V, 1, 221. *none so small advantage shall s. forth to check his reign*, John III, 4, 151. *let's s. into the shadow*, R2 III, 4, 25. *s. aside*, H4A II, 4, 36. *—ed forth before the king*, V, 2, 46. *—s me a little higher*, IV, 3, 75. *to s. out of these dreary dumps*, Tit. I, 391. *s. aside*, Rom. I, 1, 162. *by whose death he's —ed into a great estate*, Tim. II, 2, 232. *who, in hot blood, hath —ed into the law, which is past depth to those*, III, 5, 12. *what judgement would s. from this to this?* Hml. III, 4, 71. *s. between her and her fighting soul*, 113. *this gentleman —s in to Cassio and entreats his pause*, Oth. II, 3, 229. *s. you forth*, Cymb. V, 5, 130.

Scarcely to be distinguished from to go, to walk, to march: *since we are —ed thus far in*, Shr. I, 2, 83. *wherein we s. after a stranger*, John V, 2, 27. *we should not s. too far*, H4B I, 3, 20. *if well, he —ed before me, happily for my example*, H8 IV, 2, 10. *not —ing o'er the bounds of modesty*, Rom. IV, 2, 27. *I am in blood —ed in so far*, Mcb. III, 4, 137. *whose naked breast —ed before targes of proof*, Cymb. V, 5, 5.

**Step-dame**, stepmother: Mids. I, 1, 5. Troil. III, 2, 201. Cymb. I, 6, 1. II, 1, 63.

**Stephano** (*Stéphano* in Tp. V, 277; *Stepháno* in Merch.) name in Tp. II, 2, 65. 100. 104. 113. III, 2, 161. IV, 221 (allusion to a popular ballad; cf. Oth. II, 3, 92). V, 277. 286. Merch. V, 28. 51.

**Stephen**, name: Shr. Ind. 2, 95 (*S. Sly*). John III, 1, 143 (*S. Langton*). R2 III, 3, 28 (*Sir S. Scroop*).

Tit. IV, 4, 42 *(Saint S.).* Oth. II, 3, 92 (old ballad: *King S. was a worthy peer).*

**Stepmother,** a mother by marriage only: Cymb. I, 1, 71.

**Steppe,** a vast uninhabited plain(?): *from the farthest s. of India,* Mids. II, 1, 69 (Q2 Ff *steepe).*\*

**Sterile,** barren, not fertile: Tp. IV, 69. H4B IV, 3, 129. Caes. I, 2, 9. Hml. II, 2, 310. Oth. I, 3, 328.

**Sterility,** barrenness: Lr. I, 4, 300.

**Sterling,** adj. of full value: *if my word be s. yet in England,* R2 IV, 264. *with s. money,* H4B II, 1, 131. *you have ta'en these tenders for true pay, which are not s.* Hml. I, 3, 107.

**Stern,** subst. the hind part of a ship where the rudder is placed: *sit at chiefest s. of public weal,* H6A I, 1, 177. *turn our s. upon a rock,* H6B III, 2, 91. *skip from stem to s.* Per. IV, 1, 64.

**Stern,** adj. 1) severe, austere, gloomy, sullen, grim: *the s. and direful god of war,* Ven. 98. *though men can cover crimes with bold s. looks,* Lucr. 1252. *I would outstare the —est eyes that look,* Merch. II, 1, 27. *therefore put I on the countenance of s. commandment,* As II, 7, 109. *the s. brow and waspish action,* IV, 3, 9. *he hath a s. look, but a gentle heart,* John IV, 1, 88. *swearing and s. looks,* H5 V, 2, 61. *let thy looks be s.* H6A I, 2, 62. *why look you still so s. and tragical?* III, 1, 125. *Suffolk's imperial tongue is s. and rough,* H6B IV, 1, 121. *our s. alarums changed to merry meetings,* R3 I, 1, 7. *I have seen thee s.* Cor. IV, 1, 24. *the fatal bellman which gives the —est good-night,* Mcb. II, 2, 4.

2) unkind, hard-hearted, pitiless: *but he, like you, would not have been so s.* Meas. II, 2, 66. *pierced through the heart with your s. cruelty,* Mids. III, 2, 59. *will you —er be than he that dies and lives by bloody drops?* As III, 5, 6. *you are cold and s.* All's IV, 2, 8. *s., obdurate, flinty,* H6C I, 4, 142. *that I am s. and love them not,* R3 I, 3, 44. *ambition should be made of —er stuff,* Caes. III, 2, 97. *attend you here the door of our s. daughter?* Cymb. II, 3, 42.

3) fierce and rude; cruel, ferocious: *there we will unfold to creatures s. sad tunes, to change their kinds,* Lucr. 1147. *how many lambs might the s. wolf betray,* Sonn. 96, 9. *we cannot deal but with the very hand of s. injustice and confused wrong,* John V, 2, 23. *teaching s. murder how to butcher thee,* R2 I, 2, 32. *the s. tyrant war,* H4B Ind. 14. *rough deeds of rage and s. impatience,* H6A IV, 7, 8. *thy mother took into her blameful bed some s. untutored churl,* H6B III, 2, 213. *s. Falconbridge commands the narrow seas,* H6C I, 1, 239. *murder, s. murder,* R3 V, 3, 197. *what s. ungentle hands have ... made thy body bare,* Tit. II, 4, 16. *more s. and bloody than the Centaurs' feast,* V, 2, 204. *lest with this piteous action you convert my s. effects,* Hml. III, 4, 129. *if wolves had at thy gate howled that s. time,* Lr. III, 7, 63.

**Sternage,** stern, steerage: *grapple your minds to s. of this navy,* H5 III Chor. 18.

**Sternness,** severity of look: *how should I behold the s. of his presence?* Wint. IV, 4, 24.

**Sterve,** see *Starve.*

**Stew,** 1) a vessel in which things are stewed or seethed(?): *I have seen corruption boil and bubble, till it o'er-run the s.* Meas. V, 321.

2) a house of prostitution: *to mart as in a Roman*

s. Cymb. I, 6, 152. Plur. *—s in the same sense:* R2 V, 3, 16. H4B I, 2, 60.

**Steward,** one who manages the affairs of another: *they are the lords and owners of their faces, others bu —s of their excellence,* Sonn. 94, 8. Tw. II, 3, 77. 123. II, 5, 169. Wint. V, 2, 28. R2 IV, 126. H4B V, 3, 136. R3 III, 7, 133. Tim. I, 1, 288. II, 2, 18. 31. III, 4, 41. 109. IV, 2, 1. 50. IV, 3, 487. 496. 505. V, 1, 8. Hml. IV, 5, 173. *high s.* (title of an officer of state): H8 IV, 1, 18. 41.

**Stewardship,** the office of a steward: R2 II, 2, 59. III, 3, 78.

**Stewed,** seethed in a slow moist heat: *more than half s. in grease,* Wiv. III, 5, 121. *in the rank sweat of an enseamed bed, s. in corruption,* Hml. III, 4, 93. *s. in his haste,* Lr. II, 4, 31. *whipped with wire, and s. in brine,* Ant. II, 5, 65. *s. prunes,* a favourite dish in brothels: Wiv. I, 1, 296. Meas. II, 1, 92. H4A III, 3, 128 (*there's no more faith in thee than in a s. prune,* i. e. than in any thing to be found in a brothel). H4B II, 4, 158. *sodden business! there's a s. phrase indeed,* Troil. III, 1, 44 (quibbling: a phrase becoming a stew or a brothel).

**Stick,** subst. 1) a staff; a rod: Tp. I, 2, 472. H6B IV, 10, 52. Lr. II, 4, 125.

2) any stem of a tree broken or cut for fuel or another purpose: *I'll bear him no more —s,* Tp. II, 2, 167. *he that breaks a s. of Gloster's grove,* H6B I, 2, 33.

**Stick,** vb. (impf. and partic. *stuck*) 1) tr. a) to stab, to pierce: *you were best s. her,* Gent. I, 1, 108 (= kill, slay; quibbling). *to s. the heart of falsehood,* Troil. III, 2, 202.

b) to thrust in: *thou —est a dagger in me,* Merch. III, 1, 115. *in his anointed flesh s. boarish fangs,* Lr. III, 7, 58 (Qq *rash*).

c) to fix by piercing: *a codpiece to s. pins on,* Gent. II, 7, 56. *s. it in thy cap,* H5 IV, 7, 161.

d) to fasten, to attach in any manner: *to s. it* (the rod) *in their children's sight,* Meas. I, 3, 25. *with two pitch-balls stuck in her face for eyes,* LLL III, 199. *s. musk-roses in thy sleek smooth head,* Mids. IV, 1, 3. *he stuck them* (wands) *up before the fulsome ewes,* Merch. I, 3, 87. *a thing stuck on with oaths upon your finger,* V, 168. *in mine ear I durst not s. a rose,* John I, 142. *s. your rosemary on this fair corse,* Rom. IV, 5, 79.

e) to fix, to place, to settle: *millions of false eyes are stuck upon thee,* Meas. IV, 1, 61. *I stuck my choice upon her,* All's V, 3, 45. *that he might s. the smallest opinion on my least misuse,* Oth. IV, 2, 108. *we must not rend our subjects from our laws, and s. them in our will,* H8 I, 2, 94.

f) Followed by *with,* = to set with, to furnish or adorn with on the surface: *a lemon stuck with cloves,* LLL V, 2, 654. *my shroud of white, stuck all with yew,* Tw. II, 4, 56. *stuck and spangled with your flatteries,* Tim. III, 6, 101. Similarly: *suspicion all our lives shall be stuck full of eyes,* H4A V, 2, 8.

2) intr. a) to be fastened to something by piercing, or by cleaving to the surface, or by adhering in any manner: *the green plum —s fast,* Ven. 527. *Lucretia's glove, wherein her needle —s,* Lucr. 317. *a born devil, on whose nature nurture can never s.* Tp. IV, 189. *I am a kind of burr; I shall s.* Meas. IV, 3, 190. *there stuck no plume in any English crest,* John II, 317. *on*

the sheets his hair is —ing, H6B III, 2, 174. they are burrs; they'll s.where they are thrown, Troil. III, 2, 120. wherein thou —est up to the ears, Rom. I, 4, 42. when every feather —s in his own wing, Tim. II, 1, 30. Amen stuck in my throat, Mcb. II, 2, 33. his secret murders —ing on his hands, V, 2, 17. which now, like fruit unripe, —s on the tree, Hml. III, 2, 200. the slime that ·—s on filthy deeds, Oth. V, 2, 149.

b) to be fixed, not to move: that thou mayst s. i' the wars like a great sea-mark, Cor. V, 3, 73. his sword seemed in the air to s. Hml. II, 2, 501.

c) to adhere; in a moral sense: —ing together in calamity, John III, 4, 67. the knave will s. by thee, H4B V, 3, 70 (i. e. thou wilt ever be a knave). constantly thou hast stuck to the bare fortune of that beggar, Cymb. III, 5, 119. s. to your journal course, IV, 2, 10.

d) to be fixed; in a moral sense: so deep —s it in my penitent heart, Meas. V, 480. my father's rough and envious disposition —s me at heart, As I, 2, 254.* this drum —s sorely in your disposition, All's III, 6, 46. our fears in Banquo s. deep, Mcb. III, 1, 50. this avarice —s deeper, grows with more pernicious root than lust, IV, 3, 85. his speech —s in my heart, Ant. I, 5, 41.

e) to be placed, to be set, to be settled: maidens' eyes stuck over all his face, Compl. 81; the mouths, the tongues, the eyes and hearts of men ... that numberless upon me stuck as leaves do on the oak, Tim. IV, 3, 263; opinion that so —s on Marcius, Cor. I, 1, 275. all their other senses stuck in ears, Wint. IV, 4, 621. a' saw a flea s. upon Bardolph's nose, H5 II, 3, 43. it (honour) stuck upon him as the sun in the grey vault of heaven, H4B II, 3, 18. therein (in his face) stuck a sun and moon, Ant. V, 2, 79. With off, = to be set off, to be prominent: your skill shall, like a star, s. fiery off, Hml. V, 2, 268.

f) to hesitate, to scruple (always followed by an inf.): 'gainst thyself thou —est not to conspire, Sonn. 10, 6. she will not s. to round me i' the ear, Pilgr. 349. H4B I, 2, 26. H8 II, 2, 127. Cor. II, 3, 17. Hml. IV, 5, 93.

**Sticking-place**, the place in which the peg of a stringed instrument remains fast; the proper degree of tension: screw your courage to the s. Mcb. I, 7, 60.

**Stickler-like**, like an arbitrator or umpire in a combat: the dragon wing of night o'erspreads the earth, and s. the armies separate*, Troil. V, 8, 18.

**Stiff**, 1) rigid, not pliant: clap their female joints in s. unwieldy arms, R2 III, 2, 115. with s. unbowed knee, H6B III, 1, 16. how s. is my vile sense, that I stand up, Lr. IV, 6, 286. Used of limbs made rigid and inflexible by weariness, age or death: Err. I, 2, 15. H4A V, 3, 42. Cor. I, 1, 245. Rom. IV, 1, 103. IV, 5, 26. Cymb. III, 3, 32.

2) hard, strong: in a s. tempest, H8 IV, 1, 72. make you ready your s. bats and clubs, Cor. I, 1, 165. this is s. news, Ant. I, 2, 104 (hard to digest? or, according to Johnson, = asserted with good evidence?).

**Stiff-borne**, carried on with unpliant constancy: none of this could restrain the s. action, H4B I, 1, 177. cf. Hml. I, 5, 95.

**Stiffen**, to make stiff and unpliant: s. the sinews, summon up the blood, H5 III, 1, 7.

**Stiffly**, so as not to bend: and you, my sinews, ... bear me s. up, Hml. I, 5, 95.

**Stifle**, 1) tr. to suffocate: Ven. 934. John IV, 3,

113. H6C II, 6, 83. H8 IV, 1, 58. Rom. IV, 3, 33. With up: John IV, 3, 133.

2) intr. to be suffocated or choked: you shall s. in your own report, Meas. II, 4, 158.

**Stigmatic**, one branded by nature with deformity: foul s. H6B V, 1, 215. H6C II, 2, 136.

**Stigmatical**, branded by nature with deformity: s. in making, worse in mind, Err. IV, 2, 22.

**Stile**, a step or set of steps to get over a fence: Wiv. III, 1, 33. Wint. IV, 3, 133. Lr. IV, 1, 58. Quibbling in Ado V, 2, 6 and LLL I, 1, 201. IV, 1, 98. 99.

**Still**, adj. 1) silent; calm and quiet; motionless (three different significations, but mostly combined in one or another manner): pure thoughts are dead and s. Lucr. 167. deeper sin than bottomless conceit can comprehend in s. imagination, 702. s. swine eat all the draff, Wiv. IV, 2, 109 (Ray's Proverbs: the still sow eats up all the draught). at s. midnight, IV, 4, 30. how s. the evening is, Ado II, 3, 40. s. and contemplative in living art, LLL I, 1, 14. the heart's s. rhetoric, II, 229. as ever s. sleep mocked death, Wint. V, 3, 20. in the calmest and most —est night, H4B III, 1, 28. as dead midnight s. H5 III Chor. 19. the air is s. I, 1, 48. s. and motionless, IV, 2, 50. H6A V, 4, 174. H6B V, 2, 29. R3 IV, 4, 18 (Ff s. and mute, Qq mute and dumb). H8 Prol. 11. III, 2, 380. Troil. I, 3, 200. IV, 4, 92. Cor. III, 2, 11. IV, 6, 37. Tit. III, 1, 264. III, 2, 14. Rom. I, 1, 187 (s. waking sleep). Caes. I, 2, 14. Hml. III, 4, 214. Oth. I, 3, 95. V, 2, 94. Ant. II, 6, 131. IV, 11, 1. IV, 15, 28. Cymb. V, 4, 69 (—er). be s., imperatively, = be silent: LLL I, 2, 188. H4A III, 1, 244. H6B I, 1, 248. III, 1, 304. III, 2, 207. H6C II, 2, 122. Oth. V, 2, 46. = be pacified, be contented: Caes. V, 5, 50. to lie s.: John IV, 1, 50. H4A III, 1, 238. H4B IV, 5, 212. Caes. IV, 3, 201. Ant. I, 2, 114. V, 2, 299. Cymb. II, 3, 70. to sit s.: Tp. I, 2, 170. Cor. IV, 6, 37. to stand s.: Sonn. 104, 11. As III, 2, 329. Wint. V, 3, 95. H4B IV, 2, 98. H6C II, 3, 30. R3 IV, 4, 445. Hml. II, 2, 506. to stay s. As III, 2, 348. my tongue-tied Muse in manners hold her s. (= is silent) Sonn. 85, 1. hold you s. Err. III, 2, 69. I cannot, nor I will not, hold me s. IV, 2, 17.

2) continual, constant (?): s. use of grief makes wild grief tame, R3 IV, 4, 229. I of these will wrest an alphabet and by s. practice learn to know thy meaning, Tit. III, 2, 45 (or = silent, calm, patient?).

**Still**, vb. 1) to silence: s. thy deafening thunders, Per. III, 1, 4. Mostly used in speaking of crying babes: the froward infant —ed with dandling, Ven. 562. the nurse, to still her child, will tell my story, Lucr. 813. Sonn. 143, 14. Ado III, 3, 70. H6A II, 3, 17.

2) to appease, to calm: to s. my beating mind, Tp. IV, 163. whose advice hath often —ed my brawling discontent, Meas. IV, 1, 9.

**Still**, adv. 1) always, ever, constantly: s. she entreats, ... s. is he sullen, s. he lours and frets, Ven. 73. 75. 358. she will never rise, so he will kiss her s. 480. 512. 593. whose tushes never sheathed he whetteth s. 617. her anthem s. concludes in woe, 839. 964. knows no pity, but is s. severe, 1000. 1106. thy hasty spring s. blasts, and ne'er grows old, Lucr. 49. like s. pining Tantalus he sits, 858. his naked armour of s. slaughtered lust, 188. thou left'st me more than I did crave: for why I craved nothing of thee s. Pilgr. 140. the s. vexed Bermoothes, Tp. I, 2, 229. the s. closing waters, III, 3, 64. you'll s. be too forward, Gent. II, 1, 11. love *is s. most precious in itself*, II, 6, 24. *a most unholy match, which heaven and fortune s. rewards with plagues*, IV, 3, 31. *did not I bid thee s. mark me and do as I do?* IV, 4, 39. *'tis the curse in love, and s. approved*, V, 4, 43. *as you trip, s. pinch him*, Wiv. V, 5, 96. *on whom it will, it will; on whom it will not, so; yet s. 'tis just*, Meas. I, 2, 127. *pardon is s. the nurse of second woe*, II, 1, 298. *a life whose very comfort is s. a dying horror*, II, 3, 42. *him thou labourest by thy flight to shun and yet runnest toward him s.* III, 1, 13. *his friends s. wrought reprieves for him*, IV, 2, 140. *measure s. for measure*, V, 416. *one so wise as you have s. appeared*, 476. *their business s. lies out o' door*, Err. II, 1, 11. *wilt thou s. talk?* IV, 4, 46. *s. did I tell him it was vile and bad*, V, 67. *I see we s. did meet each other's man*, 386. *the summer s. doth tend upon my state*, Mids. III, 1, 158. *if it stand as you yourself s. do, within the eye of honour*, Merch. I, 1, 136. *the s. discordant wavering multitude*, H4B Ind. 19. *which (peace) she shall purchase with s. lasting war*, R3 IV, 4, 344. *this thy countenance, s. locked in steel, I never saw till now*, Troil. IV, 5, 195. *thou s. hast been the father of good news*, Hml. II, 2, 42. *nothing is at a like goodness s.* IV, 7, 117. *a s. soliciting eye*, Lr. I, 1, 234. *but s. the house-affairs would draw her hence*, Oth. I, 3, 147. *s. close as sure*, Cymb. I, 6, 139 etc. etc.

*S. and anon* = ever and anon: *s. and anon cheered up the heavy time*, John IV, 1, 47. Corrupted to *s. an end: a slave that s. an end turns me to shame*, Gent. IV, 4, 67.

2) to this time; even now; now no less than before: *to hearken if his foes pursue him s.* Ven. 699. *such seems your beauty s.* Sonn. 104, 3. *for s. 'tis beating in my mind*, Tp. I, 2, 176. *thy shape invisible retain thou s.* IV, 185. *and s. I see her beautiful*, Gent. II, 1, 73. *she holds them prisoners s.* II, 4, 92. *your old vice s.* III, 1, 283. *and youthful s.* Wiv. III, 1, 46. *I am s. attorneyed at your service*, Meas. V, 389 etc.

3) in future (no less than formerly); for ever: *thou dost survive, in that thy likeness s. is left alive*, Ven. 174. *as they last, their verdure s. endure*, 507. *let him keep his loathsome cabin s.* 637. *bids them s. consort with ugly night*, 1041. *to give away yourself keeps yourself s.* Sonn. 16, 13. *hourly joys be s. upon you*, Tp. IV, 108. *let grief and sorrow s. embrace his heart that doth not wish you joy*, V, 214. *since thou lovest, love s. and thrive therein*, Gent. I, 1, 9. *if the fat knight shall be any further afflicted, we two will s. be the ministers*, Wiv. IV, 2, 234. *he would give't thee, from this rank offence, so to offend him s.* Meas. III, 1, 101. *I could find in my heart to stay here s. and turn witch*, Err. IV, 4, 160. *as I have ever found thee honest-true, so let me find thee s.* Merch. III, 4, 47. *whether I be as true begot or no, that s. I lay upon my mother's head*, John I, 76. *thou shalt be placed as viceroy under him, and s. enjoy thy regal dignity*, H6A V, 4, 132. *for France, 'tis ours; and we will keep it s.* H6B I, 1, 106 etc.

4) even after all that has happened or has been said; nevertheless, all the same: *if nothing but the very smell were left me, yet would my love to thee be s. as much*, Ven. 442. *they fright him, but he s. pursues his fear*, Lucr. 308. *though thou repent, yet I have s. the loss*, Sonn. 34, 10. *yet seemed it winter s.* 98, 13. *so you may continue and laugh at nothing s.* Tp. II, 1, 179.

*give me thy favour s.* IV, 204. *this proves me s. a sheep*, Gent. I, 1, 82. *keep tune there s.* I, 2, 89. *thou shalt find me tractable to any honest reason: thou seest I am pacified s.* H4A III, 3, 196 (i. e. even without any honest reason. Some M. Edd. *I am pacified. Still?*). Gent. IV, 2, 15. Wiv. III, 4, 19. Meas. III, 2, 206. Err. II, 1, 110. LLL V, 2, 301. Mids. I, 1, 194. II, 2, 110. Cymb. II, 3, 97 etc.

5) Accompanying words denoting increase of degree, to imply a gradation beyond what would have seemed sufficient: *to whom I wish long life, s. lengthened with all happiness*, Lucr. Dedic. 5. *the guilt being great, the fear doth s. exceed*, Lucr. 229. Before comparatives: Lucr. 98. Sonn. 119, 10. Meas. V, 8 etc.

**Stillatory** or **Stillitory**, an alembic: *from the s. of thy face comes breath perfumed*, Ven. 443.

**Still-born**, dead at the birth: H4B I, 3, 64.

**Still-breeding**, continually propagating: R2 V, 5, 8.

**Still-closing** (not hyphened in O. Edd.) always coalescing again: *the s. waters*, Tp. III, 3, 64.

**Still-gazing**, continually gazing, or silently gazing: *in silent wonder of s. eyes*, Lucr. 84.

**Stillness**, silence; taciturnity; calmness, quiet: *do a wilful s. entertain*, Merch. I, 1, 90. *soft s. and the night*, V, 56. *modest s. and humility*, H5 III, 1, 4. *in patient s. while his rider mounts him*, III, 7, 24. *the gravity and s. of your youth*, Oth. II, 3, 191.

**Still-peering**, motionless in appearance (?): *move the s. air, that sings with piercing; do not touch my lord*, All's III, 2, 113 (Emendations proposed: *still-pierced, still-piercing, still-pacing, still-piecing* etc.).

**Still-stand**, a halt, a stop; absence of motion: *the tide swelled up unto his height, that makes a s., running neither way*, H4B II, 3, 64.

**Still-vexed**, see *Still* and *Vex*.

**Stilly**, softly, lowly: *the hum of either army s. sounds*, H5 IV Chor. 5.

**Sting**, subst. 1) a sharp point with which some animals are armed: Lucr. 364. 493. Gent. I, 2, 107. Shr. II, 211. 215. H4B IV, 5, 206. H5 I, 2, 193. H6B III, 2, 267. H6C II, 2, 15. 138. Troil. V, 10, 43. Caes. II, 1, 16. Mcb. IV, 1, 16. Ant. IV, 15, 26.

2) the thrust made with it: H6B III, 2, 47. 325. Applied to other things giving acute pain: *killed by death's sharp s.* Pilgr. 134. *thou bitter sky, thy s. is not so sharp*, As II, 7, 188. *what sharp —s are in her mildest words*, All's III, 4, 18. *slander, whose s. is sharper than the sword's*, Wint. II, 3, 86.

3) impulse, incitement: *vow, bond, nor space, in thee (love) hath neither s., knot, nor confine*, Compl. 265. Especially sexual desire: *the wanton —s and motions of the sense*, Meas. I, 4, 59. *the brutish s.* As II, 7, 66. *our carnal —s*, Oth. I, 3, 335.

**Sting**, vb. (impf. and partic. *stung*) to hurt with a point darted out; absol.: Tp. I, 2, 329. Mids. III, 2, 73. H6B IV, 2, 89. H6C II, 6, 94. H8 III, 2, 56. Tit. V, 1, 14. Caes. V, 1, 38. With an object: Merch. IV, 1, 69. R2 III, 2, 131. V, 3, 58. H4A I, 3, 240. II, 1, 16. H6B III, 1, 229. 344. III, 2, 127. Tit. II, 3, 132. Hml. I, 5, 36. 39. 88. Lr. V, 1, 56. Used of other things causing a similar pain: *—ing nettles*, R2 III, 2, 18. Figuratively, = to pain acutely: *envy did s. his high-pitched thoughts*, Lucr. 40. *there's something in't that —s his nature*, All's IV, 3, 4. *these things s. his mind so venomously*, Lr. IV, 3, 47. cf. Hml. I, 5, 88.

**Stingless,** having no sting: Caes. V, 1, 35.

**Stink** (impf. *stunk*, partic. not found) to emit an offensive smell: Tp. I, 2, 3. Wiv. III, 5, 115. Meas. III, 2, 29. All's V, 2, 13. H4A II, 4, 394. H6A IV, 7, 76. 90. H6B IV, 7, 12. 13. Cor. II, 1, 252. IV, 6, 131. Caes. I, 2, 248. Lr. I, 4, 126. II, 4, 72. Cymb. I, 6, 110. IV, 2, 59. Per. II, 4, 10. IV, 6, 145. cf. *O'erstink.*

**Stinkingly,** disgustingly: *so s. depending,* Meas. III, 2, 28.

**Stint,** subst. check, constraint (?): *and with the s. of war will look so huge, amazement shall drive courage from the state,* Per. I, 2, 25 (M. Edd. *ostent*).

**Stint,** vb. 1) tr. to check, to stop, to cause to cease: *we must not s. our necessary actions, in the fear to cope malicious censurers,* H8 I, 2, 76. *the combatants being kin half —s their strife before their strokes begin,* Troil. IV, 5, 93. *he can at pleasure s. their melody,* Tit. IV, 4, 86. *make war breed peace, make peace s. war,* Tim. V, 4, 83.

2) intr. to cease: *it —ed and said Ay,* Rom. I, 3, 48. 57. *and s. thou too,* 58. *wherefore she does, and swears she'll never s., make raging battery upon shores of flint,* Per. IV, 4, 42.

**Stir,** subst. 1) the state of being in motion or in action: *what s. keeps good old York there with his men of war?* R2 II, 3, 51. *there is no s. or walking in the streets,* Caes. I, 3, 127. *chance may crown me without my s.* Mcb. I, 3, 144. *what you shall know of —s abroad,* Ant. I, 4, 82 (= of things happening, of enterprises attempted abroad).

2) commotion, tumult, uproar: *the strumpet that began this s.* Lucr. 1471. *what halloing and what s. is this to-day?* Gent. V, 4, 13. *what s. is this?* H6A I, 4, 98.

3) agitation, excitement: *what recketh he his rider's angry s.?* Ven. 283. *as the fits and —s of's mind could best express,* Cymb. I, 3, 12.

**Stir,** vb. 1) trans. a) to disturb: *my mind is troubled, like a fountain —ed,* Troil. III, 3, 311. *a bubbling fountain —ed with wind,* Tit. II, 4, 23. *s. no embers up,* Ant. II, 2, 13.

b) to move: *they are heavier than all thy woes can s.* Wint. III, 2, 210. *he would not s. his pettitoes,* IV, 4, 619. *or s. thy foot,* John IV, 3, 96. *dares s. a wing,* H6C I, 1, 47. *we may as well push against Powle's as s. 'em,* H8 V, 4, 16.

c) to awaken: *let none of your people s. me,* Mids. IV, 1, 43. *'tis time to s. him from his trance,* Shr. I, 1, 182. *you ever have wished the sleeping of this business; never desired it to be —ed,* H8 II, 4, 164.

d) to excite, to raise: *this flower's force in —ing love,* Mids. II, 2, 69. *—s good thoughts in any breast,* John II, 112. *to s. a mutiny in the mildest thoughts,* Tit. IV, 1, 85. With *up: careless lust —s up a desperate courage,* Ven. 556. *I will s. up in England some black storm,* H6B III, 1, 349. *the thoughts of them would have —ed up remorse,* H6C V, 5, 64.

e) to excite, to move, to rouse, to agitate: *never could the strumpet ... once s. my temper,* Meas. II, 2, 185. *so shall we pass along and never s. assailants,* As I, 3, 116. *I am sorry I have thus far —ed you,* Wint. V, 3, 74. *he was —ed with such an agony,* H8 II, 1, 32. *'twill s. him strongly,* III, 2, 218. *Antony will be himself. But —ed by Cleopatra,* Ant. I, 1, 43. *I could not s. him,* Cymb. IV, 2, 38. With *up: s. De-*

*metrius up with bitter wrong,* Mids. III, 2, 361. *whose worthiness would s. it up* (the king's virtue) All's I, 1, 10. *—ing my subjects up,* H6C V, 5, 15. *you do yourselves but wrong to s. me up,* Tim. III, 4, 53. *the senate hath —ed up the confiners,* Cymb. IV, 2, 337. *lest you s. up mine* (impatience) V, 4, 112. *men must s. you up,* Per. IV, 2, 98. 156.

f) to incite, to impel, to instigate: *—ed by a painted beauty to his verse,* Sonn. 21, 2. As I, 1, 170. John II, 63. 415. R3 I, 3, 331. H8 III, 2, 418. Caes. III, 2, 126. Hml. V, 2, 256. Lr. II, 4, 277. With *on:* LLL V, 2, 695. Tw. III, 2, 63. With *up:* Mids. I, 1, 12. John II, 55. R2 IV, 133. H6B III, 1, 163. H6C IV, 8, 12. R3 IV, 4, 468. Caes. II, 1, 176. III, 2, 214. Hml. IV, 7, 9.

2) intr. a) to move one's self: *he starts at —ing of a feather,* Ven. 302. *s. not!* Ado III, 3, 103. As IV, 3, 117. Wint. V, 3, 98. John IV, 1, 81. H4A III, 2, 46. H4B IV, 5, 32. H6B II, 4, 18. R3 I, 4, 164. Troil. III, 3, 184. Rom. V, 3, 147. Caes. V, 1, 26. Mcb. V, 5, 12. Hml. I, 1, 10. IV, 1, 9. Lr. I, 1, 128. V, 3, 265. Oth. II, 3, 173. 207. IV, 1, 56. V, 2, 95.

b) to change place; to go or be carried in any manner: *if I did not think it had been Anne Page, would I might never s.* Wiv. V, 5, 199 (Slender's speech. cf. John I, 145). *s. not you till you have well determined on these slanderers,* Meas. V, 258 (= do not go away). *I will not let him s. till I have used the approved means,* Err. V, 102. *I will determine this before I s.* 167. Mids. III, 1, 125. Wint. V, 3, 101. 103. John I, 145. 172. H6A I, 4, 55. H6C I, 1, 100. V, 1, 96. Rom. I, 1, 11. 87. Caes. II, 2, 9. **38.** Hml. I, 1, 161 (Qq *dares s.,* Ff *can walk*). Lr. I, 2, 186. Oth. III, 1, 30 (*if she will s. hither;* quibbling). V, 1, 107 (Qq *an you s.,* Ff *if you stare*). *look how thou —est now!* Per. II, 1, 16 (= how awkward you are!). *how thou —est, thou block,* III, 2, 90.

c) to be in motion; to be enlivened: *now in the —ing passage of the day,* Err. III, 1, 99. *a merry, nimble, —ing spirit,* LLL V, 2, 16. *the blood more —s to rouse a lion,* H4A I, 3, 197. *now is the mad blood —ing,* Rom. III, 1, 4.

d) to be roused, to be excited: *the wrongs I have done thee s. afresh within me,* Wint. V, 1, 148. *that for which the people s.* Cor. III, 1, 53. With *against: to s. against the butchers of his life,* R2 I, 2, 3. *a man that more detests, more —s against defacers of a public peace,* H8 V, 3, 39. With *at:* (blood) *unapt to s. at these indignities,* H4A I, 3, 2. *nor s. at nothing till the axe of death hang over thee,* H6B II, 4, 49.

e) to be active; to be busy: *be —ing as the time,* John V, 1, 48. *Mortimer doth s. about his title,* H4A II, 3, 84. *s. not to-night,* IV, 3, 5. *all hell shall s. for this,* H5 V, 1, 72. *a —ing dwarf we do allowance give before a sleeping giant,* Troil. II, 3, 146. Cor. I, 3, 13. IV, 5, 233. Rom. IV, 2, 39. IV, 4, 3. Hml. I, 5, 34. IV, 4, 54. Ant. II, 1, 36.

f) to be on foot; to exist: *no ill luck —ing but what lights on my shoulders,* Merch. III, 1, 99. *what wisdom —s amongst you?* Wint. II, 1, 21. *there's no equity —ing,* H4A II, 2, 106. *I will keep where there is wit —ing,* Troil. II, 1, 130.

g) to be already out of bed in the morning; to be up: *myself was —ing ere the break of day,* Lucr. 1280. *you are early —ing,* R3 III, 2, 36. *s. with the lark to-morrow,* V, 3, 56. Troil. I, 2, 52. Caes. II, 2, 110 *(are you —ed).* Mcb. II, 3, 47. 50. Oth. III, 1, 27. 30. Per. III, 2, 12.

**Stirrer,** a riser in the morning: *an early s.* H4B III, 2, 3. H5 IV, 1, 6.

**Stirrup,** that in which the horseman sets his foot in mounting and riding: Shr. III, 2, 50. IV, 1, 124. H6B IV, 1, 53. Cor. III, 2, 119. Tim. I, 1, 82.

**Stitchery,** needlework: Cor. I, 3, 75.

**Stitches,** a sharp lancinating pain: *will laugh yourselves into s.* Tw. III, 2, 73. cf. *Side-stitches.*

**Stith** (Ff *styth,* Qq *stithy*) anvil: *as foul as Vulcan's s.* Hml. III, 2, 89.

**Stithy,** subst. smithy: Hml. III, 2, 89 (Ff *styth*).

**Stithy,** vb. to forge: *by the forge that —ed Mars his helm,* Troil. IV, 5, 255.

**Stoccado,** a thrust in fencing: *your passes, —es,* Wiv. II, 1, 234.

**Stoccata,** the same: *alla s. carries it away,* Rom. III, 1, 77 (O. Edd. *Alla Stucatho*).

**Stock,** subst. 1) the trunk, the main body of a tree: Lucr. 1063. Wint. IV, 4, 93. H5 III, 5, 7. H6B III, 2, 213. R3 III, 7, 127. H8 V, 1, 22. Hml. III, 1, 119. Cymb. V, 4, 143.

2) race, lineage, parentage: Merch. IV, 1, 296. H5 I, 2, 71. II, 4, 63. H6A II, 5, 41. H6B II, 2, 58. R3 III, 7, 122. H8 IV, 2, 49. Cor. II, 3, 245. Tit. I, 300. Rom. I, 5, 60. Cymb. I, 6, 128. Per. V, 1, 68.

3) a log, a post; the emblem of a senseless person: *no stoics nor no —s,* Shr. I, 1, 31. cf. *Flouting-stock, Laughing-stock, Pointing-stock.*

4) plur. *—s,* a machine consisting of two logs, in which the legs of mean offenders were confined by way of punishment: All's IV, 3, 122. 273. Wint. IV, 3, 22. Cor. V, 3, 160. Lr. II, 2, 132. 135. 140. 146. II, 4, 88. 201. *to put in the —s,* Lr. II, 4, 185. *to set in the —s,* Wiv. IV, 5, 123. All's IV, 3, 127. Lr. II, 4, 65. *to sit in the —s,* Gent. IV, 4, 33. All's IV, 3, 117. R2 V, 5, 26. *a pair of —s,* Err. III, 1, 60. Shr. Ind. 1, 2. *the common —s,* Wiv. IV, 5, 123. The singular, in quibbling: Gent. III, 1, 311.

5) a stocking: Gent. III, 1, 312. Shr. III, 2, 67. Tw. I, 3, 144. *nether —s,* H4A II, 4, 130. Lr. II, 4, 11.

6) = stoccado, thrust in fencing: *to see thee pass thy punto, thy s.* Wiv. II, 3, 26.

**Stock,** vb. to set in the stocks: *—ing his messenger,* Lr. II, 2, 139 (Qq *stopping*). *who —ed my servant?* II, 4, 191 (Qq *struck*). III, 4, 140 (Ff *—ed, punished;* Qq *stock-punished*).

**Stock-fish,** dried cod: *I'll make a s. of thee,* Tp. III, 2, 79.*he was begot between two —es,* Meas. III, 2, 116. *you s.* H4A II, 4, 271. Name in H4B III, 2, 35.

**Stockings,** coverings for the feet and legs: Wiv. III, 5, 92. Shr. Ind. 2, 10. IV, 1, 50. Tw. II, 5, 166. III, 2, 78. III, 4, 53. V, 346. H4B II, 2, 18. Hml. II, 1, 79. *tall —s* (i. e. reaching above the knees) H8 I, 3, 30.

**Stockish,** insensible: *nought so s., hard and full of rage, but music for the time doth change his nature,* Merch. V, 81.

**Stock-punished,** punished by being set in the stocks: Lr. III, 4, 140 (Ff *stocked, punished*).

**Stoic,** a rigorist: *let's be no —s nor no stocks,* Shr. I, 1, 31.

**Stokesly,** name in H8 IV, 1, 101.

**Stole,** a long garment worn by women: *my white s. of chastity I daffed,* Compl. 297.

**Stomach,** subst. 1) the organ of digestion: Tp. II, 2, 118. III, 3, 41. Ado I, 1, 52. LLL I, 2, 154 (*on a full s.*). IV, 3, 294. Mids. II, 2, 138. Merch. III, 5, 54. Shr. V, 2, 9 (*to close our —s up*). All's I, 1, 156. John I, 191. H6A II, 3, 80. H6B IV, 10, 10. Tit. V, 3, 29. Tim. IV, 3, 294. Oth. III, 4, 104. Per. III, 2, 54. IV, 1, 29. Quibbling in Gent. I, 2, 68. H5 II Chor. 40. III, 7, 166.

= power of digestion, figuratively: *in despite of his quick wit and his queasy s., he shall fall in love with Beatrice,* Ado II, 1, 399. *we'll not offend one s. with our play,* H5 II Chor. 40 (quibbling). *all goodness is poison to thy s.* H8 III, 2, 283. *this rudeness is a sauce to his good wit, which gives men s. to digest his words with better appetite,* Caes. I, 2, 305. *my great revenge had s. for them all,* Oth. V, 2, 75.

2) appetite: *that you might kill your s.* Gent. I, 2, 68 (satisfy your appetite). *what is't that takes from thee thy s.* H4A II, 3, 44. *she* (Fortune) *either gives a s. and no food,* H4B IV, 4, 105. *our —s will make what's homely savoury,* Cymb. III, 6, 32. *graze as you find pasture. Ay, or a s.* V, 4, 2. *to have a s.,* and *to have s.* = to have appetite: Ado I, 3, 16. Merch. III, 5, 92 (quibbling). Shr. IV, 1, 161. *to have no s.:* Err. I, 2, 49. Ado II, 3, 265.

3) inclination, disposition: *you cram these words into mine ears against the s. of my sense,* Tp. II, 1, 107. *let me praise you while I have a s.* Merch. III, 5, 92 (quibbling). *it goes much against my s.* As III, 2, 22. *fall to them* (metaphysics) *as you find your s. serves you,* Shr. I, 1, 38. *if you have a s., to't,* I, 2, 195. All's III, 6, 67. *I begin to love with no s.* III, 2, 18. *their villany goes against my weak s.* H5 III, 2, 57. *they have only —s to eat and none to fight,* III, 7, 166. *call some knight to arms that hath a s.* Troil. II, 1, 137. *you may have every day enough of Hector, if you have s.* IV, 5, 264. *when you have —s,* Caes. V, 1, 66. *make the wars against my s.* Ant. II, 2, 50. *With to: he which hath no s. to this fight,* H5 IV, 3, 35. *my little s. to the war,* Troil. III, 3, 220.

4) anger, resentment: *kill your s. on your meat and not upon your maid,* Gent. I, 2, 68. *these nobles should such —s bear,* H6A I, 3, 90. *how will their grudging —s be provoked to wilful disobedience, and rebel,* IV, 1, 141. *the winds grow high; so do your —s,* H6B II, 1, 55. *to ease their —s with their bitter tongues,* Tit. III, 1, 234. *else I should answer from a full-flowing s.* Lr. V, 3, 74. cf. *High-stomached.*

5) stubborn courage: *which raised in me an undergoing s.* Tp. I, 2, 157. *the bloody Douglas ... 'gan vail his s.* H4B I, 1, 129. *some enterprise that hath a s. in't,* Hml. I, 1, 100.

6) pride, arrogance: *vail your —s and place your hands below your husbands' foot,* Shr. V, 2, 176. *a man of an unbounded s., ever ranking himself with princes,* H8 IV, 2, 34.

**Stomach,** vb. to be angry at, to resent: *believe not all; or, if you must believe, s. not all,* Ant. III, 4, 12. *'tis not a time for private —ing,* II, 2, 9.

**Stomacher,** an ornamental covering of the breast, worn by women: Wint. IV, 4, 226. Cymb. III, 4, 86.

**Stomach-qualmed,** sick at heart, qualmish: Cymb. III, 4, 193.

**Stone,** subst. 1) concreted earthy matter, neither ductile nor soluble; the substance as well as a single piece of it: Lucr. 177. 592. Sonn. 65, 2. Gent. I, 2,

111 (cf. R2 I, 2, 69). II, 7, 28. Wiv. I, 4, 119. IV, 1, 33. Meas. I, 3, 53. Mids. V, 162. 182. 192. Merch. I, 1, 30. V, 80. As II, 1, 17. All's II, 1, 76 *(to breathe life into a s.)*. Tw. I, 5, 92 *(has no more brain than a s.)*. Wint. II, 3, 90 *(as ever oak or s. was sound.* cf. Mcb. III, 4, 22). R2 III, 3, 26. H5 II, 3, 26 *(as cold as any s.)*. IV, 7, 64. H6A III, 1, 89. H6C V, 1, 84. H8 V, 3, 104 *(when we first put this dangerous s. a rolling)* etc. etc. = a monument of stone: Sonn. 55, 4. Wint. I, 2, 360. Denoting the glass of a mirror: *if that her breath will mist or stain the s.* Lr. V, 3, 262. *The philosopher's s.* (a substance supposed to have the property of turning any thing into gold): H4B III, 2, 355. Tim. II, 2, 117.

Adjectively: *s. jugs,* Shr. Ind. 2, 90. *hunger broke s. walls,* Cor. I, 1, 210 (proverb).

Symbol of hardness and of insensibility: Ven. 200. 211. Lucr. 959. 978. Sonn. 94, 3. Gent. I, 1, 149. II, 3, 11. III, 2, 79. Tw. III, 4, 221. H6B V, 2, 50. R3 III, 7, 25. Caes. I, 1, 40. III, 2, 147. Oth. IV, 1, 193 etc. Peculiar use of the plural: *I am not made of —s,* R3 III, 7, 224 (M. Edd. *s.*). *you are men of —s,* Lr. V, 3, 257. Symbol of dumbness: *your considerate s.* Ant. II, 2, 112. Mcb. III, 4, 123.*

2) a precious stone, a gem: Sonn. 52, 7. Compl. 216. Meas. II, 2, 150. Merch. II, 8, 20. 21. 24. Wint. IV, 4, 609. R2 II, 1, 46. H6C III, 1, 63. R3 I, 4, 27. V, 3, 250. Lr. V, 3, 190. Cymb. I, 4, 84. II, 4, 40. 46.

3) the hard covering which encloses the seed of some fruits: *cracking the --s of the prunes,* Meas. II, 1, 110.

4) a thunderbolt: *are there no —s in heaven but what serve for the thunder?* Oth. V, 2, 234. *the gods throw —s of sulphur on me,* Cymb. V, 5, 240.

5) a hail-stone: Ant. III, 13, 160.

6) a testicle: Wiv. I, 4, 118. H4B III, 2, 355. Rom. I, 3, 53. Tim. II, 2, 117. Perhaps also, by way of quibbling, in Gent. I, 1, 149 and As II, 4, 47.

**Stone,** vb. 1) to pelt or kill with stones: Lucr. 978. Wint. IV, 4, 807. 835.

2) to make like stone, to harden: *thou dost s. my heart,* Oth. V, 2, 63.

**Stone-bow,** a cross-bow, from which stones or bullets were shot: Tw. II, 5, 51.

**Stone-cutter,** one who cuts figures in stone: Lr. II, 2, 63.

**Stone-hard,** hard as a stone: R3 IV, 4, 227.

**Stone-still,** still as a stone, without any motion: Lucr. 1730. John IV, 1, 77.

**Stonish,** = to astonish, to amaze: *—ed as night-wanderers often are, their light blown out,* Ven. 825. *O wonderful son, that can so s. a mother,* Hml. III, 2, 340 (Ff *astonish*).

**Stony,** 1) made of stones: Tit. III, 1, 259. Rom. II, 2, 67. V, 3, 141. Caes. I, 3, 93.

2) hard, pitiless: Merch. IV, 1, 4. H4B IV, 5, 108. H6B V, 2, 51.

**Stony-hearted,** hard-hearted: H4A II, 2, 28.

**Stony-Stratford,** place in England: R3 II, 4, 2.*

**Stool,** any chair: *a s. and a cushion for the sexton,* Ado IV, 2, 2. *fetch me a s. hither,* H6B II, 1, 142. 144. 149. *thou s. for a witch,* Troil. II, 1, 46 (an instrument of torture). *each man to his s.* Tim. III, 6, 73. *you look but on a s.* Mcb. III, 4, 68. *push us from our —s,* 82. *rise from thy s.* Ant. II, 7, 62. *a three-*

*foot s.* Mids. II, 1, 52. Cymb. III, 3, 89. *a three-legged s.* Shr. I, 1, 64. cf. *Footstool, Jointstool.*

**Stoop** or **Stoup,** subst. a drinking vessel (of uncertain size): *Marian, I say! a s. of wine!* Tw. II, 3, 14. 129. *fetch me a s. of liquor,* Hml. V, 1, 68. *set me the —s of wine upon that table,* V, 2, 278. *I have a s. of wine; and here without are a brace of Cyprus gallants that would fain have a measure,* Oth. II, 3, 30 (O. Edd. *stope*).

**Stoop,** adj. (?), crooked: *as upright as the cedar. S., I say; her shoulder is with child,* LLL IV, 3, 89.

**Stoop,** vb. 1) intr. a) to bend the body down: *the grass —s not, she treads on it so light,* Ven. 1028. *the cedar —s not to the base shrub's foot,* Lucr. 664. *—ing to relieve him,* Tp. II, 1, 121. Gent. I, 2, 72. Meas. II, 1, 24. V, 420; cf. H6B IV, 1, 125 and H6C V, 5, 6. Shr. III, 2, 164. Tw. II, 2, 16. R2 I, 1, 74. III, 4, 31. H4B IV, 2, 42. H6A III, 1, 169. V, 4, 26. Caes. III, 1, 105. Hml. II, 2, 498. Cymb. III, 3, 2, IV, 2, 176. = to get the habit of bending, to become crooked: *a straight back will s.* H5 V, 2, 168.

Figuratively, = to bow down, to yield, to submit: *bend the dukedom to most ignoble —ing,* Tp. I, 2, 116. *till she s. she must not be full-gorged,* Shr. IV, 1, 194. *grief is proud and makes his owner s.* John III, 1, 69 (a passage justly suspected. Some M. Edd. *stout;* but perhaps = is master of its owner). V, 4, 55. R2 III, 3, 48. H6A III, 1, 119. V, 1, 61. H6B IV, 1, 119. H6C I, 1, 108. II, 2, 151. Cor. V, 6, 29. Tit. II, 1, 11. V, 2, 118. Ant. II, 2, 98. With *to: and s. to honour, not to foul desire,* Lucr. 574. *a golden mind —s not to shows of dross,* Merch. II, 7, 20. *make you s. unto the sovereign mercy of the king,* R2 II, 3, 156. *you should s. unto a Frenchman's mercy,* H6B IV, 8, 50. *before he should thus s. to the herd,* Cor. III, 2, 32. *—ing to your clemency,* Hml. III, 2, 160. *when majesty —s to folly,* Lr. I, 1, 151 (Ff *falls*). cf. H4B IV, 2, 42 and H6C V, 5, 6.

b) to come down on prey, to pounce: *forthwith they fly chickens, the way which they —ed eagles,* Cymb. V, 3, 42. *the holy eagle —ed, as to foot us,* V, 4, 116. cf. Shr. IV, 1, 194 (quibbling). And in general, = to alight from the wing: *though his affections are higher mounted than ours, yet, when they s., they s. with the like wing,* H5 IV, 1, 112.

2) trans. to bow down: *have —ed my neck under your injuries,* R2 III, 1, 19. *the king before the Douglas' rage —ed his anointed head as low as death,* H4B Ind. 32. With *to,* = to humiliate, to subdue to: *before his sister should her body s. to such pollution,* Meas. II, 4, 182. *I will s. and humble my intents to your directions,* H4B V, 2, 120.

**Stop,** subst. 1) cessation of progressive motion: *my restless discord loves no — s nor rests,* Lucr. 1124 (perhaps quibbling; cf. sign. 5). *what course, what s. he makes,* Compl. 109. *he hath rid his prologue like a rough colt; he knows not the s.* Mids. V, 120 (quibbling; cf. sign. 3). *yea, without s., didst let thy heart consent, and consequently thy rude hand to act the deed,* John IV, 2, 239. *time, that takes survey of all the world, must have a s.* H4A V, 4, 83. *no care, no s.* Tim. II, 2, 1. *let's teach ourselves that honourable s., not to outsport discretion,* Oth. II, 3, 2. *then began a s. in the chaser,* Cymb. V, 3, 40.

2) cessation of speech, interruption: *where did I leave? At that sad s., where rude hands* etc. R2 V, 2, 4. *these —s of thine fright me,* Oth. III, 3, 120.

3) mark in writing, to show the proper pauses in reading or reciting: Mids. V, 120 (see sub 1). *come, the full s.* Merch. III, 1, 17 (= speak the whole sentence out).

4) hinderance, obstacle: *these be the —s that hinder study quite,* LLL I, 1, 70. *thy kinsmen are no s. to me,* Rom. II, 2, 69 (the surreptitious Q1 and some M. Edd. *let*). *more impediments than twenty times your s.* Oth. V, 2, 264.

5) In music, a) that by which the sounds of wind instruments are regulated: *a pipe of so easy and so plain a s.* H4B Ind. 17. *they are not a pipe for fortune's finger to sound what s. she please,* Hml. III, 2, 76. *these are the —s,* 376. 381. b) regulation of musical chords by the fingers: *his jesting spirit is now crept into a lute-string and now governed by —s,* Ado III, 2, 62.*

6) the act of filling up and making whole again: *a breach that craves a quick expedient s.* H6B III, 1, 288.

**Stop,** vb. 1) trans. a) to close by filling up or obstructing: *an oven that is —ed burneth more hotly,* Ven. 331. *s. that* (the keyhole) As IV, 1, 165. *s. this gap of breath with dust,* John III, 4, 32. *tears do s. the flood-gates of her eyes,* H4A II, 4, 435. *s. all sight-holes,* IV, 1, 71. *the obstructions which begin to s. our very veins of life,* H4B IV, 1, 65. *so much wit as will s. the eye of Helen's needle,* Troil. II, 1, 87. *like an oven —ed,* Tit. II, 4, 36. *—ing a bung-hole,* Hml. V, 1, 225. *s. a beer-barrel,* 235. 237. Applied particularly to the ear, mouth and nose: *my ears are —ed,* Gent. III, 1, 205. *I'll s. mine ears against the mermaid's song,* Err. III, 2, 169. Merch. II, 5, 34. Shr. IV, 3, 76. Wint. V, 1, 201. John IV, 2, 120. H4B I, 1, 79. H6C IV, 8, 39. Troil. V, 3, 2. Cor. V, 3, 5. Per. IV, 2, 86. cf. *my adder's sense to critic and to flatterer —ed are,* Sonn. 112, 11; *the suspicious head* (= ear) *of theft is —ed,* LLL IV, 3, 336; *s. the vent of hearing,* H4B Ind. 1. — *Why dost thou s. my mouth?* Gent. II, 3, 50. *s. his mouth with a kiss,* Ado II, 1, 321. V, 4, 98. John III, 1, 299. R2 V, 1, 95. H4B I, 2, 48. H5 V, 2, 297. H6B III, 2, 396. H8 II, 2, 9. Troil. III, 2, 141. Tit. II, 3, 185. V, 1, 151. V, 2, 162. 168. Tim. II, 2, 156. Lr. V, 3, 155. Oth. II, 3, 308. V, 2, 71. cf. *'gins to chide, but soon she —s his lips,* Ven. 46. — *to s. your nose,* All's V, 2, 11. 14. *heaven —s the nose at it,* Oth. IV, 2, 77. *against the blown rose may they s. their nose,* Ant. III, 13, 39.

Applied to wounds or any hurts, = to dress; to make whole, to heal: *some surgeon … to s. his wounds, lest he do bleed to death,* Merch. IV, 1, 258. *where this breach now in our fortunes made may readily be —ed,* H6B V, 2, 83. *now civil wounds are —ed, peace lives again,* R3 V, 5, 40. *s. those maims of shame,* Cor. IV, 5, 92. With *up: to s. up the displeasure he hath conceived,* All's IV, 5, 79.

With *in,* = to shut or cram in: *s. in your wind,* Err. I, 2, 53 (= keep your breath, be silent a while). *to be —ed in, like a strong distillation, with stinking clothes,* Wiv. III, 5, 114. *the envious flood —ed in my soul,* R3 I, 4, 38 (Qq *kept*).

b) to fill entirely: *it* (his ear) *is —ed with other sounds,* R2 II, 1, 17. *—ing my greedy ear with their bold deeds,* H4B I, 1, 78. *s. their mouths with stubborn bits,* H8 V, 3, 23.

c) to encumber, to obstruct, to render impassable: *distance should not s. my way,* Sonn. 44, 2. *let me s. this way first* (i. e. the door) Wiv. III, 3, 174. *the*

*proudest he that —s my way,* Shr. III, 2, 237. *my father's blood hath —ed the passage where thy words should enter,* H6C I, 3, 22. *nor you … should s. my way,* Troil. V, 3, 57. *why you s. our way with such prophetic greeting,* Mcb. I, 3, 77. *he'll s. the course by which it might be known,* Per. I, 2, 23. With *up: s. up the access and passage to remorse,* Mcb. I, 5, 45.

d) to hinder from proceeding, to arrest, to keep back: *to s. the loud pursuers in their yell,* Ven. 688. *her eyelids, who, like sluices, —ed the crystal tide,* 956. *those bars which s. the hourly dial,* Lucr. 327. *s. his speed,* 501. *a gentle flood, being —ed, the bounding banks o'erflows,* 1119. *counsel may s. a while what will not stay,* Compl. 159. *the current being —ed,* Gent. II, 7, 26. *s. the air by which he should revive,* Meas. II, 4, 25. *proceeded well, to s. all good proceeding,* LLL I, 1, 95. *no bar to s. the foreign spirits,* Merch. II, 7, 46. *—ing the career of laughter with a sigh,* Wint. I, 2, 286. *whose counsel shall s. or spur me,* II, 1, 187. *to s. their marches,* John V, 1, 7. *but s. no wrinkle in his pilgrimage,* R2 I, 3, 230. *do you mean to s. any of William's wages,* H4B V, 1, 24. *turn head, and s. pursuit,* H5 II, 4, 69. *force those waters from me which I would have —ed,* IV, 6, 29. *who in proud heart doth s. my cornets,* H6A IV, 3, 25. *to s. devoted charitable deeds,* R3 I, 2, 35. *he —ed the fliers,* Cor. II, 2, 107. *your good tongue might s. our countryman,* V, 1, 38. *s. thine unhallowed toil,* Rom. V, 3, 54. *the fountain of your blood is —ed,* Mcb. II, 3, 104 (has ceased to flow). *s. it, Marcellus,* Hml. I, 1, 139; cf. Lr. II, 1, 38 and III, 6, 57. *whose disposition will not be rubbed nor —ed,* Lr. II, 2, 161. *send to darkness all that s. me,* Ant. III, 13, 182. *what both you spur and s.* Cymb. I, 6, 99. *to s. the air,* Per. I, 1, 100. *how I might s. this tempest ere it came,* I, 2, 98.

= to hinder from utterance, to put to silence: *her voice is —ed,* Ven. 1061. *to blow the grief away that —s his answer so,* Lucr. 1664. *but she … the protestation —s,* 1700. *Philomel —s her pipe in growth of riper days,* Sonn. 102, 8. *we shall s. her exclamation,* John II, 558. *vexation almost —s my breath,* H6A IV, 3, 41. *death shall s. his dismal sound,* H6C II, 6, 58. *fills mine eyes with tears and —s my tongue,* III, 3, 14. *to s. the rumour,* H8 II, 1, 152. *it —s me here,* Oth. II, 1, 199.

= to suppress: *to s. posterity,* Sonn. 3, 8. *to s. Arthur's title in the whole,* John II, 562. *send succours, and s. the rage betime,* H6B III, 1, 285. *s. the rising of blood-sucking sighs,* H6C IV, 4, 22. *his deafened parts, which now are midway —ed,* Per. V, 1, 48.

Hence = to put an end to, to finish: *revenge on him that made me s. my breath,* Lucr. 1180, i. e. end my life, kill myself; cf. Rom. V, 3, 211 and Oth. V, 2, 202. *to s. effusion of our Christian blood,* H6A V, 1, 9. *to s. all hopes,* R3 IV, 2, 60. *to s. the inundation of her tears,* Rom. IV, 1, 12. *whoso please to s. affliction,* Tim. V, 1, 213.

2) intr. a) to cease to go forward, to stand still: Ven. 706. John V, 7, 67. H4B I, 1, 38. R3 IV, 2, 45. H8 III, 2, 114. 116. Cor. III, 1, 32. Caes. IV, 1, 32. = to cease to flow: *now —s thy spring,* H6C IV, 8, 55. b) to cease to speak: Tp. I, 2, 34. V, 198. Gent. III, 1, 364. H6C III, 2, 52. R3 III, 5, 3. IV, 3, 16. Rom. II, 4, 98. 99. Per. V, 1, 162.

**Store,** subst. (used only in the sing.; therefore in Sonn. 136, 10. *store's,* not *stores',* which is the writing of

M. Edd.) 1) property, possession, having: *poor chastity is rifled of her s.* Lucr. 692. *if s. of crowns be scant,* Pilgr. 409. *I am debating of my present s.* Merch. I, 3, 54. *aid me with that s. of power you have,* All's V, 1, 20. *your s. is not for idle markets,* Tw. III, 3, 45. *many a pound of mine own proper s.* H6B III, 1, 115. *this man may be possessed with some s. of crowns,* H6C II, 5, 57.

In *s.* = a) laid up, hoarded: *how many sons of mine hast thou* (the tomb) *in s., that thou wilt never render to me more,* Tit. I, 94; cf. *Store-house* in Mcb. II, 4, 34. b) at one's disposal, in readiness, prepared for use: *I have better news in s. for you,* Merch. V, 274. *if heaven have any grievous plague in s.* R3 I, 3, 217. *I have an hour's talk in s. for you,* Caes. II, 2, 121. *the vengeance that they had in s.* Per. II, 4, 4.

2) plenty, abundance, great number or quantity: *poorly rich, so wanteth in his s.* Lucr. 97. *heaven's fair sun that breeds the fat earth's s.* 1837. *I make my love engrafted to this s.* Sonn. 37, 8. *increasing s. with loss and loss with s.* 64, 8. *in whose confine immured is the s. which should example where your equal grew,* 84, 3. *in thy —'s account I one must be,* 136, 10. *the sea ... receives rain still and in abundance addeth to his s.* 135, 10. *to aggravate thy s.* 146, 10. *too small a pasture for such s. of muttons,* Gent. I, 1, 105. *thou callest for such s., when one is one too many,* Err. III, 1, 34. *to your huge s. wise things seem foolish,* LLL V, 2, 377. *great s. of wedding cheer,* Shr. III, 2, 188. *s. of parting tears,* R2 I, 4, 5. H4A II, 2, 94 (= warehouse?). H4B IV, 3, 131. H6B III, 1, 169. R3 I, 2, 155. H8 V, 4, 77. Cor. I, 9, 32. Rom. I, 1, 222. I, 2, 22. Caes. IV, 1, 30. Ant. IV, 1, 15. Cymb. I, 4, 107.

3) increase of men, fertility, population: *let those whom Nature hath not made for s., harsh, featureless and rude, barrenly perish,* Sonn. 11, 9. *truth and beauty shall together thrive, if from thyself to s. thou wouldst convert,* 14, 12. cf. the verb in Oth. IV, 3, 86.

Doubtful passage: *whose warped looks proclaim what s. her heart is made on,* Lr. III, 6, 57 (Collier *stone).*

**Store,** vb. 1) to preserve, to lay up, to hoard: *him she —s, to show what wealth she had in days long since,* Sonn. 67, 13. *him as for a map doth nature s., to show false art what beauty was of yore,* 68, 13. *five hundred crowns, which I did s. to be my foster-nurse,* As II, 3, 40. *all the —d vengeances of heaven,* Lr. II, 4, 164. With *up: which he bade me s. up, as a triple eye,* All's II, 1, 111.

2) to stock with people, to populate: *to new s. France with bastard warriors,* H5 III, 5, 31. *as many to the vantage as would s. the world they played for,* Oth. IV, 3, 86.

Partic. *—d* = furnished, supplied, provided: *their tables were —d full,* Per. I, 4, 28. *a cup that's —d unto the brim,* II, 3, 50. With *of: whereof the city is well —d,* Cor. I, 1, 194. Oftener *with: so —d with friends,* John V, 4, 1. *—d with all* (faults) Cor. II, 1, 20. *—d with ill,* Per. I, 1, 77. *—d with corn,* I, 4, 95.

**Store-house,** a magazine: Cor. I, 1, 83. 137. III, 1, 114. Applied to a burying-place: *Colmekill, the sacred s. of his predecessors,* Mcb. II, 4, 34; cf. *store* in Tit. I, 94.

**Storm,** subst. a tempest (usually a violent wind attended with rain): Tp. I, 1, 15. II, 2, 19. 39. 43. 114. 116. Err. I, 1, 81. Shr. III, 2, 174. V, 2, 150.

Wint. III, 2, 214. III, 3, 49. John IV, 2, 108. R2 II, 1, 35. 264. H6B III, 2, 103. V, 1, 206. H6C V, 3, 13. R3 II, 3, 35. 44. H8 I, 1, 90. III, 1, 164. Troil. I, 1, 37 (O. Edd. *scorn).* Tit. II, 3, 23. II, 4, 54. IV, 4, 71. Tim. IV, 3, 266. Mcb. I, 2, 26. Hml. II, 2, 505. Lr. II, 4, 82. 290. 312. III, 1, 49. III, 4, 6. 29. III, 7, 59. IV, 1, 34. IV, 3, 30. Ant. I, 2, 154 *(—s and tempests).* III, 13, 165. Cymb. III, 3, 62. Per. III Prol. 53. III, 1, 19. IV, 1, 21.

Figuratively, = commotion, tumult, disturbance, violent excitement, extreme danger: Lucr. 966. 1518. 1589. Compl. 101. Ado V, 4, 42. Mids. I, 2, 29. Shr. I, 1, 177. John V, 1, 20. V, 2, 55. R2 II, 4, 22. H6B III, 1, 349. V, 1, 198. H6C III, 3, 38. 47. IV, 1, 38. IV, 6, 98. IV, 7, 43 *(in his time of s.).* H8 IV, 2, 21. Troil. I, 3, 47 *(—s of fortune).* Tit. I, 154. II, 1, 25. Rom. III, 2, 64. Caes. V, 1, 68. Oth. I, 3, 250 *(my downright violence and s. of fortune;* Q1 *scorn).* Ant. IV, 4, 13.

**Storm,** vb. 1) intr. a) to blow with violence: *then s. venomously,* Per. III, 1, 7 (M. Edd. *thou —est,* or *thou s. thou).*

b) to be passionate, to chafe, to fume: *why, look you, how you s.* Merch. I, 3, 138. *to be so baited, scorned and —ed at,* R3 I, 3, 109 (Qq *thus taunted, scorned and baited at).* *now is a time to s.* Tit. III, 1, 264. *the ocean swells not so as Aaron —s,* IV, 2, 139. *wherefore s. you so?* Rom. I, 5, 62.

2) tr. to agitate, to infest, to disquiet: *—ing her world with sorrow's wind and rain,* Compl. 7.

**Storm-beaten,** violently blown against and struck by a storm: *to dry the rain on my s. face,* Sonn. 34, 6.

**Stormy,** 1) tempestuous, full of wind and rain: *like a s. day, now wind, now rain,* Ven. 965. *s. blustering weather,* Lucr. 115. *the s. gusts of winter's day,* Sonn. 13, 11. *a s. day, which makes the rivers drown their shores,* R2 III, 2, 106. *a s. night,* Per. III, 2, 4.

2) violent, passionate: *if you give o'er to s. passion,* H4B I, 1, 165. *his s. hate,* H6B III, 1, 155.

**Story,** subst. 1) history, account of memorable events: *he that can endure to follow with allegiance a fallen lord does conquer him that did his master conquer, and earns a place i' the s.* Ant. III, 13, 46.

2) any tale of true or fabulous events: *she told him —es to delight his ear,* Pilgr. 47. *some shallow s. of deep love,* Gent. I, 1, 21. *the s. of the Prodigal,* Wiv. IV, 5, 8 and H4B II, 1, 157. *the s. shall be changed: Apollo flies, and Daphne holds the chase,* Mids. II, 1, 230. *love's —es,* II, 2, 122. *Pyramus and Thisbe, says the s., did talk through the chink of a wall,* III, 1, 65. *tell sad —es of the death of kings,* R2 III, 2, 156. *our author will continue the s.* H4B V, 5, 144. *those that have not read the s.* H5 V Chor. 1. Epil. 2. H8 Prol. 26. I, 1, 36. II, 3, 90. Tit. III, 2, 83. V, 3, 83. Rom. I, 3, 92. V, 3, 309. Mcb. III, 4, 65. Hml. III, 2, 273. Cymb. II, 2, 27 and II, 4, 69 (= the subject represented by a picture; cf. Wiv. IV, 5, 8 and H4B II, 1, 157). Per. IV Prol. 19. IV, 4, 9. V Prol. 2.

3) report, account given about a matter or person; recital of facts and incidents: *the light will show, charactered in my brow, the s. of sweet chastity's decay,* Lucr. 808. *the nurse, to still her child, will tell my s.* 813. *I can set down a s. of faults concealed,* Sonn. 88, 6. *that tongue that tells the s. of thy days,* 95, 5. *the s. of my life,* Tp. V, 304. 312. *to hear the s. of your*

*loves discovered*, Gent. V, 4, 171. *to tell sad —es of my own mishaps*, Err. I, 1, 121. 138. *all the s. of the night told over*, Mids. V, 23. *which makes her s. true*, All's IV, 3, 66 (i. e. that which is told about her). H5 IV, 3, 56. H6C I, 4, 160. R3 I, 2, 161. IV, 3, 8 (Ff *s.*, Qq —es). IV, 4, 280 (Ff *letter*). Hml. V, 2, 360. Oth. I, 3, 129. Ant. V, 2, 364. Cymb. III, 6, 92. Per. V, 1, 135. 166.

4) that which a person says or tells: *where did I leave? No matter where, quoth he, leave me, and then the s. aptly ends*, Ven. 716. *their (lovers') copious —es oftentimes begun ... are never done*, 845. *whose (Sinon's) enchanting s. the credulous old Priam after slew*, Lucr. 1521. *he that writes of you ... so dignifies his s.* Sonn. 84, 8. *could make me any summer's s. tell*, 98, 7 (i. e. praise the delights of summer). *reworded a plaintful s.* Compl. 2. *without the which this s. were most impertinent*, Tp. I, 2, 137. 306. V, 117. *make me not your s.* Meas. I, 4, 30 (= make me not your theme, i. e. don't make a fool of me). Err. V, 356. Ado I, 1, 313. IV, 1, 124. As IV, 3, 154. All's V, 3, 229. R2 V, 2, 2. H4A III, 3, 191 (*it appears so by the s.*, i. e. there is no denying it after what has been said). H4B II, 4, 272. H6C II, 1, 44. Caes. I, 2, 92. Mcb. V, 5, 29. Hml. I, 1, 32. Oth. I, 3, 158. 165. IV, 1, 135. Cymb. III, 3, 55. 91. V, 5, 286. Hence almost = matter, subject, business: *when Prospero is destroyed. That shall be by and by: I remember the s.* Tp. III, 2, 156. *who hath a s. ready for your ear*, Meas. IV, 1, 56. *let us from point to point this s. know*, All's V, 3, 325. *as index to the s. we late talked of*, R3 II, 2, 149. *I must read this paper; I fear, the s. of his anger*, H8 III, 2, 209.

**Story**, subst. = floor, see *Clear-stories*.

**Story**, vb. to relate, to give an account of: *—es his victories, his triumphs and his glories*, Ven. 1013. *he —es to her ear her husband's fame*, Lucr. 106. *how worthy he is I will leave to appear hereafter, rather than s. him in his own hearing*, Cymb. I, 4, 34.

**Stoup**, see *Stoop*, subst.

**Stout**, 1) strong, firm: *rifted Jove's s. oak*, Tp. V, 45. *rocks impregnable are not so s. ... but time decays*, Sonn. 65, 7.

2) vigorous, full of life: *pluck s. men's pillows from below their heads*, Tim. IV, 3, 32.

3) proud, overbearing: *I will be strange, s.* Tw. II, 5, 185. *as s. and proud as he were lord of all*, H6B I, 1, 187. *correcting thy s. heart*, Cor. III, 2, 78.

4) bold and resolute: *with dreadful pomp of s. invasion*, John IV, 2, 173. *this earth ... bears not alive so s. a gentleman*, H4A V, 4, 93. *the s. Lord Talbot*, H6A I, 1, 106. *s. Pendragon*, III, 2, 95. *a —er champion never handled sword*, III, 4, 19. *the s. Parisians do revolt*, V, 2, 2. *s. kerns*, H6B IV, 9, 26. *s. Diomede*, H6C IV, 2, 19. *a wise s. captain*, IV, 7, 30. *s. resolved mates*, R3 I, 3, 340. *the s. Earl Northumberland*, H8 IV, 2, 12. *s. Mercutio*, Rom. III, 1, 174. *s. Tybalt*, 178. *the s. Norweyan ranks*, Mcb. I, 3, 95.

**Stoutly**, 1) strongly, firmly: *his bark is s. timbered*, Oth. II, 1, 48.

2) boldly, resolutely, obstinately: *faint not, faint heart, but s. say: so be it*, Lucr. 1209. *thou that so s. hast resisted me*, H6C II, 5, 79. *she speaks for you s.* Oth. III, 1, 47.

**Stoutness**, overbearing and unbending pride: *let thy mother rather feel thy pride than fear thy dangerous*

*s.* Cor. III, 2, 127 (the stress seems to be on the words *feel* and *fear*. Let thy mother rather be in person offended by thy pride than be further solicitous about its dangerous consequences). *his s. when he did stand for consul*, V, 6, 27.

**Stover**, fodder for cattle, as hay, straw, and the like: *the turfy mountains, where live nibbling sheep, and flat meads thatched with s., them to keep*, Tp. IV, 63.

**Stow**, to bestow, to place, lo lodge, to lay up: *night ... in her vaulty prison —s the day*, Lucr. 119. *the mariners all under hatches —ed*, Tp. I, 2, 230. *safely —ed*, Hml. IV, 2, 1. *where hast thou —ed my daughter?* Oth. I, 2, 62.

**Stowage**, state of being laid up: *to have them in safe s.* Cymb. I, 6, 192.

**Strachy**, a name or title not yet satisfactorily explained: *the lady of the S. married the yeoman of the wardrobe*, Tw. II, 5, 45.

**Straggler**, rover, vagabond: *let's whip these —s o'er the seas again*, R3 V, 3, 327.

**Straggling**, roving dispersedly and apart from the main body: *s. slaves for pillage fighting*, Lucr. 428. *he enriched poor s. soldiers with great quantity*, Tim. V, 1, 7.

**Straight** (cf. *Strait*) adj. passing from one point to another by the nearest way, right, direct, not crooked: *s. legs and passing strong*, Ven. 297. *I may be s, though they themselves be bevel*, Sonn. 121, 11. Shr. II, 256. Tw. II, 3, 148. H4A I, 1, 82. II, 4, 164. H5 V, 2, 168. Rom. II, 1, 19. Cymb. III, 1, 38. Per. V, 1, 110.

**Straight**, adv. 1) straight-forward, not by a deviating course: *bear thine eyes s., though thy proud heart go wide*, Sonn. 140, 14. *floating s., obedient to the stream*, Err. I, 1, 87. *lo, he is tilting s.* LLL V, 2, 483 (not breaking his spear across; cf. *Across*). *he runs s. and even*, H4A III, 1, 114.

2) immediately, without delay: *the steed breaketh his rein, and to her goes he s.* Ven. 264. *and s., in pity of her tender years, they both would strive who first should dry his tears*, 1091. *what fond beggar, but to touch the crown, would with the sceptre s. be strucken down?* Lucr. 217. *as one shifts, another s. ensues*, 1104. 1299. 1634. Sonn. 45, 14. 89, 3. 100, 5. 129, 5. 145, 5. Wiv. I, 1, 118. IV, 2, 85. 103. IV, 4, 75. IV, 6, 32. Meas. I, 2, 166. I, 4, 85. II, 2, 1. Err. III, 2, 190. IV, 1, 102. IV, 2, 63. IV, 4, 59. 143. LLL V, 2, 277. Mids. III, 2, 403. IV, 1, 65. Merch. I, 1, 31. I, 2, 65. I, 3, 175. II, 4, 25. II, 6, 50. II, 9, 1. As II, 1, 68. III, 5, 136. Wint. II, 3, 144. R2 II, 1, 215. V, 3, 139. H6A IV, 1, 73. IV, 4, 40. V, 4, 47. H6B II, 1, 141. III, 2, 15. 244. H6C I, 2, 71. R3 I, 3, 355. H8 III, 2, 115. Hml. II, 2, 451. Oth. IV, 1, 58 etc. etc.

**Straight-pight**, straight-fixed, erect: *for feature, laming the shrine of Venus, or s. Minerva*, Cymb. V, 5, 164.

**Straightway**, immediately, on the spot: Tp. V, 235. Mids. III, 2, 34. V, 204. H6A I, 5, 7. H6B IV, 9, 33. Caes. II, 2, 127. Ant. III, 11, 20. Cymb. III, 5, 83.

**Strain**, subst. 1) effort of thought (as if by violent stretching of the mind): *and, in the publication, make no s., but that Achilles ... will find Hector's purpose pointing on him*, Troil. I, 3, 326 (= make no difficulty, no doubt).

2) motion of the mind, internal action, impulse, feeling (German: *Regung*): *other —s of woe, which now seem woe, compared with loss of thee will not seem*

*so*, Sonn. 90, 13. *unless he know some s. in me, that I know not myself, he would never have boarded me in this fury*, Wiv. II, 1, 91. *measure his woe the length and breadth of mine, and let it answer every s. for s., as thus for thus, and such a grief for such*, Ado V, 1, 12. *love is full of unbefitting —s*, LLL V, 2, 770. *if it did infect my blood with joy, or swell my thoughts to any s. of pride*, H4B IV, 5, 171. *do not these high —s of divination in our sister work some touches of remorse?* Troil. II, 2, 113. *can it be that so degenerate a s. as this should once set footing in your generous bosoms?* 154. *thou hast affected the fine —s of honour, to imitate the graces of the gods*, Cor. V, 3, 149. *praise his most vicious s., and call it excellent*, Tim. IV, 3, 213. *it is no act of common passage, but a s. of rareness*, Cymb. III, 4, 95. *O noble s.!* IV, 2, 24.

3) natural disposition: *I would all of the same s. were in the same distress*, Wiv. III, 3, 197. *he is of a noble s., of approved valour and confirmed honesty*, Ado II, 1, 394. *you have shown to-day your valiant s.* Lr. V, 3, 40.

4) stock, race: *he is bred out of that bloody s. that haunted us in our familiar paths*, H5 II, 4, 51. *the s. of man's bred out into baboon and monkey*, Tim. I, 1, 259. *if thou wert the noblest of thy s.* Caes. V, 1, 59. *I do shame to think of what a noble s. you are, and of how coward a spirit*, Per. IV, 3, 24.

5) note, tune, song: *I at each sad s. will strain a tear*, Lucr. 1131. *the s. of strutting chanticleer*, Tp. I, 2, 385. *play false —s*, As IV, 3, 68. *that s. again!* Tw. I, 1, 4. *touch thy instrument a s. or two*, Caes. IV, 3, 257.

**Strain**, vb. 1) tr. a) to press, to squeeze: *our king has all the Indies in his arms, and more and richer, when he —s that lady*, H8 IV, 1, 46.

b) to extend, to stretch: *I am to pray you not to s. my speech to grosser issues nor to larger reach than to suspicion*, Oth. III, 3, 218. Absol.: *you s. too far*, H4A IV, 1, 75 (you go too far in your apprehensions).

c) to exert, to ply hard, to put to the utmost strength: *to strange sores strangely they s. the cure*, Ado IV, 1, 254. *my breast I'll burst with —ing of my courage*, H6A I, 5, 10. *our hope in him is dead: let us return, and s. what other means is left unto us*, Tim. V, 1, 230. *he sweats, —s his young nerves*, Cymb. III, 3, 94. *to s. courtesy* = to insist on the precedence of others, to decline to go first: *they all s. courtesy who shall cope him first*, Ven. 888; and hence = to remain behind: *my business was great; and in such a case as mine a man may s. courtesy*, Rom. II, 4, 55. Partic. *—ed* = excessive: *this —ed passion doth you wrong*, H4B I, 1, 161. *with —ed pride to come between our sentence and our power*, Lr. I, 1, 172 (Qq *strayed*).

d) to urge: *note, if your lady s. his entertainment with any strong or vehement importunity*, Oth. III, 3, 250.

e) to wrench; to force, to constrain: *s. their cheeks to idle merriment*, John III, 3, 46. *nor aught so good but —ed from that fair use revolts from true birth*, Rom. II, 3, 19. *it —s me past the compass of my wits*, IV, 1, 47. Partic. *—ed* = forced, constrained: *what —ed touches rhetoric can lend*, Sonn. 82, 10. *on what compulsion must I? The quality of mercy is not —ed*, Merch. IV, 1, 184.

f) to filter: *I at each sad strain will s. a tear*, Lucr. 1131. *I love thee in so —ed a purity*, Troil. IV,

4, 26 (Ff *strange*). *faith and troth, —ed purely from all hollow bias-drawing*, IV, 5, 169.

g) to tune (?): *it is the lark that sings so out of tune, —ing harsh discords*, Rom. III, 5, 28.

2) intr. to make efforts, to exert one's self: *more —ing on for plucking back*, Wint. IV, 4, 476 (like a hound in the leash). *like greyhounds in the slips, —ing upon the start*, H5 III, 1, 32. *to build his fortune I will s. a little*, Tim. I, 1, 143. *I do not s. at the position, — it is familiar, — but at the author's drift*, Troil. III, 3; 112 (I do not put my brains on the rack; I see no difficulty in the position. cf. subst. *Strain* 1. Ff *s. it at*). Remarkable expression: *with what encounter so uncurrent I have —ed to appear thus*, Wint. III, 2, 51 (perhaps = brought about, contrived. Dyce: with what unwarrantable familiarity of intercourse I have so far exceeded bounds, or gone astray, that I should be forced to appear thus in a public court as a criminal. — Collier *strayed*, Johnson *have I been stained*).

**Strait**, subst. 1) a narrow passage: *the tide ... boundeth ... back to the s. that forced him on so fast*, Lucr. 1670. *honour travels in a s. so narrow, where one but goes abreast*, Troil. III, 3, 154.

2) difficulty, distress: *I know into what —s of fortune she is driven*, As V, 2, 71.

**Strait**, adj. (cf. *Straight*) 1) narrow: *flying through a s. lane*, Cymb. V, 3, 7. 11.

2) tight, close: *you rode, like a kern of Ireland, your French hose off, and in your s. strossers*, H5 III, 7, 57.

3) parsimonious, niggardly: *I do not ask you much, I beg cold comfort; and you are so s. and so ingrateful, you deny me that*, John V, 7, 42.

4) strict: *whom I believe to be most s. in virtue*, Meas. II, 1, 9. *some s. decrees that lie too heavy on the commonwealth*, H4A IV, 3, 79. *such a s. edict*, H6B III, 2, 258. *his means most short, his creditors most s.* Tim. I, 1, 96.

Adverbially: *proceed no —er 'gainst our uncle Gloster than ...*, H6B III, 2, 20.

**Straited**, put to difficulty, at a loss: *if your lass should call this your lack of love or bounty, you were s. for a reply*, Wint. IV, 4, 365.

**Straitly**, strictly: *his majesty hath s. given in charge that no man shall have private conference with his brother*, R3 I, 1, 85. IV, 1, 17 (Ff *strictly*).

**Straitness**, strictness, severity: *if his own life answer the s. of his proceeding*, Meas. III, 2, 269

**Strand**, see *Strond*.

**Strange**, *Lord S. of Blackmere*, one of Talbot's baronial titles: H6A IV, 7, 65.

**Strange**, adj. 1) of another country, foreign: *one of the s. queen's lords*, LLL IV, 2, 134. *wear s. suits, disable all the benefits of your country*, As IV, 1, 34. *as by s. fortune it came to us*, Wint. II, 3, 179 (as the child of a foreigner). *studies his companions like a s. tongue*, H4B IV, 4, 69. H8 III, 1, 45. *he (my man) is s. and peevish*, Cymb. I, 6, 54. *I am something curious, being s., to have them in safe stowage*, 191.

2) not one's own, belonging to another: *the impression of s. kinds is formed in them by force*, Lucr. 1242. *millions of s. shadows on you tend*, Sonn. 53, 2. *in him a plenitude of subtle matter, applied to cautels, all s. forms receives*, Compl. 303. *some such s. bull leaped your father's cow*, Ado V, 4, 49. *s. fowl light upon neighbouring ponds*, Cymb. I, 4, 97. cf. *Strange* achieved.

3) unknown; unused before; new: *to new-found methods and to compounds s.* Sonn. 76, 4. *what s. fish hath made his meal on thee?* Tp. II, 1, 112; cf. II, 2, 28. 32 (and H8 V, 4, 34). *the signet is not s. to you,* Meas. IV, 2, 209. *thy complexion shifts to s. effects, after the moon,* III, 1, 24. *as s. as the thing I know not,* Ado IV, 1, 271. *learned without opinion, and s. without heresy,* LLL V, 1, 6 (new and original). *love to Richard is a s. brooch in this all-hating world,* R2 V, 5, 66. *you did devise s. tortures,* H6B III, 1, 122. *I stalk about her door, like a s. soul upon the Stygian banks,* Troil. III, 2, 10 (newly arrived). *these s. flies, these fashion-mongers,* Rom. II, 4, 34. *new honours come upon him, like our s. garments,* Mcb. I, 3, 145.

4) not knowing, unacquainted: *I will acquaintance strangle and look s.* Sonn. 89, 8. *as s. unto your town as to your talk,* Err. II, 2, 151. *why look you s. on me? you know me well,* V, 295. *to put a s. face on his own perfection,* Ado II, 3, 49 (= not to seem to know his own accomplishment). *am become as new into the world, s., unacquainted,* Troil. III, 3, 12. *I know thee well, but in thy fortunes am unlearned and s.* Tim. IV, 3, 56. *you make me s. even to the disposition that I owe,* Mcb. III, 4, 112 (you make me not to know myself, not to know whether I am a brave man or a coward).

5) reserved, distant, estranged, not familiar: *in many's looks the false heart's history is writ in moods and frowns and wrinkles s.* Sonn. 93, 8. *look s. and frown,* Err. II, 2, 112. *thy self I call it, being s. to me,* 123. *you grow exceeding s.* Merch. I, 1, 67. *why do you look so s. upon your wife?* All's V, 3, 168. *I will be s., stout,* Tw. II, 5, 184. *you throw a s. regard upon me,* V, 219. *if he were proud, or covetous of praise, or s. or self-affected,* Troil. II, 3, 250. *those that have more cunning to be s.* Rom. II, 2, 101. *I should have been more s.* 102. *s. love, grown bold,* III, 2, 15. *you bear too stubborn and too s. a hand over your friend,* Caes. I, 2, 35.

6) extraordinary, enormous, remarkable, singular: *against s. maladies a sovereign cure,* Sonn. 153, 8. *with good life and observation s.* Tp. III, 3, 87. *he is sick of a s. fever,* Meas. V, 152. *to s. sores strangely they strain the cure,* Ado IV, 1, 254. *we will with some s. pastime solace them,* LLL IV, 3, 377. *thou'lt show thy mercy and remorse more s. than is thy s. apparent cruelty,* Merch. IV, 1, 20. *he hath s. places crammed with observation,* As II, 7, 40. *full of s. oaths and bearded like the pard,* 150. *impossible be s. attempts to those that weigh their pains in sense,* All's I, 1, 239. *I see a s. confession in thine eye,* H4B I, 1, 94. *a s. tongue makes my cause more s., suspicious,* H8 III, 1, 45. *this (murder) most foul, s. and unnatural,* Hml. I, 5, 28. *s. and fastened villain,* Lr. II, 1, 79 (Qq *strong*). *there is some s. thing toward,* III, 3, 20. *'tis a s. truth,* Oth. V, 2, 189. *he hath laid s. courtesies and great of late upon me,* Ant. II, 2, 157. *all s. and terrible events are welcome,* IV, 15, 3. *nature wants stuff to vie s. forms with fancy,* V, 2, 98. *she doth think she hath s. lingering poisons,* Cymb. I, 5, 34. *fame answering the most s. inquire,* Per. III Prol. 22.

*To make it s.* = to do as if something extra-ordinary had happened; to seem to be shocked: *she makes it s., but she would be best pleased to be so angered with another letter,* Gent. I, 2, 102. *why makest thou it so s.?* Tit. II, 1, 81.

7) surprising, wonderful, odd: Ven. 791. 985. Tp.

I, 2, 178. 401. II, 1, 199. 213. 318. II, 2, 28. 32. 41. III, 3, 95. IV, 143. 234. V, 117. 228. 232. 242. 289. Meas. IV, 2, 216. V, 38. 39. 42. 44. Err. I, 1, 52. III, 1, 97. Ado II, 3, 22. IV, 1, 270. LLL V, 2, 210. Mids. III, 1, 90. 107. V, 59. Merch. I, 1, 51. II, 8, 13. IV, 1, 177. Shr. I, 1, 85 (*will you be so s.?*). Tw. I, 3, 120. V, 70. John I, 44 etc. etc. Followed by *should:* Wint. V, 1, 114. John V, 7, 20. Caes. II, 2, 35. Ant. III, 7, 58.

Adverbially: *how s. or odd soe'er I bear myself,* Hml. I, 5, 170. *she will speak most bitterly and s. Most s., but yet most truly,* Meas. V, 36. 37 (the suffix *ly* belonging to both adverbs; cf. Appendix).

**Strange-achieved,** gained and yet not enjoyed; acquired not for one's own self, but for the benefit of others: *for this they have engrossed and piled up the cankered heaps of s. gold,* H4B IV, 5, 72.

**Strange-disposed,** of a remarkable disposition or nature: *it is a s. time,* Caes. I, 3, 33.

**Strangely,** 1) as something not one's own, as a thing belonging to another country or to other people: *that thou commend it s. to some place where chance may nurse or end it,* Wint. II, 3, 182.

2) in the manner of one who does not know another or pretends not to know him; in a distant and reserved manner: *when thou shalt s. pass and scarcely greet me,* Sonn. 49, 5. *I have looked on truth askance and s.* 110, 6. *you all look s. on me,* H4B V, 2, 63. *which of the peers have uncontemned gone by him, or at least s. neglected?* H8 III, 2, 11. *to pass s. by him,* Troil. III, 3, 39. *they pass by s.* 71.

3) extraordinarily, uncommonly: *thou hast s. stood the test,* Tp. IV, 7. *O mischief s. thwarting,* Ado III, 2, 135. *to strange sores s. they strain the cure,* IV, 1, 254. *the herds were s. clamorous,* H4A III, 1, 40. *s. visited people, ... the mere despair of surgery, he cures,* Mcb. IV, 3, 150.

4) in a manner to cause wonder and surprise: Tp. III, 3, 40. V, 160. 313. Meas. I, 4, 50. IV, 2, 120. John IV, 2, 144. H8 III, 2, 29. IV, 1, 81. IV, 2, 112. V, 3, 94. Mcb. III, 6, 3. Hml. V, 1, 172. 173. Cymb. V, 2, 17. V, 5, 272. Per. II, 2, 53.

**Strangeness,** 1) distant behaviour, reserve: *she puts on outward s.* Ven. 310. *measure my s. with my unripe years,* 524. *ungird thy s.* Tw. IV, 1, 16. *the s. of his altered countenance,* H6B III, 1, 5. *the savage s. he puts on,* Troil. II, 3, 135. *between your s. and his pride,* III, 3, 45. *put on a form of s.* 51. *he shall in s. stand no farther off than in a politic distance,* Oth. III, 3, 12 (Qq in *strangest*).

2) wonderfulness, power of exciting surprise: Tp. I, 2, 306. V, 247. Meas. V, 386. Lr. IV, 6, 66.

**Stranger,** 1) one of another country or place: Err. I, 2, 60. IV, 2, 9. LLL V, 2, 174. 218. Merch. III, 3, 27. As IV, 3, 153. Shr. II, 87. 90. V, 1, 111. All's IV, 1, 17. Tw. III, 3, 9. John V, 2, 27 (O. Edd. *stranger, march;* M. Edd. *stranger march*). R2 II, 3, 3. H8 I, 4, 53. II, 2, 102. II, 4, 15. Tit. IV, 2, 33. Oth. I, 1, 137. Cymb. I, 6, 59. 151. II, 1, 35. 37. 44. II, 4, 126. Per. I, 4, 25. II, 2, 42. 52. II, 5, 46. V, 1, 114.

Adjectively: *the s. queen,* LLL IV, 2, 143. *to seek new friends and s. companies,* Mids. I, 1, 219 (O. Edd. *strange companions*). *swearing allegiance to s. blood,* John V, 1, 11. *the s. paths of banishment,* R2 I, 3, 143. *my s. soul,* R3 I, 4, 48. *a s. knight,* Per. II, 3, 67. II, 5, 16.

2) one unknown or, at least, not familiar; one not belonging to the house, a guest: *lends embracements unto every s.* Ven. 790. *in the interest of thy bed a s. came,* Lucr. 1620. *count the world a s.* Gent. V, 4, 70. Err. IV, 1, 36. Merch. I, 2, 135. III, 2, 240. As III, 2, 275. All's II, 5, 91. V, 3, 26. Tw. I, 4, 4. R2 I, 3, 239. H6B I, 3, 82. H8 II, 3, 17. V, 1, 170. Rom. I, 5, 146. Mcb. IV, 3, 163. Hml. I, 5, 165. Cymb. I, 4, 30. 111. Per. II, 5, 77. With *to: we are but —s to him,* Tim. III, 2, 4. metaphorically: *and to my state grew s.* Tp. I, 2, 76. *to make us —s to his looks of love,* H4A I, 3, 290. Mcb. IV, 3, 125. Lr. I, 1, 117. Oth. III, 3, 144.

Adjectively: *never coped with s. eyes,* Lucr. 99. *a s. cur,* Merch. I, 3, 119.

3) any other person, not one's self: *when shall he think to find a s. just, when he himself himself confounds,* Lucr. 159. Adjectively: *she thought they* (her words) *touched not any s. sense,* All's I, 3, 114 (= were not overheard by any other person).

4) one unacquainted, not knowing: *a s. to those most imperial looks,* Troil. I, 3, 224. *my child is yet a s. in the world,* Rom. I, 2, 8.

**Strangered,** estranged, alienated: *dowered with our curse, and s. with our oath,* Lr. I, 1, 207.

**Strangle,** to choke, to kill by stopping respiration: *—ing a snake,* LLL V, 1, 142. V, 2, 595. *the smallest thread will serve to s. thee,* John IV, 3, 129. H4A II, 4, 547. H6B II, 3, 8. III, 2, 170. R3 IV, 4, 138. Rom. IV, 3, 35 (= to suffocate). Oth. IV, 1, 220.

Metaphorically, = to hinder from appearance, to suppress, to extinguish: *I will acquaintance s. and look strange,* Sonn. 89, 8. *it is the baseness of thy fear that makes thee s. thy propriety,* Tw. V, 150 (disown what thou art). *s. such thoughts,* Wint. IV, 4, 47. *vapours that did seem to s. him,* H4A I, 2, 227 (i. e. the sun). *he has —d his language in his tears,* H8 V, 1, 157. *—s our dear vows even in the birth of our own labouring breath,* Troil. IV, 4, 39. *dark night —s the travelling lamp,* Mcb. II, 4, 7.

**Strangler,** that which chokes and destroys: *the band that seems to tie their friendship together will be the very s. of their amity,* Ant. II, 6, 130.

**Strap,** a slip of leather attached to boots to make their putting on more easy: *an they* (boots) *be not, let them hang themselves in their own —s,* Tw. I, 3, 13.

**Strappado,** a species of torture, in which a person was drawn up by his arms tied behind his back, and then suddenly let down with a jerk: *an I were at the s.* H4A II, 4, 262.

**Stratagem,** 1) an artifice in war, a trick to deceive the enemy (a deed as well as a practice): All's III, 6, 37. 68 (*your mystery in s.*). IV, 1, 55 (*it was in s.*). H5 IV, 8, 113. H6A III, 2, 18. IV, 5, 2. Lr. IV, 6, 188.

2) any artifice or trick: H4B II, 4, 22. R3 III, 5, 11. Tit. II, 1, 104. II, 3, 5.

3) a dreadful deed, anything amazing and appalling: *fit for treasons, —s and spoils,* Merch. V, 85. *every minute now should be the father of some s.* H4B I, 1, 8. *what —s, how fell, how butcherly, this deadly quarrel daily doth beget,* H6C II, 5, 89. *that heaven should practise —s upon so soft a subject,* Rom. III, 5, 211.

**Strato,** name in Caes. V, 5, 32. 33. 44. 48. 50. 53. 64.

**Straw,** subst. 1) the stalk on which corn grows, and from which it is thrashed: *when shepherds pipe on oaten —s,* LLL V, 2, 913. *those that with haste will make a mighty fire, begin it with weak —s,* Caes. I, 3, 108. Emblem of weakness and insignificance: *our lances are but —s,* Shr. V, 2, 173. *oaths are —s,* H5 II, 3, 53. *start at wagging of a s.* R3 III, 5, 7. *spurns enviously at —s,* Hml. IV, 5, 6. *a pigmy's s. does pierce it,* Lr. IV, 6, 171. Hence = trifle: *I force not argument a s.* Lucr. 1021. *I prize it not a s.* Wint. III, 2, 111. *shall blow each dust, each s., each little rub, out of the path,* John III, 4, 128. *will not debate the question of this s.* Hml. IV, 4, 26. *find quarrel in a s.* Hml. IV, 4, 55.

2) a mass of stalks of grain cut and thrashed: *a platted hive of s.* Compl. 8. *stuff me out with s.* H4B V, 5, 88. *a wisp of s. were worth a thousand crowns to make this shameless callet know herself,* H6C II, 2, 144 ("a wisp, or small twist, of straw or hay, was often applied as a mark of opprobrium to an immodest woman, a scold, or similar offenders; even the showing it to a woman was, therefore, considered as a grievous affront." Nares). *first thrash the corn, then after burn the s.* Tit. II, 3, 123. Proverbially combustible: *she burned with love, as s. with fire flameth,* Pilgr. 97. *the strongest oaths are s. to the fire i' the blood,* Tp. IV, 52. = bed-straw, litter: Meas. IV, 3, 38. All's IV, 3, 289. Lr. III, 2, 69. III, 4, 45. IV, 7, 40.

**Straw,** vb. = strew; see *O'erstrawed.*

**Strawberry,** the fruit of the plant Fragaria: H5 I, 1, 60. R3 III, 4, 34. 49. Oth. III, 3, 435.

**Straw-colour,** of a light yellow: *your s. beard,* Mids. I, 2, 95.

**Strawy,** resembling straw: *the s. Greeks, ripe for his edge, fall down before him, like the mower's swath,* Troil. V, 5, 24 (Ff *straying*).

**Stray,** subst. 1) dereliction, aberration: *I would not from your love make such a s.* Lr. I, 1, 212.

2) a straggler, a vagabond: *impounded as a s. the king of Scots,* H5 I, 2, 160. *to seize me for a s.* H6B IV, 10, 27.

Collectively, = stragglers: *pursue the scattered s.* H4B IV, 2, 120.

**Stray,** vb. 1) intr. to wander from a direct course or from company: Ven. 234. Tp. I, 2, 417. III, 3, 9. Gent. I, 1, 74. II, 7, 31. Mids. V, 409. Merch. II, 7, 35. V, 30. R2 I, 3, 206. H6B III, 1, 211. H6C III, 2, 176. Troil. V, 5, 24 (Ff *—ing*, = straggling; Qq and M. Edd. *strawy*). Tit. III, 1, 88. V, 1, 20. Ant. IV, 14, 47. Metaphorically: *love is ... skipping and vain, ... full of —ing shapes, ... varying in subjects,* LLL V, 2, 773 (*—ing* monosyll., like many similar participles; M. Edd. *stray or strange*). In a moral sense, = to go astray, to deviate from the right: Sonn. 41, 10. H8 V, 3, 64. Lr. I, 1, 172 (Ff *—ed,* Qq *strained*). Per. I, 1, 104.

2) tr. to mislead: *hath not else his eye —ed his affection in unlawful love?* Err. V, 51.

**Streak,** subst. a line of colour different from the ground: *chequering the eastern clouds with —s of light,* Rom. II, 3, 2. *what envious —s do lace the severing clouds in yonder east,* III, 5, 7. *the west yet glimmers with some —s of day,* Mcb. III, 3, 5.

**Streak,** vb. to overspread, to anoint: *with the juice of this I'll s. her eyes,* Mids. II, 1, 257.

**Streaked**, variegated with lines of a different colour, dappled: *the eanlings which were s. and pied,* Merch. I, 3, 80. *s. gillyvors,* Wint. IV, 4, 82.

**Stream**, subst. any current of water: *in vain you strive against the s.* Ven. 772. *left me to the mercy of a rude s.* H8 III, 2, 364. *a vagabond flag upon the s.* Ant. I, 4, 45.

= a current in the sea: *floating straight, obedient to the s.* Err. I, 1, 87. *my boat sails freely, both with wind and s.* Oth. II, 3, 65. = a river, brook, or rivulet: *the petty —s that pay a daily debt to their salt sovereign,* Lucr. 649. Gent. II, 7, 34. Ado III, 1, 27. As II, 1, 46. IV, 3, 80. John II, 443. R2 V, 3, 62. H5 I, 2, 209. Caes. I, 1, 64. Hml. IV, 7, 168. Oth. IV, 3, 45. Cymb. IV, 2, 184.

Figuratively, = a moving throng of people: *the rich s. of lords and ladies,* H8 IV, 1, 62. *we will be there before the s. o' the people,* Cor. II, 3, 269. cf. *to forswear the full s. of the world,* As III, 2, 440.

Applied to tears and to blood flowing plentifully: Lucr. 1078. Compl. 285. Merch. III, 2, 46. Lucr. 1774. R2 I, 1, 103. H6A III, 3, 55. R3 V, 5, 37. To full beams of light: *thy* (the moon's) *gracious, golden, glittering —s,* Mids. V, 279 (Qq F1 *beams*). To copious language: *that we must lave our honours in these flattering —s,* Mcb. III, 2, 33 (= streams of flattery).

In a moral sense, = course, drift, bent, tendency: *the very s. of his life ... must give him a better proclamation,* Meas. III, 2, 150. *he that in this action contrives against his own nobility, in his proper s. o'erflows himself,* All's IV, 3, 29. *what relish is in this? how runs the s.?* Tw. IV, 1, 64. *we see which way the s. of time doth run,* H4B IV, 1, 70. *which swims against your s. of quality,* V, 2, 34. *the s. of his dispose,* Troil. II, 3, 174. *that 'gainst the s. of virtue they may strive,* Tim. IV, 1, 27. *offend the s. of regular justice,* V, 4, 60.

Sometimes = water, flood in general: *gilding pale —s with heavenly alchemy,* Sonn. 33, 4. *turns into yellow gold his* (Neptune's) *salt green —s,* Mids. III, 2, 393. *would scatter all her spices on the s.* Merch. I, 1, 33. *bubbles in a late disturbed s.* H4A II, 3, 62. *as plays the sun upon the glassy —s,* H6A V, 3, 62. *the s. to cool this heat,* Tit. II, 1, 133. *suffocating —s,* Oth. III, 3, 389.

**Stream**, vb. 1) intr. to flow like a current; used only figuratively: *round about her tear-distained eye blue circles —ed, like rainbows in the sky: these watergalls in her dim element foretell new storms,* Lucr. 1587 (cf. All's I, 3, 157). *to imperial Love do my sighs s.* All's II, 3, 82. *her eyes in heaven would through the airy region s. so bright,* Rom. II, 2, 21 (cf. the subst. in Mids. V, 279).

2) tr. to emit, to pour out: *as they* (thy wounds) *s. forth thy blood,* Caes. III, 1, 201. = to unfurl, to display fully in the wind: *—ing the ensign of the Christian cross against black pagans,* R2 IV, 94.

**Streamer**, ensign, flag: *his brave fleet with silken —s the young Phoebus fanning,* H5 III Chor. 6.

**Street**, a public way in a town: Lucr. 1834. Wiv. IV, 2, 40 *(at s. end; cf. End).* LLL IV, 3, 278. 281. Merch. II, 5, 32. Shr. I, 2, 233. V, 1, 149. Tw. III, 3, 25. John IV, 2, 148. V, 1, 39. R2 V, 5, 77. H4A III, 2, 68. H4B III, 2, 329. H6A III, 1, 84. H6B II, 4, 8 etc. etc. *in the s.*: Meas. IV, 4, 12. Err. III, 1, 36. III, 2, 188. IV, 1, 106. V, 225. Ado III, 3, 36. Merch. II, 8, 14. All's IV, 3, 89. Tw. V, 67. John

IV, 2, 185. H4A I, 2, 95. 98. 100. H6A I, 6, 13 etc. *through the —s*: Wiv. IV, 5, 32. Err. V, 140. H6B II, 4, 14. IV, 7, 144. Cor. V, 3, 115. Ant. II, 2, 234.

**Strength**, 1) power of the body, vigour, force: Ven. 42. 111. 280. Lucr. 124. Sonn. 23, 4. Gent. II, 4, 193. Meas. II, 2, 108. Err. II, 2, 178. Ado IV, 1, 200. LLL I, 2, 180. As I, 2, 182. 185. Tw. III, 4, 254. Wint. III, 2, 107 (cf. *Limit*). IV, 4, 414. John II, 330. V, 2, 63. 137. R2 I, 1, 73. III, 2, 180. 181. H4A III, 3, 7. H4B II, 3, 55. III, 1, 42. IV, 4, 8. IV, 5, 44. 218. H5 IV, 7, 90. V, 2, 141. H6A I, 5, 1. 15. II, 3, 63. III, 2, 112. V, 5, 32. H6B III, 2, 173. IV, 10, 53. H6C I, 4, 21. II, 3, 4. II, 6, 24. III, 2, 145. V, 2, 8. V, 4, 9. 68. Troil. I, 1, 7. I, 3, 114. 137. Cor. I, 3, 87. IV, 5, 118. Tit. II, 3, 117. 238. 241. 242. III, 2, 2. Rom. V, 1, 78. Hml. IV, 4, 45. Lr. IV, 6, 235. V, 3, 131. Ant. IV, 14, 49. IV, 15, 33. Cymb. IV, 2, 160. V, 1, 31. V, 5, 150. Per. I, 4, 49. Abstr. pro concr.: *conferring them on younger —s,* Lr. I, 1, 41; cf. Cor. IV, 7, 55.

In a relative sense, = any degree of personal force: *little s. rings out the doleful knell,* Lucr. 1495. *your swords are now too massy for your —s,* Tp. III, 3, 67. *what s. I have's mine own,* Epil. 2. As I, 2, 206. Shr. V, 2, 174.

2) power of resisting, fastness, solidity: *seven walled towns of s.* H6A III, 4, 7. *for s. and safety of our country,* H6C III, 3, 211. *the king's name is a tower of s.* R3 V, 3, 12. *thy country's s. and weakness,* Cor. IV, 5, 146. *all the policy, s. and defence, that Rome can make against them,* IV, 6, 127. *our castle's s. will laugh a siege to scorn,* Mcb. V, 5, 2.

3) power of mind; moral or intellectual force: *though she strive to try her s.* Pilgr. 317. *all advice my s. can give you,* Meas. I, 1, 7. *a charge too heavy for my s.* All's III, 3, 4. *we will, according to your —s and qualities, give you advancement,* H4B V, 5, 73 (Ff s.). *I have no s. in measure,* H5 V, 2, 140. *women may fall, when there's no s. in men,* Rom. II, 3, 80. *thou hast the s. of will to slay thyself,* IV, 1, 72. 125. *retentive to the s. of spirit,* Caes. I, 3, 95. *you do unbend your noble s., to think so brainsickly of things,* Mcb. II, 2, 45. *with all the s. and armour of the mind,* Hml. III, 3, 12.

4) force, efficiency, weight; energy: *no object but her passion's s. renews,* Lucr. 1103. *a power I have, but of what s. and nature I am not yet instructed,* Meas. I, 1, 80. *thy threats have no more s. than her weak prayers,* Mids. III, 2, 250. *with all religious s. of sacred vows,* John III, 1, 229. *those prisoners were not with such s. denied,* H4A I, 3, 25. *arguments of mighty s.* H6C III, 1, 49. *disguise the holy s. of their command,* Troil. II, 3, 136. *a proof of s. she could not publish more,* V, 2, 113 (= she could not publish a stronger proof; cf. *Of*). *this boy does reason our petition with more s. than thou hast to deny it,* Cor. V, 3, 176. *by the s. of their illusion,* Mcb. III, 5, 28. *whose* (circumstances') *s. I will confirm with oath,* Cymb. II, 4, 63. *whose wisdom's s.* Per. I, 2, 119.

5) power, sway, authority: *s. by limping sway disabled,* Sonn. 66, 8. *to leave poor me, thou hast the s. of laws,* 49, 13. *if thou wouldst use the s. of all thy state,* 96, 12. *in the very refuse of thy deeds there is such s. and warrantise of skill,* 150, 7. *ere they can behold bright Phoebus in his s.* Wint. IV, 4, 124. *to give him s. to make a more requital of your love,* John

II, 33. *bidding me depend upon thy stars, thy fortune and thy s.* III, 1, 126. *it shall be so i' the right and s. o' the commons,* Cor. III, 3, 14. *they stand in their ancient s.* IV, 2, 7. *no more deep will I endart mine eye than your consent gives s. to make it fly,* Rom. I, 3, 99. *our arms, in s. of malice, and our hearts of brothers' temper, do receive you in,* Caes. III, 1, 174 (having full power of doing you harm). *make your own purpose, how in my s. you please,* Lr. II, 1, 114. *grown to s.* Ant. I, 3, 48.

6) high degree, vehemence: *dishonoured me even in the s. and height of injury,* Err. V, 200. *you would abate the s. of your displeasure,* Merch. V, 198. *I'll wrestle with you in my s. of love,* Ant. III, 2, 62.

7) number, amount of force: *of what s. they are a-foot,* All's IV, 3, 181. *to descry the s. o' the enemy,* Lr. IV, 5, 14. V, 1, 52. Ant. II, 2, 164.

8) armed force, body of troops, army: *dissever your united —s,* John II, 388. *should draw his several —s together,* H4B I, 3, 76. *all France with their chief assembled s.* H6A I, 1, 139. *gather s. and march unto him straight,* IV, 1, 73. *leader of our English s.* IV, 3, 17. *then from Ireland come I with my s.* H6B III, 1, 380. H6C V, 3, 22. R3 IV, 3, 50 (Qq *army*). IV, 4, 449. V, 3, 26 (Ff *power*). Tit. I, 43. 194. Ant. II, 1, 17.

**Strengthen,** 1) tr. to make stronger or more efficacious: Sonn. 102, 1. All's II, 4, 51. Tw. V, 162. John III, 1, 103. H4B II, 2, 30. H6C I, 2, 58 (*s. themselves*). II, 6, 7. III, 1, 52. IV, 1, 37. H8 V, 3, 118. Tit. I, 214. Caes. II, 1, 248 (*to s. that impatience*). Hml. V, 1, 317. Per. IV, 6, 114.

2) to grow stronger and stronger: *they s. from strange to stranger,* Tp. V, 227.

**Strengthless,** wanting strength, weak: Ven. 153. Lucr. 709. H4B I, 1, 141. H6A II, 5, 13.

**Stretch,** 1) tr. a) to extend (German: *recken,* and *strecken*): *the duke dare no more s. this finger of mine than he dare rack his own,* Meas. V, 316; cf. *would upon the rack of this tough world s. him out longer,* Lr. V, 3, 315. *their (groans') discharge did s. his leathern coat almost to bursting,* As II, 1, 37. *—ed along like a wounded knight,* III, 2, 253. *if both gain, all the gift doth s. itself as 'tis received, and is enough for both,* All's II, 1, 4. *upon uneasy pallets —ing thee,* H4B III, 1, 10. *my grief —es itself beyond the hour of death,* IV, 4, 57. *he —ed him, and, with one hand on his dagger, ... he did discharge a horrible oath,* H8 I, 2, 204 (he rose to his full height). *if you might please to s. it* (your cheveril conscience) II, 3, 33. *reverend for thy —ed out life,* Troil. I, 3, 61. *leave nothing out for length, and make us think rather our state's defective for requital than we to s. it out,* Cor. II, 2, 55 (to extend, i. e. to show or offer it). *thus far having —ed it* (your hand) III, 2, 74. *my sinews shall be —ed upon him,* V, 6, 45. *I s. it out for that word 'broad',* Rom. II, 4, 89. *have I in conquest —ed mine arm so far,* Caes. II, 2, 66. *would s. thy spirits up into the air,* Lr. IV, 2, 23. *Caesar's ambition, which swelled so much that it did almost s. the sides o' the world,* Cymb. III, 1, 50.

b) to open wide: *how shall we s. our eye when capital crimes appear before us,* H5 II, 2, 55. *s. the nostril wide,* III, 1, 15. *his nostrils —ed with struggling,* H6B III, 2, 171.

c) to strain, to put to the utmost strength or efficacy: *the ox hath —ed his yoke in vain,* Mids. II, 1, 93. *s. thy chest,* Troil. IV, 5, 10. *let our alliance be combined, our best friends made, our means —ed,* Caes. IV, 1, 44. *ducking observants that s. their duties nicely* Lr. II, 2, 110. *since your kindness we have —ed thus far,* Per. V, 1, 55. cf. Cor. V, 6, 45. *—ed =* strained, constrained, affected, exaggerated: *—ed metre of an antique song,* Sonn. 17, 12. *extremely —ed and conned with cruel pain,* Mids. V, 80. *to hear the wooden dialogue and sound 'twixt his —ed footing and the scaffoldage,* Troil. I, 3, 156.

2) intr. a) to be extended, to be drawn out: *there's not a minute of our lives should s. without some pleasure now,* Ant. I, 1, 46.

b) to reach, to extend to: *the —ing of a span buckles in his sum of age,* As III, 2, 139. *had it* (his skill) *—ed so far,* All's I, 1, 22. *so far as my coin would s.* H4A I, 2, 62. *which* (his lust) *—ed to their servants,* R3 III, 5, 82. *it* (his will) *—es beyond you, to your friends,* H8 I, 2, 141. *that the precipitation might down s. below the beam of sight,* Cor. III, 2, 4. *a wit of cheveril, that —es from an inch narrow to an ell broad,* Rom. II, 4, 87. *his means may well s. so far as to annoy us all,* Caes. II, 1, 159. *will the line s. out to the crack of doom?* Mcb. IV, 1, 117.

**Stretch-mouthed,** open-mouthed: Wint. IV, 4, 196.

**Strew** (spelling of O. Edd.) or **Strow** (rhyming to *dew* in Rom. V, 3, 12; to *so* in Cymb. IV, 2, 287. Impf. *—ed* in Per. I, 4, 23, a rather doubtful passage; partic. *strewn* in Tw. II, 4, 61; everywhere else *strewed*) 1) to scatter, to spread by scattering: *rushes —ed,* Shr. IV, 1, 48. *not a flower on my coffin let there be —n,* Tw II, 4, 61. *has —ed repentant ashes on his head,* John IV, 1, 111. R3 I, 3, 242. Cor. V, 5, 3. Caes. I, 1, 55. Cymb. III, 6, 50. IV, 2, 287. Per. I, 4, 23 (?). Metaphorically: *s. good luck on every sacred room,* Wiv. V, 5, 61. *so I have —ed it in the common ear,* Meas. I, 3, 15. *she may s. dangerous conjectures in ill-breeding minds,* Hml. IV, 5, 14. *smooth success be —ed before your feet,* Ant. I, 3, 101.

2) to spread by being scattered over, to cover with things scattered: *—ing her way with flowers,* LLL IV, 3, 380. *whose delay is —ed with sweets,* All's II, 4, 45. *to s. him o'er and o'er,* Wint. IV, 4, 129. John I, 216. R2 I, 3, 289. V, 2, 47. H8 IV, 2, 168. Troil. IV, 5, 166. Rom. V, 3, 12. 17. 36. 281. Hml. V, 1, 269. Cymb. IV, 2, 390. Per. IV, 1, 15.

**Strewings,** things strewed: *s. fittest for graves,* Cymb. IV, 2, 285.

**Strewments,** the same: *she is allowed her virgin crants, her maiden s.* Hml. V, 1, 256.

**Strict,** 1) tight, close: *she wildly breaketh from their s. embrace,* Ven. 874.

2) exact, accurate, rigorously nice; a) used of things: *keep the obsequy so s.* Phoen. 12. *s. statutes and most biting laws,* Meas. I, 3, 19. *a more s. restraint,* I, 4, 4. *other s. observances,* LLL I, 1, 36. *the —est decrees,* 117. *with what s. patience have I sat,* IV, 3, 165 (German: *mit peinlicher Geduld*). *my s. fast,* R2 II, 1, 80. *I will call him to so s. account,* H4A III, 2, 149. *keep aloof from s. arbitrement,* IV, 1, 70. *your s. preciseness,* H6A V, 4, 67. *such s. and severe covenants,* 114. *you undergo too s. a paradox, striving to make an ugly deed look fair,* Tim. III, 5, 24 (= what is too strictly, too positively a paradox?). *law is s.*

85. *this s. and most observant watch*, Hml. I, 1, 71. *take no — er render*, Cymb. V, 4, 17. *our s. edict*, Per. I, 1, 111. *this s. charge*, II, 1, 131. — b) of persons, = 1) severe, proceeding by exact rules: *the s. deputy*, Meas. I, 2, 186. *this s. court of Venice*, Merch. IV, 1, 204. *I was too s. to make mine own away*, R2 I, 3, 244. *this fell sergeant, death, is s. in his arrest*, Hml. V, 2, 348. 2) rigorous, hard, cruel: *the s. fates*, Per. III, 3, 8.

**Strictly**, exactly, severely, without remission or indulgence: *the king hath s. charged the contrary*, R3 IV, 1, 17 (Qq *straitly*). *she has so s. tied her to her chamber*, Per. II, 5, 8.

**Stricture**, strictness: *a man of s. and firm abstinence*, Meas. I, 3, 12.

**Stride**, subst. a step; especially a long and proud step: *turn two mincing steps into a manly s.* Merch. III, 4, 68. *every tedious s.* R2 I, 3, 268. *every s. he makes upon my land is dangerous treason*, III, 3, 92. *a s. and a stand*, Troil. III, 3, 252. *follow his —s*, Tim. I, 1, 80. *the —s they victors made*, Cymb. V, 3, 43. In Mcb. II, 1, 55 M. Edd. *—s*, O. Edd. *sides.*

**Stride**, vb. (cf. *Bestride*) 1) to step over: *a debtor, that not dares to s. a limit*, Cymb. III, 3, 35.

2) to mount as a rider: *I mean to s. your steed*, Cor. I, 9, 71. *—ing the blast*, Mcb. I, 7, 22.

**Strife**, 1) endeavour: *one that, above all other —s, contended especially to know himself*, Meas. III, 2, 246. *with s. to please you*, All's V, 3, 338. *I'll do my best to woo your lady: yet, a barful s.! whoe'er I woo, myself would be his wife*, Tw. I, 4, 41. *I do beseech thee to cease thy s., and leave me to my grief*, Rom. II, 2, 152 (M. Edd. *suit*).

2) endeavour to excel another, emulation: *his art with nature's workmanship at s.* Ven. 291. *the red blood reeked, to show the painter's s.* Lucr. 1377 (cf. 1374). *then son and father weep with equal s. who should weep most*, 1791. *artificial s. lives in these touches, livelier than life*, Tim. I, 1, 37.

3) contrariety, contradiction, variance: *as if between them twain (life and death) there were no s.* Lucr. 405. *for the peace of you I hold such s. as 'twixt a miser and his wealth is found*, Sonn. 75, 3. *if thou keep promise, I shall end this s.* (of being ashamed to be my father's child), Merch. II, 3, 20. *both here and hence pursue me lasting s.* Hml. III, 2, 232.

4) discord, contention, contest, combat, fight: *nature, with herself at s.* Ven. 11. *civil home-bred s.* 764. Lucr. 143. 236. 689. 899. Err. III, 2, 28. Mids. V, 228. Shr. II, 343. III, 1, 21. All's II, 3, 308. John II, 63. R2 V, 6, 27. H6A I, 3, 70. III, 1, 88. IV, 1, 123. 151. IV, 4, 39. V, 1, 13. V, 5, 63. H6B II, 1, 58. H6C I, 2, 4. R3 II, 1, 74. Troil. IV, 5, 93. Tit. III, 1, 193. Rom. I Chor. 8. III, 1, 183. Caes. I, 3, 11. III, 1, 263. Lr. I, 1, 45. V, 3, 42. Oth. II, 3, 258. Ant. II, 2, 80.·

**Strike**. Impf. *struck:* H6A I, 4, 80. IV, 6, 10. H6B IV, 7, 84. H6C II, 1, 132. Cor. II, 2, 99. 117. Caes. IV, 3, 22. Mcb. III, 1, 123. *stroke* (M. Edd. *struck):* Shr. II, 1, 154. Tw. IV, 1, 38. Troil. I, 2, 35. Lr. II, 4, 162 (Ff *strooke*). *strook* or *strooke* (M. Edd. *struck):* Tp. II, 1, 313. Err. II, 1, 52. H4A I, 3, 139. H4B I, 1, 44. IV, 5, 152. V, 2, 80. R3 I, 4, 19. Troil. I, 2, 6. Cor. IV, 2, 19. Rom. II, 5, 1. Caes. III, 1, 182. V, 1, 44. Lr. II, 4, 162 (Qq *stroke*). Ant. III, 11, 36. Cymb. V, 3, 9. 70. V, 5, 154. — Partic. *struck:* Wint.

I, 2, 358. John IV, 2, 235. R2 IV, 277. H4A IV, 2, 21. V, 4, 107. H5 II, 4, 54. H6A I, 1, 134. I, 4, 75. H6B I, 1, 54. IV, 2, 28. IV, 7, 86. 87. R3 I, 4, 228. Tit. II, 1, 93 (Q1 *strooke*).. II, 3, 117 (Ff Q2 *strook*). III, 1, 258. Cor. V, 6, 149. Caes. I, 2, 177. Hml. V, 2, 25 (Qq *strooke*). *stroke* (M. Edd. *struck*): Wiv. V, 5, 1. R3 V, 3, 217. Troil. II, 2, 7. Tit. I, 364. Hml. III, 2, 339 (Qq *strooke*). Ant. III, 1, 1. *strook* or *strooke* (M. Edd. *struck*): Tp. V, 25. Wiv. V, 2, 11. Err. III, 1, 56. Shr. II, 362. H4B V, 4, 11. H5 IV, 8, 27. R3 I, 1, 92. H8 V, 1, 1. Cor. I, 6, 4. II, 2, 80. IV, 1, 8. IV, 5, 230. Tit. II, 1, 93 (Ff Q2 *struck*). II, 3, 117 (Q1 *struck*). Rom. I, 1, 167. Tim. I, 1, 23. Mcb. IV, 3, 225. Hml. I, 1, 7. I, 4, 4. II, 2, 620. III, 2, 339 (Ff *stroke*). V, 2, 25 (Ff *struck*). 378. Ant. I, 2, 87. Cymb. III, 4, 117. IV, 2, 320. *strucken:* Lucr. 217. Err. I, 2, 45. Caes. II, 2, 114. Hml. III, 2, 282 (Qq *strooken*; the surreptitious Q1 and M. Edd. *stricken*). Lr. I, 4, 94 (Qq *struck*). *stroken:* Cor. IV, 5, 156. Caes. III, 1, 209. *strooken:* LLL IV, 3, 224 Rom. I, 1, 238. Hml. III, 2, 282 (Ff *strucken*). *stricken:* R2 V, 1, 25 (Qq *thrown*). Caes. II, 1, 192.

1) to make to disappear, to efface, to blot (Germ. *streichen*): *that thou didst love her, —s some scores away from the great compt*, All's V, 3, 56. *all damage else ... shall be stroke off*, Troil. II, 2, 7. *her presence shall quite s. off all service I have done*, III, 3, 29. *I shall s. off this score of absence*, Oth. III, 4, 179.

As a naval term, used of sails, = to lower, to let down: *must s. sail to spirits of vile sort*, H4B V, 2, 18 (= do them homage). *now Margaret must s. her sail and learn a while to serve*, H6C III, 3, 5. Absol.: *we see the wind sit sore upon our sails, and yet we s. not*, R2 II, 1, 266. *than bear so low a sail, to s. to thee*, H6C V, 1, 52.

2) to make or give a blow; absol.: *s. now, or else the iron cools*, H6C V, 1, 49. *thou hast stroke upon my crest*, Tit. I, 364. *s. on the tinder*, Oth. I, 1, 141. With an obj.: *the fire i'the flint shows not till it be strook*, Tim. I, 1, 23.

= to beat (with the hand or a stick); absol.: *shall I s.?* Gent. III, 1, 199. *he strook so plainly*, Err. II, 1, 52. *now you s. like the blind man*, Ado II, 1, 205. *I'll cuff you, if you s. again*, Shr. II, 221. *as he is —ing, holds his infant up*, H4B IV, 1, 212. *thou canst s., canst thou?* Troil. II, 1, 20. With an obj.: *he —s her on the cheeks*, Ven. 475. *who wouldst thou s.?* Gent. III, 1, 200. *let him not s. the old woman*, Wiv. IV, 2, 190. Mids. II, 1, 205. III, 2, 269. 303. Shr. II, 154. 223. Tw. III, 2, 88. IV, 1, 38. R2 V, 2, 85. H4A II, 2, 76. H4B I, 2, 63. V, 2, 80. V, 4, 11. H5 IV, 7, 184. IV, 8, 32. 43. H6B I, 3, 150. H8 III, 2, 117. Troil. I, 2, 6. II, 1, 24. 40. Cor. IV, 5, 156. Tit. III, 2, 14. Lr. I, 3, 1. I, 4, 94. 277. Oth. IV, 1, 193. 283. IV, 3, 91. Ant. II, 5, 42. 82. Per. V, 1, 192. With *at*, = to offer a blow: *to s. at me*, Lr. II, 2, 124. Oth. II, 1, 280.

Used of any hurt inflicted or offered with any weapon; absol.: *what needs a second —ing?* Ven. 250. *makest a show but darest not s.* Tp. I, 2, 470. *well strook! there was blow for blow!* Err. III, 1, 56. *s. home*, Meas. I, 3, 41. *his sword did ne'er leave —ing in the field*, H6A IV, 4, 81. *he stirs: shall I s.?* R3 I, 4, 164. *struck home to show my strength*, Tit. II, 3, 117. *I s. quickly, being moved*, Rom. I, 1, 7. 8. *foes that s. beside us*, Mcb. V, 7, 29. *in rage —s wide,*

Hml. II, 2, 494. *he dies that —s again,* Lr. II, 2, 53. *shall I s. now?* Ant. IV, 14, 93. *nor feel him* (death) *where he strooke,* Cymb. V, 3, 70. With *at,* = to aim at, to direct or point one's weapon at: *it cannot be, seeing his beauty, thou shouldst s. at it,* Ven. 938. *though you have ta'en a special stand to s. at me, your arrow hath glanced,* Wiv. V, 5, 248. *myself would s. at thy life,* Ado IV, 1, 129. *she —s at the brow,* LLL IV, 1, 119. *the heavens do s. at my injustice,* Wint. III, 2, 148. R2 III, 2, 86. Cor. I, 1, 70. 244. V, 6, 20. Tit. III, 2, 52. Tim. III, 5, 114. Caes. IV, 3, 105. Mcb. V, 7, 17. Hml. I, 1, 140. II, 2, 491. Transitively (sometimes = to kill): *he* (the boar) *—s whate'er is in his way,* Ven. 623. 624. *doth bend his bow to s. a doe,* Lucr. 581. *the deer that thou shouldst s.* Pilgr. 300. *calumny the whitest virtue —s,* Meas. III, 2, 198. *thousands that had struck anointed kings,* Wint. I, 2, 358 (= killed). *death hath not struck so fat a deer to-day,* H4A V, 4, 107. *a struck fowl,* IV, 2, 21. *s. those that hurt,* H6A III, 3, 53. *as if they struck their friends,* H6C II, 1, 132. *s. her* (this dainty doe) *home by force, if not by words,* Tit. II, 1, 118. *hast not thou full often struck a doe,* 93. *s. me the counterfeit matron,* Tim. IV, 3, 112. 152. *when I strooke him* (Caesar) Caes. III, 1, 182. *a deer, stroken by many princes,* 209. *struck the foremost man of all this world,* IV, 3, 22. V, 1, 44. Mcb. III, 3, 225. Hml. III, 2, 282. V, 2, 378. Lr. II, 4, 162. Oth. II, 3, 243. Ant. III, 11, 36. IV, 14, 68. Cymb. III, 3, 74.

The instrument as object: *he struck his hand upon his breast,* Lucr. 1842. *when I s. my foot upon the bosom of the ground,* John IV, 1, 2. *strooke his heels against the sides,* H4B I, 1, 44. *s. in their bare arms pins,* Lr. II, 3, 15.

The effect produced as object: *when from the Dauphins crest thy sword struck fire,* H6A IV, 6, 10. *that my words have struck but thus much show of fire from Brutus,* Caes. I, 2, 177. cf. *who strooke this heat up?* H4A I, 3, 139. Especially *blow* or *stroke* as object: R2 IV, 277. H6B IV, 7, 84. Cor. IV, 1, 8. IV, 2, 19. Per. I, 2, 59. H5 II, 1, 68. H6A I, 1, 134. I, 5, 35. Troil. V, 7, 3. Ant. IV, 14, 91. The effect expressed by a double accus.: *to s. a person dead,* Ven. 250. 948. Sonn. 86, 6. Mids. IV, 1, 86. As III, 3, 14. John IV, 3, 98. H6B IV, 7, 87. R3 I, 2, 64. 151. I, 4, 228. Troil. I, 3, 115. Rom. I, 5, 61. Ant. IV, 14, 108. *s. flat the thick rotundity of the world,* Lr. III, 2, 7 (Qq *smite*). By an accus. with an adverb or a prepositional expression: *would with the sceptre straight be strucken down,* Lucr. 217. *now subscribe your names, that his own hand may s. his honour down that violates ...,* LLL I, 1, 20. *a new world's crown, which our profane hours here have stricken down,* R2 V, 1, 25 (Qq *thrown*). *then is sin struck down like an ox,* H6B IV, 2, 28. *stroke him down,* Troil. I, 2, 35. *wail his fall who I myself struck down,* Mcb. III, 1, 123. *strooke down some mortally,* Cymb. V, 3, 9. *one of thy eyes and thy cheek's side struck off,* H6A I, 4, 75. *s. off his head,* H6B IV, 1, 69. IV, 7, 116. Hml. V, 2, 25. *I will s. it out soundly* (the glove in his cap) H5 IV, 7, 135. *who did s. out the light?* Mcb. III, 3, 19. *strooke me overboard,* R3 I, 4, 19. *let the mutinous winds s. the proud cedars 'gainst the fiery sun,* Cor. V, 3, 60. *hath from this most bravest vessel of the world strooke the main-top,* Cymb. IV, 2, 320. *struck him on his knee,* Cor. II, 2, 99 (so that he fell on his knee). *I'll s.*

*thee to my foot,* R3 I, 2, 41. *to s. me to death with mortal joy,* Cymb. V, 5, 235.

3) to use one's weapons, to be active in fight or on any occasion of employing force: *to those Italian fields, where noble fellows s.* All's II, 3, 308. *s.! down with them!* H4A II, 2, 87. *since we have begun to s.* H6C II, 2, 167. *smile, gentle heaven! or s., ungentle death!* II, 3, 6. *the still and mental parts, that do contrive how many hands shall s.* Troil. I, 3, 201. *when thou art forth in the incursions, thou —st as slow as another,* II, 1, 32. *s., fellows, s.* V, 8, 10. *clubs, bills, and partisans! s.!* Rom. I, 1, 80. *if we and Caius Marcius chance to meet, 'tis sworn between us we shall ever s. till one can do no more,* Cor. I, 2, 35. *s., you slave,* Lr. II, 2, 44. 45. *he'll s., and quickly too,* V, 3, 285. *woo't thou fight well? I'll s. and cry 'Take all,'* Ant. IV, 2, 8. *if thou fear to s. and to make me certain it is done,* Cymb. III, 4, 31. *do his bidding, s.* 73. *that —ing in our country's cause fell bravely,* V, 4, 71. *the sinful father seemed not to s., but smooth,* Per. I, 2, 78. *he should have struck, not spoke,* IV, 2, 69. Quite = to fight: *God's arm s. with us!* H5 IV, 3, 5. *whiles we have strooke,* Cor. I, 6, 4. *s. not by land,* Ant. III, 8, 3. Even actively: *when Cressy battle fatally was struck,* H5 II, 4, 54; cf. the subst. *stroke* in Cymb. V, 5, 468.

Hence in general, = to act not by fair means, but by force: *such as will s. sooner than speak,* H4A II, 1, 85. *there speak, and s., brave boys,* Tit. II, 1, 129 (cf. 118). *speak, s., redress!* Caes. II, 1, 47. 55. 56. cf. Per. I, 2, 78; IV, 2, 69, and the subst. *Striker;* and *stroke* in Caes. V, 1, 29.

4) to afflict, to punish, to chastise: *to s. and gall them for what I bid them do,* Meas. I, 3, 36. *whose cruel —ing kills for faults of his own liking,* III, 2, 281. *oft have I struck those that I never saw,* H6B IV, 7, 86. *it —s where it doth love,* Oth. V, 2, 22. *now, darting Parthia, art thou stroke,* Ant. III, 1, 1. *pardon me, or s. me, if you please,* Per. I, 2, 46. *there to s. the inhospitable Cleon,* V, 1, 253.

Applied to superhuman powers, especially to the influence of planets, = to blast, to destroy, to confound: *a bawdy planet, that will s. where 'tis predominant,* Wint. I, 2, 201. *armies of pestilence, and they shall s. your children,* R2 III, 3, 87. *struck Corioli like a planet,* Cor. II, 2, 117. *the red pestilence s. all trades in Rome,* IV, 1, 13. *some planet s. me down,* Tit. II, 4, 14. *then no planets s.* Hml. I, 1, 162. *s. her young bones, you taking airs, with lameness,* Lr. II, 4, 165. *so had you* (Gods) *... strooke me,* Cymb. V, 1, 10.

5) to affect in a particular manner by a sudden impression: *his meaning struck her ere his words begun,* Ven. 462. *it strooke mine ear most terribly,* Tp. II, 1, 313. *I am strook to the quick,* V, 25. *a savour that may s. the dullest nostril,* Wint. I, 2, 421. *thou —st me sorely,* V, 1, 17. *s. all that look upon with marvel,* V, 3, 100. *how cold it strooke my heart,* H4B IV, 5, 152. *some sudden qualm hath struck me at the heart,* H6B I, 1, 54. *I am struck with sorrow,* Cor. V, 6, 149. *guilty creatures have been strook so to the soul,* Hml. II, 2, 620. *with this ungracious paper s. the sight of the death-practised duke,* Lr. IV, 6, 283. *a Roman thought hath strooke him,* Ant. I, 2, 87. *Pompey's name —s more than could his war resisted,* I, 4, 54. *high events as these s. those that make them,* V, 2, 364. *your cause doth s. my heart with pity,* Cymb. I, 6, 118. *mine ear, therein false strooke,* III, 4, 117. *it —s me, past the*

*hope of comfort*, IV, 3, 8. *fairness which —s the eye*, V, 5, 168.

The effect produced as object: *should s. such terror to his enemies*, H6A II, 3, 24. *shadows have stroke more terror to the soul of Richard*, R3 V, 3, 217. *will s. amazement to their drowsy spirits*, Troil. II, 2, 210. *—s life into my speech*, Cymb. III, 3, 97. The effect expressed by a double accus.: *strooken blind*, LLL IV, 3, 224. *I will ... s. the Dauphin blind to look on us*, H5 I, 2, 280. *strooken blind*, Rom. I, 1, 238. *s. the wise dumb*, Ven. 1146. *this parting —s poor lovers dumb*, Gent. II, 2, 21. *deep shame had struck me dumb*, John IV, 2, 235. *with this dear sight struck pale and bloodless*, Tit. III, 1, 258. *which struck her sad*, Lucr. 262. *things to s. honour sad*, H8 I, 2, 126. By a prepositional expression: *which —s him into melancholy*, Ado II, 1, 154. *your behaviour hath stroke her into amazement*, Hml. III, 2, 339.

6) to cause to sound by percussion: *how one string ... —s each in each*, Sonn. 8, 10. *clamorous groans which s. upon my heart, which is the bell*, R2 V, 5, 56. *she s. upon the bell*, Mcb. II, 1, 32. *new sorrows s. heaven on the face that it resounds*, IV, 3, 6. Hence used of clocks, trans. and intr.: *it* (the watch) *will s.* Tp. II, 1, 13. *it hath strooke ten o' clock*, Wiv. V, 2, 11. V, 5, 1. Err. I, 2, 45. 67. IV, 2, 54. H6A I, 2, 42. R3 IV, 2, 115. 116. H8 V, 1, 1. Rom. I, 1, 167. II, 5, 1. Caes. II, 1, 192. II, 2, 114. Hml. I, 1, 7. I, 4, 4. Cymb. V, 5, 154. Of mill-wheels: *as fast as mill-wheels s.* Tp. I, 2, 281.

Used of drums, trans. and intr.: *s. alarum, drums!* R3 IV, 4, 148. *s., I say*, 150. *when the alarum were strooke*, Cor. II, 2, 80. *s. drum*, Rom. I, 4, 114. *s.! Tim.* IV, 3, 175. *let our drums s.* V, 4, 85. Lr. V, 3, 81. Figuratively: *his beating heart, alarum —ing*, Lucr. 433. With *up: s. up the drums*, John V, 2, 164. 179. H4B IV, 2, 120. *whilst any trump did sound, or drum struck up*, H6A I, 4, 80. *s. up drums*, H6C II, 1, 204. *drummer, s. up*, IV, 7, 50. *s. up the drum*, V, 3, 24. R3 IV, 4, 179. *you shall have the drum strooke up*, Cor. IV, 5, 230. *s. up the drum towards Athens*, Tim. IV, 3, 169.

And hence of any music: *s. up, pipers*, Ado V, 4, 130. *come on, s. up!* Wint. IV, 4, 161. 165. *music, awake her, s.!* V, 3, 98. *s. a free march to Troy*, Troil. V, 10, 30. *that heaven and earth may s. their sounds together*, Ant. IV, 8, 38.

7) particular significations: *we shall play a set shall s. his father's crown into the hazard*, H5 I, 2, 263 (= set on the hazard. German: *in die Schanze schlagen*). *s. the vessels*, Ant. II, 7, 103 (= tap, broach). *struck in years* = of an advanced age: *myself am strooke in years*, Shr. II, 362. *well strooke in years*, R3 I, 1, 92.

**Striker**, one who is ready to use force: *no foot land-rakers, no long-staff sixpenny —s*, H4A II, 1, 82 (*striker*, as well as the verb *to strike*, seem to have been technical terms in the slang of thieves and highwaymen, for robber and to rob. cf. Nares' and Dyce's Glossaries).*

**String**, subst. any thin line or cord: *I'll knit it* (the hair) *up in silken —s*, Gent. II, 7, 45. *spiders' —s*, Meas. III, 2, 289. *good —s to your beards*, Mids. IV, 2, 36 (to tie them fast). *hast had my purse as if the —s were thine*, Oth. I, 1, 3.

= fibre, nerve, tendon (cf. *Heart - string*): John

V, 7, 55. H8 III, 2, 105. Hml. III, 3, 70. Lr. V, 3, 216. Ant. III, 11, 57.

= the cord of a musical instrument: Sonn. 8, 9. Gent. IV, 2, 60. R2 V, 5, 46. H4A II, 4, 6. H6B II, 1, 57. R3 IV, 4, 364 (*harp not on that s.*). Troil. I, 3, 109. Tit. II, 4, 46 (*silken —s*). Caes. IV, 3, 292. Per. I, 1, 81.

**String**, vb., used only in the partic. *strung* = furnished with strings: *Orpheus' lute was strung with poets' sinews*, Gent. III, 2, 78. LLL IV, 3, 343.

**Stringless**, having no strings or cords: *a s. instrument*, R2 II, 1, 149.

**Strip**, 1) to pull off: *then will he s. his sleeve*, H5 IV, 3, 47. *she —ed it from her arm*, Cymb. II, 4, 101.

2) to make naked, to deprive of covering: *how, in —ing it, you more invest it*, Tp. II, 1, 225. *s. myself to death*, Meas. II, 4, 102. *there —ed himself*, As IV, 3, 147. *to drown my clothes, and say I was —ed*, All's IV, 1, 58. *s. your sword stark naked*, Tw. III, 4, 274. *s. thine own back*, Lr. IV, 6, 165.

2) Metaphorically, = a) to take away: *all the temporal lands would they s. from us*, H5 I, 1, 11. b) to deprive: *—ed her from his benediction*, Lr. IV, 3, 45. *if such tricks s. you out of your lieutenantry*, Oth. II, 1, 173.

**Stripe**, a stroke made with a lash: Tp. I, 2, 345. Wint. IV, 3, 60. Cor. V, 6, 108. Ant. III, 13, 152.

**Stripling**, a youth, a lad: Shr. I, 2, 144. R3 I, 3, 101. Cymb. V, 3, 19.

**Strive** (impf. *strived*: Lucr. 52. Per. V Prol. 16. *strove*: All's I, 1, 241. Lr. IV, 3, 18. Partic. *strove*: H8 II, 4, 30) 1) to make efforts, to do one's best, to endeavour: *s., man, and speak*, Cymb. V, 5, 152. With *for*, = to make efforts to attain: *for enlargement —ing*, H4A III, 1, 31. *s. by factions ... for rule and empery*, Tit. I, 18. Usually with an inf.: *crows that s. to overfly them*, Ven. 324. *nor sun nor wind will ever s. to kiss you*, 1082. Lucr. 504. 1665. Sonn. 103, 9. 112, 5. Tp. I, 2, 459. III, 1, 23. Meas. III, 1, 22. LLL IV, 1, 37. V, 2, 518. All's I, 1, 241. II, 3, 152. III, 3, 5. Tw. V, 417. Wint. IV, 4, 543. John IV, 2, 28. R2 III, 2, 97. 114. V, 1, 100. H6B IV, 1, 98. R3 I, 4, 36. H8 II, 4, 30. Cor. III, 2, 20. Rom. I Chor. 14. Tim. III, 3, 32. III, 5, 25. Lr. I, 1, 87. I, 4, 369. II, 1, 110. III, 1, 10. Oth. II, 3, 364. Ant. I, 1, 50. Per. II Prol. 19. V Prol. 16. In H8 I, 2, 169 O. Edd. *bid him s. to the love o'the commonalty;* F4 and M. Edd. *s. to gain the love.*

2) to try (without the notion of effort): *I did s. to prove the constancy and virtue of your love*, Sonn. 117, 13. *though she s. to try her strength*, Pilgr. 317. *if I did think I were well awake, I'ld s. to tell you*, Tp. V, 230. *thou wrongest thyself, if thou shouldst s. to choose*, All's II, 3, 153. *I'll s. to take a nap*, R3 V, 3, 104.

3) to contend, to struggle, to resist: *mastering what not —s*, Compl. 240. *but if thou s., poor soul, what art thou then?* LLL IV, 1, 94. *nay, if thou s.* Oth. V, 2, 81. With *against*: *in vain you s. against the stream*, Ven. 772. *I know I love in vain, s. against hope*, All's I, 3, 207. *do not s. against my vows*, IV, 2, 14. *that 'gainst the stream of virtue they may s.* Tim. IV, 1, 27. *to s. with* = to struggle against: *think women still to s. with men, to sin and never for to saint*, Pilgr. 341. *so —s the woodcock with the gin*, H6C I, 4, 61. *vex not yourself, nor s. not with your breath,*

R2 II, 1, 3 (i. e. your want of breath imposing the necessity of being silent). *now bid me run, and I will s. with things impossible; yea, get the better of them,* Caes. II, 1, 325.

4) to quarrel, to be in contention or dispute: *do as adversaries do in law, s. mightily, but eat and drink as friends,* Shr. I, 2, 279. *you do me double wrong, to s. for that which resteth in my choice,* III, 1, 17. *the fatal colours of our — ing houses,* H6C II, 5, 98. *s. no more,* Tit. III, 1, 178.

5) to emulate, to vie: *variable passions throng her constant woe, as — ing who should best become her grief,* Ven. 968. *they both would s. who first should dry his tears,* 1092. *within whose face beauty and virtue —d which of them both should underprop her fame,* Lucr. 52. *adoption —s with nature,* All's I, 3, 151. *daughter and mother so s. upon your pulse,* 175. *patience and sorrow s. who should express her goodliest,* Lr. IV, 3, 18. *a piece of work so bravely done, so rich, that it did s. in workmanship and value,* Cymb. II, 4, 73 (it was doubtful, which of the two, workmanship or value, was greatest). cf. Lr. I, 1, 87.

**Stroke,** subst. 1) any sudden act of one body upon another: *oared himself with his good arms in lusty s. to the shore,* Tp. II, 1, 119. *wounds the unsisting postern with these —s,* Meas. IV, 2, 92. *the oars, which to the tune of flutes kept s.* Ant. II, 2, 200. *amorous of their —s,* 202.

= blow: *as you love —s,* Err. II, 2, 8. *enraged him on to offer —s,* H4B IV, 1, 211. Cor. III, 3, 79. 97. Oth. IV, 1, 285. Cymb. III, 5, 40.

= a cut or thrust made with a weapon: *one s. shall free thee,* Tp. II, 1, 292. *with bloodless s.* Tw. II, 5, 117. *without s. or wound,* John II, 418. H6C II, 1, 54 (allusion to the proverb: *many —s fell great oaks*). II, 3, 3. R3 V, 3, 90. Troil. IV, 5, 93. Cor. I, 4, 58. Caes. V, 1, 29. 30. Mcb. I, 2, 38. V, 4, 20. V, 7, 15. Lr. IV, 2, 77. Ant. IV, 14, 117. *to give a s.* H6A IV, 1, 22. *to strike a s.* H5 II, 1, 68. H6A I, 1, 134. I, 5, 35. Troil. V, 7, 3. Ant. IV, 14, 91. = death-blow: *the Destinies will curse thee for this s.* Ven. 945. *the bloodiest shame, the wildest savagery, the vildest s.* John IV, 3, 48. R2 III, 1, 31. R3 I, 2, 178. Rom. III, 3, 23. Ant. V, 1, 64. V, 2, 298.

3) the agency of any hostile and pernicious power: *free from oppression or the s. of war,* H6A V, 3, 155. *Henry ... all that made me happy at one s. has taken,* H8 II, 1, 117. *when the greatest s. of fortune falls,* II, 2, 36. *'tis fond to wail inevitable —s,* Cor. IV, 1, 26. *what not done, that thou hast cause to rue, wherein I had no s. of mischief in it,* Tit. V, 1, 110. *your potent and infectious fevers heap on Athens, ripe for s.* Tim. IV, 1, 23. *their fears of hostile —s,* V, 1, 202. *nor all deserve the common s. of war,* V, 4, 22. *virtue itself scapes not calumnious —s,* Hml. I, 3, 38. *whom the heavens' plagues have humbled to all —s,* Lr. IV, 1, 68. *the nimble s. of quick cross lightning,* IV, 7, 34. *some distressful s. that my youth suffered,* Oth. I, 3, 157. *thou art past the tyrant's s.* Cymb. IV, 2, 265.

4) the sound of a clock announcing a full hour: *upon the s. of four,* R3 III, 2, 5. IV, 2, 115. V, 3, 235. *thou keepest the s.* IV, 2, 117.

5) fighting, giving battle: *ere the s. of this battle,* Cymb. V, 5, 468 (cf. *strike* in H5 II, 4, 54).

6) a line (as made with a pen): *his life is parallel'd even with the s. and line of his great justice,* Meas. IV, 2, 83.

**Stroke,** vb. to rub gently with the hand: Ven. 45. Tp. I, 2, 333. Ado V, 1, 15. As I, 2, 75. H4B II, 4, 106. Troil. I, 3, 165. V, 2, 51.

**Strond** (most M. Edd. *strand*) the shore, the beach: Lucr. 1436. Merch. I, 1, 171. Shr. I, 1, 175 (F4 *strand*). H4A I, 1, 4. H4B I, 1, 62. H8 V, 4, 55 (a quarter of London. F4 *Strand*).

**Strong,** 1) vigorous, of great physical power: *so s. a prop to support so weak a burden,* Ven. Ded. 2. *his — er strength,* Ven. 111. *straight legs and passing s.* 297. *the colt ... never waxeth s.* 420. *with his s. course opens them again,* 960. *the —est body shall it make most weak,* 1145. Lucr. 1646. 1767. Sonn. 65, 4. 11. Err. II, 2, 177. Ado IV, 1, 127. V, 1, 25. As I, 2, 224. II, 3, 6. IV, 3, 152. John IV, 2, 82. R3 V, 3, 311. Cor. I, 1, 62 etc.

Hence = acting by physical force: *from me by s. assault it is bereft,* Lucr. 835. *if by s. hand you offer to break in,* Err. III, 1, 98. *I wot not by what s. escape he broke from those,* V, 148. *to tie thee to my s. correction,* R2 IV, 77. *the busy meddling fiend that lays s. siege unto this wretch's soul,* H6B III, 3, 22. *to recover of us, by s. hand, those foresaid lands,* Hml. I, 1, 102. *yet must not we put the s. law on him,* Hml. IV, 3, 3.

2) endowed with great force of mind or will: *divert s. minds to the course of altering things,* Sonn. 115, 8. *had women been so s. as men,* Pilgr. 321. *we are made to be no —er than faults may shake our frames,* Meas. II, 4, 132. *crouching marrow in the bearer s.* Tim. V, 4, 9. *O constancy, be s. upon my side,* Caes. II, 4, 6.

3) powerful, mighty: *high winds, s. pirates, shelves and sands,* Lucr. 335. *your charter is so s. that you yourself may privilege your time,* Sonn. 58, 9. *I s. o'er them, and you o'er me being s.* Compl. 257. *to thy s. bidding task Ariel,* Tp. I, 2, 192. *one so s. that could control the moon,* V, 269. *what king so s. can tie the gall up in the slanderous tongue,* Meas. III, 2, 198. *in any breast of s. authority,* John II, 113. *in place and in account nothing so s. and fortunate as I,* H4A V, 1, 38. *the s. Illyrian pirate,* H6B IV, 1, 108. *a word devised to keep the s. in awe,* R3 V, 3, 310. *s. thief (i. e. gold)* Tim. IV, 3, 45. *your voice shall be as s. as any man's,* Caes. III, 1, 177. *Pompey is s. at sea,* Ant. I, 4, 36 etc.

Especially = supplied with forces, having sufficient troops: *his forces s.* John II, 61. *with s. and mighty preparation,* H4A IV, 1, 93. *'tis but wisdom to make s. against him,* IV, 4, 39. *we are a body s. enough,* H4B I, 3, 66. *the marshal and the archbishop are s.* II, 3, 42. *our armour all as s.* IV, 1, 156. *think we King Harry s.* H5 II, 4, 48. *s. enough to issue out,* H6A IV, 2, 20. *s. rescue,* IV, 6, 3. *is he but retired to make him s.* H6B IV, 9, 9. In a relative sense, when preceded by numerals, = amounting to, powerful to the extent of: *how many horse the duke is s.* All's IV, 3, 149. *seven thousand s.* H4A IV, 1, 88. *he was not six and twenty s.* IV, 3, 56. H4B III, 1, 96. H6A IV, 1, 20. H6C II, 1, 177. V, 3, 14. Jocularly: *I have been dear to him, lad, some two thousand s., or so,* Tw. III, 2, 59 (Sir Toby's speech).

4) firm, solid: *nor gates of steel so s., but time decays,* Sonn. 65, 8. *though the ship were no —er than a nutshell,* Tp. I, 1, 50. *not on a band, but on a —er thing, a chain,* Err. IV, 2, 50. *by Cupid's —est bow,*

Mids. I, 1, 169. *a s. mast*, Tw. I, 2, 14. *it* (my leg) *is s*. I, 3, 143 (i. e. thick, bulky). *what —er breastplate than a heart untainted*, H6B III, 2, 232. *s. staves*, H8 V, 4, 8. *s. as the axletree on which heaven rides*, Troil. I, 3, 66. *s. fetters*, Ant. I, 2, 120. Metaphorically, = fixed, firm, constant: *which makes thy love more s.* Sonn. 73, 13. *her mother, even s. against that match*, Wiv. IV, 6, 27. *the s. statutes stand like the forfeits in a barber's shop*, Meas. V, 322. *any vice whose s. corruption inhabits our frail blood*, Tw. III, 4, 390. *our s. possession and our right for us*, John I, 39. 40. *thou ever s. upon the —er side*, III, 1, 117. *s. reasons make s. actions*, III, 4, 182. *the s. warrant of an oath*, R2 IV, 235. *s. as a tower in hope*, I, 3, 102. *makes one pardon s.* V, 3, 135. *the s. course of my authority*, H8 V, 3, 35. *to steel a s. opinion to themselves*, Troil. I, 3, 353. *he will stand very s. with us*, Caes. II, 1, 142. *be s. in whore*, Tim. IV, 3, 141. *things bad begun make themselves s. by ill*, Mcb. III, 2, 55. *my —er guilt defeats my s. intent*, Hml. III, 3, 40. *cannot remove nor choke the s. conception that I do groan withal*, Oth. V, 2, 55. *we are s. in custom*, Per. III, 1, 52. *hath built Lord Cerimon such s. renown as time shall ne'er decay*, III, 2, 48.

Hence, in a good sense, = sure, to be relied on, certain: *how is this justified? The —er part of it by her own letters*, All's IV, 3, 65. *there is no English soul more —er to direct you than yourself*, H8 I, 1, 147. *I held Epicurus s. and his opinion*, Caes. V, 1, 77. *whose death indeed's the —est in our censure*, Per. II, 4, 34 (= most certain).

In a bad sense, = obdurate, reckless: *O heinous, s. and bold conspiracy*, R2 V, 3, 59. *s. and fastened villain*, Lr. II, 1, 79 (Ff *strange*).

5) affecting the senses forcibly: *to be stopped in, like a s. distillation*, Wiv. III, 5, 114. *poor suitors have s. breaths*, Cor. I, 1, 61 (bad breaths. cf. All's V, 2, 5).

In a general sense, = working forcibly, forcible, effectual, powerful: *assailed by night with circumstances s. of present death*, Lucr. 1262. *far the weaker with so s. a fear*, 1647. *to him that bears the s. offence's cross*, Sonn. 34, 12. *I will drink potions of eisel 'gainst my s. infection*, 111, 10. *my s. imagination sees a crown dropping upon thy head*, Tp. II, 1, 208. *the —est suggestion*, IV, 26. *the —est oaths are straw to the fire i'the blood*, 52. *in my heart the s. and swelling evil of my conception*, Meas. II, 4, 6. *the fiend is s. within him*, Err. IV, 4, 110. *with the force and s. encounter of my amorous tale*, Ado I, 1, 327. *messengers of s. prevailment*, Mids. I, 1, 35. *lost with their fears thus s.* III, 2, 27. *such tricks hath s. imagination*, V, 18. *the spirit of my father grows s. in me*, As I, 1, 75. *let gentleness my s. enforcement be*, II, 7, 118. *the oath of a lover is no —er than the word of a tapster*, III, 4, 34. *my reasons are most s.* All's IV, 2, 59. *to tell, he longs to see his son, were s.* Wint. I, 2, 34. *s. matter of revolt and wrath*, John III, 4, 167. *s. reasons*, 182. *think them* (reasons) *s.* IV, 2, 41. 42. *know the —est and surest way to get*, R2 III, 3, 201. *had not God, for some s. purpose, steeled the hearts of men*, V, 2, 34. *s. poison*, H6B III, 3, 18. *reasons s. and forcible*, H6C I, 2, 3. *O instance, s. as Pluto's gates*, Troil. V, 2, 153. *I am his kinsman and his subject, s. both against the deed*, Mcb. I, 7, 14. *my —er guilt defeats my s. intent*, Hml. III, 3, 40. *which drives o'er your content these s. necessities*, Ant. III, 6, 83. *the sore terms we*

*stand upon with the gods will be s. with us for giving over*, Per. IV, 2, 38 etc.

6) of a high degree, great, violent: *night doth nightly make grief's strength seem —er*, Sonn. 28, 14. *whose inward pinches therefore are most s.* Tp. V, 77. *folly in fools bears not so s. a note as foolery in the wise*, LLL V, 2, 75. *so s. a liking*, As I, 3, 28. *love's s. passion*, All's I, 3, 139. *her* (Fortune's) *s. displeasure*, V, 2, 6. *so s. a passion*, Tw. II, 4, 97. *the verity of it is in s. suspicion*, Wint. V, 2, 31. *a s. disease*, John III, 4, 112. *the fit is —est*, 114. *my pains and s. endeavours*, H5 V, 2, 25. *I'll amerce you with so s. a fine*, Rom. III, 1, 195. *s. shudders*, Tim. IV, 3, 137. *nor our s. sorrow upon the foot of motion*, Mcb. II, 3, 130. *I am weak with toil, yet s. in appetite*, Cymb. III, 6, 37 etc.

7) severe (German: *strenge*)? cf. the passages quoted above: Meas. V, 322. LLL V, 2, 75. H8 V, 3, 35. Hml. IV, 3, 3. Ant. III, 6, 83.

Adverbial use: *smell somewhat s.* All's V, 2, 5. *I have the back-trick simply as s. as any man in Illyria*, Tw. I, 3, 132. *though it do work as s. as aconitum*, H4B IV, 4, 47. *violenteth in a sense as s. as that which causeth it*, Troil. IV, 4, 4. *I am armed so s. in honesty*, Caes. IV, 3, 67. *conceit in weakest bodies —est works*, Hml. III, 4, 114. *he that builds —er than the mason*, V, 1, 46. 54.

**Strong-barred**, shut with strong bolts: *s. gates*, John II, 370.

**Strong-based**, standing on a firm foundation: *the s. promontory*, Tp. V, 46.

**Strong-besieged**, besieged by a mighty force, hard-beset: *s. Troy*, Lucr. 1429.

**Strong-bonded**, imposing a strong obligation: *that s. oath*, Compl. 279.

**Strong-fixed**, firmly established: *s. is the house of Lancaster*, H6A II, 5, 102.

**Strong-framed**, of a strong make: *tut, I am s., he* (the devil) *cannot prevail with me*, R3 I, 4, 154 (Qq *strong in fraud*).

**Strong-jointed**, having strong limbs: *s. Samson*, LLL I, 2, 77.

**Strong-knit**, firmly joined or compacted: *s. limbs*, H6A II, 3, 21. *s. sinews*, H6C II, 3, 4.

**Strongly**, 1) firmly, in such a manner as not easily to be shaken or removed: *thy merit hath my duty s. knit*, Sonn. 26, 2. *you are so s. in my purpose bred*, 112, 13. *I am affianced this man's wife as s. as words could make up vows*, Meas. V, 227.

2) with great force and power, in such a manner as not easily to be forced or resisted: *too s. embattled against me*, Wiv. II, 2, 260. *s. guarded*, John III, 3, 2. *who s. hath set footing in this land*, R2 II, 2, 48. *look you s. arm to meet him*, H5 II, 4, 49. *fortify it s. 'gainst the French*, III, 3, 53. *'tis s. wedged up in a blockhead*, Cor. II, 3, 30. *Dunsinane he s. fortifies*, Mcb. V, 2, 12.

3) with energy; forcibly: *our late edict shall s. stand in force*, LLL I, 1, 11. *which each to other hath so s. sworn*, 309. *which was so s. urged past my defence*, John I, 258. *we all have s. sworn to give him aid*, R2 II, 3, 150. *delivered s. through my fixed teeth*, H6B III, 2, 313. *all these accused him s.* H8 II, 1, 24. *she for him pleads s. to the Moor*, Oth. II, 3, 361. *do s. speak to us*, Ant. I, 2, 188. *this will witness outwardly, as s. as the conscience does within*, Cymb. II, 2, 36. *'tis*

*not sleepy business, but must be looked to speedily and s.* III, 5, 27.

4) in a high degree, much, violently: *what did he note but s. he desired?* Lucr. 415. *some passion that works him s.* Tp. IV, 144. *your charm so s. works 'em,* V, 17. *which appears most s. in bearing thus the absence of your lord,* Merch. III, 4, 3. *if it smell so s.* All's V, 2, 8 (cf. 5). *possessed with fear so s. that they dare not meet each other,* H4A II, 2, 113. *though s. apprehended,* H4B I, 1, 176. *'twill stir him s.* H8 III, 2, 218. *to satisfy my remembrance the more s.* Mcb. V, 1, 38. *suspects, yet s. loves,* Oth. III, 3, 170 (Ff *soundly*).

**Strong-necked,** having a strong neck: Ven. 263.

**Strong-ribbed,** having strong ribs: Troil. I, 3, 40.

**Strong-tempered,** very hard (cf. *Temper*): *s. steel,* Ven. 111.

**Strong-winged,** having strong wings: Ant. IV, 15, 35.

**Strossers** (most M. Edd. *trossers;* cf. Nares' and Dyce's glossaries) tight drawers or breeches: *in your strait s.* H5 III, 7, 57.

**Strow, Strowings,** and **Strowments,** see *Strew* etc.

**Stroy,** destroy: *what I have left behind —ed in dishonour,* Ant. III, 11, 54.

**Struggle,** vb. to strive, to make efforts in order to escape from the grasp of a superior force: Ven. 227. 710. 1047 (*—ing for passage*). John IV, 1, 77. H6B III, 2, 171. H6C I, 4, 62. Hml. III, 3, 68.

**Strumpet,** a prostitute: Lucr. 1471. Meas. II, 2, 183. Err. IV, 4, 127. All's II, 1, 174. V, 3, 293. Wint. III, 2, 103. H6A I, 5, 12. V, 4, 84. R3 III, 4, 73. 76. Tit. V, 2, 191. Hml. II, 2, 240. Oth. IV, 1, 97. IV, 2, 81. 82. 85. V, 1, 34. 78. 121. 122. V, 2, 77. 79. Ant. I, 1, 13. V, 2, 215. Cymb. III, 4, 22. 116. *the s. wind,* Merch. II, 6, 16. 19. *that s. Fortune,* John III, 1, 61. Hml. II, 2, 515.

**Strumpeted,** made a strumpet, debauched, defiled: Sonn. 66, 6. Err. II, 2, 146.

**Strung,** see *String,* vb.

**Strut,** to walk with a proud gait or affected dignity: Tp. I, 2, 385. Wiv. I, 4, 31. R3 I, 1, 17. Troil. I, 3, 153. Mcb. V, 5, 25. Hml. III, 2, 36. Ant. III, 13, 114. Cymb. III, 1, 33.

**Stubble,** the part of corn-stalks left in the ground by the reaper: *like a s. land at harvest-home,* H4A V, 3, 35 (courtiers' beards, at that time, would not be closely shaved, but trimmed with a pair of scissors). *to kindle their dry s.* Cor. II, 1, 274.

**Stubborn,** 1) stiff, hard, not flexible: *are you more s. hard than hammered iron?* John IV, 1, 67 (M. Edd. *stubborn-hard*). *stop their mouths with s. bits,* H8 V, 3, 23. *his s. buckles, with these your white enchanting fingers touched, shall more obey than to the edge of steel,* Troil. III, 1, 163. *bow, s. knees,* Hml. III, 3, 70.

2) unreasonably obstinate, contumacious, headstrong: *proud, disobedient, s., lacking duty,* Gent. III, 1, 69. *turned her obedience to s. harshness,* Mids. I, 1, 38. *leaving his wealth and ease, a s. will to please,* As II, 5, 55. *the queen is obstinate, s. to justice,* H8 II, 4, 122. *to s. spirits they* (the hearts of princes) *swell,* III, 1, 163. *your s. answer about the giving back the great seal,* III, 2, 346. *as she is s., chaste against all suit,* Troil. I, 1, 100 (M. Edd. *stubborn-chaste*).

3) rough, rude, rugged, harsh: *I fear these s. lines lack power to move,* LLL IV, 3, 55. *that I may appear s. to him,* Tw. III, 4, 74. *upon some s. and uncourteous parts,* V, 369. *though authority be a s. bear,* Wint. IV, 4, 832. *your s. usage of the pope,* John V, 1, 18. *created with a s. outside,* H5 V, 2, 244. *this s. Cade,* H6B III, 1, 360. *you bear too s. and too strange a hand over your friend,* Caes. I, 2, 35. *you s. ancient knave, you reverend braggart,* Lr. II, 2, 133. *to slubber the gloss of your new fortunes with this more s. and boisterous expedition,* Oth. I, 3, 228.

4) ruthless, insensible: *thou art said to have a s. soul, that apprehends no further than this world,* Meas. V, 485. *pluck commiseration from s. Turks and Tartars,* Merch. IV, 1, 32. *it is the —est young fellow of France,* As I, 1, 148. *the sepulchre in s. Jewry,* R2 II, 1, 55. *free from a s. opposite intent,* H6B III, 2, 251. *do not give advantage to s. critics, apt, without a theme, for depravation,* Troil. V, 2, 131.

**Stubborn-chaste,** see *Stubborn* sub 2.

**Stubborn-hard,** see *Stubborn* sub 1.

**Stubbornly,** obstinately: *when s. he did repugn the truth,* H6A IV, 1, 94.

**Stubbornness,** 1) obstinacy, contumacy: *to persever in obstinate condolement is a course of impious s.* Hml. I, 2, 94.

2) roughness, harshness: *translate the s. of fortune into so quiet and so sweet a style,* As II, 1, 19. *even his s., his checks, his frowns ... have grace and favour in them,* Oth. IV, 3, 20.

**Stuck,** stoccado, thrust in fencing: *he gives me the s. in with such a mortal motion, that it is inevitable,* Tw. III, 4, 303 (most M. Edd. *stuck-in* or *stuckin*). *if he by chance escape your venomed s.* Hml. IV, 7, 162.

**Stud,** an ornamental knob or protuberance: *coral clasps and amber —s,* Pilgr. 366. *two letters for her name fairly set down in —s,* Shr. III, 2, 63.

**Studded,** adorned with shining knobs: *the s. bridle,* Ven. 37. *their harness s. with gold and pearl,* Shr. Ind. 2, 44.

**Student,** one devoted to books, a scholar: Wiv. III, 1, 38. LLL II, 64. III, 36. Tw. IV, 2, 9.

**Studied,** 1) studious, intent, inclined: *a prince should not be so loosely s. as to remember so weak a composition* (viz small beer) H4B II, 2, 10. *your graces have been more than could my s. purposes requite,* H8 III, 2, 168. *I have heard it, and am well s. for a liberal thanks which I do owe you,* Ant. II, 6, 48.

2) With *in,* = having made a thing one's study; well versed, practised: *one well s. in a sad ostent,* Merch. II, 2, 205. *as one that had been s. in his death, to throw away the dearest thing he owed, as 'twere a careless trifle,* Mcb. I, 4, 9.

**Studious,** 1) diligent, eager to attain a thing: *be wary in thy s. care,* H6A II, 5, 97.

2) given to books and learning: *the s. universities,* Gent. I, 3, 10.

**Studiously,** diligently, carefully: *written pamphlets s. devised,* H6A III, 1, 2.

**Study,** subst. 1) any endeavour of the mind: *it is my s. to seem despiteful and ungentle to you,* As V, 2, 85. *to be more thankful to thee shall be my s.* Wint. IV, 2, 21. *I have laboured, and with no little s., that my teaching and ... my authority might go one way,* H8 V, 3, 34. Tit. V, 2, 12. Lr. I, 1, 279. Plur. *—es: your safety, for the which myself and them bend their best —es,* John IV, 2, 51. H4A I, 3, 228. H8 III, 1, 123. 174.

2) application to books and learning: Pilgr. 61. Tp. III, 1, 20. Meas. I, 4, 61. LLL I, 1, 55. 58. 67. 68. 70. 84. 143. I, 2, 53. II, 23. IV, 2, 113. IV, 3, 300. 311. Mids. I, 2, 69 (*I am slow of s.*; Snug's speech). H4B I, 2, 132. H5 I, 1, 57. H6A II, 4, 56. V, 1, 22. Plur. —*es*: Tp. I, 2, 77. Gent. I, 1, 67. LLL I, 1, 172. As V, 4, 32. Shr. I, 1, 9. III, 1, 12.

3) the object of such application: *those* (liberal arts) *being all my s.* Tp. I, 2, 74. H5 I, 1, 42. Lr. III, 4, 163. Peculiar expression: *an he were* (in my books), *I would burn my s.* Ado I, 1, 81.

4) an apartment appropriated to literary employment: H6B I, 3, 62. Tit. V, 2, 5. Rom. III, 3, 76. Caes. II, 1, 7. Figuratively: *the idea of her life shall sweetly creep into his s. of imagination*, Ado IV, 1, 227 (cf. *my bosom's shop* in Sonn. 24, 7).**⁕**

**Study,** vb. 1) to fix the mind on a subject, to dwell on in thought, to be intent: *the state whereon I —ed*, Meas. II, 4, 7. *to s. where I well may dine*, LLL I, 1, 61. *hath mine uncle Beaufort and myself ... —ed so long, sat in the council-house*, H6B I, 1, 90. *how to s. for the people's welfare*, H6C IV, 3, 39. With an inf.: *or s. where to meet some mistress fine*, LLL I, 1, 63. *s. to break it*, 66. 80. 144. *then I'll s. how to die*, As IV, 3, 63. *as had she —ed to misuse me so*, Shr. II, 160. *who —es day and night to answer all the debt he owes to you*, H4A I, 3, 184. *who should s. to prefer a peace*, H6A III, 1, 110.

Transitively, = to meditate; to devise; to think on; to be intent on: *s. help for that which thou lamentest*, Gent. III, 1, 242. *I have —ed eight or nine wise words t speak to you*, Ado III, 2, 73. *what —ed torments hast for me?* Wint. III, 2, 176. *as I have watched the night ... in —ing good for England*, H6B III, 1, 111. *to s. fashions to adorn my body*, R3 I, 2, 258. *I shall s. deserving*, Lr. I, 1, 32. *'tis a —ed, not a present thought*, Ant. II, 2, 140.

2) to apply the mind to books and learning: *to live and s. here three years*, LLL I, 1, 35. 48. 51. 59. 108. 181. I, 2, 37. 56. IV, 3, 292. 296. As III, 2, 339. Shr. I, 1, 17. II, 80.

Trans., = to apply to for the purpose of learning: *he hath —ed her will*, Wiv. I, 3, 54. *do you s. them both?* (the sword and the word) III, 1, 45. *s. what you most affect*, Shr. I, 1, 40. H4B IV, 4, 68. Per. III, 2, 32.

Hence = to learn by heart: *painted cloth, from whence you have —ed your questions*, As III, 2, 291. *where did you s. all this goodly speech?* Shr. II, 264. *I can say little more than I have —ed*, Tw. I, 5, 190. 206. *s. a speech of some dozen lines*, Hml. II, 2, 566. cf. the subst. in Mids. I, 2, 69.

3) to meditate, to muse, to ponder: *—es my lady? mistress, look on me*, LLL V, 2, 847. *I have been —ing how I may compare this prison unto the world*, R2 V, 5, 1. With *of: you make me s. of that*, Tp. II, 1, 82. With *on: bids thee s. on what fair demands thou meanest to have him grant thee*, Ant. V, 2, 10.

4) to make out by scientific research: *here is three —ed*, LLL I, 2, 54.

**Stuff,** subst. 1) that of which a thing is made; materials: *we are such s. as dreams are made on*, Tp. IV, 156. *nature never framed a woman's heart of prouder s.* Ado III, 1, 50. *what s. 'tis made of*, Merch. I, 1, 4. *ambition should be made of sterner s.* Caes. III, 2, 97. *if it be made of penetrable s.* Hml. III, 4, 36. *that we are made of s. so flat and dull*, IV, 7, 31. *nature wants*

*s. to vie strange forms with fancy*, Ant. V, 2, 97. *great nature moulded the s. so fair*, Cymb. V, 4, 49. Specially, = cloth, texture of any kind: *I gave him the s.* Shr. IV, 3, 119. *what s. wilt have a kirtle of?* H4B II, 4, 297.

2) matter, substance, thing; in a physical sense: *he'll make us strange s.* Tp. IV, 234. *I never knew man hold vile s. so dear*, LLL IV, 3, 276. *youth's a s. will not endure*, Tw. II, 3, 53. *there's a whole merchant's venture of Bourdeaux s. in him*, H4B II, 4, 69. *who in spite put s. to some she beggar*, Tim. IV, 3, 272. *cleanse the stuffed bosom of that perilous s.* Mcb. V, 3, 44. *did compound for her a certain s.* Cymb. V, 5, 255 (a potion).

In a moral or intellectual sense: *there's in him s. that puts him to these ends*, H8 I, 1, 58. *you are full of heavenly s.* III, 2, 137. *serves as s. for these two to make paradoxes*, Troil. I, 3, 184. *thy verse swells with s. so fine and smooth*, Tim. V, 1, 87. *there was no such s. in my thoughts*, Hml. II, 2, 324. *yet do I hold it very s. o' the conscience to do no contrived murder*, Oth. I, 2, 2. *I do not think so fair an outward and such s. within endows a man but he*, Cymb. I, 1, 23.

Especially, things spoken or recited: *it is more pleasing s.* Shr. Ind. 2, 142 (i. e. a comedy). Usually in contempt: *what s. is this! how say you?* Tp. II, 1, 254. *O heavens! what s. is here?* Meas. III, 2, 5. *this is the silliest s. that ever I heard*, Mids. V, 212. *such a deal of skimble-skamble s.* H4A III, 1, 154. *here's goodly s. toward*, H4B II, 4, 214. *at this fusty s. ... Achilles laughs*, Troil. I, 3, 161. *O proper s.!* Mcb. III, 4, 60. *such s. as madmen tongue*, Cymb. V, 4, 146.

3) furniture; goods; utensils: *rich garments, linens, —s and necessaries*, Tp. I, 2, 164. *household s.* Shr. Ind. 2, 143. III, 2, 233. *what masking s. is here?* IV, 3, 87. *his treasure, rich —s, and ornaments of household*, H8 III, 2, 126. *such boiled s. as well might poison poison*, Cymb. I, 6, 125; cf. *the s. we have, a strong wind will blow it to pieces*, Per IV, 2, 19. = luggage: *fetch our s. from thence*, Err. IV, 4, 153. 162. V, 408. 409.

**Stuff,** vb. 1) to fill very full, to cram: *till gorge be —ed*, Ven. 58. *a maid, and —ed!* Ado III, 4, 65. *a hulk better —ed in the hold*, H4B II, 4, 70. *cleanse the —ed bosom*, Mcb. V, 3, 44. *I will s. your purses full of crowns*, H4A I, 2, 146. Followed by *with: they* (the lines) *are —ed with protestations*, Gent. IV, 4, 134. *to s. my head with more ill news*, John IV, 2, 133. *with a foul traitor's name s. I thy throat*, R2 I, 1, 44. H4B Ind. 8. Cor. V, 1, 53. Oth. I, 1, 14. Per. I, 4, 67. 93.

Applied to empty things swelled out by putting something in: *a —ed man*, Ado I, 1, 59. *—ed tennis-balls*, III, 2, 47. *parsley to s. a rabbit*, Shr. IV, 4, 101. John I, 141. H4A II, 4, 497. Cor. II, 1, 98. Rom. V, 1, 43. With *out: —s out his vacant garments with his form*, John III, 4, 97. H4B V, 5, 87.

Figuratively, = to make full, to complete: *it will s. his suspicion more fully*, Lr. III, 5, 22. With *up: his servile powers, who, flattered by their leader's jocund show, s. up his lust, as minutes fill up hours*, Lucr. 297. Partic. —*ed* = full, complete: *whom you know of —ed sufficiency*, Wint. II, 1, 185. —*ed with* = full of: —*ed with all honourable virtues*, Ado I, 1, 56. —*ed with honourable parts*, Rom. III, 5, 183.

2) to press or thrust in: *in ivory coffers I have —ed my crowns*, Shr. II, 352.

3) —*ed* = unable to smell in consequence of a cold: Ado III, 4, 64.

**Stuffing**, that which is used to fill any thing: Ado I, 1, 59.

**Stumble**, 1) to trip in walking, to be near falling: Shr. III, 2, 59. IV, 1, 79. R2 V, 5, 87. H4B I, 1, 131. R3 I, 4, 18. III, 4, 86. With *at: s. at the threshold,* H6C IV, 7, 11. Rom. V, 3, 122. —*ing caused by darkness: it grows dark, he may s.* LLL V, 2, 633. *before the* —*ing night did part our weary powers,* John V, 5, 18 (the night in which there is no safe walking or acting). Applied to the tongue: *his tongue, all impatient to speak and not see, did s. with haste,* LLL II, 239. *my tongue should s. in mine earnest words,* H6B III, 2, 316.

In a moral sense, = to err: *so you s. not unheedfully,* Gent. I, 2, 3. *she'll not s.* Wint. II, 3, 52. *blind reason* —*ing without fear,* Troil. III, 2, 77. *they s. that run fast,* Rom. II, 3, 94. *I* —*ed when I saw,* Lr. IV, 1, 21.

2) With *on,* = to light on by chance or inadvertently: *what man art thou that thus bescreened in night so* —*st on my counsel?* Rom. II, 2, 53. *nor aught so good but strained from that fair use revolts from true birth,* —*ing on abuse,* II, 3, 20.

**Stumbling-block**, that which obstructs the way: *I would remove these tedious* —*s and smooth my way upon their headless necks,* H6B I, 2, 64.

**Stump**, a part remaining after the rest is amputated or destroyed: H8 I, 3, 49 (of a tooth). Tit. II, 4, 4. III, 2, 42. V, 2, 22. 183.

**Stupid**, dull, wanting sensibility and apprehension: *s. with age,* Wint. IV, 4, 409.

**Stupify**, to make insensible, to benumb: *will s. and dull the sense awhile,* Cymb. I, 5, 37. Partic. —*ed* = stupid; *or* —*ed or seeming so in skill,* Wint. II, 1, 165.

**Sturdy**, 1) stout, strong: *the forceless flowers like s. trees support me,* Ven. 152.

2) brutally relying on one's strength: *look where the s. rebel sits,* H6C I, 1, 50.

**Sty**, subst. an inclosure for swine: R3 IV, 5, 2. Ant. IV, 15, 62. Figuratively, a place of bestial debauchery: Hml. III, 4, 94. Per. IV, 6, 104.

**Sty**, vb. to lodge as in a sty: *here you s. me in this hard rock,* Tp. I, 2, 342.

**Stygian**, pertaining to the infernal river Styx: *upon the S. banks,* Troil. III, 2, 10.

**Style**, 1) manner of writing with regard to language: Sonn. 32, 14. 78, 11. 84, 12. Ado V, 1, 37. V, 2, 6.

2) manner of expression appropriate to particular characters: *I can construe the action of her familiar s.* Wiv. I, 3, 51. LLL I, 1, 201. IV, 1, 98. As II, 1, 20. IV, 3, 31. H6A IV, 1, 50. R3 IV, 4, 360.

3) title, appellation: *Ford's a knave, and I will aggravate his s.; thou, Master Brook, shalt know him for knave and cuckold,* Wiv. II, 2, 297. *count's master is of another s.* All's II, 3, 205. *here is a silly stately s. indeed! the Turk, that two and fifty kingdoms hath, writes not so tedious a s. as this,* H6A IV, 7, 72. 74. *King Reignier, whose large s. agrees not with the leanness of his purse,* H6B I, 1, 111. *a queen in title and in s.* I, 3, 51.

As for plays on the word, see *Stile.*

**Styled**, titled: *thou wert dignified enough, to be s. the under-hangman of his kingdom,* Cymb. II, 3, 134.

**Styx**, the infernal river: Troil. V, 4, 20. Tit. I, 88. Alluded to in R3 I, 4, 45.

**Sub-contracted**, contracted after a former contract, betrothed for the second time: *she* (my wife) *is s. to this lord,* Lr. V, 3, 86.

**Subdue**, 1) to overcome, to overpower, to vanquish: *their cheer is the greater that I am* —*d,* Ado I, 3, 74. *a peace is of the nature of a conquest, for then both parties nobly are* —*d,* H4B IV, 2, 90. *you fly from your oft* —*d slaves,* H6A I, 5, 32. *tugged for life and was by strength* —*d,* H6B III, 2, 173. *by many hands your father was* —*d,* H6C II, 1, 56. *if he do resist, s. him at his peril,* Oth. I, 2, 81. *thou hast* —*d his judgement too,* Ant. III, 13, 36. *with those hands ... s. my worthiest self,* IV, 12, 47. *could this carl have* —*d me,* Cymb. V, 2, 5.

2) to bring into subjection: *having* —*d the Saxons,* H5 I, 2, 46. 62. *John of Gaunt, which did s. the greatest part of Spain,* H6C III, 3, 82.

In a moral sense, = to prevail over, to subjugate, to render submissive; absol.: *his* —*ing tongue,* Compl. 120. With an object: *the accident ... did her force s.* Compl. 248. *pensived and* —*d desires,* 219. *this virtuous maid* —*s me quite,* Meas. II, 2, 186. IV, 2, 84. LLL I, 2, 187. IV, 1, 40. Wint. IV, 4, 587. H6A I, 2, 109. Oth. I, 3, 112. II, 3, 346. V, 2, 348. Cymb. I, 1, 136. With *to: her infinite cunning* —*d me to her rate,* All's V, 3, 217. *his large fortune ... —s and properties to his love and tendance all sorts of hearts,* Tim. I, 1, 57. *'twould s. my father entirely to her love,* Oth. III, 4, 59. —*d to* = subject to, subjugated by: *my nature is* —*d to what it works in, like the dyer's hand,* Sonn. 111, 6. *this man's threats, to whom I am* —*d,* Tp. I, 2, 489. *my heart's* —*d even to the very quality of my lord,* Oth. I, 3, 251. *his face* —*d to penetrative shame,* Ant. IV, 14, 74 (not showing any trace of its former pride).

3) to crush, to oppress, to tame, to disable: *being once* —*d in armed tail,* Troil. V, 10, 44. *to make him worthy whose offence* —*s him,* Cor. I, 1, 179. *nothing could have* —*d nature to such a lowness but his unkind daughters,* Lr. III, 4, 72.

**Subduement**, conquest, victory: *despising many forfeits and* —*s,* Troil. IV, 5, 187.

**Subject**, subst. 1) one under the dominion of another: Ven. 1045. Lucr. 616. 722. Tp. I, 2, 341 (*I am all the* —*s that you have*). II, 1, 165. II, 2, 131. 157. III, 2, 41. V, 167. Gent. II, 6, 8. Meas. V, 317. Err. II, 1, 19. Ado III, 3, 33. 35. Merch. II, 2, 49. Shr. V, 2, 155. H6A III, 1, 182. IV, 1, 166. IV, 2, 7. V, 4, 160. H6B I, 3, 52 (*to*). II, 2, 8. IV, 9, 5. 6. H6C III, 1, 70. 78. 81. R3 IV, 4, 356. Lr. V, 3, 60 (*I hold you but a s. of this war, not as a brother*; i. e. one who ought to obey, not to command). Ant. I, 3, 92 (*your royalty holds idleness your s.*) etc. etc.

2) the people under the dominion of a sovereign: *the general s. to a well-wished king quit their own part,* Meas. II, 4, 27 (M. Edd. *the general, s.*). *the greater file of the s. held the duke to be wise,* III, 2, 145. *let the s. see, to make them know ...,* V, 14. *one that indeed physics the s., makes old hearts fresh,* Wint. I, 1, 43. *why this watch so nightly toils the s. of the land,* Hml. I, 1, 72. *the levies ... are all made out of his s.* I, 2, 33. *how from the finny s. of the sea these fishers tell the infirmities of men,* Per. II, 1, 52. cf. also H6B IV, 1, 82.

3) creature, being; that which is in existence: *our very priests must become mockers, if they shall encounter*

such *ridiculous* —*s as you are*, Cor. II, 1, 94. *that heaven should practise stratagems upon so soft a s. as myself*, Rom. III, 5, 212 (perhaps collectively in Per. II, 1, 52; see sub 2). Hence the following expression: *thoughts are no* —*s; intents but merely thoughts*, Meas. V, 458; i. e. thoughts are no real, existing things.

4) he who, or that which, is exposed or liable to something: *have I scaped love-letters in the holiday-time of my beauty, and am I now a s. for them?* Wiv. II, 1, 3. *leaves his part-created cost a naked s. to the weeping clouds*, H4B I, 3, 61. *we are time's* —*s, and time bids be gone*, 110. *to be shame's scorn and s. of mischance*, H6A IV, 6, 49. *I am too mean a s. for thy wrath*, H6C I, 3, 19. *live each of you the* —*s to his hate*, R3 I, 3, 302. *proved the s. of my own soul's curse*, IV, 1, 81. *beauty, wit, high birth, ... are* —*s all to envious and calumniating time*, Troil. III, 3, 173.

5) that which is spoken or thought or treated of; theme, argument: *how can my Muse want s. to invent*, Sonn. 38, 1. *the wits of former days to* —*s worse have given admiring praise*, 59, 14. 82, 4. 84, 6. 100, 4. 103, 10. Meas. II, 4, 2. Err. V, 65. Ado V, 1, 137. LLL I, 2, 120. V, 2, 774. H6C III, 2, 91. H8 Prol. 7. Tim. IV, 3, 272. Caes. I, 2, 92.

6) he who, or that which, is the cause or occasion of something: *I am the unhappy s. of these quarrels*, Merch. V, 238. *I could be sad. Very hardly upon such a s.* H4B II, 2, 47. *I cannot fight upon this argument; it is too starved a s. for my sword*, Troil. I, 1, 96. *none so noble whose life were ill bestowed or death unfamed where Helen is the s.* II, 2, 160. *the dry serpigo on the s.* (of the quarrel) II, 3, 81. *near approaches the s. of our watch*, Mcb. III, 3, 8.

**Subject**, adj. 1) being under the dominion of another: *let me have no s. enemies*, John IV, 2, 171 (i. e. no enemies among my subjects). *I, her sovereign, am her s. love*, R3 IV, 4, 355 (Qq *s. low*). *the eastern tower, whose height commands as all the vale*, Troil. I, 2, 3. With *to*: *I am s. to a tyrant*, Tp. III, 2, 48. Meas. II, 4, 27 (O. Edd. *the general s.*, M. Edd. *the general, s.*). John II, 43. H5 I, 2, 242. H8 II, 4, 26. Tim. IV, 3, 347. Hml. I, 3, 18. Cymb. I, 1, 172.

2) exposed, liable, obnoxious: *s. to the tyranny of mad mischances*, Ven. 737. *s. and servile to all discontents*, 1161. *s. to Time's love or to Time's hate*, Sonn. 124, 3. *be s. to no sight but thine and mine*, Tp. I, 2, 301. Wiv. III, 5, 117. Err. V, 54. Merch. III, 1, 64. John III, 1, 14. R2 III, 4, 103. H4B III, 2, 325. IV, 4, 54. H5 IV, 1, 251.

**Subject**, vb. 1) to put under the power of another: *s. his coronet to his crown*, Tp. I, 2, 114.

2) to expose, to make liable: *I rather will s. me to the malice of ... a bloody brother*, As II, 3, 36.

**Subjected**, adjectively, 1) having the qualities of a subject: *s. thus, how can you say to me, I am a king?* R2 III, 2, 176.

2) due from a subject, becoming in a subject: *needs must you lay your heart at his dispose, s. tribute to commanding love*, John I, 264.

**Subjection**, the state of being a subject; service: *brought in s. her immortality, and made her thrall to living death*, Lucr. 724. (the horse) *proud of s.*, noble by the sway, Compl. 108. *his majesty ... to whom I am now in ward, evermore in s.* All's I, 1, 6. *to whom I do bequeath my faithful services and true s. everlastingly*, John V, 7, 105. *whom to disobey were against all pro-*

*portion of s.* H5 IV, 1, 153. *I dare be bound he's true and shall perform all parts of his s. loyally*, Cymb. IV, 3, 19. *I'll tame you, I'll bring you in s.* Per. II, 5, 75.

**Submerged**, put under water, drowned: *so half my Egypt were s. and made a cistern for scaled snakes*, Ant. II, 5, 94.

**Submission**, 1) the act of submitting, delivery of one's self to the authority of another: *s., Dauphin! 'tis a mere French word*, H6A IV, 7, 54. *proclaim a pardon to the soldiers fled that in s. will return to us*, R3 V, 5, 17.

2) humble behaviour, reverence: *to whom, with all s., I do bequeath my services*, John V, 7, 103. *give sorrow leave awhile to tutor me to this s.* R2 IV, 167. *tell her I return great thanks, and in s. will attend on her*, H6A II, 2, 52. *all the court admired him for s.* H6B III, 1, 12. *I commend this kind s.* V, 1, 54. *in all s. and humility*, 58.

3) acknowledgment of a fault, confession of error: *be not as extreme in s. as in offence*, Wiv. IV, 4, 11. *I may ... find pardon on my true s.* H4A III, 2, 28. *O calm, dishonourable, vile s.* Rom. III, 1, 76.

**Submissive**, testifying submission or inferiority; humble: LLL IV, 1, 92. Shr. Ind. 1, 53. H6A III, 4, 10. IV, 7, 53.

**Submit**, 1) trans. to subject, to yield or resign to the power of another: *I s. my fancy to your eyes*, All's II, 3, 174. Refl.: *we should s. ourselves to an unknown fear*, All's II, 3, 6. *s. thee, boy*, John II, 159. III, 1, 194. H5 II, 2, 77. H6A V, 4, 130. Cor. III, 3, 44. Caes. I, 3, 47 (= expose). Ant. III, 12, 17.

2) intr. to yield, to give up resistance, to acknowledge the power of another: *what must the king do now? must he s.?* R2 III, 3, 143. *he shall s., or I will never yield*, H6A III, 1, 118. With *to*: H6A V, 1, 56. Cymb. V, 5, 460. Per. II, 4, 39.

**Suborn**, to procure by secret collusion, to abet: *thou hast* —*ed the goldsmith to arrest me*, Err. IV, 4, 85. *what peer hath been* —*ed to grate on you?* H4B IV, 1, 90. *whom I did s. to do this ruthless piece of butchery*, R3 IV, 3, 4. *they* (the murderers of Duncan) *were* —*ed*, Mcb. II, 4, 24. Applied especially to false witnesses: Sonn. 125, 13. Meas. V, 106. 308. H6A V, 4, 21. H6B III, 1, 180. Oth. III, 4, 153.

**Subornation**, the crime of procuring one to do a bad action, and specially to bear false witness: *guilty of perjury and s.* Lucr. 919. *wear the detested blot of murtherous s.* H4A I, 3, 163. *the duchess by his s. began her devilish practices*, H6B III, 1, 45. *foul s. is predominant*, 145.

**Subscribe**, 1) to underwrite (one's name); absol.: *my uncle's fool* —*d for Cupid*, Ado I, 1, 41. *write to him; I will s.* Ant. IV, 5, 14. With *to*: *s. to your deep oaths, and keep it too*, LLL I, 1, 23. *if my tongue did e'er solicit, or my hand s. to any syllable that made love to you*, Per. II, 5, 69. Transitively, = to write or place underneath: *s. your names*, LLL I, 1, 19. *they shall s. them for large sums of gold*, R2 I, 4, 50 (underwrite their names).

2) to sign and attest with one's own hand: *he hath not yet* —*d this*, H5 V, 2, 363. —*d by the consuls*, Cor. V, 6, 82. —*d it*, Hml. V, 2, 52.

3) to become surety, to guaranty; with *for*: *I know thou'rt valiant; and, to the possibility of thy soldiership, will s. for thee*, All's III, 6, 89 (I warrant that **thou**

wilt do all that thou possibly canst). *I will s. for thee, thou art both knave and fool,* IV, 5, 34.

4) to admit of, to grant, to acknowledge: *as I s. not that, nor any other, but in the loss of question,* Meas. II, 4, 89. *I will s. him a coward,* Ado V, 2, 59. *will you s. his thought?* Troil. II, 3, 156. With *to,* in the same sense: *plead a new state in thy unrivalled merit, to which I thus s.: Sir Valentine, thou art a gentleman* etc., Gent. V, 4, 145. *but when I had —d to mine own fortune and informed her fully,* All's V, 3, 96 (acknowledged, confessed the state of my affairs).

5) to yield, to confess one's self to be in the wrong, to submit: *if I have fewest* (roses), *I s. in silence,* H6A II, 4, 44. *which fear if better reasons can supplant, I will s. and say I wronged the duke,* H6B III, 1, 38. *all cruels else s.,* Lr. III, 7, 65. With *to,* = to submit to, to acknowledge the superiority of, to pay respect to, to obey: *death to me —s, since spite of him I'll live in this poor rhyme,* Sonn. 107, 10. *to your pleasure humbly I s.* Shr. I, 1, 81. *Hector in his blaze of wrath —s to tender objects,* Troil. IV, 5, 105. *we will all s. to thy advice,* Tit. IV, 2, 130. Transitively, = to make to be inferior, to reduce to the state of dependency: *the king gone to-night! —d his power!* Lr. I, 2, 24 (Ff *prescribed*).

**Subscription,** submission, obedience: *you owe me no s.* Lr. III, 2, 18.

**Subsequent,** following: *small pricks to their s. volumes,* Troil. I, 3, 344.

**Subsidy,** a tax imposed on a particular occasion: H6B IV, 7, 25. Pl. —*es:* H6C IV, 8, 45.

**Subsist,** to live, to continue: *so long as brain and heart have faculty by nature to s.* Sonn. 122, 6. *no more infected with my country's love than when I parted hence, but still —ing under your great command,* Cor. V, 6, 73.

**Substance,** 1) matter; that of which things consist: *if the dull s. of my flesh were thought,* Sonn. 44, 1. *what is your s., whereof are you made?* 53, 1. *so much as makes it light or heavy in the s.* Merch. IV, 1, 328. *all of one nature, of one s. bred,* H4A I, 1, 11. *the purpose is perspicuous even as s., whose grossness little characters sum up,* Troil. I, 3, 324 (as the material world, which seems immense, but is calculated and defined by means of little figures. According to others, it means here wealth, treasure, estate). *as thin of s. as the air,* Rom. I, 4, 99. *thou dost breathe, hast heavy s.* Lr. IV, 6, 52.

2) any thing existing by itself, of which we can say that it is; a being: *you murdering ministers, wherever in your sightless —s you wait on nature's mischief,* Mcb. I, 5, 50. *all the noble s.* Hml. I, 4, 37 (corr. pass.). *that little seeming s.* (Cordelia) Lr. I, 1, 201. *earthly man is but a s. that must yield to you,* Per. II, 1, 3.

3) that which constitutes the thing itself, and not only a vain semblance of it (usually opposed to *shadow*): *flowers distilled leese but their show; their s. still lives sweet,* Sonn. 5, 14. *since the s. of your perfect self is else devoted, I am but a shadow,* Gent. IV, 2, 124. 127. *my s. should be statue in thy stead,* IV, 4, 206. *so far this shadow* (a picture) *doth limp behind the s.* Merch. III, 2, 130. *each s. of a grief hath twenty shadows,* R2 II, 2, 14. *there* (in my soul) *lies the s.* (of my grief) IV, 299. *much of the father's s.!* H4B III, 2, 142. *now the s. shall endure the like* (as the picture, viz hang) H6A II, 3, 38. *then have I s. too,* 49. *my s. is not here,* 51. *these are his s., sinews, arms and strength,*

63. *the s. of that great shadow I did represent,* H6B I, 1, 13. *shadows have struck more terror to the soul of Richard than can the s. of ten thousand soldiers,* R3 V, 3, 218. *he takes false shadows for true —s,* Tit. III, 2, 80. *despised s. of divinest show,* Rom. III, 2, 77. *the very s. of the ambitious is merely the shadow of a dream,* Hml. II, 2, 264.

Hence = the main and essential part of a thing: *dear father, soul and s. of us all,* Tit. I, 374. *conceit, more rich in matter than in words, brags of his s., not of ornament,* Rom. II, 6, 31.*

4) material means and resources: *grows strong and great in s. and in power,* R2 III, 2, 35. *and yet, in s. and authority, retain but privilege of a private man,* H6A V, 4, 135. Hence = goods, means of living, treasure: *this shadow doth such s. give that I in thy abundance am sufficed,* Sonn. 37, 10. *you take the sum and s. that I have,* Gent. IV, 1, 15. *he is of s. good,* Wiv. I, 3, 40. *love like a shadow flies when s. love pursues,* II, 2, 215. *he shall not knit a knot in his fortunes with the finger of my s.* III, 2, 77. *thy s. cannot amount unto a hundred marks,* Err. I, 1, 24. *he hath put all my s. into that fat belly of his,* H4B II, 1, 81. *the sixth part of his s. to be levied without delay,* H8 I, 2, 58. *you have sent innumerable s. ... to furnish Rome,* III, 2, 326.

5) contents, purport: *how far the s. of my praise doth wrong this shadow in underprizing it,* Merch. III, 2, 127. *their* (the letters') *cold intent, tenour and s., thus,* H4B IV, 1, 9. *unto your grace do I in chief address the s. of my speech,* 32.

**Substantial,** 1) material, corporeal, bulky: *to draw with idle spiders' strings most ponderous and s. things,* Meas. III, 2, 290. cf. *Self-substantial.*

2) real, solid, not merely seeming, not illusive: *your reason was not s.* Err. II, 2, 105. *acquitted by a true s. form,* H4B IV, 1, 173.* *a dream, too flattering-sweet to be s.* Rom. II, 2, 141.

**Substitute,** one acting with delegated power in the place of another: Meas. III, 1, 192. IV, 2, 198. V, 133. 140. Merch. V, 94. R2 I, 2, 37. I, 4, 48. H4B IV, 2, 28. IV, 4, 6. H6A V, 3, 5. H6B III, 1, 371. R3 III, 7, 133. 181. Oth. I, 3, 224. Per. V, 3, 51.

**Substituted,** 1) put in the place of another: *how their child shall be ... s. in the place of mine,* Tit. IV, 2, 159.

2) invested with delegated authority: *who is s. 'gainst the French, I have no certain notice,* H4B I, 3, 84.

**Substitution,** the office of a substitute, delegated authority: Tp. I, 2, 103.

**Substractor,** detractor, slanderer: Tw. I, 3, 37.

**Subtile** and **Subtilty,** see *Subtle, Subtlety.*

**Subtle,** 1) thin, fine, nice, delicate: *it must needs be of s., tender and delicate temperance,* Tp. II, 1, 41. *some joy too fine, too s., potent,* Troil. III, 2, 25 (M.Edd. *subtle-potent*). *a point as s. as Ariachne's broken woof,* V, 2, 151.

2) sly, artful, cunning: *am I politic? am I s.?* Wiv. III, 1, 103. *s. as Sphinx,* LLL IV, 3, 342. *a s. traitor needs no sophister,* H6B V, 1, 191. *Warwick is a s. orator,* H6C III, 1, 33. *incensed by his s. mother to taunt and scorn you,* R3 III, 1, 152. *nor sweeten talk, nor play at s. games,* Troil. IV, 4, 89. *bolder, though not so s.* (as the devil) Cor. I, 10, 17. *the s. queen of Goths,* Tit. I, 392. *the swift, the slow, the s.* (dog)

Mcb. III, 1, 96. *s. as the fox for prey*, Cymb. III, 3, 40.

3) acting under the cover of a false appearance; being other than in seeming; deceptious, treacherous: *the s. shining secrecies writ in the glassy margents of such books*, Lucr. 101 (secrecies hid under a false show, but well discernible to the eye of a man of experience). *swift s. post*, 926 (moving imperceptibly and approaching unawares). *to mock the s. in themselves beguiled*, 957. *as s. Sinon here is painted, so sober, sad, so weary and so mild*, 1541. *in him a plenitude of s. matter, applied to cautels, all strange forms receives*, Compl. 302. *smooth not thy tongue with filed talk, lest she some s. practice smell*, Pilgr. 307. *a delicate wench. Ay, and a s.* Tp. II, 1, 44. *thou s., perjured, false, disloyal man*, Gent. IV, 2, 95. *she is too s. for thee, and her smoothness, her very silence and her patience speak to the people*, As I, 3, 79. *I feel these youth's perfections with an invisible and s. stealth to creep in at mine eyes*, Tw. I, 5, 316 (i. e. imperceptible; or rather not sufficiently guarded against, as not seeming dangerous at first). *this s. king*, H4A I, 3, 169. *a s. knave! but yet it shall not serve*, H6B II, 1, 104 (playing the innocent). *s., false and treacherous*, R3 I, 1, 37. *the s. traitor this day had plotted ... to murder me*, III, 5, 37. *thy age confirmed, proud, s., bloody*, IV, 4, 171. *he is equal ravenous as he is s.* H8 I, 1, 160. *like to a bowl upon a s. ground, I have tumbled past the throw*, Cor. V, 2, 20 (seeming smooth and even, but in fact uneven and treacherous). *what s. hole is this, whose mouth is covered with rude-growing briers*, Tit. II, 3, 198. *when s. Greeks surprised King Priam's Troy*, V, 3, 84. *suck the s. blood o' the grape, till the high fever seethe your blood to froth*, Tim. IV, 3, 432 (running glibly over the palate, but heating the blood. German: *heimtückisch*). *is not thy kindness s.* 515. *let our hearts, as s. masters do, stir up their servants to an act of rage, and after seem to chide 'em*, Caes. II, 1, 175. *a slipper and s. knave*, Oth. II, 1, 246. *this is a s. whore*, IV, 2, 21.

**Subtlety,** 1) cunning; stratagem: *the fox which lives by s.* Ven. 675. *by gins, by snares, by s.* H6B III, 1, 262.

2) false appearance, deception, illusion: *unlearned in the world's false —es*, Sonn. 138, 4. *you do yet taste some —es of the isle, that will not let you believe things certain*, Tp. V, 124 (Steevens: "this is a phrase adopted from ancient cookery and confectionary. When a dish was so contrived as to appear unlike what it really was, they called it a *subtlety*. Dragons, castles, trees etc. made out of sugar, had the like denomination". A remark furnishing a new instance for the peculiar use of the word, but hardly illustrative of the above passage). *'tis the king's s. to have my life*, Per. II, 5, 44.

**Subtle-witted,** crafty: *the s. French conjurers*, H6A I, 1, 25.

**Subtly,** deceitfully: *thou proud dream, that playest so s. with a king's repose*, H5 IV, 1, 275. *and danger, like an ague, s. taints even then when we sit idly in the sun*, Troil. III, 3, 232. *a poison, which the friar s. hath ministered to have me dead*, Rom. IV, 3, 25 (Ff *subtilly*).

**Subtractor,** writing of some M. Edd. for *substractor*, q. v.

**Suburbs,** the parts of a city that lie without the walls: Meas. I, 2, 98. 105. II, 1, 65. Tw. III, 3, 39. H6A I, 4, 2. 9. H8 V, 4, 76. Metaphorically: *dwell I but in the s. of your good pleasure?* Caes. II, 1, 285 ("the s. were the general resort of disorderly persons in fortified towns, and in London also. It was the same in ancient times". Nares).

**Subversion,** destruction: *seek s. of thy harmless life*, H6B III, 1, 208.

**Subvert,** to destroy: *—s your towns*, H6A II, 3, 65.

**Succeed,** 1) to follow, to come after, to be subsequent or consequent; absol.: *a most harsh one* (language), *and not to be understood without bloody —ing*, All's II, 3, 199 (= consequence). *after summer evermore —s barren winter*, H6B II, 4, 2. *a pattern to all princes living with her, and all that shall s.* H8 V, 5, 24. *the effects he writes of s. unhappily*, Lr. I, 2, 157 (come to pass after his prediction). *not another comfort like to this —s in unknown fate*, Oth. II, 1, 195. *bethought me what was past, what might s.* Per. I, 2, 83. *—ing* = later, living in after-times: *sung by children in —ing times*, Lucr. 525. *beauty's pattern to —ing men*, Sonn. 19, 12. *to God, my king, and my —ing issue*, R2 I, 3, 20. *—ing ages*, R3 III, 1, 71. *to the —ing royalty he leaves the healing benediction*, Mcb. IV, 3, 155.

Trans.: *the curse of heaven and men s. their evils*, Per. I, 4, 104.

2) to take the place which another has left; to become heir; absol.: *no woman shall s. in Salique land*, H5 I, 2, 39. H6B II, 2, 52. H6C I, 1, 146. 227. H8 II, 1, 112. Tit. I, 40 (Hanmer: *—ed*). Mcb. III, 1, 64. IV, 3, 49. Per. I, 4, 64.

Trans., = a) to be heir or successor to: *s. thy father in manners as in shape*, All's I, 1, 70. *not Amurath an Amurath —s*, H4B V, 2, 48. H5 Epil. 10. H6A II, 5, 83. H6C II, 2, 94. b) to inherit: *if not a fedary, but only he owe and s. thy weakness*, Meas. II, 4, 123.

3) to come down by order of succession, to descend, to devolve: *a ring, that downward hath —ed in his house from son to son*, All's III, 7, 23. *seize upon the fortunes of the Moor, for they s. on you*, Oth. V, 2, 367 (Qq *s. to you*). *hope, —ing from so fair a tree as your fair self, doth tune us otherwise*, Per. I, 1, 114.

**Succeeder,** successor, heir: R3 IV, 4, 128. V, 5, 30.

**Success,** 1) succession: *our parents' noble names, in whose s. we are gentle*, Wint. I, 2, 394. *and so s. of mischief shall be born, and heir from heir shall hold this quarrel up*, H4B IV, 2, 47.

2) issue, result, fortune (as a vox media): *let me hear of thy s. in love*, Gent. I, 1, 58. *I'll send him certain word of my s.* Meas. I, 4, 89. *s. will fashion this event in better shape*, Ado IV, 1, 236. *to try s.* All's I, 3, 253. *when your lordship sees the bottom of his s. in it*, III, 6, 39. *we cannot greatly condemn our s.* 59. *I know not what the s. will be*, 86. *so thrive I in my enterprise and dangerous s. of bloody wars*, R3 IV, 4, 236 (Qq *dangerous attempt of hostile arms*). *the s. shall give a scantling of good or bad unto the general*, Troil. I, 3, 340. *lead their —es as we wish our own*, Cor. I, 6, 7. *I shall ere long have knowledge of my s.* V, 1, 62. *my speech should fall into such vile s. as my thoughts aim not at*, Oth. III, 3, 222. *Caesar and Lepidus have made wars upon Pompey. What is the s.?* Ant. III, 5, 6. *bad s.* H6C II, 2, 46. Troil. II, 2, 117. *good s.* H6C III, 3, 146. Cor. I, 1, 264. Lr. V, 3, 194. Ant. II, 4, 9. *best s.* H6C II, 2, 74. *well found s.* Cor. II, 2, 48.

3) prosperous termination of an enterprise, good fortune: *greets heaven for his s.* Lucr. 112. *on a love-book pray for my s.* Gent. I, 1, 19. Merch. III, 2, 243. All's IV, 3, 100. Wint. V, 1, 166. H5 II, 2, 24. H6A I, 2, 82. I, 6, 5. IV, 7, 62. V, 2, 8. H6C I, 2, 76. II, 1, 125. R3 IV, 4, 193. V, 3, 165. Troil. I, 3, 183. IV, 5, 149. Cor. I, 9, 75. Caes. II, 2, 6. V, 3, 65. Mcb. I, 3, 90. 132. I, 5, 1. I, 7, 4. Ant. I, 3, 100. V, 2, 103. Cymb. I, 1, 32. IV, 2, 352.

**Successantly,** successfully? or following after another (viz Aemilius, who had gone before)? *then go s., and plead to him,* Tit. IV, 4, 113 (some M. Edd. *successfully;* Capell *incessantly*).

**Successful,** effective, prosperous, fortunate: Shr. I, 2, 158. Wint. III, 1, 12. H4B IV, 4, 1. H6C II, 2, 41 *(fortune).* Tit. I, 66. 172.

**Successfully,** fortunately: As I, 2, 162 *(he looks s.;* cf. *Look).* Shr. IV, 1, 192. Tit. I, 194.

**Succession,** 1) the act of following, of doing as another has done before: *example, that so terrible shows in the wreck of maidenhood, cannot for all that dissuade s.* All's III, 5, 25.

2) that which is to come; futurity: *slander lives upon s., for ever housed where it gets possession,* Err. III, 1, 105 (feeds on futurity, makes all that is to come its prey). *he hath put me off to the s. of new days this month,* Tim. II, 2, 20. *their writers do them wrong, to make them exclaim against their own s.* Hml. II, 2, 368.

3) the act or right of succeeding or coming to the inheritance of ancestors: Sonn. 2, 12. Tp. II, 1, 151. All's IV, 3, 314. Wint. IV, 4, 440. 491. R2 II, 1, 199. H4A III, 2, 99. H6C II, 1, 119. 172. IV, 6, 56. Hml. III, 2, 356.

4) successors, heirs, descendants: *Cassibelan ... for him and his s. granted Rome a tribute,* Cymb. III, 1, 8. *thinking to bar thee of s., as thou reft'st me of my lands,* III, 3, 102.

**Successive** (*successive* in Meas. II, 2, 98), 1) following in order or uninterrupted course: *what future evils, either now or by remissness new-conceived, and so in progress to be hatched and born, are now to have no s. degrees, but, ere they live, to end,* Meas. II, 2, 98 (viz the degrees of being conceived, of being hatched, and of being born). *an union richer than that which four s. kings in Denmark's crown have worn,* Hml. V, 2, 284.

2) having or giving the right of succeeding to an inheritance; hereditary, legitimate: *now is black beauty's s. heir,* Sonn. 127, 3. *as next the king he was s. heir,* H6B III, 1, 49. *plead my s. title with your swords,* Tit. I, 4.

**Successively,** 1) in uninterrupted order, one following another: *is it upon record, or else reported s. from age to age?* R3 III, 1, 73.

2) by order of succession and inheritance: *so thou the garland wearest s.* H4B IV, 5, 202. *but as s. from blood to blood, your right of birth,* R3 III, 7, 135.

**Successor** (*successor*), one that follows in the place of another: Wint. V, 1, 48. = descendant: Wiv. I, 1, 14. H8 I, 1, 60.

**Succour,** subst. any kind of relief or assistance: As II, 4, 75. R2 III, 2, 32. H4A V, 4, 45. H6A I, 2, 50. IV, 3, 30. H8 II, 1, 109. Per. I, 1, 171. *far from his s.* H8 III, 2, 261 (from the possibility of coming to his assistance). *draw to her s.* V, 4, 55. Plur. —*s* = auxiliary troops: H5 III, 3, 45. H6A IV, 4, 23. H6B III, 1, 285.

**Succour,** vb. (used only in the inf. pres.). to relieve, to help, to assist: *shine sun to s. flowers,* Pilgr. 203. *God will s. us,* H6B IV, 4, 55. H6C III, 3, 41. 207. IV, 7, 56. Tit. IV, 4, 80.

**Such,** 1) of that or the like kind or degree: *some of us are gentlemen, s. as the fury of ungoverned youth thrust from the company of awful men,* Gent. IV, 1, 45. *a spare mast, s. as seafaring men provide,* Err. I, 1, 81. *s. is the simplicity of man,* LLL I, 1, 219. *though the devil lead the measure, s. are to be followed,* All's II, 1, 58. *s. as to my claim are liable,* John V, 2, 101. *s as thou,* Mcb. IV, 2, 82. *s. the adornment of her bed,* Cymb. II, 2, 25 etc. Adjectively: *four s. lamps,* Ven. 489. *s. nectar,* 572. 949. Lucr. 102. 155. 363. 460. 896. 1555. Tp. I, 2, 28. 372. 465. V, 184. Cor. III, 3, 19 (*s. time* = then) etc. etc. *s. time-beguiling sport,* Ven. 24. *s. distilling showers,* 66. *s. petty bondage,* 394. 638. Lucr. 832. 999. 1347. 1825. Tp. II, 1, 174. The ind. art. placed between it and the noun: *s. a park,* Ven. 239. 522. *s. a weak and silly mind,* 1016. *s. a peerless dame,* Lucr. 21. 464. 1540. Tp. I, 2, 101. 457. 493. III, 2, 37. Gent. I, 1, 161. Ado V, 1, 7 (*s. a one*) etc. *s. a coloured periwig,* Gent. IV, 4, 196 (see *A*). *s. another proof,* Gent. I, 1, 97; and, on the other hand, *another s. offence,* Meas. II, 3, 14. As for a particular signification of *s. another,* see *Another.*

Followed by the conjunction *that: s. disdain that they have murdered this poor heart,* Ven. 501. *the birds s. pleasure took, that some would sing,* 1101. Lucr. 19. 1265. 1385. 1403. 1433. 1532. 1561 etc. By *as,* in the same sense: *such signs of rage they bear ... as it seemed they would debate with angry swords,* Lucr. 1419. *I feel s. sharp dissension in my breast as I am sick,* H6A V, 5, 84 etc. (cf. *As*). By an inf., in the same sense (viz of an effect): *I would with s. perfection govern, to excel the golden age,* Tp. II, 1, 167. *s. is the simplicity of man to hearken after the flesh,* LLL I, 1, 219.

*As,* correlatively, before the thing related to or compared with: *with s. black payment as thou hast pretended,* Lucr. 576. *who so base would s. an office have as slanderous death's man to so base a slave,* 1000. *in me thou seest the twilight of s. day as after sunset fadeth in the west,* Sonn. 73, 5. Tp. III, 3, 16. Gent. IV, 1, 45. Err. I, 1, 81. John V, 2, 101. Mcb. IV, 2, 82 etc. etc. *s. as it is* = of whatever kind: *every man has business and desire, s. as it is,* Hml. I, 5, 131. *I have other holy reasons, s. as they are,* All's I, 3, 35.

The relative pronoun in the same sense: *no man well of s. a salve can speak, that heals the wound and cures not the disgrace,* Sonn. 34, 7. *in me thou seest the glowing of s. fire that on the ashes of his youth doth lie,* 73, 9. *s. a man that can do my business,* Gent. IV, 4, 70. *with s. gifts that heaven shall share with you,* Meas. II, 2, 147. *s. things that want no ear but yours,* IV, 3, 108. *whose state is s. that cannot choose but lend and give where it is sure to lose,* All's I, 3, 220. *s. allowed infirmities that honesty is never free of,* Wint. I, 2, 263. *s. words that are but roted in your tongue,* Cor. III, 2, 55. *to s. a man that is no fleering tell-tale,* Caes. I, 3, 116. *s. suffering souls that welcome wrongs,* II, 1, 130. *her offence must be of s. unnatural degree that monsters it,* Lr. I, 1, 222. *put upon him s. a deal of man that worthied him,* II, 2, 127. *to confound s. time that drums him from his sport,* Ant. I, 4, 28. *they are people s. that mend upon the world*, Cymb. II, 4, 25. *purchased by s. sin, for which the pardoner himself is in*, Meas. IV, 2, 111. *in s. forms which here were presupposed upon thee*, Tw. V, 358. *s. an affection, which cannot choose but branch now*, Wint. I, 1, 26. *s. a part which never I shall discharge to the life*, Cor. III, 2, 105. *such I will have, whom I am sure he knows not from the enemy*, All's III, 6, 24. *for the most part s. to whom as great a charge as little honour he meant to lay upon*, H8 I, 1, 76.

*Such like* = of the like kind, of the same sort: *others, they think, delight in s. like circumstance, with s. like sport*, Ven. 844. *with s. like flattering*, Pilgr. 413. *even with s. like valour men hang and drown their proper selves*, Tp. III, 3, 59. *and I for s. like petty crimes as these*, Gent. IV, 1, 52. *and many s. like liberties of sin*, Err. I, 2, 102. *s. like toys as these*, R3 I, 1, 60. *plate, jewels, and s. like trifles*, Tim. III, 2, 23. *and many s. like Ases*, Hml. V, 2, 43. At the close of enumerations, = and so forth: *virtue, youth, liberality, and s. like*, Troil. I, 2, 277 (Ff *and so forth*). cf. *according to Fates and Destinies and s. odd sayings*, Merch. II, 2, 65.

2) By omission of the correlative, = so great, emphatically; very great, very much, very considerable: *frame some feeling line that may discover s. integrity*, Gent. III, 2, 77. *I could come to s. honour!* Wiv. II, 1, 45. *this creature's no s. thing*, Ant. III, 3, 44. *your daughter, whom she bore in hand to love with s. integrity, she did confess was as a scorpion to her sight*, Cymb. V, 5, 44. Tw. III, 4, 395. = very bad: *I shall have s. a life!* Troil. IV, 2, 22. cf. *so* Lr. II, 2, 41.

3) of the same kind, not other: *my songs and praises be to one, of one, still s., and ever so*, Sonn. 105, 4. *the canker-blooms have full as deep a dye as the perfumed tincture of the roses, hang on s. thorns and play as wantonly*, 54, 7. *it hath s. senses as we have, s.* Tp. I, 2, 412. *in the self-same inn a meaner woman was delivered of s. a burthen*, Err. I, 1, 56. *as his your case is s.* LLL IV, 3, 131. *let their beds be made as soft as yours, and let their palates be seasoned with s. viands*, Merch. IV, 1, 97.

4) Used to hint in a general and indefinite manner at persons or things, that could very well be distinctly indicated and pointed out, if the speaker pleased: *that s. a one and s. a one were past cure*, Meas. II, 1, 114. *you spurned me s. a day*, Merch. I, 3, 128. *if you repay me not on s. a day, in s. a place, s. sum*, 147. *I'ld venture the well-lost life of mine on his grace's cure by s. a day and hour*, All's I, 3, 255. *at s. and s. a sconce, at s. a breach, at s. a convoy*, H5 III, 6, 75. *we died at s. a place*, IV, 1, 144. *I saw him yesterday, ... with s., or s.* Hml. II, 1, 57. *this might be my lord s. a one, that praised my lord s. a one's horse*, V, 1, 92. *how I would think on him at certain hours s. thoughts and s.* Cymb. I, 3, 28. *s. and s. pictures*, II, 2, 25.

**Such-a-one**, and **Such-like**, see *Such*.

**Suck**, subst. *to give s.* = to suckle; abs.: Mcb. I, 7, 54. With a dat.: *she that gave thee s.* Troil. II, 3, 252.

**Suck**, vb. 1) absol. to draw in with the mouth: *where the bee — s, there s. I*, Tp. V, 88. *to s., to s.* H5 II, 3, 58. Especially = to draw the breast: *to see my lambs s.* As III, 2, 81. *at their mothers' moist eyes babes shall s.* H6A I, 1, 49. *—ing on her bosom*, Rom. II, 3, 12. = to be at the breast: *when Hector's grandsire —ed*, Troil. I, 3, 292. *—ing*: Merch. II, 1, 29. H6A

III, 1, 197. H6B III, 1, 71. Bottom even says: *as gently as any —ing dove*, Mids. I, 2, 85. Figuratively, = to draw in as a whirlpool, to absorb: *England his approaches makes as fierce as waters to the —ing of a gulf*, H5 II, 4, 10.

2) tr. to draw in, to draw out; a) the matter imbibed as object: *such nectar from his lips she had not —ed*, Ven. 572. *a wasp —ed the honey that thy chaste bee kept*, Lucr. 840. Err. II, 2, 194. As II, 5, 13. Shr. I, 1, 28. R2 III, 4, 38. H5 II, 3, 58. IV, 4, 68. H6B IV, 1, 109. Rom. V, 3, 92. Tim. IV, 3, 432. Caes. II, 2, 87. Hml. III, 1, 164. = to draw from the breast as a suckling: *thy valiantness was mine, thou —edst it from me*, Cor. III, 2, 129. *the milk thou —edst from her*, Tit. II, 3, 144. *hadst —ed wisdom from my breast*, Rom. I, 3, 68. With *up*: *all the infections which the sun —s up from bogs*, Tp. II, 2, 1. Mids. II, 1, 89. R2 III, 2, 14. Caes. II, 1, 262. Cymb. III, 1, 22.

b) that from which matter is drawn as object: *as the weasel —s eggs*, As II, 5, 14. *I s. my teeth*, John I, 192. *—s her princely eggs*, H5 I, 2, 171. Applied to the breast: *a son that —ed an earthly mother*, Ven. 863. *the —ed and hungry lioness*, As IV, 3, 127. *when thou —edst her breast*, H6A V, 4, 28. Tit. IV, 2, 178. Hml. V, 2, 196.

c) the accus. denoting the effect: *the ivy that —ed my verdure out on't*, Tp. I, 2, 87. *your fair show shall s. away their souls*, H5 IV, 2, 17. *my sea shall s. them dry*, H6C IV, 8, 55. *more spongy to s. in the sense of fear*, Troil. II, 2, 12. *my baby at my breast, that —s the nurse asleep*, Ant. V, 2, 313.

**Suckle**, to nurse at the breast: Cor. I, 3, 44. Oth. II, 1, 161.

**Sudden**, 1) happening without previous notice, coming unexpectedly: *a s. pale usurps her cheek*, Ven. 589. *their secret and s. arrival*, Lucr. Arg. 8. *the s. surprise of my powers*, Wiv. V, 5, 130. *s. breaking out of mirth*, LLL V, 1, 121. *the s. hand of death close up mine eye*, V, 2, 825. *whose s. sight hath thralled my wounded eye*, Shr. I, 1, 225. *his s. approach, so out of circumstance and s.* Wint. V, 1, 90. *on some great s. hest*, H4A II, 3, 65. *s. sorrow serves to say thus ...*, H4B IV, 2, 83. *this s. mischief never could have fallen*, H6A II, 1, 59. *one s. foil shall never breed mistrust*, III, 3, 11. *somewhat too s., sirs, the warning is*, V, 2, 14. *some s. qualm hath struck me*, H6B I, 1, 54. *his s. death*, III, 2, 133. *what makes you in this s. change*, H6C IV, 4, 1. *this s. stab of rancour*, R3 III, 2, 89. *by s. floods*, IV, 4, 512. *what s. anger's this*, H8 III, 2, 204. *that's somewhat s.* 394. *that mirth fate turns to s. sadness*, Troil. I, 1, 40. *with a s. reinforcement*, Cor. II, 2, 117. *this my s. choice*, Tit. I, 318. *too rash, too unadvised, too s.* Rom. II, 2, 118. *no s. mean of death*, III, 3, 45. *sorted out a s. day of joy*, III, 5, 110. *this so s. business*, IV, 3, 12. *such a s. flood of mutiny*, Caes. III, 2, 215. *s. push gives them the overthrow*, V, 2, 5. *with a s. vigour it doth curd ... the wholesome blood*, Hml. I, 5, 68. *this s. sending him away*, IV, 3, 8. *my s. and more strange return*, IV, 7, 47. *they for s. joy did weep*, Lr. I, 4, 191.

Adverbially: *report that I am s. sick*, Ant. I, 3, 5.

Substantively; *of a s.*: Shr. I, 1, 152. Tit. I, 393. *on a s.*: Wiv. IV, 4, 51. H8 III, 2, 114. Rom. II, 3, 50. *on such a s.* As I, 3, 27. *on the s.*: Ven. 749. H4B IV, 2, 80. H6A II, 2, 23. H8 IV, 2, 96. Cor. I, 4, 50. II, 1, 237. Ant. I, 2, 86. V, 2, 347.

2) unprepared, not provided for, extemporal: *all her s. quips*, Gent. IV, 2, 12. *that you might the better arm you to the s. time*, John V, 6, 26. *never was such a s. scholar made*, H5 I, 1, 32. *as I with s. and extemporal speech purpose to answer*, H6A III, 1, 6. *you were ever good at s. commendations*, H8 V, 3, 122.

3) happening immediately, speedy: *to-morrow! O, that's s.* Meas. II, 2, 83. *join not with grief ... to make my end too s.* R2 V, 1, 17. *none durst come near for fear of s. death*, H6A I, 4, 48. *to-morrow is too s.* R3 III, 4, 45. *this tempest aboded the s. breach of it* (the peace) H8 I, 1, 94. *which reformation must be s. too*, V, 3, 20. *who, raging with thy tears, and they with them, without a s. calm, will overset thy tempest-tossed body*, Rom. III, 5, 137. *should the bearers put to s. death*, Hml. V, 2, 46. *returned me expectations and comforts of s. respect and acquaintance*, Oth. IV, 2, 192.

4) quick, hasty: *let us both be s.* Tp. II, 1, 306. *lest my liking might too s. seem*, Ado I, 1, 316. *my s. wooing, nor her s. consenting*, As V, 2, 8. *there was never any thing so s.* 33. *therefore I will be s. and dispatch*, John IV, 1, 27. *how thou shalt escape by s. flight*, H6A IV, 5, 11. *it will excuse this s. execution of my will*, V, 5, 99. *he's s., if a thing comes in his head*, H6C V, 5, 86. *be s. in the execution*, R3 I, 3, 346. *I stand on s. haste*, Rom. II, 3, 93. *Casca, be s., for we fear prevention*, Caes. III, 1, 19.

5) rash, inconsiderate: *I am too s. bold*, LLL II, 107 (M. Edd. *sudden-bold*). *some s. mischief may arise of it*, H5 IV, 7, 186 (a mischief caused by rashness). *revoke your s. approbation*, Cor. II, 3, 259.

6) violent; impetuous; passionate: *s. and quick in quarrel*, As II, 7, 151. *small showers last long, but s. storms are short*, R2 II, 1, 35. *as humorous as winter and as s. as flaws congealed in the spring of day*, H4B IV, 4, 34. *false, deceitful, s., malicious*, Mcb. IV, 3, 59. *he is rash and very s. in choler*, Oth. II, 1, 279. In R2 I, 3, 227 Ff s. sorrow, Qq sullen sorrow.

**Sudden-bold,** see *Sudden* 5.

**Suddenly,** 1) unexpectedly, all at once: *and withal s. stabbed herself*, Lucr. Arg. 21. *muse not that I thus s. proceed*, Gent. I, 3, 64. *when I s. call you, come forth*, Wiv. III, 3, 11. *Hero s. died*, Ado IV, 2, 66. *you were best to tell Antonio what you hear; but do not s., for it may grieve him*, Merch. II, 8, 34. *your argosies are come to harbour s.* V, 277. As IV, 3, 111. All's III, 6, 24. John V, 6, 30. R2 I, 4, 55. H5 III, 5, 8. H6A I, 4, 72. III, 3, 59. IV, 7, 12. V, 3, 40. H6B II, 1, 45. III, 2, 370. H8 IV, 2, 15. V, 4, 58. Troil. V, 3, 65. Tit. II, 3, 104. V, 1, 23. 38. Caes. II, 1, 239. Lr. II, 1, 58. IV, 3, 1. Cymb. I, 4, 131.

2) without premeditation, extempore: *do it without invention*, s. H6A III, 1, 5. *but s. to nominate them all, it is impossible*, H6B II, 1, 129. *how to make ye s. an answer*, H8 III, 1, 70.

3) within a short time, quickly: *a shining gloss that vadeth s.* Pilgr. 170. *was ever match clapped up so s.?* Shr. II, 327.

4) presently, immediately: *be s. revenged on my foe*, Lucr. 1683. *Mistress Ford desires you to come s.* Wiv. IV, 1, 6. *and s. resolve me in my suit. I will, if s. I may*, LLL II, 110. 111. *his malice 'gainst the lady will s. break out*, As I, 2, 295. *do this s.* II, 2, 19. *I will buy it right s.* II, 4, 100. *the great Apollo s. will have the truth of this appear*, Wint. II, 3, 200. *when time is ripe, which will be s.* H4A I, 3, 294. *I'll re-*

pent, *and that s.* III, 3, 5. H5 V, 2, 81. H6B II, 2, 67. H6C IV, 2, 4. R3 IV, 2, 19. 20. IV, 4, 76. 450 (Qq *presently*). H8 V, 4, 83. Troil. IV, 4, 35. Hml. II, 2, 215. Per. III, 1, 70. IV, 1, 96.

**Sue,** to beg, to entreat, to petition; 1) absol.. *when maidens s., men give like gods*, Meas. I, 4, 80. Err. I, 1, 146. LLL III, 191. 206. R2 I, 1, 196. R3 I, 2, 171. IV, 4, 94 (Ff *who —s and kneels*, Qq *who —s to thee*). 101. Troil. I, 2, 317. Ant. III, 12, 24. As a term of law, = to prosecute, to make legal claim: *how can this be true, that you stand forfeit, being those that s.?* LLL V, 2, 427 (punning).

An inf. following: *to s. to live, I find I seek to die* Meas. III, 1, 42. *I will s. to be rid of it* (life) 174. R2 V, 3, 129. H6C III, 2, 61. Lr. I, 1, 30. Oth. II, 3, 278.

2) With *for* (before the thing requested): *I s. for exiled majesty's repeal*, Lucr. 640. *I s. for yours* (acquaintance) Wiv. II, 2, 170. Meas. II, 4, 163. H8 II, 1, 70. Cor. II, 3, 216. Ant. II, 1, 5. *to whom I —d for my dear son's life*, Tit. I, 453.

With *to* (before the person applied to): *her eyes petitioners to his eyes —ing*, Ven. 356. *my master —s to her*, Gent. II, 1, 143. H6A I, 2, 112. V, 1, 4. H6B I, 3, 42. R3 I, 2, 168. II, 1, 106. IV, 4, 94 (see sub 1). 101. Tit. I, 453 (see sub 2). Oth. II, 3, 276. III, 3, 79. Ant. III, 12, 13.

3) trans. = to beg, to ask for: *to s. and be denied such common grace*, Tim. III, 5, 95. *when you —d staying*, Ant. I, 3, 33. As a term of law, = a) to lay legal claim to: *the statute of thy beauty thou wilt take, thou usurer, that put'st forth all to use, and s. a friend came debtor for my sake*, Sonn. 134, 11. *by his attorneys-general to s. his livery*, R2 II, 1, 203. II, 3, 129. H4A IV, 3, 62 (cf. *Livery*). b) to seek for in law: *that therefore such a writ* (of a praemunire) *be —d against you, to forfeit all your goods*, H8 III, 2, 341.

**Sueno,** see *Sweno.*

**Suffer,** 1) to bear with patience or constancy; to support, not to sink under; absol.: *if wisdom be in —ing*, Tim. III, 5, 51. *with patience more than savages could s.* Ant. I, 4, 61. *a Roman with a Roman's heart can s.* Cymb. V, 5, 81. *thou art a man, and I have —ed like a girl*, Per. V, 1, 138. Trans.: *s. question*, All's II, 5, 42. *the one part —ed, the other will I do*, Cor. II, 3, 131. *can wisely s. the worst that man can breathe*, Tim. III, 5, 31. *to s. the slings and arrows of fortune*, Hml. III, 1, 57. *my duty cannot s. to obey your daughter's hard commands*, Lr. III, 4, 153.

2) to undergo or bear with a lively sense of pain; absol., = to be in pain and distress: *how once I —ed in your crime*, Sonn. 120, 8. *her —ing ecstasy*, Compl. 69. *the —ing pangs it bears*, 272. *my —ing youth*, 178. *I have —ed with those that I saw s.* Tp. I, 2, 5. 6. *I do as truly s. as e'er I did commit*, Gent. V, 4, 76. Wiv. III, 3, 233. IV, 5, 113. Ado V, 1, 40. LLL I, 1, 313. All's IV, 4, 30. V, 3, 163. Tw. I, 5, 284. Wint. II, 1, 128. H4B IV, 1, 101 (cf. *To*). Cor. I, 1, 69 (*your —ing in this dearth*). IV, 6, 6. Mcb. III, 2, 16.* III, 6, 48. Hml. III, 1, 37. Lr. II, 4, 110. III, 6, 111. Oth. III, 3, 54. Cymb. V, 5, 335. Per. IV, 4, 23.

Trans.: *let me s. the imprisoned absence of your liberty*, Sonn. 58, 5. *what I have —ed*, Wiv. III, 5, 97. *that you have —ed all this*, 126. *I —ed the pangs of three deaths*, 109. IV, 5, 110. V, 5, 177. *the wrongs I s.* Err. III, 1, 16. V, 398. Ado III, 3, 3. Merch. IV, 1,

12. All's IV, 4, 27. Wint. IV, 4, 800. H4B IV, 1, 68. H8 IV, 2, 8. Mcb. IV, 3, 48. Hml. II, 2, 191. III, 2, 71. Lr. II, 4, 45. Oth. I, 3, 158. IV, 2, 182.

3) to be injured, to sustain loss or damage: *it —s not in smiling pomp*, Sonn. 124, 6. *that —s under probation*, Tw. II, 5, 142. *your jewel hath —ed under praise*, Tim. I, 1, 165. *our naked frailties, that s. in exposure*, Mcb. II, 3, 133. *who hast not in thy brows an eye discerning thine honour from thy —ing*, Lr. IV, 2, 53 (what does you honour from what is detrimental to you). *things outward do draw the inward quality after them, to s. all alike*, Ant. III, 13, 34.

4) to be put to death: *hath lately —ed by a thunderbolt*, Tp. II, 2, 38. *sure as I live, he had —ed for it*, Gent. IV, 4, 17. 36. *so must you be the first that gives this sentence, and he, that —s*, Meas. II, 2, 107 (or = —s it?). *to let him s.* II, 4, 97. cf. All's IV, 4, 30.

5) to undergo, to be affected by, to experience (in a good or a bad sense): *why dost thou pine within and s. dearth*, Sonn. 146, 3. *their —ed labour*, Tp. I, 2, 231. *doth s. a sea-change into something rich and strange*, 400. *he shall not s. indignity*, III, 2, 42. *for which of my good parts did you first s. love for me? S. love! a choice epithet! I do s. love indeed, for I love thee against my will*, Ado V, 2, 65. 67 (cf. *sufferance* in Troil. II, 1, 104). *no motion of the liver, but the palate, that s. surfeit, cloyment and revolt*, Tw. II, 4, 102. *Hermione hath —ed death*, Wint. III, 3, 42. *if your settled project may s. alteration*, IV, 4, 536. R2 II, 1, 267. H5 IV, 8, 56. H6A V, 5, 8. H8 I, 2, 51. Troil. IV, 1, 74. Cor. I, 10, 18. III, 3, 46. V, 2, 72. Caes. II, 1, 68. III, 2, 44. Hml. III, 2, 141. V, 2, 117. Ant. I, 2, 139. II, 2, 159. IV, 2, 23.

6) to bear, to allow, to let, not to hinder; absol. (= to acquiesce, to put up with anything): *such —ing souls that welcome wrongs*, Caes. II, 1, 130. *thou hast no weapon, and perforce must s.* Oth. V, 2, 256. Transitively: *that they will s. these abominations ...from forth her fair streets chased*, Lucr. 1832. *would s. her poor knight surprised*, All's I, 3, 119. *how long shall tender duty make me s. wrong?* R2 II, 1, 164. *—ing so the causes of our wreck*, 269. *he that hath —ed this disordered spring*, III, 4, 48. *detraction will not s. it*, H4A V, 1, 142. *s. them now, and they'll o'ergrow the garden*, H6B III, 1, 32. H6C I, 1, 59. R3 I, 3, 271. H8 V, 3, 24. Cor. III, 1, 40. 303. V, 2, 19. Lr. I, 2, 54. Cymb. I, 4, 59. Cymb. IV, 2, 143. The passive *to be —ed* = to be allowed to have one's own way, not to be hindered or interfered with: *affection is a coal that must be cooled; else, —ed, it will set the heart on fire*, Ven. 388. *so did your son* (try himself); *he was so —ed*, H4B II, 3, 57. *being —ed in that harmful slumber*, H6B III, 2, 262. *being —ed with the bear's fell paw*, V, 1, 153 (cf. *With*). *a little fire is quickly trodden out, which, being —ed, rivers cannot quench*, H6C IV, 8, 8.

Followed by an inf., a) without *to: to s. the flesh-fly blow my mouth*, Tp. III, 1, 62. *never —s matter of the world enter his thoughts*, Troil. II, 3, 196. b) with *to: —ing my friend for my sake to approve her*, Sonn. 42, 8. *would s. him to spend his youth at home*, Gent. I, 3, 5. Err. IV, 4, 113. V, 157. LLL I, 2, 133. Mids. III, 2, 327. Merch. V, 213. Tw. V, 349. R2 I, 2, 30. H4A IV, 3, 93. H4B II, 4, 372. H6A I, 5, 9. III, 1, 97. V, 4, 127. R3 IV, 1, 16. H8 V, 2, 29. V, 3, 106. Cor. I, 1, 82. IV, 5, 83. Tit. I, 375. II, 1, 124. IV,

4, 83. Rom. II, 4, 163. Hml. V, 1, 109. Lr. IV, 2, 44. Cymb. I, 1, 170. V, 4, 63. Per. V, 1, 79. The inf. omitted: Shr. II, 31. Wint. IV, 4, 863. John II, 559. Troil. IV, 2, 31.

**Sufferance,** 1) a bearing with patience; moderation, patience: *if not a present remedy, at least a patient s.* Ado I, 3, 10. *s. is the badge of all our tribe*, Merch. I, 3, 111. *if a Christian wrong a Jew, what should his s. be by Christian example?* III, 1, 73. *England shall ... admire our s.* H5 III, 6, 132. *our yoke and s. show us womanish*, Caes. I, 3, 84.

2) pain, torment: *shall his death draw out to lingering s.* Meas. II, 4, 167. *the beetle ... in corporal s. finds a pang as great*, III, 1, 80. *'tis a s. panging as soul and body's severing*, H8 II, 3, 15. *her s. made almost each pang a death*, V, 1, 68.

3) distress, misery, suffering: *patience, tame to s., bide each check*, Sonn. 58, 7. *your sorrow hath eaten up my s.* Wiv. IV, 2, 2. *made a push at chance and s.* Ado V, 1, 38. *the seeming —s that you had borne*, H4A V, 1, 51. *of s. comes ease*, H4B V, 4, 28. *patience herself... doth lesser blench at s.* Troil. I, 1, 28. *our s. is a gain to them*, Cor. I, 1, 22. *thy nature did commence in s.* Tim. IV, 3, 268. *breathed our s. vainly*, V, 4, 8. *the s. of our souls*, Caes. II, 1, 115. *then the mind much s. doth o'erskip*, Lr. III, 6, 113.

3) damage, loss: *a noble ship of Venice hath seen a grievous wreck and s. on most part of their fleet*, Oth. II, 1, 23.

4) death by execution: *which I in s. heartily will rejoice*, H5 II, 2, 159.

5) permission, allowance, connivance; negative consent by not hindering: *some villains of my court are of consent and s. in this*, As II, 2, 3. *lest example breed, by his s., more of such a kind*, H5 II, 2, 46 (i. e. by his being suffered). *thou shalt reign but by their s.* H6C I, 1, 234. *your last service was s., 'twas not voluntary: no man is beaten voluntary*, Troil. II, 1, 104. *they do prank them in authority, against all noble s.* Cor. III, 1, 24. *we have been too slight in s.* Cymb. III, 5, 35.

**Suffering,** see *Suffer* 2 & 3.

**Suffice,** 1) absol. to be enough: *if the love of soldier can s.* Wiv. II, 1, 12. *if that will not s.* Merch. IV, 1, 210. 213. Shr. I, 2, 66. Wint. I, 2, 235. H4B III, 2, 178. 180. H6B III, 3, 71. Ant. IV, 14, 117 (*—ing strokes for death*). Per. II, 1, 78. Followed by an inf.: *let it then s. to drown one woe*, Lucr. 1679. *to know thee shall s.* Pilgr. 63 and LLL IV, 2, 115. By a clause: *it —th that Brutus leads me on*, Caes. II, 1, 333. V, 1, 125. The pron. *it* omitted: *—th, my reasons are good*, Shr. I, 1, 252. III, 2, 108. *—th that I have maintains my state*, H6B IV, 10, 24. *—th not that we are brought to Rome?* Tit. I, 109. *—th a Roman with a Roman's heart can suffer*, Cymb. V, 5, 80.

2) trans. a) to satisfy, to content: *true sorrow then is feelingly —d when with like semblance it is sympathised*, Lucr. 1112. *I in thy abundance am —d*, Sonn. 37, 11. *till he be first —d, I will not touch a bit*, As II, 7, 131. *when my knightly stomach is —d*, John I, 191.

b) to be enough for (though not quite adequate to the want or demand): *it shall s. me*, LLL II, 167. *let it s. the greatness of your powers to have bereft a prince of all his fortune*, Per. II, 1, 8. Used especially to express that enough has been said: *let it s. thee ...*

*that I love thee,* Wiv. II, 1, 10. As I, 3, 57. Troil. II, 3, 73. Oth. III, 4, 131.

3) refl. to content one's self (Germ. *sich begnügen*): *let's return again, and s. ourselves with the report of it,* All's III, 5, 10.

**Sufficiency,** adequate qualification, ability: *then no more remains but that to your s.* Meas. I, 1, 8. *but no man's virtue nor s. to be so moral when he shall endure the like himself,* Ado V, 1, 29. *whom you know of stuffed s.* Wint. II, 1, 185. *a substitute of most allowed s.* Oth. I, 3, 224.

**Sufficient,** 1) adequate to the end proposed, enough: Gent. V, 4, 75. Shr. IV, 4, 45. H5 I, 2, 141. III, 2, 64. H6A II, 3, 56. V, 5, 13. 92. H6C I, 3, 26. Tim. III, 5, 61. Cymb. I, 4, 161.

2) fit, able: *are there not men in your ward s. to serve it?* Meas. II, 1, 281. 287. *some s. honest witnesses,* Shr. IV, 4, 95. *half a dozen s. men,* H4B III, 2, 102. *you'll never meet a more s. man,* Oth. III, 4, 91. *all in all s.* IV, 1, 276.

In the language of Shylock, = capable of paying, solvent, rich: *my meaning in saying he is a good man is to have you understand me that he is s.* Merch. I, 3, 17. *the man is, notwithstanding, s.* 27.

**Sufficiently,** to a degree answering the purpose, satisfactorily, so as to have or to be enough: *businesses which none without thee can s. manage,* Wint. IV, 2, 16. *we will be revenged s.* H6A I, 4, 58. *his sealed commission doth speak s. he's gone to travel,* Per. I, 3, 14.

**Suffigance,** Dogberry's blunder for *sufficient:* Ado III, 5, 56.

**Suffocate,** to kill by stopping respiration, to choke: *let not hemp his windpipe s.* H5 III, 6, 45. — *ing streams,* Oth. III, 3, 389. Unchanged in the partic.: *for Suffolk's duke, may he be s.* H6B I, 1, 124. *this chaos, when degree is s., follows the choking,* Troil. I, 3, 125.

**Suffocation,** death caused by choking: Wiv. III, 5, 119.

**Suffolk,** name of an English county: H6C I, 1, 156. IV, 8, 12. *Earl* or *Duke of S.* the baronial title of several peers famous in English history: H5 IV, 6, 10. 11. 15. 24. IV, 8, 108. H6A V, 3, 53. 132 etc. H6B I, 1, 17. 45. 64. 124 etc. H8 IV, 1, 17. 41. V, 1, 8.

**Suffrage,** a voice given in the choice of a man for an office: *entreat them to give their s.* Cor. II, 3, 142. Plur. —*s:* Lucr. Arg. 3. Tit. I, 218. IV, 3, 19. Per. II, 4, 41.

**Sugar,** subst. the sweet substance made from Saccharum officinarum: Wiv. II, 2, 70. LLL V, 2, 231. As III, 3, 31. Wint. IV, 3, 40. R2 II, 3, 6. H4A I, 2, 126. II, 4, 25. 34. 65. R3 I, 3, 242. Adjectively, = sweet: *severed lips, parted with s. breath,* Merch. III, 2, 119. *there is more eloquence in a s. touch of them* (your lips) H5 V, 2, 303.

**Sugar,** vb. to sweeten (in a metaphorical sense), to embellish, to colour: *these sentences, to s., or to gall, being strong on both sides, are equivocal,* Oth. I, 3, 216. *with devotion's visage and pious action we do s. o'er the devil himself,* Hml. III, 1, 48. Partic. —*ed* = sweetly tempting, enticing: *wouldst have ... followed the —ed game before thee,* Tim. IV, 3, 259. *thy —ed tongue* (turns) *to bitter wormwood taste,* Lucr. 893. —*ed words,* H6A III, 3, 18. H6B III, 2, 45. R3 III, 1, 13.

**Sugar-candy,** sugar clarified and crystallized: *one poor penny-worth of s. to make thee long-winded,* H4A III, 3, 180.*

**Sugarsop,** name of a servant in Shr. IV, 1, 92.

**Suggest,** 1) to insinuate, to intimate, to infuse: (jealousy) *gives false alarms, —eth mutiny,* Ven. 651. *what spirit, what devil, —s this imagination?* Wiv. III, 3, 230. *if secret powers s. but truth to my divining thoughts,* H6C IV, 6, 69. *this, as you say, —ed at some time when his soaring insolence shall touch the people,* Cor. II, 1, 269.

2) to prompt or inform underhand, to whisper: *two loves I have of comfort and despair, which like two spirits do s. me still,* Sonn. 144, 2. *he did s. his soon-believing adversaries,* R2 I, 1, 101. *we must s. the people in what hatred he still hath held them,* Cor. II, 1, 261.

3) to tempt, to seduce: *his boast of Lucrece' sovereignty —ed this proud issue of a king,* Lucr. 37. *tender youth is soon —ed,* Gent. III, 1, 34. *those heavenly eyes, that look into these faults, —ed us to make,* LLL V, 2, 780. *to s. thee from thy master,* All's IV, 5, 47. *what Eve, what serpent, hath —ed thee to make a second fall of cursed man?* R2 III, 4, 75. *all other devils that s. by treasons,* H5 II, 2, 114. *—s the king to this last costly treaty,* H8 I, 1, 164. *they* (devils) *do s. at first with heavenly shows,* Oth. II, 3, 358.

**Suggestion,** 1) any intimation or insinuation: *who* (the heart) *like a king perplexed in his throne, by their* (the eyes') *s. gives a deadly groan,* Ven. 1044.

2) a prompting to do evil, secret incitement, temptation, seduction: *they'll take s. as a cat laps milk; they'll tell the clock to any business that we say befits the hour,* Tp. II, 1, 288. *the most opportune place, the strongest s. our worser genius can, shall never melt mine honour into lust,* IV, 26. —*s are to others as to me,* LLL I, 1, 159. *a filthy officer he is in these —s for the young earl,* All's III, 5, 18. *arm thy constant and thy nobler parts against these giddy loose —s,* John III, 1, 292. *Arthur, whom they say is killed on your s.* IV, 2, 166. *misled by your s.* H4A IV, 3, 51. *that the united vessel of their blood, mingled with venom of s., ... shall never leak,* H4B IV, 4, 45. *then was I going prisoner to the Tower, by the s. of the queen's allies,* R3 III, 2, 103. *one that, by s., tied all the kingdom,* H8 IV, 2, 35 (an expression taken from Holinshed, meaning perhaps any underhand practice). *why do I yield to that s. whose horrid image doth unfix my hair,* Mcb. I, 3, 134. *I'ld turn it all to thy s., plot, and damned practice,* Lr. II, 1, 75.

**Suit,** subst. 1) attendance: *which late her noble s. in court did shun,* Compl. 234. *give notice to such men of sort and s. as are to meet him,* Meas. IV, 4, 19 (such as owed attendance to the prince as their liege lord. cf. the term of feudal law: *suit and service*). Hence the phrase: *out of —s with fortune,* As I, 2, 258 (no more in the service and attendance of fortune). Quibbling in LLL V, 2, 275.

2) a prosecution at law, an action brought against a person: *the client* (the heart) *breaks, as desperate in his s.* Ven. 336 (quibbling). *hast thou no s. against my knight?* Wiv. II, 1, 220. *I do arrest you, sir; you hear the s.* Err. IV, 1, 79. *that I follow thus a losing s. against him,* Merch. IV, 1, 62. *of a strange nature is the s. you follow,* 177. *to arrest a p. at the s. of another:* Err. IV, 1, 69. IV, 2, 43. 44. IV, 4, 134. Tw.

III, 4, 360. H4B II, 1, 48. 77. *in durance, at Malvolio's s.* Tw. V, 283; cf. Meas. IV, 3, 10. *—s of durance,* quibbling: Err. IV, 3, 26.

3) petition, address of entreaty: *if opportunity and humblest s. cannot attain it,* Wiv. III, 4, 20; *not a man of them shall have the grace, despite of s.,* to see a *lady's face,* LLL V, 2, 129; *and might by no s. gain our audience,* H4B IV, 1, 76; *be not you spoke with, but by mighty s.* R3 III, 7, 46; *at my s. pardon what is past,* Tit. I, 431; *whose life I have spared at s. of his grey beard,* Lr. II, 2, 68. *where his s. may be obtained,* Lucr. 898. *the king of Naples ... hearkens my brother's s.* Tp. I, 2, 122. *moneys is your s.* Merch. I, 3, 120. II, 2, 145. 146. *thou hast obtained thy s.* 153. As IV, 1, 87. 89 (quibbling). *if this s. be won, that you express content,* All's Epil. 336. Wint. I, 2, 402. R2 IV, 154. H6A II, 2, 47. V, 3, 19. H6B IV, 1, 124. H6C III, 3, 142. H8 V, 3, 161. Cor. II, 3, 231. V, 2, 94. V, 3, 6. 17. 136. Oth. I, 1, 9. III, 3, 26. 80. III, 4, 87. 110. IV, 1, 108. Per. V, 1, 262. *to make s.* H8 I, 2, 197. Tit. I, 223. Cymb. V, 5, 71. With *to* before the person applied to: *many a wooer does commence his s. to her he thinks not worthy,* Ado II, 3, 52. *I have a s. to you,* Merch. II, 2, 186. *we will make it our s. to the duke that the wrestling might not go forward,* As I, 2, 192. H4B V, 1, 79. H6B IV, 7, 4. Cor. II, 1, 254. Caes. II, 4, 27. Oth. III, 1, 36.

Specially = a) *a request made to a prince, a court-solicitation:* Tp. I, 2, 79. III, 2, 44. Meas. II, 2, 28. II, 4, 70. V, 460. LLL II, 110. V, 2, 749. Wint. IV, 4, 828. John IV, 2, 62. 84. R2 V, 3, 130. H4A I, 2, 80. H6A V, 1, 34. H6B I, 3, 42. IV, 7, 4. H6C III, 2, 4. 8. 13. 16. 81. 117. IV, 8, 40. R3 III, 7, 63. 140 (Ff *cause*). 148. 203. 214 and 221 (*accept*). H8 I, 2, 10. II, 3, 85 (*for any s. of pounds*). Rom. I, 4, 78 (*she gallops o'er a courtier's nose, and then dreams he of smelling out a s.*). Caes. II, 4, 27. 42. III, 1, 5. 6. 28. Hml. I, 2, 43. Cymb. V, 5, 71.

b) *amorous solicitation, courtship;* sometimes proposal of marriage: *what great danger dwells upon my s.?* Ven. 206. *tender my s.* Lucr. 534. *I attended a youthful s.* Compl. 79 (= the suit of a youth). *in thy s. be humble true,* Pilgr. 330. Gent. IV, 2, 102. IV, 4, 186. V, 2, 1. Wiv. I, 4, 153. II, 1, 98. III, 5, 126. Err. IV, 2, 14. Ado II, 1, 78. 365. II, 3, 52. III, 2, 103. LLL V, 2, 275. 756. 849. Merch. I, 2, 113. II, 7, 73. All's I, 3, 204. II, 3, 82. III, 5, 74. Tw. I, 2, 45. I, 5, 116. III, 1, 119. John I, 254. H5 V, 2, 132. H6A V, 3, 75. 150. R3 I, 2, 236. Troil. I, 1, 100. Rom. I, 2, 6. Hml. I, 3, 129. Oth. IV, 1, 26. IV, 2, 201. Cymb. III, 4, 92. V, 5, 185.

4) *dress, apparel: some four —s of satin,* Meas. IV, 3, 11. *gives them —s of durance,* Err. IV, 3, 26 (quibbling). *in a s. of buff,* IV, 2, 45. *a page's s.* Merch. II, 4, 33. As II, 7, 44 (quibbling). IV, 1, 34. Shr. Ind. 1, 59. 106 (*see him dressed in all —s like a lady*). Tw. V, 242. H4A I, 2, 81 (quibbling). II, 4, 213. 228. H5 III, 6, 81. IV, 2, 57. Hml. I, 2, 78. III, 2, 137. Lr. III, 4, 141. Cymb. III, 2, 78. III, 5, 128. 141. Metaphorically: *to put on your boldest s. of mirth,* Merch. II, 2, 211. *these but the trappings and the —s of woe,* Hml. I, 2, 86.

**Suit,** vb. 1) tr. a) *to clothe, to dress: that I did s. me all points like a man,* As I, 3, 118. *I'll s. myself as does a Briton peasant,* Cymb. V, 1, 23. Partic. *—ed* = dressed: Merch. I, 2, 79. All's I, 1, 170. Tw. V,

241. Troil. Prol. 24. Lr. IV, 7, 6. Metaphorically: *therefore my mistress' brows are raven black, her eyes so —ed,* Sonn. 127, 10. *and s. thy pity like in every part,* 132, 12. *description cannot s. itself in words,* H5 IV, 2, 53. Similarly: *there's one meaning well —ed,* Ado V, 1, 231 (German: *eingekleidet*).

b) *to fit, to adapt: O dear discretion, how his words are —ed,* Merch. III, 5, 70. *but therein —s his folly to the mettle of my speech,* As II, 7, 81. *s. the action to the word,* Hml. III, 2, 19. *his whole function —ing with forms to his conceit,* Hml. II, 2, 582 (fitting, by means of external forms, his whole action to the image of his mind).

c) *to be adapted to, to become: what he is indeed, more —s you to conceive than I to speak of,* As I, 2, 279. *such furniture as —s the greatness of his person,* H8 II, 1, 99

2) intr. *to agree, to accord: such a one whose wrongs do s. with mine,* Ado V, 1, 7. Tw. I, 2, 50. III, 4, 6. H5 I, 2, 17. Tim. II, 2, 23. Mcb. II, 1, 60. *let him be so entertained amongst you as —s with gentlemen of your knowing, to a stranger of his quality,* Cymb. I, 4, 29 (as it agrees with, as it becomes, gentlemen of your breeding towards a stranger etc.).

**Suitable,** fit: *what is amiss in them, you gods, make s. for destruction,* Tim. III, 6, 92.

**Suitor** (pronounced like *shooter* in LLL IV, 1, 110) 1) *a petitioner:* LLL II, 34. All's V, 3, 151. H4B II, 1, 138 (*I will not be your s.,* i. e. submissive to you). H6C III, 1, 19. R3 I, 3, 64. H8 I, 2, 9. Cor. I, 1, 61 (*they say poor —s have strong breaths*). Tit. I, 44. Caes. II, 3, 12. II, 4, 15. 35. III, 1, 227 (*am moreover s. that I may produce his body*). Oth. III, 1, 51. III, 3, 42. With *to: I am a woeful s. to your honour,* Meas. II, 2, 27. *she hath been a s. to me for her brother,* V, 34. Cor. V, 3, 78. Tim. III, 5, 7. Ant. II, 1, 4.

2) *one who follows women: no heretics burned, but wenches' —s,* Lr. III, 2, 84. *she that could ... see —s following and not look behind,* Oth. II, 1, 158.

3) *a wooer, a lover:* Ven. 6. Gent. II, 1, 143. Ado I, 1, 130. LLL IV, 1, 110. Merch. I, 1, 169. I, 2, 38. As III, 2, 438. Shr. I, 1, 189. I, 2, 243. 261. 272. II, 8. 336. Wint. V, 3, 109. With *to: —s to her,* Shr. I, 2, 122. *are you a s. to the maid?* 230. II, 91. Cymb. I, 6, 2.

**Sullen,** 1) *sad, melancholy, dismal: you shall hear the surly s. bell give warning to the world,* Sonn. 71, 2. *be thou the trumpet of our wrath and s. presage of your own decay,* John I, 28. *shorten my days thou canst with s. sorrow,* R2 I, 3, 227 (Ff *sudden*). *the s. passage of thy weary steps,* 265. *put on s. black,* V, 6, 48. *a s. bell, remembered tolling a departing friend,* H4B I, 1, 102. *our solemn hymns to s. dirges change,* Rom. IV, 5, 88. In Oth. III, 4, 51 Qq *a salt and s. rheum,* Ff *sorry.*

2) *morose, peevish, waspish: still is he s., still he lours and frets,* Ven. 75. *she is peevish, s., froward,* Gent. III, 1, 68. *I love to cope him in these s. fits,* As II, 1, 67. *rough and coy and s.* Shr. II, 245. *froward, peevish, s., sour,* V, 2, 157. *rude ragged nurse, old s. playfellow for tender princes,* R3 IV, 1, 102. *like a misbehaved and s. wench,* Rom. III, 3, 143. Apemantus, *if thou wert not s., I would be good to thee,* Tim. I, 2, 242. *I am sick and s.* Ant. I, 3, 13.

3) *gloomy, dark: like to the lark at break of day arising from s. earth,* Sonn. 29, 12. *like bright metal*

on a s. ground, H4A I, 2, 236. why are thine eyes fixed to the s. earth? H6B I, 2, 5.

**Sullens,** moroseness, dumps: let them die that age and s. have, R2 II, 1, 139.

**Sully,** subst. stain, blemish: laying these slight —es on my son, Hml. II, 1, 39.

**Sully,** vb. 1) tr. to soil, to stain, to tarnish: where wasteful time debateth with decay, to change your day of youth to —ed night, Sonn. 15, 12. that may not s. the chariness of our honesty, Wiv. II, 1, 102. s. the purity and whiteness of my sheets, Wint. I, 2, 326. H6A IV, 4, 6.

2) intr. to be soiled, to get dirty: your white canvas doublet will s. H4A II, 4, 84.

**Sulphur,** brimstone: Oth. III, 3, 329. V, 2, 279 (cf. Sulphurous). Considered as that of which lightning consists: to charge thy s. with a bolt that should but rive an oak, Cor. V, 3, 152. the gods throw stones of s. on me, Cymb. V, 5, 240, i. e. thunderbolts.

**Sulphurous,** made of brimstone, or impregnated with it; considered as a quality of thunder and lightning: the fire and cracks of s. roaring, Tp. I, 2, 204. thy sharp and s. bolt, Meas. II, 2, 115. you s. and thought-executing fires, Lr. III, 2, 4. he came in thunder; his celestial breath was s. to smell, Cymb. V, 4, 115. thy nimble s. flashes, Per. III, 1, 6. Applied to the flames of hell (cf. sulphur in Oth. V, 2, 279): when I to s. and tormenting flames must render up myself, Hml. I, 5, 3. there's hell, there's darkness, there's the s. pit, Lr. IV, 6, 130.

**Sultan,** the Turkish emperor: Merch. II, 1, 26.

**Sultry,** oppressively hot: Hml. V, 2, 101. 103.

**Sum,** subst. 1) the aggregate or whole of several numbers or quantities added: when as thy love hath cast his utmost s., called to that audit by advised respects, Sonn. 49, 3. to your audit comes their distract parcels in combined —s, Compl. 231. how much the gross s. of deuce-ace amounts to, LLL I, 2, 49.

2) the whole abstracted, abridgment, amount, upshot: that is the s. of all, Ado I, 1, 147. 'confess' and 'love' had been the very s. of my confession, Merch. III, 2, 36. the full s. of me is s. of something which ..., 159. this is the very s. of all, John II, 151. the s. of all is that the king hath won, H4B I, 1, 131. the s. of all our answer is but this, H5 III, 6, 172. the s. of all I can I have disclosed, R3 II, 4, 46. grates me: the s. Ant. I, 1, 18. the s. of this, brought hither to Pentapolis, Per. III Prol. 33.

3) the whole number or quantity: to leave for nothing all thy s. of good, Sonn. 109, 12. the s. and substance that I have, Gent. IV, 1, 15. giving thy s. of more to that which had too much, As II, 1, 48. the stretching of a span buckles in his s. of age, III, 2, 140. produce the grand s. of his sins, H8 III, 2, 293. were the s. of these (kisses) countless, Tit. V, 3, 158. I cannot s. up s. of half my wealth, Rom. II, 6, 34. your s. of parts did not together pluck such envy from him, Hml. IV, 7, 74. forty thousand brothers could not, with all their quantity of love, make up my s. V, 1, 294. parcel the s. of my disgraces by addition of his envy, Ant. V, 2, 163.

4) number, quantity (of money): a s. of money, H5 IV, 1, 159. H6A V, 1, 52. H6B III, 1, 61. —s of gold, All's IV, 3, 204. R2 I, 4, 50. H6B I, 1, 129. Caes. IV, 3, 70. heaps and —s of love and wealth, Tim. V, 1, 155. s., alone, = a quantity of money:

Wiv. III, 4, 16. Err. I, 1, 154. IV, 1, 1. 7. 38. 72. IV, 4, 136. V, 131. 284. LLL II, 131. 134. 162. Merch. I, 1, 179. I, 3, 104. 148. III, 2, 289. 299. IV, 1, 210. Shr. III, 2, 137. John IV, 2, 142. H4B I, 1, 78. 91. H5 I, 1, 79. I, 2, 133. II Chor. 33. H6B IV, 1, 22. Tim. I, 2, 238. II, 1, 2. III, 3, 22. III, 4, 30. 49. 93. V, 1, 9. Cymb. I, 1, 147. I, 6, 186. profitless usurer, why dost thou use so great a s. of —s, Sonn. 4, 8 (= so immense a sum).

**Sum,** vb. to compute, to cast up: this fair child of mine shall s. my count, Sonn. 2, 11. —ed the account of chance, H4B I, 1, 167. will you with counters s. the past proportion of his infinite? Troil. II, 2, 28. With up: whose grossness little characters s. up, Troil. I, 3, 325. Rom. II, 6, 34. Cymb. V, 4, 170.

**Sumless,** inestimable: as rich with praise as is the ooze and bottom of the sea with sunken wreck and s. treasuries, H5 I, 2, 165.

**Summary,** abridged account, abstract: Merch. III, 2, 131. H4B IV, 1, 73.

**Summer,** the warmest part of the year: Ven. 91. 802. Lucr. 837. Sonn. 5, 5. 6, 2. 54, 8. 104, 14. Pilgr. 160. Wiv. II, 1, 127. Ado II, 3, 75. LLL I, 1, 102. Mids. II, 1, 82. 111. Merch. II, 9, 94. III, 1, 66. V, 264. All's IV, 4, 31. Tw. I, 5, 21. Wint. I, 1, 6. IV, 4, 80. 107. V, 3, 51. John V, 7, 30 (there is so hot a s. in my bosom, that all my bowels crumble up to dust). R2 I, 3, 299. H4B III, 2, 144. H5 I, 2, 194. V, 2, 340. H6B I, 1, 81. II, 4, 2. H6C II, 2, 164. V, 7, 18. R3 I, 1, 2. III, 1, 94 (short —s lightly have a forward spring). Tit. II, 3, 94. V, 2, 172. Rom. I, 3, 77. II, 2, 121. Mcb. I, 6, 3. Cymb. IV, 2, 219. IV, 4, 29. Per. II, 5, 36. With the def. art., in a general sense: the s. still doth tend upon my state, Mids. III, 1, 158. show not their mealy wings but to the s. Troil. III, 3, 79.

Compounded with other words: s. air, LLL V, 2, 293. Rom. II, 6, 19. their s. beauty, R3 IV, 3, 13. s. bird, H4B IV, 4, 91. Tim. III, 6, 34. s. buds, Mids. II, 1, 110. s. butterflies, Cor. IV, 6, 94. s. corn, R2 III, 3, 162. s. days, Per. IV, 1, 18. s. grass, H5 I, 1, 65. s. fields, R3 V, 2, 8. s. flies, LLL V, 2, 408. H6C II, 6, 17. Oth. IV, 2, 66 (Qq —'s flies). s. house, H4A III, 1, 164. s. leaves, R2 I, 2, 20. s. morn, Pilgr. 159. s. news, Cymb. III, 4, 12. s. smocks, LLL V, 2, 916. s. songs, Wint. IV, 2, 11.

On the other hand: a —'s bower, H4A III, 1, 210. a —'s cloud, Mcb. III, 4, 111. —'s corn, H6B III, 2, 176. a —'s day, Ven. 32. Sonn. 18, 1. Mids. I, 2, 89. H5 III, 6, 67. IV, 8, 23. Tit. V, 1, 14. in —'s drought, Tit. III, 1, 19. the —'s dust, R2 III, 3, 43. on a —'s evening, Caes. III, 2, 176. —'s flies, Oth. IV, 2, 66 (Ff s. flies). as clear as is the —'s sun, H5 I, 2, 86. —'s time, Sonn. 97, 5. any —'s story, Sonn. 98, 7.

All-hallown s. H4A I, 2, 178 (= late summer; as an emblem of an old man with the passions of youth). expect Saint Martin's s. H6A I, 2, 131 (see Martin). on the bat's back I do fly after s. merrily, Tp. V, 92; cf. the swallow follows not s. more willing, Tim. III, 6, 31.

S. implying the idea of all that is pleasant and gratifying: could make me any —'s story tell, Sonn. 98, 7. thou art a s. bird, which ever in the haunch of winter sings the lifting up of day, H4B IV, 4, 91. to those men that sought him sweet as s. H8 IV, 2, 54. if 't *be s. news, smile to't before*, Cymb. III, 4, 12. *as one shall see in a —'s day* = it would be a lucky hit, if you should happen to see the like: *a proper man, as one shall see in a —'s day*, Mids. I, 2, 89 (Quince's speech). *uttered as brave words at the bridge as you shall see in a —'s day*, H5 III, 6, 67. *a most contagious treason come to light, as you shall desire in a —'s day*, IV, 8, 23 (Fluellen's speeches).

Used for the whole year: *five —s*, Err. I, 1, 133. cf. R2 I, 3, 141. H8 III, 2, 360. Rom. I, 2, 10. Per. I, 4, 39 (O. Edd. *savours*).

**Summered,** carried through the summer, kept warm: *maids, well s. and warm kept, are like flies at Bartholomew-tide*, H5 V, 2, 335.

**Summer-seeming,** appearing like summer; seeming to be the effect of a transitory and short-lived heat of the blood: *this avarice sticks deeper, grows with more pernicious root than s. lust*, Mcb. IV, 3, 86.

**Summer-swelling,** growing up in summer: *the s. flower*, Gent. II, 4, 162.

**Summit** (O. Edd. *somnet*) highest point, top: Hml. I, 4, 70 (Ff *sonnet*). III, 3, 18. Lr. IV, 6, 57.

**Summon,** 1) to call on, to warn: *coal-black clouds ... do s. us to part*, Ven. 534. *s. the town*, Cor. I, 4, 7 (i. e. to surrender).

2) to call, to cite, to give notice to appear: *s. a session*, Wint. II, 3, 202. *what lusty trumpet thus doth s. us?* John V, 2, 117. *s. a parley*, H6A III, 3, 35. *I'll knock once more to s. them*, H6C IV, 7, 16. With an inf.: *the people ... are —ed to meet*, Cor. II, 3, 151. The place of destination added: *why hath thy queen —ed me hither?* Tp. IV, 83. *those sounds that ... s. him to marriage*, Merch. III, 2, 53. *some trumpet s. hither to the walls these men of Angiers*, John II, 198. H6A IV, 2, 2. H6B II, 4, 70. R3 III, 1, 172. Mcb. II, 1, 64. Oth. IV, 2, 169.

With *up*: *when to the sessions of sweet silent thought I s. up remembrance of things past*, Sonn. 30, 2. *s. up your dearest spirits*, LLL II, 1. *s. up the blood*, H5 III, 1, 7 (O. Edd. *commune*). *they —ed up their meiny*, Lr. II, 4, 35.

**Summoners,** persons employed to warn offenders to appear in court: *close pent-up guilts, rive your concealing continents, and cry these dreadful s. grace*, Lr. III, 2, 59.

**Summons,** a call, warning, citation: *on this green land answer your s.* Tp. IV, 131. *stays but the s. of the appellant's trumpet*, R2 I, 3, 4. *to make this present s.* H8 II, 4, 219. *a heavy s. lies like lead upon me, and yet I would not sleep*, Mcb. II, 1, 6. *black Hecate's s.* III, 2, 41. *it started like a guilty thing upon a fearful s.* Hml. I, 1, 149. *why you answer this present s.* Lr. V, 3, 121. *what is the reason of this terrible s.?* Oth. I, 1, 82.

**Sumpter,** a pack-horse: *to be slave and s. to this detested groom*, Lr. II, 4, 219.

**Sumptuous,** costly, splendid: H4A III, 2, 58. H6A V, 1, 20. H6B I, 3, 133. IV, 7, 106.

**Sumptuously,** splendidly: Tit. I, 351.

**Sun** (usually masc.: Ven. 856. 859. Lucr. 781. Sonn. 33, 9. Err. II, 2, 30. Wint. IV, 4, 105. 819. R2 III, 2, 42. III, 3, 63. H4A I, 2, 10. 221. H6C V, 3, 5. R3 V, 3, 277. Caes. II, 1, 106. 110. Neut. in Sonn. 148, 12: *the s. itself*), 1) the luminary that makes the day: Ven. 1. Sonn. 59, 6. Tp. II, 1, 248. V, 42. Gent. I, 3, 86. II, 6, 10. V, 1, 1. Wiv. I, 3, 70. IV, 4, 7. Meas.

IV, 3, 92. Err. I, 1, 28. 89. LLL IV, 3, 369 (*get the s. of them*). Mids. III, 2, 50. Shr. IV, 5, 3. Wint. IV, 3, 52 (*raisins o'the s.*) H4A II, 4, 135. H6A V, 4, 87. H6B II, 4, 39 (*enjoy the s.* = live). H6C II, 1, 35. R3 V, 3, 282. Tim. IV, 3, 69. Oth. II, 3, 382 etc. Without the article: *when s. doth melt their snow*, Lucr. 1218. *to —'s parching heat displayed my cheeks*, H6A I, 2, 77. *as s. and showers there had made a lasting spring*, H8 III, 1, 7. *ere the set of s.* Mcb. I, 1, 5. *never shall s. that morrow see*, I, 5, 62. *a huge eclipse of s. and moon*, Oth. V, 2, 100.

*The blessed s.* Shr. IV, 5, 17. 18. H4A I, 2, 10. II, 4, 449. *the cheerful s.* Tit. II, 3, 13; cf. Rom. I, 1, 140. *the fair s.* Ven. 483. Err. II, 2, 56. LLL IV, 3, 69. R2 IV, 35. R3 I, 2, 263. *the glorious s.* LLL I, 1, 84. Tw. IV, 3, 1. John III, 1, 77. H6B III, 1, 353. H6C II, 1, 22. 26. *the golden s.* LLL IV, 3, 26. H5 II, 4, 58. Tit. II, 1, 5. *the holy s.* Cymb. IV, 4, 41; cf. Rom. I, 1, 125. III, 2, 25. Lr. I, 1, 111. *the s. arises*, Ven. 856. Caes. II, 1, 106. *the s. rises*, Wint. IV, 4, 105. Troil. I, 2, 8. V, 10, 25. Tit. V, 2, 56. *the —'s uprise*, Tit. III, 1, 159. Ant. IV, 12, 18. *the s. sets*, Tp. III, 1, 22. Err. I, 2, 7. Shr. Ind. 2, 122. John V, 5, 1. R2 II, 1, 12. II, 4, 21. R3 II, 3, 34. H8 III, 2, 416. Troil. V, 8, 5. Tim. I, 2, 150 etc. *the sun hath made a golden set*, R3 V, 3, 19. *ere the set of s.* Mcb. I, 1, 5. *five hundred courses of the s.* (= years) Sonn. 59, 6. H8 II, 3, 6. Troil. IV, 1, 27. *by the fifth hour of the s.* Troil. II, 1, 134. *as many lies as may be hollaed from s. to s.* R2 IV, 55 (in the course of a day? According to commentators, = from sunrise till sunset. O. Edd. *from sin to sin*). *one score* (of miles) *'twixt s. and s.* Cymb. III, 2, 70. *show thy descent by gazing 'gainst the s.* H6C II, 1, 92. *could behold the s. with as firm eyes as he*, Cymb. I, 4, 12. *worse than the s. in March, this praise doth nourish agues*, H4A IV, 1, 111. *all the infections that the s. sucks up from bogs* etc. Tp. II, 2, 1. *some meteor that the s. exhales*, Rom. III, 5, 13 (cf. *Exhale*).

Emblem of supreme beauty: Lucr. 780. Most excellent things compared with it; as eyes: Ven. 198. Lucr. 1224. Sonn. 49, 6. persons: Sonn. 33, 14. H8 I, 1, 6. 33. Badge of the house of York: H6B IV, 1, 98. H6C II, 1, 40. R3 I, 1, 2.

2) a sunny place; sunshine: *tempest after s.* Ven. 800. *parch in Afric s.* Troil. I, 3, 370. *in the s.* (= where the rays of the sun fall): Meas. II, 2, 166. As II, 7, 15. Tw. II, 5, 20. Wint. I, 2, 67. R3 I, 1, 26. Troil. III, 3, 233. Hml. II, 2, 185. Used to express careless idleness: *who doth ambition shun and loves to live i'the sun*, As II, 5, 41. *the spinsters and the knitters in the s. do use to chant it*, Tw. II, 4, 45. *I had rather have one scratch my head i'the s. when the alarum were struck*, Cor. II, 2, 79. *thy dog that hath lain asleep in the s.* Rom. III, 1, 29. *how is it that the clouds still hang on you? Not so, my lord; I am too much i'the s.* Hml. I, 2, 67 (I am more careless and idle than I ought to be).\* Proverb: *thou out of heaven's benediction comest to the warm s.* Lr. II, 2, 169 (= out of the frying-pan into the fire. cf. *Benediction*).

Plays on the words *sun* and *son*, see sub *Son*.

**Sunbeam,** a ray of the sun: Cymb. IV, 2, 350.

**Sunbeamed,** radiant like the sun: *your s. eyes*, LLL V, 2, 168 (a ridiculed expression).

**Sun-bright,** resembling the sun in brightness: *her s. eye*, Gent. III, 1, 88.

**Sun-burning,** the tanning effect of the sun: *whose face is not worth s.* H5 V, 2, 154.

**Sun-burnt,** tanned by the sun: *you s. sicklemen,* Tp. IV, 134. *thus goes every one to the world but I, and I am s.* Ado II, 1, 331. *the Grecian dames are s. and not worth the splinter of a lance,* Troil. I, 3, 282.

**Sunday,** the Lord's day: *sigh away —s,* Ado I, 1, 204. Shr. II, 299. 300. 324. 326. 395. 397. Troil. I, 1, 79. Hml. I, 1, 76. *velvet-guards and S. citizens,* H4A III, 1, 261 (citizens apparelled in their sunday finery). *there's rue for you, and here's some for me: we may call it herb-grace o' Sundays,* Hml. IV, 5, 182 (when we mean to speak with elegance).

**Sunder,** subst. *in s.* = in two: *who* (the pillow) *seems to part in s., swelling on either side,* Lucr. 388. *gnawing my bonds in s.* Err. V, 249 (F2.3.4 *asunder*). *cut my lace in s.* R3 IV, 1, 34 (Ff *asunder*).

**Sunder,** vb. 1) to separate: *that vile wall which did these lovers s.* Mids. V, 133. *so sweet a bar should s. such sweet friends,* Merch. III, 2, 120. *shall we be —ed,* As I, 3, 100. H6A IV, 3, 42. H6C IV, 1, 23. R3 V, 3, 100. Troil. V, 10, 27. With *from: the sea that —s him from thence,* H6C III, 2, 138. Peculiar expression: *what more favour can I do to thee, than with that hand that cut thy youth in twain to s. his that was thine enemy,* Rom. V, 3, 100 (i. e. to cut it in twain too, to separate the soul from the body).

2) intr. to be separated, to quit each other, to part: *strangers and foes do s., and not kiss,* All's II, 5, 91. *even as a splitted bark, so s. we,* H6B III, 2, 411.

**Sundry,** manifold: *revolving the s. dangers of his will's obtaining,* Lucr. 128. *it is a melancholy of mine own, compounded of many simples, extracted from many objects, and indeed the s. contemplation of my travels,* As IV, 1, 17. *masking the business from the common eye for s. weighty reasons,* Mcb. III, 1, 126. *my poor country shall have more vices than it had before, more suffer and more s. ways than ever,* IV, 3, 48. *s. blessings hang about his throne, that speak him full of grace,* 158.

**Sun-expelling,** keeping the sun off: *her s. mask,* Gent. IV, 4, 158.

**Sun-like,** resembling the sun: *s. majesty,* H4A III, 2, 79.

**Sunny,** 1) proceeding from the sun: *sweet moon, I thank thee for thy s. beams,* Mids. V, 277 (Pyramus' speech).

2) bright: *my decayed fair a s. look of his would soon repair,* Err. II, 1, 99. *her s. locks hang on her temples like a golden fleece,* Merch. I, 1, 169.

**Sunrise,** the first appearance of the sun above the horizon: Meas. II, 2, 153.

**Sunrising,** the same: R3 V, 3, 61.

**Sunset,** the descent of the sun below the horizon: Sonn. 73, 6. John III, 1, 110. H6C II, 2, 116. Rom. III, 5, 127.

**Sunshine,** the light of the sun, or the place where it shines: Ven. 799. All's V, 3, 33. Lr. IV, 3, 20. Metaphorically, = anything that has a genial and beneficial influence, or that makes happy: *vouchsafe to show the s. of your face,* LLL V, 2, 201. *send him many years of s. days,* R2 IV, 221. *ripens in the s. of his favour,* H4B IV, 2, 12. *ne'er may he live to see a s. day,* H6C II, 1, 187. *even then that s. brewed a shower for him,* II, 2, 156. *our s. made thy spring,* 163.

**Sup,** 1) intr. to eat the evening meal: Pilgr. 186.

Gent. II, 4, 141. Meas. IV, 3, 159. Err. IV, 3, 66. Merch. II, 4, 18. Wint. V, 2, 112. H4A I, 2, 216. H4B II, 1, 201. II, 2, 159. II, 4, 14. H6B I, 4, 84. V, 1, 214. 216. R3 III, 1, 199. V, 3, 48. Troil. III, 1, 89. 94. Cor. IV, 2, 49. 50 (*I s. upon myself*). Rom. I, 2, 88. Caes. I, 2, 292. Mcb. I, 7, 29. V, 5, 13 (*I have —ed full with horrors*). Oth. IV, 1, 172. 273. IV, 2, 239. V, 1, 117. 119. Ant. IV, 8, 33. Cymb. III, 1, 6, 91.

2) tr. to treat with supper, to feed: *if a' have no more man's blood in's belly than will s. a flea,* LLL V, 2, 698. *s. them* (the dogs) *well and look unto them all,* Shr. Ind. 1, 28.

**Superbus,** surname of the last Roman king Tarquin: Lucr. Arg. 1.

**Super-dainty,** highly delicate, lovely: *my s. Kate,* Shr. II, 189.

**Superficial,** shallow, slight: *a very s., ignorant, unweighing fellow,* Meas. III, 2, 147. *this s. tale is but a preface of her worthy praise,* H6A V, 5, 10.

**Superficially,** shallowly, slightly: *you have glozed, but s.* Troil. II, 2, 165. *you know me, do you not? Faith, sir, s.* III, 1, 10.

**Superfinical,** spruce, foppish in the highest degree: *s. rogue,* Lr. II, 2, 19 (Ff *superserviceable, finical*).

**Superfluity,** more than enough, plenty beyond what is wanted: *s. comes sooner by white hairs, but competency lives longer,* Merch. I, 2, 8. *one* (shirt) *for s., and another for use,* H4B II, 2, 20. *if they would yield us but the s.* Cor. I, 1, 17. *then we shall ha' means to vent our musty s.* 230.

**Superfluous,** 1) overflowing, exuberant: *the love I dedicate your lordship is without end; whereof this pamphlet, without beginning, is but a s. moiety,* Lucr. Ded. 2 (a part, as it were, running over). *that their hot blood may spin in English eyes, and dout them with s. courage,* H5 IV, 2, 11.

2) exuberant, too great: *a proper title of a peace, and purchased at a s. rate,* H8 I, 1, 99.

3) more than enough; unnecessary, useless: *I have no s. leisure,* Meas. III, 1, 158. *that s. case that hid the worse and showed the better face,* LLL V, 2, 387. *this abundance of s. breath,* John II, 148. *this 'once again' was once s.* IV, 2, 4. *s. branches we lop away,* R2 III, 4, 63. *why thou shouldst be so s. to demand the time of the day,* H4A I, 2, 12. *it were s.* H4B III, 2, 154. *our s. lacqueys,* H5 IV, 2, 26. *this, like to a murdering-piece, in many places gives me s. death,* Hml. IV, 5, 96. *which had s. kings for messengers,* Ant. III, 12, 5. *to say you're welcome were s.* Per. II, 3, 2.

4) having more than enough, living in abundance: *cold wisdom waiting on s. folly,* All's I, 1, 116. *our basest beggars are in the poorest thing s.* Lr. II, 4, 268. *let the s. and lust-dieted man ... feel your power,* IV, 1, 70. *their s. riots,* Per. I, 4, 54.

**Superfluously,** in a degree beyond what is necessary, needlessly: H5 III, 7, 80.

**Superflux,** more than enough, superfluity: *that thou mayst shake the s. to them,* Lr. III, 4, 35.

**Superior,** one higher in rank than another: *that meaner men should vaunt that golden hap which their —s want,* Lucr. 42. *every step, exampled by the first pace that is sick of his s.* Troil. I, 3, 133.

**Supernal,** placed above, heavenly: *that s. judge,* John II, 112.

**Supernatural,** not produced according to the

laws of nature, miraculous: *to make modern and familiar, things s. and causeless*, All's II, 3, 3. *this s. soliciting cannot be ill*, Mcb. I, 3, 130.

**Superpraise**, to overpraise: Mids. III, 2, 153.

**Superscript**, the direction of a letter: LLL IV, 2, 135.

**Superscription**, the same: H6A IV, 1, 53. Tim. II, 2, 81.

**Superserviceable**, over-officious: Lr. II, 2, 19 (Ff. *s., finical;* Qq *superfinical*).

**Superstition**, belief in, and reverence of, things which are no proper objects of worship: Wint. V, 3, 43. Per. III, 1, 50.

**Superstitious**, 1) addicted to superstition: Wiv. IV, 4, 36. Troil. V, 3, 79. Caes. II, 1, 195.

2) devoted with idolatry: *been, out of fondness, s. to him*, H8 III, 1, 131.

**Superstitiously**, in a superstitious manner, with erroneous religion: Wint. III, 3, 40. Per. IV, 3, 49.

**Supersubtle**, cunning, crafty in an excessive degree: Oth. I, 3, 363.

**Supervise**, subst. inspection; *on the s.* = at sight: *that, on the s., no leisure bated, no, not to stay the grinding of the axe, my head should be struck off*, Hml. V, 2, 23.

**Supervise**, vb. to inspect, overlook: *let me s. the canzonet*, LLL IV, 2, 124 (Holofernes' speech).

**Supervision**, inspection: *would you the s. grossly gape on? behold her topped?* Oth. III, 3, 395 (Q1 *supervisor*).

**Supervisor**, a looker-on: *would you, the s., grossly gape on?* Oth. III, 3, 395 (Ff and later Qq *supervision*).

**Supper**, the evening meal (its time at five or six o' clock: LLL I, 1, 240. Merch. II, 2, 122; but cf. R3 V, 3, 47): Ado I, 3, 44. 72. II, 1, 156 *(will eat no s.).* LLL I, 1, 240. Merch. II, 2, 122. II, 5, 11. As III, 2, 102 *(dinners and — s)*. Shr. IV, 1, 47. 142. John I, 204. R2 IV, 333. H4A I, 2, 144. H4B II, 1, 172. H6B II, 2, 2. R3 III, 2, 123. Cor. IV, 3, 43. Rom. I, 2, 78. I, 3, 100. I, 4, 105. II, 4, 135. Tim. III, 1, 26. Mcb. III, 1, 26. Lr. III, 6, 90. Oth. I, 1, 99. IV, 1, 166. IV, 2, 169. Ant. II, 2, 225. IV, 2, 44. *we hold a solemn s.* Mcb. III, 1, 14. *to make a s.* H6C V, 5, 85. H8 I, 3, 52. *after s.* Lucr. Arg. 6. Lucr. 122. Gent. III, 2, 96. H4A I, 2, 3. II, 4, 589. H4B III, 2, 332. *soon at after s.* R3 IV, 3, 31 (Ff *soon, and after s.).* *at s.* Gent. II, 1, 47. Ado I, 1, 279. II, 1, 1. H4A I, 2, 210. II, 1, 62. H4B II, 1, 177. II, 2, 173. V, 3, 15. R3 II, 4, 10. Troil. II, 1, 84. Caes. II, 1, 238. Hml. IV, 3, 18. Oth. III, 3, 57. *soon at s.* Merch. II, 3, 5 (cf. *Soon).* With the def. article: *his daughter is to be brought by you to the s.* Shr. IV, 4, 86.

**Supper-time**, the time of the evening meal: Tp. III, 1, 95. Shr. IV, 3, 192. V, 2, 128. H6A I, 4, 59. R3 V, 3, 47 *(it's s., my lord; it's nine o' clock).* Mcb. III, 1, 44. Oth. IV, 2, 249. *at s.* Merch. II, 2, 215. *soon at s.* Err. III, 2, 179 (cf. *Soon). in s.* Merch. II, 4, 1.

**Supplant**, to displace, to remove, to make away with: *you did s. your brother Prospero*, Tp. II, 1, 271. *I will s. some of your teeth*, III, 2, 56 (Stephano's speech). *you three from Milan did s. good Prospero*, III, 3, 70. *we must s. those rough rug-headed kerns*, R2 II, 1, 156. *which fear if better reasons can s.* H6B III, 1, 37. *lest the people ... s. you for ingratitude*, Tit. I, 447.

**Supple**, pliant, flexible; in a physical and moral sense: *that are of —r joints*, Tp. III, 3, 107. *the tribute of his s. knee*, R2 I, 4, 33. *I'll knead him, I'll make him s.* Troil. II, 3, .231. *s. knees feed arrogance*, III, 3, 48. *s. and courteous to the people*, Cor. II, 2, 29. *when we have stuffed these pipes, ... we have —r souls*, V, 1, 55. *each part, deprived of s. government*, Rom. IV, 1, 102. *contract and starve your s. joints*, Tim. I, 1, 257.

**Suppliance**, satisfaction, gratification, pastime, diversion (cf. *Supply*): *for Hamlet and the trifling of his favour, hold it a fashion and a toy in blood, a violet in the youth of primy nature, forward, not permanent, sweet, not lasting, the perfume and s. of a minute*, Hml. I, 3, 9.

**Suppliant**, subst. an humble petitioner (dissyll. also in the middle of the line): Lucr. 897. All's V, 3, 134. R2 V, 3, 75. R3 I, 2, 207. Cor. III, 1, 44. Tit. IV, 3, 117. With *for: when she for thy repeal was s.* Gent. III, 1, 234. *heard ye not what an humble s. Lord Hastings was to her for his delivery?* R3 I, 1, 74.

**Suppliant**, adj. *(suppliant)*, suppletory, auxiliary: *whereunto our levy must be s.* Cymb. III, 7, 14.

**Supplicant**, adj. beseeching submissively: *and s. their sighs to you extend*, Compl. 276.

**Supplication**, humble petition: H6B I, 3, 3. 16. IV, 4, 48. Cor. V, 3, 31. Tit. IV, 3, 107. 109.

**Supply**, subst. a furnishing with what is wanted, aid, support, relief: *for the which s , admit me Chorus to this history*, H5 Chor. 31 (i. e. to have the assistance of 'your imaginary forces'). *my relief must not be tossed and turned to me in words, but find s. immediate*, Tim. II, 1, 27. *to use 'em toward a s. of money*, II, 2, 201. *to expend your time with us awhile, for the s. and profit of our hope*, Hml. II, 2, 24.

Especially = succours, additional forces: *the great s. that was expected by the Dauphin here, are wrecked*, John V, 3, 9. *your s., which you have wished so long, are cast away*, V, 5, 12. *looks he not for s.?* H4A IV, 3, 3. *eating the air on promise of s.* H4B I, 3, 28. *the Earl of Salisbury craveth s.* H6A I, 1, 159. *delays my promised s. of horsemen*, IV, 3, 10. *the prince shall follow with a fresh s.* H6C III, 3, 237. *with a s. of Roman gentlemen*, Cymb. IV, 3, 25. Plur. *—es*, in the same sense: *our —es live largely in the hope of great Northumberland*, H4B I, 3, 12. *we have —es to second our attempt*, IV, 2, 45. *with new —es of men*, Mcb. I, 2, 32. *'tis their fresh —es*, Cymb. V, 2, 16.

**Supply**, vb. 1) to fill (a place): *to s. the places at the table*, Shr. III, 2, 249. *when these sovereign thrones are all —ed*, Tw. I, 1, 38. *the chairs of justice —ed with worthy men*, Cor. III, 3, 35. Particularly applied to places that have become vacant: *our absence to s.* Meas. I, 1, 19. *I fill up a place, which may be better —ed when I have made it empty*, As I, 2, 205. *you shall s. the bridegroom's place*, Shr. III, 2, 251. *thy place ..., which by thy younger brother is —ed*, H4A III, 2, 33. *instead whereof let this s. the room*, H6C II, 6, 54. *s. his place*, IV, 6, 50. *s. the place*, Lr. IV, 6, 273. *I being absent and my place —ed*, Oth. III, 3, 17.

2) to furnish with what is wanted: *no man will s. thy want*, Pilgr. 410. *to s. the ripe wants of my friend*, Merch. I, 3, 64. *s. your present wants*, 141. *to s. your wants*, R2 I, 4, 51. *a hundred almshouses right well —ed*, H5 I, 1, 17. *an empty box, which ... I come to entreat your honour to s.* Tim. III, 1, 18. *nor has he*

*with him to s. his life*, IV, 2, 47. *if he care not for't, he will s. us easily*, IV, 3, 407. Followed by *with: s. me with the habit*, Meas. I, 3, 46. *well —ed with noble counsellors*, H5 II, 4, 33. *requesting your lordship to s. his instant use with so many talents*, Tim. III, 2, 40. *s. it with one gender of herbs*, Oth. I, 3, 326. *—est me with the least advantage of hope*, IV, 2, 178. *—ing every stage with an augmented greeting*, Ant. III, 6, 54.

3) to strengthen by additional troops, to succour, to reinforce: *Macdonald ... from the western isles of kerns and gallowglasses is —ed*, Mcb. I, 2, 13 (*of* = *by*).

4) to gratify the desire of, to content: *and did s. thee at thy garden-house*, Meas. V, 212. *knaves be such abroad, who having, by their own importunate suit, or voluntary dotage of some mistress, convinced or —ed them*, Oth. IV, 1, 28.

**Supplyant,** see *Suppliant*, adj.

**Supplyment,** additional assistance (?): *I will never fail beginning nor s.* Cymb. III, 4, 182 (Dyce: a continuance of supply).

**Support,** subst. maintenance, means of sustenance: *a thousand pound a year, annual s., out of his grace he adds*, H8 II, 3, 64.

**Support,** vb. 1) to prop, to sustain, to keep from falling or sinking: *so strong a prop to s. so weak a burden*, Ven. Ded. 2. *these forceless flowers like sturdy trees s. me*, Ven. 152. *s. him by the arm*, As II, 7, 199. *here am I left to underprop this land, who, weak with age, cannot s. myself*, R2 II, 2, 83. *these feet ... unable to s. this lump of clay*, H6A II, 5, 14.

2) to uphold by aid or countenance: *to s. so dissolute a crew*, R2 V, 3, 11. *to strengthen and s. King Edward's place*, H6C III, 1, 52. *make edicts for usury, to s. usurers*, Cor. I, 1, 84. *'tis not enough to help the feeble up, but to s. him after*, Tim. I, 1, 108. *kept his credit with his purse, —ed his estate*, III, 2, 76. *for —ing robbers*, Caes. IV, 3, 23. *wherefore darest thou s. a published traitor?* Lr. IV, 6, 236.

3) to maintain, to sustain: *and in the most exact regard s. the worships of their name*, Lr. I, 4, 287.

4) to bear, to endure: *his flawed heart, too weak the conflict to s.* Lr. V, 3, 197. *I a heavy interim shall s. by his dear absence*, Oth. I, 3, 259.

**Supportable,** bearable, endurable: *and s. to make the dear loss, have I means much weaker*, Tp. V, 145.

**Supportance,** 1) that which keeps from falling or sinking, support, prop: *give some s. to the bending twigs*, R2 III, 4, 32.

2) that which keeps up and preserves from failing; an upholding: *he will fight with you for's oath sake; ... therefore draw, for the s. of his vow*, Tw. III, 4, 329.

**Supporter,** a prop: *come, Escalus, you must walk by us on our other hand; and good —s are you*, Meas. V, 18. *he'll stand at your door like a sheriff's post, and be the s. to a bench*, Tw. I, 5, 158. *no s. but the huge firm earth can hold it up*, John III, 1, 72.

**Supposal,** opinion: *holding a weak s. of our worth*, Hml. I, 2, 18.

**Suppose,** subst. supposition, presumption, opinion: *have by marriage made thy daughter mine, while counterfeit —s bleared thine eye*, Shr. V, 1, 120. *we come short of our s. so far that after seven years' siege yet Troy walls stand*, Troil. I, 3, 11. *lose not so noble a friend on vain s.* Tit. I, 440.

**Suppose,** vb. 1) to lay down or state as a pro-

position or fact that may be true, for the sake of argument: *you must lay down the treasures of your body to this —d*, Meas. II, 4, 97. *s. they take offence without a cause*, H6C IV, 1, 14. *s. he did it unconstrained*, H6C I, 1, 143.

2) to form in the mind, to figure to one's self, to imagine; absol.: *in your —ing once more put your sight of heavy Pericles*, Per. V Prol. 21. With an object: *nor dare I question with my jealous thought where you may be, or your affairs s.* Sonn. 57, 10 (form an idea of your affairs). Passively: *when great treasure is the meed proposed, though death be adjunct, there's no death —d*, Lucr. 133. *whether it is that she reflects so bright, that dazzleth them, or else some shame —d*, 377. *a vulgar comment will be made of it and that —d by the common rout ... that may ...* Err. III, 1, 101. *more furious raging broils than yet can be imagined or —d*, H6A IV, 1, 186. Hence *—d* = imaginary: *the sight which makes —d terror true*, Lucr. 455. *make such wanton gambols with the wind, upon —d fairness*, Merch. III, 2, 94. — With a clause: *s. within the girdle of these walls are now confined two mighty monarchies*, H5 Prol. 19. *s. that you have seen the king embark his royalty*, III Prol. 3. *that you aptly will s. what pageantry ... the regent made in Mytilene*, Per. V, 2, 5.

3) to imagine, to fancy, to think (erroneously): *he shall s. no other but that he is carried ...*, All's III, 6, 26. With a double accus.: *all hearts, which I by lacking have —d dead*, Sonn. 31, 2. *so many have —d them mistress of his heart*, Compl. 142. *he —s me travelled to Poland*, Meas. I, 3, 14. *s. the singing birds musicians*, R2 I, 3, 288. *he doth s. my sleep my death*, H4B IV, 5, 61. *which vainly I —d the Holy Land*, IV, 5, 239. *they s. me mad*, Tit. V, 2, 142. *to s. her chaste*, Oth. IV, 1, 73. Passively: *how easy is a bush —d a bear*, Mids. V, 22. *I am —d dead*, All's IV, 4, 11. *idly —d the founder of this law*, H5 I, 2, 59. *—d dead*, Per. V, 3, 35. cf. *—d as forfeit to a confined doom*, Sonn. 107, 4. *s. him now at anchor*, Per. V Prol. 16. Hence *—d* = pretended: *let my unsounded self, —d a fool, now set thy wit to school*, Lucr. 1819. *let the —d fairies pinch him*, Wiv. IV, 4, 61. *—d Lucentio must get a father, called —d Vincentio*, Shr. II, 409. *if you should tender your —d aid*, All's I, 3, 242. *wounding —d peace*, H4B IV, 5, 196. *so termed of our —d father*, H6B IV, 2, 33. *tell false Edward, thy —d king*, H6C III, 3, 223. IV, 1, 93. *these —d evils*, R3 I, 2, 76. *to his foe —d he must complain*, Rom. II Chor. 7. *in this —d distress of his*, Tim. V, 1, 15. *Edmund, —d Earl of Gloster*, Lr. V, 3, 113.

With an inf.: *whom he —s to be a friar*, All's IV, 3, 125. With a clause: *s. thou dost defend me from what is past*, Lucr. 1684. *so shall I live, —ing thou art true, like a deceived husband*, Sonn. 93, 1. *—ing that they saw the king's ship wrecked*, Tp. I, 2, 236. *whom they s. is drowned*, III, 3, 92. *I hear that Valentine is dead. And so s. am I*, Gent. IV, 2, 114. *s. what hath been cannot be*, All's I, 1, 240. *I did s. it should be on constraint*, John V, 1, 28. *s. devouring pestilence hangs in our air*, R2 I, 3, 283. *if you s. as fearing you it shook*, H4A III, 1, 23. *they —d I could rend bars of steel*, H6A I, 4, 51. *s. this arm is for the duke of York*, H6C II, 4, 2. *s. that I am now my father's mouth*, V, 5, 18. *—d their state was sure*, R3 III, 2, 86. *those wrongs which thou —st I have done to thee*, IV, 4, 252. *—ing that I lacked it*, Ant. II, 2, 86.

4) to be of opinion, to think, to presume: *I s. we are made to be no stronger*, Meas. II, 4, 132. *eldest son, as I s., to Robert Faulconbridge*, John I, 1, 52. *who would e'er s. they had such courage*, H6A I, 2, 35. *if he s. that I have pleaded truth*, II, 4, 29. *as little joy as you s. you should enjoy*, R3 I, 3, 151. 153. *after conflict such as was —d the wandering prince and Dido once enjoyed*, Tit. II, 3, 21. *it is —d he that meets Hector issues from our choice*, Troil. I, 3, 346. *I aimed so near, when I —d you loved*, Rom. I, 1, 211. *with which grief, it is —d, the fair creature died*, V, 3, 51. *bid him s. some good necessity touches his friend*, Tim. II, 2, 236. With a double accus., = to think, to hold to be: *—ing it a thing impossible*, Shr. I, 2, 123. *I s. him virtuous*, Tw. I, 5, 277. *which some s. the soul's frail dwelling-house*, John V, 7, 3. *—d sincere and holy in his thoughts*, H4B I, 1, 202. *would you not s. your bondage happy*, H6A V, 3, 110.

Confounded with *depose* by Pompey in Meas. II, 1, 162.

**Supposition,** 1) hypothesis, imagination unproved: *yet his means are in s.: he hath an argosy bound to Tripolis, ... but ships are but boards*, Merch. I, 3, 18. In H4A V, 2, 8 O. Edd. *s.*, M. Edd., for the sake of the metre, *suspicion*.

2) imagination, conceit: *and in that glorious s. think he gains by death that hath such means to die*, Err. III, 2, 50.

3) opinion: *the s. of the lady's death will quench the wonder of her infamy*, Ado IV, 1, 240. *only to seem to deserve well, and to beguile the s. of that lascivious young boy the count, have I run into this danger*, All's IV, 3, 333.

**Suppress,** 1) to keep in, to keep under, to restrain, to stifle, to stop, to quell: *his rage of lust ... slacked, not —ed*, Lucr. 425. *on both sides thus is simple truth —ed*, Sonn. 138, 8. *the mercy that was quick in us but late, by your own counsel is —ed and killed*, H5 II, 2, 80. *well didst thou, Richard, to s. thy voice*, H6A IV, 1, 182. *to bridle and s. the pride of Suffolk*, H6B I, 1, 200. *yet heavens are just, and time —eth wrongs*, H6C III, 3, 77. *till Warwick or himself be quite —ed*, IV, 3, 6. *to s. his further gait herein*, Hml. I, 2, 30. *to s. his nephew's levies*, II, 2, 61.

2) to supplant, to displace: *to crown himself king and s. the prince*, H6A I, 3, 68. *thus the Mortimers, in whom the title rested, were —ed*, II, 5, 92.

**Supremacy,** highest place and power: Shr. V, 2, 109. 163. John III, 1, 156. Per. II, 3, 42. With *over*: *o'er my spirit thy full s. thou knewest*, Ant. III, 11, 59.

**Supreme** (*súpreme* or *supréme*; cf. Grammatical Observations p. 1413) highest: *the life of purity, the s. fair*, Lucr. 780. *s. head*, John III, 1, 155. *s. magistrates*, H6A I, 3, 57. *the s. King of kings*, R3 II, 1, 13. *the s. seat*, III, 7, 118. *two authorities, neither s.* Cor. III, 1, 110. *s. Jove*, V, 3, 71. *my s. crown of grief*, Cymb. I, 6, 4.

Substantively: *imperious s. of all mortal things*, Ven. 996.

**Sur-addition,** additional title, surname: *so gained the s. Leonatus*, Cymb. I, 1, 33.

**Surance,** assurance, surety, warrant: *now give some s. that thou art Revenge, stab them*, Tit. V, 2, 46.

**Surcease,** subst. cessation, stop: *if the assassination could trammel up the consequence, and catch with his* (i. e. the consequence's) *s. success*, Mcb. I, 7, 4.

**Surcease,** vb. to cease: *O time, cease thou thy course and last no longer, if they s. to be that should survive*, Lucr. 1766. *I will not do't, lest I s. to honour mine own truth*, Cor. III, 2, 121. *no pulse shall keep his native progress, but s.* Rom. IV, 1, 97.

**Sure,** adj. 1) secure, safe: *if we recover that* (the forest), *we are s. enough*, Gent. V, 1, 12. *are you s. of your husband now?* Wiv. IV, 2, 6 (*of* = from). *supposed their state was s.* R3 III, 2, 86. *a s. and safe one* (way) H8 III, 2, 439. *to guard s. their master*, Tim. III, 3, 40.

2) affording security and safety; no more able to do harm: *I have made him s.* H4A V, 3, 48 (i. e. I have killed him). *I'll make him s.* V, 4, 127. *hold him s.* H4B II, 1, 27. *see you guard him s.* IV, 3, 81. *guard him s.* H6B III, 1, 188. *we will make that s.* Tit. II, 3, 133. *see that you make her s.* 187. *whilst I at a banquet hold him s.* V, 2, 76. *bind them s.* 161. *is he s. bound?* 166. *I'll make him s. enough*, Per. I, 1, 169.

3) firm, stable, steady: *there is no s. foundation set on blood*, John IV, 2, 104. *consent upon a s. foundation*, H4B I, 3, 52. *though thou standest more s. than I could do*, IV, 5, 203. *in justice' equal scales, whose beam stands s.* H6B II, 1, 205. *let Caesar seat him s.* Caes. I, 2, 325. *thou s. and firm-set earth*, Mcb. II, 1, 56 (O. Edd. *sowre*). *horses swift and s. of foot*, III, 1, 38. *great tyranny, lay thou thy basis s., for goodness dare not check thee*, IV, 3, 32.

Hence = indissolubly united, betrothed, married: *she and I ... are now so s. that nothing can dissolve us*, Wiv. V, 5, 237. *Dumain is mine, as s. as bark on tree*, LLL V, 2, 285. *you and you are s. together, as the winter to foul weather*, As V, 4, 141.

4) unfailing, infallible: *s. ones* (reasons) Err. II, 2, 94. 95. *s. wit, follow me this jest now*, Rom. II, 4, 65 (the spurious Q1 and most M. Edd. *well said*). *you are too s. an augurer*, Ant. V, 2, 337. *than be cured by the s. physician death*, Cymb. V, 4, 7.

*To be s.*, followed by an infinitive, synonymous to infallibly, certainly: *I'll be s. to keep him above deck*, Wiv. II, 1, 94 (= I'll certainly keep him etc.). *where she is s. to lose*, All's I, 3, 221. *so should I be s. to be heart-burned*, H4A III, 3, 58. *so should he be s. to be ransomed*, H5 IV, 1, 127. *if we both stay, we both are s. to die*, H6A IV, 5, 20. H6C IV, 4, 35. *be s. to hear some news*, V, 5, 48. *thou art s. to lose*, Ant. II, 3, 26. *I would I were so s. to win the king*, Cymb. II, 4, 1. *I am s. to be hanged at home*, Per. I, 3, 3.

*Be s.*, followed by a subjunctive, = do not fail: *be s. you be not loose*, H8 II, 1, 127. *be s. thou prove my love a whore, be s. of it*, Oth. III, 3, 359.

With *of*, = assured, certain of meeting or obtaining: *I would I were as s. of a good dinner*, Shr. I, 2, 218. *the poor chicken should be s. of death*, H6B III, 1, 251. *then am I s. of victory*, H6C IV, 1, 147. *that's s. of death without it*, Cor. III, 1, 155. *thou art s. of me*, Oth. I, 3, 371 (i. e. of my help). *ply Desdemona well, and you are s. on't*, V, 1, 107. *we will awake him and be s. of him*, Caes. I, 3, 164. *such friends as thought them s. of you*, Cor. V, 3, 8. Similarly: *I will be s. my Katharine shall be fine*, Shr. II, 319 (= assured).

5) certain, not liable to failure, doubtless: *until I know this s. uncertainty*, Err. II, 2, 187. *nothing so s.* LLL IV, 3, 283. *uncertain life and s. death*, All's II, 3, 20. *that know the strongest and —st way to get*, R2 III, 3, 201. *as s. as day*, H4A III, 1, 255. *certain, 'tis*

*certain; very s., very s.* H4B III, 2, 40. *linger not our s. destructions on,* Troil. V, 10, 9. *a s. destruction,* Cor. II, 1, 259. *'tis s. enough, an you knew how,* Tit. IV, 1, 95 (?). *if money were as certain as your waiting, 'twere s. enough,* Tim. III, 4, 48. *there might be thought, though nothing s., yet much unhappily,* Hml. IV, 5, 13. *most s. and vulgar,* Lr. IV, 6, 214. *it is as s. as you are Roderigo,* Oth. I, 1, 56. *where death is s.* Ant. III, 10, 10.

6) to be relied on: *in s. wards of trust,* Sonn. 48, 4. *you are both s., and will assist me?* Ado I, 3, 71. *these promises are fair, the parties s.* H4A III, 1, 1. *you are no —r than is the coal of fire upon the ice,* Cor. I, 1, 176. *he is your brother by the —r side,* Tit. IV, 2, 126. *as s. a card as ever won the set,* V, 1, 100. *I'll make assurance double s.* Mcb. IV, 1, 83. *still close as s.* Cymb. I, 6, 139.

7) certainly knowing, assured: *s. I am, the wits of former days to subjects worse have given admiring praise,* Sonn. 59, 13. *I am s. she is not buried,* Gent. IV, 2, 108. *meed, I am s., I have received none,* Wiv. II, 2, 212. *in my house I am s. he is,* IV, 2, 154. Err. V, 119. Ado II, 1, 138. III, 1, 36. V, 4, 84. Mids. III, 2, 154. IV, 1, 197. Merch. I, 1, 97. II, 2, 86. As III, 2, 110 (*be s.* = know for certain; certainly). III, 5, 26. All's II, 3, 310. Tw. I, 5, 37. Wint. I, 2, 30. Cor. II, 3, 173. Tim. IV, 3, 514. Oth. I, 1, 102. Cymb. I, 6, 96 etc. With *of: he was not s. of it,* Gent. V, 2, 40. Meas. I, 2, 72. 73. II, 1, 55. Tim. III, 6, 63 (*be s. of it* = know it for certain). Lr. IV, 5, 24. Ant. III, 13, 62. Oth. IV, 1, 238.

8) having full confidence, persuaded: *and, to be s. that is not false I swear, a thousand groans ... do witness bear thy black is fairest,* Sonn. 131, 9. *for this, be s., to-night thou shalt have cramps,* Tp. I, 2, 325. *less than this, I am s., you cannot give,* Gent. V, 4, 25. *I am s. you both of you remember me,* Err. V, 291. 303. *his discretion, I am s., cannot carry his valour,* Mids. V, 239. *I am s. thou wilt not take his flesh,* Merch. III, 1, 53. *I am s. the duke will never grant ...,* III, 3, 24. *I am s. care's an enemy to life,* Tw. I, 3, 2. *be s. I count myself in nothing else so happy,* R2 II, 3, 45. *be thou s. I'll well requite thy kindness,* H6C IV, 6, 10. *I would be s. to have all well,* Tit. V, 3, 31 etc. With *of: you two would marry. Be s. of that, — two other husbands,* Wiv. III, 2, 16. Merch. V, 229. Shr. II, 76. All's I, 3, 261. Mcb. V, 1, 54. Lr. V, 3, 194. Oth. I, 2, 11 (Ff *assured*). Ant. II, 5, 103 (*that art not what thou'rt s. of;* viz an honest man?).

**Sure,** adv. 1) safely: *and open perils —st answered,* Caes. IV, 1, 47.

2) firmly: *the sooner to effect and —r bind this knot of amity,* H6A V, 1, 16. *I found a friend, and s. as death I swore I would not part a bachelor from the priest,* Tit. I, 487.

3) unfailingly, infallibly: *this brain ... hunts not the trail of policy so s. as it hath used to do,* Hml. II, 2, 47.

4) assuredly, certainly: *I know most s. my art is not past power,* All's II, 1, 160. *how s. you are my daughter,* Per. V, 1, 228. *God and his angels guard your sacred throne. S., we thank you,* H5 I, 2, 8 (= be sure, be assured? cf. *he shall, s. on't,* Cor. III, 1, 273). *revenged I will be, as s. as his guts are made of puddings,* Wiv. II, 1, 31. *as s. as I have a thought,* Ado IV, 1, 333. *as s. as I do see your grace,* Err. V,

279. *as s. as English Harry lives ... so s. I swear to get the town,* H6A III, 2, 80. *so s. as this beard's grey,* Wint. II, 3, 162. *s. as I live, he had suffered for't,* Gent. IV, 4, 17. Simply inserted by way of asseveration: *and s. it waits upon some god o'the island,* Tp. I, 2, 388. *most s. the goddess on whom these airs attend,* 421. *s. it was the roar of a whole herd,* II, 1, 315. *he is s. i'the island,* 325. Gent. II, 4, 92. III, 1, 63. IV, 2, 127. Wiv. II, 1, 77. 90. III, 2, 31. IV, 1, 3. IV, 2, 223. IV, 4, 77. Meas. III, 1, 110. V, 68. Err. II, 1, 3. 57. 59. IV, 3, 10. V, 176. Ado II, 1, 161. II, 3, 125. III, 1, 56. As II, 4, 29. III, 5, 11. IV, 3, 30. V, 4, 35. Tw. III, 4, 9. Wint. IV, 4, 691. H4B II, 2, 135. V, 2, 29. H6A II, 1, 47. V, 3, 85. H6B I, 3, 8. II, 4, 50. III, 2, 283. V, 1, 13. R3 III, 7, 80. H8 I, 3, 15. III, 2, 141. Troil. V, 2, 126. V, 3, 6. Hml. II, 2, 281. V, 2, 79. Oth. III, 1, 45 etc.

**Surecard** (Qq *Soccard*), name in H4B III, 2, 95 (cf. Tit. V, 1, 100).*

**Surely,** 1) firmly: *that I may s. keep mine oath,* Shr. V, 2, 36. *by this knot thou shalt so s. tie thy now unsured assurance to the crown,* John II, 470.

2) certainly, undoubtedly: *and s. as I live, I am a maid,* Ado V, 4, 64. *none are so s. caught,* LLL V, 2, 69. *he pays you as s. as your feet hit the ground,* Tw. III, 4, 305. *as s. as I live,* R2 IV, 102. *as s. as my soul intends to live ... I do believe,* H6B III, 2, 153. Simply inserted by way of asseveration: *and s. it is a sleepy language,* Tp. II, 1, 210. *s. I think you have charms,* Wiv. II, 2, 107. Meas. I, 2, 175. III, 2, 137. IV, 2, 34. Err. IV, 4, 89. 156. Ado II, 3, 180. III, 2, 103. IV, 1, 261. 317. 319. LLL I, 2, 92. As II, 2, 16. Shr. IV, 2, 65. All's III, 5, 58. H4B III, 2, 77. H5 III, 2, 126 (Captain Jamy: *suerly*). H6A IV, 6, 50. H6B III, 1, 77. V, 1, 216. H6C II, 6, 41. H8 I, 1, 57. II, 2, 124. III, 2, 356 (*full s.*). V, 4, 62. Troil. III, 2, 138. Tim. III, 4, 32. IV, 3, 500. Hml. III, 2, 351 (Ff *freely*). Oth. I, 1, 158. II, 3, 244. Cymb. V, 5, 92.

**Surety,** subst. 1) security, confidence of safety: *the wound of peace is s., s. secure,* Troil. II, 2, 14.

2) certainty: *but I, for mere suspicion in that kind, will do as if for s.* Oth. I, 3, 396.

3) foundation of stability, support, trust: *what s. of the world, what hope, what stay, when this was now a king, and now is clay?* John V, 7, 68. *with s. stronger than Achilles' arm,* Troil. I, 3, 220.

4) confirmation, warrant, guarantee: *in s. of the which one part of Aquitaine is bound to us,* LLL II, 135. *she called the saints to s. that she would never put it from her finger,* All's V, 3, 108. *makest an oath the s. for thy truth against an oath,* John III, 1, 282. *givest such sarcenet s. for thy oaths,* H4A III, 1, 256. *he is a man who with a double s. binds his followers,* H4B I, 1, 191. *we'll take your oath ... for s. of our leagues,* H5 V, 2, 400. *give me some token for the s. of it,* Troil. V, 2, 60.

5) bail; hostage: *I'll be his s.* Tp. I, 2, 475. *the Frenchman became his s.* Merch. I, 2, 89. V, 254. All's IV, 4, 3. *procure your —es for your days of answer,* R2 IV, 159. *let there be impawned some s. for a safe return again,* H4A IV, 3, 109. *the bastard boys of York shall be the s. for their father,* H6B V, 1, 116. *bane to those that for my s. will refuse the boys,* 121.

**Surety,** vb. to be evidence for; to bail: *the jeweller that owes the ring is sent for, and he shall s. me,* All's V, 3, 298. *we'll s. him,* Cor. III, 1, 178.

**Surety-like,** like a bondsman or bail: Sonn. 134, 7.

**Surfeit,** subst. excess in eating and drinking, gluttony; and sickness and satiety caused by it; in a physical and a moral sense: *s. is the father of much fast,* Meas. I, 2, 130. *as a s. of the sweetest things the deepest loathing to the stomach brings,* Mids. II, 2, 137. *thou, my s. and my heresy,* 141. *now comes the sick hour that his s. made,* R2 II, 2, 84. *to cure thy o'er-night's s.* Tim. IV, 3, 227. *—s, imposthumes, grief,* Ven. 743. *suffer s., cloyment and revolt,* Tw. II, 4, 102. *by s. die your king,* R3 I, 3, 197. *thou art too full of the wars' —s,* Cor. IV, 1, 46. *the —s of our own behaviour,* Lr. I, 2, 130. *full —s,* Ant. I, 4, 27.

**Surfeit,** vb. 1) tr. to feed to excess, to cloy (used only in the partic. *—ed): the never —ed sea,* Tp. III, 3, 55. *the — ed grooms,* Mcb. II, 2, 5. *my hopes, not —ed to death, stand in bold cure,* Oth. II, 1, 50.

2) intr. a) to indulge one's appetite to excess, to gluttonize, to revel: *whereon they s., yet complain on drouth,* Ven. 544. *as poor birds, deceived with painted grapes, do s. by the eye and pine the maw,* 602. *thus do I pine and s. day by day, or gluttoning on all, or all away,* Sonn. 75, 13. *with our —ing and wanton hours have brought ourselves into a burning fever,* H4B IV, 1, 55. *as one that —s thinking on a want,* H6B III, 2, 348. *what authority —s on would relieve us,* Cor. I, 1, 16. *voluptuously s. out of action,* I, 3, 28. *this the banquet she shall s. on,* Tit. V, 2, 194.

b) to feel uneasy and sick in consequence of excess: *love —s not, lust like a glutton dies,* Ven. 803. *the profit of excess is but to s.* Lucr. 139. *excess of it will make me s.* Gent. III, 1, 220. Meas. V, 102. Merch. I, 2, 6. III, 2, 115. All's III, 1, 18 *(s. on their ease).* Tw. I, 1, 2. H4A III, 2, 71. H4B I, 3, 88. H6B I, 1, 251.

**Surfeiter,** glutton, reveller: *this amorous s.* Ant. II, 1, 33.

**Surfeit-swelled,** tumefied by gluttony: H4B V, 5, 54.

**Surfeit‧taking,** surfeiting, cloyed: Lucr. 698.

**Surge,** a large wave: Tp. II, 1, 114. 117. Tw. V, 236. H4B III, 1, 20. H5 III Chor. 13. Tit. III, 1, 96. Tim. IV, 2, 21. IV, 3, 442. V, 1, 221. Lr. IV, 6, 20. Oth. II, 1, 13. Cymb. III, 1, 28. Per. III, 1, 1. Only once in prose, in a passage justly suspected: *to be thrown into the Thames, and cooled, glowing hot, in that s., like a horse-shoe,* Wiv. III, 5, 123 (Capell proposes *forge,* with little probability).

**Surgeon,** one who cures by manual operation: Mids. V, 316. Merch. IV, 1, 257. Tw. V, 175. 202. H5 IV, 1, 145. H6A II, 4, 53. III, 1, 146. Troil. V, 1, 12. Rom. III, 1, 97. Caes. I, 1, 27. Mcb. I, 2, 44. Lr. IV, 6, 196. Oth. II, 3, 253. V, 1, 30. 100. Per. IV, 6, 29.

**Surgery,** the art and practice of a surgeon; cure by manual operation: *tarred over with the s. of our sheep,* As III, 2, 64. *skill in s.* H4A V, 1, 135. H4B II, 4, 56. Mcb. IV, 3, 152. Oth. II, 3, 260.

**Surly,** 1) gloomy, dismal: *than you shall hear the s. sullen bell give warning to the world,* Sonn. 71, 2. *that s. spirit, melancholy,* John III, 3, 42.

2) gloomily morose, sullen, crabbed: *'tis like you'll prove a jolly s. groom,* Shr. III, 2, 215. *s. with servants,* Tw. II, 5, 163. *the sad-eyed justice, with his s. hum,* H5 I, 2, 202. *under the s. Gloster's governance,* H6B I, 3, 50. *see how the s. Warwick mans the wall,* H6C V, 1, 17. *covetous of praise, or s. borne,* Troil. II, 3,

249. *it would have galled his s. nature,* Cor. II, 3, 203. *who glared upon me and went s. by,* Caes. I, 3, 21.

**Surmise,** 1) reflection, thought: *that praise which Collatine doth owe enchanted Tarquin answers with s., in silent wonder of still-gazing eyes,* Lucr. 83 (by thinking to himself, how much Collatine's praise had come short of Lucrece's beauty). *being from the feeling of her own grief brought by deep s. of others' detriment,* 1579.

2) speculation, imagination, conjecture: *in a theme so bloody-faced as this conjecture, expectation, and s. of aids incertain should not be admitted,* H4B I, 3, 23. *function is smothered in s.* Mcb. I, 3, 141.

3) suspicion: *book both my wilfulness and errors down and on just proof s. accumulate,* Sonn. 117, 10. *if I shall be condemned upon —s,* Wint. III, 2, 113. *rumour is a pipe blown by —s, jealousies, conjectures,* H4B Ind. 16. *if any here, by false intelligence or wrong s., hold me a foe,* R3 II, 1, 54. *to behold the thing whereat it trembles by s.* Tit. II, 3, 219. *such exsufflicate and blown —s,* Oth. III, 3, 182. *I speak not out of weak —s,* Cymb. III, 4, 24.

**Surmise,** vb. to imagine, to conjecture: *it (my grief) is but —d whiles thou art standing by,* H6B III, 2, 347. *that unbodied figure of the thought that gave't (the action) —d shape,* Troil. I, 3, 17. *now gather and s.* Hml. II, 2, 108.

**Surmount,** to surpass, to exceed: *as I all other in all worths s.* Sonn. 62, 8. *this Hector far —ed Hannibal,* LLL V, 2, 677. *your presence makes us rich, ... and far —s our labour to attain it,* R2 II, 3, 64. Absol., = to be surpassing: *bethink thee on her virtues that s., and natural graces that extinguish art,* H6A V, 3, 191.

**Surname,** appellation added to the original name: *my s. Coriolanus,* Cor. IV, 5, 74. 77. V, 3, 170.

**Surnamed,** having an appellation added to the original name: Lucr. Arg. 1. LLL V, 2, 553. 555. Tit. I, 23.

**Surpass,** to go beyond in excellence, to excel: Ven. 289. Tp. III, 2, 110. Wint. III, 1, 2.

**Surplice,** a white garment worn by the clergy: Phoen. 13. All's I, 3, 99 (it must be remembered that the Puritans objected to the use of the surplice and substituted for it the black gown).

**Surplus,** overplus, more than suffices: *it is a s. of your grace,* Wint. V, 3, 7. *he hath faults, with s., to tire in repetition,* Cor. I, 1, 46.

**Surprise,** subst. a state of being overpowered; extreme confusion and perplexity caused by something extraordinary: *the guiltiness of my mind, the sudden s. of my powers, drove the grossness of the foppery into a received belief,* Wiv. V, 5, 131. *the very principals did seem to rend, and all to topple; pure s. and fear made me to quit the house,* Per. III, 2, 17.

**Surprise,** vb. 1) to fall on, to attack or take suddenly: *now serves the season that they may s. the silly lambs,* Lucr. 166. *you'll be —d,* LLL V, 2, 84. *I will s. him,* All's III, 6, 24. *we had not been thus shamefully —d,* H6A II, 1, 65. *suddenly —d by bloody hands,* V, 3, 40. *—d our forts,* H6B IV, 1, 89. *we may s. and take him,* H6C IV, 2, 17. 25. *by his foe —d at unawares,* IV, 4, 9. *when with a happy storm they were —d,* Tit. II, 3, 23. *when subtle Greeks —d King Priam's Troy,* V, 3, 84. *the castle of Macduff I will s.* Mcb. IV, 1, 150. IV, 3, 204.

Used of an assault made on the chastity of a woman: *how she* (Io) *was beguiled and —d*, Shr. Ind. 2, 57. *would suffer her poor knight —d*, All's I, 3, 120. *Lavinia is —d*, Tit. I, 284. *wert thou thus —d, ravished and wronged*, IV, 1, 51.

2) to seize, to take prisoner: *the prisoners which he in this adventure hath —d*, H4A I, 1, 93. *—d and taken prisoners*, H6A IV, 1, 26. *to s. me*, H6B IV, 8, 61. *is the traitor Cade —d?* IV, 9, 8. *I rushed upon him, —d him suddenly*, Tit. V, 1, 38. *how easily she may be —d*, Ant. V, 2, 35.

3) to overpower, to perplex, to confound: *this dismal cry rings sadly in her ear, through which it enters to s. her heart*, Ven. 890. *this mutiny each part doth so s. that from their dark beds once more leap her eyes*, 1049. *so glad of this as they I cannot be, who are —d withal*, Tp. III, 1, 93. *s. her with discourse of my dear faith*, Tw. I, 4, 25. *the ear-deafening voice o'the oracle ... so —d my sense, that I was nothing*, Wint. III, 1, 10. *I am —d with an uncouth fear*, Tit. II, 3, 211. *you witch me in it, s. me to the very brink of tears*, Tim. V, 1, 159.

**Sur-reined**, overridden, knocked up: *a drench for s. jades*, H5 III, 5, 19.

**Surrender**, subst. cession, resignation: *the s. of those lands*, Hml. I, 2, 23. *if our father carry authority with such dispositions as he bears, this last s. of his will but offend us*, Lr. I, 1, 309.

**Surrender**, vb. to resign, to yield: *that in common view he may s.* R2 IV, 156. *to whom ... I would s. it* (this place) H8 I, 4, 81.

**Surrender-up**, subst. cession: *about s. of Aquitaine to her father*, LLL I, 1, 138.

**Surrey**, name: R2 IV, 65. 74. H4B III, 1, 1. R3 V, 3, 2. 69. 273. H8 II, 1, 43. III, 2, 253. 274. IV, 1, 39. Name of a horse: R3 V, 3, 64.

**Survey**, subst. 1) sight, look: *whose beauty did astonish the s. of richest eyes*, All's V, 3, 16. *time, that takes s. of all the world*, H4A V, 4, 82.

2) inspection, examination: *I leave it to your honorable s.* Ven. Ded. 6. *make but an interior s. of your good selves*, Cor. II, 1, 44. *lest the people, and patricians too, upon a just s., take Titus' part*, Tit. I, 446.

**Survey**, vb. 1) to look on: *the which* (treasure) *he will not every hour s.* Sonn. 52, 3. *my love's sweet face s., if time have any wrinkle graven there*, 100, 9. *which here thou viewest, beholdest, —est, or seest*, LLL I, 1, 247 (Armado's letter). *I will s. the inscriptions*, Merch. II, 7, 14. *s. with thy chaste eye ... thy huntress' name*, Ant. III, 2, 2. *to the furthest verge that ever was —ed by English eye*, R2 I, 1, 94. *to s. his dead and earthy image*, H6B III, 2, 147.

2) to inspect, to examine: *we first s. the plot*, H4B I, 3, 42. 50. *—s the singing masons*, H5 I, 2, 197. *I am come to s. the Tower*, H6A I, 3, 1. *to s. the bodies of the dead*, IV, 7, 57. *let us s. the vantage of the field*, R3 V, 3, 15.

3) to see, to perceive: *the Norweyan lord —ing vantage*, Mcb. I, 2, 31. cf. sub 1: R2 I, 1, 94.

**Surveyor**, (*survéyor*; in H8 I, 1, 222 *súrveyor*), an overseer: H6B III, 1, 253. H8 I, 1, 115. 222. I, 2, 172. II, 1, 19. = a measurer of land: H4B I, 3, 53.

**Survive**, 1) tr. to outlive: *if thou s. my well-contented day*, Sonn. 32, 1. Shr. II, 125. H6A III, 2, 37. Tit. V, 3, 41.

2) intr. to live after the death of another or after any

thing else that has happened: *and so, in spite of death, thou dost s.* Ven. 173. Lucr. 204. 223. 519. 1766. Sonn. 81, 2. Gent. IV, 2, 110. H4A III, 2, 154 (Ff *if I perform and do s.*, Qq *if He be pleased I shall perform*). H4B V, 2, 125. Tit. I, 82. 102. 133. 173.

**Survivor**, one who outlives another: Cor. V, 6, 19. Hml. I, 2, 90.

**Susan**, female name in Rom. I, 3, 18. 19. I, 5, 10.

**Suspect**, subst. suspicion: *her rash s. she doth extenuate*, Ven. 1010. *the ornament of beauty is s., a crow that flies in heaven's sweetest air*, Sonn. 70, 3. Err. III, 1, 87. H6B I, 3, 139. III, 1, 140 (O. Edd. *suspence*). III, 2, 139. H6C IV, 1, 142 (*have you in s.*). R3 I, 3, 89 (*—s*). III, 5, 32 (Ff *—s*). Tim. IV, 3, 519. 521. With *of: if some s. of ill masked not thy show*, Sonn. 70, 13.

**Suspect**, vb. to imagine guilt or danger, to mistrust; absol.: *it shall s. where is no cause of fear*, Ven. 1153. Wiv. III, 3, 159. IV, 2, 138. Oth. III, 3, 170. With a subord. clause: *whether that my angel be turned fiend s. I may, yet not directly tell*, Sonn. 144, 10. *thou dost s. that I have been disloyal*, R2 V, 2, 104. H6B III, 2, 190. R3 III, 7, 111. Rom. V, 2, 9. Oth. II, 1, 304. V, 1, 78. Ant. IV, 14, 122. Per. I, 2, 21.

Trans., = to regard with mistrust; to fear: *little —eth the false worshipper*, Lucr. 86. *teaches them s. the thoughts of others*, Merch. I, 3, 162. *that truth should be —ed*, All's I, 3, 187. *who would have —ed an ambush?* IV, 3, 335. *he will s. us still*, H4A V, 2, 6. John IV, 2, 26. IV, 3, 134. H6B III, 1, 152. H6C V, 4, 44. Tit. II, 3, 213. Tim. II, 2, 164. IV, 3, 333. Lr. I, 2, 197. Oth. I, 3, 404. IV, 2, 2. Cymb. I, 5, 31. Double accus.: *if you my father do s. an instrument of this your calling back*, Oth. IV, 2, 44. With *as* or *for: s. these noblemen as guilty*, H6B III, 2, 186. *thy friends s. for traitors*, R3 I, 3, 223. cf. *lest she s. her children not her husband's*, Wint. II, 3, 107. With an inf.: *you may s. him to be no true man*, Ado III, 3, 53. *I do s. this trash to be a party*, Oth. V, 1, 85. With a clause: *should s. me that I mean no good to him*, R3 III, 7, 89. With prepositions: *if you s. me in any dishonesty*, Wiv. IV, 2, 140. *most —ed of this murder*, Rom. V, 3, 224. *to be —ed of more tenderness*, Cymb. I, 1, 94. *lest I be —ed of your carriage from the court*, III, 4, 189. *I rather will s. the sun with cold than thee with wantonness*, Wiv. IV, 4, 7. *to s. me with the Moor*, Oth. IV, 2, 147.

Confounded with *respect* by Dogberry: Ado IV, 2, 76. 77.

**Suspence**, reading of O. Edd. in H6B III, 1, 140: *that you will clear yourself from all s.*; M. Edd. rightly *suspect*.

**Suspend**, to delay, to stay, to hinder from proceeding: *to s. your indignation against my brother till you can derive from him better testimony of his intent*, Lr. I, 2, 86. *s. thy purpose, if thou didst intend to make this creature fruitful*, I, 4, 298.

**Suspicion**, imagination and apprehension of something ill: Ven. 448. Wiv. III, 3, 108. IV, 2, 36. Ado I, 1, 201. Wint. II, 1, 160. III, 2, 152. V, 3, 149. R2 IV, 157. H4A IV, 2, 8 (O. Edd. *supposition*). H4B I, 1, 84. H5 II, 2, 140. H6B III, 2, 25. H6C V, 6, 11. V, 7, 13. R3 II, 1, 94. III, 5, 8. H8 III, 1, 53. 128. Rom. V, 3, 222 (*the parties of s.* = the suspicious parties). Oth. I, 3, 395. III, 3, 179. 220. IV, 2, 215. *to bear s.* = to suspect: Lucr. 1321. *to take s.* (= to conceive s.): Wint. I, 2, 460. *in s.* = suspicious: *so like an old tale, that the verity of it is in strong s.* Wint. V, 2, 31. *out of s.* = without, free from s.: *out of all s., she is virtuous,* Ado II, 3, 166. The object of apprehension added with *in* or *of: because in York this breeds s.* H6B I, 3, 210. *have some special s. of Falstaff's being here,* Wiv. III, 3, 200. *which puts upon them s. of the deed,* Mcb. II, 4, 27. The possessive pronoun usually subjective (f. i. Wint. IV, 2, 36. Wint. I, 2, 460), but also objective: *they shall be ready at your highness' will to answer their s. with their lives,* Tit. II, 3, 298 (i. e. the s. conceived against them). *if I find him comforting the king, it will stuff his s. more fully,* Lr. III, 5, 22. Abstr. pro concr.: *we took this mattock and this spade from him. A great s.* Rom. V, 3, 187 (= suspicious circumstance).

**Suspicious,** 1) entertaining suspicion or inclined to suspect, apprehensive: *the s. head of theft,* LLL IV, 3, 336. *that any one should be s. I more incline to Somerset than York,* H6A IV, 1, 153.

2) giving reason to imagine ill: *even so s. is this tragedy,* H6B III, 2, 194. *a black, s., threatening cloud,* H6C V, 3, 4. *a strange tongue makes my cause more strange, s.* H8 III, 1, 45.

**Suspiration,** respiration, breathing: *nor windy s. of forced breath,* Hml. 1, 2, 79.

**Suspire,** to breathe: *did he s., that light and weightless down perforce must move,* H4B IV, 5, 33. = to be born, to come into life: *since the birth of Cain, the first male child, to him that did but yesterday s., there was not such a gracious creature born,* John III, 4, 80.

**Sustain,** 1) to support, to uphold: *the prop that doth s. my house,* Merch. IV, 1, 376. *your need to s.* Tw. IV, 2, 135. *and the gored state s.* Lr. V, 3, 320. *s. me, O!* Ant. III, 11, 45.

2) to afford the means of subsistence, to maintain, to keep; absol.: *the idle weeds that grow in our —ing corn,* Lr. IV, 4, 6 (nourishing). Trans.: *an hundred knights, by you to be —ed,* Lr. I, 1, 136. *if she s. him and his hundred knights,* I, 4, 355. *nor any way s. him,* III, 3, 6.

3) to endure, to bear up against sth.; absol.: *their —ing garments not a blemish,* Tp. I, 2, 218 (according to others, the garments that bore them up in the sea). Trans.: *spending his manly marrow in her arms, which would s. the bound and high curvet of Mars's fiery steed,* All's II, 3, 299. *the sides of nature will not s. it,* Ant. I, 3, 17.

4) to maintain; refl. = to maintain one's place (?): *a better (weapon) never did itself s. upon a soldier's thigh,* Oth. V, 2, 260 (= maintained its place on account of its excellent quality?).

5) to suffer, to undergo: *the profit of excess is but to surfeit, and such griefs s., that they prove bankrupt in this poor-rich gain,* Lucr. 139. *if thou dost weep for grief of my —ing,* 1272. *short time seems long in sorrow's sharp —ing,* 1573. *let me s. no scorn,* Tw. I, 5, 186. *pricked on by public wrongs —ed in France,* H6A III, 2, 78. *to do them good, I would s. some harm,* H6C III, 2, 39. *you shall s. moe new disgraces,* H8 III, 2, 5. *with other incident throes that nature's fragile vessel doth s. in life's uncertain voyage,* Tim. V, 1, 204. *what loss your honour may s.* Hml. I, 3, 29. *I doubt not you s. what you're worthy of* (viz a repulse) Cymb. I, 4, **125.**

**Sustenance,** food: *let him receive no s.* Tit. V, 3, 6. *nor taken s. but to prorogue his grief,* Per. V, 1, 25.

**Sutler,** one who sells provisions and liquors in a camp: H5 II, 1, 116.

**Sutton-Cophill,** name of a place in England: H4A IV, 2, 3. Hanmer *Sutton-Colfield,* Cambridge Editors *Sutton-Co'fil'.* *

**Suum,** sound imitative of the whistling of the wind: *through the hawthorn blows the cold wind: says s., mun, ha, no, nonny,* Lr. III, 4, 103.

**Swabber,** one whose office it is to clean the deck of a vessel: Tp. II, 2, 48. Tw. I, 5, 217.

**Swaddling-clouts** (Ff *swathing-clouts*) linen bandages wrapped round new-born children: Hml. II, 2, 401.

**Swag-bellied,** having a large overhanging belly: *your s. Hollander,* Oth. II, 3, 80.

**Swagger,** to rant, to be noisy and boisterous: *what hempen homespuns have we —ing here?* Mids. III, 1, 79. *will he s. himself out on's own eyes?* Troil. V, 2, 136. *the —ing upspring,* Hml. I, 4, 9. Especially = to bluster, to bully: *a terrible oath, with a —ing accent sharply twanged off,* Tw. III, 4, 197. *when I came to wive, ... by —ing could I never thrive,* V, 408. *hang him, —ing rascal!* H4B II, 4, 76. 79. 84. 102. 112. 113 (very imperfectly understood by Mrs Quickly). *an I should have been —ed out of my life,* Lr. IV, 6, 243 (Edgar, in the character of a peasant: *zwaggered*). *squabble, s., swear,* Oth. II, 3, 281. *With before the person bullied: he'll not s. with a Barbary hen,* H4B II, 4, 107. *a rascal that —ed with me last night,* H5 IV, 7, 131.

**Swaggerer,** a blusterer, a bully: As IV, 3, 14. H4B II, 4, 81. 83. 91. 104. 105. 117.

**Swain,** 1) a peasant, particularly a shepherd: *onward to Troy with the blunt —s he goes,* Lucr. 1504 (shepherds in v. 1502). *all our pleasure known to us poor —s,* Pilgr. 289. *that young s. that you saw here,* As II, 4, 89. *a —'s wearing,* Wint. IV, 4, 9. 30. 166. 377. 402. *to be no better than a homely s.* H6C II, 5, 22.

2) any person of low rank: *Costard the s. and he shall be our sport,* LLL I, 1, 180. 250. 277. III, 5. 50. 66. V, 1, 134. V, 2, 538. *like this transformed scalp from off the head of this Athenian s.* Mids. IV, 1, 70. Used as a term of contempt: *a s.! a most simple clown!* LLL IV, 1, 142. *too light for such a s. as you to catch,* Shr. II, 205. *you peasant s.!* IV, 1, 132. *a hedge-born s.* H6A IV, 1, 43. *begotten of a shepherd s.* V, 4, 37. *obscure and lowly s.* H6B IV, 1, 50. *shall I stab the forlorn s.?* 65.

3) a youth given to thoughts of love; a lover: *what is she, that all our —s commend her?* Gent. IV, 2, 40. *cherish thy forlorn s.* V, 4, 12. *true —s in love shall in the world to come approve their truths by Troilus,* Troil. III, 2, 180.

**Swallow,** subst. the bird Hirundo: Wint. IV, 4, 119. H4B IV, 3, 36. R3 V, 2, 23. Tit. II, 2, 24. IV, 2, 172. Tim. III, 6, 31. Ant. IV, 12, 4.

**Swallow,** vb. 1) to receive through the gullet into the stomach: *a —ed bait,* Sonn. 129, 7. *had —ed snow-balls for pills,* Wiv. III, 5, 24. LLL III, 15. V, 1, 45. Caes. IV, 3, 156. Hml. IV, 2, 20. Lr. III, 4, 137. Ant. V, 2, 348. Cymb. III, 5, 58. V, 5, 381. Metaphorically: *now s. down that lie,* R2 I, 1, 132 (and try to digest it). *capital crimes, chewed, —ed and digested,* H5 II, 2, 56 (gone through all the stages of concoction). *I'll make thee ... s. my sword*, H6B IV, 10, 31 (receive it into your body; cf. *Eat*).

2) to devour, to englut, to engulf; absol.: *what is thy body but a —ing grave, seeming to bury that posterity*, Ven. 757. *a —ing gulf*, Lucr. 557. *the —ing gulf of blind forgetfulness*, R3 III, 7, 128. *the —ing womb of this deep pit*, Tit. II, 3, 239. Trans.: *these lovely caves ... opened their mouths to s. Venus' liking*, Ven. 248. *they that lose half with greater patience bear it than they whose whole is —ed in confusion*, Lucr. 1159. *ere it should the good ship so have —ed*, Tp. I, 2, 12. *sea-swallowed*, II, 1, 251. *—ed his vows whole*, Meas. III, 1, 235 (retracted, disavowed them; cf. *to eat one's word*, sub *Eat*). *—ed with yest and froth*, Wint. III, 3, 94. *with open mouth —ing a tailor's news*, John IV, 2, 195. *being daily —ed by men's eyes, they surfeited with honey*, H4A III, 2, 70. *for fear of —ing*, V, 1, 64. *shall be —ed in this controversy*, H5 II, 4, 109. *for —ing the treasure of the realm*, H6B IV, 1, 74. *may that ground gape and s. me alive*, H6C I, 1, 161. *half our sailors —ed in the flood*, V, 4, 5. *the interview, that —ed so much treasure*, H8 I, 1, 166. *they have —ed one another*, Troil. V, 4, 36. *some envious surge will s. him*, Tit. III, 1, 97. *s. her own increase*, V, 2, 192. *the earth hath —ed all my hopes but she*, Rom. I, 2, 14. *let prisons s. 'em*, Tim. IV, 3, 537. *it englut and —s other sorrows*, Oth. I, 3, 57. *they've —ed the whole parish*, Per. II, 1, 37. 43. *Thetis ... —ed some part o' the earth*, IV, 4, 39.

With *up: seemed to s. up his sound advice*, Lucr. 1409 (to listen to it eagerly). *the sea whose envious gulf did s. up his life*, H6C V, 6, 25. *as thou (the earth) dost s. up this good king's blood*, R3 I, 2, 66. *blind oblivion —ed cities up*, Troil. III, 2, 194. *though the yesty waves confound and s. navigation up*, Mcb. IV, 1, 54. *till that a capable and wide revenge s. them* (my thoughts) *up*, Oth. III, 3, 460 (make an end of them).

**Swan**, the bird Cygnus: Lucr. 1011. Wiv. V, 5, 7. H6A V, 3, 56. H6C I, 4, 19 (fem.). Tit. IV, 2, 102 (fem.). Rom. I, 2, 92. Ant. III, 2, 48. Cymb. III, 4, 142. Sacred to Juno: As I, 3, 77. Singing shortly before its death: *and now this pale s. in her watery nest begins the sad dirge of her certain ending*, Lucr. 1611. *let the priest in surplice white, that defunctive music can, be the death-divining s.* Phoen. 15. *this pale faint s. who chants a doleful hymn to his own death*, John V, 7, 21. *I will play the s. and die in music*, Oth. V, 2, 247.

**Swan-like**, like a swan: *he makes a s. end, fading in music*, Merch. III, 2, 44.

**Swarm**, subst. infinite number: *this s. of fair advantages*, H4A V, 1, 55.

**Swarm**, vb. 1) to throng in multitudes: *our peasants, who in unnecessary action s. about our squares of battle*, H5 IV, 2, 27. *the plebeians —ing at their heels*, H5 Chor. 27. *the common people by numbers s. to us*, H6C IV, 2, 2. *the multiplying villanies of nature do s. upon him*, Mcb. I, 2, 12. Inserted in H6C II, 6, 8 by M. Edd. from the surreptitious Qq.

2) to be crowded, to be overrun: *her wholesome herbs —ing with caterpillars*, R2 III, 4, 47.

**Swart**, black, dark (of complexion): *what complexion is she of? S., like my shoe*, Err. III, 2, 104. *lame, foolish, crooked, s., prodigious*, John III, 1, 46. *I was black and s. before*, H6A I, 2, 84.

**Swart-complexioned**, black, dark: *the s. night*, Sonn. 28, 11.

**Swarth**, subst. swath: *cons state without book and utters it by great —s*, Tw. II, 3, 162.

**Swarth**, adj. black (of complexion): *your s. Cimmerian*, Tit. II, 3, 72 (Qq *swarty*).

**Swarthy**, the same: *a s. Ethiope*, Gent. II, 6, 26.

**Swarty**, the same: Tit. II, 3, 72 (Ff *swarth*).

**Swasher**, a braggart, a bully: *I have observed these three —s*, H5 III, 2, 30.

**Swashing**, swaggering, hectoring, dashing, smashing: *we'll have a s. and a martial outside, as many other mannish cowards have*, As I, 3, 122. *remember thy s. blow*, Rom. I, 1, 70 (German: *deinen Schwadronenhieb*).

**Swath**, subst. (cf. *Swarth*) that which the mower cuts down with one sweep of the scythe: Troil. V, 5, 25.

**Swath**, subst. the bandages wrapped round new-born children: *from our first s.* Tim. IV, 3, 252.

**Swathe**, vb. in *Enswathed*, q. v.

**Swathing-clothes**, the bandages wrapped round new-born children: H4A III, 2, 112 (Qq *swathling clothes*). Cymb. I, 1, 59.

**Swathing-clouts**, the same: Hml. II, 2, 401 (Qq *swaddling clouts*).

**Swathling-clothes**, see *Swathing-clothes*.

**Sway**, subst. 1) direction, manage, government: *strength by limping s. disabled*, Sonn. 66, 8 (by being misdirected). *proud of subjection, noble by the s.* Compl. 108 (the manege of the rider). With *of*; a) subjectively: *proceed i'the s. of your own will*, Lr. IV, 7, 20. b) objectively: *this s. of motion, this Commodity*, John II, 578 (cf. the verb in Mids. I, 1, 193). *should not our father bear the great s. of his affairs with reasons*, Troil. II, 2, 35. *a place of potency and s. o'the state*, Cor. II, 3, 190. *when all the s. of earth shakes like a thing unfirm*, Caes. I, 3, 3 (all the government and established order of the earth. Johnson: the whole weight or momentum of this globe. Craik: all the balanced swing of earth).

2) rule, dominion: *so dry he was for s.* Tp. I, 2, 112. *to behold his s.* Meas. I, 3, 43. *you would bear some s.* Err. II, 1, 28 (*bear* = have). *mercy is above this sceptred s.* Merch. IV, 1, 193. Shr. V, 2, 163. R2 IV, 206. H4A V, 1, 57. V, 5, 41 (Ff *way*). H6C IV, 6, 32. Troil. I, 3, 60. Rom. IV, 1, 10. Mcb. I, 5, 71. Lr. I, 1, 139. II, 4, 193.

**Sway**, vb. 1) to govern, to direct, to manage, to influence, to rule; a) trans.: *when thou gently —est the wiry concord*, Sonn. 128, 3. *with insufficiency my heart to s.* 150, 2. *let my counsel s. you*, Ado IV, 1, 203. *with what art you s. the motion of Demetrius' heart*, Mids. I, 1, 193. *the will of man is by his reason —ed*, II, 2, 115. *affection, master of passion, —s it to the mood of what it likes or loathes*, Merch. IV, 1, 51. *a thing not in his power to bring to pass, but —ed and fashioned by the hand of heaven*, I, 3, 94. *thy huntress' name that my full life doth s.* As III, 2, 4. *M, O, A, I, doth s. my life*, Tw. II, 5, 118. 121. *she could not s. her house*, IV, 3, 17. *the sword which —s usurpingly these several titles*, John I, 13. *this hand ... that —s the earth this climate overlooks*, II, 344. *usurpers s. the rule awhile*, H6C III, 3, 76. *minds —ed by eyes are full of turpitude*, Troil. V, 2, 112. *nought but humour —s him*, Tim. III, 6, 122. *s. our great designs,*

Ant. II, 2, 151. With *from,* = to turn away from: *them that so much have —ed your majesty's good thoughts away from me,* H4A III, 2, 130. *was —ed from the point, by looking down on Caesar,* Caes. III, 1, 219.

b) absol. to rule, to have dominion: *so —s she level in her husband's heart,* Tw. II, 4, 32. *let thy fair wisdom s.* IV, 1, 56. *no one should s. but he,* H6A III, 1, 37. *a gentler heart did never s. in court,* III, 2, 135. *hadst thou —ed as kings should do,* H6C II, 6, 14. *I had rather be their servant in my way than s. with them in theirs,* Cor. II, 1, 220. *his affections —ed more than his reason,* Caes. II, 1, 20. *who —s, not as it hath power,* Lr. I, 2, 53. *you gods that s. in love,* Per. I, 1, 19.

2) intr. to be biassed, to be directed, to move: *he seems indifferent, or rather —ing more upon our part,* H5 I, 1, 73.* *now —s it this way, like a mighty sea,... now —s it that way,* H6C II, 5, 5. *the mind I s. by and the heart I bear shall never sag with doubt,* Mcb. V, 3, 9. *to s. on* = not to yield to doubt and fear, but rather go on: *let us s. on and face them in the field,* H4B IV, 1, 24.

**Swayed,** a term of veterinary science, = stained and weakened in the hinder parts of the body; substituted by some M. Edd. for *waid* of O. Edd. in Shr. III, 2, 56.*

**Swear** (impf. usually *swore,* partic. *sworn;* impf. *sware:* H4B III, 2, 342. Tit. IV, 1, 91. Ff *sware,* Qq *swore:* Tit. I, 487. Partic. *swore,* for the sake of the rhyme, in LLL I, 1, 114) 1) to declare or affirm in a solemn manner: *—ing I slew him,* Lucr. 518. *one would s. he saw them quake,* 1393. *Lucrece —s he did her wrong,* 1462. *his scarlet lust came evidence to s. that my poor beauty had purloined his eyes,* 1650. *s. that brightness doth not grace the day,* Sonn. 150, 4. *s. how thou escapedst,* Tp. II, 2, 132. *whether this be or be not, I'll not s.* V, 123. Gent. IV, 3, 12. Wiv. II, 1, 60. IV, 2, 31. 88. Meas. IV, 3, 62. V, 208. 516. Err. III, 2, 145. IV, 2, 9. Ado I, 1, 152. LLL IV, 1, 58. V, 2, 359. Mids. II, 1, 56. Merch. I, 1, 56. III, 1, 119. IV, 2, 15. All's II, 5, 54. Tw. I, 5, 147. H4B III, 2, 342. H6A IV, 4, 31. IV, 5, 28. Oth. III, 3, 336 etc. etc. With an accus.: *I heard him s. his affection,* Ado II, 1, 175. *tells a lie and —s it,* IV, 1, 325. *s. the lies he forges,* All's IV, 1, 26. *as you s. them lordship,* V, 3, 156. *to s. false allegations,* H6B III, 1, 180. *he swore consent to your succession,* H6C II, 1, 172. *if something thou wilt s. to be believed,* R3 IV, 4, 372. *the truest princess that ever swore her faith,* Cymb. V, 5, 417 etc. Double accus.: *I have sworn thee fair,* Sonn. 147, 13 and 152, 13. *those unproper beds which they dare s. peculiar,* Oth. IV, 1, 70. Followed by prepositions or adverbs: *made them s. against the thing they see; for I have sworn thee fair; more perjured I, to s. against the truth so foul a lie,* Sonn. 152, 12—14. *he'll be hanged yet, though every drop of water s. against it,* Tp. I, 1, 62. *procure knaves to s. against you,* H8 V, 1, 134. *I'll s. for 'em,* Wint. IV, 4, 155 (= answer, be surety for them). *to s. to sth.* = to s. sth.: *he knows I am no maid, and he'll s. to't,* All's V, 3, 291. *to s. to a person,* = to give a. p. a solemn assurance: *although I s. it to myself alone,* Sonn. 131, 8. *s. to thy blind soul that I was thy Will,* 136, 2. *that's to ye sworn to none was ever said,* Compl. 180. *—ing to my friends you were good soldiers,* Wiv. II, 2, 9. *I have heard him s. to Tubal that he would rather have Antonio's flesh,* Merch. III, 2, 286. *I s. to*

*thee by the white hand of Rosalind, I am that he,* As III, 2, 413. Wint. V, 2, 168. H6C III, 2, 93. Cymb. III, 3, 67. Per. IV, 3, 50 etc. *there did this perjured goldsmith s. me down that I received...,* Err. V, 227 (cf. *Down*). *s. his thought over by each particular star,* Wint. I, 2, 424 (cf. *Over*). With an accus. and a prepositional expression denoting an effect: *though they would s. down each particular saint,* Meas. V, 243. *Biron did s. himself out of all suit,* LLL V, 2, 275.

2) to promise in a solemn manner: *love made me s.* Gent. II, 6, 6. *—s he will shoot no more,* Tp. IV, 100. *he —s he'll turn me away,* Wiv. III, 3, 32. *swore that he would labour my delivery,* R3 I, 4, 252. *'tis sworn between us we shall ever strike till one can do no more,* Cor. I, 2, 35. *I swore I would not part a bachelor from the priest,* Tit. I, 487. *s. with me... as Brutus sware ... that we will prosecute mortal revenge,* IV, 1, 89. 91 etc. *my hand hath sworn ne'er to pluck thee from thy thorn,* Pilgr. 237. *I'll s. to be thy true subject,* Tp. II, 2, 130. *have sworn to live with me,* LLL I, 1, 16. 51. 59. 111. Merch. V, 170. H6A V, 4, 129. Ant. IV, 14, 81 etc. *surfeits... s. nature's death,* Ven. 744. *though I had sworn the contrary,* Ado I, 1, 198. *so much I have already sworn,* LLL I, 1, 34. *I'll keep what I have swore,* 114. *to whom you swore a secret pilgrimage,* Merch. I, 1, 120. *what to your sworn counsel I have spoken,* All's III, 7, 9. *I have heard her s. it,* Tw. I, 3, 117. *let us s. our resolution,* Caes. II, 1, 113 (i. e. to perform what we have resolved). John III, 1, 1. 268. V, 1, 10. R2 I, 1, 134. H4A IV, 3, 65. V, 1, 46. R3 II, 1, 8. Troil. V, 2, 62 etc. *I'll s. myself thy subject,* Tp. II, 2, 156. *our general has sworn you out of reprieve and pardon,* Cor. V, 2, 53. *— I had no judgment when to her I swore,* Mids. III, 2, 134. *I s. to thee,* Merch. V, 242. 247. *I s. to thee... tomorrow will I meet with thee,* Mids. I, 1, 169. *you swore to me that you would wear it,* Merch. V, 152. *thou didst s. to me to marry me,* H4B II, 1, 98. *to me love —ing,* Sonn. 152, 2. *that which each to other hath so strongly sworn,* LLL I, 1, 309. *where we swore to you dear amity,* John V, 4, 19. *s. allegiance to his majesty,* H6A V, 4, 169. *— To s. to sth.* = to vow sth.; to promise adherence on oath: *when they had sworn to this advised doom,* Lucr. 1849. *s. to that,* Tp. II, 2, 145. *you swore to that,* LLL I, 1, 53. *what you first did s. unto,* IV, 3, 291. *to these injunctions every one doth s.* Merch. II, 9, 17. *hath sworn unto the practices of France, to kill us here,* H5 II, 2, 90. *to the which this knight hath likewise sworn,* 93. *two yoke-devils sworn to either's purpose,* 106. *it is great sin to s. unto a sin,* H6B V, 1, 182. *had I so sworn as you have done to this,* Mcb. I, 7, 58. *though I s. to silence,* Per. I, 2, 19. With *out,* = to renounce solemnly, to forswear: *your grace hath sworn out housekeeping,* LLL II, 104.

That to which reference is made, in order to make the assurance or vow more forcible, preceded by the preposition *by:* Ven. 80. Tp. II, 2, 125. Gent. IV, 2, 100. Ado IV, 1, 278. 330. Merch. IV, 1, 36. V, 142. 245. 247. Tw. III, 1, 169. V, 129. Wint. I, 2, 424. II, 3, 168. R2 I, 1, 78. R3 IV, 4, 366. 368. 373 etc. With the omission of *by,* the verb used transitively in the same sense: *thou —est thy gods in vain,* Lr. I, 1, 163 (?). That on which the hand is placed in taking an oath (usually *a book,* i. e. a bible, or a sword, as representing and resembling the holy Cross), preceded by on: to s. on a book, Wiv. I, 4, 156. Tp. II, 2, 130. Merch. II, 2, 168. V, 301. Wint. III, 2, 125. H4A II, 4, 371. Hml. I, 5, 145 etc.

3) With the words oath or vow as objects, = to make, to take: that (vow) they swore, Lucr. 1848. I have sworn deep oaths, Sonn. 152, 9. Pilgr. 92. LLL I, 1, 65. II, 97. V, 2, 451. Merch. III, 3, 5. As III, 4, 44. All's IV, 3, 252. H4A III, 1, 258. H6A I, 1, 162. H6C III, 1, 72 etc. The word vow subject of the active verb: God keep all vows unbroke that s. to thee, R2 IV, 215 (Ff are made).

4) to put to an oath, to cause to take an oath: were you sworn to the duke or to the deputy? Meas. IV, 2, 196. s. me to this, LLL I, 1, 69. the first inter'gatory that my Nerissa shall be sworn on, Merch. V, 301. to s. him in the justice of his cause, R2 I, 3, 10. swore the devil his true liegeman upon the cross, H4A II, 4, 371. whom after under the confession's seal he solemnly had sworn, H8 I, 2, 165. s. priests and cowards, Caes. II, 1, 129. unto bad causes s. such creatures as men doubt, 131. then I swore thee ... that thou shouldst ..., V, 3, 38.

Hence to be sworn = a) to have sworn: if you are armed to do as sworn to do, LLL I, 1, 22. my hand is sworn ne'er to pluck thee, IV, 3, 111. yet am I sworn and I did purpose, boy, with this same very iron to burn them out, John IV, 1, 124. whom thou wert sworn to cherish, R3 I, 4, 213. thou art sworn as deeply to effect what we intend as ..., III, 1, 158. I am sworn not to give regard to you, Tim. I, 2, 251. thou art sworn that, when the exigent should come, ... thou then wouldst kill me, Ant. IV, 14, 62. I am sworn to do my work with haste, Per. IV, 1, 70. to Bolingbroke are we sworn subjects now, R2 V, 2, 39. we his subjects sworn in all allegiance, H6C III, 1, 70. you were sworn true subjects unto me, 78. I am sworn of the peace, Wiv. II, 3, 55 (have taken an oath as justice of peace). the sworn twelve, Meas. II, 1, 20 (the jury). I should blush to see you so attired, sworn, I think, to show myself a glass, Wint. IV, 4, 13. Madam, as thereto sworn by your command, I tell you this, Ant. V, 2, 198. Thus the participle passed into the sense of closely tied, engaged, intimate (the idea of an oath taken, however, never quite lost sight of): the king is my love sworn, LLL V, 2, 282. be but sworn my love, Rom. II, 2, 35. being sworn my soldier, John III, 1, 125. being my sworn servant, the duke retained him his, H8 I, 2, 191. her attendants are all sworn and honorable, Cymb. II, 4, 125. now my sworn friend, Wint. I, 2, 167. friends now fast sworn, Cor. IV, 4, 12. commit not with man's sworn spouse, Lr. III, 4, 84. Especially in the phrase sworn brother (cf. the mediaeval fratres jurati), originally one of two who have covenanted to share each other's fortunes; = bosom friend (cf. they shook hands and swore brothers, As V, 4, 107): he hath every month a new sworn brother, Ado I, 1, 73. trust, his sworn brother, Wint. IV, 4, 607. I am sworn brother to grim Necessity, R2 V, 1, 20. I am sworn brother to a leash of drawers, H4A II, 4, 7. H4B III, 2, 345. H5 II, 1, 13 (we'll be sworn brothers to France; quibbling). III, 2, 47. Cor. II, 3, 102. Applied, in the same manner, to the contrary: thy sworn enemy, Tw. III, 4, 187. his sworn and mortal foe, H6C III, 3, 257. And to inveterate propensities: a sworn rioter, Tim. III, 5, 68.

b) to swear, in the phrases I dare be sworn and I'll be sworn (= I protest): I dare be sworn for him he would not leave it, Merch. V, 172. I can swim like a duck, I'll be sworn, Tp. II, 2, 134. I'll be sworn 'tis true, III, 3, 26. Gent. IV, 4, 33. Wiv. I, 4, 156. II, 2, 39. III, 3, 29. Err. V, 259. Ado II, 1, 308. II, 3, 25 (I will not be sworn). LLL V, 2, 720. Merch. II, 2, 97. Tw. I, 5, 86 (Sir Toby will be sworn). Wint. II, 1, 63. H4A II, 4, 55. III, 1, 61. Troil. I, 2, 188 etc.

5) to use profane language (f. i. zounds, 'sblood etc.): another smothered seems to pelt and s. Lucr. 1418. he would not s. Wiv. II, 1, 58. this would make mercy s. and play the tyrant, Meas. III, 2, 207. Merch. II, 2, 200. Shr. II, 290. III, 2, 169. IV, 1, 81. 187. Tw. III, 4, 196. H4A III, 1, 253. II, 4, 490. H6B I, 1, 188. H6C II, 6, 76. R3 I, 4, 140. III, 7, 220. Tim. IV, 3, 122 (cf. Object). Cymb. II, 1, 5 etc. Transitively, or rather with an accusative expressing the effect: being thus frighted —s a prayer or two and sleeps again, Rom. I, 4, 87 (utters some profaneness which must serve him for a prayer). —est grace o'erboard, Tp. V, 219. Perhaps Lr. I, 1, 163.

**Swearer,** 1) one who takes an oath, or who calls God to witness for the truth of his declaration: I'll be sworn, as my mother was (a maid), the first hour I was born. I do believe the s. Wiv. II, 2, 41. what is a traitor? Why, one that swears and lies ... Then the liars and —s are fools, Mcb. IV, 2, 55. 56.

2) one who uses profane language: she'll disfurnish us of all our cavaliers, and make our —s priests, Per. IV, 6, 13.

**Swearings,** oaths, vows: all those s. keep as true in soul, Tw. V, 277.

**Sweat,** subst. the moisture excreted from the skin: Lucr. 396 (cf. the verb in Ven. 25). 1381. As III, 2, 58. Shr. I, 2, 203. H4A II, 3, 61. H8 Prol. 28. Tit. II, 3, 212. Hml. III, 4, 92. Ant. I, 4, 21. Emblem of toil and labour: without s. or endeavour, Tp. II, 1, 160. the ploughman lost his s. Mids. II, 1, 94. saved your husband so much s. Cor. IV, 1, 19. the s. of industry would dry and die, but for the end it works to, Cymb. III, 6, 31. Considered as the chief specific in the venereal disease: what with the war, what with the s., ... I am custom-shrunk, Meas. I, 2, 84. Falstaff shall die of a s. H4B V, 5, 147. Used of blood, metaphorically: drops bloody s. from his war-wearied limbs, H6A IV, 4, 18.

**Sweat,** vb. (impf. sweat: Merch. III, 2, 205. As II, 3, 58. H8 II, 1, 33. partic. sweat: Tim. III, 2, 28. sweaten, in rhyming: Mcb. IV, 1, 65) 1) intr. to excrete moisture from the skin: his —ing palm, the precedent of pith and livelihood, Ven. 25 (cf. Moist). the love-sick queen began to s. 175. —ing with guilty fear, Lucr. 740. Wiv. III, 3, 93. Err. III, 2, 105. As III, 2, 57. H4A II, 2, 115. H4B II, 4, 234. 388. H8 I, 1, 24. II, 1, 33. Cor. I, 4, 27. Mcb. II, 3, 7. Lr. V, 3, 55. Oth. II, 3, 85. Cymb. III, 3, 93. —ing Lust usurped his (Love's) name, Ven. 794. cf. a young and —ing devil, that commonly rebels, Oth. III, 4, 42. —ing considered as a cure of the venereal disease: till then I'll s. and seek about for eases, Troil. V, 10, 56.

= to toil, to labour: did make my foe to s. LLL V, 2, 556. why s. they under burthens? Merch. IV, 1, 95. when service s. for duty, As II, 3, 58. none will s. but for promotion, 60. for that England's sake with burden of our armour here we s. John II, 92. s. in this business and maintain this war, V, 2, 102. I mean not *to s. extraordinarily*, H4B I, 2, 235. *shall I s. for you?* IV, 3, 13. —*s in the eye of Phoebus*, H5 IV, 1, 290. *if you do s. to put a tyrant down*, R3 V, 3, 255. *I have s. to see his honour*, Tim. III, 2, 28. *to groan and s. under the business*, Caes. IV, 1, 22. *if arguing make us s.* V, 1, 48. *to grunt and s. under a weary life*, Hml. III, 1, 77. *'tis —ing labour to bear such idleness*, Ant. I, 3, 93. cf. Merch. III, 2, 205. H4B V, 5, 26. R3 III, 1, 24.

2) trans. to emit, to exude, to shed: *whiles a more frosty people s. drops of gallant youth in our rich fields*, H5 III, 5, 25. *it is no little thing to make mine eyes to s. compassion*, Cor. V, 3, 196. *grease that's —en from the murderer's gibbet*, Mcb. IV, 1, 65.

**Sweaty**, moist with sweat: *their s. night-caps*, Caes. I, 2, 247. = toilsome: *this s. haste*, Hml. I, 1, 77.

**Sweep**, subst. probably = a pompous passing along, a dashing motion: *what a s. of vanity comes this way!* Tim. I, 2, 137.

**Sweep**, vb. (partic. *swept*, impf. not found) 1) tr. a) to drive away or to clean as with a besom: *to s. the dust behind the door*, Mids. V, 397. *cobwebs swept*, Shr. IV, 1, 49. *thy lips that kissed the queen shall s. the ground*, H6B IV, 1, 75. *I am the besom that must s. the court clean of such filth*, IV, 7, 34. *they must s. my way*, Hml. III, 4, 204. *some friends that will s. your way for you*, Ant. III, 11, 17.

b) to brush, to carry off as with a brushing stroke: *ears that s. away the morning dew*, Mids. IV, 1, 126. *thus have we swept suspicion from our seat*, H6C V, 7, 13. *unless we s. 'em from the door with cannons*, H8 V, 4, 13. *I could with barefaced power s. him from my sight*, Mcb. III, 1, 119.

c) to drag along, to carry with pride: *let Talbot like a peacock s. along his tail*, H6A III, 3, 6.

d) to pass over or along with swiftness: (choughs) *madly s. the sky*, Mids. III, 2, 23.

2) intr. a) to pass with swiftness: *s. on, you fat and greasy citizens*, As II, 1, 55. *Harry England, that —s through our land with pennons ...*, H5 III, 5, 48. *lo, where George of Clarence —s along*, H6C V, 1, 76. *that I ... may s. to my revenge*, Hml. I, 5, 31.

b) with a superfluous *it*, = to pass with pomp (like a peacock): *she —s it through the court with troops of ladies*, H6B I, 3, 80.

**Sweepstake**, see *Swoopstake*.

**Sweet**, adj. pleasing to any sense; as to the taste: *one s. kiss*, Ven. 84. *for one s. grape who will the vine destroy?* Lucr. 215. *s. honey*, Gent. I, 2, 106. Troil. V, 10, 45. Rom. II, 6, 11. *a surfeit of the —est things*, Mids. II, 2, 137. *s. hay*, IV, 1, 37. —*est nut hath sourest rind*, As III, 2, 115. *things s. to taste prove in digestion sour*, R2 I, 3, 236. *have their palates both for s. and sour*, Oth. IV, 3, 96. *s. fish*, Cymb. IV, 2, 36 etc. Peculiar expression: *she hath a s. mouth* (= she has a sweet tooth, is dainty-mouthed) Gent. III, 1, 330. Agreeable to the smell, fragrant: *the fields' chief flower, s. above compare*, Ven. 8. *the flowers are s.* 1079. *s. issue of a more s. smelling sire*, 1178. *their* (flowers') *substance still lives s.* Sonn. 5, 14. *s. musk-roses*, Mids. II, 1, 252. *s. breath*, IV, 2, 44. *wrapped in s. clothes*, Shr. Ind. 1, 38. *burn s. wood to make the lodging s.* 49. *I smell s. savours*, 2, 73. *s. marjoram*, All's IV, 5, 17 and Lr. IV, 6, 94. *s. beds of flowers*, Tw. I, 1, 40. *very s. and contagious* (breath) II, 3, 57. *gloves as s. as damask roses*, Wint. IV, 4, 222. 253.

*call for s. water, wash thy hands*, Tit. II, 4, 6 (i. e. perfumed water); cf. *which with s. water nightly I will dew*, Rom. V, 3, 14. *as s. as balm*, Ant. V, 2, 314 etc. etc. Pleasing to the ear: *marvellous s. music*, Tp. III, 3, 19. Gent. II, 7, 28. *s. air*, Tp. I, 2, 393. III, 2, 145. Mids. I, 1, 183. *with some s. concert*, Gent. III, 2, 84. *such s. complaining grievance*, 86 (some M. Edd. *sweet-complaining*). *s. harmony*, Merch. V, 57. *s. sounds*, 84. *silver hath a s. sound*, Rom. IV, 5, 134. *s. instruments hung up in cases*, Tim. I, 2, 102. *s. bells jangled*, Hml. III, 1, 166 etc. To the touch (= soft): *s. bottom-grass*, Ven. 236. *a s. embrace*, 539. 811. *when the s. wind did gently kiss the trees*, Merch. V, 2. *the air most s.* Wint. III, 1, 1. Troil. III, 2, 54.

Hence in general = pleasing, delightful, lovely, charming: *that s. coral mouth*, Ven. 542. *s. lips*, 633. *the s. channel of her bosom*, 958. *s. beginning, but unsavoury end*, 1138. *to make the breach and enter this s. city*, Lucr. 469. *the story of s. chastity's decay*, 808. *such s. observance in this work was had*, 1385. *loathsome canker lives in —est bud*, Sonn. 35, 4. *s. fire* (of the eye) Pilgr. 68 and LLL IV, 2, 120. *these s. thoughts*, Tp. III, 1, 14. *'twas a s. marriage*, II, 1, 72. *no s. aspersion shall the heavens let fall*, IV, 18. *in the —est bud the eating canker dwells*, Gent. I, 1, 42. *hear s. discourse*, I, 3, 31. *omitting the s. benefit of time to clothe mine age with angel-like perfection*, II, 4, 65. *a s. virtue in a maid*, III, 1, 277. *give up your body to such s. uncleanness*, Meas. II, 4, 54. *either death or life shall thereby be the —er*, III, 1, 6. *'tis a physic that's bitter to s. end*, IV, 6, 8. *my s. hope's aim*, Err. III, 2, 63. *s. recreation barred*, V, 78. *so s. and voluble is his discourse*, LLL II, 76 (cf. *a Roman sworder murdered s. Tully*, H6B IV, 1, 136). *so s. a changeling*, Mids. II, 1, 23. *s. are the uses of adversity*, As II, 1, 12. *the s. sound that breathes upon a bank of violets*, Tw. I, 1, 5. *'tis not so s. now as it was before*, 8. *nature's own s. and cunning hand*, I, 5, 258. *so s. a breath to sing*, II, 3, 21. *this affliction has a taste as s. as any cordial comfort*, Wint. V, 3, 76. *the s. milk of concord*, Mcb. IV, 3, 98. *'tis most s., when in one line two crafts directly meet*, Hml. III, 4, 209 etc.

= kind, gentle, mild, meek: *welcomes the warm approach of s. desire*, Ven. 386. *for one s. look*, 371. *chiding that tongue that ever s. was used in giving gentle doom*, Sonn. 145, 6. *the s. glances of thy honoured love*, Gent. I, 1, 4. *some other mistress hath thy s. aspects*, Err. II, 2, 113. *this most patient, s. and virtuous wife*, Shr. III, 2, 197. *that their souls may make a peaceful and a s. retire*, H5 IV, 3, 86. *plant Christian-like accord in their s. bosoms*, H5 V, 2, 382 (a prolepsis, cf. Appendix; = in their bosoms which thus may become kind). *to those men that sought him s. as summer*, H8 IV, 2, 54. *s. mercy is nobility's true badge*, Tit. I, 119. *let me report to him your s. dependency*, Ant. V, 2, 26 etc. In a bad sense, = feigning kindness and friendship, smooth, hypocritical: *a blister on his s. tongue!* LLL V, 2, 335. *that there should be small love 'mongst these s. knaves*, Tim. I, 1, 258. *s. words, low-crooked courtesies*, Caes. III, 1, 42. *he* (death) *hides him in fresh cups, soft beds, s. words*, Cymb. V, 3, 72.

With *to*, = dear: *a something s. to thee*, Sonn. 136, 12. *thy life to me is s.* H6A IV, 6, 55.

Hence a general word of endearment: *s. boy*, Ven. 155. 583. 613. *s. seals*, 511. *s. Death, I did but jest*, 997. *s. sprites, the burthen bear*, Tp. I, 2, 381. *s. lord*, *you play me false*, V, 172. *s. heart*, LLL V, 1, 115; cf. V, 2, 1 and Tit. I, 481 (see *Sweetheart*). Gent. I, 1, 11. 56. I, 3, 45. II, 1, 4. II, 4, 37. II, 5, 3. III, 2, 90. Wiv. II, 1, 155. Meas. III, 1, 133. V, 435. 442. Err. V, 197 etc. *pardon me*, *s. one*, Tw. V, 221. *to the s. Julia*, Gent. I, 2, 125. *aiming at Silvia as a —er friend*, II, 6, 30. *the s. woman leads an ill life with him*, Wiv. II, 2, 92. *my s. love*, Ven. 1188. *his s. uplocked treasure*, Sonn. 52, 2. *thy s. beloved name*, 89, 10. *my —est friend*, 133, 4. *my s. mistress*, Tp. III, 1, 11. Gent. IV, 4, 182. *for thy more s. understanding*, LLL I, 1, 267 (Armado's letter). *set not thy s. heart on proud array*, Lr. III, 4, 85. *s. my child* LLL I, 2, 71. *s. my lord*, V, 2, 882. *s. my coz*, As I, 2, 1. *s. my lord*, Troil. IV, 2, 2. Applied even to heaven and celestial things: *s. welkin*, LLL III, 68. *is there not rain enough in the s. heavens to wash it white as snow*, Hml. III, 3, 45. *and s. religion makes a rhapsody of words*, III, 4, 47. *let me not be mad*, *s. heaven*, Lr. I, 5, 50. *broke them* (oaths) *in the s. face of heaven*, III, 4, 91. *Amen to that*, *s. powers*, Oth. II, 1, 197 (cf. in German: *der liebe Himmel*).

Substantively, in the same sense: *bid my s. prepare to chide*, Rom. III, 3, 162. *—s to the s.* Hml. V, 1, 266. *liegers for her s.* Cymb. I, 5, 80. Especially in the vocative: *thus far for love my love-suit*, *s.*, *fulfil*, Sonn. 136, 4. *s.*, *now*, *silence!* Tp. IV, 124; cf. Err. IV, 2, 29. *s.*, *except not any*, Gent. II, 4, 154. Err. III, 2, 66. Ado V, 4, 55. LLL IV, 1, 109. V, 2, 329 *(the ladies call him s.)*. Mids. II, 2, 45. III, 2, 247. V, 99. Merch. II, 6, 44. II, 9, 77. As III, 2, 264. Wint. IV, 4, 136. R2 V, 1, 20. Troil. III, 1, 172. III, 2, 137. III, 3, 222. Tit. I, 431. Rom. II, 2, 120. 183. Hml. III, 2, 225. Oth. III, 3, 56. Ant. III, 7, 24 etc. *O my s.* Compl. 239. LLL IV, 2, 145. V, 2, 132. Oth. II, 1, 207. *gentle s.* Mids. V, 87. LLL V, 2, 373. *good s.* Merch. III, 5, 76. *dear my s.* Tw. II, 5, 192.

**Sweet**, subst. (cf. the last section of the preceding article) 1) anything agreeable and luscious to the taste: *the bottom poison*, *and the top o'erstrawed with —s*, Ven. 1144. *the —s we wish for turn to loathed sours*, Lucr. 867. *honey*, *and milk*, *and sugar; ... metheglin*, *wort*, *and malmsey; ... there's half a dozen —s*, LLL V, 2, 234. *culling from every flower the virtuous —s*, H4B IV, 5, 76. *let them not lick the s. which is their poison*, Cor. III, 1, 157. *a choking gall and a preserving s.* Rom. I, 1, 200. *have their palates both for s. and sour*, Oth. IV, 3, 96.

2) agreeable smell, perfume: *whence didst thou steal thy s. that smells*, *if not from my love's breath?* Sonn. 99, 2. *but s. or colour it had stolen from thee*, 15.

3) any thing pleasing and delightful: *—s with —s war not*, Sonn. 8, 2. *—s and beauties do themselves forsake*, 12, 11. *the wide world and all her fading —s*, 19, 7. *in what —s dost thou thy sins enclose*, 95, 4. *—s grown common lose their dear delight*, 102, 12. *for compound s. forgoing simple savour*, 125, 7. *to be forbod the —s that seem so good*, Compl. 164. *youth so apt to pluck a s.* Pilgr. 240 and LLL IV, 3, 114. *to suck the —s of s. philosophy*, Shr. I, 1, 28. *whose want and whose delay is strewed with —s*, All's II, 4, 45. *the bitter past*, *more welcome is the s.* V, 3, 334. *then comes in the s. o'the year*, Wint. IV, 3, 3; cf. *now comes in the s. o'the night*, H4B V, 3, 53 (cf. II, 4, 396). *the setting sun*, *and music at the close*, *as the last taste of —s*, *is —est last*, R2 II, 1, 13. *nor with thy —s comfort*

*his ravenous sense*, III, 2, 13. *my unblown flowers*, *new-appearing —s*, R3 IV, 4, 10. *tempering extremities with extreme s.* Rom. II Chor. 14. *— s to the s.* Hml. V, 1, 266. *melt their —s on blossoming Caesar*, Ant. IV, 12, 22.

**Sweet**, adv. 1) in a manner agreeable to the senses; as a) to the smell: *smell so s.* H4A I, 3, 54. Rom. II, 2, 44. Oth. IV, 2, 68. b) to the ear: *how silver s. sound lovers' tongues*, Rom. II, 2, 166.

2) softly, gently, blandly, benignly: *as oft 'twixt May and April is to see*, *when winds breathe s.*, *unruly though they be*, Compl. 103. *look s.*, *speak fair*, Err. III, 2, 11. *how s. the moonlight sleeps upon this bank*, Merch. V, 54. *sleep with it now! yet not so sound and half so deeply s. as he ...*, H4B IV, 5, 26. *s. rest his soul*, H6C V, 2, 48. *so s. to rest*, Rom. II, 2, 188. *what early tongue so s. saluteth me?* II, 3, 32.

**Sweet-and-twenty**, a term of endearment: *then come kiss me*, *s.* Tw. II, 3, 52 (cf. *good even and twenty*, *good Master Page!* Wiv. II, 1, 202. *tricks eleven and twenty long*, Shr. IV, 2, 57).

**Sweeten**, to make sweet or to perfume; and, metaphorically, to make grateful and pleasing, to soften: *—s the aloes of all forces*, Compl. 272. *the face to s. of the whole dungy earth*, Wint. II, 1, 156. *theirs* (travel) *is —ed with the hope*, R2 II, 3, 13. *to s. which name of Ned*, *I give thee this pennyworth of sugar*, H4A II, 4, 24. *s. the bitter mock*, H5 II, 4, 122. *I cannot sing*, *... nor s. talk*, Troil. IV, 4, 88. *s. with thy breath this neighbour air*, Rom. II, 6, 26. *all the perfumes of Arabia will not s. this little hand*, Mcb. V, 1, 57. *an ounce of civet*, *to s. my imagination*, Lr. IV, 6. 133. *with fairest flowers I'll s. thy sad grave*, Cymb. IV, 2, 220.

**Sweet-faced**, handsome: *a s. youth*, Err. V, 418. Mids. I, 2, 88.

**Sweetheart**, 1) mistress: *take your —'s hat*, Wint. IV, 4, 664.

In all the other passages, where the word is found, it is used as a tender address, and ought to be written in two words (which is, indeed, the prevalent spelling of O. Edd.): Wiv. IV, 2, 12. V, 5, 26. All's II, 3, 285. 288. Tw. I, 3, 75. III, 4, 33. H4B II, 4, 24. 197. H8 I, 4, 94. Rom. IV, 5, 3 (cf. *Sweet*).

2) Name of a dog: *the little dogs and all*, *Tray*, *Blanch*, *and S.*, *see*, *they bark at me*, Lr. III, 6, 66.

**Sweeting**, 1) a kind of sweet apple: *thy wit is a very bitter s.; it is a most sharp sauce*, Rom. II, 4, 83.

2) a word of endearment: Shr. IV, 3, 36. Tw. II, 3, 43. H6A III, 3, 21. Oth. II, 3, 252.

**Sweetly**, 1) in a manner agreeable to the senses: *the air breathes upon us here most s.* Tp. II, 1, 46. *the air nimbly and s. recommends itself ...*, Mcb. I, 6, 2. *smelling so s.* Wiv. II, 2, 67. *it smells most s. in my sense*, Per. III, 2, 60. Metaphorically: *my conversion so s. tastes*, As IV, 3, 138.

2) gratefully, delightfully, gently; so as to please: *th' one s. flatters*, *th' other feareth harm*, Lucr. 172. *they do but s. chide thee*, Sonn. 8, 7. *which time and thoughts so s. doth deceive*, 39, 12. *so many have s. supposed them mistress of his heart*, Compl. 142. *at my parting s. did she smile*, Pilgr. 187. *that so s. were forsworn*, Meas. IV, 1, 2. *how s. you do minister to love*, Ado I, 1, 314. *so you walk softly and look s.* II, 1, 91. *the idea of her life shall s. creep into his study of imagination*, IV, 1, 226. *when tongues speak s.*, *then they name her name*, LLL III, 167. *how most s. a' will swear*,

IV, 1, 148. *the epithets are s. varied*, IV, 2, 9. *the crow doth sing as s. as the lark*, Merch. V, 102. *she sings as s. as a nightingale*, Shr. II, 172. *riddle-like lives s. where she dies*, All's I, 3, 223. *speak s., although thy looks be sour*, R2 III, 2, 193. *brought s. forth the freckled cowslip*, H5 V, 2, 48. *words s. placed*, H6A V, 3, 179. *from whence that tender spray did s. spring*, H6C II, 6, 50. *all which secure and s. he enjoys*, II, 5, 50. *s. in force unto her fair life's end*, R3 IV, 4, 351. *s. showed a noble patience*, H8 II, 1, 35. *O trespass s. urged*, Rom. I, 5, 111. *he and myself have travail'd in the great shower of your gifts, and s. felt it*, Tim. V, 1, 74. *to sound more s. in great Caesar's ear*, Caes. III, 1, 50.

**Sweet-marjoram**, see *Marjoram*.

**Sweetmeats**, fruits preserved with sugar, especially perfumed sugar-plums: Mids. I, 1, 34. Rom. I, 4, 76 (alias *kissing-comfits*).

**Sweetness**, the quality of being sweet, in its proper and its figurative sense: *having felt the s. of the spoil*, Ven. 553. *thy looks should nothing thence but s. tell*, Sonn. 93, 12. *being full of your s., to bitter sauces did I frame my feeding*, 118, 5. *they surfeited with honey and began to loathe the taste of s.* H4A III, 2, 72. *how hast thou with jealousy infected the s. of affiance*, H5 II, 2, 127. *some joy too fine, tuned too sharp in s.* Troil. III, 2, 25. *our lives' s.* Lr. V, 3, 184. (joys) *drown me with their s.* Per. V, 1, 196. Peculiar expression: *to remit their saucy s. that do coin heaven's image in stamps that are forbid*, Meas. II, 4, 45; i. e. the sweet pleasure in which they saucily indulged.

**Sweet-savoured**, having a sweet taste: *meat s. in thy taste*, Err. II, 2, 119.

**Sweet-seasoned**, well tempered, soft, gentle: *so are you to my thoughts as food to life, or as s. showers are to the ground*, Sonn. 75, 2.

**Sweet-smelling**, fragrant: Ven. 1178.

**Sweet-suggesting**, sweetly tempting, seductive: Gent. II, 6, 7.

**Swell**, subst. the highest rise of the water, high-tide: *the swan's down-feather, that stands upon the s. at full of tide*, Ant. III, 2, 49. Subst. or verb in All's II, 3, 134? O. Edd. *where great additions swell's, and virtue none. Is this: where great additions' swell is*, or: *where great additions swell us?*

**Swell**, vb. (impf. *swelled:* Wiv. III, 5, 18. H4B II, 3, 63. Cymb. V, 5, 162. *swollen* or *swoln:* Ven. 325. Tp. II, 1, 117. H4A II, 4, 496. H4B Ind. 13. Mcb. IV, 3, 151) 1) trans. to make bigger, to make tumid, to cause to rise (as waves): *the water —s a man*, Wiv. III, 5, 16. *when I had been —ed*, 18. *bids the wind ... s. the curled waters 'bove the main*, Lr. III, 1, 6. *s. his sail with thine own powerful breath*, Oth. II, 1, 78. Metaphorically, = to inflate: *where great additions swell's, and virtue none*, All's II, 3, 134 (*swell us?* or subst.?). *if it did ... s. my thoughts to any strain of pride*, H4B IV, 5, 171. *beauty that made barren the —ed boast of him that best could speak*, Cymb. V, 5, 162. = to inflate with anger: *not to s. our spirit, he shall be executed presently*, Tim. III, 5, 102.

2) intr. a) to grow bigger, to grow turgid: *all swoln with chafing*, Ven. 325. *whose —ing dugs do ache*, 875. *that swollen parcel of dropsies*, H4A II, 4, 496. *ten thousand —ing toads*, Tit. II, 3, 101. *people swoln and ulcerous*, Mcb. IV, 3, 151. *'twould appear by external —ing*, Ant. V, 2, 349. Applied to women

with child: *Polixenes has made thee s. thus*, Wint. II, 1, 62. *the big year, swoln with some other grief, is thought with child by the stern tyrant war*, H4B Ind. 13. *unless it s. past hiding*, Troil. I, 2, 294.

Used of waters, = to rise above the ordinary level, or to be agitated and driven into waves: *a river stayed ... —eth with more rage*, Ven. 332. *my uncontrolled tide ... —s the higher by this let*, Lucr. 646. *their understanding begins to s., and the approaching tide will shortly fill the reasonable shore*, Tp. V, 80. *so high above his limits —s the rage of Bolingbroke*, R2 III, 2, 109. *'tis with my mind as with the tide —ed up unto his height*, H4B II, 3, 63. *my sea shall s. so much the higher by their ebb*, H6C IV, 8, 56. *the higher Nilus —s, the more it promises*, Ant. II, 7, 23. *Cydnus —ed above the banks*, Cymb. II, 4, 71. *whose waves to imitate the battle sought with —ing ridges*, Lucr. 1439. *breasted the surge most swoln*, Tp. II, 1, 117. *the —ing Adriatic seas*, Shr. I, 2, 74. *float upon the —ing tide*, John II, 74. *the waters s. before a boisterous storm*, R3 II, 3, 44. *the ocean —s not so as Aaron storms*, Tit. IV, 2, 139. *I have seen the ambitious ocean s.* Caes. I, 3, 7. *s. billow*, V, 1, 67.

In a sense half physical, half moral (cf. below): *who (the pillow), therefore angry, seems to part in sunder, —ing on either side to want his bliss*, Lucr. 389. *they (his veins) s. in their pride*, 432. *emptying our bosoms of their counsel —ed*, Mids. I, 1, 216 (i. e. brimful of secrets. O. Edd. *sweld*, M. Edd. *sweet*). *—est thou, proud heart?* R2 III, 3, 140. *here he comes, —ing like a turkey-cock*, H5 V, 1, 15. *from that spring whence comfort seemed to come, discomfort —s*, Mcb. I, 2, 28. *how this mother —s up toward my heart*, Lr. II, 4, 56. *s., bosom, with thy fraught*, Oth. III, 3, 449. *the silken tackle s. with the touches of those hands*, Ant. II, 2, 215. *Caesar's ambition, which —ed so much that it did almost stretch the sides o'the world*, Cymb. III, 1, 50.

b) to rise and increase gradually, to gather and grow: *the maid with —ing drops gan wet her circled eyne*, Lucr. 1228. *the tears that s. in me*, LLL IV, 3, 36. *these —ing heavens*, H4A III, 1, 202 (i. e. eyes filling with tears). *that same dew, which sometime on the buds was wont to s. like round and orient pearls*, Mids. IV, 1, 59. *the summer-swelling flower*, Gent. II, 4, 162. cf. above: Tp. V, 80.

c) Followed by *with*, = to be full of: *flowing and —ing o'er with arts and exercise*, Troil. IV, 4, 80. *thy verse —s with stuff so fine and smooth*, Tim. V, 1, 87. cf. above: Mids. I, 1, 216.

d) In a metaphorical and moral sense, = 1) to grow in the mind and fill the soul: *—ing passion doth provoke a pause*, Ven. 218. *in my heart the strong and —ing evil of my conception*, Meas. II, 4, 6. *the unseen grief that —s with silence in the tortured soul*, R2 IV, 298. *my mildness hath allayed their —ing griefs*, H6C IV, 8, 42. *here no envy —s*, Tit. I, 153. cf. above: Mcb. I, 2, 28. Cymb. III, 1, 50. 2) to be inflated: *imagined worth holds in his blood such swoln and hot discourse*, Troil. II, 3, 183. *noble —ing spirits*, Oth. II, 3, 57 (cf. *—ing like a turkey-cock*, H5 V, 1, 15; and Ant. II, 2, 215). Hence *—ing* = grand, pompous, magnificent: *a more —ing port than my faint means would grant continuance*, Merch. I, 1, 124. *monarchs to behold the —ing scene*, H5 Prol. 4. *as happy prologues to the —ing act of the imperial theme*, Mcb. I, 3, 128. 3) to be inflated with anger or passion: *to stubborn spirits they* (the hearts of princes) *s.* H8 III, 1, 164. *the —ing difference of your settled hate*, R2 I, 1, 201. *from envious malice of thy —ing heart*, H6A III, 1, 26. *these —ing wrong-incensed peers*, R3 II, 1, 51. *the venomous malice of my —ing heart*, Tit. V, 3, 13. cf. above: Lucr. 389. 432. R2 III, 2, 109. III, 3, 140. Oth. III, 3, 449.

**Swelter**, to breed by internal heat, to exsude: *toad, that under cold stone days and nights has thirty one —ed venom sleeping got*, Mcb. IV, 1, 8.

**Sweno**, name of the Norwegian king in Mcb. I, 2, 59.

**Swerve**, to leave the due or intended course, to go astray, to be inconstant: *the cause of this fair gift in me is wanting, and so my patent back again is —ing*, Sonn. 87, 8. *the fairest youth that ever made eye s.* Wint. IV, 4, 385. *constant in spirit, not —ing with the blood*, H5 II, 2, 133. *I have offended reputation, a most unnoble —ing*, Ant. III, 11, 50. *but, alas, I s.* Cymb. V, 4, 129. With *from,* = to deviate from: *that you s. not from the smallest article of it*, Meas. IV, 2, 107. *if I be false, or s. a hair from truth*, Troil. III, 2, 191.

**Swerver**, in *Bed-swerver*, q. v.

**Swift**, adj. 1) rapid, quick, speedy: Ven. 1190. Lucr. 46. 926. 1215. 1691. Sonn. 45, 4. 10. 51, 6. 65, 11. 143, 3. Tp. I, 2, 450. Gent. I, 3, 23. II, 6, 42. Meas. III, 1, 58. IV, 3, 107. LLL V, 2, 261. Mids. III, 2, 379. As II, 1, 42. III, 2, 324. Shr. Ind. 2, 49. All's III, 2, 76. Wint. I, 2, 289. III, 2, 164. IV, 1, 5. John II, 448. R2 I, 3, 79. H4A I, 3, 103. H4B I, 1, 109. H5 II 4, 6. III Chor. 1. III, 5, 33. V Chor. 15. H6A IV, 5, 9. R3 IV, 1, 49. V, 2, 23. Troil. III, 2, 12. IV, 2, 14. Cor. III, 1, 3. Rom. II, 5, 13. III, 1, 170. V, 1, 35. Tim. V, 1, 231. Mcb. I, 4, 17. II, 4, 15. III, 1, 38. 96. III, 6, 47. Hml. I, 5, 29. Lr. III, 7, 12. Oth. II, 3, 232. III, 3, 477. Ant. III, 7, 37. IV, 6, 35. Cymb. II, 4, 27. *s. celerity*, Mcb. V, 399. *—est expedition*, Gent. III, 1, 164. *in all s. haste*, Troil. I, 1, 119. *the —er speed*, Wint. IV, 4, 683. John II, 233. R2 V, 1, 54. Substantively: *too s. arrives as tardy as too slow*, Rom. II, 6, 15.

2) rapidly passing, of short continuance: *how s. and short his time of folly*, Lucr. 991. *the —est hours*, Compl. 60. *s. as a shadow, short as any dream*, Mids. I, 1, 144. *make s. the pangs of my queen's travails*, Per. III, 1, 13.

3) ready, prompt, quick: *having so s. and excellent a wit*, Ado III, 1, 89. *he is very s. and sententious*, As V, 4, 65. With a quibble: *I say lead is slow. You are too s. to say so*, LLL III, 62 (= too rash). *Lucentio slipped me like his greyhound ... A good s. simile, but something currish*, Shr. V, 2, 54. *his evasion, winged thus s. with scorn, cannot outfly our apprehensions*, Troil. II, 3, 123.

**Swift**, adv. swiftly, rapidly: *Away! As s. as lead*, LLL III, 58. *courses as s. as thought*, IV, 3, 330. *my eyes can look as s. as yours*, Merch. III, 2, 199. *skirr away as s. as stones*, H5 IV, 7, 64. *another would fly s., but wanteth wings*, H6A I, 1, 75. *light boats sail s.* Troil. II, 3, 277. V, 10, 29. Tit. IV, 1, 3. IV, 2, 172. V, 2, 51. Hml. I, 5, 66. Cymb. I, 3, 14. II, 2, 48. Compar. *—er: I do wander every where, —er than the moon's sphere*, Mids. II, 1, 7. *about the wood go —er than the wind*, III, 2, 94. 101. IV, 1, 103. H4B I, 1, 123. III, 2, 282. Troil. III, 2, 170.

**Swift-footed**, fleet, rapid: *s. time*, Sonn. 19, 6.

**Swiftly**, speedily, quickly: Ven. 321. Tp. III, 3, 107. As II, 3, 9. Shr. V, 1, 1. Wint. I, 2, 409. H4B III, 2, 287. H6A II, 2, 29. H6C II, 1, 109.

**Swiftness**, speed, celerity: Tw. II, 5, 186. H5 I, 2, 306. H8 I, 1, 142. Cor. III, 1, 313.

**Swift-winged**, fleet as if borne on wings: *yet are these feet ... s. with desire to get a grave*, H6A II, 5, 15. *that our s. souls may catch the king's*, R3 II, 2, 44.

**Swill**, to drink grossly and greedily, to gulp down: *his* (the rock's) *confounded base, —ed with the wild and wasteful ocean*, H5 III, 1, 14. *the boar that ... —s your warm blood like wash*, R3 V, 2, 9.

**Swim** (impf. *swam*, Tp. III, 2, 16. *swom*, Gent. I, 1, 26. partic. *swam*, As IV, 1, 38. *swom*, Tp. II, 2, 133), to move in water by the motion of the limbs: Tp. I, 2, 191. II, 1, 238. II, 2, 133. 134. 136. III, 2, 16. Gent. I, 1, 26 (*you never swom the Hellespont.* cf. *he trots the air*, H5 III, 7, 16). Mids. II, 1, 174. H4A I, 3, 194. H6C I, 4, 20. V, 4, 29. H8 III, 2, 359. Troil. V, 4, 21. Cor. I, 1, 184. Caes. I, 2, 104. Lr. III, 4, 116. 134.

= to float, to be borne and carried by the water: *you have swam in a gondola*, As IV, 1, 38. *s. bark!* Caes. V, 1, 67.

Metaphorically: *which she, with pretty and with —ing gait following*, Mids. II, 1, 130 (with a waving motion, in imitation of the ships). *which —s against your stream of quality*, H4B V, 2, 34.

**Swimmer**, one who swims: Lucr. 1097. Ado V, 2, 31. Mcb. I, 2, 8.

**Swine**, the animal Sus scrofa: Ven. 616. 1115. LLL IV, 2, 91 (*pearl for a s.*). Shr. Ind. 1, 34. R3 V, 2, 10. Plur. *s.:* Wiv. IV, 2, 109 (*still s. eat all the draff*). John V, 2, 142. Tim. V, 1, 52. Mcb. I, 3, 2. Lr. IV, 7, 39.

**Swine-drunk**, drunk in a beastly manner: All's IV, 3, 286.

**Swine-herd**, keeper of swine: Wint. IV, 4, 332.

**Swine-keeping**, keeping of swine, as a swineherd: H4A IV, 2, 38.

**Swing**, subst. vibratory motion of a thing suspended and hanging loose: *the great s. and rudeness of his* (a ram's) *poise*, Troil. I, 3, 207.

**Swing**, vb. (impf. *swong*; M. Edd. *swung*), to brandish, to flourish: *which* (sword) *he swong about his head*, Rom. I, 1, 118.

**Swinge**, to whip: *you —d me for my love*, Gent. II, 1, 88. *now will he —d for reading my letter*, III, 1, 392. *I would have —d him*, Wiv. V, 5, 197. *I had —d him soundly*, Meas. V, 130. *s. me them soundly forth unto their husbands*, Shr. V, 2, 104. *saint George, that —d the dragon*, John II, 288. *I will have you soundly —d*, H4B V, 4, 21. 23.

**Swinge-buckler**, a riotous fellow, a roisterer: H4B III, 2, 24.

**Swinish**, beastly, gross: *when in s. sleep their drenched natures lie*, Mcb. I, 7, 67. *they clepe us drunkards, and with s. phrase soil our addition*, Hml. I, 4, 19.*

**Swinstead** (corrupted from *Swineshead*), place in England: John V, 3, 8, 16. Lincolnshire, near Spalding.

**Swissers**, see *Switzers*.

**Switch**, a flexible twig, a rod: *fetch me crab-tree staves, and strong ones: these are but —es to 'em*, H8 V, 4, 9. *s. and spurs*, Rom. II, 4, 73 (O. Edd. *swits*).

**Swithald** or **Swithold**, contraction of *Saint*

*Withold* (who was invoked against the nightmare): *S. footed thrice the old*, Lr. III, 4, 125. Most M. Edd. *Saint Withold.*

**Switzers** (Qq *Swissers*), hired guards from Switzerland: Hml. IV, 5, 97.

**Swoon**, to sink into a fainting fit; a word differently spelt in O. Edd.: 1) *swoon*: As IV, 3, 159. R3 IV, 1, 35 (Qq *sound*). 2) *swoond*: H4B IV, 5, 234. Cor. V, 2, 72. 107. Tim. IV, 3, 373 (F3.4 *swound*). Ant. IV, 9, 26. 3) *swoun* or *swown*: Mids. II, 2, 154 (F1 *sound*, Q2 and later Ff *swound*). H6C V, 5, 45. 4) *swound*: Lucr. 1486 (rhyming to *wounds*). Meas. II, 4, 24. Mids. II, 2, 154 (Q1 *swoun*, F1 *sound*). As III, 5, 17. Wint. V, 2, 99. John V, 6, 22 (F4 *swoon*). Caes. I, 2, 249. 253. 5) *sound*: Compl. 305. 308. LLL V, 2, 392. Mids. II, 2, 154 (Q1 *swoun*, Q2 and later Ff *swound*). As V, 2, 29 (F4 *swound*). R3 IV, 1, 35 (Ff *swoon*). Troil. III, 2, 24. Tit. V, 1, 119 (later Ff *swooned*). Rom. III, 2, 56. Hml. V, 2, 319.

**Swoond**, see *Swoon*.

**Swoop**, the sudden pouncing of a bird on its prey: *all my pretty chickens at one fell s.* Mcb. IV, 3, 219.

**Swoopstake** (O. Edd. *soopstake*, most M. Edd. *sweepstake*), winning and taking all stakes at once; by wholesale, indiscriminately: *is't writ in your revenge, that s. you will draw both friend and foe, winner and loser?* Hml. IV, 5, 142.

**Sword**, a weapon worn at the side, and used by hand either for thrusting or cutting: Lucr. 1421. 1640. Sonn. 55, 7. Tp. II, 1, 161. III, 3, 62. 67. Wiv. II, 1, 135. III, 1, 112. Ado V, 1, 54. 57. LLL V, 2, 276. 481. 701. Mids. III, 1, 19. V, 350. As II, 3, 32. II, 4, 47. All's II, 1, 40 etc. etc. *no s. worn but one to dance with*, All's II, 1, 32. *kept his s. like a dancer*, Ant. III, 11, 36 (cf. *Dancing-rapier*). *my long s.* Wiv. II, 1, 236. Rom. I, 1, 82. *thy two-hand s.* H6B II, 1, 46. *six French —s*, Hml. V, 2, 168. *my Spanish s.* All's IV, 1, 52. *a s. of Spain, the ice-brook's temper*, Oth. V, 2, 253. *playing at s. and dagger*, Wiv. I, 1, 295 (cf. *Dagger*). *s. against s.* Ant. III, 13, 27. *s. to s.* Cor. III, 1, 13. *to die on one's s.* (= by one's s.): Mids. II, 2, 107. Caes. V, 1, 58. Mcb. V, 8, 2. *to measure —s*, As V, 4, 91. *to eat a s.* (= to receive it into the body, to be wounded or killed): *I will make him eat it*, Ado IV, 1, 279. *I would make him eat a piece of my s.* H4A V, 4, 157. *a' should eat —s first*, Troil. II, 3, 228. cf. *swallow my s. like a great pin*, H6B IV, 10, 31. *to put to the s.* = to kill: As V, 4, 164. H6B III, 1, 284. *avarice hath been the s. of our slain kings*, Mcb. IV, 3, 87 (= the death, ruin). *to draw the s.:* Lucr. 626. Tp. II, 1, 292. Err. V, 151. 262. LLL I, 2, 62. Mids. III, 1, 11. III, 2, 411. Tw. I, 3, 66. 68. III, 4, 429. IV, 1, 45. V, 191. Rom. III, 1, 9 (*draws him on the drawer;* where *him* is the dativus ethicus: most M. Edd., following the surreptitious Q1, *draws it*) etc. etc. *I hide my s.* (= I sheathe it) As II, 7, 119. *to put up the s.:* Tp. I, 2, 469. Tw. III, 4, 343. 354. John IV, 3, 79. 98. H5 II, 1, 46. Cor. V, 6, 136. Rom. I, 1, 72. 75. Caes. I, 3, 19 etc. cf. *up, s.!* Hml. III, 3, 88. *to sheathe the s.* H5 III, 1, 21. Tit. I, 85. 204. *here sheathe thy s.* (i. e. in my body) H6C V, 5, 70. *to unsheathe the s.* H6C II, 2, 59. *strip your s. stark naked*, Tw. III, 4, 274. *naked —s*, Err. IV, 4, 148. *when I see a s. out* (= drawn): Wiv. II, 3, 47. Lr. II, 1, 40. IV, 6, 233. Oth. II, 3, 183. *out, s.!* Mids. V, 301. Cymb. IV, 1, 24. *forth, my s.!* Oth. V, 1, 10.

Symbol of combat and war: *the s. should end it*, Wiv. I, 1, 41. *the world's mine oyster, which I with s. will open*, II, 2, 3. *I wooed thee with my s.* Mids. I, 1, 16. *awake our sleeping s. of war*, H5 I, 2, 22. *—s our law*, R3 V, 3, 311. *he had rather see the —s*, Cor. I, 3, 60. *I will use the olive with my s.* Tim. V, 4, 82. *since yet thy cicatrice looks raw and red after the Danish s.* Hml. IV, 3, 63. Joined to *fire* and *famine: thou hadst fire and s. on thy side*, H4A II, 4, 348. *famine, s. and fire*, H5 Prol. 7. *with blood and s. and fire*, I, 2, 131. *I fear neither s. nor fire*, H6B IV, 2, 63. Opposed to the word (= gospel): Wiv. III, 1, 44. H4B IV, 2, 10. cf. Mids. II, 2, 107. H4B III, 2, 83.

Emblem of power and authority: *not the king's crown, nor the deputed s.* Meas. II, 2, 60. *he who the s. of heaven will bear*, III, 2, 275. *to lay aside the s. which sways usurpingly these several titles*, John I, 12. *and blunt the s. that guards the peace and safety of your person*, H4B V, 2, 87. *still bear the balance and the s.* 103. *the s., the mace, the crown*, H5 IV, 1, 278. *I gird thee with the valiant s. of York*, H6A III, 1, 171. *we here create thee the first duke of Suffolk, and gird thee with the s.* H6B I, 1, 65. *the mayor's s.* IV, 3, 16. *except a s. or sceptre balance it*, V, 1, 9. *is the s. unswayed?* R3 IV, 4, 470. *persuade justice to break her s.* Oth. V, 2, 17.

Solemn oaths taken upon a sword: *you shall swear upon this s. of justice*, Wint. III, 2, 125. *lay on our royal s. your banished hands*, R2 I, 3, 179. *upon my s.* Hml. I, 5, 147. *swear by this s.* Wint. III, 2, 168. *swear by my s.* Hml. I, 5, 154. 160. cf. Ado IV, 1, 276. R2 I, 1, 78. H4A V, 3, 26. H5 II, 1, 105. H6B V, 3, 15.

A sword hung over the grave of a knight: *no trophy, s., nor hatchment o'er his bones*, Hml. IV, 5, 214.

**Sword-and-buckler**, formerly the most common weapons of fencers, but supplanted, in the poet's time, by the rapier and dagger, and accounted fitting for the vulgar only; hence used with some contempt: *that same s. Prince of Wales*, H4A I, 3, 230.

**Sworder**, a gladiator: *a Roman s. and banditto slave murdered sweet Tully*, H6B IV, 1, 135. *and be staged to the show against a s.* Ant. III, 13, 31.

**Sword-hilts**, the handle of a sword: *hold thou my s., whilst I run on it*, Caes. V, 5, 28.

**Sword-men**, soldiers: *like to prove most sinewy s.* All's II, 1, 62 (Parolles' speech).

**Swoun** and **Swound**, see *Swoon*.

**Swounds**, an exclamation contracted from *God's wounds*, used as an oath (cf. *Zounds*): Hml. II, 2, 604 (Ff *why*). V, 1, 297 (Ff *come*).

**Sycamore**, the tree Ficus sycomorus: LLL V, 2, 89. *the grove of s.* Rom. I, 1, 128.\*a *s. tree*, Oth. IV, 3, 41.

**Sycorax**, name of Caliban's mother: Tp. I, 2, 258. 263. 290. 331. 340. III, 2, 109. 110.

**Syenna** (most M. Edd. *Sienna*) name in Cymb. IV, 2, 341.\*

**Sylla**, the celebrated Roman dictator, proverbial for cruelty: *like ambitious S. overgorged with gobbets of thy mother's bleeding heart*, H6B IV, 1, 84.

**Syllable,** 1) that which is uttered by one articulation; the smallest part of speech: *do all points of my command. To the s.* Tp. I, 2, 500. *which you shall find by every s. a faithful verity*, Meas. IV, 3, 131. *who dare speak one s. against him*, H8 V, 1, 39. *every s. that here was spoke*, Troil. V, 2, 117. *if thou deniest* *the least* s. *of thy addition*, Lr. II, 2, 25. *I heard each* s. Oth. IV, 2, 5. *subscribe to any* s. *that made love to you*, Per. II, 5, 70. *I will believe you by the* s. *of what you shall deliver*, V, 1, 169.

Metaphorically, = the smallest particle, a little, a jot: *the duke will extend to you what further becomes his greatness, even to the utmost* s. *of your worthiness*, All's III, 6, 75. *wish he were something mistaken in't. No, not a* s. H8 I, 1, 195.

2) = word: *I can't say your worships have delivered the matter well, when I find the ass in compound with the major part of your —s*, Cor. II, 1, 65. *with such words that are but roted in your tongue, though but bastards and —s of no allowance to your bosom's truth*, III, 2, 56. *it* (heaven) *resounds as if it felt with Scotland and yelled out like* s. *of dolour*, Mcb. IV, 3, 8. Metaphorically: *creeps in this petty pace to the last* s. *of recorded time*, Mcb. V, 5, 21.

**Syllogism**, the logical form of reasoning, consisting of two premises and the conclusion: Tw. I, 5, 55.

**Symbol**, emblem, type: *were't to renounce his baptism, all seals and —s of redeemed sin*, Oth. II, 3, 350.

**Symet**, reading of O. Edd. in John V, 7, 21; M. Edd. *cygnet*.

**Sympathize**, 1) intr. to agree, to be of the same disposition: *we* s. Troil. IV, 1, 26. Followed by *with*: *the southern wind ... foretells a tempest. Then with the losers let it* s. H4A V, 1, 7. *the men do* s. *with the mastiffs in robustious and rough coming on*, H5 III, 7, 158. *the thing of courage, as roused with rage, with rage doth* s. *and with an accent tuned in selfsame key retorts to chiding fortune*, Troil. I, 3, 52.

2) trans. to answer to, to correspond with: *true sorrow then is feelingly sufficed when with like semblance it is —d*, Lucr. 1113 (when it meets with the semblance of the same suffering). *yet when they have devised what strained touches rhetoric can lend, thou truly fair wert truly —d in true plain words by thy true-telling friend*, Sonn. 82, 11 (my plain words were most suitable to, expressed best, thy fair nature). *all that are assembled in this place, that by this —d one day's error have suffered wrong, go keep us company*, Err. V, 397 (entered into, shared). *a message well — d: a horse to be ambassador for an ass*, LLL III, 52. *the senseless brands will* s. *the heavy accent of thy moving tongue and in compassion weep the fire out*, R2 V, 1, 46.

**Sympathy**, any conformity; agreement of disposition, or of fortune, or of rank, or of age etc.: *no flower was nigh ... but stole his blood and seemed with him to bleed. This solemn* s. *poor Venus noteth*, Ven. 1057. *even so the maid with swelling drops gan wet her circled eyne, enforced by* s. *of those fair suns set in her mistress' sky, who in a salt-waved ocean quench their light*, Lucr. 1229 (s. *of*, objectively, = s. with; cf. the verb). *you are not young, no more am I; go to then, there's a* s.: *you are merry, so am I; ha, ha! then there's more* s.: *you love sack, and so do I; would you desire better* s.? Wiv. II, 1, 7. 9. 10. *if there were a* s. *in love*, Mids. I, 1, 141 (i. e. no difference in blood, or rank, or age). *if that thy valour stand on* s. R2 IV, 33 (equality of blood and rank. Ff —es). *if* s. *of love unite our thoughts*, H6B I, 1, 23. *what a* s. *of woe is this*, Tit. III, 1, 148 (not fellow-feeling, not a state of being affected by the sufferings of another, but correspondence, similarity of suffering). *he is even in my mistress' case, just in her case! O woful* s.! Rom. III, 3, 85. s. *in years, manners and beauties*, Oth. II, 1, 232. *be what it is, the action of my life is like it, which I'll keep, if but for* s. Cymb. V, 4, 151 (as I am in the same situation).

**Synagogue**, a house appropriated to the religious worship of Jews: Merch. III, 1, 135. 136.

**Synod**, assembly of a legislative body: *it hath in solemn —s been decreed, both by the Syracusians and ourselves*, Err. I, 1, 13. Particularly an assembly of the gods: *thus Rosalind of many parts by heavenly* s. *was devised*, As III, 2, 158. *the glorious gods sit in hourly* s. *about thy particular prosperity*, Cor. V, 2, 74. *all you gods, in general* s., *take away her power*, Hml. II, 2, 516. *gods and goddesses, all the whole* s. *of them*, Ant. III, 10, 5. *we poor ghosts will cry to the shining* s. *of the rest against thy deity*, Cymb. V, 4, 89.

**Syracusa** (O. Edd. *Siracusa*) town in Sicily: Err. I, 1, 3. 37. V, 320. 325.

**Syracuse** (O. Edd. *Siracuse*) the same: Err. V, 363.

**Syracusian** (O. Edd. *Siracusian*) 1) subst. a native of Syracuse: Err. I, 1, 14. 29. V, 285. 326. 2) adj. pertaining to Syracuse: Err. I, 1, 18. I, 2, 3. V, 124.

**Syria**, country in Asia: Ant. I, 2, 106. III, 1, 18. III, 6, 10. 16. V, 2, 200. Per. Prol. 19.

**Syrup**, a decoction for medicinal purposes: *with wholesome —s, drugs and holy prayers*, Err. V, 104. *not poppy, nor mandragora, nor all the drowsy —s of the world, shall ever medicine thee to that sweet sleep*, Oth. III, 3, 331.

# T.

**T**, the twentieth letter of the English alphabet: LLL V, 1, 24. Tw. II, 5, 96. 99. Ant. IV, 7, 7.

**Ta**, in *wo't ta*, corrupted from *wouldst thou:* H4B II, 1, 63 (Ff *thou wilt not?*).

**Table**, 1) that on which a picture is painted: *mine eye hath played the painter and hath stelled thy beauty's form in t. of my heart*, Sonn. 24, 2 (the heart itself being the table; cf. *Of*). *to sit and draw his arched brows ... in our heart's t.* All's I, 1, 106. *I beheld myself drawn in the flattering t. of her eye*, John II, 503. 504.

2) that on which something is written: *who art the t. wherein all my thoughts are charactered*, Gent. II, 7, 3. *unclasp the —s of their thoughts to every ticklish reader*, Troil. IV, 5, 60. *you* (seals) *clasp young Cupid's —s* (i. e. letters) Cymb. III, 2, 39. *from the t. of my memory I'll wipe away all trivial fond records*, Hml. I, 5, 98. Used a) of the boards containing the ten commandments: *scraped one* (commandment) *out of the t.* Meas. I, 2, 9. *the great King of kings hath in the —s of his law commanded*, R3 I, 4, 201 (Ff *t.*). b) plur. —s = memorandum-book: *thy*

*gift, thy —s, are within my brain full charactered with lasting memory*, Sonn. 122, 1. *to trust those —s that receive thee more*, 12. *his master's old —s, his note-book, his counsel-keeper*, H4B II, 4, 289. *therefore will he wipe his —s clean*, IV, 1, 201. *my —s, — meet it is I set it down*, Hml. I, 5, 107. c) the palm of the hand, in the language of chiromancy: *if any man in Italy have a fairer t. which doth offer to swear upon a book*, Merch. II, 2, 167.

3) the article of furniture usually consisting of boards supported by four legs: H4B II, 1, 95 *(at the round t.)*. Rom. III, 1, 7. Hml. V, 2, 278. Particularly used for meals: Gent. IV, 4, 20. Wiv. I, 1, 270. Err. III, 1, 23. Merch. III, 5, 65 *(cover the t.)*. 67. As II, 7, 105. Shr. III, 2, 249. Wint. IV, 4, 59. H4B II, 2, 190. Troil. I, 1, 29. II, 3, 45. Cor. IV, 5, 205. IV, 7, 4 *(at t.)*. Rom. I, 5, 29. Tim. I, 2, 30. 132. III, 6, 88. Mcb. III, 4, 12. 46. III, 6, 34. Hml. I, 2, 181. IV, 3, 26. IV, 5, 44 *(God be at your t.)*. Per. I, 4, 28. *T. and bed the symbols of conjugal life* (cf. *Board*): H6C I, 1, 248. *to set foot under a person's t.* = to live upon his charity: *your father were a fool to give thee all, and in his waning age set foot under thy t.* Shr. II, 404.

4) a company sitting together at a table: *it shall please you to gratify the t. with a grace*, LLL IV, 2, 161. *you may worst of all this t. say so*, H8 V, 3, 79. *a perfecter giber for the t.* Cor. II, 1, 91. *by the entreaty and grant of the whole t.* IV, 5, 213. *I drink to the general joy o' the whole t.* Mcb. III, 4, 89. *to set the t. on a roar*, Hml. V, 1, 211.

5) —s = backgammon: *when he plays at —s, chides the dice in honourable terms*, LLL V, 2, 326.

**Table-book**, memorandum-book: Wint. IV, 4, 610. Hml. II, 2, 136.

**Tabled**, set down in writing: *though the catalogue of his endowments had been t. by his side and I to peruse him by items*, Cymb. I, 4, 6.

**Table-sport**, the object of diversion at table; standing-butt: *let me for ever be your t.* Wiv. IV, 2, 169.

**Tablet**, a small table to write on: *this t. lay upon his breast*, Cymb. V, 4, 109.

**Table-talk**, conversation at table: Merch. III, 5, 93.

**Tabor**, a small drum used for festivity: Tp. IV, 175. LLL V, 1, 161. Cor. I, 6, 25. V, 4, 53. Accompanied by a pipe: *I have known when there was no music with him but the drum and the fife; and now had he rather hear the t. and the pipe*, Ado II, 3, 15. *you would never dance again after a t. and pipe*, Wint. IV, 4, 183. Used by fools: Tw. III, 1, 2. 10.

**Taborer**, a player on the tabor: Tp. III, 2, 160.

**Tabourines**, drums: *beat loud the t., let the trumpets blow, that this great soldier may his welcome know*, Troil. IV, 5, 275. *trumpeters, make mingle with our rattling —s*, Ant. IV, 8, 37.

**Taciturnity**, silence, discretion: *the secrets of nature have not more gift in t.* Troil. IV, 2, 75.

**Tacked**, stitched together: *the half shirt is two napkins t. together*, H4A IV, 2, 47.

**Tackle**, the ropes of a ship, cordage, rigging: Tp. I, 2, 147. John V, 7, 52. H5 III Chor. 8. H6C V, 4, 15. Cor. IV, 5, 67. Ant. II, 2, 214 (F1 *the silken t. swell*, later Ff *swells*). cf. *Ladder-tackle*.

**Tackled**; *a t. stair* = rope-ladder: *bring thee cords made like a t. stair*, Rom. II, 4, 201.

**Tackling**, cordage, rigging: *the friends of France our shrouds and —s*, H6C V, 4, 18 (trisyll.?). *a poor bark, of sails and t. reft*, R3 IV, 4, 233.

**Taddle**, see *Tiddle taddle*.

**Tadpole**, a frog in its first state from the spawn: Tit. IV, 2, 85. Lr. III, 4, 135 (O. Edd. *tod-pole*).

**Taffeta**, a fine and smooth stuff of silk: *beauties no richer than rich t.* LLL V, 2, 159. *t. phrases, silken terms precise*, 406. *your t. punk*, All's II, 2, 23. *a snipt t. fellow*, IV, 5, 2. *the tailor make thy doublet of changeable t.* Tw. II, 4, 77. *a fair hot wench in flame-coloured t.* H4A I, 2, 11.

**Tag**, the rabble: *will you hence, before the t. return?* Cor. III, 1, 248.

**Tag-rag people**, the same: *if the t. did not clap him and hiss him*, Caes. I, 2, 260.

**Tah**, in *rah tah tah*, an exclamation expressive of nimbleness: H4B III, 2, 303.

**Tail**, 1) the part of an animal which terminates its body behind: Ven. 298. 305. 314. 923. Gent. II, 5, 37. Merch. II, 2, 101. 103. 104. Shr. II, 215. Wint. I, 2, 329. H6A III, 3, 6. H6B V, 1, 154. Troil. V, 8, 21. V, 10, 4. 44. Rom. I, 4, 79. Mcb. I, 3, 9. Oth. I, 1, 156. Metaphorically: *this body hath a t. more perilous than the head*, Cymb. IV, 2, 144. As for *dragon's t.*, Lr. I, 2, 140, see *Dragon*.

2) backside, arse: *if they* (his eyes) *were set in his t.* Tp. III, 2, 13. *where should I lose my tongue? In thy tale. In thy tail?* Gent. II, 3, 55. *with my tongue in your t.* Shr. II, 219.

3) the yard: Troil. V, 10, 44 (quibbling). Rom. II, 4, 101. 105.

Quibbling between *t.* and *tale:* Gent. II, 3, 55. Rom. II, 4, 101. Oth. III, 1, 8 *(thereby hangs a t.)*.

**Tailor**, one whose occupation is to make clothes: Tp. II, 2, 55. Err. IV, 3, 7. Mids. I, 2, 60. Merch. III, 1, 30. As V, 4, 48. Shr. IV, 3, 59. 61. 86. 92. 166. 168. All's II, 5, 18. 21. Tw. II, 4, 76. John IV, 2, 195. H4A II, 4, 273. H4B III, 2, 164 *(a man's t.)*. 161 and 169 *(a woman's t.)*. R3 I, 2, 257. H8 I, 3, 20. Cor. IV, 5, 235. Rom. I, 2, 40. III, 1, 30. Mcb. II, 3, 15. Lr. III, 2, 83. Oth. II, 3, 95. Ant. I, 2, 170. Cymb. II, 3, 84. IV, 2, 84. (to sing) *'tis the next way to turn t.* H4A III, 1, 264. *this secrecy of thine shall be a t. to thee and shall make thee a new doublet and hose*, Wiv. III, 3, 34. *a t. made thee*, Lr. II, 2, 60. 61. 63 (as the best thing about thee is thy clothes). *knowest me not by my clothes? No, nor thy t., who is thy grandfather: he made those clothes, which, as it seems, make thee*, Cymb. IV, 2, 81 (cf. *whose mother was her painting*, III, 4, 52). cf. the poor jest of Cloten, IV, 1, 4.

Peculiar use: *down topples she and 'tailor' cries*, Mids. II, 1, 54 (the custom of crying tailor at a sudden fall backwards, Johnson 'thinks he remembers' to have observed. Emendations proposed: *rails or; tailsore*).*

**Taint**, subst. 1) stain, spot, blemish: *any t. of vice whose strong corruption inhabits our frail blood*, Tw. III, 4, 390. *the —s and blames I laid upon myself*, Mcb. IV, 3, 124. *they may seem the —s of liberty*, Hml. II, 1, 32. *his —s and honours waged equal with him*, Ant. V, 1, 30.

2) corruption, infection: *commotions, uproars, with a general t. of the whole state*, H8 V, 3, 28.

3) disparagement, disgrace, discredit: *we did our*

*main opinion crush in t. of our best man*, Troil. I, 3, 374. *your fore-vouched affection fallen into t.* Lr. I, 1, 224.

**Taint,** vb. (*t.* for *—ed* in H6A V, 3, 183; cf. V, 5, 81), 1) trans. a) to imbue, to touch: *a pure un-spotted heart, never yet t. with love, I send the king*, H6A V, 3, 183. *Nero will be —ed with remorse*, H6C III, 1, 40. cf. *attaint* in H6A V, 5, 81.

b) to soil, to stain: *which I will not t. my mouth with*, H8 III, 2, 332. *their breaths with sweetmeats —ed are*, Rom. I, 4, 76. In H5 I, 2, 173 some M. Edd. *taint*, others *tear*; O. Edd. corruptly *tame.*

c) to infect with a disease: *whether thou art —ed or free*, Meas. I, 2, 44. *I am a —ed wether of the flock*, Merch. IV, 1, 114. Applied to diseases of the mind: *pray heaven his wisdom be not —ed*, Meas. IV, 4, 5. *wise men, folly-fallen, quite t. their wit*, Tw. III, 1, 75. *the man is —ed in's wits*, III, 4, 14. *pride, which out of daily fortune ever —s the happy man*, Cor. IV, 7, 38. Absol.: *danger, like an ague, subtly —s even then when we sit idly in the sun*, Troil. III, 3, 232.

d) to injure, to prejudice, to impair, to take from: *travel-tainted as I am*, H4B IV, 3, 40 (weakened, exhausted by travelling). *that my disports corrupt and t. my business*, Oth. I, 3, 272. *his unkindness may defeat my life, but never t. my love*, IV, 2, 161.

e) to stain in a moral sense, to defile, to corrupt: *by our ears our hearts oft —ed are*, Lucr. 38. *which (blood) by him —ed shall for him be spent*, 1182. *corrupt and —ed in desire*, Wiv. V, 5, 94. *bear a fair presence, though your heart be —ed*, Err. III, 2, 13. *her foul —ed flesh*, Ado IV, 1, 145. *what plea so —ed and corrupt*, Merch. III, 2, 75. *a very —ed fellow, and full of wickedness*, All's III, 2, 89. *let no quarrel t. the condition of this present hour*, Tw. V, 365. *corrupt and —ed with a thousand vices*, H6A V, 4, 45. *t. not thy mind, nor let thy soul contrive against thy mother aught*, Hml. I, 5, 85. *if thy faith be not —ed with the breach of hers*, Cymb. III, 4, 27. *to t. his nobler heart and brain with jealousy*, V, 4, 65.

f) to disgrace, to discredit, to expose to blame: *punish my life for —ing of my love*, Tw. V, 141. *my age was never — ed with such shame*, H6A IV, 5, 46. *to t. that honour every good tongue blesses*, H8 III, 1, 55. *brought him, as a man sorely —ed, to his answer*, IV, 2, 14. *speaking too loud, or —ing his discipline*, Oth. II, 1, 275.

2) intr. a) to be affected with incipient putrefaction, to be corrupted: *you cannot preserve it* (flesh) *from —ing*, Cymb. I, 4, 148.

b) to be infected and corrupted in a moral sense: *I cannot t. with fear*, Mcb. V, 3, 3.

c) to be impaired, to become stale and tasteless: *lest the device take air and t.* Tw. III, 4, 145

**Taintingly,** so as to put to shame: Cor. I, 1, 114 (M. Edd. *tauntingly*).

**Tainture,** defilement: H6B II, 1, 188.

**Take** (impf. *took*, partic. *took, taken, ta'en*), I) trans. in its original sense = to touch; to strike in a beneficial or pernicious manner; 1) to charm, to captivate: *which must t. the ear strangely*, Tp. V, 313. *devised and played to t. spectators*, Wint. III, 2, 38. *t. the winds of March with beauty*, IV, 4, 119. *to t. your imagination*, Per. IV, 4, 3. 2) to destroy; absol.: *here, there, and everywhere, he leaves and —s*, Troil. V, 5, 26 (= he spares or kills). *his sword, death's*

*stamp, where it did mark, it took*, Cor. II, 2, 112. *t. or lend*, Cymb. III, 6, 24 (cf. *Lend*). With an object: *how soon confusion may ... t. the one by the other*, Cor. III, 1, 111. *whose plots have broke their sleep to t. the one the other*, IV, 2, 20. *consumed with fire, and took what lay before them*, IV, 6, 78. *not fear still to be —n*, Lr. I, 4, 353. Used of the malignant influence of superhuman powers: *he blasts the tree and —s the cattle*, Wiv. IV, 4, 32. *then no planet strikes, no fairy —s*, Hml. I, 1, 163. *strike her young bones, you —ing airs, with lameness*, Lr. II, 4, 166. *bless thee from whirlwinds, star-blasting and —ing*, III, 4, 61. *now the witch t. me*, Ant. IV, 2, 37. = to strike, to give a blow: *t. him over the costard with the hilts*, R3 I, 4, 159. With a dat. and accus.: *he took you a box o' the ear*, Meas. II, 1, 189. *took him such a cuff*, Shr. III, 2, 165. *does not Toby t. you a blow o' the lips?* Tw. II, 5, 75. *I will t. thee a box on the ear*, H5 IV, 1, 231. IV, 7, 133.

= to seize, to lay hold of: *she —s him by the hand*, Ven. 361. 1124. *t. hands*, Tp. I, 2, 377. As V, 4, 134. *t. a serpent by the tongue*, Ado V, 1, 90. *let me t. you a button-hole lower*, LLL V, 2, 706. *till you t. her hand before this friar*, Ado IV, 4, 56. *t. him by the arm*, As IV, 3, 163. *I t. her hand*, All's II, 3, 183. *your fathers —n by the silver beards*, H5 III, 3, 36. *the worst is filthy and would not hold —ing*, Tim. I, 2, 159. cf. Wiv. I, 1, 308. IV, 6, 37. Meas. IV, 1, 55 etc. Metaphorically: *many a man would t. you at your word*, Err. I, 2, 17. LLL II, 217. Rom. II, 2, 49.

= to have recourse to, to betake one's self to: *run, master, run; for God's sake t. a house*, Err. V, 36 (enter, take refuge in, a house). *he took this place for sanctuary*, 94. *shouldst thou t. the river Styx, I would swim after*, Troil. V, 4, 20 (go, plunge into). *I t. the earth to the like*, R2 IV, 52 (I apply to the earth, by throwing down my glove. Q1 *task*; Ff om.). *make you t. the hatch*, John V, 2, 138 (leap over it). Hence the phrases: *to t. horse*, H4A I, 1, 60. H6B IV, 4, 54. R3 III, 2, 16. *let me t. my horse*, H4A IV, 1, 119 (the earlier Qq *taste*). *ere he t. ship for France*, H5 II Chor. 30. *t. shipping*, H6A V, 5, 87. *lest the device t. air and taint*, Tw. III, 4, 145 (= get public). *to t. one's way*, Sonn. 48, 1. All's II, 5, 69. Cymb. I, 5, 31. *t. the instant way*, Troil. III, 3, 153. *every fairy t. his gait*, Mids. V, 423. *t. thy flight*, Mids. V, 310. *t. the start*, Merch. II, 2, 6. *t. a travel*, R2 I, 3, 262. *I'll t. my heels*, Err. I, 2, 94. *t. sanctuary*, R3 III, 1, 28. *I will t. the wall of any man*, Rom. I, 1, 15 (cf. *Wall*).

= to come upon unexpectedly, to catch by surprise, to find at advantage or disadvantage: *I will t. him*, Wiv. III, 2, 41. *I will now t. the lecher*, III, 5, 146. *where we may t. him*, IV, 4, 16. *he vows if he can t. you, to scorch your face*, Err. V, 182. *to be —n with a wench*, LLL I, 1, 290. 291. 299. *that girl that I took with the hind Costard*, I, 2, 123. *—n napping*, IV, 3, 130. *you took the moon at full, but now she's changed*, V, 2, 214. *when I did him at this advantage t.* Mids. III, 2, 16. *I took him sleeping*, 38. *let not me t. him*, Merch. V, 236. *you shall never t. her without her answer, unless you t. her without her tongue*, As IV, 1, 175. *I have ta'en you napping*, Shr. IV, 2, 46. *though I took him at's prayers*, All's II, 5, 45. *when at Bohemia you t. my lord*, Wint. I, 2, 40. *were I ta'en here it would scarce be answered*, Tw. III, 3, 28. *half my power ... are —n by the tide*, John V, 6, 40. *wert*

*—n with the manner*, H4A II, 4, 346 (cf. *Manner*). *we took him setting of boys' copies*, H6B IV, 2, 95. *to t. her in her heart's extremest hate*, R3 I, 2, 232. *be not ta'en tardy by unwise delay*, IV, 1, 52. *you have ta'en a tardy sluggard here*, V, 3, 225. *he was not —n well; he had not dined*, Cor. V, 1, 50. *let the county t. you in your bed*, Rom. IV, 5, 10. *you t. us even at the best*, Tim. I, 2, 157. *he took my father grossly, full of bread*, Hml. III, 3, 80. *you may t. him at your pleasure*, Oth. IV, 2, 243 etc. = to find (but in a tone of reproach): *I thought to have ta'en you at the Porpentine*, Err. III, 2, 172.

= to seize, to make prisoner, to catch (as animals), to get into one's power (as towns etc.): *his master goeth about to t. him*, Ven. 319. *Valentine, if he be ta'en, must die*, Gent. III, 1, 232. *she's ta'en* (like a bird), *I warrant you*, Ado III, 1, 104 (Qq limed). *ha' ta'en a couple of knaves*, III, 5, 34. *John is ta'en in flight*, V, 4, 127. *well ta'en*, Shr. II, 207. *he has —n their greatest commander*, All's III, 5, 5. *ta'en*, John III, 2, 7. *t. purses*, H4A I, 2, 15. 110. II, 4, 452. *in his flight was took*, H4B I, 1, 131. *slaughtered or took*, H6A I, 1, 147. *Talbot is ta'en*, I, 2, 14. *he is ta'en or slain*, IV, 4, 42. *what prisoners thou hast ta'en*, IV, 7, 56. *if you be ta'en*, H6B V, 2, 78. *had he been ta'en*, H6C II, 1, 4. *Henry is ta'en*, III, 2, 118. *t. another Troy*, 190. *if Troy be not —n till these two undermine it*, Troil. II, 3, 9. *a new-ta'en sparrow*, III, 2, 36. *a prisoner, yesterday took*, III, 3, 19. *the town is ta'en*, Cor. I, 10, 1. *—s it* (fish) *by sovereignty of nature*, IV, 7, 34. *ta'en or slain*, Caes. V, 5, 3. *Antony be took alive*, Ant. IV, 6, 2 etc. *to t. prisoner:* Lucr. 1608. John III, 4, 7. H4B I, 1, 126. H6A I, 1, 145 etc.

Applied to diseases, = to seize, to attack: *a fit of madness took him*, Err. V, 139. *being —n with the cramp*, As IV, 1, 104. *old John of Gaunt is grievous sick, suddenly —n*, R2 I, 4, 55. *a grievous sickness took him*, H6B III, 2, 370.

= to lay hands on and carry away: *when death —s one* (babe) Lucr. 1161. *the devil t. one party*, Wiv. IV, 5, 108. Tp. III, 2, 89. As III, 2, 226. R2 V, 5, 103. Troil. IV, 2, 77 etc. *then Lucifer t. all*, Wiv. I, 3, 84. *her brother's ghost would t. her hence in horror*, Meas. V, 441. *nay, then, a shame t. all!* H6B III, 1, 307. *a bugbear t. him*, Troil. IV, 2, 34. *Lucina sent not me her aid, but took me in my throes*, Cymb. V, 4, 44 etc.

= to bring out of the power or possession of another; absol.: *that opportunity which they had to t. from us, to resume we have again*, Cymb. III, 1, 15. *and all in war with Time for love of you, as he —s from you, I engraft you new*, Sonn. 15, 14. With an object: *when your highness took his dukedom*, As I, 3, 61. *t. but my shame*, R2 I, 1, 175. *when they did t. his eyes*, Lr. IV, 2, 89. *what cannot be preserved, when fortune —s, patience her injury a mockery makes*, Oth. I, 3, 206 (= when fortune —s what cannot be preserved). *and ta'en the treasure of her honour*, Cymb. II, 2, 41. *to t. a person's life:* Tp. I, 2, 267. V, 274. Meas. II, 4, 53. As I, 1, 158. H6A III, 1, 22. Ant. III, 12, 23 etc. With *away*: *to t. away the edge of that day's celebration*, Tp. IV, 28. *a cloud —s all away*, Gent. I, 3, 87. *to t. away a life true made*, Meas. II, 4, 47. III, 2, 122. Wint. III, 2, 16. John III, 1, 178. V, 1, 41. Hml. II, 2, 516 etc. With *from*: *unless thou t. that honour from thy name*, Sonn. 36, 12. *me from myself thy cruel eye hath —n*, 133, 5; cf. Hml. V, 2, 245.

*which* (island) *thou —st from me*, Tp. I, 2, 332. III, 2, 73. Gent. III, 1, 343. Meas. V, 211 (*the body that took away the match from Isabel*). Err. II, 1, 89. V, 117. 352. Mids. III, 2, 177. As I, 1, 19. II, 7, 95. Tw. III, 3, 34. Wint. IV, 3, 65. V, 3, 41. R2 I, 1, 183. H4A II, 4, 179. H6B II, 4, 17. H6C II, 5, 58. R3 I, 4, 223. IV, 4, 294. H8 II, 2, 7. Cor. II, 2, 150. II, 3, 222. Rom. V, 3, 185. Ant. III, 7, 12. Cymb. III, 4, 62 etc. With *off*: *you t. it off again* (the consulship) Cor. III, 3, 61. *who by self and violent hands took off her life*, Mcb. V, 8, 71. *it would cost you a groaning to t. off my edge*, Hml. III, 2, 259. *your power and your command is —n off*, Oth. V, 2, 331. *the heaviness and guilt within my bosom —s off my manhood*, Cymb. V, 2, 2. *whose life she had ta'en off by poison*, V, 5, 47. *that monster envy ... Marina's life seeks to t. off*, Per. IV Prol. 14. Hence to t. off = to kill, to make away with: *the deep damnation of his —ing off*, Mcb. I, 7, 20. *whose execution —s your enemy off*, III, 1, 105. *let her who would be rid of him devise his speedy —ing off*, Lr. V, 1, 65. *I must have your maidenhead —n off, or the common hangman shall execute it*, Per. IV, 6, 136.

= to deduct, to subtract: *cannot t. two from twenty and leave eighteen*, Cymb. II, 1, 60.

= to bear, or carry, or lead along: *t. with you your companions*, Tp. V, 292. *t. him to prison*, Meas. III, 2, 32. *t. him hence*, V, 313. 382. 526. *t. him to thy custody*, Err. I, 1, 156. *t. the stranger to my house, and with you t. the chain*, IV, 1, 36. *t. away this villain*, LLL I, 2, 158. *how I shall t. her from her father's house*, Merch. II, 4, 31. *t. her to thee*, As III, 5, 63. *t. them to the buttery*, Shr. Ind. 1, 102. *a sword ta'en out of the town-armoury*, III, 2, 47. *t. in your love*, IV, 2, 71. *t. the fool away*, Tw. I, 5, 42. 43. 58. 60. *to have ta'en it away yourself*, II, 2, 6. *t. this fellow in*, H6B I, 3, 36. *t. her to thee*, I, 4, 55. *with your holy load, —n from Paul's*, R3 I, 2, 30. *Furies, t. him to your torments*, I, 4, 57. *I'll t. her to my guard*, Ant. V, 2, 67 etc.

Metaphorically: *I would your grace would t. me with you*, H4A II, 4, 506 (i. e. would be clear and explicit, that I might be able to follow and understand your meaning). *soft! t. me with you*, Rom. III, 5, 142.

= to choose and make to be one's own: *to t. a wife*, Gent. III, 1, 76. *if he t. her, let him t. her simply*, Wiv. III, 2, 77. *I will never t. you for my love again*, V, 5, 121. *I t. thee for pity*, Ado V, 4, 93. *do it for thy true-love*, Mids. II, 2, 28. *I t. thee for wife*, As IV, 1, 135. *I take thee for my husband*, 139. *a woman that Brutus took to wife*, Caes. II, 1, 293. Mids. III, 2, 459. As III, 3, 69. All's II, 3, 109. 112. Tw. II, 4, 30. H6C III, 2, 89 etc.

= to catch (as a disease): *he hath ta'en the infection*, Ado II, 3, 126. *his very genius hath —n the infection of the device*, Tw. III, 4, 142. *t. cold*, Shr. IV, 1, 11. *to t. a cold*, H4A II, 3, 9. *his corruption being ta'en from us*, V, 2, 22. *as men t. diseases one of another*, H4B V, 1, 85. *t. some new infection to thy eye*, Rom. I, 2, 50. ct. I, 5, 110. *t. corruption from that particular fault*, Hml. I, 4, 35. Similarly: *I will t. my death, I never meant him any ill*, H6B II, 3, 90. *let me pray before I t. my death*, H6C I, 3, 35. *will this wood t. fire?* Wiv. V, 5, 92. Absol. *to t.* = to t. fire: *I can t., and Pistol's cock is up*, H5 II, 1, 55.

= to seize on, to catch, to choose, not to neglect: *conspiracy his time doth t.* Tp. II, 1, 302. *have no leisure —n to weigh how once I suffered,* Sonn. 120, 7. *to t. an ill advantage of his absence,* Wiv. III, 3, 116. *the next advantage will we t. throughly,* Tp. III, 3, 14. *He that might the vantage best have took,* Meas. II, 2, 74. *t. time to pause,* Mids. I, 1, 83. *let's t. the instant by the forward top,* All's V, 3, 39. *you might t. occasion to kiss,* As IV, 1, 75. *if you t. not the heat,* H4B II, 4, 324. *t. the time, kneel down,* H6C V, 1, 48. *a tide which, —n at the flood,* Caes. IV, 3, 219. *we must t. the current when it serves,* 223. *who, having some advantage, took it too eagerly,* V, 3, 7. *t. thy fair hour,* Hml. I, 2, 62. *took once a pliant hour,* Oth. I, 3, 151.

= to receive into the hand, to begin to hold: *he —s it* (a glove) *from the rushes,* Lucr. 318. *t. the paper,* Gent. I, 2, 46. *you t. the sum and substance that I have,* IV, 1, 15. *the jewel that we find, we stoop and t. it,* Meas. II, 1, 24. *he hath ta'en his bow and arrows,* As IV, 3, 4. *t. it to you,* Shr. IV, 1, 168. *t. my sword,* Mcb. II, 1, 4. *t. thee that too,* 5 etc. etc.

= to receive into the mind; 1) to hear, to learn: *t. this of me, ... myself am moved to woo thee for my wife,* Shr. II, 191. *'twill not be well, t. it of me,* H8 V, 1, 30. *no, t. more,* Cor. III, 1, 140. *t. this of me: Lucrece was not more chaste,* Tit. II, 1, 108. *t. it of my soul, my lord leans to discontent,* Tim. III, 4, 70. *t. this note: my lord is dead; Edmund and I have taken,* Lr. IV, 5, 29. *I would not t. this from report,* IV, 6, 144. *t. that of me, who have the power to seal the accuser's lip,* 173. 2) to understand; to interpret; to suppose to mean: *would not t. her meaning,* Pilgr. 154. *you have —n it wiselier than I meant you should,* Tp. II, 1, 21. *good Lord, how you t. it,* 80. *if thou beest a devil, t. it as thou list,* III, 2, 138. *in what key shall a man t. you, to go in the song?* Ado I, 1, 188. *let me t. you a buttonhole lower,* LLL V, 2, 706. *O, t. the sense of my innocence,* Mids. II, 2, 45. *love —s the meaning in love's conference,* 46. *our sport shall be to t. what they mistake,* V, 90. *noble respect —s it in might, not merit,* 92. *was this —n by any understanding pate but thine?* Wint. I, 2, 222. *choler, if rightly —n,* H4A II, 4, 356. *t. it in what sense thou wilt,* Rom. I, 1, 31. *t. our good meaning,* I, 4, 46. *very well took,* II, 4, 131. *you t. me in too dolorous a sense,* Ant. IV, 2, 39. 3) to consider, to take into view: *the whole world cannot pick out five such, t. each one in his vein,* LLL V, 2, 548. *he was a man, t. him for all in all,* Hml. I, 2, 187. 4) to hold, to think; with an infinitive: *what the best is,* (my eyes) *t. the worst to be,* Sonn. 137, 4. *I took him to be killed with a thunderstroke,* Tp. II, 2, 112. *we t. him to be a thief,* Meas. III, 2, 17. *I t. him to be valiant,* Ado II, 3, 195. *which I t. to be either a fool or a cipher,* As III, 2, 308. *I t. my young lord to be a very melancholy man,* All's III, 2, 3. *which I t. to be too little for pomp to enter,* IV, 5, 54. *so* (a shepherdess) *he then took her to be,* Wint. V, 2, 127 etc. With a double accus.: *the empress' sons I t. them,* Tit. V, 2, 154. With *for* (whether the opinion be erroneous or not): *the doors ... he —s for accidental things of trial,* Lucr. 326. *to t. this drunkard for a god,* Tp. V, 296. *a better woodman than thou —st him for,* Meas. IV, 3, 171. *I was ta'en for him,* Err. V, 387. *not the men you took them for,* Ado III, 3, 51. *t. salve for l'envoy,* LLL III, 79. *I took three threes for nine,* V, 2, 495. *I t. him for the better dog,* Shr. Ind. 1, 25. *to be generous, guiltless, and of free disposition,*

*is to t. those things for bird-bolts,* Tw. I, 5, 99. Merch. III, 5, 46. All's II, 5, 6. Tw. III, 4, 410. John IV, 2, 209. H6A III, 2, 62. H6B I, 3, 14. 82. R3 I, 3, 224. III, 5, 25. Cor. I, 5, 3. Tit. II, 3, 71. Hml. III, 4, 32. Lr. IV, 6, 78. Cymb. III, 3, 104 etc. *to t. it* = to think, to believe: *howe'er it pleases you to t. it so, the ring was never hers,* All's V, 3, 88. *you overween to t. it so,* H4B IV, 1, 149. *one would t. it ... the spavin reigned among 'em,* H8 I, 3, 11. *who hath got, as I t. it, an ague,* Tp. II, 2, 68. *Sir Proteus, as I t. it,* Gent. IV, 2, 90. *as I t. it, it is almost day,* Meas. IV, 2, 109. *who, as I t. it, have stolen his birds' nest,* Ado II, 1, 237. *whither is he gone? Marry, as I t. it, to Rousillon,* All's V, 1, 28. Wint. II, 1, 198. H4B I, 2, 126. H5 IV, 7, 22. H8 I, 1, 175. Hml. V, 2, 156. Oth. V, 1, 51. Ant. IV, 11, 2. *I t. it, your own business calls on you,* Merch. I, 1, 63. *and here, I t. it, is the doctor come,* IV, 1, 168. *I t. it there's but two ways,* H4B V, 3, 114. H8 I, 3, 33. IV, 1, 51. V, 3, 88. Mcb. II, 1, 3. Hml. I, 1, 104 etc. 5) to conceive, to form in the mind, to feel: *the birds such pleasure took,* Ven. 1101. *—s delight to see his active child,* Sonn. 37, 1. *I t. all my comfort of thy worth and truth,* 4. *save what* (delight) *must from you be took,* 75, 12. *I should t. a displeasure against you,* Tp. IV, 202. *there will be pity —n on you,* Meas. I, 2, 112. *wherein I t. pride,* II, 4, 10. *—s pity on decayed men,* Err. IV, 3, 25. *you t. pleasure in the message,* Ado II, 3, 262. *she cannot love, nor t. no shape nor project of affection,* III, 1, 55. *t. comfort,* Mids. I, 1, 202. *when thou —st true delight in ...,* III, 2, 454. *hath ta'en displeasure 'gainst his niece,* As I, 2, 290. *I t. some joy to say you are,* IV, 1, 90. *t. thou no scorn to wear the horn,* IV, 2, 14. *t. a good heart and counterfeit to be a man,* IV, 3, 174. *t. no unkindness of his hasty words,* Shr. IV, 3, 169. *wondering how thou tookest it* (wonder) All's II, 1, 93. *his ill ta'en suspicion,* Wint. I, 2, 460. *t. mercy on the poor souls,* H5 III, 4, 103. *and t. foul scorn to fawn on him,* H6A IV, 4, 35. *hence I took a thought, this was a judgment on me,* H8 II, 4, 193. *took some pride to do myself this wrong,* Cor. V, 6, 37. *t. thought and die for Caesar,* Caes. II, 1, 187. *now I have —n heart thou vanishest,* IV, 3, 288. *t. patience,* Lr. II, 4, 140. *t. to you no hard thoughts,* Ant. V, 2, 116. *their father took such sorrow,* Cymb. I, 1, 37. cf. the articles *Comfort, Delight, Displeasure, Heart, Joy, Liking, Mercy, Offence, Pity, Pleasure, Scorn, Sorrow.*

= to submit to the hazard of, to be contented with: *you must t. your chance,* Merch. II, 1, 38. *t. thy fortune,* Hml. III, 4, 32. *he might have took his answer long ago,* Tw. I, 5, 282. *wilt t. thy chance with me?* Cymb. IV, 2, 382. *t. the lot,* Ant. II, 6, 63. Hence = to acquiesce in, to put up with: *swounds, I should t. it,* Hml. II, 2, 604. *an they will t. it* (the truth), *so; if not, he's plain,* Lr. II, 2, 106. Modified in sense by adverbs or other additions: *unless I took all patiently, I should not live,* Lucr. 1641. *my daughter —s his going grievously,* Gent. III, 2, 14. *and t. the shame with joy,* Meas. II, 3, 36. *I'll t. it as a peril to my soul,* II, 4, 65. *if you t. it not patiently,* III, 2, 79. *he —s it ill,* Err. II, 1, 12. *t. them* (my cates) *in good part,* III, 1, 28. *you'll mar the light by —ing it in snuff,* LLL V, 2, 22. *since you do t. it so much at heart,* Merch. V, 145. *how he —s it at heart,* Tw. III, 4, 112. *to t. the death of her brother thus,* I, 3, 2. *to tell me how he —s it,* I, 5, 301. *to report your lord's —ing of this,* II, 2, 11. *t. it how you will,*

II, 3, 204. *took it deeply*, Wint. II, 3, 14. *t. thy correction mildly*, R2 V, 1, 32. *I will t. it as a sweet disgrace*, H4B I, 1, 89. *I t. it kindly*, H6B III, 1, 346. *that you t. with unthankfulness his doing*, R3 II, 2, 90. *which he'll t. in gentle part*, III, 4, 21. *if you t. it as a pleasure to you in being so*, Cor. II, 1, 34. *you'll t. it ill*, Tim. V, 1, 93. *how the people t. the cruel issue*, Caes. III, 1, 293. *t. it to heart*, Hml. I, 2, 101. *I t. it much unkindly*, Oth. I, 1, 1. *you t. things ill*, Ant. II, 2, 29. *you must not t. my former sharpness ill*, III, 3, 38. *how he —s my death*, IV, 13, 10. *to try your —ing of a false report*, Cymb. I, 6, 173.

= to receive and swallow as a drink or medicine: *the thing she took to quench it*, Wint. IV, 4, 61. *I have —n my last draught*, H6B II, 3, 73. *t. physic*, Lr. III, 4, 33. *have you ta'en of it?* Cymb. V, 5, 258 etc. cf. *t. a taste of my finding him*, As III, 2, 246. Tp. II, 1, 288.

= to assume: *he —s and leaves, in either's aptness, as it best deceives, to blush at speeches rank, to weep at woes, or to turn white*, Compl. 305. *t. this shape*, Tp. I, 2, 303. *t. any shape but that*, Mcb. III, 4, 102. *t. you, as 'twere, some distant knowledge of him*, Hml. II, 1, 13 (= pretend). With *upon* and the refl. pronoun, = 1) to charge one's self with; to undertake: *to t. a fault upon me that he did*, Gent. IV, 4, 15. *she'll t. the enterprise upon her*, Meas. IV, 1, 66. *if you will t. it on you to assist him*, IV, 2, 10. *you must t. Thisby on you*, Mids. I, 2, 46. *do not seek to t. your change upon you*, As I, 3, 104. *this way will I t. upon me to wash your liver clean*, III, 2, 442. *I t. the fault on me*, Tw. III, 4, 344. *I'll t. it upon me*, Wint. II, 2, 32. *I should t. on me the hostess-ship o' the day*, IV, 4, 71. *'twere no good part to t. on me to keep and kill thy heart*, R2 V, 1, 98. *t. on himself the sovereignty*, R3 III, 7, 79. *to t. on you the charge*, 131. *we shall t. upon's what else remains to do*, Mcb. V, 6, 5. 2) to assume; to appropriate to one's self: *that I have took upon me such an immodest raiment*, Gent. V, 4, 105. *to t. upon you another man's name*, Shr. V, 1, 37. *have —n the shapes of beasts upon them*, Wint. IV, 4, 26. *that dread King that took our state upon him*, H6B III, 2, 154. *fear not yet to t. upon you what is yours*, Mcb. IV, 3, 70. 3) to pretend; to arrogate: *I now t. upon me, in the name of Time, to use my wings*, Wint. IV, 1, 3. *—s on him to reform some edicts*, H4A IV, 3, 78. *why the devil ... took he upon him to appoint who should attend on him?* H8 I, 1, 73. 4) to pretend to a quality or to a knowledge, to profess: *one that —s upon him to be a dog indeed*, Gent. IV, 4, 13. *this slave took on him as a conjurer*, Err. V, 242. *I told him you were sick; he —s on him to understand so much*, Tw. I, 5, 149. *how comes that? says he that —s upon him not to conceive*, H4B II, 2, 123. *I t. not on me here as a physician*, IV, 1, 60. *she —s upon her to spy a white hair on his chin*, Troil. I, 2, 153. *t. upon's the mystery of things*, Lr. V, 3, 16. *you must either be directed by some that t. upon them to know, or do t. upon yourself that which I am sure you do not know*, Cymb. V, 4, 186. 5) without an object, or with *it*, = to play one's part, to cut a figure: *you'll prove a jolly surly groom, that t. it on you at the first so roundly*, Shr. III, 2, 216. *look that you t. upon you as you should*, IV, 2, 108. *she —s upon her bravely at first dash*, H6A I, 2, 71.

= to receive, or to get possession of, as of a thing desired or claimed: *I will not t. too much for him*, Tp. II, 2, 80. *and much less t. what I shall die to want*, III,

1, 78. *t. my daughter*, IV, 1, 14. *turn her out to who will t. her in*, Gent. III, 1, 77. *t. all, pay all, ... all is as she will*, Wiv. II, 2, 123. *t. your places*, Mids. V, 84. *by —ing or by giving of excess*, Merch. I, 3, 63. *t. interest*, 76. *and such assurance ta'en*, Shr. IV, 4, 49. *t. the Highest to witness*, All's IV, 2, 24. *t. and give back affairs*, Tw. IV, 3, 18. *t. not, good cousin, further than you should*, R2 III, 3, 16. *let us t. any man's horses*, H4B V, 3, 141. *we render you the tenth, to be ta'en forth at your only choice*, Cor. I, 9, 34. *let us t. the law of our sides*, Rom. I, 1, 44. *t. all myself*, II, 2, 49. *I'll t. the ghost's word for a thousand pound*, Hml. III, 2, 297. *or that you will t. longer time*, V, 2, 207. *t. the shadow of this tree for your good host*, Lr. V, 2, 1. *to have bought what I have took*, Cymb. III, 6, 48. *I having ta'en the forfeit*, V, 5, 208 etc. *t. all*, a proverbial phrase, properly, as it seems, = the French *va tout: I'll strike and cry T. all*, Ant. IV, 2, 8. *the longer liver t. all*, Rom. I, 5, 17 (German: *wer zuletzt lacht, lacht am besten*). *unbonneted he runs, and bids what will t. all*, Lr. III, 1, 15 (bids defiance to any thing). — *To t. sth. upon one's death*, or *upon one's honour* etc., = to give an assurance, to protest by one's honour, or by the certainty of death: *I took it upon mine honour thou hadst it not*, Wiv. II, 2, 12. *took it on his death that this my mother's son was none of his*, John I, 110. *—s on the point of honour to support so dissolute a crew*, R2 V, 3, 11. *they t. it already upon their salvation, that ... I am the king of courtesy*, H4A II, 4, 9. *I'll t. it upon my death, I gave him this wound*, V, 4, 154.

= to make a mark or copy of a thing, to note down: *although his (the star's) height be —n*, Sonn. 116, 8. *the character I'll t. with wax*, Tim. V, 3, 9. *they t. the flow o'the Nile by certain scales i'the pyramid*, Ant. II, 7, 20. *t. the marks of her*, Per. IV, 2, 61. = to set down in writing: *his confession is —n*, All's IV, 3, 130. cf. below: *to t. measure, to t. an inventory, to t. a note*.

= to receive as a thing in any way given or communicated: *as new-fallen snow —s any dint*, Ven. 354. *which (well) from love's fire took heat perpetual*, Sonn. 154, 10. *that horse his mettle from his rider —s*, Compl. 107. *which any print of goodness wilt not t.* Tp. I, 2, 352. *t. thou that* (i. e. a blow), III, 2, 84; cf. Err. I, 2, 92; II, 2, 23; Shr. IV, 1, 151; R3 I, 4, 276. *t. it for your pains*, Gent. I, 1, 124. *t. this again* (a writing) II, 1, 124. *t. your honours*, Meas. I, 1, 53. *to t. life from thine own sister's shame*, Meas. III, 1, 139. *t. my defiance*, 143. *took deep scars to save thy life*, Err. V, 192. *a stag that had ta'en a hurt*, As II, 1, 34. *to t. dust*, Tw. I, 3, 135. *hob, nob, is his word; give 't or t. 't*, III, 4, 263. *as you shake off one* (misery) *to t. another*, Wint. IV, 4, 580. *then t. my king's defiance from my mouth*, John I, 21. *t. his mother's thanks*, Mids. II, 32. *heaven t. my soul*, IV, 3, 10. *heaven will t. our souls*, R2 III, 1, 33. *those mouthed wounds which valiantly he took*, H4A I, 3, 97. *let this acceptance t.* H5 Epil. 14. *t. him, and use him well*, H8 V, 3, 154. *there's laying on, t. it off who will, as they say: there be hacks*, Troil. I, 2, 224 (cf. Tw. III, 4, 263). *telling how I took the blow*, 294. *I took him, made him joint-servant with me*, Cor. V, 6, 31 (cf. H8 V, 3, 154.). *from forth the fatal loins ... a pair of lovers t. their life*, Rom. Prol. 6. *then have my lips the sin that they have took*, I, 5, 110. *the spurns that patient merit of the unworthy —s*, Hml. III, 1, 74. *have took their discharge*, Lr. V, 3, 105. *make death proud to t. us*, Ant. IV, 15, 88. *if thou please to t. me to thee*, V, 1, 10. *can t. no greater wound*, Cymb. III, 4, 117. *home art gone, and ta'en thy wages*, IV, 2, 261 etc.

*To t.* and *leave* joined, as contradistinctive, in different significations: *he —s and leaves, in either's aptness, as it best deceives, to blush ... or to turn white*, Compl. 305 (he chooses or forbears). *as though I knew not what to t. and what to leave*, Shr. I, 1, 104 (what to do and what not). *t. her or leave her*, Lr. I, 1, 208. *every where he leaves and —s*, Troil. V, 5, 26 (spares or kills). Perhaps also in Cymb. III, 6, 24 (O. Edd. *t. or lend*).

*To t. the sacrament*, properly = to receive the communion, to partake of the Lord's supper, in the sense of to make a vow: *shall I set down your answer so? Do: I'll t. the sacrament on't, how and which way you will*, All's IV, 3, 156. *that they and we, perusing o'er these notes, may know wherefore we took the sacrament, and keep our faiths firm and inviolable*, John V, 2, 6. *you shall not only t. the sacrament to bury mine intents*, R2 IV, 328. *a dozen of them here have ta'en the sacrament, to kill the king*, V, 2, 97. *ten thousand French have ta'en the sacrament to rive their artillery upon no soul but Talbot*, H6A IV, 2, 28. *as we have ta'en the sacrament, we will unite the white rose and the red*, R3 V, 5, 18; cf. I, 4, 208. This may contribute to explain the use of *to take an oath* (administered by another) = to make an oath: Merch. II, 9, 2. Shr. IV, 2, 32. H6C I, 1, 196. I, 2, 22 etc. (*to t. an oath of* = to administer an oath to: Lucr. Arg. 20). And hence perhaps the following expressions: *betwixt mine eye and heart a league is took*, Sonn. 47, 1 (= a peace is concluded). *till he t. truce with her contending tears*, Ven. 82. *with my vexed spirits I cannot t. a truce*, John III, 1, 17. *offences 'gainst me, that I cannot t. peace with*, H8 II, 1, 85. *the seas and winds, old wranglers, took a truce*, Troil. II, 2, 75. *could not t. truce with the unruly spleen of Tybalt*, Rom. III, 1, 162 (cf. *his present reconciliation t.* Oth. III, 3, 47?).

= to accept, not to refuse: *they'll t. suggestion, as a cat laps milk*, Tp. II, 1, 288. *t. no repulse, whatever she doth say*, Gent. III, 1, 100. *I t. your offer*, IV, 1, 70. *t. the honour*, Wiv. II, 1, 46. *I may t. his bond*, Merch. I, 3, 28. *if he will t. it* (my friendship), so, 170. *proffers not took reap thanks for their reward*, All's II, 1, 150. *would you t. the letter of her*, III, 4, 1. *we'll t. your offer kindly*, III, 5, 104. *will you t. eggs for money? No, I'll fight*, Wint. I, 2, 161 (cf. *Egg*). *such offers ... as we may t.* John V, 7, 85. *t. this compact of a truce*, H6A V, 4, 163. *I will t. thy word*, Rom. II, 2, 91 (i. e. believe thee). *I was a fine fool to t. it*, Oth. IV, 1, 155. *t. I your wish* (i. e. the crown), *I leap into the seas*, Per. II, 4, 43 etc. = believe: Lr. IV, 6, 144.

Joined with adverbs or prepositional phrases to express any change of place or state produced by any action or manipulation: *first red as roses that on lawn we lay, then white as lawn, the roses took away*, Lucr. 259. *which* (twilight) *black night doth t. away*, Sonn. 73, 7. *t. those lips away*, Meas. IV, 1, 1. *t. away the grief of a wound*, H4A V, 1, 134. *let me still t. away the harms I fear*, Lr. I, 4, 352 (remove). *an a' speak any thing against me, I'll t. him down*, Rom. II, 4, 159 (= I will put him down, i. e. baffle, crush him. The nurse's speech). *t. thy face hence*, Mcb. V, 3, 19. *and t. unmingled thence that drop again*, Err. II, 2, 129. *t.*

*in the top-sail*, Tp. I, 1, 7. *or t. off thine* (wonder) All's II, 1, 92 (remove it, make an end of it). *to t. off so much grief from you*, Wint. V, 3, 55. *should t. it* (sentence of banishment) *off again*, R2 III, 3, 135. *it sets him on, and it —s him off*, Mcb. II, 3, 36 (pulls him back, restrains him). *speak, man: thy tongue may t. off some extremity, which to read would be even mortal to me*, Cymb. III, 4, 17. *I'll have my brains ta'en out and buttered*, Wiv. III, 5, 7. *their stings and teeth newly ta'en out*, H4B IV, 5, 206. *the fairest votary took up that fire*, Sonn. 154, 5. *what is't that you took up so gingerly?* Gent. I, 2, 70. 134. *t. up those clothes*, Wiv. III, 3, 155. *t. it* (the basket) *up*, IV, 2, 114. *they three were —n up by fishermen*, Err. I, 1, 111. *by men of Epidamnum all were —n up*, V, 350. *why had I not took up a beggar's issue?* Ado IV, 1, 134. Lr. I, 1, 256. *t. him up*, Shr. Ind. 1, 45. 72. *as he stooped to t. it up*, III, 2, 164. *t. it* (the gown) *up unto thy master's use. T. up my mistress' gown for thy master's use?* IV, 3, 160. 161. 164. *t. it up straight*, Wint. II, 3, 135. 183. *t. up the corse*, R3 I, 2, 226. *t. up those cords*, Rom. III, 2, 132. *— the shame that from them no device can take*, Lucr. 535. *to t. this poor maid from the world*, Meas. III, 1, 240. *t. me from the world*, H6C I, 4, 167 (= kill me). *something that does t. your mind from feasting*, Wint. IV, 4, 356. *I am sorry to see you ta'en from liberty*, H8 I, 1, 205. *and from these shoulders ta'en a load*, III, 2, 382. *your loves took from you the apprehension of his present portance*, Cor. II, 3, 231. *his own impatience —s from Aufidius a great part of blame*, V, 6, 147. *t. this from this* (head from shoulder) Hml. II, 2, 156. *if Hamlet from himself be ta'en away*, V, 2, 245. *t. the present horror from the time*, Mcb. II, 1, 59. *t. me from this world with treachery*, Oth. IV, 2, 220. *with his own sword I have ta'en his head from him*, Cymb. IV, 2, 150. *t. this charm from off her sight*, Mids. II, 1, 183. *the other —s in hand no cause, but company, of her drops' spilling*, Lucr. 1235 (cf. *Hand*). *he hath ta'en you newly into his grace*, Ado I, 3, 23. *t. the cork out of thy mouth*, As III, 2, 213. *to t. our brother Clarence to your grace*, R3 II, 1, 76. *t. to your royal self this proffered benefit of dignity*, III, 7, 195 (cf. Shr. IV, 1, 168. Wint. III, 2, 232. H8 V, 1, 105. Cor. II, 1, 34. II, 2, 147. Ant. V, 1, 10. V, 2, 116) etc.

Peculiar use of some adverbs: *to t. in* = to conquer, to subdue, to take: *affliction may subdue the cheek, but not t. in the mind*, Wint. IV, 4, 588. *to t. in many towns*, Cor. I, 2, 24. *to t. in a town with gentle words*, III, 2, 59. *t. in that kingdom*, Ant. I, 1, 23. *t. in Toryne*, III, 7, 24. *mused of —ing kingdoms in*, III, 13, 83. *such assaults as would t. in some virtue*, Cymb. III, 2, 9. *swore with his own single hand he'ld t. us in*, IV, 2, 121.

*To t. out* = 1) to ask to dance: *I were unmannerly, to t. you out, and not to kiss you*, H8 I, 4, 95. 2) to copy: *I'll have the work ta'en out*, Oth. III, 3, 296. *t. me this work out*, III, 4, 180. IV, 1, 156. 159. 161.

*To t. up* = 1) to occupy, to take: *t. up some other station*, Cor. IV, 5, 32. 2) to trip: *he took up my legs sometime*, Mcb. II, 3, 45. 3) to intercept, to obstruct: *such a keech can t. up the rays o' the sun*, H8 I, 1, 56. *schoolboys' tears t. up the glasses of my sight*, Cor. III, 2, 116. 4) to seize, to have recourse to: *dare not t. up arms like gentlemen*, H6A III, 2, 70. 5) to adopt, to acknowledge, to be contented to receive: *fear not, Cesario, t. thy fortunes up; be that thou knowest thou* art, Tw. V, 151. *t. up this mangled matter at the best*, Oth. I, 3, 173. 6) to make up, to settle: *how was that* (quarrel) *ta'en up?* As V, 4, 50. *seven justices could not t. up a quarrel*, 104. *I have his horse to t. up the quarrel*, Tw. III, 4, 320. *to t. up a matter of brawl betwixt my uncle and one of the emperial's men*, Tit. IV, 3, 92. 7) to obtain on trust, to borrow: *if a man is through with them in honest —ing up, they stand upon security*, H4B I, 2, 46. cf. the quibbles: *to prove a goodly commodity, being —n up of these men's bills*, Ado III, 3, 191. *t. up commodities upon our bills*, H6B IV, 7, 135. 8) to levy: *you are to t. soldiers up in counties*, H4B II, 1, 199. *you have ta'en up the subjects of his substitute*, IV, 2, 26. 9) to rebuke, to rate, to scold: *I was —n up for laying them down*, Gent. I, 2, 135. *t. this shadow up, for 'tis thy rival*, IV, 4, 202 (quibbling). *yet art thou good for nothing but —ing up*, All's II, 3, 218. *a whoreson jackanapes must t. me up for swearing*, Cymb. II, 1, 4. 10) to oppose, to encounter, to cope with: *a third must t. up us*, H4B I, 3, 73. *t. up the English short*, H5 II, 4, 72. *I will t. up that* (proverb) *with 'Give the devil his due'*, III, 7, 126. *I could myself t. up a brace o' the best of them*, Cor. III, 1, 244. Senses 9 and 10 joined in the clown's speech: *how it* (the sea) *chafes, how it rages, how it —s up the shore*, Wint. III, 3, 90.

Various periphrastical use with substantives (cf. the resp. nouns): *—s no account how things go from him*, Tim. II, 2, 3. *to t. a new acquaintance of thy mind*, Sonn. 77, 12. *a certain aim he took*, Mids. II, 1, 157. *t. thy breath*, H6A IV, 6, 4. Troil. IV, 5, 192. V, 8, 3. *let no man t. care for himself*, Tp. V, 257. *had I a sister were a Grace, he should t. his choice*, Troil. I, 2, 258. Cor. I, 6, 65. Tit. IV, 1, 34. *t. counsel of their friends*, Ven. 640. *to fast like one that —s diet*, Gent. II, 1, 25. *shall I not t. mine ease in mine inn?* H4A III, 3, 92. *a potion, which so took effect as I intended*, Rom. V, 3, 244. *by water shall he die and t. his end*, H6B I, 4, 36. *t. their examination*, Ado III, 5, 53. *lest he should t. exceptions to my love*, Gent. I, 3, 81. V, 2, 3. *let him t. his haste*, Tim. V, 1, 213. *makes it t. head from all indifferency*, John II, 579. *for —ing so the head*, R2 III, 3, 14. *t. heed*, Tp. IV, 22. Merch. II, 2, 8. *there t. an inventory of all I have*, H8 III, 2, 452. *his —n labours*, All's III, 4, 12. Hml. II, 2, 83. *let us t. our leave*, Gent. I, 1, 56. IV, 4, 38. Meas. I, 4, 90. *took measure of my body*, Err. IV, 3, 9. *to t. a note of what I stand in need of*, Gent. II, 7, 84. Meas. II, 2, 94. IV, 1, 38. V, 80. H8 II, 3, 59. *—ing no notice that she was so nigh*, Ven. 341. *to t. order*, Shr. I, 2, 126. R2 V, 1, 53. *to t. the pain*, Pilgr. 192. *to t. pains*, Tp. I, 2, 354. IV, 190. Gent. I, 1, 123. Err. V, 393. Mids. I, 2, 111. Merch. IV, 1, 7. Tim. III, 5, 26. *t. your patience to you*, Wint. III, 2, 232. H8 V, 1, 105. *t. your place*, Merch. IV, 1, 170. *with my nobler reason against my fury do I t. part*, Tp. V, 27. Meas. V, 435. Mids. III, 2, 322. 333. *t. but possession of her with a touch*, Gent. V, 4, 130. *when she will t. the rein I let her run*, Wint. II, 3, 51. *—s no rest*, Ven. 647. 1185. Tp. II, 1, 197. V, 301. Wint. II, 3, 10. H6C II, 5, 32. *might have ta'en revenge*, Meas. IV, 4, 33. *unwholesome weeds t. root with precious flowers*, Lucr. 870. Ado I, 3, 24. H8 I, 2, 87. *I must t. like seat*, H6C III, 3, 10. *I trust to t. of truest Thisby sight*, Mids. V, 280 (Ff *taste*). *you have ta'en a special stand*, Wiv. V, 5, 247. cf., besides, the substantives *Course, Farewell, Harm, Hold*,

*Muster, Nap, Occasion, Render, Rouse, Survey, Turn, Vantage, Vengeance, Wreak.*

II. refl. = to betake one's self: *ere these eyes of mine t. themselves to slumber*, H5 III, 2, 123. *t. you to your tools*, Tit. IV, 3, 6. *a vestal livery will I t. me to*, Per. III, 4, 10. *t. away thyself* = go away: Tim. IV, 3, 283. As for the clown's speech in Wint. IV, 4, 751: *your worship had like to have given us one* (i. e. a lie), *if you had not —n yourself with the manner*, see *Manner*.

III. intr. 1) to betake one's self, to have recourse, to apply: *have you any thing to t. to? Nothing but my fortune*, Gent. IV, 1, 42.

2) to have the intended effect (German: *sich machen): I know a way, if it t. right, in spite of fortune, will bring me off again*, H8 III, 2, 219. Partic. *—n: whatsome'er he is, he's bravely —n here*, All's III, 5, 55 (he has done well here, has behaved bravely). *never greater* (shows and pageants), *nor, I'll assure you, better —n*, H8 IV, 1, 12 (of a better effect, better executed).

3) With *on*, = to be furious, to chafe, to fret: *t. on as you would follow, but yet come not*, Mids. III, 2, 258. Followed by *with: she does so t. on with her men*, Wiv. III, 5, 40. *he so —s on yonder with my husband*, IV, 2, 22. *how will my mother for a father's death t. on with me*, H6C II, 5, 104.

**Taker,** 1) one who catches a disease: *he is sooner caught than the pestilence, and the t. runs presently mad.* Ado I, 1, 88.

2) one who swallows something: *a swallowed bait on purpose laid to make the t. mad*, Sonn. 129, 8. *that the life-weary t. may fall dead*, Rom. V, 1, 62.

**Taking,** subst. state of extreme alarm, agony of fear: *what terror 'tis! but she, in worser t.* Lucr. 453. *what a t. was he in when your husband asked me was in the basket*, Wiv. III, 3, 191. As for *t.* = malignant influence, witchery (Lr. III, 4, 61), and *t. off* = cutting off, killing (Mcb. I, 7, 20. Lr. V, 1, 65), see *Take*.

**Talbonites,** name given in contempt to the English by the Pucelle: H6A III, 2, 28. Hanmer *Talbotines*, most M. Edd. *Talbotites*.

**Talbot,** 1) name of the renowned English general in the French wars of the fifteenth century: H5 IV, 3, 54. H6A I, 1, 106. 121. 128 (a *T.!* a *T.!* cf. *A*). I, 4, 23. II, 2, 37 and III, 3, 20 (the *T.*). IV, 2, 3 (*John T.*). IV, 7, 61 (his various titles enumerated) etc. etc. 2) his son John T.: H6A IV, 3, 35. IV, 5, 1 etc. 3) Sir Gilbert T., a partisan of Richmond: R3 IV, 5, 10.

**Talbotites,** see *Talbonites*.

**Tale,** 1) any thing told, a story, a narrative: Lucr. 1078. 1496. Pilgr. 93. Tp. I, 2, 106. 140. Wiv. IV, 4, 28. 38. Meas. V, 370. Ado I, 1, 218 (*like the old t.* cf. Dyce's Glossary). II, 1, 135 (the *Hundred Merry —s*; a book lately reprinted). III, 3, 157. Mids. I, 1, 133. Merch. IV, 1, 276. As I, 2, 128. Shr. IV, 1, 65. 74. Wint. II, 1, 23. 25. IV, 1, 14. V, 2, 30. 66. John I, 98. III, 4, 108. IV, 2, 18. 202. R2 III, 4, 10. V, 1, 41. 44 (Ff *fall*). H4A II, 4, 281. V, 4, 158. H5 IV, 7, 45. H6A II, 5, 62. V, 5, 10. H6C II, 1, 120. Cor. I, 1, 93. 98. Tit. II, 3, 105. III, 2, 27. 47. IV, 1, 47. V, 3, 94. Mcb. V, 5, 26. Hml. I, 5, 15. II, 2, 468 (Qq *talk*). 522. Lr. I, 4, 35. V, 3, 12. 214. Oth. I, 3, 90. 171. IV, 1, 85. Cymb. II, 2, 45. III, 3, 14. V, 5, 297. Per. I, 4, 2. *vows as light as —s*, Mids. III, 2. 133. *truths would be —s, where now half —s be truths*, Ant. II, 2, 136. cf. Pilgr. 93. *to tell —s* = to communicate things not much to the credit of a person: Tp. V, 129. Meas. IV, 3, 175. Tw. II, 1, 43. Lr. II, 4, 231. cf. Err. IV, 3, 89. Ado III, 2, 63. H4A III, 2, 23. Cymb. I, 6, 143. H8 V, 3, 110. Proverbial phrase: *thereby hangs a t.* Wiv. I, 4, 159. As II, 7, 28. Shr. IV, 1, 60. Oth. III, 1, 8.

2) any thing that is or has been said or spoken: *to a pretty ear she tunes her t.* Ven. 74. *she trembles at his t.* 591. *she wispers in his ears a heavy t.* 1125. *when thou comest thy t. to tell,* Pilgr. 305 (to say that thou lovest her). *my amorous t.* Ado I, 1, 327. *they are both in a t.* IV, 2, 33 (both say the same). *thou canst not ... devise a name so slight ... as the pope. Tell him this t.* John III, 1, 152. *my death's sad t. may yet undeaf his ear,* R2 II, 1, 16 (what I say in death). *that his t. to me may be nothing but 'Anon',* H4A II, 4, 35. *I should have told your grace's t.* H6B III, 1, 44 (I should have said the same as you). *to end a t. of length,* Troil. I, 3, 136 (a long speech). Compl. 4. Tp. III, 2, 56. 91. Gent. II, 3, 54. II, 4, 126. Wiv. I, 1, 79. I, 4, 85. Meas. V, 84. Ado III, 3, 109. 151. LLL II, 74. V, 2, 729. Mids. II, 1, 51. Merch. I, 2, 52. Shr. II, 71. IV, 2, 67. V, 2, 24. John III, 1, 5. 25. 26. IV, 2, 234. R2 III, 2, 121. V, 3, 37. H4A I, 3, 256. II, 3, 51. II, 4, 135. V, 2, 91. R3 III, 7, 31. IV, 4, 327. 358. 359. 462. V, 3, 194. Troil. I, 2, 91. Cor. V, 6, 58. Tit. III, 1, 40. Rom. I, 5, 25. II, 4, 99. II, 5, 34. V, 3, 230. Mcb. I, 3, 97 *(as thick as t. came post with post;* perhaps = as fast as words, as speech can utter it. M. Edd. *hail).* Oth. V, 1, 125. Ant. I, 2, 102.

Usually joined with the verb *to tell,* except in the following passages: *my tongue hath but a heavier t. to say,* R2 III, 2, 197 (rhyming). *I will a round unvarnished t. deliver,* Oth. I, 3, 90. *I could a t. unfold,* Hml. I, 5, 15. The case is another in the phrase *short t. to make,* H6C II, 1, 120. Hml. II, 2, 146.

Punning upon *t.* and *tail:* Gent. II, 3, 54. Rom. II, 4, 99.

**Talent,** 1) a sum of money among the ancient Greeks: Tim. I, 1, 95. 141. I, 2, 6. II, 2, 202. 208. 235. 238. III, 1, 19. III, 2, 13. 26. 43. III, 4, 94. *in you, which I account his beyond all —s,* Cymb. I, 6, 80 (exceeding any price. Read: *which I account's,* i. e. is).

2) 'a locket consisting of hair platted and set in gold' (Malone): *behold these —s of their hair, with twisted metal amorously impleached,* Compl. 204.*

3) a natural gift, faculty: *a rare t.* LLL IV, 2, 64. *those that are fools, let them use their —s,* Tw. I, 5, 16.

4) see *Talon.*

**Tale-porter,** name in Wint. IV, 4, 273.

**Talk,** subst. 1) the act of speaking: *sometime it* (her grief) *is mad and too much t. affords,* Lucr. 1106. *so she sleep not in her t.* Gent. III, 1, 335. *crossing the plain highway of t.* Merch. III, 1, 13. *practise rhetoric in your common t.* Shr. I, 1, 35. *to be cross in t.* II, 251. *our argument is all too heavy to admit much t.* H4B V, 2, 24. R3 III, 1, 126. Troil. IV, 4, 88. 141. Tim. V, 2, 14. Hml. III, 2, 300. Ant. V, 2, 50.

2) something spoken: *mine ears, that to your wanton t. attended,* Ven. 809. *mingling my t. with tears,* Lucr. 797. *smooth not thy tongue with filed t.* Pilgr. 306. *as strange unto your town as to your t.* Err. II, 2, 151. Meas. IV, 3, 188. Ado III, 1, 20. R2 IV, 14. H6C III, 3, 158. Troil. V, 1, 17. Tit. III, 2, 31. V, 2, 17.

3) mutual discourse, conversation: *what sad t. was that,* Gent. I, 3, 1. *break their t.* Wiv. III, 4, 22. *our t. must only be of Benedick,* Ado III, 1, 17. *spent an hour's t.* LLL II, 68. *I would not have my father see me in t. with thee,* Merch. II, 3, 9. As II, 4, 21. Wint IV, 4, 317. H6A I, 2, 118. III, 1, 63. H6C IV, 1, 6 R3 III, 1, 177. Cor. IV, 7, 4. Caes. II, 2, 121. IV, 3, 226. 289 *(hold).* Hml. I, 3, 134 *(to give words or t. with the Lord Hamlet).* Lr. III, 3, 16 *(maintain). to have t. of* = to converse about: *we had an hour's t. of that wart,* Wiv. I, 4, 162. II, 1, 172. *I had t. of you last night,* All's V, 2, 56. *to have more t. of these sad things,* Rom. V, 3, 307.

**Talk,** vb. 1) to speak, to utter words; absol.: *canst thou t.?* Ven. 427. *begins to t.* Lucr. 1783. *he will be —ing,* Tp. II, 1, 27. *without any more —ing,* II, 2, 178. *she doth t. in her sleep,* Gent. III, 1, 333. Err. III, 1, 38. IV, 4, 46. Ado I, 1, 117. LLL IV, 3, 274. As V, 2, 57. H4A V, 2, 92 etc. In a bad sense, = to speak impertinently, to prattle: *to babble and to t.* Ado III, 3, 37. *he will be —ing,* III, 5, 36. *to prate and t. for life,* Wint. III, 2, 42. *I do not t. much,* H8 II, 1, 146. *this —ing lord,* III, 2, 265. *poor prattler, how thou —est,* Mcb. IV, 2, 64. *come, come, you t.* Oth. IV, 3, 25. Modified by an adverb or prepositional expression: *to t. in deeds,* Lucr. 1348. *does not t. after the wisest,* Tp. II, 2, 76. *love —s with better knowledge,* Meas. III, 2, 159. *you t. greasily,* LLL IV, 1, 139. Merch. II, 2, 200. As I, 3, 26. III, 5, 110. H6A III, 2, 4. V, 3, 108.

With *of:* —*ed of virtue,* Lucr. 846. *when you t. of war,* Gent. V, 2, 16. Wiv. I, 1, 301. IV, 2, 30. 94. Ado III, 2, 107. V, 1, 317. LLL III, 119. Merch. I, 2, 45. II, 2, 50. V, 151. As III, 5, 94. H4B I, 1, 54 etc. With *on:* *this Sir Proteus that we t. on,* Gent. IV, 2, 73. Rom. II, 5, 43. Ant. II, 2, 85. Cymb. II, 4, 132. With *to,* = to address words to: *t. not to me,* Wiv. IV, 6, 1. Gent. IV, 2, 104. As III, 4, 1. Shr. II, 35. John III, 4, 91. IV, 1, 25. H4A I, 3, 234. III, 1, 163. Rom. III, 5, 204. Oth. III, 3, 296. IV, 2, 102. With *to* and *of: what —est thou to me of the hangman?* H4A II, 1, 73. R3 III, 4, 77 (Ff —*est thou to me of ifs?* Qq *tellest thou me of ifs?).*

With a clause: *we were —ing that our garments seem fresh,* Tp. II, 1, 96.

With an accus. denoting an effect: *thou dost t. nothing to me,* Tp. II, 1, 170. *all tongues to t. their bitterest,* Wint. III, 2, 217. Double accus.: *they would t. themselves mad,* Ado II, 1, 369. *t. thy tongue weary,* Cymb. III, 4, 115. Accus. and prepositional expression: *t. us to silence,* H8 I, 4, 45. *t. him out of patience,* Oth. III, 3, 23.

2) to converse: *to t. and greet,* LLL V, 2, 144. *Pyramus and Thisby did t. through the chink of a wall,* Mids. III, 1, 65. *the very time Aumerle and you did t.* R2 IV, 61. *we must out and t.* Caes. V, 1, 22. *Edmund and I have —ed,* Lr. IV, 5, 30 (have spoken of the matter and come to an agreement). *we shall t. before we fight,* Ant. II, 6, 2. Followed by *with: t. with her,* Tp. IV, 32. Meas. I, 4, 36. V, 348. Err. II, 2, 192. Ado V, 1, 340. Merch. I, 3, 37. H6A III, 3, 35. Lr. III, 4, 159 etc. *I must t. a word with you,* R3 IV, 4, 198 (accus. of measure. Qq *speak). I'll t. a word with this Theban,* Lr. III, 4, 162.

**Talker,** one who talks much, a prattler: *I'll grow a t.* Merch. I, 1, 110. —*s are no good doers,* R3 I, 3, 352. *I be not found a t.* H8 II, 2, 79.

**Tall,** 1) high in stature: *how t. was she? About

*my stature*, Gent. IV, 4, 162. *if t., a lance ill-headed; if low, an agate*, Ado III, 1, 64. *which is the greatest lady, the highest? The thickest and the —est*, LLL IV, 1, 47. *few —er are so young*, V, 2, 846. *the cowslips t. her pensioners be*, Mids. II, 1, 10. *her t. personage, her height*, III, 2, 292. As I, 2, 284 (M. Edd. *smaller*, or *lesser*, or *lower*). I, 3, 117. III, 5, 118. Tw. IV, 2, 7. H4B V, 1, 65. V, 3, 36. Ant. II, 5, 118. III, 3, 14. Applied to stockings, = long, high: *t. stockings, short blistered breeches*, H8 I, 3, 30.

2) large and strong, stout: *I am a worthless boat, he of t. building, and of goodly pride*, Sonn. 80, 12. *many a t. ship*, Merch. III, 1, 6. R2 II, 1, 286. Oth. II, 1, 79. *yond t. anchoring bark*, Lr. IV, 6, 18.

3) stout, sturdy, lusty, spirited (German *tüchtig*): *and carry back to Sicily much t. youth that else must perish here*, Ant. II, 6, 7. Except this passage, the word, in this sense, is either used with irony, as by Falstaff: *good soldiers and t. fellows*, Wiv. II, 2, 11; by Sir Toby: *he's as t. a man as any*, Tw. I, 3, 20; and by Percy: *which many a good t. fellow had destroyed*, H4A I, 3, 62; or with braggardism, as by Shallow: *I would have made you four t. fellows skip like rats*, Wiv. II, 1, 237; or ridiculed, as by Mercutio: *a very good blade! a very t. man!* Rom. II, 4, 31; or only put in the mouth of mean persons: *anon comes Pyramus, sweet youth and t.* Mids. V, 145 (in the play of Pyramus and Thisbe). *a —er man than I will take cold*, Shr. IV, 1, 11 (Grumio's speech). *thou'rt a t. fellow*, IV, 4, 17 (Tranio's speech). *Sir John Falstaff, a t. gentleman*, H4B III, 2, 67 (Bardolph's speech). *spoke like a t. fellow that respects his reputation*, R3 I, 4, 156 (the second murderer's speech). Pistol even says: *thy spirits are most t.* H5 II, 1, 72. As for the phrase *a t. man of his hands* (Wiv. I, 4, 26. Wint. V, 2, 177. 179. 181. 185), employed by Simple and the clown, see *Hand*.

**Tallow**, the grease or fat of an animal: Wiv. V, 5, 16 (a phrase properly applied to bucks growing lean after rutting-time). Err. III, 2, 100. H4A II, 4, 125. H4B I, 2, 179. Rom. III, 5, 158 (*t. face*, i. e. pale face). Cymb. I, 6, 110.

**Tallow-catch**, reading of O. Edd. in H4A II, 4, 252; supposed by some to be = tallow-ketch, i. e. a vessel filled with tallow; by others = tallow-keech, i. e. fat rolled up in a round lump.

**Tally**, subst. a stick on which notches or scores are cut, to keep accounts by: *our fore-fathers had no other books but the score and the t.* H6B IV, 7, 39. *nor need I —es thy dear love to score*, Sonn. 122, 10.

**Talon** (O. Edd. *talent;* cf. Dull's pun in LLL IV, 2, 65) the claw of a bird of prey: H4A II, 4, 363. H6B III, 2, 196. H6C I, 4, 41. Per. IV, 3, 48.

**Tame**, adj. 1) having lost its native wildness, accustomed to man, domestic: Ven. 1096. Tp. II, 2, 71. 80. Gent. III, 2, 80. All's II, 5, 50. Wint. I, 2, 92 (*make's fat as t. things;* cf. *Thing*). R2 I, 1, 174. H4A V, 2, 10. *I'll watch him t.* Oth. III, 3, 23 (like a hawk). *you must be watched ere you be made t.* Troil. III, 2, 46. Used of things, = wonted, accommodated to one's habits, grown into a custom: *sequestering from me all that time, acquaintance, custom and condition made t. and most familiar to my nature*, Troil. III, 3, 10.

2) subdued: *how t. a meacock wretch can make the curstest shrew*, Shr. II, 314. With *to*, = bearing patiently: *patience, t. to sufferance, bide each check*, Sonn.

58, 7. *make them t. to their obedience*, John IV, 2, 262. *made t. to fortune's blows*, Lr. IV, 6, 225 (Qq *made lame by fortune's blows*).

3) Metaphorically, either in a good sense, = free from passion, mild, gentle, meek; or in a bad sense, = heartless, spiritless, insensible, dull: *fair nature is both kind and t.* Compl. 311. *youth is wild, and age is t.* Pilgr. 164. *to be what I would not shall not make me t.* Wiv. III, 5, 153. *you could not with more t. a tongue desire it*, Meas. II, 2, 46. *you are a t. man, go!* Mids. III, 2, 259. *I see love hath made thee a t. snake*, As IV, 3, 70. *yet can I not of such t. patience boast*, R2 I, 1, 52. *he's no swaggerer; a t. cheater*, H4B II, 4, 105. *their (horses') courage with hard labour t. and dull*, H4A IV, 3, 23. *still use of grief makes wild grief t.* R3 IV, 4, 229. *weaker than a woman's tear, —r than sleep, fonder than ignorance*, Troil. I, 1, 10. *be not too t. neither*, Hml. III, 2, 18. *start not so wildly from my affair. I am t., sir*, 322. *at your age the hey-day in the blood is t.* III, 4, 69.

In a physical sense, = harmless, ineffectual, impotent: *his remedies are t. in the present peace and quietness of the people*, Cor. IV, 6, 2.

**Tame**, vb. 1) to reduce from a wild to a domestic state, to make gentle: Ven. 560. Lucr. 956. H8 V, 3, 21. Troil. I, 3, 391. III, 2, 84.

2) to subdue, to crush, to depress: *continuance —s the one (woe)* Lucr. 1097. *if justice cannot t. you*, Ado V, 1, 210. *to t. you Kate*, Shr. II, 278. IV, 1, 213. IV, 2, 53. 58. V, 2, 188. *winter —s man, woman and beast*, IV, 1, 24. 25. *t. the savage spirit of wild war*, John V, 2, 74. *—d the king and made the dauphin stoop*, H6C II, 2, 151. *I'll t. you, I'll bring you in subjection*, Per. II, 5, 75. With *to: —ing my wild heart to thy loving hand*, Ado III, 1, 112.

Peculiar expressions: *would drink up the lees and dregs of a flat —d piece*, Troil. IV, 1, 62 (not *unmanned*, as Juliet calls herself in Rom. III, 2, 14, but resembling a hawk grown too familiar with man. Perhaps *flat-tamed*, i. e. tamed to flatness or staleness). *if that the heavens do not their visible spirits send quickly down to t. these vile offences*, Lr. IV, 2, 47 (= to restrain).

**Tamely**, with a subdued spirit, with unresisting submission: H4B IV, 2, 42. H8 III, 2, 279. Lr. II, 4, 279.

**Tameness**, 1) state of being reclaimed from wildness: Lr. III, 6, 19. 2) meekness, gentleness: *any madness ... seemed but t., civility and patience*, Wiv. IV, 2, 27.

**Taming-school**, a school in which the art is taught of subduing a contumacious spirit: Shr. IV, 2, 54. 55.

**Tamora**, name of the queen of the Goths in Tit. I, 139 etc.

**Tamworth**, place in Warwickshire: R3 V, 2, 13.

**Tan**, 1) to make (leather) firm and impervious to water: *his (a tanner's) hide is so —ed with his trade, that he will keep out water a great while*, Hml. V, 1, 186.

2) to make brown, to deprive of the freshness of youth: *beated and chopped with —ed antiquity*, Sonn. 62, 10. *time, whose accidents ... t. sacred beauty*, 115, 7.

**Tang**, subst. a shrill sound, a twang: *she had a tongue with a t.* Tp. II, 2, 52.

**Tang**, vb. to ring, to twang: *let thy tongue t. argu-*

*ments of state*, Tw. II, 5, 163. *let thy tongue t. with arguments of state*, III, 4, 78 (F1 *langer*).

**Tangle**, 1) to implicate, to ravel: *his speech was like a —d chain*, Mids. V, 125.

2) to ensnare: *how a bird lies —d in a net*, Ven. 67. *lay lime to t. her desires*, Gent. III, 2, 68. *she means to t. my eyes too*, As III, 5, 44. *with the snares of war to t. thee*, H6A IV, 2, 22. *have all limed bushes, and ... they'll t. thee*, H6B II, 4, 55. *my king is —d in affection to a creature of the queen's*, H8 III, 2, 35.

**Tanling**, one tanned or scorched by the sun: *to be still hot summer's —s and the shrinking slaves of winter*, Cymb. IV, 4, 29.

**Tanner**, one whose occupation is to tan leather: H6B IV, 2, 24. Hml. V, 1, 183.

**Tantalus**, the fabulous king condemned to be placed in water and beneath a fruit-tree, without the power of reaching either: Ven. 599. Lucr. 858.

**Tap**, subst. a slight blow: *this is the right fencing grace, my lord; t. for t., and so part fair*, H4B II, 1, 206.

**Tap**, vb. to pierce or broach a cask: *he shall draw, he shall t.* Wiv. I, 3, 11. With *out,* = to draw, to let out (liquor): *that blood ... hast thou —ed out and drunkenly caroused*, R2 II, 1, 127.

**Tape**, a narrow fillet or band of linen: Wint. IV, 4, 322. 610.

**Taper**, a candle: Wiv. IV, 4, 50. 62. LLL V, 2, 267. R2 I, 3, 223. Cor. I, 6, 32. Tit. I, 324. II, 3, 228. IV, 2, 89 *(by the burning —s of the sky)*. Caes. II, 1, 7. 35. IV, 3, 164. 275. Oth. I, 1, 142. 167. Cymb. II, 2, 5. 19. cf. *Night-taper*.

**Taper-light**, candle-light: John IV, 2, 14. Per. Prol. 16.

**Tapestry**, woven hangings: *the desk that's covered o'er with Turkish t.* Err. IV, 1, 104. *the shaven Hercules in the smirched worm-eaten t.* Ado III, 3, 146. *my hangings all of Tyrian t.* Shr. II, 351. *to pawn the t. of my dining-chambers*, H4B II, 1, 154. 159 *(—es)*. *hanged with t. of silk and silver*, Cymb. III, 4, 69.

**Taphouse**, alehouse: Meas. II, 1, 219.

**Tapster**, one who draws beer and serves the customers of an alehouse (= the modern *waiter*): *shrill-tongued —s answering every call*, Ven. 849. Wiv. I, 3, 17. 19. Meas. I, 2, 112. 115. II, 1, 63. 207. 215. 223. 224. 232. LLL I, 2, 43 *(I am ill at reckoning; it fitteth the spirit of a t.)*. As III, 4, 34. H4A IV, 2, 31. H4B I, 2, 193. Troil. I, 2, 123. Tim. IV, 3, 215.

**Tar**, subst. a resinous substance obtained from pine and fir-trees: Tp. II, 2, 54. As III, 2, 65. 70.

**Tar**, vb. to smear with tar: *—ed over with the surgery of our sheep*, As III, 2, 63.

**Tardily**, slowly: *could speak low and t.* H4B II, 3, 26.

**Tardiness**, slowness, or rather a habit of being behindhand in sth.: *a t. in nature which often leaves the history unspoke that it intends to do*, Lr. I, 1, 238.

**Tardy**, adj. slow and behindhand in one's business, being too late, laggard: *is your t. master now at hand?* Err. II, 1, 44. *an you be so t., come no more in my sight*, As IV, 1, 51. *whose manners still our t. apish nation limps after*, R2 II, 1, 22 (being always in the rear, behindhand with others). *these t. tricks of yours will ... break some gallows' back*, H4B IV, 3, 31. *some t. cripple bore the countermand*, R3 II, 1, 89. *be not ta'en t. by unwise delay*, IV, 1, 52. *you have ta'en a t.*

*sluggard here*, V, 3, 225. *you're t.* H8 I, 4, 7. *the prince must think me t. and remiss*, Troil. IV, 4, 143. *however he puts on this t. form*, Caes. I, 2, 303 (the contrary to 'quick mettle', 300). *this overdone, or come t. off*, Hml. III, 2, 28 (cf. *Come* and *Lag*). *your t. son to chide*, III, 4, 106.

Adverbially: *too swift arrives as t. as too slow*, Rom. II, 6, 15 (and perhaps in Hml. III, 2, 28).*

**Tardy**, vb. to retard, to render slow: *Camillo —ed my swift command*, Wint. III, 2, 163.

**Tardy-gaited**, slow, laggard: *the cripple t. night who ... doth limp so tediously away*, H5 IV Chor. 20.

**Tarentum**, town in Italy: Ant. III, 7, 22.

**Targe**, a shield: LLL V, 2, 556 *(with t. and shield. Holofernes' poetry)*. Ant. II, 6, 39. Cymb. V, 5, 5.

**Target**, the same: H4A II, 4, 224. H6C II, 1, 40. H8 Prol. 15. Cor. IV, 5, 126. Hml. II, 2, 334. Ant. I, 3, 82. IV, 8, 31. Per. I, 1, 140. II, 1, 143.

**Tarpeian**, pertaining to the rocky steep in ancient Rome, from which criminals were precipitated: *bear him to the rock T.* Cor. III, 1, 213. *the T. rock*, 266. III, 2, 3. *the steep T. death*, III, 3, 88. *the rock T.* 103.

**Tarquin**, name of the last king of Rome and of his sons: Lucr. Arg. 22. 25. Lucr. 3 and passim. Cor. II, 1, 166. II, 2, 92. 98. V, 4, 46. Tit. III, 1, 299. IV, 1, 63. Caes. II, 1, 54 *(the T.)*. Mcb. II, 1, 55. Cymb. II, 2, 12.

**Tarquinius**, the same: Lucr. Arg. I. 5. 12.

**Tarre**, to set on (dogs): *and like a dog that is compelled to fight, snatch at his master that doth t. him on*, John IV, 1, 117. *pride alone must t. the mastiffs on, as 'twere their bone*, Troil. I, 3, 392. *and the nation holds it no sin to t. them to controversy*, Hml. II, 2, 370.

**Tarriance**, 1) the act of remaining in a place, of not going away: *I am impatient of my t.* Gent. II, 7, 90. 2) the act of waiting, of staying in expectation: *Cytherea a longing t. for Adonis made under an osier*, Pilgr. 74.

**Tarry**, 1) intr. a) to stay, to abide, to lodge: *thou knowest where I will t.* Merch. IV, 2, 18.

b) to continue in a place, to remain, not to go away: *t. I here, I but attend on death*, Gent. III, 1, 186. *I t. too long*, Wiv. I, 4, 64. 93. 117. *farewell. T., sweet Beatrice*, Ado IV, 1, 294. 327. *t., rash wanton*, Mids. II, 1, 63. *t., Jew*, Merch. IV, 1, 346. *I'll t. no longer with you: farewell*, As III, 2, 309. *I chafe you, if I t.: let me go*, Shr. II, 243. *I cannot t.* IV, 4, 99. *if you t. longer, I shall give worse payment*, Tw. IV, 1, 20. *if you will not (go), t. at home and be hanged*, H4A I, 2, 147. 162. *leave me, or t., Edward will be king*, H6C IV, 1, 65. *better do so (go along) than t. and be hanged*, IV, 5, 26. *I will not t.* H8 II, 4, 131. *there is no —ing here*, Troil. II, 3, 269. *prithee, t.; you men will never t.* IV, 2, 15. 16. *I might have still held off, and then you would have —ed*, 18. *those that go or t.* V, 1, 85. 86. *t. with him till I turn again*, Tit. V, 2, 141. *fly; there is no —ing here*, Caes. V, 5, 30. *there is nor flying hence nor —ing here*, Mcb. V, 5, 48. *if you will measure your lubber's length again, t.; but away!* Lr. I, 4, 101. *but I will t., the fool will stay*, II, 4, 83.

c) to stay in expectation, to wait: *nay, t., I'll go along with thee*, Meas. IV, 3, 174. *Thisby, —ing in mulberry shade*, Mids. V, 149. *it stands so that I may hardly t. so long,* Shr. Ind. 2, 127. 129. *t., Petruchio, I must go with thee,* I, 2, 117. *if you will t., but till the troops come by, I will conduct you,* All's III, 5, 42. *I'll t. till my son come,* Wint.III,3,78. *t., dear cousin,* H5 IV, 6, 15. *have I not —ed?* Troil. I, 1, 17. 19. 21. *t. till they push us,* Caes. V, 5, 25. *t. and take the fool with thee,* Lr. I, 4, 338. With *for: I brought you word an hour since that the bark Expedition put forth to-night; and then were you hindered by the sergeant to t. for the hoy Delay,* Err. IV, 3, 40. *we'll rest us and t. for the comfort of the day,* Mids. II, 2, 38. *t. for the mourners, and stay dinner,* Rom. IV, 5, 150.

d) to delay: *you'll lose the tide, if you t. any longer,* Gent. II, 3, 39. *I pray you, t.* Merch. III, 2, 1. *t. a little; there is something else,* IV, 1, 305.

2) trans. to wait for, to remain till: *here's a Bohemian Tartar —es the coming down of thy fat woman,* Wiv. IV, 5, 21. *I cannot t. dinner,* H4B III, 2, 204 (= stay dinner). *he that will have a cake out of the wheat must needs t. the grinding,* Troil. I, 1, 16. 18. 20.

**Tarsus,** see *Tharsus.*

**Tart,** subst. in *Apple-tart,* q. v.

**Tart,** adj. sour, harsh, crabbed; *another way, the news is not so t.* Lr. IV, 2, 87. *so t. a favour to trumpet such good tidings,* Ant. II, 5, 38.

**Tartar,** 1) a native of Tartary: *here's a Bohemian T. tarries the coming down of thy fat woman,* Wiv.IV, 5, 21. *swifter than arrow from the —'s bow,* Mids. III, 2, 101. *out, tawny T., out!* 263. *stubborn Turks and —s,* Merch. IV, 1, 32. *through flinty —'s bosom,* All's IV, 4, 7. *bearing a —'s painted bow of lath,* Rom. I, 4, 5. *nose of Turk and —'s lips,* Mcb. IV, 1, 29.

2) Tartarus, hell: *he's in T. limbo, worse than hell,* Err. IV, 2, 32. *follow me. To the gates of T., thou most excellent devil of wit,* Tw. II, 5, 225. *he might return to vasty T. back and tell the legions ...,* H5 II, 2, 123.

**Tartly,** sourly, crabbedly: *how t. that gentleman looks! I never can see him but I am heart-burned an hour after,* Ado II, 1, 3.

**Tartness,** sourness, asperity: *they (letters of commendations) cannot be too sweet for the King's t.* All's IV, 3, 96. *the t. of his face sours ripe grapes,* Cor. V, 4, 18.

**Task,** subst. 1) business imposed, work to be done: (the sun) *his day's hot t. hath ended,* Ven. 530. *her husband's shallow tongue in that high t.* (of praising her) *hath done her beauty wrong,* Lucr. 80. *then be this all the t. it* (the tongue) *hath to say,* 1618. *she, that yet her sad t. hath not said,* 1699. *this my mean t.* (of bearing logs) Tp. III, 1, 4. Err. I, 1, 32. Ado I, 1, 301. LLL I, 1, 47 *(keep).* V, 2, 862. John III, 55. R2 II, 2, 145*(undertake).* III, 2, 191. H6A I, 1, 152. H6B I, 1, 9 *(perform).* III, 1, 318. H6C II, 1, 200. III, 2, 52. 53. R3 III, 7, 246 (Ff *work*). Tit. III, 1, 276 *(do).* V, 2, 58 *(do).* V, 3, 150. Oth. IV, 1, 196. IV, 2, 112. Ant. IV, 14, 35 *(do).* Cymb. IV, 2, 260 *(do).* Per. I, 1, 2 *(undertake).*

2) work, labour, toil: *the heavy ploughman snores, all with weary t. fordone,* Mids. V, 381. *why such impress of shipwrights, whose sore t. does not divide the Sunday from the week,* Hml. I, 1, 75.

3) *at t.* = censured, blamed: *you are much more at t. for want of wisdom than praised for harmful mildness,* Lr. I, 4, 366 (Q2 and M. Edd. *attask'd.* cf. the modern *to take to t.*).

**Task,** vb. 1) to impose a business to, to employ,

*to charge: while other sports are —ing of their minds,* Wiv. IV, 6, 30 (cf. *Of*). *to t. the tasker,* LLL II, 20. *some things of weight that t. our thoughts,* H5 I, 2, 6. *therefore let every man now t. his thought, that this fair action may on foot be brought,* 309. *a harvest-man that's —ed to mow or all or lose his hire,* Cor. I, 3, 39. With *to,* = to challenge, to summon, to command to do: *lest the world should t. you to recite what merit lived in me,* Sonn. 72, 1. *to thy strong bidding t. Ariel and all his quality,* Tp. I, 1, 192. *what earthy name to interrogatories can t. the free breath of a sacred king?* John III, 1, 148. *I t. the earth to the like,* R2 IV, 52 (the later Qq *take,* q. v.) *t. me to my word, approve me,* H4A IV, 1, 9 (challenge me to act up to my word).

Hence = to put to the proof, to test, to try: *the gallants shall be —ed,* LLL V, 2, 126. *I am unfortunate in the infirmity, and dare not t. my weakness with any more,* Oth. II, 3, 43.

2) = to tax (as *ask* was sometimes spelt *ax*): *—ed the whole state,* H4A IV, 3, 92. *I t. not you, you elements, with unkindness,* Lr. III, 2, 16 (Ff *tax*).

3) In H4A V, 2, 51 Qq and M. Edd. *how showed his —ing? seemed it in contempt?* i. e. his challenge. The rest of O. Edd. *talking.*

**Tasker,** one that imposes a task: *but now to task the t.* LLL II, 20.

**Tassel,** an ornamental bunch of silk: *thou t. of a prodigal's purse,* Troil. V, 1, 36.

**Tassel-gentle,** properly *tiercel-gentle,* the male goshawk: *for a falconer's voice, to lure this t. back again,* Rom. II, 2, 160. cf. *Tercel.\**

**Taste,** subst. 1) the sense of which are the organs of which are the tongue and the palate, and by which we perceive the relish of things: *what banquet wert thou to the t.* Ven. 445. *nor t., nor smell, desire to be invited,* Sonn. 141, 7. *never meat sweet-savoured in thy t.* Err. II, 2, 119. *love's tongue proves dainty Bacchus gross in t.* LLL IV, 3, 339. *come to my natural t.* Mids. IV, 1, 179. *sans teeth, sans eyes, sans t.* As II, 7, 166. *the ear, t., touch and smell,* Tim. I, 2, 132. *will the cold brook ... caudle thy morning t.* IV, 3, 226. *inventions to delight the t.* Per. I, 4, 40.

Applied to the mind, = intellectual relish and discernment: *which we of t. and feeling are,* LLL IV, 2, 30 (Sir Nathaniel's speech).

2) the particular manner in which this sense is affected; the sensation which a thing produces on the tongue and palate: *that sweet coral mouth, whose precious taste her thirsty lips well knew,* Ven. 543. *the petty streams ... add to his* (the ocean's) *flow, but alter not his t.* Lucr. 651. *his t. delicious, in digestion souring, devours his will,* 699. *thy sugared tongue* (turns) *to bitter wormwood t.* 893. *began to loathe the t. of sweetness,* H4A III, 2, 72. *this bitter t. yield his engrossments to the ending father,* H4B IV, 5, 79. *do you like the t.?* H6A III, 2, 44. *when, both your voices blended, the greatest t. most palates theirs,* Cor. III, 1, 103. *till the fresh t. be taken from that clearness,* Tit. III, 1, 128.

In a moral sense: *thou shalt not know the stained t. of violated troth,* Lucr. 1059. *thou didst rob it* (our house) *of some t. of tediousness,* Merch. II, 3, 3. *this affliction has a t. as sweet as any cordial comfort,* Wint. V, 3, 76. *bitter shame hath spoiled the sweet world's t.* John III, 4, 110. *not palating the t. of her dishonour,* Troil. IV, 1, 59. *whose qualification shall come into no true t. again but by the displanting of Cassio*, Oth. II, 1, 283 (all will be distasted, though they should seem appeased for the moment. Qq *trust*). cf. sub 6 Mcb. V, 5, 9.

3) a flavour of something extraneous to the thing itself; a relish, a tang, a tincture: *nor hath love's mind of any judgment t.* Mids. I, 1, 236. *my father did something smack, something grow to, he had a kind of t.* Merch. II, 2, 19. *my negation hath no t. of madness,* Troil. V, 2, 127. Hence *in some t. =* in some sort: *and in some t. is Lepidus but so,* Caes. IV, 1, 34.

4) the act of trying by the tongue; gustation; metaphorically: *take a t. of my finding him, and relish it with good observance,* As III, 2, 246. *now I begin to relish thy advice, and I will give a t. of it forthwith to Agamemnon,* Troil. I, 3, 389.

5) trial, experiment; proof; specimen: *for a t.* As III, 2, 106. *till that the nobles ... have of their puissance made a little t.* H4B II, 3, 52. *have we not had a t. of his obedience?* Cor. III, 1, 318. *I do beseech you, as in way of t., to give me now a little benefit,* Troil. III, 3, 13 (cf. As III, 2, 106). *give us a t. of your quality,* Hml. II, 2, 452. *he wrote this but as an essay or t. of my virtue,* Lr. I, 2, 47.

6) the act of eating or drinking: *the sweetest honey is loathsome in his own deliciousness and in the t. confounds the appetite,* Rom. II, 6, 13. Metaphorically = the act of feeling or experiencing sth.; a) enjoyment: *but yet be blamed, if thou thyself deceivest by wilful t. of what thyself refusest,* Sonn. 40, 8. *the setting sun, and music at the close, as the last t. of sweets, is sweetest last,* R2 II, 1, 13. b) painful sense, suffering: *that man is not alive might so have tempted him as you have done, without the t. of danger and reproof,* H4A III, 1, 175. *if you give him life, after the t. of much correction,* H5 II, 2, 51. *the t. whereof* (death) *God of his mercy give you patience to endure,* 179. *I have almost forgot the t. of fears,* Mcb. V, 5, 9.

**Taste,** vb. 1) trans. a) to perceive by means of the tongue and palate: *being early plucked, is sour to t.* Ven. 528. *man's hand is not able to t., his tongue to conceive ... what my dream was,* Mids. IV, 1, 218 (Bottom's speech). *things sweet to t. prove in digestion sour,* R2 I, 3, 236. *when that the watery palate —s indeed love's thrice repured nectar,* Troil. III, 2, 22. *when it did t. the wormwood,* Rom. I, 3, 30.

b) to try by the tongue: *who did t. to him?* John V, 6, 28 ("allusion to the royal *taster*, whose office was to taste and declare the goodness of the wine and dishes." Dyce). *t. of it first, as thou art wont to do,* R2 V, 5, 99. *to t. sack and drink it,* H4A II, 4, 501.

c) to try, to prove in general: *some kind of men that put quarrels purposely on others, to t. their valour,* Tw. III, 4, 267. *here the Trojans t. our dearest repute with their finest palate,* Troil. I, 3, 337. *praise us as we are —d, allow us as we prove,* III, 2, 98. Sir Toby, with purposed affectation: *t. your legs, sir; put them to motion,* Tw. III, 1, 87; cf. 91.

d) to have a particular relish as of something extraneous to the thing itself: *you do yet t. some subtilties of the isle,* Tp. V, 123.

e) to eat or drink; properly and figuratively: *shows thee unripe; yet mayst thou well be —d,* Ven. 128. *dainties are made to t.* 164. *the one a palate hath that needs will t.* Compl. 167. *you are sick of self-love and t. with a distempered appetite,* Tw. I, 5, 98. *they might have lived to bear and he to t. their fruits of duty,* R2 III, 4, 62. *gall, worse than gall, the daintiest that they t.* H6B III, 2, 322. *let them not live to t. this land's increase,* R3 V, 5, 38. *this, being smelt, with that part cheers each part; being —d, slays all senses with the heart,* Rom. II, 3, 26. *go in and t. some wine with me,* Caes. II, 2, 126. *I'll prove it on thy heart, ere I t. bread,* Lr. V, 3, 94. *to t. the fruit of yon celestial tree,* Per. I, 1, 21.

With *of*, in a partitive sense: *he shall t. of my bottle,* Tp. II, 2, 77. *will't please you t. of what is here?* III, 3, 42. *t. of these conserves,* Shr. Ind. 2, 3. *that we may t. of your wine,* H6A II, 3, 79. *which she ... shall be assured to t. of too,* Cymb. I, 5, 82. *I'll now t. of thy drug,* IV, 2, 38.

f) to feel, to experience, to undergo, to suffer, to enjoy: *of this book this learning mayst thou t.* Sonn. 77, 4. *so shall I t. at first the very worst of fortune's might,* 90, 11. *—ing it* (grief), *their counsel turns to passion,* Ado V, 1, 22. *I trust to t. of truest Thisby sight,* Mids. V, 280 (Qq take). *never to t. the pleasures of the world,* John IV, 3, 68. *feel want, t. grief,* R2 III, 2, 176. *look to t. the due meet for rebellion,* H4B IV, 2, 116. *not a man of them that we shall take shall t. our mercy,* H5 IV, 7, 68. *never have you —d our reward,* H6A III, 4, 22. *the grief is fine, full, perfect, that I t.* Troil. IV, 4, 3. *and t. Lord Timon's bounty,* Tim. I, 1, 285. *hath put himself from rest and must needs t. his folly,* Lr. II, 4, 294. *all friends shall t. the wages of their virtue, and all foes the cup of their deservings,* V, 3, 302. *if the general camp had —d her sweet body,* Oth. III, 3, 346. *that you have —d her in bed,* Cymb. II, 4, 57. *let them be joyful too, for they shall t. our comfort,* V, 5, 403. *t. gentlemen of all fashions,* Per. IV, 2, 83. And thus even: *let me t. my horse,* H4A IV, 1, 119 (Ff and later Qq take). *I never —d Timon in my life, nor came any of his bounties over me,* Tim. III, 2, 84.

With *of* (partitively): *whose every word deserves to t. of thy most worst,* Wint. III, 2, 180. *how much salt water thrown away in waste, to season love that of it doth not t.* Rom. II, 3, 72. *all that of his bounties t.* Tim. I, 2, 129. V, 1, 61. *the valiant never t. of death but once,* Caes. II, 2, 33. *by —ing of our wrath,* Cymb. V, 5, 308. *those cities that of plenty's cup and her prosperities so largely t.* Per. I, 4, 53.

2) intr. to have a smack, to produce a particular sensation on the palate; properly and figuratively: *since my conversion so sweetly —s,* As IV, 3, 138. *for conspiracy, I know not how it —s,* Wint. III, 2, 73. *how —s it? is it bitter?* H8 II, 3, 89. *she will t. as like this as a crab does to a crab,* Lr. I, 5, 18. With *of*, to denote the particular smack: *every idle, nice and wanton reason shall to the king t. of this action,* H4B IV, 1, 192.

**Tattered** (sometimes *tottered*) torn; ragged: *thy youth's proud livery ... will be a t. weed,* Sonn. 2, 4. *puts apparel on my t. loving,* 26, 11. *from this castle's t. battlements,* R2 III, 3, 52 (Q1. 2 tottered). *a hundred and fifty t. prodigals,* H4A IV, 2, 37 (Qq and earlier Ff tottered). *in t. weeds,* Rom. V, 1, 39. *through t. clothes small vices do appear,* Lr. IV, 6, 168.

**Tattering** (M. Edd.) or **Tottering** (O. Edd.), hanging in rags: *and wound our t. colours clearly up,* John V, 5, 7.

**Tatters** (Ff) or **Totters** (Qq), fluttering rags: *tear a passion to t.* Hml. III, 2, 11.

**Tattle,** 1) to talk idly, to prate: *peace your —ings,* Wiv. IV, 1, 26 (Evans' speech). *like my lady's eldest son, evermore —ing,* Ado II, 1, 11. *let the ladies t. what they please,* Tit. IV, 2, 168,

2) to tell tales, to blab: *she shall not see me, ... she's a very —ing woman,* Wiv. III, 3, 99.

**Taunt,** subst. scoff, insulting mockery: *to stand at the t. of one who makes fritters of English,* Wiv. V, 5, 151. Usually in the plur. *—s:* H6A I, 4, 39. H6C II, 1, 64. II, 6, 66 *(give).* R3 I, 3, 106. Cor. I, 1, 259. Ant. II, 2, 73.

**Taunt,** vb. to scoff, to mock; 1) trans.: *did not her kitchen-maid rail, t. and scorn me?* Err. IV, 4, 77. Mids. IV, 1, 62. Tw. III, 2, 47. H6A III, 2, 54. R3 I, 3, 109 (Qq —*ed, scorned and baited at;* Ff *baited, scorned and stormed at*). III, 1, 134. 153. Ant. I, 2, 111. 2) absol.: *I'll write to him a very —ing letter,* As III, 5, 134. 3) with *at: to t. at slackness,* Ant. III, 7, 28 (cf. R3 I, 3, 109).

**Tauntingly** (O. Edd. *taintingly,* q. v.): Cor. I, 1, 114.

**Taurus,** name of 1) a chain of mountains in Asia: *high —' snow,* Mids. III, 2, 141.

2) the sign of the zodiac next to Aries: Tit. IV, 3, 69. *shall we set about some revels? What shall we do else? were we not born under T.? T.! that's sides and heart. No, sir: it is legs and thighs,* Tw. I, 3, 147 (The medical astrology of that time referred the affections of particular parts of the body to the predominance of particular constellations. According to Hopton's Concordancy of Years, 1615, Taurus 'governeth the neck, throat and voice').

3) a general of Octavius Caesar: Ant. III, 7, 79. III, 8, 1.

**Tavern,** a house where liquors are sold and drinkers entertained: Wiv. V, 5, 167. R2 V, 3, 5. H4A I, 2, 45. 54. II, 2, 59. III, 3, 49. 230. H4B II, 4, 388. H6A III, 1, 148. Rom. III, 1, 6. Lr. I, 4, 266.

**Tavern-bill,** a bill made out in a tavern: Cymb. V, 4, 161.

**Tavern-reckoning,** the same: H4A III, 3, 178.

**Tawdry-lace,** a rustic necklace: Wint. IV, 4, 253 (said to be corrupted from *Saint Audrey,* i. e. Saint Ethelreda, on whose day, the 17th of October, a fair was held in the isle of Ely, where gay toys of all sorts were sold).

**Tawny,** of a yellowish-dark colour: *the ground indeed is t.* Tp. II, 1, 54. *from t. Spain,* LLL I, 1, 174. *out, t. Tartar,* Mids. III, 2, 263. *we shall your t. ground with your red blood discolour,* H5 III, 6, 170. *blue coats to t. coats,* H6A I, 3, 47. 56. III, 1, 74 (the usual livery of ecclesiastical apparitors). *peace, t. slave, half me and half thy dam,* Tit. V, 1, 27. *turn ... their view upon a t. front,* Ant. I, 1, 6. cf. *Orange-tawny.*

**Tawny-finned** (O. Edd. *tawny fine*), having dark fins: *I will betray t. fishes,* Ant. II, 5, 12.

**Tax,** subst. 1) impost, tallage: *the commons hath he pilled with grievous —es,* R2 II, 1, 246.

2) reproach, charge: *t. of impudence,* All's II, 1, 173.

**Tax,** vb. 1) to load with imposts: *I would not t. he needy commons,* H6B III, 1, 116.

2) to load with any charge; to charge, to demand: *t. not so bad a voice to slander music any more than once,* Ado II, 3, 46 (perhaps confounded with *task,* q. v.).

3) to censure, to reproach, to inveigh against:

*thus wisdom wishes to appear most bright when it doth t. itself,* Meas. II, 4, 79. *you t. Signior Benedick too much,* Ado I, 1, 46. *who cries out on pride, that can therein t. any private party?* As II, 7, 71. *my —ing like a wild-goose flies,* 86. *never —ed for speech,* All's I, 1, 77. *they t. our policy,* Troil. I, 3, 197. *both —ing me,* V, 1, 46. *traduced and —ed of other nations,* Hml. I, 4, 18. *she'll t. him home,* III, 3, 29. Followed by *of: my fore-past proofs shall t. my fears of little vanity,* All's V, 3, 122. By *with: to t. him with injustice,* Meas. V, 312. *so many giddy offences as he hath generally —ed their whole sex withal,* As III, 2, 368. *with all the spots o'the world —ed and deboshed,* All's V, 3, 206. *I t. not you, you elements, with unkindness,* Lr. III, 2, 16 (Qq *task*).

**Taxation,** 1) the act of loading with imposts: R2 II, 1, 260. H8 I, 2, 30. 37. 38. 40.

2) demand, claim (cf. *tax* vb. 2): *I bring no overture of war, no t. of homage,* Tw. I, 5, 225.

3) censure, satire, invective: *you'll be whipped for t. one of these days,* As I, 2, 91.

**Teach** (impf. and partic. *taught*) to make to learn, to instruct, to inform, to communicate knowledge or skill; absol.: *to follow mine own —ing,* Merch. I, 2, 19. *the manner of his —ing,* Shr. IV, 2, 5. *a mistress to most that t.* Wint. IV, 4, 594. H4A I, 1, 96. H8 V, 3, 16. 34. Trans.; as object the thing which one is made to learn: *thou didst t. the way,* Lucr. 630. *not learning more than the fond eye doth t.* Merch. II, 9, 27. *t. lavoltas high,* H5 III, 5, 33. *maintain the thing you t.* H6A III, 1, 129. *that we but t. bloody instructions, which, being taught, return,* Mcb. I, 7, 8; cf. Shr. III, 1, 69. Oth. II, 3, 2 (*ourselves* nom. or accus.?). Per. IV, 6, 199 etc. The person instructed as object: *his proceedings t. thee,* Ven. 406. *I have taught him, even as one would say precisely, thus I would t. a dog,* Gent. IV, 4, 5. 6. *my love is thine to t.* Ado I, 1, 293. *to t. a teacher ill beseemeth me,* LLL II, 108. *highly fed and lowly taught,* All's II, 2, 4. Shr. I, 1, 197. Caes. IV, 1, 35. Oth. IV, 2, 111. V, 1, 33 etc. Double accus.: *hath taught them scornful tricks,* Ven. 501. *your love taught it this alchemy,* Sonn. 114, 4. *if I might t. thee wit,* 140, 5. *taught thee one thing or other,* Tp. I, 2, 354. *you taught me language,* 363. *the catch you taught me,* III, 2, 127. Wiv. IV, 1, 67. IV, 5, 61. Meas. II, 4, 19. Err. III, 2, 14. LLL V, 1, 49. V, 2, 99. 431. Mids. I, 1, 152. 195. Merch. III, 1, 74. R2 I, 4, 13. H6C V, 6, 19. Hml. II, 2, 293 etc. The passive with the thing as subject and the person as object: *it hath been taught us from the primal state,* Ant. I, 4, 41. With the person as subject and the thing as object: *they are taught their manage,* As I, 1, 13. *you would be taught your duty,* R3 I, 3, 250. *where I was taught of your chaste daughter the wide difference twixt amorous and villanous,* Cymb. V, 5, 193. The person placed after the thing: *he was a fool that taught them* (these manners) *me,* H4B II, 1, 205. Preceded by *to* in this case: *creatures that by a rule in nature t. the act of order to a peopled kingdom,* H5 I, 2, 188.

Followed by a subordinate clause: *I'll t. you how you shall arraign your conscience,* Meas. II, 3, 21. *t. me how you look, and with what art you sway the motion of Demetrius' heart,* Mids. I, 1, 192. *t. twenty what were good to be done,* Merch. I, 2, 17. IV, 1, 440. As I, 3, 99. Rom. I, 1, 232. Mcb. I, 6, 12. Lr. II, 4, 69. By an infinitive: *those eyes that taught all other eyes to see*, Ven. 952. *t. the fool to speak*, 1146. —*ing decrepit age to tread the measures*, 1148. Lucr. 996. Sonn. 50, 3. 64, 11. 78, 5. 86, 5. 145, 8. Pilgr. 320. Gent. II, 1, 143. 174. II, 6, 8. Wiv. I, 4, 115. II, 2, 214. III, 3, 44. Err. IV, 1, 101. LLL IV, 3, 13. Merch. IV, 1, 439. As I, 1, 32. III, 2, 362. Shr. IV, 5, 79. H6C I, 4, 124. Hml. I, 2, 175 etc. The inf. preceded by *how: thou —est how to make one twain*, Sonn. 39, 13. *I t. thee how to make him seem ...*, 101, 13. Tp. I, 2, 334. II, 1, 222. Merch. III, 2, 10. As III, 2, 388. John V, 2, 88 etc. The inf. without *to: whose own hard dealings —es them suspect the thoughts of others*, Merch. I, 3, 162. *To it* in the place of a preceding infinitive: *I believe you: your honour and your goodness t. me to't*, Per. III, 3, 26 (i. e. to believe you; which in modern English would be: *t. me so*, or *t. me to*).

Sometimes not so much = to make to learn, as to make to know, to tell, to show: —*ing the sheets a whiter hue than white*, Ven. 398. *where is any author in the world —es such beauty as a woman's eye?* LLL IV, 3, 313. *she doth t. the torches to burn bright*, Rom. I, 5, 46 (i. e. she shows the torches, by her own radiance, what it is to burn bright). *he learned to sin, and thou didst t. the way*, Lucr. 630. cf. Meas. II, 4, 19. R2 IV, 301. All's II, 4, 35. John III, 1, 120. *who is the suitor? Shall I t. you to know?* LLL IV, 1, 110 (= shall I tell you?). *to what end, my lord? That you must t. me*, Hml. II, 2, 293.

Sometimes = to induce, to prevail on, to set on to: *him that thou taughtest this ill*, Lucr. 996. *how angerly I taught my brow to frown*, Gent. I, 2, 62. *I could have taught my love to take thy father for mine*, As I, 2, 12. *his false cunning taught him to face me out of his acquaintance*, Tw. V, 91. *if thou ... t. thy hasty spleen to do me shame*, John IV, 3, 97. *they whom youth and ease have taught to glose*, R2 II, 1, 10. *this is his uncle's —ing*, H4A I, 1, 96. *t. not thy lips such scorn*, R3 I, 2, 172. *the bloody proclamation to escape, ... taught me to shift into a madman's rags*, Lr. V, 3, 186. cf. Cor. II, 1, 271 (some M. Edd. *touch*).

**Teacher**, instructor, preceptor: LLL II, 108. H4A III, 1, 265. H8 I, 2, 113. Cymb. III, 4, 87.

**Team**, horses, or things serving in their stead, drawing the same carriage: Ven. 179. Gent. III, 1, 265 (*a t. of horse*). Mids. V, 391. All's I, 3, 48. H4A III, 1, 221. Rom. I, 4, 57 (*a t. of atomies*).

**Tear**, subst. a drop of water secreted by the eye: Ven. 49. 82. 192. 360. 425. 491. 949. 961. 962. 966. 979. 1071 (*salt —s*). 1092. 1176. Lucr. 570. 588. 594. 682 etc. cf. the articles *Drop, Fall, Shed, Salt*. Applied to other fluids in the form of drops: *purple —s* = drops of blood, Ven. 1054. H6C V, 6, 64. *dewy —s* = dew-drops: R3 V, 3, 284.

**Tear**, vb. (impf. *tore*, partic. *torn*) 1) to draw by violence, to pull: *to t. his hair*, Lucr. 981. Ado II, 3, 153. John III, 4, 45. Troil. IV, 2, 113. Rom. III, 3, 68. Lr. III, 1, 7. *stab them, or t. them on thy chariot-wheels*, Tit. V, 2, 47. With adverbs: *that I'll t. away*, Gent. I, 2, 125. *do not t. away thyself from me*, Err. II, 2, 126. *the lioness had torn some flesh away*, As IV, 3, 148. *with their teeth the walls they'll t. down*, H6A I, 2, 40. *the bear tore out his shoulder-bone*, Wint. III, 3, 97. —*ing his country's bowels out*, Cor. V, 3, 102. With prepositions: *from thy cheeks my image thou hast torn*, Lucr. 1762. *will you t. impatient answers from*

*my gentle tongue*, Mids. III, 2, 286. *I tore them* (hairs) *from their bonds*, John III, 4, 70. *from my own windows torn my household coat*, R2 III, 1, 24. *I tore it* (the paper) *from the traitor's bosom*, V, 3, 55. *I will t. the reckoning from his heart*, H4A III, 2, 152. *to t. the garter from thy craven's leg*, H6A IV, 1, 15. *they will by violence t. him from your palace*, H6B III, 2, 246. *t. the crown from the usurper's head*, H6C I, 1, 114. *honour torn from Hector*, Troil. IV, 5, 145. *torn from forth that pretty hollow cage*, Tit. III, 1, 84. *t. the stained skin of my harlot brow*, Err. II, 2, 138 (M. Edd. *off my h. b.*). *him will I t. out of that cruel eye*, Tw. V, 130. *t. the lions out of England's coat*, H6A I, 5, 28. *mandrakes torn out of the earth*, Rom. IV, 3, 47.

2) to pull in pieces, to rend: —*ing of papers*, Compl. 6. *which she tore*, 44; 51; Gent. I, 2, 105; IV, 4, 136; Ado II, 3, 148; LLL IV, 3, 57; 200; Merch. IV, 1, 234; Rom. II, 2, 57; Mcb. III, 2, 49; Lr. V, 3, 157. *when their thundering shock at meeting —s the cloudy cheeks of heaven*, R2 III, 3, 57; *to t. with thunder the wide cheeks o''he war*, Cor. V, 3, 151. *for —ing a poor whore's ruff*, H4B II, 4, 156. *my arms torn and defaced*, H6B IV, 1, 42. *did so set his teeth and t. it* (a butterfly) Cor. I, 3, 70. *though thy tackle's torn*, IV, 5, 67. *t. a passion to tatters*, Hml. III, 2, 11. *a part to t. a cat in*, Mids. I, 2, 32 (proverbial phrase, particularly applied to theatrical ranting). *France should have torn and rent my very heart*, H6B I, 1, 126. *a tempest, which his mortal vessel —s*, Per. IV, 4, 30. *t. me, take me*, Tim. III, 4, 100. *t. him for his bad verses*, Caes. III, 3, 34. *woo't t. thyself*, Hml. V, 1, 298. *to dislocate and t. thy flesh and bones*, Lr. IV, 2, 65. *I will t. thee joint by joint*, Rom. V, 3, 35. *to t. her limb-meal*, Cymb. II, 4, 147. *torn to pieces with a bear*, Wint. V, 2, 68. *to t. us all to pieces*, R2 II, 2, 139. H8 V, 4, 80. Cor. V, 6, 121. Caes. III, 3, 30. Oth. III, 3, 431. Hence = to lacerate, to laniate; to hurt or destroy in a savage manner: *enforced hate ... shall rudely t. thee*, Lucr. 669. *she with her nails her flesh doth t.* 739. *that with my nails her beauty I may t.* 1472. 1564. *through his teeth, as if the name he tore*, 1787; cf. *a —ing groan did break the name of Antony*, Ant. IV, 14, 31. *these hands shall t. her*, Ado IV, 1, 193. *torn with briers*, Mids. III, 2, 443. —*ing the Thracian singer in their rage*, V, 49. *my teeth shall t. the slavish motive of recanting fear*, R2 I, 1, 192. *I could t. her*, H4B II, 4, 167. *did he not straight in pious rage the two delinquents t.* Mcb. III, 6, 12. *as this mouth should t. this hand*, Lr. III, 4, 15.

With an accus. denoting the effect: *these nails may t. a passage through the flinty ribs*, R2 V, 5, 20.

3) to burst, to break: *they seemed almost, with staring on one another, to t. the cases of their eyes*, Wint. V, 2, 14. *patient fools, whose children he hath slain, their base throats t. with giving him glory*, Cor. V, 6, 53. *else would I t. the cave where Echo lies ... with repetition of my Romeo's name*, Rom. II, 2, 162. cf. Ant. IV, 14, 31. = to break, in a moral sense: *new faith torn*, Sonn. 152, 3. *our faith not torn*, LLL IV, 3, 285.

A difficult passage (though not pointed out as such by most commentators): *though you think that all, as you have done, have torn their souls by turning them from us, and we are barren and bereft of friends*, R2 III, 3, 83 (it cannot mean the same as in H6B I, 1,

126. Perhaps = destroyed, doomed to perdition; with a licence accounted for by the consonance with *turning*).

**Tear-distained**, stained by tears: Lucr. 1586.

**Tear-falling**, shedding tears: R3 IV, 2, 66.

**Tearful**, weeping: *t. eyes*, H6C V, 4, 8.

**Tearsheet**, name of a loose girl in H4B II, 1, 176. II, 2, 167. II, 4, 13. 416. H5 II, 1, 81 etc.

**Tear-stained**, stained by tears: H6B II, 4, 16.

**Teat**, the nipple of the female breast: Tit. II, 3, 145. Rom. I, 3, 68.

**Teder**, see *Tether*.

**Tedious**, 1) wearisome, tiresome, too long: Ven. 841. Lucr. 1379. Gent. I, 1, 31. Meas. II, 1, 119. II, 4, 9. Ado III, 5, 20. Mids. II, 2, 112. III, 2, 431. V, 56. 58. 64. Merch. II, 6, 11. II, 7, 77. As III, 2, 19. 163. Shr. III, 2, 107. John III, 4, 108. R2 I, 3, 268. V, 1, 40. V, 2, 26. H4A III, 1, 159. H6A I, 2, 53. IV, 7, 74. H6C III, 1, 9. R3 I, 4, 90. III, 1, 5. III, 2, 6. Rom. III, 2, 28. V, 3, 230. Tim. IV, 3, 374. Hml. II, 2, 223. III, 2, 237. Oth. III, 4, 175. Per. IV, 1, 69. V, 1, 28. *that is the brief and the t. of it*, All's II, 3, 34 (instead of: *the short and the long of it*. Parolles' speech).

2) full of annoyance, odious: *my woes are t., though my words are brief*, Lucr. 1309. *heavy t. penury*, As III, 2, 342. *within me grief hath kept a t. fast*, R2 II, 1, 75. *to sport would be as t. as to work*, H4A I, 2, 229. *I would remove these t. stumbling-stocks*, H6B I, 2, 64. *brief abstract and record of t. days*, R3 IV, 4, 28. *a man's life is a t. one*, Cymb. III, 6, 1. cf. Mids. II, 2, 112. John III, 4, 108.

3) laborious: *can trace me in the t. ways of art*, H4A III, 1, 48. *my brain more busy than the labouring spider weaves t. snares to trap mine enemies*, H6B III, 1, 340. *and in a t. sampler sewed her mind*, Tit. II, 4, 39. *I am in blood stepped in so far that, should I wade no more, returning were as t. as go o'er*, Mcb. III, 4, 138. *it were a t. difficulty to bring them to that prospect*, Oth. III, 3, 397.

Misapplied by Dogberry in Ado III, 5, 23.

**Tediously**, so as to weary; longer or more slowly than is desired: *the cripple tardy-gaited night who, like a foul and ugly witch, doth limp so t. away*, H5 IV Chor. 22. *night hath been too brief. Beshrew the witch! with venomous wights she stays as t. as hell*, Troil. IV, 2, 13 (Ff *hideously*).

**Tediousness**, tiresomeness, irksomeness, prolixity: Ado III, 5, 26. Merch. II, 3, 3. R2 II, 3, 12. Hml. II, 2, 91.

**Teem**, 1) trans. to bring forth: *the even mead ... conceives by idleness and nothing —s but hateful docks*, H5 V, 2, 51. *whose (nature's) womb and breast —s and feeds all*, Tim. IV, 3, 179. *each minute —s a new one* (grief) Mcb. IV, 3, 176.

2) intr. to bear fruit or children, to be fruitful: *the —ing autumn, big with rich increase*, Sonn. 97, 6. *—ing foison*, Meas. I, 4, 43. *this —ing womb of royal kings*, R2 II, 1, 51. *is not my —ing date drunk up with time*, V, 2, 91. *the —ing earth*, H4A III, 1, 28. *if she must t., create her child of spleen*, Lr. I, 4, 303. Followed by *with*, = a) to conceive by: *if that the earth could t. with woman's tears, each drop she falls would prove a crocodile*, Oth. IV, 1, 256. b) to be big with, to bring forth: *t. with new monsters*, Tim. IV, 3, 190.

**Teen**, vexation, pain, grief: *my face is full of shame, my heart of t.* Ven. 808. *or my affection put to the smallest t.* Compl. 192. *to think o'the t. that I have turned you to*, Tp. I, 2, 64. *of sighs, of groans, of sorrow and of t.* LLL IV, 3, 164. *each hour's joy wrecked with a week of t.* R3 IV, 1, 97. *I'll lay fourteen of my teeth, — and yet, to my t. be it spoken, I have but four*, Rom. I, 3, 13.

**Telamon**, the father of Ajax, confounded with his son (in consequence of the latter being surnamed *Telamonius*): *he is more mad than T. for his shield*, Ant. IV, 13, 2 ("i. e. for the armour of Achilles, the most valuable part of which was the shield." Steevens).

**Telamonius**, son of Telamon: *now, like Ajax T., on sheep or oxen could I spend my fury*, H6B V, 1, 26.

**Tell** (impf. and partic. *told*) 1) to count, to number: *sometime he trots, as if he told the steps*, Ven. 277. *are they* (ten hundred touches) *not quickly told?* 520. *t. o'er the sad account of fore-bemoaned moan*, Sonn. 30, 10. *age in love loves not to have years told*, 138, 12. *one: t.* Tp. II, 1, 15. *they'll t. the clock to any business*, 289. *how many is one thrice told?* LLL I, 2, 41. *the measure then of one is easily told*, V, 2, 190. *you may t. every finger I have with my ribs*, Merch. II, 2, 114 (Launcelot's speech). *faster than you'll t. money*, Wint. IV, 4, 185. *you t. a pedigree of threescore and two years*, H6C III, 3, 92. *shall we* (instead of numbering Ave-Maries) *on the helmets of our foes t. our devotion?* II, 1, 164. *while one would t. twenty*, R3 I, 4, 122. *t. the clock there*, V, 3, 276. *and front but in that file where others t. steps with me*, H8 I, 2, 43. *longer than I have time to t. his years*, II, 1, 91. *t. out my blood*, Tim. III, 4, 95. *while they have told their money*, III, 5, 107. *while one with moderate haste might t. a hundred*, Hml. I, 2, 238. *as many dolours as thou canst t. in a year*, Lr. II, 4, 55. *when usurers t. their gold i' the field*, III, 2, 89. cf. the following phrases: *when I do count the clock that —s the time*, Sonn. 12, 1. *the iron tongue of midnight hath told twelve*, Mids. V, 370. *the sound that —s what hour it is*, R2 V, 5, 55. *till the bell have told eleven*, Oth. II, 2, 11. *To t. over* = to reckon up, to sum up: *but all the story of the night told over, and all their minds transfigured so together, more witnesseth than fancy's images*, Mids. V, 23. *t. o'er your woes again*, R3 IV, 4, 39. *what damned minutes —s he o'er who dotes, yet doubts*, Oth. III, 3, 169.

2) to narrate: *I'll t. you my dream*, Wiv. III, 3, 171. *t. Mistress Anne the jest, how my father stole two geese*, III, 4, 40. *I t. this tale vilely*, Ado III, 3, 157. *to t. sad stories*, Err. I, 1, 121. *t. her the process of Antonio's end*, Merch. IV, 1, 274. 276. *t. us the manner of the wrestling*, As I, 2, 118. *to t. this story*, IV, 3, 154. *t. us a tale*, Wint. II, 1, 23. *we'll t. tales*, R2 III, 4, 10. *a tale told by an idiot*, Mcb. V, 5, 27 etc.

3) to communicate, to inform, to show by words: *thou told'st me thou wouldst hunt the boar*, Ven. 614. *shall t. my loving tale*, Lucr. 486. *that we before have heard them told*, Sonn. 123, 8. *t. your piteous heart there's no harm done*, Tp. I, 2, 14. 34. 43. 100 (see *Into*. As for the construction, cf. Wint. I, 2, 337: *and thereby for sealing the injury* etc. = for sealing thereby). 117. 260. III, 2, 48. Gent. I, 3, 1. II, 4, 87. II, 7, 5. Wiv. I, 1, 137. III, 4, 9. IV, 4, 60. Err. IV,

3, 89 etc. etc. *to t. fortune*, Sonn. 14, 5. Ant. I, 2, 43. 55. *to t. a lie*, Tp. I, 2, 248. III, 2, 32. Wiv. I, 1, 69. Ado IV, 1, 324. Merch. III, 4, 69 etc. *to t. one's mind*, Gent. I, 1, 148. Err. II, 1, 48 (cf. *Mind*). *to t. tales* (see *Tale*), Tp. V, 129. Meas. IV, 3, 175. Tw. II, 1, 43 etc. cf. Sonn. 76, 7. 89, 12. R3 I, 3, 113 (*threat you me with —ing of the king?* a construction only possible in the supposition, that in the phrase *to tell the king* the latter word is accus., not dative). *he —s you rightly. Ye t. me what you wish for both, my ruin*, H8 III, 1, 97. 98 (i. e. he counsels you well). With *of: —s him of trophies*, Ven. 1013. *not to t. of good or evil luck*, Sonn. 14, 3. Tp. III, 3, 96. IV, 168. Wiv. III, 3, 31. Meas. II, 4, 186. Err. II, 2, 18. Mids. III, 2, 310. As I, 2, 243. John II, 348. R2 V, 3, 1. H4A V, 2, 37. Ant. II, 2, 78 (*I told him of myself*, i. e. I gave him an account of my manner of living). III, 6, 45 etc. *To* before the person: *nor can I fortune to brief minutes tell*, Sonn. 14, 5. *she —s to your highness simple truth*, Err. V, 211. *I heard him t. it to one of his company*, H4A II, 1, 62. *I could t. to thee, as to one it pleases me to call my friend*, H4B II, 2, 44. *t. this heavy message to the king*, H6B III, 2, 379. *no jocund health ... but the great cannon to the clouds shall t.* Hml. I, 2, 126. The person subject of the passive: *I was told you were in a consumption*, Ado V, 4, 96. *I have been told so of many*, As III, 2, 361. *has been told so*, Tw. I, 5, 156. *he must be told on't*, Wint. II, 2, 31. John IV, 2, 114. H5 III, 7, 113 (*I was told that*). Troil. II, 3, 88. Tim. IV, 3, 214. The thing subject of the passive: *my tale is told*, LLL V, 2, 729. Merch. IV, 1, 276. *'twas told me you were rough*, Shr. II, 245. Wint. III, 3, 121. *were it but told you*, V, 3, 116. *the news was told*, H4A I, 1, 58. *this shall be told our lovers*, Troil. I, 3, 284. *two truths are told*, Mcb. I, 3, 127. *'tis told me he hath oft given private time to you*, Hml. I, 3, 91. *when 'tis told*, Lr. V, 3, 182. *our ills told us*, Ant. I, 2, 114. *what by me is told*, Per. III Prol. 57.

Peculiar phrases: a) *I can t. you* = you shall see; trust me; you may rely on it; take warning: *this will shake your shaking, I can tell you*, Tp. II, 2, 88. *there are pretty orders beginning, I can t. you*, Meas. II, 1, 250. *you will take little delight in it, I can t. you*, As I, 2, 169. *'tis in request, I can t. you*, Wint. IV, 4, 297. *it jumps with my humour, ... I can t. you*, H4A I, 2, 79. *you shall find no boys' play there, I can t. you*, V, 4, 76. *he'll lay about him to-day, I can t. them that*, Troil. I, 2, 58. *let them take heed of Troilus, I can t. them that too*, 61. *I can t. you*, III, 2 120. Cor. IV, 3, 26. Similarly: *you are a churchman, or, I'll t. you, cardinal, I should judge now unhappily*, H8 I, 4, 88. *when his disguise and he is parted, t. me what a sprat you shall find him*, All's III, 6, 113. b) *I cannot t.* = I don't know what to say or what to do: *I cannot t.; I make it breed as fast*, Merch. I, 3, 97. *good Grumio, fetch it me. I cannot t.; I fear 'tis choleric*, Shr. IV, 3, 22. *I cannot t., but I had as lief take her dowry with this condition*, I, 1, 135. IV, 4, 91. *and yet, in some respects, I grant I cannot go: I cannot t.; virtue is of so little regard*, H4B I, 2, 190. *she did you wrong, for you were troth-plight to her. I cannot t.: things must be as they may*, H5 II, 1, 22. *I cannot t., the world is grown so bad*, R3 I, 3, 70. *I cannot t.; we must proceed as we do find the people*, Cor. V, 6, 15. c) *when? can you tell?* an expression of contemptuous defiance or refusal: *have at

you with a proverb — shall I set in my staff? Have at you with another; that's — when? can you tell?* Err. III, 1, 52. *lend me thine. Ay, when? canst t.?* H4A II, 1, 43. cf. *we have French quarrels enow, if you could t. how to reckon*, H5 IV, 1, 241. *proud and ambitious tribune, canst thou t.?* Tit. I, 201. d) *t. not me* = go to; nonsense! *t. not me; when the butt is out, we will drink water*, Tp. III, 2, 1. *but t. not me: I know, Antonio is sad to think upon his merchandise*, Merch. I, 1, 39. *t. not me of mercy*, III, 3, 1. *tilly-fally, Sir John, ne'er t. me*, H4B II, 4, 90. *tush! never t. me; I take it much unkindly*, Oth. I, 1, 1. Cor. IV, 6, 55.

4) to say, to speak: *wilt thou make the match? He —s her, no*, Ven. 587. *more I could t., but more I dare not say*, 805. *as if they heard the woeful words she told*, 1126 (rhyming). *marking what he —s with trembling fear, as fowl hear falcon's bells*, Lucr. 510 (rhyming). *remember what I told you: if the prince do solicit you, you know your answer*, Ado II, 1, 69. *but t. me then, 'tis so*, All's I, 3, 182. *my dear dear love to your proceeding bids me t. you this*, Caes. II, 2, 103 (i. e. my love bids me say this to, i. e. with respect to, your proceeding). *to t. true, to t. truly, to t. truth, to t. plain* etc. (cf. the resp. words) = to speak truth etc.: Gent. II, 5, 35. Wiv. III, 4, 11. LLL IV, 3, 272. Mids. III, 2, 68. All's I, 3, 181. 191. Tw. IV, 2, 121. H4A III, 1, 59 etc. — In Cor. II, 1, 67 O. Edd. *t. you have.*

5) to explain, to solve: *whoso asked her for his wife, his riddle told not, lost his life*, Per. Prol. 38.

**Teller**, one who tells or communicates: *the nature of bad news infects the t.* Ant. I, 2, 99.

**Tell-tale**, one who gives mischievous information about the concerns of other persons: Gent. I, 2, 133. Wiv. I, 4, 12. Merch. V, 123. H4B IV, 1, 202. Caes. I, 3, 117. Adjectively: *the t. day*, Lucr. 806. *these t. women*, R3 IV, 4, 149.

**Tellus**, the earth, personified: *Neptune's salt wash and —' orbed ground*, Hml. III, 2, 166. *I will rob T. of her weed*, Per. IV, 1, 14.

**Temnest**, reading of Qq (Ff om.) in Lr. II, 2, 150; M. Edd. *contemned'st.*

**Temper**, subst. 1) the state of a metal as to its hardness; the quality of a sword: *to stain the t. of my knightly sword*, R2 IV, 29. *a sword, whose t. I intend to stain with the best blood*, H4A V, 2, 94. *which (blade) bears the better t.* H6A II, 4, 13. *sword, hold thy t.* H6B V, 2, 70. *it is a sword of Spain, the ice-brook's t.* Oth. V, 2, 253.

2) disposition, constitution, temperament: *never could the strumpet ... once stir my t.* Meas. II, 2, 185. *a hot t. leaps o'er a cold decree*, Merch. I, 2, 20. *you know your father's t.* Wint. IV, 4, 478. *a noble t. dost thou show in this*, John V, 2, 40. *he holds your t. in a high respect*, H4A III, 1, 170. *what man of good t. would endure this tempest of exclamation?* H4B II, 1, 87. *his t. must be well observed*, IV, 4, 36. *O that the living Harry had the t. of him*, V, 2, 15. *if thou canst love a fellow of this t.* H5 V, 2, 153. *hearts of most hard t. melt and lament for her*, H8 II, 3, 11. *you have a gentle, noble t.* III, 1, 165. *in whom the —s and the minds of all should be shut up*, Troil. I, 3, 57. *you keep a constant t.* Cor. V, 2, 100. *thy beauty hath made me effeminate and in my t. softened valour's steel*, Rom. III, 1, 120. *his comfortable t. hath forsook him*, Tim. III, 4, 71. *a man of such a feeble t.* Caes. I, 2, 129. *our hearts of brothers' t.* III, 1, 175. *that dauntless t. of

*his mind*, Mcb. III, 1, 52. *after the noble t. of your lordship*, Cymb. II, 3, 6.

Emphatically, = wonted disposition, freedom from excess or extravagance, equanimity: *keep me in t.: I would not be mad*, Lr. I, 5, 51 (cf. *Distemper*). *his captain's heart ... reneges all t.* Ant. I, 1, 8.

**Temper**, vb. 1) trans. to bring to a proper or desired state or quality: *lack of —ed judgment*, Meas. V, 478. *never durst poet touch a pen to write until his ink were —ed with love's sighs*, LLL IV, 3, 347. Particular significations: a) to compound, to mix: *the poison of that lies in you to t.* Ado II, 2, 21. *—ing extremities with extreme sweet*, Rom. II Chor. 14. *if you could find out a man to bear a poison, I would t. it*, III, 5, 98. *it is a poison —ed by himself*, Hml. V, 2, 339. *to t. poisons for her*, Cymb. V, 5, 250.

b) to wet, to moisten (dry things): *the kerns of Ireland are in arms and t. clay with blood of Englishmen*, H6B III, 1, 311. *and cast you (the eyes) with the waters that you lose, to t. clay*, Lr. I, 4, 326. *let me go grind their bones to powder small and with this hateful liquor t. it*, Tit. V, 2, 200 (or = mix it).

c) to warm: *what wax so frozen but dissolves with —ing?* Ven. 565.

d) to make hard by cooling: *the elements, of whom your swords are —ed*, Tp. III, 3, 62 (or = compounded?). cf. *strong-tempered* in Ven. 111, and *mistempered* in Rom. I, 1, 94.

e) to fashion, to mould, to dispose: *where you may t. her by your persuasion to hate young Valentine*, Gent. III, 2, 64. *he (the devil) that —ed thee bade thee stand up, gave thee no instance why thou shouldst do treason*, H5 II, 2, 118. *'tis she that —s him to this extremity*, R3 I, 1, 65 (Ff *tempts*). *and t. him with all the art I have, to pluck proud Lucius from the warlike Goths*, Tit. IV, 4, 109.

The partic. *—ed*, adjectively, = 1) disposed: *when you are better —ed to attend*, H4A I, 3, 235. *when was my lord so much ungently —ed, to stop his ears against admonishment?* Troil. V, 3, 1. *when grief and blood ill —ed vexeth him*, Caes. IV, 3, 115. 116. 2) having a certain state or quality; conditioned: *if the truth of thy love to me were so righteously —ed as mine is to thee*, As I, 2, 14. *took fire and heat away from the best —ed courage of his troops*, H4B I, 1, 115. *were your days as green as Ajax' and your brain so —ed*, Troil. II, 3, 265. *I thought thy disposition better —ed*, Rom. III, 3, 115.

2) intr. to have or get a proper or desired state or quality: *I have him already —ing between my finger and my thumb, and shortly will I seal with him*, H4B IV, 3, 140 (becoming warm and soft like wax). *few men rightly t. with the stars*, H6C IV, 6, 29 (act and think in conformity with their fortune). cf. *untempering* in H5 V, 2, 241.

**Temperality**, Mrs Quickly's word for temper: H4B II, 4, 25.

**Temperance**, 1) agreeable temperature, mild climate: *it (the island) must needs be of subtle, tender and delicate t.* Tp. II, 1, 42.

2) moderation; calmness: *a gentleman of all t.* Meas. III, 2, 251. *are you chafed? ask God for t.* H8 I, 1, 124. *being once chafed, he cannot be reined again to t.* Cor. III, 3, 28. *justice, verity, t., stableness*, Mcb. IV, 3, 92. *in the whirlwind of passion you must acquire and beget a t.* Hml. III, 2, 8. *I doubt not of his t.* Lr.

IV, 7, 24 (cf. *Distemperance*). *O t., lady*, Ant. **v**, 2, 48.

3) chastity: *thou makest the vestal violate her oath; thou blowest the fire when t. is thawed*, Lucr. 884. *though you can guess what t. should be, you know not what it is*, Ant. III, 13, 121.

4) female name: *T. was a delicate wench*, Tp. II, 1, 43 (Taylor: *though bad they be, they will not bate an ace to be called Prudence, Temp'rance, Faith, or Grace*).

**Temperate**, 1) of a mild temperature: *shall I compare thee to a summer's day? thou art more lovely and more t.* Sonn. 18, 2. cf. H5 III, 3, 30.

2) moderate, calm: *peace, lady! pause, or be more t.* John II, 195. *such t. order in so fierce a cause*, III, 4, 12. *my blood hath been too cold and t.* H4A I, 3, 1. *whiles yet the cool and t. wind of grace o'erblows the ... clouds*, H5 III, 3, 30. *there was more t. fire under the pot of her eyes*, Troil. I, 2, 160. *who can be ... t. and furious in a moment*, Mcb. II, 3, 114.

3) chaste: *come, t. nymphs*, Tp. IV, 132. *she is not hot, but t. as the morn*, Shr. II, 296.

**Temperately**, moderately, calmly: Cor. II, 1, 240. III, 1, 219. III, 3, 67. Hml. III, 4, 140.

**Tempest**, a violent storm: Ven. 238. 454. 800. Lucr. 1788. Sonn. 116, 6. Tp. I, 2, 194. V, 6. 153. Wiv. II, 1, 64. V, 5, 23. Mids. I, 1, 131 (*the t. of my eyes*, i. e. tears). Tw. III, 4, 419. John III, 4, 1. IV, 3, 156. V, 1, 17. V, 2, 50. R2 I, 3, 187. II, 1, 263. III, 3, 46. H4A V, 1, 6. H4B II, 1, 87. II, 4, 392. H5 II, 4, 99. H6B III, 1, 351. III, 2, 102. 176. IV, 9, 32. V, 1, 197. H6C II, 5, 86. V, 6, 46. R3 I, 4, 44. IV, 4, 523. H8 I, 1, 92. IV, 1, 72 (*in a stiff t.*). Troil. I, 3, 26. Tit. I, 458 (*dies in t. of thy angry frown*). IV, 2, 160. Caes. I, 3, 5. 10. Hml. III, 2, 7. Lr. III, 2, 62. III, 4, 12. 24. Oth. II, 1, 21. 34. 68. 187. Ant. I, 2, 154. Per. I, 2, 98. III Prol. 48. IV, 1, 19. IV, 4, 30. V, 3, 33.

**Tempest-dropping-fire**, reading of O. Edd. in Caes. I, 3, 10; M. Edd. *tempest dropping fire*; perhaps *tempest-dropping fire*, i. e. fire dropping with the fury of a tempest.

**Tempest-tossed**, tossed or thrown about by a tempest: Rom. III, 5, 138. Mcb. I, 3, 25.

**Tempestuous**, blowing with violence: *t. gusts*, H6A V, 5. Tit. V, 3, 69.

**Temple**, 1) an edifice appropriated to public worship: Tp. IV, 153. Ado III, 3, 172. Mids. II, 1, 238. IV, 1, 185. 202. IV, 2, 16. Merch. II, 1, 44. As III, 3, 50. Wint. II, 1, 183. III, 1, 2. H6A II, 2, 12. Cor. III, 3, 36. IV, 6, 85. V, 3, 67. 207. Cymb. V, 4, 106. V, 5, 398. 482. Per. III, 4, 13. V, 1, 241. V, 2, 17. V, 3, 25. Used of man and of the human body as the habitation of the soul: Lucr. 719. 1172. Tp. I, 2, 457. Tim. V, 1, 51. Mcb. II, 3, 73. Hml. I, 3, 12. Cymb. II, 1, 69. IV, 2, 55. V, 5, 220.

2) name of the two inns of court in London: H6A II, 5, 19. *T. garden*, H6A II, 4, 125. *T. hall*, H4A III, 3, 223. H6A II, 4, 3.

**Temple**, the upper part of the sides of the head where the pulse is felt: *lays his finger on his t.* H8 III, 2, 115. Plur. *—s*: Mids. IV, 1, 56. Merch. I, 1, 170. John II, 108. R2 III, 2, 161. H6A V, 4, 134. H6C I, 4, 104. R3 IV, 4, 383. V, 5, 5. Tit. II, 3, 62. Oth. IV, 1, 53.

**Temple-garden**, see *Temple*.

**Temple-hall**, see *Temple*.

**Temple-haunting**, resorting to, and dwelling about, temples: *the t. martlet*, Mcb. I, 6, 4.

**Temporal**, 1) pertaining to this life or this world, not spiritual, not eternal: *my library was dukedom large enough: of t. royalties he thinks me now incapable*, Tp. I, 2, 110. *whose minds are dedicate to nothing t.* Meas. II, 2, 155. *his sceptre shews the force of t. power*, Merch. IV, 1, 190. *is this an hour for t. affairs?* H8 II, 2, 73. *much better she ne'er had known pomp: though 't be t., yet if that quarrel fortune do divorce it from the bearer, 'tis a sufferance panging*, II, 3, 13. *so children t. fathers do appease; gods are more full of mercy*, Cymb. V, 4, 12.
2) secular, not ecclesiastical: *all the t. lands which men devout by testament have given to the church*, H5 I, 1, 9.

**Temporary**, temporal, respecting things not spiritual: *I know him* (Friar Lodowick) *for a man divine and holy; not scurvy, nor a t. meddler*, Meas. V, 145 (meddling with things which do not concern his spiritual profession. Henley: one who introduces himself, as often as he can find opportunity, into other men's concerns)

**Temporize**, to come to terms, to compromise: *thou wilt quake for this shortly. I look for an earthquake too, then. Well, you will t. with the hours*, Ado I, 1, 276. *the Dauphin is too wilful-opposite and will not t. with my entreaties*, John V, 2, 125. *if I could t. with my affection, or brew it to a weak and colder palate, the like allayment could I give my grief*, Troil. IV, 4, 6. *all's well, and might have been much better, if he could have —d*, Cor. IV, 6, 17.

**Temporizer**, one who seeks to come to terms with anybody and anything: *a mindless slave, or else a hovering t., that canst with thine eyes at once see good and evil, inclining to them both*, Wint. I, 2, 302.

**Tempt**, 1) as a vox media, a) when a person is object, = to call on, to invite, to induce: *who but today hammered of this design, but durst not t. a minister of honour*, Wint. II, 2, 50. *withhold thine indignation, mighty heaven, and t. us not to bear above our power*, John V, 6, 38. *how often have I —ed Suffolk's tongue ... to sit and witch me*, H6B III, 2, 114. *who —ed me to walk upon the hatches*, R3 I, 4, 12. *t. him with speed aboard*, Hml. IV, 3, 56. b) when a thing is object, = to try, to risk, to venture on: *nor t. the danger of my true defence*, John IV, 3, 84. *let grow thy sinews till their knots be strong, and t. not yet the brushes of the war*, Troil. V, 3, 34. *when we will t. the frailty of our powers*, IV, 4, 98. *and t. the rheumy and unpurged air to ·add unto his sickness*, Caes. II, 1, 266.
2) to try to seduce, to entice; absol.: *thy —ing lip*, Ven. 127. *the —ing tune*, 778. *now, to t., all liberty procured*, Compl. 252. *nor doth she t.* Meas. II, 2, 165. LLL IV, 3, 257. Mids. III, 2, 140. Shr. Ind. 1, 118. Troil. IV, 4, 93. Trans.: Compl. 251. Gent. II, 6, 8. Meas. II, 1, 17. II, 2, 163. Err. IV, 2, 1. 13. IV, 3, 48. Ado IV, 1, 53. LLL I, 2, 179. V, 2, 322. Merch. II, 2, 3. John III, 1, 208. R3 IV, 4, 418. 419. Troil. IV, 4, 98. Cor. V, 3, 20. Lr. IV, 6, 222. Oth. IV, 1, 8. With prepositions following, = to seduce: *my female evil —eth my better angel from my side*, Sonn. 144, 6. *his eye unto a greater uproar —s his veins*, Lucr. 427. *thy beauty —ing her to thee*, Sonn. 41, 13. *mine ear hath —ed judgment to desire*, H6C III, 3, 133. *'tis she that —s him to this harsh extremity*, R3 I, 1, 65 (Q1

*tempers him to this extremity). whom corrupting gold would t. unto a close exploit of death*, IV, 2, 35. *gold will t. him to any thing*, 39. *t. me no more to folly*, Troil. V, 2, 18. *let the bloat king t. you again to bed*, Hml. III, 4, 182. *if it t. you toward the flood*, I, 4, 69.
3) to provoke; to defy: *t. not too much the hatred of my spirit*, Mids. II, 1, 211. *do not t. my misery*, Tw. III, 4, 383. *if thou darest t. me further, draw thy sword*, IV, 1, 45. *you t. him overmuch*, Wint. V, 1, 73. *that man is not alive might so have —ed him*, H4A III, 1, 174. *you t. the fury of my three attendants*, H6A IV, 2, 10. *in —ing of your patience*, H8 I, 2, 55. *he —s judgment*, Troil. V, 7, 22. *t. not a desperate man*, Rom. V, 3, 59. *t. the heavens*, Caes. I, 3, 53. *t. me no further*, IV, 3, 36. 59. 62. *they t. heaven*, Oth. IV, 1, 8. *t. him not so too far*, Ant. I, 3, 11.

**Temptation**, motive to ill, enticement: Sonn. 41, 4. 94, 4. Meas. II, 2, 158. 182. Merch. I, 2, 106. Wint. I, 2, 77.

**Tempter**, one who entices to evil: Compl. 318. Meas. II, 2, 163. H6A I, 2, 123. Cymb. II, 2, 9.

**Ten**, twice five: Ven. 22. 519 (*t. hundred*). 1008. Tp. I, 1, 61. II, 1, 247. II, 2, 34. III, 1, 8. Gent. IV, 1, 2. IV, 4, 62. Wiv. I, 3, 8. II, 2, 86. III, 5, 54. V, 2, 11. Meas. I, 2, 8 (*the t. Commandments*). II, 1, 252. 254. II, 4, 128. V, 1, 42. 45 etc. etc. *one to t.* (cf. *To*): H6A I, 2, 34. *t. to one*: H6A IV, 1, 21. H6C I, 2, 75. V, 4, 60. *'tis t. to one =* it is very probable: Shr. V, 2, 62. H4B I, 1, 182. H6A V, 4, 157. H6B II, 1, 4. H6C V, 1, 46. H8 Epil. 1. cf. Ado I, 3, 171. *by these t. bones!* (i. e. the ten fingers) H6B I, 3, 193. *I'ld set my t. commandments in your face*, 145 (i. e. the ten fingers with their nails). *as fit as t. groats is for the hand of an attorney*, All's II, 2, 22 (the customary fee to an attorney). *hail, royal prince! Thanks, noble peer; the cheapest of us is ten groats too dear*, R2 V, 5, 72 (cf. *Noble* and *Royal*). Substantively: *the value of one t.* Troil. II, 2, 23. *thou shalt have more than two —s to a score*, Lr. I, 4, 140. Denoting a playing-card with ten spots: H6C V, 1, 43. cf. Shr. II, 407.

**Tenable**, probably = capable to be retained, not let out, not uttered (cf. *Intenible*). *if you have hitherto concealed this sight, let it be t. in your silence still*, Hml. I, 2, 248 (Ff *treble*).

**Tenant**, 1) one who holds of another, vassal; servant: *those proud lords, to blame, make weak-made women —s to their shame*, Lucr. 1260. *a quest of thoughts, all —s to the heart*, Sonn. 46, 10. *you may have drawn together your —s, friends and neighbouring gentlemen*, H4A III, 1, 90. *where are thy —s and thy followers?* R3 IV, 4, 481. *you were the duke's surveyor, and lost your office on the complaint o'the —s*, H8 I, 2, 173. *I have been your t., and your father's t., these fourscore years*, Lr. IV, 1, 14.
2) dweller, inhabitant: *that frame outlives a thousand —s*, Hml. V, 1, 50.

**Tenantius**, name of a king of ancient Britain: Cymb. I, 1, 31. V, 4, 73.

**Tenantless**, unoccupied: *leave not the mansion so long t.* Gent. V, 4, 8. *the graves stood t.* Hml. I, 1, 115.

**Tench**, the fish Cyprinus tinca: *I am stung like a t.* H4A II, 1, 17.

**Tend**, 1) to have a tendency, to move in a certain direction: *his affections do not that way t.* Hml. III, 1, 170. With *to,* = to be directed to, to aim at, to contribute to: *to no other pass my verses t. than of your* *graces and your gifts to tell*, Sonn. 103, 11. *the diamond, 'twas beautiful and hard, whereto his invised properties did t.* Compl. 212. *whereto —s all this?* Mids. III, 2, 256. *where doing —s to ill*, John III, 1, 272. *—s that thou wouldst speak to the Duke of Hereford?* R2 II, 1, 232. *thoughts —ing to ambition*, V, 5, 18. 23. *any thing that —s to laughter*, H4B I, 2, 9. *any choice —s to God's glory*, H6A V, 1, 27. *—ing to the good of their adversaries*, Cor. IV, 3, 44. *that our request did t. to save the Romans*, V, 3, 132. *writings all —ing to the great opinion*, Caes. I, 2, 322. *his speech —ing to Caesar's glories*, III, 2, 63. *whereto we see in all things nature —s*, Oth. III, 3, 231. *that you in all obey her, save when command to your dismission —s*, Cymb. II, 3, 57. *—s to vice*, II, 5, 21.

2) = to attend (q. v.); a) to be ready for service, to be in waiting: *the time invites you; go; your servants t.* Hml. I, 3, 83. *the associates t., and every thing is bent for England*, IV, 3, 47. *give him —ing* (= attendance) Mcb. I, 5, 38.

b) with *on*, = to wait on: *millions of strange shadows on you t.* Sonn. 53, 2. *what should I do but t. upon the hours and times of your desire?* 57, 1. *and t. on no man's business*, Ado I, 3, 17. *the summer still doth t. upon my state*, Mids. III, 1, 158. *from whence thou camest, how —ed on*, All's II, 1, 210. *a lord that twenty such rude boys might t. upon*, III, 2, 84. *three months this youth hath —ed upon me*, Tw. V, 102. *threefold vengeance t. upon your steps*, H6B III, 2, 304. *let us address to t. on Hector's heels*, Troil. IV, 4, 148. *Ajax commands the guard to t. on you*, V, 1, 79. *you spirits that t. on mortal thoughts*, Mcb. I, 5, 42. *hitherto doth love on fortune t.* Hml. III, 2, 216. *the knights that t. upon my father*, Lr. II, 1, 97.

c) with *to*, = to be attentive to, to listen to: *t. to the master's whistle*, Tp. I, 1, 8.

d) trans. 1) to attend, to wait on, to serve: *four or five women that —ed me*, Tp. I, 2, 47. *in a house where twice so many have a command to t. you*, Lr. II, 4, 266. *t. me to-night*, Ant. IV, 2, 24. 32. 2) to do homage: *worthier than himself here t. the savage strangeness he puts on*, Troil. II, 3, 135. *her gentlewomen ... —ed her i'the eyes*, Ant. II, 2, 212. 3) to guard, to take care of: *whc didst thou leave to t. his majesty?* John V, 6, 32. *cherish Duke Humphrey's deeds, while they do t. the profit of the land*, H6B I, 1, 204. *so many hours must I t. my flock*, H6C II, 5, 31. *good angels t. thee!* R3 IV, 1, 93 (Qq *guard*). 4) to accompany: *they* (cares) *t. the crown*, R2 IV, 199. 5) to expect? *—s service*, Ff in Lr. II, 4, 103.

**Tendance**, attendance; 1) waiting on, attention, care: *subdues and properties to his love and t. all sorts of hearts*, Tim. I, 1, 57. *she purposed, by watching, weeping, t., kissing, to o'ercome you with her show*, Cymb. V, 5, 53. With *to: nature does require her times of preservation, which perforce I, her frail son, ... must give my t. to*, H8 III, 2, 149.

2) persons attending: *his lobbies fill with t.* Tim. I, 1, 80.

**Tender**, subst. 1) an offer for acceptance: *such welcome as honour without breach of honour may make t. of to thy true worthiness*, LLL II, 171. *which* (debt) *now in some slight measure it* (sleep) *will pay, if for his t. here I make some stay*, Mids. III, 2, 87. *the like t. of our love we make*, John V, 7, 106. *and then to have a wretched puling fool ... in her fortune's t., to*

*answer 'I'll not wed'*, Rom. III, 5, 186. *which is material to the t. of our present*, Cymb. I, 6, 208. Especially a proposal of marriage or of love: *there is, as 'twere, a t., a kind of t., made afar off by Sir Hugh*, Wiv. I, 1, 215. *if she should make t. of her love*, Ado II, 3, 186. *I will make a desperate t. of my child's love*, Rom. III, 4, 12. *he hath of late made many —s of his affection to me*, Hml. I, 3, 99. *do you believe these —s, as you call them?* 103. 106.

2) a thing offered: *of pensived and subdued desires the t.* Compl. 219 (= present). Especially something offered for payment: *the barren t. of a poet's debt*, Sonn. 83, 4; cf. Mids. III, 2, 87. *that you have ta'en these —s for true pay*, Hml. I, 3, 106 (perhaps = tokens representing money).

**Tender**, subst. regard, care: *hast showed thou makest some t. of my life*, H4A V, 4, 49. *nor the redresses sleep, which, in the t. of a wholesome weal, might in their working do you that offence*, Lr. I, 4, 230.

**Tender**, adj. 1) soft, smooth and weak in a physical sense, not rough or hard: *t. hide*, Ven. 298. *her t. hand*, 352. *his —er cheek*, 353. *Love's t. spring*, 656. *the t. leaves*, 798. *unruly blasts wait on the t. spring*, Lucr. 869. *the t. inward of thy hand*, Sonn. 128, 6. *the soft and t. fork of a poor worm*, Meas. III, 1, 16. *wisdom and blood combating in so t. a body*, Ado II, 3, 171. *those t. limbs of thine*, All's III, 2, 107. *thy t. lambkin*, H4B V, 3, 121. *my t. lambs*, H6A I, 2, 76. *thy t. side*, V, 3, 49. *my t. feet*, H6B II, 4, 34. *that t. spray*, H6C II, 6, 50. *the t. leaves of hopes*, H8 III, 2, 353. *too great oppression for a t. thing*, Rom. I, 4, 24. *with t. Juliet matched*, II Prol. 4. Oth. I, 2, 66. Especially applied to immature youth: *the t. boy*, Ven. 32. *the t. spring upon thy lip*, 127. *his t. years*, 1091. Sonn. 1, 4. 12. Pilgr. 53. Gent. I, 3. 47. III, 1, 34. LLL I, 2, 8. 12. 14. 16. As I, 1, 135. Wint. III, 2, 197. John IV, 2, 58. R2 II, 3, 42. H6A III, 1, 71. IV, 1, 149. V, 4, 50. V, 5, 81. H6C II, 2, 115. R3 III, 1, 28. IV, 1, 4. 99. 103. IV, 4, 9. 224. 342. 383. 385. V, 3, 95. Tit. III, 2, 22. 48. 50. V, 3, 167. Hml. IV, 4, 48. *in protection of their t. ones* (= their young) H6C IV, 2, 28.

2) delicate, in a physical and moral sense; a) gentle, kind: *never trained to offices of t. courtesy*, Merch. IV, 1, 33. *thou art she in thy not chiding, for she was as t. as infancy and grace*, Wint. V, 3, 26. b) easily impressed, very susceptible of any sensation: *the snail, whose t. horns being hit*, Ven. 1033. LLL IV, 3, 338. *your affections would become t.* Tp. V, 19. *her t. shame will not proclaim against her maiden loss*, Meas. IV, 4, 26. *I am such a t. ass, if my hair do but tickle me, I must scratch*, Mids. IV, 1, 27. *corrupt the t. honour of a maid*, All's III, 5, 75. *your soft and t. breeding*, Tw. V, 331. *her frights and griefs, which never t. lady hath borne against*, Wint. II, 2, 24. *I will devise a death as cruel for thee as thou art t. to't*, IV, 4, 452. *t. womanish tears*, John IV, 1, 36. *put in her t. heart the aspiring flame of golden sovereignty*, R3 IV, 4, 328. *come, seeling night, scarf up the t. eye of pitiful day*, Mcb. III, 2, 47. *why should we be t. to an arrogant piece of flesh threat us*, Cymb. IV, 2, 126. With *of: so t. of rebukes that words are strokes to her*, Cymb. III, 5, 40. With *over: you that are thus t. o'er his follies*, Wint. II, 3, 128. *thou that hast a heart so t. o'er it*, 133. *a page so kind, so t. over his occasions*, Cymb. V, 5, 87 (so nicely sensible of his wants). c) ef-

feminate: *the many will be too chill and t., and they'll be for the flowery way,* All's IV, 5, 56. d) quick, keen, sharp: (a hound) *unapt for t. smell,* Lucr. 695. *nor are mine ears with thy tongue's tune delighted, nor t. feeling,* Sonn. 141, 6.

3) loving, fond: *which I will keep so chary as t. nurse her babe,* Sonn. 22, 12. *gone in t. embassy of love,* 45, 6. *a t. fatherly regard,* Shr. II, 288. *how long shall t. duty make me suffer wrong?* R2 II, 1, 164. *prick my t. patience to those thoughts,* 207. *in their dear care and t. preservation of our person,* H5 II, 2, 59. *I thank them for their t. loving care,* H6B III, 2, 280. H6C IV, 6, 66. *the t. love I bear your grace,* R3 III, 4, 65. *I do love my country's good with a respect more t. than mine own life,* Cor. III, 3, 112. *a t. kiss,* Rom. I, 5, 98. *whom Fortune's t. arm with favour never clasped,* Tim. IV, 3, 250.

4) making a soft impression, mild: *of subtle, t. and delicate temperance,* Tp. II, 1, 41. *embrace by a piece of t. air,* Cymb. V, 4, 140. V, 5, 437. 446. *soft and t. flattery,* Per. IV, 4, 45.

5) exciting kind feelings: *subscribes to t. objects,* Troil. IV, 5, 106. *I know how t. 'tis to love the babe that milks me,* Mcb. I, 7, 55. With *to,* = dear: *whose life's as t. to me as my soul,* Gent. V, 4, 37.

**Tender,** vb. 1) to offer, to present: *the honey fee of parting —ed is,* Ven. 538. *—ed the humble salve which wounded bosoms fits,* Sonn. 120, 11. *who once again I t. to thy hand,* Tp. IV, 5. *those (tears) at her father's churlish feet she —ed,* Gent. III, 1, 225. *if hearty sorrow be a sufficient ransom for offence, I t.'t here,* V, 4, 76. *some t. money to me,* Err. IV, 3, 4. *t. me affection,* Mids. III, 2, 230. *never any thing can be amiss, when simpleness and duty t. it,* V, 83. *here I t. it* (money) *for him,* Merch. IV, 1, 209. *if you should t. your supposed aid,* All's I, 3, 242. *I come to t. it,* II, 1, 116. *to t. it* (the petition) *herself,* V, 3, 132. *the faithfullest offerings that e'er devotion —ed,* Tw. V, 118. *I t. you my service,* R2 II, 3, 41. *to your highness' hand I t. my commission,* H8 II, 2, 104. *what kind of my obedience I should t.* II, 3, 66. *loving kiss for kiss thy brother Marcus —s on thy lips,* Tit. V, 3, 157. *'tis not amiss we t. our loves to him,* Tim. V, 1, 14. *I crave no more than hath your highness offered, nor will you t. less,* Lr. I, 1, 198. *let me my service t. on your lips,* Cymb. I, 6, 140. *those duties which you t. to her,* II, 3, 56. *why —est thou that paper to me?* III, 4, 11. *nor to us hath —ed the duty of the day,* III, 5, 31. With *down: had he twenty heads to t. down on twenty bloody blocks,* Meas. II, 4, 180. *t. down their services to Lord Timon,* Tim. I, 1, 54. Reflexively: *be but duteous, and true preferment shall t. itself to thee,* Cymb. III, 5, 160.

2) to show: *who* (jewels) *—ing their own worth from where they were glassed, did point you to buy them,* LLL II, 244. *I'll bring you where he is aboard, t. your persons to his presence,* Wint. IV, 4, 826 (= show, or introduce? Autolycus' speech, in his assumed character of a courtier). *t. yourself more dearly, or ... you'll t. me a fool,* Hml. I, 3, 109 (you will show me a fool, i. e. a fool).

**Tender,** vb. to regard or treat with kindness; to like; to hold dear; to take care of: *t. my suit,* Lucr. 534. *how does your content t. your own good fortune?* Tp. II, 1, 270. *I thank you that you t. her,* Gent. IV, 4, 145. *if any friend will pay the sum for him, he shall not die; so much we t. him,* Err. V, 132. *by my life, I do; which I t. dearly,* As V, 2, 77. *t. well my hounds,* Shr. Ind. 1, 16. *your minion, whom ... I t. dearly,* Tw. V, 129. *—ing the precious safety of my prince,* R2 I, 1, 32. H5 II, 2, 175. H6B III, 1, 277. R3 I, 1, 44. *and so betide me as well I t. you and all of yours,* II, 4, 72. *if with pure heart's love ... I t. not thy beauteous princely daughter,* IV, 4, 405. *you t. more your person's honour than your high profession spiritual,* H8 II, 4, 116. *—ing our sister's honour,* Tit. I, 476. *which name I t. as dearly as my own,* Rom. III, 1, 74. *t. yourself more dearly,* Hml. I, 3, 107. *for thine especial safety, which we do t.* IV, 3, 43. Strange expression: *when my angry guardant stood alone, —ing my ruin and assailed of none,* H6A IV, 7, 10 (the same as tender over my ruin, i. e. my fall; cf. Wint. II, 3, 128. 133; full of pity and grief at my fall).

**Tender-bodied,** having a tender body, very young: Cor. I, 3, 6.

**Tender-dying,** dying in early youth: *when death doth close his t. eyes,* H6A III, 3, 48 (M. Edd. *tender dying*).

**Tender-feeling,** very sensible: *her t. feet,* H6B II, 4, 9.

**Tender-hearted,** having great sensibility: R2 III, 3, 160.

**Tender-hefted:** *thy t. nature shall not give thee o'er to harshness,* Lr. II, 4, 174 (Qq *tender hested*). Steevens: "*t.* = tender-heaved, i. e. whose bosom is agitated by tender passions." Edinb. Rev. Jul. 1869, p. 106: "*heft* is a well-known older English word for handle, that which holds or contains, and *tender-hefted* is simply delicately-housed, daintily-bodied, finely-sheathed. *Heft* was in this way applied proverbially to the body, and Howel has a phrase quoted by Halliwell: *loose in the heft,* to designate an ill habit of life, a person of dissipated ways". But is *haft* or *heft,* i. e. handle, indeed that which holds or contains, or not rather that by which a thing is held? *Loose in the handle,* applied to a person, could not possibly mean any thing else than what *loose in the heft* is said to have designated. Perhaps *tender-hefted,* i. e. tender-handled, is = tender, gentle, to touch or to approach; of an easy and winning address, affable.

**Tender-hested,** lection of Qq in Lr. II, 4, 174, defended by Nares as meaning 'giving tender hests or commands'. Ff and M. Edd. *tender-hefted.*

**Tenderly,** 1) softly, gently: *t. apply to her some remedies for life,* Wint. III, 2, 153. *O, good sir, t., O!* IV, 3, 74. *will as t. be led by the nose as asses are,* Oth. I, 3, 407.

2) kindly, fondly: *so t. officious to save this bastard's life,* Wint. II, 3, 159. *my stooping duty t. shall show,* R2 III, 3, 48. *that so t. and entirely loves him,* Lr. I, 2, 104.

**Tender-minded,** susceptible of soft passions, compassionate: *to be t. does not become a sword,* Lr. V, 3, 31.

**Tenderness,** 1) the state or quality of being soft and weak: *the t. of her nature became as a prey to her grief,* All's IV, 3, 60. Abstr. pro concr.: *go, t. of years,* LLL III, 4 (= tender boy. Armado's speech). *think you I can a resolution fetch from flowery t.?* Meas. III, 1, 83 (from a tender woman, 'whose action is no stronger than a flower', Sonn. 65, 4).

2) sensibility, delicacy: *doing these fair rites of t.*

H4A V, 4, 98. *my conscience first received a t., scruple and prick*, H8 II, 4, 170. *her delicate t. will find itself abused*, Oth. II, 1, 235. Especially lively sympathy, susceptibility of soft passions, particularly of love and pity: *nature will betray its folly, its t.* Wint. I, 2, 152. *make blind itself with foolish t.* H4A III, 2, 91. *tears ... which nature, love and filial t. shall pay thee*, H4B IV, 5, 39. *your t. of heart*, R3 III, 7, 210. *melting with t. and kind compassion*, IV, 3, 7. *not of a woman's t. to be*, Cor. V, 3, 129. *more t. than doth become a man*, Cymb. I, 1, 94.

**Tender-smelling,** having a delicate smell: *your nose smells 'no' in this, most t. knight*, LLL V, 2, 569.

**Tending:** Mcb. I, 5, 36; see *Tend.*

**Tenedos,** an island near Troy: Troil. Prol. 11.

**Tenement,** a house or any property held by a tenant or vassal: *leased out like to a t. or pelting farm*, R2 II, 1, 60. *to forfeit all your goods, lands, —s*, H8 III, 2, 342.

**Tenfold,** adj. and adv. ten times greater; ten times more: *our t. grief*, Tit. III, 2, 6. *I will reward thee ... t. for thy good valour*, Ant. IV, 7, 15.

**Tennis,** a play at which a ball is driven with a racket: H8 I, 3, 30. Hml. II, 1, 59.

**Tennis-ball,** a ball used in the play of tennis: Ado III, 2, 47. H5 I, 2, 258.

**Tennis-court,** a place for playing at tennis: Per. II, 1, 64. *t. keeper:* H4B II, 2, 21.

**Tenour** (O. Edd. *tenor,* and oftener *tenure*) sense contained, purport: Gent. III, 1, 56. Meas. IV, 2, 216. Ado IV, 1, 169. Merch. IV, 1, 235. As IV, 3, 11. Wint. V, 1, 38. H4A IV, 4, 7. H4B IV, 1, 9. V, 5, 75. H5 V, 2, 72 (pl.). H8 I, 2, 206. Troil. II, 1, 100. Caes. IV, 3, 171. Cymb. II, 4, 36. III, 7, 1. Per. I, 1, 111. III Prol. 24. *here folds she up the t. of her woe*, Lucr. 1310 (i. e. her letter).*to find out shames and idle hours in me, the scope and t. of thy jealousy*, Sonn. 61, 8 (= the aim and substance of etc.). *misuse the t. of thy kinsman's trust*, H4A V, 5, 5 (the meaning, the intention which he had in confiding the matter to thee).

**Tent,** subst. a pavilion: *costly apparel, —s and canopies*, Shr. II, 354. Especially the portable lodge of soldiers: Ven. 108. Lucr. Arg. 5. Lucr. 15. Meas. II, 1, 263. LLL IV, 3, 373. V, 2, 307. 309. 311. Merch. V, 5. All's III, 6, 29. IV, 3, 232. John II, 544. III, 2, 6. H4A II, 3, 54. V, 4, 8. V, 5, 22. H5 III, 7, 74. 136. IV, 1, 304. H6A I, 4, 110. IV, 7, 51. H6B V, 1, 55. H6C IV, 2, 20. IV, 3, 10. R3 V, 3, 1. 7. 23. 303 (cf. *On*). Caes. III, 2, 176. IV, 2, 46. 51. Ant. IV, 6, 23. V, 1, 73 etc. etc. (*at* and *in* indiscriminately before it).

**Tent,** subst. a probe for searching a wound: *the t. that searches to the bottom of the worst*, Troil. II, 2, 16. Punning: *who keeps the t. now? The surgeon's box, or the patient's wound*, V, 1, 11.

**Tent,** vb. to lodge as in a tent, to tabernacle: *the smiles of knaves t. in my cheeks*, Cor. III, 2, 116 (the soldier Coriolanus' speech).

**Tent,** vb. 1) to search, to probe (as a wound): *I'll observe his looks, I'll t. him to the quick*, Hml. II, 2, 626. *mine ear, therein false struck, can take no greater wound, nor t. to bottom that*, Cymb. III, 4, 118 (cannot find the bottom of it).

2) to cure: *well might they* (your wounds) *fester 'gainst ingratitude, and t. themselves with death*, Cor. I, 9, 31 (cure themselves, be cured by dying).*'tis a sore upon us you cannot t. yourself*, III, 1, 236. cf. *un-*

*tented* = incurable in Lr. I, 4, 322.

**Tented,** covered with tents: *the t. field*, Oth. I, 3, 85.

**Tenth,** the ordinal of ten: Sonn. 38, 9. H5 I, 2, 77. H6A I, 1, 110. Troil. III, 2, 95. Lr. I, 1, 179. Substantively, = 1) one out of ten: *if we have lost so many —s of ours*, Troil. II, 2, 21. *take thou the destined t.* Tim. V, 4, 33 (by decimation). 2) the tenth part: *the t. of mankind would hang themselves*, Wint. I, 2, 199. *we render you the t., to be ta'en forth*, Cor. I, 9, 34. *who of their broken debtors take a third, a sixth, a t.* Cymb. V, 4, 20. 3) a tithe: *among the people gather up a t.* H6A V, 5, 93.

**Ten-times-barred-up,** writing of some M. Edd. in R2 I, 1, 180; not hyphened in O. Edd.

**Tent-royal,** the tent of a king: H5 I, 2, 196.

**Tenure,** the manner of holding lands and tenements of a superior: *where be his quiddities, his quillets, his cases, his —s and his tricks*, Hml. V, 1, 108.

**Tercel,** the male hawk: *the falcon* (i. e. the female hawk) *as the t., for all the ducks in the river*, Troil. III, 2, 56 (i. e. Cressida will be as good for hawking as Troilus; cf. the German phrase: *sie geht ins Wasser,* properly = she takes the water well). cf. *Tassel-gentle.*

**Tereu,** a sound imitative of the voice of the nightingale: Pilgr. 386.

**Tereus,** a Thracian king, who ravished his sister-in-law Philomele and then cut out her tongue: Lucr. 1134. Tit. II, 4, 26. 41. IV, 1, 48. Cymb. II, 2, 45.

**Term,** subst. 1) the time in which a court is held for the trial of causes: *they* (lawyers) *sleep between t. and t.* As III, 2, 350. *the wearing out of six fashions, which is four —s, or two actions*, H4B V, 1, 90.

2) time in general: *for t. of life thou art assured mine*, Sonn. 92, 2. *buy —s divine in selling hours of dross*, 146, 11. *have sworn for three years' t. to live with me*, LLL I, 1, 16. *not to see a woman in that t.* 37. *within the t. of three years*, 131. *you shall this twelvemonth t. ... visit the sick*, V, 2, 860. *till t. of eighteen months be full expired*, H6B I, 1, 67. *expire the t. of a despised life*, Rom. I, 4, 109. *for some t. to do obsequious sorrow*, Hml. I, 2, 91. *doomed for a certain t. to walk the night*, I, 5, 10. *taking leave as long a t. as yet we have to live*, Cymb. I, 1, 107.

3) expression, word: *stand under the adoption of abominable —s*, Wiv. II, 2, 309. 310. *I cannot woo in festival —s*, Ado V, 2, 41. *chides the dice in honourable —s*, LLL V, 2, 327. *taffeta phrases, silken —s*, 406. *she in mild —s begged my patience*, Mids. IV, 1, 63. *I like not fair —s and a villain's mind*, Merch. I, 3, 180 (or = conditions?). *as you would say in plain —s*, II, 2, 68. *to have defended it with any —s of zeal*, V, 205. As II, 7, 16. Shr. II, 159. 271. Tw. II, 4, 5. IV, 2, 36. R2 I, 1, 57. H4A I, 3, 46. II, 3, 52. IV, 1, 85. IV, 3, 63. V, 4, 162. H4B IV, 4, 73. H5 II, 1, 32. IV, 8, 44. V, 2, 99. H6A I, 2, 93. II, 5, 47. IV, 1, 97. H6B I, 1, 30. III, 2, 311. IV, 9, 44. IV, 10, 38. V, 1, 25. H6C I, 1, 265. II, 2, 85. R3 IV, 4, 359 (Qq in plain —s tell her my loving tale; Ff plainly to her tell my l. t.). Troil. I, 3, 159. V, 2, 38. Tit. II, 3, 110. Rom. I, 1, 218. III, 1, 64. Caes. III, 1, 203. Mcb. V, 8, 8. Hml. I, 3, 132. Oth. I, 2, 7. IV, 2, 116. 121. Ant. II, 2, 24. III, 4, 7.

4) condition (only in the plur.); a) stipulation, proposition stated and offered for acceptance: *if we can make our peace upon such large —s and so absolute*

*as our conditions shall consist upon*, H4B IV, 1, 186. *we have consented to all —s of reason*, H5 V, 2, 357. Perhaps also in Merch. I, 3, 180 (see above).

b) relation, footing: *shall I so much dishonour my fair stars, on equal —s to give him chastisement*, R2 IV, 22. *that you and I should meet upon such —s as now we meet*, H4A V, 1, 10. *did not we send grace, pardon and —s of love to all of you?* V, 5, 3. *to close in —s of friendship with thine enemies*, Caes. III, 1, 203 (or = expressions?). *parted you in good —s?* Lr. I, 2, 171. *in quarter and in —s like bride and groom*, Oth. II, 3, 180. *if you seek us afterwards in other —s* (i. e. as an enemy), *you shall find us in our salt-water girdle*, Cymb. III, 1, 80. *the sore —s we stand upon with the gods*, Per. IV, 2, 37.

c) state, situation, circumstances: *long upon these —s I held my city*, Compl. 176 (= in this state). *what —s the enemy stood on*, H5 III, 6, 78 (what was the position of the enemy). *the —s of our estate may not endure hazard so dangerous*, Hml. III, 3, 5. Used with some latitude: *were I under the —s of death*, Meas. II, 4, 100 (= were I to die). *now to deliver her possession up on —s of base compulsion*, Troil. II, 2, 153 (= in consequence of compulsion; by compulsion). *to recover of us, by strong hand and —s compulsatory, those lands*, Hml. I, 1, 103. *a sister driven into desperate —s*, IV, 7, 26.

d) mode of being or of acting; sometimes used in a quite periphrastical way: *may any —s acquit me from this chance?* Lucr. 1706 (any thing that I might do). *to keep the —s of my honour precise*, Wiv. II, 2, 22 (all that concerns my honour; or, in short, = my honour); cf. *but in my —s of honour I stand aloof*, Hml. V, 2, 257. *so rushling in silk and gold, and in such alligant —s*, Wiv. II, 2, 69 (= in so fine a style; Mrs Quickly's speech). *in —s of choice I am not solely led by nice direction of a maiden's eye*, Merch. II, 1, 13 (with respect to the choice; in my choice). *both my revenge and hate loosing on thee without all —s of pity*, All's II, 3, 173 (= without any pity). *whom thou in —s so bloody and so dear hast made thine enemies*, Tw. V, 74 (in so bloody a manner). *if you grow foul with me, I will scour you with my rapier, as I may, in fair —s*, H5 II, 1, 60 (Nym's speech). 74. *lest your displeasure should enlarge itself to wrathful —s*, Troil. V, 2, 38 (= to wrath; or = words). *be judge yourself, whether I in any just t. am affined to love the Moor*, Oth. I, 1, 39 (justly in any respect; the only instance of the singular). Peculiar passage: *our city's institutions and the —s for common justice*, Meas. I, 1, 11 (the conditions on which common justice proceeds; the proceedings at law).

**Term**, vb. to name, to call: Sonn. 17, 11. Tp. V, 15. Err. I, 1, 100. Ado III, 2, 44. Merch. III, 2, 160. Wint. III, 1, 5. H6A II, 1, 20. H6B III, 2, 196. IV, 2, 33. IV, 7, 66. IV, 9, 30. R3 III, 4, 41. III, 5, 79. Troil. I, 1, 44. Cor. IV, 5, 164. 221. Lr. II, 4, 200. Cymb. I, 4, 106. V, 5, 448.

**Termagant**, an imaginary God of the Mahometans, represented as a most violent character in the old Miracle-plays and Moralities: *'twas time to counterfeit, or that hot t. Scot had paid me scot and lot too*, H4A V, 4, 114. *I would have such a fellow whipped for o'erdoing T.; it outherods Herod*, Hml. III, 2, 15. Very impertinently substituted by M. Edd. for *armgaunt* of O. Edd. in Ant. I, 5, 48.

**Termination**, term, word: *she speaks poniards, and every word stabs: if her breath were as terrible as her —s, there were no living near her*, Ado II, 1, 256.

**Termless**, inexpressible, indescribable: *like unshorn velvet on that t. skin*, Compl. 94. cf. *Phraseless.*

**Terrene**, terrestrial, earthly: *our t. moon is now eclipsed*, Ant. III, 13, 153. (accentuated on the first syllable, as preceding the subst.).

**Terrestrial**, pertaining to the earth, earthly, *give me thy hand, t.* Wiv. III, 1, 108 (the host's speech) *this t. ball* (i. e. the earth) R2 III, 2, 41.

**Terrible**, 1) causing fear, formidable: Tp. I, 2, 264. Ado II, 1, 256. All's III, 5, 23. IV, 1, 3. Tw. III, 4, 197. R2 III, 2, 133. H4B I, 2, 244. H5 II, 4, 35. III, 1, 9. H6A IV, 5, 8. H6B III, 3, 6. R3 I, 4, 63. H8 III, 1, 164. Cor. I, 4, 57. Tim. V, 4, 2. Caes. I, 3, 130. II, 2, 47. Mcb. I, 2, 51. I, 7, 80. II, 3, 62. III, 2, 18. III, 4, 78. Lr. IV, 7, 34. Oth. I, 1, 82. V, 2, 203 (Ff *horrible*). Ant. IV, 15, 3. Cymb. III, 1, 27. Per. III, 1, 57.

2) fearful, affrighted: *what paper were you reading? Nothing, my lord. No? what needed, then, that t. dispatch of it into your pocket?* Lr. I, 2, 32.

**Terribly**, formidably: Tp. II, 1, 313. Mids. I, 2, 76. Tim. IV, 3, 136.

**Territory**, the land under the dominion of a prince or state: As III, 1, 8. Lr. I, 1, 51. Plur. *—es:* Gent. III, 1, 163. John I, 10. V, 2, 136. R2 I, 3, 139. H6A V, 3, 146. V, 4, 139. H6B III, 1, 84. III, 2, 245. Cor. IV, 5, 140. IV, 6, 40. 77.

**Terror**, 1) great fear or fright felt: *which with cold t. doth men's minds confound*, Ven. 1048. *coward-like with trembling t. die*, Lucr. 231. *what t. 'tis*, 453. *effects of t. and dear modesty*, Compl. 202. Wiv. IV, 4, 23. Tw. III, 4, 207. R2 V, 4, 9. H4B IV, 5, 177. R3 III, 5, 4. V, 3, 170. Lr. IV, 2, 12. *to strike t. to:* H6A II, 3, 24. R3 V, 3, 217.

2) fear communicated, dreadfulness: *lent him our t.* Meas. I, 1, 20. *to stick it in their children's sight for t.* I, 3, 26. *to our perjury to add more t.* LLL V, 2, 470. *meet with no less t. than the elements*, R2 III, 3, 55. R3 I, 4, 7. H8 V, 1, 89. V, 5, 48. Cor. II, 2, 109. Rom. III, 3, 13. IV, 3, 38. Caes. II, 1, 199. IV, 3, 66.

3) the cause of fear: *their perch and not their t.* Meas. II, 1, 4. *we make trifles of —s*, All's II, 3, 4. *both joy and t. of good and bad*, Wint. IV, 1, 1. *beating and hanging are —s to me*, IV, 3, 30. *thou hate and t. to prosperity*, John III, 4, 28. *here is the t. of the French*, H6A I, 4, 42. II, 2, 17. IV, 2, 16. IV, 7, 78. H6B III, 2, 328. Tit. I, 29. V, 1, 10. Lr. II, 4, 285. Cymb. IV, 2, 111.

**Tertian**, a fever returning every other day: *a burning quotidian t.* H5 II, 1, 124 (Mrs Quickly's speech).

**Test**, subst. proof; 1) trial, examination: *thou hast strangely stood the t.* Tp. IV, 7. *let there be some more t. made of my metal*, Meas. I, 1, 49. *bring me to the t.* Hml. III, 4, 142.

2) testimony, evidence: *an esperance so obstinately strong, that doth invert that t. of eyes and ears*, Troil. V, 2, 122 (Q *the attest*). *to vouch this is no proof, without more wider and more overt t.* Oth. I, 3, 107.

**Testament**, a will, a writing by which a person disposes of his property after his death: Lucr. 1183. As I, 1, 78. II, 1, 47. All's V, 3, 197. H5 I, 1, 10.

IV, 6, 27. H6A I, 5, 17. Tim. V, 1, 30. Caes. III, 2, 135. 158. Per. IV, 2, 107. *he is come to open the purple t. of bleeding war,* R2 III, 3, 94, i. e. he is come to try, who will become heir of England by the decision of war.

**Tested,** tried by a test, refined, pure: *the t. gold,* Meas. II, 2, 149.

**Tester,** a coin of the value of sixpence: *hold, there's a t. for thee,* H4B III, 2, 296. For money in general: *t. I'll have in pouch when thou shalt lack,* Wiv. I, 3, 96 (Pistol's speech). cf. *Testril.*

**Testern,** to present with a tester: *you have —ed me,* Gent. I, 1, 153 (Speed's speech).

**Testify** (used only in the infinitive) to give evidence, to witness, to prove: *to t. your bounty, I thank you, you have testerned me,* Gent. I, 1, 152. *here is the note of the fashion to t.* Shr. IV, 3, 131. *her mother can t. she was the first fruit of my bachelorship,* H6A V, 4, 12. *the bricks are alive at this day to t. it,* H6B IV, 2, 158. *no warmth, no breath, shall t. thou livest,* Rom. IV, 1, 98. *some natural notes about her body above ten thousand meaner moveables would t.* Cymb. II, 2, 30. *as yon grim looks do t.* Per. Prol. 40.

**Testimonied,** attested, witnessed, proved by testimony: *let him be but t. in his own bringings forth,* Meas. III, 2, 153.

**Testimony,** declaration of a witness, proof by witness, evidence given: Meas. II, 4, 131. V, 244. 470. Ado IV, 1, 318. As IV, 3, 171. All's II, 5, 5. Tw. V, 164. Wint. II, 3, 137. III, 2, 25. H5 IV, 8, 38 (*bear.* Fluellen's speech). Tit. V, 3, 8. Lr. I, 2, 88. Cymb. I, 4, 161. III, 4, 22. *very reverend sport, truly; and done in the t. of a good conscience,* LLL IV, 2, 2 (with the approbation of conscience. Sir Nathaniel's speech).

**Testiness,** fretfulness, peevishness: Cymb. IV, 1, 23.

**Testril,** a sixpence (cf. *Tester*): Tw. II, 3, 34.

**Testy,** easily angry, fretful, peevish: Ven. 319. Lucr. 1094. Sonn. 140, 7. Gent. I, 2, 58. Mids. III, 2, 358. R3 III, 4, 39. Cor. II, 1, 47. Caes. IV, 3, 46. Per. I, 1, 17.

**Tetchy,** touchy, fretful, peevish: *t. and wayward was thine infancy,* R3 IV, 4, 168. *he's as t. to be wooed to woo, as she is stubborn-chaste,* Troil. I, 1, 99. *to see it t. and fall out with the dug,* Rom. I, 3, 32.

**Tether** (Qq *teder* or *tider;* cf. the low German *tidern*) a rope by which a beast is confined within certain limits: *with a larger t. may he walk than may be given you,* Hml. I, 3, 125.

**Tetter,** subst. a cutaneous disease; scab, scurf: Troil. V, 1, 27. Hml. I, 5, 71.

**Tetter,** vb. to affect with tetter: *those measles, which we disdain should t. us,* Cor. III, 1, 79.

**Tewksbury,** town in England: *his wit's as thick as T. mustard,* H4B II, 4, 262. Last battle-field of Queen Margaret: H6C V, 3, 19. R3 I, 2, 242. I, 3, 120. I, 4, 56. II, 1, 111. V, 3, 120.

**Text,** 1) something written for instruction: *and t. underneath, 'Here dwells Benedick the married man,'* Ado V, 1, 185. *fair as a t. B in a copy-book,* LLL V, 2, 42. *what shall be next, pardon old Gower, — thus long's the t.* Per. II Prol. 40.

2) that on which a comment is written: *the t. is old,* Ven. 806. *what is your t.?* Tw. I, 5, 237. 240. 251. *that's a certain t.* Rom. IV, 1, 21. *no more; the t. is foolish,* Lr. IV, 2, 37.

3) a passage of Scripture: *society, saith the t., is the happiness of life,* LLL IV, 2, 168. 169. *approve it with a t.* Merch. III, 2, 79. *your exposition on the holy t.* H4B IV, 2, 7.

**Thaisa** (trisyll.; accentuated now on the first, now on the second syll.), female name in Per. II, 3, 57. V, 1, 212. 213. V, 3, 4. 27. 34. 35. 46. 55. 70.

**Thaliard,** name in Per. I, 1, 151. 170. I, 3, 31. II Prol. 23.

**Thames,** the river on which London lies: *to be thrown into the T.* Wiv. III, 5, 6. 122. *thrown into T.* 129. H5 IV, 1, 120. H6B IV, 8, 3. *by the T. side,* Wiv. III, 3, 16. *the T. water,* Wiv. III, 5, 23.

**Than** (spelt *then* in O. Edd., as the modern *then* is sometimes spelt *than,* and rhymes to *ran* and *began* in Lucr. 1440) the particle used after comparatives, to introduce the second member of the comparison: Ven. 7. 9. 10. 92. 200. 398. 599. 661. 764. 776. 909. Lucr. 77. 105. 299. 418. 537 etc. Tp. I, 1, 21. 48. 50. I, 2, 20. 45 etc. etc. Correlative to *so:* LLL III, 180. = than that: *nor could she moralize his wanton sight, more than his eyes were opened to the light,* Lucr. 105. *we are made to be no stronger than faults may shake our frames,* Meas. II, 4, 133. *hath amazed me more than I dare blame my weakness,* All's II, 1, 88. *I had rather glib myself than they should not produce fair issue,* Wint. II, 1, 149. Cor. I, 4, 17. Omitted (?): *moe thousand deaths,* Meas. III, 1, 40.

**Thane,** an old Scottish title of honour, nearly equivalent to Earl: Mcb. I, 2, 45. 48. 53. I, 3, 48. 49. 71. 72. 87. 105. 108. 109. 116. 119. 122. 133. I, 4, 35 and passim.

**Thank,** vb. to express gratitude to; with an accus.: Tp. I, 2, 175. 293. II, 1, 198 (*I* omitted, cf. *I*). III, 2, 43. IV, 164. Gent. II, 1, 88. II, 4, 35. IV, 2, 24. IV, 4, 143. 145. Wiv. I, 1, 85. III, 4, 60. Meas. IV, 5, 11. Ado I, 1, 158. 240. As I, 2, 252. II, 5, 25. 28. Shr. V, 1, 78. H4B V, 3, 69. Caes. V, 1, 45 etc. etc. Passively: *you shall find yourself to be well —ed,* All's V, 1, 36. *he (Jove) is to be —ed,* Tw. III, 4, 92. *God be —ed,* Ado V, 1, 190. Merch. II, 2, 55. Shr. Ind. 2, 99. John V, 1, 29. H4A III, 3, 214. H5 II, 2, 158. R3 III, 7, 165. With *for: t. him not for that which he doth say,* Sonn. 79, 13. *heavens t. you for it,* Tp. I, 2, 175. II, 1, 123. Gent. III, 1, 161. IV, 2, 86. Wiv. II, 2, 84. Merch. II, 1, 22. III, 4, 43. IV, 1, 341. Shr. Ind. 2, 99. All's V, 1, 33. H4A III, 3, 214. H5 II, 2, 158 etc. etc. *a thing to t. God on,* H4A III, 3, 133. *t. me no thankings, nor proud me no prouds,* Rom. III, 5, 153. Ironically: *so that my errand, due unto my tongue, I t. him, I bare home upon my shoulders,* Err. II, 1, 73. *nay, I have verses too, I t. Biron,* LLL V, 2, 34. *and Lord Biron, I t. him, is my love,* 457. cf. Tp. II, 1, 123. Caes. V, 1, 45 etc. Used to decline a request: *will't please your worship to come in? No, I t. you,* Wiv. I, 1, 277. 280. 293. 315 etc. cf. H4B V, 3, 69.

**Thankful,** 1) grateful: Ado V, 1, 324. LLL IV, 2, 29. As III, 2, 221. All's II, 3, 43. IV, 3, 366. V, 1, 17. Tw. III, 4, 83. H8 V, 5, 73. Cor. I, 6, 9 (*t. sacrifice,* i. e. the sacrifice of thanks). Tit. I, 215. Rom. III, 5, 147. Ant. I, 2, 167 (*give the gods a t. sacrifice,* i. e. a thank-offering). With *to:* Gent. II, 4, 52. Wint. IV, 2, 20. H8 I, 1, 150. With *for:* LLL IV, 2, 74. Shr. II, 166. Rom. III, 5, 149. With *to* and *for:* Tw. IV, 2, 89.

2) earning thanks, thankworthy: *that he can hither come so soon, is by your fancy's t.* doom, Per. V, 2, 20.

**Thankfully,** with thanks, gratefully: Merch. I, 1, 152. IV, 2, 9. Tim. I, 2, 162. V, 1, 94. Lr. III, 6, 2. Cymb. I, 6, 28. 79. Per. IV, 6, 65.

**Thankfulness,** 1) gratitude: Ado IV, 1, 31. H5 II, 2, 32. H6B I, 1, 20. Tim. III, 6, 80.

2) thanks: *accept my t.* Cor. V, 4, 62. *take from my heart all t.* Per. III, 3, 4.

**Thanking,** subst. gratitude: *the charge and t. shall be for me,* All's III, 5, 101. Plur. —s = thanks: *many and hearty —s to you both,* Meas. V, 4. *thank me no —s,* Rom. III, 5, 153. *and graced the —s of a king,* Cymb. V, 5, 407.

**Thankless,** ungrateful: Cor. IV, 5, 76. Tim. V, 1, 63. Lr. I, 4, 311.

**Thanks,** gratitude expressed, kindness acknowledged: Gent. IV, 4, 53. Meas. I, 1, 41. I, 4, 28. IV, 2, 191. V, 7. Ado II, 3, 259. 271. LLL V, 2, 748. Shr. IV, 3, 41. 45. R2 II, 3, 61 etc. etc. *to con t.* = to be thankful: All's IV, 3, 174. Tim. IV, 3, 428. *to give t.* = to thank: Sonn. 38, 5. Err. IV, 3, 5. Ado I, 1, 242. III, 3, 20. Mids. V, 89. Merch. IV, 1, 288. Shr. II, 178. All's II, 1, 133. John V, 7, 108. H6A V, 3, 163. R3 I, 1, 127 etc. *give t. you have lived so long* (= thank God) Tp. I, 1, 26; cf. *t. be given, she's very well,* All's II, 4, 4. *to give t.* = to say grace: Shr. IV, 1, 162. cf. Cor. IV, 7, 4. *to have t.* = to receive t., to be thanked: Mids. I, 1, 249. All's IV, 3, 195. Cor. V, 1, 46. Ant. IV, 14, 140 etc. *to render t.* As II, 5, 29. *to return t.* H6A II, 2, 51. *t.,* absol.: Meas. III, 1, 106. V, 534. Ado V, 3, 28. LLL V, 2, 559. Mids. I, 1, 21. V, 179. Merch. I, 1, 111. H6A II, 4, 132. H6B I, 1, 68. H6C I, 1, 31. Hml. I, 1, 8.

In spite of the phrase *a thousand t.* (Shr. II, 85. H5 IV, 4, 64. H6C III, 2, 56. H8 I, 4, 74. cf. the German *tausend Dank*), always used as a singular: *much t. for my good cheer,* Err. V, 392. *little t.* Merch. IV, 1, 288. *must have that t. from Rome,* Cor. V, 1, 46. *t. to men of noble minds is honourable meed,* Tit. I, 215. *else is his t. too much,* Rom. II, 6, 23. *much t.* Hml. I, 1, 8. *well studied for a liberal t.* Ant. II, 6, 48.

**Thanksgiving,** 1) thanking: *I cannot stay t.* LLL II, 193. 2) a short prayer, grace said at table: *in the t. before meat,* Meas. I, 2, 15.

**Tharborough,** corrupted from *thirdborough,* = constable: LLL I, 1, 185.*

**Tharsus** (M. Edd. mostly *Tarsus*) name of a town (Tarsus in Cilicia?): Per. I, 2, 115. I, 4, 21. 55. II Prol. 11 etc. Changed to *Thasos* or *Thassos* by M. Edd. in Caes. V, 3, 104, more in congruity, perhaps, with history than with the principles of textual criticism. It seems too probable that Sh. took *Tarsus* and *Thasos* for the same.

**That,** demonstr. pron. (plur. *those*), used to indicate and point to an object of perception (either seen, or —in which case it is called a determinative pronoun — only imagined) as separated from the subject; and therefore distinguished from *this*: *applying this to that,* Ven. 713. *that time offered sorrow, this, general joy,* H8 IV, 1, 6. *two ships, of Corinth that, of Epidaurus this,* Err. I, 1, 94. *that gold* (i. e. the crown on thy head) *must round engirt these brows of mine,* H6B V, 1, 99. *to the boy Caesar send this* (i. e. my) *grizzled head. That* (i. e. your) *head, my lord?* Ant. III, 13, 19. *my ears would love that* (i. e.

thy) *inward beauty,* Ven. 434. *that hard heart of thine,* 500. 631. *she hath spied him already with those sweet eyes,* Mids. V, 328. *thy lips, those kissing cherries,* III, 2, 140. *what means that hand upon that breast of thine?* John III, 1, 21. *bind up those tresses,* III, 4, 61 (v. 68: *bind up your hairs*). *Surrey durst better have burnt that tongue than said so,* H8 III, 2, 254. *teach me, Alcides, thy rage, ... and with those hands that grasped the heaviest club, subdue my worthiest self,* Ant. IV, 12, 46 etc.

Used absolutely as well as adjectively; a) adjectively: *that sweet coral mouth,* Ven. 542. *to bury that posterity which ...,* 758. *at that time,* Tp. I, 2, 70. *wherefore did they not that hour destroy us? My tale provokes that question,* 139. 140. *that man,* 169. *no hope that way,* II, 1, 240 etc. *those fair lips of thine,* Ven. 115. *if those hills be dry,* 233. *love made those hollows,* 243 etc. *not that devoured, but that which doth devour, is worthy blame,* Lucr. 1256. *foretell new storms to those already spent,* 1589. *out of that 'no hope',* Tp. II, 1, 239. *that most deeply to consider is the beauty of his daughter,* III, 2, 106. *that to come,* Ant. II, 3, 6. *the names of those their nobles that lie dead,* H5 IV, 8, 96. *that her hand,* Troil. I, 1, 55. *that their fitness does unmake you,* Mcb. I, 7, 53. *thy demon, that thy spirit which keeps thee,* Ant. II, 3, 19 (M. Edd. unnecessarily: *that's thy spirit*). *threats the throat of that his officer that murdered Pompey,* III, 5, 19. *draw that thy honest sword,* IV, 14, 79. *those poor number saved with you,* Tw. I, 2, 10. *for those of old and the late dignities,* Mcb. I, 6, 18.

b) absolutely; with reference to things: *begged for that which thou unasked shalt have,* Ven. 102. *the bettering of my mind with that which ... o'erprized all popular rate,* Tp. I, 2, 91. *if he were that which now he's like,* II, 1, 282. *those* (liberal arts) *being all my study,* Tp. I, 2, 74. *those* (tears) *at her father's churly feet she tendered,* Gent. III, 1, 225 etc. Plural form of the subject caused by that of the predicate: *those are pearls that were his eyes,* Tp. I, 2, 398. Merch. IV, 1, 254. Cor. I, 6, 66. *the armour that I saw in your tent, are those stars or suns upon it?* H5 III, 7, 74. Referring to sentences, or to things thought or acted: *what of that?* Ven. 717. Mids. I, 1, 228 (cf. *What*). *but that I do not,* Tp. I, 2, 52. Caes. IV, 3, 298. *take thou that* (blows) Err. II, 2, 23. *it is not that that hath incensed the duke,* H6A III, 1, 36. *mark but my fall, and that that ruined me,* H8 III, 2, 440. *what's that?* (i. e. what you say) Troil. I, 2, 42 etc. *that is* = that is to say: Tp. II, 1, 282. Meas. II, 4, 135 etc. *and that,* used to explain or add to what is said: *I heard a humming, and that a strange one,* Tp. II, 1, 318. *he shall pay for him that hath him, and that soundly,* II, 2, 81. *to deliver all the intelligence against you, and that with the divine forfeit of his soul,* All's III, 6, 33. *I find it, and that to the infection of my brains,* Wint. I, 2, 145. *I'll repent, and that suddenly,* H4A III, 3, 5. *scarce half made up, and that so lamely,* R3 I, 1, 22. *given hostile strokes, and that not in the presence of dreaded justice,* Cor. III, 3, 97. *so 'tis put on me, and that in way of caution,* Hml. I, 3, 95. *heard others praise, and that highly,* III, 2, 33. *you have been talked of, ... and that in Hamlet's hearing,* IV, 7, 73. *his voice was propertied as all the tuned spheres, and that to friends,* Ant. V, 2, 84. Sometimes for the modern *so: trim it handsomely. Ay, that I will,* Tp. V, 294.

*was there a wise woman with thee?* Ay, *that there was,* Wiv. IV, 5, 60. *knowest thou not the duke hath banished me? That he hath not,* As I, 3, 97. *you saw the ceremony? That I did,* H8 IV, 1, 60. cf. Dogberry's phrase: *gifts that God gives,* Ado III, 5, 47.

Referring to persons; not only in the plural: *those that I saw suffer,* Tp. I, 2, 6. *let it lie for those that it concerns,* Gent. I, 2, 76. *those that betray them do no treachery,* Wiv. V, 3, 24. *God punish me with hate in those where I expect most love,* R3 II, 1, 35. *who are those at the gate?* Err. III, 1, 48. *me they left with those of Epidamnum,* V, 353. *my loving greetings to those of mine in court,* All's I, 3, 259. *combined with those of Norway,* Mcb. I, 3, 112. *those of his chamber had done it,* II, 3, 106 etc. But also in the singular: *who is that that spake?* Gent. IV, 2, 87. *who is that at the door that keeps all this noise?* Err. III, 1, 61. *who's that which calls?* Meas. I, 4, 6. *the contents dies in the zeal of that which it presents,* LLL V, 2, 519. *he; that with the plume,* All's III, 5, 81. *then thou art as great as that thou fearest,* Tw. V, 153 (= as he whom thou fearest). *who's that that bears the sceptre?* H8 IV, 1, 38. *shall he be worshipped of that we hold an idol more than he?* Troil. II, 3, 199 (= worshipped by him whom we hold etc.) *who's that at door?* IV, 2, 36. *that, with his sons, a terror to our foes, hath yoked a nation strong,* Tit. I, 29. *who is that you love?* Rom. I, 1, 205 (= she whom). *who's that which rings the bell?* Oth. II, 3, 160 (Qq *that that rings*).

Sometimes pointing not so much to persons or things as to their qualities, and almost = such, or things of such a nature: *that's to ye sworn to none was ever said,* Compl. 180. *thy vile race had that in't which good natures could not abide to be with,* Tp. I, 2, 359. *and that* (will be) *supposed ... that may dwell upon your grave,* Err. III, 1, 101. *had you that craft, to reave her ...,* All's V, 3, 86. *a heart of that fine frame to pay this debt of love,* Tw. I, 1, 33. *there's that in this fardel will make him scratch his beard,* Wint. IV, 4, 727. *hast thou that holy feeling ... to counsel me ...,* R3 I, 4, 257. *I will put that business in your bosoms, whose execution takes your enemy off,* Mcb. III, 1, 104. *there cannot be that vulture in you, to devour so many ...,* IV, 3, 74. *whose love was of that dignity that it went hand in hand with the vow,* Hml. I, 5, 48. *there cannot be those numberless offences 'gainst me that I cannot take peace with,* H8 II, 1, 84. *think us those we profess, peace-makers,* III, 1, 167. cf. Cor. V, 1, 46. Lr. I, 4, 231. II, 4, 259. Mcb. V, 1, 66. In this sense, sometimes followed by *as* as its correlative: *those as sleep and think not on their sins,* Wiv. V, 5, 57. *I could not answer in that course of honour as she had made the overture,* All's V, 3, 98. *bear that proportion to my flesh and blood as did the fatal brand,* H6B I, 1, 233. *wish his mistress were that kind of fruit as maids call medlars,* Rom. II, 1, 35. *that gentleness ... as I was wont to have,* Caes. I, 2, 33. *I return those duties back as are right fit,* Lr. I, 1, 99. *entertained with that ceremonious affection as you were wont,* I, 4, 63. 314 (Ff). *those arts they have as I could put into them,* Cymb. V, 5, 338.

Used emphatically, either in dislike or in praise: *between that sun and thee,* Ven. 194. *jealousy, that sour unwelcome guest,* 449. *the boar, that bloody beast,* 999. *she's fled unto that peasant Valentine,* Gent. V, 2, 35. *by that most famous warrior, Duke Menaphon,*

Err. V, 367. *that angel knowledge,* LLL I, 1, 113. *that pure congealed white, high Taurus' snow,* Mids. III, 2, 141. *making that idiot laughter keep men's eyes,* John III, 3, 45. *then was that noble Worcester ta'en prisoner,* H4B I, 1, 125. *that furious Scot,* 126. *that wretched Anne, thy wife,* R3 V, 3, 159. *till death, that winter, kill it,* H8 III, 2, 179. *the fool will not; he there, that he,* Troil. II, 1, 91 etc. Similarly *that is,* with a predicate, by way of applause and encouragement, = there is, i. e. thou art, you are: *why, that's my spirit!* Tp. I, 2, 215. *that's my noble master,* 299. *why, that's my dainty Ariel,* V, 95. *why, that's my bawcock,* Wint. I, 2, 121. *sweet queen! that's a sweet queen, i' faith,* Troil. III, 1, 77. *that's my brave boy,* Cor. V, 3, 76. *ay, that's my boy,* Tit. IV, 1, 110. *that's my good son,* Rom. II, 3, 47. *that's my brave lord,* Ant. III, 13, 177. cf. *I would have men of such constancy put to sea, that their business might be every thing and their intent every where; for that's it that always makes a good voyage of nothing,* Tw. II, 4, 80.

Elliptically, = so it is, yes: *she found Benedick and Beatrice between the sheet? That.* Ado II, 3, 145. *crown him? that.* Caes. II, 1, 15.

By the omission of the following relative, *that* = a) he who, she who: *who is that calls so coldly?* Shr. IV, 1, 13. *as great as that thou fearest,* Tw. V, 153. *the shaft confounds not that it wounds, but tickles still the sore,* Troil. III, 1, 129 (i. e. kills not her, whom it wounds. M. Edd. *confounds, not that* etc.). *who is that you love,* Rom. I, 1, 205. *who's that knocks?* Caes. II, 1, 309. *woe that too late repents,* Lr. I, 4, 279 (= woe to him who). b) = what, that which: *great grief grieves at that would do it good,* Lucr. 1117. *I joy in that I honour most,* Sonn. 25, 4. *I am that I am,* 121, 9. *seem you that you are not?* Gent. II, 4, 10. *cease to lament for that thou canst not help,* III, 1, 241. *throw us that you have about ye,* IV, 1, 3. *the knave bragged of that he could not compass,* Wiv. III, 3, 212. *over and above that you have suffered,* V, 5, 177. *be that you are,* Meas. II, 4, 134. *gather the sequel by that went before,* Err. I, 1, 96. *the meat wants that I have,* II, 2, 57. *consent to pay thee that I never had,* IV, 1, 74. *have you that I sent you for?* IV, 4, 9. *let me be that I am,* Ado I, 3, 38. *aim better at me by that I now will manifest,* III, 2, 100. *if you dare not trust that you see, confess not that you know,* 122. *here's that shall drive some of them to a noncome,* III, 5, 67. *let me go with that I came,* V, 2, 47. *'tis strange, that these lovers speak of,* Mids. V, 1. *we are accomplished with that we lack,* Merch. III, 4, 62. *that they call compliment is like the encounter of two dog-apes,* As II, 5, 26. *I earn that I eat, get that I wear,* III, 2, 77. *I will continue that I broached in jest,* Shr. I, 2, 84. *I read that I profess,* IV, 2, 8. *seeks not to find that her search implies,* All's I, 3, 222. *is it possible he should know what he is, and be that he is?* IV, 1, 49. *I am not that I play,* Tw. I, 5, 196. *the heavens with that we have in hand are angry,* Wint. III, 3, 5. *do you almost think, although you see, that you do see?* John IV, 3, 44. *doth that I would not have it do,* H4A III, 2, 90. *meditating that shall dye your white rose in a bloody red,* H6A II, 4, 60 (thinking on what shall dye etc., i. e. combat. A passage strangely misinterpreted). *answer that I shall ask,* H6B I, 4, 29. *be that thou hopest to be,* III, 1, 333. *'tis true that Henry told me of,* H6C V, 6, 69. *on him I lay that you would lay on me*, R3 III, 7, 171 (Qq *what*). *I am possessed of that is mine*, Tit. I, 408. *where liest o' nights? Under that's above me*, Tim. IV, 3, 292. *now follows that you know*, Hml. I, 2, 17. *followed that I blush to look upon*, Ant. III, 11, 12. *that you did fear is done*, V, 2, 338.

By the omission of the following conjunction, *in that* = considering that, inasmuch as, since, as: *in spite of death thou dost survive, in that thy likeness still is left alive*, Ven. 174. *pardon me, in that my boast is true*, Compl. 246. *my brother had but justice, in that he did the thing for which he died*, Meas. V, 454. *but in that thou art like to be my kinsman, live unbruised*, Ado V, 4, 111. *in that each of you have forsworn his book, can you still dream and pore and thereon look*, LLL IV, 3, 297. *my better, in that you are the first-born*, As I, 1, 50. *brook such disgrace well as he shall run into, in that it is a thing of his own search*, 141. *thou dost consent in some large measure to thy father's death, in that thou seest thy wretched brother die*, R2 I, 2, 27. *for thy treachery, what's more manifest? in that thou laid'st a trap to take my life*, H6A III, 1, 22. *I like it not, in that he bears the badge of Somerset*, IV, 1, 177. *let him die, in that he is a fox*, H6B III, 1, 257. *coal-black is better than another hue, in that it scorns to bear another hue*, Tit. IV, 2, 100. *to suppress his further gait herein, in that the levies are all made out of his subject*, Hml. I, 2, 31. Coming near the sense of *because: I love thee well, in that thou likest it not*, Shr. IV, 3, 83. *entreat her not the worse in that I pray to use her well*, H6B II, 4, 81. *in that you brook it ill, it makes him worse*, R3 I, 3, 3. *happy, in that we are not over-happy*, Hml. II, 2, 232.

**That,** relat. pron., chiefly used to introduce a distinctive clause: *rain added to a river that is rank perforce will force it overflow the bank*, Ven. 71. *thus he that overruled I oversswayed*, 109. *mastering her that foiled the god of fight*, 114. *flowers that are not gathered in their prime rot and consume themselves*, 131. *the sun that shines from heaven shines but warm*, 193 (opposed to the earthly son, i. e. Adonis). *none that I love more than myself*, Tp. I, 1, 22. *I have suffered with those that I saw suffer*, I, 2, 6. 43. 46. 47. 64. 82. 135. 194. 214. 282. 292. 313. 336. 341. 398. 399. 407. 429. 445 etc. etc. Hence the phrases: *unhappy that I am; naught that I am*, Gent. V, 4, 28. Mcb. IV, 3, 225 etc. (never *which I am*). A difference apparently observed between *that* and other relatives: *my heart bleeds to think o' the teen that I have turned you to, which is from my remembrance*, Tp. I, 2, 64. *hail, many-coloured messenger that ne'er dost disobey the wife of Jupiter, who with thy saffron wings ... diffusest honey-drops*, IV, 76. *it was the swift celerity of his death, which I did think with slower foot came on, that brained my purpose*, Meas. V, 401. *I to the world am like a drop of water that in the ocean seeks another drop, who, falling there to find his fellow forth, unseen, inquisitive, confounds himself*, Err. I, 2, 36. *you have oft enquired after the shepherd that complained of love, who you saw sitting by me on the turf*, As III, 4, 51. *that eyes, that are the frailest and softest things, who shut their coward gates on atomies, should be called tyrants*, III, 5, 12. *here's a prophet that I brought with me, ... whom I found with many hundreds treading on his heels*, John IV, 2, 147. *now sir, the sound that tells what hour it is are clamorous groans, which* (Ff *that*) *strike upon my heart, which is the bell*, R2 V, 5, 55.

*like one that draws the model of a house beyond his power to build it; who, half through, gives o'er*, H4B I, 3, 58. *and such other gambol faculties a' has, that show a weak mind and an able body, for the which the prince admits him*, II, 4, 273. *the jades that drag the tragic melancholy night, who with their drowsy wings clip dead men's graves*, H6B IV, 1, 4. *it was he that made the overture of thy treasons to us, who is too good to pity thee*, Lr. III, 7, 89.

But often quite = who or which, in appositional and merely descriptive clauses: *nature that made thee ... saith that the world hath ending with thy life*, Ven. 11. *there they hoist us, to cry to the sea that roared to us*, Tp. I, 2, 149. *some food we had and some fresh water, that a noble Neapolitan, Gonzalo, did give us*, 160. *stained with grief that's beauty's canker*, 415. *a single thing, as I am now, that wonders to hear thee speak of Naples*, 432. *breasted the surge most swoln that met him*, II, 1, 117. *oared himself to the shore, that o'er his wave-worn basis bowed*, 120. *you may thank yourself, ... that would not bless our Europe with your daughter*, 124. *my foolish rival, that her father likes only for his possessions are so huge, is gone with her*, Gent. II, 4, 174. *one Julia, that his changing thoughts forget, would better fit his chamber*, IV, 4, 124. *alas, their love may be called appetite, no motion of the liver, but the palate, that suffer surfeit*, Tw. II, 4, 102. *cut off the heads of too fast growing sprays, that look too lofty in our commonwealth*, R2 III, 4, 35. *as if it were Cain's jaw-bone, that did the first murder*, Hml. V, 1, 85 etc. Alternating with *who* and *which*, without any perceptible difference (but never, like *which*, referring to a whole sentence): *you, brother mine, that entertain ambition, expelled remorse and nature; who, with Sebastian, would have here killed your king*, Tp. V, 75. *sometime like apes that mow and chatter at me and after bite me, then like hedgehogs which lie tumbling in my way, ... sometime am I all wound with adders who with cloven tongues do hiss me into madness*, II, 2, 9. *to her whose state is such that cannot choose but lend and give where she is sure to lose; that seeks not to find that her search implies*, All's I, 3, 222. *it is an heretic that makes the fire, not she which burns in't*, Wint. II, 3, 115. *the weeds which his broad-spreading leaves did shelter, that seemed in eating him to hold him up, are plucked up*, R2 III, 4, 51. *there are other Trojans that thou dreamest not of, the which for sport sake are content to do the profession some grace: that would ... make all whole*, H4A II, 1, 77. *he doth sin that doth belie the dead, not he which says the dead is not alive*, H4B I, 1, 98 (cf. John II, 511). *milk-livered man, that bearest a cheek for blows, a head for wrongs; who hast not ... an eye discerning thine honour ...; that not knowest ...*, Lr. IV, 2, 51. cf. III, 4, 134. I, 4, 232. Cor. V, 6, 108.

Correlative to *so* and *such: no perfection is so absolute, that some infirmity doth not pollute*, Lucr. 854. *no man well of such a salve can speak that heals the wound and cures not the disgrace*, Sonn. 34, 8. *such fire that on the ashes of his youth doth lie*, 73, 10. *a witch and one so strong that could control the moon*, Tp. V, 270. *sail so expeditious that shall catch your royal fleet*, 315. *such a youth that can with some discretion do my business*, Gent. IV, 4, 70. *whose state is such that cannot choose but ...*, All's I, 3, 220. *such allowed infirmities that honesty is never free of*, Wint.

I, 2, 263. *who's so gross, that seeth not this palpable device?* R3 III, 6, 11. *such words that are but roted in your tongue*, Cor. III, 2, 55. *such a man that is no fleering tell-tale*, Caes. I, 3, 116. *who so firm that cannot be seduced?* I, 2, 316. *such things were that were most precious to me*, Mcb. IV, 3, 223. *such an act that blurs the grace and blush of modesty*, Hml. III, 4, 41. *put upon him such a deal of man that worthied him*, Lr. II, 2, 128. *a kind of men so loose of soul that in their sleeps will mutter their affairs*, Oth. III, 3, 417. *a prohibition so divine that cravens my weak hand*, Cymb. III, 4, 80 etc.

**That,** conj. 1) serving to introduce a clause which is, logically, either the subject of the principal sentence, f i.: *'tis childish error that they are afraid*, Ven. 898. *this is my spite, that, thou being dead, the day should yet be light*, 1134. *how is it that this lives in thy mind?* Tp. I, 2, 49. *my brother's suit, which was ... that he should presently extirpate me*, 123. or the object: *saith that the world hath ending*, Ven. 12. *say that the sense of feeling were bereft me*, 439. 521. *whispers in mine ear that if I love thee, I thy death should fear*, 660. *hoping that Adonis is alive*, 1009. *now thinks he that her husband's tongue ... hath done her beauty wrong*, Lucr. 78. *nought knowing ... that I am no better than Prospero*, Tp. I, 2, 19. (at the end of the verse in H8 I, 1, 106). or a necessary complement of an essential part of the principal sentence; f. i.: *taking no notice that she is so nigh*, Ven. 341. *prays her that he may depart*, 578. *envy ... did sting his thoughts, that meaner men should vaunt that golden hap*, Lucr. 41. *I conjure thee that thou neglect me not*, Meas. V, 50. *thy father's wealth was the first motive that I wooed thee*, Wiv. III, 4, 14. *flatter themselves that they are not the first of fortune's slaves*, R2 V, 5, 24. *I have incensed the lords that he is a most arch heretic*, H8 V, 1, 43 etc. etc.

The principal sentence omitted, and the subordinate clause (with *should*) expressing indignant surprise: *that a brother should be so perfidious!* Tp. I, 2, 67 (i. e. it is strange, or incredible; or can it be that etc.). *that a monster should be such a natural!* III, 2, 36. *'mongst all foes that a friend should be the worst!* Gent. V, 4, 72. *that a lady ... should be abused!* Mids. II, 2, 133. *that right should thus overcome might!* H4B V, 4, 27. H6A I, 3, 57. R3 II, 2, 27. Rom. I, 1, 175. 177. Tim. IV, 3, 176. Cymb. II, 1, 57 etc. (cf. the complete periods in Ven. 156 and 205: *may it be that thou shouldst think it heavy unto thee? what am I that thou shouldst contemn me this?*).

Used, by means of a similar ellipsis, as an optative particle: *that god forbid ... I should in thought control your times of pleasure*, Sonn. 58, 1. *O, that record could with a backward look show me your image*, 59, 5. *O, that our night of woe might have remembered my deepest sense, how hard true sorrow hits*, 120, 9. *Ah, that I had my lady at this bay*, Pilgr. 155. *O, that you bore the mind that I do*, Tp. II, 1, 266. *O heavens, that they were living both in Naples*, V, 149. Gent. II, 1, 76. III, 1, 374. Wiv. II, 1, 103. Meas. III, 2, 40. Err. IV, 4, 62. Ado IV, 1, 305. LLL V, 2, 61. Mids. I, 1, 195 *(would).* 197. Merch. II, 9, 41. As II, 4, 23. II, 7, 42. Tw. I, 2, 41. John V, 7, 44. H6A IV, 3, 24. H6B I, 4, 31 *(that I had said and done!).* II, 1, 134. III, 1, 193. H6C II, 5, 95 *(would).* R3 I, 3, 257. Tim. IV, 3, 281 etc.

Likewise the use of *not that* to be explained by an ellipsis (originally: I do not say, I do not pretend that); a) *not that* = not because, not inasmuch as: *she would have me as a beast: not that, I being a beast, she would have me, but that she, being a very beastly creature, lays claim to me*, Err. III, 2, 87. *we have been called so of many; not that our heads are some brown, some black, ... but that our wits are so diversely coloured*, Cor. II, 3, 20. *if then that friend demand why Brutus rose against Caesar, this is my answer: not that I loved Caesar less, but that I loved Rome more*, Caes. III, 2, 22. *words before blows: is it so, countrymen?* Not that we love words better, V, 1, 28. b) *not that I know* = not to my knowledge, not for aught I know: *charges she more than me? Not that I know*, Meas. V, 200. *hath there been such a time that I have positively said 'Tis so, when it proved otherwise? Not that I know*, Hml. II, 2, 155. Perhaps also *that I know* = for aught I know: *there's nine that I know*, Cor. II, 1, 168 (but it may be = which I know).

2) correlative to *so* and *such*: *taught them such disdain that they have murdered this poor heart of mine*, Ven. 502. *doth pitch the price so high, that she will draw his lips' rich treasure dry*, 552. 858. 970. 1050. 1064. 1102. Lucr. 20. 70. 98. 1561. Tp. I, 2, 29. 207. Meas. II, 4, 41. Ant. IV, 15, 44 etc. etc. Used for *as*, the subject of the principal and subordinate sentences being the same: *who are of such sensible and nimble lungs that they always use to laugh at nothing*, Tp. II, 1, 174. *which pierces so that it assaults mercy*, Epil. 17. *she so loves the token ... that she reserves it evermore*, Oth. III, 3, 295. *you love your child so ill that you run mad, seeing that she is well*, Rom. IV, 5, 76 etc.

3) denoting a consequence, = so that: *at this Adonis smiles as in disdain, that in each cheek appears a pretty dimple*, Ven. 242. *he will not manage her, although he mount her: that worse than Tantalus' is her annoy*, 599. *and now she beats her breast, whereat it groans, that all the neighbour caves make verbal repetition of her moans*, 830. *ne'er settled equally, but high or low, that all love's pleasure shall not match his woe*, 1140. *hiding base sin in plaits of majesty, that nothing in him seemed inordinate*, Lucr. 94. *his falchion on a flint he softly smiteth, that from the cold stone sparks of fire do fly*, 177. 467. 1353. 1524. 1738. 1764. Sonn. 76, 7. 98, 4. Compl. 127. 309. Tp. I, 2, 85. 371. III, 2, 151. IV, 183. Gent. II, 1, 32. III, 1, 109. 112. III, 5, 4, 169. Wiv. III, 5, 92. Meas. IV, 2, 204. Err. V, 140. LLL V, 2, 9. Mids. II, 1, 105. Shr. Ind. 2, 60. All's I, 3, 218. Wint. I, 1, 31. IV, 4, 146. H4B I, 1, 197. IV, 1, 216. H6B I, 1, 55. III, 1, 12. 123. H6C III, 1, 47. H8 I, 1, 25. Tit. III, 1, 240. Rom. IV, 3, 48. Caes. I, 1, 50. Mcb. I, 2, 58. I, 7, 8. II, 2, 7. 24. Cymb. V, 4, 45 etc.

Noting not so much a consequence as a fact supposed to be in connexion with what precedes, = seeing that, it being the case that: *what am I, that thou shouldst contemn me this?* Ven. 205. *dost thou drink tears, that thou provokest such weeping?* 949. *what uncouth ill event hath thee befallen, that thou dost trembling stand*, Lucr. 1599. *where art thou, Muse, that thou forget'st so long to speak ...*, Sonn. 100, 1. *what foul play had we, that we came from thence?* Tp. I, 2, 60. *what is she, that all our swains commend her?* Gent. IV, 2, 40. *I doubt he be not well, that he comes not home*, Wiv. I, 4, 43. *what an unweighed behaviour hath he* picked out of my conversation, that he dares in this manner assay me? II, 1, 25. have I laid my brain in the sun and dried it, that it wants matter ..., V, 5, 144. do I love her, that I desire to hear her speak again, Meas. II, 2, 178. there is something in the wind, that we cannot get in, Err. III, 1, 69. these hands do lack nobility, that they strike a meaner than myself, Ant. II, 5, 82. Err. II, 2, 12. Ado I, 1, 106. 181. IV, 1, 63. V, 1, 233. V, 4, 41. Mids. I, 1, 207. As I, 1, 42. Tw. I, 1, 10. H6B IV, 7, 107. H6C IV, 1, 10. R3 IV, 3, 45. Tit. IV, 4, 82 etc.

4) denoting a reason, = in as much as: her eyes are mad that they have wept till now, Ven. 1062. if it be poisoned, 'tis the lesser sin that mine eye loves it and doth first begin, Sonn. 114, 14. that he does I weep, Tp. I, 2, 434. do not smile at me that I boast her off, IV, 9. I have entertained thee, partly that I have need of such a youth, Gent. IV, 4, 69. the reason that I gather he is mad, Err. IV, 3, 87. I wonder that you will still be talking, Ado I, 1, 117. their cheer is the greater that I am subdued, I, 3, 74. he who shall speak for her is afar off guilty but that he speaks, Wint. II, 1, 105. refuge their shame, that many have and others must sit there, R2 V, 5, 27. is he gracious in the people's eye? The more that Henry was unfortunate, H6C III, 3, 118. how goes the world with thee? The better that your lordship please to ask, R3 III, 2, 99. only poor, that when she dies with beauty dies her store, Rom. I, 1, 222 etc. Especially, when preceded by but: thou hadst been gone ere this, but that thou told'st me thou wouldst hunt the boar, Ven. 614 etc. cf. But.

5) denoting a purpose, = in order that; particularly when followed by may (see May), but also with the simple subjunctive and with shall, should, and even will (cf. the resp. verbs): that they were (living), I wish myself were mudded ..., Tp. V, 150. you will the sooner (resolve me) that I were away, LLL II, 112. I should wish it dark, that I were couching with the doctor's clerk, Merch. V, 305 (only in Q1; the rest of O. Edd. till). wipe the dim mist from thy doting eyne, that thou shalt see thy state and pity mine, Lucr. 644. watch the door with pistols, that none shall issue out, Wiv. IV, 2, 53. I will teach you how to humour your cousin, that she shall fall in love with Benedick, Ado II, 1, 396. that thou shalt see the difference of our spirits, I pardon thee thy life, Merch. IV, 1, 368. that you shall surely find him, lead to the Sagittary the raised search, Oth. I, 1, 158. was Milan thrust from Milan, that his issue should become kings of Naples? Tp. V, 205. that you should think we come not to offend, Mids. V, 109. I speak not this that you should bear a good opinion of my knowledge, As V, 2, 59. hath my sword therefore broke through London gates, that you should leave me at the White Hart? H6B IV, 8, 24. in fierce tempest is he coming, ... that, if requiring fail, he will compel, H5 II, 4, 101. there is so much (money) that thou wilt kill me straight, Caes. V, 4, 13 (?).

6) supplying the place of a relative preceded by a preposition (as the pronoun that cannot have a preposition before it): now the happy season once more fits, that love-sick Love by pleading may be blest, Ven. 328. so, till the judgment that yourself arise, you live in this, Sonn. 55, 13. this is the hour that Madam Silvia entreated me to call, Gent. IV, 3, 1. V, 1, 3. in the instant that I met with you he had of me a chain, Err. IV, 1, 9. upon the instant that she was accused,

Ado IV, 1, 217. now thy image doth appear in the rare semblance that I loved it first, V, 1, 260. upon the next occasion that we meet, LLL V, 2, 143. is not this the day that Hermia should give answer of her choice? Mids. IV, 1, 141. now it is the time of night that the graves ... every one lets forth his sprite, V, 387. who riseth from a feast with that keen appetite that he sits down? Merch. II, 6, 9. in the instant that your messenger came, IV, 1, 152. thou lovest me not with the full weight that I love thee, As I, 2, 9. since Pythagoras' time, that I was an Irish rat, III, 2, 187. this is the time that the unjust man doth thrive, Wint. IV, 4, 688. the morn that I was wedded to her mother, H6A V, 4, 24. shall rue the hour that ever thou wast born, H6C V, 6, 43. I was your mother much upon these years that you are now a maid, Rom. I, 3, 73. hath there been such a time ... that I have positively said ..., Hml. II, 2, 154 etc.

Similarly now that = now when: now that their souls are topful of offence, John III, 4, 180. now that God and friends have shaken Edward from the regal seat, H6C IV, 6, 1 (cf. Now). then that = then when: and then that Henry Bolingbroke and he, being mounted and both roused in their seats, ... then, then, when there was nothing ... H4B IV, 1, 117. cf. unsafe the while that we must lave our honours in these flattering streams, Mcb. III, 2, 32.

7) supplying the place of other conjunctions in the second part of a clause: as if between them twain there were no strife, but that life lived in death, and death in life, Lucr. 406 (= but as if). if frosts and fasts nip not the gaudy blossoms of your love, but that it bear this trial and last love, LLL V, 2, 813. but since he stands obdurate and that no lawful means can carry me out of his envy's reach, Merch. IV, 1, 9. sith wives are monsters to you, and that you fly them, All's V, 3, 156. since you to non-regardance cast my faith, and that I partly know the instrument ..., Tw. V, 125. The offences we have made you do we'll answer, if you first sinned with us and that with us you did continue fault and that you slipped not with any but with us, Wint. I, 2, 84. if he think it fit to shore them again and that the complaint they have to the king concerns him nothing, let him call me rogue, IV, 4, 869. if we have entrance ... and that we find the watch but weak, H6A III, 2, 7. when but in all I was six thousand strong and that the French were almost ten to one, IV, 1, 21. before we met or that a stroke was given, 22. I am not your king till I be crowned and that my sword be stained with heart-blood of the house of Lancaster, H6B II, 2, 65. if all obstacles were cut away, and that my path were even to the crown, R3 III, 7, 157. if this law of nature be corrupted, and that great minds ... resist the same, Troil. II, 2, 178. when he had carried Rome and that we looked for no less spoil than glory, Cor. V, 6, 43. if the measure of thy joy be heaped like mine and that thy skill be more to blazon it, Rom. II, 6, 25. whether he was combined with those of Norway, ... or that with both he laboured in his country's wreck, I know not, Mcb. I, 3, 113. though yet of Hamlet our dear brother's death the memory be green, and that it us befitted to bear our hearts in grief, Hml. I, 2, 2. if he be now returned as checking at his voyage, and that he means no more to undertake it, IV, 7, 63. if this should fail, and that our drift look through our bad performance, 152. when you are hot and dry, ... and that he calls for drink, 160. since thy outside looks so fair and warlike, and that thy

*tongue some say of breeding breathes*, Lr. V, 3, 143. *nothing can or shall content my soul till I am evened with him, wife for wife, or failing so, yet that I put the Moor at least into a jealousy*, Oth. II, 1, 309. *if you think fit, or that it may be done*, III, 1, 54. *if e'er my will did trespass 'gainst his love, or that mine eyes ... delighted them in any other form, or that I do not ...* IV, 2, 154. *as if the world should cleave, and that slain men should solder up the rift*, Ant. III, 4, 31. *howsoe'er 'tis strange, or that the negligence may well be laughed at, yet is it true*, Cymb. I, 1, 66. *I love and hate her, for she's fair and royal, and that she hath all courtly parts more exquisite than lady*, III, 5, 71. *if you ... accept my rhymes, and that to hear an old man sing may to your wishes pleasure bring*, Per. Prol. 13. Placed in the second part of a conditional clause, *if* being omitted in the first: *were it not thy sour leisure gave sweet leave to entertain the time ... and that thou teachest how to make one twain*, Sonn. 39, 13. *had time cohered with place or place with wishing, or that the resolute acting of your blood could have attained the effect*, Meas. II, 1, 12.

8) Added to other conjunctions and relative adverbs, without modifying their sense: *after that the holy rites are ended*, Ado V, 4, 68. *after that things are set in order here, we'll follow them*, H6A II, 2, 32. *because that I familiarly sometimes do use you for my fool, your sauciness will jest upon my love*, Err. II, 2, 26. *Oberon is wrath, because that she hath a lovely boy*, Mids. II, 1, 21. As I, 3, 117. John V, 2, 96. R3 III, 1, 130. IV, 2, 117. Cor. III, 2, 52. *a little time before that Edward sicked and died*, H4B IV, 4, 128. *take my soul, before that England give the French the foil*, H6A V, 3, 23. *the breath no sooner left his father's body, but that his wildness ... seemed to die too*, H5 I, 1, 26. *all this ... could not take truce with the unruly spleen of Tybalt, but that he tilts ... at bold Mercutio's breast*, Rom. III, 1, 163. *when by no means he could persuade me ..., but that I told him, the revenging gods 'gainst parricides did all their thunders bend, ... he charges home my unprovided body*, Lr. II, 1, 47. *to be diseased ere that there was true needing*, Sonn. 118, 8. *ere that we will suffer such a prince ... to be disgraced, we all will fight*, H6A III, 1, 97. *for that I love your daughter, ... I must advance the colours of my love*, Wiv. III, 4, 82. Mids. II, 1, 220. Mcb. IV, 3, 185. *hearing how that every day men of great worth resorted to this forest*, As V, 4, 160. *marked you not how that the guilty kindred of the queen looked pale*, R3 II, 1, 135. H8 III, 2, 32. *if that from him there may be aught applied ..., 'tis promised*, Compl. 68. *what would you with her, if that I be she?* Gent. IV, 4, 115. *if that I am I*, Err. III, 2, 41. *to try if that our own be ours or no*, H6A III, 2, 63. *to say if that the boys of York shall be the surety*, H6B V, 1, 115. LLL IV, 3, 252. Mids. I, 2, 81 (Qq *if you should*). Merch. II, 6, 54. III, 2, 224. As I, 3, 45. 51. II, 4, 71. II, 7, 191. IV, 3, 84. Tw. I, 5, 54. 324. V, 375. John II, 89. 484. III, 3, 48. III, 4, 163. IV, 3, 59. R2 II, 3, 123. IV, 33. H4A IV, 1, 58. H4B IV, 1, 32. H5 I, 2, 167. H6A I, 3, 28. II, 5, 61. H6B IV, 4, 23. R3 II, 2, 7. IV, 4, 141. 221 *(as if that)*. V, 1, 7. Troil. V, 5, 41 *(as if that)*. Cor. IV, 2, 13. Rom. II, 2, 143. Caes. IV, 3, 103. Hml. IV, 4, 5. Lr. IV, 2, 46. V, 3, 262. *lest that my mistress hear my song*, Pilgr. 348. *lest that our goods be confiscate*, Err. I, 2, 2. Tw. III, 4, 384. Wint. II, 1, 195. John III, 1, 91. 196. H5

II, 4, 141. H6C I, 1, 98. Cor. IV, 4, 5. Rom. II, 2, 111. Caes. III, 1, 92. Lr. IV, 6, 237. Per. I, 3, 22. *I force not argument a straw, since that my case is past the help of law*, Lucr. 1022. Sonn. 92, 10. Err. II, 1, 114. Merch. III, 3, 30. As III, 5, 94. H5 IV, 1, 321. R3 I, 1, 82. V, 3, 202. Cor. III, 2, 50. V, 3, 98. Mcb. IV, 3, 106. Lr. I, 1, 251. *'tis no sin, sith that the justice of your title to him doth flourish the deceit*, Meas. IV, 1, 74. Lr. II, 4, 242. *so that* (= on condition that; if) *you had her wrinkles and I her money, I would she did as you say*, All's II, 4, 20. Wint. II, 1, 9. R2 III, 4, 102. *does it not flow as hugely as the sea, till that the weary very means do ebb?* As II, 7, 73. H4B II, 3, 51. IV, 4, 40. H6B III, 1, 362. R3 IV, 4, 231. Mcb. I, 2, 54. Hml. IV, 7, 182. Oth. III, 3, 459. V, 2, 336. Ant. II, 7, 113. Per. I, 2, 107. *though that nature with a beauteous wall doth oft close in pollution, yet of thee I will believe ...*, Tw. I, 2, 48. John III, 3, 57. Cor. I, 1, 144. Lr. IV, 6, 219. Oth. I, 1, 71. III, 3, 261. *when that mine eye is famished for a look, ... with my love's picture then my eye doth feast*, Sonn. 47, 3. LLL IV, 3, 145. As II, 7, 75. IV, 3, 117. Tw. V, 398. John I, 95. II, 405. H4A V, 4, 39. H4B IV, 2, 5. IV, 5, 135. R3 I, 4, 241. III, 5, 86. Troil. III, 2, 22. IV, 5, 193. Tit. V, 2, 198. Rom. III, 3, 62. Caes. III, 2, 96. Hml. V, 1, 310. *and where that you have vowed to study, ... can you still dream ...*, LLL IV, 3, 296. *where that his lords desire him to have borne his helmet*, H5 V Chor. 17. *and whether that my angel be turned fiend suspect I may, yet not directly tell*, Sonn. 144, 9. Meas. I, 2, 163. As IV, 3, 59. H6A IV, 1, 28. *while that the armed hand doth fight abroad, the advised head defends itself at home*, H5 I, 2, 178. V, 2, 46. *whiles that his mountain sire ... smiled to see him*, II, 4, 57. *so then I am not lame, ... whilst that this shadow doth such substance give*, Sonn. 37, 10. R2 IV, 238. Tit. V, 2, 183. *what impediment there is, why that the naked, poor and mangled peace should not ... put up her lovely visage*, H5 V, 2, 34.

9) Omitted: *nor could she moralize his wanton sight, more than his eyes were opened to the light*, Lucr. 105. *we are made to be no stronger than faults may shake our frames*, Meas. II, 4, 133. *hath amazed me more than I dare blame my weakness*, All's II, 1, 88 (my astonishment has been too great to be laid to the charge of my weakness, or to be called weakness). *I'ld give bay Curtal and his furniture, my mouth no more were broken than these boys'*, II, 3, 66 (= that my mouth etc.). *I had rather glib myself than they should not produce fair issue*, Wint. II, 1, 149. *direct mine arms I may embrace his neck*, H6A II, 5, 37. *have we some strange Indian ... come to court, the women so besiege us?* H8 V, 4, 35 etc. Omitted in the first part of the clause and placed in the second: *'tis best we stand upon our guard, or that we quit this place*, Tp. II, 1, 322. *would face me down he met me on the mart and that I beat him*, Err. III, 1, 7. *but now I am returned and that war-thoughts have left their places vacant*, Ado I, 1, 303. *she says I am not fair, that I lack manners*, As IV, 3, 15. *think I am dead and that even here thou takest thy last leave*, R2 V, 1, 38.

**Thatch,** subst. roof: *let us not hang like roping icicles upon our houses' t.* H5 III, 5, 24 (the French constable's speech).

**Thatch,** vb. to cover as with a roof of straw: *t. your poor thin roofs with burthens of the dead*, Tim.

IV, 3, 144 (i. e. with false hair). —*ed* = having a roof covered with straw: *my visor is Philemon's roof ... Why, then, your visor should be —ed*, Ado II, 1, 102. *ill-inhabited, worse than Jove in a —ed house*, As III, 3, 11. In Tp. IV, 63: *flat meads —ed with stover*, it seems = covered in general, which is the original signification of the word.

**Thaw**, subst. the melting of things frozen: *a man of continual dissolution and t.* Wiv. III, 5, 119. *that I was duller than a great t.* Ado II, 1, 252.

**Thaw**, vb. to melt, to dissolve; 1) trans.: *favour, savour, hue and qualities ... are on the sudden wasted, —ed and done*, Ven. 749. *thou blowest the fire when temperance is —ed*, Lucr. 884. *now my love is —ed*, Gent. II, 4, 200. *where Phoebus' fire scarce —s the icicles*, Merch. II, 1, 5. *a fire to t. me*, Shr. IV, 1, 9. *—ing cold fear*, H5 IV Chor. 45. *t. the consecrated snow*, Tim. IV, 3, 386. *—ed from the true quality with that which melteth fools*, Caes. III, 1, 41.

2) intr.: *that this too too solid flesh would melt, t. and resolve itself into a dew*, Hml. I, 2, 130.

**The** (often apostrophized before vowels, f. i. *th'one sweetly flatters, th'other feareth harm*, Lucr. 172. *i'th' air or th'earth*, Tp. I, 2, 387. *the other* abbreviated to *t'other* or *tother: she vaunted 'mongst her minions t'other day*, H6B I, 3, 87. *here comes sleeve and t'other*, Troil. V, 4, 19 (Ff *th'other*). *I'll lean upon one crutch and fight with tother*, Cor. I, 1, 246. *I saw him yesterday, or tother day*, Hml. II, 1, 56 etc. In R2 II, 2, 112 and 113 Qq *t'one, t'other*, Ff *th'one, th'other*. In Troil. V, 4, 10 even: *o' th'tother side;* a vulgarism very frequent in contemporary writers. cf. *Other*), the definite article, employed in general as at present: *the sun*, Ven. 1. *the weeping morn*, 2. *hied him to the chase*, 3. *the field's chief flower*, 8. *the world*, 12. *the god of fight*, 114. *so shall the day seem night*, 122. *my beauty as the spring doth yearly grow*, 141 (cf. *Spring*). *the earth's increase*, 169. *the fire that burneth me*, 196. *the time is spent*, 255. *when a painter would surpass the life*, 289. *her eyes wooed still, his eyes disdained the wooing*, 358. *she takes him by the hand*, 361. *the sense of feeling*, 439. *what banquet wert thou to the taste*, 445. *as the wolf doth grin*, 459. *as the berry breaks*, 460. *he strikes her on the cheeks*, 475. *all the earth*, 484. *in the west*, 530. *fall to the earth*, 546. *the night is spent*, 717. *on the sudden*, 749. *confounded in the dark she lay*, 827. *catch her by the neck*, 872. *strike the wise dumb and teach the fool to speak*, 1146. *from the besieged Ardea*, Lucr. 1. *his eye commends the leading to his hand*, 436. *the flesh being proud, desire doth fight with grace*, 712 etc. etc.

Sometimes instead of the possessive pronoun: *hang the head*, Ven. 666 (cf. *Head*). *to put the finger in the eye and weep*, Err. II, 2, 206. *hard in the palm of the hand*, III, 2, 124 (Rowe: *her hand*). *for putting the hand in the pocket*, Meas. III, 2, 49. *to shake the head*, Merch. III, 3, 15. *you shake the head*, Ado II, 1, 377. *he bites the lip*, R3 IV, 2, 27 (Ff *he gnaws his lip*). *he hangs the lip at something*, Troil. III, 1, 152. *he drops down the knee before him*, Tim. I, 1, 61. *at the feet sat*, Ant. III, 6, 5. Caes. II, 4, 34. Mcb. I, 7, 58.

Before gerunds: *worth the eating*, Caes. I, 2, 296. *have hanged a man for the getting a hundred bastards*, Meas. III, 2, 125. *in the delaying death*, IV, 2, 174. *be cunning in the working this*, Ado II, 2, 53. *you need not fear the having any of these lords*, Merch. I, 2, 109.

*in the cutting it if thou dost shed one drop*, IV, 1, 309. *for the better increasing your folly*, Tw. I, 5, 85. *whose state so many had the managing*, H5 Epil. 11. *the giving back the great seal to us*, H8 III, 2, 347. *what she doth cost the holding*, Troil. II, 2, 52 (cf. Hml. V, 1, 100). *nothing in his life became him like the leaving it*, Mcb. I, 4, 8. *what can man's wisdom in the restoring his bereaved sense*, Lr. IV, 4, 9. *I will attempt the doing it*, Oth. III, 4, 22. *the seeing these effects*, Cymb. I, 5, 25. *the locking-up the spirits a time*, 41. (*of* after the gerund, f. i. As II, 4, 49. Caes. III, 1, 51).

Before proper names: *the Hero that here lies,* Ado V, 3, 4 (punning upon the appellative noun *hero?* cf. IV, 1, 101. At least the female form *heroine* is unknown to Sh.). *else the Puck a liar call*, Mids. V, 442. *at the Saint Francis here*, All's III, 5, 39 (i. e. at an inn called so). *the Douglas*, H4A II, 3, 28. IV, 1, 3. H4B Ind. 31. *the Douglas and the Hotspur*, H4A V, 1, 116. *the Talbot*, H6A II, 2, 37. III, 3, 20. 31. *the Burgundy*, III, 3, 37. *the Tarquin*, Caes. II, 1, 54. Similarly: *the Count Claudio*, Ado II, 2, 1. 34. IV, 1, 331. *the Count Rousillon*, All's I, 2, 18. I, 3, 161. II, 3, 200. *the Count Orsino*, Tw. I, 5, 109. II, 1, 44. *the Prince Florizel*, Wint. IV, 2, 29. *the Count Melun*, John IV, 3, 15. V, 4, 9. *the Lieutenant Cassio*, Oth. III, 4, 1 (Ff *Lieutenant Cassio*). *the great Apollo*, Wint. II, 3, 200. III, 2, 138 (III, 1, 14 and III, 2, 129 *great Apollo*). *the good Camillo*, III, 2, 157. *the old Andronicus*, Tit. IV, 4, 89. *the young Romeo*, Rom. II, 4, 125.

Before abstract terms seemingly used in a general sense, but in fact restricted by their particular application: *torches are made to light, ... fresh beauty for the use*, Ven. 164 (Venus has a certain use in mind). *doth not the appetite alter?* Ado II, 3, 247 (i. e. with respect to marriage). *the fashion wears out more apparel than the man*, III, 3, 148 (quite personified; cf. v. 140 sq.). *when the age is in, the wit is out*, III, 5, 37 (Dogberry's proverbial saying, specially applied to his colleague Verges and the wit which he once was master of). *the mathematics and the metaphysics, fall to them as you find your stomach serves you*, Shr. I, 1, 37 (i. e. the studies about which you make so much fuss). *so is running away, when fear proposes the safety*, All's I, 1, 217 (which before was recommended by advantage). *smacks it not something of the policy?* John II, 396 (which you make so much of). *to live but by the spoil*, H6B IV, 8, 41 (read this together with what follows: *by robbing of your friends*). *but say it were not registered, methinks the truth should live from age to age*, R3 III, 1, 76. *the leisure and the fearful time cuts off the ceremonious vows of love*, V, 3, 97. *what will you give us? No money, but the gleek*, Rom. IV, 5, 115 (the one that I know). *all is the fear, and nothing is the love; as little is the wisdom, where the flight so runs against all reason*, Mcb. IV, 2, 12. *their dear causes would to the bleeding and the grim alarm excite the mortified man*, V, 2, 4. Cor. IV, 6, 41. Hml. I, 1, 84. *if it be not now, yet it will come; the readiness is all*, V, 2, 234 (i. e. of leaving or dying). *that Venus where we see the fancy outwork nature*, Ant. II, 2, 206 (i. e. that fancy which we are wont to place so far below nature. But cf. *imagination, understanding* etc. in their present use). see *the death* sub *Death*.

The same point of view perhaps admissible in the following cases: *who is so faint, that dare not be so bold to touch the fire, the weather being cold?* Ven. 402. i. e. the flame). *in the Ocean drenched, or in the fire,* 494. *air and water do abate the fire,* 654. *to swim, to dive into the fire,* Tp. I, 2, 191. *the fire seven times tried this,* Merch. II, 9, 63. *a death that I abhor; for the water swells a man,* Wiv. III, 5, 16. *what is she in the white?* LLL II, 197. *the April's in her eyes,* Ant. III, 2, 43 (i. e. tears). *I have a poor penny-worth in the English,* Merch. I, 2, 77 (which is the only language he understands). *skill in the weapon is nothing without sack,* H4B IV, 3, 123 (opposed to learning). *how dare the plants look up to heaven, from whence they have their nourishment?* Per. I, 2, 55 (not plants in general, but we that are like plants).

In the predicate: *am I the man yet?* As III, 3, 3 (cf. *Man*). *live you the marble-breasted tyrant still,* Tw. V, 127. *made his majesty the bawd to theirs,* John III, 1, 59. *he was the wretched'st thing when he was young,* R3 II, 4, 18. *they are the poorest,* H8 IV, 2, 148. *if he return the conqueror,* Lr. IV, 6, 271. *I am alone the villain of the earth,* Ant. IV, 6, 30. *thy father was the duke of Milan,* Tp. I, 2, 54. *that they were living both in Naples, the king and queen there,* V, 150. *I'll make you the queen of Naples,* I, 2, 449. *were I but now the lord of such hot youth,* R2 II, 3, 99 (Qq lord. cf. *Lord*). *the Marchioness of Pembroke!* H8 II, 3, 94 (cf. 63).

Before the vocative: *the wild waves, whist!* Tp. I, 2, 379. *brother, my lord the duke!* III, 3, 51. *my lord the king!* Wint. III, 2, 143. *my lord the emperor, resolve me this,* Tit. V, 3, 35. *farewell, the latter spring,* H4A I, 2, 177 (M. Edd. *thou latter spring*). *O the father, how he holds his countenance,* II, 4, 432. *the Roman gods, lead their successes, ... that we may give you thankful sacrifice!* Cor. I, 6, 6 (M. Edd. *ye Roman gods;* or: *the Roman gods lead.*) *O the gods!* II, 3, 60. IV, 1, 37. *hark, Tamora, the empress of my soul,* Tit. II, 3, 40. *the last of all the Romans, fare thee well!* Caes. V, 3, 99. *the gods! it smites me beneath the fall I have,* Ant. V, 2, 171. 221. Lr. II, 4, 171. *as you, O the dearest of creatures, would even renew me with your eyes,* Cymb. III, 2, 43. *exposing it — O, the harder heart! alack! no remedy! — to the greedy touch of Titan,* III, 4, 164. *the god of this great vast, rebuke these surges,* Per. III, 1, 1 (most M. Edd. *thou god*). cf. *the venom clamours of a jealous woman, poisons more deadly than a mad dog's tooth!* Err. V, 69 (most M. Edd. *the venom clamours of a jealous woman poison* etc.). Lr. I, 1, 271.

The following differences from modern or common usage easily accounted for: *the one so like the other,* Err. I, 1, 52. *the one of them contains my picture,* Merch. II, 7, 11. *which is the wiser here? Justice or Iniquity?* Meas. II, 1, 180. *a! the first sight they have changed eyes,* Tp. I, 2, 440. *for urging it the second time to me,* Err. II, 2, 47. *bad news, by'r lady; seldom comes the better,* R3 II, 3, 4. *by that you love the dearest in the world,* H8 IV, 2, 155. *as common as any the most vulgar thing to sense,* Hml. I, 2, 99. *never will I undertake the thing wherein thy counsel and consent is wanting,* H6C II, 6, 101; cf. *in this rapture I shall surely speak the thing I shall repent,* Troil. III, 2, 139. *when he might act the woman in the scene,* Cor. II, 2, 100. *we shall buy maidenheads by the hundreds,* H4A II, 4, 398. *knock 'em down by the dozens,* H8 V, 4, 33. *should by the minute feed on life,* Cymb. V, 5, 51. cf. the articles *Heaven, Day, Night, Which* etc.

Before two comparatives, denoting corresponding gradation (cf. *Much*): *the mightier man, the mightier is the thing that makes him honoured,* Lucr. 1004. *the more she saw the blood his cheeks replenish, the more she thought he spied in her some blemish,* 1357. *the sooner the better,* H6B I, 4, 17. Tp. III, 1, 80. Gent. II, 7, 24. IV, 2, 14. Err. II, 2, 89. As IV, 1, 162. R2 I, 1, 41. H4A V, 2, 15. H5 IV, 3, 22. H6C V, 1, 70 etc. The first comparative replaced by another form of expression, or supplied in thought: *her words are done, her woes the more increasing,* Ven. 254. *and that his beauty may the better thrive, with Death she humbly doth insinuate,* 1011. *never did he bless my youth with his; the more am I accurst,* 1120. *swells the higher by this let,* Lucr. 646. *the baser is he ... to shame his hope,* 1002. *you swinged me for my love, which makes me the bolder to chide you for yours,* Gent. II, 1, 89. *if you turn not, you will return the sooner,* II, 2, 4. III, 1, 95. III, 2, 19. IV, 4, 29. 63. V, 4, 136. Wiv. II, 1, 56. 186. III, 2, 86. IV, 6, 39. Meas. I, 4, 22. II, 1, 233. III, 1, 6. IV, 3, 48. 50. Err. I, 2, 103. Mids. II, 1, 202. All's I, 1, 161. H6A V, 1, 15. H6B I, 1, 29. H6C IV, 1, 83. IV, 8, 56. Mcb. III, 1, 26. IV, 3, 184. Ant. III, 2, 52 etc. The article before the second comparative omitted: *who taught thee how to make me love thee more the more I hear and see just cause of hate?* Sonn. 150, 10. Comparative omitted: *the more you beat me, I will fawn on you,* Mids. II, 1, 204. The article seemingly superfluous: *what were thy lips the worse for one poor kiss?* Ven. 207. *let them alone till they are sober: if they make you not then the better answer, you may say they are not the men you took them for,* Ado III, 3, 49. *how much the better to fall before the lion than the wolf,* Tw. III, 1, 139. *I am the worse, when one says 'swagger'* H4B II, 4, 112.

Omitted with the liberty peculiar to poetical language and still more common in ancient than in modern poetry: *to cabin!* Tp. I, 1, 18. *safely in harbour is the king's ship,* I, 2, 226. *stealing unseen to west,* Sonn. 33, 8. *ere I went to wars,* Ado I, 1, 307. *the smallest mouse that creeps on floor,* Mids. V, 223. *milk comes frozen home in pail,* LLL V, 2, 925. *sticks me at heart,* As I, 2, 254. *with spectacles on nose and pouch on side,* II, 7, 159. *no man at door,* Shr. IV, 1, 123. Wint. IV, 4, 352. *he be at palace,* IV, 4, 731. *their grace 'fore meat, their talk at table, and their thanks at end,* Cor. IV, 7, 3. *on one and other side,* Troil. Prol. 21. *foamed at mouth,* Caes. I, 2, 255. *performed at height,* Hml. I, 4, 21. *I will be thrown into Etna, as I have been into Thames,* Wiv. III, 5, 129. *from the banks of Wye and sandy-bottomed Severn,* H4A III, 1, 65. *from Trent and Severn hitherto,* 74. *you shall have Trent turned,* 136. *from the waves of Tiber,* Caes. I, 2, 114. *all the worms of Nile,* Cymb. III, 4, 37. *if Marcius should be joined with Volscians,* Cor. IV, 6, 89. *King of Pont,* Ant. III, 6, 72. *ear's deep-sweet music, and heart's deep-sore wounding,* Ven. 432. *proving from world's minority their right,* Lucr. 67. *wilt thou be glass wherein it shall discern authority for sin,* 619. *greatest scandal waits on greatest state,* 1006. *to drown in ken of shore,* 1114. *when sun doth melt their snow,* 1218. *eclipses stain both moon and sun, and loathsome canker lives in sweetest bud,* Sonn. 35, 3. *more tuneable than lark to shepherd's ear,* Mids. I, 1, 184. *plain as way to parish church,* As II, 7, 52. *he that can assure my daughter greatest dower,* Shr. II, 345. *if thou proceed as high as word*, All's II, 1, 213. *mightst never draw sword again*, Tw. I, 3, 66. *longest way shall have the longest moans*, R2 V, 1, 90. *to sun's parching heat displayed my cheeks*, H6A I, 2, 77. *where is best place to make our battery next*, I, 4, 65. *this jarring discord of nobility*, IV, 1, 188. *York is meetest man to be your regent*, H6B I, 3, 163. *as salt as sea*, III, 2, 96. *while heart is drowned in cares*, III, 3, 14. *in humblest manner*, H8 II, 4, 144. *I propend to you in resolution to keep Helen still*, Troil. II, 2, 191. *as false ... as fox to lamb*, III, 2, 200. *fallen in first rank*, III, 3, 161. *that* (love) *which dearest father bears his son*, Hml. I, 2, 111. *best safety lies in fear*, I, 3, 43. *left me bare to weather*, Cymb. III, 3, 64. *as nurse said*, Per. IV, 1, 53 etc. Very often omitted before substantives followed by *of*: *o'ercharged with burden of mine own love's might*, Sonn. 23, 8. *in table of my heart*, 24, 2. *our dear love lose name of single one*, 39, 6. *in pride of all his growth*, 99, 12. *in process of the seasons*, 104, 6. *some beauty peeped through lattice of seared age*, Compl. 14. *by help of her ministers*, Tp. I, 2, 275. *in absence of thy friend*, Gent. I, 1, 59. *sink in apple of his eye*, Mids. III, 2, 104. *with splendour of his precious eye*, John III, 1, 79. *to crouch in litter of your stable planks*, V, 2, 140. *we at time of year do wound the bark*, R2 III, 4, 57. *in reproof of many tales devised*, H4A III, 2, 23. *rock his brains in cradle of the rude surge*, H4B III, 1, 20. *in shadow of such greatness*, IV, 2, 15. H5 I, 1, 15. I, 2, 58. 110. III Chor. 18. III, 5, 22. IV, 7, 81. V, 2, 400. H6A III, 2, 77. H6B I, 2, 36. 79. II, 3, 71. H6C I, 4, 13. II, 1, 133. II, 5, 8. III, 2, 6. III, 3, 211. IV, 1, 68. IV, 6, 51. IV, 7, 18. R3 III, 5, 81. III, 7, 35 (Ff *at lower end of the hall;* cf. Cor. IV, 5, 205; Qq *at the lower end* etc.). V, 3, 176. H8 III, 2, 128. IV, 1, 10. 16. Troil. I, 1, 38. I, 3, 178. Cor. III, 3, 121. IV, 5, 205. Tit. I, 197. 458. Rom. I, 2, 106. III, 2, 82. Caes. I, 2, 301. III, 1, 216. Hml. I, 5, 65. Lr. I, 2, 120. II, 2, 68. Oth. II, 1, 24. Ant. II, 2, 160. Cymb. III, 5, 61. IV, 2, 190.

**Theatre,** a playhouse: As II, 7, 137. John II, 375. R2 V, 2, 23. Caes. I, 2, 263. I, 3, 152. Hml. III, 2, 31.

**Theban,** a native of Thebes: Lr. III, 4, 162.

**Thebes,** town in ancient Greece: Mids. V, 51.

**Thee,** see *Thou.*

**Theft,** 1) the act of stealing: Ven. 160. Lucr. 838. 918. Sonn. 99, 12. Wiv. I, 3, 28. Err. IV, 2, 61. All's II, 1, 34. H4A IV, 2, 67 (= practice of stealing). H6A III, 1, 48. Troil. II, 2, 92. V, 3, 21. Cor. I, 9, 22. Tim. IV, 3, 430. 447. Mcb. II, 3, 151. Lr. IV, 6, 44. Cymb. V, 5, 341. Abstr. pro concr.: *when the suspicious head of theft is stopped*, LLL IV, 3, 336 (= the ears of thieves).

2) the thing stolen: *if he steal aught the whilst this play is playing, ... I will pay the t.* Hml. III, 2, 94.

3) (for the sake of quibbling) the act of withdrawing privily: *I'll steal away. There's honour in the t.* All's II, 1, 34. *shift away; there's warrant in that t. which steals itself, when there's no mercy left*, Mcb. II, 3, 151.

**Their,** poss. pron. of the third pers. plur.: Ven. 20. 44 (*each leaning on their elbows*). 131. 165. 216. 248. 418. 488. 503. 506. 507. 532 etc. *God send every one their heart's desire*, Ado III, 4, 61. *Picardy hath slain their governors*, H6B IV, 1, 89. Superfluous: *tears show their love, but want their remedies*, R2 III, 3, 203.

**Theirs,** absol. poss. pron. of the third pers. plur.: *a mischief worse than civil home-bred strife, or theirs*

*whose desperate hands themselves do slay*, Ven. 765 (= the mischief of them whose etc.). *an eye more bright than t.* Sonn. 20, 5. 32, 14. Tp. I, 1, 58. Gent. III, 1, 24 (*this love of t.* = this their love). Meas. I, 4, 82. LLL V, 2, 138. John II, 35. R2 II, 3, 13. H4B IV, 2, 46. H6B III, 2, 385. Cor. II, 1, 220. III, 1, 211. V, 6, 4 (*in theirs and in the commons' ears;* cf. *yours* in Tp. II, 1, 254). Tim. V, 1, 156. Mcb. I, 6, 26 (*your servants ever have theirs, themselves, and what is theirs, in compt)* etc. etc.

**Them,** see *They.*

**Theme,** 1) a subject on which one speaks or writes: *leave this idle t.*, *this bootless chat*, Ven. 422. *you will fall again into your idle over-handled t.* 770. *if that* (my good name) *be made a t. for disputation, the branches of another root are rotted*, Lucr. 822. *fair, kind and true, ... three —s in one*, Sonn. 105, 12. *I am your t.* Wiv. V, 5, 170. *to me she speaks; she moves me for her t.* Err. II, 2, 183. *this weak and idle t., no more yielding but a dream*, Mids. V, 434. *a son who is the t. of honour's tongue*, H4A I, 1, 81. *it is a t. as fluent as the sea*, H5 III, 7, 36. *she is a t. of honour and renown*, Troil. II, 2, 199. *O deadly gall, and t. of all our scorns*, IV, 5, 30. *she's a deadly t.* 181. *handle not the t., to talk of hands*, Tit. III, 2, 29. *that is the very t. I came to talk of*, Rom. I, 3, 63. *to reason most absurd, whose common t. is death of fathers*, Hml. I, 2, 103. *big of this gentleman our t.* Cymb. I, 1, 39. *will to ears and tongues be t. and hearing ever*, III, 1, 4. *when a soldier was the t.* III, 3, 59.

2) discourse on a certain subject: *it was the subject of my t.* Err. V, 65. *your writing now is colder than that t., 'She had not been, nor was not to be equalled'; thus your verse flowed with her beauty once*, Wint. V, 1, 100; cf. above Err. II, 2, 183 (most commentators: colder than dead Hermione, the former subject of your praise).

3) subject, question, cause, matter: *have just our t. of woe*, Tp. II, 1, 6. *shall I to this lady? Ay, that's the t.* Tw. II, 4, 125. *the gracious queen, part of his t., but nothing of his ill-ta'en suspicion*, Wint. I, 2, 459.*in a t. so bloody-faced as this, conjecture ... should not be admitted*, H4B I, 3, 22. *you are pleasant. With your t. I could o'ermount the lark*, H8 II, 3, 93. *stubborn critics, apt, without a t., for depravation*, Troil. V, 2, 131. *it will in time win upon power and throw forth greater —s for insurrection's arguing*, Cor. I, 1, 224. *to honour and advance the t. of our assembly*, II, 2, 61 (him for whose sake we are assembled, i. e. Coriolanus). *here he comes, and I must ply my t.* Tit. V, 2, 80 (that which I am about). *happy prologues to the swelling act of the imperial t.* Mcb. I, 3, 129. *I will fight with him upon this t.* Hml. V, 1, 289. 291. *their contestation was t. for you; you were the word of war*, Ant. II, 2, 44 (a matter, an enterprise undertaken in your interest).

**Themselves,** 1) they or them in contradistinction to others: *things growing to t.* Ven. 166. *if pleased t., others, they think, delight in such-like circumstance*, 843. Tp. II, 1, 192. V, 32. Wiv. IV, 1, 69. Meas. I, 1, 34. I, 3, 28. I, 4, 83. II, 2, 177. Tw. III, 4, 391 (*O heavens t.!*) etc. etc. Refl.: Ven. 132. 765. 810. 1032. Wiv. II, 2, 257. Meas. II, 4, 125. H6C I, 2, 58 etc. etc.

2) each other: *each in her sleep t. so beautify, as if between them twain there were no strife, but that life lived in death, and death in life*, Lucr. 404. *if they were but a week married, they would talk t. mad,*

Ado II, 1, 369. *that for a toy, a thing of no regard, King Henry's peers and chief nobility destroyed t. and lost the realm of France,* H6A IV, 1, 147. *valour and pride excel t. in Hector; the one almost as infinite as all, the other blank as nothing,* Troil. IV, 5, 79. cf. *Ourselves.*

**Then** (originally spelt *than,* and sometimes found in this form in Sh., f. i. Merch. II, 2, 200. H6C II, 5, 9. rhyming to *began:* Lucr. 1440) 1) at that time: *then thou wast not out three years old,* Tp. I, 2, 40. *how I cried out then,* 133. 152. 162. 212. 213. 271. 281. II, 1, 274. III, 2, 148. Gent. V, 4, 47 etc. Adjectively: *our t. dictator,* Cor. II, 2, 93. Substantively: *then call me husband, but in such a then I write a never,* All's III, 2, 62.

2) after that: *mark his condition and the event; then tell me, if this might be a brother,* Tp. I, 2, 117. *hear a little further, and then I'll bring thee to the present business,* 136. 201. 336. 377. II, 1, 185. III, 2, 123. V, 317. Gent. I, 1, 33. Meas. III, 2, 86 etc. = *further, besides:* Shr. II, 358. Ant. II, 2, 75. III, 6, 26 etc. *now and then* = sometimes: Merch. II, 2, 200. As III, 5, 103. H5 III, 6, 71. Lr. IV, 3, 14 etc. *first ... then:* Err. IV, 2, 15. H8 V, 3, 15. *first ... then ... then:* Meas. IV, 3, 4. 9. 13. Err. IV, 2, 7. 9. 11. H8 III, 2, 310. 313. 316. 326. *first ... and then:* R3 III, 2, 8. 10. *first ... and then ... and lastly:* H6C III, 3, 52. 53. 54. *now ... then:* H6C II, 5, 10. *sometime ... then:* Tp. II, 2, 10. *sometime ... and then:* H6C II, 5, 9. *sometimes ... and sometime ... and then:* Tp. III, 2, 149. *then ... then* (= *now ... now*): As III, 2, 436.

3) if it is so; in that case: *work you then,* Tp. I, 1, 45. *my affections are then most humble,* I, 2, 482. *then wisely weigh our sorrow with our comfort,* II, 1, 8. *why doth it not then our eyelids sink?* 201. 244. 306. II, 2, 56. 132. 157. III, 1, 87. III, 2, 59. IV, 1, 32. V, 288. Gent. I, 1, 72. 77. 79 *(why t.).* I, 2, 2. 72. 76. 85. II, 1, 85. II, 5, 17 *(how t.?).* II, 7, 33. 62. III, 1, 195 and 197 *(who t.? what t.?* cf. As II, 7, 83. H6C I, 1, 136). IV, 2, 49. Meas. III, 2, 85. Err. II, 1, 97. Merch. I, 1, 158. I, 3, 115 etc. Transposed: *how comes it that thou art then estranged from thyself?* Err. II, 2, 122 (= *how comes it then that* etc., a liberty very common in German. Most M. Edd., adopting Rowe's emendation, *that thou art thus estranged*).

4) on the other hand; in return: *thou shalt be as free as the mountain winds: but then exactly do all points of my command,* Tp. I, 2, 499. *he is then a giant to an ape; but then is an ape a doctor to such a man,* Ado V, 1, 205.

Difficult passage: *more* (reasons), *more strong, then lesser is my fear, I shall indue you with,* John IV, 2, 42 (explained by some as meaning 'then when my fear is less', and emended by others to *when lesser* etc. Perhaps it ought to be: *the lesser*).

**Thence,** 1) from that place, from there: Ven. 582. Lucr. 736. 743. 1552. 1724. 1850. Sonn. 48, 13. 51, 3. Tp. I, 2, 62. 131. 393. II, 1, 108. V, 310. Gent. I, 2, 122. III, 1, 37. IV, 1, 23. IV, 2, 117. Meas. IV, 3, 66. Err. II, 2, 129. V, 143. 246. Mids. I, 1, 218. All's III, 2, 55. Wint. II, 2, 60. H6A I, 4, 12. H6C II, 2, 107 etc. *whate'er thy thoughts or thy heart's workings be, thy looks should nothing t. but sweetness tell,* Sonn. 93, 12. *in the great hand of God I stand, and t. against the undivulged pretence I fight of treasonous malice,* Mcb. II, 3, 136.

Preceded by *from,* in the same sense: Ven. 195. 227. 488. Lucr. 760. Sonn. 86, 12 *(I was not sick of any fear from t.).* Compl. 34. Tp. I, 2, 60. Gent.

II, 4, 53. Meas. IV, 3, 103. Err. IV, 4, 79. 153. Mids. III, 2, 368. H6A IV, 1, 171. H6B II, 3, 6. H6C III, 2, 138 *(chides the sea that sunders him from t.)* etc.

2) from this, out of this; from that source, for that reason: *but t. I learn,* Sonn. 118, 13. *in nothing art thou black save in thy deeds, and t. this slander, as I think, proceeds,* 131, 14. *t. comes it that my name receives a brand, and almost t. my nature is subdued to what it works in,* Sonn. 111, 5, 6. *t. it came that ...,* All's V, 3, 52. *t. it is, that I to your assistance do make love,* Mcb. III, 1, 123.

3) not there, elsewhere, absent: *who would be t. that has the benefit of access?* Wint. V, 2, 118. *'tis not the land I care for, wert thou t.* H6B III, 2, 359. *they prosper best of all when I am t.* H6C II, 5, 18. *when fair Cressid comes into my thoughts, — so, traitor! When she comes! when is she t.?* Troil. I, 1, 31. *From t.,* in the same sense: *to feed were best at home; from t. the sauce to meat is ceremony,* Mcb. III, 4, 36 (= from home, as another's guest).

**Theoric,** theory (opposed to practice): *had the whole t. of war in the knot of his scarf, and the practice in the chape of his dagger,* All's IV, 3, 162. *the art and practic part of life must be the mistress to this t.* H5 I, 1, 52. *the bookish t., wherein the toged consuls can propose as masterly as he,* Oth. I, 1, 24.

**There,** 1) in or at that place: Ven. 119. 245. 301. 691. 915. 1035. Lucr. 114 etc. etc. Superfluous: *and in a dark and dankish vault at home there left me,* Err. V, 248. *the County Paris at Saint Peter's Church shall happily make thee there a joyful bride,* Rom. III, 5, 116. *so that my speed to Mantua there was stayed,* V, 2, 12. *if at Philippi we do face him there,* Caes. IV, 3, 211. *Here and there,* see *Here.*

2) to or into that place: *will not let a false sound enter there,* Ven. 780. *there they hoist us,* Tp. I, 2, 148. *the rarest that e'er came there,* II, 1, 99 etc.

3) Multifariously employed to point to, and single out, persons and things; applied to persons (present or absent): *his testy master goeth about to take him; when lo, the unbacked breeder, full of fear, jealous of catching, swiftly doth forsake him, with her the horse, and left Adonis there,* Ven. 322 (not = left Adonis in that place, but = left Adonis where he stood). *he ran upon the boar with his sharp spear, who did not whet his teeth at him again, but by a kiss thought to persuade him there,* 1114 (him who ran on him). *for, in conclusion, he did beat me there,* Err. II, 1, 74 (i. e. he there, your husband, my master). *that goldsmith there,* V, 219. *he dined with her there, at the Porpentine,* 275. *Lady Margery, your midwife there,* Wint. II, 3, 160. *away toward Bury, to the Dauphin there,* John IV, 3, 114. *knock him down there,* H6B IV, 6, 9. *that good man of worship, Anthony Woodville, her brother there,* R3 I, 1, 67. *the haughty prelate Bishop of Exeter, his brother there,* IV, 4, 503 *(Ff his elder brother).* *the fool will not, he there, that he: look you there,* Troil. II, 1, 91. *loves the whore there,* V, 4, 7. *ha, art thou there?* V, 6, 8 (art thou come, thou, whom I am seeking?). *who's there?* Hml. I, 1, 1 (challenge of a sentinel). Used as a call to servants or other inferior persons: *what, ho! Abhorson! where's Abhorson there!* Meas. IV, 2, 21. *where are you there?* H6B I, 2, 68. *who is there? Take this fellow in,* I, 3, 36. *within there! Flaminius! Servilius!* Tim. II, 2, 194. *come in, without there!* Mcb. IV, 1, 135. *louder the music there!*

Lr. IV, 7, 25. *from Sicyon, ho, the news! speak there,* Ant. I, 2, 117. *on, there! pass along,* III, 1, 37. *approach, there!* III, 13, 89. *some wine, within there, and our viands!* III, 11, 73. *set on there!* Cymb. V, 5, 484. In other cases also, the person not expressly named, but understood: *keep tune there still,* Gent. I, 2, 89 (i. e. you, to whom I am speaking). *what is he of basest function that says his bravery is not on my cost, thinking that I mean him, but therein suits his folly to the mettle of my speech? There then; how then? what then?* As II, 7, 83 (i. e. to such a person as this what am I to reply?).

Pointing to things: *there, take the paper,* Gent. I, 2, 46. *try me in thy paper. There, and Saint Nicholas be thy speed,* III, 1, 300. *there, take it* (the diamond) Err. V, 392. *what letter are you reading there,* Gent. I, 3, 51. *toward Swinstead, to the abbey there,* John V, 3, 8. *there is my hand,* H4B V, 2, 117. Or to actions or occurrences: *what a blow was there given!* Tp. II, 1, 180. *there spake my brother; there my father's grave did utter forth a voice,* Meas. III, 1, 86. *there, take you that* (blows) Err. I, 2, 92. *there's for you. Why, there's for thee, and there, and there,* Tw. IV, 1, 27; cf. Troil. II, 1, 127. *how now there!* Wint. III, 2, 148. *there's a bargain made,* Caes. I, 3, 120. *there's a great spirit gone,* Ant. I, 2, 126 (by Fulvia's death). *why, there then: thus I do escape the sorrow of Antony's death,* IV, 14, 94. *there; my blessing with thee,* Hml. I, 3, 57.

Hence often = this, that: *thou art thy father's daughter; there's enough,* As I, 3, 60. *you shall read it in — what do ye call there?* All's II, 3, 26. *there was the weight that pulled me down,* H8 III, 2, 408. *why, there's the privilege your beauty bears,* Tit. IV, 2, 116. *there's a fearful point,* Rom. IV, 3, 32. *how that might change his nature, there's the question,* Caes. II, 1, 13. *you and I must part, but that's not it: Sir, you and I have loved, but there's not it,* Ant. I, 3, 88. *it was not brought me, my lord; there's the cunning of it,* Lr. I, 2, 63. *but when to my good lord I prove untrue, I'll choke myself: there's all I'll do for you,* Cymb. I, 5, 87.

And = in this, by this: *what I will, I will, and there an end,* Gent. I, 3, 65. II, 1, 168. R2 V, 1, 69 (cf. *End*). *there she lost a noble and renowned brother,* Meas. III, 1, 227. *serve God, love me, and mend. There will I leave you too,* Ado V, 2, 95 (with these words). *there all is marred; there lies a cooling card,* H6A V, 3, 84. *you break no privilege nor charter there,* R3 III, 1, 54. *thy Juliet is alive, for whose dear sake thou wast but lately dead; there art thou happy; Tybalt would kill thee, but thou slewest Tybalt; there art thou happy too,* Rom. III, 3, 137; cf. 140. *there stand I in much peril,* Oth. V, 1, 21. *dost thou hold there still?* Ant. II, 5, 92. *you have been a great thief by sea. And you by land. There I deny my land service,* II, 6, 98 (in this point). *there was our error,* Cymb. V, 5, 260.

= on this occasion; at this point; almost = then: *his passion ... even there resolved my reason into tears, there my white stole of chastity I daffed,* Compl. 296. *Herne the hunter ... doth walk round about an oak, with great ragged horns; and there he blasts the tree and takes the cattle and makes milch-kine yield blood,* Wiv. IV, 4, 32. *and there indeed let him name his name,* Mids. III, 1, 46. *and even there he put his hand behind him,* Merch. II, 8, 46. *and there put on him what forgeries you please,* Hml. II, 1, 19. *there she shook the*

*holy water from her heavenly eyes,* Lr. IV, 3, 31. *when the rain came, ... there I found 'em, there I smelt 'em out,* IV, 6, 104.

Emphatically, by way of applause: *ay, touch him; there's the vein,* Meas. II, 2, 70 (= that's the right way). *there's a girl goes before the priest,* As IV, 1, 140. *why, there's a wench,* Shr. V, 2, 180. *there's a good grandam,* John II, 163. H4B V, 3, 24. Troil. I, 2, 217. 218. 223. 248. Ant. II, 7, 94. and with irony: *you leer upon me, do you? there's an eye wounds like a leaden sword,* LLL V, 2, 480. Or = to the point; that's the point: *now prove our loving lawful, and our faith not torn. Ay, marry, there! some flattery for this evil,* LLL IV, 3, 286. *why, there, there, there, there! a diamond gone,* Merch. III, 1, 87 (= that touches to the core). *why, there 'tis; so say I too,* All's II, 3, 17. *you are so fretful, you cannot live long. Why, there is it,* H4A III, 3, 15. *ay, there's the question,* H6B IV, 2, 149. *there thou hast it,* R3 IV, 2, 73 (Ff *then*). *there was it,* Cor. V, 6, 44. *there thou say'st,* Hml. V, 1, 29. *O ho, are you there with me?* Lr. IV, 6, 148. *there's the point,* Ant. II, 6, 31.

Used as a cry of encouragement: *Silver! there it goes, Silver! Fury, Fury, there! Tyrant, there!* Tp. IV, 257. *there, there, Hortensio, will you any wife?* Shr. I, 1, 56. *his blows are well disposed: there, Ajax,* Troil. IV, 5, 116. *Troilus, thou coward Troilus! Ay, there, there!* V, 5, 43. *why, there it goes,* Tit. IV, 3, 76. *so, so, there! aches contract and starve your supple joints,* Tim. I, 1, 256.

4) Very frequently placed before the verb, when there is inversion of the subject: *where there are but twain,* Ven. 123. *there wanteth but a mean,* Gent. I, 2, 95. *let there be some more test made,* Meas. I, 1, 49. Ven. 863. 1187. Lucr. 133. 143. 976. Tp. I, 2, 15. 29. 238. 242. II, 1, 257. III, 3, 22. 44. Meas. I, 2, 28. Err. III, 2, 185. As I, 3, 121 etc. *there is no hiding you* = it is impossible to hide you, Wiv. IV, 2, 64. *there is no following her,* Mids. III, 2, 82. Ado III, 2, 41. All's II, 3, 251. H4A IV, 1, 39. H8 I, 3, 43. Cymb. IV, 4, 9.

Omitted: *whose wraths to guard you from ... is nothing but heart-sorrow,* Tp. III, 3, 81. *sigh for the tooth-ache? where is but a humour or a worm,* Ado III, 2, 27. *satisfaction can be none,* Tw. III, 4, 261. *was never subject longed to be a king,* H6B IV, 9, 5. *remaineth nought but to inter our brethren,* Tit. I, 146 etc.

**Thereabout,** 1) near that number, not much more or less: *O for a fine thief of the age of two and twenty* or *t.* H4A III, 3, 212 (Qq *thereabouts*).

2) concerning that: *'twas Aeneas' tale to Dido, and t. of it especially, where he speaks of Priam's slaughter,* Hml. II, 2, 468.

**Thereabouts,** 1) near that number: *five or six thousand horse, ... or t.* All's IV, 3, 171. H4A III, 3, 212 (Ff *thereabout*).

2) of that import, or aiming at that: *how! dare not! do not. Do you know and dare not? Be intelligent to me; 'tis t.: for to yourself, what you do know, you must and cannot say, you dare not,* Wint. I, 2, 378. *he has given example for our flight, most grossly, by his own. Ay, are you t.? why, then, good night indeed,* Ant. III, 10, 29.

**Thereafter,** according: *how a scores of ewes now? T. as they be: a score of good ewes may be worth ten pounds,* H4B III, 2, 56.

**Thereat,** at it, at that: *not for Bohemia, nor the*

*pomp that may be t. gleaned*, Wint. IV, 4, 500 (at or in possessing it). *that this sight should make so deep a wound, and yet detested life not shrink t.* Tit. III, 1, 248. *t. enraged*, Lr. IV, 2, 75.

**Thereby,** 1) annexed to that: *t. hangs a tale*, Wiv. I, 4, 159. As II, 7, 28. Shr. IV, 1, 60. Oth. III, 1, 8.

2) by that, by means of that: *from fairest creatures we desire increase, that t. beauty's rose might never die*, Sonn. I, 2. Gent. III, 1, 31. Meas. III, 1, 6. Mids. IV, 1, 162. LLL IV, 3, 283. Tw. IV, 1, 60. Wint. I, 2, 337. John III, 1, 276. R2 I, 3, 218. H4A V, 4, 119. H6A V, 4, 115. H6B II, 1, 187. III, 2, 218. IV, 2, 171. H6C II, 5, 25. R3 I, 3, 68. Cor. V, 3, 133. Tit. II, 3, 207. Mcb. V, 4, 5. *she carved thee for her seal, and meant t. thou shouldst print more*, Sonn. 11, 13. As V, 1, 38. Tit. IV, 4, 84.

**Therefore,** 1) for that: *t. my son i' the ooze is bedded*, Tp. III, 3, 100 (in punishment for this). *what should I get t.?* Mids. III, 2, 78. *t. we meet not now*, H4A I, 1, 30 (for this purpose). *lament t.* H4B V, 3, 112. *we are t. provided*, H6B I, 4, 3 (we are provided with what is necessary to perform this). *hath my sword t. broke through London gates, that you should leave me at the White Hart?* IV, 8, 24. *thou wilt revolt and fly to him, I fear. No, mighty liege; t. mistrust me not*, R3 IV, 4, 479 (as for this; concerning this). *often have you thanks t.* Troil. III, 3, 20. Cor. II, 3, 225.

2) on that account, accordingly, consequently: Ven. 390. 733. 751. 807. 1087. Tp. I, 2, 360. II, 1, 23. III, 2, 2. IV, 22. 206. V, 77. Gent. I, 1, 90. I, 3, 89. III, 1, 84. 276. 323. 370. III, 2, 36. 51. 90. IV, 4, 62. 169 etc. etc.

**Therein,** 1) in it or in them; in this; a) referring to nouns: *and therein* (in a just show) *so ensconced his secret evil*, Lucr. 1515. *to gaze t.* (in my breast) *on thee*, Sonn. 24, 12. Mids. V, 67. R2 I, 3, 181. II, 1, 81. III, 3, 168. IV, 276. H5 III Chor. 25. H6A III, 2, 127. V, 4, 140. Troil. I, 2, 124. Hml. II, 2, 80 etc.

b) referring to sentences, = in this, in this point, in this respect: *I prattle something too wildly and my father's precepts I t. do forget*, Tp. III, 1, 59. *since thou lovest, love still and thrive t.* Gent. I, 1, 9. IV, 1, 34. Meas. II, 1, 100. Ado V, 1, 33. Merch. III, 2, 90. As II, 7, 71. All's II, 3, 72. Tw. V, 269. Wint. I, 2, 247. IV, 2, 22. IV, 4, 447. 698. H6C IV, 6, 57. R3 I, 3, 96. III, 4, 18. H8 III, 2, 143. Tim. III, 1, 21. Caes. I, 3, 91. 92. Ant. III, 2, 35 etc.

2) by this (cf. *In*): *and t. heartens up his servile powers*, Lucr. 295. *so doest thou too, and t. dignified*, Sonn. 101, 4. *who hast by waning grown, and t. showest thy lovers withering as thy sweet self growest*, 126, 3. *since t. she doth shun a thousand cursed hours*, Wiv. V, 5, 241. *and t. do account myself well paid*, Merch. IV, 1, 417. *but t. suits his folly to the mettle of my speech*, As II, 7, 81. *t. thou wrongest thy children*, H6C III, 2, 74. *he is my son, yea, and t. my shame*, R3 II, 2, 29. *t. thou hast undone*, Tit. IV, 2, 77. *comforting t., that when old robes are worn out, there are members to make new*, Ant. I, 2, 170.

**Thereof,** 1) of it, of that: *she dares not t. make discovery*, Lucr. 1314. *in the praise t. spends all his might*, Sonn. 80, 3. *maiden-tongued he was, and t. free*, Compl. 100. *the loss t. still fearing*, Pilgr. 94. *in lieu t.* Gent. II, 7, 88. *on the receipt t.* Err. IV, 1, 38. *to*

*have spoke t.* Mids. I, 1, 112. LLL I, 1, 191. III, 130. Wint. I, 2, 396. IV, 4, 384. H4B V, 3, 106. H6A II, 4, 79. H6B V, 1, 207. H6C I, 1, 58. I, 3, 41. I, 4, 129. 133. IV, 7, 64. R3 I, 3, 154. 308. III, 1, 48. III, 2, 47. III, 7, 79. 86. 175. 234. 236 (Ff *of this*). V, 3, 268. Rom. III, 5, 99. Hml. IV, 3, 61 etc. Often = its, even when referring to the subject of the sentence: *all the power t. it* (wit) *doth apply to prove, by wit, worth in simplicity*, LLL IV, 2, 77 (i. e. all its own power). *meaning his house, which, by the sign t., was termed so*, R3 III, 5, 79.

2) from that (cf. *Of*): *t. comes the proverb*, Gent. III, 1, 305. Err. IV, 3, 53. V, 68. 72. *t. the raging fire of fever bred*, 75.

**Thereon,** on it, on that: *shall t. fall and die*, Lucr. 1139. *promise-breach t. dependent*, Meas. V, 411. *and t. look*, LLL IV, 3, 298. *t. his execution sworn*, Wint. I, 2, 445. *t. I pawn my credit*, H6C III, 3, 116. *t. engrave Edward and York*, R3 IV, 4, 272. *from his reason fallen t.* Hml. II, 2, 165. *if t. you rely*, Ant. V, 2, 133.

**Thereto,** 1) to it, to that; governed by verbs: *accords t.* Gent. I, 3, 90. *adding t.* LLL V, 2, 446. All's V, 3, 133. Tw. V, 83. Wint. II, 1, 67. H5 V, 2, 90. H6A V, 3, 138. Cor. III, 2, 97. IV, 5, 73. Mcb. IV, 1, 33. Hml. I, 1, 83. Lr. I, 4, 361. Ant. V, 2, 198. By an adjective: *if my reason will t.* (to my fancy) *be obedient*, Wint. IV, 4, 494.

2) besides, over and above, to boot (cf. *To*): *you are certainly a gentleman, t. clerkly experienced*, Wint. I, 2, 391. *if she be black, and t. have a wit*, Oth. II, 1, 133. *so out of thought, and t. so o'ergrown*, Cymb. IV, 4, 33.

**Thereunto,** to it; for it; besides: *points of ignorance pertaining t.* H8 I, 3, 27. *asking your pardon t.* Hml. IV, 7, 46. *there's none so foul and foolish t.* Oth. II, 1, 142.

**Thereupon,** on this; in consequence of this; therefore (always referring to sentences): *and t. I drew my sword on you*, Err. V, 262. *and t. these errors are arose*, 388. *and t. I will kiss thee*, Ado V, 2, 50. *and t. thou speakest the fairest shoot*, LLL V, 1, 12. *and t. I drink unto your grace*, H4B IV, 2, 68. *and t. give me your daughter*, H5 V, 2, 375. *and t. he sends you this good news*, R3 III, 2, 48. *I dare t. pawn the moiety of my estate to your ring*, Cymb. I, 4, 118.

**Therewith,** with it: *t. angry*, H4A I, 3, 40. *dry her weeping eyes t.* R3 IV, 4, 278 (Ff *withal*). *t. satisfied*, Oth. I, 2, 88

**Therewithal,** with it, with that; at the same time (cf. *Withal*): *give her that ring and t. this letter*, Gent. IV, 4, 90. *moved t.* 175. *thy slanders I forgive, and t. remit thy other forfeits*, Meas. V, 525. *showed me silks ... and t. took measure of my body*, Err. IV, 3, 9. *and t. to win me*, LLL V, 2, 858. *did buy a poison, and t. came to this vault to die*, Rom. V, 3, 289. *but of that to-morrow, when t. we shall have cause of state craving us jointly*, Mcb. III, 1, 34. *not alone the imperfections of long-engraffed condition, but t. the unruly waywardness*, Lr. I, 1, 301. *your lady is one of the fairest that I have looked upon. And t. the best*, Cymb. II, 4, 33.

**Thersites,** name of the railer in the Trojan war: Troil. I, 3, 73 etc. Cymb. IV, 2, 252.

**Theseus,** the fabulous king of Athens: Gent. IV, 4, 173. Mids. I, 1, 20, and passim in this play.

**Thessalian**, pertaining to Thessaly: *dew-lapped like T. bulls*, Mids. IV, 1, 127.

**Thessaly**, country of ancient Greece: *a cry more tuneable was never holla'd to, nor cheered with horn, in Crete, in Sparta, nor in T.* Mids. IV, 1, 131. *the boar of T. was never so embossed*, Ant. IV, 13, 2.

**Thetis**, a sea-goddess; mother of Achilles: Troil. I, 3, 212. III, 3, 94. Confounded with Tethys, the wife of Oceanus, and used for the sea, the ocean: *let the ruffian Boreas once enrage the gentle T.* Troil. I, 3, 39. *T., being proud, swallowed some part o'the earth*, Per. IV, 4, 39. Cleopatra called so by Antony in their naval war against Octavius: Ant. III, 7, 61.

**Thewes** or **Thews**, muscles and sinews, bodily strength: *care I for the limb, the t., the stature, bulk, and big assemblance of a man?* H4B III, 2, 276. *Romans now have t. and limbs like to their ancestors*, Caes. I, 3, 81. *nature, crescent, does not grow alone in t. and bulk*, Hml. I, 3, 12.

**They** (obj. case *them*, often mutilated to *'em*, f.i. Tp. I, 2, 82. 83. 330. 417. II, 2, 7. III, 1, 76. V, 265. 280. Wiv. I, 1, 311. *I will leave 'em them*, H5 IV, 3, 124), personal pronoun of the third pers. plur.; *they:* Ven. 66. 116. 176. 184. 192 etc. etc. *them:* Ven. 20. 21. 52. 176 etc. etc. Indefinitely, = people, men: *they say there's but five upon this isle*, Tp. III, 2, 6. Gent. II, 4, 96. Wiv. II, 2, 135. 174. Err. I, 2, 97. Ado IV, 1, 254 *(to strange sores strangely they strain the cure)*. H6B I, 2, 100 etc. Determinatively: *they of those marches*, H5 I, 2, 140. *they of Rome are entered in our counsels*, Cor. I, 2, 2. *they in France of the best rank and station*, Hml. I, 3, 73. *they that level at my abuses*, Sonn. 121, 9. *the best of them that speak this speech*, Tp. I, 2, 429. Gent. I, 2, 31. Err. II, 1, 33. Ado II, 3, 237. H6A III, 3, 75 etc. Superfluous: *poor birds they are not set for*, Mcb. IV, 2, 36. *they for them: what stays had I but they?* R3 II, 2, 76. *hast not the soft way which were fit for thee to use as they to claim*, Cor. III, 2, 83. *them for they: for the which myself and them bend their best studies*, John IV, 2, 50. *here's them in our country of Greece gets more with begging*, Per. II, 1, 68 (the fisherman's speech). *them for themselves*, refl.: *unto the wood they hie them*, Ven. 323 (cf. *Hie*). *little stars may hide them when they list*, Lucr. 1008. *old woes bear them mild*, 1096. Compl. 142. Gent. II, 4, 123. Ado III, 3, 46. Mids. II, 1, 31. Shr. IV, 1, 5. H4A I, 3, 173. Cor. III, 1, 23. V, 3, 8. Rom. II, 3, 27. IV, 5, 90. Mcb. II, 2, 25. Hml. I, 2, 56. Oth. II, 3, 181 etc.

**Thick**, adj. 1) having a great circumference, not thin or slender: *his short t. neck*, Ven. 627. *the —est and the tallest* (lady) LLL IV, 1, 47. 48. 51. *smite flat the t. rotundity o' the world*, Lr. III, 2, 7. = having or producing more depth or extent than usual; laid on so as to increase the bulk: *this shoulder was ordained so t. to heave*, H6C V, 7, 23. *if this cursed hand were —er than itself with brother's blood*, Hml. III, 3, 44. And adverbially: *let her paint an inch t.* Hml. V, 1, 214.

2) dense, close, set with things close to each other, or being close to each other: *thin mane, t. tail*, Ven. 298 (having much hair). *in the —est troop*, H6C II, 1, 13. *though perils did abound, as t. as thought could make 'em*, H8 III, 2, 195. *the dews of heaven fall t. in blessings on her*, IV, 2, 133. *where you perceive them t.* Caes. I, 1, 76. *a retire, anon a rout, confusion t.* Cymb. V, 3, 41.

Adverbially: *thou shalt be pinched as t. as honey-comb*, Tp. I, 2, 329. *the floor of heaven is t. inlaid with patines of bright gold*, Merch. V, 59. *bears his blushing honours* (blossoms) *t. upon him*, H8 III, 2, 354.

3) inspissated, crass: *had baked thy blood and made it heavy, t.* John III, 3, 43. *his wit's as t. as Tewksbury mustard*, H4B II, 4, 262. *make t. my blood*, Mcb. I, 5, 44. *make the gruel t. and slab*, IV, 1, 32. *their eyes purging t. amber*, Hml. II, 2, 200. In a moral sense, = heavy, dull: *t. slumber hangs upon mine eyes*, Per. V, 1, 235. see above: John III, 3, 43. H4B II, 4, 262. Mcb. I, 5, 44.

4) not transparent, not clear; turbid (of fluids); dense, dark (of vapours and clouds): *let thy misty vapours march so t.* Lucr. 782. *come, t. night*, Mcb. I, 5, 51. *their t. breaths, rank of gross diet*, Ant. V, 2, 211. *dissolve, t. cloud, and rain*, 302. *a fountain troubled, muddy, ill-seeming, t.* Shr. V, 2, 143. cf. the quibble: *thine* (desert) *is too t. to shine*, H4B IV, 3, 64. In a moral sense: *the people muddied, t. and unwholesome in their thoughts and whispers*, Hml. IV, 5, 82 (cloudy in mind).

Applied to eyes, = dim, short-sighted: *his dimensions to any t. sight were invincible*, H4B III, 2, 336. *my sight was ever t.* Caes. V, 3, 21. cf. *your eyeglass is —er than a cuckold's horn*, Wint. I, 2, 269.

5) following each other in quick succession, rapid, quick: *through his lips do throng weak words, so t. come in his poor heart's aid, that no man could distinguish what he said*, Lucr. 1784. *he furnaces the t. sighs from him*, Cymb. I, 6, 67 (or = dense, vaporous?).

Adverbially: *O Lord, sir! t., t., spare not me*, All's II, 2, 47 (fast, quickly!). *and speaking t., which nature made his blemish, became the accents of the valiant; for those that could speak low and tardily would turn their own perfection to abuse*, H4B II, 3. 24.*my heart beats —er than a feverous pulse*, Troil. III, 2, 38. *as t. as tale* (M. Edd. *hail*) *came post with post*, Mcb. I, 3, 97. *why do you send so t.?* Ant. I, 5, 63. *say, and speak t.* Cymb. III, 2, 58.

**Thick**, adv. (see *Thick*, adj.): Lucr. 782. 1784. Tp. I, 2, 329. Merch. V, 59. All's II, 2, 47. H4B II, 3, 24. H8 III, 2, 354. Troil. III, 2, 38. Mcb. I, 3, 97. Hml. V, 1, 214. Ant. I, 5, 63. Cymb. III, 2, 58.

**Thick**, vb. to thicken, to inspissate: *thoughts that would t. my blood*, Wint. I, 2, 171.

**Thick-coming**, crowding: *not so sick, as she is troubled with t. fancies*, Mcb. V, 3, 38.

**Thicken**, 1) tr. to strengthen, to confirm: *this may help to t. other proofs that do demonstrate thinly*, Oth. III, 3, 430.

2) intr. to grow dim, to become dark: *light —s, and the crow makes wing to the rooky wood*, Mcb. III, 2, 50. *thy lustre —s, when he shines by*, Ant. II, 3, 27.

**Thicket**, a close wood or copse: Gent. V, 3, 11. LLL IV, 2, 60. V, 2, 94. H6C IV, 5, 3. Troil. II, 3, 270 *(keeps t.)*.

**Thick-eyed**, having dim eyes: *and given my treasures and my rights of thee to t. musing and cursed melancholy*, H4A II, 3, 49.

**Thick-grown**, dense: *this t. brake*, H6C III, 1, 1.

**Thick-lipped**, having thick lips: Tit. IV, 2, 175.

**Thick-lips**, one having thick lips: Oth. I, 1, 66. As to the form of the word, cf. *Chops, Fatguts, Jackanapes, Pots, Ribs*.

**Thick-pleached**, thickly interwoven: *a t. alley in mine orchard*, Ado I, 2, 10.

**Thick-ribbed**, having strong ribs; enclosing so as not to be broken through (cf. *Rib*): *to reside in thrilling region of t. ice*, Meas. III, 1, 123.

**Thick-sighted**, short-sighted, purblind: Ven. 136. cf. H4B III, 2, 336. Caes. V, 3, 21.

**Thick-skin**, an insensible fellow, a blockhead: *what wouldst thou have, boor? what, t.?* Wiv. IV, 5, 2. *the shallowest t. of that barren sort*, Mids. III, 2, 13.

**Thidias**, name in Ant.; M. Edd., following Plutarch, *Thyreus*, q. v.

**Thief**, one who steals: Lucr. 305. 693. 888. 997. Sonn. 48, 8. 99, 2. Wiv. II, 2, 319. Meas. II, 1, 20. III, 2, 17. IV, 2, 47. 49. 50. Err. III, 2, 16. IV, 2, 59. Ado III, 3, 53. 57. 62. 134. LLL IV, 3, 187. Mids. III, 2, 283 (*you t. of love*). Merch. III, 1, 97. 98. As III, 2, 345. All's II, 5, 86. III, 2, 132. Tw. V, 77. 121. R2 III, 2, 47. H4A I, 2, 70. II, 1, 103. II, 2, 10. II, 4, 452. III, 3, 212. H6B IV, 10, 36. H6C V, 6, 12. Cor. II, 1, 32. Tim. II, 2, 100. IV, 3, 45. 439 sq. Mcb. V, 2, 22. Lr. III, 7, 23. IV, 6, 156. Oth. I, 2, 57. 62. I, 3, 208. Ant. II, 6, 96. Cymb. I, 4, 100. II, 3, 76. IV, 2, 75. 86. Per. IV, 6, 121. Plur. *thieves:* Ven. 724. 1086. Lucr. 126. Tp. IV, 187. Wiv. II, 1, 126. Meas. II, 1, 23. II, 2, 176. Merch. II, 6, 23. As I, 3, 112. Tw. V, 404. R2 III, 2, 39. IV, 123. H4A I, 2, 28 (*of*). 75. II, 2, 29. II, 4, 99. III, 3, 63. H5 I, 2, 177. H6C I, 4, 42. 63. Troil. II, 2, 94. Tim. IV, 3, 35. 415 sq. V, 1, 187. Lr. I, 2, 133. Oth. I, 1, 79. 81. Ant. II, 6, 100. Cymb. I, 4, 107.

Sometimes equivalent to robber: *so full of fear as one with treasure laden, hemmed with thieves*, Ven. 1022. *draw forth thy weapon, we are beset with thieves*, Shr. III, 2, 238. *notable pirate, thou salt-water t.* Tw. V, 72. *a foul felonious t. that fleeced poor passengers*, H6B III, 1, 129. *where be these bloody thieves?* Oth. V, 1, 63. cf. Lucr. 693. 888. 997. As I, 3, 112. Tw. V, 121. H4A II, 2, 98. 99. 112. H6C I, 4, 63. Hml. IV, 6, 21. Per. IV, 2, 97.

Used as a term of reproach: *Angelo is an adulterous t.* Meas. V, 40 (or = a secret fornicator). *what a deformed t. this fashion is*, Ado III, 3, 131. 140. *lie still, ye t.* H4A III, 1, 238. *my little tiny t.* H4B V, 3, 60. *ay me, most credulous fool, egregious murderer, t., any thing that's due to all the villains past, in being, to come*, Cymb. V, 5, 211. *caused a lesser villain than myself, a sacrilegious t., to do't*, 220. cf. IV, 2, 86.

**Thief-stolen**, stolen by thieves: Cymb. I, 6, 5.

**Thievery**, 1) theft: *it's an honourable kind of t.* Gent. IV, 1, 40. *I'll example you with t.* Tim. IV, 3, 438. 2) that which is stolen: *crams his rich t. up*, Troil. IV, 4, 45.

**Thievish**, 1) practising theft: *that rich jewel he should keep unknown from t. ears*, Lucr. 35. *like a t. dog*, 736. *truth proves t. for a price so dear*, Sonn. 48, 14.

Applied to violent robbery: *with a base and boisterous sword enforce a t. living on the common road*, As II, 3, 33. *walk in t. ways*, Rom. IV, 1, 79 (ways infested by robbers).

2) moving stealthily: *time's t. progress to eternity*, Sonn. 77, 8. *hath told the t. minutes how they pass*, All's II, 1, 169.

**Thigh**, that part of the body which is between the trunk and the knee: Ven. 873. Pilgr. 127. Mids.

III, 1, 172. As I, 3, 119. Tw. I, 3, 149. H4A IV, 1, 105. V, 4, 131. 155. H4B IV, 5, 77 (plur. *—es*, dissyll.). H6B III, 1, 362. Cor. II, 1, 167. Rom. II, 1, 19. Caes. II, 1, 301. Oth. III, 3, 425. V, 2, 261. Cymb. IV, 2, 310.

**Thill-horse**, see *Fill-horse*.

**Thimble**, a metal cover for the finger, used to secure it from the needle in sewing: Shr. IV, 3, 108. 149. John V, 2, 156.

**Thin**, adj. 1) lean, slender: *my face so t.* John I, 141. *you t. man*, H4B V, 4, 20. 34. Metaphorically, = scanty: *a t. and slender pittance*, Shr. IV, 4, 61.

2) having little extent from one of the two surfaces to the other: *the mure that should confine it in so t. that life looks through*, H4B IV, 4, 120. Used of light clothes: *if your garments were t.* Err. III, 1, 70. *t. weeds*, LLL V, 2, 811. *gave himself, all t. and naked, to the numb cold night*, R3 II, 1, 117 (lightly dressed). Metaphorically, = not sufficient for a covering, slight, easily seen through: *we will not line his t. bestained cloak with our pure honours*, John IV, 3, 24. *they* (flatteries) *are too t. and bare to hide offences*, H8 V, 3, 125. *wider and more overt test than these t. habits and poor likelihoods*, Oth. I, 3, 108.

3) not closely set; used of hair: *t. mane*, Ven. 298. *his beard grew t.* Shr. III, 2, 177. *their t. and hairless scalps*, R2 III, 2, 112. *thatch your poor t. roofs*, Tim. IV, 3, 144. *with this t. helm*, Lr. IV, 7, 36 (a bald head).

4) rare, not dense; used of the air and of fluids: *from his lips did fly t. winding breath*, Lucr. 1407. *melted into air, t. air*, Tp. IV, 150. *fantasy, which is as t. of substance as the air*, Rom. I, 4, 99. *the t. and wholesome blood*, Hml. I, 5, 70. *t. drink*, abhorred by Falstaff and recommended by King Henry VI: H4B IV, 3, 98. 134. H6C II, 5, 48.

**Thin-belly**, a lean belly (characteristic of a man in love): *with your arms crossed on your t. doublet like a rabbit on a spit*, LLL III, 19 (O. Edd. *thinbellies doublet* and *thinbellie doublet;* M. Edd. *thin belly-doublet*).

**Thine**, possessive pronoun of the second pers. sing.; 1) adjectively before vowels: Ven. 145. Lucr. 483. 516. Tp. I, 2, 25. 37. 318. 408. II, 1, 229. II, 2, 139. V, 121. Gent. III, 1, 22. Meas. IV, 3, 158. Err. II, 2, 116. Mids. III, 2, 298 etc. before *h: thine host, thine Ephesian calls*, Wiv. IV, 5, 19. with *own:* Ven. 157. Tp. I, 2, 356. IV, 13. Wiv. II, 1, 15. Meas. I, 2, 39. III, 1, 29. 140. Err. I, 2, 61. II, 2, 200 etc. Perhaps throughout unemphatical, *thy*, not *thine*, being used, where some stress is laid on the pronoun: *why, Suffolk, England knows thine insolence. And thy ambition, Gloster*, H6B II, 1, 31. cf. Ven. 170. LLL IV, 3, 28.

2) without a noun, but with reference to one preceding: *to no sight but t. and mine*, Tp. I, 2, 302. V, 63. Gent. III, 1, 131. IV, 2, 118. Wiv. II, 1, 74. Meas. V, 210 etc. with *own:* Tp. IV, 218. Ven. 117 etc. *of t.*, following a noun, not only = one of those whom or which thou hast: *some worthless slave of t. I'll slay*, Lucr. 515. 1632. *misbegotten blood I spill of t.* H6A IV, 6, 22. but as often = of thee, thy: *those fair lips of t.* Ven. 115. *that hard heart of t.* 500. 631. Sonn. 92, 4. 142, 5. Err. II, 2, 175. John III, 1, 21. H6A II, 3, 39. R3 IV, 4, 516. Tit. I, 306. Mcb. V, 3, 16 etc.

3) substantively, = a) thy property: *thou mine, I t.* Sonn. 108, 7. Gent. V, 4, 135. LLL IV, 1, 109 etc.

Tp. IV, 32. Gent. V, 4, 151. Meas. I, 1, 31 etc. b) thy relations, thy children, thy family: *that t. may live, when thou thyself art dead*, Ven. 172. *lasting shame on thee and t. I will inflict*, Lucr. 1630. Sonn. 10, 14. Tit. I, 49. 115. Lr. I, 1, 81 etc.

**Thin-faced**, having a thin face: *a t. knave, a gull*, Tw. V, 213.

**Thing**, any substance; whatever is: *—s growing to themselves are growth's abuse*, Ven. 166. *t. like a man, but of no woman bred*, 214. *if springing —s be any jot diminished, they wither in their prime*, 417. *what canst thou boast of —s long since, or any t. ensuing*, 1078. *all —s in common nature should produce*, Tp. II, 1, 159. *I will requite you with as good a t.* V, 169. *bears no impression of the t. it was*, Gent. II, 4, 202. *good —s should be praised*, III, 1, 353. *of another t. she may* (be liberal) 359. *you would have them always play but one t.* IV, 2, 71. *the t. is to be sold*, As II, 4, 96. *we will have rings and —s and fine array*, Shr. II, 325. IV, 3, 56. *I can hardly forbear hurling —s at him*, Tw. III, 2, 87. *has this t. appeared again?* Hml. I, 1, 21 etc. etc.

Applied to men and animals, = being, creature: *imperious supreme of all mortal —s*, Ven. 996. *we leave to be the —s we are for that which we expect*, Lucr. 149. *some fierce t. replete with too much rage*, Sonn. 23, 3. *in pursuit of the t. she would have stay* (a hen) 143, 4. *thou liest, malignant t.* Tp. I, 2, 257. *dull t., I say so*, 285. *gabble like a t. most brutish*, 357. *I might call him a t. divine*, 418. *a single t., as I am now*, 432. *good —s will strive to dwell with it*, 459. *these be fine —s*, II, 2, 120. *but this t. dare not*, III, 2, 63. *what —s are these*, V, 264. *this t. of darkness*, 275. *this is as strange a t. as e'er I looked on*, 289. *sweet ornament that decks a t. divine*, Gent. II, 1, 4. *she excels each mortal t. upon the dull earth dwelling*, IV, 2, 51. *they* (bears) *are very ill-favoured rough —s*, Wiv. I, 1, 312. *I hold you as a t. enskyed and sainted*, Meas. I, 4, 34. *wake when some vile t. is near*, Mids. II, 2, 34. *vile t., let loose*, III, 2, 260. *a poor virgin, an ill-favoured t.* As V, 4, 60. *you are idle shallow —s*, Tw. III, 4, 137. *make us as fat as tame —s*, Wint. I, 2, 92. *O thou t.!* II, 1, 82. *poor t., condemned to loss*, III, 3, 192. *such goodly —s as you*, V, 1, 178. *go, you t., go. Say, what t., what t.?* H4A III, 3, 131. *see, sons, what —s you are*, H4B IV, 5, 65. *have you dispatched this t?* H6B III, 2, 6. *he was the wretched'st t. when he was young*, R3 II, 4, 18. *every man ... was a t. inspired*, H8 I, 1, 91. *the t. of courage ... with rage doth sympathize*, Troil. I, 3, 51. *hence, rotten t.* Cor. III, 1, 179. *thou noble t.* IV, 5, 122. *vows revenge as spacious as between the youngest and oldest t.* IV, 6, 68. *such —s as you*, V, 2, 109. *none serve with him but constrained —s*, Mcb. V, 4, 13. *no cataplasm ... can save the t. from death*, Hml. IV, 7, 146. *the king is a t. A thing, mylord! Of nothing*, IV, 2, 31 (Nares: *a t. of nothing*, a common phrase to express any thing very worthless. cf. *a t. of naught* in Mids. IV, 2, 14). *—s that love night*, Lr. III, 2, 42. *leaving free —s and happy shows behind*, III, 6, 112. *he is a t. too bad for bad report*, Cymb. I, 1, 16. *thou basest t.* 125. *the same dead t. alive*, V, 5, 123 etc.

Supplying abstract notions, = matter, affair, circumstance, fact, action, story etc.: *—s out of hope are compassed oft with venturing*, Ven. 567. *in hand with all —s, nought at all effecting*, 912. *for one t. she*

*did they would not take her life*, Tp. I, 2, 266. *taught thee each hour one t. or other*, 355. *I would by contraries execute all —s*, II, 1, 148. *will not let you believe —s certain*, V, 125. *think of each t. well*, V, 251. *I see —s too, although you judge I wink*, Gent. I, 2, 139. *are all these —s perceived in me?* II, 1, 34. *three —s that women highly hold in hate*, III, 2, 33. *'tis a foul t. when a cur cannot keep himself in all companies*, IV, 4, 11. *to be a dog at all —s*, 14. *there's no such t. in me*, Wiv. III, 3, 72. *they can tell you how —s go better than I can*, III, 4, 69. *I would not have —s cool*, IV, 2, 240. *you shall hear how —s go*, IV, 5, 126. *'tis one t. to be tempted, another t. to fall*, Meas. II, 1, 17. *it is the only t. for a qualm*, Ado III, 4, 75. *a little t. would make me tell them ...*, Tw. III, 4, 332. *rob the exchequer the first t. thou dost*, H4A III, 3, 205. *—s are often spoke and seldom meant*, H6B III, 1, 268. *—s have fallen out so unluckily*, Rom. III, 4, 1. *I fear some ill unlucky t.* V, 3, 136. *where, both in time, form of the t., each word made true and good, the apparition comes*, Hml. I, 2, 210. *—s standing thus unknown*, V, 2, 356. *to scan this t. no further*, Oth. III, 3, 245. *it is a common t. to have a foolish wife*, 302. *the breaking of so great a t. should make a greater crack*, Ant. V, 1, 14 etc. etc. cf. *All-thing, Any, Every, Some* etc. the *t.* often = that: *'twas I did the t. you wot of*, Gent. IV, 4, 30; cf. *past cure of the t. you wot of*, Meas. II, 1, 115. *presume not that I am the t. I was*, H4B V, 5, 60. *never will I undertake the t. wherein thy counsel is wanting,* H6C II, 6, 101. *I shall surely speak the t. I shall repent*, Troil. III, 2, 139 etc. *a t.* = something: *should I have wished a t., it had been he*, Gent. II, 4, 82. *I will do a greater t. than that*, Wiv. I, 1, 248. *I shall discover a t. to you*, II, 2, 190. *when shall you see me write a t. in rhyme?* LLL IV, 3, 181. *shall I tell you a t.?* V, 1, 152. *there is a t. within my bosom tells me ...*, H4B IV, 1, 183. *a t. devised by the enemy*, R3 V, 3, 306. *I told you a t. yesterday*, Troil. I, 2, 185. *thou wilt undertake a t. like death*, Rom. IV, 1, 74. *I should undertake a t.*, Hml. V, 2, 92. *I have a t. for you*, Oth. III, 3, 301 etc.

**Think** (impf. and partic. *thought; thoughten* in Per. IV, 6, 115 not partic.) 1) to have the mind occupied, to revolve ideas in the mind, to meditate: *hath he any eyes? hath he any —ing?* Wiv. III, 2, 31. *when I would pray and t.* Meas. II, 4, 1. *an bad —ing do not wrest true speaking*, Ado III, 4, 33. *I cannot speak nor t.* Wint. IV, 4, 462. *on —ing on no thought I t.* R2 II, 2, 31. *I t., but dare not speak*, Mcb. V, 1, 87. *there is nothing either good or bad, but —ing makes it so*, Hml. II, 2, 256. *to put him to ill —ing*, Oth. III, 4, 29. *what shall we do, Enobarbus? T. and die*, Ant. III, 13, 1 etc. With an accus. denoting the effect: *if I would t. my heart out of —ing*, Ado III, 4, 84. Trans., with the object of thought, = to form or harbour in the mind, to conceive, to imagine, to devise: *I t. good thoughts, whilst other write good words*, Sonn. 85, 5. *nimble thought can jump both sea and land as soon as t. the place where he would be*, 44, 8. *what his heart —s his tongue speaks*, Ado III, 2, 14. *may this be so? I will not t. it*, 121. *t. but this ... that you have but slumbered here*, Mids. V, 431. *to t. so base a thought*, Merch. II, 7, 50. *that we might show what we alone must t.* All's I, 1, 199. *what might you t.?* Tw. III, 1, 128. *all the unmuzzled thoughts that tyrannous heart can t.* 131. *'tis powerful, t. it, from east, west, north* and south, Wint. I, 2, 202. where I may t. the remnant of my thoughts in peace, John V, 4, 46. thoughts which honour and allegiance cannot t. R2 II, 1, 208. these deeds must not be thought after these ways, Mcb. II, 2, 33. I saw 't not, thought it not, it harmed not me, Oth. III, 3, 339 etc. to t. no harm, LLL I, 1, 44. R3 I, 3, 51. never thought offence, Per. I, 2, 28. t. no shame of me, Lucr. 1204. to t. scorn, see sub Scorn. With a clause: dost thou t., Claudio? if I would yield him my virginity, thou mightst be freed, Meas. III, 1, 97. sleep I now and t. I hear all this? Err. II, 2, 185 (imagine only). that little —s she has been sluiced, Wint. I, 2, 194. I tremble to t. your father should pass this way, IV, 4, 19. I am afraid to t. what I have done, Mcb. II, 2, 51. yet have I fierce affections, and t. what Venus did with Mars, Ant. I, 5, 17 etc.

2) to consider: she bids me t. how I have been forsworn, Gent. IV, 2, 10. bid her t. what a man is, Wiv. III, 5, 51. do thou but t. what 'tis to cram a maw from such a vice, Meas. III, 2, 22. t. you question with the Jew, Merch. IV, 1, 70. I was —ing with what manners I might safely be admitted, All's IV, 5, 93. t. with thyself how more unfortunate than all living women are we come hither, Cor. V, 3, 96 etc. With on: these things further thought on, Tw. V, 324. now I t. on't, they should be good men, H8 III, 1, 21. t. on that, and fix most firm thy resolution, Oth. I, 1, 4 etc.

3) With of or on, = to call to mind, to recollect, to dwell or to light on by meditation: to t. o'the teen that I have turned you to, Tp. I, 2, 64. t. of that, a man of my kidney, t. of that, Wiv. III, 5, 116. what we do not see we tread upon, and never t. of it, Meas. II, 1, 26. and t. no more of this night's accidents but as the fierce vexation of a dream, Mids. IV, 1, 73. I should t. of shallows, Merch. I, 1, 26. made me to t. of this, All's I, 3, 238. bid Gloster t. of this, R3 I, 4, 245. the most convenient place that I can t. of, H8 II, 2, 138 etc. haply I t. on thee, Sonn. 29, 10. 30, 13. if —ing on me then should make you woe, 71, 8. —ing on thy face, 131, 10. 149, 3. t. on thy Proteus, Gent. I, 1, 12. urge not my father's anger, but t. upon my grief, IV, 3, 28. —ing on it makes me cry 'alas', IV, 4, 89. to t. upon her woes, 149. I weep myself to t. upon thy words, 180. Wiv. II, 1, 166. V, 5, 12. 57. Meas. II, 2, 77. Ado V, 4, 43. 129. Merch. I, 1, 37. II, 2, 178. II, 8, 31. All's I, 1, 90. Tw. III, 1, 114. R2 I, 3, 295. H4A III, 3, 35. H6A IV, 1, 148. H6B II, 4, 41. III, 2, 344. 348. IV, 7, 15. H6C I, 4, 173. R3 I, 1, 141. V, 3, 126. Cor. II, 3, 196. Hml. I, 2, 6. Lr. I, 1, 144. Oth. V, 2, 191 etc.

4) to be of opinion: others, they t., delight in such-like circumstance, Ven. 843. she —s he could not die, 1060. I do not t. thou canst, Tp. I, 2, 40. I do t., a king, III, 1, 60. when I shall t. Phoebus' steeds are foundered, IV, 30. dost thou t. so? V, 19. you speak not as you t. Mids. III, 2, 191. Gent. I, 1, 141. II, 7, 62. Meas. II, 1, 143. Err. I, 1, 88. Ado II, 3, 24. 179. III, 4, 81. V, 4, 43. All's V, 3, 210. Oth. V, 2, 192 etc. etc. to my —ing, = in my opinion: H4B V, 5, 114. Caes. I, 2, 240. Trans., with a pronoun as object, = to believe: I t. it well, Meas. II, 4, 130. would heart of man once t. it? Hml. I, 5, 121. do you t. this? II, 2, 151 (Ff think 'tis this). I'll hit him now. I do not t. it, V, 2, 306. I t. it freely, Oth. II, 3, 335.

With a double accus., = to esteem, to hold to be: shouldst t. it heavy, Ven. 156. he —s me now incapable,

Tp. I, 2, 111. may I be bold to t. these sprites, IV, 120. Gent. I, 2, 21. 24. II, 1, 33. Meas. I, 1, 72. Tw. V, 325. H4B IV, 1, 146 (every thing set off that might so much as t. you enemies) etc. etc. to t. long = to expect with impatience, to long for: but long she —s till he return again, Lucr. 1359. have I thought long to see this morning's face, Rom. IV, 5, 41. to t. much = to hold it to be a great thing (cf. Lr. III, 4, 6): —est it much to tread the ooze, Tp. I, 2, 252. Acc. c. inf.: —ing his prattle to be tedious, R2 V, 2, 26. I t. this lady to be my child Cordelia, Lr. IV, 7, 69 etc.

With for: the conceit is deeper than you t. for, Shr. IV, 3, 163. dost not t. me for the man I am, Cor. IV, 5, 62 (cf. H4B I, 2, 6, and see For). With as: Caes. II, 1, 32.

5) to judge, to form an opinion; with of or on: to t. nobly of my grandmother, Tp. I, 2, 119. t. of each thing well, V, 251. perchance you t. too much of so much pains, Gent. II, 1, 119 (estimate them at too high a rate). I shall t. the worse of fat men, Wiv. II, 1, 56. as you hear of me, so t. of me, Ado IV, 1, 338. I t. nobly of the soul, Tw. IV, 2, 59. t. of me as you please, V, 317. an honest woman and well thought on, H4B II, 4, 100 (of good fame. Mrs Quickly's speech). to make us no better thought of, a little help will serve, Cor. II, 3, 15. —ing too precisely on the event, Hml. IV, 4, 41 etc. Trans., with what as object: what —est thou of the fair Sir Eglamour? Gent. I, 2, 9. V, 4, 164. Wiv. II, 1, 85. Meas. I, 1, 22. Tw. I, 5, 79. II, 5, 32. IV, 2, 58. H8 II, 3, 107. Caes. I, 2, 214 etc.

6) to mean, to intend: I thought all for the best, Rom. III, 1, 109. With an inf.: he did t. to reprehend her, Ven. 470. he thought to kiss him, 1110. 1114. if you t. well to carry this, Meas. III, 1, 267. I thought to close mine eyes, LLL V, 2, 90. thou thoughtest to help me, All's II, 1, 133. I thought to stay him, R3 I, 4, 19. —ing to bar thee of succession, Cymb. III, 3, 102 etc. Inf. of the perfect (cf. Have): here thought they to have done some wanton charm, Tp. IV, 94. I thought to have told thee of it, 168. I did t. to have beaten thee, Ado V, 4, 111. thought to have spoke thereof, Mids. I, 1, 112 etc. I had thought, see Thought subst.

7) to expect; to hope: I thought to have ta'en you at the Porpentine, Err. III, 2, 172. I did never t. to marry, Ado II, 3, 236. you t. to dine with me, Shr. III, 2, 187. that I should love a star and t. to wed it, All's I, 1, 98. when men t. least I will, H4A I, 2, 241. all goes well. As heart can t. IV, 1, 84. he little thought of this divided friendship, R3 I, 4, 244. I did not t. to shed a tear in all my miseries, H8 III, 2, 429. he that will t. to live till he be old, Lr. III, 7, 69. I did not t. to draw my sword 'gainst Pompey, Ant. II, 2, 156.

8) to bear in mind, to have regard to, to pay attention to, to provide for: always thought that I require a clearness, Mcb. III, 1, 132. With on: that likewise have we thought upon, and thus, Wiv. IV, 4, 46. t. upon patience, All's III, 2, 50. the heavens have thought well on thee, to bring forth this discovery, V, 3, 150. have you thought on a place whereto you'll go? Wint. IV, 4, 547. if any order might be thought upon, H5 IV, 5, 21. when I have chased all thy foes from hence, then will I t. upon a recompense, H6A I, 2, 116. I'll t. upon the questions, H6B I, 2, 82. not a thought but —s on dignity, III, 1, 338. well thought upon, R3 I, 3, 344 and Lr. V, 3, 250. what ever have been thought on in this state, that could be brought to bodily act ere Rome had circumvention? Cor. I, 2, 4.

9) Impersonally, *it —s* = it seems (cf. *Methinks* and *Methought*): *where it —s best unto your royal self*, R3 III, 1, 63 (Ff *where it think'st best;* Q1.2 *where it seems best*). *does it not, thinks 't thee, stand me now upon*, Hml. V, 2, 63 (Ff *thinkst thee*, Qq *think thee*. cf. *methinkst* in All's II, 3, 269). Perhaps *thinks* for *methinks: what largeness thinks in Paradise was sawn*, Compl. 91.

**Thinking**, subst. (cf. *Think*), thought: *I am wrapped in dismal —s*, All's V, 3, 128. *his —s are below the moon*, H8 III, 2, 134. *speak to me as to thy —s*, Oth. III, 3, 131. cf. Wiv. III, 2, 31. As V, 2, 55. Cor. IV, 6, 31. Tim. I, 1, 219. Oth. I, 2, 76. II, 3, 344. Cymb. I, 4, 157.

**Thinly**, 1) not thickly, not closely or numerously: *like stones of worth they* (feasts) *t. placed are.* Sonn. 52, 7. *about his shelves a beggarly account of empty boxes ... were t. scattered*, Rom. V, 1, 48.

2) slightly, insufficiently: *this may help to thicken other proofs that do demonstrate t.* Oth. III, 3, 431 (cf. *thin* in I, 3, 108).

**Third**, the ordinal of three; 1) the first after the second: Sonn. 99, 10. Tp. I, 2, 445. V, 311. Gent. IV, 4, 24. Wiv. V, 1, 2. Ado V, 1, 276. LLL V, 1, 56. V, 2, 113. Merch. I, 3, 20. 75. II, 7, 8. III, 1, 11. 81. As I, 2, 137. V, 4, 98. Shr. Ind. I, 13. 57. Tw. I, 5, 141. 143. II, 3, 189 (*let the fool make a t.;* cf. H6B III, 2, 303). V, 40 (*the old saying is*, the *t. pays for all*). Wint. II, 1, 145. III, 2, 99. H4A I, 2, 207. H4B I, 3, 72. III, 2, 330. H5 I, 2, 248 (*Edward the T.*) etc. *the poor t. is up*, Ant. III, 5, 12 (i. e. Lepidus, the last of the three triumvirs).

2) as a fractional number, = one of three equal (parts): *the t. part of a minute*, Mids. II, 2, 2. *a full t. part*, Cor. V, 6, 78. Substantively: Lr. I, 1, 82. 88. Ant. II, 2, 63. Cymb. V, 4, 19. *three —s* (i. e. the whole, all) All's II, 5, 32. In Tp. IV, 3 O. Edd. *I have given you here a t. of mine own life;* M. Edd. *thread* or *thrid.*

**Thirdborough**, a kind of constable; substituted (on account of Sly's answer) by M. Edd. for *headborough* of O. Edd. in Shr. Ind. I, 12. Corrupted to *tharborough* in LLL I, 1, 185.

**Thirdly**, in the third place: Ado V, 1, 222.

**Thirst**, subst. want and desire of drink: *to quench his t.* Shr. I, 1, 24. *unstanched t.* H6C II, 6, 83. = any desire: *not in t. for revenge*, Cor. I, 1, 25.

**Thirst**, vb. 1) to feel want and desire of drink: *to all, and him, we t.* Mcb. III, 4, 91. With *for: t. for drink*, Ven. 92. *for blood*, H6A III, 1, 117. With *after: and more* (blood) *—s after*, All's III, 1, 4.

2) to have any vehement desire: *whom I so much t. to see*, Wint. IV, 4, 524. *dost thou t. to have me fold up Parca's fatal web?* H5 V, 1, 20 (Pistol's speech). With *after: —ing after prey*, H6B IV, 4, 51.

**Thirsty**, feeling want and desire of drink: *her t. lips*, Ven. 543. *our natures do pursue, like rats that ravin down their proper bane, a t. evil; and when we drink we die*, Meas. I, 2, 134 (*a t. evil* = an evil of thirst, a thirst-evil, i. e. an evil thirsted for. cf. *their hungry prey* in H6A I, 2, 28; and see Appendix). LLL V, 2, 372. Shr. V, 2, 144. H4A I, 1, 5. H6C II, 3, 15. *my heart is t. for that noble pledge*, Caes. IV, 3, 160. *to be t. after tottering honour*, Per. III, 2, 40.

**Thirteen**, ten and three: Tw. V, 252. 255. John II, 460. H6A I, 4, 78. Tim. II, 2, 120.

**Thirtieth**, the ordinal of thirty: *ere the t. of May*, H6B I, 1, 49.

**Thirty**, three times ten: Tp. III, 2, 17. Err. V, 400. Shr. Ind. 2, 116. I, 2, 33 (cf. *Pip*). All's IV, 1, 63. IV, 5, 86. John II, 530. H4A I, 2, 211. III, 3, 54. 221. IV, 1, 130. H4B II, 1, 111. II, 4, 179. IV, 1, 22. H6C II, 1, 177. II, 2, 68. III, 3, 96. V, 3, 14. Rom. I, 5, 35. 41. Caes. V, 1, 53. Mcb. IV, 1, 7. Hml. III, 2, 165. 167. V, 1, 177. Lr. III, 7, 16. Oth. I, 3, 37. Ant. III, 3, 31. Plur. *—es: thirty dozen moons with borrowed sheen about the world have times twelve —es been*, Hml. III, 2, 168.

**This** (plur. *these. This is* sometimes contracted to *this: this a good friar, belike*, Meas. V, 131. *this a heavy chance 'twixt him and you*, Shr. I, 2, 46. *this a good block*, Lr. IV, 6, 187. *this* or *these* abbreviated to *'s: my father died within's two hours*, Hml. III, 2, 134; M. Edd. *these*), demonstrative pronoun used to point to something that is present or near in place or time, or to something that is just mentioned or about to be mentioned; adjectively: *deign this favour*, Ven. 15. *pay this countless debt*, 84. *upon this promise did he raise his chin*, 85. *for this good turn*, 92. *this primrose bank*, 151. *these violets whereon we lean*, 125. *these forceless flowers support me*, 152. *these lovely caves ... opened their mouths*, 247. *would root these beauties*, 636. *pursue these creatures*, 677. *these mine eyes*, 503. *this her mother's plot*, Wiv. IV, 6, 32. *this her easy-held imprisonment*, H6A V, 3, 139 etc. etc. *within this mile* = within a mile of this place: Cor. I, 4, 8. Mcb. V, 5, 37. Absolutely, with reference either to single things or to whole sentences or speeches: *with this she seizeth on his palm*, Ven. 25. 811. 1121. *this said*, 217. 865. *at this Adonis smiles*, 241. *this I do to captivate the eye*, 281. *what hour is this?* 495. *how is it that this lives in thy mind?* Tp. I, 2, 49. *tell me if this might be a brother*, 118. *is not this true?* 267. *for this thou shalt have cramps*, 325. *didst thou offer her this* (dog) *from me?* Gent. IV, 4, 58. *your nose smells 'no' in this* (Nathaniel's nose) LLL V, 2, 569. *O Antony, I have followed thee to this*, Ant. V, 1, 36. *that our stars should divide our equalness to this*, 48 (= to this point, this extremity). *take this from this, if it be otherwise*, Hml. II, 2, 156. *when thou shalt have overlooked this*, IV, 6, 13 etc. etc. Opposed to *that: applying this to that, and so so*, Ven. 713. *two ships, of Corinth that, of Epidaurus this*, Err. I, 1, 94 etc. (cf. *That*). Plur. *these: tired with all these, for restful death I cry*, Sonn. 66, 1 (i. e. the following considerations). *these are they*, Tp. II, 2, 109. *nor the lover's* (melancholy) *which is all these*, As IV, 1, 15. *there lie, and there thy character; there these*, Wint. III, 3, 47. *one of these is true*, IV, 4, 586. *all these and more we hazard by thy stay*, H6A IV, 6, 40. *these indeed seem*, Hml. I, 2, 83. *last, and as much containing as all these*, IV, 5, 87. *where virtue is, these are more virtuous*, Oth. III, 3, 186. *are letters brought, the tenour these*, Per. III Prol. 24. Emphatically (evidently explained by a gesture, as *this* in Hml. II, 2, 156): *O could this kiss be printed in thy hand, that thou mightst think upon these by the seal, through whom a thousand sighs are breathed for thee*, H6B III, 2, 344 (i. e. my lips). The plural attracted by the form of the predicate: *these are devils*, Tp. II, 2, 91. *these be fine things*, 120. III, 3, 30. V, 259. Gent. II, 7, 72. IV, 1, 5. V, 4, 14. Err. IV, 3, 10. LLL I, 1, 47. 70. III, 22. Mids.

II, 1, 81. As IV, 1, 107. H6B III, 1, 64. H8 IV, 2, 154 etc.

Not only *these,* but also *this,* absol. with reference to persons: *to the most of men this is a Caliban,* Tp. I, 2, 480. *which is that Barnardine? This, my lord,* Meas. V, 483. *Hymen now with luckier issue speed's than this for whom we rendered up this woe,* Ado V, 3, 33. *Hector was but a Troyan in respect of this,* LLL V, 2, 640. *there be fools alive, I wis, silvered o'er; and so was this,* Merch. II, 9, 69. *we'll make an instrument of this,* Wint. IV, 4, 637. *they are both hanged, and so would this be,* H5 IV, 4, 78. *he was a man; this in respect a child,* H6C V, 5, 56. *a son some year elder than this,* Lr. I, 1, 20.

Applied to notions of time, *this* = 1) the present; *this day* = to-day: Meas. I, 2, 182. Err. V, 204. Merch. II, 2, 154. IV, 1, 409. H4A II, 4, 176. H6C II, 6, 20. H8 IV, 1, 75. Tit. I, 235 etc. *This,* absolutely, = the present time, now: *between this and supper,* Cor. IV, 3, 43. *the time 'twixt this and supper,* Mcb. III, 1, 26. *and as a stranger ... hold thee from this for ever,* Lr. I, 1, 118. Particularly in the phrases *by this* and *ere this;* cf. *By* and *Ere.* 2) = last; *this other day* = very lately: *writ to me this other day,* All's IV, 3, 226. *you denied to fight with me this other day,* Wint. V, 2, 140. *and said this other day,* H4A III, 3, 152. *did but try us this other day,* Tim. III, 6, 3. *when your lordship this other day sent to me,* 46. *a prediction I read this other day,* Lr. I, 2, 153. *this even* = last evening: *she did intend confession at Patrick's cell this even; and there she was not,* Gent. V, 2, 42. *this night* = last night: *my troublous dream this night doth make me sad,* H6B I, 2, 22. *this month, this week* etc. = last month, since a month etc.: *whereon this month I have been hammering,* Gent. I, 3, 18. *where have you been these two days?* IV, 4, 48. *have done any time these three hundred years,* Wiv. I, 1, 13. *this week he hath been heavy,* Err. V, 45. *these fifteen years you have been in a dream,* Shr. Ind. 2, 81. *have been so any time these four hours,* Wint. V, 2, 147. *the language I have learned these forty years,* R2 I, 3, 159. *within these forty hours Surrey durst better have burnt that tongue,* H8 III, 2, 253. *he hath put me off to the succession of new days this month,* Tim. II, 2, 20. *how does your honour for this many a day?* Hml. III, 1, 91. H4A II, 3, 41. H6A I, 4, 16. H6B IV, 2, 2. IV, 10, 3. 41. Troil. V, 2, 182. Cor. I, 1, 59. Caes. II, 1, 88. Lr. IV, 1, 14. Cymb. IV, 2, 66 etc. Often *this* for *these* (the sum being reckoned up, as it were, in a total): *which for this nineteen years we have let slip,* Meas. I, 3, 21. *has been a vile thief this seven year,* Ado III, 3, 134. *who for this seven years hath esteemed him ...,* Shr. Ind. 1, 122. *I have forsworn his company this two and twenty years,* H4A II, 2, 17. *that I did not this seven year,* II, 4, 343. *I have maintained that salamander this two and thirty years,* III, 3, 54. *this seven years did not Talbot see his son,* H6A IV, 3, 37. *have ventured this many summers in a sea of glory,* H8 III, 2, 360. *for this many hundred years,* Rom. IV, 3, 40 (only in Q2; the rest *these* ). *hath lain this two days,* V, 3, 176 (only Q2). *this three years I have taken a note of it,* Hml. V, 1, 150 (Ff *these* ). *I have not seen him this two days,* Lr. I, 4, 77. *this twenty years ... these demesnes have been my world,* Cymb. III, 3, 69. *who for this three months hath not spoken,* Per. V, 1, 24. 3) = next to come: *this night I'll waste in sorrow,* Ven.

583. *this night he meaneth to climb ...,* Gent. II, 6, 33. *he's safe for these three hours,* Tp. III, 1, 21. *'twill be this hour ere I have done weeping,* Gent. II, 3, 1. *within these three days his head to be chopped off,* Meas. I, 2, 69. *within these two days he will be here,* IV, 2, 213. *within these two months ... I expect return,* Merch. I, 3, 158. *within these ten days if that thou be'st found,* As I, 3, 45. *for these two hours I will leave thee,* IV, 1, 180. *within these three hours 'twill be time,* All's IV, 1, 27. *there shall not these seven years be born another such,* Wint. IV, 4, 589. *I must leave you within these two hours,* H4A II, 3, 39. *nor shall we need his help these fourteen days,* III, 1, 88. *the first of this next month,* H6B II, 4, 71. *are like to dance these three days,* H8 V, 4, 68. *shall hold ye play these two months,* 90 etc. *this for these: he cannot draw his power this fourteen days,* H4A IV, 1, 126. *within this three hours will fair Juliet wake,* Rom. V, 2, 25.

In other cases, likewise, now pointing to what has preceded, now to what is to follow: *this it is to be a peevish girl,* Gent. V, 2, 49 (German: *so geht's, wenn* etc.). *this it is, when men are ruled by women,* R3 I, 1, 62. *why, this it is, see, see!* H8 II, 3, 81. *this it is to have a name,* Ant. II, 7, 12. *Hector's opinion is this in way of truth* ( = as I said ), Troil. II, 2, 189. *this for him,* Ant. III, 12, 15. On the other hand: *why, this it is: my heart accords thereto, and yet a thousand times it answers 'no',* Gent. I, 3, 90. *marry, this it is, sir,* Ado III, 5, 7 ( = I shall tell you). *your reason? This it is: ...,* Caes. IV, 3, 198. *but this it is: our foot shall stay with us,* Ant. IV, 10, 4. *this above all: to thine own self be true,* Hml. I, 3, 78. *if thou fall, O then imagine this, the earth ... thy footing trips,* Ven. 721. *this is my spite, that, thou being dead, the day should yet be light,* 1133. *at last she smilingly with this gives o'er: Fool, fool, quoth she,* Lucr. 1567. *let this be done: put them ...,* Meas. IV, 3, 90. *what was his cause of anger? the noise goes, this: there is among the Greeks ...,* Troil. I, 2, 12. *nor will he yield me this, to show him ...,* Tim. I, 2, 200 etc.

Used, not to define or point to something, but to designate things or persons as sufficiently known in their qualities; sometimes in a good, oftener in a bad sense: *shall cool the heat of this descending sun,* Ven. 190. *whether doth my mind ... drink up the monarchs' plague, this flattery,* Sonn. 114, 2. *where should they find this grand liquor that hath gilded 'em?* Tp. V, 280. *alas! this parting strikes poor lovers dumb,* Gent. II, 2, 21. *what should it be that he respects in her, ... if this fond Love were not a blinded god?* Gent. IV, 4, 201. *as these black masks proclaim an enshield beauty,* Meas. II, 4, 79 (cf. Rom. I, 1, 236). *how will you do to content this substitute?* III, 1, 192. *she should this Angelo have married,* 221. *her combinate husband, this well-seeming Angelo,* 231. *this Angelo was not made by man and woman,* III, 2, 111. *this Claudio is condemned for untrussing,* 189. *what is the news from this good deputy?* IV, 1, 27. *get you some of this distilled Carduus Benedictus,* Ado III, 4, 73. *for men's sake, the authors of these women,* LLL IV, 3, 359. *Lord, what fools these mortals be,* Mids. III, 2, 115. *where are these lads? where are these hearts?* IV, 2, 25. *now will I stir this gamester,* As I, 1, 170. *this duke hath ta'en displeasure 'gainst his gentle niece,* I, 2, 289. *O this learning, what a thing it is!* Shr. I, 2, 160. *as we watch these kites that bate and beat,* Shr. IV, 1, 198.

*shall we hear this dialogue between the fool and the soldier?* All's IV, 3, 112. *out of this nettle danger we pluck this flower safety*, H4A II, 3, 10. *like one of these harlotry players*, II, 4, 436. *how subject we old men are to this vice of lying!* H4B III, 2, 326. *these fellows of infinite tongue, that can rhyme themselves into ladies' favours, they do always excuse themselves out again*, H5 V, 2, 163. *these women are shrewd tempters*, H6A I, 2, 123. *where be these warders*, I, 3, 3. *have you dispatched this thing?* H6B III, 2, 6. *where are these porters, these lazy knaves?* H8 V, 4, 73. *where is this Hector?* Troil. V, 5, 44. *this peace is nothing but to rust iron*, Cor. IV, 5, 234. *these happy masks that kiss fair ladies' brows*, Rom. I, 1, 236 (cf. Meas. II, 4, 79). *where's this girl? what, Juliet*, I, 3, 4. *these tedious old fools!* Hml. II, 2, 223. *when I have stolen upon these sons-in-law*, Lr. IV, 6, 190. *the untuned and jarring senses, O, wind up of this child-changed father*, IV, 7, 17. *the ingratitude of this Seleucus does even make me wild*, Ant. V, 2, 153. Hence *these* sometimes found, where *those* would be expected: *with these nails I'll pluck out these* (i. e. thy) *false eyes*, Err. IV, 4, 107. *why have these banished and forbidden legs dared once to touch a dust of England's ground?* R2 II, 3, 90 (Qq *those*). *if I shall return once more to kiss these lips, I will appear in blood*, Ant. III, 13, 174. *will I cause these of Cyprus to mutiny*, Oth. II, 1, 281. cf. especially Meas. II, 4, 79 and Rom. I, 1, 236, with the notes of the commentators.

Peculiarities of use: = such: *would run to these and these extremities*, Caes. II, 1, 31. *with arms encumbered, thus, or this head-shake*, Hml. I, 5, 174 (shown by a gesture). *these many* = so many: *these many shall die*, Caes. IV, 1, 1. Having *as* for its correlative: *do me this courteous office as to know of the knight what my offence to him is*, Tw. III, 4, 278. *under these hard conditions as this time is like to lay upon us*, Caes. I, 2, 174.

= thus or so: *what am I that thou shouldst contemn me this?* Ven. 205. *further I will not flatter you ... than this, that nothing do I see in you ... should merit any hate*, John II, 518. *this long's the text*, Per. II Prol. 40 (perhaps *long* substantively. Ff. *thus long*).

**Thisbe** (O. Edd. *Thisby* or *Thisbie*, a form retained by M. Edd. only in the speeches of the clowns) the mistress of Pyramus: Mids. I, 2, 13. 46. III, 1, 10. III, 2, 18. IV, 2, 40. V, 57. 131. 267. 271. 319. 366 etc. Merch. V, 7. Rom. II, 4, 45.

**Thisby**, see *Thisbe*.

**Thisne**, Bottom's blunder for *Thisbe:* Mids. I, 2, 55.*

**Thistle**, a prickly plant of the class Syngenesia (*Cirsium*): Ado III, 4, 76. 80. Mids. IV, 1, 12. H5 V, 2, 52.

**Thither**, to that place: Lucr. 113. Sonn. 153, 12. Pilgr. 190. Gent. I, 1, 55. I, 3, 29. III, 1, 128. 145. Wiv. III, 5, 77. IV, 4, 27. 44. Meas. III, 2, 67. Err. IV, 1, 112. V, 224. Ado I, 3, 67. II, 1, 267. III, 2, 3. LLL II, 96. IV, 3, 374. V, 2, 312. Mids. I, 1, 251. Merch. IV, 1, 455. As IV, 3, 162. Shr. IV, 3, 188. All's III, 2, 75. Wint. IV, 2, 57. R2 III, 2, 78. H4A II, 3, 118. H6A III, 1, 51. H6B I, 4, 78. III, 1, 290. IV, 5, 11. H6C III, 1, 30. V, 3, 21. V, 6, 67. R3 I, 2, 107. II, 4, 69. V, 2, 13. H8 I, 1, 112. Oth. II, 1, 216 (Qq *hither*) etc. Seemingly = to that (but the idea of change of place always retained): *nothing remains but*

*that I kindle the boy t.* As I, 1, 179. *let your wedding be to-morrow: t. will I invite the duke*, V, 2, 16. *you are transported by calamity t. where more attends you*, Cor. I, 1, 78. cf. Wiv. III, 5, 77.

**Thitherward**, in that direction: *he's gone to serve the duke of Florence: we met him t.* All's III, 2, 55.

**Thoas**, see *Thous*.

**Thomas**, Christian name of several persons: T. of Woodstock Duke of Gloster, sixth son of Edward III, R2 I, 2, 16. H6B II, 2, 16. T. of Clarence, son of Henry IV, H4B IV, 4, 16. 19. 21. 41. Sir T. More, Lord chancellor in the reign of Henry VIII, H8 III, 2, 393. Sir T. Bullen, father of the second wife of Henry VIII, H8 I, 4, 92. Sir T. Erpingham, R2 II, 1, 283. H5 IV, 1, 13. 24. 96. Sir T. Gargrave, H6A I, 4, 63. 88. Sir T. Grey, H5 II Chor. 25. II, 2, 150. Sir T. Lovell, R3 IV, 4, 520. H8 I, 2, 185. I, 3, 16. 49. 64. I, 4, 10. II, 1, 82. V, 1, 5. 7. 10. 22. 27 etc. T. Mowbray Duke of Norfolk, R2 I, 1, 6. 29. 110. I, 3, 16. 38. 110. H4B III, 2, 31. T. Earl of Surrey, R3 V, 3, 69. Sir T. Vaughan, R3 II, 4, 43. T. Cromwell, H8 IV, 1, 108. T. Horner, H6B I, 3, 29. T. Page, Wiv. I, 1, 46. T. Wart, H4B III, 2, 147. Rice ap T. R3 IV, 5, 12.

*T.* a name commonly applied to tapsters: Pompey addressed as *T.* tapster by Mrs Overdone: Meas. I, 2, 115.

**Thong**, a leathern strap (part of a bridle): *throwing the base t. from his bending crest*, Ven. 395; cf. 392.

**Thorn**, 1) a sharp prickle growing from the stem of a plant; a spine: Lucr. 492. Sonn. 35, 2. All's I, 3, 135. IV, 2, 19. IV, 4, 32. Wint. I, 2, 329. R2 IV, 323. H6A II, 4, 69. H6C III, 2, 175. V, 5, 13. Rom. I, 4, 26. The nightingale or Philomel supposed to lean, in singing, her breast against a thorn, to make her song more doleful: *whiles against a t. thou bearest thy part, to keep thy sharp woes waking*, Lucr. 1135. *she leaned her breast up-till a t., and there sung the dolefullest ditty*, Pilgr. 382. Figurative use: *those —s that in her bosom lodge*, Hml. I, 5, 87. *the —s we stand upon!* Wint. IV, 4, 596; and quibbling: *the roses fearfully on —s did stand*, Sonn. 99, 8 (felt very uneasy).

2) a tree or shrub armed with spines: *the cankerblooms hang on such —s*, Sonn. 54, 7. *ne'er to pluck thee from thy t.* Pilgr. 238 and LLL IV, 3, 112. *through ... pricking goss and —s*, Tp. IV, 180. *withering on the virgin t.* Mids. I, 1, 77. *a bush of —s*, III, 1, 61. *briers and —s*, III, 2, 29. *bush of t.* V, 136. *plant this t., this canker*, H4A I, 3, 176. H6A II, 4, 33. H6B III, 1, 67. H6C III, 2, 175. Figuratively: *among the —s and dangers of this world*, John IV, 3, 141.

**Thorn-bush**, a shrub that has thorns: Mids. V, 263.

**Thorny**, full of thorns, or pricking like thorns; properly and metaphorically: *t. brambles*, Ven. 629. *t. hedgehogs*, Mids. II, 2, 10. *the t. point of bare distress*, As II, 7, 94. *a t. wood*, Shr. Ind. 2, 59. H6C III, 2, 174. V, 4, 67. *the sharp t. points of my alleged reasons*, H8 II, 4, 224. *the steep and t. way to heaven*, Hml. I, 3, 48. *a —er piece of ground*, Per. IV, 6, 153.

**Thorough**, prep. through: *to show her bleeding body t. Rome*, Lucr. 1851. *go t. the streets*, Wiv. IV, 5, 32. *t. bush, t. brier, ... t. flood, t. fire*, Mids. II, 1, 3. 5 (Q2 Ff *through*). *and t. this distemperature we see the seasons alter*, 106 (Q2 F1.4 *through*). *how he glisters t. my rust*, Wint. III, 2, 172 (O. Edd. *through*). *with*

*Cain go wander t. shades of night*, R2 V, 6, 43 (Qq *through*; Ff *through the shades*). *the false revolting Normans t. thee disdain to call us lord*, H6B IV, 1, 87. *be led t. our streets*, Cor. V, 3, 115 (F1 *through*). *whose eyes do never give but t. laughter*, Tim. IV, 3, 492. *these words become your lips as they pass t. them*, V, 1, 198. *will follow the fortunes and affairs of noble Brutus t. the hazards of this untrod state*, Caes. III, 1, 136. *to be led t. the streets of Rome*, V, 1, 110. *t. tattered clothes small vices do appear*, Lr. IV, 6, 168 (Qq *through*).

**Thorough**, adv. through: *who, half t., gives o'er*, H4B I, 3, 59 (Ff *through*). *it pierced me t.* Per. IV, 3, 35.

**Thorough**, adj. complete, full, perfect: *all his behaviours did make their retire to the court of his eye, peeping t. desire*, LLL II, 235 (Q2 *through*).

**Thoroughfare**, writing of some M. Edd. in Cymb. I, 2, 11; see *Throughfare*.

**Thoroughly** (cf. *Throughly*) fully, completely: *would t. woo her, wed her and bed her and rid the house of her*, Shr. I, 1, 149. *to look into this business t.* H6B II, 1, 202. *we shall heat you t. anon*, V, 1, 159. *these are almost t. persuaded*, Cor. I, 1, 205.

**Thou** (apostrophized: *th'art:* Shr. IV, 4, 17. All's II, 4, 28. III, 6, 88. Tw. III, 3, 128. Cor. IV, 5, 100. Tim. I, 2, 34. II, 2, 58. IV, 3, 481 etc. M. Edd. *thou'rt.* O. Edd. *thou'rt* in Wint. I, 2, 211. Meas. I, 2, 33 etc. *th'hast*, Tim. IV, 3, 394. Lr. V, 3, 35. 173. *th'hadst:* Tim. IV, 3, 309; M. Edd. *thou hadst*), objective case *thee;* personal pronoun of the second person in the singular number; oftener used than at present, as being the customary address from superiors to inferiors, and expressive, besides, of any excitement of sensibility; of familiar tenderness as well as of anger; of reverence as well as of contempt. (Thus the constant address of Venus to Adonis in Ven. is *thou*, of Adonis to Venus *you*. Tarquin and Lucrece, being both in a state of extreme emotion, constantly address each other with *thou*. The swaggering host in Wiv. uses *thou* to every body, as long as he is in his pride, but *you*, when he is crestfallen, Wiv. IV, 6, 6. In a solemn style even princes are addressed with *thou:* Err. V, 191. H5 IV, 7, 74. H8 V, 1, 162. Cymb. III, 1, 5; whereas Falstaff uses *you* even to Jove: Wiv. V, 5, 6. cf. Abbott's Shakespearian Grammar p. 153 sq.). *Thou* and *you* alternating: *for you, most wicked sir, ... I do forgive thy rankest fault, and require my dukedom of thee*, Tp. V, 133. *sir, by your leave; hast thou or word or wit* etc. Meas. V, 368. *what is in you? why doest thou tear it?* LLL IV, 3, 200. *what wilt thou do? ... get you in*, As I, 1, 80. *your father were a fool to give thee all*, Shr. II, 403. *you notorious villain, didst thou never see thy master's father?* V, 1, 54. *come you, my lord, to see my open shame? now thou dost penance too*, H6B II, 4, 20 (*you* in the first sentence preferred on account of the appellative 'my lord'). *seal you this league with thy embracements*, R3 II, 1, 29 (Qq *thou;* cf. *my peace we will begin*, Cymb. V, 5, 459). *thou wouldst be gone to join with Richmond; I will not trust you, sir*, IV, 4, 491 ('when the appellative *sir* is used, even in anger, *thou* generally gives place to *you'*. Abbott). *if you plead as well for them as I can say nay to thee for myself*, III, 7, 53. *you play the spaniel, ... but whatsoever thou takest me for, thou hast a cruel nature*, H8 V, 3, 128. *you are kindly met, sir: fare thee well*, Tim. III, 2, 31. *if thou beest not immortal,*

*look about you*, Caes. II, 3, 7. *as in the rest you said thou hast been godlike perfect,* Per. V, 1, 208 etc. Joined with other words; with an adjective: *by cruel cruel thee quite overthrown*, Rom. IV, 5, 57. *good thou, save me a piece of marchpane*, I, 5, 9. With substantives in the vocative case: *thou dearest Perdita*, Wint. IV, 4, 40. *thou Icarus*, H6A IV, 6, 55. *fellow thou, awake*, Caes. IV, 3, 301. *thou drone, thou snail*, Err. II, 2, 196. *O thou thing*, Wint. II, 1, 82. *thou dotard*, II, 3, 74. *why, thou loss upon loss*, Merch. III, 1, 96. *thou unadvised scold*, John II, 191. *thou full dish of fool*, Troil. V, 1, 10. *thou disease of a friend*, Tim. III, 1, 56. Preceding and following terms of reproach (in O. Edd. without the comma employed by M. Edd.): *thou deboshed fish thou*, Tp. III, 2, 29. *thou jesting monkey thou*, 52. *thou drunkard thou*, Err. III, 1, 10. *thou gaoler thou*, IV, 4, 112. *thou dissembler thou*, Ado V, 1, 53. *thou knave thou*, H4A III, 3, 141. 147. *thou thing of no bowels thou*, Troil. II, 1, 54. *I shall forestall thee, Lord Ulysses thou*, IV, 5, 230. *thou damnable box of envy thou*, V, 1, 29. *thou tassel of a prodigal's purse thou*, 36 etc.

Redundant after imperatives: *wipe thou thine eyes*, Tp. I, 2, 25. *know thou, for this I entertain thee*, Gent. IV, 4, 75. *follow thou thy desperate sire*, H6A IV, 6. 54 etc. As a dativus commodi: *although thou steal thee all my poverty*, Sonn. 40, 10. *made thee no mistakings*, Tp. I, 2, 248. *thou wilt never get thee a husband*, Ado II, 1, 20. *I'll devise thee brave punishments for him*, V, 4, 130. *get thee a sword*, H6B IV, 2, 1 etc.

*Thee* reflexively: *withdraw thee*, Gent. V, 4, 18. *get thee away*, Err. I, 2, 16. *bear thee well*, Ado III, 1, 13. *set thee down*, LLL IV, 3, 4. *prepare thee*, Merch. IV, 1, 324. *till thou canst quit thee*, As III, 1, 11. *scratch thee but with a pin*, III, 5, 21. *warm thee*, Shr. Ind. 1, 10. *uncase thee*, I, 1, 212. *betake thee to't*, Tw. III, 4, 240. *disease thee*, Wint. IV, 4, 648. *yield thee to my hand*, John II, 156. *submit thee*, 159. *cloister thee*, R2 V, 1, 23. *unbuttoning thee*, H4A I, 2, 3. *to hide thee*, II, 4, 291. *thou bearest thee like a king*, V, 4, 36. *employ thee for our good*, H6A III, 3, 16. *no way canst thou turn thee*, IV, 2, 25. *hide thee from their looks*, H6B II, 4, 23. *hast thought thee happy*, IV, 1, 55. *hide thee from the bear*, V, 2, 2. *address thee instantly*, 27. *resolve thee*, H6C I, 1, 49. *bethink thee*, I, 4, 44. *hie thee to hell*, R3 I, 3, 143 (cf. *Hie*). *defend thee*, III, 5, 19. *guard thee well*, Troil. V, 5, 253. *do not chafe thee*, 260. *speed thee*, Cor. IV, 5, 93. *hast thou hurt thee*, Tit. II, 3, 203. *calm thee*, IV, 1, 83. *lay thee all along*, Rom. V, 3, 3 etc.

*Thou for thee: nothing this wide universe I call, save thou, my rose*, Sonn. 109, 14. *Thee for thou: to breed another thee*, Sonn. 6, 7. *'tis thee, myself, that for myself I praise*, 62, 13. *if this should be thee*, Tw. II, 5, 113. *how agrees the devil and thee?* H4A I, 2, 127. *here's none but thee and I*, H6B I, 2, 69. *it is thee I fear*, IV, 1, 117. *I am not thee*, Tim. IV, 3, 277. *I would not be thee*, Lr. I, 4, 204. Particularly after imperatives: *look thee*, Gent. II, 5, 30. Wint. III, 3, 116. Cor. V, 2, 77. Tim. IV, 3, 530. *hark thee*, Gent. III, 1, 127. *run thee to the parlour*, Ado III, 1, 1.*stand thee close*, III, 3, 110. IV, 1, 24. *sit thee down*, LLL I, 1, 317. Mids. IV, 1, 1. *hear thee*, Merch. II, 2, 189. *hold thee that to drink*, Shr. IV, 4, 17. All's IV, 5, 46. *hang thee*, Tw. II, 5, 114. *return thee*, H6A III, 3, 56. *stay thee*, H6C III, 2, 58. *take thee that*, Mcb. II, 1, 5. *break thee off*, Hml. I, 1, 40. *come thee on*, Ant. IV, 7, 16 etc. cf. *fare thee well*, sub *Fare*.

*Thou* easily omitted, as the second person is sufficiently indicated by the inflexion of the verb: *then camest in smiling*, Tw. V, 357. *pratest*, Rom. IV, 5, 135. 138 (Q2 *prates;* the surreptitious Q1 and most M. Edd. *pretty*). *shouldst have kept one to thyself*, Tim. I, 1, 275. Particularly in questions: *why dost abhor me?* Ven. 138. *why didst not tell me sooner?* Gent. III, 1, 390. *art not ashamed?* Ado III, 4, 28. *hast any philosophy in thee?* As III, 2, 22. *wast ever in court?* 34. *wast born in the forest here?* V, 1, 24. *art rich?* 27. All's IV, 1, 10. Tw. II, 3, 26. 122. V, 202. Wint. I, 2, 121. 325. III, 2, 176. III, 3, 81. IV, 3, 78. IV, 4, 262. H4A II, 1, 34. II, 4, 3. H6A I, 3, 22. V, 3, 68. H8 I, 2, 202. Tit. II, 3, 209. II, 4, 21. V, 1, 46. Tim. I, 1, 206. 223. 226. 235. II, 2, 84. IV, 3, 221. 480. Caes. I, 1, 31. Hml. III, 2, 298. V, 2, 83. Lr. II, 2, 1. 114. II, 4, 196. III, 4, 4. Oth. II, 1, 260. III, 3, 110. Ant. V, 2, 296. Cymb. III, 5, 125. IV, 2, 81. 382. V, 5, 110 etc.

**Thou**, vb. to address with the pronoun *thou* (which was thought indecent, when done to strangers): *if thou —est him some thrice, it shall not be amiss*, Tw. III, 2, 48.

**Though**, conj. 1) notwithstanding that, however: *travellers ne'er did lie, t. fools at home condemn 'em*, Tp. III, 3, 27. *t. the seas threaten, they are merciful*, V, 178. Gent. II, 1, 178. II, 4, 64. V, 4, 20. Wiv. I, 1, 174. II, 1, 148. Err. I, 1, 70 etc. etc. Elliptically: *governed him in strength, t. not in lust*, Ven. 42. *thou art no man, t. of a man's complexion*, 215. *lovers' hours are long, t. seeming short*, 842. Tp. II, 1, 251. Gent. III, 1, 103. Ado II, 1, 215. Wint. I, 2, 284 etc.

Followed by the indicative, in speaking of things founded on fact: *my woes are tedious, t. my words are brief*, Lucr. 1309. *thy vile race, t. thou didst learn, had that in't ...*, Tp. I, 2, 359. *t. thou canst swim like a duck, thou art made like a gourse*, II, 2, 135. *t. I am struck to the quick, yet ... 'gainst my fury do I take part*, V, 25. *I do forgive thee, unnatural t. thou art*, 79. *thy letters may be here, t. thou art hence*, Gent. III, 1, 248. *t. Page stands so firmly on his wife's frailty, yet I cannot put off my opinion*, Wiv. II, 1, 241. *t. we are justices ..., we have some salt of our youth in us*, II, 3, 48. *the law hath not been dead, t. it hath slept*, Meas. II, 2, 90. *t. he hath fallen by promptures of the blood, yet hath he in him such a mind of honour*, II, 4, 178. *not of this country, t. my chance is now to use it*, III, 2, 230. Err. I, 1, 147. V, 3. Merch. II, 3, 18. As I, 2, 48. Wint. II, 1, 189. IV, 4, 732. R2 I, 2, 24. H6A I, 4, 82. H6B III, 2, 230. H6C II, 2, 166 etc.

Followed by the subjunctive in hypothetical cases: *t. they be outstripped by every pen, reserve them for my love*, Sonn. 32, 6. *t. thou repent, yet I have still the loss*, 34, 10. *which t. it alter not love's sole effect, yet doth it steal sweet hours*, 36, 7. *the summer's flower is to the summer sweet, t. to itself it only live and die*, 94, 10. *I love not less, t. less the show appear*, 102, 2. *I'll warrant him for drowning, t. the ship were no stronger than a nutshell*, Tp. I, 1, 49. *he'll be hanged yet, t. every drop of water swear against it*, 62. *t. this island seem to be desert*, II, 1, 35. IV, 213. V, 41. Wiv. II, 1, 4. II, 2, 230. Meas. II, 2, 134. Err. III, 1, 28. III, 2, 13. IV, 2, 28. Mids. II, 2, 84. III, 1, 138. Merch. I, 1, 56. Tw. II, 5, 136. H6A IV, 1, 102. Lr. III, 3, 18 etc. The subjunctive also expressing real things founded on

fact: *tears harden lust, t. marble wear with raining*, Lucr 560. *t. his false finger have profaned the ring, mine shall not do his Julia so much wrong*, Gent. IV, 4, 141. cf. below *t. that* in Tw. I, 2, 48. Lr. IV, 6, 219. *Be* and *were* often found so (but cf. *Be*, with respect to their being used as indicative forms), f. i.: *only Collatinus finds his wife, t. it were late in the night, spinning amongst her maids*, Lucr. Arg. 9. *by whose aid, weak masters t. ye be, I have bedimmed the sun*, Tp. V, 41. *and true he swore, t. yet forsworn he were*, Err. IV, 2, 10. V, 311. Mids. III, 2, 325. Merch. IV, 1, 198. H6C II, 6, 34 etc.

*No marvel t.* (with the subjunctive) = it is not strange that: *no marvel t. thy horse be gone*, Ven. 390. *no marvel then t. I mistake my view*, Sonn. 148, 11. *no marvel t. he pause*, Err. II, 1, 32. Mids. II, 2, 96. R3 I, 4, 63. Troil. II, 2, 33. Lr. II, 1, 100.

*I care not* or *I reck not t.* (with the subjunctive) = it is all one to me, it does not signify: *I care not t. he burn himself in love*, Gent. II, 5, 55. *I reck not t. I end my life to-day*, Troil. V, 6, 26. Elliptically, *what t.* = what should I care? never mind; and hence = *though* alone: *what t. the rose have prickles, yet 'tis plucked*, Ven. 574. *what t. her frowning brows be bent, her cloudy looks will calm*, Pilgr. 311. *what t. she strive to try her strength, her feeble force will yield*, 317. *what t. care killed a cat, thou hast mettle enough in thee to kill care*, Ado V, 1, 132. *what t. he love your Hermia? Lord, what t.?* Mids. II, 2, 109. *what t. I be not so in grace as you, ... this you should pity rather*, III, 2, 232. As III, 5, 37. H6A V, 3, 101. H6B I, 1, 158. H6C V, 4, 3. R3 I, 1, 154. H8 III, 2, 97. Ant. III, 13, 4. *what t.* alone, without a following clause, = I do not care; it is all the same to me: *I keep but three men, ... but what t.? yet I live like a poor gentleman born*, Wiv. I, 1, 286. *but what t.? courage!* As III, 3, 51. *by chance but not by truth; what t.?* John I, 169. *it* (my iron) *is a simple one, but what t.? it will toast cheese*, H5 II, 1, 9.

*T. that* = though (cf. *That*): *t. that nature with a beauteous wall doth oft close in pollution, yet of thee I will believe ...*, Tw. I, 2, 48. John III, 3, 57. Cor. I, 1, 144. Lr. IV, 6, 219. Oth. I, 1, 71. III, 3, 261.

2) *as t.* = as if: *I thank you as much as t. I did*, Wiv. I, 1, 291. *shall I be appointed hours, as t. I knew not what to leave and what to take?* Shr. I, 1, 104. *I'll give her thanks, as t. she bid me stay by her a week*, II, 179.

**Though**, adv. however, yet: *your hands than mine are quicker for a fray, my legs are longer t. to run away*, Mids. III, 2, 343. *would Katharine had never seen him t.* Shr. III, 2, 26. *I would not be so sick t. for his place*, H8 II, 2, 83.

**Thought**, 1) any thing formed in the mind; an idea, a conception, a reflection, a fancy, an opinion, a recollection, an expectation, a design etc.: *the engine of her —s*, Ven. 367; i. e. her tongue; cf. Tit. III, 1, 82. *all my mind, my t., my busy care, is how to get my palfrey from the mare*, Ven. 383. *whose vulture t. doth pitch the price so high*, 551. *the t. of it doth make my faint heart bleed*, 669. *the one* (hope) *doth flatter thee in —s unlikely, in likely —s the other* (despair) *kills thee quickly*, 989. *even in this t. through the dark night he stealeth*, Lucr. 729. *within his t. her heavenly image sits*, 288. *I think good —s whilst other write good words*, Sonn. 85, 5. *more to know did never meddle with my —s*, Tp. I, 2, 22. *I wish mine eyes* *would ... shut up my —s*, II, 1, 192. *thy —s I cleave to*, IV, 165. *I do begin to have bloody —s*, 220. *every third t. shall be my grave*, V, 311. *the table wherein all my —s are charactered*, Gent. II, 7, 3. *his —s immaculate*, 76. *my —s do harbour with my Silvia nightly*, III, 1, 140. *one Julia, that his changing —s forget*, IV, 4, 124. *heaven make you better than your —s*, Wiv. III, 3, 219. *I was three or four times in the t. they were not fairies*, V, 5, 129. *throw away that t.* Meas. I, 3, 1. *let it not sound a t. upon your tongue against my brother's life*, II, 2, 140. *—s are no subjects*, V, 458. *let this be duly performed, with a t. that more depends on it*, IV, 2, 127. *I speak my t.* Ado I, 1, 226. *to think so base a t.* Merch. II, 7, 50. *punish me not with your hard —s*, As I, 2, 196. *never so much as in a t. unborn did I offend your highness*, I, 3, 53. *there was no t. of pleasing you when she was christened*, III, 2, 283. *let your highness lay a more noble t. upon mine honour*, All's V, 3, 180. *I come to whet your gentle —s on his behalf*, Tw. III, 1, 116. *all the unmuzzled —s that tyrannous heart can think*, 130. *with t. of such affections, step forth mine advocate*, Wint. V, 1, 220. *where I may think the remnant of my —s in peace*, John V, 4, 46. *those —s which honour and allegiance cannot think*, R2 II, 1, 207. *on no t. I think*, II, 2, 31. *swayed your majesty's good —s away from me*, H4A III, 2, 131. *a power much smaller than the smallest of his —s*, H4B I, 3, 30 (= hopes, expectations). *I think you are Sir John Falstaff, and in that t. yield me*, IV, 3, 19. *question your royal —s*, V, 2, 91. *we have now no t. in us but France*, H5 I, 2, 302. *a name that in my —s becomes me best*, III, 3, 6. R3 I, 1, 59. Troil. I, 1, 30. II, 3, 156. IV, 1, 53. Tit. III, 1, 204 (later Ff t.). Caes. III, 1, 176. V, 5, 71. *with more offences at my beck than I have —s to put them in*, Hml. III, 1, 128. *the main descry stands on the hourly t.* Lr. IV, 6, 218 (= is hourly expected). *if we make t. of this, we must not think the Turk is so unskilful.* Oth. I, 3, 26. *prove such a wife as my —s make thee*, Ant. III, 2, 26. *will their good —s call from him*, III, 6, 21. Cymb. I, 3, 28. IV, 4, 33 etc. etc.

*I had thought* (followed by the perf. inf.) = I intended, I supposed, I was going: *I had t. to have held my peace*, Wint. I, 2, 28. *I had t. to have learned his health of you*, R2 II, 3, 24. H4B II, 2, 2. H6B II, 3, 107. Cor. IV, 5, 155. Mcb. II, 3, 20. Lr. I, 4, 224. Oth. I, 2, 5. Ant. III, 13, 186. cf. Oth. II, 3, 266 (Qq and M. Edd. *I thought*). H8 V, 3, 135.

Plur. *—s* sometimes = the manner of thinking, the disposition of the mind: *whose high imperious —s have punished me*, Gent. II, 4, 130. *manage it against despairing —s*, III, 1, 247. *your own good —s excuse me*, LLL II, 176. *bear free and patient —s*, Lr. IV, 6, 80. *to put my father in impatient —s*, Oth. I, 3, 243. *fair —s* and *good —s* (i. e. joy, happiness), as a kind wish: *fair —s and happy hours attend on you!* Merch. III, 4, 41. *good —s possess thee!* R3 IV, 1, 94. *fair —s be your fair pillow*, Troil. III, 1, 49 (Yorkshire tragedy I, 4: *never look for prosperous hour, good —s, quiet sleep, contented walks*). cf. *holy and heavenly —s still counsel her*, H8 V, 5, 30.

In this first as well as in the second sense, often applied to love, as a passion bred and nourished in the mind: *bending all my loving —s on thee*, Sonn. 88, 10. *made wit with musing weak, heart sick with t.* Gent. I, 1, 69. *a little time will melt her frozen —s*, III, 2, 9. *whose* (lust's) *flames aspire as — s do blow them*, Wiv.

V, 5, 102. *to steal your —s*, Merch. II, 1, 12. *that same wicked bastard of Venus, that was begot of t., conceived of spleen, and born of madness*, As IV, 1, 217. *for his —s, would they were blanks, rather than filled with me*, Tw. III, 1, 114. *she pined in t.* II, 4, 115. *to angle for your —s*, Troil. III, 2, 162.

2) the act and operation of thinking, the forming of ideas, meditation: *those parts of thee that the world's eye doth view want nothing that the t. of hearts can mend*, Sonn. 69, 2. *t. is free*, Tp. III, 2, 132. Tw. I, 3, 73 (proverb). *if I in t. felt not her very sorrow*, Gent. IV, 4, 177. *those that lawless and incertain t. imagine howling*, Meas. III, 1, 127. *now he's there, past t. of human reason*, Err. V, 189. *it is past the infinite of t.* Ado II, 3, 106. *when such bad dealing must be seen in t.* R3 III, 6, 14. *sicklied o'er with the pale cast of t.* Hml. III, 1, 85. *had he been where he thought, by this had t. been past*, Lr. IV, 6, 45. *she deceives me past t.* Oth. I, 1, 167. Ant. I, 2, 150. III, 6, 87. Almost = mind, faculty of thinking, of forming ideas: *whereon the t. might think sometime it saw the carcass of a beauty spent*, Compl. 10. *as sure as I have a t. or a soul*, Ado IV, 1, 333. *how far dost thou excel, no t. can think, nor tongue of mortal tell*, LLL IV, 3, 42. *shall I have the t. to think on this, and shall I lack the t. that such a thing bechanced would make me sad?* Merch. I, 1, 36. *thou hast a perfect t.* John V, 6, 6.

Used of sad contemplations, almost = sorrow, melancholy: *take t. and die for Caesar*, Caes. II, 1, 187.*t. and affliction, passion, hell itself, she turns to favour and to prettiness*, Hml. IV, 5, 188. *if swift t. break it not* (the heart), *a swifter mean shall outstrike t.; but t. will do't*, Ant. IV, 6, 35. Similarly of single sorrowful reflections: *hence I took a t., this was a judgment on me*, H8 II, 4, 193. *there is pansies, that's for —s*, Hml. IV, 5, 177. *take to you no hard —s*, Ant. V, 2, 116. *make not your —s your prisons*, 185. cf. *Thought-sick.*

*T.* swifter than any thing: Sonn. 44, 1. H4B IV, 3, 37. H5 V Chor. 15. Rom. II, 5, 4 etc. *as swift as t.* LLL IV, 3, 330. *fleeter than t.* V, 2, 261. *faster than t.* Wint. IV, 4, 565. *fly like t.* John IV, 2, 175. *of no less celerity than t.* H5 III Chor. 3. *with a t.* = in a twinkling, in no time: *come with a t.* Tp. IV, 164. *with a t. seven of the eleven I paid*, H4A II, 4, 242. *I will be here again, even with a t.* Caes. V, 3, 19. *even with a t. the rack dislimns*, Ant. IV, 14, 9. *upon a t.*, in the same sense: *upon a t. he will again be well*, Mcb. III, 4, 55.

3) the least imaginable degree or quantity; an atom, a trifle: *if the hair were a t. browner*, Ado III, 4, 14. *not Neoptolemus ... could promise to himself a t. of added honour torn from Hector*, Troil. IV, 5, 145.

**Thoughted,** in *Holy-thoughted* and *Sick-thoughted*, q. v.

**Thoughten,** having a thought; thinking: *for me, be you t. that I came with no ill intent*, Per. IV, 6, 115.

**Thought-executing,** doing execution in the same moment as it is thought of; rapid like thought: *you sulphurous and t. fires*, Lr. III, 2, 4.

**Thoughtful,** mindful, careful: *for this they have been t. to invest their sons with arts*, H4B IV, 5, 73.

**Thought-sick,** uneasy with sad reflections, sorrowful: *this solidity and compound mass, with tristful visage, as against the doom, is t. at the act*, Hml. III, 4, 51.

**Thous** (M. Edd. *Thoas*), name in Troil. V, 5, 12.

**Thousand,** ten hundred; often used to denote any great number: *a t. furlongs*, Tp. I, 1, 69. III, 2, 146. Gent. I, 3, 91. II, 7, 69. IV, 4, 139. V, 3, 3. V, 4, 48. Wiv. II, 2, 84. 259. Err. I, 1, 22. II, 1, 61 etc. etc. *a t. good-morrows*, Gent. II, 1, 102. IV, 3, 6. Cor. IV, 5, 151 etc. *poor a t. crowns*, As I, 1, 2. *two t.* Gent. II, 1, 107. Wiv. II, 2, 44. *three t.* Meas. I, 2, 50. *five t.* Gent. II, 5, 10 etc. *a t. t.* Lucr. 963. Tp. III, 1, 91. Tw. II, 4, 64. Oth. IV, 1, 203. *the t. marks*, Err. I, 2, 81. *a t. of these letters*, Wiv. II, 1, 76. *many t. on's* (= of us) Wint. I, 2, 206. H4B III, 1, 4. *many a t. grains*, Meas. III, 1, 20. *a many t. warlike French*, John IV, 2, 199. *some t. verses*, LLL V, 2, 50. Without an article: *t. escapes of wit*, Meas. IV, 1, 63. *the general throng of t. friends*, H8 Prol. 29. *cast t. beams upon me*, IV, 2, 89. *that's t. to one good one*, Cor. II, 2, 83. *from t. dangers*, Tit. III, 1, 196. *with t. doubts*, Per. I, 2, 97.

Plur. —*s:* Tw. II, 5, 196. Wint. I, 2, 389. H6B III, 1, 152. H8 II, 3, 97. Cor. I, 1, 203 (*of*). Mcb. IV, 3, 44. Cymb. V, 4, 170 etc. *some —s of these logs*, Tp. III, 1, 10. *many —s*, Wint. I, 2, 8. *that, and —s more of semblable import*, Ant. III, 4, 2 (= a thousand things more).

**Thousand-fold**, multiplied by a thousand: *brings a t. more care*, H6C II, 2, 52. *a t. it doth*, II, 5, 46. *a t. more bitter*, H8 II, 3, 8. *but more in Troilus t. I see*, Troil. I, 2, 310.

**Thousandth** (O. Edd. *thousand*), the ordinal of thousand: As IV, 1, 46. Per. V, 1, 136.

**Thracian**, adj. native of, or pertaining to, Thrace: *the T. singer* (Orpheus) Mids. V, 49. Tit. II, 4, 51. *the T. fatal steeds*, H6C IV, 2, 21 (the horses of King Rhesus). *the T. tyrant*, Tit. I, 138 (Polymestor, who had murdered Priam's son Polydore). *the T. king Adallas*, Ant. III, 6, 71.

**Thraldom**, bondage, slavery: *he delivers thee from this world's t. to the joys of heaven*, R3 I, 4, 255.

**Thrall**, subst. 1) a slave, one subject to another: *I, my mistress' t.* Sonn. 154, 12. *look gracious on thy prostrate t.* H6A I, 2, 117. *long time thy shadow hath been t. to me, for in my gallery thy picture hangs*, II, 3, 36. *make me die the t. of Margaret's curse*, R3 IV, 1, 46. *that were the slaves of drink and —s of sleep*, Mcb. III, 6, 13.

2) slavery: *love hath forlorn me, living in t.* Pilgr. 266.

**Thrall**, adj. enslaved, bound in servitude: *love makes young men t. and old men dote*, Ven. 837. *brought in subjection her immortality, and made her t. to living death and pain perpetual*, Lucr. 725.

**Thrall**, vb. to enslave: *nor falls under the blow of —ed discontent*, Sonn. 124, 7. *that maid whose sudden sight hath —ed my wounded eye*, Shr. I, 1, 225. *sense to ecstasy was ne'er so —ed but it reserved some quantity of choice*, Hml. III, 4, 74. cf. *Enthralled*, which is, almost exclusively, used of the servitude of love.

**Thrash**, to beat out from the husk with a flail: *first t. the corn*, Tit. II, 3, 123. = to drub: *thou art here but to t. Trojans*, Troil. II, 1, 50.

**Thrasher**, one who thrashes grain: H6C II, 1, 131.

**Thrasonical**, boastful, hectoring: *his general behaviour vain, ridiculous and t.* LLL V, 1, 14. *Caesar's t. brag of 'I came, saw, and overcame'*, As V, 2, 34.

**Thread,** subst. a small twist drawn out to considerable length: *golden —s*, Lucr. 400. *a silken t.* Ado V, 1, 25. Rom. II, 2, 181. *thou t.* Shr. IV, 3, 108. *a skein of t.* 111. *with needle and t.* 121. *a bottom of brown t.* 138. *weave their t. with bones*, Tw. II, 4, 46. *any silk, any t.* Wint. IV, 4, 325. *the smallest t. that ever spider twisted*, John IV, 3, 127. *one t., one little hair*, V, 7, 54. Emblem of life, as being spun and cut by the Parcae: *you have shore with shears his t. of silk*, Mids. V, 348 (Thisbe's speech). *O Fates, come, come, cut t. and thrum*, 291 (Pyramus' speech). *let not Bardolph's vital t. be cut*, H5 III, 6, 49 (Pistol's speech). *his t. of life had not so soon decayed*, H6A I, 1, 34. *their t. of life is spun*, H6B IV, 2, 31. *grief shore his old t. in twain*, Oth. V, 2, 206. *cut his t. of life*, Per. I, 2, 108. Figuratively: *he draweth out the t. of his verbosity*, LLL V, 1, 18. In Tp. IV, 3 O. Edd. *I have given you here a third of mine own life;* M. Edd. *a thread* or *thrid.*

**Thread**, vb. to pass as a thread through the eye of a needle: *for a camel to t. the postern of a needle's eye*, R2 V, 5, 17. *they would not t. the gates*, Cor. III, 1, 124. —*ing dark-eyed night*, Lr. II, 1, 121 (the adjective *dark-eyed* evidently formed in allusion to the eye of a needle. cf. *unthread the rude eye of rebellion*, John V, 4, 11).

**Threadbare**, having the nap worn off, shabby: *a t. juggler*, Err. V, 239. *'tis t.* H6B IV, 2, 8.

**Threaden**, made of thread: *her t. fillet*, Compl. 33. *the t. sails*, H5 III Chor. 10.

**Threat**, subst., used only in verse and in the plur. —*s* = menaces: Tp. I, 2, 488. Gent. III, 1, 236 (*with many bitter —s of biding there*). Mids. III, 2, 250. As IV, 3, 110. Wint. III, 2, 92. H6C I, 1, 72. 101. Troil. IV, 5, 261. Tim. III, 5, 43. Caes. IV, 3, 66. Hml. IV, 1, 14. Lr. IV, 2, 57.

**Threat**, vb. (used only in verse and in the present time), to menace, to threaten; absol.: *no more than he that —s*, John III, 1, 347. —*est where's no cause*, H6B I, 4, 51. Tim. IV, 2, 21. Caes. V, 1, 38. Mcb. II, 1, 60. An inf. following: *who —s to do as much as ever Coriolanus did*, Tit. IV, 4, 67. A clause: *whose crooked beak —s if he mount he dies*, Lucr. 508. Transitively, a) the person menaced as object: *that ever t. his foes*, Ven. 620. Lucr. 331. 547. R2 III, 3, 90. Tit. II, 1, 40. Ant. III, 5, 19. Cymb. IV, 2, 127. *t. you me with telling of the king?* R3 I, 3, 113. *and t. me I shall never come to bliss*, Tit. III, 1, 273. b) the evil to be inflicted as object: *every one did t. to-morrow's vengeance on the head of Richard*, R3 V, 3, 205.

**Threaten**, to menace; absol.: *though the seas t., they are merciful*, Tp. V, 178. Meas. I, 3, 24. Err. I, 1, 10. Merch. II, 7, 18. III, 2, 105. Shr. V, 2, 136. John III, 4, 120. V, 2, 73. R2 III, 3, 51. H5 II, 4, 110. H6B IV, 1, 107. H6C I, 3, 17. II, 6, 58. V, 3, 4. Tit. I, 134. II, 1, 4. IV, 2, 94. Tim. V, 1, 169. Caes. I, 3, 8. Hml. III, 4, 57. Ant. I, 3, 52. III, 13, 171. With an inf.: *hath —ed to put me into everlasting liberty*, Wiv. III, 3, 30. IV, 2, 89. Lr. II, 1, 68. Transitively; 1) the thing or person menaced as object: *the twigs that t. them*, All's III, 5, 56. Wint. III, 2, 165. John II, 225. 481. V, 1, 49. H4A V, 4, 42. H5 II, 4, 70. IV Chor. 10. Cor. I, 6, 36. Tit. III, 1, 224. Caes. II, 2, 10. Mcb. II, 4, 6. Per. V, 1, 201. An inf. following: —*ed me to strike me*, Mids. III, 2, 312. With following: —*ing Ilion with annoy*, Lucr. 1370. Wint. V, 1, 201. H6C V 4, 23. R3 I, 4, 193. Rom. V, 3, 276. Hml. II, 2, 528. Cymb. V, 5, 77. 2) the evil to be inflicted as object:

*the skies t. present blusters*, Wint. III, 3, 4. *the law that —ed death*, Rom. III, 3, 139. *no less is —ed me*, Lr. III, 3, 19. *—s life or death*, Per. I, 3, 25.

**Threatener,** one who menaces: John V, I, 49.

**Threateningly,** in a menacing manner: All's II, 3, 87.

**Three,** two and one: Ven. 1064. Sonn. 104, 3. Pilgr. 211. Tp. I, 2, 41. II, 1, 283. III, 2, 7. III, 3, 53. 104. V, 136. 272. Gent. III, 2, 33. IV, 4, 4. 19. V, 1, 11. Wiv. I, 1, 13. II, 2, 327. III, 5, 110. Meas. I, 2, 50. V, 362. Err. I, 1, 111. Ado II, 1, 278. Mids. III, 2, 193. H4A I, 3, 102. Lr. I, 1, 39 etc. etc. *the picture of 'we t.'* Tw. II, 3, 17 (Malone: a common sign, in which two wooden heads are exhibited with this inscription under it, *'We three loggerheads be'*; the spectator being supposed to make the third).

Substantively: *now here is t. studied*, LLL I, 2, 54. *I always took t. —s for nine*, V, 2, 495. *by twos and —s*, Wint. I, 2, 438. *these four —s of herdsmen*, IV, 4, 344. *one t. of them hath danced before the king*, 345. *by ones, by twos, and by —s*, Cor. II, 3, 47.

Misapplied by Evans for *third*: Wiv. I, 1, 142.

**Three-farthings:** *my face so thin that in my ear I durst not stick a rose lest men should say 'Look where t. goes'*, John I, 143. Dyce: an allusion to the three-farthing silver pieces of Queen Elizabeth, which were very thin, and had the profile of the sovereign with a rose at the back of her head: and we must remember that in Shakespeare's time sticking roses in the ear was a court-fashion.

**Three-farthing-worth,** a quantity of the value of three farthings: *t. of silk*, LLL III, 150 (Ff Q2 *three farthings worth*).

**Threefold,** three-double, thrice repeated, triple; 1) adj.: *a torment thrice t.* Sonn. 133, 8. *this t. perjury*, Gent. II, 6, 5. *with t. love*, LLL V, 2, 835. *according to our t. order ta'en*, H4A III, 1, 71. *t. vengeance*, H6B III, 2, 304. *a t. death*, H6C V, 4, 32. *the t. world divided*, Caes. IV, 1, 14.

2) adv.: *'tis t. too little*, Gent. I, 1, 116. *t. renowned*, H6C V, 7, 5. *t. distressed*, R3 II, 2, 86.

**Three-foot,** having three legs: *t. stool*, Mids. II. 1, 52. Cymb. III, 3, 89.

**Three-headed,** having three heads: *Cerberus, that t. canis*, LLL V, 2, 593.

**Three-hooped:** *the t. pot shall have ten hoops*, H6B IV, 2, 72. Douce: the old drinking-pots, being of wood, were bound together, as barrels are, with hoops; whence they were called hoops. Cade promises that every can which now had three hoops shall be increased in size so as to require ten.

**Three-hours,** of three hours' standing: *thy t. wife*, Rom. III, 2, 99.

**Three-inch,** three inches high: *you t. fool*, Shr. IV, 1, 27.

**Three-legged,** having three legs: *to comb your noddle with a t. stool*, Shr. I, 1, 64.

**Three-man:** *t. song-men*, Wint. IV, 3, 44 (i. e. singers of songs in three parts). *a t. beetle*, H4B I, 2, 255 (a rammer managed by three men).

**Three-nooked,** having three corners: *the t. word shall bear the olive freely*, Ant. IV, 6, 6 (cf. *the three corners of the world*, John V, 7, 116).

**Three-pence,** a coin of three times the value of a penny: Meas. II, 1, 95. 107. 255. H8 II, 3, 36 (*a t. bowed would hire me*). cf. Cor. II, 1, 80.

**Three-pile,** the richest and most costly kind of velvet (called so probably from a richer accumulation of the pile): *and in my time wore t.* Wint. IV, 3, 14. Name: *Master T. mercer*, Meas. IV, 3, 11.

**Three-piled,** set with a thick, rich pile; of first-rate quality: *thou art good velvet; thou 'rt a t. piece*, Meas. I, 2, 33 (perhaps with a hidden meaning similar to the German *dreihärig*, or with an allusion to *peeled*, i. e. stripped of hair). Metaphorically, = superfine, exaggerated: *t. hyperboles*, LLL V, 2, 407.

**Threescore,** sixty: Sonn. 11, 8. Ado I, 1, 201. H4A II, 4, 467. H5 IV, 3, 3 (*t. thousand*). H6C III, 3, 93. Hml. II, 2, 73 (Ff *three*). *t. and ten*, H4A II, 2, 27. Mcb. II, 4, 1.

**Three-suited:** *a base, proud, shallow, beggarly, t. ... knave*, Lr. II, 2, 16. Three suits as well as "a hundred pounds a year" (the smallest income of a juryman) and "*worsted stockings*" seem to have been proverbial to denote what might have been an object of envy to extreme poverty (cf. Lr. III, 4, 141 and Ado IV, 2, 88) but of contempt in a wouldbe gentleman who sought the society of the great. See Ben Jonson's Epicoene A. III Sc. I: "*who allows you ... your three suits of apparel a year? your four pair of stockings, one silk, three worsted?*

**Threne** (the following superscription has the Greek form *threnos*) lamentation, funeral song: *whereupon it made this t. to the phoenix and the dove*, Phoen. 49.

**Thresh** and **Thresher,** see *Thrash* and *Thrasher*.

**Threshold,** the plank that lies at the bottom of a door: Lucr. 306. LLL III, 118. Merch. I, 3, 120. H6C IV, 7, 11. Cor. I, 3, 82. IV, 5, 124.

**Thrice,** three times: Gent. I, 2, 117. III, 1, 365. Wiv. II, 1, 26. V, 5, 54. Ado III, 2, 11. LLL I, 2, 41. 54. Merch. II, 2, 173. IV, 1, 227. 234. 318. Shr. III, 2, 44. All's II, 5, 33. Tw. III, 2, 48. Wint. III. 3, 24. V, 2, 115. H4A III, 1, 137. III, 2, 112. H4B IV, 4. 125. H5 I, 2, 217. IV, 6, 4. V, 1, 79. Cor. II, 3, 135. Rom. I, 1, 98. Tim. III, 3, 22. Caes. I, 2, 226. 228. II, 2, 2. III, 2, 101. 102. Mcb. I, 3, 35. IV, 1, 1. 2. Hml. I, 2, 202. II, 1, 93. III, 2, 269. Lr. III, 4, 125. *three times and t. alternating*: H4A III, 1, 65. H6B V, 3, 9. H6C I, 4, 10. *three times t.* LLL V, 2, 488. H6B III, 2, 358. *t. three times*, Merch. I, 3, 160. *the t. three Muses*, Mids. V, 52.

Used by way of general amplification: *makes summer's welcome t. more wished*, Sonn. 56, 14. *gain by ill t. more than I have spent*, 119, 14. *a torment t. threefold*, 133, 8. *he is t. a villain*, As I, 1, 61. *my limbs are t. themselves*, H4B I, 1, 145. *t. is he armed that hath his quarrel just*, H6B III, 2, 233.

Often before adjectives and participles (sometimes hyphened by O. and M. Edd., but without consistency): *t. blessed*, Mids. I, 1, 74. *t. crowned queen of night*, As III, 2, 2 ('alluding to the triple character of Proserpine, Cynthia, and Diana.' Johnson). *a t. double ass*, Tp. V, 295. *my t. driven bed of down*, Oth. I, 3, 232. *t. fair lady*, Merch. III, 2, 147. *t. fairer than myself*, Ven. 7. *t. famed*, H6B III, 2, 157. Troil. II, 3, 254. *t. gentle*, Oth. III, 4, 122. *t. gorgeous*, H5 IV, 1, 283. *t. gracious*, R2 II, 2, 24. H4A III, 2, 92. *t. noble*, Shr. Ind. 2, 120. R2 III, 3, 103. H6B III, 1, 266. Tit. I, 120. *t. nobler*, Ant. IV, 14, 95. *t. puissant*, H5 I, 2, 119. *t. renowned*, R3 IV, 2, 13. *t. repured*, Troil. III, 2, 23 (Ff *t. reputed*). *t. valiant*, H5 IV, 6, 1. Tit. V, 2, 112. *t. victorious*, H6A IV, 7, 67. *t. welcome*, Tw. V, 248. H6A I, 2, 47. *t. wider*, H4B V, 5, 58. *t. worse*, R2 III,

2, 132. *t. worthy*, LLL V, 1, 151. H5 IV, 4, 66. Troil. II, 3, 200.

**Thrid**, writing of some M. Edd. for *third* of O. Edd. in Tp. IV, 3; others *thread*, q. v.

**Thrift**, 1) frugality, good husbandry: *t., t., Horatio! the funeral baked meats did coldly furnish forth the marriage tables*, Hml. I, 2, 180.

2) profit, gain: *I am now about no waste, I am about t.* Wiv. I, 3, 47. *French t., you rogues,* 93.* *my bargains and my well-won t.* Merch. I, 3, 51. *t. is blessing, if men steal it not,* 91. *to see alike mine honour as their profits, their own particular —s,* Wint. I, 2, 311. *how, i' the name of t., does he rake this together!* H8 III, 2, 109. *from my first have been inclined to t.* Tim. I, 1, 118. *where t. may follow fawning,* Hml. III, 2, 67. *the instances that second marriage move are base respects of t.* 193.

3) success, prosperity in any way: *I have a mind presages me such t.* Merch. I, 1, 175. *you snatch some hence for little faults; that's love, to have them fall no more: you some permit to second ills with ills, each elder worse, and make them dread it, to the doers' t.* Cymb. V, 1, 15 (= to their advantage).

**Thriftless**, 1) prodigal, extravagant: *he shall spend mine honour with his shame, as t. sons their scraping fathers' gold,* R2 V, 3, 69. *t. ambition, that wilt ravin up thine own life's means,* Mcb. II, 4, 28.

2) unprofitable: *an all-eating shame and t. praise,* Sonn. 2, 8. *what t. sighs shall poor Olivia breathe!* Tw. II, 2, 40.

**Thrifty**, frugal, economical, intent on profit: *like a t. goddess, she determines herself the glory of a creditor, both thanks and use,* Meas. I, 1, 39. *a proverb never stale in t. mind,* Merch. II, 5, 55. *the t. hire I saved under your father,* As II, 3, 39.* *they are t. honest men,* H6B IV, 2, 196. *a t. shoeing-horn in a chain,* Troil. V, 1, 61.

**Thrill**, 1) to affect with a sharp, shivering sensation running through the system: *to reside in —ing region of thick-ribbed ice,* Meas. III, 1, 123. *—ed with remorse,* Lr. IV, 2, 73.

2) to have a shivering sensation running through the system, to be chilled: *to t. and shake even at the crying of your nation's crow,* John V, 2, 143. *doth not thy blood t. at it?* H4A II, 4, 407. *I have a faint cold fear —s through my veins,* Rom. IV, 3, 15.

**Thrive** (impf. —*d*, Per. V, 2, 9. partic. —*d*, Ant. I, 3, 51) 1) to grow, to increase, to flourish, to take well (German *gedeihen*): *love —s not in the heart that shadows dreadeth,* Lucr. 270. *truth and beauty shall together t.* Sonn. 14, 11. *honours t., when rather from our acts we them derive,* All's II, 3, 142. *wholesome berries t. and ripen best,* H5 I, 1, 61. *why should it* (meat) *t. and turn to nutriment,* Tim. III, 1, 61. *let copulation t.* Lr. IV, 6, 116.

2) to prosper in business, to increase in goods and estate: *blessed bankrupt, that by love so —th,* Ven. 466. *I will t.* Wiv. I, 3, 22. 81. *this was a way to t.* Merch. I, 3, 90. *now t. the armourers,* H5 II Chor. 3. *do well t. by them,* Oth. I, 1, 53. *such as have not —d upon the present state,* Ant. I, 3, 51. *letting them* (debtors) *t. again,* Cymb. V, 4, 20.

3) to prosper, to succeed in any way, to be fortunate, to be happy: *they that t. well take counsel of their friends,* Ven. 640. *that his beauty may the better t.* 1011. *if he t. and I be cast away,* Sonn. 80, 13. *love still and t. therein,* Gent. I, 1, 9. *if these four Worthies in their first show t.* LLL V, 2, 541. *here do I choose, and t. I*

*as I may,* Merch. II, 7, 60. *to wive and t.* Shr. I, 2, 56. *he cannot t., unless her prayers . . . reprieve him,* All's III, 4, 26. *by foolery t.* IV, 3, 374. *would not have knaves t. long,* V, 2, 34. *by swaggering could I never t.* Tw. V, 408. *the unjust man doth t.* Wint. IV, 4, 689. *my innocency and Saint George to t.* R2 I, 3, 84. *as York —s to beat back Bolingbroke,* II, 2, 144. *as I intend to t. in this new world,* IV, 78. *ill mayst thou t., if thou grant any grace,* V, 3, 99. *we shall t., I trust,* H4A I, 3, 300. *say that he t.* H6B III, 1, 379. *if we mean to t. and do good,* IV, 3, 17. *if you t. well, bring them to Baynard's castle,* R3 III, 5, 98. *a jolly —ing wooer,* IV, 3, 43. *who —s and who declines,* Cor. I, 1, 197. *live and t.* IV, 6, 23. *if I t. well, I'll visit thee again,* Tim. IV, 3, 170. *seek to t. by that which has undone thee,* 210. *to have us t. in our mystery,* 457. *if ever thou wilt t., bury my body,* Lr. IV, 6, 253. *t. by other means,* V, 3, 34. *how I did t. in this fair lady's love,* Oth. I, 3, 125. *Pompey —s in our idleness,* Ant. I, 4, 76. *if you t.* Per. II, 1, 157. *so he —d, that he is promised to be wived to fair Marina,* V, 2, 9. = to be victorious, to conquer: *if Lord Percy t. not,* H4A IV, 4, 36. *as I intend to t. to-day,* H6B V, 2, 17. *if we t.* H6C II, 3, 52. R3 V, 3, 267. Lr. V, 2, 2. Ant. IV, 3, 10. IV, 4, 9. *so t. I,* as a form of solemn assurance: *so t. I as I truly swear the like,* R3 II, 1, 11. *so t. I and mine,* 24. *so t. I in my enterprise,* IV, 4, 235. 398. cf. *so t. it* (greatness) *in your game,* John IV, 2, 95. *so t. Richard as thy foes may fall,* H6A III, 1, 174. *so t. my soul,* Rom. II, 2, 153.

4) to succeed (used of things), to go on or turn out well, to have a good issue: *how —s your love?* Gent. II, 4, 125. *your undertaking cannot miss a —ing issue,* Wint. II, 2, 45. *I will not wish thy wishes t.* John III, 1, 334. *I wish your enterprise may t.* Caes. III, 1, 13. *if this letter speed, and my invention t.* Lr. I, 2, 20. *his comforts t., his trials well are spent,* Cymb. V, 4, 104.

**Thriver**, one who makes profit: *pitiful —s, in their gazing* (Staunton *gaining*) *spent,* Sonn. 125, 8.

**Throat**, the forepart of the neck, which is the passage for food and breath (oftenest used as the best assailable part of an enemy): Tp. I, 1, 43. III, 3, 45. Meas. II, 4, 153. IV, 3, 26. LLL III, 15. As I, 1, 63. Tw. I, 3, 42. H5 II, 1, 24. IV, 4, 15. H6C V, 6, 9. R3 I, 3, 189. Troil IV, 4, 56 (*my heart will be blown up by my t.; Ff. by the root*). Cor. IV, 5, 102. V, 4, 8. 59. V, 6, 31. 53. Tit. V, 2, 197. Tim. I, 2, 53. V, 1, 182. Hml. V, 1, 283. Lr. I, 1, 168. Ant. II, 5, 35. II, 6, 144. III, 5, 19. Cymb. IV, 2, 150. *in the t. of death =* in the jaws of death: LLL V, 2, 865. R3 V, 4, 5. *to cut one's t. =* to kill, to murder him: Wiv. I, 4, 115. H4A II, 2, 88. H5 II, 1, 73. 96. III, 2, 119. IV, 4, 34. IV, 7, 10. 66. H6B IV, 1, 20. IV, 2, 29. Troil. IV, 4, 131. Tit. V, 2, 182. Rom. I, 4, 83. Tim. III, 5, 44. IV, 1, 10. IV, 3, 121. 452. Caes. I, 2, 268. Mcb. III, 4, 16. Hml. IV, 7, 127. Cymb. III, 4, 35. *fly . . . to our enemies' —s,* H6A I, 1, 98. *fall to their —s,* Ant. II. 7, 78. *catch each other by the t.* R3 I, 3, 189. Oth. V, 2, 355. Lies or slanders thrown back into the throat from which they proceeded: *until it had returned these terms of treason doubled down his t.* R2 I, 1, 57. *as low as to thy heart, through the false passage of thy t., thou liest,* 125. *I'll turn my part thereof into thy t.* H6A II, 4, 79. *the solus in thy teeth, and in thy t.* H5 II, 1, 51. *thrust these reproachful speeches down his t.* Tit. II, 1, 55. *till all these mischiefs be returned again even in their —s that have committed them,* III, 1, 275. *that it did*

(give me the lie) *i'the very t. on me,* Mcb. II, 3, 43. *gives me the lie i'the t.,* as deep as to the lungs, Hml. II, 2, 601. *even in his t.* . . *I return the lie,* Per. II, 5, 56. Hence the following phrases: *I lie in my t.* LLL IV, 3, 13. Shr. IV, 3, 133. Tw. III, 4, 172. H4B I, 2, 94. R3 I, 2, 93. Oth. III, 4, 13. *that's a lie in thy t.* H5 IV, 8, 17 (Fluellen's speech). *with a foul traitor's name stuff I thy t.* R2 I, 1, 44.
= voice: *and turn his merry note unto the sweet bird's t.* As II, 5, 4. *my t. of war be turned ... into a pipe small as an eunuch,* Cor. III, 2, 112. *the cock... with his lofty and shrill-sounding t.* Hml. I, 1, 151. *whose rude —s Jove's dreadful clamours counterfeit,* Oth. III, 3, 355.

**Throb,** to beat violently (as the heart), to palpitate: Ven. 1186. H6B IV, 4, 5. Tit. V, 3, 95. Mcb. IV, 1, 101.

**Throe** (O. Edd. *throwe*) subst. extreme pain, pang, agony: *that gave to me many a groaning t.* H8 II, 4, 199. *other incident —s that nature's fragile vessel doth sustain,* Tim. V, 1, 203. *Lucina took me in my —s,* Cymb. V, 4, 44.

**Throe,** vb. (O. Edd. *throw* or *throwe*) to pain, to put in agony: *a birth indeed which —s thee much to yield,* Tp. II, 1, 231. *with news the time's with labour, and —s forth each minute some,* Ant. III, 7, 81 (but this may be *throws forth* = brings forth).

**Throne,** subst. a royal seat: Lucr. 413. Tp. III, 3, 23. Meas. V, 295. All's IV, 3, 4. Tw. I, 1, 38. John III, 1, 74. H6A I, 1, 149. II, 5, 69. H6B II, 3, 38. IV, 9, 1. H6C I, 1, 74. II, 1, 93. 193. Cor. IV, 6, 32. Oth. III, 3, 448 etc. Preceded by *in*: Ven. 1043. H6A III, 1, 44. H6C I, 1, 22. 84. 124. IV, 3, 64. V, 7, 1. R3 II, 2, 100. III, 7, 216. Rom. V, 1, 3 etc. By *on*: H5 I, 2, 117. IV, 1, 281. Troil. V, 10, 7.

**Throne,** vb. 1) intr. to be enthroned: *he wants nothing of a god but eternity and a heaven to t. in,* Cor. V, 4, 26.
2) trans. to enthrone: *as who have not, that their great stars —d and set high?* Lr. III, 1, 23. Partic. *—d: a —d queen,* Sonn. 96, 5. *a fair vestal —d by the west,* Mids. II, 1, 158. Merch. IV, 1, 189. Tw. II, 4, 22. H8 I, 1, 11. Tim. I, 1, 64. Ant. I, 3, 28.

**Throng,** subst. a crowd pressing forward to some purpose: *a short knife and a t.* Wiv. II, 2, 18 (cf. Lr. III, 2, 88). *so play the foolish —s with one that swoons,* Meas. II, 4, 24. *strange fantasies which, in their t. and press to that last hold, confound themselves,* John V, 7, 19. *nor the t. of words that come with such more than impudent sauciness from you,* H4B II, 1, 122. *troop in the —s of military men,* IV, 1, 62. *to smother up the English in our —s,* H5 IV, 5, 20. *I'll to the t.* 22. *followed with the general t. and sweat of thousand friends,* H8 Prol. 28. *flamens do press among the popular —s,* Cor. II, 1, 230. *be abhorred all feasts, societies, and —s of men,* Tim. IV, 3, 21. *fellow, come from the t.* Caes. I, 2, 21. *the t. that follows Caesar at the heels,* II, 4, 34. *nor cutpurses come not to —s,* Lr. III, 2, 88.

**Throng,** vb. 1) intr. to crowd and press forward to some purpose: *which (her breath) —ing through her lips, so vanisheth as smoke from Aetna,* Lucr. 1041. *much like a press of people at a door, t. her inventions, which shall go before,* 1302. *through his lips do t. weak words, so thick come...,* 1783. *wherefore t. you hither?* Err. V, 38. *in their rooms come —ing soft and delicate desires,* Ado I, 1, 305. *they t. who should buy first,* Wint. IV, 4, 612. *where be the —ing troops that followed thee?* R3

IV, 4, 96. *to the shore t. many doubtful friends,* 435. *all several sins ... t. to the bar,* V, 3, 199. *many mazed considerings did t. and pressed in with this caution,* H8 II, 4, 185. *I have seen the dumb men t. to see him,* Cor. II, 1, 278. *I'll say th'hast gold: thou wilt be —ed to,* Tim. IV, 3, 395.
2) trans. a) to press (in a crowd): *here one being —ed bears back, all bollen and red,* Lucr. 1417.
b) to crowd about: *variable passions t. her constant woe, as striving who should best become her grief,* Ven. 967. Hence = to fill with a crowding multitude: *t. our large temples with the shows of peace, and not our streets with war,* Cor. III, 3, 36 (O. Edd. *through*). *the blind mole casts copped hills towards heaven, to tell the earth is —ed by men's oppression,* Per. I, 1, 101 (the earth is completely taken up and filled by the encroaching avidity of man). With *up,* = to fill completely, to possess entirely: *a man —ed up with cold,* Per. II, 1, 77.

**Throstle,** the thrush, Turdus musicus: Mids. III, 1, 130. Merch. I, 2, 65 (O. Edd. *trassell*).

**Throttle,** to choke: *t. their practised accent in their fears,* Mids. V, 97.

**Through,** prepos. 1) in all, throughout; locally and temporally: *fear t. all her sinews spread,* Ven. 903. *t. the length of times he stands disgraced,* Lucr. 718. *t. all the signories it was the first,* Tp. I, 2, 71. *this is enough to be the decay of lust t. the realm,* Wiv. V, 5, 153. *t. Athens I am thought as fair as she,* Mids. I, 1, 227. I, 2, 5. *seek t. this grove,* II, 1, 259. *a merchant of great traffic t. the world,* Shr. I, 1, 12. *seek t. your camp to find you,* H5 IV, 1, 303. *so much applauded t. the realm of France,* H6A II, 2, 36. *we will make thee famous t. the world,* III, 3, 13. *levy great sums of money t. the realm,* H6B III, 1, 61. *proclaimed a coward t. the world,* IV, 1, 43. *those maims of shame seen t. thy country,* Cor. IV, 5, 93 etc.
2) Denoting way or passage from end to end, or from side to side: *two doves will draw me t. the sky,* Ven. 153. *he .. t. the dark laund runs apace,* 813. *conveyed t. the empty skies,* 1191. *wandered t. the forest,* Gent. V, 2, 38. *roaming clean t. the bounds of Asia,* Err. I, 1, 134. *he hurried t. the street,* V, 140. *followed t. toothed briars,* Tp. IV, 179 etc. Emphatically reduplicated: *thy slander hath gone t. and t. her heart,* Ado V, 1, 68. *I'll t. and t. you,* Troil. V, 10, 26. *carries them t. and t. the most fond and winnowed opinions,* Hml. V, 2, 200.
3) Denoting a medium passed: *a dive-dapper peering t. a wave,* Ven. 86. *t. his mane and tail the high wind sings,* 305. *hers (eyes) which t. the crystal tears gave light,* 491. *the brambles ... t. whom he rushes,* 630. *the many musets t. the which he goes,* 683. *this dismal cry rings sadly in her ear, t. which it enters,* 890. *t. the floodgates breaks the silver rain,* 959. *t. little vents... the wind wars with his torch,* Lucr. 310. *the very eyes of men t. loopholes thrust,* 1383. *might I but t. my prison once a day behold this maid,* Tp. I, 2, 490. *here's a maze trod indeed t. forth-rights and meanders,* III, 3, 3. *these follies are within you and shine t. you like the water in an urinal,* Gent. II, 1, 40. *I'll convey thee t. the city-gate,* III, 1, 252. *go you t. the town to Frogmore,* Wiv. II, 3, 78. *do but behold the tears that swell in me, and they thy glory t. my grief will show,* LLL IV, 3, 37. *thrust thy sharp wit quite t. my ignorance,* V, 2, 398. *half his face must be seen t. the lion's neck,* Mids. III, 1, 38. *that the moon may t. the centre creep,* III, 2, 54.

*pierced t. the heart*, 59. *some that will evermore peep t. their eyes*, Merch. I, 1, 52. *thy casement I need not open, for I look t. thee*, All's II, 3, 226. *thrust t. the doublet*, H4A II, 4, 185. *these* (i. e. lips) *t. whom a thousand sighs are breathed for thee*, H6B III, 2, 345 etc.

4) Denoting instrumentality, = by means of, by: *so him I lose t. my unkind abuse*, Sonn. 134, 12. *falls t. wind, before the fall should be*, Pilgr. 136. *my master t. his art foresees the danger*, Tp. II, 1, 297. *sluiced out his innocent soul t. streams of blood*, R2 I, 1, 103. *thou wouldst have me drowned on shore, with tears as salt as sea, t. thy unkindness*, H6B III, 2, 96. *begun t. malice of the bishop's men*, H6A III, 1, 76. *whether it be t. force of your report*, V, 5, 79. *the interview betwixt England and France might, t. their amity, breed him some prejudice*, H8 I, 1, 181. *make sacred even his stirrup, and t. him drink the free air*, Tim. I, 1, 82. *something you may deserve of him t. me*, Mcb. IV, 3, 15. *when Antony is gone, t. whom I might command it* (Herod's head) Ant. III, 3, 6 etc.

Hence denoting a source, a cause, = out of, on account of: *thou art like enough, t. vassal fear, to fight against me*, H4A III, 2, 124. *some falling merely t. fear*, Cymb. V, 3, 11. *if this law of nature be corrupted t. affection*, Troil. II, 2, 177. *I love the king and t. him what is nearest to him*, Wint. IV, 4, 533. *I am pressed to death t. want of speaking*, R2 III, 4, 72. *the subjects' grief comes t. commissions*, H8 I, 2, 57 etc.

**Through**, adv. 1) from side to side, from beginning to end, to the end: *who, half t., gives o'er*, H4B I, 3, 59. *the happiest youth, viewing his progress t.* III, 1, 54. *give the word t.* H5 IV, 6, 38. *I am half t.* Cor. II, 3, 130. *my good intent may carry t. itself to that full issue*, Lr. I, 4, 3. *I ran it t.* Oth. I, 3, 132. *when shall I hear all t.?* Cymb. V, 5, 382. *with sighs shot t.* Per. IV, 4, 26. *to go t.* = to do one's utmost, not to stick at any thing: *I do it for some piece of money, and go t. with all*, Meas. II, 1, 285. *I have gone t. for this piece*, Per. IV, 2, 47. Similarly: *if a man is t. with them in honest taking up, then they must stand upon security*, H4B I, 2, 45 (i. e. if a man does his utmost in borrowing, or rather if a man condescends to borrow, in an honourable manner). Sometimes = fully, completely: *he's not yet t. warm*, Troil. II, 3, 232. *I would revenges ... would seek us t. and put us to our answer*, Cymb. IV, 2, 160.

Emphatically reduplicated: *I will t. and t. cleanse the foul body of the infected world*, As II, 7, 59. *blasts of January would blow you t. and t.* Wint. IV, 4, 112. *my buckler cut t. and t.* H4A II, 4, 186.

2) Denoting a way or passage: *were beauty under twenty locks kept fast, yet love breaks t.* Ven. 576. *he himself must speak t.* (t. the lion's skin) Mids. III, 1, 39. *show me thy chink, to blink t. with mine eyne*, V, 178. *our soldiers shall march t.* H4A IV, 2, 3. *life looks t. and will break out*, H4B IV, 4, 120. *he had made two holes... and so peeped t.* II, 2, 89. *in this place ran Cassius' dagger t.* Caes. III, 2, 178. *giants may jet t.* Cymb. III, 3, 5.

**Throughfare**, a thoroughfare, an open and unobstructed passage: *the vasty wilds of wide Arabia are as —s now for princes to come view fair Portia*, Merch. II, 7, 42. *his body's a passable carcass, if he be not hurt: it is a t. for steel*, Cymb. I, 2, 11.

**Throughly**, thoroughly: *the next advantage will we take t.* Tp. III, 3, 14. *till thy wound be t. healed*,

Gent. I, 2, 115. *if he had been t. moved*, Wiv. 1, 4, 95. *we'll do it t.* Meas. V, 260. *to quit me of them t.* Ado IV, 1, 202. *I am informed t. of the cause*, Merch. IV, 1, 173. *now do your duty t.* Shr. IV, 4, 11. *you scarce can right me t. then*, Wint. II, 1, 99. *most t. to be winnowed*, H8 V, 1, 111. *I'll be revenged most t.* Hml. IV, 5, 136. *my point and period will be t. wrought*, Lr. IV, 7, 97. *Lucius will do's commission t.* Cymb. II, 4, 12. *I am t. weary*, III, 6, 36.

**Throughout**, prep. in every part of, in all: *a man well known t. all Italy*, Shr. II, 69. *every sovereign state t. the world*, John V, 2, 82. *ne'er t. the year to church thou goest*, H6A I, 1, 42. *t. the town*, I, 6, 11. *t. every town proclaim them traitors*, H6B IV, 2, 186. *follow thee t. the world*, Rom. II, 2, 148.

**Throughout**, adv. in every place, from first to last: *tell my friends, tell Athens, in the sequence of degree from high to low t.* Tim. V, 1, 212.

**Throw**, subst. a cast of dice or of a bowl in gaming: *abate t. at novum*, LLL V, 2, 547. *if Hercules and Lichas play at dice, the greater t. may turn from the weaker hand*, Merch. II, 1, 33. Metaphorically: *like to a bowl upon a subtle ground, I have tumbled past the t.* (in praising Coriolanus) Cor. V, 2, 21. *you can fool no more money out of me at this t.* Tw. V, 45 (by this device, by this trick).

**Throw**, vb. (impf. *threw*, partic. *thrown*) 1) to fling, to cast, to drive to a distance: *which one by one she in a river threw*, Compl. 38. *I t. thy name against the bruising stones*, Gent. I, 2, 111. *t. it thence into the raging sea*, 122. *t. us that you have about ye*, IV, 1, 3. *a stone to t. at his dog*, Wiv. I, 4, 119; cf. As I, 3, 3. 5. *t. foul linen upon him*, Wiv. III, 3, 139. —*ing him into the water*, 194. III, 5, 6. 37. 122. 128. *they threw me off from behind one of them*, IV, 5, 68. *how far that little candle —s his beams*, Merch. V, 90. *he will t. a figure in her face*, Shr. I, 2, 114. *threw the sops in the sexton's face*, III, 2, 175. *burs —n upon thee in holiday foolery*, As I, 3, 13. *the name of her that threw it*, All's V, 3, 95. *you threw it him out of a casement*, 229. *you peevishly threw it to her*, Tw. II, 2, 14. *I'll t. your dagger o'er the house*, IV, 1, 30. *there I t. my gage*, R2 I, 1, 69. IV, 46. *t. down your gage*, I, 1, 161. 162. 186 (Qq t. up). IV, 84. *t. the rider headlong in the lists*, I, 2, 52. *the king hath —n his warder down*, I, 3, 118; H4B IV, 1, 125. 126. *threw dust on Richard's head*, R2 V, 2, 6. 30; H4B I, 3, 103. *t. the quean in the channel*, H4B II, 1, 51. *t. none away*, H5 V, 1, 56. *threw it* (a jewel) *towards thy land*, H6B III, 2, 108. *t. them into Thames*, IV, 8, 2. *he that —s not up his cap for joy*, H6C II, 1, 196; Cor. IV, 6, 135; Caes. I, 2, 246. *they threw their caps*, Cor. I, 1, 216. *our masters may t. their caps at their money*, Tim. III, 4, 101 (whistle for it, give it up for lost). *I t. my infamy at thee*, H6C V, 1, 82. *I'll t. thy body in another room*, V, 6, 92. *I will t. my glove to Death himself*, Troil. IV, 4, 65; Tim. V, 4, 49. *t. it* (my dust) *against the wind*, Cor. III, 2, 104. *in the poisoned entrails t.* Mcb. IV, 1, 5. 66. *your leafy screens t. down*, V, 6, 1. —*n out his angle for my proper life*, Hml. V, 2, 66. *to t. my sceptre at the injurious gods*, Ant. IV, 15, 76. *threw her in the sea*, Per. III, 2, 80. V, 3, 19 etc.

Applied to dice: *I had rather be in this choice than t. ames-ace for my life*, All's II, 3, 84. *set less than thou —est*, Lr. I, 4, 136. Figuratively: *who sets me else? by heaven, I'll t. at all*, R2 IV, 57.

Used of fluids, = to cast, to pour: *they threw on him great pails of puddled mire*, Err. V, 172. *t. cold water on thy choler*, Wiv. II, 3, 89. *upon thy eyes I t. all the power this charm doth owe*, Mids. II, 2, 78. Metaphorically: *t. this report on their incensed rage*, John IV, 2, 261.

Often implying the idea of haste, or of negligence and contempt: —*ing the base thong from his bending crest*, Ven. 395. *now he —s that shallow habit by*, Lucr. 1814. *in so profound abysm I t. all care of others' voices*, Sonn. 112, 9. *threw her sun-expelling mask away*, Gent. IV, 4, 158. *t. away that thought*, Meas. I, 3, 1. *I'ld t. it* (life) *down for your deliverance as frankly as a pin*, III, 1, 105. *the grosser manner of these world's delights he —s upon the gross world's baser slaves*, LLL I, 1, 30. *t. away that spirit*, V, 2, 877. *unregarded age in corners —n*, As II, 3, 42. *the duke hath … —n into neglect the pompous court*, V, 4, 188. *off with that bauble, t. it under foot*, Shr. V, 2, 122. *these warlike principles do not t. from you*, All's II, 1, 2. *I will t. thee from my care for ever*, II, 3, 169. *some achieve greatness, and some have greatness —n upon them*, Tw. V, 379. *what reverence he did t. away on slaves*, R2 I, 4, 27. *t. away respect, tradition*, III, 2, 172. *I have —n a brave defiance in king Henry's teeth*, H4A V, 2, 42; cf. Oth. III, 4, 184. *thus king Henry —s away his crutch*, H6B III, 1, 189. *wilt thou, O God, fly from such gentle lambs and t. them in the entrails of the wolf?* R3 IV, 4, 23. *the remainder viands we do not t. in unrespective sieve*, Troil. II, 2, 71. *meal and bran together he —s without distinction*, Cor. III, 1, 323. *how much salt water —n away in waste*, Rom. II, 3, 71. *you would t. them off* (my accounts) Tim. II, 2, 143. *were I like thee, I'ld t. away myself*, IV, 3, 219. *to t. away the dearest thing he owed* (viz. life) Mcb. I, 4, 10. *t. physic to the dogs*, V, 3, 47. *t. to earth this unprevailing woe*, Hml. I, 2, 106. *there has been much —ing about of brains*, II, 2, 375. *thy dowerless daughter, —n to my chance*, Lr. I, 1, 259. *I see that nose of yours, but not that dog I shall t. it to*, Oth. IV, 1, 147. *t. your vile guesses in the devil's teeth*, III, 4, 184 (cf. H4A V, 2, 42). *threw a pearl away*, V, 2, 347. *you therein t. away the absolute soldiership you have by land*, Ant. III, 7, 42. *now t. me again*, Cymb. V, 5, 263. With *up*, = to give up, to resign: *t. up your gage*, R2 I, 1, 186 (Ff *t. down*).

2) to drive with force: *what tempest threw this whale ashore*, Wiv. II, 1, 65. Per. II Prol. 38. V, 3, 23. *t. him* (the devil) *out*, Hml. III, 4, 169. —*n from Leonati seat*, Cymb. V, 4, 59.

3) to bring down from an erect station: *Charles in a moment threw him and broke three of his ribs*, As I, 2, 135. *t. their power i'the dust*, Cor. III, 1, 171. *Cimber —s before thy feet an humble heart*, Caes. III, 1, 34. With *down*, in a proper and figurative sense: *my better parts are all —n down*, As I, 2, 262. *the crown, which waste of idle hours hath quite —n down*, R2 III, 4, 66. *to t. down Hector*, Troil. III, 3, 208. *hath —n down so many enemies*, Tit. III, 1, 164. Refl.: *Lucrece' father … himself on her body threw*, Lucr. 1733. *myself I t. … at thy foot*, R2 I, 1, 165. *then threw he down himself*, H4B IV, 1, 127. *threw him on my father*, Lr. V, 3, 213.

4) to direct, to turn, to cast: *'I hate' from hate away she threw, and saved my life, saying 'not you'*, Sonn. 145, 13 (= turned off, averted; made it to be no bate). *I t. my hands, mine eyes, my heart to thee*,

H6C II, 3, 36. *to t. out our eyes for brave Othello*, Oth. II, 1, 38. Applied to the eye, = to cast: *she —s her eyes about the painting round*, Lucr. 1499. *how mine eyes t. gazes to the east*, Pilgr. 193. —*ing it* (your eye) *on any other object*, Meas. V, 23. *he threw his eye aside*, As IV, 3, 103. *you t. a strange regard upon me*, Tw. V, 219. *t. thine eye on yon young boy*, John III, 3, 59. *threw many a northward look*, H4B II, 3, 13. H6B II, 4, 22. H6C I, 4, 37. II, 5, 85 (*up*). Cymb. V, 5, 394.

5) to lay or put in haste:' *on his neck her yoking arms she —s*, Ven. 592. *over Suffolk's neck he threw his wounded arm*, H5 IV, 6, 25. —*ing his mantle rudely o'er his arm*, Lucr. 170. *he comes and —s his mantle by*, Pilgr. 79. Often quite = to put (particularly in speaking of articles of dress, but also in other cases): *threw my affections in his charmed power*, Compl. 146. *t. in the frozen bosoms of our part hot coals of vengeance*, H6B V, 2, 35. *t. it* (the veil) *o'er my face*, Tw. I, 5, 175. *tacked together and —n over the shoulders*, H4A IV, 2, 48. *t. off this sheet*, H6B II, 4, 105. *shall we go t. away our coats of steel*, H6C II, 1, 160. *t. over her the veil of infamy*, R3 IV, 4, 208. *I have seen her t. her night-gown upon her*, Mcb. V, 1, 5. *before my body I t. my warlike shield*, V, 8, 33. Metaphorically: *threw off his spirit, his appetite, his sleep*, Wint. II, 3, 16. *when this loose behaviour I t. off*, H4A I, 2, 232. cf. Lucr. 1814. Gent. IV, 4, 158.

Used of snakes casting their skins: *there the snake —s her enamelled skin*, Mids. II, 1, 255.

6) With *forth*, = to utter, to produce, to bring to light: *with a sigh … she —s forth Tarquin's name*, Lucr. 1717. *it will in time t. forth greater themes for insurrection's arguing*, Cor. I, 1, 224. Perhaps also: *with news the time's with labour, and —s forth each minute some*, Ant. III, 7, 81; M. Edd. *throes*, q. v. (cf. *to thrust forth*).

7) With the prep. *on*, either in a good sense, = to bestow on, to impart to, to give; or in a bad sense, = to inflict on, to lay on: (her eyes) *threw unwilling light upon the wide wound*, Ven. 1051. *to t. a perfume on the violet*, John IV, 2, 12. *an act that very chance doth t. upon him*, Troil. III, 3, 131; cf. Tw. V, 379. *I threw the people's suffrages on him*, Tit. IV, 3, 19. —*ing but shows of service on their lords*, Oth. I, 1, 52. *opinion … —s a more safer voice on you*, I, 3, 226. *begin to t. Pompey the Great and all his dignities upon his son*, Ant. I, 2, 194. —*ing favours on the low Posthumus*, Cymb. III, 5, 75. (cf. Mids. II, 2, 78. John IV, 2, 261). *the wrong that she hath —n on me*, Err. V, 202. *a lurking adder whose double tongue may with a mortal touch t. death upon thy sovereign's enemies*, R2 III, 2, 22. *though that his joy be joy, yet t. such changes of vexation on't*, Oth. I, 1, 72. —*ing restraint upon us*, IV, 3, 91. —*n such despite and heavy terms upon her*, IV, 2, 116.

**Thrower-out**, one who exposes, casts out to chance: *made thy person for the t. of my poor babe*, Wint. III, 3, 29.

**Thrum**, the tufted end of weavers' threads: *O Fates, come, come, cut thread and t.* Mids. V, 291 (Pyramus' speech).*

**Thrummed**, composed of coarse ends or tufts: *her t. hat*, Wiv. IV, 2, 80.

**Thrush**, the bird Turdus musicus: Wint. IV, 3, 10. cf. *Throstle*.

**Thrust**, subst. an attack with the point of a sharp

weapon; opposed to blow: H4B II, 1, 21. Rom. III, 1, 173. Oth. V, 1, 24. *to make a t.* H4B II, 4, 228. H5 II, 1, 105. *interchanging —s and blows*, Rom. I, 1, 120. *at blow and t.* Oth. II, 3, 238.

**Thrust,** vb. (impf. and partic. *thrust*) 1) trans. a) to throw, to put in haste: *as you'ld t. a cork into a hogshead*, Wint. III, 3, 95. *slippers which his nimble haste had falsely t. upon contrary feet*, John IV, 2, 198. *these affairs thus t. disorderly into my hands*, R2 II, 2, 110.

b) to put (the idea of haste dropped): *there would appear the very eyes of men through loopholes t.* Lucr. 1383 (put forth, advanced; cf. Merch. II, 5, 32). *each trifle under truest bars to t.* Sonn. 48, 2. *an thou wilt needs t. thy neck into a yoke*, Ado I, 1, 203. *nor t. your head into the public street*, Merch. II, 5, 32. *betwixt the firmament and it you cannot t. a bodkin's point*, Wint. III, 3, 87. *thou shalt t. thy hand as deep into the purse of rich prosperity*, John V, 2, 60. *to t. his icy fingers in my maw*, V, 7, 37. *the lion dying —eth forth his paw*, R2 V, 1, 29. *you might have t. him and all his apparel into an eel-skin*, H4B III, 2, 350 (Ff truss'd). *by —ing out a torch from yonder tower*, H6A III, 2, 23. *to t. his hand between his* (a cur's) *teeth*, H6C I, 4, 57.

Figuratively: *craft and perjury should t. into so bright a day such black-faced storms*, Lucr. 1517. *you ... acquainted me with interest of this land, yea, t. this enterprise into my heart*, John V, 2, 90. *can t. me from a level consideration*, H4B II, 1, 124. *—ing this report into his ear*, Caes. V, 3, 74.

With *forth*, = to put forth: *where doth the world t. forth a vanity*, R2 II, 1, 24. *if the time t. forth a cause for thy repeal*, Cor. IV, 1, 40. *who ... —s forth his horns again into the world*, IV, 6, 44.

With the preposition *on* (cf. *to throw on*), = to impart to, to bestow on, to present with gratuitously: *understand what advice shall t. upon thee*, All's I, 1, 225. *some achieve greatness and some have greatness t. upon 'em*, Tw. II, 5, 158. III, 4, 49 (in V, 379 *thrown*).

Refl., = to place one's self, to enter, to mingle: *I have t. myself into this maze, haply to wive and thrive*, Shr. I, 2, 55. *go and t. thyself into their companies*, John IV, 2, 167. In a bad sense, = to intrude: *an unmannerly slave, that will t. himself into secrets*, Gent. III, 1, 393. *he —s me himself into the company of three or four gentlemanlike dogs*, IV, 4, 18. *how dare you t. yourselves into my private meditations?* H8 II, 2, 65.

c) to push; to drive with force: *backward she pushed him, as she would be t.* Ven. 41; cf. *women ... are ever t. to the wall*, Rom. I, 1, 20. 22. *which was t. forth of Milan*, Tp. V, 160. *was Milan t. from Milan*, 205. *such as the fury of ungoverned youth t. from the company of awful men*, Gent. IV, 1, 46. *though we would have t. virtue out of our hearts by the head and shoulders*, Wiv. V, 5, 155. *t. but these men away*, John IV, 1, 83. *t. him down stairs*, H4B II, 4, 202. *thou be t. out like a fugitive*, H6A III, 3, 67. *so wish I, I might t. thy soul to hell*, H6B IV, 10, 85. *the house of York, t. from the crown*, IV, 1, 94. *unless he seek to t. you out perforce*, H6C I, 1, 34. *I come to have thee t. me out of doors*, Tim. I, 2, 25. *t. him out at gates*, Lr. III, 7, 93.

Figuratively: *not a dangerous action can peep out his head but I am t. upon it*, H4B I, 2, 239 (forced upon it against my inclination). *as if we were ... all that we are evil in, by a divine —ing on*, Lr. I, 2, 137

(forcing on, incitement). *shall join to t. the lie unto him*, Cor. V, 6, 110 (to make him swallow it perforce). *till I have ... t. these reproachful speeches down his throat*, Tit. II, 1, 55.

d) to attack with the point of a weapon; absol.: *these four t. at me*, H4A II, 4, 223. *every minute of his being —s against my nearest of life*, Mcb. III, 1, 117. With an object; 1) the hurt person object: *eight times t. through the doublet*, H4A II, 4, 184. *t. Talbot with a spear into the back*, H6A I, 1, 138. *he was t. in the mouth with a spear*, H6B IV, 7, 10. *as I t. thy body with my sword*, IV, 10, 84 (O. Edd. *t. in thy body*). 2) the weapon object: *the bloody spur ... that sometimes anger —s into his side*, Sonn. 50, 10. *t. thy sharp wit quite through my ignorance*, LLL V, 2, 398. *I'll t. my knife in your mouldy chaps*, H4B II, 4, 138.

2) intr. with *in*, = to intrude: *that never may ill office, or fell jealousy ... t. in between the paction of these kingdoms*, H5 V, 2, 393.

**Thumb,** the short strong finger answering to the other four: LLL V, 1, 138. Mcb. I, 3, 28. *another, with his finger and his t., cried 'Via! we will do't, come what will come'*, LLL V, 2, 111. *'twixt his finger and his t. he held a pouncet-box*, H4A I, 3, 38. *I have him already tempering between my finger and my t.* H4B IV, 3, 141. *he turned me about with his finger and his t.* Cor. IV, 5, 160. *govern these ventages with your finger and t.* Hml. III, 2, 373. *I will bite my t. at them*, Rom. I, 1, 49. 51. 52. 53. 57. 58 (an insult performed by putting the nail of the thumb between the teeth and 'making it to knack'. Cotgrave). *by the pricking of my —s, something wicked this way comes*, Mcb. IV, 1, 44.

**Thumb-ring,** a ring worn on the thumb (as was the custom of grave personages. Nares : *I could have crept into any alderman's t.* H4A II, 4, 365.

**Thumb,** name in H6B II, 3, 84.

**Thump,** vb. to beat with something blunt, to cuff (cf. *Bethump*): *jump her and t. her*, Wint. IV, 4, 196. *see thou t. thy master well*, H6B II, 3, 85. *whom our fathers have beaten, bobbed and —ed*, R3 V, 3, 334. *thus I t. it* (my heart) *down*, Tit. III, 2, 11. Applied to the stroke of a bird-bolt: *proceed, sweet Cupid: thou hast —ed him with thy bird-bolt under the left pap*, LLL IV, 3, 24. And used as an interjection: *I shoot thee at the swain. T. then and I flee*, LLL III, 66.

**Thunder,** subst. the loud noise following a flash of lightning: Ven. 268. Sonn. 14, 6. Pilgr. 67. Tp. III, 3, 97. V, 44. Meas. II, 2, 113. 114. LLL IV, 2, 119. Shr. I, 2, 96. Wint. III, 1, 10. John III, 1, 124. III, 4, 38. V, 2, 173. H5 II, 4, 100. Troil. II, 3, 209. Cor. I, 6, 25. II, 1, 283. V, 3, 151. Mcb. I, 2, 26 (—s). IV, 1, 86. Hml. II, 2, 508. Lr. III, 2, 15. 46. III, 4, 160. IV, 6, 103. IV, 7, 33. Ant. V, 2, 86. Cymb. V, 4, 114. Per. II Prol. 30. II, 1, 2. III, 1, 5 (—s). IV, 2, 154 (*t. shall not so awake the beds of eels*). V, 1, 201. Joined with lightning: *secure of —'s crack or lightning flash*, Tit. II, 1, 3. *in t., lightning, or in rain*, Mcb. I, 1, 2. Its effect confounded with that of lightning: *let thy blows ... fall like amazing t. on the casque ...*, R2 I, 3, 81. H6B IV, 1, 104. Lr. II, 1, 48 (Qq —s). III, 2, 6. Oth. V, 2, 235. Used of other mighty sounds: *the t. of my cannon*, John I, 26. II, 411. Hml. I, 2, 128. *that forced t. from his heart did fly*, Compl. 325. *such sweet t.* (of barking dogs) Mids. IV, 1, 123. *that engenders t. in his breast and makes* *him roar these accusations forth*, H6A III, 1, 39. *thy voice is t.* R3 I, 4, 172.

**Thunder,** vb. to make thunder, to make a sound as after a flash of lightning; impersonally: *if it should t.* Tp. II, 2, 22. *let it t.* Wiv. V, 5, 21. Personally: *could great men t.* Meas. II, 2, 110. *have I not heard ... heaven's artillery t. in the skies?* Shr. I, 2, 205. R2 III, 3, 56 (the poet's theory expounded here). H6A III, 2, 59. Troil. IV, 5, 136. Cor. III, 1, 257. Ant. III, 13, 85. Used of a loud and threatening voice: *the youths that t. at a playhouse*, H8 V, 4, 63. —*est with thy tongue*, Tit. II, 1, 58. *a man ... that* —*s, lightens*, Caes. I, 3, 74. *what act that roars so loud and* —*s in the index?* Hml. III, 4, 52. Trans., = to utter with a loud voice: *with groans that t. love*, Tw. I, 5, 275. *who* —*s to his captives blood and death*, H6C II, 1, 127.

**Thunder-bearer,** he in whose hands is the thunder; Jove: *I do not bid the t. shoot*, Lr. II, 4, 230.

**Thunderbolt,** a bolt or arrow supposed to be sent down in lightning: Tp. II, 2, 38. As I, 2, 226. H4A IV, 1, 120. Caes. IV, 3, 81. Lr. III, 2, 5. Ant. II, 5, 77.

**Thunder-claps,** bursts, peals of thunder: Tp. I, 2, 202.

**Thunder-darter,** he who darts the thunder; Jove: Troil. II, 3, 11.

**Thunderer,** he who thunders, Jove: Cymb. V, 4, 95.

**Thunder-like,** resembling thunder: Cor. I, 4, 59.

**Thunder-master,** master of the thunder, Jove: Cymb. V, 4, 30.

**Thunder-stone,** = thunderbolt: *have bared my bosom to the t.* Caes. I, 3, 49. *the all-dreaded t.* Cymb. IV, 2, 271.

**Thunder-stroke,** the effect of a thunderbolt, a blast of lightning: *they dropped as by a t.* Tp. II, 1, 204. *killed with a t.* II, 2, 112.

**Thurio,** name in Gent. II, 4, 3. 23 etc.

**Thursday,** the fifth day of the week: H4A II, 4, 74. III, 2, 174. H4B II, 4, 298. Rom. III, 4, 20. 28. 29. 30. III, 5, 113. 154. 162. IV, 1, 1. 20. 42. 49. IV, 2, 36.

**Thus,** 1) in this manner, or in this state; a) pointing to something that is present and in view, and usually accompanied by a gesture explaining its meaning: *'even thus', quoth she, 'the warlike god embraced me', and then she clipped Adonis in her arms; 'even thus', quoth she, 'the warlike god unlaced me', as if the boy should use like loving charms; 'even thus'* etc. Pilgr. 147. *whiles you, doing thus, to the perpetual wink for aye might put this ancient morsel*, Tp. II, 1, 284 (the words being accompanied by the gesture of stabbing). *with his royal finger, thus, dally with my excrement*, LLL V, 1, 109. *thus must thou speak, and thus thy body bear*, V, 2, 100 (as I show thee to do it). *one rubbed his elbow, thus*, 109. *thus did he strangle serpents*, 595. *let him hold his fingers thus*, Mids. III, 1, 72. *hood mine eyes thus with my hat*, Merch. II, 2, 203. *I extend my hand to him thus*, Tw. II, 5, 72. *but now a king, now thus*, John V, 7, 66 (dead, as you see him before you). *traverse; thus, thus, thus*, H4B III, 2, 291. *a' would manage you his piece thus*, 302. *why lifts she up her arms in sequence thus?* Tit. IV, 1, 37. *the cap plays in the right hand thus*, Tim. II, 1, 19. *waving thy head, which often thus correcting thy stout*

*heart*, Cor. III, 2, 78. *with a kind of smile, ... even thus*, I, 1, 112. *to Aufidius thus* (bleeding as I am) *I will appear and fight*, I, 5, 20. *let him ... wave thus*, I, 6, 74. *dismissed me thus with his speechless hand*, V, 1, 67. *he put it by with the back of his hand thus*, Caes. I, 2, 222. *thus, Brutus, did my master bid me kneel; thus did Mark Antony bid me fall down*, III, 1, 123. *for so much trash as may be grasped thus*, IV, 3, 26. *with arms encumbered thus*, Hml. I, 5, 174. *with his other hand thus o'er his brow*, II, 1, 89. *do not saw the air with your hand thus*, III, 2, 6. *how long hath she been thus?* IV, 5, 66 (in the state we see her. F1 *this*). *I should e'en die with pity, to see another thus*, Lr. IV, 7, 54. *wear your eye thus, not jealous nor secure*, Oth. III, 3, 198. *the nobleness of life is to do thus*, Ant. I, 1, 37 (explained by an embrace). *were we to fight, I should do thus*, II, 2, 27 (i. e. greet you). *he's walking in the garden thus*, III, 5, 17. *thy master thus with pleached arms*, IV, 14, 73. cf. besides: Tp. III, 3, 9. IV, 231. V, 188. Gent. I, 2, 19. 116. Meas. I, 2, 83. II, 4, 20. III, 2, 56. Err. II, 1, 83. II, 2, 48. 155 etc.

Frequent in this sense before adjectives and adverbs, and not to be confounded with *so: my mistress, dearest; and I thus humble ever*, Tp. III, 1, 87 (i. e. on my knees). *up, cousin, up; your heart is up, I know, thus high at least, although your knee be low*, R2 III, 3, 195 (as high as the crown on my head, to which I am pointing). *when a' was a crack not thus high*, H4B III, 2, 34 (not the height from the ground to my hand). *thus high ... is Richard seated*, R3 IV, 2, 3 (on this throne). *go to them, with this bonnet in thy hand; and thus far having stretched it, here be with them*, Cor. III, 2, 74. *his evasions have ears thus long*, Troil. II, 1, 75. *thus much of this will make black white*, Tim. IV, 3, 28 (the quantity which I am grasping here with my hand). *to his good friends thus wide I'll ope my arms*, Hml. IV, 5, 145. *she hath bought the name of whore thus dearly*, Cymb. II, 4, 128 (for this jewel here). *though trained up thus meanly*, III, 3, 82. Judge by these of the following passages: *muse not that I thus suddenly proceed*, Gent. I, 3, 64. *according to your ladyship's impose, I am thus early come*, IV, 3, 9. *thy life ... should be thus foolishly lost at a game of tick-tack*, Meas. I, 2, 195. *to counterfeit thus grossly with your slave*, Err. II, 2, 171. *the chain unfinished made me stay thus long*, III, 2, 173. *why are you thus out of measure sad?* Ado I, 3, 2. *how come you thus estranged?* LLL V, 2, 213. *we shall be rich, if fairings come thus plentifully in*, V, 2, 2. *their sense thus weak, lost with their fears thus strong*, Mids. III, 2, 27. *we are amazed, and thus long have we stood to watch the fearful bending of thy knee*, R2 III, 3, 72. *a subject speaks ... thus boldly for his king*, IV, 133. *that rise thus nimbly*, 318. *why are you thus alone?* H4A II, 3, 40. *that you ... thus contumeliously should break the peace*, H6A I, 3, 58. *we had not been thus shamefully surprised*, II, 1, 65. *noble uncle, thus ignobly used*, II, 5, 35. *whose maiden blood, thus rigorously effused*, V, 4, 52. *makes them thus forward in his banishment*, H6B III, 2, 253. *to be thus bold in terms before thy sovereign*, H6C II, 2, 85. *stand you thus close, to steal the bishop's deer?* IV, 5, 17. *it is his policy to haste thus fast*, V, 4, 63. *to be thus opposite with heaven*, R3 II, 2, 94. *to taunt and scorn you thus opprobriously*, III, 1, 153. *that we would ... proceed thus rashly to the villain's death*, III, 5, 43. *have I lived thus long ... a wife, a true one?* H8 III, 1, 125 (to be *a curse like this*). *if we live thus tamely, to be thus jaded*, III, 2, 279. *his evasion, winged thus swift with scorn*, Troil. II, 3, 123. *temperately proceed to what you would thus violently redress*, Cor. III, 1, 220. *I am most fortunate thus accidentally to encounter you*, IV, 3, 40. *the sorrow that delivers us thus changed*, V, 3, 39 (not = so much changed, but as you see us). *that have been thus forward in my right*, Tit. I, 56. *after that he came thus sad away*, Caes. I, 2, 279. *why stands Macbeth thus amazedly?* Mcb. IV, 1, 126. *tell me why thou art thus incensed*, Hml. IV, 5, 126. *thus out of season*, Lr. II, 1, 121. *that discarded fathers should have thus little mercy on their flesh*, III, 4, 75. *our general cast us thus early for the love of Desdemona*, Oth. II, 3, 14.

Oftenest before *far* and *much*, not in the sense of 'to such a point, to such a degree', but = to this point, to this degree, demonstratively, and never followed by a correlative *as* or *that: thus far the miles are measured from thy friend*, Sonn. 50, 4. *thus far for love my love-suit, sweet, fulfil*, 136, 4. *since we are stepped thus far in, I will continue that I broached in jest*, Shr. I, 2, 83. *thus far, with rough and all unable pen, our bending author has pursued the story*, H5 Epil. 1. *yet thus far fortune maketh us amends*, H6C IV, 7, 2. *thus far our fortune keeps an upward course*, V, 3, 1. *thus far into the bowels of the land have we marched on without impediment*, R3 V, 2, 3. *you that thus far have come to pity me*, H8 II, 1, 56. *I speak my good lord cardinal to this point, and thus far clear him*, II, 4, 167. *and thus far I confirm you*, Tim. I, 2, 98. *having thus far proceeded, ... is it not meet ...*, Cymb. I, 5, 15. *thus far, and so farewell*, III, 5, 1. *since your kindness we have stretched thus far, let us beseech you*, Per. V, 1, 55. *are you not ashamed ... to be thus much o'ershot?* LLL IV, 3, 160. *you would not do me thus much injury*, Mids. III, 2, 148. *I have spoke thus much to mitigate the justice of thy plea*, Merch. IV, 1, 202. *thus much for greeting*, Shr. IV, 1, 115. *I am glad that my weak words have struck but thus much show of fire from Brutus*, Caes. I, 2, 177. *when your mistress hears thus much from you*, Lr. IV, 5, 34.

b) pointing to what immediately follows: *teaching them thus to use it in the fight, when shame assailed, the red should fence the white*, Lucr. 62. *and justly thus controls his thoughts unjust: 'Fair torch' etc.* 189. *'it cannot be' she in that sense forsook, and turned it thus, 'It cannot be, I find, but such a face should bear a wicked mind'*, 1539. *if I lose them, thus find I by my loss: for Valentine myself, for Julia Silvia*, Gent. II, 6, 21. *to which I thus subscribe: Sir Valentine, ... take thou thy Silvia*, V, 4, 145. *were he my kinsman, it should be thus with him: he must die to-morrow*, Meas. II, 2, 82. *I have heard herself come thus near, that, should she fancy, it should be one of my complexion*, Tw. II, 5, 29. *because they speak no English, thus they prayed to tell your grace, that they could ...*, H8 I, 4, 65. *the end of all is bought thus dear, the breath is gone ...*, Per. I, 1, 98. Lucr. 477. Sonn. 42, 5. 46, 13. 51, 1. 99, 1. 117, 1. 145, 8. Compl. 177. Wiv. IV, 4, 46. IV, 6, 34. Meas. I, 4, 39. III, 1, 6. Err. II, 2, 107. LLL IV, 1, 26. R2 III, 3, 121. H4B IV, 2, 84. H6A IV, 2, 5. R3 III, 7, 32. H8 II, 4, 169. V, 3, 87. I, 1, 188. Cor. I, 1, 100. Tim. V,

1, 171. Caes. III, 1, 125. Hml. I, 2, 199. V, 1, 231. Ant. II, 7, 20. III, 13, 53. Cymb. IV, 2, 347 etc. Elliptically: *thus, sir: although this lord* etc. Tp. II, 1, 231. *as thus: to study where I well may dine*, LLL I, 1, 61. *thus in plain terms*, Shr. II, 271. *then thus*, R2 II, 1, 277. *marry, sir, thus*, H4B V, 1, 14 (= I have something to tell you). *then thus*, H6B II, 2, 9. *but, marry, thus, my lord*, Troil. III, 1, 68. *as thus: I know his father*, Hml. II, 1, 14 etc.

Often before *far* and *much: yet with the fault I thus far can dispense: myself was stirring ere the break of day* etc. Lucr. 1279. *know thus far forth*, Tp. I, 2, 177. *thus far I witness with him, that he dined not at home, but was locked out*, Err. V, 254. *thus far can I praise him: he is of a noble strain*, Ado II, 1, 393. *let me buy your friendly help thus far*, All's III, 7, 15. *yet thus far I will boldly publish her: she bore a mind* etc. Tw. II, 1, 29. *thus far come near my person: tell them* etc. R3 III, 5, 85. *thus far we are one in fortunes: both fell by our servants*, H8 II, 1, 121. *and thus far hear me*, III, 2, 432. *thus far give me leave to speak him: he was a man* etc. IV, 2, 32. *thus far may it like your grace to let my tongue excuse all*, V, 3, 147. *thus far you shall answer: if you make* etc. Cymb. I, 4, 169. *were thus much overheard: the prince discovered to Claudio that he loved my niece*, Ado I, 2, 10. *thus much I have learnt: he rather means to lodge you in the field*, LLL II, 84. *at least thus much: I'll pawn the little blood, Wint. II, 3, 165. *add thus much more, that no Italian priest shall tithe or toll in our dominions*, John III, 1, 153. *dost thou understand thus much English: canst thou love me?* H5 V, 2, 205. *tell 'em thus much from me*, H8 I, 4, 77. *but thus much, they are foul ones*, III, 2, 300. *I'll say thus much for him*, V, 3, 155. *only thus much I give your grace to know*, Tit. I, 413. *so much for him. Now for ourself, ... thus much the business is*, Hml. I, 2, 27.

c) pointing to what precedes or has been said: *thus chides she death*, Ven. 932. *thus weary of the world, away she hies*, 1189. *thus graceless holds he disputation*, Lucr. 246. *thus cavils she with every thing she sees*, 1093. *thus by day my limbs, by night my mind, for thee and for myself no quiet find*, Sonn. 27, 13. 64, 11. 69, 5. Phoen. 37. Tp. I, 2, 89. 97. II, 1, 225. Gent. I, 3, 78. II, 4, 198. III, 1, 15. Wiv. V, 5, 40. Meas. II, 2, 68. II, 4, 78. III, 1, 109. V, 119. Err. I, 1, 84. LLL IV, 3, 153. Mids. II, 1, 74. III, 2, 327. 363. IV, 2, 19. H6B II, 2, 29. III, 1, 89. 191. III, 2, 56. Mcb. II, 2, 44 etc. etc.

Joined to *so: wast thou mad, that thus so madly thou didst answer me?* Err. II, 2, 12. *you that are thus so tender o'er his follies*, Wint. II, 3, 128. *thy spirit within thee hath been so at war and thus hath so bestirred thee in thy sleep*, H4A II, 3, 60.

d) = accordingly, in consequence, so (leading over from what precedes to what follows): *thus hoping that Adonis is alive, her rash suspect she doth extenuate*, Ven. 1009. *thus is his cheek the map of days outworn*, Sonn. 68, 1. *thus for my duty's sake I rather chose to cross my friend*, Gent. III, 1, 17. *thus fail not to do your office*, Meas. IV, 2, 129. *thus when I shun Scylla, your father, I fall into Charybdis, your mother*, Merch. III, 5, 18. *thus we are agreed*, Ant. II, 6, 58.

2) Denoting degree or quality, = so: *let me be thus bold with you to give you over at this first encounter*, Shr. I, 2, 104. *I am thus bold to put your grace in*

*mind* etc. R3 IV, 2, 113. *if study's gain be thus and this be so*, LLL I, 1, 67. *I have before-time seen him thus*, Cor. I, 6, 24. *yet will I still be thus to them*, III, 2, 6. *to be thus is nothing, but to be safely thus*, Mcb. III, 1, 48. *'tis in ourselves that we are thus or thus*, Oth. I, 3, 323. *he approves the common liar, who thus speaks of him at Rome*, Ant. I, 1, 61. With to be, to say, and to do = to be so, to do so etc. Meas. II, 2, 68. As I, 3, 54. H4B IV, 3, 34. H6A II, 4, 87. H6C III, 1, 53. H8 I, 1, 171. Troil. I, 1, 61. Mcb. III, 1, 84. Ant. III, 6, 19. Cymb. III, 5, 28. *thus did he answer me*, Cymb. IV, 2, 41 (= the same answer he made to me).

3) Used indefinitely (the manner or quality not defined, but left to the imagination of the hearer): *for these courtesies I'll lend you thus much moneys*, Merch. I, 3, 130. *though the wisdom of nature can reason it thus and thus*, Lr. I, 2, 114. *wounding his belief in her renown with tokens thus and thus*, Cymb. V, 5, 203.

**Thwack**, to beat, to bang: *he shall not stay, we'll t. him hence with distaffs*, Wint. I, 2, 37. *he that was wont to t. our general*, Cor. IV, 5, 189. 190. 192.

**Thwart**, adj. perverse, cross-grained: *create her child of spleen, that it may live and be a t. disnatured torment to her*, Lr. I, 4, 305.

**Thwart**, vb. to cross; 1) to pass over: *Pericles is now again —ing the wayward seas*, Per. IV, 4, 10. 2) to counteract, to interfere with, to hinder: *in this aim there is such —ing strife*, Lucr. 143. *if crooked fortune had not —ed me*, Gent. IV, 1, 22. *to t. me in my mood*, Err. II, 2, 172. *O mischief strangely —ing*, Ado III, 2, 135. Merch. III, 1, 59. H6C IV, 6, 22. Troil. I, 3, 15. V, 1, 42 (*from*). Rom. V, 3, 154. In Cor. III, 2, 21 M. Edd. *—ings*, O. Edd. *things*.

**Thy**, poss. pron. of the second pers. sing. (cf. *Thou*): Ven. 12. 13. 15. 19. 48. 113 etc. etc. Before vowels: Ven. 500. Lucr. 522. 579. 841. 912. 1067. Sonn. 4, 13. Tp. I, 2, 66. III, 2, 10. Gent. IV, 2, 112. Wiv. IV, 4, 8. Meas. V, 526. Err. III, 2, 10. V, 73. Mids. II, 2, 32. 81. Caes. III, 1, 197 etc. More emphatical, in this case, than *thine: upon the earth's increase why shouldst thou feed, unless the earth with thy increase be fed?* Ven. 170. *yet for thy honour did I entertain him*, Lucr. 842. *so sweet a kiss the golden sun gives not ... as thy eye-beams*, LLL IV, 3, 28. *England knows thine insolence. And thy ambition, Gloster*, H6B II, 1, 32.

**Thymbria** (Ff *Timbria*; M. Edd. *Tymbria*) one of the gates of Troy: Troil. Prol. 16.

**Thyme**, the plant Thymus: *where the wild t. blows*, Mids. II, 1, 249. *set hyssop and weed up t.* Oth. I, 3, 326 (O. Edd. *time*).

**Thyreus** (O. Edd. *Thidias*) name in Ant. III, 12, 31. III, 13, 73.

**Thyself** (O. Edd. in two words), 1) thy own person: *be of t. rejected*, Ven. 159. *an image like t.* 664. *so in t. art made away*, 763. *t. thou gavest*, Sonn. 87, 9. Tp. I, 2, 68. III, 2, 116. Gent. III, 1, 32. 167. 255. IV, 2, 110. IV, 3, 18. Wiv. III, 4, 3. Meas. III, 1, 19. III, 2, 24. Err. IJ, 2, 122 etc. etc. As it is written in two words in O. Edd., *self* being considered as a substantive (cf. *Self*), the verb may follow in the third person: *thy self is self-misused*, R3 IV, 4, 376 (Qq *thy self thy self misusest*). *thy self should govern Rome and me*, Tit. IV, 4, 60.

2) in thy own person: *when thou t. art dead*, Ven. 172. *what he owes thee thou t. dost pay*, Sonn. 79, 14. *as thou reportest t.* Tp. I, 2, 271. *thou t. art a wicked villain*, Meas. I, 2, 26 etc. 3) refl.: *woo t.* Ven. 159. *make t. like a nymph*, Tp. I, 2, 301. 454. III, 2, 137. IV, 70. Gent. II, 5, 3. Meas. I, 1, 32. Err. II, 2, 126. 131 etc. etc.

**Tib**, a cant term for a low, common woman: *as fit as —'s rush for Tom's forefinger*, All's II, 2, 24. *every coistrel that comes inquiring for his T.* Per. IV, 6, 176.

**Tiber**, the river of Rome; fem. and without article: *I would they were in T.* Cor. III, 1, 262. *T. trembled underneath her banks*, Caes. I, 1, 50. *draw them to T. banks*, 63. *from the waves of T.* I, 2, 114. *on this side T.* III, 2, 254. *let Rome in T. melt*, Ant. I, 1, 33. *the troubled T. chafing with her shores*, Caes. I, 2, 101. = Tiber-water: *with not a drop of allaying T. in't*, Cor. II, 1, 53.

**Tiberio**, name in Rom. I, 5, 131.

**Tice**, vb. to entice: *these two have —d me hither to this place*, Tit. II, 3, 92. In Wint. I, 2, 416 some M. Edd. *t.* for *vice* of O. Edd.

**Tichfield**: *Baron of T.*, one of the baronial titles of the Earl of Southampton, Ven. and Lucr. Ded.

**Tick**, the insect Ixodes: *I had rather be a t. in a sheep than such a valiant ignorance*, Troil. III, 3, 315.

**Tickle**, adj. unstable, precarious, ticklish: *thy head stands so t. on thy shoulders that a milkmaid ... may sigh it off*, Meas. I, 2, 177. *the state of Normandy stands on a t. point*, H6B I, 1, 216. cf. *Sere*.

**Tickle**, vb. to titillate, to affect with a prurient sensation: *which is as bad as die with —ing*, Ado III, 1, 80. *if my hair but t. me, I must scratch*, Mids. IV, 1, 28. *if you t. us, do we not laugh?* Merch. III, 1, 68. *the trout that must be caught with —ing*, Tw. II, 5, 26. *to t. our noses with spear-grass*, H4A II, 4, 340. *she —d his chin*, Troil. I, 2, 150. *—s still the sore*, III, 1, 130. *let wantons ... t. the senseless rushes with their heels*, Rom. I, 4, 36. *—ing a parson's nose*, 80. *the clown shall make those laugh whose lungs are —d o'the sere*, Hml. II, 2, 337 (cf. *Sere*). *smiling, as some fly had —d slumber*, Cymb. IV, 2, 210.

Metaphorically, = 1) to gratify in any manner, to cajole, to flatter, to stir up to pleasure or to lust; absol.: *mock with thy —ing beams eyes that are sleeping*, Lucr. 1090 (cf. Cymb. IV, 2, 210). *that smooth-faced gentleman, —ing commodity*, John II, 573. (the blood) *which else runs —ing up and down the veins, making that idiot laughter keep men's eyes*, John III, 3, 44. *unclasp the tables of their heart to every —ing reader*, Troil. IV, 5, 61 (every reader who knows how to handle them. Q and M. Edd. *ticklish*). *how fine this tyrant can t. where she wounds*, Cymb. I, 1, 85. With an object: *to be so —d, they* (my eyes) *would change their state with those dancing chips*, Sonn. 128, 9. *expectation, —ing skittish spirits*, Troil. Prol. 20. *the devil Luxury ... —s these together*, V, 2, 56. *such a nature, —d with good success, disdains the shadow which he treads on*, Cor. I, 1, 264. 2) to nettle, to vex: *she's —d now; her fume needs no spurs*, H6B I, 3, 153. 3) to serve one right, to make one pay for it: *if he had not been in drink, he would have —d you othergates than he did*, Tw. V, 198. *I'll t. ye for a young prince*, H4A II, 4, 489. *I'll t. your catastrophe*, H4B II, 1, 66. *he'll t. it for his concupy*, Troil. V, 2, 177.

**Tickle-brain,** a species of strong liquor: *peace, good pint-pot; peace, good t.* H4A II, 4, 438.

**Ticklish,** easily tickled, wanton, prone to lust: *unclasp the tables of their heart to every t. reader,* Troil. IV, 5, 61 (Ff *tickling*).

**Tick-tack,** a game at tables, a sort of backgammon (Fr. *tric-trac*); used in a wanton sense: *thy life ... should be thus foolishly lost at a game of t.* Meas. I, 2, 196.

**Tiddle taddle,** tattling: H5 IV, 1, 71 (Fluellen's speech). cf. *Tittle-tattle.*

**Tide,** subst. 1) time; season: *set among the high —s in the calendar,* John III, 1, 86. With a pun: *flow this way! he keeps his —s well,* Tim. I, 2, 57. Perhaps also in the broken speech of Capulet: *day, night, hour, t., time, work, play, ... my care hath been ...,* Rom. III, 5, 178.

2) the alternate ebb and flow of the sea: *a' parted even just between twelve and one, even at the turning o' the t.* H5 II, 3, 14 (according to the old superstition that people die only in the time of ebb). *his ebbs, his flows, as if the passage and whole carriage of this action rode on his t.* Troil. II, 3, 141. *marks the waxing t.* Tit. III, 1, 95. *there is a t. in the affairs of men, which, taken at the flood, leads on to fortune,* Caes. IV, 3, 218. *lackeying the varying t.* Ant. I, 4, 46. *at full of t.* III, 2, 49. More especially the flow: *as through an arch the violent roaring t. outruns the eye,* Lucr. 1667 (masc. 1670. cf. Cor. V, 4, 50). *would thou mightst lie drowning the washing of ten —s,* Tp. I, 1, 61. *the approaching t. will shortly fill the reasonable shore,* V, 80. *the t. is now,* Gent. II, 2, 14. *you'll lose the t.* II, 3, 39. 43. *both wind and t. stays for this gentleman,* Err. IV, 1, 46. *whose foot spurns back the ocean's roaring —s,* John II, 24. *a braver choice of dauntless spirits ... did never float upon the swelling t.* 74. *I was amazed under the t., but now I breathe again aloft the flood,* IV, 2, 138. *half my power ... are taken by the t.* V, 6, 40. H4B II,3,63. H5 I, 2, 149. IV, 1, 101. H6A V, 5, 6. H6C I, 4, 20. II, 5, 6. III, 3, 48; IV, 3, 59 and V, 1, 53 *(wind and t.).* V, 4, 31. H8 V, 4, 18. Troil. III, 3, 159. Cor. V, 4, 50.

Metaphorically; denoting a) a state of being at the height or in superabundance: *my uncontrolled t.* (of desire) *turns not, but swells the higher by this let,* Lucr. 645. *what a t. of woes,* R2 II,2,98. *turn the t. of fearful faction,* H4A IV, 1, 67. *the t. of blood in me hath flowed in vanity,* H4B V, 2, 129. *the t. of pomp that beats upon the high shore of this world,* H5 IV, 1, 281. *I have important business the t. whereof is now,* Troil. V, 1, 90. *let in the t. of knaves,* Tim. III, 4, 118. Used of copious tears: Ven. 957. 979. Lucr. 1789. Gent. II, 2, 14. H6A I, 1, 83. — b) a regular course and process: *the noblest man that ever lived in the t. of times,* Caes. III, 1, 257.

**Tide,** vb. to betide: *t. life, t. death, I come without delay,* Mids. V, 205 (Thisbe's speech).

**Tider,** see *Tether.*

**Tidings,** news, intelligence: Lucr. 254. As III, 2, 214. All's II, 1, 63. R2 II, 4, 3. III, 4, 71. H4B I, 1, 35. IV, 2, 106. V, 3, 99. H6A V, 2, 10. H6B II, 1, 165 *(what t. with our cousin Buckingham?* cf. H4B I, 1, 33). H6B IV, 9, 7. R3 IV, 1, 37. H8 V, 1, 160. Cor. V, 4, 61. Tit. IV, 3, 78. V, 1, 120. Mcb. IV, 3, 181. Oth. II, 2, 2. Ant. II, 5, 24. 39. Cymb. IV, 3, 39. With *of:* Ven. 867. R2 III, 2, 105. H4A I, 1, 47. H6A I,

1, 58. H6C II, 1, 7. 109. R3 I, 4, 237. Tit. III, 1, 159. Rom. III, 3, 8. V, 3, 287. Caes. V, 3, 78. Oth. II, 1, 88. Cymb. II, 4, 19. V, 5, 10. Used indiscriminately as a sing. and plur.; as a sing.: *this t.* R2 III, 4, 80. R3 IV, 3, 22 (later Ff *these t.*). Ant. IV, 14, 112. *that t.* Caes. IV, 3, 155. *the t. comes,* John IV, 2, 115. *how near the t. of our comfort is,* R2 II, 1, 272. *that's the worst t.* H4A IV, 1, 127. *what good t. comes with you?* H4B I, 1, 33. *is colder t.* R3 IV, 4, 536 (Ff *news*). *what is your t.?* Mcb. I, 5, 31. *it is t. to wash the eyes of kings,* Ant. V, 1, 27. As a plural: *these t.* Wiv. IV, 5, 57. As V, 4, 159. John IV, 2, 132. H6A I, 1, 83. Tit. IV, 4, 70. Caes. V, 3, 54. *t. were brought me,* H6C II, 1, 109. *joyful t. ... What are they?* Rom. III, 5, 105. *let ill t. tell themselves when they be felt,* Ant. II, 5, 87. *t. to the contrary are brought,* Per. II, Prol. 15.

**Tidy,** used in a scarcely ascertainable (and at any rate improper) sense by Doll Tearsheet in addressing Falstaff: *thou whoreson little t. Bartholomew boar-pig,* H4B II, 4, 250.

**Tie,** subst. knot, fastening: *to the which my duties are with a most indissoluble t. for ever knit,* Mcb.III,1,17.

**Tie,** vb. to bind, to fasten with a knot: *to t. the rider she begins to prove,* Ven. 40. *if the —d* (viz. dog) *were lost,* Gent. II, 3, 41. 42. 44. *Ill t. them* (horses) *in the wood,* H4A I, 2, 199. II, 2, 12. *horses are —d by the heads,* Lr. II, 4, 8. *—ing his new shoes with old ribands,* Rom. III, 1, 31. *one that —s his points,* Ant. III, 13, 157. *her hair, nor loose, nor —d in formal plat,* Compl. 29. *shave the head and t. the beard,* Meas. IV, 2, 187 (some M. Edd. *tire,* others *dye*). Metaphorically: *sin and obstinacy t. thy tongue,* All's I, 3, 186. *—d it by letters-patents,* H8 III, 2, 250 (fastened, confirmed it). *one that by suggestion —d all the kingdom,* IV, 2, 36 (cf. *suggestion*). *Cressid is mine, —d with the bonds of heaven,* Troil. V, 2, 154. *—ing her duty, beauty .... in an extravagant stranger,* Oth. I, 1, 136. *the band that seems to t. their friendship together,* Ant.II,6,129. With *to: the steed, being —d unto a tree,* Ven. 263. 391. *have their provender —d to their mouth,* H6A I, 2, 11. Troil. V, 8, 21. Cor. III, 1, 314. Tit. II, 1, 17. Mcb. V, 7, 1. Lr. III, 7, 54. Ant. III, 11, 57. Metaphorically, = to bind to: *whereto all bonds do t. me,* Sonn. 117, 4. 137, 8. *their* (the eyes') *poor balls are —d to the orbed earth,* Compl. 24 (fixed). *t. the wiser souls to thy false seeming,* Meas. II, 4, 14. Shr. III, 1, 19. John II, 470. R2 IV, 77. H4A I, 3, 238. H6C IV, 1, 66. H8 II, 2, 90. Cor. II, 3, 205. Lr. IV, 2, 14. Cymb. I, 6, 23. III, 7, 15. Per. II, 5, 8 (*she has so strictly —d her to her chamber,* = confined). With an infinitive: *will t. the hearers to attend each line,* Lucr. 818. *I am —d to be obedient,* Shr. I, 1, 217 (obliged). R2 I, 1, 63. Cor. II, 2, 69. *Here and* where = hereto, whereto: *his liking, where you were —d in duty,* Wint. V, 1, 213. *she hath —d sharp-toothed unkindness, like a vulture, here,* Lr. II, 4, 136. *to t. over to* = to put off to or till: *this moral —s me over to time and a hot summer,* H5 V, 2, 339.

With *up,* = to bind completely, so as to hinder from any motion: *to unloose this —d up justice,* Meas. I, 3, 32. *if 'twill t. up thy discontented sword,* Ant. II, 6, 6. *t. up the libertine in a field of feasts,* II, 1, 23. *my horse is —d up safe,* Cymb. IV, 1, 24. *t. my treasure up in silken bags,* Per. III, 2, 41. Used of the tongue: *t. up my love's tongue,* Mids. III, 1, 206. *death ... —s up my tongue,* Rom. IV, 5, 32. cf. *this thy praise cannot be so thy praise, to t. up envy evermore enlarged,* Sonn. 70, 12 (= to put it to silence). *what king so strong can t. the gall up in the slanderous tongue?* Meas. III, 2, 199.

**Tiger,** the animal Felis tigris; proverbially ferocious: Ven. 1096. Lucr. 955. 980. Sonn. 19, 3. Gent. III, 2, 80. Mids. II, 1, 233. John III, 1, 260. H5 III, 1, 6. H6C I, 4, 137. 155. III, 1, 39. R3 II, 4, 50. Troil. I, 3, 49. III, 2, 84. Cor. V, 4, 31 *(a male t.).* Tit. III, 1, 54. 55. V, 3, 5. Rom. V, 3, 39. Tim. IV, 3, 189. Mcb. III, 4, 101. IV, 1, 33. Unchanged in the fem. (the form *tigress* unknown to Sh.): *when did the —'s young ones teach the dam?* Tit. II, 3, 142. *that heinous t. Tamora,* V, 3, 195. —*s, not daughters,* Lr. IV, 2, 40.

Name of an inn: Err. III, 1, 95. of a ship: Tw. V, 65. Mcb. I, 3, 7.

**Tiger-footed,** moving in bounds, hastening to seize one's prey: *this t. rage,* Cor. III, 1, 312.

**Tight,** sound, able, fit, in a good state: *our ship ... is t. and yare and bravely rigged,* Tp. V, 224. *my father hath ... twelve t. galleys,* Shr. II, 381. *my queen's a squire more t. at this than thou,* Ant. IV, 4, 15.

**Tightly,** ably, adroitly, soundly: *bear you these letters t.* Wiv. I, 3, 88. *he will clapper-claw thee t.* II, 3, 67.

**Tike,** dog, cur: *bobtail t. or trundle-tail,* Lr. III, 6, 73. Term of reproach: *base t., callest thou me host?* H5 II, 1, 31 (Pistol's speech). In Wiv. IV, 5, 55 the surreptitious Qq and some M. Edd. *ay, sir tike;* Ff *ay, sir; like* etc.

**Tile,** a plate of baked clay used to cover the roofs of buildings: *his brains are forfeit to the next t. that falls,* All's IV, 3, 217.

**Till,** 1) prepos. to the time of: *from morn t. night,* Ven. 154. *must not die t. mutual overthrow of mortal kind,* 1018. *and t. action, lust is perjured,* Sonn. 129, 2. *farewell t. half an hour hence,* Tp. III, 1, 91. *never t. this day,* IV, 144. *t. the perpetual doom,* Wiv. V, 5, 62. *t. that I'll view the manners of the town,* Err. I, 2, 12. *t. bed-time,* 28. *t. a merrier hour,* 69. *I never saw her t. this time,* II, 2, 164. *t. doomsday,* III, 2, 101. *t. this present hour,* V, 401. *not t. a hot January,* Ado I, 1, 94. *not t. Monday,* II, 1, 374. *wonder not t. further warrant,* III, 2, 115. *t. the break of day,* Mids. III, 2, 446. *fight t. the last gasp,* H6A I, 2, 127. *t. the point of death,* III, 1, 168. *t. further trial,* H8 V, 1, 104. *not t. Thursday,* Rom. IV, 2, 36. *be patient t. the last,* Caes. III, 2, 12. *from the first corse t. he that died to-day,* Hml. I, 2, 105 *(he* for *him)* etc. etc. Before adverbs of time and prepositional expressions: *I knew not what 'twas to be beaten t. lately,* Wiv. V, 1, 28. *t. now,* Ven. 1062. Meas. IV, 2, 141. V, 233. Err. I, 1, 124. Mids. V, 73. Merch. III, 1, 90. *t. soon,* R3 IV, 3, 35 (Ff t. *then). t. then,* Err. I, 2, 30. V, 422. LLL I, 1, 317. H5 II Chor. 41 *(not t. then). t. when,* Tp. V, 250. *t. after supper,* Gent. III, 2, 96. *t. after Theseus' wedding-day,* Mids. II, 1, 139 etc. Seemingly = to: *sleep and feeding may prorogue his honour even t. a Lethe'd dullness,* Ant. II, 1, 27. cf. *Whereuntil* and *Up-till.*

2) conj. to the time when: *t. breathless he disjoined,* Ven. 541. *t. they have singled the cold fault out,* 693. *t. the wild waves will have him seen no more,* 819. *t. time had made them for us,* Meas. I, 2, 157. *stay there t. I come to thee,* Err. I, 2, 10. cf. Tp. I, 2, 347. Meas.

V, 321. Err. V, 153 etc. etc. Followed by the indicative, in speaking of matters of fact, as well as in hypothetical cases: *claps her pale cheek; t. clapping makes it red,* Ven. 468. *on the grass she lies as she were slain, t. his breath breatheth life in her again,* 474. *thus stands she in a trembling ecstasy, till ... she tells them 'tis a causeless fantasy,* 896. *who with a lingering stay his course doth let, t. every minute pays the hour his debt,* Lucr. 329. *the wolf hath seized his prey, the poor lamb cries, t. with her own white fleece her voice controlled entombs her outcry,* 678. *no exclamation ... can rein his rash desire, t. like a jade self-will himself doth tire,* 707 etc. *some good conceit of thine ... will bestow it, t. whatsoever star that guides my moving points on me graciously ... and puts apparel on my tattered loving,* Sonn. 26, 9. *I will peg thee in his entrails, t. thou hast howled away twelve winters,* Tp. I, 2, 295. *I will resist such entertainment t. mine enemy has more power,* 465. *do not approach t. thou dost hear me call,* IV, 50. *lead him on with a fine-baited delay, t. he hath pawned his horses,* Wiv. II, 1, 99. *t. 'tis one o'clock, our dance of custom let us not forget,* V, 5, 78. *I will never mistrust my wife again, t. thou art able to woo her in good English,* 142. *let him continue in his courses t. thou knowest what they are,* Meas. II, 1, 196. *that stays but t. her owner comes aboard,* Err. IV, 1, 86. *lead them thus, till o'er their brows ... sleep ... with leaden legs ... doth creep,* Mids. III, 2, 364. *till Lionel's issue fails, his should not reign,* H6B II, 2, 56 etc.

Followed by the subjunctive in hypothetical and problematical cases: *as an empty eagle tires with her beak on feathers, flesh and bone, ... t. either gorge be stuffed or prey be gone,* Ven. 58. *she swears ... never to remove, t. he take truce with her contending tears,* 82. *Cynthia for shame obscures her silver shine, t. forging nature be condemned of treason,* 729. *to wrong the wronger t. he render right,* Lucr. 943. *and with my trespass never will dispense, t. life to death acquit my forced offence,* 1071. *die I will not t. my Collatine have heard the cause,* 1177. *but long she thinks t. he return again,* 1359. *this windy tempest, t. it blow up rain, held back his sorrow's tide, to make it more,* 1788. *when a woman woos, what woman's son will sourly leave her t. she have prevailed?* Sonn. 41, 8. *till each to razed oblivion yield his part of thee, thy record never can be missed,* 122, 7. *yet this shall I ne'er know ... t. my bad angel fire my good one out,* 144, 14. *blow t. thou burst thy wind,* Tp. I, 1, 8. II, 1, 249. II, 2, 42. IV, 97. Gent. I, 2, 115. II, 5, 5. 6. II, 7, 14. 36. III, 2, 75. Wiv. II, 1, 68. IV, 4, 60. Meas. II, 1, 3. III, 2, 110. V, 162. 266. Err. II, 1, 31. III, 1, 58. III, 2, 156. IV, 1, 108. Ado II, 1, 373. II, 3, 137. LLL I, 2, 131. Mids. II, 2, 61. V, 129. As II, 7, 89. John II, 29. H6B I, 1, 67. I, 4, 30. II, 1, 149. II, 4, 49. Rom. II, 2, 172 etc. *not t.* Ado II, 1, 62. LLL II, 121 (not before) etc.

Elliptically: *he will not hear t. feel,* Tim. II, 2, 7. Peculiar passages: *I long t. Edward fall by war's mischance,* H6C III, 3, 254. *as in the common course of all treasons, we still see them reveal themselves, t. they attain to their abhorred ends,* All's IV, 3, 27 (= in the time before they etc., or simply = before). cf. above: Sonn. 41, 8. *Till that,* see *That.*

**Till,** vb. to husband, to cultivate, to plough and prepare for seed: *manured, husbanded and —ed,* H4B IV, 3, 130.

**Tillage,** the practice of ploughing and preparing

for seed: *where is she so fair whose uneared womb disdains the t. of thy husbandry?* Sonn. 3, 6.

**Tilly-fally** (Mrs. Quickly) or **Tilly-vally** (Sir Toby), an exclamation of contempt at what has been said: *am I not of her blood? t., lady!* Tw. II, 3, 83. *dost thou hear? it is mine ancient. T., Sir John, ne'er tell me,* H4B II, 4, 90.

**Tilt,** subst. a tournament, a military game in the time of knighthood, at which the combatants ran against each other with lances on horseback: *practise —s and tournaments,* Gent. I, 3, 30. *break a lance, and run a t. at death,* H6A III, 2, 51. *thou ran'st a t. in honour of my love,* H6B I, 3, 54.

**Tilt,** vb. 1) to run in a tournament and thrust with a lance: *lo, he is —ing straight,* LLL V, 2, 483.

2) to fight, to thrust in general: *this is no world to play with mammets and to t. with lips,* H4A II, 3, 95. *he —s with piercing steel at bold Mercutio's breast,* Rom. III, 1, 163. *swords out, and —ing one at other's breast,* Oth. II, 3, 183.

3) to toss, to play unsteadily: *what observation madest thou in this case of his heart's meteors —ing in his face?* Err. IV, 2, 6.

**Tilter,** one who runs with a lance in a tournament: *a puisny t., that spurs his horse but on one side,* As III, 4, 46. In Meas. IV, 3, 17 probably = fighter, fencer: *Master Forthlight the t.*

**Tilth,** tillage, husbandry: *contract, succession, bourn, bound of land, t., vineyard, none,* Tp. II, 1, 152. *her plenteous womb expresseth his full t. and husbandry,* Meas. I, 4, 44. In Meas. IV, 1, 76 some M. Edd. *t.,* O. Edd. *tithes.*

**Tilt-yard,** a place for tilting: H4B III, 2, 347. H6B I, 3, 62.

**Timandra,** name of a courtesan in Tim. IV, 3, 81. 88. V, 1, 6.

**Timber,** wood fit for building: *one of you will prove a shrunk panel and like green t. warp,* As III, 3, 90. *we take from every tree lop, bark, and part o'the t.* H8 I, 2, 96. In Merch. II, 7, 69 O. Edd. *gilded t. do worms infold;* M. Edd. *gilded tombs.*

**Timbered,** built, framed, shaped: *my arrows, too slightly t. for so loud a wind, would have reverted,* Hml. IV, 7, 22. *his bark is stoutly t.* Oth. II, 1, 48.

**Timbria,** one of the six gates of Troy: Troil. Prol. 16.

**Time,** subst. 1) the general idea of successive existence; the measure of duration: *as the riper should by t. decease,* Sonn. 1, 3. *what seest thou else in the dark backward and abysm of time?* Tp. I, 2, 50. *have more t. for vainer hours,* 173. *t. goes upright with his carriage,* V, 2 (does not sink under its load, but carries all into execution). *wherefore waste I t.* Gent. I, 1, 51. *for want of idle t.* II, 1, 172. *omitting the sweet benefit of t.* II, 4, 65. *t. is the nurse and breeder of all good,* III, 1, 243. *t. wears,* Wiv. V, 1, 8. *till t. had made them for us,* Meas. I, 2, 157. *the tooth of t.* V, 12. *t. shall try,* Ado I, 1, 262. *spite of cormorant devouring t.* LLL I, 1, 4. *spend a minute's t. in pruning me,* IV, 3, 182. *take t. to pause,* Mids. I, 1, 83. *who t. trots withal* etc. As III, 2, 328. *t. lost,* V, 3, 41. *what else may hap to t. I will commit,* Tw. I, 2, 60. *O t., thou must untangle this,* II, 2, 41. *faster than thought or t.* Wint. IV, 4, 565. *the yet unbegotten sin of —s,* John IV, 3, 54. *fill up chronicles in t. to come,* H4A I, 3, 171. *I have a young conception in my brain; be you my t. to*

bring it to some shape, Troil. I, 3, 313 (play the part of time, whose office is to develop things) etc. etc. *in little t.* Ven. 132. *long t.* (= a long t.) R2 II, 1, 77. H6A II, 3, 36. *in short t. after,* H4A IV, 3, 90. *t. out of mind,* Meas. IV, 2, 17. Rom. I, 4, 69. Considered as serving for particular purposes: *we shall lose our t.* Tp. IV, 248. *let him spend his t. no more at home,* Gent. I, 3, 14. *here he means to spend his t. awhile,* II, 4, 80. *give me so much of your t. in exchange,* Wiv. II, 2, 242. *heaven so speed me in my t. to come,* III, 4, 12 etc. etc. *In t.* = one day or other; by degrees: *in t. the rod becomes more mocked than feared,* Meas. I, 3, 26. *he in t. may come to clear himself, but at this instant he is sick,* V, 150. *in t. the savage bull doth bear the yoke,* Ado I, 1, 263. *you will try in t.* As I, 3, 25. *in t. I may believe, yet I mistrust,* Shr. III, 1, 51. *I did in t. collect myself,* Wint. III, 3, 38. *likely in t. to bless a regal throne,* H6C IV, 6, 74. *in t. will find their fit rewards,* H8 III, 2, 245. *it will in t. win upon power,* Cor. I, 1, 223. *which will in t. break ope the locks o'the senate,* III, 1, 137. *that in t. will venom breed,* Mcb. III, 4, 30. *you may do then (hear of it) in t.* Lr. II, 1, 14. *in t. we hate that which we often fear,* Ant. I, 3, 12. *wrinkled deep in t.* I, 5, 29. *dost thou think in t. she will not quench,* Cymb. I, 5, 46. *and in t. may make some stronger head,* IV, 2, 138. *and in t. to work her son into the adoption of the crown,* V, 5, 54 etc.

Personified as masc.: *mis-shapen T.* etc. Lucr. 925. *nothing 'gainst —'s scythe can make defence save breed, to brave him,* Sonn. 12, 13. *wasteful T.* 15, 11. 13. *his scythe and crooked knife,* 100, 14. *his bending sickle,* 116, 10. — *'s fickle glass, his sickle hour,* 126, 2. *where shall —'s best jewel from —'s chest lie hid?* 65, 10 (i. e. from the coffin). *the plain bald pate of father T. himself,* Err. II, 2, 71. *T. himself is bald,* 107. *if T. were in debt,* IV, 2, 57. 58. 60. 61. *I (t.) turn my glass,* Wint. IV, 1, 16. 32. *old T. the clocksetter, that bald sexton,* John III, 1, 324. *thy word is current with him (T.) for my death,* R2 I, 3, 231. *T. hath a wallet at his back, wherein he puts* etc. Troil. III, 3, 145.

2) a particular part of duration, conceived either as a space or as a point; a period as well as a moment: *the t. is spent,* Ven. 255. *now stole upon the t. the dead of night,* Lucr. 162. *these lets attend the t., like little frosts that sometime threat the spring,* 330 (i. e. are natural, when one has such business before one). *the clock that tells the t.* Sonn. 12, 1. *not with the t. exchanged,* 109, 7 (i. e. the time of absence). *canst thou remember a t. before we came unto this cell?* Tp. I, 2, 39. *at that t. it was the first,* 70. *the t. 'twixt six and now,* 240. *before the t. be out,* 246. *since Dido's t.* II, 1, 76. *I was the man i'the moon when t. was,* II, 2, 142. *at that t. I made her weep,* Gent. IV, 4, 170. *in these —s you stand on distance,* Wiv. II, 1, 233. *I have seen the t.* 236. *the t. was once when thou wouldst vow ...,* Err. II, 2, 115. *his word might bear my wealth at any t.* V, 8. *to take the present t. by the top,* Ado I, 2, 15. *in eaning t.* Merch. I, 3, 88. *by this t.* Merch. II, 6, 59; cf. John II, 219. *the t. I linger here,* Merch. II, 9, 74. *many that have at —s made moan to me,* III, 3, 23. *music for the t. doth change his nature,* V, 82. *the t. was that I hated thee,* As III, 5, 92. *did I never speak of all that t.?* Shr. Ind. 2, 84 (= in all that t. Sly's speech). *t. was, I did him a desired office,* All's

IV, 4, 5. *the t. will bring on summer*, 31 (i. e. not time in general, but that period of time which is immediately before us; hence the article). *at this t. of night*, Tw. II, 3, 95. *the t. hath been ...*, R2 III, 3, 11. *what t. do you mean to come to London?* H4A II, 1, 46. *the t. was that you broke your word*, H4B II, 3, 10. *the t. of night when Troy was set on fire, the t. when screech-owls cry*, H6B I, 4, 20. *where and what t. your majesty shall please*, R3 IV, 4, 490. *and when such t. they have begun to cry, let them not cease*, Cor. III, 3, 19. *the — s have been, that, when the brains were out, the man would die*, Mcb. III, 4, 78. *the t. has been, my senses would have cooled*, V, 5, 10. *in the fatness of these pursy — s*, Hml. III, 4, 153. *that t. — O — s! — I laughed him out of patience*, Ant. II, 5, 18. *the locking-up the spirits a t.* Cymb. I, 5, 41 etc. etc. *from t. to t.* Wiv. IV, 6, 8. As IV, 1, 107. Cor. III, 3, 94. Rom. III, 3, 170. *upon this t.* Meas. IV, 1, 17. *upon a t.* Cymb. III, 5, 137. *one t. or other*, Tw. II, 4, 73. H4B IV, 3, 32. H5 II, 1, 73. *nature hath framed strange fellows in her t.* Merch. I, 1, 51. *have I not in my t. heard lions roar?* Shr. I, 2, 201. *and in my t. wore threepile*, Wint. IV, 3, 13. *any t. these three hundred years*, Wiv. I, 1, 12. *hourly any t. this two and twenty years*, H4A II, 2, 17. III, 3, 54. *dinner t., supper t., winter t.* etc. Tp. III, 1, 95. Wiv. IV, 4, 30 (cf. the resp. articles). *good t. =* good hap: *good t. encounter her*, Wint. II, 1, 20 (i. e. a happy delivery). *I wish my brother make good t. with him*, Cymb. IV, 2, 108 (may acquit himself well). cf. *O t. most accurst, 'mongst all foes that a friend should be the worst*, Gent. V, 4, 71. *What is the t. o' the day?* = what o' clock is it: Tp. I, 2, 239. H4A I, 2, 1 etc.; used as a ludicrous question to change the theme: LLL II, 122; cf. As III, 2, 318. *fair t. of day, good t. of day*, used as a salutation: LLL V, 2, 339. H4B I, 2, 107. H5 V, 2, 3. R3 I, 1, 122. I, 3, 18. II, 1, 47. IV, 1, 6. Tim. III, 6, 1 etc. *when every one will give the t. of day* (= greet) H6B III, 1, 14. *a malkin not worth the t. of day* (= not worth greeting) Per. IV, 3, 35.

3) season proper or appropriated to something: *make use of t., let not advantage slip*, Ven. 129. *'tis t. I should inform thee farther*, Tp. I, 2, 22. *the truth you speak doth lack some gentleness and t. to speak it in*, II, 1, 138. *conspiracy his t. doth take*, 302. *the t. now serves not to expostulate*, Gent. III, 1, 251. *when you see your t.* Wiv. V, 3, 2. *when they see t. they'll go or come*, Err. II, 1, 8. *there's a t. for all things*, II, 2, 66. *'tis high t. that I were hence*, III, 2, 162. *lest I come not t. enough*, IV, 1, 41 (cf. H4A II, 1, 48). *'tis t. that I were gone*, IV, 2, 53. *'tis t. you were ready*, Ado III, 4, 53. *stay the riping of the t.* Merch. II, 8, 40. *if I break t.* All's II, 1, 190. *is there no respect of place, persons, nor t. in you?* Tw. II, 3, 99. *we have landed in ill t.* Wint. III, 3, 3. *we as t. of year do wound the bark*, R2 III, 4, 57. *t. enough to go to bed with a candle*, H4A II, 1, 48. *wizards know their — s*, H6B I, 4, 18. *take the t.* H6C V, 1, 48. *take t. to do him dead*, I, 4, 108. *take your t.* Ant. II, 6, 23. *my occasions have found t. to use 'em*, Tim. II, 2, 200. *in best t. we will require her welcome*, Mcb. III, 4, 5 etc. etc. *in t.* = at the right moment; before it is too late: *look to't in t.* H6B I, 3, 147. *that gentle physic, given in t., had cured me*, H8 IV, 2, 122. *come in t.* Mcb. II, 3, 6. Lr. V, 3, 247. Ant. V, 1, 72. *just to the t.* Sonn. 109, 7. *In good t., in happy t.* = a) at the right mo-

ment, in good season, not too early and not too late: *to jest in good t.* Err. II, 2, 65. *we stood to't in good t.* Cor. IV, 6, 10. *and in good t. you gave it*, Lr. II, 4, 253. b) fortunately, happily, upon a wish (Fr. *à propos*): *here comes the rascal I spoke of. In very good t.* Meas. V, 286. *come in happy t.* Shr. Ind. 1, 90. *were now the general of our gracious empress, as in good t. he may, from Ireland coming*, H5 V Chor. 31. *and in good t. here comes the noble duke*, R3 II, 1, 45. III, 1, 24. 95. III, 4, 22. IV, 1, 12. *the king and queen and all are coming down. In happy t.* Hml. V, 2, 214. cf. the pun in Ado II, 1, 73. hence = well met: Gent. I, 3, 44. All's V, 1, 6. Rom. I, 2, 45. Oth. III, 1, 32 etc. c) = the French *à la bonne heure*, used either to express acquiescence, or astonishment and indignation: *and sowing the kernels of it in the sea, bring forth more islands. Ay. Why, in good t.* Tp. II, 1, 95. *pray you, use your patience: in good t.* Wiv. III, 1, 84. *leave me awhile with the maid ... In good t.* Meas. III, 1, 183. *I think the meat wants that I have. In good t., sir, what's that?* Err. II, 2, 58. *myself am moved to woo thee for my wife. Moved! in good t., let him that moved you hither remove you hence*, Shr. II, 196. *marry, garlic, to mend her kissing with! Now, in good t.* Wint. IV, 4, 163. *hath sorted out a sudden day of joy, that thou expectest not. Madam, in happy t., what day is that?* Rom. III, 5, 112. *he, in good t., must his lieutenant be*, Oth. I, 1, 32.

4) season, moment, mentioned with reference to repetition: *another t. mine eye is my heart's guest*, Sonn. 47, 7. Tp. III, 2, 85. *but one fiend at a t.* (= at once) III, 3, 102. *any man living may be drunk at a t.* Oth. II, 3, 319 (= once. Qq *at some t.*). *a greater sum than ever at one t. the clergy yet did part withal*, H5 I, 1, 80. I, 2, 134 (= at once). *it were fit that all the plagues of hell should at one t. encounter such revolt*, Cymb. I, 6, 111. *at all — s* = always, All's I, 1, 9. *for this t.* Gent. II, 4, 30. Meas. II, 1, 265. Cymb. I, 1, 178. *this one t.* Wiv. IV, 2, 168. *yet one t. he did call me by my name*, Cor. V, 1, 9. *how mightily some other — s we drown our gain in tears*, All's IV, 3, 79. *another — s to see ...*, H4B III, 1, 49. *many a t.* Tp. III, 1, 40. *many a t. and oft*, Merch. I, 3, 107. H4A I, 2, 56. *at many — s I brought in my accounts*, Tim. II, 2, 142. *every t. gentler than other*, Caes. I, 2, 230. *urging it the second t.* Err. II, 2, 47. *a second t.* H4A V, 2, 101. *this is the third t.* Wiv. V, 1, 2. *the last t.* IV, 2, 32. *last t.* 98 etc.

Hence simply used by way of multiplication: *'ay me' she cries, and twenty — s 'woe, woe'*, Ven. 833. *a thousand — s*, 1130. *he ten — s pines*, Lucr. 1115. 1604. Sonn. 6, 8. Tp. III, 1, 8. Gent. I, 3, 91. Wiv. V, 5, 129. Meas. II, 4, 80. V, 42. 45. LLL III, 48. Merch. II, 6, 5. Wint. IV, 4, 802. H4A I, 3, 102. II, 4, 184. H6B II, 4, 60. 61. H8 V, 4, 46 etc. etc.

5) eternal duration, eternity: *when in eternal lines to t. thou growest*, Sonn. 18, 12. *to keep your name living to t.* Cor. V, 3, 127.

6) duration of a being, age: *a youth of greater t. than I shall show to be*, Gent. II, 7, 48. *tough senior, as an appertinent title to your old t.* LLL I, 2, 18. *when old t. shall lead him to his end*, H8 II, 1, 93. *all the learnings that his t. could make him the receiver of*, Cymb. I, 1, 43.

7) life: *not of this country, though my chance is now to use it for my t.* Meas. III, 2, 231. *the great*

*debts wherein my t. something too prodigal hath left me gaged*, Merch. I, 1, 129. *I like this place, and willingly would waste my t. in it*, AsII,4,95. *he hath persecuted t. with hope*, All's I, 1, 17 (cf. *Persecute*). *the purest treasure mortal —s afford is spotless reputation*, R2 I, 1, 177. *out of thy long-experienced t. give me some counsel*, Rom. IV, 1, 60. *his right arm might purchase his own t. and be in debt to none*, Tim. III, 5, 77. *upon this bank and school of t.* Mcb. I, 7, 6. *the best and soundest of his t. hath been but rash*, Lr. I, 1, 298. *makes the world bitter to the best of our —s*, I, 2, 50. *what's to come of my despised t. is nought but bitterness*, Oth. I, 1, 162. *the t. shall not outgo my thinking on you*, Ant. III, 2, 60 (= my life shall not last longer than etc.). *where I have paid more pious debts to heaven than in all the fore-end of my t.* Cymb. III, 3, 73. Caes. III, 1, 99.

8) the present state of things; circumstances: *that the —'s enemies may not have this to grace occasions*, John IV, 2, 61. *I am not glad that such a sore of t. should seek a plaster by contemned revolt*, V, 2, 12. *that you might the better arm you to the sudden t.* V, 6, 26. *let us pay the t. but needful woe*, V, 7, 110. *but t. will not permit*, R2 II, 2, 121. *I would the state of t. had first been whole ere he by sickness had been visited*, H4A IV, 1, 25. *the ragged'st hour that t. and spite dare bring*, H4B I, 1, 151. *thus we play the fools with the t.* II, 2, 155. *to beguile the t.* (cf. Tw. III, 3, 41), *look like the t.* Mcb. I, 5, 64. *as I shall find the t. to friend, I will* (redress) IV, 3, 10. *the t. is free*, V, 8, 55. *the t. is out of joint*, Hml. I, 5, 188. *beyond him in the advantage of the t.* Cymb. IV, 1, 12.

Hence almost equivalent to the present moment, the present: *as bombast and as lining to the t.* LLL V, 2, 791 (to fill up the emptiness of the present moment). *that what in t. proceeds may token to the future our past deeds*, All's IV, 2, 62. *it spoils the pleasure of the t.* Mcb. III, 4, 98. *this was sometime a paradox, but now the t. gives it proof*, Hml. III, 1, 115. Cor. IV, 7, 50. Ant. II, 7, 106.

9) men, the world: *that posterity which by the rights of t. thou needs must have*, Ven. 759 (the claim which the world has on thee). *wonder of t.* 1133. *if all were minded so, the —s should cease, and threescore year would make the world away*, Sonn. 11, 7. *slander doth but approve thy worth the greater, being wooed of t.* 70, 6. *that I have frequent been with unknown minds and given to t. your own dear-purchased right*, 117, 6. *the fashion of the t. is changed*, Gent. III, 1, 86. *picked from the chaff and ruin of the —s*, Merch. II, 9, 48. *they wear themselves in the cap of the t.* All's II, 1, 55. *mock the t. with fairest show*, Mcb. I, 7, 81. *you may convey your pleasures in a spacious plenty, and yet seem cold, the t. you may so hoodwink*, IV, 3, 72. *live to be the show and gaze o'the t.* V, 8, 24. *who would bear the whips and scorns of t.* Hml. III, 1, 70. *to show the very age and body of the t. his form and pressure*, III, 2, 27. *a fixed figure for the t. of scorn to point his slow and moving finger at it*, Oth. IV, 2, 54 (*t. of scorn* = scornful world; cf. *Of*).

10) musical measure: *distress likes dumps when t. is kept with tears*, Lucr. 1127. *he kept not t.* Wiv. I, 3, 29. As V, 3, 39. Tw. II, 3, 100. R2 V, 5, 42. Rom. II, 4, 21. Hml. III, 4, 140. Oth. IV, 1, 93 (figuratively). *pinch him to your t.* Wiv. V, 5, 96. *the fault will be in the music, if you be not wooed in good t.* Ado II, 1, 73 (quibbling). *when t. is broke*, R2 V, 5, 43. *sweet bells*

*jangled, out of t. and harsh*, Hml. III, 1, 166 (Ff *tune*). In Mcb. IV, 3, 235 O. Edd. *this t. goes manly*, M. Edd. *this tune*.

**Time-beguiling**, making the time pass quickly: *t. sport*, Ven. 24.

**Time-bettering**, improving the state of things, full of innovations: *some fresher stamp of the t. days*, Sonn. 82, 8.

**Time-bewasted**, consumed, used up by time: *my oil-dried lamp and t. light*, R2 I, 3, 221.

**Timed**, measured as in music, regulated by giving the time: *whose every motion was t. with dying cries*, Cor. II, 2, 114.

**Time-honoured**, being of a venerable age: *old John of Gaunt, t. Lancaster*, R2 I, 1, 1.

**Timeless**, 1) unseasonable, unseemly: *some untimely thought did instigate his all too t. speed*, Lucr. 44.

2) untimely, premature, unnatural: *a pack of sorrows which would press you down ... to your t. grave*, Gent. III, 1, 21. *who performed the bloody office of his t. death*, R2 IV, 5. *must I behold thy t. cruel death?* H6A V, 4, 5. *guilty of Duke Humphrey's t. death*, H6B III, 2, 187. *their parents' t. death*, H6C V, 6, 42. *the causer of the t. deaths of these Plantagenets*, R3 I, 2, 117. *the complot of this t. tragedy*, Tit. II, 3, 265 (the murder of Bassianus). *poison hath been his t. end*, Rom. V, 3, 162.

**Timely**, adj. early, soon attained: *happy were I in my t. death*, Err. I, 1, 139. *to gain the t. inn*, Mcb. III, 3, 7.

**Timely**, adv. early: *bright orient pearl, alack, too t. shaded*, Pilgr. 133. *he did command me to call t. on him*, Mcb. II, 3, 51. *called me —er than my purpose hither*, Ant. II, 6, 52. *certainties either are past remedies, or, t. knowing, the remedy then born*, Cymb. I, 6, 97.

**Timely-parted**, having died in time (cf. *Untimely*), i. e. having died a natural death: *oft have I seen a t. ghost*, H6B III, 2, 161.

**Time-pleaser**, one who complies with prevailing opinions, whatever they may be, and sets up his sail to every wind: *the devil a puritan that he is, or any thing constantly, but a t.* Tw. II, 3, 160. *scandaled the suppliants for the people, called them —s, flatterers*, Cor. III, 1, 45.

**Timon**, the celebrated misanthrope of antiquity: *and critic T. laugh at idle toys*, LLL IV, 3, 170. Tim. I, 1, 13 and passim.

**Timorous**, full of fear, timid: *the t. flying hare*, Ven. 674. *the t. yelping of the hounds*, 881. *like a t. thief*, All's II, 5, 86. *sings heavy music to my t. soul*, H6A IV, 2, 40. *t. deer*, 46. *t. wretch*, H6C I, 1, 231. *his t. dreams*, R3 IV, 1, 85. *with like t. accent and dire yell*, Oth. I, 1, 75.

**Timorously**, timidly: *heard the traitor speak and t. confess ...*, R3 III, 5, 57.

**Tinct**, 1) dye, colour: *there I see such black and grained spots as will not leave their t.* Hml. III, 4, 91. *white and azure laced with blue of heaven's own t.* Cymb. II, 2, 23.

2) tincture, the grand elixir of the alchemists: *Plutus himself, that knows the t. and multiplying medicine*, All's V, 3, 102. *that great medicine hath with his t. gilded thee*, Ant. I, 5, 37.

**Tincture**, dye, colour: *the perfumed t. of the roses*, Sonn. 54, 6. *the lily t. of her face*, Gent. IV, 4, 160. *if you can bring t. or lustre in her lip, her eye*, Wint.

III, 2, 206. *press for —s, stains,* Caes. II, 2, 89 (by dipping their handkerchiefs in the blood of Caesar).

**Tinder,** something very inflammable used for kindling fire from a spark: *strike on the t.* Oth. I, 1, 141. Falstaff calls Bardolph *t. box,* Wiv. I, 3, 27, on account of his fiery face.

**Tinder-like,** like tinder, easily catching fire: *hasty and t. upon too trivial motion,* Cor. II, 1, 55.

**Tine,** see *Tiny.*

**Tingling,** a pricking sensation: *a kind of sleeping in the blood, a whoreson t.* H4B I, 2, 128.

**Tinker,** a mender of old brass: Mids. I, 2, 63. IV, 1, 208. Shr. Ind. 2, 22. 75. Tw. II, 3, 95. Wint. IV, 3, 19. 103. H4A II, 4, 20. H6B III, 2, 277. Proverbial tipplers and would-be politicians.

**Tinsel,** a kind of shining cloth: *skirts, round underborne with a bluish t.* Ado III, 4, 22.

**Tiny** (O. Edd. *tine* or *tyne*), small, puny (always joined with *little,* by way of giving the expression some tenderness): *when that I was and a t. little boy,* Tw. V, 398. *any pretty little t. kickshaws,* H4B V, 1, 29. *my little t. thief,* V, 3, 60. *he that has and a little t. wit,* Lr. III, 2, 74.

**Tip,** subst. point, end, extremity: *on the t. of his subduing tongue,* Compl. 120. *in love, to the very t. of the nose,* Troil. III, 1, 138.

**Tip,** vb. to furnish or cover on the end or top: *we'll t. thy horns with gold,* Ado V, 4, 44. *there is no staff more reverend than one —ed with horn,* 126. *by yonder blessed moon I swear that —s with silver all these fruit-tree tops,* Rom. II, 2, 108.

**Tippling,** quaffing: *to sit and keep the turn of t. with a slave,* Ant. I, 4, 19.

**Tipsy,** intoxicated, fuddled: *the riot of the t. Bacchanals,* Mids. V, 48.

**Tip-toe,** on the end of the toes: *jocund day stands t. on the misty mountain tops,* Rom. III, 5, 10. = on the alert, awake, attentive: *will stand a t. when this day is named, and rouse him at the name of Crispian,* H5 IV, 3, 42.

**Tire,** subst. 1) furniture of any kind (?): *I much marvel that your lordship, having rich t. about you, should at these early hours shake off the golden slumber of repose,* Per. III, 2, 22.

2) head-dress: *on Helen's cheek all art of beauty set, and you in Grecian —s are painted new,* Sonn. 53, 8. *if I had such a t., this face of mine were full as lovely,* Gent. IV, 4, 190. *thou hast the right arched beauty of the brow that becomes the ship t., the t. valiant, or any t. of Venetian admittance,* Wiv. III, 3, 60. *I like the new t. within excellently, if the hair were a thought browner,* Ado III, 4, 13. *put my —s and mantles on him,* Ant. II, 5, 22.

**Tire,** vb. to attire, to dress, to adorn: *imitari is nothing: so doth the hound his master, the ape his keeper, the —d horse his rider,* LLL IV, 2, 131 (the horse adorned with ribbons or trappings). In Err. II, 2, 99 some M. Edd. *the money that he spends in —ing;* O. Edd. *trying;* some M. Edd. *trimming.* In Ven. 177: *Titan, —d in the midday heat, with burning eye did hotly overlook them; —d* may be dressed, but is explained by most as meaning weary.

**Tire,** vb. 1) trans. a) to fatigue, to weary; absol.: *he hath faults ... to t. in repetition,* Cor. I, 1, 47. *witness the —ing day and heavy night,* Tit. V, 2, 24. With an object: Lucr. 1363. LLL IV, 3, 307. R2 V, 5, 94. R3

IV, 4, 188. H8 I, 1, 134. Oth. II, 1, 65. *—d* = weary: Ven. 561. Lucr. 1617. Sonn. 27, 2. Err. IV, 3, 24. Shr. IV, 1, 1. 56. Tw. III, 4, 152 *(—d out of breath).* R2 IV, 178. H4A III, 1, 160. H5 II, 1, 26. Troil. III, 2, 183. Cor. I, 9, 91. Caes. I, 2, 115. Refl.: *self-will himself doth t.* Lucr. 707. *when thou hast —d thyself in base comparisons,* H4A II, 4, 276. *I have —d myself,* Cymb. III, 6, 2.

b) to fill with satiety, to make sick of sth., to disgust: *the beast that bears me, —d with my woe,* Sonn. 50, 5. *—d with all these, for restful death I cry,* 66, 1. *and t. the hearer with a book of words,* Ado I, 1, 309. *I have stayed to t. your royalty,* Wint. I, 2, 15. *to prove more fortunes thou art —d,* Cor. IV, 5, 100. *then should not we be —d with this ado,* Tit. II, 1, 98. *within a dull, stale, —d bed,* Lr. I, 2, 13. *Fortune, —d with doing bad,* Per. II Prol. 37.

2) intr. to be fatigued, to become weary: *your wit will t.* LLL II, 120. *as truest horse that yet would never t.* Mids. III, 1, 98. 105. *your sad (heart) —s in a mile,* Wint. IV, 3, 135. *he —s betimes that spurs too fast,* R2 II, 1, 36. *the posts come —ing on,* H4B Ind. 37.*

**Tire,** vb. 1) intr. to tear a prey, to seize and feed on it ravenously (used of birds of prey): *as an empty eagle, sharp by fast, —s with her beak on feathers, flesh and bone,* Ven. 56.* *will like an empty eagle t. on the flesh of me,* H6C I, 1, 269. Metaphorically: *upon that were my thoughts —ing,* Tim. III, 6, 5 (eagerly intent and busy). *when thou shalt be disedged by her that now you —st on,* Cymb. III, 4, 97. cf. *Womantired.*

2) tr. to make to feed ravenously, to glut: *in his will his wilful eye he —d,* Lucr. 417.

**Tire-valiant,** a fanciful head-dress: Wiv. III, 3, 60.

**Tiring-house,** the dressing-room of a theatre: Mids. III, 1, 4.

**Tirra-lyra,** a sound imitative of the note of a lark: Wint. IV, 3, 9.

**Tirrel,** see *Tyrrel.*

**Tirrits,** a word from the vocabulary of Mrs. Quickly, probably meaning *terrors:* H4B II, 4, 220.

**Tisick,** phthisic, or perhaps hectic; the complaint of Pandarus in Troil. V, 3, 101. Name in H4B II, 4, 92.

**Tissue,** cloth interwoven with gold or silver: *cloth of gold, of t.* Ant. II, 2, 204. cf. *Inter-tissued.*

**Titan,** the god of the sun: Ven. 177. H4A III, 4, 133 (in v. 134 it ought perhaps to be: *pitiful-hearted butter*). Troil. V, 10, 25. Tit. I, 226. II, 4, 31. Rom. II, 3, 4. Cymb. III, 4, 166.

**Titania,** the queen of the fairies: Mids. II, 1, 60. 74. 119. 177. 253. III, 2, 1. 34. IV, 1, 80.

**Tithe,** 1) subst. the tenth part: *the t. of a hair was never lost in my house before,* H4A III, 3, 66 (O. Edd. *tight*). *a slave that is not twentieth part the t. of your precedent lord,* Hml. III, 4, 97.

2) adj. tenth: *every t. soul, 'mongst many thousand dismes, hath been as dear as Helen,* Troil. II, 2, 19. cf. *the t. woman* in All's I, 3, 89.

In Meas. IV, 1, 76 O. Edd. unintelligibly: *our corn's to reap, for yet our —s to sow,* Some M. Edd. *tilth's.*

**Tithe,** vb. 1) to levy the tenth part: *no Italian priest shall t. or toll in our dominions,* John III, 1, 154.

2) to decimate: *by decimation and a —d death ... take thou the destined tenth,* Tim. V, 4, 31.

**Tithe-pig**, a pig given to a priest as a church-rate: Rom. I, 4, 79.

**Tithe-woman**, not hyphened in O. Edd.; the tenth woman, and a woman that pays the tithe: *we'ld find no fault with the t., if I were the parson*, All's I, 3, 89.

**Tithing**, a decennary, a district: *whipped from t. to t.* Lr. III, 4, 140.

**Titinius**, name in Caes. I, 2, 127. IV, 2, 52 etc.

**Title**, 1) an inscription put over any thing as a name by which it is distinguished: *tell me once more what t. thou* (a casket) *dost bear*, Merch. II, 9, 35. cf. *Title-leaf* and *Title-page*.

2) an appellation of dignity and honour: Lucr. 892. Sonn. 25, 2. Meas. V, 56. LLL IV, 1, 85. All's II, 3, 124. 138. 209. John II, 492. R2 II, 1, 226. II, 3, 72. 75. III, 3, 11. IV, 255. H4A V, 3, 23. H5 IV, 1, 271. 280. H6A IV, 7, 85. V, 4, 151. V, 5, 38. H6B I, 2, 73. I, 3, 51. H6C II, 2, 140. III, 3, 8. 28. IV, 1, 68. 72. R3 I, 4, 78. 82. III, 1, 99. IV, 1, 20. IV, 4, 348. H8 II, 3, 39. 63. III, 1, 140. IV, 2, 112. Troil. III, 1, 17. Cor. III, 1, 144. Tit. V, 1, 5. Tim. IV, 3, 36. Mcb. I, 2, 65. I, 5, 8. Lr. I, 4, 163. V, 3, 48. 81. Oth. I, 2, 31. Cymb. I, 1, 31. V, 2, 7.

3) any appellation or name: *what a happy t. do I find, happy to have thy love, happy to die*, Sonn. 92, 11 (= how am I to be called happy). *this deceit loses the name of craft, of disobedience, or unduteous title*, Wiv. V, 5, 240 (*unduteous t.* = name of undutifulness). *it may be I go under that t.* (the prince's fool) Ado II, 1, 212. *think you of a worse t., and I will fit her to it*, III, 2, 114. *tough senior, as an appertinent t. to your old time*, LLL I, 2, 18. *I will love her everlastingly. But how long shall that t. 'ever' last?* R3 IV, 4, 350. *a proper t. of a peace*, H8 I, 1, 98 (= a peace properly called so). *Romeo would, were he not Romeo called, retain that dear perfection which he owes without that t.* Rom. II, 2, 47. *the devil himself could not pronounce a t. more hateful to mine ear* (than Macbeth) Mcb. V, 7, 8. LLL IV, 2, 39. Merch. III, 1, 15. Shr. I, 2, 130. III, 2, 125. Wint. II, 1, 94. IV, 4, 872. R2 I, 1, 24. H4A II, 4, 307. III, 2, 110. V, 4, 79. H6B III, 1, 359. R3 IV, 4, 300. 340. H8 IV, 1, 96. V, 3, 138. Tim. I, 2, 94. Cymb. I, 4, 96. Per. V, 1, 205.

4) a claim, a right: Sonn. 46, 9. Mids. I, 1, 92. John II, 192. 200. 277. H4A II, 3, 85. IV, 3, 104. H5 I, 2, 16. 72. 87. 89. 94. H6A II, 5, 92. H6B III, 1, 92. V, 1, 176. H6C I, 1, 130. 134. 159. 169. II, 2, 160. III, 1, 48. III, 2, 129. IV, 7, 57. Tit. I, 4. Tim. IV, 3, 154. Mcb. IV, 3, 34. With *in: to have his t. live in Aquitaine*, LLL II, 146. *Arthur's t. in the whole*, John II, 562. *my t. in the queen*, H6B I, 1, 12. With *to: the justice °of your t. to him*, Meas. IV, 1, 74. *his —s to some dukedoms*, H5 I, 1, 87. *my t. to England's crown*, H6B II, 2, 4. H6C I, 1, 102. 104. III, 3, 145. IV, 7, 46. H8 I, 2, 144. Ant. V, 2, 291. *to make t.* = to lay claim: *she may lawfully make t. to as much love as she finds*, All's I, 3, 107. *make claim and t. to the crown of France*, H5 I, 2, 68. With an inf.: *having so great a t. to be more prince*, John IV, 1, 10. With *of: lost that t. of respect which the proud soul ne'er pays but to the proud*, H4A I, 3, 8.

5) property, possession (as founding a right): *to say nothing, to do nothing, to know nothing, and to have nothing, is to be a great part of your t.* All's II, 4, 27. *the sword which sways usurpingly these severai —s*, John

I, 13. *to guard a t. that was rich before*, IV, 2, 10. *for ever should they be expulsed from France and not have t. of an earldom here*, H6A III, 3, 26. *so much interest have I in thy sorrow as I had t. in thy noble husband* (as his mother) R3 II, 2, 48. *to leave his wife, to leave his babes, his mansion and his —s in a place from whence himself does fly*, Mcb. IV, 2, 7. *now does he feel his t. hang loose about him*, V, 2, 20; cf. IV, 3, 34.

**Titled**, having a name: *t. goddess*, All's IV, 2, 2 (= having the name of a goddess, by being called Diana). *as amply t. as Achilles is*, Troil. II, 3, 203 (great as Achilles' name is).

**Title-leaf**, the leaf of a book which contains its title: *this man's brow, like to a t., foretells the nature of a tragic volume*, H4B I, 1, 60. "In the time of the poet the title-page to an elegy, as well as every intermediate leaf, was totally black". Steevens.

**Titleless**, having no name: Cor. V, 1, 13.

**Title-page**, the page which contains the title of a book: Per. II, 3, 4.

**Tittles**, trifles: *what shalt thou exchange for rags? robes; for t.?* titles, LLL IV, 1, 85 (Armado's letter).

**Tittle-tattling**, prating, talking idly: *you must be t. before all our guests*, Wint. IV, 4, 248. cf. *Tiddle taddle.*

**Titus**, name: Tw. V, 66. Cor. I, 1, 243. I, 4, 25. I, 5, 12. I, 9, 89. Tit. I, 38 and passim. Tim. III, 4, 1. 85.

**To**, adv. (often spelt *too* in O. Edd.) 1) forward, on: *to, Achilles! to, Ajax, to!* Troil. II, 1, 119. *very well, go to! I cannot go to, man*, Oth. IV, 2, 195. *go to,* imperatively, very frequently used as an expression of exhortation or of reproof (cf. *Go*, and add to the instances quoted there Tp. IV, 253 and Oth. IV, 2, 194). *to and fro* = forward and backward, up and down: H6A II, 1, 69. H6B IV, 8, 57. *debating to and fro,* H6B I, 1, 91. *the to and fro conflicting wind and rain,* Lr. III, 1, 11. *to and back,* in the same sense: *goes to and back, lackeying the varying tide*, Ant. I, 4, 46.

2) Denoting motion towards a thing for the purpose of laying hold of it; particularly applied to food: *to fall to* = to help one's self, to eat freely: As II, 7, 171. R2 V, 5, 98. H5 V, 1, 38. Tit. III, 2, 34. *to stand to*, in the same sense: *I will stand to and feed*, Tp. III, 3, 49. 52. Similarly: *lay to your fingers*, Tp. IV, 251. *any flax-wench that puts to before her troth-plight,* Wint. I, 2, 277.

3) Denoting direction: *my wind cooling my broth would blow me to an ague*, Merch. I, 1, 23 (= would blow an ague towards me. *Me* dat., not accus.).

4) Denoting junction: *can honour set to a leg?* H4A V, 1, 133 (rejoin a leg to the body from which it is cut off). Hence *to clap to* = to shut hastily: *clap to the doors*, H4A II, 4, 305. *who upon the sudden clapped to their gates*, Cor. I, 4, 51. cf. *grow to*, Merch. II, 2, 18.

5) Denoting an aim proposed in doing something: *thou rather shalt enforce it with thy smile than hew to it with thy sword*, Tim. V, 4, 46 (= than shape it for thy purpose by hewing or cutting it).

**To**, prepos. 1) Denoting motion towards a place or a state, f. i.: *hasteth to his horse*, Ven. 258. *to her straight goes he*, 264. *she came stealing to the wayward boy*, 344. *the sheep are gone to fold, birds to their nest*, 532. *fall to the earth*, 546. *driven to doubt*, 692. *the path ... leadeth on to danger*, 788. *love to heaven is fled*, 793. *she hasteth to a myrtle grove*, 865. *she coasteth to the cry*, 870. *clapping their tails to the ground,*

923. *holding their course to Paphos*, 1193. *they all posted to Rome*, Lucr. Arg. 8. *departed to the camp*, 13. *to cabin!* Tp. I, 1, 18. *off to sea again*, 53. *the teen I have turned you to*, I, 2, 64. *brought to this shore*, 180. *I shall no more to sea*, II, 2, 44. *to Milan let me hear from thee*, Gent. I, 1, 57 (later Ff *at*). *must I go to him?* III, 1, 386. *welcome to Milan*, II, 5, 1 (cf. *Welcome*). *come to me soon at night*, Wiv. II, 2, 295. *bring me to the sight of Isabella*. Meas. I, 4, 18. *I shall beat you to your tent*, II, 1, 262. *go you to Angelo*, III, 1, 253. *first go with me to church*, ... *and then away to Venice to your friend*, Merch. III, 2, 305. 306. *I part with him to one that I would have* ...., II, 5, 50. *take her to thee*, As III, 5, 63. *to him will I*, V, 4, 190. *take it to you*, Shr. IV, 1, 168. *bid him repair to us to Ely House*, R2 II, 1, 216. *I see thy glory fall to the base earth*, II, 4, 20. *to shoot me to the heart*, H6A I, 4, 56. *stoop to the block*, H6B IV, 1, 125. *a cockatrice hast thou hatched to the world*, R3 IV, 1, 55. *came to the bar*, H8 II, 1, 12. *when the planets to disorder wander*, Troil. I, 3, 95. *to him!* Cor. I, 5, 10. *go you to the senators*, Tim. II, 2, 205. *take it to heart*, Hml. I, 2, 101. *hell itself breathes out contagion to this world*, III, 2, 408. *to hell, allegiance! vows, to the blackest devil!* IV, 5, 131. *I am cut to the brains*, Lr. IV, 6, 197. *sold to slavery*, Oth. I, 3, 138. *'tis easy to't*, Ant. III, 10, 32 (i. e. to go there). *shall uplift us to the view*, V, 2, 211. *he takes the babe to his protection*, Cymb. I, 1, 41. *she'll home to her father*, III, 2, 77. *if you'll back to the court*, III, 4, 133.

2) Denoting motion towards a work to be done or a question to be treated: *Adonis hied him to the chase*, Ven. 3. *I'll bring thee to the present business*, Tp. I, 2, 136. *to thy strong bidding task Ariel*, 192 (cf. *task*). *I'll to my book*, III, 1, 94. *to prayers!* I, 1, 54. *only to the plain form of marriage*, Ado IV, 1, 1. *but to the place where*, LLL I, 1, 247. *so to your pleasures!* As V, 4, 198. *now to your younger daughter*, Shr. II, 334. *once more to this Captain Dumain*, All's IV, 3, 276. *but to your protestation*, Wint. IV, 4, 379. *to work!* John II, 37. *now to our French causes*, H5 II, 2, 60. *now, sir, to you*, H6A III, 4, 28. *then to breakfast*, H8 III, 2, 202. *but to the sport abroad*, Troil. I, 1, 118. *to our sport!* Tit. II, 2, 19. *to our work alive*, Caes. IV, 3, 196. *beware of entrance to a quarrel*, Hml. I, 3, 66. *now to you*, Lr. III, 1, 34 etc. etc. Often *to it* = to work: *fall to't*, Tp. I, 1, 3. *they will to't then*, Meas. II, 1, 246; in an obscene sense; cf. IV, 3, 161 and Lr. IV, 6, 119 (cf. besides *Go*). *to't they go like lightning*, Rom. III, 1, 177. *we shall to't presently* (i. e. to dinner) Tim. III, 6, 38. *we'll e'en to't like French falconers*, Hml. II, 2, 449. *to it*, absolutely and imperatively: Gent. II, 7, 89. IV, 2, 25. Shr. I, 2, 195. All's III, 6, 67. Tw. III, 4, 340. H4A I, 3, 257. II, 4, 275. V, 4, 75. H6C II, 1, 165. V, 4, 72. Tit. IV, 3, 58. Lr. IV, 6, 119. Hml. V, 1, 56. Oth. III, 1, 17 etc. Similarly with designations of persons: *as he fell to her, so fell she to him*, Pilgr. 146 (as he assailed her, took hold of her). *to her, boy*, Wiv. I, 3, 61 (assail her, make at her). *to her, coz*, III, 4, 36. Meas. II, 2, 43. 47. 124. Merch. II, 2, 119. Shr. V, 2, 33. Tw. IV, 2, 20. Troil. III, 3, 274. Ant. III, 11, 25 etc.

3) Denoting a point or limit reached in space, time, or degree, = as far as; till; no less than; not even excepted: *the turtle's loyal breast to eternity doth rest*, Phoen. 58. *the sea mounting to the welkin's cheek*, Tp.

I, 2, 4. *performed to point the tempest*, I, 2, 194; cf. *to every article*, 195; *to the syllable*, 500; *even to the utmost syllable of your worthiness*, All's III, 6, 74; *to a hair*, Troil. III, 1, 157. *struck to the quick*, Tp. V, 25. *punish them to your height of pleasure*, Meas. V, 240. *Time ... to the world's end will have bald followers*, Err. II, 2, 108. *from the hour of my nativity to this in stant*, IV, 4, 31. *she would infect to the north star*, Ado II, 1, 258. *command me any service to the world's end*, 272. *being two hours to day*, Merch. V, 303. *I'll pull off all my raiment, to my petticoat*, Shr. II, 5. *from below your duke to beneath your constable*, All's II, 2, 32. *to the possibility of thy soldiership, I will subscribe for thee*, III, 6, 88. *'tis long to night*, Tw. III, 3, 21. *incensed againt you, even to a mortal arbitrement*, III, 4, 286. *to be her advocate to the loudest*, Wint. II, 2, 39. *since the birth of Cain ... to him that did but yesterday suspire*, John III, 4, 80. *like the watchful minutes to the hour*, IV, 1, 46 (cf. *hour*). *to the furthest verge*, R2 I, 1, 93. *as low as to thy heart*, 124. *pierced to the soul* 171. *up to the ears in blood*, H4A IV, 1, 117. *what may the king's whole battle reach unto? To thirty thousand*, 130. *we ready are to try our fortunes to the last man*, H4B IV, 2, 44. *Mars his true moving ... to this day is not known*, H6A I, 2, 2. *all I have, to the last penny*, H8 III, 2, 453. *I was a chaste wife to my grave*, IV, 2, 170. *they came to the broomstaff to me*, V, 4, 57. *knows the youth even to his inches*, Troil. IV, 5, 111. *applaud it to the clouds*, Hml. IV, 5, 107. *invades us to the skin*, Lr. III, 4, 7. *he cried almost to roaring*, Ant. III, 2, 55. *round even to faultiness*, III, 3, 33. *divide our equalness to this*, V, 1, 48. *how far it is to this same blessed Milford*, Cymb. III, 2, 61. *skipped from sixteen years of age to sixty*, IV, 2, 199. *her stature to an inch*, Per. V, 1, 110. *credit thy relation to points that seem impossible*, 125 etc. etc.

Hence signifying a result or effect produced; f. i.: *dashed to pieces*, Tp. I, 2, 8 (cf. *tear to pieces, cut to pieces* etc. sub *Piece*). *I shall laugh myself to death*, II, 2, 158. *bite him to death*, III, 2, 38. *attached with weariness to the dulling of my spirits*, III, 3, 6. *I will plague them even to roaring*, IV, 193. *dissolves to water*, Gent. III, 2, 8. *I shall have law in Ephesus, to your notorious shame*, Err. IV, 1, 84; Ado V, 1, 248; LLL V, 2, 358; Cor. IV, 5, 106. *if he love me to madness*, Merch. I, 2, 69. *to the world's pleasure*, All's II, 4, 37. *to the full arming of the verity*, IV, 3, 72. *I find it, and that to the infection of my brains*, Wint. I, 2, 145. *then shall this hand and seal witness against us to damnation*, John IV, 2, 218. *to our heart's great sorrow*, H6C I, 1, 128. *spread they shall be to thy foul disgrace*, 253. *and in devotion spend my latter days, to sin's rebuke and my Creator's praise*, IV, 6, 44. *what may befall him, to his harm and ours*, 95. *to our grief*, R3 III, 1, 98. *God hold it, to your honour's good content*, III, 2, 107. *they shall breed selves of themselves, to our recomforture*, IV, 4, 425. *to the mere undoing of all the kingdom*, H8 III, 2, 329. *God safely quit her of her burthen ... to the gladding of your highness*, V, 1, 71. *she shall be, to the happiness of England, an aged princess*, V, 5, 57. *of whom, even to the state's best health, I have deserved this hearing*, Tim. II, 2, 206. *this embalms and spices* (her) *to the April day again*, IV, 3, 41. *to all our lamentation*, Cor. IV, 6, 34. *worthy to be a rebel, for to that the multiplying villanies of nature do swarm upon him*, Mcb. I, 2, 10 (= to that effect). *to the amazement of mine eyes*, II, 4, 19. *the moist star ... was sick almost to doomsday with eclipse*, Hml. I, 1, 120. *did your letters pierce the queen to any demonstration of grief?* Lr. IV, 3, 11. *I am hurt to danger*, Oth. II, 3, 197. *to your so infinite loss*, Cymb. I, 1, 120. *make her go back, even to the yielding*, 1, 4, 115. *this will witness ... to the madding of her lord*, II, 2, 37. *love's counsellor should fill the bores of hearing to the smothering of the sense*, III, 2, 60. *that we have taken no care to your best courses*, Per. IV, 1, 39. cf. *to laugh to scorn; to chance, to turn,* and similar verbs.

4) Denoting direction, tendency and application: *her eyes petitioners to his eyes suing*, Ven. 356; *the suit I made to thee*, Tp. III, 2, 45; *that's my business to you*, III, 3, 69. *I am an humble suitor to your virtues*, Tim. III, 5, 7; *my business is to the king. What advocate hast thou to him?* Wint. IV, 4, 765; *tell me what you have to the king*, 824; *to give me your good report to the prince*, V, 2, 162; *do my service to his majesty*, H8 III, 1, 179; *I have business to my lord*, Troil. III, 1, 63. *my love to thee*, Ven. 442; Gent. II, 6, 28; III, 2, 48; *my hate to Marcius*, Cor. I, 10, 24; Tim. IV, 1, 40; *my good will is to it*, Tp. III, 1, 30; *his appetite is more to bread than stone*, Meas. I, 3, 53; *to feel my affection to your honour*, Lr. I, 2, 94; *my zeal to Valentine is cold*, Gent. II, 4, 203; *have respect to mine honour*, Caes. III, 2, 15; *let mild women to him lose their mildness*, Lucr. 979; *treachery used to Valentine*, Gent. II, 6, 32; *arms her with the boldness of a wife to her allowing husband*, Wint. I, 2, 185. *look well to her heart*, Ven. 580; *mine ears that to your wanton talk attended*, 809; *treason can but peep to what it would*, Hml. IV, 5, 124 (cf. the verbs *to hearken, to listen* etc.). *applying this to that*, Ven. 713; *if I had self-applied love to myself*, Compl. 77; *gold that's put to use*, Ven. 768; *and to him put the manage of my state*, Tp. I, 2, 69. *he puts transgression to't*, Meas. III, 2, 101. *to cry to the sea that roared to us*, Tp. I, 2, 149; *then to Silvia let us sing*, Gent. IV, 2, 49; *clamorous to the frighted fields*, H4A III, 1, 40; *to whom by oath he menaced revenge upon the cardinal*, H8 I, 2, 137; *few words to fair faith*, Troil. III, 2, 103 (cf. the verbs *to say, to speak, to talk, to write* etc.). *inclined to sleep*, Tp. I, 2, 185; *hath no stomach to this fight*, H5 IV, 3, 35; *he was disposed to mirth*, Ant. I, 2, 86; *to inure thyself to what thou art like to be*, Tw. II, 5, 160; *unused to the melting mood*, Oth. V, 2, 349. *you were kneeled to*, Tp. II, 1, 128; II, 2, 123; *your knees to them, not arms, must help*, Cor. I, 1, 76; *off goes his bonnet to an oyster-wench*, R2 I, 4, 31; *bow to any*, H6B IV, 1, 125; *bowed her to the people*, H8 IV, 1, 85; *bending to your state*, Oth. I, 3, 236. *doth mistake in her gifts to women*, As I, 2, 38; *by thy help to this distressed queen*, H6C III, 3, 213. *is't possible that my deserts to you can lack persuasion?* Tw. III, 4, 382; H6B I, 4, 50; Tit. I, 24. *command me any service to her thither*, LLL V, 2, 312; *be eloquent in my behalf to her*, R3 IV, 4, 357; *what wouldst thou have to Athens?* Tim. IV, 3, 287 (cf. *I would to God*, sub *Will*); *if you'll employ me to him*, Ant. V, 2, 70. *no man hath any quarrel to me*, Tw. III, 4, 248; Ado I, 1, 244; Cor. IV, 5, 133; cf. *the king does whet his anger to him*, H8 III, 2, 92. *the phrase is to the matter*, Meas. V, 90; *speak to the business*, H8 V, 3, 1; *that's to't indeed*, Troil. III, 1, 32; *to prove upon thy heart whereto I speak, thou liest*, Lr. V, 3, 140. *no thought ... save those to God*, H5 I, 2, 303; *my integrity to heaven*, H8 III, 2, 454; *'tis a fault to*

heaven, Hml. I, 2, 101; *I hold my duty, as I hold my soul, both to my God and to my gracious king*, II, 2, 45; *the assault you have made to her chastity*, Cymb. I, 4, 175. *bending his sword to his master*, Lr. IV, 2, 75.

Hence denoting destination, aim, design and purpose (almost = for): *called him all to naught*, Ven. 993. *tutor both to good and bad*, Lucr. 995. *that to my use it might unused stay*, Sonn. 48, 3. *one midnight fated to the purpose*, Tp. I, 2, 129. *swear to that*, II, 2, 145. *destined to a drier death*, Gent. I, 1, 158. *pray her to a fault for which I chid her*, 1, 2, 52. *would not force the letter to my view*, 54. *lay their swords to pawn*, Wiv. III, 1, 113. *spirits are not finely touched but to fine issues*, Meas. I, 1, 37. *strip myself to death*, II, 4, 102. *prepare yourself to death*, III, 1, 169. *the beggary he was never born to*, III, 2, 100. *that you are thus bound to your answer*, Ado V, 1, 233. *let me go no farther to mine answer*, 236. *wherefore was I to this keen mockery born?* Mids. II, 2, 123. *I shall hardly spare a pound of flesh ... to my bloody creditor*, Merch. III, 3, 34. *to good wine they do use good bushes*, As Epil. 5. *I have a hundred milch-kine to the pail*, Shr. II, 359. *naturally born to fears*, John III, 1, 15. *arm you to the sudden time*, John V, 6, 26. *well sinewed to our defence*, V, 7, 88. *to this we swore our aid*, H4A V, 1, 46. *doth offer him ... with her to dowry some petty dukedoms*, H5 III, Chor. 30. *give signal to the fight*, H6C V, 4, 72. *he is franked up to fatting*, R3 I, 3, 314. *fashioned to much honour*, H8 IV, 2, 50. *follow to thine answer*, Cor. III, 1, 177. *to this your son is marked*, Tit. I, 125. *a pig prepared to the spit*, IV, 2, 146. *pawn me to this your honour*, Tim. I, 1, 147. *you have my voice to it*, III, 5, 1. *disbursed ten thousand dollars to our general use*, Mcb. I, 2, 62. *giving to you no further personal power to business with the king*, Hml. I, 2, 37. *a command to parley*, Hml. I, 3, 123. *I am native here and to the manner born*, I, 4, 15. *arm you to this speedy voyage*, III, 3, 24. *do but blow them to their trial*, V, 2, 202. *hath had three suits to his back*, Lr. III, 4, 141. *sounds a parley to provocation*, Oth. II, 3, 23 (Qq. *of*). *is it not an alarum to love?* 27. *a special purpose, which wrought to his desire*, V, 2, 323 etc. etc. (cf. *to boot* sub *Boot*).

Hence = in the quality of, as, for: *Tunis was never graced before with such a paragon to their queen*, Tp. II, 1, 75. *Destiny, that hath to instrument this lower world*, III, 3, 54. *therefore would I have thee to my tutor*, Gentl. III, 1, 84. *have a woman to your lord*, As V, 4, 140. *for my thoughts, you have them ill to friend*, All's V, 3, 182. Caes. III, 1, 143. Mcb. IV, 3, 10. Cymb. I, 4, 116. *I have a king here to my flatterer*, R2 IV, 308. *I had rather have my horse to my mistress*, H5 III, 7, 62. 67. *this fellow had a Volscian to his mother*, Cor. V, 3, 178. *has a fool to his servant*, Tim. II, 2, 103. *a yeoman that has a gentleman to his son*, Lr. III, 6, 14. *to have to wife:* As IV, 1, 130. Shr. II, 121. 282. *having an honest man to your husband*, Wiv. III, 3, 107. IV, 2, 137. *to take to wife:* Caes. II, 1, 293. Hml. I, 2, 14. Ant. II, 2, 130. *to crave to wife:* H6C III, 1, 31. cf. *thou shalt have more than two tens to a score*, Lr. I, 4, 140.

5) Denoting addition: *rain added to a river*, Ven. 71. 994. *foretel new storms to those already spent*, Lucr. 1589 (= besides). *if I had his* (shape) *...*, *and, to his shape, were heir to all this land*, John I, 144. *a greater gift! O that's the sword to it* (the dagger) R3 III, 1, 116. *the Greeks are strong and skilful to their*

*strength, fierce to their skill, and to their fierceness valiant,* Troil. I, 1, 7. *where he hath won a name to Caius Marcius,* Cor. II, 1, 181. *seek happy nights to happy days,* Rom. I, 3, 106. *those* (honours) *of old, and the late dignities heaped up to them,* Mcb. I, 6, 19. *and to that dauntless temper ... he hath a wisdom ...,* III, 1, 52. *to the felt absence now I feel a cause,* Oth. III, 4, 182. *to them the legions garrisoned in Gallia ... have crossed the sea,* Cymb. IV, 2, 333. Lr. IV, 1, 40?

6) Denoting junction: *rein his proud head to the saddle-bow,* Ven. 14. *tied to the tree,* 391. *face grows to face,* 540. *his grief may be compared well to one sore sick,* 702. 1172. *bound him to her breast,* 812. *his breath and beauty set gloss on the rose, smell to the violet,* 936. *put fear to valour, courage to the coward,* 1158. *kings might be espoused to more fame,* Lucr. 20. *do not marry me to yond fool,* Wiv. III, 4, 87. *thy thoughts I cleave to,* Tp. IV, 165. *my very lips might freeze to my teeth,* Shr. IV, 1, 7. *as if she would pin her to her heart,* Wint. V, 2, 84. *false blood to false blood joined,* John III, 1, 2. *have woe to woe, sorrow to sorrow joined,* R2 II, 2, 66. *grow to the ground,* V, 3, 106. *thy son's blood cleaving to my blade,* H6C I, 3, 50. *what lies heavy to't* (the heart) Cor. IV, 2, 48; cf. *this gentle and unforced accord of Hamlet sits smiling to my heart,* Hml. I, 2, 124. *to-night she's mewed up to her heaviness,* Rom. III, 4, 11 (= together with); cf. *confined, bound in to saucy doubts and fears,* Mcb. III, 4, 25. *hold thee to my heart,* I, 4, 32. *screwed to my memory,* Cymb. II, 2, 44. (an air) *with rich words to it,* II, 3, 20. *thou hast stuck to the bare fortune of that beggar Posthumus,* III, 5, 119. *this fierce abridgment hath to it circumstantial branches,* V, 5, 383 etc. etc.

Hence *to be to =* to belong to (cf. *Be*); *to stand to =* to side with, or to persist in (cf. *Stand*).

Nearly related is its use in comparisons, = in comparison of: *thou, to whom my jewels trifles are,* Sonn. 48, 5. *to the most of men this is a Caliban, and they to him are angels,* Tp. I, 2, 480. *who in this kind of fooling am nothing to you,* II, 1, 178. *there is no woe to his* (Love's) *correction, nor to his service no such joy on earth,* Gent. II, 4, 138. *all I can is nothing to her whose worth makes other worthies nothing,* 166. *any madness I ever beheld seemed but tameness to this his distemper,* Wiv. IV, 2, 28. *the weariest life ... is a paradise to what we fear of death,* Meas. III, 1, 132. *I to the world am like a drop of water,* Err. I, 2, 35. *he is then a giant to an ape, but then is an ape a doctor to such a man,* Ado V, 1, 205. LLL II, 63. As III, 2, 98. Shr. III, 2, 159. All's II, 3, 300. 309. III, 5, 62. Wint. IV, 1, 15. H4A III, 3, 130. H4B IV, 3, 56. H6A III, 2, 25. H6B III, 1, 64. IV, 10, 51. Troil. I, 2, 259. Cor. II, 1, 128. Tit. V, 1, 90. Rom. II, 4, 41. III, 5, 221. Mcb. III, 4, 64. Hml. I, 2, 140. I, 5, 52. III, 1, 52. Oth. III, 3, 81. Ant. III, 12, 8. Cymb. III, 2, 10. III, 3, 26.

Hence, in general, denoting opposition and contrast: *Saint Denis to Saint Cupid! what are they that charge their breath against us?* LLL V, 2, 87. *set'st oath to oath, thy tongue against thy tongue,* John III, 1, 264. *face to face, and frowning brow to brow,* R2 I, 1, 15. H8 V, 3, 47. *will I make good against thee, arm to arm,* R2 I, 1, 76. *one half-penny worth of bread to this intolerable deal of sack,* H4A II, 4, 592. *Harry to Harry shall, hot horse to horse, meet and ne'er part,* IV, 1, 122. *blue coats to tawny coats,* H6A I, 3, 47.

*set limb to limb, and thou art far the lesser,* H6B IV, 10, 50. *match to match I have encountered him,* V, 2, 10. *will you set your wit to a fool's?* Troil. II, 1, 94. *were half to half the world by the ears,* Cor. I, 1, 237. *if e'er again I meet him beard to beard,* I, 10, 11. *true sword to sword,* 15. III, 1, 13. *dares me to personal combat, Caesar to Antony,* Ant. IV, 1, 4. Numbers thus opposed: *we have ten proofs to one that blood hath the victory,* Ado II, 3, 171. *there's five to one; besides, they all are fresh,* H5 IV, 3, 4. H6A I, 2, 34. IV, 1, 21. H6C I, 2, 72. 75. I, 4, 60. Used in betting: *my hat to a half-penny, Pompey proves the best Worthy,* LLL V, 2, 563. *for heaven to earth, some of us never shall a second time do such a courtesy,* H4A V, 2, 100. *to win her, all the world to nothing,* R3 I, 2, 238. Rom. III, 5, 215. *my dukedom to a beggarly denier,* R3 I, 2, 252. *my horse to yours,* Cor. I, 4, 2. *it is lots to blanks,* V, 2, 10. *his cocks win the battle ... when it is all to naught,* Ant. II, 3, 37. *I pawn the moiety of my estate to your ring,* Cymb. I, 4, 119. *I will lay you ten thousand ducats to your ring,* 139. *I will wage against your gold, gold to it,* 144. *twenty to one then he is shipped already,* Gent. I, 1, 72. *'tis ten to one it maimed you,* Shr. V, 2, 62. Ado III, 3, 84. Tw. I, 3, 113. H4B I, 1, 182. H6A V, 4, 157. H6B II, 1, 4. H6C V, 1, 46. H8 Epil. 1.

Contrariety implied also in the phrases: *to one's eyes, to one's face, to one's teeth,* = in presence and defiance of: *her shall you hear disproved to her eyes,* Meas. V, 161. *even to the eyes of Richard gave him defiance,* H4B III, 1, 64. *to see your wives dishonoured to your noses,* Cor. IV, 6, 83. *that I shall live and tell him to his teeth 'Thus didest thou',* Hml. IV, 7, 57. *being spoke ... to your face,* Rom. IV, 1, 28. 34. *weepest thou for him to my face?* Oth. V, 2, 77.

7) Denoting measure and proportion: *task me to the word,* H4A IV, 1, 9. *construe the times to their necessities,* H4B IV, 1, 104. *made us pay one shilling to the pound,* H6B IV, 7, 25. *that to the pace of it I may spur on my journey,* Cor. I, 10, 32.

Hence = according to, in congruity or harmony with: *just to the time,* Sonn. 109, 7. *even to my wish,* Wiv. IV, 6, 12. *pinch him to your time,* V, 5, 96. *set all hearts to what tune pleased his ear,* Tp. I, 2, 85. *that I might sing it to a tune,* Gent. I, 2, 80. *fashion your demeanour to my looks,* Err. II, 2, 33. *what we have we prize not to the worth whiles we enjoy it,* Ado IV, 1, 220. *my lady, to the manner of the days, in courtesy gives undeserving praise,* LLL V, 2, 365. *love and simplicity in least speak most, to my capacity,* Mids. V, 105. *fortune now to my heart's hope!* Merch. II, 9, 20. *you to his love must accord,* As V, 4, 139. *according to the fashion and the time,* Shr. IV, 3, 95. *I did not bid you mar it to the time,* 97. *if it be aught to the old tune,* Tw. V, 111. *here's one to a very doleful tune,* Wint. IV, 4, 265. *I will prove so to my power,* V, 2, 182. *to my thinking* (= in my opinion) H4B V, 5, 114. *I never did her any, to my knowledge,* R3 I, 3, 309. *as loud, and to as many tunes,* H8 IV, 1, 73. *when I am hence, I'll answer to my lust,* Troil. IV, 4, 134. *to her own worth she shall be prized,* 135. *a soldier even to Cato's wish,* Cor. I, 4, 57. *that to his power he would have made them mules,* II, 1, 262 (as far as it lay in his power). *to my poor unworthy notice, he mocked us,* II, 3, 166. *remedied to your public laws,* Tim. V, 4, 62 (M. Edd. rendered to). *to my thinking,* Caes. I, 2, 240. *went it not so? To the selfsame tune and words,* Mcb. I, 3, 88. *he* delivers our offices ... to the direction just, III, 3, 4. to my mind (= in my opinion) Hml. I, 4, 14. to my judgement, Lr. I, 4, 62. they wear their faces to the bent of the king's looks, Cymb. I, 1, 13. welcomed and settled to his own desire, Per. IV Prol. 2. when he shall come and find our paragon to all reports thus blasted, IV, 1, 36 etc.

Similarly denoting correspondency and simultaneousness (cf. to-day, to-night): to jig off a tune at the tongue's end, canary to it with your feet, LLL III, 12. to dance our ringlets to the whistling wind, Mids. II, 1, 86 (cf. to cry to the sea that roared to us, Tp. I, 2, 149, i. e. to cry to the roaring of the sea, which roared to our cries). sung to the harp, V, 45. sung to her lute, H4A III, 1, 211. to his music plants and flowers ever sprung, H8 III, 1, 6. she dances to her lays, Per. V, Prol. 4. cf. if it be summer news, smile to't before, Cymb. III, 4, 13. he went to bed to her very description, Per. IV, 2, 109. Cor. IV, 5, 209.

8) Denoting relation, = concerning, as to (or more properly: on occasion of, on starting the question): to make you answer truly to your name, Ado IV, 1, 80 (i. e. concerning the appellation which you deserve); once more to this Captain Dumain: you have answered to his reputation with the duke and to his valour: what is his honesty? All's IV, 3, 277; where we may leisurely each one demand and answer to his part performed in this wide gap of time, Wint. V, 3, 153. what's this to my Lysander? where is he? Mids. III, 2, 62 (= what has this to do with etc.). he shall be none; we'll keep him here: then what is that to him? R2 V, 2, 100. where to his accusations he pleaded still not guilty, H8 II, 1, 12. Hector is not Troilus in some degrees. 'Tis just to each of them; he is himself, Troil. I, 2, 75. few words, but, to effect, more than all yet, Lr. III, 1, 52. though I am bound to every act of duty, I am not bound to that all slaves are free to, Oth. III, 3, 135 (concerning which all slaves are free. Ff all slaves are free, without to). what say you to = what do you think about: what sayst thou to this? R2 I, 1, 110. what shall be said to thee? Oth. V, 2, 293 (cf. Say). my love to your proceeding bids me tell you this, Caes. II, 2, 103 (on occasion of, concerning, your proceeding). guilty to, originally = guilty concerning sth., and then = guilty of, see sub Guilty.

9) Supplying, in an infinity of cases, the place of the dative of other languages; as dativus commodi et incommodi: stain to all nymphs, Ven. 9. to a pretty ear she tunes her tale, 74. things growing to themselves are growth's abuse, 166. what banquet wert thou to the taste, 445. wreck to the seaman, 454. thy beauty hath ensnared thee to this night, Lucr. 485. die to themselves, Sonn. 54, 11. I to all the world must die, 81, 6. the summer's flower is to the summer sweet, though to itself it only live and die, 94, 9. 10. Meas. I, 3, 28. LLL I, 1, 31. Cymb. III, 4, 133. fresh to myself, Compl. 76. drink to me, Tp. III, 2, 4 (cf. Drink); here's to my love, Rom. V, 3, 119. this will prove a brave kingdom to me, Tp. III, 2, 153. Meas. II, 1, 263. that's more to me than my wetting, Tp. IV, 211. what's that to you? Shr. II, 305. IV, 1, 72. John V, 2, 92. V, 6, 4. Lr. III, 4, 7. Oth. III, 3, 315. Ant. II, 2, 36. make me fear misfortune to my ventures, Merch. I, 1, 21. more (joy) than to us wait in your royal walks, Mids. V, 30. my heart is to her but as guest-wise sojourned, III, 2, 171. this is a dear manakin to you, Tw. III, 2, 57. the queen

is spotless in the eyes of heaven and to you, Wint. II, 1, 132. hath made us by-words to our enemies, H6C I, 1, 42. for his trial and fair purgation to the world, H8 V, 3, 152. your secrecy to the king and queen moult no feather, Hml. II, 2, 306. ere I could make a prologue to my brains, they had begun the play, V, 2, 30 etc. etc.

Denoting, after substantives, the state of being appertinent, = of: the bawd to lust's abuse, Ven. 792. true leaders to their queen, 503. thou lackey to eternity, Lucr. 967. my reason, the physician to my love, Sonn. 147, 5. being an enemy to me inveterate, Tp. I, 2, 122. rich scarf to my proud earth, IV, 82. the best comforter to an unsettled fancy, V, 59. she is daughter to this duke, V, 192. to be my fellow-servant to your ladyship, Gent. II, 4, 105. slaves they are to me, III, 1, 141. the fair sister to her unhappy brother Claudio, Meas. I, 4, 20. I am confessor to Angelo, III, 1, 168. melancholy, kinsman to despair, Err. V, 80. foes to life, 82. being a professed tyrant to their sex, Ado I, 1, 170. reason becomes the marshal to my will, Mids. II, 2, 120. though I am daughter to his blood, I am not to his manners, Merch. II, 3, 18. she is issue to a faithless Jew, II, 4, 38. son to some man else, As I, 2, 236. I am shepherd to another man, II, 4, 78. he was a brother to your daughter, V, 4, 29. they are bastards to the English, All's II, 3, 100. and be the supporter to a bench, Tw. I, 5, 158. this child was prisoner to the womb, Wint. II, 2, 59 (never of after prisoner). heir to all this land, John I, 144. the honourable father to my foe, R2 I, 1, 136. third son to the third Edward, H6A II, 4, 84. the third son to king Edward, II, 5, 76. a prophet to the fall of all our foes, III, 2, 32. as procurator to your excellence, H6B I, 1, 3. foe to the public weal, Cor. III, 1, 176. 191. the grandchild to her blood, V, 3, 24. the cock that is the trumpet to the morn, Hml. I, 1, 150. my news shall be the fruit to that great feast, II, 2, 52. we still retain the name and all the additions to a king, Lr. I, 1, 138. I cannot speak any beginning to this peevish odds, Oth. II, 3, 185 etc. etc.

Indicating, after adjectives, the person or thing, with respect to which, or in whose interest, a quality is shown or perceived (whereas, in general, of serves to designate the object or material, in or by which the quality shows itself; f. i. she is too liberal of her tongue, Gent. III, 1, 355, = she spends her tongue too liberally; you are liberal of your loves, H8 II, 1, 126; but liberal to mine own children in good bringing up, Shr. I, 1, 98; free of speech, Oth. III, 3, 185; but free and bounteous to her mind, I, 3, 266): servile to my coy disdain, Ven. 112. to thine own face affected, 157. subject to the tyranny of mischances, 737. contrary to the Roman laws, Lucr. Arg. 2. correspondent to command, Tp. I, 2, 297. invisible to every eye-ball, 303. my father's loss, the wreck of all my friends ... are but light to me, 489. I will be thankful to any happy messenger, Gent. II, 4, 53. constant to myself, II, 6, 31 etc. etc. cf. accessary, advantageous, apparent, appertinent, attributive, auspicious etc. etc.

The same difference between the accusative and dative after verbs (the near and distant objects of grammarians): mud not the fountain that gave drink to thee, Lucr. 577. left me to a bootless inquisition, Tp. I, 2, 35. subject his coronet to his crown, 114. give a name to every fixed star, LLL I, 1, 89 etc. etc. To omitted: when dreams do show thee me, Sonn. 43, 14 (= thee to me). I'll yield him thee asleep, Tp. III, 2, 68. did *bring them me*, Err. V, 385. *as God did give her me*, Ado IV, 1, 27. *seek to spill the poor deer's blood, that my heart means no ill*, LLL IV, 1, 35. *whose unwished yoke my soul consents not to give sovereignty*, Mids. I, 1, 81. *wilt thou give him me?* III, 2, 63. *happier the man, whom favourable stars allot thee for his lovely bedfellow*, Shr. IV, 5, 40. *those that vulgars give boldest titles*, Wint. II, 1, 94. *he was a fool that taught them* (manners) *me*, H4B II, 1, 205. *you will give them me*, H6B III, 1, 345. *I may ere night yield both my life and them to some man else, as this dead man doth me*, H6C II, 5, 60. *the law I bear no malice for my death*, H8 II, 1, 62. *a stirring dwarf we do allowance give before a sleeping giant*, Troil. II, 3, 146. *now play him me*, I, 3, 170. *you'll give him me*, III, 2, 113. *I give him you*, Tit. I, 102. *he hath left them you*, Caes. III, 2, 254. *the man that gave them thee*, Cymb. IV, 2, 85. cf. *Apply*. Of its omission, when the dative is placed before the accusative, every page offers instances.

Placed after the noun: *what to?* Rom. III, 1, 15. *my father did something smack, something grow to*, Merch. II, 2, 18. As for Wint. I, 2, 437: *your followers I will whisper to the business*, cf. *Whisper*.

**To**, the infinitival particle, used in general as at present. The infinitive having the force of the subject of the sentence, f. i. *to get it is thy duty*, Ven. 168. *to die and go we know not where, ... 'tis too horrible*, Meas. III, 1, 118. of the predicate: *to speak on the part of virginity is to accuse your mothers*, All's I, 1, 148. of the object: *'gins to woo him*, Ven. 6. *learned to sport*, 105 etc. etc. of the preposition *of* (or a genitive): *despair to gain*, Lucr. 131. *take the pains to go with us*, Err. V, 394. *your power to draw*, Mids. II, 1, 197. *the art to love*, Shr. IV, 2, 8. *this is no month to bleed*, R2 I, 1, 157. *I'll give thee scope to beat*, III, 3, 140. *easy ways to die*, Ant. V, 2, 359. *some falls are means the happier to arise*, Cymb. IV, 2, 403 etc. of the prepos. *for* or *to: earth's sovereign salve to do a goddess good*, Ven. 28. *unapt to toy*, 34. *to bid the wind a base he now prepares*, 303. *bound to stay*, Sonn. 58, 4 etc. etc. preceded by *so* or *such* (= as to): Tp. II, 1, 168. H4A I, 2, 240 etc.; cf. Cymb. IV, 2, 200. = in order to: Ven. 227. 238. 281. Tp. I, 2, 107 etc. etc. Serving, in short, as at present, to give a special determination to any general notions, negative as well as positive. To treat this matter thoroughly, would almost be as much as to write an English grammar; therefore, referring the reader to the several words, which are followed by an infinitive with *to*, we confine ourselves to such cases as have found no place in other articles.

1) Referring not to single words, to individualize a general notion, but to the whole sentence, and denoting the particular circumstance under which the matter takes, or is to take, place; a) equivalent to a gerund preceded by *in* or *by: poor queen of love, in thine own law forlorn, to love a cheek that smiles at thee in scorn*, Ven. 252. *what dost thou mean to stifle beauty and to steal his breath*, 934. *thou art well appaid as well to hear as grant what he has said*, Lucr. 915. *poor hand, why quiverest thou at this decree? honour thyself to rid me of this shame*, 1031. *shake hands to torture me, the one by toil, the other to complain how far I toil*, Sonn. 28, 7. *mine own true love that doth my rest defeat, to play the watchman ever for thy sake*, 61, 12. *I have*

*broke your hest to say so*, Tp. III, 1, 37. *what do you mean to dote thus on such luggage?* IV, 231. *to think upon her woes, I have wept a hundred several times*, Gent. IV, 4, 149. *I weep myself to think upon thy words*, 180. *I'll make you amends next, to give you nothing for something*, Err. II, 2, 54. *may he not do it by fine and recovery? Yes, to pay a fine for a periwig and recover the lost hair of another man*, 76. *you wrong me much to say so*, IV, 1, 66. *certain stars shot madly from their spheres, to hear the sea-maid's music*, Mids. II, 1, 154. *I'll follow thee and make a heaven of hell, to die upon the hand I love so well*, 244. *you would not use a gentle lady so, to vow and swear and superpraise my parts*, III, 2, 153. *thou but offendest thy lungs to speak so loud*, Merch. IV, 1, 140. *I will not shame myself to give you this*, 431. *lie not, to say mine eyes are murderers*, As III, 5, 19. *thou strikest me sorely to say I did*, Wint. V, 1, 18. *thou art not holy to belie me so*, John III, 4, 44. *I was too strict to make mine own away*, R2 I, 3, 244. *I shall grieve you to report the rest*, II, 2, 95. *no worse can come to fight*, III, 2, 183. *thou canst make no excuse current, but to hang thyself*, R3 I, 2, 84. *my hair doth stand on end to hear her curses*, I, 3, 304. *what meanest thou to curse thus?* Troil. V, 1, 30. *yet to bite his lip and hum at good Cominius, much unhearts me*, Cor. V, 1, 48 (= that he bites, or his biting). *to answer that, I should confess to you*, Rom. IV, 1, 23. *what mean these masterless and gory swords to lie discoloured by this place of peace?* V, 3, 143. *never mind was to be so unwise, to be so kind*, Tim. II, 2, 6. *to fright you thus, methinks, I am too savage*, Mcb. IV, 2, 70. *to know my deed, 'twere best not know myself*, II, 2, 73. *what mean you, sir, to give them this discomfort?* Ant. IV, 2, 34. *I the truer, so to be false with her*, Cymb. I, 5, 44. *the wandering wind blows dust in others' eyes to spread itself*, Per. I, 1, 97. Peculiar passage: *and suffer the condition of these times to lay a heavy and unequal hand upon our honours*, H4B IV, 1, 102 (i. e. to suffer from these times laying etc.).

b) equivalent to a conditional clause: *to clear this spot by death, at least I give a badge of fame to slander's livery*, Lucr. 1053. *to die, I leave my love alone*, Sonn. 66, 14. *I should sin to think but nobly of my grandmother*, Tp. I, 2, 119. *a Jew would have wept to have seen our parting*, Gent. II, 3, 13. *to leave my Julia, shall I be forsworn; to love fair Silvia, shall I be forsworn; to wrong my friend, I shall be much forsworn*, II, 6, 1. *I fly not death, to fly this deadly doom*, III, 1, 185. *mine were the very cipher of a function, to fine the faults ... and let go by the actor*, Meas. II, 2, 40. *I may make my case as Claudio's, to cross this in the smallest*, IV, 2, 178. *I should wrong it* (your desert), *to lock it in the wards of covert bosom*, V, 10. *I should be guiltier than my guiltiness, to think I can be undiscernible*, 373. *to be ruled by my conscience, I should stay with the Jew*, Merch. II, 2, 23. *you might have saved me my pains to have taken it away yourself*, Tw. II, 2, 6. *you scarce can right me throughly then to say you did mistake*, Wint. II, 1, 99. *I know not what I shall incur to pass it*, II, 2, 57. *would you not suppose your bondage happy, to be made a queen?* H6A V, 3, 111. *Nero will be tainted with remorse, to hear and see her plaints*, H6C III, 1, 41. *you shall have better cheer ... and thanks to stay and eat it*, Cymb. III, 6, 68. *thou'lt torture me to leave unspoken that which, to be spoke, would torture thee*, V, 5, 139. The infinitive not referring to the subject of the principal sentence: *my laments would be drawn out too long, to tell them all with one poor tired tongue,* Lucr. 1617. *your falsehood shall become you well to worship shadows,* Gent. IV, 2, 131. *I'll give you a pottle of burnt sack to give me recourse to him,* Wiv. II, 1, 223. *so to study, three years is but short,* LLL I, 1, 181. *ill to example ill, would from my forehead wipe a perjured note,* IV, 3, 124. *to crush this a little, it would bow to me,* Tw. II, 5, 152. *so that, conclusions to be as kisses, if your four negatives make your two affirmatives, why then, the worse for my friends,* V, 23. *to do this deed, promotion follows,* Wint. I, 2, 356. *to keep them here, they would but stink,* H6A IV, 7, 89. *thus to have said, ... had touched his spirit,* Cor. II, 3, 198. *to pay five ducats, I would not farm it,* Hml. IV, 4, 20. *to seek through the regions of the earth for one his like, there would be something failing in him that should compare,* Cymb. I, 1, 20. *disguise that which, to appear, itself must not yet be,* Cymb. III, 4, 148 (O. and M. Edd. *that which to appear itself, must* etc.). The subject of the infinitive preceded by *for* (cf. *For*): Cor. II, 2, 13. 34. II, 3, 10. Hml. III, 2, 317. Per. I, 1, 93.

c) equivalent to a causal clause: *who* (the pillow) *therefore angry, seems to part in sunder, swelling on either side to want his bliss,* Lucr. 389. *the beast that bears me, tired with my woe, plods dully on, to bear that weight in me,* Sonn. 50, 6. *who can blame me to piss my tallow?* Wiv. V, 5, 16. *his tongue, all impatient to speak and not see,* LLL II, 238. *nor do I now make moan to be abridged from such a noble rate,* Merch. I, 1, 126. *why blame you me to love you?* As V, 2, 109. *I cannot blame thee now to weep,* Shr. III, 2, 27. *he is grown too proud to be so valiant,* Cor. I, 1, 263. *who then shall blame his pestered senses to recoil,* Mcb. V, 2, 23. Caes. IV, 3, 10.

2) Employed, conformably to common usage, to denote a) destination; f. i. *Adonis had his team to guide,* Ven. 179. *we all were ... by that destiny to perform an act,* Tp. II, 1, 252. *his forward voice now is to speak well of his friend,* II, 2, 94. *a very virtuous maid, and to be shortly of a sisterhood,* Meas. II, 2, 21. b) futurity, f. i.: *tongues to be,* Sonn. 81, 11. *ages yet to be,* 101, 12. *what is to come,* Tp. II, 1, 253. *I am to break with thee of some affair,* Gent. III, 1, 59. *and so in progress to be hatched and born,* Meas. II, 2, 97. *I am to discourse wonders,* Mids. IV, 2, 29. *whereof it is born, I am to learn,* Merch. I, 1, 5; cf. *are you yet to learn what late misfortune is befallen King Edward?* H6C IV, 4, 2. *yet is the hour to come that e'er I proved thee false,* H6B III, 1, 204. c) possibility, f. i. *he's not to be found,* Meas. I, 2, 180. LLL I, 2, 118. *she is a woman, therefore to be won,* H6A V, 3, 79. *that's not suddenly to be performed,* H6B II, 2, 67. d) obligation or necessity; f. i.: *thou art to post after,* Gent. II, 3, 37. *she is not to be kissed fasting,* III, 1, 326. *now am I ... to plead for that which I would not obtain,* IV, 4, 105. *you are not to go loose any longer,* Wiv. IV, 2, 128. *thou art to continue now,* Meas. II, 1, 200. *then have you lost a sight, which was to be seen, cannot be spoken of,* Wint. V, 2, 47. *why a king of years should be to be protected,* H6B II, 3, 29. *thou art to die,* Oth. V, 2, 56. adjectively: *such to be pitied and o'erwrested seeming,* Troil. I, 3, 157.

Used also, in a peculiar manner, e) to denote quality and capacity: *not gross to sink,* Ven. 150. *not an eye that sees you but is a physician to comment on*

*your malady,* Gent. II, 1, 42. *that which seems the wound to kill,* Troil. III, 1, 132 (= deadly wound). *wert thou an oracle to tell me so,* IV, 5, 252. cf. *he could not see to garter his hose,* Gent. II, 1, 82 (could not see so as to be able to garter etc.). *the approbation of those ... are wonderfully to extend him,* Cymb. I, 4, 21. Cor. II, 3, 182. III, 1, 81. f) periphrastically, after *to be: I am to entreat you, to con them,* Mids. I, 2, 101. *he hath been all this day to look you,* As II, 5, 34 (= looking for you). *I have been to seek you,* Oth. V, 1, 81. *never mind was to be so unwise, to be so kind,* Tim. II, 2, 6. *where there is advantage to be given, both more and less have given him the revolt,* Mcb. V, 4, 11. *courtesies, which I will be ever to pay and yet pay still,* Cymb. I, 4, 39. cf. *Come.*

3) The active inf. instead of the passive· *savage, extreme, rude, cruel, not to trust,* Sonn. 129, 4. *such a storm as oft 'twixt May and April is to see,* Compl. 102. *that most deeply to consider is the beauty of his daughter,* Tp. III, 2, 106. *too hard to keep,* LLL I, 1, 47. *what's to do?* Tw. III, 3, 18. *were I to get again,* John I, 259. *O that it were to do,* H6B III, 2, 3. *the lustre of the better yet to show shall show the better,* Troil. I, 3, 361. *why was my Cressid then so hard to win?* III, 2, 124. *what's to do?* Caes. II, 1, 326. *little is to do,* Mcb. V, 7, 28. V, 8, 64. *this thing's to do,* Hml. IV, 4, 44. *'tis yet to know,* Oth. I, 2, 19. *that's the next to do,* Ant. II, 6, 60.

4) The accus. with the inf. common to a far greater extent than even in Latin; f. i. *think women still to strive with men,* Pilgr. 341. *thou shalt find those children nursed ... to take a new acquaintance of thy mind,* Sonn. 77, 12. *when I saw myself to win,* 119, 4. *whom I believe to be most strait in virtue,* Meas. II, 1, 9. *shall we thus permit a blasting and a scandalous breath to fall on him so near us?* V, 122. *who heard me to deny it or forswear it?* Err. V, 25. *will never grant this forfeiture to hold,* Merch. III, 3, 25. *this to be true, I do engage my life,* As V, 4, 171. *I feel this youth's perfections ... to creep in at mine eyes,* Tw. I, 5, 317. *I had rather hear you to solicit that,* III, 1, 120. *I have deserved all tongues to talk their bitterest,* Wint. III, 2, 217. *we profess ourselves to be the slaves of chance,* IV, 4, 551. *which to prove fruit, hope gives not so much warrant,* H4B I, 3, 39. *myself have heard a voice to call him so,* H6B II, 1, 94. *would ye not think his cunning to be great,* 132. *they would not have you to stir forth to-day,* Caes. II, 2, 38. *and the remainder, that shall still depend, to be such men as may besort your age,* Lr. I, 4, 272.

But quite idiomatically, also a nominative and inf. joined: *it is the lesser blot, modesty finds, women to change their shapes than men their minds,* Gent. V, 4, 109. *a heavier task could not have been imposed than I to speak my griefs unspeakable,* Err. I, 1, 33. *what he is indeed, more suits you to conceive than I to speak of,* As I, 2, 279. *thou this to hazard needs must intimate skill infinite or monstrous desperate,* All's II, 1, 186. *which that it shall, is all as monstrous ... as my Antigonus to break his grave,* Wint. V, 1, 42. *to beg of thee, it is my more dishonour than thou of them,* Cor. III, 2, 124. cf. 83. *I to bear this ... is some burden,* Tim. IV, 3, 266. *nature so preposterously to err, ... sans witchcraft could not,* Oth. I, 3, 62. *which he to seek of me again perforce, behoves me keep at utterance,* Cymb. III, 1, 72.

5) Elliptical expressions: *I know not where to hide my head*, Tp. II, 2, 23 (= where I am to hide). *I know not what to say*, Mids. III, 2, 344. R2 II, 2, 100. *the king knows at what time to promise, when to pay*, H4A IV, 3, 53 etc. *and he to die for it!* Meas. II, 2, 6. *and I to sigh for her!* LLL III, 202. *O hateful hands, to tear such loving words! injurious wasps, to feed on such sweet honey*, Gent. I, 2, 105. *my own flesh and blood to rebel!* Merch. III, 1, 37. *I, that killed her husband, to take her in her heart's extremest hate*, R3 I, 2, 231. *if my shirt were bloody, then to shift it*, Cymb. I, 2, 6 (cf. the German inf. as imper.). *now, the gods to bless your honour!* Per. IV, 6, 23 (i. e. now for the gods and their power, to bestow blessings on you; the bawd's speech. M. Edd. *to-bless*).

6) Repeated before a second infinitive: *I am fain to shuffle, to hedge, and to lurch*, Wiv. II, 2, 25. *he teaches him to hick and to hack*, IV, 1, 68. *to scorch your face and to disfigure you*, Err. V, 183. *I come by note, to give and to receive*, Merch. III, 2, 141. *it is as easy to count atomies as to resolve the propositions of a lover*, As III, 2, 245. *to leave the Talbot and to follow us*, H6A III, 3, 20. *to see Caesar and to rejoice in his triumph*, Caes. I, 1, 35 etc. Partially repeated: *learned to sport and dance, to toy, to wanton, dally, smile and jest*, Ven. 105. *I have no one to blush with me, to cross their arms and hang their heads with mine, to mask their brows and hide their infamy*, Lucr. 792 etc.

Omitted in the second and following places: *neither eyes nor ears, to hear nor see*, Ven. 437. *as well to hear as grant*, Lucr. 915. *to live or die*, 1154. *to stand in thy affairs, fall by thy side*, Sonn. 151, 12. *to stead up your appointment, go in your place*, Meas. III, 1, 261. *grace to stand, and virtue go*, III, 2, 278. *I am come to advise you, comfort you and pray with you*, IV, 3, 55. *unfit to live or die*, 68. *to go with us into the abbey here and hear at large discoursed all our fortunes*, Err. V, 395. *to disgrace Hero ... and not marry her*, Ado IV, 2, 57. *not to see ladies, study, fast, not sleep*, LLL I, 1, 48. *to speak and not see*, II, 238. *to jig off a tune, ... canary to it* etc. III, 12. *to lean upon my shoulder and dally with my excrement*, V, 1, 109. *to excuse or hide the liberal opposition*, V, 2, 742. *to pity and be pitied*, As II, 7, 117. *to chat as well as eat*, Shr. V, 2, 11. *as good to die and go, as die and stay*, John IV, 3, 8. *to insinuate, flatter, bow, and bend my limbs*, R2 IV, 165. *to wake a wolf is as bad as smell a fox*, H4B I, 2, 175 (Ff to smell). *to quell the Dauphin or bring him in obedience*, H6A I, 1, 164. *to crown himself king and suppress the prince*, I, 3, 68. *not to wear, handle, or use any sword*, 78. *the sooner to effect and surer bind this knot*, V, 1, 15 etc.

7) Placed before the second infinitive, though omitted, conformably to grammar, before the first: *I should control your times of pleasure, or at your hand the account of hours to crave*, Sonn. 58, 3. *to make him much outlive a gilded tomb, and to be praised of ages yet to be*, 101, 12. *would no more endure this wooden slavery than to suffer the flesh-fly blow my mouth*, Tp. III, 1, 62. *heaven would that she these gifts should have, and I to live and die her slave*, As III, 2, 162. *that you'll marry me, or else refusing me, to wed this shepherd*, V, 4, 22. *dares better be damned than to do't*, All's III, 6, 96. *bade me come smiling, to put on yellow stockings*, Tw. V, 346. *hadst thou rather be a Falconbridge and like thy brother to enjoy thy land*, John I, 135. *didst let thy heart consent, and consequently thy rude hand to act the deed*, IV, 2, 240. *make you take the hatch, to dive like buckets*, etc. V, 2, 139. *bids you ... deliver up the crown and to take mercy on the poor souls*, H5 II, 4, 103. *I desire you do me right and justice, and to bestow your pity on me*, H8 II, 4, 14. *who would be so mocked with glory, or to live but in a dream of friendship?* Tim. IV, 2, 33. *Brutus had rather be a villager than to repute himself a son of Rome*, Caes. I, 2, 173 (cf. Rom. IV, 1, 77). *I had rather coin my heart ... than to wring ...*, IV, 3, 73. *make thy two eyes start from their spheres, thy knotted and combined locks to part*, Hml. I, 5, 18. *how we may steal from hence, and for the gap ... to excuse*, Cymb. III, 2, 66. *makes both my body pine and soul to languish*, Per. I, 2, 31. *she'll wed the stranger knight, or never more to view nor day nor light*, II, 5, 17. Cor. II, 1, 256.

Passages unnecessarily emended by M. Edd.: *then let them all encircle him about and fairy-like to pinch the unclean knight*, Wiv. IV, 4, 57 (M. Edd. *to-pinch*). *let it be rather thought you affect a sorrow than to have*, All's I, 1, 60 (M. Edd. *than have it*). *where these two Christian armies might combine the blood of malice in a vein of league, and not to spend it so unneighbourly*, John V, 2, 39 (M. Edd. *to-spend*). *you must either be directed by some that take upon them to know, or to take upon yourself that which I am sure you do not know*, Cymb. V, 4, 187 (M. Edd. *or do take*; some *or take*).

8) Great differences from modern usage in inserting or omitting it after certain verbs: *they would not have you to stir forth*, Caes. II, 2, 38. *I durst to wager she is honest*, Oth. IV, 2, 12. *still losing when I saw myself to win*, Sonn. 119, 4. 64, 10. LLL IV, 3, 168. *thou shalt find those children ... to take a new acquaintance of thy mind*, Sonn. 77, 12. *who heard me to deny it?* Err. V, 25. Tw. III, 1, 120. H6B II, 1, 94. *I feel this youth's perfections ... to creep in at mine eyes*, Tw. I, 5, 317. cf. besides the verbs *to bid, dare, make, need* etc.

On the other hand: *how long within this wood intend you stay?* Mids. II, 1, 138. *your betters have endured me say my mind*, Shr. IV, 3, 75; cf. *suffer* in Tp. III, 1, 62. *will you be so good as eat it?* H5 V, 1, 31. *to pray Achilles see us at our tent*, Troil. V, 9, 8. *you were wont be civil*, Oth. II, 3, 190 (Ff to be). cf. the verbs *to behove, beteem, cause, chance, charge, come, command, constrain, desire, enforce, entreat, forbid, 'gin, go, help, know, list, have need, ought, perceive, persuade, please, pray, teach, vouchsafe, will, wish* etc.

9) *For to*, = *to*, see sub *For* conj. 4, and add to the passages quoted there: *though bride and bridegroom wants for to supply the places at the table*, Shr. III, 2, 249.

**Toad**, a paddock, Bufo; emblem of loathsomeness: Tp. I, 2, 340. Wint. IV, 4, 268. R3 IV, 4, 81. 145. Troil. II, 3, 170. V, 1, 67. Tit. IV, 2, 68. Rom. II, 4, 215. Tim. IV, 3, 181. 375. Lr. III, 4, 135. Oth. III, 3, 270. IV, 2, 61. Cymb. IV, 2, 90. Thought to be venomous: Lucr. 850. As II, 1, 13. R2 III, 2, 15. H6C II, 2, 138. R3 I, 2, 19. 148. I, 3, 246. Tit. II, 3, 101. Mcb. IV, 1, 6. Having a precious stone in its head: As II, 1, 13. Changing eyes with the lark: Rom. III, 5, 31.

**Toad-spotted**, tainted and polluted with venom like the toad: *from the extremest upward of thy head to the descent and dust below thy foot a most t. traitor*, Lr. V, 3, 138 (with a play on the word: spotted like Bufo variabilis).

**Toadstool**, a poisonous mushroom, Agaricus; Thersites called so by Ajax: Troil. II, 1, 22.

**To-and-fro-conflicting**, writing of M. Edd. in Lr. III, 1, 11; not hyphened in O. Edd.; see *Fro* and *To*.

**Toast**, subst. dried and scorched bread, dipped in melted butter or put into liquor: *fetch me a quart of sack; put a t. in 't*, Wiv. III, 5, 3. *I pressed me none but such —s and butter*, H4A IV, 2, 22 (effeminate fellows).* *as rheumatic as two dry toasts*, H4B II, 4, 63 (Mrs. Quickly's speech). *made a t. for Neptune*, Troil. I, 3, 45 (a rich morsel to be swallowed).

**Toast**, vb. to dry and scorch at a fire; applied only to cheese: Wiv. V, 5, 147. H5 III, 1, 9. H6B IV, 7, 13. Lr. IV, 6, 90.

**Toasting-iron**, an iron used for toasting cheese; a sword called so in contempt: John IV, 3, 99.

**Toaze**, probably = to touse, i. e. to pull, to tear: *thinkest thou, for that I insinuate, or t. from thee thy business, I am therefore no courtier?* Wint. IV, 4, 760.

**To-be-pitied**, pitiful, paltry: Troil. I, 3, 157; not hyphened in O. Edd.

**To-bless**, writing of M. Edd. in Per. IV, 6, 23; O. Edd. *now the gods to bless your honour!* see *To*, inf. part. 5.

**Toby**; *Sir T. Belch*, name in Tw. I, 3, 4. 47 etc.

**Tod**, subst. twenty eight pounds of wool: *every t. yields pound and odd shilling*, Wint. IV, 3, 34.

**Tod**, vb. to yield a tod: *every 'leven wether —s*, Wint. IV, 3, 33.

**To-day**, the present day, or on the present day: Sonn. 56, 3. 105, 5. Tp. III, 2, 31. Gent. V, 4, 13. Wiv. I, 4, 166. Meas. IV, 1, 17. Err. I, 2, 52. II, 2, 209. III, 1, 40. IV, 3, 47. IV, 4, 4. Ado II, 3, 93. LLL IV, 1, 5. Merch. I, 1, 121. III, 4, 84. As II, 1, 29. Shr. Ind. 1, 24. All's I, 2, 33. Tw. V, 294 (*t. morning*). Wint. I, 2, 64. John IV, 1, 28. R2 I, 3, 57. II, 1, 197. H4A II, 3, 119. H4B II, 3, 44. H5 II, 2, 63. H6A II, 4, 124. IV, 6, 34. H6B II, 1, 161. H6C II, 2, 127 etc.

**Todpole**, see *Tadpole*.

**Toe**, one of the extremities of the foot, corresponding to a finger on the hand: Tp. IV, 46. LLL V, 2, 114. Shr. Ind. 2, 12. Tw. I, 3, 44. H4B I, 2, 274. Troil. II, 1, 116. IV, 5, 15. Cor. I, 1, 159. 160. Rom. I, 5, 18. Mcb. IV, 1, 14 (*t. of frog*). Hml. V, 1, 152. Lr. III, 2, 31. *from t. to crown*, Tp. IV, 233. *from the crown to the t.* Mcb. I, 5, 43. *from the top to t.* R3 III, 1, 156. *from top to t.* Hml. I, 2, 228.

**Toe**, vb., see *Top*, vb. 1.

**Tofore**, previously; formerly: *to make plain some obscure precedence that hath t. been sain*, LLL III, 83 (Armado's speech). *O would thou wert as thou t. hast been*, Tit. III, 1, 294.

**Toge** or **Togue**, a gown, a Roman toga; a word conjecturally introduced into the modern texts: *why in this woolvish t. should I stand here*, Cor. II, 3, 122. F1 *wooluish tongue;* later Ff *woolvish gown.* A passage yet to be set to rights.

**Toged**, wearing a toga, gowned; lection of Q1 in Oth. I, 1, 25: *wherein the t. consuls can propose as masterly as he;* the rest of O. Edd. *tongued*.

**Together**, 1) in a state of union, blent in one, not divided or separated: *were never four such lamps t. mixed*, Ven. 489. *milk and blood mingled t.* 902. *every something, being blent t.* Merch. III, 2, 183. *let nature crush the sides o'the earth t.* Wint. IV, 4, 489. *mingle their spurs t.* Cymb. IV, 2, 58 etc.

2) so as to be closely joined: *their lips t. glued*, Ven. 546. *I'll manacle thy neck and feet t.* Tp. I, 2, 461. *that set together is noddy*, Gent. I, 1, 122. *do no more adhere and keep place t. than the hundredth psalm to the tune of Green Sleeves*, Wiv. II, 1, 63. *if it were chained t.* Err. IV, 1, 26 etc. *to join t.* (trans.): As III, 3, 88. H6C II, 1, 37. IV, 1, 22. R3 II, 2, 118. Per. III Prol. 18. intr.: Ven. 971. H5 IV, 1, 143. H6B I, 1, 199. *as idle as she may hang t.* (without dissolving) Wiv. III, 2, 13; cf. *as well as one so great and so forlorn may hold t.* Wint. II, 2, 23.

3) in company, one with the other; or into company, one to the other: *all t. lost*, Lucr. 147. *all which t. ... beat at thy heart*, 589. *crabbed age and youth cannot live t.* Pilgr. 157. *they fell t. all*, as by consent, Tp. II, 1, 203. *draw t.* 294. *confined t. in the same fashion*, V, 7. *brought us thus t.* 188. *get your apparel t.* Mids. IV, 2, 36. Gent. II, 4, 63. Wiv. II, 1, 193. III, 2, 40. III, 3, 247. IV, 5, 129. V, 3, 5. Meas. I, 1, 82. IV, 1, 73. Err. V, 208. Ado I, 1, 162. LLL IV, 3, 192. Mids. IV, 1, 136. Merch. III, 4, 12. IV, 1, 157. As V, 2, 44. 122. Ant. III, 13, 79 (*wisdom and fortune combating t.*). Cymb. I, 2, 32 (*her beauty and her brain go not t.*) etc. *to meet t.:* Err. V, 361. Mids. III, 2, 11. Shr. II, 133. All's IV, 5, 92. H4B IV, 4, 64. Tim. III, 4, 3. Mcb. II, 3, 140. Per. V, 1, 243.

4) each other; with each other: *their breaths embraced t.* Oth. II, 1, 266. *I cannot hope Caesar and Antony shall well greet t.* Ant. II, 1, 39. *we have known t.* Cymb. 1, 4, 36. *let's consult t.* Wiv. II, 1, 111. *we'll pluck a crow t.* Err. III, 1, 83. *reason and love keep little company t.* Mids. III, 1, 147. *they have conspired t.* Merch. II, 5, 22. *we have 'greed so well t.* Shr. II, 299. *when last we spake t.* R2 II, 3, 29. *would we had spoke t.* Ant. II, 2, 167. *you should not speak t.* Cymb. I, 1, 83. *fought t.* Cor. I, 1, 236.

5) without intermission: *for ten year t.* Meas. II, 1, 252. 277. As III, 2, 101. Wint. III, 2, 212. V, 3, 71. *a year t.* As III, 5, 64. *an hour t.* Ado V, 1, 172. *two hours t.* H4A II, 4, 183. Cor. I, 3, 64. Hml. II, 2, 160. Lr. I, 2, 170. *three market-days t.* H6B IV, 2, 62. *two nights t.* Hml. I, 2, 196. Cymb. III, 6, 2. *urged it twice t.* R2 V, 4, 5.

**Toil**, subst. net, snare: LLL IV, 3, 2 (*they have pitched a t.*). Caes. II, 1, 206. Hml. III, 2, 362. Ant. V, 2, 351.

**Toil**, subst. labour, exertion, effort: Sonn. 27, 1. 28, 7. 60, 4. Tp. I, 2, 242. LLL IV, 3, 326. Shr. V, 2, 166. John II, 93. V, 5, 6. H4A I, 3, 31. H5 I, 1, 16. IV, 1, 296. H6A III, 4, 21. H6C II, 3, 1. R3 I, 4, 79. Troil. I, 3, 203. Rom. I Chor. 14. V, 3, 54. Mcb. IV, 1, 10. 20. 35. Cymb. III, 3, 49. III, 6, 37. Per. I, 3, 24.

**Toil**, vb. 1) intr. to labour, to exert one's strength, to make efforts: Sonn. 25, 12. 28, 8. Ado IV, 1, 191. LLL IV, 3, 3. H4B III, 1, 62. H5 II, 2, 36. H6C III, 2, 178. H8 I, 1, 24. Rom. II, 5, 77.

2) trans. a) to put to pains and labour, to strain: *have —ed their memories*, Mids. V, 74. *t. his wits*, H6B I, 1, 83. *why this watch ... so nightly —s the subject*, Hml. I, 1, 72.

b) to weary, to fatigue: *—ed with works of war*, R2 IV, 96.

**Token**, subst. 1) any sign by which something is perceived: *to expound the meaning or moral of his signs and —s*, Shr. IV, 4, 80 (i. e. winks and gestures; cf.

Tit. II, 4, 5). *in t. of which duty ... my hand is ready*, V, 2, 178. *I follow him not by any t. of presumptuous suit*, All's I, 3, 204. *do you not read some —s of my son in the large composition of this man?* John I, 87. *that all their eyes may bear those —s home of our restored love*, H4B IV, 2, 64. *this t. serveth for a flag of truce*, H6A III, 1, 138. *gives t. of a goodly day to-morrow*, R3 V, 3, 21 (Qq *signal*). *by the same t. you are a bawd*, Troil. I, 2, 307. *in t. of the which my noble steed I give him*, Cor. I, 9, 60. *how with signs and —s she can scrowl*, Tit. II, 4, 5. *when the most mighty gods by —s send such dreadful heralds*, Caes. I, 3, 55. *wounding his belief in her renown with —s thus and thus*, Cymb. V, 5, 203.

2) a sign of infection: *corrupted blood some watery t. shows*, Lucr. 1748. Especially spots indicating the infection of the plague: *you are not free, for the Lord's —s on you do I see*, LLL V, 2, 423 (with a pun on the word. cf. *death-token* in Troil. II, 3, 187, and *tokened*).

3) a sign by which one proves the legitimacy of a commission or demand; whether an action or a thing produced: *to pinch her by the hand, and on that t. the maid hath given consent to go with him*, Wiv. IV, 6, 44. *are there no other —s between you 'greed concerning her observance?* Meas. IV, 1, 41. *say, by this t., I desire his company*, IV, 3, 144. *either send the chain or send me by some t.* Err. IV, 1, 56. *by this t. I would relieve her*, All's V, 3, 85 *go by this t.* R3 IV, 2, 80. *send thy t. of reprieve*, Lr. V, 3, 250.

4) a pledge of faith: *give me some t. for the surety of it*, Troil. V, 2, 60. *throw the glove, or any t. of thy honour else*, Tim. V, 4, 50.

5) a pledge or memorial of love or friendship, a love-token, a keepsake: *give her no t. but stones*, Gent. I, 1, 148. *it seems you loved not her, to leave her t.* IV, 4, 79. *gave these —s to us*, LLL V, 2, 424. *promises, enticements, oaths, —s*, All's III, 5, 20. III, 6, 123. V, 3, 68. H6A V, 3, 181 (*loving t.*). 186. Troil. I, 2, 306. V, 1, 45. Hml. II, 2, 144. Oth. III, 3, 293. III, 4, 181. IV, 1, 159. V, 2, 61. 216. Ant. V, 2, 168.

**Token**, vb. to be a sign and memorial of: *what in time proceeds, may t. to the future our past deeds*, All's IV, 2, 63.

**Tokened**, spotted, denoting the infection of the plague (cf. *Token*, subst. 2): *the t. pestilence, where death is sure*, Ant. III, 10, 9.

**Toledo**, Spanish town: H8 II, 1, 164.

**Tolerable**, supportable? or passable, not contemptible? *thou didst make t. vent of thy travel; it might pass*, All's II, 3, 212. Misapplied for *intolerable* by Dogberry in Ado III, 3, 37.

**Toll**, vb. 1) to pay toll or tallage: *I will buy me a son-in-law in a fair, and t. for this: I'll none of him*, All's V, 3, 149 (= pay a tax for the liberty of selling. The later Ff and some M. Edd. *and t. him: for this, I'll none of him*).

2) to take toll, to raise a tax: *no Italian priest shall tithe or t. in our dominions*, John III, 1, 154. Trans., = to raise; to levy, to collect, to glean: *like the bee, —ing from every flower the virtuous sweets*, H4B IV, 5, 75 (Ff *culling*).

**Toll**, vb. to sound or ring, as a bell: *the clocks do t.* H5 IV Chor. 15. Trans., = to sound or ring for: *a sullen bell, —ing a departing friend*, H4B I, 1, 103.

**Tom**, diminutive of *Thomas*, a favourite name among the common people: *and T. bears logs into the hall*, LLL V, 2, 924. *T. Snout the tinker*, Mids. I, 2, 63. *as Tib's rush for —'s forefinger*, All's II, 2, 24. *good T. Drum, lend me a handkercher*, V, 3, 322 (cf. *Drum*). *I prithee, T., beat Cut's saddle*, H4A II, 1, 6. *their* (the drawers') *christen names, as T., Dick and Francis*, II, 4, 9. *here, T., take all the money*, H6B II, 3, 76. *T. o'Bedlam*, Lr. I, 2, 148, the common name of vagabond beggars, either mad or feigning to be so; the name and part assumed by Edgar in his disguise: Lr. II, 3, 20. III, 4, 43. 51. 59 etc.

**Tomb**, subst. 1) a grave, a place where a dead body is deposited (never in prose): Ven. 244. Sonn. 3, 7. 83, 12. 86, 4. Mids. V, 335. All's II, 3, 147. Tw. V, 241 (*his watery t.*). H4B V, 2, 124. H6A IV, 5, 34. H6B III, 2, 78. H6C I, 4, 16. Cor. IV, 7, 52. Tit. II, 3, 196. Rom. II, 3, 9. III, 5, 56. Hml. IV, 4, 64. Cymb. IV, 2, 217. Per. I, 2, 5.

2) a monument erected to enclose, and preserve the memory of, the dead: Ven. 1013. Sonn. 17, 3. 101, 11. 107, 14. Ado V, 1, 70. 293. V, 2, 80. V, 3, 9. 15. LLL I, 1, 2. Mids. III, 1, 99. V, 139. 204. 268. Merch. II, 7, 69 (O. Edd. *timber*). All's I, 2, 49. II, 3, 145. R2 III, 3, 105. V, 1, 12. H5 I, 2, 103. H6A II, 2, 13. H6B IV, 10, 73. H8 III, 2, 399. Tit. 1, 116. 159. 349. 388. Rom. IV, 3, 30. V, 2, 30. V, 3, 73. 201. 262. 283. Tim. V, 3, 5. Lr. II, 4, 133.

**Tombed**, entombed, buried: *thy unused beauty must be t. with thee*, Sonn. 4, 13.

**Tombless**, destitute of a sepulchral monument: H5 I, 2, 229.

**Tomboy**, a strumpet, a drab: *partnered with —s hired ...* Cymb. I, 6, 122.

**To-morrow**, the day, or on the day, after the present: Ven. 585. Sonn. 56, 4. 105, 5. Pilgr. 185. 204. 210. Gent. I, 3, 39. 70. IV, 2, 78. Wiv. III, 3, 210 (*t. eight o'clock*). 245 (*t. morning*). IV, 3, 2. Meas. II, 1, 34 (*t. morning*). II, 2, 7. IV, 2, 7 (*t. morning*). 23. 56 (*t. four o'clock*). IV, 3, 162. Err. III, 1, 5. Ado II, 1, 372. II, 3, 88 (*t. night*) III, 1, 101. V, 1, 295 (*t. morning*). LLL II, 166. Mids. I, 1, 164; 247; I, 2, 103 (*t. night*). IV, 1, 93 (*t. midnight*). Merch. III, 3, 34. As V, 2, 16. John V, 5, 22. R2 II, 1, 197. 217 (*t. next*). H4A II, 4, 564 (*by t. dinner-time*). H5 III, 6, 181 (*on t. bid them march away*). IV, 1, 230 (*after t.*). H6A IV, 6, 35. H6B I, 4, 84 (*t. night*). V, 1, 46. R3 V, 3, 45. Troil. III, 2, 149 (*till t. morning*). V, 1, 43 (*in —'s battle*). Tim. V, 1, 189. Hml. IV, 5, 48. Oth. III, 3, 58 (*t. dinner*). Ant. IV, 2, 42 (*I hope well of t.*) etc.

**Tomyris**, the queen of the Massagetae, by whom Cyrus was slain: *as famous ... as Scythian T. by Cyrus' death*, H6A II, 3, 6.

**Ton**, see *Tun*.

**Tongs**, *let's have the t. and the bones*, Mids. IV, 1, 32; a musical instrument unknown at present. Dyce: The music of the tongs was produced, I believe, by striking them with a key, while the bones were played upon by rattling them between the fingers.

**Tongue**, subst. 1) the limb within the mouth: *a neat's t.* Merch. I, 1, 112. *t. of dog*, Mcb. IV, 1, 15. *adders with cloven —s*, Tp. II, 2, 13. *a serpent with forked t.* H6B III, 2, 259. *snakes with double t.* Mids. II, 2, 9. III, 2, 72. R2 III, 2, 21. *hold a serpent by the t.* Ado V, 1, 90. John III, 1, 258. *aspics' —s*, Oth. III, 3, 450. *with my t. in your tail*, Shr. II, 219; cf. Gent. II, 3, 52. *lolling the t. with slaughtering*, Cymb.

V, 3, 8. In man, an instrument of taste: *love's t. proves dainty Bacchus gross in taste*, LLL IV, 3, 339. Oftener the instrument of speech: Ven. 217. 775. Lucr. 78. Sonn. 89, 9. Tp. II, 1, 24. II, 2, 52. III, 1, 41. III, 2, 14. III, 3, 38. IV, 59. Gent. II, 6, 14. III, 1, 104. 356. Meas. I, 1, 46. I, 4, 33 *(t. far from heart)*. II, 2, 46. 140. II, 4, 173. V, 413. Err. II, 1, 72. III, 2, 10. V, 308. Ado II, 1, 284 *(my Lady T.)*. IV, 1, 323. LLL I, 2, 101. V, 2, 242. 382. 727. 852. H5 V, 2, 164. H6C II, 1, 44 etc. *keep a good t. in your head*, Tp. III, 2, 39. 120 (take care what you say). *to scape the serpent's t.* Mids. V, 440 (not to be hissed). *I have ne'er a t. in my head*, Merch. II, 2, 166 (I cannot speak). *I as one that am the t. of these*, John IV, 2, 47 (spokesman). *I must find that title in your t.* R2 II, 3, 72. *have not well the gift of t.* H4A V, 2, 78. *which action's self was t. to*, H8 I, 1, 42. *none stands under more calumnious —s*, V, 1, 113. *put not your worthy rage into your t.* Cor. III, 1, 241. *had t. at will*, Oth. II, 1, 150. *which you shall never have t. to charge me with*, Ant. II, 2, 83. *to bite one's t.* = to be silent, H6B I, 1, 230. H6C I, 4, 47. *to find one's t.* = to be able to speak, H4B I, 1, 74. *to keep one's t.* = to keep silence, Shr. I, 1, 214. *to hold one's t.*, in the same sense: Sonn. 102, 13. Err. IV, 4, 22. As II, 5, 31. John IV, 1, 97. H6A III, 1, 61. V, 3, 42. Troil. III, 2, 137. Rom. III, 5, 171. Mcb. II, 3, 125. Hml. I, 2, 159. Lr. I, 4, 214. *to tie one's t.* = to put to silence: *sin and hellish obstinacy tie thy t.* All's I, 3, 186. *to tie up*, in the same sense: Mids. III, 1, 206. Rom. IV, 5, 32. *to wag one's t.* = to speak unseasonably: H8 I, 1, 33. V, 3, 127. Hml. III, 4, 39. *a double t.* = double-dealing, duplicity: Ado V, 1, 170. LLL V, 2, 245. Mids. III, 2, 72. *this knave's t. begins to double* (= to speak brokenly) H6B II, 3, 94.

2) the manner of speaking; a) with respect to sound, = voice: *the t. of Isabel*, Meas. IV, 3, 111. *I know your t.* Merch. II, 6, 27. *with soft low t.* Shr. Ind. I, 114. *knowest my t. so well*, John V, 6, 8. *the sound of Marcius' t.* Cor. I, 6, 26. *I hear a t., shriller than all the music, cry Caesar*, Caes. I, 2, 16. *dull of t.* Ant. III, 3, 19. b) with respect to meaning or expression: *I have no t. but one: gentle my lord, let me entreat you speak the former language*, Meas. II, 4, 139. 173. *a bird of my t.* Ado I, 1, 140. *he speaks the common t., which all men speak with him*, Tim. I, 1, 174. *is't not possible to understand in another t.?* Hml. V, 2, 132. *mince not the general t.* Ant. I, 2, 109.

3) a language (as used by a particular nation): Wiv. II, 3, 62. As V, 4, 38. All's IV, 1, 82. Tw. I, 3, 97. H4A III, 1, 125. H4B IV, 4, 69. H5 V, 2, 203. 313. H6B IV, 2, 181. H8 I, 4, 57. III, 1, 45. *have you the —s*, (= do you know foreign languages?) Gent. IV, 1, 33. Ado V, 1, 167.

4) a vote: *your sued-for —s*, Cor. II, 3, 216. *disclaim their —s*, III, 1, 35.

5) the clapper of a bell: *the iron t. of midnight hath told twelve*, Mids. V, 370. *the midnight bell, with his iron t. and brazen mouth*, John III, 3, 38. cf. *he hath a heart as sound as a bell, and his t. is the clapper*, Ado III, 2, 13.

**Tongue**, vb. 1) to speak: *such stuff as madmen t. and brain not*, Cymb. V, 4, 147. cf. *out-tongue*.

2) to speak of: *but that her tender shame will not proclaim against her maiden loss, how might she t. me*, Meas. IV, 4, 28.

**Tongued**, having a tongue, loquacious: *the t. consuls*, Oth. I, 1, 25 (Q1 and most M. Edd. *toged*).

**Tongueless**, 1) having no tongue, speechless, silent: *the t. caverns of the earth*, R2 I, 1, 105. *our grave ... shall have a t. mouth, not worshipped with a waxen epitaph*, H5 I, 2, 232. *what t. blocks were they! would they not speak?* R3 III, 7, 42.

2) not mentioned, not spoken of: *one good deed dying t. slaughters a thousand*, Wint. I, 2, 92.

**Tongue-tied**, keeping silence: *art made t. by authority*, Sonn. 66, 9. *a better spirit doth use your name ... to make me t.* 80, 4. *my t. Muse in manners holds her still*, 85, 1. *do not press my t. patience with too much disdain*, 140, 2. *love and t. simplicity in least speak most*, Mids. V, 104. *t. our queen? speak you*, Wint. I, 2, 27. H6A II, 4, 25. H6C III, 3, 22. R3 III, 7, 145. IV, 4, 132. Troil. III, 2, 219. Caes. I, 1, 67.

**To-night**, 1) this, or in this, present night: Ado II, 1, 177. III, 3, 100. 154. Tw. II, 3, 142 *(for t.)*. John V, 5, 15. 20. H4A II, 4, 306. H6A II, 1, 61. II, 2, 9. R3 V, 3, 216. H8 V, 1, 56. Rom. III, 4, 5. 11. IV, 3, 2. Mcb. III, 3, 16 etc.

2) last night: Wiv. III, 3, 171. Ado III, 5, 33. Merch. II, 5, 18. Wint. II, 3, 10. John IV, 2, 85. 165. H4A II, 4, 392 (Ff *by night*). H5 III, 7, 74. H6B III, 2, 31. R3 II, 1, 71. III, 2, 11. Rom. I, 4, 50 etc.

3) in the night after the present day, next night: Pilgr. 210. Tp. I, 2, 325. III, 3, 14. 17. Wiv. III, 4, 103 *(once t.)*. IV, 6, 19. V, 5, 180. 259. Meas. III, 2, 292. IV, 3, 145. Err. III, 2. 154. IV, 3, 35. IV, 4, 161. Ado I, 1, 322. LLL V, 2, 270. 737. Mids. II, 1, 18. Merch. I, 2, 139. II, 2, 180. 208. II, 4, 18. II, 5, 37. II, 6, 68. IV, 2, 2. H4A IV, 2, 3. H6B V, 1, 214. R3 V, 3, 7. 48 etc. Opposed to last night: Shr. IV, 1, 201. R3 II, 4, 2.

**Too**, (often spelt *to* in O. Edd.) 1) more than enough, or more than is suitable: *too delicate to act her commands*, Tp. I, 2, 272. *lest too light winning make the prize too light*, 451. II, 1, 249. III, 1, 42 etc. etc. *all too short a date*, Sonn. 18, 4 (cf. *All*). *too rash a trial*, Tp. I, 2, 467. Gent. I, 1, 105. I, 2, 94. II, 4, 106. Wiv. III, 2, 74. Meas. III, 2, 106. 175. LLL II, 49 etc. Reduplicated: *too too oft*, Lucr. 174. *too too much*, Gent. II, 4, 205. Wiv. II, 2, 260. LLL V, 2, 532. Merch. II, 6, 42. Hml. I, 2, 129 etc. too much substantively: *goodness, growing to a plurisy, dies in his own too much*, Hml. IV, 7, 119. *another, to amplify too much, would make much more*, Lr. V, 3, 206. cf. Rom. I, 1, 195.

2) likewise, also, at the same time: Tp. II, 1, 80. 87. 109. 155. 220. 318. II, 2, 57. III, 2, 87. Gent. I, 2, 139. II, 4, 157. II, 5, 30. III, 1, 342. Wiv. IV, 5, 42. Err. I, 2. II, 2, 131. H8 V, 4, 72 etc. etc. Before the word to which it refers: *you that have so fair parts of woman on you, have too a woman's heart*, H8 II, 3, 28. *and too* = and at the same time: *it shall be sparing and too full of riot*, Ven. 1147. *it shall be merciful and too severe*, 1155. *wild and yet too gentle*, Err. III, 1, 110. *then you scratched your head, and too impatiently stamped with your foot*, Caes. II, 1, 244.

**Tool**, any instrument of manual operation: *sirs, take you to your —s*, Tit. IV, 3, 6. *some coiner with his —s made me a counterfeit*, Cymb. II, 5, 5.

Hence, or rather originally, = weapon: *this no slaughterhouse no t. imparteth to make more vent for passage of her breath*, Lucr. 1039. *draw thy t.* Rom. I, 1, 37. *lolling the tongue with slaughtering, having work more plentiful than —s to do't,* Cymb. V, 3, 9. Euphemistically = the yard: *have we some strange Indian with the great t. come to court, the women so besiege us?* H8 V, 4, 35. cf. Rom. I, 1, 37 and Cymb. II, 5, 5.

**Tooth,** bony substance growing out of the jaws: Err. V, 70. Shr. I, 2, 80 *(with ne'er a t. in her head).* All's II, 3, 48. Wint. IV, 3, 7 *(doth set my pugging t. on edge; cf.* H4A III, 1, 133*).* IV, 4, 375. John I, 213. III, 1, 260. H4A II, 2, 26. H4B IV, 5, 133. H6C I, 4, 112. R3 I, 3, 291. II, 4, 29. Mcb. III, 2, 15. IV, 1, 22 etc. Plur. *teeth:* Ven. 269. 1113. Lucr. 1787. Sonn. 19, 3. Tp. III, 2, 57. Gent. III, 1, 344. 348. Err. V, 249. Ado V, 1, 116. LLL V, 2, 332. Merch. I, 1, 55. As I, 1, 88. H6A I, 2, 39. III, 1, 90. H6C V, 6, 53 etc. *to pick one's teeth,* All's III, 2, 8. Wint. IV, 4, 780 (the custom indicating a person of quality). *chill pick your teeth,* Lr. IV, 6, 250. *I suck my teeth,* John I, 192. *to tug and scamble and to part by the teeth the unowed interest of state,* IV, 3, 146. *your colt's tooth is not cast yet,* H8 I, 3, 48 (you are still like a boy). *'tis a secret must be locked within the teeth and the lips,* Meas. III, 2, 143. *to fix one's teeth,* H6B III, 2, 313. *to set one's teeth,* H5 III, 1, 15. Cor. I, 3, 70. Ant. III, 13, 181. *'Tarquin' was pronounced plain, but through his teeth, as if the name he tore,* Lucr. 1787. *when the best hint was given him, he not took 't or did it from his teeth,* Ant. III, 4, 10 (not from his heart, only for form's sake and with reluctance). *in despite of the teeth of all rhyme and reason,* Wiv. V, 5, 133 (in open defiance of). *dost thou jeer and flout me in the teeth,* Err. II, 2, 22 (= directly to my face). *I have thrown a brave defiance in King Henry's teeth,* H4A V, 2, 43. *Puff in thy teeth,* H4B V, 3, 96. *the solus in thy teeth,* H5 II, 1, 51. *conned by rote, to cast into my teeth,* Caes. IV, 3, 99. *defiance hurl we in your teeth,* V, 1, 64. *throw your vile guesses in the devil's teeth, from whence you have them,* Oth. III, 4, 184. *daring the event to the teeth,* H8 I, 2, 36. *compelled, even to the teeth and forehead of our faults, to give in evidence,* Hml. III, 3, 63. *that I shall live and tell him, to his teeth, 'thus didest thou',* IV, 7, 57. Metaphorically: *the tooth of time,* Meas. V, 12. *thy* (winter's) *tooth is not so keen,* As II, 7, 177. *fell sorrow's tooth,* R2 I, 3, 302. *sweet love is food for fortune's tooth,* Troil. IV, 5, 293. *live out of the teeth of emulation,* Caes. II, 3, 14. *by treason's tooth bare-gnawn,* Lr. V, 3, 122. *so sharp are hunger's teeth,* Per. I, 4, 45.

**Tooth-ache,** pain in the teeth: Ado III, 2, 21. 26. 72. V, 1, 36. Cymb. V, 4, 178.

**Tooth-drawer,** one whose business is to extract teeth: *worn in the cap of a t.* LLL V, 2, 622.

**Toothed,** having teeth: *had I been t. like him,* Ven. 1117. In botany, = dentate, thorny: *t. briers,* Tp. IV, 180.

**Toothpick,** an instrument for cleaning the teeth: *like the brooch and the t., which wear not now,* All's I, 1, 171. *now your traveller, he and his t. at my worship's mess,* John I, 190. cf. All's III, 2, 8 and Wint. IV, 4, 780.

**Toothpicker,** the same: *I will fetch you a t. now from the furthest inch of Asia,* Ado II, 1, 274 (to use toothpicks being a foreign fashion, introduced by travellers).

**Top,** subst. 1) the highest part of any thing: *the bottom poison, and the t. o'erstrawed with sweets,* Ven. 1143. *skins vice o'the t.* Meas. II, 2, 136. *on the t. of*

*the mountain* (cf. *Mountain-top*) LLL V, 1, 87. Mids. IV, 1, 114. H4A II, 2, 8. Rom. III, 5, 10. Tit. II, 1, 1. Tim. I, 1, 86. Lr. IV, 6, 1. *the highest promontory t.* Tit. II, 2, 22. *on the t. of a thistle,* Mids. IV, 1, 12. *to wag their* (pines') *high —s,* Merch. IV, 1, 76. As IV, 3, 106. R2 III, 2, 42. R3 I, 3, 264. Rom. II, 2, 108. Cymb. IV, 2, 175. Per. I, 2, 29. II, 2, 43 *(a branch ... only green at t.).* (a ship) *vailing her high t. lower than her ribs,* Merch. I, 1, 28. *had I seen the vaulty t. of heaven figured quite o'er,* John V, 2, 52. *rude hands from windows' —s threw dust,* R2 V, 2, 5. *take the ruffian billows by the t.* H4B III, 1, 22. *I will have it on't,* IV, 3, 53. *on this turret's t.* H6A I, 4, 26. Troil. IV, 5, 220. Hml. II, 2, 497. III, 4, 193. *they use to write it on the t. of letters,* H6B IV, 2, 107. *on the chimney's t.* H6C V, 6, 47. Caes. I, 1, 44.

Metaphorically, = the highest point or degree: *now stand you on the t. of happy hours,* Sonn. 16, 5. *the t. of admiration,* Tp. III, 1, 38. *He, which is the t. of judgement,* Meas. II, 2, 76. *this is the very t., the height, the crest ... of murder's arms,* John IV, 3, 45. *from t. of honour to disgrace's feet,* H6B I, 2, 49. *which, to the spire and t. of praises vouched,* Cor. I, 9, 24. *bears upon his baby brow the round and t. of sovereignty,* Mcb. IV, 1, 89 (interpreted by the commentators as meaning the upper part of the crown). *sound me from my lowest note to the t. of my compass,* Hml. III, 2, 383. *they fool me to the t. of my bent,* 401. *the art o'the court ... whose t. to climb is certain falling,* Cymb. III, 3, 47. *our griefs are risen to the t.* Per. II, 4, 23. *in t. of* = in the height of: *in t. of rage the lines she rents,* Pilgr. 55. *in —s of all their pride,* H6C V, 7, 4. *my competitor in t. of all design,* Ant. V, 1, 43. *in the t. of* = higher than, above: *whose judgements cried in the t. of mine,* Hml. II, 2, 459. cf. *cry out on the t. of question,* 355 (see IV, 7, 28, and *Question*).

2) Applied to men, = the crown of the head: *from the t. to toe,* R3 III, 1, 156. *from t. to toe,* Hml. I, 2, 228. Pars pro toto, = the head: *bowed his eminent t. to their low ranks,* All's I, 2, 43. *all the stored vengeances of heaven fall on her ingrateful t.* Lr. II, 4, 165. *what trunk is here without his t.?* Cymb. IV, 2, 354. Totum pro parte, = the forelock: *to take the present time by the t.* Ado I, 2, 16. *let's take the instant by the forward t.* All's V, 3, 39.

3) the inverted conoid which children play with by setting it to turn on the point: *since I whipped t.* Wiv. V, 1, 27. *not big enough to bear a schoolboy's t.* Wint. II, 1, 103. *as one would set up a t.* Cor. IV, 5, 161. cf. *Parish-top.*

**Top,** vb. 1) to rise above, to surpass: *—ing all others in boasting,* Cor. II, 1, 23. *a devil more damned in evils to t.* Macbeth, Mcb. IV, 3, 57. *so far he —ed my thought,* Hml. IV, 7, 89 (Ff *past). would make much more and t. extremity,* Lr. V, 3, 207. In Lr. I, 2, 21 most M. Edd. *Edmund the base shall t. the legitimate;* Ff *to',* Qq *tooth';* some M. Edd. *toe,* a pretended provincialism, = to pluck up by the root.

2) to crop, to lop: *like to groves, being —ed, they higher rise,* Per. I, 4, 9.

3) to tup, to cover, to copulate with: *would you ... behold her —ed?* Oth. III, 3, 396. *Cassio did t. her,* V, 2, 136 (some M. Edd. *tup).*

**Topas,** name of a curate in Tw. IV, 2, 2 etc.

**Top-branch,** the highest branch: H6C V, 2, 14.

**Top-full**, full to the brim: *their souls are t. of offence*, John III, 4, 180. *fill me ... t. of direst cruelty*, Mcb. I, 5, 43.

**Top-gallant**, the top-gallant-sail above the topsail; metaphorically = the summit, the pinnacle: *cords made like a tackled stair, which to the high t. of my joy must be my convoy*, Rom. II, 4, 202.

**To - pinch**, writing of M. Edd. in Wiv. IV, 4, 57; see *To*, inf. part. 7.*

**Topless**, without a superior, supreme (or immeasurably high?): *thy t. deputation he puts on*, Troil. I, 3, 152.

**Topmast**, the mainmast: Tp. I, 1, 37. I, 2, 199. H6C V, 4, 14. Cymb. III, 1, 22.

**Topple**, 1) intr. to tumble, to fall down: *down —s she*, Mids. II, 1, 53. *though castles t. on their warders' heads*, Mcb. IV, 1, 56. *lest my brain turn, and the deficient sight t. down headlong*, Lr. IV, 6, 24. *the very principals did seem to rend and all to t.* Per. III, 2, 17 (cf. *All-to*).
2) to throw down, to overturn: *—s down steeples*, H4A III, 1, 32 (Ff *tumbles*).

**Top-proud**, proud to the highest degree: *this t. follow*, H8 I, 1, 151.

**Top-sail**, a sail extended across the topmast: *take in the t.* Tp. I, 1, 7.

**Topsy-turvy**, with the top downward and the bottom upward: *we shall o'erturn it* (the kingdom) *t. down*, H4A IV, 1, 82.

**Torch**, a big wax light that may be used in the open air as well as in a chamber; often equivalent to candle: Ven. 163. Lucr. 178 (*a waxen t.*). 190. 311. 448. Tp. IV, 97 (*Hymen's t.*). Meas. I, 1, 33. Ado V, 3, 24. H4A III, 3, 48. H6A II, 5, 122. III, 2, 23. 26 (*wedding t.*). 30. Troil. V, 1, 92. V, 2, 5. Rom. I, 4, 11. 35. I, 5, 46. 127. V, 3, 1. 21. 125. 171. Caes. I, 3, 17. Lr. II, 1, 34. Ant. IV, 2, 41. IV, 14, 46. Per. II, 2, 32.

**Torch - bearer**, one who attends another with a torch: Merch. II, 4, 5. 24. 40. II, 6, 40. Rom. III, 5, 14.

**Torcher**, one who gives light: *ere twice the horses of the sun shall bring their fiery t. his diurnal ring*, All's II, 1, 165.

**Torch-light**, light of a torch; a signal given with lighting a torch: *Statilius showed the t.* Caes. V, 5, 2.

**Torch-staves**, staves to fix candles on: *the horsemen sit like fixed candlesticks, with t. in their hand*, H5 IV, 2, 46.

**Torment**, subst. extreme pain, anguish, torture: Lucr. 861. Sonn. 39, 9. 133, 8. Tp. I, 2, 251. 287. 289. V, 104. Gent. III, 1, 170. Ado II, 3, 130. LLL V, 2, 353. Merch. III, 2, 37. Wint. III, 2, 176. John IV, 1, 84. H6A I, 4, 57. H6C III, 2, 180. R3 I, 4, 57. IV, 4, 163 (Qq *anguish*). Troil. V, 2, 43. Tit. V, 2, 42. Lr. I, 4, 305. Oth. I, 3, 309. V, 2, 305. Cymbl. III, 5, 143.

**Torment**, vb. to put to extreme pain: Ven. 202. Lucr. 151. Sonn. 132, 2. Tp. II, 2, 15. 58. 66. 74. Gent. II, 2, 12. IV, 1, 26. Ado II, 3, 163. Mids. II, 1, 147. John IV, 1, 84. R2 IV, 270 (O. Edd. —*s*, M. Edd. —*st*). H6C I, 1, 270. I, 3, 31. R3 I, 3, 226. Tit. V, 1, 150. Rom. I, 2, 57. II, 4, 5. III, 2, 43. Tim. IV, 3, 335. Hml. I, 5, 3. Oth. V, 2, 334. Cymb. V, 5, 142. Refl.: H6B III, 2, 329. H6C III, 2, 179. R3 II, 2, 35.

**Tormentor**, he who or that which gives pain: *these words hereafter thy —s be*, R2 II, 1, 136.

**Torrent**, a violent and rapid stream, a strong current: *enforced from our quiet by the rough t. of occasion*, H4B IV, 1, 72. *the t. roared*, Caes. I, 2, 107. *in the very t., tempest, and ... whirlwind of passion*, Hml. III, 2, 6.

**Tortive**, twisted, turned aside: *divert his* (the pine's) *grain t. and errant from his course of growth*, Troil. I, 3, 9.

**Tortoise**, animal of the order Chelonii: Tp. I, 2, 316. Rom. V, 1, 42.

**Torture**, subst. 1) torment judicially inflicted: All's II, 1, 177. IV, 3, 137. Wint. II, 3, 181. III, 2, 178. IV, 4, 796. H6B III, 1, 122. H6C II, 6, 72. Rom. I, 1, 93. Mcb. III, 2, 21 (*on the t. of the mind to lie*). Oth. V, 2, 369. Cymb. IV, 3, 12. IV, 4, 14. V, 5, 133.
2) excruciating pain: Lucr. 1287. John IV, 1, 34. H4B II, 4, 171. H6A V, 4, 58. H6B III, 2, 401. Rom. III, 2, 44. III, 3, 18. 29. Ant. IV, 14, 46.

**Torture**, vb. 1) to punish with torture: All's II, 1, 36. H6B II, 1, 146. III, 1, 131. 376. III, 2, 247. III, 3, 11. Ant. III, 13, 150. Cymb. V, 5, 139.
2) to excruciate, to torment: Sonn. 28, 6. 133, 3. Wiv. III, 2, 41. Ado IV, 1, 186. LLL V, 2, 60. Mids. V, 37. Merch. III, 1, 122. 125. Tw. V, 226. John IV, 3, 138. R2 IV, 298. R3 IV, 4, 108. Tit. II, 3, 285. Oth. III, 3, 368. Cymb. V, 5, 140.

**Torturer**, one who tortures: Merch. III, 2, 37. R2 III, 2, 198. Cymb. V, 5, 215.

**Toryne**, place in ancient Epirus: Ant. III, 7, 24. 56.

**To-spend**, writing of some M. Edd. in John V, 2, 39; see *To*, inf. part. 7.

**Toss**, 1) to throw: *my relief must not be —ed and turned to me in words, but find supply immediate*, Tim. II, 1, 26. *back do I t. these treasons to thy head*, Lr. V, 3, 146. *even now did the sea t. up upon our shore this chest*, Per. III, 2, 50 (M. Edd. *t. upon our shore*). *so huge a billow as —ed it upon shore*, 59. Especially, = to throw upward: *I will t. the rogue in a blanket*, H4B II, 4, 240. And = to throw up and down, to cause to rise and fall, to move to and fro: *what book is that she —eth so?* Tit. IV, 1, 41. particularly used of the rolling and tumbling motion of waves (cf. *Seatost*): *he by waves from coast to coast is —ed*, Per. II Prol. 34. *on the sea tumbled and —ed*, V Prol. 13 (Q1 *we there him left*, most M. Edd. *we there him lost*). participle and gerund passively: *your mind is —ing on the ocean*, Merch. I, 1, 8. *after your late —ing on the breaking seas*, R2 III, 2, 3. Metaphorically: *madly —ed between desire and dread*, Lucr. 171. *such a deal of spleen as you are —ed with*, H4A III, 1, 82. *often up and down my sons were —ed*, R3 II, 4, 58. *thou hadst been —ed from wrong to injury*, Per. V, 1, 131.
2) to carry triumphantly on a pike or anything similar: *good enough to t.* H4A IV, 2, 71. *a sceptre ... on which I'll t. the flower-de-luce of France*, H6B V, 1, 11. *the soldiers should have —ed me on their pikes*, H6C I, 1, 244.

**Toss-pot**, a toper: Tw. V, 412.

**Total**, adj. complete, entire: *head to foot now is he t. gules*, Hml. II, 2, 479.

**Total**, subst. the whole sum or amount: *may soon bring his particulars to a t.* Troil. I, 2, 124.

**Totally**, completely: *he doth but mistake the truth t.* Tp. II, 1, 57.

**Tother**, see *Other*.

**Totter**, 1) to shake so as to threaten a fall, to vacillate, to stagger: *if th' other two be brained* *like us, the state —s,* Tp. III, 2, 8. *our —ing state,* R3 III, 2, 37.

2) to waver, to balance, to be uncertain: *many likelihoods ... which hung so —ing in the balance that I could neither believe nor misdoubt,* Alls I, 3, 129. *to be thirsty after —ing honour,* Per. III, 2, 40.

**Tottering** (M. Edd. *tattered* or *tattering*) hanging in rags: *wound our t. colours clearly up,* John V, 5, 7.

**Tottered,** (M. Edd. *tattered*) torn, ragged: *from this castle's t. battlements,* R2 III, 3, 52 (Ff *tattered*). *an hundred and fifty t. prodigals,* H4A IV, 2, 37.

**Totters** (Ff *tatters*) rags: *tear a passion to t.* Hml. III, 2, 11.

**Touch,** subst. 1) contact, reach of any thing so that there is no space between: *scape the dreadful t. of merchant-marring rocks,* Merch. III, 2, 273. *the t. of holy bread,* As III, 4, 15. *whose simple t. is powerful to araise King Pepin,* All's II, 1, 78. *their t. affrights me as a serpent's sting,* H6B III, 2, 47. 325. Rom. I, 5, 98. Mcb. IV, 3, 143. Hml. V, 2, 297. Ant. II, 2, 215. Cymb. I, 6, 100.

2) the act of touching, a contact sought and performed; either for an injurious purpose: *let go that rude uncivil t.* Gent. V, 4, 60. 130. *a sweet t., a quick venue of wit,* LLL V, 1, 62 (= hit? cf. Hml. V, 2, 297. Armado's speech). *whose (adders') double tongue may with a mortal t. throw death upon ...,* R2 III, 2, 21. *the least word that might be to the prejudice of her present state, or t. of her good person,* H8 II, 4, 155. or out of love: *what is ten hundred —es* (i. e. kisses) *unto thee?* Ven. 519. *enforced hate, instead of love's coy t., shall rudely tear thee,* Lucr. 669. *— es so soft still conquer chastity,* Pilgr. 50. Err. II, 2, 118. H5 V, 2, 303. Oth. IV, 3, 39. Cymb. III, 4, 165.

Hence euphemistically, = sexual commerce: *to base — es prone,* Sonn. 141, 6. *from their beastly —es I drink, I eat,* Meas. III, 2, 25. *free from t. or soil with her,* V, 141. *to preserve this vessel from every other foul unlawful t.* Oth. IV, 2, 84.

3) the sense of feeling: *the ear, taste, t. and smell,* Tim. I, 2, 132. *might I but live to see thee in my t.* Lr. IV, 1, 25.

4) affection, sensation, feeling: *hast thou a t., a feeling of their afflictions,* Tp. V, 21. *didst thou but know the inly t. of love,* Gent. II, 7, 18. *have you no modesty, no maiden shame, no t. of bashfulness,* Mids. III, 2, 286. *this she delivered in the most bitter t. of sorrow that e'er I heard virgin exclaim in,* All's I, 3, 122. *no beast so fierce but knows some t. of pity,* R3 I, 2, 71. *some —es of remorse,* Troil. II, 2, 115. *I know no t. of consanguinity,* IV, 2, 103. *he wants the natural t.* Mcb. IV, 2, 9. *the death of Fulvia, with more urgent —es, do strongly speak to us,* Ant. I, 2, 187. *I am senseless of your wrath; a t. more rare subdues all pangs, all fears,* Cymb. I, 1, 135.

5) touchstone: *to-morrow is a day wherein the fortune of ten thousand men must bide the t.* H4A IV, 4, 10. *now do I play the t., to try if thou be current gold indeed,* R3 IV, 2, 8. *thou t. of hearts* (viz. gold) Tim. IV, 3, 390.

Hence =test, proof: *hast thou killed him sleeping? O brave t.! could not a worm, an adder, do so much?* Mids. III, 2, 70 (= test or proof of bravery). *my friends of noble t.* Cor. IV, 1, 49 (of tried nobleness).

6) any single act in the exercise of an art; a) a stroke of a pen: *what strained —es rhetoric can lend,*

Sonn. 82, 10. b) the act of the hand on a musical instrument: *whose heavenly t. upon the lute doth ravish human sense,* Pilgr. 107. *Orpheus' lute, whose golden t. could soften steel and stones,* Gent. III, 2, 79. *stillness and the night become the —es of sweet harmony,* Merch. V, 57. *with sweetest —es pierce your mistress' ear,* 67. *put into his hands that knows no t. to tune the harmony,* R2 I, 3, 165. *I know no t. of it* (a recorder) Hml. III, 2, 371. c) a stroke of a pencil: *such heavenly —es ne'er touched earthly faces,* Sonn. 17, 8. *here is a t., is't good?* Tim. I, 1, 36. *artificial strife lives in these — es,* 38.

7) trait: *to have the —es dearest prized,* As III, 2, 160. *some lively —es of my daughter's favour,* V, 4, 27. *one of the prettiest —es of all,* Wint. V, 2, 89. *one t. of nature makes the whole world kin, that all with one consent praise new-born gawds,* Troil. III, 3, 175.*

Hence 8) a dash, a spice, a smack: *I perceive in you so excellent a t. of modesty,* Tw. II, 1, 13.* *behold ... a little t. of Harry in the night,* H5 IV Chor. 47. *I have a t. of your condition, which cannot brook the accent of reproof,* R3 IV, 4, 157. *give your friend some t. of your late business,* H8 V, 1, 13 (= hint).

**Touch,** vb. 1) to come in contact with in any manner, but particularly by means of the hand: *t. but my lips with those fair lips of thine,* Ven. 115. *to t. the fire,* 402. *though neither eyes nor ears, to hear nor see, yet should I be in love by —ing thee,* 438. *but to t. the crown,* Lucr. 216. *the boy for trial needs would t. my breast,* Sonn. 153, 10. Pilgr. 49. Tp. II, 2, 105. V, 286. Wiv. V, 5, 88. Err. II, 1, 111. II, 2, 120. Ado III, 3, 60. Merch. I, 1, 32. Shr. IV, 1, 96. Tw. II, 5, 171. R2 I, 3, 43. II, 3, 91. H4B IV, 1, 17 (*t. ground and dash themselves to pieces*). H5 III Chor. 33. III, 7, 17. H6A II, 5, 39. V, 3, 47. H8 I, 4, 75. Troil. I, 3, 304. III, 1, 164. Rom. I, 5, 53. 101. II, 2, 25. Caes. I, 2, 7. 8. Ant. V, 2, 246. Cymb. V, 3, 78. Per. I, 1, 28. 80. 87. V, 3, 75. Used of kissing and other amorous actions: *that you have — ed his queen forbiddenly,* Wint. I, 2, 416. *t. her soft mouth and march,* H5 II, 3, 61. *the sun no sooner shall the mountains t.* Hml. IV, 1, 29 (cf. below def. 8). *that I might t.! but kiss, one kiss,* Cymb. II, 2, 16. *on the —ing of her lips,* Per. V, 3, 42.

2) to take as food or drink, to taste: *she —ed no unknown baits,* Lucr. 103. Pilgr. 53. *to t. no food,* LLL I, 1, 39. *he dies that —es any of this fruit,* As II, 7, 98. *I will not t. a bit,* 133. *I am forbid to it* (burnt meat) Shr. IV, 1, 174. *before you t. the meat,* IV, 3, 46. *or t. one drop of it,* V, 2, 145. *ready to starve and dare not t. his own,* H6B I, 2, 229. Similarly: *never durst poet t. a pen to write,* LLL IV, 3, 346.

3) to strike, to hurt, to injure: *no loss shall t. her by my company,* Meas. III, 1, 181. *that no particular scandal once can t.* IV, 4, 30. *this —es me in reputation,* Err. IV, 1, 71. *t. her whoever dare,* Shr. III, 2, 235. *they shall not t. thee,* 240. *do not t. my lord,* All's III, 2, 114. *he will not t. young Arthur's life,* John III, 4, 160. *I will not t. thine eye,* IV, 1, 122. *the lion will not t. the true prince,* H4A II, 4, 300. *that face of his the hungry cannibals would not have — ed,* H6C I, 4, 153. *he would not then have — ed them,* Tit. II, 4, 47. *he that —es this my son,* IV, 2, 92. *I have —ed thee to the quick,* IV, 4, 36. *t. not the boy,* V, 1, 49. *seeing his reputation — ed to death,* Tim. III, 5, 19. *shall no man else be —ed but only Caesar?* Caes. II, 1, 154. *what villain —ed his body,* IV, 3, 20. *nor steel, nor poison*

... can t. him further, Mcb. III, 2, 26. he hath not —ed you yet, IV, 3, 14. they cannot t. me for coining, Lr. IV, 6, 83. with shame — the first that ever —ed him —, Cymb. III, 1, 25. heavens, how deeply you at once do t. me, IV, 3, 4. some mortally, some slightly —ed, V, 3, 10.

4) to hit, to come near: a loss in love that —es me more nearly, Sonn. 42, 4. ay, t. him, there's the vein, Meas. II, 2, 70. you — ed my vein at first, As II, 7, 94. when his holy state is — ed so near, H6A III, 1, 58. to t. his growth nearer than he — ed mine, R3 II, 4, 25. there you —ed the life of our design, Troil. II, 2, 194. t. me not so near, Oth. II, 3, 220.

5) to land, to come to shore; absol.: our ship hath — ed upon the deserts of Bohemia, Wint. III, 3, 1. Trans.: by his command have I here —ed Sicilia, Wint. V, 1, 139. shortly mean to t. our northern shore, R2 II, 1, 288. he —ed the ports desired, Troil. II, 2, 76.

6) to reach, to attain: — ing now the point of human skill, Mids. II, 2, 119. where fathom-line could never t. the ground, H4A I, 3, 204. I have — ed the highest point of all my greatness, H8 III, 2, 223. if he will t. the estimate, Tim. I, 1, 14 (pay the price at which it is estimated). hills whose heads t. heaven, Oth. I, 3, 141. thy thoughts t. their effects in this, Ant. V, 2, 333 (are realized).

7) to test by the touchstone, to probe, to try: which, being — ed and tried, proves valueless, John III, 1, 100. had —ed his spirit and tried his inclination, Cor. II, 3, 199. they have all been — ed and found base metal, Tim. III, 3, 6. t. them with several fortunes, IV, 3, 5. a suit wherein I mean to t. your love indeed, Oth. III, 3, 81.

8) to handle in a skilful manner; a) to play on as a musician: before you t. the instrument, Shr. III, 1, 64. t. thy instrument a strain or two, Caes. IV, 3, 257. b) to paint or to form as an artist: such heavenly touches ne'er —ed earthly faces, Sonn. 17, 8. spirits are not finely — ed but to fine issues, Meas. I, 1, 36. cf. whose beard the silver hand of peace hath —ed, H4B IV, 1, 43; the sun no sooner shall the mountains t. Hml. IV, 1, 29 (gild their summits. In both the latter passages a combination of different significations).

9) to mention in speaking: but t. this sparingly, R3 III, 5, 93. — ed you the bastardy of Edward's children? III, 7, 4. nearer than your particular demands will t. it, Hml. II, 1, 12. t. you the sourest points with sweetest terms, Ant. II, 2, 24.

10) to relate to, to concern: some affairs that t. me near, Gent. III, 1, 60. the contempts thereof are as — ing me, LLL I, 1, 191. it — eth us both ... to labour and effect one thing specially, Shr. I, 1, 118. to treat of high affairs — ing that time, John I, 101. the quarrel — eth none but us alone, H6A IV, 1, 118. R3 I, 3, 262. II, 3, 26. III, 2, 23. Troil. II, 2, 9. 126. Cor. III, 1, 123. Caes. III, 1, 7. 8. Hml. I, 3, 89. III, 2, 252. IV, 5, 207 (if they find us —ed; i. e. accessary to the deed). Lr. V, 1, 25. Oth. IV, 1, 209.

—ing = concerning: we may soon our satisfaction have — ing that point, Meas. I, 1, 84. H5 II, 2, 174. H6A III, 1, 50. H6B II, 2, 89. H6C II, 1, 119. III, 3, 136. Cor. I, 1, 155. Hml. I, 1, 25. I, 5, 137. Oth. II, 1, 32. Cymb. III, 5, 100. as — ing, in the same sense: LLL IV, 1, 123. H5 I, 1, 79. III, 2, 102. 107. R3 V, 3, 271.

11) to affect in any manner: a) applied to the senses: if any air of music t. their ears, Merch. V, 76 (is heard by them). they (her words) —ed not any stranger sense, All's I, 3, 114. my name hath — ed your ears, Cor. V, 2, 11. if the drink ... t. my palate adversely, II, 1, 61.

b) = to infect: that I am —ed with madness, Meas. V, 51. to be —ed with so many giddy offences, As III, 2, 366. — ed with that malignant cause, All's II, 1, 113. the life of all his blood is —ed corruptibly, John V, 7, 2. I'll t. my point with this contagion, Hml. IV, 7, 147. cf. sub d: Ado III, 2, 19. Shr. I, 1, 166.

c) to move, to rouse: which — ed the very virtue of compassion in thee, Tp. I, 2, 26. my patience here is —ed, Meas. V, 235. their familiarity, which was as gross as ever — ed conjecture, Wint. II, 1, 176.

d) to make an impression on, to move, to strike mentally, to fill with passion or a tender feeling: how seems he to be — ed? Meas. IV, 2, 148. how dearly would it t. thee to the quick, Err. II, 2, 132. if love have —ed you, nought remains but so, Shr. I, 1, 166. he is —ed to the noble heart, Wint. III, 2, 222. this deep disgrace in brotherhood —es me deeper than you can imagine, R3 I, 1, 112. his curses and his blessings t. me alike, H8 II, 2, 54. insupportable and — ing loss, Caes. IV, 3, 151. how Antony is —ed with what is spoke already, Ant. II, 2, 142. Caesar is —ed, V, 1, 33. I think the king be — ed at very heart, Cymb. I, 1, 10. Followed by with, to denote the passion or feeling inspired: —ed with anger, Tp. IV, 145. if so your heart were —ed with that remorse, Meas. II, 2, 54. to be truly —ed with love, Ado III, 2, 19. — ed with human gentleness and love, Merch. IV, 1, 25. —ed with choler, H5 IV, 7, 188. t. me with noble anger, Lr. II, 4, 279. —es us not with pity, V, 3, 232.

**Touching,** concerning, see Touch vb. 10.

**Touchstone,** a stone by which gold is tried: gold that's by the t. tried, Per. II, 2, 37.

Name of the clown in As II, 4, 19. III, 2, 12. 46.

**Tough,** 1) not soft and flexible, but stiff and unimpressible: my t. senior, LLL I, 2, 10. 11. 17. 18.

2) not easily worn or broken: we are — er than you can put us to't, Wint. I, 2, 15. thy t. commixture melts, H6C II, 6, 6. O sides, you are too t. Lr. II, 4, 200. upon the rack of this t. world, V, 3, 314.

**Toughness,** strength of texture, durability: cables of perdurable t. Oth. I, 3, 343.

**Touraine,** French province: John I, 11. II, 152. 487. at T., in Saint Katharine's churchyard, H6A I, 2, 100.

**Tournament,** tilt, joust: tilts and —s, Gent. I, 3, 30.

**Tourney,** vb. to tilt in the lists: to just and t. for her love, Per. II, 1, 116. wilt thou t. for the lady? 150.

**Tours,** French town: H6A IV, 3, 45. H6B I, 1, 5. I, 3, 53.

**Touse** (cf. toaze), to pull, to tear, to rend: to the rack with him! we'll t. you joint by joint, Meas. V, 313.

**Tow,** to drag through the water by means of a rope; writing of M. Edd. in Ant. III, 11, 58: thou knewest too well my heart was to thy rudder tied by the strings, and thou shouldst t. me after. O. Edd. stowe.

**Toward,** adj. 1) willing, apt, ready to do; opposed to froward: perverse it (love) shall be where it shows most t. Ven. 1157. then fell she on her back, fair queen and t. Pilgr. 55. 'tis a good hearing when children are t. Shr. V, 2, 182.

2) forward, bold: *that is spoken like a t. prince,* H6C II, 2, 66.

**Toward,** adv. in preparation and expectation, near at hand: *a play t.* Mids. III, 1, 81. *there is, sure, another flood t.* As V, 4, 35. *here's some good pastime t.* Shr. I, 1, 68. *some cheer is t.* V, 1, 14. *here's goodly stuff t.* H4B II, 4, 214. *here's a noble feast t.* Tim. III, 6, 68. *what might be t.* Hml. I, 1, 77. *what feast is t.* V, 2, 376. *have you heard of no likely wars t.* Lr. II, 1, 11. *there is some strange thing t.* III, 3, 21. *do you hear aught of a battle t.* IV, 6, 213. *four feasts are t.* Ant. II, 6, 75.

**Toward,** prep. (usually monosyll., sometimes dissyll.), 1) in a direction to: *leads t. Mantua,* Gent. V, 2, 47. *runnest t. him still,* Meas. III, 1, 13. *t. that shade address,* LLL V, 2, 92. *sighed his soul t. the Grecian tents,* Merch. V, 5; cf. *I have t. heaven breathed a secret vow,* III, 4, 27. *my father's (house) bears more t. the market-place,* Shr. V, 1, 10. *the clear stones t. the south north,* Tw. IV, 2, 41. *what incidency of harm is creeping t. me,* Wint. I, 2, 404. H6B IV, 2, 198. R3 I, 4, 13. H8 II, 4, 165. Mcb. II, 1, 34. Ant. III, 10, 31. Cymb. II, 2, 20 etc.

Often quite equivalent to *to: and then go I t.* Arragon, Ado III, 2, 2. *I must away this night t.* Padua, Merch. IV, 1, 403. *fly t. Belmont,* 457. *his big manly voice, turning again t. childish treble,* As II, 7, 162. *once more t. our father's,* Shr. IV, 5, 1. *go thou t. home,* All's II, 5, 95. *upon which errand I now go t. him,* Wint. V, 1, 232. *it draws t. supper in conclusion so,* John I, 204. *away t. Bury, to the Dauphin there,* IV, 3, 114. *tell him, t. Swinstead, to the abbey there,* V, 3, 8. *arrows fled not swifter t. their aim,* H4B I, 1, 123. *now dispatch we t. the court,* IV, 3, 82. *it now draws t. night,* H5 III, 6, 179. *in travel t. his warlike father,* H6A IV, 3, 36. *to-morrow t. London back again,* H6B II, 1, 201. *marched t. Saint Albans,* H6C II, 1, 114. *they hold their course t. Tewksbury,* V, 3, 19. *post t. the north,* R3 III, 2, 17. *shall we t. the Tower?* 91.119 (Qq *to*). *when mine oratory drew t. end,* III, 7, 20 (Qq *grew to an end*). *let us t. the king,* Mcb. I, 3, 152 etc.

2) tending to, aiming at and contributing to; for: *t. the education of your daughters I here bestow a simple instrument,* Shr. II, 99. *to use 'em t. a supply of money,* Tim. II, 2, 200. *if it be aught t. the general good,* Caes. I, 2, 85. *by doing every thing safe t. your love and honour,* Mcb. I, 4, 27. cf. H5 IV, 8, 4 and Tim. V, 1, 23.

3) to, in a moral sense: *no love t. others in that bosom sits,* Sonn. 9, 13. *in his love t. her ever most kind and natural,* Meas. III, 1, 229. *wherein t. me my homely stars have failed,* All's II, 5, 80. *this was a great argument of love in her t. you,* Tw. III, 2, 13. *disobedience and ingratitude to you and t. your friend,* Wint. III, 2, 70. *have misdemeaned yourself t. the king,* H8 V, 3, 15. *they confess t. thee forgetfulness,* Tim. V, 1, 147. *cold-hearted t. me,* Ant. III, 13, 158.

4) Denoting a person referred to in a question, = with: *I will be thy adversary t. Anne Page,* Wiv. II, 3, 99. *your loving motion t. the common body, to yield what passes here,* Cor. II, 2, 57 (cf. *towards:* Cor. V, 1, 41. Cymb. II, 3, 68).

**Towardly,** ready to do or learn, docile, tractable: *I have observed thee always for a t. prompt spirit,* Tim. III, 1, 37.

**Towards,** adv. in preparation, at hand: *we have a trifling foolish banquet t.* Rom. I, 5, 124.

**Towards,** prep. (usually monosyll., sometimes dissyll.), 1) in a direction to: *t. thee I'll run and give him leave to go,* Sonn. 51, 14. *as the waves make t. the pebbled shore,* 60, 1. *cutting the clouds t. Paphos,* Tp. IV, 93. *always bending t. their project,* 175. *his intent t. our wives,* Wiv. II, 1, 181. *if he should intend this voyage t. my wife,* 189. *was carried t. Corinth,* Err. I, 1, 88. *some unborn sorrow is coming t. me,* R2 II, 2, 11. *with what wings shall his affections fly t. fronting peril,* H4B IV, 4, 66. *blow t. England's blessed shore,* H6B III, 2, 90. *threw it t. thy land,* 108. *glided t. your majesty,* 260. *we'll forward t. Warwick,* H6C IV, 7, 82 (i. e. to oppose him). *it ripens t. it,* Ant. II, 7, 103 etc.

Equivalent to *to: a reverend man ... t. this afflicted fancy drew,* Compl. 61. *if you can carry her your desires t. her,* Wiv. I, 1, 245 (Evans' speech). *t. Florence is he?* All's III, 2, 71. *pace softly t. my kinsman's,* Wint. IV, 3, 121. *I t. the north, ... my wife to France,* R2 V, 1, 76. *you ... t. York shall bend you,* H4A V, 5, 36. *the king is now in progress t. Saint Albans,* H6B I, 4, 76. *let's march t. London,* IV, 3, 20. *t. Berwick post amain,* H6C II, 5, 128. *he comes t. London,* IV, 4, 26. *now t. Chertsey,* R3 I, 2, 29. 226. *the mayor t. Guildhall hies him,* III, 5, 73. *t. London they do bend their course,* IV, 5, 14. *gallop apace ... t. Phoebus' lodging,* Rom. III, 2, 2. *strike up the drum t. Athens,* Tim. IV, 3, 169. *we first address t. you,* Lr. I, 1, 193. *and t. himself ... we must extend our notice,* Cymb. II, 3, 64 etc.

2) tending to, aiming at, for: *t. our assistance we do seize to us the plate,* R2 II, 1, 160. *quick is mine ear to hear of good t. him,* 234. *certain issue strokes must arbitrate, t. which advance the war,* Mcb. V, 4, 21.

3) to, in a moral sense: *which sorrow is always t. ourselves, not heaven,* Meas. II, 3, 32. *what warmth is there in your affection t. any of these suitors?* Merch. I, 2, 37. *there is some ill a brewing t. my rest,* II, 5, 17. *the rather will I spare my praises t. him,* All's II, 1, 106. *if the duke continue these favours t. you,* Tw. I, 4, 1. *the manner of your bearing t. him,* Wint. IV, 4, 569. *a heart that wishes t. you honour and plenteous safety,* H8 I, 1, 103. *like her true nobility, she has carried herself t. me,* II, 4, 143. *his malice t. you,* Cor. II, 3, 197. *Rome, whose gratitude t. her deserved children,* III, 1, 292. *our graces t. him,* Mcb. I, 6, 30. *if there be any good meaning t. you,* Lr. I, 2, 190. *our intents, which t. you are most gentle,* Ant. V, 2, 127. *the malice t. you,* Cymb. V, 5, 419.

4) with (cf. *toward,* prep. 4): *make trial what your love can do for Rome t. Marcius,* Cor. V, 1, 41. *we shall have need to employ you t. this Roman,* Cymb. II, 3, 68.

5) about: *t. three or four o'clock,* R3 III, 5, 101.

**Tower,** subst. 1) a very high and strong building: Lucr. 945. 1382. Sonn. 64, 3. Pilgr. 327. Tp. IV, 152. Gent. III, 1, 35. 119. John II, 325. H4A III, 1, 33. H6A I, 4, 11. 76. III, 2, 23. IV, 2, 13. Troil. I, 2, 2. IV, 5, 220. Rom. IV, 1, 78. Tim. V, 4, 25. Caes. I, 1, 44. I, 3, 93. Lr. III, 4, 187. Per. I, 4, 24. Symbol of strength: *strong as a t. in hope,* R2 I, 3, 102. *the king's name is a t. of strength,* R3 V, 3, 12.

2) name of the ancient castle of London used as a citadel, an arsenal, and a state-prison: R2 IV, 316.

V, 1, 52. H6A I, 1, 167. I, 3, 1. 61. H6B IV, 5, 5. IV, 6, 17. IV, 9, 38. H6C III, 2, 120. IV, 8, 57. V, 5, 50. R3 I, 1, 45. H8 I, 1, 207. I, 2, 194. V, 1, 107. V, 3, 54 etc. *at the T.* H6A III, 1, 23. R3 III, 1, 65. 139 etc. *in the T.* H6B V, 1, 41. R3 IV, 2, 76. V, 3, 151 etc. Said to have been built by Julius Caesar: R2 V, 1, 2. R3 III, 1, 68.

**Tower,** vb. to fly high, to soar as a bird of prey: *which like a falcon —ing in the skies coucheth the fowl below,* Lucr. 506. *ha, majesty! how high thy glory —s,* John II, 350. *and like an eagle o'er his aery —s,* V, 2, 149. *my lord protector's hawks do t. so well,* H6B II, 1, 10. *a falcon —ing in her pride of place,* Mcb. II, 4, 12. *—ing =* very high: *the bravery of his grief did put me into a —ing passion,* Hml. V, 2, 80.

**Towered,** having towers: *a t. citadel,* Ant. IV, 14, 4.

**Towerhill,** meeting-place of the Puritans in the poet's time: *the tribulation of T.* H8 V, 4, 65.

**Town,** a collection of houses larger than a village: Pilgr. 327. Gent. V, 4, 3. Wiv. I, 1, 299. I, 3, 39. II, 1, 149. II, 2, 198. II, 3, 78. V, 5, 112. Err. I, 1, 15. I, 2, 6. 12. 22. 97. II, 2, 151. Ado III, 4, 102. LLL I, 1, 147. Mids. I, 1, 165. II, 1, 238. As III, 3, 59. V, 4, 149. 152. H6A I, 1, 63. 91. H6B I, 3, 138. II, 1, 164. III, 1, 63. H6C IV, 2, 15 etc. etc. *the peasant —s,* H4B Ind. 33 (German: *Landstädte*). *our —s of war,* H5 II, 4, 7. Oth. II, 3, 213. *through every market t.* H6B II, 1, 159. Lr. III, 6, 78. *seven walled —s of strength,* H6A III, 4, 7. *—s of garrison,* V, 4, 168. *this enemy t.* Cor. IV, 4, 24. With *of:* *our t. of Cicester,* R2 V, 6, 3. *the t. of Orleans,* H6A I, 6, 9. H6C I, 4, 180. II, 2, 1. R3 V, 2, 12. *Leicester t.* R3 V, 5, 10. *Lud's t.* Cymb. III, 1, 32. IV, 2, 99. V, 5, 481. Without the article: *at —'s end,* H4A IV, 2, 10 (Ff *at the —'s end*). *in field and t.* Mids. III, 2, 398. *there's a nobleman in t.* Rom. II, 4, 213. Oth. I, 3, 44. *what good sport is out of t.* Troil. I, 1, 116. *come to t.* Wiv. IV, 5, 78. Shr. I, 1, 47. H4B II, 2, 108. 177. Distinguished from city: *razeth your cities and subverts your —s,* H6A II, 3, 65. III, 3, 45. III, 4, 7. R3 I, 4, 146. Confounded with city: Tw. III, 3, 19. 24. Cor. IV, 4, 1. 24. = the inhabitants of the town: *the t. will rise,* Oth. II, 3, 161. *the t. might fall in fright,* 232.

Compounds: *t. armoury,* Shr. III, 2, 47. *t. bull,* H4B II, 2, 172. *t. crier,* Hml. III, 2, 4. *t. gate,* LLL I, 2, 75. *t. way,* Wiv. III, 1, 7.

**Town-crier,** a public crier who makes proclamation: Hml. III, 2, 4.

**Township,** the body of the inhabitants of a town: *I am but a poor petitioner of our whole t.* H6B I, 3, 27.

**Townsmen,** the inhabitants of a town: John II, 361. H6B II, 1, 68.

**Toy,** subst. 1) any thing liked and affected, though of little worth; a bawble: *haply your eye shall light upon some t. you have desire to purchase,* Tw. III, 3, 44. *any silk, any thread, any —s for your head,* Wint. IV, 4, 326. cf. Ant. V, 2, 166.

2) a futile thing, a nothingness: *sells eternity to get a t.* Lucr. 214. (set) *as little by such —s as possible,* Gent. I, 2, 82. *I do not like des —s,* Wiv. I, 4, 46 (Dr. Caius' speech). *silence, you airy —s,* V, 5, 46. *critic Timon laugh at idle —s,* LLL IV, 3, 170. *a t., my liege,* 201. *I never may believe these antique fables nor these fairy —s,* Mids. V, 3. *even a t. in hand here,* As III, 3, 77. *tut, a t.!* Shr. II, 404 (= nonsense!). *a*

*knack, a t., a trick, a baby's cap,* IV, 3, 67. *a foolish thing was but a t.* Tw. V, 400. *dreams are —s,* Wint. III, 3, 39. *shall we fall foul for —s?* H4B III, 4, 183. *for a t., a thing of no regard,* H6A IV, 1, 145. *being but a t., which is no grief to give,* R3 III, 1, 114. *there's nothing serious in mortality; all is but —s,* Mcb. II, 3, 99. *each t. seems prologue to some great amiss,* Hml. IV, 5, 18. *light-winged —s of feathered Cupid,* Oth. I, 3, 269 (cf. the verb *to toy*). *some lady trifles, ... immoment —s,* Ant. V, 2, 166. *triumphs for nothing and lamenting —s is jollity for apes and grief for boys,* Cymb. IV, 2, 193.

3) an idle fancy, an odd conceit, a folly: *the tricks and —s that in them* (women) *lurk,* Pilgr. 337. *there's —s abroad,* John I, 232 (there are follies in the world). *such like —s as these have moved his highness to commit me now,* R3 I, 1, 60. *if no inconstant t. nor womanish fear abate thy valour in the acting it,* Rom. IV, 1, 119. *hold it a fashion and a t. in blood,* Hml. I, 3, 6. *the very place puts —s of desperation ... into every brain,* I, 4, 75. *no conception nor no jealous t. concerning you,* Oth. III, 4, 156.

**Toy,** vb. to trifle, to dally amorously: *with leaden appetite, unapt to t.* Ven. 34. *to t., to wanton,* 106.

**Toze,** see *Toaze.*

**Trace,** subst. mark left, vestige: *no t. of him,* Cymb. V, 5, 12.

Plur. *—s* = harness for beasts of draught: *the —s of the smallest spider's web,* Rom. I, 4, 61.

**Trace,** vb. 1) to follow by footsteps or other marks left: *why may not imagination t. the noble dust of Alexander?* Hml. V, 1, 224. *the search so slow, that could not t. them,* Cymb. I, 1, 65.

2) to follow: *can t. me in the tedious ways of art,* H4A III, 1, 48. *all my joy t. the conjunction,* H8 III, 2, 45. *his wife, his babes, and all unfortunate souls that t. him in his line,* Mcb. IV, 1, 153.

3) to put on the track: *this poor trash of Venice, whom I t. for his quick hunting,* Oth. II, 1, 312 (most M. Edd. *trash*).

4) to delineate, to draw: *who else would t. him, his umbrage, nothing more,* Hml. V, 2, 125 (or = follow?).

5) to walk over, to pace: *as we do t. this alley up and down,* Ado III, 1, 16. *to t. the forests,* Mids. II, 1, 25.

**Track** (Ff *tract*) course, way; used of the sun: *the envious clouds are bent to dim his glory and to stain the t. of his bright passage to the occident,* R2 III, 3, 66. *the weary sun hath made a golden set and, by the bright t. of his fiery car, gives signal of a goodly day,* R3 V, 3, 20.

**Tract,** 1) trace, track: *flies an eagle flight, bold and forth on, leaving no t. behind,* Tim. I, 1, 50 (by which to trace and follow it).

2) course, way (of the sun): *the eyes now converted are from his low t.* Sonn. 7, 12. R2 III, 3, 66 and R3 V, 3, 20 (Qq and M. Edd. *track*).

3) course, proceeding: *the t. of every thing would by a good discourser lose some life,* H8 I, 1, 40.

**Tractable,** manageable, governable, compliant: *thou shalt find me t. to any honest reason,* H4A III, 3, 194. *if thou dost find him t. to us,* R3 III, 1, 174. *this t. obedience,* H8 I, 2, 64. Troil. II, 3, 160. Tit. I, 470. Per. IV, 6, 211.

**Trade,** subst. 1) traffic, commerce: *the t. and profit of the city consisteth of all nations,* Merch. III, 3,

30. *others, like merchants, venture t. abroad,* H5 I, 2, 192.

2) frequent resort and intercourse: *some way of common t.* R2 III, 3, 156. *where most t. of danger ranged,* H4B I, 1, 174. *stands in the gap and t. of moe preferments,* H8 V, 1, 36.

3) business of any kind: *if your t. be to her,* Tw. III, 1, 83. *have you any further t. with us?* Hml. III, 2, 346.

4) business pursued for procuring subsistence; occupation, profession, particularly mechanical employment: Wiv. I, 3, 18. Meas. I, 2, 111. II, 1, 237. 238. 270. IV, 2, 53. 58. IV, 3, 20. Shr. III, 1, 69. Troil. V, 10, 52. Cor. III, 2, 134. IV, 1, 13. Tim. IV, 1, 18. IV, 3, 133. 460. Caes. I, 1, 13. Mcb. II, 3, 121. Hml. V, 1, 187. Lr. IV, 1, 40. IV, 6, 15. Oth. I, 2, 1. Per. IV, 2, 12. 42. IV, 6, 74. 76. *what t. are you of?* Meas. II, 1, 206. *what t. art thou?* H4B III, 2, 160. Caes. I, 1, 5. 9. 12. *had been but two hours at the t.* Lr. II, 2, 65. *how long have you been at this t.?* Per. IV, 6, 73.

5) standing practice, custom, habit: *thy sin's not accidental, but a t.* Meas. III, 1, 149.

**Trade,** vb. to traffic, to carry on commerce, to deal: *they shall be my East and West Indies, and I will t. to them both,* Wiv. I, 3, 79. *the common ferry which* —*s to Venice,* Merch. III, 4, 54. *we shall have good* —*ing that way,* H4A II, 4, 401. *how did you dare to t. and traffic with Macbeth in riddles and affairs of death,* Mcb. III, 5, 4. *music, moody food of us that t. in love,* Ant. II, 5, 2.

**Traded,** professional: *villany is not without such rheum* (tears)*, and he, long t. in it, makes it seem like rivers of remorse,* John IV, 3, 109. *eyes and ears, two t. pilots 'twixt the dangerous shores of will and judgment,* Troil. II, 2, 64.

**Trade-fallen,** fallen, brought low in one's business: *revolted tapsters and ostlers t.* H4A IV, 2, 32.

**Traders,** persons engaged in trade or commerce: *I'll view the manners of the town, peruse the t., gaze upon the buildings,* Err. I, 2, 13. *the embarked t. on the flood,* Mids. II, 1, 127. *t. riding to London with fat purses,* H4A I, 2, 141. *good t. in the flesh,* Troil. V, 10, 46 (= dealers).

**Tradesman,** probably a shopkeeper: *I meddle with no* —*'s matters, nor women's matters, but with awl,* Caes. I, 1, 25. Plur. *tradesmen: it* (lying) *becomes none but tradesmen,* Wint. IV, 4, 745. *our tradesmen singing in their shops,* Cor. IV, 6, 8.

**Tradition,** old custom: *the courtesy of nations allows you my better, . . . but the same t. takes not away my blood,* As I, 1, 51. *throw away respect, t., form and ceremonious duty,* R2 III, 2, 173. *will you mock at an ancient t., begun upon an honourable respect,* H5 V, 1, 74.

**Traditional,** attached to old customs, old-fashioned: *too ceremonious and t.* R3 III, 1, 45.

**Traduce,** to censure, to decry, to defame: *a divulged shame* —*d by odious ballads,* All's II, 1, 175. —*d by ignorant tongues,* H8 I, 2, 72. —*d and taxed of other nations,* Hml. I, 4, 18. *beat a Venetian and* —*d the state,* Oth. V, 2, 354. *he is already* —*d for levity,* Ant. III, 7, 14.

**Traducement,** obloquy: *'twere a concealment worse than a theft, no less than a t., to hide your doings,* Cor. I, 9, 22.

**Traffic,** subst. 1) trade, commerce: *having t. with*

*thyself alone, thou of thyself thy sweet self dost deceive,* Sonn. 4, 9. *no kind of t. would I admit,* Tp. II, 1, 148. *to admit no t. to our adverse towns,* Err. I, 1, 15. *a merchant of great t. through the world,* Shr. I, 1, 12. *which for* —*'s sake most of our city did,* Tw. III, 3, 34. *my t. is sheets,* Wint. IV, 3, 23. *t. confound thee,* Tim. I, 1, 244. 246. 247.

2) business, transaction: *I give thee kingly thanks, because this is in t. of a king,* H6A V, 3, 164. *the fearful passage of their love . . . is now the two hours' t. of our stage,* Rom. Prol. 12.

**Traffic,** vb. 1) to practise commerce: *despair to gain doth t. oft for gaining,* Lucr. 131.

2) to have business, to deal, to have to do: *since dishonour* —*s with man's nature, he is but outside,* Tim. I, 1, 158. *to trade and t. with Macbeth in riddles and affairs of death,* Mcb. III, 5, 4.

**Trafficker,** trader, merchant: Merch. I, 1, 12.

**Tragedian,** an actor of tragedy (or actor, player, in general?): *has led the drum before the English* —*s,* All's IV, 3, 299. *I can counterfeit the deep t.* R3 III, 5, 5. *those you were wont to take delight in, the* —*s of the city,* Hml. II, 2, 342.

**Tragedy,** 1) a dramatic representation of a serious action: Mids. V, 367. Hml. II, 2, 416. III, 2, 159.

2) a mournful and dreadful event: Lucr. 766. H5 I, 2, 106. H6A I, 4, 77. H6B III, 1, 153. III, 2, 194. H6C II, 3, 27. R3 III, 2, 59. Tit. II, 3, 265. IV, 1, 60.

**Tragic,** of the nature of tragedy, mournful, calamitous: Compl. 308. Phoen. 52. Err. I, 1, 65. H4B I, 1, 61. H6B IV, 1, 4. H6C V, 6, 28. R3 II, 2, 39. IV, 4, 68 (Ff *frantic*). Tit. IV, 1, 47. Oth. V, 2, 363.

**Tragical,** the same: Mids. V, 57. 66. H6A III, 1, 125. R3 IV, 4, 7. *tragical-historical, tragical-comical-historical-pastoral,* Hml. II, 2, 417. 418.

**Trail,** subst. trace, track, scent: *if I cry out thus upon no t.* Wiv. IV, 2, 208 (if I bark, like a hound, on a wrong scent). *or else this brain of mine hunts not the t. of policy so sure,* Hml. II, 2, 47. *how cheerfully on the false t. they cry,* IV, 5, 109. *this is an aspic's t., and these fig-leaves have slime upon them,* Ant. V, 2, 354.

**Trail,** vb. to draw along the ground: —*est thou the puissant pike?* H5 IV, 1, 40 (Pistol's speech). *along the field I will the Trojan t.* Troil. V, 8, 22. *beat thou the drum, that it speak mournfully: t. your steel pikes,* Cor. V, 6, 152.

**Train,** subst. 1) something drawn along behind; the end of a robe: Gent. II, 4, 159. H6B I, 3, 88. H8 II, 3, 98 (*honour's t. is longer than his foreskirt*). IV, 1, 51. the tail of a peacock: *we'll pull his plumes and take away his t.* H6A III, 3, 7. Applied to the tail of a comet: *stars with* —*s of fire,* Hml. I, 1, 117.

2) a retinue, a number of attendants: Tp. V, 300. LLL III, 166. Mids. II, 1, 25. Wint. II, 1, 33. V, 1, 92. 163. H6A V, 4, 100. R3 II, 2, 120. H8 IV, 1, 37. Tit. II, 3, 75. Caes. I, 2, 184. Lr. I, 4, 270. 274. 285. II, 4, 64 (Ff *number*). 161. 177. 207. 308. = company: *which of this princely t. call ye the warlike Talbot?* H6A II, 2, 34. = troops, army: *let our* —*s march by us,* H4B IV, 2, 93.

3) something used to allure and entice; a bait: *Macbeth by many of these* —*s hath sought to win me into his power,* Mcb. IV, 3, 118.*

**Train,** vb. 1) to draw, to entice, to allure: *t. me not with thy note, to drown me,* Err. III, 2, 45. *t. our* *intellects to vain delight*, LLL I, 1, 71. *as a call to t. ten thousand English to their side*, John III, 4, 175. *we did t. him on*, H4A V, 2, 21. *for that cause I —ed thee to my house*, H6A II, 3, 35. *you t. me to offend you*, Troil. V, 3, 4. *I —ed thy brethren to that guileful hole*, Tit. V, 1, 104.

2) to bring up, to educate, to teach: *never —ed to offices of courtesy*, Merch. IV, 1, 32. *you have —ed me like a peasant*, As I, 1, 72. *they were —ed together*, Wint. I, 1, 24. *Henry the Fifth he first —ed to the wars*, H6A I, 4, 79. *nobly —ed*, Rom. III, 5, 182 (Ff and later Qq *allied*). *he must be taught and —ed*, Caes. IV, 1, 35. *by Cleon —ed in music*, Per. IV Prol. 7. With *up*: *I was —ed up in the English court*, H4A III, 1, 122. *he was never —ed up in arms*, R3 V, 3, 272. Tit. I, 30. Cymb. III, 3, 82. V, 5, 338. *Training* = education: H8 I, 2, 112. Per. III, 3, 16. IV, 6, 119.

**Traitor**, one guilty of treason: Lucr. 361. 877. 888. 1686. Tp. I, 2, 460. 469. V, 128. Meas. I, 4, 77. LLL IV, 3, 212. V, 2, 604. As I, 3, 54. All's I, 1, 50. H6A I, 3, 15. II, 1, 19. II, 4, 97. IV, 3, 27. H6B I, 3, 177. 182. 197. I, 4, 44. II, 3, 103. III, 1, 174. IV, 2, 115. 177. R3 III, 4, 77. H8 I, 2, 214. Tit. V, 2, 178 etc. With *to* before the person or cause betrayed: Gent. IV, 4, 110. Err. III, 2, 167. As II, 3, 13. Shr. V, 2, 160. R2 I, 3, 24. 39. IV, 135. H6C I, 1, 79. R3 I, 4, 210. Cor. III, 3, 66.

Used as a feminine: As I, 3, 58. 74. Shr. V, 2, 160. All's II, 1, 99. Wint. II, 1, 89. In Wiv. III, 3, 65 the spurious Qq and M. Edd. *t.*, Ff *tyrant*.

Adjectively: *his t. eye*, Lucr. 73. *a t. coward*, R2 I, 1, 102. *a t. villain*, H6A IV, 3, 13. *their t. father*, H6B V, 1, 116. *the t. murderer*, Rom. III, 5, 85 (Ff and later Qq om. *murderer*).

**Traitorly**, treacherous: Wint. IV, 4, 821 (Autolycus' speech).

**Traitorous**, treacherous: H6A IV, 1, 173. H6B III, 2, 240. Cor. III, 1, 175. Tit. I, 302. 452. IV, 1, 93. IV, 4, 53. Hml. I, 5, 43. Lr. III, 7, 8.

**Traitorously**, treacherously, perfidiously: All's IV, 3, 339. H6B II, 2, 27. III, 2, 123. IV, 7, 35.

**Traitress**, a woman who betrays; apparently used as a term of endearment: *a counsellor, a t. and a dear*, All's I, 1, 184.

**Trammel up**, either to tie up or to net up (a trammel meaning both a kind of long net and a contrivance used for regulating the motions of a horse): *if the assassination could t. up the consequence and catch with his surcease success*, Mcb. I, 7, 3.

**Trample**, to stamp, to paw: *a breeding jennet ... Adonis' —ing courser doth espy*, Ven. 261. With *on*, = to tread on in contempt: *—ing contemptuously on thy disdain*, Gent. I, 2, 112. *t. on their sovereign's head*, R2 III, 3, 157. *o'errun and —d on*, Troil. III, 3, 163. Trans. in the same sense: *which with usurping steps do t. thee*, R2 III, 2, 17.

**Trance**, want of self-consciousness, a state of being beside one's self; 1) ecstasy: *'tis time to stir him from his t.* Shr. I, 1, 182. 2) bewilderment: *disturb his hours of rest with restless —s*, Lucr. 974. *both stood, like old acquaintance in a t.*, *met far from home, wondering each other's chance*, 1595.

**Tranced**, seemingly dead, insensible: Lr. V, 3, 218. cf. *Entranced*.

**Tranect**, a word probably corrupted from the Italian *traghetto* (= ferry): *bring them ... unto the t.*,

to the common *ferry which trades to Venice*, Merch. III, 4, 53. (*see: traject.*).

**Tranio**, name in Shr. I, 1, 1. 17 etc.

**Tranquil**, peaceful, calm: *t. mind*, Oth. III, 3, 348.

**Tranquillity**, ease, freedom from care: *with nobility and t., burgomasters and great oneyers*, H4A II, 1, 84.

**Transcend**, to be superior to others: *that praise, sole pure, —s*, Troil. I, 3, 244.

**Transcendence**, supereminence: *in a most weak and debile minister great power, great t.* All's II, 3, 40.

**Transfer**, to transport or remove from one situation to another, to transform, to change: *in things right true my heart and eyes have erred, and to this false plague* (i. e. this plague of being false) *are they now —ed*, Sonn. 137, 14.

**Transfigure**, to transform, to metamorphose: *all their minds —d so together*, Mids. V, 24.

**Transfix**, to transplace, to remove: *time doth t. the flourish set on youth*, Sonn. 60, 9.

**Transform**, to metamorphose: Wiv. IV, 5, 98. Err. II, 2, 197. III, 2, 40. LLL IV, 3, 82. Mids. IV, 1, 69 (*this —ed scalp*, i. e. this scalp by which a transformation is effected): R2 V, 1, 27. Tit. II, 3, 64. Tim. V, 4, 19. Caes. I, 3, 24. With *from*: *the power of beauty will sooner t. honesty from what it is to a bawd*, Hml. III, 1, 112. *these dispositions that of late t. you from . . .* (Ff *transport*) Lr. I, 4, 242. With *into*: As II, 7, 1. Oth. II, 3, 293. Ant. I, 1, 12. With *to*: Wiv. V, 5, 86. Err. III, 2, 151. Ado II, 3, 25. LLL IV, 3, 166. Merch. II, 6, 39. R3 IV, 4, 322. Hml. III, 1, 112. Ant. IV, 2, 36. With a double accus.: *if the fat villain have not —ed him ape*, H4B II, 2, 77.

**Transformation**, change of appearance, metamorphosis: Wint. IV, 4, 31. H4A I, 1, 44. H4B II, 2, 194. Tim. IV, 3, 349. Hml. II, 2, 5. = the shape to which one is changed: *how my t. hath been washed and cudgelled*, Wiv. IV, 5, 98. *the goodly t. of Jupiter there, his brother, the bull*, Troil. V, 1, 59.

**Transgress**, to offend, to sin: *let sin, alone committed, light alone upon his head that hath —ed so*, Lucr. 1481. *before he* (Adam) *—ed*, Ado II, 1, 260. *you —ing slave*, LLL I, 2, 159. *virtue that —es is but patched with sin*, Tw. I, 5, 53. *my —ing boy*, R2 V, 3, 96. With *against*: *I have then sinned against his experience and —ed against his valour*, All's II, 5, 11.

**Transgression**, offence, crime: Lucr. 634. Sonn. 120, 3. Gent. II, 4, 197. Meas. III, 2, 101. Ado II, 1, 229. 232. 233. LLL V, 2, 431. John I, 256. Rom. I, 1, 191.

**Transilvanian**, see *Transylvanian*.

**Translate**, 1) to transform, to change: *so are those errors that in thee are seen to truths —d*, Sonn. 96, 8. *how many lambs might the stern wolf betray, if like a lamb he could his looks t.* 10 (i. e. change his shape so as to look like a lamb). *were the world mine, Demetrius being bated, the rest I'ld give to be to you —d*, Mids. I, 1, 191 (I would give the rest, to be changed to you, i. e. if, in return, I were you). Bottom, *thou art —d*, III, 1, 122. *left sweet Pyramus —d there*, III, 2, 32. *t. thy life into death, thy liberty into bondage*, As V, 1, 58. *would t. his malice towards you into love*, Cor. II, 3, 197. *whose present grace to present slaves and servants —s his rivals*, Tim. I, 1, 72. *than the force of honesty can t. beauty into his likeness*, Hml. III, 1, 113.

2) to render into another language (or rather to change by rendering into another language): —*d her will out of honesty into English,* Wiv. I, 3, 54. *can t. the stubbornness of nature into so quiet and so sweet a style,* As II, 1, 19. *wherefore do you so ill t. yourself out of the speech of peace that bears such grace into the harsh and boisterous tongue of war?* H4B IV, 1, 47.

3) to interpret, to explain: *that any thing he sees, which moves his liking, I can with ease t. it to my will,* John II, 513. *Aeneas ... did in great Ilion thus t. him to me,* Troil. IV, 5, 112. *there's matter in these sighs; these profound heaves you must t.; 'tis fit we understand them,* Hml. IV, 1, 2.

**Translation,** interpretation, explication, analysis: *some thousand verses of a faithful lover, a huge t. of hypocrisy,* LLL V, 2, 51 (a huge commentary on the nature of hypocrisy).

**Transmigrate,** to pass from one body into another: *the elements once out of it, it* —*s,* Ant. II, 7, 51.

**Transmutation,** change into another state: *by education a card-maker, by t. a bear-herd,* Shr. Ind. 2, 21 (Sly's speech).

**Transparent,** 1) pervious to the light, pellucid: *nor shines the silver moon one half so bright through the t. bosom of the deep,* LLL IV, 3, 31. *t. Helena, nature shows art, that through thy bosom makes me see thy heart,* Mids. II, 2, 104. *bay windows t. as barricadoes,* Tw. IV, 2, 40.

2) bright: *the glorious sun's t. beams,* H6B III, 1, 353. *t. heretics* (the eyes), *be burnt for liars,* Rom. I, 2, 96.

**Transport,** vb. 1) to bear or carry from one place to another: *the winds which should t. me farthest from your sight,* Sonn. 117, 8. *the scene is now* —*ed to Southampton,* H5 II Chor. 35. *for costs and charges in* —*ing her,* H6B I, 1, 134. Applied to letters, messages and the like borne or sent: *I shall not need t. my words by you; here comes his grace in person,* R2 II, 3, 81. *a servant* —*ing a sum of money,* H5 IV, 1, 159. *which* (conditions of peace) *shall .be* —*ed presently to France,* H6A V, 1, 40. *when I came hither to t. the tidings,* Mcb. IV, 3, 181. *might not you t. her purposes by word?* Lr. IV, 5, 20 (instead of by letter).

2) to bear, to carry: *her ashes ...* —*ed shall be at high festivals before the kings and queens of France,* H6A I, 6, 26. *he cannot temperately t. his honours from where he should begin and end,* Cor. II, 1, 240 (= from where he should begin to where he should end. cf. *the gap that we shall make in time, from our hence-going and our return,* Cymb. III, 2, 65). *whose whisper ... as level as the cannon to his blank,* —*s his poisoned shot,* Hml. IV, 1, 43. —*ed ... to the gross clasps of a lascivious Moor,* Oth. I, 1, 125.

3) to remove from this world to the next, to kill (euphemistically): *to t. him in the mind he is were damnable,* Meas. IV, 3, 72. *he cannot be heard of; out of doubt he is* —*ed,* Mids. IV, 2, 4 (Starveling's speech).

4) to put beside one's self; to hurry away by violence of passion: *being* —*ed by my jealousies to bloody thoughts,* Wint. III, 2, 159. *you are* —*ed by calamity thither where more attends you,* Cor. I, 1, 77.

b) to bear away the soul in ecstasy, to ravish: *being* —*ed and rapt in secret studies,* Tp. I, 2, 76. *my lord's almost so far* —*ed that he'll think anon it lives,* Wint. V, 3, 69. *thy letters have* —*ed me beyond this ignorant present,* Mcb. I, 5, 57. — Lr. I, 4, 242 Ff t., Qq *transform.*

**Transportance,** conveyance, waftage: *be thou my Charon and give me swift t. to those fields,* Troil. III, 2, 12.

**Transpose,** to change: *things base and vile, holding no quantity, love can t. to form and dignity,* Mids. I, 1, 233. *that which you are my thoughts cannot t.* Mcb. IV, 3, 21.

**Trans-shape,** to shape into another form, to distort, to caricature: *thus did she ... t. thy particular virtues,* Ado V, 1, 172.

**Transylvanian,** a native of Transylvania: Per. IV, 2, 23.

**Trap,** subst. an engine shutting with a spring, used for taking mice: H5 I, 2, 177. Figuratively, an insidious stratagem: Ado III, 1, 106. *to lay a t.* H6A III, 1, 22. H8 V, 1, 143. *I will say 'marry t.' with you,* Wiv. I, 1, 170 ('exclamation of insult when a man was caught in his own stratagem.' Johnson).

**Trap,** vb. 1) to catch insidiously, to ensnare: *snares to t. mine enemies,* H6B III, 1, 340. cf. *Entrap.*

2) to dress (a horse) with ornaments: *thy horses shall be* —*ed,* Shr. Ind. 2, 43. *horses* —*ed in silver,* Tim. I, 2, 189.

**Trapping,** ornaments of horse furniture: *rich caparisons or t. gay,* Ven. 286. Plur. —*s* = any ornamental appendages: *we are some of her* —*s,* Tw. V, 10. *these but the* —*s and the suits of woe,* Hml. I, 2, 86.

**Trash,** subst. worthless matter, dross, lumber: *it is but t.* Tp. IV, 223. *lay hands upon these traitors and their t.* H6B I, 4, 44. Troil. II, 1, 138. Caes. I, 3, 108. IV, 3, 26. 74. Oth. III, 3, 157. Used of worthless persons: *this poor t. of Venice,* Oth. II, 1, 312. *I do suspect this t. to be a party in this injury,* V, 1, 85.

**Trash,** vb. to lop, to crop: *who to advance and who to t. for overtopping,* Tp. I, 2, 81.* Substituted by M. Edd. for *brach* in Shr. Ind. 1, 17, and for *trace* in Oth. II, 1, 312, and explained as meaning 'to restrain a dog by a trash, i. e. a strap or rope, fastened to his neck'; a signification applied by some commentators also to the passage in Tp.

**Trassell,** lection of O. Edd. in Merch. I, 2, 65; M. Edd. *throstle.*

**Travail** or **Travel,** subst. (O. Edd. not making the distinction observed at present, but using the two forms indiscriminately in each of the following significations) 1) labour, toil: *weary with toil, I haste me to my bed, the dear repose for limbs with t. tired,* Sonn. 27, 2. *deserves the t. of a worthier pen,* 79, 6. *is all our t. turned to this effect?* H6A V, 4, 102. *I have had my labour for my t.* Troil. I, 1, 70. *as honour, loss of time, t., expense,* II, 2, 4. *what he learns by this may prove his t., not her danger,* Cymb. III, 5, 103.

2) labour in childbirth: *thirty three years have I but gone in t. of you, my sons,* Err. V, 400. *on this t. look for greater birth,* Ado IV, 1, 215. *God safely quit her of her burthen, and with gentle t.* H8 V, 1, 71. *the lady ... does fall in t. with her fear,* Per. III Prol. 52. *make swift the pangs of my queen's* —*s,* III, 1, 14.

3) much walking, and fatigue caused by it: *as if with grief or t. he had fainted,* Lucr. 1543. *now they are oppressed with t.* Tp. III, 3, 15. *with long t. I am stiff and weary,* Err. I, 2, 15. *would he not be a comfort to our t.?* As I, 3, 133. *a young maid with t. much oppressed,* II, 4, 74.

4) a wandering, rambling: *after a demure t. of regard,* Tw. II, 5, 59.* *jealousy what might befall your*

*t.* III, 3, 8. *in my —s' history,* Oth. I, 3, 139 *(Ff traveller's).*

5) a journey or voyage: Sonn. 50, 2. Gent. I, 1, 13. I, 3, 16. Err. I, 1, 140. LLL V, 2, 197. As IV, 1, 18. All's II, 3, 213. Tw. I, 2, 23. R2 I, 3, 262 *(take).* II, 3, 12. H4B V, 5, 25. H6A IV, 3, 36. Hml. IV, 7, 72. Ant. I, 2, 161. II, 1, 31. Per. I, 2, 116. I, 3, 14 *(gone to t.).* 35. II, 4, 56.

6) the act of travelling: *my youthful t. therein made me happy,* Gent. IV, 1, 34. *a man of t.* LLL V, 1, 114. *those types of t.* H8 I, 3, 31.

**Travail** or **Travel**, vb. (the two forms used indiscriminately in O. Edd.) 1) to labour, to toil: *obey our will, which —s in thy good,* All's II, 3, 165. *to load our purposes with what they t. for,* Tim. V, 1, 17.

2) to walk, to wander: *time—s in divers paces,* As III, 2, 326. *toward my grave I have —ed but two hours,* Tw. V, 166. *if I t. but four foot farther afoot,* H4A II, 2, 12. *not able to t. with her furred pack,* H6B IV, 2, 51. *speculation turns not to itself, till it hath —ed and is married, there where it may see itself,* Troil. III, 3, 110. *honour —s in a strait so narrow,* 154. *he and myself have —ed in the great shower of your gifts,* Tim. V, 1, 73. *how chances it they t.?* Hml. II, 2, 343 (= stroll).

3) to make a journey or voyage: *t. forth without my cloak,* Sonn. 34, 2. *his youthful morn hath —ed on to age's steepy night,* 63, 5. *like him that —s, I return again,* 109, 6. *whither t. you?* Gent. IV, 1, 16. *he supposes me —ed to Poland,* Meas. I, 3, 14. LLL V, 2, 557. As I, 3, 111 *(forth).* IV, 1, 29. Shr. Ind. 1, 76 *(—ing some journey).* IV, 2, 73. IV, 5, 51. All's IV, 3, 50. John IV, 2, 143. R2 V, 5, 73. H8 I, 3, 19 *(our —ed gallants).* Mcb. II, 4, 7 *(dark night strangles the —ing lamp).* Lr. II, 2, 162. II, 4, 90. Cymb. III, 3, 33. Per. I, 2, 106.

**Travailer** or **Travailor** or **Traveiler** or **Travellour** or **Traveller** (the last form alone used by M. Edd.), 1) a labourer: *as fast locked up in sleep as guiltless labour when it lies starkly in the —'s bones,* Meas. IV, 2, 70. *as motion and long-during action tires the sinewy vigour of the t.* LLL IV, 3, 308.

2) one who goes a journey, a wayfarer: Gent. IV, 1, 6. As II, 4, 18. Shr. IV, 5, 72. H4A II, 2, 35. Mcb. III, 3, 6. Hml. III, 1, 80. Oth. I, 3, 139 (Qq *travels).* Cymb. I, 4, 47. Per. IV, 2, 123.

3) one who has seen foreign countries: Tp. III, 3, 26. Meas. IV, 3, 18. LLL I, 1, 164. IV, 2, 97. As IV, 1, 21. 33. All's II, 3, 277. II, 5, 30. John I, 189.

**Travel-tainted**, fatigued with travelling: H4B IV, 3; 40.

**Travers**, name in H4B I, 1, 28. 33. 55.

**Traverse**, vb. a military word of command, = march, go on: *hold, Wart, t.; thus, thus, thus,* H4B III, 2, 291. *t., go, provide thy money,* Oth. I, 3, 378. Used of fencing, probably = to make a thrust: *to see thee fight, to see thee foin, to see thee t.* Wiv. II, 3, 25 (the host's speech).

**Traverse**, adv. across: *swears brave oaths and breaks them bravely, quite t., athwart the heart of his lover,* As III, 4, 45.

**Traversed**, crossed, folded: *have wandered with our t. arms and breathed our sufferance vainly,* Tim. V, 4, 7.

**Tray**, name of a dog in Lr. III, 6, 66.

**Tray-trip**, a game at dice ('in which success de-

---

pended upon throwing a trois'. Nares): *shall I play my freedom at t. and become thy bond-slave?* Tw. II, 5, 207.

**Treacher** (Ff) or **Treacherer** (Qq), traitor: *knaves, thieves and —s by spherical predominance:* Lr. I, 2, 133.

**Treacherous**, committing treason, faithless, perfidious: Tp. I, 2, 128. Gent. V, 4, 63. Ado III, 1, 28. As I, 1, 157. I, 3, 67. John V, 4, 38. R2 III, 2, 16. IV, 54. V, 3, 60. H4A V, 4, 57. H5 II Chor. 22. H6A I, 4, 35. II, 2, 16. H6C II, 2, 114. R3 I, 1, 37. I, 4, 211. II, 1, 38. IV, 4, 171 (not in Ff). Tit. IV, 2, 117. Rom. IV, 1, 58. Mcb. IV, 3, 18. Hml. II, 2, 609. V, 2, 327. Lr. III, 7, 87. Oth. V, 1, 58. Cymb. IV, 2, 317. *sheep run not half so t. from the wolf ... as you fly from your oft-subdued slaves,* H6A I, 5, 30. (some M. Edd. *timorous.* But in the opinion and language of a man like Talbot cowardice is treachery; cf. I, 4, 35, and see *trusty* in IV, 1, 23). cf. also Merch. III, 2, 83.

**Treacherously**, perfidiously: Lucr. Arg. 15. H6C II, 1, 72.

**Treachery**, treason, perfidy: Gent. IV, 1, 29. Ado V, 1, 257. Wint. II, 1, 195. John V, 4, 37. R2 I, 1, 11. V, 2, 75. H5 II, 2, 11. H6A I, 1, 69. III, 1, 21. III, 2, 37. IV, 1, 61. V, 4, 109. H6B I, 2, 47. H6C II, 5, 45. Mcb. III, 3, 17. IV, 2, 84. Hml. V, 2, 318. 323. Lr. I, 2, 123. IV, 2, 6. Oth. IV, 2, 221. *to do t.* Wiv. V, 3, 24. *to use t.* Gent. II, 6, 32. H6A I, 1, 68.

**Tread**, subst. footing, stepping with the foot: *her feet were much too dainty for such t.* LLL IV, 3, 279. *the quaint mazes ... for lack of t. are undistinguishable,* Mids. II, 1, 100. *it no more merits the t. of a man's foot,* All's II, 3, 292. *list if thou canst hear the t. of travellers,* H4A II, 2, 35.

**Tread**, vb. (impf. *trod;* partic. *trod,* used to form active and passive tenses; *trodden,* used to form passive tenses, and joined adjectively to substantives. In H4A I, 3, 135 Qq *down-trod Mortimer,* Ff *downfall* or *downfaln)* 1) to set the foot; a) intr.: *t. softly,* Tp. IV, 194. *bid me be advised how I t.* H6B II, 4, 36. *the ground shrinks before his —ing,* Cor. V, 4, 20. With *on,* in a physical sense, = to step on, to set the foot on: *she —s on it* (the grass) *so light,* Ven. 1028. *my mistress, when she walks, —s on the ground,* Sonn. 130, 12. *what we do not see we t. upon,* Meas. II, 1, 26. III, 1, 79. LLL V, 2, 330. R2 I, 3, 289. H4A II, 4, 442. V, 4, 13. H5 IV, 7, 149. H6C II, 2, 17. Cor. I, 1, 265. I, 3, 50. V, 6, 135. Per. IV, 1, 79. Peculiar expression: *he ne'er drinks but Timon's silver —s upon his lip,* Tim. III, 2, 78. *to t. on the heels of* = to follow close: *with many hundreds —ing on his heels,* John IV, 2, 149. Rom. I, 2, 28. Hml. IV, 7, 164. *to t. on,* in a moral sense, = to trample, to set the foot on in contempt: *misery is trodden on by many,* Ven. 707. *this down-trodden equity,* John II, 241. *on my heart they t. now whilst I live,* R2 III, 3, 158. *you t. upon my patience,* H4A I, 3, 4. V, 2, 86. Cor. V, 3, 116. 123. 127. Tim. IV, 3, 95. Mcb. IV, 3, 45.

b) trans. (or rather with an accus. and an adverbial expression denoting the effect); in a physical sense: *swear by her foot, that she may t. out the oath,* H5 III, 7, 103. *t. it under foot,* H6B V, 1, 209. *a little fire is quickly trodden out,* H6C IV, 8, 7. *I will t. this villain into mortar,* Lr. II, 2, 71. In a moral sense, *to t. down* = to trample under one's feet: John III, 1, 58. 215. 216. R2 II, 3, 126. H6C III, 3, 8.

2) to walk, to go, to move; a) intr.: *any emperor that ever trod on neat's leather,* Tp. II, 2, 73. Caes. I, 1, 29. *why in their so sacred paths he dares to t.* Wiv. IV, 4, 59. *where her shoe ... doth t.* LLL I, 2, 174. *wheresoe'er this foot of mine doth t.* John III, 3, 62. *by this heavenly ground I t. on,* H4B II, 1, 152 (Mrs. Quickly's speech). *any that —s but on four pasterns,* H5 III, 7, 12. *a far-off shore where he would t.* H6C III, 2, 136. *t. on the sand, why, there you quickly sink,* V, 4, 30. *so shall no foot upon the churchyard t., but ...,* Rom. V, 3, 5. *the land bids me t. no more upon 't,* Ant. III, 11, 1. *joy to see him t.* Per. II, 1, 165. cf. *Mistreadings.*

b) trans. to walk in or on: *she —s the path that she untreads again,* Ven. 908. *one encompassed with a winding maze, that cannot t. the way out readily,* Lucr. 1152. *to t. the ooze of the salt deep,* Tp. I, 2, 252. *he trod the water,* II, 1, 115. *here's a maze trod indeed,* III, 3, 2. *as strange a maze as e'er man trod,* V, 242. *may t. the groves,* Mids. III, 2, 390. *a kinder gentleman —s not the earth,* Merch. II, 8, 35. *if we walk not in the trodden paths,* As I, 3, 15. *we t. in warlike march these greens,* John II, 241. *t. the stranger paths of banishment,* R2 I, 3, 143. *to t. them* (the streets) *with her tender-feeling feet,* H6B II, 4, 9. *t. the path that thou shalt ne'er return,* R3 I, 1, 117. *would I had never trod this English earth,* H8 III, 1, 143. *trod the ways of glory,* III, 2, 436. *himself the path of dalliance —s,* Hml. I, 3, 50. *I'll t. these flats,* Cymb. III, 3, 11. *you should t. a course pretty and full of view,* III, 4, 149. Applied to dancing: *to t. a measure,* Ven. 1148. LLL V, 2, 185. 187. As V, 4, 45.

3) to copulate as birds; intr.: *when turtles t.* LLL V, 2, 915. trans.: *the cock that —s them,* Pilgr. 338.

**Treason,** 1) any perfidy; insidious and deceitful practice, or breach of fidelity: *thus t. works ere traitors be espied,* Lucr. 361. (night) *whispering conspirator with close-tongued t. and the ravisher,* 770. *'tis thou that executest the traitor's t.* 877. *wrath, envy, t., rape,* 909. 920. *I do betray my nobler part to my gross body's t.* Sonn. 151, 6. Tp. II, 1, 160. Ado III, 3, 113. LLL IV, 3, 190. 194. Merch. III, 2. 27. 28. V, 85. All's IV, 3, 26. H5 IV, 1, 245. H6A III, 2, 36. IV, 1, 74. V, 3, 189. V, 4, 109. H6B III, 1, 54. H6C V, 2, 18. Troil. II, 2, 150 *(to)* etc.

2) a crime committed against the safety or dignity of the state or king: As I, 3, 63. R2 II, 3, 109. H4B IV, 2, 123. H5 II Chor. 29. II, 2, 119 *(do)*. H6A II, 4, 91. 92. 97. H6B I, 3, 180. II, 3, 97. III, 1, 169. 174. IV,.6, 6. H8 I, 2, 7. Cymb. V, 5, 345 etc. With *to*: H6B III, 1, 70. 102. *capital t.* R2 IV, 151. H4B IV, 2, 109. H6B V, 1, 107. *high t.* (a crime that immediately affects the king): Wint. III, 2, 14. R2 I, 1, 27. H4B IV, 2, 107. H5 II, 2, 145. 147. 149. H6B I, 3, 185. III, 1, 97. H8 I, 1, 201. II, 1, 27. Figuratively: *till forging nature be condemned of t. for stealing moulds from heaven that were divine,* Ven. 729. *by their* (the eyes') *high t. is his heart misled,* Lucr. 369. *flat t. 'gainst the kingly state of youth,* LLL IV, 3, 293.

**Treasonable,** involving the crime of treason: *his t. abuses,* Meas. V, 347.

**Treasonous,** treacherous, perfidious: *this top-proud follow ... I know to be corrupt and t.* H8 I, 1, 156. *against the undivulged pretence I fight of t. malice,* Mcb. II, 3, 138.

**Treasure,** subst. 1) wealth accumulated: Ven.

767. Lucr. 1056. Sonn. 52, 2. 75, 6. Gent. IV, 1, 75. R3 II, 4, 69. Cor. III, 3, 115 (*t. of my loins,* i. e. the hoarded riches of my loins, viz my children). Hml. I, 1, 137. Ant. I, 5, 44 (*this t. of an oyster,* i. e. a pearl). Per. III, 2, 41. = money in store for public use: H6B III, 3, 2. IV, 1, 74. H6C III, 3, 36. V, 4, 79.

2) riches, property; properly and figuratively: *she will draw his lips' rich t. dry,* Ven. 552. *enrich the poor with —s,* 1150. *unlocked the t. of his happy state,* Lucr. 16. *all the t. of thy lusty days,* Sonn. 2, 6. *treasure thou some place with beauty's t.* 6, 4. *mine be thy love, and thy love's use their t.* 20, 14. *stealing away the t. of his spring,* 63, 8. *she may detain, but not still keep, her t.* 126, 10. *for all the t. that thine uncle owes,* John IV, 1, 123. *my —s and my rights of thee,* H4A II, 3, 48. *the t. in this field achieved,* Cor. I, 9, 33. *the gods have sent thee t.* Tim. IV, 3, 532. *though the t. of nature's germens tumble all together,* Mcb. IV, 1, 58. *pour our —s into foreign laps,* Oth. IV, 3, 89. *my t.'s in the harbour,* Ant. III, 11, 11. 21. *hath after thee sent all thy t.* IV, 6, 21. *I have picked the lock and ta'en the t. of her honour,* Cymb. II, 2, 42.

Often almost = money: *as one with t. laden,* hemmed with thieves, Ven. 1022. *you have an exchequer of words, and no other t. to give your followers,* Gent. II, 4, 44. *I have writ my letters, casketed my t.* All's II, 5, 26. *the interview that swallowed so much t.* H8 I, 1, 166. *his plate, his t., rich stuffs, and ornaments of household,* III, 2, 125. *want t.* Tim. II, 2, 214. cf. Tim. IV, 3, 404. Caes. IV, 1, 24. Ant. IV, 5, 10. 12. Per. III, 2, 74.

3) any thing very much valued: *what t. hast thou lost,* Ven. 1075. *when great t. is the meed proposed,* Lucr. 132. *lay down the —s of your body,* Meas. II, 4, 96. *our copper buys no better t.* LLL IV, 3, 386. *in Baptista's keep my t. is,* Shr. I, 2, 118. *she is your t.* II, 32. *to deck thy body with my ruffling t.* IV, 3, 60. *you waste the t. of your time with a foolish knight,* Tw. II, 5, 85. *have taken t. from her lips,* Wint. V, 1, 54. *the purest t. mortal times afford,* R2 I, 1, 177. *this tun of t. ... What t., uncle? Tennis-balls,* H5 I, 2, 255. 258. *thine eyes and thoughts beat on a crown, the t. of thy heart,* H6B II, 1, 20. *my soul's t.* III, 2, 382. *this t. in mine arms,* Tit. IV, 2, 173. *the precious t. of his eyesight,* Rom. I, 1, 239. *your chaste t.* Hml. I, 3, 31. *what a t. hadst thou,* II, 2, 423. 424. *that rarest t. of your cheek,* Cymb. III, 4, 163.

4) treasury: *Will will fulfil the t. of thy love, ay, fill it full with wills, and my will one,* Sonn. 136, 5.

**Treasure,** vb. to enrich, to make precious: *t. thou some place with beauty's treasure,* Sonn. 6, 3.

**Treasure-house,** a house where treasures are kept: *then to thee, thou silver t.* Merch. II, 9, 34.

**Treasurer,** one who has charge of treasure: Ant. V, 2, 142.

**Treasury,** 1) a place where stores of wealth are reposited: (heaven) *the t. of everlasting joy,* H6B II, 1, 18.

2) treasure: *I would have ransacked the pedlar's silken t. and have poured it to her acceptance,* Wint. IV, 4, 361. *all my t. is yet but unfelt thanks,* R2 II, 3, 60. *as rich as is the ooze and bottom of the sea with sunken wreck and sumless —es,* H5 I, 2, 165. *have cost a mass of public t.* H6B I, 3, 134 (later Ff *treasure*). *revel in Lavinia's t.* Tit. II, 1, 131. *conceit may rob the t. of life,* Lr. IV, 6, 43.

**Treat,** vb. to discourse, to speak, to have for subject: *say what the play —s on,* Mids. I, 2, 9. *that part of philosophy that —s of happiness,* Shr. I, 1, 19. *—s of Tereus' treason,* Tit. IV, 1, 48. *to t. with* = to negotiate with: *there with the emperor to t. of high affairs,* John I, 101.

**Treatise,** discourse, talk, tale: *your t. makes me like you worse and worse,* Ven. 774. *lest my liking might too sudden seem, I would have salved it with a longer t.* Ado I, 1, 317. *my fell of hair would at a dismal t. rouse and stir,* Mcb. V, 5, 12.

**Treaty,** 1) negotiation: *suggests the king to this last costly t., the interview, that swallowed so much treasure,* H8 I, 1, 165.

2) an agreement relating to public affairs: *what good condition can a t. find i'the part that is at mercy?* Cor. I, 10, 6. *making a t. where there was a yielding,* V, 6, 68. *thy father would ne'er have made this t.* Ant. II, 6, 85.

3) a proposal tending to an agreement: *why answer not the double majesties this friendly t. of our threatened town?* John II, 481. *we are convented upon a pleasing t. and have hearts inclinable to honour and advance the theme of our assembly,* Cor. II, 2, 59. *I must to the young man send humble —es,* Ant. III, 11, 62.

**Treble,** subst. the highest of the four principal parts in music: As II, 7, 162. Shr. III, 1, 39. H4B III, 2, 351 *(a t. hautboy).*

**Treble,** adj. threefold: Ven. 329. Meas. III, 2, 205. 283. H4B IV, 5, 129. Tit. V, 1, 8. Mcb. IV, 1, 121. Hml. V, 1, 269. 270.

**Treble,** vb. to make thrice as much: *which to do —s thee o'er,* Tp. II, 1, 221 (makes thee thrice what thou art, i. e. a king). *for you I would be —d twenty times myself,* Merch. III, 2, 154. *double six thousand, and then t. that,* 302. *our battalion —s that account,* R3 V, 3, 11. *—s their confusion,* Per. IV, 1, 65. In Hml. I, 2, 248 Ff. unintelligibly *t.,* Qq *tenable.*

**Treble-dated,** living thrice as long as man: *t. crow,* Phoen. 17.

**Treble-sinewed,** having thrice the strength of other times: *I will be t., hearted, breathed,* Ant. III, 13, 178 (the word *t.* belonging also to *hearted* and *breathed*).

**Trebonius,** name in Caes. I, 3, 148. II, 1, 94. II, 2, 120 etc.

**Tree,** a plant with a woody and perennial stem: Ven. 152. 263. 391. Sonn. 12, 5. Pilgr. 135. 378. Phoen. 2 *(the sole Arabian t.).* Tp. II, 2, 128. III, 2, 40. III, 3, 23 *(one t., the Phoenix' throne).* Wiv. IV, 4, 32. V, 5, 83. LLL IV, 3, 341. V, 2, 285 *(Dumain is mine, as sure as bark on t.).* 908. Merch. V, 2. 80. As II, 1, 16. II, 3, 63. III, 2, 9. 249 *(Jove's t.,* i. e. the oak). R2 II, 3, 53. H4A II, 4, 471 *(the t. may be known by the fruit).* H4B II, 4, 41. H6B II, 1, 96. H6C II, 5, 49. V, 2, 14 *(Jove's spreading t.).* Tit. II, 3, 2. V, 1, 47. 138. Oth. V, 2, 15. 350 *(Arabian —s).* Cymb. III, 3, 60. V, 5, 264. Per. I, 1, 114 etc. cf. *Cypress, Elder, Medlar, Pomegranate, Willow* etc.

**Tremble,** to shake involuntarily, to quake, to quiver; as the effect of cold: Wint. IV, 4, 81. of a fever: Cor. I, 4, 61; or of different emotions; as of amorous desire: Ven. 27. Ant. II, 5, 30. of mad rage: Err. IV, 4, 54. of anger: Rom. I, 5, 92. of grief and anguish: Lucr. 1599. H6B II, 1, 166. Hml. V, 2, 345. Oth. IV, 1, 40. in most cases of fear: Ven. 642. 895.

Lucr. 231. 261. 457. 511. 1020. 1391. Tp. I, 2, 205. II, 2, 83. Wiv. III, 1, 12. Ado II, 3, 203. LLL V, 2, 693. Mids. III, 1, 43. V, 224. As V, 1, 63. John II, 294. R2 I, 1, 69. H6B I, 1, 227. III, 1, 19. H6C I, 1, 242. V, 6, 14. R3 I, 2, 43. I, 3, 160. Cymb. IV, 2, 87 etc. Followed by *at,* to denote the external cause: Ven. 591. 668. Tp. I, 2, 371. Wint. III, 2, 33 *(tyranny shall t. at patience,* i. e. in looking on patience). R2 III, 2, 46 *(at themselves).* 53. H4A I, 3, 144. H5 I, 2, 154. H6B I, 4, 29. Tit. II, 1, 11. Hml. V, 2, 345. Oth. IV, 1, 40. Cymb. IV, 2, 90. By *with,* to denote the internal motive: R2 II, 2, 12. Cymb. IV, 2, 303. *a —ing contribution,* H8 I, 2, 95, i. e. a contribution attended by trembling (*—ing* being the gerund); cf. *all-obeying breath, unrecalling crime, feeling sorrows.*

**Tremblingly,** so as to shake: *t. she stood and on the sudden dropped,* Ant. V, 2, 346.

**Trench,** subst. a ditch cut and earth thrown up for defence; used only in the plural: *of —es, tents,* H4A II, 3, 54. *retire into your —es,* H6A I, 5, 33. Cor. I, 4, 42. I, 6, 12. 40. Figuratively, = wrinkles, furrows: *when forty winters shall besiege thy brow and dig deep —es in thy beauty's field,* Sonn. 2, 2. *these —es made by grief and care,* Tit. V, 2, 23.

**Trench,** vb. to cut: *the wide wound that the boar had —ed in his soft flank,* Ven. 1052. *a figure —ed in ice,* Gent. III, 2, 7. *with twenty —ed gashes on his head,* Mcb. III, 4, 27. cf. *Entrench.* = to dig, to make furrows: *no more shall —ing war channel her fields,* H4A I, 1, 7.* = to drain by digging, to turn off and divert from the usual channel: *a little charge will t. him here* (the river Trent) H4A III, 1, 112.

**Trenchant,** cutting, sharp: *let not the virgin's cheek make soft thy t. sword,* Tim. IV, 3, 115.

**Trencher,** a plate: *nor scrape t., nor wash dish,* Tp. II, 2, 187. *he steps me to her t. and steals her capon's leg,* Gent. IV, 4, 10. *holding a t.* LLL V, 2, 477. *take it to you, —s, cups and all,* Shr. IV, 1, 168. *fed from my t.* H6B IV, 1, 57. *serve with thy t.* Cor. IV, 5, 54. *he shift a t.? he scrape a t.?* Rom. I, 5, 2. *one which holds a t.* Tim. I, 1, 120 (= is a servant). *I found you as a morsel cold upon dead Caesar's t.* Ant. III, 13, 117.

**Trencher-friends,** spongers, parasites: Tim. III, 6, 106.

**Trencher-knight,** a serving-man attending at table: LLL V, 2, 464; cf. 476.

**Trencher-man,** a feeder, eater: *he is a very valiant t.* Ado I, 1, 51.

**Trent,** a river in England: H4A III, 1, 74. 79. 102 *(the smug and silver T.).* 136.

**Trespass,** subst. offence, sin, crime: Lucr. 524. 632. 812. 1070. 1476. 1613. Sonn. 35, 6. 120, 13. Tp. III, 3, 99. Wint. I, 2, 265. II, 2, 63. III, 2, 190. R2 I, 1, 138. V, 2, 89. H4A V, 2, 16. H5 II, 4, 125. H6A II, 4, 94. H6B III, 1, 132. Rom. I, 5, 111. Hml. III, 4, 146. Lr. II, 2, 151. II, 4, 44. Oth. III, 3, 64. *to do t.: have paid down more penitence than done t.* Wint. V, 1, 4. *if e'er my will did t. 'gainst his love,* Oth. IV, 2, 152. *his wife did —es to Caesar,* Ant. II, 1, 40. *to make t.: sorry for my t. made,* H6C V, 1, 92.

**Tressel,** name in R3 I, 2, 222.

**Tresses,** knots or curls of hair: Sonn. 68, 5. John III, 4, 61. H6A I, 1, 3.

**Trey,** a three at cards: *honey, milk, and sugar; there is three. Nay then, two —s, ... metheglin, wort, and malmsey,* LLL V, 2, 232.

**Trial,** 1) examination, probation, test: *the doors, the wind, the glove, he takes for accidental things of t.* Lucr. 326. *the boy for t. needs would touch my breast,* Sonn. 153, 10. *all thy vexations were but my —s of thy love,* Tp. IV, 1, 6. *with t. fire touch his finger-end,* Wiv. V, 5, 88. *a t., come,* 92. *if it* (your love) *bear this t.* LLL V, 2, 813. *let us teach our t. patience,* Mids. I, 1, 152. *whose t. shall better publish his commendation,* Merch. IV, 1, 165. *was rather meant for his t. and fair purgation to the world,* H8 V, 3, 151. *the protractive —s of great Jove to find persistive constancy in men,* Troil. I, 3, 20. *in the t. of his several friends,* Tim. III, 6, 6. *sink in the t.* Caes. IV, 2, 27. *blow them to their t.* Hml. V, 2, 202. *stands an honourable t.* Ant. I, 3, 75. *'tis a punishment or t.* Cymb. III, 6, 11. *his —s well are spent,* V, 4, 104. *to make t. or a t. of: to make t. of that which every one had avouched,* Lucr. Arg. 9. *make not too rash a t. of him,* Tp. I, 2, 467. *he made t. of you only,* Meas. III, 1, 202. *make the t. of it in any constant question,* Tw. IV, 2, 52. *before thou make a t. of her love,* H6A V, 3, 76. *make t. what your love can do,* Cor. V, 1, 40.

2) judicial examination: Meas. V, 304. 377. LLL I, 1, 279. Wint. II, 3, 205. III, 2, 122. R2 IV, 153. H6B III, 1, 114 *(t. day).* 138. III, 3, 8. H8 I, 2, 211. II, 1, 111. 118. II, 2, 92. III, 1, 96. IV, 1, 5. V, 1, 104. V, 3, 53. Cor. III, 1, 268. Lr. III, 6, 26 *(at t.).* 37.

3) a combat decisive of the merits of a cause: *challenge thee to t. of a man,* Ado V, 1, 66. *let your gentle wishes go with me to my t.* As I, 2, 199. *in dreadful t. of our kingdom's king,* John II, 286 (i. e. a battle which was to decide which of two was the legitimate king). *in this hot t.* 342. *'tis not the t. of a woman's war, the bitter clamour of two eager tongues, can arbitrate this cause,* R2 I, 1, 48. *I'll answer thee in any fair degree of knightly t.* 81. *to assign our t. day,* 151. *order the t., marshal,* I, 3, 99. IV, 56. 71. 90. 106. *to wage an instant t. with the king,* H4A IV, 4, 20 (= battle). *if once they join in t.* V, 1, 85. *by this one bloody t. of sharp war,* R3 V, 2, 16. *in the t. much opinion dwells,* Troil. I, 3, 336. *it would come to immediate t.* Hml. V, 2, 175. *the opposition of your person in t.* 179.

4) a state of being tried and known by experience; proof, verification: *they will scarcely believe this without t.* Ado II, 2, 41. *all purity, all t., all observance,* As V, 2, 104 (Schlegel very well: *ganz Bewährung*). *do not plunge thyself too far in anger, lest thou hasten thy t.* All's II, 3, 223 (= lest thou be found out too soon). *sith every action ... t. did draw bias and thwart,* Troil. I, 3, 14 (= proof, experience). cf. Merch. IV, 1, 165 and H8 V, 3, 151.

**Trial-day,** see *Trial* sub 2 and 3.
**Trial-fire,** see *Trial* sub 1.

**Tribe,** 1) the Roman *tribus:* *have you collected them by —s?* Cor. III, 3, 11. V, 5, 2.
2) race; a body of people as having a particular descent: *he* (death) *insults o'er dull and speechless —s,* Sonn. 107, 12. *cursed be my t., if I forgive him,* Merch. I, 3, 52. *a wealthy Hebrew of my t.* 58. *sufferance is the badge of all our t.* 111. *here comes another of the t.* III, 1, 80. *thy t. before him,* Cor. IV, 2, 24. *six Aufidiuses, or more, his t.* V, 6, 130. *to the creating a whole t. of fops,* Lr. I, 2, 14. *too hard for my wits and all the t. of hell,* Oth. I, 3, 364. *the souls of all my t. defend from jealousy,* III, 3, 175. *richer than all his t.* V, 2, 348.

**Tribulation,** a very common name among the Puritans; applied to the whole sect: *that no audience, but the t. of Tower-hill, or the limbs of Lime-house, their dear brothers, are able to endure,* H8 V, 4, 65 (a passage not yet satisfactorily explained).

**Tribunal,** an elevated place, a tribune: *i'the market-place, on a t. silvered, Cleopatra and himself in chairs of gold were publicly enthroned,* Ant. III, 6, 3. In Tit. IV, 3, 92 the clown says *t. plebs* for *tribunus plebis.*

**Tribune,** an officer of ancient Rome, chosen by the plebeians to defend their liberties against the nobility: Cor. I, 1, 219. I, 9, 6. II, 2, 155. III, 1, 21. 31 etc. Tit. I, 46. 63. 181 etc. Cymb. III, 7, 8. Invested with the office of judges: Cor. II, 1, 77. Tit. III, 1, 23.

**Tributary,** adj. paying tribute, subject; or paid in tribute: *that face ... to which Love's eyes pay t. gazes,* Ven. 632. *whereat each t. subject quakes,* 1045. *at this tomb my t. tears I render,* Tit. I, 159. III, 1, 270. *your t. drops belong to woe,* Rom. III, 2, 103. *poor t. rivers,* Cymb. IV, 2, 36.

**Tributary,** subst. one that pays tribute, a vassal: Caes. I, 1, 38. Hml. V, 2, 39. Ant. III, 13, 96.

**Tribute,** stated payment made in acknowledgment of submission, or as the price of peace, or by virtue of a treaty: Tp. I, 2, 113. 124. II, 1, 293. Merch. III, 2, 56. Shr. V, 2, 152. H4B III, 2, 331. H6A V, 4, 130. H6B IV, 7, 128. Tit. I, 251. Hml. III, 1, 178. Cymb. II, 4, 13. 20. III, 1, 8. 34. 42. 45. 46. 49. V, 5, 69. 462. Figuratively = any thing done or given out of devotion: *paying more slavish t. than they owe,* Lucr. 299 (being more submissive than necessary). *what —s wounded fancies sent me,* Compl. 197. *take some remembrance of us, as a t., not as a fee,* Merch. IV, 1, 422. *needs must you lay your heart at his dispose, subjected t. to commanding love,* John I, 264. *had the t. of his supple knee,* R2 I, 4, 33. *his majesty shall have t. of me,* Hml. II, 2, 333.

**Trice,** a very short time, a moment: *in this t. of time,* Lr. I, 1, 219. *in a t.* Tw. IV, 2, 133. Cymb. V, 4, 171. *on a t.* Tp. V, 238.

**Trick,** subst. 1) artifice, stratagem, device: *the —s and toys that in them* (women) *lurk,* Pilgr. 337. *I'll quickly cross by some sly t. blunt Thurio's dull proceeding,* Gent. II, 6, 41. *this can be no t.* Ado II, 3, 229. *some —s, some quillets, how to cheat the devil,* LLL IV, 3, 288. *I see the t. on't: here was a consent,* V, 2, 460. *teacheth —s eleven and twenty long,* Shr. IV, 2, 57. *I smell the t. on't,* Wint. IV, 4, 657. *I know a t. worth two of that,* H4A II, 1, 41. *what t., what device, what starting-hole,* II, 4, 290. *at this instant he bores me with some t.* H8 I, 1, 128. *that t. of state was a deep envious one,* II, 1, 44. *I abhor this dilatory sloth and —s of Rome,* II, 4, 237. *all his —s founder,* III, 2, 40. *raised only, that the weaker sort may wish good Marcius home again. The very t. on't,* Cor. IV, 6, 70. *with twenty popish —s,* Tit. V, 1, 76. *is it your t. to make me ope the door?* V, 2, 10. *there are no —s in plain and simple faith,* Caes. IV, 2, 22. *there's —s i'the world,* Hml. IV, 5, 5. *his cases, his tenures, and his —s,* V, 1, 109. *—s of custom,* Oth. III, 3, 122. *this is a t. to put me from my suit,* III, 4, 87. *the —s in war,* Cymb. III, 3, 15.

2) a knack, art, a dexterous contrivance: *knows the t. to make my lady laugh,* LLL V, 2, 465. *such —s hath strong imagination,* Mids. V, 18. *the sly whoresons*

*have got a speeding t. to lay down ladies*, H8 I, 3, 40. *here is fine revolution, an we had the t. to see it*, Hml. V, 1, 99. *to prince it much beyond the t. of others*, Cymb. III, 3, 86. *if such —s as these strip you out of your lieutenantry*, Oth. II, 1, 172. R3 I, 1, 14. = a sleight of hand, the legerdemain of a juggler: *have we devils here? do you put — s upon us with savages and men of Ind?* Tp. II, 2, 60. *I must use you in such another t.* IV, 37. *a juggling t., to be secretly open*, Troil. V, 2, 24. *in forgery of shapes and —s*, Hml. IV, 7, 90. cf. *Back-trick* and *Tumbling-trick*.

3) particular habit, custom, character: *is the world as it was, man? which is the way? is it sad, and few words, or how? the t. of it?* Meas. III, 2, 55. *I spoke it but according to the t.* V, 510 (= to act in character). *it was alway yet the t. of our English nation, if they have a good thing, to make it too common*, H4B I, 2, 240. *it is our t.* (viz. to weep) Hml. IV, 7, 188. *you laugh when boys or women tell their dreams; is't not your t.?* Ant. V, 2, 75.

4) a peculiarity: *heart too capable of every line and t. of his sweet favour*, All's I, 1, 107. *the t. of his frown*, Wint. II, 3, 100. *he hath a t. of Cordelion's face*, John I, 85. *a villanous t. of thine eye*, H4A II, 4, 446. *the t. of that voice I do well remember*, Lr. IV, 6, 108.

5) a touch, a dash, a trait of character: *yet I have a t. of the old rage: bear with me, I am sick*, LLL V, 2, 416. *a man that had this t. of melancholy sold a goodly manor for a song*, All's III, 2, 9. *put thyself into the t. of singularity*, Tw. II, 5, 164. III, 4, 79. (the fox) *will have a wild t. of his ancestors*, H4A V, 2, 11.

6) any thing done not deliberately, but out of passion or caprice; a vicious or foolish action or practice: *thy eyes' shrewd tutor, that hard heart of thine, hath taught them scornful —s*, Ven. 501. *this glove to wanton —s is not inured*, Lucr. 320. *played some —s of desperation*, Tp. I, 2, 210. *didst thou ever see me do such a t.?* Gent. IV, 4, 43. *that were a t. indeed!* Wiv. II, 2, 117. *plays such fantastic —s before high heaven*, Meas. II, 2, 121. *why would he for the momentary t. be perdurably fined?* Meas. III, 1, 114. *it was a mad fantastical t. of him to steal from the state*, III, 2, 98. *these tardy —s of yours*, H4B IV, 3, 31. *this t. may chance to scathe you*, Rom. I, 5, 86. *these are unsightly —s*, Lr. II, 4, 159. *how comes this t. upon him?* Oth. IV, 2, 129. *'tis one of those odd — s which sorrow shoots out of the mind*, Ant. IV, 2, 14. *jade's tricks:* Ado I, 1, 145. All's IV, 5, 64. Troil. II, 1, 21.

7) any thing mischievously and roguishly done to cross and disappoint another: *the t. you served me*, Gent. IV, 4, 38. *I'll never be drunk whilst I live again, but in honest company, for this t.* Wiv. I, 1, 188. *we will yet have more —s with Falstaff*, III, 3, 203. *if I be served such another t.* III, 5, 7. As IV, 1, 40. *if I put any —s upon 'em*, All's IV, 5, 63. *as good a t. as ever hangman served thief*, Tim. II, 2, 99.

8) Plur. *—s* = pranks, frolics, jokes: *stands on —s, when I am undisposed*, Err. I, 2, 80. *I have within my mind a thousand raw —s of these bragging Jacks*, Merch. III, 4, 77. *let my horses be well looked to, without any —s*, All's IV, 5, 62. *—s he hath had in him, which gentlemen have*, V, 3, 239. *I'll question you of my lord's —s and yours when you were boys*, Wint. I, 2, 61. *what need these —s?* Troil. V, 1, 15. *you are never without your —s*, Cor. II, 3, 38. cf. *Rope-tricks*.

9) a toy, a trifle, a plaything: *a knack, a toy, a t.,*

*a baby's cap*, Shr. IV, 3, 67. *I remain a pinched thing, yea, a very t. for them to play at will*, Wint. II, 1, 51. *by some chance, some t. not worth an egg, shall grow dear friends*, Cor. IV, 4, 21. *for a fantasy and t. of fame*, Hml. IV, 4, 61.

**Trick**, vb. to dress out, to adorn: *in the phrase of war, which they t. up with new-tuned oaths*, H5 III, 6, 80. *head to foot now is he total gules, horridly —ed with blood of fathers, mothers* etc. Hml. II, 2, 479 (Dyce: 'this is properly an heraldic term, = blazoned, *trick* meaning a delineation of arms, in which the colours are distinguished by their technical marks, without any colour being laid on').

**Tricking**, dresses, ornaments: *properties and t. for our fairies*, Wiv. IV, 4, 79.

**Trickling**, flowing down gently: *t. tears are vain*, H4A II, 4, 431 (Falstaff's tragi-comedy). cf. *Trill*.

**Tricksy**, 1) full of tricks and devices: *my t. spirit*, Tp. V, 226. 2) quaint (see *trick* vb. and *trick* subst. 9): *I do know a many fools ... garnished like him, that for a t. word defy the matter*, Merch. III, 5, 74.

**Trident**, the three-forked sceptre of Neptune: Tp. I, 2, 206. Cor. III, 1, 256.

**Trier**, that which brings to the test: *extremity was the t. of spirits*, Cor. IV, 1, 4.

**Trifle**, subst. a thing of no moment: Ven. 1023. Sonn. 48, 2. 5. Tp. II, 2, 8. Wiv. II, 1, 46. 47. Merch. II, 2, 170 (*a small t. of wives*). IV, 1, 430. All's II, 2, 36. Wint. IV, 3, 26. IV, 4, 368. V, 1, 222. 224. H4A II, 4, 121. III, 3, 119. H6A IV, 1, 150. R3 III, 7, 9. Tim. I, 2, 213. III, 2, 24. Mcb. I, 3, 125. I, 4, 11. Lr. I, 3, 7. V, 3, 295. Oth. III, 3, 322. V, 2, 228. Ant. V, 2, 165. Cymb. I, 1, 120. I, 4, 88. Per. II, 3, 92. *to make —s of* = to make light of: All's II, 3, 4. Wint. II, 3, 62.

Sometimes = a toy, a pleasing bawble: *some enchanted t. to abuse me*, Tp. V, 112. *knacks, —s, nosegays*, Mids. I, 1, 34. *to fetch me —s*, II, 1, 133. cf. Ant. V, 2, 165 and Cymb. I, 1, 120.

**Trifle**, vb. 1) intr. to act or talk without the becoming seriousness: *this is —ing*, Tp. III, 1, 79. *for Hamlet and the —ing of his favour*, Hml. I, 3, 5. *I feared he did but t. and meant to wreck thee*, II, 1, 112. Followed by *with*, = to play with: *how love can t. with itself*, Gent. IV, 4, 188. *the cardinals t. with me*, H8 II, 4, 236. *I do t. thus with his despair*, Lr. IV, 6, 33. *I thus would play and t. with your reverence*, Oth. I, 1, 133.

2) trans. a) to make a trifle of, to make trivial: *this sore night hath —d former knowings*, Mcb. II, 4, 4. b) to waste in levity: *we t. time*, Merch. IV, 1, 298. *we t. time away*, H8 V, 3, 179.

**Trifler**, one who acts or talks with levity: H4A II, 3, 93.

**Trifling**, adj. insignificant: *if it were not for one t. respect*, Wiv. II, 1, 45. *we have a t. foolish banquet towards*, Rom. I, 5, 124. *some t. present*, Tim. II, 2, 145.

**Trigon**, triangle: *look whether the fiery T. be not lisping to his master's old tables*, H4B II, 4, 288. Nash: 'The twelve signs in astrology are divided into four *trigons*, or triplicities, each denominated from the connatural element: so they are three fiery (Aries, Leo, Sagittarius), three airy, three watery, and three earthly. When the three superior planets met in Aries, Leo, or Sagittarius, they formed *a fiery trigon*.'

**Trill,** to trickle: *an ample tear —ed down her delicate cheek,* Lr. IV, 3, 14.

**Trim,** subst. ornamental dress: *proud-pied April dressed in all his t.* Sonn. 98, 2. *their purposed t. pieced not his grace, but were all graced by him,* Compl. 118. *they come like sacrifices in their t.* H4A IV, 1, 113. *our hearts are in the t.* H5 IV, 3, 115 (notwithstanding our outward slovenry). *my noble steed I give him, with all his t. belonging,* Cor. I, 9, 62. *a thousand ... have on their riveted t.* Ant. IV, 4, 22. *forget your laboursome and dainty —s,* Cymb. III, 4, 167.

In speaking of ships = the state of being fully prepared for sailing: *where we in all her t. freshly beheld our royal ship,* Tp. V, 236. *the ship is in her t.* Err. IV, 1, 90.

**Trim,** adj. nice, fine; mostly used with irony: *the flowers are sweet, their colours fresh and t.* Ven. 1079. *men are only turned into tongue, and t. ones too,* Ado IV, 1, 323. *t. gallants, full of courtship and of state,* LLL V, 2, 363. *a t. exploit,* Mids. III, 2, 157. *a t. reckoning,* H4A V, 1, 137. *these t. vanities,* H8 I, 3, 38. *there's a t. rabble let in,* V, 4, 75. *O, this is t.* Troil. IV, 5, 33. *'twas t. sport for them,* Tit. V, 1, 96.

Adverbially: *he that shot so t.* Rom. II, 1, 13.

**Trim,** vb. 1) to put in due order, to adjust in any way; to make neat, to cleanse, to prune: *t. it* (the cell) *handsomely,* Tp. V, 293. *the house—ed, rushes strewed,* Shr. IV, 1, 48. *that he had not so —ed and dressed his land as we this garden,* R2 III, 4, 56. *help to t. my tent,* Troil. V, 1, 50. *cut her hands and —ed her as thou sawest,* Tit. V, 1, 93. 94. 95. With *up: the lustful bed on purpose —ed up for Semiramis,* Shr. Ind. 2, 41. *—ing up the diadem,* Ant. V, 2, 345.

Used of ships, = to fit out: *a vessel that is new —ed,* H8 I, 2, 80. *—ed with rich expense,* Per. V. Prol. 19.

2) to dress up, to deck, to array: *needy nothing —ed in jollity,* Sonn. 66, 3. *I was —ed in Julia's gown,* Gent. IV, 4, 166. *—ed like a younker,* H6C II, 1, 24. *—ed in forms and visages of duty,* Oth. I, 1, 50. *one another's glass to t. them by,* Per. I, 4, 27. With *up: —ed up your praises with a princely tongue,* H4A V, 2, 57. *go and t. her up,* Rom. IV, 4, 24. Peculiar passage: *being now —ed in thine own desires,* H4B I, 3, 94, = having fully obtained thy desires; cf. *Attire, Dress, Enwrap, Wrap.*

**Trimly,** nicely, finely, sprucely: *neat and t. dressed,* H4A I, 3, 33.

**Trinculo,** name of the jester in Tp. II, 2, 105 etc.

**Trinkets,** 1) toys, small ornaments: *as if my t. had been hallowed,* Wint. IV, 4, 613.

2) implements, tools, tackle: *we'll see your t. here all forthcoming,* H6B I, 4, 56.

**Trip,** subst. a stroke or catch by which a wrestler supplants his antagonist: *or will not else thy craft so quickly grow, that thine own t. shall be thine overthrow?* Tw. V, 170 (that thou wilt be caught in thy own snare).

**Trip,** vb. 1) intr. a) to walk or run with quick, short and light steps; used of women: *t. and go, my sweet,* LLL IV, 2, 144. *t. Audrey,* As V, 1, 68. *t. no further, pretty sweeting,* Tw. II, 3, 43. *your own ladies ... come —ing after drums,* John V, 2, 155. of nymphs, fairies, and the like: *like a fairy t. upon the green,* Ven. 146. *many nymphs came —ing by,* Sonn. 154, 4. *—ing on his toe,* Tp. IV, 46. *t., t., fairies,* Wiv. V, 4, 1. 4. *as you t., still pinch him,* V, 5, 96. *t. we after the*

*night's shade,* Mids. IV, 1, 101. *t. away, make no stay,* V, 428 (cf. *Night-tripping*). Used of dancing: *the triplex is a good —ing measure,* Tw. V, 41. *all the Greekish girls shall —ing sing,* Troil. III, 3, 211. *excellent in making ladies t.* Per. II, 3, 103. cf. Wiv. V, 5, 96.

b) to stumble, to fall, to offend: *you have —ed since,* Wint. I, 2, 76.

2) trans. to supplant, to cause to fall by striking the feet suddenly from under the person: *the earth, in love with thee, thy footing —s,* Ven. 722. *then t. him, that his heels may kick at heaven,* Hml. III, 3, 93. Lr. I, 4, 95. II, 2, 126. *to t. up a person's heels:* As III, 2, 224. Lr. II, 2, 32.

Metaphorically: *to t. the course of law,* H4B V, 2, 87. *these her women can t. me, if I err,* Cymb. V, 5, 35 (refute me, give me the lie).

**Tripartite,** drawn up in three correspondent copies: *our indentures t. are drawn,* H4A III, 1, 80.

**Tripe,** entrails prepared for food: *how say you to a fat t. finely broiled?* Shr. IV, 3, 20.

**Tripe-visaged,** an epithet applied by Doll Tearsheet to the beadle, in a sense probably not quite clear to herself (pale? sallow?): *thou damned t. rascal,* H4B V, 4, 9.

**Triple,** 1) threefold: *by the t. Hecate's team,* Mids. V, 391 (in allusion to her threefold character, — Luna in heaven, Diana on earth, and Hecate in the nether world). *the t. crown* (of the pope) H6B I, 3, 66.

2) third: *which ... he bade me store up as a t. eye, safer than mine own two, more dear,* All's II, 1, 111. *you shall see in him the t. pillar of the world transformed into a strumpet's fool,* Ant. I, 1, 12.

**Triple-turned,** three times faithless: *t. whore,* Ant. IV, 12, 13.

**Triplex,** triple time: *the t. is a good tripping measure,* Tw. V, 41.

**Tripolie** (Shr.) or **Tripolis** (Merch.), town in Africa: Merch. I, 3, 18.* III, 1, 106 * III, 2, 271.* Shr. IV, 2, 76.

**Trippingly,** with a light step; nimbly: *sing and dance it t.* Mids. V, 403. *speak the speech ... t. on the tongue,* Hml. III, 2, 2.

**Tristful,** sad, sorrowful: *this solidity and compound mass, with t. visage, as against the doom, is thought-sick at the act,* Hml. III, 4, 50 (Qq *heated*). In H4A II, 4, 434 O. Edd. *trustful,* M. Edd. *tristful.*

**Triton,** a sea-god, the trumpeter of Neptune: *hear you this T. of the minnows?* Cor. III, 1, 89.

**Triumph,** subst. 1) the solemn procession of a victorious general and his army in ancient Rome: *Pompey, ... art thou led in t.?* Meas. III, 2, 47. Caes. V, 1, 109. Ant. V, 2, 109. *to beautify thy —s,* Tit. I, 110. *safer t. is this funeral pomp,* 176. *to rejoice in his t.* Caes. I, 1, 36. *comes in t. over Pompey's blood,* 56. *thy conquests, glories, —s, spoils,* III, 1, 149. Ant. III, 13, 136. IV, 12, 33. V, 1, 66. Applied to modern times: *grace the t. of great Bolingbroke,* R2 III, 4, 99. Figuratively: *let thy dauntless mind still ride in t. over all mischance,* H6C III, 3, 18.

2) victory, conquest: *his victories, his —s and his glories,* Ven. 1014. *life's t. in the map of death,* Lucr. 402.

3) exultation: *whose worthiness gives scope, being had, to t., being lacked, to hope,* Sonn. 52, 14. *t. is become an alehouse guest,* R2 V, 1, 15. *which I will bear in t. to the king,* H6B IV, 10, 89. Tit. II, 1, 14.

Rom. II, 6, 10. III, 1, 127. Caes. III, 2, 54. Hml. I, 4, 12. Oth. II, 2, 4. Cymb. IV, 2, 193.

4) pomp of any kind: *let those who are in favour with their stars of public honour and proud titles boast, whilst I, whom fortune of such t. bars,* ... Sonn. 25, 3. *when thou didst ride in t. through the streets,* H6B II, 4, 14.

5) a public festivity or exhibition of any kind, particularly a tournament: *we will include all jars with —s, mirth and rare solemnity,* Gent. V, 4, 161. *with pomp, with t. and with revelling,* Mids. I, 1, 19. *hold those justs and —s?* R2 V, 2, 52. *for gay apparel 'gainst the t. day,* 66. *those —s held at Oxford,* V, 3, 14. *thou art a perpetual t., an everlasting bonfire-light,* H4A III, 3, 46. *at a t. having vowed to try his strength,* H6A V, 5, 31. *spend the time with stately —s, mirthful comic shows,* H6C V, 7, 43. *this day of t.* (viz of coronation) R3 III, 4, 44. *to begin the t.* Per. II, 2, 1. 5. 53. *honouring of Neptune's —s,* V, 1, 17.

6) a trump-card (?): *packed cards with Caesar and false-played my glory unto an enemy's t.* Ant. IV, 14, 20.

**Triumph,** vb. (usually *tríumph; triúmph* in Lucr. 1388. LLL IV, 3, 35. H4A V, 4, 14. V, 3, 15. R3 III, 4, 91. IV, 4, 59. Ant. IV, 8, 16) 1) to return home and enter publicly as a victorious general: *weepest to see me t.* Cor. II, 1, 194.

2) to be victorious: *he may t. in love,* Sonn. 151, 8. With *in,* to denote the conquered enemy: *t. in so false a foe,* Lucr. 77. With *on* and *over,* in the same sense: *I never had —ed upon a Scot,* H4A V, 3, 15 (Ff *o'er*). *Antony's* (valour) *hath —ed on itself,* Ant. IV, 15, 15. *—s over chance,* Tit. I, 178.

3) to exult: *air, quoth he, thy cheeks may blow; air, would I might t. so,* Pilgr. 236 and LLL IV, 3, 110. *how will he t., leap and laugh at it,* LLL IV, 3, 148. *let frantic Talbot t. for a while,* H6A III, 3, 5. *do you t., Roman?* Oth. IV, 1, 121. With *at: as 'twere —ing at mine enemies,* R3 III, 4, 91 (Ff *as too —ing, how* etc.). With *in: so ridest thou —ing in my woe,* LLL IV, 3, 35. *rebels' arms t. in massacres,* H4A IV, 4, 14. *France, t. in thy glorious prophetess,* H6A I, 6, 8. *here's the heart that — s in their death,* H6C II, 4, 8. *t. in thy day of doom,* V, 3, 260. *t. not in my woes,* R3 IV, 4, 59. With *over: I, with mine enemies, will t. o'er my person,* H8 V, 1, 125. With *upon* or *on: t. thus upon my misery,* Shr. IV, 3, 34. *so t. thieves upon their conquered booty,* H6C I, 4, 63. *to t. ... upon their woes whom fortune captivates,* 114. *and there ride on the pants —ing,* Ant. IV, 8, 16.

4) to shine forth (German: *prangen*): *the clear unmatched red and white which —ed in that sky of his delight,* Lucr. 12. *in great commanders grace and majesty you might behold, —ing in their faces,* 1388. *the blood of twenty thousand men did t. in my face,* R2 III, 2, 77.

**Triumphant,** 1) celebrating victory, pertaining to a triumph in the Roman style: *a t. car,* H6A I, 1, 22. *with t. march,* H6C II, 6, 87. *with t. garlands,* R3 IV, 4, 333. *make t. fires,* Cor. V, 5, 3. *on t. chariots,* Ant. III, 1, 10.

2) victorious: *doth point out thee as his t. prize,* Sonn. 151, 10 (= as the prize of his triumph, his victory). *that which his t. father's hand had won,* R2 II, 1, 181. *t. death,* H6A IV, 7, 3.

3) exulting: *think you, but that I know our state secure, I would be so t. as I am?* R3 III, 2, 84.

4) glorious, of supreme magnificence and beauty: *my sun one early morn did shine with all t. splendour on my brow,* Sonn. 33, 10. *the red rose on t. brier,* Mids. III, 1, 96 (Thisbe's speech). *England, bound in with the t. sea,* R2 II, 1, 61. *I'll bury thee in a t. grave,* Rom. V, 3, 83. *a most t. lady,* Ant. II, 2, 189.

**Triumphantly,** 1) in the manner of a victorious conqueror: *banners ... t. displayed,* John II, 309. *or else t. tread on thy country's ruin,* Cor. V, 3, 116.

2) festively, rejoicingly: *dance in Duke Theseus' house t.* Mids. IV, 1, 94.

**Triumpher,** (*triúmpher*) one who returns as a victorious general: Tit. I, 170. Tim. V, 1, 199.

**Triumpherate** (Ant.) or **Triumphery** (LLL), M. Edd. *triumvirate* etc., the union of three men who divided among them the Roman empire: Ant. III, 6, 28. *thou makest the t., the corner-cap of society,* LLL IV, 3, 53.

**Trivial,** trifling, worthless, inconsiderable: *make t. price of serious things,* All's V, 3, 61. *we have but t. argument, more than mistrust, that shows him worthy death,* H6B III, 1, 241. *the respects thereof are nice and t.* R3 III, 7, 175. *hasty and tinder-like upon too t. motion,* Cor. II, 1, 55. *I'll wipe away all t. fond records,* Hml. I, 5, 99. *when we debate our t. difference loud,* Ant. II, 2, 21. *of so slight and t. a nature,* Cymb. I, 4, 45.

**Troian,** see *Trojan.*

**Troien,** one of the six gates of Troy: Troil. Prol. 16.

**Troilus** or **Troylus,** a son of Priam's, lover of Cressida: Lucr. 1486. Ado V, 2, 31. Merch. V, 4. As IV, 1, 97. Tw. III, 1, 59. Troil. I, 1, 5 and passim. Name of a spaniel: Shr. IV, 1, 153.

**Trojan** (O. Edd. *Troian* or *Troyan*) 1) subst. a native of Troy: Lucr. 1551. Mids. I, 1, 174. H6A V, 5, 106. Troil. I, 1, 4. I, 3, 233 etc.

Used as a cant term for persons of a doubtful character: *Hector was but a T. in respect of this,* LLL V, 2, 640. *unless you play the honest T., the poor wench is cast away,* 681. *there are other —s than thou dreamest not of,* H4A II, 1, 77. *base T.* H5 V, 1, 20. 32.

2) adj. pertaining to Troy: Lucr. 1431. Merch. V, 4. H4B II, 4, 181. Troil. Prol. 21. I, 2, 13 etc. Per. I, 4, 93.

**Troll,** to warble, to sing gaily: *will you t. the catch,* Tp. III, 2, 126.

**Troll-my-dames,** the French game of *Trou-madame:* Wint. IV, 3, 92.

**Troop,** subst. 1) a number of people, a company: *to whose weak ruins muster —s of cares,* Lucr. 720. *to this t. come thou not near,* Phoen. 8. *in —s I have dispersed them 'bout the isle,* Tp. I, 2, 220. *her t. of fairies,* Wiv. V, 3, 12. *a huge infectious t. of pale distemperatures,* Err. V, 81. *a jolly t. of huntsmen,* John II, 321. *is not the Lady Constance in this t.?* 540. R2 IV, 231. H6C II, 1, 13 (*in the thickest t.*). R3 III, 7, 85. H8 I, 4, 53. III, 2, 412. IV, 2, 87. V, 4, 89. Troil. IV, 5, 64. Cor. I, 1, 208. Mcb. V, 3, 25. Oth. I, 2, 54. = retinue: *with —s of ladies,* H6B I, 3, 80. *where be the thronging —s that followed thee?* R3 IV, 4, 96. *unfurnished of her well beseeming t.* Tit. II, 3, 56. *your populous —s,* Ant. III, 6, 50. *Dido and her Aeneas shall want —s,* IV, 14, 53.

2) a body of soldiers: *the t. is past,* All's III, 5, 96. *with a t. of Florentines,* III, 6, 23. *having full scarce six thousand in his t.* H6A I, 1, 112. *amongst the —s*

*of armed men*, II, 2, 24. *unite your —s of horsemen with his bands of foot*, IV, 1, 165. *two mightier —s*, IV, 3, 7. *a t. of kerns*, H6B III, 1, 361. *they have —s of soldiers*, H6C I, 1, 68. *some —s pursue the queen*, II, 6, 33. *with a puissant t.* V, 1, 6. *from t. to t.* R3 V, 3, 70. *whether yon —s are friend or enemy*, Caes. V, 3, 16. 18. *a t. of horse*, Lr. IV, 6, 189. *the plumed t.* Oth. III, 3, 349 (Ff —s). Plur. *— s* = army: All's III, 5, 43. IV, 3, 152. John V, 2, 133. H4B Ind. 25. H6A I, 5, 2. 22. III, 3, 32. H6C II, 3, 49. IV, 8, 4. Tit. V, 1, 20. Tim. III, 5, 115. Lr. IV, 5, 16. Cymb. V, 2, 14.

**Troop,** vb. to march in a body, to march in company: *I second thee; t. on*, Wiv. I, 3, 114 (Pistol's speech). *at whose approach ghosts ... t. home to churchyards*, Mids. III, 2, 382. *nor do I as an enemy to peace t. in the throngs of military men*, H4B IV, 1, 62. *there will the lovely Roman ladies t.* Tit. II, 1, 113. *a snowy dove —ing with crows*, Rom. I, 5, 50. *all the large effects that t. with majesty*, Lr. I, 1, 134.

**Trophy,** 1) a sign and token of victory: *giving full t., signal and ostent quite from himself to God*, H5 V Chor. 21. *let no images be hung with Caesar's —es*, Caes. I, 1, 74 (cf. I, 2, 288: *Marullus and Flavius, for pulling scarfs off Caesar's images, are put to silence.* Sueton. Caes. 79: *coronam lauream candida fascia praeligatam*).

2) memorial; monument: *tells him of —es, statues, tombs*, Ven. 1013. *hung with the —es of my lovers gone*, Sonn. 31, 10. *all these —es of affections hot*, Compl. 218. *the mere word's a slave deboshed on every tomb, on every grave a lying t.* All's II, 3, 146. *worn as a memorable t. of predeceased valour*, H5 V, 1, 76. *it* (blood) *more becomes a man than gilt his t.* Cor. I, 3, 43 (= his sepulchral monument). *till we with —es do adorn thy tomb*, Tit. I, 388. *that these great towers, —es and schools should fall for private faults in them*, Tim. V, 4, 25. *no t., sword, nor hatchment o'er his bones*, Hml. IV, 5, 214. *when down her weedy —es and herself fell in the weeping brook*, IV, 7, 175 (i. e. a garland of flowers gathered to hang them over her father's grave).

**Tropically,** figuratively: *the mouse-trap. Marry, how? t.* Hml. III, 2, 247.

**Trossers,** see *Strossers.*

**Trot,** subst. a decrepit old woman: *an old t. with ne'er a tooth in her head*, Shr. I, 2, 80. Lucio calls Pompey so: Meas. III, 2, 53.

**Trot,** vb. to move with a high jolting pace: Ven. 277. Wiv. I, 3, 7. LLL III, 188. As III, 2, 328. 330. 331 (the *trotting* pace represented, in these passages, as disagreeable to the rider). H5 III, 7, 83. 86. Tit. V, 2, 55. Lr. III, 4, 57. 104. Peculiar passage: *he —s the air*, H5 III, 7, 16 (not transitively; the air being an accus. denoting the space passed over; cf. *you never swum the Hellespont*, Gent. I, 1, 26, and see *Wing* vb.)

**Troth,** 1) truth: *to speak t.* Mids. II, 2, 36. *to say the t. on't*, Cor. IV, 5, 198. *I'll speak t.* Cymb. V, 5, 274.

2) faith: *she conjures him ... by holy human law and common t.* Lucr. 571. *thou smotherest honesty, thou murderest t.* 885. *thou shalt not know the stained taste of violated t.* 1059. *that strong-bonded oath that shall prefer and undertake my t.* Compl. 280. *and not break my t.* LLL I, 1, 66. *break faith and t.* IV, 3, 143. *virtue's office never breaks men's t.* V, 2, 350.

*two bosoms and one t.* Mids. II, 2, 42. 50. *one man holding t.* III, 2, 92. *violation of all faith and t. sworn to us*, H4A V, 1, 70. *faith and t.* Troil. IV, 5, 168. *bid her alight and her t. plight*, Lr. III, 4, 128. *the loyallest husband that did e'er plight t.* Cymb. I, 1, 96. Used to express a slight oath: *t.!* Wiv. I, 4, 154. II, 2, 177. Meas. II, 1, 228. III, 2, 59. Ado II, 1, 220. III, 4, 6. V, 4, 77. Tw. III, 1, 27. H8 II, 3, 34 (*yes, t. and t.*) etc. *good t.* Mids. II, 2, 129. H8 II, 3, 33. Cymb. III, 6, 48. *in t.* H4B II, 2, 12 (Qq *by my t.*). *in good t.* Troil. III, 1, 124. *o' my t.* Tp. II, 2, 36. LLL IV, 1, 144. Oftenest *by my t.:* Wiv. I, 1, 199. 297. Meas. IV, 3, 163. 187. Err. III, 1, 62. Ado I, 1, 226. 228 (*by my two faiths and —s*). II, 1, 19. 355. II, 3, 77. 242. III, 4, 9. 18. V, 1, 230. LLL IV, 1, 131. V, 2, 450. Merch. I, 2, 1. As I, 2, 94. III, 2, 303. IV, 1, 192. V, 1, 12. All's III, 2, 3. John III, 3, 55. H4B II, 2, 12 (Ff *in t.*). H6C III, 2, 64. R3 III, 4, 23. III, 7, 43. H8 II, 3, 23. Troil. III, 1, 116 etc.

**Trothed,** betrothed: *my new t. lord*, Ado III, 1, 38 (*new t.* hyphened by M. Edd.).

**Troth-plight,** betrothment, affiance: *puts to before her t.* Wint. I, 2, 278.

**Troth-plight,** betrothed, affianced: *is t. to your daughter*, Wint. V, 3, 151. *you were t. to her*, H5 II, 1, 21.

**Trouble,** subst. 1) disturbance, perplexity, embarrassment, affliction, suffering: *mark the poor, to overshoot his —s*, how he outruns the wind, Ven. 680. *all torment, t., wonder and amazement inhabits here*, Tp. V, 104. *—s of the marriage-bed*, Err. II, 1, 27. *that you would put me to this shame and t.* V, 14. *is it your dear friend that is thus in t.?* Merch. III, 2, 293. *prompted by your present t.* Tw. III, 4, 377. *I would his —s likewise were expired*, H6A II, 5, 31. H6B V, 1, 70. H6C V, 5, 16. H8 II, 2, 16. III, 1, 1. Caes. I, 2, 38. Mcb. IV, 1, 18. V, 1, 80. V, 3, 42. Hml. III, 1, 59. Oth. III, 3, 150. Per. II Prol. 7. II, 4, 44.

2) molestation: *what t. was I then to you*, Tp. I, 2, 151. *you are come to meet your t.* Ado I, 1, 97. 99. 100. *forgive me your t.* Tw. II, 1, 35. Wint. I, 2, 26. V, 3, 9. H8 IV, 2, 162. Mcb. I, 6, 11. 14.

3) pains, labour: *is twenty hundred kisses such a t.?* Ven. 522. *unapt to toil and t. in the world*, Shr. V, 2, 166. *double toil and t.* Mcb. IV, 1, 10. 20. 35. *this is a joyful t. to you*, II, 3, 53. *you lay out too much pains for purchasing but t.* Cymb. II, 3, 93.

**Trouble,** vb. 1) to put into agitation, to disturb, to disorder: *like a —d ocean*, Lucr. 589. *a woman moved is like a fountain —d*, Shr. V, 2, 142. *the meteors of a —d heaven*, H4A I, 1, 10. cf. Mcb. II, 4, 5. *whose filth and dirt —s the silver spring where England drinks*, H6B IV, 1, 72. *the —d Tiber chafing with her shores*, Caes. I, 2, 101. *a mote it is to t. the mind's eye*, Hml. I, 1, 112.

2) to come in one's way, not to let alone, to interrupt: *hence, t. us not*, Tp. I, 1, 19. R3 I, 2, 50. *if you t. him any more in's tale*, Tp. III, 2, 55. *my father and the gentleman are in sad talk, and we'll not t. them*, Wint. IV, 4, 317. *t. me no more with vanity*, H4A I, 2, 91. *I will be gone, sir, and not t. you*, Rom. V, 3, 40 (cf. Err. IV, 3, 71). *t. him not, his wits are gone*, Lr. III, 6, 94. *t. him no more till further settling*, IV, 7, 81. Hence = to hinder, to make an end of by interruption: *to t. your joys with like relation*, Wint. V, 3, 129 *t. not the peace*, Cor. V, 6, 129.

3) to perplex, to vex, to disquiet, to afflict, to distress: *all the neighbour caves, as seeming —d, make verbal repetition of her moans,* Ven. 830. *her —d brain,* 1040. 1068. *—d minds,* Lucr. 126. *this —d soul,* 1176. *my old brain is —d,* Tp. IV, 159. *t. not yourself,* Wiv. III, 4, 92. *with pure love and —d brain,* As IV, 3, 3. *your husband, being —d with a shrew,* Shr. V, 2, 28. *fresh expectation —d not the land with any longed-for change,* John IV, 2, 7. *a much —d breast,* 73. H5 II, 3, 22. V, 2, 392. H6B V, 1, 34. R3 IV, 3, 49. V, 3, 104. Troil. III, 3, 311. Tit. II, 2, 9. IV, 4, 3. Rom. I, 1, 127. Tim. III, 6, 42. Mcb. V, 3, 38. Hml. I, 2, 224. V, 2, 226. Ant. III, 6, 82.

4) to molest: *t. deaf heaven with my bootless cries,* Sonn. 29, 3. *this babble shall not henceforth t. me,* Gent. I, 2, 98. *I have a bag of money here —s me,* Wiv. II, 2, 178. *your town is —d with unruly boys,* Err. III, 1, 62. *I'll be gone, sir, and not t. you,* Err. IV, 3, 71 (cf. Rom. V, 3, 40). Ado I, 1, 130. Merch. I, 2, 112. IV, 1, 44. As I, 1, 82. II, 7, 171. Wint. II, 1, 1. R2 IV, 303. H4A V, 1, 113. H4B IV, 5, 128. H6A II, 3, 25. III, 1, 144. IV, 1, 127. V, 3, 180. H6B I, 1, 141. I, 3, 94. III, 1, 324. IV, 5, 8. H6C III, 3, 155. V, 5, 5. R3 I, 3, 61. IV, 2, 122. Cor. II, 3, 76. 117. Tit. I, 367. Tim. III, 3, 1. V, 1, 216. Caes. II, 1, 87. Lr. I, 4, 275. II, 4, 222. Per. III, 2, 19.

Applied to diseases: *—d with the lampass,* Shr. III, 2, 52. *this fever, that hath —d me so long,* John V, 3, 3. H4B I, 2, 139. Troil. V, 3, 102. Oth. III, 3, 414. Ant. III, 2, 5. 57.

5) to put to pains and labour: *meaning henceforth to t. you no more,* Gent. II, 1, 125. *I would not by my will have —d you,* Tw. III, 3, 1. H6A I, 4, 22. H8 IV, 2, 77. Troil. IV, 2, 3. V, 1, 75. Tit. I, 189. Rom. IV, 4, 18. Caes. IV, 3, 259. Refl.: *t. not yourself,* Troil. IV, 2, 1. Oth. IV, 3, 1. Ant. II, 4, 1.

**Troubler,** disturber: *the t. of the poor world's peace,* R3 I, 3, 221. *not to be a t. of your peace,* Per. V, 1, 153.

**Troublesome,** giving trouble: *I'll rather be unmannerly than t.* Wiv. I, 1, 325. *this act is as an ancient tale new told, and in the last repeating t.* John IV, 2, 19. *and be like them* (the times) *to Percy t.* H4B II, 3, 4. *so t. a bedfellow* (the crown) IV, 5, 22. *how t. it sat upon my head,* 187. *you are strangely t.* H8 V, 3, 94. Cor. IV, 5, 17. *the time is t.* Cymb. IV, 3, 21.

**Troublous,** disturbed, restless, turbulent: *my t. dream this night doth make me sad,* H6B I, 2, 22. *in this t. time,* H6C II, 1, 159. *in this t. world,* V, 5, 7. *'twill prove a t. world,* R3 II, 3, 5 (Ff *giddy*). 9.

**Trough,** a piece of timber excavated to give swine their food in: R3 V, 2, 9.

**Trout,** the fish Salmo trutta or Salmo fario: Meas. I, 2, 91. Tw. II, 5, 25 (*the t. that must be caught with tickling*).

**Trow,** 1) to trust, to believe: *learn more than thou —est,* Lr. I, 4, 135 (don't believe all that thou learnest or hearest). 2) to think, to suppose: *—est thou that e'er I'll look upon the world?* H6B II, 4, 38. *—est thou that Clarence is so harsh,* H6C V, 1, 85. 3) to know: *he privily deals with our cardinal; and as I t.,* — which *I do well,* etc. H8 I, 1, 184. *you t., nuncle, the hedgesparrow* etc. Lr. I, 4, 234 (Ff *know*).

*I t.* = I dare say, certainly: *I t. this is his house,* Shr. I, 2, 4. *'tis time, I t.* R2 II, 1, 218. *'twas time, I t., to wake and leave our beds,* H6A II, 1, 41. *now*

*Winchester will not submit, I t.,* or *be inferior to the proudest peer,* V, 1, 56. *'twas no need, I t., to bid me trudge,* Rom. I, 3, 33. *are you so hot? marry, come up, I t.* II, 5, 64.

*t. you* = can you tell? do you know? guess!: *and t. you what he called me?* LLL V, 2, 279. *t. you who hath done this?* As III, 2, 189. *t. you whither I am going?* Shr. I, 2, 165.

*I t.* or *t.* alone, added to questions, expressive of contemptuous or indignant surprise (nearly = I wonder): *who's there, I t.?* Wiv. I, 4, 140. *what tempest, I t., threw this whale ... ashore?* II, 1, 64. *what means the fool, t.?* Ado III, 4, 59. *what is the matter, t.?* Cymb. I, 6, 47.

**Trowel,** the mason's tool used to take up mortar and spread it on the bricks: *well said: that was laid on with a t.* As I, 2, 112 (a proverbial phrase, probably = without ceremony).

**Troy,** the famous town besieged and destroyed by the Greeks: Lucr. 1367. 1382. 1429. 1547. Wiv. I, 3, 83. LLL V, 2, 537. 890. Merch. III, 2, 56. All's I, 3, 75. R2 V, 1, 11. H4B I, 1, 73. II, 4, 237. H6B I, 4, 20. III, 2, 118. H6C II, 1, 51. 52. III, 2, 190. IV, 8, 25. Troil. Prol. 1 etc. I, 3, 12 (*T. walls*). 135 (fem.) etc. Tit. I, 136. III, 1, 69. III, 2, 28. IV, 1, 20. V, 3, 84. 87. Caes. I, 2, 113.

**Troyan,** see *Trojan.*

**Troylus,** see *Troilus.*

**Truant,** an idler, one neglecting his duty: *myself have been an idle t.,* omitting the sweet benefit of time, Gent. II, 4, 64. *since I played t. and whipped top,* Wiv. V, 1, 27 (stayed from school). *I will never be a t., love, till I have learned thy language,* H4A III, 1, 207. *I have a t. been to chivalry,* V, 1, 94. *I have been a t. in the law,* H6A II, 4, 7. *I am not such a t. since my coming, as not to know the language I have lived in,* H8 III, 1, 43. *you are no t.* Hml. I, 2, 173.

Hence = a trifler, a rover (German: *Springinsfeld*): *I hope he be in love. Hang him, t.! there's no true drop of blood in him,* Ado III, 2, 18. *aged ears play t. at his tales,* LLL II, 74.

Adjectively: *O t. Muse, what shall be thy amends for thy neglect of truth in beauty dyed?* Sonn. 101, 1. *chid thee t. youth,* H4A V, 2, 63. *with t. vows to her own lips,* Troil. I, 3, 270. *a t. disposition,* Hml. I, 2, 169.

**Truant,** vb. to play the truant, to be inconstant: *'tis double wrong, to t. with your bed and let her read it in thy looks,* Err. II, 2, 17.

**Truce,** 1) armistice, temporary cessation of hostilities: *I have awhile given t. unto my wars,* H6A III, 4, 3. *in this dull and long-continued t.* Troil. I, 3, 262. *the seas and winds ... took a t.* II, 2, 75. *during all question of the gentle t.* IV, 1, 11.

2) peace: *keep then fair league and t. with thy true bed,* Err. II, 2, 147. *before this t.* John III, 1, 233 (231 and 235 *peace*). *make compromise, insinuation, parley and base t. to arms invasive,* V, 1, 68. *in the next parliament called for the t. of Winchester and Gloster,* H6A II, 4, 118. *this token serveth for a flag of t. betwixt ourselves and all our followers,* III, 1, 138. *peaceful t. shall be proclaimed in France,* V, 4, 117. *take this compact of a t.* 163. *excitements to the field, or speech for t.* Troil. I, 3, 182. *to take t.* = to make peace: *till he take t. with her contending tears,* Ven. 82. *with my vexed spirits I cannot take a t.* John III, 1, 17.

*all this ... could not take t. with the unruly spleen of Tybalt,* Rom. III, 1, 162.

**Truckle-bed,** a bed that runs on wheels and may be pushed under another: Wiv. IV, 5, 7. Rom. II, 1, 39. cf. *Standing-bed.*

**Trudge,** to trot, to run (hastily and heavily): *vanish like hailstones, go, t., plod away o'the hoof,* Wiv. I, 3, 91. *t. with it in all haste and carry it among the whitsters in Datchet-mead,* III, 3, 13. *'tis time to t., pack and be gone,* Err. III, 2, 158. *night-walking heralds that t. betwixt the king and Mistress Shore,* R3 I, 1, 73. *go, sirrah, t. about through fair Verona,* Rom. I, 2, 34. *'twas no need to bid me t.* I, 3, 34.

**True,** 1) conformable to fact: Ven. 658. Tp. I, 2, 267. II, 1, 50. 255. 271. III, 3, 26. Epil. 3. Gent. I, 1, 25. 83. II, 1, 87. V, 2, 13. V, 4, 110. Wiv. I, 1, 162. II, 1, 132. Meas. V, 43. 44. Mids. I, 1, 95. III, 2, 280. All's IV, 3, 66 etc. etc. *to say t.* Sonn. 114, 3. Wiv. II, 2, 49. All's IV, 3, 171. Tw. II, 5, 213. H4A I, 3, 250 etc. *to speak t.* Tp. II, 1, 20. III, 1, 70. LLL V, 2, 364. As V, 4, 82. H6B III, 1, 183. Troil. III, 2, 105 etc. *to tell* (one) *t.* Gent. II, 5, 35. Wiv. III, 4, 11. Meas. II, 1, 233. Err. V, 180. Ado II, 1, 121. 223. LLL I, 1, 227. IV, 1, 18. Mids. III, 2, 68. Merch. III, 2, 259. All's I, 3, 181. 225. IV, 3, 183. V, 3, 234. H4A V, 3, 6. Troil. I, 1, 60 *(as t. thou tellest me).* IV, 1, 51. Cor. V, 2, 33. Tim. I, 2, 223. IV, 3, 513. Ant. I, 2, 102. IV, 6, 26 etc. *and t. he swore, though yet forsworn he were,* Err. IV, 2, 10. Substantively: *my false o'erweighs your t.* Meas. II, 4, 170.

2) veracious, free from falsehood, not lying, not mistaken, not feigned: *these mine eyes, t. leaders to their queen,* Ven. 503. *sweets that shall the —st sight beguile,* 1144. *my t. eyes have never practised how to cloak offences,* Lucr. 748. *with soft slow tongue, t. mark of modesty,* 1220. *what eyes hath love put in my head, which have no correspondence with t. sight,* Sonn. 148, 2. *love's eye is not so t. as all men's No,* 8. 9. *give the lie to my t. sight,* 150, 3. *if these be t. spies which I wear in my head,* Tp. V, 259. *with t. prayers, that shall be up at heaven,* Meas. II, 2, 151. *my t. complaint,* V, 24. *there are no faces —r than those that are so washed,* Ado I, 1, 27. *fair she is, if that mine eyes be t.* Merch. II, 6, 54. *with many vows of faith and ne'er a t. one,* V, 20. *you have deserved high commendation, t. applause and love,* As I, 2, 275. *if sight and shape be t.* V, 4, 126. *is there no exorcist beguiles the —r office of mine eyes,* All's V, 3, 306. *it is with me, as the very t. sonnet is,* Tw. III, 4, 24. *prove t., imagination,* 409. *as yet the glass seems t.* V, 272 (?). *the t. acquaintance of mine ear,* John V, 6, 15. *your spirit is too t., your fears too certain,* H4B I, 1, 92. *from t. evidence,* H6B III, 2, 21. *his napkin, with his t. tears all bewet,* Tit. III, 1, 146. *the last t. duties of thy noble son,* V, 3, 155. *O t. apothecary,* Rom. V, 3, 119. *but a sickly part of one t. sense could not so mope,* Hml. III, 4, 80. *I am —st speaker,* Cymb. V, 5, 376 etc. Adverbially: *the plain simple vow that is vowed t.* All's IV, 2, 22.

3) honest: *rich preys make t. men thieves,* Ven. 724. *my t. preserver,* Tp. V, 69. *mark but the badges of these men: then say if they be t.* 268. *though the priest o'the town commended him for a t. man,* Wiv. II, 1, 149. *every t. man's apparel fits your thief,* Meas. IV, 2, 46. 47. *if you meet a thief, you may suspect him ... to be no t. man,* Ado III, 3, 54. *a t. man or a thief that*

*gallops so?* LLL IV, 3, 187. *as t. we are as flesh and blood can be,* 214. *the t. man's put to death,* R2 V, 3, 73. *cried 'Stand' to a t. man,* H4A I, 2, 122. *as I am a t. man,* II, 1, 101. *to turn t. man and to leave these rogues,* II, 2, 24. *the thieves have bound the t. men,* 98. *it was the blood of t. men,* II, 4, 343. *now for a t. face and good conscience,* 550. *as I am a t. woman,* III, 3, 82. *so t. men yield, with robbers so o'ermatched,* H6C I, 4, 64. *I thought to crush him in an equal force, t. sword to sword,* Cor. I, 10, 15. *there is no time so miserable but a man may be t.* Tim. IV, 3, 463. *I am no t. man,* Caes. I, 2, 263. *makes the t. man killed and saves the thief,* Cymb. II, 3, 76. 77.

In a general sense, = trustworthy, to be depended on, not failing: *each trifle under —st bars to thrust,* Sonn. 48, 2. *strong joints, t. swords,* Troil. I, 3, 238. *with your t. sword,* V, 3, 56 (cf. Cor. I, 10, 15, and see *Steel*). *as t. a dog as ever fought at head,* Tit. V, 1, 102.

4) faithful: *the death of this t. wife,* Lucr. 1841. *the t. concord of well-tuned sounds,* Sonn. 8, 5. *mine own t. love,* 61, 11. *supposing thou art t.* 93, 1. *fair, kind and t.* 105, 9. *my most t. mind thus makes mine eye untrue,* 113, 14. *neither t. nor trusty,* Pilgr. 86. *t. or fair,* Phoen. 64. *to be thy t. subject,* Tp. II, 2, 130. *look thou be t.* IV, 51. 84. Gent. II, 2, 8. 17. II, 7, 74. IV, 2, 5. 7. Wiv. II, 1, 15. Err. II, 2, 147. Mids. II, 1, 197 *(t. as steel).* V, 280. Merch. III, 2, 49. All's II, 5, 79. H4B IV, 5, 148. H6C IV, 1, 40. Troil. III, 2, 106. Hml. IV, 5, 120 etc. *(t. and faithfully,* in LLL V, 2, 841 = truly and faithfully. cf. Appendix). With *to:* Compl. 34. Wiv. III, 3, 28. LLL V, 2, 783. Mids. III, 2, 50. IV, 1, 181. V, 200. Wint. V, 1, 124. John V, 7, 118. R2 I, 3, 86. H6B V, 1, 82. *t. love* often = love: *who sees his t. love in her naked bed,* Ven. 397. *do it for thy t. love take,* Mids. II, 2, 28. Gent. IV, 2, 126. IV, 3, 20. LLL IV, 3, 122. Mids. III, 2, 89. Tw. II, 3, 41 etc.

5) genuine, real, not factitious, but being indeed so: *let me, t. in love, but truly write,* Sonn. 21, 9. *to find where your t. image pictured lies,* 24, 6. *so t. a fool is love,* 57, 13 (quibbling). *his rose is t.* 67, 8. *beauty ... without all ornament, itself and t.* 68, 10. *to be deceived are that there was t. needing,* 118, 8. *the t. gouty landlord which doth owe them,* Compl. 140. *how t. a twain seemeth this concordant one,* Phoen. 45. *her t. perfection,* Gent. II, 4, 197. *that is my t. humour,* Wiv. I, 3, 112. *as I am a t. spirit,* V, 5, 33. *how I may bear me like a t. friar,* Meas. I, 3, 48. *it is impossible you should take t. root,* Ado I, 3, 25. *in a false quarrel there is no t. valour,* V, 1, 120. *takest t. delight,* Mids. III, 2, 455. *I thought you lord of more t. gentleness,* II, 2, 132. *gleaned from the t. seed of honour,* Merch. II, 9, 47. *the —st poetry is the most feigning,* As III, 3, 19. *there is no t. cuckold but calamity,* Tw. I, 5, 56. *as I am t. knight,* II, 3, 54. R2 I, 3, 34. *never call a t. piece of gold a counterfeit,* H4A II, 4, 539. *acquitted by a t. substantial form,* H4B IV, 1, 173. *prince, as thou art t.,* [for blood of ours shed blood of Montague, Rom. III, 1, 153 (= as thou art truly a prince). *ne'er did poor steward wear a —r grief,* Tim. IV, 3, 487. *let our just censures attend the t. event,* Mcb. V, 4, 15. *all men's faces are t. ... but there is never a fair woman has a t. face,* Ant. II, 6, 102. 105 (quibbling). *is this letter t.?* Cymb. III, 5, 106 (not counterfeited) etc. Adverbially: *a dear, a t. industrious friend,* H4A I, 1, 62.

6) conformable to reason or to rules; just, right, correct, exact: *here comes the almanac of my t. date,* Err. I, 2, 41. *establish him in his t. sense again,* IV, 4, 51. *she cannot be so much without t. judgment,* Ado III, 1, 88. *an bad thinking do not wrest t. speaking,* III, 4, 34. *as it appears in the t. course of all the question,* V, 4, 6. *the numbers t.* LLL V, 2, 35. *the throstle with his note so t.* Mids. III, 1, 130 (cf. *as duly, but not as truly, as bird doth sing on bough,* H5 III, 2, 19). *it is not enough to speak, but to speak t.* Mids. V, 121. *knew the t. minute when exception bid him speak,* All's I, 2, 39. *so long as out of limit and t. rule you stand against anointed majesty,* H4A IV, 3, 39. *in t. English, I love thee,* H5 V, 2, 237. *by t. computation of the time,* R3 III, 5, 89 (Qq *just*). *deaf to the voice of any t. decision,* Troil. II, 2, 173. *manifests the t. knowledge he has in their disposition,* Cor. II, 2, 15. *your dishonour mangles t. judgment,* III, 1, 158. *let me still remain the t. blank of thine eye,* Lr. I, 1, 161 (straitly within the aim of thy eye). *if it be a sin to make a t. election, she is damned,* Cymb. I, 2, 30. Adverbially: *chance as fair and choose as t.* Merch. III, 2, 133. *my dial goes not t.* All's II, 5, 6. *how t. he keeps the wind,* H6C III, 2, 14.

7) conformable to law and justice, rightful, legitimate: *your t. rights be termed a poet's rage,* Sonn. 17, 11. *upon a t. contract I got possession of Julietta's bed,* Meas. I, 2, 149. *'tis all as easy falsely to take away a life t. made as to put metal in restrained means to make a false one,* II, 4, 47. *screws me from my t. place in your favour,* Tw. V, 126. *as t. begot,* John I, 75. *his father never was so t. begot,* II, 130. *he that steeps his safety in t. blood,* III, 4, 147. *nor tempt the danger of my t. defence,* IV, 3, 84. *the t. prince,* H4A I, 2, 173. II, 4, 298. 300. *his t. titles to some dukedoms,* H5 I, 1, 87. *in honour of a t. Plantagenet,* H6A II, 5, 52. *to conquer France, his t. inheritance,* H6B I, 1, 82. *an oath ... not took before a t. and lawful magistrate,* H6C I, 2, 23. *Caesar shall have all t. rites and lawful ceremonies,* Caes. III, 1, 241. *the —st issue of thy throne,* Mcb. IV, 3, 106.

8) conformable to nature, due, natural: *that will ask some tears in the t. performing of it,* Mids. I, 2, 27. *he shall think by our t. diligence he is no less than what we say he is,* Shr. Ind. 1, 70. *I can give his humour the t. bent,* Caes. II, 1, 210. = of due proportions, well-shaped: *no shape so t., no truth of such account,* Sonn. 62, 6. *my mind as generous and my shape as t. as honest madam's issue,* Lr. I, 2, 8.

**True-anointed**, writing of M. Edd. in H6C III, 3, 29; not hyphened in O. Edd.

**True-begotten** (not hyphened in O. Edd.) legitimate: *my t. father,* Merch. II, 2, 36 (Launcelot's speech).

**True-betrothed** (not hyphened in O. Edd.) lawfully affianced: Tit. I, 406.

**True-born**, having a right by birth to a title: *a t. Englishman,* R2 I, 3, 309. *a t. gentleman,* H6A II, 4, 27.

**True-bred**, of a right breed, genuine: *she's a beagle, t.* Tw. II, 3, 195. *t. cowards,* H4A I, 2, 206. *a' (the knave) will not out; he is t.* H4B V, 3, 71. *O, t.!* Cor. I, 1, 247.

**True-confirmed** (not hyphened in O. Edd.) not to be shaken in faith: *I am my master's t. love,* Gent. IV, 4, 108.

**True-derived**, of lawful descent, legitimate: *to draw forth your noble ancestry from the corruption of abusing times unto a lineal t. course,* R3 III, 7, 200.

**True-devoted**, full of true devotion and honest zeal: *a t. pilgrim,* Gent. II, 7, 9.

**True-disposing**, justly ordaining, just: *O upright, just and t. God,* R3 IV, 4, 55.

**True-divining**, having a true presentiment: Tit. II, 3, 214.

**True-fixed**, (not hyphened in O. Edd.) steadily and immovably settled: *whose t. and resting quality,* Caes. III, 1, 61.

**True-hearted**, faithful, honest: H6C IV, 8, 9. H8 V, 1, 155. Lr. I, 2, 126.

**True-love** (hyphened or not hyphened, indiscriminately; cf. *True*): *t. knots,* Gent. II, 7, 46. Mids. III, 2, 89. R2 V, 1, 10. Hml. IV, 5, 39.

**True-man** (cf. *Man* and *True*), an honest man: Cymb. II, 3, 76. 77.

**True-meant**, really intended: *his givings-out were of an infinite distance from his t. design,* Meas. I, 4, 55.

**True-penny**, an honest fellow: *art thou there, t.?* Hml. I, 5, 150.

**Truer-hearted**, more faithful and honest: *but an honester and t. man,* H4B II, 4, 414.

**Truest-mannered**, most honestly and faithfully disposed: Cymb. I, 6, 166.

**True-sweet**: *the flowers are sweet, their colours fresh and trim; but t. beauty lived and died with him,* Ven. 1080 (not hyphened in O. Edd.).

**True-telling**, veracious: Sonn. 82, 12.

**Trull**, a lewd and worthless woman, a drab: H6A II, 2, 28. H6C I, 4, 114. Tit. II, 3, 191. Ant. III, 6, 95. Cymb. V, 5, 177.

**Truly**, 1) according to truth, in agreement with fact: *let me, true in love, but t. write,* Sonn. 21, 9. *the wrinkles, which thy glass will t. show,* 77, 5. *most strange, but yet most t., will I speak,* Meas. V, 37. Mids. IV, 1, 154. All's I, 3, 224. John IV, 3, 92. R2 I, 3, 14. H4A I, 2, 106. Hml. IV, 4, 17. *tell me t. how thou likest her,* Ado I, 1, 180. Shr. IV, 5, 28. All's I, 3, 191. H5 IV, 7, 86. Lr. V, 1, 8. *bid her answer t.* Ado IV, 1, 76. 80. All's IV, 3, 147. Caes. III, 3, 13. 17. 29. *as I am t. given to understand,* H4A IV, 4, 11. *in every branch t. demonstrative,* H5 II, 4, 89. *more t. now may this be verified,* H6A I, 2, 32. *as I t. swear,* R3 II, 1, 11. *God shall be t. known,* H8 V, 5, 37. *to us that give you t.* Cor. I, 9, 55. *if you report him t.* V, 4, 27. *there's none can t. say he gives,* Tim. I, 2, 11. *shapes of grief, that can denote me t.* Hml. I, 2, 83. *all this can I t. deliver,* V, 2, 397. *as t. as to heaven I do confess the vices of my blood,* Oth. I, 3, 122. *swear thou art honest. Heaven doth t. know it,* IV, 2, 38. 39. *by her election may be t. read what kind of man he is,* Cymb. I, 1, 53. *report should render him hourly to your ear as t. as he moves,* III, 4, 154. *or more t., woman its pretty self,* 159. *than I did t. find her,* V, 5, 188.

2) really, not only in appearance: *thou t. fair,* Sonn. 82, 11. *I do as t. suffer as e'er I did commit,* Gent. V, 4, 76. *to be t. touched with love,* Ado III, 2, 19. *they were never so t. turned over and over in love,* V, 2, 34. As II, 7, 195. III, 2, 434. All's IV, 4, 17. H4A I, 2, 5. 6. H5 V, 2, 203. H6B III, 1, 330. V, 2, 37. H8 II, 1, 112. III, 2, 289. 377. Cor. III, 1, 218.

Rom. II, 3, 68. Tim. III, 5, 31. Mcb. IV, 3, 131. Oth. III, 3, 48.

3) rightly, correctly, justly: *if I read it* (your face) *not t., my ancient skill beguiles me*, Meas. IV, 2, 164. *as duly, but not as t., as bird doth sing on bough*, H5 III, 2, 19 (cf. *true* in Mids. III, 1, 130). *fears make devils of cherubins; they never see t.* Troil. III, 2, 75. *if Pisanio have mapped it t.* Cymb. IV, 1, 2.

4) honestly, faithfully: *we have always t. served you*, Wint. II, 3, 147. H4B V, 1, 52. V, 2, 7. Lr. I, 4, 15. II, 1, 119. Cymb. IV, 2, 373. *thou worshippest Saint Nicholas as t. as a man of falsehood may*, H4A II, 1, 71. *if like a Christian thou hadst t. borne betwixt our armies true intelligence*, V, 5, 9. (a good heart) *keeps his course t.* H5 V, 2, 173. *all masters cannot be t.* followed, Oth. I, 1, 44. *it shall safe be kept and t. yielded you*, Cymb. I, 6, 210. *what villany soe'er I bid thee do, to perform it directly and t.* III, 5, 113.

5) conformably to law and justice, legitimately: *and him by oath they t. honoured*, Lucr. 410. *his innocent babe t. begotten*, Wint. III, 2, 135. *to pay that duty which you t. owe to him that owes it*, John II, 247. *that which thou hast sworn to do amiss is not amiss when it is t. done*, III, 1, 271 (in a lawful manner). *as I t. fight, defend me heaven*, R2 I, 3, 25. *to give obedience where 'tis t. owed*, Mcb. V, 2, 26.

6) according to nature, duly, naturally: *his effigies ... most t. limned and living in your face*, As II, 7, 194. *a pageant t. played*, III, 4, 55. *'tis beauty t. blent*, Tw. I, 5, 257. *to make us say 'This is put forth too t.'* Wint. I, 2, 14.

7) indeed; a slight affirmation, sometimes almost expletive: Sonn. 132, 5. Gent. I, 1, 141. Wiv. I, 1, 322. I, 3, 4. II, 2, 121. 125. III, 2, 11. III, 4, 65. IV, 1, 4. Meas. I, 4, 3. II, 1, 194. 234. IV, 2, 61. IV, 3, 43. Ado I, 1, 112. II, 1, 67. III, 1, 34. 84. III, 3, 59. V, 4, 83. LLL IV, 2, 1. Mids. I, 1, 178. IV, 1, 35. 153. V, 272. 367. Merch. III, 5, 1. As I, 2, 19. III, 2, 35. All's II, 3, 22. H6A II, 2, 54. R3 V, 3, 245. H8 II, 1, 8. Lr. IV, 6, 4 etc. etc.

**Trump,** trumpet: H6A I, 4, 80. Troil. III, 3, 210. Tit. I, 275. Tim. I, 2, 120. Oth. III, 3, 351.

**Trumpery,** things fallaciously splendid, showy trifles: Tp. IV, 186. Wint. IV, 4, 608.

**Trumpet,** subst. 1) a wind instrument of music, chiefly used for military purposes and for making signals: Lucr. 470. LLL V, 2, 157. Merch. V, 122. Shr. Ind. 1, 74. I, 2, 207 (*—s' clang*). All's III, 5, 9. V, 2, 55. John II, 198. 205. III, 1, 303 (*braying —s*). V, 2, 117. R2 I, 3, 4. H4B IV, 1, 52. 122. H5 IV, 7, 59. R3 IV, 4, 148 etc. *o'the —s' sound*, Tim. III, 6, 37. *twice have the —s sounded*, Meas. IV, 6, 12. Merch. V, 75. R2 I, 3, 117. H6B V, 3, 32. H6C I, 1, 118. II, 1, 200. IV, 7, 69. R3 V, 3, 269. H8 IV, 1, 36. Troil. V, 3, 13. Lr. V, 1, 41. V, 3, 108. 110. *the t. sounds retreat*, H4A V, 4, 163. H5 III, 2, 94. *let the —s sound the tucket sonance*, H5 IV, 2, 34. *sound, —s, alarum*, H6B II, 3, 95. V, 2, 3. Summoning to the last judgment: *let the general t. blow his blast*, H6B V, 2, 43. *dreadful t., sound the general doom*, Rom. III, 2, 67. *till the last t.* Hml. V, 1, 253.

Metaphorically, = he who, or that which, publishes and proclaims: *to be the t. of his own virtues*, Ado V, 2, 87. *let my tongue blister and never to my red-looked anger be the t. any more*, Wint. II, 2, 35. *be thou the t. of our wrath*, John I, 27. *the southern wind doth play the t. to his purposes*, H4A V, 1, 4. *pride is his own glass, his own t., his own chronicle*, Troil. II, 3, 166. *what's the business, that such a hideous t.* (viz the alarm-bell) *calls to parley the sleepers*, Mcb. II, 3, 87. *the cock, that is the t. to the morn*, Hml. I, 1, 150.

2) a trumpeter: *let the bird of loudest lay herald sad and t. be*, Phoen. 3. *bring the —s to the gate*, Meas. IV, 5, 9. *I will the banner from a t. take*, H5 IV, 2, 61. *go, t., to the walls and sound a parle*, H6C V, 1, 16. *thou, t., there's my purse*, Troil. IV, 5, 6.

**Trumpet,** vb. to publish, to proclaim: *that I did love the Moor to live with him, my downright violence and storm of fortunes may t. to the world*, Oth. I, 3, 251. *so tart a favour to t. such good tidings*, Ant. II, 5, 39. *he must not live to t. forth my infamy*, Per. I, 1, 145.

**Trumpet-clangor,** the sound of trumpets: H4B V, 5, 42.

**Trumpeter,** one who sounds a trumpet: H6A IV, 2, 1. Cor. I, 1, 121. Ant. IV, 8, 35. Metaphorically, one who proclaims and publishes: *to be —s of our unlawful intents*, All's IV, 3, 32.

**Trumpet-tongued,** proclaiming loudly as with the voice of a trumpet: *will plead like angels, t., against* etc. Mcb. I, 7, 19.

**Truncheon,** subst. 1) a short staff, a club, a cudgel: *thy leg a stick compared with this t.* H6B IV, 10, 52.

2) a staff of command: Meas. II, 2, 61. Troil. V, 3, 53. Hml. I, 2, 204. Oth. II, 1, 280 (not in Ff).

**Truncheon,** vb., a word of Doll Tearsheet's making: *an captains were of my mind, they would t. you out, for taking their names upon you*, H4B II, 4, 154; i. e. probably: they would cudgel you out of your usurped title with their truncheons.

**Truncheoner,** one armed with a club: H8 V, 4, 54.

**Trundle-bed,** = truckle-bed; reading of the surreptitious Qq in Wiv. IV, 5, 7 and Rom. II, 1, 39.

**Trundle-tail,** a dog with a curling tail: *or bobtail tike or t.* Lr. III, 6, 73.

**Trunk,** 1) the stem of a tree (as an image of the human body): *the ivy which had hid my princely t. and sucked my verdure out on't*, Tp. I, 2, 86. *would bark your honour from that t. you bear*, Meas. III, 1, 72. *health ... is flown from this bare withered t.* H4B IV, 5, 230.

2) the body of an animal, especially of man: *souls of animals infuse themselves into the —s of men*, Merch. IV, 1, 133. *my honesty, that lies enclosed in this t.* Wint. I, 2, 435. *this frail and worthless t.* H5 III, 6, 163. *his dumb deaf t.* H6B III, 2, 144. *leaving thy t.* (without the head) *for crows to feed upon*, IV, 10, 90. *until my mis-shaped t. that bears this head be round impaled with a glorious crown*, H6B III, 2, 170. *the honoured mould wherein this t. was framed*, Cor. V, 3, 23. *make his dead t. pillow to our lust*, Tit. II, 3, 130. *to shed obsequious tears upon this t.* V, 3, 152. *that the t. may be discharged of breath*, Rom. V, 1, 63. *the creatures ... whose bare unhoused —s ... answer mere nature*, Tim. IV, 3, 229. *thy banished t.* Lr. I, 1, 180. *what t. is here without his top?* Cymb. IV, 2, 353.

3) a chest: Wiv. IV, 2, 62. John V, 2, 141. Cymb. I, 6, 196. 209. II, 2, 47. *t. work* (work made on a chest) Wint. III, 3, 75. Metaphorical use, essentially influenced by the preceding signification: *the beauteous-*

*evil are empty —s o'erflourished by the devil*, Tw. III, 4, 404. *that t. of humours*, H4A II, 4, 495.

**Trunk sleeve,** a large wide sleeve: Shr. IV, 3, 142.

**Truss,** to pack close: *you might have —ed him and all his apparel into an eel-skin*, H4B III, 2, 350 (Q *thrust*).

**Trust,** subst. 1) confidence, reliance; actively or subjectively: *Priam's t. false Sinon's tears doth flatter*, Lucr. 1560. *love's best habit is in seeming t.* Sonn. 138, 11. *serve always with assured t.* Pilgr. 329. *my t., like a good parent, did beget of him a falsehood*, Tp. I, 2, 93 (Johnson finds here an allusion to the proverb: *heroum filii noxae*). 96. *wilt thou make a t. a transgression?* Ado II, 1, 232. *give me t., the count he is my husband*, All's III, 7, 8. *wrangle with my reason that persuades me to any other t. but that I am mad*, Tw. IV, 3, 15 (nearly = opinion, belief). *grafted in my serious t.* Wint. I, 2, 246. *honesty, and t., his sworn brother*, IV, 4, 607. H4A V, 1, 11. V, 5, 5. H4B I, 3, 100. H8 III, 1, 89. Mcb. I, 4, 14. Hml. III, 2, 228. Lr. II, 1, 71 (*reposal of any t. in thee*). Cymb. I, 6, 25. 158. *to have t. in:* H6B IV, 4, 59. Cymb. I, 4, 165. *to lay t. on:* H4A IV, 1, 34. Lr. III, 5, 25.

2) passively or objectively, the state of being confided in, of being relied on: *so I, for fear of t., forget to say the perfect ceremony of love's rite*, Sonn. 23, 5 (doubting of being trusted). *on my t.* Meas. V, 147 (= upon my faith). *I no question make to have it* (money) *of my t.* Merch. I, 1, 185 (= on credit). *you never had a servant to whose t. your business was more welcome*, All's IV, 4, 15 (who was more glad to be trusted with it). *thou shalt have charge and sovereign t.* H4A III, 2, 161. *what is the t. or strength of foolish man?* H6A III, 2, 112 (how far can he be trusted?). *his minority is put unto the t. of Richard Gloster*, R3 I, 3, 12. *there's no t., no faith, no honesty in men*, Rom. III, 2, 85. *the t., the office, I do hold of you*, Oth. I, 3, 118. *have entertainment, but no honourable t.* Ant. IV, 6, 18. *to put in t.* = to trust with important business: Lr. I, 4, 15. Oth. II, 3, 131. *this was his gentleman in t.* H8 I, 2, 125 (his confident). *of t.* = reliable: *in sure wards of t.* Sonn. 48, 4. *their men of t.* Cor. I, 6, 52. *their bands i'the vaward are the Antiates, of their best t.* 54. *natures of such deep t. we shall much need*, Lr. II, 1, 117. *a man he is of honesty and t.* Oth. I, 3, 285. *O slave, of no more t. than love that's hired*, Ant. V, 2, 154.

Abstr. pro concr., = one confided in and relied on: *by me, their tribune and their t.* Tit. I, 181. *you, his false hopes, the t. of England's honour*, H6A IV, 4, 20.

3) a state of being confided to another's care and guard: *he's here in double t.* Mcb. I, 7, 12. *his sealed commission left in t. with me*, Per. I, 3, 13.

**Trust,** vb. 1) to confide; a) absol.: *more to know could not be more to t.* All's II, 1, 209. *safer than t. too far*, Lr. I, 4, 351. *have no use for —ing*, Ant. V, 2, 15. b) intr.; with *in: in them I t.* H6C I, 2, 42. *he that —s in the tameness of a wolf*, Lr. III, 6, 19. With *to: 'tis no —ing to yond foolish lout*, Gent. IV, 4, 71. *a man is well holp up that —s to you*, Err. IV, 1, 22. *never will I t. to speeches penned*, LLL V, 2, 402. Wint. IV, 4, 547. John V, 2, 174. R3 I, 4, 148. Cor. I, 1, 174. III, 2, 136. Tim. IV, 3, 139. Lr. V, 3, 103. Ant. III, 7, 63. *t. to it* = depend on it: *t. to it, thou shalt not*, Cor. V, 3, 124. *t. to it; bethink you*, Rom. III, 5, 197. c) trans. (= to confide in): *to t. those tables that*

*receive thee more*, Sonn. 122, 12. *rude, cruel, not to t.* 129, 4 (= *not to be —ed* in Ant. V, 2, 267). *not daring t. the office of mine eyes*, Pilgr. 196. *we dare t. you in this kind*, Gent. III, 2, 56. V, 4, 67. 69. Wiv. II, 2, 315. IV, 2, 209. Meas. IV, 3, 152. Err. IV, 4, 5. Ado I, 1, 197. 246. I, 3, 34 (*I am —ed with a muzzle*, i. e. when I am muzzled). II, 1, 186. II, 3, 220. IV, 1, 167. LLL V, 2, 804. Mids. III, 2, 268. 340. Merch. II, 2, 206. V, 88. As I, 3, 57. All's I, 1, 73. John II, 231. III, 1, 7. H6A I, 2, 150. III, 3, 63. 84. H6B IV, 4, 57. 58. H6C I, 2, 59. IV, 1, 42. R3 IV, 4, 492. H8 III, 1, 173. Cor. I, 1, 185. Tim. I, 2, 66. IV, 3, 434. Lr. V, 3, 96. Ant. V, 2, 13. Per. I, 1, 46 etc. *never t. me then* = God forbid! of course not: *but you'll not deliver it? Never t. me then*, Tw. III, 2, 62. *you may not despise her suit. Ne'er t. me then*, H6A II, 2, 48.

With an adverb or a prepositional expression, = to venture confidently: *how darest thou t. so great a charge from thine own custody?* Err. I, 2, 60. *my ventures are not in one bottom —ed*, Merch. I, 1, 42. *I wonder men dare t. themselves with men*, Tim. I, 2, 44. *no man's life was to be —ed with them*, Mcb. II, 3, 111 (= committed to them). *t. me here*, Cymb. IV, 2, 14 (= leave me confidently here).

*To t. a person* (or a thing personified) *with sth.* = to commit sth. confidently to a person: *I will rather t. a Fleming with my butter*, Wiv. II, 2, 316. Mids. II, 1, 217. Wint. I, 2, 235. II, 2, 37. R2 IV, 83. Tit. IV, 2, 169. Tim. I, 2, 66—69. Cymb. I, 5, 35.

2) With an infinitive or a clause, = to hope confidently (used only in the first person of the present, *I t.*): *I t. to take of truest Thisby sight*, Mids. V, 280. *I t. ere long to choke thee*, H6A III, 2, 46. *I t. it will grow to a most prosperous perfection*, Meas. III, 1, 271. *I t. you will be ruled by your father*, Ado II, 1, 53. As I, 3, 52. V, 4, 204. John II, 555. III, 1, 7. H6A V, 2, 16. R3 III, 4, 27 (Qq *I hope*). *I t.* inserted in the sentence: *but thus, I t., you will not marry her*, Shr. III, 2, 117. H4A I, 3, 300. H5 IV, 3, 96. Ant. I, 5, 7. Cymb. I, 1, 161. II, 4, 36.

3) to believe; with a clause: *I never wished to see you sorry; now I t. I shall*, Wint. II, 1, 124. With an accus. expressing the thing believed: *if you dare not t. that you see*, Ado III, 2, 122 (i. e. that which you see). *if he be credulous and t. my tale*, Shr. IV, 2, 67. *when saucy —ing of the cozened thoughts defiles the pitchy night*, All's IV, 4, 23 (cf. *Of*). *t. it, he shall not rule me*, Wint. II, 3, 49. *to t. the mockery of unquiet slumbers*, R3 III, 2, 27. *that —ed home might yet enkindle you unto the crown*, Mcb. I, 3, 120. The person believed with *to: t. to me, Ulysses, our imputation shall be oddly poised*, Troil. I, 3, 338. Simple accus. in the phrase *t. me* = truly, indeed: *now t. me, 'tis an office of great worth*, Gent. I, 2, 44. *now t. me, madam, it came hardly off*, II, 1, 115. *no, t. me*, III, 1, 68. *t. me, I think 'tis almost day*, IV, 2, 138. *t. me, I was going to your house*, Wiv. II, 1, 33. *t. me, a mad host*, III, 1, 115. II, 1, 165. III, 2, 52. III, 3, 244. IV, 2, 212. Err. I, 1, 143. Mids. V, 99. Shr. Ind. 1, 25. Tit. I, 261 etc. Similarly *never t. me*, after conditional phrases: *if my lady have not ..., never t. me*, Tw. II, 3, 79. *if I do not, never t. me*, 204. *I will, la; never t. me else*, Troil. V, 2, 59. *never t. me, if I be afeard*, Shr. V, 2, 17. cf. Wiv. IV, 2, 209. Merch. II, 2, 206.

**Truster,** 1) believer: *to make it* (mine ear) *t. of your own report against yourself*, Hml. I, 2, 172.

2) creditor: *bankrupts, ... out with your knives, and cut your —s' throats,* Tim. IV, 1, 10.

**Trustful,** faithful: *convey my t. queen,* H4A II, 4, 434 (M. Edd. unnecessarily *tristful*).

**Trustless,** faithless, fallacious: *borne by the t. wings of false desire,* Lucr. 2.

**Trusty,** fit to be depended on, faithful, honest: *neither true nor t.* Pilgr. 86. *the t. knight was wounded with disdain,* 221. *adieu, t.* Pompey, Meas. III, 2, 80. *a t. villain,* Err. I, 2, 19. *the t. Thisby,* Mids. V, 141. 146. *like Limander am I t. still,* 198. *come, t. sword,* 350. *my t. servant,* Shr. I, 1, 7. I, 2, 47. *thou t.* Welshman, R2 II, 4, 5. *our t. brother-in-law,* V, 3, 137. *like to a t. squire did run away,* H6A IV, 1, 23 (cf. *treacherous* in I, 5, 30). *our t. friend,* H6C IV, 7, 41. *choose t. sentinels,* R3 V, 3, 54. *a t. Goth,* Tit. V, 1, 34. *be t.* Rom. II, 4, 204. *this t. servant,* Lr. IV, 2, 18. *your t. servitor,* Oth. I, 3, 40.

Peculiar passage: *he might at some great and t. business in a main danger fail you,* All's III, 6, 16 (*a t. business* = a business of trust, one in which faith and honesty are required. cf. Appendix).

**Truth,** 1) conformity to fact or reality: *into t. by telling of it,* Tp. I, 2, 100 (cf. *Into*). *their eyes do offices of t.* V, 156. *I would have sworn his disposition would have gone to the t. of his words,* Wiv. II, 1, 61. *fewness and t., 'tis thus,* Meas. I, 4, 39. V, 226. Ado II, 2, 49 (Qq *t.,* Ff *—s*). Mids. II, 1, 200. As V, 4, 136. H8 II, 4, 84. III, 1, 39. Mcb. IV, 3, 130 etc. *in t.* = in fact, really: Wiv. I, 4, 148. II, 2, 108. Err. V, 254. Mids. V, 185. Merch. I, 2, 61 etc. *in good t.* H4B II, 4, 28. H5 III, 6, 39. *in very t.* H4B III, 2, 237. *in most comely t.* Ado V, 2, 8.

2) any thing conformable to fact or reality: *t. I must confess,* Ven. 1001. *bring t. to light,* Lucr. 940. *to hide the t. of this false night's abuses,* 1075. *uttering bare t.* Sonn. 69, 4. *my thoughts and my discourse as madmen's are, at random from the t. vainly expressed,* Sonn. 147, 12. *mistake the t. totally,* Tp. II, 1, 57. *hear the t. of it,* Wiv. I, 4, 80. V, 5, 233. *did deliver to our age this tale for a t.* IV, 4, 38. Meas. II, 1, 131. 138. I, 2, 82. V, 45. Err. IV, 4, 146. Ado II, 3, 239. LLL I, 1, 75. Merch. II, 2, 83. All's V, 3, 326. Wint. II, 1, 167. R3 III, 1, 76. Ant. II, 2, 136. 137 etc. *to say the t.* Meas. I, 2, 137. IV, 6, 2. Mids. III, 1, 146 etc. *the t. you speak doth lack some gentleness,* Tp. II, 1, 137. *speak the t. by her,* Gent. II, 4, 151. *you speak t.* Ado III, 1, 59. Ant. V, 2, 144 etc. *till he tell the t.* Wiv. IV, 4, 60. *I will tell t.* All's I, 3, 226. Err. V, 211. H4A III, 1, 58. *tell us —s,* Mcb. I, 3, 124. 127. *tell me for t.* H6C III, 3, 120. *hast thou read t.?* Wint. III, 2, 139 (i. e. that which is really written in the paper).

3) veracity, purity from falsehood: *love is all t., lust full of forged lies,* Ven. 804. *more praise ... than niggard t. would willingly impart,* Sonn. 72, 8. *do you think there is t. in them?* Wiv. II, 1, 178. *against my soul's pure t. why labour you to make it wander in an unknown field?* Err. III, 2, 37. *syllables of no allowance to your bosom's t.* Cor. III, 2, 57. *lest I surcease to honour mine own t.* 121. *if I may trust the flattering t. of sleep,* Rom. V, 3, 1 (some M. Edd., following the spurious Q1, *the flattering eye of sleep*). *to you they have showed some t.* Mcb. II, 1, 21. *thy t. then be thy dower,* Lr. I, 1, 110. *t.'s a dog must to kennel,* I, 4, 124.

4) genuineness, the state of not being counterfeited or adulterated: *I take all my comfort of thy worth and t.* Sonn. 37, 4 (*thy worth and t.* = thy genuine, real worth). (time) *feeds on the rarities of nature's t.* 60, 11 (*nature's t.* = true nature). *no shape so true, no t. of such account,* 62, 6. *so are those errors that in thee are seen to —s translated and for true things deemed,* 96, 8 (cf. *True*). *she, having the t. of honour in her,* Meas. III, 1, 166. *if the t. of thy love were so righteously tempered as mine is to thee,* As I, 2, 13. *it is the show and seal of nature's t., where love's strong passion is impressed in youth,* All's I, 3, 137. *thou art framed of the firm t. of valour,* H5 IV, 3, 14.

5) faith, honesty, righteousness: *where is t., if there be no self-trust?* Lucr. 158. *such signs of t. in his plain face she spied,* 1532. *t. proves thievish for a prize so dear,* Sonn. 48, 14. *thy face and thy behaviour, which ... witness good bringing up, fortune and t.* Gent. IV, 4, 74. *I have spirit to do any thing that appears not foul in the t. of my spirit,* Meas. III, 1, 214. *there is scarce t. enough alive to make societies secure,* III, 2, 240. *what authority and show of t. can cunning sin cover itself withal,* Ado IV, 1, 36. *the errors that these princes hold against her maiden t.* 166. *malice bears down t.* Merch. IV, 1, 214. *even so void is your false heart of t.* V, 189. *I will follow thee ... with t. and loyalty,* As II, 3, 70. *there is no t. in him,* III, 4, 22. *now will I charge you in the band of t.* All's IV, 2, 56. *by maidhood, honour, t.* Tw. III, 1, 162. *the t. is then most done not doing it,* John III, 1, 273. *the life, the right and t. of all this realm is fled to heaven,* IV, 3, 144. R2 I, 3, 19. 96. IV, 171. H4A III, 3, 125. 128. 174. H4B V, 2, 39. R3 I, 3, 52. III, 2, 94. Cor. III, 3, 18. Mcb. IV, 3, 117 etc.

6) faithfulness, fidelity: *his t. and lasting fealty to the new made king,* R2 V, 2, 44. *long since we were resolved of your t.* H6A III, 4, 20. *in thy face I see the map of honour, t. and loyalty,* H6B III, 1, 203. *in sign of t. I kiss your highness' hand,* H6C IV, 8, 26. 29. *briefly die their joys that place them on the t. of girls and boys,* Cymb. V, 5, 107. Particularly = faithfulness in love: *forced to break a twofold t.* Sonn. 41, 12. 54, 2. 14. 101, 2. 3. 6. 7. Gent. II, 2, 18. II, 7, 81. IV, 2, 88. Tw. III, 1, 170. IV, 3, 33. Troil. III, 2, 181—187. Cymb. III, 2, 7.

**Try,** subst. trial, test: *this breaking of his has been but a t. for his friends,* Tim. V, 1, 11.

**Try,** vb. 1) to purify, to refine as gold: *—ed gold,* Merch. II, 7, 53. *the fire seven times —ed this; seven times —ed that judgment is,* II, 9, 63. 64.

2) to prove by a test, to evince, to find or show by experience what a person or a thing is; absol.: *as time shall t.* Ado I, 1, 262. As IV, 1, 204. trans.: *thus my strength is —ed,* Ven. 280. cf. Lucr. 353. *let the end t. the man,* H4B II, 2, 50. *we have —ed the utmost of our friends,* Caes. IV, 3, 214. *—ed =* approved: *he hath still been —ed a holy man,* Rom. IV, 3, 29. *he's a —ed and valiant soldier,* Caes. IV, 1, 28. *those friends thou hast, and their adoption —ed,* Hml. I, 3, 62.

3) to examine by a test: *to t. an older friend,* Sonn. 110, 11. *not being —ed and tutored in the world,* Gent. I, 3, 21. *I will t. thee,* III, 1, 293. 299. *and t. your penitence, if it be sound,* Meas. II, 3, 22. Shr. II, 220. All's III, 6, 19. Wint. IV, 1, 1. V, 2, 144. John III, 1, 100. R2 II, 2, 85. H4B II, 3, 56. II, 4, 334. H6A I, 2, 60. 89. H6C III, 2, 33. R3 IV, 2, 9. Cor. II, 3,

200. Tim. II, 2, 187. 192. III, 6, 3. Hml. III, 2, 218. Oth. IV, 2, 48. Ant. II, 7, 133. Per. II, 2, 37.

4) to examine, to inquire into in any manner: *I will lay a plot to t. that*, Wiv. III, 3, 202. *that's a question: how shall we t. it?* Err. V, 421. *to t. whose right, of thine or mine, is most in Helena*, Mids. III, 2, 336. *I wish you had only in your silent judgement —ed it*, Wint. II, 1, 171. *to t. if that our own be ours or no*, H6A III, 2, 63. *if my actions were —ed by every tongue*, H8 III, 1, 35. *here shall I t. how the people take the cruel issue of these men*, Caes. III, 1, 292. *how may we t. it further?* Hml. II, 2, 159. 167. *t. honour's cause, forbear your suffrages*, Per. II, 4, 41 (M. Edd. *for honour's cause*).

Especially, = to examine judicially: *guiltier than him they t.* Meas. II, 1, 21. *the party —ed the daughter of a king*, Wint. III, 2, 2. *we intend to t. his grace to-day, if he be guilty*, H6B III, 2, 16. *disdainful to be —ed by it* (justice) H8 II, 4, 123. *I gave ye power as he was a counsellor to t. him*, V, 3, 143. *would t. him to the utmost*, 146. *defying those whose great power must t. him*, Cor. III, 3, 80.

And = to settle and decide by combat: *to t. with it* (the crown), *as with an enemy, the quarrel of a true inheritor*, H4B IV, 5, 167. *no king, if it come to the arbitrement of swords, can t. it out with all unspotted soldiers*, H5 IV, 1, 169. *let this dissension first be —ed by fight*, H6A IV, 1, 116. *to see this quarrel — ed*, H6B II, 3, 53. *fight for a plot whereon the number cannot t. the cause*, Hml. IV, 4, 63. cf. Mids. III, 2, 337. H6A III, 2, 63.

5) to make an experiment: *bring her to t. with main-course*, Tp. I, 1, 38.•*I will marry one day, but to t.* Err. II, 1, 42. *I have —ed* (to make verses) Ado V, 2, 36. *you will t. in time*, As I, 3, 24. H6A I, 2, 149. Troil. III, 2, 154. Cymb. II, 3, 16. With a clause: *t. what my credit can in Venice do*, Merch. I, 1, 180. *I would t. if I could cry hem*, As I, 3, 19. *I will t. how you can ...*, Shr. I, 2, 17. *t. upon yourselves what you have seen me*, Cor. III, 1, 225. Wint. III, 2, 74. H6A I, 4, 111. V, 3, 32. H6B III, 1, 309. Cor. III, 1, 251. Rom. IV, 2, 4. 5. Hml. III, 3, 65. Lr. IV, 6, 246.

Transitively, = to make experiment of; a) a person: *how god Mars did t. her*, Pilgr. 145. *t. all the friends thou hast in Ephesus*, Err. I, 1, 153. *if he were living, I would t. him yet*, All's I, 2, 72. *he might have —ed Lord Lucius*, Tim. III, 2, 2. *t. many* (masters) Cymb. IV, 2, 373. b) a thing: *thoughts are but dreams till their effects be —ed*, Lucr. 353. *that mother —es a merciless conclusion*, 1160; cf. Merch. II, 2, 39 and Hml. III, 4, 195. *though she strive to t. her strength*, Pilgr. 317. *to t. their fortune*, Gent. I, 3, 8. Wiv. IV, 2, 96. Meas. V, 76. Merch. II, 1, 24. All's I, 3, 253. II, 1, 137. 188. Tit. II, 3, 69 (*to t. experiments*). Ant. III, 12, 26. 31. Cymb. I, 5, 18. 21. I, 6, 173.

Especially applied to any kind of combats ventured on in order to settle a question: *we'll t. no manhood here*, Mids. III, 2, 412 (= we'll not fight here). *to t. a fall*, As I, 1, 132. I, 2, 216. *to t. with him the strength of my youth*, 181. *when thy father and myself in friendship first —ed our soldiership*, All's I, 2, 26. *to t. the fair adventure of to-morrow*, John V, 5, 22. *mine honour let me t.* R2 I, 1, 184. *to t. his honour*, IV, 85. *will t. fortune with him in a single fight*, H4A V, 1, 100. *to t. our fortunes*, H4B IV, 2, 43. *to t. his strength*, H6A V, 5, 32. *t. your hap against the Irish-*

men, H6B III, 1, 314. *we shall t. fortune in a second fight*, Caes. V, 3, 110. *yet I will t. the last*, Mcb. V, 8, 32. *to t. a larger fortune*, Ant. II, 6, 34. cf. Pilgr. 317. H6A I, 2, 60. 89.

**Tub,** an open wooden vessel: *that satiate yet unsatisfied desire, that t. both filled and running*, Cymb. I, 6, 48 (evident allusion to the cask of the Danaides). Sweating in a heated tub the usual cure of lues venerea: *she is herself in the t.* Meas. III, 2, 60. *the powdering t. of infamy*, H5 II, 1, 79. *season the slaves for — s and baths*, Tim. IV, 3, 86.

**Tubal,** name of a Jew in Merch. I, 3, 58. III, 1, 83. 111. III, 2, 287 etc.

**Tub-fast** (O. Edd. *fubfast*), strict abstinence observed during the cure of the tub: Tim. IV, 3, 87.

**Tuck,** a rapier: *dismount thy t.* Tw. III, 4, 244. *you vile standing t.* H4A II, 4, 274.

**Tucked,** in *Untucked,* q. v.

**Tucket,** a flourish on a trumpet: *let the trumpets sound the t. sonance and the note to mount*, H5 IV, 2, 35.

**Tuesday,** the third day of the week: Meas. V, 229. Ado V, 1, 170. All's II, 2, 25 (*Shrove T.*). H4A I, 2, 40. H4B I, 1, 29. Mcb. II, 4, 11. Oth. III, 3, 60.

**Tuffe,** a knot, a bunch: *and 'Honi soit qui mal y pense' write in emerald —s, flowers purple, blue, and white*, Wiv. V, 5, 74 (M. Edd. *tufts*).

**Tuft,** cluster, clump: *at the t. of olives*, As III, 5, 75. *behind the t. of pines*, Wint. II, 1, 34. *by yon t. of trees*, R2 II, 3, 53. In LLL IV, 2, 90 O. Edd. *turf.*

**Tug,** 1) trans. to pull, to draw, to drag, to haul along: *I mean to t. it* (your beard) H6A I, 3, 48. *so weary with disasters, —ed with fortune*, Mcb. III, 1, 112 (drawn and hauled about by fortune in my attempt to grapple with her; cf. Wint. IV, 4, 508). *t. him away*, Ant. III, 13, 102.

2) intr. to pull, to strive, to struggle, to grapple: *let myself and fortune t. for the time to come*, Wint. IV, 4, 508. *England now is left to t. and scamble*, John IV, 3, 146. *one that grasped and —ed for life*, H6B III, 2, 173. *both* (flood and wind) *—ing to be victors*, H6C II, 5, 11.

**Tuition,** protection: *and so I commit you — To the t. of God*, Ado I, 1, 283.

**Tullius;** *Servius T.*, name of the sixth king of Rome: Lucr. Arg. 2.

**Tullus,** *T. Aufidius,* the general of the Volscians in Cor. I, 1, 233. I, 8, 7. IV, 5, 60. V, 6, 133.

**Tully,** the family name of Cicero: H6B IV, 1, 136. Tit. IV, 1, 14.

**Tumble,** 1) intr. a) to roll about by turning one way and another: *hedgehogs which lie —ing in my barefoot way*, Tp. II, 2, 11. *into the —ing billows of the main*, R3 I, 4, 20. *when I saw the porpus how he bounced and —d*, Per. II, 1, 27. *a'* (the whale) *plays and —s, driving the poor fry before him*, 34. In a lascivious sense: *while we lie —ing in the hay*, Wint. IV, 3, 12. *it is not amiss to t. on the bed of Ptolemy*, Ant. I, 4, 17.

b) to lose footing and totter or fall downward: *they all did t. on the ground*, LLL V, 2, 115. *now Phaethon hath —d from his car*, H6C I, 4, 33. *ready, with every nod, to t. down into the fatal bowels of the deep*, R3 III, 4, 102. *sometimes, like to a bowl upon a subtle ground, I have —d past the throw*, Cor. V, 2, 21. *though the treasure of nature's germens t. all together*, Mcb. IV, 1, 59.

2) trans. a) to roll about: *a little snow, —d about, anon becomes a mountain,* John III, 4, 176.

b) to toss: *where we left him at sea, —d and tost,* Per. V Prol. 13 (Qq *we there him left;* M. Edd. *we there him lost*).

c) to rumple (as a bed; cf. *Betumble*); in a lascivious sense: *before you —d me,* Hml. IV, 5, 62.

d) to make to totter and fall, to throw down: *—s down steeples,* H4A III, 1, 32 (Qq *topples*). *to t. down thy husband and thyself from top of honour to disgrace's feet,* H6B I, 2, 48. *as many coxcombs as you threw caps up will he t. down,* Cor. IV, 6, 135. *t. me into some loathsome pit,* Tit. II, 3, 176.

**Tumbler,** one who plays mountebank tricks by various librations and movements of the body; a harlequin: *wear his colours like a —'s hoop,* LLL III, 190 ('tumblers' hoops are to this day bound round with ribbons of various colours'. Harris).

**Tumbling-trick,** a trick performed by a tumbler: *a Christmas gambold or a t.* Shr. Ind. 2, 140 (Sly's speech).

**Tumult,** commotion, agitation, uproar: *peeping forth this t. to behold,* Lucr. 447. *hostility and civil t. reigns between my conscience and my cousin's death,* John IV, 2, 247. *here's a goodly t.* H4B II, 4, 219. *what t.'s in the heavens?* H6A I, 4, 98. *what t.'s this,* III, 1, 74. *what hath broached this t. but thy pride?* H6C II, 2, 159.

**Tumultuous,** full of commotion and disorder: *t. wars,* R2 IV, 140. *strife,* H6A I, 3, 70. *clamour,* H6B III, 2, 239. *broils,* H6C V, 5, 1.

**Tun,** 1) a large cask: *a t. of man is thy companion,* H4A II, 4, 493. *sends you ... this t. of treasure,* H5 I, 2, 255. *—s of blood,* Cor. IV, 5, 105.

2) a certain measure: *with so many —s of oil in his belly,* Wiv. II,1,65. *is that a t. of moys?* H5 IV,4,23.

**Tunable,** see *Tuneable.*

**Tun-dish,** a tunnel, a funnel: *for filling a bottle with a t.* Meas. III, 2, 182.

**Tune,** subst. 1) sound of voice, accent; sound in general: *heavenly t. harsh-sounding,* Ven. 431. *nor are mine ears with thy tongue's t. delighted,* Sonn. 141, 5. *such a noise arose as the shrouds make at sea in a stiff tempest, as loud, and to as many —s,* H8 IV, 1, 73. *if it may stand with the t. of your voices that I may be consul,* Cor. II,3,92. *the t. of Imogen,* Cymb. V, 5, 238.

2) state of giving the due sounds: *both in a t.* As V, 3, 16. *in t.* = well tuned, giving the due sounds: *'tis no matter how it be in t.* As IV, 2, 9. Shr. III, 1, 24. 38. 46. *out of t.: out of t. on the strings,* Gent. IV, 2, 60. Tw. II, 3, 122. Rom. III, 5, 27. Hml. III, 1, 166 (Qq *time*). Ant. V, 2, 216. Cymb. IV, 2, 241.

Metaphorically, = disposition, temper, humour: *what sayest thou to this t., matter and method?* Meas. III, 2, 51. *do you speak in the sick t.?* Ado III, 4, 42. *I will fit it with some better t.* John III, 3, 26 (M. Edd. *time*). *is he not in this t., is he?* Troil. III, 3, 301. *this t. goes manly,* Mcb. IV, 3, 235 (O. Edd. *time*). *only got the t. of the time,* Hml. V, 2, 198. *who sometime, in his better t., remembers what we are come about,* Lr. IV, 3, 41. *in t.* Oth. III, 4, 123. *out of t.* Ado III, 4, 43. Troil. III, 3, 302. Oth. V, 2, 115.

3) note, air, melody: *from mine ear the tempting t. is blown,* Ven. 778. *your —s entomb within your breasts,* Lucr. 1121. *we will unfold to creatures stern sad —s,* 1147. *this is a very scurvy t.* Tp. II, 2, 46.

57. III, 2, 133. 135. Gent. I, 2, 89. 90. Wiv. II, 1, 64. LLL I, 2, 119. III, 12. 22. As III, 2, 262. Tw. II, 4, 14. 20. Wint. IV, 4, 184. 186. 216. 300. 619. H4A II, 2, 49. H4B III, 2, 340. H6B III, 2, 41. Caes. IV, 3, 267. Hml. IV, 7, 178. *set all hearts to what t. pleased his ear,* Tp. I, 2, 85. *that I might sing it to a t.* Gent. I, 2, 80. *to the t. of Green Sleeves,* Wiv. II, 1, 64. V, 5, 21. *if it be aught to the old t.* Tw. V, 111. Wint. IV, 4, 265. 295. Mcb. I, 3, 88. Ant. II, 2, 200.

**Tune,** vb. 1) to put (instruments) into a state adapted to produce music; absol.: *let's t., and to it lustily awhile,* Gent. IV, 2, 25. *his lecture will be done ere you have —d,* Shr. III, 1, 23. *come on, t.* Cymb. II, 3, 15. Trans.: *t. your instrument,* Shr. III, 1, 25. Metaphorically: *these means ... shall t. our heartstrings to true languishment,* Lucr. 1141. *who had even —d his bounty to sing happiness to him,* All's IV, 3, 12. *some joy too fine, too subtle-potent, —d too sharp in sweetness,* Troil. III, 2, 25 (Ff *and*). *you are well —d now,* Oth. II, 1, 201. *hope ... doth t. us otherwise,* Per. I, 1, 115. cf. *Tuned,* adj.

2) to give utterance by musical sounds, to sing, to play (and metaphorically, to give utterance, to express): *to a pretty ear she —s her tale,* Ven. 74. *feast-finding minstrels, —ing my defame,* Lucr. 817. *the little birds that t. their morning's joy,* 1107. *I'll t. thy woes with my lamenting tongue,* 1465. *to their instruments t. a deploring dump,* Gent. III, 2, 85. *and to the nightingale's complaining notes t. my distresses and record my woes,* V, 4, 6. *to t. a jig,* LLL IV, 3, 168. *knows no touch to t. the harmony,* R2 I, 3, 165. *the fingers of the powers above do t. the harmony of this peace,* Cymb. V, 5, 466.

**Tuneable,** musical, harmonious: *more t. than lark to shepherd's ear,* Mids. I, 1, 184. *a cry more t. was never hollaed to,* IV, 1, 129.

**Tuned,** adj. having a tune, sounding: *and wish her* (Philomela's) *lays were t. like the lark,* Pilgr. 198. *new t. oaths,* H5 III, 6, 80. *with an accent t. in selfsame key,* Troil. I, 3, 53. *his voice was propertied as all the t. spheres,* Ant. V, 2, 84. cf. *Sad-tuned,* Compl. 4, and *Well-tuned.*

**Tuner,** one who tunes or utters: *these new —s of accents,* Rom. II, 4, 30.

**Tunis,** town in Africa: Tp. II, 1, 71. 82. 83. 246. V, 209 etc.

**Tup,** to cover as a ram: *an old black ram is —ing your white ewe,* Oth. I, 1, 89. In III, 3, 396 and V, 2, 136 some M. Edd. *—ed and t.;* O. Edd. *topped and t.*

**Turband** (F1 *turbonds*), a turban: *giants may jet through and keep their impious —s on,* Cymb. III, 3, 6 ('the idea of a giant was, among the readers of romances, always confounded with that of a Saracen.' Johnson).

**Turbaned,** wearing a turban: *a malignant and a t. Turk,* Oth. V, 2, 353 (Ff *Turbond-Turke*).

**Turbulence,** tumult, commotion: *I have dreamed of bloody t.* Troil. V, 3, 11.

**Turbulent,** tumultuous, uproarious: *the t. surge,* Tim. V, 1, 221. *with t. and dangerous lunacy,* Hml. III, 1, 4. *a t. and stormy night,* Per. III, 2, 4.

**Turf,** a piece of earth covered with short grass: *one t. shall serve as pillow for us both,* Mids. II, 2, 41. *sitting by me on the t.* As III, 4, 52. H5 IV, 1, 15. Hml. IV, 5, 31. Cymb. V, 3, 14. Holofernes says *a t. of earth* for a clod of earth: LLL IV, 2, 90.

**Turfy,** covered with short grass: *thy t. mountains, where live nibbling sheep,* Tp. IV, 62.

**Turk,** a native of Turkey (appellatively = an infidel): Wiv. I, 3, 97 (*base Phrygian T.;* Pistol's speech). Ado III, 4, 57 (fem.). Merch. IV, 1, 32 (*stubborn —s and Tartars*). As IV, 3, 33. R2 IV, 95. 139. H4A V, 3, 46 *(T. Gregory;* cf. *Gregory*). R3 III, 5, 41. Mcb. IV, 1, 29. Oth. II, 1, 21. 115. 204. II, 3, 170. V, 2, 353. *to turn T.*, proverbially, = to undergo a complete change for the worse: *an you be not turned T., there's no more sailing by the star*, Ado III, 4, 57. *if the rest of my fortunes turn T. with me*, Hml. III, 2, 287.

The *T.*, by way of eminence, = the grand Turk, the sultan: *I would send them to the T., to make eunuchs of*, All's II, 3, 94. *duer paid than the —'s tribute*, H4B III, 2, 331. *take the T. by the beard*, H5 V, 2, 222. *the T., that two and fifty kingdoms hath*, H6A IV, 7, 73 (supposed to allude to an ostentatious letter of Sultan Solyman the Magnificent to the Emperor Ferdinand). *out-paramoured the T.* Lr. III, 4, 94. Oth. I, 3, 20. 22. 27. 210. 221.

**Turkey,** 1) subst. the bird Meleagris: H4A II, 1, 29. 2) adjectively = Turkish: *T. cushions*, Shr. II, 355 (cf. Err. IV, 1, 104). *a t. cock*, Tw. II, 5, 36. H5 V, 1, 16 (the male of Meleagris, representative of foolish vanity and pride).

**Turkish,** pertaining to the Turks: *covered o'er with T. tapestry*, Err. IV, 1, 104 (cf. Shr. II, 355). *this is the English, not the T. court*, H4B V, 2, 47. *like T. mute*, H5 I, 2, 232. *a T. fleet*, Oth. I, 3, 8. 14. II, 1, 10. 17. 32. II, 2, 4.

**Turkois,** see *Turquoise*.

**Turlygod** (Ff) or **Turlygood** (Qq), seemingly a name given to bedlam-beggars; derived by some from the French *turlupin:* Lr. II, 3, 21.

**Turmoil,** subst. tumult, commotion, harassing trouble: *there I'll rest, as after much t. a blessed soul doth in Elysium*, Gent. II, 7, 37.

**Turmoiled,** harassed with commotion and trouble: *who would live t. in the court*, H6B IV, 10, 18.

**Turn,** subst. 1) a walk to and fro: *a t. or two I'll walk*, Tp. IV, 162. *you and I must walk a t. together*, H8 V, I, 94. *I'll fetch a t. about the garden*, Cymb. I, 1, 81.

2) change, vicissitude: *O world, thy slippery —s!* Cor. IV, 4, 12.

3) successive course; time at which, by successive vicissitudes, some thing is to be had or done: *would sing her song and dance her t.* Wint. IV, 4, 58. *there speak and strike, brave boys, and take your —s*, Tit. II, 1, 129. *by t. to serve our lust*, IV, 2, 42. *shall our abode make with you by due t.* Lr. I, 1, 137 (Qq —s). *keep the t. of tippling with a slave*, Ant. I, 4, 19. *then 'twas my t. to fly, and now 'tis thine*, H6C II, 2, 105. V, 6, 90. Tit. V, 3, 119.

4) occasion, exigence: *if you have occasion to use me for your own t.* Meas. IV, 2, 60. *and neigh and bark ... like horse, hound ... at every t.* Mids. III, 1, 114 (according as occasion will require). *for learning and behaviour fit for her t.* Shr. I, 2, 170. *she is not for your t.* II, 63. *I am a husband for your t.* 274. *we'll fit him to our t.* III, 2, 134. *I'll meet you at the t.* Tim. V, 1, 50 (as soon as it will seem proper). *he does well to commend it himself; there are no tongues else for's t.* Hml. V, 2, 192. *to serve the t.* = to be just the thing required; to do: Gent. III, 1, 131. 389. III, 2, 93. Shr. IV, 2, 62. All's IV, 1, 51. Tit. II, 1, 96. III, 1, 165. *to serve one's t.:* Wiv. V, 5, 108. LLL

I, 1, 300. 301. I, 2, 184. As V, 2, 54. Wint. IV, 4, 520. R2 III, 2, 90. Troil. III, 1, 81. Cor. IV, 5, 94. Tit. II, 1, 96. Hml. III, 3, 52. *I must serve my t. out of mine own*, Tim. II, 1, 20. *I follow him to serve my t. upon him*, Oth. I, 1, 42. *I have enough to serve mine own t.* Mids. III, 1, 154. Meas. IV, 2, 60.

5) an action of kindness or malice: *never did passenger more thirst for drink than she for this good t.* (viz a kiss) Ven. 92. *see what good —s eyes for eyes have done*, Sonn. 24, 9. *each doth good —s now unto the other*, 47, 2. Meas. IV, 2, 62 (perhaps with a quibble, = a turn off the ladder). Shr. II, 166. Tw. III, 3, 15. Tit. I, 397. Tim. III, 2, 67. Hml. IV, 6, 22. Per. IV, 2, 151. *this young maid might do her a shrewd t., if she pleased*, All's III, 5, 71. *do my lord of Canterbury a shrewd t., and he is your friend for ever*, H8 V, 3, 178. *this sight would make him do a desperate t.* Oth. V, 2, 207. *nor did ill t. to any living creature*, Per. IV, 1, 76. *spare your arithmetic: never count the —s; once, and a million*, Cymb. II, 4, 142; cf. *he's bound unto Octavia. For what good t.? For the best t. i'the bed*, Ant. II, 5, 58. 59.

**Turn,** vb. 1) trans. a) to put into a circular motion, to move round: *t. the giddy round of Fortune's wheel*, Lucr. 952. Lr. II, 2, 180. *do not t. me about*, Tp. II, 2, 118. Wiv. V, 5, 105. Ado III, 3, 140. Cor. IV, 5, 159. *have —ed spit*, Ado II, 1, 261.

b) to form on a lathe by moving round: *I had rather hear a brazen canstick —ed*, H4A III, 1, 131.

c) to form, to shape in any manner: *every object ... the other —s to a mirth-moving jest*, LLL II, 71. *we will t. it finely off*, V, 2, 511 (Costard's speech). *the poet's pen —s them to shapes*, Mids. V, 16. *and t. his merry note unto the sweet bird's throat*, As II, 5, 3 (some M. Edd. *tune*).

Hence = to change or alter from one purpose or effect to another: *and —ed it thus 'It cannot be'* etc. Lucr. 1539. *let us confess and t. it to a jest*, LLL V, 2, 390. *great Apollo t. all to the best*, Wint. III, 1, 15. *in her right we came, which we have —ed another way, to our advantage*, John II, 549. *wouldst thou t. our offers contrary*, H4A V, 5, 4. *I will t. diseases to commodity*, H4B I, 2, 278. *t. all to a merriment*, II, 4, 324. *that blind priest, like the eldest son of fortune, —s what he list*, H8 II, 2, 22. *you t. the good we offer into envy*, III, 1, 113. *t. all her mother's pains and benefits to laughter and contempt*, Lr. I, 4, 308. *I'ld t. it all to thy suggestion*, II, 1, 74. *my mother shall t. all into my commendations*, Cymb. IV, 1, 23.

And in general, = to change, to transform: *O day untowardly —ed*, Ado III, 2, 134. Cymb. V, 2, 17. *her favour —s the fashion of the days*, LLL IV, 3, 262. *else nothing in the world could t. so much the constitution of any constant man*, Merch. III, 2, 249. *will nothing t. your unrelenting hearts*, H6A IV, 4, 59. H8 V, 2, 15. *some news is come that —s their countenances*, Cor. IV, 6, 59. *he has —ed his colour*, Hml. II, 2, 542. *t. thy complexion*, Oth. IV, 2, 62. With a double accus.: *it almost —s my dangerous nature wild*, Tim. IV, 3, 499. With *into:* *to t. all beauty into thoughts of harm*, Ado IV, 1, 108. *men are only —ed into tongue*, 323. *—s into yellow gold his salt green streams*, Mids. III, 2, 393. *mountains —ed into clouds*, IV, 1, 193. Merch. III, 4, 67. Tw. I, 1, 21. Wint. IV, 4, 284. H4B V, 1, 76. H5 Prol. 30. III, 7, 36. V, 2, 348. H6A IV, 7, 79. Cor. II, 2, 109. III, 2, 112. Caes. III, 1, 38. Oth.

II, 3, 366. Cymb. IV, 2, 200. With *to: the night of sorrow now is —ed to day,* Ven. 481. *mine eyes are —ed to fire,* 1072. *three beauteous springs to yellow autumn —ed,* Sonn. 104, 5. *all be —ed to barnacles,* Tp. IV, 249. *the young and tender wit is -- ed to folly,* Gent. I, 1, 48. Mids. I, 1, 37. 207. Merch. V, 78. John III, 1, 79. V, 7, 54. H4B I, 1, 201. II, 3, 27. IV, 1, 50. IV, 2, 10. IV, 4, 78. H5 I, 2, 282. IV, 1, 212. H6B IV, 10, 62. V, 2, 50. H6C III, 3, 199. 261. IV, 6, 3. R3 I, 3, 266. H8 II, 4, 73. Troil. I, 1, 40. II, 2, 83. III, 1, 133. V, 1, 64. V, 10, 18. Tit. IV, 2, 102. Rom. II, 3, 92. III, 3, 27. 140. Hml. IV, 5, 189. V, 1, 236. Lr. III, 2, 34. III, 4, 80. Oth. IV, 1, 193. Cymb. V, 3, 33. V, 4, 80. Per. II, 1, 125.

d) to change or shift with regard to the sides; to put the upper side downward, or one side in the place of the other: *he knows how to t. his girdle,* Ado V, 1, 142. *I t. my glass,* Wint. IV, 1, 16. *this house is —ed upside down,* H4A II, 1, 11. *t. the tables up,* Rom. I, 5, 29. *—s up the white o'the eye,* Cor. IV, 5, 208; cf. *—ing up your eyelids,* LLL III, 13. *a torch that's —ed upside down,* Per. II, 2, 32. *to t. one's back* = to show the back instead of the face: *that ever —ed their backs to mortal views,* LLL V, 2, 161. *make mouths upon me when I t. my back,* Mids. III, 2, 238. As IV, 3, 128. Cor. III, 3, 134. Tim. IV, 2, 8. Caes. II, 1, 25. Mcb. III, 6, 41. Lr. I, 1, 178. = to fly: *t. thy back and run,* Rom. I, 1, 41. H4B I, 1, 130. *to t. back* = to fly: H4A I, 2, 206. H6C I, 4, 4. II, 1, 185. Caes. V, 3, 3. *t. thy face in peace* = go in peace: John V, 2, 159. *t. thy false face* = look me in the face, stand, face me, Troil. V, 6, 6; cf. *whereto the climber-upward —s his face,* Caes. II, 1, 23. *to t. head* = to stand, to meet the enemy, not to fly: *—s head against the lion's armed jaws,* H4A III, 2, 102. *t. head and stop pursuit,* H5 II, 4, 69. *to t. the key* = 1) to lock the door: R2 V, 3, 36. 2) to unlock the door: Meas. I, 4, 8. Mcb. II, 3, 2. Lr. II, 4, 53. III, 7, 64. Oth. IV, 2, 94. *to t. the leaf,* = to read from leaf to leaf: *where every day I t. the leaf to read them,* Mcb. I, 3, 151. *how busily she —s the leaves,* Tit. IV, 1, 45. *we —ed o'er many books together,* Merch. IV, 1, 156. *—ing o'er authorities,* Per. III, 2, 33. *is not the leaf —ed down?* Caes. IV, 3, 273 (folded or doubled down). Cymb. II, 2, 45. *the coldest that ever — ed up ace,* Cymb. II, 3, 2. Applied to clothes, = to bring the inside out: *a pair of old breeches thrice —ed,* Shr. III, 2, 45. *how quickly the wrong side (of the glove) may be —ed outward,* Tw. III, 1, 14. figuratively: *so —s she every man the wrong side out,* Ado III, 1, 68. *to dress the commonwealth and t. it,* H6B IV, 2, 6. *—ed the wrong side out,* Lr. IV, 2, 9. Oth. II, 3, 54. IV, 2, 146.

e) to change with respect to direction: *—s his lips another way,* Ven. 90. *her tears began to t. their tide,* 979. H4A IV, 1, 67. *she —s away the face,* Lucr. 1711. LLL V, 2, 148. Merch. II, 8, 47. R2 I, 1, 111. Tit. II, 4, 28. Rom. I, 4, 103. Caes. V, 5, 47. *from my face she —s my foes* (viz her eyes) Sonn. 139, 11. *from Athens t. away our eyes,* Mids. I, 1, 218. Cor. II, 1, 42. Cymb. I, 3, 22. *t. your forces from this paltry siege,* John II, 54. *have torn their souls by —ing them from us,* R2 III, 3, 83. *you shall have Trent —ed,* H4A III, 1, 136. *to t. and wind a fiery Pegasus,* IV, 1, 109. *to t. your looks of favour from myself,* V, 1, 30. *t. thy sword another way,* H6A III, 3, 52. *t. the force of them upon thyself,* H6B III, 2, 332. *so shouldst thou t.*

*my flying soul,* 397. *and to my brother t. my blushing cheeks,* H6C V, 1, 99. *hath —ed my feigned prayer on my head,* R3 V, 1, 21. *he'll t. your current in a ditch,* Cor. III, 1, 96. *—s our swords into our own proper entrails,* Caes. V, 3, 95. *with his head over his shoulder —ed,* Hml. II, 1, 97. *enterprises ... their currents t. awry,* III, 1, 87. *t. their halcyon beaks with every gale,* Lr. II, 2, 84. *t. our impressed lances in our eyes which do command them,* V, 3, 50. *fly and t. the rudder,* Ant. III, 10, 3. *t. from me that noble countenance,* IV, 14, 85. *to her father t. our thoughts again,* Per. V Prol. 12.

= to bend from a perpendicular or horizontal direction: *this news hath —ed your weapon's edge,* H6B II, 1, 180 (blunted it). *steel, if thou t. the edge,* IV, 10, 59. *a feather will t. the scale,* Meas. IV, 2, 32. *the weight of a hair will t. the scales,* H4B II, 4, 276. *a mote will t. the balance,* Mids. V, 324. *till our scale t. the beam,* Hml. IV, 5, 157.

Refl.: *t. you where your lady is,* Merch. III, 2, 138. *thus I t. me from my country's light,* R2 I, 3, 176. *t. thee back and tell thy king,* H5 III, 6, 148. *t. thee, Benvolio, look upon thy death,* Rom. I, 1, 74. *the foul practice hath —ed itself on me,* Hml. V, 2, 329.

f) to bend, to direct: *t. another (eye) into the register of your own (follies)* Wiv. II, 2, 193. *no more t. me to him,* III, 4, 2. *that ever —ed their eyes to mortal views,* LLL V, 2, 163. *t. face to face and bloody point to point,* John II, 390. *t. thou the mouth of thy artillery against these walls,* 403. *—ed an eye of doubt upon my face,* IV, 2, 233. *if I t. mine eyes upon myself,* R2 IV, 247. H4A I, 3, 143. *t. not thy scorns this way,* H6A II, 4, 77. *or t. our stern upon a dreadful rock,* H6B III, 2, 91. *t. you all your hatred now on me?* R3 I, 3, 190. II, 1, 32. *to t. their own points on their masters' bosoms,* V, 1, 24. *why such unplausive eyes are bent, why —ed on him,* Troil. III, 3, 43. *t. the dregs of it (your wrath) upon this varlet,* Cor. V, 2, 83. *—s deadly point to point,* Rom. III, 1, 165. *Caesar is —ed to hear,* Caes. I, 2, 17. *I t. the trouble of my countenance merely upon myself,* 38. *such mirrors as will t. your hidden worthiness into your eye,* 56. *thou —est mine eyes into my very soul,* Hml. III, 4, 89. *when I shall t. the business of my soul to such ... surmises,* Oth. III, 3, 181. *t. the office and devotion of their view upon a tawny front,* Ant. I, 1, 4. *t. your displeasure that way,* III, 4, 34. *t. your eyes upon me,* Per. V, 1, 102. *toward Ephesus t. our blown sails,* 256. Refl.: *no way canst thou t. thee for redress,* H6A IV, 2, 25. *circle me about, that I may t. me to each one of you,* Tit. III, 1, 278.

g) to get, to put, to bring, to place in a state or condition: *I would t. her loose to him,* Wiv. II, 1, 189 (= let loose). *I would be loth to t. them together,* 193. *t. him going* (= send him packing) As III, 1, 18. Caes. III, 3, 38. *—ed my daughter into green,* Wiv. V, 5, 214. *so truly —ed over and over in love,* Ado V, 2, 35. *you are a fool and —ed into the extremity of love,* As IV, 3, 23. *it cannot but t. him into a notable contempt,* Tw. II, 5, 223. *first I'll t. yon fellow in his grave,* R3 I, 2, 261. *on your head —ing the widows' tears,* H5 II, 4, 106. *to t. to* = to put to: *nothing could be used to t. them both to gain,* Pilgr. 220. *the teen that I have —ed you to,* Tp. I, 2, 64. *a slave, that still an end —s me to shame,* Gent. IV, 4, 67. *the flame will t. him to no pain,* Wiv. V, 5, 90. *hate —s one or both to worthy danger and deserved death,* R2 V, 1, 67. *t. him to any cause of policy,* H5 I, 1, 45. *all the trouble thou hast*

—ed me to, H6C V, 5, 16. which shall t. you to no further harm, Cor. III, 1, 284. —ed her to foreign casualties, Lr. IV, 3, 45.

With away, off, out, and similar words, = to discard: I must t. away some of my followers, Wiv. I, 3, 4. III, 3, 32. IV, 3, 12. Tw. I, 5, 18. 21. H4B V, 5, 62. H8 II, 4, 42. Ant. IV, 2, 30. t. melancholy forth to funerals, Mids. I, 1, 14. I am the —ed forth, Tit. V, 3, 109. have —ed off a first so noble wife, All's V, 3, 220. Caes. IV, 1, 25. Ant. III, 6, 94. t. her out to who will take her in, Gent. III, 1, 77. Tit. V, 3, 105. Lr. III, 7, 96. With out of, = to drive out, to expel: I'll t. my mercy out o' doors, Tp. III, 2, 78. Wiv. I, 4, 131. Tw. II, 3, 78. John IV, 1, 34. H4B II, 4, 229. Cor. I, 3, 120. —ing these jests out of service, As I, 3, 25. H5 IV, 3, 119. I'll t. you out of my kingdom, Tp. IV, 253. to t. him out o'the band, All's IV, 3, 227. t. this day out of the week, John III, 1, 87. it is —ed out of all towns, R3 I, 4, 145.

h) to return, to give or send back: I will t. thy falsehood to thy heart, R2 IV, 39. Umfrevile —ed me back with joyful tidings, H4B I, 1, 34. I'll t. my part thereof (thy scorns) into thy throat, H6A II, 4, 79. we t. not back the silks upon the merchant, Troil. II, 2, 69. my relief must not be tossed and —ed to me in words, Tim. II, 1, 26.

2) intr. a) to have a circular motion, to move round: we in your motion t. and you may move us, Err. III, 2, 24. made me t. i'the wheel, 151. the fourth —ed on the toe, LLL V, 2, 114. the world —s round, Shr. V, 2, 20. go, wind, to wind, there t. and change together, Troil. V, 3, 110. t. giddy, and be holp by backward —ing, Rom. I, 2, 48. Applied to the brain, = to grow giddy: till his brains t. o'the toe, Tw. I, 3, 44. lest my brain t. Lr. IV, 6, 23. my wits begin to t. III, 2, 67.

b) to move the face to another side: gentle my lord, t. back, Meas. II, 2, 143. 145. Err. IV, 2, 56. 62. t., good lady; our Perdita is found, Wint. V, 3, 120. from the one side to the other —ing, R2 V, 2, 18. all the rest —ed on themselves, H4B I, 1, 118. so did he t. H5 IV, 6, 24. he —s away, Cor. V, 3, 168. H6B III, 2, 74. R3 I, 3, 163. did Romeo t. and fly, Rom. III, 1, 179. t. aside and weep for her, Ant. I, 3, 76.

Hence = not to fly, but to face an enemy: t., slave, and fight, Troil. V, 7, 13. Rom. III, 1, 70. Mcb. V, 8, 3. should I t. upon the true prince? H4A III, 4, 297. t. on the bloody hounds, H6A IV, 2, 51. the smallest worm will t. being trodden on, H6C II, 2, 17 (= offer resistance). he'll not swagger with a Barbary hen, if her feathers t. back in any show of resistance, H4B II, 4, 108. cf. your own reasons t. into your bosoms, as dogs upon their masters, H5 II, 2, 82.

Applied to a throw at dice: the greater throw may t. by fortune from the weaker hand, Merch. II, 1, 34.

c) to return: t. back to me, Sonn. 143, 11. Rom. II, 1, 2. Caes. III, 1, 21. his voice, —ing again toward childish treble, As II, 7, 162. or t. thou no more to seek a living in our territory, III, 1, 7. ere from this war thou t. a conqueror, R3 IV, 4, 184. tarry with him till I t. again, Tit. V, 2, 141. you did wish that I would make her t. Oth. IV, 1, 263.

d) to change direction: my tide —s not, but swells the higher by this let, Lucr. 646. now doth it t. and ebb back, H4B V, 2, 131. at the —ing of the tide, H5 II, 3, 13. if the scale do t. but in the estimation of a hair, Merch. IV, 1, 330.

e) to be changed, to alter; applied to milk, = to become sour: has friendship such a faint and milky heart, it —s in less than two nights, Tim. III, 1, 58. In a moral sense, = to be fickle and inconstant: she bade love last, and yet she fell a —ing, Pilgr. 100. her fancy fell a —ing, 214. if you t. not, you will return the sooner, Gent. II, 2, 4. some true love —ed, Mids. III, 2, 91. she is —ing and inconstant, H5 III, 6, 35. done like a Frenchman; t. and t. again, H6A III, 3, 85. she can t. and t., and yet go on, and t. again, Oth. IV, 1, 264. 265. triple —ed whore, Ant. IV, 12, 13. cf. Troil. V, 3, 110. to t. from = to fall off from; to t. to = to go over to: when he saw the fortune of the day quite —ed from him, H4A V, 5, 18. the stout Parisians do revolt and t. again unto the warlike French, H6A V, 2, 3. 6. all will revolt from me and t. to him, H6C I, 1, 151. his friends will t. to us, R3 V, 2, 19 (Qq fly). ere my true heart t. to another, Rom. IV, 1, 59.

Followed by a predicate, quite = to become: sweetest things t. sourest by their deeds, Sonn. 94, 13. whether that my angel be —ed fiend, 144, 9. to t. white, Compl. 308. —ing mortal for thy love, Pilgr. 244 and LLL IV, 3, 120. you will t. good husband now, Meas. III, 2, 74. Err. IV, 4, 160. Ado I, 1, 196. II, 3, 21. III, 4, 57. LLL I, 2, 190. V, 2, 70. Mids. III, 2, 91. Merch. I, 3, 179. III, 1, 82. As I, 2, 23. II, 5, 53. V, 1, 101. All's V, 3, 59. Tw. III, 2, 74. H4A II, 2, 24. II, 4, 393. III, 1, 264. III, 3, 114. H4B I, 2, 192. H5 V, 1, 90. V, 2, 168. Troil. V, 2, 114. V, 3, 81. Rom. I, 2, 48. II, 3, 21. Tim. IV, 1, 3. IV, 3, 217. Caes. V, 3, 2. Mcb. II, 4, 16. Hml. III, 2, 287. Lr. II, 4, 85. III, 7, 102. Oth. II, 3, 170. Ant. I, 3, 39. Cymb. V, 3, 35. Per. II, 1, 92. IV, 3, 4.

With the prepos. to, in the same sense: the sweets ... t. to loathed sours, Lucr. 867. thy honey —s to gall, 889. 890. all things t. to fair, Sonn. 95, 12. every scope by the immoderate use —s to restraint, Meas. I, 2, 132. their counsel —s to passion, Ado V, 1, 23. day would t. to night, LLL IV, 3, 233. falsehood —s to grace, V, 2, 786. that pure white ... —s to a crow, Mids. III, 2, 142. Merch. III, 2, 184. III, 4, 78 (quibbling; see below). V, 78. As IV, 3, 40. Wint. I, 2, 417. 420. John III, 1, 344. R2 III, 2, 136. H6A II, 2, 45. II, 3, 44. H8 I, 2, 117. Tit. II, 3, 144. Rom. I, 2, 94. I, 5, 106. IV, 5, 85. Tim. III, 1, 61. 62. Caes. V, 1, 49. Hml. III, 2, 228. Ant. II, 5, 79. II, 6, 108. Cymb. III, 4, 84. III, 6, 54. Per. II, 1, 125. With into: the best grace of wit will shortly t. into silence, Merch. III, 5, 49.

f) to take a way or direction; to be bent or directed: (eyes) quick in —ing, Ven. 140. which way shall she t.? 253. then shalt thou see the dew-bedabbled wretch t. and return, 704. t. up or your right hand at the next turning, Merch. II, 2, 42. t. of no hand, 44. t. down, 45. now, Thomas Mowbray, do I t. to thee, R2 I, 1, 35. t. this way, H6C I, 1, 189. speculation —s not to itself, Troil. III, 3, 109. I know not where to t. Cor. II, 1, 197. With to, 1) applied to females, = to suffer to be covered: the ewes —ed to the rams, Merch. I, 3, 82. shall we t. to men? III, 4, 78 (quibbling). 2) to fall into: she —ed to folly, Oth. V, 2, 132. to rage the city t. Per. V, 3, 97. cf. Gent. I, 1, 48. 3) to have a consequence, to result or terminate in: is all our travail —ed to this effect? H6A V, 4, 102. who knows how that may t. back to my advancement, Wint. IV, 4, 867.

**Turnbull Street,** 'now, and indeed originally,

**Turnmill-Street**, near Clerkenwell, anciently the resort of bullies, rogues, and other dissolute persons' (Nares): H4B III, 2, 329.

**Turncoat**, one who forsakes his party or principles: Ado I, 1, 125. Tim. IV, 3, 143.

**Turning**, a place at which one way is left for another: *I will leave them at the next t.* Ado II, 1, 160. *turn up on your right hand at the next t.* Merch. II, 2, 43. 44.

**Turnip**, the root of Brassica rapa: *bowled to death with —s*, Wiv. III, 4, 91.

**Turph**, name in Shr. Ind. 2, 96.

**Turpitude**, extreme baseness and depravity: *minds swayed by eyes are full of t.* Troil. V, 2, 112. *my t. thou dost so crown with gold*, Ant. IV, 6, 33.

**Turquoise**, a precious stone of a bluish-green colour: Merch. III, 1, 126.

**Turret**, a tower erected for purposes of fortification: Lucr. 441. 1372. H6A I, 4, 26. III, 2, 30.

**Turtle**, the bird Columba turtur: LLL V, 2, 915. Shr. II, 208. Emblem of chaste and faithful love: Phoen. 23. 31. 57. Wiv. II, 1, 83. III, 3, 44 (*to know —s from jays*). LLL IV, 3, 211. Wint. IV, 4, 154. V, 3, 132. Troil. III, 2, 185.

**Turtle-dove**, the same: H6A II, 2, 30.

**Tuscan**, pertaining to Tuscany: All's I, 2, 14. II, 3, 290.

**Tush**, interjection expressive of contempt for what has been said by another: Ado III, 3, 130. V, 1, 58. V, 4, 44. LLL IV, 3, 158. Shr. I, 1, 130. I, 2, 211. H4A IV, 2, 73. H6A IV, 1, 178. V, 3, 89. 107. V, 5, 10. H6C IV, 7, 13. R3 I, 2, 188. I, 3, 350 (Ff *tut*). H8 I, 2, 182. Cor. III, 2, 45. Rom. IV, 2, 39. V, 1, 29. Hml. I, 1, 30. Oth. I, 1, 1.

**Tusk**, the long pointed tooth of the boar: Ven. 1116. Plur. *tushes:* 617. 624 (dissyll.).

**Tut**, interjection expressing contempt of what has been said by another: Gent. II, 3, 46. Wiv. I, 1, 117. II, 1, 232. Shr. II, 404. III, 1, 79. III, 2, 159. IV, 4, 13. Tw. I, 3, 117. R2 II, 3, 86. H4A I, 2, 198. II, 1, 76. IV, 2, 64. 71. IV, 3, 89. H5 III, 7, 1. H6A II, 1, 49. II, 4, 19. H6B I, 2, 32. III, 1, 64. H6C II, 6, 108. III, 2, 195. R3 I, 3, 350 (Qq *tush*). I, 4, 154. III, 5, 5. IV, 2, 22. 121. Tit. V, 1, 89. V, 2, 150. Rom. I, 1, 203. I, 2, 99. Caes. V, 1, 7. Lr. I, 2, 142.

**Tutor**, subst. one who teaches and instructs, a master: *thy eyes' shrewd t., that hard heart of thine, hath taught them scornful tricks*, Ven. 500. *O time, thou t. both to good and bad, teach me to curse him*, Lucr. 995 (cf. the verb in R2 IV, 166). Tp. I, 2, 174. 469 *(my foot my t.?)*. Gent. II, 1, 144. III, 1, 84. LLL IV, 3, 323 (*beauty's —s*, i. e. those who taught you what beauty was). Shr. II, 111. H4B V, 5, 66. H6C I, 3, 2. Troil. II, 3, 32. 253. Tit. V, 1, 98. Hml. III, 2, 19. Lr. III, 2, 83 (*when nobles are their tailors' —s*, i. e. are able to instruct them in their art, are their masters).

**Tutor**, vb. to teach, to instruct: Gent. I, 3, 21. LLL IV, 2, 77. As V, 4, 31. H4B IV, 1, 44 (*whose learning and good letters peace hath —ed*). H6A IV, 5, 2. Troil. II, 1, 49. Rom. V, 3, 243. Tim. I, 1, 37. With *to:* *to t. me to this submission*, R2 IV, 166 (cf. the subst. in Lucr. 995). With *from: thou wilt t. me from quarrelling*, Rom. III, 1, 32 (wilt lesson me how to avoid quarrelling).

**Tu-whit, tu-who**, a sound imitative of the cry of the owl: LLL V, 2, 928. 937.

**Twain**, two (never before a substantive): Ven. 123. 210. 1067. Lucr. 405. 1154. Sonn. 39, 13 (*to make one t.* = to unite two in one). Phoen. 25. Tp. I, 2, 438. LLL V, 2, 48. Mids. V, 151. Merch. III, 2, 329. Shr. II, 306. Wint. IV, 4, 674. R2 I, 1, 50. V, 3, 134. H6B V, 1, 55. H6C IV, 1, 135. Troil. I, 3, 185. IV, 5, 123. Mcb. III, 1, 28. Hml. III, 2, 238. Lr. IV, 1, 44. IV, 6, 211. V, 3, 319. Ant. I, 4, 73. II, 1, 35. III, 4, 30. Cymb. III, 6, 87. V, 4, 70. *to cleave a heart in t.* Meas. III, 1, 63. *yourself in t. divide*, H6A IV, 5, 49. *this staff was broke in t.* H6B I, 2, 26. Troil. I, 3, 256. Rom. V, 3, 99. Hml. III, 4, 156. Lr. II, 2, 80 (Ff *a-twain*). Oth. V, 2, 206 (Q1 *a-twain*). *we two must be t.* Sonn. 36, 1 (parted, separated). *they two are t.* Troil. III, 1, 111. Rom. III, 5, 241. *both t.* = both, the one as well as the other: *both find each other, and I lose both t.* Sonn. 42, 11. *I remit both t.* LLL IV, 2, 459.

Substantively, = pair, couple: *how true a t. seemeth this concordant one*, Phoen. 45. *to bless this t.* Tp. IV, 104. *when such a mutual pair and such a t. can do't*, Ant. I, 1, 38.

**Twanged**, uttered with a shrill and sharp sound: *a terrible oath, with a swaggering accent sharply t. off*, Tw. III, 4, 198. cf. *Tang*.

**Twangling**, shrill-sounding, jingling, noisy: *sometimes a thousand t. instruments will hum about mine ears*, Tp. III, 2, 146. *she did call me rascal fiddler and t. Jack*, Shr. II, 159.

**Tweak**, to twitch: *—s me by the nose*, Hml. II, 2, 601.

**'Tween**, prepos. (never adv.) = between (O. Edd. sometimes *'tween*, usually *tween*): Ven. 269. Lucr. 247. Merch. III, 2, 31. 104. H4B IV, 1, 226. R3 III, 7, 95 (Qq *between*). Tit. V, 2, 183. Caes. II, 4, 7. IV, 3, 235. Hml. V, 2, 42. Lr. I, 2, 15. IV, 6, 118. Oth. II, 3, 10. Ant. III, 6, 61. Cymb. IV, 2, 249. V, 4, 24 etc.

**Twelfe** (M. Edd. *twelfth*), twelfth: Tw. II, 3, 90. cf. the title of the comedy '*Twelfe Night*'.

**Twelve**, twice six, a dozen: Tp. I, 2, 53. 296. Wiv. IV, 6, 19. V, 5, 1. Meas. II, 1, 20 (*the sworn twelve*, i. e. the jury). Err. I, 2, 45. Ado IV, 1, 85. LLL V, 2, 807. Mids. V, 370. Merch. I, 3, 105. Shr. I, 2, 258. II, 381. Wint. IV, 4, 347. R2 III, 2, 70. IV, 170. H4A II, 4, 107. III, 2, 177. H5 II, 3, 13. III, 2, 46. IV, 8, 67. H6A III, 4, 7. IV, 1, 24 (*t. hundred*). H6B I, 8. Cor. IV, 5, 128. 135. Rom. I, 3, 2. II, 5, 10. Tim. III, 6, 87. Mcb. II, 1, 3. Hml. I, 1, 7. I, 2, 252. I, 4, 3. III, 2, 168. V, 2, 174. Lr. I, 2, 5. Oth. IV, 2, 243. Ant. II, 2, 184. III, 7, 60. Per. II, 5, 10. III, 3, 2. *t. score*, elliptically, = so many yards: *as easy as a cannon will shoot point-blank t. score*, Wiv. III, 2, 34. *his death will be a march of t. score*, H4A II, 4, 598. *clapped i'the clout at t. score*, H4B III, 2, 52.

**Twelvemonth**, a year: Ado IV, 1, 151. LLL V, 2, 831. 837 (*a t. and a day*). 843. 860. 880. 881. 887 (*a t. and a day*). Merch. III, 4, 76. As III, 1, 7. III, 2, 86. Tw. I, 2, 37. H4A I, 1, 28 (Ff *a t.*, Qq *twelve month*). R3 III, 2, 57. Per. II, 4, 45. II, 5, 3.

**Twelve-score**, see *Twelve* and *Score*.

**Twentieth**, the ordinal of twenty: Merch. IV, 1, 329. Hml. III, 4, 97.

**Twenty**, twice ten: Wiv. II, 2, 73. V, 5, 117. Err. V, 326. Merch. III, 4, 84. As I, 3, 46. V, 1, 21. Shr. IV, 4, 4. V, 2, 70. All's II, 1, 168. Wint. III, 3, 60. H4A I, 1, 68. H6C I, 2, 72. R3 I, 4, 122. Rom. IV

**2, 2** etc. Indefinitely, = a considerable number, never so many: *one* (kiss) *long as t.* Ven. 22. *t. hundred kisses*, 522. *under t. locks kept fast*, 575. *t. thousand tongues*, 775. *t. times 'Woe, woe'*, 833. *t. echoes*, 834. *why of two oaths' breach do I accuse thee, when I break t.?* Sonn. 152, 6. Tp. II, 1, 278. Gent. I, 1, 31. 72 (*t. to one*). II, 4, 95. 170. II, 6, 16. II, 7, 46. Wiv. I, 1, 3. 307. II, 1, 82. III, 2, 33. IV, 4, 30. V, 5, 82. Meas. II, 4, 180. Err. III, 2, 177. Ado II, 3, 136. V, 2, 76. LLL V, 2, 265. Merch. I, 2, 17. 67. II, 6, 66. III, 2, 154. 289. 309. III, 4, 74. As I, 1, 52. Shr. V, 2, 73. All's III, 2, 84. Tw. V, 92. R2 II, 2, 14. IV, 38. V, 2, 101. H4B II, 2, 149. II, 4, 385. H6B II, 4, 60. III, 2, 206. 268. R3 I, 2, 162. IV, 2, 38. H8 I, 4, 30. Tit. V, 1, 76. Rom. II, 2, 72. 170. II, 4, 160. II, 5, 50. III, 3, 153. Caes. I, 3, 17. Mcb. III, 4, 27. Lr. II, 2, 109. II, 4, 72 (Qq *a hundred*). Oth. V, 2, 166. Ant. III, 13, 96 etc. *good even and t.* Wiv. II, 1, 203. *tricks eleven and t. long*, Shr. IV, 2, 57. *sweet and t.* Tw. II, 3, 52.

**Twice**, two times: Lucr. 567. Sonn. 17, 14. 152, 2. Pilgr. 315. Tp. IV, 45. V, 103. 177. Gent. I, 2, 117. 123. III, 1, 365. Wiv. III, 5, 103. Meas. IV, 1, 41. IV, 3, 92. IV, 6, 12. Err. I, 1, 101 (*t. five*). III, 2, 177. Ado III, 2, 10. LLL V, 2, 227. Merch. IV, 1, 69. 210. As IV, 3, 128. Shr. Ind. 1, 24. II, 382. All's II, 1, 164. John II, 275 (*t. fifteen thousand*). R2 I, 3, 141 (*t. five*). H4A IV, 2, 18. H6A IV, 6, 6. H6B III, 2. 83. H6C I, 4, 50 (*t. two*). R3 V, 3, 210. Cor. II, 3, 220. 252. Hml. III, 2, 135 (*t. two*). Ant. II, 7, 68. Cymb. IV, 2, 392. Per. III Prol. 31 (*t. six*) etc. Used by way of enforcement, = doubly, thoroughly: *a victory is t. itself*, Ado I, 1, 8. *offending is as much*, LLL IV, 3, 132. *bolted t. o'er*, Wint. IV, 4, 376. *all our service in every point t. done and then done double*, Mcb. I, 6, 15. *an old man is t. a child*, Hml. II, 2, 403. *thou art t. her love*, Lr. II, 4, 263. *his soldiership is t. the other twain*, Ant. II, 1, 35. *two boys, an old man t. a boy*, Cymb. V, 3, 57. Before adjectives and participles (hyphened by some M. Edd.): *t. treble shame on Angelo*, Meas. III, 2, 283. *t. sod simplicity*, LLL IV, 2, 23. *t. blest*, Merch. IV, 1, 186. *to make the world t. rich*, Per. III, 2, 103.

**Twice-sod**, see *twice* and *seethe*.

**Twice-told**: *life is as tedious as a t. tale*, John III, 4, 108.

**Twig**, a branch, a shoot: Meas. I, 3, 24. All's III, 5, 26. III, 6, 115. R2 III, 4, 32. H5 V, 2, 44.

**Twiggen**, cased in twigs or wicker-work: *I'll beat the knave into a t. bottle*, Oth. II, 3, 152 (Qq *wicker bottle*).

**Twilight**, the faint light after sunset: Sonn. 73, 5.

**Twilled**, a word not yet satisfactorily explained; according to some = hedged; more probably = covered with reeds or sedges (*twills* a provincialism for reeds): *thy banks with pioned and t. brims*, Tp. IV, 64.*

**Twin**, one of two children born at a birth: *the t. Dromio*, Err. V, 350. Plur. —s: Err. I, 1, 56. 82. H8 IV, 2, 58. Ant. III, 10, 12. *t. brother*, Wiv. II, 1, 74. *O hard condition, twin-born with greatness*, H5 IV, 1, 251.

Adjectively, = perfectly resembling: *an apple, cleft in two, is not more t. than these two creatures*, Tw. V, 230. Perhaps also in Per. V Prol. 8.

**Twin**, vb. 1) to be born at a birth: *we were as —ed lambs*, Wint. I, 2, 67 (O. Edd. *twyn'd*). — ed *brothers of one womb*, Tim. IV, 3, 3. *though he had —ed with me, both at a birth*, Oth. II, 3, 212. —ed = perfectly resembling each other: *distinguish 'twixt the fiery orbs above and the —ed stones upon the numbered beach*, Cymb. I, 6, 35.

2) to be like twins, either in love or in perfect resemblance: *who t., as 'twere, in love unseparable*, Cor. IV, 15. *her inkle, silk, t. with the rubied cherry*, Per. V Prol. 8 (O. Edd. *twine*).

**Twin-born**, see *Twin*, subst.

**Twin-brother**, see *Twin*, subst.

**Twine**, subst. a twisted thread: *the smallest t. may lead me*, Ado IV, 1, 252.

**Twine**, vb. to wind round, to embrace, to cling to: *from her —ing arms*, Ven. 256. *some t. about her thigh*, 873. Trans.: *let me t. mine arms about that body*, Cor. IV, 5, 112.

In Cor. IV, 4, 15 the later Ff *who twine, as 'twere, in love*; F1 *twin*.

**Twink**, a twinkling, an instant: *Presently? Ay, with a t.* Tp. IV, 43. *in a t. she won me*, Shr. II, 312.

**Twinkle**, to sparkle, to shine with a quivering light; used of the stars: Lucr. 787. Gent. II, 6, 9. Rom. II, 2, 17. Lr. I, 2, 144. With an accus. denoting the effect: *as plays the sun upon the glassy streams, —ing another counterfeited beam*, H6A V, 3, 63.

*In the —ing of an eye* = in a moment: Merch. II, 2, 177 (Launcelot's speech).

**Twinned**, see *Twin*.

**Twire**, to shine at intervals, or with an unsteady light: *when sparkling stars t. not thou gildest the even*, Sonn. 28, 12.

**Twist**, subst. a thread, a string: *breaking his oath like a t. of rotten silk*, Cor. V, 6, 96.

**Twist**, vb. to form into a thread by convolution: *with —ed metal amorously impleached*, Compl. 205. *the smallest thread that ever spider —ed from her womb*, John IV, 3, 128. *a poor prisoner in his —ed gyves*, Rom. II, 2, 180. Figuratively: *began'st to t. so fine a story*, Ado I, 1, 313.

**Twit**, to reproach sneeringly: *she —s me with my falsehood to my friend*, Gent. IV, 2, 8. *and t. with cowardice a man half dead*, H6A III, 2, 55. *there's for —ing me with perjury*, H6C V, 5, 40. Partic. *twit*: *hath he not t. our sovereign lady here with ignominious words*, H6B III, 1, 178.

**'Twixt**, prepos. (never adv.) = betwixt (q. v.): Ven. 76. 1160. Sonn. 75, 4. 115, 6. Compl. 102. Pilgr. 105. Phoen. 31. Tp. I, 2, 240. II, 1, 256. 279. V, 43. Wiv. III, 5, 132. IV, 6, 19. 49. Meas. I, 4, 71. II, 2, 33. Err. I, 1, 12. Merch. III, 2, 329. As III, 2, 142. Shr. I, 2, 46. 65. II, 306. IV, 2, 84. 118. Wint. I, 2, 134. IV, 4, 563. V, 1, 132. V, 2, 79. John III, 1, 111. IV, 2, 78. 216. R2 V, 1, 72. 74. H4A I, 3, 37. III, 1, 219. H5 I, 2, 52. V, 2, 383. 390. H6A II, 5, 46. H6B III, 1, 221. IV, 9, 31. H8 I, 1, 7. Troil. I, 3, 156. II, 1, 135. II, 3, 184. IV, 5, 123. Cor. II, 2, 19. Rom. III, 1, 172. IV, 1, 62. Tim. IV, 3, 383. Caes. IV, 3, 204. Mcb. III, 1, 26. Hml. I, 2, 252. Ant. III, 4, 20. Cymb. I, 6, 34. III, 2, 70 etc.

**Two**, one and one: Tp. I, 1, 52. I, 2, 240. 298. 421. II, 1, 196. II, 2, 93. 117. III, 1, 75. III, 2, 7. V, 274. Gent. II, 1, 106. IV, 4, 48. V, 4, 50. 118. Wiv. III, 3, 250. IV, 2, 234. IV, 4, 55. V, 3, 4. Meas. II, 4, 112 (*ignomy in ransom and free pardon are of t. houses*). Err. I, 1, 51. Ado II, 1, 397 (*with your t* *helps;* cf. *Both).* Mids. III, 2, 213 ( *t. of the first;* cf. *First).* Merch. III, 4, 64 etc. etc. *he shall kill t. of us,* Ado V, 1, 80. H6B III, 2, 303. Caes. I, 3, 138 (cf. *Of). t. and t., Newgate fashion,* H4A III, 3, 104. *by —s and threes,* Wint. I, 2, 438. Cor. II, 3, 47. *t. and thirty, a pip out,* Shr. I, 2, 33 (cf. *Pip). in t.* = into two parts, asunder: Err. V, 289. Tw. V, 230. Oth. V, 1, 72. cf. Per. I, 1, 70. Used to denote a little number: *the t. hours' traffic of our stage,* Rom. Prol. 12. *t. charming words,* Cymb. I, 3, 35. *t. or three,* Mids. IV, 2, 16. All's III, 6, 106. Mcb. IV, 1, 141. Oth. V, 1, 42 (cf. Falstaff's *t. or three and fifty,* H4A II, 4, 206). *one or t.* Rom. I, 5, 5. *some month or t.* Merch. III, 2, 9. R3 III, 1, 64. *a turn or t.* Tp. IV, 162. *a word or t.* Gent. I, 3, 52. 73. Wiv. II, 2, 43. Meas. II, 1, 20. III, 1, 48. Ado II, 1, 153. Mids. IV, 1, 41. Merch. III, 2, 1. Tw. III, 4, 412. IV, 1, 47 etc.

**Twofold,** adj. double; a) as consisting of two of the same kind: *to break a t. truth* (hers and thine) Sonn. 41, 12. *you violate a t. marriage,* R2 V, 1, 72. *sherris-sack hath a t. operation in it,* H4B IV, 3, 104. *t. balls,* Mcb. IV, 1, 121. *what's in prayer but this t. force, to be forestalled ... or pardoned,* Hml. III, 3, 48. b) as being twice so great: *doth with a t. vigour lift me up,* R2 I, 3, 71.

**Two-hand,** wielded with both hands: *come with thy t. sword,* H6B II, 1, 46.

**Two-headed,** having two heads ( or rather two faces): *by t. Janus,* Merch. I, 1, 50.

**Two-legged,** having two legs: H4A II, 4, 207.

**Two-pence,** a coin of the value of two pence: *if you do not all show like gilt —s to me,* H4B IV, 3, 55.

**Tybalt,** name in Rom., passim. *Tybert or Tybalt* was the name of the cat in the History of Reynard the Fox; this circumstance alluded to: *what is T.? More than prince of cats,* Rom. II, 4, 18. *T., thou rat-catcher,* III, 1, 78. *good king of cats,* 80.

**Tyburn,** the usual place of execution in Middlesex: *the shape of Love's T.* LLL IV, 3, 54 ( the triangular form of the gallows).

**Tymbria,** writing of M. Edd. in Troil. Prol. 16; Ff *Timbria,* Qq *Thymbria.*

**Type,** distinguishing mark, sign, badge: *so* (loyal) *am I now: O no, that cannot be; of that true t. hath Tarquin rifled me,* Lucr. 1050. *thy father bears the t. of king of Naples,* H6C I, 4, 121 (i. e. the crown). *the high imperial t. of this earth's glory,* R3 IV, 4, 244. *tall stockings, short blistered breeches, and those —s of travel,* H8 I, 3, 31.

**Typhon,** Typhoeus, a giant of ancient fable, who attempted to dethrone Jove, but was defeated and imprisoned under Mount Aetna: *roaring T.* Troil. I, 3, 160. *his threatening band of —'s brood,* Tit. IV, 2, 94.

**Tyrannical,** despotic, arbitrary: *t. power,* Cor. III, 3, 2. *power t.* 65.

**Tyrannically,** dreadfully, violently: *and are most t. clapped for it,* Hml. II, 2, 356.

**Tyrannize,** to play the tyrant, to be cruel, to inflict pain and torment: *shame folded up in blind concealing night, when most unseen, then most doth t.* Lucr. 676. *there the poison is as a fiend confined to t. on unreprievable condemned blood,* John V, 7, 47. *this poor right hand of mine is left to t. upon my breast,* Tit. III, 2, 8. *on him that thus doth t. o'er me,* IV, 3, 20.

**Tyrannous,** 1) despotic, unjustly severe: *were he mealed with that which he corrects, then were he t.* Meas. IV, 2, 87. *fear you his t. passion more,* Wint. II, 3, 28. *let us be cleared of being t.* III, 2, 5.

2) cruel, inhuman, pitiless: *thou art as t. ... as those whose beauties proudly make them cruel,* Sonn. 131, 1. *it is excellent to have a giant's strength, but it is t. to use it like a giant,* Meas. II, 2, 108. *all the thoughts that t. heart can think,* Tw. III, 1, 131. *the t. and bloody deed is done,* R3 IV, 3, 1. *that love ... should be so t. and rough,* Rom. I, 1, 176. *lend a t. and damned light to their lord's murder,* Hml. II, 2, 482. *this t. night,* Lr. III, 4, 156. *to t. hate,* Oth. III, 3, 449. *and like the t. breathing of the north shakes all our buds from growing,* Cymb. I, 3, 36. *I knew him t.* Per. I, 2, 84.

**Tyranny,** 1) hard and arbitrary exercise of power: *with a bitter invective against the t. of the king,* Lucr. Arg. 24. *that part of t. that I do bear I can shake off at pleasure,* Caes. I, 3, 99. *so let high-sighted t. range on,* II, 1, 118. Wint. II, 3, 120. III, 2, 32. 180. H6A II, 5, 100. H6B IV, 1, 96. R3 II, 4, 51. V, 2, 2. Caes. III, 1, 78. Mcb. IV, 3, 32. 67. V, 8, 67. Lr. I, 2, 52. Oth. I, 3, 197.

2) cruelty, injurious violence: *subject to the t. of mad mischances,* Ven. 737. *why, fearing of time's t., might I not then say,* Sonn. 115, 9. *whether the t. be in his place or in his eminence,* Meas. I, 2, 167. *'twould be my t. to strike and gall them for what I bid them do,* I, 3, 36. *to suffer ... the very t. and rage of his,* Merch. IV, 1, 13. *the t. of her sorrows takes all livelihood from her cheek,* All's I, 1, 57. *waste for churlish winter's t.* H4B I, 3, 62. *t. which never quaffed but blood, would have washed his knife with gentle eye-drops,* IV, 5, 86. H6A II, 3, 40. IV, 2, 17. IV, 7, 19. H6B III, 1, 123. 149. III, 2, 49. R3 III, 7, 9. V, 3, 168. Cor. V, 3, 43. Tit. II, 3, 145. 267. III, 2, 55. Lr. III, 4, 2.

**Tyrant,** 1) a hard, despotic, or lawless ruler: Sonn. 107, 14. Tp. II, 2, 166. III, 2, 49. Meas. II, 114. Mids. I, 2, 24. 31. 42. As II, 1, 61. Wint. II, 116. 122. III, 2, 135. 176. 208. H5 I, 2, 241. H6C III, 3, 69. 71 (= the Greek τύραννος, usurper? cf. As II, 1, 61). 206. IV, 4, 29. R3 V, 3, 246. 255. 256. Tit. I, 138. Tim. III, 5, 9. Caes. I, 3, 92. 103. III, 2, 74. V, 4, 5. Mcb. III, 6, 22. 25. IV, 3, 12. 36. 45. 104. 178. 185 etc. Lr. IV, 6, 63. Oth. I, 3, 230 (*the t. custom*). Cymb. IV, 2, 265. Per. I, 2, 79. 84. 103.

2) one pitiless and cruel: *which* (beauty) *the hot t.* (lust) *stains,* Ven. 797. *hard-favoured t.* (death) 931. *make war upon this bloody t. Time,* Sonn. 16, 2. *and I, a t., have no leisure taken to weigh how once I suffered in your crime,* 120, 7. *when I forgot am of myself, all t., for thy sake,* 149, 4. Meas. III, 2, 207. LLL IV, 3, 349. As III, 5, 14. IV, 3, 39. Tw. V, 127. H4B Ind. 14 (*the stern t. war*). H6B V, 2, 54. R3 I, 3, 185. IV, 4, 52 (*that excellent grand t. of the earth*). Troil. III, 2, 127. Rom. I, 1, 26. III, 2, 75. Hml. II, 2, 502. Cymb. I, 1, 84. In Wiv. III, 3, 65 Ff *thou art a t.* to say so, perhaps with a pun on the preceding *tire;* the spurious Qq and M. Edd. *traitor.*

With *to:* *those hours ... will play the —s to the very same,* Sonn. 5, 3. *I'll prove a t. to him,* Meas. II, 4, 169. *a professed t. to their sex,* Ado I, 1, 170.

Adjectively: *or t. folly lurk in gentle breasts,* Lucr. 851. *fowl of t. wing,* Phoen. 10. As I, 2, 300. John V, 3, 14.

Name of a dog: Tp. IV, 258.

**Tyre**, the town of Tyrus in Phoenicia: Per. I, 1, 1. 156. I, 2, 115 etc.

**Tyrian**, pertaining to Tyrus: *T. tapestry*, Shr. II, 351. *our T. ship*, Per. V Prol. 18.

**Tyrrel** or **Tirrel**, name in R3 IV, 2, 40. 68. 80. 85. IV, 3, 24.

**Tyrus**, town in Phoenicia: Per. III Prol. 26. III, 1, 80. III, 3, 2. IV, 4, 36. V, 3, 82.

**Tythe** and **Tything**, see *Tithe* and *Tithing*.

# U.

**U**, the fifth vowel of the English alphabet: LLL V, 1, 60 (pronounced like *you*). Tw. II, 5, 96.

**Udder**, teat, dug: *a lioness, with —s all drawn dry*, As IV, 3, 115.

**Ugly**, deformed; contrary to beautiful, in a moral as well as a physical sense: Ven. 931. 1041. Lucr. 459. 925. 1082. Sonn. 33, 6. Tp. IV, 191 *(—er)*. Mids. II, 2, 94. Merch. III, 2, 28. As II, 1, 13. John III, 1, 37. 44. IV, 3, 123. R2 I, 1, 42 *(—er)*. H4A I, 2, 226. H4B I, 1, 66 *(—est)*. IV, 1, 39. H5 IV Chor. 11. H6A V, 3, 34. 189. R3 I, 2, 23. I, 3, 227. I, 4, 3. 23. H8 I, 2, 117. Troil. V, 8, 6. Tim. III, 5, 25. 100. Hml. III, 1, 52. Lr. I, 4, 289. Oth. V, 1, 20. Ant. II, 5, 97. Cymb. V, 3, 70.

**Ulcer**, an open sore: Troil. I, 1, 53. Hml. IV, 7, 124.

**Ulcerous**, 1) having the nature of an ulcer: *u. sores*, Tim. IV, 3, 39. 2) affected with an ulcer: *people all swoln and u.* Mcb. IV, 3, 151. *the u. place*, Hml. III, 4, 147.

**Ullorxa**, an apocryphal name which has been a whetstone to the sagacity of emendators: Tim. III, 4, 112 (Globe: *all, sirrah, all;* Collier *all, look, sir;* Walker *Valerius, all,* etc.).*

**Ulysses**, the famous king of Ithaca: Lucr. 1394. 1399. H6C III, 2, 189. IV, 2, 19. Troil. I, 3, 58. 69 etc. Cor. I, 3, 93. Not mentioned by name, but spoken of in Tit. I, 380.

**Umber**, a species of ochre, of a brown colour: *with a kind of u. smirch my face*, As I, 3, 114.

**Umbered**, embrowned, darkened: *through their paly flames each battle sees the other's u. face*, H5 IV, Chor. 9.

**Umbrage**, shadow: *his semblable is his mirror, and who else would trace him, his u., nothing more*, Hml. V, 2, 125 (a speech tainted with Euphuism).

**Umfrevile**, name in H4B I, 1, 34.

**Umpire**, one to whose arbitration a question is referred: Wiv. I, 1, 139. LLL I, 1, 170. H6A IV, 1, 151. Applied to death as the general peace-maker: H6A II, 5, 29. Rom. IV, 1, 63.

**Unable**, 1) with an inf., = not having the power or means: *u. to support this lump of clay*, H6A II, 5, 14. *we are u. to resist*, Per. I, 4, 84.

2) absol. weak, impotent: *making both it* (the heart) *u. for itself*, Meas. II, 4, 21. *you froward and u. worms*, Shr. V, 2, 169. *with rough and all u. pen*, H5 Epil. 1. *sapless age and weak u. limbs*, H6A IV, 5, 4. *a love that makes breath poor, and speech u.* Lr. I, 1, 61.

**Unaccommodated**, unsupplied with conveniences: *u. man is no more but such a poor, bare, forked animal*, Lr. III, 4, 111.

**Unaccompanied**, without a companion: *which honour must not u. invest him only*, Mcb. I, 4, 40.

**Unaccustomed**, unusual, extraordinary, strange: *leave this peevish broil and set this u. fight aside*, H6A

III, 1, 93. *what u. cause procures her hither?* Rom. III, 5, 68. *shall give him such an u. dram, that he shall soon keep Tybalt company*, 91. *an u. spirit lifts me above the ground*, V, 1, 4. *the u. terror of this night*, Caes. II, 1, 199.

**Unaching**, not giving pain: Cor. II, 2, 152.

**Unacquainted**, 1) not having familiar knowledge of things: *am become as new into the world, strange, u.* Troil. III, 3, 12.

2) not familiarly known, strange, foreign: *kiss the lips of u. change*, John III, 4, 166. *follow u. colours*, V, 2, 32.

**Unacted**, not executed: *the fault unknown is as a thought u.* Lucr. 527.

**Unactive**, not doing any thing, idle: *it did remain i'the midst o'the body, idle and u.* Cor. I, 1, 102.

**Unadvised**, 1) not directed by certain knowledge, ignorantly done: *friend to friend gives u. wounds*, Lucr. 1488 (not seeing whom he strikes).* *I have u. delivered you a paper that I should not*, Gent. IV, 4, 127 (without previously looking at it).

2) inconsiderate, rash, imprudent: *stay for an answer to your embassy, lest u. you stain your swords with blood*, John II, 45. *thou u. scold*, 191. *this harnessed mask and u. revel*, V, 2, 132. *although our mother u. gave you a dancing-rapier*, Tit. II, 1, 38. *it is too rash, too u., too sudden*, Rom. II, 2, 118.

**Unadvisedly**, inconsiderately: *men shall deal u. sometimes*, R3 IV, 4, 292.

**Unagreeable**, unsuitable, not adapted: *the time is u. to this business*, Tim. II, 2, 41.

**Unaneled**, not having received extreme unction: *unhouseled, disappointed, u.* Hml. I, 5, 77.

**Unanswered**, not replied to: *your petition is yet u.* Wint. V, 1, 229.

**Unappeased**, not pacified: *that so the shadows be not u.* Tit. I, 100.

**Unapproved**, not justified and confirmed by proof: *what u. witness dost thou bear*, Compl. 53.

**Unapt**, 1) unfit: *the full-fed hound or gorged hawk, u. for tender smell or speedy flight*, Lucr. 695. *why are our bodies soft and weak and smooth, u. to toil and trouble in the world*, Shr. V, 2, 166.

2) not propense or ready: *with leaden appetite, u. to toy*, Ven. 34. *my blood hath been too cold and temperate, u. to stir at these indignities*, H4A I, 3, 2 (cf. *Apt* sub 2). *I am a soldier and u. to weep*, H6A V, 3, 133. *we pout upon the morning, are u. to give or to forgive*, Cor. V, 1, 52.

**Unaptness**, disinclination: Tp. II, 2, 140.

**Unarm**, 1) tr. to disarm, to strip of armour or arms; absol.: *u., Eros*, Ant. IV, 14, 35 (take off my armour). With an accus.: *to help u. our Hector*, Troil. III, 1, 163. Refl.: *there he —s him*, Troil. I, 2, 300. *u. thee*, V, 3, 35.

2) intr. to put off one's arms: *I'll u. again*, Troil. I, 1, 1. *u. and do not fight to-day*, V, 3, 3. 25.

**Unarmed**, having no arms, not furnished with weapons: *he leaves his back u.* H4B I, 3, 79. *our bare u. heads*, II, 4, 394. R3 IV, 4, 436. Troil. I, 3, 235. III, 3, 237. 276. IV, 5, 153. V, 8, 9.

**Unasked**, not begged, not sought by entreaty: *begged for that which thou u. shalt have*, Ven. 102.

**Unassailable**, not to be tempted and seduced: *that u. holds on his rank*, Caes. III, 1, 69.

**Unassailed**, not attacked: H6B V, 2, 18.

**Unattainted**, not infected, sound: *with u. eye compare her face with some that I shall show*, Rom. I, 2, 90.

**Unattempted**, not tempted: *my hand, as u. yet, like a poor beggar, raileth on the rich*, John II, 591.

**Unattended**, unaccompanied, left alone: *your constancy hath left you u.* Mcb. II, 2, 69.

**Unauspicious**, unfavourable, not propitious: *to whose ingrate and u. altars my soul the faithfullest offerings hath breathed out*, Tw. V, 116.

**Unauthorized**, unjustifiable: *an u. kiss*, Oth. IV, 1, 2.

**Unavoided**, 1) not avoided or shunned: *whose u. eye is murderous*, R3 IV, 1, 56.

2) inevitable: *and u. is the danger now*, R2 II, 1, 268. *a terrible and u. danger*, H6A IV, 5, 8. *all u. is the doom of destiny*, R3 IV, 4, 217.

**Unaware**, inadvertently: *as one that u. hath dropped a precious jewel in the flood*, Ven. 823. *nuzzling in his flank, the loving swine sheathed u. the tusk in his soft groin*, 1116. cf. *Unwares*.

**Unawares**, unexpectedly, by surprise: *Pucelle ... hath wrought this hellish mischief u.* H6A III, 2, 39. *take the great-grown traitor u.* H6C IV, 8, 63. *at u., in the same sense: so we ... at u. may beat down Edward's guard*, H6C IV, 2, 23. *or by his foe surprised at u.* IV, 4, 9. *like vassalage at u. encountering the eye of majesty*, Troil. III, 2, 40 (Q *at unwares*).

**Unbacked**, never mounted, not taught to bear a rider: Ven. 320. Tp. IV, 176.

**Unbaked**, not baked: *whose villanous saffron would have made all the u. and doughy youth of a nation in his colour*, All's IV, 5, 3.

**Unbanded**, having no band: *your bonnet u.* As III, 2, 398.

**Unbar**, to unfasten, to open: *the key to u. these locks*, Cymb. V, 4, 8.

**Unbarbed**, unharnessed, bare: *must I go show them my u. sconce?* Cor. III, 2, 99.

**Unbashful**, shameless: As II, 3, 50.

**Unbated**, 1) undiminished: *doth untread again his tedious measures with the u. fire that he did pace them first*, Merch. II, 6, 11.

2) unblunted (without a button on the point): *you may choose a sword u.* Hml. IV, 7, 139. V, 2, 328.

**Unbattered**, not bruised or injured by blows: *or else my sword with an u. edge I sheathe again undeeded*, Mcb. V, 7, 19.

**Unbecoming**, improper, indecorous: Mcb. III, 1, 13.

**Unbefitting**, unbecoming: *love is full of u. strains*, LLL V, 2, 770.

**Unbegot**, not yet generated: *your children yet unborn and u.* R2 III, 3, 88.

**Unbegotten**, the same: *the yet u. sin of times*, John IV, 3, 54.

**Unbelieved**, not finding credit: *as I, thus wronged, hence u. go*, Meas. V, 119.

**Unbend**, to free from flexure (as a bow); to remit from a strain, to relax: *you do u. your noble strength, to think so brainsickly of things*, Mcb. II, 2, 45. The physical and moral significations joined: *why hast thou gone so far, to be unbent when thou hast ta'en thy stand, the elected deer before thee?* Cymb. III, 4, 111. *a brow unbent* = a brow not knit, not frowning: Lucr. 1509.

**Unbewailed**, not lamented: Ant. III, 6, 85.

**Unbid**, (*únbid*, because placed before the subst.) uninvited, unwelcome: *O u. spite! is sportful Edward come?* H6C V, 1, 18.

**Unbidden**, uninvited: *u. guests are often welcomest when they are gone*, H6A II, 2, 55.

**Unbind**, to untie, to loose: *now am I Dromio and his man unbound*, Err. V, 290 (or = not bound?). *u. my hands*, Shr. II, 4. *unbound the rest*, H4A II, 4, 201. *u. my sons*, Tit. III, 1, 24.

**Unbitted**, unbridled: *our u. lusts*, Oth. I, 3, 335.

**Unbless**, to neglect to make happy; to make unhappy: *thou dost beguile the world, u. some mother*, Sonn. 3, 4. Partic. or adj. *unblessed* or *unblest* = unhappy, cursed, wretched: *every inordinate cup is unblessed*, Oth. II, 3, 311. *your unblest fate hies*, V, 1, 34.

**Unbloodied**, not made bloody: *u. beak*, H6B III, 2, 193.

**Unblowed** (F1) or **Unblown** (the rest of O. Edd.) not blown, not having the bud expanded: *my u. flowers*, R3 IV, 4, 10.

**Unbodied**, not having a corporeal shape: *that u. figure of the thought that gave't surmised shape*, Troil. I, 3, 16.

**Unbolt**, to unfasten, to open: *he shall u. the gates*, Troil. IV, 2, 3. Figuratively, = to open, to reveal: *I will u. to you*, Tim. I, 1, 51.

**Unbolted**, unsifted, coarse: *I will tread this u. villain into mortar*, Lr. II, 2, 71.

**Unbonneted**, having no bonnet on: *u. he runs*, Lr. III, 1, 14. Difficult passage: *my demerits may speak u. to as proud a fortune as this that I have reached*, Oth. I, 2, 23. Stevens: *'unbonneted* may signify, without taking the cap off' (cf. the verb *Bonnet*). The common explanation is: without the addition of patrician or senatorial dignity; the bonnet, as well as the toge, being at Venice a badge of aristocratic honours. But nowhere, not even in those plays, the scene of which is Venice, the word *bonnet* is found in this sense. Perhaps the meaning of *unbonneted* is simply: I may say so with all courtesy and humility; and Othello's words must perhaps be accompanied by a corresponding gesture, as the writing of O. Edd. seems to imply, by placing the word *unbonneted* in a parenthesis.

**Unbookish**, ignorant, unskilled: *his u. jealousy must construe poor Cassio's smiles ... quite in the wrong*, Oth. IV, 1, 102.

**Unborn** (*unbórn*; but when placed before the subst., *únborn*) 1) not born, not brought into life, not existing: *never so much as in a thought u. did I offend your highness*, As I, 3, 53. *the accusation which they have often made against the senate, all cause u.* Cor. III, 1, 129.

2) not yet born, future, to come: *some u. sorrow, ripe in fortune's womb, is coming towards me*, R2 II, 2,

10. III, 3, 88. IV, 322. H4A V, 1, 21. H5 I, 2, 287. Caes. III, 1, 113. Per. IV Prol. 45.

**Unbosom**, to disclose, to reveal: *their several counsels they u. shall*, LLL V, 2, 141.

**Unbound**, not bound; with a quibble: *thy precious book of love, this u. lover, to beautify him, only lacks a cover*, Rom. I, 3, 87. cf. Err. V, 290.

**Unbounded**, unlimited, infinite: H8 IV, 2, 34.

**Unbowed**, not bent: *with stiff u. knee*, H6B III, 1, 16. In a moral sense, = not put under the yoke, not subjugated: *bend the dukedom yet u. to most ignoble stooping*, Tp. I, 2, 115.

**Unbraced**, loosened, ungirt, unbuttoned: *thus u. have bared my bosom to the thunder-stone*, Caes. I, 3, 48. *to walk u. and suck up the humours of the dank morning*, II, 1, 262. *with his doublet all u.* Hml. II, 1, 78.

**Unbraided**, perhaps = not counterfeit, sterling, but probably the clown's blunder for *embroidered: has he any u. wares?* Wint. IV, 4, 204.

**Unbreathed**, unexercised, unpractised: *have toiled their u. memories*, Mids. V, 74 (*únbreathed*, because placed before the subst.).

**Unbred**, unbegot, unborn: *hear this, thou age u.; ere you were born was beauty's summer dead*, Sonn. 104, 13.

**Unbreeched**, wearing no breeches: Wint. I, 2, 155.

**Unbridle**, to free from the bridle, to let loose: *u. all the sparks of nature, to quit this horrid act*, Lr. III, 7, 86 (Ff and M. Edd. *enkindle*).

**Unbridled**, unruly: *rash and u. boy*, All's III, 2, 30. *my thoughts were like u. children, grown too headstrong for their mother*, Troil. III, 2, 130.

**Unbroke**, not broken, not violated: R2 IV, 215.

**Unbruised**, unhurt, undamaged: *live u. and love my cousin*, Ado V, 4, 112. *helmets all u.* John II, 254. *the fresh and yet u. Greeks*, Troil. Prol. 14. *too full of the wars' surfeits, to go rove with one that's yet u.* Cor. IV, 1, 47. *where u. youth with unstuffed brain doth couch his limbs, there golden sleep doth reign*, Rom. II, 3, 37.

**Unbuckle**, to loose from buckles, to unfasten, to take off (clothes): *u., u.* Wint. IV, 4, 661. = to pluck off in a scuffle: *we have been down together in my sleep, —ing helms, fisting each other's throat*, Cor. IV, 5, 131. *he that —s this, till we do please to daff't for our repose, shall hear a storm*, Ant. IV, 4, 12.

**Unbuild**, to raze, to destroy: *to u. the city and to lay all flat*, Cor. III, 1, 198.

**Unburden**, see *Unburthen*.

**Unburied**, not interred: Cor. III, 3, 122. Tit. I, 87.

**Unburnt**, not consumed by fire: Cor. V, 1, 27.

**Unburthen**, to unload, to free from a burden: *while we —ed crawl toward death*, Lr. I, 1, 42. Figuratively, = to disclose (what lies heavy on the mind): *to u. all my plots and purposes*, Merch. I, 1, 133. *Buckingham —s with his tongue the envious load that lies upon his heart*, H6B III, 1, 156.

**Unbutton**, to loose any thing buttoned: H4A I, 2, 3. Lr. III, 4, 114.

**Unbuttoned**, not fastened with buttons: *your sleeve u., your shoe untied*, As III, 2, 399.

**Uncapable**, incapable (q. v.); not susceptible; unable; with *of: u. of pity*, Merch. IV, 1, 5. *making him u. of Othello's place*, Oth. IV, 2, 235.

**Uncape**, probably = to uncouple (hounds): *I'll warrant we'll unkennel the fox. Let me stop this way*

*first. So, now u.* Wiv. III, 3, 176 (Warburton: to dig out the fox when earthed; Steevens: to turn the fox out of the bag).*

**Uncase**, to undress: *Pompey is —ing for the combat*, LLL V, 2, 707. *u. thee*, Shr. I, 1, 212.

**Uncaught**, not caught, not taken: Lr. II, 1, 59. Ant. IV, 8, 18.

**Uncertain** (cf. *Incertain*) 1) doubtful, not to be relied on: *the u. glory of an April day*, Gent. I, 3, 85. *u. life and sure death*, All's II, 3, 20. *the friends ... u.* H4A II, 3, 12. *u. way of gain*, R3 IV, 2, 64. *the end of war's u.* Cor. V, 3, 141. *in life's u. voyage*, Tim. V, 1, 205. *u. favour*, Cymb. III, 3, 64.

2) not knowing what to think or do: *the u. sickly appetite*, Sonn. 147, 4. *be not u.* Wint. I, 2, 441. *the people will remain u.* Cor. V, 6, 17. With *of: u. of the issue*, H4A I, 1, 61.

**Uncertainly**, not distinctly, not so as to convey certain knowledge: *her certain sorrow writ u.* Lucr. 1311.

**Uncertainty**, 1) want of reliability; doubtfulness, precariousness (of things); inconsistency, inconstancy (of persons): *our fortunes ... which now we hold at much u.* H4A I, 3, 299. *and here remain with your u.* Cor. III, 3, 124.

2) something not certainly and exactly known: *until I know this sure u.* Err. II, 2, 187.

**Unchain**, to let loose: *u. your spirits now*, H6A V, 3, 31.

**Unchanging**, unalterable: *thy face is, visard-like, u.* H6C I, 4, 116.

**Uncharge**, to acquit of blame, not to accuse: *even his mother shall u. the practice and call it accident*, Hml. IV, 7, 68.

**Uncharged**, unassailed: *open your u. ports*, Tim. V, 4, 55.

**Uncharitably**, not with Christian love and kindness: R3 I, 3, 275.

**Uncharmed**, not worked upon, not fascinated by magic power: *from love's weak childish bow she lives u.* Rom. I, 1, 217 (the surreptitious Q1 and M. Edd. *unharmed*).

**Unchary**, heedless: *laid mine honour too u. on't*, Tw. III, 4, 222 (M. Edd. *out for on't*).

**Unchaste** (*únchaste* or *unchaste*; always before the subst.) not pure, lewd: Wiv. V, 5, 100. All's IV, 3, 22. Lr. I, 1, 231. Cymb. V, 5, 284.

**Unchecked**, 1) unrestrained: *the laws ... have u. theft*, Tim. IV, 3, 447.

2) not contradicted: *it lives there u. that Antonio hath a ship wrecked*, Merch. III, 1, 2.

**Uncheerful**, joyless, ungenial: *u. night*, Lucr. 1024.

**Unchild**, to deprive of children: *he hath widowed and —ed many a one*, Cor. V, 6, 153.

**Uncivil**, ill-mannered, impolite, rude: *u. outrages*, Gent. V, 4, 17. *that rude u. touch*, 60. *this u. rule*, Tw. II, 3, 132. *this is as u. as strange*, III, 4, 277. *this u. and unjust extent against thy peace*, IV, 1, 57. *u. lady*, V, 115. *with civil and u. arms*, R2 III, 3, 102. *the u. kerns*, H6B III, 1, 310. cf. *Incivil*.

**Unclaimed**, not claimed, not pretended to: *my taxing like a wild-goose flies, u. of any man*, As II, 7, 87.

**Unclasp**, 1) tr. to open what is shut with clasps: *I have —ed to thee the book even of my secret soul*, Tw.

I, 4, 13. *I will u. a secret book*, H4A I, 3, 188. *u. the tables of their thoughts*, Troil. IV, 5, 60.

Hence = to disclose, to reveal: *in her bosom I'll u. my heart*, Ado I, 1, 325. *he ... to my kingly guest —ed my practice*, Wint. III, 2, 168.

2) absol. to leave joining hands: *u.* Per. II, 3, 107.

**Uncle,** subst. the brother of one's father or mother: Tp. I, 2, 66. 77. Wiv. III, 4, 38. 39. 41. 66. Err. V, 368. Ado I, 1, 18. 40. II, 1, 15. 66. 353. II, 3, 173. IV, 1, 114. 115. V, 2, 97. 106. V, 4, 75. Merch. I, 3, 72. As I, 1, 116. I, 2, 9. 286. I, 3, 44. 52. 109. III, 2, 362. 387. V, 4, 32 etc. etc. The name sometimes following with *of*: *u. of Exeter*, H5 I, 2, 39. *—s of Gloster and of Winchester*, H6A III, 1, 65. *u. of Winchester*, H6B I, 1, 56.

**Uncle,** a verb coined by York in R2 II, 3, 87: *grace me no grace, nor u. me no uncle;* i. e. do not call me uncle.

**Unclean** (before the subst. *únclean*, behind *uncleán*) foul, dirty: As III, 3, 36. All's V, 2, 22. Rom. I Prol. 4. In a moral sense, = impure: Wiv. IV, 4, 57. All's I, 1, 48.

**Uncleanliness,** impurity or indecency: Meas. II, 1, 82 (Elbow's speech).

**Uncleanly,** foul, filthy: *the very u. flux of a cat*, As III, 2, 70. *the u. savours of a slaughterhouse*, John IV, 3, 112. In a moral sense, = indecent, unbecoming: *courtesy would be u., if courtiers were shepherds*, As III, 2, 51. *u. scruples fear not you*, John IV, 1, 7. *some u. apprehension ... in session sit with meditations lawful*, Oth. III, 3, 139.

**Uncleanness,** impurity, defilement: Lucr. 193. Meas. II, 4, 54.

**Uncle-father,** one that is at the same time uncle and father of the same person: Hml. II, 2, 393.

**Unclew,** see *Unclue.*

**Unclog,** to disencumber, to unload: *it would u. my heart of what lies heavy to't*, Cor. IV, 2, 47.

**Unclue** (O. Edd. *unclew*), to unwind; metaphorically, = to leave bare, to ruin (?): *if I should pay you for't as 'tis extolled, it would u. me quite*, Tim. I, 1, 168.

**Uncoined:** *take a fellow of plain and u. constancy, for he perforce must do thee right, because he hath not the gift to woo in other places*, H5 V, 2, 161. Explained by some as = not counterfeit, real, true; by others as implying that Katharine was the first woman that ever made an impression on Henry. But what follows seems to show, that by *uncoined constancy* a constancy is meant which has not the current stamp on it (viz insinuating words etc.) and, being therefore unfit for circulation, must for ever remain in one and the same place.

**Uncolted,** deprived of one's horse; a word coined by Prince Henry for the sake of a pun: H4A II, 2, 42.

**Uncomeliness,** indecency: *gave such orderly and well-behaved reproof to all u.* Wiv. II, 1, 60.

**Uncomfortable,** cheerless, joyless: *u. time*, Rom. IV, 5, 60.

**Uncompassionate,** pitiless: Gent. III, 1, 231.

**Uncomprehensive,** incomprehensible, mysterious: *finds bottom in the u. deeps*, Troil. III, 3, 198.

**Unconfinable,** unrestrainable, not to be kept in check by any considerations: *thou u. baseness*, Wiv. II, 2, 21.

**Unconfirmed,** inexperienced, raw: *I wonder at it. That shows thou art u.* Ado III, 3, 124. *after his undressed, unpolished, uneducated, unpruned, untrained, or rather, unlettered, or ratherest, u. fashion*, LLL IV, 2, 19.

**Unconquered,** not vanquished or subdued: Lucr. 408. H6A IV, 2, 32. H6B IV, 10, 69.

**Unconsidered,** not attended to, not thought of: *a snapper-up of u. trifles*, Wint. IV, 3, 26. *not u. leave your honour*, H8 I, 2, 15.

**Unconstant,** unsteady, fickle: Shr. IV, 2, 14. John III, 1, 243. H6C V, 1, 102. Lr. I, 1, 304.

**Unconstrained,** free from constraint; 1) voluntary: *with free and u. soul*, Ado IV, 1, 25. *he did it u.* H6C I, 1, 143. 2) not put on in opposition to nature and inclination, and therefore imposing no constraint: *playing patient sports in u. gyves*, Compl. 242 (cf. Cymb. V, 4, 15).

**Uncontemned,** not despised: H8 III, 2, 10.

**Uncontrolled,** unchecked, unrestrained; and hence irresistible: *never did captive with a freer heart ... embrace his golden u. enfranchisement*, R2 I, 3, 90.* *his u. crest*, Ven. 104. *my u. tide turns not*, Lucr. 645.

**Uncorrected,** not set right, not kept in order: *the even mead ... wanting the scythe, all u., rank*, H5 V, 2, 50.

**Uncounted,** innumerable: *the blunt monster with u. heads* (i. e. the multitude) H4B Ind. 18.

**Uncouple,** to loose hounds from their couples, to set loose: *u. in the western valley; let them go*, Mids. IV, 1, 112. *u. here*, Tit. II, 2, 3. With *at*: *u. at the timorous flying hare*, Ven. 674.

**Uncourteous,** not complaisant, uncivil: Tw. V, 369.

**Uncouth** (úncouth; always before the subst.), properly = not known, not familiar, strange, and hence (= the German *unheimlich*) perplexing, filling the soul with dismal apprehensions: *what u. ill event hath thee befallen, that thou dost trembling stand?* Lucr. 1598. *if this u. forest yield any thing savage*, As II, 6, 6. *I am surprised with an u. fear*, Tit. II, 3, 211.

**Uncover,** to remove the cover: *u., dogs, and lap*, Tim. III, 6, 95.

**Uncovered,** not covered, open, bare: *with public accusation, u. slander, unmitigated rancour*, Ado IV, 1, 307. *stand u. to the vulgar groom*, H6B IV, 1, 128 (bare-headed). *in thy best robes u. on the bier thou shalt be borne*, Rom. IV, 1, 110 (cf. Hml. IV, 5, 164: *they bore him barefaced on the bier*). *to answer with thy u. body this extremity of the skies*, Lr. III, 4, 106 (unclothed, naked).

**Uncropped,** not plucked: *a fresh u. flower*, All's V, 3, 327.

**Uncrossed,** not struck out, not cancelled, not erased: *such gain the cap of him that makes 'em fine, but keeps his book u.* Cymb. III, 3, 26 (Collier: the tradesman's book was crossed when the account was paid).

**Uncrown,** to deprive of the crown, to dethrone: H6C III, 3, 232. IV, 1, 111.

**Unction,** a salve: *lay not that flattering u. to your soul*, Hml. III, 4, 145. *I bought an u. of a mountebank so mortal*, IV, 7, 142.

**Unctious** (M. Edd. *unctuous*) fat, oily: *with liquorish draughts and morsels u.* Tim. IV, 3, 195.

**Uncuckolded,** not made a cuckold: Ant. I, 2, 76.

**Uncurable,** incurable; irremediable: H6B III, 1, 286. V, 2, 86.

**Uncurbable**, unrestrainable: Ant. II, 2, 67.

**Uncurbed**, not refrained, not kept back: *with frank and with u. plainness tell us the Dauphin's mind*, H5 I, 2, 244.

**Uncurl**, to fall from a curled state, to become straight: *my fleece of woolly hair that now —s even as an adder when she doth unroll*, Tit. II, 3, 34.

**Uncurrent**, 1) not having currency, not passing in common payment: *oft good turns are shuffled off with such u. pay*, Tw. III, 3, 16 (viz with thanks). *pray God, your voice, like a piece of u. gold, be not cracked within the ring*, Hml. II, 2, 448.

2) objectionable: *with what encounter so u. I have strained to appear thus*, Wint. III, 2, 50.

**Uncurse**, to free from curses uttered: *again u. their souls*, R2 III, 2, 137.

**Undaunted**, fearless, intrepid: H6A I, 1, 127. III, 2, 99. V, 5, 70. Mcb. I, 7, 73.

**Undeaf**, to free from deafness: *my death's sad tale may yet u. his ear*, R2 II, 1, 16.

**Undeck**, to divest, to undress: *to u. the pompous body of a king*, R2 IV, 250.

**Undeeded**, not signalized by action, having done nothing: *my sword ... I sheathe u.* Mcb. V, 7, 20.

**Under**, prepos. below, beneath; so as to be lower than or covered by; f. i.: *u. her other* (arm) *was the tender boy*, Ven. 32. *u. whose brim the gaudy sun would peep*, 1088. *he learned but surety-like to write for me u. that bond*, Sonn. 134, 8. *the mariners all u. hatches stowed*, Tp. I, 2, 230. *I saw him beat the surges u. him*, II, 1, 114. *creep u. his gaberdine*, II, 2, 40. 115. *merrily shall I live now u. the blossom*, V, 94. *asleep u. the hatches*, 99. *you may bear it u. a cloak*, Gent. III, 1, 130. *u. the duke's table*, IV, 4, 19. *lie u. Mount Pelion*, Wiv. II, 1, 81. *u. the shade of melancholy boughs*, As II, 7, 111. *u. heaven's eye*, Err. II, 1, 16 etc. etc. Placed after the subst.: *her lily hand her rosy cheek lies u.* Lucr. 386.

Modifications of the same notion: *born u. a charitable star*, All's I, 1, 204. 206. 207. 210. *born u. Taurus*, Tw. I, 3, 147 (below, and hence influenced by). *now is the jerkin u. the line*, Tp. IV, 236. *when the false Troyan u. sail was seen*, Mids. I, 1, 174. *u. that colour* (= ensign) *am I come to scale thy fort*, Lucr. 481. *were beauty u. twenty locks kept fast*, Ven. 575. *each trifle u. truest bars to thrust*, Sonn. 48, 2. *keep thy friend u. thy own life's key*, All's I, 1, 76. *had he Duncan's sons u. his key*, Mcb. III, 6, 18. *u. the degree of a squire*, Wiv. III, 4, 48. *matched in mouth like bells, each u. each*, Mids. IV, 1, 129.

Denoting a state of being loaded, or oppressed, or overwhelmed by: *u. whose sharp fangs ... doth lie an image*, Ven. 663. *so u. his insulting falchion lies Lucretia*, Lucr. 509. *falls u. the blow of thralled discontent*, Sonn. 124, 7. *u. my burthen groaned*, Tp. I, 2, 156. *fainting u. the pleasing punishment*, Err. I, 1, 46. *I shall perish u. device and practice*, H8 I, 1, 204. *none stands u. more calumnious tongues*, V, 1, 113. *sinking u. them* (burthens) Cor. II, 1, 269. *to groan and sweat u. the business*, Caes. IV, 1, 22. *an exploit ... u. the which he shall not choose but fall*, Hml. IV, 7, 66. *I fall u. this plot*, Ant. IV, 12, 49 etc. Similarly: *u. him my genius is rebuked*, Mcb. III, 1, 55. *my better cunning faints u. his chance*, Ant. II, 3, 35. cf. also the following expressions: *if I could speak so wisely u. an arrest*, Meas. I, 2, 135. *which else would stand*

*u. grievous imposition*, 194. *he must die. U. your sentence?* II, 4, 37. *were I u. the terms of death*, 100. *if this sweet lady lie not guiltless here u. some biting error*, Ado IV, 1, 172. *u. your hard construction must I sit*, Tw. III, 1, 126. *u. this conjuration speak*, H5 I, 2, 29. *your jewel hath suffered u. praise*, Tim. I, 1, 165.

Denoting the predicament, or the semblance and form of a state or action: *u. whose* (love's) *simple semblance he* (lust) *hath fed upon fresh beauty*, Ven. 795. *u. what colour he commits this ill*, Lucr. 476. *u. the colour of commending him I have access ...*, Gent. IV, 2, 3. *what's brought to pass u. the profession of fortunetelling*, Wiv. IV, 2, 184. *it may be I go u. that title*, Ado II, 1, 212. *which indeed is not u. white and black*, V, 1, 313 (Dogberry's speech). *unless she do it u. this excuse*, Merch. II, 4, 37. *he does it u. name of perfect love*, Shr. IV, 3, 12. *all these engines of lust are not the things they go u.* All's III, 5, 22. *what your highness suffered u. that shape*, H5 IV, 8, 56. *u. pretence to see*, H8 I, 1, 177. *yet go we u. our opinion still that we have better men*, Troil. I, 3, 383. *like those that u. hot ardent zeal would set whole realms on fire*, Tim. III, 3, 33. *this villain of mine comes u. the prediction*, Lr. I, 2, 119 etc.

Denoting inferiority or subordination: *to come u. one body's hand*, Wiv. I, 4, 105. *profit very greatly u. you*, LLL IV, 2, 78. *I have eyes u. my service*, Wint. IV, 2, 40. *as we, u. heaven, are supreme head, so u. Him that great supremacy ... we will uphold*, John III, 1, 155. *I am, sir, u. the king, in some authority*, H4B V, 3, 116. *u. his master's command transporting a sum of money*, H5 IV, 1, 158. *substitutes u. the lordly monarch of the north*, H6A V, 3, 6. *the noble senate, who, u. the gods, keeps you in awe*, Cor. I, 1, 191 (= next to the Gods). *to be commanded u. Cominius*, 267. *would prevail u. the service of a child as soon*, Ant. III, 13, 24. *my youth I spent much u. him*, Cymb. III, 1, 71.

Denoting protection and authorisation: *and u. thee their poetry disperse*, Sonn. 78, 4. *as u. privilege of age to brag*, Ado V, 1, 60. *u. whose* (God's) *warrant I impeach thy wrong*, John II, 116. *u. whose countenance we steal*, H4A I, 2, 33. *u. the countenance and confederacy of Lady Eleanor*, H6B II, 1, 168. *am boldened u. your promised pardon*, H8 I, 2, 56. *proceeded u. your hands and seals*, II, 4, 222 (see above: John III, 1, 155. H4B V, 3, 116. Cor. I, 1, 191). cf. the phrases *u. allowance*, *u. your correction*, *u. favour*, *u. leave*, *u. your patience*, *u. pardon*: Lr. II, 2, 112. Meas. II, 2, 10. Tim. III, 5, 40. Caes. III, 2, 86. Tit. II, 3, 66. LLL IV, 2, 103. Caes. IV, 3, 213. Lr. I, 4, 365 (see the resp. articles).

**Under**, adv. below: *sealed u. for another*, Merch. I, 2, 89. *to bring u.* = to bring down, to bring low: *the least of all these maladies ... brings beauty u.* Ven. 746. Similarly: *the wars have so kept you u.* All's I, 1, 209, an expression used by way of quibbling, like Launce's grammatical observation: *stand u. and understand is all one*, Gent. II, 5, 33.

**Under**, adj. lower; 1) infernal: *a spirit raised from depth of u. ground*, H6B I, 2, 79. II, 1, 174 (M. Edd. *underground*). *with the spleen of all the u. fiends*, Cor IV, 5, 98. 2) sublunary: *each u. eye doth homage to hi new appearing light*, Sonn. 7, 2. *thou beacon to this u globe*, Lr. II, 2, 170 (cf. *this beneath world*, Tim. I, 1, 44). *the u.* substituted, with great probability, by M. Edd. for *yond* in Meas. IV, 3, 93: *ere twice the sun hath made his journal greeting to the u. generation.*

**Underbear,** 1) to guard, to face, to trim: *skirts round underborne with a bluish tinsel,* Ado III, 4, 21.*

2) to bear, to endure: *leave those woes alone which I alone am bound to u.* John III, 1, 65. *with the craft of smiles and patient —ing of his fortune,* R2 I, 4, 29.

**Undercrest,** to wear as on the crest: *I mean ... at all times to u. your good addition to the fairness of my power,* Cor. I, 9, 72.

**Underfoot,** so as to be trodden on: *throw it u.* Shr. V, 2, 122 (most M. Edd. in two words).

**Undergo** (impf. *underwent,* partic. *undergone*) 1) to endure with firmness, to sustain without fainting, to bear up against: *some kinds of baseness are nobly —ne,* Tp. III, 1, 3. *—es, more goddess-like than wife-like, such assaults as would take in some virtue,* Cymb. III, 2, 7. Absol.: *which raised in me an —ing stomach,* Tp. I, 2, 157.

2) to experience; a) in a bad sense, = to suffer, to bear: *than you should such dishonour u.* Tp. III, 1, 27. *Claudio —es my challenge,* Ado V, 2, 57. *much danger do I u. for thee,* John IV, 1, 134. *is't not I that u. this charge?* V, 2, 100. *that you a world of curses u.* H4A I, 3, 164. *for whom these shames ye underwent,* 179. *I will not u. this sneap without reply,* H4B II, 1, 133.

b) in a good sense, = to partake of, to enjoy: *to u. such ample grace and honour,* Meas. I, 1, 24. *as infinite (virtues) as man may u.* Hml. I, 4, 34.

3) to take upon one's self, to undertake, to perform: *what dangerous action would I not u.* Gent. V, 4, 42. *thrice blessed they that master so their blood to u. such maiden pilgrimage,* Mids. I, 1, 75. *any thing that my ability may u.* Wint. II, 3, 164. *if you will u. this flight,* IV, 4, 554. *how able such a work to u.* H4B I, 3, 54. *to u. any difficulty imposed,* Troil. III, 2, 86. *you u. too strict a paradox, striving to make an ugly deed look fair,* Tim. III, 5, 24. *to u. with me an enterprise of consequence,* Caes. I, 3, 123. *I am the master of my speeches, and would u. what's spoken,* Cymb. I, 4, 153. *to u. those employments ... with a serious industry,* III, 5, 110.

**Under-ground,** writing of some M. Edd. in H6B I, 2, 79: *a spirit raised from depth of u.* (i. e. the space beneath the surface of the earth); not hyphened in O. Edd.; cf. II, 1, 174.

**Underhand,** 1) private: *have by u. means laboured to dissuade him from it, but he is resolute,* As I, 1, 146.

2) fraudulent, insidious: *all that have miscarried by u. corrupted foul injustice,* R3 V, 1, 6.

**Under-hangman,** a subordinate hangman: Cymb. II, 3, 135.

**Under-honest,** too little considering what is becoming; a word used antithetically: *we think him over-proud and u.* Troil. II, 3, 133.

**Underlings,** mean fellows: *the fault is ... in ourselves, that we are u.* Caes. I, 2, 141.

**Undermine,** to sap: All's I, 1, 130. Troil. II, 3, 9. Figuratively: H6B I, 2, 98.

**Underminer,** a sapper: All's I, 1, 131.

**Underneath,** prepos. under, beneath: *u. thy black all-hiding cloak,* Lucr. 801. *u. that consecrated roof,* Tw. IV, 3, 25. *till these rebels come u. the yoke of government,* H4B IV, 4, 10. *the strawberry grows u. the nettle,* H5 I, 1, 60. *if u. the standard of the French she carry armour,* H6A II, 1, 23. *u. her wings,* V, 3, 57. *u. an alehouse' paltry sign,* H6B V, 2, 67. *u. the*

*belly of their steeds,* H6C II, 3, 20. *bruised u. the yoke of tyranny,* R3 V, 2, 2. *I heard a child cry u. a wall,* Tit. V, 1, 24. *u. the grove of sycamore,* Rom. I, 1, 128. *u. whose arm an envious.thrust from Tybalt hit the life of stout Mercutio,* III, 1, 172. *Tiber trembled u. her banks,* Caes. I, 1, 50. *groaning u. this age's yoke,* I, 2, 61.

**Underneath,** adv. below, under it: *and text u., 'here dwells Benedick'* etc. Ado V, 1, 185.

**Underpeep,** to cast a look under: *the flame ... would u. her lids,* Cymb. II, 2, 20.

**Underpraise,** a word not used by the poet, but apparently thought of by the jeweller in mistaking the words of Timon: *your jewel hath suffered under praise. What, my lord! dispraise?* Tim. I, 1, 165.

**Underprize,** to undervalue: Merch. III, 2, 128.

**Underprop,** to support, to uphold: *which of them both should u. her fame,* Lucr. 53. *what penny hath Rome borne ... to u. this action?* John V, 2, 99. *here am I left to u. his land, who, weak with age, cannot support myself,* R2 II, 2, 82.

**Under-skinker,** an under-drawer, one that serves liquors: H4A II, 4, 26.

**Understand,** (impf. and partic. *understood*) 1) to perceive the meaning of, to comprehend: Tp. II, 1, 268. Gent. II, 5, 25. 28. 31. 33. Wiv. I, 1, 140. 216. 219. II, 2, 133. 251. Err. II, 1, 49. 54. II, 2, 153. IV, 3, 21. Ado V, 1, 234. LLL IV, 2, 101. V, 1, 158. V, 2, 762. 764. Mids. III, 2, 236. Merch. I, 2, 74. I, 3, 16. III, 2, 7. III, 5, 63. As III, 3, 12. Shr. I, 1, 240. All's I, 1, 69. 224. II, 2, 72. II, 3, 198. IV, 1, 4. 5. 81. IV, 3, 123. Tw. I, 5, 286. III, 1, 60. 89. 90. Wint. I, 2, 229. III, 2, 81. IV, 4, 684. John III, 3, 63. IV, 2, 237. R2 V, 3, 124. H4A III, 1, 119. 201. 205. 233. H5 I, 2, 266. III, 6, 52. V, 2, 135. 205. H6B I, 4, 75. H8 V, 3, 72. Troil. III, 1, 29. IV, 5, 240. V, 10, 11. Cor. IV, 7, 17. Tit. III, 1, 143. Tim. I, 1, 51. IV, 3, 316. Caes. I, 2, 285. Mcb. I, 3, 43. III, 4, 122 (*augurs and understood relations*). Hml. I, 3, 96 (*you do not u. yourself so clearly*). III, 2, 365. IV, 1, 2. IV, 2, 24. V, 1, 41. V, 2, 131. Lr. I, 2, 43. I, 4, 260. II, 4, 100. Oth. I, 2, 52. IV, 2, 32. V, 2, 153. Ant. V, 2, 75. Cymb. II, 3, 80. Per. IV, 2, 133.

The gerund substantively: *their —ing begins to swell,* Tp. V, 79 (they begin to perceive, to become conscious of, their situation). *hast thou no —ings for thy cases,* Wiv. IV, 1, 72 (Evans' speech). *for thy more sweet —ing,* LLL I, 1, 267 (that thou mayst better understand. Armado's letter). *to thy better —ing,* As V, 1, 57. H5 V, 2, 126. H6C II, 6, 60. Hml. I, 2, 250 (*give it an —ing, but no tongue*). II, 2, 9 (*from the —ing of himself*).

Absol., = to have the faculty of perception and discernment, to be wise and judicious: *now let us u.* Wiv. I, 1, 138 (Evans' speech). *and u. again like honest men,* H8 I, 3, 32. The partic. adjectively: *was this taken by any —ing pate but thine?* Wint. I, 2, 223. *will leave us never an —ing friend,* H8 Prol. 22.

The gerund substantively = intellectual faculty, judgment: *a man's good wit seconded with the forward child —ing,* As III, 3, 14. *I am only old in judgment and —ing,* H4B I, 2, 215. *I had thought I had had men of some —ing and wisdom of my council,* H8 V, 3, 135. *an —ing simple and unschooled,* Hml. I, 2, 97.

2) to interpret mentally, to conceive with respect to meaning: *figuring that they their passions likewise lent me of grief and blushes, aptly understood in blood*

*less white and the encrimsoned mood,* Compl. 200. *what must we u. by this* (a bloody napkin)? As IV, 3, 95. *on the winking of authority to u. a law,* John IV, 2, 212.

3) to hear, to be told, to learn: *—ing that the curate and yourself are good at such eruptions,* LLL V, 1, 119. *you must u. he goes but to see a noise,* Mids. III, 1, 93. *I u. moreover upon the Rialto he hath a third at Mexico,* Merch. I, 3, 19. *your grace shall u. that ... I am very sick,* IV, 1, 150. *give me your hand and let me all your fortunes u.* As II, 7, 200. *u. you this of me,* Shr. I, 2, 259. *my suit, as I do u., you know,* All's V, 3, 160. *but by bad courses may be understood that their events can never fall out good,* R2 II, 1, 213. *as more at large your grace shall u.* H6B II, 1, 177. *you shall u. from me her mind,* R3 IV, 4, 429. *the king shall u. it presently,* H8 V, 2, 10. *u. more clear,* Troil. IV, 5, 165. *he —s you are in arms,* Tit. V, 1, 158. *as I u. how all things go,* Tim. III, 6, 20. *you shall u. what hath befallen,* Oth. V, 2, 307. *since my landing I have understood your lord has ...,* Per. I, 3, 34.

*To give to u.* = to tell, to inform: *if you give me directly to u. you have prevailed,* Cymb. I, 4, 171. *here I give to u.* Per. III, 2, 68. *to be given to u.* = to be told, to be informed: Merch. II, 8, 7. As I, 1, 130. H4A IV, 4, 11. *to have to u.* = to learn, to be informed: *and as I further have to u., is new committed to the Bishop of York,* H6C IV, 4, 10. *to let u.* = to tell, to inform: Wiv. II, 2, 171. Meas. III, 2, 144. Shr. IV, 2, 115. H6C V, 4, 33. *to make u.,* in the same sense: Meas. III, 2, 255. Tim. II, 2, 43.

4) to know: *we u. it, and thank heaven for it,* All's II, 3, 71. *he takes on him to u. so much,* Tw. I, 5, 149. *you are well understood to be a perfecter giber,* Cor. II, 1, 90. *to let* and *to make u.* = to let know: *to make you u. this in a manifested effect, I crave but four days' respite,* Meas. IV, 2, 169. *and let ourselves again but u. that as it more concerns the Turk than Rhodes, so may he with more facile question bear it,* Oth. I, 3, 21.

The gerund substantively = knowledge: *the assault that Angelo hath made to you, fortune hath conveyed to my —ing,* Meas. III, 1, 190. *I speak as my —ing instructs me,* Wint. I, 1, 20. *I speak in —ing; you are, I know it,* Lr. IV, 5, 28.

The partic. adjectively: *or nicely charge your—ing soul with opening titles miscreate,* H5 I, 2, 15 (= knowing better).

5) For the sake of quibbling, in a quite physical sense, = to stand under sth.: *my staff —s me,* Gent. II, 5, 28; cf. *my legs do better u. me than I u. what you mean,* Tw. III, 1, 89. *I scarce could u. it,* Err. II, 1, 49.

**Understanding,** subst. see *Understand.*

**Undertake** (impf. *undertook;* partic. *undertook:* Merch. II, 4, 7. Oth. V, 2, 311. *underta'en:* Wint. III, 2, 79) 1) to take upon one's self; a) to assume: *his name and credit shall you u.* Shr. IV, 2, 106.

b) to have to do with: *you'll u. her no more,* Wiv. III, 5, 127. *I would not u. her in this company,* Tw. I. 3, 61. *Sir Nicholas Vaux, who —s you to your end,* H8 II, 1, 97 (takes charge of you). *it is not fit your lordship should u. every companion that you give offence to,* Cymb. II, 1, 29 (give him satisfaction). *for this twelvemonth she'll not u. a married life,* Per. II, 5, 3.

c) to engage one's self to, to charge one's self with, to promise to perform (German: *übernehmen*); with an accus.: *—s them* (quarrels) *with a most Christian-like*

*fear,* Ado II, 3, 199. *you must needs play Pyramus. Well, I will u. it,* Mids. I, 2, 92. *you will be schoolmaster and u. the teaching of the maid,* Shr. I, 1, 197. *I undertook it* (to tender a petition) All's V, 3, 132. *to u. the business for us,* Wint. IV, 4, 836. *your beauty, which did haunt me in my sleep to u. the death of all the world, so I might live one hour in your sweet bosom,* R3 I, 2, 123 (i. e. to charge my conscience with the death of all the world). *since first he undertook this cause of Rome,* Tit. I, 31. *and do u. these present wars against the Ottomites,* Oth. I, 3, 234. *the one of them imports the death of Cassio to be undertook by Roderigo,* V, 2, 311. *wherefore then didst u. it?* Cymb. III, 4, 105. *full weak to u. our wars against the Britons,* III, 7, 5.

With an inf.: *then you must u. to slander him,* Gent. III, 2, 38. *will u. to woo curst Katharine,* Shr. I, 2, 184. *which you hear him so confidently u. to do,* All's III, 6, 22. *will you u. to betray the Florentine?* IV, 3, 326. *I'll show it the king and u. to be her advocate,* Wint. II, 2, 38. *what you have underta'en to do,* III, 2, 79. *who undertook to sit and watch by you,* H4B IV, 5, 53. *I'll u. to make thee Henry's queen,* H6A V, 3, 117. *will they u. to do me good?* H6B I, 2, 77. *I'll u. to land them on our coast,* H6C III, 3, 205. *I'll go to him and u. to bring him where he shall answer,* Cor. III, 1, 324. *I will u. all these to teach,* Per. IV, 6, 196.

d) to warrant, to answer for, to guarantee: *that strong-bonded oath that shall prefer and u. my troth,* Compl. 280. *I will u. your ben venuto,* LLL IV, 2, 163. *those two counties I will u. your grace shall well and quietly enjoy,* H6A V, 3, 158. *those ... I'll u. may see away their shilling richly,* H8 Prol. 12. *on mine honour dare I u. for good Lord Titus' innocence,* Tit. I, 436.

2) to attempt, to do, to perform; absol. (= to act, to be active): *it is the cowish terror of his spirit that dares not u.* Lr. IV, 2, 13. *I will beseech the virtuous Desdemona to u. for me,* Oth. III, 3, 337. *either he so —ing, or they so suffering,* Cymb. IV, 2, 142. With an accus.: *how I may u. a journey to ...,* Gent. II, 7, 6. 60. *I will u. one of Hercules' labours,* Ado II, 1, 380. *and better in my mind not undertook,* Merch. II, 4, 7. All's III, 6, 76. 94. IV, 1, 37. Tw. III, 1, 119. III, 4, 272. John III, 3, 56. R2 II, 2, 145. H4A II, 3, 7. H6C II, 6, 101. R3 I, 4, 197. V, 3, 42. Troil. III, 3, 36. Cor. V, 1, 47. Rom. IV, 1, 73. Hml. IV, 7, 64. 125. Per. I, 1, 2.

**Undertaker,** one who takes a business upon himself, charges himself with sth.: *for Cassio, let me be his u.* Oth. IV, 1, 224 (let me take charge of him, dispatch him. German: *ich will ihn übernehmen.* cf. *Undertake* 1 b). Absolutely, = one who makes any thing his own business, a meddler: *nay, if you be an u., I am for you,* Tw. III, 4, 349.

**Undertaking,** 1) that which one takes on himself and promises to perform; engagement: *nor nothing monstrous neither? Nothing but our —s; when we vow to weep seas* etc. Troil. III, 2, 83.

2) beginning, attempt, enterprise: Meas. III, 2, 239. All's IV, 3, 59. Wint. II, 2, 44. Troil. II, 2, 131. Hml. II, 1, 104.

**Undervalued,** with *to,* = inferior in value to: *her name is Portia, nothing u. to Cato's daughter, Brutus' Portia,* Merch. I, 1, 165. *silver ... ten times u. to tried gold,* II, 7, 53.

**Underwork,** to undermine: *thou hast underwrought his lawful king,* John II, 95.

**Underwrite,** 1) to write under sth.: *painted upon a pole, and underwrit: Here can you see the tyrant,* Mcb. V, 8, 26. cf. Sonn. 134, 7.

2) to subscribe, to submit to: *u. in an observing kind his humorous predominance,* Troil. II, 3, 137.

**Underwrought,** see *Underwork.*

**Undescried,** unperceived, undiscovered: Wint. IV, 4, 669.

**Undeserved,** not deserved, not merited: Lucr. 824. Merch. II, 9, 40. Shr. IV, 1, 202. All's II, 3, 273. John IV, 1, 108.

**Undeserver,** one of no merit: *the u. may sleep, when the man of action is called on,* H4B II, 4, 406. *your great graces heaped upon me, poor u.* H8 III, 2, 175. *to sell and mart your offices to —s,* Caes. IV, 3, 12.

**Undeserving,** adj. not deserving, unworthy: *your favours done to me, u. as I am,* Gent. III, 1, 7.

**Undeserving,** subst. (cf. *Deserving*) want of merit, unworthiness: *my lady, to the manner of the days, in courtesy gives u. praise,* LLL V, 2, 366 (*u.* the dative; not = undeserved, as it is generally explained).

**Undetermined,** not decided, not settled (or = indeterminable?): *mousing the flesh of men in u. differences of kings,* John II, 355.

**Undinted,** not impressed by blows, unbattered: *bear back our targes u.* Ant. II, 6, 39.

**Undiscernible,** undiscoverable, not to be seen through: *to think I can be u.* Meas. V, 373.

**Undiscovered,** not detected, not found out: Wint. V, 2, 130. H6B III, 1, 369. Hml. III, 1, 79.

**Undishonoured,** not disgraced: Err. II, 2, 148.

**Undisposed,** not inclined (to merriment): *stands on tricks when I am u.* Err. I, 2, 80.

**Undistinguishable,** not to be distinctly seen: Mids. II, 1, 100. IV, 1, 192.

**Undistinguished,** not discernible in its peculiar form and nature: *as often shrieking u. woe, in clamours of all size, both high and low,* Compl. 20. *O u. space of woman's wit!* (Ff *O indistinguished space of woman's will*); *a plot upon her virtuous husband's life; and the exchange my brother,* Lr. IV, 6, 278 (i. e. incalculable, unaccountable; German: *unberechenbar.* The general interpretation is: boundless, unlimited).

**Undividable,** not separable (or not divided, not separate; cf. *Dividable*): *thyself I call it, being strange to me, that u., incorporate, am better than thy dear self's better part,* Err. II, 2, 124.

**Undivided,** not disunited: *our u. loves are one,* Sonn. 36, 2.

**Undivulged,** secret, hidden: *against the u. pretence I fight of treasonous malice,* Mcb. II, 3, 137. *hast within thee u. crimes,* Lr. III, 2, 52.

**Undo,** (impf. *undid,* partic. *undone*) 1) to reverse what has been done, to annul: Tp. I, 2, 291. Mids. IV, 1, 67. Tw. II, 1, 38. H6B I, 1, 103. Tit. IV, 2, 75. Mcb. V, 1, 75. Oth. IV, 3, 71. Ant. III, 4, 17. Per. IV, 3, 1. 6. Sometimes = to make not to be or happen, to hinder from coming into existence: *and u. a great deal of honour,* Tim. III, 2, 53. *distribution should u. excess,* Lr. IV, 1, 73. *she's able to freeze the god Priapus and u. a whole generation,* Per. IV, 6, 4. Joined, in contradistinction, with *to do* (and in this case usually accented on the first syllable): *what to your wisdoms seemeth best, do or u., as if ourself were here,* H6B III, 1, 196. *Warwick, as ourself, shall do and u. as him pleaseth best,* H6C II, 6, 105. *and what they undid did,* Ant. II, 2, 210. *what can it not do and u.* Cymb. II, 3, 78. Singular expressions: *—es description to do it,* Wint. V, 2, 63 (strikes description dumb, beggars it). *if you would put me to verses …. you undid me,* H5 V, 2, 138 (you would baffle my whole love-suit). *equivocation will u. us,* Hml. V, 1, 149 (will put us to silence).

2) to untie, to loose: *to bind me, or u. me,* Ado V, 4, 20 (quibbling). *u. this button,* Lr. V, 3, 309. Metaphorically, = to solve: *if by which time our secret be —ne,* Per. I, 1, 117 (our riddle be guessed).

3) to ruin: Ven. 783. Gent. II, 5, 5. IV, 1, 5. Wiv. III, 3, 103. 117. IV, 2, 42. IV, 5, 93. Ado II, 2, 29. IV, 1, 315. V, 4, 20 (quibbling). LLL V, 2, 425. Merch. III, 1, 129. As V, 4, 47. Shr. V, 1, 44. 70. All's I, 1, 95. II, 3, 284. III, 2, 22. IV, 1, 80. IV, 3, 358. V, 3, 147. Tw. I, 3, 14. Wint. I, 2, 312. IV, 4, 452. 464. 471. R2 IV, 203. H4A II, 2, 91. 93. V, 2, 3. H4B II, 1, 25. III, 2, 124. IV, 3, 25. V, 5, 120. H6B IV, 2, 88. H6C I, 1, 232. H8 II, 1, 159. III, 2, 210. Troil. III, 1, 120. III, 3, 258. Cor. I, 1, 64. 65. IV, 6, 107. Tit. II, 1, 62. IV, 2, 55. 76. 78. Rom. III, 2, 38. Tim. IV, 2, 2. 38. IV, 3, 211. 488 (*his —ne lord*). Mcb. V, 5, 50. Oth. II, 3, 365. V, 1, 54. V, 2, 76. Ant. II, 5, 106. Cymb. IV, 2, 123. V, 5, 307. Per. IV, 6, 132. 158.

The gerund substantively, = ruin, destruction: *his master's —ing,* All's II, 4, 24. *to the mere —ing of all the kingdom,* H8 III, 2, 329. *'tis my —ing,* V, 3, 62. *by the —ing of yourself,* Ant. V, 2, 44.

**Undone,** not done, not performed: *leaves nothing u.* Cor. II, 2, 22. IV, 7, 24. Oth. III, 3, 204. Ant. III, 1, 14. *to wish things done u.* Caes. IV, 2, 9. Mcb. I, 5, 26. Lr. I, 1, 17.

**Undoubted,** 1) indubitable: *till it be u., we do lock our former scruple in our .. gates,* John II, 369.

2) unsuspected: *rest unquestioned welcome and u. blest,* All's II, 1, 211.

3) free from fear; a) subjectively, = fearless: *hardy and u. champions,* H6C V, 7, 6. b) objectively, not feared for, unallayed by apprehensions: *brave Burgundy, u. hope of France,* H6A III, 3, 41 (a hope mingled with no fear).

**Undoubtedly,** without doubt, indubitably: H8 IV, 2, 49.

**Undoubtful,** indubitable, evident: *his fact came not to an u. proof,* Meas. IV, 2, 142.

**Undreamed,** not dreamt or thought of: *to unpathed waters, u. shores,* Wint. IV, 4, 578 (accented on the first syllable, on account of its place before the subst.).

**Undress,** to strip of clothes: *u. you,* Shr. Ind. 2, 119.

**Undressed,** not put in order, not trimmed, formless: *his u., unpolished, uneducated … fashion,* LLL IV, 2, 17.

**Undrowned,** not drowned: Tp. II, 1, 237. 239.

**Unduteous,** undutiful, not obedient: *this deceit loses the name of craft, of disobedience, or u. title,* Wiv. V, 5, 240 (= title, name of undutifulness. cf. Appendix).

**Undutiful,** not acting up to duty: *I know my duty; you are all u.* H6C V, 5, 33.

**Uneared,** untilled, unploughed: Sonn. 3, 5.

**Unearned,** undeserved: *if we have u. luck now to 'scape the serpent's tongue,* Mids. V, 439.

**Unearthly,** superterrestrial: Wint. III, 1, 7.

**Uneasiness**, want of content, care: H5 II, 2, 27.

**Uneasy**, 1) difficult: *this swift business I must u. make, lest too light winning make the prize light,* Tp. I, 2, 451. *from whose simplicity I think it not u. to get the cause of my son's resort thither,* Wint. IV, 2, 56.

2) incommodious, uncomfortable: *upon u. pallets stretching thee,* H4B III, 1, 10. *u. lies the head that wears a crown,* 31.

**Uneath**, not easily, difficultly: *u. may she endure the flinty streets,* H6B II, 4, 8.

**Uneducated**, untaught, illiterate: *undressed, unpolished, u.* LLL IV, 2, 17 (Holofernes' speech).

**Uneffectual**, inefficacious: *the glow-worm shows the matin to be near and 'gins to pale his u. fire,* Hml. I, 5, 90 (by a prolepsis, = the fire which loses its effect by the approach of the morning).

**Unelected**, not chosen: Cor. II, 3, 207.

**Unequal**, 1) not equal, not of the same size, or weight or power: H6A V, 5, 34. H6C III, 2, 159. Hml. II, 2, 493.

2) unjust, unfair: *to lay a heavy and u. hand upon our honours,* H4B IV, 1, 102. *to punish me for what you make me do seems much u.* Ant. II, 5, 101.

**Uneven**, 1) not level, not smooth, rugged: *fallen am I in dark u. way,* Mids. III, 2, 417. R2 II, 3, 4. H4A II, 2, 26.

2) not uniform; not straight, not direct: *every letter he hath writ hath disvouched other. In most u. and distracted manner,* Meas. IV, 4, 3. *you say you do not know the lady's mind; u. is the course, I like it not,* Rom. IV, 1, 5.

3) intricate, full of difficulties, embarrassing: *all is u., and every thing is left at six and seven,* R2 II, 2, 121. *u. and unwelcome news,* H4A I, 1, 50.

**Unexamined**, not interrogated judicially: R3 III, 6, 9.

**Unexecuted**, not put in practice, not set at work (German: *unbethätigt*): *leave u. your own renowned knowledge,* Ant. III, 7, 45.

**Unexpected**, not looked for, sudden: John II, 80. V, 7, 64.

**Unexperienced**, having gained no knowledge, ignorant: *which now shall die in oblivion and thou return u. to thy grave,* Shr. IV, 1, 86 (Grumio's speech).

**Unexperient**, inexperienced: *that the u. gave the tempter place,* Compl. 318.

**Unexpressive**, inexpressible, ineffable: *the fair, the chaste and u. she,* As III, 2, 10.

**Unfair**, vb. to deprive of beauty: *those hours ... will play the tyrants ... and that u. which fairly doth excel,* Sonn. 5, 4.

**Unfaithful**, faithless, illoyal: As IV, 1, 199.

**Unfallible**, quite certain: *believe my words, for they are certain and u.* H6A I, 2, 59.

**Unfamed**, inglorious: *death u.* Troil. II, 2, 159.

**Unfashionable**, shapeless, deformed: *so lamely and u. that dogs bark at me,* R3 I, 1, 22.

**Unfasten**, to unfix, to loose: *plucking to unfix an enemy, he doth u. so and shake a friend,* H4B IV, 1, 209.

**Unfathered**, fatherless; and hence produced contrary to the course of nature; not to be accounted for: *this abundant issue seemed to me but hope of orphans and u. fruit,* Sonn. 97, 10. *if my dear love were but the child of state, it might for Fortune's bastard be u.* 124, 2 (as not born in the natural way). *the*

*people fear me, for they do observe u. heirs and loathly births of nature,* H4B IV, 4, 122 (= unnatural procreations; cf. *Heir.* The genitive of *nature* governed by both the preceding substantives).

**Unfed** *(únfed)* not supplied with food: Lr. III, 4, 30 *(u. sides).*

**Unfeed**, unpaid: *an u. lawyer,* Lr. I, 4, 142.

**Unfeeling**, insensible, in a physical as well as moral sense: *u. fools can with such wrongs dispense,* Err. II, 1, 103. *thou u. man,* Merch. IV, 1, 63. *dull u. barren ignorance,* R2 I, 3, 168. *and with my fingers feel his hand u.* H6B III, 2, 145.

**Unfeigned**, not feigned, sincere: Shr. IV, 2, 32. H6C III, 3, 51. 202.

**Unfeignedly**, sincerely: All's II, 3, 259. John II, 526. R3 II, 1, 22.

**Unfellowed**, having no equal: Hml. V, 2, 150.

**Unfelt**, *(unfélt* or *únfelt,* according as the following subst. is accentuated: *unfélt imaginátion; únfelt sórrow* etc.)* 1) not felt, not affecting the heart: *for u. imagination they often feel a world of restless cares,* R3 I, 4, 80. *to show an u. sorrow is an office which the false man does easy,* Mcb. II, 3, 142.

2) not perceived, not affecting the senses: *O unseen shame, invisible disgrace, O u. sore, crest-wounding private scar,* Lucr. 828. *all my treasury is yet but u. thanks,* R2 II, 3, 61 (perhaps with intentional ambiguity).

**Unfenced**, defenceless: *till u. desolation leave them as naked as the vulgar air,* John II, 386.

**Unfilial**, unbecoming in a child, undutiful: Wint. IV, 4, 417.

**Unfilled**, empty: Tw. II, 3, 7. Cor. V, 1, 51.

**Unfinished**, not finished, incomplete, half done: Ven. 415. Err. III, 2, 173. R3 I, 1, 20. H8 IV, 2, 61.

**Unfirm**, (three times *unfírm,* once *únfirm* before the subst.) not strongly fixed, or loosened: *all the sway of earth shakes like a thing u.* Caes. I, 3, 4. *loose, u. with digging up of graves,* Rom. V, 3, 6. In a moral sense, = inconstant: *our fancies are more giddy and u.* Tw. II, 4, 34. = weak: *so is the u. king in three divided,* H4B I, 3, 73.

**Unfit**, not fit, unsuitable, unqualified: Tp. III, 3, 58. Meas. IV, 3, 68. All's V, 1, 26. H6C III, 2, 92. R3 I, 2, 109. III, 7, 205. H8 I, 2, 34. II, 2, 61. Troil. II, 2, 167. Oth. III, 3, 33.

**Unfitness**, inconvenience: Lr. I, 4, 356.

**Unfitting**, unbecoming: *a passion most u. such a man,* Oth. IV, 1, 78. Ff *resulting,* M. Edd. *unsuiting.*

**Unfix**, to unsettle, to move from a place: *whose horrid image doth u. my hair,* Mcb. I, 3, 135 (cf. Hml. I, 5, 18). = to unroot: H4B IV, 1, 208. Mcb. IV, 1, 96.

**Unfledged**, young and unripe: Wint. I, 2, 78. Hml. I, 3, 65. Cymb. III, 3, 27.

**Unfold**, 1) to release from a fold or pen: *the —ing star calls up the shepherd,* Meas. IV, 2, 218.

2) to open the folds or plaits of, to spread out; metaphorically: *crush him together rather than u. his measure duly,* Cymb. I, 1, 26. cf. Lr. I, 1, 283. Applied to a folded letter, = to open: *to u. their grand commission,* Hml. V, 2, 17 (Ff *unseal*).

3) to bring forth from any ward: *by new —ing his imprisoned pride* (i. e. his wardrobe) Sonn. 52, 12.

4) to discover, to reveal, to bring to light, to betray (what has been hidden): *they their guilt with weeping will u.* Lucr. 754. *u. the evil which is here wrapt up*

*in countenance*, Meas. V, 117. *never to u. to any one which casket 'twas I chose*, Merch. II, 9, 10. *makes and —s error*, Wint. IV, 1, 2. *his contrary proceedings are all —ed*, H8 III, 2, 27. *time shall u. what plaited cunning hides*, Lr. I, 1, 283. *O heaven, that such companions thou'ldst u.* Oth. IV, 2, 141. *the Moor may u. me to him*, V, 1, 21. *must I be —ed with* (= by) *one that I have bred?* Ant. V, 2, 170.

5) to display, to show: *there we will u. to creatures stern sad tunes*, Lucr.1146. *that* (lightning) *in a spleen —s both heaven and earth*, Mids. I, 1, 146. *stand and u. yourself*, Hml. I, 1, 2 (make yourself known). *I shall u. equal discourtesy to your best kindness*, Cymb. II, 3, 101.

6) to disclose, to tell, to communicate; absol.: *to my —ing lend your prosperous ear*, Oth. I, 3, 245. Trans.: *I to Ford shall eke u. how* ... Wiv. I, 3, 105. *as you hear them* (my follies) *—ed*, II, 2, 193. *to what purpose have you —ed this to me?* 227. Meas. I, 1, 3. 30. Mids. I, 1, 208. All's I, 1, 127. Tw. I, 2, 19. I, 4, 24. V, 155. R2 III, 1, 7. III, 2, 94. H4B Ind. 4. IV, 1, 77. H5 I, 2, 10. III, 6, 124. H6B II, 1, 166. III, 2, 117. R3 II, 4, 39 (Ff *report*). Rom. II, 6, 28. Caes. II, 1, 274. 330. Mcb. III, 6, 46. Hml. I, 5, 6. 15. Oth. III, 3, 243. Cymb. V, 5, 313.

**Unfool**, to make satisfaction for calling one a fool, to make the reproach of folly undone: *have you any way to u. me again?* Wiv. IV, 2, 120.

**Unforced**, not constrained: *this gentle and u. accord of Hamlet*, Hml. I, 2, 123. = easy, natural: *it is a most pregnant and u. position*, Oth. II, 1, 239.

**Unforfeited**, kept, maintained, not lost: *to keep obliged faith u.* Merch. II, 6, 7.

**Unfortified**, not strengthened against attacks, weak: *a heart u., a mind impatient*, Hml. I, 2, 96.

**Unfortunate**, not prosperous, not favoured by fortune: As III, 2, 414. All's III, 2, 28. H6A I, 4, 4. H6C III, 3, 118. Cor. V, 3, 97. Tim. III, 6, 47. Mcb. IV, 1, 152. Lr. IV, 6, 68. Oth. II, 3, 42 (Ff *infortunate*). V, 2, 283 (Qq *infortunate*). Cymb. IV, 2, 39.

**Unfortunately**, by ill fortune: Ven. 1029.

**Unfought**, not fought: *if they march along u. withal*, H5 III, 5, 12.

**Unfrequented**, rarely visited, solitary: Gent. V, 4, 2. Tit. II, 1, 115.

**Unfriended**, destitute of friends: Tw. III, 3, 10. Lr. I, 1, 206.

**Unfriendly**, unkind, unfavourable: Per. III, 1, 58.

**Unfruitful**, not producing good effects, empty, vain: *his u. prayer*, Lucr. 344.

**Unfurnish**, to deprive, to leave destitute: *thy speech will bring me to consider that which may u. me of reason*, Wint. V, 1, 123. *Rome's royal empress, —ed of her well-beseeming troop*, Tit. II, 3, 56.

**Unfurnished**, unprovided, unsupplied with what is necessary: *having made one* (eye), *methinks it should have power to steal both his and leave itself u.* Merch. III, 2, 126 (for no face would be beautiful with only one eye, the one being a necessary and indispensable supplement and addition to the other). *empty lodgings and u. walls*, R2 I, 2, 68 (untapestried). *his u.kingdom*, H5 I, 2, 148 (unprepared for defence). *we shall be much u. for this time*, Rom. IV, 2, 10.

**Ungained**, not yet gained: Troil. I, 2, 315. 319.

**Ungalled**, unhurt, uninjured: *your yet u. esti-*

*mation*, Err. III, 1, 102. *let ... the hart u. play*, Hml. III, 2, 283.

**Ungartered**, wearing or having no garters (a sign of being in love): Gent. II, 1, 79. As III, 2, 398. Hml. II, 1, 80.

**Ungenitured**, wanting the power of propagation, impotent: Meas. III, 2, 184.

**Ungentle**, unkind, harsh, rude: Err. IV, 2, 21. As V, 2, 86. Wint. III, 3, 34. V, 1, 154. H4A V, 1, 13. 60. H6B III, 2, 290. H6C II, 3, 6. Tit. II, 4, 16. Caes. I, 1, 242. Ant. V, 1, 60. Per. IV, 6, 103.

**Ungentleness**, unkindness: *you have done me much u.* As V, 2, 83.

**Ungently**, unkindly: Tp. I, 2, 444. Troil. V, 3, 1. Caes. II, 1, 237.

**Ungird**, to loose from a girdle, to open: *u. thy strangeness and tell me*, Tw. IV, 1, 16 (German: *sei nicht so zugeknöpft*).

**Ungodly**, impious, sinful: *this u. day*, John III, 1, 109.

**Ungored**, unwounded, unhurt: *to keep my name u.* Hml. V, 2, 261.

**Ungot**, not begotten: Meas. V, 142.

**Ungotten**, the same: H5 I, 2, 287.

**Ungoverned**, 1) without government or rule, anarchical: *the state is green and yet u.* R3 II, 2, 127. *all good men of this u. isle*, III, 7, 110. = uninstructed, untutored: *the children live, whose parents thou hast slaughtered, u. youth*, R3 IV, 4, 392.

2) uncontrolled, unbridled: *the fury of u. youth*, Gent. IV, 1, 45. *his u. rage*, Lr. IV, 4, 19.

**Ungracious**, wanting grace; 1) odious, hateful: *u. wretch*, Tw. IV, 1, 51. *thy most u. head*, H6B IV, 10, 88. *you u. clamours*, Troil. I, 1, 92. *this u. paper*, Lr. IV, 6, 283.

2) impious, wicked: *that word grace in an u. mouth is but profane*, R2 II, 3, 89. *swearest thou, u. boy?* H4A II, 4, 490. *nor I u. speak unto myself for him*, R3 II, 1, 127. *as some u. pastors do*, Hml. I, 3, 47.

**Ungrateful**, unthankful: Mids. III, 2, 195. R3 II, 2, 91. Cor. IV, 5, 136. Tit. IV, 1, 111. IV, 3, 17. Tim. III, 2, 80. cf. *Ingrateful*.

**Ungravely**, without dignity, indecently: *which most gibingly, u., he did fashion after the inveterate hate he bears you*, Cor. II, 3, 233.

**Ungrown** (*úngrown*, as preceding its subst.) not yet full-grown, young: Ven. 526. H4A V, 4, 23.

**Unguarded**, not guarded, not defended or protected against enemies: H5 I, 2, 170. Mcb. I, 7, 70. Cymb. V, 3, 46.

**Unguided**, 1) having no guide: *a stranger u. and unfriended*, Tw. III, 3, 10. 2) ungoverned, anarchical: *the u. days and rotten times that you shall look upon*, H4B IV, 4, 59.

**Unhacked**, not hacked, not blunted by blows: *with u. swords and helmets all unbruised*, John II, 254. *to part with u. edges*, Ant. II, 6, 38.

**Unhair**, to strip of hair: *I'll u. thy head*, Ant. II, 5, 64.

**Unhaired**, writing of M. Edd. in John V, 2, 133; O. Edd. *un-heard*, q. v.

**Unhallowed**, 1) not kept holy, not celebrated: *let never day nor night u. pass*, H6B II, 1, 85.

2) unholy, impious, wicked: Lucr. 192. 392. 552. Meas. V, 307. Merch. IV, 1, 136. H6A III, 1, 59. Tit. II, 3, 210. V, 2, 191. V, 3, 14. Rom. V, 3, 54. Per. IV, 6, 107.

**Unhand,** to loose from the hand, to let go: *u. me, gentlemen,* Hml. l, 4, 84.

**Unhandled,** 1) not treated, not touched: *has left the cause o'the king u.* H8 III, 2, 58.

2) not managed, not trained, not broken in: *youthful and u. colts,* Merch. V, 72.

**Unhandsome,** 1) wanting beauty: *were she other than she is, she were u.* Ado l, 1, 177.

2) improper, indecent: *it is no more u. than to see the lord the prologue,* As Epil. 2. *a slovenly u. corse,* H4A I, 3, 44.

3) unfair, illiberal: *u. warrior as I am,* Oth. III, 4, 151.

**Unhanged,** not hanged, not executed by the halter, H4A II, 4, 144.

**Unhaply,** reading of O. Edd. in Lucr. 8; M. Edd. *unhappily.*

**Unhappied,** depraved: *a happy gentleman in blood and lineaments, by you u. and disfigured clean,* R2 III, 1, 10.

**Unhappily,** 1) unfortunately, with regret be it said: *With child, perhaps? U. even so,* Meas. l, 2, 160.

2) mischievously, evilly: *haply that name of chaste u. set this bateless edge on his keen appetite,* Lucr. 8 (O. Edd. *unhaply*). *purest faith u. forsworn,* Sonn. 66, 4. *you are a churchman, or, I'll tell you, cardinal, I should judge now u.* H8 l, 4, 89. *would make one think there might be thought, though nothing sure, yet much u.* Hml. IV, 5, 13. *the effects he writes of succeed u.* Lr. l, 2, 157.

**Unhappiness,** evilness: *she hath often dreamed of u. and waked herself with laughing,* Ado II, 1, 361 (i. e. wanton or mischievous tricks. cf. *unhappy* in All's IV, 5, 66). *and that be heir to his u.* R3 l, 2, 25.

**Unhappy,** 1) unfortunate, miserable, wretched, poor: Gent. IV, 4, 104. V, 4, 15. 28. 29. 31. 84. Meas. l, 4, 20. 21. IV, 3, 126. Err. I, 2, 40. As II, 3, 16. II, 7, 136. Tw. II, 5, 172. Wint. III, 2, 36. IV, 2, 30. IV, 4, 523. H4A I, 3, 148. H6B III, 2, 70. R3 II, 2, 4. V, 3, 158. H8 III, 1, 147. Tit. II, 3, 250. Lr. I, 1, 93. Oth. I, 1, 164. III, 4, 102 (*u. in the loss of it*). Ant. III, 4, 12. Per. I, 4, 69.

2) disastrous, calamitous: *u. day,* Err. IV, 4, 127. R2 III, 2, 71. Rom. IV, 5, 43. *u. fortune,* Rom. V, 2, 17.

3) evil, mischievous, fatal, pernicious (but often in a somewhat milder sense; cf. the German *unselig* and the French *malheureux*): *comparing him to that u. guest,* Lucr. 1565. *O most u. strumpet!* Err. IV, 4, 127. *a shrewd u. gallows,* LLL V, 2, 12. *I am the u. subject of these quarrels,* Merch. V, 238. *be thou armed for some u. words,* Shr. II, 140. *a shrewd knave and an u.* All's IV, 5, 66 (= roguish, full of tricks; cf. *unhappiness* in Ado II, 1, 361). *thou old u. traitor,* Lr. IV, 6, 232. *I have poor and u. brains for drinking,* Oth. II, 3, 35. *a most u. one* (division) IV, 1, 243. *u. was the clock that struck the hour,* Cymb. V, 5, 153.

**Unhardened,** soft, sensible: *messengers of strong prevailment in u. youth,* Mids. l, 1, 35.

**Unharmed,** reading of the surreptitious Q1 and M. Edd. in Rom. I, 1, 217; Q2,3 etc. and Ff *uncharmed.*

**Unhatched,** 1) not yet disclosed from the egg; unripe; not yet brought to light: *each u., unfledged comrade,* Hml. I, 3, 65 (Qq and M. Edd. *new-hatched*). *some u. practice made demonstrable here in Cyprus to him,* Oth. III, 4, 141.

2) unhacked, not blunted by blows (cf. *hatched* in Troil. I, 3, 65): *dubbed with u. rapier and on carpet consideration,* Tw. III, 4, 257 (most M. Edd. *unhacked*).

**Unheard,** 1) not perceived by the ear: *the seaman's whistle is as a whisper in the ears of death, u.* Per. III, 1, 10.

2) not admitted to audience, not listened to: *that Marcius return me u.* Cor. V, 1, 43. *she shall not sue u.* Ant. III, 12, 24.

3) not learned, not received by communication: *let the worst u. fall on your head,* John IV, 2, 136.

4) unheard of, unprecedented: *this u. sauciness and boyish troops,* John V, 2, 133 (M. Edd. *unhaired,* in the sense of unbearded, in which the poet would hardly have used the word; cf. *Hair* and its derivatives). *

**Unheart,** to dishearten, to discourage: Cor. V, 1, 49.

**Unheedful,** rash, inconsiderate: *u. vows may heedfully be broken,* Gent. II, 6, 11. *this u., desperate, wild adventure,* H6A IV, 4, 7.

**Unheedfully,** inattentively, inconsiderately: *so you stumble not u.* Gent. I, 2, 3.

**Unheedy,** inattentive, inconsiderate: *wings and no eyes figure u. haste,* Mids. I, 1, 237.

**Unhelpful,** affording no help, unprofitable, unavailing: *bewails good Gloster's case with sad u. tears,* H6B III, 1, 218.

**Unhidden,** not hidden, open, manifest: *the several and u. passages of his true titles to some certain dukedoms,* H5 I, 1, 86.

**Unholy,** not holy, profane, impious, wicked: *a most u. match,* Gent. IV, 3, 30. *this u. braggart,* Cor. V, 6, 119. *u. suits,* Hml. I, 3, 129. *her u. service,* Per. IV, 4, 50.

**Unhoped,** not hoped for: *such as fill my heart with u. joys,* H6C III, 3, 172.

**Unhopeful,** unpromising: *Benedick is not the —est husband that I know,* Ado II, 1, 392.

**Unhorse,** to throw from the saddle: *he would u. the lustiest challenger,* R2 V, 3, 19.

**Unhospitable,** unkind to strangers: Tw. III, 3, 11.

**Unhoused,** 1) having no house to seek shelter in: *bare u. trunks, to the conflicting elements exposed,* Tim. IV, 3, 229. 2) homeless, unsettled, not tied to a household and family: *I would not my u. free condition put into circumscription and confine,* Oth. I, 2, 26.

**Unhouseled,** not having received the sacrament: Hml. I, 5, 77.

**Unhurtful,** wanting the power of doing harm: *you imagine me too u. an opposite,* Meas. III, 2, 175.

**Unicorn,** a fabulous animal with a single horn, of proverbial ferocity: *to tame the u. and lion wild,* Lucr. 956. *I will believe that there are —s,* Tp. III, 3, 22. *wert thou the u.,* pride and wrath would confound thee,* Tim. IV, 3, 339. *—s may be betrayed with trees,* Caes. II, 1, 204 (running on them in their blind fury and sticking their horn fast in them).

**Unimproved,** not yet used for advantage, not turned to account, unemployed, unactive: *young Fortinbras, of u. mettle hot and full,* Hml. I, 1, 96. cf. *Improve.**

**Uninhabitable,** unfit to be the residence of men: Tp. II, 1, 37.

**Unintelligent,** not perceiving, not aware: *we will give you sleepy drinks, that your senses, u. of our insufficiency, may* etc. Wint. I, 1, 16.

**Union,** 1) junction (especially by marriage): *the true concord of well-tuned sounds by —s married,* Sonn.

8, 6. *the u. of your bed*, Tp. IV, 21. *an u. in partition*, Mids. III, 2, 210. *this u. shall do more than battery can*, John II, 446.

2) a fine pearl: *in the cap an u. shall he throw*, Hml. V, 2, 283 (Qq *unice* or *onyx*). 337.

**Unite**, 1) trans. to join: *your —d strengths*, John II, 388. *like a broken limb —d*, H4B IV, 1, 222. *the —d vessel of their blood*, IV, 4, 44. *u. your troops of horsemen with his bands of foot*, H6A IV, 1, 164. *if sympathy of love u. our thoughts*, H6B I, 1, 23. *continue this u. league*, R3 II, 1, 2. *we will u. the white rose and the red*, V, 5, 19. *Hymen did our hands u. commutual in most sacred bands*, Hml. III, 2, 170. *our vrincely eagle ... should again u. his favour with the radiant Cymbeline*, Cymb. V, 5, 474.

2) intr. to join, to act together: *if you will now u. in your complaints*, H8 III, 2, 1.

**United**, adjectively, = pertaining to union: *to give our hearts —d ceremony*, Wiv. IV, 6, 51 (i. e. the ceremony of union, of marriage).

**Unity**, 1) oneness, the state of being one: *if there be rule in u. itself, this is not she*, Troil. V, 2, 141 (i. e. if one is one).

2) concord, agreement: *these contraries such u. do hold*, Lucr. 1558. *such u. in the proofs*, Wint. V, 2, 35. *make me happy in your u.* R3 II, 1, 31. *the unity the king thy brother made*, IV, 4, 379. *the u. and married calm of states*, Troil. I, 3, 100. *confound all u. on earth*, Mcb. IV, 3, 100. *to divine of this u.* Ant. II, 6, 124.

**Universal**, 1) general, pertaining to all or to the whole: *u. plodding poisons up the nimble spirits in the arteries*, LLL IV, 3, 305 (perpetual ? or pervading the whole system?). *u. shout*, Merch. III, 2, 144. *this wide and u. theatre*, As II, 7, 137. *the woe had been u.* Wint. V, 2, 100. *a largess u. like the sun*, H5 IV Chor. 43. *appetite, an u. wolf*, Troil. I, 3, 121. *make an u. prey*, 123. *an u. shout*, Caes. I, 1, 49. *the u. peace*, Mcb. IV, 3, 99. *the u. landlord*, Ant. III, 13, 72. *u. peace*, IV, 6, 5.

2) whole, total: *in the u. world*, H5 IV, 1, 66 and IV, 8, 11 (Fluellen's speeches). *sole monarch of the u. earth*, Rom. III, 2, 94.

**Universe**, the world: *nothing this wide u. I call, save thou*, Sonn. 109, 13. *the poring dark fills the wide vessel of the u.* H5 IV Chor. 3.

**University**, a school in which all branches of learning are taught: Gent. I, 3, 10. Shr. V, 1, 72 (*at the u.*). Hml. III, 2, 104 (*i'the u.*).

**Unjointed**, wanting joints, incoherent: *this bald u. chat*, H4A I, 3, 65.

**Unjust**, (once *únjust*, before a subst.: Gent. IV, 4, 173) 1) not conforming or not conformable to law and justice: Meas. V, 302. 315. H4A I, 3, 173. H6A II, 5, 68. Tit. I, 292. Mcb. IV, 3, 83.

2) not founded in fact, untrue: *they have verified u. things*, Ado V, 1, 223.

3) dishonest: *this is the time that the u. man doth thrive*, Wint. IV, 4, 688. *discarded u. serving-men*, H4A IV, 2, 30.

4) groundless, unjustified: *in this u. divorce of us*, Err. I, 1, 105. *this uncivil and u. extent against thy peace*, Tw. IV, 1, 57. *say my request's u.* Cor. V, 3, 164.

5) faithless, false, perfidious: *and justly thus controls his thoughts u.* Lucr. 189. *foul hope and fond mistrust ... as servitors to the u.* 285. *now I must be as u. to Thurio*, Gent. IV, 2, 2. *our displeasures, to*

*ourselves u., destroy our friends*, All's V, 3, 63. *his honour is as true in this appeal as thou art all u.* R2 IV, 45. *thou art an u. man in saying so*, H4A III, 3, 146. *O passing traitor, perjured and u.* H6C V, 1, 106. *a most u. knave*, Troil. V, 1, 96. Used of faithlessness in love: *wherefore says she not she is u.?* Sonn. 138, 9. *unless thy lady prove u.* Pilgr. 331. *Theseus' perjury and u. flight*, Gent. IV, 4, 173. *his u. unkindness, that in all reason should have quenched her love*, Meas. III, 1, 249.

**Unjustice** (Ff *injustice*) want of equity: Tit. IV, 4, 18.

**Unjustly**, 1) in a manner contrary to law and justice, wrongfully: R2 I, 1, 83. H5 I, 2, 40. R3 II, 1, 125. III, 3, 22. Oth. IV, 2, 186. Cymb. III, 3, 100.

2) faithlessly; dishonestly: *this chaste blood so u. stained*, Lucr. 1836. *to cozen him that would u. win*, All's IV, 2, 76.

**Unkennel**, to drive from his hole: *we'll u. the fox*, Wiv. III, 3, 174. Metaphorically, = to discover: *if his occulted guilt do not itself u. in one speech*, Hml. III, 2, 86 (Qq *discover*).

**Unkept**, not guarded, not tended: As I, 1, 9.

**Unkind**, subst. (?), unnaturalness, averseness to the works of love (?): *let no u. no fair beseechers kill; think all but one, and me in that one Will*, Sonn. 135, 13.

**Unkind**, adj. (*unkind*; but when placed before the subst., usually *únkind*: Gent. I, 2, 109. Err. II, 1, 38. Shr. V, 2, 136. H4A V, 1, 69. H6B III, 2, 87. Rom. V, 3, 145. Lr. III, 4, 73. Oth. IV, 1, 238) 1) wanting a race or generation: *had thy mother borne so hard a mind, she had not brought forth thee, but died u.* Ven. 204 (= childless).*

2) destitute of benevolence and amiable qualities, ungentle, hard-hearted, rough: Gent. I, 2, 109. II, 3, 42. 43. Err. IV, 2, 21. Mids. III, 2, 162. Merch. V, 175. Shr. V, 2, 136. Tw. III, 4, 402. John V, 6, 12. H4A V, 1, 69. H6B III, 2, 87. IV, 9, 19. Troil. III, 2, 156. Rom. V, 3, 145. Tim. IV, 1, 36. V, 4, 21. Caes. III, 2, 187. Used of coldness in love: *young and so u.?* Ven. 187. *she puts on outward strangeness, seems u.* 310. *that you were once u. befriends me now*, Sonn. 120, 1. *so him I lose through my u. abuse*, 134, 12. Err. II, 1, 38. Tw. IV, 2, 81. Hml. III, 1, 101. Oth. IV, 1, 238.

In the following passages some commentators have interpreted it as meaning unnatural: *blow, blow, thou winter wind, thou art not so u. as man's ingratitude*, As II, 7, 175. *when envy breeds u. division*, H6A IV, 1, 193. *Titus, u. and careless of thine own*, Tit. I, 86. *what hast thou done, unnatural and u.* V, 3, 48. *bid them farewell, Cordelia, though u.* Lr. I, 1, 263. *his u. daughters*, III, 4, 73.

**Unkindly**, adv. in a harsh and ungentle manner: Mids. III, 2, 183. Tit. V, 3, 104. Caes. III, 2, 184. *take it not u.* (= don't take it ill) Shr. III, 1, 57. *I take it much u.* Oth. I, 1, 1. *I hope it remains not u. with your lordship*, Tim. III, 6, 39 (you owe me no grudge). cf. *Unkindness 2.*

**Unkindness**, 1) want of love and tenderness: Ven. 478. Sonn. 120, 5. 139, 2. Meas. II, 4, 166. III, 1, 250. Err. II, 1, 93. Wint. IV, 4, 563. R2 II, 1, 133. H6B III, 2, 96. Cor. V, 1, 45. Tim. IV, 3, 176. Mcb. III, 4, 42. Lr. I, 4, 76. II, 4, 137. III, 2, 16. IV, 3, 44. Oth. III, 4, 152. IV, 2, 159. 160. Ant. I, 2, 138 (*an u.*).

2) ill-will, grudge, a disposition to fall out and quarrel: *we shall drink down all u.* Wiv. I, 1, 204. *take no u. of his hasty words,* Shr. IV, 3, 169. *is there any u. between my lord and you?* All's II, 5, 35. *in this I bury all u.* Caes. IV, 3, 159.

**Unkinged,** deprived of royalty, dethroned: R2 IV, 220. V, 5, 37.

**Unkinglike,** unbecoming in a king: Cymb. III, 5, 7.

**Unkiss,** to annul by a kiss: *let me u. the oath 'twixt thee and me,* R2 V, 1, 74.

**Unkissed,** not kissed: Ado V, 2, 54.

**Unknit** (partic. *unknit*), 1) to untie, to loose (a knot): *will you again u. this churlish knot of all-abhorred war?* H4A V, 1, 15. *I would he had ... not u. himself the noble knot he made,* Cor. IV, 2, 31. *u. that sorrow-wreathen knot,* Tit. III, 2, 4.

2) to unwrinkle, to smoothe: *u. that threatening unkind brow,* Shr. V, 2, 136.

**Unknowing,** not knowing, ignorant: Hml. V, 2, 390.

**Unknown** (*únknown*, when placed before a substantive: Lucr. 103. Sonn. 117, 5. Meas. V, 392. Err. III, 2, 38. Ado IV, 1, 137. Wint. IV, 4, 65. 502. R3 I, 2, 218. Troil. III, 3, 125. Mcb. I, 5, 69. Lr. V, 3, 153. Oth. II, 1, 195. Per. I, 3, 35), 1) not known: Lucr. 34. 103. 527. Meas. V, 392. Err. III, 2, 38. Ado IV, 1, 137. Mids. V, 15. Wint. IV, 4, 65. 395. H5 III, 7, 40. H6A IV, 5, 23. H6B III, 1, 64. Rom. I, 5, 141. Caes. III, 1, 113. V, 1, 33. Mcb. IV, 1, 69. Hml. V, 2, 356. Lr. V, 3, 153. Oth. II, 1, 195. III, 3, 204. Cymb. IV, 4, 43. V, 1, 27. Per. I, 3, 35. With *to:* Gent. III, 1, 61. Err. III, 1, 91. Merch. I, 1, 122. Shr. I, 2, 241. II, 93. All's I, 3, 14. Wint. IV, 2, 35. R3 II, 4, 48. Cor. I, 1, 58. III, 1, 329. Mcb. IV, 3, 126 (*I am yet u. to woman*). Hml. II, 2, 17. *we make trifles of terrors, ensconcing ourselves into seeming knowledge, when we should submit ourselves to an u. fear,* All's II, 3, 6 (an unknown object of fear, or the fear of something unknown).

2) that is not to be expressed or communicated: *that I have frequent been with u. minds,* Sonn. 117, 5 (such as I should be ashamed to mention). *for divers u. reasons, I beseech you, grant me this boon,* R3 I, 2, 218 (such as I must not tell).

Hence = inexpressible, incalculable, immense: *it* (love) *is the star to every wandering bark, whose worth's u., although his height be taken,* Sonn. 116, 8. *my affection hath an u. bottom, like the bay of Portugal,* As IV, 1, 212. *for all ... the profound sea hides in u. fathoms,* Wint. IV, 4, 502.

3) Adverbially, *u. to* = without the knowledge of: *that he u. to me should be in debt,* Err. IV, 2, 48. *when as a lion's whelp shall to himself u. without seeking find,* Cymb. V, 4, 139. V, 5, 436. *who, even now, ... u. to you, unsought, were clipped about with this most tender air,* 451.

Hence, adjectively in appearance, but in fact adverbially, before nouns, = meant, hinted at without one's knowledge; unconscious: *to the u. beloved,* Tw. II, 5, 101 (beloved without knowing it). *and apprehended here immediately the u. Ajax. Heavens, what a man is there! a very horse, that has he knows not what,* Troil. III, 3, 125 (hinted at unintentionally and unconsciously).

**Unlace,** 1) to unfasten, to loose (a woman's dress): *even thus the warlike god —d me,* Pilgr. 149.

2) to strip of ornaments, to disgrace: *that you u. your reputation thus,* Oth. II, 3, 194.

**Unlaid,** not exorcised: *ghost u. forbear thee,* Cymb. IV, 2, 278.

**Unlaid ope,** not laid open, undiscovered, unbetrayed: *to keep his bed of blackness u.* Per. I, 2, 89.

**Unlawful,** 1) illegitimate: *u. issue,* Ant. III, 6, 7.

2) contrary to law, illicit: Meas. IV, 2, 16. Wint. V, 3, 96. H6A V, 5, 30. R3 I, 4, 193. III, 7, 190. Applied to illicit love: Err. V, 51. All's III, 5, 73. IV, 3, 32. Oth. IV, 2, 84. 202.

**Unlawfully,** in violation of law: Meas. III, 1, 196. R3 IV, 4, 30. Oth. V, 2, 70.

**Unlearned,** 1) not learned, not acquired by instruction: *that an invisible instinct should frame them to royalty u., honour untaught, civility not seen from other,* Cymb. IV, 2, 178.

2) uninstructed in science, illiterate: LLL IV, 2, 165. All's I, 3, 246.

3) ignorant, unacquainted; with *in: u. in the world's false subtleties,* Sonn. 138, 4. *but in thy fortunes am u. and strange,* Tim. IV, 3, 56.

**Unless,** except, but for: *we must not seem to understand him, u. some one among us whom we must produce for an interpreter,* All's IV, 1, 15. *my tongue cleave to my roof ... u. a pardon ere I rise or speak,* R2 V, 3, 32 (but for a pardon; or = except if a pardon rises or speaks sooner than I). *nor knows he how to live but by the spoil, u. by robbing of your friends and us,* H6B IV, 8, 42. *have no delight to pass away the time, u. to spy my shadow in the sun,* R3 I, 1, 26. *u. for that, my liege, I cannot guess,* IV, 4, 475. 476. *all hope is vain, u. his noble mother and his wife,* Cor. V, 1, 71. *here nothing breeds u. the nightly owl,* Tit. II, 3, 97. *u. the bookish theoric,* Oth. I, 1, 24.

Usually with a clause, = except if: Sonn. 72, 5. 121, 13. Gent. III, 1, 180. IV, 4, 110. 193. V, 4, 50. Wiv. IV, 2, 68. Meas. I, 4, 69. II, 1, 115. Err. II, 2, 120. V, 176. Ado IV, 1, 30. LLL II, 220. V, 2, 681. Mids. V, 79. Merch. I, 2, 113. II, 4, 6. As IV, 1, 176. All's III, 4, 27. V, 3, 268. H6B IV, 2, 103. H6C I, 4, 126. Per. II, 1, 73. Hml. II, 2, 539 etc. Followed by the subjunctive: Ven. 170. 410. Lucr. 961. 1635. Sonn. 7, 14. 36, 12. 65, 13. 120, 4. Pilgr. 331. Tp. II, 1, 248. II, 2, 7. Epil. 16. Gent. I, 2, 78. II, 7, 56. III, 1, 176. 237. V, 1, 5. Wiv. II, 1, 90. II, 2, 122. Err. I, 1, 22. II, 2, 169. Ado II, 1, 122. 340. III, 2, 32. Merch. I, 2, 117. II, 4, 37. III, 1, 81. III, 2, 237. IV, 1, 105. V, 283. As I, 2, 5. III, 3, 29. IV, 3, 73. Shr. I, 2, 159. H4A V, 2, 54. V, 3, 10. H6A II, 4, 56. H6B III, 1, 96. 128. III, 2, 244. IV, 7, 80. H6C II, 2, 128. Cor. III, 2, 27 (= lest?) etc. Rarely by the indicative: *u. the fear of death doth make me dote, I see my son Antipholus,* Err. V, 195. *u. thou tellest me where thou hadst this ring, thou diest within this hour,* All's V, 3, 284. *thou canst not die by traitors' hands, u. thou bringest them with thee,* Caes. V, 1, 57. *u. thou thinkest me devilish,* Cymb. I, 5, 16.

**Unlessoned,** untaught, uninstructed: Merch. III, 2, 161.

**Unlettered,** illiterate, ignorant; Sonn. 85, 6. LLL I, 1, 253. IV, 2, 18. H5 I, 1, 55.

**Unlicensed,** not permitted, without having leave:

*why, as it were u. of your loves, he would depart,* Per. I, 3, 17.

**Unlicked,** not licked: *an u. bear-whelp,* H6B III, 2, 161 (the bear being supposed to bring forth shapeless lumps of flesh, which she licked into the form of bears).

**Unlike,** 1) adj. and adv. not like, dissimilar, different or differently from: *u. myself thou hearest me moralize,* Ven. 712. *how much u. my hopes,* Merch. II, 9, 57. *sent you hither so u. yourself,* Shr. III, 2, 106. H6B I, 1, 189. III, 1, 8. Troil. II, 2, 166. Oth. I, 1, 143. Ant. I, 5, 35. Cymb. I, 6, 178. V, 4, 136. With *to: how much u. art thou to Portia,* Merch. II, 9, 56.

2) unlikely, improbable: *make not impossible that which but seems u.* Meas. V, 52. *she is a most sweet lady. Not u., sir, that may be,* LLL II, 208. *you are like to do such business. Not u. each way to better yours,* Cor. III, 1, 48. *the service that you three have done is more u. than this thou tellest,* Cymb. V, 5, 354.

**Unlikely,** improbable: Ven. 989. R2 V, 5, 19. H6C III, 2, 151. Cor. IV, 6, 72.

**Unlimited,** undefined, not to be circumscribed by peculiar terms: *scene individable, or poem u.* Hml. II, 2, 419.

**Unlineal,** not coming in the direct order of succession, not hereditary: *a barren sceptre ... to be wrenched with an u. hand, no son of mine succeeding,* Mcb. III, 1, 63.

**Unlink,** to untwist, to disjoin: *it* (the snake) *—ed itself,* As IV, 3, 112.

**Unlived,** deprived of life: *where shall I live now Lucrece is u.?* Lucr. 1754.

**Unload,** 1) to discharge of a load, to disburden: Meas. III, 1, 28. H4A IV, 2, 40. Ant. IV, 6, 24.

2) to throw off like a load, to disclose and vent what lies heavy on the heart: *Humphrey must u. his grief,* H6B I, 1, 76. *nor can my tongue u. my heart's great burthen,* H6C II, 1, 81.

**Unlock,** 1) to open what is shut with a lock; properly and figuratively: Lucr. 16. LLL I, 1, 109. Merch. I, 1, 139. II, 9, 52. Mcb. V, 1, 6.

2) to unfasten in general, to loose: *I'll frush it and u. the rivets all,* Troil. V, 6, 29.

**Unlooked** (*únlooked,* placed before the subst.) unexpected: *by some u. accident cut off,* R3 I, 3, 214.

**Unlooked-for,** 1) unexpected: Lucr. 846. John II, 79. 560. R2 I, 3, 155. H6C V, 1, 14. Rom. I, 5, 31.

2) not sought after: *whilst I, whom fortune of such triumph bars, u. joy in that I honour most,* Sonn. 25, 4 (neglected by the world). *if not, honour comes u., and there's an end,* H4A V, 3, 64.

3) unwished, unwelcome: *Clarence, Henry, and his son young Edward, and all the u. issue of their bodies,* H6C III, 2, 131.

**Unlooked on,** unnoticed, not cared for: *so thou, thyself out-going in thy noon, u. diest, unless thou get a son,* Sonn. 7, 14.

**Unloose,** to loose; to untie; to set at liberty: *they scatter and u. it from their bond,* Lucr. 136. *to u. this tied-up justice,* Meas. I, 3, 32. *the Gordian knot he will u.* H5 I, 1, 46. *u. thy long-imprisoned thoughts,* H6B V, 1, 88. *where I am robbed and bound, there must I be —d,* H8 II, 4, 147. *shall from your neck u. his amorous fold,* Troil. III, 3, 223. *the holy cords which are too intrinse t' u.* Lr. II, 2, 81.

**Unloved,** not loved: Mids. III, 2, 234. *the ostentation of our love, which, left unshown, is often left u.* Ant. III, 6, 53 (i. e. not felt; *to love a love* being a similar phrase as f. i. *to think a thought.* cf. *what ruins are in me ... by him not ruined?* Err. II, 1, 96. *the want that you have wanted,* Lr. I, 1, 282).

**Unloving,** devoid of love: H6C II, 2, 25.

**Unluckily,** unfortunately: Err. V, 125. Shr. IV, 5, 25. Wint. III, 2, 100. Rom. III, 4, 1. Tim. III, 2, 51. Peculiar use: *if like an ill venture it come u. home,* H4B V, 5, 128 (in an unlucky plight or state). *things u. charge my fantasy,* Caes. III, 3, 2 (in an unlucky manner, so as to foreshow some misfortune. cf. *we have safely found our king,* Tp. V, 221. 236. *if a son do sinfully miscarry,* H5 IV, 1, 155. see Appendix. Most M. Edd. *unlucky;* others *unlikely*).

**Unlucky,** unfortunate: H4A V, 1, 53. Tit. II, 3, 251. Rom. III, 1, 148. V, 3, 136 (Q2 *unthrifty*). Oth. V, 2, 341.

**Unlustrous,** a needless emendation of M. Edd. for *illustrious* in Cymb. I, 6, 109; cf. such words as *facinerious, robustious, dexteriously* etc.

**Unmade** (*únmade,* because placed before the subst.) not made: *taking the measure of an u. grave,* Rom. III, 3, 70.

**Unmake** (*únmake* and *unmáke*) to deprive of quality or being: *they have made themselves, and that their fitness now does u. you,* Mcb. I, 7, 54. *she may make, u., do what she list,* Oth. II, 3, 352.

**Unmanly,** unbecoming in a man: H6C I, 1, 186. H8 I, 3, 4. Tim. IV, 3, 203. Hml. I, 2, 94.

**Unmanned,** 1) not accustomed to man (a term of falconry): *hood my u. blood, bating in my cheeks, with thy black mantle,* Rom. III, 2, 14.

2) deprived of the qualities of a man: *quite u. in folly,* Mcb. III, 4, 73.

**Unmannered,** uncivil, rude: Shr. IV, 1, 169. R3 I, 2, 39.

**Unmannerly,** adj. uncivil; indecent: Gent. III, 1, 393. Wiv. I, 1, 325. Merch. I, 2, 54. John V, 2, 131. H4A I, 3, 43. H8 I, 2, 27. I, 4, 95. IV, 2, 105. Tit. II, 3, 65. Hml. III, 2, 364. Lr. I, 1, 147.

**Unmannerly,** adv. uncivilly; indecently: H8 III, 1, 176. Mcb. II, 3, 122.

**Unmarried,** not married: Wint. IV, 4, 123.

**Unmask** (*unmásk; únmask* in Lucr. 940) 1) tr. to strip of a mask; to lay open: *to u. falsehood and bring truth to light,* Lucr. 940. *u. this moody heaviness and tell thy grief,* 1602. *if she u. her beauty to the moon,* Hml. I, 3, 37.

2) intr. to put off a mask, to unveil one's self: *now I will u.* Meas. V, 206.

**Unmastered,** uncontrolled, unbridled: *his u. importunity,* Hml. I, 3, 32.

**Unmatchable,** matchless, incomparable, unparalleled: Tw. I, 5, 181. John IV, 3, 52. H5 III, 7, 151. Ant. II, 3, 20.

**Unmatched** (always before the subst.; *unmátched,* when trisyllabic; *únmatched,* when dissyll.), unequalled, matchless: Lucr. 11. John I, 265. H8 II, 4, 47. Tim. IV, 3, 523. Hml. III, 1, 167.

**Unmeasurable,** infinite, boundless: Wiv. II, 1, 109. Tim. IV, 3, 178.

**Unmeet,** not proper, unfit: Pilgr. 239 and LLL IV, 3, 113. Meas. IV, 3, 71. Ado IV, 1, 184. H6B I, 3, 167. 168.

**Unmellowed,** not ripe: Gent. II, 4, 70.

**Unmerciful,** pitiless, cruel: Lr. III, 7, 33.

**Unmeritable,** devoid of merit: *my desert u. shuns your high request,* R3 III, 7, 155. *a slight u. man,* Caes. IV, 1, 12.

**Unmeriting,** the same: Cor. II, 1, 47.

**Unminded,** not taken notice of, not cared for: *a poor u. outlaw,* H4A IV, 3, 58.

**Unmindful,** careless, negligent: R3 IV, 4, 444.

**Unmingled,** having no foreign admixture: *take u. thence that drop again,* Err. II, 2, 129. *lies rich in virtue and u.* Troil. I, 3, 30 (quadrisyll. at the end of the line).

**Unmitigable,** unappeasable, implacable: Tp. I, 2, 276.

**Unmitigated,** not softened in harshness: Ado IV, 1, 308.

**Unmixed,** not mingled: Hml. I, 5, 104.

**Unmoaned,** not lamented: R3 II, 2, 64.

**Unmoved,** 1) not roused, not excited, not exasperated: *patience u., no marvel though she pause,* Err. II, 1, 32.

2) not susceptible of excitement: *u., cold, and to temptation slow,* Sonn. 94, 4.

**Unmoving,** having no motion: *his slow u. finger,* Oth. IV, 2, 55 (Ff *slow and moving*).

**Unmusical,** not pleasing to the ear: *a name u. to the Volscians' ears,* Cor. IV, 5, 64.

**Unmuzzle,** to loose from a muzzle, to free from restraint: *u. your wisdom,* As I, 2, 74. *—d thoughts,* Tw. III, 1, 130.

**Unnatural,** 1) contrary to the laws and order of nature: R3 I, 2, 23. 61. Cor. V, 3, 184. Rom. V, 3, 152 (*come from that nest of death, contagion, and u. sleep,* i. e. where it is unnatural to sleep). Mcb. II, 4, 10. V, 1, 80. Oth. III, 3, 233. V, 2, 42.

2) contrary to the feelings of human nature, violating the first principles of nature, inhuman in the highest degree; used of persons: *u. though thou art,* Tp. V, 79. *the most u. that lived amongst men,* As IV, 3, 123. 125. *a most unworthy and u. lord,* Wint. II, 3, 113. John II, 10. H6C I, 1, 218. V, 1, 86. Cor. III, 1, 293. V, 3, 84. Tit. V, 3, 48. Hml. III, 2, 413. Lr. I, 2, 81. II, 4, 281. Cymb. IV, 4, 6. Of things or actions: *grow like savages ... to swearing and stern looks, and every thing that seems u.* H5 V, 2, 62. *the most u. wounds which thou thyself hast given her woful breast,* H6A III, 3, 50. V, 1, 12. H6C II, 5, 90. R3 I, 2, 60. 134. H8 II, 1, 123. Mcb. V, 1, 79. Hml. I, 5, 25. 28. V, 2, 392. Lr. I, 1, 222. II, 1, 52. III, 1, 38. III, 3, 2. 7. Per. IV, 4, 36.

**Unnaturally,** in opposition to natural feelings: H6C I, 1, 193.

**Unnaturalness,** a state contrary to the feelings of nature: *u. between the child and the parent,* Lr. I, 2, 157.

**Unnecessarily,** superfluously: *can prate as amply and u. as this Gonzalo,* Tp. II, 1, 264.

**Unnecessary,** not wanted, needless, useless: H5 IV, 2, 27. Lr. II, 2, 69. II, 4, 157.

**Unneighbourly,** adv. in a manner not suitable to neighbours or countrymen: John V, 2, 39.

**Unnerved,** strengthless, weak: Hml. II, 2, 496.

**Unnoble,** ignoble: Ant. III, 11, 50.

**Unnoted,** 1) not perceived, or imperceptible: *with such sober and u. passion he did behave his anger,* Tim. III, 5, 21.

2) not taken notice of: *gnats are u. wheresoe'er they fly,* Lucr. 1014. *till their own scorn return to them u.* All's I, 2, 34.

**Unnumbered,** innumerable: Caes. III, 1, 63. Lr. IV, 6, 21.

**Unordinate,** irregular, excessive; reading of Q1 in Oth. II, 3, 311; the rest of O. Edd. *inordinate.*

**Unowed,** having no owner: *the u. interest of proud-swelling state,* John IV, 3, 147 (*únowed,* because placed before the subst.).

**Unpack,** to unload (in contempt): *must like a whore u. my heart with words,* Hml. II, 2, 614.

**Unpaid,** not paid: *there remains u. a hundred thousand more,* LLL II, 134. *rustling in u. for silk,* Cymb. III, 3, 24. *she should that duty leave u. to you,* III, 5, 48. *the worth thou art u. for,* V, 5, 307.

**Unparagoned,** matchless: Cymb. I, 4, 87. II, 2, 17.

**Unparalleled,** unequalled, matchless: Wint. V, 1, 16. Cor. V, 2, 16. Ant. V, 2, 319.

**Unpardonable,** irremissible, not to be forgiven: H6C I, 4, 106.

**Unpartial,** impartial: H8 II, 2, 107.

**Unpathed** (*únpathed,* because placed before the subst.) trackless: *u. waters,* Wint. IV, 4, 578.

**Unpaved,** a word applied by Cloten to a eunuch, = having no stones (cf. *Stone*): Cymb. II, 3, 34.

**Unpay,** to annul by payment, to make undone: *pay her the debt you owe her, and u. the villany you have done her,* H4B II, 1, 130.

**Unpeaceable,** quarrelsome: Tim. I, 1, 280.

**Unpeeled,** stripped, desolate: *to let you enter his u. house,* LLL II, 88 (reading of Q1; the other O. Edd. *unpeopled*).

**Unpeg,** to open by loosing a peg: *u. the basket,* Hml. III, 4, 193.

**Unpeople,** 1) to deprive of people; with *of: which if he take, shall quite u. her of liegers for her sweet,* Cymb. I, 5, 79.

2) to deprive of inhabitants, to depopulate: Lucr. 1741. Meas. III, 2, 184. H6C I, 1, 126. Ant. I, 5, 78.

**Unpeopled,** uninhabited, desolate: LLL II, 88 (Q1 *unpeeled*). As III, 2, 134. R2 I, 2, 69.

**Unperceived,** not perceived, not seen: Lucr.1010.

**Unperfect,** deficient, not exactly knowing one's part: Sonn. 23, 1.

**Unperfectness,** imperfection, deficiency: Oth. II, 3, 298.

**Unpicked,** unplucked, ungathered, unenjoyed: *now comes in the sweetest morsel of the night, and we must hence and leave it u.* H4B II, 4, 397.

**Unpin,** to loose from pins: Oth. IV, 3, 21. 34.

**Unpinked,** not pierced with eyelet-holes: *Gabriel's pumps were all u. i'the heel,* Shr. IV, 1, 136.

**Unpitied,** 1) not pitied, not regarded with sympathetic sorrow: All's II, 1, 191. R3 IV, 4, 74. Ant. I, 3, 98.

2) unmerciful: *with an u. whipping,* Meas. IV, 2, 13.

**Unpitifully,** unmercifully: Wiv. IV, 2, 215.

**Unplagued,** not plagued, not afflicted: *toes u. with corns,* Rom. I, 5, 19.

**Unplausive,** displeased, disapproving: *why such u. eyes are bent on him,* Troil. III, 3, 43.*

**Unpleasantest,** saddest, most disagreeable: *the u. words that ever blotted paper,* Merch. III, 2, 254.

**Unpleased,** displeased: R2 III, 3, 193.

**Unpleasing,** disagreeable, offensive: LLL V, 2

912. 921. John :II, 1, 45. R2 III, 4, 74. R3 IV, 1, 37. Rom. III, 5, 28.

**Unpolicied,** devoid of policy, stupid: Ant.V,2,311.

**Unpolished,** unrefined, rude: Ven. Ded. 1. LLL IV, 2, 17. Shr. IV, 1, 128. H6B III, 2, 271.

**Unpolluted,** undefiled, pure: Hml. V, 1, 262.

**Unpossessed,** having no possessor: R3 IV,4,471.

**Unpossessing,** not coming to an estate (cf. *landless*): *thou u. bastard,* Lr. II, 1, 69.

**Unpossible,** impossible: R2 II, 2, 126 (Ff *impossible*).

**Unpractised,** wanting experience, unskilful: Lucr. 1098. Merch. III, 2, 161. Troil. I, 1, 12.

**Unpregnant,** unapt for business: *this deed unshapes me quite, makes me u. and dull to all proceedings,* Meas. IV, 4, 23. With *of,* = having no lively sense of, indifferent to: *u. of my cause,* Hml. II, 2, 595.

**Unpremeditated,** without premeditation, extempore: *I will answer u.* H6A I, 2, 88.

**Unprepared,** not prepared, not made ready, not provided: Meas. IV, 3, 71. John II, 560. R3 III, 2, 65. Mcb. II, 1, 17. Oth. V, 2, 31.

**Unpressed,** not pressed, not lain on: *have I my pillow left u. in Rome,* Ant. III, 13, 106.

**Unprevailing,** unavailing: *throw to earth this u. woe,* Hml. I, 2, 107.

**Unprevented,** not obviated, not frustrated: Gent. III, 1, 21.

**Unprizable,** 1) invaluable, inestimable: *your brace of u. estimations,* Cymb. I, 4, 99.

2) not to be valued highly, valueless: *a bawbling vessel ... for shallow draught and bulk u.* Tw. V, 58.

**Unprized** (*únprized,* because placed before its noun) not valued or invaluable? Lr. I, 1, 262.

**Unprofitable,** yielding no gain or advantage, serving no purpose, useless: Lucr. 1017. Meas. V, 460. H4A III, 1, 63. H5 III Chor. 31. Hml. I, 2, 133. Per. IV, 1, 26.

**Unprofited,** profitless: *leap all civil bounds rather than make u. return,* Tw. I, 4, 22.

**Unproper,** 1) not peculiar to an individual, not one's own, common; 2) indecent; with a double meaning: *lie in those u. beds which they dare swear peculiar,* Oth. IV, 1, 69.

**Unproperly,** improperly, unsuitably: *and u. show duty,* Cor. V, 3, 54.

**Unproportioned,** disorderly, unsuitable: *give thy thoughts no tongue, nor any u. thought his act,* Hml. I, 3, 60.*

**Unprovide,** to deprive of what is necessary: *lest her body and beauty u. my mind again,* Oth. IV, 1, 218 (divest it of resolution).

**Unprovided,** unprepared, not supplied with what is necessary; as not in sufficient preparation to meet an enemy: H6C V, 4, 63. unarmed: R3 III, 2, 75. Lr. II, 1, 54. not decently dressed: Shr. III, 2, 101. wanting money: H4A III, 3, 213. not duly prepared for death: H5 IV, 1, 183. With *of: I yet am u. of a pair of bases,* Per. II, 1, 166.

**Unprovident,** not careful in preparing for future exigencies: *deny that thou bearest love to any, who for thyself art so u.* Sonn. 10, 2.

**Unprovoke,** to counteract an incitement or impulse given, to frustrate: *lechery it* (drink) *provokes and —s,* Mcb. II, 3, 32 (the porter's speech).

**Unpruned,** not trimmed, not lopped: R2 III, 4, 45. H5 V, 2, 42. Metaphorically: LLL IV, 2, 18.

**Unpublished,** unknown, secret: *all blest secrets, all you u. virtues of the earth,* Lr. IV, 4, 16.

**Unpurged,** impure, unwholesome: *the rheumy and u. air,* Caes. II, 1, 266.

**Unpurposed,** not intended: *or thy precedent services are all but accidents u.* Ant. IV, 14, 84.

**Unqualitied** (O. Edd. *unqualited*) deprived of one's character and faculties: *he is u. with very shame,* Ant. III, 11, 44.

**Unqueened,** divested of the dignity of queen: H8 IV, 2, 171.

**Unquestionable,** averse to talk and conversation: *an u. spirit* (a mark of love) As III, 2, 393.

**Unquestioned,** unexamined, not inquired into: Meas. I, 1, 55. All's II, 1, 211.

**Unquiet,** subst. disturbance, agitation: *thunder above and deeps below make such u.* Per. II Prol. 31.

**Unquiet,** adj. not tranquil, restless: Err. V, 74. Merch. III, 2, 308. IV, 1, 294. H4B I, 2, 170. H5 I, 1, 4. R3 II, 4, 55. III, 2, 27.

**Unquietly,** in a disturbed and agitated manner: *one minded like the weather, most u.* Lr. III, 1, 2.

**Unquietness,** want of tranquillity, uneasiness, agitation: Ado I, 3, 50. Oth. III, 4, 133.

**Unraised,** not lifted up to a higher place, not elevated, remaining below: *the flat u. spirits,* H5 Prol. 9 (opposed to the '*Muse of fire that would ascend the brightest heaven of invention*' in v. 1).

**Unraked,** not raked together: *where fires thou findest u.* Wiv. V, 5, 48.

**Unread,** unlearned, illiterate: *the wise and fool, the artist and u.* Troil. I, 3, 24.

**Unready,** undressed: H6A II, 1, 39. 40.

**Unreal,** not real, only imaginary: Wint. I, 2, 141. Mcb. III, 4, 107.

**Unreasonable,** 1) not endowed with reason, irrational: *u. creatures feed their young,* H6C II, 2, 26.

2) not agreeable to reason, absurd, foolish: Wiv. IV, 2, 147. Merch. V, 203. Rom. III, 3, 111.

**Unreasonably,** in a manner contrary to reason: Cor. I, 3, 84.

**Unrecalling,** past recall, not capable of being repealed: *his u. crime,* Lucr. 993 (not the partic., but the gerund used adjectively; cf. *trembling contribution; feeling sorrows; his all-obeying breath; unrecuring wound*).

**Unreclaimed,** untamed: *a savageness in u. blood,* Hml. II, 1, 34.

**Unreconciled,** not reconciled, not restored to favour: *any crime u. as yet to heaven and grace,* Oth. V, 2, 27.

**Unreconciliable,** not capable of being brought to peace and friendship; incompatible: *that our stars u. should divide our equalness to this,* Ant. V, 1, 47.

**Unrecounted,** untold: H8 III, 2, 48.

**Unrecuring,** past cure, incurable: *the deer that hath received some u. wound,* Tit. III, 1, 90 (cf. *Unrecalling*).

**Unregarded,** not noticed, neglected: As II, 3, 42.

**Unregistered,** not recorded: Ant. III, 13, 119.

**Unrelenting,** pitiless: H6A V, 4, 59. H6C II, 1, 58. Tit. II, 3, 141 (cf. *Relent*).

**Unremoveable,** not to be removed, firmly fixed: *how u. and fixed he is in his own course,* Lr. II, 4, 94.

**Unremoveably,** in a manner that admits no

removal, fixedly: *his discontents are u. coupled to nature*, Tim. V, 1, 227.

**Unreprievable,** not to be reprieved or saved: *to tyrannize on u. condemned blood*, John V, 7, 48.

**Unresisted,** irresistible: *heedful fear is almost choked by u. lust*, Lucr. 282.

**Unresolved,** not determined: R3 IV, 4, 436.

**Unrespected,** unnoticed, unregarded: *when most I wink, then do mine eyes best see, for all the day they view things u.* Sonn. 43, 2. *they live unwooed and u. fade*, 54, 10.

**Unrespective,** 1) devoid of respect and consideration, regardless, unthinking: *I will converse with iron-witted fools and u. boys*, R3 IV, 2, 29.

2) seemingly = not attended with regard, used at random: *the remainder viands we do not throw in u. sieve*, Troil. II, 2, 71; i. e. we do not throw them unrespectively into the sewer.

**Unrest,** disquiet: Lucr. 1725. Sonn. 147, 10. R2 II, 4, 22. R3 IV, 4, 29. V, 3, 320. Tit. II, 3, 8. IV, 2, 31. Rom. I, 5, 122.

**Unrestored,** not given back: Ant. III, 6, 27.

**Unrestrained,** licentious: R2 V, 3, 7.

**Unrevenged,** not revenged: H4A V, 3, 44. H6B I, 3, 150.

**Unreverend** or **Unreverent** (used indiscriminately; cf. *Reverend*) irreverent, disrespectful: Gent. II, 6, 14. Meas. V, 307. Shr. III, 2, 114. John I, 227. R2 II, 1, 123. H6A III, 1, 49. Lr. II, 2, 133 (Ff. *reverend*).

**Unreversed,** not revoked, not repealed: Gent. III, 1, 223.

**Unrewarded,** not rewarded: Tp. IV, 242.

**Unrighteous,** not honest and upright, insincere, false: *ere yet the salt of most u. tears had left the flushing in her galled eyes, she married*, Hml. I, 2, 154.

**Unrightful,** illegitimate: R2 V, 1, 63.

**Unrip,** to rip, to cut open: *—edst the bowels of thy sovereign's son*, R3 I, 4, 212.

**Unripe** (before the subst. *únripe*, behind *unrípe*) not ripe, not mature: Ven. 128. 524. Pilgr. 51. Hml. III, 2, 200.

**Unrivalled,** peerless: Gent. V, 4, 144.

**Unroll,** to unfold or uncoil itself: *as an adder when she doth u.* Tit. II, 3, 35.

**Unrolled,** struck off the roll or register (of thieves): *let me be u. and my name put in the book of virtue*, Wint. IV, 3, 130.

**Unroof,** to strip of the roof, to ravage: *the rabble should have first —ed the city*, Cor. I, 1, 222.

**Unroosted,** driven from the roost, hen-pecked: *u. by thy dame Partlet here*, Wint. II, 3, 74.

**Unroot,** to tear up by the root, to deracinate: Alls V, 1, 6.

**Unrough** (*únrough*, because placed before the subst.) smooth, unbearded: *many u. youths that even now protest their first of manhood*, Mcb. V, 2, 10 (O. Edd. *unruffe*).

**Unruly,** not submitting to rules, disregarding restraint, ungovernable: Ven. 326. Gent. I, 2, 96. Meas. III, 1, 252. Err. II, 1, 100. III, 1, 62. John III, 4, 135 (*a sceptre snatched with an u. hand*). R2 III, 3, 179. III, 4, 30. V, 2, 110. Rom. III, 1, 162. Tim. V, 1, 183. Lr. I, 1, 301. Applied to the elements, = turbulent, tempestuous: Lucr. 869. Compl. 103. H4A III, 1, 30. Mcb. II, 3, 59.

**Unsafe** (*unsáfe; únsafe* before a subst.), 1) exposed to danger: Mcb. III, 2, 32. Oth. V, 1, 43.

2) dangerous, not to be trusted: *no incredulous or u. circumstance*, Tw. III, 4, 88. *these dangerous u. lunes i' the king*, Wint. II, 2, 30 (or = unsound, crazy? cf. *Safe* 1).

**Unsalted,** not salted, unseasoned: *speak then, thou u. leaven*, Troil. II, 1, 15 (Ff. *whinid'st*, M. Edd. *vinewedst*).

**Unsaluted,** not saluted, not greeted: Cor. V, 3, 50.

**Unsanctified,** 1) not consecrated: *she should in ground u. have lodged*, Hml. V, 1, 252.

2) profane, wicked: *in no place so u. where such as thou mayst find him*, Mcb. IV, 2, 81. *the post u. of murderous lechers*, Lr. IV, 6, 281.

**Unsatiate,** insatiate, greedy: R3 III, 5, 87 (Ff. *insatiate*). III, 7, 7 (Qq. *insatiate*).

**Unsatisfied,** 1) not contented, not gratified to the full: *we think ourselves u.* H4A I, 3, 287. *u. in getting*, H8 IV, 2, 55. *wilt thou leave me so u.?* Rom. II, 2, 125. *that satiate yet u. desire*, Cymb. I, 6, 48.

2) unpaid: *that one half which is u.* LLL II, 139.

3) not fully informed and settled in opinion: *report me and my cause aright to the u.* Hml. V, 2, 351.

**Unsavoury,** having a bad taste: *sweet beginning, but u. end*, Ven. 1138. *O bitter conduct, come, u. guide*, Rom. V, 3, 116. *all viands seem u.* Per. II, 3, 31. Metaphorically, = displeasing: *the most u. similes*, H4A I, 2, 89. *u. news*, H6C IV, 6, 80.

**Unsay,** to deny something declared, to retract: Mids. I, 1, 181. R2 IV, 9. H4A I, 3, 76. H8 V 1, 177.

**Unscaleable,** not climbable: Cymb. III, 1, 20.

**Unscanned,** inconsiderate: *the harm of u. swiftness*, Cor. III, 1, 313 (*únscanned*, because placed before the subst.).

**Unscarred** (*únscarred* before the subst.; in another collocation *unscárred*) not wounded, unhurt: *live u. of bleeding slaughter*, R3 IV, 4, 209 (Qq. *u. from*). *the u. braggarts of the war*, Tim. IV, 3, 161.

**Unschooled,** not educated, not developed by study: Merch. III, 2, 161. Hml. I, 2, 97.

**Unscissared,** unshorn: Per. III, 3, 29 (O. Edd. *unsistered*).

**Unscorched,** not scorched, not affected by fire: Caes. I, 3, 18.

**Unscoured** (*únscoured*, because placed before the subst.) not scoured, not cleaned by rubbing: Meas. I, 2, 171.

**Unscratched,** not scratched: John II, 225.

**Unseal,** to break the seal of, to open: Merch. V, 275. H8 III, 2, 79. Hml. V, 2, 17 (Qq. *unfold*). Lr. IV, 5, 22.

**Unsealed,** having no seal, not ratified, not confirmed, not sanctioned: *your oaths are words and poor conditions, but u.* Alls IV, 2, 30.

**Unseam,** to rip, to cut open: *he —ed him from the nave to the chaps*, Mcb. I, 2, 22.

**Unsearched,** not searched, not looked through and examined: Tit. IV, 3, 22.

**Unseasonable,** 1) not being in the proper season or time, untimely, ill-timed: *at any u. instant of the night*, Ado II, 2, 16. *at a time u.* John IV, 2, 20.

2) not agreeable to the season: *to strike the poor u. doe*, Lucr. 581. *like an u. stormy day*, R2 III, 2, 106.

**Unseasonably,** at an improper time: As III, 2, 258.

**Unseasoned,** 1) unseasonable, ill-timed: *emboldened me to this u. intrusion,* Wiv. II, 2, 174. *these u. hours must add unto your sickness,* H4B III, 1, 105.

2) unripe, imperfect: *'tis an u. courtier; good my lord, advise him,* Alls I, 1, 80.

**Unseconded,** not assisted: H4B II, 3, 34.

**Unsecret,** not discreet, not close: *who shall be true to us, when we are so u. to ourselves?* Troil. III, 2, 133.

**Unseduced,** not corrupted, not enticed to a surrender of chastity: Cymb. I, 4, 173.

**Unseeing,** not seeing: Sonn. 43, 8. Gent. IV, 4, 209.

**Unseeming,** not seeming: *you wrong the reputation of your name in so u. to confess receipt of that which hath so faithfully been paid,* LLL II, 156.

**Unseemly,** uncomely: *u. woman in a seeming man,* Rom. III, 3, 112.

**Unseen** (*unseén;* but *únseen,* when placed before a subst.: Lucr. 753. 763. 827. R2 IV, 297. Hml. IV, 1, 12. Only once in prose: Ant. I, 2, 159) 1) not seen, not perceived or discovered: Lucr. 676. 753. 763 (*the u. secrecy of night,* i. e. the quality of hiding unseen secrets). 827. Sonn. 33, 8. 118, 3. Pilgr. 232 and LLL IV, 3, 106. Gent. V, 4, 4. Err. I, 2, 38. LLL V, 2, 358. All's II, 3, 296. Wint. I, 2, 292. R2 III, 2, 39. IV, 187. 297. H5 I, 1, 66. Rom. III, 2, 7. Hml. III, 1, 33. III, 4, 149. IV, 1, 12. Ant. I, 2, 159.

2) invisible: *himself behind was left u. save to the eye of mind,* Lucr. 1426. *O jest u., inscrutable,* Gent. II, 1, 141.

**Unseminared,** destitute of seed or sperm: Ant. I, 5, 11.

**Unseparable,** inseparable, not to be parted: Cor. IV, 4, 16.

**Unserviceable,** not fit for service: *five or six thousand, but very weak and u.* All's IV, 3, 152.

**Unset,** unplanted: *many maiden gardens yet u.* Sonn. 16, 6.

**Unsettle,** to become unfixed, to give way, to be disordered: *his wits begin to u.* Lr. III, 4, 167.

**Unsettled,** 1) not firmly resolved: *prepared I was not for such a business; therefore am I found so much u.* All's II, 5, 68. *to rectify what is u. in the king,* H8 II, 4, 64.

2) unhinged, disturbed, troubled, contrary to calm and composed: *the best comforter to an u. fancy,* Tp. V, 59. *he something seems u.* Wint. I, 2, 147. *dost think I am so muddy, so u.* 325 (properly = turbid). *all the u. humours of the land,* John II, 66 (restless).

**Unsevered,** inseparable: *like u. friends,* Cor. III, 2, 42.

**Unsex,** to unwoman: Mcb. I, 5, 42.

**Unshaked,** not shaken, firm, steady: Caes. III, 1, 70 (cf. *Motion* and *Of*). Cymb. II, 1, 68.

**Unshaken,** 1) without being shaken and put into a vibrating motion: *but fall u. when they mellow be,* Hml. III, 2, 201.

2) firm, steady: *stand u. yours,* H8 III, 2, 199.

**Unshape,** to deprive of shape, to derange: *this deed —s me quite,* Meas. IV, 4, 23.

**Unshaped** (*unsháped* before the subst., because trisyll.) having no shape, formless, confused: *her speech is nothing, but the u. use of it doth move the hearers to collection,* Hml. IV, 5, 8.

**Unshapen,** shapeless, deformed: *that halt and am u. thus,* R3 I, 2, 251. (Ff *misshapen*).

**Unsheathe,** to draw from the scabbard: Lucr. 1724. H4B IV, 4, 86. H6C II, 2, 59. 80. 123.

**Unshorn** (*únshorn,* because placed before the subst.) not shorn, not clipped with shears: *like u. velvet,* Compl. 94.

**Unshout,** to undo what has been done by shouting: *u. the noise that banished Marcius,* Cor. V, 5, 4.

**Unshown,** not shown: Ant. III, 6, 52.

**Unshrinking,** not recoiling, not falling back with fear: Mcb. V, 8, 42.*

**Unshrubbed** (*únshrubbed,* because placed before the subst.) not set with shrubs: Tp. IV, 81.

**Unshunnable,** inevitable: Oth. III, 3, 275.

**Unshunned,** the same: *an u. consequence,* Meas. III, 2, 63.

**Unsifted,** untried: *you speak like a green girl, u. in such perilous circumstance,* Hml. I, 3, 102.

**Unsightly,** displeasing to the eye: Lr. II, 4, 159.

**Unsinewed** (reading of the later Ff; the earlier Ff and Qq *unsinnowed*) strengthless, weak: *two special reasons, which may to you perhaps seem much u., but yet to me they are strong,* Hml. IV, 7, 10.

**Unsistered,** reading of O. Edd. in Per. III, 3, 29; M. Edd. *unscissored.*

**Unsisting,** perhaps = unresting, but probably a misprint: *that spirit's possessed with haste that wounds the u. postern with these strokes,* Meas. IV, 2, 92. The proposed emendations are all of them very unsatisfactory.

**Unskilful,** 1) wanting art or knowledge: Wiv. I, 3, 29. H6C V, 4, 19. With *in: u. in the world's false forgeries,* Pilgr. 4.

2) destitute of discernment: *though it make the u. laugh,* Hml. III, 2, 29. *we must not think the Turk is so u. to leave that latest* etc. Oth. I, 3, 27.

**Unskilfully,** without knowledge and discernment: *therefore you speak u., or if your knowledge be more it is much darkened in your malice,* Meas. III, 2, 156.

**Unslipping,** not liable to slipping, to escaping from: *to knit your hearts with an u. knot,* Ant. II, 2, 129. cf. *Unrecalling.*

**Unsmirched,** unsoiled, unstained: Hml. IV, 5, 119.

**Unsoiled** (*únsoiled,* because before the subst. and dissyll.), unstained: Meas. II, 4, 155.

**Unsolicited,** not applied to, unasked, unpetitioned: *u. I left no reverend person in this court,* H8 II, 4, 219. *there's not a god left u.* Tit. IV, 3, 60.

**Unsorted,** unfit, unsuitable: *the time itself u.* H4A II, 3, 13.

**Unsought,** 1) not sought, not searched for: *unknown to you, u.* Cymb. V, 5, 451.

2) not pursued, not solicited: *love sought is good, but given u. is better,* Tw. III, 1, 168.

3) not searched (?): *loath to leave u. or that or any place that harbours men,* Err. I, 1, 136. cf. H6A V, 4, 3.

**Unsound,** not sound in character, not really virtuous, unprincipled: *lest that it make me so u. a man as to upbraid you with those kindnesses that I have done for you,* Tw. III, 4, 384.

**Unsounded,** not sounded, not explored: Lucr. 1819. Gent. III, 2, 81. H6B III, 1, 57.

**Unspeak,** to unsay, to retract: Mcb. IV, 3, 123.

**Unspeakable**, ineffable, unutterable: Err. I, 1, 33. Wint. I, 1, 37. IV, 2, 46. Tit. I, 256. V, 3, 126.

**Unspeaking**, wanting power of speech: *his description proved us u. sots*, Cymb. V, 5, 178.

**Unsphere**, to remove from its orb: *to u. the stars with oaths*, Wint. I, 2, 48.

**Unspoke**, not uttered, untold: Lr. I, 1, 239.

**Unspoken**, the same: Cymb. V, 5, 139.

**Unspotted**, spotless, unstained: Lucr. 821. H5 IV, 1, 169. H6A V, 3, 182. H6B III, 1, 100. H8 V, 5, 62. Per. I, 1, 53.

**Unsquare** (Q) or **Unsquared** (Ff), not suitable, not shaped and adapted to the purpose: *with terms u.* Troil. I, 3, 159.

**Unstable**, not fixed, inconstant: Cor. III, 1, 148.

**Unstaid** (*unstaid* in R2 II, 1, 2, where it is placed immediately before a subst.) thoughtless, volatile, giddy-headed: *for undertaking so u. a journey*, Gent. II, 7, 60. *u. and skittish in all motions else*, Tw. II, 4, 18. *in wholesome counsel to his u. youth*, R2 II, 1, 2.

**Unstained** (*unstained*, when dissyll. and placed before the subst.), spotless: Lucr. 87. 366. Sonn. 70, 8. Wint. IV, 4, 149. John II, 16. H4B V, 2, 114. Rom. IV, 1, 88.

**Unstanched** or **Unstaunched**, 1) insatiate, unquenched, unquenchable: *whose u. thirst York and young Rutland could not satisfy*, H6C II, 6, 83.

2) incontinent (? Nares) or urinae incontinens (? Dyce) or being in her terms (?): *as leaky as an u. wench*, Tp. I, 1, 51.

**Unstate**, to deprive or divest of estate and dignity: *I would u. myself, to be in a due resolution*, Lr. I, 2, 108. *Caesar will u. his happiness*, Ant. III, 13, 30.

**Unsteadfast**, not fixed, not standing firm: *on the u. footing of a spear*, H4A I, 3, 193.

**Unstooping**, unbending: *the u. firmness of my upright soul*, R2 I, 1, 121.

**Unstringed**, having no strings: *an u. viol*, R2 I, 3, 162.

**Unstuffed** (*unstuffed*, because dissyll. and placed before a subst.) not crammed, not overcharged: *where unbruised youth with u. brain doth couch his limbs*, Rom. II, 3, 37.

**Unsubstantial**, immaterial, incorporeal: *that u. death is amorous*, Rom. V, 3, 103. *thou u. air that I embrace*, Lr. IV, 1, 7.

**Unsuitable**, unbecoming, unfit, unadapted: *richly suited, but u.* Alls I, 1, 170. *which will now be so u. to her disposition*, Tw. II, 5, 221.

**Unsuiting**, not becoming; writing of M. Edd. in Oth. IV, 1, 78: *a passion most u. such a man.* Q1 *unfitting*, Ff *resulting*.

**Unsullied**, unstained: LLL V, 2, 352.

**Unsunned** (dissyll. and placed before the subst.; therefore *unsunned*) not having been exposed to the sun: *as chaste as u. snow*, Cymb. II, 5, 13.

**Unsure** (*unsure*; but before a subst. either *unsure* or *unsure*, according as the subst. is accentuated: *unsure hopes*; *unsure observance*) 1) unsafe, liable to danger: *an habitation giddy and u.* H4B I, 3, 89. *exposing what is mortal and u. to all that fortune, death and danger dare*, Hml. IV, 4, 51.

2) not assured, not certainly knowing, liable to error: *the truth thou art u. to swear*, John III, 1, 283. *his scattering and u. observance*, Oth. III, 3, 151.

3) uncertain, doubtful: *what's to come is still u.* Tw. II, 3, 50. *their u. hopes*, Mcb. V, 4, 19.

**Unsured**, made uncertain or unsafe: *by this knot thou shalt so surely tie thy now u. assurance to the crown*, John II, 471.

**Unsuspected**, not mistrusted: Shr. I, 2, 137. R3 III, 5, 23.

**Unswayable**, ungovernable, not to be influenced by others: Cor. V, 6, 26.

**Unswayed**, not governed, not managed: *who (my heart) leaves u. the likeness of a man, thy proud heart's slave to be*, Sonn. 141, 11. *is the chair empty? is the sword u.?* R3 IV, 4, 470.

**Unswear**, 1) to recant by oath what is sworn: *u. faith sworn*, John III, 1, 245. 2) to deny by oath: *hath he said anything? He hath; but be you well assured, no more than he'll u.* Oth. IV, 1, 31.

**Unswept** (*unswept*; but *unswept* before a subst.) not swept, not brushed, not cleaned: Sonn. 55, 4. Wiv. V, 5, 48. Cor. II, 3, 126.

**Unsworn**, not having taken an oath: Meas. I, 4, 9.

**Untainted**, 1) undefiled: Lucr. 1710. 1749. Meas. III, 1, 264. H6B III, 2, 232. R3 III, 1, 7.

2) uninjured: *him in thy course u. do allow for beauty's pattern to succeeding men*, Sonn. 19, 11.

3) not charged with a crime: *u., unexamined, free, at liberty*, R3 III, 6, 9.

**Untalked of**, not spoken of: Rom. III, 2, 7.

**Untangle**, to unravel, to disentangle: Tw. II, 2, 41. Rom. I, 4, 91.

**Untasted**, not tasted, not eaten: Troil. II, 3, 130.

**Untaught** (*untaught*; before a subst. *untaught*) 1) not communicated and imparted by instruction: *royalty unlearned, honour u.* Cymb. IV, 2, 178.

2) not instructed, not accustomed: *used to command, u. to plead for favour*, H6B IV, 1, 122.

3) unmannerly: *their u. love must needs appear offence*, Meas. II, 4, 29. *called them u. knaves*, H4A I, 3, 43. *O thou u., what manners is in this*, Rom. V, 3, 214.

**Untempering**, not producing the desired effect, not disposing another in one's favour, not winning (or = not fit for the occasion? cf. *Temper*): *the poor and u. effect of my visage*, H5 V, 2, 241.

**Untender**, unkind, ungentle: Lr. I, 1, 108. Cymb. III, 4, 12.

**Untendered**, not offered, unpaid: Cymb. III, 1, 10.

**Untent**, to bring out of the tent: *why will he not u. his person?* Troil. II, 3, 178.

**Untented**, not to be probed by a tent; incurable: *the u. woundings of a father's curse*, Lr. I, 4, 322.

**Unthankful**, ungrateful: H4A I, 3, 136.

**Unthankfulness**, ingratitude: Alls I, 1, 226. R3 II, 2, 90. Rom. III, 3, 24. Per. I, 4, 102.

**Unthink**, to retract in thought: *I do beseech you to u. your speaking and to say so no more*, H8 II, 4, 104.

**Unthought**, with *of* or *on*, not thought of: *I leave my duty a little u. of*, Tw. V, 318. *the u. on accident*, Wint. IV, 4, 549. *your u. of Harry*, H4A III, 2, 141.

**Unthread**, to draw out a thread from; metaphorically: *u. the rude eye of rebellion*, John V, 4, 11 (German: *entfädelt die roh eingefädelte Empörung.* cf. *to thread the postern of a needle's eye*, R2 V, 5, 17. *threading dark-eyed night*, Lr. II, 1, 121. The constant combination of the words *thread* and *eye* in all these passages is sufficient to refute the different emendations proposed by the commentators (as f. i. *untread the roadway* etc.).

**Unthrift,** subst. 1) a prodigal: *what an u. in the world doth spend shifts but his place,* Sonn. 9, 9. 13, 13. 2) one good for nothing: *my rights and royalties plucked from my arms perforce and given away to upstart —s,* R2 II, 3, 122.

**Unthrift,** adj. 1) prodigal: *what man didst thou ever know u. that was beloved after his means?* Tim. IV, 3, 311. 2) good for nothing: *and with an u. love did run from Venice,* Merch. V, 16.

**Unthrifty,** 1) not economical, not intent on profit: *u. loveliness, why dost thou spend upon thyself thy beauty's legacy?* Sonn. 4, 1. *our absence makes us u. to our knowledge,* Wint. V, 2, 121 (not intent on increasing, and hence not increasing, our knowledge). 2) unprofitable, unfortunate: *much I fear some ill u. thing,* Rom. V, 3, 136 (reading of Q2; the rest of O. Edd. *unlucky*). 3) good for nothing: *my house left in the fearful guard of an u. knave,* Merch. I, 3, 177. *can no man tell me of my u. son?* R2 V, 3, 1.

**Untie,** to unbind, to unfasten, to loosen: *u. my hands,* Shr. II, 21. *too hard a knot for me to u.* Tw. II, 2, 42. *the amity that wisdom knits not, folly may easily u.* Troil. II, 3, 111. *though you u. the winds,* Mcb. IV, 1, 52. *this knot of life at once u.* Ant. V, 2, 308. = to solve (a riddle): *a speaking such as sense cannot u.* Cymb. V, 4, 149. = to break (a charm): *u. the spell,* Tp. V, 253.

**Untied,** not bound, not tied: *your shoe u.* As III, 2, 399. The negative form producing an incorrectness of expression: *u. I still my virgin knot will keep,* Per. IV, 2, 160, i. e. not untied, not loosed.

**Until,** = till, 1) prepos.: *u. this time,* Err. IV, 4, 69. *u. last night,* Ado IV, 1, 150. *u. to-morrow morning,* V, 1, 337. *things growing are not ripe u. their season,* Mids. II, 2, 117. *u. the break of day,* V, 408. Merch. III, 4, 26. 30. H5 I, 2, 57. IV, 7, 59. H6A I, 1, 8. H6B III, 1, 138. IV, 7, 143. H6C II, 2, 162. Tit. V, 2, 57. Caes. V, 1, 26 etc. cf. *whereuntil.*

2) conj.: Lucr. 263. Err. II, 2, 187. V, 115. Ado IV, 1, 306. LLL III, 92. 98. IV, 3, 347. V, 2, 807. Merch. III, 2, 205. V, 191. All's III, 2, 103 (*u. he has no wife*). Wint. I, 2, 28. II, 3, 22. H6B III, 2, 129. Mcb. IV, 1, 92. Ant. I, 4, 42 etc. Followed by the subjunctive: Sonn. 45, 9. Meas. IV, 2, 93. V, 170. Merch. V, 95. 283. R2 V, 3, 95. H6A II, 4, 110. H6B I, 2, 10. II, 4, 56. III, 1, 352. IV, 1, 143. IV, 4, 40. IV, 9, 40. H6C I, 1, 249. R3 I, 4, 288. Cor. V, 3, 181 etc. Elliptically: *u. confirmed, signed, ratified by you,* Merch. III, 2, 149.

**Untimbered,** not furnished with timber, weak: Troil. I, 3, 43.

**Untimeable,** writing of some M. Edd. in As V, 3, 37; O. Edd. *untuneable.*

**Untimely,** adj. 1) not done or happening in the right season: *u. storms make men expect a dearth,* R3 II, 3, 35. *death lies on her like an u. frost upon the sweetest flower,* Rom. IV, 5, 28. 2) ill-timed, inopportune: *an u. ague,* H8 I, 1, 4. *O u. death!* Lr. IV, 6, 256. 3) happening before the natural time; applied to violent death: *my u. death,* Lucr. 1178. Rom. I, 4, 111. V, 3, 234. *this u. bier,* R2 V, 6, 52. *the u. fall*

of virtuous Lancaster, R3 I, 2, 4. *die by u. violence,* I, 3, 201. *it hath been the u. emptying of the happy throne,* Mcb. IV, 3, 68.

4) unsuitable, unfitting, improper: *some u. thought did instigate his all too timeless speed,* Lucr. 43. *she conjures him ... by her u. tears,* 570 (i. e. which she ought not to have shed). *and his u. frenzy thus awaketh,* 1675. *after many accents and delays, u. breathings,* 1720 (as hindering and retarding her purpose). *by your u. claspings with your child,* Per. I, 1, 128.

**Untimely,** adv. 1) not at the right time, unseasonably, amiss: *what's u. done,* Hml. IV, 1, 40. *u. comes this hurt,* Lr. III, 7, 98.

2) before the natural time: *fair flower u. plucked,* Pilgr. 131. *prodigious, and u. brought to light,* R3 I, 2, 22. *from his mother's womb u. ripped,* Mcb. V, 8, 16. Especially used of violent death: *my father came u. to his death,* H6C III, 3, 187. *how sweet a plant have you u. cropped,* V. 5, 62. *u. smothered,* R3 IV, 4, 70. *which too u. here did scorn the earth,* Rom. III, 1, 123. *here u. lay the noble Paris and true Romeo dead,* V, 3, 258.

**Untirable,** indefatigable: Tim. I, 1, 11.

**Untired** (*untired; untired* before a subst.) not fatigued, not exhausted: R3 IV, 2, 44. Caes. II, 1, 227.

**Untitled,** having no claim or right, illegitimate: *an u. tyrant,* Mcb. IV, 3, 104.

**Unto,** = to, prepos. (never adv. or infinitival particle; the accent usually on the second syllable) denoting, quite as *to* (q. v.) motion towards a place or state or work proposed, a point or limit reached, direction and tendency, application, addition, junction, opposition, correspondence and simultaneousness, and all those relations which in other languages are expressed by the dative: *Venus makes amain u. him,* Ven. 5. *u. the wood they hie them,* 323. Lucr. 120. 337. 671. Pilgr. 201. Tp. I, 2, 39. 376. Gent. I, 2, 121. II, 4, 187. IV, 1, 51. IV, 2, 74. IV, 4, 93. V, 2, 35. Err. I, 1, 68. IV, 4, 123. Mids. II, 1, 191. III, 2, 310. As IV, 3, 146. Shr. II, 316. R2 V, 1, 52. H6A III, 3, 30. IV, 1, 73 (*march u. him,* = against) etc. etc. *feasts of love I have been called u.* Compl. 181. *his eye ... u. a greater uproar tempts his veins,* Lucr. 427. *he hath turned a heaven u. a hell,* Mids. I, 1, 207 (Q2 Ff *into*). *our wars will turn u. a peaceful sport,* H6A II, 2, 45. *which humbleness may drive u. a fine,* Merch. IV, 1, 372. *I'll follow you u. the death,* John I, 154. *send danger from the east u. the west,* H4A I, 3, 195. *what may the king's whole battle reach u.?* IV, 1, 129. *amount u. a hundred marks,* Err. I, 1, 25. *my nails can reach u. thine eyes,* Mids. III, 2, 298. *I can tell her age u. an hour,* Rom. I, 3, 11. *he neighs u. her,* Ven. 307. *that eye ... u. a view so false will not incline,* Lucr. 292. *those thine eyes betray thee u. mine,* 483. *exposed u. the sea ... him and his child,* Tp. III, 3, 71. *your letter u. the nameless friend,* Gent. II, 1, 111. *to write u. her lover,* 174. *not hate u. my friend,* III, 1, 46. *promised by her friends u. a youthful gentleman,* 107. *what dear good will I bear u. Valentine,* IV, 3, 15. *if Falstaff have committed disparagements u. you,* Wiv. I, 1, 32. *complain u. the duke of this indignity,* Err. 113. *speak u. the same Aemilia,* 345 (Wiv. IV, 5, 10). *my inwardness and love is very much u. the prince,* Ado IV, 1, 248. Mids. III, 2, 309. *I am prest u. it,* Merch. I, 1, 160. *committing me u. my brother's love,* As IV, 3, 145. *I drink u. your grace,* H4B IV, 2, 68. *have con-*

*tented u. Henry's death,* H6A I, 1, 5. *his power u. Octavia,* Ant. II, 2, 146. *all my right of her I do estate u. Demetrius,* Mids. I, 1, 98. *I will seal u. this bond,* Merch. I, 3, 172. *to grow u. himself was his desire,* Ven. 1180. *u. our shame perpetual,* Wint. III, 2, 238. *I should have given him tears u. entreaties,* As I, 2, 250 (in addition to). *this is ... the crest, or crest u. the crest, of murder's arms,* John IV, 3, 46. *this slave, u. his honour, has my lord's meat in him,* Tim. III, 1, 60 (i. e. besides his honourable rank, abstractedly from his being called 'your honour', which alone should induce him to act otherwise). *tied u. a tree,* Ven. 263. *near allied u. the duke,* Gent. IV, 1, 49. *wed u. a woman,* Err. I, 1, 38. *fastened him u. a mast,* 80. *my heart u. yours is knit,* Mids. II, 2, 47. *my wretchedness u. a row of pins,* R2 III, 4, 26. *wilt thou flout me thus u. my face?* Err. I, 2, 91. *u. my mother's prayers I bend my knee,* R2 V, 3, 97. *bear that proportion ... as did the fatal brand ... u. the prince's heart of Calydon,* H6B I, 1, 235. *therefore must his voice be circumscribed u. the voice and yielding of that body,* Hml. I, 3, 23 (according to). *u. thy value I will mount myself upon a courser,* Per. II, 1, 163. *heavy u. thee,* Ven. 1256. *sorrow u. shepherds, woe u. the birds,* 455. *what is ten hundred touches u. thee?* 519. *lends embracements u. every stranger,* 790. *my honour I'll bequeath u. the knife,* Lucr. 1184. *Lucrece' cheeks u. her maid seem so,* 1217. *her sighs u. the clouds bequeathed her sprite,* 1727. *each does good turns now u. the other,* Sonn. 47, 2. *I gave this u. Julia,* Gent. V, 4, 97. *my errand, due u. my tongue,* Err. II, 1, 72. *as strange u. your town as to your talk,* II, 2, 151. *known u. these, and to myself disguised,* 216. *as it may appear u. you,* Ado III, 5, 55. *now u. thy bones good night,* V, 3, 22. *every one his love-feat will advance u. his mistress,* LLL V, 2, 124. *ere I will yield my virgin patent up u. his lordship,* Mids. I, 1, 81. *the sun was not so true u. the day,* III, 2, 50. *good night u. you all,* V, 443. *like a shifted wind u. a sail,* John IV, 2, 23 (= a wind shifted to a sail) etc. etc. *a suitor to your daughter, u. Bianca,* Shr. II, 92. *as deputy u. that gracious king,* H6A V, 3, 161. *daughter u. Reignier,* H6B I, 1, 47. *heir u. the English crown,* I, 3, 187. II, 2, 44. *sole daughter u. Lionel,* II, 2, 50 etc. etc.

**Untold,** 1) not numbered: *then in the number let me pass u.* Sonn. 136, 9.

2) not related, not revealed: Lucr. 753. Per. V, 3, 84.

**Untouched,** 1) uninjured: *depart u.* Caes. III, 1, 142. 2) not mentioned: *left nothing u.* R3 III, 7, 19.

**Untoward,** refractory, unmannerly: *if she be froward, then hast thou taught Hortensio to be u.* Shr. IV, 5, 79. *what means this scorn, thou most u. knave?* John I, 243.

**Untowardly,** unaptly, unsuitably (?): *O day u. turned,* Ado III, 2, 134.

**Untraded,** not used in common practice, unhackneyed: *mock not that I affect the u. oath,* Troil. IV, 5, 178.

**Untrained,** uneducated, uninstructed: LLL IV, 2, 18. H6A I, 2, 73.

**Untread,** to retrace: *she treads the path that she —s again,* Ven. 908. *the horse that doth u. again his tedious measures,* Merch. II, 6, 10. *we will u. the steps of damned flight,* John V, 4, 52.

**Untreasured,** deprived as of a treasure: *they found the bed u. of their mistress,* As II, 2, 7.

**Untried,** unexamined, unnoticed: Wint. IV, 1, 6.

**Untrimmed,** stripped of ornamental dress: *every fair from fair sometime declines, by chance or nature's changing course u.* Sonn. 18, 8. *the devil tempts thee here in likeness of a new u. bride,* John III, 1, 209 (a bride recently divested of her wedding-gown).

**Untrod** (*úntrod*, because placed before the subst.), not trodden, untraced: *thorough the hazards of this u. state,* Caes. III, 1, 136.

**Untrodden,** not trodden, not visited: *unpeopled offices, u. stones,* R2 I, 2, 69.

**Untroubled,** tranquil: R3 V, 3, 149.

**Untrue,** 1) not true, contrary to fact: *if it appear not plain and prove u.* All's V, 3, 318.

Substantively: *my most true mind thus maketh mine u.* Sonn. 113, 14 (some M. Edd. *makes mine eye u.*). Adverbially: *that you for love speak well of me u.* 72, 10 (contrary to truth).

2) faithless, not to be trusted: *this man's u.* Compl. 169. *to make us thus u.* LLL V, 2, 473. *he that steeps his safety in true blood shall find but bloody safety and u.* John III, 4, 148. *when to my good lord I prove u.* Cymb. I, 5, 86.

**Untrussing,** unpacking: *this Claudio is condemned for u.* Meas. III, 2, 190.

**Untruth,** 1) falsehood: Ado V, 1, 220. H8 IV, 2, 38.

2) disloyalty, want of fidelity: *so my u. had not provoked him to it,* R2 II, 2, 101. *let all —s stand by thy stained name, and they'll seem glorious,* Troil. V, 2, 179.

**Untucked,** dishevelled: Compl. 31.

**Untunable,** unharmonious, discordant: *they (my news) are harsh, u. and bad,* Gent. III, 1, 208. *though there was no great matter in the ditty, yet the note was very u.* As V, 3, 37 (some M. Edd. *untimeable,* more logically indeed, but not to the improvement of the jest).

**Untune,** to deprive of sound or harmony: *u. that string, and, hark, what discord follows!* Troil. I, 3, 109.

*Untuned,* either partic., = deprived of harmony, or of the usual sound: *with —d tongue she hoarsely calls her maid,* Lucr. 1214. *here my only son knows not my feeble key of —d cares?* Err. V, 310 (my voice which has become soundless by giving utterance to nothing but sorrow. The accent on the first syllable, as the word is placed immediately before the subst.). *the —d and jarring senses,* Lr. IV, 7, 16.

Or adj., = unharmonious: *roused up with boisterous —d drums,* R2 I, 3, 134.

**Untutored,** untaught, uninstructed, rude, raw: *my u. lines,* Lucr. Ded. 3. *she might think me some u. youth,* Sonn. 138, 3. *some stern u. churl,* H6B III, 2, 213. *u. lad, thou art too malapert,* H6C V, 5, 32. *thou speakest like him's u. to repeat,* Per. I, 4, 74.

**Untwine,** to cease winding round and clinging to: *let the stinking elder, grief, u. his perishing root with the increasing vine,* Cymb. IV, 2, 59 (cf. *With*). Used nonsensically by Pistol: *let grievous, ghastly, gaping wounds u. the Sisters Three,* H4B II, 4, 213 (a mutilated scrap of poetry).

**Unurged,** unsolicited, voluntary, of one's own accord: *the time was once when thou u. wouldst vow,* Err. II, 2, 115. *we swear a voluntary zeal and an u. faith to your proceedings,* John V, 2, 10.

**Unused,** (*únused* before a subst.). 1) not put to

use, not employed: Sonn. 4, 13. 9, 12. 48, 3. Hml. IV, 4, 39.

2) not accustomed: Sonn. 30, 5. Oth. V, 2, 349 (*u. to the melting mood*).

**Unusual,** not customary, uncommon: *at an u. hour,* Meas. V, 463. *some comet or u. prodigy,* Shr. III, 2, 98. *these your u. weeds,* Wint. IV, 4, 1. *strange u. blood, when man's worst sin is, he does too much good,* Tim. IV, 2, 38. *in u. pleasure,* Mcb. II, 1, 13. *u. vigilance,* Lr. II, 3, 4.

**Unvalued,** 1) not valued, not prized, mean: *he may not, as u. persons do, carve for himself,* Hml. I, 3, 19.

2) invaluable, inestimable: *u. jewels,* R3 I, 4, 27.

**Unvanquished,** not conquered: H6A V, 4, 141.

**Unvarnished,** not overlaid with varnish, not artificially adorned: *a round u. tale,* Oth. I, 3, 90.

**Unveil,** to uncover, to disclose to view: Troil. III, 3, 200.

**Unvenerable,** not worthy of veneration, contemptible: Wint. II, 3, 77.

**Unvexed,** not troubled, not molested: *a blessed and u. retire,* John II, 253.

**Unviolable,** (Ff *inviolable*) not to be violated or broken: R3 II, 1, 27.

**Unviolated,** not violated, uninjured: Err. III, 1, 88.

**Unvirtuous,** destitute of virtue: Wiv. IV, 2, 232.

**Unvisited,** not visited: LLL V, 2, 358.

**Unvulnerable:** Cor. V, 3, 73.

**Unwares,** undesignedly: *whom in this conflict I u. have killed,* H6C II, 5, 62. *At u.* Q in Troil. III, 2, 40.

**Unwarily,** unexpectedly: *were in the Washes all u. devoured,* John V, 7, 63.

**Unwashed,** not washed, unclean: *another lean u. artificer,* John IV, 2, 201. *rob me the exchequer the first thing thou doest, and do it with u. hands too,* H4A III, 3, 206 (without staying to wash your hands). *when good manners shall lie all in one or two men's hands and they u. too, 'tis a foul thing,* Rom. I, 5, 5.

**Unwatched** (*únwatched*) not observed with vigilance: Hml. III, 1, 196.

**Unwearied,** indefatigable: Merch. III, 2, 295.

**Unweave,** to undo what is woven: *she —s the web that she hath wrought,* Ven. 991.

**Unwed,** unmarried: Pilgr. 304. Err. II, 1, 26.

**Unwedgeable,** not to be split with wedges: Meas. II, 2, 116.

**Unweeded,** not cleared of weeds: Hml. I, 2, 135.

**Unweighed,** inconsiderate, unguarded: *what an u. behaviour,* Wiv. II, 1, 23.

**Unweighing,** thoughtless: *a very superficial, ignorant, u. fellow,* Meas. III, 2, 147.

**Unwelcome,** not welcome, not gladly received: Ven. 449. Gent. II, 4, 81. H4A I, 1, 50. H4B I, 1, 100. Troil. IV, 1, 45. Mcb. IV, 3, 138.

**Unwept,** not mourned: R3 II, 2, 65.

**Unwhipped,** not whipped: Lr. III, 2, 53.

**Unwholesome,** 1) not sound, diseased; and in a moral sense, = tainted, impaired, defective: *this u. humidity* (viz Falstaff) Wiv. III, 3, 42. *they're too u.* Per. IV, 2, 22. *the people muddied, thick and u. in their thoughts and whispers,* Hml. IV, 5, 82. *bear some charity to my wit; do not think it so u.* Oth. IV, 1, 125.

2) unfavourable to health, insalubrious: Lucr. 779. 870. Tp. I, 2, 322. H5 II, 3, 59. Troil. II, 2, 129. Cor. IV, 6, 130.

**Unwieldy,** moved or moving with difficulty, too heavy: R2 III, 2, 115. IV, 205. Rom. II, 5, 17.

**Unwilling,** 1) not willing, disinclined, reluctant: Ven. 365. Lucr. 309. Gent. II, 1, 112. Err. I, 1, 61. R2 1, 3, 245. H4B III, 2, 240. R3 III, 1, 176. H8 IV, 2, 60.

2) undesigned, involuntary: *and being opened, threw u. light upon the wide wound,* Ven. 1051. *'twas a fault u.* Shr. IV, 1, 159.

**Unwillingly,** against one's wish, reluctantly: Tp. I, 2, 368. Gent. II, 1, 129. Merch. V, 196. As II, 7, 147. Wint. IV, 4, 477. *I have, and most u., of late heard many grievous complaints of you,* H8 V, 1, 98 (= with regret).

**Unwillingness,** reluctance, loathness: *with some u.* R2 I, 3, 149. *with dull u.* R3 II, 2, 92. *with all u.* IV, 1, 58 (Qq *in all u.*).

**Unwind,** 1) to untwine, to untwist: *as you u. her love from him, ... you must provide to bottom it on me,* Gent. III, 2, 51.

2) to display: *u. your bloody flag,* H5 I, 2, 101.

**Unwiped,** not wiped, not cleaned by rubbing: Mcb. II, 3, 108.

**Unwise,** not wise, defective in judgment: R3 IV, 1, 52. Cor. III, 1, 91. Tim. II, 2, 6.

**Unwisely,** not wisely, imprudently: Lucr. 10. Tim. II, 2, 183.

**Unwish,** to wish away, to make away with by wishing: *now thou hast —ed five thousand men,* H5 IV, 3, 76.

**Unwished,** not desired, unwelcome: Mids. I, 1, 81.

**Unwit,** to deprive of understanding: *as if some planet had —ed men,* Oth. II, 3, 182.

**Unwitnessed,** not perceived: *trifles u. with eye or ear thy coward heart with false bethinking grieves,* Ven. 1023.

**Unwittingly,** without consciousness, involuntarily: R3 II, 1, 56. H8 III, 2, 123.

**Unwonted,** uncommon, unusual: Tp. I, 2, 497. Meas. IV, 2, 120.

**Unwooed,** not wooed, not courted: Sonn. 54, 10.

**Unworthily,** undeservedly; in a good as well as a bad sense: *and so u. disgrace the man,* Gent. III, 1, 29. *because u. thou wast installed in that high degree,* H6A IV, 1, 16

**Unworthiness,** want of worth and merit: Sonn. 150, 13. Tp. III, 1, 77. All's III, 7, 41. H5 IV Chor. 46. Cymb. I, 1, 127.

**Unworthy,** 1) not deserving; absol.: Gent. I, 2, 18. Mids. II, 1, 207. Merch. II, 1, 37 (*—er*). As II, 7, 76. All's III, 4, 26. H5 Prol. 10. H6B III, 2, 230. 286. Rom. I, 5, 95 (*—est*). III, 3, 31. III, 5, 145. Ant. III, 13, 84. With an inf.: *I am u. to be Henry's wife,* H6A V, 3, 122. 123. H6B IV, 4, 18. H8 III, 2, 414. Troil. IV, 4, 127. With *for,* in the same sense: *I am u. for her schoolmaster,* Per. II, 5, 40 (reading of Q1; the other O. Edd. *to be her s.*). With *of:* As IV, 1, 197. All's III, 4, 30. H6B I, 3, 108. Troil. II, 2, 94. Oth. II, 3, 104. With a simple accus.: *how much he is u. so good a lady,* Ado II, 3, 217 (Ff *to have to good a lady*). *as one u. all the former favours,* Shr. IV, 2, 30. *u. this good gift,* All's II, 3, 158. *u. thee,* Wint. IV, 4, 448. *as u. fight,* H6A IV, 7, 43.

2) wanting merit, worthless, vile: *thou worthy lord of that u. wife,* Lucr. 1304. *a poor u. brother of yours,* As I, 1, 36. Wint. II, 3, 113. John III, 1, 150. H5 I,

2, 228 *(in an u. urn)*. Troil. I, 3, 84 *(—est)*. Cor. II, 3, 166. Tit. I, 346. Hml. III, 1, 74. III, 2, 379. IV, 7, 77 *(—est)*. Cymb. I, 4, 157 *(your u. thinking)*.

3) not deserved, not justified: *doing worthy vengeance on thyself, which didst u. slaughter upon others,* R3 I, 2, 88.

**Unwrung,** not pinched, not galled: *let the galled jade wince, our withers are u.* Hml. III, 2, 253.

**Unyielding,** not surrendering: *remove your siege from my u. heart,* Ven. 423.

**Unyoke,** 1) to free from a yoke: *like youthful steers —d,* H4B IV, 2, 103. Absol.: *ay, tell me that, and u.* Hml. V, 1, 59 (= and then your day's work is done; German: *dann kannst du ausspannen.* The grave-digger's speech).

2) disjoin: *shall these hands ... u. this seizure,* John III, 1, 241.

**Unyoked,** licentious: *the u. humour of your idleness,* H4A I, 2, 220 *(únyoked,* as preceding the subst.).*

**Up,** prepos. denoting motion from a lower to a higher place, opposed to down: *runs o' horseback up a hill perpendicular,* H4A II, 4, 378. *as you go up the stairs into the lobby,* Hml. IV, 3, 39. *you do climb up it now,* Lr. IV, 6, 2 (Qq *climb it up*). Applied to a horizontal direction: *up Fish Street! down Saint Magnus' Corner!* H6B IV, 8, 1. *she says up and down the town that her eldest son is like you,* H4B II, 1, 114 (cf. *Down*).

**Up,** adv. 1) aloft, on high: *the lark ... mounts up on high,* Ven. 854. *true prayers that shall be up at heaven,* Meas. II, 2, 152. *your heart is up thus high at least,* R2 III, 3, 194. *thy seat is up on high,* V, 5, 112. *his mountain sire, on mountain standing, up in the air,* H5 II, 4, 58. *shall we stand up here?* Troil. I, 2, 193. *some two months hence up higher toward the north he* (the sun) *first presents his fire,* Caes. II, 1, 109. Applied to a level direction (in consequence of the natural illusion produced by distance): *up higher to the plain,* John II, 295. Metaphorically: *which first she'll prove on cats and dogs, then afterward up higher,* Cymb. I, 5, 39.

Denoting any direction from a lower to a higher place: *hold up thy head,* Ven. 118. *she heaveth up his hat,* 351. *a purple flower sprung up,* 1168. *his guilty hand plucked up the latch,* Lucr. 358 (cf. *Pluck*). *all the infections that the sun sucks up,* Tp. II, 2, 1. Mids. II, 1, 89. *what is't that you took up,* Gent. I, 2, 70. 73. *hang him up,* IV, 4, 24. *look up,* V, 4, 87 (cf. *Look*). *I'll creep up into the chimney,* Wiv. IV, 2, 56. *run up,* 81. *pluck up thy spirits,* Shr. IV, 3, 38. *piled up heaps of gold,* H4B IV, 5, 71 (cf. Tp. III, 1, 10). *those of old, and the late dignities heaped up to them,* Mcb. I, 6, 19. *when they shall see his crest up again,* Cor. IV, 5, 225. *he wore his beaver up,* Hml. I, 2, 230. *awhile they* (her clothes) *bore her up,* IV, 7, 177 etc. etc. Often followed by *to: dancing up to the chins,* Tp. IV, 183. *we will up to the mountain's top,* Mids. IV, 1, 114. *up to the ears in blood,* H4A IV, 1, 117. *in Thames up to the neck,* H5 IV, 1, 120. *bathe our hands in Caesar's blood up to the elbows,* Caes. III, 1, 107. *you lie up to the hearing of the gods,* Ant. V, 2, 95. *up to yond hill,* Cymb. III, 3, 10 etc. By *with: up with your fights,* Wiv. II, 2, 142. *up with it* (= take it from the ground) Wint. III, 3, 128. *up with my tent,* R3 V, 3, 7 (= pitch it) etc. As for *up and down,* see *Down.*

2) upright, erect; opposed to any state of recum-

bency, or prostration, or repose in general; a) = out of bed: *ere I was up,* Lucr. 1277. *where once thou calledst me up at midnight,* Tp. I, 2, 228. *to be up early and down late,* Wiv. I, 4, 108. Ado II, 3, 136. Tw. II, 3, 2. H4A II, 1, 64. H6B IV, 2, 2 (punning). R3 V, 3, 211. Troil. I, 2, 50. IV, 2, 18. V, 2, 1. Rom. III, 5, 64. 66. IV, 3, 10 *(sit up)*. V, 3, 188 (punning). Caes. II, 1, 88. II, 2, 117. Mcb. II, 3, 82. Cymb. II, 3, 37.

b) standing on one's feet; not sitting or lying, or kneeling: *to stay him up,* John III, 4, 138. *up, cousin, up,* R2 III, 3, 194; Cor. II, 1, 188; Lr. IV, 6, 65. *stand close up,* H8 V, 4, 92. 93. *over and over he comes, and up again,* Cor. I, 3, 68. *set up a top,* IV, 5, 161. *my sinews, bear me stiffly up,* Hml. I, 5, 95. cf. *to bear up against what should ensue,* Tp. I, 2, 157 (not to sink under it). *so long as nature will bear up with this exercise,* Wint. III, 2, 242; etc. etc.

c) on foot, agoing, in motion or action: *lust stirs up a desperate courage,* Ven. 556. *cheering up her senses,* 896. *Philip, make up,* John III, 2, 5. *blew this tempest up,* V, 1, 17. *the day shall not be up so soon as I,* V, 5, 21 (= stirring, in activity). *to pluck a kingdom down and set another up,* H4B I, 3, 50 (cf. *Set*). *since gentlemen came up,* H6B IV, 2, 10 (began to exist and be active. Holland's speech). *when two authorities are up,* Cor. III, 1, 109. *the hunt is up,* Tit. II, 2, 1. *the citizens are up,* Rom. III, 1, 138. *what misadventure is so early up?* V, 3, 188. *the storm is up,* Caes. V, 1, 68. *the game is up,* Cymb. III, 3, 107. *why then do I put up that womanly defence, to say I have done no harm?* Mcb. IV, 2, 78 (= assert, urge). *up from my cabin,* Hml. V, 2, 12. Elliptically, as a word of incitement or exhortation: *up, gentlemen, follow me,* Wiv. III, 3, 179. *up once again,* John V, 4, 2. *up and away,* H4A V, 3, 28. *up, princes!* H5 III, 5, 38. IV, 2, 1. *up, vanity! down, royal state!* H4B IV, 5, 120. *up, sir, go with me,* Rom. III, 1, 144 etc.

Often = in arms: *Percy, Northumberland, ... capitulate against us and are up,* H4A III, 2, 120. *the archbishop of York is up with well-appointed powers,* H4B I, 1, 189. *rebels there are up,* H6B III, 1, 283. IV, 1, 100. IV, 2, 2. 187. R3 IV, 4, 530.

3) Denoting an approach or coming to a place or person: *bear up and board 'em,* Tp. III, 2, 3. *certain horse are not yet come up,* H4A IV, 3, 20 (cf. *Come*). *make up, lest your retirement do amaze your friends,* V, 4, 5. 58 (= join our troops). *to see his father bring up his powers,* H4B II, 3, 14. *bring up your army,* Cor. I, 2, 29. *whither should they come? Up,* Rom. I, 2, 76 (i. e. to our house. The servant's speech). *bring up the brown bills,* Lr. IV, 6, 91 etc.

4) Denoting a state of due preparation and readiness for use: *he's winding up the watch,* Tp. II, 1, 12. Tw. II, 5, 66. Mcb. I, 3, 37. Lr. IV, 7, 16. *what he ... will make up full clear,* Meas. V, 157. *make up that,* Tw. II, 5, 133 (make that intelligible). *bring him up to liking,* Wint. IV, 4, 544. *Pistol's cock is up,* H5 II, 1, 55. *help to deck up her,* Rom. IV, 2, 41. *to prepare him up against to-morrow,* 45. *go and trim her up,* IV, 4, 24 (cf. H4A V, 2, 57. Ant. V, 2, 345). *draw up your powers,* Lr. V, 1, 51 etc.

5) Denoting a state of being reposited in a place where a thing is kept when not used: *the steed is stalled up,* Ven. 39. *put thy sword up,* Tp. I, 2, 469; *the sword goes up again,* Caes. V, 1, 52; *up, sword,* Hml. III, 3,

88; *keep up your bright swords*, Oth. I, 2, 59. *put up this letter*, LLL IV, 1, 109. *thy threatening colours now wind up*, John V, 2, 73. V, 5, 7. *keep up thy quillets*, Oth. III, 1, 25. *'tis up again*, Cymb. II, 4, 97 etc. Hence implying the notion of laying together and of closing: *an adder wreathed up in fatal folds*, Ven. 879. *here folds she up the tenour of her woe* (i. e. the letter) Lucr. 1310. *the sleeves should be cut out and sewed up again*, Shr. IV, 3, 148. *heavy sleep had closed up mortal eyes*, Lucr. 163 (cf. *Close*). *to stop up the displeasure he hath conceived*, All's IV, 5, 80.

6) Denoting confinement or concealment: *draws up her breath*, Ven. 929. *there, all smothered up, in shade doth sit*, 1035. *shame folded up in blind concealing night*, Lucr. 675 (cf. John II, 229. R3 I, 3, 269). *that shall pen thy breath up*, Tp. I, 2, 326. *my spirits are all bound up*, 486. *mine enemies are all knit up in their distractions*, III, 3, 89. *shorten up their sinews with aged cramps*, IV, 260. *I wish mine eyes would shut up my thoughts*, Tp. II, 1, 192 (cf. Mids. III, 2, 435, and see *Shut*). *tie up my love's tongue*, Mids. III, 1, 206; *tie my treasure up in silken bags*, Per. III, 2, 41 (cf. *Tie*). *could trammel up the consequence*, Mcb. I, 7, 3. *here in the sands thee I'll rake up*, Lr. IV, 6, 281. *the locking up the spirits a time*, Cymb. I, 5, 41. *sands that will ... suck them up to the topmast*, III, 1, 22 etc. *so the poor third is up*, Ant. III, 5, 13 (= in confinement).

7) Imparting to verbs the sense of completion, by indicating that the action expressed by them is fully accomplished: *dries up his oil*, Ven. 756. *I would the lightning had burnt up those logs*, Tp. III, 1, 17; cf. Tim. IV, 3, 141 and Oth. IV, 2, 75. *to make up the sum*, Err. I, 1, 154 (cf. *Make*, and *made up* = finished, accomplished, R3 I, 1, 21 etc.). *he that sets up his rest to do more exploits*, Err. IV, 3, 27 (bets all his rest, is firmly resolved; cf. *Rest* and *Set*). *poisons up the nimble spirits*, LLL IV, 3, 305. *to kill them up in their native dwelling-place*, As II, 1, 62. *to stifle such a villain up*, John IV, 3, 133. *winding up days with toil and nights with sleep*, H5 IV, 1, 296. *how many days will finish up the year*, H6C II, 5, 28. *all princely graces that mould up such a mighty piece*, H8 V, 5, 27. *'as true as Troilus' shall crown up the verse*, Troil. III, 2, 189. *the enemy by them shall make a fuller number up*, Caes. IV, 3, 208 (cf. H8 I, 1, 75). *shut up in measureless content*, Mcb. II, 1, 16 etc. cf. *to eat up, to drink up, to devour up, to swallow up* etc. sub *Eat, Drink* etc. The same signification discernible in *to break up*, *to rip up* (q. v.), where it becomes synonymous to open; and in *to give up, to render* and *surrender up, to yield up*, though it sometimes might be called a mere expletive scarcely modifying the sense.

**Upbraid**, to reproach, 1) with an accusative of the person: *I did u. her and fall out with her*, Mids. IV, 1, 55. H4B IV, 5, 159. H5 III, 6, 117. H6B III, 1, 175. Oth. V, 2, 325. The cause of reproach preceded by *about*: —*ed me about the rose I wear*, H6A IV, 1, 91. By *on*: *himself* —*s us on every trifle*, Lr. I, 3, 6. Oftenest by *with*: Err. III, 1, 113. Tw. III, 1, 141. III, 4, 385. H6A II, 5, 48. IV, 1, 156. Cor. V, 1, 35.

2) with an accus. of the thing; the person implied by a possessive pronoun: *this Sir Prudence, who should not u. our course*, Tp. II, 1, 287. *I had many living to u. my gain of it by their assistances*, H4B IV, 5, 193.

*let memory ... u. my falsehood*, Troil. III, 2, 198. *minutely revolts u. his faith-breach*, Mcb. V, 2, 18.

**Upbraidings**, reproaches: Err. V, 73. R3 I, 3, 104.

**Up-cast**, a cast, a throw (a term peculiar to the game of bowls): *when I kissed the jack, upon an u. to be hit away!* Cymb. II, 1, 2 (O. Edd. *when I kissed the jack upon an u., to be hit away*).

**Upfill**, to fill completely: *ere the sun advance his burning eye, I must u. this osier cage of ours with baleful weeds*, Rom. II, 3, 7.

**Upheave**, to raise: *her two blue windows* (i. e. her eyes) *faintly she —th*, Ven. 482.

**Uphoard**, to store, to hoard up: *if thou hast —ed in thy life extorted treasure in the womb of earth*, Hml. I, 1, 136.

**Uphold** (used only in the present) to keep from falling or declining, to support, to sustain, to maintain: *who lets so fair a house fall to decay, which husbandry in honour might u.* Sonn. 13, 10. *the noble lord most honourably doth u. his word*, LLL V, 2, 449. *even he that did u. the very life of my dear friend*, Merch. V, 214 (Ff Q2.3.4 *had held up*). *so under Him that great supremacy, where we do reign, we will alone u.*, *without the assistance of a mortal hand*, John III, 1, 157. *that which —eth him that thee —s, his honour*, 315. *Faulconbridge ... alone —s the day*, V, 4, 5. *and will awhile u. the unyoked humour of your idleness*, H4A I, 2, 219. *for —ing the nice fashion of your country*, H5 V, 2, 299. *while life —s this arm, this arm —s the house of Lancaster*, H6C III, 3, 106. 107. *whate'er I forge to feed his brain-sick fits, do you u. and maintain in your speeches*, Tit. V, 2, 72.

**Uplift**, to lift, to raise: *your swords are now too massy ... and will not be —ed*, Tp. III, 3, 68. *with —ed arms*, R2 II, 2, 50. *hands —ed in my right*, Mcb. IV, 3, 42. *slaves ... shall u. us to the view*, Ant. V, 2, 211. *your low-laid son our godhead will u.* Cymb. V, 4, 103. Metaphorically = to exalt, to elevate with joy: *how were I then —ed!* Troil. III, 2, 175.

**Up-locked**, locked up, kept under lock and key: Sonn. 52, 2.

**Upmost**, uppermost, highest: *when he once attains the u. round*, Caes. II, 1, 24.

**Upon**, prepos. denoting contact with the surface of a thing: *I will trip u. the green*, Ven. 146. *his mane u. his compassed crest now stand on end*, 272. *lawn being spread u. the blushing rose*, 590. *whose blood u. the fresh flowers being shed*, 665. *poor Wat, far off u. a hill*, 697. *u. the Mediterranean flote*, Tp. I, 2, 234. *if you remain u. this island*, 423. *hast put thyself u. this island as a spy*, 455; cf. III, 2, 6. *this music crept by me u. the waters*, I, 2, 391.*sees a crown dropping u. thy head*, II, 1, 209. *the earth he lies u.* 281. *wrecked u. this shore*, V, 137. *u. the altar of her beauty*, Gent. III, 2, 73. *each mortal thing u. the dull earth dwelling*, IV, 2, 52. *u. whose grave thou vowedst pure chastity*, IV, 3, 21. *u. his place governs Lord Angelo*, Meas. I, 4, 55 (i. e. sitting in his chair). *I'll meet with you u. the mart*, Err. I, 2, 27. *the penalty which here appeareth due u. the bond*, Merch. IV, 1, 249. *carved u. these trees*, As III, 2, 182. *appeared u. the coast*, Wint. IV, 4, 280. *to die, u. the bed my father died*, 466. *when I strike my foot u. the bosom of the ground*, John IV, 1, 3. *sets his foot u. her back*, H6C II, 2, 16. *rages u. our territories*, Cor. IV, 6, 77. *so shall no foot u. the churchyard tread*, Rom. V, 3, 5. *our foot u. the hills ... shall* stay with us, Ant. IV, 10, 5. rest u. your banks of flowers, Cymb. V, 4, 98 etc. etc. Transposed: the cold ground u. Alls III, 4, 6. — Hence used to express multiplicity (of things heaped one over another): jest u. jest, Ado II, 1, 252. thou loss u. loss, Merch. III, 1, 96.

Applied to articles of dress covering the body or part of it, and to what is like them; f. i. how well my garments sit u. me, Tp. II, 1, 272. let me feel thy cloak u. me, Gent. III, 1, 136. thrust u. contrary feet, John IV, 2, 198. new honours come u. him like our strange garments, Mcb. I, 3, 144. with that suit u. my back, Cymb. III, 5, 141. to set a gloss u. his bold intent, H6A IV, 1, 103. Likewise to any thing borne about one; f. i. we have found u. him a strange picklock, Meas. III, 2, 18. she hath the stones u. her and the ducats, Merch. II, 8, 22. with instruments u. them, Rom. V, 3, 200. And to any external mark or peculiarity seen in a person or thing: the tender spring u. thy tempting lip, Ven. 127. he hath no drowning mark u. him, Tp. I, 1, 31. the white cold virgin snow u. my heart, IV, 55. there is none of my uncle's marks u. you, As III, 2, 387. hadst thou not the privilege of antiquity u. thee, All's II, 3, 221. I have some wounds u. me, Cor. I, 9, 28. II, 1, 170. 'tis a sore u. us, III, 1, 235. can show for Rome her enemies' marks u. me, III, 3, 111. as u. thee, Macbeth, their speeches shine, Mcb. III, 1, 7. these evils thou repeatest u. thyself, IV, 3, 112. the gashes do better u. them, V, 8, 3. since I saw you last, there is a change u. you, Ant. II, 6, 54. he wears the rose of youth u. him, III, 13, 21. you do remember this stain u. her? Cymb. II, 4, 139 etc.

Placed before that by which a thing is borne or supported; f. i. leaves Love u. her back. Ven. 814. to run u. the sharp wind of the north, Tp. I, 2, 254. ride u. their backs, II, 1, 115. I escaped u. a butt of sack, II, 2, 126. u. her knees, Gent. III, 1, 226. what passion hangs these weights u. my tongue? As I, 2, 269. u. the foot of fear, H4A V, 5, 20. u. the foot of motion, Mcb. II, 3, 131. u. the next tree shalt thou hang, V, 5, 39. Similarly: hang u. his gown, Meas. II, 2, 44. hangs and lolls and weeps u. me, Oth. IV, 1, 143. Hence, metaphorically, denoting charge, dependence, reliance: the government I cast u. my brother, Tp. I, 2, 75. the present business which now's u. us, 137. a torment to lay u. the damned, 290. one that takes u. him to be a dog indeed, Gent. IV, 4, 13. wishing a more strict restraint u. the sisterhood, Meas. I, 4, 5. accusations ... more strong than are u. you yet, Cor. III, 2, 141. thou hast years u. thee, IV, 1, 45. what (cannot we) put u. his spongy officers, Mcb. I, 7, 70. I will lay trust u. thee, Lr. III, 5, 25. his death's u. him, but not dead, Ant. IV, 15, 7. my zenith doth depend u. a most auspicious star, Tp. I, 2, 181. much u. this riddle runs the wisdom of the world, Meas. III, 2, 242. much u. this it is, LLL V, 2, 472. nor is my whole estate u. the fortune of this present year, Merch. I, 1, 44. it stood u. the choice of friends, Mids. I, 1, 139. it stands your grace u. to do him right, R2 II, 3, 138; cf. R3 IV, 2, 59; Hml. V, 2, 63; Ant. II, 1, 50 (see Stand). u. such terms, H4A V, 1, 10. u. all hazards, John V, 6, 7. u. condition I may quietly enjoy mine own, H6A V, 3, 153. V, 4, 129 etc. you stand u. your honour, Wiv. II, 2, 20. rely u. it till my tale be heard, Meas. V, 370. I have it u. his own report, Wint. IV, 4, 170. we may boldly spend u. the hope of what is to come in, H4A IV, 1, 54; cf. Caes. III, 1, 221. upon the

witness of, Hml. I, 2, 194. stand u. security, H4B I, 2, 42; cf. Err. IV, 1, 68; Cor. 1, 9, 39, and see Stand. In asseverations and obsecrations: u. mine honour, Tp. II, 1, 317. Gent. III, 1, 48. Meas. V, 524. u. my faith and honour, 224. u. my life, Wiv. V, 5, 200. Err. I, 2, 95. V, 180. Shr. III, 2, 22. Hml. I, 1, 170. u. my blessing, I command thee go, H6A IV, 5, 36. u. my reputation, Alls IV, 3, 153. u. the love you bear me, get you in, Troil. V, 3, 78. Cymb. III, 2, 12. u. my soul, a lie, Oth. V, 2, 181. I'll swear u. that bottle, Tp. II, 2, 130. thou didst swear to me u. a parcel-gilt goblet, H4B II, 1, 94. my soul u. the forfeit, Merch. V, 252. my life u. it, Tw. II, 4, 23. my life u. her faith, Oth. I, 3, 295 etc.

Used, in consequence, to express the ground or occasion of any thing done: u. this promise did he raise his chin, Ven. 85. thy great gift, u. misprision growing, Sonn. 87, 11. I must pile them up u. a sore injunction, Tp. III, 1, 11. this pride of hers, u. advice, hath drawn my love from her, Gent. III, 1, 73. will you u. good dowry marry her? Wiv. I, 1, 246. I will do a greater thing than that u. your request, 248. heaven may decrease it u. better acquaintance, 255. u. a true contract I got possession, Meas. I, 2, 149. let me not find you before me again u. any complaint, II, 1, 260. if any thing fall to you u. this, IV, 2, 190. condemned u. the act of fornication, V, 70. u. what bargain do you give it me? Err. II, 2, 25. u. what cause? V, 123. if he do not dote on her u. this, Ado II, 3, 219. she died u. his words, IV, 1, 225. IV, 2, 56. and u. the grief of this suddenly dead, 65. the lady is dead u. mine and my master's false accusation, V, 1, 249. fled he is u. this villany, 258. accused her u. the error that you heard debated, V, 4, 3. I yield u. great persuasion, 95. make such wanton gambols with the wind u. supposed fairness, Merch. III, 2, 94. u. my power I may dismiss this court, IV, 1, 104. that u. knowledge of my parentage I may have welcome, Shr. II, 96. I am yours u. your will to suffer, Alls IV, 4, 30. kings break faith u. commodity, John II, 597. it frowns more u. humour than advised respect, IV, 2, 214. blew this tempest up u. your stubborn usage of the pope, V, 1, 18. thy son is banished u. good advice, R2 I, 3, 233. u. compulsion, H4A II, 4, 261. you ran away u. instinct, 331. the thing that's heavy in itself, u. enforcement flies with greatest speed, H4B I, 1, 120. to love their present pains u. example, H5 IV, 1, 19. u. my death the French can little boast, H6A IV, 5, 24. I am come hither u. my man's instigation, H6B II, 3, 88. u. what cause? R3 I, 1, 46. u. the like devotion, R3 IV, 1, 9. condemned u. it, H8 II, 1, 8. nor ever more u. this business my appearance make, II, 4, 132. a good quarrel to draw emulous factions and bleed to death u. Troil. II, 3, 80. they u. their ancient malice will forget ... these his new honours, Cor. II, 1, 244. this is no time to lend money, especially u. bare friendship, Tim. III, 1, 45. u. what sickness (dead)? Caes. IV, 3, 152. to strike at me u. his misconstruction, Lr. II, 2, 124. to do u. respect such violent outrage, II, 4, 24. u. malicious bravery doest thou come, Oth. I, 1, 100. such as have not thrived u. the present state, Ant. I, 3, 52. u. my mended judgement ... my quarrel was not altogether slight, Cymb. I, 4, 49. Passages leading over to the temporal use: u. their sight we two will fly, Wiv. IV, 4, 54. to render it u. his death, Merch. IV, 1, 384. what may chance or breed u. our absence, Wint. I, 2, 12. lo, u. thy wish, our messenger is arrived, John II, 50. he comes u. a wish, Caes. III, 2, 271. Lord Cloten, u.

*my lady's missing, came to me*, Cymb. V, 5, 275. *stole these children u. my banishment*, 342.

Temporal use: *the accident … u. the moment did her force subdue*, Compl. 248. *as it fell u. a day*, Pilgr. 373. *u. All-hallowmas last*, Wiv. I, 1, 211. *much u. this time have I promised here to meet*, Meas. IV, 1, 17. *u. the heavy middle of the night*, 35. *u. that day prepare to die*, Mids. I, 1, 86. *you shall hence u. your wedding-day*, Merch. III, 2, 313; Wint. IV, 4, 55; John I, 235; R2 I, 1, 199. *I was your mother much u. these years*, Rom. I, 3, 72. *you come most carefully u. your hour*, Hml. I, 1, 6.* *she said u. a time*, Cymb. III, 5, 137. V, 5, 153. Similarly: *u. our spiritual convocation*, H5 I, 1, 76 (but perhaps = in pursuance of the decrees passed there).

The idea of collateral position originating in that of contiguity: *u. thy side against myself I'll fight*, Sonn. 88, 3. *u. the left hand of the even field*, Caes. V, 1, 17 etc. Hence the following expressions: *till she had kindled all the world u. the right and party of her son*, John I, 34. *whose (my hand's) protection is most divinely vowed u. the right of him it holds*, II, 237. *u. his aid to wake Northumberland*, Mcb. III, 6, 30.

Denoting the direction given to an action: *there is no day for me to look u.* Gent. III, 1, 181. III, 2, 201 (cf. *Gaze, Look* etc.). *you have too much respect u. the world*, Merch. I, 1, 74. *turn the office of their view u. a tawny front*, Ant. I, 1, 6. *to turn thy hated back u. our kingdom*, Lr. I, 1, 179. *till sable night … u. the world dim darkness doth display*, Lucr. 118 (as it were, in the face of the world). *u. a homely object love can wink*, Gent. II, 4, 98. Similarly: *to shut the door u. a person*, which may be either = to shut out (Err. IV, 4, 66. V, 204. Merch. I, 2, 147. H8 II, 4, 43) or to shut in (As IV, 1, 163. Hml. III, 1, 135. cf. *you shall not now be stolen, you have locks u. you*, Cymb. V, 4, 1).

Expressing motion towards an object, either in a hostile sense, as of something coming down in a threatening manner and without having been sufficiently guarded against: *he ran u. the boar*, Ven. 1112. *shall I come u. thee with an old saying*, LLL IV, 1, 121. *u. them, lords!* IV, 3, 367; cf. R3 V, 3, 351. *to rush u. your peace*, John II, 221. *a hundred u. poor four of us*, H4A II, 4, 180. *the Scot who will make road u. us*, H5 I, 2, 138. *thus comes the English with full power u. us*, II, 4, 1. *they will not come u. us now*, III, 6, 177. *go down u. him*, III, 5, 53. *the last hour of my long weary life is come u. me*, H8 II, 1, 133. *we turn not back the silks u. the merchant*, Troil. II, 2, 69. *hope to come u. them in the heat of their division*, Cor. IV, 3, 18. *swoon for what's to come u. thee*, V, 2, 73. *fear comes u. me*, Rom. V, 3, 135. *press not so u. me*, Caes. III, 2, 171. *come down u. us with a mighty power*, IV, 3, 169. *it comes u. me*, 278. *if you make your voyage u. her*, Cymb. I, 4, 170 etc. Or implying the notion of imperceptibleness: *now stole u. the time the dead of night*, Lucr. 162. *I have an exposition of sleep come u. me*, Mids. IV, 1, 44 (Bottom's speech). *the morning comes u. us*, Caes. II, 1, 221. *the deep of night is crept u. our talk*, IV, 3, 226. cf. *the eye of reason may pry in u. us*, H4A IV, 1, 72.

Hence used to express an advantage gained over another: *begin you to grow u. me?* As I, 1, 91. *I never had triumphed u. a Scot*, H4A V, 3, 15. *sickness growing u. our soldiers*, H5 III, 3, 56. *the rabble … will in time win u. power*, Cor. I, 1, 224. *this sorrow … would*

*usurp u. my watery eyes*, Tit. III, 1, 269. *you'll win two days u. me*, Ant. II, 4, 9. *have got u. me a nobleness in record*, IV, 14, 98. *people such that mend u. the world*, Cymb. II, 4, 26.

Placed before the person or thing aimed at or suffering in an action: *this desire might have excuse to work u. his wife*, Lucr. 235. *got by the devil himself u. thy wicked dam*, Tp. I, 2, 320. *the air breathes u. us here most sweetly*, II, 1, 46. *for every trifle are they set u. me*, II, 2, 8. *do you put tricks u. us?* 60. *now Prosper works u. thee*, 84. *to have done some wanton charm u. this man and maid*, IV, 95. *that you might kill your stomach on your meat, and not u. your maid*, Gent. I, 2, 69. *huddling jest upon jest u. me*, Ado II, 1, 253. *I beg the law u. his head*, Mids. IV, 1, 160. *scolding would do little good u. him*, Shr. I, 2, 110. *to break a jest u. the company*, IV, 5, 73. *to breathe themselves u. thee*, All's II, 3, 272. *you drew your sword u. me*, Tw. V, 191. *sets spies u. us*, Wint. V, 1, 203. *done a rape u. the maiden virtue of the crown*, John II, 98. *make work u. ourselves*, 407. *denouncing vengeance u. John*, III, 4, 159. *will maintain u. his bad life to make all this good*, R2 I, 1, 99. *thou hast done much harm u. me*, H4A I, 2, 103 (reading of Q1; the rest of O. Edd. *unto*). *one that no persuasion can do good u.* III, 1, 200. *thy cruelty in execution u. offenders*, H6B I, 3, 136. *didst unworthy slaughter u. others*, R3 I, 2, 88. *they that I would have thee deal u.* IV, 2, 75. *I will beget mine issue u. your daughter*, IV, 4, 298. *the part my father meant to act u. the usurper Richard*, H8 I, 2, 195. *and with his deed did crown his word u. you*, III, 2, 156. *try u. yourselves what you have seen me*, Cor. III, 1, 225. *my sinews shall be stretched u. him*, V, 6, 45. *that my sword u. thee shall approve*, Tit. II, 1, 35. *we are too bold u. your rest*, Caes. II, 1, 86. *what cannot you and I perform u. the unguarded Duncan*, Mcb. I, 7, 69. *I must draw my sword u. you*, Lr. II, 1, 31. *I have o'erheard a plot of death u. him*, III, 6, 96. *the goodness I intend u. you*, V, 1, 7. *I follow him to serve my turn u. him*, Oth. I, 1, 42. *'tis a monster begot u. itself*, III, 4, 162. *there is mettle in death, which commits some loving act u. her*, Ant. I, 2, 148. *demuring u. me*, IV, 15, 29. *our care and pity is so much u. you*, V, 2, 188. *to be revenged u. her*, Cymb. III, 5, 79. *they will but please themselves u. her*, Per. IV, 1, 101 etc. (cf. such imprecations and good wishes as: *a plague u. this howling*, Tp. I, 1, 39. *out u. thee*, Err. III, 1, 77. *thyself u. thyself*, Troil. II, 3, 30. *mercy u. us*, Tp. III, 2, 141. *hourly joys be still u. you*, IV, 108. *a good wish u. you*, As I, 3, 24. R3 I, 3, 218. Lr. II, 4, 171. Oth. I, 2, 35. Per. III, 3, 5 etc.). Particularly placed after verbs implying the idea of feeding and consuming: *u. the earth's increase why shouldst thou feed*, Ven. 169. *lives u. his gains*, Sonn. 67, 12. *live thou u. thy servant's loss*, 146, 9. *dine, sup and sleep u. the very naked name of love*, Gent. II, 4, 141. *I have fed u. this woe already*, III, 1, 219. *feast u. her eyes*, Meas. II, 2, 179. *that I'll live u.* As III, 5, 104. *to feast u. whole thousands of the French*, John V, 2, 178. *preys u. itself*, R2 II, 1, 39. *live u. the vapour of a dungeon*, Oth. III, 3, 271. *he is vaulting variable ramps … u. your purse*, Cymb. I, 6, 135 (= at your expense) etc. Similarly after some expressions of amorous affection, f. i. *thou seest me dote u. my love*, Gent. II, 4, 173 (cf. *Dote*). *more fond on her than she u. her love*, Mids. II, 1, 266 etc. Thus even: *can thy right hand seize love u. thy left?* Ven. 158. *my birth-place hate I, and my love's u. this enemy town,* Cor. IV, 4, 23.

Direction and tendency implied also in the phrase *to call u. a person:* Sonn. 79, 1. Meas. IV, 1, 36 etc. (cf. *Call*). cf. *cried in fainting u. Rosalind,* As IV, 3, 150. H5 IV, 1, 145 (cf. *Cry*) etc. No less in the following expressions: *have some malignant power u. my life,* Gent. III, 1, 238. *I have no power u. you,* Ant. I, 3, 23. *let your highness command u. me,* Mcb. III, 1, 16.

Denoting a design or business in which a person is employed: *u. some book I love I'll pray for thee,* Gent. I, 1, 20. *when 'tis u. ill employment,* Wiv. V, 5, 135. *set forth u. his Irish expedition,* H4A I, 3, 150. *in what fashion ... he goes u. this action,* Cor. I, 1, 283. *we are convented u. a pleasing treaty,* II, 2, 59. *are summoned to meet anon u. your approbation,* II, 3, 152. *I have myself resolved u. a course which has no need of you,* Ant. III, 11, 9. *that they will waste their time u. our note,* Cymb. IV, 4, 20 etc. Hence the expressions: *'tis best we stand u. our guard,* Tp. II, 1, 321. *work for bread u. Athenian stalls,* Mids. III, 2, 10. *will stay u. your leisure,* All's III, 5, 48. *thine eye hath stayed u. some favour,* Tw. II, 4, 24. *it waits u. some god o' the island,* Tp. I, 2, 388. *shall wait u. your father's funeral,* John V, 7, 98. *what danger dwells u. my suit?* Ven. 206 (cf. the resp. articles). For the same reason after expressions of thought or speech: *love can comment u. every woe,* Ven. 714. *think u. my grief,* Gent. IV, 3, 28. *I have ta'en a due and wary note u. it,* Meas. IV, 1, 38. *do prophesy u. it dangerously,* John IV, 2, 186. *examine me u. the particulars of my life,* H4A II, 4, 414. *I'll make my heaven to dream u. the crown,* H6C III, 2, 168. *think u. what hath chanced,* Mcb. I, 3, 153. *some words u. that business,* II, 1, 23. *my first false speaking was this u. myself,* IV, 3, 131 etc.

Singular use: *I judge their number u. or near the rate of thirty thousand,* H4B IV, 1, 22 (= at). *it was u. this fashion bequeathed me* etc. As I, 1, 1. *this shepherd's passion is much u. my fashion,* II, 4, 62 (cf. Euphues' Golden Legacy, ed. Collier, p. 64: *he returned them a salute on this manner.* Greene's Pandosto, p. 36: *began to parley with her on this manner*). *to die u. the hand I loved so well,* Mids. II, 1, 244 (cf. *on* in Gent. II, 4, 113. Mids. II, 2, 107. Caes. V, 1, 58).

**Upon,** adv. 1) expressing a state of being placed on the surface of a thing: *that's insculped u.* Merch. II, 7, 57.

2) Expressing direction, in the phrase *to look u.* = to be a spectator or witness: *strike all that look u. with marvel,* Wint. V, 3, 100. *all of you that stand and look u., whilst that my wretchedness doth bait myself,* R2 IV, 237 (Ff *look u. me*). *and look u. as if the tragedy were played in jest,* H6C II, 3, 27. *he is my prize: I will not look u.* Troil. V, 6, 10.

3) Joined with other adverbs, to express progress and approach in time: *and very near u. the duke is entering,* Meas. IV, 6, 14. *the hour prefixed ... comes fast u.* Troil. IV, 3, 3. *it followed hard u.* Hml. I, 2, 179.

Seemingly adverbial, but indeed prepositional in the phrase *it stands me u.;* see *Stand.*

**Upper,** higher: *I nightly lodge her in an u. tower,* Gent. III, 1, 35. *at u. end o' the table,* Wint. IV, 4, 59 and Cor. IV, 5, 205. *let my woes frown on the u. hand,* R3 IV, 4, 37. *the u. Germany,* H8 V, 3, 30. *keep the hills and u. regions,* Caes. V, 1, 3.

**Up-pricked,** erected, pointed, pricked: *his ears u.* Ven. 271.

**Uprear,** to raise: *and this my hand against myself u.* Sonn. 49, 11. H4B IV, 1, 214. *high —ed and abutting fronts,* H5 Prol. 21. *his hair —ed,* H6B III, 2, 171.

**Upright,** 1) adj. and adv. (*úpright* and *upríght* indiscriminately), straight up, erect: *he rears u.* Ven. 279. *time goes u. with his carriage,* Tp. V, 3 ('brings forward all the expected events, without faltering under his burden'. Steevens). *as u. as the cedar,* LLL IV, 3, 89. *you whoreson u. rabbit,* H4B II, 2, 91. *I have seen him caper u.* H6B III, 1, 365. *it* (his hair) *stands u.* III, 3, 15. *it* (the world) *will never stand u.* R3 III, 2, 39. *u. he held it* (the sceptre) Tit. I, 200. *set them u. at their dear friends' doors,* V, 1, 136. *who dares in purity of manhood stand u. and say,* Tim. IV, 3, 14. *would I not leap u.* Lr. IV, 6, 27 (= straight up. cf. H6B III, 1, 365).

2) adj. (*úpright* before the subst., *upríght* behind) righteous, just, honest: *live an u. life,* Merch. III, 5, 79. *O wise and u. judge,* IV, 1, 250. 313. *the unstooping firmness of my u. soul,* R2 I, 1, 121. I, 3, 87. IV, 118. H4B V, 2, 39. H6A III, 1, 95. H6C V, 1, 78. R3 IV, 4, 55. Cymb. V, 5, 214.

**Uprighteously,** righteously, in a just and honourable manner: *you may most u. do a poor wronged lady a merited benefit,* Meas. III, 1, 205.

**Uprightness,** righteousness, integrity, virtue: Tit. I, 48.

**Uprise,** subst. (*upríse* and *úprise*) the appearance (of the sun) above the horizon: Tit. III, 1, 159. Ant. IV, 12, 18.

**Uprising,** rising, ascent: *spurred his horse so hard against the steep u. of the hill,* LLL IV, 1, 2.

**Uproar,** subst. (*úproar*) commotion, disturbance, tumult: *his eye ... unto a greater u. tempts his veins,* Lucr. 427. *an u. begun through malice of the bishop's men,* H6A III, 1, 74. *are all in u.* H8 I, 2, 36. *commotions, —s,* V, 3, 28. *by —s severed,* Tit. V, 3, 68 (later Ff *u.*).

**Uproar,** vb. (*uproár*) to stir up to tumult, to disturb: *u. the universal peace,* Mcb. IV, 3, 99.

**Uproused,** roused from sleep: Rom. II, 3, 40.

**Upshoot,** a word used by Costard with an indecent pun upon upshot and a shooting upward: LLL IV, 1, 138.

**Upshot,** final issue, conclusion: *I cannot pursue this sport to the u.* Tw. IV, 2, 76. *and in this u. purposes mistook,* Hml. V, 2, 395.

**Upside down,** with the lower part above the higher: *a burning torch that's turned u.* Per. II, 2, 32. Metaphorically, = in complete disorder: *this house is turned u.* H4A II, 1, 11.

**Upspring,** a sort of dance (according to Elze, a translation of the German *Hüpfauf:* but *Hüpfauf* is an apocryphal dance and may as well be translated from *upspring*): *keeps wassail and the swaggering u. reels,* Hml. I, 4, 9. According to others, = upstart.

**Up-stairs,** see *Stair.*

**Up-staring,** standing on end: *with hair u.* Tp. I, 2, 213.

**Upstart,** subst. used indefinitely (certainly not in the modern sense of one suddenly raised to honour): *I think this u. is old Talbot's ghost,* H6A IV, 7, 87.

**Upstart**, adj. suddenly raised to honour: *my rights and royalties ... given away to u. unthrifts*, R2 II, 3, 122.

**Up-swarm**, to raise in swarms: *have here —ed them* (his subjects) H4B IV, 2, 30.

**Up-till**, prepos. on: *leaned her breast u. a thorn*, Pilgr. 382.

**Upturned**, turned up: *the white u. wondering eyes of mortals*, Rom. II, 2, 29.

**Upward**, adv. 1) towards a higher place, higher up: *a Spaniard from the hip u.* Ado III, 2, 36. *what u. lies the street should see*, LLL IV, 3, 280. H5 II, 3, 27. Mcb. IV, 2, 24. Lr. II, 4, 75 (Qq *up the hill*).
2) more (used of time): *I have lived fourscore years and u.* Wiv. III, 1, 56. *fourscore and u.* Lr. IV, 7, 61. *u. of* = more than: *u. of twenty years*, H8 II, 4, 36.

**Upward**, adj. directed or turned to a higher place: *our fortune keeps an u. course*, H6C V, 3, 1. *thy u. face*, Tim. IV, 3, 190. *Titinius' face is u.* Caes. V, 3, 93.

**Upward**, subst. top: *from the extremest u. of thy head*, Lr. V, 3, 136.

**Upwards**, adv. so as to be turned to a higher place, and not to the ground: *she shall be buried with her face u.* Ado III, 2, 71.

**Urchin**, 1) a hedgehog: *—s shall forth at vast of night that they may work all exercise on thee*, Tp. I, 2, 326 (cf. II, 2, 10: *like hedgehogs which lie tumbling in my barefoot way and mount their pricks at my footfall*). *they'll nor pinch, fright me with u. shows*, II, 2, 5. *a thousand hissing snakes, ten thousand swelling toads, as many —s*, Tit. II, 3, 101.
2) a goblin, a sort of fairy: *like —s, ouphes and fairies, green and white*, Wiv. IV, 4, 49.

**Urchinfield**; Lord Talbot of Goodrig and U. H6A IV, 7, 64. [Castle of Uryshay, Herefordshire.]

**Urchin-show**, the sight of hedgehogs or of goblins like them: Tp. II, 2, 5. cf. *Urchin*.

**Urchin-snouted**, having a snout like that of a hedgehog (?), or having a goblin-like, demoniac snout (?): *this foul, grim, and u. boar*, Ven. 1105.

**Urge**, 1) to press, to ply hard, to impel, to solicit, to move: *and to his protestations —d the rest, who, wondering at him, did his words allow*, Lucr. 1844. *give Helen this and u. her to a present answer back*, All's II, 2, 67. *u. them while their souls are capable of this ambition*, John II, 475. *what I have done my safety —d me to*, H4A V, 5, 11. *downright oaths, which I never use till —d, nor never break for —ing*, H5 V, 2, 151. 152. *then he was —d to tell my tale again*, R3 III, 7, 31. *u. the king to do me this last right*, H8 IV, 2, 157. *the oath which by that god he swears, to that I'll u. him*, Tit. V, 1, 81. *an earnest inviting, which many my near occasions did u. me to put off*, Tim. III, 6, 12. *I —d you further*, Caes. II, 1, 243.
2) to stimulate, to incite, to irritate: *to make our appetites more keen, with eager compounds we our palates u.* Sonn. 118, 2. *wilt know again, being ne'er so little —d, another way to pluck him ... from the throne*, R2 V, 1, 64. *I'll in, to u. his hatred more to Clarence*, R3 I, 1, 147. *—ing me to fury*, Rom. V, 3, 63. *u. me no more, I shall forget myself*, Caes. IV, 3, 35. With *on*: *murder, as hating what himself hath done, doth lay it open to u. on revenge*, John IV, 3, 38.
3) to ask, to question with more or less earnestness and importunity: *but she with vehement prayers —th still under what colour he commits this ill*, Lucr. 475. *you —d me as a judge*, R2 I, 3, 237. *if you u.*

*me farther than to say 'do you in faith'? I wear out my suit*, H5 V, 2, 131.
4) to demand, to request with more or less earnestness, to claim, to insist on: *and from her twining arms doth u. releasing*, Ven. 256. *speed more than speed but dull and slow she deems: extremity still —th such extremes*, Lucr. 1337. *so thou ... with —ing helpless patience wouldst relieve me*, Err. II, 1, 39. *as thou —st justice*, Merch. IV, 1, 315. *to u. the thing held as a ceremony*, V, 206. *she —d conference*, As I, 2, 270. *my dear offence, which was so strongly —d past my defence*, John I, 258. *may bring that right in peace which here we u. in war*, II, 47. *u. it no more*, R2 IV, 271. *when I —d the ransom of my wife's brother*, H4A I, 3, 141. *therefore I u. thy oath*, Tit. V, 1, 78. *I should not u. thy duty past thy might*, Caes. IV, 3, 261. *the time will not allow the compliment which very manners —s*, Lr. V, 3, 234. *to u. sth. to or on a person* = to demand from, to insist on with: *they did u. it* (Clarence's death) *still unto the king*, R3 II, 1, 137. *your haste is now —d on you*, Lr. V, 1, 54 (you are earnestly summoned to make haste).

Intr., with *for*: *was with the Lord Lucullus to borrow so many talents, nay, —d extremely for't and showed what necessity belonged to't*, Tim. III, 2, 14.
5) to speak; a) absol. to produce arguments, to alledge proofs as an accuser: *the king's attorney ... —d on* (prepos.) *the examinations, proofs, confessions of divers witnesses*, H8 II, 1, 16. *that my accusers ... may stand forth face to face and freely u. against me*, V, 3, 48.
b) trans. to allege, assert: *and with good thoughts makes dispensation, —ing the worser sense for vantage still*, Lucr. 249 (always alleging, and placing in an advantageous light, what could be said against them in a bad sense). *u. not my amiss, lest guilty of my fault thy sweet self prove*, Sonn. 151, 3. *she hath —d her height*, Mids. III, 2, 291. *he knows not what I can u. against him*, Cor. IV, 7, 19. *if his occasion were not virtuous, I should not u. it half so faithfully*, Tim. III, 2, 46.
Hence = to speak of, to mention, to bring upon the carpet: *what have you —d that I cannot reprove?* Ven. 787. *u. not my father's anger, but think upon my grief*, Gent. IV, 3, 27. *for —ing it the second time to me*, Err. II, 2, 47. *he slept not for my —ing it*, V, 63. *besides her —ing of her wreck at sea*, 359. *I u. this childhood proof*, Merch. I, 1, 144. *patience once more, whiles our compact is —d*, As V, 4, 5. *an ancient tale new told, and in the last repeating troublesome, being —d at a time unseasonable*, John IV, 2, 20. *why —st thou so oft young Arthur's death*, 204. *u. doubts to them that fear*, R2 II, 1, 299. *I will not vex your souls ... with too much —ing your pernicious lives*, III, 1, 4. *he spake it twice, and —d it twice together*, V, 4, 5. *a challenge —d more modestly*, H4A V, 2, 53. *that self bill is —d*, H5 I, 1, 1 (= brought in). *this bill —d by the commons*, 71. *the peace which you before so —d, lies in his answer*, V, 2, 76 (on which you expatiated so eloquently). *a woman's voice may do some good, when articles too nicely —d be stood on*, 94. *well —d, H6A III, 1, 152. u. it no more*, H6C I, 1, 98. *in those busy days which here you u. to prove us enemies*, R3 I, 3, 146. *u. neither charity nor shame to me*, 274. *the —ing of that word judgement*, I, 4, 109. *how canst thou u. God's dreadful name to us?* 214. *it should be*

*put to no apparent likelihood of breach, which haply by much company might be —d*, II, 2, 137 (= might be spoken of in consequence of too great an attendance). *thou knowest our reasons —d upon the way*, III, 1, 160. *u. his hateful luxury*, III, 5, 80. *u. the necessity and state of times*, IV, 4, 416. *I —d our old acquaintance*, Cor. V, 1, 10. *wherefore dost thou u. the name of hands?* Tit. III, 2, 26. *word ill —d to one that is so ill*, Rom. I, 1, 209. *O trespass sweetly —d*, I, 5, 111. *and —d withal your high displeasure*, III, 1, 159. *u. it no more, on height of our displeasure*, Tim. III, 5, 86. *Decius, well —d*, Caes. II, 1, 155. *u. you your petitions in the street?* III, 1, 11. *my brother never did u. me in his act*, Ant. II, 2, 46. *whom he may at pleasure whip ... to quit me: u. it thou*, III, 13, 151.

**Urgent**, pressing, cogent: *to take the u. hour*, Wint. I, 2, 465. *with more u. touches*, Ant. I, 2, 187.

**Urinal**, a bottle in which urine is kept for inspection: Gent. II, 1, 41. Wiv. III, 1, 14. 91. cf. *Castalion.*

**Urine**, animal water: Meas. III, 2, 118. Merch. IV, 1, 50. Mcb. II, 3, 32.

**Urn**, 1) a vessel in which the ashes of the dead were kept: Phoen. 65. H6A I, 6, 24.

2) a grave: *lay these bones in an unworthy u., tombless, with no remembrance over them*, H5 I, 2, 228. *the most noble corse that ever herald did follow to his u.* Cor. V, 6, 146. cf. *Inurned.*

In Tit. III, 1, 17 M. Edd. **urns**, in the un-Shakespearian sense of waterpots; O. Edd. *ruins.*

**Ursula**, female name (particularly of servants): Gent. IV, 4, 122. Ado III, 1, 4 (Q *Ursley*). 15. 34. III, 4, 1. 104. V, 4, 78. H4B I, 2, 269.

**Urswick**, name: *Sir Christopher U.*, R3 IV, 5, 1 (*U*. only in the stage-direction).

**Usage**, 1) treatment: Tw. I, 5, 188. Wint. II, 3, 117. V, 1, 153. John V, 1, 18. H4A V, 1, 69. H6A V, 3, 58. H6C IV, 5, 6. Troil. IV, 4, 121. Tit. I, 266. Lr. II, 4, 26. Cymb. IV, 1, 22.

2) manners, behaviour: *heaven me such u. send, not to pick bad from bad, but by bad mend*, Oth. IV, 3, 105 (only in Q1; the rest of O. Edd. *uses*).

**Usance**, interest paid for money: *brings down the rate of u.* Merch. I, 3, 46. *my moneys and my —s*, 109. *take no doit of u. for my moneys*, 142.

**Use**, subst. 1) the act of employing a thing: *torches are made to light, ... fresh beauty for the u.* Ven. 164. *who (the tongue) mad that sorrow should his u. control*, Lucr. 1781. *mine be thy love, and thy love's u. their treasure*, Sonn. 20, 14. *all corners else o'the earth let liberty make u. of*, Tp. I, 2, 492. *u. of service none*, II, 1, 151. *no u. of metal*, 153. *they want the u. of tongue*, III, 3, 38. *he hath no u. of them* (his eyes) Wiv. III, 2, 32. *every scope by the immoderate u. turns to restraint*, Meas. I, 2, 131. *I know not what u. to put her to*, Err. III, 2, 97. *thy jealous fits have scared thy husband from the u. of wits*, V, 86. *you have forsworn the u. of eyes*, LLL IV, 3, 310. *for u. of that which is mine own*, Merch. I, 3, 114. *be able for thine enemy rather in power than u.* All's I, 1, 75. *can serve the world for no honest u.* IV, 3, 341. *can such sweet u. make of what they hate*, IV, 4, 22. *I put you to the u. of your own virtues*, V, 1, 16. *mine own purse, which I had recommended to his u.* Tw. V, 94. *the time is worth the u. on't*, Wint. III, 1, 14 (= the time is worth having been used, i. e. spent most usefully). *creatures of note for mercy-lacking —s*, John IV, 1, 121. *my tongue's u. is to me no more*

*than an unstringed viol*, R2 I, 3, 161. *when we need your u. and counsel*, H4A I, 3, 21 (= the use of your counsel; cf. *And*). *I make as good u. of it*, III, 3, 33. *another for u.* H4B II, 2, 21. *things that are mouldy lack u.* III, 2, 119. *more perfect in the u. of arms*, IV, 1, 155. *sets it in act and u.* IV, 3, 126. *comes to no u.* IV, 4, 72. *Davy serves you for good —s*, V, 3, 11. *what u. we made of them*, H5 I, 2, 268. *thou makest u. of any thing*, III, 7, 70. *many hands, and no u.* Troil. I, 2, 30. *served me to effectless u.* Tit. III, 1, 76. *strained from that fair u.* Rom. II, 3, 19. *dignities which vacant lie for thy best u. and wearing*, Tim. V, 1, 146. *if thou hast any sound or u. of voice*, Hml. I, 1, 128. *to what base ... we may return*, V, 1, 223. *we must have u. of your advice*, Lr. II, 1, 123. *craves the instant u.* 130. *having made u. of him*, Ant. III, 5, 7. *have no u. for trusting*, V, 2, 15 (don't know what to do with it) etc.

Often preceded by *to* instead of *for: for terror, not to u.* Meas. I, 3, 26. *what I saw, to my good u. I remembered*, Wint. IV, 4, 616. *spare mine eyes, though to no u. but still to look on you*, John IV, 1, 103. *to one's u.* = in order to be at one's disposal: *take it up unto thy master's u.* Shr. IV, 3, 159 (quibbling). *my fair name ... to dark dishonour's u. thou shalt not have*, R2 I, 1, 169 (that disgrace may dispose of it, deal with it, at pleasure). *the prisoners ... to his own u. he keeps*, H4A I, 1, 94. *hath here distrained the Tower to his u.* H6A I, 3, 61. *till he disbursed ... ten thousand dollars to our general u.* Mcb. I, 2, 62. *to u., without a genitive*, = at command: *o'er whom both sovereign power and father's voice I have to u.* All's II, 3, 61. *any thing I have is his to u.* H6B V, 1, 53.

2) utility, advantage, profit: *make u. of time*, Ven. 129 (= improve the moment). *made u. and fair advantage of his days*, Gent. II, 4, 68. *can you make no u. of your discontent?* Ado I, 3, 40 (= derive advantage from it). *sweet are the —s of adversity*, As II, 1, 12. *which should give us a further u. to be made than alone the recovery of the king*, All's II, 3, 41. *I must lose the u. of all deceit*, John V, 4, 27. *I rather of his absence make this u.* H4A IV, 1, 76. *a good wit will make u. of any thing*, H4B I, 2, 277. *made her serve your —s*, II, 1, 127. *practised on me for thy u.* H5 II, 2, 99. *any groat I hoarded to my u.* H6B III, 1, 113. *make u. now, and provide for thine own future safety*, H8 III, 2, 421 (= let not advantage slip). *what things there are most abject in regard and dear in u.* Troil. III, 3, 128. *make u. of thy salt hours*, Tim. IV, 3, 85.

3) present possession, usufruct: *so he will let me have the other half in u., to render it, upon his death, unto the gentleman*, Merch. IV, 1, 383. *my full heart remains in u. with you*, Ant. I, 3, 44.

4) interest paid for borrowed money: *gold that's put to u. more gold begets*, Ven. 768. *thou usurer, that put'st forth all to u.* Sonn. 134, 10. *that u. is not forbidden usury which happies those that pay the willing loan*, 6, 5. *she* (nature) *determines herself the glory of a creditor, both thanks and u.* Meas. I, 1, 41. *he lent it me awhile, and I gave him u. for it*, Ado II, 1, 288. *being kept together and put to u.* Tw. III, 1, 57.

5) occasion or need of employment, necessity, exigency: *should we ne'er have u. for 'em* (friends) Tim. I, 2, 101. *my —s cry to me*, II, 1, 20. *to supply his instant u. with so many talents*, III, 2, 41. *here is no u. for gold*, IV, 3, 290. *that mine own u. invites me to cut down*, V, 1, 209. *I have u. for it*, Oth. III, 3, 319.

*receive us for barbarous and unnatural revolts during their u. and slay us after,* Cymb. IV, 4, 7.

6) practice, habitual exercise: *every alien pen hath got my u.* Sonn. 78, 3. *how u. doth breed a habit in a man,* Gent. V, 4, 1. *to give fear to u. and liberty,* Meas. I, 4, 62 (= to the practice of liberty, or to licentious practice). *my dull deaf ears* (have) *a little u. to hear,* Err. V, 316. *still u. of grief makes wild grief tame,* R3 IV, 4, 229. *my arms are out of u.* Troil. V, 6, 16. *a brain that leads my u. of anger to better vantage,* Cor. III, 2, 30. *to the u. of actions fair and good he* (custom) *likewise gives a frock or livery that aptly is put on,* Hml. III, 4, 163. *her speech is nothing, yet the unshaped u. of it doth move the hearers to collection,* IV, 5, 8. *our laws, whose u. the sword of Caesar hath too much mangled,* Cymb. III, 1, 56. *custom what they did begin was with long u. account no sin,* Per. Prol. 30.

Hence = custom (habitual practice as well as common occurrence): *his u. was to put a ducat in her clack-dish,* Meas. III, 2, 134. *it is still her* (Fortune's) *u. to let the wretched man outlive his wealth,* Merch. IV, 1, 268. *with more haste than is his u.* All's V, 1, 24. *made impudent with u. of evil deeds,* H6C I, 4, 117. *a return exceeding all u. of quittance,* Tim. I, 1, 291. *the deed of saying is quite out of u.* V, 1, 28. *these things are beyond all u.* Caes. II, 2, 25. *blood and destruction shall be so in u.* III, 1, 265. *out of u. and staled by other men,* IV, 1, 38. *against the u. of nature,* Mcb. I, 3, 137. *cleave not to their mould but with the aid of u.* 146. *my strange and self-abuse is the initiate fear that wants hard u.* III, 4, 143. *u. almost can change the stamp of nature,* Hml. III, 4, 168. *is it his u.?* Oth. IV, 1, 285. *though tongues were out of u.* V, 1, 110.

Plur. *—s* = manners, ways, doings: *how weary, stale, flat and unprofitable seem to me all the —s of this world,* Hml. I, 2, 134. *heaven me such —s send, not to pick bad from bad, but by bad mend,* Oth. IV, 3, 105 (Q1 *usage*).

**Use,** vb. 1) trans. a) to make use of, to employ: *he hath it when he cannot u. it,* Lucr. 862. *who heaven itself for ornament doth u.* Sonn. 21, 3. *I cannot blame thee for my love thou —st,* 40, 6. *a better spirit doth u. your name,* 80, 2. 82, 3. 133, 12. 139, 4. 145, 7. Tp. I, 1, 25. IV, 36. Gent. II, 4, 214. II, 7, 73. III, 1, 123. V, 3, 14 (*will not u. a woman lawlessly;* cf. Tim. IV, 3, 83. Oth. V, 2, 70). Wiv. II, 1, 5. II, 2, 244. 285. V, 5, 77. Meas. II, 2, 109. 113. IV, 2, 26. 60. Err. II, 2, 27. V, 103. Ado I, 2, 28. II, 1, 184. IV, 1, 324. V, 1, 124. V, 2, 20. LLL I, 1, 177. Merch. II, 2, 5. IV, 1, 81. 92. As V, 4, 111. Epil. 5. Shr. I, 1, 36. All's II, 3, 114. II, 5, 32. Tw. I, 5, 15. Wint. II, 1, 72. 85. II, 2, 52. IV, 1, 4. IV, 4, 215. John III, 3, 11. IV, 1, 108. 118. IV, 2, 159. V, 1, 6. R2 III, 3, 42. H4A I, 3, 11. H4B III, 2, 309. V, 2, 115. V, 5, 134. H5 III, 7, 71. IV, 2, 62. V, 2, 151. H6A I, 3, 43. 78. II, 1, 81. H6C II, 2, 65. IV, 1, 42. V, 5, 45. R3 I, 3, 353. IV, 4, 396. V, 3, 309. Troil. V, 1, 104. Tim. I, 2, 87 (*that you would once u. our hearts*). II, 2, 188. 200 (*my occasions have found time to u. 'em toward a supply of money*). III, 1, 39. III, 2, 56 (*I was sending to u. Lord Timon myself,* i. e. to borrow money of him). IV, 3, 83 (*they love thee not that u. thee;* cf. Gent. V, 3, 14 and Oth. V, 2, 70). Mcb. II, 1, 43. V, 5, 29. Hml. II, 2, 3. Oth. V, 2, 70. Cymb. III, 5, 111 etc.

b) to practise customarily, to make a practice of: *do nothing but u. their abuses,* Meas. II, 1, 42 (Elbow's speech). *he hath not —d it before,* IV, 2, 121. *borrows money in God's name, the which he hath —d so long,* Ado V, 1, 320. *I do never u. it,* Merch. I, 3, 71 (viz to lend or borrow upon advantage). *so long I daily vow to u. it* (this exercise) Wint. III, 2, 243. *thou hast caused printing to be —d,* H6B IV, 7, 39. *all several sins, all —d in each degree,* R3 V, 3, 198. *if thou u. to beat me, I will ... tell what thou art,* Troil. II, 1, 52. *to give forth the corn o'the storehouse gratis, as 'twas —d sometime in Greece,* Cor. III, 1, 114. *a trade that I may u. with a safe conscience,* Caes. I, 1, 14. *shows a most pitiful ambition in the fool that —s it,* Hml. III, 2, 50. *I have —d it* (to be full of songs) *ever since thou madest thy daughters thy mothers,* Lr. I, 4, 187. *going shall be —d with feet,* III, 2, 94. *they have —d their dearest action in the tented field,* Oth. I, 3, 84.

Hence *—d* = accustomed: *a beggar that was —d to come so smug upon the mart,* Merch. III, 1, 48. *your greatness hath not been —d to fear,* Wint. IV, 4, 18. *—d to command, untaught to plead for favour,* H6B IV, 1, 122. *the people were not —d to be spoke to,* R3 III, 7, 29 (Qq *wont*). *the madams too, not —d to toil,* H8 I, 1, 24. *they were —d to bend,* Troil. III, 3, 71. *o'erbear what they are —d to bear,* Cor. III, 1, 250. *he hath been —d ever to conquer,* III, 3, 25. *you were —d to say extremity was the trier of spirits,* Cor. IV, 1, 3. 9. *my so —d a guest,* Per. I, 2, 3.

c) to practise in general, to do, to make, to apply to; joined with the most different nouns almost periphrastically: *so thou wilt buy and pay and u. good dealing,* Ven. 514. *they that fawned on him before u. his company no more,* Pilgr. 422. *more mickle was the pain that nothing could be —d to turn them both to gain,* 220. *they cannot u. such vigilance,* Tp. III, 3, 16. *treachery —d to Valentine,* Gent. II, 6, 32. *u. your patience,* Wiv. III, 1, 83 (Evans' speech). *an you u. these blows long,* Err. II, 2, 37. *you u. this dalliance to excuse your breach of promise,* IV, 1, 48. *I make all use of it* (my discontent), *for I u. it only,* Ado I, 3, 41 (= harbour it, have it). *this civil war of wits were much better —d on Navarre,* LLL II, 226. *she should not u. a long one* (passion) *for such a Pyramus,* Mids. V, 322. *u. all the observance of civility,* Merch. II, 2, 204. *u. your pleasure,* III, 2, 323 (do as you please). *u. thou all the endeavour of a man in speed to Padua,* III, 4, 48. *you may as well u. question with the wolf,* IV, 1, 73. *therefore u. thy discretion,* As I, 1, 152 (do as you please). *the stern brow and waspish action which she did u. as she was writing of it,* IV, 3, 10. *u. your manners discreetly in all kind of companies,* Shr. I, 1, 247. *u. a more spacious ceremony to the noble lords,* All's II, 1, 51. *do not u. it oft* (tempting him thus) H4A III, 1, 176. *rendered such aspect as cloudy men u. to their adversaries,* III, 2, 83 (Ff *u. to do to*). *u. lenity,* H5 III, 2, 26. *u. mercy to them all,* III, 3, 54. *to u. his good pleasure,* III, 6, 57. *what treachery was —d?* H6A I, 1, 68. *u. no entreaty, for it is in vain,* V, 4, 85. *words and threats shall be the war that Henry means to u.* H6C I, 1, 73. *while I u. further conference with Warwick,* III, 3, 111. *if we u. delay, cold biting winter mars our hoped-for hay,* IV, 8, 60. *u. careful watch,* R3 V, 3, 54. *we are ready to u. our utmost studies in your service,* H8 III, 1, 174. *to u. so rude behaviour,* IV, 2, 103. *we must u. expostulation kindly,* Troil. IV, 4, 62. *thou dost affect my manners and dost u. them,* Tim. IV, 3, 199. *that thou wilt u. the wars as thy redress and not as our confusion*, V, 4, 51. *nor with such free and friendly conference as he hath —d of old*, Caes. IV, 2, 18. *the rest is labour, which is not —d for you*, Mcb. 1, 4, 44. *—ing those thoughts which should indeed have died*, III, 2, 10. *u. all gently*, Hml. III, 2, 6. *to u. some gentle entertainment to Laertes before you fall to play*, V, 2, 215. *knavery's plain face is never seen till —d*, Oth. II, 1, 321. *Antony will u. his affection where it is*, Ant. II, 6, 139.

d) to treat: *how Tarquin must be —d*, Lucr. 1195. *I have —d thee with humane care*, Tp. I, 2, 345. V, 72. Gent. IV, 4, 207. Wiv. III, 3, 42 (*we'll u. this unwholesome humidity*; with reticence of the adverb). 215. iV, 4, 26. V, 5, 173. Err. II, 2, 155. III, 2, 6. Mids. II, 1, 205. 210. III, 2, 45. 152. Shr. I, 1, 65. I, 2, 32. II, 111. All's I, 1, 229. V, 2, 23. Tw. II, 5, 31. III, 4, 171. IV, 2, 37. John IV, 1, 55. H4B II, 2, 150. V, 1, 33. H5 III, 2, 138. 139. H6A II, 5, 35. H6B II, 4, 82. H6C III, 2, 123. 124. IV, 3, 36. 38. R3 III, 2, 33. IV, 1, 103. Tit. IV, 2, 40. Tim. III, 1. 39. Cymb. III, 3, 8 etc.

e) to have, possess, occupy or enjoy for a time: *why dost thou u. so great a sum of sums, yet canst not live?* Sonn. 4, 7. *some necessaries that I needs must u.* Gent. IV, 4, 188. *not of this country, though my chance is now to u. it for my time*, Meas. III, 2, 231. *I then did u. the person of your father; the image of his power lay then in me*, H4B V, 2, 73. *having great and instant occasion to u. fifty talents*, Tim. III, 1, 19. *heaven's bounty towards him might be —d more thankfully*, Cymb. I, 6, 79. cf. Ado I, 3, 41.

2) refl. to behave: *forgive me, if I have —d myself unmannerly*, H8 III, 1, 176.

3) intr. a) to be accustomed, to be wont: *where Adon —d to cool his spleen*, Pilgr. 76. *the unstained sword that you have —d to bear*, H4B V, 2, 114. Tp. II, 1, 175. Wiv. IV, 2, 58. As II, 3, 23. Tw. II, 4, 47. II, 5, 104. H4A III, 2, 83 (Ff *u. to do to their adversaries*, Qq *u. to their a.*). H5 IV, 7, 70. H6B IV, 2, 107. 109. H6C V. 5, 75. Troil. III, 3, 73. Rom. II Chor. 10. III, 5, 191. Caes. I, 2, 72. 262. Hml. II, 2, 48. Ant. II, 5, 32. III, 7, 66. Per. II, 1, 66 etc.

b) to do, to deal, to dispose: *brought him hither, to use as you think needful of the man*, Tit. V, 1, 39.

**Useful**, profitable, helpful: *u. serving-man*, John V, 2, 81. Adverbially: *which thou hast worn most u. for thy country*, Ant. IV, 14, 80.

**Useless**, answering no purpose, unserviceable: Tp. V, 60. Adverbially: *and u. barns the harvest of his wits*, Lucr. 859.

**User**, one who uses (cf. the verb *use*): *beauty's waste hath in the world an end, and kept unused, the u. so destroys it*, Sonn. 9, 12.

**Usher**, subst. one whose business is to walk before and introduce another: Cor. II, 1, 174. Ant. III, 6, 44.

**Usher**, vb. to introduce as a forerunner or harbinger: *that full star that —s in the even*, Sonn. 132, 7. *in —ing mend him who can*, LLL V, 2, 328. *no sun shall ever u. forth mine honours*, H8 III, 2, 411.

**Usual**, customary, common: Mids. V, 35. Merch. IV, 1, 72. Shr. III, 1, 12. H6C IV, 5, 11. H8 I, 2, 132. Hml. II, 1, 22.

**Usually**, customarily, ordinarily: H6B IV, 7, 43. Mcb. III, 3, 12.

**Usurer**, one who lends money and takes interest for it (which was thought disreputable, at any rate,

in the poet's time): Sonn. 4, 7. 134, 10. Ado II, 1, 197 (*like an —'s chain*). Merch. III, 1, 50. Wint. IV, 4, 266. 271. H6A III, 1, 17. Cor. I, 1, 84. Rom. III, 3, 123. Tim. II, 2, 62. 97. 101. 103. IV, 3, 112. Lr. III, 2, 89. IV, 6, 167.

**Usuring**, usurious: *the balsam that the u. senate pours into captains' wounds*, Tim. III, 5, 110. *a u. kindness*, IV, 3, 516.

**Usurp**, 1) intr. to be in a place contrary to right: *if aught possess thee from me, it is dross, —ing ivy*, Err. II, 2, 180. *it mourns that painting and —ing hair should ravish doters*, LLL IV, 3, 259 (= false hair). *the treacherous feet which with —ing steps do trample thee*, R2 III, 2, 17. With *on*, = to enter on illegitimately, to encroach on, to intrude: *this sorrow is an enemy and would u. upon my watery eyes*, Tit. III, 1, 269. *thy natural magic ... on wholesome life u. immediately*, Hml. III, 2, 271. *death may u. on nature many hours*, Per. III, 2, 82.

Especially = to hold regal power without right: As I, 2, 286. II, 1, 27. John II, 119. 121. III, 1, 61: R2 III, 3, 81. H6A I, 3, 31. H6C I, 1, 81. 169. II, 2, 165. III, 3, 79. R3 V, 2, 7. V, 3, 112. H8 II, 1, 108.

2) trans. to seize or take or assume falsely or against right: *a sudden pale —s her cheek*, Ven. 591. *sweating lust —ed his (love's) name*, 794. *thou doest here u. the name thou owest not*, Tp. I, 2, 453. *to steal from the state and u. the beggary he was never born to*, Meas. III, 2, 99. *the boy will well u. the grace, voice, gait and action of a gentlewoman*, Shr. Ind. 1, 131 (= counterfeit). *—ing his spurs so long*, All's IV, 3, 119. *are you the lady of the house? If I do not u. myself, I am*, Tw. I, 5, 198. 200. *my masculine —ed attire*, V, 257. R2 IV, 257. V, 5, 89. H6A IV, 1, 40. H6C II, 2, 12. R3 I, 3, 173. IV, 4, 27. Hml. I, 1, 46. Lr. IV, 2, 28. V, 3, 317. Oth. I, 3, 346 (*an —ed beard* = a false beard).

Especially applied to regal rights: John II, 118. 175. III, 1, 160. R2 V, 1, 65. H5 I, 2, 69. 95 (*—ed from you*; cf. *From*). H6A V, 4, 151. H6B I, 1, 244. H6C I, 1, 23. I, 2, 25. III, 3, 28. IV, 7, 66. V, 4, 77. V, 5, 37. V, 6, 73. R3 IV, 4, 109. 110. 367. 371. V, 5, 4.

**Usurpation**, illegal occupation: *so looks the strand whereon the imperious flood hath left a witnessed u.* H4B I, 1, 63. Especially illegal possession of royalty: John II, 9. H6A II, 5, 68.

**Usurper**, one who occupies a place, especially a throne, without right: Lucr. 412. As II, 1, 61. John II, 120. H5 I, 2, 78. H6B I, 3, 35. 188. IV, 4, 30. H6C I, 1, 114. III, 3, 76. H8 I, 2, 196. Mcb. V, 8, 55.

**Usurpingly**, by usurpation, illegitimately: John I, 13.

**Usury**, the practice of taking interest for money: *that use is not forbidden u.* Sonn. 6, 5. *like u. applying wet to wet*, Compl. 40. *'twas never merry world since of two — es the merriest was put down, and the worser allowed by order of law a furred gown*, Meas. III, 2, 7. *make edicts for u.*, *to support usurers*, Cor. I, 1, 84. *banish u., that makes the senate ugly*, Tim. III, 5, 99. *did you but know the city's —es and felt them knowingly*, Cymb. III, 3, 45.

**Ut**, the first note in Guido's musical scale: *ut, re, sol, la, mi, fa*, LLL IV, 2, 102. Shr. III, 1, 76.

**Utensil**, a household implement, any thing for daily use: Tp. III, 2, 104. Tw. I, 5, 264.

**Utility**, usefulness: H5 V, 2, 53.

**Utis** (from the French *huit*; originally the time between a festival and the eighth day after it) merriment, fun: *here will be old u.* H4B II, 4, 22 (the drawer's speech).

**Utmost,** 1) being at the furthest point, extreme: *that u. corner of the west,* John II, 29. *here is my butt and very sea-mark of my u. sail,* Oth. V, 2, 268. Substantively: *that's the u. of his pilgrimage,* Meas. II, 1, 36.

2) being in the highest degree or quantity: *use our commission in his u. force,* John III, 3, 11. *six or seven thousand is their u. power,* R3 V, 3, 10. H8 III, 1, 174. Cor. III, 1, 326. Per. V, 1, 76 (Ff and later Qq *uttermost*). Substantively: *try him to the u.* H8 V, 3, 146. *though he perform to the u. of a man,* Cor. I, 1, 272. *that's the u. of your having,* V, 2, 61. *we have tried the u. of our friends,* Caes. IV, 3, 214.

3) most accurate, computed with absolute exactness; last: *when as thy love hath cast his u. sum,* Sonn. 49, 3. *how much your chain weighs to the u. carat,* Err. IV, 1, 28. *what they weigh, even to the u. scruple,* Ado V, 1, 93. *extend to you what further becomes his greatness, even to the u. syllable of your worthiness,* All's III, 6, 74. *the very list, the very u. bound of all our fortunes,* H4A IV, 1, 51. *that we now possessed the u. man of expectation,* H4B I, 3, 65. *he weighs time even to the u. grain,* H5 II, 4, 138. *given to captivity me and my u. hopes,* Oth. IV, 2, 51 (none excepted, Qq om.).

**Utter,** adj. complete, total: *the son of u. darkness,* H4A III, 3, 42. *I foresee with grief the u. loss of all the realm of France,* H6A V, 4, 112. *to thy foul disgrace and u. ruin of the house of York,* H6C I, 1, 254.

**Utter,** vb. 1) to emit, to send forth (German: *von sich geben*): *pecks up wit ... and —s it again,* LLL V, 2, 316. *—ing such dulcet and harmonious breath,* Mids. II, 1, 151. *eat no onions, for we are to u. sweet breath,* IV, 2, 44. *cons state without book and —s it by great swarths,* Tw. II, 3, 161. *he —s them* (tunes) *as he had eaten ballads,* Wint. IV, 4, 185. *—ed such a deal of stinking breath,* Caes. I, 2, 247.

2) to cause to pass from one hand to another (not exactly = to sell, as the commentators explain it, but the German *unter die Leute bringen,* or *an den Mann bringen*): *beauty is bought by judgement of the eye, not —ed by base sale of chapmen's tongues,* LLL II, 16. *money's a medler, that doth u. all men's ware-a,* Wint. IV, 4, 330. *Mantua's law is death to any he that —s them,* Rom. V, 1, 67.

3) to disclose, not to keep secret: *my tongue shall u. all,* Lucr. 1076. *to u. that which else no worldly good should draw from me,* Gent. III, 1, 8. *the vile conclusion I now begin with grief and shame to u.* Meas. V, 96. Err. I, 1, 36. Ado I, 1, 217. III, 3, 112. IV, 1,

14. H4A II, 3, 114. H4B V, 3, 115. H8 I, 2, 167. Hml. II, 1, 119. Oth. III, 3, 136. Cymb. V, 5, 141.

4) to pronounce, to speak: *she —s this,* Lucr. 1721. *—ing foolish things,* 1813. *—ing bare truth,* Sonn. 69, 4. *his backward voice is to u. foul speeches,* Tp. II, 2, 95. *there is not chastity enough in language, without offence to u. them,* Ado IV, 1, 99. *I have drunk poison whiles he uttered it,* V, 1, 253. *graves, yawn and yield your dead, till death be —ed, heavily, heavily,* V, 3, 20 (i. e. the cry *'graves, yawn'* etc. shall be raised till death). LLL V, 2, 524. Merch. II, 8, 14. Shr. II, 177. All's V, 3, 208. Wint. I, 2, 104. 410. 443. John III, 4, 43. V, 7, 56. H4A I, 1, 107. II, 4, 272. H4B V, 3, 138. H5 III, 6, 66. H6A V, 5, 13. H6C IV, 1, 98. H8 I, 2, 136. II, 4, 171. V, 5, 16. Troil. II, 1, 75. Cor. II, 1, 58. II, 2, 87. V, 2, 25. Tit. V, 2, 169. V, 3, 89. Rom. II, 2, 59 ( *—ing;* most M. Edd., following the surreptitious Q1, *utterance*). III, 1, 160. III, 5, 175. Caes. III, 1, 235. Hml. III, 4, 142. Lr. I, 4, 354. Ant. I, 2, 113. II, 2, 133. With *forth: there my father's grave did u. forth a voice,* Meas. III, 1, 87. *that my tongue may u. forth the 'malice of my heart,* Tit. V, 3, 12.

**Utterance,** extremity (Fr. *outrance*): *come fate into the list, and champion me to the u.* Mcb. III, 1, 72. *which* (honour) *he to seek of me again perforce, behoves me keep at u.* Cymb. III, 1, 73.

**Utterance,** 1) emission, a sending forth (of sound): *these cannot I command to any u. of harmony,* Hml. III, 2, 378.

2) the act of speaking or expressing: *I speak ... as mine honesty puts it to u.* Wint. I, 1, 22. *the u. of a brace of tongues must needs want pleading for a pair of eyes,* John IV, 1, 98. *he has a merit to choke it in the u.* Cor. IV, 7, 49. *floods of tears will ... break my very u.* Tit. V, 3, 91. *the voice and u. of my tongue,* Caes. III, 1, 261. In Rom. II, 2, 59 the spurious Q1 and most M. Edd. *u.,* the authentic O. Edd. *uttering.*

3) elocution: *with all the gracious u. thou hast,* R2 III, 3, 125. *I have neither wit, nor words, nor worth, action, nor u.* Caes. III, 2, 226.

**Utterly,** completely, entirely: Wiv. IV, 2, 43. H4A II, 4, 516. H4B IV, 5, 218. H6A I, 1, 163. H6B III, 1, 85. H8 II, 4, 81. III, 1, 160. Ant. II, 2, 238. Per. III, 1, 59.

**Uttermost,** extreme, being in the highest degree, last, utmost: *my u. power,* H5 III, 6, 9 (Fluellen's speech). *my u. skill,* Per. V, 1, 76 (Q1. 2 *utmost*).

Everywhere else substantively: *making question of my u.* Merch. I, 1, 156 (doubting that I will do my utmost). *that shall be racked even to the u.* 181. *I will be free even to the u.* Shr. IV, 3, 80. *to the u.* Troil. IV, 5, 91. *by the eighth hour: is that the u.?* Caes. II, 1, 213. 214 (= latest). *to effect it to my u.* Oth. III, 4, 167.

# V.

**Vacancy,** 1) empty space, vacuity: *that you do bend your eye on v.* Hml. III, 4, 117. *whistling to the air, which, but for v., had gone to gaze on Cleopatra too and made a gap in nature,* Ant. II, 2, 221.

2) empty and idle time: *if he filled his v. with his voluptuousness,* Ant. I, 4, 26.

3) intermission: *no interim, not a minute's v., but day and night did we keep company,* Tw. V, 98.

**Vacant,** empty, not filled: *the v. leaves thy mind's imprint will bear,* Sonn. 77, 3. *war-thoughts have left their places v.* Ado I, 1, 304. *stuffs out his v. garments with his form,* John III, 4, 97. *with a body filled and* *v. mind*, H5 IV, 1, 286. *special dignities, which v. lie for thy best use and wearing*, Tim. V, 1, 145. With *of* = devoid of: *being of those virtues v.* H8 V, 1, 126.

**Vacation**, the time of nonterm: As III, 2, 349.

**Vade**, to fade: *untimely plucked, soon —d, plucked in the bud, and —d in the spring*, Pilgr. 131. 132. *a shining gloss that —th suddenly*, 170. *a gloss ... —d*, 174. 176. *his summer leaves all —d*, R2 I, 2, 20 (Qq *faded*).

**Vagabond**, subst. one who wanders about without a settled habitation, a vagrant: All's II, 3, 277. R2 II, 3, 120. R3 V, 3, 316.

**Vagabond**, adj. vagrant, wandering: *v. exile*, Cor. III, 3, 89. *a v. flag upon the stream*, Ant. I, 4, 45.

**Vagrom**, Dogberry's blunder for *vagabond*: Ado III, 3, 26.

**Vail**, subst. a going down, a sinking, setting: *with the v. and darking of the sun*, Troil. V, 8, 7. (or does the termination *ing* belong to both words? *vail and darking* for *vailing and darking?*).

**Vail**, vb. 1) tr. to lower, to let fall: *he —s his tail*, Ven. 314. *she —ed her eyelids*, 956. *v. your regard upon a wronged maid*, Meas. V, 20. *—ing her high-top lower than her ribs*, Merch. I, 1, 28. *France must v. her lofty-plumed crest*, H6A V, 3, 25. *do not for ever with thy —ed lids seek for thy noble father in the dust*, Hml. I, 2, 70. *did v. their crowns to his supremacy*, Per. II, 3, 42. Metaphorically: *v. your stomachs*, Shr. V, 2, 176. *Douglas ... 'gan v. his stomach*, H4B I, 1, 129. *if he have power, then v. your ignorance*, Cor. III, 1, 98.*

Doubtful passage: *fair ladies ... dismasked ... are angels —ing clouds*, LLL V, 2, 297 (Johnson: letting those clouds which obscured their brightness sink from before them. Could it not possibly be = clouds letting down, bearing down, angels? As for the construction, cf. Hml. I, 2, 2. Lr. II, 2, 129).

2) intr. to bow, to stoop, to do homage: *when she would with rich and constant pen v. to her mistress Dian*, Per. IV Prol. 29.

**Vailful**, available, advantageous; writing of some M. Edd. in Meas. IV, 6, 4; O.Edd. *to vail full purpose;* some M. Edd. *to veil full purpose.*

**Vails**, money given to servants: *there are certain condolements, certain v.* Per. II, 1, 157 (the fisherman's speech).

**Vain**, 1) empty, idle, unsatisfying, frivolous (German: *nichtig*): *beauty is but a v. and doubtful good*, Pilgr. 169. *have more time for —er hours and tutors not so careful*, Tp. I, 2, 174. *I will not hear thy v. excuse*, Gent. III, 1, 168. *train our intellects to v. delight*, LLL I, 1, 71. *brings in the champion Honour on my part against your v. assault*, All's IV, 2, 51. *leave thy v. bibble babble*, Tw. IV, 2, 105. *the want of which v. dew* (i. e. tears), Wint. II, 1, 109. *thy word is but the v. breath of a common man*, John III, 1, 8. *if heart's presages be not v.* R2 II, 2, 142. *how these v. weak nails may tear a passage*, V, 5, 19. *his addiction was to courses v.* H5 I, 1, 54. *your oath is v. and frivolous*, H6C I, 2, 27. *poor painted queen, v. flourish of my fortune*, R3 I, 3, 241. *a v. prophecy*, H8 I, 2, 147. *v. pomp and glory of this world*, III, 2, 365. *lose not so noble a friend on v. suppose*, Tit. I, 440. *hands, to do Rome service, are but v.* III, 1, 80 (idle, answering no purpose, superfluous). *begot of*

nothing but *v. fantasy*, Rom. I, 4, 98. *not with v. thanks*, Oth. III, 3, 470. *O v. boast*, V, 2, 264.

2) unwise, foolish, silly: *my father would enforce me marry v.* Thurio, Gent. IV, 3, 17. *school-maids change their names by v. though apt affection*, Meas. I, 4, 48. *there's no man is so v. that would refuse so fair an offered chain*, Err. III, 2, 185. *one whom the music of his own v. tongue doth ravish*, LLL I, 1, 167. *it would ill become me to be v., indiscreet, or a fool*, IV, 2, 31. *O v. petitioner, beg a greater matter*, V, 2, 207. *love is ... all wanton as a child, skipping and v.* 771. *every beardless v. comparative*, H4A III, 2, 67. *speak to that v. man*, H4B V, 5, 48. *a v., giddy, shallow, humorous youth*, H5 II, 4, 28. *O v. fool*, Lr. IV, 2, 61.

3) not true; used a) of things, = fallacious: *all hope is v., unless his noble mother and his wife*, Cor. V, 1, 70. b) of persons, = false, deceitful: *'tis holy sport to be a little v., when the sweet breath of flattery conquers strife*, Err. III, 2, 27 (placed in the rhyme).

4) proud of petty things, conceited: *his general behaviour v., ridiculous and thrasonical*, LLL V, 1, 13. *the schoolmaster is exceeding fantastical, too too v.* V, 2, 532. *infusing him with self and v. conceit*, R2 III, 2, 166. *any rebel or v. spirit of mine*, H4B IV, 5, 172 (But in all these passages the word may have another meaning; cf. *Vanity*).

5) answering no purpose, ineffectual: All's III, 4, 25. R2 III, 2, 214. H4B II, 4, 431. H5 III, 3, 24. Hml. I, 1, 146. Lr. V, 3, 293.

Substantively, *for v.* = to no purpose, idly: *which the air beats for v.* Meas. II, 4, 12. Oftener *in v.* = to no purpose, ineffectually: Ven. 607. 771. 772. Lucr. 1023. 1044. 1665. Pilgr. 391. Tp. IV, 97. Meas. III, 1, 199. IV, 1, 6. LLL I, 1, 140. Mids. II, 1, 88. 93. All's I, 3, 207 (*I love in v.*). Wint. V, 3, 140. R2 II, 1, 4. 7. H4B III, 3, 14. H6A V, 4, 85. H6B II, 1, 146. III, 2, 146. IV, 1, 77. 92. H6C I, 3, 21. II, 1, 135. Tit. I, 455. II, 3, 163. III, 1, 27. 73. Rom. I, 4, 45. *it is in v.* Rom. II, 1, 41. Tim. V, 1, 119. 187. Per. V, 1, 41.

**Vain-glory**, vanity: *I dare say without v.* H8 III, 1, 127. *if Hector break not his neck i'the combat, he'll break 't himself in v.* Troil. III, 3, 260. *these feasts, pomps and —es*, Tim. I, 2, 249. *it is not v. for a man and his glass to confer in his own chamber*, Cymb. IV, 1, 8.

**Vainly**, 1) idly, unreasonably: *v. thinking that she thinks me young*, Sonn. 138, 5. *my thoughts and my discourse as madmen's are, at random from the truth v. expressed*, 147, 12. *shall tax my fears of little vanity, having v. feared too little*, All's V, 3, 123.

2) falsely, erroneously: *which v. I supposed the Holy Land*, H4B IV, 5, 239.

3) to no purpose, ineffectually, in vain, idly: *this article is made in vain, or v. comes the admired princess hither*, LLL I, 1, 141. *our cannons' malice v. shall be spent against the invulnerable clouds of heaven*, John II, 251. *benefit no further than v. longing*, H8 I, 2, 81. *what torch is yond that v. lends his light to grubs*, Rom. V, 3, 125. *breathed our sufferance v.* Tim. V, 4, 8.

**Vainness**, 1) falseness: *I hate ingratitude more in a man than lying, v., babbling drunkenness*, Tw. III, 4, 389.

2) vanity, empty pride: *free from v. and self-glorious pride*, H5 V Chor. 20.

**Valance,** (O. Edd. *Vallens*) fringes of drapery: *v. of Venice gold in needlework,* Shr. II, 356.

**Valanced,** fringed: *thy face is v. since I saw thee last,* Hml. II, 2, 442 (decorated with a beard).

**Valdes,** name of a pirate in Per. IV, 1, 97 (it has been observed by the commentators that an admiral in the Spanish Armada bore the same name).

**Vale,** low ground (used only in verse): Compl. 2. Err. V, 120. H8 I, 1, 7. Troil. I, 2, 3. Tit. II, 3, 93. V, 2, 36. Ant. IV, 11, 3. Cymb. IV, 2, 176. Metaphorically, a place and state of misery or decline: *his comfort in this earthly v.* H6B II, 1, 70. *I am declined into the v. of years,* Oth. III, 3, 266.

**Valence,** *Earl of V.,* one of Talbot's baronial titles: H6A IV, 7, 63.

**Valencius** (M. Edd. *Valentinus*) name in Meas. IV, 5, 8.

**Valentine,** name 1) of the saint, on whose day (Febr. 14) birds began to couple and mates were chosen by the different sexes: *Saint V. is past: begin these wood-birds but to couple now?* Mids. IV, 1, 144. *to-morrow is Saint —'s day,* Hml. IV, 5, 48. *to be your V.* 51 (i. e. your true-love). cf. *there's not a hair on's head but 'tis a V.* Gent. III, 1, 192. *no V. indeed for sacred Silvia,* 211.

2) of different persons in Gent. I, 1, 11. 18. 55 etc. Tit. V, 2, 151. Rom. I, 2, 70.

**Valentinus,** another form of Valentine in Gent. I, 3, 67 (later Ff *Valentino*). Some M. Edd. *V.* in Gent. II, 4, 196 (O. Edd. *Valentine's*) and Meas. IV, 5, 8 (O. Edd. *Valencius*).

**Valentio,** name in Rom. I, 2, 72.

**Valeria,** female name in Cor. I, 3, 29. 46. V, 3, 67.

**Valerius,** 1) Publius V. (Publicola), the celebrated friend of the elder Brutus: Lucr. Arg. 19. 2) name of a robber in Gent. V, 3, 8.

**Valiant** (sometimes trisyll.: Gent. IV, 3, 13. R2 I, 3, 83. R3 I, 2, 245) brave, courageous: Compl. 245. Tp. III, 2, 27. 53. Gent. IV, 3, 13. Meas. II, 1, 270. III, 1, 15. Ado I, 1, 51. II, 1, 64. II, 3, 195. IV, 1, 324. Merch. II, 1, 9. As II, 3, 6. V, 4, 83. 99. All's I, 1, 127. II, 5, 3. 9. III, 6, 88. Tw. I, 5, 279. III, 4, 164. 312. John III, 1, 116. V, 3, 5. R2 I, 3, 83. H4A I, 1, 54. I, 3, 107. II, 4, 52. 309. 523. 524. III, 1, 167. V, 4, 62. H4B II, 3, 25 (trisyll.?). II, 4, 225. III, 2, 170. IV, 1, 132. IV, 3, 127. 132. H5 I, 2, 115. III, 5, 20 etc. etc.

**Valiantly,** bravely: H4A I, 3, 97. H5 III, 6, 12. IV, 3, 12. Troil. I, 2, 137. Ant. IV, 15, 58.

**Valiantness,** bravery: Cor. III, 2, 129.

**Valiant-young,** writing of M. Edd. in H4A V, 1, 90; in O. Edd. not hyphened.

**Validity,** 1) strength, efficacy: *purpose is but the slave to memory, of violent birth, but poor v.* Hml. III, 2, 199.

2) value: *this ring, whose high respect and rich v. did raise a parallel,* All's V, 3, 192. *nought enters there, of what v. and pitch soe'er,* Tw. I, 1, 12. *more v. ... lives in carrion-flies than Romeo,* Rom. III, 3, 33. *no less in space, v. and pleasure,* Lr. I, 1, 83.

**Valley,** low ground between hills: Pilgr. 355. Mids. IV, 1, 112. Wint. V, 1, 206. H5 III, 5, 51. Tit. II, 3, 84. Cymb. III, 3, 78. Denoting a certain part of the human face: *the whole matter and copy of the father, eye, nose, lip, the trick of 's frown, his forehead, nay, the v., the pretty dimples of his chin and cheek,* Wint. II, 3, 100 (depth, cavity; apparently explained by *the pretty dimples* as its apposition).

**Valley-fountain,** a fountain in a valley: Sonn. 153, 4.

**Valorous,** brave: H4B II, 4, 236. IV, 3, 43. H5 III, 2, 81. IV, 4, 66. Troil. III, 3, 275.

**Valorously,** bravely: H5 III, 2, 125 (Captain Jamy's speech).

**Valour,** bravery: Lucr. 201. Tp. III, 3, 59 (*I have made you mad; and even with such-like v. men hang and drown their proper selves*). IV, 172. Gent. V, 2, 19. Wiv. II, 3, 63. Ado II, 1, 395. III, 1, 96. IV, 1, 322. V, 1, 120. LLL I, 2, 187. III, 69. IV, 3, 340. Mids. II, 1, 234. V, 234. 236. 240. Merch. III, 2, 87. All's I, 1, 217. II, 5, 11. IV, 3, 80. 201. 278. Tw. III, 2, 21. 31. 33. 36. 41. III, 4, 210. 267. 292. John II, 138. R2 I, 3, 15. 37. IV, 33. V, 5, 114. H4A II, 2, 107. V, 4, 121. 153. V, 5, 29. H4B I, 2, 192 etc. etc.

**Valuation,** estimation: *our v. shall be such that every slight and false-derived cause ... shall to the king taste of this action,* H4B IV, 1, 189. *since of your lives you set so slight a v.* Cymb. IV, 4, 49.

**Value,** subst. worth; price: Wiv. III, 4, 15. Meas. I, 1, 56. Ado IV, 1, 222. Merch. I, 3, 160. II, 7, 25. II, 9, 91. III, 2, 289. IV, 1, 366. 434. V, 151. R2 II, 3, 19. H6A V, 1, 44. H8 V, 3, 108 (*how much more is his life in v. with him*). Troil. II, 2, 23. 53. Cor. I, 9, 21. II, 2, 63 (*a kinder v. of the people than he hath hereto prized them at*). Tim. I, 1, 79. 170. Caes. I, 2, 50. Cymb. I, 4, 16. I, 6, 190 (—*s*). II, 4, 74. Per. II, 1, 163. II, 4, 8.

**Value,** vb. 1) to rate, to prize, to estimate: *rich or poor, as fancy —s them,* Meas. II, 2, 151. *thy substance, —d at the highest rate,* Err. I, 1, 24. *her wit —s itself so highly,* Ado III, 1, 53. *I myself was to myself not mine, —ing of her,* IV, 1, 141 (estimating what she was to me. cf. *Of*). LLL II, 457. V, 2, 445. Merch. IV, 1, 451 (*let his deservings and my love withal be —d 'gainst your wife's commandment*). As I, 3, 73. John III, 1, 343. H4A III, 2, 177. V, 2, 60 (*making you ever better than his praise by still dispraising praise —d with your worth*; i. e. compared with your worth). H5 I, 1, 11. H6C V, 3, 14. Troil. II, 2, 52. Lr. I, 1, 58. II, 2, 153. II, 4, 141. Ant. V, 2, 139. Cymb. I, 6, 24.

2) to rate at a high price, to esteem: *we never —d this poor seat of England,* H5 I, 2, 169. *which of the dukes he —s most,* Lr. I, 1, 5. cf. II, 2, 153.

3) to be worth: *the peace between the French and us not —s the cost that did conclude it,* H8 I, 1, 88. *it —s not your asking,* II, 3, 52.

**Valued,** adj. pertaining to the value of things, appreciative: *the v. file distinguishes the swift, the slow, the subtle,* Mcb. III, 1, 95 (= the list of prices, the price-current).

**Valueless,** worthless: John III, 1, 101.

**Vambrace,** see *Vantbrace.*

**Van,** the first line, vanguard: Ant. IV, 6, 9.

**Vane,** weathercock: Ado III, 1, 66. III, 3, 138. LLL IV, 1, 97.

**Vanish,** (conjugated with *to be*) to disappear: Sonn. 63, 7. Tp. III, 3, 40. Gent. III, 1, 216. Wiv. I, 3, 90. LLL V, 2, 598. Mids. V, 275. R2 II, 1, 67. R3 I, 4, 52. Caes. I, 1, 67. II, 2, 12. IV, 3, 288. Mcb. I, 3, 80. I, 5, 5. Hml. I, 2, 220. Oth. III, 1, 21. Ant. IV, 12, 32. V, 2, 300 (= to die; cf. R2 II, 1, 67). Cymb. IV, 2, 350. V, 5, 473. —*ed* = gone, past: *he runs and chides his —ed loathed delight,* Lucr. 742. *moan the expence of many a —ed sight,* Sonn. 30, 8.

*picked from the worm-holes of long —ed days,* H5 II, 4, 86.

Used of breath issuing from the mouth: *which, thronging through her lips, so vanisheth as smoke from Aetna,* Lucr. 1041. Hence, pèrhaps, the singular expression: *a gentler judgement —ed from his lips,* Rom. III, 3, 10.

**Vanity,** 1) empty and vain pursuit, frivolity; subjectively and objectively: *for your writing and reading, let that appear when there is no need of such v.* Ado III, 3, 22. *where doth the world thrust forth a v.* R2 II, 1, 24. *light v., insatiate cormorant, consuming means, soon preys upon itself,* 38. *trouble me no more with v.* H4A I, 2, 92. *that v. in years,* II, 4, 500. *there's honour for you! here's no v.* V, 3, 33. *if I were much in love with v.* V, 4, 106. *up, v.! down, royal state!* H4B IV, 5, 120. *the tide of blood in me hath proudly flowed in v.* V, 2, 130. *matching to his youth and v.* H5 II, 4, 130. *to stay him from the fall of v.* R3 III, 7, 97. *what did this v. but minister communication of a most poor issue?* H8 I, 1, 85. *O heavy lightness, serious v.* Rom. I, 1, 184. *so light is v.* II, 6, 20. *what a sweep of v. comes this way,* Tim. I, 2, 137. *take v. the puppet's part against the royalty of her father,* Lr. II, 2, 39. *to do the act ... not the world's mass of v. could make me,* Oth. IV, 2, 164. Plur. *—es: thy violent —es can never last,* Lucr. 894. *I can no longer brook thy —es,* H4A V, 4, 74. *you shall find his —es forespent were but the outside of the Roman Brutus,* H5 II, 4, 36. *what had he to do in these fierce —es,* H8 I, 1, 54. *these trim —es,* I, 3, 38. *nor my wishes more worth than empty —es,* II, 3, 69. R2 III, 4, 86.

2) empty and vain conceit, illusion, deception: *I must bestow upon the eyes of this young couple some v. of mine art,* Tp. IV, 41 (some illusion produced by my art. Or simply = trifle?). *O heaven, the v. of wretched fools,* Meas. V, 164. *my fore-past proofs ... shall tax my fears of little v., having vainly feared too little,* All's V, 3, 122. *even now he sung. O v. of sickness! fierce extremes in their continuance will not feel themselves,* John V, 7, 13.

**Vanquish,** to overcome, to conquer; absol.: *if thou —est, thy words are true,* H6A I, 2, 96. With an object: Lucr. 75. Pilgr. 280. Gent. I, 1, 35. Ado IV, 1, 47. H6A III, 2, 96. III, 3, 78. IV, 7, 38. H6B II, 1, 183. 184. IV, 8, 44. 45. IV, 10, 80. H6C II, 1, 72. 73. Caes. III, 2, 190. Mcb. IV, 1, 92. Lr. V, 3, 153. Ant. IV, 15, 58. Cymb. III, 4, 10. Per. I, 2, 27. With *to,* = to prevail on, to persuade, to determine to: *I undertook it, —ed thereto by the fair grace and speech of the poor suppliant,* All's V, 3, 133.

**Vanquisher,** conqueror, victor: Cor. III, 1, 17. Hml. I, 1, 93.

**Vantage,** subst. = advantage; 1) profit, gain: *the injuries that to myself I do, doing thee v.* Sonn. 88, 12. *which though thou wouldst deny, denies thee v.* Meas. V, 418. *in her right we came, which we ... have turned to our own v.* John II, 550. *little v. shall I reap thereby,* R2 I, 3, 218. *O happy v. of a kneeling knee,* V, 3, 132. *to match with her that brings no —s,* H6B I, 1, 131. *you have all the v. of her wrong,* R3 I, 3, 310. *to win some v.* Cor. I, 1, 164. *a brain that leads my use of anger to better v.* III, 2, 31. *for my v. excellent,* Cymb. V, 5, 198.

*Of v.* = to boot, besides: *'tis meet that some more audience than a mother .. should o'erhear the speech*

*of v.* Hml. III, 3, 33. *to the v.,* in the same sense: *and as many* (women) *to the v. as would store the world,* Oth. IV, 3, 86.

2) condition favourable to success; good opportunity: *having thee at v.* Ven. 635. *with the v. of mine own excuse hath he excepted most against my love,* Gent. I, 3, 82. *I slew him ... without false v.* IV, 1, 29. *when the doctor spies his v. ripe,* Wiv. IV, 6, 43. *He that might the v. best have took,* Meas. II, 2, 74. *where you may have such v. on the duke, he shall not pass you,* IV, 6, 11. *my v. to exclaim on you,* Merch. III, 2, 176. *watch our v.* Shr. III, 2, 146. *if I have any v. of ground to get up,* H4B II, 1, 85. *till time and v. crave my company,* II, 3, 68. *you fled for v.* H6A IV, 5, 28 (to take your time). *it is war's prize to take all —s,* H6C I, 4, 59. III, 2, 25. *at your meetest v. of the time,* R3 III, 5, 74 (Qq advantage). *thus I took the v. of those few,* III, 7, 37. *all for our v.* V, 2, 22. *let us survey the v. of the field,* V, 3, 15. *I am unarmed; forego this v.* Troil. V, 8, 9. *answer the v. of his anger,* Cor. II, 3, 268. *at your v. ... let him feel your sword,* V, 6, 54. *some single —s you took,* Tim. II, 2, 138. *surveying v.* Mcb. I, 2, 31. *did line the rebel with hidden help and v.* I, 3, 113. *coign of v.* I, 6, 7 (= advantageous c.). *which* (rights) *now to claim my v. doth invite me,* Hml. V, 2, 401. *take v., heavy eyes, not to behold this shameful lodging,* Lr. II, 2, 178. *these offers, which serve not for his v., he shakes off,* Ant III, 7, 34. *when v. like a pair of twins appeared,* III, 10, 12. *when shall we hear from him? With his next v.* Cymb. I, 3, 24. *lets go by no —s,* II, 3, 50.

3) superiority: *urging the worser sense for v. still,* Lucr. 249 (placing it in a more advantageous light). *my fortunes as fairly ranked, if not with v., as Demetrius',* Mids. I, 1, 102. *'tis no wisdom to confess so much unto an enemy of craft and v.* H5 III, 6, 153 (to a cunning enemy, who is besides favoured by circumstances). *to get v. of* = to get the better of: *if they get ground and v. of the king,* H4B II, 3, 53. *such a wretch ... had the forehand and v. of a king,* H5 IV, 1, 297.

**Vantage,** vb. in *Double-vantage,* q. v.

**Vantbrace,** (Q *vambrace*), armour for the arm: *and in my v. put this withered brawn,* Troil. I, 3, 297.

**Vapians,** an apocryphal people in Sir Andrew's geography: Tw. II, 3, 24.

**Vaporous,** full of vapours or exhalations: Lucr. 771. Meas. IV, 1, 58. *upon the corner of the moon there hangs a v. drop profound,* Mcb. III, 5, 24; cf. Tim. IV, 3, 442.

**Vapour,** a visible fluid floating in the atmosphere: Ven. 184. 274. 1166. Lucr. 550. 782. Pilgr. 37. 39; cf. LLL IV, 3, 68. 70. Err. I, 1, 90. H4A I, 2, 227. H4B II, 4, 393. IV, 3, 106. H5 IV, 2, 24 (*the v. of our valour,* i. e. our breath). H6A II, 2, 27. H6C V, 3, 12. R3 III, 7, 164. Tim. III, 6, 107. Hml. II, 2, 315. Oth. III, 3, 271. Ant. IV, 14, 3. V, 2, 213.

**Vara,** Costard's pronunciation of *very:* LLL V, 2, 487.

**Variable,** 1) changeable, inconstant: *lest that thy love prove likewise v.* Rom. II, 2, 111.

2) changing, various, different: *v. passions throng her constant woe,* Ven. 967. *I never heard a passion so confused, so strange, so outrageous, and so v.* Merch. II, 8, 13. *ridges horsed with v. complexions,* Cor. II, 1, 228. *countries different with v. objects,* Hml. III, 1, 180. *your fat king and your lean beggar is but v. ser-*

vice, IV, 3, 25. *whiles he is vaulting v. ramps*, Cymb. I, 6, 134.

**Variance,** dissension, quarrel: *shall prove the author of their v.* Ant. II, 6, 138.

**Variation,** change, variety: *why is my verse so barren of new pride, so far from v. or quick change?* Sonn. 76, 2. *stained with the v. of each soil,* H4A I, 1, 64. Misapplied by Fluellen: H5 III, 6, 36. IV, 7, 19.

**Variety,** succession of different things, multi-fariousness: *making them red and pale with fresh v.* Ven. 21. *age cannot wither her, nor custom stale her infinite v.* Ant. II, 2, 241.

**Varlet,** 1) a servant to a knight: *my horse, v.! laquais, ha!* H5 IV, 2, 2. *call here my v., I'll unarm again,* Troil. I, 1, 1.

Used in a kind of hermaphroditical form, between *varlet* and *harlot* (to denote a person being in his forepart a varlet, and in his hindpart a harlot): *thou art thought to be Achilles' male varlot. Male varlot, you rogue! what's that? Why, his masculine whore,* Troil. V, 1, 18. 19 (some M. Edd. *harlot,* not considering that a plain and intelligible word would not provoke the question what was meant by it).

2) a term of reproach, = knave, rascal: Tp. IV, 170. Wiv. I, 3, 104. Meas. IV, 2, 104. Meas. II, 1, 174. 182. Ado IV, 2, 74. H4A II, 2, 25 (*I am the veriest v. that ever chewed with a tooth*). II, 4, 474. H4B II, 1, 50. Troil. V, 1, 106. V, 4, 3. Cor. V, 2, 84. Lr. II, 2, 30. II, 4, 190. Cymb. IV, 2, 83. Used coaxingly by Shallow (cf. *Knave*) in praising his servant Davy: *a good v.* H4B V, 3, 13. 14. 15. Misapplied by Elbow in Meas. II, 1, 88.

**Varletry,** rabble, mob: *the shouting v. of censuring Rome,* Ant. V, 2, 56.

**Varletto,** the host's Italianated form of *varlet* in Wiv. IV, 5, 66.

**Varnish,** subst. that which gives a gloss and sets a thing off to the best advantage: *they are both the v. of a complete man,* LLL I, 2, 46. *set a double v. on the fame the Frenchman gave you,* Hml. IV, 7, 133.

**Varnish,** vb. to set a gloss on, to give a fair and fresh appearance to: *beauty doth v. age,* LLL IV, 3, 244 (makes old people appear young again). *Christian fools with —ed faces,* Merch. II, 5, 33 (= painted). *to be new —ed,* II, 9, 49. *only painted, like his —ed friends,* Tim. IV, 2, 36.

**Varrius,** name in Meas. IV, 5, 11. 13. Ant. II, 1, 27.

**Varro,** name: Tim. II, 1, 1. II, 2, 9. 27. III, 4, 2. In Caes. IV, 3, 244 and 290 M. Edd. *V.,* O. Edd. *Varrus.*

**Varrus,** see *Varro.*

**Vary,** subst. variation, change: *turn their halcyon beaks with every gale and v. of their masters,* Lr. II, 2, 85.

**Vary,** vb. 1) tr. a) to change, to make unlike itself: *once more I'll mark how love can v. wit,* LLL IV, 3, 100.

b) to diversify by change: *every —ed object in his glance,* LLL V, 2, 775. Used of musical variations: *it sung sweet —ed notes,* Tit. III, 1, 86. Of modifications of expression by language: *'fair, kind and true' is all my argument, 'fair', kind and true' —ing to other words,* Sonn. 105, 10. *this was no damsel neither; she was a virgin. It is so —ed too, for it was proclaimed 'virgin',* LLL I, 1, 296. *the epithets are sweetly*

—ed, IV, 2, 9. *the man hath no wit that cannot, from the rising of the lark to the lodging of the lamb, v. deserved praise on my palfrey,* H5 III, 7, 35.

2) intr. a) to differ: *thou —est no more from picking of purses than giving direction doth from labouring,* H4A II, 1, 55.

b) to change, to alter, to turn: *fortune's mood —es again,* Per. III Prol. 47. Partic. *—ing =* full of changes and variations: *—ing in subjects as the eye doth roll to every —ed object in his glance,* LLL V, 2, 774. *with his —ing childness cures in me thoughts that would thick my blood,* Wint. I, 2, 170. *lackeying the —ing tide,* Ant. I, 4, 46. *darkling stand the —ing shore of the world,* IV, 15, 11.

**Vassal,** 1) a subject, a dependant: Lucr. 666. Tp. I, 2, 374. Meas. V, 391. All's II, 1, 202. H4B IV, 5, 176. Ant. V, 2, 29. Cymb. V, 5, 113.

2) a servant: *the duteous v. scarce is gone,* Lucr. 1360. *being your v., bound to stay your leisure,* Sonn. 58, 4. LLL IV, 1, 65. All's I, 3, 165. H5 III, 2, 8. R3 II, 1, 121 (*waiting —s*). Ant. II, 6, 57.

3) a low wretch, a slave: *like straggling slaves for pillage fighting, obdurate —s fell exploits effecting,* Lucr. 429. *that shallow v.* LLL I, 1, 256. *presumptuous —s,* H6A IV, 1, 125. H6B IV, 1, 111. R3 I, 4, 200. Cor. III, 2, 9. Lr. I, 1, 163.

Adjectively, in the different senses: *no outrageous thing from v. actors can be wiped away,* Lucr. 608. *thy proud heart's slave and v. wretch to be,* Sonn. 141, 12. *through v. fear,* H4A III, 2, 124. LLL IV, 3, 224. R2 III, 3, 89. H5 III, 5, 51.

**Vassalage,** the state of a subject or servant: Sonn. 26, 1. Abstr. pro concr., = subjects: *like v. at unawares encountering the eye of majesty,* Troil. III, 2, 40.

**Vast,** adj. boundless, having an extent not to be surveyed or ascertained: *more devils than v. hell can hold,* Mids. V, 9. *to seek the empty, v. and wandering air,* R3 I, 4, 39. *we shall not send o'er the v. world to seek a single man,* Cor. IV, 1, 42. *wert thou as far as that v. shore washed with the farthest sea,* Rom. II, 2, 83. Used of the sea: *the sun ... robs the v. sea,* Tim. IV, 3, 440. *to make v. Neptune weep for aye,* V, 4, 78. *in that v. tennis-court,* Per. II, 1, 64. Of darkness and dark places not to be taken in at a view: *v. sin-concealing chaos* (viz night) Lucr. 767. *forced in the ruthless, v. and gloomy woods,* Tit. IV, 1, 53. *no v. obscurity or misty vale,* V, 2, 36. *antres v. and deserts idle,* Oth. I, 3, 140. Hence = indiscriminate, ranging at large and striking at random: *v. confusion waits ... the imminent decay of wrested pomp,* John IV, 3, 152.

**Vast,** subst. (cf. the adj.) 1) a boundless sea: *shook hands as over a v.* Wint. I, 1, 33 (later Ff *a v. sea*). *the god of this great v.* Per. III, 1, 1.

2) Applied to the darkness of midnight in which the prospect is not bounded in by distinct objects: *urchins shall forth at v. of night,* Tp. I, 2, 327 (O. Edd. *for that v. of night*). *in the dead v. and middle of the night,* Hml. I, 2, 198 (lection of Q1.5.6; the rest of O. Edd. *waste*).

**Vastidity,** immensity: *though all the world's v. you had,* Meas. III, 1, 69.

**Vastly,** far and wide; as far as the eye can reach: *who, like a late-sacked island, v. stood bare and unpeopled in this fearful flood,* Lucr. 1740.

**Vasty,** vast, boundless: *the v. wilds of wide Arabia,*

Merch. II, 7, 41. *I can call spirits from the v. deep,* H4A III, 1, 52. *can this cockpit hold the v. fields of France?* H5 Prol. 12. *to v. Tartar,* II, 2, 123. *for whom this hungry war opens his v. jaws,* II, 4, 105.

**Vat,** subst., see *Fat,* subst. 2.

**Vaudemont,** French name: H5 III, 5, 43. IV, 8, 105.

**Vaughan;** *Sir Thomas V.,* name in R3 I, 3, 333 (Ff *Dorset*). II, 4, 43. III, 2, 67. III, 3, 24. IV, 4, 69. 147. V, 1, 5. 3, 142.

**Vault,** subst. 1) an arched roof; used of the sky: Tp. V, 43. H4B II, 3, 19. Lr. V, 3, 259.

2) a room with an arched roof; as a cellar: Wiv. IV, 2, 62. Err. V, 247. John V, 2, 143. H6C V, 2, 44 (*sounded like a cannon in a vault;* cf. H5 II, 4, 124. The surreptitious Qq and M. Edd. *like a clamour* etc.). Tim. II, 2, 168. Mcb. II, 3, 101. a repository for the dead: Rom. IV, 1, 111. IV, 3, 33. 39. V, 1, 20, V, 3, 86. 131. 254. 276. 290.

**Vault,** vb. to leap, to jump: *—ed into his seat,* H4A IV, 1, 107. *—ing into my saddle,* H5 V, 2, 142. *—ing ambition,* Mcb. I, 7, 27. *—ing variable ramps,* Cymb. I, 6, 134. cf. *Pretty-vaulting.*

**Vaultages,** vaulted rooms: *caves and womby v. of France shall chide your trespass and return your mock in second accent of his ordnance,* H5 II, 4, 124 (cf. H6C V, 2, 44).

**Vaulted,** arched: *this v. arch* (the canopy of heaven) Cymb. I, 6, 33.

**Vaulty,** arched, concave: *in her* (night's) *v. prison,* Lucr. 119. *thy* (death's) *v. brows,* John III, 4, 30. *the v. top of heaven,* V, 2, 52. *the v. heaven,* Rom. III, 5, 22.

**Vaumond,** name in All's IV, 3, 187.

**Vaunt,** subst. the first beginning: *our play leaps o'er the v. and firstlings of those broils,* Troil. Prol. 27.

**Vaunt,** subst. boast, brag: *such high —s of his nobility,* H6B III, 1, 50.

**Vaunt,** vb. 1) intr. a) to glory, to exult: *v. in their youthful sap, at height decrease,* Sonn. 15, 7. *under the hoofs of —ing enemies,* H4A V, 3, 43. *rouse thy —ing veins,* H5 II, 3, 4 (Pistol's speech). *the foe —s in the field,* R3 V, 3, 288.

b) to boast: *make your —ing true,* Caes. IV, 3, 52. With a clause: *she —ed ... the train of her gown was better worth than* etc. H6B I, 3, 87.

2) tr. to boast, to glory in, to possess with pride: *that meaner men should v. that golden hap which their superiors want,* Lucr. 41.

**Vaunt-courier,** forerunner: *—s to oak-cleaving thunderbolts,* Lr. III, 2, 5.

**Vaunter,** a braggart: Tit. V, 3, 113.

**Vauntingly,** boastfully: R2 IV, 36.

**Vaux,** name in H6B III, 2, 367 and H8 II, 1, 96.

**Vaward,** the vanguard: *I beg the leading of the v.* H5 IV, 3, 130. *their bands i' the v. are the Antiates,* Cor. I, 6, 53. Used with some confusion in H6A I, 1, 132: *he being in the v., placed behind with purpose to relieve and follow them* (some M. Edd. *rearward*).* Metaphorically = forepart: *since we have the v. of the day, my love shall hear the music of my hounds,* Mids. IV, 1, 110. *we that are in the v. of our youth,* H4B I, 2, 199.

**Veal,** mentioned, by way of punning, as the pronunciation of *well* common among Dutchmen, and as signifying a calf at the same time: LLL V, 2, 247.

**Vegetives,** vegetables, plants: *the blest infusions that dwell in v.,* in metals, stones, Per. III, 2, 36.

**Vehemence,** violent ardour, fervour, eagerness: As III, 2, 200.

**Vehemency,** the same: Wiv. II, 2, 247. Meas. V, 109. H8 V, 1, 149.

**Vehement,** ardent, eager, urgent: Lucr. 475. Meas. I, 1, 71. Merch. V, 155. John I, 254. R3 III, 7, 139. Oth. III, 3, 251.

**Vehemently** (Evans pronounces *fehemently*) eagerly: Wiv. III, 1, 8.

**Veil,** subst. a curtain, a cover to conceal or protect the face: Ven. 1081. Tw. I, 5, 175. Metaphorically, any thing that conceals or disguises: *where beauty's v. doth cover every blot,* Sonn. 95, 11. *the borrowed v. of modesty,* Wiv. III, 2, 42. *obscured his contemplation under the v. of wildness,* H5 I, 1, 64. *these eyes, that now are dimmed with death's black v.* H6C V, 2, 16. *throw over her the v. of infamy,* R3 IV, 4, 208.

**Veil,** vb. to cover with a veil or curtain: Merch. III, 2, 99. Tw. I, 1, 28. Cor. II, 1, 231. Metaphorically, to conceal, to disguise: *and —ed in them, did win whom he would maim,* Compl. 312. *to keep your great pretences —ed,* Cor. I, 2, 20. *if I have —ed my look,* Caes. I, 2, 37. In Meas. IV, 6, 4 O. Edd. *to vail full purpose;* some M. Edd. *to v. full p.;* others to *vailful p.*

**Vein,** 1) one of the vessels or pipes which convey the blood through animal bodies: Lucr. 419 (*azure*). 427. 440 and 1454 (*blue*). Sonn. 67, 10. 99, 5. Merch. III, 2, 178. 258. Wint. V, 3, 64. John II, 431. III, 1, 278. III, 3, 44. III, 4, 132. V, 2, 38 (*combine the blood of malice in a v. of league*). H4A I, 3, 133. H4B IV, 1, 66 (*our very —s of life*). H5 I, 2, 119. II, 3, 4 (*rouse thy vaunting —s;* Pistol's speech). IV, 2, 20. H6C I, 1, 97. R3 I, 2, 59. Troil. IV, 1, 69. Cor. I, 1, 142. V, 1, 51. Rom. I, 1, 92. IV, 1, 95. IV, 3, 15. V, 1, 61. Ant. II, 5, 29 (*my bluest —s*). Cymb. IV, 2, 222 (*azured*). Per. II, 1, 77. Metaphorically, = the interior of a thing: *to do me business in the —s o'the earth,* Tp. I, 2, 255. *checks and disasters grow in the —s of actions highest reared,* Troil. I, 3, 6. *the Trojan horse was stuffed within with bloody —s expecting overthrow,* Per. I, 4, 94.

2) disposition, temper, humour: *to see you in this merry v.* Err. II, 2, 20. *the fellow finds his v.* IV, 4, 83 (humours him). *there is no following her in this fierce v.* Mids. III, 2, 82. *you touched my v. at first,* As II, 7, 94. *now to Paris in this conquering v.* H6A IV, 7, 95. *I am not in the giving v.* R3 IV, 2, 119. *I am not in the v.* 122. *he rubs the v. of him,* Troil. II, 3, 210. *I am i'the v. of chivalry,* V, 3, 32. cf. John V, 2, 38.

3) strain, style, manner of speech or action: *touch him; there's the v.* Meas. II, 2, 70. *the whole world again cannot pick out five such, take each one in his v.* LLL V, 2, 548. *this is Ercles' v., a tyrant's v.* Mids. I, 2, 42. *I will do it in King Cambyses' v.* H4A II, 4, 426. cf. *Liver-vein.*

**Velure,** velvet: Shr. III, 2, 62.

**Velutus;** Sicinius V., one of the Roman tribunes in Cor. I, 1, 221.

**Velvet,** silk covered on the outside with a short shag or nap: Compl. 94. Meas. I, 2, 31. 32. 33. 36. All's IV, 5, 100. 101. 102. H4A II, 2, 2. Adjectively: *a v. dish,* Shr. IV, 3, 65. *a v. hose,*

V, 1, 69. *my branched v. gown*, Tw. II, 5, 54. *v. coat*, Wint. I, 2, 156. *v. guards*, H4A III, 1, 261 (trimmings of velvet being a city fashion in the poet's time).* = soft, delicate: *the v. leaves*, Pilgr. 231. LLL IV, 3, 105. *a v. brow*, III, 198. *his v. friends*, As II, 1, 50.* *v. buds*, H5 I, 2, 194.

**Velvet-guards**, see *Velvet* and *Guard*.

**Vendible**, saleable: Merch. I, 1, 112. All's I, 1, 168.

**Venerable**, worthy of reverence: As II, 7, 167. Tw. III, 4, 397. Troil. I, 3, 65. Cymb. II, 5, 3.

**Venereal**, pertaining to sexual intercourse: *these are no v. signs*, Tit. II, 3, 37.

**Venetian**, 1) adj. pertaining to Venice: *any tire of V. admittance*, Wiv. III, 3, 61. Merch. III, 2, 222. IV, 1, 178. Oth. V, 2, 337.

2) subst. a native of Venice: Merch. I, 2, 124. II, 9, 87. Oth. I, 3, 363. IV, 1, 138. V, 2, 112. 354.

**Venew** or **Venue** or **Veney**, a thrust received at playing with weapons, and hence a turn or bout at fencing: *three veneys for a dish of stewed prunes*, Wiv. I, 1, 296. *a sweet touch, a quick venue of wit*, LLL V, 1, 62.

**Veney**, see *Venew*.

**Venge**, to avenge: Lucr. 1691. R2 I, 2, 36. H5 I, 2, 292. H6A III, 4, 42. H6C II, 1, 87. Rom. III, 5, 87. Lr. IV, 2, 80. Cymb. I, 6, 92.

**Vengeance**, 1) retribution of injury, retaliation, punishment: Tp. V, 28. Wint. III, 2, 202. IV, 4, 801. John III, 4, 159. R2 I, 2, 8. H4A III, 2, 10 (*hot v.*). H5 I, 2, 283. IV, 1, 178. H6A V, 4, 53. H6B V, 2, 36. H6C I, 4, 148. II, 5, 134. IV, 1, 82. R3 I, 4, 204. 206. V, 3, 206. Troil. V, 3, 47. V, 5, 31. Tit. II, 1, 121. II, 3, 38. Rom. III, 5, 88. V, 3, 55. Hml. II, 2, 510. 610. Lr. II, 1, 90. II, 4, 164 (*stored —s of heaven*). III, 7, 66. 72. Oth. III, 3, 447. Cymb. II, 5, 8. V, 1, 11. Per. II, 4, 4. *to do v. on:* R3 I, 2, 87. Troil. II, 2, 73. *render v. and revenge*, R2 IV, 67. *to take v.* Wint. I, 2, 281. *to take v. on:* II, 3, 22. Tit. IV, 3, 34. Cymb. V, 1, 8. *of:* Tit. V, 2, 63. *working wreakful ɔ. on thy foes*, Tit. V, 2, 32.

2) harm, mischief, evil: *whiles the eye of man did woo me, that could do no v. to me*, As IV, 3, 48. *this v. on me had they executed*, Tit. II, 3, 113.

Used as a curse: *this shoe is my mother, and this my father; a v. on't, there 'tis*, Gent. II, 3, 21. *v. of Jenny's case! fie on her*, Wiv. IV, 1, 64. *a v. on your crafty withered hide!* Shr. II, 406. *a plague of all cowards, and a v. too*, H4A II, 4, 128. *threefold v. tend upon your steps!* H6B III, 2, 304. *the v. on the whole camp*, Troil. II, 3, 19. *what the v.! could he not speak 'em fair?* Cor. III, 1, 262. *v. rot you all*, Tit. V, 1, 58. *v., plague, death, confusion!* Lr. II, 4, 96. Quite adverbially: *he's v. proud*, Cor. II, 2, 6 (the officer's speech).

**Vengeful**, vindictive: Sonn. 99, 13. H6B III, 2, 198. Tit. V, 2, 51.

**Venial**, pardonable: *a v. slip*, Oth. IV, 1, 9.

**Venice,** town in Italy: Ado I, 1, 274 (*if Cupid have not spent all his quiver in V.*). LLL IV, 2, 98. Merch. I, 1, 115. 180. I, 3, 46. II, 8, 23. III, 1, 119. III, 2, 241. 306. IV, 1, 204 etc. Shr. II, 316. 356 (*valance of V. gold in needlework*). IV, 2, 83. IV, 3, 15. R2 IV, 97. Oth. I, 1, 105 etc.

**Venison**, edible beasts of chase: Wiv. I, 1, 81. 84. 202 (*v. pasty*). As II, 1, 21. Cymb. III, 3, 75. IV, 4, 37.

**Venom,** poison: *the poisonous simple sometimes is compacted in a pure compound; being so applied, his v. in effect is purified*, Lucr. 532. *spiders that suck up thy* (the earth's) *v.* R2 III, 2, 14. Particularly poison discharged from animals: Wint. II, 1, 41. R2 II, 1, 157 (St. Patrick was said to have banished all venomous reptiles from Ireland). H4B IV, 4, 45. H5 V, 2, 18 (*the v. of such looks*). R3 IV, 1, 62 (Qq *poison*). Caes. IV, 3, 47. Mcb. III, 4, 30. IV, 1, 8. Hml. II, 2, 533. V, 2, 333. Sir Andrew called *V.* by Sir Toby for his pretended virulency: Tw. III, 2, 2.

Adjectively: *toads infect fair founts with v. mud,* Lucr. 850. *v. toads*, H6C II, 2, 138. R3 I, 3, 291. Metaphorically, = pernicious: *the v. clamours of a jealous woman*, Err. V, 69. *lascivious metres, to whose v. sound the open ear of youth doth always listen*, R2 II, 1, 19.

**Venomed**, 1) envenomed, infected or tainted with venom: *v. sores*, Ven. 916. *slander's v. spear*, R2 I, 1, 171. *your v. stuck*, Hml. IV, 7, 162.

2) venomous, having in it and discharging venom: *any creeping v. thing*, R3 I, 2, 20. *v. worm*, Tim. IV, 3, 182. Metaphorically, = malignant: *the v. vengeance ride upon our swords, spur them to ruthful work, rein them from ruth*, Troil. V, 3, 47.

**Venom'd-mouth'd** (M. Edd. *venom-mouthed*), venomous: *this butcher's cur is v.* H8 I, 1, 120.

**Venomous,** full of venom, poisonous: As II, 1, 13. Ant. V, 2, 308. Metaphorically = pernicious; malignant: *thy tears are ... v. to thine eyes*, Cor. IV, 1, 23. *the v. malice of my swelling heart*, Tit. V, 3, 13. Singular expression: *beshrew the witch* (Night)! *with v. wights she stays as tediously as hell*, Troil. IV, 2, 12 (Steevens: '*v. wights*, venefici, those who practise nocturnal sorcery;' which explication, strange to say, has been acquiesced in by the other commentators. Perhaps the words mean simply people thinking on evil).

**Venomously,** grievously, poignantly; malignantly, spitefully: *these things sting his mind so v.* Lr. IV, 3, 48. *thou stormest v.* Per. III, 1, 7.

**Vent,** 1) a small aperture or passage for air: *through little —s and crannies of the place the wind wars with his torch*, Lucr. 310. *this no slaughter-house no tool imparteth to make more v. for passage of her breath*, 1040.

2) any small hole or opening made for passage: *which of you will stop the v. of hearing when loud Rumour speaks*, H4B Ind. 2. *how thy wounds bleed at many —s*, Troil. V, 3, 82.

3) discharge, emission: *here, on her breast, there is a v. of blood*, Ant. V, 2, 352.

4) utterance: *free v. of words love's fire doth assuage*, Ven. 334. *thou didst make tolerable v. of thy travels*, All's II, 3, 213.

5) freedom from restraint, liberty of indulging one's animal spirits: *it* (war) *is sprightly walking, audible, and full of v.* Cor. IV, 5, 238 (according to the common interpretation, = 'full of rumour, full of materials for discourse.' If *vent* is, indeed, a technical term of sportsmen for scent, as it has been asserted in Edinb. Rev. Oct. 72, and if it could be proved to have been so in the time of Shakespeare, the explanation given there would be undoubtedly preferable to any other: 'when the hound vents anything, he pauses to verify the scent, and then, full of eager

excitement, strains in the leash to be after the game. Full of vent, therefore, means keenly excited, full of pluck and courage').

**Vent,** vb. 1) to let out, to emit: *can he v. Trinculos?* Tp. II, 2, 111. *there's none* (air) *abroad so wholesome as that you v.* Cymb. I, 2, 5. *then we shall have means to v. our musty superfluity,* Cor. I, 1, 229 (= to void; to get rid of).

2) to utter: Tp. I, 2, 280. As II, 7, 41. Shr. I, 2, 179. Tw. IV, 1, 10. 12. 14. 17. H8 I, 2, 23. Cor. I, 1, 213. III, 1, 258. Lr. I, 1, 168. Ant. III, 4, 8. Cymb. V, 3, 56.

**Ventages,** small holes for the passage of air: *govern these v. with your finger and thumb,* Hml. III, 2, 373 (= the stops in a flute).

**Ventidius,** name in Tim. I, 1, 99. I, 2, 9. II, 2, 229. 231. III, 3, 3. 8. Ant. II, 2, 16. II, 3, 31. III, 1, 5.

**Ventricle,** a place of organic function: *begot in the v. of memory, nourished in the womb of pia mater,* LLL IV, 2, 70.

**Venture,** subst. 1) a hazard, an undertaking of chance and danger, the staking of something as for a wager: *this was a v. that Jacob served for,* Merch. I, 3, 92. *but to the purpose, and so to the v.* H4B V, 5, 123. *to desperate —s and assured destruction,* R3 V, 3, 319. *thy personal v. in the rebels' fight,* Mcb. I, 3, 91 (= the v. of thy person). *at a v.* = at hazard, at random: *spoke at a v.* H4B I, 1, 59 (Ff *at adventure*).

2) a thing put to hazard: *with diseased —s that play with all infirmities for gold,* Cymb. I, 6, 123 (creatures who put their persons to hazard for gold). Particularly, that which is sent to sea in trade (German: *schwimmendes Gut*): *had I such v. forth,* Merch. I, 1, 15. *fear misfortune to my —s,* 21. *my —s are not in one bottom trusted,* 42. *other —s he hath, squandered abroad,* I, 3, 21. III, 2, 270. H4B II, 4, 69. V, 5, 127. Caes. IV, 3, 224.

**Venture,** vb. 1) absol. to try the chance, to run all hazards: *things out of hope are compassed oft with —ing,* Ven. 567. *in —ing ill we leave to be the things we are,* Lucr. 148. *I'll make a shaft or a bolt on't; 'tis but —ing,* Wiv. III, 4, 25. *before you v. for me,* Merch. III, 2, 10. As I, 2, 251. H4B I, 1, 183. 185. H6B II, 1, 101. H8 III, 2, 358. Lr. IV, 2, 20. With *at: the king will v. at it,* H8 II, 1, 156. With *on,* = to dare to attack, to dare to try: *on the lion he will v.* Ven. 628. *to v. upon the charged chambers,* H4B II, 4, 56. *I play a merchant's part, and v. madly on a desperate mart,* Shr. II, 329. *we —d on such dangerous seas,* H4B I, 1, 181.

2) trans. a) to put to hazard, to risk, to stake: *I'll v. so much of my hawk or hound, but twenty times so much upon my wife,* Shr. V, 2, 72. *I'ld v. the well-lost life of mine on his grace's cure,* All's I, 3, 253. *upon thy certainty and confidence what darest thou v.?* II, 1, 173. *so dare we v. thee,* H4A V, 1, 101. *and v. maidenhood for't,* H8 III, 3, 25. *he had rather v. all his limbs for honour,* Cor. II, 2, 84.

b) to run the hazard of: *I'll v. it,* John IV, 3, 5. *others v. trade abroad,* H5 I, 2, 192. *I'll v. one have-at-him,* H8 II, 2, 85. *for little England you'ld v. an emballing,* II, 3, 47. *I should v. purgatory for't,* Oth. IV, 3, 77. With an inf.: *I may v. to depart alone,* Gent. IV, 3, 36. *how thou darest v. to be drunk,* Wint. V, 2, 184. H8 V, 1, 40. Cor. I, 1, 94. Lr. III, 4, 157.

**Venturous,** daring, bold: Mids. IV, 1, 39. H6A II, 1, 45. H6B III, 2, 9. R3 IV, 4, 170. H8 I, 2, 54.

**Venue,** see *Venew.*

**Venus,** 1) the goddess of beauty and love: Ven. 5. 180. 187. 248. 816. 859. 1057. Lucr. 58 (*—'doves*). Pilgr. 143. Tp. IV, 87. Ado IV, 1, 61. LLL II, 256. Mids. I, 1, 171 (*— doves*). Merch. II, 6, 5 (*—' pigeons*). As IV, 1, 216. Troil. III, 1, 34. IV, 1, 22. IV, 5, 49. 179. V, 2, 165. Rom. II, 1, 11. IV, 1, 8. Ant. I, 5, 18. II, 2, 205. Cymb. V, 5, 164.

2) name of a planet, the evening star: Mids. III, 2, 61. 107. H4B II, 4, 286. H6A I, 2, 144. Tit. II, 3, 30.

**Verb,** a part of speech that expresses existence or any modification of it: H6B IV, 7, 43.

**Verbal,** 1) literal, having word answering to word: *all the neighbour caves ... make v. repetition of her moans,* Ven. 831.

2) spoken, not written: *she told me in a sweet v. brief,* All's V, 3, 137.

3) expressed or conveyed in words: *made she no v. question?* Lr. IV, 3, 26 (= did she not speak?).

4) plain-spoken, wording one's thoughts without reserve: *you put me to forget a lady's manners, by being so v.* Cymb. II, 3, 111 (according to others, = verbose).

**Verbatim,** orally: *or am not able v. to rehearse the method of my pen,* H6A III, 1, 13.

**Verbosity,** exuberance of words: *he draweth out the thread of his v. finer than the staple of his argument,* LLL V, 1, 18 (Holofernes' speech).

**Verdict,** judgment, decision: *but quickly on this side the v. went,* Compl. 113. *whereto my tongue a party v. gave,* R2 I, 3, 234. *giving my v. on the white rose side,* H6A II, 4, 48. *must your bold v. enter talk with lords?* III, 1, 63. *let us kill him, ... is't a v.?* Cor. I, 1, 11. Specially, the determination of a jury declared to a judge: *to 'cide this title is impanneled a quest of thoughts, ... and by their v. is determined ...,* Sonn. 46, 11. *what lawful quest have given their v. up unto the frowning judge?* R3 I, 4, 189. *not ever the justice and the truth o'the question carries the due o'the v. with it,* H8 V, 1, 132.

**Verdun,** Lord V. of Alton, one of Talbot's baronial titles: H6A IV, 7, 65.

**Verdure,** freshness, life and vigour: *their* (your lips') *v. still endure, to drive infection from the dangerous year,* Ven. 507. *the ivy which had hid my princely trunk and sucked my v. out on't,* Tp. I, 2, 87. *by love the young and tender wit is turned to folly, blasting in the bud, losing his v. even in the prime,* Gent. I, 1, 49.

**Vere;** Lord Aubrey V., name in H6C III, 3, 102.

**Verge,** 1) brink, edge, margin, border: *on the extremest v. of the swift brook,* As II, 1, 42. *to the furthest v. that ever was surveyed by English eye,* R2 I, 1, 93. *upon the beached v. of the salt flood,* Tim. V, 1, 219. *nature in you stands on the very v. of her confine,* Lr. II, 4, 149. *you are now within a foot of the extreme v.* IV, 6, 26.

2) compass, circle: (thy crown) *incaged in so small a v.* R2 II, 1, 102.* *whom we raise, we will make fast within a hallowed v.* H6B I, 4, 25. *the inclusive v. of golden metal that must round my brow,* R3 IV, 1, 59.

**Verges,** name of the headborough in Ado III, 5, 10. 19. 39.

**Verify,** 1) to prove to be true, to confirm: *to v. our title with their lives,* John II, 277. *then I perceive* *that will be —ed Henry the Fifth did sometime prophesy,* H6A V, 1, 30. *unless the adage must be —ed that beggars mounted run their horse to death,* H6C I, 4, 126. *the common voice is —ed of thee,* H8 V, 3, 176.

2) to back, to support the credit of: *I have ever —ed my friends ... with all the size that verity would without lapsing suffer,* Cor. V, 2, 17.

3) to affirm, to maintain: *they have — ed unjust things,* Ado V, 1, 222 (Dogberry's speech). *I will v. as much in his beard,* H5 III, 2, 75 (Fluellen's speech). *more truly now may this be —ed,* H6A I, 2, 32.

**Verily,** in truth, really: *there was a noise, that's v.* Tp. II, 1, 321 (i. e. that is to say, in fact, not only in my dream. Some M. Edd. *verity*). *I think v. he had been hanged for't,* Gent. IV, 4, 16. *I v. did think that her old gloves were on,* As IV, 3, 25. *v., I speak it in the freedom of my knowledge,* Wint. I, 1, 12. *I may not, v.* I, 2, 45. 46. 49. 50. 55. *that those veins did v. bear blood,* V, 3, 65. *v. and in truth,* H5 V, 1, 64. *v., I swear, 'tis better to be lowly born,* H8 II, 3, 18. *v., I do not jest with you,* Cor. I, 3, 103.

**Veritable,** true: *is't true? Most v.* Oth. III, 4, 76.

**Verity,** 1) truth, fact, reality: *which you shall find by every syllable a faithful v.* Meas. IV, 3, 131. *to the full arming of the v.* All's IV, 3, 73. *the v. of it is in strong suspicion,* Wint. V, 2, 31. *'twould prove the v. of certain words,* H8 I, 2, 159. *with all the size that v. would without lapsing suffer,* Cor. V, 2, 18. *by the —es on thee made good,* Mcb. III, 1, 8. *in the v. of extolment,* Hml V, 2, 121. *in v. =* in truth: Err. IV, 4, 80. *in sincere v.* Lr. II, 2, 111. — In Tp. II, 1, 321 O. Edd. *verily,* some M. Edd. *v.*

2) faith, honesty: *I think he is not a pickpurse nor a horse-stealer, but for his v. in love, I do think him as concave as a covered goblet,* As III, 4, 25 (or = his really being in love?). *justice, v., temperance,* Mcb. IV, 3, 92.

**Vermilion,** a beautiful red colour: *praise the deep v. in the rose,* Sonn. 98, 10.

**Vermin,** noxious little animals: Lr. III, 4, 164.

**Vernon;** 1) Sir Richard V.: H4A IV, 1, 86. IV, 3, 20. IV, 4, 24. V, 2, 1. V, 5, 14. 2) Master V.: H6A II, 4, 43. 128.

**Veroles,** French name in Per. IV, 2, 115.

**Verona,** town in Italy: Gent. III, 1, 81. IV, 1, 17. 47. V, 4, 129. Shr. I, 2, 1. 22. 49. 191. II, 1, 47. Rom. Prol. 2. I, 1, 99. I, 2, 35. 89. I, 3, 70. 77. I, 5, 69. III, 1, 92 (*in V. streets*). III, 3, 15. 17 (*without V. walls*). V, 1, 12. V, 3, 300.

**Veronessa,** (F1 *Verennessa,* later Ff *Veronesso,* M. Edd. *Veronesa*), a ship of Verona (or equipped by the city of Verona): Oth. II, 1, 26.

**Versal,** the nurse's blunder for *universal* in Rom. II, 4, 219.

**Verse,** 1) a metrical line: *'tis a v. in Horace,* Tit. IV, 2, 22. 24. *a blank v.* (not in rhyme): Ado V, 2, 34. As IV, 1, 32. Hml. II, 2, 339. Plur. —*s:* LLL IV, 2, 105. 156. 164. V, 2, 50. As III, 2, 119. 175. H6A I, 1, 27. —*s =* poetical compositions: *to no other pass my —s tend,* Sonn. 103, 11. *he writes —s,* Wiv. III, 2, 69. LLL V, 2, 34. Mids. I, 1, 31. As III, 2, 172. 177. 278. 411. III, 3, 12. III, 4, 44. H5 V, 2, 137. Caes. III, 3, 34.

2) a short division of a poem, a strophe, couplet: *a staff, a stanze, a v.* LLL IV, 2, 107. *but one v.* Tw. II, 4, 7.

3) poetry, poetical composition: *who will believe my v.* Sonn. 17, 1. *my love shall in my v. ever live young,* 19, 14. *stirred by a painted beauty to his v.* 21, 2. 38, 2. 54, 14. 60, 13. 71, 9. 76, 1. 78, 2. 86, 1. 103, 13. As II, 5, 48. III, 2, 1. 179. 180. Wint. V, 1, 101. Troil. III, 2, 189. IV, 4, 24. V, 10, 40. Tim. I, 1, 16. V, 1, 87.

**Versing,** telling in verse: *v. love to amorous Phillida,* Mids. II, 1, 67.

**Very,** adj. originally = veritable, true, real: *there would appear the v. eyes of men through loopholes thrust,* Lucr. 1383. *thou art v.* Trinculo indeed, Tp. II, 2, 109. *two of them have the v. bent of honour,* Ado IV, 1, 188. *here is the v. remuneration I had of thy master,* LLL V, 1, 76. *this is the v. false gallop of verses,* As III, 2, 119. *what would you say to me now, an I were your v. v. Rosalind?* IV, 1, 71. *so many of his shadows thou hast met and not the v. king,* H4A V, 4, 31. *hath the Prince John a full commission, in v. ample virtue of his father, to hear and absolutely to determine ....?* H4B IV, 1, 163. *I have found the v. cause of Hamlet's lunacy,* Hml. II, 2, 49. Cor. IV, 6, 70. *rather blamed as mine own jealous curiosity than as a v. pretence and purpose of unkindness,* Lr. I, 4, 75. *I am absolute 'twas v. Cloten,* Cymb. IV, 2, 107. *she is thy v. princess,* Per. V, 1, 220. Hence = full, complete, perfect; cf. the following instances: *a bliss in proof, and proved, a v. woe,* Sonn. 129, 11. *v. rogues,* Wiv. II, 1, 182. *you have paid ... the v. debt of your calling,* Meas. III, 2, 264. *he is a v. paramour for a sweet voice,* Mids. IV, 2, 12. *a v. fox for his valour,* V, 234. *a v. beadle to a humorous sigh,* LLL III, 177. *my master's a v. Jew,* Merch. II, 2, 112. *stay the v. riping of the time,* II, 8, 40. *thinkest thou any man is so v. a fool to be married to hell?* Shr. I, 1, 129. *such an injury would vex a v. saint,* III, 2, 28. *I find report a v. liar,* II, 246. *a v. monster in apparel,* III, 2, 71. *an I were not a v. coward,* All's IV, 3, 356. *thy mind is a v. opal,* Tw. II, 4, 77. *he's a v. fool,* I, 3, 25. *words are v. rascals since bonds disgraced them,* III, 1, 24. *he is a v. man per se, and stands alone,* Troil. I, 2, 15. *I should make v. forges of my cheeks,* Oth. IV, 2, 74 etc. Compar. and superl.: *was not my lord the —er wag o'the two?* Wint. I, 2, 66. *there are —er knaves desire to live,* Cymb. V, 4, 209. *were he the —est antic in the world,* Shr. Ind. 1, 101. *thou hast the —est shrew of all,* V, 2, 64. *I am the —est varlet that ever chewed with a tooth,* H4A II, 2, 25. *yield me to the —est hind that shall once touch my shoulder,* Cymb. V, 3, 77.

Generally placed before substantives to indicate that they must be understood in their full and unrestricted sense: *now is she in the v. lists of love,* Ven. 595. *so shall I state at first the v. worst of fortune's might,* Sonn. 90, 12. *the cry did knock against my v. heart,* Tp. I, 2, 9. *which touched you to the v. virtue of compassion in thee,* 27. *he is a stone, a v. pebble stone,* Gent. II, 3, 11. *'tis an ill office for a gentleman, especially against his v. friend,* III, 2, 41 (one who is indeed, and in the full sense of the word, his friend. cf. Merch. III, 2, 226). *he grieves my v. heart-strings,* IV, 2, 62. *whom my v. soul abhors,* IV, 3, 17. *that with his v. heart despiseth me,* IV, 4, 99. *would I might be dead if I in thought felt not her v. sorrow,* 177. *there's the point, the v. point of it,* Wiv. I, 1, 230. *the v. yea and the no is ...,* I, 4, 98. *those that know the v. nerves of state,* Meas. I, 4, 53. *a man whose blood is v. snow-*

broth, 58. *upon the v. siege of justice Lord Angelo hath professed the contrary,* IV, 2, 101. *time is a v. bankrupt,* Err. IV, 2, 58. *the v. sum of all is ...,* LLL V, 1, 115. *the v. best at a beast,* Mids. V, 232. *the Jew is the v. devil incarnal,* Merch. II, 2, 28. *the boy was the v. staff of my age, my v. prop,* 70. *'confess and love' had been the v. sum of my confession,* III, 2, 36. *I bid my v. friends and countrymen, dear Portia, welcome,* 226 (indeed my friends, though met here very unexpectedly). *to suffer ... the v. tyranny and rage of his,* IV, 1, 13. *contrived against the v. life of the defendant,* 360. *he that did uphold the v. life of my dear friend,* V, 214. *till that the weary v. means do ebb,* As II, 7, 73. *they are in the v. wrath of love,* V, 2, 44. *I came thence for v. shame,* Shr. III, 2, 182. *in pure white robes, like v. sanctity,* Wint. III, 3, 23. *this is the v. sum of all,* John II, 151. *in v. sincerity of fear,* H4A II, 3, 32. *France should have torn and rent my v. heart,* H6B I, 1, 126. *it irks my v. soul,* H6C II, 2, 6. *in the v. pangs of death he cried,* II, 3, 17. *eyes sparkling for v. wrath,* II, 5, 131. *he shall split thy v. heart with sorrow,* R3 I, 3, 300. *even of your mettle, of your v. blood,* IV, 4, 302. *a curse begin at v. root on's heart,* Cor. II, 1, 202. *I hold it v. stuff o'the conscience to do no contrived murder,* Oth. I, 2, 2. *you could not lack ... v. necessity of this thought,* Ant. II, 2, 58. *I think the king be touched at v. heart,* Cymb. I, 1, 10 etc. *very sooth,* Wint. I, 2, 17. *in v. truth,* H4B III, 2, 237. Before adjectives used substantively: *in v. brief, the suit is impertinent to myself,* Merch. II, 2, 146. *to grace him only ... a v. little I have yielded too,* Cor. V, 3, 16 (= a mere trifle).

Similarly denoting exact conformity with what is expressed by the word: *when thou reviewest this, thou dost review the v. part was consecrate to thee,* Sonn. 74, 6 (exactly that part). *even her v. words didst thou deliver to me,* Err. II, 2, 165. *Hero was in this manner accused, in this v. manner refused,* Ado IV, 2, 65. *in v. likeness of a roasted crab,* Mids. II, 1, 48. *I dote on his v. absence,* Merch. I, 2, 120 (his absence is just what I wish for). *those are the v. words,* IV, 1, 254. H6C IV, 1, 92. *I will be point-devise the v. man,* Tw. II, 5, 177. *when we have marked with blood those sleepy two and used their v. daggers,* Mcb. I, 7, 76. *to hold my v. course,* Lr. I, 3, 26. Temporally: *the hour's now come; the v. minute bids thee ope thine ear,* Tp. I, 2, 37. *spring come to you at the farthest in the v. end of harvest,* IV, 115 (as soon as the harvest is ended). *the v. instant that I saw you, did my heart fly to your service,* III, 1, 64. *when would you use it? This v. night,* Gent. III, 1, 124. *it is about the v. hour that Silvia should meet me,* V, 1, 2. *at the v. instant of Falstaff's and our meeting,* Wiv. V, 3, 16. *he this v. day receives letters,* Meas. IV, 2, 215. *that v. hour,* Err. I, 1, 54. *this v. day,* I, 2, 3. *the v. night before the wedding,* Ado II, 2, 45 etc.

Hence denoting identity: *on this grass-plot, in this v. place,* Tp. IV, 73. *I am Prospero and that v. duke which was thrust forth of Milan,* V, 159. *all the kind of the Launces have this v. fault,* Gent. II, 3, 3. *that v. person,* Wiv. I, 1, 50. *this is the v. same, the v. hand, the v. words,* II, 1, 84. *Master Troth here, this v. man,* Meas. II, 1, 104. *we do condemn thee to the v. block where Claudio stooped to death,* V, 419. *unless you were the v. man,* Ado II, 1, 123. *that v. time I saw ... Cupid all armed,* Mids. II, 1, 155. *this v. sword entrenched it,* All's II, 1, 45. *not three hours' travel from this v. place,* Tw. I, 2, 23. *whose fair flower*

*being once displayed, doth fall that v. hour,* II, 4, 40 etc. *the v. same* (cf. *Same*): Sonn. 5, 3. 108, 6. *All's* II, 3, 29. Cymb. IV, 2, 380 etc. *with this same v. iron,* John IV, 1, 125. *this same v. day,* R3 III, 2, 49.

Equivalent to the adverb *even: thou away, the v. birds are mute,* Sonn. 97, 12. *in the v. refuse of thy deeds there is such strength,* 150, 6. *the v. rats instinctively had quit it,* Tp. I, 2, 147. *a life whose v. comfort is still a dying horror,* Meas. II, 3, 41. *the v. mercy of the law cries out,* V, 412. *my v. visor began to assume life,* Ado II, 1, 248. *I do affect the v. ground ... where her shoe doth tread,* LLL I, 2, 172. *I have deceived even your v. eyes,* Ado V, 1, 238 (cf. *Even,* adv. 5). *swearing till my v. roof was dry,* Merch. III, 2, 206. *if we walk not in the trodden paths, our v. petticoats will catch them,* As I, 3, 15. *consumes itself to the v. paring,* All's I, 1, 155. *v. envy and the tongue of loss cried fame and honour on him,* Tw. V, 61. *v. infants prattle on thy pride,* H6A III, 1, 16. *the v. parings of our nails shall pitch a field,* 102. *chaste and immaculate in v. thought,* V, 4, 51. *v. force entangles itself with strength,* Ant. IV, 14, 48 etc.

Equivalent to *alone, mere: say that ... nothing but the v. smell were left me,* Ven. 441. *now can I ... dine upon the v. naked name of love,* Gent. II, 4, 142. *'tis the v. riches of thyself that now I aim at,* Wiv. III, 4, 17. *mine were the v. cypher of a function,* Meas. II, 2, 39. *the v. stream of his life ... must give him a better proclamation,* III, 2, 150. *a' turns back for v. fear,* Err. IV, 2, 56. *thou feedest me with the v. name of meat,* Shr. IV, 3, 32. *whose v. naming punishes me,* Wint. IV, 2, 24. *may we cram within this wooden O the v. casques that did affright the air at Agincourt?* H5 Prol. 13. *all our general force might with a sally of the v. town be buckled with,* H6A IV, 4, 4. *the v. train of her worst gown was better worth,* H6B I, 3, 88. *with the v. shaking of their chains they may astonish these curs,* V, 1, 145. *the v. beams will dry those vapours up,* H6C V, 3, 12. *with the v. noise I trembling waked,* R3 I, 4, 60. *this is the v. coinage of your brain,* Hml. III, 4, 137. *a v. riband in the cap of youth,* IV, 7, 78. *the v. conveyances of his lands will hardly lie in this box,* V, 1, 119. *v. nature will instruct her in it,* Oth. II, 1, 237 etc.

**Very,** adv. modifying adjectives and adverbs; originally used to signify that the resp. word is to be understood in its full and unrestricted sense, = quite, just: *is the axe upon the block, sirrah? V. ready, sir,* Meas. IV, 3, 40. Lr. V, 3, 294. *now, v. now, an old black ram is tupping your white ewe,* Oth. I, 1, 88. Usually denoting a high degree: Ven. 531. Tp. II, 1, 67. 139. 142. 189. Gent. I, 1, 74. II, 1, 114. 128. IV, 2, 129. Wiv. I, 1, 146. 199. 261. 278. 311. II, 1, 36. II, 2, 49. 93. 191. 197. 249. III, 1, 51. 101. III, 3, 98. 181. IV, 1, 4. 31. IV, 4, 81. Meas. I, 4, 50. II, 1, 23. 97. 106. 113. 116. 118. 131. 137. 157 etc. etc.

**Vesper,** the evening: *black —'s pageants,* Ant. IV, 14, 8.

**Vessel,** 1) a ship: Tp. I, 2, 31. 211. Meas. III, 1, 225. Merch. III, 2, 273. Tw. V, 57. Wint. IV, 4, 512. H8 I, 2, 79. Cor. II, 2, 110. Oth. II, 1, 37. Ant. II, 7, 77. Cymb. II, 4, 29. Per. I, 4, 67. III Prol. 44. V, 1, 23. fem.: Tp. I, 2, 6. Merch. I, 1, 32. neut.: Merch. II, 8, 30. Ant. I, 4, 53. Per. V, 1, 18. Figuratively, applied to man: *believing thee a v. of too great a burthen,* All's II, 3, 215. *though thy tackle's* *torn, thou showest a noble* v. Cor. IV, 5, 68. *from this most bravest* v. *struck the main-top,* Cymb. IV, 2, 319.

2) a cask or other utensil for holding liquors and the like: *the empty* v. *makes the greatest sound,* H5 IV, 4, 73 (proverb). *your —s and your spells próvide,* Mcb. III, 5, 18. *strike the —s,* Ant. II, 7, 103 (= tap them). Figuratively applied to human affairs: *that the united* v. *of their blood ... shall never leak,* H4B IV, 4, 44. *if I would broach the —s of my love,* Tim. II, 2, 186 (i. e. my friends). *put rancours in the* v. *of my peace,* Mcb. III, 1, 67. Hence denoting the state of man: *other incident throes that nature's fragile* v. *doth sustain,* Tim. V, 1, 204. *to preserve this* v. *for my lord from any foul touch,* Oth. IV, 2, 83. *a tempest, which his mortal* v. *tears,* Per. IV, 4, 30. And even = a person: *I never saw a* v. *of like sorrow, so filled and so becoming,* Wint. III, 3, 21. *now is that noble* v. *full of grief,* Caes. V, 5, 13. *the weaker* v. = a woman: *for Jaquenetta, — so is the weaker* v. *called ..., I keep her as a* v. *of thy law's fury,* LLL I, 1, 276. *I must comfort the weaker* v. As II, 4, 6. *you are the weaker* v., *as they say, the emptier* v. H4B II, 4, 66. 67. *women, being the weaker —s,* Rom. I, 1, 20. Strange application of a microcosmical metaphor to the macrocosm of the universe: *creeping murmur and the poring dark fills the wide* v. *of the universe,* H5 IV Chor. 3.

**Vestal,** a priestess of Vesta: Ven. 752. Lucr. 883. Ant. III, 12, 31. Per. IV, 5, 7. a chaste woman in general: *a fair* v. *throned by the west,* Mids. II, 1, 158 (viz Queen Elizabeth). Ironically: *the kitchen* v. *scorned you,* Err. IV, 4, 78.

Adjectively: *her* v. *livery,* Rom. II, 2, 8 (i. e. her chastity). *in pure and* v. *modesty,* III, 3, 38. *a* v. *livery will I take me to,* Per. III, 4, 10.

**Vestments,** garments: Err. II, 1, 94. Tim. IV, 3, 125.

**Vesture,** dress, garment: Gent. II, 4, 160. Cor. II, 1, 250. Caes. III, 2, 200. Metaphorically, the human body as that in which the soul is dressed: *this muddy* v. *of decay,* Merch. V, 64. *in the essential* v. *of creation,* Oth. II, 1, 64.

**Vetches,** the plant Vicia sativa: Tp. IV, 61.

**Vex,** 1) to plague, to harass, to afflict, to molest: *thou canst not* v. *me with inconstant mind,* Sonn. 92, 9. *more than enough am I that* v. *thee still,* 135, 3. *how can love's eye be true, that is so —ed with watching and with tears?* 148, 10. *it hath no tongue to* v. *you,* Tw. III, 4, 229. *hyperbolical fiend, how —est thou this man?* IV, 2, 29. *a twice-told tale, —ing the dull ear of a drowsy man,* John III, 4, 109. *a trespass that doth* v. *my grieved soul,* R2 I, 1, 138. III, 1, 2. H4A III, 1, 29. H6A I, 4, 13. H8 V, 3, 107. Lr. III, 4, 62. V, 3, 313.

2) to disturb, to agitate: *the still —ed Bermoothes,* Tp. I, 2, 229. *as mad as the —ed sea,* Lr. IV, 4, 2. cf. Rom. I, 1, 198 and John II, 336.

3) to afflict or agitate in mind; a) to distress: *to misuse the prince, to* v. *Claudio,* Ado III, 2, 29. *a sight to* v. *the father's soul withal,* Tit. V, 1, 52. *'twill* v. *thy soul to hear what I shall speak,* 62. *love, ... being —ed, a sea nourished with lovers' tears,* Rom. I, 1, 198. *my poor heart, so for a kinsman —ed* III, 5, 96. *to* v. *her,* Cymb. III, 5, 147. cf. *soul-vexed* in Wint. V, 1, 59. b) to disquiet: *with my —ed spirits I cannot take a truce,* John III, 1, 17. v. *not yourself,* R2 II, 1, 3.

*—ed I am of late with passions of some difference.* Caes. I, 2, 39. *when grief and blood ill-tempered —eth him,* IV, 3, 115. c) to fret, to irritate: *I am —ed,* Tp. IV, 158. *stayest thou to* v. *me here?* Gent. IV, 4, 66. *such an injury would* v. *a very saint,* Shr. III, 2, 28. All's III, 5, 92. John II, 336. H6B I, 3, 78. H6C II, 6, 68. H8 II, 4, 130. III, 2, 104. Cor. IV, 2, 2. Rom. II, 4, 170. Tim. IV, 3, 236. Ant. I, 2, 20. Cymb. II, 1, 19.

**Vexation,** 1) torment, affliction, suffering: *all thy —s were but my trials of thy love,* Tp. IV, 5. *your children were* v. *to your youth,* R3 IV, 4, 305.

2) any state of being troubled or afflicted in mind; a) agitation: *the fierce* v. *of a dream,* Mids. IV, 1, 74. b) disquiet, trouble, great uneasiness: *to appoint myself in this* v. Wint. I, 2, 326. *throw such changes of* v. *on it,* Oth. I, 1, 72. c) grief: *the deep* v. *of his inward soul,* Lucr. 1779. *it would be much* v. *to your age,* Gent. III, 1, 16. v. *almost stops my breath,* H6A IV, 3, 41. *those repeated —s of it,* Cymb. I, 6, 5. e) anger, mortification: *full of* v. *come I,* Mids. I, 1, 22. *you do me most insupportable* v. All's II, 3, 244. *give him deserved* v. Cor. III, 3, 140. *harm not yourself with your* v. Cymb. I, 1, 134.

**Via,** an interjection of encouragement (from the Italian. Florio: '*Via,* an adverb of encouraging much used by commanders, as also by riders to their horses'): *Mistress Ford and Mistress Page, have I encompassed you? go to;* v. Wiv. II, 2, 159. v., *goodman Dull! thou hast spoken no word all this while,* LLL V, 1, 156. *another, with his finger and his thumb, cried* V., *we will do't,* V, 2, 112. *the most courageous fiend bids me pack:* v., *says the fiend; away, says the fiend,* Merch. II, 2, 11. v.! *les eaux et la terre,* H5 IV, 2, 4. *why,* v., *to London will we march amain,* H6C II, 1, 182.

**Vial** (O. Edd. *viol, violl, violle;* some M. Edd. *phial),* a glass vessel or bottle: Sonn. 6, 3 (cf. 5, 10). Wint. V, 3, 122. R2 I, 2, 12. 17. Rom. IV, 1, 93. IV, 3, 20. Hml. I, 5, 62. Ant. I, 3, 63.*Per. III, 2, 90.

**Viand,** meat dressed, food, victuals: *still cupboarding the* v. Cor. I, 1, 103. Plur. *— s:* Tp. III, 3, 41. Merch. IV, 1, 97. H6C II, 5, 52. Troil. II, 2, 70. Ant. III, 11, 73. Cymb. V, 5, 156. Per. II, 3, 31.

**Vicar,** a parish priest: Wiv. IV, 6, 48. 52. As III, 3, 43. Shr. III, 2, 170.

**Vice,** subst. 1) an habitual transgression of moral duties: Lucr. 604. 1546. Sonn. 95, 9. Meas. II, 2, 5. 29. 136. II, 4, 42. III, 2, 24. 106. 109. 284. 291. IV, 2, 115. Err. III, 2, 12. LLL V, 2, 349. Merch. III, 2, 81. Tw. III, 4, 390. Wint. III, 2, 56. IV, 3, 96. 100. John II, 596. R2 V, 3, 67. H4A II, 4, 499. H4B III, 2, 326. H6A V, 4, 45. R3 II, 2, 28 (Ff *deep v.,* Qq *foul guile*). III, 5, 29. Troil. II, 3, 246. Cor. I, 1, 43. Rom. II, 3, 21. 22. Mcb. IV, 3, 47. 51. Lr. IV, 6, 168. 258. V, 3, 170. Oth. I, 3, 123. II, 3, 128. Cymb. II, 5, 21. 29. 31. Per. I, 1, 96. 103. Personified as masc.: Hml. III, 4, 154.

2) a single transgression, a sin: *rather proved the sliding of your brother a merriment than a* v. Meas. II, 4, 116. *wilt thou be made a man out of my* v.? III, 1, 138. *unless self-charity be sometimes a* v. Oth. II, 3, 202. *she holds it a* v. *in her goodness not to do more,* 326. *livest to make thine honesty a* v. III, 3, 376. *did you perceive how he laughed at his* v.? IV, 1, 181. *it is a great price for a small* v. IV, 3, 70. cf. also Wint. III, 2, 56 and R2 V, 3, 67.

3) an imperfection, a defect, a fault: *your own v. still; mistake the word*, Gent. III, 1, 283. *here follow her —s*, 324. 338. *on that v. on him* (vanity) *will my revenge find notable cause to work*, Tw. II, 3, 165. *your air of France hath blown that v. in me* (to brag) H5 III, 6, 161. *it is my v., my fault*, Troil. IV, 4, 104. *you have a v. of mercy in you*, V, 3, 37. 39. *'tis a v. to know him*, Hml. V, 2, 87. *it is a v. in her ears*, Cymb. II, 3, 33 (O. Edd. *voice*). cf. also Troil. II, 3, 246.

4) the buffoon of the old moralities (alias *Iniquity*): *like to the old V., who with dagger of lath, in his rage and his wrath, cries ah ha! to the devil*, Tw. IV, 2, 134. *now is this —'s dagger become a squire*, H4B III, 2, 343. *like the formal v., Iniquity, I moralize two meanings in one word*, R3 III, 1, 82. *a v. of kings*, Hml. III, 4, 98. cf. also H4A II, 4, 499.

**Vice**, subst. an iron press with a screw, for holding things fast: *you must put in the pikes with a v.* Ado V, 2, 21 (quibbling). *an I but fist him once, an a' come but within my v.* H4B II, 1,24 (= my grasp).

**Vice**, to screw: *as he had seen't or been an instrument to v. you to't*, Wint. I, 2, 416 (cf. *I partly know the instrument that screws me from my true place in your favour*, Tw. V, 125).

**Vicegerent**, substitute, one having a delegated power: *the welkin's v.* LLL I, 1, 222 (Armado's letter).

**Viceroy**, substitute of a king: Tp. III, 2, 116. H6A V, 4, 131. 143.

**Vicious**, 1) devoted to vice, morally corrupt: Err. IV, 2, 21. H6A V, 4, 35. H8 I, 2, 117. Tim. IV, 3, 213. Lr. I, 1, 230. V, 3, 172.

2) defective, faulty: *for some v. mole of nature in them*, Hml. I, 4, 24.

3) wrong: *though I perchance am v. in my guess, as, I confess, it is my nature's plague to spy into abuses*, Oth. III, 3, 145. *it had been v. to have mistrusted her*, Cymb. V, 5, 65 (= blameable).

**Viciousness**, state of being vicious, corruptness: Ant. III, 13, 111.

**Victor**, one who vanquishes another (never followed by an objective genitive): Lucr. 730. 1211. Sonn. 70, 10. 86, 11. Pilgr. 223 (*v. of the day*). John II, 324. R2 I, 1, 203. H4B IV, 1, 134. H6A I, 2, 4. H6C II, 3, 53. II, 5, 11. V, 2, 6. Troil. IV, 5, 67. Lr. V, 3, 132 (*thy v. sword*). Cymb. V, 3, 43. V, 5, 460.

**Victoress**, a female who conquers: *she shall be sole v., Caesar's Caesar*, R3 IV, 4, 336 (F4 and M. Edd. *victress*).

**Victorious**, 1) having conquered, or wont to conquer: John V, 2, 146. H5 II, 4, 63. H6A II, 3, 67. III, 4, 16. IV, 7, 67. H6B I, 1, 86. V, 1, 211. H6C I, 1, 21. R3 I, 4, 242. V, 5, 1. Tit. I, 70. 105. 163. Ant. IV, 2, 43.

2) emblematic of conquest: *v. wreaths*, R3 I, 1, 5.

**Victor-sword**, writing of Ff in Lr. V, 3, 132; Qq and M. Edd. in two words.

**Victory**, success in contest, conquest: Ven. 1014. Lucr. Arg. 11. Lucr. 110. Sonn. 25, 10. Compl. 258. Ado I, 1, 8. II, 3, 172 (*hath the v.*). LLL IV, 1, 75. As IV, 2, 6. John II, 307. 394. R2 I, 3, 72. H4A IV, 3, 97. H4B Ind. 23. IV, 2, 88. H6A I, 1, 20. I, 6, 31. III, 2, 117. IV, 1, 172. IV, 6, 1. 12. H6B IV, 3, 12. IV, 8, 54. IV, 10, 78. H6C I, 1, 261. I, 2, 73. II, 2, 174. II, 3, 55. II, 5, 15. IV, 1, 147. V, 1, 70. 113. V, 3, 2. R3 III, 7, 15. IV, 4, 193. V, 3, 79. 106. 114. 165.

231. 270. 351. Troil. IV, 5, 66. Cor. II, 1, 135. V, 3, 108. 186. V, 6, 98. Rom. IV, 1, 30 (*the tears have got small v.*). Tim. III, 5, 81. Caes. V, 3, 82. Mcb. I, 2, 58. Lr. V, 1, 41 (*if you have v.*). Ant. I, 3, 100. IV, 7, 12. Cymb. V, 5, 24. Per. II, 3, 10.

**Victress**, see *Victoress*.

**Victual**, subst. provisions: *he hath done good service in these wars. You had musty v., and he hath holp to eat it*, Ado I, 1, 50.

Plur. *—s* = food: *am nourished by my —s*, Gent. II, 1, 180. *eat your —s*, H5 V, 1, 35. *it eats our —s*, Cymb. III, 6, 41.

**Victual**, vb. to supply with provisions: As V, 4, 198. H6A I, 5, 14.

**Victualler** (Qq *vitlar*), a tavern-keeper: H4B II, 4, 375 (Steevens: 'the brothels were formerly screened under pretext of being victualling houses and taverns').

**Videlicet**, see Latin in the Appendix.

**Vie**, to show or practise in competition, to contend with respect to: *nature wants stuff to v. strange forms with fancy*, Ant. V, 2, 98 (to contend with, to rival, fancy in producing strange forms). *we here below recall not what you give, and therein may v. honour with you*, Per. III, 1, 26 (may contend with you, i. e. the gods, in honour). *so with the dove of Paphos might the crow v. feathers white*, IV Prol. 33. *kiss on kiss she —d so fast*, Shr. II, 311 (i. e. as if to outdo me). cf. *Outvie*.

**Vienna**, the capital of Austria: Meas. I, 1, 23. 45. I, 2, 98. I, 3, 13. II, 1, 203. 241. 254. V, 269. 319. Hml. III, 2, 249.

**View**, subst. 1) perception by the eye, sight (subjectively and objectively: the seeing as well as the being seen): *her eyes, as murdered with the v.* Ven. 1031. *at his bloody v. her eyes are fled*, 1037. *that eye which him beholds, as more divine, unto a v. so false will not incline*, Lucr. 292. *presents thy shadow to my sightless v.* Sonn. 27, 10. *that, when they see return of love, more blest may be the v.* 56, 12. *who in despite of v. is pleased to dote*, 141, 4. *no marvel then though I mistake my v.* 148, 11. *on the first v. to swear I love thee*, Mids. III, 1, 144. *then I will her charmed eye release from monster's v.* III, 2, 377. *greater than shows itself at the first v.* All's II, 5, 73. *the first v. shall kill all repetition*, V, 3, 21. *shall not behold her face at ample v.* Tw. I, 1, 27. *when the dusky sky began to rob my earnest-gaping sight of thy land's v.* H6B III, 2, 105. *I lost fair England's v.* 110. *to affright thee with the v. thereof*, V, 1, 207. *whose aspect may fright the hopeful mother at the v.* R3 I, 2, 24. *then you have lost the v. of earthly glory*, H8 I, 1, 14. *order gave each thing v.* (let it be seen indeed; set it off). *which when the people had the full v. of*, IV, 1, 71. *mine eyes are cloyed with v. of tyranny*, Tit. III, 2, 55. *love, whose v. is muffled still*, Rom. I, 1, 177. *which on more view, of many mine being one, may stand in number*, I, 2, 32. *soar above the v. of men*, Caes. I, 1, 79. *invite you to my sister's v.* Ant. II, 2, 170. *the sweet v. on't might well have warmed old Saturn*, Cymb. II, 5, 11. *we, poor unfledged, have never winged from v. o'the nest*, III, 3, 28. *you should tread a course pretty and full of v.* III, 4, 150 (offering many opportunities of seeing and observing). Applied to letters, = perusal: *would not force the letter to my v.* Gent. I, 2, 54. *on the v. and knowing of these contents*, Hml. V, 2, 44.

*In v.* = in sight: *the enemy's in v.* Lr. V, 1, 51. *they lie in v., but have not spoke as yet,* Cor. I, 4, 4 (can see each other). *to deliver the head in the v. of Angelo,* Meas. IV, 2, 177 (that Angelo may see it). *wrecked ... in the v. of the shepherd,* Wint. V, 2, 76. *have I not hideous death within my v.?* John V, 4, 22. *here in the v. of men I will unfold,* R2 III, 1, 6. *that in common v. he may surrender,* IV, 155. H6C I, 1, 138. Cor. I, 9, 85. II, 2, 97. *Hector, in v. of Trojans and of Greeks, shall make it good,* Troil. I, 3, 273. Similarly: *before this royal v.* H5 V, 2, 32 (in presence of these royal persons).

*To the v.* = so as to be seen by everybody; in public: *made myself a motley to the v.* Sonn. 110, 2. *that these bodies high on a stage be placed to the v.* Hml. V, 2, 389. *shall uplift us to the v.* Ant. V, 2, 211.

2) look, regard: *sometimes they do extend their v. right on,* Compl. 26. *the beam of her v. gilded my foot,* Wiv. I, 3, 69. *that ever turned their backs to mortal —s,* LLL V, 2, 161. 163. *gives all gaze and bent of amorous v. on the fair Cressid,* Troil. IV, 5, 282. *turn the office and devotion of their v. upon a tawny front,* Ant. I, 1, 5. *could not endure a further v.* III, 10, 18.

3) survey, inspection, examination by the eye: *she made good v. of me,* Tw. II, 2, 20. *to behold his visage, even to my full of v.* Troil. III, 3, 241. *I have with exact v. perused thee,* IV, 5, 232.

4) look, appearance, show: *you that choose not by the v.* Merch. III, 2, 132. *love, so gentle in his v.* Rom. I, 1, 175.

**View,** vb. 1) to perceive by the eye, to see: *to v. how she came,* Ven. 343. *where they —ed each other's sorrow,* 963. *what face remains alive that's worth the —ing,* 1076. *which Tarquin —ed,* Lucr. 72. 454. 632. 1101. 1261. 1526. Sonn. 3, 1. 31, 13. 43, 2. 69, 1. Meas. II, 4, 125. LLL I, 1, 246. Merch. II, 7, 43. III, 2, 59. 62. IV, 1, 270. H6B V, 1, 69. H6C I, 4, 46. II, 1, 67. R3 I, 2, 53. H8 I, 4, 71. III, 2, 405. Oth. II, 1, 16. Per. I, 1, 30. 73. II, 5, 17. Applied to writings, = to read: *v. these letters,* H6A I, 1, 89. IV, 1, 48. *the first he —ed,* H8 III, 2, 79.

2) to look on, to survey, to examine with the eye: *I'll v. the manners of the town,* Err. I, 2, 12. 31. *feed your knowledge with —ing of the town,* Tw. III, 3, 42. *to v. the sick and feeble parts of France,* H5 II, 4, 22. IV, 3, 2. IV, 7, 85. H6A I, 1, 168. I, 4, 61. 84. H6B III, 2, 132. 149. Troil. IV, 5, 238. = to survey or examine with the eye of the mind: *the happiest youth, —ing his progress through,* H4B III, 1, 54. *tell o'er your woes, again by —ing mine,* R3 IV, 4, 39. *in —ing o'er the rest o' the selfsame day,* Mcb. I, 3, 94.

**Viewless,** invisible: *to be imprisoned in the v. winds,* Meas. III, 1, 124.

**Vigil,** the eve of a holiday: *on the v.* H5 IV, 3, 45.

**Vigilance,** watchfulness: Tp. III, 3, 16. H6B I, 1, 96. Lr. II, 3, 4.

**Vigilant,** watchful: H4A IV, 2, 64. H6A II, 1, 1. Cor. I, 1, 119. Corrupted to *vigitant* by Dogberry in Ado III, 3, 100.

**Vigitant,** see *Vigilant.*

**Vigour,** 1) force, strength: Ven. 953. Tp. I, 2, 485. Err. IV, 4, 81. LLL IV, 3, 308. John III, 1, 104. R2 I, 3, 71. Troil. II, 3, 257. III, 3, 172. Tit. IV, 2, 108.

2) efficacy, efficiency: *never could the strumpet, with all her double v., art and nature, once stir my*

temper, Meas. II, 2, 184. *with a sudden v. it doth posset and curd ... the blood,* Hml. I, 5, 68. *to try the v. of them* (compounds) Cymb. I, 5, 21.

**Vild,** see *Vile.*

**Vildly,** see *Vilely.*

**Vile** (almost as often spelt *vild,* or *vil'd,* or *vilde,* in O. Edd. In some plays, f. i. Rom. and Caes., *vile* predominant, in others, f. i. Lr. and Oth., *vild.* Ff *vild,* Qq *vile:* Tit. V, 2, 201. Hml. II, 2, 111. IV, 5, 115. Oth. III, 3, 136), originally = low, mean: *'tis v., unless it may be quaintly ordered,* Merch. II, 4, 6. *in v. apparel,* H4B I, 2, 20. *why liest thou with the v. in loathsome beds,* III, 1, 15. *be he ne'er so v., this day shall gentle his condition,* H5 IV, 3, 62. *great men oft die by v. bezonians,* H6B IV, 1, 134. Sometimes = evil, mischievous: *'tis a v. thing to die,* R3 III, 2, 64. *to dare the v. contagion of the night,* Caes. II, 1, 265. *the v. blows and buffets of the world,* Mcb. III, 1, 109.

But in general used as a vague term of contempt, = base, bad, abject, villanous: Lucr. Arg. 23. Lucr. 202. 631. Sonn. 71, 4 (—*st*). 121, 1. Tp. I, 2, 358. Gent. IV, 1, 73. Wiv. I, 3, 106. III, 4, 32. V, 5, 87. Meas. V, 95. Err. I, 1, 35. V, 67. 236. Ado III, 3, 134. IV, 1, 94. LLL IV, 3, 276. 280. Mids. I, 1, 232. II, 2, 34. 107. III, 2, 260. V, 133. 144. Merch. II, 5, 30. As III, 2, 17. V, 1, 6. Shr. II, 159. V, 2, 93. All's II, 1, 177 (—*st*). II, 3, 159. III, 5, 87. Tw. III, 4, 399. Wint. II, 1, 92. John II, 509. 577. 586. III, 1, 165. III, 4, 19. 138. IV, 1, 96. IV, 2, 241. IV, 3, 48 (—*st*). R2 II, 1, 25. H4A I, 3, 63. 241. III, 2, 87. V, 4, 39. H4B II, 2, 52. II, 4, 171. V, 2, 18. V, 3, 145. H5 IV, 1, 49. 64. II, 4, 74. III, 6, 50. IV Chor. 50. H6A I, 4, 33 (*vile esteemed,* O. Edd. *pil'd esteemed* ). III, 1, 11. III, 2, 45. IV, 1, 97. IV, 3, 33. V, 3, 112. V, 4, 16. H6B V, 2, 40. R3 I, 3, 89. Troil. II, 1, 99. V, 10, 23. Cor. I, 1, 188. Tit. V, 2, 173. 201. Rom. I, 4, 111. II, 3, 17. III, 1, 76. 146. III, 2, 59. 83. III, 3, 106. V, 3, 54. Tim. I, 1, 15. IV, 3, 470 (*vilder*). Caes. I, 3, 111. III, 2, 35. IV, 3, 71. 74. V, 1, 39. 104. V, 5, 38. Hml. I, 5, 72. II, 2, 111. 483 (Ff *their vild murthers,* Qq *their lord's murder*). IV, 1, 30. IV, 5, 115. Lr. III, 2, 71. III, 4, 150. III, 7, 83. IV, 2, 38. 47. IV, 6, 286. Oth. II, 3, 256. III, 3, 136. 222. III, 4, 184. Ant. II, 2, 243 (—*st*). IV, 14, 22. Cymb. I, 1, 143. III, 4, 75. V, 4, 18. V, 5, 252. Per. III, 3, 21. IV Prol. 41.

**Vile-concluded,** basely settled or made: *v. peace,* John II, 586.

**Vile-drawing,** writing of some M. Edd. in John II, 577; O. Edd. not hyphened.

**Vile-esteemed,** writing of M. Edd. in H6A I, 4, 33; O. Edd. in two words.

**Vilely** (O. Edd. *vildly* or *vildely; vilely* only in H4A III, 3, 1. 122) 1) meanly, basely, shamefully: *he speaks most v. of you,* H4A III, 3, 122. H4B II, 4, 327. *doth it not show v. in me to desire small beer?* II, 2, 7. *they had so v. yielded the town,* Cor. III, 1, 10. *operate most v.* Cymb. V, 5, 198. *the very doors and windows savour v.* Per. IV, 6, 117.

2) in a worthless manner, badly, ill, sorrily: *let me be v. painted,* Ado I, 1, 267. *an agate very v. cut,* III, 1, 65. *I tell this tale v.* III, 3, 157. *v. compiled,* LLL V, 2, 52. *prologue v. penned,* 305. *very v. in the morning,* Merch. I, 2, 92. *his work so noble v. bound up,* Wint. IV, 4, 22. *am I not fallen away v.* H4A III, 3, 1. *how v. doth this cynic rhyme,* Caes. IV, 3, 133.

**Vileness,** baseness, badness: *good alone is good*

*without a name; v. is so; the property by what it is should go, not by the title*, All's II, 3, 136 (i. e. it is the same with badness; it is bad without a name).

**Viliaco**, see *Villiago*.

**Village**, a small assemblage of houses in the country: As III, 3, 44. 60. R2 II, 3, 94. H4A IV, 3, 69. H5 III, 6, 116. IV, 8, 118. V, 2, 184. R3 V, 3, 209 *(v. cock)*. H8 II, 4, 159 *(v. curs)*. Lr. II, 3, 18.

**Villager**, a peasant: Caes. I, 2, 172.

**Villagery**, villages: *frights the maidens of the v.* Mids. II, 1, 35.

**Villain**, originally = bondman, slave, servant: *the homely v. courtesies to her low*, Lucr. 1338. *I am no v.; I am the youngest son of Sir Rowland*, As I, 1, 59. *who should find them but the empress' v.* Tit. IV, 3, 73. *my v.* Lr. III, 7, 78.

But usually as a term of reproach, = a vile and wicked person, a wretch, a rascal: Tp. I, 2, 309. Gent. III, 1, 202. IV, 1, 5. Wiv. IV, 2, 121. Meas. V, 304. 311. Err. II, 2, 17. Ado I, 3, 34. II, 3, 272. III, 3, 121. IV, 1, 93. 303. LLL I, 2, 158. Mids. III, 2, 402. 415. Merch. I, 3, 101. 180. As I, 1, 58. Tw. III, 4, 180 etc. etc. Adjectively: *the v. Jew*, Merch. II, 8, 4. *thou v. slave*, R3 IV, 4, 144. *v. boy*, Tit. I, 290. *that v. cousin*, Rom. III, 2, 101. *some v. mountaineers*, Cymb. IV, 2, 71.

Sometimes used in a less opprobrious sense, particularly in addresses: Gent. III, 1, 337. IV, 1, 41. Wiv. IV, 5, 73. 94. Meas. I, 2, 27. Err. I, 2, 96. II, 1, 58 etc. Even as a term of endearment: *a trusty v.* Err. I, 2, 19. *sweet v.* Wint. I, 2, 136. *v., thou might'st have been an emperor*, Tit. V, 1, 30. Applied to females: *here comes the little v.* Tw. II, 5, 16 (Maria). *it is the prettiest v.* Troil. III, 2, 35 (Cressida).

**Villain-like**, adv. villanously: *v. he lies*, Lr. V, 3, 98. Cymb. V, 5, 218.

**Villanous**, 1) very vile and wicked: Wiv. II, 2, 308. Meas. V, 265. As I, 1, 151. 161. All's IV, 5, 2. H4A I, 3, 60. II, 4, 138. 140. 504. 508. III, 3, 11. Rom. V, 3, 52. Tim. II, 2, 182. Lr. I, 2, 147. Oth. I, 3, 312. II, 1, 266. IV, 2, 22. 139. V, 2, 229. Cymb. V, 5, 195.

2) pitiful, sorry, wretched: *v. smell*, Wiv. III, 5, 93. *the v. inconstancy of man's disposition*, IV, 5, 111. *the most v. house for fleas*, H4A II, 1, 15. *there's v. news abroad*, II, 4, 366. *a v. trick of thine eye*, 445. *that's v. and shows a most pitiful ambition*, Hml. III, 2, 48.

Adverbially: *foreheads v. low*, Tp. IV, 250.

**Villanously**, 1) in a vile and wicked manner: Meas. V, 149. 2) vilely, sorrily, wretchedly: *crossgartered? Most v.* Tw. III, 2, 80.

**Villany**, 1) extreme depravity and wickedness: *pinch him for his v.* Wiv. V, 5, 104. *the commendation is not in his wit, but in his v.* Ado II, 1, 146. III, 3, 120. 168. All's IV, 3, 305. Wint. I, 2, 361. John III, 1, 116. IV, 3, 108. H4A II, 4, 504. III, 3, 187. H5 III, 2, 56. R3 I, 3, 336. Tim. III, 6, 103. IV, 3, 20. Oth. V, 2, 151. Cymb. V, 2, 13 *(the v. of our fears)*. V, 4, 68. V, 5, 225. Per. IV, 4, 44. Plur. *—es: the —es of man will set him clear*, Tim. III, 3, 30. *the multiplying —es of nature do swarm upon him*, Mcb. I, 2, 11.

2) wicked practice; or a single action of deep depravity: Ado III, 3, 117. V, 1, 71. 72. 246. 258. LLL I, 1, 189. Merch. III, 1, 74. Shr. V, 1, 140.

John IV, 2, 225. H4B II, 1, 130. H5 III, 3, 32. Tit. II, 1, 116. 121. II, 3, 7. III, 1, 203. IV, 4, 51. Tim. IV, 3, 437 *(do v.)*. Hml. V, 2, 322. Oth. V, 2, 190. Ant. II, 7, 80. Cymb. III, 4, 58. III, 5, 112 *(do)*. V, 5, 142. Plur. *—es:* Ado IV, 1, 191. H6B III, 1, 370. Tit. V, 1, 66. Hml. V, 2, 29. The sense somewhat softened: *to act any v. against him*, Wiv. II, 1, 102. *the sleeves curiously cut. There's the v.* Shr. IV, 3, 145. Misapplied by Dr. Caius: Wiv. I, 4, 71. II, 3, 16.

**Villiago** (O. Edd.) or **Viliaco** (the spelling of contemporary writers, adopted by some M. Edd.), from the Italian *vigliacco*, = a base coward: *I see them (the French) lording it in London streets, crying V. unto all they meet*, H6B IV, 8, 48.

**Vincentio**, name in Shr. I, 1, 13. 14. 200. II, 104 etc.

**Vindicative** *(vindícative)*, vindictive, revengeful: *more v. than jealous love*, Troil. IV, 5, 107.

**Vine**, the plant Vitis vinifera: Lucr. 215. Tp. IV, 112. Err. II, 2, 176. H5 V, 2, 41. H6A II, 5, 11. R3 V, 2, 8. H8 V, 5, 35. 50. Tim. IV, 3, 193. Lr. I, 1, 86. Ant. II, 7, 120. Cymb. IV, 2, 60.

**Vinegar**, an acid liquor chiefly obtained from wine: H4B II, 1, 103. Emblem of sourness and asperity: *of such v. aspect*, Merch. I, 1, 54. *there's v. and pepper in it*, Tw. III, 4, 158.

**Vinewed'st**, most mouldy; writing of M. Edd. in Troil. II, 1, 15: *thou v. leaven;* Ff *whinid'st*, Qq *unsalted.*

**Vineyard**, a ground planted with vines: Tp. II, 1, 152. IV, 68. Meas. IV, 1, 29. 30. 33. H5 III, 5, 4. V, 2, 54.

**Viol** (cf. *Vial*) a sort of violin: R2 I, 3, 162. Per. I, 1, 81. cf. *Base-viol* and *Viol-de-gamboys*.

**Viola**, female name in Tw. V, 248. 251. 260.

**Violate**, to sin against; to break (a vow etc.), to dishonour, to do violence to (maiden honour): *makest the vestal v. her oath*, Lucr. 883. *—d troth*, 1059. LLL I, 1, 21. As III, 2, 141. R2 I, 3, 18. V, 1, 71. *to v. the honour of my child*, Tp. I, 2, 347. Cymb. V, 5, 284. *experience, manhood, honour, ne'er before did v. so itself*, Ant. III, 10, 24.

**Violation**, the act of sinning against sth.; infringement; ravishment: *in double v. of sacred chastity and of promise-breach*, Meas. V, 409. *the v. of my faith*, Wint. IV, 4, 488. *v. of all faith and troth*, H4A V, 1, 70. *if your pure maidens fall into the hand of hot and forcing v.* H5 III, 3, 21.

**Violator**, in *Virgin-violator*, q. v.

**Viol-de-gamboys**, a base-viol or a violoncello (a viol taken between the legs, as it is defined by some contemporary writers): *he plays o'the v.* Tw. I, 3, 27 (which was a fashionable accomplishment).

**Violence**, 1) vehemence, intensity of action or motion: *blown with restless v. round about the world*, Meas. III, 1, 125. *to make an act of tragic v.* R3 II, 2, 39. *that seal, you ask with such a v.* H8 III, 2, 246. *the v. of either grief or joy*, Hml. III, 2, 206. *pass with your best v.* V, 2, 309. *my downright v. and storm of fortunes*, Oth. I, 3, 250. *with what v. she first loved the Moor*, II, 1, 224. *be'st thou sad or merry, the v. of either thee becomes*, Ant. I, 5, 60. *the v. of action hath made you reek*, Cymb. I, 2, 2.

2) force, power exerted against consent or unjustly: *lest your justice prove v.* Wint. II, 1, 128. *offer him no v.* H6C I, 1, 33. Hml. I, 1, 144. *to prevent the*

*tyrant's v.* H6C IV, 4, 29. *die by untimely v.* R3 I, 3, 201. *unless ... to defend ourselves it be a sin when v. assails us,* Oth. II, 3, 204. *by v.* = by force: H6B III, 2, 246. *to do v.: nor shall you do mine ear that v. to make it truster of your own report against yourself,* Hml. I, 2, 171. *you would not do me v.* Per. V, 1, 101. *to do v. on:* Rom. V, 3, 264.

**Violent,** adj. 1) forcible, moving or acting with strength, vehement; a) in a physical sense: *the v. roaring tide,* Lucr. 1667. *ride upon the v. speed of fire,* All's III, 2, 112. *he cracks his sides with v. hefts,* Wint. II, 1, 45. *I am scalded with my v. motion,* John V, 7, 49. *v. fires soon burn out themselves,* R2 II, 1, 34. *by v. swiftness,* H8 I, 1, 142. *thy exercise hath been too v.* Cor. I, 5, 16. *upon a wild and v. sea,* Mcb. IV, 2, 21. *make your bouts more v.* Hml. IV, 7, 159. *foul and v. tempest,* Oth. II, 1, 34. *with v. pace,* III, 3, 457. *never was waves nor wind more v.* Per. IV, 1, 60.

b) vehement in a moral sense, fierce, passionate: *thy v. vanities can never last,* Lucr. 894. *to these v. proceedings all my neighbours shall cry aim,* Wiv. III, 2, 44. *his unkindness ... hath made it (her love) more v. and unruly,* Meas. III, 1, 252. *must it (his jealousy) be v.* Wint. I, 2, 454. *the v. carriage of it,* III, 1, 17. *proud, v., testy magistrates,* Cor. II, 1, 47. *where the disease is v.* III, 1, 222. *the v. fit o'the time,* III, 2, 33. *mature for the v. breaking out,* IV, 3, 27. *these v. delights have v. ends,* Rom. II, 6, 9. *the expedition of my v. love outrun the pauser reason,* Mcb. II, 3, 116. *v. sorrow,* IV, 3, 169. *whose (love's) v. property fordoes itself,* Hml. II, 1, 103. *of v. birth, but poor validity,* III, 2, 199. *the most v. author of his own just remove,* IV, 5, 80. *it was a v. commencement,* Oth. I, 3, 350.

2) enormous, excessive, outrageous: *he and Aufidius can no more atone than —est contrariety,* Cor. IV, 6, 73. *in a v. popular ignorance,* V, 2, 43. *to do upon respect such v. outrage,* Lr. II, 4, 24. *those v. harms that my two sisters have in thy reverence made,* IV, 7, 28.

3) acting, or produced, by force and violence: *some v. hands were laid on Humphrey's life,* H6B III, 2, 138. 156. Tit. III, 2, 22. Mcb. V, 8, 70. *v. thefts,* Troil. V, 3, 21. *they have been v. to me and mine,* Tit. V, 2, 109. *a v. death,* H6A V, 4, 64. H6B I, 4, 34. 63. Tit. V, 2, 108.

**Violent,** vb. to be violent: *the grief is fine, full, perfect, that I taste, and —eth in a sense as strong as that which causeth it,* Troil. IV, 4, 4 (Ff *and no less in a sense*).

**Violently,** 1) vehemently, forcibly, impetuously: *which being v. borne upon,* Err. I, 1, 103. *thou art v. carried away from grace,* H4A II, 4, 491. *temperately proceed to what you would thus v. redress,* Cor. III, 1, 220. *discharged of breath as v. as hasty powder fired doth hurry,* Rom. V, 1, 64. *if you v. proceed against him,* Lr. I, 2, 89.

2) by force: *v. ravished her,* Lucr. Arg. 16.

**Violet,** the plant Viola: Ven. 125. 936. Sonn. 12, 3. 99, 1. Meas. II, 2, 166. LLL V, 2, 904. Mids. II, 1, 250. Tw. I, 1, 6. Wint. IV, 4, 120. John IV, 2, 12. R2 V, 2, 46. H5 IV, 1, 106. Hml. I, 3, 7. IV, 5, 184. V, 1, 263. Cymb. I, 5, 83. IV, 2, 172. Per. IV, 1, 16.

**Viper,** the animal Vipera: *I am no v., yet I feed on mother's flesh,* Per. I, 1, 64 (cf. H6A III, 1, 72). Emblem of mischievous malignancy: R2 III, 2, 129.

H5 II, 1, 49. Troil. III, 1, 146. Cor. III, 1, 263. Oth. V, 2, 285.

**Viperous,** having the nature of a viper: *civil dissension is a v. worm that gnaws the bowels of the commonwealth,* H6A III, 1, 72 (cf. *Viper* in Per. I, 1, 64). = venomous, malignant: *this v. traitor,* Cor. III, 1, 287. *this v. slander,* Cymb. III, 4, 41.

**Virago,** see *Firago*.

**Virgilia,** name of Coriolanus' wife: Cor. I, 3, 120.

**Virgin,** subst. a maiden, a woman who has no knowledge of man: Meas. I, 4, 16. LLL I, 1, 295 — 298. All's I, 1, 133. 140. 141. 151. I, 3, 119. H6A V, 3, 178. V, 4, 50. 83. H6B V, 1, 186. H8 V, 5, 61. Tim. V, 1, 176. Per. IV, 2, 45. IV, 6, 127. Used of any young woman not yet married: Tp. I, 2, 447. Meas. I, 4, 33. LLL IV, 2, 132. Mids. II, 2, 160. Merch. II, 1, 10. As V, 4, 60. Shr. IV, 5, 37. All's I, 3, 123. 246. III, 5, 103. H5 III, 3, 14. IV, 1, 172. H6A III, 3, 16. Troil. I, 1, 11. II, 2, 104. Tim. IV, 3, 114. Per. V, 1, 141.

Adjectively, = 1) pertaining to a maiden: *the general of hot desire was sleeping by a v. hand disarmed,* Sonn. 154, 8. *this v. palm now kissing thine,* LLL V, 2, 816. *the v. tribute paid by howling Troy,* Merch. III, 2, 56 (= the tribute of a virgin). Cor. III, 2, 114. Hml. V, 1, 255. Per. II, 5, 12. 2) pure, chaste: *break her v. knot,* Tp. IV, 15. Per. IV, 2, 160. *the white cold v. snow upon my heart,* Tp. IV, 55. *thy v. knight,* Ado V, 3, 13. *withering on the v. thorn,* Mids. I, 1, 77. 80. Merch. II, 7, 22. Wint. IV, 4, 115. H5 V, 2, 323.

**Virgin,** vb., with a superfluous *it*, = to play the virgin, to be chaste: *my true lip hath —ed it e'er since,* Cor. V, 3, 48.

**Virginal,** adj. maidenly: *tears v.* H6B V, 2, 52. *the v. palms of your daughters,* Cor. V, 2, 45. *without any more v. fencing,* Per. IV, 6, 62.

**Virginalling,** playing as upon a virginal (a sort of small pianoforte), fingering: *still v. upon his palm,* Wint. I, 2, 125.

**Virginia,** the Roman virgin whom her father killed to save her from dishonour; not mentioned by name, but alluded to in Tit. V, 3, 37.

**Virginity,** maidenhood: Meas. III, 1, 98. Ado IV, 1, 48. LLL I, 1, 298. Mids. II, 1, 219. All's I, 1, 121. 124. 126. 131. 134. 138. 139. 142. 148. 151. 153. 156. 174. 179. IV, 3, 249. V, 3, 186. Tim. IV, 1, 7. Per. IV, 2, 63. IV, 6, 22 (—es). 151. Misapplied by Evans: Wiv. I, 1, 47.

**Virginius,** the Roman who killed his daughter to preserve her from slavery and dishonour: Tit. V, 3, 36. 50.

**Virgin-knot,** see *Virgin*.

**Virgin-like,** innocent: *art thou a feodary for this act, and lookest so v. without?* Cymb. III, 2, 22.

**Virgin-violator,** a ravisher of virgins: Meas. V, 41.

**Virgo,** a constellation of the zodiac: Tit. IV, 3, 64.

**Virtue,** 1) moral goodness: *talked of v.* Lucr. 846. 847. *thy mother was a piece of v.* Tp. I, 2, 56. V, 28. Gent. III, 1, 65. Wiv. V, 5, 155. Meas. II, 1, 9. 38. II, 2, 161. 183. II, 4, 145. III, 1, 164. 215. III, 2, 198. 278. V, 226. 533. Err. III, 1, 90. III, 2, 12. Ado III, 1, 69. IV, 1, 39. 83. 223. V, 1, 29. LLL III, 76. V, 2, 349. 350. Mids. II, 1, 220 etc. Abstr. pro concr.: *my poor v.* (viz Doll Tearsheet) H4B II, 4, 51. *two reverend* *cardinal —s,* H8 III, 1, 103 (the two cardinals). *I am an humble suitor to your —s,* Tim. III, 5, 7. *O infinite v.* Ant. IV, 8, 17. Personified as fem.: Hml. III, 2, 25. Cymb. V, 5, 221.

2) a particular moral excellence: *every one commended the —s of his own wife,* Lucr. Arg. 6. *love is my sin and thy dear v. hate,* Sonn. 142, 1. *if our —s did not go forth of us,* Meas. I, 1, 34. *it becomes a v.* III, 1, 136. Ado I, 1, 57. V, 1, 172. V, 2, 88. Merch. I, 1, 163 etc.

3) bravery (the predominant signification of *virtus* among the Romans; cf. *valour is the chiefest v.* Cor. II, 2, 88): *which* (viz proud) *he is, even to the altitude of his v.* Cor. I, 1, 41. *trust to thy single v.* Lr. V, 3, 103. cf. Ant. IV, 8, 17.

4) any good quality, merit, or accomplishment: *for several —s have I liked several women,* Tp. III, 1, 42. *she can milk; a sweet v. in a maid,* Gent. III, 1, 278. 314. 320. 322. 325. 339. 340. *to waste thyself upon thy virtues,* Meas. I, 1, 32. *do you think I do not know you by your excellent wit? can v. hide itself?* Ado II, 1, 127. *that's the right v. of the medlar,* As III, 2, 127. *a v. that was never seen in you,* H4A III, 1, 126. *my v. or my plague, ... she's so conjunctive to my life and soul,* Hml. IV, 7, 13. *I can sing, weave, sew and dance, with other —s,* Per. IV, 6, 195. Proverbial: *to make a v. of necessity,* Gent. IV, 1, 62 (originally = to make a merit of what cannot be helped, and hence = to yield to necessity). *there is no v. like necessity,* R2 I, 3, 278.

5) power, efficacy: *their* (his eyes') *v.* (of reflecting) *lost,* Ven. 1131. *you still shall live; such v. hath my pen,* Sonn. 81, 13. *the v. of your eye must break my oath,* LLL V, 2, 348. *thy fair —'s force,* Mids. III, 1, 143 (= the power of thy beauty). *silence bestows that v. on it* (music) Merch. V, 101. *if you had known the v. of the ring,* 199. *much v. in If,* As V, 4, 108. John V, 7, 44. R3 IV, 4, 370. Cor. V, 2, 12. Rom. II, 3, 13. Tim. IV, 3, 391. Mcb. IV, 3, 156. Hml. IV, 5, 155. IV, 7, 145. Lr. IV, 4, 16. Oth. I, 3, 320 (*it is not in my v. to amend it*). Cymb. I, 5, 23. *by v. of =* by the efficacy or authority of: *you may suspect him, by v. of your office, to be no true man,* Ado III, 3, 54. *my commission, by whose v. ... you are joined with me ...,* H8 II, 2, 104. *by v. of that ring I take my cause out of the gripes of cruel men,* V, 3, 99. cf. the following expressions: *you are a counsellor, and, by that v., no man dare accuse you,* H8 V, 3, 50. *you have some sick offence within your mind, which, by the right and v. of my place, I ought to know of,* Caes. II, 1, 269. Similarly: *in very ample v. of his father,* H4B IV, 1, 163 (in the full power and authority of his father).

6) the very substance, essence: *which touched the very v. of compassion in thee,* Tp. I, 2, 27. *all the faith, the v. of my heart, ... is only Helena,* Mids. IV, 1, 174. *the v. of this jest will be the incomprehensible lies,* H4A I, 2, 208. *pity is the v. of the law, and none but tyrants use it cruelly,* Tim. III, 5, 8.

**Virtuous,** 1) morally good; applied to persons and practices: Lucr. 252. 391 (*like a v. monument;* cf. *Monument*). Sonn. 16, 7. 72, 5. 88, 4. Gent. IV, 4, 185. Wiv. I, 1, 191. IV, 2, 136. Meas. II, 2, 20. 185. III, 2, 239 (*it is v. to be constant*). Err. V, 134. Ado II, 3, 29. 33. 166. 240. V, 1, 311. LLL II, 18. Mids. II, 2, 59. Merch. I, 2, 30. As I, 3, 83. II, 3, 5. IV, 1, 64. All's I, 1, 48 (*v. qualities*). H4A II, 4, 460. H6A

II, 2, 20. 38. IV, 1, 35. V, 1, 43 (*v. gifts*). V, 4, 39. H6B I, 2, 20. H6C II, 2, 49. H8 II, 2, 128. Cor. V, 2, 27 (*though it were as v. to lie*). V, 3, 26 (*let it be v. to be obstinate*). Tim. III, 2, 45 (*if his occasion were not v.,* i. e. caused by his virtue) etc. etc.

2) powerful, efficacious by inherent qualities, beneficial: *corrupt with v. season,* Meas. II, 2, 168. *whose liquor hath this v. property, to take from thence all error,* Mids. III, 2, 367. *culling from every flower the v. sweets,* H4B IV, 5, 76. *that by your v. means I may again exist,* Oth. III, 4, 111.

**Virtuously,** in a virtuous manner, in conformity with the moral law: Gent. IV, 3, 38. H4A III, 3, 16. Troil. II, 3, 127. Oth. IV, 1, 7. *we are so v. bound,* Tim. I, 2, 232 (= efficaciously? powerfully?).

**Visage,** face, countenance, look: *from the world his* (the sun's) *v. hide,* Sonn. 33, 7. *which fortified her v. from the sun,* Compl. 9. 90. 96. Meas. III, 1, 90. IV, 3, 79. V, 358. LLL V, 2, 144. Mids. I, 1, 210. IV, 1, 84. Merch. I, 1, 88. III, 2, 59. All's V, 3, 136. Tw. III, 2, 69. Wint. I, 2, 266. IV, 4, 456. R2 V, 2, 15. H4B II, 3, 3. H5 V, 2, 37. 241. H6B V, 1, 69. H8 III, 2, 88. Troil. III, 3, 240. Cor. I, 9, 93. Rom. I, 4, 29. Tim. II, 1, 29. Caes. II, 1, 81. Hml. I, 2, 81. II, 2, 580. III, 1, 47. III, 3, 47. III, 4, 50. Lr. I, 4, 330. II, 2, 87. Oth. I, 1, 50 (*trimmed in forms and —s of duty*). I, 3, 253. III, 3, 387. Ant. IV, 12, 38.

**Visaged,** in *Tripe-visaged,* q. v.

**Visard,** see *Vizard.*

**Viscount,** a title of nobility next in rank to an earl: H8 I, 4, 93.

**Visible,** 1) perceptible by the eye: Tim. IV, 3, 387. Lr. IV, 2, 46. Ant. IV, 14, 14. Cymb. III, 4, 152.

2) apparent, open: *Fortune, v. an enemy,* Wint. V, 1, 216.

**Visibly,** in a manner perceptible by the eye: *who art the table wherein all my thoughts are v. charactered and engraved,* Gent. II, 7, 4.

**Vision,** sight; 1) the faculty of seeing: *nor his* (my eye's) *own v. holds what it doth catch,* Sonn. 113, 8.

2) something seen; a) something seen in reality: *to a v. so apparent rumour cannot be mute,* Wint. I, 2, 270 (perhaps used here with intended ambiguity). b) a supernatural or imaginary appearance seen in waking or dreaming: Tp. IV, 118. 151. V, 176. Wiv. III, 5, 141. Mids. III, 2, 371. IV, 1, 81. 210. V, 433. H6A I, 2, 52. 79. Troil. V, 3, 63. Caes. II, 2, 84. Mcb. II, 1, 36. Hml. I, 5, 137. Cymb. IV, 2, 346. V, 5, 467. Per. V, 3, 69.

**Visit,** vb. 1) to go or come to see: Lucr. 1307. Wiv. III, 5, 50. Err. III, 2, 179. Ado V, 4, 14. LLL I, 2, 140. II, 177. V, 2, 119. 343. Merch. II, 2, 215. Shr. I, 1, 202. III, 2, 116. IV, 5, 56. Wint. I, 1, 1. II, 3, 46. III, 2, 239. V, 1, 163. V, 2, 116. V, 3, 6. R2 I, 2, 66. I, 4, 56. 63. H4B III, 2, 314. IV, 3, 139. H6A II, 2, 41. II, 3, 27. R3 I, 3, 32. III, 7, 60. IV, 1, 16. H8 IV, 2, 116. Troil. II, 3, 87 (cf. *Of*). V, 2, 74. Cor. I, 3, 29. 85. II, 1, 212. Tim. I, 2, 181. IV, 3, 170. Caes. III, 2, 270. V, 1, 9. Hml. I, 2, 253. II, I, 4. II, 2, 35. 279. Lr. II, 1, 120. Cymb. III, 5, 45, Per. III, 1, 79. Ant. V, 2, 160.

2) to go to look after; to survey; to attend for some duty: *we'll v. Caliban my slave,* Tp. I, 2, 308. *in these fits I leave them, while I v. young Ferdinand,* III, 3, 91. *to v. the afflicted spirits in the prison,* Meas. II, 3, 4. *ere long I'll v. you again,* III, 1, 46. *I am*

going to v. the prisoner, III, 2, 272. v. the speechless sick, LLL V, 2, 861. comes to v. Malvolio the lunatic, Tw. IV, 2, 25. kept in a dark house, —ed by a priest, V, 350. forth he goes and —s all his host, H5 IV Chor. 32. —ing the sick, Rom. V, 2, 7.

3) to attend, to be about, to seek, to follow: it (sleep) seldom —s sorrow, Tp. II, 1, 195. I likewise will v. thee with mine (letters) Gent. I, 1, 60. v. by night your lady's chamber-window with some sweet concert, III, 2, 83. I will, as 'twere a brother of your order, v. both prince and people, Meas. I, 3, 45. all places that the eye of heaven —s, R2 I, 3, 275. I will wish her speedy strength and v. her with my prayers, Cor. I, 3, 87. the ruddy drops that v. my sad heart, Caes. II, 1, 290. that he might not beteem the winds of heaven v. her face too roughly, Hml. I, 2, 142 (cf. visitation in H4B III, 1, 21). Absolutely: there is nothing left remarkable beneath the —ing moon, Ant. IV, 15, 68.

In a hostile sense: by day's approach look to be —ed, Mids. III, 2, 430. ere the king dismiss his power, he means to v. us, H4A IV, 4, 37. whether to knock against the gates of Rome, or rudely v. them in parts remote, Cor. IV, 5, 148.

Strange expression: please your ladyship to v. the next room, Wint. II, 2, 47 (simply = to go into).

4) to afflict; used a) of diseases: these lords are —ed, LLL V, 2, 422 (viz with the plague). ere he by sickness had been —ed, H4A IV, 1, 26. strangely —ed people, Mcb. IV, 3, 150.

b) of heavenly judgments, = to punish, to chastise: the sins of my mother should be —ed upon me, Merch. III, 5, 16. thy sins are —ed in this poor child, John II, 179. those impieties for the which they are now —ed, H5 IV, 1, 185.

**Visitation,** a visit (the subst. visit not yet used by Sh.): this v. shows it, Tp. III, 1, 32. you have lent him v. Meas. III, 2, 255. nothing but peace and gentle v. LLL V, 2, 181. in loving v. was with me a young doctor, Merch. IV, 1, 153. means to pay Bohemia the v. Wint. I, 1, 7. what colour for my v. shall I hold up, IV, 4, 566. 'tis not a v. framed, but forced by need, V, 1, 91. in cradle of the rude imperious surge and in the v. of the winds, H4B III, 1, 21 (cf. visit in Hml. I, 2, 142). neglect the v. of my friends, R3 III, 7, 107. Charles the emperor ... here makes v. H8 I, 1, 179. your queen desires your v. V, 1, 169. to give thee nightly v. Troil. IV, 4, 75. I take all and your several —s so kind to heart, Tim. I, 2, 224. what have you now to present unto him? Nothing but my v. V, 1, 20. your v. shall receive such thanks, Hml. II, 2, 25. is it a free v.? 284. this v. is but to whet thy purpose, III, 4, 110.

**Visitings,** accessions, attacks, fits: that no compunctious v. of nature shake my fell purpose, Mcb. I, 5, 46.

**Visitor,** one who comes to see another: Wint. II, 2, 11. Tim. I, 1, 42. Used of one who administers spiritual comfort: he receives comfort like cold porridge. The v. will not give him o'er so, Tp. II, 1, 11.

**Visor** or **Vizor** (cf. Vizard), a mask for men: Ado II, 1, 99. 101. 164. 248. LLL V, 2, 227. R3 II, 2, 28 (Qq vizard). Rom. I, 4, 30. I, 5, 24. Per. IV, 4, 44.

Name in H4B V, 1, 42.*45.

**Vital,** pertaining to life, being the cause or effect of life: the v. commoners and inland petty spirits, H4B IV, 3, 119. let not Bardolph's v. thread be cut, H5

III, 6, 49. bereft my v. powers, H6B III, 2, 41. I cannot give it v. growth again, Oth. V, 2, 14.

**Vitlar,** see Victualler.

**Vitruvio,** name in Rom. I, 2, 69.

**Vives,** see Fives.

**Vixen,** a quarrelsome girl: she was a v. when she went to school, Mids. III, 2, 324.

**Viz,** to whit, that is, namely: how many pair of silk stockings thou hast, v. these, and those that were thy peach coloured ones, H4B II, 2, 18.

**Vizaments,** Sir Hugh Evans' word for advisements: Wiv. I, 1, 39.

**Vizard** or **Visard** (cf. Visor), a mask: Wiv. IV, 4, 70. LLL V, 2, 242. 246. 271. 385. 386. 387. 404. H4A I, 2, 142. 199. II, 2, 55. R3 II, 2, 28 (Ff vizor). Mcb. III, 2, 34.

**Vizarded,** masked; disguised: they must all be masked and v. Wiv. IV, 6, 40. degree being v., the unworthiest shows as fairly in the mask, Troil. I, 3, 83.

**Vizard-like,** like a mask: thy face is v. unchanging, H6C I, 4, 116.

**Vizor,** see Visor.

**Vocation,** calling, profession: H4A I, 2, 116. 117. H6A I, 2, 80. H6B IV, 2, 18.

**Vocative,** the grammatical case used in calling or addressing a person: Wiv. IV, 1, 53. 55.

**Voice,** subst. 1) the sound uttered by the mouth of living creatures, particularly of man (either in speaking or singing): Ven. 134. 429. 921. 978. 1061. Lucr. 1661. Compl. 3. Pilgr. 67. Tp. II, 2, 90. 93. 94. 95. III, 2, 147. Gent. IV, 2, 89. Meas. I, 4, 7. V, 331. Err. V, 300. 307. Ado II, 3, 46. 83. LLL IV, 2, 119. IV, 3, 344. Mids. I, 1, 31. 188. I, 2, 84. III, 1, 88. III, 2, 207. 412. IV, 2, 12. V, 194. Merch. III, 4, 67. V, 110. 113. Tw. III, 1, 99. H5 IV, 4, 72. R3 I, 4, 172 etc. etc. I'll speak in a monstrous little v. Mids. I, 2, 54. to him in thine own v. Tw. IV, 2, 71. haunts poor Tom in the v. of a nightingale, Lr. III, 6, 32.

Applied, metaphorically, to lifeless things: what warlike v. is this? (viz cannon discharged) H8 I, 4, 50. thy (the trumpet's) brass v. Troil. I, 3, 257.

2) he who, or that which, speaks in the name of another: all tongues, the v. of souls, give thee that due, Sonn. 69, 3. I, now the v. of the recorded law, Meas. II, 4, 61. the imagined v. of God himself, H4B IV, 2, 19. in my v. = in my name: implore her in my v. that she make friends to the strict deputy, Meas. I, 2, 185. but what is, come see, and in my v. most welcome shall you be, As II, 4, 87. cf. in second v. we'll not be satisfied: we come to speak with him, Troil. II, 3, 149.

3) words, speech, language: the hardest v. of her behaviour, to be Englished rightly, is 'I am Sir John Falstaff's' Wiv. I, 3, 51. let me have thy v. in my behalf, I, 4, 167 (= speak for me). there my father's grave did utter forth a v. Meas. III, 1, 87. too rude and bold of v. Merch. II, 2, 190. what plea so tainted and corrupt but, being seasoned with a gracious v., obscures the show of evil? III, 2, 76. now we speak upon our cue, and our v. is imperial, H5 III, 6, 131. haply a woman's v. may do some good, V, 2, 93. well didst thou, Richard, to suppress thy v. H6A IV, 1, 182. more deaf than adders to the v. of any true decision, Troil. II, 2, 172. is there no v. more worthy than my own, Caes. III, 1, 49. my v. is in my sword, Mcb. V, 8, 7. you cannot speak of reason to the Dane and lose your v. Hml. I, 2, 45. shouldst not want my v. for thy prefer-

*ment,* Cymb. III, 5, 115. *I have drawn her picture with my v.* Per. IV, 2, 102.

*With one v.* = unanimously: H6B I, 1, 36. Troil. I, 3, 221. cf. *all the country, in a general v., cried hate upon him,* H4B IV, 1, 136. *the common v. do cry 'it shall be so',* Tit. V, 3, 140. *they answer in a joint and corporate v.* Tim. II, 2, 213. *whose —s I desire aloud with mine: 'Hail, king of Scotland',* Mcb. V, 8, 58.

4) that which is said or spoken; talk, report: *in so profound abysm I throw all care of others' —s,* Sonn. 112, 10. *in —s well divulged,* Tw. I, 5, 279. *the v. is now only about her coronation,* H8 III, 2, 406. *the v. goes,* IV, 2, 11. *the common v., I see, is verified of thee,* V, 3, 176. *buy men's —s to commend our deeds,* Caes. II, 1, 146.

5) opinion expressed, judgment: *hath got the v. in hell for excellence,* H5 II, 2, 113. *committing freely your scruple to the v. of Christendom,* H8 II, 2, 88. *who ... opinion crowns with an imperial v.* Troil. I, 3, 187. *till by some elder masters ... I have a v. and precedent of peace,* Hml. V, 2, 260.

6) vote, suffrage: *wanting your father's v.* Mids. I, 1, 54. *the offender's life lies in the mercy of the duke only, 'gainst all other v.* Merch. IV, 1, 356. *o'er whom both sovereign power and father's v. I have to use,* All's II, 3, 60. *that I'll give my v. on Richard's s.* R3 III, 2, 53. *in the duke's behalf I'll give my v.* III, 4, 20. *pronounced your part, I mean your v., for crowning of the king,* 29. *I have no farther gone in this than by a single v.* H8 I, 2, 70. *have their free —s,* II, 2, 94. *it stands agreed by all —s,* V, 3, 88. *divided by any v. or order of the field,* Troil. IV, 5, 70. *the people must have their —s,* Cor. II, 2, 144. II, 3, 1. 41 *(give).* 50 *(give).* 84. 87. 112 *(give).* 116. 119. 132. 133. 134. 136. 137. 140. 145. 147. 164 *(have).* 167. 177. 178. 179. 180. 184. 196. 219. 223 *(of no more v. than dogs).* III, 1, 30. 103. 119. 120. IV, 6, 147 etc. Tit. I, 21. 218. Rom. I, 2, 19. Tim. III, 5, 1. Caes. III, 1, 177 *(your v. shall be as strong as any man's).* IV, 1, 16. Hml. I, 3, 23. 28. V, 2, 367. 403. Oth. I, 2, 13 *(hath a v. potential).* I, 3, 226. 246.

**Voice,** vb. 1) to report, to proclaim: *is this the Athenian minion whom the world —d so regardfully?* Tim. IV, 3, 81.

2) to vote, to nominate: *to v. him consul,* Cor. II, 3, 242.

**Void,** adj. 1) empty, not occupied: *I'll get me to a place more v.* Caes. II, 4, 37 (= less crowded).

2) ineffectual, vain, null: *by this alliance to make v. my suit,* H6C III, 3, 142.

3) destitute: *v. and empty from any dram of mercy,* Merch. IV, 1, 5. With *of: v. of all profanation,* Meas. II, 1, 55 (Elbow's speech). *v. of truth,* Merch. V, 189. *v. of pity,* H6B IV, 7, 69.

**Void,** vb. 1) to evacuate, to emit (saliva and excrementitious matter): *did v. your rheum upon my beard,* Merch. I, 3, 118. *whose low vassal seat the Alps doth spit and v. his rheum upon,* H5 III, 5, 52. *to drink those men upon whose age we v. it up again,* Tim. I, 2, 143.

2) to evacuate, to leave empty, to quit: *bid them come down or v. the field,* H5 IV, 7, 62. *—ing lobby,* = anteroom, a waiting-room for persons not admitted to the presence-chamber: *how in our —ing lobby hast thou stood and duly waited for my coming forth?* H6B IV, 1, 61. cf. *Avoid.*

3) to avoid, to shun: *of all the men i'the world I would have —ed thee,* Cor. IV, 5, 88.

**Volable** (Ff Q2 *voluble*) nimble-witted: LLL III, 67 (Armado's speech).

**Volce** and **Volcian,** see *Volsce* and *Volscian.*

**Volley,** subst. a discharge of many firearms at once: John V, 5, 5. Hml. V, 2, 363. Metaphorically: *a fine v. of words, and quickly shot off,* Gent. II, 4, 33.

**Volley,** vb. to discharge or throw out as with the noise of fire-arms; to thunder forth, to roar forth another flap-mouthed mourner ... against the welkin —s out his voice,* Ven. 921. *the holding every man shall bear as loud as his strong sides can v.* Ant. II, 7, 118.

**Volquessen,** the country of Vexin in France: John II, 527.*

**Volsce,** (O. Edd. *Volce*), one of the Volsci, a Latin people, often at war with Rome: Cor. I, 4, 28. I, 10, 5. Plur. *—s:* I, 1, 228 (O. Edd. *Volscies*). 232. 253 etc.

**Volscian,** (O. Edd. *Volcian* or *Volcean*), 1) subst. = Volsce, q. v.: Cor. IV, 5, 64. 249. IV, 6, 89. V, 3, 178 (fem.). V, 6, 116. 2) adj. pertaining to the Volsci: IV, 3, 11. IV, 7, 22. V, 2, 91. V, 3, 3.

**Voltimand,** name in Hml. I, 2, 34. II, 2, 59.

**Volubility,** fluency of speech: Shr. II, 176. All's IV, 3, 284.

**Voluble,** fluent: *v. and sharp discourse,* Err. II, 1, 92. *so sweet and v. is his discourse,* LLL II, 76.

Applied to persons, = having fluency of speech and a nimble wit: *a most acute juvenal; v. and free of grace,* LLL III, 67 (Armado's speech. Q1 *volable*). *a knave very v.* Oth. II, 1, 242.

**Volume,** 1) as much printed or written paper as is folded and bound together and forms a whole book —s of report run with these false quests,* Meas. IV, 1, 61. *I am for whole —s in folio,* LLL I, 2, 191. *the hand of time shall draw this brief into as huge a v.* John II, 103. *a v. of farewells,* R2 I, 4, 18. *would make a v. of enticing lines,* H6A V, 5, 14. *will bear the knave by the v.* Cor. III, 3, 33 (will bear a whole book full of insults).

2) a book: *furnished me from mine own library with —s,* Tp. I, 2, 167. *this man's brow, like to a titleleaf, foretells the nature of a tragic v.* H4B I, 1, 61. *such indexes, although small pricks to their subsequent —s,* Troil. I, 3, 344. *read o'er the v. of young Paris' face,* Rom. I, 3, 81. 85. *threescore and ten I can remember well, within the v. of which time I have seen hours dreadful,* Mcb. II, 4, 2. *thy commandment all alone shall live within the book and v. of my brain,* Hml. I, 5, 103. *i'the world's v. our Britain seems as off it, but not in it,* Cymb. III, 4, 140. *to place upon the v. of your deeds, as in a title-page, your worth in arms,* Per. II, 3, 3.

**Volumnia,** mother of Coriolanus: Cor. V, 4, 55.

**Volumnius,** name in Caes. V, 5, 15. 16. 21. 22. 25. 31.

**Voluntary,** adj. 1) acting or done by choice and free will: *the right of v. choosing,* Merch. II, 1, 16. *have put themselves into v. exile,* As I, 1, 107. *we swear a v. zeal and an unurged faith,* John V, 2, 10. *giving myself a v. wound,* Caes. II, 1, 300.

Adverbially: *it is but v.* John V, 1, 29. *I serve here v.* Troil. II, 1, 103. *'twas not v.; no man is beaten v.* 105.

Substantively: *fiery —es*, John II, 67 (= volunteers). *Ajax was here the v.* Troil. II, 1, 106.

2) spontaneous, proceeding from an internal impulse: *by their own importunate suit, or v. dotage of some mistress*, Oth. IV, 1, 27.

3) willing, ready: *thy v. oath lives in this bosom*, John III, 3, 23. *that thou wilt be a v. mute to my design*, Cymb. III, 5, 158.

**Voluptuously,** luxuriously, with indulgence of sensual pleasure: Cor. I, 3, 27.

**Voluptuousness,** luxuriousness, intemperance in sensual gratification: Mcb. IV, 3, 61 (= lust). Ant. I, 4, 26.

**Vomit,** subst. matter thrown up from the stomach: H4B I, 3, 99. Oth. II, 3, 86.

**Vomit,** vb. to throw up from the stomach: Lucr. 703. Tit. III, 1, 232. Cymb. I, 6, 45. With *forth:* R3 V, 3, 318.

**Votaress** (trisyll. in Per.; dissyll. and spelt *votresse* in Mids.) a woman that has taken a vow: Mids. II, 1, 123. 163. Per. IV Prol. 4.

**Votarist,** votary, one who has taken a vow; masc.: Tim. IV, 3, 27. fem.: Meas. I, 4, 5. Oth. IV, 2, 190.

**Votary,** the same; masc.: Gent. I, 1, 52. III, 2, 58. LLL II, 37. IV, 2, 141, V, 2, 892. fem.: Sonn. 154, 5.

**Votress,** see *Votaress.*

**Vouch,** subst. testimony, attestation: *my v. against you*, Meas. II, 4, 156. *and make my v. as strong as shore of rock*, H8 I, 1, 157. *to beg of Hob and Dick ... their needless —es*, Cor. II, 3, 124. *one that in the authority of her merit did justly put on the v. of very malice itself*, Oth. II, 1, 147.

**Vouch,** vb. 1) to bear witness, to give testimony: *v. with me, heaven, I therefore beg it not*, Oth. I, 3, 262.

2) to warrant, to be surety for: *most fain would steal what law does v. mine own*, All's II, 5, 87. *will his vouchers v. him no more of his purchases*, Hml. V, 1, 117.

3) to answer for, to make good (cf. avouch): *we here receive it a certainty, —ed from our cousin Austria*, All's I, 2, 5. *where I will v. the truth of it*, Cor. V, 6, 5. *what villain was it spake that word? He that would v. it in any place but here*, Tit. I, 360.

4) to maintain, to assert: *almost beyond credit, as many —ed rarities are*, Tp. II, 1, 60. *a man that never yet did, as he —es, misreport your grace*, Meas. V, 148. *what can you v. against him?* 326. *which, to the spire and top of praises —ed, would seem but modest*, Cor. I, 9, 24. *which, I dare v., is more than that he hath*, III, 1, 300. *the feast is sold that is not often —ed, while 'tis a-making, 'tis given with welcome*, Mcb. III, 4, 34. *I therefore v. again that with some mixtures ... he wrought upon her*, Oth. I, 3, 103. 106. *this gentleman —ing ... his to be more fair*, Cymb. I, 4, 63 (cf. *Disvouch*).

**Voucher,** witness, attestation: *with his statutes, his recognizances, his fines, his double —s, his recoveries*, Hml. V, 1, 114. *will his —s vouch him no more*, 117. *on her left breast a mole ..., here's a v. stronger than ever law could make*, Cymb. II, 2, 39.

**Vouchsafe,** 1) with an inf., = to condescend, to deign: *v. to alight thy steed*, Ven. 13. *v. to afford some present speed*, Lucr. 1305. *wilt thou ... not once v. to hide my will in thine*, Sonn. 135, 6. *that you v. ...*

*to excuse*, LLL V, 2, 741. *that you have —d ... my poor house to visit*, Wint. V, 3, 4. *—ing here to visit me*, Ant. V, 2, 160. Err. V, 393. LLL II, 109. V, 2, 165. 201. 205. 238. John II, 416. 523. H5 V, 2, 99. H6A II, 2, 40. III, 1, 27. V, 3, 103. V, 5, 89. H6C III, 3, 55. 110. 203. R3 I, 2, 75. 78. 202. H8 II, 3, 71. Ant. I, 4, 8 (F1 *v.*, later Ff *did v.*).

2) to grant in condescension; a) with a subordinate clause: *v. my prayer may know*, Tp. I, 2, 422. *v. to those that have not read the story, that I may prompt them*, H5 V Chor. 1. *if Brutus will v. that Antony may safely come to him*, Caes. III, 1, 130.

b) with an accus.: *v. a word*, Meas. III, 1, 152. *do but v. one change*, LLL V, 2, 209. *v. some motion to it*, 216. *our ears v. it*, 217. 344. *to your own most pregnant and —d ear*, Tw. III, 1, 100. 101. *the French amazed v. a parle*, John II, 226. *that you v. your rest here in our court*, Hml. II, 2, 13. *if your lordship would v. the answer*, V, 2, 176. *she —s no notice*, Cymb. II, 3, 45.

With accus. and dative: *v. me but this loving thought*, Sonn. 32, 9. *v. me your picture*, Gent. IV, 2, 121. *v. me one fair look*, V, 4, 23. *that she v. me audience*, LLL V, 2, 313. *if you v. me hearing and respect*, H4A IV, 3, 31. *will you v. me a few disputations with you*, H5 III, 2, 101. *to v. one glance unto the ground*, H6B I, 2, 16. *will you v. me a word*, Troil. III, 1, 64. Tim. I, 2, 183. Hml. III, 2, 307. *that you'll v. me raiment*, Lr. II, 4, 158. Improperly used by Mrs Quickly: Wiv. II, 2, 42. 45.

With accus. and inf., = to allow: *v. me speak a word*, Err. V, 282. The inf. understood, though not expressed: *I'll bring you thither, if you'll v. me*, Ado III, 2, 4. cf. LLL V, 2, 888.

3) to receive or accept in condescension: *our prayers come in, if thou v. them*, John III, 1, 294. *if your back cannot v. this burthen*, H8 II, 3, 43. *v. my labour*, Tim. I, 1, 152. *v. good morrow from a feeble tongue*, Caes. II, 1, 313.

**Vow,** subst. 1) a solemn promise: Ven. 425. Lucr. 809 (*wedlock v.*). 1843. Sonn. 152, 7. Compl. 173. 179. 263. Pilgr. 35. 239. Tp. IV, 54. 96. Gent. III, 2, 70. IV, 2, 9. 98. Wiv. II, 2, 259 (*marriage v.*). Meas. III, 1, 235. IV, 2, 180 (*the v. of my order*). IV, 3, 149. V, 228. Err. II, 2, 140. LLL IV, 3, 66. 68. 70. 113. 311. 319. Mids. III, 2, 124. 130. Merch. III, 4, 27. All's II, 3, 97. III, 4, 7. IV, 2, 14. V, 3, 142. 171 (*heaven's —s*). 173. Tw. II, 4, 121. III, 4, 329. Wint. IV, 4, 497 (*it does fulfil my v.*). V, 3, 138. John III, 1, 229. 288. IV, 3, 67. H6A II, 2, 7. III, 2, 85. H6B V, 1, 184. H6C II, 3, 34. III, 3, 250 (*to pledge my v.*). IV, 1, 141. R3 III, 7, 180. H8 II, 1, 88. Troil. IV, 4, 39. V, 1, 49. V, 2, 139 V, 3, 16. 23. Tit. II, 3, 125 (*nuptial v.*). Rom. I, 1, 229. II, 2, 127. II, 3, 62. Tim. IV, 2, 11. Hml. I, 3, 114 (*all the holy —s of heaven*). 117. 127. III, 1, 164. III, 4, 44. IV, 5, 131. Lr. IV, 6, 267. Oth. I, 3, 362. III, 3, 461. Cymb. III, 2, 47. III, 4, 56. Per. III, 3, 27. The thing promised with *of: a v. of single life*, Mids. I, 1, 121. *—s of faith*, Merch. V, 19. *your —s of love*, Caes. II, 1, 272. The person to whom a promise is made, with *to: your —s to her and me*, Mids. III, 2, 132. Troil. I, 3, 270. *To break a v.*, Sonn. 152, 3 (*thy bed v. broke*). Gent. II, 6, 11. LLL IV, 3, 63. 72. 178. Mids. I, 1, 175. H4A III, 2, 159. R3 I, 4, 211. Lr. I, 1, 171. Ant. I, 3, 30. cf. Lucr. 809. *so hold your v.*

LLL V, 2, 345 (intr.? cf. Troil. V, 3, 24). *to infringe a v.* H6C II, 2, 8. Cor. V, 3, 20. *to keep a v.* John III, 1, 279. H5 IV, 7, 146. 151. *to make a v.* Lucr. 1847. LLL II, 22. IV, 3, 318. As III, 5, 73. R2 I, 1, 118. H6C IV, 3, 4. Troil. Prol. 7. I, 2, 308. Cor. I, 6, 57. Tit. III, 1, 280. Hml. II, 2, 70. Cymb. II, 4, 111. *to make a v. to:* John III, 1, 265. H4A IV, 3, 75. Hml. I, 5, 49. Cymb. III, 2, 12. *the — s we made each other,* Tw. V, 221. *to swear a v.* Rom. II Prol. 10. *to violate a v.* As III, 2, 141. *a v. vowed,* All's IV, 2, 22.

2) a solemn asseveration: *I may not, verily. Verily! you put me off with limber — s,* Wint. I, 2, 47. *as surely as my soul intends to live ....,* I *do believe that violent hands were laid upon the life of this thrice-famed duke. What instance gives Lord Warwick for his v.?* H6B III, 2, 159. *heaven, set ope thy everlasting gates, to entertain my — s of thanks and praise,* IV, 9, 14. cf. R3 II, 1, 42. V, 3, 98. Lr. I, 1, 171.

**Vow,** vb. 1) to promise in a solemn manner; absol.: *till now did ne'er invite, nor never v.* Compl. 182 (M. Edd. *woo,* for the sake of the rhyme). *when you have — ed, you must not speak with men,* Meas. I, 4, 10 (i. e. when you have made your profession). *when I v., I weep,* Mids. III, 2, 124. 153. With an accus. denoting the thing promised: *now he — s a league, and now invasion,* Lucr. 287. *that he may v. revenge on him,* 1179. Sonn. 89, 13. 123, 13. 152, 4. Gent. IV, 3, 21. All's III, 6, 87. John II, 237. R2 I, 3, 49. H6A III, 1, 167. H6B IV, 2, 70. H6C I, 1, 55. II, 1, 30. Troil. III, 2, 93. V, 5, 31. Cor. IV, 6, 67. Oth. III, 3, 21. Per. II, 5, 11. With *to* before the person to whom something is promised: *never faith could hold, if not to beauty —ed,* Pilgr. 58 and LLL IV, 2, 110. *I have — ed to Jaquenetta to hold the plough,* V, 2, 892. All's IV, 3, 260. H6C II, 3, 29. Followed by an infinitive: Ven. Ded. 3. Lucr. Arg. 22. Sonn. 154, 3. Err. V, 182. LLL IV, 3, 296. V, 2, 892. Shr. IV, 2, 28. Wint. III, 2, 243. H6A III, 2, 77. IV, 1, 14. V, 5, 31. H6B IV, 4, 31. H6C I, 1, 160. Troil. III, 2, 84. Tit. V, 1, 81. Rom. III, 3, 129. By a clause: Merch. IV, 1, 442. Shr. IV, 5, 15. H6B I, 3, 203. H6C I, 1, 24. II, 3, 29. Tit. II, 3, 296.

2) to asseverate, to protest solemnly: *or else, by Jove I v.,* I *should have scratched out your eyes,* Gent. IV, 4, 208. *when thou unurged wouldst v. that never words were music to thine ear,* Err. II, 2, 115. *she thought, I dare v. for her, they touched not any stranger sense,* All's I, 3, 113. *he heard him swear and v. to God he came but to be duke of Lancaster,* H4A IV, 3, 60. *we v. to heaven and to his highness that what we did was mildly as we might,* Tit. I, 474.

3) Partic. *—ed* = a) confirmed by oath, sworn to: *with a —ed contract,* Meas. V, 209. *heavenly oaths, —ed with integrity,* LLL V, 2, 356. *the plain single vow that is —ed true,* All's IV, 2, 22.

b) sworn, constant, inveterate: *so mighty are his —ed enemies,* H6B III, 1, 220. *you were —ed Duke Humphrey's foes,* III, 2, 182. *thy —ed friend,* H6C III, 3, 50.

**Vowel,** a letter which represents a simple sound: *the five — s,* LLL V, 1, 56. Rom. III, 2, 46.

**Vow-fellow,** one bound by the same vow: LLL II, 38.

**Vox,** in the Latin of the clown, = a full and loud voice: *I do but read madness: an your ladyship will have it as it ought to be, you must allow V.* Tw. V, 304 (cf. *voce opus est,* in Terentius).

**Voyage,** a travel by sea: Tp. V, 208. Gent. II, 3, 47. 48. 56. Err. I, 1, 41 *(make).* IV, 1, 4. Mids. II, 1, 134. As II, 7, 40. Tw. II, 1, 11. II, 4, 81. R2 V, 6, 49. H8 I, 3, 6. Hml. III, 3, 24. IV, 7, 63. Cymb. V, 3, 44. Per. IV, 1, 37. IV, 6, 49. A walk taken on land called so by the seaman Antonio: Tw. III, 3, 7. Metaphorically: *thy loving v. is but for two months victualled,* As V, 4, 197. *in life's uncertain v.* Tim. V, 1, 205. *all the v. of their life is bound in shallows,* Caes. IV, 3, 220.

Used, in jest, of any way or course taken: *if he should intend this v. towards my wife,* Wiv. II, 1, 189; cf. *if you make your v. upon her,* Cymb. I, 4, 170. *is there no young squarer now that will make a v. with him to the devil?* Ado I, 1, 83. *I am bound to your niece; I mean, she is the list of my v.* Tw. III, 1, 86.

**Vulcan,** the god who presided over the art of forging: Ado I, 1, 187. Tw. V, 56. Troil. I, 3, 168 (*V. and his wife,* i. e. Venus). V, 2, 170. Tit. II, 1, 89 (—'s *badge,* i. e. the horns of cuckoldom). Hml. III, 2, 89.

**Vulgar,** adj. common; 1) pertaining or suiting to the common people, plebeian: *he that buildeth on the v. heart,* H4B I, 3, 90 (on the heart of the people). *talk like the v. sort of market-men,* H6A III, 2, 4. *five tribunes to defend their v. wisdoms,* Cor. I, 1, 219. *puff to win a v. station,* II, 1, 231 (among the crowd). *is no less apparent to the v. eye,* IV, 7, 21.

2) low, mean: *too excellent for every v. paper to rehearse,* Sonn. 38, 4. *the prey of every v. thief,* 48, 8. *stale and cheap to the v. company,* H4A III, 2, 41. *stand uncovered to the v. groom,* H6B IV, 1, 128. *be thou familiar, but by no means v.* Hml. I, 3, 61 (German: *mache dich nicht gemein*).

3) ordinary, common-place: *'tis a v. proof,* Tw. III, 1, 135. *as common as any the most v. thing to sense,* Hml. I, 2, 99.

4) of general circulation, public: *the impression which v. scandal stamped upon my brow,* Sonn. 112, 2. *a v. comment will be made of it,* Err. III, 1, 100. *most sure and v.: every one hears that,* Lr. IV, 6, 214. *unregistered in v. fame,* Ant. III, 13, 119.

5) general, common to all: *as naked as the v. air,* John II, 387.

Misapplied by Costard: *most incony v. wit,* LLL IV, 1, 144.

**Vulgar,** subst. 1) the common people: *which the base v. do call three,* LLL I, 2, 51. *so do our v. drench their peasant limbs in blood of princes,* H5 IV, 7, 80. *drive away the v. from the streets,* Caes. I, 1, 75. *— s,* in the same sense: *as bad as those that —s give boldest titles,* Wint. II, 1, 94.

2) the common and vernacular tongue (in the language of Armado and Touchstone): *which to annothanize in the v. — O base and obscure v.!* LLL IV, 1, 69. 70. *abandon, which is in the v. leave,* As V, 1, 53.

**Vulgarly,** before all the people, publicly: *so v. and personally accused,* Meas. V, 160.

**Vulnerable,** susceptible of wounds: *let fall thy blade on v. crests,* Mcb. V, 8, 11.

**Vulture,** the bird Vultur; emblem of voracity: *there cannot be that v. in you to devour so many,* Mcb. IV, 3, 74. Adjectively: *whose v. thought doth pitch the* *price so high, that she will draw his lips' rich treasure dry*, Ven. 551. *her sad behaviour feeds his v. folly*, Lucr. 556.

Emblem of internal torments (in allusion to the fable of Prometheus): *let —s gripe thy guts*, Wiv. I,

3, 94. *let —s vile seize on his lungs*, H4B V, 3, 145. *while the v. of sedition feeds in the bosom of such great commanders*, H6A IV, 3, 47. *to ease the gnawing v. of thy mind*, Tit. V, 2, 31. *she hath tied sharp-toothed unkindness like a v. here*, Lr. II, 4, 137.

# W.

**Waddle**, to walk in a vacillating manner, to toddle: *she could have run and —d all about*, Rom. I, 3, 37.

**Wade**, to walk through a substance that yields to the feet like water: Shr. IV, 1, 80. Wint. V, 2, 50. John II, 42. R2 I, 3, 138. Mcb. III, 4, 137.

**Wafer-cake**, a thin cake: *men's faiths are —s*, H5 II, 3, 53 (i. e. very fragile. Pistol's poetry).

**Waft** (impf. and partic. *waft*: Merch.V, 11. John II, 73) 1) to beckon: *who —s us yonder?* Err. II, 2, 111. *and w. her love to come again to Carthage*, Merch. V, 11. *whom Fortune with her ivory hand —s to her*, Tim. I, 1, 70. *it —s me still*, Hml. I, 4, 78 (Qq *waves*).

2) to cast, to turn quickly: *—ing his eyes to the contrary*, Wint. I, 2, 372. cf. H6B IV, 1, 116.

3) to carry or send over the sea: *a braver choice of dauntless spirits than now the English bottoms have w. o'er*, John II, 73. *w. me safely cross the Channel. ... I must w. thee to thy death*, H6B IV, 1, 114. 116. *shalt w. them over with our royal fleet*, H6C III, 3, 253. *w. her hence to France*, V, 7, 41.

**Waftage**, passage by water: *a ship you sent me to*, *to hire w.* Err. IV, 1, 95. *a strange soul upon the Stygian banks staying for w.* Troil. III, 2, 11.

**Wafture** (O. Edd. *wafter*) the act of waving: *with an angry w. of your hand*, Caes. II, 1, 246.

**Wag**, subst. a merry droll: Gent. V, 4, 86. LLL V, 2, 108. Wint. I, 2, 66. H4A I, 2, 18. 26. 50. IV, 2, 55. H4B I, 2, 200. Perhaps also in Ado V, 1, 16: *if such a one will smile and stroke his beard, and sorrow, w.* (O. Edd. *wagge*), *cry hem, when he should groan*; i. e. and if sorrow, a merry droll, will cry hem etc. A passage variously corrected by the commentators on the supposition, that *w.* must be the homonymous verb.

**Wag**, vb. 1) to stir, to move; a) intr.: *tremble and start at —ing of a straw*, R3 III, 5, 7. *the empress never —s but in her company there is a Moor*, Tit. V, 2, 87.

b) trans.: *no discerner durst w. his tongue in censure*, H8 I, 1, 33. *think with —ing of your tongue to move me*, V, 3, 127. *let me see the proudest ... but w. his finger at thee*, 131. *what have I done, that thou darest w. thy tongue in noise so rude against me?* Hml. III, 4, 39.

2) to move up and down, or from side to side; a) intr.: *his beard ... —ed up and down*, Lucr. 1406. *'tis merry in hall when beards w. all*, H4B V, 3, 37 (when there are only men present). *when you speak best unto the purpose, it is not worth the —ing of your beards*, Cor. II, 1, 96. *until my eyelids will no longer w.* Hml. V, 1, 290.

b) trans.: *forbid the mountain pines to w. their high tops*, Merch. IV, 1, 76. *zephyrs blowing below the violet, not —ing his sweet head*, Cymb. IV, 2, 173.

3) to go one's way: *let them w.; trot, trot*, Wiv. I, 3, 7. *here, boys, here, here! shall we w.?* II, 1, 238. *I will provoke him to't, or let him w.* II, 3, 74. *let us*

*w. then*, 101 (all the mad host's speeches). *thus may we see, quoth he, how the world —s*, As II, 7, 23. As for Ado V, 1, 16, see the preceding article.●

**Wage**, 1) trans. a) to stake, to bet: *the king hath —d with him six Barbary horses*, Hml. V, 2, 154 (Qq *wagered*). *my life I never held but as a pawn to w. against thine enemies*, Lr. I, 1, 158. *I will w. against your gold, gold to it*, Cymb. I, 4, 144.

b) to hazard, to attempt, to venture on, to encounter: *against whose fury ... the aweless lion could not w. the fight*, John I, 266. *too weak to w. an instant trial with the king*, H4A IV, 4, 20. *neglecting an attempt of ease and gain, to wake and w. a danger profitless*, Oth. I, 3, 30. *dared him ... to w. this battle at Pharsalia*, Ant. III, 7, 32. Hence = to undertake, to carry on: *he hath —d new wars 'gainst Pompey*, Ant. III, 4, 3.

c) to pay wages to, to remunerate: *he —d me with his countenance, as if I had been mercenary*, Cor. V, 6, 40.

2) intr. a) to be opposed in combat, to contend, to strive: *choose to w. against the enmity o'the air*, Lr. II, 4, 212.

b) to be opposed as a stake, to be equal: *his taints and honours —d equal with him*, Ant. V, 1, 31. *the commodity —s not with the danger*, Per. IV, 2, 34.

**Wager**, subst. something staked upon a chance; a bet: Tp. II, 1, 28. 32. Shr. V, 2, 70. Cor. I, 4, 1. Hml. V, 2, 271. Cymb. I, 4, 181. III, 2, 73. *I'll hold thee any w.* Merch. III, 4, 62. *to play a w.* Hml. V, 2, 264. *to lay a w.* Hml. V, 2, 106 (*on*). Cymb. II, 4, 95. *if the gods should play some heavenly match and on the w. lay two earthly women*, Merch. III, 5, 85. *to make a w.* Hml. IV, 7, 156 (*on*). Cymb. I, 4, 120 (*against*). *to lose a w.* Hml. V, 2, 219. Cymb. I, 6, 18. *to win a w.* Shr. V, 2, 69. 112. 116. 186.

**Wager**, vb. to bet: *and w. on your heads*, Hml. IV, 7, 135. Ant. II, 5, 16. *hath —ed with him six Barbary horses*, Hml. V, 2, 154 (Ff *waged*). Cymb. V, 5, 182 (later Ff *waged*). *I durst w. she is honest*, Oth. IV, 2, 12. Per. V, 1, 43.

**Wages**, pay given for service: Gent. I, 1, 94. 95. III, 1, 270. As II, 3, 67. II, 4, 94. Wint. I, 2, 94. H4B V, 1, 25. H8 IV, 2, 150. Tim. III, 2, 77. Lr. V, 3, 303 (*all friends shall taste the w. of their virtue*). Cymb. IV, 2, 261 (*home art gone, and ta'en thy w.*).

**Waggish**, frolicsome, wanton, roguish: Mids. I, 1, 240. Cymb. III, 4, 160.

**Waggling**, wagging, shaking, moving from side to side: *I know you by the w. of your head*, Ado II, 1, 119.

**Waggon**, a carriage; a chariot: *we must away, our w. is prepared*, All's IV, 4, 34. *from Dis's w.* Wint. IV, 4, 118. *to hale thy vengeful w. swift away*, Tit. V, 2, 51. *by the w. wheel trot all day long*, 54. *her w. spokes made of long spinners' legs*, Rom. I, 4, 59.

**Waggoner,** charioteer: Tit. V, 2, 48. Rom. I, 4, 64. III, 2, 2.

**Waggon - spoke** and **Waggon - wheel,** see *Waggon.*

**Wagtail,** the bird Motacilla: *spare my gray beard, you w.?* Lr. II, 2, 73.

**Waid,** lection of O. Edd. in Shr. III, 2, 56: *w. in the back and shoulder - shotten.* M. Edd. *swayed* or *weighed.*

**Wail,** to lament, to moan, to mourn; absol.: *begins a —ing note,* Ven. 835. *buy's a minute's mirth to w. a week,* Lucr. 213. *eyes —ing still,* 1508. Sonn. 42, 3. Gent. II, 3, 7. R2 IV, 301. H6A I, 1, 86 *(—ing robes).* R3 II, 2, 34. Rom. III, 2, 128. IV, 5, 31. Hml. II, 2, 151 (Qq *mourn*). Lr. III, 6, 74 *(Tom will make them,* i. e. dogs, *weep and w.).* IV, 6, 184 (Ff *wawl*).

Trans., = to bewail: *to w. his death,* Ven. 1017. *—s his case,* Lucr. 711. 994. 1799. Sonn. 9, 4. 30, 4. Err. IV, 2, 24. LLL V, 2, 759. R2 II, 2, 22. III, 2, 178. H6A I, 1, 51. H6B II, 1, 216. H6C II, 3, 26. V, 4, 1. R3 I, 3, 204. II, 2, 11. 102. 103. III, 5, 61. IV, 4, 99. 348. 392. 394. Troil. IV, 5, 289. Cor. IV, 1, 26. Mcb. III, 1, 122. IV, 3, 8. Ant. III, 2, 58.

**Wailful,** mournful, doleful: *w. sonnets,* Gent. III, 2, 69.

**Wain,** a waggon, a cart; *Charles' w.,* a popular name of the constellation Ursa major: H4A II, 1, 2.

**Wainrope,** a cartrope: *oxen and —s cannot hale them together,* Tw. III, 2, 64.

**Wainscot,** a wooden lining of walls made in panels: As III, 3, 88.

**Waist,** 1) the small part of the human body between the thorax and hips: Lucr. 6. Wiv. I, 3, 46. Ado III, 2, 35. LLL IV, 1, 49. 50. IV, 3, 185. H4A II, 4, 364. H4B I, 2, 162. Hml. II, 2, 236. Lr. IV, 6, 126. In Troil. II, 2, 30 and Hml. I, 2, 198 O. Edd. *waste,* most M. Edd. *waist.*

2) that which is worn round the waist, a girdle: *his neck will come to your w.,* a cord, sir, Meas. III, 2, 42 (i. e. he will be hanged. Elbow's speech). *those sleeping stones, that as a w. doth girdle you about,* John II, 217. *the noble Talbot, who now is girdled with a w. of iron and hemmed about with grim destruction,* H6A IV, 3, 20.

3) the middle part of a ship: *now on the beak, now in the w., the deck,* Tp. I, 2, 197.

**Wait,** 1) trans. a) to stay in expectation of: *w. the season and observe the times,* LLL V, 2, 63. *vast confusion —s, as doth a raven on a sick - fallen beast, the imminent decay of wrested pomp,* John IV, 3, 152. *ready for the way of life or death, I w. the sharpest blow,* Per. I, 1, 55.

b) *to w. attendance,* = to be in attendance: *w. attendance till you hear further from me,* Tim. I, 1, 161.

2) intr. a) to stay or rest in expectation: *not I, but my affairs, have made you w.* Merch. II, 6, 22. *I must w., and watch withal,* Shr. III, 1, 61. H8 V, 2, 7. 17. V, 3, 139. Tim. III, 4, 47. With *for: wretches … that w. for execution,* Gent. IV, 2, 134. Ado I, 3, 16. H6B IV, 1, 62. Tim. III, 4, 20. 46. Caes. I, 2, 310. II, 2, 119.

b) to pay attendance; to do service; to be on duty: *I am to w., though —ing so be hell,* Sonn. 58, 13. *I will … never more in Russian habit w.* LLL V, 2, 401.

*—ing in the court,* H4A I, 2, 78. *to w. at my heels,* H4B I, 2, 18. *where be these warders, that they w. not here?* H6A I, 3, 3. *how often hast thou — ed at my cup,* H6B IV, 1, 56. *your —ing vassals,* R3 II, 1, 121. *the two great cardinals w. in the presence,* H8 III, 1, 17. *who —s there?* V, 2, 4. *I must hence to w.* Rom. I, 3, 103. *I will not w. piniored at your master's court,* Ant. V, 2, 53.

With *on,* = to pay attendance to, to attend as a servant; or to be at the service of: *wrath, envy, treason, rape, and murder's rages, thy heinous hours w. on them as their pages,* Lucr. 910. *I must w. on myself,* Wiv. I, 1, 208. *go w. upon my cousin Shallow,* 282. Shr. I, 1, 213. 238. All's I, 1, 116. H4B II, 2, 190. Tit. II, 1, 10. Ant. IV, 2, 20. *it* (the music) *—s upon some god o'the island,* Tp. I, 2, 388. *I w. upon his pleasure,* Gent. II, 4, 117. *we'll w. upon your grace till after supper,* III, 2, 96. *in every thing I w. upon his will,* All's II, 4, 55. *rebuke and dread correction w. on us,* H4A V, 1, 111 (are at our service). *the noble troops that —ed upon my smiles,* H8 III, 2, 412. *I purpose not to w. on fortune till these wars determine,* Cor. V, 3, 119 (not to be a slave to fortune, i. e. not to live). *to w. upon this new-made empress,* Tit. II, 1, 20. 21. *you murdering ministers, wherever … you w. on nature's mischief,* Mcb. I, 5, 51.

= to take care of, to tend: *whilst I —ed on my tender lambs,* H6A I, 2, 76.

c) to attend, to be about, to follow, to accompany: *more* (joy) *than to us w. in your royal walks,* Mids. V, 31. *w. close; I will not see him,* H4B I, 2, 65 (follow close at my heels). With *on,* = to attend, to be appendant to or united with: *it* (love) *shall be —ed on with* (= by) *jealousy,* Ven. 1137. *danger deviseth shifts, wit —s on fear,* 690. *respect and reason, w. on wrinkled age,* Lucr. 275. *unruly blasts w. on the tender spring,* 869. *greatest scandal —s on greatest state,* 1006. *summer and his pleasures w. on thee,* Sonn. 97, 11. *infirmity which —s upon worn times* (i. e. old age) Wint. V, 1, 142. *didst bring in wonder to w. on treason,* H5 II, 2, 110. *care, mistrust and treason —s on him,* H6C II, 5, 54. *impatience —eth on true sorrow,* III, 3, 42. *good digestion w. on appetite, and health on both,* Mcb. III, 4, 38. *no man on whom perfections w.* Per. I, 1, 79. *new joy w. on you!* V, 3, 102.

Hence = to be with or to go with, to join, to accompany, to follow; originally as a term of courtesy: *my father desires your worships' company. I will w. on him,* Wiv. I, 1, 272. *let us withdraw together … I'll w. upon your honour,* Meas. I, 1, 84. Ado I, 3, 77. III, 5, 61. Mids. III, 1, 202. John V, 7, 98. H4B II, 1, 196. H5 I, 1, 98. R3 I, 3, 323 (Ff *we w. upon your grace;* Qq *we will attend your grace*). II, 1, 140. III, 2, 124. Tit. I, 338. Tim. II, 2, 35. Hml. II, 2, 273. Oth. III, 2, 6. And then = to follow, to accompany in general: *the wealth I have —s on my consent,* Wiv. III, 2, 78. *w. on me home,* All's V, 3, 323. *one good deed dying tongueless slaughters a thousand —ing upon that,* Wint. I, 2, 93. *then my soul shall w. on thee to heaven,* John V, 7, 72. *thy friends are fled to w. upon thy foes,* R2 II, 4, 23. *the maiden cities you talk of may w. on her,* H5 V, 2, 354. *heralds, w. on us,* H6A I, 1, 45. *what means this armed guard that —s upon your grace,* R3 I, 1, 43. *we'll be —ed on,* Tit. IV, 1, 122. *letting 'I dare not' w. upon 'I would',* Mcb. I, 7, 44. *at your age the hey-day in the blood is tame, it's humble, and —s upon the judgment,* Hml. III, 4, 70. *I pray you, good Horatio, w. upon him,* V, 1, 316.

**Waiting-gentlewoman** (not always hyphened in O. Edd.) an upper servant attending on a lady in her chamber: Ado II, 1, 37. II, 2, 14. Wint. III, 3, 74. H4A I, 3, 55.

**Waiting-vassal** (not hyphened in O. Edd.), attendant: R3 II, 1, 121.

**Waiting-women,** upper servants attending on a lady: Troil. V, 2, 91 (*Diana's w.,* i. e. the stars). Lr. IV, 1, 65.

**Wake,** subst. 1) the state of not sleeping, of being awake: *making such difference 'twixt w. and sleep,* H4A III, 1, 219. *got 'tween a sleep and w.* Lr. I, 2, 15 (M.Edd. *asleep and w.*). *and turn his sleep to w.* III, 2, 34.

2) the feast of the dedication of a church (formerly kept by watching all night): *at —s and wassails,* LLL V, 2, 319. *he haunts —s, fairs,* Wint. IV, 3, 109. *march to —s and fairs,* Lr. III, 6, 77.

**Wake,** vb. (impf. and partic. *—d*) 1) trans. to rouse from sleep: Ven. 855. Lucr. 942. Tp. II, 1, 312. V, 49. Err. IV, 4, 35. Ado III, 3, 74. III, 4, 1. Mids. III, 1, 132. IV, 1, 143. Merch. V, 66. R2 I, 3, 132 (*to w. our peace; cf.* IV, 139. Ado V, 1, 102. R3 I, 3, 288. Cor. III, 1, 98. See *Awake*). H4B I, 2, 174. H6B III, 2, 261. R3 IV, 1, 85 (Ff *awaked*). H8 I, 1, 122. IV, 2, 82. Troil. II, 2, 213. IV, 2, 9. Tit. II, 2, 4. II, 4, 13. Rom. IV, 5, 9. Caes. IV, 3, 270. Mcb. II, 2, 24. 74. Lr. I, 2, 55. 58. IV, 7, 18. Oth. II, 2, 258. Ant. IV, 9, 31. V, 2, 323. Metaphorically, = to arouse, to excite, to put in action: *she —s her heart by beating on her breast,* Lucr. 759. *we will not w. your patience,* Ado V, 1, 102 (cf. *to w. our peace,* R2 I, 3, 132; and see *Awake*). *upon his aid to w. Northumberland,* Mcb. III, 6, 31. *to w. and wage a danger profitless,* Oth. I, 3, 30. *answer my —d wrath,* III, 3, 363.

2) refl. to be awakened: *—d herself with laughing,* Ado II, 1, 361. *he will ...find Hector's purpose pointing on him, and w. him to the answer,* Troil. I, 3, 332.

3) intr. a) to be roused from sleep, to cease to sleep, to be awakened: Lucr. 219. 450. Sonn. 87, 14. Tp. II, 1, 209. 217. Gent. I, 1, 80. Err. II, 2, 215. Mids. IV, 1, 152. Merch. I, 1, 85. Shr. Ind. 2, 82. IV, 3, 10. Wint. III, 3, 19 (*ne'er was dream so like a —ing*). H6A II, 1, 56. H6B I, 1, 26. 249. III, 1, 263. III, 2, 227. R3 V, 3, 117. H8 I, 4, 23. Troil. I, 2, 37. Rom. I, 1, 187. Lr. I, 4, 249. III, 6, 43. Cymb. IV, 2, 306. With an accus. denoting the effect: *I'll w. mine eyeballs blind first,* Cymb. III, 4, 104 (O. Edd. *I'll w. mine eyeballs first*). Metaphorically: *to keep thy sharp woes —ing,* Lucr. 1136. *all replication prompt ... for his advantage still did w. and sleep,* Compl. 123. *keep in Tunis, and let Sebastian w.* Tp. II, 1, 260.

= to sit up for amusement, to hold a nightly revel: *for thee watch I whilst thou dost w. elsewhere,* Sonn. 61, 13. *the king doth w. to-night and takes his rouse,* Hml. I, 4, 8.

**Wakefield,** the last battle-field of the Duke of York: H6C II, 1, 107.

**Waken,** to rouse from sleep: H6C IV, 3, 19. Rom. III, 1, 28. IV, 4, 24. Oth. II, 1, 188. Cymb. II, 2, 13. Metaphorically: *in your —ed hate,* Sonn. 117, 12. *your sleepy thoughts, which here we w. to our country's good,* R3 III, 7, 124. *that I might w. reverence,* Troil. I, 3, 227.

**Wales,** principality in the west of England: H4A I, 1, 37. II, 4, 370. III, 1, 45. 76. IV, 3, 95. V, 5, 39. H4B I, 2, 119. II, 1, 189. II, 4, 318. R3 IV, 5, 7. Cymb. III, 2, 62. *Prince of W.,* the title of the hereditary prince of England: R2 II, 1, 172. H4A I, 3, 230. II, 4, 11. III, 2, 1. IV, 1, 95. 121. IV, 4, 29. V, 1, 86. 101. V, 2, 46. V, 4, 12. 42. 63. 67. H4B II, 1, 146. II, 2, 131. IV, 5, 54. H5 II, 4, 56. IV, 7, 97. H6B II, 2, 11. R3 I, 3, 199. 200.

**Walk,** subst. 1) the act of walking or going on foot: *my very w. should be a jig,* Tw. I, 3, 138. *all men ... make it their w.* Mcb. III, 3, 14 (instead of riding).

Used of a tour made by two partners in a masquerade: *I am yours for the w.* Ado II, 1, 92 (cf. Rom. I, 5, 19).

2) way, course: *I will ... be absent from thy —s,* Sonn. 89, 9. *hop in his —s and gambol in his eyes,* Mids. III, 1, 168. *more* (joy) *than to us wait in your royal —s, your board, your bed,* V, 31. *who would live turmoiled in the court, and may enjoy such quiet —s as these?* H6B IV, 10, 19 (cf. the Yorkshire Tragedy I, 4: *never look for prosperous hour, good thoughts, quiet sleep, contented —s, nor anything that makes man perfect*). *let's leave her to her silent —s,* Tit. II, 4, 8. *in the day's glorious w., or peaceful night,* Per. I, 2, 4 (cf. the verb in Merch. V, 128. Tw. III, 1, 43. Hml. I, 1, 167).

3) an avenue set with trees: *Malvolio's coming down this w.* Tw. II, 5, 19.

4) a piece of ground fit to walk and wander in; particularly a park or garden: *the fellow of this w.* Wiv. V, 5, 29 (Dyce, without quoting an authority: 'district in a forest'). *in this close w.* (the Duke of York's garden) H6B II, 2, 3. *my parks, my —s, my manors,* H6C V, 2, 24. *the forest —s are wide and spacious,* Tit. II, 1, 114. *he hath left you all his —s, his private arbours and new-planted orchards,* Caes. III, 2, 252. Applied to a town: *her* (Rome's) *wide —s encompassed but one man,* Caes. I, 2, 155 (M. Edd. unanimously *walls*).

**Walk,** vb. 1) to move slowly on the feet, to step along: *when you —ed, to w. like one of the lions,* Gent. II, 1, 28. 29 (cf. Ven. 1093. H5 II, 2, 122. H6C I, 3, 14). *he would have —ed ten mile a-foot to see a good armour,* Ado II, 3, 16. *to see him w. before a lady and to bear her fan,* LLL IV, 1, 147. *as she —ed overhead,* IV, 3, 281. *let me see thee w.* Shr. II, 258. *and thither w. on foot,* IV, 3, 188. *I can stand and w.* Wint. IV, 3, 120. H4A II, 2, 83. H6C I, 3, 14. Cor. I, 1, 105. IV, 5, 238 (*it's sprightly —ing,* audible, i. e. walking in a lively manner. M. Edd. *sprightly, waking*). V, 4, 19. Lr. I, 4, 247. III, 4, 119. Oth. IV, 3, 39. Ant. I, 5, 20.

Much oftener used than in modern language = to go, to move, and even = to come: *the lion —ed along behind some hedge,* Ven. 1093. *about he —s, rolling his greedy eyeballs,* Lucr. 367. *those dancing chips, o'er whom thy fingers w. with easy gait*, Sonn. 128, 11. *my mistress, when she —s, treads on the ground*, 130, 12. *hope is a lover's staff; w. hence with that*, Gent. III, 1, 246. *as we w. along*, V, 4, 162. *I pray you, sir, w. in*, Wiv. I, 1, 292. *fear ... to w. by this Herne's oak*, IV, 4, 40. *you must w. by us on our other hand*, Meas. V, 17. *let him w. from whence he came*, Err. III, 1, 37. *pleaseth you w. with me down to his house*, IV, 1, 12. *yonder, as I think, he —s*, V, 9 (= he comes; cf. Merch. II, 2, 183). *will you w. in to see their gossiping?* 419. Ado II, 1, 93. Mids. III, 1, 126. Merch. II, 2, 183. As I, 3, 14. Shr. IV, 1, 149. Tw. III, 4, 295. Wint. IV, 4, 855. John III, 4, 94. H4A II, 2, 8. 63. 116. II, 4, 550. III, 3, 49. H4B I, 1, 4. 170. I, 2, 12. H5 II, 1, 61. IV Chor. 30. H6A I, 4, 54. H8 IV, 1, 116. Troil. III, 2, 7. 64. 107. IV, 3, 5. 12. IV, 4, 140. Rom. IV, 1, 79. IV, 2, 44. Caes. II, 2, 8. III, 1, 108. Mcb. II, 1, 57. Hml. II, 2, 185. Oth. V, 2, 30. Cymb. V, 5, 119.

Figuratively: *foolery does w. about the orb like the sun*, Tw. III, 1, 43. *how wildly then —s my estate in France*, John IV, 2, 128. *he's —ed the way of nature*, H4B V, 2, 4 (= has died). *thou hast so long —ed hand in hand with time*, Troil. IV, 5, 203 (= hast lived so long). *that craves wary —ing*, Caes. II, 1, 15. *the morn ... —s o'er the dew of yon high eastward hill*, Hml. I, 1, 167. *with a larger tether may he w. than may be given you*, I, 3, 125.

Often, like to go, = to go away, to come away, to withdraw: *will't please you w. aside?* Meas. IV, 1, 59. *come, we will w.* IV, 5, 12. *will you w.? dinner is ready*, Ado II, 3, 218. *w. aside with me*, III, 2, 73. *w. aside the true folk, and let the traitors stay*, LLL IV, 3, 212. *you may go w. and give me leave awhile*, Shr. III, 1, 59. *we two will w. and leave you to your graver steps*, Wint. I, 2, 172. *will you w. on, my lord?* Tr. IV, 5, 291. *pray you, w. near; I'll speak with you anon*, Tim. II, 2, 132 (leave me, but remain in the vicinity). *will't please your highness w.?* Lr. IV, 7, 83. *will you w., sir?* Oth. IV, 3, 4. *w., let's see if other watchmen do hear what we do*, Ant. IV, 3, 17. *pray, w. awhile*, Cymb. I, 1, 176. cf. Ff in Lr. III, 4, 121.

2) to move or go about for recreation or any other purpose: *a turn or two I'll w., to still my beating mind*, Tp. IV, 162. *I had rather w. here*, Wiv. I, 1, 293. *I love to w. by the Counter-gate*, III, 3, 85. *come, w. in the Park*, 240. *will you w. with me about the town?* Err. I, 2, 22. III, 2, 156. Ado I, 2, 9. III, 1, 5. LLL I, 1, 237. 242. Shr. Ind. 2, 42. II, 112. John V, 6, 17. H4A III, 1, 257. H6B I, 3, 156. R3 I, 4, 12. H8 V, 1, 94. 117. Troil. III, 2, 17. Rom. I, 1, 127. 130. Caes. I, 3, 40. 46. 127. II, 1, 239. III, 2, 256. Mcb. III, 6, 5. 7. Hml. II, 2, 160. 208. III, 1, 43. V, 2, 180. Lr. IV, 6, 17. Oth. III, 2, 3. III, 4, 165. IV, 3, 2. Ant. III, 5, 17. Cymb. I, 1, 104. Per. IV, 1, 28. 30. 40. 46. 49.

Used of a tour in dancing (at a masquerade): *Lady, will you w. about with your friend?* Ado II, 1, 89. 91. *ladies that have their toes unplagued with corns will w. about with you*, Rom. I, 5, 19 (the surreptitious Q1 and most M. Edd. *have a bout*). Hence applied to fighting: *Tybalt, you rat-catcher, will you w.?* Rom. III, 1, 78 (German: *willst Du einen Tanz machen?*).

3) to act and move on the feet in sleep: *when was it she last —ed*, Mcb. V, 1, 3. 13. 66.

4) to move about as a spirit or spectre: *Herne the*

*hunter ... doth at still midnight w. round about an oak* Wiv. IV, 4, 31. *the spirits o'the dead may w. again*, Wint. III, 3, 17. *were I the ghost that —ed*, V, 1, 63. 80. *spirits w.* H6B I, 4, 22. *affairs that w., as they say spirits do, at midnight*, H8 V, 1, 13. *in all shapes ... this spirit —s in*, Tim. II, 2, 121. Caes. I, 3, 25. V, 3, 95. Mcb. II, 3, 84. V, 5, 24 (*life's but a —ing shadow*). Hml. I, 1, 138. 161 (Ff *can w.*, Qq *dares stir*). I, 2, 202. 243. I, 4, 6. I, 5, 10. Lr. III, 4, 121. Similarly: *we should hold day with the Antipodes, if you would w. in absence of the sun*, Merch. V, 128. *now heaven —s on earth*, Tw. V, 100.

5) to go, to be dressed in a particular manner: *she will veiled w.* Tw. I, 1, 28. *when I have —ed like a private man*, Tit. IV, 4, 75. *you ought not w. without the sign of your profession*, Caes. I, 1, 3. *is it physical to w. unbraced*, II, 1, 262. *in his livery —ed crowns and crownets*, Ant. V, 2, 91.

6) to live and follow one's pursuits: *'tis pity that thou livest to w. where any honest men resort*, Err. V, 28. *those that w. and wot not what they* (the stars) *are*, LLL I, 1, 91. *I will buy with you, sell with you, talk with you, w. with you*, Merch. I, 3, 37. *do not then w. too open*, Tw. III, 3, 37. *who dares not stir by day, must w. by night*, John I, 172. *nor attend the foot that leaves the print of blood where'er it —s*, IV, 3, 26. *for ever will I w. upon my knees*, R2 V, 3, 93 (Ff *kneel*). *o'er whose acres —ed those blessed feet*, H4A I, 1, 25. *we w. invisible*, II, 1, 96. 99. *we petty men w. under his huge legs*, Caes. I, 2, 137. *to w. alone* = to be an outcast, to be forsaken: *to w. alone, like one that had the pestilence*, Gent. II, 1, 21. *when wert thou wont to w. alone, dishonoured thus*, Tit. I, 339. *his poor self ... —s, like contempt, alone*, Tim. IV, 2, 15. Similarly: *methinks you w. like a stranger*, Shr. II, 87.

7) Transitively, a) to pass or go through: *do not without danger w. these streets*, Tw. III, 3, 25. *if that same demon ... should with his lion gait w. the whole world*, H5 II, 2, 122. (In Tp. IV, 165. Ado II, 3, 16. Hml. I, 5, 10 not trans., but with an accus. of the measure. see *Wing* vb.).

b) to cause to step slowly, to lead or ride with a slow pace: *I will rather trust ... a thief to w. my ambling gelding*, Wiv. II, 2, 319.

**Walking-staff,** a staff carried for support in walking: *a palmer's w.* R2 III, 3, 151.

**Wall,** subst. a structure raised to enclose and defend a place: Mids. III, 1, 64. 66. 67. 69 etc. V, 133 etc. 210 (*when —s are so wilful to hear without warning*). Wint. IV, 4, 818. H6B IV, 10, 7. 37. H6C II, 4, 4 (*a brazen w.*). Tit. V, 1, 24. Rom. I, 1, 20. 22. II, 1, 5. Proverbial: *hunger broke stone —s*, Cor. I, 1, 210. *how has the ass broke the w., that thou art out of the city?* Tim. IV, 3, 354. *I will take the w. of any man or maid*, Rom. I, 1, 15 (= get the better of); cf. 21. *the weakest goes to the w.* 18 (cf. the Life and Death of Thomas Lord Cromwell, III, 3: *though the drops be small, yet have they force to force men to the wall*).

= fortification: John IV, 3, 1. R2 II, 1, 47. III, 2, 170. H5 III, 1, 2. H6A IV, 2, 2. H6C V, 1, 17. Tim. IV, 1, 1. 38. Plur. *—s*: Lucr. 1429. Tp. II, 1, 87. Merch. V, 4. Shr. II, 369 (*Pisa —s*). John II, 198. 201 etc. H5 V, 2, 349. H6A I, 2, 40. I, 6, 1. II, 1, 3. II, 2, 25. III, 2, 69. H6C V, 1, 16. R3 IV, 1, 100. Troil. I, 1, 2 etc. Cor. I, 4, 13. I, 8, 8 (*Corioli —s*) etc. Rom.

III, 3, 17 (*Verona —s*). Tim. V, 1, 170. V, 4, 22. Mcb. V, 5, 1 etc. Figuratively: *rude ram, to batter such an ivory w.* Lucr. 464. *723. they of those marches ... shall be a w. sufficient to defend our inland,* H5 I, 2, 141. *take thou my soldiers, prisoners, patrimony: dispose of them: the walls are thine,* Lr. V, 3, 77 (= I surrender at discretion. F1 *the walls is thine;* Qq om.). *the heavens hold firm the —s of thy dear honour,* Cymb. II, 1, 68.

= the structure enclosing a building and its several rooms: LLL V, 2, 922 (*when icicles hang by the w.*). Merch. II, 9, 29. R2 I, 2, 68. V, 2, 15. V, 5, 21. H4B II, 1, 156. H5 Prol. 19. III, 3, 37. H6A I, 4, 49. R3 III, 3, 11. III, 5, 17. Rom. I, 3, 27. Hml. V, 1, 239. Lr. II, 2, 72. *to hang by the w.* = not to be made use of, to be neglected: *the enrolled penalties which have, like unscoured armour, hung by the w.* Meas. I, 2, 171. *than picture-like to hang by the w.* Cor. I, 3, 12. *I am richer than to hang by the —s,* Cymb. III, 4, 54. Figuratively: *through crystal —s each little mote will peep,* Lucr. 1251. *a liquid prisoner pent in —s of glass,* Sonn. 5, 10. Used of the human body as the external part of man: *painting thy outward —s so costly gay,* Sonn. 146, 4. *nature with a beauteous w. doth oft close in pollution,* Tw. I, 2, 48. *within this w. of flesh,* John III, 3, 20. *ye white-limed —s,* Tit. IV, 2, 98. cf. *out-wall* in Lr. III, 1, 45.

**Wall,** vb. to enclose and defend with a wall: *this flesh which —s about our life,* R2 III, 2, 167. *—ed =* surrounded with walls, fortified: As III, 3, 59. H6A III, 4, 7. Lr. V, 3, 18. Cymb. V, 3, 14. *a lady —ed about with diamonds,* LLL V, 2, 3. cf. *Sea-walled.*

With *from,* = to hinder as by a wall opposed: *on either hand thee there are squadrons pitched, to w. thee from the liberty of flight,* H6A IV, 2, 24.

**Wallet,** 1) any thing protuberant and swagging: *whose throats had hanging at 'em —s of flesh,* Tp. III, 3, 46.

2) a knapsack: Troil. III, 3, 145.

**Wall-eyed,** glaring-eyed, fierce-eyed: *w. wrath or staring rage,* John IV, 3, 49. *say, w. slave,* Tit. V, 1, 44 (As for the origin of the expression, Nares observes: *Whally,* applied to eyes, means discoloured, or, what are now called wall-eyes; from *whaule,* or *whall,* the disease of the eyes called glaucoma).

**Wall-newt,** a sort of lizard: *the w. and the water,* Lr. III, 4, 135.

**Walloon** (O. Edd. *Wallon*), 1) the border-country between the Netherlands and France: *the regions of Artois, W. and Picardy,* H6A II, 1, 10. 2) a native of it: *a base W.* I, 1, 137.

**Wallow,** to roll one's body: *w. in December snow,* R2 I, 3, 298. *in the lily-beds,* Troil. III, 2, 13.

**Walnut,** the fruit of Juglans regia: Wiv. IV, 2, 171. *a w. shell,* Shr. IV, 3, 66.

**Walter,** name of 1) Sir W. Blunt: H4A I, 1, 63. 69. IV, 3, 32. 107. V, 3, 32. 63. 2) Sir W. Herbert: R3 IV, 5, 9. 3) W. Lord Ferrers: R3 V, 5, 13 (Qq *Water*). 4) W. Whitmore: H6B IV, 1, 14. 31. 38. 115. 5) a servant of Petruchio: Shr. IV, 1, 92. 138.

**Wan,** adj. pale: H4A I, 1, 1. *pale and w.* Err. IV, 4, 111. Tit. II, 3, 90.

**Wan,** vb. to turn pale: *that from her working all his visage —ned,* Hml. II, 2, 580 (Ff *warmed*). In Ant. II, 1, 21 O. Edd. *her wand lip;* M. Edd. *waned:* perhaps *wanned.*

**Wand,** 1) a small twig, a rod: Gent. II, 3, 23. Merch. I, 3, 85.

2) a staff of authority: H6B I, 2, 28.

**Wander,** to go here and there without a certain object, to roam, to ramble: *in thy weak hive a —ing wasp hath crept,* Lucr. 839. *to make it w. in an unknown field,* Err. III, 2, 38. *a —ing knight,* Mids. I, 2, 47. H4A I, 2, 16. *he gives them good leave to w.* As I, 1, 109. *when I w. here and there,* Wint. IV, 3, 17. *a grain, a dust, a gnat, a —ing hair,* John IV, 1, 93. R2 I, 3, 270. 308. II, 3, 120. V, 6, 43. H6A V, 3, 188. R3 I, 4, 39 (*the —ing air*). Troil. I, 1, 105 (*the —ing flood*). Tit. II, 3, 22. Per. I, 1, 96 (*the —ing wind*). Used of celestial bodies: *swifter than the —ing moon,* Mids. IV, 1, 103. *by Phoebus, he, the —ing knight so fair,* H4A I, 2, 16. *ruled like a —ing planet over me,* H6B IV, 4, 16. *when the planets in evil mixture to disorder w.* Troil. I, 3, 95. *conjures the —ing stars,* Hml. V, 1, 279. Used of spirits and walking ghosts: *w., a word for shadows like myself,* Pilgr. 191. *whither w. you?* (viz Puck) Mids. II, 1, 1. *I do w. every where,* 6. *ghosts —ing here and there,* III, 2, 381. *one of our souls had —ed in the air,* R2 I, 3, 195. *then came —ing by a shadow,* R3 I, 4, 52. cf. *sits Sin, to seize the souls that w. by him,* Lucr. 882. *nor shall Death brag thou —est in his shade,* Sonn. 18, 11.

Implying the idea of error, = to go astray, to deviate: *here we w. in illusions,* Err. IV, 3, 43. *how now, wit! whither w. you?* As I, 2, 59 (quibbling). *to cast thy —ing eyes on every stale,* Shr. III, 1, 90. *wherein my youth hath faulty —ed,* H4A III, 2, 27. *return, thou —ing lord,* H6A III, 3, 76. *you w. from the good we aim at,* H8 III, 1, 138.

Often = to travel, to walk, to go: *it is the star to every —ing bark,* Sonn. 116, 7. *again to make me w. thither,* Pilgr. 190. *as he in penance —ed through the forest,* Gent. V, 2, 38. *w. up and down to view the city,* Err. I, 2, 31. *the heedful slave is —ed forth in care to seek me out,* II, 2, 3. *you faint with —ing in the wood,* Mids. II, 2, 35. *and w. we to see thy honest son,* Shr. IV, 5, 69. *—ed hither to an obscure plot,* Tit. II, 3, 77. *what cursed foot —s this way?* Rom. V, 3, 19. R2 III, 2, 49. H5 IV, 7, 75. R3 IV, 1, 3. IV, 4, 514. Tim. V, 4, 7. Caes. III, 3, 3. Ant. I, 1, 53. Cymb. III, 5, 105. IV, 2, 371.

**Wanderer,** one that wanders; used of creatures stirring but by night: *I am that merry w. of the night,* Mids. II, 1, 43. *hast thou the flower there? welcome, w.* 247. *the wrathful skies gallow the very —s of the dark,* Lr. III, 2, 44. cf. *Night-wanderer* and *Night-wandering.*

**Wanderingly,** writing of some M. Edd. for *wondringly* of O. Edd. in Per. III, 3, 7.

**Wand-like,** like a rod or staff: *w. straight,* Per. V, 1, 110.

**Wane,** subst. decrease: *he is in the w.* (viz the man representing the moon) Mids. V, 258.

**Wane,** vb. to decrease; to decline: *in —ing age,* Lucr. 142. Shr. Ind. 2, 65. II, 403. *as fast as thou shalt w., so fast thou growest in one of thine,* Sonn. 11, 1. *who hast by —ing grown, and therein showest thy lovers withering as thy sweet self growest,* 126, 3. *how slow this old moon —s,* Mids. I, 1, 4. *I seek not to wax great by others' —ing,* H6B IV, 10, 22 (O. Edd. *warning. I shall interche ge my —d state for Henry's regal crown,* H6C IV, 7, 4. *to watch the —ing of my* *adversaries*, R3 IV, 4, 4. In Ant. II, 1, 21 O. Edd. *thy wand lip*; M. Edd. *waned; perhaps wanned. cf. Beauty-waning.*

**Wanion** or **Wannion,** 'used only in the phrase *with a w.*, but totally unexplained, though exceedingly common in use; seemingly equivalent to with a vengeance, or with a plague' (Nares): *come away, or I'll fetch thee with a w.* Per. II, 1, 17.

**Want,** subst. 1) the state of not having; absence of a necessary thing or quality: *spites me more than all these —s,* Shr. IV, 3, 11. *she wants nothing, to name w., if w. it be not that she is not he,* John II, 435. *what that w. might ruin,* Cor. III, 2, 69. Lr. I, 1, 282 (exclusion from the inheritance). With *of* or a genitive: *how w. of love tormenteth,* Ven. 202. *no w. of conscience hold it,* Sonn. 151, 13. *whose w. and whose delay is strewed with sweets,* All's II, 4, 45. Wint. II, 1, 109. R2 III, 4, 16. 72. H4A III, 1, 184. IV, 1, 44 (*his present w.* = the present w. of him, i. e. his being absent at present). H5 V, 2, 69. H6A I, 1, 69. H6B IV, 8, 65. H6C I, 4, 133. V, 2, 8 etc. *for w. of:* Lucr. 153. 1099. Tp. II, 1, 146. Gent. I, 1, 31. 172. Wiv. III, 2, 14. Err. II, 2, 181. LLL V, 2, 719. Mids. I, 1, 130. All's IV, 1, 77. Tw. I, 5, 70. H5 V, 2, 57. H6B III, 1, 33 etc.

2) indigence, state of being without means: *where w. cries some,* Compl. 42. *no man will supply thy w.* Pilgr. 410. *scarcity and w. shall shun you,* Tp. IV, 116. *feel w.* R2 III, 2, 175. *one that surfeits thinking on a w.* H6B III, 2, 348. Tim. II, 2, 63. Hml. III, 2, 218. Ant. III, 12, 30.

3) need, necessity, occasion for sth.: *nothing wants that w. itself doth seek,* LLL IV, 3, 237. *to supply the ripe —s of my friend,* Merch. I, 3, 64. 141. R2 I, 4, 51. *my master's —s,* Tim. II, 2, 29. 190. *your greatest w. is, you want much of meat,* IV, 3, 419. *the w. is but to put those powers in motion,* Cymb. IV, 3, 31.

**Want,** vb. 1) not to have, to be without: *that golden hap which their superiors w.* Lucr. 42. *to w. his bliss,* 389. *—ing the spring that those shrunk pipes had fed,* 1455. *eyes this cunning w. to grace their art,* Sonn. 24, 13. *how can my Muse w. subject to invent,* 38, 1. *those parts of thee ... w. nothing that the thought of hearts can mend,* 69, 2. *unripe years did w. conceit,* Pilgr. 51. *much less take what I shall die to w.* Tp. III, 1, 79. III, 3, 25. 38. IV, 58. Epil. 13. Gent. II, 4, 112. II, 6, 12. III, 1, 147. Wiv. II, 2, 268. 270. V, 5, 144. Err. I, 1, 8. II, 2, 153. IV, 1, 4. Ado III, 2, 20. LLL IV, 2, 81. Mids. I, 1, 54. II, 1, 101. Merch. V, 205. As III, 2, 26. III, 3, 64. Shr. Ind. 1, 104. III, 2, 5. All's I, 1, 81. II, 4, 4. Wint. I, 2, 128. III, 2, 56 (*—ed less,* = had less; see Appendix). IV, 2, 15. IV, 4, 617. John II, 435. R2 III, 3, 179. H4A I, 2, 225. H6A I, 1, 75. Troil. III, 3, 25. Per. I, 4, 19 etc. *did w. of what I was in the morning,* Ant. II, 2, 76 (*of* used partitively, = part of what; cf. *Of*). *—ing of thy love,* Rom. II, 2, 78 (cf. *Of*). As for the phrase *the want that you have —ed,* Lr. I, 1, 282, see *Ruin,* vb., and cf. *wrong* in Err. II, 2, 174.

2) to need, to have occasion for; abs.: *what help we have that to your —ing may be ministered,* As II, 7, 126. Trans.: *what thou —est shall be sent after thee,* Gent. I, 3, 74. *a man of such perfection as we do in our quality much w.* IV, 1, 58. Meas. IV, 2, 154. Err. II, 2, 57. III, 1, 77. LLL V, 2, 887. Mids. I, 2, 108. Wint. IV, 3, 87. John IV, 3, 187. H4A I, 2, 175. H6A

I, 2, 27. III, 2, 41. H6B III, 1, 236. H6C V, 1, 66. R3 III, 4, 5. 89. Per. I, 4, 11. II, 3, 101. Hence = to wish for: *such things that w. no ear but yours,* Meas. IV, 3, 109. *I w. more uncles here to welcome me,* R3 III, 1, 6. *those uncles which you w. are dangerous,* 12. cf. Per. II, 3, 101.

3) to suffer indigence: *but, poorly rich, so —eth in his store,* Lucr. 97. *a swallowing gulf that even in plenty —eth,* 557. *why should you w.?* Tim. IV, 3, 420. *if heaven slumber while their creatures w.* Per. I, 4, 16. With *for: he cannot w. for money,* Tim. III, 2, 10 (= he cannot want money).

4) to be wanted, to be missed, not to be in sufficient quantity: *the cause of this fair gift in me is —ing,* Sonn. 87, 7. *there —eth but a man to fill your song,* Gent. I, 2, 95. *there w. not many that do fear ... to walk by this Herne's oak,* Wiv. IV, 4, 39. *where nothing —s that want themselves,* LLL III, 3, 237. Shr. III, 2, 248. 250. All's I, 1, 11. R2 III, 4, 13. H6A I, 1, 82. H6C II, 6, 102. R3 II, 1, 43. Cor. II, 1, 217. 271. Lr. IV, 6, 269. Cymb. IV, 3, 20. (Perhaps also in LLL V, 2, 887 and R3 III, 4, 5).

**Wanton,** adj. 1) playful, sportive, frolicsome: *w. modesty,* Lucr. 401. *playing in the w. air,* Pilgr. 230 and LLL IV, 3, 104. *all w. as a child, skipping and vain,* V, 2, 771. *make such w. gambols with the wind,* Merch. III, 2, 93. *a wild and w. herd,* V, 71. Wint. I, 2, 126. John III, 3, 36. R2 V, 1, 101. H4A IV, 1, 103. H4B IV, 1, 55. H6C I, 4, 74. H8 III, 2, 359. Rom. II, 6, 19. Hml. II, 1, 22. Lr. IV, 1, 38.

2) loose, light, trifling, petulant, frivolous: *dare you presume to harbour w. lines,* Gent. I, 2, 42. *the injuries of a w. time,* H4A V, 1, 50. *every idle, nice and w. reason,* H4B IV, 1, 191. *how sleek and w. you appear in every thing may bring my ruin,* H8 III, 2, 241.

3) luxuriant; luxurious: *the quaint mazes in the w. green,* Mids. II, 1, 99. *four lagging winters and four w. springs,* R2 I, 3, 214. *on the w. rushes lay you down,* H4A III, 1, 214. *a guard too w. for the head,* H4B I, 1, 148. *yond towers whose w. tops do buss the clouds,* Troil. IV, 5, 220. *now comes the w. blood up in your cheeks, they'll be in scarlet straight at any news,* Rom. II, 5, 72. *my plenteous joys, w. in fulness,* Mcb. I, 4, 34.

4) lustful, lascivious: *bewitching like the w. mermaid's song,* Ven. 777. *mine ears that to your w. talk attended,* 809. *nor could she moralize his w. sight,* Lucr. 104. *this glove to w. tricks is not inured,* 320. *the teeming autumn ... bearing the w. burden of the prime,* Sonn. 97, 7. *to have done some w. charm upon this man and maid,* Tp. IV, 95. *the w. stings and motions of the sense,* Meas. I, 4, 59. LLL IV, 3, 58. Mids. II, 1, 129. Shr. Ind. I, 47. All's III, 7, 18. V, 3, 211. Tw. III, 1, 18. 23. H6A III, 1, 19. V, 1, 23. H6C III, 3, 210. R3 I, 1, 17. III, 7, 187 (Qq *lustful*). Troil. Prol. 10. III, 3, 222. IV, 5, 56. Cor. II, 1, 233. Oth. I, 3, 270. *let the bloat king tempt you again to bed, pinch w. on your cheek,* Hml. III, 4, 183 (cf. *Pinch*). *he hath not yet made w. the night with her,* Oth. II, 3, 16.

**Wanton,** subst. 1) one apt to play and dally; a merry rogue, a tomboy: *her hair ... played with her breath; O modest —s!* Lucr. 401. *nay then, the w. lies,* Gent. V, 2, 10. *your worship's a w.* Wiv. II, 2, 57. *a whitely w.* LLL III, 198. *tarry, rash w.* Mids. II, 1, 63. *shall we play the —s with our woes,* R2 III,

3, 164. *let —s light of heart tickle the senseless rushes,* Rom. I, 4, 35. *no further than a —'s bird,* II, 2, 178. *down, —s, down,* Lr. II, 4, 126.

2) one brought up in luxury, an effeminate boy: *a beardless boy, a cockered silken w.* John V, 1, 70. *young w. and effeminate boy,* R2 V, 3, 10. *you make a w. of me,* Hml. V, 2, 310. *not so citizen a w. as to seem to die ere sick,* Cymb. IV, 2, 8.

3) a lascivious woman: *not to knit my soul to an approved w.* Ado IV, 1, 45. *to lip a w. in a secure couch,* Oth. IV, 1, 72. Perhaps also in LLL III, 198.

**Wanton,** vb. to play, to dally: *to toy, to w., dally, smile and jest,* Ven. 106. *which (sedges) seem to move and w. with her breath,* Shr. Ind. 2, 54. *then you'ld w. with us, if we would have you,* Wint. II, 1, 18. *to w. with this queen,* Tit. II, 1, 21.

**Wantonly,** playfully, frolicksomely: *play as w. when summer's breath their masked buds discloses,* Sonn. 54, 7.

**Wantonness,** 1) sportiveness: *young gentlemen would be as sad as night, only for w.* John IV, 1, 16. *much misconstrued in his w.* H4A V, 2, 69.

2) triflingness, lightness: *how one man eats into another's pride, while pride is feasting in his w.* Troil. III, 3, 137.

3) lasciviousness, lechery: *some say thy fault is youth, some w.* Sonn. 96, 1. *the spirit of w. is scared out of him,* Wiv. IV, 2, 223. *I rather will suspect the sun with cold than thee with w.* IV, 4, 8. *the blood of youth burns not with such excess as gravity's revolt to w.* LLL V, 2, 74. *make your w. your ignorance,* Hml. III, 1, 152 (conceal your lasciviousness under the appearance of innocent simplicity).

**Want-wit,** an idiot: Merch. I, 1, 6.

**Wappened,** over-worn, stale (see the glossaries of Nares and Dyce): *this* (gold) *is it that makes the w. widow wed again,* Tim. IV, 3, 38 (Emendations proposed: *waped, wained, wappered, vapid, woepined* etc.).(*)

**War,** subst. a contest between two powers carried on by force of arms: Ven. 98. 1159. Lucr. 831. Sonn. 55, 5. Tp. V, 44. Gent. V, 2, 16. Meas. I, 2, 83. Err. V, 161. LLL II, 132. Mids. I, 1, 142. Shr. V, 2, 2, 162. All's I, 1, 209. I, 2, 3. II, 1, 44. II, 3, 307. III, 1, 2. III, 2, 108. III, 4, 8. R2 II, 1, 252. H5 II, 4, 7 (*towns of w.* = fortified towns) etc. etc. Plur. *—s* in the sense of the singular: *some to the — s, to try their fortune there,* Gent. I, 3, 8. *when I bestrid thee in the —s,* Err. V, 192. *is Signior Mountanto returned from the —s?* Ado I, 1, 31. 43. 49. *'tis brave —s,* All's II, 1, 25. *I have seen those —s,* 26. *I'll to the Tuscan —s,* II, 3, 290. 292. *in his unlucky Irish —s,* H4A V, 1, 53. *she'll to the —s,* III, 1, 195. *thou art going to the —s,* H4B II, 4, 72. *since I have entered into these —s,* H6A I, 2, 132; cf. I, 1, 74. *attend upon Cominius to these —s,* Cor. I, 1, 241 etc. etc. Even: *as —s may be said to be a ravisher,* Cor. IV, 5, 242. *this —s,* Oth. I, 3, 235. *a man of w.* = a soldier: R2 II, 1, 286. II, 3, 52. H4B V, 1, 31. *at w.* = in the state of war (figuratively): Sonn. 46, 1. Meas. II, 2, 33. H4A II, 3, 59. Caes. I, 2, 46. *at —s,* H4B III, 1, 60. *in w.,* in the same sense: Sonn. 15, 3. *to go to w.* Troil. II, 3, 145. *to go to —s,* Ado I, 1, 307. Ant. II, 2, 66. *to make w.* H6A I, 2, 17. *to make —s,* Ant. II, 2, 95; cf. II, 1, 13. *to make w. against,* Lucr. 774. Err. III, 2, 127. *to make w. on* or *upon,* Sonn. 16, 2. R2 III,

2, 133. R3 II, 4, 62. Per. I, 2, 45. *to make —s on* or *upon,* Cor. I, 4, 40. Ant. II, 2, 43. III, 5, 4. IV, 12, 15. *to make w. with,* H6C II, 2, 31. Mcb. II, 4, 18. *to make —s with,* Cor. I, 1, 239. *to wage —s,* Ant. III, 4, 3. *this civil w. of wits were much better used on Navarre,* LLL II, 226. *frowns, words and threats shall be the w. that Henry means to use,* H6C I, 1, 73. *that thou wilt use the —s as thy redress,* Tim. V, 4, 51.

Figurative use: *their silent w. of lilies and of roses,* Lucr. 71. *a w. of looks,* Ven. 355. *such civil w. is in my love and hate,* Sonn. 35, 12. *a kind of merry w.* Ado I, 1, 62. *such w. of white and red,* Shr. IV, 5, 30. Cor. II, 1, 232. *the morning's w.* H6C II, 5, 1 etc. etc. cf. above *at w.* and *in w.*

Used of a single combat: *telling the bushes that thou lookest for —s,* Mids. III, 2, 408 (rhyming). *law of w.* Lr. V, 3, 152 (Qq. *l. of arms*).

**War,** vb. to make war, to fight, to combat, to contend: *—ed he hath not,* R2 II, 1, 252. *teach them how to w.* H5 III, 1, 25. *lions w. and battle for their dens,* H6C II, 5, 74. *why should I w. without the walls of Troy,* Troil. I, 1, 2. *those that w. for a placket,* II, 3, 22. *to be opposed against the —ing winds,* Lr. IV, 7, 32 (Ff *jarring*). With *against: you w. against your reputation,* Err. III, 1, 86. *w. against your own affections,* LLL I, 1, 9. *—est thou 'gainst Athens?* Tim. IV, 3, 102. With *upon: his brother —ed upon him,* Ant. II 1, 41. With *with:* Lucr. 311. Sonn. 8, 2. Gent. I, 1, 68. Mids. II, 2, 4. As IV, 3, 45. R3 I, 4, 260. Troil. III, 2, 178. 179.

**Warble,** subst. song, melodious utterance: *Philomel had ended the well-tuned w. of her nightly sorrow,* Lucr. 1080.

**Warble,** vb. to sing: *w., child,* LLL III, 1. As II, 5, 38. *both —ing of one song,* Mids. III, 2, 206. *rehearse your song by rote, to each word a —ing note,* V, 405.

**Ward,** subst. 1) guard, preservation: *the best w. of mine honour is rewarding my dependents,* LLL III, 133 (Armado's speech).

2) guard made in fencing, posture of defence: *come from thy w.* Tp. I, 2, 471. *what —s, what blows, what extremities he endured,* H4A I, 2, 211. *thou knowest my old w.* II, 4, 215. Metaphorically: *I could drive her then from the w. of her purity,* Wiv. II, 2, 258. *he's beat from his best w.* Wint. I, 2, 33. *at all these —s I lie, at a thousand watches,* Troil. I, 2, 288.

3) state of being under a guardian: *I must attend his majesty's command, to whom I am now in w.* All's I, 1, 5.

4) one under the care of a guardian: *his son was but a w. two years ago,* Rom. I, 5, 42. *the father should be as w. to the son,* Lr. I, 2, 79.

5) custody, confinement: *ere they will have me go to w., they'll pawn their swords for my enfranchisement,* H6B V, 1, 112.

6) a prison-cell: *prison my heart in thy steel bosom's w.* Sonn. 133, 9. *if you have any thing to say to me, come to my w.* Meas. IV, 3, 66. *to lock it in the —s of covert bosom,* V, 10. *in which (prison) there are many confines, —s and dungeons,* Hml. II, 2, 252.

7) that which secures a door; a bolt: *the locks, ... each one by him enforced, retires his w.* Lucr. 303. *how careful was I ... each trifle under truest bars to thrust, that it might stay ... in sure —s of trust,* Sonn. 48, 4. *doors that were ne'er acquainted with their —s*

*many a bounteous year*, Tim. III, 3, 38. cf. Meas. V, 10.

8) a district of a town: *are there not men in your w. sufficient to serve it?* Meas. II, 1, 281. *the deputy's wife of the w.* H4A III, 3, 130. Proverbial: *one knows not at what w. you lie*, Troil. I, 2, 283.

**Ward,** vb. to protect: *God will in justice w. you as his soldiers*, R3 V, 3, 254. *if I cannot w. what I would not have hit*, Troil. I, 2, 292. *a hand that — ed him from thousand dangers*, Tit. III, 1, 195.

**Warden,** a baking-pear: *saffron to colour the w. pies*, Wint. IV, 3, 48.

**Warder,** 1) a guard, a keeper, a sentinel: *where be these —s, that they wait not here?* H6A I, 3, 3. *memory, the w. of the brain*, Mcb. I, 7, 65. *though castles topple on their —s' heads*, IV, 1, 56.

2) a sort of truncheon, by the throwing down of which further proceedings in a combat were stayed: *the king hath thrown his w. down*, R2 I, 3, 118. H4B IV, 1, 125.

**Wardrobe,** 1) a place where clothes are kept: Sonn. 52, 10. H5 II Chor. 2. *yeoman of the w.* Tw. II, 5, 45.

2) a store of clothes: Tp. IV, 222. H4A I, 2, 82. V, 3, 27.

**Ware,** subst. merchandise: *doth utter all men's ware-a*, Wint. IV, 4, 330. Plur. *—s:* LLL V, 2, 317. Wint. IV, 4, 204. Troil. I, 3, 359.

**Ware,** town in England, at an inn of which a large bed (of about eleven feet square) attracted the curiosity of travellers: *although the sheet were big enough for the bed of W. in England*, Tw. III, 2, 51.

**Ware,** vb. (used only in the imperative) to beware, to take heed of: *w. pencils, ho!* LLL V, 2, 43. *w. horns, ho!* Troil. V, 7, 12.

**Ware,** adj. aware: Troil. IV, 2, 57. Rom. II, 2, 103. With *of:* As II, 4, 58. 59. Rom. I, 1, 131.

**Warily,** cautiously: LLL V, 2, 93. H5 III, 7, 61.

**Warlike,** 1) having the qualities of a good soldier, or becoming a good soldier: Wiv. II, 2, 237. All's II, 1, 1. Wint. V, 1, 157. John V, 1, 71. V, 2, 176. R2 III, 3, 109. H4A IV, 4, 30. H5 Prol. 5. I, 2, 104. H6A II, 2, 35. II, 5, 70. III, 2, 118 *(w. and martial)*. IV, 3, 22. 36. IV, 6, 13. V, 2, 3. H6B I, 1, 125. H6C I, 1, 5. II, 1, 19. 123. R3 I, 2, 160. I, 3, 175. V, 3, 302. Troil. Prol. 13. IV, 5, 175. Tit. II, 1, 61. III, 1, 256. IV, 4, 69. Mcb. III, 6, 31. Hml. I, 1, 47. I, 2, 9. Lr. V, 3, 142. Oth. II, 1, 27. 43. II, 3, 59. Cymb. III, 1, 53. III, 3, 41. 90.

2) pertaining to war, military: *the w. band*, Lucr. 255 (= the band of warriors). *the w. god*, Pilgr. 147 (= the god of war). *unfold to us some w. resistance*, All's I, 1, 128. *in w. march*, John II, 242. *if thou receive me for thy w. mate*, H6A I, 2, 92 (= thy mate in war). *w. enterprise*, II, 1, 44. *what w. voice*, H8 I, 4, 50. *the w. service he has done*, Cor. III, 3, 49. *in a most w. preparation*, IV, 3, 17. *ten thousand w. men*, Mcb. IV, 3, 134. John IV, 2, 199. *w. appointment*, Hml. IV, 6, 15. *w. noise*, V, 2, 360. *volley*, 363. *stands not in such w. brace*, Oth. I, 3, 24. *knows a w. charge*, Ant. IV, 4, 19.

3) pertaining or belonging to a warrior: *I break my w. word*, H6A IV, 3, 31 (= soldier's word). *with thy w. sword*, IV, 6, 8. *before my body I throw my w. shield*, Mcb. V, 8, 33.

**Warm,** adj. having heat in a moderate degree:

*the sun shines w.* Ven. 193. *your cake is w.* Err. III, 1, 71. *w. distilled waters*, Shr. Ind. 1, 48. *will put thy shirt on w.* Tim. IV, 3, 223. *thou out of heaven's benediction comest to the w. sun*, Lr. II, 2, 169 (proverbial, = to quit a better thing for a worse). Oftenest used of the temperature of animal life: Sonn. 2, 14. Tp. II, 2, 35. Meas. III, 1, 120. Err. IV, 4, 34. Merch. I, 1, 83. Shr. V, 2, 151. Wint. III, 3, 76. V, 3, 35. 66. 109. John III, 4, 132. V, 2, 59. H6C V, 1, 55. R3 V, 2, 9. Troil. IV, 5, 118. Tit. II, 4, 22. III, 1, 20. V, 3, 153. Rom. II, 5, 12. V, 3, 167. 175. 197. Lr. II, 4, 271. Ant. III, 1, 6. *a furred gown to keep him w.* Meas. III, 2, 9. *if he have wit enough to keep himself w.* Ado I, 1, 69. *am I not wise? Yes; keep you w.* Shr. II, 268. *well summered and w. kept*, H5 V, 2, 335. Lr. II, 4, 273. III, 4, 179. Oth. III, 3, 78. Per. II, 1, 84.

In a moral sense, = 1) ardent, passionate: *the w. approach of sweet desire*, Ven. 386. *the w. effects which she in him finds missing*, 605. cf. Wint. III, 3, 76. 2) at ease, having or giving an agreeable sensation: *such a commodity of w. slaves*, H4A IV, 2, 19. *he's not yet through w.; force him with praises*, Troil. II, 3, 232. *he has it now, and by his looks methinks 'tis w. at's heart*, Cor. II, 3, 160.(*)

**Warm,** vb. 1) tr. to heat in a moderate degree (always applied to an influence operating on animal life): Merch. III, 1, 65. Shr. Ind. I, 32. IV, 1, 5. 10. R2 I, 3, 145. III, 2, 131. H4B IV, 3, 111. 115. H6B III, 1, 343. Cor. I, 5, 18. Proverbial: *go to thy cold bed and w. thee*, Shr. Ind. 1, 10. Lr. III, 4, 48 (allusion to a passage in Kyd's Spanish Tragedy).

Metaphorically, = a) to excite to love, to inflame: *that fire which many legions of true hearts had — ed*, Sonn. 154, 6. Compl. 191. 292. Cymb. II, 5, 12. b) to fire, to animate: *it — ed thy father's heart with proud desire of bold-faced victory*, H6A IV, 6, 11. c) to do good, to delight: *it —s the very sickness in my heart*, Hml. IV, 7, 56. *it would w. his spirits, to hear from me you had left Antony*, Ant. III, 13, 69. *the very middle of my heart is —ed by the rest*, Cymb. I, 6, 28.

2) intr. to become animated: *from her working all his visage —ed*, Hml. II, 2, 580 (Qq *wanned*).

**War-man,** warrior: LLL V, 2, 666 (Armado's speech).

**War-marked,** bearing the marks or traces of war, approved, veteran: *your army, which doth most consist of w. footmen*, Ant. III, 7, 45.

**Warming-pan,** a pan used to warm a bed: H5 II, 1, 88.

**Warmth,** gentle heat (used only of the natural temperature of a living animal body): Rom. IV, 1, 98. Tim. II, 2, 226. Lr. IV, 6, 272. Ant. V, 2, 294. Per. III, 2, 93. Metaphorically, = ardor, fervor: *what w. is there in your affection*, Merch. I, 2, 36.

**Warn,** 1) to give notice of approaching danger; to caution against danger or evil practices: *be —ed by me*, H5 III, 7, 60. *say you are well —ed*, H6A II, 4, 103. *I —ed ye*, H8 III, 1, 109. *God w. us* = God guard us, God forbid: *for lovers lacking — God w. us!* — *matter, the cleanliest shift is to kiss*, As IV, 1, 77; cf. Mids. V, 326 (O. Edd. *God warnd us*, M. Edd. *God warrant us*). With *from:* *the devil that I w. thee from*, R3 I, 3, 298. *to w. false traitors from the like attempts*, III, 5, 49.

*—ing*, substantively: Meas. III, 2, 36 *(give; cf.*

v. 205). Merch. II, 7, 8. All's II, 1, 22 (—*ings*). H6B IV, 6, 12 (*hath a fair* —*ing*). Tim. III, 1, 28 (*take*). Caes. I, 3, 70. II, 2, 80 (—*ings*).

2) to give notice, to inform previously: *his grace not being* —*ed thereof before*, R3 III, 7, 86.

—*ing*, substantively: *you shall hear the surly sullen bell give* —*ing to the world that I am fled*, Sonn. 71, 3. *at so slender* —*ing you are like to have a slender pittance*, Shr. IV, 4, 60. *somewhat too sudden, sirs, the* —*ing is*, H6A V, 2, 14. *to be on foot at an hour's* —*ing*, Cor. IV, 3, 50. *the boy gives* —*ing something doth approach*, Rom. V, 3, 18. *I come to observe; I give thee* —*ing on't*, Tim. I, 2, 33.

3) to summon: *who is it that hath* —*ed us to the walls?* John II, 201. *the Dauphin's drum, a* —*ing bell*, H6A IV, 2, 39. *sent to w. them to his royal presence*, R3 I, 3, 39. *this sight of death is as a bell, that* —*s my old age to a sepulchre*, Rom. V, 3, 207. *they mean to w. us at Philippi here*, Caes. V, 1, 5.

—*ing*, substantively: *when walls are so wilful to hear without* —*ing*, Mids. V, 211. *which as a beacon gives* —*ing to all the rest ... to arm*, H4B IV, 3, 117. *at his* (the cock's) —*ing ... the erring spirit hies to his confine*, Hml. I, 1, 152.

**Warp,** vb. 1) intr. a) to change (as timber) from the straight direction and become crooked: *one of you will prove a shrunk panel and like green timber w.*, w. As III, 3, 90.

Partic. —*ed* (like *crooked*, q. v.) = 1) perverse, unnatural: *such a* —*ed slip of wilderness ne'er issued from his blood*, Meas. III, 1, 142. 2) malignant: *here's another, whose* —*ed looks proclaim what store her heart is made on*, Lr. III, 6, 56.

b) to turn from a proper course, to deviate: *there is our commission, from which we would not have you w.* Meas. I, 1, 15.

c) to change for the worse: *my favour here begins to w.* Wint. I, 2, 365.

2) trans. to make crooked, to turn out of shape, to distort: *his scornful perspective ... which* —*ed the line of every other favour*, All's V, 3, 49. Applied to the different effects produced by the winter wind on water (which is the emblem of falseness; cf. *Water*): *though thou the waters warp, thy sting is not so sharp as friend remembered not*, As II, 7, 187 (probably = change in general, by freezing as well as by ruffling them).

**War-proof,** valor tried in war: H5 III, 1, 18.

**Warrant,** subst. that which gives credit or authority; 1) assurance given, surety, pledge: *the w. I have of your honourable disposition ... makes it assured of acceptance.* Lucr. Ded. 2. *which ... each putter-out ... will bring us good w. of*, Tp. III, 3, 49. *his worth is w. for his welcome*, Gent. II, 4, 102. *if you be one* (a woman)*, as you are well expressed by all external* —*s*, Meas. II, 4, 137. *the w. is for yourself*, V, 83. *did but convey unto our fearful minds a doubtful w. of immediate death*, Err. I, 1, 69. *wonder not till further w.* Ado III, 2, 115. *cracking the strong w. of an oath*, R2 IV, 235. *which to prove fruit, hope gives not so much w.* H4B I, 3, 40. *upon thy princely w. I descend*, H6A V, 3, 143. *nothing spake in w. from himself*, R3 III, 7, 33. *I give thee w. of thy place*, Oth. III, 3, 20. *with w. of her virginity*, Per. IV, 2, 63. *upon a w.* = in reliance on sth.: *upon this w. shall you have access*, Gent. III, 2, 60. *I do know you, and dare upon the w.*

*of my note commend a dear thing to you*, Lr. III, 1, 18. *this gentleman vouching, and upon w. of bloody affirmation, his to be more fair* Cymb. I, 4, 63.

2) any thing that authorizes or justifies an act; authorization: *authority for sin, w. for blame*, Lucr. 620. *folly, in wisdom hatched, hath wisdom's w. ... and wit's own grace to grace a learned fool*, LLL V, 2, 71. *what I shall incur to pass it, having no w.* Wint. II, 2, 58. *under whose* (God's) *w. I impeach thy wrong*, John II, 116. *there's law and w. for my curse*, III, 1, 184. *I hope your w. will bear out the deed*, IV, 1, 6. *to take their humours for a w. to break within the bloody house of life*, IV, 2, 209. *to give us w. from the hand of heaven*, V, 2, 66. *I do know the scope and w. limited unto my tongue*, 123. *follow your envious courses; you have Christian w. for 'em*, H8 III, 2, 244. *do not cry havoc, where you should but hunt with modest w.* Cor. III, 1, 276. *a pattern, precedent and lively w. for me to perform the like*, Tit. V, 3, 44.

Especially = an instrument giving power to seize or execute an offender: Meas. I, 4, 74. IV, 2, 66. 160. 167. IV, 3, 44. V, 102. 464. John IV, 2, 70. R3 I, 3, 342. I, 4, 112. 114. H8 I, 1, 216.

3) legality, right, allowance: *may we, with the w. of womanhood, ... pursue him with any further revenge?* Wiv. IV, 2, 220. *there's w. in that theft*, Mcb. II, 3, 151. *it is a fetch of w.* Hml. II, 1, 38 (= an allowed stratagem. Qq *a fetch of wit*). *arts inhibited and out of w.* Oth. I, 2, 79. *your bride goes to that with shame which is her way to go with w.* Per. IV, 2, 139. cf. Wint. II, 2, 58.

4) voucher, attestation: *in any bill, w., quittance, or obligation*, Wiv. I, 1, 10.

**Warrant,** vb. 1) to assure, to be surety; absol.; *I w. or I'll w.*, a frequent form of asseveration: *she will become thy bed, I w.* Tp. III, 2, 112. *I'll w. we'll unkennel the fox*, Wiv. III, 3, 174. II, 1, 76. III, 3, 4. IV, 2, 235. IV, 5, 101. Meas. I, 2, 176. Err. III, 2, 99. Ado III, 2, 66. III, 4, 10. Merch. IV, 2, 15. As III, 2, 407. Wint. II, 3, 71. John IV, 1, 31. R2 III, 2, 127. H6B V, 1, 122. Cor. I, 3, 71. Oth. IV, 2, 168 (Qq *I w. you*) etc. *I dare w.* H6A III, 1, 74.

With an accus. of the person to whom an assurance or surety is given: *could all my travels w. me they live*, Err. I, 1, 140. *a foolish hanging of thy nether lip that doth w. me*, H4A II, 4, 447. *said no more but what my thoughts did w. me was likely*, Per. V, 1, 135. *I w. thee, I w. you, I'll w. you*, phrases of asseveration: Tp. II, 1, 187. IV, 1, 54. Gent. II, 1, 170. V, 4, 166. Wiv. I, 1, 308. I, 4, 12. II, 2, 51. 66. 68. 72. III, 1, 70. III, 3, 40. III, 5, 49. Meas. I, 2, 33. V, 82. Err. IV, 4, 10. Ado II, 1, 378. III, 1, 14. V, 1, 199. H6A I, 4, 21. H6B IV, 3, 19. R3 I, 4, 155 etc.

The person or thing for which assurance or surety is given, as object: *I'll w. him for drowning*, Tp. I, 1, 49. *an assurance that my remembrance* —*s*, I, 2, 46. *I'll not w. that*, Meas. II, 4, 59. *which with experimental seal doth w. the tenour of my book*, Ado IV, 1, 168. *by other* —*ed testimony*, All's II, 5, 5. *my fainting words do w. death*, H6A II, 5, 95. *his wealth doth w. a liberal dower*, V, 5, 46. Hence, in asseverations, with the accus. of the person with respect to whom something is said: *I w. him, Petruchio is Kated*, Shr. III, 2, 247. *ay, is't, I w. him*, Tw. III, 4, 160. *that he knew, I w. him*, Wint. IV, 3, 117. *she shall have whipping-cheer, I w. her*, H4B V, 4, 6. *to the pot, I w.*

*him.* Cor. I, 4, 47. *a noble fellow, I w. him,* V, 2, 115. *fast, I w. her, she!* Rom. IV, 5, 1. *and I'll w. her, full of game,* Oth. II, 3, 19. Double accus.: *w. me welcome to my Proteus,* Gent. II, 7, 71. *I'll w. him heart-whole,* As IV, 1, 49. *I w. him consul,* Cor. II, 1, 238. cf. *sith true nobility —s these words in princely courtesy,* Tit. I, 272 (= as spoken in courtesy).

Two different accusatives: *the first* (death) *I w. thee,* H6B V, 1, 195. *I'll w. you all your lands,* H6C III, 2, 21. *I'll w. him that,* Cor. II, 1, 142.

Inf. following: *discover thine infirmity, that —eth by law to be thy privilege,* H6A V, 4, 61.

2) to authorize, to justify, to allow: *if I know more of any man alive than that which maiden modesty doth w.* Ado IV, 1, 181. *put me to't, I w. you,* All's II, 2, 50. *how far I have proceeded ... is —ed by a commission from the consistory,* H8 II, 4, 91. *—ed =* just: *the chance of goodness be like our —ed quarrel,* Mcb. IV, 3, 137.

Hence = to avow, to acknowledge, to make good, to defend: *that in their country did them that disgrace, we fear to w. in our native place,* Troil. II, 2, 96.

3) to secure (against danger or loss): *by the vow of mine order I w. you,* Meas. IV, 2, 180. *I'll give thee, ere I leave thee, so much money, to w. thee, as I am 'rested for,* Err. IV, 4, 3.

4) Used in a peculiar manner by Audrey in As III, 3, 5: *your features! Lord w. us! your features!* Probably she means to say: *Lord warn us* (cf. *Warn*); nevertheless this expression of a woman who is unacquainted with such words as *features,* has seduced M. Edd. to change *God warnd us* in Mids. V, 326 to *God warrant us.*

**Warranted,** adj. concerning a warrant or surety: *the very stream of his life ... must upon a w. need give him a better proclamation,* Meas. III, 2, 151 (= if a warrant is needed). cf. *Well-warranted.*

**Warrantise,** 1) surety, pledge: *in the very refuse of thy deeds there is such strength and w. of skill that in my mind thy worst all best exceeds,* Sonn. 150, 7. *break up the gates, I'll be your w.* H6A I, 3, 13.

2) authorization, allowance: *her obsequies have been as far enlarged as we have w.* Hml. V, 1, 250 (lection of F1; the rest *warranty*).

**Warranty,** authorization, allowance, permission: *from your love I have a w. to unburden all my plots and purposes,* Merch. I, 1, 132. *her obsequies have been as far enlarged as we have w.* Hml. V, 1, 250 (F1 *warrantise*). *never loved Cassio but with such general w. of heaven as I might love,* Oth. V, 2, 60.

**Warren,** a piece of ground appropriated to the keeping of beasts and fowls, especially of rabbits: *as melancholy as a lodge in a w.* Ado II, 1, 222.

**Warrener,** the keeper of a warren: *he hath fought with a w.* Wiv. I, 4, 28.

**Warrior,** a soldier: Sonn. 25, 9. Err. V, 367. Mids. II, 1, 71 (*your w. love,* i. e. the Amazon Hippolyta). H4A III, 2, 113. IV, 4, 26. V, 4, 23. H5 III, 5, 31. IV, 3, 10. 109. H6A III, 3, 82. III, 3, 22. IV, 7, 55. H6C I, 4, 14. 66. II, 1, 209. IV, 8, 64. V, 4, 51. Troil. III, 1, 162. IV, 5, 200. Cor. I, 6, 32. II, 1, 206. V, 3, 62. Tit. I, 25. IV, 2, 180. V, 1, 1. Caes. II, 2, 19. Ant. IV, 8, 24. Othello calls Desdemona, who has accompanied him on his expedition, his *fair w.,* Oth. II, 1, 184; and she, with evident allusion to this address, calls herself an *unhandsome w.* III, 4,

151. It has been alleged that English imitators of French sonneteers frequently gave their mistresses the appellation of *warriors (guerrières);* but those passages from Othello do not prove that Shakespeare was among them.

**Wart,** a hard extuberance on the skin: Wiv. I, 4, 157. 162. 171. Err. III, 2, 148. H4B III, 2, 152. Troil. I, 2, 155. Hml. V, 1, 306.

Name in H4B III, 2, 147. 150. 174. 279. 291. 295.

**War-thoughts,** thoughts of war: Ado I, 1, 303.

**War-wearied,** fatigued with fighting: *drops bloody sweat from his w. limbs,* H6A IV, 4, 18.

**Warwick,** name of an English town: H6C V, 1, 13. *Earl of W.,* baronial title of several persons celebrated in English history, particularly of the renowned king-maker: H4B III, 1, 1. IV, 5, 48. 232. V, 2, 20. H5 IV, 3, 54. IV, 7, 178. 183. IV, 8, 21. V, 2, 85. H6A II, 4, 10. 120. III, 1, 152. V, 4, 111. H6B I, 1, 70. 86. 115. 205. 210 etc. H6C I, 1, 28. 47. 52 etc. R3 I, 1, 153. I, 3, 135. I, 4, 49. II, 1, 110. IV, 1, 86.

**Warwickshire,** name of an English county: H4A IV, 2, 56. H6B III, 2, 201. H6C IV, 8, 9.

**War-worn,** worn with war: *w. coats,* H5 IV Chor. 26.

**Wary,** cautious, carefully watching: *I have ta'en a due and w. note,* Meas. IV, 1, 38. *it behoves men to be w.* Wint. IV, 4, 257. H6A II, 5, 97. III, 2, 3. Rom. III, 5, 40. Caes. II, 1, 15. Hml. I, 3, 43. V, 2, 290 (*bear a w. eye,* = be attentive). Oth. II, 3, 58. III, 3, 420. With *of: be of thyself so w.* Sonn. 22, 9 (= take cautious care of thyself).

**Wash,** subst. 1) flood (the sea as rising and overflowing the land?): *Neptune's salt w. and Tellus' orbed ground,* Hml. III, 2, 166. Plur. — *es* (= the land overflowed by the tide?): *these Lincoln —es have devoured them,* John V, 6, 41. *in the —es ... devoured by the unexpected flood,* V, 7, 63.

2) the feed of hogs gathered from washed dishes: *swills your warm blood like w.* R3 V, 2, 9.

**Wash,** vb. 1) to cleanse by ablution; absol.: *she can w. and scour,* Gent. III, 1, 313. Wiv. I, 4, 101. With an object: Tp. II, 2, 187. Gent. III, 1, 315. Wiv. IV, 5, 99. LLL IV, 3, 273. As IV, 1, 103 (*to w. him,* refl.). Wint. IV, 4, 377. H4B II, 1, 99. H6B IV, 2, 51 (*she —es bucks*). Cor. I, 9, 47. I, 10, 27. Tit. V, 1, 95. Cymb. V, 5, 485. *to w. one's face:* Ado III, 2, 56. H4B II, 1, 162. Cor. II, 3, 66. Per. IV, 2, 28. *to w. one's hands:* Shr. Ind. 2, 78. John III, 1, 234. R2 IV, 239. H4A III, 4, 116. Tit. II, 3, 45. II, 4, 6. 7. Mcb. V, 1, 33. 68. With a second accus. denoting an effect: *to w. her clean again,* Ado IV, 1, 143. As III, 2, 443. Hml. III, 3, 46.

Metaphorically, = to purify: *that what you speak is in your conscience —ed as pure as sin with baptism,* H5 I, 2, 31. With *of,* = to purify from: *I would I could w. myself of the buck,* Wiv. III, 3, 167 (punning on buck-washing). *how fain would I w. my hands of this murder,* R3 I, 4, 279.

2) to perform the act of ablution on one's own person, to wash one's self: *he will have need of —ing,* Wiv. III, 3, 194. *come, Kate, and w.* Shr. IV, 1, 157. Cor. I, 9, 68. Caes. III, 1, 111.

3) to wet, to moisten: *the moon, the governess of floods, —es all the air, that rheumatic diseases do abound,* Mids. II, 1, 104. *she looks as clear as morning roses newly —ed with dew,* Shr. II, 174 *they ne'er*

come *but I look to be —ed,* Per. II, 1, 29. Particularly applied to tears: *sometimes falls an orient drop beside ... to w. the foul face of the sluttish ground,* Ven. 983. *he, a marble to her tears, is —ed with them, but relents not,* Meas. III, 1, 239. *there are no faces truer than those that are so —ed,* Ado I, 1, 27. *speaking of her foulness, —ed it with tears,* IV, 1, 156. *my eyes are oftener —ed than hers,* Mids. II, 2, 93. R2 V, 1, 10. H4B IV, 5, 84. 87. R3 IV, 4, 389. Rom. II, 3, 70. III, 2, 130. Lr. I, 1, 271. Ant. V, 1, 28. *to w. one's brain* = to drink copiously: Ant. II, 7, 105 (cf. *Ale-washed*).

4) to overflow, to dash against: *lie drowning the —ing of ten tides,* Tp. I, 1, 61. *that vast shore —ed with the farthest sea,* Rom. II, 2, 83. *these surges which w. both heaven and hell,* Per. III, 1, 2.

5) to remove by ablution: *my blood shall wash the slander of mine ill,* Lucr. 1207. *thy tears would w. this cold congealed blood that glues my lips and will not let me speak,* H6C V, 2, 37. With *away: their colours should be —ed away,* LLL IV, 3, 271. R2 IV, 207. 242. H4A III, 2, 137. H6A III, 3, 57. H6B III, 2, 342. H6C I, 4, 158. With *off:* R2 III, 2, 55. V, 6, 50. H6C III, 1, 17. Rom. II, 3, 76. Tim. III, 6, 102. With *from:* R3 IV, 1, 68. Mcb. II, 2, 47. 60. Ant. IV, 8, 10. With *from off:* R2 III, 1, 5. With *out of:* H5 IV, 7, 111 (Fluellen's speech).

Metaphorically, = to efface, to erase: *may this be —ed in Lethe and forgotten?* H4B V, 2, 72. With *off: I will w. off gross acquaintance,* Tw. II, 5, 175. *the double gilt of this opportunity you let time w. off,* III, 2, 27. With *out of: I do w. his name out of my blood,* All's III, 2, 70. *w. every mote out of his conscience,* H5 IV, 1, 189.

6) to overwhelm and carry off as with water: *was —ed to death with fulsome wine,* R3 V, 3, 132. *w. me in steep-down gulfs of liquid fire,* Oth. V, 2, 280. With *from, forth of, off: to be —ed off the next tide,* H5 IV, 1, 101. *a shower ... that —ed his father's fortunes forth of France,* H6C II, 2, 157. *the tide will w. you off,* V, 4, 31. *wilt thou w. him from his grave with tears?* Rom. III, 5, 71. *the sea —ed me from shore to shore,* Per. II, 1, 6. *and from the ladder-tackle —es off a canvas-climber,* IV, 1, 61.

**Washer,** a laundress: Wiv. I, 2, 5 (Evans' speech).

**Washford:** Earl of W., one of Talbot's titles: H6A IV, 7, 63.*

**Wasp,** the insect Vespa: Lucr. 839. Gent. I, 2, 106. Shr. II, 214. Wint. I, 2, 329. IV, 4, 814. H8 III, 2, 55. Tit. II, 3, 132. Emblem of petulant snappishness: *come, come, you w.; i' faith, you are too angry,* Shr. II, 210.

**Waspish,** irritable, snappish, petulant: *the stern brow and w. action which she did use,* As IV, 3, 9. *if I be w., best beware my sting,* Shr. II, 211. *I'll use you for my mirth, when you are w.* Caes. IV, 3, 50.

**Waspish-headed,** irritable: *her w. son has broke his arrows,* Tp. IV, 99.

**Wasp-stung,** stung by a wasp, highly irritated: H4A I, 3, 236 (Ff *wasp-tongued*).

**Wasp-tongued,** waspish, snappish, petulant: *what a w. and impatient fool art thou to break into this woman's mood,* H4A I, 3, 236 (Q1 *wasp-stung,* later Qq *wasp-tongue*).

**Wassail,** a drinking-bout, carousing, quaffing: *at wakes and —s,* LLL V, 2, 318. *a w. candle,* H4B I, 2, 179 (a large candle lighted up at a feast). *his two chamberlains will I with wine and w. so convince,* Mcb. I, 7, 64. *takes his rouse, keeps w.* Hml. I, 4, 9. *leave thy lascivious —s,* Ant. I, 4, 56 (O. Edd. *vassailes,* some M. Edd. *vassals*).

**Waste,** subst. 1) useless expense, consumption, loss: *beauty's w. hath in the world an end,* Sonn. 9, 11. *with old woes new wail my dear time's w.* 30, 4. *which (the crown) w. of idle hours hath quite thrown down,* R2 III, 4, 66.

Particularly = dissipation, squandering, profusion: *makest w. in niggarding,* Sonn. 1, 12. *more short than w. or ruining,* 125, 4. *the expense of spirit in a w. of shame is lust in action,* 129, 1 (*w. of shame* = shameful waste). *I am now about no w.; I am about thrift,* Wiv. I, 3, 47 (the same pun on *waist* in H4B I, 2, 160). *if you had made w. of all I have,* Merch. I, 1, 157. Tw. III, 1, 141. H4B I, 2, 160. Rom. I, 1, 224 (*make*). II, 3, 71. Tim. II, 1, 4. Lr. II, 1, 102.

2) destruction, devastation: *that make such w. in brief mortality,* H5 I, 2, 28. *all fell feats enlinked to w. and desolation,* III, 3, 18.

Abstr. pro concr.; = that which is destroyed: *that thou among the —s of time must go,* Sonn. 12, 10. *and yet, incaged in so small a verge, the w. is no whit lesser than thy land,* R2 II, 1, 103. *a naked subject to the weeping clouds and w. for churlish winter's tyranny,* H4B I, 3, 62.

3) corruption (?): *he will never in the way of w. attempt us again,* Wiv. IV, 2, 226 (never again try to seduce us). cf. Sonn. 129, 1.

4) total consumption in general: *the night grows to w.* Oth. IV, 2, 250 (= is nearly past). *they have earned the w.* Ant. IV, 1, 16 (have well deserved to enjoy it without restraint).

5) Synonymous to vast (q. v.) = boundless space: *and buckle in a w. most fathomless with spans and inches,* Troil. II, 2, 30 (M. Edd. *waist*). *in the dead w. and middle of the night,* Hml. I, 2, 198 (lection of F2.3.4; Fl Q2.3.4 *wast;* most M. Edd. with Q5. 6 and the spurious Q1 *vast*).

**Waste,** adj. 1) unoccupied, void: *what thy memory cannot contain commit to these w. blanks,* Sonn. 77, 10. 2) worthless, fit only for vile uses: *having w. ground enough,* Meas. II, 2, 170.

**Waste,** vb. 1) trans. a) to expend unnecessarily, to squander, to dissipate: *but wherefore w. I time to counsel thee,* Gent. I, 1, 51. Merch. III, 4, 54. Tw. II, 5, 85. R2 V, 5, 49. H8 V, 1, 5. Hml. II, 2, 89. Cymb. IV, 4, 20 (*upon*). Per. II, 3, 93. *you but w. your words,* Meas. II, 2, 72. Mids. III, 2, 168. *help to w. his borrowed purse,* Merch. II, 5, 50. *youth, the sooner it is —d, the sooner it wears,* H4A II, 4, 443. *we w. our lights in vain,* Rom. I, 4, 45. *—s the lamps of night in revel,* Ant. I, 4, 4. With an accus. of the effect: *I have —ed myself out of my means,* Oth. IV, 2, 187.

b) to destroy; to ruin; to desolate; to wear away: *beauty within itself should not be —d,* Ven. 130. *favour, savour, hue and qualities ... are on the sudden —d,* thawed and done,* 749. *w. huge stones with little water-drops,* Lucr. 959. *faster than time —s life,* Sonn. 100, 13. *he hath —d it (my beauty)* Err. II, 1, 90. *I —d time, and now doth time w. me,* R2 V, 5, 49. *action ... may w. the memory of the former days,* H4B IV, 5, 216 (= efface it). *my lungs are —d so,* 217 (exhausted). *hast —d our country,* H6A II, 3, 41. *the *towns defaced by —ing ruin of the cruel foe,* III, 3, 46. *would he were —d, marrow, bones and all,* H6C III, 2, 125. *the fire that mounts the liquor till 't run o'er, in seeming to augment it —s it,* H8 I, 1, 145. *the —d building,* Tit. V, 1, 23. *which being took, should ... by inches w. you,* Cymb. V, 5, 52. *thus time we w. and longest leagues make short,* Per. IV, 4, 1 (= annihilate).

c) to consume, to spend: *a summer's day ... being —d in such time-beguiling sport,* Ven. 24. *this night I'll w. in sorrow,* 583. Tp. V, 302. *in the chronicle of —d time,* Sonn. 106, 1 (= past). *to w. thyself upon thy virtues, they on thee,* Meas. I, 1, 31 (to bestow all thy powers on perfectioning thyself). *a merrier hour was never —d there,* Mids. II, 1, 57. *now the —d brands do glow,* V, 382. *companions that do converse and w. the time together,* Merch. III, 4, 12. As II, 4, 95. *we will nothing w. till you return,* II, 7, 134 (eat). *wars have not —d it* (money) R2 II, 1, 252. *hath his quick wit — d in giving reckonings,* H4B I, 2, 193. *the king hath —d all his rods on late offenders,* IV, 1, 215. *March is —d fourteen days,* Caes. II, 1, 59. *so shall he w. his means, weary his soldiers,* IV, 3, 200. *till now some nine moons —d,* Oth. I, 3, 84 (= past). *I life would wish, and that I might w. it for you,* Per. Prol. 16.

2) intr. to dwindle, to wear away, to decay: *poor —ing monuments of lasting moans,* Lucr. 798. *how thy precious minutes w.* Sonn. 77, 2. *my —ing lamps* (i. e. the eyes) Err. V, 315. *let Benedick ... consume away in sighs, w. inwardly,* Ado III, 1, 78. *like lamps whose —ing oil is spent,* H6A II, 5, 8.

**Wasteful,** 1) lavish, profuse: *to add another hue unto the rainbow ... is w. and ridiculous excess,* John IV, 2, 16. *hath seized the w. king,* R2 III, 4, 55. *I have retired me to a w. cock,* Tim. II, 2, 171.

2) ruinous, destructive, consumptive: *where w. time debateth with decay,* Sonn. 15, 11. *when w. war shall statues overturn,* 55, 5. *lean and w. learning,* As III, 2, 341. *w. vengeance,* H5 I, 2, 283. *the wild and w. ocean,* III, 1, 14. *for ruin's w. entrance,* Mcb. II, 3, 120.

**Wat,** a term among sportsmen for a hare: Ven. 697.

**Watch,** subst. 1) the state of being awake, forbearance of sleep: *fell into a sadness, then into a fast, thence to a w.* Hml. II, 2, 148. *to lie in w. there and to think on him,* Cymb. III, 4, 43. cf. Rom. II, 3, 35. H5 IV, 1, 300.

2) vigilance, attention, close observation: *I shot his fellow ... with more advised w.* Merch. I, 1, 142. *with catlike w., when that the sleeping man should stir,* As IV, 3, 116. *what w. the king keeps to maintain the peace,* H5 IV, 1, 300. *at all these wards I lie, at a thousand —es,* Troil. I, 2, 289. 290. *care keeps his w. in every old man's eye,* Rom. II, 3, 35. *near approaches the subject of our w.* Mcb. III, 3, 8. *follow her close, give her good w.* Hml. IV, 5, 74.

Particularly guard kept for military purposes: *had your w. been good, this sudden mischief never could have fallen,* H6A II, 1, 58. *use careful w.* R3 V, 3, 54. *as I did stand my w. upon the hill,* Mcb. V, 5, 33. *the rivals of my w.* Hml. I, 1, 13. 71. 106. 168. *on their w.* I, 2, 197. *kept the w.* 208. *hold you the w. to-night,* 225. Oth. II, 3, 159. Ant. IV, 3, 7 (*have careful w.*).

3) one or more persons set for a guard; watchman or watchmen, sentinel, guard: Ado III, 3, 6. 24. 30. 36. 40. 87. III, 5, 33. 49. IV, 2, 36. 39. V, 1, 316.

R2 V, 3, 9. H4A II, 4, 530. H5 IV Chor. 7. 30. H6A II, 1, 61. III, 2, 7. 35. Rom. V, 3, 71. 158. 279. 285. Caes. II, 2, 16. Hml. I, 1, 66. 110. Oth. V, 1, 37. *to set the w.* Rom. III, 3, 148. 167. Oth. II, 3, 125. With *over,* Hml. V, 1, 319. In H4A I, 2, 119 Qq and M. Edd. *match.*

4) the place where a guard is kept: *we must to the w.* Oth. II, 3, 12. 340. *brave me upon the w.* V, 2, 326 (but in all these passages it may as well signify the office of a guard).

5) a period of the night (originally perhaps the time from one relief of sentinels to another), or the time of night as forming part of the day: *at this odd-even and dull w. o'the night,* Oth. I, 1, 124. *snores out the w. of night,* H4B IV, 5, 28.

6) any thing by which the progress of time is perceived and measured; a) a candle marked out into sections, each of which was a certain portion of time in burning: *give me a w.* R3 V, 3, 63.

b) any thing regularly repeated within a certain period: (Time), *base w. of woes,* Lucr. 928 (divided and marked only by woes). *withered murder, alarumed by his sentinel, the wolf, whose howl's his w.* Mcb. II, 1, 54 (similar, in this respect, to the crowing of the cock).

c) the marks of the minutes on a dial-plate: *my thoughts are minutes, and with sighs they jar their —es on unto mine eyes, the outward w.* R2 V, 5, 52. cf. the verb in Hml. I, 1, 27, and *watchful* in John IV, 1, 46.

d) a time-piece, a clock as well as one carried in the pocket: *my heart doth charge the w.* Pilgr. 194. *he's winding up the w. of his wit; by and by it will strike,* Tp. II, 1, 12. *never going a right, being a w.* LLL III, 194 (v. 192 a German clock). *wind up my w.* Tw. II, 5, 66. *since when, my w. hath told me, toward my grave I have travelled but two hours,* V, 165. *mine eyes, the outward w.* R2 V, 5, 52.

**Watch,** vb. 1) intr. a) to be awake, not to sleep: *my sick heart commands mine eyes to w.* Ven. 584. *they that w. see time how slow it creeps,* Lucr. 1575. *for thee w. I whilst thou dost wake elsewhere,* Sonn. 61, 13. *how can love's eye be true that is so vexed with —ing and with tears,* 148, 10. *to w. like one that fears robbing,* Gent. II, 1, 25. *it hath been the longest night that e'er I —ed,* IV, 2, 141. *though it cost me ten nights' —ings,* Ado II, 1, 388. *to sigh for her! to w. for her!* LLL III, 202. *she shall w. all night,* Shr. IV, 1, 208. *w. to-night, pray to-morrow,* H4A II, 4, 306. Rom. IV, 4, 8. 9. Mcb. V, 1, 12. Hml. III, 2, 284. Lr. II, 2, 162. Oth. II, 3, 135. III, 3, 285. Cymb. II, 4, 68. cf. *All-watched.*

= to be up for purposes of business or attendance: *that I might sit all night and w. with you,* John IV, 1, 30. *for sleeping England long time have I —ed; —ing breeds leanness,* R2 II, 1, 77. 78. H4A II, 3, 50. H4B IV, 5, 20. 53. H6B III, 1, 110. IV, 7, 90. H6C V, 7, 17. Cor. II, 3, 134. Mcb. V, 1, 1. Cymb. V, 5, 53.

b) to be on the look-out, to be vigilant: *I'll go w.* Wiv. I, 4, 7. *I must wait, and w. withal,* Shr. III, 1, 62. IV, 2, 59. John IV, 1, 5. H6A I, 4, 16. 18. II, 1, 7. H6B I, 1, 249. Troil. I, 2, 295. Tit. III, 1, 5. Lr. II, 1, 22.

c) to keep guard, to act as sentinel: Ado III, 3, 98. Shr. V, 2, 150. R3 V, 3, 76. Hml. I, 2, 213. 242. Lr. IV, 7, 35. Oth. II, 1, 219. 271. II, 3, 56.

d) to look with expectation, to wait: *when you*

*shall please to play the thieves for wives, I'll w. as long for you then*, Merch. II, 6, 24.

2) trans. a) to keep from sleep (a term of falconry): *to w. her, as we w. these kites that ... will not be obedient*, Shr. IV, 1, 198. *you must be —ed ere you be made tame*, Troil. III, 2, 45. *I'll w. him tame*, Oth. III, 3, 23.

b) to have in the eye, to observe closely for some purpose: Sonn. 57, 6. Tp. II, 1, 198 (= guard). Wiv. IV, 2, 53. LLL III, 195. Mids. II, 1, 177. Merch. I, 1, 150. V, 230. Shr. III, 1, 50. III, 2, 141. 146. All's V, 3, 11. H6A I, 1, 161. H6B I, 1, 174. H6C II, 1, 12. R3 IV, 4, 4. Troil. II, 3, 138. Cor. V, 1, 56. Rom. I, 5, 52. IV, 1, 116. Hml. I, 1, 27 (or intr.?). Oth. IV, 2, 241. *I'll w. you from such — ing now*, Rom. IV, 4, 12 (hinder you by my vigilance); cf. *I'll w. you for that, ... I can w. you for telling how I took the blow*, Troil. I, 2, 291. 293.

c) to take in the fact by lying in wait for; to surprise and baffle: *I think we have —ed you now*, Wiv. V, 5, 107. *I think we —ed you at an inch*, H6B I, 4, 45. *methinks you —ed her well*, 58.

d) to look for, to wait for: *thus long have we stood to w. the fearful bending of thy knee*, R2 III, 3, 73. *ten is the hour that was appointed me to w. the coming of my punished duchess*, H6B II, 4, 7. *we will stand and w. your pleasure*, Caes. IV, 3, 249.

**Watch-case,** a sentry-box: *leavest the kingly couch a w. or a common 'larum-bell*, H4B III, 1, 17.

**Watch-dog,** a dog kept for guarding the house: Tp. I, 2, 383.

**Watcher,** one who is awake: *love hath chased sleep from my enthralled eyes and made them —s of mine own heart's sorrow*, Gent. II, 4, 135 (*of* = by, from, in consequence of; see *Of*). Mcb. II, 2, 71.

**Watchful,** 1) lacking sleep: *with twenty w., weary, tedious nights*, Gent. I, 1, 31. *keepest the ports of slumber open wide to many a w. night*, H4B IV, 5, 25. *what w. cares do interpose themselves betwixt your eyes and night?* Caes. II, 1, 98.

2) vigilant, careful: R3 III, 7, 77. V, 3, 115. 224. Troil. III, 3, 196. *w. fires* = watch-fires: H5 IV Chor. 23. In a bad sense, = spying: *in despite of brooded w. day*, John III, 3, 52. *fled the snares of w. tyranny*, Mcb. V, 8, 67.

3) Applied to minutes, = marking a portion or time within an hour (cf. the subst. *Watch* 6, c): *and like the w. minutes to the hour, still and anon cheered up the heavy time*, John IV, 1, 46 (*to the hour* = till the hour is full. cf. *Hour*).

**Watching,** subst. wakefulness: Ado II, 1, 388. cf. *Watch*, vb.

**Watchman,** 1) one who is awake: *mine own true love that doth my rest defeat, to play the w. ever for thy sake*, Sonn. 61, 12 (quibbling).

2) one careful and vigilant: *the special watchmen of our English weal*, H6A III, 1, 66. *I shall the effect of this good lesson keep, as w. to my heart*, Hml. I, 3, 46.

3) a guard; a sentinel: Ado III, 3, 42. Ant. IV, 3, 17.

**Watch-word,** parole, countersign: Lucr. 370. Wiv. V, 4, 3. H4B III, 2, 231.

**Water,** subst. 1) the principal fluid (considered as a substance): Ven. 94. 654. Lucr. 592. Sonn. 109, 8. 154, 14. Compl. 287. 291. Tp. I, 1, 62. I, 2, 334.

III, 2, 2. Gent. II, 4, 171. III, 2, 8. Wiv. II, 3, 89. III, 5, 23. Err. I, 2, 35. II, 2, 128. III, 2, 107. R2 III, 3, 56. 58. Tim. IV, 3, 425. Ant. IV, 14, 11 etc. etc. *with w. and bran*, Meas. IV, 3, 159. *with bran and w.* LLL I, 1, 303. *fresh w.* Tp. I, 2, 160. *salt w.* II, 1, 64. Tw. II, 1, 32. *holy w.* Tit. I, 323 (consecrated by the priest). Lr. III, 2, 10. IV, 3, 32. Cymb. V, 5, 269. *warm distilled —s*, Shr. Ind. 1, 48. *sweet w.* Tit. II, 4, 6. Rom. V, 3, 14. *w. that doth eat in steel*, Lucr. 755. Earth and w. heavy, air and fire light elements: Sonn. 44, 11 (cf. 45, 1—7). H5 III, 7, 23. Emblem of falseness: *false ... as wind, as —s*, Wint. I, 2, 132. *fall away like w. from ye*, H8 II, 1, 130. *as false as air, as w., wind, or sandy earth*, Troil. III, 2, 199. *smoke and lukewarn w. is your perfection*, Tim. III, 6, 99. *she was false as w.* Oth. V, 2, 134. cf. As II, 7, 187. Proverbial expressions: *would run through fire and w. for such a kind heart*, Wiv. III, 4, 107. *as profitless as w. in a sieve*, Ado V, 1, 5. *fire, fire; cast on no water*, Shr. IV, 1, 21 (allusion to a popular catch: *Scotland burneth, Scotland burneth; fire, fire, fire, fire; cast on some more water*). *their virtues we write in w.* H8 IV, 2, 46. *more w. glideth by the mill than wots the miller of*, Tit. II, 1, 85.

2) a collection of water, a lake, a river, a sea: *like the moon in w. seen by night*, Ven. 492. *he trod the w.* Tp. II, 1, 115. *I am standing w.* 221 (the sea between the ebb and the flood); cf. *'tis with him in standing w., between boy and man*, Tw. I, 5, 168. *throwing him into the w.* Wiv. III, 3, 194. *the w. swells a man*, III, 5, 16. *his throwing into the w.* IV, 1, 5. *never gazed the moon upon the w.* Wint. IV, 4, 173. H6A I, 2, 133. H6B III, 1, 53. Mcb. I, 3, 79 etc. *by w.* = at sea: Ant. II, 6, 89. 94. Plur. *— s: put the wild —s in this roar*, Tp. I, 2, 2. *this music crept by me upon the —s*, 391. *the still-closing —s*, III, 3, 64. *the roaring —s*, Merch. I, 1, 34. I, 3, 25. V, 97. As II, 7, 187. Wint. IV, 4, 578. R3 I, 4, 22. II, 3, 44. Cor. III, 1, 249. Ant. I, 2, 153. Cymb. III, 1, 20. Per. II, 1, 63 etc. Proverbial: *thou requestest but moonshine in the w.* LLL V, 2, 208 (i. e. a nothing). *now will I raise the —s*, Merch. II, 2, 52 (play a great scene). *I am for all —s*, Tw. IV, 2, 68 (fit for any thing). *smooth runs the w. where the brook is deep*, H6B III, 1, 53.

3) Used of other fluids; a) of tears: *weeping w.* Compl. 304. *a devil would have shed w. out of fire*, Wint. III, 2, 194. *there will be a world of w. shed*, H4A III, 1, 94. *here's w. to quench it*, Cor. V, 2, 78. Rom. II, 3, 71. Oth. IV, 2, 104. Ant. I, 3, 64 etc. Plur. *—s: I still pour in the —s of my love*, All's I, 3, 209. *command these fretting —s from your eyes*, Meas. IV, 3, 151. John IV, 3, 107. V, 2, 56. H5 IV, 6, 29 etc. cf. Ven. 94. Compl. 287. 291. Tw. II, 1, 33. Wint. V, 2, 91. Lr. IV, 3, 32. Ant. I, 2, 153.

b) rain: *whilst on the earth I rain my —s*, R2 III, 3, 60. *by sudden floods and fall of —s*, R3 IV, 4, 512.

c) urine: *the w. in an urinal*, Gent. II, 1, 41. *carry his w. to the wise woman*, Tw. III, 4, 114. *what says the doctor to my w.?* H4B I, 2, 2. 3. *if thou couldst cast the w. of my land*, Mcb. V, 3, 51. *to make w.* = to discharge urine: Gent. IV, 4, 41. Meas. III, 2, 117. Tw. I, 3, 139.

4) the lustre of a diamond: *here is a w.* Tim. I, 1, 18. *the diamonds of a most praised w.* Per. III, 2, 102.

**Water,** vb. 1) trans. a) to irrigate, to wet: *w. her chamber with eye-offending brine*, Tw. I, 1, 29. *he —ed* *his new plants with dews of flattery*, Cor. V, 6, 23. *the tears live in an onion that should w. this sorrow*, Ant. 1, 2, 177.

b) to supply with water for drink: *I might w. an ass at it*, Troil. III, 3, 314. *his steeds to w. at those springs*, Cymb. II, 3, 23.

2) intr. a) to shed tears: *your kindred hath made my eyes w.* Mids. III, 1, 200. V, 69. *if thine eyes can w. for his death*, H6C I, 4, 82. *mine eyes began to w.* Caes. III, 1, 285.

b) to gather saliva (as a symptom of appetite): *a Spaniard's mouth so —ed*, Per. IV, 2, 108.

c) to drink: *when you breathe in your —ing, they cry hem and bid you play it off*, H4A II, 4, 17.

**Water-colours,** colours mixed with water (not with oil): *never yet did insurrection want such w. to impaint his cause*, H4A V, 1, 80.

**Water-drops,** drops of water: Lucr. 959. R2 IV, 262. Troil. III, 2, 193. Used of tears: Lr. II, 4, 280; cf. R2 IV, 262.

**Water-flowing,** flowing like water, copious: *my mercy dried their w. tears*, H6C IV, 8, 43.

**Waterfly,** an insect living on the water (Phryganea?): Ant. V, 2, 59. Emblem of emptiness and vanity: *how the poor world is pestered with such —es*, Troil. V, 1, 38. *dost know this w.?* Hml. V, 2, 84.

**Waterford;** *Earl of W.*, one of Talbot's titles: H6A IV, 7, 63. Referring to the town of W., Ireland.

**Water-gall,** a rainbow: *round about her tear-distained eye blue circles streamed, like rainbows in the sky: these —s in her dim element foretell new storms to those already spent*, Lucr. 1588.

**Waterish,** 1) abounding with water: *w. Burgundy*, Lr. I, 1, 261. 2) thin, having no alimentary substance: *such nice and w. diet*, Oth. III, 3, 15.

**Water-newt,** a lizard living in water: *the wall-newt and the water*, Lr. III, 4, 136 (the word *newt* belonging to *water* as well as to *wall*).

**Water-pot,** a vessel used to sprinkle water on plants: Lr. IV, 6, 200.

**Water-rat,** a rat living in water: Merch. I, 3, 23.

**Water-rug,** a kind of poodle: Mcb. III, 1, 94.

**Water-side,** the margin of a river: H8 II, 1, 95.

**Water-spaniel,** a sort of spaniel taking the water: *she hath more qualities than a w.* Gent. III, 1, 271.

**Water-standing,** perpetually filled with tears: *many an orphan's w. eye*, H6C V, 6, 40.

**Water-thieves,** pirates: Merch. I, 3, 24. cf. Ant. II, 6, 97.

**Waterton,** name in R2 II, 1, 284.

**Water-walled,** fenced by the sea: John II, 27.

**Water-work,** painting executed in water-colour: *the German hunting in w.* H4B II, 1, 158.

**Watery,** 1) consisting of water: *of that black blood a w. rigol goes*, Lucr. 1745. *corrupted blood some w. token shows*, 1748. Epithet of the sea: Sonn. 64, 7. Err. II, 1, 21. Merch. II, 7, 44. Tw. V, 241. R2 II, 1, 63. Per. II, 1, 10. 54. *when Phoebe doth behold her silver visage in the w. glass*, Mids. I, 1, 210.

2) filled with water: *this gross w. pumpion*, Wiv. III, 3, 43. Applied to eyes filled with tears: Compl. 281. LLL V, 2, 206. Shr. Ind. 1, 128. Tit. III, 1, 269. cf. *this pale swan in her w. nest*, Lucr. 1611. Merch. III, 2, 47.

3) moist; used of the rainbow: Tp. IV, 71. of the moon: Mids. II, 1, 162. III, 1, 203. Wint. I, 2, 1 R3 II, 2, 69. Rom. I, 4, 62.

4) watering, vehemently desiring: *when that the w. palate tastes indeed love's thrice repured nectar*, Troil. III, 2, 22.

**Wave,** subst. a swell of water raised above the level, a billow: Ven. 819. Lucr. 1438. Sonn. 60, 1. Tp. I, 2, 205. 379. II, 1, 118. Tw. I, 2, 16. III, 4, 419. V, 236. Wint. IV, 4, 141. H6C I, 4, 21. II, 6, 36. V, 4, 24. 36. Tit. III, 1, 95. Caes. I, 2, 114. Mcb. IV, 1, 53. Per. II Prol. 34. IV, 1, 60. Figuratively, a throng of people borne along together: Cymb. V, 3, 48.

In the poetical style, = water: *like a dive-dapper peering through a w.* Ven. 86. *spread o'er the silver —s thy golden hairs*, Err. III, 2, 48. In Armado's language even in prose: *by the salt w. of the Mediterraneum*, LLL V, 1, 61.

**Wave,** vb. 1) trans. a) to move loosely one way and the other; absol.: *let him w. thus* (viz his sword) Cor. I, 6, 74. *still —ing* (his handkerchief) Cymb. I, 3, 12. With an object: *thus —ing it* (his hat) *in scorn*, Cor. II, 3, 175. *—ing thy head*, III, 2, 77. Hml. II, 1, 93. *—d his handkerchief*, Cymb. I, 3, 6. Used of weapons, = to brandish: Troil. V, 5, 9. Caes. III, 1, 109. Cymb. IV, 2, 150.

b) to beckon: *it —s you to a more removed ground*, Hml. I, 4, 61. 68. 78 (Ff always *wafts*).

2) intr. a) to play loosely in the wind: Ven. 306. Shr. Ind. 2, 55. Particularly used of ensigns: H6A I, 6, 1. H6C II, 2, 173. Cor. III, 1, 8. Cymb. V, 5, 480.

b) to be uncertain, to fluctuate, to waver: *he —d indifferently 'twixt doing them neither good nor harm*, Cor. II, 2, 19.

**Waved,** indented, having on the margin a succession of arched and undulatory segments: *horns whelked and w. like the enridged sea*, Lr. IV, 6, 71.

**Waver,** to be unsettled in opinion, to fluctuate, to be fickle: Compl. 97. Merch. IV, 1, 130. Tw. II, 4, 35. R2 II, 2, 129. H4B Ind. 19. H6A IV, 1, 138.

**Waverer,** one inconstant and fickle: Rom. II, 3, 89.

**Wave-worn,** worn and undermined by the waves: Tp. II, 1, 120.

**Waw,** in *pow w.*, an exclamation of contempt: Cor. II, 1, 157 (M. Edd. *pow wow*).

**Wawl,** to cry in distress: *the first time that we smell the air, we w. and cry*, Lr. IV, 6, 184 (Qq *wail*). cf. *Catterwauling*.

**Wax,** subst. 1) the substance which bees form into cells for the reception of their honey: All's I, 2, 65. H4B IV, 5, 77. H6B IV, 2, 89. Quibbling in H4B I, 2, 180. Emblem of softness: Ven. 565. Pilgr. 88. H6C II, 1, 171. III, 2, 51. Tit. III, 1, 45. Rom. III, 3, 126. Hml. III, 4, 84. Used as a cement to attach papers to something: *set this up with w. upon old Brutus' statue*, Caes. I, 3, 145. to make impressions of things: *w. ... wherein is stamped the semblance of a devil*, Lucr. 1245. *as a form in w. by him imprinted*, Mids. I, 1, 49. *I cannot read: the character I'll take with w.* Tim. V, 3, 6. to make figures of: *which bleeds away, even as a form of w. resolveth from his figure 'gainst the fire*, John V, 4, 24. *he's a man of w.* Rom. I, 3, 76 (as pretty as if he had been modelled in wax). *thy noble shape is but a form of w. digressing from the valour of a man*, III, 3, 126. In the following passage there is probably an allusion to the ancient practice of writing on tablets coated with wax: *my free drift ... moves in a wide sea of w.* Tim. I, 1, 47.

2) sealing-wax: LLL IV, 1, 59. Tw. II, 5, 103. H6B IV, 2, 89. Lr. IV, 6, 264. Cymb. III, 2, 35. Quibbling in LLL V, 2, 10.

3) For the sake of punning, = growth: *a wassail candle, all tallow: if I did say of w., my growth would approve the truth,* H4B I, 2, 180.

**Wax,** vb. (impf. *waxed:* Gent. III, 1, 228. Err. I, 1, 92. Cor. II, 2, 103. partic. *waxed:* Tim. III, 4, 11. *waxen:* Lucr. 1663. H6B III, 2, 76) to grow; 1) to increase: *that* (to seal on his name) *was the way to make his godhead w.* LLL V, 2, 10. *he —ed like a sea,* Cor. II, 2, 103. *marks the —ing tide,* Tit. III, 1, 95. *as this temple —es,* Hml. I, 3, 12.

2) to become: *the colt that's backed and burdened being young loseth his pride and never —eth strong,* Ven. 420. *lips new —en pale,* Lucr. 1663. *as if but now they —ed pale for woe,* Gent. III, 1, 228. *the seas —ed calm,* Err. I, 1, 92. *old I do w.* H5 V, 1, 89. *a full eye will w. hollow,* V, 2, 170. 247. H6A II, 5, 9. H6B III, 2, 76. IV, 10, 22. Tit. III, 1, 223. Rom. I, 5, 128. Tim. III, 4, 11. Hml. I, 4, 87. III, 1, 101.

**Waxen,** adj. made of wax: *a w. torch,* Lucr. 178. *image,* Gent. II, 4, 201. *tapers,* Wiv. IV, 4, 50. *their* (humblebees') *w. thighs,* Mids. III, 1, 172 (used as tapers by the fairies).

Figuratively, = soft, and hence a) penetrable: *that it may enter Mowbray's w. coat,* R2 I, 3, 75. b) easily effaced: *not worshipped with a w. epitaph,* H5 I, 2, 233.* c) very impressible: *men have marble, women w. minds,* Lucr. 1240. *how easy is it ... in women's w. hearts to set their forms,* Tw. II, 2, 31.

**Waxen,** vb. to grow, to increase: *and w. in their mirth and neeze and swear a merrier hour was never wasted there,* Mids. II, 1, 56.

**Wax-red,** red as sealing wax: *set thy seal manual on my w. lips,* Ven. 516.

**Way,** 1) a place of passage; a path, a road, a street, or anything made for passengers: *some dark deep desert, seated from the w.* Lucr. 1144. *the —s are dangerous to pass,* Gent. IV, 3, 24. Wiv. III, 1, 3. 6. 9. LLL V, 2, 926 (*foul*). Mids. II, 2, 36. Merch. II, 2, 35. V, 264 (*fair*). As II, 7, 52. Shr. IV, 1, 2 (*foul*). Wint. IV, 3, 132 (*the footpath w.*). R2 II, 3, 4. III, 3, 156. H4A II, 1, 93 (*foul*). H4B I, 1, 39. II, 2, 184. Mcb. II, 3, 21. Hml. II, 2, 277 (*beaten w.*). Lr. IV, 1, 45. 57 etc.

2) passage; any place passed or to be passed through (whether intended for it or not) as well as the act of passing: *indenting with the w.* Ven. 704. *having lost the fair discovery of her w.* 828. *it is you that have chalked forth the w. which brought us hither,* Tp. V, 203. Gent. II, 4, 94. II, 7, 8. Wiv. II, 2, 175. III, 3, 175. Meas. II, 4, 19. IV, 1, 37. 41. Err. IV, 3, 92 (*shut the doors against his w.*). Mids. III, 2, 417. Shr. III, 2, 237. R2 I, 3, 206. 207. R3 III, 1, 3. Ant. II, 6, 83 (*show us the w.*) etc. Metaphorically: *perdition shall attend you and your —s,* Tp. III, 3, 79. *prevent the —s to wail,* H4B II, 2, 179. *in the tedious —s of art,* H4A III, 1, 48. *trod the —s of glory,* H8 III, 2, 436. *he's walked the w. of nature,* H4B V, 2, 4 (= he has died). *I knew there was but one w.* H5 II, 3, 16 (i. e. he must die). *'tis the next w. to turn tailor,* H4A III, 1, 264. *is the next w. to draw new mischief on,* Oth. I, 3, 205 etc.

*To bring on the w.* = to accompany in setting out on a journey or walk: *that we may bring you something on the w.* Meas. I, 1, 62. *we will bring you on your w.* LLL V, 2, 883. Wint. IV, 3, 122. R2 I, 3, 304. I, 4, 2. Oth. III, 4, 197.

*Come your w.,* and oftener *come your —s,* = come: *come your w., sir,* Meas. III, 2, 12. *come your —s, sir,* 84. As I, 2, 221. II, 3, 66. All's II, 1, 96. 97. Tw. II, 5, 1. Troil. III, 2, 47. Hml. I, 3, 135. Lr. II, 2, 42. Per. IV, 2, 44. 158. IV, 6, 134. *come on your —s,* in the same sense: Tp. II, 2, 85 (Stephano's speech).

*To give w.* = a) to make room for passing, to make or suffer to pass: *to the brightest beams distracted clouds give w.* All's V, 3, 35. *open your gates and give the victors w.* John II, 324. *give w., dull clouds, to my quick curses,* R3 I, 3, 196. *I will give you w. for these your letters,* Hml. IV, 6, 32 (Qq *make you w.*). Hence = to make room to, to step back before another: *give them w. till he take leave, and presently after him,* Tw. III, 4, 217. *so must thy grave give w. to what's seen now,* Wint. V, 1, 98. *our country manners give our betters w.* John I, 156. *if you give w. or hedge aside,* Troil. III, 3, 157. *I will fear to catch it and give w.* Tim. IV, 3, 358. *give w. there, and go on!* Cor. II, 1, 210 (cf. *w. alone: a w. there, a w. for Caesar,* Ant. V, 2, 336). *lesser enmities may give w. to greater,* Ant. II, 1, 43. *small to greater matters must give w.* II, 2, 11. b) to yield, not to resist, to let do: *'tis a good dulness, and give it w.* Tp. I, 2, 186. *I have given w. unto this course of fortune,* Ado IV, 1, 158. *give even w. unto my rough affairs,* H4B II, 3, 2. *I gave bold w. to my authority,* V, 2, 82. *now is it manhood ... to give the enemy w.* H6B V, 2, 76. *they shall no more prevail than we give w. to,* H8 V, 1, 144. *it must omit real necessities and give w. the while to unstable slightness,* Cor. II, 1, 147. *we gave w. unto your clusters,* IV, 6, 122. *gave him w. in all his own desires,* V, 6, 32. *security gives w. to conspiracy,* Caes. II, 3, 8. *must I give w. and room to your rash choler?* IV, 3, 39. *the cursed thoughts that nature gives w. to in repose,* Mcb. II, 1, 9. *for mine own good all causes must give w.* III, 4, 136. *'tis best to give him w.* Lr. II, 4, 301. *that nature thus gives w. to loyalty,* III, 5, 4. *all the power of his wits have given w. to his impatience,* III, 6, 5. *in each thing give him w., cross him in nothing,* Ant. I, 3, 9. *you must give w.* Cymb. I, 1, 158. c) to enter into another's thoughts or wishes, to favour, to humour: *though now the time gives w. to us,* H8 III, 2, 16. *if he slay me, he does fair justice; if he give me w., I'll do his country service,* Cor. IV, 4, 25. *if the peevish baggage would but give w. to customers,* Per. IV, 6, 20. *give him w.* V, 1, 232 (do as if you also heard the music which he pretends to hear).

*Go thy w., go your w.,* and oftener *go thy —s, go your —s,* = go: *go your —s and ask ...,* Wiv. I, 2, 1. *go your —s and play,* IV, 1, 81. *go your w. to her and say this to her,* As IV, 3, 70. *go thy —s, let the horses be well looked to,* All's IV, 5, 61. *go thy —s, old Jack, die when thou wilt,* H4A II, 4, 141. *go thy —s to a nunnery,* Hml. III, 1, 132. *go thy —s, good mariner,* Per. III, 1, 81. Implying reproach: *go thy w., thou shalt not from this grove,* Mids. II, 1, 146. *now, go thy w.* III, 2, 428. *go your —s, go your —s,* As IV, 1, 186. *go thy —s, I begin to be aweary of thee,* All's IV, 5, 59. *go thy —s, go, give that changing piece to him,* Tit. I, 309. And, on the other hand, used in a tone of exhortation or applause: *sayest thou so, old Jack? go thy —s*, Wiv. II, 2, 144. *Petruchio, go thy —s, the field is won*, Shr. IV, 5, 23. *well, go thy —s, old lad, for thou shalt ha't*, V, 2, 181. *well, go thy w.; if Sir Toby would leave drinking, thou wert as witty a piece of Eve's flesh as any*, Tw. I, 5, 29. *go thy —s, Kate*, H8 II, 4, 133. *go thy w., Hector, there's a brave man*, Troil. I, 2, 216. 256. *go thy —s, wench, serve God*, Rom. II, 5, 45. cf. Per. IV, 6, 71.

*To have w.* or *to have one's w.* = to have free scope: *let me have w. to find this practice out*, Meas. V, 238. *let him have his w.* All's III, 6, 2. *he'll lade it dry to have his w.* H6C III, 2, 139.

*To hold one's w.* = to keep one's course, to go on: *let determined things to destiny hold unbewailed their w.* Ant. III, 6, 85.

*To keep one's w.* = to go on, not to stop: Wiv. III, 2, 1. Ado I, 1, 144. H8 II, 4, 128.

*To lead the w.* = to go at the head, to set the example of going: Tp. II, 2, 177. 192. Wiv. I, 1, 318. Shr. IV, 4, 69. Tw. IV, 3, 34. H6B II, 4, 110. H6C V, 1, 112. H8 V, 5, 73. Troil. III, 3, 54. Oth. II, 3, 207. *lead's the w.* Per. V, 3, 84.

*There lies your w.* = go if you please; you had better go: *the door is open, sir: there lies your w.* Shr. III, 2, 212. *will you hoist sail, sir? here lies your w.* Tw. I, 5, 216. *there lies your w., due west*, III, 1, 145. cf. *here lies our w.* = let us go, Troil. IV, 1, 79.

*To make w.* = a) to give place, to make room: *make w., unruly woman*, R2 V, 2, 110. *make w. there for the princess*, H8 V, 4, 91. Cor. II, 2, 40. Tit. I, 64. 89. Ant. V, 2, 110. b) to form and prepare a passage: *when the w. was made and paved with gold*, H8 I, 1, 187. c) to open a path through obstacles: *through the instrument my pate made w.* Shr. II, 155. *my sword shall make w. for me*, H6B IV, 8, 62. *make cruel w. through ranks of Greekish youth*, Troil. IV, 5, 184. *I will make you w. for these letters*, Hml. IV, 6, 32 (Ff *give you w.*). *I have made my w. through more impediments*, Oth. V, 2, 263. d) to go, to pass: *I make w. from hence to save my life*, Shr. I, 1, 239. *making their w. with those of nobler bulk*, Troil. I, 3, 36. *follow where the game makes w.* Tit. II, 2, 24. *make a clear w. to the gods*, Tim. III, 4, 77 (die with a good conscience). e) to advance successfully: *follow me and mark what w. I make*, Wint. V, 1, 233. *the force of his own merit makes his w.* H8 I, 1, 64. *thou dost make thy w. to noble fortunes*, Lr. V, 3, 29.

*To take a w.* or *one's w.* = to set out, to go: *when I took my w.* Sonn. 48, 1. *that presently you take your w. for home*, All's II, 5, 69. *take the instant w.* Troil. III, 3, 153. *take your own w.* Cymb. I, 5, 31.

*By the w.* = a) while going along, on the route: *an intent that perished by the w.* Meas. V, 458. *by the w. we met my wife*, Err. V, 235. *which accidentally, or by the w. of progression, hath miscarried*, LLL IV, 2, 144 (Holofernes' speech). *by the w. let us recount our dreams*, Mids. IV, 1, 204. Merch. III, 2, 231. As III, 2, 452. Wint. IV, 4, 255. R3 II, 2, 148. IV, 5, 15. Troil. IV, 4, 114. b) by the by: *I can tell you that by the w.* Wiv. I, 4, 150. Shr. IV, 2, 115. Cymb. III, 2, 61. *I hear it by the w.* Mcb. III, 4, 130 (i. e. occasionally and indirectly). c) with *of*, = for the purpose of: *we come not by the w. of accusation*, H8 III, 1, 54.

*In the w.* = where one passes: *he strikes whate'er is in his w.* Ven. 623. *the bushes in the w.* 871. 879.

*lie tumbling in my barefoot w.* Tp. II, 2, 11. Gent. I, 2, 39. Err. IV, 2, 61. Merch. V, 294. H4A V, 3, 60. Noting hinderance and obstruction: *thank God, and the good wine in thy master's w.* H6B II, 3, 99.

*On the w.* = in going or travelling along: H4A IV, 2, 39. V, 1, 36. H4B I, 1, 30. R3 III, 1, 4. 21. 160. IV, 1, 51. Hml. II, 2, 330. III, 1, 17. Lr. IV, 2, 2. 14. *you should have been well on your w. to York*, H4B II, 1, 73. *every rub is smoothed on our w.* H5 II, 2, 188. *let's on our w. in silent sort*, H6C IV, 2, 28. *light thee on thy w. to Mantua*, Rom. III, 5, 15. *she is two months on her w.* LLL V, 2, 679 (i. e. with child. Costard's speech).

*Out of the w.* = a) making room, so as to be no hinderance: *out of our w., I say*, Tp. I, 1, 29. *to draw the Moor out of the w.* Oth. III, 1, 40. *nor send you out o'the w.* IV, 2, 7. b) astray; quite beside the mark: *lead me out of my w.* Tp. II, 2, 7. *we are much out o'the w.* LLL IV, 3, 76. *it is clean out of the w.* Oth. I, 3, 366. c) gone, lost: *is't lost? is't gone? speak, is it out o'the way?* Oth. III, 4, 80.

3) direction, side: *he turns his lips another w.* Ven. 90. *which w. shall she turn?* 253. *this w. she runs*, 905. *a thousand spleens bear her a thousand —s*, 907. *my consent goes not that w.* Wiv. III, 2, 79. *I am that w. going to temptation, where prayers cross*, Meas. II, 2, 158. *which w. looks he?* Ado I, 3, 55. *you that w., we this w.* LLL V, 2, 941. *that w. goes the game*, Mids. III, 2, 289 (= now I see your drift). *fairies, be gone, and be all —s away*, IV, 1, 46 (O. Edd. *always*). *I shot his fellow the selfsame w.* Merch. I, 1, 142. *this w. the coverlet, another w. the sheets*, Shr. IV, 1, 205. *I come one w. of the Plantagenets*, John V, 6, 11 (i. e. by the father's side). *turn not thy scorns this w.* H6A II, 4, 77. *turn thy edged sword another w.* III, 3, 52. *now sways it this w. ... now sways it that w.* H6C II, 5, 5. 7. *plucked all gaze his w.* Cor. I, 3, 8. *nothing, neither w.* Hml. V, 2, 312 (on neither side). *to avert your liking a more worthier w.* Lr. I, 1, 214. *though he be painted one w. like a Gorgon, the other w. 's a Mars*, Ant. II, 5, 116. *stands upon the swell ... and neither w. inclines*, III, 2, 50. *apes ... would chatter this w.* Cymb. I, 6, 40.

*This w.* often = here, hither: *this w. comes he with it presently*, Gent. III, 1, 42. *come a little nearer this —s*, Wiv. II, 2, 47. 50 (Mrs Quickly's speech). *yonder he is coming this w.* III, 1, 27. 33. Err. V, 120. Tw. I, 5, 324. Wint. IV, 4, 20. H6B I, 3, 2. H6C IV, 5, 10. Tim. I, 2, 137. Mcb. IV, 1, 45.

Metaphorically, = tendency, character, kind: *men of his w. should be most liberal*, H8 I, 3, 61. *the w. of our profession is against it*, III, 1, 157. *you're a gentleman of mine own w.* V, 1, 28.

And = respect, point of view: *you are gone both —s*, Merch. III, 5, 20. *their residence, both in reputation and profit, was better both —s*, Hml. II, 2, 345. *one w. I like this well, ... another w. the news is not so tart*, Lr. IV, 2, 83. 86. *any w.* = in any respect, at all: *if the wind blow any w. from shore*, Err. III, 2, 153. *if I can cross him any w.* Ado I, 3, 70. *uncertain of the issue any w.* H4A I, 1, 61. *if that the king have any w. your good deserts forgot*, IV, 3, 46. *will not any w. dishonour me*, H6A V, 3, 102. *nor to betray you any w. to sorrow*, H8 III, 1, 56. *every w.* = in every respect: *he will every w. be mocked*, Wiv. V, 3, 20. *I bless myself every w.* Ado I, 3, 71. *my fortunes every w. as fairly ranked*, Mids. I, 1, 101. *is the young Dau-*

*phin every w. complete*, John II, 433. *you wrong me every w.* Caes. IV, 3, 55. *no w.* = not at all: *if the gentle spirit of moving words can no w. change you*, Gent. V, 4, 56. *I think nobly of the soul and no w. approve this opinion*, Tw. IV, 2, 59. *you must in no w. say he is covetous*, Cor. I, 1, 43. *it comes from them to you and no w. from yourselves*, 158. *that w.* = in that respect, in that point: *no hope that w. is another w. so high a hope*, Tp. II, 1, 240. *he is something peevish that w.* Wiv. I, 4, 14. *too crabbed that w.* Meas. III, 2, 105. *he was not inclined that w.* 130. *all that offend that w.* II, 1, 252. *I shall lessen God's sending that w.* Ado II, 1, 24. Wint. IV, 3, 116. H4A II, 4, 401. Cymb. I, 1, 137. I, 4, 101. *this w.* = in this point: *our breach of duty this w. is business of state*, H8 II, 2, 69.

*In w. of* or *in the w. of* = 1) with respect to, in point of, concerning, the point in question being: *Hector's opinion is this in w. of truth*, Troil. II, 2, 189. *one that wouldst be a bawd, in w. of good service*, Lr. II, 2, 21. *in the w. of bargain ... I'll cavil on the ninth part of a hair*, H4A III, 1, 139. *that in the w. of loyalty ... dare mate a sounder man*, H8 III, 2, 272. *what my tongue can do i'the w. of flattery*, Cor. III, 2, 137. 2) with a view to, for the purpose of (the modern *by way of*): *a kind of insinuation ... in w. of explication*, LLL IV, 2, 14. *they'll not show their teeth in w. of smile*, Merch. I, 1, 55. *never to speak to lady ... in w. of marriage*, II, 1, 42. *never to woo a maid in w. of marriage*, II, 9, 13. *I will not open my lips so wide as a bristle may enter in w. of thy excuse*, Tw. I, 5, 3. *I do beseech you, as in w. of taste, to give me now a little benefit*, Troil. III, 3, 13. *so 'tis put on me, and that in w. of caution*, Hml. I, 3, 95. *to speak a good word for my master ... in the w. of marriage*, Wiv. I, 4, 89. *I defy all angels ... but in the w. of honesty*, II, 2, 75 (but cf. sub 6). *he will never in the w. of waste attempt us again*, IV, 2, 226. *in the w. of argument*, H5 III, 2, 104. *as a woman should not do, but in the w. of honesty*, Ant. V, 2, 253.

4) length of space, distance: *the w. is but short*, LLL III, 57. *it is not half w. to her heart*, Shr. I, 1, 62. *which is a great w. growing on the south*, Caes. II, 1, 107. *half w. down hangs one*, Lr. IV, 6, 14. *'tis but a little w. that I can bring you*, Oth. III, 4, 199. Metaphorically: *think him a great w. fool*, All's I, 1, 112 (= in a high degree). *if I cannot recover your niece, I am a foul w. out*, Tw. II, 3, 201.

5) proceeding, course, means: *to her will frame all thy —s*, Pilgr. 323. *my best w. is to creep under his gaberdine*, Tp. II, 2, 39. *the best w. is to slander Valentine*, Gent. III, 2, 31. Wiv. II, 1, 67. *have you any w. then to unfool me again?* IV, 2, 120. *admit no other w. to save his life*, Meas. II, 4, 88. *'twere the cheaper w.* 105. *my w. is now to hie home to his house*, Err. IV, 3, 93. *you go not the w. to examine*, Ado IV, 2, 35 (the sexton's speech). *this was a w. to thrive*, Merch. I, 3, 90. *indirect crooked —s*, H4B IV, 5, 185. *I think it is our w., if we will keep in favour with the king, to be her men*, R3 I, 1, 78. *those cold —s ... are very poisonous where the disease is violent*, Cor. III, 1, 220. *I knew it the most general w.* Tim. II, 2, 209. *that's the w.* Oth. II, 3, 393; cf. Meas. V, 280.

6) manner, mode: *a thousand —s he seeks to mend the hurt*, Ven. 477. *pausing for means to mourn some newer w.* Lucr. 1365. *wherefore do not you a mightier*

*w. make war ... upon time*, Sonn. 16, 1. *pity move my father to be inclined my w.* Tp. I, 2, 447. *I will one w. or other make you amends*, Wiv. III, 1, 89. *after this downright w. of creation*, Meas. III, 2, 112. *that's the w.* V, 280 (cf. Oth. II, 3, 393). *you must wear it one w.* Ado II, 1, 198. *use it* (your hand) *some other w.* IV, 1, 329. *it must appear in other —s than words*, Merch. V, 140. *and this w. will I take upon me to wash your liver as clean*, As III, 2, 442. V, 1, 63. All's V, 3, 276 (*by none of all these —s*). Wint. IV, 4, 33. 151. John I, 181 (*thou wast got in the w. of honesty*; cf. Wiv. II, 2, 75 and Ant. V, 2, 253). H4B IV, 5, 127. Troil. IV, 5, 71. Cor. V, 6, 58 (*after your w. his tale pronounced*). Tit. II, 1, 119. Tim. I, 2, 55 (*let it flow this way*, = in this manner, i. e. with full cups). Caes. II, 2, 91. III, 1, 192. Lr. IV, 3, 21 (*her smiles and tears were like, a better way; i. e.* resembled sunshine and rain, but in a more beautiful manner). Ant. I, 3, 10. V, 2, 359. Cymb. IV, 4, 4 etc. *how and which w.*, pleonastically: *how and which w. I may bestow myself*, Gent. III, 1, 87. *how and which w. you will*, All's IV, 3, 157. *how or which way to order these affairs*, R2 II, 2, 109. *how or which way should they first break in?* H6A II, 1, 71. 73.

**Waylay**, to lie in wait for, to ambush: *I will w. thee going home*, Tw. III, 4, 176. = to set an ambush for: *Falstaff ... shall rob those men that we have already waylaid*, H4A I, 2, 183.

**Wayward**, capricious and obstinate: Ven. 344. Lucr. 1095. Gent. I, 2, 57. Err. IV, 4, 4. Ado II, 1, 65. LLL III, 181. As IV, 1, 162 (*the wiser, the —er*). R2 II, 1, 142. R3 I, 3, 29. IV, 4, 168. Rom. IV, 2, 47. Mcb. III, 5, 11. Oth. III, 3, 292. Per. IV, 4, 10 (*w. seas*). V, 1, 90 (*w. fortune*).

**Waywardness**, capricious obstinacy: Lr. I, 1, 302.

**We** (obj. case *us*; often apostrophized): *let's assist them*, Tp. I, 1, 57. 67. II, 1, 323. III, 2, 157. Gent. I, 2, 88. LLL I, 1, 123. Merch. II, 7, 36. Lr. I, 2, 45 etc. *speed's* Ado V, 3, 32. *cram's, make's*, Wint. I, 2, 91. *ride's*, 94. *give's* Ant. II, 7, 134. *laugh at's*, Ant. III, 13, 114. *between's*, Wint. I, 2, 18. V, 3, 138. Ant. III, 4, 25. *from's*, Cymb. III, 1, 15. *to's*, LLL II, 25. Wint. IV, 4, 65. Ant. IV, 9, 5. *upon's*, Tp. I, 2, 137. II, 2, 60. Cymb. III, 1, 52. *with's*, Ant. III, 1, 36 etc.), personal pronoun, plural of *I*: Ven. 125. 126. 585. 586. Lucr. 144. 148. 152. 153 etc. *us*: Ven. 421. 534. Lucr. 151. 1840 etc. *We* for *us*: *to poor we thine enmity's most capital*, Cor. V, 3, 103. *let no man abide this deed, but we the doers*, Caes. III, 1, 95. *making night hideous, and we fools of nature so horridly to shake our disposition*, Hml. I, 4, 54. *hath more ministers than we that draw his knives i'the war*, Cymb. 3, 72. *Us* for *we: shall's attend you there?* Wint. I, 2, 178. *shall's to the Capitol?* Cor. IV, 6, 148. *how shall's get it?* Tim. IV, 3, 408. *where shall's lay him?* Cymb. IV, 2, 233. *for this from stiller seats we came, our parents and us twain*, V, 4, 70. *shall's have a play of this?* V, 5, 228. *shall's go hear the vestals sing?* Per. IV, 5, 7.

*We* for *I* in the royal style: Meas. V, 2. 5. 17. All's III, 1, 7. R3 IV, 4, 472. Ant. II, 7, 134 etc. *I and we* alternately: *I am about to weep, but thinking that we are a queen, ... my drops of tears I'll turn to sparks of fire*, H8 II, 4, 71. *a charge we bear i'the war, and as the president of my kingdom will appear there for a man*, Ant. III, 7, 17. *my peace we will begin*, Cymb. V, 5, 459. Sometimes used for *I* by inferior persons, f. i. All's III, 3, 5; especially in the phrase *let us see* = let me see, f. i. Gent. I, 2, 88. Merch. II, 7, 36. Lr. I, 2, 45. IV, 6, 263.

The subjunctive of the present, followed by *we*, expressing an invitation, = let us: *then go we near her, that her ear lose nothing,* Ado III, 1, 32 (= let us go). LLL I, 1, 308. *trip we after the night's shade,* Mids. IV, 1, 101. *do we so,* Merch. II, 8, 53. *but go we in ... and ceremoniously let us prepare some welcome,* V, 36. *and to cut off all strife, here sit we down,* Shr. III, 1, 21. *let me embrace with old Vincentio, and wander we to see thy honest son,* IV, 5, 69. John II, 559. R2 I, 2, 6. H4B V, 2, 134. H5 I, 1, 95. IV, 8, 118. V, 2, 398. H6A II, 1, 13. III, 2, 102. III, 3, 68. H6B I, 1, 199. II, 2, 59. 77. II, 4, 106. III, 1, 322. H6C II, 3, 56. II, 6, 31. III, 1, 8. III, 2, 121. V, 1, 62. R3 II, 2, 141. Troil. IV, 5, 272. V, 3, 10. Tit. IV, 2, 132. Mcb. II, 2, 66. IV, 1, 127. Hml. I, 1, 33. 168. IV, 5, 106 etc. We omitted: *whether we shall meet again I know not; therefore our everlasting farewell take,* Caes. V, 1, 116.

*Us* for *ourselves,* reflectively: *we'll rest us,* Mids. II, 2, 37. *we will ... disguise us,* Merch. II, 4, 2. *we could at once put us in readiness,* Shr. I, 1, 43. *we, poising us in her defective scale,* All's II, 3, 161. *it is most meet we arm us 'gainst the foe,* H5 II, 4, 15. *let's get us from the walls,* H6A III, 2, 71. *we will repose us here,* H6B II, 1, 200. *to secure us by what we can,* V, 2, 76. *will cast us down,* Tit. V, 3, 132. *we will divest us,* Lr. I, 1, 50. *we'll there secure us,* Cymb. IV, 4, 8 etc. As dative: *shall we go and kill us venison?* As II, 1, 21. *we make us comforts of our losses,* All's IV, 3, 77. *let's make us medicines of our great revenge,* Mcb. IV, 3, 214 (cf. the dat. commodi: *we have not spoke us yet of torch-bearers,* Merch. II, 4, 5. *she looks us like a thing more made of malice than of duty,* Cymb. III, 5, 32).

**Weak,** 1) having little physical strength (either by nature, or in consequence of any thing that impairs the natural force): Ven. 1145. Lucr. 555. 1242 (= soft, pliant, impressible?). 1646. 1647. Pilgr. 163. LLL I, 1, 276 (*the —er vessel; cf. Vessel*). Merch. II, 1, 34. IV, 1, 115. As II, 4, 6. II, 7, 132.* Shr. V, 2, 165. 174. All's II, 1, 140. 179. II, 3, 39. III, 4, 41. R2 III, 2, 62. H4B II, 4, 66. 67. 385. H6A II, 3, 23. Troil. I, 3, 43 (*w. untimbered sides*). Caes. I, 3, 108 (*w. straws*). Mcb. IV, 3, 16. Cymb. III, 6, 37 etc. Applied to troops too small in number or not sufficiently prepared: All's IV, 3, 151. R2 II, 3, 154. H4A IV, 4, 19. H5 III, 6, 164. H6A I, 1, 158. III, 2, 7. IV, 4, 16. H6C II, 3, 13. IV, 5, 7. cf. All's I, 1, 127. John V, 7, 78.

2) powerless in operation, inefficacious: *my will is strong, past reason's w. removing,* Lucr. 243. *w. sights* (= eyes) Compl. 214. *w. masters though ye be,* Tp. V, 41. *means much —er,* 146. *her w. prayers,* Mids. III, 2, 250. *a w. bond holds you,* 268. *w. wind,* John V, 2, 87. H4B IV, 5, 100. Cor. V, 2, 50. *so w. a composition* (small beer) H4B II, 2, 10. *a w. and niggardly projection,* H5 II, 4, 46. *their villany goes against my w. stomach,* III, 2, 56. *the w. list of a country's fashion,* V, 2, 295. *my ancient incantations are too w.* H6A V, 3, 27. *my title's w.* H6C I, 1, 134. III, 3, 145. *my w. oratory,* R3 III, 1, 37. *a w. and colder palate,* Troil. IV, 4, 7. *my w. words,* Caes. I, 2, 176. *motives,* II, 1, 116. Mcb. I, 2, 15 etc.

3) slight, inconsiderable, little: *so strong a prop to support so w. a burden,* Ven. Ded. 2. *my love is strengthened, though more w. in seeming,* Sonn. 102, 1. *this w. impress of love,* Gent. III, 2, 6. *this w. and idle theme,* Mids. V, 434. *a w. and worthless satisfaction,* H5 III, 6, 141. *such things as might offend the —est spleen,* Troil. II, 2, 128. *holding a w. supposal of our worth,* Hml. I, 2, 18. *mine own w. merits,* Oth. III, 3, 187. *one* (life) *is too poor, too w. for my revenge,* 443.

4) wanting spirit and moral power: *to whose* (his) *soul's temple) w. ruins muster troops of cares,* Lucr. 720. *in thy w. hive a wandering wasp hath crept,* 839. *to be afeard of my deserving were but a w. disabling of myself,* Merch. II, 7, 30. *w. fear,* H4A IV, 3, 11. *so w. of courage and in judgment,* H6C IV, 1, 12. *in this w. piping time of peace,* R3 I, 1, 24. *the w. wanton Cupid,* Troil. III, 3, 222. *a w. slave,* Rom. I, 1, 17.

5) feeble of mind, wanting understanding and discernment: *to be of such a w. and silly mind,* Ven. 1016. *the w. brain's forgeries,* Lucr. 460. *this lord of w. remembrance,* Tp. II, 1, 232. *made wit with musing w.* Gent. I, 1, 69. *my conceit, smothered in errors, feeble, shallow, w.* Err. III, 2, 35. *their sense thus w.* Mids. III, 2, 27. *has a most w. pia mater,* Tw. I, 5, 123. *had our w. spirits ne'er been higher reared,* Wint. I, 2, 72. *sick interpreters, once w. ones,* H8 I, 2, 82. *conceit in —est bodies* (= persons) *strongest works,* Hml. III, 4, 114 (or in a physical sense?).

Almost = stupid: *a very w. monster,* Tp. II, 2, 148. *her wit values itself so highly that to her all matter else seems w.* Ado III, 1, 54. *fancies too w. for boys,* Wint. III, 2, 182. *a w. mind and an able body,* H4B II, 4, 273. *that the —er sort may wish good Marcius home again,* Cor. IV, 6, 69. *it were very w. dealing,* Rom. II, 4, 180 (the nurse's speech). *play the god with his w. function,* Oth. II, 3, 354.

**Weak-built,** ill founded: *w. hopes,* Lucr. 130.

**Weaken,** 1) tr. to enfeeble, to debilitate: Sonn. 23, 4. R2 V, 1, 27. H4B I, 1, 144. Troil. I, 3, 195. Oth. I, 2, 75.

2) intr. to become feeble: *his notion —s, his discernings are lethargied,* Lr. I, 4, 248.

**Weak-hearted,** spiritless: *to endure more miseries and greater far than my w. enemies dare offer,* H8 III, 2, 390.

**Weak-hinged,** supported by a weak hinge, ill founded: *your own w. fancy,* Wint. II, 3, 119. cf. *hinge* in Oth. III, 3, 365.

**Weakling,** a feeble creature: Lucr. 584. H6C V, 1, 37.

**Weakly,** 1) without sufficient strength: *w. fortressed,* Lucr. 28. *w. guarded,* H6A II, 1, 74. *you are w. made,* H8 II, 3, 40.

2) indiscreetly, injudiciously, stupidly: *I will not adventure my discretion so w.* Tp. II, 1, 188.

**Weak-made,** having by nature little strength: *make w. women tenants to their shame,* Lucr. 1260.

**Weakness,** want of strength; 1) in a physical sense: Ven. 892. Tp. I, 2, 487. Err. II, 2, 177. As II, 3, 51. Shr. V, 2, 174. John V, 3, 17. H8 IV, 2, 117. Caes. I, 3, 276 (*the w. of mine eyes*). Hml. II, 2, 148. Oth. II, 3, 43. Ant. V, 2, 347. 2) in a military sense: H5 III, 6, 132. H6A III, 2, 25. Troil. I, 3, 137. Cor. IV, 5, 146. 3) in a moral sense: Sonn. 88, 5. Tp. IV, 159. Meas. II, 4, 123. All's II, 1, 88. Wint. II, 3, 1. 2. R2 III, 2, 181. H6C V, 4, 38. R3 I, 3, 28. H8 V, 3, 72. Troil. III, 2, 140.

**Weal,** 1) welfare, prosperity, happiness: *our w., on you depending, counts it your w. to have his liberty,* John IV, 2, 65. 66. *tends to God's glory and my country's w.* H6A V, 1, 27. *touching the w. o'the common,* Cor. I, 1, 155. *of him that, his particular to foresee, smells from the general w.* Tim. IV, 3, 160. *that spirit upon whose w.* (Ff *spirit*) *depend and rest the lives of many,* Hml. III, 3, 14. *in the tender of a wholesome w.* Lr. I, 4, 230. *w.* and *woe* opposed: Ven. 987. H6A III, 2, 92. Rom. III, 2, 51.

2) commonwealth, body politic, state (cf. *Commonweal*): *sit at chiefest stern of public w.* H6A I, 1, 177. *the special watchmen of our English w.* III, 1, 66. *the charters that you bear i'the body of the w.* Cor. II, 3, 189. *a foe to the public w.* III, 1, 176. *ere human statute purged the gentle w.* Mcb.III, 4, 76 (cf. Appendix, Prolepsis). *the medicine of the sickly w.* V, 2, 27.

**Weal-balanced,** kept in a state of just proportion by reasons of state: *from thence, by cold gradation and w. form, we shall proceed with Angelo,* Meas. IV, 3, 104 (not eagerly and passionately, as my personal feelings would prompt me, but with due observance of all forms, which it would be against the public interest not to observe. M. Edd. unnecessarily and somewhat flatly *well-balanced*).

**Weald,** see *Wild,* subst. 2.

**Wealsmen,** statesmen: *two such w. as you are — I cannnot call you Lycurguses,* Cor. II, 1, 59.

**Wealth,** 1) welfare, prosperity: *I once did lend my body for his w.* Merch.V, 249. *this is the imposthume of much w. and peace,* Hml. IV, 4, 27.

2) riches: Lucr. 17. 142. Sonn. 29, 13. 37, 5. 67, 13. 75, 4. 91, 2. Compl. 270. Gent. I, 2, 13. III, 1, 362. 376. IV, 1, 11. Wiv. III, 2, 78. III, 3, 232 *(the w. of Windsor Castle).* III, 4, 6. 13. Err. I, 1, 40. III, 2, 5. 6. V, 8. 49 *(lost much w.).* Ado I, 1, 70. LLL I, 1, 31. IV, 3, 149. Merch. III, 2, 257. III, 5, 62 *( the whole w. of thy wit).* IV, 1, 269. 365. 370. V, 173 *(for the w. that the world masters).* As I, 3, 136 *(get our jewels and our w. together).* II, 5, 54. Shr. I, 2, 68. IV, 2, 98. All's II, 5, 84. John IV, 1, 131 *(for the w. of all the world).* H4A II, 4, 280 *(were masters of their w.).* IV, 1, 46. H6A V, 5, 46. H6B IV, 1, 82. IV, 10, 23. H6C IV, 8, 44. H8 III, 2, 284. Tim. IV, 3, 495 *(whilst this poor w. lasts).* Lr. I, 1, 211 etc.

**Wealthily,** richly: *I come to wive it w. in Padua; if w., then happily in Padua,* Shr. I, 2, 75. 76.

**Wealthy,** rich: Merch. I, 1, 27. I, 3, 58. V, 15. Shr. IV, 2, 37. IV, 5, 65 *(her dowry w.).* All's II, 3, 72 *(—est).* H6B I, 1, 154. IV, 7, 68. H6C I, 4, 123. Tim. II, 2, 193. III, 3, 3. Oth. I, 2, 68.

**Wean,** 1) to put from the breast, to ablactate: *take all and w. it; it may prove an ox,* LLL V, 2, 250. *she was —ed,* Rom. I, 3, 24.

2) to avert, to alienate: *I the rather w. me from despair for love of Edward's offspring in my womb,* H6C IV, 4, 17 (O. Edd. *wain*). *I will restore to thee the people's hearts, and w. them from themselves,* Tit. I, 211.

**Weapon,** an instrument of offence, particularly a sword: Lucr. 1432. Tp. I, 2, 473. II, 1, 320. 322. Wiv. I, 4, 125. II, 1, 216. III, 1, 30. 31. 73. 76. Ado V, 2, 22. Mids. IV, 1, 11. Merch. III, 1, 64. Shr. III, 2, 238. H4B I, 1, 197. II, 1, 17. II, 4, 222. IV, 3, 123 *(skill in the w.).* H5 III, 2, 38. H6A I, 3, 78

*(any sword, w., or dagger).* II, 1, 81. III, 1, 79. H6B I, 3, 61. II, 1, 180. II, 3, 98. III, 1, 347. III, 2, 237. IV, 2, 131. IV, 8, 18. V, 1, 140. H6C I, 3, 51. II, 1, 129. V, 6, 26. R3 III, 1, 122. Troil. V, 7, 5. Cor. III, 1, 185. Tit. II, 1, 59. IV, 2, 11. V, 1, 37. Rom. I, 1, 39. Caes. III, 1, 109. Mcb. V, 7, 12. Hml. V, 2, 148. 151. Lr. II, 4, 280 *(women's —s, water-drops).* Oth. I, 1, 182. V, 2, 252 etc.

**Weaponed,** provided with a weapon (a sword): *be not afraid, though you do see me w.* Oth. V, 2, 266.

**Wear,** subst. fashion: *your good worship will be my bail. No, indeed, will I not, Pompey; it is not the w.* Meas. III, 2, 78. *motley's the only w.* As II, 7, 34. *the composition that your valour and fear makes in you is a virtue of a good wing, and I like the w. well,* All's I, 1, 219. *any toys for your head of the newest and finest w.* Wint. IV, 4, 327.

**Wear,** vb. (impf. *wore,* partic. *worn.* In Tit. I, 6 Qq *ware,* Ff *wore*) 1) trans. a) to carry appendant to the body; as clothes or ornaments, in a proper and metaphorical sense: Ven. 163. 415. 1081. 1107. Lucr. 680. 1222. Tp. II, 1, 103. Gent. II, 7, 51. III, 1, 135. V, 2, 6. Meas. I, 2, 173. Err. V, 17. Ado I, 1, 200. II, 1, 196. LLL IV, 3, 48. V, 2, 130. Mids. II, 2, 71. Tw. I, 5, 63. III, 4, 228. H4A IV, 3, 55 *(royalty =* crown). H6A II, 4, 72. H6B I, 3, 88 *(her worst —ing gown).* 149. R3 III, 2, 95. IV, 2, 5. Troil. V, 2, 93. 95. Tit. I, 6. Mcb. IV, 1, 88 etc. *w. their brave state out of memory,* Sonn. 15, 8 (= be forgotten). *they w. themselves in the cap of the time,* All's II, 1, 54 (not quite = are worn, but rather = they place themselves in it, pretend to be the ornaments of society and the leaders of fashion).

Used of weapons (also = to wield, to manage): Wiv. I, 3, 84. Merch. III, 4, 65. Tw. III, 4, 276. H6A I, 3, 78. H6B III, 2, 197. Caes. I, 3, 89. Hml. II, 2, 359. Lr. II, 2, 78. Oth. V, 1, 2. Ant. IV, 14, 79 etc. Figuratively: *great tyranny, ... w. thou thy wrongs; the title is affeered,* Mcb. IV, 3, 33 (handle them like weapons, perform them fearlessly),

Of parts of the body: *the web* (i. e. downy beard) *it* (the skin) *seemed to w.* Compl. 95. *if these be true spies* (the eyes) *which I w. in my head,* Tp. V, 259. *does he not w. a great round beard,* Wiv. I, 4, 20. *he should have worn the horns on his head,* Mids. V, 244. *w. beards,* Merch. III, 2, 84. V, 158. *—s a precious jewel in his head,* As II, 1, 14. *see thee w. thy heart in a scarf,* V, 2, 23. *his right cheek is worn bare,* IV, 5, 103. *where a wasp does w. his sting,* Shr. II, 214. *shall not w. a head on his shoulders,* H6B IV, 7, 127. R3 III, 2, 94. Troil. II, 1, 79. III, 3, 271. Cor. II, 1, 195. IV, 4, 13. V, 3, 38. Mcb. II, 2, 65. Oth. III, 3, 198. Cymb. I, 1, 13. III, 1, 14. III, 5, 14 etc. Hence applied to any external mark or appearance exhibited: *the impression of keen whips I'ld w. as rubies,* Meas. II, 4, 101. *w. the print of it* (a yoke) Ado I, 1, 203. *he —s his honour in a box unseen,* All's II, 3, 296. *a countenance as clear as friendship —s at feasts,* Wint. I, 2, 344. *w. the detested blot of murderous subornation,* H4A I, 3, 162. *who —s my stripes impressed upon him,* Cor. V, 6, 108. *w. the brows of grace,* Mcb. IV,3,23. *they know not how their wits to w.* Lr. I, 4, 183. *he —s the rose of youth upon him,* Ant. III, 13, 20.

b) = to bear, to carry: *w. prayer-books in my pocket,* Merch. II, 2, 201. Especially, in the same manner as *to bear* (q. v.) = to have, to own, to harbour: *bestowed her on her own lamentation, which she yet —s for his sake,* Meas. III, 1, 238. *he —s his faith but as the fashion of his hat,* Ado I, 1, 75. *let none presume to w. an undeserved dignity,* Merch. II, 9, 40. *I will deeply put the fashion* (of sorrow) *on and w. it in my heart,* H4B V, 2, 53. *to w. our mortal state to come with her,* H8 II, 4, 228 (to spend the rest of our life with her). *ne'er did poor steward w. a truer grief for his undone lord than mine eyes for you,* Tim. IV, 3, 487. *who w. our health but sickly in his life,* Mcb. III, 1, 107. *I will w. him in my heart's core,* Hml. III, 2, 77. *a slave should w. a sword who —s no honesty,* Lr. II, 2, 79. *I wore my life to spend upon his haters,* Ant. V, 1, 8. *if you could w. a mind dark as your fortune is,* Cymb. III, 4, 146. *knighthoods and honours, borne as I w. mine, are titles but of scorn,* V, 2, 7. *the worth that learned charity aye —s,* Per. V, 3, 94.

Proverbial: *win me and w. me,* Ado V, 1, 82 (= he laughs that wins), originally = win me and have or enjoy me. cf. *I earn that I eat, get that I w.* As III, 2, 78. *thou hast me, if thou hast me, at the worst; and thou shalt w. me, if thou w. me, better and better,* H5 V, 2, 250. *you may w. her in title yours,* Cymb. I, 4, 96. See also Ado II, 1, 342 and Shr. III, 2, 120.

c) to use up, to consume, to waste, to destroy by degrees: *often touching will w. gold,* Err. II, 1, 112. *a withered hermit, fivescore winters worn,* LLL IV, 3, 242. *the morning now is something worn,* Mids. IV, 1, 187 (wasted, spent). *could I repair what she will w. in me,* Shr. III, 2, 120. *infirmity which waits upon worn times,* Wint. V, 1, 142. *much rain —s the marble,* H6C III, 2, 50. *when waterdrops have worn the stones of Troy,* Troil. III, 2, 193. *sharp misery hath worn him to the bones,* Rom. V, 1, 41 (has made him a skeleton). cf. *Outwear, War-worn, Wave-worn.*

= to weary, to exhaust: *—ing thy hearer in thy mistress' praise,* As II, 4, 38 (later Ff and M. Edd. *wearying). to w. your gentle limbs in my affairs,* All's V, 1, 4. *they are worn so, that we shall hardly in our ages see their banners wave again,* Cor. II, 1, 6.

= to efface from the memory; to forget: *our fancies are ... sooner lost and worn than women's are,* Tw. II, 4, 35. *this few days' wonder will be quickly worn,* H6B II, 4, 69. cf. below *w. out.*

With a double accusative denoting an effect: *this exceeding posting must w. your spirits low,* All's V, 1, 2. *whilst some with cunning gild their copper crowns, with truth and plainness I do w. mine bare,* Troil. IV, 4, 108. With adverbs and prepositions: *well-nigh worn to pieces with age,* Wiv. II, 1, 21. *to w. away this long age of three hours,* Mids. V, 33. *age... wore us out of act,* All's I, 2, 30. *time hath worn us into slovenry,* H5 IV, 3, 114. *many years ... not wore him from my remembrance,* Cymb. IV, 4, 23. *To w. out =* 1) to waste or destroy by degrees: *w. out thy youth with shapeless idleness,* Gent. I, 1, 8. *have worn your eyes almost out in the service,* Meas. I, 2, 113. *she may w. her heart out first,* Ado II, 3, 211. *the fashion —s out more apparel than the man,* III, 3, 149. All's I, 2, 73. H4B V, 1, 89. Cor. III, 2, 18. Rom. II, 4, 66. II, 6, 17. Caes. I, 1, 33. Ant. I, 2, 171. IV, 15, 40. Cymb. II, 3, 48 (O. Edd. *w. on't*). 2) to spend completely, to come to the end of: *long he questioned with Lucrece and wore out the night,* Lucr. 123. *in the eyes of all posterity that w. this world out to the end of*

doom, Sonn. 55, 12. *let not the hours of this ungodly day w. out the day in peace,* John III, 1, 110. R2 IV, 258. *you w. out a forenoon in hearing a cause,* Cor. II, 1, 77. *—s out his time for nought but provender,* Oth. I, 1, 47. *you may not live to w. all your true followers out,* Ant. IV, 14, 133 (to have none left). *wornout =* past, gone: *this pattern of the worn-out age,* Lucr. 1350. 3) to efface or lose from the mind, to forget, to give up: *let her w. it out with good counsel,* Ado II, 3, 209. *if you urge me farther ... I w. out my suit,* H5 V, 2, 132. *their clothes are after such a pagan cut, that sure they've worn out Christendom,* H8 I, 3, 15. *we'll w. out, in a walled prison, packs and sects of great ones,* Lr. V, 3, 17. *that lady is not now living, or this gentleman's opinion by this worn out,* Cymb. I, 4, 68.

2) intr. a) to be worn, to be the fashion: *like the brooch and the tooth-pick, which w. not now,* All's I, 1, 172.

b) to become fit by wearing (like a garment); with *to: so —s she to him, so sways she level in her husband's heart,* Tw. II, 4, 31.

c) to be wasted: *never let their crimson liveries w.* Ven. 506. *though marble w. with raining,* Lucr. 560. *thy glass will show thee how thy beauties w.* Sonn. 77, 1. *what rocky heart to water will not w.?* Compl. 291. *youth, the more it is wasted the sooner it —s,* H4A II, 4, 443. *how goes the world? It —s as it grows,* Tim. I, 1, 3. With *out: this great world shall so w. out to nought,* Lr. IV, 6, 138.

d) to pass away: *time —s,* Wiv. V, 1, 8. *the morning —s,* Shr. III, 2, 113.

**Wearer,** 1) one who has something on his body: *the grave —s* (of the habits) Wint. III, 1, 6. *were I the w. of Antonius' beard,* Ant. II, 2, 7.

2) owner: *that clear honour were purchased by the merit of the w.* Merch. II, 9, 43.

**Wearily,** like one fatigued: *you look w.* Tp. III, 1, 32.

**Weariness,** state of being tired, fatigue: Lucr. 121. 845. Tp. III, 3, 5. H4B II, 2, 3. Cymb. III, 6, 33.

**Wearing,** subst. (cf. *Wear*), dress, clothes: *a swain's w.* Wint. IV, 4, 9. *my nightly w.* Oth. IV, 3, 16.

**Wearisome,** tiresome: Gent. II, 7, 8. R2 II, 3, 5. R3 III, 1, 5.

**Weary,** adj. 1) tired, fatigued: Ven. 495. 529. 559. 705. 914. Lucr. 1542. 1621. Sonn. 7, 9. 27, 1. Gent. II, 7, 35. Err. I, 2, 7. 15. LLL V, 2, 194. 196. Mids. III, 2, 442. As II, 4, 1. 3. II, 7, 130. Shr. IV, 1, 4. Tw. III, 3, 21. John V, 5, 18. R2 I, 3, 265. II, 3, 16. V, 3, 105. H4A II, 3, 87. H4B II, 2, 1. IV, 5, 3. V, 5, 149. H5 V, 1, 89. H6A IV, 6, 27. H6C II, 3, 45. R3 IV, 4, 112 (Qq *w. neck,* Ff *wearied head*). V, 3, 19. H8 III, 2, 363. IV, 2, 22. Cor. I, 9, 91. Rom. V, 3, 118. Lr. II, 2, 177. II, 4, 89. Cymb. III, 4, 115. III, 6, 36. The cause with *of: you sunburnt sicklemen, of August w.* Tp. IV, 134. *as you are w. of the weight,* R3 I, 2, 31.

2) tired, impatient of the continuance of sth.: *I am longer to live most w.* Cor. IV, 5, 101. With *of: w. of rest,* Ven. 853. *of the world,* 1189. Mids. V, 255 (Q1 *aweary*). As III, 2, 302. R2 V, 5, 104. H4B III, 1, 48. IV, 1, 197. H6A I, 2, 26. R3 V, 3, 329.

3) sick, disgusted in general: *a true-devoted pilgrim is not w. to measure kingdoms with his feeble steps,* Gent. II, 7, 9. *so w. with disasters,* Mcb. III, 1, 112.

put on *what w. negligence you please,* Lr. I, 3, 12. *wherein we are not destitute for want, but w. for the staleness,* Per. V, 1, 58. With *of: I am w. of this charge,* Tim. III, 4, 25. *life being w. of these worldly bars,* Caes. I, 3, 96. *he that keeps nor crust nor crum, w. of all, shall want some,* Lr. I, 4, 218.

4) tiresome, causing weariness: *ere he arrive his w. noontide prick,* Lucr. 781. *the w. time she cannot entertain,* 1361. *my w. travel's end,* Sonn. 50, 2. *w. night,* 61, ?. Gent. I, 1, 31. LLL V, 2, 197. Mids. III, 2, 431. V, 381. R2 I, 3, 49. H5 IV Chor. 38. R3 III, 1, 3. H8 II, 1, 133. Troil. III, 2, 123. Tit. I, 28. Mcb. I, 3, 22. Hml. III, 1, 77. *not to be w. with you* = not to weary you, not to be tedious: Meas. I, 4, 25.

5) irksome, disgusting: *the —est and most loathed worldly life,* Meas. III, 1, 129. *seek the w. beds of people sick,* LLL V, 2, 832. *how w., stale, flat ... seem to me all the uses of this world,* Hml. I, 2, 133. *O w. reckoning,* Oth. III, 4, 176. cf. H8 II, 1, 133. Hml. III, 1, 77. Hence the following expression, which has much puzzled the commentators: *doth it* (pride) *not flow as hugely as the sea, till that the w. very means do ebb?* As II, 7, 73 (irksome and hateful, as they cannot be dispensed with, and yet are so soon exhausted. German: *bis dass es mit den leidigen Mitteln selbst auf die Neige geht*).

**Weary,** vb. 1) to fatigue, to tire: Lucr. 737. 1363. 1570. Tp. III, 1, 19. Wint. IV, 4, 343. H4B I, 1, 108. II, 4, 385. R3 IV, 4, 112 (Ff —*ed head,* Qq *weary neck*). Caes. IV, 3, 200. cf. *Day-wearied, War-wearied.*

2) to make impatient of continuance; and hence to harass by any thing irksome: Gent. II, 4, 126. Merch. I, 1, 2. As II, 4, 38 (later Ff *wearying,* F1 *wearing*). III, 2, 164. V, 2, 56. Wint. IV, 4, 342. H4B IV, 5, 94.

**Weasand,** see *Wezand.*

**Weasel,** the animal Mustela vulgaris: Lucr. 307. Hml. III, 2, 396. Sucking eggs: As II, 5, 13. H5 I, 2, 170. Full of spleen and quarrelsome: H4A II, 3, 81. Cymb. III, 4, 162.

**Weather,** subst. the state of the atmosphere with respect to any meteorological phenomena: Lucr. 115. Pilgr. 159. Tp. II, 2, 19. Shr. IV, I, 11. H5 III, 2, 113. *cold w.* Ven. 402. *foul w.* Ven. 972. Tp. II, 1, 141. 142. As V, 4, 142. R2 III, 3, 161. H4A III, 1, 68. Lr. III, 1, 1. 2. *hot w.* H4B III, 2, 101. H6B IV, 10, 10. *loud w.* Wint. III, 3, 11. *rough w.* As II, 5, 8. *this w.* = in this w. Wint. III, 3, 65. H6B IV, 10, 10. Emphatically, = storm, tempest: *they are louder than the w.* Tp. I, 1, 40. *builds in the w. on the outward wall,* Merch. II, 9, 29. *'twill endure wind and w.* Tw. I, 5, 256. *roaring louder than the sea or w.* Wint. III, 3, 104. *extremity of w. continuing,* V, 2, 129. *pour down thy w.* John IV, 2, 109. *left me bare to w.* Cymb. III, 3, 64.

Metaphorical use: *being of an old father's mind, many can brook the w. that love not the wind,* LLL IV, 2, 34 (i. e. one must put up with anything. Nathaniel's speech). *fair w. after you,* I, 2, 149 (Jaquenetta's wish). *whose honesty endured all —s,* Wint. V, 1, 195. *mine honour keeps the w. of my fate,* Troil. V, 3, 26 (= has the advantage of my fate; = weather-gage, a nautical term). *to make fair w.* = to conciliate another by fair words and a show of friendship: *it is impossible you should take true root but by the fair w. that you make yourself,* Ado I, 3, 25. *my tongue shall hush again this storm of war and make fair w. in your blustering land,*

John V, 1, 21. *I must make fair w. yet awhile,* H6B V, 1, 30. cf. the proverb: *two women placed together makes foul w.* H8 I, 4, 22.

**Weather-beaten,** harassed by hard weather: H4A III, 1, 67.

**Weather-bitten,** worn by the weather: *like a w. conduit,* Wint. V, 2, 60 (F3. 4. *weather-beaten*).

**Weathercock,** a vane: Gent. II, 1, 142. Denoting a fantastical person: *where had you this pretty w.?* Wiv. III, 2, 18. *what plume of feathers is he that indited this letter? what vane? what w.? did you ever hear better?* LLL IV, 1, 97.

**Weather-fend,** to defend from the weather, to shelter: *the line-grove which —s your cell,* Tp. V, 10.

**Weave** (impf. *weaved:* Per. IV Prol. 21; partic. *weaved:* R2 IV, 229. H4A V, 4, 88. *woven:* Ven. 266. Merch. I, 1, 14. III, 2, 121. H8 IV, 1, 80), to form by texture; absol. (= to practise weaving): Mids. II, 2, 20. Per. IV, 6, 194. trans.: Ven. 266. Merch. I, 1, 14. III, 2, 4, 46. H6B III, 1, 340. Per. IV Prol. 21. Metaphorically: *must I ravel out my —d up folly,* R2 IV, 229. *ill —d ambition,* H4A V, 4, 88. *all were woven so strangely in one piece,* H8 IV, 1, 80. *this —s itself perforce into my business,* Lr. II, 1, 17. cf. *Unweave.*

**Weaver,** one whose occupation is to weave: Wiv. V, 1, 24 (cf. 1 Samuel XVII, 7). Mids. I, 2, 19. III, 1, 23. H6B IV, 2, 30. H8 I, 2, 33. —*s* supposed to be good singers and particularly given to singing psalms (being most of them Calvinists and refugees from the Netherlands): *a catch that will draw three souls out of one w.* Tw. II, 3, 61. *I would I were a w., I could sing psalms or any thing,* H4A II, 4, 147.

**Web,** 1) any thing woven, texture: Ven. 991. Compl. 95 (a downy beard called so). All's IV, 3, 83. H5 V, 1, 21. R3 I, 3, 243. H8 I, 1, 63. Troil. II, 3, 19. Rom. I, 4, 61. Oth. II, 1, 169. III, 4, 69.

2) *the pin and w.,* a disorder of the eye, consisting in a dusky film hindering the sight: *all eyes blind with the pin and w.* Wint. I, 2, 291. *he gives the w. and the pin, squints the eye,* Lr. III, 4, 122.

**Wed** (impf. *wedded:* Wint. V, 1, 13. Cymb. V, 5, 341. *wed:* H8 III, 1, 141. Hml. III, 2, 190. partic. usually *wedded; wed* in Err. I, 1, 37. Shr. I, 2, 263. H8, 289. Per. II, 5, 92. V, 1, 69. cf. *unwed*) to marry; 1) to join or give in marriage: Err. II, 1, 28. Mids. IV, 1, 97. Shr. I, 2, 263. Cymb. I, 1, 7. I, 6, 2. Per. II, 5, 92. V, 1, 69. With *to:* Err. I, 1, 37. LLL II, 211. Mids. II, 1, 72. Shr. II, 289. H6A V, 3, 137. V, 4, 24. H6B IV, 1, 79. Metaphorically: *that noble title your master w. me to,* H8 III, 1, 141. *thou art —ed to calamity,* Rom. III, 3, 3.

2) to take a husband or a wife, to contract matrimony; absol.: Ado II, 1, 76. 79. III, 2, 128. As IV, 1, 148. Shr. II, 180. III, 2, 11. 17. All's II, 3, 98. Wint. V, 1, 24. R3 IV, 1, 74. Rom. III, 5, 119. 187. 189. Tim. IV, 3, 38. Lr. I, 1, 102. trans. = to take for husband or for wife: Pilgr. 346. Gent. II, 6, 39. Err. III, 2, 5. Ado III, 2, 118. LLL V, 2, 447. Mids. I, 1, 18. 64. 88. As V, 4, 22. 130. Shr. I, 1, 149. I, 2, 92. IV, 2, 51. All's I, 1, 98. III, 2, 23. Wint. V, 1, 13. Rom. IV, 5, 39. Hml. III, 2, 190. 224. IV, 5, 63. Cymb. V, 5, 341. Per. II, 5, 16. V, 3, 3. *my —ed mistress,* Cor. IV, 5, 123. Cymb. V, 5, 261. *my —ed lord,* Per. III, 4, 9. Metaphorically: *not to woo honour, but to w. it,* All's II, 1, 15. *in wooing sorrow let's be*

*brief, since, —ing it, there is such length in grief,* R2 V, 1, 94.

**Wedded,** adj. nuptial: *my w. bed,* Rom. I, 5, 137 (Qq and M. Edd. *wedding bed*).

**Wedding,** marriage; nuptials: Ado II, 2, 46. III, 3, 99. As III, 3, 106. V, 2, 15. V, 4, 147. 173. Hml. I, 2, 178.

**Wedding-bed:** Rom. I, 5, 137 (F1 *wedded bed*). III, 2, 136.

**Wedding-cheer:** Shr. III, 2, 188. Rom. IV, 5, 87.

**Wedding-day:** Ado III, 2, 117. IV, 1, 255. Mids. I, 2, 7. II, 1, 139. Merch. III, 2, 313. Shr. II, 33. 300. 317. III, 1, 84. III, 2, 99. John III, 1, 300. H8 Prol. 32. Rom. III, 4, 32. IV, 5, 35.

**Wedding-dower,** marriage-portion: Gent. III, 1, 78.

**Wedding-garment;** Shr. IV, 1, 51.

**Wedding-ring:** Err. II, 2, 139.

**Wedding-sheets:** Oth. IV, 2, 105.

**Wedding-torch:** H6A III, 2, 26.

**Wedge,** subst. 1) a mass of metal: *—s of gold,* R3 I, 4, 26.

2) a piece of iron or wood driven into timber to cleave it: Troil. I, 3, 316.

**Wedged,** 1) cleft as with a wedge: *my heart, as w. with a sigh, would rive in twain,* Troil. I, 1, 35. cf. *Unwedgeable.*

2) driven in like a wedge: *where* (in the crowd) *a finger could not be w. in more,* H8 IV, 1, 58. *it* (your wit) *is strongly w. up in a blockhead,* Cor. II, 3, 30.

**Wedlock,** matrimony: Lucr. 809. Merch. V, 32. As III, 3, 82. V, 4, 150. Wint. V, 1, 124. John I, 117. H6A V, 5, 62. H6C III, 3, 243. H8 II, 4, 40. Oth. V, 2, 142.

**Wedlock-hymn:** As V, 4, 143.

**Wednesday,** the fourth day of the week: Err. I, 2, 55. Merch. I, 3, 127. Wint. IV, 4, 280. R2 IV, 319. H4A I, 1, 103. III, 2, 173. V, 1, 138. H4B II, 1, 96. II, 4, 94. Cor. I, 3, 64. Rom. III, 4, 17. 19. IV, 1, 90. Oth. III, 3, 61.

**Wee,** little, tiny, thin: *he hath but a little w. face,* Wiv. I, 4, 22.

**Weed,** subst. garment: *the deed that spots and stains love's modest snow-white w.* Lucr. 196. *thy youth's proud livery ... will be a tattered w.* Sonn. 2, 4. *keep invention in a noted w.* 76, 6 (not to dress it new). *w. wide enough to wrap a fairy in,* Mids. II, 1, 256. *he wore the humble w.* Cor. II, 3, 229. *I will rob Tellus of her w., to strew thy green with flowers,* Per. IV, 1, 14. Plur. *—s:* Gent. II, 7, 42. Ado V, 3, 30. LLL V, 2, 811. Mids. II, 2, 71. Tw. V, 262. 280. Wint. IV, 4, 1. H6C III, 3, 229. IV, 1, 104. Troil. III, 3, 239. Cor. II, 3, 161. Tit. I, 70. II, 1, 18. III, 1, 43. V, 3, 196. Rom. V, 1, 39. Hml. IV, 7, 81. Lr. IV, 7, 7. Cymb. V, 1, 23.

**Weed,** subst. a useless or noxious herb: *they bid thee crop a w., thou pluckest a flower,* Ven. 946. *no grass, herb, leaf or w.* 1055. *the basest w. outbraves his dignity,* Sonn. 94, 12. H5 IV, 1, 11. H8 V, 1, 52. Hml. I, 5, 32. Oth. IV, 2, 67. Plur. *— s:* Lucr. 281. 870. Sonn. 69, 12. 94, 14. 124, 4. Tp. IV, 1, 21. R2 III, 4, 38. 50. H4B IV, 4, 54. H6B III, 1, 31. H6C II, 6, 21. R3 III, 4, 13 *(small herbs have grace, great —s do grow apace).* 15. III, 1, 103. Cor. II, 2, 109 (*as —s before a vessel under sail;* i. e. water-plants). Rom. II, 3, 8. Mcb. V, 2, 30. Hml. III, 2, 268. III, 4,

151. IV, 7, 173. Lr. IV, 4, 3. 5. Ant. I, 2, 113. Cymb. IV, 2, 390. Peculiar passage: *the needful bits and curbs to headstrong —s,* Meas. I, 3, 20 (Collier: '*weed* is a term still commonly applied to an ill-conditioned horse.' Emendations proposed: *steeds* or *wills*).

**Weed,** vb. 1) to root out, to take away as noxious herbs; in a proper and a metaphorical sense: Meas. III, 2, 284. LLL I, 1, 96. R2 II, 3, 167. H6B I, 3, 102. With *up: set hyssop and w. up thyme,* Oth. I, 3, 326. With *from: but say this w. her love from Valentine,* Gent. III, 2, 49. *to w. this wormwood from your fruitful brain,* LLL V, 2, 857. *hath —ed from my heart a root of ancient envy,* Cor. IV, 5, 108.

2) to free from noxious plants; metaphorically: *he cannot so precisely w. this land,* H4B IV, 1, 205. With *of: w. your better judgements of all opinion ... that I am wise,* As II, 7, 45.

**Weeder-out,** extirpator: *a w. of his proud adversaries,* R3 I, 3, 123.

**Weeding,** weeds, noxious herbs: *he weeds the corn, but still lets grow the w.* LLL I, 1, 96.

**Weedy,** consisting of weeds: *her w. trophies,* Hml. IV, 7, 175.

**Week,** the time from Sunday to Saturday; a space of seven days: Lucr. 213. Sonn. 116, 11. Tp. II, 1, 184. Wiv. I, 3, 8. IV, 3, 12. Err. III, 2, 101. V, 45. Ado II, 1, 369. LLL I, 1, 39. 303. I, 2, 135. IV, 2, 36. 41. Shr. II, 179. IV, 2, 74. All's III, 6, 99. Wint. I, 2, 39. IV, 4, 433. John I, 113. III, 1, 87. H4A II, 2, 101. III, 3, 18. H6C II, 5, 36. R3 IV, 1, 97. H8 IV, 1, 77. Troil. IV, 1, 9. Tit. IV, 3, 82. Rom. IV, 5, 5. Tim. II, 2, 30. Oth. III, 4, 173. Cymb. III, 2, 53. = week-days, working days: *does not divide the Sunday from the w.* Hml. I, 1, 76. Proverbial: *at fourscore it is too late a w.* As II, 3, 74.* *O that I knew he were but in by the w.* LLL V, 2, 61 (an expression taken from hiring servants; = if I had him at my command).

**Weekly,** from week to week, every week: *whom I have w. sworn to marry,* H4B I, 2, 270.

**Ween,** to fancy, to hope (erroneously): *—ing to redeem and have installed me in the diadem,* H6A II, 5, 88. *w. you of better luck in perjured witness than your master?* H8 V, 1, 136. cf. *Overween.*

**Weep** (impf. and partic. *wept*) to shed tears: Ven. 221. 414. 949. 1062. 1090. Compl. 124. Tp. III, 1, 12. 76. Gent. II, 1, 23. II, 3, 2. 7. 28. 29 *(he —s on).* IV, 2, 123. IV, 4, 170. 176. Meas. I, 4, 81. II, 2, 122. Err. II, 1, 115. II, 2, 206. Ado II, 3, 153. IV, 1, 257. 258. V, 1, 175. V, 2, 82 etc. etc. *the —ing philosopher,* Merch. I, 2, 53 (Heraclitus). *—ing joys,* H6B I, 1, 34. *—ing water* (i. e. tears) Compl. 304. *many a dry drop seemed a —ing tear,* Lucr. 1375. *said with —ing tears,* As II, 4, 53. *to w. upon the tainted place,* Lucr. 1746 (to wet it with tears); cf. John V, 2, 29 and H8 III, 2, 399. *—ing after this untimely bier,* R2 V, 6, 52. Per. IV, 3, 41. *his —ing into the needless stream,* As II, 1, 46. Used of animals: *let the stricken deer go w.* Hml. III, 2, 282. *Tom will make them* (dogs) *w. and wail,* Lr. III, 6, 74. Figurative use: *purple tears that his wound wept,* Ven. 1054. *I have inly wept,* Tp. V, 200. *my heart —s,* H8 III, 2, 335. *the dank earth —s at thy languishment,* Lucr. 1130. *as the sun had ta'en his last leave of the —ing morn,* Ven. 2. *thy sun sets —ing in the lowly west,* R2 II, 4, 21. *the —ing clouds,* H4B I, 3, 61. *she is the —ing welkin, I the earth,* Tit. III, 1, 227. *a river ... upon whose —ing margent she* *was set*, Compl. 39. *fell in the — ing brook*, Hml. IV, 7, 176 (cf. Schiller's: *du wirst hingehn, wo kein Tag mehr scheinet, der Cocytus durch die Wüsten weinet*). *when our vaults have wept with drunken spilth of wine*, Tim. II, 2, 168. Peculiar expression: *the blood — s from my heart*, H4B IV, 4, 58 (cf. *— ing tears* above).

The cause expressed by a clause: *that he does I w.* Tp. I, 2, 434. *w. that Harry's dead*, H4B V, 2, 59. H6A IV, 3, 28. H6B III, 2, 121. Per. IV, 2, 129. *did w. that it foresaw*, Troil. I, 2, 10. By an infinitive: *w. to have that which it fears to lose*, Sonn. 64, 14. *would have wept to have seen our parting*, Gent. II, 3, 12. IV, 4, 150. 180. Wint. V, 2, 49. H8 III, 2, 335. Cor. II, 1, 194. Tim. I, 2, 113. Ant. III, 2, 3. Per. III, 2, 104.

Prepositions following; 1) *at: to w. at woes*, Compl. 307. *to w. at what I am glad of*, Tp. III, 1, 74. *to w. at joy*, Ado I, 1, 28. *a deed whereat valour will w.* Cor. V, 6, 134. *— ing at my woes*, Tit. III, 1, 100. cf. Lucr. 1130 above. 2) *for: dost w. for grief of my sustaining*, Lucr. 1272. *'twill w. for having wearied you*, Tp. III, 1, 19. *— ing for what she saw must come*, Err. I, 1, 72. Merch. III, 1, 11. As III, 2, 437. IV, 1, 154. John IV, 3, 106. R2 III, 2, 4 *(for joy)*. V, 1, 87. H5 II, 2, 140. R3 II, 2, 62. IV, 4, 60. H8 III, 1, 150. Tit. III, 1, 10. Rom. III, 5, 75. 77. Per. IV, 1, 80 etc. *will w. for her pardon*, Ant. IV, 14, 45 (= will seek to obtain her pardon by tears). 3) *over: w. o'er my father's death anew*, All's I, 1, 3. *seems to w. over his country's wrongs*, H4A IV, 3, 81. *the silly owner of the goods — s over them*, H6B I, 1, 226.

With an accusative denoting an effect: *wept herself blind*, Gent. II, 3, 14. *I'll w. what's left away*, Err. II, 1, 115. *— ing his welcomes forth*, Wint. IV, 4, 559. *will w. my date of life out for his sweet life's loss*, John IV, 3, 106. *w. the fire out*, R2 V, 1, 48. *your eyes w. out at Pandar's fall*, Troil. V, 10, 49. *I could w. my spirit from mine eyes*, Caes. IV, 3, 99. *w. our sad bosoms empty*, Mcb. IV, 3, 2. *he cannot w. it* (his fortune) *back again*, Ant. II, 6, 111. Tears, or in general that which is shed, as object: *purple tears that his wound wept*, Ven. 1054. *every tear that I do w.* LLL IV, 3, 33. *my heart wept blood*, Wint. V, 2, 97. *will you have them w. our horses' blood?* H5 IV, 2, 12. *he will w. millstones*, R3 I, 4, 245. *orphans' tears wept on 'em* (his bones) H8 III, 2, 399. *to w. seas*, Troil. III, 2, 84. *w. your tears into the channel*, Caes. I, 1, 63. (cf. *where I may w. my fill*, H6C II, 5, 113).

Transitively, = to lament with tears: *she — s Troy's painted woes*, Lucr. 1492. *w. love's woe*, Sonn. 30, 7. *— ing my father's wreck*, Tp. I, 2, 390. All's V, 3, 64. R2 II, 2, 25. 27. H6A I, 1, 88. H6B III, 1, 221. R3 II, 4, 59. Rom. III, 5, 78. Lr. IV, 6, 180. Cymb. I, 4, 20.

**Weeper,** one who sheds tears, a mourner: *to make the w. laugh, the laugher weep*, Compl. 124.

**Weepingly,** with tears: *their kind acceptance w. beseeched*, Compl. 207.

**Weeping-ripe,** ready to weep: LLL V, 2, 274. H6C I, 4, 172.

**Weepings,** lamentations: *the incessant w. of my wife*, Err. I, 1, 71 (later Ff *weeping*).

**Weet,** to know: *I bind, on pain of punishment, the world to w. we stand up peerless*, Ant. I, 1, 39.

**Weigh,** 1) to ascertain the weight of, to examine by the balance: *to w. the flesh*, Merch. IV, 1, 255. *will*

*take me without — ing*, H4B I, 2, 189. *they w. not every stamp*, Cymb. V, 4, 24. Metaphorically: *more nor less to others paying than by self-offences — ing*, Meas. III, 2, 280 (by examining his own offences; judging of others by himself). *he would have — ed thy brother by himself*, V, 111. *w. thy value with an even hand*, Merch. II, 7, 25. *those that w. their pains in sense*, All's I, 1, 240. Ado V, 1, 211. R2 III, 4, 84. H4B IV, 1, 67. H5 II, 4, 137. Troil. II, 2, 26. IV, 5, 81. Tit. I, 55. Caes. I, 2, 146. Hml. I, 2, 13. Lr. I, 1, 6. Oth. III, 3, 119. Cymb. I, 4, 15. Per. V, 1, 89. That by which a thing is counterbalanced, preceded by *against* or *with: in that scales let there be — ed your lady's love against some other maid*, Rom. I, 2, 101. *w. our sorrow with our comfort*, Tp. II, 1, 8. *we cannot w. our brother with ourself*, Meas. II, 2, 126. *w. oath with oath, and you will nothing w.* Mids. III, 2, 131. *I w. my friend's affection with mine own*, Tim. I, 2, 222. *w. but the crime with this*, III, 5, 58.

Hence = to consider: *to w. how once I suffered in your crime*, Sonn. 120, 8. *the fair soul herself — ed between loathness and obedience, at which end o'the beam should bow*, Tp. II, 1, 130 (in the dependant clause *she* omitted; or *should* for *she would*). *if that the injuries be justly — ed*, Tw. V, 375. *not — ing well the end*, Wint. I, 2, 258. *you w. this well*, H4B V, 2, 102. R3 III, 1, 46. H8 II, 4, 197. Caes. II, 1, 108. Mcb. I, 3, 154. Hml. I, 3, 17. 29. IV, 3, 6. IV, 7, 150. Ant. II, 6, 32. cf. *Unweighed, Unweighing*. With a double accus., = to estimate, to esteem: *her worth that he does w. too light*, All's III, 4, 32. *in cases of defence 'tis best to w. the enemy more mighty than he seems*, H5 II, 4, 43.

And = to make account of, to care for: *eternal love in love's fresh case — s not the dust and injury of age*, Sonn. 108, 10. *you w. me not? O that's you care not for me*, LLL V, 2, 27. *for life I prize it as I w. grief*, Wint. III, 2, 44. *I w. it lightly, were it heavier*, R3 III, 1, 121. *my person, which I w. not*, H8 V, 1, 125.

2) to have weight; in a proper and a figurative sense (= to be worth): *you w. equally*, Meas. IV, 2, 31. *your vows to her and me ... will even w.* Mids. III, 2, 133. *let every word w. heavy of her worth*, All's III, 4, 31. *well — ing sums of gold*, V, 3, 203. *while they w. so even*, John II, 332. *her dowry shall w. equal with a queen*, 486. *each — s nor less nor more*, Troil. IV, 1, 65. *I love them as they w.* Cor. II, 2, 78. *how heavy — s my lord*, Ant. IV, 15, 32. With an accus. of the effect: *we shall w. thee to the beam*, All's II, 3, 162. *whose white — s down the airy scale of praise*, Compl. 226. *he — s King Richard down*, R2 III, 4, 89. *thou* (sleep) *no more wilt w. my eyelids down*, H4B III, 1, 7 (close them by thy heaviness). R3 V, 3, 153. Tim. V, 1, 154. *my friends that must w. out my afflictions, they that my trust must grow to, live not here*, H8 III, 1, 88 (= outweigh; i. e. make amends for).

With *against* or *with*, = to have the same weight as, to counterbalance: *know your own estate, how able such a work to undergo, to w. against his opposite*, H4B I, 3, 55. *in every thing the purpose must w. with the folly*, H4B II, 2, 196 (as the purpose is, such the folly must be; i. e. a foolish purpose requires as foolish a behaviour). *what you bestow, in him I'll counterpoise, and make him w. with her*, Tim. I, 1, 146.

Transitively, = to be equivalent to in weight: *how much your chain — s*, Err. IV, 1, 28. *I know them, yea,* and what they w. Ado V, 1, 93. *I w. not you,* LLL V, 2, 26 (am not so heavy as you). *what four throned ones could have —ed such a compounded one?* H8 I, 1, 11. *the heads of all thy brother cardinals ... — ed not a hair of his,* III, 2, 259. *all these are portable, with other graces* —ed, Mcb. IV, 3, 90 (counterbalanced by graces; *with* = by).

3) to be heavy, to press hard: *her heart —s sadly,* All's III, 5, 70. *that perilous stuff which —s upon the heart,* Mcb. V, 3, 45. cf. H4B III, 1, 7.

4) to raise, to lift (an anchor): *from whence at first she —ed her anchorage,* Tit. I, 73.

**Weight,** 1) a measure by which the gravity of things is ascertained: *a w. of carrion flesh,* Merch. IV, 1, 41. *there was the w. that pulled me down,* H8 III, 2, 408 (by turning the scale). *from whose so many —s of baseness cannot a dram of worth be drawn,* Cymb. III, 5, 88. *by w., by the w.,* and *in w.* = according to the quantity measured by the balance, and hence in just proportion, exactly: *make us pay down for our offence by w. the words of heaven,* Meas. I, 2, 125. *purchased by the w.* Merch. III, 2, 89. *which in w. to re-answer, his pettiness would bow under,* H5 III, 6, 136. *so much by w. hate I her Diomed,* Troil. V, 2, 168. *thy madness shall be paid by w.* Hml. IV, 5, 156.

= measure in general, degree: *thou lovest me not with the full w. that I love thee,* As I, 2, 9. *that my integrity and truth to you might be affronted with the match and w. of such a winnowed purity in love,* Troil. III, 2, 173. *how much the quantity, the w. as much as I do love my father,* Cymb. IV, 2, 17 (*how* = however).

2) the quantity ascertained by the balance; gravity: *a bell, once set on ringing, with his own w. goes,* Lucr. 1494. *heavier by the w. of a man,* Ado III, 4, 26. Shr. II, 206. All's II, 3, 126. H4B II, 4, 276. Troil. IV, 1, 71. Metaphorically: *know by measure the enemies' w.* Troil. I, 3, 203.

3) heaviness, ponderousness: *grief boundeth where it falls, not with the empty hollowness, but w.* R2 I, 2, 59. H4B I, 1, 122. Ant. IV, 15, 34. V, 2, 102.

4) burden, load: *the beast that bears me, tired with my woe, plods dully on, to bear that w. in me,* Sonn. 50, 6. *burdened with lesser w.* Err. I, 1, 109. *burdened with like w. of pain,* II, 1, 36. *I would bend under any heavy w. that he'll enjoin me to,* Ado V, 1, 286. *what passion hangs these —s upon my tongue?* As I, 2, 269. John III, 1, 297. R2 III, 4, 31. IV, 204. H4A V, 3, 35. H6C IV, 6, 51. V, 1, 36. V, 7, 24. R3 I, 2, 31. H8 V, 3, 66. Lr. V, 3, 323. Ant. I, 4, 25. I, 5, 21. III, 1, 36.

5) importance, consequence: *quittance of desert and merit according to the w. and worthiness,* H5 IV, 2, 35. *full of poise and difficult w.* Oth. III, 3, 82 (Q1 *of difficulty*). *of w.* = important, momentous: Ado III, 3, 91. H5 I, 2, 5. H8 III, 1, 71. *of no less w.* LLL II, 7. *of more w.* Ant. I, 2, 71.

**Weightless,** having no weight, light: *that light and w. down,* H4B IV, 5, 33.

**Weighty,** 1) heavy, ponderous: *it is too w. for your grace to wear,* R3 III, 1, 120 (Q1 *heavy*). Metaphorically, = grievous, afflictive: *how you stand minded in the w. difference between the king and you,* H8 III, 1, 58. *if after two days' shine Athens contain thee, attend our — er judgement,* Tim. III, 5, 102.

2) important, momentous, forcible: *my reasons are both good and w.* Shr. I, 1, 253. *a w. cause of love,* IV, 4, 26. *that w. charge,* H6A II, 1, 62. *this w. business,* H6B I, 1, 170. I, 2, 86. III, 1, 289. R3 I, 1, 148. II, 2, 144. III, 1, 119. H8 Prol. 2. II, 1, 144. III, 2, 234. V, 1, 18. Mcb. III, 1, 126.

**Weird** (O. Edd. *weyard* or *weyward;* later Ff in Mcb. IV, 1, 136 *wizard.* Monosyll. in III, 1, 2; dissyll. II, 1, 20 and IV, 1, 136; dubious in I, 3, 32 & III, 4, 133) subservient to Destiny: *the w. sisters,* Mcb. I, 3, 32. I, 5, 8. II, 1, 20. III, 4, 133. IV, 1, 136. *w. women,* III, 1, 2.

**Weke,** sound imitative of the voice of a pig: Tit. IV, 2, 146.

**Welcome,** adj. (superl. —st, H6A II, 2, 56) received with pleasure, grateful, agreeable: Gent. II, 5, 4. Meas. II, 2, 26. LLL I, 1, 315. As II, 7, 198. All's II, 1, 211. H4A I, 1, 66 (*w. news*). H6A II, 2, 56. H6B II, 3, 14. Tim. I, 2, 134. Mcb. IV, 3, 138 (*w. and unwelcome things*) etc. etc. With *to* before the person gratified: Gent. II, 4, 113. II, 7, 71. V, 4, 123. Wiv. II, 2, 157. Err. II, 2, 118. Merch. IV, 2, 4. Alls IV, 4, 16. R2 III, 1, 31 etc. before the place where one is received: Gent. II, 5, 6. Tw. II, 3, 106. R3 I, 1, 124. Per. III, 1, 30 etc. Used absolutely, in saluting a new comer: Tp. V, 125. 165. Gent. II, 4, 100. Wiv. V, 5, 33. Mids. II, 1, 247. Cor. II, 1, 198. V, 5, 6. Rom. III, 5, 24 etc. etc. With *to:* LLL II, 90. As II, 7, 105. H6A I, 2, 47. Gent. II, 5, 1. Merch. V, 139. All's I, 2, 22. H4B IV, 4, 316. H6C II, 2, 1. R3 III, 1, 1 etc. With *into: w. into our territories,* H6A V, 3, 146. *you're w. into our kingdom,* H8 II, 2, 76. *w. hither:* Merch. III, 2, 223. As II, 7, 195. Wint. V, 1, 151. R2 III, 3, 122. *w. home:* Merch. V, 113. Shr. IV, 1, 109. Cor. II, 1, 197. Hml. II, 2, 85.

Used as an expression of readiness to serve another, = I am at your service: *my business is a word or two with Claudio. And very w.* Meas. III, 1, 49. *you are w., sir, adieu. Farewell to me, sir, and w. to you,* LLL II, 213. *I mean to shift my bush, and then pursue me as you draw your bow; you are w. all,* Shr. V, 2, 48. *I humbly thank your ladyship. Your honour is most w.* Oth. IV, 3, 4. *thus defied, I thank thee for myself. Thou art w.,* Caius, Cymb. III, 1, 69. *Lord Helicane, a word. With me? and w.* Per. II, 4, 22.

**Welcome,** subst. salutation or kind reception of a new comer: Meas. III, 1, 45. Err. III, 1, 23. 25. 26. Mids. V, 94. 100. Merch. V, 38. Wint. IV, 4, 560. R2 I, 3, 212. H8 III, 2, 401. Troil. III, 3, 168 (O. Edd. *the w.,* M. Edd. *w.*). Cor. II, 1, 200. V, 5, 151. Tim. I, 2, 16. Mcb. III, 4, 2 etc. With an objective genitive (i. e. expressing the thing or person received): *makes summer's w. thrice more wished,* Sonn. 56, 14. *how thou lovest us, show in our brother's w.* Wint. I, 2, 174. *repeal him with the w. of his mother,* Cor. V, 5, 5. *whose w. had poisoned mine,* Lr. II, 4, 39. With a subjective genitive: *find the w. of a noble foe,* Troil. I, 3, 309. The possessive pronoun objectively: *confirm his w.* Gent. II, 4, 101. 102. *pray God our good cheer may answer my good will and your good w. here,* Err. III, 1, 20. Shr. V, 1, 13. All's IV, 4, 14. R2 V, 2, 29. Troil. IV, 5, 276. Tim. I, 2, 135. Mcb. IV, 1, 132. Lr. II, 4, 236. Ant. II, 6, 47. subjectively: *I hold your dainties cheap and your w. dear,* Err. III, 1, 21. *weeping his —s forth,* Wint. IV, 4, 560. H8 I, 4, 37. Rom. I, 2, 37. Mcb. III, 4, 8. With *to:* Sonn. 110, 13. LLL II, 93. Wint. IV, 4, 65. H4A IV, 3, 59. H6A IV, 3, 40 *hither:* Gent. II, 4, 102. Err. III, 1, 68. John II, 11. *home:* R2 V, 2, 29. Cor. V, 6, 51. *to bid w.: to thee and thy company I bid a hearty w.* Tp. V, 111. *bid these gentlemen w.* Wiv. I, 1, 201. Err. III, 1, 68. Ado I, 1, 155. Merch. I, 2, 140. Wint. IV, 4, 65. H6A IV, 3, 40. Ant. IV, 14, 136 etc. *to give a p. w. or to give w. to a p.:* Lucr. 90. Sonn. 110, 13. Err. I, 1, 115. Merch. V, 133. Shr. Ind. 1, 103. John II, 11. 15. R2 V, 2, 29. H4A IV, 3, 59. H8 I, 4, 57. Troil. IV, 5, 59 etc. *to have w.:* Gent. II, 5, 11. LLL II, 92. Shr. II, 97. Cor. V, 6, 51. *music, make their w.* Tim. I, 2, 135. *to make society the sweeter w.* Mcb. III, 1, 43. *not paying me a w.* Mids. V, 99. *our duties did his w. pay,* Mcb. IV, 1, 132 (our duties, i. e. reverence and homage, were offered him at his visit).

**Welcome,** vb. to salute or receive with kindness; and metaphorically, to be pleased with: *thy palfrey —s the warm approach of sweet desire,* Ven. 386. *well was he —d by the Roman dame,* Lucr. 51. *a brow unbent that seemed to w. woe,* 1509. *she doth w. daylight with her ditty,* Pilgr. 199. *w. him then according to his worth,* Gent. II, 4, 83. Err. IV, 4, 18. 37 *(home).* Shr. I, 1, 47 *(to town).* 201. III, 1, 3. Wint. IV, 4, 57. John V, 3, 15. V, 4, 12 *(home).* R2 II, 2, 7. H4B V, 2, 11 *(to w. the condition of the time;* i. e. to meet it). H5 V Prol. 34. H6B I, 1, 36. R3 III, 1, 6. 139. IV, 1, 51. IV, 4, 439. V, 3, 260 *(home).* Tit. I, 147 *(to Rome).* V, 2, 33 *(to this world's light).* 43. Caes. II, 1, 131. Per. IV Prol. 2.

**Welcomer,** one who receives a new comer: *thou woful w. of glory,* R3 IV, 1, 90.

**Welfare,** 1) wellbeing, good health; *until her husband's w. she did hear,* Lucr. 263. *and sick of w., found a kind of meetness to be diseased,* Sonn. 118, 7. *we have been praying for our husbands' w.* Merch. V, 114 (Q1 *healths*).

2) prosperity, happiness: H6B III, 1, 80. H6C IV, 3, 39. Tit. V, 3, 110.

**Welked,** see *Whelked.*

**Welkin,** the sky: Ven. 921. Lucr. 116. Tp. I, 2, 4. Wiv. I, 3, 101. LLL I, 1, 221 *(the —'s vicegerent,* in Armado's letter). III, 68. IV, 2, 5. Mids. III, 2, 356. Shr. Ind. 2, 47. Tw. II, 3, 59. III, 1, 65 *(out of my w., I might say 'element', but the word is overworn).* Wint. I, 2, 136 *(look on me with your w. eye,* = heavenly; German: *mit deinem Himmelsauge,* i. e. pure and innocent like heaven. According to others, = blue). John V, 2, 172. V, 5, 2. H4B II, 4, 182. R3 V, 3, 341. Tit. III, 1, 212. 224. 227.

**Well,** subst. 1) a spring, a fountain: *this brand she quenched in a cool w. by,* Sonn. 154, 9. *clear —s spring not,* Pilgr. 281. *have emptied all their fountains in my w., and mine I pour your ocean all among,* Compl. 255. *at Saint Gregory's w.* Gent. IV, 2, 84 (or sub 2?). *make —s and Niobes of the maids and wives,* Troil. V, 10, 19 (i. e. dissolved in tears. cf. *like Niobe, all tears,* Hml. I, 2, 149).

2) a deep narrow pit of water: Wiv. IV, 2, 62. John V, 2, 139. R2 IV, 184. Rom. III, 1, 99.

**Well,** adv. and adj. (the line of demarcation hardly definable) in a good state, or in a good manner; in all the variations of sense that the word *good* is able to express.

1) = in such a state or of such a quality as one would wish: *not blame your pleasure, be it ill or w.* Sonn. 58, 14. *to mar the subject that before was w.*

103, 10. *what care I who calls me w. or ill?* 112, 3. *will't please your worship to come in? No, I thank you, I am very w.* Wiv. I, 1, 278 (I feel quite comfortable here). *if you think w. to carry this as you may,* Meas. III, 1, 267 (= good). *one woman is fair, yet I am w.; another is wise, yet I am w.* Ado II, 3, 28 (it does me no harm). *this is not so w. as I looked for,* LLL I, 1, 281. *hence, away, now all is w.* Mids. II, 2, 25. *I have a device to make all w.* III, 1, 18. *his leg is but so so, and yet 'tis w.* As III, 5, 119. *the meat was w.* Shr. IV, 1, 172. *in what he did profess, w. found,* All's II, 1, 105 (cf. Cor. II, 2, 48). *say 'tis w.* (the statue of Hermione) Wint. V, 3, 20. *hasty marriage seldom proveth w.* H6C IV, 1, 18 (cf. *Prove). his health is w.* Tim. III, 1, 12. 13. *I am not w. in health,* Caes. II, 1, 257. *each opposite that blanks the face of joy meet what I would have w. and it destroy,* Hml. III, 2, 231. *oft we mar what's w.* Lr. I, 4, 369. *I am sorry for your displeasure, but all will sure be w.* Oth. III, 1, 45. *all may be w. enough,* Ant. III, 3, 50. *all's not w.* V, 2, 326. cf. above all, the beginning of the dialogue in All's II, 4. Substantively: *I wish him w.* Meas. III, 2, 97. Ado V, 1, 333. Merch. IV, 1, 420. All's I, 1, 193. *God send him w.* All's I, 1, 190. *what would my lord and father? Nothing but w. to thee,* H4B IV, 4, 19. *w. be with you, gentlemen,* Hml. II, 2, 398. cf. such phrases as *hearing w. of your lordship,* Tim. III, 6, 29. *I hope w. of to-morrow,* Ant. IV, 2, 42.

= in good health: *your friends are w.* Gent. II, 4, 123. *I am glad to see your worships w.* Wiv. I, 1, 80. *you look not w.* Merch. I, 1, 73. Err. IV, 2, 31. Ado I, 1, 304. IV, 1, 63. Mids. III, 2, 77. Merch. III, 2, 238. IV, 1, 396. Wint. I, 2, 387. John IV, 3, 104. 139. H4B I, 1, 138. 139. III, 2, 92 (Ff *look w.,* Qq *like w.*). IV, 4, 116. R3 II, 4, 40. H8 II, 4, 204. Rom. V, 1, 16. Tim. I, 1, 1. Caes. II, 2, 53. II, 4, 13. Mcb. III, 4, 52. 56. Ant. I, 3, 72. II, 5, 31. 39. II, 7, 35 etc.

Used of the dead, = at rest, free from the cares of the world, happy: *what were more holy than to rejoice the former queen is w.* Wint. V, 1, 30. *how doth the king? Exceeding w., his cares are now all ended,* H4B V, 2, 3. *she is w.* Rom. V, 1, 17. *you love your child so ill that you run mad, seeing that she is w.* IV, 5, 76. *they were w. at peace when I did leave them,* Mcb. IV, 3, 179 (cf. 177). *we use to say the dead are w.* Ant. II, 5, 33.

2) in a good or satisfactory manner: *w. painted idol,* Ven. 212. *a w. proportioned steed,* 290. *can so w. defend her,* 472. *thrive w.* 640. *foreknowing w. ... there he could not die,* 245. *whose taste her lips well knew,* 543. *look w. to her heart,* 580. *w. demanded,* Tp. I, 2, 139. *thou hast slept w.* 305. *thou hast done w.* 494; cf. R2 III, 3, 170 and Cymb. III, 3, 54. *to speak w. of his friend,* Tp. II, 2, 95. *you shall w. be spared,* Meas. II, 2, 14 (easily; cf. Tp. II, 1, 172). *fare ye w.* Merch. I, 1, 58; R3 III, 1, 97; Ant. II, 6, 73. *thou speakest it w.* Merch. II, 2, 161 (= thou art right; cf. Cor. I, 6, 14 and H5 III, 7, 123. see *Say). w. paid,* IV, 1, 415. *shall acquit him w.* As I, 1, 134. *he is not like to marry me w.* III, 3, 93. *she's not w. married,* Rom. IV, 5, 77. *my point ... will be throughly wrought, or w. or ill, as this day's battle's fought,* Lr. IV, 7, 98. *w. said,* Ant. II, 5, 46 etc. etc. = conveniently: *yet mayst thou w. be tasted,* Ven. 128. *his grief may be compared w. to one sore sick,* 701. *as w. as w. might be,* Pilgr. 212. *nor none so bad, but it may w. be told,*

R3 IV, 4, 459 etc. = happily, fortunately: *we prosper w. in our return*, Tp. II, 1, 73. *you are w. o'erta'en*, Merch. IV, 2, 5 (cf. *Meet*). *his father ... is w. to live*, II, 2, 55 (old Gobbo's speech). *you're w. to live*, Wint. III, 3, 125 (the clown's speech). *and w. am like to do*, Ant. II, 6, 74 etc.

3) much, greatly: *I can be w. contented*, Ven. 513. *the kiss shall be thine own as w. as mine*, 117. *ne'er pleased her babe so w.* 974. *resembling w. his pale cheeks*, 1169. *that liked of her master as w. as w. might be*, Gent. I, 1, 81. *I pray she may, as w. for the encouragement of the like ... as for the enjoying of thy life*, Meas. I, 2, 192. *never touch w. welcome to thy hand*, Err. II, 2, 118. *the lady is very w. worthy*, Ado I, 1, 224. *this deed will be w. welcome to Lorenzo*, Merch. IV, 2, 4. *I am as w. in my wits as thou art*, Tw. IV, 2, 95. *all the nearest things to my heart, as w. my chamber-councils*, Wint. I, 2, 236 etc. etc.

4) Used, in replying, or in beginning a speech, not only to express satisfaction or acquiescence (f. i. Tp. II, 1, 139. IV, 1, 50. Mids. III, 1, 48), but as a mere expletive, = why: Tp. II, 1, 26. 221. II, 2, 47. III, 3, 10. Gent. I, 1, 127. III, 1, 283. Meas. I, 2, 88. II, 2, 58. Merch. IV, 1, 448. R2 III, 3, 170 etc.

**Well-accomplished**, (not hyphened in O. Edd.) furnished with good qualities: Gent. IV, 3, 13. LLL II, 56.

**Well-acquainted** (not hyphened in O. Edd.) well known: Err. IV, 3, 2.

**Well-a-day**, exclamation expressive of dislike or grief, = ah, woe, alas: *O w., Mistress Ford! having an honest man to your husband, to give him such cause of suspicion*, Wiv. III, 3, 106. *I am as well in my wits as any man in Illyria. W. that you were, sir*, Tw. IV, 2, 116. *O w., lady, if he be not drawn now*, H5 II, 1, 38. *Ah, w., he's dead*, Rom. III, 2, 37. *O w., that ever I was born*, IV, 5, 15. *when, w., we could scarcely help ourselves*, Per. II, 1, 23. Substantively: *his daughter's woe and heavy w. in her unholy service*, Per. IV, 4, 49.

**Well-advised**, see *Advise* and *Advised*.

**Well-a-near**, well-a-day, alas: *the lady shrieks and w. does fall in travail with her fear*, Per. III Prol. 51.

**Well-apparelled** (not hyphened in O. Edd.) well dressed, adorned: Rom. I, 2, 27.

**Well-appointed**, see *Appoint 3*.

**Well-armed** (not hyphened in O. Edd.) well furnished with weapons of offence or defence: *in strong proof of chastity w.* Rom. I, 1, 216. *where they boast to have w. friends*, Lr. III, 7, 20.

**Well-balanced**, see *Weal-balanced*.

**Well-behaved**, becoming, decent: *gave such orderly and w. reproof to all uncomeliness*, Wiv. II, 1, 59.

**Well-beloved**, greatly beloved: H4A I, 3, 267. H8 II, 4, 238. Caes. III, 2, 180.

**Well-beseeming** (not hyphened in O. Edd.) well becoming: H4A I, 1, 14. Tit. II, 3, 56.

**Well-born**, of good birth: John II, 278.

**Well-breathed**, long-breathed, lasting, of good bottom: *on thy w. horse*, Ven. 678.

**Well-chosen**, selected with good judgment: H6C IV, 1, 7. cf. H8 II, 2, 2.

**Well-contented**, satisfied, happy: *if thou survive my w. day*, Sonn. 32, 1.

**Well-dealing**, fair in dealing with others, honest: *to merchants, our w. countrymen*, Err. I, 1, 7.

**Well-defended** (not hyphened in O. Edd.) well guarded: *your w. honour*, Meas. V, 407.

**Well-derived** (not hyphened in O. Edd.) good by birth and nature: *corrupts a w. nature with his inducement*, All's III, 2, 90. cf. *Derive*.

**Well-deserving**, full of merit, worthy: Merch. IV, 1, 239. R2 II, 1, 194. H4A III, 1, 138. H8 III, 2, 98.

**Well-desired** (not hyphened in O. Edd.) much sought and invited: Oth. II, 1, 206.

**Well-disposed**, well affected, loyal: *you lose a thousand w. hearts*, R2 II, 1, 206.

**Well-doing**, acquitting one's self well: *whether the horse by him became his deed, or he his manage by the w. steed*, Compl. 112.

**Well-educated** (not hyphened in O. Edd.) having a good education, well instructed: *define, define, w. infant*, LLL I, 2, 99 (Armado's speech).

**Well-famed**, famous: Troil. IV, 5, 173.

**Well-favoured**, well-looking, handsome, pretty: Gent. II, 1, 54. Wiv. II, 2, 285. Ado III, 3, 15. Tw. I, 5, 169. Lr. II, 4, 259. Per. IV, 1, 86.

**Well-foughten**, bravely fought: *in this glorious and w. field* (= battle) H5 IV, 6, 18.

**Well-found**, standing the test, tried, approved: *in what he did profess, w.* All's II, 1, 105. *our w. successes*, Cor. II, 2, 48 (found to be as great as they were reported). cf. *Well-warranted*, and *Well-seen* sub *See*.

**Well-governed** (not hyphened in O. Edd.) well mannered: *a virtuous and w. youth*, Rom. I, 5, 70.

**Well-graced** (not hyphened in O. Edd.) being in favour with others, popular: *after a w. actor leaves the stage*, R2 V, 2, 24.

**Well-knit**, strongly compacted, having a firm frame: *O w. Samson! strong-jointed Samson!* LLL I, 2, 77 (Armado's speech).

**Well-known**, fully and generally known: H4B Ind. 21.

**Well-labouring**, working hard and successfully: *whose w. sword had three times slain the appearance of the king*, H4B I, 1, 127.

**Well-learned**, full of learning, versed in science: R3 III, 5, 100.

**Well-liking**, good-conditioned, plump: *w. wits they have; gross, gross; fat, fat*, LLL V, 2, 268.

**Well-lost** (not hyphened in O. Edd.) lost in a good cause: *my w. life*, All's I, 3, 254.

**Well-meaning** (not hyphened in O. Edd.) having good intentions, harmless: *plain w. soul*, R2 II, 1, 128.

**Well-meant**, sincere, not feigned: *his demand springs not from Edward's w. honest love*, H6C III, 3, 67.

**Well-minded**, well disposed: H6C IV, 8, 27.

**Well-nigh**, see *Nigh*.

**Well-ordered**, having a good organization or form of government: *there is a law in each w. nation*, Troil. II, 2, 180.

**Well-paid**, receiving good pay for service: *his w. ranks*, Ant. III, 1, 32.

**Well-painted**, 1) skilfully painted: Ven. 212. Lucr. 1443.

2) artfully feigned: *w. passion*, Oth. IV, 1, 268.

**Well-practised**, experienced: *I will stoop ... to your w. wise directions*, H4B V, 2, 121.

**Well-proportioned** (not hyphened in O. Edd.)

well shaped, well formed: *a w. steed*, Ven. 290. *his w. beard made rough*, H6B III, 2, 175.

**Well-refined** (not hyphened in O. Edd.) polished in a high degree, free from any rudeness or impropriety: *in polished form of w. pen*, Sonn. 85, 8.

**Well-reputed** (not hyphened in O. Edd.) having a good reputation, respectable: *such weeds as may beseem some w. page*, Gent. II, 7, 43.

**Well-respected**, ruled by reasonable considerations: *if w. honour bid me on, I hold as little counsel with weak fear as you*, H4A IV, 3, 10.

**Well-sailing**, passing swiftly by means of sails: *w. ships*, Per. IV, 4, 17.

**Well-seeing**, quicksighted: Sonn. 148, 14.

**Well-seeming**, having a good appearance: *this w. Angelo*, Meas. III, 1, 232. *mis-shapen chaos of w. forms*, Rom. I, 1, 185.

**Well-seen**, see *See.*

**Well-skilled**, skilful: Lucr. 1520.

**Well-spoken**, speaking with grace, eloquent: *a knight w., neat and fine*, Gent. I, 2, 10. *these fair w. days*, R3 I, 1, 29.* *Clarence is w.* I, 3, 348. cf. *better spoken* in Lr. IV, 6, 10, and *fair-spoken.*

**Well-took**, well taken, well undergone: *we thank you for your w. labour*, Hml. II, 2, 83.

**Well-tuned**, having a good sound, melodious: *Philomel had ended the w. warble*, Lucr. 1080. *the true concord of w. sounds*, Sonn. 8, 5. *the w. horns*, Tit. II, 3, 18.

**Well-warranted**, proved to be good, and trusted on good warrant (cf. *Well-found*): Meas. V, 254.

**Well-weighing**, see *Weigh.*

**Well-willers**, friends: *be ruled by your w.* Wiv. I, 1, 72 (Evans' speech).

**Well-wished**, attended by good wishes, beloved: *a w. king*, Meas. II, 4, 27.

**Well-won**, honestly gained: *my w. thrift*, Merch. I, 3, 51 (Ff. *well-worne*).

**Welsh**, pertaining to Wales, or native of Wales: Wiv. II, 1, 209. III, 1, 100. V, 3, 13. V, 5, 85. 145 (*a W. goat*). 172 (*W. flannel*). H4A II, 4, 372 (*a W. hook*, i. e. a sort of bill hooked at the end). III, 1, 247. H5 IV, 7, 112. V, 1, 82. the *W.* = the people of Wales: H4B I, 3, 79. 83. *I am W.* (= a Welshman) H5 IV, 7, 110; cf. Wiv. III, 1, 100. Substantively, = the language of Wales: H4A III, 1, 50. 120. 193. 201. 209. 233. 239.

**Welshman**, a native of Wales: Wiv. II, 2, 317. R2 II, 4, 5. H4A I, 1, 41. H5 IV, 1, 51. 86. R3 IV, 4, 477. Plur. *Welshmen*: R2 III, 2, 73. III, 3, 2. H5 IV, 7, 102. H6C II, 1, 180. R3 IV, 3, 47.

**Welshwomen**, women native of Wales: H4A I, 1, 45.

**Wen**, a fleshy excrescence: *I do allow this w.* (i. e. Falstaff) *to be as familiar with me as my dog*, H4B II, 2, 115.

**Wench**, a female person, a woman; not always in a bad sense, as at present, but used as a general familiar expression, in any variation of tone between tenderness and contempt: *know, gentle w., it small avails my mood*, Lucr. 1273. *as leaky as an unstanched w.* Tp. I, 1, 51. *well demanded, w.* I, 2, 139 (Prospero to Miranda). 412. 479. *Temperance was a delicate w.* II, 1, 43. *to weep like a young w. that had buried her grandam*, Gent. II, 1, 24. *but tell me, w.* II, 7, 59. III, 1, 312. Meas. II, 2, 124. IV, 3, 180. Err. III, 1, 34.

109. IV, 3, 53. 55. 58. LLL I, 1, 265. 285. 290. I, 2, 62. 129. II, 257. III, 24. IV, 1, 126. IV, 3, 385. V, 2, 25. 82. 256. 321. 414. 682. Merch. II, 2, 175. Shr. I, 1, 69. II, 161. 250. III, 2, 168. 240. IV, 4, 99. V, 2, 180. All's IV, 3, 123. Tw. I, 3, 45. II, 3, 194. II, 5, 120. 198. Wint. III, 3, 62. IV, 4, 318. 335. 618. H4A I, 2, 11. 46. H4B II, 1, 161. II, 2, 152. II, 4, 405. IV, 3, 101. H6A IV, 7, 41. V, 3, 34. R3 I, 1, 155. H8 III, 1, 1. 148. III, 2, 295. IV, 2, 81. 99. 167. Troil. IV, 2, 95. V, 2, 70. Tit. III, 1, 283. Rom. II, 4, 4. 14. 42. II, 5, 45. III, 3, 143. Caes. I, 2, 274. Lr. III, 2, 84. Oth. III, 3, 313. V, 2, 272. Ant. I, 2, 36. II, 2, 231. Per. IV Prol. 16.

**Wenching**, running after wenches, lecherous: Troil. V, 4, 35.

**Wenchless**, having no store of wenches: *we lost too much money this mart by being too w.* Per. IV, 2, 5.

**Wench-like**, womanish: *do not play in w. words with that which is so serious*, Cymb. IV, 2, 230.

**Wend** (the impf. *went* see sub *Go*), to go: *w. you with this letter*, Meas. IV, 3, 150. Twice employed for the sake of the rhyme: *hopeless and helpless doth Aegeon w.* Err. I, 1, 158. *back to Athens shall the lovers w.* Mids. III, 2, 372.

**West**, 1) the region where the sun sets; with the article: Sonn 132, 8. H4A I, 3, 195. H4B Ind. 3. Rom. III, 2, 3. Mcb. III, 3, 5. Oth. IV, 2, 144. *throned by the w.* Mids. II, 1, 158. *from the w.* John II, 409. *in the w.* Ven. 530. Sonn. 73, 6. Err. I, 2, 7. R2 II, 4, 21. R3 IV, 4, 486. Cymb. V, 5, 476. Without the article: *by east, w., north and south*, LLL V, 2, 566. *by east and w.* John II, 381. *from east, w., north and south*, Wint. I, 2, 203. *from east to w.* Troil. II, 3, 274. *from south to w.* Cymb. V, 5, 471. *whether for east or w.* Cor. I, 2, 10. *stealing unseen to w.* Sonn. 33, 8. Prepositions omitted: *w. of this place*, As IV, 3, 79. *there lies your way, due w.* Tw. III, 1, 145. *w. of this forest*, H4B IV, 1, 19. *they take their courses east, w., north, south*, IV, 2, 104. Cor. II, 3, 24. *east and w.* Hml. I, 4, 37. Adjectively: *the w. end of the wood*, Gent. V, 3, 9. *my East and W. Indies*, Wiv. I, 3, 79. *the w. corner*, LLL I, 1, 249.

2) the countries lying in that region: *that utmost corner of the w.*, John II, 29. *all the wealthy kingdoms of the w.* H6B I, 1, 154. *to this part of the w.* Cymb. IV, 2, 349.

3) a westerly wind: *a south w. blow on ye*, Tp. I, 2, 323. Per. IV, 1, 51. *I am but mad north north w.* Hml. II, 2, 396.

**Westerly**, coming from the west: *is this wind w.* Per. IV, 1, 51.

**Western**, being in the west: Gent. V, 1, 1. Meas. IV, 1, 29. Mids. II, 1, 166. IV, 1, 112. As III, 2, 93 (*w. Ind*). John V, 5, 2. H6C V, 3, 6. R3 IV, 4, 433. 482. Mcb. I, 2, 12.

**Westminster**, the western part of London; seat of the royal palace: H4B II, 4, 384. *abbot of W.* R2 IV, 152. V, 6, 19. The kings crowned in the cathedral: H6B I, 2, 37. IV, 4, 31. R3 IV, 1, 32.

**Westmoreland** (O. Edd. *Westmerland*); Earl of W., baronial title of several noblemen intimately allied to the royal house of England: H4A I, 1, 31. III, 2, 170 etc. H4B I, 1, 18. 135 etc. H5 II, 2, 70. IV, 3, 19. 34. H6C I, 1, 61. 88.

**Westward**, toward the west: Wint. IV, 4, 296. H4A III, 1, 76. With *from*: Rom. I, 1, 129. Hml. I, 1, 36.

**Westward-ho,** probably an exclamation often heard from the watermen on the Thames: Tw. III, 1, 146.

**Wet,** adj. consisting of water, or moistened with water (or tears); and generally opposed to dry: Ven. 83. 966. Wint. V, 3, 81. H4B III, 1, 27. V, 1, 95. Lr. IV, 7, 71. Ant. II, 7, 55. Cymb. V, 5, 35. Substantively: *applying w. to w.* Compl. 40. *messenger of w.* All's I, 3, 157.

**Wet,** vb. (partic. *wet:* R3 I, 2, 163. 216) to moisten with water (or tears): Ven. 1179. Lucr. 1228. 1548. Sonn. 9, 1. Tp. II, 1, 127. IV, 211 (*my —ing =* my becoming wet). As III, 2, 27. H6B III, 2, 341. H6C III, 2, 184. R3 I, 2, 163 (partic. or adj.?). 216. Lr. IV, 6, 102.

**Wether,** a ram castrated: Pilgr. 272. Merch. IV, 1, 114. Wint. IV, 3, 33. cf. *Bell-wether.*

**Wexford,** see *Washford.*

**Weyard** or **Weyward,** see *Weird.*

**Wezand,** the windpipe: Tp. III, 2, 99.

**Whale,** the animal Balaena: Wiv. II, 1, 65. All's IV, 3, 249. H4B IV, 4, 40. Troil. V, 5, 23. Hml. III, 2, 398. Per. II, 1, 33. 36. III, 1, 63. *this is the flower that smiles on every one, to show his teeth as white as —'s bone,* LLL V, 2, 332 (*as white as whale's bone* was a proverbial phrase, perhaps from the circumstance that 'the ivory of western Europe in the middle ages was the tooth of the walrus'. Nares. But in our passage there is perhaps some malice intended).

**Wharf,** the bank of a river: *the fat weed that roots itself in ease on Lethe w.* Hml. I, 5, 33. *from the barge a strange invisible perfume hits the sense of the adjacent — s,* Ant. II, 2, 218.

**What,** 1) interr. pron. used to inquire after quality or kind of things; a) substantively, as subject, or predicate, or object, in principal or subordinate sentences; f. i. *what am I that thou shouldst contemn me this?* Ven. 205. *what is ten hundred touches unto thee?* 519. *what is thy body but a swallowing grave?* 757. *what's the matter?* Tp. II, 1, 309. *what where these? A living drollery,* III, 3, 20. *what's the noise?* Ant. IV, 14, 104. *and what not done, that thou hast cause to rue, wherein I had no stroke of mischief in it?* Tit. V, 1, 109. *what seest thou in the ground?* Ven. 118. *what shall she say?* 253. *what should I do?* 667. 787. 933. *w. seest thou else?* Tp. I, 2, 49. *'tis you that have the reason. To do what?* Gent. II, 1, 151. *what doth our cousin lay to Mowbray's charge?* R2 I, 1, 84 etc. *canst not feel what 'tis to love?* Ven. 201. *thou knowest not what it is,* 615. *art ignorant of what thou art,* Tp. I, 2, 18. 34. *know not what we mean,* Ven. 126. *let me remember thee what thou hast promised,* Tp. I, 2, 243. *I know them, and what they weigh,* Ado V, I, 93 etc. Anglicisms: *what is the time o'the day?* Tp. I, 2, 239. *what do you think the hour?* Tim. III, 4, 8. *what is the night?* Mcb. III, 4, 126 (= how far is the night advanced?). *what is your name?* Tp. III, 1, 36. Meas. II, 1, 45. 226. Err. III, 2, 110. Ado IV, 2, 11. LLL II, 209. As I, 2, 233. Tw. I, 2, 26. H6B II, 3, 81. IV, 2, 105. R3 IV, 2, 40. *what your name is else I know not,* Err. III, 2, 29. *what do you call your knight's name?* Wiv. III, 2, 20. *what may I call your name?* Shr. II, 67. *call me what thou darest,* Gent. II, 3, 63. *trow you what he called me?* LLL V, 2, 279. *what shall I call thee?* As I, 3, 125. 128. Shr. Ind. 2, 110. H4A I, 3, 242. H4B IV, 1, 1. H6B I, 4, 52. Tit. V, 2, 61. Hml. III, 2, 246 etc.

b) adjectively: *what bare excuses makest thou,* Ven. 188. *what great danger dwells upon my suit,* 206. *what hour is this?* 495. *what bargains may I make,* 512. 565. 1076. *what cheer?* Tp. I, 1, 2. *what foul play had we?* I, 2, 60. *what impossible matter will he make easy next?* II, 1, 88. 112. *what stuff is this?* 254. III, 3, 18. *to what end are all these words?* Shr. I, 2, 250 etc. *mark ... with what care he cranks,* Ven. 681. *say in brief for what cause thou camest to Ephesus,* Err. I, 1, 31. *Jove knows what man thou mightst have made,* Cymb. IV, 2, 207 etc. With the indefinite article, contrary to modern use: *what a strange drowsiness possesses them?* Tp. II, 1, 199 (M. Edd. *possesses them!*). *what a coil is there? who are those at the gate?* Err. III, 1, 48. *that it may show me what a face I have, since it is bankrupt of his majesty,* R2 IV, 266. *what an unkind hour is guilty of this lamentable chance?* Rom. V, 3, 145 (M. Edd. *chance!*). Peculiar passage: *what is he for a fool that betroths himself to unquietness?* Ado I, 3, 49 (= what fool is he; cf. *For*). In such phrases as: *what a plague means my niece* (Tw. I, 3, 1. H4A II, 2, 39 etc.), *a plague* is parenthetical.

Used in exclamations; substantively: *O father Abram, what these Christians are!* Merch. I, 3, 161. *what mortality is!* Cymb. IV, 1, 16. Adjectively, with the ind. article: *what a sight it was!* Ven. 343. *what a war of looks!* 355. *what a mansion have those vices got,* Sonn. 95, 9. *dost thou forget from what a torment I did free thee?* Tp. I, 2, 251. II, 1, 24. 180. 267. III, 2, 71. IV, 222. V, 295. Meas. III, 1, 240. Err. V, 269. H6B II, 1, 5. H6C V, 4, 12 etc. Without the indef. article (not only before abstracts, as f. i. Gent. I, 2, 15. Meas. III, 1, 241): *what banquet wert thou to the taste!* Ven. 445. *what treasure hast thou lost!* 1075. *what trouble was I then to you!* Tp. I, 2, 151. *thou best knowest what torment I did find thee in,* 287. *out of that 'no hope' what great hope have you!* II, 1, 240. *what fool is she!* Gent. I, 2, 53 (O. Edd. '*fool,* M. Edd. *a fool*). *what fine change is in the music!* IV, 2, 68. *I'll tell the world what man thou art,* Meas. II, 4, 154. *what case stand I in!* Wint. I, 2, 352. *what dreadful noise of waters in mine ears!* R3 I, 4, 22. *what night is this!* Caes. I, 3, 42. *what thing it is that I never did see man die,* Cymb. IV, 4, 35 etc.

Various elliptical use: a) *what =* for what purpose? why? f. i. *what may a heavy groan advantage thee?* Ven. 950. *what tell you me of it?* H4B I, 2, 129. *what dares the slave come hither?* Rom. I, 5, 57. Hence, as it were by an anticipation of the expected answer, having the force of a negative: *what were thy lips the worse for one poor kiss?* Ven. 207. *what recketh he his riders angry stir?* 283. *what cares he now for curb?* 285. *what canst thou boast of things long since?* Ven. 1077. *what cares these roarers for the name of king?* Tp. I, 1, 17. *what should I don this robe and trouble you?* Tit. I, 1, 189. *what boots it thee to call thyself a sun?* V, 3, 18. *what doth her beauty serve but as a note where I may read ...,* Rom. I, 1, 241. *what should I stay?* Ant. V, 2, 316 etc. Especially before the verb *to need: what needs a second striking?* Ven. 250. *what needeth then apologies be made?* Lucr. 31. *what shall I need to draw my sword?* Cymb. III, 4, 34. Gent. II, 1, 158. Err. III, 2, 15. H8 II, 4, 128. Caes. II, 1, 123 etc. Hence

b) *what though =* the simple *though;* originally = what do I care though, no matter though (with the subjunctive): *what though the rose have prickles, yet 'tis plucked*, Ven. 574. *what though her frowning brows be bent, her cloudy looks will calm ere night*, Pilgr. 311. *what though care killed a cat, thou hast mettle enough in thee to kill care*, Ado V, 1, 132. *what though he love your Hermia? Lord, what though? yet Hermia still loves you*, Mids. II, 2, 109. *what though I be not so in grace as you, ..., this should you pity rather than despise*, III, 2, 232. *what though you have no beauty, ... must you be therefore proud?* As III, 5, 37. *what though I be enthralled? he seems a knight*, H6A V, 3, 101. H6B I, 1, 158. H6C V, 4, 3. H8 III, 2, 97 etc. *what though*, alone, = no matter, never mind, 'tis all one: *but what though? yet I live like a poor gentleman born*, Wiv. I, 1, 286. *but what though? courage!* As III, 3, 51. *by chance, but not by truth; what though?* John I, 169. H5 II, 1, 9.

Similarly: *and what an if his sorrows have so overwhelmed his wits, shall we be thus afflicted in his wreaks?* Tit. IV, 4, 9. *how canst thou believe an oath? What if I do not? ... yet I urge thy oath*, Tit. V, 1, 73.

c) *what if* = what should you say, what would be the consequence if: *what if he had said 'widower Aeneas' too?* Tp. II, 1, 79. *what if we do omit this reprobate till he were well inclined?* Meas. IV, 3, 77. *what if we assayed to steal the clownish fool out of your father's court?* As I, 3, 131. *what if her eyes were there?* Rom. II, 2, 18. *what if this mixture do not work at all? what if it be a poison?* IV, 3, 21. 24 etc.

d) *what of* = why do you mention, what follows from, what is the matter with: *there want not many that do fear in deep of night to walk by this Herne's oak. But what of this?* Wiv. IV, 4, 41. *have not your worship a wart above your eye? Yes, marry, have I; what of that?* I, 4, 158. *well, Mistress Ford; what of her?* II, 2, 55. *all this is so, but what of this, my lord?* Ado IV, 1, 73. *and what of him? did he take interest?* Merch. I, 3, 76. Shr. IV, 4, 77. 84. IV, 2, 66. All's V, 3, 204. Wint. IV, 4, 403. H6B IV, 2, 143. IV, 7, 53. Troil. I, 2, 14. Cor. V, 4, 3. Tim. I, 1, 83. 112. Caes. II, 1, 141 (*but w. of Cicero?* = what do you think of C. cf. LLL IV, 3, 282). Hml. III, 2, 311. Oth. IV, 1, 23. Cymb. V, 5, 150. 317 etc. Similarly: *what with him? he comes not like to his father's greatness*, Wint. V, 1, 88 (= what is the matter with him?). Hence *what of that* = no matter, never mind: *the night is spent. Why, what of that?* Ven. 717. *I am thought as fair as she, but what of that? Demetrius thinks not so*, Mids. I, 1, 228. *I cannot instantly raise up the gross of full three thousand ducats; what of that? Tubal ... will furnish me*, Merch. I, 3, 57. IV, 1, 260. Tw. II, 3, 196. III, 4, 23. H4B IV, 3, 43. H6A III, 1, 59. H6C IV, 1, 49. V, 4, 13. 14. 15. Cor. V, 1, 4. Rom. II, 2, 12. II, 4, 221. Hml. III, 2, 251 etc.

e) *what*, alone, superfluously introducing a question: *what, must our mouths be cold?* Tp. I, 1, 56. *what, art thou waking?* II, 1, 209. *what, are they broken?* Gent. II, 5, 19. *what, will you walk with me about the town*, Err. I, 2, 22. *what, you wrestle tomorrow?* As I, 1, 126. *what, hast thou dined?* Shr. IV, 3, 59. *what, by a horseman or a footman?* Wint. IV, 3, 67. *what, shall I find you here?* Caes. IV, 1, 10. *say, what, is Horatio there?* Hml. I, 1, 19. *what, has this thing appeared again?* 21. *what, looked he frowningly?* I, 2, 231. cf. *but what, but what, come they to*

*visit us?* LLL V, 2, 119. *what now? how chance thou art returned so soon?* Err. I, 2, 42. *what now, Lucilius, is Cassius near?* Caes. IV, 2, 3. *what now, my son, have I not ever said ...*, John I, 31.

Similarly as a word of exclamation, expressing surprise, or exultation, or impatience: *what, canst thou talk?* Ven. 427. *what, all so soon asleep!* Tp. II, 1, 191. *what, shall these papers lie like telltales here*, Gent. I, 2, 133. *what, gone without a word!* II, 2, 16. *what, didst thou offer her this from me?* IV, 4, 58. *how now, Grumio! what, Grumio!* Shr. IV, 1, 111. *now, Cinna; now, Metellus; what, Trebonius!* Caes. II, 2, 120. *what! I do bring good news*, H4B V, 3, 133. *what! we have many goodly days to see*, R3 IV, 4, 320. *what, girl! though grey do something mingle with our younger brown, yet ha' we a brain*, Ant. IV, 8, 19. *what, I say, my foot my tutor?* Tp. I, 2, 468. *what! an advocate for an impostor!* 476. *what, man! I know them!* Ado V, 1, 92. *what, courage, man!* 132. *what, this gentleman will out-talk us all*, Shr. I, 2, 248. John I, 245. H4B IV, 5, 110. H5 V, 2, 166. Cor. IV, 1, 14. Tit. IV, 2, 97. Tim. IV, 3, 30. Ant. IV, 15, 83 etc.

Employed in calling to persons, particularly when it is done with some impatience: *what, Ariel!* Tp. IV, 33. *what, John Rugby*, Wiv. I, 4, 1. 40. 41. *what, John! what, Robert!* III, 3, 1. 154. *what, wife, I say*, IV, 2, 125. Ado III, 3, 102. Merch. II, 5, 3. 4. H4A II, 1, 4. 24. H4B V, 1, 2. Troil. V, 2, 1. V, 6, 5. Rom. I, 3, 3. 4. IV, 4, 23. IV, 5, 1. Caes. II, 1, 5. V, 3, 72. Ant. II, 7, 138 (*these drums, these trumpets, flutes, what!*). IV, 12, 30. *what ho*, in the same sense: Tp. I, 2, 313. Gent. I, 2, 66. Wiv. I, 1, 74. IV, 2, 9. 174. Meas. III, 1, 44. IV, 1, 50. IV, 2, 20. IV, 3, 25. Shr. IV, 1, 152. Tw. I, 5, 318. H4A II, 1, 52. R3 III, 2, 1 (Ff *my lord*). Rom. I, 1, 90. IV, 4, 23. Caes. II, 1, 1 etc.

2) = that which; substantively: *what follows more she murders with a kiss*, Ven. 54. *so offers he to give what she did crave*, 88. *controlling what he was controlled with*, 270. 299. *lorded not only with what my revenue yielded*, Tp. I, 2, 98. *will't please you taste of what is here*, III, 3, 42. I, 2, 369. *I do fearfully believe 'tis done, what we so feared he had a charge to do*, John IV, 1, 75. *look, what I speak, my life shall prove it true*, R2 I, 1, 87. *with what his valour did enrich his wit, his wit set down to make his valour live*, R3 III, 1, 85 (= that with which). *what you have spoke, it may be so perchance*, Mcb. IV, 3, 11. *our story, what we have two nights seen*, Hml. I, 1, 33. *what our contempt doth often hurl from us, we wish it ours again*, Ant. I, 2, 127 etc. Adjectively: *paying what ransom the insulter willeth*, Ven. 550. *set all hearts i'the state to what tune pleased his ear*, Tp. I, 2, 85. *what strength I have is mine own*, Epil. 2. *for what obscured light the heavens did grant did but convey unto our minds a doubtful warrant of immediate death*, Err. I, 1, 67. *I made thee miserable what time I threw the people's suffrages on him*, Tit. IV, 3, 19 etc. With reference to a preceding substantive: *he can afford no praise to thee but what in thee doth live*, Sonn. 79, 12. *no ill luck stirring but what lights on my shoulders*, Merch. III, 1, 99. *all proofs sleeping else but what your jealousies awake*, Wint. III, 2, 114. *draw no swords but what are sanctified*, H4B IV, 4, 4. cf. *what (counsels) ever have been thought on in this state*, Cor. I, 2, 4 (a much vexed passage. Later Ff and most M. Edd. *what ever hath* etc.). cf. R3 V, 2, 20 (Qq *who*).

3) = who (but only in the predicate): *what is this maid?* Tp. V, 185. *what are you, sir? He, sir, a tapster,* Meas. II, 1, 62. *what is that Barnardine?* IV, 2, 132. *what are you?* IV, 3, 27. *one in the prison ... I have reserved alive. What's he?* V, 472. Err. III, 1, 42. III, 2, 90. Ado I, 1, 34. II, 1, 137. LLL II, 197. V, 2, 87. 304. Mids. V, 71. As II, 4, 88. II, 7, 79. Shr. V, 1, 17. 65. Tw. I, 2, 35. I, 3, 53. I, 5, 124. III, 4, 346. Wint. V, 3, 63. John II, 134. IV, 3, 34. R2 V, 5, 69. H4B I, 2, 66. H5 III, 7, 115. IV, 3, 18. H6A V, 3, 45. H6B I, 3, 183. III, 1, 107. H6C II, 1, 43. III, 3, 44. R3 I, 4, 85. Cor. I, 10, 28. Rom. I, 5, 114. Mcb. V, 7, 2. Hml. IV, 6, 1. Lr. IV, 6, 48. V, 3, 125. Oth. I, 1, 94 etc.

4) = whatever and whoever; a) whatever: *to bear up against what should ensue,* Tp. I, 2, 158. *I beyond all limit of what else i'the world do love, prize, honour you,* III, 1, 72. *call you 'em stanzos? What you will,* As II, 5, 20 (cf. the title of the comedy: *Twelfe Night,* or *What you will;* i. e. call it whatever you will). cf. I, 3, 121. *I love thee not a jar o'the clock behind what lady-she her lord,* Wint. I, 2, 44. *come what will,* H4A I, 2, 162; cf. Hml. IV, 7, 189. Cor. III, 1, 141. *wins the king from her, with promise of his daughter, and what else,* H6C III, 1, 51. *to have his pomp and all what state compounds but only painted,* Tim. IV, 2, 35. *what will hap more to-night, safe scape the king,* Lr. III, 6, 121. III, 1, 15. *what pain it cost, what danger,* Cymb. III, 6, 81. *be what it is, the action of my life is like it,* V, 4, 149. b) whoever: *be what thou wilt, thou art my prisoner,* H6A V, 3, 45. *be what they will, I heartily forgive 'em,* H8 II, 1, 65. *that my accusers, be what they will, may stand forth face to face,* V, 3, 47. *what in the world he is that names me traitor, villain-like he lies,* Lr. V, 3, 97.

5) = something, in the phrase *I tell you what,* or *I'll tell you what* = let me tell you (not by way of communicating news, but of laying some stress on what one says): Ado V, 4, 101. Merch. I, 1, 86. H4A II, 4, 214. H4B II, 4, 166. H5 III, 6, 86. Rom. III, 5, 162. Shr. I, 2, 113. John III, 3, 60. IV, 3, 120. H4A III, 1, 155. H4B I, 1, 51. V, 4, 9. 20. R3 I, 1, 78. III, 1, 89. Troil. V, 2, 21. Cor. IV, 2, 22. Similarly: *wot you what,* R3 III, 2, 92. *this trick may chance to scathe you, I know what,* Rom. I, 5, 86 (= depend on it).

6) = somewhat, in some measure, in the phrase *what with,* = partly by, partly in consequence of: *my woeful self, ... what with his art in youth, and youth in art, threw my affections in his charmed power,* Compl. 145. *thus, what with the war, what with the sweat, what with the gallows and what with proverty, I am custom-shrunk,* Meas. I, 2, 83. *I fear, what with the sickness of Northumberland, ... and what with Owen Glendower's absence thence, ... I fear the power of Percy is too weak,* H4A IV, 4, 14. *and such a flood of greatness fell on you, what with our help, what with the absent king, what with the injuries of a wanton time,* V, 1, 49. *is it not like that I, so early waking, what with loathsome smells, and shrieks like mandrakes', ... shall I not be distraught?* Rom. IV, 3, 46. Without *with: a whoreson tisick so troubles me, and the foolish fortune of this girl, and what one thing, what another, that I shall leave you one of these days,* Troil. V, 3, 103.

**Whate'er** (followed by the indicative, though

often followed by *be;* cf. *Be*), 1) no matter what; this or that or any thing that; substantively: *he strikes w. is in his way,* Ven. 623. *do w. thou wilt,* Sonn. 19, 6. *w. thy thoughts be,* 93, 11. Gent. V, 4, 151. As II, 7, 109 (*w. you are,* i. e. savage or civil). Shr. I, 2, 155. II, 382. All's IV, 4, 36. V, 1, 37. John IV, 3, 28. R2 V, 5, 38 (Qq *be,* Ff *am*). H4A I, 3, 71 (Ff *whatever*). H6A I, 1, 37. H6C I, 4, 38. II, 1, 39. III, 3, 15. Troil. IV, 5, 77 (*therefore Achilles: but w., know this;* i. e. w. your name may be). Tit. II, 3, 195. V, 2, 71. Rom. V, 3, 26. Mcb. IV, 1, 73. Oth. III, 3, 89. Ant. II, 7, 74. IV, 4, 29. Cymb. III, 6, 80. Per. III, 2, 52. IV, 2, 10 etc. Adjectively: *w. occasion keeps him from us now,* H6B III, 1, 3.

2) = whoever: *I am to get a man, — w. he be, it skills not much,* Shr. III, 2, 133 (perhaps = of what kind soever).

**Whatever,** no matter what; this or that or any thing that; all that; substantively: *take no repulse, w. she doth say,* Gent. III, 1, 100. R2 IV, 330. H4A I, 3, 71 (Qq *whate'er*). H5 V Chor. 40. Troil. II, 3, 166. Mcb. IV, 3, 31. Oth. III, 3, 8. Adjectively: *w. fortune stays him,* Shr. III, 2, 23. John IV, 1, 84.

**Whatsoe'er,** 1) = whatever: Shr. I, 2, 216. R3 I, 1, 108 (Qq *whatsoever*). H8 V, 3, 128. Tit. II, 3, 54.

2) = whoever: *rude companion, w. thou be,* H6B IV, 10, 33. *to doom the offenders, w. they be,* R3 III, 4, 67 (Ff *whosoe'er*).

**Whatsoever,** 1) whatever: *till w. star that guides my moving points on me graciously,* Sonn. 26, 9. *w. I have merited,* Wiv. II, 2, 210. *upon any complaint w.* Meas. II, 1, 261. IV, 2, 123. Err. V, 305. Ado II, 2, 6. Shr. II, 126. H5 II, 2, 111. R3 I, 1, 108 (Ff *whatsoe'er*). H8 III, 2, 343. Cor. II, 1, 235 (*as if that w. god who leads him were slily crept into his human powers*). Caes. V, 3, 39. Hml. I, 2, 249 (Q2.3 *whatsomever*). cf. *Soever.*

2) whoever: *as any man in Illyria, w. he be, under the degree of my betters,* Tw. I, 3, 124. *w. thou art, thou art but a scurvy fellow,* III, 4, 163 (Sir Andrew's speeches). *Leonatus! a banished rascal; and he's another, w. he be,* Cymb. II, 1, 43 (Cloten's speech).

**Whatsome'er,** whatever: All's III, 5, 54. Ant. II, 6, 102.

**Whatsomever,** whatever: Hml. I, 2, 249 (lection of Q2.3; the rest of O. Edd. *whatsoever*).

**What-ye-call't,** Thingumbob: *good even, good Master W.* As III, 3, 74.

**Wheat,** the plant Triticum vulgare, and the fruit of it: Tp. IV, 61. Mids. I, 1, 185. Merch. I, 1, 116. H4B V, 1, 16. 17 (*red w.*). Troil. I, 1, 15. Lr. III, 4, 123 (*white w.*). Ant. II, 6, 37.

**Wheaten,** made of stalks of wheat: *peace should still her w. garland wear,* Hml. V, 2, 41.

**Wheel,** subst. any thing circular and turning on an axis: *it* (majesty) *is a massy w. fixed on the summit of the highest mount,* Hml. III, 3, 17. *when a great w. runs down a hill,* Lr. II, 4, 73. *bound upon a w. of fire,* IV, 7, 47. *a potter's w.* H6A I, 5, 19. *she had transformed me to a curtal dog and made me turn i'the w.* Err. III, 2, 151 (i. e. to turn the spit). Instrument of torture and execution: Wint. III, 2, 177. Cor. III, 2, 2. One of the frames which support a carriage: H4A III, 1, 132. H4B II, 4, 278. H6B II, 4, 13. Tit. V, 2, 47. 54. Caes. I, 1, 39. *a carbuncle of Phoebus' w.* Cymb. V, 5, 190. Pars pro toto, = the carriage: *at* *the —s of Caesar?* *art thou led in triumph?* Meas. III, 2, 47. *the gentle day, before the —s of Phoebus*, Ado V, 3, 26. *from forth day's path and Titan's fiery —s*, Rom. II, 3, 4. Attribute of Fortune, as the emblem of mutability: Lucr. 952. H5 III, 6, 28. 34. H6C IV, 3, 47. Hml. II, 2, 517. Lr. II, 2, 180. V, 3, 174. Confounded, in this quality, with a spinning-wheel: *mock the good housewife Fortune from her w.* As I, 2, 34. Ant. IV, 15, 44 (Fortune being, probably, supposed to do the business of the ancient Parcae). Proverbial: *then may I set the world on —s, when she can spin for her living*, Gent. III, 1, 317 (= then I have all the world in a string and may drive it before me). *would it* (the world) *were all* (drunk), *that it might go on —s*, Ant. II, 7, 99.

Not yet satisfactorily explained: *how the w. becomes it!* Hml. IV, 5, 172 (Malone: allusion to the occupation of the girl who is supposed to sing the song. Steevens, without sufficient authority: = burden, refrain).

**Wheel,** vb. 1) to turn round on an axis: *thus hath the course of justice — ed about*, R3 IV, 4, 105 (Ff *whirl'd*).

2) to fetch a compass; and hence to err about: *I was forced to w. three or four miles about*, Cor. I, 6, 19. *attend me where I w.* Troil. V, 7, 2. *an extravagant and —ing stranger of here and everywhere*, Oth. I, 1, 137.

**Wheeled,** having wheels, conveyed on wheels: *the w. seat of fortunate Caesar*, Ant. IV, 14, 75.

**Wheeson,** Whitsun: H4B II, 1, 96 (Ff *Whitson*).

**Wheezing** (Q *whissing*, Ff om.) breathing with difficulty and noise: *w. lungs*, Troil. V, 1, 24.

**Whelk,** a protuberance, a pustule, a wheal: *his face is all bubukles, and —s, and knobs*, H5 III, 6, 108.

**Whelked** (O. Edd. *welk'd* or *wealk'd*) set with protuberances, embossed: *horns w. and waved like the enridged sea*, Lr. IV, 6, 71.

**Whelm,** to overwhelm: *she is my prize, or ocean w. them all*, Wiv. II, 2, 143 (Pistol's speech).

**Whelp,** subst. the young of a dog, or of a bear, or lion: H4A III, 3, 167. H5 I, 2, 109. H6A I, 5, 26. H6C III, 2, 161. Tit. IV, 1, 96. Ant. III, 13, 94. Cymb. V, 4, 138. V, 5, 435. 443. Used of the children of savage and ferocious parents: *the son that she did litter here, a freckled w. hag-born*, Tp. I, 2, 283. *how the young w. of Talbot's, raging-wood, did flesh his puny sword in Frenchmen's blood*, H6A IV, 7, 35. *two of thy —s, fell curs of bloody kind, have here bereft my brother of his life*, Tit. II, 3, 281.

**Whelp,** vb. to bring forth young: *a lioness hath —ed in the streets*, Caes. II, 2, 17. Trans.: *thou wast —ed a dog*, Tim. II, 2, 90.

**When,** 1) interrogatively, = at what time: *w. wilt thou be the humble suppliant's friend?* Lucr. 897. *w. did you lose your daughter?* Tp. V, 152. Gent. III, 1, 123. IV, 3, 42. Err. II, 2, 13. 155. LLL I, 1, 237 etc. etc. Elliptically used as an exclamation of impatience: *come, thou tortoise! when?* Tp. I, 2, 316. *why, when, I say? ... off with my boots, you rogues! you villains, when?* Shr. IV, 1, 146. 147. *when, Harry, when? obedience bids I should not bid again*, R2 I, 1, 162. *kneel down, kneel down; nay, when? strike now, or else the iron cools*, H6C V, 1, 49. *when, Lucius, when? awake, I say*, Caes. II, 1, 5. *when, can you tell?* a proverbial

phrase expressing scorn at the demand or menace of another: Err. III, 1, 52. H4A II, 1, 43. cf. As IV, 1, 133.

2) relatively, = at the time that; with a preterit tense: *w. her lips were ready for his pay, he winks*, Ven. 89. *it was mine art, w. I arrived and heard thee, that made gape the pine*, Tp. I, 2, 292. 332. II, 1, 97. III, 2, 151. III, 3, 43. Gent. II, 1, 27 etc. With a present, a) expressing an event of ordinary and natural occurrence: *he hath it w. he cannot use it*, Lucr. 862. *to do me business in the veins o'the earth w. it is baked with frost*, Tp. I, 2, 256. *it is foul weather in us all, w. you are cloudy*, II, 1, 142. 195. III, 1, 12. 34. LLL I, 1, 238. V, 2, 926. Merch. I, 1, 85 etc. b) futurity: *that thine may live w. thou thyself art dead*, Ven. 172. *be patient. W. the sea is*, Tp. I, 1, 17. I, 2, 378. II, 1, 234. 295. III, 1, 18. III, 2, 1. 9. 73. 105. 155. V, 51. Gent. I, 1, 10. II, 1, 136. Ado V, 4, 68 etc. With a future: *w. I shall see thee frown on my defects*, Sonn. 49, 2. *run w. you will, the story shall be changed*, Mids. II, 1, 230 (= w. you will run) etc.

= at which time (the subordinate clause being, logically, the main proposition): *his testy master goeth about to take him, when, lo, the unbacked breeder ... swiftly doth forsake him*, Ven. 320. *and comely-distant sits he by her side, w. he again desires her ... her grievance with his hearing to divide*, Compl. 66. *the time was once w. thou unurged wouldst vow*, Err. II, 2, 115. *marking the embarked traders on the flood, w. we have laughed to see the sails conceive*, Mids. II, 1, 128 etc.

= at the same time that, while, whereas (noting a contrast): *who is but drunken w. she seemed drowned*, Ven. 984. *thou didst smile, ... w. I have decked the sea with drops full salt*, Tp. I, 2, 155. *you rub the sore, w. you should bring the plaster*, II, 1, 139. *w. they will not give a doit to relieve a lame beggar, they will lay out ten to see a dead Indian*, II, 2, 33. Gent. I, 2, 61. II, 1, 158. Wiv. V, 5, 12. Meas. V, 11. Err. III, 1, 35. Merch. I, 1, 97 etc.

= the time that, or the fact that, after *to know* and *see: I have known w. there was no music with him but the drum and the fife*, Ado II, 3, 13. *I know when thou hast stolen away from fairy land*, Mids. II, 1, 65. *I knew w. seven justices could not take up a quarrel*, As V, 4, 103. *I have seen w. after execution judgement hath repented*, Meas. II, 2, 11. Caes. II, 1, 20.

= which time; then (relative for demonstrative), after *since* and *till: I was adopted heir by his consent, since w. his oath is broke*, H6C II, 2, 89. *till w., be cheerful*, Tp. V, 250. *till w., go seek thy fortune*, Troil. V, 6, 19.

*w. that* = when: Sonn. 47, 3. LLL IV, 3, 145. As II, 7, 75 etc. (cf. *That*).

Scarcely distinguishable from *if: w. a painter would surpass the life, ... so did this horse excel*, Ven. 289. *and for my sake, w. I might charm thee so for she that was thy Lucrece, now attend me*, Lucr. 1681. *'tis the curse in love ... w. women cannot love where they're beloved*, Gent. V, 4, 44. *when she is able to overtake seventeen years old*, Wiv. I, 1, 54 (Evans' speech). *what a thing should I have been w. I had been swelled*, III, 5, 17 (or = after). *I may say so w. I please. And w. please you to say so? W. I like your favour*, Ado II, 1, 95. *what madness rules in brainsick men, w. for so frivolous a cause such factious emula-*

tions hall arise, H6A IV, 1, 112. would 'twere come to that. Marry, w. thou darest, H6B II, 1, 39. Cor. III, 3, 53.

**Whenas**, at the time that, when: w. I met the boar ... I railed on thee, Ven. 999. w. thy love hath cast his utmost sum, Sonn. 49, 3. I in deep delight am chiefly drowned w. himself to singing he betakes, Pilgr. 114. w. thine eye hath chose the dame, ... let reason rule, 299. w. your husband all in rage to-day came to my house ... straight after did I meet him, Err. IV, 4, 140. many a battle have I won in France, w. the enemy hath been ten to one, H6C I, 2, 75. a woful looker-on, w. the noble Duke of York was slain, II, 1, 46. cried all hail, w. he meant all harm, V, 7, 34. The signification of as preponderating, = since, as: words more sweet and yet more dangerous than baits to fish or honey-stalks to sheep, w. the one is wounded with the bait, the other rotted with delicious feed, Tit. IV, 4, 92 (but cf. when in such sentences as f.i. Tp. I, 2, 355).

**Whence**, 1) interrog. from what place, from where, and metaphorically, from what source or origin: w. didst thou steal thy sweet? Sonn. 99, 2. w. hast thou this becoming of things ill, 150, 5. w. came you, Gent. IV, 1, 18. w. comes this restraint, Meas. I, 2, 128. Wiv. IV, 5, 106. Meas. V, 247. H6A I, 4, 99 etc. Preceded by from: more should I question thee ... from w. thou camest, how tended on, All's II, 1, 210. from w.? Cor. V, 2, 4. By of: nought knowing of w. I am, Tp. I, 2, 19. of w. are you? Meas. III, 2, 229. of w., I pray you? Shr. II, 103. to know of him of w. he is, Per. II, 3, 74. V, 1, 19. to ask of w. you are, Cymb. V, 5, 16.

2) relat. from which place, from where: the book of his good acts, w. men have read his fame, Cor. V, 2, 15. Mostly preceded by from: departed back to the camp, from w. he shortly after privily withdrew himself, Lucr. Arg. 14. within the gentle closure of my breast, from w. at pleasure thou mayst go and part, Sonn. 48, 12. Err. V, 264. LLL IV, 3, 304. As III, 2, 291. All's II, 4, 13. R2 V, 1, 78. H4A I, 3, 151. H6A III, 1, 166. H6B II, 1, 160. II, 2, 25. H6C V, 3, 11. R3 I, 1, 69 etc.

3) from w. = there from where: how do all from w. you came, Gent. II, 4, 122. let him walk from w. he came, Err. III, 1, 37.

w. or from w. = from there where: come thou home, Rousillon, w. honour but of danger wins a scar, as oft it loses all, All's III, 2, 124. is returned from w. he circumscribed with his sword ... the enemies of Rome, Tit. I, 68 (Ff from where). our poesy is as a gum which oozes from w. 'tis nourished, Tim. I, 1, 22. as w. the sun 'gins his reflection shipwrecking storms and direful thunders break, Mcb. I, 2, 25.

**Whencesoever**, from what place soever: R2 II, 3, 22.

**Whene'er** or **Whenever**, at what time soever: H4A III, 2, 138; Cor. IV, 7, 26. R3 II, 1, 32; Tit. IV, 2, 15.

**Whensoever**, the same: Meas. V, 158. Hml. V, 2, 210.

**Whe'r** (O. Edd. where or whe'r) contracted from whether, q. v.: and w. he run or fly they know not whether, Ven. 304. whether we are mended, or w. better they, Sonn. 59, 11. Tp. V, 111. Err. IV, 1, 60. John I, 75. II, 167. H6B III, 2, 265. III, 3, 10. Caes. I, 1, 66. V, 3, 97.

**Where**, 1) interrogatively; a) at or in what place; f.i. w. am I? Ven. 493. w. did I leave? 715. w. 's

the master? Tp. I, 1, 10. 13. w. was she born? I, 2, 260. b) to what place; f. i. w. is my judgment fled? Sonn. 148, 3. w. runnest thou so fast? Err. III, 2, 71. w. shall w. go? Mids. III, 1, 166.

2) relatively; a) at which place, or at the place at which; f. i. here come and sit, w. never serpent hisses, Ven. 17. w. she ends, she doth anew begin, 60. love keeps his revels w. there are but twain, 123. 154. 176. 234. 426 etc. I know w. you are, As V, 2, 32 (I perceive your drift, I know what you hint at; cf. Whereabout). Correlative to so: in a strait so narrow w. one but goes abreast, Troil. III, 3, 155. in no place so unsanctified w. such as thou mayst find him. Mcb. IV, 2, 82 (cf. So). b) to which place; f.i. I must go w. it fits not you to know, Wint. IV, 4, 304. he is in heaven w. thou shalt never come, R3 I, 2, 106.

Used after verbs of seeing, when there would be expected: behold w. Madam Mitigation comes, Meas. I, 2, 45. look w. he comes, Wiv. II, 1, 106. 196. IV, 1, 9. Meas. I, 1, 25. Mids. III, 2, 176. John V, 2, 65. H6B V, 3, 14. H6C I, 3, 2. Caes. II, 2, 108. look w. Beatrice like a lapwing runs, Ado III, 1, 24. look w. three-farthings go, John I, 143. look w. the sturdy rebel sits, H6C I, 1, 50. lo w. he comes, H4B IV, 5, 90. H6C V, 5, 11. H8 I, 1, 113. Hml. I, 1, 126. lo w. your son is borne, H6A IV, 7, 17. lo w. George of Charence sweeps along, H6C V, 1, 76. lo by thy side w. Rape and Murder stands, Tit. V, 2, 45. see w. she comes, Gent. V, 1, 7. Err. IV, 1, 14. V, 128. LLL V, 2, 337. H6B V, 1, 122. H6C III, 3, 43. IV, 2, 3. V, 1, 58. see you w. Benedick hath hid himself, Ado II, 3, 42. see w. he looks out of the window, Shr. V, 1, 57. see w. he lies, H6A IV, 7, 45. see w. stand his guard, H6C IV, 3, 23. R3 III, 7, 95 etc.

As the idea of place is very expansive, where is often used for in which, or in which case, on which occasion, and sometimes almost = when: thy beauty hath ensnared thee to this night, w. thou with patience must my will abide, Lucr. 486. to be in love, w. scorn is bought with groans, Gent. I, 1, 29. this is like the mending of highways in summer, w. the ways are fair enough, Merch. V, 264. thou art not for the fashion of these times, w. none will sweat but for promotion, As II, 3, 60. w. did I leave? At that sad stop, w. rude hands from windows' tops threw rubbish on Richard's head, R2 V, 2, 5. in the unshrinking station w. he fought, Mcb. V, 8, 42. in these cases, w. the aim reports, Oth. I, 3, 6. it (love) shall suspect w. is no cause of fear, Ven. 1153. 1154. we were awaked; straightway at liberty; w. we in all her trim freshly beheld our royal ship, Tp. V, 236. w. your good word cannot advantage him, your slander never can endamage him, Gent. III, 2, 42. w. you may temper her by your persuasion, 64. when women cannot love w. they're beloved, V, 4, 44. it will not lie w. it concerns, I, 2, 77. great clerks have purposed to greet me, ... w. I have seen them shiver and look pale, Mids. V, 95. drew to defend him, ... w. being apprehended, Tw. V, 89. have broken from his liking w. you were tied in duty, Wint. V, 1, 213. they have a king and officers of sorts, w. some like magistrates correct at home, H5 I, 2, 191. why sighest thou without breaking? w. he answers again ..., Troil. IV, 4, 19. and suddenly; w. injury of chance puts back leave-taking, 35. out of her favour, w. I am in love, Rom. I, 1, 174. I have heard, w. many ... have wished that noble Brutus had his eyes, Caes. I, 2, 59.

*as little is the wisdom, w. the flight so runs against all reason,* Mcb. IV, 2, 13. *she hath my letter for the purpose, w., if thou fear to strike, ... thou art the pander to her dishonour,* Cymb. III, 4, 30.

Hence = whereas: *fellowship in woe doth woe assuage, ... w. now I have no one to blush with me,* Lucr. 792. *and w. I thought the remnant of mine age should have been cherished by her child-like duty, I am now full resolved ... to turn her out,* Gent. III, 1, 74. *his ignorance were wise, w. now his knowledge must prove ignorance,* LLL II, 103. *and w. thou now exactest the penalty ... thou wilt loose the forfeiture,* Merch. IV, 1, 22. *fight and die is death destroying death, w. fearing dying pays death servile breath,* R2 III, 2, 185. *so we should, w. now remains a sweet reversion,* H4A IV, 1, 53. *w. I was wont to feed you with my blood, I'll lop a member off and give it you,* H6A V, 3, 14. *his wealth doth warrant a liberal dower, w. Reignier sooner will receive than give,* V, 5, 47. H6B III, 2, 394. R3 IV, 4, 141 (Ff *w. 't should be branded,* Qq *w. should be graven*). Cor. I, 1, 104. I, 10, 13. Lr. I, 2, 89. Per. I, 1, 127. II, 3, 43.

= wherever: *who conquers w. he comes in every jar,* Ven. 100. *feed w. thou wilt, on mountain or in dale,* 232. *w. I have come, great clerks have purposed to greet me,* Mids. V, 93. *a savour that may strike the dullest nostril w. I arrive,* Wint. I, 2, 422. *bear me w. you will,* H6B IV, 7, 64. *attend me w. I wheel,* Troil. V, 7, 2. *w. he arrives he moves all hearts against us,* Lr. IV, 5, 10. Cor. I, 10, 24.

= whence: *every word doth almost tell my name, showing their birth and w. they did proceed,* Sonn. 76, 8. *w. have they this mettle?* H5 III, 5, 15. *w. have you this? 'tis false,* Ant. II, 1, 18 (= from whom have you heard this?). cf. *Wheresoever* in Oth. IV, 1, 160.

*w. that* = where: LLL IV, 3, 296. H5 V Chor. 17 (cf. *That*, conj. 8).

Substantively: *thou losest here, a better w. to find,* Lr. I, 1, 264. As for Shr. IV, 3, 151, see *Place.*

**Whereabout,** on what purpose: *I must not have you henceforth question me whither I go, nor reason w.* H4A II, 3, 107. Substantively, = purpose: *hear not my steps, which way they walk, for fear thy very stones prate of my w.* Mcb. II, 1, 58.

**Whereagainst,** against which: Cor. IV, 5, 113.

**Whereas,** 1) at which place, where: *he spying her bounced in, w. he stood,* Pilgr. 83. *to ride unto Saint Alban's, w. the king and queen do mean to hawk,* H6B I, 2, 58. *make a conquest of unhappy me, w. no glory's got to overcome,* Per. I, 4, 70.

2) the thing being so that (referring to something different): *and w. I was black and swart before, with those clear rays ... that beauty am I blessed with which you see,* H6A I, 2, 84. H6B IV, 7, 37.

3) while, when on the contrary: H6A II, 5, 76. V, 5, 64. Per. I, 2, 42.

**Whereat,** at which: Ven. 589. 748. 823. 829. 878. 979. 1026. 1045. Lucr. 178. 264. Mids. V, 147. H6C I, 1, 4. Cor. V, 6, 134. Tit. II, 3, 219. Tim. III, 6, 113. Hml. II, 2, 65. Cymb. V, 5, 181.

**Whereby,** 1) by what: *w. hangs a tale, sir?* Oth. III, 1, 9.

2) by which: Merch. IV, 1, 377. Shr. II, 275. H4A V, 1, 67. H4B II, 1, 104. III, 2, 86. H6C I, 1, 250. H8 I, 1, 186. Cor. I, 1, 144. Tim. I, 2, 88. Mcb. III, 1, 99. Per. II, 3, 45.

**Where'er,** at whatever place: Ven. 622. Tp. II, 2, 55. John IV, 3, 26. R2 I, 3, 308. V, 3, 141. H6C II, 3, 43.

**Wherefore,** 1) interr. a) for what reason: Sonn. 67, 1. 138, 9. Tp. I, 2, 138. II, 1, 309. III, 1, 76. Gent. I, 1, 51. IV, 4, 83. V, 2, 27. Err. II, 2, 44. 45 (*every why hath a w.;* proverbial). 46. 49. III, 1, 39. 40. IV, 4, 98. As II, 3, 6. John V, 1, 44. H6A II, 1, 54. H6B I, 1, 115 etc.

b) for what, to be what: *w. was I born?* *if that my cousin king be king of England, it must be granted I am duke of Lancaster,* R2 II, 3, 122 (for what rank or dignity).

2) relat.; a) for which cause: H6A I, 4, 53. b) for which: *peace to this meeting, w. we are met,* H5 V, 2, 1.

**Wherein,** 1) in what: Meas. V, 507. As II, 7, 83. III, 2, 234 (*w. went he?* = how was he drest?). All's V, 2, 31. R2 II, 3, 107. H4A II, 4, 501. H4B IV, 1, 89. H6B III, 1, 103. IV, 7, 103. R3 I, 4, 182. IV, 4, 93. H8 I, 2, 38 etc.

2) in which: Ven. 731. 1131. 1188. Lucr. 317. 619. 697. 1246. 1526. 1815. Sonn. 24, 3. 86, 4. 88, 7. 91, 6. 117, 2. Tp. I, 2, 464. Gent. II, 2, 10. II, 7, 3. III, 1, 60. Wiv. II, 2, 190. Meas. II, 4, 10. III, 2, 270. Merch. I, 1, 129. II, 9, 5. IV, 1, 192. V, 243. As I, 2, 196. 199. II, 7, 139. III, 2, 412. Shr. Ind. 1, 92. I, 1, 113. All's I, 2, 7. II, 1, 114. II, 5, 80. IV, 3, 39. Tw. II, 2, 29. II, 3, 169. V, 105. Wint. I, 2, 237. IV, 4, 678. John V, 2, 27. R2 I, 3, 266. II, 2, 132. H4A I, 2, 191. I, 3, 169. 180. IV, 4, 9. H4B II, 3, 22. IV, 4, 69. H5 II, 2, 170. H6A I, 1, 107. II, 2, 13. H6C I, 1, 125. II, 6, 102. R3 III, 1, 180. III, 5, 27. V, 1, 16. Cor. II, 3, 48. Rom. I, 4, 42. Caes. IV, 3, 4; cf. Hml. IV, 5, 92. I, 1, 159. II, 2, 150 (Ff *whereon*) etc.

3) in that in which (implying opposition to the following principal sentence; almost = though): *w. it doth impair the seeing sense, it pays the hearing double recompense,* Mids. III, 2, 179. *w. our entertainment shall shame us we will be justified in our loves,* Wint. I, 1, 9.

**Whereinto,** into which: Oth. III, 3, 137.

**Whereof,** 1) of what: *w. are you made?* Sonn. 53, 1. Merch. I, 1, 4. Lr. I, 4, 312.

2) of which (often preceded by the subst. on which it depends): Ven. 880. Lucr. Ded. 1. Lucr. 681. 1261. Sonn. 63, 6. Tp. II, 1, 253. V, 38. Gent. I, 1, 153. III, 1, 36. IV, 2, 13. Wiv. IV, 6, 14. Meas. V, 470. Ado V, 4, 25. Merch. I, 2, 34. IV, 1, 159. 239. 410. Shr. I, 2, 275. II, 58. All's I, 3, 195. 235. Tw. V, 372. Wint. I, 2, 260. III, 2, 18. 191. John V, 4, 44. R2 I, 1, 150. I, 2, 11. I, 4, 46. II, 1, 162. IV, 70. H4A I, 2, 81. III, 2, 72. H5 I, 2, 132. II, 2, 179. III, 2, 34. H6A I, 1, 117. II, 1, 64. II, 4, 58. III, 4, 5. IV, 1, 87. H6B III, 1, 63. 106. 135. H6C II, 6, 54. III, 3, 125. R3 III, 1, 196. III, 2, 24. Troil. I, 3, 14. 139. III, 2, 61. IV, 5, 84. Tim. II, 2, 179. IV, 3, 91. 180. 194 (= by which; cf. *Of*). Lr. IV, 6, 273. Cymb. III, 1, 29 etc.

**Whereon,** 1) on what: *w. do you look?* Hml. III, 4, 124.

2) on which: Ven. 125. 151. 544. 646. 927. Sonn. 15, 4. 73, 11. 148, 5. Compl. 10. Tp. I, 2, 127. Gent. I, 3, 18. Meas. I, 2, 164. II, 4, 7. Mids. IV, 1, 91. As I, 3, 59. Wint. I, 1, 2. John IV,

2, 156. R2 I, 3, 289. H4B I, 1, 62 (Ff *when*). IV, 2, 38. V, 2, 81. H6A II, 3, 47. Cor. IV, 6, 86. Rom. V, 3, 179. Tim. IV, 3, 184. Mcb. IV, 1, 138. Hml. II, 2, 72. 150 (Qq *wherein*). III, 1, 182. IV, 4, 63. IV, 7, 161. Lr. I, 4, 312. Oth. III, 3, 84. V, 2, 326. Ant. III, 6, 59. Cymb. III, 3, 100 etc.

**Whereout,** out of which: *and make distinct the very breach w. Hector's great spirit flew,* Troil. IV, 5, 245.

**Wheresoe'er,** in what place soever: Lucr. 1014. Mids. II, 2, 90. As I, 3, 77, III, 1, 5. All's III, 5, 69. John III, 3, 62. H6B III, 2, 406. H6C II, 6, 41. V, 1, 95. Lr. III, 4, 28.

**Wheresoever,** the same: Meas. III, 2, 96. *w. you had it,* Oth. IV, 1, 160 (= whencesoever).

**Wheresomever,** the same: H5 II, 3, 7 (Bardolph's speech).

**Wherethrough,** through which: Sonn. 24, 11.

**Whereto,** 1) to what: *w. tends all this?* Mids. III, 2, 256. *w. serves mercy,* Hml. III, 3, 46.

2) to which: Sonn. 117, 4. 124, 8. 137, 8. Compl. 212. Meas. V, 542. Tw. I, 2, 20. Wint. IV, 4, 548. R2 I, 3, 234. I, 4, 49. V, 5, 53. Cor. V, 3, 108. Rom. I, 2, 21. Caes. II, 1, 23. III, 1, 250. Mcb. I, 7, 62. Hml. III, 3, 95. IV, 2, 6. V, 1, 234. Lr. II, 4, 108. V, 3, 140. Oth. III, 3, 231. Cymb. III, 5, 47 etc.

**Whereuntil,** to what: *we know w. it doth amount,* LLL V, 2, 493. 501 (Costard's speeches).

**Whereunto,** to which: Cymb. III, 4, 109. III, 7, 13.

**Whereupon,** on which: Lucr. Arg. 12. Sonn. 20, 6. Phoen. 49. Wint. IV, 4, 763. V, 2, 5. John IV, 2, 65. R2 II, 2, 58. H4A IV, 3, 42. H4B II, 2, 29. II, 4, 99. IV, 1, 12. H8 II, 4, 201. Troil. III, 2, 215. V, 4, 17. Lr. I, 1, 14. Cymb. V, 5, 208.

**Wherever** (cf. *Where'er*) in or to what place soever: Sonn. 45, 2. As II, 2, 15. III, 5, 87. H8 V, 5, 51. Tim. IV, 2, 24. Mcb. I, 5, 50.

**Wherewith,** 1) with what: LLL I, 1, 264.

2) with which: Lucr. Arg. 2. Sonn. 60, 6. Pilgr. 408. Gent. I, 3, 2. John V, 7, 53. R2 IV, 164. H6A I, 1, 102. 104. H6B IV, 7, 79. H6C III, 1, 17. Mcb. I, 6, 17.

**Wherewithal,** with which, by means of which: *thou ladder w. the mounting Bolingbroke ascends my throne,* R2 V, 1, 55. = with what: *he may, my lord; has w.* H8 I, 3, 59 (i. e. to be noble. French: *il a de quoi.* cf. *whilst thou hast wherewith to spend,* Pilgr. 408).

**Whet,** to rub for the purpose of sharpening: Ven. 617. 1113. Merch. IV, 1, 121. H4B IV, 5, 108. R3 I, 3, 244. IV, 4, 227. Metaphorically, = to excite, to stimulate, to instigate: *I come to w. your gentle thoughts on his behalf,* Tw. III, 1, 116. *w. me to be revenged,* R3 I, 3, 332. *the king does w. his anger to him,* H8 III, 2, 92. *Cassius first did w. me against Caesar,* Caes. II, 1, 61. *to w. thy almost blunted purpose,* Hml. III, 4, 111. With *on: I will w. on the king,* John III, 181. H6B II, 1, 34. H6C I, 2, 37.

**Whether,** (often monosyll., f. i. Mids. III, 1, 156. III, 2, 81. Merch. V, 302. H6A IV, 7, 25. Cor. III, 1, 251. Tit. I, 395. Caes. II, 1, 194. Hml. II, 2, 17. Oth. I, 1, 39. Contracted to *whe'er,* q. v.) which of the two (in a principal sentence): *w. he run or fly they know not w.* Ven. 304. *was this a lover or a lecher w.?* Pilgr. 101. *in scorn or friendship, nill I construe w.* 188. *w. had you rather lead mine eyes, or eye your master's heels?* Wiv. III, 2, 3. *w. dost thou profess thyself, a*

knave or a fool? All's IV, 5, 23. *w. hadst thou rather be a Faulconbridge ... or the reputed son of Cordelion,* John I, 134.

Preceding a subordinate clause expressing one part of a disjunctive question, and followed by *or: w. he run or fly they know not w.* Ven. 304. *controversy hence a question takes, w. the horse by him became his deed, or he his manage ...,* Compl. 111. Meas. I, 2, 167. Merch. V, 302. H6A V, 5, 79. H6B I, 3, 110. R3 III, 7, 141. Troil. IV, 5, 243. Cor. IV, 5, 147 etc. the second part formed by *or no:* Tp. V, 111. Wiv IV, 5, 33. LLL V, 2, 486. Merch. II, 2, 48. III, 1, 45. III, 2, 146. As III, 2, 129. H6C II, 1, 2. R3 III, 1, 23. Tit. I, 395. Caes. II, 1, 194 etc.

The correlative clauses preceded by *w... or w.: w. we are mended, or w. better they, or w. revolution be the same,* Sonn. 59, 11. *w. it be the fault and glimpse of newness, or w. that the public body be a horse ...,* Meas. I, 2, 162. 163. *w. 'twas the coldness of the king, ... or w. 'twas report of her success,* H6C II, 1, 122. 125. cf. *move these eyes? or w. seem they in motion?* Merch. III, 2, 117. *judge if I have done amiss, or w. that such cowards ought to wear this ornament,* H6A IV, 1, 28. *if his last purpose hold, or w. since he is advised ...,* Lr. V, 1, 2. *Or w. even before the first clause: or w. doth my mind ... drink up the monarchs' plague, this flattery, or w. shall I say ...,* Sonn. 114, 1. *or w. his fall enraged him, or how 'twas,* Cor. I, 3, 69.

The interrogatory form used, not to ask a question, but to express that each of two or more alternatives is irrelevant to the main purpose: *his eyes begun to wink, ... w. it is that she reflects so bright, ... or else some shame supposed,* Lucr. 376. *for w. beauty, birth, or wealth, or wit ... entitled in their parts do crowned sit, I make my love engrafted to this store,* Sonn. 37, 5. *w. unripe years did want conceit, or he refused to take her figured proffer, the tender nimbler would not touch the bait,* Pilgr. 51. *I'll be your servant, w. you will or no,* Tp. III, 1, 86. Gent. I, 1, 79. Meas. I, 2, 43. Mids. III, 1, 156. III, 2, 81. All's II, 1, 11. H6A IV, 7, 25. H6B III, 2, 265. R3 III, 7, 214 etc. see above: H6C II, 1, 122. Cor. I, 3, 69.

By the omission of the correlative clause, *w.* passing into the sense of a simple interrogative particle, = if: *examine well your blood, w... you can endure the livery of a nun,* Mids. I, 1, 69. *who knows but you ... w. I am yours,* Merch. II, 6, 31. Meas. II, 1, 14. Merch. IV, 1, 146. 277. All's IV, 3, 199. Wint. V, 2, 144. John III, 1, 26. R2 I, 4, 22. V, 6, 4. H4A III, 2, 4. H4B II, 4, 281. Cor. III, 1, 251. Caes. V, 1, 115. Hml. II, 2, 17. Oth. I, 1, 39 etc.

*w. that* = *w.* alone (cf. *That*): Sonn. 144, 9. Meas. I, 2, 163. As IV, 3, 59. H6A IV, 1, 28.

**Whetstone,** a stone on which a thing is sharpened; figuratively, that which excites and stimulates: As I, 2, 57. 58. Troil. V, 2, 75. Mcb. IV, 3, 228.

**Whew,** exclamation imitative of the sound of whistling: H4A II, 2, 30.

**Whey,** the watery part of milk, separated from the curd: Tit. IV, 2, 178.

**Whey-face,** one palefaced; in contempt: Mcb. V, 3, 17.

**Which,** rel. pron. referring to a single word or to a sentence. The single word neuter: Ven. 83. 102. 275. 360. 452. 491. 605. 632. 675. 676. 759. 797. 812.

817. 890. 904. 982. 1000. 1031. 1170. 1176. Lucr. 127 etc. etc. The single word masc. or fem. (i. e. denoting a person): *pale cowards ...w. heartless peasants did so well resemble,* Lucr. 1392. *Priam ... w. bleeding under Pyrrhus' proud foot lies,* 1449. *all those friends w. I thought buried,* Sonn. 31, 4. 35, 14. 104, 8. 106, 13. 121, 8. Compl. 140. 234. 319. Tp. I, 2, 32. 352. 413. III, 1, 6. IV, 154. 196. V, 21. 160. Wiv. I, 1, 45. Meas. I, 4, 6, II, 2, 76. 102. V, 305. Err. V, 361. Ado V, 1, 331. LLL V, 2, 124. 519. Mids. I, 2, 5. IV, 1, 65. V, 73. 298. Merch. IV, 1, 91. V, 115. 211. Wint. I, 2, 244. 455. II, 3, 116. III, 2, 39. IV, 1, 22. IV, 4, 167. V, 2, 60. John III, 1, 33. IV, 1, 4. R2 I, 4, 38. II, 1, 108. III, 2, 204. V, 1, 34. H4B I, 1, 100. H6A I, 2, 52. II, 5, 93. 110. H6B II, 3, 107. III, 1, 372. IV, 2, 188. IV, 7, 23. H6C I, 1, 90. II, 1, 102. III, 3, 82. IV, 1, 12. R3 I, 2, 62. 88. I, 3, 199 (Ff *that*). I, 4, 46. IV, 1, 70. IV, 4, 134 and 345 (Ff *that*). 385. Hml. IV, 7, 4 etc. etc. *that w. =* he who: Meas. I, 4, 6. LLL V, 2, 519 etc. (cf. *That*).

Referring to sentences: *pure shame and awed resistance made him fret, w. bred more beauty in his angry eyes,* Ven. 70. *he did think to reprehend her, w. cunning love did wittily prevent,* 471. *as when the wind .. earth's foundation shakes, w. with cold terror doth men's minds confound,* 1048. Tp. I, 2, 156. 244. 263. II, 1, 220. III, 3, 47. V, 52. 249. Gent. I, 3, 15. III, 1, 272. III, 2, 54. Err. I, 1, 52. II, 2, 19. LLL I, 2, 175. Mids. V, 64. As III, 2, 188. All's II, 3, 156. Wint. I, 2, 392. H5 II, 2, 159. H6B IV, 7, 69. Ant. II, 2, 78 etc. The relative clause preceding the principal sentence (where *what* would be expected): *there has been earls, nay, w. is more, pensioners,* Wiv. II, 2, 78. *I saw him arrested, saw him carried away, and, w. is more, within these three days his head to be chopped off,* Meas. I, 2, 68. *and, w. was strange, the one so like the other,* Err. I, 1, 52. *I am a wise fellow, and, w. is more, an officer,* Ado IV, 2, 83. 84. V, 1, 313. *and, w. is more than all these boasts can be, I am beloved of Hermia,* Mids. I, 1, 103. *and, w. became him like a prince indeed, he made a blushing cital of himself,* H4A V, 2, 61. *and, w. is worse, she is not so divine,* H6A V, 5, 16. *and, w. is worse, all you have done ...,* Mcb. III, 5, 10.

Joined to a substantive: *w. purchase if thou make,* Ven. 515. *within w. rift,* Tp. I, 2, 277. 279. II, 1, 256. V, 4. Err. V, 328. As I, 2, 134 (*w. Charles*). Wint. I, 2, 318. John I, 1, 119. III, 1, 40. R2 I, 1, 104. H6A IV, 1, 98 etc. Peculiar construction: *if by w. time our secret be undone,* Per. I, 1, 117. *if in w. time expired he not return,* II, 4, 47. Followed by a personal pronoun: *that we thankful should be, w. we of taste and feeling are,* LLL IV, 2, 30 (German: *die wir Leute von Geschmack und Zartgefühl sind*).

In all these cases sometimes preceded by the def. article; referring to a neuter: *her heart the w. he carries hence,* Ven. 581. *the many musets through the w. he goes,* 683. Lucr. 1368. Sonn. 52, 3. Wiv. II, 2, 84. Ado V, 1, 156. LLL II, 135. Merch. III, 4, 34. V, 212. As I, 1, 15. II, 7, 41. III, 2, 409. All's II, 3, 124. V, 1, 16. Tw. V, 316. John I, 68. IV, 2, 50. V, 4, 51. R2 I, 1, 90. H4B Ind. 7. I, 1, 164. H5 IV, 3, 96. H6A I, 2, 100. II, 2, 14. H6B IV, 1, 99. R3 I, 2, 95. H8 II, 3, 7. Troil. I, 3, 60. Cor. II, 3, 12. Rom. I, 5, 74. Lr. IV, 4, 13. Oth. I, 3, 324 etc. To persons: *the party 'gainst the w. he doth contrive,* Merch. IV, 1, 352.

*half of the w. dare not shake the snow from off their cassocks,* All's IV, 3, 191. *there are other Trojans ..., the w. for sport sake are content to do the profession some grace,* H4A II, 1, 78. *of the w. five hundred were but yesterday dubbed knights,* H5 IV, 8, 90. To sentences: *then I'll bring thee to the present business ... without the w. this story were most impertinent,* Tp. I, 2, 137. *I think myself in better plight for a lender than you are, the w. has emboldened me to this intrusion,* Wiv. II, 2, 173. 284. II, 3, 98. Meas. IV, 2, 170. Err. V, 229. Ado I, 1, 247. III, 2, 58. V, 1, 175. 319. V, 3, 14. LLL I, 1, 41. V, 2, 859. Mids. V, 135. Merch. I, 3, 4. All's I, 1, 222. Wint. II, 1, 128. IV, 4, 572. R2 I, 1, 172. III, 3, 45. H4B II, 4, 274. H5 II, 2, 91. R3 I, 1, 157. Caes. III, 1, 295 etc. Joined to a substantive: *for the w. blessing I am at him upon my knees,* Ado II, 1, 30. *to the w. place,* As II, 1, 33. *in the w. hope,* II, 7, 119. *in the w. better part I have saved my life,* H4A V, 4, 122. *for the w. supply,* H5 Prol. 31. *the w. immediacy may well stand up,* Lr. V, 3, 65.

As for its correlativeness to *such* (f. i. Sonn. 26, 5. Meas. IV, 2, 112. Tw. V, 358. Wint. I, 1, 26. IV, 4, 784. Cor. III, 2, 105), see *Such*.

The way in which *w.* differed from *that*, though not always discernible, may be distinctly seen in some instances: *I am all the subjects that you have, w. first was mine own king,* Tp. I, 2, 342. *this island's mine by Sycorax my mother, w. thou takest from me,* 332. *it is you that have chalked forth the way w. brought us hither,* V, 204. *I have your own letter that induced me to the semblance I put on, with the w. I doubt not but to do myself much right,* Tw. V, 316. cf. Abbott's Grammar.

Seemingly = what, i. e. that which: *more than mistress of w. comes to me in name of fault, I must not at all acknowledge,* Wint. III, 2, 61 (a passage in which there is more than one difficulty). *he says there are two councils held, and that may be determined at the one w. may make him and you to rue at the other,* R3 III, 2, 14 (perhaps *that* not conjunction, but demonstr. pronoun).

**Which,** interrog. pronoun, by which one among a definite number (mostly one of two), is inquired for; referring to things: *to live or die, w. of the twain were better,* Lucr. 1154. *w. end o'the beam should bow,* Tp. II, 1, 131. *w. had you rather, that the most just law now took your brother's life, or ... give up your body,* Meas. II, 4, 52. *I have many ill qualities? W. is one?* Ado II, 1, 107. *I cannot tell for w. of his virtues it was,* Wint. III, 3, 94 etc. To persons: *w. is worthiest love?* Gent. I, 2, 6. *from w. lord to w. lady?* LLL IV, 1, 105. Gent. V, 2, 32. Wiv. I, 3, 39. IV, 6, 46. Meas. II, 1, 180. V, 483. Err. V, 54. 333 369. LLL I, 1, 182. IV, 1, 42. 46. IV, 2, 86. Merch. II, 1, 33. IV, 1, 174. H4B III, 1, 65. III, 2, 62. H6A II, 2, 34. H6B I, 3, 104. R3 I, 3, 160. Troil. I, 3, 231. Lr. I, 1, 5. IV, 6, 157 etc. *w. of he or Adrian,* Tp. II, 1, 28 (Gallicism). *a moth will turn the balance, w. Pyramus, w. Thisbe, is the better,* Mids. V, 324 (cf. *whether ... or whether*). *I know not w. is w.* (= which is the one, and which the other) Err. V, 364. Mids. II, 1, 114. Tim. II, 2, 82. *what is the night? Almost at odds with morning, w. is w.* Mcb. III, 4, 127. *my virtue or my plague, be it either w.* Hml. IV, 7, 13 (= whichsoever).

Sometimes the number, out of which one is asked forth, not exactly limited; but the question always intended to have one definitively singled out: *who is it that says most? w. can say more than this rich praise that you alone are you?* Sonn. 84, 1 (tell me who is the one that can etc.). *w. of you will stop the vent of hearing when loud Rumour speaks?* H4B Ind. 1. *w. of your friends have I not strove to love?* H8 II, 4, 29. Hence *w. way* seemingly = what way: *w. way shall she turn?* Ven. 253. *wildly determining w. way to fly,* Lucr. 1150. *how and w. way I may bestow myself,* Gent. III, 1, 87. *go all w. way it will,* R2 II, 2, 87. Cor. II, 3, 27. Caes. II, 4, 21. Lr. II, 4, 25. Cymb. V, 4, 181. *if I discovered not w. way she was gone,* V, 5, 277.

**Whiff,** a puff of wind: *with the w. and wind of his fell sword the unnerved father falls,* Hml. II, 2, 495.

**Whiffler,** one who goes before in a procession, like a fifer: *the deep-mouthed sea, which like a mighty w. 'fore the king seems to prepare his way,* H5 V Chor. 12.

**While,** subst. (cf. *Awhile*) a short space of time, during which something is to happen or be done: *bud and be blasted in a breathing w.* Ven. 1142. *that she her plaints a little w. doth stay,* Lucr. 1364. *now the dog all this w. sheds no tear,* Gent. II, 3, 34. *a pissing w.* IV, 4, 21. *I for a w. will leave you,* Meas. V, 257. *have you wept all this w.? Yes, and I will weep a w. longer,* Ado IV, 1, 257. 258. LLL V, 1, 157. Mids. III, 2, 83. As II, 7, 127. IV, 3, 149. Shr. II, 20. V, 1, 8. Wint. I, 2, 108. H4A I, 3, 211. H6A I, 4, 54 (*walked about me every minute w.*). III, 3, 5. H6B V, 1, 30. 33. H6C IV, 3, 57. V, 4, 29. H8 Epil. 12. Caes. III, 2, 193 etc. etc. *the w.* = in the meantime: *but Tarquin's shape came in her mind the w.* Lucr. 1536. *but if the w. I think on thee, all losses are restored,* Sonn. 30, 13. *I'll bear your logs the w.* Tp. III, 1, 24. *put on the gown the w.* Wiv. IV, 2, 85. *my master preaches patience to him, and the w. his man with scissors nicks him like a fool,* Err. V, 174. Ado II, 3, 214. LLL I, 1, 75. As II, 5, 33. Tw. II, 4, 14. II, 5, 65. III, 4, 219. Wint. IV, 4, 48. R2 II, 1, 211. Cor. III, 1, 147. Mcb. II, 1, 29. III, 2, 32. Oth. II, 3, 391. Ant. II, 7, 116. Cymb. III, 4, 131 etc. *the —s,* in the same sense: *play you the —s,* Shr. III, 1, 22.

Sometimes equivalent to time: *where have you been all this w.?* As IV, 1, 39. *a great w. ago the world begun,* Tw. V, 414. *to see if I can eat grass or pick a sallet another w.* H6B IV, 10, 9 (= another time, by way of variety. Cade's speech). *I have this w. with leaden thoughts been pressed,* Oth. III, 4, 177. *all this w.* = hitherto: *who all this w. hath revelled in the night,* R2 III, 2, 48. *you have but mistook me all this w.* 174. *I do mistake my person all this w.* R3 I, 2, 253. *show duty, as mistaken all this w. between the child and parent,* Cor. V, 3, 55.

Thus used in exclamations of grief: *alas the w.* Merch. II, 1, 31. *woe the w.* Wint. III, 2, 173. H5 IV, 7, 78. Caes. I, 3, 82. *bad world the w.* John IV, 2, 100. *God help the w.! a bad world, I say,* H4A II, 4, 146. *God help the w.!* R3 II, 3, 8. *here's a good world the w.* III, 6, 10.

**While,** conj. 1) during the time that: Ven. 564. Tp. II, 1, 197. 300. III, 1, 28. III, 3, 91. Wiv. IV, 6, 22. Err. V, 205 (later Ff *whilst*). H6C IV, 6, 42 etc.
2) as long as: Ven. 786. Tp. II, 2, 65. III, 2, 120. IV, 242. Gent. III, 1, 23. H6B IV, 10, 45. H6C I, 1, 173. III, 3, 106. Cor. I, 1, 18 etc.
3) at the same time that (implying a contrast);

f. i. *he wondered that your lordship would suffer him to spend his youth at home, w. other men of slender reputation put forth their sons to seek preferment out* Gent. I, 3, 6. *painfully to pore upon a book to seek the light of truth, w. truth the while doth falsely blind the eyesight of his look,* LLL I, 1, 74. *w. as,* in the same sense: *still revelling like lords ... w. as the silly owner ... weeps,* H6B I, 1, 225. In R2 III, 1, 22 Q1 *w.,* the rest of O. Edd. *whilst.*
4) till: *let the trumpets sound w. we return these dukes what we decree,* R2 I, 3, 122. *we will keep ourself till supper-time alone: w. then, God be with you,* Mcb. III, 1, 44. (cf. *whiles* in Tw. IV, 3, 29. Euphues' Golden Legacy, ed. Collier, p. 47: *and stood there w. the next morning.* p. 89: *to pass away the night w. bedtime.* p. 110: *nothing can make me forget Phoebe, w. Montanus forget himself.* Greene's Pandosto p. 57: *I therefore award that thou shalt have thine eyes put out, and continually w. thou diest, grind in a mill like a brute beast*).

As for *w. that,* see *That.*

**While-ere,** (O. Edd. *whileare*) erewhile, not long ago: *the catch you taught me but w.* Tp. III, 2, 127 (Caliban's speech).

**Whiles,** 1) during the time that: Tp. II, 1, 217. 284. 310. Meas. IV, 3, 84. Ado V, 1, 253. Mids. III, 2, 374. As II, 7, 128. V, 4, 5. 143. Tw. III, 3, 41. Wint. V, 1, 189. H6A IV, 4, 17. H6B III, 1, 124. 320. 348. H6C II, 3, 26. R3 I, 2, 32. Tit. II, 3, 27. Oth. II, 3, 359 (Q1 *while,* Q2. 3 *whilst*) etc.

Coincidence of time implying causality, sometimes almost = when; since; if: *w. against a thorn thou bearest thy part, ... I against my heart will fix a sharp knife,* Lucr. 1135. *w. the eye of man did woo me, that could do no vengeance to me,* As IV, 3, 47. *there's comfort in't, w. other men have gates and those gates opened, as mine, against their will,* Wint. I, 2, 197. *and peace ascend to heaven, w. we, God's wrathful agent, do correct their proud contempt that beats his peace to heaven,* John II, 87. *who but Rumour, who but only I, make fearful musters and prepared defence, w. the big year, swoln with some other grief, is thought with child by the stern tyrant war, and no such matter?* H4B Ind. 13 (Ff *whilst*). *and hold their manhoods cheap w. any speaks that fought with us upon Saint Crispin's day,* H5 IV, 3, 66. *w. they each other cross, lives, honours, lands and all hurry to loss,* H6A IV, 3, 52. *w. lions war and battle for their dens, poor harmless lambs abide their enmity,* H6C II, 5, 74. *the tiger will be mild w. she doth mourn,* III, 1, 39. *such men as he are never at heart's ease w. they behold a greater than themselves,* Caes. I, 2, 209. cf. R3 III, 7, 123 (Qq *whilst*).
2) as long as: Ado IV, 1, 221. 224. V, 4, 66. Shr. III, 2, 213. John II, 593. III, 4, 132. H4B IV, 2, 49. H6A I, 4, 91. H6B III, 2, 347. H6C II, 6, 2. III, 2, 169. V, 1, 55 etc.
3) at the same time that: Tp. I, 2, 343. II, 1, 225. Merch. I, 2, 147. As IV, 3, 54. H6A II, 4, 71. H6C V, 4, 10 etc.
4) till: *he shall conceal it w. you are willing it shall come to note,* Tw. IV, 3, 29 (cf. *While* 4).

**Whilst,** 1) during the time that: Sonn. 143, 5. 154, 3. Err. I, 1, 83. 131. Mids. V, 383. Merch. IV, 1, 136. John IV, 2, 191. H6A I, 2, 76. H6B IV, 1, 9. IV, 8, 43. H6C I, 4, 108. R3 I, 2, 3. H8 II, 4, 1.

Caes. V, 1, 43. Ant. IV, 8, 9 etc. Causality implied: *nor dare I chide the world-without-end hour w. I, my sovereign, watch the clock for you,* Sonn. 57, 6. *so then I am not lame, poor, nor despised, w. that this shadow doth such substance give,* 37, 10. *pity me then and wish I were renewed, w. like a willing patient I will drink potions of eisel,* 111, 9. *you resign the supreme seat ... to the corruption of a blemished stock, w. in the mildness of your sleepy thoughts ... this noble isle doth want her proper limbs,* R3 III, 7, 123 (Ff *whiles*).

2) as long as: Sonn. 79, 1. Pilgr. 408. Wiv. I, 1, 186. Meas. I, 2, 40. Merch. V, 64. All's II, 5, 96. Wint. V, 1, 6. 169. H6A I, 4, 80. H6B II, 4, 28. IV, 8, 12. H6C I, 1, 197. Lr. I, 1, 168. Ant. V, 1, 7 etc.

3) at the same time that (denoting a contrast): Sonn. 25, 3. 61, 13. 80, 10. 119, 6. 128, 7. Meas. II, 4, 3. Err. II, 1, 88. II, 2, 207. IV, 4, 66. Mids. V, 380. Shr. V, 2, 151. R2 II, 2, 81. III, 1, 22 (Ff Q2. 3. 4 *while*). H6A I, 1, 72. 143. H6C V, 5, 20. Troil. II, 2, 212 etc. *w. as,* in the same sense: *w. as fickle Fortune smiled, thou and I were both beguiled,* Pilgr. 401.

4) *the w.* = a) while: *I saw a smith stand with his hammer thus, the w. his iron did on the anvil cool,* John IV, 2, 194. *ravens foster forlorn children, the w. their own birds famish,* Tit. II, 3, 154. *if he steal aught the w. this play is playing,* Hml. III, 2, 93. b) in the meantime: *I'll call Sir Toby the w.* Tw. IV, 2, 4. R2 V, 2, 22. Cymb. IV, 2, 254.

As for *w. that,* see *That.*

**Whine,** to make a plaintive noise, to moan in a lamentable and childish manner: LLL III, 181. As II, 7, 145. Rom. III, 5, 186. Mcb. IV, 1, 2 (*the hedge-pig —d*). Hml. V, 1, 300. Lr. II, 2, 25. Ant. III, 13, 101. With an accus. denoting an effect: *he —d and roared away your victory,* Cor. V, 6, 98.

**Whip,** subst. an instrument of correction consisting of a lash tied to a rod: Meas. II, 4, 101. As III, 2, 421. H6B II, 1, 137. Cor. IV, 6, 134. Rom. I, 4, 63. Lr. I, 4, 123. Oth. IV, 2, 142. Metaphorically: *I that have been love's w.* LLL III, 176. *his presence must be the w. of the other,* All's IV, 3, 42. *which to hinder were in your love a w. to me,* Wint. I, 2, 25. *wert thou the Hector that was the w. of your bragged progeny,* Cor. I, 8, 12 (i. e. whom your progeny used as a whip to chastise their enemies).*the laws, your curb and w.* Tim. IV, 3, 446. *the —s of heaven,* V, 1, 64. *the —s and scorns of time,* Hml. III, 1, 70.

**Whip,** vb. to strike with a lash, to punish with a whip: Gent. IV, 4, 27. 28. Meas. II, 1, 142. 264. 269. V, 512. 513. 529. Ado II, 1, 227. 228. LLL I, 2, 125. V, 2, 686. Mids. III, 2, 410. As I, 2, 91. Shr. I, 1, 136. All's II, 2, 52. II, 3, 93. IV, 3, 261. H4A I, 3, 239. H6B II, 1, 148. 158. IV, 2, 62. H6C III, 2, 28. Cor. IV, 6, 47. 53. 60. Rom. I, 2, 57. Hml. III, 2, 15. Lr. I, 4, 180. 198. 200. 201. 202. III, 4, 139. IV, 6, 167. Oth. I, 1, 49. Ant. II, 5, 65. III, 13, 88. 93. 96. 99. 102. 131. 137. 150. IV, 1, 3. Per. II, 1, 94. IV, 2, 91 (*marry, w. thee, gosling;* cf. *marry trap*).

The gerund substantively: *do you cry 'O Lord, sir' at your —ing,* All's II, 2, 55 (i. e. at your being whipped). Meas. IV, 2, 14. V, 529. H6B II, 1, 144. Hml. II, 2, 556. Per. II, 1, 93.

With an accus. denoting an effect (= to drive by lashes): *w. him out,* Gent. IV, 4, 23. 31. *—ed the offending Adam out of him,* H5 I, 1, 29. Meas. II, 1, 270. Ado V, 1, 84. All's IV, 3, 212. Wint. IV, 3, 95.

97. John V, 2, 135. R3 V, 3, 327. Rom. III, 2, 3. Lr. I, 4, 125. Oth. V, 2, 277.

Applied to a top, = to drive and make to turn with lashes: Wiv. V, 1, 27. LLL IV, 3, 167. V, 1, 69. 72.

Metaphorically, = to lash with sarcasm, to have a lash at, to put to the blush: *they would w. me with their fine wits,* Wiv. IV, 5, 101. *now step I forth to w. hypocrisy,* LLL IV, 3, 151. *our virtues would be proud, if our faults —ed them not,* All's IV, 3, 85. *wilt thou w. thine own faults in other men?* Tim. V, 1, 40.

**Whip,** vb. to move suddenly and quickly; intr. and trans.: *I —t me behind the arras,* Ado I, 3, 63 (Ff *I —t behind the arras*). *w. to our tents, as roes run o'er land,* LLL V, 2, 309. *—s out his rapier,* Hml. IV, 1, 10.

**Whipper,** one who whips another: As III, 2, 424.

**Whipping,** see *Whip* vb.

**Whipping-cheer,** strokes with the whip served up for dinner: *she shall have w. enough,* H4B V, 4, 5.

**Whipster,** one acting suddenly and quickly (?) or a little boy who sets up and whips his top (?): *I am not valiant neither, but every puny w. gets my sword,* Oth. V, 2, 244.

**Whipstock,** the handle of a whip: Tw. II, 3, 28. Per. II, 2, 51.

**Whir,** to hurry away with a whizzing noise: *this world to me is like a lasting storm, —ing me from my friends,* Per. IV, 1, 21 (Ff *hurrying*).

**Whirl,** vb. 1) tr. to turn round rapidly: *my thoughts are —ed like a potter's wheel,* H6A I, 5, 19. *I am giddy; expectation —s me round,* Troil. III, 2, 19.

2) intr. a) to be turned in quick rotation: *justice always —s in equal measure,* LLL IV, 3, 384 (a metaphor taken from Fortune's wheel. cf. R3 IV, 4, 105). *four (moons) fixed, and the fifth did w. about the other four,* John IV, 2, 183. *thus hath the course of justice —ed about,* R3 IV, 4, 105 (Qq *wheeled*). *to calm this tempest —ing in the court,* Tit. IV, 2, 160 (i. e. whirlwind). *these are but wild and —ing words,* Hml. I, 5, 133 (= giddy. Ff *hurling*).

b) to move rapidly: *in their rage, I having hold of both, they w. asunder and dismember me,* John III, 1, 330. *I'll come and be thy waggoner, and w. along with thee about the globe,* Tit. V, 2, 49.

**Whirligig,** a top; in the language of the clown, = rotation: *thus the w. of time brings in his revenges,* Tw. V, 385.

**Whirlpool,** (Qq *whirli-pool;* Ff *whirle pool*) an eddy of water, a vortex: *through ford and w.* Lr. III, 4, 53.

**Whirlwind,** a furious tempest: *my sighs, like —s, labour hence to heave thee,* Lucr. 586. *that some w. bear unto a ragged rock,* Gent. I, 2, 120. *as —s shake fair buds,* Shr. V, 2, 140. Tim. IV, 3, 288. Hml. III, 2, 7. Lr. III, 4, 60.

**Whirring,** see *Whir.*

**Whisper,** subst. a soft low voice, words spoken in the ear of another: H5 IV Chor. 7. Per. III, 1, 9. Applied to things communicated in secret and by stealth: Cor. V, 3, 7. Hml. I, 1, 80. IV, 1, 41. IV, 5, 82.

**Whisper,** vb. to speak with a soft and low voice, so as to be heard only by one; absol.: *—ing conspirator,* Lucr. 769. *to w. and conspire against my* youth, Gent. I, 2, 43. *with —ing and most guilty diligence,* Meas. IV, 1, 39. *—ing humbleness,* Merch. I, 3, 125. As II, 7, 192. Wint. I, 2, 217. Rom. I, 5, 25 (*a —ing tale,* i. e. a tale told in whispers; *—ing* gerund). Caes. II, 2, 100. *—s in mine ear,* Ven. 659. Per. V, 1, 97. With *to: and —s to his pillow,* H6B III, 2, 375. With *with: I'll w. with the general and know his pleasure,* All's IV, 3, 329.

= to converse in whispers: *Juno and Ceres w. seriously,* Tp. IV, 125. Mids. III, 1, 73. V, 135. 161. Wint. I, 2, 284. IV, 4, 250. John II, 475. H6C I, 1, 149. Oth. II, 1, 169. IV, 2, 6.

Trans.; 1) the addressed person as object: *w. her ear and tell her,* Ado III, 1, 4. *the blushes in my cheeks thus w. me,* All's II, 3, 75. *your followers I will w. to the business,* Wint. I, 2, 437. IV, 4, 827. John IV, 2, 189. R3 IV, 4, 192. H8 I, 1, 179. Troil. I, 3, 250. Mcb. IV, 3, 210. 2) the communication as object: *she —s in his ears a heavy tale,* Ven. 1125. LLL V, 2, 436. 443. John I, 42. *we'll w. o'er a couplet or two of most sage saws,* Tw. III, 4, 412. *lean-looked prophets w. fearful change,* R2 II, 4, 11. *will w. music to my weary spirit,* H4B IV, 5, 3. *some devil w. curses in mine ear,* Tit. V, 3, 11. *the —ed ones* (viz news) Lr. II, 1, 8.

The gerund substantively; *rain sacrificial —ings in his ear,* Tim. I, 1, 81. *foul —ings are abroad,* Mcb. V, 1, 79.

**Whissing,** see *Wheezing.*

**Whist,** an interjection commanding silence, = hush: *the wild waves, w.!* Tp. I, 2, 379 (cf. *The*).

**Whistle,** subst. a small wind instrument; used at sea to summon the sailors to their duty: Tp. I, 1, 8. H5 III Chor. 9. Per. III, 1, 8. Used by sportsmen: *I have been worth the w.* Lr. IV, 2, 29 (Proverb: *it is a poor dog that is not worth the whistling*).

**Whistle,** vb. to make a shrill sound, either with the mouth or a wind instrument: As II, 7, 163. Rom. V, 3, 7. Lr. II, 2, 163. Ant. II, 2, 221. Per. IV, 1, 64. With an object: *tunes ... that he heard the carmen w.* H4B III, 2, 342. Applied to the sound of winds: Mids. II, 1, 86. H4A V, 1, 5. To the call of falconers: *I'ld w. her off and let her down the wind,* Oth. III, 3, 262 (Johnson: the falconers always let fly the hawk against the wind; if she flies with the wind behind her, she seldom returns. If therefore a hawk was for any reason to be dismissed, she was let down the wind, and from that time shifted for herself and preyed at fortune). *to w. off these secrets,* Wint. IV, 4, 248 (the clown's speech, who meant to say *whisper,* but in his blunder says more than he intended). *this being done, let the law go w.* IV, 4, 715 (i. e. you are beyond its reach. Proverbial phrase).

**Whit,** point, jot; used negatively: *no w.* (= not in the least, not at all) Sonn. 33, 13. Shr. I, 2, 175. R2 II, 1, 103. Caes. II, 1, 148. Cymb. III, 1, 6. *not a w.* Gent. IV, 2, 67. Wiv. I, 1, 27. Mids. III, 1, 17. As III, 2, 46. Shr. III, 244. H4A II, 4, 408. IV, 3, 2. R3 III, 4, 82. Troil. V, 1, 76. Rom. IV, 9, 9. Hml. V, 2, 230. Cymb. II, 4, 46. *ne'er a w.* Shr. I, 1, 240. *ne'er a w. at all,* Tit. IV, 2, 53.

**White,** being of the colour of snow or milk: Ven. 10. 398. Lucr. 472. Sonn. 130, 3. Gent. II, 3, 22. Wiv. I, 1, 16. 19. IV, 4, 49. IV, 5, 116. V, 5, 41. 74. Meas. III, 2, 4 (*brown and w. bastard*). LLL I, 2, 95. III, 169. Merch. II, 4, 13. Rom. III, 2, 19. Lr. III, 4, 123 (*w. wheat*). III, 6, 33 (*w. herring*). Oth. V, 2, 4 etc. a w. rose the badge of the house of York: H6A II, 4, 30. 36 etc. H6C I, 2, 33. II, 5, 97. R3 V, 5, 19.

*W.* the colour of hair in old age: Sonn. 12, 4. Merch. I, 2, 9. Wint. IV, 4, 415. H4A II, 4, 393. 514. Lr. III, 7, 37 (*so w., and such a traitor*). Ant. III, 11, 13 etc.

Emblem of purity and innocence: *my w. stole of chastity I daffed,* Compl. 297. *the —st virtue,* Meas. III, 2, 198. *that dye is on me which makes my — st part black,* H8 I, 1, 209. cf. Lucr. 56. 65. Tp. IV, 55.

= pale: *was it not w.? sawest thou not signs of fear lurk in mine eye?* Ven. 643. *to turn w. and swoon,* Compl. 308. *let the w. death sit on thy cheek for ever,* All's II, 3, 77. Hence emblem of cowardice: *livers w. as milk,* Merch. III, 2, 86. *left the liver w. and pale,* H4B IV, 3, 113. *I shame to wear a heart so w.* Mcb. II, 2, 65. cf. *White-livered.*

Substantively: *how w. and red each other did destroy,* Ven. 346. *teaching the sheets a —r hue than w.* 398. 1053. 1168. Lucr. 11. 56. 57. 63. 394. Sonn. 12, 4. Compl. 226. Wiv. IV, 4, 72. IV, 6, 35. V, 2, 6. 10. LLL I, 2, 104. II, 197. Mids. III, 2, 141. 144. Shr. IV, 5, 30. Tw. I, 5, 257. II, 4, 56 etc. etc. *which is not under w. and black,* Ado V, 1, 314 (i. e. written down. Dogberry's speech). *'twas I won the wager, though you hit the w.* Shr. V, 2, 186 (the centre of an archery butt; alluding to the name of Bianca). *spit w.* H4B I, 2, 237 (cf. *Spit*). *the truth of it stands off as gross as black and w.* H5 II, 2, 104. *turns up the w. o'the eye,* Cor. IV, 5, 209. *she'll find a w. that shall her blackness fit,* Oth. II, 1, 134 (punning on *w.* and *wight*). Plural: *in whose comparison all —s are ink,* Troil. I, 1, 56. *—s of eggs,* Lr. III, 7, 106.

**White-beard,** an old man: R2 III, 2, 112.

**White-bearded,** having a white beard, old: Ado II, 3, 124. H4A II, 4, 509.

**White-faced,** having a white face, white: *that pale, that w. shore* (of England) John II, 23.

**White-Friars,** 'in London, was a part situated to the south of Fleet-street, and east of the Temple' (Nares): R3 I, 2, 227.

**Whitehall,** formerly York-place, the royal palace in London: H8 IV, 1, 97.

**White-handed,** having white hands: LLL V, 2, 230.

**White Hart,** a building on the east side of the Borough of Southwark: *hath my sword therefore broke through London gates, that you should leave me at the W. in Southwark?* H6B IV, 8, 25 (with a quibble: that you should desert me like cowards).

**White-limed,** whitewashed, or plastered with lime: *ye w. walls,* Tit. IV, 2, 98 (Ff *white-limb'd,* Qq *white-limbde;* Malone *white-limn'd*).

**White-livered,** cowardly: H5 III, 2, 34. R3 IV, 4, 465. cf. *Lily-livered* and *White.*

**Whitely,** whitish, pale, of faded beauty: *a w. wanton with a velvet brow,* LLL III, 198 (Qq and earlier Ff *whitly,* later Ff *whitely;* most M. Edd. *wightly*).

**Whiteness,** white colour: Ven. 1170. Gent. III, 1, 227. Err. III, 2, 130. = paleness: *the w. in thy cheek,* H4B I, 1, 68. Emblem of purity: Ado IV, 1, 163. Wint. I, 2, 327.

**White-upturned,** writing of M. Edd. in Rom. II, 2, 29; O. Edd. without hyphen.

**Whither** (often spelt *whether* in O. Edd.) 1) to which place; relatively: Gent. V, 2, 47. Err. V, 155. All's V, I, 29. R2 V, 1, 85. = to that place to which: H4A II, 3, 118. H6C II, 5, 139.

2) to what place; interrogatively: Ven. 904. Gent. I, 3, 24. IV, 1, 16. Wiv. II, 1, 153. III, 2, 9. III, 3, 162. 164. Ado II, 1, 193. Mids. II, 1, 1. Merch. II, 4, 16. As I, 2, 59. I, 3, 92. II, 3, 29. IV, 1, 168. Shr. I, 2, 165. All's III, 5, 35. V, 1, 27. Wint. IV, 4, 305. H4A II, 3, 107. H6A I, 1, 97. II, 3, 28. IV, 4, 12. H6B II, 4, 92. III, 2, 367. H6C I, 3, 1. IV, 5, 20. R3 IV, 4, 515. Cor. IV, 1, 34 (monosyll.). Rom. I, 2, 75. Per. V, 1, 178 etc. *w. away?* = where are you going: Gent. III, 1, 51. LLL IV, 3, 186. Mids. I, 1, 180. Shr. IV, 5, 38. H6A III, 2, 104. R3 II, 3, 1. IV, 1, 7. H8 II, 1, 1.

= whithersoever: *a fool go with thy soul, w. it goes*, H4A V, 3, 22. Cor. I, 2, 16.

**Whiting-time**, bleaching-time: Wiv. III, 3, 140.

**Whitmore**, name in H6B IV, 1, 14. 31. 44.

**Whitster**, bleacher: Wiv. III, 3, 14.

**Whitsun**, pertaining to Pentecost: *W. pastorals*, Wint. IV, 4, 134. *upon Wednesday in W. week*, H4B II, 1, 96 (Q *Wheeson;* Mrs. Quickly's speech). *a W. morris-dance*, H5 II, 4, 25.

**Whittle**, a small clasp-knife: Tim. V, 1, 183.

**Whizzing**, hissing: *the exhalations w. in the air*, Caes. II, 1, 44. In Lr. III, 6, 17 Qq *hissing*, Ff *hizzing*, some M. Edd. *whizzing*.

**Who**, 1) interr. pron., always referring to persons, and never adjectively; nom. *who*, f. i. Ven. 397. 401. 415. 416. 888; objective case *whom*, f. i. Tp. I, 1, 20. Gent. II, 1, 153. IV, 4, 118. Anglos. gen. *whose*, f. i. *whose tongue is music now?* Ven. 1077. Obj. case *who* instead of *whom: who'hath she to spend the night withal but idle sounds?* Ven. 847. *for who love I so much?* Merch. II, 6, 30. Ado III, 3, 9. LLL IV, 1, 74. Tw. II, 5, 108. Wint. IV, 4, 636. John V, 6, 32. H5 IV, 7, 154. H6B III, 2, 127. Troil. II, 3, 101. III, 1, 23. Cor. II, 1, 8. Tit. V, 1, 71. Mcb. IV, 3, 171. Hml. I, 2, 190 etc. Qq *who*, Ff *whom:* Tit. III, 3, 55. F1 and Qq *who*, later Ff *whom:* Tp. I, 2, 80. Gent. III, 1, 200. IV, 2, 23. Ado I, 1, 214. V, 1, 232. LLL II, 2. As III, 2, 327. H6A III, 3, 62. H6C III, 2, 112. Troil. IV, 5, 176. Hml. II, 2, 196. Lr. I, 4, 26. V, 3, 248. Oth. I, 2, 52. IV, 2, 99. Ant. III, 6, 23. Cymb. IV, 2, 76. V, 5, 27.

**Who**, relat. pron.; Anglos. genitive *whose*, f. i. Ven. 99. 189. 268. 487. 543. Tp. I, 2, 150. 182. II, 1, 116. 257. V, 77. Gent. II, 4, 130. 166. III, 1, 227. III, 2, 69. 79. IV, 1, 27. IV, 3, 21. H4A I, 1, 38 (*heavy news, whose worst was* etc.). Objective *whom*, f. i. Ven. 630. Pilgr. 30. Sonn. 128, 11. Tp. I, 2, 68. 222. III, 3, 62. Gent. III, 1, 14. 82. III, 2, 37. IV, 3, 17. Err. I, 1, 45. Mids. V, 181. As II, 4, 52. All's III, 4, 17. 27. John II, 137. H5 III, 5, 17. H6B III, 2, 345. Cor. I, 1, 268. *who for whom:* Tp. I, 2, 231. IV, 1, 4. Gent. IV, 1, 51. Wint. V, 1, 109. H5 V, 2, 260. H6A IV, 3, 35. Troil. I, 3, 186. Tim. V, 1, 220. Mcb. III, 1, 123. III, 4, 42. Lr. IV, 1, 47. Oth. II, 3, 15 etc. Qq *who*, Ff *whom:* Merch. I, 2, 25. IV, 1, 290. H4B I, 1, 28. Ff *who*, Qq *whom:* R3 I, 3, 327. IV, 3, 4. F1 *who*, later Ff *whom:* Err. V, 137. LLL I, 1, 167. As III, 4, 52. Wint. II, 2, 6. IV, 4, 510. H6B V, 1, 63. *whom for who: whom, with Sebastian, ... would here have killed your king*, Tp. V, 76 (later Ff and M. Edd.

*who*). *whom, I thank heaven, is an honest woman*, Meas. II, 1, 72 (Elbow's speech). *than whom no mortal so magnificent*, LLL III, 180. cf. *whom they say is killed to-night*, John IV, 2, 165. *whom in constancy you think stands so safe*, Cymb. I, 4, 137.

Never adjectively joined to nouns, and always referring to nouns, never to sentences. Referring to persons, f. i. Ven. 33. 100. Tp. I, 2, 17. 68. 100. 222. Gent. II, 7, 3. III, 1, 14. 82. III, 2, 37. IV, 3, 17. To things or animals (cf. *as who should say in Shall*): Ven. 87. 306. 630. 857. 891. 956. 984. 1041. 1043. Lucr. 296. 328. 388. 655. 1119. 1139. 1231. 1740. 1781. 1805. Sonn. 41, 11. 128, 11. 141, 4. 11. 145, 11. Pilgr. 30. Tp. I, 2, 7. II, 1, 127. II, 2, 13. III, 3, 62. Gent. IV, 4, 61. Err. I, 2, 37. II, 2, 181. III, 2, 140. LLL I, 1, 82. II, 244. IV, 2, 4. Mids. V, 181. Merch. I, 3, 188. II, 7, 4. As II, 4, 52. III, 5, 13. IV, 3, 110. All's III, 4, 17. 27. IV, 2, 36. Wint. IV, 4, 581. John II, 137. 575. R2 II, 2, 71. H4A I, 3, 40. H4B V, 2, 128. H5 III, 5, 17. H6A IV, 2, 12. H6B III, 2, 164. 345. R3 I, 4, 41 (Qq *which*). 45 (Ff *I*). Troil. III, 3, 120. Cor. I, 1, 268. III, 2, 119. Rom. I, 1, 119. Caes. IV, 3, 112. Lr. IV, 3, 16 etc.

Preceded by the article: *your mistress from the whom there's no disjunction to be made*, Wint. IV, 4, 539.

= he who: *and whom he strikes his cruel tushes slay*, Ven. 624. *who by repentance is not satisfied is nor of heaven nor earth*, Gent. V, 4, 79. *fixing our eyes on whom our care was fixed*, Err. I, 1, 85. *I may neither choose whom I would nor refuse whom I dislike*, Merch. I, 2, 25. *whom we raise we will make fast*, H6B I, 4, 24. *is proclamation made that who finds Edward shall have a high reward?* H6C V, 5, 9. *we are going to whom it must be done*, Caes. II, 1, 331. *who was the thane lives yet*, Mcb. I, 3, 109. *who steals my purse steals trash*, Oth. III, 3, 157. *who tells me true, though in his tale lie death, I hear him as he flattered*, Ant. I, 2, 102. *who seeks and will not take when once 'tis offered, shall never find it more*, II, 7, 89. *who does i'the wars more than his captain can becomes his captain's captain*, III, 1, 21. Caes. I, 3, 80.

= whoever: *would make proselytes of who she but bid follow*, Wint. V, 1, 109. *let it be who it is*, Caes. I, 3, 80. *make choice of whom your wisest friends you will*, Hml. IV, 5, 204.

**Whoa ho ho** or **Whoa ho hoa**, an exclamation to attract attention at a distance; used by Slender and the old shepherd in Wiv. V, 5, 187 & Wint. III, 3, 79. cf. Merch. V, 39.

**Whoe'er**, any one that; whatever person: Sonn. 133, 11. Wiv. II, 2, 103. LLL IV, 1, 4. H4A V, 4, 37. H4B IV, 3, 12. H6A I, 2, 107. I, 3, 7. Oth. I, 3, 65. Unchanged in the accus.: *w. I woo, myself would be his wife*, Tw. I, 4, 42. *w. you find attach*, Rom. V, 3, 173.

**Whoever**, the same: Lucr. 879. Sonn. 135, 1. Err. V, 339. Shr. III, 2, 235. All's III, 2, 115. V, 3, 105. John III, 1, 335. V, 5, 19. H6C II, 2, 133. R3 II, 2, 146. Cor. III, 1, 113. Mcb. IV, 1, 47. Unchanged in the accus.: *w. the king favours*, H8 II, 1, 47.

**Whole**, 1) uninjured, unhurt, unbroken, sound: *my heart all w. as thine*, Ven. 370. *are they broken? No, they are both as w. as a fish*, Gent. II, 5, 20; cf. the same quibble in H5 III, 2, 37 and Troil. III, 1, 54. *let them keep their limbs w.* Wiv. III, 1, 79. 111.

*yet all goes well, yet all our joints are w.* H4A IV, 1, 83. *men's flesh preserved so w.* H6B III, 1, 301. *w. as the marble,* Mcb. III, 4, 22 (cf. Wint. II, 3, 90). *if you'll patch a quarrel, as matter w. you have not to make it with,* Ant. II, 2, 53. *you keep by land the legions and the horse w.* III, 7, 72. 75. III, 8, 3.

2) restored to soundness: *I would the state of time had first been w. ere he by sickness had been visited,* H4A IV, 1, 25. *he was thrust in the mouth, ... and 'tis not w. yet,* H6B IV, 7, 11. Caes. II, 1, 327. 328. Ant. IV, 8, 11. In a moral sense: *all is w.* All's V, 3, 37. *this might have been ... made w.* John I, 35. H4A II, 1, 81.

3) not only in part, all, complete, entire: Lucr. Arg. 20. Tp. II, 1, 316. II, 2, 137. Meas. III, 1, 235. Err. III, 2, 102. 140. Ado I, 1, 67. II, 1, 254. III, 1, 5. III, 3, 173. V, 2, 32. LLL I, 2, 191. Mids. II, 1, 55. III, 2, 53. Merch. I, 1, 43. All's IV, 3, 162. Tw. V, 386. John V, 2, 178. H4B II, 4, 376. H6A II, 3, 54. H6B I, 1, 133. II, 1, 164. H8 IV, 2, 154. Rom. II, 4, 78. 104. Hml. III, 2, 291. Oth. IV, 3, 79. Ant. II, 2, 183 etc. Preceded by *all: all my w. device,* Merch. III, 4, 81. *all the w. army,* H6A I, 1, 126. III, 1, 164. H8 I, 1, 12. Rom. IV, 2, 32. Oth. IV, 3, 75 (Ff *for all the w. world,* Qq *for the w. world*). Ant. III, 10, 5. Per. I, 1, 33. Substantively: *they whose w. is swallowed in confusion,* Lucr. 1159. *a leg, a head, stood for the w.* 1428. *he pays the w.* Sonn. 134, 14. *Arthur's title in the w.* John II, 562. *viceroy of the w.* H6A V, 4, 143.

**Wholesome,** 1) sound, healthy: *it doth posset and curd ... the thin and w. blood,* Hml. I, 5, 70. *thy natural magic ... on w. life usurp immediately,* III, 2, 271. *like a mildewed ear, blasting his w. brother,* III, 4, 65.

Metaphorically, = a) prosperous: *in state as w. as in state 'tis fit,* Wiv. V, 5, 63. *when shalt thou see thy w. days again,* Mcb. IV, 3, 105. *in the tender of a w. weal,* Lr. I, 4, 230. b) reasonable: *an honest method, as w. as sweet,* Hml. II, 2, 465. *if it shall please you to make me a w. answer,* III, 2, 328. *I cannot ... make you a w. answer; my wit's diseased,* 333. *in w. wisdom he might not but refuse you,* Oth. III, 1, 49.

2) tending to promote health, salubrious: Meas. IV, 2, 76 (—*st*). Err. IV, 104. LLL I, 1, 235. As III, 2, 58. Shr. IV, 3, 16. Wint. I, 2, 346. R2 III, 4, 39. 46. H5 I, 1, 61. Cor. I, 1, 18. Caes. II, 1, 264. Hml. I, 1, 162. Cymb. I, 2, 4. Per. IV, 6, 28 (*w. iniquity;* ironically).

Metaphorically, = salutary, suitable, profitable: *to wail friends lost is not by much so w. profitable as to rejoice at friends but newly found,* LLL V, 2, 760. *w. counsel,* R2 II, 1, 2. H8 I, 1, 113. *not w. to those,* I, 2, 45. *not w. to our cause,* III, 2, 99. *repeal daily any w. act,* Cor. I, 1, 85. *you wear out a good w. forenoon in hearing a cause between ...,* II, 1, 77 (which might be spent more profitably). *speak to 'em ... in w. manner,* II, 3, 66. *to such w. end as clears her from all blame,* Lr. II, 4, 146. *it seems not meet, nor w. to my place,* Oth. I, 1, 146.

**Wholesome-profitable:** LLL V, 2, 760, not hyphened in O. Edd., see *Wholesome.*

**Wholly,** entirely: Wiv. III, 2, 63. LLL V, 2, 65. Troil. III, 1, 22. IV, 4, 122. Ant. I, 2, 182. Cymb. II, 2, 7.

**Whoobub,** outcry, clamour: *had not the old man*

come in with a w. against his daughter and the king's son, Wint. IV, 4, 629.

**Whoop,** an interjection of a somewhat coarse nature: *he makes the maid to answer 'w., do me no harm, good man'; puts him off, slights him, with 'w., do me no harm, good man',* Wint. IV, 4, 199. 200. *w., Jug, I love thee,* Lr. I, 4, 245.

**Whoop,** vb. see *Hoop.*

**Whore,** subst. a prostitute, a strumpet: Tp. II, 1, 166. Wiv. IV, 1, 65. Meas. III, 2, 62. IV, 2, 39. V, 521. H4B II, 4, 157. 280. III, 2, 338. H5 II, 3, 41 (*the w. of Babylon;* cf. Revelation XVII). H6A I, 3, 35. Troil. II, 3, 79. IV, 1, 66. V, 1, 20 (*his masculine w.*). V, 2, 114. 193. V, 4, 7. 26. V, 7, 22. Tit. IV, 2, 72. Rom. II, 4, 32. Tim. IV, 3, 42. 61. 83. 133. 134. 139. 141. Mcb. I, 2, 15. Hml. II, 2, 614. Lr. I, 4, 137. II, 4, 52. III, 2, 90. III, 6, 21. IV, 6, 165. Oth. III, 3, 359. IV, 1, 187 etc. Ant. I, 2, 82. III, 6, 67. IV, 12, 13. V, 2, 221. Cymb. II, 4, 128.

**Whore,** vb. 1) to fornicate: Tim. IV, 3, 146. Oth. V, 1, 116.

2) to debauch: Hml. V, 2, 64.

**Whoremaster,** one who converses with prostitutes or practises lewdness: Meas. III, 2, 37. H4A II, 4, 516. Tim. II, 2, 111. 113. Lr. I, 2, 137.

**Whoremasterly,** running after whores, lecherous: Troil. V, 4, 7.

**Whoremonger,** the same as whoremaster: Meas. III, 2, 37.

**Whoreson,** 1) bastard: Lr. I, 1, 24.

2) a term of coarse familiarity, = fellow, when used as a substantive: *the sly —s have got a speeding trick,* H8 I, 3, 39. *well said; a merry w., ha! thou shalt be loggerhead,* Rom. IV, 4, 19. Adjectively applied not only to persons, but to anything, as a term of reproach or ludicrous dislike, and sometimes (as in the language of Doll Tearsheet) used even in a tone of coarse tenderness: Tp. I, 1, 46. Gent. II, 5, 49. IV, 4, 47. Err. IV, 4, 24. LLL IV, 3, 204. Shr. IV, 1 132. 158. 160. H4A II, 2, 88. II, 4, 155. 252. III, 3, 177. H4B I, 2, 16. 40. 43. 123. 128. II, 2, 91. II, 4, 225. 235. 250. 319. 326. III, 2, 193. Troil. II, 1, 44. II, 3, 244. V, 1, 32. V, 3, 101. Hml. V, 1, 189. 193. Lr. I, 4, 89. II, 2, 19. 35. 69. Ant. V, 2, 277. Cymb. II, 1, 4. 16.

**Whorish,** addicted to lewdness: Troil. IV, 1, 63.

**Whoso,** whosoever: R2 II, 2, 130. H6A III, 4, 39. Tim. V, 1, 212. Per. Prol. 37.

**Whosoe'er,** whatever person, any body that: H6A V, 3, 52. H6C IV, 7, 74. R3 III, 4, 67 (Qq *whatsoe'er*).

**Whosoever,** the same: R2 V, 3, 83. Troil. I, 2, 208.

**Whosomever,** = whomsoever: *w. you take him to be,* Troil. II, 1, 70 (the later Ff and M. Edd. *whosoever*).

**Why,** adv. wherefore; interrogatively and relatively; f. i. Ven. 96. 120. 138. 169. 373. 951. Lucr. 1224. 1225. Tp. I, 2, 444. II, 1, 200. 308. III, 3, 94. IV, 82. Gent. I, 2, 72. II, 3, 38. IV, 2, 27. Wiv. II, 1, 4. Err. I, 1, 30. II, 2, 45 (*every why hath a wherefore*). Mids. III, 2, 43. R3 IV, 4, 19. V, 3, 185. Lr. III, 6, 30 (= for which reason; therefore a comma after *speak*). IV, 6, 33 (*why I do trifle thus with his despair, is done to cure it*). Oth. III, 3, 176 (*why, why is this? thinkest thou I'ld make a life of jealousy?*

= wherefore do you tell me this?). Ant. IV, 14, 89 *(the thing why thou hast drawn it)* etc.

*Why so?* = wherefore, for what reason: *puppet? why so? ay, that way goes the game,* Mids. III, 2, 289. *I love you better. And why so, my lord?* Wint. II, 1, 7. Cymb. I, 1, 15.

*For why* = because, for: *sorts a sad look to her lady's sorrow, for why her face wore sorrow's livery,* Lucr. 1222. *I weep for thee and yet no cause I have, for why thou left'st me nothing in thy will; and yet thou left'st me more than I did crave, for why I craved nothing of thee still,* Pilgr. 138. 140. *sorrow changed to solace, solace mixed with sorrow, for why she sighed and bade me come to-morrow,* 204. *if she do chide, 'tis not to have you gone, for why the fools are mad, if left alone,* Gent. III, 1, 99. *trembled and shook, for why he stamped and swore,* Shr. III, 2, 169. *then must my earth with her continual tears become a deluge ..., for why my bowels cannot hide her woes, but like a drunkard must I vomit them,* Tit. III, 1, 231. Peculiar passages: *the rites for why I love him are bereft me,* Oth. I, 3, 258 (= *why* alone. But Qq *for which*). *send the hearers weeping to their beds, for why the senseless brands will sympathize ... and in compassion weep the fire out,* R2 V, 1, 46 (Qq *for why,* the etc. Ff *for why?* Perhaps *why* is here the interjection, intimating that something is to be added by way of amplification; cf. Gent. II, 3, 13).

*Why that,* see sub *That. Why either,* see *Either.*

**Why**, interj., almost an expletive, merely enlivening the speech, especially when something new is perceived or comes into the mind: Ven. 246. 717. 1109. Tp. I, 2, 215. II, 1, 95. II, 1, 261. III, 2, 29. 58. 80. 95. Gent. I, 1, 33. 79. I, 3, 4. II, 1, 50. II, 3, 13. Meas. I, 2, 3 etc. etc. *Why, so,* an expression of content or of unwilling acquiescence: *no news of them? why, so; and I know not what's spent in the search; why, thou loss upon loss,* Merch. III, 1, 95. *it shall be what o'clock I say it is. Why so, this gallant will command the sun,* Shr. IV, 3, 198. *your son was gone before I came. He was? why, so! go all which way it will,* R2 II, 2, 87. *why, so! now have I done a good day's work,* R3 II, 1, 1. Cor. V, 1, 15. *unreal mockery, hence! why, so: being gone, I am a man again,* Mcb. III, 4, 107. cf. Gent. II, 1, 137, and *why, this it is,* in I, 3, 90.

Used a as call or exclamation: *why, Jessica, I say! Why, Jessica!* Merch. II, 5, 6. *why, Davy! Here, sir!* H4B V, 1, 8. *why, how now, ho, awake!* Tp. II, 1, 308. V, 285. Gent. V, 4, 86. Meas. I, 2, 128.

**Wick**, that round which the wax or tallow in a candle is applied: Hml. IV, 7, 116.

**Wicked** (superl. *—est,* Meas. V, 53.) bad, immoral: Tp. I, 2, 320. V, 130. Wiv. II, 1, 20. 68. V, 5, 165. Meas. I, 2, 27. II, 1, 174. 183. 187. 193. 199. III, 2, 20. Mids. V, 181. As III, 2, 44. V, 1, 5. All's I, 3, 37. III, 7, 45. Wint. I, 2, 292. V, 3, 91. John II, 193. III, 1, 83. IV, 2, 71. R2 V, 1, 66. H4A I, 2, 106. II, 4, 517. H4B II, 4, 346. 347. 355. 357. H6A V, 4, 16. 42. H6B II, 1, 174. 186. III, 1, 52. R3 I, 2, 103. V, 1, 23. Troil. V, 10, 28 *(a w. conscience).* Tit. IV, 3, 23. V, 2, 98. V, 3, 145. Rom. III, 5, 235. Tim. III, 3, 33. V, 4, 71. Mcb. II, 1, 50. IV, 1, 45. Hml. I, 2, 156. I, 4, 42. I, 5, 44. III, 3, 59 *(the w. prize* = the prize of wickedness). III, 4, 12 (Ff *idle*). V, 1, 271. Lr. II, 1, 41. II, 4, 259. 260. Oth. V, 2, 181. Cymb. V, 5, 463. Per. IV, 4, 33. V, 1, 173. V, 3, 95. Lucr. 1035. 1540.

Sometimes = mischievous: *as w. dew as e'er my mother brushed ... from unwholesome fen,* Tp. I, 2, 321.* *that same w. bastard of Venus,* As IV, 1, 216. cf. Mids. II, 2, 98. Troil. IV, 4, 61. Tim. III, 2, 49.

**Wickedly**, sinfully: Lucr. 365.

**Wickedness**, 1) corruption of manners, immorality: As III, 2, 44. H5 IV, 1, 156. H6A III, 1, 14. Especially used of lewdness and incontinence: Wiv. II, 2, 134. Ado III, 2, 113. All's I, 3, 40. III, 2, 89. H5 III, 3, 22.

Apparently = a state of being mischievous: *disguise, I see thou art a w., wherein the pregnant enemy does much,* Tw. II, 2, 28.

2) a bad action: *I'll never care what w. I do,* Lr. III, 7, 99. *knows he the w.?* IV, 2, 92.

**Wicker**, made of twigs: *a w. bottle,* Oth. II, 2, 152 (Ff *twiggen-bottle*).

**Wide**, adj. 1) very extensive, stretching far: *the w. world,* Sonn. 19, 7. 107, 2. 137, 10. Err. II, 1, 21. Ado IV, 1, 292. Merch. I, 1, 167. As I, 3, 134. Troil. II, 2, 206. Tit. I, 248. Rom. III, 3, 16. *w. as the ocean is,* Sonn. 80, 5. Ado IV, 1, 142. Tim. I, 1, 47. *the w. universe,* Sonn. 109, 13. *this w. and universal theatre,* As II, 7, 137. *the w. vessel of the universe,* H5 IV Chor. 3. *in the world's w. mouth,* H4A I, 3, 153. *the w. fields,* LLL II, 1, 93. *w. Arabia,* Merch. II, 7, 42. *the w. cheeks o'the air,* Cor. V, 3, 151. *the forest walks are w.* Tit. II, 1, 114. Caes. I, 2, 155. *the w. arch of the ranged empire,* Ant. I, 1, 33.

2) having a great space between the sides, forming a great opening or gap: *small head and nostril w.* Ven. 296. *the w. wound,* 1052. Rom. III, 1, 100. *gape at —st,* Tp. I, 1, 63. *that w. gap,* Wint. IV, 1, 7. V, 3, 154. *w. havoc* (i. e. a breach) *made for bloody power to rush upon your peace,* John II, 220. *the w. difference 'twixt amorous and villanous,* Cymb. V, 5, 194.

3) capacious, holding much: *weed w. enough to wrap a fairy in,* Mids. II, 1, 256. As II, 7, 160. H4B III, 1, 51. *with conscience w. as hell,* H5 III, 3, 13. *as this temple waxes, the inward service of the mind and soul grows w. withal,* Hml. I, 3, 14. *till that a capable and w. revenge swallow them up,* Oth. III, 3, 459.

4) apparent, open, obvious: *without more —r and more overt test,* Oth. I, 3, 107 (Qq *certain.* cf. the adverb in Rom. II, 4, 91).

**Wide**, adv. 1) to a great extent, far and near: *one body should be filled with all graces w. enlarged,* As III, 2, 151 (spread abroad, distributed through the whole world). *far and w.* = for all the world, apparently, plainly: *proves thee far and w. a broad goose,* Rom. II, 4, 91 (cf. the adj. in Oth. I, 3, 107).

2) so as to have a great space from one side to the other, or to form a great opening: *the door he opens w.* Lucr. 359. John II, 300. 449. *keep my drooping eyelids open w.* Sonn. 27, 7. Tp. II, 1, 214. H4B IV, 5, 24. *the graves all gaping w.* Mids. V, 387. H4B V, 5, 58. *I will not open my lips so w. as ...,* Tw. I, 5, 2. *stretch the nostril w.* H5 III, 1, 15. *the villains march w. betwixt the legs,* H4A IV, 2, 43. *his arms spread —r than a dragon's wings,* H6A I, 1, 11. *earth, gape open w.* R3 I, 2, 65. *and w. unclasp the tables of their thoughts,* Troil. IV, 5, 60. *a thing inseparate divides more —r than the sky and earth,* V, 2, 149. *thus w. I'll ope my arms,* Hml. IV, 5, 145. *her clothes spread w.* IV, 7, 176.

3) far from the mark or from the purpose, so as

to miss the aim, astray: *bear thine eyes straight, though thy proud heart go w.* Sonn. 140, 14. *is my lord well, that he doth speak so w.?* Ado IV, 1, 63. *no such matter; you are w.* Troil. III, 1, 97. *Pyrrhus at Priam drives; in rage strikes w.; but with the whiff and wind of his fell sword the unnerved father falls,* Hml. II, 2, 494. *still, still far w.* Lr. IV, 7, 50. With *of: I never heard a man ... so w. of his own respect,* Wiv. III, 1, 58. *w. o'the bowhand,* LLL IV, 1, 135 (far from the mark).

**Wide-chapped,** opening the mouth wide: Tp. I, 1, 60.

**Wide-enlarged,** see *Enlarge* and *Wide.*

**Widen,** to throw open: *now the gates are ope; ... 'tis for the followers fortune —s them, not for the fliers,* Cor. I, 4, 44.

**Wide-skirted,** having wide borders, extensive: *w. meads,* Lr. I, 1, 66.

**Wide-stretched,** largë, extensive: *w. honours,* H5 II, 4, 82.

**Widow,** subst. a woman whose husband is dead: Lucr. 906. Sonn. 9, 1. 5. 7. Tp. II, 1, 76. 77. 78. 133. Meas. II, 1, 207. V, 175. 178. 179. Ado V, 2, 82. Merch. II, 2, 171. III, 2, 312. Shr. IV, 2, 37. 50. IV, 5, 78. V, 2, 7 etc. John II, 32. 305. III, 1, 14. 108. R2 I, 2, 43. H4B II, 1, 76. 89. II, 3, 57. H6B V, 1, 188. H6C III, 2, 16. 26. V, 6, 39. R3 I, 1, 81. II, 2, 55. III, 7, 185. Tim. IV, 3, 38. Hml. III, 2, 233. Lr. V, 1, 59. Ant. III, 3, 30 etc. With *of:* H5 I, 2, 158. Rom. I, 2, 69 *(the lady w. of Vitruvio).* With *to:* H8 III, 2, 71. *w. to a woful bed,* R3 I, 2, 249). Adjectively: *a w. aunt,* Mids. I, 1, 157. *this w. lady,* John II, 548. *my w. comfort,* III, 4, 105. *your w. dolour,* R3 II, 2, 65 (Qq *your widow's dolours*).

**Widow,** vb. 1) to bereave of a husband: *—ed wombs,* Sonn. 97, 8. *hath —ed and unchilded many a one,* Cor. V, 6, 153.

2) to endow with a widow's right, to jointure: *for his possessions ... we do instate and w. you withal,* Meas. V, 429.

3) to become a widow to, to survive as a wife: *let me be married to three kings in a forenoon and w. them all,* Ant. I, 2, 27.

**Widow-comfort,** see *Widow.*

**Widow-dolour,** see *Widow.*

**Widower,** a man whose wife is dead: Tp. II, 1, 79. All's V, 3, 70. 142. H6C III, 3, 227. IV, 1, 99. Ant. II, 2, 122.

**Widowhood,** state of being a widow (? cf. *Of*), or estate settled on a widow (?): *I'll assure her of her w., be it that she survive me, in all my lands and leases whatsoever,* Shr. II, 125.

**Widow-maker,** one who bereaves women of their husbands: John V, 2, 17.

**Wield,** to use with the hand, to manage: *weapons w.* Lucr. 1432. Rom. I, 1, 101. *wilt thou the spigot w.?* Wiv. I, 3, 24. *to w. a sceptre,* H6C IV, 6, 73. *more than words can w. the matter,* Lr. I, 1, 56.

**Wieldy,** in *Unwieldy,* q. v.

**Wife,** (plur. *wives;* also the Anglos. gen. of the singular spelt so in O. Edd., f. i. Wiv. II, 1, 242. III, 2, 35. III, 5, 79. IV, 2, 148. 171. Meas. IV, 2, 4. Merch. IV, 1, 451. V, 167. As IV, 1, 170. All's I, 3, 43) 1) any woman of mature age that is or might be married: *good morrow, good w. Not so, an't please your worship. Good maid then,* Wiv. II, 2, 36. *she's a civil modest w.* 101. *never a w. in Windsor leads a better life,* 122. *wives may be merry, and yet honest too,* IV, 2, 107. *how*

like you *Windsor wives?* V, 5, 110. *the rest aloof are the Dardanian wives,* Merch. III, 2, 58. *him I love more ... than e'er I shall love w.* Tw. V, 139 (quite = woman; placed in the rhyme). *let wives with child pray,* John III, 1, 89. *as did the wives of Jewry at Herod's slaughtermen,* H5 III, 3, 40. *pales in the flood with men, with wives and boys,* V Chor. 10. *his enforcement of the city wives,* R3 III, 7, 8. *make wells and Niobes of the maids and wives,* Troil. V, 10, 19. *lest that thy wives with spits and boys with stones in puny battle slay me,* Cor. IV, 4, 5. cf. *Alewife, Goodwife, Housewife, Midwife;* and the doubtful passage in Oth. I, 1, 21.

2) a married woman considered in her relation to her husband: Tp. I, 1, 65. II, 1, 4. III, 1, 83. IV, 77. 123. V, 210. Gent. III, 1, 66. 76 *(take a w.).* Wiv. I, 1, 201. III, 3, 242. IV, 2, 125. Meas. I, 2, 151. II, 1, 69. 120. Err. I, 1, 59. I, 2, 88. II, 1, 56. III, 1, 63 etc. etc. with *to:* R3 I, 2, 10. Lr. I, 1, 69. Cymb. V, 5, 39. *asked her for his w.* Per. Prol. 37. *I take thee for w.* As IV, 1, 137. *to woo thee for my w.* Shr. II, 195. *have to w.* As IV, 1, 130. *will have Katharine to my w.* Shr. II, 282. 367. *took to w.* Caes. II, 1, 293. Hml. I, 2, 14. *take Antony Octavia to his w.* Ant. II, 2, 130. *what dowry shall I have with her to w.* Shr. II, 121.

**Wifelike,** having the qualities of the female sex, resembling a woman: *thy meekness saint-like, w. government,* H8 II, 4, 138. *more goddess-like than w.* Cymb. III, 2, 8.

**Wight,** person, being (fem. as well as masc.): *beshrew the witch (viz night)! with venomous —s she stays as tediously as hell,* Troil. IV, 2, 12. Used by Pistol: *O base Hungarian w.* Wiv. I, 3, 23. *I ken the w.* 40. *O braggart vile and damned furious w.* H5 II, 1, 64. In rhyming: Sonn. 106, 2. LLL I, 1, 178. In the style of popular poetry: *she was a w., if ever such w. were,* Oth. II, 1, 159. *he was a w. of high renown,* II, 3, 96. *so for her many a w. did die,* Per. Prol. 39 (Gower's speech).

**Wightly,** writing of some M. Edd. in LLL III, 198. see *Whitely.*

**Wild,** 1) not tame, not domestic: Ven. 560. Sonn. 102, 11. Ado III, 1, 35. 112. Merch. V, 71. Shr. II, 279. H4A IV, 1, 103. H8 V, 3, 22. Cor. III, 2, 2. In the following passages adj. and subst. hyphened by some Edd.: *w. boars,* Ant. II, 2, 183. *sleeps by day more than the w. cat,* Merch. II, 5, 48. Shr. I, 2, 197. Oth. II, 1, 111. *a w. duck,* H4A II, 2, 108. IV, 2, 21. *w. fowl,* Mids. III, 1, 33. Tw. IV, 2, 55. *my taxing like a w. goose flies,* As II, 7, 86. Rom. II, 4, 76. *w. geese,* Mids. III, 2, 20. H4A II, 4, 152. H4B V, 1, 79. Lr. II, 4, 46. *if thy wits run the w. goose chase, I have done,* Rom. II, 4, 75 (Dyce: a kind of horse-race: two horses were started together, and whichever rider could get the lead, the other was obliged to follow him over whatever ground the foremost jockey chose to go).\*

2) growing without culture: Mids. II, 1, 249. Wint. IV, 4, 93. H5 III, 5, 7. Cymb. IV, 2, 390.

3) uncultivated, uninhabited, desert: *to trace the forests w.* Mids. II, 1, 25. As V, 4, 165. *high w. hills,* R2 II, 3, 4. *a little fire in a w. field,* Lr. III, 4, 117.

4) savage, atrocious, sanguinary: Lucr. 980. Mids. II, 1, 228. 229. V, 225. John IV, 3, 48. V, 2, 74. H4A V, 2, 11. H4B IV, 5, 132. H6B V, 2, 59. Mcb. II, 4, 16.

5) turbulent, tempestuous: *w. waves,* Ven. 819. *the w. waters,* Tp. I, 2, 2. 379. Gent. II, 7, 32. Err. II, 1,

21. Merch. V, 11. H4B I, 1, 154. H5 III, 1, 14. H8 II, 4, 200. III, 2, 198. Troil. I, 1, 105. Mcb. IV, 2, 21. *a w. night,* Lr. II, 4, 311. In a moral sense, = violently agitated: *the times are w.* H4B I, 1, 9. H8 V, 1, 15. *in w. hurry,* Cor. IV, 6, 4. *while men's minds are w.* Hml. V, 2, 405. *in a town of war, yet w.* Oth. II, 3, 214.

6) ungoverned, licentious: *the w. prince and Poins,* Wiv. III, 2, 74. *my w. societies,* III, 4, 8. Meas. IV, 3, 19. Merch. II, 2, 190. 196. H4A V, 2, 72. H4B V, 2, 123.\*H5 I, 2, 267. Hml. II, 1, 18. 22. Cymb. I, 6, 103.

Sometimes not a term of reproach, = wanton, frolicsome: *youth is w. and age is tame,* Pilgr. 164. *our w. faction,* Gent. IV, 1, 37. *pretty and witty, w. and yet, too, gentle,* Err. III, 1, 110. *to move w. laughter in the throat of death,* LLL V, 2, 865. cf. Ado III, 1, 35. Merch. V, 71. H4A IV, 1, 103.

Adverbially: *if I chance to talk a little w., forgive me,* H8 I, 4, 26.

7) violent, carried headlong by passion: *w. rage,* H5 IV, 7, 82. *desperate, w. and furious,* R3 IV, 4, 169. *w. grief,* 229. Rom. III, 3, 110. Tim. V, 1, 167. 206. Ant. V, 2, 154.

8) rash, inconsiderate: *'twere most piteous to be w.* Wint. II, 1, 182. *a w. dedication of yourselves to unpathed waters,* IV, 4, 577. *this unheedful, desperate, w. adventure,* H6A IV, 4, 7. *a w. exposture to each chance,* Cor. IV, 1, 36.

9) bewildered, distracted, mad: *w. amazement,* John V, 1, 35. *your looks are pale and w.* Rom. V, 1, 28. V, 3, 240. *it almost turns my dangerous nature w.* Tim. IV, 3, 499 (*dangerous* perhaps = exposed to danger. Most M. Edd. *mild*). *w. and whirling words,* Hml. I, 5, 133.

10) wanting order and regularity, or quiet and composure in any manner; extravagant, inordinate, eccentric, fantastic, mad: *how like you this w. counsel, mighty states? smacks it not something of the policy?* John II, 395. *the irregular and w. Glendower,* H4A I, 1, 40. *like a w. Morisco,* H6B III, 1, 365. *in this w. action,* Troil. I, 3, 340. *so w. in their attire,* Mcb. I, 3, 40. *paragons description and w. fame,* Oth. II, 1, 62. *you w. bedfellow,* Ant. I, 2, 51. *the w. disguise,* II, 7, 131. *I am w. in my beholding,* Per. V, 1, 224.

**Wild,** adv. see *Wild,* adj. 6.

**Wild,** subst. 1) wilderness: *the vasty —s of wide Arabia,* Merch. II, 7, 41. Metaphorically: *a w. of nothing, save of joy,* Merch. III, 2, 184.

2) = weald: *a franklin in the w. of Kent,* H4A II, 1, 60.

**Wild-boar,** see *Wild,* adj. 1.

**Wild-cat** (*wildcat*), see *Wild,* adj. 1.

**Wild-duck,** see *Wild,* adj. 1.

**Wilderness,** 1) a tract of solitude and savageness, a desert: Lucr. 544. Gent. IV, 1, 63. Merch. III, 1, 128. R2 IV, 74. H4B IV, 5, 137. H6B III, 2, 360. Tit. III, 1, 54. 94 (*a w. of sea*).

2) wildness: *such a warped slip of w. ne'er issued from his blood,* Meas. III, 1, 142 (*slip of w.* = wild slip).

**Wildfire,** a composition of inflammable materials: Lucr. 1523. H4A III, 3, 45.

**Wild-fowl,** see *Wild,* adj. 1.

**Wild-goose,** see *Wild,* adj. 1.\*

**Wildly,** 1) without cultivation: *valour that w. grows in them,* Cymb. IV, 2, 180.

2) savagely: *prisoners w. overgrown with hair,* H5 V, 2, 43.

3) in a bewildered manner, with perturbation or distraction, madly: *she w. breaketh from their strict embrace,* Ven. 874. *w. determining which way to fly,* Lucr. 1150. *looking w.* Wiv. III, 3, 94. R2 V, 3, 25. Hml. III, 4, 119. *how w. then walks my estate in France,* John IV, 2, 128. *start not so w. from my affair,* Hml. III, 2, 321.

4) inconsiderately, foolishly: *I prattle something too w.* Tp. III, 1, 58. *he demeaned himself rough, rude and w.* Err. V, 88. *accident is guilty to what we w. do,* Wint. IV, 4, 550. *something w. by us performed,* V, 1, 129.

**Wild-mare;** *to ride the w.* = to play at see-saw: H4B II, 4, 268.

**Wildness,** 1) disorderly growth in an uncultivated state: *vineyards, fallows ... grew to w.* H5 V, 2, 55.

2) savageness, fierceness: *wilder to him than tigers in their w.* Lucr. 980.

3) irregularity of manners, licentiousness: *prate to me of the w. of his youth,* H4B III, 2, 328. IV, 5, 153. H5 I, 1, 26. 64. Caes. II, 1, 189.

4) want of sober judgment: *our youths and w. shall no whit appear,* Caes. II, 1, 148.

5) distraction, madness: *I do wish that your good beauties be the happy cause of Hamlet's w.* Hml. III, 1, 40. *put thyself into a haviour of less fear, ere w. vanquish my staider senses,* Cymb. III, 4, 9.

**Wiles,** deceitful practices, tricks, stratagems: *the w. and guiles that women work,* Pilgr. 335. *these are but imaginary w.* Err. IV, 3, 10. *upon my wit, to defend my w.* Troil. I, 2, 285.

**Wilful,** 1) willing, pleased, ready: *this beauteous combat, w. and unwilling,* Ven. 365. *a secure and w. Actaeon,* Wiv. III, 2, 44. *when walls are so w. to hear without warning,* Mids. V, 211. *patience perforce with w. choler meeting,* Rom. I, 5, 91 (ready anger, opposed to enforced and constrained patience).

2) acting with set purpose; or done by design: *from thee going he went w. slow,* Sonn. 51, 13 (hyphened by M. Edd.). *if ever I were w. negligent,* Wint. I, 2, 255 (hyphened by O. and M. Edd.). *to confess the w. abuse,* H4B II, 4, 339. *we shall see w. adultery and murder committed,* H5 II, 1, 40. Strange expression: *you are too w. blame,* H4A III, 1, 177 (blameable on purpose, on principle; indulging your faults, though conscious that they are faults. M. Edd. *wilful-blame*).

Hence = voluntarily assumed, affected, not natural: *if thou thyself deceivest by w. taste of what thyself refusest,* Sonn. 40, 8. *and do a w. stillness entertain, with purpose to be dressed in an opinion of wisdom,* Merch. I, 1, 90.

3) obstinate, stubborn, refractory: *the Dauphin is too w. opposite,* John V, 2, 124 (hyphened by M. Edd.). *what means this w. silence?* R3 III, 7, 28. *to w. men the injuries that they themselves procure must be their schoolmasters,* Lr. II, 4, 305.

4) regardless, reckless, saucy: *and in his will his w. eye he tired,* Lucr. 417. *I owe you much, and, like a w. boy, that which I owe is lost,* Merch. I, 1, 146 (i. e. like a reckless boy I confess to you). *how will their grudging stomachs be provoked to w. disobedience, and rebel,* H6A IV, 1, 142. *peace, w. boy,* H6C V, 5, 31. *the w. sons of old Andronicus,* Tit. IV, 4, 8.

**Wilful-blame,** see *Wilful* 2.

**Wilfully,** 1) willingly, readily, voluntarily: *they*

*w. themselves exile from light,* Mids. III, 2, 386. *that w. seeks her own salvation,* Hml. V, 1, 2.

2) on purpose: *still thou mistakest, or else committest thy knaveries w.* Mids. III, 2, 346 (Ff *willingly*). *who, on my soul, hath w. betrayed the souls of those ...,* H4A I, 3, 81.

3) obstinately, stubbornly: *why thou against the church ... so w. dost spurn,* John III, 1, 142.

4) saucily: *my saucy bark inferior far to his on your broad main doth w. appear,* Sonn. 80, 8.

**Wilful-negligent,** see *Wilful* 2.

**Wilfulness,** 1) intentional and premeditated way of acting and behaving: *look both my w. and errors down,* Sonn. 117, 9 (my offences committed on purpose as well as my mistakes. cf. *forsworn in will and error,* LLL V, 2, 471).

2) inclination, propensity (?): *never Hydra-headed w. so soon did lose his seat,* H5 I, 1, 35 (perverse self-indulgence, which seemed unextirpable like the heads of the Lernaean Hydra?).

**Wilful-opposite** (not hyphened in O. Edd.), see *Wilful* 3.

**Wilful-slow** (not hyphened in O. Edd.), see *Wilful* 2.

**Will,** subst. 1) the faculty of the mind by which we desire and purpose: *so true a fool is love that in your w., though you do any thing, he thinks no ill,* Sonn. 57, 13. *he wants wit that wants resolved w. to learn his wit to exchange the bad for better,* Gent. II, 6, 12. *he is the bridle of your w.* Err. II, 1, 13. *let your w. attend on their accords,* 25. *a sharp wit matched with too blunt a w.* LLL II, 49. 50. *the w. of man is by his reason swayed,* Mids. II, 2, 115. *the w. of a living daughter,* Merch. I, 2, 26. *all too late comes counsel to be heard, where w. doth mutiny with wit's regard,* R2 II, 1, 28. *so was his w. in his old feeble body,* H6B V, 3, 13. Troil. I, 3, 122. II, 2, 179. Rom. IV, 1, 72. Caes. II, 2, 71. Hml. I, 3, 95. II, 1, 104. III, 1, 80. Oth. I, 3, 324.

2) a particular operation or effect of that faculty: a) disposition, inclination, bent of mind: *what wit sets down is blotted straight with w.* Lucr. 1299 (wit and w. corresponding to the words *conceit* and *grief* in the line before). *our shows are more than w., for still we prove much in our vows, but little in our love,* Tw. II, 4, 120. *Scotland hath w. to help, but cannot help,* H6C III, 3, 34. *a slave to each incensed w.* H8 I, 2, 65. *not friended by his wish, to your high person his w. is most malignant,* 141. *value dwells not in particular w.* Troil. II, 2, 53. *the w. dotes that is attributive to ...,* 58. *my election is led on in the conduct of my w.; my w. enkindled by mine eyes and ears, two traded pilots 'twixt the dangerous shores of w. and judgment: how may I avoid, although my w. distaste what it elected, the wife I chose?* 62—66. *there is between my w. and all offences a guard of patience,* V, 2, 53. *I have no w. to wander forth of doors,* Caes. III, 3, 3. *one may smell in such a w. most rank,* Oth. III, 3, 232. *with your w. = as you choose, as you think good: then with your w. go on,* Caes. IV, 3, 224.

*Good w. = 1)* willingness; good intention: *my good w. is to it, and yours it is against,* Tp. III, 1, 30. *pray God our cheer may answer my good w.* Err. III, 1, 20. *heart and good w.* IV, 4, 88. *here with all good w... I yield you up my part,* Mids. III, 2, 164. *if we offend, it is with our good w.* V, 108. *I will do my good w.* H4B III, 2, 167 (= my best). *he that has but effected his good*

*w. hath overta'en mine act,* Cor. I, 9, 18. *your good w. must have that thanks,* V, 1, 45. Caes. V, 5, 51. Ant. II, 5, 8. Per. III, 4, 18. 2) favor, benevolence, love: *what dear good w. I bear unto Valentine,* Gent. IV, 3, 14. *to remember my good w.* IV, 4, 103. *can you carry your good w. to the maid?* Wiv. I, 1, 238 (Evans' speech). *I tell you for good w.* IV, 5, 81 & 90 (out of friendship. Evans' and Caius' speeches). *if a' could get her good w.* Ado II, 1, 18. 224. Shr. I, 1, 86. H5 IV, 8, 73. H6A IV, 1, 54. H8 III, 1, 68. Hml. II, 2, 22. *Ill w. =* enmity, hate; cf. *Ill-will.* 3) accord, consent, approbation: *I hope I have your good w., father Page,* Wiv. III, 2, 61. III, 4, 86. IV, 4, 84. *I'll fetch my sister, to get her good w.* Err. III, 2, 70. *my w. is your good w. may stand with ours,* Ado V, 4, 28. *his good w. obtained,* II, 1, 311. *with his good w.* Shr. I, 1, 6. *without asking my good w.* V, 1, 137. All's I, 3, 19. 23. II, 4, 15. Lr. V, 3, 79. *by her good w. =* of her own accord, voluntarily: Ven. 479. *of thine own good w. =* of thy own accord, R2 IV, 177. *on my free w.* Ant. III, 6, 57. *by my w. =* of my own accord, or with my consent: Ven. 639. Ado III, 3, 67. Tw. III, 3, 1. H4B IV, 1, 159. Troil. II, 3, 202.

b) arbitrary disposal, command, authority: *bidding the law make courtesy to their w.* Meas. II, 4, 175. *whose w. stands but mine?* H6A I, 3, 11. *we must not rend our subjects from our laws and stick them in our w.* H8 I, 2, 94. *every thing includes itself in power, power into w., w. into appetite,* Troil. I, 3, 120. *to curb the w. of the nobility,* Cor. III, 1, 39. *making your —s the scope of justice,* Tim. V, 4, 4. *bid my w. avouch it,* Mcb. III, 1, 120. *their law's their w.* Per. I, 1, 103.

c) divine determination: *the —s above be done,* Tp. I, 1, 71. Wint. III, 3, 7. *oppose against their —s,* V, 1, 46. *the w. of God,* H5 I, 2, 289. V, 1, 34. R2 I, 2, 6. H6B III, 1, 86. Cymb. V, 1, 16. *by God's w.!* H6A II, 4, 82. *God's w.!* Wiv. III, 1, 62. H5 IV, 3, 23. 74. IV, 8, 2. H8 II, 3, 12. Rom. III, 3, 76. Oth. II, 3, 161 (Ff *fie, fie*). *od's blessed w.* Wiv. I, 1, 273. *od's my w.* As IV, 3, 17.

d) intention, desire: *one relying on your lordship's w.* Gent. I, 3, 61. *my w. is something sorted with his wish,* 63. *how she opposes her against my w.* III, 2, 26. *my w. is even this, that ...,* IV, 2, 93. *always obedient to your grace's w.* Meas. I, 1, 26. *is it your will Claudio shall die to-morrow?* II, 2, 7. Err. III, 2, 174. IV, 1, 112. Mids. I, 1, 87. 118. All's IV, 4, 30. John II, 193. H8 I, 2, 13. Hml. III, 3, 39. III, 2, 221. Lr. I, 1, 44. Oth. I, 3, 399. Ant. IV, 6, 2. IV, 9, 14 etc. *to do one's w.* Cor. III, 2, 137. Caes. IV, 1, 27. V, 3, 48. *to have one's w.* Err. IV, 2, 18. H6C I, 4, 144. IV, 1, 16. 17. H8 II, 1, 167. Cymb. I, 6, 8. *what is your w.? =* what do you want, what is your pleasure? Gent. IV, 2, 92. Wiv. II, 2, 164. III, 4, 58. Meas. II, 2, 26. II, 3, 2. III, 1, 153. 178. Mids. IV, 1, 23. Tit. V, 2, 152. Tim. I, 2, 123 etc. *your w.?* Tw. I, 5, 180. Ant. I, 2, 7. III, 13, 46. 92. *what's your w. with me?* Gent. III, 1, 3. Shr. Ind. 2, 105. H4A II, 4, 555. Tim. II, 2, 15.

In other cases also = pleasure: *on my frailties why are frailer spies, which in their —s count bad what I think good?* Sonn. 121, 8. *to commend their service to his w.* Gent. I, 3, 42. *make their —s their law,* V, 4, 14. *is she wedded or no? To her w., sir, or so,* LLL II, 212. *wit, an't be thy w., put me into good fooling,* Tw. I, 5, 35. *I danced attendance on his w.* H6B I, 3, 174. *direct me, if it be your w., where great Aufidius lives*, Cor. IV, 4, 7. *he stays upon your w.* Ant. I, 2, 119. *at w.* = at pleasure: *a very trick for them to play at w.* Wint. II, 1, 52. Cor. I, 6, 39. Oth. II, 1, 150. *at one's w.* Caes. II, 1, 17. Hml. I, 2, 63. Cymb. IV, 3, 13.

e) carnal desire: *the sundry dangers of his —'s obtaining*, Lucr. 128. 129. *my w. is strong, past reason's weak removing*, 243. *hot-burning w.* 247. *the locks between her chamber and his w.* 302. *in his w. his wilful eye he tired*, 417. *where thou with patience must my w. abide*, 486. 487. 495. 614. *his taste delicious, in digestion souring, devours his w.* 700. *he hath studied her w. and translated her w.* Wiv. I, 3, 54. *yielding up thy body to my w.* Meas. II, 4, 164. *never could maintain his part but in the force of his w.* Ado I, 1, 239 (in the heat of lust, when he put up with what was offered). All's IV, 3, 19. H5 V, 2, 356. Rom. II, 3, 28. Hml. I, 5, 46. III, 4, 88. Lr. IV, 6, 278. Oth. III, 3, 236. Ant. III, 13, 3. Cymb. I, 6, 47. cf., above all, the various plays on the word in Sonn. 134. 135. 136.

f) a testament: Lucr. 1198. Pilgr. 138. Wiv. III, 4, 60. Merch. I, 2, 27. 101. 118. As I, 1, 2. 71. Tw. I, 5, 265. John I, 109. II, 192. R2 III, 2, 148. Troil. V, 10, 53. Rom. I, 1, 208. Tim. V, 1, 30. Caes. III, 2, 134. 140. 143. 148. 158. 160. 161. 163. 243. 244. IV, 1, 8. Ant. III, 4, 4. Per. I, 1, 47.

**Will**, diminutive of *William*: Sonn. 135. 136. 143, 13. H4B III, 2, 23. H6B II, 3, 75.

**Will**, vb. I. regular verb; impf. and partic. pass. *willed*, partic. pres. *willing*; 1) to wish, to desire, to be for: *paying what ransom the insulter —eth*, Ven. 550. *much —ing to be counted wise*, LLL II, 18. *whose will still —s it should none spare*, 50. *as w. the rest, so —eth Winchester*, H6A III, 1, 162. *what —s Lord Talbot pleaseth Burgundy*, III, 2, 130. *not —ing any longer conference*, H6C II, 2, 171. *the mother —s it so*, Tit. IV, 2, 82. Rom. III, 5, 24. *the gentleman —ing*, Hml. V, 2, 183. *wishes fall out as they're —ed*, Per. V, 2, 16.

*Willing*, adjectively, = a) desirous, pleased, inclined; and hence = forward, ready, prompt (cf. above: LLL II, 18. H6C II, 2, 171. Hml. V, 2, 183): *with a heart as —ing as bondage e'er of freedom*, Tp. III, 1, 88 (cf. *Of*). *I was as —ing to grapple*, LLL II, 218. *but one dead that is —ing to be so*, As I, 2, 201. *you will not extort from me what I am —ing to keep in*, Tw. II, 1, 14. *she is very —ing to bid you farewell*, II, 3, 108. *he shall conceal it whiles you are —ing it shall come to note*, IV, 3, 29 (= till you desire). *could be —ing to march on to Calais without impeachment*, H5 III, 6, 150. *if they be still and —ing, I'll undertake may see away their shilling*, H5 Prol. 11. *—ing to leave their burthen*, IV, 2, 3. *they that most are —ing*, Cor. I, 6, 67. *I trouble thee too much, but thou art —ing*, Caes. IV, 3, 259. *most —ing spirits*, Cymb. IV, 2, 338. cf. Lucr. 1237. Sonn. 6, 6 (*the —ing loan*, i. e. readily and gladly given). Wiv. I, 4, 10. Meas. V, 542. As V, 4, 11. Shr. IV, 4, 34. Tw. III, 3, 11. R2 IV, 108. 190. R3 V, 3, 264. H8 III, 1, 49 (*the —est sin*, i. e. committed with the greatest eagerness). The adj., where the adv. would have been expected: *what you will have, I'll give, and —ing too*, R2 III, 3, 206 (with pleasure, gladly). *I'll send them all as —ing as I live*, H6B V, 1, 51. *most —ing, madam*, H8 IV, 2, 130. *the swallow follows not summer more —ing*, Tim. III, 6, 32.

b) pleased, contented, gratified: *he strays with —ing sport to the wild ocean*, Gent. II, 7, 32. *all pride*

*is —ing pride*, LLL II, 36. *—ing misery outlives incertain pomp, is crowned before*, Tim. IV, 3, 242.

c) complying, consenting, voluntary: *like a —ing patient, I will drink potions of eisel*, Sonn. 111, 9. *not without the prince be —ing*, Ado III, 3, 86. *what —ing ransom he will give*, H5 III, 5, 63. *a —ing bondman*, Caes. I, 3, 113. *we have —ing dames enough*, Mcb. IV, 3, 73.

2) to dispose, to determine: *what so poor a man as Hamlet is may do, ... God —ing, shall not lack*, Hml. I, 5, 186.

3) to order, to bid: *he —ed me in heedfullest reservation to bestow them*, All's I, 3, 230 (= he ordered by testament? cf. the following passage). *at Worcester must his body be interred, for so he —ed it*, John V, 7, 100. *God's mother —ed me to leave my base vocation*, H6A I, 2, 80. *we do no otherwise than we are —ed*, I, 3, 10. *who —ed you?* 11. *would they speak with me? They —ed me say so*, H8 III, 1, 18.

4) to invite, to summon: *he —s you ... that you divest yourself*, H5 II, 4, 77. *—ing you overlook this pedigree*, 90. *he craves a parley, ... —ing you to demand your hostages*, Tit. V, 1, 160.

5) to require: *it shall be to him then, as our good —s, a sure destruction*, Cor. II, 1, 258. *what custom —s, in all things should we do't*, II, 3, 125.

II. irregular verb; 2d pers. pres. *wilt*, 3d pers. *will*; impf. *would*. Often contracted to one syllable with the preceding pronoun: *I'll* (O. Edd. usually *Ile*), *thou'lt* (O. Edd. sometimes *thou't*), *he'll, she'll, we'll, you'll, they'll; I'ld, he'ld, she'ld, you'ld. Wilt thou* or *wouldst thou* contracted to *wo't* or *woo't*: H4B II, 1, 63. Hml. V, 1, 298. Ant. IV, 2, 7. IV, 15, 59. *would* for *wouldst*: Wiv. II, 2, 31. H5 V, 2, 174. Tit. III, 1, 210 (Ff *wilt*). *thou't* for *thou wouldst* Cor. I, 9, 2.

1) to have a mind, to desire; followed by an infinitive expressed or understood: *one for interest, if thou wilt have twain*, Ven. 210. *feed where thou wilt*, 232. *I know not love, nor will not know it*, 409. *'tis much to borrow, and I will not owe it*, 411. *he will not manage her*, 598. *if thou needs wilt hunt*, 673. *he needs will be absolute Milan*, Tp. I, 2, 108. *I am your wife, if you will marry me*, III, 1, 83. 86. Gent. I, 1, 11. II, 7, 63. As II, 5, 20. All's II, 1, 73. R3 I, 4, 95 etc. etc. cf. *woo't* above. Impf. *would* as indicative (= volui): *the lion walked along behind some hedge, because he would not fear him*, Ven. 1094. *not to be tempted, would she be immured*, Compl. 251. *for one thing she did they would not take her life*, Tp. I, 2, 267. *you may thank yourself ... that would not bless our Europe with your daughter*, II, 1, 124. *I fear my Julia would not deign my lines, receiving them from such a worthless post*, Gent. I, 1, 160. *what a fool is she, that knows I am a maid and would not force the letter to my view*, I, 2, 54. *he would not, but by gift of my chaste body ..., release my brother*, Meas. V, 97. *why I ... would not rather make rash remonstrance of my hidden power*, 396. *she that would be your wife now ran from you*, Err. IV, 4, 152. *heaven would that she these gifts should have*, As III, 2, 161 etc. *I will rather* and *I would rather* see sub *Rather* 4.

*Would* as subjunctive (vellem); expressing a present wish in a conditional form: *backward she pushed him, as she would be thrust*, Ven. 41. *now she weeps, and now she fain would speak*, 221. *she would, he will not in her arms be bound*, 226. *for one sweet look thy help I would assure thee,* 371. *he hath won what he would lose again,* Lucr. 688. *and now she would the caged cloister fly,* Compl. 249. *nov would I give a thousand furlongs of sea for an acre of barren ground,* Tp. I, 1, 69. *I would fain die a dry death,* 72. *I would have sunk the sea within the earth or ere ...,* I, 2, 10. *he would be king on't,* II, 1, 156. *a foul bombard that would shed his liquor,* II, 2, 22. *I would not for the world,* V, 173. *you'ld be king o'the isle,* 287. *I rather would entreat thy company,* Gent. I, 1, 5. *love still and thrive therein, even as I would when I to love begin,* 10. *which they would have the profferer construe 'Ay',* I, 2, 56. *when willingly I would have had her here,* 61. *to plead for that which I would not obtain,* IV, 4, 105. *I would have been a breakfast to the beast rather than ...,* V, 4, 34. *from which we would not have you warp,* Meas. I, 1, 15. *which princes, would they, may not disannul,* Err. I, 1, 145. *I would see his own person,* LLL I, 1, 185 etc. Followed by an infinitive of the perfect, to express an intention not carried into execution: *it cannot be that so much guile, she would have said, can lurk in such a look,* Lucr. 1535 (= she was going to say). *their antique pen would have expressed even such a beauty as you master now,* Sonn. 106, 7 (= meant or intended to express). *who ... would here have killed your king,* Tp. V, 78. *you would all this time have proved there is no time for all things,* Err. II, 2, 101. *they would have stolen away,* Mids. IV, 1, 161 etc. With the infinitive of the present, on the other hand, often quite == will (in the sense of wish): *your father would speak with you,* Gent. II, 4, 116. *when would you use it?* III, 1, 123. *there's some great matter she'ld employ me in,* IV, 3, 3. *would you speak with me?* Wiv. II, 2, 161. *we would, and we would not,* Meas. IV, 4, 37. *if you would know your wronger, look on me,* Ado V, 1, 271. *to wed Demetrius, as he would,* Mids. I, 1, 88. *what wouldst thou have with me?* H4A II, 3, 98. *if thou would have such a one, take me,* H5 V, 2, 174. *would thou kneel with me?* Tit. III, 1, 210 (Ff *wilt*). *he would be crowned,* Caes. II, 1, 12 etc.

*Will* and *would* governing an accusative: *that I will,* Tp. V, 294. *what I will, I will,* Gent. I, 3, 65. *I will none of them,* II, 1, 133. *I'll no pullet-sperm in my brewage,* Wiv. III, 5, 32. *we'll none of that,* Mids. V, 46. *will you any wife?* Shr. I, 1, 56. *will you any thing with it?* All's I, 1, 177. *you will my noble grapes,* II, 1, 74. *I'll no more drumming,* IV, 3, 331. *what greeting will you to my Lord Lafeu?* 352. *she'll none of me,* Tw. I, 3, 113. 115. *I'll no more of you,* I, 5, 45. *I'll no more with thee,* III, 1, 48. *you'll nothing to my lord by me?* 148. *I'll no gainsaying,* Wint. I, 2, 19. *what your highness will,* John IV, 2, 39. *I'll no swaggerers,* H4B II, 4, 81. *I will none of you,* III, 2, 271. *she will none,* Rom. III, 5, 140. *I will no reconcilement,* Hml. V, 2, 258. *we'll no defence,* Cymb. III, 4, 81 etc. Likewise *would,* but only in the sense of vellem (I should wish, I wish): *what would my potent master?* Tp. IV, 34. Gent. I, 2, 66. *what would you with her, if that I be she?* IV, 4, 115 (what's your business with her?). *what would thou more of man?* Wiv. II, 2, 31 (most M. Edd. *wouldst*). *what would you with her?* IV, 5, 30. III, 4, 63. Ado III, 5, 1. *what wouldst?* LLL I, 1, 183. *nothing becomes him ill that he would well,* II, 46. *what would these strangers?* V, 2, 174. 178. 180. *is he yet possessed how much ye would?* Merch. I, 3, 66. *wouldst thou aught with me?* II, 2, 128. 150. II, 9, 85. As III, 2, 316. Tw.

IV, 1, 44. John I, 1. IV, 2, 38. H4B IV, 4, 18. H5 IV, 1, 32 *(I would no other company).* V, 2, 68 *(if you would the peace).* H6A IV, 2, 5 *(and thus he would: open your city gates).* H6B I, 3, 11. II, 3, 21 *(sorrow would solace and mine age would ease).* Troil. III, 3, 17 *(what wouldst thou of us?).* 57. Hml. III, 4, 104. IV, 4, 5. Lr. I, 4, 12. Oth. I, 3, 248. IV, 1, 261. Cymb. III, 1, 1. V, 5, 108. Per. I, 3, 6 etc.

*I would* optatively, followed by a subjunctive: *I would the lightning had burnt up those logs,* Tp. III, 1, 16. *I would I knew his mind,* Gent. I, 2, 33. 50. 67. IV, 2, 64. As I, 2, 243 etc. *I would, not so,* Tp. III, 1, 61 (= I were not a king). *I would to heaven I had your potency,* Meas. II, 2, 67. John III, 4, 48. IV, 1, 23. *I would to God my heart were flint,* R3 I, 3, 140. II, 1, 74. IV, 1, 59 (Ff *O would*) etc. *I* omitted: *would thou wert as I am,* Ven. 369. *O would thou hadst not,* 428. Tp. I, 2, 349. II, 1, 107. Gent. I, 2, 104. Meas. III, 2, 189. IV, 4, 35. V, 190. Err. IV, 4, 69 *(where would you had remained).* LLL IV, 3, 123. Mids. II, 1, 59. Merch. III, 1, 93. IV, 1, 296. V, 144. All's I, 2, 52. H6B II, 1, 38. H6C I, 1, 216. R3 I, 2, 151 etc.

*Might* in the optative clause: *would I might triumph so,* Pilgr. 236. *would thou mightst lie drowning,* Tp. I, 1, 60. I, 2, 168. Gent. IV, 4, 176. Wiv. I, 1, 156. IV, 5, 95. R2 V, 3, 4. Troil. I, 1, 117 *(if 'would I might' were 'may').* Rom. III, 5, 87.

*Would* in the optative clause: *I would my valiant master would destroy thee,* Tp. III, 2, 53. *I would my husband would meet him,* Wiv. IV, 2, 86. *would that alone he would detain,* Err. II, 1, 107. *would he would change,* Mids. V, 255. *I would it would make you invisible,* Tw. III, 1, 34. *would half my wealth would buy this for a lie,* Cor. IV, 6, 160. Similarly: *I wish mine eyes would ... shut up my thoughts,* Tp. II, 1, 192. *I could wish he would modestly examine himself,* Ado II, 3, 215. *entreats thou wouldst vouchsafe to visit her poor castle,* H6A II, 2, 40. *the king's request that I would visit you,* H8 IV, 2, 116. *my next petition is that his noble grace would have some pity ...,* 139. *wish that warmer days would come,* Cymb. II, 4, 6. Hence the wish itself expressed by *would: O that our fathers would applaud our loves!* Gent. I, 3, 48. *O that your frowns would teach my smiles such skill!* Mids. I, 1, 195. *now my soul's palace is become a prison: ah, would she break from hence!* H6C II, 1, 75. *O that my death would stay these ruthful deeds!* II, 5, 95. *would the nobility lay aside their ruth!* Cor. I, 1, 201.

2) to claim, to pretend: *then reason will our hearts should be as good,* H4B IV, 1, 157. *this is a riddling merchant for the nonce: he will be here, and yet he is not here,* H6A II, 3, 58 (he pretends to be here; German: *er will hier sein). art thou king and wilt be forced?* H6C I, 1, 230 (pretendest, pleadest as an excuse, to have been forced). *her mood will needs be pitied,* Hml. IV, 5, 3 (claims pity). *that would be scanned,* III, 3, 75.

3) Denoting not so much a wish or purpose as mere readiness or likelihood: *wink again, and I will wink,* Ven. 122. *I will enchant thine ear,* 145. *she, by her good will, will never rise, so he will kiss her still,* 480. *if you will say so, you shall have a kiss,* 536. *whose vulture thought doth pitch the price so high that she will draw his lips' rich treasure dry,* 552. *you will fall again into your idle theme,* 769. *my heart ... will not let a false sound enter,* 780. *if thou wilt deign this favour, ... a thousand secrets shalt thou know,* 15. *if thou wilt*

*chide, thy lips shall never open,* 48. *he hath neither Latin, French, nor Italian, and you will come into the court and swear that I have a poor pennyworth in the English,* Merch. I, 2, 75 etc. etc. Often almost periphrastical: *gazing upon a late-embarked friend, till the wild waves will have him seen no more,* Ven. 819. *abhorred slave, which any print of goodness wilt not take,* Tp. I, 2, 352. *I'll warrant him for drowning,* I, 1, 49. *will you grant with me that Ferdinand is drowned?* II, 1, 243. *they'll nor pinch nor ...,* *unless he bid 'em,* II, 2, 4. *if it will please you to show us so much gentry,* Hml. II, 2, 21. *when we were boys, who would believe that there were ...,* Tp. III, 3, 44 (which in the present would be: *I'll believe*). *as much love in rhyme as would be crammed up in a sheet of paper,* LLL V, 2, 7. cf. the following passages: *who was so firm that this coil would not infect his reason?* Tp. I, 2, 208. *he wondered that your lordship would suffer him to spend his youth at home,* Gent. I, 3, 5. *and would you take the letter of her?* All's III, 4, 1.

*It will not be* = all is in vain, it is to no effect: *but all in vain; good queen, it will not be,* Ven. 607. *I pray you, leave me. Ho! now you strike like the blind man: 'twas the boy that stole your meat, and you'll beat the post. If it will not be, I'll leave you,* Ado II, 1, 208 (if you will not leave me at my request). *it will not be: retire into your trenches,* H6A I, 5, 33. *will it not be?* an expression of impatience: *will't not be? will not a calf's-skin stop that mouth of thine?* John III, 1, 298. *madam, madam! ay, let the county take you in your bed; he'll fright you up, i'faith; will it not be? what, dressed!* Rom. IV, 5, 11.

*We will* = let us: *some dark deep desert ... will we find out,* Lucr. 1146. *we'll visit Caliban,* Tp. I, 2, 308. *we will inherit here,* II, 2, 179. *the next advantage will we take throughly,* III, 3, 14. *now will we break with him,* Gent. I, 3, 44. *why, then, we'll make exchange,* II, 2, 6. *we'll hear him. Ay, by my beard, will we,* IV, 1, 9. 10. Wiv. III, 3, 209. IV, 2, 96. Meas. IV, 5, 12. Err. V, 128. 422. Ado I, 1, 161. V, 3, 31. LLL V, 1, 85. V, 2, 127. Mids. II, 2, 37. III, 1, 5. V, 407. Merch. IV, 1, 456. V, 55. Shr. II, 112. V, 2, 69 *(shall win the wager which we will propose).* H4B I, 1, 186. H6A I, 2, 18. III, 2, 12. H6B II, 1, 200. V, 1, 55. H6C III, 1, 1. IV, 6, 97. R3 IV, 1, 11. Hml. I, 5, 156. Ant. III, 2, 38 etc.

As denoting what may be expected, sometimes equivalent to may: *I am resolved on two points. That if one break, the other will hold,* Tw. I, 5, 26. *in fierce tempest is he coming, that, if requiring fail, he will compel,* H5 II, 4, 101. *hath begg'd that I will stay at home to-day,* Caes. II, 2, 82. And in the following phrases: *in my heart he there what hidden woman's fear there will,* As I, 3, 121. *come what will,* H4A I, 2, 162. *be what thou wilt,* H6A V, 3, 45. H8 II, 1, 65. V, 3, 47. *speed how it will,* Cor. V, 1, 61. *come Pentecost as quickly as it will,* Rom. I, 5, 38. *let shame say what it will,* Hml. IV, 7, 189. *what will hap more to-night,* Lr. III, 6, 121.

The idea of probability passing into that of use and custom: *rain added to a river that is rank will force it overflow his bank,* Ven. 72. *love is a spirit all compact of fire ... and will aspire,* 150. 153. *men will kiss even by their own direction,* 216. *being ireful, on the lion he will venture,* 628. *when they will not give a doit to relieve a lame beggar, they will lay out ten*

*to see a dead Indian,* Tp. II, 2, 33. *sometimes a thousand twangling instruments will hum about mine ears,* III, 2, 147. *which ... each putter-out ... will bring us good warrant of,* III, 3, 48. *she will often praise her liquor,* Gent. III, 1, 350. *the man doth fear God, howsoever it seems not in him by some large jests he will make,* Ado II, 3, 206. *if a man will make courtesy and say nothing, he is virtuous,* H4B II, 1, 135. *grow like savages, as soldiers will that nothing do but meditate on blood,* H5 V, 2, 59. Gent. II, 1, 11. III, 1, 393. Meas. I, 2, 190. Ado II, 3, 115. As IV, 3, 159. Shr. II, 250. Tw. I, 2, 33. H6B III, 1, 14. R3 III, 1, 126 etc. *the tiger would be tame and gently hear him,* Ven. 1096. *some would sing, some other ... would bring him mulberries,* 1102. 1087—1092. *when virtue bragged, beauty would blush for shame,* Lucr. 54. Tp. I, 2, 198. 200. 333. 356. II, 2, 53. III, 2, 150. Meas. III, 2, 136. Err. II, 2, 115. Ado III, 1, 61. Mids. II, 1, 132. As III, 2, 435. All's I, 2, 52. Wint. IV, 4, 58. H8 IV, 1, 78. Tim. II, 2, 143. Hml. I, 2, 143. II, 2, 381. Oth. I, 3, 146. Ant. I, 5, 33 etc.

4) Used, in the first as well as in the second and third persons, to form the future tense: *there shall not be one minute in an hour wherein I will not kiss my sweet love's flower,* Ven. 1188. *if you can command these elements to silence, we will not hand a rope more,* Tp. I, 1, 25. *his daughter and I will be king and queen,* III, 2, 115. *I will thrive,* Wiv. I, 3, 21. *we will thrive, lads, we will thrive,* 81. *perchance I will be there as soon as you,* Err. IV, 1, 39. *an bad thinking do not wrest true speaking, I'll offend no body,* Ado III, 4, 34. *perhaps I will return immediately,* Merch. II, 5, 52. *to-morrow will we be married,* As V, 3, 2. *I will sooner have a beard grow in the palm of my hand than he shall get one on his cheek,* H4B I, 2, 23. *there's not a piece of feather in our host; good argument, I hope, we will not fly,* H5 IV, 3, 113. *there is no hope that ever I will stay, if the first hour I shrink,* H6A IV, 5, 30. *I'll do well yet,* Cor. IV, 1, 21. *I will gain nothing but my shame and the odd hits,* Hml. V, 2, 184. *perchance I will ne'er go home,* Oth. V, 2, 197. *we will yet do well,* Ant. III, 13, 188. *courtesies which I will be ever to pay,* Cymb. I, 4, 39. Instances of the 2nd and 3rd persons: Ven. 23. 424. 761. 945. 1082. Tp. I, 2, 184. II, 1, 289. II, 2, 83. III, 2, 31. Gent. I, 1, 37. Tit. IV, 1, 117 etc. etc. *you will,* imperatively: *you'll leave your noise anon,* H8 V, 4, 1.

*Would* forming the conditional tense in all the three persons: *if I did think I were well awake, I'ld strive to tell you,* Tp. V, 230. *I would resort to her by night,* Gent. III, 1, 110. *I would be loath to turn them together,* Wiv. II, 1, 192. *I would turn her loose to him,* 189. *who I would be sorry should be thus foolishly lost,* Meas. I, 2, 195. *I would be glad to receive some instruction,* IV, 2, 18. *I would have thought,* Ado II, 3, 119. *I would be sorry,* Tw. III, 1, 44. *what wouldst thou think of me? I would think thee a most princely hypocrite,* H4B II, 2, 56. 58. *if I would stand against thee, would the reposal of any trust ... in thee make thy words faithed?* Lr. II, 1, 70. cf. Wiv. II, 1, 60. Ado II, 3, 121. Mids. IV, 1, 16. Shr. Ind. 2, 128. Instances of the 2nd and 3rd persons in every page. NB. *would* seem to have us make denial, All's I, 2, 8. *as one would say,* Merch. II, 2, 134 (= as who should say, cf. *Shall*). *as who would say,* Tit. IV, 4, 20.

5) *Will* and *would*, in all their significations, joined

with adverbs and prepositional expressions, to express motion or change of place, when modern usage would require *will go, would go* or the like: *her object will away,* Ven. 255. *now I will away,* 807. *now she will no further,* 905. *I'll to my book,* Tp. III, 1, 94. *that ... will never out of my bones,* V, 283. *I'll to the alehouse,* Gent. II, 5, 8. *I'll after,* III, 1, 394. V, 2, 51. *I'll never to sea again,* Wiv. II, 1, 96. *will on,* II, 2, 176. *I will about it,* 327. *I will to my honest knight,* III, 2, 88. *I'll in,* III, 3, 145. *we'll a birding,* 246. *I'll to him,* IV, 4, 76. 84. Meas. I, 1, 68. I, 2, 196. I, 4, 85. II, 1, 246. II, 4, 177. III, 1, 276. IV, 3, 66. 124. V, 360. Err. I, 2, 104. III, 1, 114. III, 2, 189. V, 109. LLL IV, 2, 173. V, 2, 668. 737. Mids. III, 2, 375. IV, 1, 114. V, 194. 410. Merch. II, 2, 85. IV, 1, 455. IV, 2, 2. As III, 2, 109. III, 3, 106. IV, 1, 163. 168. V, 2, 44. V, 4, 190. All's IV, 3, 91. R2 II, 1, 218. H6A I, 1, 152. 167. I, 3, 84. II, 1, 33. III, 1, 146. IV, 1, 109. V, 3, 167. H6B I, 1, 142. 171. H6C I, 1, 206. II, 5, 136. IV, 3, 3. V, 1, 110. V, 4, 21. R3 I, 1, 107. 147. I, 4, 97. II, 4, 66. III, 1, 138. Cor. II, 3, 157. Rom. III, 2, 141. Mcb. III, 4, 132. 139. 142. IV, 3, 136. Hml. II, 2, 449. Oth. V, 2, 219. Ant. II, 6, 134. IV, 14, 51 etc. *I would to Valentine,* Gent. IV, 3, 22. *we would unto the Holy Land,* H4B III, 1, 108. *he is very sick and would to bed,* H5 II, 1, 87. *there were wit in this head, an 'twould out,* Troil. III, 3, 256. *I'ld with thee,* Cor. IV, 1, 57.

*Will* substantively: *I am at war 'twixt will and will not,* Meas. II, 2, 33.

**Willer,** in *Well-willer,* q. v.

**William,** Christian name of 1) the poet himself: Ven. Ded. 9. Lucr. Ded. 8. 2) W. of Hatfield, second son of Edward III: H6B II, 2, 12. 33. 3) W. of Windsor, seventh son of Edward III: H6B II, 2, 17. 4) W. de la Pole, Earl of Suffolk: H6A II, 4, 80. H6B I, 1, 44. I, 2, 30. 5) Sir W. Glansdale: H6A I, 4, 63. 6) Sir W. Lucy: H6A IV, 4, 10. 12. 7) Sir W. Stanley: H6C IV, 5, 1. R3 IV, 5, 10. 8) W. Lord Hastings: R3 III, 1, 162. 181. III, 4, 28. 9) Sir W. Courtney: R3 IV, 4, 502 (Ff *Edward*). 10) Sir W. Brandon: R3 V, 3, 22. V, 5, 14. 11) Sir W. Blomer: H8 I, 2, 190. 12) the young son of Page: Wiv. IV, 1, 17 etc. 13) the son of Justice Silence: H4B III, 2, 11. 14) Justice Shallow's cook: H4B V, 1, 12. 17. 25. 29. 15) W. Visor: H4B V, 1, 42. 16) a young country fellow in As V, 1, 22. 23. 64.

**Willing,** see *Will* vb. I, 1.

**Willingly,** 1) on purpose: *still thou mistakest, or else commit'st thy knaveries w.* Mids. III, 2, 346 (Qq *wilfully*).

2) with one's own consent, of one's own accord, voluntarily: *more praise ... than niggard truth would w. impart,* Sonn. 72, 8. *but most w. humbles himself to the determination of justice,* Meas. III, 2, 257. IV, 3, 85. John II, 563. H4A V, 3, 61. H8 III, 1, 140.

3) readily, gladly, with pleasure: *how churlishly I chid Lucetta hence, when w. I would have had her here,* Gent. I, 2, 61. *thou knowest how w. I would effect the match,* III, 2, 22. *you embrace your charge too w.* Ado I, 1, 103. *proud of employment, w. I go,* LLL II, 35. Meas. V, 481. As II, 4, 95. Shr. III, 2, 152. Tw. V, 135. Wint. IV, 2, 60. John IV, 2, 45. H4A I, 3, 111. V, 2, 34. H6B I, 3, 216. II, 3, 33. 35. IV, 9, 42. H6C I, 1, 201. I, 2, 41. Cor. II, 2, 66. IV, 6, 144. Tit. IV, 1, 28. V, 1, 142. Rom. I, 1, 161.

Tim. III, 6, 33. Hml. I, 2, 52. II, 2, 220. Ant. III, 2, 58. Cymb. I, 6, 193. IV, 2, 167. Per. IV, 2, 128.

**Willingness,** 1) readiness: *I would expend it with all w.* H6B III, 1, 150. *look to have it yielded with all w.* R3 III, 1, 198 (Ff *kindness*).

2) good will: *w. rids way,* H6C V, 3, 21 (cf. the proverb: *where the will is ready, the feet are light*).

**Willoughby;** Lord *W.,* name in R2 II, 2, 54. II, 3, 10. 57.

**Willow,** the tree Salix: Hml. IV, 7, 167. Emblem of unhappy love: Ado II, 1, 194. 225 *(w. tree).* Merch. V, 10. Tw. I, 5, 287 *(w. cabin).* H6C III, 3, 228 and IV, 1, 100 *(wear the w. garland).* Oth. IV, 3 28. 42. 44. 46. 49. 50 *(a green w. must be my garland).* 56. V, 2, 248.

**Wiltshire;** *Earl of W.* R2 II, 1, 215. 256. II, 2, 136. III, 2, 122. III, 4, 53. H6C I, 1, 14.

**Wimpled,** muffled, veiled, hoodwinked: *this w., whining, purblind, wayward boy* (Cupid) LLL III, 181.

**Win,** (impf. and partic. *won;* in H4A III, 2, 59 Qq impf. *wan,* Ff *won*), 1) to gain by success in competition or contest, to have the better; absol.: *who loses and who —s,* Lr. V, 3, 15. *they laugh that w.* Oth. IV, 1, 126. = to have the better at play: *we shall never w. at that sport,* Merch. III, 2, 219. Rom. III, 2, 12. Mcb. I, 5, 23. Hml. V, 2, 183. 222. 298. Cymb. II, 3, 7. 8. = to be conqueror in war: *I cannot pray that thou mayst w.* John III, 1, 331. 335. H4A V, 1, 8. H4B I, 1, 132. R3 V, 3, 244. Cor. V, 3, 113. Ant. III, 4, 18. With *of: I have seen ... the firm soil w. of the watery main,* Sonn. 64, 7. *he that —s of all,* John II, 569. H8 V, 1, 58. Cymb. I, 1, 121.

With an object: *w. the wager,* Shr. V, 2, 69. 116. 186. *to w. this easy match,* John V, 2, 106. Tit. V, 1, 100. *the field is won,* Shr. IV, 5, 23. *w. the day,* John V, 4, 30. H6A I, 6, 17. H6C II, 1, 136. IV, 4, 15. R3 V, 3, 145. *all's done, all's won,* H4A V, 3, 16. *thus I w. thee,* V, 4, 38 (cf. Ado V, 1, 82). *w. a battle,* H6B V, 3, 30. H6C I, 2, 74. R3 IV, 4, 538. Mcb. I, 1, 5. *a victory,* Cor. V, 3, 186. With *of: he won it of me with false dice,* Ado II, 1, 289. *those proud titles thou hast won of me,* H4A V, 4, 79. H5 II, 1, 98. Ant. II, 3, 36. Cymb. II, 1, 54. *won three fields of Sultan Solyman,* Merch. II, 1, 26.

2) to be successful in any manner: *he may w.* (i. e. choose the right casket) Merch. III, 2, 47. *to cozen him that would unjustly w.* All's IV, 2, 76. *men's flesh preserved so whole do seldom w.* H6B III, 1, 301. *how can man hope to w. by it* (ambition) H8 III, 2, 443. With *upon* = to gain on: *the rabble ... will in time w. upon power,* Cor. I, 1, 224.*

3) to gain, to obtain, to get: *her husband's fame won in the fields,* Lucr. 107. *what w. I, if I gain the thing I seek,* 211. *he hath won what he would lose again,* 688. *thou in losing me shalt w. much glory,* Sonn. 88, 8. *to w. a Paradise,* Pilgr. 42 and LLL IV, 3, 73. *make us lose the good we oft might w.* Meas. I, 4, 78. LLL I, 1, 86. II, 60. III, 153. Merch. III, 2, 244. Shr. II, 344. All's III, 2, 96. 124. V, 3, 336. John I, 174 *(well won is still well shot).* II, 158. H4A III, 1, 113. III, 2, 59. H5 I, 2, 131. III, 1, 11. 28. H6B V, 3, 6. Cor. I, 1, 164. I, 6, 50. II, 1, 231. Mcb. I, 2, 67. IV, 3, 118 *(to w. me into his power).* Ant. II, 4, 9 *(you'll w. two days upon me).* Cymb. III, 4, 112 *(to w. time).* Per. V, 1, 44 *(would w. some words of him)* etc.

= to conquer, to get possession of: *w. me and*

*wear me,* Ado V, 1, 82 (cf. H4A V, 4, 38). *'tis won as towns with fire, so won, so lost,* LLL I, 1, 147. *this —s him, liver and all,* Tw. II, 5, 106. *w. you this city without stroke,* John II, 418. *did w. what he did spend,* R2 II, 1, 180. 181. *you won it, wore it, kept it,* H4B IV, 5, 222. *if that you will France w.* H5 I, 2, 167. *how the English have the suburbs won,* H6A I, 4, 2. *Henry ... should w. all,* III, 1, 198. *myself did w. them both* (Anjou and Maine) H6B I, 1, 119. 210. *they have won the bridge,* IV, 5, 3. *some nation that won you without blows,* Cor. III, 3, 133 etc. With *from: to w. it* (the island) *from me,* Tp. I, 2, 455. *which I will w. from France,* H6B I, 1, 213. Peculiar expressions: *Poictiers and Tours are won away,* H6A IV, 3, 45 (won by the enemy, consequently lost). *till France be won into the Dauphin's hands,* H6B I, 3, 173.

4) to gain in a moral sense; to move and prevail with by persuasion or any kind of influence; absol.: *corruption —s not more than honesty,* H8 III, 2, 445. Transitively: *pray heaven she w. him,* Meas. II, 2, 125. Wint. I, 2, 21. H5 II, 2, 124. H6B III, 1, 28. H6C III, 1, 34. 35. Mcb. I, 3, 125. With *from: she is corrupted, changed, and won from thee,* John III, 1, 55. *—s the king from her,* H6C III, 1, 50. *from his mother w. the Duke of York,* R3 III, 1, 38. *from Antony w. Cleopatra,* Ant. III, 12, 27. With *to: to w. me soon to hell,* Sonn. 144, 5. *whom I with pain have wooed and won thereto,* H6A V, 3, 138. *he will not be won to aught against him,* R3 III, 1, 166. III, 7, 50. 80. Caes. I, 3, 141. Mcb. I, 3, 123. Hml. I, 5, 45. Per. II, 4, 49. 52. With an infinitive, = to prevail on: *cannot your grace w. her to fancy him?* Gent. III, 1, 67. *w. her to consent to you,* Wiv. II, 2, 245. Err. V, 116. All's V, 3, 119. R2 II, 3, 163. Lr. II, 2, 119 etc.

Especially used of success in love: *gentle thou art and therefore to be won,* Sonn. 41, 5. *did w. whom he would maim,* Compl. 312. Tp. I, 2, 451. Gent. I, 1, 141. III, 1, 89. 105. Wiv. II, 2, 71. 248. Ado II, 1, 17. LLL IV, 3, 372. V, 2, 858. Mids. I, 1, 108. Merch. I, 2, 113. II, 1, 19. 31. As IV, 1, 189. Shr. II, 312 *(won me to her love).* All's IV, 2, 64. H6A V, 3, 79. R3 I, 2, 229. Troil. III, 2, 119 etc. cf. Gent. I, 1, 32. 33. LLL III, 8. Mids. I, 1, 17.

**Wince** or **Winch** (the first form preferred by M. Edd., the latter better authorized by O. Edd.; cf. *lance* and *lanch,* and the old lection *wrenching* for *rinsing* in H8 I, 1, 167) to shrink or start from pain: John IV, 1, 81. Hml. III, 2, 253.

**Winchester;** Henry Beaufort Bishop of W.: H6A I, 3, 19. 23. II, 4, 118. III, 1, 64. 107 etc. V, 1, 28. 39. V, 4, 120. H6B I, 1, 56. 139. Gardiner, Bishop of W.: H8 III, 2, 231. IV, 1, 101. 103. V, 3, 58. 73. 123.

*W. goose,* cant term for a certain venereal sore, thought to have originated from the public stews in Southwark being under the jurisdiction of the Bishop of Winchester: H6A I, 3, 53. Troil. V, 10, 55.

**Wincot** (Shr.) or **Woncot** (H4B), usual corruptions of *Wilmecote,* a village near Stratford: Shr. Ind. 2, 23.\*H4B V, 1, 42.

**Wind,** subst. 1) a current of air: Ven. 303. 338. 458. 1046 *(the w. imprisoned in the ground* etc.; cf. H4A III, 1, 30). 1082. 1084. 1089. Lucr. 311. Tp. I, 2, 150. 254. III, 3, 63 *(may as well wound the loud —s).* V, 42. Gent. I, 2, 118. II, 3, 59 *(if the w. were down).* Meas. III, 1, 124 *(to be imprisoned in the view-*

*less —s).* Err. IV, 1, 90 *(the merry w. blows fair from land).* Ado III, 1, 66 *(a vane blown with all —s).* Merch. I, 1, 24 *(a w. too great).* Shr. II, 135 *(little w.).* Tw. I, 5, 255 *('twill endure w. and weather).* V, 399 *(with hey, ho, the w. and the rain;* cf. Lr. III, 2, 75). Wint. II, 3, 154 *(a feather for each w. that blows;* cf. IV, 4, 552). John V, 2, 87 *(weak w.).* H4A III, 1, 30 (cf. Ven. 1046). III, 3, 102 *(is the w. in that door?).* H4B IV, 5, 100 *(weak w.).* V, 3, 89 *(what w. blew you hither?).* R3 IV, 1, 53 *(O ill-dispersing w. of misery).* Tit. IV, 3, 57 *(to shoot against the w.)* Mcb. I, 3, 82 *(melted as breath into the w.).* Hml. II, 2, 495 *(with the whiff and w. of his fell sword).* Oth. III, 3, 262 *(let her down the w.; cf. Whistle)* etc. etc. *the four —s,* Merch. I, 1, 168. *carried with more speed before the w.* Err. I, 1, 110. H6C I, 4, 4. Per. V Prol. 14. *the high w. sings,* Ven. 305. Lucr. 335. H6B II, 1, 3. 55. *sits the w. in that corner?* Ado II, 3, 102. *to know where sits the w.* Merch. I, 1, 18. R2 II, 1, 265. II, 2, 123. H5 II, 2, 12. Hml. I, 3, 56. Lr. I, 4, 112. cf. *my reason sits in the w. against me,* Ant. III, 10, 37. *w. and tide:* Err. IV, 1, 46. H6C III, 3, 48. IV, 3, 59. V, 1, 53. Proverbial expressions: *I hear it sing i'the w.* Tp. II, 2, 20. Wiv. III, 2, 38; cf. Tp. III, 3, 97. *there is something in the w. that we cannot get in,* Err. III, 1, 69. *many can brook the weather that love not the w.* LLL IV, 2, 34 (cf. *Weather).* *ill blows the w. that profits nobody,* H6C II, 5, 55; cf. H4B V, 3, 90.

Emblem of swiftness: Ven. 303. 681. Sonn. 51, 7. LLL V, 2, 261. Mids. III, 2, 94. Of liberty: *as free as mountain —s,* Tp. I, 2, 499. *I must have as large a charter as the w. to blow on whom I please,* As II, 7, 48. *speak frankly as the w.* Troil. I, 3, 253. *he should be as free as is the w.* Cor. I, 9, 89. Of wantonness: *the wanton w.* Mids. II, 1, 129. *the strumpet w.* Merch. II, 6, 16. 19. *the bawdy w. that kisses all it meets,* Oth. IV, 2, 78. Of inconstancy and falseness: Wint. I, 2, 132. Troil. III, 2, 199. Rom. I, 4, 100. Of ubiquity: *her worth, being mounted on the w., through all the world bears Rosalind,* As III, 2, 95. *I have eyes upon him, and his affairs come to me on the w.* Ant. III, 6, 63 (= from every side). *slander ... whose breath rides on the posting winds and doth belie all corners of the world,* Cymb. III, 4, 38. cf. Mcb. I, 7, 25 and H4B Ind. 4.

Considered as bearing scent: *this same coxcomb that we have i'the w.* All's III, 6, 122 (= of whom we have taken the scent). *allow the w.* V, 2, 10 (= do not stand between the wind and me); cf. H4A I, 3, 45. *he knows the game: how true he keeps the w.* H6C III, 2, 14; cf. *why do you go about to recover the w. of me, as if you would drive me into a toil,* Hml. III, 2, 362. *my son and I will have the w. of you: keep there,* Tit. IV, 2, 133 (= we will keep a strict eye upon you, and stand on our guard against you).

2) breath: *blow till thou burst thy w.* Tp. I, 1, 9 (= till thou be out of breath). *if my w. were but long enough to say my prayers,* Wiv. IV, 5, 104. *words are but w.* Err. III, 1, 75. *my w. cooling my broth,* Merch. I, 1, 22. *I shall break my w.* H4A II, 2, 14. *your w. short,* H4B I, 2, 206. *obeying with my w. when I do blow,* H6C III, 1, 86. *fetches her w. so short,* Troil. III, 2, 33. *pursy insolence shall break his w. with fear and horrid flight,* Tim. V, 4, 12. *not to crack the w. of the poor phrase,* Hml. I, 3, 108. cf. Ven. 189.

Hence = a) words, speech: *sorrow ebbs, being blown with w. of words*, Lucr. 1330. *stop in your w.* Err. I, 2, 53. *foul words is but foul w., and foul w. is but foul breath*, Ado V, 2, 52. *for his death no w. of blame shall breathe*, Hml. IV, 7, 67. *then we bring forth weeds, when our quick —s lie still; and our ills told us is as our earing*, Ant. I, 2, 114 (truth frankly told is as wholesome to the hearer as fresh air. Most M. Edd. *quick minds*). cf. H5 III, 3, 30.

b) sighs: *like a stormy day, now w., now rain, sighs dry her cheeks, tears make them wet again*, Ven. 965. *at last it rains* (i. e. he weeps), *and busy —s give o'er* (and ceases to sigh) Lucr. 1790. *storming her world with sorrow's w. and rain*, Compl. 7. *puffing with w. and rain* (sighs and tears) As III, 5, 50. *where are my tears? rain, to lay this w., or my heart will be blown up by the root*, Troil. IV, 4, 56. *the —s thy sighs*, Rom. III, 5, 135. *tears shall drown the w.* Mcb. I, 7, 25 (the word used here in each of its senses). *we cannot call her —s and water sighs and tears*, Ant. I, 2, 153.

c) a flatus emitted from behind, a fart: *a man may break a word with you, sir, and words are but w., ay, and break it in your face, so he break it not behind*, Err. III, 1, 75.

**Wind**, vb. (partic. *winded*) 1) to blow: *that I will have a recheat —ed in my forehead*, Ado I, 1, 243. 2) to nose, to scent: *the dam will wake, and if she w. you once*, Tit. IV, 1, 97.

**Wind**, vb. (impf. and partic. *wound*) 1) trans. a) to turn to this or that direction: *to turn and w. a fiery Pegasus*, H4A IV, 1, 109.

b) to turn round a fixed centre, to twist: *you have wound a goodly clew*, All's I, 3, 188. With *up*, 1) used of ensigns, = to furl or roll together: John V, 2, 73. V, 5, 7. of a watch, = to put in a state of motion by turning the spring round its pin: *he is —ing up the watch of his wit*, Tp. II, 1, 12. Tw. II, 5, 66. metaphorically: *the charm's wound up*, Mcb. I, 3, 37. *the untuned and jarring senses, O, w. up of this child-changed father*, Lr. IV, 7, 16. 2) to bring round, to consummate, to pass: *—ing up days with toil and nights with sleep*, H5 IV, 1, 296.

c) to entwist, to infold, to encircle: *all wound with adders*, Tp. II, 2, 13. *I will w. thee in mine arms*, Mids. IV, 1, 45. *this hand, fast wound about thy hair*, H6C V, I, 54.

2) intr. a) to change one's direction, to turn: *w. away, be gone, I say*, As III, 3, 104. *a creature that I teach to fight, to w., to stop, to run directly on*, Caes. IV, 1, 32.

b) to have flexures or to move in flexures: *a —ing maze*, Lucr. 1151. *thin —ing breath*, 1407. *—ing nooks*, Gent. II, 7, 31. *it* (the river) *shall not w.* H4A III, 1, 104. Metaphorically, = to fetch a compass, to make an indirect advance: *spend but time to w. about my love with circumstance*, Merch. I, 1, 154. *seek him out, w. me into him*, Lr. I, 2, 106 (*me* dat. ethicus). With an accus. denoting an effect: *to w. yourself into a power tyrannical*, Cor. III, 3, 64.

**Wind-changing**, inconstant like the wind: H6C V, 1, 57.

**Windgalls**, a disease of horses consisting in enlargements in the neighbourhood of the fetlock: Shr. III, 2, 53.

**Winding-sheet**, a sheet in which a corpse is wrapped: H6C I, 1, 129. II, 5, 114.

**Wind-instrument**, an instrument of music played by the breath: Oth. III, 1, 6. 10.

**Windlasses**, indirect advances, shifts: *with w. and with assays of bias*, Hml. II, 1, 65.

**Windmill**, a mill set in motion by the wind: H4A III, 1, 162. H4B III, 2, 207.

**Wind-obeying**, obeying the wind: *the always w. deep*, Err. I, 1, 64.

**Window**, an opening in a building for the admission of light and air, or rather the frame covering it (cf. *Bay-window, Chamber-w., Church-w.*): Lucr. 1089. Sonn. 24, 8. Gent. II, 4, 181. IV, 2, 16. Ado II, 2, 18. III, 3, 144. Mids. III, 1, 58. All's II, 3, 224 (*w. of lattice*). IV, 1, 60. R2 III, 1, 24. V, 2, 5 (*from —s' tops*). 12. H4B II, 2, 87. H6A III, 1, 84. Troil. I, 2, 120 (*compassed w.*). Cor. II, 1, 226. Rom. I, 1, 126 (*the golden w. of the east*). 145. II, 2, 2. III, 5, 41. Caes. I, 1, 44. II, 1, 36. III, 2, 264. Cymb. II, 2, 25. V, 4, 81. Per. IV, 6, 117. *enter at her w.* Gent. III, 1, 113. Mids. I, 1, 30. Hml. IV, 5, 50. *in at the w.* John I, 171 (a proverbial expression applied to illegitimate children). *in at his —s*, Caes. I, 2, 320. *talk with a man out at a w.* Ado IV, 1, 85. 311. *look out at w.* Merch. II, 5, 41 (Q1 *at a w.*). *looking out at the w.* Shr. V, 1, 32. 57. *it would not out at —s nor at doors*, John V, 7, 29.

Metaphorically applied to wounds: *these —s that let forth thy life*, R3 I, 2, 12 (not the usual and natural passage; cf. John I, 171 and V, 7, 29).*to eyes: *thou through —s of thine age shalt see ... thy golden time*, Sonn. 3, 11. *the w. of my heart, mine eye*, LLL V, 2, 848. cf. Sonn. 24, 8. to eyelids: *her two blue —s faintly she upheaveth*, Ven. 482 (cf. *Blue*). *ere I let fall the —s of mine eyes*, R3 V, 3, 116. *thy eyes' —s fall*, Rom. IV, 1, 100. *downy —s, close*, Ant. V, 2, 319. *the enclosed lights, now canopied under these —s*, Cymb. II, 2, 22.

**Window-bars** (O. Edd. *window barn*) a sort of embroidery in the form of lattice-work, worn by women across the naked bosom: *those milkpaps that through the w. bore at men's eyes*, Tim. IV, 3, 116.

**Windowed**, 1) placed in a window: *wouldst thou be w. in great Rome and see thy master thus with pleached arms?* Ant. IV, 14, 72.

2) full of openings or holes: *your looped and w. raggedness*, Lr. III, 4, 31.

**Wind-pipe**, the passage for breath, the trachea: H5 III, 6, 45. Tim. I, 2, 52.

**Windring**, unintelligible lection of O. Edd. in Tp. IV, 128: *w. brooks*; some M. Edd. *winding*, others *wandering*.

**Wind-shaked**, driven and agitated by the wind: *the w. surge*, Oth. II, 1, 13.

**Wind-shaken**, trembling and tottering in the wind: *the rock, the oak not to be w.* Cor. V, 2, 117.

**Windsor**, place in England: Wiv. I, 4, 136. II, 1, 66. II, 2, 63. 103. 122. 126. III, 1, 6 (*old W. way*). III, 3, 114. 121. 232 (*W. Castle*). IV, 4, 29 (*W. forest*). 64. V, 5, 1 (*W. bell*). 14 (*a W. stag*). 47. 60 (*W. Castle*). 110 (*W. wives*). 174. 223. H4A I, 1, 104. H4B II, 1, 98. IV, 4, 14. 50. Henry VI *born at W.*, H6A III, 1, 199. *William of W.*, the seventh and last son of Edward III: H6B II, 2, 17.

**Wind-swift**, swift as the wind: Rom. II, 5, 8.

**Windy**, 1) next the wind: *it keeps on the w. side of care*, Ado II, 1, 327 (so that care cannot scent and find it).*still you keep o'the w. side o'the law*, Tw. III, 4, 181.

2) Applied, metaphorically, to words and sighs as resembling the wind (cf. *Wind*): *with her w. sighs ... to fan and blow them dry again she seeks,* Ven. 51. *this w. tempest* (inarticulate sounds), *till it blow up rain* (i. e. tears), *held back his sorrow's tide,* Lucr. 1788. *give not a w. night a rainy morrow,* Sonn. 90, 7 (a night spent in sighs). *zeal, now melted by the w. breath of soft petitions,* John II, 477. *what showers arise, blown with the w. tempest of my heart, upon thy wounds,* H6C II, 5, 86. *w. attorneys to their client woes,* R3 IV, 4, 127 (= airy words). *w. suspiration of forced breath,* Hml. I, 2, 79.

**Wine,** the fermented juice of the grape: Tp. II, 1, 146. 153. II, 2, 78. 96. 138. IV, 252. V, 278. Wiv. I, 1, 195. II, 2, 70. V, 5, 167. Err. V, 215. Ado III, 5, 57. Merch. I, 1, 81. I, 2, 104 *(rhenish w.).* III, 1, 44 *(red w. and rhenish).* As III, 2, 211. III, 5, 73 *(falser than vows made in w.).* Epil. 4 *(good w. needs no bush).* Shr. III, 2, 172. All's II, 3, 106. Tw. II, 3, 14. 129 etc. Metaphorically: *the w. of life is drawn, and the mere lees is left this vault to brag of,* Mcb. II, 3, 100.

**Wing,** subst. 1) the limb by which an animal or imaginary being flies: Ven. 57. 306. Lucr. 507. 949. 1009. Tp. IV, 78. Gent. II, 6, 42. Ado II, 1, 155. Mids. I, 1, 237. II, 2, 4. III, 1, 175. III, 2, 365. Merch. I, 1, 14 *(woven —s,* = sails). Wint. IV, 1, 4. H4A V, 1, 64. H5 III Chor. 1. IV, 1, 177. H6A I, 1, 11. 75. H6B II, 4, 54. IV, 1, 5. H6C I, 1, 47. II, 2, 29. V, 6, 14. 20. 23. R3 IV, 4, 13. V, 2, 23. Troil. III, 2, 15. III, 3, 79. IV, 2, 14. V, 8, 17. Cor. V, 4, 14. Tit. III, 2, 61. IV, 4, 85. Rom. I, 4, 17. 60. II, 2, 5, 8. III, 2, 18. Tim. II, 1, 30. Mcb. IV, 1, 17. Ant. V, 2, 157. Cymb. III, 2, 50. III, 5, 161. V, 4, 118. V, 5, 471 *(on w.).* Used to protect the young: H6A V, 3, 57. H6B I, 3, 41. cf. H8 V, 1, 163 and Hml. III, 4, 103.

Metaphorical use: *on the w. of all occasions,* Wiv. II, 2, 209. *the tailor that made the —s she flew withal,* Merch. III, 1, 30. *health with youthful —s is flown,* H4B IV, 5, 229. *when I had seen this hot love on the w.* Hml. II, 2, 132.

Emblem of swiftness: Gent. II, 7, 11. LLL V, 2, 260. All's I, 1, 218. II, 1, 96. III, 2, 76. H5 I, 2, 307. H6C II, 3, 12. H8 I, 4, 9. Troil. II, 2, 44. Mcb. I, 4, 17. Hml. I, 5, 29.

Emblem of any thing that carries the mind upwards or along: *borne by the trustless —s of false desire,* Lucr. 2. *added feathers to the learned's w.* Sonn. 78, 7. *with what —s shall his affections fly,* H4B IV, 4, 65. *knowledge the w. wherewith we fly to heaven,* H6B IV, 7, 79. R2 II, 1, 292. R3 IV, 3, 54. V, 3, 106. Troil. II, 2, 133. Rom. II, 2, 66. Caes. I, 1, 77. Ant. III, 12, 4. Cymb. I, 6, 186.◆

Pars pro toto, *w.* = bird: *to whose sound chaste —s obey,* Phoen. 4. *every fowl of tyrant w.* = of a cruel species or nature, 10.

2) flight; the act or manner of flying: *with what w. the staniel checks at it,* Tw. II, 5, 124. *hold a w. quite from the flight of all thy ancestors,* H4A III, 2, 30. *when they stoop, they stoop with the like w.* H5 IV, 1, 112. *the crow makes w. to the rooky wood,* Mcb. III, 2, 51.

3) one of the two side-bodies of an army: All's III, 6, 52. H6A IV, 2, 43. Caes. V, 2, 4. Cymb. V, 3, 5. The first and third significations combined: *shadowing their right under your — s of war,* John II, 14.

**Wing,** vb. 1) intr. to fly: *we, poor unfledged, have*

*never —ed from view o'the nest,* Cymb. III, 3, 28. With an accus. of space: *the crows and choughs that w. the midway air,* Lr. IV, 6, 13 (cf. *never swum the Hellespont,* sub *Swim; to reel the streets at noon,* sub *Reel; walk the whole world,* sub *Walk; he trots the air,* sub *Trot; gallops the Zodiac,* sub *Gallop).*

2) to transport by flying: *will w. me to some withered bough,* Wint. V, 3, 133. Partic. *—ed* = flying: *two Talbots, —ed through the lither sky,* H6A IV, 7, 21. *I saw Jove's bird ... —ed from the spongy south to this part of the west,* Cymb. IV, 2, 348.

**Winged,** 1) furnished with wings: Lucr. 1728. Sonn. 51, 8. Err. II, 1, 18. Mids. I, 1, 235. As IV, 1, 142. H4A IV, 4, 2. H5 II Chor. 7. V Chor. 8. H6B III, 3, 16. H6C I, 1, 267. R3 II, 1, 88. Troil. II, 3, 123. Rom. II, 2, 28. Lr. III, 7, 66. Cymb. III, 5, 61. Per. IV Prol. 47.

2) covered by a side body of troops: *whose puissance on either side shall be well w. with our chiefest horse,* R3 V, 3, 300.

**Wingfield;** *Lord Cromwell of W.,* one of Talbot's baronial titles: H6A IV, 7, 66.

**Wingham,** place in England: *the tanner of W.* H6B IV, 2, 24. A village in Kent. Brandl.

**Wing-led,** lection of F1 in Cymb. II, 4, 24: *their discipline, now w. with their courages;* later Ff and M. Edd. *mingled.*

**Wink,** subst. 1) the act of closing the eye: *whiles you ... to the perpetual w.* (i. e. to death) *for aye might put this ancient morsel,* Tp. II, 1, 285. *to give mine enemy a lasting w.* Wint. I, 2, 317 (cf. *to give a winking,* Hml. II, 2, 137).

2) a significant look: *her —s and nods,* Hml. IV, 5, 11 (cf. *Eye-wink).*

3) no more time than is necessary to shut the eyes; a short moment: *ambition cannot pierce a w. beyond, but doubt discovery there,* Tp. II, 1, 242. *every w. of an eye some new grace will be born,* Wint. V, 2, 119. *I have not slept one w.* Cymb. III, 4, 103.

**Wink,** vb. 1) to shut the eyes or to have them shut as not to see: *when her lips were ready for his pay, he —s and turns his lips another way,* Ven. 90.* *art thou ashamed to kiss? then w. again, and I will w.; so shall the day seem night,* 121. *his eyes begun to w., being blinded with a greater light,* Lucr. 375. *she dares not look, yet, —ing, there appears quickshifting antics,* 458. *moody Pluto —s while Orpheus plays,* 553. *against my heart will fix a sharp knife, to affright mine eye, who, if it w., shall thereon fall and die,* 1139. *when most I w.* (i. e. in sleep) *then do mine eyes best see,* Sonn. 43, 1. 56, 6. Tp. II, 1, 216. Gent. I, 2, 139. V, 2, 14. Wiv. V, 5, 52. Err. III, 2, 58. LLL I, 1, 43. John II, 215 *(your —ing gates,* = shut). R2 IV, 284. H4B I, 3, 33. H5 II, 1, 8. III, 7, 153. V, 2, 327. 332. H6B II, 1, 105. Rom. III, 2, 6. Hml. II, 2, 137 *(if I had given my heart a —ing,* i. e. if I had shut my eyes on purpose to see nothing. Qq *working.* cf. *to give a wink,* Wint. I, 2, 317). Oth. IV, 2, 77. Cymb. II, 3, 25. II, 4, 89. V, 4, 194. 198.

With *at* or *upon* = to seem not to see: *w. at me and say thou sawest me not,* Tim. III, 1, 47. *the eye w. at the hand,* Mcb. I, 4, 52. *upon a homely object love can w.* Gent. II, 4, 98. Hence *to w. at* = to connive at: *if little faults ... shall not be —ed at,* H5 II, 2, 55. *w. at the Duke of Suffolk's insolence,* H6B II, 2, 70. *—ing at your discords,* Rom. V, 3, 294.

2) to shut the eyes involuntarily by way of relieving them, and hence to spend no more time than is necessary to shut them: *now here is three studied ere ye'll thrice w.* LLL I, 2, 54. *grew a twenty years removed thing while one would w.* Tw. V, 93. *I have not —ed since I saw these sights,* Wint. III, 3, 106.

3) to give a significant look: *and on the —ing of authority to understand a law,* John IV, 2, 211. *nor w., nor nod, nor kneel, nor make a sign,* Tit. III, 2, 43. *With at or on: w. each at other,* Mids. III, 2, 240. *you saw my master w. and laugh upon you,* Shr. IV, 4, 76. *I will w. on her to consent,* H5 V, 2, 333.

**Winner,** one who wins: Shr. V, 2, 187. Wint. V, 3, 131. H5 III, 6, 120. H6B III, 1, 184. Hml. IV, 5, 143. Cymb. II, 4, 53. III, 5, 15 (= conqueror).

**Winnow,** 1) to separate, as the chaff from the grain: *distinction, with a broad and powerful fan puffing at all, —s the light away,* Troil. I, 3, 28. *bitter torture shall w. the truth from falsehood,* Cymb. V, 5, 134.

2) to sift, to try: *we shall be —ed with so rough a wind,* H4B IV, 1, 194. H8 V, 1, 111. *such a —ed purity in love,* Troil. III, 2, 174. *through the most fond and —ed opinions,* Hml. V, 2, 201 (probably = truisms. Qq *the most profane and trennowed opinions*).*

**Winter,** the cold season of the year: Lucr. 1255. Sonn. 5, 6. 56, 13. 97, 1. Tp. V, 16. Gent. II, 4, 163. Meas. II, 1, 136. Err. III, 2, 100 *(a Poland w.).* LLL V, 2, 901. Mids. II, 1, 101. 112. Merch. III, 1, 66. As II, 3, 52. II, 5, 8. Shr. IV, 1, 24 (proverb: *w. tames man, woman and beast).* Wint. II, 1, 25. III, 2, 213. IV, 3, 4. IV, 4, 75. 79. 81. R2 V, 1, 40. H4B I, 3, 62. IV, 4, 34 *(as humorous as w.).* 92. H5 III, 3, 55. H6B I, 1, 81. II, 4, 3. H6C V, 2, 15. R3 II, 3, 33. Tit. III, 1, 20. Rom. I, 2, 28. Tim. III, 6, 33. IV, 3, 264. Lr. II, 4, 46. Ant. V, 2, 87. Cymb. IV, 2, 259. IV, 4, 30. Per. IV, 3, 50. Sometimes with the article in a general sense: *you are sure together, as the w. to foul weather,* As V, 4, 142. *the —'s cold,* Caes. I, 2, 99. Lr. II, 4, 69. John V, 7, 36. H5 III, 3, 55. Hml. V, 1, 239. Adjectively: *w. meads,* Lucr. 1218. *w. weather,* Pilgr. 159. *w. time,* Wiv. IV, 4, 30. *w. wind,* As II, 7, 174. *w. cricket,* Shr. IV, 3, 110. *w. showers,* Tim. II, 2, 180. The Anglos. gen. in the same sense: *—'s day,* Sonn. 13, 11. *the —'s wind,* As II, 1, 7. *a —'s night,* H6B III, 2, 335. H6C V, 5, 25. V, 7, 17. *at a —'s fire,* Mcb. III, 4, 65. *the present —'s state,* Cymb. II, 4, 5.

Pars pro toto, = year (as passed in a cheerless manner): *when forty —s shall besiege thy brow,* Sonn. 2, 1. Tp. I, 2, 296. Meas. III, 1, 76. LLL IV, 3, 242. Wint. V, 3, 50. R2 I, 3, 211. 214. 260. IV, 258.

Emblem of old age: *lust's w. comes ere summer half be done,* Ven. 802. *let not —'s ragged hand deface in thee thy summer,* Sonn. 6, 1. Sonn. 13, 11. Err. V, 312. cf. As II, 3, 52 and Wint. IV, 4, 79. *that w. lion, who in rage forgets aged contusions,* H6B V, 3, 2 (= old lion). *I'll take that w. from your lips,* Troil. V, 5, 24 (viz Nestor's kiss). Of death: *till death, that w., kill it,* H8 III, 2, 179. Of any cheerless situation, as misfortune, poverty, destitution: *a nun of —'s sisterhood,* As III, 4, 17 (one devoted to cold and barren chastity). *that w. should cut off our spring-time so,* H6C II, 3, 47. *if we use delay, cold biting w. mars our hoped-for hay,* IV, 8, 61. *the w. of our discontent,* R3 I, 1, 1. *this goodly summer with your w. mixed,* Tit. V, 2, 172. *'tis deepest w. in Lord*

*Timon's purse,* Tim. III, 4, 14. *as poor as w.* Oth. III, 3, 173. *quake in the present —'s state,* Cymb. II, 4, 5. cf. Tim. III, 6, 33. IV, 3, 264. Ant. V, 2, 87.

**Wintered,** pertaining to winter, worn in winter: *w. garments must be lined,* As III, 2, 111 (F3. 4 and M. Edd. *winter garments,* unnecessarily; see Appendix).

**Winter-ground,** vb. to protect from the inclemency of the winter-season, like a plant covered with straw or the like: *and furred moss besides, ... to w. thy corse,* Cymb. IV, 2, 229.

**Winterly,** cheerless, uncomfortable: *if w. (news), thou needest but keep that countenance still,* Cymb. III, 4, 13.

**Wipe,** subst. a note of infamy, a brand: *worse than a slavish w. or birth-hour's blot,* Lucr. 537.

**Wipe,** vb. 1) to make clean by gentle rubbing: *w. thine eyes,* Tp. I, 2, 25. H6C I, 4, 139. R3 IV, 4, 278 (Qq *dry).* Lr. V, 3, 23. Cymb. IV, 2, 402. *to w. my shoes,* Gent. II, 1, 86. *thy lips are scarce —d since thou drunkest last,* H4A II, 4, 170. Cor. IV, 5, 232. *let me w. thy face,* H4B II, 4, 234. Hml. V, 2, 305. *—ing his bloody brow,* Cor. I, 3, 38. *I will w. thy cheeks,* Tit. III, 1, 142. *let me w. it* (my hand) *first,* Lr. IV, 6, 136. *w. his beard,* Oth. III, 3, 439. With a double accus.: *will he w. his tables clean,* H4B IV, 1, 201. With *of:* *—d our eyes of drops,* As II, 7, 122.

2) to take away, to strike off gently: *w. the dim mist from thy doting eyne,* Lucr. 643. 1213. *how may this stain be —d from me,* 1701. LLL IV, 3, 125. As II, 7, 116. H6B IV, 10, 74. Metaphorically: *from my succession w. me, father,* Wint. IV, 4, 491. *—d it from my mind.* H4B I, 1, 211. H5 IV, 1, 139. Mcb. IV, 3, 116. Ant. II, 2, 81. With *away:* Lucr. 608. H6B II, 4, 65. IV, 1, 40. H6C II, 5, 71. Tit. III, 1, 106. V, 3, 148. Hml. I, 5, 99. With *off:* John V, 2, 45. R2 II, 1, 294. H6C I, 3, 52. Troil. II, 2, 149. With *out:* Wint. IV, 2, 11. H6A II, 4, 117. Cor. V, 3, 146. Tim. V, 4, 17.

**Wire,** a thread of metal: *if hairs be —s, black —s grow on her head,* Sonn. 130, 4. *whipped with w.* Ant. II, 5, 65.

**Wiry,** pertaining to wire, or consisting of wire: *the w. concord,* Sonn. 128, 4 *(the w. concord* = the harmony of the strings). *ten thousand w. friends,* (i. e. hairs), John III, 4, 64.

**Wis,** see *I-wis.*

**Wisdom,** 1) science, knowledge: *though the w. of nature can reason it thus and thus,* Lr. I, 2, 113. *what can man's w. in the restoring his bereaved sense?* IV, 4, 8. cf. Merch. IV, 1, 409.

2) the quality of being wise (often opposed to folly); applied with great latitude to any degree of the faculty of discerning and judging what is most just and proper, from the sapience of the sage to the sound discretion of policy or common sense: *'tis not w. thus to second grief against yourself,* Ado V, 1, 2. *cold w. waiting on superfluous folly,* All's I, 1, 116. *w. cries out in the streets, and no man regards it,* H4A I, 2, 99 (cf. Proverbs I, 20. 24). Meas. II, 1, 32. II, 4, 78. LLL V, 2, 70. Merch. I, 1, 92. Wint. II, 1, 21. H6B I, 3, 33. H6B IV, 5, 171. Tim. III, 5, 51. Lr. IV, 2, 38. *herein lives w., beauty and increase,* Sonn. 11, 5. *much upon this riddle runs the w. of the world,* Meas. III, 2, 242. *show your w. in your close patience,* IV, 3, 122. *pace your w. in that*

*good path,* 137. *pray heaven his w. be not tainted,* IV, 4, 5. *your long experience of her w.* Err. III, 1, 89. *w. and blood combating in so tender a body,* Ado II, 3, 170. IV, 1, 189. V, 1, 239. LLL IV, 3, 357. V, 2, 742. Merch. II, 9, 81. As I, 2, 74. Shr. V, 2, 127. All's I, 2, 9. II, 1, 87. Tw. III, 1, 47. Wint. IV, 4, 150. H4A IV, 1, 64. H4B I, 1, 162. H6B III, 1, 195. V, 2, 75. H6C IV, 7, 60. R3 I, 4, 99. III, 7, 40. H8 I, 3, 29. Cor. I, 1, 219. Hml. I, 2, 15. Lr. I, 4, 102. 184. Ant. V, 2, 150 etc.

**Wise,** subst. manner: *in howling w.* Pilgr. 277. *in no w.* = by no means: *he is promised to be wived to fair Marina, but in no w. till he had done his sacrifice,* Per. V, 2, 11 (Gower's speech). cf. *Colossus-wise, Likewise, Otherwise.*

**Wise,** adj. 1) experienced, skilful: *take counsel of some —r head,* Pilgr. 303. *the —st beholder ... could not say if the importance were joy or sorrow,* Wint. V, 2, 18. *in these nice sharp quillets of the law ... I am no —r than a daw,* H6A II, 4, 18. (cf. Ado V, 1, 166, where the words 'the gentleman is w.' are explained by 'he hath the tongues'). *a w. woman* = a woman skilled in hidden arts, as fortune-telling, palmistry etc.: Wiv. IV, 5, 27. 59. Tw. III, 4, 114. cf. *the —st aunt,* Mids. II, 1, 51.

2) endowed with, or showing, sound judgment; sage, judicious, sensible, discreet: *the spirits of the w. sit in the clouds and mock us,* H4B II, 2, 155. *what the w. powers deny us for our good,* Ant. II, 1, 6. Meas. III, 1, 113. V, 475. Mids. III, 1, 151. Merch. I, 1, 96. R2 I, 3, 276. III, 2, 178 and H6C V, 4, 1. III, 1, 25. *strike the w. dumb and teach the fool to speak,* Ven. 1146. *old and yet not w.* Lucr. 1550. *lest the w. world should look into your moan,* Sonn. 71, 13. *be w. as thou art cruel,* 140, 1. Tp. II, 2, 77. V, 294. Gent. I, 1, 41. II, 4, 15. IV, 2, 41. IV, 3, 13. Wiv. I, 3, 32. II, 3, 10. 39. 56. IV, 5, 82. Meas. I, 2, 103. II, 1, 57. 180. II, 4, 14. III, 2, 145. 146. Err. IV, 3, 76. V, 217. Ado II, 3, 29. 32. 167. 192. 197. LLL I, 2, 143. II, 18. V, 2, 76. Merch. III, 2, 101. As I, 1, 26. Shr. II, 267 (cf. *Wit*). Wint. I, 2, 262. Troil. IV, 5, 257. Hml. I, 2, 6. Oth. II, 3, 193. Cymb. III, 4, 121 etc. etc. *a w. gentleman,* Ado V, 1, 166, according to Dyce, = wiseacre.

—*r,* adverbially: *thou speakest —r than thou art ware of,* As II, 4, 58.

**Wisely,** adv. (comp. *wiselier,* Tp. II, 1, 21) with wisdom, judiciously: Tp. II, 1, 8. 21. Wiv. I, 3, 3. Meas. I, 2, 135. Ado III, 5, 65. Merch. II, 2, 15. As I, 2, 93. II, 7, 22. 53. III, 2, 129. Tw. I, 5, 33. III, 1, 74. Wint. IV, 4, 726. H4A I, 2, 97. H4B IV, 5, 181. Troil. I, 3, 138. III, 2, 159. Rom. I, 1, 227. II, 3, 94. II, 4, 132. III, 5, 234. Tim. III, 5, 31. Caes. III, 3, 12. 17. V, 1, 38. Mcb. III, 6, 14. Hml. I, 3. III, 3, 30. Oth. V, 2, 344. Cymb. I, 6, 43.

**Wiseman** (spelt as one word in O. Edd. and accentuated on the first syllable) one not a fool or a madman: As I, 2, 93. V, 1, 35. Tw. I, 5, 95. II, 3, 45. III, 1, 73. 75. R2 V, 5, 63. Rom. III, 3, 62. Lr. I, 4, 182. III, 2, 13 (Qq *wise man*). cf. *Man.*

**Wiseness,** wisdom: *yet have I something in me dangerous, which let thy w. fear,* Hml. V, 1, 286 (Qq *wisdom*).

**Wish,** subst. a desire (optation): Ven. Ded. 7. Gent. I, 3, 60. Wiv. III, 3, 52. Mids. I, 1, 155. Merch. III, 2, 152. 189. As V, 2, 101. H5 III, 2, 16. V, 2,

355. R3 IV, 1, 72. H8 I, 2, 140. Ant. III, 13, 18 etc. *to give a p. his w.* = to fulfil it: *to whom I gave their —es,* Ant. IV, 12, 22. *to have one's w.* = to have obtained what one desired: Sonn. 37, 14. 135, 1. Gent. IV, 2, 93. V, 4, 119. LLL IV, 3, 81. 92. H6C I, 4, 143. Cor. V, 3, 113. Rom. I, 3, 62. Cymb. III, 5, 20. *have an w. but for it* = wish for it: Per. IV, 4, 2. *take I your w.* = if I accept what you wish me to: Per. II, 4, 43. *even to my w.* = exactly as I wished: Wiv. IV, 6, 12. Cor. I, 4, 57. *upon thy w.* = as thou just wished'st, very pat: John II, 50. *he comes upon a w.* Caes. III, 2, 271. *at high w.* = having all one's wishes fulfilled: Tim. IV, 3, 245; cf. Tit. II, 1, 125. Very often used of expressions of a kind interest in the welfare of others: Meas. III, 1, 45. LLL II, 179 (*thy own w. wish I thee*). Mids. II, 2, 65. Merch. III, 4, 43. As I, 2, 198. I, 3, 24 (*a good w. upon you!*). All's I, 1, 68 (*I desire your holy —es,* = your blessing). R2 I, 3, 94 (*take from my mouth the w. of happy years*). H6A V, 3, 173 etc. = imprecation: *blistered be thy tongue for such a w.* Rom. III, 2, 91.

**Wish,** vb. 1) to have a wish, to desire; absol.: *had time cohered with place and place with —ing,* Meas. II, 1, 11. *w. chastely and love dearly,* All's I, 3, 218. With *for:* *the sweets we w. for,* Lucr. 867. Ado IV, 1, 118. As V, 2, 52. H4A I, 2, 230. R3 I, 3, 245. IV, 4, 80. H8 II, 2, 101. III, 1, 98. Tit. V, 2, 160. Rom. II, 2, 132. With an inf.: *he you oft have —ed to hear from,* Gent. II, 4, 103. Meas. II, 4, 78. Tw. II, 5, 167. Wint. II, 1, 123. H6B IV, 9, 6. H8 III, 2, 89. Cor. III, 1, 153. Tim. IV, 2, 31. Per. II, 1, 118 etc. With a subjunctive following: *w. I were renewed,* Sonn. 111, 8. *I w. all good befortune you,* Gent. IV, 3, 41. *I w. he never find more cause to change a master,* Ant. IV, 5, 15. *I w. my brother make good time with him,* Cymb. IV, 2, 108. Pilgr. 198. Tp. V, 150. Meas. IV, 1, 10. LLL V, 2, 55. Merch. II, 8, 32. As III, 3, 23. H6A V, 4, 31. Tim. V, 1, 91. Mcb. V, 5, 50. Hml. III, 1, 38 etc. With *may* or *might:* Ven. Ded. 7. H4B V, 2, 104. Tit. V, 2, 203. Caes. III, 1, 13. 144. Hml. III, 1, 42. Ven. 447. All's I, 3, 4. Tw. III, 1, 156. H6B III, 2, 109. IV, 10, 85. R3 V, 1, 14. Caes. III, 1, 16. With *should: I would w. this youth should say,* Wint. IV, 4, 101. Mcb. I, 5, 26. Cymb. V, 1, 1. With *would:* Tp. II, 1, 191. Ado II, 3, 215. Oth. II, 3, 36. IV, 1, 263. Cymb. II, 4, 6. —*ed* = should w. Cor. IV, 6, 24

Transitively; a) with a simple accus.: *I would not w. any companion,* Tp. III, 1, 54. *we w. your peace,* IV, 163. *summer's welcome thrice more —ed,* Sonn. 56, 14. *their —ed sight,* Pilgr. 202. Gent. II, 4, 82. Meas. I, 4, 4. Err. I, 1, 91. Ado V, 1, 335. LLL I, 1, 106. Mids. IV, 1, 180. Merch. III, 2, 13. Shr. V, 1, 131. All's I, 2, 63. Wint. V, 1, 143. John I, 260. V, 5, 12. H5 IV, 3, 23. 30. 73. H6A III, 3, 28. H6B II, 4, 90. III, 1, 308. III, 2, 113. H6C III, 2, 140. V, 6, 65. R3 I, 2, 185. H8 IV, 2, 69. Cor. II, 1, 255. Hml. III, 1, 64. Ant. I, 4, 42 etc. b) with an accus. and inf. without *to: in that good path that I would w. it go,* Meas. IV, 3, 138. —*ed him on the barren mountains starve,* H4A I, 3, 159 (Ff *starved*). c) with a double accus.: —*ing me like to one more rich in hope,* Sonn. 29, 5. —*ed himself the heaven's breath,* Pilgr. 234. *w. me partaker in thy happiness,* Gent. I, 1, 14. Wiv. I, 1, 83. Merch. III, 2, 153. V, 304. Shr. II, 289 All's IV, 5, 84. R2 V, 5, 33. H6C IV, 1, 21. 139. R3 IV, 2, 18. Cor. I, 1, 236 etc. d) with an accus. and an adverbial or prepositional expression: *what is best, that best I w. in thee,* Sonn. 37, 13 (= that it may be in thee). *—ing me with him,* Gent. I, 3, 59. *you can w. none* (joy) *from me,* Merch. III, 2, 193 (you cannot, by your wish, deprive me of any joy). *to w. it back on you,* III, 4, 44. *we —ed your lordship here,* R3 III, 5, 67. *he could w. himself in Thames,* H5 IV, 1, 120. 124. *how often have I —ed me thus,* Troil. III, 2, 65. *may w. Marcius home,* Cor. IV, 6, 69. *those plagues that I can w. upon thee,* R3 I, 3, 218; cf. Lr. II, 4, 171. *to w. a p. well =* to attend him with kind wishes: Meas. III, 2, 97. Ado V, 1, 333. Merch. IV, 1, 420. All's I, 1, 193. 195. Per. V, 1, 16. cf. *men in rage strike those that w. them best,* Oth. II, 3, 243, and see *Well-wished.* e) with an accus. and dative: *to whom I w. long life,* Lucr. Ded. 5. *to thy sacred state w. I all happiness,* R2 V, 6, 6. Cor. II, 2, 157. *more direful hap ... than I can w. to adders,* R3 I, 2, 19. *as you w. Christian peace to souls departed,* H8 IV, 2, 156. *I w. it to you* (the good time of day) Tim. III, 6, 2. Dative without *to,* when placed between the verb and accus.: *w. you joy,* Tp. V, 215. *to w. us one,* H5 IV, 3, 77. Ado II, 1, 200. LLL V, 2, 342. 835. Merch. III, 2, 192. III, 4, 42. H4B IV, 2, 79. R3 IV, 1, 65. H8 V, 1, 76. Cor. I, 3, 123. Ant. V, 2, 281 etc. *thy own wish w. I thee,* LLL II, 179. *Towards for to: a heart that —es t. you honour and plenteous safety,* H8 I, 1, 103. The relation of the dat. and accus. peculiarly inverted: *I could not w. them to a fairer death,* Mcb. V, 8, 49.

2) to desire, to invite, to ask, to bid; with an inf. with *to: nor* (was I) *—ed to hold my peace,* Meas. V, 79. *I will w. thee never more to dance,* LLL V, 2, 400. *—ing me to permit my chaplain ... a choice hour,* H8 I, 2, 161. *when man was —ed to love his enemies,* Tim. IV, 3, 473. *this she —ed me to make known,* Cymb. III, 5, 50. without *to: to w. him wrestle with affection,* Ado III, 1, 42. *such thanks I give as one near death to those that w. him live,* All's II, 1, 134. *the rest I w. thee gather,* H6A II, 5, 96. With *to* before a noun, = to invite: *I will w. him to her father,* Shr. I, 1, 113 (invite him to offer his service to her father). *shall I ... w. thee to a shrewd ill-favoured wife? ... thou'rt too much my friend, and I'll not w. thee to her,* I, 2, 60. 64 (shall I invite thee to try thy fortune with etc.; shall I treat thee to a shrew?)

**Wisher,** one who expresses a wish: Mids. II, 2, 65. Ant. IV, 15, 37.

**Wishful,** longing: *to greet mine own land with my w. sight,* H6C III, 1, 14.

**Wishtly,** see *Wistly.*

**Wisp,** a small bundle: *a w. of straw,* H6C II, 2, 144 (cf. *Straw*).

**Wist,** impf. of a verb *to wis* unknown to Sh.; substituted by M. Edd. for *wish* of O. Edd. in H6A IV, 1, 180. Read: *and if, — I wish he did, — but let that rest;* as Johnson proposed.

**Wistly,** attentively, observingly, with scrutiny: *what a sight it was, w. to view how she came stealing to the wayward boy,* Ven. 343. *she thought he blushed as knowing Tarquin's lust, and blushing with him w. on him gazed,* Lucr. 1355. *the sun looked on the world with glorious eye, yet not so w. as this queen on him,* Pilgr. 82. *speaking it he w. looked on me, as who should say 'I would thou wert the man',* R2 V, 4, 7 (Ql. 2 *wishtly*).

**Wit,** subst. 1) mental faculty, intellectual power of any kind; understanding, judgment, imagination (the proverbial *five —s* being defined: common wit, imagination, fantasy, estimation, memory): *my five —s nor my five senses can dissuade one foolish heart from serving thee,* Sonn. 141, 9. *four of his five —s went halting off,* Ado I, 1, 66. *how fell you besides your five —s?* Tw. IV, 2, 93. *our judgment sits five times in that* (our good meaning) *ere once in our five —s,* Rom. I, 4, 47. *thou hast more of the wild goose in one of thy —s than I have in my whole five,* II, 4, 77. *bless thy five —s,* Lr. III, 4, 59. III, 6, 60. Hence the frequent use of the plural in speaking of the activity of the mind: *useless barns the harvest of his —s,* Lucr. 859. *love inhabits in the finest —s,* Gent. I, 1, 44. *his —s are not so blunt,* Ado III, 5, 11. *dainty bits make rich the ribs, but bankrupt quite the —s,* LLL I, 1, 27. *bend thoughts and —s to achieve her,* Shr. I, 1, 184. *with all my —s, my pains and strong endeavours,* H5 V, 2, 25. *did my brother Bedford toil his —s,* H6B I, 1, 83. *our —s are so diversely coloured,* Cor. II, 3, 21. 23. 28. 29. *with witchcraft of his —s,* Hml. I, 5, 43 (M. Edd. unnecessarily *wit*). *a young maid's —s should be as mortal as an old man's life,* IV, 5, 159. The safety and soundness of the —s constituting the wise or reasonable man, their loss the fool or madman: *being mad before, how doth she now for —s?* Ven. 249. *here's a fellow frights English out of his —s,* Wiv. II, 1, 143. *I will stare him out of his —s,* II, 2, 291. *I am as well in my —s as thou,* Tw. IV, 2, 95. 98. *holp madmen to their —s,* R2 V, 5, 62. *in his right —s,* H5 IV, 7, 49. Tp. III, 2, 86. Meas. V, 33. Err. V, 42. 96. Mids. I, 2, 82. Tw. III, 4, 14. H6A V, 3, 195. Cor. IV, 2, 44. Oth. IV, 1, 280 etc. etc.

Used with the same latitude in the singular, so as to come near, sometimes, to the sense of mind: *by love the young and tender w. is turned to folly,* Gent. I, 1, 47. *made w. with musing weak,* 69. *my w. untrained in any kind of art,* H6A I, 2, 73; cf. Gent. I, 1, 2. *with what his valour did enrich his w., his w. set down to make his valour live,* R3 III, 1, 85. *the moral of my w. is 'plain and true',* Troil. IV, 4, 109. *she hath Dian's w.* Rom. I, 1, 215 (= sentiments). Sometimes = imaginative and inventive faculty: *fair fall the w. that can so well defend her,* Ven. 472. *danger deviseth shifts, w. waits on fear,* 690. *conceit and grief an eager combat fight: what w. sets down is blotted straight with will,* Lucr. 1299. *each several stone, with w. well blazoned, smiled or made some moan,* Compl. 217. *my admirable dexterity of w.* Wiv. IV, 5, 121. *thousand escapes of w. make thee the father of their idle dreams,* Meas. IV, 1, 63. *hast thou no word or w. or impudence that yet can do thee office?* V, 368. *devise, w.; write, pen,* LLL I, 2, 191. *past the w. of man to say what dream it was,* Mids. IV, 1, 211. *the man hath no w. that cannot ... vary deserved praise on my palfrey,* H5 III, 7, 33 etc. At other times = common sense, understanding, judgment: *a folly bought with w., or else a w. by folly vanquished,* Gent. I, 1, 34. *he wants w. that wants resolved will to learn his w. to exchange the bad for better,* II, 6, 12. *I have the w. to think my master is a kind of a knave,* III, 1, 262. *if I had not had more w. than he,* IV, 4, 15. *see now how w. may be made a Jack-a-lent,* Wiv. V, 5, 134. *few of any w. in such matters,* Meas. II, 1, 282. Wiv. I, 3, 102. Err.

II, 2, 39. 152. Ado I, 2, 17. V, 1, 128. LLL I, 2, 93. 94. John III, 4, 102. Lr. II, 4, 42 etc. etc.

Not seldom equivalent to wisdom: *so then we do neglect the thing we have, and all for want of w., make something nothing by neglecting it,* Lucr. 153. *Brutus ... began to clothe his w. in state and pride,* 1809. *if I might teach thee w., better it were, though not to love, yet, love, to tell me so,* Sonn. 140, 5. *one that hath taught me more w. than ever I learned before,* Wiv. IV, 5, 61. *'tis wisdom to conceal our meaning. Away with scrupulous w., now arms must rule,* H6C IV, 7, 61. cf. LLL V, 2, 70. 72. Tw. V, 218. Wint. II, 2, 52. R2 II, 1, 28. H6B III, 1, 232. Oth. II, 1, 130 etc.

Often denoting the faculty of associating ideas in a new and ingenious, and at the same time natural and pleasing way, which is at present its principal signification: Tp. II, 1, 13. IV, 242. Gent. I, 1, 132. II, 4, 38. Wiv. IV, 5, 102. Meas. II, 2, 127. Err. II, 1, 91. II, 2, 86. 88. Ado I, 1, 64. II, 1, 127. 135. 145. 399. V, 1, 124. LLL I, 2, 100 (*my father's w. and my mother's tongue assist me*). Mids. III, 1, 137. As I, 2, 48. 56. 95. Tw. I, 5, 35. R3 I, 2, 115. Troil. II, 1, 94 etc.

Proverbial expressions: *more hair than w.* Gent. III, 1, 361. 367. 368. 371. Err. II, 2, 82. 84. *w. enough to keep himself warm,* Ado I, 1, 68; cf. Shr. II, 268. *when the age is in, the w. is out,* Ado III, 5, 37. *w., whither wilt?* As IV, 1, 168; cf. I, 2, 59.

2) a) as a vox media, = a person of any degree of mental capacity: *parasites ... soothing the humour of fantastic —s,* Ven. 850. *—s of no higher breeding,* H4B II, 2, 38. *among foaming bottles and ale-washed —s,* H5 III, 6, 83. b) a man of fancy or wit: *the —s of former days to subjects worse have given admiring praise,* Sonn. 59, 13. *good —s will be jangling,* LLL II, 225. *are these the breed of —s so wondered at?* V, 2, 266. *better —s have worn plain statute-caps,* 281. *the dulness of the fool is the whetstone of the —s. How now, w., whither wander you?* As I, 2, 59. *those —s that think they have thee* (viz wit) *do very oft prove fools,* Tw. I, 5, 36. *shallow jesters and rash bavin —s,* H4A III, 2, 61.

**Wit,** vb. to know: *swift-winged with desire to get a grave, as —ing I no other comfort have,* H6A II, 5, 16. *now please you w. the epitaph is for Marina writ,* Per. IV, 4, 31 (Gower's speech). *to w.* = that is to say, namely: Merch. II, 9, 90. As V, 1, 57. H5 I, 2, 50. H6C V, 6, 51.

**Witch,** subst. 1) a woman who practises sorcery: Tp. I, 2, 258. 263. V, 269. Wiv. IV, 2, 88. 100. 180. 187. 194. 201. IV, 5, 120. 124. Err. I, 2, 100. III, 2, 149. 161. IV, 3, 80. IV, 4, 151. Ado II, 1, 186. H6A I, 5, 6 (one who could draw a witch's blood was free from her power). 21. II, 1, 18. III, 2, 38. V, 3, 34. H6B I, 2, 75. 91. II, 1, 172. II, 3, 7. R3 III, 4, 72. Troil. II, 1, 46 (*thou stool for a w.*). Mcb. I, 3, 6. IV, 1, 23 (*—es' mummy*). Hml. I, 1, 163. Lr. III, 4, 129. Ant. IV, 2, 37 (*the w. take me, if I meant it thus*).

Term of reproach for an old and ugly woman: *a mankind w.* Wint. II, 3, 67. *the cripple tardy-gaited night who like a foul and ugly w. doth limp so tediously away,* H5 IV Chor. 21; Troil. IV, 2, 12. *foul wrinkled w.* R3 I, 3, 164. *the w. shall die,* Ant. IV, 12, 47.

2) a male sorcerer: *I could find in my heart to stay here still and turn w.* Err. IV, 4, 160. *out, fool, I*

*forgive thee for a w.* Ant. I, 2, 40 (cf. the proverb: *you'll never be burnt for a witch*). Cymb. I, 6, 166.

**Witch,** vb. to bewitch, to enchant: H4A IV, 1, 110. H6B III, 2, 116. 119. H6C III, 2, 150. Tim. V, 1, 158. Hml. III, 2, 406 (*the —ing time of night;* cf. Mcb. II, 1, 51).

**Witchcraft,** 1) the practices of witches, sorcery: R3 III, 4, 63. 74. Mcb. II, 1, 51. Oth. I, 3, 64. 169. II, 3, 378. III, 3, 211. Ant. II, 1, 22. Cymb. IV, 2, 277.

2) enchantment, irresistible influence, charm: Compl. 288. Tw. V, 79. Wint. IV, 4, 434. John III, 1, 169. H5 V, 2, 301. H8 III, 2, 18. Cor. IV, 7, 2. Hml. I, 5, 43. IV, 7, 86.

**Wit-cracker,** one who breaks jests, a joker: Ado V, 4, 102.

**With;** denoting a being together; f. i. *the breeder ... swiftly doth forsake him; w. her the horse,* Ven. 322. *keep w. thy hounds,* 678. *let's all sink w. the king,* Tp. I, 1, 67. *any thing ... that hath kept w. thy remembrance,* I, 2, 44. *that which good natures could not abide to be w.* 360. *wishing me w. him,* Gent. I, 3, 59. *I lingered w. you at your shop,* Err. III, 1, 3. *leave him here w. me,* V, 108. *to come w. thee,* H6C IV, 8, 13.

Peculiar use after verbs of motion or, at least, implying the idea of motion, to express the effect of it: *nay, rather damn them w. King Cerberus,* H4B II, 4, 181 (i. e. so that they may be in hell). *lay me with Juliet,* Rom. V, 3, 73. *w. dishonour laid me on the ground,* H6B III, 3, 9 (laid me on the ground, where I lie in the company of dishonour). *I have seen the ambitious ocean swell ... to be exalted w. the threatening clouds,* Caes. I, 3, 8. *give him a statue w. his ancestors,* III, 2, 55 (in that place where the statues of his ancestors stand). *I'll pluck ye* (eyes) *out and cast you w. the waters that you lose, to temper clay,* Lr. I, 4, 325 (that you may lie on the ground together with the tears which you have shed. M. Edd. erroneously: *and cast you, w. the waters* etc.) *return w. her?* II, 4, 214 (= return to be and live with her? quite = return to her). cf. *to lie* and *sit w.* in As I, 2, 213. Meas. V, 246. H6C III, 3, 2; and the similar use of *at home* in Ant. I, 2, 190: *the letters of our friends in Rome petition us at home* (= to be at home, i. e. to come home). The same principle applicable to the following passages: *who, being suffered w. the bear's fell paw, hath clapped his tail between his legs and cried,* H6B V, 1, 153 (being suffered to be w., i. e. to combat with etc.). *that the noble Moor should hazard such a place as his own second w. one of an ingraft infirmity,* Oth. II, 3, 145.

Inversely, after verbs of separation (especially *to part*) that with which a person or thing has hitherto been together, indicated by *with: let the stinking elder, grief, untwine his perishing root w. the increasing vine,* Cymb. IV, 2, 60 (= from; so as to be no more twined with). *how did thy master part w. Madam Julia?* Gent. II, 5, 11. *when you parted w. him,* R2 I, 4, 10. II, 2, 2. III, 2, 8. R3 I, 4, 251. *hath willingly departed w. a part,* John II, 563.

*I'll be w. you* = 1) I'll be in your company, I'll come to you: *I'll be w. you anon,* H4B V, 3, 28. Troil. I, 2, 304. cf. As I, 1, 89. 2) in a menacing tone, = I'll chastise you, I'll teach you good manners, you shall pay for this (Latin *quos ego!*): *I will be w. thee straight,* Mids. III, 2, 403. *what, do you grumble? I'll* be w. you straight, Shr. IV, 1, 170. I'll be w. you anon, Tw. III, 4, 353. I shall be w. you presently, good master puppy, H8 V, 4, 29. cf. I'll be w. you at your sheep-shearing too, Wint. IV, 3, 128 (i. e. I'll pick your pockets there). Cardinal, I am w. you, H6B II, 1, 48. was I w. you there for the goose? Rom. II, 4, 78 (cf. Wint. I, 2, 217. Cor. III, 2, 74).

Denoting identity of place: she looks for night, and then she longs for morrow, and both she thinks too long w. her remaining, Lucr. 1572 (=where she is). there was an old woman even now w. me, Wiv. IV, 5, 26 (in my chamber). some say he is w. the emperor of Russia, Meas. III, 2, 93. her brother's noontide w. the Antipodes, Mids. III, 2, 55. thou shalt not gormandise, as thou hast done w. me, Merch. II, 5, 4. I entreat you home w. me to dinner, IV, 1, 401. As III, 3, 43. John IV, 1, 30. V, 4, 40. Tim. III, 2, 12. Cymb. III, 5, 83 etc. he is not w. himself, Tit. I, 368 (= he is beside himself. Ff he is not himself).

The notion of locality applied to abstract ideas: w. Death she humbly doth insinuate, Ven. 1012. he w. the Romans was esteemed so, Lucr. 1811. I lie w. her, and she w. me, Sonn. 138, 13 (I tell her untruths; cf. Oth. IV, 1, 36). will you grant w. me, Tp. II, 1, 243. 'tis fresh morning w. me, III, 1, 33. 'tis a custom w. him i'th' afternoon to sleep, III, 2, 95. whose credit w. the judge, Meas. II, 4, 92. I will break w. her, Ado I, 1, 311 (cf. Break). not a word w. him but a jest, LLL II, 216. a place of high respect w. me, Mids. II, 1, 209. have all persuaded w. him, Merch. III, 2, 283. are not w. me esteemed above thy life, IV, 1, 285. to flatter w. his lord, Tw. I, 5, 322; R2 II, 1, 88. he can do all in all w. her that hateth thee, H6B II, 4, 52. your displeasure w. the king, H8 III, 2, 392. it is an accustomed action w. her, Mcb. V, 1, 32. is Caesar w. Antonius prized so light? Ant. I, 1, 56. his taints and honours waged equal w. him, V, 1, 31. a goodly day not to keep house w. such whose roof's as low as ours, Cymb. III, 3, 1. the shipman ... w. whom each minute threatens life or death, Per. I, 3, 25 etc. cf. the following phrases: what news w. your mastership? Gent. III, 1, 280 (what news have you to tell?); what tidings w. our cousin Buckingham? H6B II, 1, 165. what's your will w. me? Gent. III, 1, 3. what wouldst thou have w. me? Rom. III, 1, 79. what would you w. her? Gent. IV, 4, 115. Wiv. III, 4, 64. IV, 5, 30. LLL V, 2, 178. Merch. II, 2, 128. H4A II, 3, 98. what w. me? Wiv. II, 2, 41. Tit. IV, 2, 54. Tim. II, 2, 15. I'll no more w. thee, Tw. III, 1, 49. Thus used to designate the person whom (or the thing which) an action concerns or with respect to whom a quality is exhibited or a state expressed: to practise his judgment w. the disposition of natures, Meas. III, 1, 165. heaven doth w. us as we w. torches do, I, 1, 33. do w. 'em what thou wilt, H6A IV, 7, 94. breaking faith w. Julia, Gent. IV, 2, 11. you do not keep promise w. me, Tw. V, 106. keeping thy word w. the devil, H4A I, 2, 135. the regent hath w. Talbot broke his word, H6A IV, 6, 2. in hand w. all things, Ven. 912. how the world is changed w. you, Err. II, 2, 154. I am witness w. her that she did, IV, 4, 92. thus stands it w. me, Meas. I, 2, 149. 'tis better w. me now than when I met thee last, R3 III, 2, 100. so is it not w. me as w. that Muse, Sonn. 21, 1. Meas. I, 1, 82. II, 2, 82. All's II, 1, 152. Tw. III, 4, 97. V, 199. Wint. I, 2, 148. R2 II, 1, 72. Cor. I, 6, 33. V, 6, 10. Rom. III, 3, 93. Mcb. II, 2, 58. Hml. III, 4, 115. 116. IV, 1, 13.

Oth. III, 4, 33. Cymb. IV, 3, 1. are w. gain so fond, Lucr. 134. stands at a guard w. envy, Meas. I, 3, 51. be not angry w. me, Ado III, 1, 94. do not be so bitter w. me, Mids. III, 2, 306. in love w. a disdainful youth, II, 1, 261. bear w. me, LLL V, 2, 417. be opposite w. a kinsman, surly w. servants, Tw. II, 5, 162. be plainer w. me, Wint. I, 2, 265. be fire w. fire, John V, 1, 48. are you so choleric w. Eleanor, H6B I, 2, 52. is so pleasant w. us, H5 I, 2, 259. an a' be proud w. me, Troil. II, 3, 215. I would dissemble w. my nature, Cor. III, 2, 62. I'll be cruel w. the maids, Rom. I, 1, 27. the troubled Tiber chafing w. her shores, Caes. I, 2, 101. the world, too saucy w. the gods, I, 3, 12. that I am meek and gentle w. these butchers, Caes. III, 1, 255 etc. Peculiar expression: they're here w. me already, whispering, rounding, 'Sicilia is a so-forth', Wint. I, 2, 217 (they go so far with respect to me as to whisper. The words perhaps accompanied by a corresponding gesture emblematizing cuckoldom). go to them, w. this bonnet in thy hand, and thus far having stretched it — here be w. them — thy knee bussing the stones, Cor. III, 2, 74 (do thus in addressing them). O ho, are you there w. me? no eyes in your head? Lr. IV, 6, 148.

Denoting junction and community: the world hath ending w. thy life, Ven. 12. his smell w. others being mingled, 691. w. him is beauty slain, 1019. I have suffered w. those that I saw suffer, Tp. I, 2, 6. executing the outward face of royalty w. all prerogative, 105. confederates ... w. the king of Naples, 112. confer fair Milan w. all the honours on my brother, 127. fresh water ... that Gonzalo ... did give us, w. rich garments, 163. I would mine eyes would w. themselves shut up my thoughts, II, 1, 192. a tongue w. a tang, II, 2, 52. w. my nobler reason 'gainst my fury do I take part, V, 26. to marry w. Nan Page, Wiv. IV, 4, 85. join not w. grief, R2 V, 1, 16. to wail it w. their age, R3 IV, 4, 394 (in v. 392 Qq in). the kings your ancestors, together w. the natural bravery of your isle, Cymb. III, 1, 17 etc. etc. see Confer, Speak etc. and the burden w. heigh ho, the wind and the rain, Tw. V, 399. Wint. IV, 3, 2. Hence expressing correspondence, likeness and comparison: nothing w. his proud sight agrees, Ven. 288. lay this Angiers even w. the ground, John II, 399. wishing his foot were equal w. his eye, H6C III, 2, 137. measure my strangeness w. my unripe years, Ven. 524. weigh oath w. oath, Mids. III, 2, 131. compare w. Caesars, H4B II, 4, 180 etc. Sometimes almost = like: indenting w. the way, Ven. 704. seemed w. him to bleed, 1056. w. others thou shouldst not abhor my state, Sonn. 150, 12. of nature's gifts thou mayst w. lilies boast and w. the half-blown rose, John III, 1, 53. as if w. Circe she would change my shape, H6A V, 3, 35.* Noting simultaneousness: w. this she seizeth on his sweating palm, Ven. 25. and w. that word she spied the hunted boar, 900. w. every minute you do change a mind, Cor. I, 1, 186. to-morrow w. your earliest let me have speech w. you, Oth. II, 3, 7. w. your speediest bring us what she says, Ant. V, 1, 67. cf. Ven. 811. 1121. Lucr. 1639. 1709. Tit. V, 1, 37. Caes. III, 2, 48 etc. cf. the phrases: come w. a thought, Tp. IV, 164. he would kiss you twenty w. a breath, H8 I, 4, 30. After expressions of contest (as, for a combat, there must needs be two): w. herself at strife, Ven. 11. 291. encounter w. the boar, 672. leaden slumber w. life's strength doth fight, Lucr. 124. in rebellion w. himself, Wint. I, 2, 355. his face still combating w. tears, R2 V, 2, 32 etc.

The idea of community lost sight of after pre-positional and adverbial expressions originating in it: *to the forge w. it*, Wiv. IV, 2, 239. *to the rack w. him*, Meas. V, 313. *to prison w. her*, 121. *then to cart w. Rosalind*, As III, 2, 114. *to Bedlam w. him*, H6B V, 1, 131. *to pieces w. me*, Cymb. III, 4, 55. *away w. the rest*, Tp. IV, 247. Wiv. IV, 2, 45. Meas. III, 2, 217. V, 46. John IV, 2, 155. H6A I, 1, 86. *down w. the topmast*, Tp. I, 1, 37. Gent. IV, 1, 2. LLL IV, 3, 368. Tim. IV, 3, 157. *forward w. your tale*, Tp. III, 2, 91. *off w. Barnardine's head*, Meas. IV, 2, 222. H4B V, 1, 60. H6B II, 1, 151. *out w. it*, Gent. III, 1, 339. IV, 4, 22. Tim. IV, 1, 9. *up w. your fights*, Wiv. II, 2, 142.

Denoting that which accompanies and modifies, either as an external appearance, or as a quality: *the sun w. purple-coloured face*, Ven. 1. *w. long dishevelled hair*, 147. *w. hair up-staring*, Tp. I, 2, 213. *let him die w. every joint a wound*, Troil. IV, 1, 29. *w. this bonnet in thy hand*, Cor. III, 2, 73 etc. *w. a lazy spright*, Ven. 181. *he trots w. gentle majesty*, 278. *swelleth w. more rage*, 332. *w. disturbed mind*, 340. *w. weary gait*, 529. *w. blindfold fury*, 554. *he cranks and crosses w. a thousand doubles*, 682. Tp. I, 2, 28. 304. 346. III, 1, 40. Gent. I, 1, 8. Meas. V, 50 (*w. that opinion*) etc. etc. cf. the phrases: *that w. his very heart despiseth me*, Gent. IV, 4, 99. *my daughter's mother thinks it w. her soul*, R3 IV, 4, 256. *w. my soul I love thy daughter*, 262 etc.

Hence denoting a means: *I'll smother thee w. kisses*, Ven. 18. *not cloy thy lips w. loathed satiety*, 19. *to try w. main-course*, Tp. I, 1, 38. *the bettering of my mind w. that which ... o'erprized all popular rate*, I, 2, 91. *w. colours fairer painted their foul ends*, 143. 222. 231. 322. 369. 393. 472. II, 1, 119. 283. II, 2, 5. 13. 128. III, 2, 97. 98. IV, 158. Epil. 10. Gent. I, 1, 29. I, 2, 94. 103. IV, 2, 6 etc. etc. Peculiar passage: *since I have crept in favour w. myself, I will maintain it w. some little cost*, R3 I, 2, 259 (i. e., according to Abbott, since I have gained favour by my person). A person as means: *he did arrest me w. an officer*, Err. V, 230. *his hands were ... bloody w. the enemies of his kin*, R2 II, 1, 183. *send for his master w. a pursuivant*, H6B I, 3, 37. After expressions of providing or furnishing: *one w. treasure laden*, Ven. 1022. *w. hairy bristles armed*, 625. *replete w. too much rage*, Sonn. 23, 3. *infused w. a fortitude from heaven*, Tp. I, 2, 154. *not honoured w. a human shape*, 283. *touched w. madness*, Meas. V, 51. *her womb then rich w. my young squire*, Mids. II, 1, 131; H5 I, 2, 163. *I'll fill these dogged spies w. false reports*, John IV, 1, 129. *to possess me w. these fears*, IV, 2, 203. *I did present him w. the Paris balls*, H5 II, 4, 131. *blessed w. beauty*, H6A I, 2, 86. *arming myself w. patience*, Caes. V, 1, 106. *how Thaliard came full bent w. sin*, Per. II Prol. 23. cf. *I rather will suspect the sun w. cold*, Wiv. IV, 4, 7. *acquaint her w. the danger of my state*, Meas. I, 2, 184 etc. The phrases *w. child, w. young*, see sub *Child* and *Young*.

Before means of nourishment = on: *to dine and sup w. water and bran*, Meas. IV, 3, 159. *you shall fast a week w. bran and water*, LLL I, 1, 303. *feast w. the best*, Shr. V, 2, 8. *I live w. bread like you*, R2 III, 2, 175. *I have supped full w. horrors*, Mcb. V, 5, 13. cf. *they are as sick that surfeit w. too much as they that starve w. nothing*, Merch. I, 2, 6. Cor. III, 3, 90.

Denoting a cause: *he burns w. bashful shame*, Ven. 49. *swoln w. chafing*, 325. *a dying coal revives w.*

*wind*, 338. *pale w. fear*, Lucr. 183. *die w. terror*, 231. *forced it to tremble w. her loyal fear*, 261. *his hand smoking w. pride*, 438. *sweating w. guilty fear*, 740. 762. 1491. 1543. Sonn. 23, 2 (*who w. his fear is put besides his part*). 75, 9. 124, 12. Tp. I, 2, 212 (*afire w. me*). 258. IV, 113. 171. 191. Gent. I, 1, 69. Wiv. II, 2, 301. Err. I, 2, 20. Ado I, 1, 250. 253. LLL II, 239. Mids. II, 2, 148. Merch. I, 1, 81. II, 1, 38. Tw. III, 4, 366 (*this comes w. seeking you*). R2 II, 2, 12 (*my inward soul w. nothing trembles: at something it grieves, more than w. parting from my lord the king*). H4B IV, 5, 13. H6A II, 5, 15. II, 4, 63. R3 I, 4, 42 (*awaked you not w. this sore agony? Ff in*). IV, 3, 20 (*gone w. conscience and remorse; see Go*). Tim. IV, 3, 493 (*weep w. laughing, not w. weeping*). Caes. IV, 3, 191 (*w. meditating that she must die once I have the patience to endure it now*). Mcb. V, 3, 10. Cymb. IV, 3, 2 (*a fever w. the absence of her son*) etc. etc. Often encroaching on the function of other prepositions, f. i. *overjoyed w. finding a bird's nest*, Ado II, 1, 230. *w. that all laughed*, LLL V, 2, 107 (M. Edd. unnecessarily *w. that, all* etc.). *I feel remorse in myself w. his words*, H6B IV, 7, 111. *will forget w. the least cause these his new honours*, Cor. II, 1, 245. 3, 267.

Lastly, denoting an external agency, by which an effect is produced, and which is usually — and at present exclusively — expressed by the prepos. by: *her best work is ruined w. thy rigour*, Ven. 954. *it* (love) *shall be waited on w. jealousy*, 1137. *accompanied w. his sons*, Lucr. Arg. 4. *made glorious by his manly chivalry, w. bruised arms and wreaths of victory*, Lucr. 110. *blinded w. a greater light*, 375. *huge fires abide and w. the wind in greater fury fret*, 648. *eagles are gazed upon w. every eye*, 1015. *what wit sets down is blotted straight w. will*, 1299. *a woman's face w. nature's own hand painted*, Sonn. 20, 1. *stone besmeared w. sluttish time*, 55, 4. *crushed w. time's injurious hand*, 63, 2. *consumed w. that which it was nourished by*, 73, 12. *wounded w. a boar*, Pilgr. 126. *killed w. a thunderstroke*, Tp. II, 2, 112. *though w. their high wrongs I am struck to the quick*, V, 25. *the mean is drowned w. your unruly base*, Gent. I, 2, 96. *metamorphosed w. a mistress*, II, 1, 32. *lust is but a bloody fire kindled w. unchaste desire*, Wiv. V, 5, 100. *to be overmastered w. a piece of valiant dust*, Ado II, 1, 64. *a vane blown w. all winds*, III, 1, 66. *a better death than die w. mocks, which is as bad as die w. tickling*, 79. *had our two noses snapped off w. two old men*, V, 1, 116. *brought w. armed men back to Messina*, V, 4, 128. *we shall be dogged w. company*, Mids. I, 2, 106. *pierced through the heart w. your stern cruelty*, III, 2, 59. *hit w. Cupid's archery*, 103. *fanned w. the eastern wind*, 142. *wounded w. the claws of a lion*, As V, 2, 26. *braved in mine own house w. a skein of thread*, Shr. IV, 3, 111. *bedazzled w. the sun*, IV, 5, 46. *your son was misled w. a snipt taffeta fellow*, All's IV, 5, 1. *I saw him put down w. an ordinary fool*, Tw. I, 5, 91. *torn to pieces w. a bear*, Wint. V, 2, 68. *we are mocked w. art*, V, 3, 68. *rounded in the ear w. that purpose-changer*, John II, 567. *wars shall kin w. kin and kind w. kind confound*, R2 IV, 141. *affrighted w. their bloody looks*, H4A I, 3, 104. *was Mahomet inspired w. a dove*, H6A I, 2, 140. *if I to-day die not w. Frenchmen's rage*, IV, 6, 34. *followed w. a rabble*, H6B II, 4, 32. *w. whose sting ... your uncle ... is bereft of life*, III, 2, 267. *boarded w. a pirate*, IV, 9, 33. *w. robbers so o'ermatched*, H6C I, 4, 64. *backed w. France*,

IV, 1, 41. *marred w. traitors*, Caes. III, 2, 201. *that we can let our beards be shook w. danger*, Hml. IV, 7, 32. *must I be unfolded w. one that I have bred*, Ant. V, 2, 171. Ven. 559. Lucr. 173. 560. 1494. Sonn. 5, 7. 27, 1. 122, 2. 128, 3. Tp. I, 2, 256. 415. III, 3, 5. 15. IV, 160. Gent. III, 2, 7. IV, 1, 12. Wiv. II, 1, 22. III, 4, 5. Meas. III, 1, 26. Err. I, 2, 15. II, 1, 34. Ado I, 1, 67. LLL V, 2, 291. Mids. II, 1, 129. 167. As II, 7, 50. III, 2, 196. III, 3, 13. John II, 26. H4A I, 3, 107. H5 III, 1, 14. H6A I, 1, 136. I, 2, 85. II, 5, 4. H6B I, 3, 132. III, 1, 223. R3 IV, 4, 239. Cor. V, 6, 12 etc.

**Withal** or **Withall,** 1) with this, with it: *revealed the actor and whole manner of his dealing, and w. suddenly stabbed herself*, Lucr. Arg. 21 (with this; as soon as she had done this; see *With*). *beating her bulk that his hand shakes w.* Lucr. 467. *the boy for trial needs would touch my breast; I, sick w., the help of bath required*, Sonn. 153, 11. *so glad of this as they I cannot be, who are surprised w.* Tp. III, 1, 93. *he will scarce be pleased w.* Gent. II, 7, 67. *we do instate and widow you w.* Meas. V, 429. Err. III, 1, 113. III, 2, 178. Ado I, 2, 23. LLL V, 1, 122. V, 2, 142. Merch. II, 7, 12. III, 1, 55. III, 2, 211. As I, 1, 139. I, 2, 29. Shr. V, 1, 23. John II, 531. H5 I, 2, 216. H6A I, 1, 154. II, 1, 51. II, 4, 38. H6C I, 4, 83. 139. III, 3, 226. Cor. V, 3, 194. Rom. I, 1, 119. Mcb. II, 2, 56. Ant. III, 6, 59 etc. Peculiar expressions: *they fell sick and died; I could not do w.* Merch. III, 4, 72 (= I could not help it). *they take place, when virtue's steely bones look bleak in the cold wind: w. full oft we see cold wisdom waiting on superfluous folly*, All's I, 1, 115 (with this, i. e. from this, in consequence of this).

2) together with this, at the same time: *he struck so plainly, I too well could feel his blows, and w. so doubtfully that I could scarce understand them*, Err. II, 1, 53. *I will have you and that fault w.* LLL V, 2, 876. *let his deservings and my love w. be valued 'gainst your wife's commandment*, Merch. IV, 1, 450. *I must have liberty w. ... to blow on whom I please*, As II, 7, 48. *nothing comes amiss, so money comes w.* Shr. I, 2, 82. *I must wait, and watch w.* III, 1, 62. *though he be merry, yet w. he's honest*, III, 2, 25. IV, 5, 50. Wint. II, 1, 153. R2 IV, 18. H4A III, 1, 143. H5 II, 4, 34. H6A V, 3, 184. R3 I, 1, 103. I, 3, 133. 332. 347. III, 7, 12. Tit. I, 135. Rom. III, 1, 159. Mcb. IV, 3, 41. Hml. I, 3, 14 etc.

3) = with, as placed at the end of the sentence: *who hath she to spend the night w.?* Ven. 847. *he has brave utensils ... which, when he has a house, he'll deck w.* Tp. III, 2, 105. *an honest fellow, as ever servant shall come in house w.* Wiv. I, 4, 11 (cf. H4A V, 3, 22. H4B V, 3, 70). *these banished men that I have kept w.* Gent. V, 4, 152. *one that I am not acquainted w.* Wiv. II, 1, 90. *her cause and yours I'll perfect him w.* Meas. IV, 3, 146. *such a fellow is not to be talked w.* V, 348. Err. V, 209. 268. Ado II, 3, 264. IV, 1, 37. LLL II, 68. 147. Merch. III, 1, 30. IV, 1, 412. As III, 2, 165. 328. 329. 330. 336. 344. 348. Shr. III, 1, 3. V, 1, 21. Tw. III, 4, 255. John III, 1, 327. H4A II, 4, 566. H5 III, 5, 12. H6A IV, 2, 34. H6C II, 1, 82. III, 2, 91. Oth. V, 2, 56 etc. Once preceding the verb: *myself and all will I w. endow a child of thine*, R3 IV, 4, 249 ('on account of the *all* at the end of the previous verse'. Abbott).

**Withdraw** (impf. *withdrew*, partic. *withdrawn*) 1) trans. a) to take aside; to draw or call away: *my*

brother ... *hath withdrawn her father to break with him about it*, Ado II, 1, 162. *advantageous care withdrew me from the odds of multitude*, Troil. V, 4, 23. b) to take back, to retract: *wouldst thou w. it* (thy vow)? Rom. II, 2, 130.

2) refl. to quit a place, to absent one's self: *her eyes, as murdered with the view, like stars ashamed of day, themselves withdrew*, Ven. 1032. *from whence* (the camp) *he privily withdrew himself*, Lucr. Arg. 14. *w. thyself* (from the battle-field), *thou bleedest too much*, H4A V, 4, 2. *I'll w. me and my bloody power*, H6A IV, 2, 8. = to go: *whither* (the town of Leicester), *if it please you, we may now w. us*, R3 V, 5, 11.

Usually = to retire, to step aside: Gent. V, 4, 18. Wint. II, 2, 16. R2 V, 3, 28. H6C II, 3, 14. R3 III, 4, 43. IV, 4, 8. Tit. I, 43. Oth. IV, 1, 57.

3) intr. to quit a place, to absent one's self: *I know the cause of his —ing*, Meas. III, 2, 140 (= his travel). = to go: *let us w. together*, Meas. I, 1, 82. I, 2, 116. Tit. I, 368. Lr. II, 4, 290. Cymb. IV, 3, 32. *we will w. into the gallery*, Per. II, 2, 58. *I will w. to furnish me with some swift means of death*, Oth. III, 3, 476. = to come (imperatively): *madam, w., the prince, the count ... are come to fetch you*, Ado III, 4, 100. *if thou say so, w. and prove it too*, Mids. III, 2, 255. *w., my lord, I'll help you to a horse*, R3 V, 4, 8.

= to retire, to step aside: Ado V, 4, 11. LLL V, 2, 308. John V, 2, 29. R2 I, 3, 121. H4A IV, 3, 107. H4B IV, 5, 17. 59. H8 III, 1, 27. Cor. III, 1, 226. Rom. I, 5, 93. III, 1, 54. Hml. III, 1, 55. III, 4, 7. V, 2, 15. Oth. IV, 1, 93. *to w. with you*, Hml. III, 2, 360 (a much vexed passage, probably = to speak a word in private with you).

**Wither,** 1) intr. to become sapless, to dry, to fade; used of plants: Ven. 418. 1182. Lucr. 1168. R2 V, 1, 8. H6B IV, 10, 67. H6C II, 5, 101. R3 II, 2, 42. Rom. I, 2, 10. Hml. IV, 5, 185. Lr. IV, 2, 35. Oth. V, 2, 15. Per. IV, 4, 35. Partic. —*ed:* Lucr. 1254. Pilgr. 177. Tp. I, 2, 463. All's I, 1, 175 (*French* —*ed pears;* cf. H4A III, 3, 4. H4B IV, 4, 8). Wint. V, 3, 133. R2 II, 1, 134. II, 4, 8. H4B IV, 5, 230. H6A II, 5, 11. H6C III, 2, 156. R3 II, 2, 41. IV, 4, 394. Tit. III, 1, 113. 168. Ant. IV, 15, 64. Cymb. IV, 2, 286. Per. II, 2, 43. With *up: mine arm is like a blasted sapling* —*ed up*, R3 III, 4, 71.

Metaphorically; used of the effect of age in man: Sonn. 126, 4. Wiv. V, 5, 161. LLL IV, 3, 242. Mids. II, 1, 50. Shr. II, 239. 406. IV, 5, 43. H4B II, 4, 8. 281. H5 IV, 1, 316. V, 2, 170. H6A II, 4, 110. R3 I, 3, 215. Troil. I, 3, 297. Mcb. I, 3, 40. Of any physical or moral decay: *a —ed servingman a fresh tapster*, Wiv. I, 3, 19. *such short-lived wits do w. as they grow*, LLL II, 54. *I am —ed like an old apple-john*, H4A III, 3, 4. *shall see thee —ed, bloody, pale and dead*, H6A IV, 2, 38. *if you contend, a thousand lives must w.* H6C II, 5, 102. *O —ed truth!* Troil. V, 2, 46. —*ed murder*, Mcb. II, 1, 52 (gaunt, spectre-like).

Sometimes = to pine away, to languish, to lead an uncomfortable life: *the cedar stoops not to the base shrub's foot, but low shrubs w. at the cedar's root*, Lucr. 665. *earthlier happy is the rose distilled than that which* —*ing on the virgin thorn grows, lives and dies in single blessedness*, Mids. I, 1, 77. With an accus. denoting an effect: *a dowager long —ing out a young man's revenue*, Mids. I, 1, 6 (consuming in a lingering manner).*

2) tr. to cause to decay: *age cannot w. her*, Ant.

II, 2, 240. *let prisons swallow 'em, debts w. 'em to nothing*, Tim. IV, 3, 538.

**Withers**, the juncture of the shoulder-bones of a horse at the bottom of the neck: H4A II, 1, 8 (*wrung in the w.*). Hml. III, 2, 253 (*our w. are unwrung*).

**Withhold** (impf. not found, partic. *withheld*) to hold back: Ven. 612. H6B V, 1, 152. R3 III, 1, 30. IV, 5, 5 (Ff *holds off*). = to hinder, to restrain: H4B IV, 5, 135. Troil. V, 3, 51. Caes. III, 2, 108. Ant. III, 6, 79. IV, 14, 69 (*the gods w. me!*). = not to send, not to execute: *w. revenge, dear God!* H6C II, 2, 7. John IV, 2, 125. V, 6, 37. Per. II, 4, 4. = to keep back instead of granting: Mids. II, 1, 26. As V, 4, 174. Shr. I, 2, 121 (*from*). John I, 18. H6A IV, 4, 31.

**Within**, prep. 1) in the inner part or in the limits of: *beauty w. itself should not be wasted*, Ven. 130. *I have hemmed thee here w. the circuit of this ivory pale*, 230. 235. *thy sea w. a puddle's womb is hearsed*, Lucr. 657. Tp. I, 2, 277. V, 60. Gent. II, 1, 40. Meas. III, 2, 143. 285. Err. V, 265. Ado II, 1, 99. Mids. II, 1, 138. As II, 3, 17. John IV, 2, 254. H6A II, 4, 3. IV, 1, 140 (*that w. ourselves we disagree*, = that discord reigns in the midst of us). Mcb. V, 2, 24 etc. Temporally, = in the course of, during: *w. which space she died*, Tp. I, 2, 279. *did he send you both these letters at an instant? W. a quarter of an hour*, Wiv. IV, 4, 5. — Transposed: *'tis better thee without than he w.* Mcb. III, 4, 14.

Peculiar expressions: *some get w. him, take his sword away*, Err. V, 34 (close with him so as to be able to disarm him. cf. Locrine IV, 2: *I ran w. her and delighted her so with the sport I made* etc.). *keep yourself w. yourself*, Ant. II, 5, 75 (don't be beside yourself).

Very often quite equivalent to in: *w. whose face beauty and virtue strived*, Lucr. 52. *w. his thought her heavenly image sits*, 288. *they whose guilt w. their bosoms lie*, 1342. *against that time do I ensconce me here w. the knowledge of mine own desert*, Sonn. 49, 10. *lean penury w. that pen doth dwell*, 84, 5. *I would have sunk the sea w. the earth*, Tp. I, 2, 11. *mercy then will breathe w. your lips*, Meas. II, 2, 78. *the fraughting souls w. her* (the ship) 13. *I'll ... sleep w. mine inn*, Err. I, 2, 14. *Satan, housed w. this man*, IV, 4, 57. *the fiend is strong w. him*, 110. *your love, so rich w. his soul*, Mids. III, 2, 229. *one come not w. another's way*, 359. *I have w. my mind a thousand raw tricks*, Merch. III, 4, 76. *the spirit of my father which I think is w. me*, As I, 1, 24. *such war of white and red w. her cheeks*, Shr. IV, 5, 30. *how hollow the fiend speaks w. him*, Tw. III, 4, 101. *to spite a raven's heart w. a dove*, V, 134. Wint. V, 1, 149. *who died w. the year of our redemption four hundred twenty six*, H5 I, 2, 60. *this lies all w. the will of God*, 289. *run a tilt at death w. a chair*, H6A III, 2, 51. H6B III, 1, 199. R3 I, 4, 23. V, 3, 86. Tim. IV, 3, 117. Caes. II, 1, 280. Per. I, 1, 88 etc.

2) in the reach or compass of: *come not w. his danger by thy will*, Ven. 639. *bring me w. the level of your frown*, Sonn. 117, 11. *though rosy lips w. his bending sickle's compass come*, 116, 10. *come not w. the measure of my wrath*, Gent. V, 4, 127. *she is not w. hearing*, II, 1, 8. *take heed the queen come not w. his sight*, Mids. II, 1, 19. Err. III, 1, 87. LLL II, 51. 67. Mids. I, 1, 50. Merch. I, 1, 137. H6B IV, 7, 28. Rom. III, 3, 52. Mcb. IV, 3, 234 etc.

Used to denote distance of place or time; a) of place: *w. a mile*, Wint. IV, 3, 104. Cor. I, 4, 8 etc. With *of*: *w. a mile of my court*, LLL I, 1, 120. H5 III, 7, 136. Caes. III, 1, 286. Lr. IV, 6, 25 etc. Similarly denoting distance or difference of measure: *your title, which is w. a very little of nothing*, All's II, 4, 27. *yet will he, w. three pound, lift as much as his brother Hector*, Troil. I, 2, 126 (only three pounds less).

b) of time; 1) with respect to the present: *I come w. an hour of my promise*, As IV, 1, 42 (an hour too late). 2) to the past: *w. this hour I was his bondman*, Err. V, 288 (an hour ago). *a blind man ... w. this half-hour hath received his sight*, H6B II, 1, 64. R3 III, 6, 8. H8 III, 2, 253. Cor. I, 8, 7. 3) to the future: *broken, dead w. an hour*, Pilgr. 174. *I'll free thee w. two days*, Tp. I, 2, 421. III, 2, 122. Meas. I, 2, 69. 198. IV, 2, 213. Err. I, 2, 11. Merch. I, 3, 158. As I, 3, 45. H6B III, 1, 327 etc.

**Within**, adv. in the inner parts, internally: Sonn. 119, 2. 146, 3. 12. Wiv. V, 5, 60. Meas. III, 1, 93. V, 16. Merch. I, 1, 83. I, 2, 105. II, 7, 59. Shr. IV, 1, 51. Wint. IV, 4, 490. Rom. I, 3, 90. Cymb. V, 1, 33 etc.

Especially = 1) in the house: *there's wood enough w.* Tp. I, 2, 314. *we'll drink w.* Wiv. I, 1, 196. *who's w. there?* I, 4, 139. *who talks w. there?* Err. III, 1, 38. 71. Meas. IV, 3, 156. LLL III, 117. Merch. II, 6, 25. R3 III, 7, 61. Oth. I, 1, 84. 2) at home: *he sent me word to stay w.* Wiv. III, 5, 59. As IV, 3, 83. Shr. V, 1, 19. 20. Tw. III, 1, 54. 63. 3) in another part of the house: *I like the new tire w. excellently*, Ado III, 4, 13. *yonder is heavy news w.* All's III, 2, 35. = in the next room: *go, stand w., let me alone with him*, John IV, 1, 85. *I'll drown you in the malmsey-butt w.* R3 I, 4, 277. *I'll call upon you straight; abide w.* Mcb. III, 1, 140. Hence used in calling on servants or other persons in the vicinity: *what, ho! w., come forth*, Meas. IV, 1, 50. *holla, w.!* Shr. II, 109. *who is w. there?* R2 V, 2, 74. H6B I, 4, 82. *w. there! Flaminius! Servilius!* Tim. II, 2, 194. *who's w.?* Caes. II, 2, 3. *some wine, w. there!* Ant. III, 11, 73 etc.

**Withold**; *St. W.*, supposed to mean St. Vitalis: *S. W. footed thrice the old*, Lr. III, 4, 125 (O. Edd. *Swithald* or *Swithold*).

**Without**, 1) adv. a) on the outside, outwardly, externally: *within be fed, w. be rich no more*, Sonn. 146, 12. *if the devil be within and that temptation w.* Merch. I, 2, 106. Shr. IV, 1, 52. Troil. III, 3, 97. V, 8, 1. Rom. I, 3, 90. Cymb. III, 2, 22. V, 1, 33. = to the outside, out: *turned your wit the seamy side w.* Oth. IV, 2, 146. — *within and out* = within and without, Wiv. V, 5, 60. cf. *without or in*, Troil. III, 3, 97.

b) out of doors, not in a house or room or other place: *here w. you shall be so received*, LLL II, 173. *here stays w. a messenger*, Merch. IV, 1, 107. H8 V, 3, 5. Tim. V, 4, 39. Mcb. IV, 1, 135. Hml. IV, 3, 14. IV, 5, 112. Oth. II, 3, 31.

c) in a state of not having: *if best were as it was, or best w.* Compl. 98.

2) prepos. a) out of, on the outside of: *w. the bed her other fair hand was*, Lucr. 393. *they are all perceived w. ye*, Gent. II, 1, 35. Mids. I, 1, 165. I, 2, 104. As III, 2, 179. R2 V, 2, 56. Troil. III, 3, 82. Rom. III, 3, 17. Mcb. III, 1, 47. Cymb. IV, 2, 307. Transposed: *it* (blood) *is better thee w. than he within*, Mcb. III, 4, 14.

b) beyond, not in the reach of: *and deal in her*

(the moon's) *command w. her power*, Tp. V, 271 (without being subject to her pernicious influence). *w. the peril of the Athenian law*, Mids. IV, 1, 158.

c) except: *businesses which none w. thee can sufficiently manage*, Wint. IV, 2, 16 (or = wanting thee and thy help?).

d) not with; in the state of not having or not being with: Ven. 846. 1008. Tp. I, 2, 74. 137. II, 1, 160. 184. II, 2, 177. III, 2, 100. V, 179. Gent. II, 1, 36. 37. II, 2, 16. II, 4, 57. 208. III, 1, 116. IV, 1, 29. V, 4, 62. Wiv. I, 1, 288. III, 3, 12. Err. I, 2, 67. II, 2, 88. 130 etc. etc.

3) conj., used by Speed, Dromio and Dogberry, = unless: *w. you were so simple, none else would*, Gent. II, 1, 38. *such a one as a man may not speak of w. he say 'Sir-reverence'*, Err. III, 2, 92. *he may stay him; marry, not w. the prince be willing*, Ado III, 3, 86.

**Without-door**, outward, external: *her w. form*, Wint. II, 1, 69.

**Withstand** (partic. *withstood*) to oppose, to resist: R2 I, 1, 173. H6B IV, 5, 4. H6C IV, 1, 146.

**Witless** (cf. *Wit*) unwise; unwitty; deranged: Meas. I, 3, 10. Shr. II, 266. Troil. V, 3, 86.

**Witness**, subst. (plur. —*es*; but *to be w.*, in the sense of testify, unchanged after plural nouns: Merch. II, 6, 32. Shr. IV, 2, 24. H6A II, 3, 9. H6B IV, 8, 65. R3 III, 4, 69. Tit. V, 1, 103. Tim. IV, 3, 486. cf. *to this I w. call the fools of time*, Sonn. 124, 13), 1) testimony, attestation: Ado IV, 2, 82. Merch. I, 3, 100. H6A III, 4, 37 (*in w.*). H6B III, 1, 168. H8 V, 1, 137. Cor. V, 3, 204. Tit. II, 3, 116. Mcb. II, 2, 47. With *of* subjectively: *may we, with the warrant of womanhood and the w. of a good conscience, pursue him*, Wiv. IV, 2, 220. *in foul mouth and in the w. of his proper ear to call him villain*, Meas. V, 310. *upon the w. of these gentlemen*, Hml. I, 2, 194. Objectively: *it is the w. still of excellency to put a strange face on his own perfection*, Ado II, 3, 48. *in w. of my love*, As III, 2, 1; Troil. III, 2, 61. H5 IV, 3, 97. H6B I, 3, 204. 213. Cor. IV, 5, 78. *to bear w.*: Sonn. 131, 11. Compl. 53. Gent. V, 4, 119. Wiv. II, 3, 36. Err. IV, 4, 80. 93. Ado V, 2, 89. H5 IV, 8, 38. H8 II, 1, 59. III, 2, 425. *to bear a p. w.*: Ado II, 3, 240. H5 V, 2, 385. Ant. IV, 9, 5. *to bear w. to something:* Tp. III, 1, 68. Wint. IV, 4, 395. V, 1, 72.

2) one who, or a thing which, bears testimony: Sonn. 124, 13. Gent. IV, 2, 110. Wiv. IV, 2, 139. Meas. V, 167. 193. Err. V, 317. Ado III, 2, 132. LLL V, 2, 33. Merch. II, 6, 24. Shr. II, 322. IV, 4, 95. All's IV, 2, 24 (*take the Highest to w.*). Tw. V, 140. Wint. IV, 4, 288. 401. John II, 274. R2 II, 1, 130. H6A II, 3, 9. H6B I, 3, 192. IV, 8, 65. H6C III, 3, 138. H8 II, 1, 17. V, 1, 108. Troil. III, 2, 205. Tit. V, 3, 78. Tim. IV, 3, 486. Caes. V, 1, 74. Mcb. V, 1, 21. Oth. III, 4, 153. With *of*, objectively: Shr. II, 52. IV, 2, 24. R3 I, 2, 234. III, 4, 69. Tit. V, 1, 103. With *to:* *be w. to it*, Wint. IV, 4, 380. *your mother lives a w. to that vow*, R3 III, 7, 180. IV, 4, 5. Ant. IV, 9, 7. Cymb. II, 3, 156 (*call w. to it*). *I am w. with her* = I bear her w. Err. IV, 4, 92.

*With a w.* = palpably, grossly: *here's packing with a w.* Shr. V, 1, 121.

**Witness**, vb. to bear testimony: Err. I, 1, 34. Merch. V, 271. Shr. II, 338. John IV, 2, 218. H6A IV, 5, 43. H8 III, 2, 269. V, 3, 30. Tit. V, 1, 5. V, 3, 114. 124. Tim. I, 1, 137 (*I call the gods to w.;*

vb.?). III, 2, 56. III, 4, 25. Oth. III, 3, 463. Cymb. II, 2, 35. The subjunctive imperatively or optatively: *heaven w., I have been …*, H8 II, 1, 22. *thy conscience w.* Cymb. III, 4, 48. with inversion: *w. this primrose bank*, Ven. 151. *w. the entertainment that he gave*, 1108. *w. heaven*, Gent. II, 6, 25. *w. you that he is borne about invisible*, Err. V, 186. *ever w. for him those twins of learning*, H8 IV, 2, 57. H5 II, 4, 53. IV, 8, 54. H6B II, 4, 86. III, 1, 292. H6C V, 7, 32. R3 I, 3, 267. Troil. IV, 1, 8. Tit. III, 1, 119. V, 2, 22—25. V, 3, 63. Caes. V, 1, 31. Hml. IV, 4, 47. Lr. V, 3, 77.

With *to:* *I w. to the times that brought them in*, Wint. IV, 1, 11. *thereto w. may my surname*, Cor. IV, 5, 73.

With *with: thus far I w. with him, that he dined at home*, Err. V, 254. 324. *God w. with me … how cold it struck my heart*, H4B IV, 5, 150. R2 IV, 63. R3 IV, 4, 60.

With an object, transitively, = to give testimony to, to attest: *that my two ears can w.* Err. II, 1, 46. *comes not that blood as modest evidence to w. simple virtue*, Ado IV, 1, 39. *all the story … more —eth than fancy's images*, Mids. V, 25. *mine eye doth his effigies w. most truly limned and living in your face*, As II, 7, 193. *shall see thy virtue —ed*, III, 2, 8. *the strond whereon the imperious flood hath left a —ed usurpation*, H4B I, 1, 63 (= a witness of its usurpation, the traces of the ravage caused by it). *—ing the truth on our side*, H6A II, 4, 63. *w. my obedience*, Cymb. III, 4, 68. Err. V, 220. All's V, 3, 200. H4A II, 4, 515. H6B I, 3, 176. R3 III, 7, 70. Mcb. IV, 3, 184. Oth. I, 3, 170. Per. I, 4, 51. II, 5, 66.

Sometimes almost = to prove, to show: *to thee I send this written embassage, to w. duty, not to show my wit*, Sonn. 26, 4. *letters … whose contents shall w. to him I am near at home*, Meas. IV, 3, 99. *the sun sets weeping in the lowly west, —ing storms to come*, R2 II, 4, 22. Gent. IV, 4, 74. LLL IV, 1, 81.

**Wit-old**, a word coined by Moth in derision of Armado and in allusion to *wittol:* LLL V, 1, 66.

**Wit-snapper**, one hunting after wit: Merch. III, 5, 55.

**Witted**, in *blunt-witted*, H6B III, 2, 210.

**Wittenberg**, town in Germany, seat of a university: Hml. I, 2, 113. 119. 164. 168.

**Wittily**, cunningly, sagaciously, ingeniously: *which cunning love did w. prevent*, Ven. 471. *as the old hermit of Prague … very w. said*, Tw. IV, 2, 16.

**Wittingly**, with knowledge, by design, on purpose: *nor w. have I infringed my vow*, H6C II, 2, 8. *if I drown myself w.* Hml. V, 1, 11. 13. cf. *Unwittingly.*

**Wittol**, a cuckold: Wiv. II, 2, 313.

**Wittolly**, cuckoldly: *the jealous w. knave*, Wiv. II, 2, 283.

**Witty**, 1) wise, discreet: *it is the —est partition that ever I heard discourse*, Mids. V, 168. *better a w. fool than a foolish wit*, Tw. I, 5, 39. *she'll come straight, you must be w. now*, Troil. III, 2, 32.

2) cunning, artful: *a marvellous w. fellow*, Ado IV, 2, 27. *the deep-revolving w. Buckingham*, R3 IV, 2, 42.

3) possessed of wit, full of pleasant conceits: Err. III, 1, 110. LLL V, 1, 4. Shr. II, 266. All's II, 4, 32. Tw. I, 5, 30. III, 2, 46. H4B I, 2, 11. H6C I, 2, 43. H8 Epil. 6. Tit. IV, 2, 29. Oth. II, 1, 132.

**Wive**, to marry: *hanging and —ing goes by destiny*, Merch. II, 9, 83. *to w. and thrive*, Shr. I, 2, 56. *when I came to w.* Tw. V, 406. *when my fate would have me w.* Oth. III, 4, 64 (Ff —*d*). *that hook of —ing, fairness*, Cymb. V, 5, 167.*With a superfluous it: to w. it wealthily*, Shr. I, 2, 75.

Trans.: *I had rather he should shrive me than w. me*, Merch. I, 2, 145. *manned, horsed and —d*, H4B I, 2, 61. *is your general —d?* Oth. II, 1, 60. *to be —d to fair Marina*, Per. V, 2, 10.

**Wizard**, a conjurer; a soothsayer: Err. IV, 4, 61. H6B I, 4, 18. V, 2, 69. R3 I, 1, 56.

**Wo**, interj.; *wo ha ho!* a cry to attract attention: Merch. V, 39.

**Wodde** or **Wode**, see *Wood.*

**Woe**, extreme calamity and grief: Ven. 254. 455. Lucr. 928. Compl. 18. Tp. II, 1, 3. 6. Gent. II, 4, 138. III, 1, 219. 228. IV, 4, 149. V, 4, 6. Meas. II, 1, 298. IV, 1, 13. V, 118. Err. I, 1, 2. 28. 109. II, 1, 15. II, 2, 207. Ado II, 3, 70. V, 1, 11. Mids. III, 2, 442. V, 384. Wint. III, 2, 210. John III, 4, 55. H6C I, 4, 115 etc. etc. *weal and w.* Ven. 987. H6A III, 2, 92. Rom. III, 2, 51.

Used as an exclamation of grief or a denunciation of calamity: *w. to that land that's governed by a child!* R3 II, 3, 11 (cf. Ecclesiastes X, 16). H4B V, 3, 144. Caes. III, 1, 258. *w. upon ye*, H8 III, 1, 114. Oth. III, 3, 366. *a Helen and a w.!* Troil. II, 2, 111. *cry w.* Wint. III, 2, 201. R2 III, 2, 102. IV, 149. R3 III, 3, 7. Lr. III, 2, 33. *w. that too late repents*, Lr. I, 4, 279. *but w. 'tis so*, Ant. IV, 15, 17. *w.!* Ven. 833. *w. for England!* R3 III, 4, 82. *w. to her chance!* Tit. IV, 2, 78. *O w.!* Rom. IV, 5, 49. V, 3, 13. *w., alas!* Mcb. II, 3, 92. *alas, and w.* Ant. IV, 14, 107. *alack for w.* LLL IV, 1, 15. R2 III, 3, 70.

*To* after it omitted: *w. is me!* Compl. 78. H6B III, 2, 72. Tit. III, 1, 240. Hml. III, 1, 168. III, 2, 173. *w. me!* Meas. I, 4, 26. *w. is my heart*, Cymb. V, 5, 2. *O w. the day*, Tp. I, 2, 15. *w. the while!* Wint. III, 2, 173. H5 IV, 7, 78. Caes. I, 3, 82.

Hence adjectively: *I am w. for it*, Tp. V, 139. *be w. for me*, H6B III, 2, 73. *w. are we*, Ant. IV, 14, 133. *should make you w.* Sonn. 71, 8.

The exclamation rechanged to a substantive, = lamentation: *this for whom we rendered up this w.* Ado V, 3, 33. *let us pay the time but needful w.* John V, 7, 110. *whose guiltless drops are every one a w., a sore complaint*, H5 I, 2, 26.

**Woe-begone**, overwhelmed with grief: H4B I,1,71.

**Woeful**, (superl. —*est*: R2 IV, 146. H6B III, 2, 409. Tit. III, 1, 290) 1) distressed with grief, afflicted: Lucr. 1125. Sonn. 145, 4. Compl. 143. Meas. II, 2, 27. LLL V, 2, 818. R2 II, 2, 99. V, 1, 42. H6A I, 4, 71. III, 3, 51. H6B III, 2, 409. H6C II, 1, 45. II, 5, 124. R3 I, 3, 193. IV, 1, 90. Troil. IV, 4, 58. Tit. III, 1, 290. IV, 1, 89. V, 2, 82. V, 3, 50. Rom. III, 3, 85 (*w. sympathy* = sympathy of woe). Mcb. II, 3, 64. Per. IV Prol. 3.

2) expressing grief: *a w. ditty*, Ven. 836. 1126. As II, 7, 148. H6B III, 2, 342. Per. III, 2, 88.

3) causing grief, calamitous, afflictive: As II, 7, 138. R2 IV, 146. 321. H6A I, 4, 77. H6C II, 5, 107. R3 I, 2, 249. H8 II, 1, 167. Rom. IV, 5, 30. 49. Caes. III, 2, 204. Lr. V, 3, 202.

**Woe-wearied**, tired by continual lamentations: *my w. tongue is mute and dumb*, R3 IV, 4, 18.

**Wold**, writing of most M. Edd. for *old* of O. Edd. in Lr. III, 4, 125; see *Old.*

**Wolf**, the animal Canis lupus: Ven. 459. 1097. Lucr. 677. 878. Sonn. 96, 9. Err. IV, 2, 36. Mids. II, 1, 180. V, 379 (behowls the moon). Merch. IV, 1, 73. 134. Tw. III, 1, 140. Wint. III, 3, 67. H4B I, 2, 174 (*wake not a sleeping w.* = do not revive the memory of what, fortunately for you, is past and forgotten). 175. H6A I, 3, 55. I, 5, 30. V, 4, 31. H6B III, 1, 78 (*ravenous*). H6C II, 4, 13. V, 4, 80. V, 6, 7. R3 IV, 4, 23. H8 I, 1, 159. Troil. I, 3, 121. III, 2, 200. Cor. II, 1, 8. IV, 6, 110. Tim. IV, 3, 336. 337 (*greedy*). Caes. I, 3, 104. Mcb. II, 1, 53. IV, 1, 22. Lr. II, 4, 213. III, 1, 13. III, 4, 96 (*greedy*). III, 6, 20 (*trusts in the tameness of a w.*). Cymb. III, 3, 41 (warlike).

Plur. *wolves:* Lucr. 165 (*owls' and —ves' death-boding cries*). Tp. I, 2, 288. Ado V, 3, 25. As V, 2, 119 (*'tis like the howling of Irish —ves against the moon*). Wint. II, 3, 187. H4B IV, 5, 138 (*thy,* i. e. England's, *old inhabitants*). H5 III, 7, 162 (*eat like—ves*). H6B III, 1, 192. IV, 1, 3. H6C I, 2, 242. I, 4, 5. 111 (—*ves of France*). Tim. III, 6, 105. IV, 1, 2. IV, 3, 189. Lr. III, 7, 63. Oth. III, 3, 404 (*as salt as —ves in pride*).

**Wolfish**, see *Wolvish.*

**Wolsey;** Cardinal W., Henry VIII 's lord chancellor: H8 I, 1, 173. 179. II, 2, 74. 141. III, 2, 436. IV, 2, 6.

**Wolvish** (most M. Edd. *Wolfish*) resembling a wolf: Merch. IV, 1, 138. Lr. I, 4, 330. Doubtful passage: *why in this woolvish tongue should I stand here?* (F1) Cor. II, 3, 122. Later Ff *in this woolvish gown.* M. Edd. *woolish gown, woolless toge* etc. cf. *Toge.*

**Wolvish-ravening**, greedily devouring like a wolf: *w. lamb*, Rom. III, 2, 76.

**Woman**, subst. the female of the human race, grown to adult years (cf. Meas. III, 2, 49 & LLL IV, 1, 125): Sonn. 144, 4. Tp. III, 1, 49. III, 2, 108. Gent. II, 3, 31. II, 7, 40. III, 1, 91. 105. Wiv. IV, 2, 77. 87. Err. I, 1, 38 etc. etc. Used as an address: Wiv. I, 4, 142. II, 1, 43. 44. III, 3, 114. IV, 2, 21. Cor. IV, 1, 12 etc. *to play the —'s part*, Gent. IV, 4, 165. *act the w. in the scene*, Cor. II, 2, 100. *the wise w.* Tw. III, 4, 114 (cf. *Wise*). *to play the w.* = to weep: H8 III, 2, 431; cf. Hml. IV, 7, 190. *a w. of the world* = a married w. As V, 3, 5 (cf. *World*). *a —'s reason; I think him so, because I think him so*, Gent. I, 2, 23 (cf. *wherefore not afield? Because not there: this —'s answer sorts*, Troil. I, 1, 109). *a —'s longing*, Wint. IV, 4, 681. Troil. III, 3, 237. *a —'s war*, R2 I, 1, 48. *this —'s mood*, H4A I, 3, 237. *a —'s fault*, III, 1, 245. *a —'s tailor*, H4B III, 2, 161. 169. *my —'s heart*, R3 IV, 1, 79. *my —'s breasts*, Mcb. I, 5, 48. *a —'s story*, III, 4, 65 etc. In a general sense without the article: Tw. II, 2, 39. III, 2, 40. Wint. IV, 4, 191. Tim. IV, 3, 501. Mcb. IV, 1, 80. IV, 3, 126. Lr. III, 4, 94 etc. Plur. *women:* Ven. 1008. Tp. I, 2, 47. II, 1, 155. III, 1, 43. Gent. III, 2, 33. IV, 1, 72. IV, 4, 95. V, 4, 44. 109. Wiv. I, 1, 309. 310 etc. etc.

= wife: *the hell of having a false w.* Wiv. II, 2, 305. *a banished w. from my Harry's bed*, H4A II, 3, 42. cf. Cor. V, 3, 130.

= female attendant: All's I, 3, 20. H8 V, 1, 63. 68. Cymb. II, 2, 1. II, 3, 143. 145. III, 2, 76. Wint.

II, 1, 124. II, 2, 12. H8 I, 4, 93. IV, 2, 140. Ant. III, 13, 38. IV, 13, 1. IV, 15, 62. V, 2, 360. Cymb. I, 5, 74. II, 3, 71 etc.

**Woman**, vb.: *I have felt so many quirks of joy and grief, that the first face of neither, on the start, can w. me unto't,* All's III, 2, 53; i. e. according to Johnson, make pliant like a woman, or, as Steevens expresses it, affect me suddenly and deeply. But as the speaker is herself a woman, and the words *unto't* also must have a meaning, it may perhaps be = to make a servant, to subdue.

**Womaned**, accompanied by a woman: *to have him see me w.* Oth. III, 4, 195.

**Womanhood**, the particular character of woman in a good sense: Wiv. IV, 2, 220. H4A III, 3, 125. 129. 139. Troil. V, 2, 129. Tit. II, 3, 174. 182.

**Womanish**, suitable to a woman in a bad sense, effeminate: John IV, 1, 36. R3 I, 4, 264. H8 II, 1, 38. Troil. I, 1, 110. Rom. III, 3, 110. IV, 1, 119. Caes. I, 3, 84.

**Womankind** (Shr.) or **Womenkind** (Per.) the female sex: Shr. IV, 2, 14. Per. IV, 6, 159.

**Womanly**, 1) pertaining to a woman: *as prisoners to her w. persuasion,* Shr. V, 2, 120.
2) suitable to a woman, resembling a woman, womanish: *why do I put up that w. defence, to say I have done no harm?* Mcb. IV, 2, 78. *nor the queen of Ptolemy more w. than he,* Ant. I, 4, 7.

**Woman-post**, a female post: John I, 218.

**Woman-queller**, one who kills women: *thou art ... a man-queller, and a w.* H4B II, 1, 58 (Mrs Quickly's speech).

**Woman-tired**, hen-pecked: *thou art w., unroosted by thy dame Partlet here,* Wint. II, 3, 74.

**Womb**, subst. the uterus of a female, or what resembles it (particularly applied to the earth as conceiving and producing things): Sonn. 3, 5. 97, 8. Tp. I, 2, 120. Meas. I, 4, 43. Mids. II, 1, 131. Tw. V, 245. Wint. II, 2, 59. John II, 182. III, 1, 44. IV, 3, 128 *(the smallest thread that ever spider twisted from her w.).* V, 2, 152. R2 I, 2, 22. II, 1, 51. II, 2, 10 *(some unborn sorrow, ripe in fortune's w.).* H4A I, 1, 23. H4B V, 4, 15. H6A IV, 5, 35. V, 4, 63. H6C III, 2, 153. IV, 4, 18. R3 I, 3, 231. IV, 1, 54. IV, 4, 47. 54. 138. 296. 423. H8 II, 4, 188. Cor. I, 3, 7. III, 3, 114. V, 3, 124. Tit. IV, 2, 124. Rom. II, 3, 10. Tim. IV, 3, 3. 178. 187. Mcb. V, 8, 15. Lr. I, 4, 300. Oth. I, 3, 377 *(there are many events in the w. of time which will be delivered).* Ant. I, 2, 38. III, 13, 163. Cymb. V, 4, 37. Per. I, 1, 107. III, 1, 34. Applied to the brain as conceiving thoughts: Sonn. 86, 4. LLL IV, 2, 71. Metaphorically, any thing hollow that receives or contains sth.: *thy sea within a puddle's w. is hearsed,* Lucr. 657. *a hill whose concave w. reworded a plainful story,* Compl. 1. *the earth ... whose hollow w. resounds,* Ven. 268. Lucr. 549. H4A III, 1, 31. Hml. I, 1, 137. *gaunt as a grave, whose hollow w. inherits nought but bones,* R2 II, 1, 83. Tit. II, 3, 239. Rom. V, 3, 45. *through the foul w. of night,* H5 IV Chor. 4. *as hasty powder fired doth hurry from the fatal cannon's w.* Rom. V, 1, 65.

Jocularly applied by Falstaff to his belly as more becoming a woman than a man: *an I had but a belly of any indifferency, I were simply the most active fellow in Europe: my w., my w., my w. undoes me,* H4B IV, 3, 25.

**Womb**, vb. to enclose, to contain: *for all the sun sees or the close earth —s,* Wint. IV, 4, 501.

**Womby**, hollow, capacious: *caves and w. vaultages of France,* H5 II, 4, 124.

**Womenkind**, see *Womankind.*

**Woncot**, see *Wincot.*

**Wonder**, subst. 1) a miracle: *but* (= except) *in them it were a w.* Phoen. 32. *by what w. you do hit of mine* (name) Err. III, 2, 30. *a w., master! here's a costard broken in a shin,* LLL III, 71. *I am to discourse —s,* Mids. IV, 2, 29. *Lucentio must get a father, ... and that's a w.; fathers commonly do get their children,* Shr. II, 411. *here is a w.* V, 2, 106. *a thing impossible to compass —s but by helps of devils,* H6A V, 4, 48. *there's some w. in this handkerchief,* Oth. III, 4, 101. John II, 497. R2 V, 5, 19.
2) matter of surprise: *O w., how many goodly creatures are there here!* Tp. V, 181. 170. *you shall see —s,* Wiv. V, 1, 13. Ado V, 4, 70. LLL I, 2, 144. Mids. V, 154. As V, 2, 31. Shr. III, 2, 193 *(make it no w.).* V, 2, 189 *('tis a w.).* Wint. V, 2, 26. John II, 50. H5 I, 1, 53. H6A I, 1, 122. H6B II, 4, 46. R3 V, 4, 2. H8 V, 5, 56. Troil. III, 3, 195. 242. Caes. II, 2, 34. Lr. IV, 7, 41 *('tis w.)* etc.
3) anything exciting admiration, a prodigy: *vouchsafe, thou w., to alight thy steed,* Ven. 13. *w. of time,* 1133. *this composed w. of your frame,* Sonn. 59, 10. Tp. I, 2, 426. 427. II, 2, 170. Gent. I, 1, 6. Err. III, 2, 32. LLL I, 1, 12. IV, 3, 85. H5 III, 7, 43. H6A IV, 7, 48. H8 I, 1, 18. I, 2, 119. V, 5, 41. Rom. III, 3, 36. Cymb. IV, 2, 176 etc.
4) surprise, astonishment: *torment, trouble, w. and amazement inhabits here,* Tp. V, 104. *I am so attired in w. I know not what to say,* Ado IV, 1, 146. As V, 4, 145. All's II, 3, 7. Tw. IV, 3, 3. Wint. V, 2, 17. H5 II, 2, 110. II, 4, 135. H6A V, 3, 195. Caes. I, 3, 60. Mcb. III, 4, 112. Hml. IV, 5, 89. Oth. II, 1, 185 *(it gives me w.)* etc. With *of: will quench the w. of her infamy,* Ado IV, 1, 241. *I stood rapt in the w. of it,* Mcb. I, 5, 6. Proverbial: *a w. lasts nine days;* cf. As III, 2, 185. H6B II, 4, 69. H6C III, 2, 113. 114.
5) admiration: *in silent w. of still-gazing eyes,* Lucr. 84. *too much w. of his eye,* 95. *all ignorant that soul that sees thee without w.* Pilgr. 65 & LLL IV, 2, 117. *that we with thee may spend our w. too,* All's II, 1, 92. *how thou tookest it* (viz wonder) 93. *the mute w. lurketh in men's ears,* H5 I, 1, 49. Tw. II, 1, 29. Wint. V, 1, 133. V, 3, 22. Mcb. I, 3, 92.

**Wonder**, vb. 1) to be surprised, to marvel: Ado III, 2, 115. Mids. V, 129. As I, 1, 164. Shr. IV, 5, 63. With an inf.: *—s to hear thee speak of Naples,* Tp. I, 2, 432. With a clause: Gent. I, 3, 4. Err. V, 13. Ado I, 1, 117. I, 3, 11. II, 3, 8. Merch. III, 3, 8. All's V, 3, 155. H4A IV, 3, 16. R3 III, 2, 26. H8 I, 1, 54. III, 2, 374 etc. The clause with an interrog. pronoun or adverb: Gent. V, 4, 169. Meas. II, 2, 187. As III, 2, 181. All's II, 1, 93. Tw. III, 4, 165. Wint. V, 2, 184. H6C IV, 5, 2. Troil. IV, 5, 211 etc. With *at:* Lucr. 1845. Wiv. IV, 6, 13. Meas. III, 1, 191. Err. IV, 2, 47. Ado III, 3, 123. Mids. II, 2, 6. V, 128. 135. All's IV, 1, 95. Tw. I, 5, 210. H4A III, 2, 29. H6C I, 4, 131. V, 4, 57. Tit. III, 1, 135. Rom. III, 5, 119. Cymb. V, 3, 53. 54 etc. Per. II, 3, 63.(*)
With *of: I w. of their being here together,* Mids. IV, 1, 136 (Q2 Ff *of this being* etc.). *on't* = of it: *I w. on't,* Tim. III, 4, 10.

Trans.: —*ing each other's chance*, Lucr. 1596.
2) to admire: *have eyes to w., but lack tongues
to praise*, Sonn. 106, 14. *grown in grace equal with
—ing*, Wint. IV, 1, 25. *her words ... makes me from
—ing fall to weeping joys*, H6B I, 1, 34. With *at:
whereat the impartial gazer late did w.* Ven. 748. *nor
did I w. at the lily's white*, Sonn. 98, 9. *not —ing at
the present nor the past*, 123, 10. *are these the breed
of wits so —ed at?* LLL V, 2, 266. *that he* (the sun)
*may be more —ed at*, H4A I, 2, 225. *w. at him*, H5
III, 7, 41.
3) *I w.* = I should like to know: *and w. what
they were*, LLL V, 2, 304. *I w. if Titania be awaked*,
Mids. III, 2, 1. *I w. if the lion be to speak*, V, 153. *I
w. what it bodes*, Shr. V, 2, 107. *a boy or a child, I
w.?* Wint. III, 3, 71. *I w. how the king escaped our
hands*, H6C I, 1, 1. II, 1, 1. *he —s to what end you
have assembled such troops*, R3 III, 7, 84.
**Wondered**, having the power of performing
miracles, wonder-working: *so rare a w. father*, Tp.
IV, 123 (cf. *A*).
**Wonderful**, surprising, marvellous: Wiv. II, 2,
62. III, 1, 39. Ado II, 3, 98 (followed by *should*).
As III, 2, 201. Shr. IV, 2, 15. Tw. III, 4, 290. V, 232.
John III, 4, 178. H4B V, 1, 72. H5 III, 6, 83. IV, 8,
117. R3 I, 2, 73. 74. III, 1, 135. Caes. I, 3, 14. Hml.
I, 5, 118. III, 2, 340. Ant. I, 2, 159.
Adverbially: *w. froward*, Shr. I, 1, 69. *a w. sweet
air*, Cymb. II, 3, 19. cf. As III, 2, 201.
**Wonderfully**, in a surprising manner: Cymb. I,
4, 21.
**Wonder-wounded**, struck with surprise: *conjures the wandering stars and makes them stand like
w. hearers*, Hml. V, 1, 280.
**Wondringly:** *your shafts of fortune, though they
hurt you mortally, yet glance full w. on us*, Per. III, 3,
7. M. Edd. *wanderingly.* Perhaps *woundingly.*
**Wondrous**, wonderful, marvellous, admirable:
635. Lucr. 1528. Sonn. 105, 6. 12. Tp. II, 2, 168.
Merch. I, 1, 163. Shr. III, 50. III, 2, 97. John II, 497.
IV, 2, 184. H4B II, 3, 32. H6A I, 2, 64. V, 3, 190
(*her w. praise* = the praise of her wondrous qualities,
the praise which makes a wonder of her). Cor. II, 1,
152. Tit. II, 3, 112. 286. V, 1, 55. Hml. III, 4, 170.
IV, 7, 87.
Adverbially (before adjectives and adverbs) = in
a strange degree: Tp. II, 1, 198. Err. III, 2, 94. Mids.
V, 59. Merch. II, 8, 48. All's III, 6, 121. V, 3, 311.
John III, 2, 1. H4A I, 3, 277 (Ff *it will do w. well*,
Qq *it will do well*). III, 1, 168. H6A V, 5, 1. H6C II,
1, 33. IV, 8, 17. Cor. I, 1, 91. II, 1, 40. Rom. IV, 2,
46. Hml. I, 5, 164. Oth. I, 3, 161. Per. II, 5, 36.
III, 2, 53.
**Wondrously**, in a strange degree: Tim. III, 4, 71.
**Wont**, subst. custom: *'tis not his w. to be the
hindmost man*, H6B III, 1, 2. *the season wherein the
spirit held his w. to walk*, Hml. I, 4, 6.
**Wont**, vb. (originally impf. of the obsol. *won*,
and therefore not inflected in the third person) to be
accustomed: *my curtal dog, that w. to have played*,
Pilgr. 273. *I bear it on my shoulders, as a beggar w.
her brat*, Err. IV, 4, 39. *Talbot is taken, whom we w.
to fear*, H6A I, 2, 14. *how the English w. through
a secret grate ... to overpeer the city*, I, 4, 10.
Partic. *wont* = accustomed, habituated, doing
customarily; used only in the predicate with the vb.

*to be;* in the present tense only when speaking of
things not liable to change: *ten times faster Venus'
pigeons fly to seal love's bonds new-made, than they
are w. to keep obliged faith unforfeited*, Merch. II, 6,
6. *greet in silence, as the dead are w.* Tit. I, 90. Imperfect: *where thou wast w. to rest thy weary head*,
Lucr. 1621. *when I was w. to greet it with my lays*,
Sonn. 102, 6. *you were w. to be a follower*, Wiv. III,
2, 2. Gent. II, 1, 27. 78. II, 4, 126. 204. Err. II, 2,
155. Ado II, 3, 19. III, 2, 56. LLL I, 1, 44. Mids.
IV, 1, 59. 76. 77. Merch. II, 5, 8. III, 1, 50. Wint.
IV, 4, 359. R2 II, 1, 65. H6A V, 3, 14. H6C I, 4,
77. II, 6, 76. R3 I, 4, 121. III, 7, 29 (Ff used). IV,
2, 17. V, 3, 74. Cor. IV, 1, 16. II, 1, 130. III, 2, 8.
IV, 5, 188. Tit. III, 4, 10. Caes. I, 2, 34.
Hml. II, 2, 341. V, 1, 210. Lr. I, 4, 64. 185. Oth. V,
2, 110. Cymb. II, 4, 40. In R2 V, 5, 99 Qq *taste of
it first, as thou art w. to do;* Ff, conformably to the
use of the poet, *as thou wert w.* In Oth. II, 3, 190 Qq
*you were w. be civil*, Ff *w. to be civil.* — With the
adverb *often:* Mids. I, 1, 215. As II, 2, 9.
Partic. or adj. *wonted* = customary; always before a subst.: *whose —ed lily white with purple tears
was drenched*, Ven. 1053. *if thou wilt permit the sun
to climb his —ed height*, Lucr. 776. *change their —ed
liveries*, Mids. II, 1, 113. III, 2, 369. H4B V, 5, 104.
H6A III, 1, 32. V, 3, 21. H6C II, 5, 49. H8 IV, 2,
102. Hml. II, 2, 354. III, 1, 41. Cymb. V, 5, 462.
**Woo**, to solicit, to seek to gain (persons) or to
obtain (things); absol.: *sing, and let me w. no more*,
Ado II, 3, 50. *I should w. hard but be your groom*,
Cymb. III, 6, 70. With *for: w. for leave to do him
good*, Hml. III, 4, 155. Trans.: *being —ed of time*,
Sonn. 70, 6 (*of* = by). *leave me alone to w. him*, As
I, 3, 135. *—ing poor craftsmen with the craft of smiles*,
R2 I, 4, 28. *I must w. you to help unarm our Hector*,
Troil. III, 1, 162. *he's tetchy to be —ed to w.* I, 1, 99.
*his occasions might have —ed me first*, Tim. III, 3,
15. *rather w. those that would mischief me*, IV, 3, 474.
*so did we w. transformed Timon to our city's love*, V,
4, 18. *hath a hundred times —ed me to steal it*, Oth.
III, 3, 293. *our king himself doth w. me oft for my con-
fections*, Cymb. I, 5, 14. *having —ed a villain to
attempt it*, Per. V, 1, 174. *nor did with unbashful forehead w. the means of weakness*, As II, 3, 50. *your poor
friends must w. your company*, II, 7, 10. not to w.
*honour, but to wed it*, All's II, 1, 15. *in —ing sorrow
let's be brief*, R2 V, 1, 93. *you took occasion to be
quickly —ed*, H4A V, 1, 56. *w. your own destruction*,
H8 V, 1, 141. *reflecting gems, which —ed the slimy
bottom of the deep*, R3 I, 4, 32; cf. *the wind, who —es
even now the frozen bosom of the north*, Rom. I, 4, 100.
Usually = to court, to solicit in love; absol.:
Ven. 358. 570. Sonn. 41, 7. Gent. IV, 4, 111. Wiv.
II, 2, 244. III, 2, 86. III, 4, 51. Ado III, 3, 51. 53. V,
2, 41. LLL V, 2, 135. 884. Mids. V, 139. Merch. II,
9, 75. Shr. I, 1, 148. I, 2, 68. Tw. III, 1, 166. H5
V, 2, 125. Troil. I, 1, 99 etc. Trans.: Ven. 6. 97.
159. 309. Sonn. 142, 10. 144, 8. Pilgr. 144. Gent.
II, 1, 154. V, 4, 57. Wiv. II, 1, 117. II, 3, 92. III,
4, 14. V, 5, 142. LLL IV, 3, 371. Mids. I, 1, 16. II,
1, 242. II, 2, 130. Shr. I, 1, 149. II, 195. IV, 2, 51.
H6A V, 3, 65. 124. 138. R3 I, 2, 228. Troil. I, 2,
312. Oth. I, 3, 166 (*I should but teach him how to
tell my story, and that would w. her;* i. e. woo and
win her) etc. etc.

**Wood,** subst. 1) a forest: Ven. 323. 826. Gent. V, 3, 9. V, 4, 2. Mids. I, 1, 165. 214. 247. I, 2, 104. II, 1, 138. 192. 223. II, 2, 35. III, 1, 153. III, 2, 94. 310. IV, 1, 118 etc. As II, 1, 3. 32. III, 3, 50. V, 4, 165. Shr. Ind. 2, 59. R2 III, 1, 23 *(my forest —s)*. H4A I, 2, 199. H6B IV, 10, 3. H6C III, 2, 174. V, 4, 67. Tit. II, 1, 128. II, 2, 2. IV, 1, 53. Rom. I, 1, 132. Tim. IV, 1, 35. IV, 3, 208. 538. Mcb. III, 2, 51. IV, 1, 93. V, 2, 5. V, 3, 2. V, 4, 3 and passim in this play.
2) the hard substance of trees: Sonn. 128, 2 (the key of a piano). Tp. I, 2, 312. 314. II, 2, 16. 75. 165. Wiv. V, 5, 92. LLL IV, 3, 248. 249. Shr. Ind. 1, 49 *(sweet w.)*. R2 III, 3, 150. H6A V, 3, 90. Tit. I, 128. Caes. III, 2, 147. Hml. IV, 7, 20.

**Wood,** adj. mad, frantic: *frenzies w.* Ven. 740. *here am I, and w. within this wood,* Mids. II, 1, 192 (Q1 *wodde). how the young whelp of Talbot's, raging w., did flesh his sword,* H6A IV, 7, 35. Conjectured by M. Edd. in Gent. II, 3, 30 (O. Edd. *would),* but not quite convincingly.

**Woodbine,** honeysuckle: Ado III, 1, 30. Mids. II, 1, 251. IV, 1, 47.*

**Wood-bird,** a bird living in woods: Mids. IV, 1, 145.

**Woodcock,** the bird Scolopax rusticola: Tw. IV, 2, 64. H6C I, 4, 61. Hml. I, 3, 115. V, 2, 317. Emblem of stupidity: Ado V, 1, 158. LLL IV, 3, 82. Shr. I, 2, 161. All's IV, 1, 100. Tw. II, 5, 92.

**Wooden,** made of wood: H5 Prol. 13. IV, 4, 77. H6A I, 1, 19. Lr. II, 3, 16. II, 4, 10. Per. IV, 6, 183. *this w. slavery,* Tp. III, 1, 62 (piling wood at command). *the w. dialogue and sound 'twixt his stretched footing and the scaffoldage,* Troil. I, 3, 155. *that's a w. thing,* H6A V, 3, 89 ('an awkward business, not likely to succeed'. Steevens).

**Woodland,** land covered with wood: *I am a w. fellow that always loved a great fire,* All's IV, 5, 49.

**Wood-leaves,** leaves gathered in the wood: *with wild w. and weeds,* Cymb. IV, 2, 390.

**Woodman,** a huntsman: Lucr. 580. Wiv. V, 5, 30. Cymb. III, 6, 28. In a wanton sense: *he's a better w. than thou takest him for,* Meas. IV, 3, 170.

**Woodmonger,** one who deals in wood: H5 V, 1, 69 (Fluellen's speech).

**Woodstock;** Thomas of W. Duke of Gloster, sixth son of Edward III: R2 I, 2, 1 (Ff. *Gloster's*). H6B II, 2, 16.

**Woodvile,** name of 1) the lieutenant of the Tower in H6A I, 3, 22. 2) Antony W., brother of Edward IV's queen Elizabeth: R3 I, 1, 67. II, 1, 68 (omitted in Qq and most M. Edd.).

**Wooer,** one who solicits in love: Wiv. I, 4, 173. Ado II, 1, 365. II, 3, 52. LLL V, 2, 838. Merch. I, 2, 119. 147. Shr. I, 1, 252. I, 2, 244. II, 252. Tw. I, 3, 17. H6C III, 2, 83. R3 IV, 3, 43. IV, 4, 327. Tim. IV, 3, 385. Oth. I, 3, 176. Cymb. II, 1, 64.

**Woof,** the cross thread in weaving: *a point as subtle as Ariachne's* (i. e. the spider's) *broken w.* Troil. V, 2, 152.

**Wooingly,** invitingly: *the heaven's breath smells w. here,* Mcb. I, 6, 6.

**Wool,** the soft hair growing on sheep: Wint. IV, 3, 35. Lr. III, 4, 109. *w. of bat,* Mcb. IV, 1, 15.

**Woollen,** made of wool: *a w. bagpipe,* Merch. IV, 1, 56 (the Lowland bagpipe commonly having the bag or sack covered with woollen cloth of a green colour. Johnson *wooden,* Capell *wawling,* Steevens *swollen,* Collier *bollen). w. vassals,* Cor. III, 2, 9 (= coarse).
Substantively, = cloth made of wool: *I could not endure a husband with a beard on his face: I had rather lie in the w.* Ado II, 1, 33 (between the blankets without sheets; a beard affecting the skin, in kissing, as disagreeably).

**Woolly,** 1) having wool instead of hair: *these w. breeders* (i. e. sheep) Merch. I, 3, 84. 2) resembling wool: *my fleece of w. hair,* Tit. II, 3, 34.

**Woolsack,** a sack of wool: H4A II, 4, 148.

**Woolward,** in wool only, without linen, a dress often enjoined as a penance by the church of Rome *I have no shirt, I go w. for penance,* LLL V, 2, 717.

**Woosel,** see *Ousel.*

**Woo't,** see *Will.*

**Worcester,** town in England: John V, 7, 99. H4A IV, 1, 125. Thomas Percy Earl of W.: R2 II, 2, 58. II, 3, 22. H4A I, 1, 96. I, 3, 15. II, 4, 392 etc. H4B I, 1, 125.

**Word,** subst. 1) a single component part of the language; f. i. *the w. 'noddy',* Gent. I, 1, 131. *blow not a w. away,* I, 2, 118. *mistake the w.* III, 1, 284. *is so from w. to w.* Alls III, 7, 10. *speaks four languages w. for w. without book,* Tw. I, 3, 28. Wiv. IV, 1, 68. LLL IV, 3, 4. Mids. II, 2, 106. Merch. III, 5, 48. Tw. III, 1, 17. 66. R3 I, 4, 109. III, 1, 83. Tim. II, 2, 161 etc. Used for the idea expressed by it: *for wisdom's sake, a w. that all men love, or for love's sake, a w. that loves all men,* LLL IV, 3, 357. *life is as bitter as a twice-told tale vexing the dull ear of a drowsy man, and bitter shame hath spoiled the sweet word's* (viz life) *taste, that it yields nought but shame and bitterness,* John III, 4, 110 (M. Edd. perhaps rightly *world's*).
A single part of speech considered as sufficient for the communication of thought: *but one w.* Tp. II, 1, 296. *interrupt the monster one w. further,* III, 2, 77. *one w., good friend. Lucio, a w. with you,* Meas. I, 2, 146. As III, 2, 237. 239. *hear me but one w.* H6C I, 1, 170. *a w., good sir,* Tp. I, 2, 442. 443. Gent. III, 1, 204. IV, 1, 38. Caes. IV, 2, 13. *a w. or two,* Gent. I, 3, 52. Wiv. II, 2, 42. *in a w.* = in short: Gent. II, 4, 71. Merch. I, 1, 35. III, 2, 99 etc. *with a w.,* in the same sense, H4A II, 4, 283. *at a w.* (German: *kurz und gut*): *he hath wronged me; indeed he hath; at a w. he hath, believe me,* Wiv. I, 1, 109. *at a w., hang no more about me,* II, 2, 16. *you are Signior Antonio. At a w., I am not ... You are he, you are he. At a w., I am not,* Ado II, 1, 118. 125. *go with us. No, at a w., madam,* Cor. I, 3, 122. *I am at a w., follow,* Wiv. I, 3, 15 (= I am not of many words; so said, so done). *I have spoke at a w.,* H4B III, 2, 319. Caes. I, 2, 270.
2) a watch-word, a parole, a motto: *cover is the w.* Merch. III, 5, 57. *hob nob is his w.* Tw. III, 4, 263. *the w. of peace is rendered,* H4B IV, 2, 87. *couple a gorge, that is the w.* H5 II, 1, 76. II, 3, 51. *our ancient w. of courage, fair St. George,* R3 V, 3, 349. *the w. is 'mildly',* Cor. III, 2, 142. *slaying is the w.* Caes. V, 5, 4. *now to my w. .... it is 'remember me',* Hml. I, 5, 110. *antiquity forgot, custom not known, the ratifiers and props of every w.* IV, 5, 105 (of every thing that is to serve for a watch-word and shibboleth to the multitude. All the proposed emendations quite un-

necessary). *his w. was still Fie, foh and fum*, Lr. III, 4, 188. *give the w.* IV, 6, 93. *death's the w.* Ant. I, 2, 139. *you were the w. of war*, II, 2, 44. *his name, that magical w. of war*, III, 1, 31. *hanging is the w.* Cymb. V, 4, 155. V, 5, 422. *the w. Lux tua vita mihi*, Per. II, 2, 21. 30. 33 (in v. 27. 38 and 44 *motto*).

3) speech, language: *speak fair —s*, Ven. 208. *her —s are done*, 254. *free vent of —s*, 334. *ere his —s begun*, 462. *foul —s and frowns*, 573. *I endowed thy purposes with —s*, Tp. I, 2, 358. *their —s are natural breath*, V, 156. Gent. I, 2, 105. II, 1, 164. III, 1, 91. Meas. V, 225. 368. Ado I, 1, 159. LLL IV, 1, 19. H6B I, 2, 89. R3 IV, 4, 126. Troil. IV, 1, 73. Hml. III, 2, 20. Lr. I, 2, 172 etc. Opposed to deeds: Tp. V, 71. Gent. II, 2, 18. H6A III, 2, 49. H8 III, 2, 154. Troil. IV, 5, 259. Mcb. II, 1, 61. Per. II Prol. 4. cf. *to fill the world with —s*, H6C V, 5, 44. to matter: H4A II, 4, 479. Troil. V, 3, 108. Rom. II, 6, 30. Lr. I, 1, 56. III, 2, 81. to writing: *might not you transport her purposes by w.?* Lr. IV, 5, 20. *by w. of mouth*, Tw. II, 3, 141. III, 4, 209. Caes. III, 1, 280. to a musical tune (= text): Mids. V, 405. Wint. IV, 4, 216. 620. Mcb. I, 3, 88. Cymb. II, 3, 20. IV, 2, 237.

*Good w.* or *good —s* = kindness expressed, commendation, praise: *where your good w. cannot advantage him*, Gent. III, 2, 42. *to speak a good w. to Mistress Anne Page for my master*, Wiv. I, 4, 88. *good —s went with her name*, Meas. III, 1, 220. *weeping-ripe for a good w.* LLL V, 2, 274. *neither my good w. nor princely favour*, R2 V, 6, 42. *neither gave to me good w. nor look*, Troil. III, 3, 144. *we have ever your good w. He that will give good —s to thee will flatter beneath abhorring*, Cor. I, 1, 170. 171. *you gave good —s of a bay courser*, Tim. I, 2, 217. *in your bad strokes you give good —s*, Caes. V, 1, 30.

= speech exchanged, conversation: *if you spend w. for w. with me*, Gent. II, 4, 41. *the friar and you must have a w. anon*, Meas. V, 364. *a man may break a w. with you*, Err. III, 1, 75. *to change a w.* LLL V, 2, 238; cf. Ado IV, 1, 185. *maintain no —s with him*, Tw. IV, 2, 107. *some —s there grew 'twixt Somerset and me*, H6A VI, 5, 46. *the generals would have some —s*, Caes. V, 1, 25. *to give —s or talk with the Lord Hamlet*, Hml. I, 3, 134. *that first we come to —s*, Ant. II, 6, 3 etc. cf. *to bandy w. for w.* Shr. V, 2, 172. H6C I, 4, 49.

4) anything said or pronounced: *with that w. she spied the hunted boar*, Ven. 900. *even at this w. she hears a merry horn*, 1025. *the woeful —s she told*, 1126. *w. of denial in thy labras here*, Wiv. I, 1, 166. *would take you at your w.* Err. I, 2, 17. Rom. II, 2, 49. Caes. I, 2, 270. *I will not eat my w.* As V, 4, 155, i. e. retract; cf. Ado IV, 1, 280. H4B II, 2, 150. *the hopeless w. of 'never to return'*, R2 I, 3, 152. *upon the w.* Caes. I, 2, 104 etc. = saying: *hath planted in his memory an army of good —s*, Merch. III, 5, 72. *dun's the mouse, the constable's own w.* Rom. I, 4, 40. = assurance; promise: *his w. is more than the miraculous harp*, Tp. II, 1, 86. *you have an exchequer of —s*, Gent. II, 4, 44. 46. *his —s are bonds*, II, 7, 75. *his w. might bear my wealth*, Err. V, 8. *engaged a prince's w.* 162. *we arrest your w.* LLL II, 160. *I'll not trust your w.* Mids. III, 2, 268. *if thou proceed as high as w.* Alls II, 1, 213 etc. *on my w.* Wiv. IV, 2, 61. 79. Meas. V, 269. *o'my w.* Rom. I, 1, 1. *first, of my w.* Ado V, 4, 123 (*of* for *on*; cf. *Of*). Tit. IV,

3, 59. *I'll be as good as my w.* (cf. *Good*): Wiv. III, 4, 112. Tw. III, 4, 357. H4A III, 3, 164. H4B V, 5, 90. *if my gossip Report be an honest woman of her w.* Merch. III, 1, 8. *they are not men o'their —s*, Lr. IV, 6, 106. *to break one's w.* H4B II, 3, 10. H5 III, 2, 37 (*breaks —s*; quibbling). H6A IV, 3, 31. IV, 6, 2 (*with*). *his sons shall give their —s for him*, H6B V, 1, 137. *to Master Brook you yet shall hold your w.* Wiv. V, 5, 258. *to keep one's w.* Mids. I, 1, 222. III, 2, 266 (*with*). Shr. III, 2, 108. John V, 1, 5. H4A I, 2, 135. H5 IV, 1, 238. Lr. III, 4, 83. *he will not pass his w.* Tw. I, 5, 87. *to take him at his w.* LLL II, 217. *I take your princely w.* H4B IV, 2, 66 etc. etc.

= communication, information, message: *I must carry her w. quickly*, Wiv. III, 5, 48. *I brought you w. that ...*, Err. IV, 3, 37. Merch. I, 2, 138. V, 28. Tw. IV, 2, 72. Wint. II, 3, 136. H4A V, 1, 109. H4B II, 4, 20. H5 III, 5, 68. H6A I, 4, 19. Cor. I, 10, 31. Mcb. IV, 1, 141. Ant. II, 5, 114. 118. Cymb. I, 5, 49. *Achilles shall have w. of this intent*, Troil. I, 3, 306. *he sent me w. to stay within*, Wiv. III, 5, 59. *to send him w. they'll meet him*, IV, 4, 18. *I'll send him certain w. of my success*, Meas. I, 4, 89. As V, 4, 74. 76. 78. Shr. V, 2, 80. John V, 3, 7 (*by*). H4A I, 1, 94. III, 2, 164. H6B III, 2, 243 & H6C II, 1, 206 (*by*). Tit. III, 1, 151. Caes. I, 3, 38. Ant. IV, 13, 4 etc.

= order, command: *when your —s are done*, Err. I, 1, 27. *every soldier kill his prisoner; give the w. through*, H5 IV, 6, 38. *the w. of Caesar might have stood against the world*, Caes. III, 2, 123. *stand, ho! give the w., ho! and stand*, IV, 2, 2 (i. e. the order to stand). *stand, ho! speak the w. along*, 33. *Brutus gave the w. too early*, V, 3, 5.

5) the Scripture, or any part of it: *the sword and the w., do you study them both, master parson?* Wiv. III, 1, 44. *make us pay down ... the —s of heaven*, Meas. I, 2, 126. *set the w. itself against the w.* R2 V, 5, 13 (Ff *faith ... faith*). *turning the w. to sword*, H4B IV, 2, 10.

**Word**, vb. 1) to pronounce, to speak: *say that the last I spoke was 'Antony', and w. it piteously*, Ant. IV, 13, 9. Opposed to singing: *I cannot sing: I'll weep and w. it with thee*, Cymb. IV, 2, 240.

2) to express, to represent, to let appear: *this matter of marrying his king's daughter, wherein he must be weighed rather by her value than his own, —s him, I doubt not, a great deal from the matter*, Cymb. I, 4, 16 (sets him in a light very different from reality).

3) to flatter with words, to cajole: *he —s me, girls, he —s me, that I should not be noble to myself*, Ant. V, 2, 191.

**Wordless**, without words: *her joy with heaved-up hand she doth express and w. so greets heaven for his success*, Lucr. 112.

**Work**, subst. 1) employment, labour, toil, task imposed: *when body's w.'s expired*, Sonn. 27, 4. *there's more w.* Tp. I, 2, 238. V, 5. *you do their w.* Mids. II, 1, 41. All's I, 1, 24. Wint. IV, 4, 687. 702. John II, 93. R2 III, 1, 44. H4A II, 4, 118. H5 IV, 3, 18. H8 III, 1, 74 (*set at w.*). Troil. V, 5, 21. V, 8, 3. V, 10, 38. Rom. III, 5, 178. Caes. I, 1, 34. Cymb. I, 5, 57.

2) Passing, by imperceptible degrees, into the general idea of any thing done or to be done by voluntary activity, sometimes synonymous to deed or doing, sometimes to business: *let's follow it, and after do*

*our w.* Tp. III, 2, 158. *no man their* (the fairies') —*s must eye*, Wiv. V, 5, 52. *when the w. of generation was ... in the act*, Merch. I, 3, 83. *you would be prouder of the w.* (viz of bearing with patience the absence of Bassanio) III, 4, 8. *I have w. in hand that you yet know not of*, 57. *this is not Fortune's w.* As I, 2, 54. *he that of greatest* —*s is finisher*, All's II, 1, 139. *to w.!* John II, 37. *who by the hand of France this day hath made much w. for tears in many an English mother*, 303. *make w. upon ourselves*, 407. *it is a damned and a bloody w.* IV, 3, 57. *if that it be the w. of any hand*, 59. 60. *knew you of this fair w.?* 116. *you look but on the outside of this w.* V, 2, 109. *toiled with* —*s of war*, R2 IV, 96. H4A I, 3, 48. 54. H5 I, 2, 114. III, 2, 93. 120. IV, 2, 19. IV, 3, 97. H6A I, 3, 83. H6B I, 4, 15. 23. R3 I, 4, 158 (Ff *shall we fall to w.*, Qq *shall we to this gear*). II, 1, 1. III, 2, 116. III, 7, 246 (Qq *task*). H8 V, 1, 18. Troil. I, 3, 18. V, 3, 48. Cor. I, 1, 56. I, 4, 10. 20. I, 5, 18. I, 8, 9. I, 9, 1. II, 2, 49. III, 1, 261. IV, 6, 88. 95. 100. V, 1, 15. V, 3, 62. Tit. V, 2, 150. Rom. II, 6, 35 (*we will make short w.*). V, 3, 261. Caes. I, 3, 129. II, 1, 327. IV, 3, 196. V, 1, 114. Mcb. II, 3, 134. III, 1, 135. III, 6, 33. Hml. III, 2, 251. V, 2, 333 (*venom, do thy w.*). Lr. V, 3, 39. Oth. V, 2, 213. 364. Ant. IV, 7, 2 (*Caesar himself has w.* = has to do, is in great straits). IV, 14, 105. V, 2, 328 (*what w. is here?* = what business have we here?). Cymb. V, 3, 8. Per. IV, 1, 71. *to go to w. with* = to proceed with respect to: *I will go darkly to w. with her*, Meas. V, 279. *I'll go another way to w. with him*, Tw. IV, 1, 36. *I went round to w.* Hml. II, 2, 139. Sometimes = agency, operation: *those hours that with gentle w. did frame the lovely gaze*, Sonn. 5, 1. *a most miraculous w. in this good king*, Mcb. IV, 3, 147.

3) Any thing made by nature or art: *her* (nature's) *best w. is ruined with thy rigour*, Ven. 954. H5 II, 4, 60. R3 IV, 3, 18. Tim. I, 1, 202. Hml. II, 2, 316. Ant. I, 2, 160. *such sweet observance in this w.* (a painting) *was had*, Lucr. 1385. Wint. V, 2, 107. Tim. I, 1, 160. V, 1, 40. 116. Cymb. II, 4, 72. *a very good piece of w.* (a play) Mids. I, 2, 14. Shr. I, 1, 258. Wint. IV, 4, 21. Tim. I, 1, 19. 43. 228. Hml. III, 2, 52. *some stair w., some trunk w.* Wint. III, 3, 75. *graves only be men's* —*s*, Tim. V, 1, 225. Especially used of embroidery: Wint. IV, 4, 212. Oth. III, 3, 296. III, 4, 72. 180. 189. IV, 1, 156. 157.

4) fortification: *let 'em win the w.* H8 V, 4, 61. *I will be walking on the* —*s*, Oth. III, 2, 3.

**Work**, vb. (impf. and partic. always *wrought;* therefore *worked* for *work* in Tim. V, 1, 116 an inadmissible substitution of M. Edd.) 1) to be employed, to labour, to toil: *my nature is subdued to what it* —*s in*, Sonn. 111, 7. *w. you then*, Tp. I, 1, 45. *w. for bread*, Mids. III, 2, 10. Tp. III, 1, 12. 16. Mids. V, 72. H4A I, 2, 229. H5 I, 2, 187. H6B IV, 7, 57. H8 III, 1, 2. Hml. I, 5, 162. II, 1, 40. Oth. II, 1, 116. III, 3, 383. Cymb. III, 6, 32. Per. II, 1, 69. Applied to an artist: *wrought he not well that painted it?* Tim. I, 1, 200. 201.

Trans., = to produce by exertion and labour (of nature or art): *now she unweaves the web that she hath wrought*, Ven. 991. *Nature, as she wrought thee, fell a doting*, Sonn. 20, 10. *so much of earth and water wrought*, 44, 11. *a princess wrought it me* (a handkerchief) John IV, 1, 43. *great business must be wrought*

*ere noon*, Mcb. III, 5, 22. *so rarely and exactly wrought*, Cymb. II, 4, 75.

2) to be in action or motion: *what me your minister, for you obeys*, —*s under you*, Compl. 230. *no more remains but that to your sufficiency, as your worth is able, and let them w.* Meas. I, 1, 10. *to swear by him whom I protest to love, that I will w. against him*, All's IV, 2, 29. *never did base and rotten policy colour her* —*ing with such deadly wounds*, H4A I, 3, 109. *by whose fell* —*ing I was first advanced*, H4B IV, 5, 207. *many things, having full reference to one consent, may w. contrariously*, H5 I, 2, 206. —*ing so grossly in a natural cause*, II, 2, 107. *not* —*ing with the eye without the ear*, 135. *how I will w. to bring this matter to the wished end*, H6A III, 3, 27. *limbs are his instruments, in no less* —*ing than are swords and bows*, Troil. I, 3, 355. *that you w. not in holier shapes*, Tim. IV, 3, 429. *our will ... which else should free have wrought*, Mcb. II, 1, 19. *the instruments, who wrought with them*, III, 1, 82. *in what particular thought to w. I know not*, Hml. I, 1, 67. *briefness and fortune, w.* Lr. II, 1, 20. *the better shall my purpose w. on him*, Oth. I, 3, 397 (cf. Lucr. 235 sub 3). *we w. by wit and not by witchcraft*, II, 3, 378. *the sea* —*s high*, Per. III, 1, 48 (the sailor's speech). *have you a* —*ing pulse?* V, 1, 155. cf. Lucr. 361. Sonn. 124, 10. Meas. III, 2, 222. Merch. I, 3, 74. All's III, 7, 3. H8 II, 2, 24. Caes. II, 1, 209 (*let me w.* = let me do). Hml. III, 4, 205 (*let it w.* = let things take their course). Lr. I, 4, 231. IV, 7, 1. Ant. II, 2, 94. Cymb. I, 5, 48. IV, 3, 41 (*the heavens still must w.*). With an accus. denoting an effect: *to w. her son into the adoption of the crown*, Cymb. V, 5, 55. cf. Rom. III, 5, 145.

The gerund often applied to the motions or labours of the mind: *whate'er thy thoughts or thy heart's* —*ings be*, Sonn. 93, 11. *in the* —*ing of your own affections*, Meas. II, 1, 10. *we bend to that the* —*ing of the heart*, LLL IV, 1, 33. *his will hath in it a more modest* —*ing*, As I, 2, 215. *intelligencer between the grace, the sanctities of heaven and our dull* —*ings*, H4B IV, 2, 22 (= affections). *till that his passions ... confound themselves with* —*ing*, IV, 4, 41. *I am sick with* —*ing of my thoughts*, H6A V, 5, 86. *or given my heart a* —*ing mute and dumb*, Hml. II, 2, 137 (Ff *winking*). *from her* (his soul's) —*ing all his visage wann'd*, 580. Similarly with an accus. of the effect: *the incessant care ... hath wrought the mure so thin*, H4B IV, 4, 119.

Transitively, = to do, to perform, to act: *the wiles and guiles that women w.* Pilgr. 335. *that they may w. all exercise on thee*, Tp. I, 2, 327. *thou hast wrought a deed of slander*, R2 V, 6, 34. *rather to wonder at the things you hear than to w. any*, Cymb. V, 3, 55. The gerund substantively: *mock your* —*ings in a second body*, H4B V, 2, 90 (= actions, doings).

3) to operate, to produce an effect: *so from himself impiety hath wrought, that for his prey to pray he doth begin*, Lucr. 341. *it* —*s*, Tp. I, 2, 493. *my high charms w.* III, 3, 88. Wiv. IV, 2, 185. Meas. III, 2, 33. LLL I, 2, 10. All's I, 3, 190. Shr. III, 2, 220. Wint. III, 2, 181. H6B II, 1, 7. H8 Prol. 3. III, 2, 37. Caes. III, 2, 265. Hml. III, 4, 114. IV, 7, 20 (Ff *would*). Oth. III, 3, 123. V, 2, 323. Ant. IV, 14, 125. With *on* or *upon*: *this desire might have excuse to w. upon his wife*, Lucr. 235 (almost = to practise; cf. Tw. II, 3, 166 and Oth. I, 3, 397). *now Prosper* —*s upon thee*, Tp. II, 2, 84. *on that vice in him will my*

*revenge find notable cause to w.* Tw. II, 3, 166. *does it w. upon him?* II, 5, 213. H5 Prol. 18. II, 2, 112. H8 II, 2, 58. Tit. III, 2, 79. Tim. III, 1, 63. Caes. II, 1, 253. Hml. V, 1, 308. Oth. IV, 1, 286. Used of medicaments and poisons: Tp. III, 3, 105. Wint. I, 2, 320. H4B IV, 4, 47. Rom. IV, 3, 21. Oth. IV, 1, 45. Per. III, 2, 10. with *upon: with some mixtures he wrought upon her,* Oth. I, 3, 106. Cymb. I, 5, 28. with *with: my physic will w. with him,* Tw. II, 3, 188. II, 5, 215.

Transitively, = a) to produce by operation, to effect: *force must w. my way,* Lucr. 513. *why —est thou mischief in thy pilgrimage?* 960. *one silly cross wrought all my loss,* Pilgr. 258. *if you can . . . , w. the peace of the present,* Tp. I, 1, 24. *to w. mine end upon their senses,* V, 53. *his friends still wrought reprieves for him,* Meas. IV, 2, 140. Err. I, 1, 35. Ado II, 2, 54. Merch. III, 2, 90. As IV, 3, 53. Shr. V, 1, 127. John III, 4, 179. IV, 2, 236. R2 IV, 4. H6A I, 2, 49. III, 2, 39. V, 4, 41. 66. H6B I, 3, 70. II, 1, 186. III, 1, 73. V, 1, 70. H6C V, 7, 25. Troil II, 2, 114. Cor. V, 3, 201. Tit. I, 264. V, 2, 8. 32. Rom. V, 3, 245 *(it wrought on her the form of death).* Lr. II, 1, 86. IV, 7, 97. Per. III, 2, 38. With an infinitive: *you wrought to be a legate,* H8 III, 2, 311. *that hath beside well in his person wrought to be set high in place,* Cor. II, 3, 254. *that we have wrought so worthy a gentleman to be her bridegroom,* Rom. III, 5, 145 (not = induced, prevailed upon, but brought about, effected).

b) to act upon, to operate upon: *then begins a journey in my head, to w. my mind, when body's work's expired,* Sonn. 27, 4. *some passion that —s him strongly,* Tp. IV, 144. V, 17. *if I had thought the sight of my poor image would thus have wrought you,* Wint. V, 3, 58. *w. your thoughts, and therein see a siege,* H5 III Chor. 25. *have wrought the easy-melting king like wax,* H6C II, 1, 171. *my dull brain was wrought with things forgotten,* Mcb. I, 3, 149. *not easily jealous, but being wrought, perplexed in the extreme,* Oth. V, 2, 345.

With prepositional expressions denoting the result and change produced by operation or influence: *will w. us all from princes into pages,* H8 II, 2, 47. *what you would w. me to, I have some aim,* Caes. I, 2, 163. *thy honourable metal may be wrought from that it is disposed,* 313. *I will w. him to an exploit,* Hml. IV, 7, 64. *to w. her to your manage,* Per. IV, 6, 69.

With *out,* = to make out, to solve: *did not I say he would w. it out?* Tw. II, 5, 139. = to carry as a prize by endeavour, to gain, to save: *if we wrought out life, 'twas ten to one,* H4B I, 1, 182.

**Worker,** in *Half-worker,* q. v.

**Working,** see *Work* vb. 2.

**Working-day,** a day on which work is performed, not a holiday: Ado II, 1, 341. H5 I, 2, 277. IV, 3, 109. Adjectively, = common, ordinary, trivial, vulgar: *how full of briers is this w. world,* As I, 3, 12. cf. *Worky-day.*

**Working-house,** a house in which any manufacture is carried on: *in the quick forge and w. of thought,* H5 V Chor. 23.

**Workman,** pl. *workmen;* 1) one who is employed in any labour: *the king's council are no good workmen,* H6B IV, 2, 16 (Bevis' speech). *do villany . . . like workmen,* Tim. IV, 3, 438.

2) a skilful artificer, an artist: *the well-skilled w.*

*this mild image drew,* Lucr. 1520. *who's his tailor? he's a good w.* All's II, 5, 21. *when workmen strive to do better than well,* John IV, 2, 28. *excellent w., thou canst not paint a man so bad as is thyself,* Tim. V, 1, 32. *in respect of a fine w., I am but . . . a cobbler,* Caes. I, 1, 10. *thou shouldst see a w. in't* (the art of war) Ant. IV, 4, 18. *therein I must play the w.* Cymb. IV, 1, 7.

**Workmanly,** skilfully, with art: *so w. the blood and tears are drawn,* Shr. Ind. 2, 62.

**Workmanship,** skill, mastership: Ven. 291. 734. Cymb. II, 4, 74.

**Worky-day,** common, trivial: *a w. fortune,* Ant. I, 2, 55. cf. *Working-day.*

**World,** 1) the universe; all that has existence considered as a whole: *the w. hath ending with thy life,* Ven. 12. *from —'s minority,* Lucr. 67. *with thy daring folly burn the w.* Gent. III, 1, 155. *though all the —'s vastidity you had,* Meas. III, 1, 69. Err. II, 2, 108. III, 2, 102. Ado II, 1, 272. Tw. V, 414. R2 II, 1, 109. H5 IV, 3, 58 etc.

Emblem of immensity: *weakly fortressed from a w. of harms,* Lucr. 28. *what a w. of vile faults . . . ,* Wiv. III, 4, 32. *a w. of torments though I should endure,* LLL V, 2, 353. *nor doth this wood lack —s of company,* Mids. II, 1, 223. *his youthful hose a w. too wide,* As II, 7, 160. *with a w. of pretty, fond, adoptious christendoms,* All's I, 1, 187. *a w. of curses,* H4A I, 3, 164. *a w. of figures,* 209. *there will be a w. of water shed,* III, 1, 94. *when a w. of men could not prevail,* H6A II, 2, 48. *yields up his life unto a w. of odds,* V, 4, 25. *a w. of earthly blessings,* H6B I, 1, 22. *called forth from out a w. of men,* R3 I, 4, 186. *a w. of care,* III, 7, 223. *all that w. of wealth,* H8 III, 2, 211. *with such a hell of pain and w. of charge,* Troil. IV, 1, 57. *a w. of sighs,* Oth. I, 3, 159.

The same idea prevalent in the following expressions: *can the w. buy such a jewel!* Ado I, 1, 183. *I would not for the w.* Tp. V, 173. Gent. II, 4, 168. Ado IV, 1, 292. LLL II, 99. *by the w.!* LLL IV, 3, 19. V, 1, 107. 111. Shr. II, 161. *in the w.* = possible, imaginable; and hence, with negatives, = at all: *I would not wish any companion in the w. but you,* Tp. III, 1, 55. 72. *my son profits nothing in the w.* Wiv. IV, 1, 15. Meas. II, 1, 56. Ado II, 1, 17. Mids. V, 78. As V, 1, 9. All's III, 6, 105. Hml. III, 2, 245. Oth. V, 1, 103 etc. cf. *an I had but one penny in the w.* LLL V, 1, 74 (all in all). *never suffers matter of the w. enter his thoughts save such as do revolve and ruminate himself,* Troil. II, 3, 196 (not any at all). *offended, and with you chiefly i'the w.* Ant. II, 2, 33. *the least wind i'the w. will blow them down,* II, 7, 3.

*For all the w.,* in comparisons, = exactly: *whose posy was for all the w. like cutler's poetry upon a knife,* Merch. V, 149. *his lackey for all the w. caparisoned like the horse,* Shr. III, 2, 66. *for all the w. as thou art to this hour was Richard then,* H4A III, 2, 93. *he was for all the w. like a forked radish,* H4B III, 2, 334. Evans says: *it is that very person for all the w.* Wiv. I, 1, 50.

*It is a w. to see* = it is a treat to see: *when the age is in, the wit is out: God help us! it is a w. to see,* Ado III, 5, 38 (Dogberry's speech). *O, you are novices! 'tis a w. to see how tame . . . a meacock wretch can make the curstest shrew,* Shr. II, 313.

2) the whole sphere of any individual existence;

that which is the all to a particular being; f. i. the earth: *the —'s comforter* (the sun) Ven. 529. *the sun ... who doth the w. so gloriously behold that cedar-tops and hills seem burnished gold,* 857. *how the —'s poor people are amazed at apparitions,* 925. *blown round about the pendent w.* Meas. III, 1, 126. *lords of the wide w. and wild watery seas,* Err. II, 1, 21. *the three corners of the w.* John V, 7, 116. R2 I, 3, 269. III, 2, 38. Mcb. II, 1, 49. Hml. IV, 1, 41 etc. Considered as the scene of human life, almost = life: *must sell her joy, her life, her —'s delight,* Lucr. 385. *weary of the w.* Ven. 1189. *to take this poor maid from the w.* Meas. III, 1, 241. *he hath released him from the w.* IV, 3, 119. *there is another comfort than this w.* V, 49. 486. *we came into the w. like brother and brother,* Err. V, 424. John I, 112. *when in the w. I lived, I was the —'s commander,* LLL V, 2, 565. *take me from the w.* H6C I, 4, 167. *I am peppered for this w.* Rom. III, 1, 103. *the sweet degrees that this brief w. affords,* Tim. IV, 3, 253 etc. This present or earthly sphere of life opposed to another: *destiny, that hath to instrument this lower w. and what is in't,* Tp. III, 3, 54. *fleet the time carelessly, as they did in the golden w.* As I, 1, 125. *win a new —'s crown,* R2 V, 1, 24. *this beneath w.* Tim. I, 1, 44. *let both the —s suffer,* Mcb. III, 2, 16. *both the —s I give to negligence,* Hml. IV, 5, 134.

Any part of the earth: *a pair of maiden —s unconquered,* Lucr. 408. *this little w.* (England) R2 II, 1, 45. *for thy w. enjoying but this land,* 111. *there is a w. elsewhere,* Cor. III, 3, 135. *Britain is a w. by itself,* Cymb. III, 1, 13. *these demesnes have been my w.* III, 3, 70. cf. *O brave new w. that has such people in't,* Tp. V, 183. *one of the greatest in the Christian w.* All's IV, 4, 2. *where am I? where's my lord? what w. is this?* Per. III, 2, 106.

The microcosm of man: *storming her w. with sorrow's wind and rain,* Compl. 7. *in his little w. of man,* Lr. III, 1, 10. And opposed to it, all that is without: *the w.'s mine oyster, which I with sword will open,* Wiv. II, 2, 2. *to see the wonders of the w. abroad,* Gent. I, 1, 6. *I to the w. am like a drop of water,* Err. I, 2, 35. *hath seen the w.* LLL V, 1, 114. Shr. I, 2, 58. *comest thou from the —'s great snare uncaught?* Ant. IV, 8, 18.

Oftenest = society, the people among whom one lives: *whose full perfection all the w. amazes,* Ven. 634. *the lamp that burns by night dries up his oil to lend the w. his light,* 756. *the w. will hold thee in disdain,* 761. 1075. *not mine own fears nor the prophetic soul of the wide w. dreaming on things to come,* Sonn. 107, 2. *all the w. besides methinks are dead,* 112, 14. Tp. I, 2, 69. III, 1, 39. Gent. I, 1, 68. I, 3, 21. II, 7, 59. V, 4, 70. Wiv. II, 1, 21. II, 2, 136. IV, 5, 95. Meas. I, 2, 120. II, 2, 53. II, 4, 153. III, 2, 3. 234. Err. I, 1, 34. Ado I, 1, 98. 200. II, 1, 216. Mids. II, 1, 224. All's I, 3, 36. Troil. III, 2, 180 (*in the w. to come* = with future generations). Tim. I, 1, 138. Hml. V, 2, 390. Oth. II, 3, 192. Cymb. II, 4, 26 etc. etc. Particularly with respect to their manner of living and thinking: *in a better w. than this I shall desire more love and knowledge of you,* As I, 2, 296 (in a better state of things). *as I intend to thrive in this new w.* R2 IV, 78 (in this new state of things). *deliver them like a man of this w.* H4B V, 3, 102. *upon this riddle runs the wisdom of the w.* Meas. III, 2, 243.

*the grosser manner of these—'s delights,* LLL I, 1, 29. *to shield thee from diseases of the w.* Lr. I, 1, 177. *little of this great w. can I speak,* Oth. I, 3, 86. *the pleasures of the w.* Cymb. IV, 2, 296. cf. Meas. IV, 3, 127. John II, 561. IV, 3, 68. 141. H6B II, 4, 38. R3 II, 3, 5. H8 III, 2, 365. Cor. IV, 4, 12. IV, 5, 234. Mcb. III, 1, 109 etc. Hence, with contempt, that which engrosses the interest of most people: *you have too much respect upon the w.* Merch. I, 1, 74. *Fortune reigns in gifts of the w., not in the lineaments of nature,* As I, 2, 44.

Peculiar phrases: *to go to the w.* = to marry: Ado II, 1, 331. All's I, 3, 20. *a woman of the w.* = a married woman: As V, 3, 5.

Let *the w. slide,* and *let the w. slip,* Sly's philosophy in Shr. Ind. 1, 6 and 2, 146 (cf. *Slide*). Similarly in a popular rhyme: *so runs the w. away,* Hml. III, 2, 285. *To set the w. on wheels,* Gent. III, 1, 317 (cf. *Wheel*).

*How goes the w.* = how do you do? Shr. IV, 1, 36. Tim. I, 1, 2. Mcb. II, 4, 21. *how goes the w. with thee?* R3 III, 2, 98. cf. *as this w. goes,* Wint. II, 3, 72. *bring me word thither how the w. goes,* Cor. I, 10, 32. *we make his friends blush that the w. goes well,* IV, 6, 5. *how goes the w. that I am thus encountered with clamorous demands,* Tim. II, 2, 36 (= how comes it, how is it). *thou seest the w. how it goes; our enemies have beat us to the pit,* Caes. V, 5, 22. *the w. may laugh again,* H6B II, 4, 82 (= I may be fortunate again). *then the w. goes hard,* H6C II, 6, 77 (= then he is poorly off).

Similarly: *'twas never merry w. since of two usuries the merriest was put down,* Meas. III, 2, 6. Tw. III, 1, 109. H6B IV, 2, 9. *how the w. is changed with you,* Err. II, 2, 154 (= how you are changed). *bad w. the while!* John IV, 2, 100. *here's a good w.!* IV, 3, 116. R3 III, 6, 10. *is the w. as it was?* Meas. III, 2, 53 (are you the same man as you were?).

**Worldlings,** as it seems, = people of this our world, men: *poor deer, thou makest a testament as w. do, giving thy sum of more to that which had too much,* As II, 1, 48. *deliver them like men of this world. A foutre for the world and w. base; I speak of Africa and golden joys,* H4B V, 3, 103 (Pistol's speech).

**Worldly,** being of the world, in the world, pertaining to the world: *my duty pricks me on to utter that which else no w. good should draw from me,* Gent. III, 1, 9 (= no good in the world). *the weariest and most loathed w. life ... is a paradise to what we fear of death,* Meas. III, 1, 129 (= earthly). *the breath of w. men cannot depose the deputy elected by the Lord,* R2 III, 2, 56 (= mortal). *upon thy sight my w. business makes a period,* H4B IV, 5, 231 (my life ends). *hast thou not w. pleasure at command,* H6B I, 2, 45 (pleasures of the world). *with his soul fled all my w. solace,* III, 2, 151. *in common w. things 'tis called ungrateful, with dull unwillingness to repay a debt,* R3 II, 2, 91. *O momentary grace of w. men, which we more hunt for than the grace of God,* III, 4, 98 (Ff *mortal*). *in no w. suit would he be moved, to draw him from his holy exercise,* III, 7, 63 (no suit in the world). *secure from w. chances and mishaps,* Tit. I, 152. *we w. men have miserable, mad, mistaking eyes,* V, 2, 65. *life being weary of these w. bars* (dungeons, irons etc.) *never lacks power to dismiss itself,* Caes. I, 3, 96. *thou thy w. task hast done,* Cymb. IV, 2, 260. = pertaining to the state or society in which one lives, opposed to private or personal: *neglecting w. ends* (the government of the state), *all dedicated to closeness and the bettering of my mind,* Tp. I, 2, 89. *the worst is w. loss thou canst unfold,* R2 III, 2, 94. *of w. matters and direction,* Oth. I, 3, 300.

**World-sharers,** persons who have divided the world among them: Ant. II, 7, 76.

**World-wearied,** weary of life: Rom. V, 3, 112.

**World-without-end,** infinite, eternal: *nor dare I chide the w. hour whilst I watch the clock for you,* Sonn. 57, 5. *a time too short to make a w. bargain in,* LLL V, 2, 799.

**Worm,** 1) any small creeping animal: Lucr. 1248. Mids. II, 2, 23. H6C II, 2, 17. Mcb. IV, 2, 32. Per. IV, 1, 79. breeding in and destroying buds: Lucr. 848. Tw. II, 4, 114. Rom. I, 1, 157. feeding on human bodies after death: Sonn. 6, 14. 71, 4. 74, 10. 146, 7. Merch. II, 7, 69. As III, 2, 67. IV, 1, 108. John III, 4, 31. R2 III, 2, 145. H4A V, 4, 87. H4B IV, 5, 117. R3 IV, 4, 386. H8 IV, 2, 126. Rom. III, 1, 112. V, 3, 109 (*—s that are thy chamber-maids*). Hml. IV, 3, 21.* 22. 28. 30. V, 1, 97 (*now my Lady Worm's*). Cymb. IV, 2, 218. Per. IV, 2, 26. causing the toothache: Ado III, 2, 27. *pricked from the lazy finger of a maid,* Rom. I, 4, 65. producing silk: Lr. III, 4, 108. Oth. III, 4, 73.

Emblem of remorse gnawing the mind: *if Don W., his conscience, find no impediment,* Ado V, 2, 86. *the w. of conscience still begnaw thy soul,* R3 I, 3, 222.

Expression of pity: *poor w., thou art infected,* Tp. III, 1, 31. *the poor w.* (the mole) *doth die for it,* Per. I, 1, 102. of contempt: *vile w., thou wast o'erlooked even in thy birth,* Wiv. V, 5, 87. LLL IV, 3, 154. Shr. V, 2, 169. cf. Lr. IV, 1, 35.

2) a snake: *dost fear the soft and tender fork of a poor w.* Meas. III, 1, 17 (the tongue being supposed the instrument with which the serpent did offence). *could not a w., an adder, do so much?* Mids. III, 2, 71. H6A III, 1, 72. H6B III, 2, 263. Tim. IV, 3, 182. Mcb. III, 4, 29. Ant. V, 2, 243. 256. 258. 261. 264. 266. 268. 282. Cymb. III, 4, 37. It is in this sense undoubtedly that Venus calls Death *grim-grinning ghost, earth's w.* Ven. 933.

**Worm-eaten,** gnawed by worms: Ado III, 3, 145. As III, 4, 27. H4B Ind. 35.

**Worm-hole,** a hole made by the gnawing of a worm: *to fill with —s stately monuments,* Lucr. 946. *picked from the —s of long-vanished days,* H5 II, 4, 86.

**Worms-meat,** food for worms: As III, 2, 67. Rom. III, 1, 112.

**Wormwood,** Artemisia absinthium, proverbial for bitterness: Lucr. 893. LLL V, 2, 857. Rom. I, 3, 26. 30. Hml. III, 2, 191.

**Wormy,** full of worms: *damned spirits ... already to their w. beds are gone,* Mids. III, 2, 384.

**Worn-out,** past, gone: *this pattern of the w. age* Lucr. 1350.

**Worry,** to tear, to lacerate, to pull to pieces: *then again —es he his daughter with clipping her,* Wint. V, 2, 58. *if we cannot defend our own doors from the dog, let us be —ed,* H5 I, 2, 219. II, 2, 83. R3 IV, 4, 50.

**Worse,** adj. and adv., the comparative of bad and ill; adj.: *what were thy lips the w. for one poor kiss?*

Ven. 207. *w. than a slavish wipe,* Lucr. 537. *to subjects w.* Sonn. 59, 14. 84, 10. 110, 8. Tp. III, 3, 36. 77. Gent. V, 4, 51. Wiv. I, 4, 33. Meas. V, 365. Err. IV, 2, 22. 26. Mids. V, 214. Merch. I, 2, 94. H6C V, 5, 58. Rom. V, 1, 80. Tim. IV, 3, 247 etc. *w. and w.* Merch. III, 2, 250. Shr. V, 2, 93. Oth. II, 1, 135. Per. IV, 6, 141. cf. Meas. III, 2, 56. Hml. III, 2, 261. Substantively: *or a w.* Shr. I, 2, 71. *there will a w. come in his place,* Caes. III, 2, 116. *set in w. than gold,* Merch. II, 7, 55. *gives but the greater feeling to the w.* R2 I, 3, 301. Gent. II, 1, 169. Troil. III, 2, 79. Hml. III, 4, 179.

Adv.: *lilies that fester smell far w. than weeds,* Sonn. 94, 14. Tp. I, 2, 59. Wiv. II, 1, 56. Meas. V, 341. Err. IV, 2, 20. 32. Mids. III, 2, 45. V, 218. Wint. IV, 1, 30. H6B II, 3, 56. Lr. II, 2, 155 (*my sister may receive it much more w.* = may take it more ill) etc.

= more sick: *I am the w., when one says swagger,* H4B II, 4, 113. *it makes him w.* R3 I, 3, 3.

= in a more bad situation, more ill off: *they were no w. than now they are,* Tp. II, 1, 261. *to be w. than worst of those that lawless and uncertain thought imagine howling,* Meas. III, 1, 126. *thou shalt not be the w. for me,* Tw. V, 30. *long to know each other w.* Troil. IV, 1, 31 (quibbling). *I am w. than e'er I was.* Lr. IV, 1, 28.

= less worth: *I was w. than nothing,* Merch. III, 2, 263 (possessed less than nothing). *many a many foot of land the w.* John I, 183. *thy master is a wise and valiant Roman; I never thought him w.* Caes. III, 1, 139 (= less). *he were the w. for that* (a cloud in his face) *were he a horse,* Ant. III, 2, 52.

Likewise as an adverb, = less: *your treatise makes me like you w. and w.* Ven. 774. *the more one sickens the w. at ease he is,* As III, 2, 25. *if you please to like no w. than I,* Shr. IV, 4, 33. *how is it less or w. that it* (policy) *shall hold companionship in peace with honour?* Cor. III, 2, 48. *the gods ... love thee no w. than thy old father Menenius does,* V, 2, 75. *if I like thee no w. after dinner,* Lr. I, 4, 44.

With notions of evil, on the contrary, = greater; more; adj.: *w. than Tantalus' is her annoy,* Ven. 599. *a mischief w. than civil home-bred strife,* 764. *they are w. fools to purchase mocking so,* LLL V, 2, 59. Adv.: *he would ... torment the poor lady w.* Ado II, 3, 163. *hated w. than the greatest infection,* Wint. I, 2, 423. *that honourable grief which burns w. than tears drown,* II, 1, 112. *w. than the sun in March this praise doth nourish agues,* H4A IV, 1, 111. *fear the report of a caliver w. than a struck fowl,* IV, 2, 21. *I'll startle you w. than the sacring bell,* H8 III, 2, 295. *who is of Rome w. hated than of you,* Cor. I, 2, 13. *I do hate thee w. than a promise-breaker,* I, 8, 2. *keep me from their w. than killing lust,* Tit. II, 3, 175. *I hate thee w.* Tim. IV, 3, 234.

**Worser,** = worse; 1) adj.: Lucr. 249. 294. 453. Sonn. 144, 4. Tp. IV, 27. Gent. II, 3, 19. Meas. III, 2, 7. Mids. II, 1, 208. Shr. I, 2, 91. H6A V, 3, 36. R3 I, 3, 102. Rom. II, 3, 29. III, 2, 108. Hml. III, 4, 157. Lr. IV, 6, 222. IV, 7, 7. Ant. I, 2, 64.

2) adv.: *how do you now, lieutenant? The w. that you give me the addition,* Oth. IV, 1, 105. = less (cf. *Worse*): *the w. welcome,* Oth. I, 1, 95. = more: *I cannot hate thee w. than I do,* Ant. II, 5, 90.

**Worship,** subst. 1) reverence and homage paid

to a higher being: Rom. III, 2, 25. Tim. V, 1, 55. With *of*, subjectively: *the slightest w. of his time*, H4A III, 2, 151. *that noble countenance wherein the w. of the whole world lies*, Ant. IV, 14, 86. With the poss. pron., objectively: *entame my spirits to your w.* As III, 5, 48.

2) honour, dignity: *whom I from meaner form have benched and reared to w.* Wint. I, 2, 314. *till I have set a glory to this hand by giving it the w. of revenge*, John IV, 3, 72 (ennobling it by revenge). *give me w. and quietness; I like it better than a dangerous honour*, H6C IV, 3, 16 (otium cum dignitate, or rather dignitatem cum otio). *that good man of w.*, Anthony Woodville, R3 I, 1, 66. *as I belong to w.* H8 I, 1, 39.* *this double w., where one part does disdain with cause, the other insult without all reason*, Cor. III, 1, 142 (i. e. the dignity and authority divided between the patricians and plebeians). *and in the most exact regard support the —s of their name*, Lr. I, 4, 288.

3) a title of honour given to persons of respectable character: Wiv. I, 1, 80. 271. John I, 190. H4B III, 2, 91. H5 III, 2, 89. R3 I, 1, 88. Cor. II, 1, 62. 104. 160. Rom. III, 1, 62. Mostly used by inferior persons in addressing their betters: Gent. II, 1, 10. Wiv. I, 4, 157. 171. II, 3, 10. IV, 5, 56. Meas. II, 1, 185. 191. III, 2, 76. Err. I, 2, 85. Ado III, 5, 25. LLL III, 151. 161. Mids. III, 1, 182. 183. Merch. I, 3, 61. II, 2, 58. 127. II, 5, 8. As I, 1, 94. 168. Shr. I, 2, 7. III, 2, 132. IV, 3, 63. H4B I, 2, 57. V, 1, 47. V, 3, 46. H6B II, 1, 80 etc. Used with irony: Alls I, 3, 33. Tim. IV, 4, 61. Caes. I, 2, 273.

**Worship**, vb. 1) to adore: Sonn. 149, 11. Tp. V, 297. Gent. II, 4, 144. II, 6, 10. IV, 2, 131. IV, 4, 204. Ado III, 5, 43. LLL V, 2, 202. Merch. II, 2, 98. As V, 2, 88. John II, 598. III, 1, 177. H4A II, 1, 70. H6A I, 2, 145. H6B III, 2, 80. IV, 2, 81 (*w. me their lord;* Cade's speech). Troil. II, 3, 198. III, 3, 182. Rom. I, 1, 125. Tim. III, 1, 51. V, 1, 51. Cymb. III, 6, 56.

2) to honour, to dignify: *our grave ... not —ed with a waxen epitaph*, H5 I, 2, 233.

**Worshipful**, 1) claiming respect, honorable: Shr. V, 1, 56. John I, 205. H4B II, 1, 75. II, 2, 65. R3 III, 7, 138.* Cor. I, 1, 254.

2) full of reverence: *his master's son, as w. he terms it*, R3 III, 4, 41 (Ff *worshipfully*).

**Worshipfully**, with reverence: *his master's son, as w. he terms it*, R3 III, 4, 41 (Qq *worshipful*).

**Worshipper**, adorer: Lucr. 86. Alls I, 3, 212. H5 IV, 1, 259.

**Worst**, 1) adj. most bad: Lucr. 324. Gent. V, 4, 72. Wiv. I, 4, 13. Meas. II, 1, 163. LLL I, 1, 283. III, 196. 197. Mids. V, 214. As III, 2, 301. Shr. I, 2, 130. IV, 2, 104. R2 IV, 115 (*w. in this royal presence may I speak*, i. e. I may be the meanest and most unfit to speak). H6B I, 3, 88. Rom. II, 4, 131 etc.

= in the most evil or afflictive state: *when he is w., he is little better than a beast*, Merch. I, 2, 95. *to be w., the lowest and most dejected thing of fortune, stands still in esperance*, Lr. IV, 1, 2. cf. *to be worse than w. of those that lawless and incertain thought imagine howling*, Meas. III, 1, 126.

Substantively: *the w. is but denial and reproving*, Lucr. 242. *so shall I taste at first the very w. of fortune's might*, Sonn. 90, 12. 80, 14. 137, 4. 150, 8. Mids. I, 1, 63. Merch. I, 2, 96. Shr. I, 2, 14. 35. IV, **4**, 60. Alls II, 1, 176 (cf. *Extend*). R2 III, 2, 94. 103.

139. H6A IV, 1, 66. 67. H6C IV, 1, 128. Troil. III, 2, 78. Cymb. II, 3, 159. 160 etc. *at the w.* = in the most evil state, or at the greatest disadvantage: *thou hast me, if thou hast me, at the w.* H5 V, 2, 250. *things at the w. will cease or else climb upward to what they were before*, Mcb. IV, 2, 24. *I am at the w.* Lr. IV, 1, 27. *let him take 't at w.* Tim. V, 1, 181 (let him interpret my declaration, that I care not, in the worst sense). *one's w.* = the utmost evil that one can do: *to taste of thy most w.* Wint. III, 2, 180. *defy us to our w.* H5 III, 3, 5. *give thy w. of thoughts the w. of words*, Oth. III, 3, 132. *to do one's w.*: Sonn. 19, 13. 92, 1. Cor. V, 2, 112. Mcb. III, 2, 24. Lr. IV, 6, 140. Oth. V, 2, 159.

2) adv. = least or most, according to the sense of the verb (cf. *Worse*): *you may w. of all this table say so*, H8 V, 3, 78 (M. Edd. erroneously: *you may, w. of all this table, say so*). *the gods do like this w.* Per. IV, 3, 21. *when thou didst hate him w.* Caes. IV, 3, 106.

**Worsted-stocking**, wearing stockings of woollen yarn: *w. knave*, Lr. II, 2, 17.

**Wort**, 1) colewort, cabbage: *pauca verba, Sir John, goot worts. Good worts! good cabbage*, Wiv. I, 1, 124.

2) new beer unfermented; the sweet infusion of malt: *metheglin, w. and malmsey*, LLL V, 2, 233.

**Worth**, subst. 1) value, price: *not valued to the money's w.* LLL II, 137. *twenty times his w.* H6B III, 2, 268. *a silly time to make prescription for a kingdom's w.* H6C III, 3, 94. *not for the w. that hangs upon our quarrel*, Troil. II, 3, 217. *I should have lost the w. of it in gold*, Cymb. II, 4, 42. *had it been all the w. of's car*, V, 5, 191. *a crown's w.* (cf. *Pennyworth*) = as much as is worth a crown: *a crown's w. of good interpretation*, H4B II, 2, 99.

2) that which one is worth; substance, wealth: *to trust the opportunity of night ... with the rich w. of your virginity*, Mids. II, 1, 219. *were my w. as is my conscience firm, you should find better dealing*, Tw. III, 3, 17. *they are but beggars that can count their w.* Rom. II, 6, 32. *he that helps him take all my outward w.* Lr. IV, 4, 10. *for the sea's w.* Oth. I, 2, 28.

3) valuable quality, worthiness, excellence: *not the w. of my untutored lines*, Lucr. Ded. 2. *of small w. held*, Sonn. 2, 4. 16, 11. 62, 7. 83, 8. 116, 8. Compl. 210. Gent. II, 4, 71. 102. 166. III, 1, 65. III, 2, 55. Meas. I, 1, 9. V, 244. 502. Ado IV, 1, 28. 220. LLL V, 2, 78. Merch. I, 1, 62. Alls III, 4, 15. R2 I, 1, 107. H6A IV, 5, 23. V, 3, 151. R3 IV, 5, 13. Troil. I, 3, 46. II, 2, 151. Cor. III, 3, 26 (*he hath been used ever to have his w. of contradiction*, i. e to gain reputation — or to gain his point? — by contradiction. Steevens' interpretation 'his full quota of contradiction', though plausible enough, is not sufficiently borne out by the collocation of the phrase). Cymb. III, 5, 89. Per. II, 4, 51 etc. *of w.* = precious; worthy: *stones of w.* Sonn. 52, 7. *an office of great w.* Gent. I, 2, 44. *a gentleman of w.* III, 1, 107. II, 4, 56. H6B III, 2, 410. Per. II, 1, 142.

4) desert, merit; that which gives worthiness: *as I all other in all —s surmount*, Sonn. 62, 8. *the w. of that* (the body) *is that which it contains*, 74, 13. *if any be of w. to undergo such ample grace*, Meas. I, 1, 23 (= if any deserve). *wilt thou undo the w. thou art unpaid for*, Cymb. V, 5, 307. Caes. III, 2, 225.

**Worth**, adj. 1) equal in price to: *a score of good*

*ewes may be w. ten pounds*, H4B III, 2, 57. Gent. II, 7, 55. Err. IV, 3, 84. H4A III, 3, 95. Tim. I, 2, 238. In a moral sense: *prove nothing w.* Ven. 418. *w. the viewing*, 1076. Sonn. 72, 14. Compl. 267. Tp. III, 1, 38. Gent. II, 5, 58. Meas. I, 2, 61. V, 208. 502. Merch. II, 6, 33. As III, 2, 217. Tw. I, 2, 57. 59. II, 2, 16. II, 4, 28. III, 4, 328. Wint. III, 1, 14. H5 III, 1, 28. Lr. I, 4, 321 etc.

2) equal in possession to, possessing: *time owes more than he's w. to season*, Err. IV, 2, 58. *even now w. this, and now w. nothing*, Merch. I, 1, 35. *to ennoble those that scarce, some two days since, were w. a noble*, R3 I, 3, 82.

3) deserving: *are w. the want that you have wanted*, Lr. I, 1, 282. *found this trespass w. the shame*, II, 4, 44. *wretch more w. your vengeance*, Cymb. V, 1, 11.

4) valuable: *his health was never better w. than now*, H4A IV, 1, 27. *the very train of her worst wearing gown was better w. than all my father's lands*, H6B I, 3, 89. *to guard a thing not ours nor w. to us*, Troil. II, 2, 22.

**Worthily,** 1) in a worthy manner, excellently or at least suitably: *thou and thy fellows your last service did w. perform*, Tp. IV, 36. *he hath deserved w. of his country*, Cor. II, 2, 27. IV, 1, 53. Ant. II, 2, 102.

2) deservedly, according to merit; a) in a good sense: *thine own acquisition w. purchased*, Tp. IV, 14. *whom w. you would have now succeed*, Tit. I, 40. Tim. I, 2, 191. Ant. II, 2, 188. Per. IV, 6, 56.

b) in a bad sense, = justly, on good cause: *I had not now w. termed them merciless*, Err. I, 1, 100. *if he appeal the duke on ancient malice, or w. ... on some known ground of treachery*, R2 I, 1, 10. *that you are w. deposed*, IV, 227. *wherefore the king most w. hath caused every soldier to cut his prisoner's throat*, H5 IV, 7, 9. *how may he wound, and w., my falsehood*, H8 II, 4, 97.

**Worthiness,** 1) excellence, dignity, virtue: Sonn. 52, 13. LLL II, 28. 63. 171. Merch. V, 200. Alls I, 1, 10. III, 6, 75. H5 II, 2, 35. 69. H6A IV, 1, 99. Cor. III, 1, 278. Caes. I, 2, 57. I, 3, 160. Oth. II, 1, 212. Cymb. IV, 2, 25.

2) the quality of being well deserved or well founded: *the w. of praise distains his worth, if that the praised himself bring the praise forth*, Troil. I, 3, 241 (well deserved praise confounds itself, if etc.).

**Worthless,** 1) having no value: *a w. boat*, Sonn. 80, 11. *my w. gifts*, Gent IV, 2, 6. *this frail and w. trunk*, H5 III, 6, 163. In a moral sense, = a) mean, contemptible: *some w. slave*, Lucr. 515. *some w. song*, Sonn. 100, 3. *such a w. post*, Gent. I, 1, 161. *a w. mistress*, II, 4, 113. 115. *w. Valentine*, III, 2, 10. *my w. self*, Merch. II, 9, 18. *w. peasants*, H6A V, 5, 53. *the daughter of a w. king*, H6B V, 1, 81. b) futile, vain, idle: *as a flattering dream or w. fancy*, Shr. Ind. 1, 44. *his own person, kneeling at our feet, but a weak and w. satisfaction*, H5 III, 6, 141. *keep off aloof with w. emulation*, H6A IV, 4, 21. *how I scorn his w. threats*, H6C I, 1, 101. *citing my w. praise*, Tit. V, 3, 117.

2) unworthy, not deserving: *w. of such honour*, Caes. V, 1, 61.

**Worthy,** adj. 1) valuable: *most w. comfort, now my greatest grief*, Sonn. 48, 6. *I have done thee w. service*, Tp. I, 2, 247. Alls III, 5, 51. *a walled town is more —er than a village*, As III, 3, 60. *boasts himself to have a w. feeding*, Wint. IV, 4, 169. *no —er*

*than the dust*, Caes. III, 1, 116. *I'll give my reasons, more —er than their voices*, Cor. III, 1, 120.

2) deserving praise, excellent (implying all the shades of meaning between simple approval and the highest veneration): *deserves the travail of a —er pen*, Sonn. 79, 6. *of worth and w. estimation*, Gent. II, 4, 56. *endued with w. qualities*, V, 4, 153. *we shall employ thee in a —er place*, Meas. V, 537. *the lady is very well w.* Ado I, 1, 224. 231. *common speech gives him a w. pass*, Alls II, 5, 58. *in that and all your —est affairs*, III, 2, 99. *w. policy*, H6B III, 1, 235. *a w. pioner*, Hml. I, 5, 163. Shr. IV, 5, 65. H4A II, 4, 505. Troil. II, 3, 134. Cymb. IV, 2, 94. 355 etc. *thou w. Lord*, Lucr. 1303. *w. Sebastian*, Tp. II, 1, 205. IV, 221. *to have a look of such a w. mistress*, Gent. II, 4, 108. *know, w. prince*, III, 1, 10. IV, 3, 7. 25. V, 4, 157. Meas. V, 1. 28. 159. 309. Ado V, 1, 278. Mids. I, 1, 52. Merch. IV, 1, 236. Wint. III, 2, 12. H6A IV, 7, 69 (*w. Saint Michael*). Ant. III, 7, 61. Cymb. I, 6, 160. 162 etc.

3) well deserved; in a good as well as in a bad sense: *with many things of w. memory*, Shr. IV, 1, 84. *this superficial tale is but a preface of her w. praise*, H6A V, 5, 11. *he has much w. blame laid upon him*, All's IV, 3, 7. *hate turns one or both to w. danger and deserved death*, R2 V, 1, 68. *doing w. vengeance on thyself*, R3 I, 2, 87.

4) well founded, legitimate: *till you compound whose right is —est*, John II, 281. *he hath more w. interest to the state than thou*, H4A III, 2, 98. *put not your w. rage into your tongue*, Cor. III, 1, 241. *hath given me some w. cause to wish things done undone*, Caes. IV, 2, 8. *as w. cause I have to fear*, Oth. III, 3, 254.

5) deserving; a) absol.; 1) in a good sense: *though twenty thousand —er come to crave her*, Wiv. IV, 4, 90. Mids. I, 1, 55. II, 2, 116. Merch. I, 1, 61. Wint. V, 1, 48. John II, 282. H6B I, 3, 110. 111. 2) in a bad sense: *and with those hands ... subdue my —est self*, Ant. IV, 12, 47.

b) with an inf.; 1) in a good sense: *more w. I to be beloved of thee*, Sonn. 150, 14. LLL V, 1, 131. Tw. II, 5, 170. H6A IV, 1, 42. H6B IV, 7, 50. H8 IV, 2, 92. Ant. III, 13, 87. V, 1, 6. Cymb. V, 5, 351. 2) in a bad sense: *w. to be whipped*, Ado II, 1, 227. *w. to be hanged*, Wint. II, 3, 109.

c) with *of;* 1) in a good sense: *w. of thy sweet respect*, Sonn. 26, 12. Gent. V, 4, 141. Merch. I, 2, 133. Alls II, 5, 84. Wint. IV, 4, 384. H6C IV, 6, 32. H8 V, 3, 154. Tim. I, 1, 233. Caes. II, 1, 303. Per. IV, 6, 101. 2) in a bad sense: *thou art w. of it* (indignity) All's II, 3, 231. *w. of present death*, Cor. III, 1, 211. *what you're w. of* (a repulse) Cymb. I, 4, 126.

d) with an accus.: 1) in a good sense: *if aught in me w. perusal stand against thy sight*, Sonn. 38, 6. *which is —est love?* Gent. I, 2, 6. *w. the owner, and the owner it*, Wiv. V, 5, 64. *w. the note*, Alls III, 5, 104. III, 6, 13. Wint. IV, 4, 446. V, 1, 176. John II, 517. H6B III, 1, 68. 278. H8 I, 4, 79. II, 4, 195. Cor. I, 1, 251. Tit. I, 250. Caes. I, 2, 181. II, 1, 317. Oth. V, 2, 160. Cymb. II, 4, 23. 135. 2) in a bad sense: *w. blame*, Lucr. 1257. Pilgr. 301. H6C V, 5, 54. *w. death*, H6B III, 1, 242. Cor. III, 1, 298. *a cause w. my spleen*, Tim. III, 5, 113. *w. shameful check*, Ant. IV, 4, 31.

6) suitable, convenient: *every exercise w. his youth and nobleness of birth*, Gent. I, 3, 33. *w. for an em-*

*press' love*, II, 4, 76. *it is more w. to leap in ourselves than tarry till they push us*, Caes. V, 5, 24. *w. to be a rebel*, Mcb. I, 2, 10. cf. Tit. I, 250.

**Worthy**, subst. 1) any thing excellent: *to her whose worth makes other —es nothing*, Gent. II, 4, 166. *in her fair cheek where several —es make one dignity*, LLL IV, 3, 236.

2) a hero: *he is not quantity enough for that —'s thumb*, LLL V, 1, 138. *I know not the degree of the w.* V, 2, 508. 564. *w. of arms*, Troil. IV, 5, 163 (hero of war). *the Nine —es* (among whom Sh. mentions Joshua, Judas Maccabaeus, Pompey the Great, Hercules, Hector, and Alexander the Great): LLL V, 1, 125. 130. 149. 161. V, 2, 486. 505. 537. 541. 588. 703. 730. H4B II, 4, 238.

**Worthy**, vb. to exalt into a hero: *put upon him such a deal of man, that —ed him*, Lr. II, 2, 128.

**Wot**, vb. (used only in the present tense and the partic. *—ing*) to know: *those that walk and w. not what they* (the stars) *are*, LLL I, 1, 91. *the gods themselves, —ing no more than I, are ignorant*, Wint. III, 2, 77. *'tis nameless woe, I w.* R2 II, 2, 40. II, 3, 59. *little —s what watch the king keeps*, H5 IV, 1, 299. *we w. not what it means*, H6A IV, 7, 55. *you w. well my hazards still have been your solace*, Cor. IV, 1, 27. *more water glideth by the mill than —s the miller of*, Tit. II, 1, 86. *I w. well where he is*, Rom. III, 2, 139. *—'st thou whom thou movest?* Ant. I, 5, 22. *well I w.* Mids. III, 2, 422. R2 V, 6, 18. H6A IV, 6, 32. H6C II, 2, 134. IV, 7, 83. V, 4, 71. Tit. II, 1, 48. III, 1, 139. V, 2, 87. *w. you what?* = let me tell you: *w. you what, my lord? to-day the lords you talk of are beheaded*, R3 III, 2, 92. *w. you what I found?* H8 III, 2, 122. *and I w. not what* (at the end of enumerations): R2 II, 1, 250. *I w. not by what strong escape*, Err. V, 148. Mids IV, 1, 169. *the thing you w. of*, a phrase of mean persons endeavouring at decency: Gent. IV, 4, 30. Meas. II, 1, 115. cf. *you may come and see the picture, she says, that you w. of*, Wiv. II, 2, 90. *a greater soldier than he you w. one*, Cor. IV, 5, 171 (some M. Edd. *you w. on*). *God w.* (subjunctive): *God w., it was defect of spirit*, Lucr. 1345. Pilgr. 254. R3 II, 3, 18 (Ff *no, no, good friends, God w.*; Qq. *no, good my friend, not so*). Hml. II, 2, 435.

**Wound**, subst. (rhyming to *ground*, R2 III, 2, 139; the verb to *sound*, Per. IV. Prol. 23) a hurt consisting in a breach of the skin and flesh of an animal body: Ven. 915. 1052. 1054. 1064. Lucr. 1116. 1466. Sonn. 34, 8. Pilgr. 129. Mids. II, 2, 101. Merch. III, 2, 268. IV, 1, 258. John II, 418. V, 2, 14. R2 III, 2, 139. III, 3, 44 etc. *a green w.* H4B II, 1, 106. H5 V, 1, 44. *to give a w.* Lucr. 1488. 1722. Sonn. 133, 2. H6A II, 5, 110. III, 3, 50. Troil. III, 3, 229. Caes. II, 1, 300. Cymb. V, 1, 21. *to make a w.* Lucr. 1201. As III, 5, 20. 30. R2 IV, 279. R3 I, 2, 11. Tim. III, 5, 66. *to lend —s*, H6A I, 1, 87. *to have* (= to receive) *a w.* H5 IV, 3, 48. (= to have received, to bear on one's body: Cor. II, 3, 174). *to receive a w.* Cor. II, 3, 113. *to take a w.* H4A I, 3, 97. Cymb. III, 4, 117. *to bind up a w.* As IV, 3, 151. R3 V, 3, 177.

Figuratively, any hurt or pain: *bearing away the w. that never healeth*, Lucr. 731. *that deep w. it gives my friend and me*, Sonn. 133, 2. *the private w. is deepest*, Gent. V, 4, 71. *show me the very w. of this ill news*, John V, 6, 21. *the long-grown —s of my in-*

*temperance*, H4A III, 2, 156. *civil —s are stopped*, R3 V, 5, 40. *the w. of peace is surety*, Troil. II, 2, 14. Especially applied to the pangs of love: Ven. 370. Gent. I, 2, 115. Mids. II, 1, 167. As II, 4, 44. III, 5, 30 etc.

**Wound**, vb. to hurt by breaking the skin and flesh: Lucr. 1185. Tp. III, 3, 63. Ado III, 1, 23. LLL IV, 1, 27. 28. Mids. V, 301. As III, 2, 254. III, 5, 16. V, 2, 25. John V, 4, 9. V, 7, 114. R2 II, 1, 99. H4B I, 1, 14 etc. Applied to senseless things: *the bearing earth with his hard hoof he —s*, Ven. 267. *—s the unsisting postern with these strokes*, Meas. IV, 2, 92. *rebels w. thee* (the earth) *with their horses' hoofs*, R2 III, 2, 7. V, 1, 30. *w. the bark*, III, 4, 58. *the sea which they ear and w. with keels*, Ant. I, 4, 49. *with sharp needle w. the cambric*, Per. IV Prol. 23.

In a moral sense: *never w. the heart with looks again*, Ven. 1042. Lucr. 466. Sonn. 120, 12. 139, 3. LLL V, 2, 481. 854. Shr. V, 2, 138. H4A V, 4, 80. H6A I, 4, 35. H6B III, 2, 51. H8 II, 2, 75. II, 4, 96. *thou wrongest his honour, —est his princely name*, Lucr. 599. 831. Ado IV, 1, 243. John I, 65. R2 I, 1, 191. H6B III, 2, 68. Hml. V, 2, 355. *the trusty knight was —ed with disdain*, Pilgr. 221. R2 III, 2, 216. Ant. V, 2, 159. Cymb. V, 5, 202. *whose sudden sight hath thralled my —ed eye*, Shr. I, 1, 225. Gent. I, 2, 114. Rom. II, 3, 50. *then we w. our modesty, when of ourselves we publish them* (our deservings) All's I, 3, 5. *the mind, the which he pricks and —s with many legions of strange fantasies*, John V, 7, 17. *while covert enmity under the smile of safety —s the world*, H4B Ind. 10. IV, 4, 196. R3 V, 5, 39. *disorder —s where it should guard*, H6B V, 2, 32. *the —ed chance of Antony*, Ant. III, 10, 36. *the chastity he —ed*, Cymb. II, 2, 14 etc. Peculiar expression: *how attentiveness —ed his daughter, till, from one sign of dolour to another, she did, I would fain say, bleed tears*, Wint. V, 2, 94. cf. *like wonder-wounded hearers*, Hml. V, 1, 280.

The gerund substantively: Ven. 432. 465. Lr. I, 4, 322.

**Woundless**, invulnerable: *hit the w. air*, Hml. IV, 1, 44.

**Wow**, in *pow w.*, an exclamation of contempt: Cor. II, 1, 157 (O. Edd. *pow waw*).

**Wrack**, (such throughout the spelling in O. Edd. of the subst. and vb.; never *wreck*; rhyming to *alack*: Per. IV Prol. 12. to *back*: Ven. 558. Lucr. 841. 965. Sonn. 126, 5. Mcb. V, 5, 51) subst. 1) destruction, ruin; loss, decay: *honour's w.* Ven. 558. Lucr. 841. *I could prevent this storm and shun thy w.* 966. *beauty's w.* 1451. R3 I, 2, 127. *nature, sovereign mistress over w.* Sonn. 126, 5. *in the w. of maidenhood*, All's III, 5, 24. *hence grew the general w. and massacre*, H6A I, 1, 135. *compassion of my country's w.* IV, 1, 56. Mcb. I, 3, 114. *Hume's knavery will be the duchess' w.* H6B I, 2, 105. *the commonwealth hath daily run to w.* I, 3, 127. *found thee a way out of his w., to rise in*, H8 III, 2, 438. *rejoices in the common w.* Tim. V, 1, 195. *what w. discern you in me deserves your pity?* Cymb. I, 6, 84. *what's thy interest in this sad w.* IV, 2, 366 (the dead body of Cloten). *envy, oft the w. of praise*, Per. IV Prol. 12.

2) destruction by sea, shipwreck: Ven. 454. Tp. I, 2, 26. 390. 414. 488. Gent. I, 1, 156. Err. V, 49 (*by w. of sea*). 359. Merch. III, 1, 110. Tw. V, 273. John III, 1, 92. R2 II, 1, 267. 269 (figuratively).

H6C II, 2, 5. V, 4, 23. Mcb. V, 5, 51 (figuratively). Oth. II, 1, 23. Per. III, 2, 51.

3) that which is lost in a shipwreck: *a w. past hope he was*, Tw. V, 82. *rich ... as is the ooze and bottom of the sea with sunken w.* H5 I, 2, 165. *methought I saw a thousand fearful —s*, R3 I, 4, 24.

**Wrack**, vb. to ruin, to destroy: *each hour's joy —ed with a week of teen*, R3 IV, 1, 97. *I feared he did but trifle and meant to w. thee*, Hml. II, 1, 113. Partic. *—ed* (ancient orthogr. *wrackt*) = shipwrecked: Sonn. 80, 11. Tp. I, 2, 236. 436. V, 137. 161. Meas. III, 1, 225. Merch. III, 1, 3. Wint. V, 2, 75. John V, 3, 11. H5 IV, 1, 100. H6B III, 2, 82. Mcb. I, 3, 29. Per. II Prol. 32.

**Wrackful**, destructive: *the w. siege of battering days*, Sonn. 65, 6.

**Wrack-threatening**, threatening ship-wreck and ruin: *thy rocky and w. heart*, Lucr. 590.

**Wrangle**, to quarrel, to brawl: *for a score of kingdoms you should w., and I would call it fair play*, Tp. V, 174 (Staunton proposes *wrong me*). *ready to w. with mine own honesty*, Wiv. II, 1, 88. LLL IV, 1, 119. As V, 4, 197. Shr. III, 1, 4. Alls II, 2, 27. Tw. IV, 3, 14. H6A II, 4, 6. H6C II, 2, 176. R3 I, 3, 158. II, 4, 55. Caes. IV, 2, 45. Oth. III, 4, 144. Ant. I, 1, 48. II, 2, 106.

**Wrangler**, opponent, adversary: *he hath made a match with such a w. that all the courts of France will be disturbed with chaces*, H5 I, 2, 264. *the seas and winds, old —s, took a truce*, Troil. II, 2, 75.

**Wrap**, to involve, to cover with something thrown or wound round; with *in*: Lucr. 48. Mids. II, 1, 256. Shr. Ind. 1, 38. Alls V, 3, 94. John II, 227. H6C I, 4, 137. II, 1, 161. Tit. IV, 2, 58. *weapons —ed about with lines*, 27. With *up*, = to cover, to hide: *the evil which is here —ed up in countenance*, Meas. V, 117. *will in concealment w. me up a while*, Lr. IV, 3, 54.

Metaphorically: *—ed and confounded in a thousand fears*, Lucr. 456 (plunged, overwhelmed). *how are they —ed in with infamies*, 636. *I am —ed in dismal thinkings*, Alls V, 3, 128. *my often rumination —s me in a most humorous sadness*, As IV, 1, 19 (cf. *Enwrap* and *Attire* vb.). Euphuism: *why do we w. the gentleman in our more rawer breath?* Hml. V, 2, 128 (i. e. why do we speak of him?).

**Wrath**, subst. 1) anger: Lucr. 909. 1474. Compl. 293. Tp. III, 3, 79 (*—s*). Gent. III, 1, 166. V, 4, 81. 127. Alls III, 4, 28. Tw. IV, 2, 137. Wint. II, 3, 139. John II, 210. III, 1, 340. III, 4, 167. IV, 3, 49. H5 IV, 7, 37 (*—s;* Fluellen's speech). H6A II, 3, 70. H6B III, 2, 292. V, 1, 157. V, 2, 55. H6C I, 3, 19. I, 4, 53. IV, 1, 82. R3 I, 4, 71. II, 1, 106 (Qq *rage*). 118. V, 3, 110. Cor. I, 4, 27. V, 2, 83. Tit. I, 419. II, 3, 143. V, 3, 184. Tim. IV, 3, 339. V, 1, 206. V, 4, 41. Caes. II, 1, 164. Mcb. V, 5, 36. Lr. I, 1, 124. III, 7, 26. IV, 1, 24. Oth. II, 3, 298. III, 3, 363. Ant. V, 2, 290 (*their after w.*). Cymb. I, 1, 86. 135. III, 2, 40. V, 5, 308. Per. I, 1, 17. IV Prol. 44.

2) rage, extreme passion, impetuosity: *they are in the very w. of love and they will together*, As V, 2, 44. *pervert the present w. he hath against himself*, Cymb. II, 4, 151. Applied to impetuosity in combat: Tw. III, 4, 254. John I, 27. H4B Ind. 30. I, 1, 109. H6C II, 5, 131. R3 I, 3, 268. Troil. I, 2, 11. IV, 5, 105. Cor. I, 9, 86. I, 10, 16. Hml. II, 2, 483.

**Wrath**, adj. angry: *Oberon is passing fell and w.* Mids. II, 1, 20 (placed in the rhyme).

**Wrathful**, 1) angry: John II, 87. H6A IV, 3, 28. H6B III, 2, 155. IV, 2, 134. Troil. V, 2, 38. Lr. III, 2, 43.

2) raging, furious, impetuous: *grating shock of w. iron arms*, R2 I, 3, 136. *valiant as the w. dove or most magnanimous mouse*, H4B III, 2, 171. *his sparkling eyes, replete with w. fire*, H6A I, 1, 12. *barren winter with his w. nipping cold*, H6B II, 4, 3. *your w. weapons drawn*, III, 2, 237. *heart, be w. still*, V, 2, 70. *a wayward son, spiteful and w., who ... loves for his own ends*, Mcb. III, 5, 12.

**Wrathfully**, angrily: Caes. II, 1, 172.

**Wrath-kindled**, angry: R2 I, 1, 152.

**Wreak**, subst. resentment, vengeance: *if thou hast a heart of w. in thee*, Cor. IV, 5, 91. *take w. on Rome*, Tit. IV, 3, 33. *shall we be thus afflicted in his —s?* IV, 4, 11.

**Wreak**, vb. 1) to revenge: *be —ed on him*, Ven. 1004. *to w. our wrongs*, Tit. IV, 3, 51. *to w. the love I bore my cousin upon his body that hath slaughtered him*, Rom. III, 5, 102.

2) to reck, to care for; spelt *reck* in this signification by M. Edd.; see *Reck*.

**Wreakful**, resenting, revengeful: *working w. vengeance on thy foes*, Tit. V, 2, 32. *live in all the spite of w. heaven*, Tim. IV, 3, 229.

**Wreakless**, see *Reckless*.

**Wreath**, garland: *—s of victory*, Lucr. 110. H6C V, 3, 2. R3 I, 1, 5. Caes. V, 3, 82. Per. II, 3, 10. *the w. of radiant fire on flickering Phoebus' front*, Lr. II, 2, 113. *a w. of chivalry*, Per. II, 2, 29.

**Wreathe**, to twine; to fold: *an adder —d up in fatal folds*, Ven. 879. *to w. your arms*, Gent. II, 1, 19. *about his neck a snake had —d itself*, LLL IV, 3, 135. As IV, 3, 109. *each —d in the other's arms*, Tit. II, 3, 25. cf. *Sorrow-wreathen*.

**Wreck**, subst. and vb., see *Wrack*.

**Wreckful**, see *Wrackful*.

**Wreck-threatening**, see *Wrack-threatening*.

**Wren**, the bird Troglodytes parvulus: Mids. III, 1, 131. Merch. V, 106. H6B III, 2, 42. R3 I, 3, 71. Mcb. IV, 2, 9. Lr. IV, 6, 114. Cymb. IV, 2, 305. Per. IV, 3, 22. Sir Toby calls Maria *the youngest w. of mine* (M. Edd. *of nine*), Tw. III, 2, 70, on account of her short stature.

**Wrench**, subst. a violent pull, a sprain: *a noble nature may catch a w.* Tim. II, 2, 218.

**Wrench**, vb. to pull by violence, to wrest: *w. awe from fools*, Meas. II, 4, 14. *your manner of —ing the true cause the false way*, H4B II, 1, 120. *w. up thy power to the highest*, Cor. I, 8, 11. *the —ing iron*, Rom. V, 3, 22. *thence to be —ed with an unlineal hand*, Mcb. III, 1, 63. *like an engine —ed my frame of nature from the fixed place*, Lr. I, 4, 290. *w. his sword from him*, Oth. V, 2, 288 (Q1 *wring*). *w. it open straight*, Per. III, 2, 53. In H8 I, 1, 167 O. Edd. *—ing*, M. Edd. *rinsing;* cf. *lance* and *lanch*, *wince* and *winch*.

**Wrest**, subst. a tuning-key: *Antenor is such a w. in their affairs that their negotiations all must slack, wanting his manage*, Troil. III, 3, 23.

**Wrest**, vb. 1) to pull and take with violence: *the imminent decay of —ed pomp*, John IV, 3, 154 (struggled for? Perhaps *wretched*). *that doit that e'er I —ed from the king*, H6B III, 1, 112. *I of these (signs) will w. an alphabet*, Tit. III, 2, 44.

2) to turn the wrong way, to misinterpret: *an bad thinking do not w. true speaking*, Ado III, 4, 33. *w. once the law to your authority*, Merch. IV, 1, 215 (*to = according to*). *have too lavishly —ed his meaning and authority*, H4B IV, 2, 58. *fashion, w. or bow your meaning*, H5 I, 2, 14. *he'll w. the sense*, H6B III, 1, 186. cf. *Ill-wresting* and *O'erwrested*.

**Wrestle,** to contend who shall throw the other down: As I, 1, 99. 126. 132. 167. As I, 2, 116. 118. 133 (*with*). 151. 154. 165. 193. 266. 282. III, 2, 244. Troil. IV, 5, 194. Metaphorically: *w. with affection*, Ado III, 1, 42. As I, 3, 21. *great affections —ing in thy bosom*, John V, 2, 41. *I'll w. with you in my strength of love*, Ant. III, 2, 62.

**Wrestler,** one who wrestles: As I, 1, 95. 178. I, 2, 134. 179. I, 3, 22. II, 2, 13 (trisyll.?). III, 2, 225.

**Wretch,** a miserable creature; a term in which now pity, now contempt, now abhorrence is predominant. Expressing pity: Ven. 680. 703. Wint. III, 3, 49. H5 II, 2, 53. IV, 3, 87. H6B III, 1, 211. III, 3, 20. 22. H6C I, 3, 12. III, 1, 47. R3 II, 2, 6. Troil. IV, 2, 32. Rom. V, 1, 52. Hml. II, 2, 168. IV, 7, 183. Lr. III, 4, 28. 34. IV, 1, 8. Cymb. V, 4, 127. Applied to sick persons: LLL V, 2, 862. Mids. V, 384. H4B I, 1, 140. to convicts and prisoners: Gent. IV, 2, 133. Wint. V, 1, 199. H5 I, 2, 243.

Expressing contempt: Lucr. 269. Sonn. 50, 7. 74, 11. 141, 12 (*thy proud heart's slave and vassal w. to be*). Meas. III, 1, 137. IV, 3, 85. 139. V, 105. Err. V, 27. 240. Merch. IV, 1, 44. Shr. II, 315. Tw. IV, 1, 51. John III, 1, 115. R2 III, 4, 80. H5 II, 2, 178. IV Chor. 41. IV, 1, 295. IV, 5, 8. H6A II, 3, 44. V, 4, 7. H6B III, 2, 307. H6C I, 1, 231. Cor. I, 9, 48. III, 1, 164. Tit. III, 4, 59. V, 3, 64. Rom. III, 5, 161. Hml. I, 5, 51. Lr. II, 2, 150. IV, 6, 208. Oth. I, 1, 115. Cymb. II, 3, 118. V, 1, 11. V, 5, 181.

Abhorrence: Wint. IV, 4, 469. H6B IV, 10, 83. R3 I, 2, 17. IV, 4, 139. V, 5, 5. H8 II, 1, 110. Tit. V, 2, 181. V, 3, 177. Lr. I, 1, 215. III, 2, 51. Oth. IV, 2, 15. V, 2, 296.

Used as a word of tenderness (mixed with pity): *the pretty w. left crying and said Ay*, Rom. I, 3, 44. *excellent w.!* Oth. III, 3, 90. *come, thou mortal w.* Ant. V, 2, 306.

**Wretched** (superl. *—est*, R3 II, 4, 18) 1) miserable, very unhappy: Lucr. 161. 1136. 1501. 1662. Sonn. 91, 13. 14. Meas. IV, 3, 126. Err. II, 1, 34. IV, 4, 118. Merch. IV, 1, 269. As II, 1, 36. II, 4, 68. III, 5, 37. IV, 3, 107. All's V, 3, 158. R2 I, 2, 27. H6A I, 48. I, 4, 70. 97. H6B III, 2, 72. 73. IV, 9, 49. H6C II, 5, 76. R3 I, 2, 18. I, 3, 203. II, 1, 93. III, 4, 95. 107. IV, 4, 8. V, 3, 159. H8 III, 1, 106. Mcb. IV, 3, 141. Hml. III, 1, 163. III, 3, 67. Oth. V, 1, 41. Ant. III, 6, 76 etc.

2) sorry, paltry, contemptible: Sonn. 119, 5. 126, 8. Meas. V, 132. 164. LLL IV, 3, 80. H4A IV, 3, 57. H5 III, 7, 142. IV, 1, 285. H6C I, 1, 216. R3 II, 4, 18. Rom. III, 1, 135. III, 5, 185. Tim. V, 5, 70. Caes. I, 2, 117. Mcb. V, 7, 17. Hml. III, 4, 31.

3) hateful, abominable: *such w. hands* (as Tarquin's) *such w. blood should spill* (as his own) Lucr. 999. *the w., bloody and usurping boar*, R3 V, 2, 7.

**Wretchedness,** misery, extreme unhappiness: Lucr. 900. Mids. V, 85. R2 III, 4, 26. IV, 238. H8 III, 1, 123. IV, 2, 84. Rom. V, 1, 68. Tim. IV, 2, 30. Lr. IV, 6, 61. Cymb. III, 4, 63.

**Wright,** in *Shipwright*, q. v.

**Wring** (impf. and partic. *wrung*) 1) to press, to squeeze: *you hurt my hand with —ing*, Ven. 421. Merch. II, 8, 49. Oth. III, 3, 421. *he —s her nose*, Ven. 475. H6B III, 2, 34. *wrung in the withers*, H4A II, 1, 7 (injured by pressing. cf. *Unwrung*). cf. *wrung with wrongs more than our backs can bear*, Tit. IV, 3, 48.

2) to press by turning and straining, as clothes in washing: *I wash, w., brew* etc. Wiv. I, 4, 101 (O.Edd. *ring*). *to w. one's hands*, a gesture of distress: Gent. II, 3, 8. III, 1, 227. H6B I, 1, 226. R3 II, 2, 3 (Qq *w. your hands*, Ff *weep so oft*). Rom. III, 2, 36. Hml. III, 4, 34.

3) to press on, to ply hard: *dangers, doubts, —ing of the conscience*, H8 II, 2, 28. *let me w. your heart*, Hml. III, 4, 35. With *to*, = to force to: *it is a hint that —s mine eyes to't*, Tp. I, 2, 135.

4) With *from*, = to take with violence, to extort, to force from: *must either punish me ... or w. redress from you*, Meas. V, 32. *your over-kindness doth w. tears from me*, Ado V, 1, 302. *to w. the widow from her customed right*, H6B V, 1, 188 (= to w. the right from the widow; cf. Appendix). *w. the sceptre from his fist*, H6C II, 1, 154. *thy sceptre wrung from thee*, III, 1, 16. *which God defend that I should w. from him*, R3 III, 7, 173. *to w. from the hard hands of peasants their vile trash*, Caes. IV, 3, 73. *he hath wrung from me my slow leave*, Hml. I, 2, 58. *w. his sword from him*, Oth. V, 2, 288 (Ff *wrench*).

5) intr. to writhe in pain, to suffer in a high degree: *those that w. under the load of sorrow*, Ado V, 1, 28. *whose sense no more can feel than his own —ing*, H5 IV, 1, 253. *he —s at some distress*, Cymb. III, 6, 79.

**Wringer** (O. Edd. *ringer;* cf. Wiv. I, 4, 101) one who wrings the water out of clothes: Wiv. I, 2, 5 (Sir Hugh's speech).

**Wrinkle,** subst. a furrow in the skin of the face: Ven. 139. Lucr. 562. 1452. Sonn. 3, 12. 63, 4. 77, 5. 93, 8. 100, 10. 108, 11. Merch. I, 1, 80. All's II, 4, 20. John II, 505. R2 I, 3, 230. II, 1, 170. IV, 277. H6C V, 2, 19. Troil. I, 1, 38. Tit. III, 1, 7. Tim. IV, 3, 148. Lr. I, 4, 306. Ant. I, 2, 19.

**Wrinkle,** vb. to give wrinkles to, to make old and ugly: *a Grecian queen whose youth and freshness —s Apollo's*, Troil. II, 2, 79.

**Wrinkled,** having wrinkles: Ven. 133. Lucr. 275. Meas. I, 3, 5. Merch. IV, 1, 270. Shr. IV, 5, 43. Wint. V, 3, 28. John IV, 2, 192. R3 I, 1, 9. I, 3, 164. Troil. II, 2, 104. Tim. IV, 1, 5. Hml. II, 2, 200. Ant. I, 5, 29. III, 11, 37.

**Wriothesley,** family name of the Earl of Southampton: Ven. and Lucr. Ded.

**Wrist,** the joint by which the hand is joined to the arm: John IV, 2, 190. Hml. II, 1, 87. Cymb. V, 4, 9.

**Writ,** subst. 1) Scripture: *holy w. in babes hath judgment shown*, All's II, 1, 141. H6B I, 3, 61. R3 I, 3, 337. Oth. III, 3, 324. *each man thinks all is w. he spoken can*, Per. II Prol. 12 (= a gospel). Jestingly: *let's see the devil's w.* H6B I, 4, 60.

2) a mandate, a precept issued from the proper authority: *ere the —s go forth*, H6B V, 3, 26 (to convoke the parliament). *that therefore such a w.* (of a praemunire) *be sued against you*, H8 III, 2, 341. *folded the w. up*, Hml. V, 2, 51. *my w. is on the life*

*of Lear*, Lr. V, 3, 245. *this is the tenour of the emperor's w.* Cymb. III, 7, 1.

3) any document: *this fatal w., the complot of this timeless tragedy*, Tit. II, 3, 264.

Doubtful passages: *I have neither w., nor words, nor worth*, Caes. III, 2, 225 (later Ff and M. Edd. *wit*). *for the law of w. and the liberty, these are the only men*, Hml. II, 2, 421 (explained as meaning exact recitation of what the author had written. In O. Edd. the words *for the law of writ and the liberty* are joined to what precedes).*

**Write,** (impf. seldom *wrote:* Tit. V, 1, 106. Hml. V, 2, 32. 37. Cymb. IV, 3, 37: usually *writ;* partic. seldom *wrote:* Ant. III, 5, 11. Cymb. III, 5, 2. 21; in Lr. I, 2, 93 Qq *wrote*, Ff *writ;* usually *writ* or *written*); 1) to form characters representing words on paper or other materials: *I writ at random*, Gent. II, 1, 117. *w. till your ink be dry*, III, 2, 75. *they can w. and read*, Ado III, 3, 12. LLL III, 206. Merch. II, 4, 13. Tw. V, 340 (*w. from it*, i. e. otherwise). H6B IV, 2, 92 etc. Gerund *—ing* = handwriting: LLL IV, 3, 203.

2) to cover with characters representing words: *till she have writ a sheet of paper*, Ado II, 3, 138. *a paper written in his hand*, V, 4, 86. *a sheet of paper writ o'both sides the leaf*, LLL V, 2, 8. *a written scroll*, Merch. II, 7, 64. *a scroll, and written round about*, Tit. IV, 2, 18.

3) to set down, to form by means of letters (in a proper and figurative sense): *to cipher what is writ in learned books*, Lucr. 811. *a letter writ to your grace*, H6A IV, 1, 12. Lucr. 102. 1183. 1295. Sonn. 23, 13. 71, 6. 115, 1. Gent. I, 2, 109. 113. 123. II, 1, 93. 110. 132. III, 1, 249. Wiv. I, 3, 65. II, 1, 76. V, 5, 73. Meas. IV, 4, 1. Err. IV, 3, 55 (*it is written*). Ado V, 4, 89. LLL I, 1, 117. 156 (*to the laws I w. my name*). IV, 1, 58. Mids. II, 2, 122. As V, 2, 84. Tw. III, 4, 43. V, 293. 370. John IV, 1, 37. R2 IV, 275. H4A I, 3, 263. H5 I, 2, 98 (*it is writ*). H6B IV, 1, 99. H6C I, 1, 169 (*over the chair of state ... w. up his title*). H8 III, 2, 287. Cor. V, 2, 96. Tit. IV, 1, 70. 84. V, 1, 106. Rom. I, 2, 36. 39 (*it is written*). 43. I, 3, 82. 86. II, 2, 57. IV, 2, 1. V, 3, 82. Caes. I, 2, 126. Hml. V, 2, 32 (*wrote it fair*). Lr. I, 2, 93. Ant. II, 6, 4. III, 5, 11 etc. With *down:* Gent. I, 2, 117. III, 1, 357. Ado IV, 2, 13. 17. 33. 73. 78. 90. John V, 2, 4. Cymb. II, 2, 24 etc. Opposed to speaking by word of mouth: Sonn. 26, 3. Mids. I, 2, 68. Shr. III, 1, 70. All's III, 2, 98. H6A III, 1, 2. 10. Cor. V, 1, 68. Rom. V, 2, 4.

The gerund *—ing* substantively = any thing written, as a letter, a note, a schedule: *I'll read the —ing*, Merch. II, 7, 64. *this is not my —ing*, Tw. V, 353. *let me see the —ing*, R2 V, 2, 57. 59. V, 3, 49. *—ings all tending to the great opinion*, Caes. I, 2, 322. *how calm and gentle I proceeded in all my —ings*, Ant. V, 1, 76. *peruse this —ing*, Per. II, 5, 41.

Metaphorical use: *let him but copy what in you is writ*, Sonn. 84, 9. *in many's looks the false heart's history is writ*, 93, 8. *the stealth of our most mutual entertainment with character too gross is writ on Juliet*, Meas. I, 2, 159. *there is written in your brow honesty and constancy*, IV, 2, 162. *have written strange defeatures in my face*, Err. V, 299. *the last taste of sweets ... writ in remembrance*, R2 II, 1, 14. *whose memory is written on the earth with yet appearing blood*, H4B

IV, 1, 81. *that I'll w. upon thy burgonet*, H6B V, 1, 200. *—ing destruction on the enemy's castle*, Tit. III, 1, 170. *raze out the written troubles of the brain*, Mcb. V, 3, 42. *that self hand which writ his honour in the acts it did*, Ant. V, 1, 22. *the record of injuries ... written in our flesh*, V, 2, 118 etc. With *down: that are written down old with all the characters of age*, H4B I, 2, 202. *opinion, who hath writ me down after my seeming*, V, 2, 128. cf. *set down* in Troil. IV, 5, 61 and Tim. IV, 3, 118.

Compare with the phrase *it is written* (Err. IV, 3, 55. H5 I, 2, 98. Rom. I, 2, 39) the following expressions: *we did think it writ down in our duty to let you know of it*, Hml. I, 2, 222. *is't writ in your revenge that you will draw both friend and foe?* IV, 5, 141.

4) to make a communication by letter: *some love of yours hath writ to you*, Gent. I, 2, 79. Meas. I, 1, 56. Gent. II, 3, 150. LLL IV, 2, 138. R2 I, 3, 186. Caes. III, 1, 278 (*Caesar did write for him to come to Rome*). Oth. I, 3, 46 etc. = to communicate, to tell by letter: Gent. I, 3, 56. Meas. IV, 2, 218. All's IV, 3, 102. 226. Cor. V, 6, 63. Rom. V, 3, 246. Cymb. III, 5, 2. 21. IV, 3, 37 etc.

5) to express, to define in black and white: *if I could w. the beauty of your eyes*, Sonn. 17, 5. *the bill that —s them all alike*, Mcb. III, 1, 101.

6) to compose, to produce as an author; absol.: Sonn. 116, 14. Wint. V, 1, 99. Ant. III, 2, 17. with *of:* Sonn. 84, 7. R3 I, 4, 46. with *on: the star-gazers, having writ on death*, Ven. 509 (?). Transitively: Gent. II, 1, 97. Wiv. III, 2, 69. Ado V, 1, 37 (*writ the style of gods*). V, 2, 4. LLL I, 2, 120. IV, 3, 99. Mids. I, 1, 18. 25. IV, 1, 220. V, 365. All's IV, 3, 355. H5 III, 7, 42. H6B IV, 7, 65. Hml. III, 2, 274 etc. *the —ing* = the text: *it would neither serve for the —ing nor the tune*, LLL I, 2, 119.

7) to subscribe: *he learned to w. for me under that bond*, Sonn. 134, 7. LLL I, 1, 117. 156. *I w., good creature, wheresoe'er she is, her heart weighs sadly*, All's III, 5, 69 (later Ff *I right;* most M. Edd. *ay, right;* some *I warrant*). *who —s himself armigero*, Wiv. I, 1, 9. *the Turk ... —s not so tedious a style*, H6A IV, 7, 74 (does not use so long a title). *this hand of mine hath writ in thy behalf*, H6B IV, 1, 63 (has underwritten orders tending to thy good).

Hence = a) to declare: *out on thee, seeming! I will w. against it*, Ado IV, 1, 57. *I'll w. against them, detest them, curse them*, Cymb. II, 5, 32. b) to claim a title, to call one's self: *I w. man*, All's II, 3, 208. *as if he had writ man ever since his father was a bachelor*, H4B I, 2, 30. *w. happy when thou hast done*, Lr. V, 3, 35. cf. *my mouth no more were broken than these boys', and writ as little beard*, All's II, 3, 67.

**Writer,** 1) a clerk: Ado III, 5, 68. H4A III, 1, 143.

2) an author: Sonn. 82, 3. Gent. I, 1, 42. 45. As V, 1, 47. H4A II, 4, 455. H5 I, 2, 64. Hml. II, 2, 366.

**Writhled,** wrinkled: *this weak and w. shrimp*, H6A III, 3, 23.

**Writing,** subst. see *Write*.

**Wroath,** see *Wroth*.

**Wrong,** subst. 1) anything not right and becoming, or done by mistake; error: *construe Cassio's smiles ... quite in the w.* Oth. IV, 1, 104. *a man of compléments, whom right and w. have chose as umpire*, LLL I, 1, 169. *pardon love this w., that sings heaven's praise* *with such an earthly tongue,* IV, 2, 121. cf. the quibble: *you will not pocket up w.* H4A III, 3, 184 and H5 III, 2, 55.

2) anything unjust: *you do him the more w.; 'twas I,* Gent. IV, 4, 29. *it cannot be that she hath done thee w.* Err. V, 135. *what judgment shall I dread, doing no w.?* Merch. IV, 1, 89. *to do a great right, do a little w.* 216. All's II, 3, 317. John III, 1, 186. R2 II, 1, 164. 238. H4A IV, 3, 101. H6A III, 2, 78. Troil. II, 2, 187. Caes. III, 1, 47 etc. *to be in the w.* = to be unjust: *we were i'the w. when we banished him,* Cor. IV, 6, 156. *to have w.* = to suffer injustice: *an you do not make him hanged among you, the gallows shall have w.* H4B II, 2, 105. *w. hath but w.* R3 V, 1, 29. *Caesar has had great w.* Caes. III, 2, 115. *to do w.* sometimes = not to do justice, not to give a person his due: *hath done her beauty w.* Lucr. 80 (in underpraising it). *do him not that w. to bear a hard opinion of his truth,* Gent. II, 7, 80. Meas. I, 2, 41. III, 2, 137. Ado II, 1, 214. Merch. V, 142. All's V, 3, 189 etc. With a kind of irony: *I fear you have done yourself some w.* Tp. I, 2, 443 (you have pretended to be what you are not). Sometimes *w.* quite = injustice: *law itself is perfect w.* John III, 1, 189. *fears attend the steps of w.* IV, 2, 56. *with the very hand of stern injustice and confused w.* V, 2, 23. *now breathless w. shall sit and pant,* Tim. V, 4, 10. *right* and *w.* opposed: *hooking both right and w. to the appetite,* Meas. II, 4, 176. *to find out right with w.* R2 II, 3, 145. Troil. I, 3, 116. II, 2, 171. Tim. IV, 3, 29.

3) any injury: *assailed by night with circumstances strong ... to do her husband w.* Lucr. 1264 (by adultery). *what w. else may be imagined ... might be done to me,* 1622. *for thy right myself will bear all w.* Sonn. 88, 14. *I shall receive this villanous w.* Wiv. II, 2, 308. *shall not do his Julia so much w.* Gent. IV, 4, 142. Err. II, 1, 103. II, 2, 174. III, 1, 16. III, 2, 17. V, 201. Ado I, 1, 245. LLL II, 154. Mids. II, 2, 129. Merch. I, 1, 155. II, 2, 141. All's I, 1, 74. II, 3, 96. Tw. V, 143. 336. Wint. V, 1, 148. John III, 1, 13. III, 3, 41. H6C IV, 1, 102 (*she had the w.* = she suffered the injury); cf. R3 I, 3, 307 and H8 III, 1, 48. Tim. III, 5, 36 etc. With an Anglosaxon genitive or a possessive pronoun, either subjectively, = an injury done by one: *to bear love's w.* Sonn. 40, 12. *his grandam's —s,* John II, 168. *to bear every knave's w.* H4B II, 1, 41. Hml. III, 1, 71. *with their high —s I am struck to the quick,* Tp. V, 25. 119. Mids. II, 1, 240. H6C III, 3, 197. Tim. V, 1, 156. Mcb. IV, 3, 33 etc. or objectively, = an injury done to one: *my husband's —s,* R2 I, 2, 47. *England's private —s,* II, 1, 166. H4A I, 3, 149. H6A III, 1, 161. R3 IV, 4, 377. Oth. V, 1, 32. *complained her —s to us,* Lucr. 1840. 1691. Meas. V, 26. Err. V, 217. Ado V, 3, 5. Shr. IV, 3, 2. John III, 1, 182. R2 II, 3, 116. 128. H6A I, 3, 59. II, 5, 22. R3 I, 3, 310. V, 3, 144. Tim. III, 5, 32 etc.

= offence, trespass: *answering one foul w., lives not to act another,* Meas. II, 2, 103. *you are i'the w. to speak before your time,* V, 86. *who I believe was packed in all this w.* Ado V, 1, 308. *forgive me this enforced w.* Merch. V, 240. Wint. IV, 4, 416. V, 1, 9. John II, 116. R2 IV, 120. R3 V, 1, 19.

= disgrace, insult: *'tis he that hath done thee w.; I did but act, he's author of thy slander,* Ven. 1005. *I will not do you that w.* (to go first) Wiv. I, 1, 323.

326. *you do yourself mighty w.,* Master Ford, III, 3, 221. *received w. by some person,* III, 1, 53. *stir Demetrius up with bitter w.* Mids. III, 2, 361. *make some reservation of your —s,* All's II, 3, 260. LLL V, 2, 733. Shr. II, 59. III, 1, 16. Tw. III, 4, 241. John III, 1, 200. R2 I, 1, 191. H4B I, 1, 90. II, 3, 39. H5 III, 2, 55 (quibbling). Hml. I, 1, 143. Lr. IV, 2, 51. Oth. I, 1, 129 etc.

= mischief, harm, hurt, pain, damage: *fiery eyes blaze forth her w.* Ven. 219. *the heart hath treble w. when it is barred the aidance of the tongue,* 329. *thy mermaid's voice hath done me double w.* 429. *despite thy* (time's) *w. my love shall ever live,* Sonn. 19, 13. *to justify the w. that thy unkindness lays upon my heart,* 139, 1. *the winds whose pity, sighing back again, did us but loving w.* Tp. I, 2, 151. Meas. II, 1, 280. II, 2, 53. Err. II, 2, 173. V, 19. 146. 398. Ado V, 1, 7. Mids. II, 2, 11. III, 2, 28. As I, 2, 202. All's V, 3, 15. John IV, 1, 118. R2 I, 3, 246. III, 2, 215. H4A I, 3, 75. IV, 3, 82. H4B Ind. 40 (*comforts false, worse than true —s*). I, 1, 161. III, 2, 273. V, 1, 58 (*he shall have no w.*). Cor. V, 6, 38. Tim. III, 4, 53. Caes. III, 1, 170 (*the general w. of Rome*). 242. Hml. II, 2, 367. Lr. I, 2, 180. Ant. V, 2, 40. Per. V, 1, 131 etc.

**Wrong,** adj. 1) not right, not that which was intended or ought to be: *I have directed you to w. places,* Wiv. III, 1, 110. *you took the w.* V, 5, 201. *to turn the w. side out:* Ado III, 1, 68. Tw. III, 1, 14. Lr. IV, 2, 9. Oth. II, 3, 54.

2) false, mistaken, erring: *that my steeled sense or changes right or w.* Sonn. 112, 8 (cf. *Right,* adj. 2). *she's in a w. belief,* H6A II, 3, 31. *the argument you held was w. in you,* II, 4, 57. *by false intelligence or w. surmise,* R3 II, 1, 54. *opinion, whose w. thought defiles thee,* Lr. III, 6, 119. *w. imaginations,* IV, 6, 290.

3) unjust, illegitimate: *if his cause be w.* H5 IV, 1, 138. *be thy title right or w.* H6C I, 1, 159. *we have your w. rebuke,* Oth. I, 1, 131.

Adverbially: *if you choose w.* Merch. II, 1, 40. III, 2, 2. *it must go w. with you and me,* John I, 41. *we go w.* Troil. V, 1, 74. *how you were w. led,* Ant. III, 6, 80.

**Wrong,** vb. 1) to do injustice to: *I w. him to call him poor,* Wiv. II, 2, 282. *I should w. it* (your desert) *to lock it in the wards of covert bosom,* Meas. V, 9. *you gave me none; you w. me much to say so,* Err. IV, 1, 66. 67. *if they speak but truth of her, these hands shall tear her; if they w. her honour, the proudest of them shall well hear of it,* Ado IV, 1, 193. 262. Meas. V, 119. Merch. I, 3, 171. III, 2, 127. Shr. II, 46. Tw. IV, 2, 32. V, 310. H4B II, 4, 353. H6C III, 2, 75. H8 III, 1, 81. 156. Rom. I, 5, 99. IV, 1, 32. Caes. III, 2, 156. IV, 2, 38. 39. IV, 3, 55. Ant. I, 4, 40. Cymb. I, 6, 145 etc.

2) to do harm, to injure in any manner: *how Tarquin —ed me,* Lucr. 819. *to w. the wronger till he render right,* 943. *the —ed Duke of Milan,* Tp. V, 107. *to w. my friend, I shall be much forsworn,* Gent. II, 6, 3. IV, 2, 112. IV, 4, 146. Wiv. I, 1, 105. 108. 110. II, 1, 133. Meas. II, 3, 24. 25. III, 1, 206. 260. V, 21. 406. Err. V, 330. Ado V, 1, 52. 53. LLL II, 155. Mids. III, 2, 308. Merch. III, 1, 69. 71. 73. Shr. II, 27. All's IV, 4, 1 (almost = to deceive). Wint. III, 3, 62. H6A II, 5, 109. H6C III, 2, 74. R3 IV, 4, 421. Rom. IV, 1, 32. Lr. I, 3, 3. Oth. II, 3, 224. **Ant.**

III, 6, 65. Per. I, 2, 112. II, 4, 25. 26 etc. Peculiar expression: *w. not that wrong with a more contempt,* Err. II, 2, 174 (= make it not worse. cf. *what ruins are in me ... by him not ruined?* II, 1, 96. *the want that you have wanted,* Lr. I, 1, 282. *love, which, left unshown, is often left unloved,* Ant. III, 6, 52).

= to give offence, to affront: *you w. me, sir, thus still to haunt my house,* Wiv. III, 4, 73. 80. *till that time I do receive your offered love like love and will not w. it,* Hml. V, 2, 263. 244. 246. *you w. this presence; therefore speak no more,* Ant. II, 2, 111. Caes. IV, 3, 1.

= to disgrace: *thou —est his honour, woundest his princely name,* Lucr. 599. *be contented; you w. yourself too much,* Wiv. III, 3, 178. IV, 2, 161. *is any woman —ed by this lewd fellow?* Meas. V, 515. 531. Shr. II, 1. H6A II, 1, 16. IV, 7, 50. R3 IV, 4, 211. H8 III, 1, 168. Tit. I, 8. Caes. IV, 3, 6 etc.

**Wronger,** one who wrongs or injures: Lucr. 943. Ado V, 1, 271. Oth. III, 3, 168. Cymb. II, 4, 54.

**Wrongful,** unfair, unjust: *I despise thee for thy w. suit,* Gent. IV, 2, 102. *in w. quarrel you have slain your son,* Tit. I, 293.

**Wrongfully,** unjustly: Sonn. 66, 7. Meas. V, 140. Ado IV, 2, 51. R2 I, 2, 39. II, 1, 201. H6B II, 3, 107. Tit. IV, 4, 55. 76 *(Lucius' punishment was w.).*

**Wrong-incensed** (not hyphened in O. Edd.) perversely exasperated: R3 II, 1, 51.

**Wrongly,** unjustly: *and yet wouldst w. win,* Mcb. I, 5, 23.

**Wroth** (O. Edd. *wroath*) ruth, misery, sorrow: *I'll keep my oath, patiently to bear my w.* Merch. II, 9, 78.

**Wry,** vb. to go obliquely, to swerve: *murder wives much better than themselves for —ing but a little,* Cymb. V, 1, 5.

**Wry-necked,** having a crooked and distorted neck: *the vile squealing of the w. fife,* Merch. II, 5, 30.

**Wye,** river in Wales: H4A III, 1, 65. H5 IV, 7, 29. 111 *(all the water in W.).*

# X.

**Xanthippe** (F1 *Zentippe,* later Ff *Zantippe*) the wife of Socrates, proverbial for a scold: Shr. I, 2, 71.

# Y.

**Yard,** 1) a measure of three feet: Shr. IV, 3, 109. 113. H4A II, 4, 273 *(tailor's y.).* Rom. I, 2, 40. Hml. III, 4, 208. Lr. IV, 6, 89 *(a clothier's y.).* two —s, Wiv. I, 3, 44. 46. *eight* —s, H4A II, 2, 26. H4B I, 2, 50. *four y.* H5 III, 2, 66 (Fluellen's speech). *loves her by the foot. He may not by the y.* LLL V, 2, 676 (with an indecent quibble).

2) a piece of timber by which a sail is extended: Tp. I, 2, 200.

**Yare,** adj. and adv. ready, active, brisk, nimble: *cheerly, my hearts, y., y.* Tp. I, 1, 7. *down with the top-mast! y., lower, lower!* 37. *our ship ... is tight and y. and bravely rigged,* V, 224. *if you have occasion to use me for your own turn, you shall find me y.* Meas. IV, 2, 61. *dismount thy tuck, be y. in thy preparation,* Tw. III, 4, 244. *their ships are y., yours heavy,* Ant. III, 7, 39. *a haltered neck which does the hangman thank for being y. about him,* III, 13, 131. *y., y., good Iras, quick,* V, 2, 286.

**Yarely,** readily, actively, briskly: *fall to it y.* Tp. I, 1, 4. *those flower-soft hands, that y. frame the office,* Ant. II, 2, 216.

**Yarn,** woollen thread: *the web of our life is of a mingled y.* All's IV, 3, 84. *all the y. she spun,* Cor. I, 3, 93.

**Yaughan,** name in Hml. V, 1, 68.*

**Yaw,** to move on unsteadily (as a ship), to steer out of the line of the course: *to divide him inventorially would dizzy the arithmetic of memory, and yet but y. neither, in respect of his quick sail,* Hml. V, 2, 120 (lection of Q2; the other Qq *raw,* Ff om. As for *but neither* = nevertheless, see *Neither.* It must be considered that the whole speech of Hamlet is intentionally affected, and calculated to puzzle his interlocutor).

**Yawn,** to open wide: *graves, y. and yield your dead,* Ado V, 3, 19. Caes. II, 2, 18. *the gashes, that bloodily did y. upon his face,* H5 IV, 6, 14. *when churchyards y.* Hml. III, 2, 407. Applied to the mouth, = to gape; 1) with greediness: *now will I dam up this thy —ing mouth,* H6B IV, 1, 73. 2) with drowsiness: *the lazy —ing drone,* H5 I, 2, 204. *the shard-borne beetle with his drowsy hums hath rung night's —ing peal,* Mcb. III, 2, 43. 3) with surprise and bewilderment: *to y., be still and wonder, when one but of my ordinance stood up,* Cor. III, 2, 11. *they y. at it and botch the words up fit to their own thoughts,* Hml. IV, 5, 9 (Ff *aim). that the affrighted globe should y. at alteration,* Oth. V, 2, 101.

**Yclad,** clad: *her words y. with wisdom's majesty,* H6B I, 1, 33.

**Ycleped** or **Ycliped,** called (used by Armado and Holofernes): LLL I, 1, 242. V, 2, 602.

**Ye,** pers. pron. of the 2nd person plur.; not differing from *you;* nominative: Tp. V, 33. 41. Gent. I, 2, 49. II, 4, 54. Wiv. III, 4, 29. Meas. IV, 3, 173. Mids. III, 2, 243. Merch. I, 1, 58. 103. II, 2, 212 (Ff and later Qq *you*). Tw. II, 1, 40. John V, 2, 91. H4A II, 2, 33. H6A II, 2, 35. III, 1, 70. 117. III, 2, 41. IV, 1, 8. V, 3, 2. 3. H6B I, 1, 137. I, 3, 141. II, 1, 132. III, 1, 4. H6C V, 4, 71. 75. R3 I, 1, 74 (Ff *you*). IV, 2, 85. Caes. I, 3, 91. Mcb. I, 3, 54 etc. Objective: Sonn. 42, 5. 111, 13. Tp. V, 170. Gent. I, 2, 28. II, 1, 104. V, 4, 58. LLL IV, 2, 10. V, 1, 101. Merch. III, 5, 3 (Ff and later Qq *you*). As II, 7, 135. V, 1, 16. Shr. I, 1, 90. H4A II, 2, 55. H6B I, 1, 141. IV, 6, 11. IV, 7, 126. H6C V, 5, 27. 35. R3 I, 2, 101 (Qq *yea*). Caes. III, 1, 157. Ant. II, 6, 78. Cymb. II, 2, 10 etc. After prepositions: Tp. I, 2, 323. Gent. II, 1, 35. IV, 1, 3. Wint. IV, 4, 663. H4B IV, 2, 75. H8 I, 4, 50. III, 1, 102 etc. *ye will* contracted to *ye'll:* LLL I, 2, 54 (Q2 Ff *you'll). ye are con-*

tracted to *y'are* in O. Edd.: All's III, 2, 94. III, 7, 14. IV, 3, 160. Wint. IV, 4, 108. Tim. I, 1, 203 etc. In Per. II, 1, 60 Ff *y'may see,* Qq *may see.*

**Yea,** particle of affirmation, = yes: Sonn. 40, 1. Tp. III, 2, 68. Meas. II, 2, 8. II, 4, 38. Err. IV, 2, 3. Mids. IV, 1, 201. R3 I, 1, 52. IV, 4, 526 etc. Substantively: *receives the scroll without or yea or no,* Lucr. 1340. *by yea and no,* Wiv. I, 1, 88. *the very yea and the no is,* I, 4, 98. *by yea and no,* IV, 2, 202. H4B II, 2, 142. *by the yea and no of general ignorance,* Cor. III, 1, 145. *by yea and nay,* LLL I, 1, 54. H4B III, 2, 10 (Qq *by yea and no*). *in russet yeas and honest kersey noes,* LLL V, 2, 413.

Often used = nay, to reprove, or notice, or amplify what has gone before: *yea, though I die, the scandal will survive,* Lucr. 204. *yea, the illiterate ... will quote my trespass,* 810. *make his bold waves tremble, yea, his dread trident shake,* Tp. I, 2, 206. *incensed the seas and shores, yea, all the creatures,* III, 3, 74. *the great globe itself, yea, all which it inherit,* IV, 154. *the state ... yea, my gravity,* Meas. II, 4, 9. *yea, dost thou jeer and flout me?* Err. II, 2, 22. *one that composed your beauties, yea, one to whom you are but as a form in wax,* Mids. I, 1, 48. *yea, art thou there?* III, 2, 411. *I tender it, ... yea, twice the sum,* Merch. IV, 1, 210. *yea, say you so?* Wint. IV, 4, 588. *yea, brother Richard, are you offended too?* H6C IV, 1, 19. *yea, are you so brief?* R3 I, 4, 88 (Ff *what*). *yea, so familiar!* Troil. V, 2, 8. *yea, Troilus! O, well fought!* V, 6, 12. *yea, is it come to this?* Lr. I, 4, 326. *yea, mistress, are you so peremptory?* Per. II, 5, 73 etc.

**Yead,** diminutive of *Edward* or rather *Yedward:* Wiv. I, 1, 160.

**Yea-forsooth:** *a rascally y. knave,* H4B I, 2, 41 (one saying to anything yea and *forsooth,* which latter was not a phrase of genteel company).

**Yean,** see *Ean.*

**Year,** the time in which the earth completes a revolution: Ven. 508. Tp. I, 2, 250. Meas. IV, 2, 25 (compound with him by the y.); cf. Shr. II, 371. 374. Err. IV, 1, 21. Merch. II, 5, 26. H6C II, 5, 28. etc. etc. Plur. —*s:* Tp. I, 2, 41. 279. Meas. II, 1, 277. IV, 2, 135. Err. V, 309. H6A II, 3, 40. IV, 3, 37 (this seven —s). H6B II, 1, 2 (these seven —s' day). H6C II, 5, 29. 38 etc. etc. Often unchanged in the plural, particularly in the language of low persons: Sonn. 11, 8. Tp. I, 2, 53. Meas. II, 1, 252. 254. 274. Ado III, 3, 134 (this seven y.; Ff —s). LLL V, 2, 11 and 894 (lection of Q1). Merch. II, 5, 27. As III, 2, 335. V, 2, 66. Shr. Ind. 2, 115. All's I, 1, 159. H4A II, 4, 343 (this seven y.; Ff —s). H4B III, 2, 224 (Ff —s). H6A I, 3, 91. Cor. V, 4, 17. Rom. I, 3, 2. Hml. V, 1, 183. Lr. III, 4, 145 etc.

—*s* equivalent to age: *my unripe —s,* Ven. 524. *his tender —s,* 1091. *thy beauty and thy —s,* Sonn. 41, 3. Gent. II, 4, 69. Meas. IV, 3, 76. Err. I, 1, 126 (at eighteen —s = at the age of etc.). III, 1, 90. As IV, 3, 86. Shr. II, 362 (struck in —s); cf. R3 I, 1, 92. H6A II, 5, 107. III, 1, 71. IV, 1, 149. V, 1, 21 etc. etc. *thou heapest a —s' age on me,* Cymb. I, 1, 133 (an age advanced in years, old age. M. Edd. *a —'s age,* which would not matter much). *of —s =* of age: *a king of —s,* H6B II, 3, 28. *till my infant fortune comes to —s,* R2 II, 3, 66 (= becomes of age). *in —s =* old: H4A II, 4, 500. Rom. III, 5, 46. *smiles his cheek in —s,* LLL V, 2, 465 (= smiles his cheek

old, i. e. makes it seem old by its continual wrinkles). Sometimes = time: *await for wretched —s,* H6A I, 1, 48. *Hector shall not have his wit this y.* Tr. I, 2, 92 (it will take some time).

**Yearly,** adj. annual: *the y. course that brings this day about,* John III, 1, 81. *five hundred poor I have in y. pay,* H5 IV, 1, 315.

**Yearly,** adv. annually, every year: *my beauty as the spring doth y. grow,* Ven. 141. Ado V, 3, 23. H5 IV, 3, 45. Cymb. III, 1, 9.

**Yearn,** 1) tr. to grieve, to vex (O. Edd. *yern* or *yearn*): *she laments for it, that it would y. your heart to see it,* Wiv. III, 5, 45. R2 V, 5, 76. *it —s me not when men my garments wear,* H5 IV, 3, 26.

2) intr. to grieve (O. Edd. *ern* or *earn*): *my heart doth y.* H5 II, 3, 3. *Falstaff he is dead, and we must y. therefore,* 6. *that every like is not the same, the heart of Brutus —s to think upon,* Caes. II, 2, 129.

**Yeast,** see *Yest.*

**Yedward,** familiar corruption of *Edward:* H4A I, 2, 149.

**Yell,** subst. a loud and alarming cry: *to stop the loud pursuers* (hounds) *in their y.* Ven. 688. *with like timorous accent and dire y. as when ... the fire is spied,* Oth. I, 1, 75. = scream of distress and agony: *nor —s of mothers, maids, nor babes,* Tim. IV, 3, 124.

**Yell,** vb. to cry out; to howl: *the dogs did y.* LLL IV, 2, 60. *as if it felt with Scotland and —ed out like syllable of dolour,* Mcb. IV, 3, 7.

**Yellow,** having the colour of gold or of withered leaves: *y. autumn,* Sonn. 104, 5. *sands,* Tp. I, 2, 376. Mids. II, 1, 126. *hair,* Gent. IV, 4, 194. *beard,* Wiv. I, 4, 23. *cuckoo-buds,* LLL V, 2, 906. *gold,* Mids. III, 2, 393. Tim. IV, 3, 26. 33. *these y. cowslip cheeks,* Mids. V, 339 (Thisbe's speech). *stockings,* Tw. II, 5, 166. 180. 185. 218. III, 4, 28. 52. V, 346. *cheek,* H4B I, 2, 204 (sign of old age). *y. chapless skulls,* Rom. IV, 1, 83. *this y. Iachimo,* Cymb. II, 5, 14. The colour of grief: *with a green and y. melancholy,* Tw. II, 4, 116. Of age and decay: *fallen into the sear, the y. leaf,* Mcb. V, 3, 23; cf. Sonn. 73, 2.

Substantively: *your perfect y.* Mids. I, 2, 98. *'mongst all colours no y. in it,* Wint. II, 3, 107 (as the colour of jealousy). *a long motley coat guarded with y.* H8 Prol. 16. *the —s, blues, the purple violets,* Per. IV, 1, 15 (yellow flowers).

**Yellowed,** grown yellow: *my papers y. with their age,* Sonn. 17, 9.

**Yellowing,** lection of Qq in Tit. II, 3, 20: *let us sit down and mark their y. noise;* Ff *yelping,* some M. Edd. *yelling.*

**Yellowness,** jealousy, in the language of Nym: *I will possess him with y.* Wiv. I, 3, 111.

**Yellows,** jaundice in horses: Shr. III, 2, 54.

**Yelping,** partic. and gerund: barking without courage: *the timorous y. of the hounds appals her senses,* Ven. 881. *a y. kennel of French curs,* H6A IV, 2, 47. In Tit. II, 3, 20 Ff *let us sit down and mark their y. noise;* Qq *yellowing.*

**Yeoman,** 1) one not advanced to the rank of a gentleman: *we grace the y. by conversing with him,* H6A II, 4, 81. *spring crestless yeomen from so deep a root?* 85. *till thou be restored, thou art a y.* 95. *a gentleman or a y.* Lr. III, 6, 11. 13. 14.

2) a freeholder, a farmer: *not so wealthy as an*

*English y.* H6C I, 4, 123. *good householders, --'s sons,* H4A IV, 2, 16.

3) appellation given in courtesy to common soldiers: *you, good yeomen, whose limbs were made in England,* H5 III, 1, 25. *fight, gentlemen of England! fight, bold yeomen!* R3 V, 3, 338.

4) a gentleman servant: *the lady of the Strachy married the y. of the wardrobe,* Tw. II, 5, 45. *now it did me —'s service,* Hml. V, 2, 36.

= a kind of under-bailiff: *where's your y.? is't a lusty'y.? will a' stand to't?* H4B II, 1, 4 (Mrs. Quickly's speech).

**Yerk,** to jerk, to thrust with a sudden and quick motion: *their wounded steeds ... y. out their armed heels at their dead masters,* H5 IV, 7, 83. *to have —ed him here under the ribs,* Oth. I, 2, 5.

**Yes,** the word of affirmation opposed to *no:* Ven. 939. Tp. I, 2, 284. 437. V, 174. Gent. II, 1, 128. II, 3, 18. Wiv. II, 2, 108. Meas. I, 4, 3. II, 2, 49. II, 3, 25. III, 1, 64. 87. 100. 108. Err. II, 2, 76. IV, 2, 56. Merch. I, 3, 34. All's II, 5, 90 (rhyming to *kiss*) etc. etc. Peculiarly used in replying to a negative proposition: *it never yet did hurt to lay down likelihoods and forms of hope. Yes, if this present quality of war, indeed the instant action, a cause on foot, lives so in hope,* H4B I, 3, 36, **i.** e. yes, it did hurt in such a case as ours, when that which is to be done immediately, depends on uncertain hopes. Similarly Cor. IV, 6, 61. V, 4, 27 and: *my quarrel was not altogether slight. Faith, yes, to be put to the arbitrement of swords,* Cymb. I, 4, 52. Used as a word of enforcement: *I say, take heed; yes, heartily beseech you,* H8 I, 2, 176.

**Yest,** spume or foam of water: Wint. III, 3, 94.

**Yesterday,** 1) on the day before to-day: Wiv. IV, 2, 152. V, 1, 14. Merch. II, 8, 27. As II, 5, 49. III, 4, 38. Tw. I, 3, 15. John III, 4, 80. H5 II, 2, 40. III, 7, 51. IV, 8, 91. V, 1, 9. 36. Troil. I, 1, 46. I, 2, 34. 185. III, 3, 19. Cor. IV, 5, 211. Caes. I, 3, 26. III, 2, 123. Mcb. III, 1, 74. Hml. II, 1, 56. Oth. III, 3, 333. IV, 1, 52. Ant. V, 2, 251.

2) substantively, = the day before to-day: *call back y., bid time return,* R2 III, 2, 69. *all our —s,* Mcb. V, 5, 22.

**Yesternight,** last night: Meas. V, 134. Ado IV, 1, 84. 184. H4A I, 1, 32. 36. II, 1, 59. R3 III, 6, 6. Troil. I, 1, 32. Tit. IV, 2, 153. Rom. V, 3, 251. Caes. II, 1, 238. Hml. I, 2, 189.

**Yesty,** foamy, frothy: *the y. waves,* Mcb. IV, 1, 53. *a kind of y. collection,* Hml. V, 2, 199 (light, frivolous, unsolid).

**Yet,** 1) now, by this time: *what if my house be troubled with a rat and I be pleased to give ten thousand ducats to have it baned? what, are you answered yet?* Merch. IV, 1, 46 (i. e. after my alleging this instance). *whose party do the townsmen yet admit?* John II, 361 (after we have measured our strengths in fight). *how yet resolves the governor of the town?* H5 III, 3, 1. *know you me yet?* Cor. IV, 3, 5 (after what I have said to put you in mind). *prepare thy brow to frown: knowest thou me yet?* IV, 5, 69. *have you done yet?* Ant. III, 13, 153. *whence are you? A poor Egyptian yet, the queen my mistress ... desires instruction,* Ant. V, 1, 52 (i. e. my queen, who is now no more than a poor Egyptian. M. Edd. *a poor Egyptian yet. The queen* etc.).

2) already: *not one of them that yet looks on me,*

*or would know me,* Tp. V, 83. *no more yet of this, for 'tis not ... befitting this first meeting,* 162. *she's come to know, if yet her brother's pardon be come hither,* Meas. IV, 3, 112. *hath yet the deputy sent my brother's pardon?* 118. *hast thou yet latched the Athenian's eyes ... as I did bid thee do?* Mids. III, 2, 36. *is he come home yet?* IV, 2, 2. *is he yet possessed how much ye would?* Merch. I, 3, 65. *is my master yet returned?* V, 34. *did you yet ever see Baptista's daughter?* Shr. I, 2, 252. *is he won yet?* Wint. I, 2, 86. *have you inquired yet who picked my pocket?* H4A III, 3, 61. *no word to your master that I am yet come to town,* H4B II, 2, 177. *heard he the good news yet?* IV, 5, 11. *is that letter ... yet sent away?* H8 IV, 2, 128. *is Caesar yet gone to the Capitol?* Caes. II, 4, 24. *yet to be known shortens my made intent,* Lr. IV, 7, 9.

*As yet,* in the same sense: *hast thou as yet conferred with Margery Jourdain?* H6B I, 2, 74. *I will not trouble you as yet,* As II, 7, 172 (Latin: *nonjam*). *as hardly will he endure your sight as yet,* Wint. IV, 4, 481.

3) still, to this time, now as formerly: *which yet are green,* Sonn. 104, 8. *grew a seething bath, which yet men prove ... a sovereign cure,* 153, 7. *all's hushed like midnight yet,* Tp. IV, 207. *you do yet taste some subtilties o' the isle,* V, 123. *will they yet look after thee?* Wiv. II, 2, 146. *yet there want not many that do fear ... to walk by this Herne's oak,* IV, 4, 39. *bestowed her on her own lamentation, which she yet wears for his sake,* Meas. III, 1, 238. *this maid hath yet in her the continuance of her first affection,* 248. *yet I have a trick of the old rage,* LLL V, 2, 416. *are you yet living?* Ado I, 1, 120. *yet it lives there unchecked that Antonio hath a ship wrecked,* Merch. III, 1, 2. *she was the fairest creature in the world, and yet she is inferior to none,* Shr. Ind. 2, 69. *I am yet so near the manners of my mother,* Tw. II, 1, 41. *they will talk of mad Shallow yet,* H4B III, 2, 16. *with yet appearing blood,* IV, 1, 82. *her mother liveth yet,* H6A V, 4, 12. *for yet is hope of life and victory,* H6C II, 3, 55. *some dregs of conscience are yet within me,* R3 I, 4, 125. *live you yet?* Cor. II, 1, 197. *thou art mighty yet,* Caes. V, 3, 94. *yet here, Laertes?* Hml. I, 3, 55. *or that I do not yet, and ever did, and ever will ... love him dearly,* Oth. IV, 2, 156. *I see her yet,* Cymb. II, 4, 101. *we wept after her hearse, and yet we mourn,* Per. IV, 3, 42.

*As yet,* in the same sense: *I might as yet have been a spreading flower,* Compl. 75.

4) hitherto: *like a red morn that ever yet betokened wreck to the seaman,* Ven. 453. *her yet unstained bed,* Lucr. 366. *bend the dukedom yet unbowed,* Tp. I, 2, 115. *thou dost me yet but little hurt,* II, 2, 82. *there are yet missing some few odd lads,* V, 254. *'tis but her picture I have yet beheld,* Gent. II, 4, 209. *a rashness that I ever yet have shunned,* III, 1, 30. *I keep but three men and a boy yet, till my mother be dead,* Wiv. I, 1, 285. *that madness that I ever yet beheld,* IV, 2, 27. *you are yet unsworn,* Meas. I, 4, 9. *your yet ungalled estimation,* Err. III, 1, 102. *in time I may believe, yet I mistrust,* Shr. III, 1, 51 etc.

*As yet,* in the same sense: *that's not five weeks old yet,* LLL IV, 2, 36. *as yet I cannot truly say how I came here,* Mids. IV, 1, 152. *things as yet not come to life,* H4B III, 1, 84. *as yet I do not (know)* R3 I, 1, 53. *have not spoke as yet,* Cor. I, 4, 4. *although as yet the face of it be covered,* Lr. III, 1, 20. *unreconciled as yet to heaven,* Oth. V, 2, 27.

*Not yet:* Tp. I, 2, 36. 244. Meas. I, 1, 81. LLL V, 2, 212 etc. Sometimes *yet* placed before *not: news that you yet dreamt not of*, Ado I, 2, 4. *yet I have not seen so likely an ambassador of love*, Merch. II, 9, 91. *the time was that I hated thee, and yet it is not that I bear thee love*, As III, 5, 93. *his powers are yet not ready*, H5 III, 3, 46. *full sick, and yet not well*, H8 II, 4, 204. *my work hath yet not warmed me*, Cor. I, 5, 18. *stained as meadows, yet not dry*, Tit. III, 1, 125. *my ears have yet not drunk a hundred words*, Rom. II, 2, 58 (the surreptitious Q1 and M. Edd. *not yet*). *we yet not know*, Ant. II, 1, 49. *yet they are not joined*, IV, 12, 1. *I yet not understand the case myself*, Cymb. II, 3, 80. Lr. II, 4, 284. cf. *never yet* and *yet never: never woman yet could rule them*, Ven. 1007. *duty never yet did want his meed*, Gent. II, 4, 112. *for yet his honour never heard a play*, Shr. Ind. 1, 96. *the nature of our quarrel yet never brooked parle*, I, 1, 116.

5) before or till some future time: *he'll be hanged yet*, Tp. I, 1, 61. *I'll to my book, for yet ere supper-time must I perform much business*, III, 1, 95. *the time is yet to come*, Meas. II, 1, 175. *we may effect this business yet ere day*, Mids. II, 2, 395. *you, Diana, under my poor instructions yet must suffer some thing in my behalf*, Alls IV, 4, 27. *yet, I pray you*, 30. *if I like thee no worse after dinner, I will not part from thee yet*, Lr. I, 4, 45 (not so soon). *you shall be yet far fairer than you are*, Ant. I, 2, 16.

6) still; before comparatives: *yet more quarrelling with occasion*, Merch. III, 5, 61. Similarly *yet again* = once more: *yet again, what do you here?* Tp. I, 1, 41. *peace yet again*, Caes. I, 2, 14. *let our wives yet once again ... appoint a meeting*, Wiv. IV, 4, 14. *yet once again proclaim it publicly*, Err. V, 130. *whom, yet once more, I hold my most malicious foe*, H8 II, 4, 82. *nor yet* = nor even: *Helen, the mother of great Constantine, nor yet Saint Philip's daughters are like thee*, H6A I, 2, 143.

7) after all; as matters stand; though the case be such: *that* (my mind) *... still pure doth in her poisoned closet yet endure*, Lucr. 1659. *I killed a man whose death I much repent, but yet I slew him manfully in fight*, Gent. IV, 1, 28. *what's yet in this that bears the name of life?* Meas. III, 1, 38. *hast thou or word or wit or impudence, that yet can do thee office?* V, 369. *yet have I left a daughter*, Lr. I, 4, 276. 327. *there's nothing in her yet*, Ant. III, 3, 21.

Sometimes = at least; though nothing else: *if not divine, yet let her be a principality*, Gent. II, 4, 152. *if your heart be so obdurate, vouchsafe me yet your picture for my love*, IV, 2, 121. *the duke yet would have dark deeds darkly answered*, Meas. III, 1, 187. *sweet Isabel, do yet but kneel by me; hold up your hands, say nothing*, V, 442. *since you could not be my son-in-law, be yet my nephew*, Ado V, 1, 297. *but tell me yet, dost thou not know my voice?* Err. V, 300. *lie further off yet*, Mids. II, 2, 44. *hear me yet*, Merch. III, 3, 3.

8) nevertheless, still: *I'll smother thee with kisses, and yet not cloy thy lips with loathed satiety*, Ven. 19. *who conquers where he comes ..., yet hath he been my captive*, 101. *this is my spite, that, thou being dead, the day should yet be light*, 1134. *I shall miss thee, but yet thou shalt have freedom*, Tp. V, 96. Ven. 112. 116. 128. 148. 406. 438. 442. 574. 576. 610. 778. 867. 986. 1070. Tp. II, 1, 26. 156. 206. 215. II, 2, 4. III, 2, 23. Gent. I, 1, 26. 133. II, 1, 123 — 126.

IV, 2, 61. IV, 4, 111. Wiv. II, 2, 138. III, 4, 19. V, 5, 258. Meas. II, 1, 4. III, 1, 92. Err. IV, 2, 10 etc. etc.

10) = the adversative particle but: Ven. 94. 544. 548. 911. 981. 998. Tp. I, 1, 20. II, 1, 38. II, 2, 55. III, 3, 31 etc. After a negation: *I sold not Maine, I lost not Normandy, yet, to recover them, would lose my life*, H6B IV, 7, 71.

Seemingly = though (cf. the German *trotzdem* = *obgleich*): *for my soul, yet I know not why, hates nothing more than he*, As I, 1, 171. *I cannot speak to her, yet she urged conference*, I, 2, 270.

**Yew**, the tree Taxus baccata (planted in church-yards, and therefore emblem of death): *my shroud of white, stuck all with y.* Tw. II, 4, 56. *bows of double-fatal y.* R2 III, 2, 117. *would bind me here unto the body of a dismal y.* Tit. II, 3, 107. *slips of y. slivered in the moon's eclipse*, Mcb. IV, 1, 27. In Rom. V, 3, 3 and 137 the spurious Q1 and M. Edd. *yew-trees*, the authentic O. Edd. *young trees.*

**Yield**, 1) trans. a) to produce, to give in return for labour or as profit: *for fear it y. me still so bad a harvest*, Ven. Ded. 6. *what my revenue —ed*, Tp. I, 2, 98. *the bees that y. it* (honey) Gent. I, 2, 107. Wiv. IV, 4, 33. Mids. V, 435. As II, 3, 64. II, 6, 6. III, 2, 123. Wint. IV, 3, 34. IV, 4, 702. V, 1, 55. John III, 4, 111. R2 III, 2, 18. H4B IV, 5, 80. H5 IV, 3, 125. Tim. III, 6, 58. Hml. IV, 4, 21. Cymb. IV, 2, 180. Per. IV, 1, 4.

= to bear, to bring forth: *a birth which throes thee much to y.* Tp. II, 1, 231. *that such a crafty devil as is his mother should y. the world this ass*, Cymb. II, 1, 58. *she was —ed there*, Per. V, 3, 48.

b) to afford, to offer, to give: *the portal ... which to his speech did honey passage y.* Ven. 452. *each unwilling portal —s him way*, Lucr. 309. *to their hope they such odd action y.* 1433. *the earth can y. me but a common grave*, Sonn. 81, 7. *the pleasures that hill and valleys ... y.* Pilgr. 356. *who never —s us kind answer*, Tp. I, 2, 309. *y. me a direct answer*, Meas. IV, 2, 7. *our soul cannot but y. you forth to public thanks*, V, 7 (= y. public thanks to you). *as much* (love) *as may be —ed to a man*, Ado III, 1, 48. *ere further leisure y. them farther means*, R2 I, 4, 40. *the means that heaven —s must be embraced*, III, 2, 29. *thy own hand —s thy death's instrument*, V, 5, 107. *O earth, y. us that king again*, H4B I, 3, 106. *he'll y. the crow a pudding*, H5 II, 1, 91. *didst y. consent to disinherit him*, H6C II, 2, 24. IV, 6, 36. 46. *if France can y. relief*, III, 3, 20. *all kindness that your estate requires and mine can y.* 150. *Burgundy will y. him help*, IV, 6, 90. *more pain ... than death can y. me here*, R3 I, 3, 169. *look to have it —ed with all willingness*, III, 1, 198. *as thou canst y. a melancholy seat*, IV, 4, 32. *day, y. me not thy light*, 401. *if they would y. us but the superfluity*, Cor. I, 1, 17. *to y. your voices*, II, 3, 184. III, 1, 34. *earth, y. me roots*, Tim. IV, 3, 23. 185. *they botch the words up fit to their own thoughts; which, as her winks and nods and gestures y. them, indeed would make one think ...*, Hml. IV, 5, 11. *that self exhibition which your own coffers y.* Cymb. I, 6, 123. *who did promise to y. me often tidings*, IV, 3, 39. *wherein my death might y. her any profit*, Per. IV, 1, 81. *this city will y. many scholars*, IV, 6, 198.

c) to grant, to allow, to admit: *the noblemen —ed Collatinus the victory*, Lucr. Arg. 11. *were not his requests so far from reason's —ing, your fair self should*

## Y

make a —ing ... in my breast, LLL II, 151. 152. I y. all this, Wint. IV, 4, 421. shall y. the other in the right opinion, H6A II, 4, 42. nor will he know his purse or y. me this, to show him what a beggar his heart is, Tim. I, 2, 200. your loving motion to the common body, to y. what passes here, Cor. II, 2, 58.

d) to deliver, to exhibit: the reasons of our state I cannot y. All's III, 1, 10. I can y. you none (reason) without words, Tw. III, 1, 27. III, 2, 4. but well and free, if thou so y. him, there is gold, Ant. II, 5, 28.

e) to emit; to give up: graves, yawn and y. your dead, Ado V, 3, 19. y. the ghost (= die) H6A I, 1, 67. R3 I, 4, 37. ere thou y. thy breath, H6A IV, 7, 24. R3 V, 3, 172. With up: graves —ed up their dead, Caes. II, 2, 18.

f) to deliver, to render, to give up, to surrender: I'll y. him thee asleep, Tp. III, 2, 68. if I would y. him my virginity, Meas. III, 1, 98. y. thee to my hand, John II, 156. H4A V, 3, 10. H4B IV, 3, 19. here he is, and here I y. him, 49. we y. our town and lives to thy soft mercy, H5 III, 3, 48. I'll y. myself to prison, H6B IV, 9, 42. I must y. my body to the earth, H6C V, 2, 9. the sheep doth y. his fleece and next his throat unto the butcher's knife, V, 6, 8. they had so vilely —ed the town, Cor. III, 1, 11. y. thee, coward, Mcb. V, 8, 23. mine honour was not — ed, but conquered merely, Ant. III, 13, 61. it shall safe be kept and truly —ed you, Cymb. I, 6, 210. y. thee, thief, IV, 2, 75. V, 3, 77. therefore briefly y. her, Per. III, 1, 53. With a double accus.: to y. myself his wife who wins me by that means, Merch. II, 1, 18. the man entire upon the next encounter —s him ours, Caes. I, 3, 156. With up: y. them up where I myself must render, Compl. 221. the law of Athens —s you up ... to death, Mids. I, 1, 119. he'ld y. them up (twenty heads) Meas. II, 4, 181. hath —ed up his body to the grave, R2 V, 6, 21. your northern castles are —ed up, III, 2, 201. is Rouen —ed up? H6A I, 1, 65. —s up his life unto a world of odds, IV, 4, 25. y. me up the keys, H6C IV, 7, 37. that reason which denies the —ing of her up, Troil. II, 2, 25. so she will y. us up, Ant. III, 13, 16. I y. thee up my life, V, 1, 12. y. up their deer to the stand o'the stealer, Cymb. II, 3, 74.

= to resign (cf. above: Meas. III, 1, 98. H6C V, 2, 9. V, 6, 8. R2 V, 6, 21. H6A IV, 4, 25): till each to razed oblivion y. his part of thee, Sonn. 122, 7. shall I now give o'er the —ed set? John V, 2, 107 (almost = lost, or at least given up for lost). —ed upon compromise that which his ancestors achieved, R2 II, 1, 253. who ... his sceptre —s to the possession of thy royal hand, V, 109. I'll make him y. the crown, H6B I, 1, 258. H6C II, 2, 101. Milo his addition y. to sinewy Ajax, Troil. II, 3, 258. Err. IV, 4, 58. Mids. I, 1, 91. H6C II, 5, 59. III, 3, 16. With up: ere I'ld y. my body up to shame, Meas. II, 4, 103. 164. LLL II, 160. Mids. I, 1, 80. III, 2, 165. John IV, 2, 157. V, 1, 1. Tit. I, 191. Oth. III, 3, 448.

g) to give a reward, to bless: the gods y. you for it, Ant. IV, 2, 33 (cf. Godild).

2) intr. a) to give place: y. day to night, H6A I, 1, 1. let York be regent, I will y. to him, H6B I, 3, 109. I yield to thee, or to the meanest groom, II, 1, 184.

b) to give way; to succumb: soldiers, when their captain once doth y., they basely fly, Ven. 893. Hercules himself must y. to odds, H6C II, 1, 53. so true men y., with robbers so o'ermatched, I, 4, 64. —ing to

another (wind) when it blows, III, 1, 87. thus —s the cedar to the axe's edge, V, 2, 11. why do I y. to that suggestion, Mcb. I, 3, 134. I bear a charmed life, which must not y. to one of woman born, V, 8, 12. a substance that must y. to you, Per. II, 1, 3.

c) to give way, not to oppose or to discontinue opposition: Ven. 547. Lucr. 339. 526. 1036. Compl. 149. Pilgr. 319. Ado V, 4, 95. Merch. IV, 1, 425. All's III, 7, 36. R2 III, 3, 58. H4A V, 1, 110. H4B II, 1, 125. H5 V, 2, 301. H6A III, 1, 112. 118. V, 3, 99. V, 5, 77. Cor. V, 3, 17 (I have —ed too; some M. Edd. unnecessarily —ed to). Tit. I, 449. With to: Ven. 566. Err. IV, 4, 84. LLL II, 168. Merch. III, 3, 15. H6A III, 1, 134. H6B V, 1, 40. R3 III, 7, 207. Troil. V, 3, 76. Tit. V, 2, 140. Caes. II, 2, 106.

d) to submit: heart, ... y. to my hand, Lucr. 1210. to your power I'll y. Err. III, 2, 40. must y. to such inevitable shame as to offend, being himself offended, Merch. IV, 1, 57. so she —s to me, Shr. II, 137. all Kent hath —ed, John V, 1, 30. I must not y. to any rites of love, H6A I, 2, 113. made me almost y. upon my knees, III, 3, 80. y. or die, H6B IV, 2, 135. all his powers do y. IV, 9, 10. what he will, I humbly y. unto, H6C III, 1, 101. to y. to his conditions, Cor. V, 1, 69. making a treaty where there was a —ing, V, 6, 69. all places y. to him, IV, 7, 28. life would not y. to age, Lr. IV, 1, 12. to wisdom he's a fool that will not y. Per. II, 4, 54.

= to surrender: R2 III, 3, 20. H4A V, 3, 11 (Ff to y.; Qq a yielder). H4B IV, 3, 13. 44. H5 III, 3, 42. IV, 2, 37. IV, 4, 1. V, 2, 327. Cor. III, 1, 215. Caes. V, 4, 12. Mcb. V, 8, 27. Lr. II, 1, 33. Ant. III, 10, 35. V, 1, 1. Cymb. I, 4, 115 (go back even to the —ing). IV, 2, 100. With to: y. to my love, Lucr. 668. the coward ... doth y. to those two armies, 75. I'll force thee y. to my desire, Gent. V, 4, 59. Meas. V, 101. H6B IV, 8, 12. H6C I, 4, 30. Ant. IV, 12, 11. Cymb. IV, 2, 80.

e) to comply, to assent: inclined to accessary —ings, Lucr. 1658. how well this —ing rescues thee from shame, LLL I, 1, 118. I would not y. to be your house's guest, V, 2, 354. if you y. not to your father's choice, Mids. I, 1, 69. I see a —ing in the looks of France, John II, 474. before I would have —ed to this league, H6B I, 1, 127. that is more than I will y. unto, H6C III, 2, 96. will not y. to our complots, R3 III, 1, 192. —ed to bear the golden yoke of sovereignty, III, 7, 145. not impute this —ing to light love, Rom. II, 2, 105. therefore must his choice be circumscribed unto the voice and —ing of that body whereof he is the head, Hml. I, 3, 23. will y. to see his daughter, Lr. IV, 3, 43. when life itself —s to the theft, IV, 6, 44. he'll never y. to that, nor must not then be —ed to in this, Ant. III, 6, 37. 38. you shall not say I y. being silent, Cymb. II, 3, 99.

**Yielder,** 1) one who allows or suffers: briers and thorns at their apparel snatch; some sleeves, some hats, from —s all things catch, Mids. III, 2, 30. 2) one who surrenders: I was not born a y. H4A V, 3, 11 (Ff to yield). 3) a y. up, = one who gives up: some guard these traitors to the block of death, treason's true bed and y. up of breath, H4B IV, 2, 123 (y. up of breath, as it were, adjectively added to bed, the sense being: treason's true bed, as it is a dying bed, a death-bed).

**Yielding,** subst. see Yield.

**Yoke**, subst. 1) the curvated piece of timber placed on the necks of draught oxen: Ado I, 1, 263. Mids. II, 1, 93. Emblem of servitude and slavery: Lucr. 409. Ado I, 1, 203. Mids. I, 1, 81. R2 II, 1, 291. H4B IV, 4, 10. H6A I, 1, 164. R3 V, 2, 2. Tit. I, 69. 111. IV, 1, 109. Caes. I, 2, 61. I, 3, 84. Mcb. IV, 3, 39. Cymb. III, 1, 52. III, 5, 5. *of sufferance in general: can I bear this shameful y.* H6B II, 4, 37. *yield not thy neck to fortune's y.* H6C III, 3, 17. *to bear the golden y. of sovereignty*, R3 III, 7, 146. *now thy proud neck bears half my burthened y.* IV, 4, 111. *and shake the y. of inauspicious stars from this world-wearied flesh*, Rom. V, 3, 111. *I shall with aged patience bear your y.* Per. II, 4, 48. of connection and unity: *whose souls do bear an equal y. of love*, Merch. III, 4, 13.

2) a pair, a couple: *a y. of his discarded men*, Wiv. II, 1, 181. *how a good y. of bullocks?* H4B III, 2, 42.

Doubtful passage: *do not these fair —s become the forest better than the town?* Wiv. V, 5, 111 (the horns worn by Falstaff called so on account of their shape? Later Ff *oaks*).

**Yoke**, vb. (cf. *Unyoke*) 1) trans. to put under a yoke: Ven. 1190. Metaphorically, = a) to bring into bondage, to subdue: Gent. I, 1, 40. H6A II, 3, 64. Troil. II, 1, 116. Tit. I, 30. b) to couple, to join: *unless thou y. thy liking to my will*, Lucr. 1633. *may my name be —d with his that did betray the Best*, Wint. I, 2, 419. *ever may your highness y. together ... my doing well with my well saying*, H8 III, 2, 150. *you are —d with a lamb*, Caes. IV, 3, 110. *every bearded fellow that's but —d may draw with you*, Oth. IV, 1, 67 (= married). *if it be sin to say so, I y. me in my good brother's fault*, Cymb. IV, 2, 19. *nobly he —s a smiling with a sigh*, 51.

2) intr. to join, to be coupled: *on his neck her —ing arms she throws*, Ven. 592. *to sunder them that y. so well together*, H6C IV, 1, 23. *we'll y. together*, IV, 6, 49. *nor y. with him for tribune*, Cor. III, 1, 57.

**Yoke-devils**, two devils coupled together: H5 II, 2, 106.

**Yoke-fellow**, companion: *—s in arms*, H5 II, 3, 56. *by his bloody side, y. to his honour-owing wounds, the noble Earl of Suffolk also lies*, IV, 6, 9. *thou, his y. of equity*, Lr. III, 6, 39.

**Yon**, 1) demonstr. pron., used in pointing at something: Mids. III, 2, 188. Merch. III, 2, 240. 246. John II, 472. III, 3, 60. H4A V, 1, 2. H5 IV, 2, 16. 39. IV, 7, 60. R3 I, 2, 261. Rom. III, 5, 19. Caes. II, 1, 103. Hml. I, 1, 167. Ant. III, 10, 10. Per. Prol. 40. I, 1, 21. 37. II, 3, 37. 54. Qq *yon*, Ff *yond:* R2 II, 3, 53. III, 3, 26. 135. III, 4, 29. Troil. IV. 5, 220. Lr. IV, 6, 18. 120. 155.

2) adv. there: *y. methinks he stands*, R2 III, 3, 91 (Ff *yond, methinks, he is*).

**Yond**, 1) demonstr. pron., used in pointing to a person or thing at a distance (not always within view): Tp. II, 2, 20. 21. 24. Gent. IV, 2, 71. Wiv. III, 4, 87. As II, 4, 64. Tw. I, 5, 147. II, 4, 83. III, 2, 73. Wint. II, 1, 31. H6A II, 1, 33. Troil. V, 3, 99. Cor. III, 1, 50. IV, 5, 110. V, 4, 1. Rom. I, 5, 130. III, 5, 4. 12. V, 3, 3. Tim. I, 2, 29. IV, 3, 465. Caes. I, 2, 194. V, 3, 18. Hml. I, 1, 36. Oth. III, 3, 460. Ant. III, 9, 1. IV, 12, 1. Cymb. III, 3, 10. IV, 2, 292. Ff *yond*, Qq *yon:* R2 II, 3, 53. III, 3, 26. 135. III, 4, 29. Troil.

IV, 5, 220. Lr. IV, 6, 18. 120. 155. In Meas. IV, 3, 93 O. Edd. *y. generation*, M. Edd. *the under generation.*

2) adv. there: *say what thou seest y.* Tp. I, 2, 409. *y. 's that same knave*, All's III, 5, 85. *y., methinks, he is*, R2 III, 3, 91 (Qq *yon methinks he stands*). *is not y. Diomed*, Troil. IV, 5, 13 (Ff *young*). *by all Diana's waiting-women y.* V, 2, 91. *what torch is y.* Rom. V, 3, 125. Oth. I, 2, 28 (Qq *yonder*).

**Yonder**, = yon or yond; 1) pron.: Meas. I, 2, 87. LLL IV, 1, 9. Mids. III, 2, 61. Merch. V, 142. R2 I, 3, 7. 26. H5 IV, 7, 123. H6A I, 4, 11. III, 2, 23. R3 I, 3, 289. Troil. IV, 5, 211. 219. V, 6, 23. Rom. I, 5, 44. 51. II, 2, 2. 107. III, 5, 8. IV, 1, 78. Caes. I, 2, 104. V, 3, 16. Hml. III, 2, 393 (Ff *that*). IV, 5, 64.

2) adv.: Gent. V, 4, 125. Wiv. II, 1, 163. III, 1, 27. 52. IV, 2, 22. V, 5, 194. Meas. I, 2, 60. Err. II, 2, 111. IV, 4, 42. V, 9. Ado I, 3, 44. V, 2, 98. Mids. III, 2, 176. 380. V, 188. Merch. II, 2, 183. As I, 1, 28. I, 2, 137. 156. 160. Shr. V, 1, 113. All's III, 2, 35. IV, 5, 99. Tw. II, 5, 20. III, 4, 310. H4B II, 1, 41. H5 IV, 1, 88. 91. H6C II, 2, 2. V, 4, 67. 80. Troil. I, 2, 229. 231. 246. 247. IV, 5, 64. 191. V, 1, 74. V, 5, 23. Cor. I, 4, 1. I, 6, 21. Tit. IV, 4, 41. Tim. III, 2, 27. IV, 3, 356. Caes. V, 3, 92. Oth. I, 2, 28 (Ff *yond*). V, 2, 106. Ant. II, 2, 14. IV, 12, 11. Per. II, 3, 23.

**Yore**; *of y.* = times ago: *what beauty was of y.* Sonn. 68, 14.

**Yorick**, name of a jester, lamented by Hamlet: Hml. V, 1, 198. 203.*

**York**, English town: R2 V, 5, 73. H4A V, 5, 36. H4B IV, 3, 80. H6C I, 4, 179 (*on Y. gates*). 180. II, 1, 65. II, 2, 1. IV, 7, 8. H8 IV, 2, 13 etc. *archbishop of Y.* H4A I, 3, 269. III, 2, 119. H4B I, 1, 189. H6C IV, 3, 53. IV, 4, 11 (*bishop of Y.*) etc. *Cardinal of Y.* (Wolsey): H8 I, 1, 51. II, 2, 106. III, 1, 62.

*Edmund Langley Duke of Y.*, son of Edward III: R2 I, 2, 62. 67 etc. H4A I, 3, 245. H6A II, 5, 85. H6B II, 2. 15 etc. His title inherited by his descendants: H6A II, 4, 119. II, 5, 41. III, 1, 165. 171 etc. His son Edward Duke of York slain in the battle of Agincourt: H5 IV, 3, 131. IV, 6, 3. IV, 8, 108. His grandson Richard Duke of Y. claiming the crown and kindling the war of the Roses: H6A III, 4, 30. H6B I, 1, 65. H6C I, 4, 180 etc. etc. The second son of Edward IV bearing the title: R3 III, 1, 101 etc.

**York-place**, a palace in London, afterwards called Whitehall: H8 IV, 1, 94. 95.

**Yorkshire**, English county: H4B IV, 4, 99. R3 IV, 4, 521.

**You**, pers. pron. of the 2nd pers. plur., the usual address to one as well as to several persons (its difference from *thou* sub *Thou*); nom. as well as objective case (as for the ancient orthography *y'are* for the modern *you're*, see *Ye*): Ven. 382. 421. 771. 774. 1082. 1084. Tp. I, 1, 14. 41 etc. etc. With an adjective: *for the prize of all too precious you*, Sonn. 86, 2. Reflexively: *rest you*, Tp. III, 1, 18. *hie you home*, Gent. IV, 2, 94. *bethink you of some conveyance*, Wiv. III, 3, 135. *hold you ever to our special drift*, Meas. IV, 5, 4. Ado V, 1, 92. *get you to heaven*, II, 1, 47. *that you should here repent you*, Mids. V, 115. *prepare you*, Merch. II, 4, 23. H6C V, 4, 60. Caes. V, 1, 12. *put you in your best array*, As V, 2, 79. *undress*

Y

*you*, Shr. Ind. 2, 119. *content ye*, I, 1, 90. *keep you warm*, II, 268. *betake you to your guard*, Tw. III, 4, 253. *to your own bents dispose you*, Wint. I, 2, 179. *dismantle you*, IV, 4, 666. *arm you*, John IV, 2, 249. *bear you well*, R2 V, 2, 50. *you towards York shall bend you*, H4A V, 5, 36. *furnish you fairly*, Troil. III, 3, 33. *fit you to the custom*, Cor. II, 2, 146 etc. etc.

Superfluous; 1) as dativus ethicus: *I'll do you your master what good I can*, Wiv. I, 4, 97. *I will find you twenty lascivious turtles*, II, 1, 82. *will not miss you morning nor evening prayer*, II, 2, 102. *what offence hath this man made you?* Meas. III, 2, 15. *she will sit you*, Ado II, 3, 116. *I will roar you as gently*, Mids. I, 2, 84 (Ff om.). *John lays you plots*, John III, 4, 146. *a' shall charge you and discharge you with the motion of a pewterer's hammer*, H4B III, 2, 280. *they will learn you by rote where services are done*, H5 III, 6, 74. *he will weep you*, Troil. I, 2, 188. *he will last you some eight year*, Hml. V, 1, 183 etc. 2) after the imperative (not only when stress is laid on it, as in Tp. I, 1, 45. Meas. I, 4, 8. II, 2, 13 etc.): *take you this*, Gent. II, 2, 6. *fear not you*, IV, 2, 82. V, 2, 45. Wiv, III, 3, 39. Meas. II, 1, 222. Err. I, 2, 92. Ado II, 2, 22. 25. III, 1, 31. V, 1, 295. Merch. I, 3, 69. Tw. I, 5, 92. Wint. IV, 3, 126. IV, 4, 52. H6B I, 4, 6. 13. Tim. III, 2, 11. Ant. II, 2, 24 etc. cf. *soft you:* Ado V, 1, 207. Hml. III, 1, 88. Oth. V, 2, 338. 3) before and after a vocative: *you madcap*, Gent. II, 5, 8. *you hag you*, Wiv. IV, 2, 188. *you minion you*, Err. IV, 4, 63. *you puppet you*, Mids. III, 2, 288. *you juggler you*, H4B II, 4, 141. *you candle-mine you*, 326. *mistress minion you*, Rom. III, 5, 152 (cf. *Thou*) etc.

Used indefinitely, = one, they: *in these times you stand on distance*, Wiv. II, 1, 233.

**Young**, being in the first part of life, not old: Ven. 187. 260. 419. 837. 1152. Lucr. 1769. Sonn. 19, 4. 138, 5. Tp. II, 2, 176. III, 3, 92. IV, 1, 40. Gent. I, 1, 22. 47. II, 1, 24. III, 2, 65. IV, 2, 26. Wiv. I, 1, 40. 77. Meas. II, 3, 13. IV, 3, 4. Err. I, 1, 125. Ado V, 1, 119. Merch. I, 2, 90. As I, 1, 57 (*you are too y. in this*). 59. Shr. Ind. 2, 147 (*we shall ne'er be —er*). II, 237. All's III, 1, 17. Tw. III, 2, 70. John I, 71 (*—er born*). H4A I, 3, 7 (*soft as y. down*). H6B II, 2, 52. H6C I, 2, 1. IV, 1, 118. R3 I, 1, 153. Lr. I, 1, 41 etc. etc. *his years but y.* Gent. II, 4, 69. H6A II, 5, 107. V, 1, 21. *thy y. days*, LLL I, 2, 15. Tit. IV, 3, 91. *such a y. one*, Shr. II, 236. John II, 521. H8 V, 3, 180. Per. IV, 2, 144. Metaphorically: *is the day so y.?* Rom. I, 1, 166. *in your —er enterprise*, H4A V, 1, 71 (when it was in the beginning). *thus Eleanor's pride dies in her —est days*, H6B II, 3, 46 (in the very beginning). *lowliness is y. ambition's ladder*, Caes. II, 1, 22. *this is yet but y.* H8 III, 2, 47 (just happened). *we are yet but y. in deed*, Mcb. III, 4, 144 (inexperienced, raw).

Substantively: *the —er rises when the old doth fall*, Lr. III, 3, 26. *how like a —er and a prodigal the scarfed bark puts from her native bay*, Merch. II, 6, 14 (a younger son; cf. S. Luke XV, 12. M. Edd. *younker*). *—er than she are happy mothers made*, Rom. I, 2, 12. I, 3, 69. *he did in the bosom reign of y., of old*, Compl. 128. *he wooes ... both y. and old*, Wiv. II, 1, 118. Mids. I, 1, 138. R2 III, 2, 119. V, 2, 13. Cor. III, 1, 228. Per. IV, 1, 42. = offspring; applied to men: *he leaves it to be mastered by his y.* Lucr. 863. to animals:

As I, 2, 100. H6C II, 2, 14. 26. 32. II, 5, 35 (*have been with y.* = pregnant). V, 6, 17. Lr. I, 4, 236. *y. one in the same sense: she feels her y. one kick*, All's V, 3, 303. *her harmless y. one*, H6B III, 1, 215. Tit. II, 3, 142. Mcb. IV, 2, 11..

**Young-eyed**, having the fresh look of youth: *y. cherubins*, Merch. V, 62. cf. Wiv. III, 2, 68.

**Youngling**, a stripling, a novice, a greenhorn: *she told the y. how god Mars did try her*, Pilgr. 145. *y., thou canst not love so dear as I*, Shr. II, 339. *y., learn thou to make some meaner choice; Lavinia is thine elder brother's hope*, Tit. II, 1, 73. *I tell you, —s*, IV, 2, 93.

**Youngly**, early in life: *that fresh blood which y. thou bestowest*, Sonn. 11, 3. *how y. he began to serve his country*, Cor. II, 3, 244.

**Young-man**, see *Man.*

**Youngster**, a youth, a lad: *for Adon's sake, a y. proud and wild*, Pilgr. 120.

**Younker**, a stripling: *will you make a y. of me?* H4A III, 3, 92 (i. e. a novice). *trimmed like a y. prancing to his love*, H6C II, 1, 24. In Merch. II, 6, 14 M. Edd. unnecessarily *y.*, O. Edd. *younger;* see *Young.*

**Your**, poss. pron., = belonging or pertaining to you: Ven. Ded. 1. 3. 6. 7. 9. Ven. 381. 423. 425. 770. 774. 776. 789. 809 etc. *good y. graces*, H8 III, 1, 78. Oth. I, 3, 52. *good y. highness*, Ant. II, 5, 106 (see *Good*). *your increasing in love Leonatus*, Cymb. III, 2, 47 (subscription under a letter).

Used indefinitely, not with reference to the person addressed, but to what is known and common: *in these times you stand on distance, your passes, stoccadoes*, Wiv. II, 1, 233. *ever your fresh whore and your powdered bawd*, Meas. III, 2, 62. *your beggar of fifty*, 133. IV, 2, 39. *every true man's apparel fits your thief*, 46. 47. 49. 50. *your hangman is a more penitent trade than your bawd*, 53. *I will discharge it in either your straw-colour beard, your orange-tawny beard etc.* Mids. I, 2, 95. *there is not a more fearful wild-fowl than your lion*, III, 1, 33. *I could munch your good dry oats*, IV, 1, 36. *your chestnut was ever the only colour*, As III, 4, 12. *all your writers do consent that ipse is he*, V, 1, 47. *as your pearl in your foul oyster*, V, 4, 63. 107. *your marriage comes by destiny, your cuckoo sings by kind*, All's I, 3, 66. II, 2, 23. 32. II, 3, 31. IV, 5, 107. Tw. V, 23. Wint. IV, 3, 135. John I, 189. H4A II, 1, 22. 33. II, 4, 82. H4B I, 2, 187. H5 III, 2, 27. Cor. II, 1, 222. V, 2, 81 (*I have been blown out of your gates with sighs;* unnecessarily corrected by some M. Edd.). V, 4, 12. Rom. I, 2, 52. Hml. III, 2, 131. IV, 3, 22. 24. 25. V, 1, 188. Oth. II, 3, 79. 82. 84. 86. Ant. II, 7, 29 etc.

**Yours**, absol. poss. pron. = that or those belonging or pertaining to you; 1) with reference to a preceding noun: *my good will is to it, and yours it is against*, Tp. III, 1, 31. *his brother and yours*, V, 12. Gent. II, 1, 2. 89. II, 4, 124. IV, 2, 92. V, 4, 172. Wiv. II, 2, 170. Meas. IV, 3, 109. 145. V, 502. Merch. IV, 1, 96. All's I, 3, 13. R3 IV, 1, 89 etc.

2) without reference, = your property: *you are no longer yours than you yourself here live*, Sonn. 13, 2. *what's mine is yours and what is yours is mine*, Meas. V, 543. All's IV, 4, 29. H8 III, 2, 199. Ant. III, 4, 28. *yours, yours*, a courteous phrase in parting, Hml. V, 2, 190. Peculiar expression: *we are yours in the garden*, Wint. I, 2, 178 (= we are at your

service); cf. *I have wounds to show you, which shall be yours in private,* Cor. II, 3, 83.

= the persons belonging to you, your friends or relations: *doth turn his hate on you or yours,* R3 II, 1, 33. 132. *as well I tender you and all of yours,* II, 4, 72. *beggared yours for ever,* Mcb. III, 1, 91. *mine will now be yours, and should we shift estates, yours would be mine,* Ant. V, 2, 151.

3) with reference to a following noun, from which it is separated: *in yours and my discharge,* Tp. II, 1, 254. cf. *in theirs and in the commons' ears,* Cor. V, 6, 4.

4) *of yours* = of you: *were some child of yours alive,* Sonn. 17, 13. *gentle breath of yours my sails must fill,* Tp. Epil. 11. *some love of yours,* Gent. I, 2, 79. IV, 4, 62. Err. I, 2, 82. Cor. V, 3, 68. Hml. III, 1, 93 etc. And even: *advance of yours that phraseless hand,* Compl. 225. *the nameless friend of yours,* Gent. II, 1, 111. *that merry sconce of yours,* Err. I, 2, 79. *she hath that ring of yours,* All's V, 3, 209. *that flattering tongue of yours,* As IV, 1, 189. H4A III, 3, 53. H6A IV, 6, 43. Caes. IV, 2, 40 etc.

**Yourself** (written in two words in O. Edd.; hence in R3 II, 1, 18: *your self is not exempt in this;* Qq are; see *Self*), plur. *yourselves;* 1) your own person or persons: *O that you were yourself!* Sonn. 13, 1. *then you were yourself again after yourself's decease,* 7. *till the judgment that yourself arise,* 55, 13. *how answer you for yourselves?* Ado IV, 2, 25. Tp. III, 1, 57. Gent. II, 1, 148. 154. II, 4, 37. IV, 3, 7. Wiv. I, 1, 320. Meas. IV, 1, 24. Err. III, 2, 175 LLL V, 1, 133 etc. Ado V, 4, 11. LLL V, 2, 430. Mids. I, 1, 126. III, 1, 31. R2 I, 3, 181. H6A IV, 1, 131. V, 4, 118. H6B IV, 7, 122. Tit. II, 1, 124 etc.

2) in your own person: *no longer than you yourself here live,* Sonn. 13, 2. 83, 6. Wiv. II, 2, 195. H6B I, 1, 85 etc. *carry your letters yourself,* Gent. I, 1, 154. Meas. V, 30. Err. III, 1, 96. LLL V, 2, 224 etc.

3) refl. pron.: *make yourself ready,* Tp. I, 1, 27. *spread yourselves,* Mids. I, 2, 17. Tp. I, 2, 443. III, 1, 20. Meas. II, 4, 91. III, 1, 169. As V, 4, 144. H6A IV, 1, 115. V, 4, 91. H6B IV, 2, 193. IV, 9, 19 etc. Emphatically: *you may thank yourself,* Tp. II, 1, 123. *love not yourselves: away, rob one another,* Tim. IV, 3, 447.

**Youth,** 1) early age, the part of life between childhood and manhood: Ven. 393. 1120. Lucr. 222. Sonn. 37, 2. Pilgr. 157—165. Gent. I, 1, 8. I, 2, 43. I, 3, 5. 16. 33. III, 1, 34. IV, 1, 45. Wiv. II, 3, 50. III, 2, 68. Meas. I, 2, 187. I, 3, 6. 10. II, 3, 11. III, 1, 32. 91. IV, 4, 32. Mids. I, 1, 35. Hml. III, 4, 84 etc. etc. plur. —*s:* Caes. II, 1, 148. Per. IV, 2, 35.

= freshness, novelty: *the y. of my new interest here,* Merch. III, 2, 224.

2) a young man: Sonn. 138, 3. Gent. II, 5, 3. II, 7, 47. IV, 2, 58. IV, 4, 69. 178. Wiv. IV, 2, 122 (*y. in a basket,* probably a proverbial phrase). Err. V, 418. Ado II, 1, 39. LLL II, 56. Mids. II, 1, 261. III, 2, 112. Merch. III, 4, 69. IV, 1, 141. IV, 2, 11; cf. Cymb. V, 5, 118. All's I, 2, 19. plur. —*s:* H8 V, 4, 63. Troil. IV, 4, 78. Mcb. V, 2, 10.

3) young people: Lucr. 1389. Gent. I, 1, 2. IV, 4, 165. Meas. II, 1, 243. LLL V, 1, 87. Mids. I, 1, 12. H4A II, 2, 89. H4B II, 3, 22. H5 II Chor. 1. H6B IV, 7, 36. R3 IV, 4, 392 etc. etc.

**Youthful,** 1) young: Lucr. 1432. Sonn. 15, 7. Gent. I, 3, 26. III, 1, 41. 107. Err. V, 52. Merch. V, 72. All's II, 3, 58. John III, 4, 125. R2 I, 3, 83. H4A IV, 1, 103. H4B I, 2, 163. IV, 2, 103. IV, 5, 229. H6A V, 3, 99. V, 5, 104. H6C V, 5, 11. Troil. I, 3, 230. II, 2, 113. Rom. II, 5, 12. III, 5, 182. IV, 2, 25. Applied to time: *his y. morn,* Sonn. 63, 4. *y. April,* Tit. III, 1, 18. *the y. season of the year,* Caes. II, 1, 108.

2) having the manners of youth: *and y. still!* Wiv. III, 1, 46.

3) pertaining to youth: *quickened with y. spleen,* H6A IV, 6, 13.

4) = of or in youth (cf. Appendix): *I attended a y. suit,* Compl. 79 (the suit of a youth). *my y. travel,* Gent. IV, 1, 34 (my travels made in my youth). *thy y. wages,* As II, 3, 67 (received and saved in thy youth). *his y. hose,* II, 7, 160 (worn in his youth). *whose y. spirit, in me regenerate, doth ... lift me up,* R2 I, 3, 70 (as it was in his youth).

**Yravish,** to ravish, to delight: Per. III Prol. 35 (Gower's speech).

**Yslake,** to slake, to abate, to silence: *now sleep —d hath the rout,* Per. III Prol. 1 (Gower's speech).

# Z.

**Zantippe,** see *Xanthippe.*

**Zany,** a subordinate buffoon whose office was to make awkward attempts at mimicking the tricks of the professional clown: *some please-man, some slight z.* LLL V, 2, 463. *I take these wise men, that crow so at these set kind of fools, no better than the fools' —es,* Tw. I, 5, 96.

**Zeal,** intense and eager interest or endeavour, ardor: *faith so infringed, which such z. did swear,* LLL IV, 3, 146. *what z., what fury hath inspired thee now?* 229. *where z. strives to content, and the contents dies in the z. of that which it presents,* V, 2, 518. 519 (*that which* = him who). John II, 244. 477 (cf. Gent. III, 2, 6—9). 565. III, 4, 150. H4A V, 4, 95. H4B V, 5, 14. H5 II, 2, 31. R3 III, 7, 208. H8 III, 1, 63. III, 2, 456. Tim. I, 2, 89 *(—s).* Applied to matters of

religion: Wint. V, 1, 107. H4B II, 4, 357. R3 III, 7, 103. H8 II, 2, 25. Troil. IV, 4, 28. Tim. III, 3, 33. Synonymous to earnestness: *to have defended it with any terms of z.* Merch. V, 205. *let not my cold words here accuse my z.* R2 I, 1, 47. *ours* (prayers, full) *of true z. and deep integrity,* V, 3, 108. *with tears of innocency and terms of z.* H4A IV, 3, 63.

Followed by *of: under the counterfeited z. of God,* H4B IV, 2, 27. Usually by *to: my z. to Valentine is cold,* Gent. II, 4, 203. *intend a kind of z. both to the prince and Claudio,* Ado II, 2, 36. *'twill make them cool in z. unto your grace,* H6B III, 1, 177. John V, 2, 10. H6C V, 1, 78. R3 II, 1, 40 (Ff *love*). Tit. I, 419. Tim. IV, 3, 523.

**Zealous,** fervent, eager, earnest: *with such a z. laughter, so profound,* LLL V, 2, 116. *upon thy cheek* *lay I this z. kiss*, John II, 19. Implying the idea of religious piety: *intend a z. pilgrimage to thee*, Sonn. 27, 6. *whilst I from far his name with z. fervour sanctify*, All's III, 4, 11. *if z. love should go in search of virtue*, John II, 428. *so sweet is z. contemplation*, R3 III, 7, 94.

**Zechin**, see *Chequin*.

**Zed**, name of the letter Z: *thou whoreson zed! thou unnecessary letter!* Lr. II, 2, 69.

**Zenelophon**, Armado's blunder for Penelophon: LLL IV, 1, 67.

**Zenith**, the highest point in the visible celestial hemisphere; metaphorically, = the highest point of one's fortune: *my z. doth depend upon a most auspicious star*, Tp. I, 2, 181.

**Zentippe**, see *Xanthippe*.

**Zephyr**, a soft and gentle wind: *as gentle as —s blowing below the violet*, Cymb. IV, 2, 172.

**Zodiac**, the twelve signs through which the sun passes: *nineteen —s have gone round*, Meas. I, 2, 172 (= years). *the sun ... gallops the z. in his glistering coach*, Tit. II, 1, 7.

**Zone**, the sphere, the orbit in which the sun moves: *let them throw millions of acres on us, till our ground, singeing his pate against the burning z., make Ossa like a wart*, Hml. V, 1, 305.

**Zounds**, an oath contracted from *God's wounds* (cf. *Swounds*): John II, 466. Evidently thought indecent, and therefore either omitted or changed in Ff: H4A I, 2, 112. I, 3, 131 (Ff *yes*). II, 1, 87. II, 2, 68. II, 3, 23 (Ff *by this hand*). II, 4, 159. 261 (Ff *no*). IV, 1, 17. V, 4, 123. 156. R3 I, 4, 128 (Ff *come*). 149. III, 7, 219. V, 3, 208. Tit. IV, 2, 72 (Ff *out*). Rom. III, 1, 52 (Ff *come*). 104 (Ff *what*). Oth. I, 1, 86. 108. II, 3, 150. 163. IV, 1, 36. V, 2, 219 (Ff *come*).

# APPENDIX.

# I. Grammatical Observations.

**1. Changeable accent of dissyllabic adjectives and participles.** In the article *Complete* a difference of sense is made between *cómplete* and *compléte*. There may some exist indeed, but it would not be sufficiently proved by the Shakespearian instances, as it constantly coincides there with a difference of place. The form *cómplete* always precedes a noun accented on the first syllable, *compléte* is always in the predicate.

> *Believe not that the dribbling dart of love*
> *Can pierce a cómplete bosom.* Meas. I, 3, 3.
> *A maid of grace and cómplete majesty,* LLL I,
> 1, 137.
> *Than all the cómplete armour that thou wearest.*
> R3 IV, 4, 189.

cf. H6A I, 2, 83. Troil. III, 3, 181. IV, 1, 27. Hml. I, 4, 52.

On the other hand:

> *He is compléte in feature and in mind.* Gent. II,
> 4, 73.
> *Is the young Dauphin every way compléte.* John
> II, 433.
> *How many make the hour* (dissyll.) *full compléte.*
> H6C II, 5, 26.

cf. H8 III, 2, 49. Tim. IV, 3, 244.

One verse only seems to make an exception:

> *Than ever they were fair. This man so complete.*
> H8 I, 2, 118.

But in consideration of the many metrical irregularities caused by a full stop in the middle of a verse, there can no serious difficulty be found in this seeming anomaly.

A similar mistake has been committed in the article *Humane.* It is true that the spelling of O. Edd. is invariably *humane,* never *human;* but it is not evident that Shakespeare invariably accented the first syllable. The passage in Wint. III, 2, 166 may possibly be scanned thus:

> *Not dó|ing ít* | *and béing* (monosyll.) | *done; hé,* |
> *most húmane;*

but the much more natural scansion would be:

> *Not dóing* (monosyll.) | *it ánd* | *being* (monosyll.)
> *dóne;* | *he, móst* | *humáne.*

The fact is that this is the only passage in which the word is placed after the noun; everywhere else it precedes a substantive.

> *By holy húmane law and common troth.* Lucr. 571.
> *Upon the lute doth ravish húmane sense.* Pilgr. 108.
> *I have used thee,*
> *Filth as thou art, with húmane care, and lodged*
> *thee.* Tp. I, 2, 346.

> *Lie further off, in húmane modesty.* Mids. II, 2, 57.
> *But touched with húmane gentleness and love.*
> Merch. IV, 1, 25.

cf. the rest of the passages cited sub *Humane.*

And thus it may be stated as a general rule, that dissyllabic oxytonical adjectives and participles become paroxytonical before nouns accented on the first syllable. A few instances will suffice.

Advérse and ádverse:

> *Though time seem so advérse and means unfit,*
> All's V, 1, 26.
> *Of thy advérse pernicious enemy,* R2 I, 3, 82.
> *Thy ádverse party is thy advocate.* Sonn. 35, 10.
> *He speak against me on the ádverse side.* Meas.
> IV, 6, 6.
> *To admit no traffic to our ádverse towns.* Err.
> I, 1, 15.

cf. Tw. V, 87. John II, 57. IV, 2, 172. H6A I, 1, 54. R3 IV, 4, 190. V, 3, 13.

Benign, only once found in Shakespeare:

> *A better prince and bénign lord.* Per. II Prol. 3.

Confíned and cónfined:

> *Therefore my verse to constancy confíned,* Sonn.
> 105, 7.
> *A god in love, to whom I am confíned.* 110, 12.
> *whose honour cannot*
> *Be measured or confíned.* Tp. V, 122.
> *Supposed as forfeit to a cónfined doom.* Sonn.
> 107, 4.

The same word, trisyllabic, retains its natural accent before a subst.:

> *Looks fearfully in the confíned deep.* Lr. IV, 1, 77.

Contrívèd and cóntrived:

> *Have you conspired, have you with these contrívèd.*
> Mids. III, 2, 196.
> *By whom this great assembly is contrívèd.* H5
> V, 2, 6.
> *To do no cóntrived murder.* Oth. I, 2, 3.

Corrúpt and córrupt:

> *If eyes corrúpt by over-partial looks.* Sonn. 137, 5.
> *Corrúpt, corrúpt, and tainted in desire.* Wiv. V,
> 5, 94.
> *at what ease*
> *Might córrupt minds procure knaves as corrúpt*
> *To swear against you?* H8 V, 1, 133.

Despísed and déspised:

> *So then I am not lame, poor, nor despísed.* Sonn.
> 37, 9.
> *Of our despísed nobility, our issues.* H8 III,
> 2, 291.

*Is yond despísed and ruinous man my lord?* Tim.
    IV, 3, 465.
*The pangs of déspised love, the law's delay.* Hml.
    III, 1, 72.
Trisyllabic:
    *And ostentation of despísed arms.* R2 II, 3, 95.
    *Despísed substance of divinest show.* Rom. III,
    2, 77.
Dispérsed and dísperse d:
    *And not the puddle in thy sea dispérsed.* Lucr.
    658.
    *To gather our soldiers scattered and dispérsed.*
    H6A II, 1, 76.
    *'My daughter' aud 'my wife' with clamours filled
    The dispersed air,* Lucr. 1805.
Distínct and dístinct:
    *Two distíncts, division none.* Phoen. 27.
    *And make distínct the very breach.* Troil. IV,
    5, 245.
    *To offend and judge are dístinct offices.* Merch.
    II, 9, 61.
    *With dístinct breath and cónsigned kisses to them.*
    Troil. IV, 4, 47.
Distráct and dístract:
    *The fellow is distráct, and so am I.* Err. IV, 3, 42.
    *To see thy noble uncle thus distráct.* Tit. IV, 3, 26.
    *Their dístract parcels in combined sums.* Compl.
    231.
Exáct and éxact:
    *O royal knavery! an exáct commánd,* Hml. V,
    2, 19.
    *And in the most exáct regárd support.* Lr. I, 4, 287.
    *To set the éxact wealth of all our states.* H4A
    IV, 1, 46.
    *I have with éxact view perused thee, Hector.*
    Troil. IV, 5, 232.
Exháled and éxhaled:
    *Let their exháled unwhólesome breath make sick
    The life of purity, the súpreme fair.* Lucr. 779.
    *And be no more an éxhaled meteor.* H4A V, 1, 19.
Exíled and éxiled:
    *Both you and I; for Romeo is exíled.* Rom. III,
    2, 133.
    *To be exíled, and thrown etc.* Cymb. V, 4, 59.
    *I sue for éxiled majesty's repeal.* Lucr. 640.
    *As calling home our éxiled friends abroad.* Mcb.
    V, 8, 66.
Expíred and éxpired:
    *To work my mind, when body's work's expíred.*
    Sonn. 27, 4.
    *Your time's expíred.* Per. I, 1, 89.
    *An éxpired date, cancelled ere well begun.* Lucr. 26.
Expréss and éxpress:
    *To the contrary I have expréss commándment.*
    Meas. II, 2, 8.
    *From him I have expréss commandment.* H6A I,
    3, 20.
    *Let me have your expréss opínions.* H6A I, 4, 64.
    *As bid me tell my tale in éxpress words.* John
    IV, 2, 234.
Extréme and éxtreme:
    *Savage, extréme, rude, cruel, not to trust.*
    *Had, having, and in quest to have, extréme.* Sonn.
    129, 4. 10.
    *And éxtreme fear can neither fight nor fly.* Lucr.
    230.

*But qualify the fire's* (dissyll.) *éxtreme rage.*
    Gent. II, 7, 22.
*The éxtreme parts of time extremely forms etc.*
    LLL V, 2, 750.
Forlórn and fórlorn:
    *And whom she finds forlórn she doth lament.*
    Lucr. 1500.
    *To some forlórn and naked hermitage,* LLL V,
    2, 805.
    *And from the fórlorn world his visage hide.* Sonn.
    33, 7.
    *Poor fórlorn Proteus, passionate Proteus.* Gent.
    I, 2, 124.
Insane, undoubtedly an oxytonon, accented on
the first syllable in the only passage in which it occurs:
    *Or have we eaten on the ínsane root.* Mcb. I, 3, 84.
Likewise invise d:
    *Whereto his ínvised properties did tend.* Compl.
    212.
Mispláced and mísplaced:
    *And gilded honour shamefully mispláced.* Sonn.
    66, 5.
    *Ere I will see the crown so foul mispláced.* R3
    III, 2, 44.
    *The mísplaced John should entertain an hour.*
    John III, 4, 133.
Mísprised:
    *You spend your passion on a mísprised mood.*
    Mids. III, 2, 74.
Obscúre and óbscure:
    *Round rising hillocks, brakes obscúre and rough.*
    Ven. 237.
    *Obscúre and lowly swain,* H6B IV, 1, 50.
    *To rib her cerecloth in the óbscure grave,* Merch.
    II, 7, 51.
    *His means of death, his óbscure funeral.* Hml.
    IV, 5, 213.
Profáne and prófane:
    *Lest I, too much profáne, should do it wrong,*
    Sonn. 89, 11.
    *In their so sacred paths he dares to tread
    In shape profáne.* Wiv. IV, 4, 60.
    *Which our profáne hours here have stricken
    down,* R2 V, 1, 25 (no exception, as *hours*
    is in the thesis; lection of Qq: *which our*
    (dissyll.) *prófane hours here have thrown
    down*).
    *What prófane wretch art thou?* Oth. I, 1, 115.
    *A pantler, not so eminent. Prófane fellow!* Cymb.
    II, 3, 129.
Profóund and prófound:
    *In so profóund abysm I throw all care.* Sonn.
    112, 9.
    *Vilely compiled, profóund simplicity.* LLL V,
    2, 52.
    *And prófound Solomon to tune a jig,* LLL IV,
    3, 168.
    *There's matter in these sighs, these prófound
    heaves,* Hml. IV, 1, 1.
In Wint. IV, 4, 501 *profóund sea,* because *sea* is in
the thesis.
Remíss and rémiss:
    *He means, my lord, that we are too remíss.* R2
    III, 2, 33.
    *The prince must think me tardy and remíss.* Troil.
    IV, 4, 143.

*That thus we die, while remiss traitors sleep.*
H6A IV, 3, 29.

Secúre and sécure:

*Whilst thou liest warm at home, secúre and safe.*
Shr. V, 2, 151.

*Open the door, secúre, fool-hardy king.* R2 V, 3, 43.

*Upon my sécure hour thy uncle stole.* Hml. I, 5, 61.

*To lip a wanton in a sécure couch,* Oth. IV, 1, 72.

Sevére and sévere:

*Which knows no pity, but is still sevére.* Ven. 1000. 1155.

*With eyes sevére and beard of formal cut.* As II, 7, 155.

*O just but sévere law!* Meas. II, 2, 41.

*It shall be with such strict and sévere covenants.*
H6A V, 4, 114.

Sincére and síncere:

*His love sincére, his thoughts immaculate.* Gent. II, 7, 76.

*Supposed sincére and holy in his thoughts.* H4B I, 1, 202.

*From síncere motions, by intelligence,* H8 I, 1, 153.

*Sir, in good sooth, in síncere verity.* Lr. II, 2, 111.

Supréme and súpreme:

*Neither supréme; how soon confusion etc.* Cor. III, 1, 110.

*The life of purity, the súpreme fair,* Lucr. 780.

*But as we, under heaven* (monosyll.), *are súpreme head.* John III, 1, 155.

Terrene:

*alack, our térrene moon*
*Is now eclipsed.* Ant. III, 13, 153.

But no other class of adjectives and participles offers so many and so striking proofs for this law of prosody as those with the prefix *un*.

*When, lo, the únbacked breeder, full of fear.*
Ven. 320.

*At which, like únbacked colts, they pricked their ears.* Tp. IV, 176.

*O únbid spite! is sportful Edward come?* H6C V, 1, 18.

*My únblown flowers, new-appearing sweets.* R3 IV, 4, 10.

*Some únborn sorrow, ripe in fortune's womb.* R2 II, 2, 10.

*Of broached mischief to the únborn times.* H4A V, 1, 21.

*This precious book of love, this únbound lover.*
Rom. I, 3, 87.

*And now have toiled their únbreathed memories.*
Mids. V, 74.

*No únchaste action or dishonoured step.* Lr. I, 1, 231.

*Have únchecked theft,* Tim. IV, 3, 447.

*And fairy-like to pinch the únclean knight.* Wiv. IV, 4, 57.

*What úncouth ill event.* Lucr. 1598.

*To únpathed waters, úndreamed shores.* Wint. IV, 4, 578.

*For where is she so fair whose úneared womb Disdains etc.* Sonn. 3, 5.

*How shall your houseless heads and únfed sides etc.* Lr. III, 4, 30.

*O únfelt sore! crest-wounding private scar!*
Lucr. 828.

The rule may seem sufficiently established by these instances. The reader will find it throughout observed. But it must always be remembered, that the following syllable must be in the arsis, and that participles, when used as trisyllabic (as f. i. *unfeigned* in H6C III, 3, 51 and 202), are out of the question.

**2. Adjectives substantively.** Mr. Abbott in his Grammar p. 20 treats of the case when adjectives supply the place of substantives denoting a quality, as *pale* for *paleness*, *bad* for *badness* etc., but does not touch upon the use no less contrary to modern grammar of adjectives placed by themselves with reference to single persons. At present *the good* signifies either that which is good, or all good people, but in Shakespeare's time it could also mean a single good man or woman. *He that did betray the Best* (i. e. the Redeemer) Wint. I, 2, 419. *Then the bold and coward, the wise and fool, the artist and unread, the hard and soft, seem all affined and kin,* Troil. I, 3, 23. *What the declined is he shall as soon read in the eyes of others as feel in his own fall,* III, 3, 76. *'Tis not enough to help the feeble up, but to support him after,* Tim. I, 1, 107. *Edmund the base shall top the legitimate,* Lr. I, 2, 19. *The younger rises when the old doth fall,* III, 3, 26. *The good in conversation is still at Tarsus,* Per. II Prol. 9. There was, consequently, no occasion to question the correctness of the passage: *And added feathers to the learned's wing,* Sonn. 78, 7.

It is the same with the indefinite article, at least before comparatives: *Whiles they behold a greater than themselves,* Caes. I, 2, 209. *I fear there will a worse come in his place,* III, 2, 116. *They strike a meaner than myself,* Ant. II, 5, 83.

Oftenest the vocative is used thus (cf. the articles *Fair, Gentle, Good, Sweet*): *Graceless, wilt thou deny thy parentage?* H6A V, 4, 14. *Most mighty for thy place and sway, and thou most reverend for thy stretched-out life,* Troil. I, 3, 60. *Let it please both, thou great, and wise, to hear Ulysses speak,* 69. *What hast thou done, unnatural and unkind?* Tit. V, 3, 48. *How now, my headstrong! where have you been gadding?* Rom. IV, 2, 16. *Noble and young, when thy first griefs were but a mere conceit, we sent to thee,* Tim. V, 4, 13. *Shaking the bloody fingers of thy foes, most noble, in the presence of thy corse,* Caes. III, 1, 199. *Infirm of purpose! give me the daggers,* Mcb. II, 2, 52. *Come, high or low; thyself and office deftly show,* IV, 1, 67. *High and mighty, you shall know I am set naked on your kingdom,* Hml. IV, 7, 43. *Well, my legitimate,* Lr. I, 2, 19. *Thou perjured,* III, 2, 54. *Reverend and gracious,* Oth. I, 3, 33. *Cold in blood, to say as I said then,* Ant. I, 5, 74.

The plural without the article: *He did in the general bosom reign of young, of old,* Compl. 128. *Meaner than myself have had like fortune,* H6C IV, 1, 71. *Mid-age and wrinkled old,* Troil. II, 2, 104 (Q *elders*, some M. Edd. *eld*). *Worthier than himself here tend the savage strangeness he puts on,* II, 3, 134. *Help him, young and old,* Cor. III, 1, 228. Rom. I, 3, 69.

**3. Adjectives doing the office of the first parts of compound nouns.** As the English adjective has no inflexion, it was formerly apt to form a looser connexion with its substantive than in other languages, and, instead of expressing a quality or degree pertaining to the latter, to be employed to limit the extent and sphere of it. Thus *a bloody fire* in Wiv. V, 5, 99 is not a fire that has the quality, or increases to the degree, of being bloody, but, as it were, a blood-fire, a fire in the blood. *A thirsty evil* in Meas. I, 2, 134, *a hungry prey* in H6A I, 2, 28, is an evil thirsted for, a prey hungered for. *Lovers' absent hours* in Oth. III, 4, 174 = absence hours, hours of absence or separation. *A fruitful prognostication* in Ant. I, 2, 53 = a prognostication of fruitfulness. *Their sterile curse* in Caes. I, 2, 9 = curse of sterility.

These instances will sufficiently explain the following passages, some of which have caused much unnecessary doubt and perplexity. *Old woes, not infant sorrows, bear them mild,* Lucr. 1096 (= woes of old people). *This fair child of mine shall sum my count and make my old excuse,* Sonn. 2, 11 (the excuse of my being old. Hazlitt *my whole excuse!*). *With mirth and laughter let old wrinkles come,* Merch. I, 1, 80 (the wrinkles of age). *Who in rage forgets aged contusions and all brush of time,* H6B V, 3, 3 (the contusions of age). *When old time shall lead him to his end,* H8 II, 1, 93. *The aged wrinkles in my cheeks,* Tit. III, 1, 7. *Too early I attended a youthful suit,* Compl. 79 (the suit of a youth). *my youthful travel therein made me happy,* Gent. IV, 1, 34 (travels made in youth). *Ere we have thy youthful wages spent,* As II, 3, 67 (wages earned and saved in thy youth). *His youthful hose, well saved, a world too wide for his shrunk shank,* II, 7, 160 (worn in his youth). *Blushing red no guilty instance gave,* Lucr. 1511 (no sign of guilt). *Thus can my love excuse the slow offence of my dull bearer,* Sonn. 51, 1 (the offence of slowness). *'Gainst death and all-oblivious enmity shall you pace forth,* 55, 9 (the enmity of entire oblivion). *I see brass eternal slave to mortal rage,* 64, 4 (the rage of mortality, i. e. of death. cf. Hml. III, 1, 67). *You to your beauteous blessings add a curse,* 84, 13 (the blessings of your beauty). *What a happy title do I find, happy to have thy love, happy to die,* 92, 11 (a title to be called happy). *This time removed was summer's time,* 97, 5 (this time of being removed). *Bearing the wanton burden of the prime,* 7 (the burden brought forth by the wantonness of the spring). *Worse essays proved thee my best of love,* 110, 8 (trials made of worse lovers). *The humble salve which wounded bosoms fits,* 120, 12 (the salve of humility, i. e. of kindness). *The just pleasure lost which is so deemed by others' seeing,* 121, 3 (the pleasure of being just). *Beauty slandered with a bastard shame,* 127, 4 (shame, disgrace of bastardy). *The wiry concord that mine ear confounds,* 128, 4 (the concord of wire-strings). *To this false plague are they now transferred,* 137, 14 (plague of being false). *doth point out thee as his triumphant prize,* 151, 10 (as the prize of his victory). *He did in the general bosom reign,* Compl. 127 (in the hearts of all people). *Which may her suffering ecstasy assuage,* 69 (the ecstasy of her suffering). *This deceit loses the name of craft, of disobedience, or unduteous title,* Wiv. V, 5, 240 (the title or name of undutifulness). *They can be meek that have no other cause,* Err. II, 1, 33 (no cause to be otherwise). *Which with experimental seal doth warrant the tenour of my book,* Ado IV, 1, 168 (the seal of experience). *Preceptial medicine to rage,* V, 1, 24 (the medicine of precepts; precepts as a medicine). *All hid, an old infant play,* LLL IV, 3, 78 (a play of

children). *My virgin patent,* Mids. I, 1, 80 (the patent of my virginity). *Thy fair virtue,* III, 1, 143 (the virtue or force of thy beauty). *Fish not with this melancholy bait for this fool gudgeon,* Merch. I, 1, 101 (this bait of melancholy). *The virgin tribute paid by howling Troy,* III, 2, 56 (virgins offered as a tribute). *Oppressed with two weak evils, age and hunger,* As II, 7, 132 (evils of weakness). *When we should submit ourselves to an unknown fear,* Alls II, 3, 6 (fear of something unknown). *Some great and trusty business,* III, 6, 16 (a business of trust, requiring trust). *Put myself into my mortal preparation,* 81 (preparation for death). *You need but plead your honourable privilege,* IV, 5, 95 (the privilege of your rank as a lord, being addressed with the title 'your honour'). *Natural rebellion done in the blaze of youth,* V, 3, 6 (rebellion of nature). *Leap all civil bounds,* Tw. I, 4, 21 (bounds of civility or good manners). *The quality of the time and quarrel might well have given us bloody argument,* III, 3, 32 (a subject or cause of shedding blood). *Nothing of that wonderful promise, to read him by his form,* III, 4, 290 (promise of something wonderful and extraordinary). *He that hears makes fearful action,* John IV, 2, 191 (the gesture of fear). *Ere my tongue shall wound my honour with such feeble wrong,* R2 I, 1, 191 (a wrong caused by feebleness). *A partial slander sought I to avoid,* I, 3, 241 (reproach of partiality). *To take advantage of the absent time,* II, 3, 79 (the time of the king's absence). *Mock not my senseless conjuration,* III, 2, 23 (conjuration of a senseless thing, viz. the earth). *Judged by subject and inferior breath,* IV, 128 (the voice of subjects and inferiors). *Thou takest thy last living leave,* V, 1, 39 (the last in life). *Hast lost thy princely privilege with vile participation,* H4A III, 2, 87 (community and intercourse with vile and base companions). *We come within our aweful banks again,* H4B IV, 1, 176 (the banks, i. e. limits or restraints, of awe and submission). *This law and female bar,* H5 I, 2, 42 (exclusion of women from succession). *Crammed with distressful bread,* IV, 1, 287 (the bread of poverty). *Solicit Henry with her wondrous praise,* H6A V, 3, 190 (the praise of her wonderful qualities). *The envious load that lies upon his heart,* H6B III, 1, 157 (the load of envy). *These hands are free from guiltless blood-shedding,* IV, 7, 108 (from shedding the blood of guiltless persons). *A drunken slaughter,* R3 II, 1, 122 (committed in drunkenness). *Our fatherless distress was left unmoaned,* II, 2, 64 (our misfortune of losing our father). *I wish no other speaker of my living actions,* H8 IV, 2, 70 (the actions of my life). *An envious fever,* Troil. I, 3, 133. *Such a precious loss,* IV, 4, 10 (loss of a precious thing). *May give you thankful sacrifice,* Cor. I, 6, 9; cf. Ant. I, 2, 167. *Against the hospitable canon,* Cor. I, 10, 26 (the law of hospitality). *Plead my successive title with your swords,* Tit. I, 4 (my title to succession). *Heart-sick groans,* Rom. III, 3, 72. *Artificial strife lives in these touches,* Tim. I, 1, 37 (emulation of art). *The monstrousness of man when he looks out in an ungrateful shape,* III, 2, 80 (in the shape of ingratitude). *A prodigal course is like the sun's,* III, 4, 12. *Filled the time with all licentious measure,* V, 4, 4. *With such familiar instances,* Caes. IV, 2, 16 (signs of familiarity). *This eternal blazon must not be to ears of flesh and blood,* Hml. I, 5, 21 (publication of eternal things). *When we have shuffled off this mortal coil,*

III, 1, 67 (coil or turmoil of mortal life). *The wicked prize itself buys out the law*, III, 3, 59 (the prize of wickedness). *Gave you such a masterly report*, IV, 7, 97 (such a report of mastership). *Mark the high noises*, Lr. III, 6, 118 (the rumours among the great ones). *In thy just proof*, 120 (in the proof of thy justness and honesty). *The main descry stands on the hourly thought*, IV, 6, 218 (the discovery of the main army is expected every hour). *To pluck the common bosom on his side*, V, 3, 49 (cf. above: Compl. 127). *Confine yourself but in a patient list*, Oth. IV, 1, 76. *He comes too short of that great property which still should go with Antony*, Ant. I, 1, 58 (that quality of greatness). *A Roman thought has struck him*, I, 2, 87 (a thought of Rome). *With brazen din blast you the city's ears*, IV, 8, 36 (din of brass instruments). *Give me the penitent instrument to pick that bolt*, Cymb. V, 4, 10. *Testy wrath could never be her mild companion*, Per. I, 1, 18 (the companion of her mildness).

Hence it comes that sometimes the relation of the adjective and its noun seems inverted and confounded: *murderous shame* = shameful murder, Sonn. 9, 14; *a separable spite* = a spiteful separation, 36, 6; *swift extremity* = extreme swiftness, 51, 6; *shady stealth* = stealing shadow, 77, 7; *living torment* = painful life, Gent. III, 1, 170; *a credent bulk* = a weighty credit, Meas. IV, 4, 29; *a good outward happiness* = a happy, pleasing exterior, Ado II, 3, 190; *virtuous property* = peculiar virtue, Mids. III, 2, 367; *brief and plain conveniency* = convenient briefness and plainness, Merch. IV, 1, 82; *aged honour* = honourable age, Alls I, 3, 216; *valiant approof* = approved valour, II, 5, 3; *estimable wonder* = admiring estimation, Tw. II, 1, 28; *the bloodiest shame* = most shameful bloodshed, John IV, 3, 47; *fiery indignation* = indignant fire, IV, 1, 63; *silken dalliance* = dallying silks, H5 II Chor. 2. *Ingrateful injury* = injurious, wicked ingratitude, Cor. II, 2, 35; *paly ashes* = ashy paleness, Rom. IV, 1, 100; *excellent differences* = different excellent qualities, Hml. V, 2, 112; *expert allowance* = allowed, acknowledged expertness, Oth. II, 1, 49; *in negligent danger* = dangerous negligence, Ant. III, 6, 81.

One class of adjectives, derived from nouns by means of the suffix *ed*, deserve particular attention, as they have often been mistaken for participles and misinterpreted accordingly. Even so sagacious a grammarian as Mr. Abbott speaks 'of an indefinite and apparently not passive use of passive participles.' That there are a great many words in *ed*, which are no participles, f. i. *aged, wicked, wretched* etc., there can be no doubt. Therefore we must take heed of supposing all words in *ed*, which, from the existence of homonymous verbs, might possibly be participles, always to be so indeed. Thus when we read in Compl. 146: *my woeful self threw my affections in his charmed power*, it would be quite preposterous to say that the passive participle *charmed* is used here in an active sense, for charming, but *charmed* is an adjective derived from the substantive *charm*, or from the common root of the substantive and verb, and meaning 'furnished, supplied, endowed with a charm.' Near as this may come to the sense of charming, no confusion of different verbal functions has taken place. In the same or a similar manner the following expressions must be explained: *All the whole army stood

*agazed on him*, H6A I, 1, 126 (furnished with gazes, i. e. gazing). *Be simple-answered, for we know the truth*, Lr. III, 7, 43 (furnished with a simple answer. Qq *simple answerer*). *Your favour is well appeared by your tongue*, Cor. IV, 3, 9 (your countenance has the due appearance, is well discernible, may well be recognized, by the help of your voice. Hanmer *affeered*, Warburton *appealed*, Jackson *apparelled* etc.). *Beguiled with outward honesty, but yet defiled with inward vice*, Lucr. 1544 (guilefully furnished, dressed in outward honesty). *And gave him what becomed love I might*, Rom. IV, 2, 26 (furnished with that which becomes; becoming). *How have I been behaved*, Oth. IV, 2, 108 (having a behaviour). *She concludes the picture was belied*, Lucr. 1533 (full of lies, disfigured by lies). *With fair blessed beams*, Mids. III, 2, 392 (beneficial). *Such force and blessed power*, IV, 1, 79. *It is twice blessed; it blesses him that gives and him that takes*, Merch. IV, 1, 186. *the blest infusions that dwell in vegetives*, Per. III, 2, 35. *The answer is as ready as a borrowed cap*, H4B II, 2, 125 (perhaps a salutation or obeisance made for the purpose of borrowing money. But we would not insist on the correctness of the passage. M. Edd. *borrower's*). *Divide me like a bribed buck*, Wiv. V, 5, 27 (given as a bribe. M. Edd. *bribe-buck*. The poet maybe chose to write *bribed* for the sake of euphony). *In despite of brooded watchful day*, John III, 3, 52 (having a brood to guard, sitting on brood. Pope *broad-eyed*, Mitford *broad* and, Collier *the broad*, Anon. *broody*). *Now thy proud neck bears half my burthened yoke*, R3 IV, 4, 111 (= burdenous, heavy). *The caged cloister*, Compl. 249 (like a cage or prison). *To be commanded under Cominius*, Cor. I, 1, 266 (having a command). *Careful hours with time's deformed hand have written strange defeatures in my face*, Err. V, 298 (not an ugly hand, as it is explained by some, but a hand that causes deformity, spoils beauty). *And the delighted spirit to bathe in fiery floods*, Meas. III, 1, 121 (the spirit whose nature it is to be full of delight, to enjoy its existence. Variously corrected or rather corrupted by M. Edd. The best commentary on Shakespeare's expression has been written by the Emperor Hadrianus in the verses: *Animula vagula, blandula, Hospes comesque corporis, Quae nunc abibis in loca Pallidula, rigida, nudula, Nec ut soles dabis jocos*). *Revenge the jeering and disdained contempt of this proud king*, H4A I, 3, 183 (full of disdain). *When I did speak of some distressed stroke*, Oth. I, 3, 157 (full of distress. Ff *distressful*). *Some enchanted trifle to abuse me*, Tp. V, 112 (cf. above: *charmed*). *Enforced hate, instead of love's coy touch, shall rudely tear thee*, Lucr. 668 (hate armed with force). *The fated sky gives us free scope*, Alls I, 1, 232 (heaven which makes or ordains the fate of man). *In these feared hopes*, Cymb. II, 4, 6 (hopes mingled with fear, if not hopes for which I am in fear). *Furred moss*, IV, 2, 228 (fur-like). *Ornament is but the guiled shore to a most dangerous sea*, Merch. III, 2, 97 (full of guile). *The imprisoned absence of your liberty*, Sonn. 58, 6 (= prison-like). *O knowledge ill inhabited*, As III, 3, 10 (having a bad habitation). *No, misconceived!* H6A V, 4, 49 (having a wrong conception). *Of pensived and subdued desires the tender*, Compl. 219 (= pensive, melancholy). *Till each to razed oblivion yield his part of thee*, Sonn. 122, 7 (oblivion whose office it is to raze and obliterate all). *The ravined salt-sea *shark*, Mcb. IV, 1, 24 (= ravenous). *Wash away thy country's stained spots*, H6A III, 3, 57 (spots which are stains, and to the dishonour of thy country). *A prince should not be so loosely studied as to remember so weak a composition*, H4B II, 2, 10 (studious, inclined). *Two traded pilots 'twixt the dangerous shores*, Troil. II, 2, 64 (professional). *I'll strive with troubled noise, to take a nap*, R3 V, 3, 104 (I'll try in spite of the noise caused around me by the troubles of war. Qq *with troubled thoughts*). *Playing patient sports in unconstrained gyves*, Compl. 242 (imposing no constraint). *Hardy and undoubted champions*, H6C V, 7, 6 (fearless). *An unpitied whipping*, Meas. IV, 2, 13 (pitiless). *Make unprofited return*, Tw. I, 4, 22 (profitless). *With the whiff and wind of his fell sword the unnerved father falls*, Hml. II, 2, 496 (strengthless). *Wintered garments should be lined*, As III, 2, 111 (M. Edd. *winter-garments.* cf. above: *bribed buck*). *So rare a wondered father*, Tp. IV, 123 (endowed with the faculty of performing miracles).

Now these adjectives in *ed*, too, are employed for the kind of hypallage treated of above: *As for the rest appealed*, R2 I, 1, 142 (the rest of the accusation). *His banished years*, I, 3, 210 (the years of his banishment). *Forfeit to a confined doom*, Sonn. 107, 4 (to the fate of a limited existence, to death). *At our more considered time we'll read*, Hml. II, 2, 81 (a time fitter for consideration). *The dedicated words which writers use of their fair subject*, Sonn. 82, 3 (words of dedication). *Bring them with imagined speed unto the tranect*, Merch. III, 4, 52 (with the speed of imagination, of thought). *Thus with imagined wing our swift scene flies*, H5 III Chor. 1 (with the wing of imagination). *To make you understand this in a manifested effect*, Meas. IV, 2, 169 (so as to effect it to be manifest, in effected manifestation). *It was married chastity*, Phoen. 61 (chastity in marriage). *Unpleasing to a married ear*, LLL V, 2, 912 (to the ear of a married man). *I can interpret all her martyred signs*, Tit. III, 2, 36 (the signs of her martyrdom). *Would from my forehead wipe a perjured note*, LLL IV, 3, 125 (note of perjury). *Ere she with blood had stained her stained excuse*, Lucr. 1316 (the excuse of her stain, of her defilement). *Nor falls under the blow of thralled discontent*, Sonn. 124, 7 (discontent of thralls). *To give our hearts united ceremony*, Wiv. IV, 6, 51 (the ceremony of union, i. e. of marriage). *The valued file distinguishes the swift, the slow, the subtle*, Mcb. III, 1, 95 (the catalogue of the different prices). *The very stream of his life ... must upon a warranted need give him a better proclamation*, Meas. III, 2, 151 (upon need of a warrant; when a warrant is needed). *Widowed wombs*, Sonn. 97, 8 (wombs of widows). *My grave is like to be my wedded bed*, Rom. I, 5, 137 (my bed of marriage. Qq *wedding*).

Much rarer is the use of the participial form in *en* in a similar adjectival and seemingly active sense: *Fair-spoken* and *well-spoken* = eloquent, R3 I, 3, 348. H8 IV, 2, 52. *The nomination of the party written to the person written unto*, LLL IV, 2, 138 (M. Edd. *the nomination of the person writing*). *I am all forgotten*, = forgetful, Ant. I, 3, 91. *Surly borne* = having a surly bearing, Troil. II, 3, 249. cf. *Thoughten*.

**4. Adverbs for adjectives**, or, in other words, the adverb not expressing a manner or degree, but a state and condition: *So shall these slaves be king, and*

*thou their slave, thou nobly base, they basely dignified*, Lucr. 660 (thou, though being of noble birth, shalt be base etc.). *Those hours ... will play the tyrants ... and that unfair which fairly doth excel*, Sonn. 5, 4 (fairly = by being fair or beautiful). *That fresh blood which youngly thou bestowest thou mayst call thine*, 11, 3 (= when young). *The best news is that we have safely found our king and company*, Tp. V, 221 (in a safe state; safe). *Where we in all her trim freshly beheld our royal, good and gallant ship*, 236 (in a fresh state; fresh, unimpaired, as if she were new). *Puts the drowsy and neglected act freshly on me*, Meas. I, 2, 175. *In Belmont is a lady richly left*, Merch. I, 1, 161 (= rich). *Those that she makes honest she makes very ill-favouredly*, As I, 2, 41 (ugly). *In what he did profess, well found*, All's II, 1, 105 (found good). *When you have our roses, you barely leave our thorns to prick ourselves*, IV, 2, 19 (in a bare state; bare). *Commend it strangely to some place where chance may nurse or end it*, Wint. II, 3, 182 (in the situation of a stranger; so as not to be known there). *O, thus she stood, even with such life of majesty, warm life, as now it coldly stands*, V, 3, 36. *if like an ill venture it come unluckily home*, H4B V, 5, 128. *You may stroke him as gently as a puppy greyhound*, II, 4, 106 (i. e. it will be as harmless to stroke him, he will be as gentle as a puppy). *If a son that is by his father sent about merchandise do sinfully miscarry upon the sea*, H5 IV, 1, 155 (in the state of sinfulness). *It lies as coldly in him as fire in a flint*, Troil. III, 3, 257. *O noble fellow, who sensibly outdares his senseless sword*, Cor. I, 4, 53 (though having sense and feeling). *How youngly he began to serve his country*, II, 3, 243. *You shall hear from me still, and never of me aught but what is like my former*, IV, 1, 53 (in my former condition; as I was formerly). *He is your brother, lords, sensibly fed of that self blood that first gave life to you*, Tit. IV, 2, 122 (as a sensible being). *Lucius' banishment was wrongfully*, IV, 4, 76. *Things unluckily charge my fantasy*, Caes. III, 3, 2 (M. Edd. *unlucky*). *Why stands Macbeth thus amazedly?* Mcb. IV, 1, 126. *The air nimbly and sweetly recommends itself unto our gentle senses*, I, 6, 2 (= by being nimble and sweet). *The funeral baked meats did coldly furnish forth the marriage tables*, Hml. I, 2, 181 (in the state of having become cold). *He took my father grossly, full of bread*, III, 3, 80. *It will stuff his suspicion more fully*, Lr. III, 5, 22.

**5. The gerund in a passive sense.** Such expressions as that in Hamlet: *the whilst this play is playing*, are in use to this day. *The table is serving, the house is building*, for *being served, being built*, or rather for *in serving, in building (a-building)*, are very common phrases. But with Shakespeare the gerund may have a passive sense even when it is not in the predicate. *The unbacked breeder, full of fear, jealous of catching, swiftly doth forsake him*, Ven. 321 (fearing to be caught). *to watch like one that fears robbing*, Gent. II, 1, 26 (being robbed). *Excuse his throwing into the water*, Wiv. III, 3, 206 and IV, 1, 5 (his having been thrown). *That's more to me than my wetting*, Tp. IV, 211. *Not a sore, till now made sore with shooting*, LLL IV, 2, 59. *This very instant disaster of his setting in the stocks*, All's IV, 3, 127. *more straining on for plucking back*, Wint. IV, 4, 476. *our love durst not come near your sight for fear of swallowing*, H4A V, 1, 64. *If you mean to save yourself from whipping,*

H6B II, 1, 144; cf. Hml. II, 2, 556 and Per. II, 1, 93. *I will take order for her keeping close*, R3 IV, 2, 53. *Women are angels, wooing*, Troil. I, 2, 312. *How 'scaped I killing when I crossed you thus?* Caes. IV, 3, 150. *And 'scape detecting*, Hml. III, 2, 94. *Or else shall he suffer not thinking on, with the hobby-horse*, 142. *An instrument of this your calling back*, Oth. IV, 2, 45.

These instances will explain the following which have much puzzled the commentators: *Let his unrecalling crime have time to wail the abusing of his time*, Lucr. 993 (a crime for which there is no recalling, which cannot be made undone). *By deed-achieving honour newly named*, Cor. II, 1, 190 (an honour the achieving or obtaining of which lies in deeds). *From his all-obeying breath I hear the doom of Egypt*, Ant. III, 13, 77 (a voice attended by a general obeying or obedience). In LLL V, 2, 366: *my lady in courtesy gives undeserving praise*, which has been interpreted in a similar manner, *undeserving* may be a dative governed by *gives*. cf. Rom. III, 5, 75. Hml. II, 2, 182.

**6. Suffixes and prefixes omitted.** Very often, when two or more adverbs are placed together, the adverbial termination *ly* is only appended to the last: *Feat and affectedly enswathed*, Compl. 48. *Most strange, but yet most truly, will I speak*, Meas. V, 37. *Looked he sad or merrily?* Err. IV, 2, 4 and H4A V, 2, 12. *He demeaned himself rough, rude and wildly*, Err. V, 88. *Sixt and lastly*, Ado V, 1, 221. *I'll serve thee true and faithfully*, LLL V, 2, 841. *Most jocund, apt and willingly*, Tw. V, 135. *Fair and evenly*, H4A III, 1, 103. *Plain and bluntly*, H6A IV, 1, 51. *Secure and sweetly*, H6C II, 5, 50. *Look fresh and merrily*, Caes. II, 1, 224. *What safe and nicely I might well delay*, Lr. V, 3, 144. *Cold and sickly he vented them*, Ant. III, 4, 7. *How honourable and how kindly we determine for her*, V, 1, 58.

Sometimes the suffix is appended to the first and omitted in the last adverb: *She will speak most bitterly and strange*, Meas. V, 36. *Sprightfully and bold*, R2 I, 3, 3. *Patiently and yielding*, H5 V, 2, 300. *His grace looks cheerfully and smooth*, R3 III, 4, 50. *Most dangerously you have with him prevailed, if not most mortal to him*, Cor. V, 3, 189. *Why do you speak so startingly and rash?* Oth. III, 4, 79.

It is the same with inflections: *I fast and prayed for their intelligence*, Cymb. IV, 2, 347. *Earth and sea's rich gems*, Sonn. 21, 6. *Nor child nor woman's face*, Cor. V, 3, 130. *Nor near nor farther off*, R2 III, 2, 64. *A weak and colder palate*, Troil. IV, 4, 7. *The humble as the proudest sail*, Sonn. 80, 6. *The generous and gravest citizens*, Meas. IV, 6, 13. *To make me blest or coursedst among men*, Merch. II, 1, 49. *Without or grudge or grumblings*, Tp. I, 2, 249. *Half sleep, half waking*, Mids. IV, 1, 152. It would not, therefore, be safe to infer the existence of a substantive *vail* from the passage in Troil. V, 8, 7: *with the vail and darking of the sun.*

Prefixes thus omitted are of rarer occurrence: *That need to be revived and breathed in me*, H4B IV, 1, 114. *'Tween asleep and wake*, Lr. I, 2, 15. Perhaps also in *belee'd and calmed*, Oth. I, 1, 30.

But in two or more compound words, which have one part in common, this is more frequently appended to one only: *How much in having, or without or in*, Troil. III, 3, 97 (= without or within). *Search Wind-*

sor Castle, elves, within and out, Wiv. V, 5, 60. *The Athenians both within and out that wall*, Tim. IV, 1, 38. *My East and West Indies*, Wiv. I, 3, 79. *Come cut and long tail*, III, 4, 47. *Furred with fox and lambskins*, Meas. III, 2, 9. *Cannot my body or blood-sacrifice entreat you*, H6A V, 3, 20. *In Buckingham, Northampton and in Leicestershire*, H6C IV, 8, 14. *The wall-newt and the water*, Lr. III, 4, 135. *Bobtail tike or trundletail*, III, 6, 73. *A closet lock and key*, Oth. IV, 2, 22. *Shrill-tongued or low*, Ant. III, 3, 15. *Treble-sinewed, hearted, breathed*, III, 13, 178. *As poisonous-tongued as handed*, Cymb. III, 2, 5. The following expression is very curious: *like bride and groom* = like bride and bridegroom, Oth. II, 3, 180.

**7. Zeugma and Syllepsis**, i. e. a word joined to two other or more words, but having a natural reference only to one.

a) Zeugma of the verb: *Or in the ocean drenched or in the fire*, Ven. 494. *Blushing red no guilty instance gave, nor ashy pale the fear that false hearts have*, Lucr. 1511. *Nor Mars his sword nor war's quick fire shall burn the living record of your memory*, Sonn. 55, 7. *I had rather hear them scold than fight*, Wiv. II, 1, 239 (= than see them fight). *She hath directed how I shall take her from her father's house, what gold and jewels she is furnished with, what page's suit she hath in readiness*, Merch. II, 4, 30 (= and has communicated what gold and jewels etc.). *You may as well forbid the mountain pines to wag their high tops and to make no noise*, IV, 1, 75 (= and command them to make no noise). *To see him shine so brisk and smell so sweet*, H4A I, 3, 54.

b) Zeugma of the noun: *She was not, sure. Most sure she was. Why, my negation hath no taste of madness. Nor mine, my lord: Cressid was here but now*, Troil. V, 2, 128 (= nor my affirmation). *Your hearts will throb and weep to hear him speak*, Tit. V, 3, 95. *A sister I bequeath you, whom no brother did ever love so dearly*, Ant. II, 2, 152 (= whom I love as never brother loved his). *She would, he will not in her arms be bound*, Ven. 226 (= she would be bound in his arms, but not he in hers).

c) Syllepsis of the auxiliary verb: *Ambition cannot pierce a wink beyond, but doubt discovery there*, Tp. II, 1, 242 (= but must doubt). *You must be so too, if heed me*, 220 (= if you will heed me). *My master and his man are both broke loose, beaten the maids a-row, and bound the doctor*, Err. V, 169 (= have beaten). *My loyalty, which ever has and ever shall be growing*, H8 III, 2, 178 (= has been). *Which I am not worthy yet to wear: I shall assuredly*, IV, 2, 92 (= I shall be). *That means not, hath not, or is not to love*, Troil. I, 3, 288. *Home art gone and ta'en thy wages*, Cymb. IV, 2, 261. Inversely: *Many have and others must sit there*, R2 V, 5, 27. (= many have sat).

d) Syllepsis of the preposition: *From whence at pleasure thou mayst come and part*, Sonn. 48, 12 (where thou mayst come and from whence thou mayst part). *I will follow, more to cross that love than hate for Silvia*, Gent. V, 2, 55 (= than out of hate). *I think and pray to several subjects*, Meas. II, 4, 1 (= I think of and pray to). *That more for praise than purpose meant to kill*, LLL IV, 1, 29 (= than on purpose). *Love and languish for his sake*, Mids. II, 2, 29 (= love him and etc.). *Secure and confident from foreign purposes*, John II, 27. *Send fair play orders and make compromise to arms invasive*, V, 1, 67. *He cannot temperately transport his honours from where he should begin and end*, Cor. II, 1, 240 (= from where he should begin to where he should end). *He hath given up himself to the contemplation, mark and devotement of her parts and graces*, Oth. II, 3, 323 (M. Edd. unnecessarily *denotement* for *devotement*). *But first of all, how we may steal from hence, and for the gap that we shall make in time, from our hence-going and our return, to excuse*, Cymb. III, 2, 65 (= from our hence-going to our return). cf. Caes. I, 2, 314.

**8. Prolepsis or anticipation,** that is, an effect to be produced represented as already produced, by the insertion of an epithet: *My tongue-tied Muse in manners holds her still*, Sonn. 85, 1 (= my Muse holds her still and is tongue-tied). *To chase the ignorant fumes that mantle their clearer reason*, Tp. V, 68 (their reason which by the chasing of the fumes becomes clearer). *The approaching tide will shortly fill the reasonable shore that now lies foul and muddy*, 81 (fill the shore and make it reasonable again. But *reasonable shore* may be = shore of reason). *Such short-lived wits do wither as they grow*, LLL II, 54 (wither, and are short-lived in consequence). *Weed your better judgments of all opinion that is rank in them*, As II, 7, 44 (weed your judgments and make them better). *What is infirm from your sound parts shall fly*, Alls II, 1, 170 (what is infirm shall fly from your parts, which will become sound thereby). *To break within the bloody house of life*, John IV, 2, 210 (to break within the house of life, viz the body, and make it bloody, shed its blood). *The crown, which waste of idle hours hath quite thrown down*, R2 III, 4, 66 (the waste of hours, which are made idle by this waste. Qq *waste and idle hours*). *The strand whereon the imperious flood hath left a witnessed usurpation*, H4B I, 1, 62 (a usurpation which may be witnessed in consequence). *Here shall they make their ransom on the sand, or with their blood stain this discoloured shore*, H6B IV, 1, 11 (which thus will become discoloured). *Flaky darkness breaks within the east*, R3 V, 3, 86 (breaks and becomes flaky). *I'ld make a quarry with thousands of these quartered slaves*, Cor. I, 1, 203. *take our friendly senators by the hands*, IV, 5, 138 (take them by the hand and show thus that you consider them as friends). *Hang his poison in the sick air*, Tim. IV, 3, 109. *It almost turns my dangerous nature wild*, 499 (makes it wild and thus dangerous. M. Edd. *mild* for *wild*). *Now breathless wrong shall sit and pant in your great chairs of ease*, V, 4, 10. *The air nimbly and sweetly recommends itself unto our gentle senses*, Mcb. I, 6, 3 (senses made gentle by its touch and influence. Becket *gentle unto our sense;* Warburton *general sense*). *Ere human statute purged the gentle weal*, III, 4, 76 (the body politic, which became gentle by law. Theobald *general*, Seymour *ungentle* for *gentle*). *The glow-worm shows the matin to be near and 'gins to pale his uneffectual fire*, Hml. I, 5, 90 (the fire which becomes uneffectual, loses its brightness). *The expectancy and rose of the fair state*, III, 1, 160 (the state which was to be adorned by him). *His silence will sit drooping*, V, 1, 311 (he will sit drooping and be silent). *I will piece her opulent throne with kingdoms*, Ant. I, 5, 45. *'tis well for thee that ... thy freer thoughts may not fly forth of Egypt*, 12. *Grow, patience! and let the stinking elder, grief, untwine his*

*perishing root with the increasing vine*, Cymb. IV, 2, 60 (let grief untwine its root from patience, in consequence of which grief will perish and patience increase). cf. Lr. IV, 2, 87.

**9. Double negative.** To join two negatives properly called so (as *nor not, nor never* etc.) and even three (*nor never none*, Tw. III, 1, 171), where one would not only have been sufficient, but more logical, was so general a custom with all the writers of Shakespeare's time, that it could not escape the notice of grammarians (cf. negative prefixes before words of a negative sense: *disannul* = annul, *dissever* = sever; thus perhaps *inexecrable* = execrable in Merch. IV, 1, 128). Less frequent, but no less remarkable was the duplication of negative words of another kind. Mr. Abbott adduces two instances of the verb *to deny*: *first he denied you had in him no right*, Err. IV, 2, 7; *you may deny that you were not the cause*, R3 I, 3, 90. Add to these the following passages, some of which have sorely tried the sagacity of critics: *To mend the hurt which his unkindness marred*, Ven. 478 (marred for made). *Let his lack of years be no impediment to let him lack a reverend estimation*, Merch. IV, 1, 162 (= either: no motive to let him lack; or: no impediment to let him have). *It is most expedient for the wise, if Don Worm, his conscience, find no impediment to the contrary, to be the trumpet of his own virtues*, Ado V, 2, 87. *I ne'er heard yet that any of these bolder vices wanted less impudence to gainsay what they did than to perform it first*, Wint. III, 2, 56 (wanted less = had less). *Who cannot want the thought how monstrous it was for Malcolm and for Donalbain to kill their gracious father?* Mcb. III, 6, 8 (Hanmer *you cannot want;* Jennens *who cannot have;* Jackson *who care not, want;* Keightley *we cannot want*). *Patience herself, what goddess e'er she be, doth lesser blench at sufferance than I do*, Troil. I, 1, 28 (= does less bear up against sufferance, or does more recoil at it). *Tullus Aufidius, is he within your walls? No, nor a man that fears you less than he, that's lesser than a little*, Cor. I, 4, 14 (Keightley *but a man;* Johnson *but fears you less;* Capell *that fears you more*). *You less know how to value her, than she to scant her duty*, Lr. II, 4, 142 (= you are apter to undervalue her than she to scant her duty. Qq *slack her duty.* Hanmer *scan her duty*). *Taking a beggar without less quality*, Cymb. I, 4, 23 (Rowe *without more quality;* Jackson *with doughtiless quality;* Grant White *with less quality;* Lloyd *without other quality*). *Lesser had been the thwartings of your dispositions, if you had not showed them how ye were disposed ere they lacked power to cross you*, Cor. III, 2, 23 (but this passage admits of another interpretation). *The cease of majesty dies not alone*, Hml. III, 3, 15 (= majesty when ceasing dies not alone); cf. *this crack of your love shall grow stronger than it was before*, Oth. II, 3, 330 (= this love now cracked); and: *the broken rancour of your high-swoln hearts, but lately splintered, knit and joined together, must gently be preserved*, R3 II, 2, 117.

Such irregularities may be easily accounted for. The idea of negation was so strong in the poet's mind, that he expressed it in more than one place, unmindful of his canon that 'your four negatives make your two affirmatives.' Had he taken the pains of revising and preparing his plays for the press, he would perhaps have corrected all the quoted passages. But he did not write them to be read and dwelt on by the eye, but to be heard by a sympathetic audience. And much that would blemish the language of a logician, may well become a dramatic poet or an orator.

Similar perplexity has been caused by some other passages, in which a negative seems to be wanting, as being borne in mind, though not expressed: *He that hath learned no wit by nature nor art may complain of good breeding or comes of a very dull kindred*, As III, 2, 31 (i. e. he may complain of good breeding as a thing not bestowed on him. Hanmer *bad breeding;* Warburton *gross breeding*). *All out of work and cold for action*, H5 I, 2, 114 (cold in as much as action did not warm them; not heated by fighting. Some M. Edd. *All out of work for want of action*). *Who almost dead for breath, had scarcely more than would make up his message*, Mcb. I, 5, 37. *I was at point to sink for food*, Cymb. III, 6, 17. cf. *leisure* in R3 V, 3, 97, and see *Leisure*.

**10. Ambiguity caused by using a word in two different senses.** We do not mean to speak of intentional plays on words, in which the comical parts of the dramas abound, but of involuntary obscurities caused by the confusion of different significations of the same word. *Fast* used in the senses swiftly and firmly at the same time: *Give my love fame faster than time wastes life*, Sonn. 100, 13 (a fame whose stability is greater, deserves a more emphatic predicate, than the swiftness of time). *Ten times faster Venus' pigeons fly to seal love's bonds new-made, than they are wont to keep obliged faith unforfeited*, Merch. II, 6, 5 (their swiftness in sealing bonds is greater than their firm constancy in keeping them). *O'er and o'er divides him 'twixt his unkindness and his kindness; the one he chides to hell and bids the other grow faster than thought or time*, Wint. IV, 4, 565 (take a firmer root than thought or time, which are proverbially fast, that is swift). *Sound* = healthy, and shrill, clear-sounding: *so sound as things that are hollow*, Meas. I, 2, 56. *he hath a heart as sound as a bell*, Ado III, 2, 13. *Heavy* = melancholy and sleepy: *though woe be heavy, yet it seldom sleeps*, Lucr. 1574. *State* = condition in general, and high rank, pomp, power: *When I have seen such interchange of state, and state itself confounded to decay*, Sonn. 64, 9. *Error* = offence and wrong opinion: *So are those errors that in thee are seen to truths translated and for true things deemed*, Sonn. 96, 7. *Arms* = the upper limbs of the human body, and weapons: *And dare avouch her beauty and her worth in other arms than hers*, Troil. I, 3, 271. *Reason* = right and reasoning: *Love hath reason, reason none, if what parts can so remain*, Phoen. 47. *Figure* = shape, and a character denoting a number: *Yet doth beauty, like a dial-hand, steal from his figure*, Sonn. 104, 10. *Spring* = vernal season and source: *Here stands the spring whom you have stained with mud, this goodly summer with your winter mixed*, Tit. V, 2, 171. *Kind* = sort and benevolent: *He says they can do nothing in this kind. The kinder we to give them thanks for nothing*, Mids. V, 88. *Open* = not shut (liberal) and not confined: *A hand open as day*, H4B IV, 4, 32. *Fruitful* = fertile and bountiful: *A hand as fruitful as the land that feeds us*, H8 I, 3, 56; cf. Oth. II, 3, 347. *More* = in a higher degree, and greater: *Excusing thy sins more than thy*

*sins are*, Sonn. 35, 8. *To fear* = to dread, and to be concerned about: *If any fear lesser his person than an ill report*, Cor. I, 6, 69. *To keep* = to retain, and to cause to be: *To keep her still and men in awe*, Per. Prol. 36 (to retain her and to keep men in awe, i. e. to deter suitors). *To undo* = to ruin and to untie: *to bind me or undo me*, Ado V, 4, 20. *For* = on account of and to the advantage of: *Thus by day my limbs, by night my mind, for thee and for myself no quiet find*, Sonn. 27, 14. *Late* = after the expected time, and lately: *I did give that life which she too early and too late hath spilled*, Lucr. 1801 (= too lately; and nevertheless opposed to too early). *O boy, thy father gave thee life too soon, and hath bereft thee of thy life too late*, H6C II, 5, 92 (a much controverted passage. In fact, there is no real antithesis between *soon* and *late*, for both words are employed in another sense than that in which they form contraries: thy father gave thee life too readily, too rashly, and bereft thee of it too lately. A similar antithesis, not in sense, but in words, see R3 I, 2, 120: *thou art the cause and most accurst effect. Cause* and *effect* being standing contraries, the poet opposed them to each other also in a sense in which they are rather synonyms: author or contriver, and executor).

Particular notice must be taken of the custom of Shakespeare of abstracting nouns from preceding verbs, and inversely: *They that have power to hurt and will do none*, Sonn. 94, 1 (= will do no hurt). *If thou dost love fair Hero, cherish it*, Ado I, 1, 310 (cherish the love). *You are loved, sir; they that least lend it you shall lack you first*, All's I, 2, 68 (= they that least lend you love, i. e. love you). *The king loves you; beware you lose it not*, H8 III, 1, 172. *As much as child e'er loved, or father found*, Lr. I, 1, 60 (found love). *Yet longest, but in a fainter kind: O, not like me, for mine's beyond beyond*, Cymb. III, 2, 56 (my longing is beyond extremity). *The codpiece that will house before the head has any*, Lr. III, 2, 27 (any house). *And bid me, when my fate would have me wive, to give it her*, Oth. III, 4, 64 (to give it my wife). *For doing I am past, as I will by thee*, All's II, 3, 246 (as I will pass by thee). *Love loving not itself none other can*, R2 V, 3, 88 (can love none else). *That bill which was like, and had indeed against us passed*, H5 I, 1, 3 (was like, or likely, to pass). *You were as flowers, now withered: even so these herblets shall*, Cymb. IV, 2, 286.

Sometimes one noun is implied by another: *Who are the late commissioners? I one, my lord: your highness bade me ask for it to-day*, H5 II, 2, 61 (ask for the commission). *Of ashy semblance, meagre, pale and bloodless, being all descended to the labouring heart*, H6B III, 2, 162 (the blood being all descended). *No lesser of her honour confident than I did truly find her*, Cymb. V, 5, 187 (than I found her truly honest or honourable).

**11. The Abstract for the Concrete.** The kind of metonymy called Abstractum pro Concreto is common to all languages and scarcely to be numbered among the peculiarities of poetical license, but no poet has been nearly so bold in it as Shakespeare.

*Adversity* = loathsome fellow: *well said, adversity*, Troil. V, 1, 14.

*Admiration* = admirable, wonderful person: *bring in the admiration*, Alls II, 1, 91.

*Affliction* = afflicted, grieved woman: *O fair affliction, peace!* John III, 4, 36.

*Age* = old man: *age, thou hast lost thy labour,* Wint. IV, 4, 787. *pity not honoured age for his grey beard,* Tim. IV, 3, 111. cf. *let me embrace thine age,* Tp. V, 121.

*Ambition* = that which is coveted by the ambitious: *I am still possessed of effects for which I did the murder, my crown, mine own ambition, and my queen,* Hml. III, 3, 55.

*Ancientry* = old people: *wronging the ancientry, stealing, fighting,* Wint. III, 3, 63.

*Baseness* = base fellow, or base thing: *thou unconfinable baseness,* Wiv. II, 2, 21. *fly, damned baseness, to him that worships thee,* Tim. III, 1, 50.

*Blasphemy* = blasphemer: *now, blasphemy, that swearest grace o'erboard, not an oath on shore?* Tp. V, 218.

*Charm* = charmer: *when I am revenged upon my charm,* Ant. IV, 12, 16.

*Chastity* = chaste woman: *ere he wakened the chastity he wounded,* Cymb. II, 2, 14.

*Clearness* = something clear: *in the fountain shall we gaze so long till the fresh taste be taken from that clearness and made a brine-pit with our bitter tears,* Tit. III, 1, 128.

*Conduct* = that which conducts: *extinguishing his conduct* (a light) Lucr. 313. *there is in this business more than nature was ever conduct of,* Tp. V, 244.

*Counsel* = counsellors: *this land was famously enriched with politic grave counsel,* R3 II, 3, 20.

*Cruelty* = cruel person: *farewell, fair cruelty,* Tw. I, 5, 307. *get thee to yond same sovereign cruelty,* II, 4, 83.

*Damnation* = sinner: *ancient damnation! O most wicked fiend!* Rom. III, 5, 235.

*Decay* = one decayed and fallen: *what comfort to this great decay may come shall be applied,* Lr. V, 3, 297.

*Diligence* = diligent and officious servant: *bravely, my diligence!* Tp. V, 241.

*Divorce* = that which divorces: *hateful divorce of love, — thus chides she Death,* Ven. 932. *O thou sweet king-killer and dear divorce 'twixt natural son and sire,* Tim. IV, 3, 382. [*The long divorce of steel,* H8, II, 1, 76.]

*Empire* = emperor: *a maid too virtuous for the contempt of empire,* All's III, 2, 34.

*Enchantment* = enchanter: *and you, enchantment, worthy enough a herdsman,* Wint. IV, 4, 445.

*Encounter* = encounterer, adversary: *encounters mounted are against your peace,* LLL V, 2, 82.

*End* = that which makes an end: *this apoplexy will certain be his end,* H4B IV, 4, 130. *either of you to be the other's end,* R3 II, 1, 15.

*Estimation* = something esteemed or valued: *beggar the estimation which you prized richer than sea and land,* Troil. II, 2, 91. *your ring may be stolen too: so your brace of unprizable estimations,* Cymb. I, 4, 99.

*Excellence* = something excellent: *and she a fair divided excellence,* John II, 439.

*Exchange* = something given in exchange: *there's my exchange,* Lr. V, 3, 97 (a glove).

*Fancy* = a woman in love: *a reverend man towards this afflicted fancy fastly drew,* Pilgr. 61.

*Fear* = a dreaded object: *imagining some fear,* Mids. V, 21. *we will fetters put upon this fear,* Hml. III, 3, 25.

*Feasts* = feasters: *feasts are too proud to give thanks to the gods,* Tim. I, 2, 62.

*Filth* = that which, or one who, is filthy and debased: *filths savour but themselves,* Lr. IV, 2, 39. *filth, thou liest,* Oth. V, 2, 231.

*Gall* = a rancorous person: *out, gall!* Troil. V, 1, 40.

*Gaze* = an object gazed on: *the lovely gaze where every eye doth dwell,* Sonn. 5, 2. *to be the show and gaze of the time,* Mcb. V, 8, 24.

*Grace* = a graceful person: *lascivious grace, in whom all ill well shows, kill me with spites,* Sonn. 40, 13.

*Humour* = one humorous: *all the unsettled humours of the land, rash, inconsiderate, fiery voluntaries,* John II, 66. *Romeo! humours! madman!* Rom. II, 1, 7.

*Ignorance* = an ignorant or stupid person: *I had rather be a tick in a sheep than such a valiant ignorance,* Troil. III, 3, 316. *fools as gross as ignorance made drunk,* Oth. III, 3, 405.

*Information* = informer: *to whip your information,* Cor. IV, 6, 53.

*Iniquity* = one iniquitous: *wholesome iniquity, have you that a man may deal withal?* Per. IV, 6, 28.

*Illusion* = phantom: *stay, illusion!* Hml. I, 1, 127.

*Joy* = that which, or he who, causes delight: *yea, joy, our chains and our jewels,* H4B II, 4, 52.

*Judgment* = judge, one able to judge: *he's one of the soundest judgments in Troy,* Troil. I, 2, 208.

*Liberty* = libertine: *disguised cheaters, prating mountebanks, and many such-like liberties of sin,* Err. I, 2, 102.

*Life* = living man: *whilst I see lives, the gashes do better upon them,* Mcb. V, 8, 2.

*Loveliness* = lovely person: *unthrifty loveliness, why dost thou spend upon thyself thy beauty's legacy?* Sonn. 4, 1.

*Malice* = one malignant: *shruggest thou, malice?* Tp. I, 2, 367.

*Mettle* = a man of mettle: *he was quick mettle, when we went to school,* Caes. I, 2, 300.

*Motive* = author: *nor are they living who were the motives that you first went out,* Tim. V, 4, 27.

*Perfection* = something perfect: *divine perfection of a woman,* R3 I, 2, 75.

*Passion* = one passionate, filled with the passion of love: *madman! passion, lover!* Rom. II, 1, 7.

*Perfume* = a perfumed woman: *hug their diseased perfumes,* Tim. IV, 3, 207.

*Pestilence* = one infected with pestilence: *a most arch heretic, a pestilence that does infect the land,* H8 V, 1, 45.

*Poverty* = poor people: *you houseless poverty.* Lr. III, 4, 26.

*Prudence* = wiseacre: *hold your tongue, good p., smatter with your gossips,* Rom. III, 5, 172.

*Quarrel* perhaps = quarreller: *if that quarrel, fortune, divorce it* (greatness) *from the bearer,* H8 II, 3, 14.

*Report* = reporter: *I have my learning from some true reports that drew their swords with you,* Ant. II, 2, 47.

*Rudeness* = rude fellow: *Mars his idiot, do, rudeness, do, camel,* Troil. II, 1, 58.

*Sickness* = one sick: *like a sickness did I loathe this food,* Mids. IV, 1, 178 (M. Edd. *like in sickness*).

*Silence* = one silent: *my gracious silence, hail!* Cor. II, 1, 192.

*Sin* = sinner: *cardinal sins and hollow hearts I fear ye*, H8 III, 1, 104. *thou scarlet sin*, III, 2, 255.

*Solidity* = solid mass: *yea, this solidity and compound mass, with tristful visage, as against the doom, is thought-sick at the act*, Hml. III, 4, 49.

*Sore* = a person afflicted with a sore: *she whom the spital-house and ulcerous sores would cast the gorge at*, Tim. IV, 3, 39.

*Speculation* = a speculator, i. e. spy: *servants, which are to France the spies and speculations intelligent of our state*, Lr. III, 1, 24.

*Speed* = speeder, assistant: *Saint Nicholas be thy speed*, Gent. III, 1, 301. *Hercules be thy speed*, As I, 2, 222.

*Tenderness* = one yet of tender age: *go, tenderness of years*, LLL III, 4.

*Untruth* = one faithless: *O false Cressid! let all untruths stand by thy stained name, and they'll seem glorious*, Troil. V, 2, 179.

*Valour* = one valiant, a brave: *and at this sport Sir Valour dies*, Troil. I, 3, 176.

*Virtue* = a virtuous person: *grant that, my poor virtue*, H4B II, 4, 51. *holy men I thought ye, two reverend cardinal virtues*, H8 III, 1, 103.

*Wrong* = wronger: *to rouse his wrongs and chase them to the bay*, R2 II, 3, 128. *now breathless wrong shall sit and pant in your great chairs of ease*, Tim. V, 4, 10. [Cf. *Beauty, Medicine, Soul, Spirit.*]

**12. The Concrete for the Abstract,** or rather a thing or person designated instead of the prominent quality inherent in them: *Our people begin to throw Pompey the Great and all his dignities upon his son*, Ant. I, 2, 195 (all the glorious and endearing ideas associated with the name of Pompey). *His complexion is perfect gallows*, Tp. I, 1, 32 (he has a hanging look). *To take the indisposed and sickly fit for the sound man*, Lr. II, 4, 113 (for that which is natural to him in a good state of health). *He echoes me, as if there were some monster in his thought*, Oth. III, 3, 107 (= monstrosity). *He preached pure maid*, Compl. 315 (virginity and innocence). *He speaks nothing but madman*, Tw. I, 5, 115. *I speak to thee plain soldier*, H5 V, 2, 156. *To speak parrot*, Oth. II, 3, 281. *Much fool may you find in you*, Alls II, 4, 36. *Leave those remnants of fool and feather that they got in France*, H8 I, 3, 25. *This is not altogether fool*, Lr. I, 4, 165. *They will not let me have all fool to myself*, 169.

**13. The whole for a part.** We do not mean to speak of the figure called totum pro parte in rhetoric (f. i. *head* for *ear*), but of a peculiarity which would perhaps have received a denomination of its own, if it had been known to ancient rhetoricians. Shakespeare very frequently uses the name of a person or thing itself for a single particular quality or point of view to be considered, in a manner which has seduced great part of his editors into needless conjectures and emendations. *How with this rage shall beauty hold a plea, whose action is no stronger than a flower?* Sonn. 65, 4 (= no stronger than the action of a flower). *Her lays were tuned like the lark*, Pilgr. 198 (= the lays of the lark). *He makes a July's day short as December*, Wint. I, 2, 169 (as a December's day). *Iniquity's throat cut like a calf*, H6B IV, 2, 29. *And be her sense but as a monument thus in a chapel lying*, Cymb. II, 2, 32

(as the sense of a monumental statue, i. e. insensible). *Holy seems the quarrel upon your grace's part, black and fearful on the opposer*, Alls III, 1, 6 (Hanmer *opposer's*). *Whose veins bound richer blood than Lady Blanch?* John II, 431. *Her dowry shall weigh equal with a queen*, 486 (= that of a queen). *Thou canst not, cardinal, devise a name so slight, unworthy and ridiculous, to charge me to an answer, as the pope*, III, 1, 151 (Keightley *the pope's*). *Mine hair be fixed on end as one distract*, H6B III, 2, 318 (= as that of one distract). *Sleep give as soft attachment to thy senses as infants empty of all thought*, Troil. IV, 2, 6 (= as to those of infants). *They call him Troilus, and on him erect a second hope as fairly built as Hector*, IV, 5, 109 (= as that on Hector). *Prosperity be thy page, thy friend no less than those she placeth highest*, Cor. I, 5, 25 (= than the friend of those). *I know the sound of Marcius' tongue from every meaner man*, I, 6, 27. *His ascent is not by such easy degrees as those who, having been supple and courteous to the people, bonneted into their estimation*, II, 2, 29. *My throat of war be turned into a pipe small as an eunuch*, III, 2, 114. *Your master's confidence was above mine*, Tim. III, 4, 31 (= that of mine). *An eye like Mars, a station like the herald Mercury*, Hml. III, 4, 57. *With a sigh like Tom o' Bedlam*, Lr. I, 2, 148. *His life, with thine, and all that offer to defend him, stand in assured loss*, III, 6, 101 (= the lives of all). *That the noble Moor should hazard such a place as his own second with one of an ingraft infirmity*, Oth. II, 3, 144. *His goodly eyes, that o'er the files and musters of the war have glowed like plated Mars*, Ant. I, 1, 4 (= like those of plated Mars). *Where's Fulvia's process? Caesar's I would say? both?* I, 1, 28 (= the process of both); cf. *high in name and power, higher than both in blood and life*, I, 2, 197. *His soldiership is twice the other twain*, II, 1, 35. These instances will suffice to place a much controverted passage in its proper light: *And mercy then will breathe within your lips, like man new made*, Meas. II, 2, 78, i. e. as within the lips of man new made, redeemed and regenerated by the grace of Heaven.

**14. Transposition of words.** To invert the relation of notions by transferring an epithet from the agent to the object or means of acting, and, in general, to apply to one part of a sentence what strictly belongs to another, is a liberty taken by all poets, and to trace it through every line in Shakespeare would be a task of infinite and perhaps unprofitable labour. But it would be interesting to compare to what lengths different poets have gone, and for Shakespeare especially, whose text has been subject to so much controversy, such a comparison might be a matter of some practical consequence. Here it must suffice to call the attention of others to the question and to show its nature by some single instances (cf. what has been said of the adjectival use of adverbs sub 3).

Transposition of epithets from the subject or predicate to the object: *Which happies those that pay the willing loan*, Sonn. 6, 6 (= that willing, or willingly, pay the loan). *What willing ransom he will give*, H5 III, 5, 63. *The thrifty hire I saved under your father*, As II, 3, 39 (= the hire which I, being thrifty, or thriftily, saved). *Held a late court at Dunstable*, H8 IV, 1, 27 (= lately held a court).

Epithets of governing and governed substantives confounded: *In me thou seest the twilight of such day as after sunset fadeth in the west*, Sonn. 73, 5 (= such a twilight of the day as etc.). *Give notice to such men of sort and suit as are to meet him*, Meas. IV, 4, 19 (= to men of such sort). *The manner of my pity-wanting pain*, Sonn. 140, 4 (= the pity-wanting manner of my pain). *My only son knows not my feeble key of untuned cares*, Err. V, 310 (my untuned key of enfeebling cares). *The world's large tongue*, LLL V, 2, 852 (= the large world's tongue). *With the divine forfeit of his soul upon oath*, All's III, 6, 33 (= with the forfeit of his divine soul). *To fill the mouth of deep defiance up*, H4A III, 2, 116 (= the deep mouth of defiance). *Dear men of estimation and command in arms*, IV, 4, 31 (= men of dear estimation). *Ere the glass finish the process of his sandy hour*, H6A IV, 2, 36 (= ere the sand-glass finish its hour). *That I may give the local wound a name*, Troil. IV, 5, 244 (= give the wound a local name). *The whole ear of Denmark is rankly abused*, Hml. I, 5, 36 (the ear of all Denmark is abused). *Course of direct session*, Oth. I, 2, 86 (= direct course of session). Similarly: *the hope to have the present benefit which I possess*, R2 II, 3, 14 (= the benefit which I possess at present).

The manner of logical dependence changed (subst. for adj., and adj. for subst.): *Time feeds on the rarities of nature's truth*, Sonn. 60, 11 (= the rarities of true nature). *Drove the grossness of the foppery into a received belief*, Wiv. V, 5, 131 (= the gross foppery). *The folded meaning of your words' deceit*, Err. III, 2, 36 (= of your deceitful words). Inversely: *Unless this general evil they maintain*, Sonn. 121, 13 (= this generality of evil). *When he most burned in heart-wished luxury*, Compl. 314 (= in the desire of luxury). *Our absence to supply*, Meas. I, 1, 19 (= us in our absence). *Provided that my banishment repealed and lands restored again be freely granted*, R2 III, 3, 40 (= the repeal of my banishment and the restoration of my lands). *What with our help, what with the absent king*, H4A V, 1, 49 (= the absence of the king). *The strand whereon the imperious flood hath left a witnessed usurpation*, H4B I, 1,

63 (a witness, traces, of usurpation. cf. above: Prolepsis).

The whole relation of ideas inverted: *You 've passed a hell of time*, Sonn. 120, 6 (= a time of hell). *Mine eye my heart the picture's sight would bar, my heart mine eye the freedom of that right*, 46, 4 (the right of that freedom). *The basest weed outbraves his dignity*, 94, 12 (= outvalues its bravery). *More to know did never meddle with my thoughts*, Tp. I, 2, 22 (= my thoughts never meddled with, cared for, knowing more). *Our soul cannot but yield you forth to public thanks*, Meas. V, 7 (= but yield public thanks to you). *Impose me to what penance your invention can lay upon my sin*, Ado V, 1, 282 (= impose to me what penance etc.). *You to your former honour I bequeath*, As V, 4, 192 (= I bequeath your former honour to you). *That malignant cause wherein the honour of my dear father's gift stands chief in power*, All's II, 1, 114 (= wherein the power ... stands chief in honour). *Till we assign you to your days of trial*, R2 V, 106 (= assign your days of trial to you). *This is the latest glory of thy praise that I, thy enemy, due thee withal*, H6A IV, 2, 33 (the last praise of thy glory). *To wring the widow from her customed right*, H6B V, 1, 188 (= to wring her customed right from the widow. Compare *stripped her from his benediction*, Lr. IV, 3, 45, with: *all the temporal lands would they strip from us*, H5 I, 1, 11). *To entail him and his heirs unto the crown*, H6C I, 1, 235. *To see you ta'en from liberty*, H8 I, 1, 205. *We must not rend our subjects from our laws, and stick them in our will*, I, 2, 93. *I would not wish them to a fairer death*, Mcb. V, 8, 49. *Every thing is sealed and done that else leans on the affair*, Hml. IV, 3, 59. *We will resign ... you to your rights*, Lr. V, 3, 300. *Be ever known to patience*, Ant. III, 6, 98.

A liberty so extended will easily explain how it came that *put fear to valour* meant the same as *put valour to fear*, *put to him all the learnings* the same as put him to all the learnings (cf. *Put*), and that in some cases (f. i. in the verb *become*) what was originally a poetical licence, in time grew so familiar as to modify and change the signification of words.

# II. Provincialisms.

In general it can be said that Shakespeare abstains from the use of provincial dialects as characteristic of his dramatical persons. He has, indeed, introduced people of all sorts speaking English very imperfectly, among whom his Welshmen are conspicuous in their substituting the literae tenues for the mediae, and the mediae for the tenues, omitting or confounding the aspiratae, and exchanging the sibilants one for another, but these must be called corruptions of the English language, not provincialisms. It is only on one occasion that he seems to imitate the peculiar speech of a certain district, Lr. IV, 6, 239—251. Concerning the particular county there referred to English scholars have been of different opinion. Steevens pleads for Somersetshire, in the dialect of which rustics were commonly introduced by ancient writers; Collier inclines to decide in favour of the north. But in trying to settle the question, it must not be forgotten, that it is not a real peasant from a particular locality, with whom we have to do, but the disguised Edgar, who strives to conceal his true character by affected rusticity. His words are, in the spelling of F1, as follows:

*Chill* (= I will) *not let go Zir* (Qq *sir*), *without vurther* (Qp om.) *'casion* (Qq *cagion*). *Good Gentleman, goe your gate, and let poore volke passe: and chud* (= if I should) *ha'* (Qq *have*) *bin zwaggerd* (Qq *zwaggar'd*) *out of my life, 'twould* (Qq *it wold* or *it would*) *not ha' bin zo* (Q2 *so*) *long as 'tis* (Qq om. *as 'tis*) *by a vortnight* (Q2 *fortnight*). *Nay, come not neere th' old man; keepe out, che vor'ye* (= I warn you. Qq *chevore ye*), *or ice* (= I shall. Qq *ile*) *try whither* (Qq *whether*) *your Costard* (Q2 *coster*) *or my Ballow* (Qq *bat*) *be the harder; chill* (= I will. Q2 *ile*) *be plaine with you. Chill picke your teeth Zir* (Q2 *sir*): *come, no matter vor* (Qq *for*) *your foynes.*

[The following words and phrases, which occur in Shakespeare, are, according to Northall's Warwickshire Wordbook, characteristic of the Warwickshire or Midland dialect (cf. Edith E. Knott, Literature 1900 I, 435).

*barm* (= yeast), *baste* (= to flog, thrash), *beetle* (= heavy iron-bound mallet), *bin* (= are, is), *bolter, bug* (= fright, alarm), *cock-sure, colly* vb., *come your ways, fettle* (= prepare, arrange), *fill-horse, gravelled, grime, honeystalks, inkle* (= coarse tape), *jowl* vb. (= to knock the head against an obstacle), *keech, kex* (kecksies), *kindle* (= to bring forth young), *ladysmocks, lone woman, loose* vb. (= to discharge fire-arms), *mammock, malkin, meddle and make, mortal* (= very), *old* (= great, abundant), *pash* vb. (to strike), *potch* (= to push, poke, thrust), *pun* (= to pound), *quat, reckon* (= to account, estimate), *shog, sliver, slop, sneap* (sbst.), [*squench* (First Part of the Contention),] *tang* (sbst.), *wall-eyed, while* (= till), *worser.*

J. Walter (Shakespeare's True Life p. 47) adds the following Warwickshire words: *batlet, bavin, bow* (= yoke), *brize* (= gadfly), *claw* (= to flutter), *cob-loaf, commit* (= to cohabit), *dout, doxy, eanlings, fardels, feeders* (= good-for-nothing servants), *forwearied, jet* (= to strut), *inkles, irk, lated, loon, pickthank, pugging tooth,* (= peg tooth), *sag, shive, squashes.*]

# III. Words and sentences taken from foreign languages.

**1. Greek.** *Misanthropos:* Tim. IV, 3, 53. *Threnos* (= funeral song) as superscription in Pilgr. 53, whereas *threne* in v. 49. *Action*, lection of F1 in Ant. III, 7, 52; later Ff and M. Edd. *Actium.* cf. *Epitheton.*

**2. Latin.** a) Single words:

*Accommodo: Accommodated! it comes of Accommodo*, H4B III, 2, 78 (Shallow's speech).

*Accusativo* (in the accusative case): *accusativo, hung, hang, hog*, Wiv. IV, 1, 49.

*Adsum* (= I am here): H6B I, 4, 26.

*Aer* (= air), see *Mollis.*

*Alias* (= otherwise, having also the name of): Alls IV, 5, 44. Cor. II, 1, 48.

*Armigero* for *armiger* (Slender's speech; = esquire) Wiv. I, 1, 10, 11.

*Ave*, a reverential salutation: Meas. I. 1, 71. cf. *Ave-Mary.*

*Benedicite*, used as an ecclesiastical salutation; in parting: Meas. II, 3, 39. in meeting: Rom. II, 3, 31.

*Caelo* (O. Edd. *celo*), abl. of caelum (sky): *like a jewel in the ear of caelo, the sky*, LLL IV, 2, 5 (Holofernes' speech).

[*Et caetera: an open et caetera* Rom. II, 1, 38.]

*Candidatus* (= candidate for an office): *be candidatus then*, Tit. I, 185.

*Canis* (= dog): *Cerberus, that three-headed canis,* LLL V, 2, 593 (Holofernes' poetry).

*Caret* (= is wanting): *but for the elegancy, facility, and golden cadence of poesy, caret,* LLL IV, 2, 127. [Misapplied and misunderstood in Wiv. IV, 1, 54: *focative is caret;* cf. Lilly's Grammar B. IV: *Nominatiuo hic, haec, hoc, Genitiuo huius .... Vocatiuo caret.*]

*Caveto* (= take heed, be cautious): *therefore Caveto be thy counsellor*, H5 II, 3, 55 (Pistol's speech).

*Circum circa* (round about), conjectured by M. Edd. in LLL V, 1, 72; O. Edd.: *I will whip about your infamy unum cita.*

*Coram* (in presence of), taken for a title by Slender: Wiv. I, 1, 6.

*Cubiculo*, ablative of cubiculum (apartment): *at the cubiculo*, Tw. III, 2, 56 Sir Toby's speech).

*Custàlorum*, corrupted from Custos Rotulorum (keeper of records): Wiv. I, 1, 7.

*Dives*, the rich man of the parable: H6A III, 3, 36.

*Ergo* (consequently, therefore), used by the pedant Holofernes and inferior persons: Err. IV, 3, 57. LLL V, 2, 597. Merch. II, 2, 63. Shr. IV, 3, 129. All's I, 3, 53. Misapplied by Launcelot: Merch. II, 2, 59. Corrupted to *argo:* H6B IV, 2, 31. to *argal:* Hml. V, 1, 13 sq.

*Facere* (to make): *facere, as it were, replication,* LLL IV, 2, 15 (Holofernes' speech).

*Fatuus*, see *Ignis.*

*Gallia*, ancient name of Gaul and Wales; see the art. *Gallia.*

*Genitivo* (in the genitive case): Wiv. IV, 1, 45.

*Hic haec hoc*, demonstr. pron., Wiv. IV, 1, 43. Gen. *hujus*, 45. Accus. *hunc hanc hoc*, 49. Gen. plur. *horum harum horum*, 63.

*Hiems* (winter); LLL V, 2, 901.

*Homo* (man): H4A II, 1, 104.

*Hysterica passio* (hysterics): Lr. II, 4, 57.

*Ignis fatuus* (will o'the wisp): H4A III, 3, 45.

*Imitari* (to imitate): LLL IV, 2, 129.

*Imprimis* (as signifying 'in the first place, firstly'): *imprimis, she can fetch and carry*, Gent. III, 1, 274. 302. *imprimis, we came down a foul hill*, Shr. IV, 1, 68. *imprimis, a loose-bodied gown*, IV, 3, 135. *imprimis, it is agreed, .... item*, .... H6B I, 1, 43.

*Ipse* (ohne's self): *all your writers do consent that ipse is he: now, you are not ipse, for I am he.* As V, 1, 48 (Touchstone's speech).

*Item* (likewise; again, in enumerations): Gent, III, 1, 277. 304 sq. LLL I, 1, 119, 130. Tw. I, 5, 265. H4A II, 4, 585. H6B I, 1, 50. 57. H8 III, 2, 320. Substantively: *though the catalogue of his endowments had been tabled by his side and I to peruse him by items,* Cymb. I, 4, 7.

*Lapis* (stone): Wiv. IV, 1, 32.

*Leo-natus*, etymologized in Cymb. V, 5, 445.

*Major*, see *Ursa.*

*Manus* (hand): LLL V, 2, 595.

*Mehercle* (in faith): LLL IV, 2, 80.

*Minime* (by no means): LLL III, 61.

*Mollis aer* (soft air): Cymb. V, 5, 447.

*Mons* (mountain): LLL V, 1, 89.

*Mulier* (woman): Cymb. V, 5, 448.

*Nominativo*, in the nominative case: Wiv. IV, 1. 42. 44.

*Ostentare* (to show): LLL IV, 2, 16.

*Passio*, see *Hysterica passio.*

*Pauca* (few, i. e. words): Wiv. I. 1, 134. H5 II, 1, 83. *pauca verba:* Wiv. I, 1, 123. LLL IV, 2, 171.

*Perge* (continue, go on): LLL IV, 2, 54.

*Pia mater* (= the brain [originally a membrane enclosing part of the brain]): LLL IV, 2, 71. Tw. I, 5, 123. Troil. II, 1, 77.

*Praemunire*, see the resp. article.

*Primo* (firstly): Tw. V, 39.

*Pueritia* (boyhood): LLL V, 1, 52.

*Pulcher* (beautiful): Wiv. IV, 1, 28.

*Quare* (wherefore): LLL V, 1, 36.

*Quasi* (as it were): LLL IV, 2, 85.

*Qui quae quod*, relat. pron.: Wiv. IV, 1, 79.

*Quis* (who): LLL V, 1, 55.

*Quondam: this quondam day* = the other day: LLL V, 1, 7.

*Quoniam* (because): LLL V, 2, 596.

*Ratolorum*, corrupted from *rotulorum*, Wiv. I, 1, 8; see *Custalorum.*

*Sanguis* (blood): LLL IV, 2, 3.

*Secundo* (secondly): Tw. V, 39.

*Sine* (without), Hertzberg's conjecture in LLL V, 1, 22: *to speak dout, sine b, when he should say doubt* (O. and M. Edd. *to speak dout, fine, when* etc.).

*Singulariter* (in the singular number): Wiv. IV, 1, 42.

*Solus* (alone): H5 II, 1, 48. 49. 50. 51. 54.

*Stuprum* (rape, violation): Tit. IV, 1, 7̇8̇.

*Terra* (earth): LLL IV, 2, 7.

*Tertio* (thirdly): Tw. V, 39.

*Triplex* (triple time): *the triplex is a good tripping measure*, Tw. V, 41.

*Unguem* (the nail), in the phrase *ad unguem* (accurately, nicely; used as signifying at the fingers' ends): LLL V, 1, 84.

*Ursa major* (the Greater Bear): Lr. I, 2, 141.

*Ver* (the spring): LLL V, 2, 901.

*Verba*, see *Pauca.*

*Verbatim* (verbally, orally, by word of mouth): *think not, although in writing I preferred the manner of thy vile outrageous crimes, that therefore I have forged, or am not able verbatim to rehearse the method of my pen*, H6A III, 1, 13.

*Videlicet* (viz, that is to say): Wiv. I, 1, 140. LLL IV, 1, 70. As IV, 1, 97. Hml. II, 1, 61. Once used in the classical sense, = one may behold; as you see: *and thus she means, videlicet*, Mids. V, 330.

*Vocativo*, in the vocative case: Wiv. IV, 1, 54.

*Vocatur* (is called): *neighbour vocatur nebour*, LLL V, 1, 25 (Holofernes' speech).

*Vox* (voice): Tw. V, 304 (cf. the resp. art.).

b) Phrases and sentences or verses quoted from divers authors:

*Vilia miretur vulgus, mihi flavus Apollo Pocula Castalia plena ministret aqua;* the motto of Ven. (Ovid, Amores I, 15, 35, translated by Jonson in his Poetaster: Kneel hinds to trash: me let bright Phoebus swell With cups full flowing from the Muses' well).

*Fauste, precor gelida quando pecus omne sub umbra Ruminat*, LLL IV, 2, 95 (I pray thee, Faustus, while all our cattle are ruminating in the cool shade. From the Eclogues of Baptista Spagnolus Mantuanus).

*Redime te captum quam queas minimo*, Shr. I, 1, 167 (redeem thyself from captivity as cheaply as possible. Terence, Eunuch. I, 1, 30: *Quid agas? nisi ut te redimas captum quam queas' Minimo*. The Shakespearian form of the verse is from Lilly's grammar).

*Hic ibat Simois, hic est Sigeia tellus; hic steterat Priami regia celsa senis*, Shr. III, 1, 28 (here the river Simois was running; here is the Sigeian country; here stood the high palace of old Priam. Ovid's Heroid. I, 33).

*In terram Salicam mulieres ne succedant*, H5 I, 2, 38 ('No woman shall succeed in Salique land'. Taken

from Holinshed). *Praeclarissimus filius noster Henricus, Rex Angliae, et Heres Frarviae*, V, 2, 369.

*Ajo te, Aeacida, Romanos vincere posse*, H6B I, 4, 65 (the ambiguous oracle which Pyrrhus received at Delphi before his war against the Romans; meaning as well: I say that thou mayst conquer the Romans, as: I say that the Romans may conquer thee. Ennius in Cicero, de divinatione II, 56).

*Tantaene animis coelestibus irae?* H6B II, 1, 24 (is such resentment found in celestial minds? Virg. Aen. I, 15).

*Medice, te ipsum*, H6B II, 1, 53 ('physician, heal thyself'; from the Vulgata; S. Luke IV, 23).

*Gelidus timor occupat artus*, H6B IV, 1, 117 (cold fear runs through the limbs; in Virg. Aen. VII, 446: *subitus tremor occupat artus*).

*Di faciant laudis summa sit ista tuae*, H6C I, 3, 48 (the Gods grant that this be the pinnacle of thy glory. Ovid's Heroid. II, 66).

*Per Styga, per Manes vehor*, Tit. II, 1, 135 (I am borne through the Styx, through the kingdom of the dead. From what author?).

*Magni dominator poli, tam lentus audis scelera? tam lentus vides:* Tit IV, 1, 82 (great ruler of the skies, doest thou so tardily hear and see crimes committed? Seneca, Hippol. II, 671).

*Integer vitae scelerisque purus Non eget Mauri jaculis nec arcu*, Tit. IV, 2, 20 (a man of spotless life and untainted with crime does not want the darts and bow of the Moor. Horace, Carm. I, 22). [The lines are quoted in Lilly's Grammar (1574) P. III.]

*Terras Astraea reliquit*, Tit. IV, 3, 4 (Astraea left the earth. Ovid's Metam. I, 150).

*Ira furor brevis est*, Tim. I, 2, 28 (anger is a short madness. Horace, Epist. I, 2, 62).

*Bonum quo antiquius eo melius*, Per. Prol. 9 (the good is the better for age). *Lux tua vita mihi*, Per. II, 2, 21 (thy light is my life). *Me pompae provexit apex*, 30 (Wilkins: the desire of renown drew me to this enterprise). *Quod me alit, me extinguit*, 33 (Wilkins: that which gives me life, gives me death). *Sic spectanda fides*, 38 (Wilkins: so faith is to be looked into). *In hac spe vivo*, 44 (Wilkins: in that hope I live). All these sentences and devices are not found in Gower.

c) Popular and proverbial phrases:

*Respice finem*, Err. IV, 4, 43 (think of the end; the last words of the well-known verse: *quidquid agis, prudenter agas, et respice finem;* sometimes changed to *respice funem*, 'beware the rope's end'; think of the halter).

*Cucullus non facit monachum*, Mcas. V, 263. Tw. I, 5, 62 (translated in H8 III, 1, 23: *'all hoods make not monks'*).

*Veni vidi vici*, LLL IV, 1, 68 (the celebrated inscription on Caesar's trophies; translated by Don Armado: *I came, saw and overcame*).

*Cum privilegio ad imprimendum solum*, Shr. IV, 4, 93; cf. *cum privilegio*, H8 I, 3, 34 (with exclusive copy-right).

*Hic jacet*, All's III, 6, 66 (here lies; the usual commencement of epitaphs).

*Diluculo surgere, viz saluberrimum est*, Tw. II, 3, 2 ('early to rise, makes a man healthy'). [Cp. Lilly's Grammar (1574) D. III: *Diluculo surgere saluberrimum est.*]

*Tremor cordis*, Wint. I, 2, 110 (throbbing of the heart).

*Ecce signum*, H4A II, 4, 187 (behold the token).

*Memento mori*, H4A III, 3, 35 (a remembrance of death).

*Semper idem, for obsque hoc nihil est*, H4B V, 5, 30 (sentences corrupted and nonsensically quoted by Pistol). [The phrase *obsque hoc = absque hoc* (without this) seems to be a corrupted legal term; cf. Ch. Allen, Notes on the Bacon-Shakespeare Question, Boston and New York 1900, p. 65.]

*Non nobis, and Te Deum*, H5 IV, 8, 128; cf. H8 IV, 1, 92 (the first words of Latin hymns).

*Quid for Quo* (all English prepositions governing the ablative of Latin words) in the sense of tit for tat: H6A V, 3, 109.

*Invitis nubibus*, H6B IV, 1, 99 (in despite of the clouds).

*In capite*, H6B IV, 7, 131 (holding of the king).

*Sancta majestas*, H6B V, 1, 5 (sacred majesty).

*Viva voce*, H8 V, 4, 67 (in the sense of speaking, appearing in person).

*In limbo Patrum*, H8 V, 4, 67, i. e. in confinement. Originally the place where the patriarchs of the Old Testament are waiting for resurrection).

*Per se*, Troil. I, 2, 15 (by one's self. cf. Nares' Glossary, p. 1).

*Suum cuique*, Tit. I, 280 (to every man his due).

*Sit fas aut nefas*, Tit. II, 1, 133 (with right or with wrong).

*Et tu, Brute*, Caes. III, 1, 77 (Caesar's last words).

*Se offendendo*, the gravedigger's blunder for *se defendendo*, in self-defence, Hml. V, 1, 9. [Perhaps an allusion to the law case of Hales v. Petit, published in Plowden's Reports in 1578 (cf. John Lord Campbell, Shakespeare's Legal Acquirements Considered, London 1859 p. 84, Ch. Allen, Notes on the Bacon-Shakespeare Question, Boston and New York 1900 p. 33). The phrase 'se offendendo' would then be equivalent to the legal term 'felo de se'.]

d) Latin apparently composed by the poet himself [or taken from Lilly's Grammar or the Sententiae Pueriles]:

*Haud credo*, LLL IV, 2, 11 (I do not believe).

*In via, 'in way, of explication'*, 14.

*Bis coctus, 'twice sod'*, 23.

*Omne bene*, 33 (all well).

*Vir sapit qui pauca loquitur*, 82 (the man is wise that speaks little). [The sentence is no doubt taken from Lilly's Grammar D. III.]

*Lege, domine*, 108 (read, sir).

*Satis quod sufficit*, V, 1, 1 (sufficiency is enough).

*Novi hominem tanquam te*, 10 (I know the man as well as I know you). [From Lilly's Grammar O. 1.]

*Anne intelligis, domine?* 28 (do you understand, sir?).

*Laus deo, bone, intelligo. Bone for bene; Priscian a little scratched*, V, 1, 30. 31 (Theobald's emendation for: *Laus deo, bene intelligo. Bome boon for boon prescian; a little scratcht.* Nathaniel employs *bone* as the vocative of *bonus*, but Holofernes thinks it to be a mistake for *bene*).

*Videsne quis venit? Video et gaudeo*, 33. 34 (do you see who comes? I see and am glad).

*Bonos dies*, the clown's blunder for *bonus dies*, good day: Tw. IV, 2, 14.

*Bona terra, mala gens*, H6B IV, 7, 61 (a good land, a bad people).

*Tanta est erga te mentis integritas, regina serenissima*, H8 III, 1, 40 (such 'is the integrity of mind towards you, most illustrious queen).

*Ego et rex meus*, III, 2, 314 (I and my king).

*Ad manes fratrum*, Tit. I, 98 (to the departed souls of the brothers).

*Ad Jovem, .... ad Apollinem, .... ad Martem*, Tit. IV, 3, 53 (to Jove, to Apollo, to Mars).

*Hic et ubique*, Hml. I, 5, 156 (here and everywhere).

**3. Spanish.** *Bilbo* = blade (so called from the town of Bilboa): Wiv. I. 1, 165. III, 5, 112.

*Labras*, Pistol's blunder for *labios* (lips): Wiv. I, 1, 166.

*Cavaleiro* and *Cavaleire*, instead of *Caballero*: Wiv. II, 1, 201. 221.

*Palabras* = senseless prattle, nonsense: Ado III, 5, 18.

*Don Adriano de Armado*: LLL I, 1, 280. IV, 1, 89.

*Fortuna delaguar*, LLL V, 2, 533 (M. Edd. *de la guerra*, which does not sufficiently suit with the context. Perhaps *fortuna del agua*, fortune or chance of the water, with allusion to the old saying, that swimming must be tried in the water; or *fortuna de la guarda*, Fortune of guard, i. e. guarding Fortune).

*Paucas pallabris*, Sly's blunder for *pocas palabras*, few words, Shr. Ind. 1, 5.

*Castiliano vulgo*, Spanish of Sir Toby's own making, good enough to impose on Maria and Sir Andrew, and very unnecessarily changed to *Castiliano volto* by some M. Edd: Tw. I, 3, 45.

*Figo*, the fig, and the female pudenda; hence a term of opprobrious contempt, accompanied by an obscene gesture (see *Fig*): H5 III, 6, 60. *Fico* in Wiv. I, 3, 33 is Italian.

*Malhecho* (O. Edd. *mallico* or *malicho*) = mischief: Hml. III, 2, 146.

*Diablo* = devil: Oth. II, 3, 160.

*Pue per doleera kee per forsa*, Per. II, 2, 27; corrected by M. Edd. to *Piu por dulzura que por fuerza*; but *piu* is no Spanish word. Perhaps the author of Pericles confounded Spanish and Italian, and the sentence ought to be written *Più per dolcezza chè per forza* (more by lenity than by force. Hertzberg's conjecture).

**4. Italian.** *Via* ('an adverb of encouragement'. Florio): Wiv. II, 2, 159. LLL V, 1, 156. V, 2, 112. Merch. II, 2, 11. H5 IV, 2, 4. H6C II, 1, 182.

*Coragio*: Tp. V, 258. All's II, 5, 97.

*Capriccio* (O. Edd. *caprichio*): All's II, 3, 310.

*Ben venuto* (O. Edd. *bien venuto* or *been venuto* or *bien vonuto*): LLL IV, 2, 164. Shr. I, 2, 282.

*Basta* (enough): Shr. I, 1, 203.

*Fico* (a fig; Spanish *figo*): Wiv. I, 3, 33.

*Bonaroba*, cf. the resp. article.

*Capocchia* (O. Edd. *chipochia*), 'the feminine form of capocchio, which signifies a fool; coaxingly applied by Pandarus to Cressida' (Nares): Troil. IV, 2, 33.

*Mercatante*; O. Edd. *marcantant*, q. v.

*Mi perdonate* (Ff *me pardonato*, Q *mi pardinato*): Shr. I, 1, 25.

*Con tutto il cuore ben trovato* (O. Edd. *contutti le core bene trobatto*): Shr. I, 2, 24.

*Alla nostra casa ben venuto, molto honorato signor*

*mio Petruchio* (O. Edd. *alla nostra casa bene venuto multo honorata signior Petruchio*): Shr. l, 2, 25.

*Venetia, Venetia, chi non ti vede non ti pretia*, or: *Venegia, Venegia, chi non te vede, non te pregia* (O. Edd. *Vemchie, Vencha, que non te vede, que non te perreche;* or *perroche;* later Ff *piaech.* Restituted by M. Edd. from Florio's Second Frutes) LLL IV, 2, 99. [Florio, Second Fruites (1592), p. 106: *Venetia, chi non ti vede non ti pretia; ma chi ti vede ben gli costa.* James Sandford, The Garden of Pleasure (1576), p. 217: *Venetia, chi non ti vede, non ti pretia.* Cf. Wolfg. Keller, Shakespeare-Jahrbuch XXXV, 263.]

Pistol's motto: *Si fortune me tormente, sperato me contente*, H4B II, 4, 195; or: *si fortuna me tormento, spera me contento*, V, 5, 102, is a medley of French and Italian, changed to pure Italian by some M. Edd., to pure French by others.

**5. French,** in the writing of the first Folio. Wiv. l, 4, 47: *unboyteene vert* (M. Edd. *un boitier vert*). 53: *mai foy, il fait fort chando, Je man voi a le Court la grand affaires* (M. Edd. *ma foi, il fait fort chaud. Je m'en vais à la cour — la grande affaire*). 57: *Ouy mette le au mon pocket, de-peech quickly* (M. Edd. *oui; mette le au mon pocket: depêche, quickly*). 65: *que ay ie oublie* (M. Edd. *qu'ai-je oublié*). 70: *O diable, diable.* II: *La-roone* (M. Edd. *larron*). III, 1, 93: *Diable!* 120: *sot.* V, 5, 73: *Hony Soit Qui Mal-y-Pence.* 218: *oon garsoon* (M. Edd. *un garçon*). *oon pesant* (un paysan).

LLL III, 71 etc.: *Lenuoy* (M. Edd. *l'envoy*). IV, 3, 383: *alone, alone* (M. Edd. *allons! allons!*) cf. V, 1, 159.

As I, 2, 104: *Boon-iour Monsieur le Beu* (M. Edd. *bon jour, Monsieur le Beau*).

All's II, 3, 50: *mor du vinager* (M. Edd. *mort du vinaigre*). III, 5, 37: *S. Iaques la grand* (M. Edd. *Saint Jaques le Grand*). [IV, 3, 311; V, 2, 35: *cardecue* (M. Edd. *quart d'*écu); cf. the resp. article.]

Tw. I, 3, 95: *pur-quoy* (M. Edd. *pourquoi*). III, 1, 78: *Dieu vou guard Monsieur. Et vouz ousie vostre serviture* (M. Edd. *dieu vous garde, monsieur. Et vous aussi; votre serviteur*).

John V, 2, 104: *Vive le Roy.*

R2 V, 3, 119: *Pardon'ne moy* (rhyming to *destroy*).

H4A II, 3, 74: *Esperance.*

H4B II, 4, 195: *si fortune me tormente, sperato me contente;* Pistol's French, italianated by most M. Edd. cf. V, 5, 102: *si fortuna me tormente, spera me contento.*

H5 II, 1, 75: *couple a gorge* (Pistol's speech). III, 4: *Alice, tu as este en Angleterre, et tu bien parlas le Language* (M. Edd. *Alice, tu as été en Angleterre, et tu parles bien le langage*). *En peu Madame* (un peu, Madame). *Ie te prie m'ensigniez, il faut que ie apprend a parlen: Comient appelle vous le main en Anglois?* (je te prie, m'enseignez; il faut que j'apprenne à parler. Comment appelez-vous la main en Anglais?). *Le main il et appelle de Hand* (la main? elle est appelée de hand). *E le doyts?* (et les doigts?). *Le doyts, ma foy Je oublie, e doyt mays, ie me souemeray le doyts ie pense qu'ils ont appelle de fingres, ou de fingres* (les doigts? ma foi, j'ai oublié les doigts, mais je me souviendrai. Les doigts? Je pense qu'ils sont appelés de fingres; oui, de fingres). *Le main de Hand, le doyts le Fingres, ie pense ie suis le bon escholier. I'ay gaynie diux mots d'Anglois vistement, coment appelle vous le ongles?* (la main de hand, les doigts de fingres. Je pense que

je suis le bon écolier; j'ai gagné deux mots d'Anglais vîtement. Comment appelez-vous les ongles?). *Le ongles, les appellons de Nayles* (les ongles? nous les appelons de nails). *De Nayles escoute: dites moy, si e parle bien: de Hand, de Fingres, e de Nayles* (de nails. Écoutez etc.). *C'est bien dict Madame, il et fort bon Anglois. Dites moy l'Anglois pour le bras. De Arme, Madame. E de coudee* (et le coude)? *D'Elbow. D'Elbow: Je men fay le repiticio de touts les mots que vous maves, apprins des a present* (je m'en fais la répétition de tous les mots que vous m'avez appris dès à présent). *Il et trop difficile Madame, comme Ie pense. Excuse moy Alice escoute, d'Hand, de Fingre, de Nayles, d'Arma, de Bilbow. D'Elbow, Madame. O Seigneur Dieu, ie men oublie d'Elbow, coment appelle vous le col. De Nick, Madame. De Nick, e le menton. De Chin. De Sin: le col de Nick, le menton de Sin. Oui. Sauf vostre honneur en verite vous pronouncies les mots ausi droict, que le Natifs d'Angleterre. Je ne doute point d'apprendre par de grace de Dieu, et en peu de temps. N'ave vos y desia oublie ce que ie vous a ensignie?* (n'avez-vous pas déjà oublié ce que je vous ai enseigné?). *Nome ie recitera a vous promptement, d'Hand, de Fingre, de Maylees. De Nayles, Madame. De Nayles, de Arme, de Ilbow. Sans vostre honeus d'Elbow. Ainsi de ie d'Elbow; de Nick, et de Sin: coment appelle vous les pied et de roba. Le Foot Madame, et le Count. Le Foot, et le Count: O Seigneur Dieu, il sont les mots de son mauvais corruptible grosse et impudique, et non pour le Dames de Honeur d'user. Ie ne voudray pronouncer ce mots devant le Seigneurs de France, pour toute le monde, fo le foot et le Count, neant moys, Ie recitera un autrefoys ma lecon ensemble, d'Hand, de Fingre, de Nayles, d'Arme, d'Elbow, de Nick, de Sin, de Foot, le Count. Excellent, Madame. C'est asses pour une foyes, alons nous a diner.*

H5 III, 5, 5: *O Dieu vivant.* 11: *Mort du ma vie.* 15: *Dieu de Battailes.* III, 7, 13: *ch'ha* (M. Edd. *ça! ha!*). 14: *le Cheval volante.* 15: *ches les narines de feu* (M. Edd. *qui a les* etc.). 68: *le chien est retourne a son proper vomissement est la leuye lavee au bourbier* (M. Edd. *le chien est retourné à son propre vomissement, et la truie lavée au bourbier*). [Quotation from the Geneva Bible (1588), 2 Peter, II, 22.] IV, 1, 35: *che vous la?* (M. Edd. *qui va là?*). 49: *Harry le Roy.* IV, 2, 2: *Monte Cheval: . . . Verlot Lacquay* (M. Edd. *montez à cheval, . . . valet! laquais!*). 4: *les ewes et terre* (M. Edd. *les eaux et la terre*). 5: *Rien puis le air et feu* (M. Edd. *rien puis? l'air et le feu*). 6: *Cein, Cousin Orleans* (M. Edd. *ciel! cousin Orléans*). IV, 4, 2: *Ie pense que vous estes le Gentilhome de bon qualitee.* 6: *O Seigneur Dieu.* 12: *O prennes misericordie aye pitez de moi* (O, prenez miséricorde! ayez pitié de moi). 17: *Est il impossible d'eschapper le force de ton br ʋs.* 22: *O perdonne moy.* 26: *Escoute comment estes vous appelle? Mounsieur le Fer.* 35: *Que dit il Mounsieur? Il me commande a vous dire que vous faite vous prest, car ce soldat icy est disposee tout asture de couppes vostre gorge* (est disposé tout à cette heure de couper votre gorge). 42: *O le vous supplie pour l'amour de Dieu: ma pardonner, Ie suis le Gentilhome de bon maison, garde ma vie, et Ie vous donneray deux cent escus.* 52: *Petit Monsieur que dit il? Encore qu'il et contra son Iurement, de pardonner aucune prisonner: neant-mons pour les escues que vous layt a promets, il est content a vous donnes le liberte le franchisement.*

57: *Sur mes genoux se vous donnes milles remercious, et Ie me estime heurex que Ie intombe, entre les main. d'un Chevalier Ie peuse le plus brave valiant et tres distinie signieur d'Angleterre* (Sur mes genoux je vous donne mille remercîments, et je m'estime heureux que je suis tombé entre les mains d'un chevalier, je pense, le plus brave, vaillant, et très distingué seigneur d'Angleterre). 70: *Saaue* (suivez) *le grand Capitaine.*

H5 IV, 5, 1: *O Diable. O signeur le iour et perdia, toute et perdie. Mor Dieu ma vie.* 5: *O meschante Fortune.*

H5 V, 2, 108: *pardonne moy.* 112: *que dit il que Ie suis semblable a les Anges? Ouy verayment, sauf vostre Grace, ainsi dit il.* 118: *O bon Dieu, les langues des hommes sont plein de tromperies.* 135: *sauf vostre honeur.* 191: *Ie quand sur le possession de Fraunce, et quand vous aves le possession de moi, ... donc vostre est Fraunce, et vous estes mienne.* 199: *Sauf vostre honeur, le Francois ques vous parleis, il et melieus que l'Anglois le quel Ie parle.* 230: *la plus belle Katherine du monde mon trescher et devin deesse.* 267: *de Roy mon pere.* 273: *Laisse mon Seigneur, laisse, laisse, may foy: Ie ne veus point que vous abbaisse vostre grandeus, en baisant le main d'une nostre Seigneur indignie seruiteur excuse moy. Ie vous supplie mon tres-puissant Seigneur.* 279: *Les Dames et Da-moisels pour estre baisee devant leur nopcese il net pas le costume de Fraunce.* 192: *ouy verayment.* 367: *Nostre trescher filz Henry Roy d'Angleterre Heretere de Fraunce.*

H6A III, 2, 13: *Che la. Peasauns la pouvre gens de Fraunce* (M. Edd. *Qui est là? Paysans, pauvres gens de France*).

H6B l, 1, 123: *Mort Dieu.* V, 2, 28: *La fin Corrone les eumenes* (M. Edd. *la fin couronne les oeuvres*).

Rom. II, 4, 46: *bon iour.*

**6. Irish.** In H5 IV, 4, 4 Pistol echoes the speech of his French prisoner with the words: *Qualtitie calmie custure me,* in which Malone and Boswell have thought to recognize the burden of an Irish song: *Calen O custure me,* i. e. little girl of my heart, for ever and ever. ["Boswell found the tune — — — including the words by Mr. Samuel Lover, in the Lyrics of Ireland (1858). The words are a corrupt, but more or less phonetic rendering of the Keltic *Caileno* (Irish-Gaelic *Cailin*) 'a little girl'; *ogh*, 'young' (whence *callino*), and *a stor mi*, 'my treasure, or 'little young girl, my treasure'." C. Mackay, Obscure Words.]

**7. Dutch**: *Lustique* (some M. Edd. *lustig*), *as the Dutchman says*, Alls II, 3, 46.

# IV. List of the words forming the latter part in compositions.

Abhor: All-abhorred.
Ability: disability.
Able: disable; unable.
About: hereabout; thereabout; whereabout. Hereabouts; thereabouts.
Absent: present-absent.
Absolver: sin-absolver.
Abuse: self-abuse.
Accessible: inaccessible.
Accommodate: unaccommodated.
Accompany: unaccompanied.
Accomplish: well-accomplished.
Accustomed: old-accustomed; unaccustomed.
Ace: ames-ace; deuce-ace.
Ache: bone-ache; heart-ache; tooth-ache; unaching.
Achieve: deed-achieving; half-achieved.
Acorn: full-acorned.
Acquaint: unacquainted; well-acquainted.
Act: coact; enact; unacted.
Active: coactive; unactive.
Actor: enactor.
Acture: enacture.
Add: new-added.
Addition: sur-addition.
Admire: all-admiring.
Admission: self-admission.
Adopt: new-adopted.
Advantage: disadvantage.
Adventure: misadventure; misadventured; peradventure.
Advise: fore-advised; unadvised; well-advised.
Affair: house-affairs; love-affairs; self-affairs; state-affairs.
Affect: self-affected.
Affright: self-affrighted.
After: hereafter; thereafter.
Against: whereagainst.
Age: nonage.
Aged: gentle-aged.
Agree: disagree.
Agreeable: unagreeable.
Aidible: inaidible.
Ale: bottle-ale; holy-ales.
All: be-all; end-all; withal.
Allow: disallow.
Alone: let-alone.
Already: fat-already.
Ambulate: preambulate.

Amel: enamel.
Amour: enamoured.
Anchor: holding-anchor.
Anele: unaneled.
Angel: she-angel.
Angle: quadrangle.
Angry: ever-angry.
Animate: disanimate.
Annex: ill-annexed.
Annul: disannul.
Anoint: true-anointed.
Answer: not answering; quick-answered; reanswer; simple-answered; unanswered.
Ape: dog-ape; Jackanapes.
Apparel: mean-apparelled; new-apparelled; well-apparelled.
Apparent: heir-apparent.
Appear: new-appearing.
Appearance: not-appearance.
Appease: unappeased.
Apply: misapply; self-applied.
Appoint: disappointed; well-appointed.
Approach: here-approach.
Approve: unapproved.
Apt: unapt.
Aptness: unaptness.
Arm: disarmed; short-armed; unarm; well-armed.
Arse: open-arse.
As: whenas; whereas.
Ask: unasked.
Asperate: exasperate.
Aspire: sky-aspiring.
Assail: unassailed.
Assailable: unassailable.
Assumption: self-assumption.
At: thereat; whereat.
Atlas: demi-Atlas.
Attaint: unattainted.
Attempt: unattempted.
Attend: sad-attending; unattended.
Audible: inaudible.
Auspicious: inauspicious; unauspicious.
Authorize: unauthorized.
Avoid: unavoided.
Aware: unaware and unawares.
Away: castaway; runaway.
Awe: overawe.
Axe: battle-axe; curtle-axe; pick-axe; pole-axe.
Babe: cradle-babe.

Baby: aglet-baby.
Back: bow-back; bunch-backed; crook-back; horseback; hunchbacked; unbacked. Goer-back; keeper-back.
Backward: goer-backward.
Badge: office-badge.
Bag: cloak-bag; honey-bag; money-bag.
Baily: bum-baily.
Bait: bear-baiting. Fine-baited.
Bake: unbaked.
Balance: weal-balanced.
Ball: emballing; eye-ball; foot-ball; pitch-ball; snow-ball; tennis-ball.
Balm: embalm.
Band: unbanded.
Bane: ratsbane.
Bank: mountebank; sea-bank.
Baptize: new-baptized.
Bar: buttery-bar; window-bar. Debar; imbar; strong-barred; ten-times-barred-up; unbar.
Barb: unbarbed.
Bare: threadbare.
Bark: embark; disembark.
Barrel: beer-barrel.
Base: abase; debase. Strong-based.
Bash: abashed.
Bashful: unbashful.
Basket: alms-basket; buck-basket.
Bate: breed-bate; debate; debatement. Abate; abatement; journey-bated; rebate; unbated.
Batter: unbattered.
Battle: embattle; high-battled.
Bawd: parcel-bawd.
Bay: embay.
Be: albeit; howbeit.
Beam: daughter-beamed; eye-beam; moonbeam; sunbeam; sunbeamed.
Bear: bugbear; forest-bear. Bull-bearing; forbear; just-borne; now-borne; o'erbear; over-bear; shard-borne; stiff-borne; underbear.
Beard: greybeard; lackbeard; scarce-bearded; white-bearded.
Bearer: ape-bearer; cup-bearer; purse-bearer; thunder-bearer; torch-bearer.
Beast: horn-beast.
Beat: bold-beating; dry-beat; ne'er-yet-beaten; new-beaten; o'erbeat; storm-beaten; weather-beaten.
Become: king-becoming; misbecome; unbecoming.
Bed: abed; bride-bed; childbed; day-bed; death-bed; down-bed; feather-bed; field-bed; lily-bed; love-bed; marriage-bed; slug-a-bed; standing-bed; truckle-bed; trundle-bed; wedding-bed.
Bedabble: dew-bedabbled.
Bee: honey-bee; humblebee.
Beef: bull beeves; ox-beef.
Beer: double-beer.
Befit: unbefitting.
Before: new-before.
Beg: fool-begged.
Beget: first-begotten; misbegot; misbegotten; new-begot; true-begotten; unbegot; unbegotten.
Beggar: she-beggar.
Begone: woe-begone.
Beguile: time-beguiling.
Behave: misbehaved; well-behaved.
Behold: sad-beholding.

Believe: hard-believing; misbelieving; soon-believing; unbelieved.
Believer: misbeliever.
Bell: alarum-bell; harebell; market-bell; passing-bell.
Belly: big-bellied; gorbellied; great-bellied; swag-bellied.
Beloved: dear-beloved; new-beloved; well-beloved.
Bemoan: fore-bemoaned.
Bench: church-bench; disbench.
Bent: new-bent; unbend; unbent.
Berry: bilberry; blackberry; dewberry; Dogberry; gooseberry; mulberry; strawberry.
Beseem: ill-beseeming; well-beseeming.
Besiege: strong-besieged.
Bespot: blood-bespotted.
Betray: fore-betrayed; late-betrayed.
Betroth: fair-betrothed; true-betrothed.
Better: time-bettering.
Between: broker-between; go-between; goer-between.
Bewail: unbewailed.
Bewaste: time-bewasted.
Bid: forbid; outbid; unbid; unbidden.
Bide: abide.
Bill: tavern-bill.
Bind: brow-bound; earth-bound; gold-bound; un-bind; unbound.
Bird: cuckoo-bird; lady-bird; night-bird; summer-bird; wood-bird.
Bishop: archbishop.
Bit: unbitted.
Bite: backbite; canker-bit; fly-bitten; sheep-biter; sheep-biting; weather-bitten.
Black: coal-black; hell-black.
Blade: shoulderblade.
Blank: pointblank.
Blast: star-blasting.
Blaze: emblaze.
Bleed: new-bleeding.
Bless: cursed-blest; special-blest; thrice-blest; unbless; unblest.
Blessing: marriage-blessing.
Blind: high-gravel-blind; hoodman-blind; purblind; sand-blind.
Block: stumbling-block.
Blood: half-blooded; heart-blood; hot-blooded; life-blood; 'sblood; sober-blooded.
Bloody: unbloodied.
Bloom: canker-bloom.
Blossom: canker-blossom; peas-blossom.
Blow: fly-blowing; fly-blown; half-blown; high-blown; o'erblow; overblown; unblowed, unblown.
Boar: wild-boar.
Board: aboard; council-board; cupboard; o'er-board, overboard; shipboard; shovel-board.
Boat: long-boat.
Bode: abode; abodement; death-boding; fairest-boding; false-boding; ill-boding.
Body: embody; loose-bodied; nobody, somebody; tender-bodied; unbodied.
Bold: overbold; sudden-bold.
Bolden: embolden.
Bolt: bird-bolt; dread-bolted; thunderbolt; unbolt; unbolted.
Boltered: blood-boltered.

Bond: strong-bonded.
Bone: barebone; bareboned; big-boned; burly-boned; jaw-bone; Pickbone; raw-boned; shoulder-bone.
Bonnet: unbonneted.
Book: absey-book; copy-book; horn-book; love-book; muster-book; note-book; prayerbook; table-book.
Bookish: unbookish.
Born: base-born; bawd-born; eldest-born; first-born; fool-born; forest-born; hag-born; hedge-born; hell-born; high-born; latter-born; low-born; mean-born; new-born; now-born; self-born; still-born; true-born; twin-born; unborn; well-born.
Borough: headborough; third-borough.
Borrow: easy-borrowed.
Bosom: unbosom.
Boss: embossed.
Bottle: blue-bottle; twiggen-bottle; wicker-bottle.
Bottom: sandy-bottomed.
Bound: embounded; unbounded. Rebound.
Bounty: self-bounty.
'Bout: about.
'Bove: above.
Bow: cross-bow; rainbow; saddle-bow; stone-bow; unbowed.
Bowel: embowel.
Bowl: standing-bowl.
Box: pepperbox; pouncetbox; tinderbox.
Boy: bow-boy; footboy; schoolboy; seaboy; ship-boy; tomboy.
Brace: unbraced.
Brag: outbrag.
Braid: unbraided. Upbraid.
Brain: clay-brained; deep-brained; dull-brained; fat-brained; hare-brained; lackbrain; mad-brain; mad-brained; Ticklebrain.
Branch: disbranch; top-branch.
Brand: firebrand.
Brave: air-braving; outbrave.
Brawler: night-brawler.
Breach: before-breach; faith-breach; promise-breach.
Bread: ginger-bread; pepper-gingerbread.
Breadth: hair-breadth.
Break: date-broken; heart-break; heart-breaking; oath-breaking; outbreak; rib-breaking; unbroke.
Breaker: horseback-breaker; law-breaker; promise-breaker.
Breast: abreast; marble-breasted; redbreast; Robin-redbreast.
Breath and breathe: lust-breathed; mortal-breathing; outbreathed; rebreathe; self-breath; treble-breathed; unbreathed; well-breathed.
Breech: Patch-breech; unbreeched.
Breed: bate-breeding; heaven-bred; home-bred; ill-breeding; mad-bred; soldier-breeder; still-breeding; true-bred; unbred.
Bridge: drawbridge; London-bridge.
Bridle: unbridle; unbridled.
Bright: silver-bright; sun-bright.
Broach: abroach.
Broad: abroad.
Broider: embroider.
Broker: love-broker.
Brook: fresh-brook; ice-brook. Abrook.
Broth: barley-broth; hell-broth; snow-broth.
Brother: twin-brother.

Brow: baby-brow; beetle-brows; black-browed; eyebrow.
Bruise: unbruised.
Buckle: unbuckle.
Buckler: swinge-buckler; sword-and-buckler.
Bud: cuckoo-bud; hawthorn-bud; Mary-bud.
Build: all-building; new-built; rich-built; unbuild; weak-built.
Bulk: overbulk.
Bullet: cannon-bullet.
Burden: disburden; unburden.
Burly: hurlyburly.
Burn: bright-burning; ever-burning; furnace-burning; heart-burned; heart-burning; hot-burning; new-burned; outburn; sun-burning; sun-burnt; unburnt.
Burse: disburse.
Bury: unburied.
Bush: hawthorn-bush; thorn-bush.
Buss: ear-bussing.
Butt: malmsey-butt. Abut.
Butter: salt-butter.
Buttock: pin-buttock; quatch-buttock.
Button: crystal-button; unbutton; unbuttoned.
Buy: dear-bought; overbuy.
By: aby. Hereby; stander-by; thereby; whereby.
Cage: incaged.
Cake: oatcake; Shortcake; wafer-cake.
Calf: bull-calf; moon-calf.
Call: miscall; recall; what-ye-call-it.
Camp: encamp.
Can: half-can.
Candle: rush-candle.
Candy: discandy; sugar-candy.
Cannon: demi-cannon.
Canopy: overcanopied.
Cantation: incantation; recantation.
Cap: blue-cap; cloud-capped; corner-cap; half-cap; madcap; night-cap; off-cap; sea-cap; statute-cap.
Capable: incapable; uncapable.
Cape: uncape.
Card: discard.
Cardinal: count-cardinal; king-cardinal.
Careful: overcareful.
Carnal: incarnal.
Carnardine: incarnardine.
Carnation: incarnation (incarnate).
Carrack: land-carrack.
Carrier: ring-carrier.
Carry: miscarry.
Case: bow-case; candle-case; discase; lute-case; uncase; watch-case.
Cast: forecast; o'ercast; outcast; overcast; rough-cast; upcast.
Caster: counter-caster.
Cat: gib-cat; musk-cat; polecat; wildcat.
Catch: coney-catch; uncaught. Tallow-catch.
Catcher: gull-catcher; rat-catcher.
Cause: because; love-cause.
Cave: concave; encave.
Cease: surcease.
Cern: concern.
Certain: incertain; uncertain.
Certainly: uncertainly.
Certainty: incertainty; uncertainty.
Cess: incessant.

Chafe: angry-chafing; enchafe.
Chain: enchain; interchain; unchain.
Chamber: bedchamber; dining-chamber; Star-chamber.
Chance: bechance; mischance; perchance.
Change: all-changing-word; child-changed; counterchange; exchange; interchange: ne'er-changing; sea-change; shallow-changing; unchanging; wind-changing.
Changer: purpose-changer.
Chant: enchant.
Chap: wide-chapped.
Charge: discharge; double-charge; full-charged; o'ercharge; overcharge; uncharge; uncharged.
Charitable: incharitable; uncharitably.
Charity: self-charity.
Charm: uncharmed.
Chary: unchary.
Chase: enchase.
Chaste: stubborn-chaste; unchaste.
Check: countercheck; half-checked; unchecked.
Cheek: half-cheek; rose-cheeked.
Cheer: wedding-cheer; whipping-cheer. All-cheering.
Cheerful: uncheerful.
Chick: March-chick.
Child: birth-child; grandchild; maid-child; man-child; unchild.
Chipper: bread-chipper.
Choose: well-chosen.
Christen: new-christened.
Christian: even-Christian.
Cipher: decipher.
Circle: encircle; semicircle; semicircled.
Cite: accite; excite; fore-recited; incite; recite.
Civil: incivil; uncivil.
Civility: incivility.
Clad: yclad.
Claim: disclaim; exclaim; proclaim; reclaim; unclaimed.
Clangor: trumpet-clangor.
Clap: shoulder-clapper; thunder-clap.
Clasp: unclasp.
Claw: clapper-claw.
Clean etc.: unclean; uncleanliness; uncleanly; uncleanness.
Cleave: oak-cleaving.
Clepe: ycleped.
Climber: canvas-climber.
Clip: inclip; pole-clipt.
Clog: enclog; unclog.
Close: disclose; enclose; fast-closed; still-closing.
Cloth: bearing-cloth; cerecloth; footcloth; sackcloth.
Clothes: bedclothes; cradle-clothes.
Cloud: enclouded.
Clout: dishclout; swaddling-clouts.
Cloy: never-cloying; o'ercloyed.
Clue: unclue.
Coal: sea-coal.
Coat: grey-coated; leather-coats; party-coated; petticoat; silken-coated; skin-coat; turncoat.
Cock: bawcock; meacock; peacock; Pelicock (?); turkey-cock; weathercock; woodcock.
Cod: peascod.
Coffin: custard-coffin.
Cognizance: recognizance.
Coin: cleanly-coined; uncoined.

Cold: a-cold; key-cold; scarce-cold; sour-cold.
Collect: recollect.
Colour: amber-coloured; Cain-coloured; discolour; divers-coloured; ebon-coloured; flame-coloured; freestone-coloured; high-coloured; many-coloured; party-coloured; peach-coloured; purple-coloured; raven-coloured; ruby-coloured; sable-coloured; straw-colour; water-colour; whey-coloured.
Colt: uncolted.
Comb: coxcomb; honey-comb.
Come: forthcoming; income; new-come; noncome; o'ercome; overcome; thick-coming; welcome.
Comeliness: uncomeliness.
Comfit: discomfit; recomfiture; kissing-comfits.
Comfort: discomfort; recomforture; widow-comfort.
Comfortable: discomfortable; uncomfortable.
Commend: discommend; recommend.
Commit: new-committed.
Communicate: excommunicate; excommunication.
Company: accompany.
Comparable: incomparable.
Comparison: self-comparison.
Compass: encompass.
Compassionate: uncompassionate.
Compense: recompense.
Complain: sweet-complaining.
Complexion: swart-complexioned.
Complice: accomplice.
Complish: accomplish; accomplishment.
Compose: ill-composed.
Compound: foolish-compounded.
Comprehensible: incomprehensible.
Comprehensive: uncomprehensive.
Compt: accompt.
Conceal: sin-concealing.
Conceit: liberal-conceited; odd-conceited.
Conceive: first-conceived; misconceived; new-conceived; quick-conceiving; sin-conceiving.
Conciliation: reconciliation.
Conclude: vile-concluded.
Condition: best-conditioned.
Conduct: safe-conduct.
Conduit: pissing-conduit.
Confinable: unconfinable.
Confirm: soul-confirming; true-confirmed; unconfirmed.
Conquer: half-conquered; never-conquered; unconquered.
Conscience: soft-conscienced.
Consider: unconsidered.
Considerate: inconsiderate.
Consolate: disconsolate.
Constancy: inconstancy.
Constant: inconstant; marble-constant; unconstant.
Constrain: unconstrained.
Construction: misconstruction.
Construe: misconstrue.
Consume: blood-consuming; sap-consuming.
Contemn: uncontemned.
Contemplative: deep-contemplative.
Contempt: court-contempt.
Contend: skill-contending.
Content: discontent; malcontent.
Contented: discontented; well-contented.
Continency: incontinency.

Continent: incontinent.
Continue: discontinue; long-continued.
Contract: precontract; sub-contracted.
Control: uncontrolled.
Convenience: inconvenience.
Convenient: inconvenient.
Cool: overcool.
Corn: peppercorn.
Corner: black-cornered; park-corner; Pie-corner.
Corporal: incorporal.
Corporate: incorporate.
Corpse: incorpsed.
Correct: incorrect; uncorrected.
Cote: dovecote; sheepcote.
Council: chamber-council.
Count: account; o'ercount; recount; uncounted. Viscount.
Counter: encounter, encounterer; hunt-counter; span-counter.
Counterfeit: death-counterfeiting.
Couple: uncouple.
Courage: encourage.
Courier: vaunt-courier.
Course: discourse; main-course; recourse.
Court: tennis-court.
Courteous: uncourteous.
Courtesy: discourtesy; kill-courtesy.
Cousin: cater-cousins.
Cover: discover; o'ercover; re-cover; self-covered; uncover; uncovered.
Cracker: wit-cracker.
Craft: handicraft; witchcraft.
Crafty: outcrafty.
Cram: news-crammed; promise-crammed.
Crants: Rosencrantz.
Craze: care-crazed.
Create: miscreate; new-create; part-created; pro-creant; procreation; recreate; recreation.
Creature: serving-creature.
Credible: incredible.
Credit: discredit.
Credulous: incredulous; over-credulous.
Creep: false-creeping.
Crest: undercrest.
Crier: town-crier.
Crimson: encrimsoned.
Crook: knee-crooking; low-crooked.
Crop: uncropped.
Cross: across; Charing-cross; high-cross; market-cross; star-crossed; uncrossed.
Crow: night-crow; o'ercrow; scarecrow.
Crown: new-crowned; thrice-crowned; uncrown.
Cruel: holy-cruel.
Cry: hue and cry; outcry.
Cuckold: uncuckolded.
Cumber: encumber.
Cup: sneak-cup.
Cupboard: court-cupboard.
Cur: village-cur.
Curable: incurable; uncurable.
Curb: uncurbed.
Curbable: uncurbable.
Cure: past-cure; recure.
Curer: body-curer; soul-curer.
Curl: uncurl.
Current: uncurrent.

Curse: accursed; uncurse.
Customed: accustomed.
Cut: new-cut-off.
Cutter: stone-cutter.
Dabble: bedabble; dew-bedabbled.
Dainty: super-dainty.
Damage: endamage.
Dame: beldame; stepdame.
Damn: condemn; double-damned; drug-damned; land-damn.
Dance: morris-dance.
Danger: endanger; self-danger.
Dangerous: honourable-dangerous.
Dare: outdare; overdaring.
Dart: death-darting; endart; thunder-darter.
Dash: bedash.
Date: new-dated; treble-dated.
Daub: bedaub.
Daughter: baby-daughter; god-daughter.
Daunt: never-daunted; undaunted.
Day: all-souls'-day; ascension-day; Ash-Wednes-day; birthday; chair-days; dog-days; doomsday; fasting-day; Friday; good-Friday; heyday; high-day; holiday; hoyday; judgment-day; law-day; love-day; market-day; marriage-day; May-day; midday; Monday; noonday; nowadays; playing-day; Saturday; schoolday; sealing-day; Shrove-Tuesday; summer-day; Sunday; Thursday; trial-day; Tuesday; wedding-day; Wednesday; well-a-day; working-day; worky-day; yesterday.
Dazzle: bedazzle.
Deacon: archdeacon.
Dead: living-dead; pale-dead.
Deadly: imminent-deadly.
Deaf: undeaf.
Deafen: ear-deafening.
Deal: double-dealing; plain-dealing; well-dealing.
Dealer: double-dealer; plain-dealer.
Dear: endear; heart-dear; precious-dear.
Death: 'sdeath.
Debt: after-debt; indebted.
Decease: late-deceased; predecease.
Deck: bedeck; undeck.
Decline: low-declined.
Deed: alms-deed; good-deed; indeed; misdeed; un-deeded.
Deem: misdeem.
Deep: breast-deep; knee-deep; pottle-deep.
Defend: well-defended.
Deign: disdain.
Delicate: moving-delicate.
Deliver: ditch-delivered; new-delivered; re-deliver.
Delve: earth-delving.
Demean: misdemean.
Demeanour: misdemeanour.
Den: digyouden; godgigoden; goodden.
Dent: indent.
Dependance: by-dependance.
Derive: false-derived; true-derived; well-derived.
Descend: condescend.
Descry: undescried.
Deserve: undeserved; undeserving; well-deserving.
Deserver: undeserver.
Desire: well-desired.
Desperate: shameless-desperate.
Destinate: predestinate.

Determine: undetermined.
Devil: demi-devil; yoke-devil.
Devise: new-devised; point-devise.
Devote: true-devoted.
Devour: love-devouring.
Dew: bedew; field-dew; honey-dew; mildew.
Diction: benediction; jurisdiction; malediction.
Die: never-dying; tender-dying.
Diet: lust-dieted.
Differency: indifferency.
Different: indifferent; indifferently.
Digest: indigest.
Dignity: indignity.
Dim: bedim.
Dinner: after-dinner.
Dint: undinted.
Direct, directly, direction: indirect etc.
Discernible: undiscernible.
Discordant: still-discordant.
Discourse: love-discourse.
Discoursive: dumb-discoursive.
Discover: undiscovered.
Discreet, discretion: indiscreet etc.
Disgrace: all-disgraced.
Dish: clackdish; fruit-dish; tundish.
Dishonour: undishonoured.
Disperse: ill-dispersing.
Dispose: ill-disposed; indisposed; true-disposing; undisposed; well-disposed.
Disposition: indisposition.
Dissoluble: indissoluble.
Distain: tear-distained:
Distant: comely-distant.
Distinguish: indistinguished; undistinguished.
Distinguishable: indistinguishable; undistinguishable.
Distinct: indistinct.
Disturb: late-disturbed.
Ditch: castle-ditch; Moorditch.
Dividable: individable; undividable.
Divide: undivided.
Divine: death-divining; ill-divining; true-divining.
Divorce: deep-divorcing.
Divulge: undivulged.
Do: ado; fordo; harm-doing; ill-doing; o'erdo; outdo; overdone; self-doing; undo; undoing; undone; well-doing.
Dock: bur-dock.
Dog: ban-dog; ditch-dog; jack-dog; night-dog; puppy-dog; watch-dog.
Dolour: widow-dolour.
Dominant, dominate: predominance, predominant, predominate.
Doom: foredoomed.
Door: adoor, adoors; back-door; behind-door-work; chamber-door; garden-door; hold-door; in-a-door; without-door.
Dote: a-doting.
Double: redouble; thrice-double.
Doublet: belly-doublet.
Doubt: misdoubt; redoubt; undoubted.
Doubtful: undoubtful.
Dove: turtle-dove.
Dower: wedding-dower.
Down: adown; Keepdown; plucker-down; puller-down; steep-down.

Dowry: marriage-dowry.
Dragon: flap-dragon.
Drake: firedrake.
Draw: air-drawn; bias-drawing; choice-drawn; cub-drawn; deep-drawing; dove-drawn; right-drawn; self-drawing; vile-drawing; withdraw.
Drawer: tooth-drawer.
Dread: all-dreaded; misdread.
Dream: dismal-dreaming; John-a-dreams; undreamed.
Drench: bedrench; deep-drenched; horse-drench; indrenched.
Dress: address; redress; undress; undressed.
Drink: alms-drink; blood-drinking; by-drinkings; swine-drunk.
Drive: thrice-driven.
Drop: dewdrop; dew-dropping; eyedrop; honey-drop; tempest-dropping; waterdrop.
Dropper: eavesdropper.
Drown: undrowned.
Drum: kettle-drum.
Dry: oil-dried.
Dubitate: indubitate.
Duck: wild-duck.
Due: indue.
Dull: pale-dull.
Dung: cow-dung.
Durance: endurance; indurance.
Dure: endure; ever-during; long-during.
Dust: o'erdusted.
Duteous, dutiful: unduteous etc.
Dwarf: giant-dwarf.
Dwell: outdwell.
Dye: new-dyed; o'erdyed.
Ear: crop-ear; flap-eared; prick-eared; shag-eared. Uneared.
Earn: unearned.
Earnest: over-earnest.
Earthly: unearthly.
Ease: disease; heart-easing; heart's-ease.
Easiness: uneasiness.
East: north-east; north-north-east.
Easy: uneasy.
Eat: all-eating; marrow-eating; mouse-eaten; o'er-eaten; worm-eaten.
Eater: garlic-eater; pork-eater.
Eath: uneath.
Eaves: house-eaves.
Eclipse: cloud-eclipsed.
Edge: disedge; keen-edged.
Edify: re-edify.
Educate: uneducated; well-educated.
Effectual: uneffectual.
Egg: finch-egg; pigeon-egg.
Ele: anele.
Elect: unelected.
Embark: disembark; late-embarked.
Embrace: rash-embraced.
Embroider: rich-embroidered.
Eminence: preeminence.
Employ: pre-employ.
End: all-ending; an-end; butt-end; finger-end; fore-end; lag-end; never-ending; noble-ending; world-without-end.
Endear: self-endeared.
Enemy: arch-enemy.

Enforce: reinforce.
Engender: high-engendered.
Engraff: long-engraffed.
Enkindle: new-enkindled.
Enlarge: wide-enlarged.
Enquiry: after-enquiry.
Enter: man-entered.
Equal: coequal; unequal.
Equality: inequality.
Ere: while-ere.
Erect: ill-erected.
Errant: knight-errant; she-knight-errant.
Esteem: best-esteemed; ever-esteemed.
Estimable: inestimable.
Eve: ember-eaves; Lammas-eve.
Even: odd-even; uneven.
Ever: however, soever, whatever etc.
Evil: beauteous-evil.
Evitable: inevitable.
Examine: unexamined.
Example: self-example.
Execrable: inexecrable.
Execute: thought-executing; unexecuted.
Exorable: inexorable.
Expect: unexpected.
Expel: sun-expelling.
Experienced: long-experienced; unexperienced.
Experient: unexperient.
Explicable: inexplicable.
Explication: self-explication.
Expressive: unexpressive.
Eye: after-eye; blue-eyed; dark-eyed; dizzy-eyed; dull-eyed; evil-eyed; fire-eyed; green-eyed; grey-eyed; hollow-eyed; o'ereye; onion-eyed; open-eyed; overeye; sad-eyed; sour-eyed; thick-eyed; wall-eyed; young-eyed.
Face: barefaced; blackfaced; bloody-faced; bold-faced; boneface; brazen-face; brazen-faced; cream-faced; deface; defacer; fair-faced; false-faced; foul-faced; glass-faced; good-faced; half-face; half-faced; ill-faced; lean-faced; old-faced; outface; pale-faced; paper-faced; red-faced; sad-faced; shame-faced; smooth-faced; sour-faced; sweet-faced; tallow-face; thin-faced; whey-face; white-faced.
Fair: thrice-fair; unfair.
Fairy: meadow-fairies.
Faithful: unfaithful.
Fall: befall; chap-fallen; crest-fallen; downfall; down-fallen; fast-falling; folly-fallen; footfall; new-fallen; pit-fall; sick-fallen; tear-falling; trade-fallen.
Fallible: infallible; infallibly; unfallible.
False: proper-false; secret-false.
Fame: defame; thrice-famed; unfamed; well-famed.
Famous: infamous.
Fane: profane.
Fangled: new-fangled.
Far: afar; overfar.
Fare: throughfare; welfare; sea-farer; sea-faring.
Farm: fee-farm.
Farthing: three-farthings.
Fashionable: unfashionable.
Fast: handfast; holdfast; steadfast. Breakfast; tub-fast.
Fasten: unfasten.
Fatal: double-fatal.

Father: forefather; godfather; grandfather; great-grandfather; uncle-father; unfathered.
Fault: default; find-fault.
Favour: hard-favoured; ill-favoured; well-favoured.
Fawn: spaniel-fawning.
Fear: afeard; begger-fear; not-fearing; soul-fearing.
Feast: marriage-feast; sheep-shearing-feast.
Feat: love-feat.
Feather: dove-feathered; down-feather.
Feature: defeature.
Fee: unfee'd.
Feeble: enfeeble.
Feed: bacon-fed; bean-fed; full-fed; o'erfed; unfed.
Feel: tender-feeling; unfeeling; unfelt.
Feign: unfeigned.
Fellow: bedfellow; coach-fellow; Goodfellow; pew-fellow; play-fellow; schoolfellow; unfellowed; vow-fellow; yoke-fellow.
Fence: unfenced.
Fend: defend; forefend; weather-fend.
Feoff: enfeoff.
Fet: deep-fet; far-fet.
Fetter: enfetter.
Field: a-field; corn-field; summer-field.
Fight: sea-fight; unfought; well-foughten.
Figure: disfigure; prefigure; refigure; self-figured; transfigure.
File: muster-file. Defile.
Filial: unfilial.
Fill: fulfil; mouth-filling; unfilled; upfill.
Fin: tawny-finned.
Find: feast-finding; new-found; well-found.
Finder: hare-finder.
Fine: define. Refined.
Finger: five-finger-tied; forefinger.
Finical: superfinical.
Finish: unfinished.
Finite: infinite.
Fire: afire; bonfire; cannon-fire; ever-fired; hell-fire; new-fired; trial-fire; wildfire.
Firm: affirm; confirm; infirm; unfirm.
Fish: dogfish; fresh-fish; land-fish; stockfish.
Fit: befit; unfit. Ague-fit.
Fitness: unfitness.
Fix: confixed; ever-fixed; infix; prefix; strong-fixed; transfix; true-fixed; unfix.
Flame: inflame.
Flash: lightning-flash.
Flaw: honour-flawed.
Fledged: unfledged.
Float: afloat.
Flourish: o'erflourish.
Flow: full-flowing; o'erflow; overflow; water-flowing.
Flower: crow-flower; cuckoo-flower; deflower.
Flux: superflux.
Fly: outfly; overfly. Butterfly; carrion-fly; flesh-fly; night-fly; summerfly; waterfly.
Foal: filly-foal.
Foe: night-foe.
Fog: south-fog.
Fold: bi-fold; fifty-fold; five-fold; manifold; nine-fold; seven-fold; tenfold; thousand-fold; threefold; twofold. Blindfold; infold; infoldings; unfold. Pinfold.
Folk: gentle-folks; market-folks.
Fond: overfond; peevish-fond.

Fool: unfool.

Foolish: childish-foolish.

Foot: afoot; barefoot; dryfoot; fiery-footed; fleet-foot; forefoot; free-footed; hasty-footed; high-foot; mountain-foot; nimble-footed; 'sfoot; swift-footed; three-foot; tiger-footed; underfoot.

For: hoped-for; longed-for; sued-for; unlooked-for; unpaid-for; therefore; wherefore.

Force: enforce; perforce; reinforce; unforced.

Fore: afore; aforehand; aforesaid; before; tofore.

Foreigner: mountain-foreigner.

Forfeit: unforfeited.

Form: deform; inform; new-form; perform; platform; preformed; reform; transform.

Formal: informal.

Formation: information; reformation; transformation.

Forsooth: yea-forsooth.

Forth: bringing-forth; henceforth; so-forth.

Fortify: unfortified.

Fortunate: infortunate; unfortunate.

Fortune: befortune; full-fortuned; misfortune.

Forward: henceforward.

Fountain: valley-fountain.

Fowl: bat-fowling; wild-fowl.

Fox: dog-fox; kid-fox; she-fox.

Frame: strong-framed.

Franchise: enfranchise.

Fraught: full-fraught; o'erfraught.

Fray: afraid; affray.

Free: enfree; fancy-free; shot-free.

Freedom: enfreedom.

Frequent: unfrequented.

Fresh: afresh; fertile-fresh; refresh.

Friar: Blackfriars; Whitefriars.

Friday: good-friday.

Friend: back-friend; mouth-friend; trencher-friend. Befriend; unfriended.

Friendly: unfriendly.

Fright: affright.

Frog: leap-frog.

From: falling-from.

Front: affront; afront; broad-fronted; confront.

Frown: outfrown.

Fruit: first-fruits.

Fruitful: unfruitful.

Full: belly-ful; bookful; brimful; handful; mouthful; pailful; topful.

Baleful, awful, barful, bashful, beautiful, blameful, boastful, bountiful, careful, changeful, chargeful, cheerful, crimeful, dareful, deathful, delightful, despiteful, direful, disdainful, disgraceful, distasteful, distressful, distrustful, doleful, doubtful, dreadful, dutiful, easeful, eventful, faithful, faultful, fearful, fitful, forceful, forgetful, fraudful, fretful, frightful, fruitful, gleeful, graceful, grateful, guileful, harmful, hateful, healthful, heedful, helpful, hopeful, increaseful, ingrateful, ireful, joyful, lawful, lustful, manfully, merciful, mightful, mindful, mirthful, mistful, mistrustful, mournful, needful, offenceful, over-careful, overfull, painful, peaceful, pitiful, plaintful, plentiful, powerful, praiseful, preyful, regardfully, remorseful, reproachful, restful, revengeful, rightful, ruthful, scathful, scornful, shameful, sinful, skilful, slothful, sorrowful, spiteful, spleenful, sportful, sprightful, successful, tearful, thankful, thoughtful, tristful, trustful, un-bashful, uncheerful, undoubtful, undutiful, unfaithful, unfruitful, ungrateful, unheedful, unhelpful, unhopeful, unhurtful, unlawful, unmerciful, unmindful, unpitifully, unrightful, unskilful, unthankful, useful, vailful, vengeful, wailful, wasteful, watchful, wilful, wishful, woeful, wonderful, worshipful, wrackful, wrathful, wreakful, wrongful, youthful.

Fume: perfume.

Function: defunction.

Furnish: disfurnish; unfurnish.

Gage: engage; ingaged; mortgage.

Gain: ungained.

Gait: heavy-gaited; slow-gaited; tardy-gaited.

Gall: o'ergalled; spur-galled; ungalled. Watergall; windgall.

Gallant: top-gallant.

Gaol: engaol.

Gape: earnest-gaping.

Garden: Paris-garden; Temple-garden.

Garment: wedding-garment.

Garnet: pomgarnet.

Garter: caddis-garter; cross-gartered; cross-gartering; ungartered.

Gate: abbey-gate; city-gate; Counter-gate; court-gate; floodgate; hell-gate; Newgate; Northgate; palace-gate; park-gate; six-gated. Othergates; runagate.

Gather: altogether; together.

Gawd: nicely-gawded.

Gay: nosegay.

Gaze: agazed; glass-gazing; steadfast-gazing; still-gazing.

Gazer: star-gazer.

Gender: engender.

General: captain-general.

Generate: regenerate.

Genitive: primogenitive.

Geniture: ungenitured.

Gentle: ever-gentle; thrice-gentle; ungentle.

Gentleness: ungentleness.

Gentlewoman: waiting-gentlewoman.

Gently: ungently.

German: cousin-german. Cozen-German.

Get: beget; forget; ill-got; ungot; ungotten.

Gift: nothing-gift.

Gig: whirligig.

Gild: engild; parcel-gilt.

Gill: flirt-gill.

Gin: begin.

Gird and girt: ungird; engirt.

Give: forgive; gain-giving; health-giving; honour-giving; misgive; thanksgiving.

Giver: direction-giver; lie-giver.

Glance: o'erglance, overglance.

Glass: burning-glass; eye-glass; hour-glass; looking-glass.

Glorious: inglorious; self-glorious.

Glory: vain-glory.

Glut: englut.

Gnaw: bare-gnawn; begnaw.

Go: ago; agone; begone; by-gone; forego; hence-going; o'ergo; outgo; overgo; undergo.

Goat: mountain-goat.

Goblin: hobgoblin.

God: demigod; love-god.

Godly: ungodly.

Goer: foregoers.

Gold: marigold.

Good: agood; curious-good; first-good.

Goose: wild-goose.

Gore: ungored.

Gorge: disgorge; full-gorged; overgorge; shrill-gorged.

Gorgeous: thrice-gorgeous.

Govern: hell-governed; misgoverned; misgoverning; ungoverned; well-governed.

Government: misgovernment.

Gown: night-gown; sea-gown.

Grace: disgrace; herb-grace; well-graced.

Graceful: disgraceful.

Gracious: disgracious; self-gracious; thrice-gracious; ungracious.

Graff and graft: engraffed; engraft; ingraft; long-engraffed; long-engrafted; misgraffed.

Grain: purple-in-grain.

Granate: pomegranate.

Grandfather and grandsire: great-gr.

Grass: bottom-grass; knot-grass; short-grassed; spear-grass.

Grateful: ingrateful; ungrateful.

Gratitude: ingratitude.

Gratulate: congratulate.

Grave: engrave.

Gravely: ungravely.

Great: o'ergreat.

Gree: agree; congree.

Greedy: overgreedy.

Green: deep-green; grass-green; o'ergreen.

Greet: congreet; regreet.

Grief: aggrieved; fee-grief; heart-grief.

Grime: begrime.

Grin: grim-grinning.

Grind: sharp-ground.

Gripe: guts-griping.

Groat: shove-groat.

Groom: bridegroom.

Gross: engross.

Ground: aground; underground; winter-ground.

Grove: broom-grove; line-grove.

Grow: fast-growing; great-grown; high-grown; long-grown; moss-grown; o'ergrow; outgrow; overgrown; rough-grown; rude-growing; thick-grown; ungrown.

Growth: o'ergrowth.

Guard: enguard; safeguard; unguarded; velvet-guards.

Guerdon: reguerdon.

Guide: misguide; unguided.

Guile: beguile.

Guise: disguise; disguiser.

Gunner: master-gunner.

Guts: calves-guts; fat-guts.

Gyve: down-gyved.

Habit: dishabit; inhabit; inhabitant.

Habitable: inhabitable.

Hack: unhacked.

Hackney: common-hackneyed.

Hail: all-hail.

Hair: horse-hair; shag-haired; unhair.

Hale: exhale; new-haled.

Hall: Guildhall; Katehall; Temple-hall; Whitehall.

Hallow: All-hallond-eve; All-hallowmas; All-hallown; unhallowed.

Halt. spring-halt.

Hand: beforehand; bow-hand; court-hand; deadly-handed; dial-hand; doughty-handed; even-handed; forehand; hand-in-hand; hard-handed; large-handed; right-hand; sleeve-hand; two-hand; underhand; unhand; white-handed.

Handle: overhandled; unhandled.

Handsome: unhandsome.

Hang: bed-hangings; chamber-hanging; heavy-hanging; o'erhang; unhanged.

Hangman: underhangman.

Hap: mishap; perhaps.

Happiness: unhappiness.

Happy: overhappy; unhappied; unhappily; unhappy.

Hard: rocky-hard; stone-hard; stubborn-hard.

Harden: heart-hardening; unhardened.

Hardiness: fool-hardiness.

Hardy: daring-hardy; fool-hardy.

Harm: life-harming; self-harming; unharmed.

Harmless: ever-harmless.

Harness: heavenly-harnessed.

Hart: White-hart.

Haste: post-haste; post-post-haste.

Hasty: o'erhasty.

Hatch: new-hatched; unhatched.

Hate: hell-hated; rival-hating.

Haunt: temple-haunting.

Have: behave; more-having.

Haviour: behaviour.

Haven: Milford-haven.

Head: ass-head; bare-headed; beetle-headed; behead; blockhead; cittern-head; deaths-head; fool's-head; forehead; heavy-headed; hoary-headed; hogshead; Hydra-headed; idle-headed; ill-headed; jolt-head; loggerhead; loggerheaded; mad-headed; many-headed; overhead; oxhead; puppy-headed; rowel-head; rug-headed; sleek-headed; three-headed; two-headed; waspish-headed.

Heal: new-healed.

Hear: mishear; never-heard-of; o'erhear; overhear; unheard.

Hearse: inhearse. Rehearse.

Heart: cruel-hearted; dishearten; dog-hearted; empty-hearted; faint-hearted; false-heart; false-hearted; flint hearted; free-hearted; full-hearted; gentle-hearted; hard-hearted; hollow-hearted; honest-hearted; kind-hearted; marble-hearted; pale-hearted; pitiful-hearted; proud-hearted; sad-hearted; shallow-hearted; soft-hearted; stony-hearted; sweetheart; tender-hearted; treble-hearted; true-hearted; truer-hearted; unheart; weak-hearted.

Heave: upheave.

Heaviness: heart-heaviness.

Heavy: honey-heavy.

Heedful: unheedful.

Heedy: unheedy.

Heel: lighter-heeled.

Heft: tender-hefted.

Heir: co-heir.

Helpful: unhelpful.

Hemp: crack-hemp.

Hen: double-henned; guinea-hen.

Hence: sithence.

Herb: nose-herb.

**Herd:** bearherd; neat-herd; shepherd; shepherdess; swine-herd.
**Heretic:** arch-heretic.
**Herod:** out-herod.
**Herring:** pickle-herring.
**Hest:** behest.
**Hew:** rough-hew.
**Hide:** all-hiding; long-hid; unhidden.
**High:** Olympus-high.
**Hill:** dunghill; molehill; Towerhill.
**Hilt:** basket-hilt; sword-hilts.
**Him:** have-at-him.
**Hind:** behind.
**Hinge:** weak-hinged.
**Hip:** red-hipped.
**Hive:** beehive.
**Hoard:** uphoard.
**Hog:** hang-hog; hedgehog.
**Hold:** ahold; behold; easy-held; household; over-hold; uphold; withhold.
**Holder:** candle-holder; house-holder.
**Hole:** auger-hole; bench-hole; bung-hole; button-hole; dog-hole; keyhole; kiln-hole; loop-hole; sight-hole; starting-hole; worm-hole.
**Holy:** devilish-holy; unholy.
**Home:** harvest-home.
**Honest:** dishonest; underhonest.
**Honestly:** dishonestly.
**Honesty:** dishonesty.
**Honour:** all-honoured; dishonour; mouth-honour; time-honoured.
**Honourable:** dishonourable.
**Hoof:** round-hoofed.
**Hook:** nuthook; sheep-hook.
**Hoop:** cock-a-hoop; inhoop; three-hooped.
**Hope:** unhoped.
**Hopeful:** unhopeful.
**Hopper:** grasshopper.
**Horn:** dishorn; ink-horn; shoeing-horn.
**Horse:** fill-horse; forehorse; hobbyhorse; malt-horse; packhorse; post-horse; stalking-horse; un-horse.
**Hose:** boot-hose.
**Hospitable:** inhospitable; unhospitable.
**Hot:** full-hot; red-hot.
**Hound:** bloodhound; greyhound; hell-hound.
**Hour:** after-hour; birth-hour; half-hour; marriage-hour; sleeping-hour; three-hours.
**House:** alehouse; almshouse; Asher-house; bawdy-house; brew-house; brothel-house; charge-house; charnel-house; council-hose; dove-house; dwelling-house; farm-house; father-house; garden-house; hot-house; jewel-house; leaping-house; Lime-house; manor-house; parliament-house; pent-house; play-house; prison-house; senate-house; slaughter-house; spital-house; store-house; summer-house; taphouse; tiring-house; treasure-house; unhoused; working-house.
**Housel:** unhouseled.
**Howl:** behowl; loud-howling.
**Hue:** heaven-hued; mustachio-purple-hued.
**Humane:** inhumane.
**Hungry:** a-hungry; an-hungry.
**Hunt:** bloody-hunting; mouse-hunt.
**Hurt:** all-hurting.
**Hutch:** bolting-hutch.

**Hymn:** wedlock-hymn.
**Idleness:** love-in-idlenes.
**Imperial:** crown-imperial.
**Imprison:** long-imprisoned.
**Improve:** unimproved.
**In:** coming-in; herein; therein; wherein; within.
**Incense:** fell-incensed; wrong-incensed.
**Inch:** four-inched; three-inch.
**Inflame:** heart-inflaming.
**Inhabitable:** uninhabitable.
**Inherit:** disinherit; one-trunk-inheriting.
**Inspire:** new-inspired.
**Instrument:** wind-instrument.
**Intelligent:** unintelligent.
**Interpret:** misinterpret.
**Into:** whereinto.
**Iron:** andiron; plough-iron; toasting-iron.
**It:** albeit; howbeit; what-ye-call-it.
**Iterate:** reiterate.
**Jack:** flap-jack; minute-jack.
**Jealous:** loving-jealous.
**Jest:** outjest.
**Jewel:** rich-jewelled.
**John:** apple-John; poor-John.
**Join:** adjoin; cojoin; conjoin; disjoin; enjoin; interjoin.
**Joindure:** rejoindure.
**Joint:** disjoint; injoint; short-jointed; strong-jointed; unjointed.
**Jointly:** conjointly.
**Joy:** enjoy; overjoy; o'erjoyed. Marriage-joys.
**Joyer:** enjoyer.
**Judge:** adjudge; high-judging.
**Judicate:** prejudicate.
**Juice:** love-juice; precious-juiced.
**Junction:** disjunction; injunction.
**Junior:** senior-junior.
**Juror:** grand-juror.
**Juryman:** grand-juryman.
**Just and justly:** unjust, unjustly.
**Justice:** chief-justice; guest-justice; injustice; un-justice.
**Keep:** cave-keeping; counsel-keeping; hard-a-keeping; homekeeping; housekeeping; promise-keeping; swine-keeping; unkept.
**Keeper:** cave-keeper; counsel-keeper; crow-keeper; doorkeeper; house-keeper; innkeeper; tennis-court-keeper.
**Kennel:** unkennel.
**Kercher and kerchief:** handkercher etc.
**Kidney:** fat-kidneyed.
**Kill:** comfort-killing; dead-killing; new-killed; self-killed; soul-killing.
**Killer:** child-killer; king-killer.
**Kiln:** lime-kiln.
**Kind:** gentle-kind; overkind; unkind. Mankind womankind.
**Kindle:** enkindle; fiery-kindled; love-kindling; wrath-kindled.
**Kindly:** unkindly.
**Kindness:** overkindness; unkindness.
**Kine:** milch-kine.
**King:** unking.
**Kinglike:** unkinglike.
**Kinsman:** great-kinsman.
**Kirtle:** half-kirtle.

**Kiss:** cloud-kissing; common-kissing; ear-kissing; heaven-kissing; unkiss; unkissed.

**Kitchen:** privy-kitchen.

**Kite:** hell-kite.

**Knee:** crook-kneed.

**Knife:** paring-knife; penknife.

**Knight:** she-knight-errant; trencher-knight.

**Knit:** strong-knit; unknit; well-knit.

**Knot:** curious-knotted; virgin-knot.

**Know:** acknown; foreknow; unknowing; well-known.

**Knowledge:** acknowledge; foreknowledge.

**Labour:** o'erlaboured; well-labouring.

**Labourer:** joint-labourer.

**Lace:** interlace; unlace. Necklace; tawdry-lace.

**Lack:** love-lacking; mercy-lacking.

**Lackey:** Starve-lackey.

**Lamb:** she-lamb.

**Lament:** dire-lamenting; new-lamenting.

**Land:** Cumberland; England; fairy-land; foot-land-raker; headland; Iceland; inland; Ireland; island; Lapland; Netherlands; Northumberland; Scotland; stubble-land; woodland.

**Lane:** Datchet-lane; long-lane.

**Lapse:** relapse.

**Lard:** enlard.

**Large:** enlarge.

**Last:** everlasting.

**Late:** alate.

**Lattice:** red-lattice.

**Law:** brother-in-law; daughter-in-law; father-in-law; outlaw; outlawry; son-in-law.

**Lawful:** unlawful.

**Lay:** allay; delay; inlay; low-laid; unlaid; way-lay.

**Layer:** bricklayer.

**Lead:** mislead; wing-led.

**Leader:** misleader; ringleader.

**Leaf:** fig-leaves; myrtle-leaf; title-leaf; wood-leaves.

**League:** co-leagued.

**Lean:** lank-lean.

**Leap:** o'erleap.

**Learned:** unlearned; well-learned.

**Leather:** dog's-leather; overleather.

**Leave:** rich-left.

**Leaven:** o'erleaven.

**Leaver:** master-leaver.

**Lee:** belee.

**Leech:** horse-leech.

**Leg:** long-legged; near-legged; short-legged; three-legged; two-legged.

**Legitimate:** illegitimate.

**Lent:** Jack-a-lent.

**Less:** ne'ertheless; unless.

**Lesson:** unlessoned.

**Letter:** love-letter; unlettered.

**Levy:** rash-levied.

**License:** all-licensed; unlicensed.

**Lick:** unlicked; foot-licker.

**Lid:** cofferlid; eyelid.

**Lie:** chamber-lie. Rely. Belie.

**Lief:** alderliefest.

**Lift:** uplift.

**Light:** bonfire-light; daylight; Forthlight; moonlight; new-lighted; starlight; taper-light; torchlight; twilight. Alight.

**Lighten:** enlighten.

**Like:** dislike; mislike. Well-liking.

**Alike;** angel-like; Basilisco-like; bear-like; beast-like; belike; brother-like; calf-like; cat-like; child-like; Chorus-like; Christian-like; church-like; clerk-like; court-like; coward-like; death-like; doctor-like; dragon-like; drone-like; fairy-like; fiend-like; fish-like; gentleman-like; giant-like; glutton-like; goddess-like; godlike; gossip-like; guilty-like; Indian-like; infant-like; jewel-like; Juno-like; justice-like; lazar-like; man-like; merchant-like; mermaid-like; mist-like; monster-like; Nestor-like; nurse-like; penthouse-like; pertaunt-like; picture-like; priest-like; prince-like; prologue-like; prophet-like; pupil-like; rascal-like; rebel-like; riddle-like; saint-like; sea-like; serpent-like; slave-like; soldier-like; spider-like; squire-like; star-like; stickler-like; suchlike; sun-like; surety-like; swan-like; thunder-like; tinder-like; unking-like; unlike; villain-like; virgin-like; vizard-like; wand-like; warlike; wench-like; wife-like.

**Likely:** unlikely.

**Liken:** disliken.

**Limb:** good-limbed.

**Lime:** birdlime; white-limed.

**Limit:** unlimited.

**Limn:** dislimn.

**Line:** bowline; fathom-line; love-line.

**Lineal:** unlineal.

**Linen:** lack-linen.

**Link:** enlink; unlink.

**Lip:** hare-lip; oxlip; rose-lipped; thick-lipped; thick-lips.

**Literate:** illiterate.

**Live:** alive; ever-living; long-lived; long-living; mortal-living; outlive; overlive; relive; short-lived; unlived.

**Liver:** lily-livered; milk-livered; pigeon-livered; white-livered.

**Load:** unload.

**Loaf:** cobloaf.

**Lock:** belocked; double-lock; picklock; unlock; up-locked; wedlock. Elf-lock: fetlock.

**Lodge:** dislodge; new-lodged.

**Loft:** henloft; aloft.

**Logic:** chop-logic.

**Lone:** alone; high-lone.

**Long:** along: flatlong; furlong; headlong; livelong; overlong; prolong. Belong. Nice-longing.

**Loof:** aloof.

**Look:** grim-looked; lean-looked; o'erlook; outlook; overlook; red-looked; sharp-looking; unlooked; unlooked-for.

**Loose:** unloose.

**Lord:** landlord.

**Lorn:** forlorn; lass-lorn.

**Lose:** fast-lost; new-lost; well-lost.

**Loss:** after-loss.

**Lot:** allot.

**Loud:** aloud.

**Love:** beloved; beloving; brother-love; dear-loved; lack-love; light-o'love; after-love; self-love; true-love; unloved; unloving.

**Low:** below.

**Loyal, loyalty:** disloyal, disloyalty.

**Luce:** flower-de-luce.

**Lucky:** unlucky.

**Lug:** head-lugged.

**Luminate, lumine:** illuminate, illumine; relume.

**Lure:** allure.
**Lurk:** fell-lurking.
**Lust:** never-lust-wearied.
**Lustre:** lack-lustre; outlustre.
**Lustrous:** inlustrous.
**Lusty:** overlusty.
**Maculate:** immaculate.
**Mad:** bemad; cuckold-mad; frantic-mad; horn-mad; raging-mad.
**Maid:** beggar-maid; bondmaid; chamber-maid; hand-maid; kitchen-maid; market-maid; mermaid; milkmaid; schoolmaid; sea-maid; servant-maid.
**Main:** amain.
**Make:** grave-making; mouth-made; new-made; unmade; unmake; weak-made.
**Maker:** ballad-maker; card-maker; coach-maker; comfit-maker; cuckold-maker; gallows-maker; gibbet-maker; grave-maker; horn-maker; jigmaker; noise-maker; peace-maker; rope-maker; sailmaker; shoemaker; widow-maker.
**Malkin:** greymalkin; kitchen-malkin.
**Man:** alderman; almsman; apron-man; arts-man; beadsman; beggar-man; bellman; blindman; bondman; bookman; carman; chapman; churchman; clergyman; countryman; craftsman; deadman; deathsman; drayman; Dutchman; Englishman; ferryman; fisherman; foeman; footman; freeman; Frenchman; gentleman; goodman; grand-juryman; great-kinsman; handicraftman; hangman; harvest-man; headsman; henchman; herdsman; hoodman; horseman; huntsman; Irishman; journeyman; Kentishman; kinsman; landmen; liegeman; log-man; madman; marketmen; markman; Merriman; nobleman; pleaseman; ploughman; roundman; seaman; seedsman; servingman; shearman; shipman; sickleman; silkman; singing-man; slaughterman; songman; spokesman; statesman; swordman; threeman; townsman; tradesman; trencher-man; true-man; underhangman; warman; watchman; wealsman; Welshman; wiseman; woman; woodman; workman; yeoman.
**Manly:** unmanly.
**Manned:** full-manned; unmanned.
**Manner:** truest-mannered; unmannered.
**Mannerly:** unmannerly.
**Mantle:** dismantle.
**Manual:** seal-manual.
**Mar:** merchant-marring.
**Mare:** night-mare; wild-mare.
**Marge:** sea-marge.
**Mark:** death-marked; elvish-marked; remarkable; remarked; sea-mark; war-marked.
**Marry:** new-married; unmarried.
**Mart:** co-mart.
**Mary:** ave-Maries.
**Mask:** dismask; immask; unmask.
**Mass:** Christmas; Hallowmas; Martlemas; Michaelmas.
**Mast:** mainmast; topmast.
**Master:** burgomaster; o'ermaster; overmaster; postmaster; schoolmaster; thundermaster; unmastered; whoremaster.
**Masterly:** whoremasterly.
**Match:** o'ermatched; overmatch; unmatched.

**Matchable:** unmatchable.
**Mate:** bedmate; bookmate; comate; copesmate; skainsmate.
**Material:** immaterial.
**Matter:** state-matter.
**Maze:** amaze.
**Me:** pardonmees.
**Mead:** Datchet-mead.
**Meal:** fishmeal. Inch-meal, limb-meal. Pealmeal.
**Mean:** double-meaning; true-meant; well-meaning; well-meant.
**Measurable:** unmeasurable.
**Measure:** overmeasure.
**Meat:** baked-meats; roast-meat; spoon-meat; sweetmeats; worms-meat.
**Meddle:** comeddle.
**Mediate:** immediate.
**Meditate, meditation:** premeditate, premeditation.
**Meet:** bemeet; unmeet.
**Meeting:** after-meeting.
**Mell:** pell-mell.
**Mellow:** unmellowed.
**Melt:** easy-melting.
**Member:** dismember.
**Mend:** amend; amends; bellows-mender.
**Merciful:** unmerciful.
**Mercury** she-Mercury.
**Mercy:** God-a-mercy; gramercy.
**Merge:** submerge.
**Merit:** demerit; unmeriting.
**Meritable:** unmeritable.
**Merry:** overmerry.
**Mesh:** enmesh.
**Mete:** bemete.
**Mettle:** lion-mettled; muddy-mettled; self-mettle.
**Mew:** emmew.
**Mid, midst:** amid, amidst.
**Mighty:** almighty.
**Migrate:** transmigrate.
**Mill:** city-mill; paper-mill; windmill.
**Mind:** bloody-minded; high-minded; motley-minded; noble-minded; noblest-minded; proud-minded; tender-minded; unminded; well-minded.
**Mindful:** unmindful.
**Mine:** candle-mine; countermine; undermine.
**Miner:** underminer.
**Mingle:** intermingle; unmingled.
**Minister:** administer; fellow-minister.
**Ministration:** administration.
**Mirable:** admirable.
**Mire:** pismire; quagmire.
**Miss:** amiss.
**Mistress:** country-mistress; master-mistress.
**Misuse:** self-misused.
**Mitigable, mitigate:** unmitigable etc.
**Mix:** commix; intermix; unmixed.
**Moan:** bemoan; fore-bemoaned; unmoaned.
**Mock:** arch-mock; bemock.
**Moderate:** immoderate.
**Modest:** immodest.
**Moil:** bemoil.
**Moment:** immoment.
**Monday:** black-Monday.
**Money:** press-money.
**Mong:** among.

**Monger:** ballad-monger; barber-monger; carpet-monger; costermonger; fancy-monger; fashion-monger; fishmonger; fleshmonger; love-monger; newsmonger; whoremonger; woodmonger.

**Monging:** fashion-monging.

**Monster:** bemonster; bully-monster; man-monster; sea-monster; servant-monster.

**Month:** twelvemonth.

**Moon:** half-moon.

**Moor:** blackamoor.

**More:** evermore; furthermore.

**Morn:** May-morn.

**Morrow:** good-morrow; to-morrow.

**Mortal, mortality:** immortal etc.

**Most:** almost; foremost; highmost; hindmost; inmost; upmost; utmost; uttermost.

**Mother:** aunt-mother; grandmother; stepmother.

**Motion:** promotion; remotion.

**Mould:** self-mould.

**Mount:** amount; dismount; o'ermount; overmount; surmount.

**Mountain:** cat o'mountain.

**Mouse:** dormouse; rearmice.

**Mouth:** deep-mouthed; flap-mouthed; foul-mouthed; honey-mouthed; humble-mouthed; narrow-mouthed; stretch-mouthed; venom-mouthed.

**Move:** best-moving; cold-moving; heaven-moving; mirth-moving; remove; unmoved; unmoving.

**Much:** insomuch; overmuch.

**Munerate:** remunerate

**Mure:** circummured; immure.

**Musical:** unmusical.

**Musket:** eyas-musket.

**Mutation:** transmutation.

**Mutual:** commutual.

**Muzzle:** unmuzzle; unmuzzled.

**Nail:** door-nail; hobnail.

**Name:** forenamed; nickname; overname; surname; surnamed.

**Natural:** supernatural; unnatural; unnaturally.

**Naturalness:** unnaturalness.

**Nature:** demi-natured; disnatured; honestnatured; sourest-natured.

**Nay:** denay.

**Near:** well-a-near.

**Necessary:** unnecessary.'

**Neck:** break-neck; strong-necked; wry-necked.

**Neglect:** self-neglecting.

**Negligent:** wilful-negligent.

**Neighbourly:** unneighbourly.

**Nerve:** unnerved.

**Net:** benet.

**New:** anew; firenew; fresh-new; renew.

**News:** love-news; mumble-news.

**Newt:** wall-newt; water-newt.

**Nigh:** well-nigh.

**Night:** a-night; fortnight; good-night; midnight; o'ernight; outnight; overnight; se'nnight, sevennight; to-night; yesternight.

**Noble:** ennoble; ignoble; thrice-noble; unnoble.

**Nobly:** ignobly.

**Nominate:** prenominate.

**Nook:** three-nooked.

**Noon:** afternoon; forenoon.

**North:** south-north.

**Nose:** hook-nosed; malmsey-nose; red-nose.

**Note:** denote; denotement; unnoted.

**Noun:** pronoun.

**Nourishment:** after-nourishment.

**Novation:** innovation.

**Noyance:** annoyance.

**Numb:** benumb.

**Number:** short-numbered; unnumbered.

**Numerable:** innumerable.

**Nurse:** foster-nurse.

**Nurture:** ill-nurtured.

**Nut:** chesnut; hazelnut; pignut; walnut.

**Nymph:** sea-nymph.

**Oath:** book-oath.

**Obedience, obedient:** disobedience etc.

**Obey:** all-obeying; disobey; wind-obeying.

**Oblation:** night-oblation.

**Oblivious:** all-oblivious.

**Obstinate:** senseless-obstinate.

**Occupy:** preoccupy.

**Oculate:** inoculate.

**Odour:** court-odour.

**Of:** hereof; never-heard-of; untalked-of; unthought-of; thereof; whereof.

**Off:** cutter-off; fallen-off; falling-off; far-off; new-cut-off; taking-off.

**Offence:** self-offence.

**Offend:** eye-offending; heart-offending.

**Offer:** proffer.

**Office:** o'eroffice.

**Old:** wit-old; wrinkled-old.

**On:** coming-on; ill-thought-on; looker-on; putter-on; unlooked-on; unthought-on; upon; thereon; whereon.

**One:** such-a-one.

**Open:** new-opened.

**Opposite:** wilful-opposite.

**Oppress:** black-oppressing; heat-oppressed.

**Oration:** peroration.

**Orb:** disorbed.

**Order:** disorder; disordered; misordered; well-ordered.

**Orderly:** disorderly.

**Ordinance:** preordinance.

**Ordinary, ordinarily:** extraordinary etc.

**Ordinate:** inordinate; unordinate.

**Other:** another.

**Out:** finder-out; giving-out; putter-out; stretched-out; throughout; thrower-out; weeder-out; whereout; without; worn-out.

**Outrun:** sight-outrunning.

**Over:** moreover.

**Owe:** honour-owing; unowed.

**Owl:** night-owl; screech-owl.

**Ox:** draught-oxen.

**Pace:** apace; cinquepace or sink-a-pace; giddy-paced; lazy-pacing; snail-paced.

**Pack:** unpack.

**Page:** title-page.

**Pain:** hell-pains.

**Painful:** feeling-painful.

**Paint:** bepaint; impaint; nose-painting; well-painted.

**Pair:** impair.

**Pale:** cold-pale; maid-pale. Impale.

**Pan:** brain-pan; Potpan; warming-pan.

**Pannel:** impanneled.

Pap: milkpap.

Paradise: demi-paradise.

Paragon: unparagoned.

Parallel: unparalleled.

Paramour: outparamour.

Pardonable: unpardonable.

Pare: cheese-paring.

Park: dispark.

Part: apart; counterpart; half-part; impart; o'er-parted; tripartite.
   Depart; departure; long-parted; peace-parted; timely-parted.

Partial: impartial; overpartial; unpartial.

Particular: door-particulars.

Partner: copartner.

Pass: overpass; repass; surpass; trespass.

Passion, passionate: compassion etc.

Past: by-past; forepast; o'erpast.

Paste: impasted.

Pasture: repasture.

Pate: baldpate, baldpated; crooked-pated; curled-pate; knotty-pated; not-pated; periwig-pated; russet-pated; smooth-pate.

Path: by-path; footpath; unpathed.

Patience, patient: impatience etc.

Patron: enpatron.

Pave: unpaved.

Pawn: impawn.

Pay: appay; new-pay; o'erpay, overpay; repay; un-paid, unpaid-for, unpay; well-paid.

Payment: nonpayment.

Peace: appease; make-peace.

Peaceable: unpeaceable.

Peach: appeach; impeach.

Pear: appear.

Peel: unpeeled.

Peep: bo-peep; by-peep; underpeep.

Peer: compeer; fellow-peer.
   Highest-peering; o'erpeer; outpeer; overpeer; still-peering.

Peg: unpeg.

Pen: goose-pen.

Pence: eleven-pence; mill-sixpence; sixpence; two-pence; threepence.

Penetrable: impenetrable.

Penny: eight-penny; half-penny; sixpenny; true-penny.

People: unpeople; unpeopled.

Perceive: unperceived.

Perch: o'erperch.

Perfect: imperfect; unperfect.

Perfection: imperfection.

Perfectness: unperfectness.

Perform: love-performing.

Performance: nonperformance.

Peril: apperil.

Perseverant: imperseverant.

Pert: malapert.

Pertain: appertain.

Pertinency: impertinency.

Pertinent: appertinent; impertinent.

Pervert: new-pervert.

Pick: bare-picked; toothpick, toothpicker; un-picked.

Picture: o'erpicture.

Pie: maggot-pie.

Piece: a-piece; birding-piece; chimney-piece; cod-piece; headpiece; master-piece; mortar-piece; murdering-piece.

Pied: proud-pied.

Pierce: ear-piercing; enpierced; side-piercing.

Piety: impiety.

Pig: boar-pig; tithe-pig.

Pigeon: cock-pigeon.

Pight: straight-pight.

Pike: morris-pike.

Pile: Threepile; threepiled.

Pin: pushpin; unpin.

Pinch: belly-pinched.

Pine: repine.

Pinion: nimble-pinioned.

Pink: unpinked.

Pint: half-pint.

Pious: impious.

Pipe: bagpipe; clyster-pipe; horn-pipe; organ-pipe; windpipe.

Piper: bagpiper.

Piss: horse-piss.

Pit: cherry-pit; cockpit; sawpit.

Pitch: high-pitched.

Piteous: dispiteous.

Pitifully: unpitifully.

Pity: to-be-pitied; unpitied.

Placable: implacable.

Place: baiting-place; birth-place; burying-place; displace; dwelling-place; high-placed; judgment-place; lurking-place; market-place; meeting-place; misplace; show-place; sporting-place; sticking-place; York-place.

Plague: unplagued.

Plain, plaint: complain, complaint.

Plant: displant; new-planted; replant; sky-planted; supplant.

Plate: breastplate.

Plausive: unplausive.

Play: fair-play; false-play.

Pleach: even-pleached; impleached; thick-pleached.

Plead: pity-pleading.

Pleasant: unpleasant.

Please: displease; time-pleaser; unpleased; unplea-sing.

Pleasure: displeasure; marriage-pleasure.

Plenish: replenish.

Plight: troth-plight.

Plot: grass-plot. Complot; fatal-plotted.

Pluck: plume-plucked.

Plume: lofty-plumed.

Plus: overplus; surplus.

Ply: apply; imply; reply.

Point: appoint; counterpoint; fiery-pointed; sharp-pointed.

Poise: counterpoise.

Poison: empoison; life-poisoning.

Pole: May-pole. Clodpole.

Policy: unpolicied.

Polish: unpolished.

Pollute: unpolluted.

Pond: fishpond.

Pool: whirlpool.

Poor: kingly-poor.

Port: Cinque-ports. Import; support; transport.

Porter: devil-porter. Tale-porter.

**Portion:** proportion.

**Pose:** compose; dispose; expose; impose; interpose; propose; repose; suppose; transpose.

**Position:** disposition; exposition; imposition; proposition; supposition.

**Possess:** dispossess; repossess; unpossessed; unpossessing.

**Possibility:** impossibility.

**Possible:** impossible; unpossible.

**Post:** hovel-post; Soundpost. O'erpost; woman-post.

**Postulate:** expostulate.

**Posture:** exposture.

**Pot:** chamber-pot; pint-pot; pottle-pot; toss-pot; water-pot.

**Potency:** impotence.

**Potent:** impotent; multipotent; omnipotent.

**Pouch:** Spanish-pouch.

**Pound:** impound. Hundred-pound.

**Powder:** gunpowder.

**Power:** o'erpower.

**Practise:** death-practised; unpractised; well-practised.

**Praise:** all-praised; dispraise; superpraise; underpraise.

**Prate:** love-prate.

**Fray:** bepray; outpray.

**Pregnable:** impregnable.

**Pregnant:** unpregnant.

**Premeditate:** deep-premeditated; unpremeditated.

**Prepare:** unprepared.

**Present:** represent.

**Preserve:** ever-preserved; life-preserving; nice-preserved.

**Press:** depress; express; impress; o'erpress; oppress; suppress; unpressed.

**Presser:** bed-presser.

**Pression:** impression; oppression.

**Pressure:** expressure; impressure.

**Prevail:** unprevailing.

**Prevent:** unprevented.

**Prick:** uppricked.

**Price:** market-price. Disprize; misprize; o'erprize; outprize; underprize; unprized.

**Priest:** hedge-priest.

**Print:** imprint.

**Prison:** imprison.

**Prizable:** unprizable.

**Probable:** improbable.

**Probate:** reprobate.

**Probation:** approbation; reprobation.

**Profit:** unprofited.

**Profitable:** unprofitable; wholesome-profitable.

**Promise:** break-promise.

**Proof:** ague-proof; approof; high-proof; pistol-proof; plot-proof; reproof; shame-proof; war-proof.

**Prop:** underprop.

**Proper:** appropriation; improper; unproper.

**Properly:** unproperly.

**Property:** disproperty.

**Proportion:** disproportion; disproportioned; past-proportion; unproportioned; well-proportioned.

**Protectorship:** lord-protectorship.

**Proud:** high-proud; misproud; overproud; top-proud.

**Prove:** approve; disprove; improve; reprove.

**Provide:** sharp-provided; unprovide; unprovided.

**Provident:** improvident; unprovident.

**Provoke:** unprovoked.

**Prune:** unpruned.

**Pry:** narrow-prying.

**Publish:** unpublished.

**Pudding:** hodge-pudding.

**Pudency:** impudency.

**Puff:** lazy-puffing.

**Puissant:** thrice-puissant.

**Punish:** stock-punished.

**Puppet:** demi-puppet.

**Purchase:** dear-purchased; repurchase.

**Pure:** impure; repured.

**Purge:** unpurged.

**Purity:** impurity.

**Purple:** mustachio-purple-hued.

**Purpose:** unpurposed.

**Purse:** cutpurse; dispurse; pickpurse.

**Purtenance:** appurtenance.

**Quake:** earthquake.

**Qualify:** constant-qualified.

**Quality:** unqualitied.

**Qualm:** stomach-qualmed.

**Quantity:** disquantity.

**Quean:** cotquean.

**Queen:** mother-queen; unqueen.

**Queller:** boy-queller; man-queller; woman-queller.

**Quench:** never-quenching.

**Quest:** request. Bequest.

**Question:** unquestioned.

**Questionable:** unquestionable.

**Quicken:** requicken.

**Quiet:** disquiet; unquiet.

**Quietly:** disquietly; unquietly.

**Quietness:** unquietness.

**Quill:** goose-quill; sharp-quilled.

**Quit:** acquit; requit; requite.

**Quittance:** acquittance.

**Quote:** misquote.

**Rag:** tag-rag.

**Rage:** enrage.

**Raise:** araise; quick-raised; unraised.

**Rake:** unraked; foot-land-raker.

**Ramsey:** Peg-a-Ramsey.

**Rank:** enrank; fore-rank.

**Rapier:** dancing-rapier.

**Rapt:** enrapt.

**Rash:** heady-rash.

**Rat:** land-rat; water-rat.

**Rate:** low-rated; o'errate.

**Rattle:** berattle.

**Raven:** night-raven.

**Ravening:** wolvish-ravening.

**Ravish:** yravish.

**Raze:** down-razed.

**Reach:** high-reaching; o'erreach, overreach.

**Read:** o'erread, overread; unread.

**Ready:** already; unready.

**Real:** unreal.

**Reap:** new-reaped.

**Rear:** high-reared; uprear.

**Reasonable:** unreasonable.

**Reave:** bereave.

**Recall:** unrecalling.

**Recite:** fore-recited.

**Reckoning:** tavern-reckoning.

Reclaim: unreclaimed.
Reconcile: irreconciled; unreconciled.
Reconciliable: unreconciliable.
Recount: unrecounted.
Recoverable: irrecoverable.
Recure: unrecuring.
Red: fiery-red; overred; ripe-red; wax-red.
Redbreast: Robin-redbreast.
Reek: foul-reeking.
Refined: well-refined.
Regard: best-regarded; unregarded.
Regardance: nonregardance.
Register: unregistered.
Regular, regulous: irregular etc.
Rein: surreined.
Relent: unrelenting.
Religious: irreligious.
Relish: disrelish.
Remain: here-remain.
Removable: irremovable; unremovable.
Render: life-rendering; surrender.
Renowned: thrice-renowned.
Repair: new-repair.
Reparable: irreparable.
Repent: high-repented.
Replete: full-replete.
Report: misreport.
Reprievable: unreprievable.
Reprove: self-reproving.
Repured: thrice-repured.
Repute: thrice-reputed; well-reputed.
Resist: unresisted.
Resolve: high-resolved; unresolved.
Resolute: irresolute.
Resound: harsh-resounding; ill-resounding.
Respect: unrespected; well-respected.
Respective: unrespective.
Responsive: corresponsive.
Rest: never-resting; night-rest; unrest.
Restore: unrestored.
Restrain: unrestrained.
Return: back-return; home-return.
Revenge: unrevenged.
Reverend: unreverend.
Reverse: unreversed.
Revocable: irrevocable.
Revolve: deep-revolving.
Reward: unrewarded.
Rhyme: berhyme; love-rhyme.
Rib: bare-ribbed; strong-ribbed; thick-ribbed.
Rich: enrich; poor-rich.
Rid: bedrid.
Ride: outride; override.
Ridge: enridged.
Right: aright; bedright; birthright; downright; forthright; outright; upright.
Righteous: unrighteous.
Rightful: unrightful.
Rightness: uprightness.
Ring: agate-ring; enring; horn-ring; joint-ring; seal-ring; thumb-ring; wedding-ring.
Rip: unrip.
Ripe: sinking-ripe; unripe; weeping-ripe.
Ripen: overripened.
Rise: arise; new-risen; sunrise; sunrising; uprise; uprising.

Rival: corival; unrivalled.
Road: inroad.
Roar: outroar; uproar.
Roast: ill-roasted; overroasted.
Robe: disrobe; enrobe; fire-robed; riding-robe; wardrobe.
Rod: riding-rod.
Roll: enrolled; unroll.
Rood: Holyrood.
Roof: unroof.
Rook: bully-rook.
Room: bedroom; by-room; elbow-room; sea-room.
Roost: unroosted.
Root: enrooted; ill-rooted; shallow-rooted; unroot.
Rope: wain-rope. Down-roping.
Rose: muskrose; primrose; red-rose.
Rotten: dirt-rotten.
Rough: boisterous-rough; unrough.
Round: enround.
Rouse: arouse; uprouse.
Row: a-row; cross-row.
Royal: face-royal; tent-royal.
Rude: giant-rude.
Rug: water-rug.
Rule: hard-ruled; night-rule; o'errule; overrule.
Ruly: unruly.
Run: ever-running; forerun; o'errun; outrun; over-run; sight-outrunning.
Runner: forerunner.
Sack: woolsack. Sherris-sack. Late-sacked; ransack.
Sacrifice: blood-sacrifice.
Sad: heavy-sad; new-sad; sober-sad.
Saddle: pack-saddle.
Safe: unsafe; vouchsafe.
Sail: top-sail; well-sailing.
Sainted: outward-sainted.
Salt: sea-salt; unsalted.
Salute: resalute; unsaluted.
Same: selfsame.
Sand: quicksand.
Sanctify: unsanctified.
Sane: insane.
Satiate: insatiate; unsatiate.
Satisfy: unsatisfied.
Sauce: jack-sauce.
Save: past-saving.
Savour: sweet-savoured.
Savoury: unsavoury.
Saw: handsaw.
Say: assay. Foresaid; foresay; gainsay; hearsay; soothsay; soothsayer; unsay.
Scaleable: unscaleable.
Scan: unscanned.
Scar: unscarred.
Scent: rank-scented.
Sceptre: bloody-sceptred.
Schedule: enschedule.
Scholar: fellow-scholar.
School: dancing-school; grammar-school; taming-school; unschooled.
Schoolmaster: fellow-schoolmaster.
Science: prescience.
Scissars: unscissared.
Scold: outscold.
Sconce: insconce.
Scorch: unscorched.

Score: fivescore; fourscore; ninescore; sixscore; threescore; twelvescore.
Scorn: outscorn.
Scour: unscoured.
Scratch: unscratched.
Screen: bescreen.
Scribe: circumscribe; describe; inscribe; prescribe; subscribe.
Scroll: inscrolled.
Scrutable: inscrutable.
Sculp: insculp; insculpture.
Scutch: overscutched.
Sea: salt-sea; south-sea.
Seal: counterseal; unseal; unsealed.
Seam: enseamed; unseam.
Sear: ensear.
Search: bitter - searching; deep - searched; unsearched.
Season: sweet-seasoned; unseasoned.
Seasonable: unseasonable.
Seat: dark-seated; disseat.
Second: unseconded.
Secret: unsecret.
Seduce: saint-seducing; unseduced.
See: all-seeing; foresee; oversee; unseeing; unseen; well-seeing.
Seed: fern-seed; hag-seed; hemp-seed; honeyseed; mustard-seed; nettle-seed.
Seek: beseech; beseek; unsought.
Seem: beseem; ill-beseeming; ill-seeming; summer-seeming; unseeming; well-seeming.
Seemly: unseemly.
Seer: all-seer.
Seethe: twice-sod.
Self: herself, himself, itself etc.
Sell: outsell.
Seller: fosset-seller.
Seminared: unseminared.
Send: resend.
Sensible: insensible.
Separable: inseparable; unseparable.
Separate: inseparate.
Sequence: consequence.
Sequent: consequent; subsequent.
Servant: fellow-servant; joint-servant.
Server: process-server.
Service: land-service; sick-service.
Serviceable: superserviceable; unserviceable.
Set: beset; firm-set; inset; o'erset; onset; overset; sad-set; sunset; unset.
Setter: clock-setter.
Settle: unsettle.
Sever: dissever; unsevered.
Sex: unsex.
Shade: o'ershade, overshade.
Shaft: buttshaft; love-shaft.
Shake: all-shaking; a-shaking; head-shake; love-shaked, unshaked, unshaken; windshaked, windshaken.
Shame: ashamed.
Shape: ill-shaped; misshaped, misshapen; transshape; unshape; unshaped, unshapen.
Sharer: world-sharer.
Shear: sheep-shearing; unshorn.
Sheathe: ill-sheathed; missheathed; unsheathe.
Shed: bloodshed; new-shed.

Sheet: Tearsheet; wedding-sheets; winding-sheet.
Shell: eggshell; inshelled; muscle-shell; nutshell; walnut-shell.
Shelter: enshelter.
Shield: enshield.
Shift: quick-shifting.
Shine: bright-shining; fair-shining; moonshine; o'ershine; outshining; overshine; sunshine.
Ship: inshipped.
Shire: Carnarvonshire; Devonshire; Dorsetshire; Glostershire; Herefordshire; Leicestershire; Northamptonshire; Oxfordshire; Staffordshire; Warwickshire; Wiltshire; Yorkshire.
Shoe: horseshoe; slipshod.
Shoot: grief-shot; nook-shotten; o'ershoot; shoulder-shotten; upshoot.
Shore: ashore.
Shot: cannonshot; upshot.
Shout: unshout.
Shovel: fire-shovel.
Show: dumbshow; foreshow; seld-shown; unshown; urchin-show.
Shower: o'ershower.
Shrew: beshrew.
Shriek: night-shriek; shrill-shrieking.
Shrine: enshrine.
Shrink: custom-shrunk; unshrinking.
Shrub: unshrubbed.
Shun: all-shunned; unshunned.
Shunnable: unshunnable.
Shut: cockshut.
Sick: brain-sick; crafty-sick; fancy-sick; heart-sick; lion-sick; love-sick; sea-sick; thought-sick.
Sickness: falling-sickness; greensickness.
Side: aside; backside; beside; both-sides; broadside; Cheapside; inside; outside; seaside; shipside; upside; waterside.
Siege: besiege.
Sift: unsifted.
Sight: eagle-sighted; eyesight; foresight; high-sighted; oversight; thick-sighted.
Sightly: unsightly.
Sign: assign; consign; ensign.
Silk: sleave-silk.
Silver: quicksilver.
Simple: fee-simple.
Sinew: ensinewed; treble-sinewed; unsinewed.
Sinuate: insinuate.
Sire: butcher-sire; grandsire; great-grandsire.
Sisting: unsisting.
Sixpence: mill-sixpence.
Size: great-sized. O'ersized.
Skilful: unskilful.
Skill: well-skilled.
Skin: calves-skin; eel-skin; elf-skin; lamb-skin; sheepskin; sow-skin; thick-skin.
Skinker: underskinker.
Skip: o'erskip.
Skirt: foreskirt; wide-skirted.
Sky: enskyed.
Slake: yslake.
Slaughter: manslaughter; self-slaughter.
Slave: bond-slave; jack-slave.
Sleep: asleep; gentle-sleeping; outsleep.
Sleeve: down-sleeves; side-sleeves.
Slip: o'erslip, overslip; unslipping.

Slow: fly-slow; foreslow; sly-slow; snail-slow; soft-slow; wilful-slow.
Slubber: beslubber.
Smear: besmear.
Smell: sweet-smelling; tender-smelling.
Smirch: besmirched; unsmirched.
Smith: goldsmith.
Smock: lady-smock.
Snapper: wit-snapper.
Snare: ensnare.
Snout: urchin-snouted.
Snow: mountain-snow; o'ersnowed.
Snuff: scent-snuffing.
So: also; howsoever; insomuch; whoso.
Soar: high-soaring.
Sober: perpetual-sober.
Sociable: insociable.
Soft: flower-soft.
Soil: unsoiled.
Soldier: fellow-soldier.
Sole: single-soled.
Solicit: unsolicited.
Solve: absolve; dissolve; resolve.
Son: godson; whoreson.
Song: love-song; plain-song; prick-song.
Soon: eftsoons.
Sooth: forsooth.
Sop: milksop; Sugarsop.
Sore: deep-sore; eye-sore; heart-sore; plague-sore.
Sorrow: heart-sorrow; heart-sorrowing; sea-sorrow.
Sort: besort; consort; resort; unsorted.
Sot: besotted.
Soul: All-souls-day.
Sound: unsound. Unsounded. Harsh-sounding; ill-resounding; resound; shrill-sounding.
Sovereignty: self-sovereignty.
Spaniel: water-spaniel.
Spare: none-sparing
Sparrow: hedge-sparrow.
Speak: bespeak; better-spoken; fair-spoken; false-speaking; forspeak; foul-spoken; misspeak; out-speak; respeak; unspeak; unspeaking; unspoke; unspoken; well-spoken.
Speakable: unspeakable.
Spear: boar-spear.
Speed: soon-speeding.
Spend: expend; forespend.
Sperm: pullet-sperm.
Sperse: aspersion; disperse.
Sphere: unsphere.
Spial, spy: espial; espy.
Spice: bespice.
Spin: home-spun.
Spire: aspire; conspire; expire; inspire; suspire.
Spirit: barren-spirited; frosty-spirited; ill-spirited; low-spirited; pleasant-spirited.
Spite: despite.
Spoil: despoil.
Spoke: waggon-spoke.
Sponge: disponge.
Sport: disport; outsport; table-sport.
Spot: bespot; cinque-spotted; pinch-spotted; toad-spotted; unspotted.
Spouse: espouse.
Spread: broad-spreading; o'erspread, overspread.

Spright: softly-sprighted.
Spring: gallant-springing; love-spring; mountain-spring; new-sprung; offspring; upspring.
Spur: coldspur; copper-spur; forespurrer; Hotspur.
Spy: espy.
Square: unsquared.
Squint: asquint.
Squire: esquire; mountain-squire.
Stable: unstable.
Stablish: establish.
Stack: hay-stack.
Staff: broomstaff; cowl-staff; long-staff; torch-staff; walking-staff.
Staid: unstaid.
Stain: bestain; blood-stained; distain; lust-stained; neighbour-stained; overstain; tear-stained; un-stained.
Stair: downstairs; upstairs.
Stake: swoopstake.
Stalk: honey-stalk.
Stall: forestall; head-stall; install.
Stanch: unstanched.
Stand: still-stand. Deadly-standing; notwithstand-ing; outstand; understand; understanding; water-standing; withstand.
Star: ill-starred; lodestar.
Stare: mortal-staring; o'erstare; outstare; up-staring.
Start: upstart.
Starve: hunger-starved; hungry-starved.
State: estate; instate; unstate.
Statue: state-statue.
Stay: outstay.
Stead: bested; instead.
Steadfast: unsteadfast.
Steal: thief-stolen.
Stealer: horse-stealer.
Steep: ensteep; insteep.
Stem: restem.
Step: footstep; o'erstep.
Steward: high-steward.
Stick: candlestick; canstick; fiddlestick; poking-stick.
Still: bestill; distill. Stone-still.
Sting: wasp-stung.
Stink: o'erstink.
Stir: bestir; spirit-stirring.
Stitch: side-stitches.
Stock: flouting-stock; laughing-stock; linstock; pointing-stock; whipstock. Nether-stocks.
Stocking: puke-stocking; worsted-stocking.
Stomach: high-stomached.
Stone: agate-stone; brimstone; cherry-stone; corner-stone; grave-stone; grindstone; gun-stone; hail-stone; London-stone; millstone; thunder-stone. touchstone; whetstone.
Stool: closestool; footstool; jointstool; toadstool.
Stoop: unstooping.
Stop: spell-stopped.
Store: new-store. Clear-stores.
Storm: sea-storm.
Stow: bestow.
Strain: constrain; distrain; restrain.
Strange: estrange.
Strangle: birth-strangled.
Straw: rye-straw.

Stray: astray.
Street: Fish-street.
Stress: distress.
Stretch: outstretch; wide-stretched.
Stride: bestride.
Strike: heart-struck; new-struck; outstrike.
Strew: bestrew; o'erstrawed.
String: base-string; bow-string; eye-string; hamstring; heart-strings; lute-string; unstringed.
Strip: outstrip.
Stroke: thunder-stroke.
Strong: headstrong.
Stroy: destroy.
Student: fellow-student.
Stuff: household-stuff; unstuffed.
Subdue: oft-subdued; self-subdued.
Subjugate: assubjugate.
Substantial: insubstantial; self-substantial; unsubstantial.
Subtle: supersubtle.
Suck: blood-sucking; fen-sucked.
Sucker: blood-sucker; rabbit-sucker.
Sue: ensue; pursue; pursuer.
Sufficience: insufficience, insufficiency.
Suggest: sweet-suggesting.
Suit: love-suit; nonsuit; pursuit; unsuiting. Riding-suit; sober-suited; three-suited.
Suitable: unsuitable.
Sully: unsullied.
Summer: midsummer.
Sun: unsunned.
Sunder: asunder.
Sup: half-supped.
Supper: after-supper.
Supportable: insupportable.
Suppose: presupposed.
Suppressive: insuppressive.
Supreme: co-supreme.
Sure: assure; cocksure; unsure; unsured.
Surfeit: never-surfeited.
Surmise: presurmise.
Surprise: fear-surprised.
Survey: resurvey.
Suspect: unsuspected.
Swain: boatswain.
Swallow: sea-swallowed.
Sward: greensward.
Swarm: upswarm.
Swathe: enswathed.
Sway: o'ersway; oversway; unswayed.
Swayable: unswayable.
Swear: deep-sworn; forswear; outswear; overswear; unswear; unsworn.
Sweep: unswept.
Sweeper: chimney-sweeper.
Sweet: deep-sweet; flattering-sweet; honey-sweet; silver-sweet; true-sweet.
Sweeten: outsweeten.
Swell: big-swoln; high-swoln; hollow-swelling; o'erswell; outswell; proud-swelling; summer-swelling; surfeit-swelled.
Swerver: bed-swerver.
Swift: momentary-swift; wind-swift.
Sword: backsword; half-sword; victor-sword.
Tackle: ladder-tackle.

Tail: bobtail; horse-tail; long-tail; red-tailed trundle-tail; wagtail. Entail.
Taint: attaint; travel-tainted; untainted.
Take: betake; ill-ta'en; leave-taking; mistake; new-ta'en; o'ertake, overtake; partake, partaker; purse-taking; surfeit-taking; undertake, undertaker, undertaking; well-took.
Tale: carry-tale; half-tale; tell-tale.
Talk: out-talk; table-talk; untalked-of.
Tame: entame.
Tangle: entangle; untangle.
Taper: night-taper.
Tart: apple-tart.
Task: attask.
Taste: distaste; untasted.
Tattle: tittle-tattle.
Tawny: orange-tawny.
Teach: untaught.
Teacher: parrot-teacher.
Tear: plough-torn.
Tedious: overtedious.
Teem: beteem; o'erteemed.
Tell: all-telling; foretel; fortune-tell; new-told; retell; true-telling; twice-told; untold.
Teller: fortune-teller.
Temn: contemn, contempt.
Temper: best-tempered; distemper; ill-tempered, mistempered; strong-tempered; untempering.
Temperance: distemperance; intemperance.
Temperate: intemperate.
Temperature: distemperature; intemperature.
Temporal: extemporal.
Tempt: attempt.
Ten: thirteen, fourteen etc.
Tend: attend; contend; extend; intend.
Tendance: attendance.
Tender: ram-tender. Untender. Untendered.
Tenible: intenible.
Tent: untent. Untented.
Tenuate: extenuate.
Term: mistermed.
Termination: determination.
Test: attest.
Testate: intestate.
Text: Mar-text.
Thankful, thankfulness: unthankful etc.
Thanks: pickthanks.
Thee: prithee.
Thick: heavy-thick; inch-thick.
Thief: land-thief; water-thief.
Thing: anything; all-thing; something; nothing.
Think: bethink; forethink; ill-thought-on; methinks, methought; misthink; unthink; unthought.
Thirsty: bloodthirsty.
Thistle: holy-thistle.
Thorn: hawthorn.
Though: although.
Thought: love-thought; war-thoughts; holy-thoughted; sick-thoughted.
Thrall: enthrall.
Thread: packthread; unthread.
Threaten: wrack-threatening.
Thrift: spendthrift; unthrift.
Thrifty: unthrifty.
Throat: cut-throat.
Throne: enthroned.

Through: wherethrough.
Throw: o'erthrow, overthrow.
Thump: bethump.
Thwart: athwart.'
Tice: entice.
Tide: betide; Lammas-tide; noontide; Shrovetide.
Tie: five-finger-tied; shoe-tie; tongue-tied; untie; untied.
Till: until; uptill.
Timber: clean-timbered; hardest-timbered; un-timbered.
Time: after-times; bed-time; beforetime; betime; betimes; dinner-time; holiday-time; leaping-time; lifetime; meantime; milking-time; oftentimes, ofttimes; pastime; ring-time; rut-time; striving-time; sometime, sometimes; spring-time; supper-time; whiting-time; winter-time.
Timeless: all-too-timeless.
Timely: untimely.
Tirable: untirable.
Tire: attire; ship-tire. Woman-tired. Untired.
Tissue: intertissued.
Title: entitle; untitled.
To: hereto; hitherto; unto; thereto; whereto.
Toe: pettitoe; tiptoe.
Tofore: heretofore.
Together: altogether.
Token: betoken; death-token; love-token.
Tolerable: intolerable.
Tomb: entomb.
Tongue: close-tongued; honey-tongued; lewd-tongued; long-tongued; maiden-tongued; out-tongue; poisonous-tongued; shrill-tongued; trum-pet-tongued; wasp-tongued.
Tooth: sharp-toothed.
Top: cedar-top; chimney-top; main-top; mountain-top; o'ertop, overtop; parish-top.
Torch: wedding-torch.
Toss: betoss; sea-tost; tempest-tost.
Touch: ne'er-touched; untouched.
Toward: untoward, untowardly.
Town: Free-town; market-town; peasant-town.
Trade: hold-door-trade; untraded.
Train: untrained.
Trance: entranced.
Transform: new-transformed.
Trap: entrap; mousetrap.
Tread: down-trod, down-trodden; earth-treading; mistreadings; untread; untrod, untrodden.
Treasure: entreasured; intreasured; untreasured.
Treat: entreat.
Tree: axle-tree; bay-tree; box-tree; crab-tree; elder-tree; fruit-tree; olive-tree; palm-tree; plum-tree; willow-tree; yew-tree.
Trench: entrench; intrenched.
Trenchant: intrenchant.
Tribune: fellow-tribune.
Tribute: attribute; distribute.
Trick: backtrick; rope-trick; tumbling-trick.
Trim: betrim; new-trimmed; untrimmed.
Trip: night-tripping; o'ertrip. Traytrip.
Troth: betroth; new-trothed.
Trouble: untroubled.
True: honest-true; untrue.
Trull: kitchen-trull.
Trunk: one-trunk-inheriting.

Truss: untrussing.
Trust: distrust; mistrust; self-trust.
Truth: untruth.
Try: untried.
Tuck: standing-tuck. Untucked.
Tuesday: Shrove-Tuesday.
Tumble: betumble.
Tune: care-tuned; ill-tuned; new-tuned; sad-tuned; untune; untuned; well-tuned.
Tuneable: untuneable.
Turn: o'erturn, overturn; return; triple-turned; up-turned; white-upturned.
Tutor: untutored.
Twain: atwain.
Tween: between.
Twenty: sweet-and-twenty.
Twig: hazel-twig; lime-twig.
Twine: untwine.
Twist: entwist.
Twixt: betwixt.
Unable: self-unable.
Uncle: great-uncle.
Under: stand-under.
Unfold: new-unfolding.
Unhappy: fortunate-unhappy.
Unite: disunite; reunite.
Until: whereuntil.
Unto: thereunto; whereunto.
Untrimmed: new-untrimmed.
Up: blower-up; bringing-up; hunts-up; layer-up; made-up; sealed-up; setter-up; snapper-up; start-up; steep-up; surrender-up; ten-times-barred-up; tied-up.
Upon: hereupon; thereupon; whereupon.
Upward: climber-upward.
Ure: inure.
Urge: unurged.
Urn: inurned.
Use: abuse, abuser; ill-used; misuse; unused.
Usual: unusual.
Utter: ill-uttering.
Vade: evade; invade.
Valiant: ever-valiant; thrice-valiant; tire-valiant.
Value: dearest-valued; disvalue; o'ervalue; under-value; unvalued.
Vanish: long-vanished.
Vanquish: unvanquished.
Vantage: advantage; double-vantage.
Varnish: new-varnished; unvarnished.
Vassal: waiting-vassal.
Vault: pretty-vaulting.
Veil: overveil; unveil.
Vein: blue-veined; liver-vein.
Venerable: unvenerable.
Venge: avenge; revenge.
Venom: envenom; outvenom.
Venture, venturous: adventure etc.
Verb: no-verb; proverb; proverbed.
Verberate: reverberate (reverb).
Verdict: party-verdict.
Vest: invest.
Vestal: kitchen-vestal.
Vex: earth-vexing; soul-vexed; still-vexed; unvexed.
Vice: high-viced.
Victorious: thrice-victorious.
Vie: outvie.

View: interview; overview; review.
Vile: revile.
Villain: arch-villain; outvillain.
Vincible: invincible.
Viol: base-viol.
Violable: inviolable; unviolable.
Violate: unviolated.
Violator: virgin-violator.
Virtuous: seeming-virtuous; unvirtuous.
Visage: grim - visaged; humble - visaged; pale-visaged; tripe-visaged.
Visible: invisible.
Visit: revisit; unvisited.
Voice: low-voiced; outvoice; shrill-voiced; silver-voiced.
Void: avoid; devoid.
Vouch: avouch; disvouch; forevouch.
Vow: avow; bed-vow; break-vow; Deep-vow; marriage-vow.
Vulnerable: invulnerable.
Wail: bewail.
Wait: await.
Wake: awake; night-waking; still-waking.
Walk: late-walking; night-walking; o'erwalk.
Wall: abbey-wall; castle-wall; outwall; sea-walled; water-walled.
Wander, wanderer: night-wandering, night-wanderer.
Wane: beauty-waning.
Want: pity-wanting.
War: closet-war; man-of-war.
Ward: award. Bearward; foreward; rearward; vaward. Afterward, afterwards; awkward; backward; bedward; downward, downwards; eastward; forward; froward; goer-backward; henceforward; hitherward, hitherwards; homeward, homewards; inward; nayward; northward; onward; outward; Parisward; parkward; Pittieward; southward; thitherward; toward; upward; wayward; westward; woolward.
Ware: beware; unwares; unwarily.
Warm: lukewarm.
Warn: forewarn.
Warp: moldwarp.
Warrant: well-warranted.
Wash: ale-washed; buck-washing; unwashed.
Waste: bewaste.
Waster: candle-waster.
Watch: all-watched; night-watch; o'erwatched, overwatched; unwatched.
Water: holy-water; mock-water; pomewater; rain-water; rose-water; salt-water; sea-water.
Wave: salt-waved.
Wawl: catterwauling.
Wax: ear-wax. New-waxen.
Way: alway, always; away; church-way; crossway; halfway; highway; horse-way; midway; pathway; roadway; runaway; straightway.
Weaken: fever-weakened.
Weal, wealth: commonweal, commonwealth.
Wear: o'erworn; outwear; overworn; war-worn; wave-worn.
Weary: aweary; day-wearied; dog-weary; forwearied; life-weary; lust-wearied; ne'er-lust-wearied; unwearied; war-wearied; woe-wearied; world-wearied.
Weather: overweather.

Weave: ill-weaved; unweave.
Web: cobweb.
Wed: unwed.
Wedgeable: unwedgeable.
Wednesday: Ash-Wednesday.
Weed: furrow-weeds; unweeded.
Ween: o'erween, overween.
Weep: beweep; unwept.
Weigh: o'erweigh; outweigh; overweigh; unweighed; unweighing; well-weighing.
Welcome: unwelcome.
Well: ill-well.
Wench: flax-wench; kitchen-wench; oyster-wench.
West: north-north-west; south-west.
Wet: bewet.
Wether: bellwether.
What: somewhat.
Wheel: chariot-wheel; enwheel; mill-wheel; waggon-wheel.
Whelm: o'erwhelm, overwhelm.
Whelp: bearwhelp.
Where: anywhere; elsewhere; everywhere; nowhere; otherwhere; somewhere.
While: awhile; breathing-while; erewhile; meanwhile; otherwhiles.
Whip: unwhipped.
Whistle: sheep-whistling.
White: lily-white; milk-white; silver-white; snow-white.
Whither: somewhither.
Whole: heart-whole.
Wholesome: unwholesome.
Whore: bewhore.
Wide: thrice-wider.
Widow: maiden-widowed.
Wieldy: unwieldy.
Wife: ale-wife; goodwife; housewife; loose-wived; midwife; orange-wife.
Wig: periwig.
Will: good-will; ill-will; nill; self-will; self-willed; unwilling; well-willer.
Willingness: unwillingness.
Win: feast-won; well-won.
Wind: long - winded; shortwinded; southwind; whirlwind.—Unwind.
Window: bay-window; chamber-window; church-window.
Wine: pipe-wine.
Wing: clip-winged; eagle-winged; fleet-winged; full-winged; lapwing; light-winged; sea-wing; slow-winged; strong-winged swift-winged.
Wink: eyewink; hoodwink.
Wipe: unwiped.
Wise: unwise. Burdenwise; Colossus-wise; guest-wise; likewise; otherwise.
Wisely: unwisely.
Wish: heart-wished; unwish; unwished; well-wished.
Wit: beef-witted; blunt-witted; fat-witted; hasty-witted; high-witted; iron-witted; lean-witted; mother-wit; quick-witted; sodden-witted; subtle-witted; unwit; want-wit.
Witch: bewitch.
With: forthwith; therewith; wherewith.
Withal: therewithal; wherewithal.
Wither: never-withering.
Withstand: notwithstanding.

Witness: unwitnessed.
Wittingly: unwittingly.
Witty: foolish-witty.
Wolf: bitch-wolf; demi-wolf; she-wolf.
Woman: beggar-woman; butter-woman; city-woman; country-woman; day-woman; distaff-woman; Englishwoman; Frenchwoman; gentle-woman; herb-woman; kinswoman; madwoman; tithe-woman; waiting-woman; Welshwoman.
Womb: enwombed; round-wombed.
Wont: unwonted.
Woo: new-woo; unwooed.
Wood: greenwood; Ringwood; wormwood. Raging-wood.
Word: all-changing-word; ayword; by-word; court-word; nayword; reword; watch-word.
Work: a-work; bed-work; behind-door-work; dark-working; firework; handiwork; high-wrought; needle-work; night-work; outwork; sale-work; stair-work; underwork; water-work.
Worker: half-worker.
World: all-the-world; half-world.
Worm: blindworm; glow-worm; malt-worm.
Worse: thrice-worse.
Worshipper: idiot-worshipper.

Worth: halfpenny-worth; outworth; pennyworth; three-farthing-worth.
Worthiness: unworthiness.
Worthy: all-worthy; death-worthy; note-worthy; praiseworthy; thrice-worthy; unworthy.
Wound: back-wounding; crest-wounding; deep-wounded; gogs-wounds; love-wounded; 'swounds; wonder-wounded; Zounds.
Wrap: enwrap.
Wrath: after-wrath.
Wreathe: sorrow-wreathen.
Wreck: shipwreck.
Wrest: ill-wresting; o'erwrested.
Wright: shipwright.
Wring: unwrung.
Write: handwriting; underwrite.
Wrong: self-wrong.
Wry: awry.
Yard: churchyard; half-yard; mete-yard; tilt-yard; vineyard.
Year: good-year; half-year; new-year.
Yield: easy-yielding; unyielding.
Yoke: unyoke; unyoked.
Yond: beyond.
Young: valiant-young.

# SUPPLEMENT

## A SELECTION

### OF NEW RENDERINGS AND INTERPRETATIONS.

**Abject**: *the queen's abjects* R3, I, 1, 106, i. e. "the most servile of her subjects". Herford.

**Absolute**: *you are too absolute* Cor. III, 2, 39 i. e. "uncompromising, unqualified".
Chambers, Warwick Sh.

**Accept**: *pass our accept and peremptory answer* H5, V, 2, 82, i. e. "(probably) give the answer upon which we definitely and finally agree. 'Accept' has commonly been understood 'acceptance'; but the French king does not guarantee that he will accept the articles, merely that he will give a definite decision. Hence Mr. W. A. Wright's proposal to understand 'accept' as a participle, — 'the answer which we have accepted as decisive') is preferable". Herford.

**Accord**: *and, Jove's accord, nothing so full of heart* Troil. I, 3, 238 i. e. "having Jove on their side, they are of unmatched valour". Herford.

**Accost**, vb.: *that give accosting welcome ere it comes* Troil. IV, 5, 59: "*accosting*, Monk Mason's emendation of Q F, *a coasting*, which Schmidt explains 'as the first step taken to meet the hesitating approach of a wooer.' But there is no example of the use of *coasting* for the *wooer's* approach; whereas *accost*, as we know from *Twelfth Night*, meant 'front her, board her, woo her, assail her". Herford.

**Act**, subst.: *smiling extremity out of act*, Per. V, 1, 140, i. e. "smiling frantic sorrow into self-control". Herford.

**Action**: *his whole action grows not in the power on't* Ant. III, 7, 69 i. e. "his plans have been formed without regard to his military strength". Herford.

**Adonis**: *thy promises are like Adonis' gardens that one day bloomed and fruitful were the next* H6A I, 6, 6. Cp. Spenser, F. Qu. III. VI, 42:
There [*viz.* in the Garden of Adonis] is continuall
      spring, and harvest there
Continuall, both meeting at one tyme:
For both the boughes doe laughing blossoms beare,
And with freshe colours decke the wanton pryme,
And eke attonce the heavy trees they clyme,
Which seeme to labour under their fruites lode. [S.]

**Affeered**: *the title is affeered* Mcb. IV, 3, 34 = "settled, confirmed". NEDict. "'To affeer' says Ritson, himself a lawyer, 'is to assess, or reduce to certainty.'"
Clark & Wright, Clar. Press Ed.

**After-supper** Mids. V, 34, "not a separate meal from supper, but the last course of it, the rere-supper or dessert". E. K Chambers Warwick Shakespere, cp. W. A. Wright, Clar. Press Ed.

**Again**: *sitting on a bank, weeping a. the king my*

*father's wreck* Tp. I, 2, 390. "Weighing the various pros and cons, I am inclined to side with Malone, and to conclude that in the line from the Tempest..... *again* is an old form of the preposition *against* in the sense of 'in expectation of', 'in view of', 'angesichts', for which sense see Al. Schmidt's quotations i. v. *against* prep. 1 b ...." Stoffel, Engl. Stud. 29, 105. [?]

**Aged**: *aged night* R3, IV, 4, 16. "Schmidt explains = 'night of old age'. This is hardly adequate. "Hath dimmed your infant morn to night" would naturally mean 'hath slain you in your infancy'; and that is the sense required by the context. Some confusion, however is caused by the epithet *aged*, which is introduced for the sake of antithesis to *infant*. The two do not really balance one another. *Your infant* morn means 'your bright young lives'; *aged night* might be paraphrased as 'the darkness that death brings upon the aged'."
Macdonald, Warwick Shakespeare.

**A-hold**: *lay her a.; set her two courses off to sea again* Tp. I, 1, 52, i. e. "bring her close to the wind by hauling up the main-sail, and set her two lowest sails (*courses*) on the other tack, to try to clear the land that way." Herford.

**Aids**: Compl. 117. "The manage had not only its needful corrections, but its helps and cherishing, by hand, leg, and voice. Shakespeare calls them 'aids' and 'terms of manage'."
D. H. Madden, Diary of William Silence.

**All**: *all to all* Mcb. III, 4, 92, "a drinking formula: 'all good wishes to all'."
E. K. Chambers, Warwick Shakespeare.

**All-hallown Summer** H4A I, 2, 178 "the bright warm weather which sometimes comes about all Saints' day, and so a figure of Falstaff, who preserved his youthful passions to a late period of life".
Wright, Clar. Press Ed.

**Almost**: *ye cannot reason almost with a man* R3 II, 3, 39 = 'can scarcely reason'. Wright, Clar. Press. Ed., Franz, Shakespeare Gramm.

**Amble**: "The word amble did not then, as now, denote a slow and easy trot. It was an artificial pace, in which the horse moved simultaneously the fore and hind legs on each side ..." D. H. Madden.

**Ancientry**: *.. a measure, full of state and a.* Ado II, 1, 80, i. e. "old-fashioned formality".
Wright, Clar. Press. Ed.

**Andirons** (Cymb. II, 4, 88) = "fire-dogs". Wyatt, Warwick Sh.
"A utensil consisting of an iron bar sustained horizontally at one end by an upright pillar or support

usually ornamented or artistically shaped, at the other by a short foot; a pair of these, also called '*fire-dogs*', being placed one at each side of the hearth or fire-place, with the ornamental ends to the front, to support burning wood.'"                            NEDict.

**Angel:** *Brutus was Caesar's a.* Caes. III, 2, 185; *i. e.* "his 'good genius'; alluding to the belief which evidently coloured Shakespeare's psychology, that every man has his 'daemon' or spirit which keeps him, whose voice speaks through his highest intelligence (II, 1, 66). But the belief shaded off into metaphor, and at times he can speak of 'our worser genius', the source of temptations".                                    Herford.

**Angel:** *an ancient a.* Shr IV, 2, 61 "a colloquial name for worthy old men of somewhat formal cut; probably from the coin".                            Herford.

**Angus:** H4A I, 1, 73, "George Douglas, only son of William first Earl of Douglas. His mother, Margaret Stewart, was Countess of Angus in her own right". Wright, Clar. Press Ed.

**Appertainment(s):** Troil II. 3, 87, *i. e.* "prero-gatives".                                            Herford.

**Appointment:** *to stead up your a.* Meas. III, 1, 261 *i. e.* to "supply the place you have engaged to fill".                                            Herford.

**Arden:** (As I, 1, 121 etc.) "The real forest of Ardennes lies partly in the French department of that name, but chiefly in Namur, Liege, and Luxemburg. But Shakespeare's forest is in fairyland — an English fairyland with glimpses of the classical Arcadia. The name 'Arden' also belonged to the wooded part of Warwickshire, and this may have been in Shakespeare's mind as well".
J. C. Smith, Warwick Shakespeare.

**Arm-gaunt:** *an arm-gaunt steed* Ant. I, 5, 48. "The context requires the horse to have been vigorous and high-spirited; the epithet may suggest this indi-rectly, the horse being 'lean from bearing arms in battle', hence warlike."                            Herford.

**Aroint:** *a. thee witch* Mcb. I, 3, 6, Lr. III, 4, 129. "Rynt thee" is used by milkmaids in Cheshire to a cow, when she has been milked, to bid her get out of the way. Ray in his Collection of English Words gives '*Rynt ye*: By your leave, stand handsomly. As Rynt you witch, quoth Besse Locket to her mother. Proverb, Chesh.'"                            Clark & Wright, Clar. Pr. Ed.
"The local nature, the meaning, and form of the phrase [sc. *rynt you, rynd-ta*], seem all opposed to its identity with Shakespeare's *Aroynt.*"            NEDict.

**Artificial:** *artificial gods* Mids. III, 2, 203, "that is, I suppose, gods whose creative power works in the sphere of art, not nature".
E. K. Chambers, Warwick Shakespeare.

**As:** *But if thy love were ever like to mine* — *as sure I think did never man love so* ...... As II, 4, 29. "As introduces a statement "qualifying or even contra-dicting what goes before" (Ingleby). This use seems to have escaped Schmidt. Cf III, 5, 38."
J. C. Smith, Warwick Shakespeare.

**As:** *and many such - like Ases of great charge* Hml. V, 2, 43
'A quibble is intended between "as", the conditional particle, and "ass" the beast of burden.'
Johnson, quoted in Clark & Wright's Clar. Press Ed.

**Asmath,** H6B I, 4, 27, "an evil spirit, Asmodeus Tob. III, 8)".                                        Herford.

**Ass:** *the ass in compound with the major part of your syllables* Cor. II, 1, 64, *i. e.* "nearly every word a foolish one".                    Chambers, Warwick Sh.

**Attorneyship** H6A V, 5, 56, "discretional agency of another".                        Gollancz, Temple Sh.

**Austerity** Mids. I, 1, 90 == "severe self - morti-fication; used technically of the religious discipline of a nun".                        W. A. Wright, Clar. Press Ed.

**Babble:** *and a babbled of green fields* H5 II, 3, 17 (Theobald conj.). Lock Richardson compares Ps. 23. *The Lord is my shepherd; I shall not want. He maketh me to lie down in green pastures, he leadeth me beside the still waters.* (Shakespeare Studies, New York 1896.)

**Baby:** *protest me the b. of a girl* Mcb. III, 4, 106. "The infant of a very young mother would be likely to be puny and weak. Sidney Walker however under-stands 'baby' here to mean 'doll', quoting two passages from Sir Philip Sydney, and referring to Ben Jonson's Bartholomew Fair *passim*; but the word is not used elsewhere in this sense by Shakespeare."
Clark & Wright, Clar. Press Ed.

**Bagot:** R2 I, 4, 23 etc. == "Sir William Bagot, sometime Sheriff of Leicestershire".            Herford.

**Bald:** *these b. tribunes* Cor. III, 1, 164, *i. e.* "witless".                                            Herford.

**Balk:** Lucr. 696 == "to turn aside from, as when a horse refuses".                                    Wyndham.

**Banish:** *as 't were to banish their affects with him* R2 I, 4, 30 "bear their affections into banishment with him".                    Herford, Warwick Shakespeare.

**Bank:** *within our awful banks* H4 B, IV 1, 176, *i. e.* "the bounds of loyal obedience".        Herford.

**Barbed:** R3, I, 1, 10. R2 III, 3, 117 "a form of 'barbed' == 'armed with a *barb* or *bard*'. From Fr. *barde* == 'horse-armour', which is perhaps ultimately an Arabic word (Murray). The '*barde*' was the covering that protected the chest and sides of the horse when caparisoned for battle."
Macdonald, Warwick Shakespeare.

**Bare,** adj.: *a. b. petition,* Cor. V, 1, 20 *i. e.* "a request unaccompanied by any promise of atonement or restitution."                                        Herford.

**Bare,** vb, (Fol. beare): *bare the raven's eye* Cymb II, 2, 49.
[Theobald's emendation 'bare' instead of 'beare' is not quite convincing. I should prefer: *clear(e) the raven's eye* cf. Err. III, 2, 57: *Gaze where you should, and that will clear your sight.* S.]

**Bargulus:** H6B IV, 1, 108; "his proper name was Bardylis; he was originally a collier, and ultimately became King of Illyria; he was defeated and slain in battle by Philip of Macedon".
Gollancz, Temple Sh.

**Barkloughly,** R2, III, 2, 1 == "Harlech. The name is due to a mere scribal or printer's blunder in Holinshed, standing for 'Hertlowle', or Hertlow, the last an Anglicised form of the Old Welsh 'Harddlech'".
Herford.

**Barnacles** Tp. IV, 249, "geese which were suppos-ed to breed out of certain shellfish which grew upon trees".                            Boas, Warwick Sh.

**Barson:** H4B V, 3, 94 == "Barston, Warwicksh.".
Brandl, Schlegel-Tieck.

**Base:** *to bid the wind a base* Ven. 303 = "prisoner's base or county base". Wyndham.

**Baseness:** *nursed by b.* Meas. III, 1, 15 *i. e.* "due to the labour of mean men". Herford.

**Basilisks** (H4A II, 3, 56) "were the largest kind of ordnance, weighing nine thousand pounds and having a bore of 8³/₄ inches". Wright, Clar. Press Ed.

**Basingstoke:** H4B, II, 1, 182 "near Reading, Hants". Brandl, Schlegel-Tieck.

**Basket-hilt:** *you b. stale juggler* H4B II, 4, 141, *i. e.* "a worn-out practiser of sword-tricks". Herford.

**Bastardly:** *thou b. rogue* H4B II, 1, 55; "Mrs. Quickly blunders between 'bastard' and 'dastardly'". Herford.

**Bat-fowling:** *go a b.* Tp. II, 1, 185 *i. e.* "the hunting of bats by night, they were scared with flames and knocked down with poles". Herford.

**Bawcock** Tw. III, 4, 125 etc. = "fine fellow. Fr. *beau coq.*" A. D. Innes, Warwick Sh.

**Bawd** (Rom. II, 4, 134) = "*hare* (quibbling). Cf. NE. Dict., Wright, Engl. Dial. Dict." Max Förster.

**Bawd** subst. Hml. I, 3, 130, see Bond.

**Bawl:** *you bawling blasphemous dog* Tp. I,1 , 43 ... "the bawling, the babbling, and the overtopping hound... 'If they be to busie before they finde the Sent good, we say they Bawle', says the author of the Noble Arte. . . The bawler who cries upon no scent is a degree worse than the babbler". D. H. Madden.

**Bay** subst., Meas. II, 1, 255, "an architectural term for a certain division of a building, usually the space included between successive beams or buttresses. Coles' Latin Dictionary (quoted by Singer) defines 'a bay of building, *mensura 24 pedum*'". Herford.

**Bay:** *at a bay* Ven. 877 "a term of venery for the action of hounds baying in a circle round the exhausted stag or boar". Wyndham.

**Be** (II, 2, f): *tke king by this is set him down to sleep*, H6C IV, 3, 2.
The anomaly is explained by taking 'is set' as equivalent to 'is sate' and 'him' as a refl. dative. Franz, Shakespeare-Grammatik S. 350.

**Beam:** *the beam of sight* Cor. III, 2, 5, *i. e.* "the distance sight can reach, as if a beam of light proceeded from the eye". Chambers, Warwick Sh.

**Bear** vb.: *here's neither bush nor shrub, to b. off any weather at all* Tp. II, 2, 18. "a pregnant phrase, equivalent to 'bear and so keep off me'". Boas, Warwick Sh.

**Bear** vb.: *Caesar doth bear me hard, but he loves Brutus* Caes. I, 2, 317 cf. Caes. II, 1, 215, III, 1, 157. "The phrase *to bear one hard* occurs three times in this play, but nowhere else in Shakespeare. It seems to have been borrowed from horsemanship, and to mean *carries a tight rein,* or *reins hard,* like one who *distrusts* his horse." Henry N. Hudson (Joseph Crosby).

**Bear** vb.: *therefore bear up, and board 'em* Tp. III, 2, 3 "a nautical phrase, meaning to 'put the helm up, and keep a vessel off her course'". Boas, Warwick Sh.

**Beat** vb: *beated and chopped with tann'd antiquity* Sonn. 62, 10; *i. e.* "flayed. Properly an agricultural term (still used in Devonshire) for paring away the sods from moorland". Herford.

**Beauty:** *let not us ... be called thieves of the day's beauty* H4A, I, 2, 28. "The 'day's beauty' being the sun, the only meaning which can be attached to these words is 'let us not be called thieves by the sun', that is in broad daylight." Wright Clar. Press Ed.

**Benevolence** R2 II, 1, 250. "This name (which soon became ironical) for a *forced loan* was first introduced under Edward IV. in 1473." Herford, Warwick Shakespeare.

**Bennet:** *the bells of Saint B.* Tw. V, 42, *i. e.* "St. Benedict's, just opposite the Globe Theatre." Herford.

**Berown(e):** LLL I, 1, 15 etc., very likely identical with (Armand Gontaut de) Biron. He "was well known by repute and highly popular in England; the English contingent sent by Elizabeth in 1589 [? 1591] usually serving under his command, and finding him 'very respective to her Majesty and loving to her people'". Herford, cf. S. Lee, Life of Sh., Sarrazin, Shakespeare-Jahrbuch XXXI, 206.

**Bezonian:** H6B IV, 1, 134. "First, therefore, let every man understand, that this title of Husbandmen is not tyed onely to the ordinarie tillers of the earth, such as we call husbandmen; in France peasants; in Spaine, Besonyans, and generall the cloutshoo." Markham's English Husbandman, quoted by Sp. Baynes, Shakespeare Studies p. 284.

**Bias** (R2, III, 4, 5) "was a technical term in bowls (originally meaning *slant, oblique*) and applied alike to the construction or form of the bowl imparting an oblique motion, the oblique line in which it runs and the kind of impetus given to cause it to run obliquely". Herford, Warwick Shakespeare, Murray, N. E. Dict.

**Bigot:** John IV, 2, 162 etc. "*Lord Bigot* is called in the old play Richard earle of Bigot, and in Holinshed Richard earle de Bigot. Whether this is an error for Roger Bigod Earl of Norfolk it is difficult to say." W. A. Wright, Clar. Press Ed.

**Bill:** *set up his bills* Ado I, 1, 39 = "issued a public challenge". Wright, Clar. Press Ed.

**Billingsgate** (H4B II, 1, 182) "'was not originally a fish market exclusively, but in Elizabeth's reign was an open place for the landing and bringing in of any fish, corn, salt stores, victuals and fruit (grocery wares excepted)'". Harrison (Furnivall).

**Birnam** (Mcb. IV, 1, 93 etc.) "is a high hill near Dunkeld, twelve miles W. N. W. of Dunsinnan, which is seven miles N. E. of Perth. On the top of the latter hill are the remains of an ancient fortress, popularly called Macbeth's Castle". Clark & Wright, Clar. Press Ed.

**Bladed:** *b. corn* Mcb. IV, 1, 55, "corn in the blade, before it is in the ear". Clark & Wright, Clar. Press Ed.

**Blame:** *the king my uncle is to(o) blame for this* R3 II, 2, 13 = "too blameable'. Murray Oxf. Diction. s. v. *blame,* cf. Franz, Shakespeare-Grammatik s. v. *too.*

**Blazon:** *thy tongue, thy face ..... give thee five-fold b.* Tw. I, 5, 312. = "the heraldic proclamation of the armorial bearings." A. D. Innes, Warwick Sh.

**Blue-eyed:** *this b. hag* Tp. I, 2, 269.
"This may refer to (1) the *pupil* of the eye, and denote the 'pale-blue, fish-like, malignant eye which is

often seen in hag-like women' (Grant White); or (2) the livid colour of the *eyelid*, which was a sign of pregnancy. Wright, who suggests this view, compares Webster's *Duchess of Malfi*, II, 1: 'The fins of her eyelids look most teeming blue.'"

Boas, Warwick Sh.

**Blunt:** *what a blunt fellow is this grown* to be! Caes. I, 2, 299 '*Blunt* here means, apparently, *dull* or *slow*.'

Henry N. Hudson.

**Body:** *the body is with the king, but the king is not with the body* Hml. IV, 2, 28.

"To the courtiers his [=Hamlet's] words are nonsense; for himself they mean 'the body lies in death with the king my father, but my father walks disembodied'".

Dowden, Hamlet.

**Body:** *Body a me* H8, V, 2, 22.

"The origin of this nonsensical oath is not explained in the N. E. Dict. It is a literal translation of the French *corps de moi*, equally meaningless to those who are not versed in French oath-lore. . . . . . . . A disguise of a *corps* oath, *cordieu*, appears in Roger de Collerye's Monologue du Résolu: Corps de moy."

F. Adams, Notes & Quer. 8 Ser. Vol. 3.

**Bond:** *sanctified and pious b—s* Hml. I, 3, 130 = "troth-plights" (Verlöbnisse).

Schröer, Sh. Jahrb. XXXI, 366.

**Bone:** *Strike her young bones, you taking airs, with lameness* Lr. II, 4, 165, *i. e.* "her unborn infant".

W. A. Wright, Clar. Press Ed. [?]

**Bosom:** *our bosom interest* Mcb. I, 2, 64 = "close and intimate affection".

Clark & Wright, Clar. Pr. Ed.

**Bowl,** sbst.: *gossip's bowl* Mids. II, 1, 47, "probably filled with 'lamb's wool', a compound of ale, nutmeg, sugar, toast, and roasted crabs or apples".

E. K. Chambers, Warwick Shakespeare.

**Bowl** vb.: . . . . . . . *some that know little but—ing* Wint. IV, 4, 338 *i. e.* "the smooth, even motion of ordinary dancing, as distinguished from the jumps and capers of the 'Satyrs'".

Herford.

**Bow-string:** *hold or cut bow-strings* Mids. I, 2, 114.

"This is clearly a metaphor from archery, though it is diversely explained. I think it means 'Hold (*i. e.* keep your promises) or give up the play'. To cut bowstrings for archers would be much the same as burning their ships for seamen. . . . . . . . The only near parallel is in Chapman and Shirley's *The Ball* (1639) —".

"*Scutilla.* — — have you devices
To jeer the rest?
*Lucia.* All the regiment on 'em, or I'll break
my bow-strings."

E. K. Chambers, Warwick Shakespeare.

**Branch:** *a branch of victory*, As IV, 2, 5.

"Jaques probably intends a pun; *branch* is used for the antlers of the deer."

J. C. Smith, Warwick Shakespeare.

**Brand,** sbst.: *two winking Cupids, nicely depending on their brands* Cymb. II, 4, 91.

"*Brands* is explained in two ways: (1) = brandirons, *i. e.* the horizontal bars at the back of the andirons on which the logs actually rest. The fact that the Cupids would not stand without the support of these 'brands' favours this interpretation. (2) *Brands*

= the Cupids' firebrands or torches, by resting on which they seemed to be maintaining their poise."

Wyatt, Warwick Sh.

**Brawl:** *I do the wrong, and first begin to brawl* R3, I, 3, 324, "raise an outcry".

Macdonald, Warwick Shakespeare.

**Brawn** H4A II, 4, 124 "in the East Anglian, Cumberland and Lowland Scotch dialects, means a boar. See 2 Henry IV, 1, 1, 19".

Wright, Clar. Press Ed.

**Bread:** *holy bread* As III, 4, 15 "probably sacramental bread, though Barron Field says it was "merely one of the ceremonies which Henry VIII.'s Articles of Religion pronounced good and lawful".

J. C. Smith, Warwick Shakespeare.

**Break,** vb. (II, 5): *the broken rancour of your high-swoln hearts* R3 II, 2, 117, *i. e.* "the wound caused by the rancour of . . .".

Herford.

**Break:** *broken music* As I, 2, 150 "part music arranged for different instruments".

J. C. Smith, Warwick Shakespeare.

**Breath:** *almost dead for b.* Mcb. I, 5, 37 "*i. e.* for want of breath". Clark & Wright, Clar. Press Ed.

= "dying for breath".

Koppel, Shakespeare-Studien.

**Bribed,** adj.: *a. b. buck* Wiv. V, 5, 27 "was a buck cut up into portions (Old French *bribes*) = 'portions of meat to be given away'".

Gollancz.

**Broil:** *the great Myrmidon who —s in loud applause* Troil I, 3, 379 *i. e.* who "is wrought into a fever of conceit by" —.

Herford.

**Brown:** *he's in for a commodity of brown paper* etc. Meas. IV, 3, 5. "Usurers were accustomed to increase their profits by making their loans partly in cheap commodities reckoned far above their value, which the borrower then realised at a heavy loss. Usurers were thence known as 'brown-paper merchants' ".

Herford.

**Bulk:** Oth V, 1, 1, Cor. II, 1, 226, "the projecting part of a shop on which goods were exposed for sale".

Gollancz.

**Bully:** *bully Bottom* Mids. III, 1, 8, "a term of familiarity addressed by his companions to a jolly blustering fellow . . . . . . . It probably was a slang word which had come into use not long before 1600. Florio (Ital. Dict.) gives 'Bullo, a swaggerer, a swashbuckler'".

W. A. Wright, Clar. Press Ed.

**Burn:** *b. some sack* Tw. II, 3, 206 "*i. e.* 'mull'".

A. D. Innes, Warwick Sh.

**Burton-heath** Shr. Ind. 2, 19, "is Barton-on-the Heath, the home of Shakespeare's aunt Edmund Lambert's wife, and of her sons".

Sidney Lee, Shakespeare.

**Bushy,** R2 I, 4, 23 etc. = "Sir John Bushy, Speaker of the House of Commons in 1394".

Herford.

**Butt,** sbst.: *a rotten carcass of a b.* Tp. I, 2, 146.

"It is evident that *butt* cannot here have its modern meaning of 'cask', as there would be no sense in the words, 'not rigg'd, nor tackle, sail, nor mast'. Brinsley Nicholson suggests that it is a nautical term, borrowed by Shakespeare from an Italian original to give local colouring to the tale, and that it may be a version of *Botto*, a sort of sloop with very rounded ribs, very little run, and flattish bottom."

Boas, Warwick Sh.

**Buttock**: *the buttock of the night* Cor. II, 1, 56 "*i. e.* the small hours of the night".
Chambers, Warwick Sh.

**Buzz**: *buzz, buzz* Hml. II, 2, 412, "according to Blackstone an interjection used at Oxford, equivalent to 'Stale news' ".
Chambers, Warwick Sh.

**Calf**: *hang a calf's skin on those recreant limbs* John III, 1, 129 etc. "Sir John Hawkins says, 'When fools were kept for diversion in great families, they were distinguished by a calf's-skin coat, which had the buttons down the back'."
Wright, Clar. Press Ed.

**Campeius** H8 II, 1, 160 etc. = "Campeggio".
Wright, Clar. Press Ed.

**Candle - holder** Rom I, 4, 38. "A common name for a mere looker-on."
White, quoted by Furness, Var. Ed.

**Candy**: *the c—ied tongue* Hml. III, 2, 65 = "covered with a coating of hypocrisy".
Clark & Wright, Clar. Press Ed.

**Canker-bloom** Sonn. 54, 5 = "a blossom eaten by canker" (Wyndham).

**Canon**: *from the c.* Cor. III. 1, 90 "means exactly 'irregular' "
Chambers, Warwick Sh.

**Canonized**: *c. bones* Hml I, 4, 47 not 'sainted', but buried 'according to the *canon* or ordinance of the church'.
Chambers, Warwick Sh.

**Canopy**, subst.: *bore the c.* Sonn. 125, 1, "*i. e.* rendered outward homage".
Herford.

**Canterbury**: *my Lord of Canterbury* H8 II, 4, 218 "William Warham, who died 23rd of August, 1532, and was succeeded by Cranmer — — — ".
Wright, Clar. Press Ed.

**Cap**: *such gain the c. of him* Cymb. III, 3, 25; *i. e.* "receive obsequious salutations (from the supplier of the 'unpaid-for silk', who nevertheless remains unpaid)".
Herford.

**Cape** Shr. IV, 3, 140. "The word 'cape' had in Shakespeare's day the meaning of a narrow band encircling the neck".
D. H. Madden.

**Captivity**: *triumphant Death, smear'd with captivity* H6A, IV, 7, 3, "(probably) smeared with the blood of the mortal wounds which bring men into thy power".
Herford.

Cf. H6A I, 1, 20:
And Death's dishonourable victory
We with our stately presence glorify,
Like captives bound to a triumphant car.
Cp. the use of 'Captivity' = "those who are in captivity, captives collectively", Murray NED. [S.]

**Carbonado**, subst.: H4A V, 3, 61, Cor. IV, 5, 199 "was a rasher or steak slashed for broiling on the coals".
Wright, Clar. Press Ed.

**Career**: *he passes some humours and—s* H5, II, 1, 132. "'The short turning of a nimble horse, now this way, nowe that way' (Baret Alvearie); *transf.* a frisk, gambol."
Murray, NED.

**Career**: *if misfortune miss the first career* R2, I, 2, 49. . . "Used technically of the *charge* in a tournament or combat."
Herford, Warwick Shakespeare.

**Carnal**: *carnal cur* R3, IV, 4, 56 = "carnivorous, *i. e.* cruel. No other instance of this sense is quoted in the *New English Dictionary*".
Macdonald, Warwick Shakespeare.

**Case**, subst.: Wint. IV, 4, 844. "The fox's skin was in hunting language his case."
D. H. Madden.

**Catch**, subst.: (Tp.III, 2, 126 etc.) "Catch, round, or roundelay, and canon in unison are in music nearly the same thing.
In all, the harmony is to be sung by several persons, and is so contrived that, though each sings precisely the same notes as his fellows, yet by beginning at stated periods of time from each other, there results a harmony of as many parts as there are singers. The catch differs only in that the words of one part are made to answer or *catch* the other . . .."
Chappell, Popular Music of the Olden time, quoted by Wright.

**Catercousins** (Merch. II, 2, 139) = "friends, a familiar term answering to the modern chums. The origin of the word is obscure, but it most probably means those who were related or connected, by being 'catered - for together, tablemates . . . . . . . . The old derivation from *quatre* is almost certainly wrong".
H. L. Withers, Warwick Shakesp., Merch. of Ven. p. 132. Cf. NEDict.

**Cause**, subst.: *as c. will be obeyed* Cor. I, 6, 83 *i. e.* "as occasion shall arise".
Chambers, Warwick Sh.

**Ceremony**: *I never stood on ceremonies, but now they fright me* Caes. II, 2, 13.
"*Ceremonies* is here put for the ceremonial or sacerdotal interpretation of prodigies and omens."
Henry N. Hudson.

**Chain**: *rub your chain with crumbs* Tw. II, 3, 129 "*i. e.* polish up your badge of office; 'mind your own business' ".
A. D. Innes, Warwick Sh.

**Chair.** "In the well-known passage in Coriol. IV, 7, 52, over which many have stumbled, the whole sense comes out at once by simply calling to mind that *chair*, in Tudor English, was sometimes used in the sense of 'pulpit'. . . . . . . The general sense is just this: 'Power however commendable it may seem to itself, can find no tomb so conspicuous, no tomb so obvious, as when it chooses for itself a pulpit whence to declaim its own praises.' "
W. W. Skeat, Notes & Queries, VII Ser., Vol. IX.

**Changeable**: *ch. taffeta* Tw, II, 4, 76 "is silk that changes colour as the light varies".
A. D. Innes, Warwick Sh.

**Character**: *reserve their character* Sonn. 85, 3 = "preserve or treasure up their style by labouring it preciously, with a secondary suggestion of fastidious restraint".
Wyndham.

**Charbon**: *young Charbon the puritan and old Poysam the papist* All's I, 3, 55. "'Charbon' possibly for 'Chair-bonne', and 'Poysam' for 'Poisson', alluding to the respective lenten fares of the Puritan and Papist."
Gollancz (Herford).

**Charge**: *answering us with our own ch.* Cor. V, 6, 68, *i. e.* "bringing us back nothing except our expenses to meet".
Chambers, Warwick Sh.

**Charity**: *of charity, what kin are you to me* Tw. V, 237 = 'for charity's sake'
Wright, Clar. Press Ed.

**Charm**, vb.: *ch—ing words*, Cymb. I, 3, 35; *i. e.* "words which should give him [sc. Posthumus] a charmed security from evil influences".
Herford.

**Charmingly**: *this is a most delightful vision, and harmonious ch.* Tp. IV, 119 *i. e.* "magically".
                                                        Herford.
**Charneco**: H6B II, 3, 63 "a kind of sweet wine, made at a village near Lisbon".
                                        Gollancz, Temple Sh.
**Chase**, subst. (H5 II, 4, 68). "A chase at tennis is the duration of a contest between the players, in which the endeavour on each side is to keep the ball up."                                        Hudson.
**Check**, vb.: *that thou mayst be a queen and c. the world* John II, 123; "an allusion to the queen at chess."                                        Herford.
**Check**, vb.: *if he be now returned, as —ing at his voyage, and that he means no more to undertake it* Hml. IV, 7, 64.
"The metaphor is taken from falconry, and is technically applied to a falcon that forsakes her proper game to fly after some other bird."
                                Clark & Wright, Clar. Press Ed.
**Cheer**, sbst: *an anchor's cheer* Hml. III, 2, 229 *i. e.* "anchoret's chair. So Bishop Hall, Satires IV, 2, 103: Sit seaven yeares pining in anchores cheyre".
                                        Dowden, Hamlet.
**Chertsey** (R3, I, 2, 29 etc.), "a market town in Surrey, 25 miles W. S. W. of London".
                                Macdonald, Warwick Shakespeare.
**Child-changed**: Lr. IV, 7, 17, *i. e.* "changed by the unnatural conduct of his children. Some understand it as meaning changed to a child, but Lear's malady was insanity, not childishness".
                                Wright, Clar. Press Ed. [?]
**Chops** H4A I, 2, 151 "fat chops; not as Schmidt oddly defines it, 'a person resembling a piece of meat' (Shakespeare Lexicon)".
                                Wright, Clar. Press Ed.
**Chough**: *'t is a chough* Hml. V, 2, 89 "probably 'chuff', a wealthy churl."                        Herford.
**Christopher**: *Sir C.* (Urswick) R3, IV, 5, 1, "a priest in the service of the Countess of Richmond, employed by her in confidential communications with her son".                                        Herford.
**Circumstance**: *c—s shortened* Ado III, 2, 105 *i. e.* "cutting short the details". Wright, Clar. Press Ed.
**Circumvention**: *ere Rome had c.* Cor. I, 2, 6 "*i. e.* had sufficient warning to be able to circumvent us".                        E. K. Chambers, Warwick Sh.
**Civil**: *a civil doctor* Merch. V, 210 = "a Doctor of Civil Law".
                Furness Var. Ed.; H. L. Withers, Warwick Sh.
**Clamour**, vb.: *c. your tongues* Wint. IV, 4, 250 *i. e.* "constrain, repress. This expression, a puzzle to the older commentators, has been almost certainly identified with M. E. *clameren*, 'thrust closely together', cognate with Scand. *klome*, a screw, Germ. *Klamm*, narrow defile; O. E. *clom*, fetter; *clamber*, cling closely".
                                Herford, cf. NEDict s. v. *clamour*.
**Cleanly** adj.: *the cleanliest shift is to kiss* As IV, 1, 77, = "the best way out of it".
                                J. C. Smith, Warwick Shakespeare.
**Clear**, vb.: *the imposition clear'd hereditary ours*, Wint. I, 2, 74 *i. e.* "setting aside the 'original sin' we inherit as men".                                        Herford.
**Clearly**: *and wound our tattering colours clearly up* John V, 5, 7 = "quite, entirely".
        W. Franz, Shakespeare-Grammatik, cf. Murray, Dict.

**Clifton** H4A V, 4, 46 "was Sir John Clifton, Knight of the Shire of Nottingham 4 Henry IV".
        (French, Shakspereana Generalogica, quoted by
                W. A. Wright, Clar. Press Ed.)
**Clip**: *Who with their drowsy, slow and flagging wings c. dead men's graves* H6B IV, 1, 6 (Ff. *cleap*); .. "I believe 'clip' to be wrong, and 'clap' to be right, because the word 'clap' was by the writers of the sixteenth and seventeenth centuries applied specifically to the stroke given by wings."
                        H. H. Vaughan, New Readings.
**Close** (*music at the close* R2 II, 1, 12) "was used as a special term for the harmonious chords which habitually end a piece of music".
                        Herford, Warwick Shakespeare.
**Clutch**: *in thy hands c—ed as many millions* Cor. III, 3, 71 "passive, 'were there clutched'".
                        Chambers, Warwick Sh.
**Coast**, vb.: Troil. IV, 5, 59 see *Accost* vb.
**Coat** (As I, 3, 16) "petticoat. Shakespeare does not use it elsewhere in this sense; but it is common enough in ballad-poetry".
                        J. C. Smith, Warwick Shakespeare.
**Cobbler**: *in respect of a fine workman, I am but —a c.* Caes I, 1, 17. *Cobbler* "it seems, was used of a coarse workman, or a botcher, in any mechanical trade. So that the Cobbler's answer does not give the information required".                        Henry N. Hudson.
**Cock**, sbst.: *I have retired me to a wasteful cock, and set mine eyes at flow*, Tim. II, 2, 171. "Of the many suggested emendations 'wakeful cock' (Jackson's) seems the best, meaning a cockloft where Flavius remained sleepless. The text may, however, be understood in the sense that he sat by a running wine-cock, shedding tears as fast as the wine was wasted".
                                        Herford.
**Cock-a-hoop**: *you will set cock-a-hoop* Rom. I, 5, 83 *i. e.* "give a loose to all disorder, set all by the ears", originally = "to turn on the tap and let the liquor flow".                                Murray, NED.
**Cockney**: *Cry to it, nuncle, as the cockney did to the eels* Lr. II, 4, 123; *i. e.* "a squeamish, overnice, wanton, or affected woman".                Murray, NEDict.
**Cock-shut-time**: R3 V, 3, 70. "Dr. Murray (NED.) inclines to the opinion that it meant simply the time for shutting up the fowls."
                                Macdonald, Warwick Sh.
**Cognizance**: *great men shall press for tinctures, stains, relics, and cognizance* Caes II, 2, 89. *Cognizance* is here used in a heraldic sense, as meaning any badge or token to show whose friends or servants the owners or wearers were".                Henry N. Hudson.
**Collop**: *most dear'st! my collop*: Wint. I, 2, 137. "It was a proverbial saying that 'it is a dear collop that is cut out of thy own flesh'".        Herford.
**Come**: *come Lammas Eve*, Rom. I, 3, 17 (cp. Meas. III. 2, 214, H4B II, 4, 413).
'Come', in such phrases, was originally the subj. mood, as in Fr. *viennent les Pâques*, cf. New Engl. Dict. *come*, 35, p. 654, W. Franz Shakespeare-Grammatik §. 503, Anmerk. 2.                                [S.]
**Comma** (Hml. V, 2, 42 cf. Tim. I, 1, 48). "No emendation is required; the obscurity has arisen through forgetting an earlier meaning of *comma*, a phrase or group of words forming a short member of a sentence or period. . . . Here amity begins and amity ends the

period, and peace stands between like a dependent clause." Dowden, Hamlet.

**Commodity**: *a commodity of good names* H4A I, 2, 93, "a consignment, a store or stock". Wright, Clar. Press Ed.

**Complement**: *captain of c—s* Rom. II, 4, 20, *i. e.* "master of etiquette". Herford.

**Complement**: *garnished and decked in modest complement* H5 II, 2, 134, *i. e.* "*accomplishment* or *completeness*, quite distinct from compliment". H. N. Hudson.

**Composition** Mcb. I, 2, 59 = "terms of peace". Clark & Wright, Clar. Press Ed.

**Con**: *an affectioned ass, that cons state without book* Tw. II, 3, 161, *i. e.* "gets up rules of dignified deportment". Herford.

**Conceit**: *conceit in weakest bodies strongest works* Hml. III, 4, 114; *conceit upon her father* Hml. IV, 5, 45 = "a (morbid) affection or seizure of the body or mind". Murray, NED., Schröer, Sh. Jahrb. XXXI, 367.

**Conclusion**: *there must be conclusions* H5, II, 1, 27: *i. e.* "attempts. Nym cautiously avails himself of the antiquity of the word". Herford.

**Consequence**: *but Edward lives. True, noble prince. O bitter c., that Edward still should live*, R3 IV, 2, 15. *i. e.* "conclusion of the sentence". Herford.

**Consistory**: *my counsel's c.*, R3 II, 2, 151, *i. e.* "'the assembly of whose deliberations my counsels are the issue'. The Consistory was properly an ecclesiastical court". Herford.

**Corin ... Phillida.** Mids. II, 1, 66—68. "These are traditional names of lovers in pastoral poetry. The first genuine English pastoral appeared in *Tottel's Miscellany* (1557) with the title, *Harpalus' Complaint of Phillida's Love bestowed on Corin that loved her not, and denied him that loved her*." E. K. Chambers, Warwick Shakespeare.

**Corinthian**: *a C.* H4A II, 4, 13, "a cant term for a profligate; a 'fast man', loose liver". Herford.

**Corn**: *pipes of corn* Mids. II, 1, 67 = "made of oat straw". W. A. Wright, Clar. Press Ed.

**Corner-cap**: *the c. of society* LLL IV, 3, 53, "the beretta or three-cornered cap of the Catholic priest". Herford.

**Courageous** Merch. II, 2, 10, probably Launcelot Gobbo's blunder instead of 'outrageous'. (Delius.)

**Course** (Mcb. II, 2, 39). "Schmidt and editors generally assume that course belongs to the metaphor of 'life's feast', and means a course in a meal. Why sleep should be the second course they do not explain. ... Shakespeare's word for a course in a meal was s e r v i c e, as in Haml. IV, 3, 25. ... Nature (*i. e.* life, existence) is here compared to a race with two courses or rounds, which are respectively the waking state and sleep". [?] Arthur Gray, Notes & Quer. VII. Ser. Vol. 6.

**Courser**: *breeding, which, like the —s hair, hath yet but life, and not a serpent's poison* Ant. 1, 2, 200 "alluding to the popular notion that horsehair put into water will turn into a snake or worm". Gollancz (Herford).

**Court**: *our great c.*, Cymb. III, 5, 50; *i. e.* "this important court-meeting". Herford.

**Courtesy** Merch. V, 217 = "the desire to show gratitude". H. L. Withers, Warwick Shakespeare.

**Courtesy**: *the courtesy of nations* As I, 1, 49, = "the usage of the civilized world, *jus gentium*: viz. the law of primogeniture". J. C. Smith, Warwick Shakespeare.

**Court-gate**: H8 I, 3, 18. "In Ralph Agas's Map of London' about 1560, one of the gates of Whitehall is called the court-gate. It is probably that which was designed by Holbein, and stood facing Charing Cross a little south of the banqueting house". Wright, Clar. Press Ed.

**Cozen-Germans**: Wiv. IV, 5, 79. "In Q, this allusion is more specific: For there is three sorts of cosen garmombles, Is cosen all the Host of Maidenhead and Readings. There is little doubt that *garmombles* is a thin disguise for Mömpelgard, the Count of Mömpelgard having ... visited Windsor in 1592." Herford.

**Cozier**: *your —s' catches* Tw. II, 3, 97 = "'tailors' of the class previously referred to as 'botchers', *i. e.* patchers or menders". Innes, Warwick Sh.

**Craze**: *crazed title* Mids. I, 1, 92 = 'a title with a flaw in it'. W. A. Wright, Clar. Press Ed.

**Crop**, subst: *the rich crop of sea and land* Cymb. I, 6, 33,. "Crosby proposed *scope*; I retain *crop* which I take to be a bold metaphor for the wide expanse or prospect of sea and land, suggesting the thought of a harvest." A. J. Wyatt, Warwick Sh.

**Cross**, subst: *the c. of a Welsh hook* H4A II, 4, 372 *i. e.* "the point where the shaft of a halberd was crossed by the steel head which formed an axe on one side and a spike on the other". Herford.

**Cross**, vb.: *I am that way going to temptation, where prayers c.* Meas. II, 2, 159 *i. e.* "cross one's path, bar the way; Isabel's deferential leave-taking being in effect a prayer for his [Angelo's] honour". Herford.

**Cross-bow**: *c—s* H5 IV, 8, 99, H6C III, 1, 6; *i. e.* "cross-bow men". Herford.

**Crown** vb.: *crowned* Sonn. 37, 7 "blazoned beneath the crown, a technical term of Heraldry". Wyndham.

**Crum**(b) see *Chain*.

**Crush**, vb.: *that is but a —ed necessity* H5 I, 2, 175 *i. e.* "one that is overborne, annihilated, by contrary reasons". Herford.

**Cuckoo-buds.** "Shakespeare's cuckoo-buds may safely be assumed to be the same as the 'buttercups' of to-day, especially the Ranunculus acris". Grindon, the Shakespeare Flora, cp. H. N. Ellacombe, Plant-Lore of Shakespeare.

**Cure**, subst.: *my hopes, not surfeited to death, stand in bold cure* Oth. II, 1, 51: *i. e.* "not having extravagantly indulged his hopes he has a good prospect of their fulfilment". Herford.

**Currish**: *his c. riddles* H6C V, 5, 26, *i. e.* "fables about beasts". Herford.

**Curvet**, subst. All's II, 3, 299. "Among these salts and leaps the corvette, or curvet, was highly esteemed. It was 'a certaine continuall pransing and dansing up and downe still in one place, like a beare at a stake and sometimes sideling to and fro, wherein the horse maketh as though he would faine run, and cannot be suffered'." D. H. Madden, quoting Gervase Markham.

**Cushion**: *And this c. my crown* H4A II, 4, 416. "Country people in Warwickshire used a cushion for a crown in their harvest-home diversions." Dr. Letherland, quoted by W. J. Rolfe (Friendly Edition of Shakespeare) and Ch. Allen (Notes on the Bacon-Shakespeare Question).

**Cuttle**: *an you play the saucy cuttle with me* H4B II, 4, 139 *i. e.* "cut-purse".                    Herford.

**Dainty**: *grows d. of his worth* Troil. I, 3, 145, *i. e.* "idly preoccupied, puffed up with his dignity".                                                    Herford.

**Damn**: *A fellow almost —ed in a fair wife* Oth. I, 1, 21. "The most plausible interpretation is 'almost married' to Bianca; the epithet indicating either the disreputableness of this match or Jago's scorn for marriage in general".                    Herford.

**Danger**: *do danger* Caes. II, 1, 17. "That is, do *mischief*, and so *be* or *prove dangerous*.                                            Henry N. Hudson.

**Dauphin** see *Dolphin*.

**Dear**: *my —est foe* Hml. I, 2, 182. "'Dear' is used of whatever touches us nearly either in love or hate, joy or sorrow".
                    Clark & Wright, Clar. Press Ed.
[Cf. H4A III, 2, 123, Tit. III, 1, 257, R2, I, 3, 151 (*dear* = Ags. *déor*).]

**Debase**: *debase ... on me* R3 I, 2, 247 = "lower to my level".
                    Macdonald, Warwick Shakespeare.

**Debitor and Creditor** Oth. I, 1, 31 "the title of certain ancient treatises on book-keeping; here used as a nick-name".            Clarke, Gollancz.

**Deflower**: *Since lion vile hath here deflour'd my dear* Mids. V, 297, Pyramus-Bottom's blunder for 'devoured'.                    (Delius.)

**Defuse**: *defused attire* H5 V, 2, 61. "It appears from Florio's *Dictionary*, that *diffused*, or *defused*, was used for *confused*. *Defused attire* is therefore *disordered* or *dishevelled attire*".        H. N. Hudson.

**Delate**: *these delated articles* Hml. I, 2, 38 "is 'articles setting forth what powers are delated, delegated, or made over to you'".
                    Chambers, Warwick Sh.

**Demise**: R3, IV, 4, 247 "make transference of".
                    Macdonald, Warwick Shakespeare.

**Deputy**: *the deputy's wife of the ward* H4A, III, 3, 130. "The deputy of a ward is the common-councilman who is appointed to act for the alderman in his absence, and is therefore a man of position and respectability".        Wright, Clar. Press Ed.

**Descry**: *to d. the strength o' the enemy* Lr. IV, 5, 13 *i. e.* "reconnoitre. So in Richard III, V, 3, 9: 'Who hath descried the number of the foe?'"
                    W. A. Wright, Clar. Press Ed.

**Desk**: *If I had play'd the desk or tablebook* Hml. II, 2, 136 = "if I had been the agent of their correspondence".        Clark & Wright, Clar. Press Ed.

**Determinate**, Sonn 87, 4 = 'expired' Malone, Wyndham.

**Dewlap**: *her withered dewlap* Mids. II, 1, 50 "is properly the loose skin which hangs from the throat of cattle".        W. A. Wright, Clar. Press Ed.

**Dian**: *Dian's Bud* Mids. IV, 1, 78. "It can be nothing but Shakespeare's translation of Artemisia, the herb of Artemis or Diana, a herb of wonderful virtue according to the writers before Shakespeare's day".            Ellacombe, Plant-Lore.

**Die**, vb.: *that strain again! it had a dying fall* Tw. I, 1, 4, "*i. e.* it sank softly to silence".
                    A. D. Innes, Warwick Sh.

**Die**, vb.: *a dying debt* R3, IV, 4, 21 = "a debt that can only be paid by death".
                    Macdonald, Warwick Shakespeare.

**Diet**, subst.: *an evil diet*, R3, I, 1, 139 = "manner of life".        Macdonald, Warwick Shakespeare.

**Digest**: *we'll digest the abuse of distance* H5 II Chor. 31 *i. e.* "manage, dispose of, the awkwardness imposed by the vast and rapid movements of the action. Others interpret 'arrange, or contrive, the illusion of distance'".                    Herford.

**Dim**, adj.: *violets d.* Wint. IV, 4, 120 "probably 'of quiet colour, not showy'".        Gollancz.

**Disable**: *disable not thyself* H6A, V, 3, 67 "means 'use not language which impeaches your own competency'. 'To disable' in this sense was a term of frequent forensic use in the sixteenth century."
                    H. H. Vaughan, New Readings.

**Disaster**: *disasters in the sun* Hml. I, 1, 118. "A term derived from the ancient astrology, and denoting the malevolent influences of the heavenly bodies. Here the reference is to the extraordinary paleness of the sun mentioned by Plutarch which was followed by the products of the earth."
                    Clark & Wright, Clar. Press Ed.

**Discovery**: *such preposterous —ies* Troil. V, 1, 28. "Thersites probably means the rank abuses which disclosed themselves to his censorious eye in the Greek camp at large".            Herford.

**Dishonest** Tw. I, 5, 46 "badly behaved".
                    A. D. Innes, Warwick Sh.

**Dispatch**, vb: *nay, now dispatch* R3 I, 2, 182. "Schmidt takes this = 'put to death'. But it need mean no more than 'make haste' as in I, 3, 356 ..."
                    Macdonald, Warwick Shakespeare.

**Distemperature**: *this distemperature* Mids II, 1, 106. "This disturbance between Oberon and Titania; not the perturbation of the elements. Compare . . . . . . Romeo and Juliet II, 3, 40:
'Therefore thy earliness doth me assure
Thou art uproused by some distemperature.'
                    W. A. Wright, Clar. Press Ed.

**Division** H4A III, 1, 211, Rom III, 5, 29, Mcb. IV, 3, 96 "means roughly a brilliant passage of short notes, which is founded on a much simpler passage of longer notes".
Naylor, Shakespeare and Music p. 26. cf. Wright, Clar. Press Ed.

**Dolphin**: *D. my boy* Lr. III, 4, 104. "Apparently the words of a song. Farmer quotes from B. Jonson's Bartholomew Fair [V, 3]: 'Od's my life! I am not allied to the sculler yet; he shall be Dauphin my boy.' Steevens on the authority of an old gentleman gives a stanza from a ballad written on some battle or tournament in France:
'Dolphin my boy, my boy
Cease, let him trot by;
It seemeth not that such a foe
From me or you would fly.'
But nothing more is known about it."
                    Wright, Clar. Press Ed.

**Down**: *d. sleeves* Ado III, 4, 20 ..... "Mr. Grant White remarks: 'The dress was made after a fashion which is illustrated in many old portraits. Beside a sleeve which fitted more or less closely to the arm and extended to the wrist, there was another, for ornament, which hung from the shoulder, wide or open'. The 'down sleeves' were probably those that fitted more closely". Wright, Clar. Press Ed.

**Drollery**: Tp. III, 3, 21 "A d., in Shakespeare's time meant 'a puppet-show'. A living drollery is a show in which the figures are not wooden dolls, but living persons". Boas, Warwick Sh.

**Drossy**: *the d. age* Hml. V, 2, 197. = "pinchbeck, imitative". E. K. Chambers, Warwick Sh.

**Drum**: *if you give him not John —'s entertainment* All's III, 6, 41 *i. e.* "the entertainment that a drum gets, a 'drumming'; hence, an unceremonious expulsion. Holinshed relates of a hospitable Mayor of Dublin that 'his porter, or any other officer, durst not, for both his ears, give the simplest man that resorted to his house Tom Drum's entertainment, which is, to hale a man in by the head and thrust him out by both the shoulders'. The phrase was thus proverbial. There is no reason to suppose that Marston's Interlude, Jack Drum's Entertainment (1601) is specially alluded to". Herford (Gollancz).

**Dry-foot**: Err. IV, 2, 39. " 'To draw dry-foot' was a phrase in constant use. It is used, in contradistinction to tracking footsteps in wet or moist ground, to signify hunting with nothing to guide the hound but the scent, where the object of pursuit has passed along dry-foot". H. D. Madden.

**Ducdame** (As II, 5, 56). "Perhaps the old game of Tom Tidler's Ground may throw some light on the matter... It was the custom for the boy who temporarily held the hill or *tom* to assert that the ground or circle belonged to him of right, and dare the invaders to dispossess him by the exclamation of Duc da mé... The word .. resolves itself into the Keltic or Gaelic, *Duthaich*, the *t* silent before the aspirate (pronounced *du-haic*, and signifying a country, an estate, a territory, a piece of land; *do* signifying to, and *mi* me — *i. e.*, this territory or ground is to me; it is my land or estate". Mackay, Obscure Words.

**Dudgeon**: *I see thee still, and on thy blade and d. gouts of blood*, Mcb. II, 1, 46. Cf. (Kyd's) Solim. & Pers. (ed Boas) I, 3, 160: *swear upon my Dudgin dagger*, *i. e.* "a dagger with a hilt made of 'dudgin', a particular kind of wood, probably boxwood". Boas.

**Dull**: *this is a d. sight* Lr. V, 3, 282 = "this is a sorry sight (with reference to Cordelia's corpse)". Koppel, Verbesserungsvorschläge zu Lear.

**Dumain**, name in LLL "is a common anglicised version of that Duc de Maine or Mayenne whose name was so frequently mentioned in popular accounts of French affairs in connection with Navarre's movements that Shakespeare was led to number him also among his supporters". Sidney Lee, Shakespeare.

**Dunsmore** H6C V, 1, 3. "Dunsmoor Heath lies southeast of Coventry". Ch. Allen, Notes on the Shakespeare-Bacon Question p. 176.

**Duty**: *your highness' part is to receive our duties* Mcb, I, 4, 24

= "obedience, loyalty, service owed by (or due from) a person to another". Koppel, Shakespeare Studien.

**Duty**: *Think'st thou that d. shall have dread to speak* ..... Lr. I, 1, 149, "feeling of duty, conscientiousness" (Pflichtgefühl, Pflichtbewusstsein, Pflichttreue"). Koppel, Verbesserungsvorschläge zu Lear.

**Earthly**: *earthlier happy* Mids. I, 1, 76 = "happier on earth. The phrase is really the comparative of the compound adjective 'earthly happy'". E. K. Chambers, Warwick Shakespeare.

**Eastcheap** "was chiefly occupied by butchers, tavern-keepers, and cooks. The 'Boar's Head' immortalized by Shakspeare as the chosen resort of Jack Falstaff and his roystering companions, was situated in the Great Eastcheap ... It did in fact stand about the spot now occupied by the statue of William IV". Harrison-Furnivall.

**Egg**: *will you take —s for money* Wint. I, 2, 161. "A proverb, meaning: 'Will you submit to be paid in eggs instead of coin?' 'will you put up with an affront?' ". Herford.

**Elder**, subst.: *an elder gun* H5 IV, 1, 210 "is a *popgun*; so called because made by punching the pith out of a piece of elder". H. N. Hudson.

**Elder** adj.: *(to second ills with ills)*, *each e. worse* Cymb. V, 1, 14. "The words must mean 'each ill or crime worse than the one which had preceded it', the crime being termed *elder* because committed at a more advanced age". Wyatt, Warwick Sh.

**Ely**: *Ely House* R2 I, 4, 58, II, 1, 216 = "the Bishop of Ely's palace, in Holborn". Herford.

**Embarguement**: *e—s all of fury*, Cor. I, 10, 22; *i. e.* "impediments. The word seems to be suggested by the Sp. 'embargamientos' in the same sense. The vulgate 'embarquements' is an easy corruption. L.". Herford.

**Emboss'd**: *Brach Merriman, the poor cur is emboss'd* Shr. Ind. I, 17 "Merriman is sorely fatigued, or (in the language of Venery) embossed". D. H. Madden.

**Enactures** Hml. III, 2, 207 = "enactments, resolutions. Perhaps it may have the further meaning of carrying purposes into execution". Clark & Wright, Clar. Press Ed.

**Enceladus**: Tit IV, 2, 93. The name is probably taken from Lodge's poem The Honour of the Garter, cf. Ch. Crawford, Sh. Jahrbuch XXXVI, 115.

**Enforcement**: *your mere enforcement* R3, III, 7, 233 = "the simple fact that you have compelled me". Macdonald, Warwick Shakespeare.

**Engage**: *suffered his kinsman March to be —ed in Wales, there without ransom to lie forfeited* H4A IV, 3, 95 *i. e.* "kept as a hostage". Wright, Clar. Press Ed.

**Enswathe**: *enswathed and seal'd to curious secrecy* Lov. Compl. 49 = "envelop with sealing thread". Wyndham. — 'Anciently the ends of a piece of narrow ribbon were placed under the seals of letters, to connect them more closely'. Steevens.

**Entertainment**: *already in the e.* Cor. IV, 3, 49 *i. e.* "in receipt of pay and rations". Chambers, Warwick Sh. [?]

**Entitled** cf. Intituled.

**Entreatment**: *set your entreatments at a higher rate* Hml. I, 3, 122 = "conversation, interview". Murray NED., cf. Schröer, Sh. Jahrb. XXXI, 364.

**Equivocator** Mcb. II, 3, 9 "probably an allusion to the doctrine of 'equivocation' — Newman's 'economy' of truth — taught by the Jesuits; and perhaps in especial to the trial, in March 1606, of Garnet, Superior of the order in England". Chambers, Warwick Sh., cf. Clark & Wright, Clar. Press Ed.

**Estridge** (H4A IV, 1, 98 Ant. III, 13, 197). "A dove pecking an ostrich is not a lively image, and I doubt that the idea would ever have occurred to a commentator, had he been aware, that a kind of hawk in common use was known as an estridge". D. H. Madden.

**Eternal**: *an eternal plant* H6C III, 3, 124. "Eternal means here 'of a quality which transcends things of this world, and belongs to the supernatural'. We have a similar use of 'eternal' in Hamlet:

But this eternal blazon must not be
To ears of flesh and blood. — Act I, 5, 21.

Where 'eternal' is applied to the temporary pains of purgatory". H. H. Vaughan, New Readings & Renderings.

**Eternal**: *th' eternal Devil* Caes. I, 2, 160. "The Poet has *eternal* several times for *infernal*". Henry N. Hudson.

**Evil**: *all the embossed sores and headed e—s* As II, 7, 67. "*Headed evils* are boils grown to a head". J. C. Smith, Warwick Shakespeare.

**Expense**: *moan the expense of many a vanish'd sight* Sonn. 30, 8 = "pay my account of moans for". Wyndham.

**Exposure**: *to weaken and discredit our exposure* Troil. I, 3, 195 *i. e.* "weaken, by discrediting us, our ability to resist the assaults to which we are exposed". Herford.

**Extend**: *ne worse of worst extended* All's II, 1, 176 "it is probably used here simply in the sense of 'meted out to me', or merely used for the purpose of emphasising 'worse of worst'". Gollancz.

**Extent**: *in this uncivil and unjust e. against thy peace* Tw. IV, 1, 57, = "'attack', a legal term... The full legal term is a writ of '*extendi facias*'". A. D. Innes, Warwick Sh.

**Eye**: *this same bias .... clapp'd on the outward eye of fickle France* John II, 583. "According to Staunton the eye of a bowl was 'the aperture on one side which contains the bias or weight'". Wright, Clar. Press Ed.

**F**aint, adj.: *upon f. primrose-beds* Mids. I, 1, 215. "The epithet is probably a variation upon the more familiar *pale* applied to the colour of the primrose, as in 'pale primroses that die unmarried' (Wint. Tale IV, 4, 121)". Herford.

**Falconbridge**: *Stern F. commands the narrow seas* H6C I, 1, 239. "This detail is taken from a later period, and belongs to an essentially different political situation. Halle relates, under date 1471, that 'Thomas Nevel, bastard son of Lord Fauconbridge.... was before this time [but not earlier than 1470, when Warwick broke with York] appointed by the earl of Warwick to be vice-admiral of the sea', with the charge to guard the passage between Dover and Calais lest any *adherents of Edward* should attempt to cross". Herford.

**Fast**: *to f. in fires* Hml. I, 5, 11. "'Fast' appears to be used here in the very general sense of undergoing penance". Chambers, Warwick Sh.

**Fat**: *fat room* H4A II, 4, 1 "probably 'vat-room' — the air of the room reeking with the fumes of beer. 'Fat' was an Elizabethan spelling of 'vat'". Herford.

**Favour**: *and stain my f—s in a bloody mask* H4A III, 2, 136. "*My favours* is interpreted by Warburton and Johnson to mean my features, but although the singular 'favour' has this sense, the plural is not used of a single person. 'Favours' were the ornaments — such as scarfs or gloves, which knights wore, as tokens in the first instance of their mistresses' favour". Wright, Clar. Press Ed.

**Favour**: *in this case of favour* Cymb. I, 6, 42 *i. e.* in this "question of relative beauty". Herford.

**Fear**, vb.: *like a good thing being often read, grown fear'd and tedious* Meas. II, 4, 9. "If this is right, the 'tedium' is the reason of the 'fear'. But *fear'd* is not improbably an error for *sear'd*, *sered*, withered, stale". Herford.

**Feat**, vb.: *to the more mature a glass that f—ed them* Cymb. I, 1, 49 *i. e.* "constrained them to propriety". New Engl. Diction., Wyatt, Warwick Sh.

**Fee**: *a lover's fee* Mids. III, 2, 113. "Halliwell explains this as meaning proverbially three kisses. He quotes an old ballad —

How many? says Batt;
Why, three, says Matt,
For that 's a maiden's fee".
E. K. Chambers, Warwick Shakespeare.

**Fillip**: *if I do, f. me with a three-man beetle* H4B I, 2, 255. "It was a common sport of Warwickshire boys to put a toad on one end of a short board, placed across a small log, and then to strike the other end with a bat, thus throwing the toad high in the air. This is called filliping the toad. A three-man beetle is a heavy rammer with three handles, used in driving piles. This might be used to fillip a heavy weight like Falstaff". Ch. Allen, Notes on the Bacon-Shakespeare Question (citing Rolfe's and Steevens' editions).

**Fire-drake**: H8 V, 4, 45. "A f., or fiery dragon, sometimes denoted a meteor or fiery exhalation, such as a will o' the wisp, and sometimes an artificial firework or rocket". Wright, Clar. Press Ed.

**Flame**, vb.: *I —d amazement* Tp. I, 2, 198, *i. e.* "I caused amazement by appearing in the form of flame". Boas, Warwick Sh.

**Flaw**, subst.: *observe how Antony becomes his flaw* Ant. III, 12, 34 *i. e.* "adapts himself to the collapse of his fortunes". Herford.

**Flesh**, vb.: *fleshed villains*, R3, IV, 3, 6. "To 'flesh' a dog or falcon was to reward it with a portion of the first game which it killed". Wright, Clar. Press Ed.

**Flibbertigibbet**: Lr. III, 4, 120. "Percy quotes from Harsnet, p. 49: 'Frateretto, Fliberdigibbet, Hoberdidance, Tocobatto, were four deuils of the round, or Morrice, whom Sara in her fits, tuned together, in measure and sweet cadence'". Wright, Clar. Press Ed.

**Follow**: *The love that follows us sometime is our trouble* Mcb. I, 6, 11 = "to be after, to pursue". Koppel, Shakespeare Studien.

**Fondling** Ven. 229. "The word is descriptive of Venus' action, not a term of endearment applied to Venus". "Fondling, she saith: 'Since etc.'". Wyndham.

**Forehand**: *a forehand shaft* H4B III, 2, 52. "The exact character of this arrow is doubtful; but Ascham (Toxoph. p. 126) implies that it was one with which the archer shot 'right afore him'; it was preferably made, according to Ascham, with a 'big breast', in order 'to bear the great weight of the bow'". Herford.

**Forestall**: *a ragged and —ed remission* H4B V, 2, 38 *i. e.* "a pardon asked for before it could have been spontaneously granted, and thus granted with contempt as to a beggar". Herford.

**Forfeit**, subst.: *despising many forfeits and subduements* Troil. IV, 5, 187, *i. e.* "disdaining to slay and vanquish many whose lives were in his power". Herford.

**Formal**: *the formal vice Iniquity* R3 III, 1, 82 = „conventional" Macdonald, Warwick Shakespeare.

**Fosset-seller**: Cor. II, 1,79 (forset-seller Fol. 1 — 3, fauset-seller Fol. 4)... "Mr. A. P. Paton found from Gouldman's Dictionary that Forset is the equivalent of Cistella, Arcella & c., 'a little Chest, Casket, or Coffer'". Chambers, Warwick Sh.

**Frank** subst.: H4B II, 2, 160 "was a pen for fattening cattle, pigs, or fowls". Macdonald, Warwick Sh., Rich. III.

**Frontlet**: *What makes that f. on?* Lr. I, 4, 208 = "What makes you wear that frown, like a frontlet or forehead cloth?". W. A. Wright, Clar. Press Ed.

**Fulsome**: *wash'd to death with fulsome wine* R3 V, 3, 132. "Malone explains *fulsome* as 'unctuous', and Schmidt as 'nauseous'. Neither explanation seems quite adequate. The word meant originally 'full'. The signification of 'nauseous', which the word now has, must have come through an intermediate sense of 'overmuch' ('too full'), 'cloying with excess' and this intermediate sense best suits the context here". Macdonald, Warwick Shakespeare.

**Fur**, vb.: *her —ed pack* H6B, IV, 2, 51 *i. e.* "the pedlar's wallet of hide with the hair turned outwards". Herford.

**Gadshill** H4A I, 2, 139 etc., "between Gravesend and Rochester, was in Shakespeare's time a noted place for highway robberies". Wright, Clar. Press Ed.

**Gall**, vb.: *a galled rock* H5 III, 1, 12 *i. e.* "chafed, lashed by the spray". Moore Smith, Warwick Sh.

**Gallop** (Ado III, 4, 94; As III, 2, 119). 'The false gallop, or artificial canter, was denoted by the Latin term *succussatura*, and the idea of jolting would be naturally associated with that pace in the case of the straight-pasterned, thickset horse.' .... D. H. Madden, Diary of Master William Silence p. 296.

**Galloway nags** (H4B II, 4, 205). "There is a certain race of little horses in Scotland, called Galway Nagges, which I have seene hunt the Buck and stagge exceeding well, and indure the chase with good courage".

Gervase Markham, quoted by D. H. Madden.

**Gardiner**: H8 II, 2, 109 etc. "Stephen Gardiner, afterwards (1531) bishop of Winchester, was appointed Secretary 28 July, 1529". Wright, Clar. Press Ed.

**Gawsey** H4A V, 4, 45. "*Sir Nicholas G.* appears to have been Sir Nicholas Goushill of Hoveringham, co. Notts, who with his son Sir Robert was killed at Shrewsbury". W. A. Wright, Clar. Press Ed.

**Genius**: *The genius and the mortal instruments are then in council* Caes. II, 1, 66. "As Brutus is speaking with reference to his own case, he probably intends *genius* in a good sense; for the spiritual or immortal part of himself. If so, then he would naturally mean by *mortal*, his perishable part, or his ministerial faculties, which shrink from executing what the directive power is urging them to". Henry Hudson.

**Giddy**: H6A III, 1, 83 *That many have their giddy brains knock'd out.* "'Giddy' here means 'wild with fury' not simply 'foolish'". Cp. H5 I, 2, 145 *Who hath been still a giddy neighbour to us.* H. H. Vaughan, New Readings & new Renderings.

**Gild**: *g—ed pale looks* Cymb. V, 3, 34 *i. e.* "brought the colour back to faces blanched through fear". Wyatt, Warwick Sh.

**Gimmal(ed)-bit** ('jymold bitt') H5 IV, 2, 49. "A bit in which two parts or links were united as in the gimmal ring". Nares, quoted by D. H. Madden.

**Glance**, subst: *squandering glances* As II, 7, 57 = "random shots". J. C. Smith' Warwick Shakespeare.

**Glimpse**: *the fault and g. of newness* Meas. I, 2, 162 *i. e.* "the imperfect vision due to novelty". Herford.

**Gloss**: *your painted gloss* H8 V, 3, 71. "A 'painted gloss' is a highly coloured, artificial comment, which conceals the real meaning of the speaker as a painted mask conceals the face". Wright, Clar. Press Ed.

**Gloucester**: *the Duke of Gloucester's death* R2 I, 1, 100, *i. e.* "Thomas of Woodstock, youngest son of Edward III, and uncle of Richard and of Bolingbroke. Mowbray was, in reality, himself concerned, with Gloucester and with Bolingbroke, in a plot to seize the King (June 1397); he betrayed it to Richard, and was charged to put Gloucester to death". Herford.

**Go (off)**: *Some must go off* Mcb. V, 8, 36, "a singular euphemism for 'die'". Clark & Wright, Clar. Press Ed.

**Good-year**: what the good-year! Ado I, 3, 1, etc. "The expletive use in questions is equivalent to, and possibly adopted from, the early mod. Du. wat goedtjaar. ... The Du. lexicographers suggest that the idiom probably arose from an elliptical use of *good year* as an exclamation, = 'as I hope for a good year'". Murray, NEDict.

**Good-year**: *what the good-year!* Ado I, 3, 1 etc, "an interjectional expression of frequent occurrence, but unknown origin. Hanmer invented a French equivalent for it, which has apparently no other existence than in his invention; *goujère* a disease contracted from a *gouge* or camp-follower. It may possibly be a corruption of *quad-yere* = bad year, which occurs in Chaucer, and would so be equivalent to the Italian, imprecation *mal' anno!* Or it may be a euphemism for the latter". Wright, Clar. Press Ed.

**Grain**: *your purple in grain beard* Mids. 1, 2, 97 *"purple-in-grain*, the dye obtained from the *Kermes*, (whence Fr. *cramoisi* and English *crimson*), an insect which attached itself to the leaves of the Kermes oak (*Quercus coccifera*), a tree found in the south of Europe, especially in Spain, and also in India and Persia". W. A. Wright, Clar. Press Ed.

**Gratify**: *gratify this gentleman* Merch: IV, 1, 406 = 'thank and reward'. H. L. Withers, Warwick Shakespeare; cp. Furness, Var. Ed.

**Gratulate**: *and g. his safe return to Rome* Tit. I, 221; *i. e.* "mark our satisfaction at". Herford.

**Greece** Shr. Ind. 2, 95 "whence 'old John Naps' derived his cognomen, is an obvious misreading of Greet, a hamlet by Winchmere in Gloucestershire, not far removed from Shakespeare's native town". Sidney Lee, W. Shakespeare.

**Green**, name in R2 I, 4, 23 etc. = "Sir Henry Green, son of a judge of the Court of Queen's Bench". Herford.

**Grossness**: *perspicuous even as substance, whose g. little characters sum up* Troil. I, 3, 325" *i. e.* just as the bulk of a large mass can be expressed in a few little figures, so the meaning of the large undefined challenge is expressed by the single implicit challenge to Achilles". Herford.

**Grow**: *the sun arises, which is a great way growing on the south* Caes. II, 1, 107 "that is, verging or inclining towards the South (in accordance with the early time of the year)". Henry N. Hudson.

**Grow**: *begin you to grow upon me?* As I, 1, 91 "encroach upon me, 'put out your horns' as we might say". J. C. Smith, Warwick Shakespeare.

**Guerdon**, LLL III, 170. "In a little book entered on May 13, 1598 and published in that year as written by J. M. .... and entitled 'a Health to the Gentlemanly Profession of Serving-Men' one finds on signatures I, &c., the following: '..... Now the Servant payd no deerer for the Guerdon then he did for the Remuneration, though *the Guerdon was XI. d. better*, for it was a Shilling, and the other but a Threefarthinges'. The words that I have italicized show, as seems to me, that one borrowed from the other, or both from a common source, and the more probable conclusion is that Shakespeare introduced into his play a story then newly current. .....". Br. Nicholson, Notes & Quer. VII. Ser. Vol. 9.

**Gyves**: *would concert his g. to graces* Hml. IV, 7. 21. "I suppose the idea in 'gyves' is 'faults which should be fetters on his popularity'. Clarke interprets, "turn all my attempts to restrain him into so many injuries perpetrated against his innocence and good qualities". Theobald proposed *gybes*, Daniel *gyres*". E. K. Chambers, Warwick Sh.

**Hackney** LLL III, 1, 33 .. (The word) "was used in the English language ... to denote a small useful nag, of the kind usually employed on the road. This being the class of horse commonly let out on hire, the secondary meaning of a hired animal, in common use, became attached to the word". D. H. Madden.

**Half-checked** *bit* Shr. III, 2, 57. "It may have been the vulgar stable equivalent of one of the many terms of art enumerated by Blundevill; possibly the half-scatch bit". D. H. Madden.

**Hang**: *you must rise and be hanged* Meas. IV, 3, 24, *i. e.* "executed. The verb, like the noun 'hangman', was used with reference to the block as well as the gallows". Herford.

**Hangman**: *the little h.* Ado III, 2, 11 *i. e.* "the little rogue" (Cf. Gentl. IV, 4, 60 *the h. boys*). Wright, Clar. Press Ed.

**Happy**: *those happy smilets* Lr. IV, 3, 21: "pleasant, graceful" (*liebliches, holdes Lächeln*). Koppel, Verbesserungsvorschläge zu Lear.

**Hardiment**: *in changing h. with great Glendower* H4A I, 3, 101, "in valorous exchange of blows". Wright, Clar. Press Ed.

**Hardock** (hordock): Lr. IV, 4, 4. "I find 'hardhake' is given as the equivalent of *Jacea nigra* (or Knapweed) in a MS. herbal in the library of Trinity College Cambridge [R. 14. 32]); and in John Russell's Boke of Nurture (Early English Text Society, 1868), p. 183, is mentioned 'yardehok', which is apparently a kind of hock or mallow. If the botanists could identify the plants mentioned under these names, either of them could easily be corrupted into 'Hardokes' or 'hordocks'". Wright, Clar. Press Ed.

**Harpier** Mcb. IV, 1, 3 "presumably the familiar of the Third Witch". E. K. Chambers, Warwick Sh.

**Hatched**: *venerable Nestor hatch'd in silver* Troil. I, 3, 65 *i. e.* "silver-haired, from the analogy of the fine parallel lines *hatched*, as a ground or ornament in metal engraving". Herford.

**Hawk**, subst.: *when the wind is southerly, I know a hawk from a handsaw* Hml. II, 2, 397. "The word *hawk* was and is used for a plasterer's tool, but no example has been found earlier than 1700. [Cf. Murray NED. S.] *Hack*, however, is an Elizabethan name for a tool for breaking or chopping, and for agricultural tools of the mattock, hoe, and pick-axe type (New Eng. Diction.). *Handsaw* might suggest hack, for we find in 1 Henry IV II, 4, 187, 'My sword hackt like a handsaw'". Dowden, Hamlet.

**Hazard**: *a set shall strike his father's crown into the the hazard* H5 1, 2, 263. "A tennis court was divided by a net into two equal parts, of which one was called the *hazard*". Moore Smith, Warwick Sh. [Cf. Murray NEDict.: "*Hazard side*, the side of the court into which the ball is served".]

**Headland**: *shall we sow the h. with wheat?* H4B V, 1, 16 "the strip of unploughed land left at the end of the furrows, where the plough was turned. As this became available for sowing later than the field, it was often sowed with a later species of wheat". Vaughan, Herford.

**Heath**: *long h.* Tp. I, 1, 70, "a variety of heath, 'which beareth his flowers alongst the stemmes', was then so called". Herford.

**Hebenon (Hebona)** (Hml. 1, 5, 62) "Dr. Brinsley Nicholson (New Sh. Soc. Transactions, 1880—2) argues that the plant meant is the yew. He shows that the name *ebenus* was applied to the yew; that Spenser's mention of a "heben bow" and a "heben lance" require a tough wood, and that ... the yew was supposed to curdle the blood, and so produce a kind of leprosy". E. K. Chambers, Warwick Sh. (Cp. L. H. Grindon, Shakespeare's Flora.)

**Hem**, vb. *I would try, if I could cry 'hem' and have him* As. I, 3, 19 "Rosalind probably said *ha' im* or *hae'm*, this colloquial pronunciation of *have* and its parts being occasionally used by Shakespeare even in verse, where the fuller form is written". Herford.

**Hent**: *a more horrid hent* Hml. III, 3, 88 "grip; or perhaps 'way', 'course'. The word is used in western counties for the course of a ploughshare". Chambers, Warwick Shakespeare.

**Heritage**: *service is no heritage* All's I, 3, 26; the idea seems to be that, 'if service is no blessing, children are'; Psalm CXXVII. 3. has been appropriately cited in connection with this expression: — 'Lo, children are an heritage of the Lord'". Gollancz.

**Hick**: Wiv. IV, 1. 68, *i. e.* "leap, probably used in a coarse sense". Herford.

**High**: *the high East* Caes. II, 1, 110 "is the *perfect* East". Henry N. Hudson.

**High**, sbst.: *the highest of the field*, H4A V, 4, 164 "the highest ground from which the whole field of battle could be seen. It would have been unnecessary to note this, had not Schmidt (Shakespeare Lexicon) interpreted highest to mean 'the farthest visible part (as the horizon seems to be raised)'". Wright, Clar. Press Ed.

**Hilts** (II5 II Chor. 9). "Mr. Deighton writes: 'This word is commonly explained in dictionaries as the *handle* of the sword. It is, however, not the handle itself, but the protection of the handle... Formerly it consisted of a steel bar projecting at right angles to the blade on each side. This form of the two transverse projections explains the use of the plural'". Moore Smith, Warwick Sh.

**Holmedon** H4A I, 1, 55 etc., "Humbleton in Northumberland, near Wooler". Wright, Clar. Press Ed.

**Honorificabilitudinitatibus** LLL V, 1, 44. The word is probably (directly or indirectly) taken from Joannes de Balbi's Catholicon (ed. Venetiis 1497) or from Dante's De Vulgari Eloquio. Cf. Borinski, Anglia XVIII, 450, XIX, 135, M. Herrmann, Euphorion I, 283, A. v. Mauntz, Shakespeare-Jahrbuch XXXIII, 271. [S.]

**Hope**, sbst.: *times in hope* Sonn. 60, 13 = "future times". Dowden.

**Hose**: *you, being in love, cannot see to put on your hose* Gent. II, 1, 84. "Probably 'unable to see to put on one's hose' was a proverbial expression meaning 'unable to tell which leg to put into one's hose first', *i. e.* 'not to have one's wits about one'". Gollancz.

**Hospitable**: *the h. canon* Cor. I, 10, 26, *i. e.* "the laws of hospitality". Chambers, Warwick Sh.

**House**: *how this becomes the h.* Lr. II, 4, 155 *i. e.* "suits the relations of the family. The phrase seems to have been common. Steevens quotes from Chapman's Blind Beggar of Alexandria (Works I, 29), 'come up to supper it will become the house wonderfull well'". W. A. Wright, Clar. Press Ed.

**Household**: *from my own windows torn my household coat*, R2 III, 1, 24 *i. e.* "my arms blazoned in the stained glass". Herford. [?]

**Hue** (hew) Sonn. 20, 7 = "shape, embodiment." Dowden, Wyndham.

**Hull**: *there they hull* R3, IV, 4, 438 = "float about with sails furled, *i. e.* lie to". Macdonald, Warwick Shakespeare.

**Humorous**: *the humorous man* Hml. II, 2, 335 "the character part of the piece". Chambers, Warwick Sh.

**Humour**, sbst.: *Do what you will, dishonour shall be humour* Caes. IV, 3, 109. "Whatever dishonourable thing you may do, I will set it down to the humour or infirmity of the moment". Henry N. Hudson.

**Humour**, sbst.: *the h. of forty fancies*, Shr. III, 2, 70, "either some collection of the short poems called *Fancies*, or a bunch of ribbons, also sometimes so called". Herford.

**Humour**, vb.: *If I were Brutus now, and he were Cassius, He should not humour me*, Caes. I, 2, 319. "To humour a man, as the word is here used, is to turn and wind and manage him by watching his moods and crotchets, and touching him accordingly". Henry N. Hudson.

**Ignorant**: *imprison't not in i. concealment* Wint. I, 2, 397, *i. e.* "concealment under the pretext of ignorance". Herford.

**Illness**: *art not without ambition, but without the i. should attend it* Mcb. I, 5, 21. "The word is generally explained as 'wickedness', but I am inclined to think it is rather 'discontent', 'nervous irritability', 'unwillingness to follow the common herd, and refrain from realizing ambition'". E. K. Chambers, Warwick Sh.

**Image**: *the great doom's image* Mcb. II, 3, 83 = "a sight as terrible as the Last Judgement". Clark & Wright, Clar. Pr. Ed.

**Imbar**: *and rather choose to hide them in a net than amply to i. their crooked titles usurped from you* H 5, I, 2, 94. "Mr. Wright takes 'imbar' = 'bar in, defend'. 'They prefer to involve themselves in contradictions rather than thoroughly to defend their own titles'. I can hardly believe that Shakespeare would have used 'bar' and 'imbar' so near together in opposite senses, and I believe the passage to be corrupt". Moore Smith, Warwick Sh.

[The reading of Qu. A. B *imbace = embase*, i. e. *disannul*, seems to me quite correct, cf. North's Plutarch, Coriolanus, § 46: 'their Tribuneship, which most manifestly is the embasing of the Consulship'. S.]

**Impare**: *nor dignifies an impare thought with breath* Troil. IV, 5, 103; *i. e.* "imperfect, immature, 'improportioned'. The word appears to be Shakespeare's coinage. It is probably suggested by Lat. *impar*, not by the verb *impair*; but the emendator of the Folio text, after his wont, assimilated it to the familiar word [impair]. The best commentary is Polonius' charge to Laertes: 'Give thy thoughts no tongue, nor any unproportioned thought his act'". Herford.

**Importantly**: Cymb. IV, 4, 19; *i. e.* "importunately". Herford.

**Imprese**: R 2 III, 1, 25 "device, emblem on an escutcheon". Herford, Warwick Shakespeare.

**Indeed**: *yes, if this present quality of war, indeed the instant action* H 4 B I. 3, 36. "The error probably lies in the word 'indeed'; the simplest substitute for which is 'induced' (Monck Mason). This gives an excellent sense. Lord Bardolph replies: 'Yes (*i. e.* it did hurt to lay down likelihoods, etc.), if the momentary aspect of the war, so arrived at, induced immediate action; since a cause once se

on foot has always more chances against it, than
for it".                                    Herford.
[Perhaps the word 'indued' would suit the context
just as well, or even better. Cp. Oth. III, 4, 146 'let
our finger ache, and it indues our other healthful
members even to that sense of pain'.          S.]
**Indenture** (Hml. V, 1, 119 etc.). "Indentures were
agreements made out in duplicate, of which each party
kept one. Both were written on the same sheet of
paper, or parchment, which was cut in two in a crooked
or indented line (whence the name), in order that the
fitting of the two parts might prove the genuineness
of both in case of dispute".
                        Clark & Wright, Clar. Press Ed.
**Infant**: *infant state* John II, 97 = "the state that
belongs to an infant".     Wright, Clar. Press Ed.
**Intendment**: *we do not mean the coursing snatchers only, but fear the main i. of the Scot* H5 I, 2,
144 i. e. "collective purpose, combined attack". Moore
Smith, Warwick Sh.
**Interessed**, see *Interest*.
**Interest**: *to whose young loves the vines of France
and milk of Burgundy strive to be interest* Lr. I, 1, 87
*i. e.* "interess'd . . . . For the form of the word see
Cotgrave (Fr. Dict.): 'Interessé . . . . Interessed, or
touched in; dishonoured, hurt, or hindered by . . . . .
Steevens quotes . . . . . from Ben Jonson's Sejanus
III, 1:
          'But that the dear republic,
          Our sacred laws, and just authority
          Are interess'd therein, I should be silent'".
                                Wright, Clar. Pr. Ed.
**Intermit**: *pray to the gods to intermit the plague*
Caes. I, 1, 59. *"Intermit* is here equivalent to *remit*;
that is, *avert*, or *turn back*." Henry N. Hudson.
**Intituled** (intitled, entitled): *intituled in their
parts do crowned sit* Sonn. 37, 7 (cf. Lucr. 57) = "formally blazoned (term of Heraldry)". Wyndham.
**Iron**: *bruising irons* R3 V, 3, 110, *i. e.* "battle
maces".                                     Herford.
**Isbel**: *Isbels of the country* All's III, 2, 13 (14) *i. e.*
"waiting women generally".               Gollancz.
**Issue**, subst.: *interjoin their i—s* Cor. IV, 4, 22
*i. e.* "unite their designs, as Coriolanus proposes that
he and Aufidius shall do. Rolfe explains, 'let their
children intermarry'". Chambers, Warwick Sh.

**Jack-sauce** H5 IV, 7, 148, "an impudent fellow.
'Jack-sauce' occurs in *How a Man may Choose a Good
Wife from a Bad* (1602) V, 1, 8 — — —"
                                    Moore Smith, Warwick Sh.
**Jade**, subst.: *the j—s that drag the tragic melan-
choly night* H6 B IV, 1, 3, *i. e.* "(here) dragons".
                                            Herford.
**Jaunce**, vb.: *jauncing Bolingbroke* R2. V, 5. 94
"From Fr. *jancer*; explained by Cotgrave (as used of
a horse) "to stirre a horse in the stable till hee fret
withall" i. e. to fret the horse to make him prance".
Wright, Clar. Press. Ed., Herford, Warwick Shake-
speare.
**Jaw-bone**: *Cain's jaw-bone* Hml.V,1,85, "alluding
to the ancient tradition that Cain slew Abel with the
jaw-bone of an ass".                      Herford.
**Jet**: *tyranny begins to jet upon the aweless throne*
R3 II, 4, 51 = "encroach".
                        Macdonald, Warwick Shakespeare.

**Jewel**: *mine eternal* j. Mcb. III, 1, 68
"Delius interprets 'eternal jewel' to mean eternal
happiness. But does it not rather mean 'immortal
soul', which Macbeth has sold to the Evil one?".
                        Clark & Wright, Clar. Press Ed.
**Jig**: *he's for a jig or a tale of bawdry*, Hml. II, 2,
522 = "a humorous performance by a clown, given
after the fall of the curtain. It included music, dancing,
and coarse humour, and probably resembled some of
the 'turns' at a modern music-hall more than anything else".     Chambers, Warwick Shakespeare.
**Jump** vb.: *to j. a body with a dangerous physic*
Cor. III, 1, 154, *i. e.* "apply a violent stimulus that
may galvanise it back into life".
                                Chambers, Warwick Sh.
**Juno**: *J—s swans*, As I, 3, 77, "a slip (or possibly
a misprint) for *Venus' swans*".            Herford.

**Kildare** H8 II, 1, 41 = "Gerald Fitz Gerald,
earl of Kildare, then Deputy of Ireland".
                                Wright, Clar. Press Ed.
**Kiln-hole**: *or k., to whistle off these secrets* Wint.
IV, 4, 247 "probably the fire-place used in making
malt; a noted gossiping place".           Gollancz.
**Kimbolton** H8 IV, 1, 34 = "Kimbolton Castle,
in Huntingdonshire".     Wright, Clar. Press Ed.
**Kind**: *a little more than kin, and less than kind*
Hml. I, 2, 65 = "more than related, but less than son
(mehr als verwandt, doch weniger als Sohn)". Schröer,
Sh. Jahrb. XXXI, 362.
**Kiss**, vb.: *when Ik—ed the jack* Cymb. II, 1, 2.
"In the game of bowls to which Shakespeare has
several allusions, the object of each player is to roll
his bowls so that they come to rest as near as possible
to the jack, the small bowl towards which aim is taken.
The most successful stroke is to "kiss the jack" *i. e.*
to play one's bowl alongside and touching the jack.
From this position, however one may be dislodged, as
Cloten was, by the 'upcast' (delivery) of a following
player's bowl".        A. J. Wyatt, Warwick Sh.
**Knot-grass** (Mids. III, 2, 329) "is the Polygonum
aviculare, a British weed, low, straggling, and many-
jointed, hence its name of Knot-grass."
          H. N. Ellacombe, Plant-Lore of Shakespeare.
. . . "a low-growing herb of the Buckwheat familly.
It is probably called 'hindering' because it was supposed to stunt the growth of children. Cf. Beaumont
and Fletcher, *The Knight of the Burning Pestle*,
"Should they put him into a straight pair of gaskins,
't were worse than Knotgrass, he would never grow
after it" — — —. But the 'Knot-grass' also 'hinders'
the plough, and is called in the north the Deil's-
lingels'".
                        E. K. Chambers, Warwick Shakespeare.

**Lampass**: Shr. III, 2, 52 "a swelling of the palate".                                      Herford.
**Lancaster**: (the Duke of) Lancaster H4B I, 1,
134, I, 3, 82 "*i. e.* Prince John of Lancaster. In reality, he never possessed this title, remaining Prince
John until his brother's accession, when he was made
Duke of Bedford".                        Herford.
**Land-damn**: Wint. II, 1, 143. "The word has
also been regarded as a quibbling variation of landan
— a dialectical word still current for the rustic punishment inflicted in various Districts upon 'slan-

derers and adulterers'; it consisted of the public announcement of the delinquents' names to an audience previously summoned by a blowing of horns and trumpets along the country side. ..... Notes and Queries III, 464 (quot. Ingleby)". Herford.

**Lapwing:** *with maids to seem the l.* Meas. I, 4, 32 *i. e.* "to delude them by pretences, as the lapwing tries to divert the sportsman from the direction of its nest". Herford.

**Late:** *O boy, thy father gave thee life too soon, And hath bereft thee of thy life too late* H6C II, 5, 93. "The force of the crude couplet seems to be: — O boy, too soon thy father gave thee life (better thou had'st never been born!); too late he discovers that the fatal blow was aimed at thee .... others explain *'too late'* = *'too recently'*." Gollancz, Temple Sh.

**Laugher:** Caes. I, 2, 72 "if it be the right word, must mean *jester* or *buffoon.*" Henry N. Hudson.

**Laughter:** Tp. II, 1, 33, "It is just possible, as Ingleby has suggested, that *a laughter* may be 'the cant name for some small coin commonly laid in betting'". Boas, Warwick Sh.

**Laund** (lawnd) Ven. 813 = "an open space of untilled ground in a wood." Wyndham.

**Law:** *the l. of arms is such* H6A, III, 4, 38. "By the ancient law before the Conquest, fighting in the king's palace, or before the king's judges, was punished with death. And by Statute 33, Henry VIII., malicious striking in the king's palace, whereby blood is drawn, is punishable by perpetual imprisonment and fine at the king's pleasure and also with loss of the offender's right hand". Blackstone, quoted in Gollancz' Temple Sh.

**Learnedly:** *much he spoke, and learnedly, for life* H8 II, 1, 28 *i. e.* "like a counsel 'learned in the law', not merely skilfully like a practised orator". Wright, Clar. Press Ed.

**Leiger** (lieger): *which shall quite unpeople her of —s for her sweet* Cymb. I, 5, 80 = "shall deprive her of her husband's only ambassador at this court. 'Liegers for her sweet' is a sarcastically exaggerated equivalent of 'agent for his master' in l. 76, as if Imogen's 'sweet' were a foreign power". A. J. Wyatt, Warwick Sh.

**Lethe:** *crimsoned in thy lethe* (Caes. III, 1, 206). "Steevens quotes Heywood's Iron Age II, 1632. "The proudest nation that great Asia nurs'd Is now extinct in lethe." Capell says *lethe* is a technical term for the deer's life-blood, but no instance has been offered". Arthur D. Innes, Warwick Shakespeare.

**Letters-patents:** H8 III, 2, 250 etc. "or *literae patentes,* according to Cowell (Law Dictionary, ed. 1607), 'be writings sealed with the broad Seale of England, whereby a man is authorised to do or enioy any thing that otherwise of himself he could not'". Wright, Clar. Press Ed.

**Level,** subst.: *by line and l.* Tp. IV, 239; *i. e.* "methodically." Herford.

**Likelihood:** *apparent likelihood* R3 II, 2, 136 = "clear prospect". Macdonald, Warwick Shakespeare.

**Limbo Patrum** H8 V, 4, 67, "a cant name for a prison". Wright, Clar. Press Ed.

**Lime:** (H4A II, 4, 137, 140), "according to Sir Richard Hawkins, was put in sack to preserve it (Ob-servations p. 153, Hakluyt Soc. ed.); but for whatever purpose it may have been employed in making the wine it is evident that lime was used to adulterate it". Wright, Clar. Press Ed.

**Limekiln:** *—s in the palm* Troil. V, 1, 25 *i. e.* "gouty lumps". Herford.

**Lincoln:** *my Lord of L.* H8 II, 4, 207 "John Longland, the king's confessor, was Bishop of Lincoln from 1521 to 1547". Wright, Clar. Press Ed.

**Line,** subst. (Tp. IV, 193) "may be explained in two ways — (1) *lime-tree,* in which case Prospero refers to a tree of 'the line-grove which weather-fends his cell' — — — (2) *Clothes-line,* the alternative interpretation is, *a priori,* less probable, for it is incongruous to suppose that such an appliance of civilization should be hanging outside of Prospero's cell. Yet it must be allowed that this interpretation gives more points to Stephano's jests — — —" Boas, Warwick Sh.

**Linen** Lucr. 680 "probably-linen sheets". Wyndham.

**Lingare:** H5 I, 2, 74. "Holinshed has 'Lingard'. Her actual name was Liutgard". Herford.

**Lipsbury:** *if I had thee in L. pinfold, I would make thee care for me,* Lr. II, 2, 9. "Farmer supposed 'Lipsbury pinfold' to be 'a cant phrase, with some corruption, taken from a place where the fines were arbitrary'. Others have conjectured that it was a boxing ring. Nares thinks that a pun on 'lips' is intended, and that the phrase denotes 'the teeth'. This appears the most probable explanation which has yet been given". Wright, Clar. Press Ed.

**Livery:** *to sue his l.* R2 II, 1, 204. II, 3, 129. H4A IV, 3, 62. "This, as described by Campbell, was a proceeding to be taken by a ward of the crown, on coming of age, to obtain possession of his lands, which the king had held as guardian in chivalry during his minority". Ch. Allen, Notes on the Shakespeare-Bacon Question.

**Livery:** *nature's l.* Hml. I, 4, 32 *i. e.* "a blemish they were born with". Herford.

**Lob:** *thou l. of spirits,* Mids. II, 1, 16 *i. e.* "thou lubber of the spirit world; Puck's rough, shaggy enterior being contrasted with the dainty and delicate make of the elves". Herford. ['Lob' is by Skeat identified with the Welsh *llob,* a dolt, blockhead]. S.

**Lockram:** Cor. II, 1, 225, "a coarse linen, so called from the town of Lokrenan in Brittany, where it was made". Chambers, Warwick Sh., Skeat.

**Loggats** (Hml. V, 1, 100). — — "The game so called resembles bowls, but with notable differences. First is it played not on a green, but on a floor strewed with ashes. The Jack is a wheel of lignum-vitae or other hard wood, nine inches in diameter and three or four inches thick. The loggat, made of apple-wood is a truncated cone 26 or 27 inches in length — — — Each player has three loggats which he throws, holding lightly the thin end. The object is to lie as near the Jack as possible. — — — Perhaps Hamlet meant to compare the skull to the Jack at which the bones were thrown". Clark & Wright, Clar. Press Ed.

**Longaville,** name in LLL. = (Duc de) Longueville, cf. Sidney Lee, Gentleman's Mag. Oct. 1878, Sarrazin, Shakespeare-Jahrbuch XXXI, 200.

**Loss**: *the tongue of l.* Tw. V, 61. *i. e.* "the voices of the losers".        A. D. Innes, Warwick Sh.

**Love**: *O injurious love, that respites me a life, whose very comfort is still a dying horror,* Meas. II, 3, 40, *love* = "the indulgence of the law. But *law*, as suggested by Hanmer is very likely Shakespeare's word".        Herford.

**Lug**: *a lugged bear* H4A I, 2, 83, "a dancing bear dragged about by the head".
        Wright, Clar. Press Ed.

**Lure** Shr. IV, 1, 195. "This was a sham bird, usually constructed of pigeon's wings, to which was attached food for the hawk, known as a train."
        D. H. Madden.

**Lust-dieted** Lr. IV, 1, 70 = 'feeding on lust, voluptuous' ('der Wollust fröhnend').
        Koppel, Verbesserungsvorschläge zu Lear.

**Lute**: *he capers nimbly in a lady's chamber to the lascivious pleasing of a l.* (Qu. *love* R3) I, 1, 13. "To the Folio reading *Lute* there is one fatal objection, viz. that the adoption of it renders the word *pleasing* utterly unintelligible. It is true, that, for example, Alexander Schmidt in his Lexicon claims for *pleasing* in this passage the sense of 'pleasure, arbitrary will, command', but we feel that this sense is forced upon the word *pour le besoin de la cause*, for the express purpose of enabling the student to explain this passage, other instances of a substantive *pleasing* with this sense being absolutely wanting. On reflection, however, the Quarto reading appears to be quite intelligible: *chamber* in Sh. usually, if not invariably, means 'bed-chamber', sometimes with the suggestion of sexual indulgence; *to the lascivious pleasing of* (=for the purpose of pleasing . . . . . in a lascivious way) is a construction that has nothing abnormal in it; and to parallel the phrase *a love*, we would cite, for inst., M. of Ven. IV, 1, 277, although it is true that the reference there is to a young *man*".
Van Dam, Shakespeare, Prosody and Text, p. 368.
[The Folio reading 'lute' is, however, supported by the parallel of Marlowe's lines in Tamberlaine, Part II, I, 4 (v. 2590):

Their fingers made to quaver on a Lute,
Their armes to hang about a Ladies necke,
Their legs to dance and caper in the aire.
                                S.]

**Lym** (Lr. III, 6, 72). „This was a purebred bloodhound, used in those days for finding and harbouring the deer. He was so called because he was held in hand by means of a leather strap called a liam; a Norman-French term of venery, derived from *ligamen*. He was all nose and no cry, being used to hunt absolutely mute".        D. H. Madden.

**Mab** (Rom I, 4. 53 etc.). "Beaufort, in his 'Antient Topography of Ireland', mentions *Mabh* as the chief of the Irish fairies. In speaking of the chief of the genii, he says, 'when presiding over the forests and chief of the *Fiodh Rhehe* — — — it was denominated *Mabh* by the Irish, by the Greeks *Diana*, and by the Romans *Pan*' ".
        Thoms, quoted by Furness, Var. Ed.

**Mace**: *O murderous slumber, layest thou thy leaden m. upon my boy?* Caes. IV, 3. 268. "Cf. Spenser, F. Qu. I, 4, 44:

'But whenas Morpheus had with leaden mace
Arrested all that courtly company.'
In both cases, the mace is the club borne by an officer of justice, not, as Steevens and Hudson explain it, the sceptre of a monarch".
        W. J. Rolfe.

**Machine**: *whilst this m. is to him* Hml. II, 2, 124. "T. Bright, in *A Treatise of Melancholy* (1586), explains the nature of the body as that of a machine, connected with the 'soul' by the intermediate 'spirit'. He compares (p. 66) its action to that of a clock."
        Dowden.

**Maiden**: *a m. battle* Troil. IV, 5, 87, *i. e.* "bloodless".        Herford.

**Maintenance**: *lustier maintenance* H4A V, 4, 22, "stouter endurance or resistance".
        Wright, Clar. Press Ed.

**Malt-horse** (Err. III, 1, 32, Shr. IV, 1, 132).
"The Welsh, or Kymric, branch of the Keltic languages spoken in the British Isles, supplies *mallt*, which in all the Welsh dictionaries is explained as 'devoid of energy, dull, spiritless, stupid'. — — — Thus, *Malt-horse* as used by Shakespeare does not mean the horse that draws the malt for the brewer; but a dull, heavy, stupid horse".
        C. Mackay, Obscure Words. [?]

**Mankind**: *a m. witch* Wint. II, 3, 67 *i. e.* "violent, ferocious".        Herford.

**Manner**: *I was taken with the manner* LLL. I, 1, 204 *i. e.* "'with the thing stolen upon him', a legal phrase".        Herford.

**Margarelon**, Troil. V, 5, 7 = *Margareton* in Caxton's Recuyell (cf. Small, Stage-Quarrel p. 157).

**Marish**, see *Nourish*.

**Mark**: *God save the mark* H4A I, 3, 56 etc. "Whatever be the origin of this expression, it is used as a kind of apology for mentioning a disagreeable subject. — — — Perhaps the 'mark' is the sign of the cross made to avert the evil omen, and the expression is a kind of prayer that it may be effectual".
        Wright, Clar. Press Ed.

**Mastic(k)**: *when rank Thersites opes his m. jaws,* Troil. I, 3, 73 *i. e.* "vituperative. The epithet is interesting as possibly containing a reference to the Histriomastix. The Greek μάστιξ was the ultimate source of a word; but Shakespeare had probably met with the Latin derivative *mastigia*, 'scourge', in Plautus".
        Herford.

**Material**: *which is m. to the tender of our present* Cymb. I, 6, 207 = "affects, *i. e.* causes delay in".
        Herford.

**Mean**, sbst.: *our —s secure us,* Lr. IV, 1, 22, *i. e.* "things we think meanly of, our mean or moderate condition, are our security".
        Wright, Clar. Press Ed.

**Medlar**: *the rotten medlar* Meas. IV, 3, 184 "used wantonly for 'woman' ".        Gollancz.

**Memphis**: *a statelier pyramis to her I'll rear than Rhodope's or —' ever was* H6A I, 6, 22. "Capell's '*of Memphis*' has been generally adopted. Pliny, writing of the pyramids near Memphis, records that 'the fairest and most commended for workmanship was built at the cost and charges of *one Rhodope*, a verie strumpet' ".        Gollancz, Temple Sh.

**Menteith** H4A I, 1, 73 "was one of the titles of Murdach Earl of Fife, whose mother Margaret Graham

was Countess of Menteith in her own right (French, Shakespeareana Genealogica p. 73)".
Wright, Clar. Press Ed.

**Metheglin** LLLV, 2, 233 "a drink made of honey and water fermented". Gollancz, Temple Sh.

**Milch** (Hml. II, 2, 540): "milk-giving, thence 'moist'. Steevens quotes from Drayton's Polyolbion [XIII, 171], 'Exhaling the milch dewe'".
Clark & Wright, Clar. Press Ed.

**Mind,** subst. see *Month.*

**Mind,** vb.: *m—ing true things by what their mockeries be* H5 IV Chor. 53 "*Minding,* here, is the same as *calling to mind.*
H. N. Hudson, Moore Smith, Warwick Sh.

**Minister,** vb.: H8, I, 1, 86. "It would seem that 'minister communication of a most poor issue' meant 'furnish occasion for a conference which led to a poor result'". Wright, Clar. Press Ed.

**Misprision**: *m. in the highest degree* Tw. I, 5, 61, = "misapprehension. *In the highest degree* introduces a play upon the legal use of the term in 'misprision of treason' or 'of felony', *i. e.* Knowledge of the crime coupled with concealment of it".
A. D. Innes, Warwick Sh.

**Miss,** subst. Ven. 53 = "*error*". Wyndham.

**Mistress**: *for her only mistress' death,* Per. IV, 1, 11. "Perhaps *mistress* is a corruption of *minion's*".
Herford.

**Mock,** vb.: *it is the green-eyed monster which doth m. the meat it feeds on* Oth. III, 3, 166, "*i. e.* makes its sport with its prey (like a cat), torturing him with 'damned minutes' of doubt, instead of making him 'certain of his fate' at once". Herford.

**Model**: *O England, m. to thy inward greatness, like little body with a mighty heart* H5 II Chor. 16. *i. e.* "visible form in which dwells a mighty spirit. Mr. Vaughan points out that 'model' does not here imply likeness, but is parallel to 'little body' in the next line. For 'model' = a mould or envelope, cp. Richard II, III, 2, 153, where the grave is called 'that small model of the barren earth Which serves as paste and cover to our bones'".
Moore Smith, Warwick Sh.

**Modern:** *her modern grace* All's V, 3, 216; "this word in Shakespeare always means 'ordinary'. If it is right, Bertram can only mean that Diana has the charm of a prevailing, *i. e.* fashionable, type of beauty. But his point is, on the contrary, that she is rare and therefore precious. The most probable emendation is *modest*". Herford.

**Modest**: *humbly entreating from your royal thoughts a modest one,* All's II, 1, 131 *i. e,* "of moderate approval, a simple admission that her (Helena's) offer, though declined, was not out of place". Herford.

**Modo**: *M. he's call'd and Mahu* Lr. III, 4, 149. "Both these names are found in Harsnet p. 46".
Wright, Clar. Press Ed.

**Montacute**: H8 I, 1, 217. "Lord M., or Montague, was Henry Pole, son of the Countess of Salisbury, and grandson of George, Duke of Clarence".
Wright, Clar. Pr. Ed.

**Month**: *I see you have a month's mind to them* Gent. I, 2, 137; *i. e.* "a violent desire. The phrase originally meant the service of *reminder* or 'commemoration', which a testator directed to be performed a month (or, in other cases, a week, or a year) after

his decease. But a commoner sense of *mind,* 'inclination', 'wish', superseded this, the phrase, though now meaningless, remaining unchanged in form".
Herford.

**Mordake** the Earl of Fife (H4A I, 1, 71 etc.) "was Murdach Stewart, eldest son of Robert Duke of Albany, Regent of Scotland".
Wright, Clar. Press Ed.

**Morris**: *nine men's morris* Mids. II, 1, 98.
"A rustic game, which is still extant in some parts of England, so called from the counters (Fr. *merelles*), with which it is played. It is described by James in the Variorum Shakespeare as follows: 'In that part of Warwickshire where Shakespeare was educated, and the neighbouring parts of Northamptonshire, the shepherds and other boys dig up the turf with their Knives to represent a sort of imperfect chess-board. It consists of a square, sometimes only a foot diameter, sometimes three or four yards. Within this is another square, every side of which is parallel to the external square; and these squares are joined by lines drawn from each corner of both squares, and the middle of each line. One party, or player, has wooden pegs, the other stones, which they move in such a manner as to take up each other's men, as they are called, and the area of the inner square is called the pound, in which the men taken up are impounded. These figures are by the country people called *Nine Men's Morris,* or *Merrils*; and are so called because each party has nine men. These figures are always cut upon the green turf or leys, as they are called, or upon the grass at the end of ploughed land, and in rainy seasons never fail to be choked up with mud'. Another variety of the game as described by Alchorne in the Variorum Shakespeare corresponds with what I have seen in Suffolk. — — — 'A figure is made on the ground by cutting out the turf; and two persons take each nine stones, which they place by turns in the angles, and afterwards more alternately, as at chess or draughts. He who can play three in a straight line may then take off any one of his adversary's, where he pleases, till one, having lost all his men loses the game'".
W. A. Wright, Clar. Press Ed.
[The latter variation seems to be very much the same as the game called 'Mühleziehen' in Germany. S.]

**Mortify**: *the —ed man* Mcb. V, 2, 5 *i. e.* "(even) the devout ascetic, dead to all natural sympathies".
Herford.

**Mose,** vb. (Shr. III, 2, 51) "a disease akin to glanders, the name of which is 'borrowed of the French tongue, wherein it is called Mortdeschien [= mort d'eschine], that is to say, the death of the backe'".
D. H. Madden, quoting from Blundevill, The foure chiefest Offices belonging to Horsemanship.

**Mot** Lucr. 830 = "the motto on the scroll".
Wyndham.

**Moth**: *all the yarn she spun in Ulysses' absence did but fill Ithaca full of —s* Cor. I, 3, 94. "The word was pronounced 'motts'. There is thence, apparently, a play upon the cant meaning 'lovers', a sense still current in Ireland. The *Slang Dict.* gives 'mot', a girl of indifferent character. L." Herford.

**Moth,** name in LLL. "Mothe or la Mothe, the name of the pretty ingenious page, was that of a

French ambassador who was long popular in London".
                    Sidney Lee, Shakespeare [?]

**Motion** (Meas. III, 1, 120). "The word motion is sufficiently common in the dramatists in the sense of puppet, automaton, and in the expression 'the perpetual motion' retains that meaning even to-day. Schmidt gives numerous examples, but curiously misinterprets 'Meas. f. Meas'. III, 1, 120 — — — — :

This sensible warm motion to become
A kneaded clod

The human body is a motion or automaton; not however, an insensate, cold piece of mechanism, but sensible and warm. If motion here means 'sense, perceptivity' (Schmidt), how can it become a 'kneaded clod'?"

Arthur Gray, Notes & Quer. VII. Ser. Vol. 6.

**Mouse**: *well moused, lion* Mids. V, 274 = 'torn in pieces; as a cat tears a mouse'.
                              W. A. Wright, Clar. Press Ed.

**Mover**: *see here these m — s* Cor. I, 5, 5. "The term is, I think, ironical — 'these idle fellows who are loitering when they should be moving".
                              E. K. Chambers, Warwick Sh.

**Muddy**: *you muddy knave* H4A II, 1, 106, = "thick-witted".                   Wright, Clar. Press Ed.

**Murray** H4A I, 1, 73, "Thomas Dunbar, second Earl of Moray".
                              Wright, Clar. Press Ed.

**Mutual**: *mutual ranks* H4A I, 1, 14 "are ranks in which all are combined".
                              Wright, Clar. Press Ed.

**Narrow**: *the Narrow Seas* Merch III, 1, 4 = "the English Channel".
                    Clar. Press Ed., Furness Var. Ed.

**Native**: *the head is not more n. to the heart* Hml. I, 2, 47 = "connected by nature with".
                              Clark & Wright, Clar. Press Ed.

**Nayword** (O. Edd. *an ayword*) Tw. II, 3, 146. "The sense here seems to be 'byeword'."
                              A. D. Innes, Warwick Sh.

**Neat**: *neat's leather* Caes I, 1, 29 "is what we call cowhide or calfskin".           Henry N. Hudson.

**Neoptolemus** Troil. IV, 5, 142 = "Achilles. Shakespeare seems to have been led to give him this name either from the mention in the *Troyboke* of a Neoptolemus beside Achilles among the Greeks at Troy, or from the name of his son, Pyrrhus Neoptolemus, as if Neoptolemus were a family name. Pyrrhus Neoptolemus cannot be meant, as he has been referred to as a boy 'at home', III, 3, 209".     Herford.

**New-reaped**: *his chin new-reap'd* H4A I, 3, 34, "not new shaven, for then the resemblance to a stubble land after harvest would be lost. The beard was trimmed and close cut, not long and flowing".
                              Wright, Clar. Press Ed.

**Nice**: *hence, thou n. crutch*, H4B I, 1, 45 *i. e.* "effeminate".                     Herford.

**Noble**: *n. sufferance* Cor. III, 1, 24, *i.e.* "sufferance by men who are noble".
                              Chambers, Warwick Sh.

**Nourish**, subst.: *our isle be made a nourish of salt tears* H6A I, 1, 50. Pope's emendation *marish* for Ff. 'nourish' has been adopted by Herford and others. 'Nourish' "can be defended as equivalent to 'nourice' or 'nurse'; and Steevens asserts that 'nourish'

is an old term for a stew or fish-preserve. But there is slight evidence of this, and the use of so rare a word would not be in keeping with the straight forward, incurious style of the author of 1. Hen. VI".
                                          Herford.

**Number**, subst.: *that shall convert those tears by n. into hours of happiness* H4B V, 2, 61 "*i. e.* tear for tear".                     Herford.

**Nun**: *the livery of a nun* Mids. I, 1, 70. "For the word 'nun' applied to a woman in the time of Theseus see North's Plutarch (1631), p. 2. 'But Aegeus desiring (as they say) to know how he might haue children, went into the city of Delphes, to the Oracle of Apollo: where, by a Nunne of the temple, this notable prophecie was given him for on answer'.     W. A. Wright, Clar. Press Ed.

**O**: *and O shall end* Tw. II, 5, 144, "*i. e.* a halter".
                                          Herford.

**Obsequious** (tear) Sonn. 31, 5 = "funereal".
                                Dowden, Wyndham.

**O'erlook**: Merch. III, 2, 15 *beshrew your eyes, they have o'erlooked me and divided me.* "To 'overlook' was to cast a spell upon, by means of the 'glamour' or power of the eye".
                    H. L. Withers, Warwick Shakespeare.

**Offer**, vb: *offer'd mercy* Cymb. I, 3, 4 "has been explained as 'the pardon of a condemned criminal', which does not reach him. To me, the most probable reference is to the Divine mercy, offered and not accepted".             Wyatt, Warwick Sh.

**Office**, vb.: *a Jack guardant cannot o. me from my son Coriolanus* Cor. V, 2, 68, *i. e.* "Keep me by virtue of his office".             Chambers, Warwick Sh.

**Omittance**: *omittance is no quittance* As. III, 5, 133 "evidently a proverb 'a debt is not cancelled because you omit to exact it' ".
          Cf. Milton P. L. X, 53: Forbearance no acquittance.
                    J. C. Smith, Warwick Shakespeare.

**Oneyers**: *Burgomasters and great oneyres* H4A II, 1, 84. "The nearest companion I can find here [sc. in Dutch] for such dignities as burgomasters is *oneer groot* = infinitely great. Whether *oneer groot* may have travelled by way of groot oneer in to English slang -- — — -- — is a question about which I have an opinion which may or may not be that of others". W. Watkiss Lloyd, Notes & Quer. VII. Ser. Vol. 3. [?]

**Open**, adj.: *an o. room* Meas. II, 1, 135, "probably 'sunny'".                     Herford.

**Ore (Or)** *Virtue would stain that or(e)* (Mod. Edd. *o'er*) *with silver white*, Lucr. 56; *i. e.* "Virtue, by an admixture of 'silver white': — the blazon of chastity with 'that' = Beauty's blushes = 'Beauty's red' of l. 59: — obtained, in accordance with Heraldry, the 'mixed colour', *gold*, which is 'blazed' by the name of *Or*. Virtue's *white*, mixed with Beauty's *red*, has now produced heraldic *or*".           Wyndham.

**Ornament**, see *Substance*.

**Orphan**: *hope of orphans* Sonn. 97, 10 = "hope of leaving posthumous offspring".           Tyler.

**Other**: *Vaulting ambition which o'erleaps itself and falls on the other* Mcb. I, 7, 27.
Vordieck (Engl. Stud. 28, 312) proposes to read "th' author".                     [S.]

**Out**, adv.: *more is to be said and to be done than out of anger can be uttered* H4A I, 1, 107 *i. e.* "without" anger. Delius, W. Franz, Shakespeare-Grammatik p. 266.

**Out**, prepos.: *those that bawl out the ruins of thy linen* H4B II, 2, 27. "The allusion is to Poins" illegitimate children, who 'bawl' in swaddling-clothes made out of his old shirts". Herford.

**Outward**: *and with sighs they jar their watches on unto mine eyes, the o. watch* R2, V, 5, 52. Shakespeare wrote: „unto mine eyes y̌ watch"; the compositor set up *the watch* (confusion between y̌ and y̌), and the editor took upon him to make this clear in his own way by inserting *outward* between *the* and *watch*. And this nonsense editors and readers have been content to sit down to for three centuries past!" Van Dam, William Shakespeare, Prosody and Text p. 320. [?]

**Overscutched**: *o. huswives* H4B III, 2, 340 "'Huswives' could be used ironically, and Ray's statement, that 'over-switch'd huswife' meant 'strumpet', makes the reading 'overswitched' (adopted by Grant White) plausible". Herford.

**Overtop**: *'who to trash for overtopping'* Tp. I, 2. 81. "The overtopping hound is not necessarily a bawler, or even a brabbler. His fault is that his hunting is too quick for the rest of the pack. — — — the huntsman would level him down to the body of his companions by a process known as trashing". D. H. Madden.

**Oxlip**. 'The Oxelip, or the small kind of white Mulleyn, is very like to the c̆owslip aforesaid, sauing that his leaues be greater and larger, and his floures be of a pale or faint yelow colour, almost white and without sauour.' Lyte's Herball (1595), p. 134. See W. A. Wright, Clar. Press Ed., Note to Mids II, 1, 250. — — — "the plant commonly so called is a hybrid between the primrose and the cowslip" E. K. Chambers, Warwick Shakespeare.

**Pajock**: *a very, very p.* Hml. III, 2, 295. "Mr. McGrath in Notes and Queries conjectures that the word is the same as 'patchocke' which occurs in Spenser's View of the Present State of Ireland. It is said of the English in that country that 'some in Leinster and Ulster are degenerate, and growen to be as very patchockes as the wild Irish'." Clark & Wright, Clar. Press Ed.

**Pallid** Compl. 198.
The reading 'palyd' or 'palid' of O. Edd. is supported by the following line from the Returne from Parnassus, First Part (edd. Macray 1886) p. 28, I, 1, 90: — — To youre leane followers, youre palied ghosts. [S.]

**Parmaceti** H4A I, 3, 58. "Reed quotes from Sir Richard Hawkins' Voyage into the South Sea, 1593, where it is said of the whale, 'The fynnes are also esteemed for many and sundry uses, as is his spawne for divers purposes: this wee corruptly call *parmacettie;* of the Latine word, Sperma-ceti'". Wright, Clar. Press Ed.

**Part**, vb.: *part his function*, Sonn. 113, 3 = "depart, abandon". Wyndham.

**Partlet**: *how now, Dame Partlet the hen*, H4A III, 3, 60. A quibble seems to be intended. "A partlet was a gorget or handkerchief for the neck and throat, not exclusively worn by women". Wright, Clar. Press Ed.

**Parts**: *intituled (entitled) in their parts do crowned sit.* Sonn. 37, 7 "the technical terms for the places in a shield on which armorial devices are borne". Wyndham.

**Party-verdict** R2 I, 3, 234 "a decision to which you were a party". Herford, Warwick Shakespeare.

**Pass**: *p —ed in probation with you* Mcb. III, 1, 80 = "I proved to you in detail, point by point. The word 'passed' is used in the same sense as in the phrase 'pass in review'". Clark & Wright, Clar. Press Ed.

**Passage**: *passages of grossness* Tw. III, 2, 77 = "'gross impositions'. 'Passage' practically = imposition." A. D. Innes, Warwick Sh.

**Passage**: *unhidden passages of his true titles* H5 I, 1, 86 = "the clear and indisputable courses by which his titles descended". G. C. Moore Smith, Warwick Sh.

**Pasture**: *the mettle of your pasture* H5 III, 1, 27 i. e. "the fine quality of your rearing. A writer in the *Edinburgh Review* for Oct. 1872 traces a reference here to the belief that the strength and other qualities of stags were much affected by the nature of their pasture. He quotes from the *Noble Art of Venerie*: 'harts beare their heads according to the pasture and feede of the country where they are bred'". Moore Smith, Warwick Sh.

**Patines** Merch. V, 59 "small plates of gold in which the consecrated wafer or bread is presented to communicants" H. L. Withers Warwick Shakespeare (Cp. Furness' Var. Ed. of the Merch of Ven. p. 246).

**Peasant**: *through the peasant towns* H4B Ind. 33, i. e. "country, provincial" towns. Herford.

**Peascod**: *I remember the wooing of a peascod instead of her* As II, 4, 52. "A country lass, when she finds a pod with nine peas, will still place it above the door, and the first man who enters is to be her husband. In Shakespeare's time in was a favourite love token. The peascod must mean here the whole plant which Touchstone mistakes for his sweetheart, as he mistakes a stone for his rival". J. C. Smith, Warwick Shakespeare.

**Peel**, see *pill*.

**Pegasus**: *in Genoa, where we were lodgers at the Pegasus* Shr. IV, 4, 5. Cf. Returne from Parnassus, 2 d Part (edd. Macray) p. 88: "meete me an houre hence, at the signe of the Pegasus in Cheapside". [S.]

**Pen**, vb.: *p. thy breath up* Tp. I, 2, 326 i. e. "make thee gasp for breath". Wyatt, Warwick Sh.

**Penker** (R3, III, 5, 104). "Friar P. was Provincial of the Austin friars". Herford.

**Pennon** H5 III, 5, 49. "A p. was a small triangular flag at the head of a knight's lance, having on it his armorial bearing". (Fairholt, Costume in England).

**Pennyworth**: *We'll fit the kid-fox with a pennyworth* Ado II, 3, 44, i. e. "a bargain. Compare Winter's Tale, IV, 4, 650: 'Though the pennyworth on his side be the worst'. To fit one with a pennyworth is therefore to sell him a bargain in which he will get the worst". Wright, Clar. Press Ed.

**Peremptory** H4A I, 3, 17, "self-asserting, imperious". Wright, Clar. Press Ed.

**Perkes**, see *Woncot*.

**Person**: *if any fear lesser his p.* Cor. I, 6, 70 *"i. e.* danger to his person".

Chambers, Warwick Sh.

**Perspective** (R2 II, 2, 18) "in Elizabethan English was a general term for various artificial means of producing *optical illusion* — — —: But it was specially applied to a kind of *relief* in which the surface was so modelled as to produce, when seen from the side, the impression of a continuous picture, which, when seen from the front, disappeared".

Herford, Warwick Shakespeare.

**Pertaunt-like** LLL V, 2, 67. "It is perhaps worth while suggesting that the phrase (*tant*) *pour tant* (*quasi* 'tit for tat') perhaps underlies the word: it may well have been used in some game: Mr. Marshall quotes *pur Tant* from a poetical description of an old game, but no explanation has as yet been advanced".

Gollancz, Temple Sh.

**Pertaunt-like** LLL V, 2, 67: "an obscure phrase, possibly containing an allusion to the game of 'post and pair', and denoting absolute and unexpected subjection of one player to another. The phrase 'pur tant' was apparently used in this sense in that game".

Herford.

**Philip**: *P. and Jacob* Meas. III, 2, 214 *i. e.* "the day of these saints, 1st May".

Herford.

**Philosophy**: *in your p.* Hml. I, 5, 167 = "natural philosophy", ("Naturphilosophie, Naturwissenschaft".

(Kluge.)

**Phoebus** H4A I, 2, 16. "Falstaff refers to The Knight of the Sun (El Donzel del Febo), as Steevens pointed out, who was known in Shakespeare's time from an English translation of the Spanish romance called the Mirror of Knighthood, Espejo de Caballerias, one of the books found by the curate and the barber in Don Quixote's library".

Wright, Clar. Press Ed.

**Phoebus**: *the young P. fanning* H5 III, Chor. 6; *i. e.* "fluttering in the morning sun".    Herford.

**Pig-nuts** Tp. II, 2, 172: "the tuber or root-stock of the plant known as the *Bunium flexuosum*. It is round and brown, white inside, and pleasant to the taste. It cannot be pulled up by force, but needs to be "dug" for".

F. S. Boas, Warwick Shakespeare.

**Pill** (Most mod. editions *peel*) = *peel* Merch. I, 3, 85. Cf. "Jacob took him rods of green poplar, and pilled white strakes in them" Gen XXX, 37.

**Pick-thanks** (H4A III, 2, 25 "are those who seek to win favour for themselves by telling tales of others".    Wright, Clar. Press Ed.

**Pioned**: *thy banks with p. and twilled brims* Tp. IV, 64. "— — The words more probably do not refer to flowers at all, for the banks seem to be spoken of as 'pioned and twilled' *before* April 'betrims' them. In this case some agricultural operations are alluded to. *Pioning* is used by Spenser in the sense of 'digging', Faerie Queene II, 10 — — *Twilled* may be connected with the French *touiller*, to begrime or besmear, and the passage, according to Henley, refers 'to the repairing of the brims of banks, which have given way, by opening the trenches from whence the banks themselves were at first raised, and facing them up afresh with the mire those trenches contain'".

Boas, Warwick Sh.

**Placket**: *those that war for a p.* Troil. II, 3, 22,

*i. e.* for "a woman (properly a portion of a woman's dress)".    Herford.

**Plague**: *stand in the plague of custom* Lr. I, 2, 3. "Capell explains this as meaning, 'be subject or exposed to the vexation of custom'. I cannot help thinking that Shakespeare had in his mind a passage in the Prayer-book Version, of Psalm XXXVIII, 17, 'And I truly am set in the plague'; where 'plague' is used in a sense for which I have found no parallel. The version evidently follows the Latin of Jerome's translation, 'Quia ego ad plagam paratus sum'.

W. A. Wright, Clar. Press Ed.

**Plain-song**: *plain-song cuckoo* Mids. III, 1, 134. "Mr. Chappell defines plain-song as song in which "the descant rested with the will of the singer", as opposed to "prick-song", *i. e.* "harmony written or pricked down." But is not the real point rather that plain-song is unvarying traditional melody, whereas in prick-song elaborate variations were introduced? Plain-song was a term originally applied to grave, simple, ecclesiastical chants. This distinction exactly fits the difference between the monotonous note of the cuckoo, and the richly-varied music — "brave prick-song" Lyly calls it — of the nightingale".

E. K. Chambers, Warwick Shakespeare.

**Play**, vb.: *play the men* Tp. I, 1, 11, *i. e.* "act with spirit".    Boas, Warwick Sh.

**Pleasing**, see *Lute*.

**Pleasure**: *common pleasures* Caes. III, 2, 255 *i. e.* "pleasaunces, pleasure-grounds".    Herford.

**Point**: *a point of wisdom* R3 I, 4, 99 = "a procedure which shows wisdom".

Macdonald, Warwick Shakespeare.

**Pole**: *painted upon a pole* Mcb. V, 8, 26 "*i. e.* painted on a cloth suspended on a pole, as in front of a wild beast show".

Clark & Wright, Clar. Press Ed.

**Politician**: *I had as lief be a Brownist as a politician* Tw. III, 2, 34, *i. e.* "one belonging to the party of Liberal Catholics". H. S. Bowden, The Religion of Shakespeare London 1899 p. 191, cf. Brandl, Shakespeare-Jahrb. XXXVI, 291.

**Politician**: *the pate of a p.* Hml. V, 1, 86; *i. e.* "plotter. The word in Shakespeare suggests Machiavelism".    Herford.

**Pompey**: *P.'s blood*, Caes. I, 1, 56; "*i. e.* his [sc. the great Pompejus'] son, Cneius, who had fallen in the battle of Munda, the immediate occasion of Caesar's Triumph".    Herford.

**Poprin**: *poprin pear* Rom. II, 1, 38. "*Poperingue* is a town in French Flanders two leagues distant from Ypres, from whence the Poperin pear was brought into England. — — — The word was chosen, I believe, merely for the sake of a quibble which it is not necessary to explain."

Dyce, quoted by Furness, Var. Ed.

**Porch**: *in Pompey's p.* Caes. I, 3, 126. *i. e.* "'one of the porches about the theatre [of Pompey], in which there was a certain place full of seats for men to sit in; where also was set up the image of Pompey' (North). This porch was the actual scene of the assassination, which Shakespeare places on the Capitol; and the 'image' is that which he nevertheless makes Caesar's body stain with blood (III, 2, 192)".    Herford.

**Pore**: *the poring dark* H5 IV Chor. 2, *i. e.* "persystently brooding over the earth. The word has no etymological connection with 'purblind' and seems to mean 'to poke or linger over a thing.'"

Moore Smith, Warwick Sh.

**Portage**: *thy loss is more than can thy portage quit, with all thou canst find here*, Per. III, 1, 35 *i. e.* "the child's loss even at the outset is such that all that it inherits by birth falls short of what its birth has cost. This seems to be the clear meaning, irregularly expressed."
Herford.

**Portage**: *let it* (the eye) *pry through the p. of the head like the brass cannon*, H 5, III, 1, 10; "*i. e.* eye-sockets".
Herford.

**Portugal**: *the bay of Portugal*, As IV, 1, 213 a name "still used by sailors to denote that portion of the sea off the coast of Portugal from Oporto to the headland of Cintra"
Wright.

**Possess**: *which art possess'd now to depose thyself* R2, II, 1 108 = "seized with a mad impulse."
Herford, Warwick, Shakespeare.

**Posture**: *the posture of your blows* Caes. V, 1, 33 "for *nature* or *character* probably".
H. N. Hudson.
= "where you will succeed in planting your blows".
A. D. Innes.

**Practisants**: *here entered Pucelle and her p.* H6A III, 2, 20; = "fellow-plotters".
Gollancz, Temple Sh.

**Precious**: *you p. winners* Wint. V, 3, 131 *i. e.* "winners of what gon prize".
Herford.

**Precious**: *the most p. square of sense* Lr. I, I, 76, = sensitive, scrupulous („das empfindlichste, schärfste, genaueste oder peinlichste Vernunftmaass"). Cp. Cymb. I, 6, 37, John IV, 1, 94.
Koppel, Verbesserungsvorschläge zu Lear.

**Prefer**: *Ay, if Messala will p. me to you* Caes. V, 5, 61 = "recommend".
Henry N. Hudson, Arthur D. Innes, Warwick Shakespeare.

**Prester**: *P. John*, Ado II, 1, 276 "was a fabulous Christian King of vast wealth and power who was supposed to live in some inaccessible region in the east of Asia. Marco Polo identifies the original Prester John with Unc Khan, the chief of the Keraits, a Mongol tribe said to have professed Christianity. In the sixteenth century the name was applied to the King of Abyssinia, whose title *Prestegian* was according to Purchas (Pilgrimage ed. 1614 p. 670), was 'easily deflected and altered to *Priest John*".
W. A. Wright, Clar. Press Ed. (cf. Fr. Zarncke, Ueber die Sage vom Priester Johannes. Bang, Engl. Stud. XXVIII, 214). S.

**Pretty**: (*a course pretty and full of view* Cymb. III, 4, 150) "is often glossed 'apt, suitable for the purpose". The whole expression, 'You should tread a pretty course', seems to me rather to mean: 'You would have a part to play that would be novel, full of interest, and likely to succeed'. Collier suggested the reading *privy*".
Wyatt, Warwick Sh.

**Print**, vb: *the story that is —ed in her blood* Ado IV, 1. 124; "that is, as Johnson explains it, 'the story which her blushes discover to be true', for the Friar, although Hero had swooned, observed 'a thousand blushing apparitions To start into her face'. This is a more natural explanation than that given by Schmidt———". W. A. Wright, Clar. Press Ed.

**Probable**: *it is spoke freely out of many mouths* . *— how p. I do not know* Cor. IV, 6, 65 *i. e.* "capable of proof".
Chambers, Warwick Sh.

**Profess**: *that I p. myself in banqueting to all the rout* Caes. I, 2, 77; *i. e.* "make professions of friendship".
Herford.

**Profound**: *a vaporous drop profound* Mcb. III, 5, 24 "with deep or hidden qualities' Johnson — — But the Clarendon Press editors explain it as deep, and therefore ready to fall".
E. K. Chambers, Warwick Shak.

**Property**, vb.: *his. voice was —ed as all the tuned spheres* Ant. V, 2, 83, *i. e.* "harmonious as the spheres".
Herford.

**Proverbed**: *I am p. with a grandsire phrase*, Rom. I, 4, 37; *i. e.* "the old proverb fits my case, viz. that it is well to leave off when the game is at the fairest".
Herford.

**Provincial**: *P. roses* Hml. III, 2, 288, *i. e.* "rosettes resembling the damask rose, called 'provincialis' (from Provins, near Paris)".
Herford.

**Psalteries** Cor. V, 4, 52. "The psaltery seems to have resembled the modern dulcimer, a small hollow chest with strings stretched across it".
Chambers, Warwick Sh.; cf. Naylor, Shakespeare and Music p. 176.

**Publish**: *thus far I will boldly p. her* Tw. II, 1, 30 *i. e.* 'speak of her openly'.
A. D. Innes, Warwick Sh.

**Pugging tooth** Wint. IV, 3, 7 "means (not as the glossary explains it, thievish) but pegging, peg tooth, *i. e.*, the canine, or dog tooth. 'The child hasn't its pegging teeth', old women will say.
J. Walter, Shakespeare's True Life.

**Puke-stocking**: H4 A II, 4, 78. "It is not certain whether 'puke' here denotes a colour or a material: probably the latter, for the next epithet, 'caddis-garter', is derived from the material of which garters were made. As a colour 'puke' appears to have been something between grey and black, and in Baret's Alvearie is given as the equivalent of the Latin *pullus*. 'Puke' as a material was a kind of dark-coloured cloth — —".
W. A. Wright, Clar. Press Ed.

**Pull**: *I p. in resolution* Mcb. V, 5, 42 = "check, rein in". Clark & Wright, Clar. Press Ed.

**Purchase**, subst.: *fourteen years' purchase* Tw. IV, 1, 24 "*i. e.* purchase at the price of fourteen years' returns; from which it is clear that this was a high rate for the purchase of land in Shakespeare's day, though it would be low now".
A. D. Innes, Warwick Sh.

**Push**, subst.: *the present push* Hml. V, 1, 318 = "the instant test". Clark & Wright, Clar. Press Ed.

**Put**: *this is put forth too truly* Wint. I, 2, 14 *i. e.* "this foreboding is too well justified". Herford.

**Pyramid**: *Time — — —, thy pyramids* Sonn. 123, 2 *i. e.* "'all that Time piles up from day to day', new structures of event".
Herford.

**Quality** (Hml. II, 2, 363) "was especially used of the theatrical profession".
Wright, Clar. Press Ed.

**Quality**: *without less quality* Cymb. I, 4, 24 *i. e.* "with no other than a beggar's position".
Wyatt, Warwick Sh.

**Queasy**: *I have one thing of q. question* Lr. II, 1, 19 *i. e.* "easily disturbed, unsettled, and therefore requiring delicate management".
W. A. Wright, Clar. Press Ed.

**Question**: *little eyases that cry out on the top of q.* Hml. II, 2, 356.
"This is generally interpreted as 'cry out in a high childish treble' or 'cry out, dominating conversation'. I believe it really means, 'cry out on the burning question of the day, the question that is at the top, most prominent'".
Chambers, Warwick Sh.

**Questionable**: *in such a questionable shape* Hml. I, 4, 43 "*i. e.* arousing obstinate questionings or problems in Hamlet's mind that need an answer".
Chambers, Warwick Shakespeare.

**Quill**: *in the q.* H6B I, 3, 4.
— — "Halliwell and others explain it also as 'all together in a body'. This interpretation is borne out by a passage in '*The Devonshire Damsel's Frolic*', one of the 'Songs and Sonnets' in the collection called 'Choyce Drollery', &c (1656): —
'Thus those females were all in a quill
And following on their pastimes still'.
No satisfactory explanation has yet been given of the origin of the phrase. The following solution is suggested: — 'the quill' I take to be a popular elaboration of the more correct phrase 'a quill' which occurs in the ballad quoted; the latter seems to be a corruption of French *accueil*, O. F. *acueil, acoil, akel, achoil*, &c., 'a gathering together'".
Gollancz, Temple Sh.

**Quintessence** As III, 2, 147. "Over and above the four elements (fire, air, earth, and water) the mediaeval alchemists figured a fifth essence, *quinta essentia*, or other, purer even than fire. This quintessence is to the world as the spirit to the body. Hence it is used loosely for the concentrated essence of anything, perhaps with a confused idea that the name means "essence five times distilled".
J. C. Smith, Warwick Shakespeare.

**Quirk** (Tw. III, 4, 268) "'temper', 'turn of mind': from Celtic root meaning 'turn'.
A. D. Innes, Warwick Sh.

**Quoif**: *thou sickly quoif* H4B I, 1, 147 "the invalid's headbandage or 'Kerchief'".
Herford.

**Random**: *at random* Ven. 940 (Qu. *randon*). "The old form from Old French *randon*, French *randonée*. 'Terme de chasse. Tour, circuit fait sur un même lieu par une bête qu'on a lancée'. Littré".
Wyndham.

**Rank**, subst.: *the right butter-women's rank* As III, 2, 103 = "the regular jog-trot of butter-women going to market in a row. — — — Wright plausibly conjectures *rack*, which, as appears from Holme, is a pace between trot and an amble".
J. C. Smith, Warwick Shakespeare.

**Ransom**: R3 V, 3, 265 = "the price to be paid in the event of failure".
Macdonald, Warwick Shakespeare.

**Rapture**: Cor. II, 1, 223. "The emendation (sc. *rupture*)" is supported by the following quotation from *Phioravante's Secrets* (1582): 'To helpe yong Children of the Rupture. The Rupture is caused

two waies, the one through weaknesse of the place, and the other through much crying'".
Chambers, Warwick Sh.

**Rascal** (Haml. II, 2, 594). "'A rascal was a lean and worthless deere'".
D. H. Madden.

**Ravenspurgh** H4A I, 3, 248, "formerly on the coast between Hull and Bridlington. It has disappeared for many years". Wright, Clar. Press Ed.

**Readiness**: *let's briefly put on manly readiness* Mcb. II, 3, 139.
"Here the phrase means first 'complete armour' in contrast to the 'naked frailties' just mentioned, and involves also the corresponding habit of mind".
Clark & Wright, Clar. Press Ed.

**Recognizance** (Hml. V, 1, 113). "Recognisance . . . . . is as a Bond or Obligation Record testifying the Recognisor to owe to the Recognisee a certain sum of money".
Cowel's Law Dictionary, quoted in Clark & Wright's Clarendon Press Ed.

**Recorder** Mids. V, 123, "a flute with a hole bored in the side and covered with gold-beater's skin, so as to approach the effect of the human voice. See Chappell, *Popular Music of the Olden Time*, p. 246".
E. K. Chambers, Warwick Shakespeare.

**Recover**: *why do you go about to r. the wind of me, as if you would drive me into a toil?* Hml. III, 2, 361.
"In order to drive a deer into the toils it was needful to get to windward of him, so that, having you in the wind, he might break in the opposite direction".
D. H. Madden.

**Recovery**: *fine and r.* Wiv. IV, 2, 225 "were part of the legal mechanism for converting a conditional tenure of land into ownership".
Herford.

**Regard**, subst.: *regards of safety and allowance* Hml. II, 2, 79, "terms securing the safety of the country and regulating the passage of the troops through it".
Clark & Wright, Clar. Press Ed.

**Regard**: *your loss is great, so your r. should be* H6A IV, 5, 22, "*i. e.* care for your own safety".
Gollancz, Temple Sh.

**Relapse**: *killing in relapse of mortality* H5, IV, 3, 107, *i. e.* "in the very act of being resolved into their mortal elements; as they decompose. L".
Herford.

**Religious**: *an old religious uncle of mine* As III, 2, 362 "probably = belonging to a religious order".
J. C. Smith, Warwick Shakespeare.

**Remainder**: *cut the entail from all remainders* All's IV, 3, 313 "(a legal term) = something limited over to a third person on the creation of an estate less than that which the grantor has".
Gollancz.

**Remembrancer**: (Cymb. I, 5, 77), "in law was the name of an officer in the exchequer".
A. J. Wyatt, Warwick Sh.

**Reputation**: *answer in the effect of your reputation* H4B II, 1, 142, *i. e.* "respond to her suit in the manner conformable to your position". Herford.

**Resolution** (*and r. thus fobbed as it is with the rusty curb of old father antic the law?*) H4A I, 2, 67 "is to be interpreted here by the 'purse of gold most resolutely snatched' in line 28".
Wright, Clar. Press Ed.

**Respite**, subst.: *the determined r. of my wrongs* R3 V, 1, 19, *i. e.* "the appointed limit to my exemption from the impending punishment of my misdeeds". Herford.

**Rest**: *that is my rest* H5, II, 1, 17 *i. e.* "undertaking. According to Nares' *Glossary*, a phrase from a game at cards called Primero. By *rest* was meant the cards on which you stood to win (as in the modern game Nap). 'To set up one's rest' was to complete one's hand of cards, and stand on it; so, metaphorically 'to set up one's rest to do anything' meant to take upon one to do it". Moore Smith, Warwick Sh. Cp. Err. IV, 3, 37, Rom. IV, 5, 6 etc.

**Resty**: *rise, resty muse* Sonn. 100, 9 *i. e.* "jibbing (term of manege)". Wyndham.

**Retirement**: *a comfort of retirement lives in this* H4A IV, 1, 56, *i. e.* "a support to fall back upon". Herford.

**Revenue**: *my ripe revenue* R3, III, 7, 158 = "something which I have a right to, and which the time has come for me to enjoy". Macdonald, Warwick Shakespeare.

**Rheumatic**: H4B II, 4, 62, H5, II, 3, 40 "is a Quicklyism for lunatic". H. N. Hudson.

**Rheumatic**: *rheumatic diseases* Mids. II, 1, 105 "says Malone, 'signified in Shakespeare's time, not what we now call rheumatism, but distillations from the head, catarrhs, &c' — — — It would be more correct to say that the term included all this in addition to what is now understood by it". Wright, Clar. Press Ed.

**Richard**: *Sir R. Grey* H6C III, 2, 2. "'Richard' is an oversight; Holinshed calls him (rightly) Sir John Gray, and reports that he received his Knighthood on the very battlefield of St. Albans at which he fell". Herford.

**Ring**, subst.: *cracked within the ring (like a piece of uncurrent gold)* Hml. II, 2, 448 'There was a ring or circle on the coin, within which the sovereign's head was placed: if the crack extended from the edge beyond the ring the coin was rendered unfit for currency'. Douce, quoted by Clark & Wright.

**Ring**, subst.: *you are full of pretty answers. Have you not been acquainted with goldsmiths' wives and conned them out of rings?*, As III, 2, 289, "*i. e.* out of the mottoes or 'posies' of rings". Herford.

**Road**: Gent. I, 1, 53, II, 4, 187 *i.e.* "wharf, harbour" Herford (cf. Shakespeare-Jahrbuch XXXVI, 96).

**Roam**: *and not to crack the wind of the poor phrase, roaming it thus* Hml. I, 3, 109 = "beating the field, pursuing" (durchstreifen, verfolgen). Schröer, Sh. Jahrb. XXXI, 364.

**Rochford**, H8 I, 4, 93. "Sir Thomas Bullen was not created Viscount Rochford till 18 June, 1525". Wright, Clar. Press Ed.

**Romano**: *Julio Romano*, Wint. V, 2, 106. "Giulio Pippi, known as Giulio R. was born in 1492, and died in 1546; his fame as a painter" [and sculptor, cf. Sarrazin, Shakespeare's Lehrjahre P. 124] "was widespread". Gollancz.

**Room**: *if room enough* Tp. I, 1, 9 *i. e.* "if there be sea-room enough". Boas, Warwick Sh.

**Rose**: H8 I, 2, 152. "The manor of the Red Rose belonged to the Duke of Buckingham — —. The subsequent fortunes of the house are told by Stow in his Survey of London. 'In this [Suffolk] Lane is one notable grammar school, founded in the year 1561 by the master, wardens, and assistants of the Merchant-Tailors in the parish of St. Laurence Poultney; Richard Hilles, sometime master of that company, having before given 500 *l.* towards the purchase of a house, called the manor of the Rose, sometime belonging to the Duke of Buckingham, wherein the said school is kept'". Wright, Clar. Press Ed.

**Royalty**: *(have seen the well-appointed king embark) his r.* H5 III Chor. 5, "taken by Schmidt = 'his majesty', *i. e.* himself. This seems to me turgid. I think 'royalty' means 'his royal state and surroundings'". Moore Smith, Warwick Sh.

**Rump-fed**: *the rump-fed ronyon* Mcb. I, 3, 6, "surely not, as some commentators assert, 'fed on offal', but rather fed on the best joints, pampered". Clark & Wright, Clar. Pr. Ed.

"I prefer to either of these the more pointed explanation of Dyce's 2nd edition. He quotes from Kilian's *Dictionary*, '*Rompe* nux myristica, vilior, cassa inanis. The reference will then be to the chestnuts which the woman was eating". E. K. Chambers, Warwick Sh.

**Run**: *runs the bushes* Ven. 871 "run a transitive verb". Wyndham.

**Runagate** R3 IV, 4, 465 "properly a doublet of *renegade*. The Middle English *renegat* means an apostate. — — It almost seems as if Shakespeare understood it in the sense of 'runaway'. For Richard nowhere accuses Richmond of trachery, though he does accuse him of cowardice in taking refuge in Brittany". Macdonald, Warwick Sh.

**Runaway**: *that runaways' eyes may wink* Rom. III, 2, 6. "No interpretation of this word is satisfactory. Those who retain it commonly explain it 'ramblers, vagabonds', whose observation Romeo could not defy till it was dark; a prosaic idea. Dyce proposed 'rude day'; Heath 'Rumour's; Halpin thought that 'Runaway' meant Cupid; Warburton that it referred to Phoebus in his chariot; and Mr. Gollancz suggests, very prettily that Runaway 'may have belonged, in the sense of "Day" to the playful phraseology of Elizabethan girls, and savours of the expressive language of children's rhymes'". Herford.

**Sacring bell**: H8 III, 2, 295 "which was rung at the elevation of the Host, or before the Sacrament as it was carried through the streets to the sick. Here probably the latter". Wright, Clar. Press Ed.

**Safety**: *scalds with safety* H4B IV, 5, 31 *i. e.* "burns while it protects". Herford.

**Sagittary**: *the S.* Oth. I, 1, 159, "either the name of an inn (cf. 'the Centaur' in *Com. of Errors*) or the official residence of the military and naval commanders, where the statue of an archer is still said to exist. It is not known however, to have been so called, and the allusions suggest that Shakespeare, in any case, thought of an inn". Herford.

**Salt**, adj.: *the s. fish is an old coat*, Wiv. I, 1, 22. "This passage has not been entirely explained. Shallow probably means to correct Evans somewhat as follows: — 'The luce is not the louse, but the freshwater fish, which, salted and "white", marks an ancient coat-of arms". Herford.

**Sanctuary**: H6C IV, 4, 31 etc., "the sanctuary at Westminster, which afforded protection from any persecution". Gollancz, Temple Sh.

**Sandal**: H6C I, 2, 63 "near Wakefield".
Herford.
**Sands**: H8 I, 3, 47 etc. "Lord Sands, or Sandys, was at this time Sir William Sandys, who was not created Baron Sandys of the Vine, near Basingstoke, till 1523". Wright, Clar. Press Ed.
**Satisfy**: *I shall be satisfied* Caes. IV, 2, 10 = "have a sufficient explanation".
Arthur D. Innes, Warwick Shakespeare.
**Sauce**, vb.: *s. his palate with thy most operant poison* Tim. IV, 3, 299. = "*bite, pepper*".
Koppel, Sh. Stud.
**Saucy**: *saucy doubts and fears* Mcb. III, 4, 25 = "pungent, sharp, gnawing". Koppel, Sh. Studien.
**Scamels** Tp. II, 2, 176. "The word may either mean (1) 'limpets', a diminutive of *scam*, shell-fish, derived from the Norse *skama* or shell; or (2) some kind of rock-breeding bird. Stevenson, in his *Birds of Norfolk*, says that the female bar-tailed Godwit is called a *scamell* by the gunners of Blakeney. But this bird is not a rock-breeder — — —. Of the numerous conjectural readings the most plausible is *sea-mells* or sea-malls (Theobald, Steevens, Malone, Harting) i. e. 'sea-gulls'. Boas, Warwick Sh.
**Scratch**: *Priscian a little scratched* LLL V, 1, 32 "alluding to the common phrase *diminuas Prisciani caput*, applied to such as speak false Latin".
Gollancz, Temple Sh.
**Scrubbed**: *a little scrubbed boy* Merch. V, 162 "short or stunted like a scrub or shrub".
H. L. Withers, Warwick Shakespeare. (Cp. Furness Var. Ed. Merch. of Ven. p. 260).
**Sea-monster**: Lr. I, 4, 283. "It is more likely that by the sea-monster he [Sh.] meant the whale".
Wright, Clar. Press Ed.
**Sear**, vb.: *and s. up my embracements from a next with bonds of death* Cymb. I, 1, 116, i. e. "cere, cover with wax; chiefly used of dipping linen cloth in melted wax, to be used as a shroud. The shroud was called a *cerecloth* or cerement (here 'bonds of death')".
A. J. Wyatt, Warwick Sh.
**Search**: *if it be a day fits you, search out of the calendar* Per. II, 1, 58. Hudson and Herford read: *steal't.* [S.]
**Season**, vb.: *all s—ed office* (Cor. III, 3, 64. "This may be explained either, with Johnson, as 'established and settled by time', or, with Schmidt, as 'qualified, tempered', as opposed to 'power tyrannical'. I prefer the former. It is true that, although certain popular rights, such as a say in the choice of consul, were of old standing, yet the tribunate was quite an innovation . . . . But the tribunes themselves were the last people to make this distinction".
Chambers, Warwick Sh., Herford.
**Season**, subst.: *the season of all natures, sleep* Mcb. III, 4, 141 = " the balm of hurt minds".
Koppel, Shakespeare Studien.
**Second**, subst.: *you have shamed me in your condemned seconds* Cor. I, 8, 15 i. e. "by seconding me in such a damned cowardly fashion".
Chambers, Warwick Sh.
**Second**, subst.: *which is not mix'd with seconds* Sonn. 125, 11 "*Seconds*, I submit = 'assistants', 'colleagues', or at least, other poets similarly engaged in conquering 'Eternity' by laboured 'Petrarchizing'".
Wyndham.

**Security**: *but s. enough to make fellow-ships accurst* Meas. III, 2, 241 i. e. "entreaties to stand surety".
Herford.
**Seel**: Oth. III, 3, 210. „It was then the custom to close the eyes of a newly-taken hawk until she had become accustomed to the hood, by drawing through the eyelids a fine silken thread".
D. H. Madden.
**Seem**: *Why do you start and seem to fear Things that do sound so fair* Mcb. I, 3, 51 = "to show, to signify" (cf. Cor. V, 1, 8, Mcb. I, 2, 47, I, 3, 43, Wint. T. IV, 4, 157): *to seem thus washing her hands* (Mcb. V, 1, 33 = "to pretend", (cf. Lear II, 1, 30, All's IV, 1, 25, Meas. II, 4, 75 etc.).
Koppel, Shakespeare Studien I, 28, 53.
**Set**: *who sets me else?* R2, IV, 57 = "'who else challenges me to a game', properly 'lays down stakes'".
Herford, Warwick Shakespeare.
**Set**: *She's e'en setting on water to scald such chickens as you are*, Tim. II, 2, 71 i. e. "she is preparing to pluck you; alluding to the custom of plunging the newly killed chicken into boiling water before plucking it. L."
Herford.
**Setebos**: Cp. Purchas his Pilgrimes based on Eden's translation of Pigafetta's Journal (publ. 1577): "they cryed upon their great Devill Setebos, to helpe them" (quoted by G. Wyndham, Fortn.Rev.LXIV, 795).
**Shake**: *he faced the slave Which ne'er shook hands nor bade farewell to him Till he unseam'd him from the nave to the chaps* Mcb. I, 2, 21 = "he faced the slave who never found time for the preliminary formalities of a duel i. e. shaking hands with and bidding farewell to the opponent, till Macbeth unseam'd him etc."
Koppel, Shakespeare Studien.
**Shape**: *fit us to our shape*, Hml. IV, 7, 151, = "enable us to act our proposed part".
Clark & Wright, Clar. Press Ed.
**Shapeless**: *s. idleness* Gentl. I, 1, 8 i. e. "devoid of definite aim".
Herford.
**Sheep-biting**: *show your sheep-biting face* Meas. V, 359 i. e. "thievish".
Gollancz. [?]
**Shift**, subst.: *when he was made a shriver, 't was for sh.* H6C III, 2, 108 i. e. "for a cunning purpose".
Herford.
**Shirley** H4A V, 4, 41 was Sir Hugh Shirley, Master of the Hawks to Henry IV (French Shakespeareana Genalogica, quoted in Wright's Clar. Press Ed.).
**Sign**: *(with) signs of war (about his aged neck)* R2, II, 2, 74 "is defined by the local description: it means the mail-gorget or throat-piece".
Herford, Warwick Shakespeare.
**Simple**, subst.: *in s. time* Wiv. III, 3, 79 i. e. "in the season when medicinal herbs were gathered".
Herford.
**Simular**: *thou s. man of virtue* Lr. III, 2, 54 i. e. "thou man who feignest virtue".
W. A. Wright, Clar. Press Ed.
**Sinel** Mcb. I, 3, 71. "The real name of Macbeth's father was Finley. In Fordun's *Scotochronicon* (IV, 44) he appears as "Finele", and of this Boethius, and Holinshed following him, make "Synele".
Chambers, Warwick Sh.
**Sinew**: *a rated sinew* H4A IV, 4, 17, "a source of strength on which they reckoned".
Wright, Clar. Press Ed.

**Single**, adj.: *yours. bond* Merch. I,3,146. „Technically, a single bond was a bond without condition; but Antonio's bond was to have a condition, and therefore it was inaccurately described as a single bond. The meaning intended appears to be, a bond without a surety". Ch. Allen, Notes on the Bacon-Shakespeare Question p. 132. cp. Furness Var. Ed.

**Single**, vb.: *s. you thither then this dainty doe* Tit. II, 1, 117. (Cp. H6C. II, 4, 12)‹ „It was in those days usual to single the harboured deer, and unharbour, or force him to break covert, by means of the liam-hound. 'When he (the hart) is hunted and doth first leave the hearde, we say that he is *syngled* or *empryned*'. (*Noble Arte*"). D. H. Madden.

**Slave**, vb.: *let the superfluons and lust-dieted man, that—s your ordinance, feel your power quickly.* Lr. IV, 1, 71 (Qq. *stands*). i. e. "that instead of obeying your law makes it a slave to his own appetite". W. A. Wright, Clarendon Press Ed.
Koppel conjectures: "*scants" your ordinance.* Verbesserungsvorschläge zu Lear p. 104.

**Sledded**: *the sledded pole-axe* Hml. I, 1, 63. May not 'sledded' be used here in a proleptical sense (= 'sliding on the ice like a sledge')? S.

**Sly** Shr. Ind. 1, 3 etc. "There was a genuine Stephen Sly, who was in the dramatist's day a self-assertive citizen of Stratford".
Sidney Lee, Shakespeare.

**Smulkin** Lr. III,4, 146. "The name is borrowed from Harsnet, p. 47, as Percy shews: 'The names of ther punie spirits cast out of Trayford were these, Hilco, Smolkin, Hillio, Hiaclito, and Lustie huffecap'." Wright Clar. Press Ed.

**Sneak-cup** (H4A III, 3, 99), "one who shirks his liquor." Wright, Clar. Press Ed.

**Snuff**, subst.: *in s—s and packings of the dukes* Lr. III, 1, 26 *i. e.* "quarrels".
W. A. Wright, Clar. Press Ed.

**Soil** (*solye* Q) Sonn. 69, 14 = "solution"
Cambr. Ed., Wyndham.

**Solve**, subst. see *soil*.

**Somerset**: but sec where S. and Clarence comes! H6C IV, 2, 3 etc. "This was doubtless meant for the third duke, Henry Beaufort. But his revolt from Edward occurred, according to Holinshed, seven years before that of Warwick [in reality 'about Christmas, 1462'], and was speedily followed by his execution after Hexham, 1464. The later history of the dramatic Somerset is rather that of his brother Edmund, who was always a staunch Lancastrian, and was beheaded after Tewkesbury". Herford.

**Soothe**: *has your king married the Lady Grey? and now, to s. your forgery and his, sends me a paper to persuade me patience?* H6C III, 3, 175 *i. e.* to "put a good face upon". Herford.

**Soul**, cf. S. Singer, Shakespeare-Jahrb. XXXVI, 71 ff.

**Sound** vb.: *pray heaven, he sound not my disgrace* H8 V, 2, 13, *i. e.* "proclaim".
Wright Clar. Press Ed.

**Southam** H6C V, 1, 9, place in Warwickshire, between Warwick and Daventry (cf. Allen, Notes on the Shakespeare-Bacon Question p. 175).

**Sovereignty** Lucr. 69 "the dignity attaching to certain dispositions of heraldic bearings".
Wyndham.

**Spanish**: *S. pouch* H4A II, 4, 79. "Perhaps the expression describes the vintner's squat thick-set figure, the epithet 'Spanish' being used because his jerkin was of Spanish leather. The Prince afterwards calls Falstaff a 'stuffed cloak-bag'. But more probably the pouch was a characteristic part of the vintner's attire, like the other articles mentioned".
W. A. Wright, Clar. Press Ed.

**Spear-grass** H4A II, 4, 340 "is in Suffolk the common name for couch-grass, called also 'quitch' or 'twitch'. Its botanical name is *Triticum repens*".
Wright, Clar. Press Ed.

**Specify**: *do not forget to sp. that I am an ass,* Ado V, 1, 264; "Dogberry can only have blundered into this correct use of so technical a word; he meant to say "testify'." Herford.

**Spit**: *I would I might never spit white again* H4B I, 2, 237; "this was regarded as a sign of health: 'The whitte spittle not knotty signifieth health', says Batman upon Bartholome, quoted by Furnivall. It was also regarded as a sign of thirst; and may hence, in Falstaff's mouth, have referred to the immediate concomitant of thirst, — drink". Herford.

**Spite** subst.: *and s. of s. needs must I rest awhile* H6C II, 3, 5, *i. e.* "for all my warlike fury". Herford.

**Sportful**: *is s. Edward come?* H6C V, 1, 18, *i. e.* "lascivious". Herford.

**Spot** vb.: *a handkerchief — ed with strawberries* Oth. III, 3, 435, *i. e.* "embroidered". Herford.

**Spot**, subst. Cor. I, 3, 56, "pattern".
Chambers Warwick Sh.

**Spring-halt** H8 I, 3, 13. "It must have been from some 'ignorant smith' that Sh. learned to miscall the affection known as stringhalt". D. H. Madden.

**Stafford** H4A V, 3, 7 etc. *The Lord of Stafford* was Edmund, fifth Earl of Stafford..... He married Ann Plantagenet, daughter of Thomas of Woodstock, Duke of Gloucester, by Eleonor daughter of Humphrey de Bohun, Earl of Hereford. His wife was therefore the King's first cousin on the father's side, and first cousin to the Prince of Wales on the mother's". Wright, Clar. Press Ed.

**Staines** H5 II, 3, 2 "was the first stage on the road from London to Southampton".
Wright, Clar. Press Ed.

**State**: *thy state of law* R2, II, 1, 114 "your legal status as King". Herford, Warwick Shakespeare.

**Steel'd** (Mod. Ed. **stelled**) = "engraved" Ven. 377, Lucr. 1444, Sonn XXIV, 1.
Wyndham, Note to Lucr. 1444.

**Stell** s. steel.

**Steppe**: *from the farthest steppe of India* Mids. II, 1, 69. "To the reading 'steppe' it is objected that the word in the sense in which it is applied to the vast plains of Central Asia was not known in Shakespeare's day, but it is dangerous to assert a proposition which may be disproved by a single instance of the contrary. — — — On the other hand, too much weight must not be attached to the spelling of the first quarto, for in III, 2. 85 'sleep' is misprinted 'slippe'."
Wright, Clar. Press Ed.

**Stick**, vb.: *my father's rough and envious disposition sticks me at heart* As. I, 2, 254 *i. e.* "stabs me to the heart".
Wright, Clar. Press Ed., Franz, Shakespeare-Grammatik S. 204.

**Stock-fish**: *I'll make a s. of thee* Tp. III, 2, 79; "*i. e.* beat thee, like dried cod".      Herford.

**Stone**: *stones have been known to move* Mcb. III, 4, 123. "Mr. Paton refers this to the 'rocking-stones' or 'Clacha breath', by which the Druids tested guilt. It was supposed that only the innocent could shake them. There is one near Glamis Castle".
     E. K. Chamber, Warwick Sh.

**Stony-Stratford** R3, II, 4, 2 "a market town in Buckinghamshire situated on Watling Street. It was a stage nearer London than Northampton".
     Macdonald, Warwick Shakespeare.

**Stop** sbst.: *his jesting spirit is now crept into a lute-string and now governed by —s.* Ado III, 2, 62. "*Stops*, or frets were the small pieces of wire or cord, fastened round the neck of a lute at intervals of a semitone, on which the strings were pressed".
     Wright, Clar. Press Ed.

**Strain**: *whith what encounter so uncurrent. I have — ed to appear thus* Wint. III, 2, 51. 'When he (the hart) runneth verie fast, then he streyneth' (*Noble Arte*); quoted by D. H. Madden.

**Streak** vb. Mids. II, 1, 257 'stroke, touch gently'.
     W. A. Wright, Clar. Press Ed.

**Striker**: *long-staff sixpenny —s* H4A II, 1, 82, *i. e.* "thieves with long staves that knock men down for sixpence. 'Striker' was a cant term for a petty thief, and in Greene's Art of Coneycatching (1592) the cutting a pocket or picking a purse is called striking. — — — In Lilly's Mother Bombie, I, 1, a medicine for a threadbare purse is 'a pike staffe to take a purse on the high way'".
     W. A. Wright, Clar. Press Ed.

**Study**, subst.: *his study of imagination*, Ado IV, 1, 227, *i. e.* "his brooding fancy".      Herford.

**Substance**: *conceit, more rich in matter than in words, brags of its s., not of ornament*, Rom. II, 6, 31, *i. e.* "rejoices in possessing, not in brilliantly describing its possession".      Herford.

**Substantial**: *acquitted by a true s. form* H4B IV, 1, 173 *i. e.* "a due and legally valid form of pardon".      Herford.

**Suffer** *let — — both the worlds suffer* Mcb. III, 2, 16 "*i. e.* perish". Clark & Wright, Clar. Press. Ed.

**Sugar-candy** (H4A III, 3, 180) "according to an authority quoted by Mr. Rushton (Shakespeare illustrated by Old Authors, p. 50) was an ingredient, in a mixture given to a fighting cock, one object of which was to 'prolong his breath'."
     Wright, Clar. Press Ed.

**Sun**: *I am too much i' the sun* Hml. I, 2, 67. "Hamlet ironically replies that he is too much in the sunshine of the royal presence to be gloomy. There may also be a play of words between *sun* and *son*: 'You call me your son, and so I am, a mere prince, who should be a king'. — — — 'To be i' the sun' appears also to be a proverbial phrase for 'to be miserable'.
     Chambers, Warwick Sh.

**Surecard** H4B III, 2, 95 "an old name for a boon companion".      Herford.

**Sutton-Cophill** H4A IV, 2, 3 = "*Sutton Co' fil* or Sutton-Coldfield" (Warwickshire).
     W. A. Wright, Clar. Press Ed., Brandl.

**Sway**: *swaying more upon our part* H5 I, 1, 73 = "inclining more to our side".
     Moore Smith, Warwick Sh.

**Swayed**: *s. in the back* Shr. III, 56 *i. e.* "a slackness in the muscles of the back through excessive strain, causing the horse to roll or falter".
     Herford.

**Swinish**: *with s. phrase* Hml. I, 4, 19, *i. e.* "by calling us swine".      Herford.

**Sycamore**: "There is no reason to doubt that with Shakspere — — — it would unquestionably be the yet nobler tree, Platanus orientalis. No tree, in its general character, is more imposing than the plane".
     Grindon, Shakespeare's Flora.

**Sycamore** Rom. I, 1, 128 = "Acer Pseudo-Platanus, great maple". Beisley, quoted by Furness, Var. Ed.

**Syenna**: *Syenna's brother* Cymb. IV, 2, 341 *i. e.* "brother of the ruler of Siena, a town and province in Tuscany".      Wyatt, Warwick Sh.

**Tailor**: *down topples she and 'tailor' cries* Mids. II, 1, 54. "Halliwell thinks that *tailor* is equivalent to 'thief', and quotes *Pasquil's Night-Cap* (1612) —
"Thieving is now an occupation made,
Though men the name of tailor do it give".
*Tailor* in this sense is probably a corruption of the older *taylard*. Furness would read *tailer*, and explain it as a fall on the tail, after the analogy of 'header'. Halliwell's explanation seems the best, as it is the victim's outcry that is in question, and not that of the bystanders".
     E. K. Chambers, Warwick Shakespeare.

**Talent**: *behold these —s of their hair* Compl. 204. "Shakespeare uses the word twice for an *accomplishment*; twelve times in its original sense of a sum or weight of Greek currency, all in *Timon of Athens*; and once, as perhaps here for a precious possession. Cf. Cymbeline, I, VI, 79 — —".      Wyndham.

**Tardy**, adj.: *now this overdone, or come tardy off* Hml. III, 2, 28, *i. e.* "feebly executed". Herford.

**Tacsel-gentle** Rom II, 2, 160. "The males of the hawks principally used in falconry — the peregrine and goshawk were called 'tiercels', or 'tercels' because (it is said) they are smaller than the females by one third; the male of the nobler species — the peregrine — being distinguished by the addition of the word 'gentle'".      D. H. Madden.

**Tenour** (tenure Q.) Lucr. 1310 "in law = a transcript or copy which implies that a correct copy is set out, and therefore that the instrument must have been set out correctly — — ^—".
     Imper. Diction., Wyndham.

**Tent** vb.: *well might they* (your wounds) . . . . . . . . *t. themselves with death* Cor. I, 9, 31 *i. e.* "probe themselves, make themselves smart, not with being spoken of, but, with death".
     Chambers, Warwick Sh. [?]

**Termless** Compl. 94 = "youthful". Wyndham.

**Tharborough** LLL I, 1, 185. "The petty constable was elected for a year only so that he could gain no experience worth having. In the country he was chosen by the freemen of the tithing or twelfth division of the hundred at a court leet; in Warwickshire only every third borough had a constable; hence his name there was thirdborough or tharborough. (See Eirenarcha or of the Office of the Justices of Peace, by Lambard, edition, a. D. 1610)".
     Grace Latham, Shakespeare Jahrb. XXXII, 137.

**Theme**: *the gracious queen, part of his t., but nothing of his ill-ta'en suspicion* Wint. I, 2, 459; *i. e.* "involved (with Polyxenes) in his suspicions, but in no wise sharing it". Herford.

**Thick**: *speaking thick* H4B II, 3, 24 *i. e.* "with indistinct abruptness". Herford.

**Thisne**: *Thisne, Thisne* Mids. I, 2. 55. "These words are printed in italic in the old copies, as if they represented a proper name, and so 'Thisne' has been regarded as a blunder of Bottom's for Thisbe. But as he has the name right in the very next line it seems more probable that 'Thisne' signifies 'in this way' and he then gives a specimen of how he would aggravate his voice. 'Thissen' is given in Wright's Provincial Dictionary as equivalent to 'in this' manner". W. A. Wright, Clar. Press Ed. [??]

**Thou**: *run thee to the parlour* Ado III, 1, 1. "'Thee' is used here redundantly, as in III, 3, 94, IV, 1, 21, 'Stand thee'. Schmidt (Shakespeare Lexicon) gives this as an instance of 'thee' for 'thou'; but in all the cases he quotes 'thee' is either redundant, representing what Latin grammarians call the *dativus commodi*, or reflexive". Wright, Clar. Press Ed. (cf. W. Franz, Shakespeare-Grammatik § 134).

**Thought**: *take thought and die for Caesar* Caes. II, 1, 187. "*Think and die* or *take thought and die* is an old phrase for *grieve one's self to death*". Henry N. Hudson.

**Thrift**: *French t.* Wiv. I, 3, 93 *i. e.* "the economical practice of employing a page instead of a band of retainers". Herford.

**Thrifty**: *thrifty hire* As. II, 3, 39 = "hire saved by thrift." J. C. Smith, Warwick Shakespeare.

**Thrum**: *cut thread and thrum* Mids. V, 291. "is the loose end of a weaver's warp, and is used of any coarse yarn. — — — — 'Thread and thrum' was end of used as an expression for everything in general. So Herrick (Hesperides I, 100):

'Thou who wilt not love, do this;
Learne of me what Woman is,
Something made of thred and thrumme
A meere Botch of all and some' ".
W. A. Wright, Clarendon Press Edition.

**Tire** vb.: *the posts come — ing on* H4B Ind. 37. "probably riding hard, without a pause". Herford.

**Tire**: Ven. 56. "a term of falconry used of a hawk tearing its food, from French *tirer*". Wyndham.

**Tithe**: *our corn's to reap, for yet our tithe's to sow* Meas. IV, 1, 76. "This may possibly be explained (with Knight) as the seed to be sown — the tenth of the harvest; but this usage has not been proved. Warburton very plausibly substituted *tilth, i. e.* land to be soon, as in Temp. II, 1, 152". Herford.

**Toast**: *I pressed me none but such toasts and butter* H4A IV, 2, 22 = "cockneys, self-indulgent fellows". Wright, Clar. Press Ed.

**Tongs**: *let's have the tongs and the bones* Mids. IV, 1, 32. "The 'tongs' appear to have been a rustic instrument, like a triangle, played with a key". E. K. Chambers, Warwick Shakespeare.

**To-pinch** (Wiv. IV, 4, 57):
Then let them all encircle him about
And, fairy-like, to-pinch the unclean knight.
"The use of the hyphen between *to* and *pinch* in the above quotation, to form a compound verb with

a conjectural meaning, is erroneous, as has been already observed in the 'Century Dictionary'. The examples that follow show that our older writers, using *let* with more than one infinitive tied to it, occasionally put *to* before the second infinitive: —
And let never myschip uppon him falle
Ne false traytoure him *to* betray.
Awdelay, quoted in Warkworth's 'Chronicle' p. XIV.
But let the wicked beare theyre shame
And in the graue to fall.
Sternhold, Psalm XXXI, 17 (ed. 1564)".
F. Adams, Notes & Queries, 8. Ser. Vol. 1.

**Touch**: Tw. II, 1, 13 = "delicate feeling". A. D. Jnnes, Warwick Sh.

**Touch**: *one touch of Nature* Troil. III, 3, 157. "I have explained that *touch* in this famous quotation means defect or bad trait, from confusion with the once common word *tache*, sometimes misspelt *touch*". W. W. Skeat, Notes & Queries. VI. Ser. Vol. 11.

**Traject**: Merch. III, 4, 53. "Rowe's correction for the printer's error 'tranect'. Hunter quotes from Coryat's *Crudities*, "There are in Venice thirteen ferries or passages, which they commonly call Traghetti". (Cp. Furness, Var. Ed. of the Merch. of Ven. p. 177.) H. L. Withers, Warwick Shak.

**Train**: *Macbeth by many of these — s hath sought to win me into his power*, Mcb. IV, 3, 118 *i. e.* "tricks". E. K. Chambers, Warwick Sh.

**Train**: *Macbeth by many of these trains hath sought to win me into his power*. Mcb. IV, 3, 118. "The lure — — — was a sham bird, usually constructed of pigeon's wings, to which was attached food for the hawk, known as a train". D. H. Madden.

**Trash** vb.: *who to trash for overtopping* Tp. I, 2, 81. "The use of the word 'trash' among terms of venery, both as a verb and as a substantive, is now clearly established. — — — It is used as a substantive by Gervase Markham in his *Country Contentments*. He mentions trashes with couples, liams, collars etc., among articles commonly kept in a huntsmans lodgings.

— — — However the trash may have been applied, it clearly appears — — — to have consisted of a long strap — — —. When the hound was running this long strap, dragged along the ground, handicapped the overtopping hound". D. H. Madden.

**Travel**: *after a demure t. of regard.* Tw. II, 5, 59 = "after allowing my gaze to travel gravely round". A. D. Innes, Warwick Sh.

**Trench**: *trenching war.* H4A I, 1, 7, "war that cuts trenches in the surface of the land to throw up earth works for defence". Wright, Clar. Press Ed.

**Tripolis**: Merch. I. 3, 18, III, 1, 106, III, 2, 271. "*not* the city in Barbary in N. Africa as is clear from a comparison with III, 265 and 266 [= III, 2, 271], but the seaport in Syria, a little to the north-east of Beyrout. — — The *Asiatic* Tripolis was on the way from Venice to the East, by the 'Euphrates valley route". It was a famous port in Crusading times, and traded with Venice in glass". H. L. Withers, Warwick Shakespeare.

**Try** vb.: *bring her to t. with main-course.* Tp. I, 1, 38 *i. e.* "Keep her close to the wind with the mainsail. To 'lie at try' is to keep as close to the wind

as possible. Cf. Hakluyts *Voyages*, 1598 I, 277: 'And when the barke had way, we cut the hawser, and so gate the sea to our friend, and tryed out al that day with our maine-course'."        Boas, Warwick Sh.
**Twilled** cf. *Pioned*.

**Ullorxa**, Tim. III, 4, 112 = "VII or X a." = "seven or ten other".
            Harold Littledale, Athenaeum No. 3839
                        (May 25, 1901).
**Unadvised**: *friend to friend gives u. wounds* Lucr. 1488 *i. e.* "involuntary".                Herford.
**Uncape** Wiv. III, 3 176. "Professor Baynes — — — points out that though no example of its technical use has yet been found, there can be little doubt that "uncape" was a sporting term locally or colloquially employed instead of uncouple".
John Monck Mason, quoted by D. H. Madden.

**Uncontrolled**: *uncontrolled enfranchisement* R2 I, 3, 90 = "enfranchisement which consists in being uncontrolled".    Herford, Warwick Shakespeare.

**Underbear**: *skirts round underborne with a bluish tinsel* Ado III, 4, 21. "It seems very improbable that a gown which was made of cloth of gold should be merely trimmed with 'a bluish tinsel', and it is more likely that this was the material either of the lining of the skirt or of a petticoat worn under it so as to set it out".            Wright, Clar. Press Ed.
**Unheard**: *this u. sauciness and boyish troops* John V, 2, 133 = "*unhair'd*, beardless. Theobald's reading — — — — is justified by the passages which he quoted from Macbeth, V, 2, 10: — — — and Venus and Adonis, 487:
Whose beams upon his hairless face are fix'd'. 'Hair' is spelt 'heare' in Spenser, Faery Queen II, 9 § 13:
Staring with hollow eies, and stiffe vpstanding heares'."            Wright, Clar. Press Ed.
**Unimproved**: *unimproved mettle* Hml I, 1, 96. "probably means here 'untutored', not chastened by the lessons of experience".
            Clark & Wright, Clar. Press Ed.
**Unkind** (unkinn'd) Ven. 201 = unkinned "without offspring".            Wyndham.
**Unplausive**: *u. eyes* Troil. III, 3, 43, *i. e.* "neglectful".            Herford.
**Unproportioned**: *give thy thoughts no tongue, nor any u. thought his act*, Hml. I, 3, 60, *i. e.* "misshapen, ugly, wicked*. Cf. Jonson, Every man out of his Humour I, 1. *To melt this unproportioned frame of nature*".
                        W. Wetz.
**Unshrinking**: *in the u. station where he fought* Mcb. V, 8, 42, *i. e.* "the post from which he did not flinch".            Clark & Wright, Clar. Press Ed.
**Unyoked** H4A I, 2, 220, "uncontrolled, like an animal, when its work is done and the yoke is taken off".            Wright, Clar. Press Ed.
**Upon**: *upon your hour* Hml. I, 1, 6. "An unusual phrase, meaning 'just as your hour is about to strike' ".
            Clark & Wright, Clar. Press Ed.
**Upon**: *this music crept by me upon the waters* Tp. I, 2, 391 *i. e.* "stole past me and hushed the waves" ("beschleicht die wilden Wogen und bringt sie zur Ruh").            Fernow, Engl. Stud. 30, 89.

**Vail**: *if he have power, then v. your ignorance* Cor. III, 1, 98. "If the text is correct, 'vail your ignorance', must mean, 'let your ignorance, which gave him power, bow down to him in submission' ".
            Chambers, Warwick Sh.
**Vantage**: *'t is meet that some more audience than a mother — — —. should o'erhear the speech of* v. Hml. III, 3, 33 — — — "That *of vantage* in the Hamlet quotation above given cannot mean 'to boot', 'besides', is clear from the fact that after 'some more audience than a mother', 'to boot' would be an almost meaningless redundancy. I find that well-nigh all the English commentators explain the phrase of vantage in a very different way. Abbott § 165, for instance, says: 'Of 'here retains its original meaning of 'from'; hence the words are equivalent to 'from the vantage-ground of concealment' — To me there is not the least doubt that this is the correct explanation".            Stoffel, Engl. Stud. 29, 98.
**Vantage**: *if not with vantage Mids.* 1, 102 = 'if I have not even an advantage over him in this respect'.    W. A. Wright, Clar. Press Ed.
**Vaward**: *he, being in the v.*, *placed behind with purpose to relieve and follow them* H6A I, 1, 132. "Theobald conj. 'rereward' (but probably 'vaward' = 'in the front line of his own troop')".
            Gollancz, Temple Sh. [?]
**Velvet**: *v. guards* H4A III, 1, 261; "*i. e.* citizens' wives in their festive costume, of which black velvet facings and trimmings were an important part".
            Herford.
**Velvet**: *his velvet friends* As II, 1, 50. "The covering of the newly-grown antlers is called 'velvet' ".            D. H. Madden.
**Verge**: *incaged in so small a verge* R2, II, 1, 102 "The use of the term verge is felicitous, since this technically described the compass about the king's court, which extended for twelve miles around".
            Wright, Clar. Press Ed., cf. Herford,
                        Warwick Shakespeare.
**Vial**: *sacred —s* Ant. I, 3, 63, "alluding to the lachrymatory vials, or bottles of tears, which the Romans sometimes put into the urn of a friend".
            Gollancz.
**View**: *invite you to my sister's view* Ant. II. 2, 170 *i. e.* "to see my sister".            Gollancz.
**Visor** H4B V, 1, 42 see *Woncot*.
**Volquessen**: John II, 527 "the ancient country of the Velocasses, whose capital was Rouen; divided in modern times into Vexin Normand and Vexin Français".            Wright, Clar. Press Ed.
**Vouch** sbst.: *one that — did justly put one the vouch of very malice itself* Oth. II, 1, 147 *i. e.* "provoke the acknowledgment".            Herford.

**Wag**: *bid sorrow wag*, Ado V, 1, 16, *i. e.* "bid it go its way, dismiss it. This is Capell's emendation for A and Ff. 'and sorrow, wag, cry hem, when he should groan'. This would make 'sorrow' the subject of 'patch grief', etc."            Herford.
**Wappened**: Tim. IV, 3, 38 *i. e.* "*wapper'd*, worn out. Misprinted 'wappen'd in F; 'unwapper'd' occurs in *Two N. Kins.* V, 4, 10, and elsewhere. L." Herford.
**Warm**: *'t is warm at's heart* Cor. II, 3, 160 *i. e.* "he's pleased at it, though he takes care not to show it".            Chambers, Warwick Sh.

**Washford** H6A IV, 7, 63 "an old name of Wexford in Ireland". Gollancz, Temple Sh.

**Waxen:** *a waxen epitaph* H5 I, 2, 233. "Explained by Gifford as a eulogy affixed to the grave with wax. In England till the present century it was common to pin poetical elegies, etc., to the hearse of a deceased person, especially at the universities. — — — Whether the words 'waxen epitaph' can mean an epitaph fastened by wax', is however, very doubtful". Moore Smith, Warwick Sh.

**Weak** = *two weak evils, age and hunger* As. II, 7, 132 = "causing weakness". J. C. Smith, Warwick Shakespeare.

**Week:** *at fourscore it is too late a week* As II, 3, 74 = "too late by a week, *i. e.* by a good deal — a proverbial expression. Wright, however, thinks *a* = in the, as in 'a night' (II, 4, 44)." J. C. Smith, Warwick Shakespeare.

**Well-spoken:** *these fair well-spoken days* R3, I, 1, 29 = 'days when fair speeches and smooth words were in vogue'. Macdonald, Warwick Shakespeare.

**Whip** sbst.: *the Hector, that was the whip of your bragged progeny* Cor. I, 8, 12. "The 'bragged progeny' is of course the Trojans, from whom the Romans claimed descent, 'progeny' being used in the general sense of 'race'. Hector was the Trojan 'whip' or champion". Chambers, Warwick Sh.

**Whist:** *courtsied when you have and kiss'd the wild waves w.* Tp. I, 2, 379; "kissed the waves into hushed stillness, *i. e.* kissed partners (immediate prelude to the dance) and thereby hushed the noisy waves into attention (Allen). This interpretation, favoured by the punctuation in Ff. and by v. 392, is more Shakespearean than the commoner one, which makes v. 379 a parenthesis". Herford.

**White** Lucr. 56, 65 = "Argent (heraldic term)". Wyndham.

**Wicked:** *thy w. dam* Tp. I, 2, 320, "probably 'having baneful qualities'". Boas, Warwick Sh.

**Wild:** *my father is gone w. into his grave* H4B V, 2, 123 "*i. e.* my wildness is buried with him". Herford.

**Wild-goose chase** Rom. II, 4, 75. "The Wild goose chase received its name from the manner of the flight which is made by Wild geese, which is generally one after another; so the two Horses after the running of Twelvescore Yards had liberty which horse soever could get the leading to ride what ground he pleased: the hindmost Horse being bound to follow him within a certain distance — — — and whichever Horse could distance the other won the match'. Nicholas Cox, Gentleman's Recreation, quoted by D. H. Madden.

**Win:** *the rabble . . . will in time w. upon power* Cor. I, 1, 224; *i. e.* "take advantage of the power already won to win more". E. K. Chambers, Warwick Sh.

**Wincot,** Shr. Ind. 2, 23 "was the familiar designation of three Warwickshire villages — — — There is a very small hamlet named Wincot within four miles of Stratford, now consisting of a single farmhouse which was once an Elizabethan mansion; it is situated on what was doubtless in Shakespeare's day, before the land there was enclosed, an open heath. This Wincot forms part of the parish of Quinton, where, according to the parochial registers, a Hacket family resided in Shakespeare's day. Yet by Warwickshire contemporaries the Wincot of the 'Taming of the Shrew' was unhesitatingly identified with Wilnecote, near Tamworth, on the Staffordshire border of Warwickshire, at some distance from Stratford. — — — It is therefore probable that Shakespeare consciously invested the home of Kit Sly and of Kit's hostess with characteristics of Wilnecote as well as cf the hamlet near Stratford". Sidney Lee, Shakespeare.

**Window:** *these windows that let forth thy life* R3 I, 2, 12 "Schmidt connects this passage with the notion of a window as an indirect or unnatural means of exit and entrance — — —. Surely it is better to interpret it in the light of the old custom of opening the windows and doors in a house that the soul of a dying person may pass out freely". Macdonald Warwick Shakespeare.

**Windy:** *it keeps on the w. side of care,* Ado II, 1, 327 *i. e.* "so as to have the advantage of it. The figure is nautical. In naval actions in the old days of sailing-ships it was always an object to get the weather-gage of the enemy. — — — Schmidt explains it as a hunting metaphor — — —. But the scent would be carried down by the wind, and this cannot be the explanation". Wright, Clar. Press Ed.

**Wing** sbst.: *the best feather of our eving* Cymb. I, 6, 186 *i. e.* "the choicest spirit of our fellowship". Wyatt, Warwick Sh.

**Wink,** vb., Ven. 90 = "to start aside, from O. Fr. *guenchir*". Wyndham.

**Winnow:** *the most fond and — — ed opinions* Hml. V, 2, 201. "So F I. — — — The F I text may stand, in the sense of 'foolish and over-refined'". E. K. Chambers, Warwick Sh.

**With:** *with Circe* H6A V, 3, 35, "means 'in competition with Circe' as in the lines of King John:
'Thou may'st with lilies boast
And with the half-blown rose'.
Act III. Sc. 1. H. H. Vaughan, New Readings.

**Wither:** *long withering out a young man's revenue* Mids. I. 1, 6 = 'causing the revenue to dwindle as she herself withers away'. W. A. Wright, Clar. Press Ed.

**Wive:** *besides that hook of w—ing, Fairness* Cymb. V, 5, 167 *i. e.* "besides that hook which catches a husband, beauty". Wyatt, Warwick Sh.

**Woncot** (Wincot) H4B V, 1, 42. "When — — the justice's factotum, Davy, asked his master 'to countenance William Visor of Woncot against Clement Perkes of the Hill', the local references are unmistakable. Woodmancote, where the' family of Visor or Vizard has flourished since the sixteenth century, is still pronounced Woncot. The adjoining Stinchcombe Hill (still familiarly known to natives as 'the Hill') was in the sixteenth century the home of the family of Perkes". Sidney Lee.

**Wonder** vb.: *princes not doing so are like to gnats, which make a sound, but kill'd are wonder'd at* Per. II, 3, 63 *i. e.* "prove, in spite of their sound, to be marvellously small". Herford.

**Woodbine:** *so doth the woodbine the sweet honeysuckle gently entwist* Mids. IV, 1, 47. "— — the parallelism of the present passage makes it clear to my mind that two plants are meant, just as the ivy and the elm are two, and Titania and Bottom are two. A point is lost if Bottom is not compared to the 'sweet honeysuckle'. What plant, then, is here intended by the woodbine? Possibly the *Convolvulus sepium*, the great white bindweed or withywind. — — — And possibly the *Clematis Vitalba*, or traveller's joy, which is called *wooden-binde* in an 11th-century Anglo-Saxon vocabulary (cf. Ellacombe, *Plant-Lore of Shakespeare*)".

E. K. Chambers, Warwick Shakespeare.

**Worm**: *a certain convocation of politic worms are e'en at him. Your worm is your only emperor for diet* Hml. IV, 3, 21. "There is a punning allusion to the Diet of Worms".                                    Herford.

**Worship** subst.: *as I belong to worship* H8 1, 1, 39 *i. e*, "as I am a nobleman".

Wright, Clar. Press Ed.

**Worshipful**: *Your very worshipful and loving friends* R3, III, 7, 138. "Schmidt explains this as if it meant 'worthy to be reverenced'; but here and in III, 4, 41 the word seems rather to imply 'full of reverence'". Macdonald, Warwick Shakespeare.

**Writ**: *for the law of w. and the liberty, these are the only men* Hml. II, 2, 421. "This means pieces written according to rules and without rules, 'classical' and 'romantic' dramas. Collier, however, explains it 'written and extemporised plays'.

Chambers, Warwick Sh.

**Yaughan** (Hml. V, 1, 68) "perhaps the name of a London tavern-keeper. The alehouse of "deaf John" is mentioned in Jonson's *Alchemist;* in Every Man out of his Humour V, 6, he mentions 'a Jew, one Yohan', but not as a tavern-keeper. Yaughan is said to be a common Welsh name". Dowden.

**Yaw**: *to divide him inventorially would dizzy the arithmetic of memory, and yet but y. neither, in respect of his quick sail*, Hml. V, 2, 120. "The explanation of the text as it stands may be: To enumerate in detail the perfections of Laertes would bewilder the computations of memory, yet for all that — in spite of the calculations — the enumeration would stagger to and fro (and so fall behind) in comparison with Laertes' quick sailing — — — —".                    Dowden.

**Yorick** (Hml. V, 1, 198, 203). "Ainger: Yorick is perhaps the Danish *Jörg* (George). — — — — Furness notes that Jerick is the name of a 'Dutch Bowr" in Chapman's Alphonsus".        Dowden.

# Addendum.

**'Gainst** (sometimes unapostrophized)=against; 1) prepos. a) denoting direction: *gazing 'g. the sun,* H6C II, 1, 92. *'g. whose shore riding,* Per. V, 3, 10. Usually with the notion of contrariety, of harm done or suffered: *this sessions pushes 'g. our heart,* Wint. III, 2, 2. *spit forth their iron indignation 'g. your walls,* John II, 212. *a piece of ordnance 'g. it I have placed,* H6A I, 4, 15. *the dread curses, like the sun 'g. glass, recoil,* H6B III, 2, 330. *let the mutinous winds strike the proud cedars g. the fiery sun,* Cor. V, 3, 60. *cracked g. our rocks,* Cymb. III, 1, 29. *which like a waxen image 'g. a fire bears no impression of the thing it was,* Gent. II, 4, 201. *as a form of wax resolveth from his figure g. the fire,* John V, 4, 25. *well might they (your wounds) fester 'g. ingratitude and tent themselves with death,* Cor. I, 9, 30 (= meeting with ingratitude).

b) temporally, = in expectation of, to be provided for: *to buy apparel 'g. the wedding day,* Shr. II, 317. *gay apparel g. the triumph day,* R2 V, 2, 66 (Ff *against). fettle your fine joints 'g. Thursday next,* Rom. III, 5, 154.

c) in opposition or repugnance to: *g. venomed sores the only sovereign plaster,* Ven. 916. *nothing g. times scythe can make defence,* Sonn. 12, 13. *I will drink potions of eisel g. my strong infection,* 111, 10. *a forted residence 'g. the tooth of time,* Meas V, 12. *dotes on what he looks 'g. law or duty,* Lucr. 497. Sonn. 10, 6. 35, 11. 55, 9. 60, 7. Compl. 157. 271. Pilgr. 30. Tp. V, 26. Meas. V, 154. 244 (F1 *against*). LLL II, 152. IV, 1, 91. IV, 3, 293 (F1 *against*). Merch. IV, 1, 205. 352. 356. 451 (F1 *against*). As 1, 2, 294. Tw. III, 3, 26. V, 404 (*g. knaves and thieves men shut their gate*). Wint. III, 2, 155 (*pardon my great profanenes 'g. thine oracle*). John II, 346. R2 I, 3, 190. II, 1, 243. 245. H4A V, 1, 43. H4B I, 3, 84 (Q *against*). IV, 5, 225. H5 I, 2, 27. II, 2, 53. H6B III, 2, 20. 165. H6C I, 4, 43. 149. IV, 1, 38. Cor. IV, 6, 66. Tim. II, 2, 147. IV, 1, 27. IV, 3, 102. Mcb. I, 2, 5 (*who fought 'g. my captivity*). Ant. III, 4, 4 etc.

2) conjunction, = in expectation of or looking forward to the time when: *see them ready g. their mother comes,* Tit. V, 2, 206 (Qq *against*). *some say that ever g. that season comes ... the bird of dawning singeth asl night long,* Hml. I, 1, 158.